SCRYE
COLLECTIBLE
CARD GAME
CHECKLIST & PRICE GUIDE

BY

JOHN JACKSON MILLER
AND JOYCE GREENHOLDT
WITH JAMES MISHLER

Published by

krause
publications

The World's Largest Hobby & Collectibles Publisher

Please, call or write us for our free catalog of collectibles publications. To place an order or receive our free catalog, call (800) 258-0929. For editorial comment and further information, use our regular business telephone at (715) 445-2214.

ISBN: 0-87349-254-4
Library of Congress Catalog Number: 00-111282
Printed in the United States of America

"The only category in any hobby that fits everything is 'miscellaneous.'"

— Chet Krause

Contents

Prices and Descriptions

Under each game, BASIC SETS appear first (in order of release)
followed by EXPANSIONS (in order of release).

Foreword
by Peter Adkison
founder, Wizards of the Coast

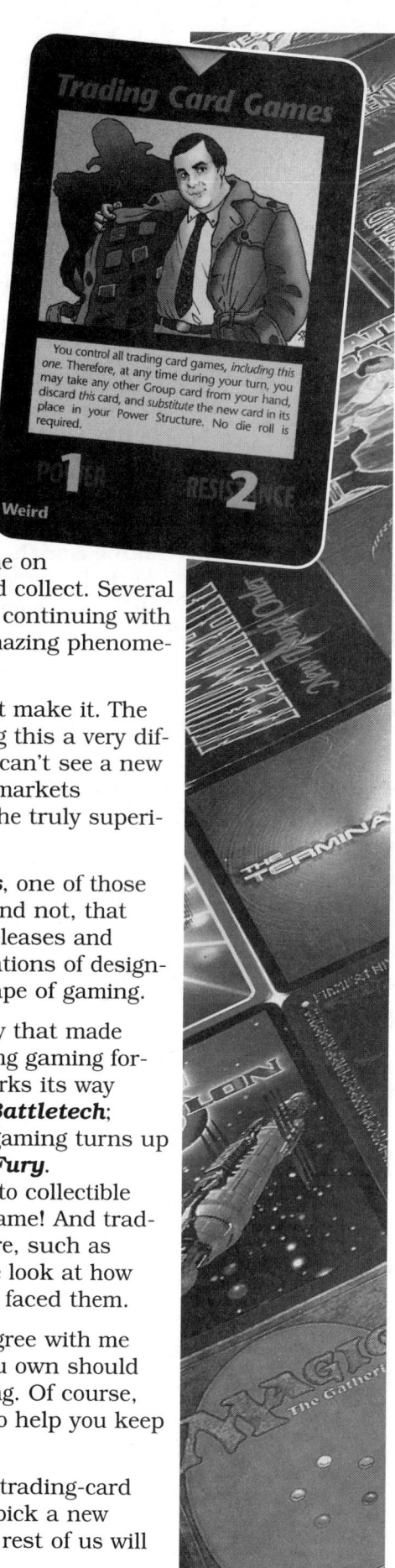

The collectible card game craze caught everyone by surprise, even those of us who were there at the beginning. When Richard Garfield initially presented **Magic: The Gathering** to me back in 1991, I knew it'd be popular. I didn't dare to dream that, within a year of its release, there would essentially be an established gaming genre. One with prestigious game companies anxiously releasing their own games; one that was developing into an intellectual sport through tournaments; and one with entire magazines springing up to cover it.

The creative breakthrough behind the concept was the idea of combining a game with trading cards. For a trading-card game to really do well, it has to make use of the best features of both products. A hot trading-card game has to be an excellent game on its own terms, but also has to be a product people like to trade and collect. Several games have fit this description, beginning with **Magic** in 1993 and continuing with (to name a few) **Star Wars**, **Legend of the Five Rings**, and the amazing phenomenon of **Pokémon**.

For every successful, "living" game, there are others that didn't make it. The game design challenges for this type of product are intense, making this a very difficult market to compete in. The genre remains a strong one, but I can't see a new game standing on its own without recognizing the needs of all the markets involved. Some trading-card game buyers game and some collect; the truly superior game inspires its fans to do both.

In this volume, **Scrye: The Guide to Collectible Card Games**, one of those magazines I was talking about, looks at all the games, successful and not, that have built this genre since 1993, with listings for more than 400 releases and 70,000 cards. Essays put these games, the products of the imaginations of designers at dozens of firms, into perspective as part of the larger landscape of gaming.

And it's the interplay with the rich history of the gaming hobby that made trading-card games become such a diverse genre so quickly. Existing gaming formats were brought forward and cultivated: Fantasy role-playing works its way through **Magic** and **Vampire**; miniatures combat transforms into **Battletech**; sports simulations inspire **MLB Showdown**; and real old-time wargaming turns up in the Civil War combat of **Dixie** and WWII battles of **Echelons of Fury**. **Illuminati: New World Order** even brought a classic card game into collectible form — and wound up transforming later editions of the original game! And trading-card games proved amazingly able to adapt ideas from elsewhere, such as comic books, movies, TV shows, and anime. Reviews in this volume look at how good a job the designers did, as well as some of the challenges that faced them.

There are prices in this book for everything, but the authors agree with me that the important thing is playing the game. Ideally, every card you own should find its home not in a notebook, but in a deck you're actively playing. Of course, with 70,000+ cards out there, it's good to have a collector's utility to help you keep track of things.

My advice? Learn all you can, from here and elsewhere, about trading-card games and the larger world of gaming they belong to. Maybe you'll pick a new game to play. Or maybe you'll come up with an idea for a game the rest of us will soon be playing!

Acknowledgments

A project this size requires more acknowledgements than we have space, but we'll give it a try anyway.

There are two people we couldn't have produced this book without. **Denise Janec** helps maintain the price guides for *Scrye* magazine and helped us find and correct a number of the lists that appear in this book. **James Mishler** came on board as *Scrye*'s Associate Editor in the middle of this project, but hit the ground running by helping us organize our collection for photography and by writing reviews of a large number of the games presented here.

Thanks go to **Maggie Thompson** and **Brent Frankenhoff** of our sister magazine, *Comics Buyer's Guide*, who provided copious amounts of proofreading. Thanks also go to *Toy Shop*'s **Tom Barstch,** who lent a hand in editing.

Jason Winter, consulting editor for *Scrye*, polled our crack team of contributors to find expert players on games new and old and helped coordinate the flow of text to us. Our other consulting editors, **Joe Alread**, **Ka-Lok Fung**, and **Bennie Smith**, took the point on some of the biggest and most complicated games, for which we're greatly appreciative. A lot of material came from *Magic Horizons* designer (and Joyce's husband) **Michael Greenholdt**, who must have been shuffling cards back in the womb.

We can't go without expressing our gratitude to **Richard Weld**, a *Scrye* columnist who's made it his mission in life to play every single CCG published in English. He graciously contributed both his gameplay insights about some of the harder games to find, as well as a number of the cards themselves for our use here. He has also independently developed his own collection of card lists, and while those presented here are ones from our own research, Weld's work served as a good "reality check" whenever we needed to compare notes on some particularly rare stuff. As Richard once noted after a long conversation with us about incorrect card names on *Banemaster*, we may yet be the only people still talking about one or two of these games!

Our retail pricing team helped immensely; they can be found on page 41. A number of stores helped us lay our hands on the cards we needed. In Madison, Wis., we found a lot at **Pegasus Games** and **The Game Haven**. Over in Appleton, Wis., **Chimera Hobby Shop** lent a hand. And in Stevens Point, Wis., **Games People Play**, **FIZZ Collectables**, and **Galaxy Hobby** helped out.

To verify the composition of a number of sets, we went to a lot of manufacturers — and we thank them for their patience while we kept asking about a lot of sets they hadn't produced in years. Some even provided cards, which came in handy. We also rang the phone off the hook at **ACD Distribution** with a lot of little questions, and they deserve note as well.

We also mustn't overlook the work of **Joanne White**, founder of *Scrye* and its editor until 1999. Her work provided us a place to start.

When it comes to patience, we can't help but think of **Debbie Bradley** and the rest of the Krause book department, which suffered our repeated delays as we figured out just *how* big this project was going to be.

A tremendous "thank you" goes to our families, who put up with our extended absences as we put this tome to bed. And, finally, thanks to the readers of *Scrye* magazine, who told us that "the great CCG Codex" was the one book they really needed. We've done our best to provide something that qualifies.

John Jackson Miller
Editorial Director,
Comics & Games Division
Krause Publications

Joyce Greenholdt
Editor,
Scrye magazine

Welcome!

People have been asking for it for years — and we're pleased to be able to provide it. ***The Scrye Collectible Card Game Checklist and Price Guide*** should serve as your "CCG Codex" for years to come — giving you a place to record your collection, check out prices, and find out more about the games all at once!

Some quick notes on what you'll find inside:

The lists. We've compiled lists for what we believe to be every CCG release in the English language during the 20th Century. Many of the lists came from the manufacturers, and we have tried to double check those lists versus the actual cards. We have made *many* revisions to the lists that manufacturers have put out — and those included here should be considered to trump even the ones that have appeared in *Scrye* magazine over the years. In a few cases, we've even been able to discover rarities where none had been known before by examining the card placement in packs.

The prices. We've printed the latest "game store" prices as of press time for almost every item in this volume. Given the age of many of the releases covered here, we expect many of the prices here to remain relevant for years to come. Prices for current and more actively traded games will, of course, change more often, and for these purposes we suggest keeping track through our magazine, *Scrye*. Even for those releases, this volume should still serve as a useful, permanent checklist.

The essays. We've gone to many insiders and tournament players to provide descriptions, historical background, and opinions on every basic and expansion set. A few notes about this material: We try to speak in terms of "the player" as much as possible, but have chosen to go with "his" and "him" where pronouns are concerned. This is for brevity's sake and is no reflection on the make-up of the audience of card gamers — in fact, *Magic* brought more women into gaming than any game since *Dungeons & Dragons*.

And, in general, in this book we speak in the present tense when describing how a game plays, and in the past tense when discussing how players reacted to the game. These shifts are necessary, we feel, to indicate that, while much of what we're writing is history, the games themselves are, in a sense, "living" things.

Changes. We have made every effort to put out the most complete and accurate product we can. But with 75,000+ entries, mistakes can happen. If you've found a card that isn't listed here and should be — or the other way around — contact us at:

scryemail@krause.com

or write to us at **Scrye Editorial**, 700 E. State St., Iola, WI 54990.

Give as complete a description as possible of what you've found, With your help, we can continue to provide you with the world's best database of CCG information!

Enjoy!

In the beginning...

Getting from 'dice and mice' to billions of collectible game cards

whirlwind synopsis by John Jackson Miller

People have been playing games forever, but games as a hobby — we like to call it hobby gaming — didn't really begin to come together until after World War II. Sure, card games and board games had been around forever — but there hadn't been a widespread impulse to give cards with something other than hearts and diamonds a try. And with depressions and wars and things going on, one can forgive a certain lack of free time to commit to such things.

Postwar affluence meant leisure time, though, and games became a bigger part of how people spent that time. Board games became a big benefactor, with games developing to appeal to the youngest children on up to the Monopoly crowd. As the Baby Boomers grew older, though, some weren't satisfied with the complexity of popular games, many of which were, to use today's phrase, "roll-your-dice-move-your-mice games." There began, a little at a time, a niche market for games a little more challenging than people were used to.

Wargames became an early favorite, from *Tactics* onward through historical simulations of ever increasing complexity in the 1960s and 1970s. A related offshoot, strategy board games, proved capable of simulating (in a fun way) an even wider variety of activities, from the abstract to the familiar. Such 3M games as *Acquire* and *Thinking Man's Golf* presented banking and sports with designs far more sophisticated than could be found rotting at the top of a typical closet.

Hobby games were being noticed, too. Allan B. Calhamer's deep but elegantly simple strategy game *Diplomacy* was rejected by Milton Bradley and Parker Brothers as being "too complex" — and Calhamer had to make sets on his own before it was picked up by a small company in 1959.* In three years, the Kennedys were said to be playing it at the White House — and Henry Kissinger called it his favorite game. Some niche!

Some fancy new card games were there, but sold all in one package. A new wrinkle had come with *Strat-O-Matic*, a game using cards with statistics for ball players. New years meant new cards — and the first real expandable card game of any kind. It got around, too: Richard Nixon's son-in-law, David Eisenhower, was said to spend a lot of time in the White House playing *Strat-O-Matic* baseball.

(*Ironic footnote: Today, Hasbro owns Milton Bradley, Parker Brothers, and, finally, **Diplomacy** — not to mention **Magic: The Gathering** and **Dungeons & Dragons**!)

As Avalon Hill, SPI, and others built the board game side of things in the 1970s, they turned to hobby shops to reach customers. Real "hobby" hobby shops — model planes, trains, and the like — had sprung up across North America, many run by veterans with an interest in things military. It was a small step from a model tank on the shelf to a wargame — and many game stores began life this way. Across town, comics shops began opening up in the 1970s, and they'd take an interest in selling games later on, too.

Onto this scene, in 1974, began to wash gaming's first major wave. *Dungeons & Dragons* came on the scene humbly — as a chapter in the wargaming rule book *Chain Mail* — but it was clear that it offered something different. Players didn't simulate the real past, they created one. (A revival of interest in Tolkien's *Lord of the Rings* gave ready inspiration.) And the goal of a player wasn't necessarily to beat the enemy and go home. It could be whatever the player imagined — and whatever a patient "dungeonmaster" would indulge.

D&D would have a rocky first decade, but it would build a sure base on college campuses, and then in high schools. By 1982, it was already pop culture — turning up in the movie *E.T.* Many other companies rose to compete with TSR with their own brands of role-playing games. By the mid-1980s, thousands of hobby shops had switched over to become full-line game stores, giving new creators a chance to reach the audience. Companies with names like Iron Crown. Steve Jackson Games. FASA, the Freedonian Air & Space Administration. Mayfair. One group of college students, calling themselves Wizards of the Coast, came up with their own photocopied role-playing game, *Castles & Conquests,* in 1983.

Cool new card games were surfacing, as well. 1965's *Nuclear War* and 1982's *Illuminati* became so popular that "expansion editions" with more cards to mix into the deck became necessary in 1983. Even Avalon Hill, maker of seemingly staid strategy boardgames saw value in increasing players' options, offering extra cards for such games as *Civilization* and *Kingmaker.*

Role-playing would see a revival in the mid-1980s as story became a major part of the mix. Rather than leaving all the imagination up to the players, companies added storylines to their games — as TSR did by adding *Dragonlance* to *Dungeons & Dragons.* White Wolf even called its line of horror games "storytelling games" — and horrified many "paper and pencil" gamers as some of its gamemasters abandoned dice entirely.

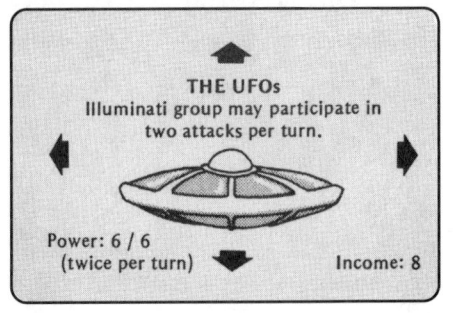

So here we were in 1992. We have hobby gamers. Hobby game shops. Fantasy worlds. Games that evolved. Games with storylines. Where could we go from here?

THE ROAD TO MAGIC

Those Seattle gamers who'd designed a game just for fun years before decided, in 1990, to start Wizards of the Coast for real as a full-fledged game manufacturer. Peter and Cathleen Adkison, Lisa Lowe, and Ken McGlothlen signed up to be the executive officers when the company was incorporated on Dec. 17 of that year.

The first offices were in basement of Peter Adkison, then a systems analyst with Boeing. The initial mission was the April 1992 launch of a new role-playing system, *The Primal Order,* which gave players of other games rules to "translate" their games to the new system. One of the makers of those other games, Palladium Books, didn't like that very much, and sued — something which could've brought an early end to the company.

But other forces were converging. After marketing guru Lisa Stevens joined Wizards of the Coast from White Wolf in 1991, Wizards also picked up the *Talislanta* role-playing line. And through a friend on the Internet, Adkison met Richard Garfield, then a doctoral student in combinatorial math (which sounds awfully hard). Garfield and friend Mike Davis had come up with a board game in 1983, *RoboRally*, and needed a manufacturer.

But Wizards of the Coast didn't yet have the resources to produce the high-end game, so in their August 1991 meeting Adkison challenged Garfield to come up with an intermediate product — a smaller one, to generate some cash flow before releasing *RoboRally*. Garfield was asked to design a game requiring minimal equipment and 15 to 20 minutes to play.

Wizards behind the curtain:
Peter Adkison, ***Lisa Stevens***,
*and **Richard Garfield** (below).*

What Garfield came up with in December 1991 was **Mana Flash**, the prototype for **Magic: The Gathering**. Playtest cards were as playtest cards usually are — really rough approximations of actual cards, just to see if the game worked.

It *did* work… and in April 1993, Garfield set up Garfield Games to attract funding to the project. It was still intended to be a Wizards of the Coast product, but this gave Garfield, by this time a math professor at Walla Walla's Whitman College, a bigger share of the company — and a better chance at finding investors, since the Palladium suit with Wizards hadn't been settled.

Funding found, in May the game was renamed **Magic** and the word began to spread. The first ad appeared on the back of *Cryptych*, a fantasy and pop culture magazine by Joanne White, along with Adkison's description of the game: "At first glance, it's not clear whether **Magic** is a fantasy-based card game or a series of fantasy trading cards.

That's because it's both. It's a game, but the cards are produced in a 'collectible' format: no given card is ever reprinted, each card has a unique name, and some cards are more common than others. Certain very rare cards are especially powerful within the game." Adkison spoke of the adaptability of the system to other genres, noting that they were working on card games for White Wolf's *Vampire* and *Werewolf*. "Eventually, Wizards of the Coast would like to cover every genre, including science fiction, horror, and historical. Who knows, maybe WotC will even do a trading card game based on baseball!"

Wizards of the Coast ordered the first printing from Carta Mundi, a Belgian printer of quality trading cards, to arrive in time for the Origins game convention in Ft. Worth, Texas. over the Fourth of July weekend. The night before the event, Joanne White learned to play from Adkison and was amazed by the game — and so were all the distributors that tried out *Magic* over the next few days of the convention. Those demonstrations literally changed lives. Within months, White would be publishing *Scrye*, a magazine devoted to this new kind of card game — and the distributors would be begging Wizards of the Coast to ship them as much *Magic* as possible. They knew they could sell it.

And sell it they did. With sales starting in August, the first shipments arrived in waves: 600,000 *Alpha* version cards, then 1.8 million more *Alpha* cards, then 7.6 million *Beta* version cards. The 10 million cards, which Wizards of the Coast expected to last six months, were gone in six weeks.

With its own tournament league starting up, nothing could stop *Magic* — or so it seemed. Disaster was averted in October 1993, when *Arabian Nights*, the first expansion, was about to go to press — in a version that few today would find familiar. Wizards of the Coast had initially decided to print each expansion set with different colored backs — pink, in the case of *Arabian Nights*. Players could strip out cards from certain expansions that way, or so the theory went. Carta Mundi was about to start printing when Lisa Stevens took a call from a retailer who put customer after customer on the phone to say that, no, this was a *terrible* idea that would stunt the game. Convinced, Stevens sold Adkison and Garfield on the view — and hurriedly, a scimitar image was pulled from *Talislanta* and faxed to Belgium to be added to the cards' black plate.

And so the expansion symbol was born — and a blow to the early vitality of the embryonic game was narrowly averted. You can still see the pink card back on the *Arabian Nights* box, if you can afford one.

What's that? Yes, cards were skyrocketing in price. The gaming world would never be the same...

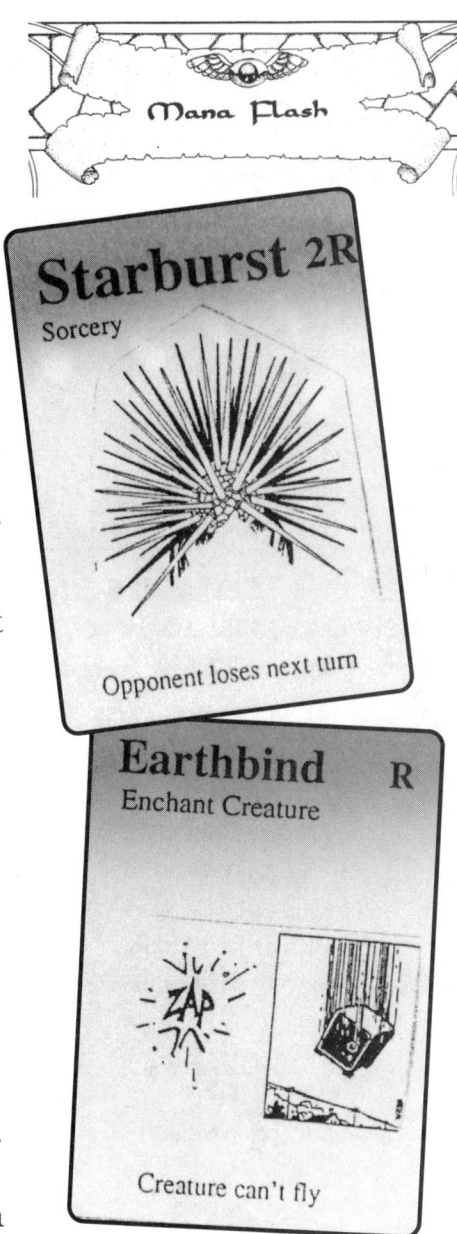

1994: "CRACK FOR GAMERS"

The above off-color reference was, by early 1994, an industry buzzword for **Magic**. So was "a license to print money." Would that only Carta Mundi had been able to print any faster!

"**Magic** is hot! We can't keep it in the store!" said Steve Sorvo of Oak Leaf Comics, Mason City, Iowa in February. "We can't get it in the store!"

At the Game Manufacturers Association trade show in New Orleans March 28, the new concept in gaming was the hot topic. Several companies announced that they, too, would get into the act. *Dungeons & Dragons* maker TSR hurried its own entry, **Spellfire**, into production, and it made it out in June as the second CCG.

Many bought it, but most *really* wanted something else: more **Magic**. The third expansion, **Legends**, was so hot it melted through the store counters. It might as well have: It was gone in an instant wherever it appeared – and where it did appear, it soon went for hundreds of dollars a box.

It was almost impossible for anyone to get **Magic**, leaving raw nerves between both customers and retailers and between retailers and their distributors. Many retailers, trying to get around the allocation mechanisms, as distributors portioned out their meager shares of scarce product, inflated their orders by enormous amounts in the hopes of getting more **Magic**.

Unfortunately for them, Wizards of the Coast finally caught up.

On November 15, Wizards of the Coast shipped **Fallen Empires**, the **Magic** set with the largest print run ever. It was bad timing all around. This was also when **Magic** made its break into mass market stores, with computer shops stocking plenty of **Fallen Empires**. Adding to the store traffic jam, that week Decipher released the **Star Trek Customizable Card Game**, coinciding with the release of *Star Trek: Generations*.

When the low-powered and over-printed **Fallen Empires** laid an egg with players, chaos followed. Retailers who'd ordered hundreds of boxes, expecting dozens, got hundreds — and soon the set was being deeply discounted all over the place. Distributors appealed to Wizards of the Coast, which allowed retailers to cancel unshipped portions of their orders, even though it had made warnings beforehand that the product might actually be there this time.

It was a hard, expensive lesson in CCG economics for all. But not the last one...

1995: GLUT AND GLORY

As happens when you have a hit, Wizards had made a lot of corporate friends: 1995 saw *Magic* comics from Acclaim, and *Magic* novels had begun from HarperCollins. A goodly chunk of those sold just to people looking to get the cards offered, but no matter: It was making *Magic* something new: a *brand*.

And being heard above the (card) pack was meaning more and more. At the GAMA Trade Show in March, every third product announced was a CCG. It wasn't just other game firms this time. Sportscard makers, who had endured a slump in sales of "non-sports" cards after the comics market peaked in 1993, found partners in many game designers. The biggest buzz at GAMA surrounded Donruss' announcement of an *X-Files* CCG, but games would also be forthcoming from card makers Upper Deck, Playoff, Fleer, FPG, Comic Images, and Topps.

The CCG market could simply no longer be ignored. In June, **Comics Retailer**, trade magazine for the comics industry, expanded its readership and coverage to become the trade magazine for the games industry, as well. It was an industry more than a little concerned about the pace of new releases. "There are *way* too many CCGs coming out," warned retailer John Waite of Gorilla Bob's in Spokane, Wash., that month. "Beware the fall!"

Capital City Distribution offered *32* new CCG products in its August catalog. Among those that shipped, *nine* new basic sets: *Banemaster, Battlelords, Gridiron Fantasy Football, Highlander, Overpower, Quest for the Grail, Star Quest, WildStorms*, and *Wing Commander*.

Starting just after Gen Con, retailers noticed a definite lull in CCG sales. And CCGs they *knew* they could sell weren't there yet. "Decipher is really blowing it by not getting the **Star Wars** CCG out before Christmas," said Clayton Ikler of Lee's Comics, Palo Alto, Calif. in November. Decipher did beat Christmas, but well after the best shopping days were past.

Too much growth, too quickly took its toll on Wizards of the Coast, which, on Dec. 7, announced a major downsizing. The "consolidation," nearly five years after the firm's incorporation, eliminated its role-playing game department, outsourced the novels, and cut more than 30 jobs.

"I'm swimming in *Magic* inventory," said retailer Mark Welch of Comic Cubicle of Williamsburg, Va. in late December. "But I refuse to dump and completely ruin the market like the convention clowns did with the sports card and comics markets."

It would take that kind of discipline from everyone in the business to keep the CCG hobby from dying young.

38 new games • **85** new releases

JANUARY
Doomtrooper: Limited
Wyvern: Premiere Limited

FEBRUARY
On the Edge: The Cut-Ups Project

MARCH
Blood Wars
Blood Wars: Rebels & Reinforcements
Doomtrooper: Unlimited
Illuminati: Unlimited
Wyvern: Limited

APRIL
Galactic Empires: New Empires
Illuminati: One With Everything
Magic: The Gathering: Fourth Edition
Star of the Guardians: Limited
Towers in Time: Limited

MAY
Dixie: Shiloh
Doomtrooper: Inquisition
Echelons of Fire: First Edition
Echelons of Fury: First Edition
On the Edge: Shadows
Rage: Limited
Sim City: Limited
Spellfire: Artifacts
Ultimate Combat: Limited

JUNE
Blood Wars: Factols & Factions
Magic: The Gathering: Ice Age
Shadowfist: Limited
Super Deck!: Slim Decks

JULY
Dixie: Gettysburg
Galactic Empires: Powers of the Mind
Hyborian Gates
Power Cardz: First Strike
Rage: Unlimited
Redemption: Limited
Super Nova: First Edition
Tempest of the Gods: Limited

AUGUST
Banemaster: The Adventure
Battlelords: Limited
Blood Wars: Powers & Proxies
Doomtrooper: Warzone
Galactic Empires: Time Gates
Gridiron Fantasy Football
Highlander: Series Edition
Illuminati: New World Order: Assassins
On the Edge: Arcana
OverPower: Marvel Limited
Quest for the Grail: Preview
Shadowfist: Netherworld
Star Quest: The Regency Wars
Vampire: The Eternal Struggle: Unlimited
Wildstorms: Limited
Wing Commander: Limited

SEPTEMBER
Guardians: Limited
Heresy: Kingdom Come Limited
Magic: Chronicles
One-on-One Hockey Challenge: Premiere
Power Cardz: Spawn
Rage: The Umbra
Spellfire: Powers
Ultimate Combat: Ancient Fighting Arts of China

OCTOBER
Doomtrooper: Mortificator
Echelons of Fire: Second Edition
Echelons of Fury: Second Edition
Red Zone: Premiere
Shadowfist: Standard
Spellfire: Third Edition
Top of the Order
Wyvern: Phoenix

NOVEMBER
Crow: Limited
Galactic Empires: Advanced Technologies
Galactic Empires: Universe Edition
Guardians: Dagger Isle
James Bond 007: Goldeneye
Kult: Limited
Legend of the Five Rings: Imperial Edition
Magic: Fallen Empires
Star Trek: Alternate Universe
Vampire: The Eternal Struggle: Dark Sovereigns

DECEMBER
Eagles: Waterloo
Echelons of Fire: Pacific Campaign
Middle-earth: The Wizards Limited
Quest for the Grail: Limited
Rage: The Wyrm
Red Zone: 1995 Expansion Teams
Ruinsworld: Limited
Spellfire: Underdark
Star Wars: Premiere Limited

1996: AFTER THE PARTY

17 new games • **70** new releases

The year didn't open much rosier for the CCG trade, as the winter's *Magic* product, *Homelands*, opened to reviews as the worst expansion in the game's history. Games that had launched in the 1995 frenzy put out releases, only to find their audiences getting smaller with each "expansion" rather than larger. Discussions of the "product life cycle" circulated, and many wondered if the CCG wasn't simply a fad whose day was done.

But others took lessons. Producing and selling CCGs to collectors was one thing, but finding *players* was everything. Releases such as factory sets and late 1995's *Magic: Chronicles* were player-friendly, even if they did drive speculators out of the market. Wizards of the Coast, in fact, fielded complaints about the effects of *Chronicles* from some dealers in the secondary market. "We call them trading-card games, not collectible card games," said Wizards' Lisa Stevens in April 1996. "We've never said that they are collectible. It's not that we don't realize what they are, it's just that collectability is not what we want to emphasize. We've taken the stand that gameplay is what's important."

As *Magic* gameplay went, so went the CCG world. So when *Alliances* appeared in June to spectacular reviews and sales, it pumped some needed life into the hobby. Sales weren't going to be at the lofty levels of 1994, it became apparent, but neither did many retailers really want them to be.

Wizards took further steps to ensure that CCGs were not just collected, but actively played, with the institution of the Arena League. On Aug. 2, tournament promoters staged simultaneous inaugural events in 10 U.S. cities. The regular events and ratings for players resembled what had long existed for the U.S. Chess Federation, and brought *Magic* closer to what Peter Adkison said he hoped it would become: "an intellectual sport."

While things were brightening somewhat for the CCG field, serious trouble was developing in Lake Geneva, Wis., home of TSR. The previous fall, having been unable to duplicate Wizards' success with *Magic*, TSR had bet the farm on *Dragon Dice*, a collectible dice game that opened to decent reviews. Unfortunately, it was hideously expensive to produce — and when sales leveled off for the game, TSR was stuck with boatloads of dice still on the way to the States. Financial problems in other areas of its business came to a head in December — and the constant flow of products from what had been the industry leader since the 1970s suddenly, and mysteriously, stopped...

1997: DAVID BUYS GOLIATH

With nothing coming from TSR, life still went on at game shops. Those who had TSR as their largest supplier noticed that, yes, products from other companies, CCGs included, were keeping their doors open. And with 20 years to build up *Dungeons & Dragons* product on their shelves, some retailers could easily handle a lapse in the role-playing side of things.

The gaming world became aware of shuttle diplomacy between Seattle and Lake Geneva, and on Apr. 10, Wizards of the Coast — the largest game manufacturer as of 1995 — announced it was buying the longtime leader. By June, the deal was done and *Dungeons & Dragons* moved under the Wizards imprint, giving Adkison and company the top-selling role-playing line they'd long been hoping to invent on their own. *Dragon Dice* and *Spellfire* were not invited to this resurrection, however.

Meanwhile, CCGs releases flowed at a slower pace than in recent years, with only seven new systems hitting the shelves. "The CCG market has finally undergone its anticipated transformation into a steady business," said gaming analyst Steve Peterson after attending the 1997 GAMA Trade Show. "The collecting madness has passed."

Decipher followed Wizards' Arena success by introducing its own sanctioned tournament program for **Star Wars** players in the spring. Wizards of the Coast opened a 32,000-square-foot Game Center in Seattle's university district May 16, a "temple to gaming" with room for 270 players and — of concern to many retailers — its own game shop. More Wizards stores would follow. And Five Rings Publishing, which had made inroads with **Legend of the Five Rings**, was bought by Wizards June 26.

By September, Wizards accounted for two-thirds of all CCG sales. Competitors grew more concerned Sept. 2 when Wizards was awarded Patent #5,662,332 for a "trading-card game method of play." It came as a surprise, despite the fact that every **Magic** release since the June 22, 1994, filing read "patent pending." Perhaps no one expected a patent to be awarded with so many CCGs on the market — and many perceived the move to be an attempt to close the barn door way too late. Indeed, **Spellfire** had shipped two days before Wizards' filing. Resentment grew on Oct. 14, when Wizards announced its plans to extract royalties from other CCG makers.

But only **Imajica**'s HarperPrism ever publicly announced it would meet Wizards' terms. To this day, there have been no public reports of Wizards taking legal action against anyone for refusing to pay royalties — or of anyone mounting a legal challenge to the patent.

7 new games • **54** new releases

JANUARY
Ani-Mayhem: Set 1
Galactic Empires: Galactic Invaders
Galactic Empires: Invaders
Mythos: Dreamlands Limited
Star Trek The Card Game: Starfleet Maneuvers
Wyvern: Kingdom

FEBRUARY
BattleTech: Unlimited
Magic: Visions
OverPower: DC JLA
OverPower: Marvel IQ

MARCH
Doomtrooper: Paradise Lost
Legend of the Five Rings: Crimson & Jade
Magic: Fifth Edition

APRIL
BattleTech: Counterstrike
Dark Eden: Limited
Galactic Empires: Allied Forces
Star Trek: First Anthology
Star Wars: Dagobah

MAY
Middle-earth: The Lidless Eye
OverPower: Marvel Monumental
Star Wars: First Anthology
Wildstorms: Legends

JUNE
Legend of the Five Rings: Obsidian Edition
Magic: Portal
Magic: Weatherlight
X-Files: The Truth is Out There

JULY
Kult: Inferno
Redemption: Women of the Bible
Star Trek: Fajo Collection
X-Files: 101361

AUGUST
Aliens/Predator
BattleTech: Mercenaries
Imajica: Limited
Legend of the Five Rings: Time of the Void
Middle-earth: Against the Shadow
Shadowrun: Limited
Spellfire: Dungeons!

SEPTEMBER
Ani-Mayhem: Dragonball Z
Magic: 1997 World Championship Decks
Warlords: Limited

OCTOBER
Dune: Eye of the Storm
Magic: Tempest
Star Wars: Cloud City
OverPower: Marvel Classic

NOVEMBER
Babylon 5: Campaign Set
Babylon 5: Premier
BattleTech: Mechwarrior
Legend of the Five Rings: Scorpion Clan Coup 1-3
Middle-earth: The White Hand
Mythos: New Aeon

DECEMBER
Star Trek: First Contact
Wildstorms: Best of Wildstorms

1998: DECK DROUGHT?

4 new games • **62** new releases

Five years into the life of CCGs, interest seemed to have levelled off. In February, every other CCG sold by game retailers was *Magic* — and there wasn't even a new release out. And when a new *Magic* release did hit, like March's *Stronghold*, it sucked all the air out of sales of other CCGs like an explosion in a coal mine.

This left little room for competition. Indeed, the only company that put out a new CCG in 1998 was Wizards of the Coast.

The number of new CCG releases for the year, 62, is deceptive due to the "Rolling Thunder" release program for products coming from Wizards' Five Rings division. *Doomtown*, *Dune*, *Legend of the Burning Sands*, *Legend of the Five Rings*, and *Rage* all spread "story-line" sets across a series of monthly "episodes," actually micro-expansions whose boosters were packaged with starters from the storyline's basic set. "Rolling Thunder" added volume to a year that otherwise would have seen only 39 traditional releases, the lowest number since 1994. "Rolling Thunder" also turned a number of gamers off, as it virtually guaranteed that the audience for the last episode would be smaller than for the first and it put many unnecessary starter decks on the market.

People were still clearly interested in gaming. August's Gen Con attracted a record 20,000 people. And the year found retailers focusing more than ever on the importance of in-store gaming to the CCG market. Two out of every three game and comic-book stores surveyed said they had space set aside for in-store CCG play.

In October, when CCG sales had, in past years, dipped, Wizards began the Urza's Cycle for *Magic*, an incredibly powerful — some said *too* powerful — set of releases which injected new life into the tournament scene.

Still, new bodies were needed. Of the four new games introduced in 1998, three belonged to the ARC System, designed by Wizards as an easy-to-learn entry point into CCGs. If *C•23*, *Hercules*, and *Xena* failed to set the world on fire, it may well been an indication that anyone already in game stores was either past that level or not interested at all. Clearly, a break-out property was needed to drag new people into gaming. But what?

At the end of 1998, Wizards of the Coast solicited to retailers a CCG for beginners based on *Pokémon*, a cartoon that had made news in the States first after giving children seizures in Japan. Most copies were earmarked for the mass market. After all, what game store would want something about an electric mouse...?

1999: DAY OF THE ELECTRIC MOUSE

Everyone *thought* 1999 would be all *Star Wars: Episode I*. **Pokémon** was regarded as a modest attempt to find more success than the Arc System games had in getting new players to try CCGs.

What Wizards of the Coast got was something else — the youth pop-cultural fad of the year. Beanie Babies, Mighty Morphin' Power Rangers, Teenage Mutant Ninja Turtles: All had their day on *every* kid's want list, and it happened that, when Pokémon's turn came, CCG cards were the most affordable way for kids to buy in.

And buy they did. In the summer of 1999, *Pokémon* became the first and only CCG to outsell **Magic**. It also brought CCGs out of the hobby shops and firmly into the mainstream. At the height of its popularity, there were references to it on the network news and late-night TV. Large department chains such as Wal-Mart and Toys 'R' Us started selling everything Pokémon, and, helped by a feature film, it dominated the 1999 Christmas season.

Wizards wasn't prepared — and game retailers, who'd passed on the kiddie game when it was first offered, grew irate when they couldn't get more. Since it had never been *meant* for the hobby, most of it was headed to the mass market, causing resentment toward Wizards among game retailers. Wizards exacerbated the situation when, in May 1999, it bought the Game Keeper chain of mall stores, causing retailers to allege preferential treatment in the availability of **Pokémon** to these stores.

Game stores still did *very* well for themselves, splitting at least $100 million from **Pokémon** alone — if the cards all sold at suggested retail price, which very few did!

Sales this big didn't go unnoticed on Wall Street. On Sept. 9 (just as this author's son was being born), Hasbro, which had earlier purchased game industry icon Avalon Hill, bought the firm started in Peter Adkison's basement for an eye-bulging $325 million. Adkison was kept on in charge of Wizards of the Coast, and a "hands-off" policy on behalf of the company's new corporate masters was intimated. Whether that would be temporary or permanent remained to be seen, but players quickly imagined what sorts of things Hasbro might be able to do for Wizards of the Coast. *Magic Monopoly?* Why not?

The CCG world had changed yet again. Even here — on Nov. 15, Krause Publications, publisher of the soon-to-be-renamed **Comics & Games Retailer**, bought **Scrye** magazine from Joanne White, naming John Jackson Miller and Joyce Greenholdt its editor and managing editor. And a big question remained: How many "Pokékids" were really playing CCGs — and how many could we teach?

6 new games • **44** new releases

JANUARY
Legend of the Five Rings: Dark Journey Home
Pokémon: 1st Edition
Pokémon: Unlimited Edition
Rage: Snake Eyes: Phase 6

MARCH
Aliens/Predator: Alien Resurrection
Doomtown: Pine Box
Highlander: The Four Horsemen
Magic: Urza's Legacy
Rage: Snake Eyes: Equinox

APRIL
Magic: Classic (6th Edition)
Star Wars: Endor

MAY
Young Jedi: Menace of Darth Maul
Legend of the Five Rings: Pearl Edition

JUNE
Doomtown: Mouth of Hell
Doomtown: Shootout at High Noon
Legend of the Five Rings: Honor Bound
Legend: Siege at Sleeping Mountain
Magic: Urza's Destiny
Redemption: The Warriors

JULY
Pokémon: Jungle 1st Edition
Pokémon: Jungle Unlimited

AUGUST
7th Sea: No Quarter
Babylon 5: Psi-Corps
Star Trek: Blaze of Glory
Tomb Raider: Premiere

SEPTEMBER
Doomtown: Reaping of Souls
Magic: 1999 World Championship Decks

OCTOBER
Magic: Mercadian Masques
Star Wars: Enhanced Cloud City
Young Jedi: Jedi Council

NOVEMBER
Babylon 5: Severed Dreams
Doomtown: Revelations
Legend of the Five Rings: Ambition's Debt
Magic: Battle Royale
Netrunner: Classic
Pokémon: Fossil 1st Edition
Pokémon: Fossil Unlimited

DECEMBER
7th Sea: Strange Vistas
Austin Powers
Star Trek: Rules of Acquisition
Star Trek: Second Anthology
Star Wars: Enhanced Jabba's Palace
Tomb Raider: Slippery When Wet
Wheel of Time: Premiere

2000: CCGs Go 3-D!

19 new games • **56** new releases

Pokémon "the fad" peaked in April, and most of the gaming hobby was prepared for it. In fact, a wave of "follow-on" games had begun to arrive in shops from manufacturers hoping to keep those players around.

A Poké-Glut was feared, but to veterans of 1995, the situation didn't seem as dire. First, there weren't nearly as many new releases: Around half as many new systems were introduced in 2000 as in 1995.

Also, the level of risk seemed lower, thanks to experience. Shops in 1995 didn't know what new CCGs people would want and ordered blindly, fearing they'd get caught without the next big thing. Shops in 2000 had a better idea what would sell, and though they still didn't like to be caught without — witness **Pokémon** — all their eggs weren't in the CCG basket. A resurgence in role-playing from *Dungeons & Dragons Third Edition* saw to that.

Further, the success of a CCG no longer seemed to depend on winning every gamer. **Wheel of Time** and **Star Trek** kept going by targeting niches of fanatical players willing to spend a *lot*. Wizards of the Coast looked for new gamers in sportscard shops with its first sports CCG, **MLB Showdown**. And even the sportscard companies who had dabbled in CCGs and ran in 1995 now looked at the market as something that might endure. Upper Deck, for example, followed up 2000's **Digimon** with two more games — and then announced four more.

New hopes were kindled with the Gen Con introduction by Wiz Kids of **Mage Knight Rebellion**, a collectible miniatures game. *(See page 508.)* A CCG in 3-D form, it had only *begun* to realize its potential by the end of 2000.

But 2000 ended on a sour note. Gamers knew *Pokémon* couldn't stay white-hot, but investors often have the collective foresight of Mr. Magoo. Hasbro, its stock bloodied in the bear market, ended its "hands-off" period with Wizards and sold off its interactive division, which had been at work with Richard Garfield on new ways to play online. Peter Adkison responded Dec. 14 with his resignation. Hasbro also cut more than 100 jobs from Wizards. Gone was Wizards' CCG magazine, as well as veteran Lisa Stevens — and **Legend of the Five Rings** was put up for sale. Early the next year, Wizards would close its centerpiece "temple to gaming," admitting that, wondrous as it was, it was unprofitable on almost every level.

The changes came nearly five years after Wizards' previous layoffs and 10 years after its founding. But considering the enormous new growth of the company following the 1995 cuts, few are willing to bet against the company scaling ever new heights in the future.

2001: THE ODYSSEY CONTINUES

Not quite three quarters of a decade had passed since those first long boxes of **Magic Alpha** cards had shipped to the waiting Wizards of the Coast team at the Origins convention in Ft. Worth when a pair of CCG milestones passed.

If you don't count **Boy Crazy** and **Flights of Fantasy** (and some don't), the 100th different CCG shipped in December 2000. It was **Age of Empires II**. And the 400th release with different cards may well have been **Young Jedi: Duel of the Fates**, which shipped right before press time. (That's a tougher one to count, as there are semi-expansions that could be added or dropped from anyone's count.)

Either way, they're out there. Since the presses first ran at Carta Mundi, more than 75,000 different CCG cards have been designed and printed. That's 10,000 different cards a year being added to an ever-more-impressive gaming library. And while we're loathe to estimate, the total number of cards printed is well into the several billions. At three cards a millimeter, it's a deck 100 miles high. And growing.

But these aren't the most important statistics. Count, rather, the number of people who've played CCGs. The number of hours of enjoyment given, of friends made, of imaginations stoked. We can't count them ourselves, so we've done the next best thing. We've provided a volume that reviews all those four-hundred plus releases and lists all those 75,000-plus cards. It's our hope we can save you enough time to put toward more important things. Like playing games!

Enough talk. Deal the cards!

A MATTER OF TIMELINES

We have tried to track down the release dates and product configurations for every product in this book. In most cases, we had the information first-hand. Where we could, we contacted the manufacturer for further infomation. But in many cases the manufacturer was no longer still around.

In these cases, we looked at past issues of **Scrye** and **Comics & Games Retailer** to see when market reports began showing up for those games — and derived release dates from there.

We have also looked at distributor catalogs and the *Games Quarterly Catalog* for when those products were solicited. We have tended to treat some of this information with a grain of salt — because many, many products missed their announced ship dates and not every distributor got games at the same time — but information in these places about product configuration (number of boosters in a box, etc.) has tended to be reasonably accurate.

It is entirely possible that some of these reports may be off by a month or two, but we believe we're in the right year for everything. There will certainly be people who remember seeing a game before a date in this volume, and if so, we'd like to hear from you. In general, we've looked for dates when games became available for sale in stores — and not available for sneak previews at conventions.

And while we've tried very hard and do believe that every single major CCG release in English appears in these pages, we have no doubt that we may have missed a few of the various configurations the CCGs were sold in. Just now we've remembered that **On the Edge** later came in something called a "Burger Box." We imagine we'll be doing that for months after this book comes out. Again, if you have something to add, please let us know.

Using this guide...
to learn about CCGs so you won't look goofy at the game store

What's a collectible card game?

A collectible card game is a card game in which each player uses his own deck using cards that are mostly sold in random assortments.

Magic: The Gathering was the first. The novelty of the game is both in its mechanics and its method of availability: Each player builds his own deck of wizard's spells from a wide selection of cards. Then, in "duels" with opponents, the player learns the weaknesses of his deck and chooses different cards to work with before entering another game.

Those cards can be acquired by trading with other players, or buying them from retailers in starter decks (usually containing 60 cards and rules) and booster packs (usually containing from 8 to 15 cards). The assortment of cards is mostly random, with cards vital to play being the most common (or fixed), more powerful cards being uncommon or rare. Later, special foil cards came along to look pretty.

That's is! Now you've got all the definitions you need to recognize a "CCG" when you see one. Just about all of the many, many others that followed conformed to the above description.

*At **Scrye** magazine, we've developed a few questions we use to determine what qualifies as a "collectible card game":*

The CCG test

- Are the game cards sold in booster packs, starter decks, or both?

- As sold by the manufacturer, it impossible to be sure of getting every card by making make only a small number of purchases of the base product?

- Does every player play with his own deck, using cards of his choice?

- Does the manufacturer market it as a "collectible card game"?

For this book, we included all games for which the answers to all four questions at lower left is "yes." There are a few exceptions, where only three out of the four conditions was met, which we included in the main section of the book. Most of the games which only met two of the criteria we have listed in **Appendix C: Semi-CCGs**.

Looking more closely at the questions:

• Are the game cards sold in booster packs, starter decks, or both?

Magic was initially sold in starter decks and booster packs, and that remains the way that most CCGs are marketed. There have been a few CCG products that have been sold in boxed sets — *Star Wars* and *Magic* beginners sets, mainly — but the principal point of entry into the game is through the starters and boosters.

We hedge on requiring both starters and boosters to allow a few

exceptions which clearly otherwise fit the CCG model. There were no boosters for **Eagles** and no starters for **The Crow**, but each fit the other three definitions perfectly: Their cards were randomly inserted, each player has his own deck, and they were both clearly marketed as CCGs.

• As presented by the manufacturer, is it impossible to be sure of getting every card by making a small number of purchases of the base product?

Before retailers began building sets of their own, getting a complete set of *Magic* in the beginning required buying a huge number of starter decks and booster packs — and there was no assurance you could *ever* complete the set. Wizards of the Coast would later offer a complete *Magic Collector's Edition*, but this was never intended — and never treated — as the base product, as the entry point to the game.

This random element is absolutely essential to driving the collectible dynamic, the thing that drove players to trade cards from *Magic* straight through to *Pokémon*. Sportscards had already established a tradition and mechanism for selling random parts of a set of cards, and CCGs readily adapted it. It's of note that

the lawyer who unsuccessfully sued Wizards of the Coast for selling random *Pokémon* cards had previously unsuccessfully sued sportscard companies for making it hard to get all the good players in a small number of purchases.

It's worth re-emphasizing that random insertion of powerful cards is not, at heart, a marketing ploy, even though it has been used as such by some. There has to be some way of controlling the usage of really powerful cards, or the game collapses as a competitive activity. Manufacturers can do this by rule or by tournament regulation, but it's often more effective to do it by controlling supply.

Games which aren't CCGs on this score include buy-one-get-them-all sets like *Age of Heroes* and *Anime Madness*. A game which is currently on the borderline is **Calorie Kids**. It was sold in starter decks, each player must have his own deck, and its makers clearly marketed it as a CCG. But the starter decks have fixed assortments of cards, such that buying the differently named theme decks gets

you the entire card set. There's nothing there to drive collectible activity. At press time, the maker was still planning to put out random booster packs. If that happens, there won't be any question that the game fits the definition. If not, then it'll be off to the "almost" section.

• Does every player play with his own deck, using cards of his choice?

Here's the burst of design genius in *Magic*. The game gave players the freedom to personalize, to pick a strategy that suited them. To develop that strategy, then to abandon it when it got boring. Compared with other games — and the relatively limited number of potential strategies, CCGs are a tactician's dream (or nightmare)! Every game becomes an experiment.

About the only concept previously close in card game form were rotisserie sports games such as *Strat-O-Matic* and Avalon Hill's *Statis Pro* games, which had cards for players on sports teams. You could mix and match teams if you wanted to, but there really wasn't any random element in terms of being able to get the cards. If you bought *Statis Pro Basketball* in 1988, you got Michael Jordan. No risk.

We've found this to be the trickiest question when it comes to looking at games on the borderline. We chose to include in the main section of this book Heartbreaker's **Super Nova**, in which players play from a common deck. The

game comes only in booster packs, cards are randomly inserted, and it was definitely marketed as a CCG. In fact, it fits the other three requirements so strongly we consider its failure to meet the "separate decks" requirement to be something of a design flaw. The company clearly wanted people to buy cards sold at random — it just forgot that personalizing decks is a competitive activity and requires both players. (Our guess is that Heartbreaker thought that, without starters, groups of players would build the necessary common deck with boosters. Given where the game is now, the strategy didn't work .)

Meanwhile, we don't count as a traditional CCG *Dragon Storm*, where the gamemaster has the deck and players just have a few cards face up, taking the place of items on a role-playing game character sheet. We treat *Dragon Storm* differently from **Super Nova** in part because of the next "test."

• Does the manufacturer market it as a "collectible card game"?

We suppose we shouldn't care what the manufacturer says — a product is what it is. Some manufacturers have produced games they called CCGs, even though they didn't meet all the first three criteria. That generally means we just take a harder look.

We do give some weight to intention. **Flights of Fantasy** and **Boy Crazy** are card games (if marginal ones) sold in random booster packs. **Flights of Fantasy** was advertised as a CCG, and **Boy Crazy** was marketed a collectible card product you can play a game with. That's enough for us: Nothing in our definitions say the game actually has to be viable as a collectible card game. (And we have a number of games in this book that certainly proved they weren't!)

On the other hand, we recall that the makers of *Dragon Storm* went to some effort in the beginning to market its product as a role-playing game with cards, taking some pride even in differentiating it from the zoo of CCGs that

"Trading-card game" versus "collectible card game" versus "customizable card game" versus "expandable card game"...

Spend much time in gaming, and you'll realize that this is a product category *no one can really decide what to call.*

"Trading-card game" is what Wizards of the Coast called the **Magic** product then and now, and it is an accurate description of the product. These are games played with trading cards — or, at least, cards that are sold the same way that trading cards are sold. It's what's on Wizards of the Coast's patent.

The authors of this volume initially preferred this to **"collectible card game,"** since the word "collectible" tended to be loaded with expectations in a world of sportscard and comics shops that had been rocked by booms and busts over things that were supposed to be "collectible." Particularly early on with sportscard retailers new to the product, our fear was that the phrase might mislead them into applying collectible sportscard logic to what was, in fact, a game. Most consumers broke open the packs and played with the cards, anathema to most sportscard dealers. And complete sets weren't nearly as vital — they just wanted the good cards.

So from the earliest days straight through to today, our **Comics & Games Retailer** magazine refers only to "trading-card games." In the meantime, we bought **Scrye** magazine, which already had "Collectible Card Games" in its trademark — and, to be honest, "collectible card game" is the phrase that seems to have won out with the general public. (Just try a Web search to prove it.) So that's the phrase we're going with.

As for other competitors, Decipher calls its own games **"customizable card games,"** and, while it's probably the most descriptive name and not "loaded" at all, it's also got about one too many syllables to trip off the tongue. And "expandable card game" (which **Age of Empires II** seems to have chosen, just to be different) seems to better describe those card games which are complete in one non-random purchase and then can be expanded in another non-random purchase. *Nuclear War* and the original *Illuminati*, with their expansion sets, come to mind.

had been loosed on the market. We were iffy enough on its classification following the "separate deck" test that we were willing to class it apart from the traditional CCGs based on that description. (Later advertising seemed to turn on that score, perhaps as the sales benefits of being included in the CCG universe were made manifest. A booster release, *Kanchaka Campaign*, even came out.)

A final note on definitions: We're not "in charge" of anything but our own books and magazines, and we don't say anything good or bad about a game by declaring it a CCG or not. We simply have to draw some boundaries about what we cover, as a label that covers everything means nothing. As the founder of our publishing company, Chet Krause, says, "The only category that fits everything in any hobby is 'miscellaneous.'"

Gaming is ever-evolving, and we expect our definitions to be subject to change. We should note an

additional new wrinkle on this score: The collectible miniatures game **Mage Knight Rebellion** is marketed identically to a CCG. It's sold in starter packs and booster packs (that are even called that); it's not possible to get all the figures in a small number of purchases (the fiigures are randomly inserted); and everyone has his own army of figures. If the figures weren't three-dimensional, it'd be a CCG for sure. That's why **Scrye** has started to consider the game on equal footing with CCGs and why we've added a **Mage Knight** checklist and price guide as **Appendix A**.

Who knows? In a while we may be bringing you the **Scrye Collectible Miniatures Game Checklist and Price Guide**...

CCG TERMINOLOGY

What does "Scrye" mean?

Scry is a Middle-English word meaning to tell the future. You'll see it in fantasy novels where people talk about using scrying pools and such.

Scrye is Krause Publications' trademark for the leading magazine in the adventure gaming industry. **Scrye** was founded soon after the invention of the collectible card game market, not just to talk about the strategies for the games (though that's a major part), but also to follow the ups and downs of the CCG secondary market.

What does "metagame" mean?

This is a word you will see in several of the essays in this volume. Sometimes called the "tournament environment," the metagame refers to how the universe of cards available for use in a CCG affects the strategies players are choosing. Because CCGs are dynamic — cards coming in through expansions or out due to being banned — certain card combinations come into favor, lose favor, or stop working altogether.

The metagame for any CCG is always changing, and there can even be said to be local metagames — even down to your own house. (If you and your brother only have certain cards in your collections, that's going to affect the strategies you're going to use.)

Scrye remains the first and best magazine for learning the latest about the metagames for **Magic**, **Star Wars**, **Star Trek**, **Pokémon**, and dozens of other CCGs.

What's a "sideboard"?

Sideboards were introduced with early tournaments for **Magic: The Gathering** as a means by which players could filter some additional cards into their decks between games — without going overboard and bringing in a whole suitcase of cards.

A typical tournament might let you bring the deck you plan to play with, plus a "sideboard" of, say, 15 cards that you can dig into between games to fine-tune your deck. Sideboards have strategies all their own — players take care that every card there might help deal with unexpected developments in the local metagame. (See? There's that word.)

Why wouldn't you just put all the cards you might need in the deck you're playing with?

Because you'd look like a rookie, because that's a rookie move in CCGs. Sure, if you hauled around a 200-card **Magic** deck, you'd be sure you had every card you might conceivably need, but the odds that you'd find the exact card you needed when you needed it would be very low.

What are "dead games" and "live games?"

These are phrases used to refer to whether CCG systems are being supported at present by their manufacturers (and, to a lesser extent, by their fans).

A "dead game" is very hard to get into, because no one's out there organizing tournament support or answering questions about rules. And because new releases are so important to the evolving "metagame," when they stop coming out, players stop playing.

The first CCG to be released, **Magic**, is very

much alive. Its manufacturer is still cranking out releases, supporting tournaments, and answering questions.

The second CCG to be released, **Spellfire**, is dead. The last release came out in 1997, when Wizards of the Coast bought its original publisher, TSR, and stopped making additions to the game. There are cells of players keeping it "alive" here and there on websites and at conventions — no game published in the millions of copies is ever *really* gone — but it is, for the moment, dead.

We — and players in general — do not use these terms to demean the systems or their designers. (In fact, there are a lot of great "dead" games.) But the distinction has an important effect on the aftermarket, and it must be made.

A side note: Sometimes when manufacturers stop supporting a game, fans and designers create their own rules and even "virtual expansions" online. We applaud their efforts but continue to regard the question of whether the manufacturer is supporting the game to be basic to the game's health — at least, when we're talking in terms of how much people are looking to pay for cards.

You said *Spellfire* is dead "for the moment." Do games ever come back to "life"?

Sure. All it takes is someone to come back and pick up the game and start supporting it again with new physical releases.

The third CCG released, **Jyhad**, is an example. **Jyhad** was published by Wizards of the Coast, renamed **Vampire**, and passed on to White Wolf, which stopped adding expansions in 1997. **Vampire** was then dead for most intents and purposes. Until CCGs got hot again, and it rose from its coffin in a new release in 2000.

How can you tell that a game has "died"?

It's hard to say. CCG necrology isn't an exact science by any means. But there are some tipoffs.

First, if the manufacturer goes away, as happened with TSR. If there is no clear successor to buy and continue the game (or if, as in **Spellfire**'s case, the new owner shows little interest), that's usually a bad sign.

Second, if the license to produce the game has been lost. Comics character Spawn went from **Spawn PowerCardz** by one company to **WildStorms** by another. Upper Deck's **Racing Challenge** only came out in late 2000, but the company at press time announced that it no longer has the license. That doesn't mean Upper Deck won't be happy to answer your questions about the game, but it does mean that you've probably seen the last of it, unless someone else picks up the license.

Since many game manufacturers stay around forever, there might be a third category added to "dead" and "alive": "dormant," or something like that. There hasn't been a new release for Columbia Games' **Dixie** in years, but Columbia is still around and will be happy to answer any of your questions and sell you cards. And there is nothing to stop them from putting out, say, **Dixie: Chancellorsville** tomorrow and putting the game back into the fully "live" column.

Fully "living" games in early 2001
(with releases or expansions from the last year and which have not been dropped by their manufacturer)

7th Sea	Pokémon
Age of Empires II	Redemption
Babylon 5	Sailor Moon
Calorie Kids	Scooby Doo
Digi-battle	Shadowfist
Dragonball Z	Star Trek
Dredd	Star Wars
Legend of the Five Rings	Terminator
Lost Colony	Vampire
Magi Nation	Wheel of Time
Magic: The Gathering	Wizard in Training
MLB Showdown	WCW Nitro
Monty Python and the Holy Grail	WWF Raw Deal
	X-Men
Pez	Young Jedi

What am I supposed to do with all the useless common cards I've got?

We'd wait a while too see how useless they really are. Every so often something will come along in a gaming system that'll revive interest in certain cards that once seemed worthless.

In the meantime, if you've got heaping gobs of land cards from *Magic*, you probably won't want to stuff them into plastic sleeves. Many of the supply companies that make the sleeves have card-sized boxes available.

If you're *sure* you don't want the cards, you can try to sell them — but note that most other active players of the game usually have the same problem that you've got. We suggest finding a friend who isn't in the game and providing him with a starter deck and your "instant collection" of extra cards. Who knows? You may have just found your next opponent.

Ain't fantasy games supposed to be satanic or dangerous or something?

Good Lord, no!

In the early 1980s, "urban legends" about college kids who played *Dungeons & Dragons* and ran off made the rounds. Televangelists who were already railing against heavy metal music and late-night television added it to their hit lists. A novelist cranked out a potboiler on the subject, *Mazes and Monsters*, and Tom Hanks played the cracked gamer from that story in the movie of the week. *60 Minutes* even sent Ed Bradley out to investigate the claims.

Problem was, there was never any problem. The Industry Watch Committee of the Game Manufacturer's Association has diligently investigated all claims to date of adventure games leading to violent activity. *None* have panned out. Again: *None* have panned out. In the few known criminal cases where games were blamed for anti-social activity, *all* the people eventually recanted. It was just a handy defense.

And concerns with the topics of certain games being "seductive" tend to deflate when people find out the broad range of subjects that games address. Yes, *Magic* features characters who dabble in magic — but the same Deckmaster game system allows those same players to play-act robots in *BattleTech* or computer programmers in *Netrunner*. Gamers have great imaginations and are exceptionally nimble at moving from game setting to game setting.

People who can turn immediately from thinking about aliens in one game to baseball in the next have no problem keeping subject matter in proper perspective. Think about how many times you've played *Monopoly*. Did you run out and become a ruthless slumlord?

OK, bottom line: We do not wish to minimize the concerns of parents interested in what their children are interested in. Some games have themes that are more appropriate for older players, and parents should keep an eye out. Better still, they should try to play a game or two with their kids. It's no coincidence that Hasbro, which advertises "Family Game Nights" on TV also owns Wizards of the Coast, the company that makes *Magic* and *Dungeons & Dragons*.

For more information, check out GAMA's website at *www.gama.org*.

I've bought a CCG and learned it. Now where can I find an opponent?

Often, right where you bought the game. Most game stores have gaming areas and regular "open gaming" times. They also usually run local tournaments for many CCGs on a regular basis. *Scrye* magazine's tournament calendar is the most comprehensive of its kind; check for the stores near you.

Also, fantasy, comic-book, science-fiction, and game conventions, from local shows all the way up to mighty Gen Con, provide wonderful formal and informal settings to play CCGs. The larger shows may be more than a day trip, but there are several that are true "celebrations of gaming" that are not to be missed. Again, check the listings in *Scrye*.

In this book, we try to provide some guidance as to which games have larger ready-made player bases. Check the ratings boxes with the individual game listings.

But often, you don't have to look far to find an opponent. One of the things that made CCGs so popular in the beginning was that, where it took four or five people to play most board games and role-playing games, it only took two people to play a CCG. *Magic*'s earliest TV ads had the slogan, "All you need is a deck — and a friend." And, since almost everyone on the planet has played some kind of card game before, you don't even have to explain character sheets or the funny-shaped dice. They're already trained on the equipment!

Where can I read more about CCGs?

Bet you know what we're going to say. You can find *Scrye* magazine — and our other books about CCGs — at your local game store. If you can't find it there, call our subscription department at (800) 258-0929. (Subscription calls only, please — sorry, but we can't answer your CCG questions at this number.)

Or visit us at *www.krause.com!*

Using this guide...
to ORGANIZE your collection and keep from drowning in a sea of cards

FINDING THINGS

Why do you list cards in alphabetical order when some cards have numbers?

To help you find them.

No, seriously. In all cases, we tried to put ourselves in the position of someone playing a game and searching for a specific card. Nobody ever takes a break between **Magic** games and says. "Man, I need to grab a copy of card #28 from **Nemesis**." No, they go looking for Air Bladder. (OK, maybe nobody ever goes looking for Air Bladder. It's gross. But you get the general idea.

But wait a minute. Here's a set over here where you listed them by number!

Alphabetical order is the rule — except when it isn't. Simple enough, huh?

There are games such as **Dixie** where the card names are such that no one in their right mind would resort to alphabetization when storing their cards. **Dixie: Shiloh**'s first four cards alphabetically are 1st Arkansas, 1st Florida Bn., and two different cards named 1st IL Lt. (Art.) — and the set runs through nearly 400 cards with numbers and slight differentiations in names. We don't imagine anyone storing these cards althabetically, when the manufacturer has so kindly provided card numbers.

Do you always treat cards with numbers in their names that way?

Only if the set has actual card numbering. Otherwise, we sort cards with numbers in their names to the top, in numerical order. That's how computers do things.

That's also why the first

game listed in this book is **7th Sea**. If it were called **Seventh Sea**, we'd list it under "S."

I thought *Magic* cards with card numbers are already in alphabetical order. Why are you jumbling them up?

We're not — we just don't think that the way they've sorted them is the way that players search for cards.

Wizards of the Coast numbers its cards alphabetically, *within colors*. They'll go from A-Z in white, then blue, then black, then red, then green — and keep on numbering. The problem with that, as we see it, is that, when the player digs out the **Magic: Prophecy** notebook looking for, say, Rhystic Study, he's got to remember that the card is blue. The Rhystics are spread across several colors, and some people have trouble keeping them straight. So it's better if all the Rhystics are in one place — with the Rs.

Clearly, there are pluses and minuses. Someone sorting by this book is not going to be able to see all the blue cards from a set in one place. On the other hand, this book is going to be more easily usable to the novice. If you're at the store and Joe Retailer's non-gaming pal is working the register, you've got a reasonable chance he or she will be able to find a price in this book for a card that's not in front of them.

There's also the small matter of savings *to you*. By listing a set straight from start to finish alphabetically and not subdividing it, we probably save you a nine-pocket page or two. Most players who *do* sort sets by color or card type have found that the subsets don't break down in nines and, more often than not, they're left with that one awful page with one or two cards in it before the next subset begins.

STORAGE

What are these little numbers about in the card lists?

They're the savior to anyone who's ever had to store a trading card set. *Any* kind of trading-card set.

Back in the days when trading cards meant just sports cards or movie cards, putting them in nine-pocket sleeves meant getting very good at your nine-times tables. A card-sorting pro quickly learns that card #53 is obvi-

> You will need
> **20**
> nine-pocket pages to store this set.
> (10 doubled up)

ously going to be the eighth card on sleeve six.

Trouble is, that gets complicated (for most of us) when a set goes out beyond a couple of hundred cards — and many sports card sets do. It gets worse when it's hard to find the number on the card.

Collectible card games made the nightmare even worse. Until a few years ago, almost all of them had no numbering at all — only names. You can imagine people trying to sort a 350-card baseball set using alphabetical order — well, that was the challenge CCGs posed. It was a natural oversight: Game designers expected people to *play* their card games and not slip them away into notebooks. But they also never envisioned that there would be more than 70,000 CCG cards floating around in a few years — or that the **Magic** player would have to contend with a possible collection of more than 7,000 different cards in less than a decade!

What we've done is had our trusty Macintoshes break every single checklist into nine-card units. But that's not all. We've put the number of the sheet a card "goes" in at the head of every nine-card section. Our method allows you to pull a card at random from a booster and automatically go to the proper page in your notebook to store it.

What are these nine-card sleeves you're talking about, and where can I get them?

There are several companies that make plastic sheets with pockets that hold nine cards (three across and three down) and can be stored in a three-ring binder. Check with your local card retailer, or look in ads in issues of **Scrye**. Most dealers carry them or can get them.

Card sheets are available which fit several sizes of cards. There are some which accommodate **Heresy** and **Sim City**, which both had oversized cards.

How many nine-pocket sheets will I need to store a set?

We've done the math for you. A box at the start of each set listing notes how many sheets are necessary so you don't have to skip to the end of the list to see.

We've also mentioned what that number will be for those who "double up" their cards — putting them back-to-back in the sleeves. We know that the number of people who do this in the CCG hobby is much higher than in other kinds

of card-collecting hobbies, for the simple reason that CCG cards are basically one-sided. You don't need to see both sides to know what a card does.

There are exceptions, of course. Some CCGs, like **Arcadia** (at right) and **Flights of Fantasy**, have double-sided cards. But take a look at them and you can see they're more closely related to regular trading cards than most CCGs.

Should I "double up" my cards in their sleeves?

It's up to you, of course, and it's usually either a financial or aesthetic decision.

Another reason that sportscard collectors don't put more than one card in a single pocket is to protect the cards from the damage that occurs when you pull one out. CCG cards have to be more durable and thinner to be usable at all and, with their rounded corners, they're generally not prone to as much damage when you put more than one in a sleeve. Some people squeeze their duplicate cards into single pockets, and for most of these folks doubling up is not the best idea. You can fit more Air Bladders into a pocket if it doesn't have to share space with a bunch of Battlefield Perchers.

Enough with the Air Bladders already.

Oh, so all the Air Bladders are going to be in your deck, right? We're performing a useful service here.

Come to think of it, those Blastoderms are pretty icky looking, too...

Using this guide...
to figure out what your collection is WORTH — or what cards will cost

PRICING

Where do you get these prices?

Scrye magazine consults each month with a team of retailers in North America who sell CCG single cards in their stores. Some of them specialize in a few games. Some of them sell everything. They help keep us ahead of the curve on market developments, and we pass along the prices they charge in volumes like this and in each issue of *Scrye*.

We don't make up prices at *Scrye*. We're not saying there are others that do. We're saying *we* don't.

With all these retailers, how do you decide what price a card is going for?

In this volume, we've taken all the reports from our panel on each given item and present the median — that is, the one charging the *middle* price when all the prices are listed. We're not running the highest price we got or the lowest price. If Abe charges $1, Bob charges $2, and Chuck charges $4, we go with Bob.

That way, you get asense for what the middle-of-the-road store is charging for cards. This is better than just taking the mean, because it helps adjust for local differences.

Let's say among 51 stores, one of them is selling **Babylon 5** uncommons for $1,000 each and *everybody* else has them at $1. If you just took the mean, that one store would drag the price for uncommons up above $20 — even though 50 stores are charging a buck! Taking the median allows you to set aside "outliers" like these: We'd look at what the store in the exact middle is charging. And in this case, the store with the 26th highest (and lowest) price for **Babylon 5** uncommons is charging $1. That's our price!

Are these the prices a store will pay for my cards?

No! This is perhaps the biggest mistake that beginning collectors make in *any* field, not just CCGs.

Our price guide is designed to tell one thing: what the typical retailer is charging customers for certain cards. That's why most retailers will not pay the full price for *any* item in *any* price guide. If they're expected to sell them again at the price that's in the guides, they make no

profit — and that's what they're in business to do. Retailers have other expenses, such as overhead, advertising, and employees, so, when they buy cards, they generally pay anywhere from cents on the dollar to up to half the guide values for cards.

Some retailers will, indeed, pay more — but only in situations of extremely high demand and short supply, when the prices are changing so fast that the price guides can't keep up. These occurrences are very rare but have happened twice in CCG history — during the **Magic** boom of 1994 and the **Pokémon** boom of 1999. These situations are rare, though, and in general you really can't count on a retailer ever giving you the prices you see in price guides.

Some retailers don't buy cards at all from customers — some because they have all they need, others because they don't want to disappoint people who don't understand the way the market works.

Price guides do serve a secondary, indirect purpose, in that they tells collectors what standards they should set when selling or trading cards to other collectors. You won't necessarily charge your friend the $20 we have listed for a certain card here, but you wouldn't want to trade it for a card that our guide says is worth $1. (Unless you really, really need it, of course.) In this way, guides like this help you make educated financial decisions with regard to your collection.

You've got one price for sets, but, when you add up all the cards in the set, it's much more! Why is that?

It's for the same reason that you pay less for a six-pack of Cokes than you would for six individual Cokes. It would be more work for a retailer to sell every single card in a set individually, so he's almost always willing to accept a lower profit on the items as a group in order to generate more cash flow. And if you buy "onesies," you're going to pay more — because the retailer has to pay his clerk at the register the same whether you're there checking out with a $1 common or a $5,000 set. Alliteratively, buying in bulk is a better bargain for both of you.

For example: At press time, our retail panelists have **Magic: Homelands** complete sets selling for $50. If you add up their prices for all

the cards in the set, it totals $141.10. But a retailer could go his entire life without selling some of the commons and uncommons in the set, and, as the set's most expensive card is only worth $6, it could take a dozen transactions before you'd reach $50. It's much easier to find one person to pay $50 and be done with it. After all, retailers run stores, not museums.

We haven't checked, but we believe this relationship holds with every single set in this book. There are cases where the set price given is very near what all the cards add up to, and that's the case for sets that are in high demand and where building a complete set involves a lot of work on the part of the seller. For example, a **Magic Beta** set runs $4,800 at press time, whereas the single cards together total $5,663.35. Those prices are close because the set is old and in short supply to begin with, and because retailers can generate good cash flow selling even the commons from the set.

I found cards at my store for a lot less than you've got in this book! What gives?

You've found what we call in the collecting game a "bargain." Buy 'em!

Seriously, there are a few reasons a price may be lower in one specific store. Maybe the retailer ordered way too many. Maybe the game never caught on in that neighborhood and the retailer got stuck with a lot of cards. Maybe the retailer is clearing space for a big new game coming out soon. Maybe the retailer needs the cash flow more than he needs the inventory.

There are a million reasons why a local price may be lower — or higher — than the ones we list. That's why we have so many stores in our retail support team: to try to capture more of these local variations.

I found cards at my store for a lot more than you've got in this book! What gives?

Same answer: There isn't just one game store in the world, there are thousands, all setting prices based on their own local needs. Maybe a game is hotter in your area than in most parts of the world. Maybe a tournament's coming up and there's a lot of demand for a given game. Maybe there's been news of a new expansion to an old system. Maybe the distributors that the retailer buys from are having trouble getting their hands on more.

Again, this is why we have so many stores in our database — to show you what's happening

in the rest of the world. Even if your local store is part of our retail support team, our prices may not exactly reflect what's going on there — but they will be that much closer for its participation.

You've got an old game in here my store couldn't give away for years — and you've got it priced at $50 a box! What's the deal?

The reason lies in a difference between the way we do things and the way some others approach price guides. Only retailers who actually sell a product are counted toward our price.

This sounds obvious, but there are subtleties to it. We didn't just go to, say, the 80% of our stores who don't sell **Terror** at all and say, "Hey, we know you don't even have any boxes of **Terror**, but if you did, what would you charge?" We might get a bunch of answers ranging from a nickel on up, but

they wouldn't mean very much. That's because there really wouldn't be a store anywhere actually charging a nickel a box, so why count that answer?

(Regard the Mercedes Benz. "I don't have a Mercedes, but if I did, I'd only charge you a buck for it." That answer won't affect what you pay at the dealership, we assure you.)

Frequently, when only a handful of retailers are carrying a game, the price tends to be higher — even when demand for the product seems to be low all around. Sometimes, stores set themselves up as specialists in the area of, say, science-fiction games.

Sometimes, the retailers who still have a slow product really need, for purposes of valuing the assets of their businesses, to continue to value a product at close to what they paid for it. (And in most cases, that's around $50 a display box.)

Maybe they're mindful of how much it would cost to restock. If five rich (and easily amused) guys in Dubuque suddenly get into **Banemaster**, it's going to be expensive for the retailer to find much more, because a lot of the original stock went into the incinerator when it didn't sell.

Finally, retailers tend to be cautious, with good reason, about declaring once and for all that a product has lost all its worth. When CCGs started hitting the shelves in a fast and furious way in 1995, many retailers found them-

selves shifting the slower-moving games to the discount rack just to gain shelf space for the newer stuff. The problem some retailers found with being too eager to do that is that their customers got into the habit of thinking they didn't have to pay sticker price — that they could just wait a month or two and pull it out of the discount bin. Taking business away from the "front-market" like that not only costs the retailer money on discounts, but it almost always means that the game will not catch on in that store. Because the people who could've been playing it and getting hooked on the game are waiting to buy it until it's on sale, the retailer's decided no one wants the game and doesn't push it or order any more.

What is certification, and does it affect the prices of CCG cards?

A definite "no" to the second question — but to understand why, we need to answer the first.

Certification, or third-party grading, came about first in the coin-collecting hobby to make it easier for buyers and sellers to agree on the condition of an item — especially important if one grade made a difference in the hundreds of dollars or more. In the mid-1990s, it spread to the sportscard hobby, where it was quickly adopted. In 2000 it was introduced for comic books, and in early 2001 it became available for action figures.

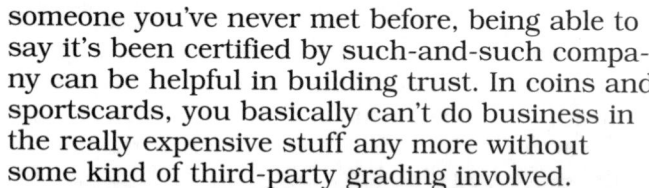

To get their collectibles graded, people send their items to one of a number of companies set up to do grading (or sometimes they take it to a store that sends it in for them). The grading service examines the item, grades it according to its own standards, and then encases it, along with a certificate of the grade, in plastic.

That's right, the whole coin, comic book, or card gets encased in plastic. This is referred to as "slabbing" and it doesn't damage the item inside. (It's just suspended so it doesn't move around. The slabs so far for comic books get pretty bulky, and the ones for action figures look like plastic bricks!)

If you open the slab, the company no longer guarantees that the comic book is the grade that they say it is. And that's important, because when you're buying a $5,000 by mail order from someone you've never met before, being able to say it's been certified by such-and-such company can be helpful in building trust. In coins and sportscards, you basically can't do business in the really expensive stuff any more without some kind of third-party grading involved.

In 1999, some of the sportscard dealers noticed the boom in **Pokémon** CCG cards and began sending them to the sportscard graders for slabbing. Everyone soon learned that slabs and CCGs really didn't mix, for a number of reasons.

One that should be obvious is that, of course, CCG cards aren't just for looking at, they're game components. Most of the valuable cards have value because they have value in a game. If you can't pop the slab open (and it's not always easy or possible without dinging the card), it's not much good.

Something more surprising has to do with the grades given to CCG cards. One reason that slabbing appealed to dealers in coins, sportscards, and comic books is that a very small percentage of items were graded as "perfect" — and these "perfect" items started selling for many, many times what unslabbed versions were going for. But, against all previous experience with sportscards, when **Pokémon** CCG cards were sent in and graded by sportscard standards, almost every one was graded as a "Perfect 10," "Gem Mint," or something like that. Unlike sportscards, CCG cards are meant to be shuffled and tend to be made of sterner stuff, if you will — and the major place where sportscards lose points with graders is their sharpened corners, something CCG cards don't have.

So grade certificaton of CCG cards has turned out, at least so far, to be a bust. It hasn't even developed as a particularly useful tool for people selling through the mail (and on eBay), possibly because CCG buyers are willing to forgive a difference between a perfect and less-than-perfect condition card. They expect that a good card has been used.

I've got some cards in this book. Can I sell them to you? And are you selling any of the cards in this book?

No and no. You'd be surprised how often we get asked one or the other of these questions. We're in business to provide information. If you need cards, there are lots of people in business to sell them to you. And we certainly don't need any more cards ourselves!

Can you e-mail me your price lists?

Sorry. We get far too many requests of this type to take care of them. Besides, we publish books. If we e-mailed everyone our price lists, we wouldn't be publishing books very long.

Online pricing — and why it's not always useful

In general, the price someone realizes for a card or set on eBay (there are other auction sites, but this is the one with the most CCG traffic) is the *highest* possible price you're going to see, since people are actually competing to see who can pay more. But it doesn't always say much about what the real market price is.

A particular auction result reflects what someone would pay at that moment, and there's no guarantee that those conditions would recur. In general, retail stores don't pay a lot of attention to these results — except for items in extremely short supply and high demand, they prefer to set fixed prices. The people most likely to consider a past online auction result in deciding what to pay are the people bidding in other online auctions, who check around to see what other buyers recently did.

Even then, it's not an exact science. Here are just some of the factors that can drive a card's closing auction price up or down:

• **What time did the auction close?** Most of the action in auctions takes place in the last few minutes. If an auction closes after midnight on the East Coast of the United States, chances are it's going to close for lower than it otherwise would. Likewise, if you see an item that closed around 9 p.m. EST, chances are that item closed for about as high a price as it could, since it's a time that people all across North America are likely to be online.

• **What day did the auction close?** Whether you can judge much from what a card auction closed at also depends on what day the auction closed. Again, the rule here is that, the greater number of potential bidders, the higher the price. It takes two to tango — and Friday, traditionally the day when the smallest number of people are sitting around looking at the Web, you're more likely to see auctions closing for their opening bids or fizzling out altogether. If you see a Beta Black Lotus close for $100 on Friday evening, it doesn't mean that the market for Black Lotuses has collapsed and they're all worth $100 now. It may just mean that everybody who might want a Black Lotus had a date. (Or, more likely, a game to play. But we can hope.)

Conversely, auctions that close Sunday or Monday, days when Web usage is highest, tend to close for more because more people are out there competing for the items. Again, this is only a general rule. Since auctioneers know that there are a lot of people out there on Sundays, they post more auctions then — and this causes more supply, and this drives prices down.

Sound confusing? It sure is. That's one of the reasons we still have price guides. We can't tell you what'll happen at 3 in the morning on eBay, but we still can have a good idea what a retailer will charge you in a store.

• **How well was the auction put together?** If you see a card that went on eBay for what you think is a lot of money, go look at the auction itself. Was the auction well designed — that is, put together with nice pictures and no annoying features? Did the auctioneer offer to take credit cards or Paypal? Did the auctioneer offer free shipping? Did he have a high feedback rating? If the answer to many of these questions was yes, then you can believe that at least part of the buyer's willingness to pay extra for a card resulted from his confidence in the seller. Another seller might not get the same price.

If a card went for lower than you would expect, look, too, to see if the auctioneer failed to do some of the "right things." A seller with a negative rating on eBay isn't going to sell the best card in the world for a good price. Who'd trust him?

• **How many more items like this closed that day?** This is the big one. A quick search will tell you whether the card you saw close was on eBay for the entire month — or perhaps one of dozens that closed that day. If supply is great in the market, all the closing prices will tend to be lower than average. If few are available, closing prices are likely to be higher.

It is not always correct to assume, however, that, if there are a bunch of a particular card for sale on eBay, it's in plentiful supply and probably not worth much. The fact is that success attracts success, and, if sellers see any card close for $400, they're more likely to put their copies of that card up than anything else. That will eventually have the net effect of dragging prices down some, but not a whole lot — especially not if the card has some practical use that made someone want to pay that much for it in the first place.

Conversely, you can't look at a situation where only one or two copies of a card are on eBay in a given month and decide that this lack of supply means that the card is scarce and, therefore, more valuable. That could be, but it could also be that previous auctions for the card didn't go for much, and that's why few are online.

Using this guide...
to find a really good game!

Concept	●●●●●
Gameplay	●●●●●
Card art	●●●●●
Player pool	●●●●●

Concept

●●●●● A great idea! A perfect fit with a CCG.
●●●●○ A pretty good basis for a CCG.
●●●○○ An average idea for a CCG.
●●○○○ A marginal idea for a CCG.
●○○○○ Really didn't need to be a CCG.
○○○○○ Aaaggh!

Here we're looking at both how strong the idea behind the game is and how naturally it makes use of the dynamics of CCGs.

Is the concept either familiar enough to players that they know about it already, or is it one so strong that people would be willing to learn about it? Topics like World War II or *Star Wars* are familiar enough to most that they don't have to be explained. A game about, say, the Punic wars or the sport of curling might have a harder time.

With **Magic**, even though the fantasy world was new, the trappings were familiar enough that most were willing to learn the details.

We also ask whether the concept behind it is one that people think would be naturally suited to a CCG. Most concepts that have two (or more) clearly delineated sides in opposition seem to have a natural advantage when it comes to easy adaptation to a CCG. Accepting a CCG about J.R.R. Tolkien's *Lord of the Rings* is a lot easier than accepting a CCG about Julian Jaynes' *The Origin of Consciousness in the Breakdown of the Bicameral Mind*.

In short, here we're looking for the reaction in the store when the game is announced. Do people want it sight unseen — or do they *not* want it sight unseen? Is it a good idea, or isn't it?

Gameplay

●●●●● Elegant, easy to learn, dynamic.
●●●●○ Enjoyable, no major rules problems that haven't been fixed. People actually play it.
●●●○○ Playable but inelegant. Small rules, balance problems.
●●○○○ Moments of fun hard to find. Play problems noticable.
●○○○○ Rough. Big rules holes. Just no fun.
○○○○○ Its designers probably don't play it.

Elegance. Ease of learning. Adaptability. Balance. Dynamic. Fun. These are just some of the positive buzzwords when it comes to evaluating a CCG's gameplay. If we found players (or ourselves) using them about a game, we took notice. Likewise, if a CCG lacks on one of more of these scores, we took notice of that, as well. Some games are easy to learn, balanced, and dynamic — but no fun. Some games can adapt to change and are fun — but are tough to learn. We noted these things.

We also took a look at the game mechanics themselves, and how they stood up to problems over the years. Some games are "broken" when certain powerful cards cause rules problems or wreck competitive balance. Some are "broken" out of the box. Did the manufacturer address these problems in later releases? We account for that. **Star Trek**, for example, was considered a broken game for some time by a lot of players — but there have been efforts to address that. That's important. Some manufacturers never get the chance.

Card art
(and general appearance)

●●●●● Outstanding!
●●●●○ More cool cards than not.
●●●○○ A few strong cards. Average.
●●○○○ Some of the cards are an active turnoff.
●○○○○ Visuals are distracting, unpleasant.
○○○○○ Bleagh!

Our philosphy is that card art should be appealing but should not interfere with the true function of a CCG, its game play. Nevertheless, strong art appeals to collectors and can certainly make the entire gaming process more rewarding. Who wants to look at lousy cards all evening?

For drafted art, we look at both quality of the pieces and appropriateness to the subject. Do we wish we could see some of the pieces larger? Do we wish we could see some of the pieces smaller, and through dark glasses? For photo art, which is found in most games adapting TV shows and movies, we look at the selection and quality of images. Are they fuzzy screen captures or the same publicity photos over and over again?

To a small extent, we look at card design here, too, as they're frequently chosen by the same people who pick the paintings or photos. Are typefaces chosen that match the art aesthetically yet convey the information they're supposed to? Sometimes it's a hard trick. The designers of **Doctor Who** wanted to go with a funky techno font to match the topic, and ended up selecting the single most illegible typeface yet seen in CCGs. (Tell a "4" from a "Y." We dare you.)

Player pool

●●●●● Opponents, tourneys everywhere.
●●●●○ Opponents, tourneys in urban areas.
●●●○○ Opponents in urban areas, tourneys only at conventions.
●●○○○ Opponents only at cons. No tourneys.
●○○○○ Lucky to find an opponent at a con.
○○○○○ Solitaire time.

This is actually the least subjective of all our measures, because we have hard evidence to draw from. We looked at current sales. We looked at programs from Gen Con. We looked at our own tournament calendar and reports in *Scrye*. We looked at fan sites on the Web. It's easy to see, from these, how easy or hard it's going to be to find a community of players for a game within easy reach.

These are *our* ratings, and, while they take into account what the reviewers who wrote our essays said, they may not exactly match those views. We purposefully chose experts on many of the games inside to write about them, and they naturally may be more enthusiastic about them than we believe the typical gamer might be. (We feel most of them kept enough balance in what they said, though.)

They also don't reflect how we feel about the people who made these games or those who play them. Others can see things that we and our reviewers can't, and that's fine. Everybody's CCG is somebody's favorite. Likewise, we're the first to admit that we like some things that others didn't when the game came out. That's one reason we wanted to do this book: to let people know about some great old games that they may have missed.

Agree or disagree with one of our reviews? Write us and let us know. We stand ready to change our minds.

CCG Identification Guide

As the number of existing Collectible Card Games grows past 100, it helps to have a guide to recognize which cards are associated with which games. As you'll see, you can't always tell from the name of the card back!

Faces and backs of sample cards from all sets follow, as well as expansion names and dates of production. When a set includes more than one card back, the individual types are shown. Page numbers with each game refer to the checklist and price guide sections elsewhere in this book.

[Brackets indicate a basic set that had no official subtitle.]

7th Sea
Alderac
1999-

Basic sets (2)
• No Quarter
• Broadsides

Expansion sets (4)
• Strange Vistas
• Shifting Tides
• Scarlet Seas
• Black Sails

page 42

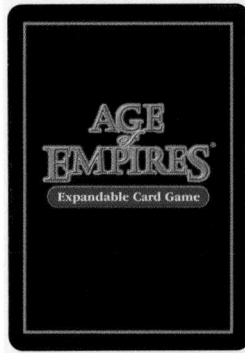 

Age of Empires II
United States Playing Card Co.
2000-

Basic sets (1)
• [Limited]

page 50

 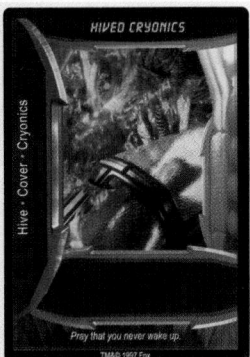

Aliens Predator
HarperPrism
1997-1999

Basic sets (1)
• [Limited]

Expansion sets (1)
• Alien Resurrection

page 52

Ani-Mayhem
Pioneer
1996-1997

Basic sets (1)
• Set 0

Expansion sets (2)
• Set 1
• Dragonball Z

page 56

Arcadia
White Wolf
1996

Basic sets (1)
• The Wyld Hunt

Expansion sets (1)
• King Ironheart's Madness

page 61

Above:
Purple-backed card

Right:
Red-backed card

Above:
Waylay cards

Right:
Character cards (merit)

Left:
Green-backed card

Austin Powers

Decipher

1999

Basic sets (1)
• [Limited]

page 66

Above:
Good deck card

Left: Evil deck card

Battlelords

New Millennium

1995

Basic sets (1)
• Limited

page 84

Battletech

Wizards of the Coast

1996-1998

Basic sets (3)
• Limited
• Unlimited
• Commander's Edition

Expansion sets (5)
• Counterstrike
• Mercenaries
• Mechwarrior
• Arsenal
• Crusade

page 86

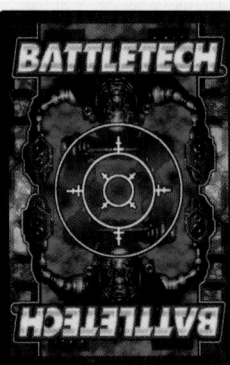

Above right:
Unlimited card
(black border)

Left:
Limited card (green
border)

Right:
Commander's
Edition card (new
format, also found
in Crusade)

Babylon 5

Precedence

1997-

Basic sets (2)
• Premier
• Deluxe

Expansion sets (6)
• The Shadows
• The Great War
• Psi-Corps
• Severed Dreams
• Wheel of Fire
• Crusade

page 67

Banemaster

Chessex

1995

Basic sets (1)
• The Adventure

page 82

Above:
Adventure deck
card

Right: Banemaster
deck card

Blood Wars

TSR

1995

Basic sets (1)
• [Limited]

Expansion sets (3)
• Escalation Pack 1:
  Rebels &
  Reinforcements
• Escalation Pack 2:
  Factols & Factions
• Escalation Pack 1:
  Powers & Proxies

page 95

Boy Crazy

Decipher

2000-

Basic sets (1)
• [Limited]

page 99

Calorie Kids

Ocean of Wisdom

2000-

Basic sets (1)
• [Limited]

page 100

The Crow

Target Games

1995

Basic sets (1)
• [Limited]

page 101

C•23

Wizards of the Coast

1998

Basic sets (1)
• [Limited]

page 102

 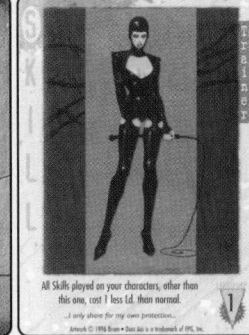

Dark Age

FPG

1996

Basic sets (1)
• Feudal Lords

page 103

Dark Eden

Target Games

1997

Basic sets (1)
• Limited

page 105

Digi-Battle

Upper Deck/Bandai

2000-

Basic sets (1)
• Series 1
Expansion sets (1)
• Series 2

page 107

Dixie

Columbia Games

1994-1995

Basic sets (2)
• Bull Run 1st Edition
• Bull Run 2nd Edition
Expansion sets (2)
• Shiloh
• Gettysburg
Various collectors sets

page 109

Doctor Who

MMG

1996

Basic sets (1)
• Series 1
Expansions (1)
• Series 2

page 107

Above:
Confederate deck card

Left:
Union deck card

Doomtown

Wizards of the Coast/Alderac

1998-2000

Basic sets (3)
• Episode 1-2
• Pine Box
• Boot Hill
Expansion sets (12)
• Episodes 3-9
• Mouth of Hell
• Reaping of Souls
• Revelations
• Ashes to Ashes
• Eye for an Eye

page 116

Doomtrooper

Target Games

1995-1997

Basic sets (2)
• Limited
• Unlimited
Expansion sets (6)
• Inquisition
• Warzone
• Mortificator
• Golgotha
• Apocalypse
• Paradise Lost

page 129

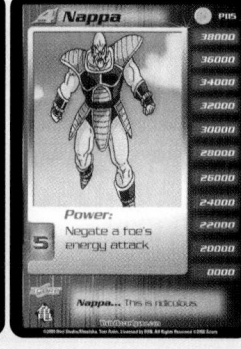

Dragonball Z

Score

2000-

Basic sets (1)
• Saiyan Saga
Expansion sets (1)
• Frieza Saga

page 137

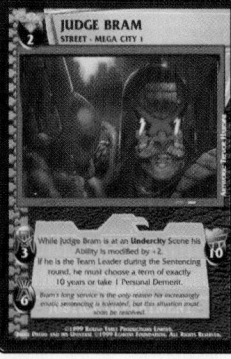

Dredd

Pinnacle

2000-

Basic sets (1)
• Limited Edition

page 140

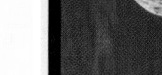

Dune

Last Unicorn

1997-1998

Basic sets (1)
• Eye of the Storm
Expansion sets (6)
• Judge of the Change
  Episodes 1-3
• Thunder at Twilight
  Episodes 1-3

page 142

Eagles

Columbia Games

1995

Basic sets (1)
• Waterloo

page 147

Echelons of Fire

Medallion Simulations

1995

Basic sets (2)
• First Edition
• Second Edition

page 150

Above:
French cards

Right:
Anglo-Dutch cards

Below:
Prussian cards

Above:
First Edition card
(darker tan border
on card face)

Right:
Second Edition card
(lighter tan border
on card face)

Rarities:
Bronze, Silver, and
Gold versions exist
of all cards. Check
the color of the oval
border and corner
boxes.

Top card: Bronze

Card above: Silver

Card at left: Gold

Echelons of Fury

Medallion Simulations

1995

Basic sets (2)
• First Edition
• Second Edition
Expansion sets (1)
• Pacific Campaign

page 151

Fantasy Adventures

Mayfair Games

1996

Basic sets (1)
• [Limited Edition]

page 154

Fastbreak

Wildstorm

1996

Basic sets (1)
• One-on-One Basketball

page 157

Above:
Encounter Deck
cards

Right:
Hero Deck cards

Flights of Fantasy

Destini

1994

Basic sets (1)
• [Limited Edition]

page 158

 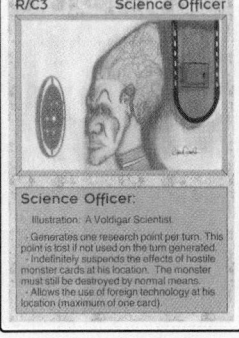

Galactic Empires

Companion Games

1994-1997

Basic sets (4)
• Alpha
• Beta
• Primary
• Universe

Expansion sets (9)
• New Empires
• Powers of the Mind
• Time Gates
• Advanced Technologies
• Piracy
• Comedy Club
• Persona
• Galactic Invaders
• Allied Forces

page 159

Above left:
Most cards
(white ship on bottom
when card is turned)

Left:
Some Allied Forces
cards (white ship on top
when card turned)

 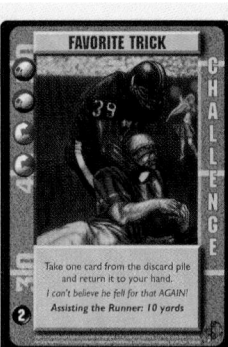

Gridiron Fantasy Football

Columbia

1995

Basic sets (2)
• Retail Edition
• Hobby Edition

page 174

Above:
Offensive Action
card

Near right:
Offensive Play card

Far right:
Team card

Near right:
Defensive Action
card

Far right:
Defensive Play card

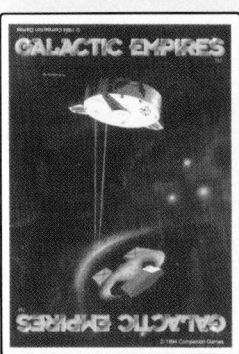 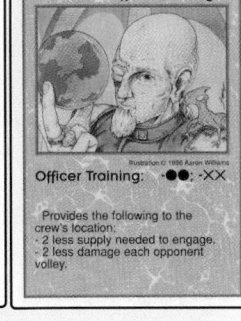

Guardians

FPG

1995-1996

Basic sets (2)
• Limited Edition
• Revised Edition

Expansion sets:
• Dagger Isle
• Drifter's Nexus
• Necropolis Park

page 178

Hercules

Wizards of the Coast

1998

Basic sets (1)
• The Legendary Journeys

page 182

Heresy

Last Unicorn

1995

Basic sets (1)
• Kingdom Come

page 183

Highlander

Thunder Castle

1995-1999

Basic sets (2)
• Series Edition
• Movie Edition
Expansion sets (4)
• The Watcher's Chronicles
• The Gathering
• Arms & Tactics
• The Four Horsemen
Special sets (2)
• Duncan Collection
• Methos Collection

page 186

Illuminati: New World Order

Steve Jackson

1994-1998

Basic sets (2)
• Limited Edition
• Unlimited Edition
Expansion sets (1)
• Assassins
Special sets (2):
• One With Everything
• SubGenius

page 196

Hyborian Gates

Cardz

1995

Basic sets (1)
• [Limited Edition]

page 194

Above left:
Blue-backed group card

Above right:
Limited Editon design

Far left:
Red-backed plot card

Left:
Unlimited Edition design

James Bond 007

Target Games

1995

Basic sets (1)
• Goldeneye

page 203

Right:
Black background design from One With Everything (near right) and SubGenius (far right)

Above:
Red-backed villain cards

Right:
Blue-backed hero cards

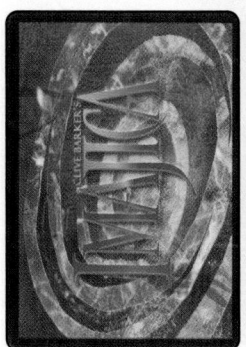

Imajica

HarperPrism

1997

Basic sets (1)
• [Limited Edition]

page 201

Jyhad

Wizards of the Coast

1994

Basic sets (1)
• Limited

page 204

 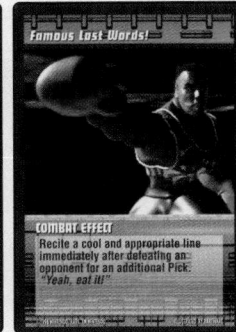

Killer Instinct

Topps

1996

Basic sets (1)
• [Limited]

page 207

Above:
Brown-backed
vampire cards

Right:
Green-backed
library cards

Kult

Target Games

1995-1997

Basic sets (1)
• Limited
Expansion sets (1)
• Inferno

page 209

Last Crusade

Chameleon
Eclectic/Pinnacle

1995

Basic sets (1)
• From Normandy to
the Rhine

page 211

Above:
U.S. unit and event
cards

Right:
German unit and
event cards

 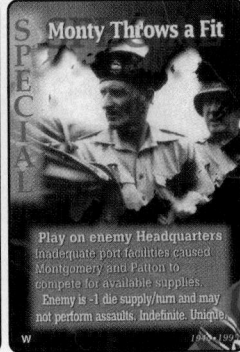

Legend of the Five Rings

Alderac/Wizards
of the Coast

1995-

Basic sets (5)
• Imperial Edition
• Emerald Edition
• Obsidian Edition
• Jade Edition
• Pearl Edition
Expansion sets (20)
• Shadowlands
• Forbidden Knowledge
• Anvil of Despair
• Crimson & Jade
• Time of the Void
• Scorpion Clan Coup
   Episodes 1-3
• The Hidden Emperor
   Episodes 1-6
• The Dark Journey Home
• Honor Bound
• Ambition's Debt
• Fire & Shadow
• Soul of the Empire
• Spirit Wars
Learner sets (3)
• Battle of Beiden Pass
• Storms Over Matsu
   Palace
• Siege at Sleeping
   Mountain

page 217

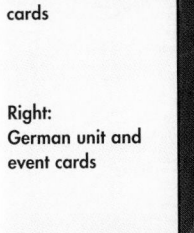 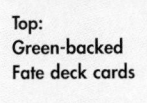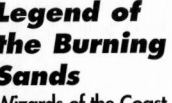

Legend of the Burning Sands

Wizards of the Coast

1998

Basic sets (1)
• Awakenings
Expansion sets (3)
• Episode 1: Shadow of
   the Tyrant
• Episode 2: Secrets and Lies
• Episode 3: Black hand,
   Black Heart

page 213

Top:
Green-backed
Fate deck cards

Above:
Black-backed
Dynasty deck cards

Right:
New card back
(begins in Spirit
Wars)

Looney Tunes

Wizards of the Coast

2000

Basic sets (1)
• [Limited]

page 242

Lost Colony

Pinnacle

2000-

Basic sets (1)
• Fear the Reaper

page 243

Left: Lost Colony cards
(Showdown is not the
generally recognized
name of this game, but
it appears on cards)

Above:
Porky-Pig backed
player cards

Right:
Bugs Bunny-backed
scene cards

Magi Nation

Interactive
Imagination

2000-

Basic sets (1)
• Duel

page 244

Magic: The Gathering

Wizards of the Coast

1993-

Basic sets (7)
• [Alpha]
• [Beta]
• Unlimited
• Revised
• Fourth Edition
• Fifth Edition
• Classic [Sixth Edition]

Expansion sets (21)
• Arabian Nights
• Antiquities
• Legends
• The Dark
• Fallen Empires
• Ice Age
• Homelands
• Alliances
• Mirage
• Visions
• Weatherlight
• Stronghold
• Exodus
• Tempest
• Urza's Saga
• Urza's Legacy
• Urza's Destiny
• Mercadian Masques
• Nemesis
• Prophecy
• Invasion

Special sets
• Collectors Edition
• Chronicles
• Vanguard 1-3
• Unglued
• The Astral Set
• Anthologies
• Rivals
• Beatdown
• Various tournament sets

Beginner sets
• Portal
• Portal: Second Age
• Portal: Three Kingdoms

page 246

Far left: Magic card back

Middle left: Magic Alpha card face

Near left: Recent Magic card face

Below: Vanguard card (3.5" x 5")

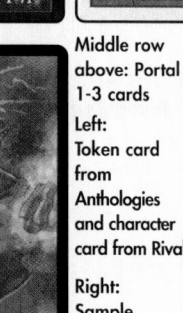

Middle row
above: Portal
1-3 cards

Left:
Token card
from
Anthologies
and character
card from Rivals

Right:
Sample
tournament
card face and
back

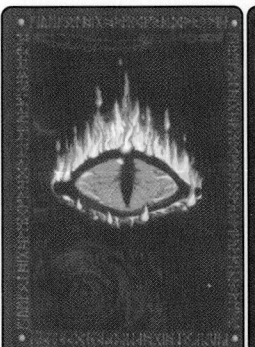 

Middle-earth

Iron Crown

1995-1998

Basic sets (2)
- The Wizards Limited
- The Wizards Unlimited

Expansion sets (6)
- The Dragons
- Dark Minions
- The Lidless Eye
- Against the Shadow
- The White Hand
- The Balrog

page 296

MLB Showdown

Wizards of the Coast

2000

Basic sets (1)
- 2000 Edition

Expansion sets (1)
- Pennant Run

page 307

Above:
Limited card (most cards)

Right:
Limited card (land cards) front and back

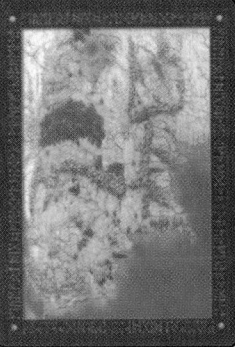 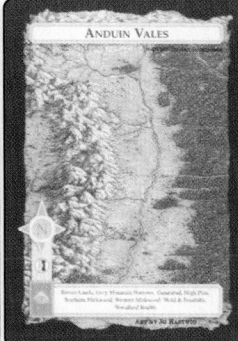

Above:
Blue-backed player cards

Right:
Red-backed strategy cards

 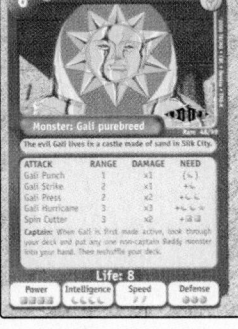

Monster Rancher

Artbox

2000-

Basic sets (1)
- [Limited]

page 310

 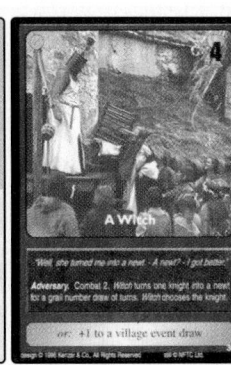

Monty Python and the Holy Grail

Kenzer

1996-

Basic sets (1)
- Premiere

Expansion sets (1)
- Taunt You a Second Time

page 311

Mortal Kombat

Brady Games

1996

Basic sets (1)
- Limited

page 314

 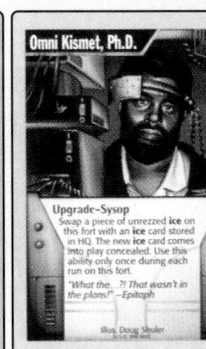

Netrunner

Wizards of the Coast

1996-1999

Basic sets (1)
- Limited

Expansion sets (2)
- Proteus
- Classic

page 322

Mythos

Chaosium

1996-1997

Basic sets (2)
- Limited
- Standard

Expansion sets (5)
- The Expeditions of Miskatonic University
- Cthulhu Rising
- Legends of the Necronomicon
- Dreamlands Limited
- New Aeon

page 316

Above:
Purple-backed corporate deck cards

Right:
Green-backed runner deck cards

On the Edge

Atlas Games

1994-1995

Basic sets (2)
• Limited
• Unlimited
Expansion sets ()
• Cut-Ups
• Shadows
• Arcana

page 326

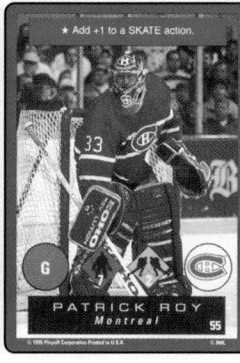

One-on-One Hockey Challenge

Playoff

1995

Basic sets (1)
• Premiere Edition

page 331

OverPower

Fleer/Marvel Interactive

1995-1998

Basic sets (4)
• Marvel Limited
• DC
• Image
• Marvel Classic

Expansion sets (6)
• Marvel Power Surge
• Marvel Mission Control
• Marvel IQ
• DC Justice League
• Marvel Monumental
• Marvel X-Men

page 333

Top right:
Marvel OverPower
cards (standard)

Right:
Marvel OverPower
cards (mission)

Pez

U.S. Games

2000-

Basic sets (1)
• [Limited]

page XXX

Pokémon

Wizards of the Coast

1999-

Basic sets (3)
• 1st Edition
• Unlimited Edition
• Base Set 2
Expansion sets (6)
• Jungle (1st & Unlimited)
• Fossil (1st & Unlimited)
• Team Rocket (1st & Unlimited)
• Gym Heroes (1st & Unlimited)
• Gym Challenge (1st & Unlimited)
• Neo Genesis (1st & Unlimited)

page 350

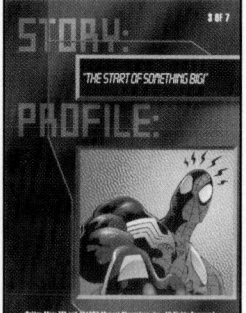

Left:
DC OverPower
cards

PowerCardz

Caliber Games Systems

1995

Basic sets (2)
• First Strike
• Spawn

page 358

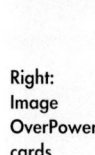

Right:
Image
OverPower
cards

Above:
First Strike cards

Right:
Spawn
cards

Quest for the Grail
Stone Ring/
Horizon
1995

Basic sets (1)
• Preview
• Limited

page 360

Racing Challenge
Upper Deck
2000-

Basic sets (1)
• 2000

page 362

Above:
Preview cards —
court deck
(lion-backed)

Right:
Limited cards —
quest deck
(unicorn-backed)

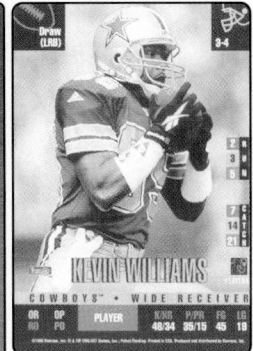

Red Zone
Donruss
1995

Basic sets (1)
• Premiere
Expansion sets (1)
• 1995 Expansion
Teams

page 373

Rage
White Wolf/
Wizards of the Coast
1995-1999

Basic sets (2)
• Limited
• Unlimited
Expansion sets (11)
• The Umbra
• The Wyrm
• War of the Amazons
• Legacy of the Tribes
• Snake Eyes: Phases 1-6
• Snake Eyes: Equinox

page 364

Redemption
Cactus Games
1995-

Basic sets (3)
• Limited
• Unlimited
• Second Edition
Expansion sets (3)
• The Prophets
• Women of the Bible
• The Warriors

page 375

Above:
Rage Sept cards

Right:
Rage Combat
cards

Ruinsworld
Medallion
Simulations
1995

Basic sets (1)
• Limited

page 378

Left:
Rage Character
cards, front and
back

Above:
Ruinsworld
character cards

Right:
Ruinsworld
play cards

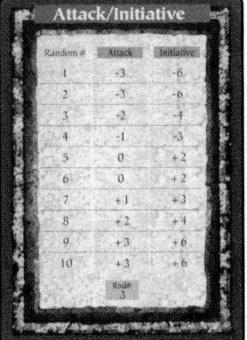

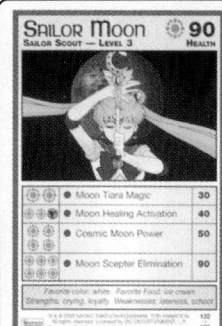

Sailor Moon
Dart Flipcards
2000-

Basic sets (1)
• [Limited]

Scooby Doo
Journeyman Press
2000-

Basic sets (1)
• [Limited]

page 379

page 380

Shadowfist
Daedelus/Z-Man
1995-

Basic sets (3)
• Limited
• Standard
• Year of the Dragon
Expansion sets (3)
• Netherworld
• Flashpoint
• Throne War

Shadowrun
FASA
1997-1998

Basic sets (1)
• Limited
Expansion sets (1)
• Underworld

page 382

page 387

Spellfire
TSR
1994-1997-

Basic sets (4)
• First-Fourth Editions
Expansion sets (12)
• Boosters #1
• #2 Ravenloft
• #3 Dragonlance
• #4 Forgotten Realms
• #5 Artifacts
• #6 Powers
• #7 Underdark
• #8 Runes & Ruins
• #9 Birthright
• #10 Draconomicon
• #11 Nightstalkers
• #12 Dungeons!

page 396

Sim City
Mayfair Games
1995-1996

Basic sets (1)
• Limited
Expansion sets (4)
• Chicago
• Washington D.C.
• New York City
• Atlanta

page 390

Above:
Standard-sized cards
Left:
Long Limited cards

Star of the Guardians
Mag Force 7
1995

Basic sets (1)
• Limited

page 416

Star Quest
Comic Images
1995

Basic sets (1)
• [Limited]

page 418

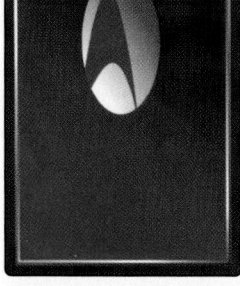

Star Trek Customizable Card Game
Decipher
1994-

Basic sets (2)
• Limited
• Unlimited
Expansion sets (8+)
• Alternate Universe
• Q Continuum
• First Contact
• The Dominion
• Blaze of Glory
• Rules of Acquisition
• Trouble with Tribbles
• Mirror Mirror

page 420

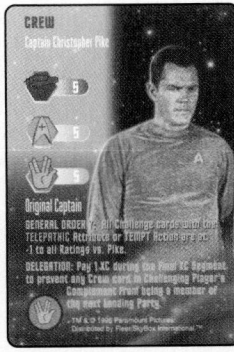

Star Trek: The Card Game
Fleer
1996-1997
Basic sets (1)
• Limited
Expansion sets (1)
• Starfleet Maneuvers

page 433

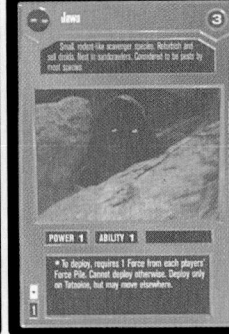

Star Wars
Decipher
1995-
Basic sets (2)
• Premiere Limited
• Premiere Unlimited
• Special Editon
Expansion sets (7)
• A New Hope
• Hoth
• Dagobah
• Cloud City
• Jabba's Palace
• Endor
• Death Star II
Special sets
• First Anthology
• Second Anthology
• Reflections
• Third Anthology
• Reflections 2
• Two-Player Sets
Repackaged sets
• Enhanced Premiere
• Enhanced Cloud City
• Enhanced Jabba's
  Palace

page 436

Super Deck!
Card Sharks
1994-1995
Basic sets (1)
• Yellow Edition
Expansion sets (1)
• Slim Decks

page 452

Top: Dark Side
Limited card

Left: Light side
Unlimited card

Super Nova
Target Games
1995
Basic sets (1)
• First Edition

page 453

Tank Commander
Moments in History
1996
Basic sets (1)
• The Eastern Front

page 454

Tempest of the Gods
Black Dragon
1995
Basic sets (1)
• Limited

page 455

The Terminator
Precedence
2000-
Basic sets (1)
• [Limited]

page 457

Terror
Kris Silver
1996
Basic sets (1)
• [Limited]

page 458

Tomb Raider
Precedence
1999-
Basic sets (1)
• Premier
Expansion sets (2)
• Slippery When Wet
• Big Guns

page 460

Top of the Order

Donruss

1995

Basic sets (1)
• [Limited]

page 463

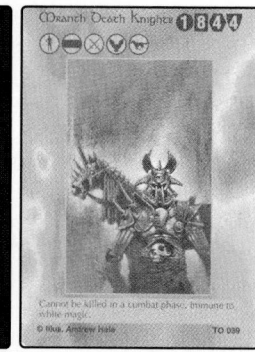

Towers in Time

Thunder Castle

1995

Basic sets (1)
• Limited

page 464

Ultimate Combat

Ultimate Games

1995

Basic sets (1)
• Limited
Expansion sets (1)
• Ancient Fighting Arts of China

page 465

Vampire

Wizards of the Coast/White Wolf

1995-

Basic sets (1)
• Unlimited
Expansion sets (4)
• Dark Sovereigns
• Ancient Hearts
• The Sabbat
• Sabbat War

page 467

Warlords

Iron Crown

1997

Basic sets (1)
• Limited

page 475

Above:
Brown-backed vampire cards

Right:
Green-backed library cards

WCW Nitro

Wizards of the Coast

2000

Basic sets (1)
• [Limited]

page 476

WildStorms

WildStorm

1995-1996

Basic sets (1)
• Limited
Expansion sets (4)
• Conflict
• Image Universe
• Legends
• Best of WildStorms

page 480

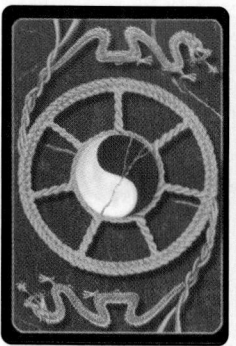

Wheel of Time

Precedence

1999-

Basic sets (1)
• Premier
Expansion sets (2)
• Dark Prophecies
• Children of the Dragon

page 477

Above:
WildStorms regular card

RightL
WildStorms Legends card

Wing Commander
Mag Force 7

1995

Basic sets (1)
• Limited

page 486

Left:
Terran
cards
Right:
Kilrathi
card
back

Wizard in Training
Upper Deck

2000-

Basic sets (1)
• [Limited]

page 488

WWF Raw Deal
Comic Images

2000-

Basic sets (1)
• [Limited]

page 489

Wyvern
U.S. Games

1995-1996

Basic sets (3)
• Premiere Limited
• Limited
• Kingdom
Expansion sets (2)
• Phoenix
• Chameleon

page 490

X-Files
USPC

1996-1997

Basic sets (2)
• Premiere
• The Truth Is Out There
Expansion sets (1)
• 101361

page 496

X-Men
Wizards of the Coast

2000-

Basic sets (1)
• [Limited]

page 499

Xena
Wizards of the Coast

1996-1997

Basic sets (1)
• [Limited]
Expansion sets (1)
• Battle Cry

page 500

Young Jedi
Decipher

1999-

Basic sets (1)
• Menace of Darth Maul
Expansion sets
• Jedi Council
• Battle of Naboo
• Duel of the Fates
Repackaged sets:
• Enhanced Darth Maul
• Enhanced Battle of Naboo

page 504

Xxxenophile
Slag-Blah Entertainment

1996

Basic sets (1)
• [Limited]

page 502

Above: Light-side cards

Right: Dark-side cards

 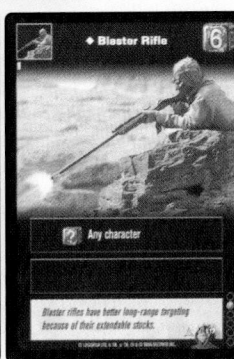

SCRYE Grading Guide

Poor	Good	Fine	Near Mint	Mint
Urza's Avenger	Mahamoti Djinn	Karma	Sivitri Scarzam	Earthcraft

This simplified grading guide gives basic categories for the condition of game cards and applies to all of the collectible card games. *Scrye* card prices are based on Near Mint or Mint condition cards.

However, with card sets that are highly collectible, such as *Magic: The Gathering Alpha* and *Beta*, Mint condition cards may command a premium price much higher than the Near Mint price, because perfect cards from those sets are extremely hard to find.

NOTE: Most tournament rules only allow play decks to have cards all in similar conditions, so that an obviously worn card cannot be easily identified from the rest of the play deck.

Mint: This is a card that is perfect in every way.

Near Mint: This (probably) unplayed card shows almost no wear. It may have a few minor scratches or slight marks on the edges. Generally, collectors seek only Mint and Near Mint cards.

Fine: This card has obviously been played, but not heavily. It lacks marks that would make it easily identifiable. It has some minor scratches and/or less than perfect edges. It will show less than 1/16" depth of white along one or two edges of one face of the card. It may have a minor crease that is only visible close up.

Good: This card has a played look to it. It will have white showing on three or four edges on both faces. It may also have more than 1/16" depth of white showing on an edge on the back face of the card. It may also be a card that looks like a Near Mint card except for one distinguishing wear feature, such as a slight tear or easily identifiable crease. It may also have permanent black marks from dirt. It is only acceptable for play if it cannot be easily distiguished from the other cards in the play deck.

Poor: Any card in less than Good condition.

Misprints & Errors: If a card is damaged in the factory by being irregularly cut or crimped, it often has no value. However, an irregularly printed card or a printing error which causes an oddity (such as a black card back or the wrong card back) may be sought-after by a collector who is focusing on oddities. If a card has a text/icon/art error that is later corrected, it may have a premium value.

Autographed Cards: So far, an autograph has not lowered a card's value; to some people, an autograph increases the card's value. A card autographed by the game's designer or the card artist is of more value to a collector. A card autographed and augmented by the game's designer is even better!

Buying cards?

When you consider buying cards from a mail-order company, always ask these questions before making a decision:
- What condition is the card in?
- How much does the company charge for shipping?
- Is the card in stock?
- How long will it take to receive it?
- What are my payment options?
- How long has this company been in business?

When you are buying cards through an on-line auction service such as eBay or a trading cards through an online site, be sure to check a seller or trader's feedback rating or references.

MAGIC: THE GATHERING Expansion Symbols

These are found on the right-hand side of black-bordered cards, beneath the illustration.

Arabian Nights: Scimitar
Antiquities: Anvil
Legends: Greek Column Top
The Dark: Crescent Moon
Fallen Empires: Crown
Ice Age: Snowflake
Homelands: Circular World Symbol
Alliances: Pennant
Mirage: Palm Tree
Visions: "V"
Astral: Shooting Star
MicroProse Computer Game: Aswan Jaguar 6x9 promo.
Portal: Circular Symbol
Weatherlight: Open Book
Tempest: Cloud with Lightning Bolt

Stronghold: Door with Portcullis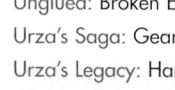
Exodus: Bridge
Unglued: Broken Egg
Urza's Saga: Gears
Urza's Legacy: Hammer
Classic Edition : Roman Numeral "6"
Urza's Destiny: Flask
Mercadian Masques: Mask
Nemesis: Halberd
Prophecy: Crystal
Invasion: Coalition Symbol
Planeshift: Galaxy Symbol

From Exodus onward, the color of the expansion symbol indicates the rarity of the card: Gold=Rare, Silver=Uncommon, Black=Common

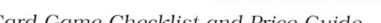

An introduction to the SCRYE price guide

The games are listed in alphabetical order, from *7th Sea* to *Young Jedi*. Core card sets are listed first, in the order they were release, followed by expansions, also organized by release date.

The checklist for each card set is divided into numbered nine-card groups to make it easier for you to organize your cards in nine-pocket pages for storage in three-ring binders.

A note on rarities: We have used the manufacturers' rarity designations in the card checklists. Occasionally, these include numbers as well as letter codes, e.g. R1, R3, U2. The number usually refers to the number of times a card appears on a press sheet. Cards with lower numbers are more rare than cards with the same letter code with a higher number (An R1 is more rare than an R2, for example).

Some manufactures subdivide rarities in other ways, for example, having Common and Very Common cards in a set.

Finally, rarities do not necessarily indicate the same thing in different games, because of differences in popularity, print runs, and other factors. Rare cards for some games are much more available than rare cards for other games.

Game Title →

Vital Stats for card set
(Publisher, number of cards, etc.)

Sample Card →

Game ratings →

Set, Box, & Pack Prices →

Storage requirements for set →

Card checklist →

Rarity codes →

Numbers indicate which nine-pocket page cards go in →

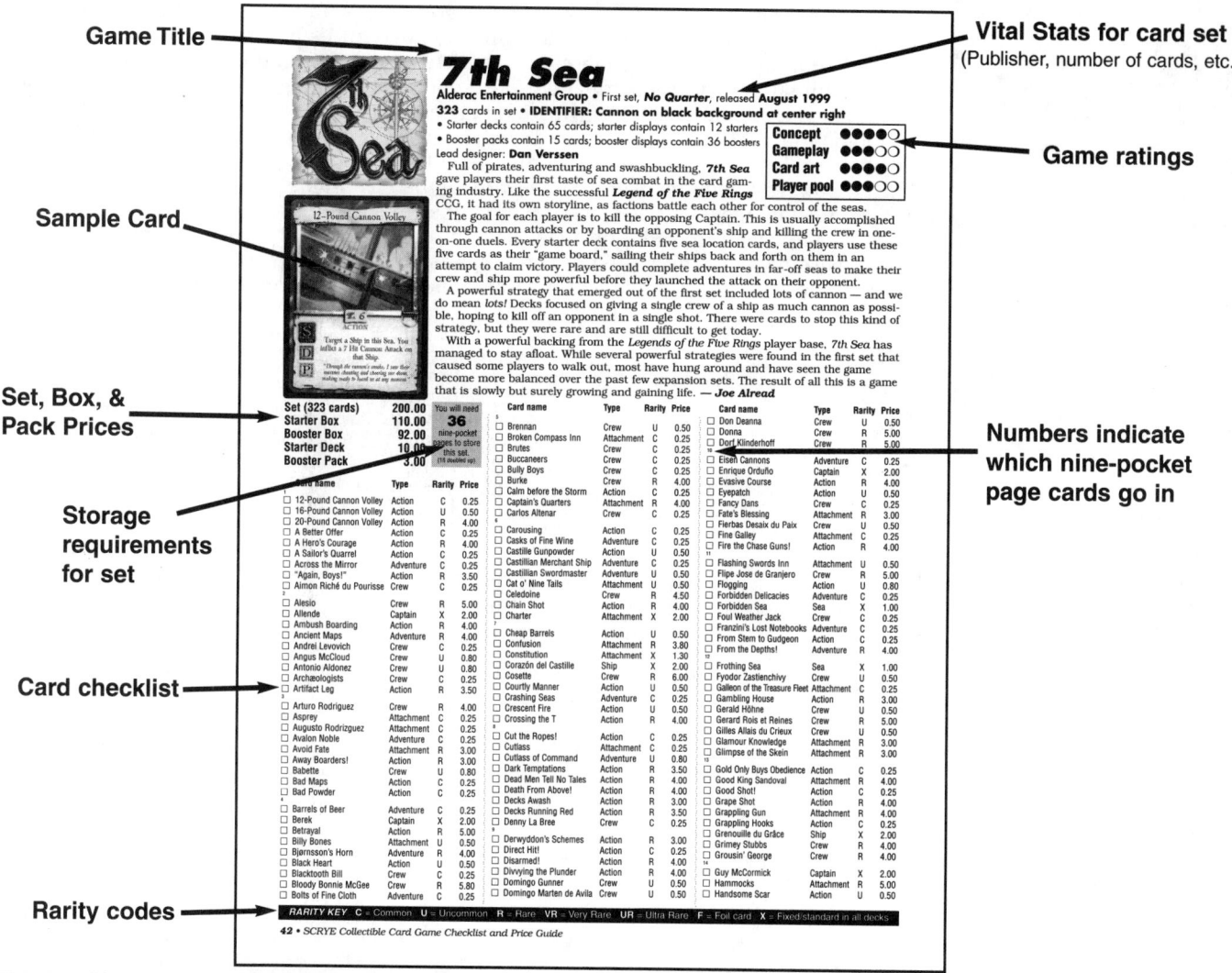

7th Sea

Alderac Entertainment Group • First set, *No Quarter*, released **August 1999**
323 cards in set • **IDENTIFIER: Cannon on black background at center right**
• Starter decks contain 65 cards; starter displays contain 12 starters
• Booster packs contain 15 cards; booster displays contain 36 boosters
Lead designer: **Dan Verssen**

Full of pirates, adventuring and swashbuckling, **7th Sea** gave players their first taste of sea combat in the card gaming industry. Like the successful *Legend of the Five Rings* CCG, it had its own storyline, as factions battle each other for control of the seas.

The goal for each player is to kill the opposing Captain. This is usually accomplished through cannon attacks or by boarding an opponent's ship and killing the crew in one-on-one duels. Every starter deck contains five sea location cards, and players use these five cards as their "game board," sailing their ships back and forth on them in an attempt to claim victory. Players could complete adventures in far-off seas to make their crew and ship more powerful before they launched the attack on their opponent.

A powerful strategy that emerged out of the first set included lots of cannon — and we do mean *lots!* Decks focused on giving a single crew of as much cannon as possible, hoping to kill off an opponent in a single shot. There were cards to stop this kind of strategy, but they were rare and are still difficult to get today.

With a powerful backing from the *Legends of the Five Rings* player base, 7th Sea has managed to stay afloat. While several powerful strategies were found in the first set that caused some players to walk out, most have hung around and have seen the game become more balanced over the past few expansion sets. The result of all this is a game that is slowly but surely growing and gaining life. — *Joe Alread*

Concept	●●●●○		
Gameplay	●●●○○		
Card art	●●●●○		
Player pool	●●●○○		

Set (323 cards)		200.00
Starter Box		110.00
Booster Box		92.00
Starter Deck		10.00
Booster Pack		3.00

You will need **36** nine-pocket pages to store this set (18 doubled up).

Card Name	Type	Rarity	Price
12-Pound Cannon Volley	Action	C	0.25
16-Pound Cannon Volley	Action	U	0.50
20-Pound Cannon Volley	Action	R	4.00
A Better Offer	Action	C	0.25
A Hero's Courage	Action	R	4.00
A Sailor's Quarrel	Action	C	0.25
Across the Mirror	Adventure	R	0.25
"Again, Boys!"	Action	R	3.50
Aimon Riché du Pourisse	Crew	C	0.25
Alesio	Crew	R	5.00
Allende	Captain	X	2.00
Ambush Boarding	Action	R	4.00
Ancient Maps	Adventure	R	4.00
Andrei Levovich	Crew	C	0.25
Angus McCloud	Crew	U	0.80
Antonio Aldonez	Crew	U	0.80
Archaeologists	Crew	C	0.25
Artifact Leg	Action	R	3.50
Arturo Rodriguez	Crew	R	4.00
Asprey	Attachment	C	0.25
Augusto Rodriguez	Attachment	C	0.25
Avalon Noble	Adventure	C	0.25
Avoid Fate	Attachment	R	3.00
Away Boarders!	Action	R	3.00
Babette	Crew	U	0.80
Bad Maps	Action	C	0.25
Bad Powder	Action	C	0.25
Barrels of Beer	Adventure	C	0.25
Berek	Captain	X	2.00
Betrayal	Action	R	5.00
Billy Bones	Attachment	U	0.50
Bjornsson's Horn	Adventure	R	4.00
Black Heart	Action	U	0.50
Blacktooth Bill	Crew	C	0.50
Bloody Bonnie McGee	Crew	R	5.80
Bolts of Fine Cloth	Adventure	C	0.25

Card name	Type	Rarity	Price
Brennan	Crew	U	0.50
Broken Compass Inn	Attachment	C	0.25
Brutes	Crew	C	0.25
Buccaneers	Crew	C	0.25
Bully Boys	Crew	C	0.25
Burke	Action	R	4.00
Calm before the Storm	Action	R	4.00
Captain's Quarters	Attachment	R	4.00
Carlos Altenar	Crew	C	0.25
Carousing	Action	C	0.25
Casks of Fine Wine	Adventure	C	0.25
Castille Gunpowder	Action	U	0.50
Castillian Merchant Ship	Adventure	C	0.25
Castillian Swordmaster	Adventure	U	0.50
Cat o' Nine Tails	Attachment	U	0.50
Celedoine	Crew	R	4.50
Chain Shot	Action	R	4.00
Charter	Attachment	X	2.00
Cheap Barrels	Action	U	0.50
Confusion	Attachment	R	3.80
Constitution	Attachment	R	1.30
Corazón del Castille	Ship	X	2.00
Cosette	Crew	R	6.00
Courtly Manner	Action	U	0.50
Crashing Seas	Adventure	C	0.25
Crescent Fire	Action	U	0.50
Crossing the T	Action	R	4.00
Cut the Ropes!	Action	C	0.25
Cutlass	Attachment	C	0.25
Cutlass of Command	Adventure	U	0.80
Dark Temptations	Action	R	3.50
Dead Men Tell No Tales	Action	R	4.00
Death From Above!	Action	R	4.00
Decks Awash	Action	R	3.00
Decks Running Red	Action	R	3.50
Denny La Bree	Crew	C	0.25
Derwyddon's Schemes	Action	R	3.00
Direct Hit!	Action	C	0.25
Disarmed!	Action	R	4.00
Divvying the Plunder	Action	R	4.00
Domingo Gunner	Crew	U	0.50
Domingo Marten de Avila	Crew	U	0.50

Card name	Type	Rarity	Price
Don Deanna	Crew	U	0.50
Donna	Crew	R	5.00
Dorf Klinderhoff	Crew	R	5.00
Eisen Cannons	Adventure	C	0.25
Enrique Orduño	Captain	X	2.00
Evasive Course	Action	R	4.00
Eyepatch	Action	U	0.50
Fancy Dans	Crew	C	0.25
Fate's Blessing	Attachment	R	3.00
Fierbas Desaix du Paix	Crew	U	0.50
Fine Galley	Attachment	C	0.25
Fire the Chase Guns!	Action	R	4.00
Flashing Swords Inn	Attachment	U	0.50
Flipe Jose de Granjero	Crew	R	5.00
Flogging	Action	U	0.80
Forbidden Delicacies	Adventure	C	0.25
Forbidden Sea	Sea	X	1.00
Foul Weather Jack	Crew	C	0.25
Franzini's Lost Notebooks	Adventure	C	0.25
From Stern to Gudgeon	Action	C	0.25
From the Depths!	Adventure	R	4.00
Frothing Sea	Sea	X	1.00
Fyodor Zastienchivy	Crew	U	0.50
Galleon of the Treasure Fleet	Attachment	U	0.50
Gambling House	Action	R	3.00
Gerald Höhne	Crew	U	0.50
Gerard Rois et Reines	Crew	R	5.00
Gilles Allais du Crieux	Crew	U	0.50
Glamour Knowledge	Attachment	R	3.00
Glimpse of the Skein	Attachment	R	3.00
Gold Only Buys Obedience	Action	C	0.25
Good King Sandoval	Attachment	R	4.00
Good Shot!	Action	C	0.25
Grape Shot	Action	R	4.00
Grappling Gun	Attachment	R	4.00
Grappling Hooks	Action	C	0.25
Grenouille du Grâce	Ship	X	2.00
Grimey Stubbs	Crew	R	4.00
Grousin' George	Crew	R	4.00
Guy McCormick	Captain	X	2.00
Hammocks	Attachment	R	5.00
Handsome Scar	Action	U	0.50

RARITY KEY C = Common U = Uncommon R = Rare VR = Very Rare UR = Ultra Rare F = Foil card X = Fixed/standard in all decks

42 • *SCRYE Collectible Card Game Checklist and Price Guide*

7th Sea

Alderac Entertainment Group • First set, **No Quarter**, released **August 1999**

323 cards in set • **IDENTIFIER: Cannon on black background at center right**

- Starter decks contain 65 cards; starter displays contain 12 starters
- Booster packs contain 15 cards; booster displays contain 36 boosters

Lead designer: **Dan Verssen**

Concept	●●●●○
Gameplay	●●●○○
Card art	●●●●○
Player pool	●●●○○

Full of pirates, adventuring and swashbuckling, **7th Sea** gave players their first taste of sea combat in the card gaming industry. Like the successful **Legend of the Five Rings** CCG, it had its own storyline, as factions battle each other for control of the seas.

The goal for each player is to kill the opposing Captain. This is usually accomplished through cannon attacks or by boarding an opponent's ship and killing the crew in one-on-one duels. Every starter deck contains five sea location cards, and players use these five cards as their "game board," sailing their ships back and forth on them in an attempt to claim victory. Players could complete adventures in far-off seas to make their crew and ship more powerful before they launched the attack on their opponent.

A powerful strategy that emerged out of the first set included lots of cannon — and we do mean *lots!* Decks focused on giving a single crew of a ship as much cannon as possible, hoping to kill off an opponent in a single shot. There were cards to stop this kind of strategy, but they were rare and are still difficult to get today.

With a powerful backing from the *Legends of the Five Rings* player base, *7th Sea* has managed to stay afloat. While several powerful strategies were found in the first set that caused some players to walk out, most have hung around and have seen the game become more balanced over the past few expansion sets. The result of all this is a game that is slowly but surely growing and gaining life. — *Joe Alread*

Set (323 cards)		200.00
Starter Box		110.00
Booster Box		92.00
Starter Deck		10.00
Booster Pack		3.00

> You will need **36** nine-pocket pages to store this set. (18 doubled up)

Card name	Type	Rarity	Price
12-Pound Cannon Volley	Action	C	0.25
16-Pound Cannon Volley	Action	U	0.50
20-Pound Cannon Volley	Action	R	4.00
A Better Offer	Action	C	0.25
A Hero's Courage	Action	R	4.00
A Sailor's Quarrel	Action	C	0.25
Across the Mirror	Adventure	C	0.25
"Again, Boys!"	Action	R	3.50
Aimon Riché du Pourisse	Crew	C	0.25
Alesio	Crew	R	5.00
Allende	Captain	X	2.00
Ambush Boarding	Action	R	4.00
Ancient Maps	Adventure	R	4.00
Andrei Levovich	Crew	C	0.25
Angus McCloud	Crew	U	0.80
Antonio Aldonez	Crew	U	0.80
Archæologists	Crew	C	0.25
Artifact Leg	Action	R	3.50
Arturo Rodriguez	Crew	R	4.00
Asprey	Attachment	C	0.25
Augusto Rodrizguez	Attachment	C	0.25
Avalon Noble	Adventure	C	0.25
Avoid Fate	Attachment	R	3.00
Away Boarders!	Action	R	3.00
Babette	Crew	U	0.80
Bad Maps	Action	C	0.25
Bad Powder	Action	C	0.25
Barrels of Beer	Adventure	C	0.25
Berek	Captain	X	2.00
Betrayal	Action	R	5.00
Billy Bones	Attachment	U	0.50
Bjørnsson's Horn	Adventure	R	4.00
Black Heart	Action	U	0.50
Blacktooth Bill	Crew	C	0.25
Bloody Bonnie McGee	Crew	R	5.80
Bolts of Fine Cloth	Adventure	C	0.25

Card name	Type	Rarity	Price
Brennan	Crew	U	0.50
Broken Compass Inn	Attachment	C	0.25
Brutes	Crew	C	0.25
Buccaneers	Crew	C	0.25
Bully Boys	Crew	C	0.25
Burke	Crew	R	4.00
Calm before the Storm	Action	C	0.25
Captain's Quarters	Attachment	R	4.00
Carlos Altenar	Crew	C	0.25
Carousing	Action	C	0.25
Casks of Fine Wine	Adventure	C	0.25
Castille Gunpowder	Action	U	0.50
Castillian Merchant Ship	Adventure	C	0.25
Castillian Swordmaster	Adventure	U	0.50
Cat o' Nine Tails	Attachment	U	0.50
Celedoine	Crew	R	4.50
Chain Shot	Action	R	4.00
Charter	Attachment	X	2.00
Cheap Barrels	Action	U	0.50
Confusion	Attachment	R	3.80
Constitution	Attachment	X	1.30
Corazón del Castille	Ship	X	2.00
Cosette	Crew	R	6.00
Courtly Manner	Action	U	0.50
Crashing Seas	Adventure	C	0.25
Crescent Fire	Action	U	0.50
Crossing the T	Action	R	4.00
Cut the Ropes!	Action	C	0.25
Cutlass	Attachment	C	0.25
Cutlass of Command	Adventure	U	0.80
Dark Temptations	Action	R	3.50
Dead Men Tell No Tales	Action	R	4.00
Death From Above!	Action	R	4.00
Decks Awash	Action	R	3.00
Decks Running Red	Action	R	3.50
Denny La Bree	Crew	C	0.25
Derwyddon's Schemes	Action	R	3.00
Direct Hit!	Action	C	0.25
Disarmed!	Action	R	4.00
Divvying the Plunder	Action	R	4.00
Domingo Gunner	Crew	U	0.50
Domingo Marten de Avila	Crew	U	0.50

Card name	Type	Rarity	Price
Don Deanna	Crew	U	0.50
Donna	Crew	R	5.00
Dorf Klinderhoff	Crew	R	5.00
Eisen Cannons	Adventure	C	0.25
Enrique Orduño	Captain	X	2.00
Evasive Course	Action	R	4.00
Eyepatch	Action	U	0.50
Fancy Dans	Crew	C	0.25
Fate's Blessing	Attachment	R	3.00
Fierbas Desaix du Paix	Crew	U	0.50
Fine Galley	Attachment	C	0.25
Fire the Chase Guns!	Action	R	4.00
Flashing Swords Inn	Attachment	U	0.50
Flipe Jose de Granjero	Crew	R	5.00
Flogging	Action	U	0.80
Forbidden Delicacies	Adventure	C	0.25
Forbidden Sea	Sea	X	1.00
Foul Weather Jack	Crew	C	0.25
Franzini's Lost Notebooks	Adventure	C	0.25
From Stem to Gudgeon	Action	C	0.25
From the Depths!	Adventure	R	4.00
Frothing Sea	Sea	X	1.00
Fyodor Zastienchivy	Crew	U	0.50
Galleon of the Treasure Fleet	Attachment	C	0.25
Gambling House	Action	R	3.00
Gerald Höhne	Crew	U	0.50
Gerard Rois et Reines	Crew	R	5.00
Gilles Allais du Crieux	Crew	U	0.50
Glamour Knowledge	Attachment	R	3.00
Glimpse of the Skein	Attachment	R	3.00
Gold Only Buys Obedience	Action	C	0.25
Good King Sandoval	Attachment	R	4.00
Good Shot!	Action	C	0.25
Grape Shot	Action	R	4.00
Grappling Gun	Attachment	R	4.00
Grappling Hooks	Action	C	0.25
Grenouille du Grâce	Ship	X	2.00
Grimey Stubbs	Crew	R	4.00
Grousin' George	Crew	R	4.00
Guy McCormick	Captain	X	2.00
Hammocks	Attachment	R	5.00
Handsome Scar	Action	U	0.50

RARITY KEY C = Common U = Uncommon R = Rare VR = Very Rare UR = Ultra Rare F = Foil card X = Fixed/standard in all decks

Card name	Type	Rarity	Price
Here There Be Monsters	Attachment	U	0.50
Hidden Knife	Attachment	U	0.50
Hiding in the Reefs	Action	C	0.25
High Seas Boarding	Action	C	0.25
Hired Swordsman	Action	R	4.00
Hole in the Hull	Action	U	0.50

15

Card name	Type	Rarity	Price
Hook	Action	U	0.50
I Fights Better Drunk	Action	C	0.25
I Told You Not to Trust Him	Action	R	4.00
Into the Fray	Action	R	3.00
Invar Andersson	Crew	U	0.50
Isabeau Dubois du Arrent	Crew	C	0.25
It's Who You Know	Action	C	0.25
Ivory Spyglass	Adventure	R	4.00
Jack Tars	Crew	C	0.25

16

Card name	Type	Rarity	Price
Jack Trades	Crew	R	4.50
Jacob Faust	Crew	U	0.50
Javier de Bejarano	Crew	R	4.00
Jemy	Crew	C	0.25
Jens Bjørn	Crew	U	0.50
Jillison Brown	Crew	C	0.25
Jimmy Bass	Crew	U	0.50
Joern Keitelsson	Crew	R	5.00
Julius Caligari	Crew	U	0.50

17

Card name	Type	Rarity	Price
Keel of Rowan Wood	Adventure	R	4.00
Korintine Nicolovich	Crew	R	5.00
La Boca	Sea	X	1.00
Lady Katerina	Adventure	C	0.25
Last Second Cannon Volley	Action	R	4.00
Leonard Pinkerton	Crew	U	0.50
Letter of Marque	Attachment	X	2.00
Leviathan Bone	Action	R	3.00
Li'll Jim	Crew	U	0.50

18

Card name	Type	Rarity	Price
Lord Windamshire	Crew	U	0.50
Louis Sices du Sices	Crew	C	0.25
Lucky Lou	Crew	U	0.50
Lucrezia	Crew	U	0.50
Luis de Rioja	Crew	C	0.25
Lyin' John Fox	Crew	C	0.25
Mad Jack O'Bannon	Attachment	R	3.00
Mad Mario	Crew	U	0.50
Maggie Malone	Crew	C	0.25

19

Card name	Type	Rarity	Price
Manuel Dejavez	Crew	U	0.50
Margaretta Orduño	Crew	R	5.00
Mark Scars	Crew	R	4.30
Marketeers	Crew	C	0.25
Master Gunner	Attachment	C	0.25
Master of the Tops	Attachment	C	0.25
Maureen Leveque	Crew	U	0.50
Mermaids	Action	U	0.50
Michael Fitzhugh	Crew	U	0.50

20

Card name	Type	Rarity	Price
Michael Rois et Reines	Crew	U	0.50
Mind Your P's and Q's	Action	R	3.80
Misfire	Action	C	0.25
Monkey's Fist	Action	U	0.50
Montaigne Puzzle Sword	Attachment	U	0.50
Montaigne Valet	Attachment	C	0.25
Mordekai's Casket	Adventure	U	0.50
Mountainous Mike	Crew	U	0.50
Mr. Briggs	Attachment	R	4.00

21

Card name	Type	Rarity	Price
Mr. Smythe	Crew	U	0.50
Musketeers	Attachment	C	0.25
Mutiny!	Action	R	4.00
Narrow Escape	Action	U	0.50
Naval Sanction	Attachment	X	2.00
Near Miss	Action	C	0.25
Needle Nose Nye	Crew	C	0.25
Nice Try!	Action	R	4.00
No Escape!	Action	R	4.00

22

Card name	Type	Rarity	Price
Off Course	Action	U	0.50
One with the Sails	Action	U	0.50
Only Two Came Out	Attachment	U	0.50
Otiro	Crew	U	0.50

Card name	Type	Rarity	Price
Out of Rum	Action	U	0.50
Padre Alfonso	Crew	R	5.00
Padre Esteban	Crew	C	0.25
Panache	Action	U	0.50
Passionate Duel	Adventure	U	0.50

23

Card name	Type	Rarity	Price
Paule du Paix	Crew	U	0.50
Peek at the Future	Attachment	R	3.50
Peg Leg	Action	U	0.50
Pepin	Crew	R	5.00
Persuasion	Attachment	R	4.00
Phelan Cole	Crew	U	0.50
Phineas Flynn	Crew	U	0.50
Piles of Skulls	Action	R	3.00
Point Blank Cannon Volley	Action	C	0.25

24

Card name	Type	Rarity	Price
Port Master	Attachment	R	4.00
Porté Knowledge	Attachment	R	4.00
Porté Ward	Attachment	R	3.00
Powder Monkeys	Crew	C	0.25
Prepare for Boarding!	Action	C	0.25
Press Gang	Action	C	0.25
Queen Elaine	Attachment	R	4.00
Queen of the Sea	Action	R	4.00
Queen of the Sidhe	Attachment	R	4.00

25

Card name	Type	Rarity	Price
Quick Reload	Action	U	0.50
Quick Sailing	Action	U	0.50
Quick Tack	Action	C	0.25
Rafael de St. Theresa	Crew	C	0.25
Ramming Speed!	Action	R	4.00
Rats!	Attachment	U	0.50
Raze the Village	Adventure	C	0.25
Reclusive Backers	Attachment	C	0.25
Red	Attachment	C	0.25

26

Card name	Type	Rarity	Price
Red Scarves	Crew	C	0.25
Red Skies at Morning	Action	R	4.00
Red Skies at Night	Action	C	0.25
Reggie Wilcox	Crew	R	4.00
Reis	Captain	X	2.00
Riant Gaucher	Crew	R	4.00
Riggers	Crew	C	0.25
Roger Gaffrin	Crew	U	0.50
Romantic Captive	Attachment	R	4.00

27

Card name	Type	Rarity	Price
Rosa Maria de Barcino	Crew	U	0.50
Rosamonde du Montaigne	Crew	C	0.25
Rose & Cross Apprentice	Adventure	C	0.25
Rough Voyage	Action	U	0.50
Rough Waters	Attachment	U	0.50
Sabotaged Sails	Action	U	0.50
Sailing under the Jolly Roger	Action	U	0.50
Sails of Wind	Adventure	R	4.00
Samuel Sanderson	Crew	C	0.25

28

Card name	Type	Rarity	Price
Samuel Smitts	Crew	C	0.25
Sandoval's Guard	Crew	C	0.25
Save the Princess	Adventure	C	0.25
Scarlet Hook of Madness	Action	R	4.00
Scott Jay	Crew	R	4.00
Scraping the Bottom	Adventure	U	0.50
Scurvy	Action	U	0.50
Seal of the Sun King	Attachment	X	2.00
Sean McCorley	Crew	U	0.50

29

Card name	Type	Rarity	Price
Seven League Striders	Attachment	U	0.50
Shellbacks	Crew	C	0.25
Sidhe Sails	Adventure	U	0.50
Sidney	Crew	U	0.50
Sinking of The Swan	Adventure	C	0.25
Slip of the Tongue	Action	C	0.25
Slippery Sal	Crew	U	0.50
Sniper	Action	U	0.50
Solomon Sails	Crew	U	0.50

30

Card name	Type	Rarity	Price
Son of a Gun	Action	R	4.00
Southern Trade Winds	Action	R	4.00
Speed Isn't Everything	Action	C	0.25
St. Roger's Blessing	Attachment	R	3.00
St. Roger's Day	Action	C	0.25

Card name	Type	Rarity	Price
Steal Their Wind	Action	U	0.50
Steering Clear	Action	C	0.25
Stirring Speech	Action	R	3.00
Stolen Guns	Adventure	U	0.50

31

Card name	Type	Rarity	Price
Storms Make Sailors	Adventure	C	0.25
Swivelling Cannon	Attachment	U	0.50
Syrneth Crystal Eye	Action	R	4.00
Tagging	Action	C	0.25
Take No Prisoners!	Attachment	U	0.50
Target Their Powder Room	Action	R	4.00
The Better Part of Valor	Action	C	0.25
The Black Dawn	Ship	X	2.00
The Calloways	Crew	U	0.50

32

Card name	Type	Rarity	Price
The Crimson Roger	Ship	X	2.00
The Discovery	Ship	X	2.00
The General	Captain	X	2.00
The Great Grey	Action	U	0.50
The Hanged Man	Ship	X	2.00
The Inquisition	Attachment	U	0.50
The Living Storm	Action	U	0.50
The Marquis d'Arrent	Attachment	R	4.00
The Mirror	Sea	X	1.00

33

Card name	Type	Rarity	Price
The Ocean's Teeth	Adventure	R	3.00
The Pact of the Crimson Rogers	Attachment	X	2.00
The Sailor's Curse	Action	U	0.50
Thom Brunner	Crew	C	0.25
Thomas Metzger	Crew	U	0.50
Through the Portal	Attachment	R	4.00
Timothy le Beau	Crew	R	4.00
Tom Toblin	Crew	U	0.50
Too Close for Comfort	Action	C	0.25

34

Card name	Type	Rarity	Price
Trade Sea	Sea	X	1.00
Treasure Hold	Attachment	U	0.50
Two-Toe Terrance	Crew	C	0.25
Unexpected Turn of Events	Action	U	0.50
Ussuran Pelts	Adventure	C	0.25
Velik	Crew	U	0.50
Vincent Rochester	Crew	C	0.25
Vincenzo Caligari	Attachment	R	3.00
Vodacce Valuables	Adventure	U	0.50

35

Card name	Type	Rarity	Price
Vodanken	Action	R	4.00
Warren Abbotsford	Crew	U	0.50
Waylaid	Attachment	C	0.25
We Needs Us an Ussuran Gunner	Adventure	U	0.50
Wee Willy	Crew	R	4.00
Wenching	Action	C	0.25
When All Else Fails	Action	C	0.25
Who Can You Trust?	Action	R	3.00
Who Shot the Albatross?	Attachment	U	0.50

36

Card name	Type	Rarity	Price
Wilhelm Dünst	Crew	R	5.00
William Fodd	Crew	U	0.50
William Toss	Crew	C	0.25
Willowed Ropes	Attachment	U	0.50
Wind at Your Back	Adventure	C	0.25
Winds of Fate	Adventure	C	0.25
Wreckers	Adventure	R	3.50
You Won't Be Needin' This!	Action	R	4.00

7th Sea tips

"Many players forget to do this, but it can be helpful to watch what your opponent discards. This gives you an insight into the makeup of his deck, as well as what he's thinking. If your opponent throws away a key boarding card, then you probably won't need to worry about being boarded for the rest of the turn."

— Kevin Wilson, Scrye 6.4 (Oct 99)

RARITY KEY C = Common U = Uncommon R = Rare VR = Very Rare UR = Ultra Rare F = Foil card X = Fixed/standard in all decks

7th Sea • Broadsides
(No Quarter, 2nd ed.)

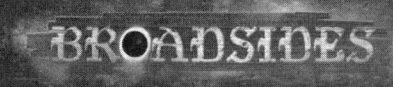

Alderac Entertainment Group • Released **January 2000**

323 cards in set • **IDENTIFIER: Skull and crossbones on green at center right**

- Starter decks contain 65 cards; starter displays contain 12 starters
- Booster packs contain 15 cards; Booster displays contain 36 boosters

Broadsides reprinted the **No Quarter** set, with a few minor changes. Starter decks contain a new type of fixed card for each faction, Figureheads, which replace six of the cards from *No Quarter*.

The specific cards omitted are **Charter, Constitution, Letter of Marque, Naval Sanction, Seal of the Sun King,** *and* **The Pact of the Crimson Rogers.**

The replacement cards are **Lumière de l'Empereur, The Gallows, The Queen's Reward, The Reaper, The Shield Man,** and **The Spear of Theus.** Some of these cards were better than others and sold appropriately.

As far as the rest of the set goes, there were only minor text changes on the cards and nothing else. — *Joe Alread*

SCRYE NOTES: *While cards of this set bear a 1999 copyright, the set did not hit stores until 2000.*

Set (323 cards)	**160.00**
Starter Box	**99.00**
Booster Box	**90.00**
Starter Deck	**9.00**
Booster Pack	**3.00**

You will need **36** nine-pocket pages to store this set. (18 doubled up)

Card name	Type	Rarity	Price
12-Pound Cannon Volley	Action	C	0.20
16-Pound Cannon Volley	Action	U	0.80
20-Pound Cannon Volley	Action	R	3.80
A Better Offer	Action	C	0.15
A Hero's Courage	Action	R	2.50
A Sailor's Quarrel	Action	C	0.15
Across the Mirror	Adventure	C	0.15
"Again, Boys!"	Action	R	2.50
Aimon Riché du Pourisse	Crew	C	0.15
Alesio	Crew	R	4.30
Allende	Captain	X	2.50
Ambush Boarding	Action	R	3.30
Ancient Maps	Adventure	R	3.30
Andrei Levovich	Crew	C	0.15
Angus McCloud	Crew	U	0.50
Antonio Aldonez	Crew	U	0.50
Archæologists	Crew	C	0.15
Artifact Leg	Action	R	2.50
Arturo Rodriguez	Crew	R	2.80
Asprey	Attachment	C	0.15
Augusto Rodrizguez	Attachment	C	0.15
Avalon Noble	Adventure	C	0.15
Avoid Fate	Attachment	R	2.80
Away Boarders!	Action	R	2.50
Babette	Crew	U	0.50
Bad Maps	Action	C	0.15
Bad Powder	Action	C	0.15
Barrels of Beer	Adventure	C	0.15
Berek	Captain	X	2.50
Betrayal	Action	R	4.80
Billy Bones	Attachment	U	0.50
Bjørnsson's Horn	Adventure	R	2.50
Black Heart	Action	U	0.50
Blacktooth Bill	Crew	C	0.15

Card name	Type	Rarity	Price
Bloody Bonnie McGee	Crew	R	3.80
Bolts of Fine Cloth	Adventure	C	0.15
Brennan	Crew	U	0.50
Broken Compass Inn	Attachment	C	0.15
Brutes	Crew	C	0.15
Buccaneers	Crew	C	0.15
Bully Boys	Crew	C	0.15
Burke	Crew	R	2.50
Calm Before the Storm	Action	C	0.15
Captain's Quarters	Attachment	R	2.50
Carlos Altenar	Crew	C	0.15
Carousing	Action	C	0.15
Casks of Fine Wine	Adventure	C	0.15
Castille Gunpowder	Action	U	1.30
Castillian Merchant Ship	Adventure	C	0.15
Castillian Swordmaster	Adventure	U	0.50
Cat O' Nine Tails	Attachment	U	1.30
Celedoine	Crew	R	3.30
Chain Shot	Action	R	4.30
Cheap Barrels	Action	U	0.50
Confusion	Attachment	R	3.00
Corazón del Castille	Ship	X	2.50
Cosette	Crew	R	4.80
Courtly Manner	Action	U	0.50
Crashing Seas	Adventure	C	0.15
Crescent Fire	Action	U	0.80
Crossing the T	Action	R	4.80
Cut The Ropes!	Action	C	0.15
Cutlass	Attachment	C	0.15
Cutlass of Command	Adventure	U	0.80
Dark Temptations	Action	R	2.50
Dead Men Tell No Tales	Action	R	3.30
Death From Above!	Action	R	3.30
Decks Awash	Action	R	2.50
Decks Running Red	Action	R	2.50
Denny La Bree	Crew	C	0.15
Derwyddon's Schemes	Action	R	3.50
Direct Hit!	Action	C	0.20
Disarmed!	Action	R	3.80
Divvying the Plunder	Action	R	2.80
Domingo Gunner	Crew	U	0.50
Domingo Marten de Avila	Crew	U	0.50
Don Deanna	Crew	U	0.80
Donna	Crew	R	3.80
Dorf Klinderhoff	Crew	R	3.30

Card name	Type	Rarity	Price
Eisen Cannons	Adventure	C	0.15
Enrique Orduño	Captain	X	2.50
Evasive Course	Action	R	3.80
Eyepatch	Action	U	0.80
Fancy Dans	Crew	C	0.15
Fate's Blessing	Attachment	R	2.50
Fierbas Desaix du Paix	Crew	U	0.80
Fine Galley	Attachment	C	0.20
Fire the Chase Guns!	Action	R	3.80
Flashing Swords Inn	Attachment	U	0.50
Flipe Jose de Granjero	Crew	R	2.50
Flogging	Action	U	0.50
Forbidden Delicacies	Adventure	C	0.15
Forbidden Sea	Sea	X	2.00
Foul Weather Jack	Crew	C	0.15
Franzini's Lost Notebooks	Adventure	C	0.15
From Stem to Gudgeon	Action	C	0.15
From The Depths!	Adventure	R	3.30
Frothing Sea	Sea	X	2.00
Fyodor Zastienchivy	Crew	U	0.50
Galleon of the Treasure Fleet	Attachment	C	0.15
Gambling House	Action	R	3.30
Gerald Höhne	Crew	U	0.50
Gerard Rois et Reines	Crew	R	3.80
Gilles Allais du Crieux	Crew	U	0.80
Glamour Knowledge	Attachment	R	2.30
Glimpse of the Skein	Attachment	R	2.50
Gold Only Buys Obedience	Action	C	0.15
Good King Sandoval	Attachment	R	2.50
Good Shot!	Action	C	0.15
Grape Shot	Action	R	4.80
Grappling Gun	Attachment	R	4.80
Grappling Hooks	Action	C	0.15
Grenouille du Grâce	Ship	X	2.50
Grimey Stubbs	Crew	R	2.50
Grousin' George	Crew	R	2.50
Guy McCormick	Captain	X	2.50
Hammocks	Attachment	R	4.00
Handsome Scar	Action	U	0.80
Here There Be Monsters	Attachment	U	0.80
Hidden Knife	Attachment	U	0.50
Hiding in the Reefs	Action	C	0.15
High Seas Boarding	Action	C	0.15
Hired Swordsman	Action	R	3.30
Hole in the Hull	Action	U	0.80

RARITY KEY   **C** = Common   **U** = Uncommon   **R** = Rare   **VR** = Very Rare   **UR** = Ultra Rare   **F** = Foil card   **X** = Fixed/standard in all decks

Card name	Type	Rarity	Price
Hook	Action	U	0.50
I Fights Better Drunk	Action	C	0.15
I Told You Not To Trust Him	Action	R	3.30
Into the Fray	Action	R	2.50
Invar Andersson	Crew	U	0.50
Isabeau Dubois du Arrent	Crew	C	0.15
It's Who You Know	Action	C	0.15
Ivory Spyglass	Adventure	R	3.80
Jack Tars	Crew	C	0.20
Jack Trades	Crew	R	3.80
Jacob Faust	Crew	U	0.80
Javier de Bejarano	Crew	R	2.50
Jemy	Crew	C	0.15
Jens Bjørn	Crew	U	0.50
Jillison Brown	Crew	C	0.15
Jimmy Bass	Crew	U	0.50
Joern Keitelsson	Crew	R	3.80
Julius Caligari	Crew	U	0.80
Keel of Rowan Wood	Adventure	R	2.50
Korintine Nicolovich	Crew	R	2.50
La Boca	Sea	X	2.00
Lady Katerina	Adventure	C	0.15
Last Second Cannon Volley	Action	R	3.30
Leonard Pinkerton	Crew	U	0.50
Leviathan Bone	Action	R	2.50
Li'll Jim	Crew	U	0.50
Lord Windamshire	Crew	U	0.50
Louis Sices du Sices	Crew	C	0.15
Lucky Lou	Crew	U	0.50
Lucrezia	Crew	U	0.50
Luis de Rioja	Crew	C	0.15
Lumière de l'Empereur	Attachment	X	3.00
Lyin' John Fox	Crew	C	0.15
Mad Jack O'Bannon	Attachment	R	3.30
Mad Mario	Crew	U	0.50
Maggie Malone	Crew	C	0.15
Manuel Dejavez	Crew	U	0.80
Margaretta Orduño	Crew	R	4.80
Mark Scars	Crew	R	3.30
Marketeers	Crew	C	0.15
Master Gunner	Attachment	C	0.15
Master of the Tops	Attachment	C	0.15
Maureen Leveque	Crew	U	1.50
Mermaids	Action	U	1.30
Michael Fitzhugh	Crew	U	0.80
Michael Rois et Reines	Crew	U	0.80
Mind Your P's and Q's	Action	R	2.50
Misfire	Action	C	0.15
Monkey's Fist	Action	U	0.50
Montaigne Puzzle Sword	Attachment	U	0.50
Montaigne Valet	Attachment	C	0.15
Mordekei's Casket	Adventure	U	0.50
Mountainous Mike	Crew	U	0.80
Mr. Briggs	Attachment	R	3.30
Mr. Smythe	Crew	U	0.80
Musketeers	Attachment	C	0.15
Mutiny!	Action	R	3.80
Narrow Escape	Action	U	0.50
Near Miss	Action	C	0.15
Needle Nose Nye	Crew	C	0.15
Nice Try!	Action	R	2.50
No Escape!	Action	R	3.80
Off Course	Action	U	0.80
One with the Sails	Action	U	0.50
Only Two Came Out	Attachment	U	0.50
Otiro	Crew	U	0.50
Out of Rum	Action	U	0.50
Padre Alfonso	Crew	R	3.30
Padre Esteban	Crew	C	0.15
Panache	Action	U	0.80

Card name	Type	Rarity	Price
Passionate Duel	Adventure	U	0.50
Paule du Paix	Crew	U	0.50
Peek at the Future	Attachment	R	2.50
Peg Leg	Action	U	1.00
Pepin	Crew	R	3.80
Persuasion	Attachment	R	2.50
Phelan Cole	Crew	U	0.80
Phineas Flynn	Crew	U	0.80
Piles of Skulls	Action	R	2.50
Point Blank Cannon Volley	Action	C	0.15
Port Master	Attachment	R	2.50
Porté Knowledge	Attachment	R	2.50
Porté Ward	Attachment	R	2.50
Powder Monkeys	Crew	C	0.15
Prepare for Boarding!	Action	C	0.15
Press Gang	Action	C	0.15
Queen Elaine	Attachment	R	2.50
Queen of the Sea	Action	R	2.50
Queen of the Sidhe	Attachment	R	2.50
Quick Reload	Action	U	0.80
Quick Sailing	Action	U	0.80
Quick Tack	Action	C	0.15
Rafael de St. Theresa	Crew	C	0.15
Ramming Speed!	Action	R	3.80
Rats!	Attachment	U	0.50
Raze the Village	Adventure	C	0.15
Reclusive Backers	Attachment	C	0.15
Red	Attachment	C	0.15
Red Scarves	Crew	C	0.15
Red Skies at Morning	Action	R	3.30
Red Skies at Night	Action	C	0.15
Reggie Wilcox	Crew	R	3.30
Reis	Captain	X	2.50
Riant Gaucher	Crew	R	2.50
Riggers	Crew	C	0.15
Roger Gaffrin	Crew	U	0.80
Romantic Captive	Attachment	R	2.50
Rosa Maria de Barcino	Crew	U	0.80
Rosamonde du Montaigne	Crew	C	0.15
Rose & Cross Apprentice	Adventure	C	0.15
Rough Voyage	Action	U	0.80
Rough Waters	Attachment	U	0.50
Sabotaged Sails	Action	U	0.80
Sailing Under the Jolly Roger	Action	U	1.30
Sails of Wind	Adventure	R	2.50
Samuel Sanderson	Crew	C	0.15
Samuel Smitts	Crew	C	0.15
Sandoval's Guard	Crew	C	0.15
Save the Princess	Adventure	C	0.15
Scarlet Hook of Madness	Action	R	3.30
Scott Jay	Crew	R	2.50
Scraping the Bottom	Adventure	U	0.50
Scurvy	Action	U	0.80
Sean McCorley	Crew	U	0.80
Seven League Striders	Attachment	U	0.80
Shellbacks	Crew	C	0.15
Sidhe Sails	Adventure	U	0.50
Sidney	Crew	U	0.80
Sinking of The Swan	Adventure	C	0.15
Slip of the Tongue	Action	C	0.15
Slippery Sal	Crew	U	0.50
Sniper	Action	U	0.50
Solomon Sails	Crew	U	0.80
Son of a Gun	Action	R	2.50
Southern Trade Winds	Action	R	2.50
Speed Isn't Everything	Action	C	0.15
St. Roger's Blessing	Attachment	R	2.50
St. Roger's Day	Action	C	0.15
Steal Their Wind	Action	U	0.50
Steering Clear	Action	C	0.15

Card name	Type	Rarity	Price
Stirring Speech	Action	R	3.00
Stolen Guns	Adventure	U	0.50
Storms Make Sailors	Adventure	C	0.15
Swivelling Cannon	Attachment	U	1.30
Syrneth Crystal Eye	Action	R	2.50
Tagging	Action	C	0.15
Take No Prisoners!	Attachment	U	0.80
Target Their Powder Room	Action	R	2.50
The Better Part of Valor	Action	C	0.15
The Black Dawn	Ship	X	2.50
The Calloways	Crew	U	0.80
The Crimson Roger	Ship	X	2.50
The Discovery	Ship	X	2.50
The Gallows	Attachment	X	3.00
The General	Captain	X	2.50
The Great Grey	Action	U	1.30
The Hanged Man	Ship	X	2.50
The Inquisition	Attachment	U	0.50
The Living Storm	Action	U	1.30
The Marquis d'Arrent	Attachment	R	2.50
The Mirror	Sea	X	2.00
The Ocean's Teeth	Adventure	R	2.50
The Queen's Reward	Attachment	X	3.00
The Reaper	Attachment	X	3.00
The Sailor's Curse	Action	U	0.50
The Shield Man	Attachment	X	3.00
The Spear of Theus	Attachment	X	3.00
Thom Brunner	Crew	C	0.15
Thomas Metzger	Crew	U	0.80
Through the Portal	Attachment	R	3.30
Timothy le Beau	Crew	R	2.50
Tom Toblin	Crew	U	0.80
Too Close for Comfort	Action	C	0.15
Trade Sea	Sea	X	2.00
Treasure Hold	Attachment	U	0.50
Two-Toe Terrance	Crew	C	0.15
Unexpected Turn of Events	Action	U	1.30
Ussuran Pelts	Adventure	C	0.15
Velik	Crew	U	1.30
Vincent Rochester	Crew	C	0.15
Vincenzo Caligari	Attachment	R	2.50
Vodacce Valuables	Adventure	U	0.50
Vodanken	Action	R	3.30
Warren Abbotsford	Crew	U	0.50
Waylaid	Attachment	C	0.15
We Needs Us An Ussuran Gunner	Adventure	U	0.50
Wee Willy	Crew	R	2.50
Wenching	Action	C	0.15
When All Else Fails	Action	C	0.15
Who Can You Trust?	Action	R	3.30
Who Shot the Albatross?	Attachment	U	0.50
Wilhelm Dünst	Crew	R	2.50
William Fodd	Crew	U	0.80
William Toss	Crew	C	0.15
Willowed Ropes	Attachment	U	0.50
Wind at Your Back	Adventure	C	0.15
Winds of Fate	Adventure	C	0.15
Wreckers	Adventure	R	2.50
You Won't be Needin' This!	Action	R	2.50

7th Sea art

7th Sea set sail with a variety of creators on board. Artists on the first release include William O'Connor, Val Mayerik, Quinton Hoover, Drew Tucker, April Lee, Ed Cox, Jonathan Hunt, Michael Phillippi, and Mark Pennington.

RARITY KEY C = Common U = Uncommon R = Rare VR = Very Rare UR = Ultra Rare F = Foil card X = Fixed/standard in all decks

7th Sea • Strange Vistas

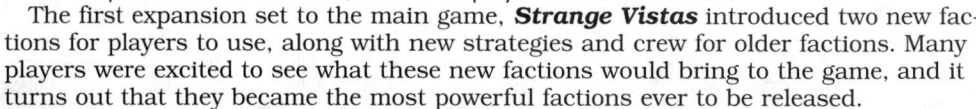

Alderac Entertainment Group • Released **December 1999**

156 cards in set • **IDENTIFIER: Ship's sail on blue at center right**

- Starter decks contain 65 cards; starter displays contain 12 starters
- Booster packs contain 15 cards; booster displays contain 36 boosters

The first expansion set to the main game, ***Strange Vistas*** introduced two new factions for players to use, along with new strategies and crew for older factions. Many players were excited to see what these new factions would bring to the game, and it turns out that they became the most powerful factions ever to be released.

With the new factions dominating deck types, many of the older factions lost some playability as a result of this expansion. Powerful strategies from ***No Quarter*** were pretty much ignored.

Through it all, though, the power of these new factions kept players interested enough to wait and see what was given to them in the next set. — **Joe Alread**

Set (156 cards)	140.00
Starter Box	77.50
Booster Box	81.50
Starter Deck	10.00
Booster Pack	3.00

You will need 18 nine-pocket pages to store this set. (9 doubled up)

Card name	Type	Rarity	Price
1			
A Gallant Stand	Adventure	C	0.25
A Sailor's First Skill	Attachment	C	0.25
Al-Katim	Crew	C	0.25
Aldana School	Attachment	U	1.00
All For One!	Action	U	0.80
Ambrogia School	Attachment	U	0.80
Ancient Training Techniques	Adventure	U	0.80
Andre Braudel	Crew	R	4.00
Andres Donovich	Crew	C	0.25
2			
Artifact Cannon	Adventure	R	3.50
Back Alley Rum	Adventure	U	0.80
Becalmed	Action	C	0.25
Belaying Pin	Attachment	C	0.25
Belit	Attachment	R	3.00
Berek's Already Done That	Action	U	0.80
Bjorn Brind	Crew	U	0.80
Boatload of Jennys	Adventure	U	0.80
Braving the Nor'wester	Adventure	R	3.00
3			
Brotherhood Pride	Action	R	3.00
Cannister Shot	Action	C	0.25
Cargo Hook	Attachment	C	0.25
Castille Pride	Action	R	3.00
Common Pier	Attachment	C	0.25
Cool Castillian Blood	Attachment	U	0.80
Corsair Pride	Action	R	3.00
Crimson Roger Pride	Action	R	3.00
Cross of Virtue	Attachment	R	3.00
4			
Crossfire	Adventure	R	3.00
Customs Check	Action	U	0.80
Dalia	Crew	U	0.80
Danger on the High Seas	Action	C	0.25
Dangerous Cargo	Adventure	U	0.80
Daniel	Crew	U	0.80
Dispatching The Scum	Action	R	3.00
Disregard	Action	R	3.00
Donovan School	Attachment	U	0.80
5			
Dredging the Trade River	Adventure	U	0.80
Drop a Boarding Net	Action	C	0.25
Dunti	Crew	U	0.80
Dupre & Hans	Crew	C	0.25
Edahgo	Crew	R	4.50
Eisenfaust School	Attachment	U	0.80
Entertainers	Crew	C	0.25
Escorting the MacDuff	Adventure	C	0.25
Espera	Crew	C	0.25
6			
Experience is the Best Teacher	Action	R	3.00
Explorer Pride	Action	R	3.00

Card name	Type	Rarity	Price
Fancy Footwork	Adventure	U	0.80
Fancy Swordplay	Action	C	0.25
Fine Rigging	Adventure	U	0.80
First Mate's Watch	Action	R	3.50
Galafré Flaubert du Doré	Crew	U	0.80
Galley Captives	Crew	C	0.25
Gaspar	Crew	R	4.00
7			
Ghouls Sneak on Board	Action	U	0.80
Giovanni Villanova	Attachment	R	3.00
Gold Earring	Attachment	C	0.25
Gosse Pride	Action	R	3.00
Grappling Cannon	Attachment	C	0.25
Gunnery at its Finest	Action	C	0.25
Hamish	Crew	R	3.50
Harpoon	Attachment	C	0.25
Helpful Advice	Action	U	0.80
8			
Henderson	Crew	C	0.25
Hernando Ochoa	Crew	C	0.25
Iken of Venderheim	Crew	R	4.00
"I'll Be Taking That"	Action	U	0.80
Imshi	Crew	R	3.50
Infection	Action	U	0.80
Inil	Crew	U	0.80
Jack-of-All-Trades	Attachment	R	3.00
Jean-Marie Rois-et-Reines	Attachment	U	0.80
9			
Jenny House	Attachment	C	0.25
Joseph Dunn	Crew	C	0.25
Julia	Crew	C	0.25
Kalem the Believer	Attachment	R	3.00
Kheired-Din	Captain	X	1.00
Kheired-Din's Secret	Attachment	R	3.00
Leegstra School	Attachment	U	0.80
Lemons	Action	C	0.25
Long Hand	Attachment	U	0.80
10			
Long Range Cannon Volley	Action	C	0.25
Low on Shot	Action	R	3.00
Mabela	Crew	U	0.80
Making of a Hero	Adventure	R	3.00
Man the Bilge Pumps!	Action	C	0.25
Martin Tytus	Crew	C	0.25
McCormick's Quest	Action	R	3.00
Melinda Gosse	Crew	R	5.00
Miguel Cortez	Crew	U	0.80
11			
Mike Fitzpatrick	Crew	U	0.80
Montaigne Pride	Action	R	3.00
Musket	Attachment	C	0.25
Old Flame	Attachment	R	3.00
Palace Raid	Adventure	C	0.25
Parting Shot	Action	C	0.25
Philip Gosse	Captain	X	1.00
Pistol	Attachment	C	0.25
Plague of Boca	Action	C	0.25
12			
Posh Quarters	Attachment	R	3.00
Prayer	Action	U	0.80
Purple Heaves	Action	R	3.00

Card name	Type	Rarity	Price
Ramming Spike	Attachment	U	0.80
Retired Smuggler	Attachment	C	0.25
Rigged for Speed	Attachment	R	3.00
Riposte	Action	C	0.25
Roger School	Attachment	U	0.80
Run 'im Through!	Action	C	0.25
13			
Safe Path	Attachment	U	0.80
Sea Dog Pride	Action	R	3.00
Secrets of the Tops	Action	C	0.25
Sergei Nyasvy	Crew	U	0.80
Seven-Color Sam	Crew	C	0.25
Shala	Crew	R	4.00
Sharp Maneuvering	Action	C	0.25
Shore Knowledge	Attachment	U	0.80
Sidhe Storm	Adventure	R	3.00
14			
Special Gift	Attachment	U	0.80
Staying Ahead of Trouble	Adventure	R	3.00
Strange Skies	Ship	X	1.00
Strength isn't Everything	Adventure	C	0.25
"Stroke, Stroke..."	Action	U	0.80
Syrneth Tiller	Adventure	C	0.25
Take it Like a Man!	Action	U	0.80
Taking the Hit	Action	C	0.25
The Captain's Word	Action	R	3.00
15			
The Code	Attachment	X	1.00
The Finest Cannons...	Adventure	C	0.25
The First Switch	Adventure	R	3.00
The General's Tactics	Action	R	3.00
The Three Fate Witches	Action	U	0.80
The Unwritten Rules	Attachment	F	1.00
The Wrath of Reis	Action	R	3.00
Théah Eats the Weak	Action	C	0.25
Their Captain's Will	Adventure	C	0.25
16			
There's More Where They Came From	Action	U	0.80
Thomas Gosse	Crew	U	0.80
Throw Me the Whip!	Action	C	0.25
Torvo Espada	Crew	R	4.00
Trinkets and Baubles	Adventure	U	0.80
Turning Enemies Into Friends	Action	U	0.80
Tyree the Worthless	Crew	R	4.00
Uncharted Course	Ship	X	1.00
Uprising!	Action	U	0.80
17			
Ussuran Intrigue	Adventure	U	0.80
Valroux School	Attachment	U	0.80
Volta	Crew	U	4.00
Wake of Estallio	Action	C	0.25
Walk the Plank!	Action	U	0.80
Warship	Attachment	R	3.00
"Warship to Port!"	Action	C	0.25
We're Doomed!	Attachment	U	0.80
Well Equipped Sick Bay	Attachment	R	3.00
18			
Well Stocked Armory	Attachment	R	3.00
Wild Party!	Action	R	3.00
X Almost Marks the Spot	Action	R	3.00

RARITY KEY C = Common U = Uncommon R = Rare VR = Very Rare UR = Ultra Rare F = Foil card X = Fixed/standard in all decks

7th Sea • Shifting Tides

Alderac Entertainment Group • Released **March 2000**
156 cards in set • **IDENTIFIER: Crown on red at center right**

- Starter decks contain 65 cards; starter displays contain 12 starters
- Booster packs contain 15 cards; booster displays contain 36 boosters

Some of the problems that **7th Sea** had were fixed with the release of **Shifting Tides**. Putting lots of cannon cards on a single crew was, all of a sudden, very risky. Two new factions were reintroduced and, while they weren't as strong as what was seen in **Strange Vistas**, they were sure to get the boosts they needed in time.

Also released with this set was a new alternative winning condition, which was implemented by a new card type called the control card. If you were able to get all five different control cards into play, you would win. These cards were easy for your opponent to get rid of, though, and didn't see much success until they got the help they needed from the next set, **Scarlet Seas**. — **Joe Alread**

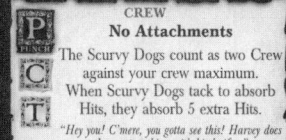

Set (156 cards)	120.00		
Starter Box	90.00		
Booster Box	90.00		
Starter Deck	9.00		
Booster Pack	2.70		

You will need 18 nine-pocket pages to store this set. (9 doubled up)

Card name	Type	Rarity	Price
Advanced Swordsmanship	Attachment	R	3.50
Adventuring Galley	Attachment	U	0.80
Aether Compass	Adventure	R	3.50
Alister McGurk	Crew	C	0.25
Allied Warship	Attachment	U	0.80
Allow Me...	Action	U	0.80
Ambroise Praisse du Richetoisse	Crew	U	0.80
Amiral Alazais Valoix-Praisse III	Captain	X	1.50
Armed Brig	Attachment	U	0.80
Armed Frigate	Attachment	U	0.80
Arnlaug Rijs Bragison	Crew	C	0.25
Augusto de Augustin	Crew	R	5.00
Barcino Fortress	Adventure	U	0.80
Barnacles	Action	U	0.80
Basic Swordsmanship	Attachment	C	0.25
Beat You To It!	Action	R	4.00
Billy "Bilge Rat" Bones	Crew	R	4.00
Blows Up In Your Face	Action	U	0.80
Boarded by Skeletons	Action	R	4.00
Botas Rojas	Crew	C	0.25
Brawny Rowers	Crew	C	0.25
Brother Mattias Brewer	Crew	U	0.80
Burn Their Sails	Action	R	4.00
Captain	Attachment	R	4.00
Castillian Navy	Attachment	U	0.80
Challenge to a Duel	Action	C	0.25
Cheap Cutlass	Attachment	C	0.25
Cheap Sails	Attachment	C	0.25
Cheap Tools	Attachment	C	0.25
Close Range Cannon Volley	Action	C	0.25
Coastal Patrols	Attachment	U	0.80
Connor Lynch	Crew	R	3.80
Corsairs Figurehead	Attachment	R	3.50
Crescent Treasures	Attachment	U	0.80
Cut Throats	Crew	C	0.25
Delaina Darling	Crew	C	0.25
Desperate Move	Action	R	4.00
Dirk	Attachment	C	0.25
"Don't Mess With Me, Boy!"	Action	R	3.50
Egil Bergljot Larrson	Crew	U	0.80
El Vago	Attachment	R	4.00
Errant Match	Action	C	0.25
Felix l'Aigle	Crew	C	0.25
Fid Blue-Eye	Crew	R	4.00
Fine Boots	Attachment	C	0.25
Fine Rope and Tackle	Adventure	C	0.25
Fire and Steel	Action	R	4.00

Card name	Type	Rarity	Price
Fresh Powder	Adventure	C	0.25
Gino Napoli	Crew	U	0.80
Good Use of Space	Attachment	C	0.25
Gosse Figurehead	Attachment	R	4.00
Graham Hapworth	Crew	C	0.25
Gris Hallisdottir	Crew	U	0.80
Gustolph Hirsch	Crew	U	0.80
Gytha Ives	Crew	C	0.25
Haunted by the Past	Action	R	3.50
Headed Out	Action	U	0.80
Herje (Ruin)	Attachment	R	3.50
Heroic Stand	Action	U	0.80
Hoskuld Hardrada	Crew	R	4.00
Into the Fog	Action	C	0.25
Jacques Renault	Crew	R	4.00
Jorund Guttormsson	Crew	U	0.80
Kedish the Crescent	Crew	R	4.00
Kirsten Blumfeld	Crew	U	0.80
Kjøtt (Flesh)	Attachment	X	0.90
Lady's Kiss	Action	C	0.25
Last Second Escape!	Action	C	0.25
Le Prédateur des Mers	Ship	X	1.50
Leila	Crew	U	0.80
Lightening the Load	Action	U	0.80
Listen!	Action	U	0.80
Long Tall Harry	Crew	R	4.00
Lowly Captives	Crew	C	0.25
Lucky Vandrad Hallvardson	Crew	C	0.25
Main Gauche	Attachment	C	0.25
Major Hull Damage	Action	R	4.00
Marcel Entour	Crew	C	0.25
Michael Rois et Reines	Crew	U	0.80
Minor Hull Damage	Action	C	0.25
Montaigne Exports	Adventure	U	0.80
Musette Falisci	Crew	R	3.50
Navigational Tools	Adventure	C	0.25
No Banter ...	Action	C	0.25
... No Barter ...	Action	U	0.80
... No Quarter!	Action	R	4.00
Nød (Intensity)	Attachment	U	0.80
Northern Allies	Attachment	U	0.80
Oar Team	Crew	C	0.25
Obscured by the Smoke	Action	U	0.80
Offensive Maneuvers	Adventure	C	0.25
Orm Greybeard	Crew	U	0.80
Pack 'em In!	Attachment	U	0.80
Panzerhand	Attachment	C	0.25
Peter Silver	Crew	U	0.80
"Please, take your time"	Action	U	0.80
Pocket Money	Attachment	C	0.25
Poor Jack	Action	C	0.25
Powder Keg Tavern	Attachment	R	4.00
Pulling Through	Attachment	R	4.00
Red the Adventurer	Crew	U	0.90
Red Thorfild	Crew	R	4.00

Card name	Type	Rarity	Price
Repel Boarders!	Action	C	0.25
Reporting Drunk	Action	C	0.25
Ring of Honor	Adventure	R	4.00
Ring of Villainy	Adventure	R	4.00
Rognvald Brandson	Crew	R	4.00
Rosamonde du Montaigne	Crew	R	5.00
Ruby Earring	Attachment	C	0.25
Runed Ship's Wheel	Adventure	R	4.00
Santino Medrano	Crew	U	0.80
Scarlet Launch	Attachment	R	3.50
Scary Tattoo	Attachment	C	0.25
Scurvy Dogs	Crew	C	0.25
Secret of the Winds	Attachment	R	3.50
Sharp Shooter	Action	U	0.80
Shot Across the Bow	Action	R	3.50
Sighted Pistol	Adventure	C	0.25
Sigvaldi Sveinson	Crew	R	4.00
Silver Earring	Attachment	C	0.25
Slashing Across the Decks	Adventure	R	4.00
Small Fortress	Attachment	U	0.80
Speedy Courier	Attachment	U	0.80
Spit in Death's Eye	Adventure	C	0.25
Stans (Calm)	Attachment	U	0.80
Sterk (Wholeness)	Attachment	U	0.80
Stolen Documents	Adventure	C	0.25
Stolen Sword	Adventure	U	0.80
Styrke (Strength)	Attachment	U	0.80
"Tar, Tar, and More Tar"	Action	R	3.50
Tarsis the Mad	Crew	R	5.00
That Hurts!	Action	U	0.80
The Gullet	Crew	U	0.80
The Kire	Crew	R	4.00
The Ogre	Attachment	U	0.80
The Revensj	Ship	X	1.50
The River	Attachment	R	4.00
The Second Switch	Adventure	R	4.00
Therein Lies a Tale	Action	C	0.25
Thordis Bjerregaard	Crew	U	0.80
Timothy le Beau	Crew	X	0.90
To Fight Another Day	Action	R	4.00
Tugging the Strands	Attachment	R	4.00
Ulf Karlssen	Crew	R	5.00
Unexpected Hero	Attachment	C	0.25
Valkyries	Crew	C	0.25
Vesten Figurehead	Attachment	R	4.00
Vesten Pride	Action	R	3.50
Victory for the Bold	Action	U	0.80
Villskap (Fury)	Attachment	U	0.80
Vivianne Étalon du Toille	Crew	C	0.25
Vodanken's Breath	Action	R	3.50
Willie Wilcox	Crew	U	0.80
Would-Be Traders	Action	C	0.25
Wounded	Action	R	3.50
Yngvild Olafssdottir	Captain	X	1.50

RARITY KEY C = Common **U** = Uncommon **R** = Rare **VR** = Very Rare **UR** = Ultra Rare **F** = Foil card **X** = Fixed/standard in all decks

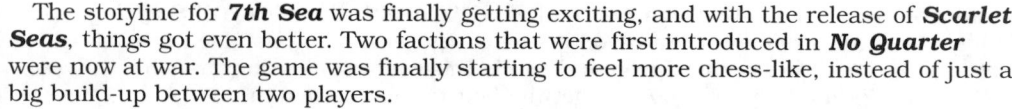

7th Sea • Scarlet Seas

Alderac Entertainment Group • Released **August 2000**
156 cards in set • **IDENTIFIER:** Swashbuckling symbol at right
- Starter decks contain 65 cards; starter displays contain 12 starters
- Booster packs contain 15 cards; booster displays contain 36 boosters

The storyline for **7th Sea** was finally getting exciting, and with the release of **Scarlet Seas**, things got even better. Two factions that were first introduced in **No Quarter** were now at war. The game was finally starting to feel more chess-like, instead of just a big build-up between two players.

Scarlet Sails has a large number of powerful cards in it, making it highly desirable. Control decks got a huge boost, and they started winning major tournaments. Many of the remaining over-powerful strategies out of **No Quarter** were all but destroyed with this set, giving the game more balance than it had ever had. — **Joe Alread**

Captain Reis card

Start: Forbidden Sea
Villainous • Swordsman +2 (Reis inflicts 2 extra Hits during Boarding Attacks)
While you have three or more other Crimson Rogers Crew on your Ship, your Cannon costs to play, cancel, discard, or sink a card are reduced by 3 (minimum 1).

Set (156 cards)	100.00
Starter Box	90.00
Booster Box	90.00
Starter Deck	9.00
Booster Pack	3.00

You will need 18 nine-pocket pages to store this set. (9 doubled up)

Card name	Type	Rarity	Price
7th Sea Eddy	Action	R	3.00
A Coward Among Us	Action	U	0.50
Adeeb Al-Amid	Crew	C	0.10
...and He Makes Witty Repartee	Action	R	3.50
...and One for All	Action	C	0.10
Andrew Littlejohn	Crew	C	0.10
Angus McCloud	Crew	R	4.00
Annie Rush	Crew	C	0.10
Babette	Crew	R	3.50
Backs to the Wall	Action	C	0.10
Bad Luck	Action	R	3.00
Barnacle Pete	Crew	U	0.50
Barracuda	Action	R	3.50
Battle of San Felipe	Adventure	C	0.10
Below the Waterline	Action	C	0.10
Best Served Cold ...	Action	U	0.80
Big Target	Action	R	3.00
Blockade	Attachment	C	0.10
Brenden Stafford	Attachment	R	3.50
Butcher Pinchot	Crew	U	0.50
By the Gods ...	Attachment	R	3.00
Cafe of Broken Dreams	Attachment	C	0.10
Call to Duty	Action	C	0.10
Cannons of la Bucca	Attachment	U	0.80
Captain Bonnie McGee	Captain	X	0.90
Captain Reis	Captain	X	0.90
Celedoine	Crew	X	0.90
Cheap Cannons	Attachment	C	0.10
Cheap Gunpowder	Action	C	0.10
Clear Skies	Action	R	3.00
Clear the Decks	Action	C	0.10
Confusion on Deck	Action	C	0.10
Cornelius van Brock	Crew	C	0.10
Dark Dreams	Action	C	0.10
Dashing Duel	Action	U	0.50
Defense of the Motherland	Attachment	R	3.00
Desperate Wages	Action	U	0.50
Destiny's Touch	Action	C	0.10
Diplomatic Envoy	Attachment	R	3.00
Disguised Ship	Action	C	0.10
Don't Make me Ask again	Action	R	4.00
Double the Rum Ration	Action	R	4.00
Down to the Nub	Action	U	0.80
Dry Docks	Attachment	R	3.50
Duel with a Castillian	Adventure	U	0.50
Eisen Cannon Balls	Adventure	C	0.10
Eisen Steel	Adventure	U	0.80

Card name	Type	Rarity	Price
Extra Watch	Action	C	0.10
Eye of the Storm	Adventure	R	3.50
Faisal	Crew	U	0.50
Fate's Web	Attachment	U	0.50
Favor for a Noble	Adventure	C	0.10
Fear and Fire	Attachment	U	0.50
Francois Gaulle dul Motte	Crew	C	0.10
Friendly Winds	Action	U	0.50
Gaspar	Crew	R	3.50
Gem of Warning	Adventure	R	3.50
Geno	Crew	U	0.50
Gerald Höhne	Crew	R	3.50
Gillian the Razor	Crew	C	0.10
Guns Blazing	Action	C	0.10
Hand of the Sirens	Attachment	U	0.50
Harsh Light of Reality	Action	R	3.00
He Fights Well ...	Action	R	3.00
... He Rides Well ...	Action	R	3.00
High Seas Cannoning	Attachment	C	0.10
Hoskuld Hardrada	Crew	R	3.50
Høst (Harvest)	Attachment	R	3.00
Hostile Harbor	Attachment	C	0.10
Howls of Vengeance	Attachment	C	0.10
I'm Not Left-Handed	Action	R	4.00
Inil	Crew	R	4.00
Inquisitor Bascalle	Crew	R	4.00
It's A Trap	Action	U	0.80
Javier de Bejarano	Crew	R	4.00
Jemy	Crew	U	0.50
Joern Keitelsson	Crew	X	0.90
Jorund's Betrayal	Action	R	3.00
King before Captain	Action	U	0.80
La Bucca Defenses	Attachment	R	3.00
Land Lubber	Action	R	3.50
Li'll Jim	Crew	R	3.50
Lightning Flash	Action	C	0.10
Livestock	Action	C	0.10
Locked In Death	Action	R	3.50
Marc Pierre	Crew	U	0.50
Maria Forlani	Crew	U	0.50
Marker Barrel	Attachment	U	0.50
Master of Wind and Tide	Attachment	U	0.50
Max Discher	Crew	C	0.10
Merchant Quarter	Attachment	C	0.10
Merchant Ship	Attachment	C	0.10
Moment of Glory	Action	U	0.80
Montaigne Ship of the Line	Attachment	R	4.00
Mother-in-Law	Attachment	U	0.80
Mumblety Peg	Crew	R	4.00
Natalia Ivanova	Crew	C	0.10
Nicole Cowbey	Crew	U	0.80
Night of Horror	Action	U	0.80
No Survivors!	Action	C	0.10
Orf Helfir	Crew	U	0.50
Out of Action	Action	U	0.80

Card name	Type	Rarity	Price
Pertruccio Garibaldi	Crew	U	0.50
Phantom Topman	Attachment	R	3.50
Phelan Cole	Crew	R	4.00
Pulled From the Sea	Action	C	0.10
Queen Eleanor	Attachment	R	3.00
Rabbit's Foot	Attachment	C	0.10
Rats in the Hold	Attachment	R	3.00
Richardo Ramos	Crew	U	0.50
Rita del Zepeda	Crew	C	0.10
Rum Runners	Attachment	C	0.10
Rune Knowledge	Attachment	U	0.50
Sabine Montjoy	Crew	C	0.10
Sea Chantey	Action	U	0.50
Sean McCorley	Crew	R	4.00
Secret Stash	Attachment	C	0.10
She's Coming Apart!	Action	U	0.50
Ship's Boat	Attachment	R	3.00
Ship's Brig	Attachment	U	0.80
Show of Force	Attachment	U	0.80
Skeletal Boarding Gang	Crew	U	0.50
Slow Tack	Action	C	0.10
Speak Softly...	Attachment	U	0.50
Succubus	Action	R	3.00
Swift Vengence	Attachment	U	0.50
Swimming with Sharks	Action	C	0.10
Swing from the Rigging	Action	C	0.10
Syrneth Guardians	Action	R	3.50
Syrneth Powder	Adventure	R	3.50
Tempting the Portal	Attachment	R	3.00
The Crow's Nest	Attachment	U	0.50
"The Few, the Proud ..."	Action	U	0.80
The Grey Queen's Price	Attachment	R	3.00
The Hurricane	Ship	X	0.90
The Right Place	Attachment	R	3.00
The Scarlet Roger	Ship	X	0.90
The Third Switch	Adventure	C	0.10
Therein Lies a Tale	Action	U	0.50
Through the Magic Mirror	Adventure	U	0.80
Tight-Knit Crew	Attachment	R	3.00
Tools of the Trade	Action	C	0.10
Top Dog	Action	R	3.00
Topaz Broach	Attachment	C	0.10
Underwater Cave	Action	U	0.50
Unreliable	Action	U	0.50
Ussuran Brawl	Adventure	U	0.50
Velda Conklin	Crew	C	0.10
Vendel Smugglers	Attachment	C	0.10
Vengeful Serpent	Attachment	U	0.80
Vestenmannavnjar Archers	Crew	C	0.10
Vestenmannavnjar Funeral	Action	R	3.00
Vile Duel	Action	U	0.50
Vodacce Pirates	Attachment	U	0.50
Will Do You No Good!	Action	C	0.10
Without a Trace ...	Action	U	0.80

RARITY KEY C = Common U = Uncommon R = Rare VR = Very Rare UR = Ultra Rare F = Foil card X = Fixed/standard in all decks

7th Sea • Black Sails

Alderac Entertainment Group • Released **November 2000** • **53** cards in set
IDENTIFIER: Black sail at center right • Starter decks contain 65 cards
• Booster packs contain 50 cards • Sold from combo displays with 5 starters and 8 booster packs

Black Sails introduces the dreaded Black Freighter into the game, bringing with it dead sailors who had once been aligned with other factions. Rather than containing random cards, *Black Sails* boosters contain 50 of the 53 cards in the set. Starters contain the three fixed cards as well as cards from other sets.

While the set is still being explored, early reports suggest that our undead sailors may not be as powerful as originally thought. Their low statistics and somewhat restrictive abilites have made them difficult to build a winning deck with. However, due to their popularity it should only be a matter of time until this faction gets the power it needs to strike some real fear into those who live in the lands of Theah. — *Joe Alread*

Set (53 cards)	20.00		
Combo Box	129.25	**6**	
Starter Deck	10.00	nine-pocket	
Booster Pack	10.00	pages to store this set. (3 doubled up)	

Card name	Type	Rarity	Price
☐ Armed Sloop	Attachment	XB	0.40
☐ Black Freighter	Ship	XS	2.00
☐ Black Heart of the Sea	Attachment	XB	0.40
☐ Black Siren	Attachment	XB	0.40
☐ Captain Necros	Captain	XS	2.00
☐ Dalia	Crew	XB	0.40
☐ Denny La Bree	Crew	XB	0.40
☐ Don Deanna	Crew	XB	0.40
☐ Feed the Hunger	Adventure	XB	0.40
☐ Gilles Allais du Crieux	Crew	XB	0.40
☐ Gold Coins	Adventure	XB	0.40
☐ High Morale	Adventure	XB	0.40
☐ Iken of Venderheim	Crew	XB	0.40
☐ Innocent Bystander	Action	XB	0.40

Card name	Type	Rarity	Price
☐ Kiss of Death	Action	XB	0.40
☐ Lord Windamshire	Crew	XB	0.40
☐ Mark Scars	Crew	XB	0.40
☐ Marooned	Action	XB	0.40
☐ Moaning Song of the Dead	Action	XB	0.40
☐ Moldy Morris	Crew	XB	0.40
☐ Never Knew Him	Action	XB	0.40
☐ No-Leg William	Crew	XB	0.40
☐ Plague Ship	Attachment	XB	0.40
☐ Power of Purity	Action	XB	0.40
☐ Reinheart the Ripper	Crew	XB	0.40
☐ "Rigger" Mortis	Crew	XB	0.40
☐ "Run 'em Down Boys!"	Action	XB	0.40
☐ Rusty Cutlass	Adventure	XB	0.40
☐ Samuel Smitts	Crew	XB	0.40
☐ Savage Storm	Attachment	XB	0.40
☐ Scarlet Gem of Death	Adventure	XB	0.40
☐ Skeletal Cannon Crew	Crew	XB	0.40
☐ Skeletal Deck Hands	Crew	XB	0.40
☐ Skeletal Sabotuers	Crew	XB	0.40

Card name	Type	Rarity	Price
☐ Skeletal Sail Crew	Crew	XB	0.40
☐ Skeletal Thugs	Crew	XB	0.40
☐ Skull Shot	Action	XB	0.40
☐ Stench	Crew	XB	0.40
☐ Tales of the Black Freighter	Action	XB	0.40
☐ The Curse	Attachment	XS	2.00
☐ Thomas Gosse	Crew	XB	0.40
☐ To the Death!	Action	XB	0.40
☐ Traitor's Scream	Attachment	XB	0.40
☐ Ulrich the Unholy	Crew	XB	0.40
☐ Victor of Luthon	Crew	XB	0.40
☐ Vile Temple	Attachment	XB	0.40
☐ Water Bloated Bill	Crew	XB	0.40
☐ Well of Purity	Adventure	XB	0.40
☐ William Toss	Crew	XB	0.40
☐ Would-Be Gunners	Action	XB	0.40
☐ Zombie Dans	Crew	XB	0.40
☐ Zombie Riggers	Crew	XB	0.40
☐ Zombie Shore Gang	Crew	XB	0.40

7th Sea • Foil promo cards

Alderac Entertainment Group

Many of the promotional cards were released in certain magazines and the **7th Sea** newsletter, *The Crow's Nest*, and can be found nowhere else. Many of these cards are fairly weak, but the few that are not command $10 and more in some places.

There are foil versions of cards from the regular sets, and these have the expansion symbol. The non-foil promo **Samuel Smitts** appeared in *Scrye 6.4* and has no expansion symbol.— *Joe Alread*

Fair Weather Friend

Card name	Type	Price
☐ A Friend in Need	Action	5.00
☐ Admiral Alazais Valoix Praisse III	Captain	8.00
☐ Allende	Captain	8.00
☐ Ambush	Action	5.00
☐ Berek	Captain	8.00
☐ Betrayal	Action	10.00
☐ Brothers in Arms	Action	5.00
☐ Calling in Favors	Action	5.00
☐ Captain Bonnie McGee	Captain	8.00
☐ Captain Necros	Captain	8.00
☐ Captain Reis	Captain	8.00
☐ Corazón del Castille	Ship	8.00
☐ Corsairs Figurehead	Attachment	5.00
☐ Enrique Ordu´no	Captain	8.00
☐ Fair Weather Friend (7th Sea Secret Society)	Ship	8.00
☐ Forbidden Sea (Tournament prize)	Sea	5.00
☐ Frothing Sea (Tournament prize)	Sea	5.00
☐ Gentleman's Agreement	Action	5.00
☐ Gosse Figurehead	Attachment	5.00

Card name	Type	Price
☐ Grenouille du Gráce	Ship	8.00
☐ Guy McCormick	Captain	8.00
☐ Hassad the Enforcer	Crew	5.00
☐ Ill Fated Journey	Attachment	5.00
☐ In the Dark of the Night (Broadsides League)	Action	5.00
☐ Indisposed (League prize)	Action	5.00
☐ Jacklyn the Black	Crew	5.00
☐ Kheired-Din	Captain	8.00
☐ La Boca (Tournament prize)	Sea	5.00
☐ Le Prédatuer des Mers	Ship	8.00
☐ Lumiére de l'Empereur	Attachment	5.00
☐ Neeman the Coward (League)	Crew	5.00
☐ Philip Gosse	Captain	8.00
☐ Plunder Redemption	Action	5.00
☐ Reis	Captain	8.00
☐ Strange Skies	Ship	8.00
☐ The Black Dawn	Ship	8.00
☐ The Black Freighter	Ship	8.00
☐ The Crimson Roger	Ship	8.00
☐ The Discovery	Ship	8.00
☐ The Gallows	Attachment	5.00
☐ The General	Captain	8.00
☐ The Hanged Man	Ship	8.00

Crew Maximum: 8
Immediately after players reveal their starting Crews, choose and sink up to 6 of the cards in your deck.
React: Tack before performing an action, to move to an adjacent Sea.

Card name	Type	Price
☐ The Homeward Arrow	Ship	8.00
☐ The Hurricane	Ship	8.00
☐ The Mirror (Tournament prize)	Sea	5.00
☐ The Moon Beckoned (7th Sea Secret Society)	Action	5.00
☐ The Queen's Reward	Attachment	5.00
☐ The Reaper	Attachment	5.00
☐ The Revensj	Ship	8.00
☐ The Scarlet Roger	Ship	8.00
☐ The Shield Man	Attachment	5.00
☐ The Spear of Theus	Attachment	5.00
☐ The Traitor's Scream	Attachment	5.00
☐ Trade Sea (Tournament prize)	Sea	5.00
☐ Uncharted Course	Ship	8.00
☐ Vesten Figurehead	Attachment	5.00
☐ What Do We Have Here? (Broadsides League prize)	Action	5.00
☐ Yngvild Olafssdottir	Captain	8.00

Age of Empires II

The United States Playing Card Co. • Released **December 2000**

269 cards in set

- Starters contain a 96-card starter deck, four Age Cards, a Civilization Card, one 12-card booster pack, and one rule book
- Starter displays contain 10 starters; two each Goths, Mongols, Persians, Celts, and Britons
- Booster packs contain 12 cards
- Booster displays contain 36 boosters

Designed by **Marcus D'Amelio** and **Ted Triebull**

The *Age of Empires II Expandable Card Game* is based one of the most popular computer games on the market, and Microsoft's Age of Empire lends itself well to conversion to an expandable card game format. As in the computer game, players struggle to advance their own civilization from the Dark Age, through the Feudal and Castle Ages, finally to the Imperial Age, holding out against the depredations of the civilizations of their opponents. Unlike the computer game, the *Age of Empires II* CCG allows for face-to-face competition without the need to lug around a computer. Also, *Age of Empires II* allows for the feel and sensibilities of a war game, yet has the relative simplicity and short learning curve of a card game, easily acting as a stepping stone between computer war games and board war games.

Players build their civilizations through the creation of villagers, the production of wood, stone, gold, and food, the development of advanced technologies, and the construction of new buildings. Villagers are produced through the expenditure of food, while the allocation of villagers to various location cards allows the collection of further resources, the research of new technologies, and the building of new locations (and so on, onward and upward). The only way to slow opponents' efforts to build their civilizations is to strike with military units, which destroy buildings and eliminate villagers. The game is won when one civilization loses all its town centers or loses all villagers, as well as the ability to produce more; or when a civilization advances to Imperial Age and constructs a Wonder of the World that lasts for six turns; or when a civilization gathers five relics and holds them for six turns.

Age of Empires II released shortly before this book went to print and too early for after-market pricing. Whether it will join the short list of successful, sustained CCGs or whether it will be lost in the howling wilderness of the Collectible Card Game Age has yet to be seen. — *James A. Mishler*

Concept	●●●●○
Gameplay	●●●○○
Card art	●●●○○
Player pool	●●●○○

Too new for pricing!
See current issues of SCRYE for the latest after-market prices!

Set (269 cards)

Starter Box	85.00
Booster Box	107.64
Starter Deck	8.50
Booster Pack	2.99

You will need 30 nine-pocket pages to store this set. (15 doubled up)

Promo cards

Card name	Type
Price	
☐ Bone Shaft Arrows	Event
☐ Celtic Battle Cry	Event
☐ Flood	Event
☐ Mystigogy	Event
☐ Rally the Workers	Event
☐ Shots in the Back	Event
☐ Spirits of the Ancestors	Event

Card name	Type	Rarity
[1]		
☐ A Branch from the Bo Tree	Relic	U
☐ Abandoned Mine	Event	C
☐ Alchemist	Event	C
☐ Arbalest	Upgrade	U
☐ Archer	Unit	C
☐ Archery Range (Arab)	Building	C
☐ Archery Range (European)	Building	C
☐ Archery Range (Far East)	Building	C
☐ Archery Range (Raider)	Building	C
[2]		
☐ Avalanche	Event	R
☐ Bad Omen	Event	C
☐ Bandits	Event	U

Card name	Type	Rarity
☐ Banking	Event	C
☐ Barracks (Arab)	Building	C
☐ Barracks (European)	Building	C
☐ Barracks (Far East)	Building	C
☐ Barracks (Raider)	Building	C
☐ Barracks Raid	Event	R
[3]		
☐ Barrel of Grog	Event	R
☐ Battering Ram	Unit	C
☐ Berries	Event	C
☐ Blacksmith (Arab)	Building	U
☐ Blacksmith (European)	Building	U
☐ Blacksmith (Far East)	Building	U
☐ Blacksmith (Raider)	Building	U
☐ Blast Furnace	Technology	R
☐ Boar	Event	C
[4]		
☐ Bodkin Arrow	Technology	U
☐ Bow Saw	Technology	U
☐ Bracer	Technology	R
☐ Briton Arbalest	Upgrade	R
☐ Briton Town Center	Building	U
☐ Brushfire	Event	R
☐ Camel	Unit	C
☐ Capped Ram	Upgrade	U
☐ Cartography	Technology	C
[5]		
☐ Castle (Arab)	Building	C
☐ Castle (European)	Building	C
☐ Castle (Far East)	Building	C
☐ Castle (Raider)	Building	C
☐ Castle Age (III)	Age	X
☐ Cavalier	Upgrade	U

Card name	Type	Rarity
☐ Cavalry Archer	Unit	U
☐ Celt Battering Ram	Unit	U
☐ Celt Capped Ram	Upgrade	U
[6]		
☐ Celt Champion	Upgrade	R
☐ Celt Heavy Scorpion	Upgrade	R
☐ Celt Long Swordsman	Upgrade	C
☐ Celt Man-at-Arms	Upgrade	C
☐ Celt Mangonel	Unit	U
☐ Celt Militia	Unit	C
☐ Celt Onager	Upgrade	U
☐ Celt Pikeman	Upgrade	U
☐ Celt Scorpion	Unit	U
[7]		
☐ Celt Siege Onager	Upgrade	R
☐ Celt Siege Ram	Upgrade	R
☐ Celt Spearman	Unit	C
☐ Celt Two-Handed Swordsman	Upgrade	R
☐ Chain Barding Armor	Technology	U
☐ Chain Mail Armor	Technology	U
☐ Champion	Upgrade	U
☐ Charlamagne's Palace at Aix la' Chapelle	Wonder	URF
☐ Charlamagne's Palace at Aix la' Chapelle	Building	R
[8]		
☐ Coinage	Event	C
☐ Conscription	Event	U
☐ Crop Rotation	Technology	R
☐ Crossbowman	Upgrade	U
☐ Dark Age (I)	Age	X
☐ Decoy	Event	U
☐ Deus Ex Machina	Event	R

RARITY KEY C = Common U = Uncommon R = Rare VR = Very Rare UR = Ultra Rare F = Foil card X = Fixed/standard in all decks

Card name	Type	Rarity
Double-Bit Axe	Technology	C
Drought	Event	C

9

Card name	Type	Rarity
Elite Huskarl	Upgrade	URF
Elite Huskarl	Upgrade	R
Elite Longbowman	Upgrade	URF
Elite Longbowman	Upgrade	R
Elite Mangudai	Upgrade	URF
Elite Mangudai	Upgrade	R
Elite Skirmisher	Upgrade	U
Elite War Elephant	Upgrade	URF
Elite War Elephant	Upgrade	R

10

Card name	Type	Rarity
Elite Woad Raider	Upgrade	URF
Elite Woad Raider	Upgrade	R
Emperor's Decree	Event	R
Epidemic	Event	R
Exposed Gold Deposit	Event	C
Fallen Tree	Event	C
Farm	Building	C
Festival Day	Event	R
Feudal Age (II)	Age	X

11

Card name	Type	Rarity
Fire Brigade	Event	C
Flaming Arrows	Event	C
Fletching	Technology	C
Followers of Tielle	Event	R
Foreign Scholar	Event	R
Forest Fire	Event	U
Forget the Past	Event	R
Forging	Technology	C
Fortified Wall	Upgrade	R

12

Card name	Type	Rarity
Fortune Favors the Foolish	Event	U
Fresh Bow String	Event	U
Gate	Building/Wall	R
Gathering Point	Event	C
Gold Mine	Building	C
Gold Mining	Technology	C
Gold Nugget	Event	C
Gold Shaft Mining	Technology	U
Golden Gonjir	Relic	U

13

Card name	Type	Rarity
Good Wind Today	Event	C
Goth Two-handed Swordsman	Upgrade	R
Goth Champion	Upgrade	R
Goth Long Swordsman	Upgrade	U
Goth Man-at-Arms	Upgrade	U
Goth Militia	Unit	U
Goth Pikeman	Upgrade	U
Goth Spearman	Unit	U
Guilds	Technology	U

14

Card name	Type	Rarity
Hand Cart	Technology	C
Heavy Camel	Upgrade	R
Heavy Cavalry Archer	Upgrade	R
Heavy Plow	Technology	U
Heavy Scorpion	Upgrade	U
Heavy Tree Cover	Event	C
High Ground	Event	U
Hoardings	Technology	C
Holy War	Event	C

15

Card name	Type	Rarity
Horse Collar	Technology	C
House (Arab)	Building	C
House (European)	Building	C
House (Far East)	Building	C
House (Raider)	Building	C
Husbandry	Event	C
Huskarl	Unit	R
Imperial Age (IV)	Age	X

16

Card name	Type	Rarity
Intimidation	Event	U
Iron Casting	Technology	U
"It's a Clever Fake!"	Event	U
Keeper of the Books	Event	R
Knight	Unit	U
Knowledge Has a Price	Event	C

Card name	Type	Rarity
Learn From Your Mistakes	Event	R
Leather Archer Armor	Technology	U
Light Cavalry	Upgrade	C
"Listen to a Story"	Event	U

17

Card name	Type	Rarity
Long Swordsman	Upgrade	C
Longbowman	Unit	R
Look to the Future	Event	R
Loom	Technology	C
Lumber Camp	Building	C
Man-at-Arms	Upgrade	C
Mangonel	Unit	C
Mangudai	Unit	R
Market (Arab)	Building	U

18

Card name	Type	Rarity
Market (European)	Building	U
Market (Far East)	Building	U
Market (Raider)	Building	U
Mercenaries	Event	U
Militia	Unit	C
Mill (Arabia)	Building	C
Mill (European)	Building	C
Mill (Far East)	Building	C
Mill (Raider)	Building	C

19

Card name	Type	Rarity
Mine Raid	Event	R
Monastery (Arab)	Building	R
Monastery (European)	Building	R
Monastery (Far East)	Building	R
Monastery (Raider)	Building	R
Mongel Cavalry Archer	Unit	U
Mongol Heavy Cavalry Archer	Upgrade	R
Mongol Light Cavalry	Upgrade	U
Mud Slide	Event	R

20

Card name	Type	Rarity
Muddy Battlefield	Event	U
Night Attack	Event	R
Onager	Upgrade	U
Outpost	Building	R
Padded Archer Armor	Technology	C
Paladin	Upgrade	U
Palisade Wall	Building/Wall	C
Persian Cavalier	Upgrade	R
Persian Knights	Unit	R

21

Card name	Type	Rarity
Persian Paladin	Upgrade	R
Persian Town Center	Building	U
Pikeman	Upgrade	C
Plate Barding Armor	Technology	R
Plate Mail armor	Technology	R
Poisoning the Well	Event	R
Poor Morale	Event	C
Population Explosion	Event	U
Putting up the Walls	Event	C

22

Card name	Type	Rarity
Quarry	Event	C
Recruiting	Event	R
Relentless Attack	Event	U
Revelation	Event	U
Ring Archer Armor	Technology	R
Robbed by Robin	Event	R
Rock Collection	Event	C
Rock of Cashel	Wonder	URF
Rock of Cashel	Building	R

23

Card name	Type	Rarity
Sandstorm	Event	R
Sappers	Event	C
Scale Barding Armor	Technology	C
Scale Mail Armor	Technology	C
Scorch the Land	Event	U
Scorpion	Unit	C
Scout Cavalry	Unit	C
Seal of Muhammed	Relic	U
Seige Sabotage	Event	C

24

Card name	Type	Rarity
Sheep	Event	C
Siege Onager	Upgrade	R
Siege Ram	Upgrade	R

Card name	Type	Rarity
Siege Workshop (Arab)	Building	U
Siege Workshop (European)	Building	U
Siege Workshop (Far East)	Building	U
Siege Workshop (Raider)	Building	U
Skirmisher	Unit	C
Slave Trade	Event	U

25

Card name	Type	Rarity
Slow Research	Event	C
Spearman	Unit	C
Spies	Event	C
Squires	Event	C
Stable (Arab)	Building	U
Stable (European)	Building	U
Stable (Far East)	Building	U
Stable (Raider)	Building	U
Stand of Trees	Event	C

26

Card name	Type	Rarity
Stealth Attack	Event	R
Stone Mine	Building	C
Stone Mining	Technology	C
Stone Shaft Mining	Technology	U
Stone Wall	Building/Wall	C
Strategist Enlisted	Event	C
Surprise Skirmish	Event	C
The Cross of Cong	Relic	U
The Final Strike	Event	R

27

Card name	Type	Rarity
The Golden Tent of the Great Khan	Wonder	URF
The Golden Tent of the Great Khan	Building	R
The Holy Grail	Relic	U
"The Jester Is Dead, Let's Get Them!"	Event	U
"The King is Dead, Long Live The King"	Event	R
The Palace of Ctesiphon on the Tigris	Wonder	URF
The Palace of Ctesiphon on the Tigris	Building	R
"They Came out of Nowhere"	Event	U
Threw a Shoe	Event	C

28

Card name	Type	Rarity
Tomb of Theodoric	Wonder	URF
Tomb of Theodoric	Building	R
Town Bell	Event	C
Town Center (Arab)	Building	C
Town Center (European)	Building	C
Town Center (Far East)	Building	C
Town Center (Raider)	Building	C
Town Patrol	Event	U
Town Watch	Event	C

29

Card name	Type	Rarity
Tracking	Event	U
Trade Cart	Event	C
Treaty From Abroad	Event	U
Trebuchet	Unit	R
Two-handed Swordsman	Upgrade	U
Two-man Saw	Technology	R
Typhoid	Event	C
Urgent Need	Event	R
War Elephant	Unit	R

30

Card name	Type	Rarity
Watch Tower	Building	R
Wheelbarrow	Technology	C
Woad Raider	Unit	R
You Are Being Attacked by Wild Animals	Event	C
Your Hunters are Waylaid	Event	C
Your Tracks Betray You	Event	U
Your Will is not Strong Enough	Event	R
Zealous Monk	Event	R

Pricing updates

See current issues of *Scrye* for recent prices for this set.

RARITY KEY C = Common   U = Uncommon   R = Rare   VR = Very Rare   UR = Ultra Rare   F = Foil card   X = Fixed/standard in all decks

FAST CLAW

Predator · Adaptable · Brave
Lethal · Veteran

5
7

12 honor.
Plus 1 to hit in Close Combat.

How can anything that big move so fast?
TM&© 1997 Fox

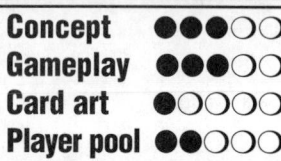

Concept	●●●○○
Gameplay	●●●○○
Card art	●○○○○
Player pool	●●○○○

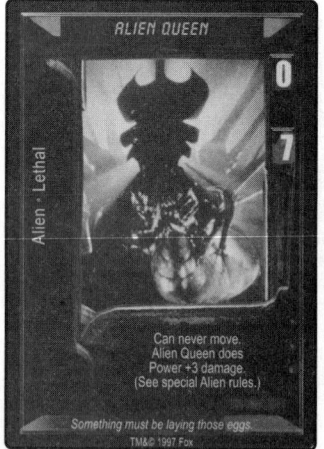

ALIEN QUEEN

Alien · Lethal

0
7

Can never move.
Alien Queen does
Power +3 damage.
(See special Alien rules.)

Something must be laying those eggs.
TM&© 1997 Fox

Terminator too

For a scenario integrating *Terminator* CCG cards with *Aliens Predator* cards, see *Scrye* 7.6 (Nov 00).

Aliens Predator

Published by **HarperPrism**, based on a design by **Precedence** • Released **August 1997**
363 cards in set • **IDENTIFIER: 1997 copyright; narrower space for art**

- Starter decks contain 60 cards, briefing sheet, rule book, tip card, and 20 cardboard counters
- Starter displays contain 12 starters: four each of Alien, Predator, and Colonial Marine decks
- Booster packs contain 15 cards
- Booster displays contain 36 boosters

Designed by **John Myler, Ran Ackels, Paul W. Brown III, David Hewitt,** and **Ted Kraver**

The ***Aliens Predator Customizable Card Game*** is based on the *Alien* and *Predator* movie franchises, and, while the crossover between the two story lines originally appeared in the Dark Horse Comics' series *Aliens vs. Predator*, a hint of the unified universe subsequently "officially" appeared in the movie *Predator 2* (unfortunately, the much-touted Aliens/Predator movie never made it out of pre-production).

The *Aliens Predator CCG* Battleground Game System was developed for HarperPrism (which had gotten into CCGs as the original publisher of the **Magic** novels) by Precedence Publishing, which later went on to release the **Terminator** CCG. **Terminator** uses the same Battleground Game System as *Aliens Predator*, and is fully compatible with the earlier game.

The science-fiction franchises are action-packed, and the CCG accurately captures the gritty, violent tone of the setting. Each of the three factions (Aliens, Predators, and Colonial Marines) have a distinct goal or set of goals to be reached during a pre-set game scenario in order to win, with an overall default victory resulting from the destruction of all opposing forces. The Aliens win by turning all game locations into part of their hive, and the Predators win by gathering "honor" from specific types of kills, while the Colonial Marines win by rescuing a set number of civilians. If a player achieves his victory goal at any time during a round, that player wins immediately.

The Battleground system was designed specifically to the needs of a game containing three factions and does an admirable job of translating the action in the movies into a card game format. All players act during the same round, in faction order: Colonial Marines, Aliens, and Predators. The game includes Location, Character, Item, and Event cards. Some cards are specific to one or two factions. Location cards are used to build player-specific battlegrounds; locations with identical names in different battlegrounds represent the same location. Characters and supporting characters are moved from location to location, seeking to fulfill the necessary victory goals.

Characters have two attributes, Speed and Power. Speed determines how fast a character can move as well as how difficult it is to hit, and Power determines how much damage the character does in close combat as well as how well it resists damage. Characters can attack opposing characters, search for items or supporting characters, and activate items. Combat is resolved by rolling a six-sided die, adding any modifiers and comparing to the target's final Speed; if the number is equaled or exceeded, the target is hit. If hit, all damage that exceeds the target's Power plus modifiers accrues as damage counters on that character. Each damage counter reduces that character's current Speed, Power, and to-hit rolls by one; when total damage counters equal Power, the character dies. Items and Events can be used to modify movement, attacks, defense, or other actions.

Aliens Predator, though heavily marketed by HarperPrism in print and at conventions, never really made a large enough splash in the CCG market to keep going. Card images were far too murky even for fans of the films to appreciate. But the *Terminator* CCG connection puts this game into the "not *entirely* dead" category. Perhaps the forthcoming *Terminator 3* and *Terminator 4* movies will generate interest in the *Terminator* CCG, spurring further interest in *Aliens Predator*. — *James A. Mishler*

	Price
Set (363 cards)	245.00
Starter Box	100.00
Booster Box	85.00
Starter Deck	9.00
Booster Pack	3.00

You will need **41** nine-pocket pages to store this set. (21 doubled up)

Card name	Type	Rarity	Price
[1]			
☐ 2 x 2 formation	Event	R	4.00
☐ A Bad Feeling	Event	R	3.30
☐ A Kill With No Honor	Event	C	0.10
☐ Access Space	Location	U	1.00
☐ Access Tunnel	Event	U	0.80

Card name	Type	Rarity	Price
☐ Acid Resistant Claws	PredatorItem	U	0.80
☐ Acid Splash	Event	C	0.10
☐ Acid Spray	Event	U	1.00
☐ Activate Self Destruct	Event	U	0.80
[2]			
☐ Adapt and Overcome	Event	R	3.50
☐ Adrenaline Rush	Event	C	0.10
☐ Advantageous Terrain	Event	C	0.10
☐ Aggravated Wound	Event	U	0.80
☐ Airlock	Location	C	0.10
☐ Alien Birth	Event	R	4.60
☐ Alien Hunter	Event	U	0.80
☐ Alien Pursuit	Event	C	0.20

Card name	Type	Rarity	Price
☐ Alien Queen	Alien	C	0.20
[3]			
☐ Alien Stealth	Event	C	0.10
☐ Alien Warrior	Alien	C	0.25
☐ Alien Wave	Event	C	0.25
☐ Ambush	Event	C	0.10
☐ Ambush Point	Location	R	4.00
☐ Armory	Location	U	1.00
☐ Ash	MarineChar	R	5.00
☐ At Any Price	Event	R	3.50
☐ At the Limit	Event	R	3.50
[4]			
☐ Atmosphere Processor	Location	C	0.10

RARITY KEY C = Common U = Uncommon R = Rare VR = Very Rare UR = Ultra Rare F = Foil card X = Fixed/standard in all decks

Card name	Type	Rarity	Price
☐ Baptism of Fire	Event	U	0.80
☐ Barracks	Location	C	0.10
☐ Battlefield Chaos	Event	U	0.90
☐ Battlefield Medicine	Event	C	0.10
☐ Bishop	MarineChar	R	7.50
☐ Black Marketeer	SupChar	R	5.00
☐ Blaze the Path	Event	U	0.80
☐ Block	Event	C	0.10
5			
☐ Body Slam	Event	C	0.10
☐ Booby Trap	Event	R	4.00
☐ Bottled Courage	MarineItem	C	0.15
☐ Breakthrough!	Event	U	0.80
☐ Breeding Chamber	Location	C	0.10
☐ Bug Hunt	Event	U	0.80
☐ Burst Pipe	Event	R	4.00
☐ Calculated Risk	Event	C	0.10
☐ Camouflage	MarineItem	R	3.80
6			
☐ Camouflage suit	PredatorItem	C	0.20
☐ Captured	Event	C	0.10
☐ Cargo Bay	Location	C	0.10
☐ Carpe Corpus	Event	U	0.90
☐ Carter Burke	MarineChar	R	4.90
☐ Ceiling Highway	Event	U	0.80
☐ Ceremonial Armor	PredatorItem	C	0.10
☐ Chemical Base	MarineItem	C	0.10
☐ Chest Burster	Alien	C	0.20
7			
☐ Child	SupChar	C	0.10
☐ Close Quarters	Event	C	0.15
☐ CN-20 Nerve Gas	MarineItem	R	4.30
☐ Cocooned Victim	SupChar	R	5.00
☐ Collapsible Spear	PredatorItem	U	0.80
☐ Combat Knife	MarineItem	U	0.80
☐ Combat Mastery	Event	R	5.00
☐ Committed Posture	Event	R	3.50
☐ Communications Array	MarineItem	U	0.90
8			
☐ Communications Center	Location	C	0.10
☐ Company Official	SupChar	C	0.10
☐ Computer Center	Location	C	0.10
☐ Concentrated Fire	Event	C	0.10
☐ Corporate Office	Location	C	0.10
☐ Corridor	Location	C	0.10
☐ Counter	Event	U	0.80
☐ Cover Formation	Event	C	0.10
☐ Covering Fire	Event	U	0.80
9			
☐ Cower	Event	C	0.10
☐ Cpl. Ackels	MarineChar	C	0.20
☐ Cpl. Brown	MarineChar	C	0.15
☐ Cpl. Hicks	MarineChar	R	10.00
☐ Cpl. Myler	MarineChar	U	1.00
☐ Crazed Civilian	Event	U	0.80
☐ Crossfire	Event	C	0.15
☐ Crude Explosives	MarineItem	C	0.10
☐ Cryonics Chamber	Location	C	0.10
10			
☐ Cunning Hunter	Predator	C	0.15
☐ Dallas	MarineChar	R	5.80
☐ Darts	PredatorItem	C	0.10
☐ Dead End	Event	R	4.00
☐ Death from Above	Event	R	3.80
☐ Defend the Hive	Event	C	0.10
☐ Demolition Charge	MarineItem	U	0.80
☐ Desperate Leap	Event	C	0.10
☐ Desperate Shot	Event	C	0.10
11			
☐ Deteriorating Situation	Event	U	0.80
☐ Dire Straits	Event	U	0.90
☐ Disarmament	Event	U	0.80
☐ Disengaging Attack	Event	C	0.15
☐ Dishonor	Event	C	0.15
☐ Display of Skill	Event	R	3.80

Card name	Type	Rarity	Price
☐ Dissection	Event	U	0.80
☐ Dock Worker	SupChar	U	0.80
☐ Docking Bay	Location	C	0.10
12			
☐ Dodge	Event	C	0.15
☐ Dodge and Roll	Event	C	0.15
☐ Double Packed Ammo	MarineItem	C	0.10
☐ Dwindling Options	Event	U	1.00
☐ Eager Youth	Predator	C	0.15
☐ Eat This!	Event	C	0.10
☐ Eat Vacuum	Event	C	0.10
☐ Egg Sack Detachment	Event	R	4.00
☐ Electronics Tech	SupChar	C	0.10
13			
☐ Elevator	Location	U	0.80
☐ Emergency Escape Vessel	Event	R	4.30
☐ Empty	Event	U	0.80
☐ End of the Line	Event	R	3.50
☐ Engineer	SupChar	C	0.10
☐ Engineering	Location	C	0.10
☐ Equipment Warehouse	Location	C	0.20
☐ Evacuation	Event	C	0.10
☐ Experimental Rifle	MarineItem	R	5.00
14			
☐ Extra Ammo	MarineItem	C	0.10
☐ Extremely Agitated	Event	R	3.50
☐ Face Hugger Attack	Event	C	0.20
☐ Facing Bad Luck	Event	R	3.50
☐ Fast Claw	Predator	U	1.00
☐ Field Pack	MarineItem	U	1.30
☐ Field Promotion	Event	R	3.80
☐ Fiery Defense	Event	U	0.80
☐ Fire Alarm	Event	R	3.50
15			
☐ Flack Jacket	MarineItem	C	0.20
☐ Flanking	Event	C	0.15
☐ Flesh Wound	Event	C	0.20
☐ Fog of War	Event	U	0.90
☐ Fortify	Event	R	3.50
☐ Found 'Em	Event	C	0.20
☐ Frenzy	Event	R	3.50
☐ Friendly Fire	Event	R	4.00
☐ Garrison Pack	MarineItem	C	0.20
16			
☐ Get Away from Her	Event	C	0.15
☐ Ghost Image	Event	U	0.90
☐ Good Shot	Event	C	0.15
☐ Got It	Event	C	0.15
☐ Grapple	Event	C	0.20
☐ Gray Stripe	Predator	C	0.15
☐ Grenade Launcher	MarineItem	U	1.00
☐ Hacker	SupChar	U	0.90
☐ Hand Welder	MarineItem	U	1.00
17			
☐ Hardpoint	Location	R	3.50
☐ Have Me Some Fun!	Event	U	0.90
☐ Head Shot	Event	U	0.90
☐ Heat Exchanger	Location	U	0.90
☐ Heat of Battle	Event	U	0.90
☐ Heroic Stand	Event	R	3.50
☐ Hidden	Event	R	3.80
☐ Hidey Hole	Event	R	3.50
☐ Hive Construction	Event	C	0.15
18			
☐ Hived Airlock	Location	U	0.90
☐ Hived Corridor	Location	U	0.90
☐ Hived Cryonics	Location	C	0.15
☐ Hived Engineering	Location	C	0.20
☐ Hived Hall	Location	C	0.15
☐ Hived Lounge	Location	C	0.15
☐ Hived Main Corridor	Location	C	0.20
☐ Hived Passage	Location	C	0.15
☐ Hived Plant	Location	C	0.15
19			
☐ Hived Processor	Location	C	0.20

Card name	Type	Rarity	Price
☐ Hived Quarters	Location	C	0.15
☐ Hived Shop	Location	C	0.20
☐ Hived Storage	Location	C	0.15
☐ Honored Elder	Predator	R	6.00
☐ Hull Breach	Event	R	3.50
☐ Hunter's Mask	PredatorItem	U	0.90
☐ Hunting Kit	PredatorItem	C	0.15
☐ Huntmaster	Predator	R	6.50
20			
☐ I Can Take It	Event	U	0.90
☐ I Can't Lock In!	Event	C	0.15
☐ I Work Best Alone	Event	R	3.50
☐ If It Bleeds	Event	C	0.15
☐ Infirmary	Location	C	0.15
☐ Instinctive Escape	Event	C	0.15
☐ Isolated Corridor	Location	U	0.90
☐ It Was a Bad Call	Event	C	0.15
☐ It's Just the Cat	Event	C	0.15
21			
☐ Juggernaut	Event	R	3.50
☐ Kane	MarineChar	R	5.00
☐ Kill and Kill Again	Event	C	0.20
☐ Kitchen	Location	C	0.20
☐ Know Your Enemy	Event	R	3.00
☐ Lab Worker	SupChar	U	0.90
☐ Lambert	MarineChar	R	4.90
☐ Landing Pad	Location	C	0.15
☐ Laser Sight	PredatorItem	C	0.15
22			
☐ Lay of the Land	Event	R	4.20
☐ Learning Experience	Event	R	3.50
☐ Let's Rock	Event	U	1.00
☐ Like a Ghost	Event	U	0.90
☐ Limb from Limb	Event	U	0.90
☐ Living Quarters	Location	C	0.15
☐ Long Range Shot	Event	C	0.20
☐ Look Sharp	Event	C	0.15
☐ Loose Formation	Event	U	0.90
23			
☐ Loss of Command	Event	U	0.90
☐ Lt Campbell	MarineChar	U	1.00
☐ Lucky Break	Event	R	3.50
☐ M240 Flame Thrower	MarineItem	U	1.00
☐ M3 Body Armor	MarineItem	C	0.15
☐ M41A Pulse Rifle	MarineItem	C	0.15
☐ M42A Scope Rifle	MarineItem	R	4.50
☐ M56 Smart Gun	MarineItem	U	1.00
☐ Machine Shop	Location	C	0.15
24			
☐ Main Corridor	Location	C	0.15
☐ Makeshift Weapon	MarineItem	C	0.15
☐ Malfunction	Event	C	0.20
☐ March of Time	Event	U	1.00
☐ Marine Private	MarineChar	C	0.15
☐ Marine Short Course	Event	R	4.00
☐ "Marines, We Are Leaving!"	Event	C	0.20
☐ Mask	PredatorItem	C	0.20
☐ Masterful Shot	Event	R	4.00
25			
☐ Mechanic	SupChar	C	0.15
☐ Medikit	MarineItem	C	0.15
☐ Meditation	Event	C	0.15
☐ Meeting Hall	Location	C	0.15
☐ Melee Claws	PredatorItem	C	0.20
☐ Mess Hall	Location	C	0.20
☐ Mk 35 Pressure Suit	MarineItem	U	0.90
☐ Mk 50 Compression suit	MarineItem	R	4.00
☐ Motion Scanner	MarineItem	C	0.15
26			
☐ Naginata	PredatorItem	R	4.00
☐ Natural Selection	Event	R	4.00
☐ New Era in Science	Event	R	4.00
☐ Nobody's Home	Event	R	3.50
☐ Not So Fast	Event	R	4.00

Card name	Type	Rarity	Price
Nowhere to Hide	Event	U	0.90
Observe the Prey	Event	U	0.90
On a Roll	Event	R	4.00
On the Move	Event	C	0.20
27			
Operations	Location	C	0.20
Opportunity	Event	R	3.80
Overconfidence	Event	C	0.15
Overkill	Event	C	0.15
Overwatch	Event	C	0.15
P-5000 Powerloader	MarineItem	U	0.90
Panic	Event	C	0.15
Parker	MarineChar	R	5.00
Passed by	Event	U	0.90
28			
Perfect Organism	Event	C	0.20
Personal Data Locator	MarineItem	R	4.00
Pet	SupChar	C	0.15
Pet Hybrid	Alien	U	1.00
Physician	SupChar	U	0.90
Pincer Grab	Event	U	0.90
Plasma Caster	PredatorItem	U	1.00
Pounce	Event	U	0.90
Pour It ON!	Event	U	0.90
29			
Power Outage	Event	R	3.50
Power Plant	Location	U	0.90
Predator Hybrid	Alien	R	6.00
Predator Medikit	PredatorItem	C	0.15
Predator Mothership	Location	R	6.00
Predator Ship	Location	U	1.00
Predator Shuttle	Location	C	0.20
Prepare Yourself	Event	R	3.50
Primal Force	Event	R	4.00
30			
Programmer	SupChar	U	0.90
Protect the Queen	Event	C	0.20
Pvt. Hewitt	MarineChar	U	1.00
Pvt. Hudson	MarineChar	R	7.00
Pvt. Masters	MarineChar	C	0.15
Pvt. McIntyre	MarineChar	C	0.20
Pvt. Rogers	MarineChar	C	0.20
Pvt. Von Gries	MarineChar	C	0.20
Quarantine	Location	U	0.90
31			
Quartermaster	SupChar	R	5.00
Ransack	Event	U	0.90
Rapid Fire	Event	U	0.90
Ravaged Chamber	Event	R	4.00
Ready for Trouble	Event	C	0.15
Recon	Event	U	0.90
Reflexive Action	Event	U	0.90
Regroup	Event	R	4.00
Remote Sensors	Event	C	0.15
32			
Rend	Event	C	0.20
Repair	Event	C	0.15
Rescue	Event	C	0.15

Card name	Type	Rarity	Price
Retreat	Event	C	0.15
Right to the Wall	Event	R	4.00
Rip Asunder	Event	U	0.90
Ripley	MarineChar	R	8.00
Rivalry	Event	R	3.50
Roll with It	Event	U	1.00
33			
Royal Guard	Alien	U	1.00
Royal Jelly	Event	C	0.20
Sacrifice	Event	R	3.50
Saturation Fire	Event	U	0.90
Scattergun	PredatorItem	C	0.20
Science Lab	Location	U	0.90
Second Chance	Event	R	4.00
Secure Position	Event	C	0.15
Security Checkpoint	Location	U	0.90
34			
Security Chief	SupChar	R	4.00
Security Doors	Event	C	0.15
Security Guard	SupChar	C	0.20
Security Station	Location	R	4.00
Self Destruct	PredatorItem	U	1.00
Self Destruct Sequence	Event	R	4.90
Sensing Weakness	Event	C	0.15
Sentry Gun Control	MarineItem	R	4.00
Settle the Score	Event	U	0.90
35			
Sgt. Bass	MarineChar	C	0.15
Sgt. Hart	MarineChar	U	1.00
Sharp Eye	Predator	U	1.00
Short, Controlled Bursts	Event	C	0.15
Shotgun	MarineItem	C	0.15
Situational Awareness	Event	C	0.15
Sleeper	SupChar	U	1.00
Slow Motion	Event	U	0.90
Small Arms	MarineItem	C	0.15
36			
Snapshot	Event	R	4.00
Somebody Wake up Hicks	Event	R	4.00
Sprint	Event	C	0.15
Staff Worker	SupChar	C	0.20
Stairwell	Location	U	0.90
Stalking the Queen	Event	C	0.15
Standoff	Event	R	3.50
Structural Damage	Event	R	4.00
Structural Repairs	Event	C	0.20
37			
Study the Enemy	Event	C	0.20
Success Breeds Success	Event	R	3.50
Superior Analysis	Event	U	0.90
Superior Species	Event	U	0.90
Sweep the Area	Event	C	0.15
Tail Lash	Event	R	4.00
Tail Spear	Event	C	0.15
Take Aim	Event	U	0.90
Take Cover	Event	C	0.15
38			
Take Him with You	Event	C	0.20

Card name	Type	Rarity	Price
Take Names	Event	U	0.90
Take the initiative	Event	U	0.90
Takedown Strike	Event	C	0.20
Taking Chances	Event	C	0.15
Tavern	Location	U	0.90
The Area Is Secure	Event	R	4.00
The Hunt	Event	C	0.20
The Strong Survive	Event	C	0.15
39			
The Will to Live	Event	R	4.00
There's Something in Here	Event	R	3.50
This Changes Everything	Event	R	3.50
Throwing Disk	PredatorItem	R	5.00
Tight Formation	Event	U	0.90
Tighten the Perimeter	Event	R	3.50
Trick of the Light?	Event	R	4.00
Trip	Event	U	0.90
Twice as Deadly	Predator	R	4.00
40			
Twitchy Artificial Person	Event	R	4.00
UA 571C Sentry Gun	MarineItem	R	5.00
Warrior Queen	Alien	R	8.00
Water Processing	Location	U	0.90
Weapon Cache	Event	C	0.20
Weapons Locker	Location	C	0.20
Welcome to the War	Event	R	4.00
Where There's One	Event	C	0.20
WO Kraver	MarineChar	C	0.15
41			
You Want Some of This?	Event	C	0.15
Young Queen	Alien	C	0.20
Young Tusk	Predator	C	0.20

Critical hits

"Most of the pictures used on the *Aliens Predator* cards are either too dark or too grainy to even make out what they are. This is the worst part of the game and it makes it less enjoyable to play...

"There is a good game hidden inside *Aliens Predator*. The trick is to get scenarios that bring out the interesting things in the game and downplay the boring parts...

"I can't strongly recommend the game unless you are a real *Aliens/Predator* fan or would like to play miniatures with cards."

— Mike Fitzgerald, writing in *Scrye* 5.2

Aliens Predator • Promo cards

Alderac Entertainment Group

Additional cards for **Aliens Predator** appeared in a number of gaming industry magazines as part of HarperPrism's support program for the game. See also the listings for the *Terminator* CCG, which also had promo cards available compatible with *Aliens Predator* (including the familiarly named **I'll Be Back**, which appeared in *Scrye* 7.6 (Nov 00).

Card name	Price
Air Control Fans	7.00
As the Queen Commands	5.50
Battle Standard	15.00
Berserk	7.00
Conestoga Class	15.00

Card name	Price
Corporate Agent	4.00
Critical Hit	15.00
Defensive Position	5.50
From Behind	0.30
High Adjudicator	6.00

Card name	Price
I Thought you were dead!	6.00
Infrared Binoculars	7.00
M237 Enhanced Silencer	4.00
Rogue Assassin	4.50
Under Its Gaze	8.00

RARITY KEY **C** = Common **U** = Uncommon **R** = Rare **VR** = Very Rare **UR** = Ultra Rare **F** = Foil card **X** = Fixed/standard in all decks

Aliens Predator •
Alien Resurrection

HarperPrism • Released **March 1999**
116 cards in set • **IDENTIFIER: Tiny "AR" in lower-right corner**
• Booster packs contain 9 cards; booster displays contain 36 boosters

At the time of its release, series fans referred to the film *Alien³* as what is know in media parlance as a "franchise killer." Dour and depressing, the movie did away with most of the elements fans had liked and rendered, for some, the drama of the previous films completely meaningless.

Somehow, they made a sequel anyway, and, in the immortal words of *Bloom County*, "Maybe it wasn't *that* bad but, Lord, it wasn't good." Equal parts clones and confusion with a little Winona Ryder thrown in made for mediocre box office in the United States, and, while it wasn't much to work with, HarperPrism and Precedence gamely (no pun intended) sallied in with this expansion to *Alien Predator*.

A new faction was added to the game, Rogues, representing Call's smugglers from the movie, and the film's oddball Aliens were added to that faction. The military figures in the film were added to the Colonial Marines faction. Predators being absent from the film, one wouldn't expect their decks would get much help, but the designers kindly threw in a supply of Items for them.

Unfortunately, by the time this set hit store shelves, the film was already a half-remembered experience for many, and it did little to stave off the game's early demise in the overall market. Pockets of loyal players do still remain, — *John Jackson Miller*

Set (116 cards)	135.00		
Booster Box	77.50		
Booster Pack	3.00		

You will need **13** nine-pocket pages to store this set. (7 doubled up)

Card name	Type	Rarity	Price
Acid Attack	Event	C	0.10
Acid Rounds	PredatorItem	U	0.50
Alien Lab	Location	U	0.50
Alien Sacrifice	Event	C	0.10
Ambushed Predator	SupChar	R	4.00
Aquatic Agility	Event	C	0.10
Avery G.	SupChar	U	0.50
Black Market	Event	U	0.50
Bloody Trophy	Event	R	4.00
Bounty Hunter	RogueChar	R	6.00
Breath Analyzer	Event	U	0.50
Call	RogueChar	R	4.00
Calling in the Favors	Event	R	3.80
Chapel	Location	R	3.00
Christie	RogueChar	R	4.00
Clear Us a Path	Event	U	0.50
Cloned Alien Warrior	AlienChar	U	1.00
Cloned Queen	AlienChar	R	6.00
Code 8	Event	R	3.00
Collapsible Shotgun	RogueItem	C	0.10
Coolant Leak	Condition	U	0.50
Creepy	RogueChar	C	0.10
Criminal Instinct	Event	R	3.00
Dark Shaman	RogueChar	R	4.00
Decompression Valves	PredatorItem	R	3.00
Desperate for Air	Event	C	0.10
Distraction	Event	U	0.50
Doctor Gediman	SupChar	U	0.50
Doctor Wren	MarineChar	R	4.00
Draco Double Burner	MarineItem	U	0.50
Egg Clutch	Event	R	4.00
Elgyn	RogueChar	R	4.00
Enhanced Cunning	Event	R	3.00
Establish the Hive	Event	U	0.50
Experimental Research	Event	R	3.00
Face Burster	Event	C	0.10

Card name	Type	Rarity	Price
Face Hugger	AlienChar	C	0.10
Fight or Flight	Event	R	3.00
Flechete Rounds	Item	C	0.10
Flooded	Event	C	0.10
Flooded Corridor	Location	C	0.10
Force Net	PredatorItem	U	0.50
Galley	Location	C	0.10
General Perez	MarineChar	R	5.00
Genetic Experiment: Accelerated Metabolism	Event	R	3.00
Genetic Experiment: Armored Exoskeleton	Event	R	3.00
Genetic Experiment: Intrinsic Flaw	Event	U	0.50
Genetic Experiment: Natural Camouflage	Event	R	5.00
Genetics Lab	Location	C	0.10
Good to Go	Condition	R	4.00
Halogen Attachment	Item	C	0.10
Hatchery	Location	R	3.00
Hillard	RogueChar	C	0.10
Hit below the Belt	Event	U	0.50
Human Cargo	Event	R	4.00
Hunter's Caster	PredatorItem	R	4.00
Hunting Cloak	PredatorItem	R	4.00
"If He Dies, You Die"	Event	R	2.80
I'm Okay…	Event	U	1.00
Into the Tunnels	Event	C	0.10
Invasive Surgery	Event	R	3.00
Item's Too Late!!!	Event	U	0.50
Johner	RogueChar	R	4.00
Keep 'em Down	Event	U	0.50
Lacrima 99	MarineItem	C	0.10
Last Stand	Event	R	4.00
Learn by doing	Event	U	0.50
Let the Army Guys Deal	Event	C	0.10
Lock the Door	Event	U	0.50
Loose Tusk	RogueChar	U	1.00
Low Light Levels	Condition	R	4.00
Lower Level Living Quarters	Location	C	0.10
M220 Uranium Grenade	MarineItem	U	0.50
M91 Flamer Unit	MarineItem	U	0.50

Card name	Type	Rarity	Price
Medical Lab	Location	U	0.50
Mirror Image	Event	C	0.10
Neuro Toxin	PredatorItem	U	0.50
Newborn	AlienChar	R	4.00
Night Shade	RogueChar	U	1.00
Non-Human Presence Detected	Event	R	3.00
Not That Way!	Event	R	4.00
Out of Breath	Event	U	0.50
Pack Tactics	Event	R	3.00
Plasma Overcharge	Event	R	3.00
Pointman Is Hit!	Event	C	0.10
Portable Data Drive	Item	C	0.10
Pressure Doors	Barrier	U	0.50
Prohibited Imports Scanner	Item	C	0.10
P.T.V. Personal Transport Vehicle	Vehicle	R	4.00
Purvis	SupChar	U	0.50
Pvt. Distephano	MarineChar	C	0.10
Quick Escape	Event	R	4.00
Recalibrate Ground Level	Event	R	4.00
Resin Barrier	Bar	U	0.50
Rig Item Up	Event	C	0.10
Ripley	RogueChar	R	8.00
Rogue Mercenary	RogueChar	C	0.10
Shadow Blade	RogueChar	U	0.50
Share the Pain	Event	C	0.10
Shortcut	Event	R	4.00
Silent Wraith	RogueChar	R	4.00
Sporting Chance	Event	R	4.00
Storage Facility	Location	R	4.00
Strong Arm Tactics	Event	R	3.00
Terrorized	Event	C	0.10
The Queen Is Dead	Event	R	3.80
The Water's Fine	Event	C	0.10
Thermos Gun	RogueItem	U	0.50
Trick Shot	Event	R	4.00
Underwater Debris	Event	C	0.10
Unexpected Benefits	Event	C	0.10
Venom Cloud Module	PredatorItem	R	4.00
Vriess		R	5.00
Waste Tank 5	Location	C	0.10
Wrist Guns	RogueItem	U	0.50
Zip Gun	RogueItem	C	0.10

RARITY KEY C = Common U = Uncommon R = Rare VR = Very Rare UR = Ultra Rare F = Foil card X = Fixed/standard in all decks

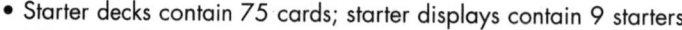

Ani-Mayhem

Pioneer Entertainment (Panime Division) • First set, **Set 0**, released **July 1996**
303 cards in set
• Starter decks contain 75 cards; starter displays contain 9 starters
• Booster packs contain 9 cards; Booster displays contain 60 boosters

Sportcard companies had published collectible card games — why not a video label? Pioneer Entertainment, the division of Pioneer Elecrtronics that produced videotapes and laser discs (those big things that came before DVDs), had experience repackaging anime titles for the American market. Trading on the popularity of anime characters, Pioneer Entertainment developed **Ani-Mayhem,** its first and only CCG to date, for release under its Panime logo. Ani-Mayhem **Set 0** consisted of images derived from four popular anime shows: *Bubblegum Crisis, El Hazard, Ranma 1/2,* and *Tenchi Muyo.*

Ani-Mayhem requires one to four players to create a playing field of location cards. On it are placed item cards (treasures) and disasters (enemies/hazards). Each player moves his characters on this field in a group and battles the disasters in an attempt to acquire items. The disasters move around the field in a pattern, and when they move off the map (and then back on) — they permanently remove items from the field. In effect, you really play against the disasters, rather than your opponents.

Ani-Mayhem did not have the best design; it was cumbersome and confusing to play, and you could do little to affect your opponent's success. On the positive side, it was original and is one of the few CCGs that can be played solitaire.

Tod Harrick served as the manager of the CCG products line for Pioneer, which produced two more sets for Ani-Mayhem. When Harrick left at the end of 1997, he was never replaced, and the game was allowed to die. — **Jack Everitt**

Concept	●●●○○
Gameplay	●●○○○
Card art	●●●○○
Player pool	●○○○○

Set (303 cards)	97.50
Starter Display Box	35.00
Booster Display Box	65.00
Starter Deck	8.00
Booster Pack	3.00

You will need **34** nine-pocket pages to store this set. (17 doubled up)

Card name	Type	Rarity	Price
33-S Sexaroid	MinorD	R	5.00
5 Yen Coin	Item	C	0.25
55-C Bodyguard Boomer	MinorD	C	0.25
7 Lucky Gods Martial Artists	MajorD	R	4.00
A.D. Police HQ	Location	U	0.80
Afura Mann	Character	C	0.25
Akane Tendo	Character	U	0.80
Akane's Cooking	MinorD	R	5.50
Akane's Rage	MinorD	R	4.00
Ambulance	Flash	C	0.25
Angel of Mercy	Flash	R	4.50
Angry Schoolgirls	MinorD	R	5.00
Assassin Disguise	Enhancemt	U	0.80
Assault/Shining Knight	Combat	C	0.25
Assisted Flight	Flash	C	0.25
Attack Pods	Equipment	C	0.25
Auntie Saotome	MinorD	R	4.00
Baby	MinorD	C	0.25
Bad Reputation	Flash	R	4.00
Barbells	Item	C	0.25
Bash/Broken Heart	Combat	U	0.80
Big Bug	MajorD	R	4.00
Big Sucker Gas Slash	Flash	U	0.80
Brian J. Mason	MajorD	U	0.80
Briefing	Global	C	0.25
BU-12B Cyberdroid	MinorD	C	0.25
Bugrom Big Raid Medal	Item	C	0.25
Bugrom Bridge Bashers	MinorD	C	0.25
Bugrom Homeland	Location	C	0.25
Bugrom Horde	MinorD	C	0.25
"Bugrom, Type I"	MinorD	R	3.50
Captured!	MinorD	C	0.25
C'est La Vie	Location	C	0.25

Card name	Type	Rarity	Price
Chang Tiger Clan Ring	Item	R	5.00
Charge/Scandal	Combat	C	0.25
Chief Servant Londs	Character	C	0.25
City of Floristica	Location	R	3.50
Class C Boomer	MinorD	C	0.25
Class C Female Boomer	MinorD	U	0.80
Clean Livin'	Enhancemt	R	4.50
Cleaning Supplies	Item	C	0.25
Cloud Monster	MinorD	U	0.80
Club/Stunning Smile	Combat	U	0.80
Combat Training	Global	U	0.80
Control Cube	Equipment	U	0.80
Crystal Tunnels	Location	C	0.25
Cute Little Dolly	Item	C	0.25
Cynthia	Item	U	0.80
Dai-Kokusei and Dai-Hakusei	MinorD	U	0.80
Dailey Wong	Character	U	0.80
DD J1 Battlemover	MajorD	R	5.50
Deception/Tied Up	Combat	C	0.25
Defense Minister Callahan	Item	U	0.80
Desert of Bleached White Bones	Location	C	0.25
Desert Skimmer	Equipment	U	0.80
Deserted Island	Location	U	0.80
Detective Kiyone	Character	R	7.00
Detective Mihoshi	Character	U	0.80
"Deva, The Bugrom Queen"	MajorD	C	0.25
Dimensional Hammer	Equipment	C	0.25
Dimensional Sleep Chamber	Item	C	0.25
Dimensional Vortex	MinorD	R	4.00
Disguise Revealed	MinorD	U	0.80
Dobermans	MajorD	C	0.25
Dodge/Puppy Dog Eyes	Combat	C	0.25
Dr. Raven	Global	U	0.80
Dr. Stingray	Global	U	0.80
Dr. Tofu	Character	R	8.00
Equipment Breakdown	Flash	U	0.80

Card name	Type	Rarity	Price
Everyone's After Me	MajorD	C	0.25
F.G. Frederick	MajorD	U	0.80
Face Slam/Beautiful Queen	Combat	C	0.25
Fatora Disguise	Enhancemt	U	0.80
Female Jealousy	Flash	U	0.80
Fire Shield	Flash	U	0.80
Floristica Marketplace	Location	R	3.50
Floristica Palace Room	Haven	R	3.50
Flying Block	Flash	C	0.25
Forceful Impact	MinorD	C	0.25
"Funaho, The Holy Tree"	Location	U	0.80
Furinkan High	Location	C	0.25
Galaxy Destroyer	MajorD	R	6.50
Galaxy Destroyer Remote	Item	R	5.00
Galaxy Police Flag	Item	U	0.80
Galaxy Police HQ	Location	C	0.25
Gas Attack/Incomparable Beauty	Combat	U	0.80
GD-42 Crab Mech	MajorD	C	0.25
Genaros Station	Location	U	0.80
Gene Doubling	Enhancemt	U	0.80
Genma Saotome	Character	R	7.00
Genom Military Lab	Location	R	3.50
Genom Research Center	Location	U	0.80
Genom Tower	Location	C	0.25
Go Board	Item	U	0.80
Go Fish	Flash	U	0.80
Hammer/Lover's Kiss	Combat	C	0.25
Hand Computer	Equipment	C	0.25
Happosai	MajorD	C	0.25
Have a Nice Trip	MinorD	C	0.25
Horned Mongoose Whistle	Item	U	0.80
Hot Legs	Location	C	0.25
Hot Springs House	Location	C	0.25
Hungry Cabbit	MinorD	C	0.25
I'm Buyin'	Enhancemt	C	0.25
Ifurita's Power Key Staff	Item	R	5.00
Ifurita's Tomb	Location	R	5.00
Interference	Global	C	0.25
Island Restaurant	Location	R	4.00

RARITY KEY **C** = Common **U** = Uncommon **R** = Rare **VR** = Very Rare **UR** = Ultra Rare **F** = Foil card **X** = Fixed/standard in all decks

Card name	Type	Rarity	Price
13			
Jail Break	Flash	C	0.25
Jinnai's Strike Squad	MajorD	U	0.80
Jump	Enhancemt	R	4.00
Juraian Battlesuit	Enhancemt	U	0.80
Juraian Guardians	MinorD	U	0.80
Juraian Royal Teardrop	Item	C	0.25
Juraian Ultra Battlesuit	Enhancemt	R	4.00
Jusenkyo	Location	C	0.25
K-12 Battlesuit	Equipment	U	0.80
14			
Kagato	MajorD	C	0.25
Kasumi	Global	C	0.25
Katsuhiko Jinnai	Character	C	0.25
Keys	Item	C	0.25
Kick/Awfully Cute	Combat	C	0.25
Kirin	MajorD	U	0.80
Kiriya	Character	R	7.00
"Kiriya, The Phantom Assassin"	MinorD	U	0.80
Knee Slam/Special Gift	Combat	C	0.25
15			
Kodachi Kuno (The Black Rose)	MinorD	C	0.25
Kodachi's School Dress	Item	C	0.25
Lab Explosion	MinorD	C	0.25
Lady Tokimi	MinorD	C	0.25
Lamp of Fire	Equipment	R	3.50
Lamp of the Winds	Equipment	R	4.50
Largo	MajorD	C	0.25
Leon McNichol	Character	C	0.25
Leon's Boomer Rifle	Equipment	R	5.00
16			
Leon's Missile Gun	Equipment	U	0.80
Lingerie	Item	C	0.25
Linna Yamazaki	Character	U	0.80
Linna's Hardsuit	Equipment	U	0.80
Lisa Vannett	Character	R	7.00
Lisa Vannett's Camera	Item	U	0.80
Little Washu	Character	C	0.25
Locked Gate	MinorD	C	0.25
Mackie Stingray	Character	R	7.00
17			
Mackie's Battlesuit	Equipment	R	5.00
Magical Girl Pretty Sammy	Character	R	7.00
Maid Disguise	Enhancemt	U	0.80
Makoto Mizuhara	Character	C	0.25
Masaki Comes Visiting	Global	C	0.25
Masaki House	Haven	R	5.00
Masaki Shrine	Location	R	5.00
Medical Disguise	Enhancemt	U	0.80
Medical Treatment	Flash	C	0.25
18			
Mega Motoslave	Global	R	4.50
Mihoshi's Driving	Flash	U	0.80
Mihoshi's Laser Pistol	Equipment	C	0.25
Mihoshi's Mothership	Haven	R	5.00
Military Disguise	Enhancemt	U	0.80
Misdirection	Flash	C	0.25
Miss Hinako	MajorD	U	0.80
Miz Mishtal	Character	U	0.80
Mountain Man	Enhancemt	C	0.25
19			
Mountain Sign Post	Item	U	0.80
Mousse	Character	R	7.00
Mr. Masamichi Fujisawa	Character	C	0.25
Mr. Panda	Character	R	9.50
Mrs. Tendo's Cookbook	Item	U	0.80
Mt. Muldoon	Location	C	0.25
Mu-Mu Chan	Character	R	7.00
Musical Instrument	Item	U	0.80
Nabiki Tendo	Character	C	0.25
20			
Najato (Phantom Prince)	MinorD	U	0.80
Nanami Jinnai	Character	U	0.80
Natsumi and Karume	MajorD	C	0.25
Nene Romanova	Character	C	0.25
Nene's Hardsuit	Equipment	U	0.80
Nobuki Inn	Location	R	4.50
Okonomiyaki (Ukyo's Pizza)	Item	C	0.25
Old Woman	MinorD	C	0.25
P-Chan	Character	U	0.80
21			
Palace Guard	Global	R	4.00
Panic/Enchanted View	Combat	C	0.25
Paralyze/Captivate	Combat	C	0.25
Parry/Handsome Lad	Combat	C	0.25
Pass Around	Enhancemt	C	0.25
Pay Attention!	Flash	R	3.50
Peeping Disguise	Enhancemt	U	0.80
Personal Training	Enhancemt	U	0.80
Piece of Cake	Item	C	0.25
22			
Planet Jurai	Location	C	0.25
Police Disguise	Enhancemt	R	3.50
Possession	Flash	R	4.00
Power Chi	Enhancemt	R	5.00
Power Gem	Item	R	4.50
Power Grip	Global	C	0.25
Princess Ayeka	Character	U	0.80
Princess Sasami	Character	U	0.80
Principal Kuno	MajorD	C	0.25
23			
Priss and the Replicants	MinorD	U	0.80
Priss Asagiri	Character	C	0.25
Priss' First Live Concert Poster	Item	R	5.00
Priss' Hardsuit	Equipment	U	0.80
Pruning Shears	Equipment	C	0.25
Punch/Lovely Hair	Combat	C	0.25
Quincy	MajorD	U	0.80
Ranma Saotome (Boy Type)	Character	C	0.25
Ranma Saotome (Girl Type)	Character	C	0.25
24			
Raven's Garage	Haven	R	4.00
Red Tape	MinorD	R	4.00
Refreshing Drink	Item	U	0.80
Reika "Vision" Chang	Character	R	7.00
Relaxing Hot Springs	Global	U	0.80
Reload	Flash	C	0.25
Restricted Area	MinorD	C	0.25
Reverse Attack	Flash	U	0.80
Ring of Water	Equipment	R	4.50
25			
Royal Flying Barge	Equipment	U	0.80
Royal Librarian	Flash	R	4.50
Royal Painting	Item	C	0.25
Royal Trees of Jurai	Location	U	0.80
Ryo-Ohki (Cabbit)	Character	C	0.25
Ryo-Ohki (Ship)	Character	C	0.25
Ryoga Hibiki	Character	U	0.80
Ryoko	Character	C	0.25
Ryoko's Prison Cave	Location	R	4.50
26			
Ryu-Oh's Seed	Item	U	0.80
Ryugenzawa	Location	U	0.80
Sake Tub	Item	C	0.25
Satellite Strike	MajorD	C	0.25
Seito Bridge	Location	C	0.25
Servant	Enhancemt	U	0.80
Sexaroid Data Disk	Item	U	0.80
Shaken Up/Singing Sensation	Combat	C	0.25
Shampoo	Character	U	0.80
27			
Shampoo (Cat)	Character	U	0.80
Shayla-Shayla	Character	U	0.80
Shi Chi Hokodan	Flash	C	0.25
Shinonome High School	Location	U	0.80
Shuttle Craft	Equipment	C	0.25
Shuttle Crash	MinorD	C	0.25
Slam/Great Service	Combat	U	0.80
Slap/Beautiful Redhead	Combat	C	0.25
Smash/Stupefaction	Combat	C	0.25
28			
Soft Bath Towel	Item	C	0.25
Soja Guardians	MinorD	C	0.25
Space Pirate Attack	MajorD	U	0.80
Space Pirate Ryoko's Hideout	Location	R	5.00
Spotlight	Flash	R	3.50
Spring of Arliman	Location	C	0.25
Spring of Life	Location	U	0.80
Spy Camera	Global	R	4.00
Stand Up Straight	Flash	C	0.25
29			
Stomp/Cool Dude	Combat	C	0.25
Supreme Battle Aura	Flash	R	4.50
Surveillance	Global	R	4.00
Survival Shot	Location	C	0.25
Sylia Stingray	Character	U	0.80
Sylia's Hardsuit	Equipment	U	0.80
Sylvie	Character	R	7.00
Tatewaki Kuno	MinorD	U	0.80
Taunt	Flash	C	0.25
30			
Teacher Disguise	Enhancemt	C	0.25
Telephone Pole	Location	C	0.25
Temporal Disturbance	Flash	R	3.50
Tenchi Masaki	Character	U	0.80
Tenchi the Master Key	Item	R	5.00
The Citadel	Location	R	3.50
The Demoness Ifurita	MajorD	C	0.25
The Masaki Van	Equipment	C	0.25
The Mass	MajorD	C	0.25
31			
The Mass Humanoid Form	MinorD	R	4.50
The Reversed World	Location	R	3.50
The Ruined City	Location	U	0.80
The Silky Doll	Haven	R	5.00
The Tendo Dojo	Haven	R	5.00
This Device	Enhancemt	U	0.80
Tokyo Mega Dome	Location	C	0.25
Toma	MajorD	U	0.80
Toma's Guards	MinorD	C	0.25
32			
Toma's Palace	Location	U	0.80
Towed Vehicle	MinorD	U	0.80
Traffic Ticket	MinorD	R	4.00
Training Ground of Cursed Springs	MinorD	C	0.25
Training Partner	Flash	R	4.00
Transmitter Bra	Equipment	R	5.00
Trapped Door	MinorD	U	0.80
Tsunami	Equipment	U	0.80
Ukyo Kuonji	Character	R	9.50
33			
Ukyo's Restaurant	Location	C	0.25
"Ura, The Armor Cat"	Equipment	U	0.80
U.S.S.D. Miltary HQ	Location	R	3.50
Vision's Private Jet	Equipment	R	5.00
Washu	Character	U	0.80
Washu's Baby Formula	Item	C	0.25
Washu's Lab	Location	U	0.80
Water Kettle	Flash	U	0.80
Water Spear	Flash	C	0.25
34			
Wedding Jewels	Enhancemt	C	0.25
Wings of the Lighthawk	Enhancemt	R	4.50
Wrath of the Eye of God	Flash	R	6.50
Yamata No Orochi	MinorD	U	0.80
Yoiko-no-taiso Step 1	Flash	U	0.80
Yukinojo	Enhancemt	U	0.80

RARITY KEY C = Common   U = Uncommon   R = Rare   VR = Very Rare   UR = Ultra Rare   F = Foil card   X = Fixed/standard in all decks

Ani-Mayhem • Set 1

Pioneer Entertainment • Released **January 1997**

220 cards in set • **IDENTIFIER:** Series names in trademark line

• Booster packs contain 9 cards; booster displays contain 60 boosters

The first expansion for **Ani-Mayhem**, mundanely titled **Set 1**, consisted of 220 cards with images derived from four more popular anime shows: *Armitage III, Dominion Tank Police, Phantom Quest Corp.,* and *Project A-ko*, with a special appearance by *Oh My Goddess!*

The set was sold in booster packs only. — **Jack Everitt**

Set (220 cards)	90.00	
Booster Display Box	36.00	
Booster Pack	2.00	

You will need 25 nine-pocket pages to store this set. (12 doubled up)

Card name	Type	Rarity	Price
3 Way Rumble	MinorD	C	0.25
A Goddess' Kiss	Enhancemt	R	3.00
Accost/Call to Arms	Combat	C	0.25
Acrophobia	Global	U	0.80
Agent "D"	Character	C	0.25
Akagiyama 23	Equip	U	0.80
Akagiyama Missiles	Enhancemt	R	3.50
A-ko Magami	Character	C	0.25
A-ko's House	Haven	C	0.25
AI	Character	C	0.25
Alarm Clock	Item	C	0.25
Alien Battleship	MajorD	U	0.80
Alien Invasion Force	MajorD	U	0.80
Alien Ship	Location	R	3.00
Ancient Pottery	Item	U	0.80
Annapuma	Character	C	0.25
Antiques	Item	C	0.25
Assassin-Bot (Aqua Augmentation)	MajorD	U	0.80
Assassin-Bot (Land Augmentation)	MajorD	U	0.80
Assault with Intent to Kill	Flash	R	4.50
Assistance/I Surrender	Combat	U	0.80
Assisted Shot	Flash	C	0.25
Asteroid	MinorD	C	0.25
Avoid/Overdoing It	Combat	C	0.25
Avoid Fire	Flash	U	0.80
Ayaka Kisaragi	Character	C	0.25
Back to Reality	Flash	R	4.00
Beauty/Knocked Out	Combat	C	0.25
Bills and Calculator	Item	U	0.80
Bio Ball	MinorD	U	0.80
Bio-Ball Remover	Equip	U	0.80
B-ko Daitokuji	Character	C	0.25
B-ko's Bath	Location	R	3.00
B-ko's English Textbook	Item	U	0.80
Blind Throw/Surprised	Combat	C	0.25
Blocking Rush/Halitosis	Combat	C	0.25
Blown Main CPU	Flash	C	0.25
Bonaparte	Equip	R	3.00
Breaking and Entering	Global	R	3.00
Breather Mask	Item	C	0.25
Broad Shoulders/It's Your Fault	Combat	U	0.80
Broken Back	Flash	R	3.50
Call to God	Flash	R	4.00

Card name	Type	Rarity	Price
Captain Napolipolita	Character	U	0.80
Cathedral	Location	R	3.00
Chaplain	Character	U	0.80
Charged Up/Ogle	Combat	U	0.80
C-ko Kotobuki	Item	U	0.80
C-ko's Cooking	MinorD	C	0.25
C-ko's Lunch	Item	C	0.25
Classy Crooks	Global	U	0.80
Comfy?/Screw Kick	Combat	C	0.25
Comm Goggles	Equip	U	0.80
Comm Phone	Equip	R	3.00
Compact	Item	U	0.80
Computer Core	Location	U	0.80
Computer Link	Equip	C	0.25
Conception Building	Location	C	0.25
Country Bar	Location	R	3.00
Crazy Eyes	Flash	U	0.80
Cross	Item	C	0.25
Danich Hill Dome	Location	R	3.00
Data Stream	Enhancemt	R	3.00
Daylight	Flash	U	0.80
Defense Forces	MinorD	R	3.00
Desert Skeletons	MinorD	C	0.25
Desperate Shot/Terror	Combat	C	0.25
Dinner with Mom and Dad	MinorD	U	0.80
Dirty Laundry	Item	R	3.00
Distraction/Toss	Combat	C	0.25
Don't Move	Flash	C	0.25
Dr. Rene D'anclaude	MajorD	U	0.80
Dracula	MajorD	C	0.25
Earrings	Item	R	3.00
Ecstasy/Take Cover	Combat	C	0.25
Eddie	Character	U	0.80
Electronic Day Planner	Equip	R	3.50
Elite Medical Staff	Global	R	3.00
Emergency Stop	Flash	C	0.25
Exorcism Circle	Enhancemt	R	4.00
Falling Debris	MinorD	R	3.00
Falling I-Beam	MinorD	C	0.25
Family Picture	Item	U	0.80
Fancy Dance/Sexy Teacher	Combat	C	0.25
Fire Fight	MinorD	C	0.25
Following Orders	Flash	U	0.80
Forceful Passage	Flash	R	3.00
Funky Muggers	MinorD	U	0.80
Get Around	Flash	R	3.00
Getting Dressed/Ninja Defense	Combat	C	0.25
Glass of Wine	Item	U	0.80
Gone Crazy/Lovely Ladies	Combat	U	0.80
Goons	MinorD	C	0.25
Grab 'n Run	Flash	C	0.25
Graviton City	Location	R	3.00
Graviton High School for Girls	Location	C	0.25
Group Photo	Item	R	3.00
Happy Students	Global	U	0.80
Happy Tanks	MinorD	R	3.00
Happy/Surprise Attack	Combat	C	0.25

Card name	Type	Rarity	Price
Hidden Weapon	Flash	U	0.80
Hounded by the Press	MinorD	R	3.00
Hu-Gite Manufacturing	Location	R	3.00
I've Been Waiting for You	Flash	R	3.50
In the Hall	MinorD	U	0.80
Inhuman Strength	Enhancemt	R	3.50
Interrogation	Global	U	0.80
Introduction	Flash	R	3.00
Jacking In	Enhancemt	U	0.80
Jet Pack	Equip	U	0.80
Julian "Pluto" Moore	Character	U	0.80
Julian's Gravesite	Location	R	3.00
Junk Yard	Location	C	0.25
Karaoke Taxi	Flash	U	0.80
Kelly McCannon Poster	Item	U	0.80
Kozo Karino	Character	C	0.25
Lab Computers	Item	U	0.80
Last Chance to Confess	Flash	U	0.80
Late for School	Global	U	0.80
Leona Ozaki	Character	C	0.25
Lovely Persuasion/Tracheotomy	Combat	C	0.25
Loving You	Flash	R	4.00
Lt. Randolph	Character	R	6.50
Lucky Shot	Flash	R	3.00
Mad Doctor	MajorD	C	0.25
Mamoru Shimesu	Character	U	0.80
Mars Shuttle	Equip	U	0.80
Martian Police Department	Location	U	0.80
Martian Security Forces	MajorD	U	0.80
Max 5000	MinorD	C	0.25
Mecha Plans	Item	R	3.00
Medical Scanner	Equip	U	0.80
Memory Bank IO Room	Location	C	0.25
Minor Injury	Flash	R	3.00
Miss Ayumi	Character	R	6.50
Missile Walk	Flash	U	0.80
Mournful Look/Southern Cross Fist	Combat	C	0.25
Murder Scene	Location	U	0.80
Murdered Music Star	MinorD	U	0.80
Museum	Location	U	0.80
Nanami Rokugo	Character	R	6.50
Naomi Armitage	Character	C	0.25
Nightmare	MajorD	R	3.00
No Way Out	MinorD	U	0.80
Observation Droid	MinorD	U	0.80
On The Move	MajorD	R	3.00
One World	MinorD	C	0.25
Over the Edge	Flash	R	3.00
Panic Attack	Flash	C	0.25
Patiently Waiting	Enhancemt	R	4.50
Pedal Copter	Equip	C	0.25
Peep Hole	Enhancemt	R	4.00
Pentacle	Flash	U	0.80
Phantom Quest Corporation	Haven	C	0.25
Phobian	Item	U	0.80
Phone Booth	Location	C	0.25

RARITY KEY C = Common U = Uncommon R = Rare VR = Very Rare UR = Ultra Rare F = Foil card X = Fixed/standard in all decks

58 • *SCRYE Collectible Card Game Checklist and Price Guide*

Card name	Type	Rarity	Price
Pleasure Treatment	Enhancemt	C	0.25
Police Forensic Expert	Enhancemt	R	4.50
Political Investigation	MajorD	C	0.25
Power Push	Flash	R	3.00
Power Suit	MinorD	R	3.00
Pretty Lady/Startled	Combat	U	0.80
[19]			
Project Greenpeace	Item	U	0.80
Ready to Go	Global	C	0.25
Red Commandos	MajorD	U	0.80
Red Dragon Spirit Capture Star Sword	Equip	U	0.80
Robot Flight Crew	Enhancemt	U	0.80
Robot Guard	Enhancemt	U	0.80
Robot Slave	Equip	R	4.50
Rock/Paper/Scissor	Flash	C	0.25
Rokkon	Character	C	0.25
[20]			
Ross Sylibus	Character	C	0.25
Ross' Apartment	Haven	C	0.25
Ross' Battle Suit	Equip	R	5.50
Run Over	MinorD	R	3.00
Runaway Elevator	MinorD	C	0.25
Running Fight	MinorD	C	0.25

Card name	Type	Rarity	Price
Running Late	MinorD	C	0.25
Sahara Demon	MajorD	U	0.80
'Scuse Us	Flash	C	0.25
[21]			
Security Camera	Global	U	0.80
Sewer	Location	U	0.80
Shinjuku Police Building	Location	R	3.00
Shinora Hospital	Location	C	0.25
Shopping Spree	MinorD	C	0.25
Short Out	MinorD	U	0.80
Shortcut	Global	U	0.80
Shot Down	MinorD	U	0.80
Space Station	Location	R	3.00
[22]			
Specs	Character	C	0.25
Speed	Enhancemt	U	0.80
Spirit Protection Tablet	Item	U	0.80
Squad Bay	Haven	C	0.25
Squad Leader Britain	Character	R	6.50
St. Lowell Spaceport	Location	U	0.80
Striptease	Flash	U	0.80
Sudden Stop	MinorD	C	0.25
Surgical Laser	MinorD	R	3.00

Card name	Type	Rarity	Price
[23]			
Swamp Boat	Equip	R	3.50
Swat Team	MinorD	U	0.80
Swimming Pool	Location	U	0.80
Take Your Best Shot	Flash	C	0.25
Tank Police HQ	Location	C	0.25
Tank Police on Patrol	MajorD	C	0.25
Tank Special	MinorD	R	3.00
Tea Room Transylvania	Location	C	0.25
Tears/Trip	Combat	U	0.80
[24]			
Tender Moment	Global	R	3.00
Tracer Bug	Equip	C	0.25
Training Book	Item	C	0.25
Turbo Boost	Enhancemt	U	0.80
Under Age Smoking	MajorD	U	0.80
Unfinished Building	Location	C	0.25
Unipuma	Character	C	0.25
Unwanted Guest	MinorD	U	0.80
Vampire Ambush	MinorD	C	0.25
[25]			
Wake Up Call	Flash	C	0.25
Wrist Lasers	Enhancemt	U	0.80
Wrong Button	MinorD	R	3.00
Young Belldandy	Character	R	6.50

Ani-Mayhem • Dragonball Z

Pioneer Entertainment • Released September 1997

233 cards in set • **IDENTIFIER:** Dragonball Z name in trademark

- Starter decks packs contain 70 cards; starter displays contain 10 starters
- Booster packs contain 9 cards; booster displays contain 60 boosters

Not to be confused with the 2000 game of the same name by Score, *Dragonball Z*, the stand-alone second expansion to *Ani-Mayhem,* features 233 cards and a completely rewritten and comprehensible rulebook. Released in September 1997 and previewed at GenCon the month before, this set focused on only one anime series and was the most successful of the three *Ani-Mayhem* products.

This set had three advantages: a hot license, very sharp images and a different team producing the product. Whereas *Set 0* and *Set 1* are going for relatively cheap prices, *Dragonball Z* often still brings premium prices — even now that it's no longer the "official" ongoing *Dragonball Z* CCG! — *Jack Everitt*

Set (233 cards)	150.00
Starter Display Box	70.00
Starter Pack	9.50
Booster Display Box	65.00
Booster Pack	2.00

You will need **26** nine-pocket pages to store this set. (13 doubled up)

Card name	Type	Rarity	Price
[1]			
2 Dragon Balls	Item	U	1.00
3 Dragon Balls	Item	R	5.00
Acid Head	MinorD	U	0.50
Adult Gohan	Character	R	5.00
Airbus	Equip	U	0.80
Algebra	Equip	R	3.50
Alien Jungle	Location	C	0.10
Alien Landing Site	Location	C	0.10
Arena	Location	C	0.10
[2]			
Asteroid Field	MinorD	U	0.50
Atlia	Character	U	0.80
Baba	Character	R	3.00
Baby Dragon	Item	U	0.50
Baby Gohan	Character	C	0.25
Baby Saiyan	MinorD	R	3.00
Back Kick/Sense of Wonder	Combat	U	0.50
Baseball Stadium	Location	C	0.10
Be with you/Hangin' Around	Combat	C	0.10
[3]			
Bench Brawl/Tantrum	Combat	U	0.50
Berserk/Disco Groove	Combat	U	0.50
Beware: Bathroom!	Location	C	0.10
Blasters	Equipment	C	0.25
Bubbles	Character	R	3.50

Card name	Type	Rarity	Price
Bulma	Character	C	0.25
Bump on the Head	Enhancemt	R	4.00
Cafe	Location	C	0.10
Campground	Location	U	0.50
[4]			
Capsule Army Knife	Item	C	0.25
Capsule Corporation	Location	U	1.00
Catch Bubbles	MinorD	R	3.00
Change Direction	Flash	C	0.25
Chi-Chi	Character	C	0.25
Chiao-Tzu	Character	R	4.00
Crushing Left/Say Cheese!	Combat	U	0.50
Demon Hordes	MinorD	U	0.50
Desert Battleground	Location	C	0.10
[5]			
Destructo Disc	Flash	R	3.50
Devastating Attack/Sinister Beauty	Combat	C	0.10
Divert Attack	Flash	R	4.00
Dodonpa	Flash	C	0.25
Dodoria	MajorD	C	0.20
Don't Be a Dummy	MinorD	C	0.20
Double Blow/Gusto	Combat	C	0.10
Dr. Weelo	MinorD	R	3.00
Dr. Weelo's Bio Men	MinorD	U	0.50
[6]			
Dr. Weelo's Fortress	Location	R	3.00
Dragon Ball	Item	C	0.25
Dragon Radar	Equipment	R	4.00
Dream Mirror	Equipment	R	4.00
Drop Kick/Sorrow	Combat	C	0.10
Ebi-Furiya	MinorD	U	0.50
Equipment Retrieval	Global	U	0.80

Card name	Type	Rarity	Price
Excessive Gravity	MinorD	U	0.50
[7]			
Fake Item	Flash	R	3.00
False Moon	Flash	R	3.00
Farmer with Shotgun	Character	C	0.25
Films about Gladiators/Dork	Combat	U	0.50
Firewood	Item	C	0.10
Floating Car	Equipment	C	0.25
Flying Kick/15 Minutes	Combat	C	0.10
Flying Nimbus	Item	R	4.00
Forest Glade	Location	U	0.50
[8]			
Freeza	MajorD	R	3.00
Freeza's Ship	Location	R	3.00
Fried/Lead Baloon	Combat	C	0.10
Frothy Mugs of Water	Global	C	0.25
Frozen Wastes	Location	C	0.10
Full Moon	MinorD	U	0.50
Future Trunks	Character	UR	9.00
Garlic Jr.	MajorD	U	0.50
Garlic Jr.'s Palace	Location	U	0.50
Genki-Dama (Spirit Ball)	Flash	R	3.50
[9]			
Giant's Toy Biplane	Equipment	U	0.80
Ginger	MajorD	C	0.20
Ginyu	MajorD	U	0.50
Gohan Is Angry	Flash	C	0.25
Gohan the Barbarian	Character	U	1.00
Gohan's Cave	Haven	C	0.25
Gohan's Supplies	Item	C	0.25
Goku	Character	C	0.25
[10]			
"Goku (better stats, different art)"	Character	R	5.00

RARITY KEY C = Common U = Uncommon R = Rare VR = Very Rare UR = Ultra Rare F = Foil card X = Fixed/standard in all decks

Card name	Type	Rarity	Price
Goku and Chi-Chi's House	Location	U	1.00
Good Deed	Enhancemt	U	0.80
Goten	Character	R	4.00
Goz	MinorD	C	0.20
Goz' Flying Machine	Equipment	R	3.50
Grace/Poise	Combat	C	0.10
Gravity Ship	Equipment	R	4.00
Great King Yemma	Global	R	3.00
Gregory	Character	R	3.50
Guardian of the Earth	Global	R	4.00
Guldo	MinorD	C	0.20
Guru	Global	R	3.80
Gut Punch/Only a Mother	Combat	C	0.10
Hand Gun	Equipment	U	1.00
Haste	Flash	U	0.80
Head Butt/Sad Eyes	Combat	C	0.10
Heavy Gravity Training	Enhancemt	R	3.00
"Hey, You're Not Dead!"	Flash	C	0.25
Hiding Out	Global	U	0.50
High Ground	Flash	C	0.25
Homework	MinorD	C	0.10
Hong Kong	Location	U	0.50
Hungry Dinosaur	MinorD	C	0.10
Ibuprofen and Quickly!	MinorD	U	0.50
Illusionary Castle	Location	C	0.10
Impending Doom	MinorD	U	0.50
In My Sights/Zen Experience	Combat	C	0.10
Incoming/Cowardice	Combat	C	0.10
Jan-Ken-Po	Flash	C	0.25
Just a Scratch	Flash	R	3.50
"Just a Trim/Say It, Don't Spray It!"	Combat	C	0.10
Kai's Dimensional Sedan	Equipment	R	3.00
Kamehameha	Flash	U	0.50
Kami	Character	R	4.00
Kami's Floating Palace	Location	U	0.50
Keen Observation	Flash	R	3.00
Kidnapped	MajorD	C	0.20
King Kai	Global	C	0.25
King Kai's Bungalow	Haven	U	0.80
King Kai's Planetoid	Location	R	3.00
King Yemma's Fruit	Item	U	0.50
King Yemma's Palace	Location	C	0.10
Kishiime	MinorD	C	0.10
Know When to Run	Flash	U	0.70
Krillin	Character	C	0.25
Laser Eyes	Flash	C	0.25
Leap of Faith	Enhancemt	U	0.80
"Leg Sweep/Why, You Little Devil"	Combat	C	0.10
Lemlia	Item	C	0.10
Light	Equipment	R	3.00

Card name	Type	Rarity	Price
Loner	MinorD	U	0.50
Lunch	Character	U	0.80
Lunch Break/All Dressed Up	Combat	U	0.50
Lunch's House	Haven	C	0.25
M.V.P.	Enhancemt	C	0.25
Makkankoupousou	Flash	R	3.00
Master Roshi	Character	U	1.00
Medical Regenerator	Global	U	0.80
Meltdown	Flash	R	3.00
Mez	MinorD	C	0.10
Mighty Fridge	Item	C	0.10
Mindtrap	Flash	R	3.00
Miso-Cutsun	MinorD	U	0.50
Moon Destruction	Flash	C	0.20
Mother Instinct	Flash	U	1.00
Mystery Foe	MinorD	R	3.00
Nail	Character	U	0.80
Namek Ship	Equipment	R	4.00
Nappa	MajorD	C	0.20
No Help!	MinorD	U	0.50
Oolong	Character	U	1.00
"Oooh, I Got Me!/Tango"	Combat	U	0.50
Otherworld Lounge	Haven	U	0.80
Out of the Frying Pan	Flash	U	0.50
Overload	MinorD	C	0.10
Ox-King	Character	U	0.80
Pendulum Training Room	Location	R	3.00
Piccolo	Character	R	5.00
"Pinned/Well, It's Like This..."	Combat	C	0.10
Planet Arlia	Location	C	0.10
Planet Freeza	Location	C	0.10
Planet Namek	Location	R	3.00
Planet Vegeta	Location	R	3.00
Power Sense	Global	U	0.80
Power Up	Global	U	1.00
Presents	Item	U	0.50
Princess Snake	MajorD	U	0.50
Princess Snake's Palace	Location	R	3.00
Property Damage	MinorD	U	0.50
Pterodactyl	MinorD	C	0.10
Pummel/What'd YOU Have For Lunch?!	Combat	C	0.10
Raditz	MajorD	C	0.20
Raiichi and Zaakro	MajorD	C	0.20
Razor Balls	Equipment	C	0.25
Recoom	MajorD	C	0.20
Refuge	Global	R	3.80
Regeneration	Flash	U	0.80
Rescue	Flash	R	3.00
Rocket Launcher	Equipment	U	0.80
Roshi's Veranda	Haven	C	0.25
Sabre-Toothed Tiger	MajorD	C	0.20

Card name	Type	Rarity	Price
Saibamen	MinorD	U	0.50
Saiyan Space Pod	Equipment	C	0.25
Samurai Gohan	Item	R	4.00
Scouter	Equipment	C	0.25
Screwed/Hero	Combat	U	0.50
"See Monkey, Do Monkey"	Mr Dis	U	1.00
Senzu Beans	Item	R	3.00
Shen Lon	Flash	UR	9.00
Shield	Flash	R	4.00
Shinseiju Tree	MinorD	R	3.00
Ship's Auto-Toilet	Item	R	3.00
Shock/Flowers	Combat	C	0.10
Sleepy Grass	Item	C	0.10
Slow Moving Traffic	Global	C	0.20
Snake Way	Location	U	0.50
Speed II	Enhancemt	C	0.25
Spirit	Enhancemt	C	0.25
Spirit Fighting	Enhancemt	C	0.30
Split Form	Flash	C	0.25
Squeeeeeeeeze!	MinorD	U	0.50
Sunshine Daydream	Flash	U	0.50
Super Saiyan Goku	Character	UR	8.50
Super Saiyan Goten	Character	UR	8.50
Super Saiyan Trunks	Character	UR	8.50
Survey	Enhancemt	R	3.50
Survival Training	Enhancemt	U	1.00
Tail Steak	Item	C	0.10
Tares	MajorD	R	3.00
Technological Artifact	Item	C	0.10
Telekinese	Flash	R	3.00
The Dead Zone	MajorD	U	0.50
The Pit	MinorD	C	0.10
Tien (Tenshinhan)	Character	C	0.25
Time Out!	Flash	C	0.25
Too Much Sun/Nabbed	Combat	C	0.10
Tortoise	Item	R	3.00
Training with Kami	Global	U	1.00
Trunks	Character	C	0.25
Ultimate Sacrifice	Flash	R	3.80
Vegeta	MajorD	U	1.00
Watch That 1st Step...	MinorD	U	0.50
Weighted Clothing	Enhancemt	U	0.80
West Side City Hospital	Haven	U	1.00
Who Sows the Wind	Flash	C	0.25
Wild Swing/Begging For Mercy	Combat	C	0.10
Willpower	MinorD	U	0.50
Yajirobe	Character	C	0.25
Yamcha	Character	C	0.25
Yipes/Happy 2 C U	Combat	C	0.10
Young Gohan	Character	U	1.00
Zarbon	MinorD	R	3.00

Attack up to 2 Locations away from the Location Character is at, at -2 from your total Attack per Location, OR Double Movement for 2 Characters without Equipment.

This powerful weapon, which can extend many times its normal length was given to Goku by his adopted grandfather, Gohan, who won it in a card game from Karin.

Card name	Type		Price
Alielle	Character	Set 1	4.00
Alliance	Global	DBZ	5.00

Ani-Mayhem • Promo cards

Pioneer Entertainment

Many of these cards appeared in magazines. **Final Stand** appeared in *Scrye* 4.4 (Nov 97).

Card name	Type		Price
Armitage	Character	Set 0	3.80
Armitage's Gun	Equipment	Set 1	4.00
Better Off Dead	Enhancemt	Set 1	4.00
Broken Bonds	Global	Set 1	4.00
Confusion/Voyeur	Combat	DBZ	5.00
Don't Touch!!	Enhancemt	Set 1	4.00
Final Stand	Global	DBZ	5.00
Frozen	Flash	DBZ	5.00
Furry Eyes	MinorD	Set 1	4.00
Galus	Character	Set 1	4.00
Gohan's Dragon Ball	Item	DBZ	5.50
Happy Ending	Global	Set 1	4.00
I Like to Watch	Enhancemt	DBZ	5.00
Immortality	Enhancemt	DBZ	5.00
Interdimensional Teleport	Enhancemt	Set 1	4.00

Card name	Type		Price
Kids These Days	MajorD	DBZ	3.80
Mind Scanner	Enhancemt	Set 1	4.00
Motorcycle Getaway	Flash	Set 1	4.00
Pioneer LDC - Mars	Location	Set 1	4.00
Plotting	Flash	Set 1	4.00
Police Reinforcements	Global	Set 1	4.00
Power Pole	Equipment	DBZ	5.00
Priss' Trailer	Location	Set 1	4.00
Puppet Bomb	MinorD	Set 1	4.00
Reference Books	Item	Set 1	4.00
Satellite Observation	Global	Set 1	4.00
Sudden Recall	Flash	Set 1	4.00
Washu's Space Time Converter	Flash	Set 0	5.00
Yajirobe's Hog	Equipment	DBZ	5.00
Yosho Masaki	Flash	Set 1	4.00

RARITY KEY C = Common U = Uncommon R = Rare VR = Very Rare UR = Ultra Rare F = Foil card X = Fixed/standard in all decks

Arcadia

White Wolf Publishing • First set, **The Wyld Hunt**, released **August 1996**

377 cards in set • **IDENTIFIER: Waylay card backs are ivory-colored**

- Character and Story booster displays each contain 24 boosters
- Character and Story booster packs each contain 15 cards
- Character booster packs contain one Character Card and 14 Merit and Flaw cards
- Story booster packs each contain one Quest card and 14 League and Waylay cards

Designed by **Mike Tinney**

    Arcadia is a character-driven collectible card game based on the *Changeling* role-playing game setting from White Wolf Publishing. Players create characters that adventure in the fantastical Changeling homeland of Arcadia, where the Seelie and Unseelie Courts do battle with dark magic. The characters travel through the troubled leagues of Arcadia, seeking to complete quests, gain power, and amass treasure.

    The Character Packs include Characters, Merits, and Flaws, while the Story Packs include Leagues, Quests, Waylays, and Treasures. Each Character card is a three-dimensional pop-up card (unique in the CCG genre) that includes the basic information on one character type. Characters include male and female Humans, Trolls, Sidhe, Redcaps, Ogres, Imps, etc. The base characters are modified by Merits such as Abilities, Advantages, Allies, Arts, and Treasures and can gain more than a base number of Merits by choosing Flaws, such as Curses, Enemies, and Weaknesses. Players then choose a Quest, which allows them to choose a certain point value of Treasures while their opponent may choose a number of Waylays (dangerous encounters).

    Each Quest chosen allows a player to choose five Leagues (lands). A game board is created from the Leagues chosen, and the Treasures and Waylays are placed beneath. Characters move from League to League, meeting different creatures or dangers (the Waylays, or special League encounters), gathering Treasures, and attempting to meet the requirements of their various Quests. A Character gains experience by completing the Quests, with which the player could improve a Character by choosing more Merits or keeping Treasures found during a game. Thus, Arcadia was singular in the CCG genre by allowing a player to create and improve a character from game to game, adding a new layer of competitive development beyond simple card collecting.

    Billed by White Wolf as both a card game and a role playing game, *Arcadia* never quite caught on with the fans of either game format. The cards, square-edged and featuring different images and text on both sides, may easily be mistaken for simple trading-cards by the unitiated. — *James A. Mishler*

The Changeling Adventure Card Game

Concept	●●●○○
Gameplay	●●○○○
Card art	●●●○○
Player pool	●○○○○

Collector alert

Many cards for *Arcadia* are double-sided, so you may not want to "double them up" in nine-pocket pages if you want to prevent damage (and see both sides, obviously.)

Set (377 cards)	220.00
Booster Display Box	60.00
Booster Pack	2.40

You will need 42 nine-pocket pages to store this set. (21 doubled up)

No rarity levels in set

Card name	Type	Price
1		
☐ Aberhold Slave Pits	League	1.00
☐ Absent-Minded	Flaw	0.20
☐ Aegis Monolith	League	1.40
☐ "Al-Kanon, the Chaos Sword"	Merit	0.20
☐ Allergies	Flaw	0.20
☐ "Althros, The Steam City"	League	1.00
☐ Amnesia	Quest	1.60
☐ Arborian Oak-kin	Waylay	0.90
☐ Arborian Willowtree Warrior	Waylay	0.70
2		
☐ Arden-Coast Junction	League	0.20
☐ Arden-Palinian Junction	League	0.60
☐ Ardenmore Guard Patrol	Waylay	0.20
☐ Ardenroad	League	0.20
☐ Ardenroad (Forest)	League	0.20
☐ Ardenroad (Hills)	League	0.20
☐ Arm-Wrestling Troll	Waylay	0.70
☐ Assault on Ebonlique	Quest	3.00
☐ Assjack	Waylay	0.70
3		
☐ Assjack's Trust	Merit	0.80
☐ Autumn Plague	Waylay	0.20
☐ Axe of the Ogre Fiend Gurrgall	Merit	0.30
☐ Bad Luck	Flaw	0.35

Card name	Type	Price
☐ Bag of Gold	Merit	0.30
☐ Balanvale	League	1.00
☐ Balath Castle	League	0.70
☐ Balm for Madness	Quest	1.10
☐ Bane Tower	League	1.40
4		
☐ Bane Tower Road	League	1.00
☐ Banek	Waylay	0.20
☐ Bell the Cat	Waylay	0.60
☐ Belt of Troll Strength	Merit	0.30
☐ Bernard Assjack	Flaw	0.15
☐ Billy Smith, 8th Grade Honor Student and Human Cartographer	Merit	0.30
☐ Blackmail	Merit	0.35
☐ Blackrock Pass	League	1.00
☐ Bloath: Ogre Bully	Waylay	0.45
5		
☐ Bog	Waylay	0.70
☐ Boil and Bubble	Merit	0.40
☐ Bottom-Heavy	Flaw	0.25
☐ Boulder	Waylay	0.20
☐ Brilliant Strategy	Merit	0.25
☐ Broad-Shouldered	Merit	0.35
☐ Bully	Merit	0.20
☐ Capture the Traitor	Quest	1.60
☐ Chameleon	Merit	0.50
6		
☐ Chimera	Waylay	2.80
☐ Circlet of Resolve	Merit	1.10
☐ Cityboy	Merit	0.30
☐ Claustrophobic	Flaw	0.20

Card name	Type	Price
☐ Clear Thinking	Merit	0.35
☐ Cog Dragoon	Waylay	2.80
☐ Cog Soldier	Waylay	2.80
☐ Coin of Clarity	Merit	0.40
☐ Colinwell	League	0.20
7		
☐ Commanding Presence	Merit	0.25
☐ Conscription	Quest	1.10
☐ Coral Palace	League	0.70
☐ Coral Trident	Merit	2.30
☐ Corporeal Ghost	Waylay	0.20
☐ Courier for the Court	Quest	3.00
☐ Court of Praxis Tynon	League	2.80
☐ Coward	Flaw	0.20
☐ Crazed	Flaw	0.20
8		
☐ Creativity	Merit	0.50
☐ Cunning	Merit	0.25
☐ Dark Reach Pass	League	0.20
☐ Darkened Glen	League	1.00
☐ Darkling Junction	League	0.20
☐ Darklingvale	League	1.40
☐ Darkreach Loche	League	1.40
☐ Darkreach Mountains	League	0.20
☐ Darkreach Spires	League	0.20
9		
☐ Davelon, Gleeful Satyr	Merit	0.50
☐ Deductive Reasoning	Merit	0.25
☐ Devilish Grin	Merit	0.60
☐ Dictum	Merit	0.40
☐ Dirty Fighter	Merit	0.25

RARITY KEY **C** = Common **U** = Uncommon **R** = Rare **VR** = Very Rare **UR** = Ultra Rare **F** = Foil card **X** = Fixed/standard in all decks

SCRYE Collectible Card Game Checklist and Price Guide • **61**

Card name	Type	Price
Dishonest	Flaw	0.25
Doppelganger	Merit	0.70
Dragonkin	Flaw	0.15
Dragonkin (female)	Character	1.50
[10] Dragonkin (male)	Character	1.50
Dreaming	Merit	0.40
Duelist	Merit	0.20
Duke Bane	Waylay	0.90
Eagle Eyes	Merit	0.35
Ebonlique	League	1.40
Effigy	Merit	0.50
Eidle Road	League	0.70
Eidolon	League	1.00
[11] Eloquent Speech	Merit	0.25
Ensnare	Merit	0.70
Escort Lady Sophia	Quest	0.60
Even Dragons Pay Taxes	Quest	0.70
Fae Armor	Merit	0.40
Fae Blade	Merit	0.50
Fair Fortune	Merit	1.10
Fancy Pants	Merit	0.40
Fealty to House Fionna	Merit	0.30
[12] Fealty to House Liam	Merit	0.30
Fianna Garou	Waylay	0.70
Fields of Rust	League	1.40
Fields of Sabine	League	0.20
Fiesole	League	0.60
Flock of Harpies	Waylay	1.40
Foresight	Merit	0.30
Forest of the Midnight Sun	League	0.60
Forest Spiders	Waylay	0.20
[13] Forestry	Merit	0.35
Frost Giant	Waylay	1.40
Frost Haven	League	0.70
Fuddle	Merit	0.50
Fugue	Merit	0.50
Gambling Knockers	Waylay	1.40
Gauntlet of Herculean Strength	Merit	0.70
Giant Eagle	Merit	0.30
Giant Hopping Toad	Merit	0.35
[14] Giant Slug	Waylay	0.20
Gimmix	Merit	0.70
Gird the Realm's Heroes	Quest	1.60
Glamour Dance	Waylay	0.90
Glamour Dust	Merit	0.40
Glass Jaw	Flaw	0.20
Gnome's Brew	Waylay	0.70
Golden Torc	Merit	0.50
Goldenreach Fields	League	0.70
[15] Gord's Knot	Waylay	0.20
Gorgeous	Merit	0.60
Grandeur	Merit	0.70
Grey Reach	League	1.00
Grey River	League	1.00
Greyview	League	0.50
Guilty As Charged	Waylay	0.90
Gullible	Flaw	0.25
Gurthdass, Troll Bodyguard	Merit	0.30
[16] Hall of the Ogre King	League	0.60
Hamlet of Bloath	League	1.00
Hamlet of Easlynn	League	0.70
Haunted Heart	Merit	2.30
Hawk Knife	Merit	0.70
Heather-Balm	Merit	0.70
Hermit's Hollow	League	0.60
Hills of Steam	League	0.20
Hopscotch	Merit	0.50

Card name	Type	Price
[17] Hound of Hades	Waylay	0.60
Human (female)	Character	1.50
Human (male)	Character	1.30
Humans	Flaw	0.20
Hungry Ettin	Waylay	0.70
Huntinglane	League	0.20
Huntsman's Snare	Waylay	0.20
Hurrgan Skurr, Ogre Henchman	Merit	0.30
Hurricane	Waylay	0.35
[18] Icarian Flying Skiff	Waylay	0.20
Imp (female)	Character	1.10
Imp (male)	Character	1.10
Imps	Flaw	0.25
Indecisive	Flaw	0.20
Innocent Smile	Merit	0.25
Ione's Temple	League	0.20
Iron Will	Merit	0.35
Irondeath Fields	League	0.70
[19] Irondew Artillery	Waylay	0.60
Irondew Keep	League	1.00
Irondew Road (Fields)	League	1.00
Irondew Road (Marsh)	League	0.20
Jailbreak	Quest	1.60
Jealous Redcap	Waylay	0.20
King Ironheart	Flaw	0.25
Knocker (female)	Character	1.00
Knocker (male)	Character	1.50
[20] Knocker's Artifact	Merit	1.10
Knockers	Flaw	0.20
Kryllian's Pond	League	0.20
Lady Kryddia, Sidhe Adventurer	Merit	0.40
Lady Sophia	Merit	0.40
Lance of Ardlanth	Merit	1.10
Lightning Quick	Merit	0.20
Lost!	Waylay	0.20
Low Moral Character	Merit	0.35
[21] Magical Barrier	Waylay	0.70
Manticora	Waylay	1.40
Map of the Land	Merit	0.20
Marauders	Quest	0.70
Maze	Waylay	0.20
Mead of Vigor	Merit	1.10
Mephisto's Seeds	Merit	0.50
Mer	Flaw	0.20
Mer (female)	Character	1.20
[22] Mer (male)	Character	3.10
Middleguard	League	1.40
Middlemarch Invaders	Quest	0.70
Middlemarch Junction	League	0.70
Midnight Falls	League	1.00
Mirror, Mirror	Merit	2.30
Mirthos Fjadal	Merit	0.20
Mountain Heritage	Merit	0.25
Mountain of the Kings	League	1.40
[23] Mounted Spidereye Goblin	Waylay	0.70
Mouth of Grey	League	1.40
Noria of Eternity	League	1.00
Nowhere Blind	League	0.70
Nowhere Glade	League	3.00
Nowhere Junction	League	0.20
Nuvorg, Imp Conman	Merit	0.20
Nymph	Character	3.10
Nymph's Wreath	Merit	0.20
[24] Nymphs	Waylay	0.20
Oakenshield	Merit	0.50
Oathfriend	Waylay	0.20

Card name	Type	Price
Oceanius	League	0.20
Ogre (female)	Character	1.30
Ogre (male)	Character	3.10
Ogre Games	Waylay	0.90
Ogre Kin	Merit	0.20
Ogre Watch Bridge	League	2.80
[25] Ogres	Flaw	0.20
Old Man of the Sea	Waylay	0.90
Orchid Isle	League	3.00
Page	Merit	0.50
Palinian Road	League	0.50
Palinian-Coast Junction	League	0.20
Pansy	Flaw	0.20
Pathetic Sniveling	Merit	0.25
Peace Mission	Quest	1.10
[26] Pearl of Wisdom	Merit	0.40
Perceptive Fighter	Merit	0.25
Perfect Body	Merit	0.30
Pesky Merchant	Waylay	0.20
Pferl	League	1.00
Pilgrim's Burden	Waylay	0.20
Pirates	Waylay	0.20
Pit of the Grubworm	Waylay	0.90
Pitha's Testing Zone	League	1.40
[27] Pixie Dust	Merit	0.40
Portal Passage	Merit	0.40
Potion of Love	Merit	0.50
Prometheus' Fist	Merit	1.10
Proper Etiquette	Waylay	0.20
Protocol	Merit	0.50
Prove Yourself	Quest	1.10
Psyche Out	Merit	0.35
Quest for Knowledge	Quest	1.10
[28] Quicksand	Waylay	0.20
Quicksilver	Merit	0.70
Raxis	League	0.50
Reconnaissance Mission	Quest	1.60
Redcap (female)	Character	1.10
Redcap (male)	Character	1.90
Redcaps	Flaw	0.10
Relentless	Merit	0.25
Renegade Dragonkin	Waylay	0.90
[29] River of Rust	League	1.40
Road to Middlemarch	League	0.60
Roc Attack	Waylay	0.70
Rockslide	Waylay	0.20
Rogue Troll	Waylay	0.70
Rosewood Bend	League	1.00
Rosewood Keep	League	1.00
Royal Cartographer	Quest	0.90
Royal Wedding Gift	Quest	0.70
[30] Ruins of Astalar	League	0.60
Runes	Merit	1.10
Runic Circle	Merit	1.10
Runs-Wild, Werewolf Traveler	Merit	0.35
Sabine Glade	League	1.00
Sadmost Bridge	League	0.20
Saining	Merit	1.10
Sandman	Waylay	0.60
Sardinium	League	0.70
[31] Satyr	Flaw	0.25
Satyr	Character	1.10
Satyr's Pipes	Merit	0.30
Save Rosewood Keep	Quest	0.90
Scorched Fields	League	1.40
Scour Darkreach Mountains	Quest	0.70
Scroll of Knowledge	Merit	0.25

RARITY KEY C = Common   U = Uncommon   R = Rare   VR = Very Rare   UR = Ultra Rare   F = Foil card   X = Fixed/standard in all decks

Card name	Type	Price
Sea Worthy	Merit	0.45
Seek the Oracle's Advice	Quest	0.60
Sense of Direction	Merit	0.20
Seraph	Waylay	0.60
Shadow Rust Vale	League	1.40
Shaebanaria, Nymph Guide	Merit	0.20
Shield	Merit	0.70
Sibylline Swamp	League	1.40
Sidhe	Flaw	0.25
Sidhe (female)	Character	1.30
Sidhe (male)	Character	1.00
Sidhe Sword	Merit	0.20
Silvernahl, Mer Debater	Merit	0.40
Sir Wrathgar	Waylay	0.70
Slavers	Quest	0.20
Slavers	Waylay	0.90
Snide Remarks	Merit	0.25
Sophia's Favor	Merit	0.35
Sophia's Hatred	Flaw	0.15
Sphinx's Riddle	Waylay	0.70
Spidereye Goblin	Waylay	0.20
Spike Trap	Waylay	0.20
Splendour Bridge	League	0.20
Splendour Lake	League	0.20
Splendour Waters	League	1.40
Splendourscale	Waylay	0.90
Steadfast	Merit	0.30
Steely Sinews	Merit	0.80
Stone Egg	Merit	0.40
Stormguard Keep	League	1.00
Sundered Copse	League	0.20
Sundered Woods	League	0.20
Sure Pass Trail	League	1.00

Card name	Type	Price
Swamp Rat	Merit	0.25
Tattletale	Merit	0.70
Tax Collector	Waylay	0.20
The City of Coral	League	2.80
The Crystal Falls	League	1.00
The Eastern Coastal Road	League	0.20
The Eastern Coastal Road (Forest)	League	0.20
The Edge of Grey Filth	League	0.20
The Flower Quest	Quest	1.60
The Graveyard of Ships	League	1.40
The Kyrrian Tower	League	0.20
The Loa-Heedron	League	2.80
The Marsh of Grey Filth	League	1.40
The Palinian Road	League	0.20
The Road to Nowhere	League	0.70
The Ruins of Plugrath	League	1.40
The Rust Mines of Toris Baalgarth	League	0.70
The Sheriff of Raxis	Flaw	0.15
The Silver Branch	Merit	0.30
The Silver Tongue	Merit	0.20
The Swamplands	League	1.40
The Wyld Hunt	Quest	1.60
The Wyld March	League	0.60
Thieves Guild	Merit	0.30
Thieves!	Waylay	1.40
Thomas the Lame Brigand	Waylay	0.20
Tiberius	Flaw	0.25
Tiberius	Waylay	0.70
Ties to Middlemarch	Merit	0.45
Tome of the Dragonkin	Merit	0.20
Traveling Papers	Waylay	0.20
Trojan Horse	Waylay	0.90
Troll (female)	Character	1.50

Card name	Type	Price
Troll (male)	Character	1.50
Trolls	Flaw	0.20
Tsu Ocean (Dif. 5)	League	1.40
Tsu Ocean (Dif. 6 Ver. A)	League	1.00
Tsu Ocean (Dif. 6 Ver. B)	League	0.70
Underdog	Merit	0.25
Unicorn	Waylay	0.20
Unseelie Knight	Waylay	0.45
Vengeful	Merit	0.25
Victory over Duke Bane	Quest	1.60
Wand of Ice	Merit	0.50
Wandering Imp	Waylay	0.30
Wanderlust	Merit	0.70
Warhorse	Merit	0.35
Warrant	Flaw	0.25
Wasteland	League	0.70
Water Elemental	Waylay	0.70
Waterrunner	Waylay	0.20
Weak Knees	Flaw	0.25
Weakling	Flaw	0.20
Wenig, Knocker Mechanic	Merit	0.35
Whirlpool	Waylay	0.20
Whiselkane's Lane	League	0.20
Will-o'-the-Wisp	Merit	0.50
Willow Light	Merit	1.10
Willow-Whisper	Merit	0.70
Willowtree Scrub	League	0.70
Willowtree Vale	League	1.00
Winged Sandals	Merit	0.35
Witch's Curse	Waylay	0.90
Witty Repartee	Merit	0.25
Wooden Horse	Merit	0.25
Writ of Carte Blanche	Merit	0.50
Wyldstone	Merit	0.70

Arcadia • King Ironheart's Madness

White Wolf Publishing • Released **December 1996**

404 cards in set • **IDENTIFIER: Waylay card backs are black**

- Character and Story booster displays each contain 24 boosters
- Character and Story booster packs each contain 15 cards
- Character booster packs contain one Character card and 14 Merit and Flaw cards

    The Wyld Hunt was designed to be the first in a trilogy of releases for the **Arcadia** line. The second installment, **King Ironheart's Madness**, with a whopping 404 cards, was released at the end of 1996 — just as the upheavals following the initial CCG glut led White Wolf to reconsider its plans.

    The concluding installment, **The Lion's Den**, never saw print, but 781 cards is still plenty for a two-release game. Only **MLB Showdown**, in 2000, would come near that mark. — *James A. Mishler*

Set (404 cards)	265.00	
Booster Display Box	90.00	
Booster Pack	2.40	

You will need 45 nine-pocket pages to store this set. (23 doubled up)

No rarity levels in set

Card name	Type	Price
Accountability	Waylay	0.50
Affectionate Oilslick	Waylay	0.50
Air Assault	Quest	3.00
Aldrich, the Mechician	Flaw	0.50
Aldrich, the Mechician	Quest	3.00
Aldrich, the Mechician	Waylay	2.00
Aldrich's Workshop	League	2.00
Alert	Merit	1.00

Card name	Type	Rarity	Price
Al-Sidan, Djinn assassin	Merit		1.00
Anal retentive	Flaw		0.50
Arborian Cog Tower	League		2.00
Arden Border	League		2.00
Arden Junction	League		2.00
Army Ant Guides	Merit		1.00
Army Ant Kommando Kit	Merit		1.00
Army Ant Platoon	Character		2.00
Army Ants	Flaw		0.50
Ash Heaps	Waylay		2.00
Assault on Mechopolis	Quest		3.00
Assembly Line	Waylay		0.50
Augury	Merit		2.50
Bag of Gold	Merit		1.50
Barnacle Armor	Merit		1.50

Card name	Type	Rarity	Price
Beguiling	Merit		1.00
Berserker	Merit		1.00
Blade of Cold Iron	Merit		3.00
Blind	Flaw		0.50
Bliss Camp	Merit		3.00
Blood Key	Merit		3.00
Bog of Ire	League		2.00
Bog Pits of Grey Filth	League		2.00
Boggan Gang Bangers	Waylay		0.50
Border Run	Quest		3.00
Bradburr's Mighty Pen	Merit		3.00
Braggart	Flaw		0.50
Brawny	Merit		1.00
Buccaneer Colony	Waylay		2.00
Bumpkin	Flaw		0.50

Card name	Type	Price
☐ Burn & Boil	Merit	2.00
☐ Buster Zoltan, Human Mechanic	Merit	2.50
☐ Capsized	Waylay	0.50
☐ Captive Heart	Merit	0.50
☐ Carnivorous Plants	Waylay	0.50
☐ Chainblade	Merit	3.00
☐ Charm	Merit	2.00
6		
☐ Charming	Merit	1.00
☐ Chasm Range Foothills	League	0.50
☐ Chasm Range Trail	League	0.50
☐ Chasm Spires.	League	2.00
☐ Cheater	Merit	2.50
☐ Clock Roaches	Waylay	2.00
☐ Clumsy	Flaw	0.50
☐ Cog Access bridge	League	0.50
☐ Cog Access Highway	League	2.00
7		
☐ Cog Autogyro	Waylay	2.00
☐ Cog Barracks	League	0.50
☐ Cog Dreadnought	Waylay	2.00
☐ Cog Exoskeleton	Merit	1.50
☐ Cog Hunter	Merit	2.50
☐ Cog Hunting Dogs	Waylay	0.50
☐ Cog Juggernaut	Waylay	2.00
☐ Cog Marauders	Waylay	2.00
☐ Cog Mortar	Waylay	2.00
8		
☐ Cog Platoon	Waylay	0.50
☐ Cog Refinery	League	2.00
☐ Cog Sniper	Waylay	0.50
☐ Cog Spider Flyers	Waylay	2.00
☐ Cog Spider Tank	Waylay	2.00
☐ Cog Squid	Waylay	2.00
☐ Cog Steed	Merit	0.50
☐ Cog Submarine	Waylay	2.00
☐ Cog Tank	Merit	2.50
9		
☐ Cog Training Grounds	League	2.00
☐ Cog Trap	Waylay	2.00
☐ Cogophobia	Flaw	0.50
☐ Commanding	Merit	1.00
☐ Coughing Break	Waylay	0.50
☐ Creative	Merit	1.00
☐ Cruel Geyser	Waylay	0.50
☐ Cutting Humor	Merit	1.00
☐ Dapper Rokea	Waylay	2.00
10		
☐ Dark Yeoman's Guidance	Merit	1.00
☐ Dark Yeoman's Quest: Cog Refinery Spill	Quest	3.00
☐ Dark Yeoman's Quest: Decoy	Quest	3.00
☐ Dark Yeoman's Quest: Jacko D'Rakk	Quest	3.00
☐ Dark Yeoman's Quest: King of the Hill	Quest	3.00
☐ "Dask, Dragonkin Knight"	Merit	1.00
☐ Dem Bones	Merit	2.50

Card name	Type	Price
☐ Despised	Flaw	0.50
☐ Dignified	Merit	1.00
11		
☐ Discerning	Merit	1.00
☐ Disciplined	Merit	1.00
☐ Djinn (female)	Character	1.00
☐ Djinn (male)	Character	1.00
☐ Djinn Scimitar	Merit	2.50
☐ Djinn Wanderers	Waylay	2.00
☐ Downtown Mechopolis	League	0.50
☐ Dreamcatcher	Merit	2.50
☐ Dunes of Remorse	League	2.00
12		
☐ Dystopian Maze	Waylay	2.00
☐ Earthquake	Merit	2.00
☐ Earthshape	Merit	2.50
☐ East Cog Access Road	League	2.00
☐ East Cog Tower	League	2.00
☐ East Gate Access	League	2.00
☐ East Watch Tower	League	2.00
☐ Egg of the Wyrd	Merit	2.50
☐ Elder Form	Merit	2.00
13		
☐ Empathetic	Merit	1.00
☐ Endurance Reserves	Merit	1.00
☐ Enslaved!	Quest	3.00
☐ Escape the Great Caliph's Wrath	Quest	3.00
☐ Eshu	Flaw	0.50
☐ Eshu (female)	Character	1.00
☐ Eshu (male)	Character	0.50
☐ Eshu Buckler	Merit	2.50
☐ Explorer	Merit	2.00
14		
☐ Fairbanks, Eshu Pirate	Merit	0.50
☐ Fallen Border	League	2.00
☐ Fashion Victim	Flaw	0.50
☐ Fate Fire	Merit	2.00
☐ Favored by Ali'i	Merit	1.00
☐ Ferocious	Merit	1.00
☐ Fianna Garou	Character	1.00
☐ Fields of Honor	League	2.50
☐ Fields of Plunder	League	2.50
15		
☐ Fields of Sludge	League	0.50
☐ Flame Lance	Merit	2.50
☐ Flash Powder	Merit	2.50
☐ Flatlands	League	2.00
☐ Fleet of Foot	Merit	2.00
☐ Flicker Flash	Merit	2.00
☐ Flood	Merit	2.00
☐ Footpad	Waylay	0.50
☐ Free the Waterfall City	Quest	3.00
16		
☐ Garden District	League	2.00
☐ Geasa	Merit	2.00
☐ General Electric	Waylay	2.00
☐ General Motors	Waylay	2.00
☐ Gremlin (female)	Character	1.00
☐ Gremlin (male)	Character	2.00
☐ Gremlins	Flaw	0.50
☐ Gremlin's Tools	Merit	2.00
☐ Grey Bog	League	2.00
17		
☐ Grey Marsh	League	0.50
☐ Grey Mire River	League	0.50
☐ Grey River	League	2.00
☐ Grey Sod Glades	League	2.00
☐ Gridlock	Waylay	2.00
☐ Griffin	Merit	1.00
☐ Gurthdass	Flaw	0.50
☐ Gurthdass, Troll Bodyguard	Merit	1.00
☐ Head Leech	Waylay	0.50
18		
☐ Hermann, Boggan Scout	Merit	0.50

Card name	Type	Price
☐ High Anxiety	Flaw	0.50
☐ Holly Strike	Merit	2.00
☐ Hunted!	Quest	3.00
☐ Hypo-Scorpions	Waylay	0.50
☐ Ill-Prepared	Flaw	0.50
☐ Industrial Accident	Waylay	2.00
☐ Inferno	Merit	2.00
☐ Ingenious	Merit	1.00
19		
☐ Insane Homesteaders	Waylay	0.50
☐ Insidious	Merit	1.00
☐ Insight	Merit	2.00
☐ Intimidating	Merit	1.00
☐ Intuitive	Merit	1.00
☐ Iron Park	League	2.00
☐ Iron Plains	League	2.00
☐ Iron Swamp	League	0.50
☐ Irondew Junction	League	0.50
20		
☐ Irondew Road	League	2.00
☐ Irondew Ruins	League	2.00
☐ Ironheart's Toll Bridge	League	0.50
☐ Ironheart's Trust	Merit	2.00
☐ Ironleaf Fields	League	2.00
☐ Ironleaf Forest	League	2.00
☐ Ironleaf Lane	League	2.00
☐ Ironleaf Vale	League	2.00
☐ Jabbermouth	Flaw	0.50
21		
☐ Jack Hammer, Rehabilitated Cog Dragon	Merit	2.00
☐ Jacko D'Rakk	Waylay	2.00
☐ Jacko's Bog	League	0.50
☐ Join the Monkeywrench Gang!	Quest	3.00
☐ Jungle Sirens	Waylay	2.00
☐ Kaihikaai	League	2.00
☐ Kelwrath's Volcano	League	2.00
☐ Kenu, Escaped Kokua Slave	Merit	2.00
☐ King Ironheart's Highway	League	0.50
22		
☐ King Ironheart's Highway (Savvy Trial)	League	0.50
☐ King Ironheart's Highway (Wasteland)	League	0.50
☐ Knowledgeable	Merit	1.00
☐ Kokua	Flaw	0.50
☐ Kokua (female)	Character	1.00
☐ Kokua (male)	Character	1.00
☐ Kokua Blowguns	Waylay	2.00
☐ Kokua Raid	Quest	3.00
☐ Lair of the Steam Drake	League	2.00
23		
☐ Lastwater Fields	League	0.50
☐ Lazy	Flaw	0.50
☐ Liberated Steam Sprites	Merit	1.00
☐ Little Hammer God	Merit	2.00
☐ Lodestone	Merit	2.00
☐ Lord Gamine	Flaw	0.50
☐ Lord Gamine's Backing	Merit	2.00
☐ Loric's Fields	League	2.00
☐ Lost City of Mirron.	League	2.00
24		
☐ Lyya, Naga Mistress of Secrets	Merit	1.00
☐ Magic Beans	Merit	2.00
☐ Magic Carpet	Merit	2.00
☐ Maria, Satyr Poet	Merit	0.50
☐ Marketplace	League	0.50
☐ Mechanical Knack	Merit	1.00
☐ Mechopolis Blueprints	Merit	2.00
☐ Mechopolis Security	Waylay	0.50
☐ Mechopolis Water Works	League	2.00
25		
☐ Mechorg (female)	Character	2.00
☐ Mechorg (male)	Character	1.00

The *Arcadia* map

There are a lot of map ("League") cards in *Arcadia*, and, for the curious wondering how they all fit together, there's help.

Scrye #17 (Nov 96) features a color centerspread map of Ardenmore, the country where *The Wyld Hunt* takes place. The map includes commentary by designer Mike Tinney. Look for it in your game retailer's back issue section or on eBay.

RARITY KEY **C** = Common **U** = Uncommon **R** = Rare **VR** = Very Rare **UR** = Ultra Rare **F** = Foil card **X** = Fixed/standard in all decks

64 • *SCRYE Collectible Card Game Checklist and Price Guide*

Card name	Type	Price
Mechorg Assassin	Waylay	2.00
Meditative Practice	Merit	2.00
Middlemarch Airfields	League	2.00
Mirage	Merit	2.00
Misdirection	Merit	1.00
Monkey Wrench	Merit	2.00
Mooch	Merit	2.00
26		
Mr. Briefcase, Human Magician	Merit	1.00
Murch, Renegade Gremlin	Merit	1.00
Music Box	Merit	2.00
Naga	Flaw	0.50
Naga (female)	Character	1.00
Naga (male)	Character	1.00
Naga Fangspear	Merit	2.00
Naga Guardians	Waylay	2.00
Naturally Aggressive	Merit	1.00
27		
Nomad	Merit	2.00
Northern Boglands	League	2.00
Northgate Fields	League	2.00
Nowhere Forest	League	2.00
Nowhere Timberlands	League	2.00
Omar's Tackle Shop	League	2.00
Overconfident	Flaw	0.50
Oyster Pearl Ring	Merit	2.00
Pacifist	Flaw	0.50
28		
Passing Kraken	Waylay	2.00
Personal Dirigible	Merit	2.00
Persuasive	Merit	1.00
Phantom Shadows	Merit	2.00
Plummet	Waylay	2.00
Polluted Water	Waylay	0.50
Pooka Mask	Merit	2.00
Porta-Sphinx	Merit	2.00
Possessed	Flaw	0.50
29		
Press Gang	Waylay	0.50
Progress	Waylay	2.00
Propaganda	Waylay	0.50
Proselytizing Velociraptors	Waylay	2.00
Qadan, The City of Clouds	League	2.00
Racoon Pooka	Character	1.00
Raid on General Motors' Workshop	Quest	3.00
Rally the Slaves	Quest	3.00
Rat Apple Fields	League	2.00
30		
Rat Apples	Waylay	0.50
Rational	Merit	1.00
Razor Hawks	Waylay	2.00
Red Herring	Merit	2.00
Reflective	Merit	1.00
Remorseless	Merit	1.00
Renegade Cog	Character	1.00
Renewed Vigor	Merit	2.00
Repeating Crossbow	Merit	1.00
31		
Residential Mechopolis	League	2.00
Reweaving	Merit	2.00
Riddle Gate	Waylay	2.00
Ring of Karma	Merit	2.00
River of Sludge	League	0.50
Road Crew	Waylay	0.50
Road of the Sleeping Giant	League	2.00
Road to Kelwrath's Volcano	League	2.00
Road to Skyeholme	League	2.00
32		
Road to the Fallen Lands	League	0.50
Robust	Merit	1.00
Rose-Colored Goggles	Merit	2.00
Rugged	Merit	1.00
Ruined Temple	Waylay	2.00
Ruins of Srissan	League	2.50

Card name	Type	Price
Rust Bucket	Merit	2.00
Salamander	Waylay	2.00
Sandman Pageant	Waylay	2.00
33		
Sands of Sleep	Merit	2.00
Sandstorm	Waylay	2.00
Schism	Merit	2.00
Secret Tunnels	League	2.00
Seductive	Merit	1.00
Selina, Alternative Sluagh	Merit	1.00
Selkie (female)	Character	1.00
Selkie Sealskin	Merit	2.00
Sewer Raft	Merit	2.00
34		
Sharktooth Sword	Merit	2.00
Ship in a Bottle	Merit	2.00
Shooting Star	Merit	2.00
Shrewd	Merit	1.00
Shrink Lamp	Merit	2.00
Side Track	Merit	2.00
Sidewinder	Waylay	2.00
Skeleton Key	Merit	2.00
Sky Ray	Merit	0.50
35		
Slammer, Triton Mercenary	Merit	0.50
Sluagh	Flaw	0.50
Sluagh (female)	Character	2.00
Sluagh (male)	Character	1.00
Sluagh Shadow Shoes	Merit	2.00
Smog Cloud	Waylay	0.50
Sociopathic Steam Sprites	Waylay	0.50
Sooper Gloo	Merit	2.00
South of Sybilline	League	2.00
36		
Southern Wastelands	League	2.00
Splendour Brook	League	0.50
Splendour River	League	2.00
Splendour Riverbed	League	2.00
Springheel Jack	Merit	2.00
Spyglass	Merit	2.00
Star Body	Merit	2.00
Steam-powered Flight Rig	Merit	2.00
Steelwing, the Steam Drake	Waylay	2.00
37		
Stilt Gators	Waylay	2.00
Stinking Rich	Merit	2.00
Storm Clouds	Merit	2.00
Storm Maker	Merit	2.00
Stowaway!	Quest	3.00
Streetwise	Merit	1.00
Stronger Than You Look	Merit	1.00
Stupid	Flaw	0.50
Submissive	Flaw	0.50
38		
Svelte	Merit	1.00
Swamp of Fingers	League	2.00
Sweatshop Heat	Waylay	2.00
Tangle Vines	Waylay	2.00
Tempest	Merit	2.00
Tempting Illusion	Waylay	0.50
Tenacious	Merit	1.00
Tenderfoot	Flaw	0.50
The 4man	Waylay	0.50
39		
The Ant Hill	League	2.00
The Dance	Merit	2.00
The Dark Yeoman's Dream Test	Quest	3.00
The Darkening	Quest	3.00
The Eastern Grey River	League	2.00
The Far Steppes	League	2.00
The Floating City	Quest	3.00
The Giant's Breath	League	2.00
The Giant's Third Eye	Merit	2.00

Card name	Type	Price
40		
The Great Caliph	Flaw	0.50
The Great Caliph's Respect	Merit	1.00
The Great Dam	League	2.00
The Lighthouse	League	2.00
The Mirage	League	2.00
The Pipeline	League	2.00
The Promenade	League	2.00
The Secret of the Sleeping Giant	Quest	3.00
The Secret Trail	League	2.00
41		
The Shipyards	League	2.00
The Skywalk	League	0.50
The Slave Pit	Quest	3.00
The Sleeping Giant	League	2.00
The Slums	League	0.50
The Steam Drake's Lair	Quest	3.00
The Third Eye	Quest	3.00
The Tower of King Ironheart	League	2.00
The Vortex	League	2.00
42		
The Wastelands	League	0.50
Thick-Skinned	Merit	2.00
Tiger Trap	Waylay	0.50
Timberlands of Grey Filth	League	0.50
Time Clock	Waylay	0.50
Tornado	Waylay	2.00
Torque Wrench	Waylay	2.00
Triton	Character	1.00
Tsu Coastline	League	0.50
43		
Tsu Ocean (Dif. 6)	League	2.00
Tsu Ocean (Dif. 7)	League	0.50
Twist, Redcap Urchin	Merit	0.50
Undercity Slave Pits	League	2.00
Unwind the Key	Quest	3.00
Uptown	League	0.50
Useless Sycophant	Flaw	0.50
Vain	Flaw	0.50
Veiled Eyes	Merit	2.00
44		
Vigorous	Merit	1.00
Volcanic Plain	Waylay	0.50
Waste Tunnels	League	0.50
Wasted Fields	League	2.00
Weapons Master	Merit	1.00
Weaver Ward	Merit	2.00
West Cog Tower	League	2.50
Western Access Tunnels	League	0.50
Western Moor	League	0.50
45		
Western Watch Tower	League	2.00
Wily	Merit	1.00
Wind Pistol	Merit	2.00
Wind Runner	Merit	2.00
Worn Out	Waylay	0.50
Wyld Boars	Waylay	0.50
Wyvern	Waylay	2.00
Zip of Zeppelins	Waylay	2.00

RARITY KEY C = Common   U = Uncommon   R = Rare   VR = Very Rare   UR = Ultra Rare   F = Foil card   X = Fixed/standard in all decks

Austin Powers

Jerry Springer
Biting Talk Show Host

Vibs 1 GROOVY

1 CREEPY

You may play this Agent and Springin' Shindig as a single action.

25 MOJO

Decipher • Released December 1999

140 cards in set

Concept	●●○○○
Gameplay	●●○○○
Card art	●●●○○
Player pool	●●○○○

- Starter decks contain 60 cards; starter displays contain 12 starters
- Booster packs contain 11 cards; booster displays contain 30 boosters

Around the video release of *The Spy Who Shagged Me*, the **Austin Powers** game tried to bring the party atmosphere of Mike Myers' spy spoofs to the CCG field.

Each player has their own set of agents, each worth a certain point value. First to 100 points wins. Character fights are simple, with each player playing "frickin' bone" attack cards, the last "Bone" played winning that fight. You're allowed two actions a turn, which involve any combination of playing a character or initiating an attack.

Powerful decks revolved around a certain main character, and were fun to play. But many players wouldn't attack unless they had a hand full of Bones, which sometime prolonged the game, because no one wanted to risk losing a major battle.

Humorous, but not a hit — and releasing as it did when more children than ever were in the hobby, its subject matter may have been a drawback. *Scrye* couldn't even print the full names of cards without complaints from parents of Pokékids! — **Joe Alread**

Set (140 cards)	100.00
Starter Display Box	100.00
Booster Display Box	95.00
Starter Deck	10.00
Booster Pack	3.00

You will need **16** nine-pocket pages to store this set. (8 doubled up)

Card name	Rarity	Price
Amanda Kisenhugg, Go-Go Dancer	C	0.25
Anita Boyd, Woody Stalker	C	0.30
Austin, From 10 Minutes From Now	R	5.00
"Austin … I AM YOUR FATHER!"	U	1.00
Austin Powers, All Shagged Out	R	7.00
Austin Powers, Astro-Naughty	R	6.00
Austin Powers, Bikini-Clad Bombshell?	R	7.00
Austin Powers, Fashion Photographer	R	6.00
Austin Powers' Kama Sutra	C	0.30
Austin Powers, M.O.D. Agent	F	2.00
Austin's Magnifying Specs	U	1.00
Balancing Act	C	0.25
Balcony Beauties	U	1.00
Barry Erman, Battering Ram Expert	C	0.25
Basil Exposition, Elder British Intelligence Superior	U	1.00
Basil Exposition, Younger British Intelligence Superior	R	5.00
Bastard Bagpipes	U	1.00
Belgian Dip	U	1.00
Booster Shot	F	0.40
Bottoms Up	C	0.30
Bridal Shower	C	0.25
Busby Queensman, Undistractable Guardsman	C	0.25
Carmen Gettit, Heinie Toucher	F	0.50
Chastity, "Shagette"	C	0.25
Cherry, "Shagette"	C	0.25
"Crikey!"	C	0.25
Cryo Chamber	C	0.25
Dance of the Randy Minx	C	0.25
"Death Star"	U	1.00
Dick, Fighter Pilot	F	0.40
Disciplinary Action	C	0.30
Divine, "Shagette"	U	1.00
"Do you swing?"	C	0.25
"Doctaaaarrrrri!"	C	0.25
"Don't go there, girlfriend."	C	0.25
Dr. Evil, Bent on World Domination	F	2.00
Dr. Evil, In Quasi-Futuristic Clothes	R	10.00
Dr. Evil, Irresistible Mojo Juggernaut	R	8.00
Dr. Evil's Secret Volcano Lair	C	0.30
Evil Egg	C	0.25
Evil Rap	U	1.00

Card name	Rarity	Price
Fat Bastard, Dead Sexy	R	8.00
Fat Bastard, Disgruntled Scottish Guard	U	1.00
Felicity Shagwell, American Woman	R	6.00
Felicity Shagwell, Astro-Very-Naughty	R	6.00
Felicity Shagwell, Bikini-Clad Bombshell	R	8.00
Felicity Shagwell, In Quasi-Futuristic Clothes	R	6.00
Felicity Shagwell, London Tourist	R	5.00
Felicity's Corvette	U	1.00
Fembot Vanessa, Kamikaze Bride	R	5.00
Flash in the Pad	U	1.00
Frau Farbissina, "Laser" Operator	R	5.00
Frau Farbissina, LPGA Cruiser	U	1.00
Frau Farbissina, Weird Momma	R	4.00
General Hawk, Presidential Advisor	R	4.00
"Get in my BELLY!"	C	0.25
Goldie, Heartthrob	F	0.40
Half Nelson	U	1.00
Homing Device	R	4.00
"Hop on the good foot and do the bad thing."	C	0.25
"How does that feel, baby?"	C	0.25
Human Shield	F	0.50
"I am a sexy bitch!"	U	1.00
"I ate a BABY!"	C	0.30
"I put the GRR in swinger, baby."	C	0.25
"I'll cover your rear."	U	1.00
"I'm even better off my feet."	C	0.25
Irritating Interrogation	R	4.00
"It got weird, didn't it?"	U	1.00
"It's just not in the cards now, is it?"	C	0.25
Ivana Humpalot, Dr.Evil's "Pawn"	R	5.00
Ivana Humpalot, Russian Tiger	U	1.00
"I've beaten Dr. Evil before and I'll beat him again."	C	0.30
Jerry Springer, Biting Talk Show Host	U	1.00
Jerry Springer, Talk Show Ringmaster	U	1.00
Joe, Bazooka Marksman	C	0.25
Johnson, Radar Operator	C	0.25
Jonas Cooper, Haz Mat Agent	C	0.25
Ménage à Trois	U	1.00
Mini-Me, In Quasi-Futuristic Clothes	R	10.00
Mini-Me, Vicious Little Chihuahua Thing	R	8.00
Mini-Me's Goodbye Card	C	0.25
Mojo Extractor	U	1.00
Mojo Vial	F	0.50
"Move over, Rover. This chick is taking over."	C	0.25
Mr. Elvis Costello, Radio Sweetheart	U	1.00
Mr. English Colonel, Weight Loss Consultant	U	1.00
Mrs. Ruth, Sex-Ed Teacher	U	1.00
Mustafa, Tri-questa-phobic Assassin	R	5.00
Nicely Packed	F	0.40
"Nobody knows what you're talking about…ass"	U	1.00

Card name	Rarity	Price
No-J	U	1.00
Number Two, Healthy and Youthful	R	5.00
Number Two, Not Dead, Just Badly Burned	R	4.00
"Oh, behave."	C	0.25
"Once you've had fat, you'll never go back."	C	0.25
"One for me… and one for my homies"	C	0.30
One-Eyed Monster, Cabbage-Scented Carney	F	0.40
"Ooo… frisky are we?"	C	0.30
"Perhaps next time you should try foreplay!"	C	0.25
Pit of Liquid Hot Magma	C	0.25
Rabbi Schlotsky, Evil Mohel	C	0.25
Rebecca Romijn, Hasn't Had "The Pleasure"	R	4.00
Remote Control	U	1.00
Roadkill	U	1.00
Robin Swallows, Determined Assassin	R	4.00
Robin Swallows, Maiden Name: Spitz	U	1.00
Rodd, Hot, Salty Nuts Vendor	C	0.25
Scott Evil, The Margarine of Evil	R	5.00
Shagette Forcefield	C	0.25
Slugfest	U	1.00
Southern California?	C	0.25
Spank You Very Much	U	1.00
Spin Doctor	U	1.00
Springin' Shindig	U	1.00
Stroking the Bishops	U	1.00
Synchronized Swinging	C	0.30
Telly Wise, Springer Fan	C	0.25
The President, Oblivious to 90s References	R	3.00
"The swinger has landed."	U	1.00
"The thought of you naked is just gross."	C	0.25
"The world is mine!"	C	0.25
Time Beetle	C	0.25
Time Machine	U	1.00
Unibrau, Hot German Birdie	U	1.00
Wanda McLuff, Pecker Watcher	C	0.25
Wang, Chinese Student	C	0.25
"What do you think of these, my man?"	C	0.25
"When a problem comes along, you must zip it … zip it good."	C	0.30
"Why won't you DIE?"	C	0.25
Willie Nelson, The Highwayman	C	0.25
Would you care for a suckle of my zipple?	C	0.25
www.shh.com … org	C	0.30
"Yeah, baby!"	C	0.25
Yellow Submarine	U	1.00
"You are hairy like ANIMAL!"	C	0.25
"You are one groovy baby … baby"	U	1.00
"You don't have to be cute with me."	C	0.25
"You gonna cry? You gonna squirt some?"	C	0.25
"Zip it!"	C	0.25

RARITY KEY **C** = Common **U** = Uncommon **R** = Rare **VR** = Very Rare **UR** = Ultra Rare **F** = Foil card **X** = Fixed/standard in all decks

Babylon 5

Precedence • First set, **Premier**, released **November 1997**

446 cards in set

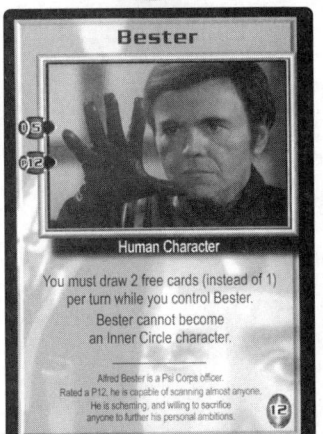

- Starter decks contain 60 cards, rulebook and playmat; displays contain 12 starters, 3 of each race
- Booster packs contain 8 cards; Booster displays contain 24 boosters

Designed by **Ran Ackels, Edi Birsan, Paul W. Brown III, John Hart, David Hewitt,** and **John Myler**

   Babylon 5 is a game of galactic control based on the TV series of the same name, about a 23rd century space station acting as a United Nations for the Centauri, Humans, Minbari, Narns, and other less powerful races. Lurking are both the Vorlons and Shadows, the elder races of the *Babylon 5* universe.

   Though playable with less or more, the CCG is at its best as a four-player game. Each player plays one of the four primary races: Centauri, Humans, Minbari, or Narn. Victory is achieved by having 20 or more Power and more Power than any other player. Power is a total of Influence and Power bonuses. Influence is used to play cards, draw cards, and for power. Each faction starts the game with four influence, the race's ambassador in play, and three cards of different types as an opening hand. (Yes, you get to choose your opening hand!) Starting at four and trying to get to 20 is not something that happens in the first few turns, preventing most opening-hand abuses.

   Each race has cards only it can play. Because of this, each race is relatively better or worse in an ability. There are five abilities: Diplomacy, Intrigue, Psi, Military, and Leadership. The Centauri, for example, are better in Intrigue but worse in Leadership.

   Babylon 5 tends to play out in three stages. The first stage is building influence. The second stage varies: Traditionally, it involves winning a number of Conflicts that give Influence. Conflicts are the interactive part of the game. Characters or fleets with the correct ability (most conflicts only allow one ability to be used in them) may participate in the conflict by rotating to provide support or opposition. If support is greater than opposition, the conflict wins; otherwise it loses. The third stage often involves playing an agenda, a type of card that decks build around, as they are the primary way to gain a power bonus over your influence total, that gives enough additional power to win. How much power is highly variable. An infinite power bonus is theoretically possible with some of the agendas. Five is excellent.

   The TV show is done, but the CCG is still going strong. Besides its American following, it has a strong following overseas. The game lends itself well to social players who enjoy politics in their CCGs. However, the political nature of the game is lost when there are too few players, yet too many players can slow the game down too much. With personality having a strong effect on who wins, competitive players can get frustrated. Nevertheless, tournament play is very common throughout the world.

   For collectors, there is quite a bit of good news. Main characters' images are found on numerous cards. Many of the main characters are found in the starters; 50 of the 60 cards in a starter are fixed. Autographed versions of main characters are also present, with a signed **Delenn Transformed** as the autographed card for *Premier*. — **Ian Lee**

Concept	●●●●○
Gameplay	●●●○○
Card art	●●●○○
Player pool	●●●●○

Set (446 cards)	300.00
Starter Display Box	85.00
Booster Display Box	41.00
Starter Deck	9.00
Booster Pack	2.00

You will need 50 nine-pocket pages to store this set. (25 doubled up)

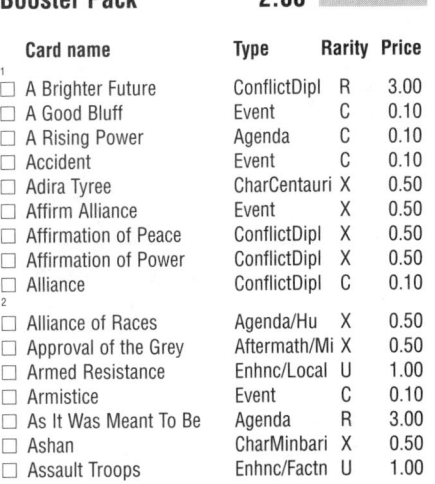

Card name	Type	Rarity	Price
A Brighter Future	ConflictDipl	R	3.00
A Good Bluff	Event	C	0.10
A Rising Power	Agenda	C	0.10
Accident	Event	C	0.10
Adira Tyree	CharCentauri	X	0.50
Affirm Alliance	Event	X	0.50
Affirmation of Peace	ConflictDipl	X	0.50
Affirmation of Power	ConflictDipl	X	0.50
Alliance	ConflictDipl	C	0.10
Alliance of Races	Agenda/Hu	X	0.50
Approval of the Grey	Aftermath/Mi	X	0.50
Armed Resistance	Enhnc/Local	U	1.00
Armistice	Event	C	0.10
As It Was Meant To Be	Agenda	R	3.00
Ashan	CharMinbari	X	0.50
Assault Troops	Enhnc/Factn	U	1.00

Card name	Type	Rarity	Price
Assigning Blame	Aftermath	X	0.50
Attacking Pawns	Conflict/Intr	C	0.10
Avert Incident	Event	C	0.10
Babylon 5 Unrest	Enhnc/B5	R	3.00
Backroom Dealing	Enhnc/Char	U	1.00
Balance	Event	X	0.50
Battle Tested	Aftermath	U	1.00
Bester	CharHuman	R	10.00
Bio-Weapon Discovery	Conflict/Intr	R	3.80
Black Market	Conflict/Intr	U	1.00
Blockade	Conflict/Milit	R	3.00
Blood Oath	Aftermath	U	1.00
Book of G'Quan	Enhnc/Na/Ch	X	0.50
Border Raid	Conflict/Milit	X	0.50
Campaign for Support	ConflictDipl	C	0.10
Carn Mollari	CharCentauri	X	0.50
Carpe Diem	Event	R	5.00
Casualty Reports	Aftermath	R	3.00
Catherine Sakai	Char/Neutral	U	1.00
Censure	Enhnc/Fleet	U	1.00
Centauri Agent	CharCentauri	X	0.50
Centauri Aide	CharCentauri	X	0.50
Centauri Captain	CharCentauri	X	0.50

Card name	Type	Rarity	Price
Centauri Prime	Loctn/Cent	X	0.50
Centauri Telepath	CharCentauri	C	0.10
Change of Plans	Event	C	0.10
Changing Opinion	Event	C	0.10
Chaos Reigns	Event	C	0.10
Chrysalis	Event/Minb	U	1.00
Colonial Fleet (Centauri)	FleetCentauri	X	0.50
Colonial Fleet (Human)	FleetHuman	X	0.50
Colonial Fleet (Minbari)	FleetMinbari	X	0.50
Colonial Fleet (Narn)	FleetNarn	X	0.50
Combat Experience	Aftermath	C	0.10
Commerce Raiding	Enhnc/Global	U	1.00
Commercial Telepaths	Group	U	1.00
Compatible Goals	ConflictDipl	U	1.00
Competing Interests	Event	R	3.00
Complete Support	ConflictDipl	U	1.00
Concealed Weapon	Enhnc/Ch	C	0.10
Concentrated Effort	Event	C	0.10
Condemn Deportations	ConflictDipl	C	0.10
Conflicting Desires	Event	R	3.00
Conflicting Loyalties	Event	R	3.00
Confusion in Chaos	Event	C	0.10
Consolidated Position	ConflictDipl	R	3.00

RARITY KEY **C** = Common   **U** = Uncommon   **R** = Rare   **VR** = Very Rare   **UR** = Ultra Rare   **F** = Foil card   **X** = Fixed/standard in all decks

Card name	Type	Rarity	Price	Card name	Type	Rarity	Price	Card name	Type	Rarity	Price
Contact with Shadows	Event	C	0.10	Fixed in Their Ways	Enhnc/Fa	U	1.00	Kalain	CharMinbari	X	0.50
Contact with Vorlons	Event	X	0.50	Fleet of the Line	FleetHuman	R	5.00	Kha'Mak	CharNarn	X	0.50
Coordinated Fire	Event	C	0.10	Fleet Support Base	Enhnc/Local	X	0.50	Kidnapping	Conflict/Intr	X	0.50
Counterintelligence	Group	R	3.80	Fleets on the Border	Event	C	0.10	Knowledge Is Power	Agenda	X	0.50
Court the Rebellious	Conflict/Intr	C	0.10	Focus Your Efforts	Aftermath	U	1.00	Knowledge of Shadows	Event	C	0.10
Covert Allies	Enhnc/Char	R	3.00	For My People	Event	C	0.10	Knowledge of the Soul	Event	U	1.00
Crisis of Self	Aftermath	U	1.00	For the Common Good	Event	C	0.10	Ko'Dath	CharNarn	X	0.50
Crusade	Conflict/Milit	R	3.30	For the Good of All	Event	X	0.50	Kosh Naranek	CharVorlon	R	7.00
Crystal Cities	Enhnc/Mi/Lo	X	0.50	Forced Commitment	Enhnc/Factn	X	0.50	Lack of Subtlety	Event	C	0.10
Cut Supply Lines	Event	C	0.10	Forced Evolution	Agenda/Majr	R	4.40	Lady Ladira	CharCentauri	U	1.00
Cynthia Torqueman	Char/Neutral	U	1.00	Forced Impairment	Conflict/Intr	R	4.00	Lady Morella	CharCentauri	X	0.50
Damage Control Team	Group	R	4.00	Forces Collide	Event	R	3.30	Lamentations	Aftermath	X	0.50
Dan Randall	Char/Neutral	C	0.10	Frederick Lantz	CharHuman	X	0.50	Latent Telepath	EnhncChar	C	0.10
Decisive Tactics	Event	X	0.50	Free the Souls	Conflict/Intr	R	3.00	Leading the Races	AgendaHum	C	0.10
Declaration of War	Event	X	0.50	Garrison Fleet	FleetCentauri	U	1.00	Learning Experience	Aftermath	C	0.10
Deep Space Fleet (Centauri)	FleetCentauri	X	0.50	G'Drog	CharNarn	C	0.25	Left Vulnerable	Aftermath	R	3.00
Deep Space Fleet (Human)	FleetHuman	X	0.50	General Franklin	CharHuman	U	1.00	Lennier	CharMinbari	X	0.50
Deep Space Fleet (Minbari)	FleetMinbari	C	0.10	General Hague	CharHuman	X	0.50	Level the Playing Field	Event	X	0.50
Deep Space Fleet (Narn)	FleetNarn	X	0.50	G'Kar	CharNarn	X	0.50	Limited Strike	ConflictMilit	X	0.50
Defame Ambassador	Event	C	0.10	Glory	Aftermath	R	3.00	Liquidating Assets	Event	C	0.10
Defense in Depth	Agenda	U	1.00	Government Opposition	Group	R	3.00	Lockdown	Event	C	0.10
Delenn	CharMinbari	X	0.50	Grey Council Fleet	FleetMinbari	R	5.00	Londo Mollari	CharCentauri	X	0.50
Delenn Transformed	CharMinbari	R	7.00	Grievance	Aftermath	U	1.00	Long Term Investment	Event	C	0.10
Demonstrative Victory	ConflictDipl	R	3.00	Growth in Chaos	Agenda/Cent	C	0.20	Lord Kiro	CharCentauri	U	1.00
Despair	Aftermath	R	3.00	G'Sten	CharNarn	R	4.30	Lord Refa	CharCentauri	U	1.00
Destiny Fulfilled	Event	X	0.50	Guilt	Aftermath	U	1.00	Lord Valo	CharCentauri	C	0.10
Develop Relationship	Aftermath	U	1.00	Gunboat Diplomacy	Conflict/Milit	X	0.50	Loss of Face	Aftermath	C	0.10
Dhaliri	CharMinbari	U	1.00	Harvest Souls	Aftermath	R	4.00	Loss of Support	ConflictDipl	U	1.00
Diplomatic Advantage	Aftermath	R	3.00	Hate Crime	Conflict/Intr	U	1.00	Lovell	CharMinbari	C	0.10
Diplomatic Blunder	Event	C	0.10	Heavy Fleet	FleetNarn	R	5.00	Luis Santiago	CharHuman	R	5.50
Diplomatic Corps	Group	C	0.10	Hedronn	CharMinbari	X	0.50	Luxuries of Homeworld	EnhncChar	U	1.00
Diplomatic Immunity	Event	C	0.10	Hidden Agent	Aftermath	X	0.50	Lyndisty	CharCentauri	C	0.10
Disaffected Centauri	Char/Neutral	R	4.00	Hidden Knowledge	Event	X	0.50	Lyta Alexander	CharNeutral	X	0.50
Disaffected Human	Char/Neutral	R	4.00	Higher Calling	Agenda	C	0.10	Maintain the Peace	Agenda	R	3.30
Disaffected Minbari	Char/Neutral	R	4.00	Hire Raiders	Event	C	0.10	Marcus Cole	CharNeutral	R	6.00
Disaffected Narn	Char/Neutral	R	4.00	Homeworld Fleet (Centauri)	FleetCentauri	X	0.50	Markab Fleet	FleetNonA	R	4.30
Disenchantment	Aftermath	U	1.00	Homeworld Fleet (Human)	FleetHuman	X	0.50	Mars Colony	LocatnHum	X	0.50
Disgrace	Aftermath	R	3.00	Homeworld Fleet (Minbari)	FleetMinbari	X	0.50	Martyr	Aftermath	R	3.00
Dishonor	Conflict/Intr	X	0.50	Homeworld Fleet (Narn)	FleetNarn	X	0.50	Mary Ann Cramer	CharNeutral	C	0.10
Draal	CharMinbari	X	0.50	Hour of the Wolf	Event	U	1.00	Mass Drivers	Enhnc/Fleet	U	1.00
Draft	Enhnc/Fa	U	1.00	Human Agent	CharHuman	X	0.50	Meddling with Others	Agenda	U	1.00
Drazi Sunhawk	Fleet/NonA	C	0.10	Human Aide	CharHuman	X	0.50	Medical Assistance	Event	X	0.50
Drigo	CharCentauri	X	0.50	Human Captain	CharHuman	X	0.50	Meditation	Event	C	0.10
Du'Nar	CharNarn	U	1.00	Humanitarian Aid	ConflictDipl	C	0.10	Merchandising B5	Event	C	0.10
Durlan	CharMinbari	C	0.10	Hunted	Aftermath	X	0.50	Miagi Hidoshi	CharHuman	X	0.50
Du'Rog	CharNarn	C	0.10	"Hunter, Prey"	Conflict/Intr	C	0.10	Michael Garibaldi	CharHuman	X	0.50
Early Warning	Event	X	0.50	Immolan V	Locatn/Cent	U	1.00	Military Cadre	Group	C	0.10
Earth	Loctn/Human	X	0.50	Immortality Serum	ConflictDipl	R	3.00	Military Telepaths	Group	U	1.00
Elric	Char/Neutral	R	5.00	Imperial Telepaths	Group/Cent	R	4.00	Minbar	LocatMinbar	X	0.50
Emergency Military Aid	Event	C	0.10	Imperialism	Agenda	C	0.10	Minbari Agent	CharMinbari	X	0.50
Emperor Turhan	CharCentauri	X	5.00	In the Line of Duty	Aftermath	U	1.00	Minbari Aide	CharMinbari	X	0.50
Energy Mines	Enhn/Na/Flt	X	0.50	Inevitable Destiny	Aftermath	R	3.00	Minbari Captain	CharMinbari	X	0.50
Enrage	Aftermath	U	1.00	Infiltrate and Exploit	Agenda	U	1.00	Minbari Protectorate	LocatMinvar	U	1.00
Establish Base	Conflict/Milit	U	1.00	Influential Lords	Group/Cent	U	1.00	Minbari Telepath	CharMinbari	X	0.50
Euphrates Treaty	ConflictDipl	X	0.50	Internal Strife	Event	C	0.10	Mines	Enhnc/Fact	U	1.00
Expeditionary Fleet (Centauri)	FleetCentauri	X	0.50	Interstellar Corporation	Group	C	0.10	Minister Malachi	CharCentauri	R	5.50
Expeditionary Fleet (Human)	FleetHuman	X	0.50	Intolerable Interference	Aftermath	U	1.00	Moral Quandary	Event	C	0.10
Expeditionary Fleet (Minbari)	FleetMinbari	X	0.50	Intrigues Mature	Event	C	0.10	Morden	CharNeutral	R	5.00
Expeditionary Fleet (Narn)	FleetNarn	X	0.50	Ipsha Battleglobe	Fleet/NonA	U	0.80	Motivated Leaders	Group	R	3.00
Exploit Opportunities	Aftermath	X	0.50	ISN	Group	U	1.00	Mr. Adams	CharNeutral	U	1.00
Exploitation	Enhnc/Local	C	0.10	Isolated	Enhnc/Char	U	1.00	Muddy the Waters	Conflict/Intr	C	0.10
Exploration	Event	C	0.10	Isolationism	Enhnc/Factn	U	1.00	Na'Far	CharNarn	U	1.00
Extended Contacts	Group	C	0.10	It Will Be His Undoing	Aftermath	R	3.00	Na'Kal	CharNarn	X	0.50
Extreme Sanction	ConflictDipl	U	1.00	Ja'Doc	CharNarn	X	0.50	Na'Ka'Leen Feeder	Conflict/Intr	C	0.10
Finish the War	Agenda/Milit	X	0.50	Jason Ironheart	CharNeutral	R	6.00	Narn Agent	CharNarn	X	0.50
First Battle Fleet (Centauri)	FleetCentauri	X	0.50	Jeffrey Sinclair	CharHuman	X	0.50	Narn Aide	CharNarn	X	0.50
First Battle Fleet (Human)	FleetHuman	X	0.50	Jha'Dur	CharNeutral	R	5.00	Narn Captain	CharNarn	X	0.50
First Battle Fleet (Minbari)	FleetMinbari	X	0.50	John Sheridan	CharHuman	R	10.00	Narn Homeworld	Locat/Narn	X	0.50
First Battle Fleet (Narn)	FleetNarn	X	0.50	Judgement by Success	Enhnc/Factn	U	1.00	Narn Rabble	Group/Narn	U	1.00
								Na'Toth	CharNarn	X	0.50

RARITY KEY C = Common • U = Uncommon • R = Rare • VR = Very Rare • UR = Ultra Rare • F = Foil card • X = Fixed/standard in all decks

68 • SCRYE Collectible Card Game Checklist and Price Guide

Card name	Type	Rarity	Price
☐ Negotiated Surrender	Aftermath	R	1.50
☐ Neroon	CharMinbari	U	1.00
☐ Neutrality Treaty	ConflictDipl	C	0.25
☐ Never Again	AgendaNarn	X	0.25
☐ News of Defeat	Aftermath	U	1.00
☐ News of Galactic Import	Event	C	0.25
☐ N'Grath	CharNeutral	X	0.25
☐ Nightmares	Aftermath	U	1.00
☐ No Escape	Aftermath	R	3.00
32			
☐ Non-Aggression Pact	ConflictDipl	C	0.10
☐ Non-Aligned Support	ConflictDipl	U	1.00
☐ Not Meant to Be	Event	R	4.00
☐ Observers	Group	R	3.00
☐ Older but Wiser	Aftermath	C	0.10
☐ Order Above All	Agenda/Majr	R	4.00
☐ Overworked	Enhnc/Char	C	0.10
☐ Parliament of Dreams	ConflictDipl	R	3.00
☐ Paying for Sins	Aftermath	R	3.00
33			
☐ Peace In Our Time	Agenda	X	0.50
☐ Peacekeeping	Conflict/Milit	U	1.00
☐ Personal Enemies	Aftermath	X	0.50
☐ Personal Involvement	Aftermath	X	0.50
☐ Personal Protection	Enhnc/Char	U	1.00
☐ Personal Sacrifice	Aftermath	X	0.50
☐ Picket Fleet (Centauri)	FleetCentauri	X	0.50
☐ Picket Fleet (Human)	FleetHuman	X	0.50
☐ Picket Fleet (Minbari)	FleetMinbari	X	0.50
34			
☐ Picket Fleet (Narn)	FleetNarn	X	0.50
☐ Planetary Defenses	Enhnc/Local	C	0.10
☐ Political Realignment	Event	U	1.00
☐ Popular Support	Event	X	0.50
☐ Power Politics	Agenda	X	0.50
☐ Power Posturing	Enhnc/Char	R	3.00
☐ Precision Strike	Conflict/Intr	U	1.00
☐ Prolonged Talks	Event	R	3.00
☐ Prophecy	Enhnc/Char	X	0.50
35			
☐ Protests	Aftermath	R	3.00
☐ Proxima III	Locat/Human	U	1.00
☐ Psi Attack	Conflict/Psi	U	1.00
☐ Psi Bodyguard	Enhnc/Char	X	0.50
☐ Psi Corps Intelligence	Group/Hum	X	0.50
☐ Psi Interrogation	Conflict/Intr	C	0.10
☐ Public Apology	Aftermath	R	3.00
☐ Pulling Strings	Enhnc/Char	C	0.10
☐ Purge the Disloyal	Conflict/Intr	U	1.00
36			
☐ Quadrant 14	Locat/Narn	X	0.50
☐ Quadrant 37	Locat/Narn	U	1.00
☐ Rabble Rousers	Group	U	1.00
☐ Racial Hatred	Aftermath	R	3.00
☐ Ragesh III	Locat/Cent	X	0.50
☐ Raid Shipping	Conflict/Milit	U	1.00
☐ Rally the People	ConflictDipl	R	3.50
☐ Rally to the Cause	Event	C	0.10
☐ Ramming	Event	R	3.00
37			
☐ Ranger Strike Team	Group	U	1.00
☐ Rangers Surveillance	Group	R	4.00
☐ Rathenn	CharMinbari	R	5.00
☐ Recalled to Service	Event	R	3.70
☐ Refugees	Aftermath	X	0.50
☐ Religious Caste	Group/Milit	U	1.00

Card name	Type	Rarity	Price
☐ Renowned Victory	Aftermath	X	0.50
☐ Repairing the Past	Aftermath	X	0.50
☐ Rescue	Aftermath	U	1.00
38			
☐ Reserve Fleet	FleetHuman	U	1.00
☐ Retribution	Aftermath	X	0.50
☐ Revenge	Agenda/Narn	X	0.50
☐ Reverse Advances	Aftermath	R	3.00
☐ Rise of the Republic	Agenda/Cent	X	0.50
☐ Rise to Power	Aftermath	X	0.50
☐ Rivalry	Aftermath	X	0.50
☐ Rogue Soul Hunter	Ch/Neutral	R	4.80
☐ Saber Rattling	ConflictDipl	U	1.00
39			
☐ Sabotage	Conflict/Intr	X	0.50
☐ Salvage Yard	Enhnc/Local	R	4.00
☐ Sanctions	Event	C	0.10
☐ Sandra Hiroshi	CharHuman	C	0.10
☐ Sarah	CharHuman	U	1.00
☐ Second Battle Fleet (Centauri)	FleetCentauri	X	0.50
☐ Second Battle Fleet (Human)	FleetHuman	X	0.50
☐ Second Battle Fleet (Minbari)	FleetMinbari	X	0.50
☐ Second Battle Fleet (Narn)	FleetNarn	X	0.50
40			
☐ Secondary Control	Enhnc/Factn	R	3.00
☐ Secondary Experience	Aftermath	X	0.50
☐ Secret Police	Group	U	1.00
☐ Secret Strike	Event	R	4.00
☐ Secret Vorlon Aid	Event	C	0.10
☐ Security Training	Enhnc/Char	U	1.00
☐ Seduction	Event	C	0.10
☐ Seizing Advantage	Agenda	R	3.00
☐ Self Doubt	Event	C	0.10
41			
☐ Senator Voudreau	CharHuman	U	1.00
☐ Servants of Order	Agenda/Milit	X	0.50
☐ Shadow Assault	Conflict/Milit	U	1.00
☐ Shadow Strike	Event	U	1.00
☐ Shakat	CharMinbari	R	5.30
☐ Shal Mayan	CharMinbari	X	0.50
☐ Short Term Goals	Event	X	0.50
☐ Short Term Investment	Event	C	0.10
☐ Shunned	Enhnc/Ch	U	1.00
42			
☐ Skeletons in the Closet	Aftermath	R	3.00
☐ Sleeper Personality	Co	X	0.50
☐ Sleeping Z'ha'dum	Lo	R	5.00
☐ Sneak Attack	Event	C	0.10
☐ Sortie	Event	C	0.10
☐ Soul Hunter	Ch/Neutral	U	1.00
☐ Special Ops	Event	C	0.10
☐ Spin Doctors	Group	R	3.30
☐ Sponsor Rebels	Conflict/Intr	U	1.00
43			
☐ Stealth Technology	Enhnc/Mi/Flt	R	4.00
☐ Stephen Franklin	CharHuman	X	0.50
☐ Stop Hostilities	ConflictDipl	X	0.50
☐ Strafing Run	Event	C	0.10
☐ Strategic Reassignment	Event	C	0.10
☐ Strength in Adversity	Agenda	U	1.00
☐ Strike Fleet	FleetNarn	U	1.00
☐ Subliminal Influence	Event	U	1.00
☐ Successful Manipulation	Aftermath	U	1.00
44			
☐ Supplement Security	ConflictDipl	X	0.50
☐ Support Babylon 5	Event	X	0.50

Card name	Type	Rarity	Price
☐ Support of the Mighty	Agenda	U	1.00
☐ Susan Ivanova	CharHuman	X	0.50
☐ Talia Winters	CharHuman	X	0.50
☐ Ta'Lon	CharNarn	X	0.50
☐ Technological Espionage	Conflict/Intr	C	0.10
☐ Telepathic Scan	Conflict/Ps	X	0.50
☐ Temptations	Conflict/Intr	C	0.20
45			
☐ Terrorist Bombings	Conflict/Intr	U	1.00
☐ Test Their Mettle	ConflictDipl	R	3.00
☐ The Eye	Enhnc/CE/Ch	R	4.00
☐ The Great Machine	Conflict	R	4.00
☐ The Hope of Peace	Agenda	U	1.00
☐ The Opposition Rises	Event	C	0.10
☐ The Price of Power	Event	X	0.50
☐ Thenta Makur	Group/Narn	R	5.00
☐ Third Battle Fleet (Centauri)	FleetCentauri	R	5.00
46			
☐ Third Battle Fleet (Minbari)	FleetMinbari	U	1.00
☐ Total War	Agenda	R	4.40
☐ Trade Pact	ConflictDipl	X	0.50
☐ Trade Windfall	Event	C	0.10
☐ Transfer Point Io	Locat/Human	U	1.00
☐ Triluminary	Enhnc/Mi/Ch	U	1.00
☐ Tu'Pari	CharNarn	R	5.00
☐ Under Pressure	Aftermath	U	1.00
☐ Underworld Connections	Event	X	0.50
47			
☐ United Front	Aftermath	X	0.50
☐ Universe Today Feature	Event	C	0.10
☐ Unrecognized Data	Event	C	0.10
☐ Upgraded Defenses	Enhnc/B5	X	0.50
☐ Urza Jaddo	CharCentauri	X	0.50
☐ Utility Fleet (Centauri)	FleetCentauri	C	0.10
☐ Utility Fleet (Human)	FleetHuman	C	0.10
☐ Utility Fleet (Narn)	FleetNarn	C	0.10
☐ Vendetta	Aftermath	R	3.00
48			
☐ Victory In My Grasp	Event	X	0.50
☐ Vir Cotto	CharCentauri	X	0.50
☐ Vital Interests	Enhnc/Factn	R	3.00
☐ Vorlon Enhancement	Enhnc/Char	R	4.00
☐ Vorlon Rescue	Event	R	3.30
☐ Vree Saucers	Fleet/NonA	R	4.00
☐ War by Popular Decree	Event	C	0.10
☐ War College	Group	C	0.10
☐ War Hero	Aftermath	X	0.35
49			
☐ Warleader Shakiri	CharMinbari	R	5.00
☐ Warleader's Fleet	FleetMinbari	R	5.50
☐ Warren Keffer	CharHuman	C	0.10
☐ Warrior Caste	Group/Milit	R	3.00
☐ Wear and Tear	Aftermath	U	1.00
☐ What Do You Want?	Event	C	0.10
☐ Who Are You?	Event	C	0.10
☐ Wind Swords	Group/Milit	U	1.00
☐ Witness Protection	Conflict/Intr	R	3.00
50			
☐ Working Relationship	Enhnc/Char	U	1.00
☐ Wounded	Aftermath	R	3.00
☐ You Are Not Ready	Event	X	0.50
☐ You Know My Reputation	Event	X	0.50
☐ Zack Allan	CharHuman	U	1.00

Babylon 5 • Campaign Set

Precendence • Released **November 1997**
- Box contains two starter decks, one Premier booster pack and oversized rule-book
- Two versions available: **Narn vs. Centauri** and **Minbari vs. Human**

The **Campaign Set** for the **Babylon 5** CCG is simply a repackaging of the **Premier** starters to allow easier entry into the game. One set includes the Minbari and Human starters; the other, Narn and Centauri starters. There was a promotion where certain sets included the **Doctor Franklin** promo card. A sticker on the outside was the tipoff. — *Ian Lee*

Narn Vs. Centauri Box	**15.00**	**Minbari vs. Human Box**	**15.00**	

Collectible Card Game

Babylon 5 • *Deluxe (Premier, 2nd Ed.)*

Precedence • Released **August 1998**

380 cards in set • **IDENTIFIER: 1998 trademark; brighter and redder than** *Premier* **cards**

• Booster packs contain 8 cards; booster displays contain 24 boosters and checklist

Deluxe, a reprint of the *Premier* set of the **Babylon 5 CCG**, became necessary when *Premier* boosters sold out. Precedence fixed many of the problems with cards abused in *Premier*, making *Deluxe* more important than just an opportunity for new players to get the base set cards.

Ten major card changes were made. Some of the changes had previously been errata to *Premier* cards. The most significant changes mainly involve agendas that proved too easy to abuse, such as **Seizing Advantage**, **As It Was Meant To Be**, and **Maintain the Peace**. One main character, **John Sheridan**, also got changed, making his new version one of the most sought after of the *Deluxe* cards.

Deluxe has some oddities for the *Babylon 5* player/collector. Fixed cards, cards only found in starters from *Premier*, are one to a pack, making the *Deluxe* versions far harder to acquire than the *Premier* versions. Some cards, but only a few, have new artwork. Most of the cards look different from the *Premier* versions because of different color correction — *Deluxe* cards are brighter and redder. The "unique" cards from *Premier* were not reprinted. A mistake was made in half the **As It Was Meant To Be** cards, causing Precedence to pull the incorrect versions, leaving the correct version twice as rare. A signed **Commander Ivanova**, unsigned as an uncommon in **The Shadows**, is the autographed card. — *Ian Lee*

Set (380 cards)	100.00
Starter Display Box	38.00
Booster Display Box	30.00
Starter Deck	8.00
Booster Pack	2.20

You will need **43** nine-pocket pages to store this set. (22 doubled up)

Card name	Type	Rarity	Price
[1]			
A Brighter Future	Conflict	R	2.40
A Good Bluff	Event	C	0.10
A Rising Power	Agenda	C	0.10
Accident	Event	C	0.10
Adira Tyree	Character	X	0.40
Affirmation of Power	Conflict	X	0.25
Alliance	Conflict	C	0.10
Approval of the Grey	Aftermath	X	0.25
Armed Resistance	Enhancement	U	0.80
[2]			
Armistice	Event	C	0.10
As It Was Meant To Be (Two versions)	Agenda	R1	2.40
Assault Troops	Enhancement	U	0.80
Attacking Pawns	Conflict	C	0.10
Avert Incident	Event	C	0.10
Babylon 5 Unrest	Enhancement	R3	2.40
Backroom Dealing	Enhancement	U	0.80
Balance	Event	X	0.25
Battle Tested	Aftermath	U	0.80
[3]			
Bester	Character	R	8.00
Bio-Weapon Discovery	Conflict	R	2.80
Black Market	Conflict	U	0.80
Blockade	Conflict	R	2.40
Blood Oath	Aftermath	U	0.80
Border Raid	Conflict	X	0.25
Campaign for Support	Conflict	C	0.10
Carpe Diem	Event	R	4.00
Casualty Reports	Aftermath	R	2.40
[4]			
Catherine Sakai	Character	U	0.80
Censure	Enhancement	U	0.80
Centauri Agent	Character	X	0.25
Centauri Aide	Character	X	0.25
Centauri Captain	Character	X	0.25
Centauri Telepath	Character	C	0.10
Change of Plans	Event	C	0.10

Card name	Type	Rarity	Price
Changing Opinion	Event	C	0.10
Chaos Reigns	Event	C	0.10
[5]			
Chrysalis	Event	U	0.80
Colonial Fleet (Centauri)	Fleet	X	0.25
Colonial Fleet (Human)	Fleet	X	0.25
Colonial Fleet (Minbari)	Fleet	X	0.25
Colonial Fleet (Narn)	Fleet	X	0.25
Combat Experience	Aftermath	C	0.10
Commerce Raiding	Enhancement	U	0.80
Commercial Telepaths	Group	U	0.80
Compatible Goals	Conflict	U	0.80
[6]			
Competing Interests	Event	R	2.40
Complete Support	Conflict	U	0.80
Concealed Weapon	Enhancement	C	0.10
Concentrated Effort	Event	C	0.10
Condemn Deportations	Conflict	C	0.10
Conflicting Desires	Event	R	2.40
Conflicting Loyalties	Event	R	2.40
Confusion in Chaos	Event	C	0.10
Consolidated Position	Conflict	R	2.40
[7]			
Contact with Shadows	Event	C	0.10
Contact with Vorlons	Event	C	0.25
Coordinated Fire	Event	C	0.10
Counterintelligence	Group	R	2.80
Court the Rebellious	Conflict	C	0.10
Covert Allies	Enhancement	R	2.40
Crisis of Self	Aftermath	U	0.80
Crusade	Conflict	R	2.40
Cut Supply Lines	Event	C	0.10
[8]			
Cynthia Torqueman	Character	U	0.80
Damage Control Team	Group	R	2.40
Dan Randall	Character	C	0.10
Declaration of War	Event	X	0.25
Deep Space Fleet (Centauri)	Fleet	X	0.25
Deep Space Fleet (Human)	Fleet	X	0.25
Deep Space Fleet (Minbari)	Fleet	C	0.10
Deep Space Fleet (Narn)	Fleet	X	0.25
Defame Ambassador	Event	C	0.10
[9]			
Defense in Depth	Agenda	U	0.80
Delenn Transformed	Character	R	5.60

Card name	Type	Rarity	Price
Demonstrative Victory	Conflict	R	2.40
Despair	Aftermath	R	2.40
Destiny Fulfilled	Event	X	0.25
Develop Relationship	Aftermath	U	0.80
Dhaliri	Character	U	0.80
Diplomatic Advantage	Aftermath	R	2.40
Diplomatic Blunder	Event	C	0.10
[10]			
Diplomatic Corps	Group	C	0.10
Diplomatic Immunity	Event	C	0.10
Disaffected Centauri	Character	R3	3.20
Disaffected Human	Character	R3	3.20
Disaffected Minbari	Character	R3	3.20
Disaffected Narn	Character	R3	3.20
Disenchantment	Aftermath	U	0.80
Disgrace	Aftermath	R	2.40
Draft	Enhancement	U	0.80
[11]			
Drazi Sunhawk	Fleet	C	0.10
Du'Nar	Character	U	0.80
Du'Rog	Character	U	0.80
Durlan	Character	C	0.10
Early Warning	Event	X	0.25
Elric	Character	R	4.00
Emergency Military Aid	Event	C	0.10
Emperor Turhan	Character	R	4.80
Energy Mines	Enhancement	X	0.25
[12]			
Enrage	Aftermath	U	0.80
Establish Base	Conflict	U	0.80
Exploit Opportunities	Aftermath	X	0.25
Exploitation	Enhancement	C	0.10
Extended Contacts	Group	C	0.10
Extreme Sanction	Conflict	U	0.80
Finish the War	Agenda	X	0.25
First Battle Fleet (Centauri)	Fleet	X	0.25
First Battle Fleet (Human)	Fleet	X	0.25
[13]			
First Battle Fleet (Minbari)	Fleet	X	0.25
First Battle Fleet (Narn)	Fleet	X	0.25
Fixed in Their Ways	Enhancement	U	0.80
Fleet of the Line	Fleet	R	4.00
Fleet Support Base	Enhancement	X	0.25
Fleets on the Border	Event	C	0.10
Focus Your Efforts	Aftermath	U	0.80
For My People	Event	C	0.10

RARITY KEY C = Common U = Uncommon R = Rare VR = Very Rare UR = Ultra Rare F = Foil card X = Fixed/standard in all decks

Card name	Type	Rarity	Price
For the Common Good	Event	C	0.10
For the Good of All	Event	X	0.25
Forced Commitment	Enhancement	R	2.40
Forced Evolution	Agenda	R	3.20
Forced Impairment	Conflict	R3	3.20
Forces Collide	Event	R3	2.40
Frederick Lantz	Character	X	0.25
Free the Souls	Conflict	R	2.40
G'Drog	Character	C	0.20
G'Sten	Character	R	2.80
Garrison Fleet	Fleet	U	0.80
General Franklin	Character	U	0.40
General Hague	Character	X	0.40
Glory	Aftermath	R	2.40
Government Opposition	Group	R	2.40
Grey Council Fleet	Fleet	R	4.00
Grievance	Aftermath	U	0.60
Growth in Chaos	Agenda	C	0.15
Guilt	Aftermath	U	0.80
Gunboat Diplomacy	Conflict	X	0.25
Harvest Souls	Aftermath	R	3.20
Hate Crime	Conflict	U	0.80
Heavy Fleet	Fleet	R	4.00
Hidden Agent	Aftermath	X	0.25
Hidden Knowledge	Event	X	0.25
Higher Calling	Agenda	C	0.10
Hire Raiders	Event	C	0.10
Hour of the Wolf	Event	U	0.80
Human Agent	Character	X	0.25
Human Aide	Character	X	0.25
Human Captain	Character	X	0.25
Humanitarian Aid	Conflict	C	0.10
Hunted	Aftermath	X	0.25
"Hunter, Prey"	Conflict	C	0.10
Immolan V	Location	U	0.80
Imperial Telepaths	Group	R	3.20
Imperialism	Agenda	C	0.10
In the Line of Duty	Aftermath	U	0.80
Inevitable Destiny	Aftermath	R	2.40
Infiltrate and Exploit	Agenda	U	0.80
Influential Lords	Group	U	0.80
Internal Strife	Event	C	0.10
Interstellar Corporation	Group	C	0.10
Intolerable Interference	Aftermath	U	0.80
Intrigues Mature	Event	C	0.10
Ipsha Battleglobe	Fleet	U	0.60
ISN	Group	U	0.80
Isolated	Enhancement	U	0.80
Isolationism	Enhancement	U	0.80
It Will Be His Undoing	Aftermath	R3	2.40
Ja'Doc	Character	X	0.40
John Sheridan	Character	R	8.00
Judgement by Success	Enhancement	U	0.80
Kha'Mak	Character	X	0.40
Knowledge is Power	Agenda	X	0.25
Knowledge of Shadows	Event	C	0.10
Knowledge of the Soul	Event	U	0.80
Kosh Naranek	Group	R	6.40
Lack of Subtlety	Event	C	0.10
Lady Ladira	Character	U	0.80
Lamentations	Aftermath	X	0.25
Latent Telepath	Enhancement	C	0.10
Leading the Races	Agenda	C	0.10
Learning Experience	Aftermath	C	0.10
Left Vulnerable	Aftermath	R	2.40
Liquidating Assets	Event	C	0.10

Card name	Type	Rarity	Price
Lockdown	Event	C	0.10
Long Term Investment	Event	C	0.10
Lord Kiro	Character	U	0.80
Lord Refa	Character	U	0.80
Lord Valo	Character	U	0.10
Loss of Face	Aftermath	C	0.10
Loss of Support	Conflict	U	0.80
Lovell	Character	C	0.10
Luis Santiago	Character	R	4.00
Luxuries of Homeworld	Enhancement	U	0.80
Lyndisty	Character	C	0.10
Maintain the Peace	Agenda	R	2.40
Marcus Cole	Character	R	4.80
Markab Fleet	Fleet	R	3.20
Martyr	Aftermath	R	2.40
Mary Ann Cramer	Character	C	0.10
Mass Drivers	Enhancement	U	0.80
Meddling with Others	Agenda	U	0.80
Medical Assistance	Event	X	0.25
Meditation	Event	C	0.10
Merchandising B5	Event	C	0.10
Military Cadre	Group	C	0.10
Military Telepaths	Group	U	0.80
Minbari Agent	Character	X	0.25
Minbari Aide	Character	X	0.25
Minbari Captain	Character	X	0.25
Minbari Protectorate	Location	U	0.80
Mines	Enhancement	U	0.80
Minister Malachi	Character	R	4.00
Moral Quandary	Event	C	0.10
Morden	Character	R	4.00
Motivated Leaders	Group	R	2.40
Mr. Adams	Character	U	0.80
Muddy the Waters	Conflict	C	0.10
Na'Far	Character	U	0.80
Na'Ka'Leen Feeder	Conflict	C	0.10
Narn Agent	Character	X	0.25
Narn Aide	Character	X	0.25
Narn Captain	Character	X	0.25
Narn Rabble	Group	U	0.80
Negotiated Surrender	Aftermath	R	0.80
Neroon	Character	U	0.80
Neutrality Treaty	Conflict	C	0.20
News of Defeat	Aftermath	U	0.80
News of Galactic Import	Event	C	0.20
Nightmares	Aftermath	U	0.80
No Escape	Aftermath	R	2.40
Non-Aggression Pact	Conflict	C	0.10
Non-Aligned Support	Conflict	U	0.80
Not Meant to Be	Event	R3	3.20
Observers	Group	R	2.40
Older but Wiser	Aftermath	C	0.10
Order Above All	Agenda	R	3.20
Overworked	Enhancement	C	0.10
Parliament of Dreams	Conflict	R	2.40
Paying for Sins	Aftermath	R	2.40
Peace In Our Time	Agenda	X	0.25
Peacekeeping	Conflict	U	0.80
Personal Enemies	Aftermath	U	0.80
Personal Involvement	Aftermath	X	0.25
Personal Protection	Enhancement	U	0.80
Personal Sacrifice	Aftermath	X	0.25
Picket Fleet (Centauri)	Fleet	X	0.25
Picket Fleet (Human)	Fleet	X	0.25
Picket Fleet (Minbari)	Fleet	X	0.25
Picket Fleet (Narn)	Fleet	X	0.25
Planetary Defenses	Enhancement	C	0.10

Card name	Type	Rarity	Price
Political Realignment	Event	U	0.80
Power Posturing	Enhancement	R1	2.40
Precision Strike	Conflict	U	0.80
Prolonged Talks	Event	R	2.40
Prophecy	Enhancement	X	0.25
Protests	Aftermath	R	2.40
Proxima III	Location	U	0.80
Psi Attack	Conflict	U	0.80
Psi Bodyguard	Enhancement	X	0.25
Psi Interrogation	Conflict	C	0.10
Public Apology	Aftermath	R	2.40
Pulling Strings	Enhancement	C	0.10
Purge the Disloyal	Conflict	U	0.80
Quadrant 14	Location	X	0.25
Quadrant 37	Location	U	0.80
Rabble Rousers	Group	U	0.80
Racial Hatred	Aftermath	R	2.40
Ragesh III	Location	X	0.25
Raid Shipping	Conflict	U	0.80
Rally the People	Conflict	R	2.80
Rally to the Cause	Event	C	0.10
Ramming	Event	R	2.40
Ranger Strike Team	Group	U	0.80
Rangers Surveillance	Group	R	2.40
Rathenn	Character	R	4.00
Recalled to Service	Event	R	2.40
Refugees	Aftermath	X	0.25
Religious Caste	Group	U	0.80
Renowned Victory	Aftermath	X	0.25
Repairing the Past	Aftermath	X	0.25
Rescue	Aftermath	U	0.80
Reserve Fleet	Fleet	U	0.80
Retribution	Aftermath	X	0.25
Reverse Advances	Aftermath	R	2.40
Rise to Power	Aftermath	X	0.25
Rivalry	Aftermath	X	0.25
Rogue Soul Hunter	Character	R	3.60
Saber Rattling	Conflict	U	0.80
Sabotage	Conflict	X	0.25
Salvage Yard	Enhancement	R	3.20
Sanctions	Event	C	0.10
Sandra Hiroshi	Character	C	0.10
Sarah	Character	U	0.80
Second Battle Fleet (Centauri)	Fleet	X	0.25
Second Battle Fleet (Human)	Fleet	X	0.25
Second Battle Fleet (Minbari)	Fleet	X	0.25
Second Battle Fleet (Narn)	Fleet	X	0.25
Secondary Control	Enhancement	R	2.40
Secondary Experience	Aftermath	X	0.25
Secret Police	Group	U	0.80
Secret Strike	Event	R	3.20
Secret Vorlon Aid	Event	C	0.10
Security Training	Enhancement	U	0.80
Seduction	Event	C	0.10
Seizing Advantage	Agenda	R	2.40
Self Doubt	Event	C	0.10
Senator Voudreau	Character	U	0.80
Servants of Order	Agenda	X	0.25
Shadow Assault	Conflict	U	0.80
Shadow Strike	Event	U	0.80
Shakat	Character	R	4.00
Shal Mayan	Character	U	0.40
Short Term Goals	Event	X	0.25
Short Term Investment	Event	C	0.10
Shunned	Enhancement	U	0.80
Skeletons in the Closet	Aftermath	R	2.40
Sleeper Personality	Conflict	X	0.25

RARITY KEY C = Common U = Uncommon R = Rare VR = Very Rare UR = Ultra Rare F = Foil card X = Fixed/standard in all decks

Card name	Type	Rarity	Price
☐ Sleeping Z'ha'dum	Location	R	4.00
☐ Sneak Attack	Event	C	0.10
☐ Sortie	Event	C	0.10
☐ Soul Hunter	Character	U	0.80
☐ Special Ops	Event	C	0.10
☐ Spin Doctors	Group	R	2.40
☐ Sponsor Rebels	Conflict	U	0.80
☐ Stealth Technology	Enhancement	R	3.20

37

Card name	Type	Rarity	Price
☐ Stop Hostilities	Conflict	X	0.25
☐ Strafing Run	Event	C	0.10
☐ Strategic Reassignment	Event	C	0.10
☐ Strength in Adversity	Agenda	U	0.80
☐ Strike Fleet	Fleet	U	0.80
☐ Subliminal Influence	Event	U	0.80
☐ Successful Manipulation	Aftermath	U	0.80
☐ Support Babylon 5	Event	X	0.25
☐ Support of the Mighty	Agenda	U	0.80

38

Card name	Type	Rarity	Price
☐ Technological Espionage	Conflict	C	0.10
☐ Telepathic Scan	Conflict	X	0.25
☐ Temptations	Conflict	C	0.15
☐ Terrorist Bombings	Conflict	U	0.80
☐ Test Their Mettle	Conflict	X	0.25

Card name	Type	Rarity	Price
☐ The Hope of Peace	Agenda	U	0.80
☐ The Opposition Rises	Event	C	0.10
☐ The Price of Power	Event	X	0.25
☐ Thenta Makur	Group	R	4.00

39

Card name	Type	Rarity	Price
☐ Third Battle Fleet (Centauri)	Fleet	R	4.00
☐ Third Battle Fleet (Minbari)	Fleet	U	0.80
☐ Total War	Agenda	R	3.40
☐ Trade Pact	Conflict	X	0.25
☐ Trade Windfall	Event	C	0.10
☐ Transfer Point Io	Location	U	0.80
☐ Triluminary	Enhancement	U	0.80
☐ Tu'Pari	Character	R	4.00
☐ Under Pressure	Aftermath	U	0.80

40

Card name	Type	Rarity	Price
☐ United Front	Aftermath	X	0.25
☐ Universe Today Feature	Event	C	0.10
☐ Unrecognized Data	Event	C	0.10
☐ Utility Fleet (Centauri)	Fleet	C	0.10
☐ Utility Fleet (Human)	Fleet	C	0.10
☐ Utility Fleet (Narn)	Fleet	C	0.10
☐ Vendetta	Aftermath	R	2.40
☐ Victory in My Grasp	Event	X	0.25
☐ Vital Interests	Enhancement	R3	2.40

41

Card name	Type	Rarity	Price
☐ Vorlon Enhancement	Enhancement	R	3.20
☐ Vorlon Rescue	Event	R	2.40
☐ Vree Saucers	Fleet	R	3.20
☐ War by Popular Decree	Event	C	0.10
☐ War College	Group	C	0.10
☐ War Hero	Aftermath	X	0.20
☐ Warleader Shakiri	Character	R	4.00
☐ Warleader's Fleet	Fleet	R	4.00
☐ Warren Keffer	Character	C	0.10

42

Card name	Type	Rarity	Price
☐ Warrior Caste	Group	R	2.40
☐ Wear and Tear	Aftermath	U	0.80
☐ What Do You Want?	Event	C	0.10
☐ Who Are You?	Event	C	0.10
☐ Wind Swords	Group	U	0.80
☐ Witness Protection	Conflict	R	2.40
☐ Working Relationship	Enhancement	U	0.80
☐ Wounded	Aftermath	R	2.40
☐ You Are Not Ready	Event	X	0.25

43

Card name	Type	Rarity	Price
☐ You Know My Reputation	Event	X	0.25
☐ Zack Allan	Character	U	0.80

Citizen G'Kar

Narn Character

Must either: replace your G'Kar; or replace another faction's G'Kar if that faction lost influence last turn from a conflict initiated by another player. Transfer all attached cards. Citizen G'Kar's controller has no Babylon 5 vote. Citizen G'Kar, or any fleet he leads, may participate in any conflict (using the appropriate ability), regardless of restrictions on which race or faction may participate.

"Everything out there has only one purpose: to distract us from ourselves, from what is truly important. There are no distractions in here. You can learn much from silence."

TM & © 1999 Warner Bros. Game Design © 1999 Precedence Publishing. Severed Dreams.

BABYLON 5

Collectible Card Game

Babylon 5 • *The Shadows*

Precedence • Released **April 1998**

203 cards in set

• Booster packs contain 12 cards; booster displays contain 18 boosters and checklist

The Shadows, the first of several expansions for the **Babylon 5 CCG,** has as its primary theme the developing battle between the Vorlons and the Shadows. With **Premier**, allying one's faction with one of the elder races was a benefit. With Shadows, it became the primary way to win.

Shadow players receive: **Mr. Morden,** more powerful replacement for **Morden,** the key character to existing Shadow decks; **Lord Mollari,** replacement for the Centauri ambassador who shores up the Centauri's leadership weakness; and Shadow Fleets, fleets which can come back repeatedly. Vorlon players receive something far more important, however. For them, there is Vorlon Space, a location which builds Vorlon influence to match the locations that build Shadow influence.

Of the 203 cards, 100 are rares and 6 of the 53 uncommons are twice as rare as other uncommons. The Shadows has been very unfriendly to the customer. As a partial compensation, boosters contain two rares, a good thing as most of the tournament level cards are rare. For the serious player, *The Shadows* is a necessary evil to own as some of the cards are still among the best in the game. A signed version of Mr. Morden is the autographed card for this set. — *Ian Lee*

Set (203 cards)	250.00
Starter Display Box	35.00
Booster Display Box	35.00
Booster Pack	2.10

You will need 23 nine-pocket pages to store this set. (12 doubled up)

Card name	Type	Rarity	Price
1			
☐ A Final Statement		R	2.30
☐ A Moment of Beauty		U	0.50
☐ Act of War		C	0.10
☐ Additional Force		R	2.80
☐ Aiding the Shadows		C	0.10
☐ Aiding the Vorlons		C	0.10
☐ Ambassador Kosh		R	6.50
☐ Ambitious Captain		C	0.10
☐ Ancient Rivals		U	0.50
2			
☐ Annex Neutral World		R	2.80
☐ Assassination Device		R	2.90
☐ Associates Revealed		U	0.50
☐ At Peak Performance		U	0.50

Card name	Type	Rarity	Price
☐ Atmospheric Fighters		C	0.10
☐ Attack Babylon 5		R	3.00
☐ Block Progress		C	0.10
☐ Bloodied but Unbowed		C	0.10
☐ Body Armor		U	0.50
3			
☐ Border World		U	0.50
☐ Brother Theo		C	0.10
☐ Build Infrastructure		U	0.50
☐ Bureaucracy		U	0.50
☐ Calenn		R	4.00
☐ Calling the Shots		R	2.90
☐ Casualties		C	0.10
☐ Catastrophic Damage		U	0.50
☐ Centauri Beta I		R	3.00
4			
☐ Change of Direction		R	2.90
☐ Commander Ivanova		U	0.60
☐ Conquered Holding		U	0.50
☐ Consumed by Shadows		R	3.00
☐ Convincing Words		C	0.10
☐ Corrupted Destiny		U	0.50

Card name	Type	Rarity	Price
☐ Coup de Grace		R	3.00
☐ Covering Weaknesses		R	3.00
☐ Damaged from Within		R	3.00
5			
☐ Debt of Gratitude		C	0.10
☐ Dedicated Follower		R	2.90
☐ Delay the War		C	0.10
☐ Directing Events		C	0.10
☐ Disciple of Light		R	3.00
☐ Disruption		C	0.10
☐ Elder Races Triumph		U	0.50
☐ Eliminate Threats		R	3.00
☐ Emergency Repairs		C	0.10

T'his, th'at, and th'e ot'her

Yes, there really are a bunch of cards for Zathras in *Babylon 5,* with the apostrophes in different places. "Either way, it is confusing to be Zathras."

RARITY KEY C = Common U = Uncommon R = Rare VR = Very Rare UR = Ultra Rare F = Foil card X = Fixed/standard in all decks

72 • *SCRYE Collectible Card Game Checklist and Price Guide*

Card name	Type	Rarity	Price
[6]			
Emperor Cartagia		R	5.00
Entil'zha		R	5.00
Extermination		U	0.50
Factional Inertia		R	3.00
Fast Learner		R	2.50
Followers of G'Quan		R	3.00
Force the Issue		C	0.10
Forging Alliances		R	3.00
Freedom of Choice		R	2.70
[7]			
Gather Rebels		R	3.00
Glitch		C	0.10
Government Aid		R	2.90
Government Hostility		U	0.50
Grey Council Servitor		U	0.50
Growing Skepticism		R	2.30
Healing Artifact		R	3.50
Heavy Resistance		R	3.00
Held Back		R	2.80
[8]			
Heralds of the Grey		R	3.00
Hidden Corruption		R	3.00
Hidden Safehouse		C	0.10
High Level Connections		U	0.50
Hollow Victory		R	3.00
Impasse		C	0.10
"In Chaos, Uncertainty"		R	2.50
In the Spotlight		R	3.00
Information Overload		R	3.00
[9]			
Internal Opposition		U	0.50
Into Their Own		U	0.50
"Knowledge, Then Action"		R	3.00
Lashing Out		R	3.00
Learn Their Weakness		R	2.30
Leaving the Past		U	0.50
Liberating Resources		U	0.50
Looking Ahead		R	2.80
Lord Mollari		R	5.00
[10]			
Lost in Shadows		R	2.90
Low Morale		U	0.50
Loyal Guardsmen		U	0.50
Managed Growth		R	3.00
Manifest Destiny		R	3.00
Military Buildup		U	0.50
Minbari Fighting Pike		U	0.50
Mindwipe		R	3.00
Minister Virini		U	0.50
[11]			
Misdirected Force		U	0.50
Mobilize Reserves		C	0.10
Modern Refit		C	0.10
Monks		R	3.00
Mr. Morden		R	5.30
Muster Support		U	0.50
Mysterious Protections		R	3.00
Na'Mel		U	0.50
New Opportunities		R	2.80
[12]			
New Priorities		R	2.90
Nightwatch Agent		C	0.10
Nightwatch Enforcers		U	0.50
No Alternatives		U	0.50
Not Alone		R	2.10
Not in Vain		C	0.10
Observation Post		U	0.50
Obstacles to Victory		R	2.80
Over the Brink		R	2.10
[13]			
Peaceful Solutions		R	2.80
Permanent Wound		R	2.30
Personal Insult		C	0.10

Card name	Type	Rarity	Price
Political Pull		R	2.50
Portents		U	0.50
PPG Rifle		U	0.60
Preeminence		R	2.90
Prejudice Grows		U	0.50
Presidential Coup		R	3.00
[14]			
Prey on the Weak		C	0.10
Prove Your Worth		R	2.10
Psionic Pacification		R	2.10
Public Outcry		C	0.10
Puppeteer		R	3.00
Raising the Stakes		R	2.50
Rampage		U	0.50
Ranger Operations		R	3.00
Rapid Recovery		C	0.10
[15]			
Rebuilding Effort		C	0.10
Recalled		R	2.50
Recover and Regroup		R	2.30
Reducing Risk		U	0.50
Reeling from the Blows		U	0.50
Refusal to Yield		R	3.00
Reluctant Allies		R	2.90
Removed from Power		C	0.10
Reverse Engineering		U	0.50
[16]			
Search for Direction		C	0.10
Sebastian		R	4.50
Seeds of Anarchy		U	0.50
Senator Young		R	3.00
Shadow Aid		U	0.50
Shadow Medallion		R	3.00
Shadow Retribution		R	2.80
Shadow Ship		U	0.50
Sigma 957		R	3.00
[17]			
Slow Poison		U	0.50
Slow Recovery		C	0.10
Sowing Unrest		C	0.10
Special Intelligence		R	3.00
Spread Unrest		R	2.30
Squandered Chances		C	0.10
Stagnation		R	2.10
Statement of Position		U	0.50
Status Quo		R	2.80
[18]			
Stim Addiction		R	2.80
Stolen Spoils		R	2.50
Stripped Bare		R	2.50
Support Fleet (Centauri)		C	0.10

Card name	Type	Rarity	Price
Support Fleet (Human)		C	0.10
Support Fleet (Minbari)		C	0.10
Support Fleet (Narn)		C	0.10
Survey In Force		U	0.50
Sworn to Shadows		R	2.80
[19]			
Taking Credit		R	3.00
Taralenn II		R	3.00
Telekinesis		R	3.00
Temporary Aid		C	0.10
Test of Merit		U	0.50
The Long Night		C	0.10
The Lure of Shadow		R	2.90
The Vorlons Respond		R	2.90
The White Star		R	5.30
[20]			
The Young Races Rise		R	2.80
Their Own Destiny		C	0.10
Things to Come		C	0.10
To Fight Legends		U	0.50
To Stand Alone		R	3.00
To the Victor		R	2.70
Tolonius VII		U	0.50
Too Predictable		U	0.50
Trivial Gains		C	0.10
[21]			
Troubles Brewing		C	0.10
Twisting the Knife		U	0.50
Uncertain Followers		C	0.10
Uncertain Futures		R	3.00
Underground Resistance		C	0.10
Undermine Trust		R	3.00
Unheralded Losses		R	2.90
Unsung Hero		R	3.00
Va'Kal		R	4.00
[22]			
Vorlon Cruiser		U	0.50
Vorlon Protection		U	0.50
Vorlon Proxy		C	0.10
Vorlon Space		R	3.00
Vorlons Ascendent		C	0.10
Walkabout		R	2.30
We Can't Allow That		C	0.10
When Duty Calls		R	3.00
William Morgan Clark		R	4.50
[23]			
Withdrawal		C	0.10
Z'ha'dum Awakened		R	3.80
Za'thras		R	3.50
Zath'ras		C	0.10
Zathras'		U	0.50

RARITY KEY C = Common U = Uncommon R = Rare VR = Very Rare UR = Ultra Rare F = Foil card X = Fixed/standard in all decks

SCRYE Collectible Card Game Checklist and Price Guide • **73**

Sheridan Reborn

Human Character

Cannot be sponsored. If John Sheridan is your ambassador, rotate Lorien to replace John Sheridan with Sheridan Reborn, transferring all enhancements and marks. Sheridan Reborn gains Diplomacy and Leadership equal to his Destiny Marks. Rotate John Sheridan as an action and play a conflict card. You must apply 3 influence (in addition to any other requirements) for each prior action you have had this turn to initiate this additional conflict.

"We began in chaos, too primitive to make our own decisions. Then, we were manipulated from outside by forces that thought they knew what was best for us. And now... now we are finally standing on our own."

The Great War. TM & © 1998 Warner Bros. Game Design © 1998 Precedence Publishing.

Babylon 5 • *The Great War*

THE GREAT WAR

Precedence • Released **October 1998**

397 cards in set • **IDENTIFIER: Set name at lower left**

- Starter decks contain 60 cards; starter displays contain 6 starters
- Booster packs contain 10 cards; booster displays contain 20 boosters

    The Great War is the largest ***Babylon 5*** expansion. Part of the reason is that it introduced two new aspects to the game: a new, fifth, faction, the League of Non-Aligned Worlds; and opposition factions, factions of the same race as the ***Premier*** races but with different ambassadors and a few different rules and cards.

    The Non-Aligned were originally far too powerful, beginning the game with two ambassadors in play instead of one. That rule has been changed, with the second ambassador moving to the opening hand. Moreover, the opposition concept turned out to be a bust. For instance, some of the multiple faction rules, used when there are two factions playing the same race, have become optional. Because the opposition starter is a non-playable starter filled with cards only applicable to situations involving multiple factions of the same race, it suffers from being mostly useless. The Non-Aligned starter, however, is necessary to play a Non-Aligned faction and has numerous valuable cards.

    As for the rest of this huge set, *The Great War* is an improvement over **The Shadows** in terms of having many quality cards, including important commons and uncommons. One uncommon, **We Are Not Impressed**, single-handedly changed the metagame, eliminating power bonuses as long as it remained in play. As with *Shadows*, *The Great War* boosters have two rares each. A signed **Prime Minister Mollari** is the autographed card. — **Ian Lee**

BABYLON 5
Collectible Card Game

Set (397 cards)	**120.00**	**You will need**
Starter Display Box	**44.50**	**45**
Booster Display Box	**34.50**	nine-pocket
Starter Deck	**8.50**	pages to store this set.
Booster Pack	**2.50**	(23 doubled up)

Card name	Type	Rarity	Price
A Good Bluff	Event	X	0.35
A Show of Guile	Aftermath	R	2.00
A Time for Heroes	Event	C	0.15
Abandoned	Aftermath	U	0.60
Acolyte	Char/Minbar	U	0.60
Advance Fleet	Fleet/Narn	U	0.60
Advanced Training	Enhnc/Char	C	0.15
Affirmation of Support	Event	C	0.15
Against the First Ones	Agenda	U	0.60
Agamemnon	Enhnc/Hu/Flt	R	2.80
Aggressive Action	Confl/Intrigue	R	3.00
All or Nothing	Event	C	0.15
Alliance	Confl/Dipl	X	0.35
Altruism	Agenda	U	0.60
Ancient Enemies	Enhnc/Gl	U	0.60
Anla'Shok	Gr/Minbar	R	3.00
Anna Sheridan	Char/Shadow	R	3.00
Arrest Dissidents	Confl/Minbar	X	0.20
At a Standstill	Aftermath	U	0.60
Attack Outpost	Confl/Minbar	U	0.60
Babylon 5 Fighters	Fleet/B5	U	0.60
Babylon 5 War Council	Enhnc/B5	U	0.60
Backlash	Aftermath	U	0.60
Battle Hardened	Aftermath	C	0.15
Battle Momentum	Event	C	0.15
Behind the Curve	Event	C	0.15
Beyond the Rim	Confl/Dipl	R	2.00
Biased Reporting	Enhnc/Fa	U	0.60
Big Guns	Event	C	0.15
Black Ops Consultant	Char/Neutral	C	0.15
Blind the Watchers	Confl/Intrigue	U	0.60
Bluff	Con	C	0.15
Bogged Down	Event	C	0.15
Bolstered Defenses	Locat/Contg	C	0.15

Card name	Type	Rarity	Price
Border Raid	Confl/Minbar	X	0.20
Brakir	Locatn/NonA	U	0.60
Brakiri Cruisers	Fleet/NonA	X	0.35
Brakiri Merchant	Char/NonA	C	0.15
Brakiri War Fleet	Fleet/NonA	X	0.35
Bureaucratic Infighting	Event	X	0.20
Buy Favor	Confl/Dipl	U	0.60
Buy New Resources	Event	R	2.80
Caliban	Char/Neutral	C	0.15
Call Intrigue a Marker	Confl/Dipl	C	0.15
Call Their Bluff	Confl/Intrigue	U	0.60
Captured Fleet	Aftermath	X	0.20
Carrier Group	Fleet/Human	U	0.60
Centauri Courtier	Char/Centari	C	0.15
Centauri Fanatic	Char/Centari	X	0.20
Chain of Command	Aftermath	U	0.60
Change of Heart	Event	X	0.20
Changeling Net	Enhnc/Char	R	2.00
Cheat Fate	Event	C	0.15
Chosen of God	Agenda/NonA	R	3.00
Civil Servants	Group	U	0.60
Cloak and Dagger	Event	C	0.15
Cloud of Doom	Event	C	0.15
Coincidence	Event	C	3.00
Combined Fleet	Fleet/NonA	R	4.00
Command Ship	Fleet/Neutral	R	3.00
Confrontation	CoCon	R	2.00
Conscription	Event	R	2.50
Consultants	Group/NonA	R	2.50
Cut Supply Lines	Event	X	0.20
Dagool	Char/NonA	R	3.00
Day of the Dead	Event	R	2.00
Death of Kosh	Confl/Intrig	R	2.50
Debt of Gratitude	Aftermath	X	0.20
Declaration of War	Event	X	0.20
Dedicated Assistant	Aftermath	C	0.15
Deep Scan	Confl/Psi	U	0.60
Defeated	Aftermath	R	2.50
Defend the Races	Agenda/Maj	R	2.50
Defensive Tactics	Enhnc/Char	C	0.15
Delegate Authority	Event	C	0.15

Card name	Type	Rarity	Price
Different Perspectives	Event/NonA	X	0.20
Diplomatic Channels	Enhnc/Ch/NA	U	0.60
Diplomatic Intrusion	Confl/Dipl	U	0.60
Diplomatic Payoff	ChCon	R	2.00
Disruption	Confl/Intrig	X	0.20
Dissent	Enhnc/Agen	U	0.60
Divert Blame	Confl/Intrig	X	0.20
Doctor Lilian Hobbs	Char/Neutral	U	0.60
Drazi Strike Fleet	Fleet/NonA	U	0.60
Drazi Sunhawk	Fleet/NonA	X	0.20
Drazi War Fleet	Fleet/NonA	X	0.35
Dust	Event	U	0.60
Efficiency	Enhnc/Fa	U	0.60
Egyptian God of Frustration	Enhnc	U	0.60
Elections	Confl/Dipl	X	0.20
Emfeeli	Enhnc/Min/Fl	R	2.50
Empire Builder	Agenda	U	0.60
Entrap	ChCon	C	0.15
Ethnocentric	Enhnc/Char	X	0.20
Exploit Opportunities	Aftermath	X	0.20
Eye for an Eye	Event/Narn	X	0.20
Eyes and Ears	Agenda	C	0.15
Eyes on the Border	Event	U	0.60
Failed Goals	Aftermath	U	0.60
Falsified Orders	Event	C	0.15
Fashar	Char/NonA	X	0.20
Fast Transport	Enhnc/Fleet	U	0.60
Fate Awaits	Enhnc/Gl	U	0.60
Fate Calls	Confl/Dipl	R	2.00
Fate Favors	Con/Conting	C	0.15
Feast of Strife	Agenda	U	0.60
Feint	Event	R	2.00
Fighter Base	Enhnc/Locat	U	0.60
Find Focus	Event	C	0.15
First One Intervention	Aftermath	R	2.40
First One Involvement	Event	R	2.90
First One Protection	Char/Conting	R	2.40
First Squadron	Enhnc/Fleet	U	0.60
First United Fleet	Fleet/Un	R	4.00
Fleets on the Border	Event	X	0.20
Force Majeure	Agenda/Maj	R	2.80

RARITY KEY C = Common **U** = Uncommon **R** = Rare **VR** = Very Rare **UR** = Ultra Rare **F** = Foil card **X** = Fixed/standard in all decks

Card name	Type	Rarity	Price		Card name	Type	Rarity	Price		Card name	Type	Rarity	Price
Fray at the Edges	Event	R	2.00		Lt. David Corwin	Char/Human	C	0.15		Power Block	Enhnc/Factn	X	0.20
From the Sidelines	Event	C	0.15		Luhf/Syhf	Char/NonA	R	3.50		Power Brokers	Group	R	2.80
Front Man	Char/Contng	C	0.15		Lurkers	Group	C	0.15		Power in Consensus	Conf/Conting	C	0.15
Fulcrum of Power	Agenda/NA	C	0.15		Lyta Empowered	Char/Vorl	R	4.50		Power Play	Event	R	2.00
Full Mobilization	Agenda/Maj	R	2.00		Machiavellian Politics	Event	C	0.15		Precise Targeting	Event	C	0.15
Further Gains	Conf/Contng	R	2.50		Maintain Control	Confl/Psi	R	2.00		Premonition	Enhnc/Factn	R	2.00
Futility	Aftermath	R	2.00		Marked Out	Event	C	0.15		Pride of the Kha'Ri	Enhnc/Na/Flt	R	2.50
Garrison Duty	Event	C	0.15		Martial Law	Enhnc/Factn	X	0.20		Prime Minister Mollari	Char/Centari	R	5.00
Gear Up for War	Enhnc/Factn	R	2.80		Master of All	Agenda/Ma	R	2.00		Propaganda	Enhnc/Factn	U	0.60
G'Kar Enlightened	Char/Narn	R	3.00		Med Lab	Enhnc/B5	C	0.15		Protecting Your Race	Enhnc/Gl	X	0.20
G'Neb	Char/Narn	U	0.80		Media Mogul	Agenda	U	0.60		Public Resentment	Aftermath	R	2.00
Good Press	Confl/Dipl	X	0.20		Medical Assistance	Event	X	0.20		Purple Files	Char/Conting	R	2.50
Grassroots Support	Confl/Dipl	X	0.20		Melat	Locatn/NonA	U	0.60		Pushed to War	Event	C	0.15
Ground Forces	Loc/Conting	C	0.15		Merciless	Enhnc/Char	R	2.00		Pushing Limits	Aftermath	U	0.60
Growing Distrust	Event	C	0.15		Milashi Voktal	Char/NonA	X	0.35		Put on the Squeeze	Confl/Intrig	C	0.15
Guarded Resource	Enh/Conting	R	2.00		Military Outpost	Locatn	C	0.15		Quality Leadership	Enhnc/Factn	U	0.60
Gunboat Diplomacy	Confl/Minbar	X	0.20		Minbari Fanatic	Char/Minbar	X	0.20		Racial Command	Event	X	0.20
Gyor	Char/Neutral	U	0.60		Minister Durano	Char/Centari	R	5.00		Racial Cooperation	Enhnc/Factn	X	0.20
Hacker	Enhnc/Char	U	0.60		Minister Verano	Char/Centari	U	0.60		Racial Ties	Enhnc/Char	X	0.20
Hand of Valen	Agenda	U	0.60		Mob Violence	Event	X	0.20		Rag-Tag Fleet	Fleet/NonA	X	0.35
Hard Lessons	Char/Conting	C	0.15		Moles	Group	X	0.20		Ranger Initiate	Char/Neutral	C	0.15
Harkar	Char/NonA	U	0.60		Momentum	Enhnc/Factn	R	2.50		Ranger Training	Enhnc/Loctn	R	2.00
Heavy Losses	Aftermath	U	0.60		Mr. Chase	Char/Neutral	C	0.15		Rapid Growth	Event	X	0.35
Heroic Aid	Event	C	0.15		Mu Tai Exhibition	Event	C	0.15		Reap the Whirlwind	Event	C	0.15
Hidden Pressures	Event	R	2.50		Munitions Convoy	Fleet/NonA	X	0.20		Reaping Iniquity	Event	U	0.60
Hidden Treasury	Agenda/Cont	R	2.50		Mutiny	Confl/Intrigue	X	0.20		Rebirth Ceremony	Event	R	2.00
Hostile Reaction	Event	C	0.15		Narn'Far	Char/Narn	X	0.20		Repairing the Past	Aftermath	X	0.20
Human Fanatic	Char/Human	X	0.20		Narn Agitator	Char/Narn	C	0.15		Reprisal	Aftermath	U	0.60
Hyach Matriarch	Char/NonA	R	3.00		Narn Fanatic	Char/Narn	X	0.20		Research Station	Enhnc/Loctn	U	0.60
Hyach Patriarch	Char/NonA	X	0.20		Neroon	Char/Minbar	X	0.20		Reservations	Enhnc/Glbl	U	0.60
Ill Fated Reverses	Confl/Dipl	C	0.15		Network Support	Group	C	0.15		Resupply Network	Group	U	0.60
Important Visitor	Event	X	0.20		Nhuk/Vrek	Char/NonA	R	4.00		Rumor Mongers	Group	U	0.60
Improvised Weapon	Char/Contng	C	0.15		No Compromises	Enhnc/Gl	U	0.60		Sacrifice Play	Event	C	0.15
Independence	Enhnc/Loca	X	0.20		No Mercy	Aftermath	U	0.60		Safety in Numbers	Agenda/NA	X	0.20
Independent Support	Enhnc/Agen	U	0.50		Non-Aligned Agent	Char/NonA	X	0.20		Sanctions	Event	X	0.20
Inflexible Plans	Event	C	0.15		Non-Aligned Aide	Char/NonA	X	0.20		Sanctuary	Aftermath	R	2.50
Insurrection	Enhnc/Globl	X	0.20		Non-Aligned Captain	Char/NonA	X	0.20		Scapegoats	Event	C	0.15
Intelligence Gathering	Char/Conting	U	0.50		Non-Aligned Fanatic	Char/NonA	X	0.20		Screened	Char/Conting	U	0.60
Interference	Event	C	0.15		Not Our Concern	Event	X	0.20		Seat of Power	Enhnc/Char	X	0.20
Internecine Struggle	Confl/Minbar	X	0.20		Officer Exchange	Confl/Dipl	U	0.60		Second Squadron	Enhnc/Fleet	U	0.60
Intervention Force	Fleet/B5	R	3.00		On All Fronts	Confl/Minbar	R	2.00		Second United Fleet	Fleet/Un	R	4.00
Intrigues Mature	Event	X	1.00		Opportunity for Chaos	Event	R	2.00		Secure the Home Front	Agenda	X	0.20
Invent the Future	Event	C	0.15		Order Maintained	Confl/Minbar	R	2.00		Security Crackdown	Event	C	0.15
ISN Reporter	Char/Neutral	C	0.15		Out of the Loop	Event	C	0.15		Security Detail	Group	C	0.15
Judgement	ChCon	X	0.20		Pak'ma'ra Lurkers	Group/NonA	C	0.15		Security Fleet (Centauri)	Fleet/Centari	X	0.35
Julie Musante	Char/Human	U	0.60		Pak'ma'ra Spacelanes	Locatn/NonA	X	0.35		Security Fleet (Human)	Fleet/Human	X	0.35
Justin	Char/Shadow	R	4.00		Paralyzing Injury	Aftermath	C	0.15		Security Fleet (Minbari)	Fleet/Minbar	X	0.35
Kalika Qwal'mizra	Char/NonA	X	0.35		Parlay Gains	Conf/Conting	C	0.15		Security Fleet (Narn)	Fleet/Narn	X	0.35
Know Your Enemy	Event	X	0.20		Patrol Fleet	Fleet/Centari	U	0.60		Security Fleet (Non-Aligned)	Fleet/NonA	X	0.35
Knowledge Is Power	Agenda	X	0.20		Peace Accord	Event	C	0.15		Security Override	Event	C	0.15
Labor Strike	Event	C	0.15		Peace Dividend	Conf/Conting	U	0.60		Seductive Arguments	Event	C	0.15
Led Astray No More	Aftermath	C	0.15		Peaceful Unification	Agenda/NA	X	0.35					
Lennan	Char/Minbar	C	0.15		Permanent Losses	Aftermath	C	0.15					
Let Them Fight	Confl/Dipl	R	2.00		Perpetual Conflict	Confl/Intrig	R	2.00					
Lethke Zum Bartrado	Char/NonA	X	0.35		Personal Growth	Aftermath	C	0.15					
Lhim/Dram	Char/NonA	U	0.60		Personal Involvement	Aftermath	X	0.20					
Life Pods	Enhnc/Fleet	C	0.15		Picket Duty	Char/Conting	C	0.15					
Light Shines	Event	U	0.60		Plague	Confl/Dipl	R	2.50					
Lobbyists	Group	C	0.15		Planet Defense Fleet	Fleet/Minbar	U	0.60					
Local Supremacy	Agenda	X	0.20		Planet-wide Unrest	Confl/Intrigue	U	0.60					
Lord Refa	Char/Centauri	X	0.20		Plans Revealed	Confl/Dipl	U	0.60					
Lorien	Char/Neutral	R	3.00		Play for Keeps	Event	C	0.15					
Lost Opportunities	Char/Conting	U	0.60		Playing Both Sides	Agenda	R	2.50					
Lou Welch	Char/Neutral	U	0.60		Pointing Fingers	Event	X	0.20					
Low Level Conflict	Event	C	0.15		Popular Tariffs	Enhnc/Globl	U	0.60					

Great changes

"The introduction of four new, opposing ambassadors in The Great War presents new opportunities for each race: A Minbari/Shadow/Warrior Caste deck is much easier to build, thanks to **Neroon** and his absence of Vorlon marks. And **William Morgan Clark** makes the Human/Shadow/Intrigue a deck archetype to be feared."

— *Wes Brown*, **Scrye** 6.2 (Jun 99)

RARITY KEY **C** = Common **U** = Uncommon **R** = Rare **VR** = Very Rare **UR** = Ultra Rare **F** = Foil card **X** = Fixed/standard in all decks

Card name	Type	Rarity	Price
☐ Severed Ties	Confl/Intrige	U	0.60
☐ Shadow Base	Enhnc/Locat	U	0.60
☐ Shadow Cloud	Confl/Minbar	R	2.90
☐ Shadow Implants	Enhnc/Char	R	2.30
☐ Shadow Scouts	Fleet/Shado	U	0.60
☐ Shadow Strike Fleet	Fleet/Shado	R	3.00
☐ Shadow Symbiont	Confl/Intrig	R	2.40
☐ Shadow Tech Upgrade	Enhnc/Fleet	R	2.90
☐ Shadow War Fleet	Fleet/Shad	R	3.00
35			
☐ Shadows Fall	Event	U	0.60
☐ Shadowwatch	Enhnc/Glbl	R	2.00
☐ Shambah III	Locatn/NonA	U	0.60
☐ She'lah	Char/NonA	X	0.35
☐ Sheridan Reborn	Char/Human	R	5.00
☐ Show the Colors	Confl/Minbar	C	0.15
☐ Silver Tongue	Event	C	0.15
☐ Skirmish	Event	C	0.15
☐ Special Ops	Event	X	0.20
36			
☐ Spirit of Cooperation	Event	C	0.15
☐ Stasis	Enhnc/Gl	U	0.60
☐ Straight Talk	Event	C	0.15
☐ Strange Bedfellows	Confl/Dipl	R	2.00
☐ Strike at the Heart	Confl/Dipl	U	0.60
☐ Suarez Cil'tlakh	Char/NonA	X	0.35
☐ Subtle Influences	Confl/Psi	U	0.60
☐ Subversion	Event	X	0.20
☐ Supply Convoy	Fleet/NonA	C	0.15
37			
☐ Taunts and Games	Event	C	0.15
☐ Techno-mage	Char/Neutral	R	3.00
☐ Telepath Block	Enhnc/Factn	U	0.60
☐ Telepath Recruit	Char/NonA	C	0.15
☐ Telepathic Scan	Confl/Psi	X	0.20
☐ Tense Situation	Event	C	0.15
☐ Tenuous Control	Event	U	0.60

Card name	Type	Rarity	Price
☐ Terra Firma	Agenda/Mj	R	2.50
☐ Terrorist Strike	Confl/Intrig	X	0.20
38			
☐ Test Their Mettle	Confl/Dipl	X	0.20
☐ The Greater Good	Event	C	0.15
☐ The Katai	Enhnc/NAI/Fl	R	3.00
☐ The Path of Conquest	Agenda/Maj	R	2.00
☐ The Price of Fame	Aftermath	U	0.60
☐ The Right Contacts	Group	X	0.20
☐ The Upper Hand	Confl/Intrig	R	2.00
☐ Third Squadron	Enhnc/Fleet	U	0.60
☐ Third United Fleet	Fleet/Un	R	3.00
39			
☐ This Was a Mistake	Event	R	2.00
☐ Ties to the Mighty	Enhnc/Char	C	0.15
☐ Time of Decision	Event	C	0.15
☐ To Make a Stand	Agenda/Maj	R	2.00
☐ Trade Pact	Confl/Dipl	X	0.20
☐ Trade Sanctions	Event	C	0.15
☐ Trade War	Event	C	0.15
☐ Truce	Event	U	0.60
☐ Tualakh Vit'lokh	Char/NonA	U	0.60
40			
☐ Ulkesh Kosh	Char/Vorlon	R	5.00
☐ Uncertain Times	Event	X	0.20
☐ Underground Telepath	Char/Neutral	U	0.60
☐ Unexpected Activity	Event	R	2.50
☐ Unexpected Return	Event	U	0.60
☐ Unfounded Rumors	Char/Conting	R	2.00
☐ Universe Today Feature	Event	X	0.20
☐ University Complex	Enhnc/Locat	U	0.60
☐ Unpopular Goals	Confl/Dipl	X	0.20
41			
☐ Unpopular Intervention	Event	C	0.15
☐ Valarius	Enhnc/Ce/Flt	R	3.00
☐ Vengeance Fleet	Fleet/Narn	R	3.00
☐ Venlesh	Char/NonA	C	0.15
☐ Vicious Blow	Char/Conting	C	0.15

Card name	Type	Rarity	Price
☐ Vicious Rumors	Aftermath	U	0.60
☐ Vizak	Char/NonA	X	0.35
☐ Vlur/Nhar	Char/NonA	X	0.35
☐ Voice of the Resistance	Group	R	2.00
42			
☐ Vorlon Allies	Enhnc/Locat	U	0.60
☐ Vorlon Dreams	Confl/Intrig	U	0.60
☐ Vorlon Order	Enhnc/Glbl	R	2.50
☐ Vorlon Planet Killer	Confl/Minbar	R	3.00
☐ Vorlon Strike Fleet	Fleet/Vorlon	R	3.00
☐ Vorlon Universe	Agenda/Maj	R	2.50
☐ Vorlon War Fleet	Fleet/Vorlon	R	3.00
☐ Vree Scouts	Fleet/NonA	X	0.70
☐ War Fever	Enhnc/Factn	U	0.60
43			
☐ War Footing	Agenda	U	0.60
☐ War Protesters	Confl/Dipl	U	0.60
☐ Wargames	Confl/Le	R	2.80
☐ We Are Not Impressed	Enhnc/Glbl	U	0.60
☐ Well Publicized	Aftermath	R	2.00
☐ What Are You?	Aftermath	C	0.15
☐ What Were You Thinking?	Aftermath	U	0.60
☐ White Star Fleet	Fleet/B5	R	2.80
☐ William Morgan Clark	Char/Human	X	0.35
44			
☐ With a Sacrifice	Aftermath	U	0.60
☐ With an Iron Fist	Confl/Minbar	X	0.20
☐ Wrong Place and Time	Aftermath	U	0.60
☐ You Didn't Mean That	Event	C	0.15
☐ You Do Not Understand	Event	C	0.15
☐ Z'athras	Char/Neutral	R	3.00
☐ Zat'hras	Char/Neutral	C	0.15
☐ Zathr'as	Char/Neutral	U	0.60
☐ Zero Sum Game	Enhnc/Glbl	X	0.20
45			
☐ Zhabar	Locatn/NonA	X	0.35

Kelsey

Human Character

Psi Corps Character. Psi Cop.
Psi Corps Ambassador's Assistant.
Kelsey cannot attack Human characters
who do not have Psi.

Kelsey is a young and ambitious Psi Cop aspiring to fill the void
left by Byron's disappearance. She volunteers for important
and dangerous missions, attempting to win Bester's
favor and join his inner circle.

TM & © 1999 Warner Bros. Game Design © 1999 Precedence Publishing. Psi Corps.

Collectible Card Game

Babylon 5 • Psi-Corps

Precedence • Released **August 1999**

196 cards in set • **IDENTIFIER: Set name at card bottom**

- Starter decks contain 60 cards, counter sheet, and revised rulebook
- Starter displays contain 6 starters
- Booster packs contain 8 cards; booster displays contain 24 boosters, checklist, and promo card

Psi Corps introduces the Psi Corps faction, an alternate faction for the Humans with **Alfred Bester** as the ambassador. In addition, there are several cards that relate to psi, including neutral telepaths and a host of new psi conflicts.

This set's impact is minimal unless you play a heavy psi deck or the Psi Corps faction. Because psi is unbalanced between the races, the new psi conflicts keep the supporting nature of the older ones. Only one conflict encourages a deck that does nothing but psi and it takes too long to win with. The idea of Psi Corps fighting against neutral telepaths hasn't worked out well, since the strategies involved never reached the strength of other, more straightforward strategies.

A change was made in autograph cards beginning with *Psi Corps*. Instead of there being one autograph card, *Psi Corps* has three: **Alfred Bester**, **Byron**, and **Zathras**. *Psi Corps* has also been one of the harder sets to get hold of. A smaller print run and the appeal of Bester (played by Walter Koenig) sold it faster than any previous set. — *Ian Lee*

Set (196 cards)	105.00	
Starter Display Box	57.50	
Booster Display Box	40.00	
Starter Deck	10.00	
Booster Pack	2.00	

You will need
22
nine-pocket
pages to store
this set.
(11 doubled up)

Card name	Type	Rarity	Price
1			
☐ A Better Place	Aftermath	R	3.50
☐ A New Era	Enhancmnt	C	0.15

Card name	Type	Rarity	Price
☐ A Time For Peace	Event	U	0.50
☐ Abbut	Character	U	0.50
☐ Acclaim	Aftermath	C	0.15
☐ Acknowledge Legitimacy	Conflict	U	0.50
☐ Administrator Drake	Character	X	0.50
☐ Afraid of The Dark	Enhancmnt	U	0.50
☐ Age of Exploration	Event	C	0.15
2			
☐ Alfred Bester	Character	R	7.00

Card name	Type	Rarity	Price
☐ Alisa Beldon	Character	C	0.15
☐ Anarchy	Conflict	R	4.00
☐ Anti-Telepath Virus	Conflict	R	4.00
☐ Arms Race	Event	C	0.15
☐ At Any Cost	Event	U	0.50
☐ Balus	Location	R	4.00
☐ Be Seeing You	Aftermath	X	0.50
☐ Bester	Character	X	1.00

Card name	Type	Rarity	Price
3			
☐ Bester's Black Omega	Enhancmnt	R	4.00
☐ Black Omega Auxiliary	Fleet	X	0.50
☐ Black Omega Fighters	Fleet	X	0.50
☐ Black Omega Pilot	Character	X	0.50
☐ Black Omega Squadron	Enhancmnt	U	0.50
☐ Blackmail	Conflict	X	0.50
☐ Block	Event	C	0.15
☐ Bloodhound	Character	X	0.50
☐ Build Bridges	Enhancmnt	C	0.15
4			
☐ Burnt From Both Ends	Event	C	0.15
☐ Burnt Out	Aftermath	C	0.15
☐ Byron	Character	R	5.00
☐ Cease-Fire	Conflict	C	0.15
☐ Centauri Festival	Contingency	U	0.50
☐ Challenge Psi Corps	Agenda	U	0.50
☐ Chen Hikaru	Character	X	0.50
☐ Come Join Us	Agenda	X	0.50
☐ Commercial Telepaths	Group	X	0.50
5			
☐ Conspiracy!	Event	C	0.15
☐ Continued Progress	Event	U	0.50
☐ Convene The Grey Council	Event	R	3.50
☐ Cyborg Reconstruction	Enhancmnt	R	3.80
☐ Cynthia & Rosa	Character	U	0.50
☐ Danger Sense	Contingency	X	0.50
☐ Dark Talia	Character	R	4.50
☐ David	Character	C	0.15
☐ Diplomatic Recognition	Enhancmnt	C	0.15
6			
☐ Direct Link	Contingency	C	0.15
☐ Divide and Conquer	Conflict	U	0.50
☐ Don't You Trust Me?	Conflict	C	0.15
☐ Doomed Conspiracy	Conflict	R	4.00
☐ Drop Your Barriers	Enhancmnt	X	0.50
☐ Dust	Event	C	0.15
☐ Earth	Location	X	0.50
☐ Ego Boost	Event	C	0.15
☐ Elite Black Omega	Fleet	R	4.00
7			
☐ Empathy	Conflict	X	0.50
☐ Exercises of the Mind	Aftermath	X	0.50
☐ Expanded Network	Event	X	0.50
☐ Expendable	Event	U	0.50
☐ Exposed	Conflict	C	0.15
☐ Forget Something?	Conflict	R	3.50
☐ Front Page Exposure	Aftermath	U	0.50
☐ Gestalt	Event	R	4.00
☐ Good to Go	Event	U	0.50
8			
☐ Gordon	Character	X	0.50
☐ Greed	Enhancmnt	U	0.50
☐ Guerillas	Enhancmnt	U	0.50
☐ Harriman Gray	Character	X	0.50
☐ Hidden Hand	Event	C	0.15
☐ Hole In Your Mind	Conflict	U	0.50
☐ Homeworld Fleet	Fleet	X	0.50
☐ Hunting the Blips	Agenda	R	4.00
☐ I'd Die First	Event	U	0.50
9			
☐ Informant	Conflict	R	3.80
☐ Insufficient Support	Event	C	0.15
☐ Internal Disruptions	Enhancmnt	U	0.50
☐ Irrelevant	Enhancmnt	R	3.50
☐ Is That the Whole Truth?	Conflict	C	0.15
☐ Isdrell	Character	R	4.00
☐ Jason's Gift	Aftermath	R	4.00
☐ Jecinda	Character	U	0.50
☐ Jonathan Harris	Character	U	0.50
10			
☐ Juphar Trkider	Character	U	0.50

Card name	Type	Rarity	Price
☐ Katz	Character	R	3.80
☐ Kelsey	Character	X	0.50
☐ Korrinine	Character	R	3.30
☐ Last Ditch Effort	Contingency	C	0.15
☐ Laurel Takashima	Character	R	4.00
☐ Lavindra	Character	R	4.00
☐ Level the Playing Field	Event	X	0.25
☐ Like Unto The Gods	Event	U	0.50
11			
☐ Lindstrom	Character	C	0.15
☐ Lise Hampton	Character	C	0.15
☐ Living Legends	Event	U	0.50
☐ Make Them Angry	Conflict	C	0.15
☐ Manipulate the Masters	Contingency	R	3.40
☐ Mass Rioting	Event	R	3.00
☐ Master Manipulation	Enhancmnt	U	0.50
☐ Master of Deception	Aftermath	U	0.50
☐ Master Plan	Enhancmnt	X	0.50
12			
☐ Matthew Stoner	Character	X	0.50
☐ Military Telepaths	Group	X	0.50
☐ Mind Games	Conflict	X	0.25
☐ Minds That Matter	Event	C	0.15
☐ Mindwalkers	Enhancmnt	U	0.50
☐ Misdirection	Aftermath	R	3.00
☐ Miss Constance	Character	C	0.15
☐ Mistaken Identity	Contingency	C	0.15
☐ Mother Ship Alpha	Fleet	R	4.00
13			
☐ Movekk	Character	U	0.50
☐ My Hands are Tied	Event	R	3.50
☐ Negotiation Deadline	Event	U	0.50
☐ Nejokk	Character	C	0.15
☐ Night of the Long Knives	Conflict	R	3.50
☐ No Surprises	Conflict	C	0.15
☐ Nobody Can Stop Us	Agenda	X	0.50
☐ Not Without a Fight	Agenda	U	0.50
☐ Nowhere but Down	Aftermath	R	3.00
14			
☐ Obey	Event	X	0.50
☐ Open Season	Event	R	3.40
☐ Oqmrritkz	Location	C	0.15
☐ Ostracized	Aftermath	U	0.50
☐ "Our Last, Best Hope"	Enhancmnt	R	3.80
☐ Overwhelming Emotions	Aftermath	R	3.30
☐ Pain	Event	X	0.50
☐ Personal Quest	Enhancmnt	C	0.15
☐ Picket Fleet	Fleet	X	0.50
15			
☐ Political Firestorm	Aftermath	C	0.15
☐ Proxima III	Location	X	0.50
☐ Psi Academy	Group	C	0.15
☐ Psi Attack	Conflict	X	0.50
☐ Psi Bodyguard	Enhancmnt	X	0.50
☐ Psi Corps Intelligence	Group	X	0.50
☐ Psi Suppressors	Conflict	C	0.15
☐ Psionic Sabotage	Event	C	0.15
☐ Psychic Blunder	Event	C	0.15
16			
☐ Pundits	Aftermath	U	0.50
☐ Punitive Sanctions	Conflict	C	0.15
☐ Religious Festival	Event	C	0.15
☐ Repairing the Past	Aftermath	X	0.50
☐ Reparations	Aftermath	R	3.50
☐ Reprogrammer	Character	U	0.50
☐ Reprogramming Team	Group	U	0.50
☐ Resigned to His Fate	Event	U	0.50
☐ Revenge is Sweet	Contingency	C	0.15
17			
☐ Rogue	Enhancmnt	C	0.15
☐ Saboteurs	Group	C	0.15

Card name	Type	Rarity	Price
☐ Sanctity of The Mind	Event	C	0.15
☐ Sara	Character	C	0.15
☐ Say What They Want	Event	C	0.15
☐ Secret Police	Group	X	0.50
☐ Sector 90	Location	U	0.50
☐ Seeing Shadows	Conflict	U	0.50
☐ Seeking Knowledge	Enhancmnt	R	3.50
18			
☐ Sh'Sak	Character	R	4.30
☐ Star Chamber	Group	U	0.50
☐ Steal Skills	Contingency	X	0.50
☐ Stealing Secrets	Conflict	R	3.00
☐ Stirring Rebuke	Event	U	0.50
☐ Strike Back!	Event	R	4.00
☐ Syria Planum	Location	X	0.50
☐ Tactical Error	Contingency	U	0.50
☐ Talia Winters	Character	X	0.50
19			
☐ Team Player	Enhancmnt	U	0.50
☐ Telepath Colony	Agenda	U	0.50
☐ Telepath for Hire	Character	C	0.15
☐ Telepath Hunter	Character	U	0.50
☐ Telepath Recruiters	Group	R	4.00
☐ Telepathic Revenge	Contingency	C	0.15
☐ Telepathic Scan	Conflict	X	0.50
☐ That's the Spirit	Event	U	0.50
☐ The Badge & The Gloves	Enhancmnt	X	0.50
20			
☐ The Corps is Mother	Agenda	X	0.50
☐ The Growing Conspiracy	Enhancmnt	U	0.50
☐ The Mind's Eye	Event	X	0.50
☐ The Spider's Web	Event	C	0.15
☐ They Are Not For You	Event	R	3.50
☐ They're Just Mundanes	Aftermath	R	3.60
☐ Thirteen	Character	R	3.50
☐ Thomas	Character	U	0.50
☐ Thought Police	Agenda	R	3.80
21			
☐ Trade Pact	Conflict	X	0.40
☐ Tunnel of Life & Death	Contingency	R	3.50
☐ Unauthorized Scan	Aftermath	C	0.15
☐ Underground Leader	Character	R	4.00
☐ Underground Railroad	Group	U	0.50
☐ Underutilized Resources	Enhancmnt	U	0.50
☐ Universal Enemy	Aftermath	R	3.00
☐ Utility Fleet	Fleet	X	0.50
☐ Visions in Time	Conflict	R	4.00
22			
☐ Wade	Character	R	3.80
☐ War of Information	Event	C	0.15
☐ Wastelands	Enhancmnt	X	0.50
☐ We Are Both Damned	Aftermath	U	0.50
☐ We Think Alike	Conflict	U	0.50
☐ William Edgars	Character	R	4.00
☐ Zathras	Character	R	4.00

Conspiracy marks

"The **Psi Corps** set fully explains the Conspiracy mark, which first appeared on **Great War**'s alternate human ambassador, William Morgan Clark. The Psi Corps faction cannot sponsor non-Psi-Corps cards loyal to any race, unless it currently controls fewer cards of that type than it has conspiracy marks. This restriction does not apply to neutral cards, and reciprocal rules exist for other factions wishing to sponsor cards loyal to Psi Corps."

— Mike Hummel, **Scrye** 6.3 (Aug 99)

RARITY KEY **C** = Common **U** = Uncommon **R** = Rare **VR** = Very Rare **UR** = Ultra Rare **F** = Foil card **X** = Fixed/standard in all decks

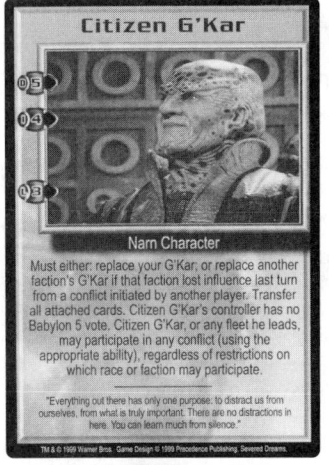

Citizen G'Kar

Narn Character

Must either: replace your G'Kar; or replace another faction's G'Kar if that faction lost influence last turn from a conflict initiated by another player. Transfer all stacked cards. Citizen G'Kar's controller has no Babylon 5 vote. Citizen G'Kar, or any fleet he leads, may participate in any conflict (using the appropriate ability), regardless of restrictions on which race or faction may participate.

"Everything out there has only one purpose: to distract us from ourselves, from what is truly important. There are no distractions in here. You can learn much from silence."

TM & © 1999 Warner Bros. Game Design © 1999 Precedence Publishing, Severed Dreams.

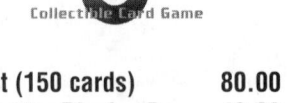

BABYLON 5™
Collectible Card Game

Babylon 5 • *Severed Dreams*
Precedence • Released **November 1999**
150 cards in set • **IDENTIFIER: Set name at lower right**
• Booster packs contain 8 cards; displays contain 24 boosters, checklist, and promo card

Following closely on the heels of *Psi Corps* due to delays in that expansion, *Severed Dreams* has three themes. Simulating a key story arc in the show, Babylon 4 cards enable mutual victories. Nightwatch adds the element of xenophobia. Then, there are alternate versions of main characters, similar to the mirror universe of *Star Trek*.

Babylon 4 decks need the agenda **Steal Babylon 4** (common); Babylon 4 conflicts (of which there are three each for diplomacy, intrigue, and military); and, someone else to claim victory. Babylon 4 decks are parasitic. Primarily, Nightwatch decks make characters stronger by converting non-Nightwatch into Nightwatch. For some of the characters introduced in *Severed Dreams*, that's sufficient to increase their abilities. For other characters, the key card is Nightwatch Collaborators. All of the necessary cards are commons. There is no Nightwatch victory; it is a way to help you win by normal means.

Every race with the exception of the Non-Aligned "race" gets new starting ambassadors and at least one main character replacement. Some new ambassadors are exceptional: extra card (opening hand) **Captain Sheridan**, extra card **G'Kar**, transformer **Delenn**, gambling **Londo Mollari**. Nevertheless, *Premier* ambassadors are still worth playing. The three autograph cards in *Severed Dreams* are **Ranger Lennier, Captain Sinclair,** and **Jane.** — ***Ian Lee***

Set (150 cards)	80.00		
Booster Display Box	42.00		
Booster Pack	2.00		

You will need 17 nine-pocket pages to store this set. (9 doubled up)

Card name	Type	Rarity	Price
☐ 50 Credits a Week	Event	C	0.20
☐ A Shot in the Dark	Event	R	4.00
☐ A World Gone Mad	Event	U	0.50
☐ Alexander	Enhncmt	R	4.00
☐ Alien Scum	Event	C	0.2
☐ Alyt	Enhncmt	U	0.5
☐ Alyt Neroon	Character	R	4.00
☐ Anti-Psi Training	Event	C	0.20
☐ Assume Authority	Conflict	R	3.00
☐ Attaché	Enhncmt	U	0.50
☐ Attaché Cotto	Character	R	3.00
☐ Attack the Underlings	Conflict	C	0.20
☐ Between You & The Abyss	Event	R	3.00
☐ Breaching Pod	Event	C	0.20
☐ Cannot Run Out of Time	Conflict	U	0.50
☐ Captain Sheridan (contngn)	Character	R	5.00
☐ Captain Sheridan (extra card)	Character	R	5.00
☐ Captain Sinclair	Character	R	5.50
☐ Carve Up the Galaxy	Conflict	U	0.50
☐ Citizen G'Kar	Character	R	5.00
☐ Cocksure	Enhncmt	U	0.50
☐ Compensation	Conflict	U	0.50
☐ Councilor Na'Far	Character	R	4.00
☐ Courtly Intrigue	Agenda	C	0.20
☐ Cult of Personality	Aftermath	U	0.50
☐ Deep Agent	Character	C	0.20
☐ Deeron	Character	C	0.20
☐ Defuse the Situation	Conflict	U	0.50
☐ Delenn (Lennier)	Character	R	5.00
☐ Delenn (promote)	Character	R	5.00
☐ Delenn (transformer)	Character	R	5.00
☐ Den'sha	Conflict	R	4.00
☐ Desperate Measures	Event	U	0.50
☐ Disinformation	Conflict	U	0.50
☐ Do as You Are Told	Enhncmt	R	3.00
☐ Dogfight	Conflict	U	0.50
☐ Domestic Concerns	Enhncmt	C	0.20
☐ Doomed Expedition	Event	U	0.50
☐ Double-cross	Contingency	C	0.20
☐ Draal the Caretaker	Character	R	3.80
☐ Dwindling Resources	Enhncmt	R	3.00
☐ Efficiency Engineers	Group	C	0.20

Card name	Type	Rarity	Price
☐ Entil'zha Delenn	Character	R	5.00
☐ Evacuation	Conflict	C	0.20
☐ Executive Aide	Enhncmt	U	0.50
☐ Eye of the Storm	Agenda	R	4.00
☐ Facing Oblivion	Event	C	0.20
☐ Fifth Column	Enhncmt	U	0.50
☐ Flashback	Aftermath	R	3.00
☐ Foiled Scheme	Aftermath	C	0.20
☐ Force Them Back	Conflict	U	0.50
☐ Friendless & Forgotten	Aftermath	C	0.20
☐ G'Kar	Character	R	5.00
☐ G'Kar Forsaken	Character	R	5.00
☐ Giant Fusion Bomb	Conflict	U	0.50
☐ Gravity Well	Event	C	0.20
☐ Handy Dandy Micro Helper	Conflict	R	4.00
☐ Head on a Pike	Aftermath	C	0.20
☐ "Hello, Old Friend "	Conflict	U	0.50
☐ Honored Position	Conflict	U	0.50
☐ How Dare You?	Contingency	U	0.50
☐ Incentives	Enhncmt	C	0.20
☐ Information Control	Conflict	U	0.50
☐ Jane	Character	R	4.00
☐ Journalistic Integrity	Aftermath	C	0.20
☐ Kha'Ri Citadel	Enhncmt	R	4.00
☐ Lady Daggair	Character	R	4.00
☐ Lady Mariel	Character	U	0.50
☐ Lady Timov	Character	U	0.50
☐ Lise Hampton Edgars	Character	U	0.50
☐ Londo Mollari (diplomat)	Character	R	4.00
☐ Londo Mollari (gambler)	Character	R	4.00
☐ Londo's Wives	Group	U	0.50
☐ Major Krantz	Character	C	0.20
☐ Malcontent	Character	C	0.20
☐ Man for All Seasons	Enhncmt	R	3.00
☐ Mass Carnage	Aftermath	R	3.00
☐ Mister Allan	Character	R	4.00
☐ Mister Welles	Character	R	3.50
☐ Mutual Understanding	Event	U	0.50
☐ Natural Born Leader	Aftermath	C	0.20
☐ Nay-Sayer	Enhncmt	C	0.20
☐ Nest of Vipers	Group	U	0.50
☐ Nightwatch Collaborators	Group	U	0.50
☐ No One Returns	Contingency	U	0.50
☐ Not The One	Event	U	0.50
☐ Now He's Ready	Aftermath	C	0.20
☐ Nuclear Bluff	Conflict	U	0.50
☐ Number One	Character	R	4.00
☐ Offer a Position	Event	C	0.20

Card name	Type	Rarity	Price
☐ Our Own People First	Agenda	C	0.20
☐ Oversight Committee	Group	U	0.50
☐ Overwhelmed	Contingency	C	0.20
☐ Paparazzi	Enhncmt	C	0.20
☐ Pariah	Aftermath	U	0.50
☐ Partnership for Peace	Conflict	C	0.20
☐ Penultimate Revenge	Conflict	U	0.50
☐ "Pestilence, Famine, Death"	Event	U	0.50
☐ Pierce Macabee	Character	U	0.50
☐ Predestination	Event	U	0.50
☐ Prime Minister Refa	Character	R	4.00
☐ Psi World	Event	R	4.00
☐ Psychopath	Character	C	0.20
☐ Quartermaster	Enhncmt	U	0.50
☐ Question Authority	Conflict	C	0.20
☐ Rapid Aging	Aftermath	U	0.50
☐ Redeemed	Event	U	0.50
☐ Resist Control	Conflict	C	0.20
☐ Right Makes Might	Event	U	0.50
☐ Rising Star	Enhncmt	U	0.50
☐ Senator King	Character	U	0.50
☐ Shining Beacon in Space	Conflict	R	3.00
☐ Silent Majority	Enhncmt	U	0.50
☐ Sniper	Character	C	0.20
☐ Snoop	Enhncmt	C	0.20
☐ Steal Babylon 4	Agenda	C	0.20
☐ Suicide Run	Event	C	0.20
☐ Sycophant	Character	C	0.20
☐ Tacticians	Group	U	0.50
☐ Taking Sides	Aftermath	C	0.20
☐ The Conspiracy Deepens	Agenda	C	0.20
☐ The Hive	Group	U	0.50
☐ The Messiah Effect	Enhncmt	R	4.00
☐ The One	Aftermath	R	4.00
☐ The Path to Peace	Agenda	C	0.20
☐ They're Killing Us!	Conflict	U	0.50
☐ Thug	Character	C	0.20
☐ Time Jump	Conflict	R	3.80
☐ Time Stabilizer	Enhncmt	C	0.20
☐ Toast to Victory	Aftermath	C	0.20
☐ Tonia Wallis	Character	C	0.20
☐ Trakis	Character	R	3.50
☐ Triple-cross	Event	R	3.00
☐ Under Our Protection	Contingency	U	0.50
☐ Unstuck in Time	Aftermath	R	4.00
☐ Valen's War	Aftermath	R	4.00
☐ VIP Involvement	Event	R	4.00

RARITY KEY **C** = Common   **U** = Uncommon   **R** = Rare   **VR** = Very Rare   **UR** = Ultra Rare   **F** = Foil card   **X** = Fixed/standard in all decks

Card name	Type	Rarity	Price
☐ War Crimes Trial	Conflict	R	3.00
☐ Warriors Council	Agenda	C	0.20
☐ Watch Your Back	Conflict	C	0.20
☐ We Die for The One	Contingency	U	0.50

Card name	Type	Rarity	Price
☐ Why Are You Here?	Enhncmt	R	3.00
☐ Why Are You Hitting Me?	Contingency	C	0.20
☐ With Us or Against Us	Event	C	0.20
☐ Written in the Stars	Event	C	0.20

(17)

Card name	Type	Rarity	Price
☐ Xenophobia	Event	C	0.20
☐ You Have a Destiny	Enhncmt	U	0.50
☐ You Three Are One	Event	R	3.50
☐ Zathras Who Was	Character	R	4.00

Babylon 5 • *Wheel of Fire*

Precedence • Released April 2000

152 cards in set • **IDENTIFIER: Set name at lower right**

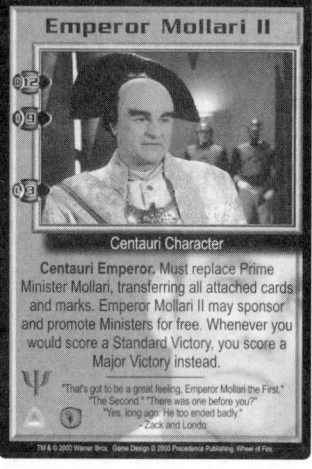

• Booster packs contain 9 cards; displays contain 24 boosters, checklist, and promo

Even with the changes that previous expansions had wrought, **Wheel of Fire** is the most revolutionary of the expansions. The new themes are the Drakh and the Interstellar Alliance (ISA). Any faction may "Drakhify" — go from a normal faction to a Drakh faction, which can only win by satisfying the requirements on a Drakh agenda. As compensation, Drakh cards are stronger, allowing a Drakh deck to achieve these more challenging goals. A political entity, the ISA forms only by having other factions agree. Once it's formed, winning becomes more difficult for non-members, as they are required to have additional power to win based on the number of members. Members are barred from certain plays, such as targeting another member with military conflicts.

The paradigm shift is towards ISA versus Drakh leaving older strategies behind, primarily Vorlons and Shadows which once dominated the metagame. The necessary cards to play ISA and Drakh are common, so a large investment is unnecessary. The three autograph cards are **President Sheridan**, **Doctor Sheridan**, and **Lieutenant Corwin**. — *Ian Lee*

Set (152 cards)	**175.00**
Booster Display Box	**65.00**
Booster Pack	**3.00**

You will need 17 nine-pocket pages to store this set. (9 doubled up)

Card name	Type	Rarity	Price
(1)			
☐ Agitation	Conflict	U	1.00
☐ Airlock Mishap	Event	C	0.25
☐ All Alone in the Night	After	C	0.25
☐ Alliance Fleet	Fleet	R	4.00
☐ And So It Begins	Contingency	U	1.00
☐ Attack the Shadows	Conflict	C	0.25
☐ Barren Worlds	Location	R	3.00
☐ Black Rose Killer	Aftermath	C	0.25
☐ Blow the Jump Gate	Conflict	U	1.00
(2)			
☐ Blue Narn	Character	R	5.00
☐ Brakiri Priest	Character	R	3.30
☐ Bread and Circuses	Aftermath	U	1.00
☐ Breaking News	Aftermath	C	0.25
☐ But We're Your Allies	Conflict	C	0.25
☐ Captain Ivanova	Character	R	6.50
☐ Chief Allan	Character	R	5.00
☐ Conquest Fleet	Fleet	U	1.00
☐ Contest the Presidency	Conflict	C	0.25
(3)			
☐ Cooperative Measure	Event	C	0.25
☐ Coplann	Character	U	1.00
☐ Corporate Connections	Contingency	R	3.50
☐ Cosmopolis	Location	U	1.00
☐ Councilor La'shan	Character	U	1.00
☐ Crawling Chaos	Event	C	0.25
☐ Dangerous Game	Event	C	0.25
☐ Dark Legacy	Enhancmnt	U	1.00
☐ Declaration of Principles	Enhancmnt	C	0.25
(4)			
☐ Destroy Them From Within	Aftermath	U	1.00
☐ Disillusioned Garibaldi	Character	R	5.00
☐ Doctor Sheridan	Character	R	5.00
☐ Drakh Armada	Fleet	R	5.00
☐ Drakh Entire	Group	U	1.00
☐ Drakh Mothership	Fleet	U	1.00
☐ Drakh Raiders	Fleet	C	0.25
☐ Drazi Merchant	Character	C	0.25
☐ Drone Fleet	Fleet	R	5.00
(5)			
☐ Elizabeth Lochley (Cost 10)	Character	R	5.00

Card name	Type	Rarity	Price
☐ Elizabeth Lochley (Nightwatch)	Character	R	5.00
☐ Emperor Mollari II (old)	Character	R	8.00
☐ Emperor Mollari II (young)	Character	R	7.00
☐ Emperor Refa	Character	R	5.00
☐ Errand of Mercy	Conflict	U	1.00
☐ Espers	Group	R	4.00
☐ Expelled	Conflict	C	0.25
☐ Feast of Lights	Aftermath	R	4.00
(6)			
☐ Flying Fortress	Fleet	U	1.00
☐ Foment Discord	Agenda	C	0.25
☐ Force Omega	Fleet	U	1.00
☐ Forell	Character	C	0.25
☐ Free Trade	Conflict	C	0.25
☐ General Na'Tok	Character	U	1.00
☐ Gerontocracy	Enhancmnt	U	1.00
☐ G'Obel	Character	R	5.00
☐ Guilds	Group	U	1.00
(7)			
☐ Hindsight	Event	R	4.00
☐ ISA President	Enhancmnt	C	0.25
☐ Interstellar Alliance	Event	C	0.25
☐ It Stops Here	Aftermath	R	4.00
☐ Ivory Towers	Enhancmnt	C	0.25
☐ Kill Them All	Event	C	0.25
☐ King Arthur	Character	R	5.00
☐ Kirrin	Character	U	1.00
☐ Kullenbrak	Character	R	5.00
(8)			
☐ Lady Na'Toth	Character	R	5.00
☐ Lazarenn	Character	U	1.00
☐ League Spokesbeing	Enhancmnt	U	1.00
☐ Legacy of Power	Aftermath	R	5.00
☐ Let the Galaxy Burn	Agenda	C	0.25
☐ Lieutenant Corwin	Character	R	5.00
☐ Llort Bodyguard	Character	C	0.25
☐ Lyta Released	Character	R	5.00
☐ Main Battlefleet	Fleet	R	5.00
(9)			
☐ Major Lianna Kemmer	Character	U	1.00
☐ Manish'tushu	Character	U	1.00
☐ Master of Darkness	Character	C	0.25
☐ Media Circus	Group	R	4.00
☐ Medical Database	Conflict	C	0.25
☐ Megalopolis	Location	U	1.00
☐ Minister Chorlini	Character	U	1.00
☐ Miziri Tal	Character	R	5.00

Card name	Type	Rarity	Price
☐ Mutual Defense	Enhancmnt	C	0.25
(10)			
☐ My Good Friend!	Event	U	1.00
☐ Napar'ishu	Character	C	0.25
☐ Newton's Third Law	Contingency	R	4.00
☐ Nug/Ulg	Character	U	1.00
☐ Open Aggression	Conflict	R	4.00
☐ Opportunism	Conflict	R	4.00
☐ Organic Technology	Enhancmnt	U	1.00
☐ Outfoxed	Contingency	C	0.25
☐ Pak'ma'ra's Hump	Enhancmnt	C	0.25
(11)			
☐ Point of No Return	Enhancmnt	C	0.25
☐ Power Supreme	Agenda	U	1.00
☐ Power of Darkness	Event	C	0.25
☐ President Sheridan	Character	R	6.50
☐ Prohibited Area	Conflict	C	0.25
☐ Proof of Genocide	Conflict	U	1.00
☐ Psychedelic Program	Conflict	C	0.25
☐ Psychic Trauma	Contingency	C	0.25
☐ Pull From Behind	Conflict	C	0.25
(12)			
☐ Renegade Telepath	Character	U	1.00
☐ Resist the Vorlons	Conflict	C	0.25
☐ Rimush	Character	R	5.00
☐ Roam the Stars	Location	U	1.00
☐ Round Table	Event	U	1.00
☐ Rule By the Masses	Agenda	U	1.00
☐ Schism	Event	R	5.00
☐ Search For a Home	Agenda	U	1.00
☐ Secret and Arrogant	Conflict	C	0.25
(13)			
☐ Seeds of Destruction	Agenda	R	4.00
☐ Shadow of a Shadow	Enhancmnt	R	4.00
☐ Shai Alyt Neroon	Character	R	5.00
☐ Shar'kali	Character	U	1.00
☐ Sharrukin	Character	R	4.00
☐ Shine in the Night	Conflict	C	0.25
☐ Shiv'kala	Character	R	5.00
☐ Signs and Portents	Contingency	U	1.00
☐ Soldier of Darkness	Character	R	4.00
(14)			
☐ Something in the Air	Enhancmnt	C	0.25
☐ Starfire Wheel	Conflict	R	4.00
☐ State Visit	Event	U	1.00
☐ Strange Happenings	Event	C	0.25
☐ Subvert the Nexus	Agenda	U	1.00

RARITY KEY C = Common   **U** = Uncommon   **R** = Rare   **VR** = Very Rare   **UR** = Ultra Rare   **F** = Foil card   **X** = Fixed/standard in all decks

Card name	Type	Rarity	Price
Surgeon of Darkness	Character	U	1.00
Surgical Strike	Conflict	R	4.00
Terror Tactics	Agenda	U	1.00
The Chosen Ones	Event	U	1.00
15			
The Corps is Father	Enhancmnt	U	1.00
The First One	Aftermath	C	0.25
The Rangers	Enhancmnt	C	0.25
The Regent	Character	R	5.00
The Secret Masters	Agenda	C	0.25
The Trap Is Sprung	Aftermath	U	1.00
"There is Danger, Remember"	Aftermath	R	4.00

Card name	Type	Rarity	Price
Touched By Vorlons	Aftermath	U	1.00
Treachery	Contingency	R	4.00
16			
Tyranny Enthroned	Conflict	R	4.00
United We Stand	Aftermath	U	1.00
Unity	Contingency	C	0.25
Universal Policeman	Conflict	C	0.25
Ur'nammu	Character	C	0.25
Vorlon	Character	R	5.00
Vorlon Renegade	Character	R	5.00
We Are One	Enhancmnt	C	0.25
We Have Always Been			

Card name	Type	Rarity	Price
Here	Enhancmnt	U	1.00
17			
We Say It's Over	Conflict	C	0.25
Wheel of Fire	Conflict	R	5.00
Who Do You Serve?	Event	U	1.00
Win-Win Schemes	Enhancmnt	C	0.25
Wisdom of G'Quan	Event	U	1.00
Work of the Wicked	Conflict	C	0.25
Wushmeshkeshlep Fo	Character	U	1.00
You Have No Power Here	Event	R	4.00

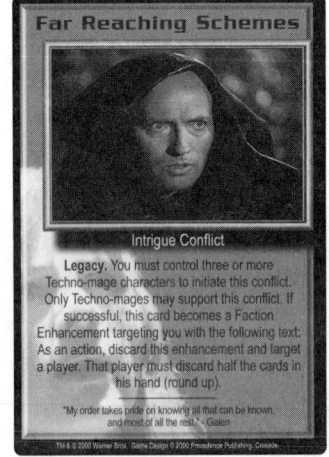

Far Reaching Schemes

Intrigue Conflict

Legacy. You must control three or more Techno-mage characters to initiate this conflict. Only Techno-mages may support this conflict. If successful, this card becomes a Faction Enhancement targeting you with the following text: As an action, discard this enhancement and target a player. That player must discard half the cards in his hand (round up).

"My order takes pride on knowing all that can be known, and most of all the rest." - Galen

TM & © 2000 Warner Bros. Game Design © 2000 Precedence Publishing, Crusade.

Babylon 5 • Crusade

Precedence • Released **December 2000**

159 cards in set • **IDENTIFIER: Set name at lower right**

• Booster packs contain 9 cards; booster displays contain 24 boosters

Designed by **Kevin Tewart** and **Mike Hummel**

Crusade expands the *Babylon 5* CCG setting by adding cards featuring characters and concepts from the very short-lived TNT *Crusade* series, the sequel to the Babylon 5 television series, as well as cards from the original series.

Crusade pumps up the Techno-mages, adding individual characters as well as Techno-mage vessels and items. The power of the *Excalibur*, the centerpiece of the television series, adds a lot of firepower to any deck. And of course, there are numerous cards based on the characters from the show, some of which are specially featured in the rare autograph cards, which are found one in every 48 booster packs.

A further expansion, *An'la'shok*, was planned at press time. — *James A. Mishler*

Set (159 cards)	167.00
Booster Display Box	65.00
Booster Pack	3.00

You will need **18** nine-pocket pages to store this set. (9 doubled up)

Card name	Type	Rarity	Price
1			
A Call For Help	Event	R	2.50
A Crusade... (for a cure)	Enhancmnt	C	0.20
A Crusade... (for a legacy)	Enhancmnt	C	0.20
A Crusade... (for knowledge)	Enhancmnt	C	0.20
A Crusade... (for profit)	Enhancmnt	C	0.20
A Dying People	Event	C	0.20
A Good Lead	Aftermath	C	0.20
A Warning	Event	R	2.50
2			
Above It All	Event	R	2.50
Accommodations	Event	C	0.20
Age of Conquest	Contingency	R	3.00
Agents Durkani & Lyssa	Character	R	3.50
Ain't I a Stinker?	Event	R	3.00
Alien Takeover	Conflict	U	0.80
All In the Cards	Event	R	2.50
Alliance Superfleet	Fleet	R	4.00
Alwyn	Character	U	0.80
Ancient Data Crystal	Aftermath	R	3.00
3			
Andre Sabbat	Character	U	0.80
Apocalypse Box	Enhancmnt	U	0.80
Apriori Flentak & Nix	Character	R	3.00
Archaeologist D. Taylor	Character	U	0.80
Arsenal of Yesterdays	Enhancmnt	C	0.20
Automated Fleet	Fleet	U	0.80
Bio-Adaptive Shielding	Enhancmnt	C	0.20
Blaylock	Character	R	3.50
Bruder	Character	U	0.80
4			
Captain Daniels	Character	U	0.80
Captain Lochley (at desk)	Character	R	4.00
Captain Lochley (close-up)	Character	R	4.00

Card name	Type	Rarity	Price
Collaboration	Conflict	R	2.50
Collar Gun	Aftermath	U	0.80
Corporations Go On	Enhancmnt	U	0.80
Death Incarnate	Enhancmnt	C	0.20
Death of a Planet	Conflict	R	3.50
5			
Death of Culture	Aftermath	U	0.80
Detailed Data Analysis	Conflict	C	0.20
Dire Consequences	Contingency	R	2.50
Dr. Sarah Chambers (brown smock)	Character	R	4.00
Dr. Sarah Chambers (purple smock)	Character	R	4.00
Duel to the Death	Event	C	0.20
Dureena Nafeel (peering)	Character	R	4.00
Dureena Nafeel (standing)	Character	R	4.00
Electron Incantation	Aftermath	U	0.80
Elizabeth Trent	Character	R	4.00
6			
EVA Salvaging	Aftermath	U	0.80
Everything Has a Price	Event	R	2.50
Excalibur	Fleet	R	5.00
Exodus	Fleet	R	3.00
Explore Vorlon Space	Conflict	R	3.50
Faces in Stone	Event	U	0.80
Far Reaching Schemes	Conflict	R	2.50
Final Destiny	Conflict	U	0.80
Fireball	Event	C	0.20
7			
First Contact Protocols	Conflict	U	0.80
Forced Down	Conflict	R	2.50
Galen (holding fire)	Character	R	5.00
Galen (hood and staff)	Character	R	5.00
Galen's Crystal Ball	Enhancmnt	U	0.80
Galen's Magic Rock	Aftermath	R	4.00
Galen's Ship	Fleet	R	4.50
Galen's Staff	Enhancmnt	C	0.20
General Ivanova	Character	R	6.50
8			
Genius Loci	Character	R	2.50
Ghost Ship	Conflict	C	0.20

Card name	Type	Rarity	Price
Goods and Services	Event	C	0.20
High-Tech Weapons	Conflict	C	0.20
Holo-Demons	Event	R	2.50
Holo-Dragon	Event	R	3.00
Homunculus	Contingency	C	0.20
How to Succeed in Business	Event	R	2.50
Hyperspace Getaway	Contingency	C	0.20
9			
Illegal Raid	Conflict	U	0.80
Invisibility	Enhancmnt	U	0.80
IPX Official	Character	C	0.20
Isabelle	Character	R	3.50
Isabelle's Quest	Aftermath	R	3.00
Jacob Redway	Character	U	0.80
John Matheson (blue/black uniform)	Character	R	4.00
John Matheson (grey/red uniform)	Character	R	4.00
Kevin Sprach	Character	U	0.80
10			
Kulan	Character	U	0.80
Lemm Uh'Ekim	Character	C	0.20
Leonard Anderson	Character	U	0.80
Lieutenant Carr	Character	U	0.80
Lieutenant Tewart	Character	U	0.20
Lise Hampton Edgars Garibaldi	Character	R	4.00
Lorkans	Character	C	0.20
"M. Garibaldi, CEO"	Character	R	5.00
Main Gun	Enhancmnt	U	0.80
11			
Marata Fleet	Fleet	C	0.20
Mars Conference	Conflict	R	2.50
Matthew Gideon (blue/black uniform)	Character	R	3.50
Matthew Gideon (grey/red uniform)	Character	R	3.50
Max Eilerson (close-up)	Character	R	3.00
Max Eilerson (on ledge)	Character	R	3.00
Meddling with the Unknown	Contingency	C	0.20

RARITY KEY C = Common   U = Uncommon   R = Rare   VR = Very Rare   UR = Ultra Rare   F = Foil card   X = Fixed/standard in all decks

Card name	Type	Rarity	Price
Monopoly	Conflict	U	0.80
"Mr. Jones"	Character	C	0.20

12

Card name	Type	Rarity	Price
Nanotech Plague	Conflict	U	0.80
Natchok Var	Character	U	0.80
Navigator Robertson	Character	C	0.20
New Team	Aftermath	C	0.20
New Uniforms	Aftermath	C	0.20
Not Dead Yet	Event	R	2.50
Nova Dreadnoughts	Fleet	R	4.00
Nowhere to Hide	Enhancmnt	R	2.50
Null Field	Event	C	0.20

13

Card name	Type	Rarity	Price
Onslaught	Agenda	U	0.80
Opportunity Knocks	Aftermath	C	0.20
Organelle Transfer	Enhancmnt	C	0.20
Out of My Sky	Conflict	C	0.20
Personal Crusade	Enhancmnt	C	0.20
Pieces of the Puzzle	Aftermath	C	0.20
Portrait of the Past	Event	C	0.20
Pro Zeta Corporation	Group	U	0.80
Probes	Conflict	C	0.20

14

Card name	Type	Rarity	Price
Protected	Contingency	C	0.20
Psychic Projection	Event	C	0.20

Card name	Type	Rarity	Price
Quarantine	Enhancmnt	U	0.80
Quick to Anger	Enhancmnt	U	0.80
Record Returns	Conflict	U	0.80
Red Tape	Aftermath	U	0.80
Refuge	Aftermath	C	0.20
Reign of Terror	Conflict	C	0.20
Relaxation	Event	R	2.50

15

Card name	Type	Rarity	Price
Repeating Lasers	Enhancmnt	U	0.80
Retributive Strike	Event	R	2.50
Robert Conner	Character	C	0.20
Samuel Drake	Character	C	0.80
Serendipity	Conflict	C	0.20
Shady Dealings	Contingency	C	0.20
Sogayu	Character	C	0.80
Something Always Happens	Contingency	U	0.80
Special Agent Kendarr	Character	R	4.00

16

Card name	Type	Rarity	Price
Surprising Allies	Enhancmnt	U	0.80
Survivor's Guilt	Aftermath	U	0.80
Tactical Nuke	Event	C	0.20
Techno-Virus	Aftermath	R	3.00
The Circle is Joined	Event	R	2.50

Card name	Type	Rarity	Price
The Fen	Event	C	0.20
The Tech	Enhancmnt	U	0.80
The Truth Is Out...	Enhancmnt	C	0.20
Thieves' Guild	Group	U	0.80

17

Card name	Type	Rarity	Price
Tomorrow's Children	Conflict	R	2.50
Trace Miller	Character	U	0.80
Trial By Fire	Conflict	U	0.80
Trulann	Character	U	0.80
Ulterior Motives	Conflict	C	0.20
Undercover Investigation	Conflict	C	0.20
Victory	Fleet	R	4.50
Warlock Destroyers	Fleet	U	0.80
Well of Forever	Conflict	U	0.80

18

Card name	Type	Rarity	Price
We'll Take Over	Enhancmnt	U	0.80
Who's Your Little Pak'ma'ra?	Enhancmnt	R	2.50
Working Together	Event	U	0.80
Yabc Ftoba	Character	R	3.50
Yellow Journalism	Enhancmnt	U	0.80
You Are Expendable	Event	C	0.20

Babylon 5 • Promo and signed cards

Precedence

Promo cards for the **Babylon 5** CCG cover the entire spectrum from cards so strong that they received errata, to cards so weak you burst out laughing, to a card that differs in only the most minor way from an existing card found in every Narn starter.

Destined to Be and **Broken Allegiance** have errata. **Destined to Be** must now target a conflict. **Broken Allegiance** must be played as your first action. For humor, try getting anything useful out of **Contact First Ones**.

There is a misimpression among some players that promos are necessary to compete. Even the best ones aren't seen that often, so don't believe it. As for value, the promos range quite a bit, largely based on what the promotion was. Play value has a very poor correlation to card value among the promos. — **Ian Lee**

SCRYE NOTES: *Not that anyone would, but you can't play with a signed card — not without putting it in a sleeve with an opaque back. Signed* **Babylon 5** *cards are "notarized" with a Precedence stamp that can easily be seen through the back of the card.*

1

Card name	Type		Price
A Meeting of Minds	Psi	Pr	3.00
Asimov Laws	GrtWr	Pr	5.00
Attack Formation	GrtWr	Pr	8.00
Blessings	Prem	Pr	3.00
Bombing Run	Prem	Pr	4.50
Brevari	SevDr	Pr	5.00
Broken Allegiance	Shdws	Pr	5.00
Bureaucratic Control	Shdws	Pr	5.00
Captain Pierce	Prem	Pr	3.00

2

Card name	Type		Price
Charting the Course	GrtWr	Pr	10.00
Contact First Ones	Prem	Pr	3.00
Credit Chip	Shdws	Pr	3.80
Cultural Connections	Prem	Pr	4.50
Defector Revealed	GrtWr	Pr	5.00
Defense Treaty	Shdws	Pr	5.00
Destined to Be	Prem	Pr	7.00
Destroy the Opposition	Prem	Pr	4.00
Disarray	GrtWr	Pr	6.00

3

Card name	Type		Price
Dodger	SevDr	Pr	2.50
Dr. Franklin	Prem	Pr	5.00
Elder Statesman	Psi	Pr	3.00
Evidence of Shadows	Shdws	Pr	4.30
Exhaustion	GrtWr	Pr	6.00

Card name	Type		Price
Flarn	WoF	Pr	4.00
For the Future	Deluxe	Pr	3.00
Gaim Merchant	GrtWr	Pr	6.00
Inconclusive Strike	Shdws	Pr	3.00

4

Card name	Type		Price
Join the Corps	Psi	Pr	3.00
Junk Food	Crusade	Pr	3.00
Lack of Direction	Prem	Pr	5.00
Monitored Deal	Prem	Pr	3.00
Na'toth (variant)	Prem	Pr	8.00
Past Victories	Shdws	Pr	10.25
Psi Arbitrators	Psi	Pr	4.00
Psi Spies	Psi	Pr	4.00
Return to Ideals	GrtWr	Pr	3.50

5

Card name	Type		Price
Rogue Telepath	Deluxe	Pr	3.00
Secrets of Success	SevDr	Pr	3.00
Shadow Contact	Shdws	Pr	3.00
Signed Alfred Bester	Psi	UR	82.50
Signed Anna Sheridan	WoF	UR	56.00
Signed Byron	Psi	UR	55.25
Signed Captain Sinclair	SevDr	UR	65.00
Signed Commander Ivanova	Deluxe	UR	82.50
Signed Delenn Transformed	Prem	UR	82.50

6

Card name	Type		Price
Signed Jane	SevDr	UR	55.00
Signed Lt. Corwin	WoF	UR	57.50
Signed Lyta Empowered	Shdws	UR	57.50
Signed Max Eilerson	Crusade	UR	53.75
Signed Mr. Morden	Shdws	UR	57.50
Signed President Sheridan	WoF	UR	82.50
Signed Prime Minister Mollari	GrtWr	UR	82.50
Signed Ranger Lennier	SevDr	UR	65.00
Signed Zathra's	Psi	UR	57.50

7

Card name	Type		Price
Solo Flight	Crusade	Pr	3.00
Spoo	Deluxe	Pr	3.00
Suppress The Media	Prem	Pr	5.00
Taree	SevDr	Pr	4.50
The Dreaming	Psi	Pr	3.00
The Just Suffer	GrtWr	Pr	9.00
The Third Age	Crusade	Pr	3.50
Tip-Top Shape	Crusade	Pr	3.00
Unrelenting Pressure	Shdws	Pr	4.00

8

Card name	Type		Price
Veteran Fleet	Shdws	Pr	8.00
Zathra's	GrtWr	Pr	3.20
Zog!	Crusade	Pr	3.50

RARITY KEY C = Common U = Uncommon R = Rare VR = Very Rare UR = Ultra Rare F = Foil card X = Fixed/standard in all decks

Banemaster: The Adventure

+5 +5
0 0
+1 +1
+4 +4
+1 +1

Mad Vampire Sheep

Concept	●●○○○
Gameplay	●○○○○
Card art	○○○○○
Player pool	○○○○○

Collector bane

Complain if you will about **Banemaster**'s misspelled cards (like **Firey Wind**), jumbled art (one **Skeleton Warriors** card has the art from **Scorpion Orcs**), and inconsistent card names on the press sheet (**Pan's Pig** also appears as **Pan's Pig Statue**).

We'll complain that the maker's only announced card list seems to have been preliminary, and dozens of the cards we've found either have changed names or aren't there at all. We've pieced a list together here, reconciling where we could. Cards with asterisks may not exist.

Banemaster

Tiger Ltd., packaged in the U.S. by **Chessex** • Released **August 1995**
At least **179** cards in set (**234** cards announced, but could be as many as **241**)
- Starter decks contain 70 cards, 36-page rulebook and order-of-play card
- Starter displays contain 10 starters
- Booster packs contain 12 cards; Booster displays contain 60 boosters
Designed by **Alexander Duncan**

Brought over from Britain into the thick of the first collectible-card game boom, **Banemaster: The Adventure** attempted to bring more of a role-playing flavor to fantasy card gaming. It's remembered now, however, more for the scale of its failure.

At some point in the distant past, the vile Banemaster threatened the villagers of Glendochy, Scotland, swiping their treasures and their children. For his amusement, the Banemaster forced his young captives to fight over the treasure in his dungeon. That rosy and not-too-kid-friendly scenario inspired the *Banemaster* Basic Game, which uses only the 45 orange-backed Adventure cards found in the starter deck. One of the simplest CCG games since **Super Deck**, the Basic Game has players compete to "claim" Treasure cards from their own hands. Simple arithmetic is the order of the day, with players placing Power cards and modifying them with Weapon, Spell, and Potion cards. The first player to accumulate 50 treasure points wins. Since ties mean both players win their treasures, draws are possible. As in most trick-taking games, much of the Basic Game strategy comes in the order of play. Using the boosters, a player could theoretically pack out his deck with cards of higher point values, but it's difficult to imagine anyone doing it just for the Basic Game.

The Advanced and Tournament Game rules use more card icons to add new dimensions. In addition to their Adventure decks, each player runs a deck of green-backed Banemaster cards. (25 are available in each starter.) In turn, each player uses this deck to run the Banemaster, stocking Place cards with dungeon-style Feature, Event, Marauder and Trap cards. Opponents build Adventure decks to fit one of four adventuring professions: alchemists, ecclesiastics, vagabonds, and warriors. (That's magic-users, clerics, thieves, and fighters to you and me.) Depending on the icons on the cards chosen by the character running the Banemaster, some professions fare better than others.

The intent, clearly, is to encourage players to tell a story. You can't play a Banemaster setting up a **Sacrifice Slab** in a **Torture Chamber** guarded by a **Fire Sprite** and a **Poison Gas Cloud** without waxing eloquent about how these items came to be together. But there are enough different kinds of cards and attributes to worry about in the Advanced and Tournament games that keeping track of them all makes strategy hard to formulate from turn to turn. The round-robin format also makes it tough to get any kind of rhythm going.

Banemaster was produced for U.S. distribution by Chessex, then the largest game distributor to hobby shops. *Magic* had meant piles of money for distributors, but most had made their money simply as middlemen. Chessex already had its own manufacturing arm, so producing its own CCG must have seemed a sure bet to even greater profits. But *Banemaster*, with its garish colors, frequent misspellings, anonymous-sounding card names, and weak art (which was often very gruesome for a kid's game), rarely left the shelf and became an early entry on the list of one-release-only CCG failures.

The only game now is making sense of the manufacturer's highly inaccurate published card list. We have taken our best shot. — *John Jackson Miller*

Set (241 cards?)	10.00		
Starter Display Box	7.00		
Booster Display Box	9.00		
Starter Deck	2.50		
Booster Pack	0.50		

You will need **27** nine-pocket pages to store this set. Maybe. (14 doubled up)

1
Card name	Type	Rarity	Price
☐ Abandoned Vault	Banemaster	Place	0.05
☐ Aladdin's Lamp*	Adventure	Treasure	0.05
☐ Ancient Necklace	Adventure	Treasure	0.05
☐ Ant Mage	Banemaster	Marauder	0.05
☐ Apathy Of Age	Adventure	Potion	0.05
☐ Armoire	Banemaster	Feature	0.05
☐ Arrow Wall Slots	Banemaster	Trap	0.05
☐ Ash Slayer	Banemaster	Marauder	0.05
☐ Attack Fog*	Adventure	Spell	0.05
2				
☐ Audience Hall	Banemaster	Place	0.05
☐ Avalanche*	Adventure	Power/Find	0.05

Card name	Type	Rarity	Price
☐ Axeman Statue	Banemaster	Trap	0.05
☐ Battle Axe	Adventure	Weapon	0.05
☐ Battle Hammer	Adventure	Weapon	0.05
☐ Battle Sickle	Adventure	Weapon	0.05
☐ Beheading Scythe*	Banemaster	Trap	0.05
☐ Belly Rip Swords	Adventure	Weapon	0.05
☐ Black Bludgeon	Adventure	Weapon	0.05
3				
☐ Blackout*	Banemaster	Event	0.05
☐ Blindness	Adventure	Potion	0.05
☐ Blood Boiling	Adventure	Spell	0.05
☐ Blood Knife*	Adventure	Weapon	0.05
☐ Blood Tonic	Adventure	Potion	0.05
☐ Blue Divvils	Banemaster	Marauder	0.05
☐ Blue Dragon Attack	Banemaster	Event	0.05
☐ Bone Handle Parang*	Adventure	Weapon	0.05
☐ Book Shelves	Banemaster	Feature	0.05
4				
☐ Brain Booster	Adventure	Potion	0.05
☐ Brain Bursting	Adventure	Spell	0.05

Card name	Type	Rarity	Price
☐ Brain Wraith	Banemaster	Marauder	0.05
☐ Brass Bludgeon	Adventure	Weapon	0.05
☐ Building Collapse	Banemaster	Event	0.05
☐ Bursting Dam	Adventure	Power/Find	0.05
☐ Carved Horn*	Adventure	Treasure	0.05
☐ Cat Skull Bollas*	Adventure	Weapon	0.05
☐ Chain of Gold	Adventure	Treasure	0.05
5				
☐ Chair*	Banemaster	Feature	0.05
☐ Chest Of Drawers*	Banemaster	Feature	0.05
☐ Claymore	Adventure	Weapon	0.05
☐ Cloth Of Gold	Adventure	Treasure	0.05
☐ Cognac Cask	Banemaster	Feature	0.05
☐ Confusion	Adventure	Potion	0.05
☐ Coronette	Adventure	Treasure	0.05
☐ Cosmic Vortex*	Adventure	Power/Find	0.05
☐ Crashing Wave	Adventure	Power/Find	0.05
6				
☐ Crumbling Walls	Banemaster	Event	0.05
☐ Crystal Cavern	Banemaster	Place	0.05

***Asterisks denote cards on the manufacturer's card list which have not yet been confirmed to exist.**

Card name	Type	Rarity	Price
Crystal Cutter	Adventure	Weapon	0.05
Cutlas*	Adventure	Weapon	0.05
Dagger Drop Gate	Banemaster	Trap	0.05
Dank Dungeon	Banemaster	Place	0.05
Dense Smoke	Adventure	Spell	0.05
Diamond Ring	Adventure	Treasure	0.05
Dirk	Adventure	Weapon	0.05

7

Card name	Type	Rarity	Price
Disorientation	Adventure	Potion	0.05
Dragon Firebreath	Adventure	Potion	0.05
Dragontooth Axe	Adventure	Weapon	0.05
Drop Blade	Banemaster	Trap	0.05
Drop Slab	Banemaster	Trap	0.05
Elven Blade*	Adventure	Weapon	0.05
Emerald Ring*	Adventure	Treasure	0.05
Entrance Hall	Banemaster	Place	0.05
Exploding Floor	Banemaster	Trap	0.05

8

Card name	Type	Rarity	Price
Exploding Force	Adventure	Spell	0.05
Exploding Handle	Banemaster	Trap	0.05
Exploding Wall	Banemaster	Trap	0.05
Explosion 1	Adventure	Power/Find	0.05
Explosion 2	Adventure	Power/Find	0.05
Explosion 3	Adventure	Power/Find	0.05
Eye Glue	Adventure	Spell	0.05
Falling Chandellier	Banemaster	Trap	0.05
Fear*	Adventure	Potion	0.05

9

Card name	Type	Rarity	Price
Feasting Chamber*	Banemaster	Place	0.05
Fighting Irons*	Adventure	Weapon	0.05
Fire Sprite	Banemaster	Marauder	0.05
Fireball	Adventure	Spell	0.05
Firedrake Diamond	Adventure	Treasure	0.05
Firewall	Adventure	Spell	0.05
Firey Wind (sic)	Banemaster	Event	0.05
Fist Crusher	Adventure	Power/Find	0.05
Fleet Of Foot	Adventure	Potion	0.05

10

Card name	Type	Rarity	Price
Flesh Disintigrate [sic]	Adventure	Spell	0.05
Flesh-eating Fog	Banemaster	Marauder	0.05
Flood*	Banemaster	Event	0.05
Floor Gives Way*	Banemaster	Event	0.05
Floor Opening*	Banemaster	Feature	0.05
Floor Sprung Spear	Banemaster	Trap	0.05
Footcrush Slab*	Banemaster	Trap	0.05
Freeze Up	Adventure	Spell	0.05
Friendship*	Adventure	Spell	0.05

11

Card name	Type	Rarity	Price
Gale Wind	Adventure	Power/Find	0.05
Garroting Cord*	Adventure	Weapon	0.05
Gash Glove	Adventure	Weapon	0.05
Geyser	Adventure	Power/Find	0.05
Giant Ruby	Adventure	Treasure	0.05
Gnarled Shillelagh	Adventure	Weapon	0.05
Gold Circlet*	Adventure	Treasure	0.05
Gold Club	Adventure	Weapon	0.05
Gold Coins*	Adventure	Treasure	0.05

12

Card name	Type	Rarity	Price
Gold Dragon Attack	Banemaster	Event	0.05
Gold Ingot Horde	Adventure	Treasure	0.05
Golden Goblet	Adventure	Treasure	0.05
Golden Mask	Adventure	Treasure	0.05
Golden Orb	Adventure	Treasure	0.05
Golden Plates	Adventure	Treasure	0.05
Granite Alter (sic)	Banemaster	Feature	0.05
Great Hall	Banemaster	Place	0.05
Gruesome Gas	Adventure	Spell	0.05

13

Card name	Type	Rarity	Price
Gutting Gauntlets	Adventure	Weapon	0.05
Hammer Headache	Adventure	Potion	0.05
Hands Of Wood*	Adventure	Spell	0.05
Head Cleaver	Adventure	Weapon	0.05
Headless Axeman*	Banemaster	Marauder	0.05
Heart's Desire*	Adventure	Power/Find	0.05
Hiccups	Adventure	Potion	0.05
Hooded Moog	Banemaster	Marauder	0.05
Horror Hatchet	Adventure	Weapon	0.05

14

Card name	Type	Rarity	Price
Ice Needle Mace	Adventure	Weapon	0.05
Icy Blast*	Banemaster	Event	0.05
Invisible Pit	Banemaster	Trap	0.05
Invisible Wall	Adventure	Spell	0.05
Iron Ball Mace	Adventure	Weapon	0.05
Iron Chest	Banemaster	Feature	0.05
Iron Tonic	Adventure	Potion	0.05
Jade Dragon*	Adventure	Treasure	0.05
Jellacidon	Banemaster	Marauder	0.05

15

Card name	Type	Rarity	Price
Katana	Adventure	Weapon	0.05
Killer Kris	Adventure	Weapon	0.05
Killer Rabbit	Banemaster	Marauder	0.05
Knee Smasher	Banemaster	Trap	0.05
Kragan*	Adventure	Weapon	0.05
Lady's Jewel Bag	Adventure	Treasure	0.05
Lamp Stand*	Banemaster	Feature	0.05
Land Crab*	Banemaster	Marauder	0.05
Lava Flow In Dark	Adventure	Power/Find	0.05

16

Card name	Type	Rarity	Price
Lengthen Arms*	Adventure	Potion	0.05
Lift Net*	Banemaster	Trap	0.05
Lightning	Adventure	Power/Find	0.05
Liquid Stone Floor	Banemaster	Trap	0.05
Lord's Jewel Bag	Adventure	Treasure	0.05
Lords Bedroom*	Banemaster	Place	0.05
Lost Party Room*	Banemaster	Place	0.05
Mad Mallet	Adventure	Weapon	0.05
Mad Vampire Sheep	Banemaster	Marauder	0.05

17

Card name	Type	Rarity	Price
Magic Necklace	Adventure	Treasure	0.05
Make Fear	Adventure	Spell	0.05
Mantis Speed*	Adventure	Potion	0.05
Mantrap	Banemaster	Trap	0.05
Master Balcony	Banemaster	Place	0.05
Metal Rain	Banemaster	Trap	0.05
Metal Rain*	Adventure	Spell	0.05
Meteor Impact	Adventure	Power/Find	0.05
Mirage Mangler	Banemaster	Marauder	0.05

18

Card name	Type	Rarity	Price
Mirror Image*	Adventure	Spell	0.05
Monarch Crown	Adventure	Treasure	0.05
Monster Strength	Adventure	Potion	0.05
Mud Gobbler	Banemaster	Marauder	0.05
Nightmare Breath	Adventure	Potion	0.05
Oak Table	Banemaster	Feature	0.05
Old Master	Adventure	Treasure	0.05
Onyx Candle Sticks	Adventure	Treasure	0.05
Orb Of State	Adventure	Treasure	0.05

19

Card name	Type	Rarity	Price
Oubliette	Banemaster	Place	0.05
Overdoor Weight	Banemaster	Trap	0.05
Pan's Pig Statue	Adventure	Treasure	0.05
Pan's Pig [sic]	Adventure	Treasure	0.05
Plague Of Locusts*	Banemaster	Event	0.05
Plasma Ball	Adventure	Power/Find	0.05
Platinum Goblet	Adventure	Treasure	0.05
Platinum Orb*	Adventure	Treasure	0.05
Poison Gas Attack	Banemaster	Event	0.05

20

Card name	Type	Rarity	Price
Precious Painting	Adventure	Treasure	0.05
Princess Tiara	Adventure	Treasure	0.05
Procession Hall*	Banemaster	Place	0.05
Quarterstaff*	Adventure	Weapon	0.05
Raging Torrent*	Adventure	Power/Find	0.05
Ramhorn Catapult	Adventure	Weapon	0.05
Razor Fingers	Adventure	Weapon	0.05
Red Dragon Strike	Banemaster	Event	0.05
Red Roarer	Banemaster	Marauder	0.05

21

Card name	Type	Rarity	Price
Reptile Skin	Adventure	Potion	0.05
Rock Fall	Banemaster	Trap	0.05
Roof Terrace	Banemaster	Place	0.05
Room Lightning	Banemaster	Event	0.05
Royal Platters	Adventure	Treasure	0.05
Ruby Ring*	Adventure	Treasure	0.05

Card name	Type	Rarity	Price
Sacrifice Slab	Banemaster	Feature	0.05
Scaley Land Squid	Banemaster	Marauder	0.05
Scarecrow*	Banemaster	Marauder	0.05

22

Card name	Type	Rarity	Price
Scorpion Orc [Green]	Banemaster	Marauder	0.05
Sea Storm	Adventure	Power/Find	0.05
Seeming Growth*	Adventure	Potion	0.05
Sideboard*	Banemaster	Feature	0.05
Silver Orb*	Adventure	Treasure	0.05
Skeleton Warriors	Banemaster	Marauder	0.05
Skeleton Warriors [Scorpion Orc image]	Banemaster	Marauder	0.05
Skull Mace	Adventure	Weapon	0.05
Skunk Smell*	Adventure	Potion	0.05

23

Card name	Type	Rarity	Price
Sloth Slowness	Adventure	Potion	0.05
Snake Pit	Banemaster	Trap	0.05
Sorcerer's Study*	Banemaster	Place	0.05
Spike Ball	Banemaster	Trap	0.05
Spike-Toed Boots	Adventure	Weapon	0.05
Spiral Stabber	Adventure	Weapon	0.05
Stabbing Sword	Adventure	Weapon	0.05
Star Burst	Adventure	Spell	0.05
Star Chamber	Banemaster	Place	0.05

24

Card name	Type	Rarity	Price
Statue	Banemaster	Feature	0.05
Steel Skin*	Adventure	Potion	0.05
Stiletto	Adventure	Weapon	0.05
Stone Corridor	Banemaster	Place	0.05
Stone Crusher	Banemaster	Marauder	0.05
Straining Face	Adventure	Power/Find	0.05
Sucking Slug*	Banemaster	Marauder	0.05
Sudden Vacuum*	Banemaster	Event	0.05
Tapestry Room*	Banemaster	Place	0.05

25

Card name	Type	Rarity	Price
Throne Room*	Banemaster	Place	0.05
Throwing Stars	Adventure	Weapon	0.05
Tomahawk	Adventure	Weapon	0.05
Tornado	Adventure	Power/Find	0.05
Tornado Blades	Banemaster	Marauder	0.05
Torture Chamber	Banemaster	Place	0.05
Trap Door	Banemaster	Trap	0.05
Trapped In Limbo	Banemaster	Event	0.05
Treacle Air*	Adventure	Spell	0.05

26

Card name	Type	Rarity	Price
Treasure Chest	Adventure	Treasure	0.05
Tree In Wind	Adventure	Power/Find	0.05
Trip Wire*	Banemaster	Trap	0.05
Trunk	Banemaster	Feature	0.05
Turn To Stone	Adventure	Spell	0.05
Twin Headed Viper	Banemaster	Marauder	0.05
Two Eye Stabber	Adventure	Weapon	0.05
Volcano	Adventure	Power/Find	0.05
Wall Niche*	Banemaster	Feature	0.05

27

Card name	Type	Rarity	Price
Water Wheel	Adventure	Power/Find	0.05
Waterfall	Adventure	Power/Find	0.05
Weapon Fumble	Adventure	Spell	0.05
Well Chamber	Banemaster	Place	0.05
Whirlpool	Adventure	Power/Find	0.05
Wild Pearl Ring	Adventure	Treasure	0.05
Zombie Big Bat*	Banemaster	Marauder	0.05

Power/find cards

Power/Find cards don't have names on them, but the manufactiurer's released list does note names like **Raging Torrent**, **Whirlpool**, and **Lava Flow in Dark**. We have done our best to reconcile the actual cards with these names by looking at the art, but we can't guarantee that our **Cosmic Vortex** is their **Cosmic Vortex**. We still wind up with a card count that does not match their announced figure of 234.

*Asterisks denote cards on the manufacturer's card list which have not yet been confirmed to exist.

Battlelords

New Millennium • Released August 1995

335 cards in set

Concept	●●●○○
Gameplay	●●●○○
Card art	●●●○○
Player pool	○○○○○

- Starter decks contain 60 cards; starter displays contain 10 starters
- Booster packs contain 15 cards; booster displays contain 36 boosters

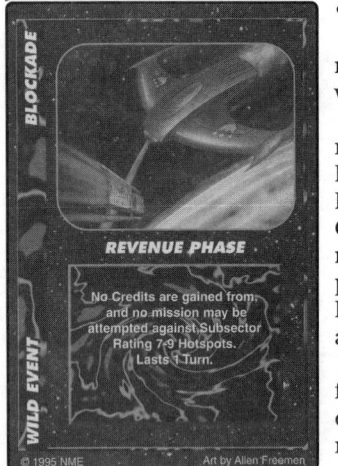

The **Battlelords** collectible card game is based on the role-playing game of the same name from Optimus Design Systems. The CCG remains very loyal to the RPG setting, which had a small but hardcore following.

Battlelords is novel in that it is one of the first (if not the first) CCG to use two separate decks in game play, the Fame deck and the Fortune deck. The Fame deck contains Hotspots, Missions, Wild cards, and Battle cards, while the Fortune deck contains Battlelords, PUDs ("Personnel Under Development"), Equipment, Matrices, and Operations. The object of the game is to gain Fame points. The Commander with the most Fame points above a preset goal at the end of a full turn wins the game. Fame points are earned by assigning Squads to complete Missions against an opponents' Hotspots, Operations, and Squads. The Skirmish system is simple and straightforward, a comparison of strength of Ranged or Melee values against Defense value of Squads.

Battlelords never really caught on beyond the core following generated by the RPG fans and vanished quickly into the 1995 CCG glut. An **Unlimited Edition** and an expansion, **Genesis**, were announced for release in September 1995 and May 1996 repetively, but we've found no eveidence that they ever came out. — *James A. Mishler*

Set (335 cards)	125.00
Starter Display Box	18.00
Booster Display Box	20.00
Starter Deck	3.50
Booster Pack	1.50

You will need **38** nine-pocket pages to store this set. (19 doubled up)

Card name	Type	Rarity	Price
Abel	Hotspot	C	0.20
Aeodronian Incursion	Wild Event	U	1.80
Aeodronian Invasion	Wild Event	R	5.30
Alliance Auxiliary	Operation	R	5.30
Alliance Crackdown	Wild Event	R	5.30
Alliance Experiment	Mission	R	5.30
Alpha-2	Hotspot	C	0.20
Ambush	Battle	R	5.30
Amperon	Equipment	R	5.30
Amplified Reflexes	Equipment	R	5.30
Analyze Defense	Matrix	U	0.60
Annogrebia	Hotspot	U	0.60
Anti-Aeodronian Sorte	Mission	R	5.30
Anti-Arachnid Sorte	Mission	U	1.30
Anti-Insurgent	Mission	C	0.20
Anti-Synthetic	Mission	U	0.60
Anti-Terrorism	Mission	C	0.20
Antidote	Wild Event	U	1.80
Arachnid Invasion	Wild Event	R	5.30
Arash-iki	Battlelord	U	0.60
Ariel	Battlelord	U	0.80
ARM Connections	Operation	R	5.30
Armorer	Operation	U	1.30
Arms Dealer	Operation	U	0.60
Artemis Raila	Battlelord	C	0.20
Assassination	Mission	U	1.80
Assizzian Palm	Matrix	C	0.20
Astral Travel	Matrix	R	5.30
Auckland	Hotspot	C	0.20
Auto Doc	Equipment	U	0.60
Balshrom	Hotspot	C	0.20
Balshrom Banshee Laser Rifle	Equipment	R	5.30
Bank Folds	Wild Event	R	5.30
Bar Room Brawl	Wild Event	R	5.30
Battlefield Promotion	Wild Event	U	1.80
BC-Blister Chaingun	Equipment	U	0.60
Berserk	Matrix	C	0.20

Card name	Type	Rarity	Price
Beta Delphis	Hotspot	U	0.80
Big Lou	Battlelord	U	1.10
Binghamton	Hotspot	C	0.20
Black Market	Operation	U	0.60
Black Widow	Battlelord	C	0.20
Blacklisted	Wild Event	R	3.50
Blessing	Matrix	C	0.20
Blockade	Wild Event	C	0.20
Bloody Pool	Battlelord	R	5.30
Blue Razor	Battlelord	U	0.80
Botch	Battlelord	Chase	8.50
Bounty Hunter	Operation	C	0.20
Brewery	Operation	R	5.30
Browning .50 Machine Gun	Equipment	C	0.20
Bunker	Equipment	U	0.80
Called Shot: Head	Battle	R	5.30
Careful Aim	Battle	U	1.00
Chainsaw	Equipment	C	0.20
Chatilian Psychic	PUD	C	0.20
Chatilian Seer	PUD	C	0.20
Chatilian Sender	PUD	C	0.20
Chilled Veins	Matrix	C	0.20
Civilian Security Sweep	Wild Event	C	0.20
Cizerack Heroine	PUD	U	0.60
Cizerack Huntress	PUD	R	5.30
Cizerack Runner	PUD	U	0.60
Cizerack Scout	PUD	U	0.60
Coandas	Hotspot	C	0.20
Cobra XM2 Omega Cannon	Equipment	R	5.30
Cole Creeg	Battlelord	U	0.60
Computer Theft	Wild Event	U	0.80
Connec	Hotspot	C	0.20
Cornered	Wild Event	C	0.20
Corporate Center	Operation	U	0.60
Cosmolakis	Battlelord	Chase	8.50
Counter Espionage: Alliance	Mission	U	1.10
Counter Espionage: Rebels	Mission	U	0.60
Cover	Battle	C	0.20
Credit Card	Wild Event	U	0.90
Critical Hit	Battle	R	5.30
Crossfire	Battle	U	1.80
Crouch	Battle	U	0.80
Cyber Ghouls	Wild Event	U	0.90
Cyber Rejection	Wild Event	U	0.80
Cyrion Zakka	Battlelord	C	0.20

Card name	Type	Rarity	Price
Dakarious	Battlelord	R	5.30
Decoy	Battle	R	5.30
Defection	Wild Event	U	0.80
Dermal Armor	Equipment	U	1.10
Desperate Evasion	Battle	U	0.60
Destroig War Chassis	Equipment	R	5.30
DFMS-401	Equipment	U	1.30
Disarm	Battle	U	0.60
Disinformation	Wild Event	U	0.90
Disruption	Matrix	U	0.60
Dodge	Battle	C	0.20
Dr. Mayhem	Battlelord	U	0.80
Draw	Battle	R	5.30
Drendlets	Hotspot	U	0.60
Drenels	Hotspot	C	0.20
Ectoplasm	Matrix	U	0.60
Edtne	Hotspot	C	0.20
EMP Grenade	Equipment	U	0.90
Energy Barrier	Matrix	C	0.20
Energy Cloud	Matrix	R	5.30
Energy Mace	Equipment	C	0.20
Eridam	Battlelord	U	0.60
Eridani Budaish	PUD	U	0.80
Eridani Budaish-Thralek	PUD	R	5.30
Eridani Kimikasous	PUD	C	0.20
Escape	Wild Event	R	5.30
Escort	Mission	U	0.80
Espionage: Alliance	Mission	U	0.80
Espionage: Dra Consulate	Mission	R	5.30
Espionage: Tecreaseans	Mission	R	5.30
Essence Transfer	Matrix	R	5.30
Evance	Hotspot	R	5.30
Executioner	Battlelord	R	5.30
Exoskeleton	Equipment	C	0.20
Exploration	Mission	R	3.10
False Lead	Wild Event	U	0.90
Fan Out	Battle	C	0.20
Fansar Essar	Battlelord	C	0.60
Faraway	Hotspot	C	0.20
Fatigued	Battle	U	0.60
Fear	Hotspot	C	0.20
Fear	Matrix	C	0.20
Feature Article	Wild Event	R	3.10
Feint	Battle	C	0.20
Field Reporter	Operation	R	5.30

Card name	Type	Rarity	Price
Financier	Operation	R	5.30
Food Broker	Operation	C	0.20
Forced Retreat	Wild Event	R	2.80
Frag Grenade	Equipment	R	5.30
Frenzy	Battle	R	5.30
Full Auto	Battle	U	0.60
Gen Human Navigator	PUD	U	0.60
Gen Human Pilot	PUD	C	0.20
Gen Human Radio Operator	PUD	C	0.20
Generation Armor	Equipment	U	1.30
Genetic Virus: Eridani	Wild Event	R	5.30
Genetic Virus: Gen Human	Wild Event	R	5.30
Genetic Virus: Orion Rogue	Wild Event	R	5.30
Genetic Virus: Phentari	Wild Event	R	3.50
Genetic Virus: Ram Python	Wild Event	R	5.30
Ghalak	Hotspot	C	0.20
Grandle Hospis	Hotspot	U	0.50
Granny	Battlelord	C	0.20
Grendel	Battlelord	Chase	8.50
Grom's Warrior	Matrix	R	5.30
Gronk	Battlelord	U	0.80
Guard Duty	Mission	U	1.00
Gun Runner	Operation	U	0.60
Gun Running	Mission	U	1.30
Hand of Fate	Wild Event	U	2.80
Harper's World	Hotspot	C	0.20
Heartless	Matrix	R	3.00
High-Tech Security Sweep	Wild Event	R	4.50
HUD-A Scan Unit	Equipment	R	4.50
Huma	Hotspot	C	0.20
Human Cyborg	PUD	C	0.20
Human Security Officer	PUD	U	0.80
Human Trader	PUD	C	0.20
Hunter Bane	Battlelord	C	0.20
Infiltration Armor	Equipment	R	5.30
Interdiction	Mission	U	1.80
Internal Security	Operation	C	0.20
Iron Will	Battle	R	5.30
Jaloon	Hotspot	C	0.10
Jam	Battle	R	5.30
Jaquassarrious (Face Shot)	Battlelord	R	5.30
Jaquassarrious (Pilot)	Battlelord	R	5.30
Jarred Makhouse	Battlelord	U	0.80
Jilleal	Hotspot	C	0.20
Just A Flesh Wound	Battle	R	5.30
Kamakazi	Battle	R	5.30
Kamo	Battlelord	U	0.80
Kasaandre	Battlelord	C	0.20
Kente	Hotspot	C	0.20
Kermadec	Hotspot	C	0.20
Killing's Asteroid	Hotspot	C	0.20
Kla	Battlelord	U	0.80
Kodiak Armor	Equipment	R	5.30
Krisr	Hotspot	C	0.20
Krytea Naval Yard	Hotspot	U	0.60
Liaison: Krakeds	Mission	R	5.30
Liaison: Sheustron	Mission	R	5.30
Line of Credit	Wild Event	U	1.80
Loan	Wild Event	R	5.30
Loan Shark	Operation	R	5.30
Loan Shark Busted	Wild Event	R	5.30
Locate Missing Person	Mission	C	0.20
Madd Mike	Battlelord	R	5.30
Madd Mike's Brochure	Wild Event	U	2.30
Maelstrom General	Wild Event	R	5.30
Makin	Hotspot	C	0.20
Malfunction	Wild Event	R	5.30
Malik Kazat	Battlelord	Chase	8.50
Mass Healing	Matrix	U	0.80
Massive BRI	Equipment	C	0.20
Maximizer Autocannon	Equipment	R	5.30
Mayday	Wild Event	U	0.60
Mazian Shapechanger	PUD	C	0.20
Mazian Spy	PUD	C	0.20
MDD-24	Equipment	R	5.30
Mechanized Battle Armor	Equipment	R	5.30
Medal of Honor	Wild Event	U	1.80
Medical Center	Operation	R	2.80
Medicine Courier	Mission	R	5.30
Mentio	Hotspot	C	0.20
Mighty Blow	Battle	U	1.80
Military Security Sweep	Wild Event	U	1.50
Mind Probe Station	Operation	C	0.20
Mind Strangle	Matrix	U	1.80
Misery	Hotspot	C	0.20
Mutzachan Beta Controller	PUD	U	0.60
Mutzachan Particle Controller	PUD	R	5.30
Mutzachan Proton Controller	PUD	C	0.20
Naxtar	Hotspot	U	0.60
Negation	Matrix	U	1.30
Nephgia 6	Hotspot	C	0.20
New Recruits	Wild Event	U	0.90
Nitros	Hotspot	U	0.60
Nrell	Hotspot	U	0.60
Odak	Battlelord	R	6.30
Off Balance	Battle	U	0.60
Omus	Hotspot	U	1.80
Ophea	Hotspot	C	0.20
Orion Rogue Cat Burglar	PUD	U	0.60
Orion Rogue Sniper	PUD	U	1.80
Orion Rogue Thief	PUD	C	0.20
Orion Rogue Traveler	PUD	U	1.80
Pain	Matrix	C	0.20
Pain Inhibition Serum	Equipment	U	0.60
Parry	Battle	C	0.20
Partial Concealment	Battle	U	1.80
Peacemaker Support	Wild Event	R	5.30
Personal Vendetta	Mission	C	0.20
Phelinssarious	Battlelord	C	0.20
Phentari Assassin	PUD	R	5.30
Phentari Gengineer	PUD	R	5.30
Phentari Militant	PUD	R	5.30
Phentari Phreak	PUD	R	5.30
Phentari Predator	PUD	R	5.30
Piracy	Mission	C	0.20
Plasma Grenade	Equipment	R	5.30
Plasmoid Devourer	Wild Event	R	5.30
Point Blank	Battle	U	0.60
Position Compromised	Wild Event	C	0.20
Power Arm	Equipment	C	0.20
Price Went Up	Wild Event	C	0.20
Prof. Hezba	Battlelord	U	0.60
Psychic Force	Matrix	R	5.30
Puringa	Hotspot	C	0.20
Python Barbarian	PUD	R	5.30
Python Cub	PUD	U	1.30
Python Demolisher	PUD	U	1.30
Python Interrogator	PUD	R	5.30
Python Punk	PUD	U	0.90
Quarmiss	Battlelord	C	0.20
Raalehr	Battlelord	R	2.80
Raise Dead	Matrix	U	1.80
Ram Berserker	PUD	R	5.30
Ram Commando	PUD	R	3.10
Ram Enforcer	PUD	R	5.30
Ram Gunner	PUD	R	5.30
Ram Halfbreed	PUD	C	0.20
Ram Runt	PUD	U	0.90
Ram Soldier	PUD	R	5.30
Rebel Negotiations	Mission	U	1.50
Rebel Sympathizer	Operation	U	0.60
Reincarnate	Matrix	R	5.30
Rescue Refugees	Mission	U	0.60
Riot	Wild Event	C	0.20
RKM Showtime Pulse Cannon	Equipment	R	5.30
Rush Axnor	Battlelord	R	2.80
Sabrine	Battlelord	C	0.20
Sarge Dowe	Battlelord	C	0.20
Scrub Mission	Wild Event	R	5.30
Search and Destroy	Mission	C	0.20
Second Chance	Wild Event	C	0.20
Seek Ancient Knowledge	Mission	C	0.20
Short Burst	Battle	U	0.60
Slagger Thunderbolt Generator	Equipment	U	1.80
Slanger	Hotspot	C	0.20
Slave License	Operation	U	0.60
Slaver	Operation	U	0.60
Smoke Grenade	Equipment	R	5.30
Smuggler	Operation	U	0.60
Snapshot	Battle	C	0.20
Spy Satellite	Operation	R	5.30
Ssithiss	Hotspot	C	0.20
Steal Arcane Secrets	Mission	C	0.20
Strike Team Omega	Mission	C	0.20
Subsector HQ	Operation	R	5.30
Sueimma	Hotspot	C	0.20
Suicide Bomb	Wild Event	R	5.30
Surprise	Battle	C	0.20
Surveillance	Mission	R	5.30
Tactics Shift	Wild Event	C	0.20
Talberma	Hotspot	C	0.20
Targeting Eye	Equipment	U	0.60
Tecreasean Incursion	Wild Event	U	0.60
Telnik Dxtar	Battlelord	C	0.20
Terrorism	Mission	C	0.20
The Bossman	Battlelord	C	0.20
The Butcher	Battlelord	U	0.80
Theft	Wild Event	U	0.60
Thwack'em Stick	Equipment	C	0.20
Time Slow	Matrix	R	5.30
Todek	Battlelord	U	0.60
Tokk	Battlelord	R	5.30
Trade Minds	Matrix	U	0.80
Trade Negotiations	Mission	U	0.60
Trader	Operation	U	0.60
Training Facility	Operation	R	5.30
Traitor	Wild Event	C	0.20
Trick Shot	Battle	U	0.60
Tsa Zen Defiler	PUD	R	5.30
Tsa Zen Hacker	PUD	U	1.80
Tsa Zen Warlock	PUD	C	0.20
Ugram	Battlelord	U	0.80
Uottre	Hotspot	C	0.20
Urgent Mission	Wild Event	U	0.60
Uro's World	Hotspot	R	5.30
Ward of Assizza	Matrix	U	1.80
Water Broker	Operation	C	0.20
Weapons Factory	Operation	U	0.60
Weapons Permit	Equipment	U	0.80
Weapons Sale	Wild Event	C	0.20
Worm Hole	Matrix	R	5.30
Wrist Rockets	Equipment	R	5.30
"Wrong Place, Wrong Time"	Wild Event	R	5.30
Xelan Peacemaker	Battlelord	U	0.60
Xxipt	Hotspot	C	0.20
Yeppter	Hotspot	C	0.20
Zen Medic	PUD	R	2.80
Zero-G Lab	Operation	R	5.30

RARITY KEY C = Common U = Uncommon R = Rare VR = Very Rare UR = Ultra Rare F = Foil card X = Fixed/standard in all decks

Battletech

Wizards of the Coast under license from **FASA** • First set, **Limited**, released **November 1996**
283 cards in set • **IDENTIFIER: Black border on cards**

- Starter decks contain 60 cards, one rulebook, one First Game Guide, and one six-sided die
- Starter displays contain 12 decks
- Booster packs contain 15 cards; booster displays contain 36 boosters

Designed by **Richard Garfield, Charlie Curita, Glenn Elliot,** and **William Jockush**

BattleTech is one of the most popular science-fiction properties ever to come from gaming. Over the years, FASA has developed an intricate setting that spawned a long line of *BattleTech* games, supplements, and adventures as well as a line of computer games. It was only natural that the property would see release as a collectible card game, and its announced production by Wizards of the Coast was heralded by many as a vision of the benefits fans would enjoy from future cooperation among game companies. (The game came out much later than the announcement, so it must not have been *that* easy.)

The ***BattleTech Trading Card Game*** that came out in late 1996 has three basic card types. The 'Mech cards represent the dozens of different combat vehicles of the BattleTech universe. Command cards provide resources, personnel, equipment, and other devices central to pursuing the overall strategic goals of the game. Finally, the Mission cards enable the player to modify the action at the tactical level by modifying the battles between the various 'Mechs during their mission runs. Play is generally similar to that of a Deckmaster game in that the Command Resource cards are played and tapped to generate resources, which are in turn used to deploy 'Mechs. 'Mech construction can take several turns, unlike the standard summoning function in ***Magic***.

'Mechs are used to attack an opponent's 'Mechs, resource locations, deck (called the Stockpile), or discard pile (called the Scrapheap). 'Mechs tap when attacking and also when defending (unlike in *Magic*) Damage from a 'Mech is reduced by armor and unless a weapon is very powerful or a 'Mech is relatively weak, damage accrues to the target through the use of counters. Each card that can be attacked has a Structure value; cards with damage counters equal to their Structure are sent to the Scrapheap. Undefended attacks against the stockpile move a number of cards from the Stockpile to the Scrapheap equal to the damage dealt; a player loses the game when they must and cannot draw a card from their deck, which includes occasions where a 'Mech damages a Stockpile and cards must go to the Scrapheap. Other rules, such as Overheat, Alpha Strike, and Missile attacks help bring the feel of the original game to the CCG format.

BattleTech eventually saw the release of five expansions and three editions over the two years of its run. It never really caught a broad audience as it was felt by many *BattleTech* players to be a "poor cousin" and by many *Magic* players to be a poor substitute. This is unfortunate, since judged on its own, it's an admirable SF-based trading card game. — *James A. Mishler*

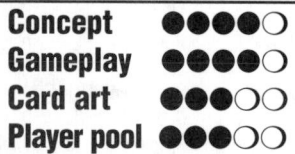

Concept	●●●●○
Gameplay	●●●●○
Card art	●●●○○
Player pool	●●●○○

Battletech • Unlimited

Wizards of the Coast, under license from **FASA** • Released **February 1997**
283 cards in set • **IDENTIFIER: Teal-blue border on cards**

- Starter decks contain 60 cards, one rulebook, one First Game Guide, and one six-sided die
- Starter displays contain 12 decks
- Booster packs contain 15 cards; booster displays contain 36 boosters

The ***Unlimited Edition*** of ***BattleTech*** differs only slightly from the **Limited Edition**.

The cards are the same, save for text changes in 37 cards. The only other difference (and the one you'll obviously use) is the border color: The *Unlimited* cards have a teal-blue border. Prices and checklists for both sets are included below.

> You will need
> **32**
> nine-pocket pages to store **EACH** set.
> (16 doubled up)

LIMITED (Black Border)		UNLIMITED (Blue Border)	
Set (283 cards)	270.00	Set (283 cards)	225.00
Starter Display Box	97.00	Starter Display Box	70.00
Booster Display Box	107.00	Booster Display Box	60.00
Starter Deck	9.50	Starter Deck	9.00
Booster Pack	3.50	Booster Pack	3.20

LIMITED	Card name	Type	Rarity	UNLIMITED
□ 0.25	Accurate Intelligence	Mission	C	0.15 □
□ 0.25	Aerospace Fighter Mission	Command	C	0.15 □
□ 8.00	Alex Mallory	Command	R	4.30 □

LIMITED	Card name	Type	Rarity	UNLIMITED
□ 0.25	Ambush!	Command	C	0.15 □
□ 1.00	Ammo Explosion	Mission	U	0.60 □
□ 4.00	Arms Reduction	Command	R	3.30 □
□ 1.00	Arrow IV Battery	Command	U	0.60 □
□ 1.00	Assassin ASN-21	Mech	U	0.60 □
□ 0.25	Atlas AS7-D	Mech	C	0.15 □
□ 5.00	Atlas AS7-K	Mech	R	4.00 □
□ 0.25	Awesome AWS-8Q	Mech	C	0.15 □
□ 0.25	Awesome AWS-9M	Mech	C	0.15 □
□ 5.50	Axman AXM-1N	Mech	R	4.30 □
□ 1.00	Banshee BNC-3E	Mech	U	0.60 □

LIMITED	Card name	Type	Rarity	UNLIMITED
0.25	Banshee BNC-5S	Mech	C	0.15
1.00	Battalion Support	Command	U	0.60
5.00	Bearer of McKennsy Hammer	Command	R	3.50
8.50	Bjorn Jorgensson	Command	R	5.00
0.25	Black Hawk A Nova	Mech	C	0.15
0.25	Black Hawk B Nova	Mech	C	0.15
0.25	Black Hawk D Nova	Mech	C	0.15
0.25	Black Hawk Prime Nova	Mech	C	0.15
1.00	Black Knight BL6-KNT	Mech	U	0.60
0.25	Blackjack BJ2	Mech	C	0.15
0.25	Caesar CES-3R	Mech	C	0.15
7.50	Candace Liao	Command	R	4.00
1.00	Cataphract CTF-3D	Mech	U	0.60
0.25	Catapult CPLT-C3	Mech	C	0.15
0.25	Caught in Hangar	Command	C	0.15
0.25	Centurion CN9-A	Mech	C	0.15
1.00	Centurion CN9-D	Mech	U	0.60
1.00	Chaparral Missile Tank	Command	U	0.60
1.00	Charger CGR-1A1	Mech	U	0.60
0.25	Cicada CDA-2A	Mech	C	0.15
0.25	Cicada CDA-3M	Mech	C	0.15
1.00	Clint CLNT-2-3T	Mech	U	0.60
1.00	Clint CLNT-2-3U	Mech	U	0.60
1.00	Combat Engineers	Command	U	0.60
0.25	Commando COM-2D	Mech	C	0.15
1.00	Communications Blackout	Command	U	0.60
4.50	Communications Failure	Mission	R	3.50
1.00	Comstar Bank Account	Command	U	0.60
5.00	Contract with Gray Death Legion	Command	R	3.30
5.00	Contract with Wolf's Dragoons	Command	R	3.80
2.70	Coventry Metal Works	Command	V	0.50
0.25	Critical Hit	Mission	C	0.15
1.00	Crockett CRK-5003-1	Mech	U	0.60
4.50	Culling	Command	R	3.80
0.25	Cyclops CP11A	Mech	C	0.15
12.00	Daishi A Dire Wolf	Mech	R	6.50
1.00	Dasher C Firemoth	Mech	U	0.60
0.25	Dasher D Firemoth	Mech	C	0.15
0.25	Dasher Prime Firemoth	Mech	C	0.15
4.50	Death Commando Strike	Command	R	3.80
1.00	Death From Above	Mission	U	0.60
0.25	Dervish DV-6M	Mech	C	0.15
0.25	Dervish DV-7D	Mech	C	0.15
5.00	DEST Pilot	Command	R	4.80
0.25	Dragon DRG-1N	Mech	C	0.15
5.00	Dragonfly A Viper	Mech	R	4.30
1.00	Dragonfly B Viper	Mech	U	0.60
1.00	Dragonfly C Viper	Mech	U	0.60
1.00	Dragonfly D Viper	Mech	U	0.60
1.00	Dragonfly Prime Viper	Mech	U	0.60
1.00	Dropship Site	Command	U	0.60
1.00	Effective Groundwork	Command	U	0.80
1.00	Elemental Point	Command	U	0.60
5.90	Elias Crichell	Command	R	4.00
4.50	Elite Infantry	Command	R	3.50
1.10	Elite MechWarrior	Command	U	0.80
0.25	Enforcer ENF-4R	Mech	C	0.15
0.25	Enforcer ENF-5D	Mech	C	0.15
5.00	Evantha Fetladral	Command	R	4.30
0.25	Expert 'Mech Technicians	Command	C	0.15
1.00	Exterminator EXT-4D	Mech	U	0.60
0.25	Extra Armor Plating	Command	C	0.15
1.00	Falcon FLC-4P	Mech	U	0.60
0.25	Feint	Mission	C	0.15
1.00	Fenris A Ice Ferret	Mech	U	0.60
0.25	Fenris C Ice Ferret	Mech	C	0.15
0.25	Fenris D Ice Ferret	Mech	C	0.15
0.25	Fenris Prime Ice Ferret	Mech	C	0.15
0.25	Ferro-Fibrous Armor	Command	C	0.15
0.25	Firestarter FS9-H	Mech	C	0.15

LIMITED	Card name	Type	Rarity	UNLIMITED
6.00	Firestarter FS9-S	Mech	R	3.80
5.00	Flashman FLS-8K	Mech	R	3.80
1.00	Flea FLE-17	Mech	U	0.60
0.25	Forged Mission Orders	Mission	C	0.15
7.30	Galen Cox	Command	R	4.80
1.00	Gladiator A Executioner	Mech	U	0.60
6.00	Gladiator B Executioner	Mech	R	4.30
1.00	Gladiator C Executioner	Mech	U	0.60
0.25	Gladiator Prime Executioner	Mech	C	0.15
0.25	Good Shooting!	Mission	C	0.15
0.25	Grand Dragon DRG-5K	Mech	C	0.15
0.25	Grasshopper GHR-5H	Mech	C	0.15
1.00	Gray Death Pilot	Command	U	0.60
7.20	Grayson Death Carlyle	Command	R	4.30
4.50	Guerrilla Support	Command	R	4.00
4.00	Guillotine GLT-5M	Mech	R	3.50
9.00	"Hanse Davion ""The Fox"""	Command	R	4.30
1.00	Hatamoto-Chi HTM-27T	Mech	U	0.60
0.25	Hatchetman HCT-3F	Mech	C	0.15
1.00	Hatchetman HCT-5S	Mech	U	0.60
1.00	Head Shot	Mission	U	0.60
1.00	Heavy Fog	Mission	U	0.60
3.10	Heavy Industry	Command	V	0.50
0.25	Helicopter Support	Command	C	0.15
0.25	Heroic Sacrifice	Mission	C	0.15
5.00	Highlander HGN-732	Mech	R	3.80
0.25	Holographic Decoy	Command	C	0.15
4.50	Hoplite HOP-4D	Mech	R	3.30
1.00	Hornet HNT-171	Mech	U	0.60
0.25	Hovertank Detachment	Command	C	0.15
0.25	Hunchback HBK-4G	Mech	C	0.15
1.00	Hussar HSR 200-D	Mech	U	0.60
1.00	Imp IMP-3E	Mech	U	0.60
1.00	Improvised Weapon	Mission	U	0.60
0.25	Inexorable Advance	Mission	C	0.15
1.00	Infantry Platoon	Command	U	0.60
0.25	Inside Job	Command	C	0.15
5.00	ISF Counterespionage	Command	R	5.00
0.25	JagerMech JM6-DD	Mech	C	0.15
0.25	JagerMech JM6-S	Mech	C	0.15
8.00	Jaime Wolf	Command	R	4.80
0.25	Javelin JVN-10N	Mech	C	0.15
0.25	Jenner JR7-D	Mech	C	0.15
1.00	Jump into Cover	Mission	U	0.60
8.50	Justin Xiang Allard	Command	R	4.50
10.00	Kai Allard-Liao	Command	R	4.80
1.00	Kamikaze MechWarrior	Command	U	0.60
0.25	Katana CRK5003-2	Mech	C	0.15
1.00	Kell Hound Pilot	Command	U	0.60
5.00	Koshi A Mist Lynx	Mech	R	4.50
0.25	Koshi B Mist Lynx	Mech	C	0.15
4.50	Koshi C Mist Lynx	Mech	R	4.30
1.00	Koshi D Mist Lynx	Mech	U	0.60
0.25	Koshi Prime Mist Lynx	Mech	C	0.15
1.00	Lance Commander	Command	U	0.60
4.50	Lancelot LNC25-01	Mech	R	3.50
1.00	Leap Before You Look	Mission	U	0.60
6.30	Leo Showers	Command	R	4.30
1.00	Loki A Hellbringer	Mech	U	0.60
1.00	Loki B Hellbringer	Mech	U	0.60
1.00	Loki Prime Hellbringer	Mech	U	0.60
0.25	Long Range Targeting System	Command	C	0.15
1.00	Long Tom Battery	Command	U	0.60
3.60	Luck of the Fox	Mission	R	3.30
1.00	Lured into Bog	Mission	U	0.60
1.00	Mad Cat A Timber Wolf	Mech	U	0.60
1.00	Mad Cat B Timber Wolf	Mech	U	0.60
6.00	Mad Cat C Timber Wolf	Mech	R	3.80
1.00	Mad Cat D Timber Wolf	Mech	U	0.60
0.25	Mad Cat Prime Timber Wolf	Mech	C	0.15

RARITY KEY C = Common U = Uncommon R = Rare VR = Very Rare UR = Ultra Rare F = Foil card X = Fixed/standard in all decks

LIMITED	Card name	Type	Rarity	UNLIMITED
5.00	Man O' War A Gargoyle	Mech	R	4.50
5.00	Man O' War B Gargoyle	Mech	R	4.30
5.50	Man O' War C Gargoyle	Mech	R	4.30
0.25	Man O' War Prime Gargoyle	Mech	C	0.15
1.00	Maneuvering Ace	Command	U	0.60
4.50	Manipulation of Romano	Command	R	3.30
3.00	Marik Arms Trade	Command	V	0.50
6.80	Marissa Morgan	Command	R	4.50
0.25	Masakari A Warhawk	Mech	C	0.15
1.00	Masakari B Warhawk	Mech	U	0.60
6.00	Masakari C Warhawk	Mech	R	4.30
4.80	Masakari Prime Warhawk	Mech	R	3.50
1.00	MASC	Command	U	0.60
4.50	Maskirovka Operatives	Command	R	3.80
0.25	Master Spy	Command	C	0.15
5.00	Mauler MAL-1R	Mech	R	4.30
1.00	Maverick Mechjock	Command	U	0.60
8.50	Melissa Steiner Davion	Command	R	4.50
1.00	Mercury MCY-97	Mech	U	0.60
1.00	Mislabeled Drop Boxes	Command	U	0.60
0.25	Misrouted Command	Command	C	0.15
1.00	Missile Spotter	Mission	U	0.60
0.25	Mobile HQ	Command	C	0.15
1.00	Mongoose MON-66	Mech	U	0.60
8.00	Morgan Hasek Davion	Command	R	4.50
8.10	Morgan Kell	Command	R	4.50
0.25	Move to Partial Cover	Mission	C	0.15
3.00	NAIS	Command	V	0.50
13.50	Natasha Kerensky	Command	R	6.50
1.00	Navigation Computer	Command	U	0.60
4.30	Open Supply Lines	Command	R	4.30
1.00	Operation Advisory Council	Command	U	0.60
1.00	Orion ON1-K	Mech	U	0.60
5.00	Orion ON1-M	Mech	R	3.80
1.00	Overwhelm	Mission	U	0.60
0.25	Panther PNT-9R	Mech	C	0.15
4.80	Perimeter Alarm	Command	R	3.50
1.00	Phantom Signal	Command	U	0.60
8.30	Phelan	Command	R	5.00
0.25	Point Defense System	Command	C	0.15
5.00	Pryde's Pride	Mission	R	4.30
0.25	Puma A Adder	Mech	C	0.15
1.10	Puma C Adder	Mech	U	0.60
0.25	Puma Prime Adder	Mech	C	0.15
1.00	Pushing the Envelope	Mission	U	0.60
0.25	Quickdraw QKD-4G	Mech	C	0.15
0.25	Quickdraw QKD-5M	Mech	C	0.15
5.00	Rampage!	Mission	R	4.50
1.10	Rapid Cool-Down	Mission	U	0.60
1.00	Raven RVN-3L	Mech	U	0.60
4.50	Reassigned Pilot	Mission	R	4.30
4.80	Report from the Watch	Command	R	4.30
1.00	Retrieve Lost 'Mech	Command	U	0.60
1.00	Retrofitted Laser System	Command	U	0.60
1.00	Retrofitted Missile Rack	Command	U	0.60
6.50	Romano Liao	Command	R	4.50
4.50	Rookie Pilot	Command	R	3.50
1.00	Running Battle	Mission	U	0.60
1.00	Ryoken A Storm Crow	Mech	U	0.60
1.00	Ryoken D Storm Crow	Mech	U	0.80

LIMITED	Card name	Type	Rarity	UNLIMITED
0.25	Ryoken Prime Storm Crow	Mech	C	0.15
0.25	Sabotage 'Mech	Command	C	0.15
4.50	Sabotaged Heat Sinks	Command	R	4.30
5.00	Sabotaged Missiles	Command	R	3.80
5.00	Sacrifice for the Dragon!	Mission	R	4.80
4.50	SAFE Report	Command	R	4.30
1.00	Salvage Strike Crew	Command	U	0.60
3.80	Satchel Charges	Mission	R	3.50
0.25	Saturation Bombing	Command	C	0.15
3.00	Scrounger Crew	Command	V	0.50
1.00	Sentinel STN-3M	Mech	U	0.60
1.00	Shady Business	Command	U	0.60
5.00	Shogun SHG-2F	Mech	R	3.50
4.10	Silver Sunburst Pilot	Command	R	3.80
1.00	Special Forces Op	Mission	U	0.60
0.25	Specialized Project Team	Command	C	0.15
1.00	Spider SDR-5V	Mech	U	0.60
0.25	Stalker STK-3F	Mech	C	0.15
1.00	Stalker STK-5M	Mech	U	0.60
4.00	Steal 'Mech	Command	R	3.80
0.25	Strength of the Pillar of Steel	Mission	C	0.15
1.00	Studied Move	Mission	U	0.60
6.00	Subhash Indrahar	Command	R	3.80
2.70	Sun Zhang MechWarrior Academy	Command	V	0.50
0.50	Support: Assembly (3 versions)	Command	V	0.30
0.50	Support: Logistics (3 versions)	Command	V	0.30
0.50	Support: Munitions (3 versions)	Command	V	0.30
0.50	Support: Politics (3 versions)	Command	V	0.30
0.50	Support: Tactics (3 versions)	Command	V	0.30
8.10	Takashi Kurita	Command	R	4.00
4.00	Teachings of the Unfinished Book	Command	R	3.80
1.00	Temporary Cease-Fire	Mission	U	0.60
7.50	Theodore Kurita	Command	R	4.50
3.00	Think Tank	Command	V	0.50
6.00	Thomas Marik	Command	R	4.50
0.25	Thor A Summoner	Mech	C	0.15
4.50	Thor B Summoner	Mech	R	4.30
0.25	Thor C Summoner	Mech	C	0.15
1.00	Thor D Summoner	Mech	U	0.60
0.25	Thor Prime Summoner	Mech	C	0.15
1.00	Thug THG-11E	Mech	U	0.60
0.25	Topple	Mission	C	0.15
0.25	Treachery!	Command	C	0.15
0.25	Trebuchet TBT-5N	Mech	C	0.15
1.00	Trebuchet TBT-7M	Mech	U	0.60
6.00	Tsen Shang	Command	R	4.10
0.25	Uller B Kit Fox	Mech	C	0.15
4.00	Uller C Kit Fox	Mech	R	3.50
1.00	Uller D Kit Fox	Mech	U	0.60
0.25	Uller Prime Kit Fox	Mech	C	0.15
0.25	UrbanMech UM-R60	Mech	C	0.15
0.25	Veteran MechWarrior	Command	C	0.15
10.00	Victor Steiner Davion	Command	R	5.00
0.25	Victor VTR-9B	Mech	C	0.15
0.25	Victor VTR-9K	Mech	C	0.15
0.25	Vindicator VND-1R	Mech	C	0.15
0.25	Vulcan VT-5M	Mech	C	0.15
0.25	Vulture A Mad Dog	Mech	C	0.15
6.00	Vulture B Mad Dog	Mech	R	3.50
0.25	Vulture C Mad Dog	Mech	C	0.15
0.25	Vulture Prime Mad Dog	Mech	C	0.15
0.25	Whitworth WTH-1	Mech	C	0.15
0.25	Whitworth WTH-2	Mech	C	0.15
1.00	Wolf Dragoons Pilot	Command	U	0.60
0.25	Wolf Trap WFT-1	Mech	C	0.15
0.25	Wolfhound WLF-2	Mech	C	0.15
5.50	Wyvern WVE-5N	Mech	R	3.50
0.25	Zeus ZEU-6S	Mech	C	0.15
0.25	Zeus ZEU-9S	Mech	C	0.15

Recipe for *BattleTech*

"Take the basic resource-building mechanic from *Magic*. Take the mechanic from *Vampire* of putting counters on face-down cards before bringing them into play. Take the mechanic from *Netrunner* of allowing almost everything in play to be attacked. Improve on these mechanics and add several very elegant new ideas, and you have the *BattleTech* CCG."

— *Mike Fitzgerald, in Scrye 4.1 (Apr 97)*

RARITY KEY C = Common U = Uncommon R = Rare VR = Very Rare UR = Ultra Rare F = Foil card X = Fixed/standard in all decks

Battletech • Commander's Edition

Wizards of the Coast, under license from **FASA** • Released **August 1998**

343 cards in set • **IDENTIFIER: New design with larger card name; stats moved to left**

- Starter decks contain 60 cards, rules, metal counters, and die; starter displays contain 8 starters
- Booster packs contain 15 cards; booster displays contain 36 boosters

The **BattleTech Commander's Edition** updates the **BattleTech** CCG with changes in both rules and appearance. The new rulebook includes rulings and changes made from **Limited** through **Arsenal**; the two versions, one written from the Clan perspective, one written from that of the Inner Sphere, are identical save in flavor text.

New card fronts better reflect card function (card backs are unchanged). Asset costs are color coded for quicker identification, faction symbols are included for fast faction identification, and all the primary statistics are included in a bar on the left side of the card for higher in-hand readability. The speed characteristic is even included in a new speedometer icon as an aid for new players in determining relative speeds.

Several new cards are included in this set, notably the Faction Box Cards, which grant powerful special abilities to specific faction decks. Each faction deck also includes a special High Command card, also usable with a specific faction. These two cards combine to give straight faction decks an incredible boost in the *Commander's Edition.*

The facelift and rules compilation did not stem the sliding popularity of the game. Only one expansion, **Crusade**, followed the release of the new edition, and that expansion had been planned even as the new edition was being designed. — *James A. Mishler*

Pre-constructed decks:

- **Clan Ghost Bear**
- **Clan Jade Falcon**
- **Clan Smoke Jaguar**
- **Clan Wolf**
- **ComStar**
- **House Davion**
- **House Kurita**
- **House Steiner**

	Price
Set (343 cards)	215.00
Starter Display Box	67.50
Booster Display Box	95.00
Starter Deck	8.00
Booster Pack	3.30

You will need 39 nine-pocket pages to store this set. (20 doubled up)

Card name	Type	Rarity	Price
1			
Accelerated Turnaround	Command	U	0.50
Adam Steiner	Command	R	3.00
Aerospace Fighter Mission	Command	C	0.20
Airstrikes Close to Home	Command	U	0.50
Albatross Revised (ALB-3U)	Unit	R	4.50
Aletha Kabrinski	Command	R	4.00
Alex Mallory	Command	R	4.00
Anastasius Focht	Command	R	4.00
Annihilator (ANH-2A)	Unit	R	4.00
2			
Anvil Revised (ANV-3M)	Unit	U	0.50
Arms Reduction	Command	R	5.00
Arrow IV Battery	Command	U	0.50
Assassin (ASN-23)	Unit	U	0.80
Assault on the Rear Echelon	Command	R	5.00
Atlas (AS7-D)	Unit	C	0.20
Atlas Revised (AS7-K)	Unit	R	4.50
Avatar (AV1-OC)	Unit	U	0.50
Awesome (AWS-8Q)	Unit	C	0.20
3			
Awesome Revised (AWS-9M)	Unit	C	0.20
Bait and Switch	Mission	U	0.50
Banshee (BNC-5S)	Unit	C	0.20
Bearer of McKennsy Hammer	Command	R	5.00
Behemoth (Stone Rhino)	Unit	R	4.00
Berserker Revised (BRZ-A3)	Unit	R	4.00
Black Hawk A (Nova)	Unit	C	0.20
Black Hawk C Revised (Nova)	Unit	U	0.50
Black Hawk D (Nova)	Unit	C	0.20
4			
Black Hawk Prime (Nova)	Unit	C	0.20
Black Knight (BL6-KNT)	Unit	U	0.50
Black Lanner Prime	Unit	R	5.00
Black Market Connections	Command	U	0.50
Blackjack (BJ-2)	Unit	C	0.20
Blackjack (BJ2-OB)	Unit	U	0.50
Blitzkrieg	Mission	R	4.00
Blood of Kerensky	Command	U	0.50
Blow the Pass!	Mission	R	4.00
5			
Booty Cache	Command	R	4.00
Brutal Punch	Mission	C	0.20
C3 Retrofit	Command	U	0.50
Caesar Revised (CES-3R)	Unit	C	0.20
Candace Liao	Command	R	5.00
Catapult (CPLT-C1)	Unit	U	0.50

Card name	Type	Rarity	Price
Catapult (CPLT-C3)	Unit	C	0.20
Cauldron-Born A	Unit	R	3.50
Centurion (CN9-D)	Unit	U	0.50
6			
Cerberus (MR-V2)	Unit	U	0.50
Charger Revised (CGR-3K)	Unit	R	4.00
Cicada (CDA-3M)	Unit	C	0.20
Civilian Settlement	Command	U	0.50
Clint Revised (CLNT-2-3U)	Unit	U	0.50
Com Guard Response Team	Mission	C	0.20
Commando (COM-5S)	Unit	C	0.20
Communications Failure	Mission	R	5.00
ComStar High Command	Command	D	3.80
7			
ComStar Investment	Command	U	0.50
ComStar Support	Command	C	0.20
Contract with 21st Centauri Lancers	Command	R	5.00
Contract with Black Thorns	Command	R	3.50
Contract with Eridani Light Horse	Command	R	5.00
Contract with Gray Death Legion	Command	R	5.00
Contract with Hansen's Roughriders	Command	R	5.00
Contract with Kell Hounds	Command	R	4.00
Contract with Northwind Highlanders	Command	U	0.50
8			
Contract with Snord's Irregulars	Command	R	4.00
Coordinator Theodore Kurita	Command	R	3.00
Corridor of Fire	Command	U	0.80
Corvis	Unit	C	0.20
Coventry Metal Works	Command	U	1.00
Creative Terraforming	Command	R	4.00
Critical Hit	Mission	C	0.20
Crockett (CRK-5003-1)	Unit	U	0.50
Cyclops (CP 10-Z)	Unit	U	0.50
9			
Daikyu (DA1-01)	Unit	U	0.50
Daimyo (DMO-1K)	Unit	C	0.20
Daishi Prime (Dire Wolf)	Unit	R	5.00
Dasher B (Fire Moth)	Unit	R	4.50
Dasher Prime (Fire Moth)	Unit	C	0.20
Davion High Command	Command	D	3.80
Death Commando Strike	Command	R	4.00
Death from Above	Mission	U	0.50
Defensive Formation	Mission	C	0.20
10			
Deploy Reinforcements	Mission	C	0.20
Dervish (DV-7D)	Unit	C	0.20
Difficult Terrain	Command	U	0.50

Card name	Type	Rarity	Price
Disguised Coordinates	Command	U	0.50
Double-Time Offense	Command	U	0.50
Dr. Ariel Reed	Command	R	4.00
Dragon (DRG-1N)	Unit	C	0.20
Dragonfly A (Viper)	Unit	R	4.00
Dragonfly B (Viper)	Unit	U	0.80
11			
Dragonfly Prime (Viper)	Unit	U	0.80
DropShip Site	Command	U	0.50
Earthwerks Limited	Command	R	4.00
ECM Retrofit	Command	R	4.00
Enforcer (ENF-5D)	Unit	C	0.20
Evantha Fetladral	Command	R	4.50
Exterminator (EXT-4D)	Unit	U	0.50
Falcon Hawk (FNHK-9K1A)	Unit	C	0.20
Falconer (FLC-8R)	Unit	R	5.00
12			
Fanatical Leader	Command	U	0.50
Feint	Mission	C	0.20
Fenris C (Ice Ferret)	Unit	C	0.20
Fenris D (Ice Ferret)	Unit	C	0.20
Field Command Post	Command	U	0.50
Firefly (FFL-4B)	Unit	U	0.50
Firestarter (FS9-OD)	Unit	U	0.50
First Circuit Summons	Command	R	4.00
Flashman (FLS-8K)	Unit	R	5.00
13			
Flea (FLE-17)	Unit	U	0.50
Fog-Shrouded Moors	Command	U	0.50
For the Chancellor!	Mission	U	0.50
Forged Mission Orders	Mission	C	0.20
Galahad (Glass Spider)	Unit	C	0.20
Gallowglas (GAL-1GLS)	Unit	R	4.00
Gearhead	Command	C	0.20
Ghost Bear High Command	Command	D	3.80
Gladiator A (Executioner)	Unit	U	0.50
14			
Gladiator B (Executioner)	Unit	R	4.00
Good Shooting!	Mission	C	0.20
Grand Dragon (DRG-5K)	Unit	C	0.20
Grand Titan Revised (T-IT-N10M)	Unit	C	0.20
Grasshopper (GHR-5H)	Unit	C	0.20
Grendel Prime	Unit	C	0.20
Grim Reaper (GRM-R-PR29)	Unit	C	0.20
Guillotine (GLT-5M)	Unit	R	3.50
Gunslinger (GUN-1ERD)	Unit	U	0.50
15			
Haakon Magnusson	Command	R	5.00
Hatamoto-Chi (HTM-27T)	Unit	U	0.50
Hatchetman Revised (HCT-5S)	Unit	U	0.50
Headhunter	Command	R	4.50
Heavy Fog	Mission	U	0.50

RARITY KEY C = Common U = Uncommon R = Rare VR = Very Rare UR = Ultra Rare F = Foil card X = Fixed/standard in all decks

Card name	Type	Rarity	Price
Heavy Woods	Command	U	0.50
Hellhound (Conjurer)	Unit	U	0.50
Hercules (HRC-LS-9000)	Unit	U	0.50
Hermes (HER-1S)	Unit	C	0.20
Hermes II (HER-5S)	Unit	C	0.20
Heroic Sacrifice	Mission	C	0.20
Hidden Reserves	Command	C	0.20
Highlander (HGN-732)	Unit	R	4.00
Hitman (HM-1)	Unit	R	4.00
Hohiro Kurita	Command	R	4.00
Holographic Decoy	Command	U	0.50
Hoplite (HOP-4D)	Unit	R	4.00
Hunchback (HBK-4G)	Unit	C	0.20
Hunchback IIC	Unit	C	0.20
Hunchback Revised (HBK-5M)	Unit	C	0.20
Huron Warrior (HUR-W0-R4L)	Unit	C	0.20
Hussar (HSR 200-D)	Unit	U	0.50
Imp Revised (IMP-3E)	Unit	U	0.50
Inside Job	Command	C	0.20
Intimidating Paint Job	Command	C	0.20
ISF Counterespionage	Command	R	3.50
Jade Falcon High Command	Command	D	3.80
Jagermech (JM6-DD)	Unit	C	0.20
Jenner (JR7-D)	Unit	C	0.20
Jenner IIC	Unit	C	0.20
Jerrard Cranston	Command	R	4.00
Jump Jet Retrofit	Command	R	3.50
"Kai, Champion of Solaris"	Command	R	5.00
Katana (CRK-5003-2)	Unit	C	0.20
Katherine Steiner-Davion	Command	R	5.00
Khan Bjorn Jorgensson	Command	R	4.50
King Crab (KGC-000)	Unit	R	4.00
Kintaro (KTO-19)	Unit	U	0.50
Kintaro (KTO-20)	Unit	C	0.20
Komodo (KIM-2)	Unit	R	5.00
Koshi B (Mist Lynx)	Unit	C	0.20
Koshi C (Mist Lynx)	Unit	R	5.00
Koshi Prime (Mist Lynx)	Unit	C	0.20
Kraken (Bane)	Unit	U	0.50
Kurita High Command	Command	D	3.80
Lance Commander	Command	U	0.50
Lancelot (LNC25-01)	Unit	R	4.00
Laser System Retrofit	Command	U	0.50
Last Stand at Hanover	Mission	U	0.50
Linebacker B	Unit	C	0.20
Linebacker Prime	Unit	C	0.20
Loki B (Hellbringer)	Unit	U	0.50
Long Range Targeting System	Command	R	5.00
Luck of the Fox	Mission	R	3.50
Mad Cat B (Timber Wolf)	Unit	U	0.50
Mad Cat Prime (Timber Wolf)	Unit	C	0.20
Man O' War B (Gargoyle)	Unit	R	5.00
Man O' War Prime (Gargoyle)	Unit	C	0.20
Mandrill	Unit	R	4.00
Marissa Morgan	Command	R	3.50
Masakari Prime (Warhawk)	Unit	R	5.00
Maskirovka Operatives	Command	R	4.00
Massive Battlefield Confusion	Mission	R	4.00
Mauler	Unit	R	5.00
'Mech Hangar	Command	C	0.20
'Mech Trap	Command	C	0.20
MedEvac Team	Command	R	4.50
Mercenary Commission Contacts	Command	R	5.00
Misrouted Command	Command	C	0.20
Missile Rack Retrofit	Command	U	0.80
Missile Spotter	Mission	U	0.50
Mongoose (MON-66)	Unit	U	0.80
Morgan Hasek-Davion	Command	R	5.00
Morgan Kell	Command	R	6.00
Move to Partial Cover	Mission	C	0.20
Naga D	Unit	U	0.50
Naga Prime	Unit	U	0.50
Naginata (NG-C3A)	Unit	U	0.50
Narrow Valley	Command	C	0.20
Night Gyr B	Unit	C	0.20
Nightsky Revised (NGS-4S)	Unit	U	0.50
Nobori-nin A (Huntsman)	Unit	U	0.50
Omi Kurita	Command	R	4.00
OmniMech-Pod Cache	Command	U	0.50
Orion (ON1-M)	Unit	R	4.00
Overrun	Mission	C	0.20
Overwhelm	Mission	U	0.50
Owens Revised (OW-1)	Unit	U	0.80
Owens Revised (OW-1D)	Unit	R	5.00
Panther (PNT-9R)	Unit	C	0.20
Penetrator Revised (PTR-4D)	Unit	U	0.50
Peregrine (Horned Owl)	Unit	C	0.20
Perimeter Alarm	Command	R	4.50
Phantom A	Unit	U	0.50
Phantom B	Unit	U	0.50
Phantom Prime	Unit	C	0.20
Phelan Ward	Command	R	4.00
Piranha	Unit	R	5.00
Point Defense System	Command	U	0.50
Pouncer B	Unit	C	0.20
Pouncer C	Unit	C	0.20
Pouncer Prime	Unit	C	0.20
Primus Sharilar Mori	Command	R	4.00
Prince Victor Steiner-Davion	Command	R	4.00
Prometheus (Dire Wolf)	Unit	R	5.00
Pryde's Pride	Mission	R	4.00
Puma A (Adder)	Unit	C	0.20
Puma C (Adder)	Unit	U	0.50
Puma D (Adder)	Unit	U	0.50
Puma Prime (Adder)	Unit	R	3.50
Pushing the Envelope	Mission	U	0.50
Quick Salvage Operation	Mission	U	0.50
Quickdraw (QKD-4G)	Unit	C	0.20
Quickdraw (QKD-5M)	Unit	C	0.20
Rakshasa (MDG-1A)	Unit	U	0.50
Rapid Cool-Down	Mission	U	0.80
Raven (RVN-3L)	Unit	U	0.50
Reactor Breach	Mission	R	5.00
Recon Pilot	Command	U	0.25
Redline Pilot	Command	C	0.20
Relentless Assault	Mission	U	0.50
Repair Facility	Command	C	0.20
Rhonda Snord	Command	R	4.50
Rhonda's Highlander (HGN-732)	Unit	R	4.00
Risky Combat Jump	Mission	U	0.50
Ristar MechWarrior	Command	R	5.00
Rocky Gorge	Command	U	0.50
Rolling Hills	Command	U	0.50
Rookie Pilot	Command	R	3.50
Ryoken B (Stormcrow)	Unit	R	5.00
Ryoken C (Stormcrow)	Unit	C	0.20
Ryoken D (Stormcrow)	Unit	U	0.50
Sacrifice for the Dragon!	Mission	R	4.00
Salamander (PPR-5S)	Unit	R	4.00
Sandhurst Royal Military Academy	Command	U	0.50
Scarabus (SCB-9A)	Unit	R	5.00
Sharpshooter	Command	C	0.20
Shin Yodama	Command	R	4.00
Shogun (SHG-2F)	Unit	R	4.00
Sibko Allegiance	Mission	R	4.50
Simone Devon	Command	R	4.00
Single Combat	Command	R	4.00
Smoke Jagua/r High Command	Command	D	3.80
Snake (SNK-1V)	Unit	C	0.20
Solaris Games Veteran	Command	R	4.50
Spider (SDR-5V)	Unit	U	0.50
Spider Revised (SDR-7M)	Unit	C	0.20
St. Ives Operations Officer	Command	U	0.50
St. Ives Salvage Crew	Command	R	4.00
Staging Ground	Command	U	0.50
Stalker (STK-3F)	Unit	C	0.20
Steal 'Mech	Command	R	3.50
Stealth (STH-1D)	Unit	C	0.20
Steiner High Command	Command	D	3.80
Strafing Run	Command	C	0.20
Strip Mining Operation	Command	C	0.20
Studied Move	Mission	U	0.50
Sun Zhang Mechwarrior Academy	Command	U	0.50
Sunder (SD1-OB)	Unit	U	0.50
Sun-Tzu Liao	Command	R	4.00
Supernova	Unit	C	0.20
Support: Assembly	Command	S	0.20
Support: Logistics	Command	S	0.20
Support: Munitions	Command	S	0.20
Support: Politics	Command	S	0.20
Support: Tactics	Command	S	0.20
Tactical Advantage	Mission	C	0.20
Tactical Nuke	Command	R	4.00
Taking the Hit	Mission	C	0.20
Targeting Ace	Command	U	0.50
Targeting Computer Retrofit	Command	U	0.50
Teachings of the Unfinished Book	Command	R	3.50
Tempest Revised (TMP-3M)	Unit	C	0.20
Temporary Cease-Fire	Mission	U	0.50
The Remembrance	Command	R	4.00
Think Tank	Command	R	0.10
Thomas Marik	Command	R	5.00
Thor B Revised (Summoner)	Unit	R	4.00
Thor D (Summoner)	Unit	U	0.50
Thorn (THE-N)	Unit	C	0.20
Thumper Battery	Command	U	0.50
Thunder (THR-1L)	Unit	C	0.20
Topple	Mission	U	0.50
Tracking System Failure	Command	C	0.20
Training Facility	Command	U	0.50
Trapped!	Mission	R	5.00
Treachery!	Command	C	0.20
Trebuchet (TBT-5N)	Unit	C	0.20
Trebuchet (TBT-7M)	Unit	U	0.50
Turkina A	Unit	U	0.50
Uller B (Kit Fox)	Unit	C	0.20
Uller D (Kit Fox)	Unit	U	0.50
Uller Prime (Kit Fox)	Unit	C	0.20
Underworld Connections	Command	U	0.50
Unnamed Sources	Command	U	0.50
Unopposed	Mission	C	0.20
UrbanMech (UM-R63)	Unit	C	0.20
UrbanMech IIC	Unit	C	0.20
Venom Revised (SDR-9K)	Unit	U	0.50
Veteran MechWarrior	Command	C	0.20
Vicious Kick	Mission	C	0.20
Victor (VTR-9B)	Unit	C	0.20
Victor (VTR-9K)	Unit	C	0.20
Vindicator Revised (VND-3L)	Unit	U	0.50
Vlad of the Wards	Command	R	4.50
Vulture C (Mad Dog)	Unit	C	0.20
Vulture Prime (Mad Dog)	Unit	C	0.20
Whitworth (WTH-1)	Unit	C	0.20
Wolf High Command	Command	D	3.80
Wolfgang Hansen	Command	R	4.50
Wolfhound (WLF-2)	Unit	C	0.20
Work Stoppage	Command	U	0.50
Wraith (TR1)	Unit	C	0.20
Wyvern (WVE-5N)	Unit	R	4.00
Wyvern IIC	Unit	C	0.20
Yen-Lo-Wang (CN9-YLW)	Unit	R	5.00
Zeus (ZEU-9S)	Unit	C	0.20

RARITY KEY C = Common U = Uncommon R = Rare VR = Very Rare UR = Ultra Rare F = Foil card X = Fixed/standard in all decks

Battletech • Counterstrike

Wizards of the Coast, under license from **FASA** • Released **April 1997**
99 cards in set • **IDENTIFIER: Large 'C' behind color text**

• Booster packs contain 15 cards; booster displays contain 36 boosters

The **Counterstrike** expansion for **BattleTech** introduced unique legendary names to *BattleTech* CCG play, including **Ulric Kerensky, Chandrasekhar Kurita, Haakon Magnussen,** and **Adam Steiner** and **Ryan Steiner,** among others.

Several new and variant 'Mechs also premiered in this set, including several House and Clan affiliated 'Mechs. The major complaint about this expansion was that it was small, weighing in at only 99 cards.

Wizards of the Coast introduced a unique way of denoting expansions on cards for *Battletech.* Cards for *Counterstrike* have a big letter 'C' in a printed-circuit font ghosted behind the color text. — *James A. Mishler*

Set (99 cards)	85.00	**11** nine-pocket pages to store this set. (6 doubled up)
Booster Display Box	70.00	
Booster Pack	3.00	

Card name	Type	Rarity	Price
Accelerate Conflict	Command	R	3.00
Accelerated Turnaround	Command	U	1.00
Adam Steiner	Command	R	6.00
Annihilator ANH-2A	Mech	R	5.00
Assassin ASN-23	Mech	U	1.00
Assassination	Command	U	1.00
Bait and Switch	Mission	U	.1.00
Berserker Warrior	Command	R	4.00
Black Hawk C Nova	Mech	U	1.00
Black Market Connections	Command	U	1.00
Blackjack BJ-1	Mech	C	0.10
Blitzkrieg	Mission	R	5.00
Blockade	Command	R	5.00
Blood of Kerensky	Command	C	0.10
Blow the Pass!	Mission	R	4.00
Bombardier BMB-12D	Mech	R	4.00
Bribed Pilot	Command	U	1.00
Catapult CPLT-C1	Mech	U	1.00
Champion CHP-1N	Mech	U	1.00
Chandrasekhar Kurita	Command	R	5.00
Charger CGR-3K	Mech	R	5.00
Commando COM-5S	Mech	C	0.10
Contract with Kell Hounds	Command	R	4.00
Cover of Night	Mission	U	1.00
Crab CRB-27	Mech	C	0.10
Cyclops CP 10-Z	Mech	U	1.00
Daishi B Dire Wolf	Mech	R	8.00
Daishi Prime Dire Wolf	Mech	R	9.00
Dasher A Firemoth	Mech	R	4.00

Card name	Type	Rarity	Price
Dasher B Firemoth	Mech	R	4.00
Defensive Formation	Mission	C	0.10
Deploy Reinforcements	Mission	C	0.10
Double-Time Offense	Command	U	1.00
Earthwerks Limited	Command	C	0.10
End Run	Mission	C	0.10
Fanatical Leader	Command	U	1.00
Fenris B Ice Ferret	Mech	C	0.10
Field Command Post	Command	C	0.10
Field Construction Site	Command	C	0.10
Firefly FFL-4B	Mech	U	1.00
For the Chancellor!	Mission	U	1.00
Gladiator D Executioner	Mech	U	1.00
Grasshopper GHR-5J	Mech	C	0.10
Guillotine GLT-3M	Mech	C	0.10
Haakon Magnussen	Command	R	5.00
Hazardous Battle Zone	Mission	U	1.00
Hermes HER-1S	Mech	C	0.10
Hermes HER-3S	Mech	C	0.10
Hip Shattered	Mission	R	5.00
Hunchback HBK-5M	Mech	C	0.10
Jenner JR7-K	Mech	U	1.00
King Crab KGC-000	Mech	R	4.00
Kintaro KTO-19	Mech	U	1.00
Kintaro KTO-20	Mech	C	0.10
Lance Diversion	Mission	C	0.10
Lance Formation	Mission	C	0.10
Lostech Cache	Command	C	0.10
Massive Battlefield Confusion	Mission	R	4.00
Master Scrounger	Command	C	0.10
Mech Hangar	Command	C	0.10
Minefield	Mission	C	0.10
Mobile Long Tom	Command	U	1.00
No Quarter	Mission	R	4.00
Oda Hideyoshi	Command	R	5.00

Card name	Type	Rarity	Price
Operations Liaison	Command	C	0.10
Orbital Bombardment	Command	R	4.00
Overrun	Mission	C	0.10
Panther PNT-10K	Mech	C	0.10
Pinpoint Air Strike	Command	U	1.00
Puma B Adder	Mech	C	0.10
Puma D Adder	Mech	U	1.00
Quick Salvage Operation	Mission	U	1.00
Recon Pilot	Command	U	1.00
Report from the Norns	Command	R	4.00
Risky Combat Jump	Mission	U	1.00
Ryan Steiner	Command	R	5.00
Ryoken B Stormcrow	Mech	R	5.00
Ryoken C Stormcrow	Mech	C	0.10
Secured Drop Site	Command	C	0.10
Sentinel STL-3L	Mech	C	0.10
Spider SDR-7M	'Mech	C	0.10
Star Diversion	Mission	C	0.10
Star Formation	Mission	C	0.10
Strafing Run	Command	C	0.10
Superior Navigation	Mission	R	5.50
Tactical Nuke	Command	R	5.50
Thor Mobile Artillery	Command	U	1.00
Thorn THE-N	Mech	C	0.10
Thumper Battery	Command	U	1.00
Tor Miraborg	Command	R	5.00
Trapped!	Mission	R	5.00
Uller A Kit Fox	Mech	C	0.10
Ulric Kerensky	Command	R	4.50
UrbanMech UM-R63	Mech	C	0.10
Veteran Officer	Command	U	1.00
Vicious Kick	Mission	C	0.10
Vindicator VND-3L	Mech	U	1.00
Vlad of the Wards	Command	R	5.00
Vulcan VT-5S	Mech	U	1.00

Battletech • Mercenaries

Wizards of the Coast, under license from **FASA** • Released **August 1997**
101 cards in set • **IDENTIFIER: Large 'M' behind color text**

• Booster packs contain 15 cards; booster displays contain 36 boosters

The **Mercenaries** expansion introduced unique 'Mechs to the **BattleTech** CCG. These 'Mechs had not been seen before in any other *BattleTech* game and thus added a level of surprise for fans new and old, and added to the collectability of the set.

For the hardcore player, the *Mercenaries* set added the ComStar faction (potent with political resources) and, of course, more Mercenary cards, which tipped the courses of battles. — *James A. Mishler*

Set (101 cards)	90.00	**12** nine-pocket pages to store this set. (6 doubled up)
Booster Display Box	70.00	
Booster Pack	3.00	

Card name	Type	Rarity	Price
Access to Extra Munitions	Command	C	0.10
Albatross ALB-3U	Unit	R	4.00
Aletha Kabrinski	Command	R	4.50
Ammo Truck	Command	U	1.00
Anastasius Focht	Command	R	6.00
Anvil ANV-3M	Unit	U	1.00

Card name	Type	Rarity	Price
Apollo APL-1M	Unit	C	0.10
Artillery Bombardment	Command	C	0.10
Assault 'Mech Specialists	Command	U	1.00

RARITY KEY C = Common   U = Uncommon   R = Rare   VR = Very Rare   UR = Ultra Rare   F = Foil card   X = Fixed/standard in all decks

Card name	Type	Rarity	Price
2			
Assault on the Rear Echelon	Command	C	0.10
Baboon Howler	Unit	R	5.00
Batchall	Mission	R	4.50
Behemoth Stone Rhino	Unit	R	6.50
Berserker BRZ-A3	Unit	R	4.80
Booty Cache	Command	R	4.80
Com Guard Response Team	Mission	C	0.10
ComStar Investment	Command	U	1.00
ComStar News Bureau	Command	R	4.00
3			
ComStar Support	Command	C	0.10
ComStar Technicians	Command	U	1.00
Contract with 21st Centauri Lancers	Command	R	5.30
Contract with Black Thorns	Command	R	4.80
Contract with Eridani Light Horse	Command	R	4.00
Contract with Northwind Highlanders	Command	U	1.00
Contract with Snord's Irregulars	Command	R	4.30
Corvis	Unit	C	0.10
Dart DRT-3S	Unit	U	1.00
4			
Difficult Terrain	Command	C	0.10
Disguised Coordinates	Command	C	0.10
Disrupted Supply Lines	Mission	U	1.00
Dr. Ariel Reed	Command	R	4.80
Expert Negotiating Team	Command	U	1.00
First Circuit Summons	Command	U	1.00
Grand Titan T-IT-N10M	Unit	C	0.10
Grim Reaper GRM-R-PR29	Unit	C	0.10
Gunslinger GUN-1ERD	Unit	U	1.00
5			
Hammer HMR-3M	Unit	C	0.10
Hellbound Conjurer	Unit	U	1.00

Card name	Type	Rarity	Price
Hercules HRC LS-9000	Unit	U	1.00
Hermes II HER-5S	Unit	C	0.10
Hidden Reserves	Command	C	0.10
High-Profile Target	Command	U	1.00
Hohiro Kurita	Command	R	5.00
Huron Warrior HUR-WO-R4L	Unit	C	0.10
Hyperpulse Generator	Command	R	4.80
6			
Intimidating Paint Job	Command	U	1.00
Jackal JA-KL-1532	Unit	C	0.10
Kraken Bane	Unit	U	1.00
Last Stand at Hanover	Mission	U	1.00
Linebacker B	Unit	C	0.10
Linebacker Prime	Unit	C	0.10
Mandrill	Unit	R	5.00
Maskirovka Headquarters	Command	U	1.00
'Mech Rotation	Command	U	1.00
7			
'Mech Trap	Command	C	0.10
Mercenary Commission Contacts	Command	U	1.00
Mercenary Contract	Command	C	0.10
Mercenary Relations Division	Command	C	0.10
Myndo Waterly	Command	R	5.50
Naga Prime	Unit	U	1.00
Nekekami Sabotage	Command	U	1.00
Nightsky NGS-4S	Unit	U	1.00
Omi Kurita	Command	R	4.50
8			
Outreach Mercenary Training	Command	C	0.10
Penetrator PTR-40	Unit	U	1.00
Phantom C	Unit	U	1.00
Phantom D	Unit	U	1.00
Phantom Prime	Unit	C	0.10
Pouncer C	Unit	C	0.10

Card name	Type	Rarity	Price
Pouncer Prime	Unit	C	0.10
Protection Racket	Command	R	4.50
Rapid Deployment	Command	C	0.10
9			
Reactor Breach	Mission	R	4.80
Redjack Ryan	Command	R	4.80
Relentless Assault	Mission	U	1.00
Repair Facility	Command	C	0.10
Rhonda Snord	Command	R	5.80
Rhonda's Highlander HGN-732	Unit	R	5.30
Salamander PPR-5S	Unit	R	5.00
Sandhurst Royal Military Academy	Command	U	1.00
Scarabus SCB-9A	Unit	R	4.80
10			
Sharilar Mori	Command	R	5.50
Snake SNK-1V	Unit	C	0.10
Stealth STH-1D	Unit	C	0.10
Strip Mining Operation	Command	C	0.10
Sun-Tzu Liao	Command	R	6.30
Tactical Advantage	Mission	C	0.10
Taking the Hit	Mission	C	0.10
Targeting Ace	Command	U	1.00
Tempest TMP-3M	Unit	C	0.10
11			
Thunder THR-1L	Unit	C	0.10
Tracking System Failure	Command	U	1.00
Transportation Delay	Command	C	0.10
Underworld Connections	Command	C	0.10
Unopposed	Mission	C	0.10
UrbanMech IIC	Unit	C	0.10
Vandervahn Chistu	Command	R	5.50
Venom SDR-9K	Unit	U	1.00
Widowmaker Daishi Dire Wolf	Unit	R	8.30
12			
Wyvern IIC	Unit	C	0.10
Yen-Lo-Wang CN9-YLW	Unit	R	6.00

Battletech • *Mechwarrior*

Wizards of the Coast, under license from **FASA** • Released **August 1997**
108 cards in set • **IDENTIFIER: Large 'MW' behind color text**

- Booster packs contain 15 cards; booster displays contain 36 boosters

The *Mechwarrior* expansion for *BattleTech* brings some heavy 'Mechs to the battlefield, including the **Prometheus Dire Wolf**, the **Cerberus**, the **Naginata**, and the Turkina class 'Mechs.

There are also some potent advanced personalities in this set, including **Khan Natasha Kerensky, Prince Victor Steiner-Davion,** and **Phelan Ward. — *James A. Mishler***

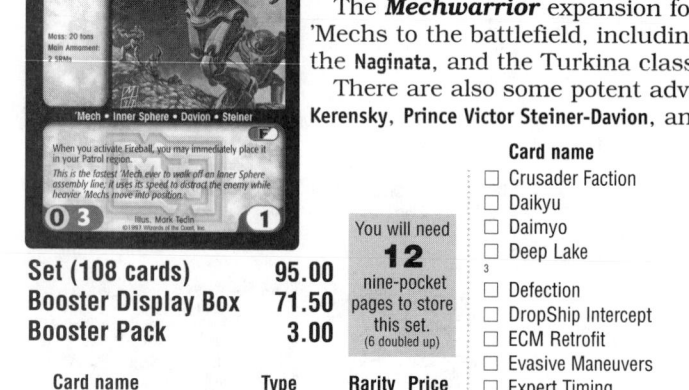

Set (108 cards)	95.00
Booster Display Box	71.50
Booster Pack	3.00

You will need **12** nine-pocket pages to store this set. (6 doubled up)

Card name	Type	Rarity	Price
1			
Accidental Collision	Mission	U	1.00
Airstrikes Close to Home	Command	U	1.00
Avatar	Unit	U	1.00
Black Lanner Prime	Unit	R	5.00
Blackjack	Unit	C	0.10
Brutal Punch	Mission	C	0.10
C3 Retrofit	Command	C	0.10
Cauldron-Born A	Unit	R	5.00
Cerberus	Unit	U	1.00
2			
Charge!	Mission	R	4.00
Civilian Settlement	Command	C	0.10
Contract with Hansen's Roughriders	Command	R	6.00
Corridor of Fire	Command	U	1.00
Creative Terraforming	Command	U	1.00

Card name	Type	Rarity	Price
Crusader Faction	Command	U	1.00
Daikyu	Unit	U	1.00
Daimyo	Unit	C	0.10
Deep Lake	Command	C	0.10
3			
Defection	Command	U	1.00
DropShip Intercept	Mission	U	1.00
ECM Retrofit	Command	C	0.10
Evasive Maneuvers	Mission	R	4.00
Expert Timing	Mission	U	1.00
Falcon Hawk	Unit	C	0.30
Falconer	Unit	R	5.00
Financial Collapse	Command	R	5.00
Fireball	Unit	C	0.10
4			
Firestarter	Unit	U	1.00
Fog-Shrouded Moors	Command	C	0.10
Fortunes of War	Mission	R	4.00
Galahad	Unit	C	0.10
Gallowglas	Unit	R	5.00
Gearhead	Command	C	0.10
Grendel Prime	Unit	C	0.10
Headhunter	Command	R	5.00
Heavy Woods	Command	C	0.10
5			
Hidden Location	Command	R	5.00
Hitman	Unit	R	5.00

Card name	Type	Rarity	Price
Hunchback IIC	Unit	C	0.10
Inferno Missile Retrofit	Command	U	1.00
Jenner IIC	Unit	C	0.10
Jump Jet Retrofit	Command	C	0.10
"Kai, Champion of Solaris"	Command	R	7.00
Katherine Steiner-Davion	Command	R	7.00
Khan Natasha Kerensky	Command	R	6.00
6			
Komodo	Unit	R	5.00
Linebacker A	Unit	U	1.00
Loremaster	Command	U	1.00
MedEvac Team	Command	R	5.00
Merchant Caste	Command	U	1.00
Naga A	Unit	U	1.00
Naga D	Unit	U	1.00
Naginata	Unit	U	1.00
NARC Retrofit	Command	C	0.10
7			
Narrow Valley	Command	C	0.10
Night Gyr A	Unit	R	5.00
Night Gyr B	Unit	C	0.30
Nobori-Nin A	Unit	U	1.00
OmniMech-Pod Cache	Command	U	1.00
Owens	Unit	C	0.10
Owens	Unit	R	5.00
Peregrine	Unit	C	0.10
Phantom A	Unit	U	1.00

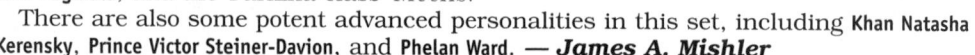

RARITY KEY **C** = Common **U** = Uncommon **R** = Rare **VR** = Very Rare **UR** = Ultra Rare **F** = Foil card **X** = Fixed/standard in all decks

Card name	Type	Rarity	Price
Phantom B	Unit	U	1.00
Phelan Ward	Command	R	7.00
Piranha	Unit	R	5.00
Pouncer A	Unit	U	1.00
Pouncer B	Unit	C	0.10
Prince Victor Steiner-Davion	Command	R	7.00
Prometheus	Unit	R	6.00
Rakshasa	Unit	U	1.00
Redline Pilot	Command	C	0.10
Ristar MechWarrior	Command	R	5.00
Rocky Gorge	Command	C	0.10
Rolling Hills	Command	C	0.10
Salvage Yard	Command	C	0.10
Scientist Caste	Command	U	1.00
Severed Supply Lines	Command	R	5.00

Card name	Type	Rarity	Price
Sharpshooter	Command	C	0.10
Shin Yodama	Command	R	5.00
Sibko Allegiance	Mission	R	5.00
Single Combat	Command	U	1.00
Sirnone Devon	Command	R	4.00
Solaris Contacts	Command	C	0.10
Solaris Games Veteran	Command	R	5.00
St. Ives Operations Officer	Command	U	1.00
St. Ives Salvage Crew	Command	R	4.50
Staging Ground	Command	U	1.00
Sunder	Unit	C	0.10
Supernova	Unit	C	0.10
Support from Home	Command	R	5.00
Tactical Superiority	Mission	C	0.10
Targeting Computer Retrofit	Command	C	0.10

Card name	Type	Rarity	Price
Technician Caste	Command	U	1.00
The Remembrance	Command	R	4.00
Thunder LRMs	Command	R	5.00
Time Bomb	Command	U	1.00
Training Facility	Command	C	0.10
Turkina A	Unit	U	1.00
Turkina C	Unit	R	5.00
Tyra Miraborg	Command	R	7.00
Unnamed Sources	Command	U	1.00
Warden Faction	Command	U	1.00
Warrior Caste	Command	U	1.00
Watchman	Unit	C	0.10
Wolfgang Hansen	Command	R	7.00
Work Stoppage	Command	U	1.00
Wraith	Unit	C	0.10

Battletech • Arsenal

Wizards of the Coast, under license from **FASA** • Released **March 1998**
108 cards in set • **IDENTIFIER: Large 'A' behind color text**

• Booster packs contain 15 cards; booster displays contain 36 boosters

The **Arsenal** expansion for **BattleTech** brings a new class of card to the game, Vehicles, including assault tanks, elementals, and helicopters. Vehicles add support to the main battle forces of the 'Mech, but are not as resilient as their more powerful and versatile cousins.

There are also a number of Mission and Command cards that improve and back up Vehicles. This set also brings out the "big guns" personality wise, including **Hanse Davion**, **Takashi Kurita, Maximillian Liao, Janos Marik,** and **Katrina Steiner.** — *James A. Mishler*

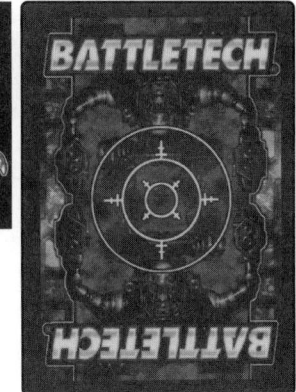

	Price
Set (108 cards)	85.00
Booster Display Box	83.00
Booster Pack	3.00

You will need **12** nine-pocket pages to store this set. (6 doubled up)

Card name	Type	Rarity	Price
Advanced Manufacturing Techniques	Command	C	0.20
Airdropped Supplies	Command	R	4.00
Bandersnatch	Unit	U	0.80
Battle Armor Squad	Unit	C	0.20
Behemoth (Flamer Variant)	Unit	U	0.80
Berserk Elemental Point	Unit	U	0.80
Black Hawk S	Unit	U	0.90
Black Lanner A	Unit	C	0.30
Blitzkrieg Elemental Point	Unit	U	0.80
Bulldog	Unit	C	0.20
Bulldog (AC/2 Variant)	Unit	C	0.20
Bulldog (LRM Variant)	Unit	C	0.20
Burke	Unit	U	1.00
Carpet Bombing	Mission	C	0.20
Castle Defense	Mission	C	0.20
Cauldron-Born Prime	Unit	C	0.20
Cavalry	Unit	C	0.30
Chameleon	Unit	U	0.80
Chaos March Veteran	Command	U	0.80
Combat Drop	Command	U	0.80
Command Circuit	Command	R	5.00
Coordinator Theodore Kurita	Command	R	5.50
Covert Elemental Point	Unit	U	0.80
Cyrano	Unit	R	5.00
Daishi S	Unit	U	1.00
Dan Allard	Command	R	5.00
Defensive Embankment	Command	U	0.80
Demolisher	Unit	C	0.20
Demon	Unit	U	0.80
Desert Wasteland	Command	C	0.20
Diamond Will's	Command	R	5.50
Doc Trevena	Command	R	5.50

Card name	Type	Rarity	Price
Elizabeth O'Bannon	Command	R	5.50
Enhanced IR Sensors	Command	U	0.80
Ferro-Fibrous Upgrade	Command	C	0.20
Final Push	Mission	U	0.80
Fire Falcon A	Unit	R	4.30
Fire Falcon C	Unit	U	1.00
Fire Falcon Prime	Unit	C	0.30
Fire From Cover	Mission	C	0.20
Front-Loaded Supply Lines	Mission	C	0.20
Galleon-3058	Unit	U	0.80
Grendel D	Unit	C	0.30
Grizzly	Unit	C	0.20
Hanse Davion's Legacy	Command	R	5.30
Holovid Frameup	Command	R	5.50
Hot-Loaded LRMs	Command	U	0.90
J. Edgar (MG Variant)	Unit	C	0.30
Jade Monkey	Command	R	5.00
Janos Marik's Legacy	Command	R	5.30
Jerrard Cranston	Command	R	4.80
Jump Troops	Command	C	0.20
Katrina Steiner's Legacy	Command	R	4.80
Keith Smith	Command	R	5.00
Kodiak	Unit	R	4.50
Lightning	Unit	R	5.50
Linebacker C	Unit	C	0.20
Mad Cat Pryde	Unit	R	4.50
Mad Cat S	Unit	U	0.80
Magi	Unit	R	4.30
Maximillian Liao's Legacy	Command	R	4.50
Mech Recall	Command	R	5.00
MechWarrior Peter	Command	U	0.80
Nice Grouping	Mission	U	0.80
Night Gyr C	Unit	C	0.20
Nightshade	Unit	R	5.00
Nobori-nin C	Unit	C	0.20
Ontos (LRM Variant)	Unit	R	4.50
Ontos-3058	Unit	C	0.20
Partisan-3058	Unit	U	0.80
Pillager	Unit	R	4.80

Card name	Type	Rarity	Price
Pinto	Unit	U	0.80
Pouncer D	Unit	U	0.90
Primus Sharilar Mori	Command	R	4.00
Puma	Unit	R	4.00
Ramming Speed!	Mission	U	0.80
Resource Broker	Command	U	0.80
Saladin	Unit	C	0.30
Schrek	Unit	C	0.20
Secret Buildup	Command	U	0.80
Shadow Cat A	Unit	C	0.20
Shadow Cat B	Unit	R	4.50
Skirmisher Elemental Point	Unit	U	0.80
Sloth Squad	Unit	U	0.80
Spartan	Unit	C	0.20
Spector	Unit	C	0.20
SRM Carrier	Unit	U	0.80
Steel Talons	Mission	R	4.80
Strength of the Bear	Mission	U	0.20
Suicide Troops	Command	U	0.80
Takashi Kurita's Legacy	Command	R	4.50
Tanya O'Bannon	Command	R	5.00
Thor M	Unit	R	4.50
Tormano Liao	Command	R	6.00
Trial of Bloodright	Command	R	4.50
Trial of Grievance	Command	C	0.20
Trial of Position	Command	U	0.80
Trial of Possession	Command	U	0.80
Trial of Refusal	Command	R	4.00
Uller S	Unit	U	0.90
Unlikely Love Affair	Command	R	4.00
Vehicle Repair Barn	Command	C	0.20
War Funds	Command	C	0.20
Warrior H-8	Unit	C	0.30
Weapons Depot	Command	C	0.20
Yellow Jacket	Unit	C	0.20
Zephyr	Unit	U	1.00
Zhanzheng de Guang	Command	U	0.80

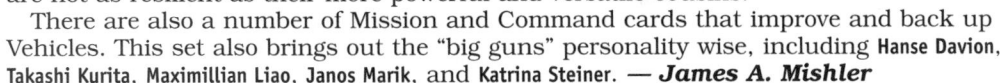

RARITY KEY C = Common U = Uncommon R = Rare VR = Very Rare UR = Ultra Rare F = Foil card X = Fixed/standard in all decks

Battletech • Crusade

Wizards of the Coast, under license from **FASA**

Released **November 1998** • **IDENTIFIER: New card design**

108 cards in set

- Booster packs contain 15 cards
- Booster displays contain 36 boosters

Crusade followed quickly on the heels of **Commander's Edition**, and takes advantage of the faction building that had been done in the new edition by adding Alliance cards.

Alliance cards allow cards from different factions to cooperate by adding or subtracting faction affiliations, most notably with the Federated Commonwealth (Steiner-Davion), the Star League (all Inner Sphere) and the Invading Clans (all Clans).

Crusade is also packed with Omni 'Mechs, includes several Vehicles, and significantly increases the forces of the Steel Vipers.

Another announced expansion, **Payback**, presumably would have included more Vehicles and continued the growing **BattleTech CCG** story line. But sales had fallen in the two years since **Limited** came out, and *Crusade* was the last released expanison for the game. — *James A. Mishler*

SCRYE NOTES: Crusade *is the one of the few expansion names to have been used by more than one CCG (apart from the ubiquitous descriptives "Limited," "Premiere," etc.). Precedence released* **Crusade** *for* **Babylon 5** *in December 2000. Confusion was unlikely anyway, and as that name was based on a TV show title, there was little choice.*

Set (108 cards)	85.00
Booster Display Box	82.50
Booster Pack	2.90

You will need 12 nine-pocket pages to store this set. (6 doubled up)

Card name	Type	Rarity	Price
[1]			
Annihilator (ANH-1A)	Unit	U	1.00
Arc-Royal Defense Cordon	Command	R	4.50
Aris Sung	Command	R	4.00
Avatar (AV1-OB)	Unit	U	1.00
Backing of the Grand Council	Command	C	0.20
Battle Attrition	Command	R	5.50
Battle Cobra A	Unit	C	0.20
Battle Cobra B	Unit	U	1.00
Battle Cobra Prime	Unit	C	0.20
[2]			
Black Hawk-KU (BHKU-O)	Unit	C	0.30
Black Hawk-KU (BHKU-OC)	Unit	U	1.00
Black Lanner D	Unit	R	5.50
Black Watch (BKW-7R)	Unit	U	1.00
Blackjack (BJ2-OA)	Unit	C	0.20
Blackjack (BJ-3)	Unit	C	0.20
Blaze of Glory	Mission	U	1.00
Breaking the Envelope	Mission	R	4.50
Cataphract (CTF-1X)	Unit	C	0.20
[3]			
Cerberus (MR-5M)	Unit	R	5.50
Cestus (CTS-6Y)	Unit	U	1.00
Champion (CHP-2N)	Unit	C	0.20
Charger (CGR-1A5)	Unit	C	0.20
Charger (CGR-1L)	Unit	U	1.00
Close Formation	Mission	C	0.20
Comstar Deep Agent	Command	U	1.00
Conquer	Mission	R	5.00
Coup de Grâce	Mission	U	1.00
[4]			
Crossbow A	Unit	C	0.20
Crossbow B	Unit	C	0.20
Cyclops (CP-11-C)	Unit	U	1.00
DEST Commando Sabotage	Command	U	1.00
Enfield (END-6Q)	Unit	C	0.20
Entrenched Holdings	Command	U	1.00

Card name	Type	Rarity	Price
Entropy-Based Warfare	Command	C	0.20
Exterminator (EXT-4A)	Unit	C	0.20
Falsified Maps	Mission	R	5.00
[5]			
Fast Deployment	Command	C	0.20
Fire Falcon B	Unit	C	0.30
Fire Falcon D	Unit	U	1.00
Fire From Partial Cover	Mission	C	0.20
Firestarter (FS9-OF)	Unit	C	0.20
Force of Will	Mission	R	4.00
Fury	Command	C	0.20
Goshawk (Vapor Eagle)	Unit	R	5.00
Grand Crusader (GRN-D-01)	Unit	R	5.00
[6]			
Grendel B	Unit	U	1.00
Grendel C	Unit	C	0.30
Hankyu C	Unit	U	1.00
Hankyu Prime	Unit	C	0.30
Hasty Alliance	Command	R	5.00
Heat of Battle	Command	C	0.20
Heat Sink Destruction	Command	U	1.00
Hollander (BZK-F3)	Unit	U	1.00
Huron Warrior (HUR-WO-R4M)	Unit	C	0.20
[7]			
Icy Terrain	Command	C	0.20
Improved Construction Facilities	Command	C	0.30
Indiscriminate Terrorism	Command	R	4.50
Intimidation Tactics	Mission	U	1.00
Isolated Forces	Command	R	5.00
It's a Trap!	Command	U	1.00
Judith Faber	Command	R	5.00
Khan Vlad Ward	Command	R	4.50
Knights of the Inner Sphere	Command	R	6.50
[8]			
Kraken 2 (Bane)	Unit	R	5.00
Loose Cannon	Command	R	4.50
Marthe Pryde	Command	R	5.50
Maskirovka Sabotage	Mission	R	5.00
'Mech Smuggling	Command	R	5.00
MechWarrior Trent	Command	R	4.50
Michael Ryan	Command	R	5.30

Card name	Type	Rarity	Price
Move to Dubious Cover	Mission	U	1.00
Naga B	Unit	R	5.80
[9]			
Natural Talent	Command	U	1.00
Nexus (NXS1-A)	Unit	C	0.30
Night Gyr D	Unit	R	5.00
Night Gyr Prime	Unit	C	0.20
Paul Moon	Unit	R	5.00
Perigard Zalman	Command	R	5.00
Perseus (P1A)	Unit	U	1.00
Political Stranglehold	Command	U	1.00
Raptor (RTX1-OA)	Unit	C	0.30
[10]			
Raptor (RTX1-OE)	Unit	U	1.00
Rhino	Unit	U	1.00
Rommel	Unit	C	0.20
Shadow Cat Prime	Unit	C	0.20
Solahma MechWarrior	Command	U	1.00
SRM Carrier-3058	Unit	U	1.00
Star Commander	Command	U	1.00
Star League Proving Grounds	Command	U	1.00
Starslayer (STY-3C)	Unit	R	5.50
[11]			
Steady...Steady...FIRE!	Mission	U	1.00
Steel Viper R&D Team	Command	U	1.00
Strategic Bombardment	Command	U	1.00
Striker (STC-2C)	Unit	U	1.00
Surprise Maneuvers	Mission	U	0.60
Task Force Serpent	Command	R	4.50
Temptation	Command	C	0.20
The Federated Commonwealth	Command	R	5.00
The Invading Clans	Command	R	5.50
[12]			
The Star League	Command	R	6.00
Thunder Hawk (TDK-7X)	Unit	R	5.00
Trojan Horse	Mission	U	1.00
Turkina Prime	Unit	C	5.00
Viper (Black Python)	Unit	R	5.00
Viper's Maw	Mission	R	4.50
War Dog (WR-DG-02FC)	Unit	U	1.00
Wolfhound (WLF-1)	Unit	C	0.20
Zhukov	Unit	C	0.20

RARITY KEY C = Common U = Uncommon R = Rare VR = Very Rare UR = Ultra Rare F = Foil card X = Fixed/standard in all decks

Blood Wars

TSR • Released March 1995
300 cards in set • **IDENTIFIER: None**
- Starter "duel decks" contain two decks of 50 cards; starter displays contain 5 starters
- Booster packs are actually part of concurrent release, **Rebels & Reinforcements**

Designed by **Steven Schend**

By late 1994, it was clear CCGs were around to stay — and it was clear to the onetime industry leader TSR it would have to broaden its presence in the field. After **Spellfire** had been rushed to press to lukewarm reviews, an interest developed in bringing out a more thoughtfully designed CCG, making better use of the *Dungeons & Dragons* mythos. For **Blood Wars**, TSR crafted a multiplayer CCG simulating political battles in its latest campaign "world," Planescape, home to vairous deities and demigods.

In **Blood Wars**, two or more players use Warlords, Legions, and Fate cards to seize Battlefields, thereby winning victory points. A "mustering period," during which no Challenges may be launched by players, is set, and players build "battle hands" ready to fight for Battlefields. In the action phase, a player may play a Battlefield card from his "command hand" and issue a challenge to try to win it, either through Intrigue or Combat, two significantly different resolution systems. If the player wins his challenge, the battle-field goes to his victory pool. There are several different ways for players in *Blood Wars* to interact, and the system rewards having using more than one set of tactics.

Blood Wars turns seemed to take forever, and not entirely due to the multiple players, either, since the busy turn sequence held perhaps one bell and one whistle too many. And while a card game featuring the subtleties of politics might be rewarding, it ran counter to CCGs' most popular feature in 1995 — quick play leading to quick resolutions so you can get another game in, quick. (This writer, in fact, led one of the playtest teams for *Blood Wars* — and this complaint was front and center in his team's report.) And while the production design improved upon the often garish look of *Spellfire* cards, the dominant browns and tans of the Planescape source material gave the game a drab appearance that did little to draw players in.

Plans were laid for at least six expansions to *Blood Wars*, but TSR caught on quickly that this was not to be the company's magic collectible bullet and only the initial set of three releases came out. — *John Jackson Miller*

Concept	●●●○○
Gameplay	●●○○○
Card art	●●○○○
Player pool	○○○○○

Set (300 cards)	127.00	**34** nine-pocket pages to store this set. (17 doubled up)	
Starter Display Box	59.75		
Starter Deck	6.00		

Card name	Type	Rarity	Price
1			
☐ Aasimar	Legion	U	0.75
☐ Abishai	Legion	C	0.20
☐ Acheron	Battlefield	C	0.20
☐ Aferoxxynomak	Warlord	U	0.50
☐ Agathinon	Legion	U	0.75
☐ Alu-Fiend	Legion	C	0.20
☐ Ambush!	Fate	C	0.20
☐ Amnizu Warden	Warlord	MC	0.05
☐ Amun-Thys	Battlefield	U	0.75
2			
☐ Animate Battlefield	Fate	U	0.75
☐ Arborea	Battlefield	C	0.20
☐ Arcadia	Battlefield	C	0.20
☐ Archon Guardian	Warlord	MC	0.05
☐ Armor of Invulnerability	Fate	C	0.25
☐ Asgard	Battlefield	U	1.00
☐ Asrai	Legion	R	3.70
☐ Assassination Plot	Fate	R	4.00
☐ Astral Conduit	Fate	C	0.20
3			
☐ Astral Plane	Battlefield	C	0.20
☐ Automata	Battlefield	U	0.75
☐ Avoral	Legion	U	0.75
☐ Azzagrat	Battlefield	VC	0.10
☐ Baator	Battlefield	MC	0.05
☐ Babau Recruiter	Legion	C	0.20
☐ Bacchae	Legion	C	0.20
☐ Bahamut	Warlord	VC	0.10
☐ Baku	Legion	U	0.75

Card name	Type	Rarity	Price
4			
☐ Balaena	Legion	R	4.30
☐ Bar-Lgura	Legion	R	4.00
☐ Barbazu	Legion	R	3.90
☐ Barghest Legionnaire	Legion	U	0.75
☐ Barghest Lord	Legion	R	4.10
☐ Bariaur	Legion	C	0.20
☐ Barnstable	Battlefield	R	4.20
☐ Battle Scarred Planes	Fate	R	4.10
☐ Beastlands	Battlefield	C	0.20
5			
☐ Bedlam	Battlefield	U	0.75
☐ Betrayal	Fate	C	0.20
☐ Bifrost the Rainbow Bridge	Battlefield	R	4.00
☐ Blade of Loyalty	Fate	C	0.20
☐ Bladeling Hero	Warlord	MC	0.05
☐ Blood War Provocation	Fate	C	0.25
☐ Blue Slaad	Legion	U	0.75
☐ Bralani Eladrin	Legion	R	4.30
☐ Buseni	Legion	C	0.20
6			
☐ Bytopia	Battlefield	C	0.20
☐ Call to Arms	Fate	C	0.20
☐ Cambion Baron	Legion	U	0.75
☐ Cambion Mercenary	Fate	U	0.75
☐ Carceri	Battlefield	MC	0.05
☐ Cat Lord	Warlord	C	0.25
☐ Caverns of Thought	Battlefield	R	4.30
☐ Cervidal	Legion	U	0.75
☐ Chaos Beast	Legion	R	4.30
7			
☐ Chaos Imps	Legion	R	4.20
☐ Charge!	Fate	C	0.20
☐ Chasme	Legion	U	0.75
☐ Chronepsis	Warlord	VC	0.10
☐ Cloak of Invisibility	Fate	U	1.00
☐ Clueless Warrior	Legion	R	4.40

Card name	Type	Rarity	Price
☐ Clueless Wizard	Legion	C	0.20
☐ Conclave of Generals	Fate	U	0.75
☐ Consolidation of Power	Fate	R	3.90
8			
☐ Cornugon Whiplord	Warlord	MC	0.05
☐ Coure Eladrin	Legion	C	0.20
☐ Court under the Stars	Battlefield	U	0.75
☐ Cranium Blast	Fate	C	0.20
☐ Cranium Rats	Legion	C	0.20
☐ Crystal Ball	Fate	U	0.75
☐ Curst	Battlefield	U	0.50
☐ Darktome the Arcanaloth	Warlord	U	0.75
☐ Decaton	Legion	U	0.75
9			
☐ Deepshaft Hall	Battlefield	U	0.75
☐ Demonweb Pits	Battlefield	VC	0.10
☐ Dergholoth	Legion	R	4.40
☐ Deva Commander	Warlord	MC	0.05
☐ Dothion	Battlefield	U	0.75
☐ Dragonscale Armor	Fate	U	1.00
☐ Dretch	Legion	C	0.20
☐ Duchess Callisto	Warlord	U	0.75
☐ Duke Lucan	Warlord	U	0.75
10			
☐ Duke Windheir	Warlord	U	0.75
☐ Dwarven Mountain	Battlefield	VC	0.10
☐ Echarus	Warlord	C	0.20
☐ Ecstasy	Battlefield	U	0.75
☐ Einheriar	Legion	U	0.75
☐ Elshava	Battlefield	R	4.00
☐ Elves of Arborea	Legion	C	0.20
☐ Elysium	Battlefield	C	0.20
☐ End Hostilities!	Fate	R	3.90
11			
☐ Equinal Guardinal	Legion	C	0.20
☐ Ercid, Avenger of Rudra	Warlord	C	0.20
☐ Erinyes	Legion	C	0.20

Card name	Type	Rarity	Price
Escape from Death	Fate	C	0.20
Excelsior	Battlefield	U	0.75
Exiraati	Warlord	C	0.20
Faaram the Slaadi King	Warlord	C	0.20
Faerie Queen Morwel	Warlord	R	4.20
Faerinaal, Queen's Consort	Warlord	U	0.75
12			
Faunel	Battlefield	U	0.75
Fensir Rakka	Legion	U	0.75
Fire Mephit	Legion	U	0.75
Firre Eladrin	Legion	U	0.75
Floating City	Battlefield	R	4.10
Forbidden Citadel	Battlefield	VC	0.10
Fortitude	Battlefield	U	0.75
Fortress of the Arcanaloth	Battlefield	U	0.75
Gaola	Battlefield	U	0.75
13			
Gate Key	Fate	U	0.75
Gates of the Moon	Battlefield	U	0.75
Gazra	Warlord	C	0.20
Gehenna	Battlefield	MC	0.05
Gelugon Overlord	Warlord	MC	0.05
Ghaele Eladrin	Legion	R	4.00
Githyanki	Legion	C	0.20
Githzerai	Legion	C	0.20
Glabrezu	Legion	U	0.75
14			
Glorium	Battlefield	U	0.75
Grandfather Oak	Battlefield	R	4.10
Gray Slaad	Legion	U	0.75
Graz'zt	Warlord	VC	0.10
Green Slaad	Legion	C	0.20
Gwynarwhyf the Veiled	Warlord	C	0.20
Hamatula	Legion	U	0.75
Hawk Lord	Warlord	MC	0.05
Honorable Passing	Fate	C	0.20
15			
Hopeless	Battlefield	U	0.75
Hound Archon	Legion	C	0.20
Hruggekolokh	Battlefield	VC	0.10
Hydroloth	Legion	U	0.75
Infinite Staircase	Battlefield	VC	0.10
Invite to Battle	Fate	C	0.20
Iron City of Dis	Battlefield	U	0.75
Jade Palace	Battlefield	VC	0.10
Jotunheim	Battlefield	U	0.75
16			
Kochrachon	Legion	C	0.20
Lance of Pain	Fate	C	0.20
Lantern Archon	Legion	C	0.20
Lazaret the Brown	Warlord	C	0.20
Leonal Guardinal	Legion	R	4.00
Light Aasimon	Legion	U	0.75
Lillend	Legion	R	4.20
Limbo	Battlefield	C	0.20
Lizard Lord	Warlord	C	0.25
17			
Lord Hwhyn	Warlord	U	0.75
Lord Rhanok	Warlord	U	0.75
Lord Tenarrus	Warlord	VC	0.10
Lord Thomstel the Maedarson	Warlord	U	0.75
Lost Comrade Returns	Fate	U	0.75
Lupinal	Legion	C	0.20
Mace of Misery	Fate	C	0.20
Madhouse	Battlefield	R	4.20
Major Transformation	Fate	C	0.20
18			
Malaetar Rider	Legion	U	0.75
Malelephant	Legion	C	0.20
Marilith Colonel	Warlord	MC	0.05
Marisa	Warlord	C	0.20
Mausoleum of Chronepsis	Battlefield	VC	0.10
Mechanus	Battlefield	C	0.20
Mellinos the Rrakkmal	Warlord	C	0.20
Merratet	Battlefield	U	0.75
Mezzoloth	Legion	U	0.75

Card name	Type	Rarity	Price
19			
Minauros the Sinking	Battlefield	U	0.75
Modron Procession	Fate	C	0.20
Molydeus Magistrate	Warlord	MC	0.05
Monodrone	Legion	R	4.20
Monster Summons	Fate	C	0.20
Mount Celestia	Battlefield	C	0.20
Mount Olympus	Battlefield	C	0.25
Movanic Deva	Legion	C	0.20
Nabassu	Legion	C	0.20
20			
Nalfeshnee Captain	Warlord	MC	0.05
Naratyr	Battlefield	U	0.75
Nic'Epona	Legion	C	0.20
Nidavellir	Battlefield	U	0.75
Night Hag	Legion	C	0.20
Norse Dwarves	Legion	U	0.75
Noviere Eladrin	Legion	C	0.20
Nupperibo	Legion	C	0.20
Nycaloth Warrior	Warlord	MC	0.05
21			
Octon	Legion	R	4.10
Old Hannirian	Warlord	VC	0.10
Oread	Legion	U	0.75
Osyluth	Legion	U	0.75
Outsider Archer	Legion	C	0.20
Palace of Judgement	Battlefield	VC	0.10
Pandemonium	Battlefield	C	0.20
Pandemonium Madness	Fate	C	0.20
Parai	Legion	R	3.90
22			
Pazrael	Warlord	R	3.90
Phylaras	Warlord	VC	0.10
Piscoloth	Legion	C	0.20
Plague-Mort	Battlefield	U	0.75
Plain of Infinite Portals	Battlefield	VC	0.10
Plains of Gallenshu	Battlefield	U	0.75
Planetar General	Warlord	MC	0.05
Political Scapegoat	Fate	C	0.20
Powers of Evil Intervene	Fate	U	0.75
23			
Powers of Good Intervene	Fate	R	4.10
Powers of Neutrality Intervene	Fate	R	3.90
Press Gang	Fate	U	0.50
Prime Summons I	Fate	C	0.20
Prime Summons II	Fate	U	0.75
Prime Summons III	Fate	U	0.75
Prime Summons IV	Fate	R	4.40
Protection vs. Fate	Fate	C	0.20
Protection vs. Legions	Fate	C	0.20
24			
Protection vs. Warlords	Fate	C	0.20
Quadrone	Legion	C	0.20
Quarton Hierarch	Warlord	MC	0.05
Quill	Legion	R	4.60
Quinton Hierarch	Warlord	MC	0.05
Rain of Fire	Fate	C	0.20
Red Slaad	Legion	C	0.20
Regulus	Battlefield	VC	0.10
Release from Care	Battlefield	R	3.70
25			
Renegotiations	Fate	C	0.20
Ribcage	Battlefield	U	0.50
Rigus	Battlefield	U	0.75
River Ma'at	Battlefield	VC	0.10
River Oceanus	Battlefield	C	0.20
River Styx	Battlefield	VC	0.10
Rogue Modron	Legion	C	0.20
Sardior	Warlord	VC	0.10
Scepter of Shekelor	Fate	R	4.20
26			
Scimitar of Valor	Fate	U	0.75
Scion of Ilsensine	Warlord	MC	0.05
Semuanya's Bog	Battlefield	VC	0.10
Sheela Peryroyl's Realm	Battlefield	U	0.75
Shield Maidens of Odin	Legion	R	4.00
Shiere Eladrin	Legion	C	0.20

Card name	Type	Rarity	Price
Shra'kt'lor	Battlefield	R	4.00
Smaragd	Battlefield	U	0.75
Sneak Attack	Fate	U	0.75
27			
Snowhair Oread	Legion	U	0.75
Soot Hall	Battlefield	U	0.50
Spawning Stone	Battlefield	R	4.20
Spell Mirror	Fate	C	0.20
Spies in the Walls	Fate	C	0.20
Spinagon	Legion	C	0.20
Spirit of the Air	Legion	C	0.20
Spirited Troops	Fate	C	0.20
Stolen Seat of Power	Fate	R	4.50
28			
Straifling	Battlefield	U	0.75
Strongale Hall	Battlefield	U	0.75
Succubus	Legion	C	0.25
Sword Archon	Legion	C	0.20
Sword of Purity	Fate	C	0.20
Sylvania	Battlefield	U	0.75
Talisid the Leonal Prince	Warlord	C	0.20
Teardrop Palace	Battlefield	VC	0.10
The Abyss	Battlefield	MC	0.05
29			
The Bladed Mace	Fate	U	1.00
The Gilded Hall	Battlefield	R	4.50
The Gray Waste	Battlefield	MC	0.05
The Harmonica	Battlefield	R	4.20
The High Grove of Alfheim	Battlefield	R	3.90
The Mines of Marsellin	Battlefield	U	0.75
The Outlands	Battlefield	VC	0.10
The Pillar of Skulls	Battlefield	U	1.00
The Ship of Chaos	Battlefield	U	0.75
30			
The Silver Sea	Battlefield	U	1.00
The Spire	Battlefield	VC	0.10
The Viper Wastes	Battlefield	U	0.75
Throne Archon	Warlord	MC	0.05
Tiamat	Warlord	R	4.30
Tide Turns!	Fate	C	0.20
Tiefling Amazon	Legion	U	0.75
Tiefling Wanderer	Legion	C	0.20
Tiefling Wizard	Legion	R	4.10
31			
Tokarrast Mercenary	Warlord	R	4.10
Torch	Battlefield	U	0.50
Torremor	Battlefield	VC	0.10
Tradegate	Battlefield	U	0.75
Trident of Corruption	Fate	U	0.75
Trumpet Archon	Legion	U	0.75
Tulani Champion	Warlord	MC	0.05
Tulani Warlord	Warlord	MC	0.05
Unified Front	Fate	U	0.50
32			
Urial, the Celestial Arrow	Warlord	R	4.40
Ursinal Guardinal	Legion	U	0.75
Vadarther the Ultroloth	Warlord	C	0.20
Valhalla	Battlefield	R	4.10
Vanaheim	Battlefield	U	0.75
Vargouilles	Legion	C	0.20
Vorkehan	Battlefield	R	4.20
Vrock	Legion	U	0.75
Warden Archon	Legion	C	0.20
33			
Wasting Tower of Khin-Oin	Battlefield	VC	0.10
Windglum	Battlefield	R	3.90
Winter's Hall	Battlefield	VC	0.10
Wolf Lord	Warlord	C	0.25
Xaos	Battlefield	U	0.50
Xerxes the Vigilant	Warlord	C	0.20
Yagnoloth	Legion	U	0.75
Yggdrasil	Battlefield	C	0.25
Ysgard	Battlefield	C	0.20
34			
Zoronor, City of Shadows	Battlefield	U	0.75
Zoveri	Legion	R	4.40
Zrintor the Viper Forest	Battlefield	U	0.75

RARITY KEY MC = Most Common **VC** = Very Common **C** = Common **U** = Uncommon **R** = Rare **X** = Fixed/standard in all decks

Blood Wars • *Rebels & Reinforcements*

TSR • Released **March 1995**

34 cards in set • **IDENTIFIER: None**

• Booster packs contain 15 cards; booster displays contain 36 packs

No, this isn't the smallest CCG expansion in history — it's actually how TSR packaged the booster packs for the initial **Blood Wars** release. As with **Spellfire**, TSR had the beginning booster packs include the 300 cards from the basic edition as well as from a special set of rares that could be found only in the boosters — in this case, 34.

Spellfire caused confusion by numbering its expansions from that initial set of boosters — a few collectors wondered where "Set 1" was before realizing it was the premiere release. *Blood Wars* fixed that by naming this first batch of boosters **Escalation Pack I: Rebels & Reinforcements** (which may puzzle people today searching for the nonexistent basic set boosters). The idea was sound: If multiple expansions on the market gave the appearance of a healthy game, it doesn't hurt to give yourself a head-start. — *John Jackson Miller*

Chase set (34 cards)	85.00	
Booster Display Box	82.50	
Booster Pack	1.50	

You will need 4 nine-pocket pages to store this set. (2 doubled up)

Card name	Type	Rarity	Price
Amulet of Protection	Fate	Ch	4.90
Bebilith Sympathizer	Fate	Ch	4.50
Bugbear Shaman	Legion	Ch	5.90
Crown of Protection	Fate	Ch	4.90
Foo Dog Pack	Fate	Ch	5.00
Gaze of the Bodak	Fate	Ch	4.90
Hruggek	Warlord	Ch	6.50

Card name	Type	Rarity	Price
Hruggek's Symbol	Fate	Ch	4.90
Legions Mutiny!	Fate	Ch	4.90
Lemure Patrol	Fate	Ch	4.60
Lower Planar Conscription	Fate	Ch	4.50
Marraenoloth Skiff	Fate	Ch	4.90
Massacre in Baator	Fate	Ch	4.90
Mephit Swarm	Fate	Ch	4.90
Mercykiller Paladin	Fate	Ch	5.50
Modron Sentries	Fate	Ch	4.90
Native of Sigil	Fate	Ch	4.90
Nupperibo Host	Fate	Ch	4.90
Peace Compact	Fate	Ch	4.50
Prisoners of War	Fate	Ch	4.90

Card name	Type	Rarity	Price
Ring of Protection	Fate	Ch	4.90
Scream of Armanites	Fate	Ch	4.90
Shamble of Rutterkin	Fate	Ch	4.90
Shekinester	Warlord	Ch	6.30
Shekinester's Symbol	Fate	Ch	4.90
Slaadi Mob	Fate	Ch	4.90
Slaughter in the Abyss	Fate	Ch	5.00
The Converted	Fate	Ch	4.90
The Lady of Pain	Warlord	Ch	21.00
Tiefling Sensate	Fate	Ch	4.90
Tutor of the Crone	Legion	Ch	5.60
Upper Planar Recruitment	Fate	Ch	4.40
Yeth Hound Pack	Fate	Ch	5.10
Yugoloth Bribery	Fate	Ch	4.90

Blood Wars • *Factols & Factions*

TSR • Released **June 1995**

134 cards in set • **IDENTIFIER: None**

• Booster packs contain 15 cards; booster displays contain 36 packs

Factols & Factions adds Warlord and Legion cards representing forces from Sigil, the nexus of the Planescape setting. Sigil Warlords can stack up to six Legion cards of various alignments if they are members of that Warlord's faction. — *John Jackson Miller*

Set (134 cards)	84.00	
Booster Display Box	70.00	
Booster Pack	1.80	

You will need 15 nine-pocket pages to store this set. (8 doubled up)

Promo card

Card name	Rarity	Price
Guardian Molydeus (Gen Con 1995)	R	3.00

Card name	Rarity	Price
Agathyn Anarchist	C	0.20
Amazon Guardian	Ch	3.00
Analchist Mark	Ch	3.50
Apothean Archer	C	0.20
Aquallorian Sensate	C	0.20
Armanite	Ch	2.50
Armory Of Sigil	U	0.35
Artus	R	1.60
Astral Searcher	U	0.45
Barber Shop Portal	R	1.50
Bladeswirl Portal	R	1.50
Bleak Battalion	R	1.60
Bleaker Mark	R	1.60
Boyles Glen	Ch	3.00
Chandlea's Portal	Ch	3.00
Chaos Men Mark	Ch	3.50
Cipher Mark	Ch	3.50
Clerk's Ward	U	0.35
Dabus	Ch	2.50
Dagger's Throw Portal	R	1.50
Dead Mark	R	1.60
Defier Mark	R	1.60
Diplomatic Treachery	Ch	3.00
Doomguard Mark	R	1.60
Doppelganger	C	0.20

Card name	Rarity	Price
Elder Beholder	C	0.20
Emerald Dragon Hatchling	R	1.50
Equipment Disintegration	Ch	3.00
Erosion Of Faith	Ch	3.00
Factol Ambar	U	0.45
Factol Darius	U	0.35
Factol Erin Darkflame Montgomery	R	1.80
Factol Hashkar	U	0.35
Factol Karan	U	0.45
Factol Lhar	U	0.35
Factol Mallin	U	0.45
Factol Pentar	U	0.45
Factol Rhys	U	0.35
Factol Rowan Darkwood	R	1.80
Factol Sarin	U	0.45
Factol Skall	U	0.35
Factol Terrance	U	0.45
Factol's Favor	U	0.45
Foecircle Portal	Ch	3.00
Foxwoman	C	0.20
Gamakar The Studious	R	1.60
Gladiator Of Sigil	C	0.20
Godsman Warrior	C	0.20
Godsmen Mark	R	1.60
Golden Portal	Ch	3.00
Great Blade Of Tasup	R	1.50
Guildhall/Market Ward	U	0.35
Guvner Bailiff	C	0.20
Guvner Mark	Ch	3.50
Halfling Cleric	C	0.20
Harbinger House	R	1.50
Hard Head Mark	Ch	3.50
Hardhead Dwarves	C	0.20

Site of the Lady's Ward of Sigil; head-quarters of the Fraternity of Order.

Card name	Rarity	Price
Harp Of Stars	R	1.50
Heartless Mark	Ch	3.50
Hezrou	Ch	3.00
Hidden Treasure	Ch	3.00
Hieracosphinx	R	1.50
Hill Giant	C	0.20
Hin Archer	C	0.20
Hive Ward	U	0.35
Hobgoblin Deader	C	0.20
Hope Incarnate	U	0.45
Indep Mark	Ch	3.50
Inkwell Portal	R	1.50
Inquisitive Kender	R	1.50
Judge Arcane	C	0.20
Larvae	Ch	2.50
Lizard Man	C	0.20
Lower Ward	U	0.35
Mane	C	0.20
Mediator	U	0.45
Mimir	Ch	3.00
Minor Magistrate	C	0.20
Moon Dog	C	0.20
Moon's Rose Patrol	Ch	3.00
Notice Of Secundus	U	0.45
Ogre Mage	C	0.20

RARITY KEY C = Common U = Uncommon R = Rare VR = Very Rare UR = Ultra Rare Ch = Chase X = Fixed/standard in all decks

Card name	Rarity	Price
☐ Orryx	R	1.60
☐ Paladin	R	1.50
☐ Portal Of Pain	Ch	3.00
☐ Quick Escape	R	1.50
☐ Ratatosk Gliders	U	0.45
☐ Red Death Mask	Ch	3.50
☐ Rest & Relaxation	Ch	3.00
11		
☐ Rogue Modron Merchant	C	0.20
☐ Sensate Mark	Ch	3.50
☐ Servant Li's Request	Ch	3.00
☐ Sigil's Sentries	U	0.45
☐ Signer Mark	Ch	3.50
☐ Streets Of Sigil	R	1.50
☐ Swords' Breath Portal	R	1.50
☐ Temple Of The Abyss	R	1.50
☐ The Aspirant	C	0.20
12		
☐ The Bleak Battalion	C	0.20

Card name	Rarity	Price
☐ The City Barracks	U	0.35
☐ The City Courts	R	1.50
☐ The Civic Festhall	R	1.50
☐ The Cynical Wizard	C	0.20
☐ The Defiant Ones	C	0.20
☐ The Dragon Bar	R	1.50
☐ The Entropy League	C	0.20
☐ The Gatehouse	U	0.35
13		
☐ The Glee-Bashers	C	0.20
☐ The Great Foundry	U	0.35
☐ The Great Gymnasium	U	0.35
☐ The Greengage	R	1.50
☐ The Hall Of Records	R	1.50
☐ The Hall Of Speakers	U	0.35
☐ The Hive	U	0.35
☐ The Key of Pain	UR/Ch	17.50
☐ The Lady's Ward	U	0.45

Card name	Rarity	Price
14		
☐ The Mazes	Ch	3.00
☐ The Mortuary	U	0.35
☐ The Perished	C	0.20
☐ The Prison	U	0.35
☐ The Scratcher	Ch	3.00
☐ The Screaming Falls	Ch	3.00
☐ The Shattered Temple	U	0.35
☐ Tiefling Mage/Thief	C	0.20
☐ Treant	C	0.20
15		
☐ Undead Host	Ch	3.00
☐ Under Arrest	U	0.35
☐ Valhalla's Finest	R	1.50
☐ Vorkehan Guard	C	0.20
☐ Wemic Shaman	R	1.50
☐ Wererat Indep	C	0.20
☐ Wererats Of Sigil	Ch	2.50
☐ Weretiger	C	0.20

Blood Wars • *Powers & Proxies*

TSR • Released **June 1995**

134 cards in set • **IDENTIFIER: None**

- Booster packs contain 15 cards; booster displays contain 36 packs

Powers & Proxies was by no means intended to be the last **Blood Wars** expansion. Three more expansions had been announced for 1996 and 1997 by the time that TSR stopped production on the game: *Escalation Pack IV: Insurgents of the Inner Planes*, *Escalation Pack V: Weapons & Warmongers*, and *Escalation Pack VI: Hand of Fates*. But a reference guide, *Warlord Tactical Manual*, did make it out before the end came.— *John Jackson Miller*

You will need **15** nine-pocket pages to store this set. (8 doubled up)

Set (134 cards)	**75.00**
Booster Display Box	**56.50**
Booster Pack	**1.80**

Card name	Rarity	Price
1		
☐ Abyssal Bats	C	0.20
☐ Ankhwugaht	R	1.90
☐ Apollo	R	1.90
☐ Apotheosis	U	0.60
☐ Archduke Dispater	Ch	3.50
☐ Ares	C	0.20
☐ Artemis	U	0.50
☐ Artemis' Bow	Ch	2.50
☐ Arumdina	Ch	2.50
2		
☐ Athena	C	0.20
☐ Avernus	C	0.20
☐ Axe Of Anarchy	C	0.20
☐ Axe Of The Dwarvin Lords	Ch	2.50
☐ Baervan Wildwanderer	R	1.90
☐ Bahamut's Charge	Ch	2.00
☐ Bahamut's Palace	C	0.20
☐ Baldur	U	0.60
☐ Baron Molikroth	U	0.60
3		
☐ Bast	R	1.90
☐ Bast's Defense	Ch	2.50
☐ Battle Axe Of Discord	U	1.40
☐ Battlefield Revolt	R	2.30
☐ "Bel, Regent Of Avernus"	C	0.20
☐ Bow Of Law	C	0.20
☐ Bow Of Order	U	0.50
☐ Cania	R	1.90
☐ Cavalry Rescue	R	2.60
4		
☐ Chaotic Holy Symbol	R	2.60
☐ Codex Of Infinite Planes	Ch	3.50
☐ Court Of Light	U	0.50
☐ Dis	C	0.20
☐ Dispater's Campaign	U	0.80
☐ Dugmaren Brightmantle	U	0.50
☐ Dumathoin	Ch	3.50
☐ Emissary Of Chaos	C	0.20
☐ Emissary Of Evil	C	0.20
5		
☐ Emissary Of Good	C	0.20
☐ Emissary Of Law	C	0.20
☐ Emissary Of Neutrality	C	0.20
☐ Evil Holy Symbol	Ch	3.50
☐ Farastu	C	0.20
☐ Flandal Steelskin	U	0.50

Card name	Rarity	Price
☐ Frey	Ch	3.50
☐ Freya	R	1.90
☐ Garl Glittergold	R	3.30
6		
☐ Garl's Faithful	R	1.90
☐ Good Holy Symbol	Ch	3.50
☐ Goristro	R	1.90
☐ Greater Coin Of Fate	Ch	3.50
☐ Gungnir	Ch	3.50
☐ Hod	U	0.50
☐ Holy Ground	Ch	3.50
☐ Howler	R	1.90
☐ Ilsensine	C	0.20
7		
☐ Kelubar	C	0.20
☐ Lawful Holy Symbol	R	1.90
☐ Legionnaires Of The Light	U	0.50
☐ Loki	R	1.90
☐ Lolth	Ch	3.50
☐ Lolth's Grove	R	1.90
☐ Maladomini	R	1.90
☐ Malbolge	U	0.50
☐ Marraenoloth Pilot	R	1.90
8		
☐ Mass Desertion	Ch	3.50
☐ Merrshaulk	R	1.90
☐ Minauros	C	0.20
☐ Minion Of Set	R	1.90
☐ Mjolnir	Ch	3.50
☐ Muamman Duathal	C	0.20
☐ Nectar Of Life	C	0.20
☐ Nephthys	U	0.50
☐ Nessus	R	2.30
9		
☐ Neutral Holy Symbol	R	1.90
☐ Nightmare	U	0.50
☐ Njord	U	0.50
☐ Occupying Forces	Ch	3.50
☐ Odin	Ch	3.50
☐ Olympus	U	0.60
☐ Order's Battalion	U	0.50
☐ Pazrael's Onslaught	C	0.20
☐ Phlegethos	U	0.50
10		
☐ Primus	Ch	3.50
☐ Prince Levistus	R	1.90
☐ Prismatic Battlesphere	R	1.90
☐ Proxy Of Chaos	C	0.20
☐ Proxy Of Chaos II	U	0.40
☐ Proxy Of Evil	C	0.20
☐ Proxy Of Evil II	U	0.50

Card name	Rarity	Price
☐ Proxy Of Good	C	0.20
☐ Proxy Of Good II	U	0.40
11		
☐ Proxy Of Law	C	0.20
☐ Proxy Of Law II	U	0.40
☐ Proxy Of Neutrality	C	0.20
☐ Proxy Of Neutrality II	U	0.40
☐ Pyrrhic Victory	Ch	3.50
☐ Ramenos	R	1.90
☐ Reenlistment	C	0.20
☐ Return To The Front	Ch	3.50
☐ Revenge Of The Exiraati	R	1.90
12		
☐ Segojan Earthcaller	C	0.20
☐ Selune	R	1.90
☐ Semuanya	U	0.50
☐ Set	Ch	3.50
☐ Shang-Ti	Ch	3.50
☐ Shator	C	0.20
☐ Sheela Peryroyl	U	0.50
☐ Sif	C	0.20
☐ Stygia	U	0.50
13		
☐ Sung Chiang	U	0.50
☐ Surtr	Ch	3.50
☐ Svartalfheim Drow	U	0.50
☐ Tabaxi	R	1.90
☐ Temporary Truce	Ch	2.00
☐ The Aegis	Ch	3.50
☐ The Defenders Harmonic	U	0.50
☐ The Floating Gods	UR/Ch	5.00
☐ The Kindred Souls	R	1.90
14		
☐ The Knights Anarchic	U	0.50
☐ The Mythcarvers	R	1.90
☐ The Oracles	R	1.90
☐ The Ruby Palace	C	0.20
☐ The Valiants Of Valhalla	R	1.90
☐ The Veterans Sanguine	U	0.50
☐ Thor	R	1.90
☐ Throne Of The Gods	Ch	3.50
☐ Thrym	Ch	3.50
15		
☐ Tiamat's Lair	C	0.20
☐ Tyr	C	0.20
☐ Uller	C	0.20
☐ Vergadain	R	1.90
☐ Wastrilith Dictator	C	0.20
☐ Wrath Of The Gods	R	3.30
☐ Yen-Wang-Yeh	R	1.90
☐ Zeus	Ch	3.50

RARITY KEY C = Common   U = Uncommon   R = Rare   VR = Very Rare   UR = Ultra Rare   F = Foil card   X = Fixed/standard in all decks

Boy Crazy

Decipher • Released **February 2000**

363 cards in set

Concept	●●○○○
Gameplay	●●○○○
Card art	●●●○○
Player pool	●○○○○

• Booster packs contain 10 cards; booster displays contain 36 boosters

Lots of girls played **Pokémon**, and one of the big challenges facing game companies in 2000 was figuring out ways to keep girls buying cards. Knowing that some of those girls were hitting the *Tiger Beat* years, Decipher released its own teen-heartthrob CCG.

Each card features a photo of a young male model, along with his favorite TV show, drink, car, and animal, and, most importantly, his ideal traits in a girl. (**Chris** from Washington is a Gemini and the captain of his baseball team, and "when he's not hitting home runs on the field and with girls, he likes to play with his cat.")

Each booster pack came with rules for a matchmaking game to be played with these images of spiky-haired teen-hunk wanna-bes, just reaching our minimal definition of a CCG. Hardcore CCG completists should find this an irresistible curiosity.

Decipher says *Boy Crazy* sold well in the mass market and overseas. In gaming, it was a dead letter. Girls may have entered game stores to buy *Pokémon*, but 95% of store managers and existing customers were still guys, and *Boy Crazy* appeared in few shops. One could argue the presence of a reverse double-standard: A set from someone portraying adolescent girls as sex symbols would've sold like "crazy" in hobby shops, but we'd worry about it sending retailers to jail! — *John Jackson Miller*

You will need **41** nine-pocket pages to store this set. (21 doubled up)

If nothing else, you'll just want to watch Vic walk. He says his walk is his best quality. His worst, his fears, is his lack of patience. But Vic is not one to dwell on the past. His motto is: "forward ever, backwards never." And, this adage comes in handy while he enjoys his favorite pastimes: hiking and biking.

Set (363 cards)	72.00
Booster Box	69.00
Booster Pack	1.95

No rarity levels in set

Card name	Price		Card name	Price		Card name	Price		Card name	Price
1 Tony	0.20		39 Dan	0.20		83 Michael	0.20		127 Mikk	0.20
2 Brendan	0.20		40 Gabriel	0.20		84 J.D.	0.20		128 Matt	0.20
3 Jason	0.20		41 Cole	0.20		85 Peter	0.20		129 Andrew	0.20
4 Octavian	0.20		42 Kevin	0.20		86 David	0.20		130 George	0.20
5 Tyler	0.20		43 Kyle	0.20		87 Kevin	0.20		131 Billy	0.20
6 Wes	0.20		44 Dominick	0.20		88 Andy	0.20		132 James	0.20
7 James	0.20		45 Luke	0.20		89 Vincent	0.20		133 Seth	0.20
8 Danny	0.20		46 Graeme	0.20		90 Brent	0.20		134 Josh	0.20
9 Olamide	0.20		47 Bo	0.20		91 Mal	0.20		135 Anthony	0.20
10 Keith	0.20		48 Daveindra	0.20		92 Carl	0.20		136 Ryan	0.20
11 Corey	0.20		49 Adam	0.20		93 Jason	0.20		137 Kenneth	0.20
12 Clarence	0.20		50 Sebastian	0.20		94 Vladimir	0.20		138 Thomas	0.20
13 Gerard	0.20		51 Joey	0.20		95 Chad	0.20		139 Tim	0.20
14 Chris	0.20		52 Justin	0.20		96 Brian	0.20		140 Ray	0.20
15 Joe	0.20		53 Majid	0.20		97 Mitchell	0.20		141 Steven	0.20
16 Justin	0.20		54 Trevor	0.20		98 Ryan	0.20		142 Eric	0.20
17 Chris	0.20		55 Kyle	0.20		99 Wes	0.20		143 Trevor	0.20
18 Jed	0.20		56 Cameron	0.20		100 Jack	0.20		144 Charles	0.20
19 Brett	0.20		57 Brian	0.20		101 Gerard	0.20		145 Matt	0.20
20 Aldo	0.20		58 Anthony	0.20		102 Kody	0.20		146 Danny	0.20
21 Stephen	0.20		59 Josh	0.20		103 Jamal	0.20		147 Mike	0.20
22 Dayne	0.20		60 Mitch	0.20		104 Josh	0.20		148 Ryan	0.20
23 Jimi	0.20		61 Adam	0.20		105 Trung	0.20		149 Lindsay	0.20
24 Corey	0.20		62 Aaron	0.20		106 Josh	0.20		150 Aaron	0.20
25 Garrett	0.20		63 Saad	0.20		107 Robert	0.20		151 Ray	0.20
26 Ryan	0.20		64 Taron	0.20		108 Vic	0.20		152 Brian	0.20
27 J.T.	0.20		65 Chris	0.20		109 Joshua	0.20		153 Chad	0.20
28 Sean	0.20		66 Tony	0.20		110 Nate	0.20		154 Jason	0.20
29 Randall	0.20		67 Mark	0.20		111 Chad	0.20		155 Simon	0.20
30 Donny	0.20		68 Collier	0.20		112 John	0.20		156 Mike	0.20
31 Brian	0.20		69 Christopher	0.20		113 William	0.20		157 Cam	0.20
32 Andy	0.20		70 Jason	0.20		114 Joshua	0.20		158 De'Garryan	0.20
33 Kevin	0.20		71 Mark	0.20		115 Vinnie	0.20		159 Destiny	0.20
34 Luke	0.20		72 Paul	0.20		116 Brian	0.20		160 Clint	0.20
35 Josh	0.20		73 Jason	0.20		117 Nate	0.20		161 Carlos	0.20
36 Randy	0.20		74 Michael	0.20		118 Graham	0.20		162 Jeremy	0.20
37 Jon-Scot	0.20		75 Leon	0.20		119 Louis	0.20		163 Jamal	0.20
38 Joshua	0.20		76 JR	0.20		120 Brandon	0.20		164 Daniel	0.20
			77 Brian	0.20		121 Vic	0.20		165 Ryan	0.20
			78 Jose	0.20		122 Cody	0.20		166 Christopher	0.20
			79 Kyle	0.20		123 Jon	0.20		167 Michael	0.20
			80 Scott	0.20		124 Kyle	0.20		168 Christian	0.20
			81 Matt	0.20		125 David	0.20		169 Mark	0.20
			82 Mark	0.20		126 Xavier	0.20		170 Dalen	0.20
									171 Matt	0.20

Card name	Price		Card name	Price		Card name	Price
172 Sal	0.20		211 Kim	0.20			
173 Nicholas	0.20		212 Jimmy	0.20			
174 John	0.20		213 Mike	0.20			
175 Kenny	0.20		214 Chris	0.20			
176 Alex	0.20		215 Kevin	0.20			
177 Michael	0.20		216 Justin	0.20			
178 Greg	0.20		217 Shane	0.20			
179 Justin	0.20		218 Chris	0.20			
180 Jesus	0.20		219 Daniel	0.20			
181 Andre	0.20		220 Tyler	0.20			
182 Brian	0.20		221 Carmine	0.20			
183 Chris	0.20		222 Jay	0.20			
184 Billy	0.20		223 Matthew	0.20			
185 Brandon	0.20		224 Sean	0.20			
186 Brandon	0.20		225 Matthew	0.20			
187 David	0.20		226 David	0.20			
188 Wade	0.20		227 Joseph	0.20			
189 Kunal	0.20		228 Britain	0.20			
190 Brian	0.20		229 Darren	0.20			
191 Marvin	0.20		230 Aaron	0.20			
192 Michael	0.20		231 Adam	0.20			
193 Bryan	0.20		232 Talib	0.20			
194 Zach	0.20		233 Tony	0.20			
195 Tyler	0.20		234 Jesse	0.20			
196 Shaun	0.20		235 Jeff	0.20			
197 Jonathan	0.20		236 Adam	0.20			
198 Jimmy	0.20		237 James	0.20			
199 Ryan	0.20		238 Chris	0.20			
200 Sean	0.20		239 Brian	0.20			
201 Casey	0.20		240 Joshua	0.20			
202 Tim	0.20		241 Damon	0.20			
203 Matt	0.20		242 Jeff	0.20			
204 Brad	0.20		243 Brandon	0.20			
205 Joe	0.20		244 Brian	0.20			
206 Kevin	0.20		245 Drew	0.20			
207 Nicholas	0.20		246 Patrick	0.20			
208 Tobias	0.20		247 Talon	0.20			
209 Joshua	0.20		248 Todd	0.20			
210 Chris	0.20		249 Zachary	0.20			
			250 Eric	0.20			

RARITY KEY C = Common U = Uncommon R = Rare VR = Very Rare UR = Ultra Rare F = Foil card X = Fixed/standard in all decks

SCRYE Collectible Card Game Checklist and Price Guide • **99**

Card name	Price	Card name	Price	Card name	Price	Card name	Price	Card name	Price	Card name	Price
251 Victor	0.20	270 Justin	0.20	289 Randall	0.20	308 Fred	0.20	327 Austin	0.20	346 Fred	0.20
252 Justin	0.20	271 Andrew	0.20	290 Kevin	0.20	309 Aaron	0.20	328 Chris	0.20	347 Matt	0.20
253 Dustin	0.20	272 Jeremiah	0.20	291 Sam	0.20	310 Miguel	0.20	329 James	0.20	348 Alex	0.20
254 Ryan	0.20	273 Eric	0.20	292 Shane	0.20	311 Matt	0.20	330 Billy	0.20	349 Adam	0.20
255 Michael	0.20	274 Matt	0.20	293 Shon	0.20	312 Jonathan	0.20	331 Robert	0.20	350 Jameson	0.20
256 Matt	0.20	275 Stephen	0.20	294 Ryan	0.20	313 Lynn	0.20	332 Jason	0.20	351 Jonathan	0.20
257 Tim	0.20	276 Aiden	0.20	295 Jonathan	0.20	314 Matt	0.20	333 Brian	0.20	352 Cody	0.20
258 Michael	0.20	277 Grant	0.20	296 Christopher	0.20	315 Joshua	0.20	334 Travis	0.20	353 David	0.20
259 J.R.	0.20	278 Gentry	0.20	297 Kevin	0.20	316 Tyler	0.20	335 Eric	0.20	354 David	0.20
260 Brooks	0.20	279 Brian	0.20	298 Richard	0.20	317 Tom	0.20	336 Brandon	0.20	355 Craig	0.20
261 Oliver	0.20	280 Brian	0.20	299 Matt	0.20	318 Caleb	0.20	337 Brett	0.20	356 Lucas	0.20
262 Loren	0.20	281 Chris	0.20	300 Tyler	0.20	319 Dan	0.20	338 Chris	0.20	357 Tony	0.20
263 Bryan	0.20	282 Jonathan	0.20	301 Sean	0.20	320 Cody	0.20	339 Luis	0.20	358 Justin	0.20
264 Drew	0.20	283 Jesse	0.20	302 Brian	0.20	321 Suresh	0.20	340 Justin	0.20	359 Tyler	0.20
265 Diego	0.20	284 Kory	0.20	303 Bryce	0.20	322 Mark	0.20	341 Sheldon	0.20	360 Blake	0.20
266 Eric	0.20	285 Vincent	0.20	304 Michael	0.20	323 Danny	0.20	342 Ted	0.20	361 John	0.20
267 Alvin	0.20	286 Jake	0.20	305 Alex	0.20	324 Juan	0.20	343 Sunil	0.20	362 Kenji	0.20
268 Rigel	0.20	287 Felipe	0.20	306 David	0.20	325 Michael	0.20	344 Tydan	0.20	363 Dan	0.20
269 Roy	0.20	288 Michael	0.20	307 Jeryd	0.20	326 Mitsunori	0.20	345 Stephen	0.20		

Calorie Kids

Ocean of Wisdom • Released **May 2000**

35 cards in set

- Starter decks contain 58 cards plus 2 holographic cards
- Starter decks are preconstructed: **Introductory Set**, **Ice & Water**, and **Flying & Magic**

Concept	●●○○○
Gameplay	●●○○○
Card art	●●●○○
Player pool	●○○○○

In the heady days of Pokémania, everyone wanted to get into the act. **Calorie Kids** is a perfect example of a good idea that went way off into left field — the berry fields, that is, right next to the orange grove and the vineyard. To call the concepts and characters odd is an understatement. Can you imagine a player's consternation at being defeated by a character named Grapewizz?

The concept behind Calorie Kids is that there are two groups of beings, the Calorie Kids and the Calorie Kids DT, the one good, the other evil. Calorie Kids travel the galaxies defending civilization from the villainous Calorie Kids DT. Both groups attempt to "attain higher stages of consciousness" by "jumping" using "caloric energy" — and maybe some fruit punch as well.

"Jumping" seems pretty much to be an excuse to play a variant of the classic game of "War." There are two basic games that can be played, each with a "pick your favorite rules and use them" style of play. Every Calorie Kid has a KAR number and every Calorie Kid DT (aka, "Bad Kids") has a RAK number, which are essentially combat values. Each basic game consists of six rounds of War, KAR against RAK, except that the cards are played from the hand instead of blind, and one player plays his card before the other. Each card is worth a number of Victory Points. A player that loses five exchanges loses the game, otherwise the winner is the player with the highest total Victory Points.

There are advanced rules that use a mix and match of "optional" rules that add complexity to the game, but overall it is still simply a fruity food fight. — *James Mishler*

SCRYE NOTES: *Booster packs were promised with the initial release of* **Calorie Kids***, and while they did not appear with the initial release, they were still in the works at press time. If they don't make it out, we won't consider* **Calorie Kids** *a true CCG in future discusions, as a set can be built from buying the three different starters.*

Transforms from Orangecee

Oranjuju — Daily intake: 40 CAL — 150 KAR

Residency: JU Universe

Molecular transformation: U-Jump
Heat magnification: 20 m
Fuel consumption: 8 Mortal Fuel Units (MFU)

Weapon: ju-hypnosis goggles. Effect: paralysis
Victory: 60, thermopower

a.k.a. Solarite, Chancellor, Federation Uph-ju

Illus. James Li — © 1999 Ocean of Wisdom

	Price
Starter Display Box	79.00
Two-player	
starter Deck (3 versions)	9.99

You will need 4 nine-pocket pages to store this set. (2 doubled up)

Card name	Type	#	Price
Bluberisaur	CalKidDT	1	0.50
Bluberiwrath	CalKidDT	2	0.25
Cherille	CalKid	5	0.05
Cherisar	CalKid	2	0.25
Cheryamor	CalKid	1	0.50
Cloaker/Supershield	Thermopower	3	0.15
Converter/Blocker	Thermopower	4	0.15
Converter/Blocker Class E	Thermopower	5	0.05
Converter/Blocker Class F	Thermopower	5	0.05
Converter/Blocker Class M	Thermopower	5	0.05

Card name	Type	Rarity	Price
Converter/Blocker Class P	Thermopower	5	0.05
Digbluberry	CalKidDT	5	0.05
Foulplum	CalKidDT	5	0.05
Grapevine	CalKid	2	0.25
Grapewizz	CalKidDT	2	0.25
Melonmelu	CalKid	4	0.15
Melonsquirtle	CalKidDT	4	0.15
Orangecee	CalKid	2	0.25
Orangeskull	CalKidDT	3	0.15
Orangezip	CalKidDT	2	0.25
Orangio	CalKid	3	0.15
Oranjuju	CalKid	1	0.50
Papayablow	CalKidDT	5	0.05
Papayakill	CalKidDT	1	0.50
Papayanerd	CalKidDT	2	0.25
Pearatle	CalKid	2	0.25

Card name	Type	Rarity	Price
Pearee	CalKid	1	0.50
Pearpaw	CalKid	5	0.05
Plumichu	CalKid	2	0.25
Plumumu	CalKid	5	0.05
Saurgrape	CalKid	5	0.05
Tatoogrape	CalKidDT	5	0.05
Witchyplum	CalKidDT	2	0.25
Wormhole/Annihilator	Thermopower	3	0.15
Zutorange	CalKidDT	F	0.50

Thermopower

Collectors note: There are multiple versions of each Thermopower card in *Calorie Kids*.

RARITY KEY # = number of cards in starter deck

The Crow

Heartbreaker Hobbies/Target Games AB
Released **November 1995**
122 cards in set

Concept	●●○○○	
Gameplay	●●●○○	
Card art	●●○○○	
Player pool	○○○○○	

• Booster packs contain 15 cards; booster displays contain 36 boosters

Based on James O'Barr's moody series, 1994's *The Crow* is regarded as one of the best comic-book adaptation films of all time. As a collectible card game released during the CCG glut of 1995, it died quicker than its title character, Eric Draven. It was one of *three* new CCGs introduced by Heartbreaker/Target in the U.S. just in the month of November — including *James Bond 007* and *Kult!*

Each player controls Angel, Devil, and Neutral Bystander cards, and sends them off into combat with opposing personalities. There are also action cards which let players pump their Personality or hinder another player's.

Each Personality has an attack and defense value, and "Virtue," equal to the highest value. Players play the card and discard cards from their hands with a Virtue equal to the card they're playing, then attack. If a player has a higher attack value than an opponent's defense value, the opponent is wounded. If a wounded personality is wounded again, it is killed. A player wins by killing 25 Virtue worth of his opponent's personalities.

While *The Crow* would have been a great game for younger kids, the subject matter was way too dark for them — and older players didn't flock to it, either. An expansion in support of the movie sequel, *Crow: City of Angels*, was announced for October 1996 but never came out. — ***Richard Weld***

You will need
14
nine-pocket pages to store this set.
(7 doubled up)

Set (122 cards)	96.75
Booster Display Box	70.00
Booster Pack	2.40

Card name	Rarity	Price
A Dead Man Visits You	C	0.20
Anarchy - Now That's Fun!	C	0.20
Arson	U	0.80
Attrition	Ch	21.50
Awareness	C	0.20
Believe In Angels	U	0.90
Big Plans	U	0.80
Blade	C	0.15
Blend In	U	0.60
Blinded	U	0.60
Bouncer	C	0.20
Brutality	U	0.80
Burdened	U	0.80
Calm Within The Storm	U	1.00
Captured	U	0.80
Change Of Heart	C	0.20
Club Trash	U	0.80
Crescendo	Ch	22.50
Crime Scene	U	0.60
Criminal Scum	U	0.80
Cut Off	U	1.00
Darla	C	0.25
"Darla's Home, Sarah's House"	U	1.00
Death Overdrive	R	4.00
Deliverance	U	1.00
Delivered Out Of Evil	C	0.15
Despair	Ch	21.50
Detective Torres	R	4.00
Determination	U	0.60
Deviation	C	0.20
Devil's Night In Detroit	U	0.90
Driving Beat	U	0.80
Dusted	U	0.80
Eat This	U	0.80
Eric Draven - The Crow	R	8.00
Eternal Sadness	U	0.80
Even Up	U	0.80
Fear	Ch	22.50
Fear And Bullets	U	0.80

Card name	Rarity	Price
Feint	U	0.80
Firepower	U	0.90
Flashback Stupor	U	0.90
Fleeting Happiness	U	0.90
Friend In Need	U	0.60
Funboy	R	3.30
Gabriel	R	6.00
Gideon	C	0.20
Gideon's Pawnshop	U	0.60
Grange	R	2.50
Graveyard	C	0.20
Healing Crow	R	6.30
Henchman	C	0.20
Hidden Away	U	0.90
Hit And Run	U	0.60
Hope Sings Eternal	U	1.40
I'm Coming Home	U	0.60
Inertia	Ch	22.50
Intimidated	C	0.20
Invincibility	U	0.60
Invulnerable Crow	R	5.50
Irony	Ch	21.50
Junked Up	U	0.60
Kind-Hearted Soul	U	0.60
Lament	Ch	21.50
Like Lightning	U	0.90
Lonely Crow	R	6.00
Looter	C	0.20
Lost In Remorse	C	0.20
Lost Opportunity	U	1.00
Love Never Dies	U	1.10
Makeshift Weapon	U	1.00
Maxi-Dogs	U	0.60
Mother Is The Name For God	U	1.10
Myca	R	2.50
Nervous	C	0.20
Not A Good Night For Bad Guys	U	0.60
Nothing Personal	U	1.00
Officer Albrecht	R	5.50
Officer Annabella	R	5.50
Pain	Ch	21.50
Pain Threshold	U	1.00
Precarious Situation	C	0.20

Card name	Rarity	Price
Power Of Vengeance	U	0.60
Resolved Crow	R	5.80
Resources	U	0.60
Righteousness	U	0.60
Running Scared	C	0.20
Ruthless Crow	R	6.00
Sarah	R	9.00
Serendipity	U	0.60
Shelly Webster	R	8.00
Shelly's Ring	U	0.60
Skank	R	2.30
Skull Cowboy	C	0.20
Sorry!	C	0.20
Soul Search	U	0.80
Spiritual Guidance	C	0.15
Superior Crow	R	7.00
Swipe	U	0.90
Tables Turn	U	0.80
T-Bird	R	2.00
The Artocity Exhibition	Ch	22.50
The Big Moby	U	0.60
The Boardroom	C	0.20
The Cathedral	U	0.60
The Loft	C	0.20
Thicker Than Water	U	1.00
Tin Tin	R	2.50
Token Of Friendship	U	0.60
Top Dollar	R	3.00
Transformation Of Tears	U	1.00
Upper Hand	U	0.60
Vantage Point	U	0.60
Velocity	Ch	22.50
Vengeful Crow	R	6.30
Viciousness	U	0.60
Victims - Aren't We All?	U	0.90
Vision Of Weakness	U	0.60
Weakness	U	0.60
Wrong Things Right	U	0.60
You Never Stop Dying For Me	U	0.90
Your Power Is Mine	C	0.20

RARITY KEY C = Common U = Uncommon R = Rare VR = Very Rare Ch = Chase card F = Foil card X = Fixed/standard in all decks

C·23 (Also known as *Jim Lee's C·23*)

Wizards of the Coast • Released **April 1998**

162 cards in set

- Starters contain 40 cards and two large rules sheets
- Starter displays contain 18 starters, three each of six different theme decks
- Booster packs contain 12 cards; booster displays contain 45 boosters

Designed by **Charlie Catinus, Mike Davis, Skaff Elias, Richard Garfield, Joe Grace, Jim Lin,** and **Joel Mick**

Wizards of the Coast had been interested for years in the comics market (where, after all, many of its products are sold). Rather than adapt an existing comic book for its first foray, Wizards worked with Image Comics star Jim Lee (whose studio had previously given us the **Wildstorms** CCG) to create a CCG world supported by a new ongoing comic book.

In the far future of *C·23*, the remnants of humanity live an underground city, "The Colony." Humanity sends cybernetically enhanced HyperShock Troops to try to reclaim the Earth's surface from the Angelans, a monstrous race of humanoid insects. Things are complicated by the factionalization of the Colony, between the evil government of Cronus and the rebels led by Corbin, who has discovered a terrible secret.

The first game released using the ARC System, *C·23* is compatible with **Hercules: The Legendary Journeys** as well as **Xena: Warrior Princess**, the other two ARC System releases. The system is a simplified Deckmaster system, similar in many respects to **Magic: The Gathering**. There are four different types of cards: Resource, Character, Combat, and Action cards. "Tapping" is a core game mechanism in the ARC System, as it is in Deckmaster. Unlike **Magic**, however, there are only three different "colors" in *C·23*: red "Military Resources" (locations such as **Armory**), green "Medical Resources" (**Biology Lab**), and blue "Political Resources" (**Council Chamber**).

Resources are played and tapped to bring Characters into play or to play Combat or Action cards. Character, Combat and Action cards each are of a single color; at least one of the resources tapped to use that card must be of the same color as the card. Characters attack an opponent; the opponent may defend with Characters, Combat, or Action cards (unlike Deckmaster, defending Characters tap). If an attacking Character is unblocked it will deal damage directly to the opponent's deck; one card discarded for every point of damage. A player that loses all cards from their deck loses the game.

With few non-gaming comic-book fans interested in reading an appendage to a game, sales of the *C·23* comic book were disappointing. (Jim Lee himself soon left the comics self-publishing biz, selling his studio to DC Comics in late 1998.) Sales of the CCG weren't much better, and the planned expansion, **Uprising**, was not produced. Perhaps if the ARC System games had been released following the **Pokémon** craze, they'd have had a better reception, as the system is a stage in complexity between *Pokémon* and *Magic.* — *James A. Mishler and John Jackson Miller*

	Rating
Concept	●●○○○
Gameplay	●●●○○
Card art	●●●○○
Player pool	●○○○○

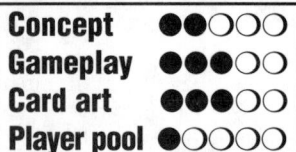

Set (162 cards)	76.00	
Starter Display Box	50.00	
Booster Display Box	50.00	
Starter Deck	5.50	
Booster Pack	2.20	

You will need **18** nine-pocket pages to store this set. (9 doubled up)

#	Card Name	Color	Type	Rar	Price
144	Added Incentives	Blu	Act	R	3.00
120	Ambush Tactics	Blu	Cbt	C	0.20
73	Angelan Autopsy	Grn	Act	U	0.60
115	Angelan Commander	Blu	Char	C	0.20
55	Angelan Garrison	Grn	Char	C	0.20
61	Angelan Guard Beast	Grn	Char	C	0.20
147	Angelan Hulkbusters	Blu	Char	R	4.00
81	Angelan Juggernaut	Grn	Char	U	0.60
58	Angelan Scouts	Grn	Char	C	0.20
145	Angelan Seers	Blu	Char	R	4.00
59	Angelan Slaves	Grn	Char	C	0.20
70	Angelan Transport	Grn	Act	U	0.60
161	Angelan War Room	Blu	Res	X	0.20
130	Armored Transport	Blu	Char	U	0.60
156	Armory	Red	Res	X	0.20
119	Artillery Support	Blu	Cbt	C	0.20
108	Automated Defenses	Blu	Char	C	0.20
47	Barrage	Red	Char	R	4.00
2	Barrage's HE Charge	Red	Act	C	0.20
40	Barrage's Homing Missile	Red	Act	R	3.00

#	Card Name	Color	Type	Rar	Price
38	Barrage's Tracking Missiles	Red	Act	R	3.00
35	Because Hemlocke Commands It	Red	Act	R	2.50
157	Biology Lab	Grn	Res	X	0.20
28	Bomb 'n' Bash Unit	Red	Char	U	0.60
158	Breeding Chamber	Grn	Res	X	0.20
14	Burn Squad	Red	Char	C	0.20
107	Carnivorous Plant	Blu	Char	C	0.20
50	Climactic Battle	Red	Cbt	R	3.00
30	Colonial Division	Red	Char	U	0.60
117	Colonial Hulkbusters	Blu	Char	C	0.20
4	Colonial Police	Red	Char	C	0.20
112	Colonial Scouts	Blu	Char	C	0.20
10	Combat-Stressed Vets	Red	Char	C	0.20
13	Convicts	Red	Char	C	0.20
48	Corbin	Red	Char	R	6.00
33	Corbin Flashes His Ion Blade	Red	Cbt	U	0.60
42	Corbin Leads the HyperShocks	Red	Act	R	3.00
39	Corbin Levels an Outpost	Red	Act	R	3.00
86	"Corbin Needs Help, Badly"	Grn	Act	R	3.00
88	Corbin Questions the Survivors	Grn	Act	R	3.00
36	Corbin Raids the Armory	Red	Act	R	2.50
71	Corbin Suddenly Remembers	Grn	Act	U	0.60
51	Corbin Trashes a Lab	Red	Cbt	R	3.00
31	Corbin's Expert Touch	Red	Cbt	U	0.60
162	Council Chamber	Blu	Res	X	0.20
150	Councilor Mariah	Blu	Char	R	4.00

#	Card Name	Color	Type	Rar	Price
105	Councilor Mariah Makes Plans	Blu	Act	C	0.20
136	Councilor Mariah Tracks Her Assets	Blu	Act	R	2.50
114	Councilor Mariah's Guard	Blu	Char	C	0.20
143	Councilor Mariah's Influence	Blu	Act	R	3.00
126	Cronus Consults the Oracle	Blu	Act	U	0.60
125	Cronus Planned Ahead	Blu	Act	U	0.60
29	Cybered-Up Gizard	Red	Char	U	0.60
121	Decoy	Blu	Act	U	0.50
32	Defensive Force Fields	Red	Cbt	U	0.60
124	Delaying Tactic	Blu	Act	U	0.50
67	Desert Nomads	Grn	Char	C	0.20
34	Desperate Gamble	Red	Act	R	2.50
103	Did You Hear Something?	Blu	Act	C	0.20
95	Ekon	Grn	Char	R	4.00
140	Ekon's Intelligence Net	Blu	Act	R	2.50
60	Ekon's Recruits	Grn	Char	C	0.20
12	Ekon's Task Force	Red	Char	C	0.20
56	Ekon's Understudy	Grn	Char	C	0.20
127	Electric Barrier	Blu	Char	U	0.60
18	Electrodart Rifle	Red	Cbt	U	0.60
44	Elite Special Forces Unit	Red	Char	R	4.00
27	EMP Platoon	Red	Char	U	0.60
135	Facade	Blu	Cbt	U	0.60
11	Fanatical Troops	Red	Char	C	0.20
134	Flank Attack	Blu	Cbt	U	0.60

RARITY KEY C = Common U = Uncommon R = Rare VR = Very Rare UR = Ultra Rare F = Foil card X = Fixed/standard in all decks

102 • SCRYE Collectible Card Game Checklist and Price Guide

Card name	Type	Rarity	Price
☐111 Forward Command Point	Blu	Char C	0.20
☐ 3 Fresh Out of the Academy	Red	Char C	0.20
☐ 96 Gamelus	Grn	Char R	4.00
☐ 80 Gamelus Corps	Grn	Char U	0.60
☐ 85 Gamelus Plots the Approach	Grn	Act R	3.00
☐ 77 Giant Scorpion	Grn	Char U	0.60
☐ 25 Goon Squad	Red	Char U	0.60
☐109 Groundpounders	Blu	Char C	0.20
☐148 Hemlocke	Blu	Char R	5.30
☐ 22 Hemlocke Gets His Hands Dirty	Red	Act U	0.60
☐106 Hemlocke Puts His Foot Down	Blu	Act C	0.20
☐113 Hemlocke's Investigators	Blu	Char C	0.20
☐131 Hemlocke's Secret Police	Blu	Char U	0.60
☐ 83 Hyper Stimulants	Grn	Cbt U	0.60
☐155 HyperShock Barracks	Red	Res X	0.20
☐141 Indiscriminate Terrorism	Blu	Act R	3.00
☐ 87 Knockout Gas	Grn	Act R	3.00
☐ 54 Lethal Porcurchin	Grn	Char C	0.20
☐ 7 Loyal Strike Force	Red	Char C	0.20
☐133 Lucky Strike	Blu	Cbt U	0.60
☐ 66 Lumbering Hulk	Grn	Char C	0.20
☐ 91 Major Offensive	Grn	Act R	3.00
☐149 Medicus	Blu	Char R	4.00
☐151 Medicus Patches Them Up	Blu	Cbt R	3.00
☐129 Medicus's Lab Workers	Blu	Char U	0.60
☐116 Mobile Sector HQ	Blu	Char C	0.20
☐ 52 Mustard Gas	Grn	Act C	0.20
☐152 Mutual Enemy	Blu	Cbt R	3.00
☐ 45 Nemesis	Red	Char R	4.50
☐ 17 Nemesis Crushes Them…	Red	Cbt C	0.20

Card name	Type	Rarity	Price
☐ 19 Nemesis Knows Counterattacks	Red	Act U	0.60
☐ 21 Nemesis Mows Down Angelans	Red	Act U	0.60
☐137 Nemesis Spots a Weakness	Blu	Act R	2.50
☐123 Outmaneuver	Blu	Act U	0.50
☐ 43 Panzer	Red	Char R	4.00
☐ 46 Phalanx	Red	Char R	5.00
☐ 1 Phalanx Busts Down the Door	Red	Act C	0.20
☐ 41 Phalanx Gets Carried Away	Red	Act R	3.00
☐ 20 Phalanx Has Just the Thing	Red	Act U	0.60
☐ 24 Phalanx Hoses Them Down	Red	Act U	0.60
☐132 Phalanx Provides Suppression Fire	Blu	Cbt U	0.60
☐138 Phalanx's Images Run Interference	Blu	Act R	2.50
☐ 23 Phalanx's Plasma Barrage	Red	Act U	0.60
☐ 97 Phyla	Grn	Char R	5.00
☐ 53 Phyla Does the Dirty Work	Grn	Act C	0.20
☐ 89 Phyla Drums Up Support	Grn	Act R	3.00
☐ 37 Phlya Filches an Ultrasound Rifle	Red	Act R	3.00
☐ 82 Phyla's Stingers	Grn	Cbt U	0.80
☐ 76 Phyla's Stoolie	Grn	Char U	0.60
☐ 74 Plague Mosquitoes	Grn	Char U	0.60
☐ 94 Plague Swarms	Grn	Char R	4.00
☐ 92 Plaguebearer	Grn	Char R	4.00
☐ 75 Poisonous Snakes	Grn	Char U	0.60
☐ 98 Razorflies	Grn	Char R	3.50
☐ 8 Rebel Rousers	Red	Char C	0.20
☐ 5 Rebel Sentry	Red	Char C	0.20
☐ 16 Rejected Experiment	Red	Char C	0.20
☐ 15 Riot Suppressors	Red	Char C	0.20

Card name	Type	Rarity	Price
☐ 65 Rioting Masses	Grn	Char C	0.20
☐ 26 Rocket Platoon	Red	Char U	0.60
☐ 99 Sand Worm	Grn	Char R	3.50
☐ 72 Scouting Mission	Grn	Act U	0.60
☐128 Sensor Station	Blu	Char U	0.60
☐ 62 Sewer Dwellers	Grn	Char C	0.20
☐ 9 Sniper Crew	Red	Char C	0.20
☐ 79 Spies in High Places	Grn	Char U	0.60
☐ 78 Stampeding Herd	Grn	Char U	0.60
☐104 Stasis Field	Blu	Act C	0.20
☐ 63 Strafing Drone	Grn	Char C	0.20
☐100 Strength in Numbers	Grn	Cbt R	2.50
☐118 Subdue	Blu	Cbt C	0.20
☐ 69 Sudden Mutation	Grn	Cbt C	0.20
☐159 Surgery Room	Grn	Res X	0.20
☐122 Tactical Database	Blu	Act U	0.50
☐ 84 Tactical Instincts	Grn	Cbt U	0.60
☐160 The Oracle	Blu	Res X	0.20
☐146 The Outcasts	Blu	Char R	4.00
☐139 The Outcasts Take Point	Blu	Act R	2.50
☐ 64 Thunder Beetle	Grn	Char C	0.20
☐ 49 Tracking Device	Red	Cbt R	3.00
☐110 Training Cadre	Blu	Char C	0.20
☐153 Trap!	Blu	Cbt R	3.00
☐ 90 Truth Serum	Grn	Act R	3.00
☐ 57 Tunnel Commando	Grn	Char C	0.20
☐101 Virus Carriers	Grn	Cbt R	2.50
☐ 6 Water Cannon Brigade	Red	Char C	0.20
☐154 Weapons Factory	Red	Res X	0.20
☐ 68 Wolvern Pack	Grn	Char C	0.20
☐142 Wrath of Hemlocke	Blu	Act R	3.00
☐ 93 Wyland	Grn	Char R	4.00
☐102 Wyland's Cocktail Surprise	Grn	Cbt R	2.50

Dark Age

FPG (Friedlander Publishing Group) • First set, ***Feudal Lords***, released **July 1996**
231 cards in set • **2** promo cards
- Starter decks contain 65 cards, sticker, and dice
- Booster packs contain 10 cards; booster displays contain 36 booster packs
- Combo display pack contains 6 starter decks and 36 booster packs
Designed by **Luke Peterschmidt**

Dark Age: Feudal Lords was the closest thing to a "Mad Max" CCG ever available on the market, capturing the essence of the post-apocalypse genre, both in appearance and in game play. The game was a showcase of art from Brom, Bradstreet and other artists from the "Gritty, Dark, Leather-and-Rubber-Clad School of Style."

The game is about combat, pure and simple. The object is to reach 10 Victory Points by looting an opponent's turf, killing his characters, or accomplishing a goal outlined on a Victory card. Each player has a specific Leader and a Controlled Location card with three areas. Leaders have Leadership and Supply points which are used to play Characters, Instants, Supplies, Skills, and Weapons. Each character has a Combat String for Distance Fire, Close Combat Attack, and Close Combat Block. The Combat String is a series of numbers against which a roll of two six-sided dice is compared. Every number in the string that is equaled or exceeded means a hit is scored; Close Combat can be blocked with a similar roll. The combat system has a gritty, post-apocalypse feel that has yet to be equalled.

Unfortunately, ***Dark Age*** came out late in the initial CCG glut and at the same time that the post-apocalypse genre hit rock bottom. A 225-card expansion set, ***The Brood***, was announced for October 1996 but was never released.— ***James A. Mishler***

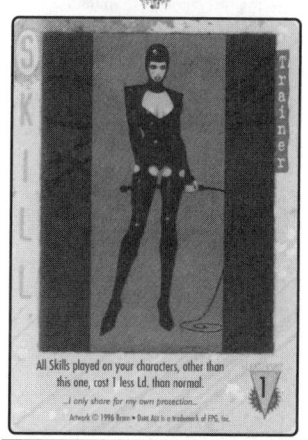

All Skills played on your characters, other than this one, cost 1 less Ld. than normal.
…I only share for my own protection.
Artwork © 1996 Brom • Dark Age is a trademark of FPG, Inc.

Concept	●●●○○	
Gameplay	●●●●○	
Card art	●●●●○	
Player pool	○○○○○	

Set (231 cards + 2 promos)	45.00	
Combo Display Box	30.00	
Booster Display Box	20.00	
Starter Deck	4.00	
Booster Pack	2.00	

You will need 26 nine-pocket pages to store this set. (13 doubled up)

☐ Artifact: Energy Bot	Promo	5.00
☐ Clergy Ann	Promo	2.00

Card name	Rarity	Price
☐ Abraham	R	2.00
☐ Acid Rain	R	1.00
☐ Acolyte	U	0.50
☐ Aggression	C	0.05
☐ Ain't Gonna Happen	U	0.50
☐ Ain't No Big Thing	U	0.50
☐ Anticipation	U	0.50
☐ Artifact - Brain Expander	Ch	5.00

Card name	Rarity	Price
☐ Artifact - Digger Bot	Ch	5.00
☐ Artifact - Organizer Bot	Ch	5.00
☐ Artifact - Pleasure Bot	Ch	5.00
☐ Artifact - Wise Leader	Ch	5.00
☐ Assassin	R	2.00
☐ Attack Shield	U	0.50
☐ Attack Wasps	U	0.50
☐ Bad Doc Leader	X	1.00

RARITY KEY C = Common **U** = Uncommon **R** = Rare **VR** = Very Rare **UR** = Ultra Rare **F** = Foil card **X** = Fixed/standard in all decks

Card name	Rarity	Price	Card name	Rarity	Price	Card name	Rarity	Price
☐ Bad Luck	C	0.05	☐ Heavy Armor	R	2.00	☐ Quick to the Punch	C	0.05
☐ Bad Reputation	R	1.00	☐ Hell Blade	R	2.00	☐ Rally Round The Carcass	R	1.00
☐ Bane	U	0.50	☐ Hell Storm	R	2.00	☐ Ravage	C	0.05
☐ Banger	C	0.05	☐ Hero	U	0.50	☐ Raze	U	0.50
☐ Banshee Warrior	C	0.05	☐ Hidden Stores	C	0.05	☐ Razor Claw	U	0.75
☐ Bar/Rooftops/Water Hole	X	0.10	☐ Hit the Seams	C	0.05	☐ Razor Wire Spring Trap	R	2.00
☐ Big Boy Must Go Down	R	1.00	☐ Holy Land Fever	U	0.50	☐ Reactive Shield	R	2.00
☐ Bio Farm/Dumping Grounds/Forest	X	0.10	☐ Holy Symbol	R	2.00	☐ Receive Council	U	0.50
☐ Black Market	R	1.00	☐ Holy Text	U	0.50	☐ Red	R	1.00
☐ Blessen	C	0.05	☐ HooDoo Leader	X	0.75	☐ Red Fungus Injection	U	0.50
☐ Blood Ritual	R	1.00	☐ HooDoo Totem	R	2.00	☐ Religious Fervor	U	0.50
☐ Bloodless Leader	U	0.50	☐ Hunter	R	2.00	☐ Riot in the Streets	C	0.05
☐ Bluff	C	0.05	☐ Hypnotism	R	1.00	☐ Rumble Time	C	0.05
☐ Bobby Gun	C	0.05	☐ I Hear Good Things	R	1.00	☐ Saboteurs	R	1.00
☐ Bounty Hunter	C	0.05	☐ Imposter	R	1.00	☐ Sacrifical Lamb	U	0.50
☐ Brain Stimm	C	0.05	☐ "In Your Face, Ace"	R	1.00	☐ Saint Mark	R	1.00
☐ Brass	R	2.00	☐ Initiate of Murk	C	0.05	☐ Scar Gang Leader	X	1.00
☐ Bravery	U	0.50	☐ Insightful Arming	U	0.50	☐ Scorched Earth	C	0.05
☐ Bribe the Recruit	U	0.50	☐ Inspiration	C	0.05	☐ Scour Battlefield	C	0.05
☐ Bribe the Trainer	C	0.05	☐ Interdiction	U	0.50	☐ Search for Crew	C	0.05
☐ Bribery	U	0.50	☐ Intimidation	C	0.05	☐ Self-Destruct Bomb	U	0.50
☐ Briggum	U	0.50	☐ Intuitive	C	0.05	☐ Shade	R	1.00
☐ Bunker	U	0.50	☐ Invest Leadership	R	1.00	☐ Shepherd	C	0.05
☐ Buster	R	2.00	☐ Kaustic	U	0.50	☐ Situational Awareness	U	0.50
☐ Can't Touch This	U	0.50	☐ Killer Instinct	U	0.50	☐ Skilled Mentor	R	1.00
☐ Cathedral/Reactor Core/Magnetic Core	X	0.10	☐ Killing Grounds/War Shelter/Sewage Plant	X	0.10	☐ Sling Net Gun	U	0.50
☐ Chastity	R	1.00	☐ Knows the Land	U	0.50	☐ Slum Lord	U	0.75
☐ Chem Mask	C	0.05	☐ Labrynth/Acrid Fields/Safety Tunnels	X	0.10	☐ Smoke Grenade	C	0.05
☐ Chop Shop	U	0.50	☐ Lady Luck Smiles	C	0.05	☐ Solitary Reflection	R	1.00
☐ City Leader	U	0.50	☐ Leadership	U	0.50	☐ Sonic Distractor	C	0.05
☐ Clean the Sewers	C	0.05	☐ Light Armor	R	2.00	☐ Sour Victory	R	1.00
☐ Coil	U	0.50	☐ Lock Out	R	1.00	☐ Speed	R	1.00
☐ Corrosive Fuel Spray	U	0.50	☐ Looter	U	0.50	☐ Spinning Spear	R	1.00
☐ Cutter Arm	C	0.05	☐ Luck	U	0.50	☐ Stimm Treatment	U	0.50
☐ Death Dervish Grenade	C	0.05	☐ Lucky Blow	C	0.05	☐ Strik	U	0.50
☐ Death Disk	R	1.00	☐ Lucky Shot	C	0.05	☐ Strike to Stun	C	0.05
☐ Defector	C	0.05	☐ Machine Core/Sewers/Great Hall	X	0.10	☐ Sucker Punch	C	0.05
☐ Defensive Posture	C	0.05	☐ Manipulate	U	0.50	☐ Sucks To Be You	R	1.00
☐ Depository/Transport Tubes/Grav Field	X	0.10	☐ Marksman	R	2.00	☐ Survivalist Leader	X	0.75
☐ Disciple of the Fall	C	0.05	☐ Martial Arts	U	0.50	☐ Targeter	C	0.05
☐ Dodge and Hide	C	0.05	☐ Maul	R	1.00	☐ Teck Ear	C	0.05
☐ Dredge Holes	U	0.50	☐ Meathook	C	0.05	☐ Terrifying Scream	C	0.05
☐ Dreg Surfer	C	0.05	☐ Meet the Charge	R	1.00	☐ Terrorist Bot	R	2.00
☐ Enhanced Optix	C	0.05	☐ Mercenary Leader	X	1.00	☐ That Thing is HUGE	R	1.00
☐ Fame	C	0.05	☐ Mesh Armor	U	0.50	☐ Threats	C	0.05
☐ Field Medic	R	2.00	☐ New Options	U	0.50	☐ Tool Kit	U	0.50
☐ Fiend	U	0.50	☐ "Nice Try, French Fry"	U	0.50	☐ Trainer	C	0.05
☐ Find Weak Spot	R	2.00	☐ "No Guts, No Glory"	U	0.50	☐ Training	R	1.00
☐ Flame Thrower	R	2.00	☐ "No Way, Jose"	U	0.50	☐ True Charisma	R	1.00
☐ Flash Grenades	R	2.00	☐ Nope	U	0.50	☐ Venousa	U	0.50
☐ Foresight	C	0.05	☐ Not in the Briar Patch	U	0.50	☐ Victory Dance	R	2.00
☐ Fortune Smiles	C	0.05	☐ Not Quite Dead	C	0.05	☐ Vision of Paradise	R	1.00
☐ Frustrate Defense	R	1.00	☐ Offensive Posture	C	0.05	☐ Viz Noise Generator	R	1.00
☐ Fuel Tank	C	0.05	☐ Once More Into the Fray	R	1.00	☐ VooDoo Doll	R	1.00
☐ Funny Little Pills	R	1.00	☐ Pale Fighter	C	0.05	☐ Warburn	U	0.50
☐ Get Out There You Big Lug	U	0.50	☐ Park/Factory/Mega Mall	X	0.10	☐ Warhead Leader	X	1.00
☐ Get Shorty	C	0.05	☐ Pastor	C	0.05	☐ Warknight Leader	X	1.00
☐ Get The Goodies	U	0.50	☐ Patcher	C	0.05	☐ Weapon Harness	C	0.05
☐ Gimme That	R	1.00	☐ Patient Leader	C	0.05	☐ Weaponsmith	R	2.00
☐ Glue Cannon	R	1.00	☐ Poisoned Blade	U	0.50	☐ White Reaver Leader	X	0.75
☐ Goliath Syndrome	R	1.00	☐ Political Bribes	R	1.00	☐ Wilderness Guide	U	0.50
☐ Good Pickins	U	0.50	☐ Politiking the Draft	R	1.00	☐ Wildeye	U	0.50
☐ Goodman	C	0.05	☐ Power Fist	U	0.75	☐ Wipeout!	C	0.05
☐ Grafter	C	0.05	☐ Preacher	U	0.50	☐ Witness Leader	X	0.75
☐ Grenade	C	0.05	☐ Preveyor	U	0.50	☐ Wrecker	U	0.50
☐ Grenade Launcher	U	0.75	☐ Prudence	R	1.00	☐ X-Cess	C	0.05
☐ Grinner	C	0.05	☐ Psychotic Intern	R	1.00	☐ X-Cite	U	0.50
☐ Grith	U	0.50	☐ Purity	C	0.05	☐ X-Otic	R	1.00
☐ Gymnasium/Acid Tunnels/Energy Core	X	0.10	☐ Pyro	C	0.05	☐ You Ain't All That	R	1.00
☐ Hail Storm	R	1.00	☐ Quatermaster	C	0.05	☐ You Ain't That Tough	R	1.00
☐ Head Gear	U	0.50	☐ Quick Shot	R	1.00	☐ You Just Try	C	0.05
☐ Heal Pouch	U	0.50	☐ Quick to React	C	0.05			

RARITY KEY   **C** = Common   **U** = Uncommon   **R** = Rare   **VR** = Very Rare   **UR** = Ultra Rare   **F** = Foil card   **X** = Fixed/standard in all decks

Dark Eden

Heartbreaker Hobbies/Target Games AB • Released **April 1997**

303 cards in set

- Starter decks contain 60 cards; starter displays contain 8 starters
- Booster packs contain 15 cards; booster displays contain 24 boosters

 Dark Eden presents the same post-apocalyptic Earth as Heartbreaker's **Doomtrooper** CCG, wherein the Four Tribes, Crescentia, the Sons of Rasputin, the Lutheran Triad, and the Templars, as well as the Dark Legion, the Brotherhood, and the Megacorporations fight to control Turf.

 Dark Eden has four card types: Commanders, Establishments, Warriors and Intrigue. The Commander has an Affiliation and produces Resources, including Gold, Food, Fuel, and Raw Materials. Establishments, which also produce Resources, are played next to the Commander, and build around him, creating a map. Warriors go in a space between the "Turf" of the players. Intrigue cards can be played out of the hand in combat, or attached to Warriors if enhancements or equipment.

 Players perform Actions, balance Resources, attack opponent's warriors, and raid opponent's Turf. Actions include playing Establishments, playing Warriors, attaching equipment, or using Intrigue cards. Warriors can be formed into Attack or Defense Groups.

 Designed to be "dark future" realistic, there are two types of combat: Attacking and Raiding. Warriors can Attack an opponent's Warrior, or Raid and, hopefully, destroy an opponent's Establishment. A player gets one Attack per turn. In the end, once players Raid and destroy 50 points of Establishments, they win.

 The basic strategy of *Dark Eden* is to build a really strong army, use it to crush any blockers, then drive over and blow up Establishments. It's a combat game, pure and simple — but it couldn't combat 1997's soft market for CCGs. Two expansions, **Genesis** and **Exodus** were announced for 1998, but were never released — *Richard Weld*

Concept	●●○○○
Gameplay	●●●○○
Card art	●○○○○
Player pool	○○○○○

Set (303 cards)	102.00	**34** nine-pocket pages to store this set. (17 doubled up)
Starter Display Box	57.00	You will need
Booster Display Box	65.00	
Starter Deck	4.75	
Booster Pack	2.25	

Card name	Group	Type	Rarity	Price
[1]				
☐ A Small Victory	Genrl	Intrig	R2	1.00
☐ Abdul IV Of The Pale Sun	Crscntia	Comndr	C1	0.10
☐ Ali II Of The Eclipse	Crscntia	Comndr	R1	2.00
☐ Ambush	Genrl	Intrig	U1	0.75
☐ Amphibious Landing	Genrl	Intrig	U1	0.75
☐ Anti-Aircraft Gun	Genrl	Intrig	U2	0.50
☐ Anti-Terrorism Headquarters	Genrl	Estab	R1	1.50
☐ Arable Land	Genrl	Estab	C2	0.05
☐ Armored Harness	Genrl	Intrig	C1	0.10
[2]				
☐ Armory	Genrl	Estab	R1	1.50
☐ Arson	Genrl	Intrig	U1	0.75
☐ Asian Skull	Genrl	Intrig	R2	2.00
☐ Assassination	Genrl	Intrig	U1	0.75
☐ Astinou	Tmplar	Comndr	U1	0.75
☐ Back From The Brink	Genrl	Intrig	R1	2.00
☐ Bait And Switch	Genrl	Intrig	R1	2.00
☐ Barricade	Genrl	Estab	U2	0.50
☐ Battering Ram	Genrl	Intrig	U1	0.75
[3]				
☐ Bazaar	Genrl	Estab	R1	1.50
☐ Behold The Future Possibilities	Crscntia	Intrig	R1	2.00
☐ Berserk	Genrl	Intrig	U2	0.50
☐ "Blessing, Or Curse?"	Genrl	Intrig	C1	0.10
☐ Blitz	Genrl	Intrig	U1	0.75
☐ Blitztank	Rasputin	Warr	R1	1.50
☐ Bloodlust	Genrl	Intrig	C1	0.10
☐ Boot Camp	Genrl	Estab	U1	0.75
☐ Brethren Unite	Genrl	Intrig	C2	0.05
[4]				
☐ Bribe	Genrl	Intrig	R1	2.00
☐ Brick By Brick	Genrl	Intrig	R1	2.00
☐ Brotherbound Sergeant	Crscntia	Warr	C1	0.10
☐ Brotherbound Trooper	Crscntia	Warr	C2	0.05

Card name	Group	Type	Rarity	Price
☐ Bumper Crop!	Genrl	Intrig	C1	0.10
☐ Butcher	Crscntia	Estab	U1	0.75
☐ Cain Mournor	Luthrn	Comndr	U1	0.75
☐ Call To Arms	Genrl	Intrig	C2	0.05
☐ Camouflage	Genrl	Intrig	R2	1.00
[5]				
☐ Cavalier	Luthrn	Warr	C1	0.10
☐ Charge	Genrl	Intrig	U1	0.75
☐ Coastline	Genrl	Intrig	U2	0.50
☐ Combined Arms	Genrl	Intrig	U1	0.75
☐ Combined Funds	Genrl	Intrig	U1	0.75
☐ Confusion	Genrl	Intrig	R2	1.00
☐ Connections	Genrl	Intrig	C1	0.10
☐ Conscript	Genrl	Warr	C2	0.05
☐ Contaminate Water Supply	Genrl	Intrig	R1	2.00
[6]				
☐ Corarius Transport	Rasputin	Warr	U1	0.75
☐ Corsair	Luthrn	Warr	U1	0.75
☐ Cossack	Rasputin	Warr	C1	0.10
☐ Cossack Kommendant	Rasputin	Warr	C1	0.10
☐ Cossack Scout	Rasputin	Warr	R1	1.50
☐ Countdown	Genrl	Intrig	R1	2.00
☐ Countess Alexandra Spetz	Rasputin	Comndr	U1	0.75
☐ Crescent Musk	Crscntia	Estab	R1	1.50
☐ Crescentia Embassy	Genrl	Estab	C1	0.10
[7]				
☐ Crescentian Twotusk	Crscntia	Warr	U2	0.50
☐ Cut Off	Genrl	Intrig	U1	0.75
☐ Dark Blessing	DkLeg	Intrig	C1	0.10
☐ DkLeg Citadel	Genrl	Estab	C1	0.10
☐ Death From Above	Genrl	Intrig	U1	0.75
☐ Deep Mine	Genrl	Estab	C2	0.05
☐ Defense Center	Genrl	Estab	U1	0.75
☐ Defensive Perimeter	Genrl	Intrig	R2	1.00
☐ Demolition Plans	Genrl	Intrig	R1	2.00
[8]				
☐ Denied	Genrl	Intrig	C1	0.10
☐ Desperate Actions	Genrl	Intrig	R1	2.00
☐ Dishonorable Discharge	Genrl	Intrig	R1	2.00
☐ Double-Barreled Shotgun	Genrl	Intrig	C2	0.05
☐ Driving Winds	Genrl	Intrig	R1	2.00
☐ Drought	Genrl	Intrig	C1	0.10

Card name	Group	Type	Rarity	Price
☐ Duke Erich Von Drier	Rasputin	Comndr	C1	0.10
☐ Duke Friedrich Rauft	Rasputin	Comndr	R1	2.00
☐ Earthshock	DkLeg	Intrig	U1	0.75
[9]				
☐ Eclipse Mammoth	Crscntia	Warr	C1	0.10
☐ Economic Planning	Genrl	Intrig	C1	0.10
☐ Efficiency	Genrl	Intrig	C1	0.10
☐ Efficient Use Of Space	Genrl	Intrig	C1	0.10
☐ Elijah Cormick	Luthrn	Comndr	R1	2.00
☐ Equalize	Genrl	Intrig	U1	0.75
☐ Espionage Agency	Genrl	Estab	C1	0.10
☐ Eureka!	Genrl	Intrig	C1	0.10
☐ European Skull	Genrl	Intrig	R1	2.00
[10]				
☐ Ezoghoul	DkLeg	Warr	R1	1.50
☐ Faithlessness	Genrl	Intrig	U1	0.75
☐ Fall Back!	Genrl	Intrig	R1	2.00
☐ False Front	Genrl	Intrig	R2	1.00
☐ False Prophet	Genrl	Intrig	U1	0.75
☐ Faulty Map	Genrl	Intrig	R1	2.00
☐ Fertile Grounds	Genrl	Estab	C1	0.10
☐ Fervor	Genrl	Intrig	C1	0.10
☐ First Things First	Genrl	Intrig	R2	1.00
[11]				
☐ Fist Of Judah	Genrl	Intrig	C2	0.05
☐ Fix The Books	Genrl	Intrig	U2	0.50
☐ Flammen Incinerator	Rasputin	Intrig	U2	0.50
☐ Flammen Soldat	Rasputin	Warr	R1	1.50
☐ Focus Inward	Genrl	Intrig	R1	2.00
☐ Food Shortage	Genrl	Intrig	R2	1.00
☐ Fortified Walls	Genrl	Intrig	C1	0.10
☐ Fortune Or Folly	Genrl	Intrig	C1	0.10
☐ Fresh Start	Genrl	Intrig	R1	2.00
[12]				
☐ Fuel Shortage	Genrl	Intrig	R2	1.00
☐ Fuel Spill	Genrl	Intrig	C1	0.10
☐ Fumble	Genrl	Intrig	U2	0.50
☐ Fusilier	Luthrn	Warr	U1	0.75
☐ Garbage Dump	Genrl	Estab	U1	0.75
☐ Gendarme	Tmplar	Warr	U1	0.75
☐ Gendarme Bestal	Tmplar	Warr	R1	1.50
☐ Gomorrian Emasculator	DkLeg	Warr	R2	1.50
☐ Grainery	Genrl	Estab	C1	0.10

Card name	Group	Type	Rarity	Price
13				
Grand Heretic Marcus	DkLeg	Comndr	U1	0.75
Grenade	Genrl	Intrig	R2	1.00
Greymourn Trench Artillery	Luthrn	Warr	U1	0.75
Grimgrind Airvessel	Luthrn	Warr	U1	0.75
Grinder	Brthrhd	Warr	U1	0.75
Grove	Genrl	Estab	C1	0.10
Gusher!	Genrl	Intrig	C1	0.10
Hang Glider	Genrl	Intrig	C1	0.10
Harding's Influence	Genrl	Intrig	R1	2.00
14				
Heavy Cavalier	Luthrn	Warr	U2	0.50
Heavy Maintenance	Genrl	Intrig	C1	0.10
Hellblaster	DkLeg	Intrig	U1	0.75
Hidden Riches	Genrl	Intrig	C1	0.10
Holy Urox	Crscntia	Warr	U2	0.50
Horde Centurion	Tmplar	Warr	C1	0.10
Horde Trooper	Tmplar	Warr	C2	0.05
Hospital	Genrl	Estab	R1	1.50
Human Shield	Genrl	Intrig	R1	2.00
15				
Hussein Of The Drowned Star	Crscntia	Comndr	U1	0.75
Hypersight	DkLeg	Intrig	U1	0.75
I Thought You Were Watching It	Genrl	Intrig	U1	0.75
I'll Take That	Genrl	Intrig	C1	0.10
Illumination	Genrl	Intrig	R1	2.00
Immobilized	Genrl	Intrig	R1	2.00
Impervious Rock Formation	Genrl	Estab	C1	0.10
Indigo	Brthrhd	Warr	U1	0.75
Inefficiency	Genrl	Intrig	C1	0.10
16				
Infiltration	Genrl	Intrig	R2	1.00
Ironshark	Genrl	Intrig	C1	0.10
Jaeger Commando	Rasputin	Warr	U1	0.75
Jihad Infantry Trooper	Crscntia	Warr	U1	0.75
Jonah Sand	Luthrn	Comndr	C1	0.10
Josef Gabriel	Luthrn	Comndr	U1	0.75
Just In Time	Genrl	Intrig	R2	1.00
Kommendant	Rasputin	Warr	C1	0.10
Kommendant Leitheusser	Rasputin	Comndr	C1	0.10
17				
Larceny	Genrl	Intrig	R1	2.00
Livery	Genrl	Estab	C2	0.05
Lost Potential	Genrl	Intrig	R1	2.00
Lutheran Disciple	Luthrn	Warr	C2	0.05
Lutheran Sergeant	Luthrn	Warr	C1	0.10
Luthrn Embassy	Genrl	Estab	C1	0.10
Malevolence	Genrl	Intrig	C1	0.10
Manufacturing Plant	Genrl	Estab	C1	0.10
Marine Serett	Tmplar	Warr	U2	0.50
18				
Martyr	Crscntia	Warr	U1	0.75
Mastermind Coup D'etat	Genrl	Intrig	U1	0.75
Mastodon	Crscntia	Warr	C1	0.10
Mastodon Handler	Crscntia	Warr	R1	1.50
Melancholy	Genrl	Intrig	R1	2.00
Memorium	Genrl	Intrig	R1	2.00
Mercenary	Genrl	Intrig	R2	1.00
Methane Pump	Genrl	Estab	C1	0.10
Militia	Genrl	Intrig	C1	0.10
19				
Minefield	Genrl	Estab	U2	0.50
Mineral Deposit	Genrl	Estab	C1	0.10
Mint	Genrl	Estab	U1	0.75
Misappropriation	Genrl	Intrig	U1	0.75
Mitch Hunter	Megacp	Warr	U1	0.75
Montàgne	Tmplar	Comndr	U1	0.75
Motivated Troops	Genrl	Intrig	U1	0.75
Motor Pool	Genrl	Estab	U1	0.75
Mounted Spikes	Genrl	Intrig	C1	0.10
20				
Munitions Dump	Genrl	Estab	U1	0.75
Nassal	DkLeg	Warr	C1	0.10
Naval Training Center	Genrl	Estab	R1	1.50
Necrobionic Mutation	DkLeg	Intrig	C1	0.10
Necrobionic Torrent	DkLeg	Intrig	R1	2.00
Nepharite Ancyrite	DkLeg	Comndr	C1	0.10
Never Again	Genrl	Intrig	R2	1.00
North American Skull	Genrl	Intrig	R1	2.00
Not So Fast	Genrl	Intrig	C1	0.10
21				
Nothing To Lose	Genrl	Intrig	R2	1.00
Notre Dame	Tmplar	Estab	R1	1.50
Oil Field	Genrl	Estab	C2	0.05
On Your Own	Genrl	Intrig	R1	2.00
Onslaught	Genrl	Intrig	U2	0.50
Ore Deposit	Genrl	Estab	C2	0.05
Our Enemy's Weakness Is Exposed	Crscntia	Intrig	R1	2.00
Our True Enemy Is Revealed	Crscntia	Intrig	R1	2.00
Our Will Is Beyond Measure	Crscntia	Intrig	U2	0.50
22				
Overtime	Genrl	Intrig	R2	1.00
Pacified	Genrl	Intrig	R1	2.00
Palanquin Airvessel	Luthrn	Warr	R1	1.50
Patriarch	Luthrn	Warr	C1	0.10
Payment Up Front	Genrl	Intrig	C1	0.10
Peacetime	Genrl	Intrig	R1	2.00
Personal Transport	Genrl	Intrig	C1	0.10
Phische	DkLeg	Warr	C1	0.10
Plague	Genrl	Intrig	R1	2.00
23				
Potential	Genrl	Intrig	C1	0.10
Predatorian	Tmplar	Warr	C1	0.10
Prefabrication Yard	Rasputin	Estab	R1	1.50
Pretorian Stalker	DkLeg	Warr	R1	1.50
Prisoner Work Camp	Genrl	Estab	U1	0.75
Prophet	Crscntia	Warr	C1	0.10
Prophetic Vision	Crscntia	Intrig	U1	0.75
Prosperity	Genrl	Intrig	R1	2.00
Pulp Plant	Luthrn	Estab	U1	0.75
24				
Purification Lab	Genrl	Estab	U1	0.75
Pyrite	Genrl	Intrig	C1	0.10
Rampage!	Genrl	Intrig	U1	0.75
Razide	DkLeg	Warr	R2	1.50
Reconstruction	Genrl	Intrig	R1	2.00
Recycle	Genrl	Intrig	U1	0.75
Refinery	Genrl	Estab	U1	0.75
Retreat	Genrl	Intrig	U1	0.75
Rich Deposit!	Genrl	Intrig	C1	0.10
25				
Rivetbull	Rasputin	Warr	U1	0.75
Robbed Blind	Genrl	Intrig	U1	0.75
Rough Seas	Genrl	Intrig	R1	2.00
Sacred Tear	Crscntia	Warr	R1	1.50
Salvage	Genrl	Intrig	R1	2.00
Samir Of The Rising Moon	Crscntia	Comndr	R1	2.00
Sanctum	Luthrn	Estab	R1	1.50
Schwerwaffe Soldat	Rasputin	Warr	U2	0.50
Scorched Earth	Genrl	Intrig	R1	2.00
26				
Scout Cavalier	Luthrn	Warr	U2	0.50
Seaman	Genrl	Warr	C2	0.05
Sebastian Crenshaw	Brthrhd	Warr	U1	0.75
Security Station	Genrl	Estab	C1	0.10
Serennel	Tmplar	Comndr	U1	0.75
Share The Wealth	Genrl	Intrig	R1	2.00
Shield	Genrl	Intrig	C1	0.10
Shock Soldat	Rasputin	Warr	R2	1.50
Shrieking Frenzy	DkLeg	Intrig	C1	0.10
27				
Silo	Genrl	Estab	C1	0.10
Sneaky Coward	Genrl	Intrig	U1	0.75
Soil Nutriture	Genrl	Estab	U1	0.75
Solar Power Generator	Tmplar	Estab	U1	0.75
Soldat	Rasputin	Warr	C2	0.05
Solidarity	Genrl	Intrig	C1	0.10
Sons Of Rasputin Embassy	Genrl	Estab	C1	0.10
Soul Siphon	DkLeg	Intrig	R1	2.00
South American Skull	Genrl	Intrig	R1	2.00
28				
Stained Crow	Genrl	Warr	C2	0.05
Steam Tunnel	Rasputin	Estab	U1	0.75
Storehouse	Genrl	Estab	R1	1.50
Strafe Attack	Genrl	Intrig	U1	0.75
Subversive	Genrl	Intrig	C1	0.10
Suffer the Consequences	Genrl	Intrig	R1	2.00
Summit Meeting	Genrl	Intrig	R1	2.00
Support Artillery Ox	Crscntia	Warr	R1	1.50
Survival Of The Fittest	Genrl	Intrig	U1	0.75
29				
Tactical Superiority	Genrl	Intrig	C2	0.05
Tailwave	Rasputin	Warr	U2	0.50
Tank	Genrl	Estab	C1	0.10
Task Force	Genrl	Intrig	R1	2.00
Tavern	Genrl	Estab	C1	0.10
Tmplar Embassy	Genrl	Estab	C1	0.10
Tmplar Legionnaire	Tmplar	Warr	U1	0.75
Tmplar Marine	Tmplar	Warr	U2	0.50
Terrorism	Genrl	Intrig	R1	2.00
30				
The Best Laid Plans	Genrl	Intrig	U1	0.75
The Blessing	Luthrn	Intrig	R1	2.00
The Calling	Luthrn	Intrig	U1	0.75
The Changeling	Luthrn	Intrig	C1	0.10
The Conviction	Luthrn	Intrig	U1	0.75
The Cost Of War	Genrl	Intrig	C1	0.10
The Defiance	Luthrn	Intrig	C1	0.10
The Howling Is Upon Us	Crscntia	Intrig	U1	0.75
The Protection	Luthrn	Intrig	U1	0.75
31				
The Sacrifice	Luthrn	Intrig	U1	0.75
The Trembling	Luthrn	Intrig	U1	0.75
Think Again!	Genrl	Intrig	C1	0.10
Torrent Battle Wagon	Crscntia	Warr	U1	0.75
Torrential Downpour	Genrl	Intrig	R1	2.00
Toxic Leak	Genrl	Intrig	R2	1.00
Trading Post	Genrl	Estab	C1	0.10
Traitor!	Genrl	Intrig	U1	0.75
Transfer Orders	Genrl	Intrig	U2	0.50
32				
Tusked Serett	Tmplar	Warr	C1	0.10
Undead Legionnaire	DkLeg	Warr	C2	0.05
Unholy Hunger	DkLeg	Intrig	R1	2.00
Upper Hand	Genrl	Intrig	U1	0.75
Valpurgius Arrives!	Genrl	Intrig	R1	2.00
Vault	Genrl	Estab	R1	1.50
Vehicle Works	Genrl	Estab	C2	0.05
Veiled Dart	Rasputin	Warr	R1	1.50
Venom Sack	DkLeg	Intrig	U1	0.75
33				
Veragé	Tmplar	Comndr	R1	2.00
Verounist Stingray	Tmplar	Warr	R1	1.50
Veterinary Hospital	Genrl	Estab	R1	1.50
Visionary Decomposition	DkLeg	Intrig	R1	2.00
Walking Tall	Genrl	Intrig	C1	0.10
War Room	Genrl	Estab	R1	1.50
Watch Tower	Genrl	Estab	U2	0.50
We Have To Eat!	Genrl	Intrig	R2	1.00
Weapons Factory	Genrl	Estab	R1	1.50
34				
Whew!	Genrl	Intrig	U1	0.75
Winds Of Change	Genrl	Intrig	R1	2.00
Work Exchange	Genrl	Intrig	U1	0.75
Wrench In The Works	Genrl	Intrig	U1	0.75
Writ Of Inquisitor Benedictus	Genrl	Intrig	R1	2.00
Zhurgon	DkLeg	Warr	U2	0.50

RARITY KEY C = Common U = Uncommon R = Rare # = Lower numbers are rarer X = Fixed/standard in all decks

Digi-Battle (also known as *Digimon*)

Upper Deck • First set, *Series 1,* released **February 2000**
128 cards in set

- Starter decks contain 62 cards and a rulebook; starter displays contain 10 decks
- Booster packs each contain 8 cards; booster Displays each contain 36 packs

The ***Digi-Battle Collectible Card Game*** is based on the *Digimon* ("digital monsters") animated television and movie series and all three, like ***Pokémon***, target a younger audience. "Like *Pokémon*" is, in fact, a phrase seldom heard apart from *Digimon*. But unlike *Pokémon*, *Digi-Battle* and the *Digimon* property in general never got the wild, broad support that *Pokémon* experienced.

The game itself features six card types. Four are different card levels of Digimon, from the weakest, basic level Rookie cards, through Champion cards and the more powerful Ultimate and Mega Level Digimon cards. Digimon are "evolved" through the use of Digivice cards, until no more digivolving is possible based on the cards in hand. Relative strengths of the Digimon attacks are compared in the Battle phase, with the Power Blast cards allowing for bonuses to an attack if targeted Digimon possess specific Special Abilities. Highest point value Digimon wins, and the winning player adds the point value of the battle (based on the relative level of the opposing Digimon) to his score. The first player to 1,000 points wins.

Poor distribution across the game trade may explain part of why *Digi-Battle* never really caught on with hardcore gamers. Upper Deck, a sportcard company, had partnered years before with Precedence on ***Gridiron Fantasy Football*** and had handled the mass-market distribution on that product; with *Digi-Battle*, their strategy also relied heavily on the mass market. (But *Digi-Battle* may have served as a CCG training ground for Upper Deck, which released two other CCGs in 2000.)

Upper Deck parted ways with Bandai, the owner of the *Digimon* property, shortly after the release of ***Digi-Battle Series 2***. There have been reports that Bandai will release its own edition of *Digi-Battle*, though whether it will use the same system and when (and even if) it will be released are unknown as of press time.— ***James A. Mishler***

Concept	●●○○○
Gameplay	●●○○○
Card art	●●●○○
Player pool	●●○○○

SCRYE NOTES: Digimon cards have separate numbering tracks depending on whether they appear in starter (ST) decks or booster (BO) packs.

Set (128 cards)	152.50
Starter Display Box	77.00
Booster Display Box	80.00
Starter Deck	10.00
Booster Pack	3.00

You will need **15** nine-pocket pages to store this set. (8 doubled up)

Card#	Card Name	Type	Rarity	Price
ST-01	Agumon	Rook.	C	0.25
BO-11	Andromon	Ult.	R	2.50
ST-14	Angemon	Champ.	C	0.25
BO-16	Angewomon	Ult.	R	3.00
ST-43S	Apemon	Champ.	F	6.50
ST-43	Apemon	Champ.	C	0.25
BO-45	Aquatic Attack	PwrBlst	C	0.25
BO-24	Asuramon	Ult.	R	2.50
ST-45S	Bakemon	Champ.	F	6.00
ST-45	Bakemon	Champ.	C	0.25
ST-04	Birdramon	Champ.	C	0.25
ST-03	Biyomon	Rook.	C	0.25
ST-52	Blitz	PwrBlst	C	0.25
BO-41	Boltmon	Mega	GS	11.50
BO-52	Bomb Dive	PwrBlst	R	2.50
ST-41S	Candlemon	Rook.	F	8.00
ST-41	Candlemon	Rook.	C	0.25
ST-17	Centarumon	Champ.	C	0.25
ST-36	Coelamon	Champ.	C	0.25
BO-44	Coral Rip	PwrBlst	U	0.50
ST-54	Counter Attack!	PwrBlst	C	0.25
BO-28	Crabmon	Rook.	C	0.25
ST-42S	DemiDevimon	Rook.	F	6.50
ST-42	DemiDevimon	Rook.	C	0.25
BO-54	Depth Charge	PwrBlst	R	2.50
BO-02	Devimon	Champ.	R	3.00
ST-58	Digi-Duel	PwrBlst	C	0.25

Card#	Card Name	Type	Rarity	Price
BO-53	Digiruption	PwrBlst	R	2.50
ST-60	Digivice Green & Yellow	Digivolve	C	0.25
ST-59	Digivice Red	Digivolve	C	0.25
ST-61	Digivice Red & Green	Digivolve	C	0.25
ST-62	Digivice Yellow	Digivolve	C	0.25
ST-55	Digivolve to Champion	Digivolve	C	0.25
ST-19	Dokugumon	Champ.	C	0.25
ST-35	Dolphmon	Champ.	C	0.25
ST-57S	Downgrade	PwrBlst	F	6.50
ST-57	Downgrade	PwrBlst	C	0.25
BO-33	Dragomon	Ult.	U	0.50
BO-10	Drimogemon	Champ.	C	0.25
BO-18	Ebidramon	Champ.	C	0.25
BO-51	Even Steven	PwrBlst	U	0.50
BO-46	Fly Away	PwrBlst	C	0.25
BO-43	Fly-Trap	PwrBlst	U	0.50
BO-07	Frigimon	Champ.	C	0.25
ST-05	Gabumon	Rook.	C	0.25
ST-06	Garurumon	Champ.	C	0.25
BO-15	Gatomon	Champ.	GS	12.50
ST-27	Gekomon	Champ.	C	0.25
BO-30	Gesomon	Champ.	C	0.25
ST-11	Gomamon	Rook.	C	0.25
BO-19	Gorillamon	Champ.	C	0.25
ST-23	Gotsumon	Rook.	C	0.25
ST-51	Green Offensive	Force FX	C	0.25
ST-02	Greymon	Champ.	C	0.25
ST-33	HerculesKabuterimon	Mega	F	6.50
ST-12	Ikkakumon	Champ.	C	0.25
BO-47	Iron Drill	PwrBlst	C	0.25
BO-26	Jagamon	Ult.	U	0.50
ST-08	Kabuterimon	Champ.	C	0.25
ST-21	Kimeramon	Ult.	C	0.25

Card#	Card Name	Type	Rarity	Price
ST-18	Kunemon	Rook.	C	0.25
BO-13	Kuwagamon	Champ.	C	0.25
BO-22	LadyDevimon	Ult.	R	3.00
BO-03	Leomon	Champ.	R	2.50
BO-17	Magnadramon	Mega	R	3.00
ST-46S	Mammothmon	Ult.	F	6.50
ST-46	Mammothmon	Ult.	C	0.25
BO-34	MarineAngemon	Mega	GS	11.50
ST-39S	MarineDevimon	Ult.	F	6.50
ST-39	MarineDevimon	Ult.	C	0.25
ST-28	MegaKabuterimon	Ult.	C	0.25
BO-31	MegaSeadramon	Ult.	U	0.50
BO-05	Meramon	Champ.	C	0.25
ST-53S	Metal Attack	PwrBlst	F	6.50
ST-53	Metal Attack	PwrBlst	C	0.25
BO-27	MetalEtemon	Mega	F	7.00
BO-01	MetalGreymon	Ult.	R	3.00
BO-35	MetalSeadramon	Mega	F	7.00
BO-21	Minotarumon	Ult.	C	0.25

Time crisis

When *Digimon* came out in Japan versus when *Pokémon* came out has been an interesting question, but don't be fooled by the dates on Upper Deck's *Digi-Battle* cards. They all read "© 1999 Bandai" — even the **Series 2** cards that came out in May of 2000. But make no mistake, future CCG archaeologists: ***Digi-Battle*** was strictly a 2000 release in the United States.

RARITY KEY C = Common U = Uncommon R = Rare VR = Very Rare UR = Ultra Rare F = Foil card X = Fixed/standard in all decks

Card#	Card Name	Type	Rarity	Price		Card#	Card Name	Type	Rarity	Price		Card#	Card Name	Type	Rarity	Price
☐ BO-14	Mojyamon	Champ.	C	0.25		☐ ST-40S	Pukumon	Mega	F	6.00		☐ BO-29	Syakomon	Rook.	C	0.25
☐ BO-12	Monochromon	Champ.	C	0.25		☐ ST-40	Pukumon	Mega	C	0.25		☐ BO-36	Tapirmon	Rook.	C	0.25
☐ ST-20	Musyamon	Champ.	C	0.25		☐ BO-37	Pumpkinmon	Ult.	U	0.50		☐ ST-07	Tentomon	Rook.	C	0.25
☐ BO-38	Myotismon	Ult.	U	0.50		☐ ST-49	Red Offensive	Force FX	C	0.25		☐ ST-10	Togemon	Champ.	C	0.25
☐ ST-15	Nanimon	Champ.	C	0.25		☐ BO-23	Roachmon	Champ.	C	0.25		☐ ST-25	Tortomon	Champ.	C	0.25
☐ ST-37	Octomon	Champ.	C	0.25		☐ ST-22	Rockmon	Champ.	C	0.25		☐ ST-29	Triceramon	Ult.	C	0.25
☐ BO-04	Ogremon	Champ.	C	0.25		☐ ST-34	SaberLeomon	Mega	F	6.50		☐ ST-56	Ultra Digivolve	Digivolve	F	6.50
☐ ST-31	Okuwamon	Ult.	C	0.25		☐ BO-32	Scorpiomon	Ult.	U	0.50		☐ ST-16	Unimon	Champ.	C	0.25
☐ BO-49	Option Eater	PwrBlst	C	0.25		☐ BO-06	Seadramon	Champ.	C	0.25		☐ BO-20	Vilemon	Champ.	C	0.25
☐ BO-48	Organic Enhancer	PwrBlst	U	0.50		☐ BO-09	Shellmon	Champ.	C	0.25		☐ ST-47S	WereGarurumon	Ult.	F	6.50
☐ ST-24	Otamamon	Rook.	C	0.25		☐ BO-08	ShogunGekomon	Ult.	U	0.50		☐ ST-47	WereGarurumon	Ult.	C	0.25
☐ ST-09	Palmon	Rook.	C	0.25		☐ ST-32	SkullGreymon	Ult.	C	0.25		☐ ST-44S	Wizardmon	Champ.	F	6.50
☐ ST-13	Patamon	Rook.	C	0.25		☐ BO-40	SkullMammothmon	Mega	R	3.00		☐ ST-44	Wizardmon	Champ.	C	0.25
☐ BO-39	Phantomon	Ult.	U	0.50		☐ ST-48S	SkullMeramon	Ult.	F	6.50		☐ ST-50	Yellow Offensive	Force FX	C	0.25
☐ BO-42	Piedmon	Mega	F	8.00		☐ ST-48	SkullMeramon	Ult.	C	0.25		☐ ST-38	Zudomon	Ult.	C	0.25
☐ ST-30	Piximon	Ult.	C	0.25		☐ BO-25	Snilmon	Champ.	C	0.25						
☐ BO-50	Power Freeze	PwrBlst	C	0.25		☐ ST-26	Starmon	Champ.	C	0.25						

Digi-Battle • *Series 2*

Upper Deck • Released **May 2000**

72 cards in set

- Booster packs contain 8 cards
- Booster displays contain 36 boosters

The **Digi-Battle Series 2** expansion increased the number of Champion, Ultimate, and Mega Level Digimon available to *Digi-Battle* players — but not by much, as it is a small expansion at 72 cards.

Series 2 also marked the last expansion for *Digi-Battle* released by Upper Deck. The game rights reverted to Bandai in the fall of 2000.

Digi-Battle, with this release, also becomes probably the only game where one can perish at the hands of a mutant cherry tree. (Although we wouldn't put it beyond the designer of **Banemaster**, a game itself filled with **Killer Rabbits** and **Mad Vampire Sheep**, to have included such a creature as well.) — ***James A. Mishler***

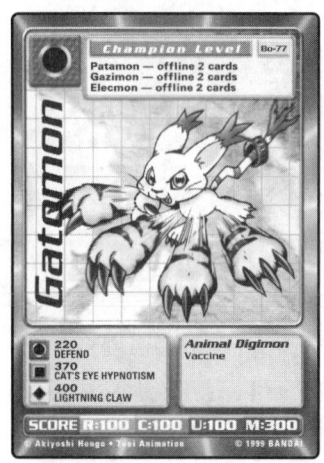

Set (72 cards)   150.00
Booster Display Box   92.50
Booster Pack   3.00

You will need

8

nine-pocket pages to store this set.
(4 doubled up)

SCRYE NOTES: *Some **Digimon** cards in this list have numbering indicating that they're from starter decks (ST). In all cases these are foil versions of cards from the Series 1 Starters.*

Card#	Card Name	Type	Rarity	Price		Card#	Card Name	Type	Rarity	Price
☐ BO-53	Digiruption	PwrBlst	R	2.50		☐ BO-74	Deltamon	Champ.	C	0.20
☐ BO-88	AeroVeedramon	Ult.	F	8.00		☐ BO-91	Deramon	Ult.	U	0.60
☐ BO-104	Black Gears	PwrBlst	R	3.00		☐ BO-70	Digitamamon	Ult.	R	3.40
☐ BO-90	Blossomon	Ult.	U	0.70		☐ BO-97	Digivice Green	Digivolve	C	0.20
☐ BO-92	Cherrymon	Ult.	R	3.00		☐ BO-98	Digivice Red & Yellow	Digivolve	C	0.20
☐ ST-36S	Coelamon	Champ.	F	5.80		☐ ST-19S	Dokugumon	Champ.	F	5.80
☐ BO-100	Crest of Courage	PwrBlst	R	3.30		☐ ST-35S	Dolphmon	Champ.	F	6.00
☐ BO-103	Crest of Friendship	PwrBlst	R	3.00		☐ BO-61	Elecmon	Rook.	C	0.20
☐ BO-101	Crest of Reliability	PwrBlst	R	3.00		☐ BO-57	Etemon	Ult.	R	3.00
☐ BO-102	Crest of Sincerity	PwrBlst	R	3.00		☐ BO-73	ExTyrannomon	Ult.	R	3.30
☐ BO-99	Crest Tag	Digivolve	R	3.30		☐ BO-105	Flood	PwrBlst	U	0.60
☐ BO-78	Cyclonemon	Champ.	C	0.20		☐ BO-81	Floramon	Rook.	C	0.20
☐ BO-79	DarkTyrannomon	Champ.	C	0.20		☐ BO-93	Garbagemon	Ult.	U	0.70
☐ BO-67	Datamon	Ult.	U	0.70		☐ BO-89	Garudamon	Ult.	U	0.70
						☐ BO-77	Gatomon	Champ.	GS	10.00
						☐ BO-60	Gazimon	Rook.	C	0.20
						☐ ST-27S	Gekomon	Champ.	F	4.80
						☐ BO-68	Giromon	Ult.	U	0.70
						☐ BO-71	Gizamon	Rook.	C	0.20
						☐ ST-23S	Gotsumon	Rook.	F	5.30
						☐ BO-95	Gryphonmon	Mega	R	2.80
						☐ ST-21S	Kimeramon	Ult.	F	5.30
						☐ BO-85	Kiwimon	Champ.	C	0.20
						☐ BO-56	Kokatorimon	Champ.	C	0.20
						☐ BO-55	Machinedramon	Mega	F	5.30
						☐ BO-64	Mamemon	Ult.	U	0.70
						☐ BO-106	Meat	PwrBlst	C	0.20
						☐ BO-69	Megadramon	Ult.	U	0.80
						☐ ST-28S	MegaKabuterimon	Ult.	F	6.00

Card#	Card Name	Type	Rarity	Price
☐ BO-80	MetalGreymon	Ult.	GS	10.00
☐ BO-65	MetalMamemon	Ult.	U	0.70
☐ BO-62	Monzaemon	Ult.	U	0.70
☐ BO-82	Mushroomon	Rook.	C	0.20
☐ ST-20S	Musyamon	Champ.	F	4.50
☐ BO-76	Myotismon	Ult.	GS	8.00
☐ BO-63	Numemon	Champ.	C	0.20
☐ ST-37S	Octomon	Champ.	F	5.80
☐ ST-31S	Okuwamon	Ult.	F	5.30
☐ ST-24S	Otamamon	Rook.	F	6.80
☐ BO-94	Phoenixmon	Mega	R	3.00
☐ ST-30S	Piximon	Ult.	F	5.30
☐ BO-108	Pluck	PwrBlst	C	0.20
☐ BO-96	Puppetmon	Mega	F	5.30
☐ BO-72	Raremon	Champ.	C	0.20
☐ BO-87	RedVegiemon	Champ.	C	0.20
☐ ST-22S	Rockmon	Champ.	F	5.30
☐ ST-32S	SkullGreymon	Ult.	F	5.80
☐ ST-26S	Starmon	Champ.	F	5.80
☐ BO-59	Sukamon	Champ.	C	0.20
☐ BO-84	Togemon	Champ.	C	0.20
☐ ST-25S	Tortomon	Champ.	F	5.00
☐ ST-29S	Triceramon	Ult.	F	6.00
☐ BO-75	Tuskmon	Champ.	C	0.20
☐ BO-66	Tyrannomon	Champ.	C	0.20
☐ BO-83	Veedramon	Champ.	C	0.20
☐ BO-107	Waterproof	PwrBlst	U	0.70
☐ BO-58	Whamon	Champ.	C	0.20
☐ BO-86	Woodmon	Champ.	C	0.20
☐ ST-38S	Zudomon	Ult.	F	5.80

Digi-Battle waves

Digimon released in complicated series of "waves," hitting various parts of the market in different amounts at different times.

A number of **Series 1** cards read "First Edition" while others don't. We have not observed any pricing variations whatsoever on this score.

"A difference which makes no difference is no difference..."

RARITY KEY   **C** = Common   **U** = Uncommon   **R** = Rare   **VR** = Very Rare   **UR** = Ultra Rare   **F** = Foil card   **X** = Fixed/standard in all decks

Dixie

Columbia Games • First release, **Bull Run 1st Ed.**, released **November 1994**
200 cards in set

- Starter decks contain 60 cards; starter displays contain 12 starters
- Booster packs do not exist

Designed by **Tom Dalgliesh**

Dixie has been described by some as the best American Civil War miniatures game ever produced. Considering that it is a card game, that says quite a bit. *Dixie* is, in fact, a hybrid game, a near-seamless combination of miniature game rules and card game rules. The care with which the authors treat the historical accuracy of the topic is evident, and, while the artwork is not Angus McBride Osprey quality, it does its duty.

The *Dixie* game system is one of the few that does not try to have some sort of "balance" between the players, instead opting for a quasi-historical setup. At the historical Bull Run, for example, the Union had an initial advantage, which is reflected in the fact that the Yankee player "musters," or starts, with 18 cards while the Rebel player starts with 15. The cards are played onto a battlefield, which consists of Left, Center, and Right positions for each player between which lies the Middle Ground (Yankee Right against Rebel Left, *etc.*). Each position may stack up to four cards, which include Terrain (one per position), Infantry, Cavalry, Artillery, and Generals (one per position; Generals give bonuses to morale and don't count for stacking purposes).

The goal of the game is to occupy, unopposed, two enemy positions with Infantry, Cavalry, or Artillery cards. The combat system is designed to accurately portray the style of combat used in the Civil War, which is aptly accented by the Morale system that reflects the true nature of battle. The combat rules are quite detailed, and include rules for Counter-Battery, Artillery Support, Melee, Enfilade (which allows for an additional victory condition through Envelopment), Engaging/Disengaging, Outflanking, and Scouting. The game can be expanded for larger battles to five positions across (Right, Right Center, Center, Left Center, Left), with the use of larger decks (victory requires capturing three positions or two plus an Envelopment).

Unfortunately, while the Civil War easily lends itself to the CCG format (especially in this hybrid design), CCG market demographics are hostile to historical simulations. This is a shame, as *Dixie* and its stand-alone sequels serve as both fine games and an introduction to the hobby's *first* genre, historical wargaming. — *James A. Mishler*

Concept	●●●●●
Gameplay	●●●●○
Card art	●●●○○
Player pool	●●○○○

Set (200 cards)	30.00	You will need **23** nine-pocket pages to store this set. (12 doubled up)
Starter Display Box	60.00	
Starter Deck	6.50	

#	Card name	Side	Type	Price
☐ 100	Davies	USA	Gen	0.50
☐ 101	Miles	USA	Gen	0.50
☐ 102	Runyon	USA	Gen	0.50
☐ 103	Blenker	USA	Gen	0.50
☐ 104	Heintzelman	USA	Gen	0.50
☐ 105	Hunter	USA	Gen	0.50
☐ 106	Burnside	USA	Gen	0.50
☐ 107	Franklin	USA	Gen	0.50
☐ 108	Howard	USA	Gen	0.50
☐ 109	Keyes	USA	Gen	0.50
☐ 110	McDowell	USA	Gen	0.50
☐ 111	Schenck	USA	Gen	0.50

After-market prices

You may notice that all *Dixie: Bull Run* cards have the same after-market price. That is, in part, because there are no rarities in the set and because every card in the set is still available for direct-order from the manufacturer, Columbia Games, both as singles and as sets.

The same is true of the other two Dixie expansions, **Shiloh** and **Gettysburg**, as well as the Napoleonic CCG from Columbia, **Eagles**.

#	Card name	Side	Type	Price
☐ 112	Tyler	USA	Gen	0.50
☐ 113	Willcox	USA	Gen	0.50
☐ 114	Porter	USA	Gen	0.50
☐ 115	Sherman	USA	Gen	0.50
☐ 116	Richardson	USA	Gen	0.50
☐ 117	1st US/G	USA	Arty	0.50
☐ 118	1st US/I	USA	Arty	0.50
☐ 119	2nd US/A	USA	Arty	0.50
☐ 120	2nd US/D	USA	Arty	0.50
☐ 121	2nd US/E	USA	Arty	0.50
☐ 122	2nd US/G	USA	Arty	0.50
☐ 123	2nd US/M	USA	Arty	0.50
☐ 124	3rd US/E	USA	Arty	0.50
☐ 125	5th US/D	USA	Arty	0.50
☐ 126	71st NY	USA	Arty	0.50
☐ 127	Brookwood's NY	USA	Arty	0.50
☐ 128	Rhode Island Art.	USA	Arty	0.50
☐ 129	US 2nd Dragoon	USA	Cav	0.50
☐ 130	US/1st	USA	Cav	0.50
☐ 131	US/2nd USA	USA	Cav	0.50
☐ 132	CT/1st	USA	Inf	0.50
☐ 133	CT/2nd	USA	Inf	0.50
☐ 134	CT/3rd	USA	Inf	0.50
☐ 135	ME/2nd	USA	Inf	0.50
☐ 136	NY/82nd	USA	Inf	0.50
☐ 137	OH/1st	USA	Inf	0.50
☐ 138	OH/2nd	USA	Inf	0.50
☐ 139	NY/13th	USA	Inf	0.50
☐ 140	NY/69th (Irish)	USA	Inf	0.50
☐ 141	NY/79th	USA	Inf	0.50
☐ 142	WI/2nd	USA	Inf	0.50
☐ 143	MA/1st	USA	Inf	0.50
☐ 144	MI/2nd	USA	Inf	0.50
☐ 145	MI/3rd	USA	Inf	0.50

#	Card name	Side	Type	Price
☐ 146	NY/12th	USA	Inf	0.50
☐ 147	NY/8th Militia	USA	Inf	0.50
☐ 148	NY/84th	USA	Inf	0.50
☐ 149	NY/27th	USA	Inf	0.50
☐ 150	US/Regulars	USA	Inf	0.50
☐ 151	US/Marines	USA	Inf	0.50
☐ 152	NH/2nd	USA	Inf	0.50
☐ 153	NY/71st	USA	Inf	0.50
☐ 154	RI/1st	USA	Inf	0.50
☐ 155	RI/2nd	USA	Inf	0.50
☐ 156	MA/5th	USA	Inf	0.50
☐ 157	MA/11th	USA	Inf	0.50
☐ 158	MN/1st	USA	Inf	0.50
☐ 159	MI/1st	USA	Inf	0.50
☐ 160	MI/4th	USA	Inf	0.50
☐ 161	NY/11th	USA	Inf	0.50
☐ 162	NY/38th	USA	Inf	0.50
☐ 163	ME/3rd	USA	Inf	0.50
☐ 164	ME/4th	USA	Inf	0.50
☐ 165	ME/5th	USA	Inf	0.50
☐ 166	VT/2nd	USA	Inf	0.50
☐ 167	NJ/1st Militia	USA	Inf	0.50
☐ 168	NJ/2nd Militia	USA	Inf	0.50
☐ 169	NJ/3rd Militia	USA	Inf	0.50
☐ 170	NJ/4th Militia	USA	Inf	0.50
☐ 171	NJ/1st Volunteer	USA	Inf	0.50
☐ 172	NJ/2nd Volunteer	USA	Inf	0.50
☐ 173	NJ/3rd Volunteer	USA	Inf	0.50
☐ 174	NY/41st Volunteer	USA	Inf	0.50
☐ 175	NY/8th	USA	Inf	0.50
☐ 176	NY/29th	USA	Inf	0.50
☐ 177	NY/39th	USA	Inf	0.50
☐ 178	PA/27th	USA	Inf	0.50
☐ 179	NY/16th	USA	Inf	0.50

RARITY KEY C = Common U = Uncommon R = Rare VR = Very Rare UR = Ultra Rare F = Foil card X = Fixed/standard in all decks

#	Card name	Side	Type	Price
☐ 180	NY/18th	USA	Inf	0.50
☐ 181	NY/31st	USA	Inf	0.50
☐ 182	NY/32nd	USA	Inf	0.50
☐ 183	NY/21st	USA	Inf	0.50
☐ 184	NY/25th	USA	Inf	0.50
☐ 185	Centreville	USA	Terr	0.50
☐ 186	Holden Hill	USA	Terr	0.50
☐ 187	Bull Run	USA	Terr	0.50
☐ 188	Stone Bridge	USA	Terr	0.50
☐ 189	Sudley Woods	USA	Terr	0.50
☐ 190	Grigsby Woods	USA	Terr	0.50
☐ 191	Sudley Ford	USA	Spec	0.50
☐ 192	Ball's Ford	USA	Spec	0.50
☐ 193	Color-Guard	USA	Spec	0.50
☐ 194	Outflank	USA	Spec	0.50
☐ 195	Force-March	USA	Spec	0.50
☐ 196	Sharpshooter	USA	Spec	0.50
☐ 197	Rally	USA	Spec	0.50
☐ 198	Double-Canister	USA	Spec	0.50
☐ 199	Uniform Confusion	USA	Spec	0.50
☐ 200	Bonham	CSA	Gen	0.50
☐ 201	Holmes	CSA	Gen	0.50
☐ 202	Cocke	CSA	Gen	0.50
☐ 203	Beauregard	CSA	Gen	0.50
☐ 204	Jones	CSA	Gen	0.50
☐ 205	Bartow	CSA	Gen	0.50
☐ 206	Ewell	CSA	Gen	0.50
☐ 207	Johnson	CSA	Gen	0.50
☐ 208	Smith	CSA	Gen	0.50
☐ 209	Elzey	CSA	Gen	0.50
☐ 210	Evans	CSA	Gen	0.50
☐ 211	Bee	CSA	Gen	0.50
☐ 212	Early	CSA	Gen	0.50
☐ 213	Longstreet	CSA	Gen	0.50
☐ 214	Jackson	CSA	Gen	0.50
☐ 215	Alexandria Light	CSA	Arty	0.50
☐ 216	Richmond Howitzer	CSA	Arty	0.50
☐ 217	"Washington, 1st"	CSA	Arty	0.50
☐ 218	"Washington, 2nd"	CSA	Arty	0.50
☐ 219	"Washington, 3rd"	CSA	Arty	0.50
☐ 220	Loudon	CSA	Arty	0.50
☐ 221	Lynchburg	CSA	Arty	0.50
☐ 222	"Washington, 4th"	CSA	Arty	0.50
☐ 223	Purcell	CSA	Arty	0.50
☐ 224	Rockbridge	CSA	Arty	0.50
☐ 225	Wise	CSA	Arty	0.50
☐ 226	Staunton	CSA	Arty	0.50
☐ 227	Culpepper	CSA	Arty	0.50

Dixie • Bull Run 2nd Edition

Columbia Games • Released March 1995

200 cards in set • IDENTIFIER: Set name at bottom, "2nd Edition" at top

- Starter decks contain 60 cards; starter displays contain 12 starters

The first **Dixie** set was reprinted four months after its release in a second edition. The only significant difference between **1st** and **2nd Edition Bull Run** is the addition of "2nd Edition" printed at the top of the card face. A new edition of the rules is also included (Version 2.0). We have observed no difference in prices between *1st* and *2nd Edition* cards. — **James Mishler**

#	Card name	Side	Type	Price		#	Card name	Side	Type	Price
☐ 228	Thomas	CSA	Arty	0.50		☐ 264	VA/5th	CSA	Inf	0.50
☐ 229	VA/30th (VA/2nd)	CSA	Cav	0.50		☐ 265	VA/27th	CSA	Inf	0.50
☐ 230	Harrison's Battalion	CSA	Cav	0.50		☐ 266	VA/33rd	CSA	Inf	0.50
☐ 231	Independent	CSA	Cav	0.50		☐ 267	GA/7th	CSA	Inf	0.50
☐ 232	VA/1st (Black Horse)	CSA	Cav	0.50		☐ 268	GA/8th	CSA	Inf	0.50
☐ 233	SC/2nd	CSA	Inf	0.50		☐ 269	AL/4th	CSA	Inf	0.50
☐ 234	SC/3rd	CSA	Inf	0.50		☐ 270	MS/2nd	CSA	Inf	0.50
☐ 235	SC/7th	CSA	Inf	0.50		☐ 271	MS/11th	CSA	Inf	0.50
☐ 236	SC/8th	CSA	Inf	0.50		☐ 272	NC/6th	CSA	Inf	0.50
☐ 237	LA/8th	CSA	Inf	0.50		☐ 273	MD/1st	CSA	Inf	0.50
☐ 238	AL/5th	CSA	Inf	0.50		☐ 274	TN/3rd	CSA	Inf	0.50
☐ 239	AL/6th	CSA	Inf	0.50		☐ 275	VA/10th	CSA	Inf	0.50
☐ 240	LA/6th	CSA	Inf	0.50		☐ 276	VA/13th	CSA	Inf	0.50
☐ 241	MS/17th	CSA	Inf	0.50		☐ 277	Matthews Hill	CSA	Terr	0.50
☐ 242	MS/18th	CSA	Inf	0.50		☐ 278	Henry Hill	CSA	Terr	0.50
☐ 243	SC/5th	CSA	Inf	0.50		☐ 279	Lookout Hill	CSA	Terr	0.50
☐ 244	NC/5th	CSA	Inf	0.50		☐ 280	Bull Run (Upper)	CSA	Terr	0.50
☐ 245	VA/1st	CSA	Inf	0.50		☐ 281	Bull Run (Lower)	CSA	Terr	0.50
☐ 246	VA/11th	CSA	Inf	0.50		☐ 282	Bull Run	CSA	Terr	0.50
☐ 247	VA/17th	CSA	Inf	0.50		☐ 283	Chinn Woods	CSA	Terr	0.50
☐ 248	VA/24th	CSA	Inf	0.50		☐ 284	Buck Woods	CSA	Terr	0.50
☐ 249	VA/8th	CSA	Inf	0.50		☐ 285	Holkum Woods	CSA	Terr	0.50
☐ 250	VA/18th	CSA	Inf	0.50		☐ 286	Cover	CSA	Spec	0.50
☐ 251	VA/19th	CSA	Inf	0.50		☐ 287	Rebel Yell	CSA	Spec	0.50
☐ 252	VA/28th	CSA	Inf	0.50		☐ 288	Rally	CSA	Spec	0.50
☐ 253	VA/49th	CSA	Inf	0.50		☐ 289	Color-Guard	CSA	Spec	0.50
☐ 254	LA/7th	CSA	Inf	0.50		☐ 290	Outflank	CSA	Spec	0.50
☐ 255	MS/13th	CSA	Inf	0.50		☐ 291	Force-March	CSA	Spec	0.50
☐ 256	VA/7th	CSA	Inf	0.50		☐ 292	Sharpshooter	CSA	Spec	0.50
☐ 257	LA/1st (Tigers)	CSA	Inf	0.50		☐ 293	Double-Canister	CSA	Spec	0.50
☐ 258	SC/4th	CSA	Inf	0.50		☐ 294	Uniform Confusion	CSA	Spec	0.50
☐ 259	AR/1	CSA	Inf	0.50		☐ 295	Manassas Gap RR	CSA	Spec	0.50
☐ 260	TN/2nd	CSA	Inf	0.50		☐ 296	Orange & Alex RR	CSA	Spec	0.50
☐ 261	Hampton's Legion	CSA	Inf	0.50		☐ 297	Blackburn's Ford	CSA	Spec	0.50
☐ 262	VA/2nd	CSA	Inf	0.50		☐ 298	Mitchell's Ford	CSA	Spec	0.50
☐ 263	VA/4th	CSA	Inf	0.50		☐ 299	Union Mills Ford	CSA	Spec	0.50

Dixie • Shiloh

Columbia Games • Released May 1995

400 cards in set • IDENTIFIER: Set name on card bottom

- Starter decks contain 60 cards; starter displays contain 12 starters
- Booster packs do not exist

The **Shiloh** expansion, covering the momentous Tennessee battle, adds a whopping 400 cards to the overall list available in **Dixie**.

Several rules changes are made in *Shiloh*, including the allowance of two Terrain cards in a single position; specific Shiloh Victory Conditions; Generals may add to the Stacking limit of Positions; two Generals may be deployed in the same position, as long as they are not of the same rank; and the historical application of card timing by dividing Shiloh into Days. Custom Battle Decks are even more potent with over 600 cards available in the *Dixie* game. — **James A. Mishler**

Set (400 cards)	50.00
Starter Display Box	67.50
Starter Deck	6.50

45 nine-pocket pages to store this set. (23 doubled up)
You will need

#	Card name	Side	Army	Price		#	Card name	Side	Army	Price
☐ 1	Grant	USA	Tenn	0.50		☐ 6	2nd Illinois (Art.)	USA	Tenn	0.50
☐ 2	15th Michigan	USA	Tenn	0.50		☐ 7	2nd Illinois (Art.)	USA	Tenn	0.50
☐ 3	14th Wisconsin	USA	Tenn	0.50		☐ 8	Ohio Light (Art.)	USA	Tenn	0.50
☐ 4	1st Illinois (Art.)	USA	Tenn	0.50		☐ 9	McClernand	USA	Tenn	0.50
☐ 5	1st Illinois (Art.)	USA	Tenn	0.50		☐ 10	4th Illinois (Cav.)	USA	Tenn	0.50
						☐ 11	Carmichael (Cav.)	USA	Tenn	0.50

RARITY KEY C = Common U = Uncommon R = Rare VR = Very Rare UR = Ultra Rare F = Foil card X = Fixed/standard in all decks

#	Card name	Side	Army	Price	#	Card name	Side	Army	Price	#	Card name	Side	Type/Army	Price
☐ 12	Stewart's IL (Cav.)	USA	Tenn	0.50	☐ 80	32nd Illinois	USA	Tenn	0.50	☐ 148	Gibson	USA	Ohio	0.50
☐ 13	2nd IL Lt. (Art.)	USA	Tenn	0.50	☐ 81	41st Illinois	USA	Tenn	0.50	☐ 149	32nd Indiana	USA	Ohio	0.50
☐ 14	1st IL Lt. (Art.)	USA	Tenn	0.50						☐ 150	39th Indiana	USA	Ohio	0.50
☐ 15	2nd IL Lt. (Art.)	USA	Tenn	0.50	☐ 82	3rd Iowa 3	USA	Tenn	0.50	☐ 151	15th Ohio	USA	Ohio	0.50
☐ 16	Ohio Light (Art.)	USA	Tenn	0.50	☐ 83	Veatch	USA	Tenn	0.50	☐ 152	49th Ohio	USA	Ohio	0.50
☐ 17	Hare	USA	Tenn	0.50	☐ 84	14th Illinois	USA	Tenn	0.50	☐ 153	Nelson	USA	Ohio	0.50
☐ 18	8th Illinois	USA	Tenn	0.50	☐ 85	15th Illinois	USA	Tenn	0.50					
☐ 19	18th Illinois	USA	Tenn	0.50	☐ 86	46th Illinois	USA	Tenn	0.50	☐ 154	1st Ohio Lt. (Art.)	USA	Ohio	0.50
☐ 20	11th Iowa	USA	Tenn	0.50	☐ 87	25th Indiana	USA	Tenn	0.50	☐ 155	Ammen	USA	Ohio	0.50
☐ 21	13th Iowa	USA	Tenn	0.50	☐ 88	Lauman	USA	Tenn	0.50	☐ 156	36th Indiana	USA	Ohio	0.50
☐ 22	Marsh	USA	Tenn	0.50	☐ 89	31st Indiana	USA	Tenn	0.50	☐ 157	6th Ohio	USA	Ohio	0.50
☐ 23	11th Illinois	USA	Tenn	0.50	☐ 90	44th Indiana	USA	Tenn	0.50	☐ 158	24th Ohio	USA	Ohio	0.50
☐ 24	20th Illinois	USA	Tenn	0.50						☐ 159	Hazen	USA	Ohio	0.50
☐ 25	45th Illinois	USA	Tenn	0.50	☐ 91	17th Kentucky	USA	Tenn	0.50	☐ 160	9th Indiana	USA	Ohio	0.50
☐ 26	48th Illinois	USA	Tenn	0.50	☐ 92	25th Kentucky	USA	Tenn	0.50	☐ 161	6th Kentucky	USA	Ohio	0.50
☐ 27	Raith	USA	Tenn	0.50	☐ 93	Sherman	USA	Tenn	0.50	☐ 162	41st Ohio	USA	Ohio	0.50
☐ 28	17th Illinois	USA	Tenn	0.50	☐ 94	4th Ill. (Cav.)	USA	Tenn	0.50	☐ 163	Bruce	USA	Ohio	0.50
☐ 29	29th Illinois	USA	Tenn	0.50	☐ 95	4th Ill. (Cav.)	USA	Tenn	0.50	☐ 164	1st Kentucky	USA	Ohio	0.50
☐ 30	43rd Illinois	USA	Tenn	0.50	☐ 96	Indiana Lt. (Art.) (2)	USA	Tenn	0.50	☐ 165	2nd Kentucky	USA	Ohio	0.50
☐ 31	49th Illinois	USA	Tenn	0.50	☐ 97	1st Ill. Lt. (Art.) 4	USA	Tenn	0.50	☐ 166	20th Kentucky	USA	Ohio	0.50
☐ 32	Wallace (1/2)	USA	Tenn	0.50	☐ 98	1st Ill. Lt. (Art.) 2	USA	Tenn	0.50	☐ 167	Crittenden	USA	Ohio	0.50
☐ 33	US 2nd/4th (Cav.)	USA	Tenn	0.50	☐ 99	4th Ill. (Art.)	USA	Tenn	0.50	☐ 168	4th U.S. (Art.)	USA	Ohio	0.50
☐ 34	2nd IL (Cav.)	USA	Tenn	0.50	☐ 100	McDowell	USA	Tenn	0.50	☐ 169	Boyle	USA	Ohio	0.50
☐ 35	1st IL Lt. (Art.)	USA	Tenn	0.50	☐ 101	40th Illinois	USA	Tenn	0.50	☐ 170	9th Kentucky	USA	Ohio	0.50
☐ 36	1st MO (Art.)	USA	Tenn	0.50	☐ 102	6th Iowa	USA	Tenn	0.50	☐ 171	13th Kentucky	USA	Ohio	0.50
☐ 37	1st MO (Art.)	USA	Tenn	0.50	☐ 103	46th Ohio	USA	Tenn	0.50	☐ 172	19th Ohio	USA	Ohio	0.50
☐ 38	1st MO (Art.)	USA	Tenn	0.50	☐ 104	Stuart	USA	Tenn	0.50	☐ 173	59th Ohio	USA	Ohio	0.50
☐ 39	Tuttle	USA	Tenn	0.50	☐ 105	55th Illinois	USA	Tenn	0.50	☐ 174	Smith	USA	Ohio	0.50
☐ 40	2nd Iowa	USA	Tenn	0.50	☐ 106	54th Ohio	USA	Tenn	0.50	☐ 175	11th Kentucky	USA	Ohio	0.50
☐ 41	7th Iowa	USA	Tenn	0.50	☐ 107	71st Ohio	USA	Tenn	0.50	☐ 176	26th Kentucky	USA	Ohio	0.50
☐ 42	12th Iowa	USA	Tenn	0.50	☐ 108	Hildebrand	USA	Tenn	0.50	☐ 177	13th Ohio	USA	Ohio	0.50
☐ 43	14th Iowa	USA	Tenn	0.50	☐ 109	53rd Ohio	USA	Tenn	0.50	☐ 178	Wood	USA	Ohio	0.50
☐ 44	McArthur	USA	Tenn	0.50	☐ 110	57th Ohio	USA	Tenn	0.50	☐ 179	Garfield	USA	Ohio	0.50
☐ 45	9th Illinois	USA	Tenn	0.50	☐ 111	77th Ohio	USA	Tenn	0.50	☐ 180	13th Michigan	USA	Ohio	0.50
☐ 46	12th Illinois	USA	Tenn	0.50	☐ 112	Buckland	USA	Tenn	0.50	☐ 181	64th Ohio	USA	Ohio	0.50
☐ 47	13th Missouri	USA	Tenn	0.50	☐ 113	48th Ohio	USA	Tenn	0.50	☐ 182	65th Ohio	USA	Ohio	0.50
☐ 48	14th Missouri	USA	Tenn	0.50	☐ 114	70th Ohio	USA	Tenn	0.50	☐ 183	Wagner	USA	Ohio	0.50
☐ 49	81st Ohio	USA	Tenn	0.50	☐ 115	72nd Ohio	USA	Tenn	0.50	☐ 184	15th Indiana	USA	Ohio	0.50
☐ 50	Sweeny	USA	Tenn	0.50	☐ 116	Prentiss	USA	Tenn	0.50	☐ 185	40th Indiana	USA	Ohio	0.50
☐ 51	7th Illinois	USA	Tenn	0.50	☐ 117	15th Iowa	USA	Tenn	0.50	☐ 186	57th Indiana	USA	Ohio	0.50
☐ 52	50th Illinois	USA	Tenn	0.50	☐ 118	16th Iowa	USA	Tenn	0.50	☐ 187	24th Kentucky	USA	Ohio	0.50
☐ 53	52nd Illinois	USA	Tenn	0.50	☐ 119	23rd Missouri	USA	Tenn	0.50	☐ 188	Spain Field	USA	Terr	0.50
☐ 54	57th Illinois	USA	Tenn	0.50	☐ 120	11th Ill. (Cav.)	USA	Tenn	0.50	☐ 189	Lick Creek	USA	Terr	0.50
☐ 55	58th Illinois	USA	Tenn	0.50	☐ 121	11th Ill. (Cav.)	USA	Tenn	0.50	☐ 190	Locust Grove	USA	Terr	0.50
☐ 56	8th Iowa	USA	Tenn	0.50	☐ 122	Ohio Light (Art.)	USA	Tenn	0.50	☐ 191	Rea Field	USA	Terr	0.50
☐ 57	Wallace (0/1)	USA	Tenn	0.50	☐ 123	Minn. Lt. (Art.)	USA	Tenn	0.50	☐ 192	Shiloh Branch	USA	Terr	0.50
☐ 58	Indiana Lt. (Art.) (3)	USA	Tenn	0.50	☐ 124	Peabody	USA	Tenn	0.50	☐ 193	Barnes Wood	USA	Terr	0.50
☐ 59	1st Mo. (Art.)	USA	Tenn	0.50	☐ 125	12th Michigan	USA	Tenn	0.50	☐ 194	Crescent Field	USA	Terr	0.50
☐ 60	Smith	USA	Tenn	0.50	☐ 126	21st Missouri	USA	Tenn	0.50	☐ 195	Owl Creek	USA	Terr	0.50
☐ 61	11th Indiana	USA	Tenn	0.50	☐ 127	25th Missouri	USA	Tenn	0.50	☐ 196	Woolf Wood	USA	Terr	0.50
☐ 62	24th Indiana	USA	Tenn	0.50	☐ 128	16th Wisconsin	USA	Tenn	0.50	☐ 197	Peach Orchard	USA	Terr	0.50
☐ 63	8th Missouri	USA	Tenn	0.50	☐ 129	Miller	USA	Tenn	0.50	☐ 198	Bloody Pond	USA	Terr	0.50
☐ 64	Thayer	USA	Tenn	0.50	☐ 130	61st Illinois	USA	Tenn	0.50	☐ 199	Hornet's Nest	USA	Terr	0.50
☐ 65	23rd Indiana	USA	Tenn	0.50	☐ 131	18th Missouri	USA	Tenn	0.50	☐ 200	Duncan Field	USA	Terr	0.50
☐ 66	1st Nebraska	USA	Tenn	0.50	☐ 132	18th Wisconsin	USA	Tenn	0.50	☐ 201	Dill Branch	USA	Terr	0.50
☐ 67	58th Ohio	USA	Tenn	0.50	☐ 133	Buell	USA	Ohio	0.50	☐ 202	Mulberry Wood	USA	Terr	0.50
☐ 68	Whittlesey	USA	Tenn	0.50	☐ 134	McCook	USA	Ohio	0.50	☐ 203	Perry Field	USA	Terr	0.50
☐ 69	20th Ohio	USA	Tenn	0.50	☐ 135	5th U.S. (Art.)	USA	Ohio	0.50	☐ 204	Tilghman Branch	USA	Terr	0.50
☐ 70	76th Ohio	USA	Tenn	0.50	☐ 136	Rousseau	USA	Ohio	0.50	☐ 205	Owl Swamp	USA	Terr	0.50
☐ 71	78th Ohio	USA	Tenn	0.50	☐ 137	6th Indiana	USA	Ohio	0.50	☐ 206	Cover	USA	Spec	0.50
☐ 72	Hurlbut	USA	Tenn	0.50	☐ 138	5th Kentucky	USA	Ohio	0.50	☐ 207	Lost Reserves	USA	Spec	0.50
☐ 73	5th Ohio (Cav.)	USA	Tenn	0.50	☐ 139	1st Ohio	USA	Ohio	0.50	☐ 208	Color Guard	USA	Spec	0.50
☐ 74	5th Ohio (Cav.)	USA	Tenn	0.50	☐ 140	15th U.S.	USA	Ohio	0.50	☐ 209	Sharpshooter	USA	Spec	0.50
☐ 75	1st Mo. Lt. (Art.)	USA	Tenn	0.50	☐ 141	16th U.S.	USA	Ohio	0.50	☐ 210	Double-Canister	USA	Spec	0.50
☐ 76	1st Mi. Lt. (Art.)	USA	Tenn	0.50	☐ 142	19th U.S.	USA	Ohio	0.50	☐ 211	Battle Confusion	USA	Spec	0.50
☐ 77	Ohio Lt. (Art.)	USA	Tenn	0.50	☐ 143	Kirk	USA	Ohio	0.50	☐ 212	Rally	USA	Spec	0.50
☐ 78	Williams	USA	Tenn	0.50	☐ 144	34th Illinois	USA	Ohio	0.50	☐ 213	Bayonet Charge	USA	Spec	0.50
☐ 79	28th Illinois	USA	Tenn	0.50	☐ 145	29th Indiana	USA	Ohio	0.50	☐ 214	Battle Smoke	USA	Spec	0.50
					☐ 146	30th Indiana	USA	Ohio	0.50	☐ 215	Supply Wagon	USA	Spec	0.50
					☐ 147	77th Pennsylvania	USA	Ohio	0.50					

RARITY KEY C = Common **U** = Uncommon **R** = Rare **VR** = Very Rare **UR** = Ultra Rare **F** = Foil card **X** = Fixed/standard in all decks

#	Card name	Side	Type/Army	Price
216	Ammo Depletion	USA	Spec	0.50
25				
217	John Barleycorn	USA	Spec	0.50
218	Field Hospital	USA	Spec	0.50
219	Stragglers	USA	Spec	0.50
220	Exploding Gun	USA	Spec	0.50
221	Exploding Caisson	USA	Spec	0.50
222	Counter Order	USA	Spec	0.50
223	Prisoner Escort	USA	Spec	0.50
224	Battle Fatigue	USA	Spec	0.50
225	Mascot	USA	Spec	0.50
26				
226	Ambulance Corps	USA	Spec	0.50
227	Last Stand	USA	Spec	0.50
228	Rearguard	USA	Spec	0.50
229	Henry Rifle	USA	Spec	0.50
230	Looting	USA	Spec	0.50
231	Johnny Shiloh	USA	Spec	0.50
232	Rain	USA	Spec	0.50
233	Pittsburg Landing	USA	Spec	0.50
234	River Transport	USA	Spec	0.50
27				
235	USS Tyler	USA	Spec	0.50
236	USS Lexington	USA	Spec	0.50
237	Johnson (2/2)	CSA	Miss	0.50
238	Beauregard	CSA	Miss	0.50
239	Polk	CSA	Miss	0.50
240	Clark	CSA	Miss	0.50
241	Russell	CSA	Miss	0.50
242	11th Louisiana	CSA	Miss	0.50
243	12th Tennessee	CSA	Miss	0.50
28				
244	13th Tennessee	CSA	Miss	0.50
245	22nd Tennessee	CSA	Miss	0.50
246	Bankhead's (Art.)	CSA	Miss	0.50
247	Stewart	CSA	Miss	0.50
248	13th Arkansas	CSA	Miss	0.50
249	4th Tennessee	CSA	Miss	0.50
250	5th Tennessee	CSA	Miss	0.50
251	33rd Tennessee	CSA	Miss	0.50
252	Stanford's (Art.)	CSA	Miss	0.50
29				
253	Cheatham	CSA	Miss	0.50
254	47th Tennessee	CSA	Miss	0.50
255	Lindsay's (Cav.)	CSA	Miss	0.50
256	Brewer's (Cav.)	CSA	Miss	0.50
257	Johnson (2/1)	CSA	Miss	0.50
258	Blythe's Miss. Bn.	CSA	Miss	0.50
259	2nd Tennessee	CSA	Miss	0.50
260	15th Tennessee	CSA	Miss	0.50
261	154th Tennessee	CSA	Miss	0.50
30				
262	Polk's (Art.)	CSA	Miss	0.50
263	Stephens	CSA	Miss	0.50
264	7th Kentucky	CSA	Miss	0.50

Dixie card numbering

While we have listed most card sets in this book in alphabetical order, the high quantity of cards names with numbers in **Dixie** leads us to make an exception. We doubt anyone would try to figure out where to put the **47th Tennessee** versus the **5th Tennessee** (a computer spreadsheet and a human would give you different answers) when there are card numbers to fall back on.

Note that **Dixie: Bull Run**'s numbering starts with #100.

#	Card name	Side	Army	Price
265	1st Tennessee Bn.	CSA	Miss	0.50
266	6th Tennessee	CSA	Miss	0.50
267	9th Tennessee	CSA	Miss	0.50
268	Smith's (Art.)	CSA	Miss	0.50
269	Bragg	CSA	Miss	0.50
270	Ruggles	CSA	Miss	0.50
31				
271	Jenkin's (Cav.)	CSA	Miss	0.50
272	Gibson	CSA	Miss	0.50
273	1st Arkansas	CSA	Miss	0.50
274	4th Louisiana	CSA	Miss	0.50
275	13th Louisiana	CSA	Miss	0.50
276	19th Louisiana	CSA	Miss	0.50
277	Anderson	CSA	Miss	0.50
278	1st Florida Bn.	CSA	Miss	0.50
279	17th Louisiana	CSA	Miss	0.50
32				
280	20th Louisiana	CSA	Miss	0.50
281	9th Texas Bn.	CSA	Miss	0.50
282	Confederate Resp.	CSA	Miss	0.50
283	Hodgson's (Art.)	CSA	Miss	0.50
284	Pond	CSA	Miss	0.50
285	16th Louisiana	CSA	Miss	0.50
286	18th Louisiana	CSA	Miss	0.50
287	38th Tennessee	CSA	Miss	0.50
288	Crescent Louisiana	CSA	Miss	0.50
33				
289	Orleans Guard	CSA	Miss	0.50
290	Ketchum's (Art.)	CSA	Miss	0.50
291	Withers	CSA	Miss	0.50
292	Clanton's (Cav.)	CSA	Miss	0.50
293	Gladden	CSA	Miss	0.50
294	21st Alabama	CSA	Miss	0.50
295	22nd Alabama	CSA	Miss	0.50
296	25th Alabama	CSA	Miss	0.50
297	26th Alabama	CSA	Miss	0.50
34				
298	1st Louisiana	CSA	Miss	0.50
299	Robertson's (Art.)	CSA	Miss	0.50
300	Chalmers	CSA	Miss	0.50
301	5th Mississippi	CSA	Miss	0.50
302	7th Mississippi	CSA	Miss	0.50
303	9th Mississippi	CSA	Miss	0.50
304	10th Mississippi	CSA	Miss	0.50
305	52nd Tennessee	CSA	Miss	0.50
306	Gage's (Art.)	CSA	Miss	0.50
35				
307	Jackson	CSA	Miss	0.50
308	17th Alabama	CSA	Miss	0.50
309	18th Alabama	CSA	Miss	0.50
310	19th Alabama	CSA	Miss	0.50
311	2nd Texas	CSA	Miss	0.50
312	Girardey's (Art.)	CSA	Miss	0.50
313	Hardee	CSA	Miss	0.50
314	Hindman	CSA	Miss	0.50
315	2nd Arkansas	CSA	Miss	0.50
36				
316	6th Arkansas	CSA	Miss	0.50
317	7th Arkansas	CSA	Miss	0.50
318	3rd Confederate	CSA	Miss	0.50
319	Miller's (Art.)	CSA	Miss	0.50
320	Swett's (Art.)	CSA	Miss	0.50
321	Cleburne	CSA	Miss	0.50
322	15th Arkansas	CSA	Miss	0.50
323	6th Mississippi	CSA	Miss	0.50
324	2nd Tenn. Provs.	CSA	Miss	0.50
37				
325	5th (35th) Tenn.	CSA		0.50
326	23rd Tennessee	CSA	Miss	0.50
327	24th Tennessee	CSA	Miss	0.50
328	Trigg's (Art.)	CSA	Miss	0.50
329	Calvert's (Art.)	CSA	Miss	0.50
330	Hubbard's (Art.)	CSA	Miss	0.50
331	Wood	CSA	Miss	0.50
332	16th Alabama	CSA	Miss	0.50

#	Card name	Side	Type/Army	Price
333	8th Arkansas	CSA	Miss	0.50
38				
334	9th (14th) AR Bn.	CSA	Miss	0.50
335	3rd Miss. Bn.	CSA	Miss	0.50
336	27th Tennessee	CSA	Miss	0.50
337	44th Tennessee	CSA	Miss	0.50
338	55th Tennessee	CSA	Miss	0.50
339	Harper's (Art.)	CSA	Miss	0.50
340	Breckinridge	CSA	Miss	0.50
341	Forrest's (Cav.)	CSA	Miss	0.50
342	Wharton's (Cav.)	CSA	Miss	0.50
39				
343	Adam's (Cav.)	CSA	Miss	0.50
344	McClung's (Art.)	CSA	Miss	0.50
345	Robert's (Art.)	CSA	Miss	0.50
346	Trabue	CSA	Miss	0.50
347	4th Alabama Bn.	CSA	Miss	0.50
348	31st Alabama	CSA	Miss	0.50
349	3rd Kentucky	CSA	Miss	0.50
350	4th Kentucky	CSA	Miss	0.50
351	5th Kentucky	CSA	Miss	0.50
40				
352	6th Kentucky	CSA	Miss	0.50
353	Crew's Bn.	CSA	Miss	0.50
354	Morgan's (Cav.)	CSA	Miss	0.50
355	Cobb's (Art.)	CSA	Miss	0.50
356	Byrne's (Art.)	CSA	Miss	0.50
357	Bowen	CSA	Miss	0.50
358	9th Arkansas	CSA	Miss	0.50
359	10th Arkansas	CSA	Miss	0.50
360	2nd Confederate	CSA	Miss	0.50
41				
361	1st Missouri	CSA	Miss	0.50
362	Thompson's (Cav.)	CSA	Miss	0.50
363	Hudson's (Art.)	CSA	Miss	0.50
364	Watson's (Art.)	CSA	Miss	0.50
365	Statham	CSA	Miss	0.50
366	15th Mississippi	CSA	Miss	0.50
367	22nd Mississippi	CSA	Miss	0.50
368	19th Tennessee	CSA	Miss	0.50
369	20th Tennessee	CSA	Miss	0.50
42				
370	28th Tennessee	CSA	Miss	0.50
371	45th Tennessee	CSA	Miss	0.50
372	Rutledge's (Art.)	CSA	Miss	0.50
373	Cover	CSA	Spec	0.50
374	Lost Reserves	CSA	Spec	0.50
375	Color Guard	CSA	Spec	0.50
376	Sharpshooter	CSA	Spec	0.50
377	Double-Canister	CSA	Spec	0.50
378	Battle Confusion	CSA	Spec	0.50
43				
379	Rally	CSA	Spec	0.50
380	Bayonet Charge	CSA	Spec	0.50
381	Battle Smoke	CSA	Spec	0.50
382	Supply Wagon	CSA	Spec	0.50
383	Ammo Depletion	CSA	Spec	0.50
384	John Barleycorn	CSA	Spec	0.50
385	Field Hospital	CSA	Spec	0.50
386	Stragglers	CSA	Spec	0.50
387	Exploding Gun	CSA	Spec	0.50
44				
388	Exploding Caisson	CSA	Spec	0.50
389	Counter Order	CSA	Spec	0.50
390	Prisoner Escort	CSA	Spec	0.50
391	Battle Fatigue	CSA	Spec	0.50
392	Rebel Yell	CSA	Spec	0.50
393	Cavalry Charge	CSA	Spec	0.50
394	Purdy Road Bridge	CSA	Spec	0.50
395	Barne's Ford	CSA	Spec	0.50
396	Bedford Forrest	CSA	Spec	0.50
45				
397	Pittsburgh-Corinth Rd.	CSA	Spec	0.50
398	Skulkers	CSA	Spec	0.50
399	Brush Fire	CSA	Spec	0.50
400	Shiloh Church	CSA	Spec	0.50

RARITY KEY C = Common   U = Uncommon   R = Rare   VR = Very Rare   UR = Ultra Rare   F = Foil card   X = Fixed/standard in all decks

Dixie • Gettysburg

Columbia Games • Released July 1995
250 cards in set •IDENTIFIER: Set name on card bottom
- Starter decks contain 60 cards; starter displays contain 12 starters
- A 250-card **Factory Set** is available

The **Gettysburg** expansion adds 250 cards to the overall list available in **Dixie**. Numerous rules changes are made in **Gettysburg**, including the addition of a Morale rating for all troops, a modifier to the Combat Value denoted by superscripting an A, B or C (Excellent, Average, Poor) to the CV; Firepower die rolls are adjusted to a more intuitive system (wherein you roll 1's, 2's, or 3's instead of 6's, 5's, or 4's); Firepower ratings are now included on the cards themselves; Horse Artillery are added to the card mix; Generals have a new Hit system; additional rules on Morale are included; and Battle of Gettysburg historical battle rules and limitations are outlined.

The greatest and most important battle of the American Civil War is a fitting finale to the Dixie series. — *James A. Mishler*

	Set (250 cards)	40.00
	Starter Display Box	57.50
	Starter Deck	6.50

You will need 28 nine-pocket pages to store this set. (14 doubled up)

#	Card name	Side	Army	Price
1	Meade	USA	Off	0.50
2	Hunt	USA	Off	0.50
3	Ransom	USA	Arty	0.50
4	McGilvery	USA	Arty	0.50
5	Taft	USA	Arty	0.50
6	Huntington	USA	Arty	0.50
7	Fitzhugh	USA	Arty	0.50
8	Hancock	USA	Off	0.50
9	Hazard	USA	Arty	0.50
10	Caldwell	USA	Off	0.50
11	NY-61	USA	Inf	0.50
12	NY-69	USA	Inf	0.50
13	NY-52	USA	Inf	0.50
14	DE-2	USA	Inf	0.50
15	Gibbon	USA	Off	0.50
16	MN-1	USA	Inf	0.50
17	PA-72	USA	Inf	0.50
18	MI-7	USA	Inf	0.50
19	Hays	USA	Off	0.50
20	OH-4	USA	Inf	0.50
21	NJ-12	USA	Inf	0.50
22	NY-111	USA	Inf	0.50
23	Reynolds	USA	Off	0.50
24	Doubleday	USA	Off	0.50
25	Wainwright	USA	Arty	0.50
26	Wadsworth	USA	Off	0.50
27	WI-6	USA	Inf	0.50
28	NY-84	USA	Inf	0.50
29	Robinson	USA	Off	0.50
30	ME-16	USA	Inf	0.50
31	MA-12	USA	Inf	0.50
32	Rowley	USA	Off	0.50
33	PA-142	USA	Inf	0.50
34	PA-149	USA	Inf	0.50
35	VT-13	USA	Inf	0.50
36	Sickles	USA	Off	0.50
37	Randolph	USA	Arty	0.50
38	Birney	USA	Off	0.50
39	PA-114	USA	Inf	0.50
40	ME-3	USA	Inf	0.50
41	MI-3	USA	Inf	0.50
42	Humphreys	USA	Off	0.50
43	MA-11	USA	Inf	0.50
44	NY-71	USA	Inf	0.50
45	NH-2	USA	Inf	0.50
46	Howard	USA	Off	0.50
47	Osborne	USA	Arty	0.50

#	Card name	Side	Type/Army	Price
48	Barlow	USA	Off	0.50
49	NY-54	USA	Inf	0.50
50	CT-17	USA	Inf	0.50
51	Von Steinwehr	USA	Off	0.50
52	PA-27	USA	Inf	0.50
53	OH-55	USA	Inf	0.50
54	Schurz	USA	Off	0.50
55	IL-82	USA	Inf	0.50
56	WI-26	USA	Inf	0.50
57	Slocum	USA	Off	0.50
58	Sykes	USA	Off	0.50
59	Martin	USA	Arty	0.50
60	Barnes	USA	Off	0.50
61	MA-18	USA	Inf	0.50
62	MI-4	USA	Inf	0.50
63	ME-20	USA	Inf	0.50
64	Ayres	USA	Off	0.50
65	US-4	USA	Inf	0.50
66	US-17	USA	Inf	0.50
67	PA-91	USA	Inf	0.50
68	Crawford	USA	Off	0.50
69	PA-13 Res.	USA	Inf	0.50
70	PA-12 Res.	USA	Inf	0.50
71	Sedgewick	USA	Off	0.50
72	Tomkins (A)	USA	Arty	0.50
73	Tomkins (B)	USA	Arty	0.50
74	Wright	USA	Off	0.50
75	NJ-15	USA	Inf	0.50
76	PA-95	USA	Inf	0.50
77	WI-5	USA	Inf	0.50
78	Howe	USA	Off	0.50
79	VT-4	USA	Inf	0.50
80	NY-43	USA	Inf	0.50
81	Newton	USA	Off	0.50
82	NY-65	USA	Inf	0.50
83	RI-2	USA	Inf	0.50
84	PA-93	USA	Inf	0.50
85	Williams	USA	Off	0.50
86	Muhlenburg	USA	Arty	0.50
87	Ruger	USA	Off	0.50
88	MD-1	USA	Inf	0.50
89	MD-3	USA	Inf	0.50
90	IN-27	USA	Inf	0.50
91	Geary	USA	Off	0.50
92	OH-66	USA	Inf	0.50
93	PA-29	USA	Inf	0.50
94	NY-102	USA	Inf	0.50
95	Pleasonton	USA	Off	0.50
96	Robertson	USA	Arty	0.50
97	Tidball	USA	Arty	0.50
98	Buford	USA	Off	0.50
99	NY-8	USA	Cav	0.50
100	WV-3	USA	Cav	0.50
101	US-5	USA	Cav	0.50

#	Card name	Side	Type/Army	Price
102	Gregg	USA	Off	0.50
103	NJ-1	USA	Cav	0.50
104	ME-1	USA	Cav	0.50
105	Kilpatrick	USA	Off	0.50
106	VT-1	USA	Cav	0.50
107	MI-5	USA	Cav	0.50
108	Ammo Depot	USA	Spec	0.50
109	Baltimore Pike	USA	Spec	0.50
110	Bayonet Charge	USA	Spec	0.50
111	Breastworks	USA	Spec	0.50
112	Color Guard	USA	Spec	0.50
113	Double-Canister	USA	Spec	0.50
114	Escort	USA	Spec	0.50
115	Extend Line	USA	Spec	0.50
116	Flank Patrol	USA	Spec	0.50
117	Friendly Fire	USA	Spec	0.50
118	Glory	USA	Spec	0.50
119	HeadQuarters	USA	Spec	0.50
120	Late Reserves	USA	Spec	0.50
121	Provost Guard	USA	Spec	0.50
122	Rally	USA	Spec	0.50
123	Rearguard	USA	Spec	0.50
124	Sharps Rifle	USA	Spec	0.50
125	Sharpshooter	USA	Spec	0.50
126	Shell Fire	USA	Spec	0.50
127	Signal Station	USA	Spec	0.50
128	Skirmishers	USA	Spec	0.50
129	Spencer Rifle	USA	Spec	0.50
130	Staff Officer	USA	Spec	0.50
131	Stone Wall	USA	Spec	0.50
132	Taneytown Rd.	USA	Spec	0.50
133	McPherson Ridge	USA	Terr	0.50
134	Herbst Woods	USA	Terr	0.50
135	Railway Cuts	USA	Terr	0.50
136	Seminary Ridge	USA	Terr	0.50
137	Oak Hill	USA	Terr	0.50
138	Gettysburg	USA	Terr	0.50
139	Little Round Top	USA	Terr	0.50
140	Devil's Den	USA	Terr	0.50
141	Wheatfield	USA	Terr	0.50
142	Peach Orchard	USA	Terr	0.50
143	Cemetary Ridge	USA	Terr	0.50
144	Cemetary Hill	USA	Terr	0.50
145	Ziegler's Grove	USA	Terr	0.50
146	The Angle	USA	Terr	0.50
147	Culps Hill	USA	Terr	0.50
148	Pardee Field	USA	Terr	0.50
149	McAllister's Woods	USA	Terr	0.50
150	Spangler's Spring	USA	Terr	0.50
151	Lee	CSA	Off	0.50
152	Alexander	CSA	Off	0.50
153	Longstreet	CSA	Off	0.50
154	Alexander	CSA	Arty	0.50
155	Eshleman	CSA	Arty	0.50

RARITY KEY C = Common U = Uncommon R = Rare VR = Very Rare UR = Ultra Rare F = Foil card X = Fixed/standard in all decks

SCRYE Collectible Card Game Checklist and Price Guide • 113

#	Card name	Side	Type/Army	Price
☐ 156	Hood	CSA	Off	0.50
☐ 157	AL-15	CSA	Inf	0.50
☐ 158	TX-1	CSA	Inf	0.50
☐ 159	GA-20	CSA	Inf	0.50
☐ 160	GA-11	CSA	Inf	0.50
☐ 161	Henry	CSA	Arty	0.50
☐ 162	McLaws	CSA	Off	0.50

19

#	Card name	Side	Type/Army	Price
☐ 163	SC-7	CSA	Inf	0.50
☐ 164	MS-17	CSA	Inf	0.50
☐ 165	GA-50	CSA	Inf	0.50
☐ 166	GA-24	CSA	Inf	0.50
☐ 167	Cabell	CSA	Arty	0.50
☐ 168	Pickett	CSA	Off	0.50
☐ 169	VA-1	CSA	Inf	0.50
☐ 170	VA-14	CSA	Inf	0.50
☐ 171	VA-18	CSA	Inf	0.50

20

#	Card name	Side	Type/Army	Price
☐ 172	Dearing	CSA	Arty	0.50
☐ 173	Ewell	CSA	Off	0.50
☐ 174	Dance	CSA	Arty	0.50
☐ 175	Nelson	CSA	Arty	0.50
☐ 176	VA-17	CSA	Cav	0.50
☐ 177	Johnson	CSA	Off	0.50
☐ 178	MD-1	CSA	Inf	0.50
☐ 179	LA-10	CSA	Inf	0.50
☐ 180	VA-4 (Stonewall)	CSA	Inf	0.50

21

#	Card name	Side	Type/Army	Price
☐ 181	VA-25	CSA	Inf	0.50
☐ 182	Latimer	CSA	Arty	0.50
☐ 183	Early	CSA	Off	0.50
☐ 184	GA-60	CSA	Inf	0.50
☐ 185	NC-57	CSA	Inf	0.50
☐ 186	LA-8	CSA	Inf	0.50
☐ 187	VA-52	CSA	Inf	0.50

#	Card name	Side	Type/Army	Price
☐ 188	Jones	CSA	Arty	0.50
☐ 189	Rodes	CSA	Off	0.50

22

#	Card name	Side	Type/Army	Price
☐ 190	NC-43	CSA	Inf	0.50
☐ 191	NC-23	CSA	Inf	0.50
☐ 192	AL12	CSA	Inf	0.50
☐ 193	GA-44	CSA	Inf	0.50
☐ 194	NC-14	CSA	Inf	0.50
☐ 195	Carter	CSA	Arty	0.50
☐ 196	A.P. Hill	CSA	Off	0.50
☐ 197	McIntosh	CSA	Arty	0.50
☐ 198	Pegram	CSA	Arty	0.50

23

#	Card name	Side	Type/Army	Price
☐ 199	Heth	CSA	Off	0.50
☐ 200	NC-26	CSA	Inf	0.50
☐ 201	MS-11	CSA	Inf	0.50
☐ 202	VA-40	CSA	Inf	0.50
☐ 203	TN-1 (Turney)	CSA	Inf	0.50
☐ 204	Garnett	CSA	Arty	0.50
☐ 205	Pender	CSA	Off	0.50
☐ 206	SC-1	CSA	Inf	0.50
☐ 207	NC-7	CSA	Inf	0.50

24

#	Card name	Side	Type/Army	Price
☐ 208	NC-22	CSA	Inf	0.50
☐ 209	GA-49	CSA	Inf	0.50
☐ 210	Poague	CSA	Arty	0.50
☐ 211	Anderson	CSA	Off	0.50
☐ 212	AL-10	CSA	Inf	0.50
☐ 213	VA-12	CSA	Inf	0.50
☐ 214	FL-5	CSA	Inf	0.50
☐ 215	MS-16	CSA	Inf	0.50
☐ 216	GA-22	CSA	Inf	0.50

25

#	Card name	Side	Type/Army	Price
☐ 217	Lane	CSA	Arty	0.50
☐ 218	Stuart	CSA	Off	0.50
☐ 219	Cobb's Legion	CSA	Cav	0.50

#	Card name	Side	Type/Army	Price
☐ 220	VA-4	CSA	Cav	0.50
☐ 221	NC-2	CSA	Cav	0.50
☐ 222	VA-18	CSA	Cav	0.50
☐ 223	Beckham	CSA	Arty	0.50
☐ 224	Ammo Depletion	CSA	Spec	0.50
☐ 225	Bayonet Charge	CSA	Spec	0.50

26

#	Card name	Side	Type/Army	Price
☐ 226	Carlisle Road	CSA	Spec	0.50
☐ 227	Cashtown Pike	CSA	Spec	0.50
☐ 228	Color Guard	CSA	Spec	0.50
☐ 229	Double-Canister	CSA	Spec	0.50
☐ 230	Escort	CSA	Spec	0.50
☐ 231	Extend Line	CSA	Spec	0.50
☐ 232	Friendly Fire	CSA	Spec	0.50
☐ 233	Glory	CSA	Spec	0.50
☐ 234	Grand Battery	CSA	Spec	0.50

27

#	Card name	Side	Type/Army	Price
☐ 235	Headquarters	CSA	Spec	0.50
☐ 236	Late Reserves	CSA	Spec	0.50
☐ 237	Provost Guard	CSA	Spec	0.50
☐ 238	Rally	CSA	Spec	0.50
☐ 239	Rebel Yell	CSA	Spec	0.50
☐ 240	Sharpshooter	CSA	Spec	0.50
☐ 241	Skirmishers	CSA	Spec	0.50
☐ 242	Staff Officer	CSA	Spec	0.50
☐ 243	Stone Wall	CSA	Spec	0.50

28

#	Card name	Side	Type/Army	Price
☐ 244	Whitworth Gun	CSA	Spec	0.50
☐ 245	Benner's Hill	CSA	Terr	0.50
☐ 246	Gettysburg	CSA	Terr	0.50
☐ 247	Seminary Ridge	CSA	Terr	0.50
☐ 248	Spangler's Wood	CSA	Terr	0.50
☐ 249	Biesecker's Wood	CSA	Terr	0.50
☐ 250	Warfield Ridge	CSA	Terr	0.50

Doctor Who

MMG • Released **April 1996**

301 cards in set; **1** promo card

- Starter decks contain 60 cards and rules; starter displays contain 12 starters
- Booster packs contain 12 cards; booster displays contain 45 boosters

Designed by **Paul Viall** and **Eamon Bloomfield**

Concept	●●○○○
Gameplay	●●○○○
Card art	○○○○○
Player pool	○○○○○

Poor **Doctor Who**. The longest-running science-fiction TV series has never gotten much respect in gaming. FASA's role-playing game featuring the Time Lord from Gallifrey faded into the mists of time, and Game Designer's Workshop's board game materialized mostly yawns. And even when CCGs went as global as the good Doctor's fan base, his own offering wound up joining the industry's jargon as an oft-invoked example of a failed CCG.

Players battle in three Time Zones, Past, Present, and Future, using Creatures and Resources. Life energy of players is represented by Time cards, which also confer card-draw bonuses. Attacks in an uncontested zone can strike Time cards — once they're gone, an opponent loses. It's a lot like playing three **Magic** games simultaneously.

If gameplay is uninspired — it's never really clear who players represent or why they're fighting each other — the cards are worse. Stuck with archival footage from TV episodes (many black-and-white), MMG resorts for many other cards to stock psychadelic moiré patterns. And the techno typeface used on the cards remains the most illegible font ever used in a CCG.

Hardcore Whovians are warned that the chances of finding an opponent for this are nil. When *Doctor Who* was released, this reviewer bought two decks at a game shop several towns away. On the next visit to that same shop, four years later (during its "going out of business" sale, no less), a *Doctor Who* CCG starter display was sitting there — complete, except for two decks. Asked if it was the same display, the retailer sighed, "Oh, *you're* the one..." — **John Jackson Miller**

You will need **34** nine-pocket pages to store this set. (17 doubled up)

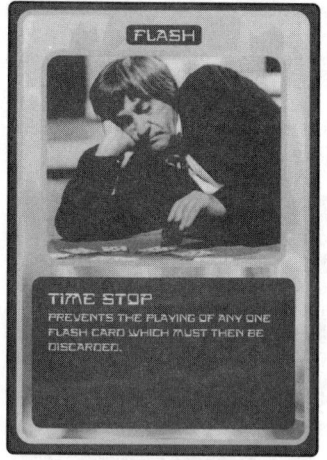

TIME STOP
PREVENTS THE PLAYING OF ANY ONE FLASH CARD WHICH MUST THEN BE DISCARDED.

Art on the above card really is in black-and-white.

Set (301 cards)	87.75	
Starter Display Box	25.00	
Booster Display Box	25.00	
Starter Deck	10.00	
Booster Pack	3.00	

Card name	Rarity	Price
☐ Exterminate	Promo	4.00
1		
☐ 76 Totters Lane	U	1.00
☐ Ace	R	4.30
☐ Adric	U	1.00
☐ Aggedon	U	1.00
☐ Alpha Centauri	U	1.00

Card name	Rarity	Price
☐ Andromeda Sleepers	C	0.25
☐ Animus	R	3.50
☐ Atlantean Fish People	U	1.00
☐ Autons	C	0.25
2		
☐ Balarium Gas	U	1.00
☐ Bannermen	C	0.25

RARITY KEY C = Common U = Uncommon R = Rare VR = Very Rare UR = Ultra Rare F = Foil card X = Fixed/standard in all decks

Card name	Rarity	Price
Barbara Wright	U	1.00
Barbed Wire	C	0.25
Bazooka	C	0.25
Ben Jackson	U	1.00
Bendalypse Gas	U	1.00
Black Dalek	R	5.30
Blindfold	U	1.00
3		
Blinovitch Limitation Effect	R	3.50
Bok	C	0.25
Brain Transformer	C	0.25
Castrovalva	R	4.00
Chameleon Circuit	C	0.25
Chumblies	C	0.25
C.I.A.	U	1.00
Cloister Bell	C	0.25
Crusades	C	0.25
4		
Cryogenics	U	1.00
Cyber Bomb	C	0.25
Cybercontroller	R	4.50
Cyberleader	R	4.50
Cybermat	C	0.25
Cybermen	C	0.25
Daemons	R	3.50
Dalekenium Bomb	C	0.25
Daleks	C	0.25
5		
Davros	UR	15.00
Death Ray	C	0.25
Demat Gun	U	1.00
DN6	C	0.25
Doctor Who 1	R	10.00
Doctor Who 2	R	10.00
Doctor Who 3	R	10.00
Doctor Who 4	UR	15.00
Doctor Who 5	R	10.00
6		
Doctor Who 6	R	10.00
Doctor Who 7	R	10.00
Dodo Chaplet	U	1.00
Doomsday Machine	UR	19.50
Double Time	R	3.50
Draconian	C	0.25
Drahvin	C	0.25
Dulciens	C	0.25
Duranium Shield	C	0.25
7		
Earthshock	R	4.00
Elixir Of Life	C	0.25
Emperor Dalek	R	6.50
Extortion	U	1.00
Exxilons	C	0.25
Fast Return Switch	R	3.50
Faster Then Light Propulsion	U	1.00
Fendahleen	C	0.25
Fenric's Flask	R	4.00
8		
Flashback	R	3.80
Force Field	C	0.25
Fusion Booster	C	0.25
Genesis Of The Daleks	R	5.30
Genocide	R	3.50
Ghostlight	R	4.30
Giant Robot	C	0.25
Glitter Gun	U	1.00
Gold Dalek	R	5.30
9		
Goth	R	6.50
Greek Hoplites	C	0.25
Green Death	U	1.00
Group Capt. Gilmore	R	4.30
Gustave Lytton	R	4.00
H.A.D.S.	C	0.25
Hal's Arrow	C	0.25
Harry Sullivan	R	4.50
Hexachromite Gas	U	1.00
10		
High Council Meeting	U	1.00
Highlanders	U	1.00
Hydromel	C	0.25
Ian Chesterton	U	1.00
Ice Warrior	C	0.25
Icthar	R	3.80
Irongron	C	0.25
Jamie McCrimmon	U	1.00
Jo Grant	U	1.00
11		
K-9	R	5.30
Kamelion	R	3.50
Kartz And Reimer Time Capsule	U	1.00
Kastrians	U	1.00
Katarina	R	4.30
Kontron Crystals	R	3.80
Kronos	R	4.00
Krotons	C	0.25
Kublai Khan	R	4.00
12		
Lazar's Disease	R	3.80
Leela	R	5.50
Linx	U	1.00
Living Power Battery	R	3.30
Liz Shaw	U	1.00
Marine Space Corps	R	3.00
Mechanoids	U	1.00
Melanie Bush	R	4.60
Menoptera	C	0.25
13		
Metamorphic Symbiosis Regenerator	C	0.25
Meteorites	U	1.00
Mind Battle	C	0.25
Mind Drain	C	0.25
Mongol	C	0.25
Monoids	U	1.00
Morgaine	U	1.00
Movellan Logic	R	4.00
Neanderthals	C	0.25
14		
Nestene	R	4.00
Neurotrope X	U	1.00
Nimon	U	1.00
Nyssa	R	4.50
Ogron	C	0.25
Particle Suppressor	C	0.25
P.C.M. Gas	C	0.25
Peking Homunculus	R	3.80
Perpugillian Brown	U	1.00
15		
Planet Of Evil	R	4.80
Policemen	C	0.25
Polly Lopez	U	1.00
Prapilus	R	4.00
Primitives	C	0.25
Prof. Clifford Jones	U	1.00
Q Capsule	C	0.25
Random Laser Beam Emitter	R	3.50
Ransom Demand	C	0.25
16		
Raston Attack	C	0.25
Raston Warrior Robot	R	4.50
Robomen	C	0.25
Robophobia	C	0.25
Robot	R	4.00
Romana	R	5.30
Romans	C	0.25
Rutans	C	0.25
Sacred Flame	U	1.00
17		
Sanctum	C	0.25
Sarah Jane Smith	U	1.00
Sea Base Four	C	0.25
Sea Devils	C	0.25
Seers	U	1.00
Sergeant Benton	R	4.00
Shrivenzales	C	0.25
Sidrat	C	0.25
Siligtone Dome	U	1.00
18		
Silurians	C	0.25
Skarasen	U	1.00
Sonic Cone	U	1.00
Sonic Screwdriver	R	3.80
Sonic Toolkit	U	1.00
Sontarans	U	1.00
Space Freighter	U	1.00
Space Pod	U	1.00
Space Special Security	C	0.25
19		
Space Station	C	0.30
Spar	U	1.00
Spectrox	U	1.00
Star Base	C	0.30
Steven Taylor	U	1.00
Susan	U	1.00
Tachyon Recreation Generator	R	3.50
TARDIS	C	0.30
Tartarus	C	0.30
20		
T.C.E.	U	1.00
Tegan Jovanka	U	1.00
Teleportation	U	1.00
Temporal Grace	U	1.00
Terileptils	C	0.30
Tetraps	R	4.00
Tharils	U	1.00
The Alliance	U	1.00
The Ambassadors	U	1.00
21		
The Ancient Law Of Gallifrey	R	4.00
The Ark In Space	R	4.80
The Aztecs	U	1.00
The Black Guardian	R	5.30
The Black Orchid	U	1.00
The Black Scorpion	U	1.00
The Brigadier	R	5.30
The Brothers Of Demnos	C	0.30
The Clanton Gang	U	1.00
22		
The Claws Of Axos	R	4.00
The Curse Of Fenric	R	4.00
The Destroyer	R	4.50
The Earp Clan	U	1.00
The Emperor Of Draconia	R	5.30
The Eye Of Harmony	R	3.50
The Eye Of Orion	C	0.30
The Faceless Ones	R	4.50
The Game Of Rasillon	U	1.00
23		
The Great Fire Of London	U	1.00
The Great Intelligence	R	4.00
The Happiness Patrol	C	0.30
The Harp Of Rasillon	R	4.00
The Keeper Of Traken	C	0.30
The Kinda Jhana's Box	U	1.00
The Malus	R	3.50
The Massacre	R	4.50
The Master	R	8.00
24		
The Master's Presence	U	1.00
The Master's Spaceship	R	3.80
The Meddling Monk	R	5.30
The Mind Of Evil	R	3.50
The Moonbase	R	4.30
The Myth Makers	U	1.00
The Oracle	R	4.00
The Rani	R	5.30
The Records Of Rasillon	C	0.30
25		
The Revenge Of The Cybermen	R	5.00
The Ring Of Rasilon	R	3.80
The Rod Of Rasilon	R	3.80
The Sash Of Rasilon	R	3.80
The Silver Nemesis	R	4.00
The Sisterhood	R	5.30
The Space Pirates	R	3.80
The Time Warrior	R	4.30
The Tomb Of Rasillon	U	1.00
26		
The Watcher 1	C	0.30
The Watcher 1	C	0.30
The Watcher 1	C	0.30
The Watcher 2	C	0.30
The Watcher 2	C	0.30
The Watcher 2	U	1.00
The Watcher 3	C	0.30
The Watcher 3	C	0.30
The Watcher 3	R	3.00
27		
The Web Of Fear	R	4.80
The White Guardian	U	1.00
Thunderbolt Missile	U	1.00
Time 1	C	0.30
Time 1	C	0.30
Time 1	C	0.30
Time 2	C	0.30
Time 2	C	0.30
Time 2	C	0.30
28		
Time 3	C	0.30
Time 3	C	0.30
Time 3	U	1.00
Time 4	C	0.30
Time 4	U	1.00
Time 4	U	1.00
Time 5	C	0.30
Time 5	C	0.30
Time 5	C	0.30
29		
Time 6	C	0.30
Time 6	U	1.00
Time 6	R	3.00
Time Acceleration Beam	U	1.00
Time Barrier	C	0.30
Time Controller	U	1.00
Time Corridor	R	4.50
Time Dam	R	3.80
Time Eddy	C	0.30
30		
Time Loop	U	1.00
Time Ram	U	1.00
Time Scoop	U	1.00
Time Stop	C	0.30
Time Travel	U	1.00
Time Winds	R	4.50
Time Worn	R	4.80
Timelash	R	4.80
T-Mat	R	3.80
31		
Total Survival Kit	U	1.00
Tranquil Repose	R	3.80
Transduction Barriers	C	0.30
Trench	U	1.00
Trionic Lock	C	0.30
Trisilicate	U	1.00
Underground Bunker	C	0.30
UNIT Corporal	C	0.30
UNIT Headquarters	U	1.00
32		
UNIT Soldier	C	0.30
Vengeance On Varos	R	4.80
Venom Gun	C	0.30
Venusian Aiki-Do	U	1.00
Vervoids	U	1.00
Vicki	U	1.00
Victoria Waterfield	U	1.00
Viral Destruction	R	3.50
Vislor Turlough	R	4.50
33		
Vorum Gas	R	3.50
V-Ship	C	0.30
Warning	R	3.50
Web Gun	C	0.30
White Dalek	U	1.00
Whomobile	R	4.00
Winifred Bambera	U	1.00
Woolfweeds	U	1.00
X-Ray Laser Cannon	C	0.30
34		
Yeti	C	0.30
Zarbi	C	0.30
Zoe Heriot	U	1.00
Zygons	U	1.00

RARITY KEY C = Common U = Uncommon R = Rare VR = Very Rare UR = Ultra Rare F = Foil card X = Fixed/standard in all decks

Doomtown (also known as *Deadlands*)

Wizards of the Coast (Five Rings division) • First set, **Episodes 1 & 2**, Released **February 1998**
156 cards in set • **IDENTIFIER: No symbol by artist name**

- Booster packs contain 15 cards; booster displays contain 48 boosters
- Starter decks contain 60 cards; combo displays contain 6 starter decks and 24 booster packs

Doomtown is based on the award-winning horror-western role-playing game, *Deadlands*. Wizards of the Coast's Five Rings Publishing divison released nine Episodes that formed the basic card set for *Doomtown* — with the first two Episodes combined in the initial release. (The card backs say Deadlands, but the name is definitely *Doomtown*).

In *Doomtown*, the players take the role of one of the outfits vying for the control the town of Gomorra and its rich veins of Ghost Rock, a sort of super-coal. The players build the town location by location during play and win by gaining more control points (from locations) and victory points (usually from actions), than their opponent has Influence points (from characters, "dudes").

Many *Doomtown* mechanics are taken from poker. Each card has a suit and value, as well as game effect text. Combat is decided by drawing cards from decks, the number based on the bullet rating (combat ability) of the dudes involved, and building the best poker hand possible. The difference in hand ranks equals the number of dudes killed. The mandatory deck size is 52 cards plus two optional jokers, no more, no less.

The three outfits released in **Episodes 1 & 2** are the Lawdogs (town sheriff and deputies), the Blackjack gang (major outlaw group) and the Collegium (mad scientists banded together to control the Ghost Rock). Both the Lawdogs and the Collegium have the ability to generate victory points apart from locations, making them the stronger outfits.

Doomtown developed a hardcore base of fans, but it wasn't enough to keep Wizards of the Coast in the game; it gave the rights back to Alderac in late 1999. Alderac dropped the line in November 2000, citing slowing sales. — *Michael Greenholdt*

Sidekick - While this dude is in a Shootout, Kenny acts as an additional dude with a zero-draw Bullet Rating.
"Oh my Gawd! They killed Kenny!"

Concept	●●●●○
Gameplay	●●●●○
Card art	●●●○○
Player pool	●●●○○

Set (156 cards)	127.00
Combo Display Box	80.00
Booster Display Box	85.00
Starter Deck	9.00
Booster Pack	3.50

You will need **18** nine-pocket pages to store this set. (9 doubled up)

Card name	Type	Rarity	Price
A Coach Comes to Town	Event	C	0.20
A Price on his Head	Action	R	3.00
Abandoned Mine	Deed	R	3.00
And Stay Down!	Action	U	3.00
Arizona Jane	Dude	U	3.00
Arson	Action	C	0.20
Bad Tequila	Action	C	0.20
Benny Hibbs	Dude	C	0.20
Black Jack	Dude	X	2.00
Blackjacks	Outfit	X	0.80
Blacksmith	Deed	C	0.20
Bluff	Action	R	3.00
Bob Bidwell	Dude	C	0.20
Brawl	Action	C	0.20
Bucket Brigade	Action	C	0.20
Bullet-Proof Vest	Goods	C	0.30
Casino Morongo	Deed	C	0.20
Cassidy Greene	Dude	C	0.20
Caught With Yer Pants Down	Action	U	3.00
Cave-in	Action	R	3.00
Charlie Landers	Dude	C	0.20
Cheatin' Varmint	Action	C	0.20
Christmas Day	Event	U	3.00
Claim Jumper	Action	C	0.20
Claims Office	Deed	R	3.00
Clean Up The Town	Action	C	0.20
Clell Miller	Dude	C	0.20
Cletus Peacock	Dude	C	0.20
Collegium	Outfit	X	0.80
Colorado Lode	Deed	R	3.00
Cordelia "Corky" Hendricks	Dude	C	0.20
Crack Shot	Action	U	3.00
Dead Man's Hand	Action	R	3.00
Deputy John Templeton	Dude	U	3.00

Card name	Type	Rarity	Price
Dispatch Office	Deed	C	0.45
Diversion	Action	C	0.20
Don't Like yer Looks!	Action	R	3.00
Double Dealin'	Action	C	0.20
Dragon's Nest Strike	Deed	R	3.50
Drawing a Bead	Action	U	3.00
Drop in the Ocean Strike	Deed	C	0.20
Dust Devil	Action	U	3.00
Dynamite Launcher	Goods	R	5.00
Earthquake	Event	U	4.50
Easter Sunday	Event	C	0.20
Eddie Bellows	Dude	U	3.00
Erik Zarkov	Dude	R	3.00
Eureka!	Event	C	0.20
Exchange Office	Deed	C	0.20
Extortion	Action	R	3.00
Fanning the Hammer	Action	C	0.20
Father Juan Navarro	Dude	C	0.20
Fineas von Landingham	Dude	R	3.00
Foale's Folly	Deed	C	0.20
Founder's Day	Event	R	3.00
Framed	Action	R	3.00
Friends in Low Places	Action	C	0.20
Fu Leng's Laundry & Tailoring	Deed	U	3.00
Full Moon	Event	R	3.00
Gatling Pistol	Goods	R	3.00
Gettin' Outta Hand	Action	U	3.00
Giddyup!	Action	C	0.20
Git!	Action	R	3.00
Golden Mare Hotel	Deed	U	3.00
Grave Robbin'	Action	R	4.00
Graveyard	Deed	R	3.00
Gremlins	Action	R	3.00
Hangin' Judge Gabriel	Dude	U	5.00
Haunting	Action	C	0.20
Head 'em Off at the Pass	Action	C	0.20
Headsman's Axe	Action	R	3.00
Heavy Rain	Event	C	0.20
Hector Casparo	Dude	C	0.20
Hell's Fury	Action	R	4.00
Henry's Hole	Deed	C	0.20
Hideout	Deed	U	3.00

Card name	Type	Rarity	Price
Humphrey Walters	Dude	U	3.00
Ignore 'im	Action	C	0.20
J.P. Coleman	Dude	X	0.50
Jail	Deed	R	3.00
Jessie Freemont	Dude	C	0.30
Joker	Special	R	5.00
Just a Graze	Action	C	0.20
Kenny	Goods	C	0.20
LAD Saloon	Deed	R	3.00
Lady Luck	Action	R	3.00
Law Dogs	Outfit	X	0.80
Lilith Vandekamp	Dude	U	3.00
Lucky Ted	Dude	C	0.20
Lynch Mob	Action	R	5.00
Marcus Perriwinkle	Dude	C	0.20
Mechanical Horse	Goods	C	0.20
Meredith Singleton	Dude	U	3.00
Mick Caples	Dude	C	0.25
Miner's Union House	Deed	R	3.00
Nash Bilton	Dude	R	3.00
Nasty Doc's	Deed	R	3.00
Nate Hunter	Dude	R	3.00
New Hat	Goods	C	0.20
"Nice Boots, Chief"	Action	U	3.00
Old Moon Saloon	Deed	C	0.20
Oswald Hardinger	Dude	X	2.00
Out of Ammo	Action	U	3.00
Pannin' for Gold	Action	R	3.00
Pearl-Handled Revolver	Goods	C	0.20
Perry's Pawnshop	Deed	R	3.00
Pharmacy	Deed	U	3.00
Photographer Shop	Deed	C	0.20
Pike's Puddle Mine	Deed	C	0.20
Pinto	Goods	C	0.20
Pony Express	Deed	C	0.20
Prof. Parnham's Miracle Elixir	Goods	C	0.20
Prof. Susan Franklin	Dude	C	0.20
Quickdraw	Action	C	0.20
Rachel Sumner	Dude	R	3.00
Raid	Action	C	0.20
Ray Gun	Goods	R	3.00
Roan	Goods	C	0.20

RARITY KEY C = Common U = Uncommon R = Rare VR = Very Rare UR = Ultra Rare F = Foil card X = Fixed/standard in all decks

Card name	Type	Rarity	Price	Card name	Type	Rarity	Price	Card name	Type	Rarity	Price
Robert Holmes	Dude	C	0.15	Spike Dougan	Dude	R	3.00	[17] The Slaughterhouse	Deed	C	0.20
Rock Ridge Mine	Deed	R	3.00	Spirit of Kentucky Shaft	Deed	C	0.20	The Tree	Deed	U	3.00
Rocket Pack	Goods	R	3.50	St. Martin's Chapel	Deed	U	3.00	The Undertaker's	Deed	C	0.20
Run Outta Town	Action	C	0.20	Still	Goods	U	3.00	Tombstone Dispatch Branch Office	Deed	C	0.20
Sam's General Store	Deed	C	0.20	[16] Sun in Yer Eyes	Action	C	0.20	Town Hall	Deed	R	3.00
San Simeon Mine	Deed	C	0.20	Sweaty Dynamite	Goods	C	0.20	Vampiric Dance Hall Girl	Dude	U	2.50
Sandra Harris	Dude	C	0.20	Tao Cheng ("TC")	Dude	C	0.20	Victor Navarro	Dude	C	0.20
Scalpin'	Action	R	3.00	The 1st Bank of Gomorra	Deed	R	3.00	Warrant	Action	C	0.20
[15] Schoolhouse	Deed	C	0.20	The Alright Corral	Deed	C	0.20	Winchester Rifle	Goods	C	0.20
Scrapyard	Deed	R	3.00	The Courthouse	Deed	R	3.00	[18] Wishing Well	Deed	C	0.20
Shortcut	Action	R	3.00	The Desert Rose Lode	Deed	C	0.20	Yellow Belly	Action	R	3.00
Silas Peacock	Dude	C	0.20	The Golden Crack	Deed	R	3.00	Yer all Chicken!	Action	R	3.00
Snake Eyes	Action	R	5.00	The Sabbath	Event	R	3.00				

Doomtown • Episode 3

Wizards of the Coast (Five Rings division) • Released **May 1998**

52 cards in set • **IDENTIFIER: No symbol by artist name**

- Booster packs contain 15 cards; booster displays contain 48 boosters
- Starter decks contain 60 cards; combo displays contain 6 starter decks and 24 booster packs

Episode 3 introduces the Sweetrock Mining Co. Outfit. Their special ability to generate more control points from strikes (mining locations outside of town) made them a dominating outfit in tournament play. In **Doomtown**, it is harder to move to an out-of-town location than one inside Gomorra. With the use of an event card, Heavy Rains, that prohibited movement to and from town, a Sweetrock player could lay down several strikes and win without possible interference from his or her opponent.

The three other outfits were strengthened, receiving more dudes. Several staple cards are in this set, including **Ambush**, a Job action card that allowed a player to attack a dude anywhere, and **It was a Mountain Lion**, a dude-killing event card that was the basis for several successful deck designs until changed by errata. — *Michael Greenholdt*

				Card name	Type	Rarity	Price	Card name	Type	Rarity	Price
Set (52 cards)	68.00			Friends in High Places	Action	R	3.00	Overtime	Action	C	0.15
Combo Display Box	80.00			Gatling Gun	Goods	R	3.00	Pinned Down	Action	C	0.15
Booster Display Box	85.00			Gerald Klippstein	Dude	C	0.15	Pistol Whip	Action	R	3.00
Starter Deck	9.00			Get a Rope	Action	R	3.00	Red Crow	Dude	R	3.00
Booster Pack	3.50			[3] Get on your Feet!	Action	C	0.15	[5] Red Hill Hotel	Deed	C	0.15

Card name	Type	Rarity	Price	Card name	Type	Rarity	Price	Card name	Type	Rarity	Price
[1] A Secret Tunnel	Action	R	3.00	Gordo Andrade	Dude	R	3.00	Refuse to Fall	Action	C	0.15
Ace in the Hole	Action	R	3.00	Government Audit	Event	C	0.15	Reverend Simon MacPherson	Dude	R	3.00
Ambush	Action	C	0.15	Gunther Hapworth	Dude	R	3.00	Robert Northrop	Dude	R	3.00
… and Scooter	Dude	R	3.00	Hell's End Mine	Deed	R	3.00	Rooftop Sniper	Action	C	0.15
Austin Stoker	Dude	C	0.15	Holy Wheel Gun	Goods	C	0.15	Scooter's Lift Winch	Deed	C	0.15
Big Jake...	Dude	C	0.15	Howard Findley	Dude	X	0.80	Sir Whitmore	Dude	R	3.00
Bob's Fix-it Shop	Deed	R	3.00	Ignacio's Excotics	Deed	C	0.15	Smiley's Shaft	Deed	C	0.15
Bomb	Goods	R	3.00	It Was a Mountain Lion	Event	R	3.00	Sweetrock Mining Co.	Outfit	X	0.80
[2] Dr. Reginald Branson	Dude	C	0.15	Jail Break	Action	R	3.00	[6] The Docks	Deed	R	3.00
Equipment Shop	Deed	R	3.00	[4] Jim MacNeil	Dude	C	0.15	The Fair Comes to Town	Event	R	3.00
Ezzie	Dude	C	0.15	Judge Henry Warwick	Dude	C	0.15	The Good Doctor	Deed	C	0.15
Flamethrower	Goods	C	0.15	Max Baine	Dude	R	3.00	The Temperance Army	Event	C	0.15
Flint Parker	Dude	R	3.00	One Eyed Ike's Weapons Locker	Deed	C	0.15	The Twitch	Dude	C	0.15
				Orphanage	Deed	R	3.00	Tom O'Reilly	Dude	C	0.15
								Top of the World Lode	Deed	R	3.00

You will need **6** *nine-pocket pages to store this set. (3 doubled up)*

Doomtown • Episode 4

Wizards of the Coast (Five Rings division) • Released **June 1998**

52 cards in set • **IDENTIFIER: Club (♣) by artist name**

- Booster packs contain 15 cards; booster displays contain 48 boosters
- Starter decks contain 60 cards; combo displays contain 6 starter decks and 24 booster packs

The Whateley outfit, a family of evil magicians (Hucksters) is introduced in **Episode 4**. Their arrival allowed for the first Influence denial decks, which won the game by temporarily reducing an opponent's Influence without otherwise affecting the opponent's dudes. Since spells cost nothing to play, The Whateley decks were the fastest yet.

Also new was the **Shotgun** item card, which allows a dude to kill an opposing dude in a shootout before the combat resolution, based on the other dude's value and the **Shotgun** wielder's combat score. It's been a staple of many decks. — *Michael Greenholdt*

				Card name	Type	Rarity	Price
Set (52 cards)	68.00			[1] Barkum & Barkum Attorneys	Deed	C	0.20
Combo Display Box	80.00			Basil Whateley	Dude	R	3.00
Booster Display Box	85.00			Billy No-Neck	Dude	R	3.00
Starter Deck	9.00			Blood Curse	Hex	R	3.00
Booster Pack	3.50			Bronco Bjork Gutmansen	Dude	C	0.20

You will need **6** *nine-pocket pages to store this set. (3 doubled up)*

Card name	Type	Rarity	Price
Buckets Nelson	Dude	C	0.20
Byron St. James	Dude	R	3.00

RARITY KEY	C = Common U = Uncommon R = Rare VR = Very Rare UR = Ultra Rare F = Foil card X = Fixed/standard in all decks	

Card name	Type	Rarity	Price
☐ Callahan's Ditch	Deed	C	0.20
☐ Circus Sideshow	Event	C	0.20
☐ Deputize	Action	C	0.20
☐ Dolores Whateley	Dude	R	3.00
☐ Eagle Rock	Dude	C	0.20
☐ Ezekiel Whateley	Dude	C	0.20
☐ Foreclosure	Action	C	0.20
☐ Forgery	Action	C	0.20
☐ Greased Lightning Pill	Goods	R	3.00
☐ Helpin' Hand	Hex	C	0.20
☐ His Back Was To Me	Action	C	0.20
☐ Independence Day	Event	R	3.00
☐ It's Just Coal...	Action	C	0.20
☐ King Willy's Mother Lode	Deed	C	0.20
☐ Lord Grimely's Manor	Deed	R	4.50

Card name	Type	Rarity	Price
☐ Manitou's Revenge	Action	R	3.00
☐ Mind Twist	Hex	R	3.00
☐ Missed Me!	Hex	R	3.00
☐ Missing Children	Event	R	3.00
☐ Moses Whateley-Braun	Dude	C	0.20
☐ Nicodemus Whateley	Dude	R	3.00
☐ Nowhere To Run	Action	C	0.20
☐ Pacific Maze Railstation	Deed	R	3.00
☐ Pierre Fontaine	Dude	C	0.20
☐ Sam Horowitz	Dude	C	0.20
☐ Samhain	Event	R	3.00
☐ Saul Whateley	Dude	C	0.20
☐ Shadow Walk	Hex	C	0.20
☐ Sheila Mirabella	Dude	R	3.00
☐ Sheriff's Watchin'	Action	C	0.20

Card name	Type	Rarity	Price
☐ Shotgun	Goods	C	0.20
☐ Smith & Robards Delivery	Action	R	3.00
☐ Soul Blast	Hex	C	0.20
☐ Stray Lead	Action	C	0.20
☐ Sunnyside Hotel	Deed	R	3.00
☐ Texas Twister	Hex	C	0.20
☐ The Clock Tower	Deed	R	3.00
☐ The Witching Hour	Action	R	3.00
☐ They Just Pay Better 'n You	Action	R	3.00
☐ Unknown Hooded Figure	Dude	R	3.00
☐ Werewolf	Dude	R	3.00
☐ Werner Braun	Dude	R	3.00
☐ Whateley Family Estate	Outfit	X	1.30
☐ Wilhelmina Whateley	Dude	X	1.30
☐ Yer Cheatin' Too!	Action	R	3.00

Doomtown • Episode 5

Wizards of the Coast (Five Rings division) • Released **July 1998**

52 cards in set • **IDENTIFIER: Club (♣) by artist name**

- Booster packs contain 15 cards; booster displays contain 48 boosters
- Starter decks contain 60 cards; combo displays contain 6 starter decks and 24 booster packs

In **Episode 5**, The Sioux Union was introduced, another spell-casting outfit, casting spirit spells rather than hexes. Unlike the Whateleys, The Sioux Union has both good fighters and potent spell casters, and an outfit ability that allows the Sioux player to forego income from his or her outfit to retrieve a Sioux dude or a spirit spell.

Although strong on paper, The Sioux Union never seemed to live up to its potential, perhaps due to a lack of really useful spells and a difficulty in casting the more difficult spells. Unlike the Hucksters or the Whateleys, The Sioux did not have access to cards or abilities that strengthened their spell-casting ability.

An important card in this set was **Shadow Man**, a hex that made the caster immune to opponent's actions, including being called out for a shootout. Combined with other hexes, this spell became the basis for several deck strategies. — **Michael Greenholdt**

Set (52 cards)	68.00
Combo Display Box	80.00
Booster Display Box	85.00
Starter Deck	9.00
Booster Pack	3.50

You will need **6** nine-pocket pages to store this set. (3 doubled up)

Card name	Type	Rarity	Price
☐ Benjamin Nightsinger	Dude	C	0.20
☐ Bounty Hunter	Action	R	3.00
☐ Bow and Arrow	Goods	C	0.20
☐ Calming Spirits	Spirit	R	3.00
☐ Charlie Flatbush	Dude	C	0.20
☐ Corporeal Twist	Hex	R	3.00
☐ Crazy Quilt	Dude	R	3.00
☐ Curse	Spirit	C	0.20
☐ Danny Hamilton	Dude	R	3.00
☐ Deadland	Deed	R	3.00
☐ Double Time	Action	C	0.20
☐ Elizabeth King	Dude	C	0.20
☐ Feather-In-His-Hair	Dude	C	0.20

Card name	Type	Rarity	Price
☐ Fish Ridge Mine	Deed	R	3.00
☐ Harold Longfellow	Dude	C	0.20
☐ Hat Gun	Action	R	3.00
☐ Hot Lead Flyin'	Action	C	0.20
☐ Human Shield	Action	C	0.20
☐ Ian Spencer-Whitney	Dude	R	3.00
☐ Icehouse	Deed	R	3.00
☐ John Bloody Knife	Dude	R	3.00
☐ Joseph Eyes-Like-Rain	Dude	X	1.80
☐ Labor Dispute	Event	R	3.00
☐ Lawrence Goodman	Dude	C	0.20
☐ Lightning Strike	Spirit	R	3.00
☐ Little Running Bear	Dude	R	3.00
☐ Medicine	Spirit	C	0.20
☐ Miss Coutreau's	Deed	C	0.20
☐ New Science Magazine	Event	C	0.20
☐ On the Side Strike	Deed	C	0.20
☐ Pembroke's Analysis of Hoyle	Goods	R	3.00
☐ Reserves	Action	R	3.00
☐ Rumors	Action	C	0.20

Card name	Type	Rarity	Price
☐ Shadow Man	Hex	R	3.00
☐ Singing Feather	Dude	C	0.20
☐ Snakebite	Action	C	0.20
☐ Strength of the Bear	Spirit	C	0.20
☐ Take Ya With Me	Action	C	0.20
☐ The 1st Bank is Robbed!	Event	R	3.00
☐ The Amazing Xemo	Dude	C	0.20
☐ The Sioux Union	Outfit	X	1.30
☐ Throw Down	Action	R	3.00
☐ Thunder Gulch Strike	Deed	C	0.20
☐ Tioga Joe	Dude	R	3.00
☐ Total Eclipse	Event	R	3.00
☐ Walkin' Dead	Dude	C	0.20
☐ Walks-in-Footprints	Dude	R	3.00
☐ War Paint	Action	R	3.00
☐ Water's Edge Strike	Deed	C	0.20
☐ Weaponsmith	Deed	R	3.00
☐ Whiskey Nick	Dude	R	3.00
☐ Wise Cloud	Dude	C	0.20

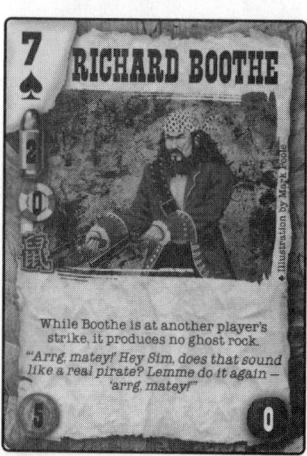

Doomtown • Episode 6

Wizards of the Coast (Five Rings division) • Released **August 1998**

52 cards in set • **IDENTIFIER: Club (♣) by artist name**

- Booster packs contain 15 cards; booster displays contain 48 boosters
- Starter decks contain 60 cards; combo displays contain 6 starter decks and 24 booster packs

Episode 6 saw the release of the Maze Rat outfit, the bane of Sweetrock Co. The Maze Rats can freely move to out-of-town locations and can take over other players' strikes. Suddenly, Sweetrock can no longer afford to sit back, but has to aggressively defend its strikes.

The Maze Rats are, however, vulnerable to outfits that stayed in Gomorra, notably the Lawdogs and the Collegium.

A card that changed the landscape of **Doomtown** makes its appearance in this set: **No Funny Stuff**. This card prohibits any reactions during a shootout, as well as any further shootout actions. Since the main bar to cheating hands (that is, those hands containing

RARITY KEY C = Common   U = Uncommon   R = Rare   VR = Very Rare   UR = Ultra Rare   F = Foil card   X = Fixed/standard in all decks

more than one card of the same suit and value) is reaction anti-cheating cards, this card allows such hands free rein. **No Funny Stuff** was later changed in errata to allow the play of anti-cheating cards and fell out of favor.— *Michael Greenholdt*

Set (52 cards)	**68.00**		
Combo Display Box	**80.00**		
Booster Display Box	**85.00**		
Starter Deck	**9.00**		
Booster Pack	**3.50**		

You will need **6** nine-pocket pages to store this set. (3 doubled up)

Card name	Type	Rarity	Price
1			
☐ Air Gun	Goods	R	3.00
☐ Becky Henrick	Dude	R	3.00
☐ Buffalo Rifle	Goods	C	0.20
☐ Bum Rush	Action	C	0.20
☐ Burn `Em Down	Action	C	0.20
☐ Buster Madison	Dude	C	0.20
☐ Captain Sim Yut-San	Dude	X	1.80
☐ Chin Wei-Lun	Dude	R	3.00
☐ Chinese Day Laborers	Action	R	3.00
2			
☐ Church Raisin'	Action	R	3.00
☐ Coleman is Killed!	Event	C	0.20
☐ Crippled	Action	C	0.20

Card name	Type	Rarity	Price
☐ Election Day	Event	R	3.00
☐ Finnegan O`Malley	Dude	C	0.20
☐ Green-Eye Saloon	Deed	C	0.20
☐ Gyonshee	Dude	R	3.00
☐ Hank Gallagher	Dude	C	0.20
☐ Harlot`s Haven Strike	Deed	C	0.20
3			
☐ Howlin' Hollow	Deed	R	3.00
☐ Hunch	Hex	R	3.00
☐ Ike`s Strike	Deed	C	0.20
☐ Jebediah Whateley	Dude	R	3.00
☐ Kidnapping	Action	C	0.20
☐ Library	Deed	R	3.00
☐ Little Mountain	Dude	R	3.00
☐ Long Arm of the Law	Event	R	3.00
☐ Luck of the Draw	Action	C	0.20
4			
☐ Marko Muscovich	Dude	C	0.20
☐ Maze Dragon	Dude	R	3.00
☐ Maze Runner	Goods	R	3.00

Card name	Type	Rarity	Price
☐ Mitobu	Dude	C	0.20
☐ Mortimer Jones	Dude	C	0.20
☐ Mustang	Goods	C	0.20
☐ Nelson Roberts	Dude	R	3.00
☐ Night Haunt	Action	R	3.00
☐ No Funny Stuff	Action	C	0.20
5			
☐ Phantom Fingers	Hex	C	0.20
☐ Po Yu	Dude	R	3.00
☐ Rain Dance	Spirit	R	3.00
☐ Red Spade	Action	R	3.00
☐ Richard Boothe	Dude	C	0.20
☐ Sacred Tomahawk	Goods	R	3.00
☐ Smiling Lizard Lode	Deed	R	3.00
☐ Speed of the Wolf	Spirit	C	0.20
☐ Stampede	Event	R	3.00
6			
☐ Sun Shu-Jen	Dude	R	3.00
☐ Tattoo	Action	R	3.00
☐ The Fear	Action	C	0.20
☐ The Lucky Dog Lode	Deed	C	0.20
☐ The Maze Rats	Outfit	X	1.30
☐ Wall Crawler	Dude	C	0.20
☐ Xiong "Wendy" Cheng	Dude	C	0.20

Doomtown • Episode 7

Wizards of the Coast (Five Rings division) • Released September 1998

52 cards in set • **IDENTIFIER: Heart (♥) by artist name**

- Booster packs contain 15 cards; booster displays contain 48 boosters
- Starter decks contain 60 cards; combo displays contain 6 starter decks and 24 booster packs

The Texas Rangers ride into town in **Episode 7**. The Rangers are very effective against Terrors (various supernatural creatures) and can ignore movement restrictions, which allows them to be competitive against most deck concepts. A new outfit card for the Blackjack gang is also added, allowing the Blackjacks to boot ("tap") to gain Ghost Rock, which really pumped up the power of this outfit.

This set introduces many experienced dudes, dudes from previous sets that were changed to reflect their experiences in Gomorra. Both the spirit and hex spell users receive a number of useful spells, and a staple of the game, **Massacre at High Noon**, appears. It allows the player to start a shootout at a location and if the player wins, all dudes at that location are killed (the initiating player's dudes went home first). — *Michael Greenholdt*

Set (52 cards)	**68.00**		
Combo Display Box	**80.00**		
Booster Display Box	**85.00**		
Starter Deck	**9.00**		
Booster Pack	**3.50**		

You will need **6** nine-pocket pages to store this set. (3 doubled up)

Card name	Type	Rarity	Price
1			
☐ Apache Devil Dancers	Spirit	R	3.00
☐ Ask the Spirits	Spirit	C	0.20
☐ Billy Iron Horse	Dude	R	3.00
☐ Blackjacks	Outfit	C	0.50
☐ Bobo LeVeux	Dude	R	3.00
☐ Cheyenne Bottoms	Dude	C	0.20
☐ Chrono Accelerator	Goods	C	0.20
☐ Death's Head Joker	Special	R	5.00
☐ Den of Eastern Delights	Deed	R	3.00
2			
☐ Derringer	Action	C	0.20
☐ Envy	Dude	C	0.20
☐ Father Juan Navarro (Exp.)	Dude	R	3.00
☐ Flophouse	Deed	C	0.20
☐ Friendly Game	Action	C	0.20
☐ Hired Guns	Action	R	3.00
☐ Holdout Knife	Goods	C	0.20
☐ "Hoyle's Book, 1769 Ed."	Goods	R	3.00
☐ Jack Guns Down Spike	Event	R	3.00
3			
☐ Joe Larson	Dude	C	0.20

Card name	Type	Rarity	Price
☐ Kansas City Kara	Dude	C	0.20
☐ Katie Karl	Dude	X	1.80
☐ Little Running Bear (Exp.)	Dude	C	0.20
☐ Los Ojos Del Dios	Dude	R	3.00
☐ Lucky Horseshoe Lode	Deed	R	3.00
☐ Marked Cards	Action	R	3.00
☐ Massacre at High Noon	Action	R	3.00
☐ Mimic	Action	C	0.20
4			
☐ Nicodemus Whateley (Exp.)	Dude	R	3.00
☐ Nicodemus' Deck	Goods	R	3.00
☐ Puppet	Hex	C	0.20
☐ Quick-draw Holster	Goods	C	0.20
☐ Rails Richardson	Dude	R	3.00
☐ Raymond Armstrong	Dude	C	0.20
☐ Repel Manitou	Spirit	C	0.20
☐ Reverend Simon MacPherson (Exp.)	Dude	R	3.00
☐ Robert Northrop (Exp.)	Dude	R	3.00

Card name	Type	Rarity	Price
5			
☐ Sacrifice	Miracle	C	0.20
☐ Spike Kills Eureka	Event	C	0.20
☐ Spirit Warrior	Spirit	R	3.00
☐ Stoker's Sabre	Goods	C	0.20
☐ Strike Experiment #1	Deed	C	0.20
☐ Summon Spirit	Spirit	R	3.00
☐ Take Cover	Action	R	3.00
☐ Tent City (Chinese Workers)	Deed	C	0.20
☐ That's Two Pair	Action	C	0.20
6			
☐ The Barber's Shop	Deed	R	3.00
☐ The Bathhouse	Deed	C	0.20
☐ The Mission House	Deed	R	3.00
☐ The Texas Rangers	Outfit	X	1.00
☐ Town Well	Deed	C	0.20
☐ Unholy Symbol	Goods	R	3.00
☐ Yellow Traitor!	Action	C	0.20
☐ Zeke Beauchamp	Dude	C	0.20

More uncommon than most

The cards marked "U" for Uncommon in *Doomtown: Episodes 1 & 2*, *Mouth of Hell*, and *Reaping of Souls* are actually probably better described as a level between traditional Uncommon and Rare card distribution frequencies. They appear more frequently than the Rare cards in the set, but not as frequently as you would expect for an Uncommon card based on the breakdowns in other games.

RARITY KEY C = Common   U = Uncommon   R = Rare   VR = Very Rare   UR = Ultra Rare   F = Foil card   X = Fixed/standard in all decks

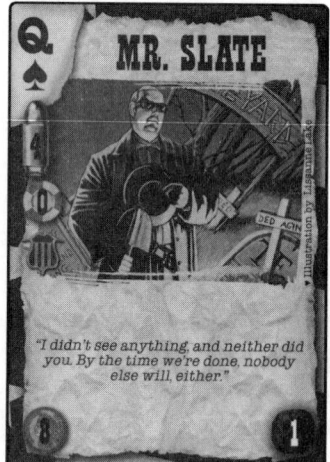

Doomtown • Episode 8

Wizards of the Coast (Five Rings division) • Released **October 1998**

52 cards in set • **IDENTIFIER: Heart (♥) by artist name**

- Booster packs contain 15 cards; booster displays contain 48 boosters
- Starter decks contain 60 cards; combo displays contain 6 starter decks and 24 booster packs

The Agency, the Union counterpart to the Texas Rangers, makes its way into Gomorra in **Episode 8**. Led by **The Ghost**, the harrowed Abraham Lincoln, the Agency gains victory points by killing Terrors. This Episode includes more harrowed dudes who have been re-animated by a manitou (demons) and are tougher than normal humans. Their main game ability was that when slain, instead of being killed, the opposing player had to draw a card from his or her deck. The harrowed dude could be sent home, discarded and was only killed if an ace was drawn.

Episode 8 also saw the release of a considerable number of the third spell type, miracles, although the outfit that uses them most appears in *Episode 9*. — *Michael Greenholdt*

Set (52 cards)	68.00
Combo Display Box	80.00
Booster Display Box	85.00
Starter Deck	9.00
Booster Pack	3.50

You will need **6** nine-pocket pages to store this set. (3 doubled up)

Card name	Type	Rarity	Price
Avarice	Dude	R	3.00
Benjamin Dean	Dude	R	4.00
Bottom Dealin'	Action	R	3.00
Call Weather	Spirit	C	0.20
Calm	Miracle	R	3.00
Captain Sim Yut-San (Exp.)	Dude	R	3.00
Censure	Miracle	R	3.00
Chester Nero	Dude	C	0.20
Chilling Effect	Action	C	0.20
Consecrate Armament	Miracle	C	0.20
Cort Williams	Dude	C	0.20
Degeneration	Action	C	0.20

Card name	Type	Rarity	Price
Drinks On The House	Action	R	3.00
Drought	Event	C	0.20
Duplicator	Goods	R	3.00
Erik Zarkov (Exp.)	Dude	R	3.00
Gomorra Gazette	Deed	C	0.20
Good Stiff Drink	Action	R	3.00
Gus Gallagher	Dude	C	0.20
Hardinger's Blueprints	Goods	R	3.00
Holy Roller	Miracle	R	3.00
Home Sweet Home	Action	R	3.00
Johnny Quaid	Dude	R	3.00
Josef Nicolai Rocescu	Dude	R	3.00
Knot Mine	Deed	C	0.20
Lay On Hands	Miracle	R	3.00
Lost Faith	Action	C	0.20
Machinist's Shop	Deed	R	3.00
Magnetic Poles Realign	Event	C	0.20
Major Earthquake	Event	R	3.00
Martyr's Cross	Goods	R	3.00
Nash Bilton (Exp.)	Dude	R	3.00

Card name	Type	Rarity	Price
Nate Hunter Is Elected Sherrif	Event	R	3.00
Pair of Six-Shooters	Goods	C	0.20
Philip Blackmoor	Dude	C	0.20
Raven's Crevasse	Deed	R	3.00
Sister Mary Jebediah	Dude	C	0.20
Smoke Signals	Action	C	0.20
Stuffed To The Gills Strike	Deed	R	3.00
Swapped Decks	Action	R	3.00
Test Of Faith	Miracle	C	0.20
That'll Leave A Scar	Action	C	0.20
The Agency	Outfit	X	1.30
The Carpenter's Shop	Deed	C	0.20
The Dentist's Office	Deed	C	0.20
The Ghost	Dude	X	1.80
The Gilded Feather	Deed	R	3.00
Tin Shield	Goods	C	0.20
Tombstone Frank	Dude	C	0.20
Turtle's Shell	Spirit	C	0.20
Will O' The Wisp	Dude	C	0.20
William Olson	Dude	C	0.20

Doomtown • Episode 9

Wizards of the Coast (Five Rings division) • Released **November 1998**

52 cards in set • **IDENTIFIER: Heart (♥) by artist name**

- Booster packs contain 15 cards; booster displays contain 48 boosters
- Starter decks contain 60 cards; combo displays contain 6 starter decks and 24 booster packs

The final episode of **Doomtown**'s initial release introduces The Flock, a group of diabolic blessed who use the third type of spell, miracles. The Flock gain extra control from strikes that already produced controls points, but have no special ability to protect or play out strikes. Their characters tend to be either good fighters or good spell users, but cost a lot to maintain.

Episode 9 also introduced of one of the most used cards in *Doomtown*, the **Jackelope Stampede**. An anti-cheating card, the **Jackelope Stampede** not only made the cheating player redraw his or her hand, only drawing five cards, but it also made the cheating player discard a card from play. It quickly became the anti-cheating card of choice and changed many deck designs so as to minimize cheating, at the expense of shootout draws. — *Michael Greenholdt*

Set (52 cards)	68.00
Combo Display Box	80.00
Booster Display Box	85.00
Starter Deck	9.00
Booster Pack	3.50

You will need **6** nine-pocket pages to store this set. (3 doubled up)

Card name	Type	Rarity	Price
Any One Of Ya!	Action	R	3.00
Babble On	Miracle	C	0.20
Barthalomew Prospectus	Dude	R	3.00
Black Jack (Exp.)	Dude	R	3.00
Blueprints	Action	R	3.00
Bolts O' Doom	Hex	C	0.20
Bowie Knife	Goods	C	0.25
Buffalo Chip Saloon	Deed	C	0.20

Card name	Type	Rarity	Price
Camille Sinclair	Dude	C	0.25
Coleman's Badge	Goods	R	3.00
Confession	Miracle	C	0.25
Dealer's Choice	Event	C	0.20
Dumb Luck	Action	C	0.20
Elijah	Dude	X	0.40
Eureka?!?	Event	C	0.25
Exorcism	Miracle	R	3.00
Flam	Dude	C	0.20
Flim	Dude	C	0.25
Gluttony	Dude	R	3.00
I Got The Pistols...	Action	C	0.20
Idleness	Dude	R	3.00

Card name	Type	Rarity	Price
Inspiration	Miracle	R	3.00
J.P. Coleman (Exp.)	Dude	R	3.00
Jack's Right Shooter	Good	R2	3.00
Jackalope Stampede	Action	C	0.25
Lechery	Dude	C	0.25
Legal Offices Of _____	Deed	R	3.00
Lonesome Willow Strike	Deed	C	0.25
Look Homeward Mine	Deed	R	3.00
Los Diablos Stampede	Event	R	3.00
Mordecai Whateley	Dude	R	3.00
Mr. Slate	Dude	C	0.20
Pox Walker	Dude	C	0.20
Pride	Dude	C	0.20

RARITY KEY   C = Common   **U** = Uncommon   **R** = Rare   **VR** = Very Rare   **UR** = Ultra Rare   **F** = Foil card   **X** = Fixed/standard in all decks

Card name	Type	Rarity	Price		Card name	Type	Rarity	Price		Card name	Type	Rarity	Price
☐ Revival Comes to Town	Event	R	3.00		☐ Sonic Destabilization Ray	Goods	C	0.20		☐ The Flock	Outfit	X	1.30
☐ Sanctify	Miracle	C	0.25		☐ Stagecoach Office	Deed	R	3.00		☐ The Gaping Maw Strike	Deed	C	0.25
☐ Seductress	Action	R	3.00		☐ Supplies From Back East	Action	R	3.00		☐ The Intelligence Shop	Deed	R	3.00
☐ Skin Shifter	Dude	C	0.25		☐ Surveyor's Office	Deed	C	0.25		☐ We've Got Ya Surrounded	Action	C	0.20
☐ Smite	Miracle	R	3.00		☐ SUZY 309	Dude	R	3.00		☐ Wrath	Dude	R	3.00
☐ Snake Handlin'	Miracle	R	3.00		☐ Tastes Like Chicken	Action	C	0.20					

Doomtown • Pine Box

Wizards of the Coast (Five Rings division) • Released **March 1999**

321 cards in set • **IDENTIFIER: Heart (♥) by artist name**

• Two-player set contains 100 cards; starter displays contain 6 sets

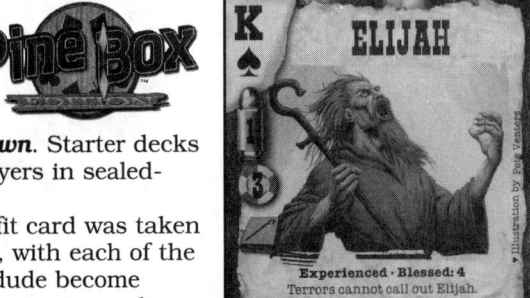

The **Pine Box** edition serves as a consolidated basic set for **Doomtown**. Starter decks come in coffin-shaped boxes and contain two faction decks, giving players in sealed-deck tournaments a choice of which faction to play.

All the original outfits were reproduced, although the Blackjack outfit card was taken from **Episode 7** instead of the original. Twenty new cards were added, with each of the 10 outfits gaining an experienced dude (although the Lawdogs had a dude become experienced and unaligned). Each outfit also gained a new card that was more-or-less slanted towards the main thrust of the outfit.

Other than the new cards, the bulk of the most useful cards were reprinted in **Pine Box**, with the notable exceptions of **Massacre at High Noon** and **Shadow Man**. The 20 special and fixed cards appear below; card backs still read © 1998. — *Michael Greenholdt*

Two-player starter set 12.00

Card name	Type	Rarity	Price		Card name	Type	Rarity	Price		Card name	Type	Rarity	Price
					☐ Danny Hamilton (Exp.)	Dude	X	3.80		☐ Jim MacNeil (Exp.)	Dude	X	4.00
					☐ Delores Whateley (Exp.)	Dude	X	4.00		☐ Nate Hunter (Exp.)	Dude	X	4.00
☐ All Saints Day	Event	XR	2.80		☐ Demon's Eye	Hex	XR	2.50		☐ Rachel Sumner (Exp.)	Dude	X	4.00
☐ Between The Shoulderblades	Action	XR	2.50		☐ Elijah (Exp.)	Dude	X	4.50		☐ Takin' Precautions	Action	XR	2.50
☐ Buckets Nelson (Exp.)	Dude	X	3.50		☐ Gerald Klippstein (Exp.)	Dude	X	3.50		☐ The Ghost (Exp.)	Dude	X	3.50
☐ Burial Ground	Deed	XR	2.50		☐ Ghost Rock Detector	Goods	XR	2.50		☐ Tioga Joe (Exp.)	Dude	X	3.50
☐ Bushwhacked	Action	XR	3.00		☐ Hell's Comin' With Me	Action	XR	2.50		☐ Unlucky Charm	Action	XR	2.50
☐ California Queen	Deed	XR	2.50										

Doomtown • Mouth of Hell

Wizards of the Coast (Five Rings division) • Released **June 1999** (cards say ©1998)

181 cards in set • **IDENTIFIER: Spade (♠) by artist name**

• Starter decks contain 60 cards; starter displays contain 12 starters

• Booster packs contain 15 cards; booster displays contain 48 boosters

The first nine episodes establish the town of Gomorra; from then on, a definite story-line influences the cards found in the **Doomtown** expansions. Three outfits receive new outfit cards in **Mouth of Hell**. The Lawdogs get a break on weapons cost and can call out any wanted dudes without restriction. The Collegium gain influence as they built gadget weapons and victory points for killing powerful opponents. Sweetrock can put a strike into play at the start of the game and gain a bullet rating at their strikes.

The event cards tend to reflect the storyline, and a new card type, harrowed powers, is introduced. The harrowed powers duplicate many effects from spells, weapons, and items, but once played, a harrowed power is discarded, altering the harrowed dude, making it much more difficult to get rid of a harrowed power. — *Michael Greenholdt*

Set (181 cards)	125.00	
Starter Display Box	99.00	You will need **21** nine-pocket pages to store this set. (11 doubled up)
Booster Display Box	135.00	
Starter Deck	9.50	
Booster Pack	3.00	

Card name	Type	Rarity	Price		Card name	Type	Rarity	Price		Card name	Type	Rarity	Price
					☐ Austin Saves Father Juan	Event	R	3.50		☐ Caught In The Crossfire	Action	C	0.20
					☐ Back To Nature	Spirit	R	3.00		☐ Choking Gas	Goods	C	0.20
☐ 1st Baptist Church of Gomorra	Deed	C	0.20		☐ Bad To The Bone	Action	C	0.20		☐ Claws	Action	C	0.20
☐ 2nd Bank of Gomorra	Deed	U	1.30		☐ Bash	Hex	C	0.20		☐ Clear Out!	Miracle	R	3.50
☐ A Few Custom Modifications	Action	R	4.00		☐ Bat's Breath Mine	Deed	C	0.20		☐ Clell Miller (Exp.)	Dude	R	5.00
☐ Acid Gun	Goods	U	1.30		☐ Battle Hymn	Miracle	C	0.20		☐ Cloak	Miracle	R	4.30
☐ Aim for the Head	Action	C	0.20		☐ Benediction	Miracle	C	0.20		☐ Clumsiness	Spirit	C	0.20
☐ "Alfred Barkum, Sr."	Dude	C	0.20		☐ Bind Spirit	Spirit	R	3.50		☐ Coleman Returns	Event	C	0.20
☐ Alice Chamberlain	Dude	C	0.20		☐ Bladed Fist	Dude	C	0.20		☐ Culling of the Blessed	Event	R	4.00
☐ Angus McFadden	Dude	C	0.20		☐ Blaze Of Glory	Action	R	4.50		☐ Dark Beast	Dude	C	0.20
☐ Arcane Protection	Action	R	4.00		☐ Blue Moon	Action	U	1.30		☐ Dark Protection	Hex	C	0.20
☐ Armor Of Righteousness	Miracle	R	4.30		☐ Bogie Man	Dude	C	0.20		☐ Darren Titus	Dude	U	1.30
☐ Auction	Action	C	0.20		☐ Bone Fiend	Dude	C	0.30		☐ Deer Eater	Dude	R	4.00
					☐ Bookstore	Deed	R	4.30		☐ Deputy Dave Montreal	Dude	U	1.80
					☐ Bottleneck Mine	Deed	C	0.20		☐ Deputy Milo Powell	Dude	C	0.20
					☐ Brownsville Jack	Dude	C	0.20		☐ Dervish	Miracle	C	0.20
					☐ Bull Whip	Goods	C	0.20		☐ Desmond Quentin	Dude	C	0.20
					☐ Burnt Offerin'	Miracle	C	0.20		☐ Devil's Plaything	Miracle	U	1.30

RARITY KEY C = Common   U = Uncommon   R = Rare   VR = Very Rare   UR = Ultra Rare   F = Foil card   X = Fixed/standard in all decks

Card name	Type	Rarity	Price
☐ Devil's Touch	Action	C	0.20
☐ Double-barreled Shotgun	Goods	C	1.30
☐ Dream Catcher	Goods	R	3.80
☐ Ectoplasmic Calcifier	Goods	R	3.50
☐ Electrostatic Pump Gun	Goods	U	1.30
☐ Elysium Fields Mine	Deed	R	3.50
☐ Extra Room	Deed	C	0.20
7			
☐ Fall Guy	Action	C	0.20
☐ False Face	Spirit	C	0.20
☐ Ferret's Eye	Dude	C	0.20
☐ Ferryman's Fee	Action	C	0.20
☐ Field Test	Action	C	0.20
☐ Fight Like A Man	Action	C	0.20
☐ Findley's Quill Pen	Goods	R	3.80
☐ Flim (Exp.)	Dude	R	4.80
☐ Fortune-Teller's Shop	Deed	R	4.50
8			
☐ Fountain	Deed	C	0.20
☐ Freddy Fast Hands	Dude	U	1.30
☐ Ghost Infestation	Event	R	4.30
☐ Ghost Train	Event	U	2.30
☐ 'Glom	Dude	U	1.30
☐ Groom	Hex	C	0.20
☐ Guard Dog House	Deed	C	0.20
☐ Hiding In The Bushes	Action	C	0.20
☐ High Noon	Action	R	4.30
9			
☐ Holmes' Workshop	Deed	R	4.00
☐ Horse Thief	Action	C	0.20
☐ Hostile Takeover	Action	C	0.20
☐ Howard Findley (Exp.)	Dude	X	3.10
☐ Hunter's Moon Strike	Deed	C	0.20
☐ Hunter's Office — Law Dogs	Outfit	X	1.60
☐ Interpret Vision	Miracle	C	0.20
☐ Invisibility	Spirit	R	4.00
☐ Ironteeth	Dude	C	0.20
10			
☐ Jacob the Healer	Dude	C	0.20
☐ James Hastings	Dude	U	1.30
☐ Jeb Parker	Dude	C	0.20
☐ John the Doomsayer	Dude	U	1.30
☐ Julius Bailey	Dude	X	3.10
☐ Katie Karl (Exp.)	Dude	R	5.50
☐ Kentucky Windage	Hex	C	0.20
☐ Lucifer Whateley	Dude	U	1.30
☐ Manitou's Control	Action	R	3.50
11			
☐ Marcus Perriwinkle (Exp.)	Dude	U	1.30
☐ Martyr's Mirror	Hex	R	4.30

Card name	Type	Rarity	Price
☐ Mary the Wanderer	Dude	C	0.20
☐ McCracken Brothers	Dude	C	0.20
☐ Melissa Thomas	Dude	C	0.20
☐ Meredith Kills The Hooded Figure	Event	R	3.50
☐ "Mirror, Mirror"	Action	R	3.80
☐ Miss Greene's Room	Deed	U	1.30
☐ Montana Holland	Dude	C	0.20
12			
☐ Mr. Bones	Dude	C	0.20
☐ Mr. Prim	Dude	C	0.20
☐ New Moon Saloon	Deed	U	1.30
☐ New Town Hall	Deed	C	0.20
☐ Night Haunt Attack	Action	C	0.20
☐ Nightmare	Action	C	0.20
☐ No End In Sight	Action	C	0.20
☐ Only Winged 'Em	Action	C	0.20
☐ Pact with Darkness	Hex	U	1.30
13			
☐ Peevie	Dude	C	0.20
☐ Phillip Goodson	Dude	R	4.30
☐ Pickpocket	Action	R	3.80
☐ Pit Wasp Swarm	Dude	C	0.20
☐ Po Yu (Exp.)	Dude	R	5.00
☐ Rachel Murders Warwick	Event	R	4.00
☐ Razor-Cliff Mine	Deed	C	0.20
☐ Red Handed	Action	C	0.20
☐ Redbrook	Dude	C	0.20
14			
☐ Riot	Event	C	0.20
☐ Ritual Scars	Action	C	0.20
☐ Robert Holmes (Exp.)	Dude	R	5.00
☐ Rocket Boots	Goods	C	0.20
☐ Run-Down Lot	Deed	C	0.20
☐ Sally Daniels	Dude	C	0.20
☐ Sauce For The Gander	Action	C	0.20
☐ Sawed-off Shotgun	Goods	C	0.20
☐ Secret Bomb	Action	C	0.20
15			
☐ Secret Identity	Action	C	0.20
☐ Secret Lab	Deed	R	4.30
☐ Shootin' From The Hip	Action	C	0.20
☐ Shouting Tom	Dude	C	0.20
☐ Singing Feather (Exp.)	Dude	R	5.00
☐ Sister Mary Jebediah (Exp.)	Dude	R	5.00
☐ Skunky Swade	Dude	C	0.20
☐ Sleeping With Shadows	Event	U	1.30
☐ Slumber Needle	Goods	C	0.20
16			
☐ Spike Dougan (Exp.)	Dude	R	5.00
☐ Sticks to Snakes	Spirit	U	1.30

Card name	Type	Rarity	Price
☐ Stitchin'	Action	U	1.80
☐ Stone Man	Dude	C	0.20
☐ Strikes A Hawk	Dude	U	1.30
☐ Sumner's Revenge	Event	U	1.30
☐ Sweetrock Smoking Lounge	Deed	R	4.50
☐ Sympathy for the Devil	Hex	R	4.00
☐ Tack and Harness Shop	Deed	C	0.20
17			
☐ Takin' Cover	Action	R	4.00
☐ Tao Cheng ("T.C.") (Exp.)	Dude	R	5.00
☐ Tapped Out	Event	C	0.20
☐ Telescopic Pistol Sight	Goods	U	1.30
☐ Terrormental	Dude	R	4.00
☐ The Back Room	Deed	C	0.20
☐ The Cooper	Deed	C	0.20
☐ The Labyrinth Mine	Deed	C	0.20
☐ The Lode	Deed	R	5.00
18			
☐ The Motherlode Is Found	Event	R	4.50
☐ The New Front — Collegium	Outfit	X	1.60
☐ The Side Pocket Billiard Hall	Deed	C	0.20
☐ The Spirits Flee	Spirit	R	4.30
☐ The Steam Tunnel Lode	Deed	C	0.20
☐ The T and Q Cattle Ranch	Deed	C	0.20
☐ Theatre	Deed	R	4.30
☐ This Round Is On Us	Action	C	0.20
☐ Throw Your Weight Around	Action	C	0.20
19			
☐ Time Vision Goggles	Goods	R	4.00
☐ "...Today, I Am"	Action	C	0.20
☐ Trick Shootin'	Action	C	0.20
☐ "Two Hands, Two Guns"	Action	C	0.20
☐ Undead Miners	Event	C	0.20
☐ Unknown Hooded Figure (Exp.)	Dude	R	5.00
☐ Unnatural Selection	Action	U	1.30
☐ Vision Quest	Spirit	C	0.20
☐ Walter Ponds	Dude	U	1.30
20			
☐ Warwick's Gavel	Goods	R	4.00
☐ Water to Wine	Miracle	C	0.20
☐ Wave Shadow	Dude	C	0.20
☐ Weapons Tax	Event	C	0.20
☐ Western Corporate Office — Sweetrock	Outfit	X	1.60
☐ Whisky Nick's Joint	Deed	C	0.20
☐ William Badson	Dude	R	4.50
☐ Xiong "Wendy" Cheng (Exp.)	Dude	X	3.40
21			
☐ You're Not Fast Enough...	Action	C	0.20
☐ You're With Me	Action	C	0.20

3 ♥
BLUE JEANS

This Dude's Influence cannot be reduced in any way.
"Nothin' comes between me and the supple feel o' denim."

1

Doomtown • Reaping of Souls

Wizards of the Coast (Five Rings) • Released **September 1999** (cards say ©1998)

181 cards in set • **IDENTIFIER: Cross (†) by artist name**

- Starter decks contain 60 cards; starter displays contain 12 starters
- Booster packs contain 15 cards; booster displays contain 48 boosters

In the **Doomtown** storyline, the Whateley family releases a powerful evil creature, the Knicknevin, which destroys much of the town. In **Reaping of Souls,** three new outfit cards are released. The Coalition represents a joining of the Texas Rangers and the Agency, which can use either or both dude affiliations freely. **The Flock, Children of Armageddon,** can sacrifice a dude to get any one card out of the deck or discard pile.

The Whateley Extended Family pays less to maintain Terrors and gains control points when the fear level in town goes above 6. *Reaping of Souls* released as many experienced dudes as new ones, as dudes became popular for more than their in-game abilities. A new type of location card, improvements, was introduced, that could only be played on existing locations. — *Michael Greenholdt*

Set (181 cards)	137.50	
Starter Display Box	99.00	
Booster Display Box	135.00	
Starter Deck	9.00	
Booster Pack	3.00	

You will need **21** nine-pocket pages to store this set. (11 doubled up)

Card name	Type	Rarity	Price
1			
☐ A Legal Deck	Action	C	0.20
☐ A Score Is Settled	Event	R	3.50
☐ A Slight Cough	Action	C	0.20
☐ A Stiff Fine	Action	C	0.20

Card name	Type	Rarity	Price
☐ Ainsley Cunningham	Dude	C	0.20
☐ All Harroweds' Eve	Event	C	0.20
☐ All Souls' Day	Event	C	0.20
☐ Ambition	Action	U	3.00
☐ Ammo Belt	Goods	C	0.20

RARITY KEY C = Common U = Uncommon R = Rare VR = Very Rare UR = Ultra Rare F = Foil card X = Fixed/standard in all decks

Card name	Type	Rarity	Price
☐ … And Scooter (Exp.)	Dude	U	4.00
☐ Armitage the Damned	Dude	R	4.30
☐ Army Of Gremlins	Event	U	3.50
☐ Assault On The Whateleys	Action	R	4.30
☐ Attitude	Action	C	0.20
☐ Austin Kills John Bloody Knife	Event	R	3.50
☐ Austin Stoker (Exp.)	Dude	R	5.50
☐ Bakery	Deed	C	0.20
☐ Balcony	Improvemt	C	0.20
☐ Bank Draft	Goods	C	0.20
☐ Bankrupt Morals	Action	C	0.20
☐ Basement	Improvemt	C	0.20
☐ Bedrock	Improvemt	C	0.20
☐ Benjamin Dean (Exp.)	Dude	R	4.50
☐ Big Jake... (Exp.)	Dude	U	3.80
☐ Black Cat	Hex	C	0.20
☐ Blue Jeans	Goods	C	0.20
☐ Bolt-Action Rifle	Goods	C	0.20
☐ Boom-Boom O'Bannon	Dude	C	0.20
☐ Bounty	Action	U	3.00
☐ Bribin' The Town Council	Action	R	3.80
☐ Bulletproof Glass	Improvemt	R	3.50
☐ Cassandra	Dude	C	0.20
☐ Chainsaw	Goods	C	0.20
☐ Chester Nero (Exp.)	Dude	U	4.00
☐ Circle K Ranch	Deed	C	0.20
☐ Collegium Sinks the Typhoon	Action	R	3.50
☐ Complaint Window	Improvemt	R	3.50
☐ Confusion	Miracle	R	3.50
☐ Conveyor Belt	Improvemt	C	0.20
☐ Coyote's Laugh	Spirit	R	3.50
☐ Cracked Bone Strike	Deed	U	3.50
☐ Dance Hall	Deed	C	0.20
☐ Dead Man's Laughter Lode	Deed	U	3.50
☐ Dead Walk The Earth	Event	C	0.20
☐ Deputy John Templeton (Exp.)	Dude	R	5.00
☐ Devil Bats	Dude	C	0.20
☐ Dexter Simpson	Dude	C	0.20
☐ Doctor Duvalier	Dude	C	0.20
☐ Dominion	Action	C	0.20
☐ Eagle's Sight	Spirit	C	0.20
☐ Elizabeth King (Exp.)	Dude	C	0.20
☐ Elmo Schacci	Dude	C	0.20
☐ Ely Parker	Dude	C	0.20
☐ Enoch Whateley	Dude	C	0.20
☐ Envy (Exp.)	Dude	R	4.30
☐ Eureka's Rage	Action	C	0.20
☐ Ezzie (Exp.)	Dude	R	4.50
☐ Fineas Von Landingham (Exp.)	Dude	R	4.50
☐ Fire And Brimstone	Miracle	U	3.00
☐ Flash Flood	Spirit	R	3.50
☐ Fleeting Memories	Hex	R	3.50
☐ Fool's Joker	Special	R	5.00
☐ Gomorra Volunteer Fire Brigade	Deed	C	0.20
☐ Good Kharma	Action	C	0.20
☐ Grace	Action	C	0.20
☐ Gypsy's Tent	Deed	U	3.50
☐ Hard Labor	Action	C	0.20
☐ Harvest Moon	Event	C	0.20
☐ Helga's Wafflehaus	Deed	C	0.20
☐ Hitched Buggy Strike	Deed	C	0.20
☐ Home Is Where Nothin' Happens	Event	C	0.20
☐ Hope In Winter	Dude	C	0.20
☐ I Want A Raise	Action	U	3.30
☐ Inheritance	Event	C	0.20
☐ Insurance Policy	Action	C	0.20
☐ Iron Gate	Improvemt	C	0.20
☐ Jessie Freemont (Exp.)	Dude	U	4.00

Card name	Type	Rarity	Price
☐ John Bloody Knife (Exp.)	Dude	R	5.00
☐ Knicknevin	Event	R	4.00
☐ Knicknevin's Deal	Hex	R	4.30
☐ Last Will	Action	C	0.20
☐ Let's Take It Outside	Action	C	0.20
☐ Light Of The Lord	Miracle	C	0.20
☐ Lighthouse	Deed	C	0.20
☐ Locust Swarm	Miracle	C	0.20
☐ Long Hallways	Improvemt	C	0.20
☐ Lord Grimely's Manor (Exp.)	Deed	R	5.00
☐ Los Ojos Del Dios (Exp.)	Dude	X	2.60
☐ Lukas Owens	Dude	C	0.20
☐ Lumberyard	Deed	C	0.20
☐ Mae Parker	Dude	C	0.20
☐ Malrog Whateley	Dude	C	0.20
☐ Max Baine (Exp.)	Dude	R	4.50
☐ Mental Hospital	Deed	U	3.00
☐ Meredith Singleton (Exp.)	Dude	U	4.00
☐ Mines Reopen	Action	U	3.00
☐ "Mirror, Mirror"	Hex	U	3.00
☐ Miss Lily	Dude	C	0.20
☐ Miss Me?	Action	R	4.00
☐ Muddy Brown Strike	Deed	C	0.20
☐ My Fight's With You	Action	C	0.20
☐ Mystical Bag	Goods	U	3.30
☐ Nemesis	Action	R	3.50
☐ Nightmare Realm	Hex	C	0.20
☐ Ninth Circle Mine	Deed	C	0.20
☐ No-Tell Hotel	Deed	R	3.50
☐ Observatory	Deed	U	3.00
☐ Pale Horse	Goods	R	4.00
☐ Paper Money	Action	C	0.20
☐ Penny Arcade	Deed	C	0.20
☐ Pocket Watch	Goods	C	0.20
☐ Poison Woman	Dude	C	0.20
☐ Polecat Saloon	Deed	C	0.20
☐ Puny Mortals!	Action	R	3.50
☐ Quarantine	Event	C	0.20
☐ Quick Reload	Action	C	0.20
☐ Radar	Goods	R	3.80
☐ Raven Smiles	Dude	C	0.20
☐ Relic	Action	U	3.00
☐ Renovations	Action	C	0.20
☐ Reserve Judgement Strike	Deed	C	0.20
☐ Rope Bridge	Improvemt	C	0.20
☐ Rough And Tumble Saloon	Deed	C	0.20
☐ Runnin' Water	Improvemt	C	0.20
☐ Sammy Childs	Dude	C	0.20
☐ Sandra Harris (Exp.)	Dude	R	4.50
☐ Saul Whateley (Exp.)	Dude	R	4.50
☐ Sea Of Sorrows Mine	Deed	C	0.20
☐ Second Story	Improvemt	U	3.00
☐ Shark's Grin Lode	Deed	R	4.00
☐ Sheriff's Shaft	Deed	C	0.20

Card name	Type	Rarity	Price
☐ Shootin' Range	Deed	C	0.20
☐ Sin Eater	Dude	C	0.20
☐ Snow In July	Miracle	R	3.50
☐ Soul In A Bottle	Hex	R	3.80
☐ Speaking With The Dead	Action	R	3.50
☐ Squish-Eye Samantha	Dude	C	0.20
☐ Strangers Among Us	Event	C	0.20
☐ Strike Experiment #2	Deed	C	0.20
☐ Sun Shu-Jen (Exp.)	Dude	R	4.50
☐ SUZY 309 (Exp.)	Dude	R	4.50
☐ Suzy Goes Berserk	Hex	C	0.20
☐ Tailor	Deed	C	0.20
☐ Teamwork	Action	C	0.20
☐ The Ammo-Matic	Goods	R	4.00
☐ The Coalition	Outfit	X	1.60
☐ The Evidence	Goods	C	0.20
☐ "The Flock, Children Of Armageddon"	Outfit	X	1.60
☐ The Gate Is Opened	Event	R	3.50
☐ The Horse Doctor	Deed	C	0.20
☐ The Jinx	Dude	C	0.20
☐ The Madman's Secret	Event	R	3.50
☐ The Taskmaster	Dude	U	3.30
☐ The Whateleys, Extended Family	Outfit	X	1.60
☐ Timmy Derrick	Dude	C	0.20
☐ Tool Belt	Goods	C	0.20
☐ Trick Deck	Goods	C	0.20
☐ Tricky Spirits	Action	C	0.20
☐ Tzipporah Whateley	Dude	U	3.50
☐ U.S. Army Enlistment Office	Deed	R	3.80
☐ Vampire Ambush	Event	C	0.20
☐ Vampiric Dance Hall Girl (Exp.)	Dude	R	4.00
☐ Vermin Problem	Action	C	0.20
☐ Victor Navarro (Exp.)	Dude	R	4.50
☐ Voice O' The Damned	Action	R	3.50
☐ Walkin' Stick	Goods	C	0.20
☐ War Of Words	Action	C	0.20
☐ War Party	Spirit	U	3.00
☐ Water Tower	Deed	R	3.50
☐ Weapons Locker	Improvemt	C	0.20
☐ Welcome To Hell	Miracle	R	3.50
☐ What Have You Done Lately?	Action	C	0.20
☐ What This Town Needs Is...	Action	C	0.20
☐ Whateley Family Bible	Goods	R	4.80
☐ Wilhelmina Whateley (Exp.)	Dude	X	2.60
☐ Windows Derek	Dude	C	0.20
☐ Wise Cloud (Exp.)	Dude	U	3.80
☐ Wither	Action	R	3.50
☐ Worse'n I Thought	Action	R	3.50
☐ Wrath (Exp.)	Dude	X	2.60
☐ Zapper	Goods	U	3.00

RARITY KEY C = Common U = Uncommon R = Rare VR = Very Rare UR = Ultra Rare F = Foil card X = Fixed/standard in all decks

Doomtown • Revelations

Wizards of the Coast (Five Rings division) • Released **November 1999**

182 cards in set • **IDENTIFIER: Omega (Ω) by artist name**

- Starter decks contain 60 cards; starter displays contain 12 starters
- Booster packs contain 15 cards; booster displays contain 45 boosters

The biblical Apocalypse is the theme of this, the last Wizards of the Coast/Five Rings **Doomtown** expansion. References to the Book of Revelations abound, including the seven bowls and the marks of the four horsemen.

Revelations continues the Knicknevin storyline as three new outfit cards rise to meet the challenge. In the Blackjack-Stoker Alliance, your wanted dudes gain influence and you get a break on one dude's maintenance. The Maze Rat, Landed Rats have lost their movement advantages, but can gain Ghost Rock from strikes they control but do not own. **Sioux Union War Party** allows shaman spellcasters to give bullet bonuses in shootouts.

The "Bullet" cards make their appearance in Revelations. A "Bullet" card can be discarded to kill a particular kind of dude, a powerful effect. Also noteworthy is the event, **Burning the Whateley Estate**, which allows a players to bring a new outfit card from the same outfit into play. — *Michael Greenholdt*

Card backs still say ©1998, but this set came out in late 1999.

	Price
Set (182 cards)	150.00
Starter Display Box	104.50
Booster Display Box	115.00
Starter Deck	9.50
Booster Pack	3.00

You will need **21** nine-pocket pages to store this set. (11 doubled up)

Card name	Type	Rarity	Price
Abel Owens	Dude	C	0.25
Alexander Whale	Dude	U	4.00
Alfred Barkum, Jr.	Dude	C	0.25
Along the Way Strike	Deed	C	0.25
Archaeological Dig	Deed	C	0.25
Arizona Jane (Exp.)	Dude	U	1.00
Audience	Action	C	0.25
Autogyro	Goods	R	3.80
Auto-Incendiary Bullets	Goods	C	0.25
Battle For Lord Grimeley's	Event	U	3.00
Battle Plan	Event	C	0.25
Billy No-Neck (Exp.)	Dude	R	4.00
Black Jack (Exp. 2)	Dude	X	4.00
Blackjacks, Stoker's Alliance	Outfit	X	2.50
Blood Oath	Spirit	U	4.00
Bloody Face	Action	R	3.50
Boardinghouse	Deed	C	0.25
Boat Yard	Deed	C	0.25
Bobo Leveux (Exp.)	Dude	R	3.30
Bone-Tipped Bullets	Goods	C	0.25
Born Under a Strange Star	Action	C	0.25
Both Barrels	Action	C	0.25
Boxin' Match	Event	C	0.25
Brewery	Improvemt	U	4.00
Burning Of The Whateley Estate	Event	R	4.00
Buster Madison (Exp.)	Dude	R	4.00
Buster's Gambling Hall	Deed	C	0.25
Cain Regen	Dude	C	0.25
Candy Shop	Deed	C	0.25
Chao Li	Dude	C	0.25
Charlie Flatbush (Exp.)	Dude	U	4.00
Chinese Ogre	Dude	C	0.25
Christopher Hill	Dude	C	0.25
Clock Strikes Thirteen	Event	R	3.50
Cobbler Shop	Deed	C	0.25
Cold-Iron Bullets	Goods	C	0.25
Con Game Gone Bad	Action	C	0.25
Cover Fire	Action	C	0.25
Deer-Stalkin' Hat	Goods	R	3.50
Denton Filmore	Dude	C	0.25
Double Or Nothin'	Action	R	3.00
Dr. Lawrence	Dude	C	0.25

Card name	Type	Rarity	Price
Dr. Reginald Branson (Exp.)	Dude	R	4.00
Dread Wolf Pack	Dude	C	0.25
Dud Round	Action	C	0.25
Eagle Rock (Exp.)	Dude	C	0.25
Embezzlement	Action	R	3.80
End of Time Lode	Deed	C	0.25
Eye Of The Storm	Event	X	
Faminite	Dude	C	0.25
Far Away Strike	Deed	U	4.00
Faro Table	Improvemt	C	0.25
Father Terrance	Dude	C	0.25
Feedin' Time	Action	U	1.00
Fifth Bowl	Miracle	C	0.25
First Bowl	Miracle	C	0.25
Flamin' Barrels	Action	C	0.25
Foreclosed Folly Strike	Deed	C	0.25
Fourth Bowl	Miracle	U	3.00
Francis Whateley	Dude	R	4.50
Fresh Horses	Action	R	3.50
Front Porch	Improvemt	C	0.25
Funeral Procession	Action	R	3.50
Gadget Warehouse	Deed	R	3.50
Gas Lamp	Improvemt	R	3.50
Ghost Rock Fever	Event	R	3.50
Glass Maker	Deed	C	0.25
Grendel's Eye Strike	Deed	C	0.25
Guide	Miracle	C	0.25
Gus Gallegher (Exp.)	Dude	R	3.50
Ham-Handed Play	Action	R	3.80
Harold Longfellow (Exp.)	Dude	X	2.00
Headless Horseman	Dude	C	0.25
Here Comes the Cavalry	Action	C	0.25
Holy Bullets	Goods	U	1.00
Homeless Joe	Improvemt	R	3.80
Hoodoo	Dude	C	0.25
Horned Owl's Fury	Spirit	C	0.25
Horse Racetrack	Deed	C	0.25
Hot-loaded Rounds	Action	C	0.25
Humphrey Walters (Exp.)	Dude	R	3.80
Idleness (Exp.)	Dude	C	0.25
Infared Spectacles	Goods	C	0.25
Intimidation	Action	R	3.50
Investment Broker	Deed	R	3.80
It's Just You and Me	Action	C	0.25
Jenny Cooper	Dude	C	0.25
Joseph Eyes-Like-Rain (Exp.)	Dude	X	2.00
Joseph's Return	Event	C	0.25
Killer Kerry	Dude	C	0.25
Last Rites	Miracle	C	0.25

Card name	Type	Rarity	Price
Lemat Pistol	Goods	C	0.25
Looking Glass	Hex	C	0.25
Lost in the Badlands	Action	C	0.25
Low Profile	Action	C	0.25
Mad Dog Campbell	Dude	C	0.25
Magic Bus	Goods	R	3.50
Magnum Bullets	Goods	C	0.25
Mark Of Death	Hex	R	3.80
Mark of Famine	Hex	C	0.25
Mark of Man	Action	C	0.25
Mark of Pestilence	Hex	C	0.25
Mark Of War	Hex	R	3.80
Mark Preston	Dude	C	0.25
Mask	Goods	C	0.25
Maze Rats, Landed Rats	Outfit	X	1.00
Misdirection	Action	C	0.25
Monopoly	Action	R	3.00
Museum	Deed	R	4.00
Nate Hunter (Exp. 2)	Dude	R	4.30
Nature's Wrath	Spirit	C	0.25
Nebuchadnezzar	Dude	C	0.25
Nelson Roberts (Exp.)	Dude	U	4.00
Nick's Never Closes	Deed	C	0.25
No Mint Juleps Here	Action	R	3.30
Panic Attack	Action	C	0.25
Papa's Lode Strike	Deed	U	1.00
Peace Pipe	Goods	R	3.50
Pennsylvania Kid	Dude	C	0.25
Piano Player	Improvemt	C	0.25
Pipe	Goods	C	0.25
Postal Fine	Action	C	0.25
Pride (Exp.)	Dude	R	4.00
Prof. Susan Franklin (Exp.)	Dude	R	3.30
Psychic Projector	Goods	U	1.00
Pump	Improvemt	U	4.00
Purging of the Golden Mare	Event	C	0.25
Rats In Gomorra	Action	C	0.25
Reckoner's Bullet	Goods	R	4.00
Reggie Cornell	Dude	C	0.25
Richard Boothe (Exp.)	Dude	R	3.50
Roll of Dimes	Goods	U	3.00
Run, You Coward!	Action	R	3.80
Saloon's on Fire	Event	C	0.25
Sam Horowitz (Exp.)	Dude	U	3.00
Scared Stiff Saloon	Deed	R	3.50
Second Bowl	Miracle	C	0.25
Seldon Harrison	Dude	C	0.25
Seventh Bowl	Miracle	R	4.00
Seventh-Sign Strike	Deed	R	4.00
Shallow Grave	Action	R	4.00

Card name	Type	Rarity	Price
Sheila Mirabella (Exp.)	Dude	R	3.50
Shigetoshi Hohiro	Dude	U	1.00
Shotgun Wedding	Action	R	3.80
[17] Sidewalk	Improvemt	C	0.25
Silas Peacock (Exp.)	Dude	C	0.25
Silver Bullets	Goods	C	0.25
Sioux Union, War Party	Outfit	X	2.00
Sixth Bowl	Miracle	U	1.00
Skunky Swade (Exp.)	Dude	R	3.50
Sleep o' the Dead	Action	U	1.00
Spare Chamber	Goods	U	4.00
Spirit's Eyes	Dude	C	0.25
[18] Spurs	Goods	C	0.25
Stained-Glass Windows	Improvemt	C	0.25

Card name	Type	Rarity	Price
"Stand Alone, Die Alone"	Event	R	4.00
Statute 32 Of The Penal Code	Event	R	3.80
Stayin' Put	Hex	C	0.25
Stoker Versus Knicknevin	Action	C	0.25
Storage Shed	Deed	R	4.00
Sun In His Eyes	Dude	C	0.25
[19] Supernatural Smarts	Action	C	0.25
Supernatural Speed	Action	C	0.25
Tailoring Shop	Deed	C	0.25
Tax Season	Event	C	0.25
Termite Infestation	Action	C	0.25
The Drifter	Dude	U	4.00
The End is Nigh	Event	C	0.25
The House Always Wins	Event	C	0.25

Card name	Type	Rarity	Price
The Missionary	Dude	U	1.00
Third Bowl	Miracle	C	0.25
[20] Thunderbird	Dude	U	1.00
Tinker	Action	C	0.25
Together At Last	Action	R	3.50
Tomb Guardian	Dude	R	3.50
Trackin' Teeth	Action	U	4.00
Trading Post	Deed	C	0.25
Two Birds Chirping	Dude	U	4.00
Wendigo Garrison	Dude	C	0.25
Western Union Offices	Deed	R	4.00
[21] White Horse	Dude	C	0.25
Wrath O' God	Event	R	4.30

Doomtown • *Boot Hill*

Alderac Entertainment Group • Released **April 2000**

318 cards in set • IDENTIFIER: Plus (✛) by artist name

- Starter decks contain 60 cards; starter displays contain 9 starters
- Booster packs contain 15 cards; booster displays contain 36 boosters

Alderac's first **Doomtown** set, **Boot Hill**, was released as the third basic set for *Doomtown*. It reprints many of the cards from the previous sets, but did not add any new cards, as **Pine Box** did.

Boot Hill reflected the changes in the storyline by unveiling the concept of "*Boot Hill*-legal" decks and tournaments. As with **Legend of the Five Rings**, Alderac planned three types of tournaments: Open, where players can use any *Doomtown* cards printed; Boot Hill-Extended, where players can only use dudes, deeds and events that have been released in *Boot Hill* or in later expansions; and Boot Hill-Strict, where players can only use cards that have been released in *Boot Hill* or in later expansions. The latter two styles were planned for tournaments relating to storyline developments. — *Michael Greenholdt*

Set (318 cards)	102.50
Starter Display Box	90.00
Booster Display Box	60.00
Starter Deck	9.00
Booster Pack	3.00

You will need **36** nine-pocket pages to store this set. (18 doubled up)

Card name	Type	Rarity	Price
[1] 2nd Bank of Gomorra	Deed	U	0.80
A Coach comes to Town	Event	C	0.15
A Legal Deck	Action	C	0.25
A Secret Tunnel	Action	U	0.80
Abandoned Mine	Deed	R	3.00
Abel Owens	Dude	C	0.35
Ace in the Hole	Action	U	0.50
Acid Gun	Goods	U	0.80
Alice Chamberlain	Dude	C	0.15
[2] Ambition	Action	U	0.80
Ambush	Action	U	0.80
...and Scooter	Dude	U	0.80
And Stay Down!	Action	R	3.00
Apache Devil Dancers	Spell	C	0.25
Arcane Protection	Action	R	4.00
Arizona Jane	Dude	U	0.80
Armor of Righteousness	Spell	R	3.00
Army of Gremlins	Event	U	0.80
[3] Arson	Action	C	0.15
Autogyro	Goods	R	3.00
Bad Tequila	Action	C	0.15
Bad to the Bone	Action	C	0.25
Bankrupt Morals	Action	C	0.15
Barkum & Barkum Attnys	Deed	U	1.00
Barthalomew Prospectus	Dude	R	4.00
Bedrock	Deed	C	0.15
Benjamin Dean	Dude	C	0.15
[4] Big Jake...	Dude	U	0.80
Billy No-Neck	Dude	R	4.00
Black Jack	Dude	C	0.35

Card name	Type	Rarity	Price
Blackjacks	Outfit	X	1.30
Blood Curse	Spell	R	4.00
Blood Oath	Spell	U	0.80
Bobo Leveux	Dude	R	3.00
Bookstore	Deed	R	4.00
Bounty Hunter	Action	R	3.00
[5] Bowie Knife	Goods	C	0.15
Brewery	Improvemt	U	0.80
Bucket Brigade	Action	C	0.15
Buckets Nelson	Dude	C	0.15
Bum Rush	Action	C	0.15
Burn 'em Down	Action	C	0.15
Burnt Offerin'	Spell	C	0.25
Buster Madison	Dude	R	4.00
Cain Regen	Dude	C	0.35
[6] Callahan's Ditch	Deed	C	0.15
Camille Sinclair	Dude	C	0.25
Captain Sim Yut San	Dude	C	0.25
Cassandra	Dude	C	0.15
Chao Li	Dude	C	0.15
Charlie Flatbush	Dude	U	0.80
Charlie Landers	Dude	C	0.15
Chester Nero	Dude	U	0.80
Claim Jumper	Action	U	0.80
[7] Claws	Action	C	0.15
Clean up the town	Action	C	0.15
Clell Miller	Dude	R	4.00
Collegium - The New Front	Outfit	X	1.30
Colorado Lode	Deed	R	4.00
Corkie's Sidearm	Goods	X	0.80
Cort Williams	Dude	C	0.35
Cover Fire	Action	C	0.15
Coyote's Laugh	Spell	R	3.00
[8] Crack Shot	Action	R	3.00
Darren Titus	Dude	U	0.80
Dead Man's Laughter Lode	Deed	U	0.80
Deadland	Deed	R	3.00

Card name	Type	Rarity	Price
Dealer's Choice	Event	C	0.15
Death's Head Joker	Action	C	4.00
Deer Eater	Dude	R	4.00
Den of Eastern Delights	Deed	C	0.15
Deputize	Action	C	0.15
[9] Deputy Dave Montreal	Dude	U	0.80
Desmond Quentin	Dude	C	0.25
Dispatch Office	Deed	C	0.15
Doctor Duvalier	Dude	C	0.15
Dolores Whateley	Dude	R	4.00
Don't Like yer Looks!	Action	R	3.00
Double Dealin'	Action	C	0.15
Dr. Reginald Branson	Dude	U	0.80
Dragon's Nest Strike	Deed	R	4.00
[10] Dragon's Tooth	Goods	X	0.80
Dread Wolf Pack	Dude	C	0.15
Dream Catcher	Goods	R	3.00
Drop in the Ocean Strike	Deed	C	0.15
Drought	Event	C	0.15
Dumb Luck	Action	C	0.15
Dust Devil	Action	R	3.00
Eagle Rock	Dude	C	0.15
Electrostatic Pump Gun	Goods	U	0.80
[11] Electrothermic Entropy Projector	Goods	X	0.60
Elysium Fields Mine	Deed	R	3.00
Erik Zarkov	Dude	R	4.00
Eureka?!?	Event	C	0.15
Eureka's Rage	Action	C	0.15
Ezzie	Dude	U	0.80
Faminite	Dude	C	0.15
Fanning the Hammer	Action	C	0.15
Father Juan Navarro	Dude	C	0.15
[12] Father Terrance	Dude	C	0.15
Fineas Von Landingham	Dude	R	4.00
Fire and Brimstone	Spell	U	0.80
Fish Ridge Mine	Deed	R	3.00

RARITY KEY **C** = Common **U** = Uncommon **R** = Rare **VR** = Very Rare **UR** = Ultra Rare **F** = Foil card **X** = Fixed/standard in all decks

Card name	Type	Rarity	Price
Flamethrower	Goods	U	0.80
Flaming Barrels	Action	C	0.15
Foale's Folly	Deed	C	0.15
Fool's Joker	Action	R	4.00
Foreclosure	Action	C	0.15
Fortune-Teller's Shop	Deed	R	4.00
Founder's Day	Event	R	3.00
Frank	Goods	X	0.50
Friends in Low Places	Action	C	0.25
Full Moon	Event	R	3.00
Funeral Procession	Action	R	4.00
Gerald Klippstein	Dude	U	0.80
Ghost Infestation	Event	R	3.00
Ghost Rock Fever	Event	R	3.00
Ghost Train	Event	U	0.80
Giddyup!	Action	C	0.15
'Glom	Dude	U	0.50
Golden Mare Hotel	Deed	R	3.00
Government Audit	Event	U	0.50
Graveyard	Deed	R	3.00
Green-Eye Saloon	Deed	C	0.15
Gus Gallagher	Dude	R	4.00
Gypsy's Tent	Deed	U	0.80
Harvest Moon	Event	C	0.15
Head 'em Off at the Pass	Action	C	0.15
Headsman's Axe	Action	R	3.00
Hell's End Mine	Deed	U	0.80
Holy Bullets	Goods	U	0.80
Homeless Joe	Improvemt	R	3.00
Hostile Takeover	Action	C	0.15
Howlin' Hollow	Deed	R	3.00
Infrared Spectacles	Goods	C	0.25
Inspiration	Spell	C	0.15
J.P. Coleman	Dude	U	0.35
Jackelope Stampede	Action	C	0.15
Jail	Deed	R	3.00
James Hastings	Dude	U	0.80
Jebediah Whateley	Dude	R	4.00
Jenny Cooper	Dude	C	0.15
Jessie Freemont	Dude	U	0.80
John Templeton	Dude	R	4.00
Just a graze	Action	C	0.15
Katie Karl	Dude	R	4.00
Kenny	Goods	C	0.15
Kentucky Windage	Spell	C	0.15
Kidnapping	Action	C	0.25
King Willy's Mother Lode	Deed	C	0.15
Knicknevin's Deal	Spell	R	3.00
LAD Saloon	Deed	R	3.00
Lady Luck	Action	R	3.00
Law Dogs - Hunter's Office	Outfit	X	1.30
Lay on Hands	Spell	C	0.25
Legal offices of _____	Deed	C	0.15
Locust Swarm	Spell	C	0.25
Long Arm of the Law	Event	R	3.00
Looking Glass	Spell	C	0.25
Los Ojos del Dios	Dude	C	0.15
Lucifer Whateley	Dude	U	0.80
Magnum Bullets	Goods	C	0.35
Manitou's Control	Action	R	3.00
Manitou's Revenge	Action	R	3.00
Marcus Perriwinkle	Dude	U	0.80
Massacre at High Noon	Action	C	0.15
Max Baine	Dude	R	4.00
Maze Rats - Landed Rats	Outfit	X	1.30
Medicine	Spell	C	0.25
Mental Hospital	Deed	U	0.80
Meredith Singleton	Dude	U	0.80
Mines Reopen	Action	U	0.80
"Mirror, Mirror"	Spell	U	0.80
Miss Greene's Room	Deed	U	0.80
Miss Me?	Action	R	4.00
Mr. Bones	Dude	C	0.15

Card name	Type	Rarity	Price
Mr. Prim's Bust	Goods	X	0.50
Nate Hunter	Dude	R	4.00
Nebuchadnezzar	Dude	C	0.15
Nelson Roberts	Dude	U	0.50
New Hat	Goods	C	0.15
New Moon Saloon	Deed	U	0.80
New Town Hall	Deed	C	0.25
"Nice Boots, Chief"	Action	R	3.00
Nicodemus Whateley	Dude	R	4.00
Nightmare Realm	Spell	C	0.15
No Funny Stuff	Action	C	0.25
No Mint Juleps Here	Action	R	3.00
Observatory	Deed	U	0.80
Only Winged 'Em	Action	C	0.15
Out of Ammo	Action	R	4.00
Pacific Maze Rail Station	Deed	R	3.00
Pact with Darkness	Spell	U	0.80
Pair of Six-shooters	Goods	C	0.25
Pearl-Handled Revolver	Goods	C	0.15
Peevie	Dude	C	0.15
Pike's Puddle Mine	Deed	C	0.15
Pinned Down	Action	R	3.00
Pistol Whip	Action	U	0.80
Po Yu	Dude	R	4.00
Pocket Watch	Goods	C	0.15
Prof. Susan Franklin	Dude	R	4.00
Pump	Improvemt	U	0.80
Puppet	Spell	C	0.25
Rachel's Sidearm	Goods	X	0.60
Raven Smiles	Dude	C	0.15
Raven's Chop	Goods	X	0.50
Ray Gun	Goods	R	3.50
Raymond Armstrong	Dude	C	0.25
Red Hill Hotel	Deed	U	0.80
Refuse to Fall	Action	U	0.80
Reggie Cornell	Dude	C	0.15
Relic	Action	U	0.80
Reserves	Action	R	3.50
Richard Boothe	Dude	R	4.00
Riot	Event	C	0.15
Roan	Goods	C	0.15
Robert Northrop	Dude	C	0.15
Rock Ridge Mine	Deed	R	4.00
Rocket Pack	Goods	R	4.00
Rumors	Action	C	0.15
Run-Down Lot	Deed	C	0.25
Running Water	Improvemt	C	0.25
Sacrifice	Spell	C	0.25
Sam Horowitz	Dude	U	0.80
San Simeon Mine	Deed	C	0.15
Saul Whateley	Dude	R	4.00
Second Story	Improvemt	U	1.00
Shallow Grave	Action	R	4.00
Shark's Grin Lode	Deed	R	3.00
Sheriff's Watchin'	Action	C	0.15
Shigetoshi Hohiro	Dude	U	0.80
Shortcut	Action	R	3.00
Shotgun	Goods	C	0.15
Shouting Tom	Dude	C	0.25
Silas Peacock	Dude	C	0.15
Singing Feather	Dude	R	4.00
Sioux Nation	Outfit	X	1.30
Sister Mary Jebediah	Dude	R	4.00
Sister Mary's Shotgun	Goods	X	0.50
Skunky Swade	Dude	R	4.00
Sleep o' the Dead	Action	U	0.80
Sleeping with Shadows	Event	U	0.80
Smiley's Shaft	Deed	R	3.00
Smiling Lizard Lode	Deed	R	3.00
Snake Eyes	Action	R	4.00
Snakebite	Action	C	0.15
Soul Blast	Spell	C	0.25
Speed of the Wolf	Spell	C	0.15

Card name	Type	Rarity	Price
Spirit of Kentucky Shaft	Deed	C	0.15
Spirit Warrior	Spell	C	0.15
St. Martin's Chapel	Deed	R	3.00
Stained Glass Windows	Deed	C	0.25
Stampede	Event	R	3.00
Sticks to Snakes	Spell	U	0.80
Stitchin'	Action	U	0.80
Strike Experiment #1	Deed	C	0.15
Strikes a Hawk	Dude	U	0.80
Stuffed to the Gills Strike	Deed	C	0.15
Summon Spirit	Spell	C	0.25
Sumner's Revenge	Event	U	1.00
Sun in yer eyes	Action	C	0.15
Surveyor's Office	Deed	C	0.15
Sweaty Dynamite	Goods	C	0.15
Sweetrock - Western Corporate Office	Outfit	X	1.30
Sympathy for the Devil	Spell	R	3.00
Take Ya With Me	Action	C	0.15
Termite Infestation	Action	C	0.15
Texas Twister	Spell	C	0.15
That'll Leave a Scar	Action	C	0.15
The 1st Bank of Gomorra	Deed	R	3.00
The Agency	Outfit	X	1.30
The Alright Corral	Deed	C	0.25
The Barber's Shop	Deed	C	0.15
The Clock Tower	Deed	R	3.00
The Courthouse	Deed	R	3.00
The Dentist's Office	Deed	C	0.15
The Docks	Deed	U	1.00
The Drifter	Dude	U	0.80
The Evidence	Goods	C	0.35
The Joker	Action	R	7.00
The Lode	Deed	R	4.00
The Mission House	Deed	C	0.15
The Sabbath	Event	R	3.00
The Scythe	Goods	X	0.60
The Slaughterhouse	Deed	C	0.25
The Spirits Flee	Spell	R	3.00
The Texas Rangers	Outfit	X	1.30
The Tree	Deed	R	4.00
The Undertaker's	Deed	C	0.25
The Whateleys - Extended Family	Outfit	X	1.30
Thunderbird	Dude	U	0.80
Tin Shield	Goods	C	0.15
Tombstone Dispatch Branch Office	Deed	C	0.25
Top of the World Lode	Deed	U	1.00
Town Well	Deed	C	0.15
Tracking Teeth	Action	U	0.80
Two Birds Chirping	Dude	U	0.80
Tzipporah Whateley	Dude	U	0.80
Unholy Symbol	Goods	C	0.15
Unknown Hooded Figure	Dude	R	4.00
Victor Navarro	Dude	R	4.00
Walkin' Dead	Dude	C	0.15
Walks-in-Footprints	Dude	R	4.00
Wall Crawler	Dude	C	0.15
Walter Ponds	Dude	U	0.80
War Paint	Action	R	4.00
Warrant	Action	C	0.15
Wendigo Garrison	Dude	C	0.15
Whateley Family Bible	Goods	R	3.00
William Olson	Dude	C	0.15
Winchester Rifle	Goods	C	0.15
Windows Derek	Dude	C	0.15
Wise Cloud	Dude	U	0.80
Wither	Action	R	4.00
Wrath of God	Event	R	4.00
Xiong "Wendy"Cheng	Dude	C	0.25
Zapper	Goods	U	0.80

RARITY KEY **C** = Common **U** = Uncommon **R** = Rare **VR** = Very Rare **UR** = Ultra Rare **F** = Foil card **X** = Fixed/standard in all decks

126 • SCRYE Collectible Card Game Checklist and Price Guide

Doomtown • Ashes to Ashes

Wizards of the Coast (Five Rings division) • Released **April 2000**
158 cards in set • **IDENTIFIER: Star (☆) by artist name**

- Starter decks contain 60 cards; starter displays contain 12 starters
- Booster packs contain 15 cards; booster displays contain 36 boosters

The race to build a transcontinental railroad is an important feature in the *Deadlands* role-playing game. Known as the Great Rail War, this conflict surfaces in **Ashes to Ashes** as three outfits gain new outfit cards. **Sweetrock, Gomorra Ltd. Rail Line** gives the player a break on the purchase price of deeds and can ace a deed to gain Ghost Rock. **Texas Rangers, Dixie Rails** receives a significant discount on purchasing and maintaining harrowed dudes. **The Agency, Union Blue** can kill harrowed dudes much more easily and can purchase gadgets without mad scientists to build them.

There are more new dudes in this expansion than in the previous few. This was probably to rebuild the available number of dudes for the Boot Hill-expanded and strict tournament formats. There are also several cards affecting skill ratings (mad scientist, huckster, shaman, blessed), most notably **Spirit Pipe** and **Hired Help**. — *Michael Greenholdt*

Set (158 cards)	150.00	
Starter Display Box	85.00	**You will need**
Booster Display Box	90.00	**18** nine-pocket pages to store this set. (9 doubled up)
Starter Deck	9.50	
Booster Pack	3.00	

Card name	Type	Rarity	Price
1			
Accountant	Deed	U	0.50
Adrian Townsend	Dude	U	0.50
Alastor The Executioner	Dude	R	4.00
Anahuac Staff	Goods	C	0.10
Army Of The Dead	Dude	C	0.10
Art Gallery	Deed	U	0.50
Astoreth Whateley	Dude	U	0.50
Astoreth's Rage	Spirit	U	0.50
Bad Blood	Hex	R	3.00
2			
Barthalomew Prospectus (Exp.)	Dude	R	4.00
Billy Iron Horse (Exp.)	Dude	R	4.00
Bleeding Vein	Deed	R	4.00
Blood Money	Goods	C	0.10
Brigadier-General Patterson	Dude	X	1.00
Brimstone	Hex	C	0.10
Calm Before The Storm	Event	C	0.10
Candlestick Maker	Deed	C	0.10
Cerulean Cove Mining Operation	Deed	R	4.00
3			
Chupacabra	Dude	R	4.00
Close Shave	Action	U	0.50
Confederate Barracks	Deed	U	0.50
Confederate Hunter	Action	R	4.00
Corporate Headquarters	Improvemt	R	4.00
Cort Williams (Exp.)	Dude	X	3.00
Cynthia Kingston	Dude	U	0.50
Deal With The Devil	Hex	U	0.50
Defendin' What's Yours	Action	R	3.00
4			
Dehydration	Action	R	3.00
Delilah Darby-Scorne	Dude	C	0.10
Demon's Den	Improvemt	C	0.10
Deputy Dave Montreal (Exp.)	Dude	R	4.00
Derailed Cafe	Deed	U	0.50
Down The Barrel...	Action	R	3.00
Drawin' A Blank	Hex	U	0.50
Dustin Halloway	Dude	U	0.50
Elijah's Parish	Deed	C	0.10
5			
Enrique Alonso	Dude	C	0.10
Erik Zarkov (Exp. 2)	Dude	R	4.00
Far-Away Fred	Dude	U	0.50
Fate's Warning Strike	Deed	R	3.00
Fine China Shop	Deed	C	0.10
Fireworks Distraction	Action	C	0.10
Fisticuffs	Action	C	0.10
Flesh Mob	Dude	R	3.50
Formal Duds	Goods	U	0.50
6			
Founder's Memorial	Improvemt	U	0.50
Freddy Fast-Hands (Exp.)	Dude	R	4.00
Gandy Dancer	Dude	C	0.10
Gareth Comes To Town	Event	R	4.00

Card name	Type	Rarity	Price
Gatling Emplacement	Improvemt	R	3.00
Greasin' Palms	Action	R	4.00
Gris-Gris	Goods	U	0.50
Guilt By Association	Action	C	0.10
Hand Cart	Goods	C	0.10
7			
Hangin' Judge	Dude	R	5.00
Harmony Of The Heavens	Spirit	C	0.10
Harvesting Plots	Improvemt	U	0.50
Heat Wave	Event	U	0.50
Higher Learning	Spirit	U	0.50
Hired Help	Action	R	3.00
Hundred Yearling Ranch	Deed	U	0.50
Hydro-Accelerator	Deed	C	0.10
I Gotcha Covered	Action	C	0.10
8			
Indoor Plumbing	Improvemt	R	3.00
Investment Machine	Goods	C	0.10
Isaiah "Holdout" Curwen	Dude	U	0.50
Jacynth Ambrose	Dude	C	0.10
Jesse Radcliffe	Dude	U	0.50
Jeweler	Deed	C	0.10
Jonah Wheeler	Dude	U	0.50
Joseph Moon	Dude	U	0.50
Juliet "Jewel" Sumner	Dude	R	4.00
9			
Knicknevin's Legacy	Action	R	4.00
Last Meal	Action	C	0.10
Lazy Sunday	Action	C	0.10
Leaning Rock Strike	Deed	C	0.10
Leather and Saddle Shop	Deed	C	0.10
Listen Up!	Action	C	0.10
Lord Ripley Scorne	Dude	C	0.10
Lost Horizon	Action	C	0.10
Lucifer Whateley (Exp.)	Dude	R	4.00
10			
Mad Wolf Striding	Dude	U	0.50
Maurice Foster	Dude	C	0.10
Max Baine (Exp. 2)	Dude	X	3.00
Megan Mallory	Dude	U	0.50
Melissa Thomas (Exp.)	Dude	R	4.00
Mesa Checkpoint	Action	C	0.10
Military Occupation	Event	C	0.10
Mosley's Maw	Deed	U	0.50
Move Along	Action	U	0.50
11			
Nadia Krasnova	Dude	C	0.10
Natalie Sherman	Dude	U	0.50
New Dunwitch Casino	Deed	R	3.00
"New Town, New Rules"	Event	R	3.00
Nick's and Nack's	Deed	R	3.00
Nolan's Smithy	Deed	C	0.10
"Oh No, You Don't!"	Action	U	0.50
One Good Turn...	Action	U	0.50
Path Of The Righteous	Miracle	R	3.50
12			
Penny Farthing	Goods	C	0.10
Personal Safe	Goods	C	0.10
Play It Again	Action	U	0.50
Printing Press	Goods	R	4.00
Prophecy	Miracle	U	0.50

Card name	Type	Rarity	Price
Publicity Stunt	Action	U	0.50
Puttin' The Heat On	Action	U	0.50
Quickdraw Sling	Goods	R	3.00
Quon Lin	Dude	U	0.50
13			
Rats In The Walls	Improvemt	C	0.10
Recall Orders	Event	R	3.00
Red Tape	Action	R	3.00
Reverend C.A. Johnson	Dude	C	0.10
Rex Handlen	Dude	U	0.50
Rhett Caufield	Dude	C	0.10
Road House	Deed	C	0.10
Roll The Dice...	Miracle	C	0.10
Rounders Diamond	Deed	U	0.50
14			
Santana Tate	Dude	R	4.00
Scott Pierce	Dude	U	0.50
Secret Passages	Improvemt	C	0.10
Sergeant Sean Slade	Dude	C	0.10
Speakin' With The Dead	Event	C	0.10
Spectral Visitors	Event	C	0.10
Spirit Pipe	Goods	R	4.00
Spiritual Pawn	Action	U	0.50
Spiritual Society Enclave	Deed	R	3.00
15			
Spit And Vinegar	Event	R	3.00
Steam-Powered Crane	Goods	R	3.00
Stumbling Into The Badlands	Event	U	0.50
"Sweetrock, Gomorra Ltd. Rail Line"	Outfit	X	1.00
Tea And Tobacco Shop	Deed	R	3.50
Texas Rangers, Dixie Rails	Outfit	X	1.00
"The Agency, Union Blue"	Outfit	X	1.00
The Crucible	Dude	U	0.50
The Jaded Jackalope	Deed	U	0.50
16			
The Lord Provides	Miracle	U	0.50
The North End	Action	C	0.10
The Snitch	Dude	C	0.10
Thedrick Whateley	Dude	C	0.10
This Don't Involve You	Action	C	0.10
Toll Bridge	Deed	U	0.50
Town Drunk	Dude	C	0.10
Toy Shop	Deed	C	0.10
Twist of Fate	Action	R	3.00
17			
Unexpected Guest	Event	U	0.50
Unfinished Business	Spirit	R	4.00
Union Armory	Improvemt	U	0.50
Union Train Depot	Deed	R	3.50
Vance Donovan	Dude	R	4.00
Waylaid!	Action	R	3.00
Weeping Crow	Dude	C	0.10
Welcome Home	Action	U	0.50
Wendigo Garrison (Exp.)	Dude	R	4.00
18			
Whiskey Flask	Goods	U	0.50
White Shire	Goods	R	3.00
"Who Are You, Again?"	Action	C	0.10
Wyrm Hill	Deed	R	3.00
Yer Not Welcome Here!	Action	R	3.00

RARITY KEY **C** = Common **U** = Uncommon **R** = Rare **VR** = Very Rare **UR** = Ultra Rare **F** = Foil card **X** = Fixed/standard in all decks

Doomtown • Eye for an Eye

Wizards of the Coast (Five Rings division) • Released **August 2000**

157 cards in set • IDENTIFIER: Four diamonds (❖) by artist name

- Starter decks contain 60 cards; starter displays contain 12 starters
- Booster packs contain 15 cards; booster displays contain 36 boosters

    In what had become the standard for **Doomtown**, three new outfit cards were released in *Eye for an Eye*. **Blackjacks, Rachel's Gang** can buy job cards (special action cards) out of the deck. **Lost Angels**, the replacement for the defunct Flock, have potent anti-spell abilities. **Sioux Spirit Warriors'** opponents cannot prevent the loss of dudes in shootouts. More "Bullet cards" appear, as well as a deed that allows the recovery of Bullets from the expended pile (Boot Hill).

    A 199-card set expansion, ***Do Unto Others***, was announced in November 2000 to be the last Doomtown offering from Alderac. — *Michael Greenholdt*

Set (157 cards)	150.00
Starter Display Box	90.00
Booster Display Box	95.00
Starter Deck	10.00
Booster Pack	3.00

You will need **18** nine-pocket pages to store this set. (9 doubled up)

Card name	Type	Rarity	Price
Abel Owens (Exp.)	Dude	R	3.80
Abomination Pit	Improvemt	U	0.80
Agoraphobia	Action	C	0.25
All God's Children	Event	R	3.30
Ammunitionist	Deed	U	0.80
Andrew Garret	Dude	C	0.25
Animate Hand	Dude	X	5.00
April Segarra	Dude	U	0.80
Auxiliumortis	Event	U	0.80
Banish	Hex	U	0.80
Barney Brash	Dude	C	0.25
Between the Cracks	Action	C	0.25
Bioengineering	Goods	R	3.30
Bites the Hand	Dude	C	0.25
"Blackjacks, Rachel's Gang"	Outfit	X	4.70
Blasted Prairie	Deed	U	0.80
Bloodsport Arena	Deed	C	0.25
Breath of the Spirits	Spirit	C	0.25
Brimstone Bullets	Goods	R	3.30
Bring It Down!	Action	U	0.80
Brush with Death	Miracle	C	0.25
Cadaverus Mobilis	Event	U	0.80
Cain Regen (Exp.)	Dude	R	3.50
Channel Fort	Deed	R	3.50
Charlie Landers (Exp.)	Dude	U	0.80
Chip	Goods	R	3.30
Claustrophobia	Action	C	0.25
Clean Getaway	Action	U	0.80
Clovis the Devilbunny	Goods	U	0.80
Confessional	Deed	U	0.80
Construction Crew	Action	U	0.80
Darren Titus (Exp.)	Dude	U	0.80
David Hope	Dude	R	3.80
Deep in the Earth Shaft	Deed	C	0.25
Deputy Tophet	Dude	C	0.25
Desperate Measures	Action	U	0.80
Distracted!	Action	R	3.00
Divided Loyalties	Action	U	0.80
Doctor Duvalier (Exp.)	Dude	R	3.50

Doomtown Promo cards

Card name	Type	Price
Big Doc's Casino	Deed	2.50
Harrowed Kenny	Dude	3.50
Jack's Left Shooter	Goods	3.00
Joker	Special	6.00
Lilith Vandekamp (Exp.)	Dude	3.50
Lucky Rabbit's Foot	Goods	3.00
Start Again	Action	4.80
Stop The Presses	Action	4.00

Card name	Type	Rarity	Price
Doctor Hardstrom	Dude	U	0.80
Draw!	Miracle	U	0.80
Eagle Bow	Goods	R	3.30
Eagle Rock (Exp. 2)	Dude	X	5.00
Elephant Hill Mausoleum	Deed	U	0.80
Elijah (Exp. 2)	Dude	X	5.00
Ethics Aside…	Action	R	3.00
Evan Childes	Dude	U	0.80
Exploratory Trench	Deed	C	0.25
Eyes That Cannot See	Action	U	0.80
Father Terrance (Exp.)	Dude	R	4.00
Faulty Pipes	Action	R	3.00
Faustian Deal	Hex	R	3.30
First To Fall	Action	U	0.80
Flashfire Bullets	Goods	C	0.25
Flight Of Angels	Action	C	0.25
Freak Show	Deed	U	0.80
Get Off My Land!	Action	C	0.25
Ghost Of My Father	Dude	U	0.80
Gnosis	Dude	C	0.25
Guardian Angel	Dude	C	0.25
Guy Fawkes Day	Event	R	3.00
Haborym	Dude	C	0.25
Hatchet	Goods	C	0.25
Hiding Out	Action	U	0.80
I Gotta Stake in This!	Action	C	0.25
Inner Strength	Action	U	0.80
Insult to Injury	Action	C	0.25
Interior Decorating	Improvemt	C	0.25
It's For Her Own Good	Action	C	0.25
Jack Brash	Dude	C	0.25
Jack Whateley	Dude	U	0.80
Jam!	Action	U	0.80
Jenny Cooper (Exp.)	Dude	R	3.80
Jolinaxas	Dude	R	3.80
Jordan Caldwell	Dude	U	0.80
Juliet "Jewel" Sumner (Exp.)	Dude	R	3.50
Just What I Need …	Action	C	0.25
Last Request	Action	R	3.00
Life Of The Party	Action	U	0.80
Lillith	Dude	U	0.80
Lost Angels	Outfit	X	4.70
Lt. Colonel Frederick Sykes	Dude	C	0.25
Lucifer's Cane	Goods	R	3.30
Lyin' In Wait	Action	R	3.00
Lynchin' Noose	Goods	U	0.80
Magic Bus V. 2.0 (Death Bus)	Goods	C	0.25
Mercy	Action	R	3.50
Midnight Snack	Action	U	0.80
Min Su Tao	Dude	C	0.25
Moloch	Dude	C	0.25
"Mr. Applegate, Esq."	Dude	U	0.80
Mr. Slate (Exp.)	Dude	R	4.50
Mysterious Ways	Miracle	R	3.00
New Pony Express Office	Deed	R	3.50
Night Sentry	Improvemt	U	0.80
No Way Out!	Improvemt	C	0.25
Nyctophobia	Action	C	0.25
O'Reilly's Five & Dime	Deed	R	4.00

Card name	Type	Rarity	Price
Old Scratch	Dude	U	0.80
One Eyed Jacks are Wild	Action	C	0.25
Oswald Hardinger (Exp.)	Dude	R	4.50
Pandora's Box	Goods	R	3.30
Perdition	Dude	R	3.50
Phantoms	Action	C	0.25
Poker Night	Event	R	3.30
Power Plant	Deed	C	0.25
Prison Factory	Deed	R	3.30
Prospectus' Secret Workshop	Deed	R	4.00
Rachel Sumner (Exp. 2)	Dude	X	5.00
Raymond Armstrong (Exp.)	Dude	U	0.80
Recruiter	Improvemt	R	4.00
Registry	Deed	U	0.80
Requiem	Dude	C	0.25
Rescue Operation	Action	R	3.00
Rooster Beenz	Dude	C	0.25
Run 'Em Down!	Action	U	0.80
Rustlers	Event	R	3.00
Sabtabiel's Remains	Goods	R	3.30
Salvage Operation	Deed	U	0.80
Screamers	Goods	U	0.80
Seeking Fury	Dude	C	0.25
Sepulcher	Improvemt	R	3.00
Sewer Tunnels	Improvemt	U	0.80
Sewing Circle	Action	C	0.25
Shave and a Haircut	Action	C	0.25
Sheriff Syn	Dude	C	0.25
Shigetoshi Hohiro (Exp.)	Dude	R	3.80
Simon Lambeth	Dude	R	4.00
Sin Je	Dude	U	0.80
"Sioux, Spirit Warriors"	Outfit	X	4.70
Sister Mercy Winters	Dude	U	0.80
Soul Blast Cannon	Goods	U	0.80
Spirit Walk	Hex	C	0.25
Spring Cleaning	Improvemt	U	0.80
Stallion	Goods	C	0.25
Strikers' Shaft	Deed	C	0.25
The Beast Within	Spirit	R	3.30
The C.S.A. Ourobouros	Deed	R	3.30
The Good Book	Goods	R	3.30
The Perch	Deed	C	0.25
This'll Teach You…	Action	R	3.50
Three-Card Monte	Goods	C	0.25
Three-Piece Suit	Goods	U	0.80
Thunderbird (Exp.)	Dude	R	3.80
"Trouble There, Buck?"	Action	R	3.30
Two Birds Chirping (Exp.)	Dude	U	0.80
Tzipporah Whateley (Exp.)	Dude	R	4.00
Under The Gun	Action	U	0.80
War Cry	Spirit	U	0.80
Watering Hole	Deed	C	0.25
Well Of Souls	Improvemt	R	3.50
We've Got Hostages	Action	R	3.30
William Rose	Dude	C	0.25
Working Out the Details	Event	C	0.25
You're Comin' With Us!	Action	R	3.50
You've Got This Comin'!	Action	C	0.25
Zeke Hillard	Dude	C	0.25

RARITY KEY   **C** = Common   **U** = Uncommon   **R** = Rare   **VR** = Very Rare   **UR** = Ultra Rare   **F** = Foil card   **X** = Fixed/standard in all decks

---

Card illustration text (left margin card):

RUN 'EM DOWN!

Shootout: All of your Dudes in this Posse with Horses attached either gain a +1 Bullet bonus or become Studs (your choice for each Dude), until the end of the shootout.

"Stop! Please! We need your help! Something's wrong at the camp! Raven's vision quest... he... he's gone! They took him!" –Deer Eater

Doomtrooper

Target Games AB/Heartbreaker Hobbies • First set, *Limited,* released **January 1995**

334 cards in set • **IDENTIFIER: Red pinstripe on outer border**

- Starter decks contain 60 cards; starter displays contain 10 starters
- Booster packs contain 15 cards; Booster displays contain 36 boosters

Designed by **Bryan Winter**

The **Doomtrooper** techno-fantasy card game is based on the *Mutant Chronicles* sci-ence-fantasy setting developed by the late Target Games AB and the former Heartbreaker Hobbies. In the future, humanity flees to Mars, Venus, and Mercury after a terrible calamity devastates Earth. Five vast Corporations control the lives of the teem-ing billions while the Brotherhood, a mystical organization, controls their souls and pro-tects them from the evils of the Dark Legion. The five Corporations are often at war with each other yet have seen the threat the Dark Legion poses and, together with the Brotherhood, formed the Cartel to battle the forces of the Dark Legion.

Doomtrooper centers on combat; the object is to have your forces battle your oppo-nent's forces for Promotion Points. The first player to 25 Promotion Points wins the game. Players put together two groups: a Squad of Cartel Doomtroopers and a Kohort of Dark Legion warriors. Warriors are brought into play by spending Destiny Points; each player starts with five Destiny, then can earn more by taking an Action to Meditate or by taking victory points from attacks as Destiny instead of Promotion Points. Slain warriors are worth Promotion Points or Destiny as are specific Missions that can be played.

A player can take three actions per turn. Actions include Add Warrior, Add Warrior in Cover (three Actions), Seek Cover, Exit Cover, Meditate, Equip Warrior, Bestow Gift, Assign Mission, or Attack (which, if taken, must be the last Action taken). Each warrior has four abilities: Fight (close combat value), Shoot (ranged combat value), Armor, and Value (cost in Destiny or value in Promotion Points if slain). Equipment can add to the warrior's abilities; weapons add to Fight or Shoot, while armor adds to Armor. The Art (Brotherhood) and the Dark Symmetry (Dark Legion) are the "magic" of **Doomtrooper**. Combat is fast, with the appropriate ability being compared to Armor (battles are either Fight or Shoot, not both), then modifier cards can be played. Both combatants might die or be wounded. Victory points may then be awarded as Promotion or Destiny Points, or a combination of both at the recipients wish.

Doomtrooper caught the flavor of the *Mutant Chronicles* setting better than most other "property"-based CCGs did. It also had some novel additions, such as being able to play cards from your collection rather than simply from your deck (like the singular Ring of Ma'ruf in Magic).

Unfortunately, while it had some initial success, the CCG did not develop a financially viable following. **Doomtrooper** continues to have a small if very fanatical following, and is one of the few "dead" CCGs that continues to have a web presence. — *James A. Mishler*

Concept	●●●●○
Gameplay	●●●●○
Card art	●●●○○
Player pool	●○○○○

Rarities note

To describe rarities for later **Doomtrooper** sets, Target abandoned R (Rare) and went with three "Common" levels and two and sometimes three "Uncommon" levels. The lower the number after the letter, the hard-er it is to find among Common or Uncommon cards from that set.

You will need **38** nine-pocket pages to store this set. (19 doubled up)

Set (334 cards)	**150.00**
Starter Display Box	**80.00**
Booster Display Box	**80.00**
Starter Deck	**6.50**
Booster Pack	**2.10**

Card name	Rarity	Price
[1]		
AC-40 "Justifier"	U	1.00
Agent Nick Michaels	C	0.25
AH/UH-19 Grapeshot Guardian	R	4.00
Airman	U	1.30
Alakhai The Cunning	R	5.00
Ambush	U	1.00
Animate Dead	R	4.00
Archangel	C	0.20
Archinquisitor Nikodemus	R	5.00
[2]		
Assassination	R	5.00
Automatic Fire	U	1.30
Bacteria Grenade	U	1.00
Bamboozled!	U	1.30
Bauhaus Blitzer	C	0.20
Bauhaus Great Infurior	R	4.00

Card name	Rarity	Price
Bayonet	C	0.25
Big Bob Watts	R	5.00
Billy	C	0.25
[3]		
Blessed Armor	R	4.00
Blessed Legionnaire	C	0.20
Blessed Vestal Laura	U	1.30
Blindness	C	0.25
Blood Beret	C	0.20
Blood Lust	C	0.20
Bogged Down	R	3.50
Born With a Silver Spoon	U	1.00
Botched Orders	R	4.00
[4]		
Cairath	R	4.00
Callistonian Intruder	U	1.50
CAP 7000P	R	4.00
Capitol Sword of Honor	U	1.00
Cardinal Dominic	R	5.00
Centurion	U	1.00
Changeling Empathy	U	1.00
Chasm!	C	0.20
Chasseur	C	0.20
[5]		
Chemiman	U	1.00

Card name	Rarity	Price
Child of Ilian	C	0.20
Chosen	R	4.00
Citadel of Algeroth	U	1.50
Citadel of Demnogonis	U	1.50
Citadel of Ilian	U	1.50
Citadel of Muawijhe	U	1.50
Citadel of Semai	U	1.50
Clan Infighting	R	4.00
[6]		
Clansman	C	0.20
Clansman Claymore	U	1.00
Combat Armor	C	0.25
Combat Warhead	U	1.00
Command	U	1.00
Composite Armor	R	5.00
Confuse	R	4.00
Control Mind	U	1.00
Corporate Shenanigans	R	3.50
[7]		
Corrupt Shield	U	4.00
Cowardice	U	1.00
Crenshaw The Mortificator	R	4.00
Cuirassier	C	0.20

Card name	Rarity	Price
Curator	U	1.00
Curator Sword	U	1.50
Cybercurity MP	C	0.25
Cybernetic Power Arm	R	4.00
Cybernetic Retinas	R	4.00
[8]		
Dark Fire	C	0.25
Dark Kohort	R	4.00
Dark Visitation	U	1.00
Deathlockdrum	R	4.00
Decay	U	1.00
Deform	U	1.50
Demolition Kit	R	5.00
Demoted	U	1.00
Desperate Measures	R	3.50
[9]		
Destroy Kohort	R	4.00
Destroy Squad	R	5.00
Dimensional Hole	U	1.50
Dimensional Warp	U	1.50
Discern Truth	U	1.30
Discovered	U	1.00
Disrupt Power	U	1.50
Distort	U	1.00

RARITY KEY **C** = Common **U** = Uncommon **R** = Rare **VR** = Very Rare **UR** = Ultra Rare **F** = Foil card **X** = Fixed/standard in all decks

SCRYE Collectible Card Game Checklist and Price Guide • **129**

Card name	Rarity	Price
Divine Inspiration	R	4.00
10		
Doomed	U	1.00
Dragoon	C	0.20
Dull Blade	C	0.25
Dutiful Service	U	1.00
Earthquake	R	5.00
Edward S. Murdoch	R	4.00
Efficiency Training	U	1.50
Elemental Ball	C	0.25
Elemental Bolt	C	0.25
11		
Elemental Empathy	U	1.00
Elemental Wall	C	0.25
Empathy	R	3.50
Essence of Clarity	R	5.00
Essence of Integrity	R	5.00
Essence of Morality	R	5.00
Essence of Purity	R	5.00
Essence of Rectitude	R	5.00
Essence of Virtue	R	5.00
12		
Establish Defensive Perimeter	R	4.00
Etoiles Mortant	C	0.20
Evasion Training	R	4.00
Evasive Action	C	0.20
Ex-Bauhaus Freelancer	C	0.25
Ex-Capitol Freelancer	C	0.25
Ex-Cybertronic Freelancer	C	0.25
Ex-Imperial Freelancer	C	0.25
Ex-Mishima Freelancer	C	0.25
13		
Exonerated Ronin	R	5.00
Exorcise Dark Influences	C	0.25
Exorcise Disease	C	0.25
Exorcise Empathy	U	1.30
Exorcise Evil Thoughts	C	0.25
Exorcise Infection	C	0.25
Exorcise Poison	C	0.25
Exorcise Self	U	1.00
Exorcise Wound	C	0.25
14		
Exorcism	U	1.00
Expedite Request	U	1.50
Explosion	R	4.00
Ezoghoul	R	4.00
Fallen From Favor	C	0.25
Fay & Klaus	U	1.30
Fifteen Minutes of Fame	R	5.00
First Aid Kit	C	0.20
Flow of Acid	R	4.00
15		
Flush Out The Coward	R	3.50
Fly	U	1.00
Forced March	U	1.00
Fortune of War	U	1.30
Foxhole	U	1.00
Framed!	U	1.00
Free Marine	C	0.20
Fukido	U	1.30
Fukimura No. 12 Kamikaze	R	5.00
16		
Fury of the Clansmen	R	4.00

Card name	Rarity	Price
Gale Force Winds	R	4.00
Gaze	R	4.00
Gehenna Puker	R	5.00
Gift of Fate	U	1.00
Golden Lion	C	0.20
Greater Domination	R	4.00
Greater Hypnosis	R	4.00
Greater Telepathy	R	4.00
17		
Grenade Launcher	R	5.00
Hand of Death	U	1.50
Hatamoto	C	0.20
Heavy Fog	C	0.20
Heimburg	U	1.50
Heretic	C	0.20
Hidden In The Shadows	C	0.20
HMG MK. XIXB Charger	R	5.00
Honorary Baptism	U	1.00
18		
Hussar	C	0.20
Illusion	U	1.50
Immaculate Fury	R	4.00
Imperial Doomlord	R	5.00
Imperial Southpaw	R	4.00
Improve Self	U	1.00
Indigestion	U	1.50
Infantry	C	0.20
Infection	U	1.50
19		
Infiltration	R	4.00
Influence	U	1.00
Initiative	C	0.20
Inquisitor	C	0.20
Inquisitor Majoris	R	5.00
Insane Dance	U	1.50
Inspire the Masses	R	3.50
Inspired	C	0.20
Installation	R	3.50
20		
Insubordination	U	1.00
Internal Affairs Crackdown	R	4.00
Invoke Frenzy	R	4.00
Invoke Pain	U	1.00
Invulnerability	U	1.00
Item Vision	U	1.00
Joy of Victory	C	0.20
Keeper of The Art	R	4.00
Kinetic Empathy	U	1.00
21		
Knighthood	U	1.00
Kratach	U	1.50
L&A Plasma Carbine	U	1.30
Lane Chung	U	1.30
Legionnaire of Semai	C	0.20
Lesser Domination	C	0.20
Lesser Hypnosis	C	0.20
Lesser Telepathy	C	0.20
Levitation	U	1.00
22		
Longshore	U	1.50
Lost Paperwork	U	1.00
Lucky Shot	C	0.20
Machinator	C	0.25
Malfunction!	C	0.20
Manifest Destiny	R	5.00
Manipulative Empathy	U	1.00
Martial Training	R	4.00
Martian Banshee	C	0.20
23		
Max Steiner	R	5.00
Mental Constitution	U	1.00
Mind Melt	U	1.50
Mind Wall	C	0.25
Miscommunication	U	1.00

Card name	Rarity	Price
Mitch Hunter	R	5.00
Mortificator	C	0.20
Mortis Sword	U	1.00
Mystic	U	1.00
24		
Mystical Training	R	4.00
Narrow Escape!	U	1.50
Necromutant	C	0.20
Necrovisual Link	R	5.00
Negative Karma	R	4.00
Nepharite Hunt	R	4.50
Nepharite of Algeroth	R	5.00
Nepharite of Demnogonis	R	5.00
Nepharite of Ilian	R	5.00
25		
Nepharite of Muawijhe	R	5.00
Nepharite of Semai	R	5.00
Nimrod Autocannon	R	5.00
Noted Efficiency	U	1.00
Out of Ammo	C	0.25
Pam Afton	U	1.30
Personal Anti-Personnel Mines	R	5.00
Phantasm	U	1.00
Portable Force Shield	R	5.00
26		
Portal of Dark Healing	R	4.00
Portal of The Great Conqueror	R	3.50
Portal of Undeath	R	5.00
Portents of Victory	U	1.00
Positive Karma	U	1.00
Possess	R	4.00
Powerful Blow	C	0.20
Premonition	U	1.50
Premonition Empathy	U	1.00
27		
Presence	C	0.25
Pretorian Stalker	R	5.00
Proficiency	C	0.25
Prove Your Valor	R	4.00
Psycho-Scanner	R	4.00
Punisher Blade	U	1.00
Punisher Handgun	U	1.00
Purple Shark	R	4.00
Radar Scanner	C	0.25
28		
Rams Air Cavalry	U	1.30
Razide	R	4.00
Recalled	R	5.00
Reinforcements	U	1.50
Reinstatement	U	1.30
Repentance	R	4.00
Reputation	R	5.00
Resist Elements	C	0.25
Resist Pain	C	0.25
29		
Retraining	U	1.50
Retreat!	C	0.25
Reverberating Sharpener	C	0.25
Reversal of Fortune	R	5.00
Revisor	C	0.20
Rogue	U	1.30
Ruthless Efficiency	R	3.50
Sabotage!	R	4.00
Sacred Warrior	C	0.20
30		
Samurai	C	0.20
San Dorado	U	1.50
Scalper	U	1.00
Screaming Legionnaire	C	0.20
Scythe of Semai	R	4.00
Sea Lion	C	0.20
Sean Gallacher	R	4.00

Card name	Rarity	Price
Secret Headquarters	R	4.00
Secret Mission	R	5.00
31		
Send Dreams	U	1.30
Sgt. Mc Bride	U	1.50
Sharpshooter	R	4.00
Sherman .74 Model 13 Bolter	U	1.30
Shield	C	0.25
Shrieketh	R	4.00
Shroud	R	4.00
Siege of The Citadel	R	3.50
Sleep	R	4.00
32		
SMG MK. III Interceptor	U	1.30
Smoke Bomb	U	1.30
Snub The Cardinal	R	4.00
Special Commendation	U	1.00
Speed	U	1.00
Spiked Barricade	C	0.25
Spoke In The Cog	U	1.00
Spy in The Ranks	R	4.00
Stigmata	R	5.00
33		
Strategic Restructuring	U	1.50
Strength of Will	C	0.25
Strike	C	0.25
Suggestion	U	1.30
Suicide Mission	R	4.00
Suicide Warhead	U	1.50
Sunset Striker	C	0.20
Surprise Attack	U	1.00
Surprise Invasion!	U	1.00
34		
T-32 "Wolfclaw" JBT	R	5.00
Tactical Advantage	U	1.00
Tainted!	R	4.00
Take Aim	C	0.25
Take Cover	C	0.25
Tatsuo	R	4.00
Telepathic Message	U	1.00
Teleportation	C	0.25
Telescopic Sight	C	0.25
35		
Templar	U	1.50
Terror	C	0.25
The Cathedral	U	1.50
The HQ	U	1.50
Ticker	C	0.25
Time Death	R	5.00
Time Rot	R	4.00
Traitor Discovered	R	5.00
Trencher	C	0.20
36		
Trevor Bartholomew	U	1.30
True Gate	R	4.00
True Path	C	0.25
Twist of Fate	U	1.30
Twitcher	C	0.25
Undead Legionnaire	C	0.20
Undercover Agents	R	4.00
Valerie Duval	R	4.00
Valkyrie	C	0.20
37		
Vassht	U	1.30
Venusian Ranger	C	0.20
Violator Sword	U	1.30
Well-rounded Squad	R	4.00
Whispers of Heresy	R	5.00
Wind of Insanity	U	1.00
Wolfbane Light Cavalry	U	1.30
Yojimbo	R	4.00
Young Guard	C	0.20
38		
Zenithian Soulslayer	U	1.50

Pinstripes

Check the border when looking at *Doomtrooper* cards. A small red pinstripe indicates that a card comes from the *Limited* set.

RARITY KEY C = Common   U = Uncommon   R = Rare   VR = Very Rare   UR = Ultra Rare   F = Foil card   X = Fixed/standard in all decks

Doomtrooper • Unlimited

Target Games AB/Heartbreaker Hobbies • Released **March 1995**
345 cards in set • **IDENTIFIER: No red pinstripe on outer border**
- Starter decks contain 60 cards; starter displays contain 10 decks
- Booster packs contain 15 cards; booster displays contain 36 packs
Designed by **Bryan Winter**

The **Doomtrooper Unlimited Edition** is differentiated from the **Limited Edition** only by the lack of the red pinstripe along the outer border of the card; both sets had white borders.

The card sets are otherwise very similar. Second Edition is a slightly larger set, with such cards as **Armored Personnel Carrier**, **At Peace with the Art**, and **At Your Service** added and cards such as **Agent Nick Michaels** and **Bamboozled!** dropped.

Target was a European firm, so it should surprise few that Swedish, Dutch, and Norse-language versions of *Doomtrooper* exist. — *James A. Mishler*

You will need **39** nine-pocket pages to store this set. (19 doubled up)

Set (345 cards)	150.00
Starter Display Box	80.00
Booster Display Box	80.00
Starter Deck	6.50
Booster Pack	2.10

Card name	Rarity	Price
A Greater Need	R	7.00
AC-40 "Justifier"	U	1.00
AH/UH-19 Grapeshot Guardian	R	4.00
Aim	C	0.25
Airman Trevor Bartholomew	U	1.30
Alakhai The Cunning	R	5.00
Ambush	U	1.00
Animate Dead	R	4.00
Archangel	C	0.25
Archinquisitor Nikodemus	R	5.00
Armored Personnel Carrier	C	0.25
Assassination	R	5.00
At Peace With The Art	U	1.30
At Your Service	U	1.30
Bacteria Grenade	U	1.00
Bauhaus Blitzer	C	0.25
Bauhaus Great Infurior	R	4.00
Better Your Reputation	C	0.30
Big Bob Watts	R	5.00
Bitter Victory	C	0.25
Blessed Armor	R	4.00
Blessed Legionnaire	C	0.25
Blessed Vestal	U	1.30
Blind Fury	U	1.30
Blood Beret	C	0.25
Blood Lust	C	0.25
Born With a Silver Spoon	U	1.00
Botched Orders	R	4.00
Budget Cuts	C	0.25
Building Boom	C	0.25
Cairath	R	4.00
Callistonian Intruder	U	1.50
CAP 7000P	R	4.00
Capitol Sword of Honor	U	1.00
Cardinal Dominic	R	5.00
Centurion	U	1.00
Chainripper	C	0.30
Changeling Empathy	U	1.00
Chasm!	C	0.25
Chasseur	C	0.25
Chemiman	U	1.00
Child of Ilian	C	0.25

Card name	Rarity	Price
Chosen	R	4.00
Citadel of Algeroth	U	1.50
Citadel of Demnogonis	U	1.50
Citadel of Ilian	U	1.50
Citadel of Muawijhe	U	1.50
Citadel of Semai	U	1.50
Clan Infighting	R	4.00
Clansman	C	0.25
Clansman Claymore	U	1.00
Combat Warhead	U	1.00
Command	U	1.00
Commitment To Service	C	0.30
Composite Armor	R	5.00
Confuse	R	4.00
Control Mind	U	1.00
Corrosive Ichor	C	0.30
Corrupt Shield	U	1.00
Cowardice	U	1.00
Crenshaw The Mortificator	R	4.00
Cuirassier	C	0.25
Curator	U	1.00
Curator Sword	U	1.50
Cybernetic Power Arm	R	4.00
Cybernetic Retinas	R	4.00
Dark Kohort	R	4.00
Dark Visitation	U	1.00
Deathlockdrum	R	4.00
Decay	U	1.00
Deform	U	1.50
Demolition Kit	R	5.00
Demoted	U	1.00
Destroy Kohort	R	4.00
Destroy Squad	R	5.00
Dimensional Hole	U	1.50
Dimensional Warp	U	1.50
Discovered	U	1.00
Disrupt Power	U	1.50
Distort	U	1.00
Divine Inspiration	R	4.00
Dizzying Aura	C	0.30
Domination	C	0.25
Doomed	U	1.00
Dragoon	C	0.25
Dutiful Service	U	1.00
Dwelling On The Past	U	1.00
Earthquake	R	5.00
Economic Disaster	R	7.00
Edward S. Murdoch	R	4.00
Efficiency Training	U	1.50
Elemental Empathy	U	1.00

Card name	Rarity	Price
Elemental Foci	C	0.30
Empathic Awareness	R	7.00
Envision Conflict	C	0.25
Essence of Clarity	R	5.00
Essence of Integrity	R	5.00
Essence of Morality	R	5.00
Essence of Purity	R	5.00
Essence of Rectitude	R	5.00
Essence of Virtue	R	5.00
Establish Defensive Perimeter	R	4.00
Etoiles Mortant	C	0.25
Evasion Training	R	4.00
Evasive Action	C	0.25
Exonerated Ronin	R	5.00
Exorcise Self	U	1.00
Exorcism	U	1.00
Exorcism Empathy	C	0.30
Expedite Request	U	1.50
Explosion	R	4.00
Ezoghoul	R	4.00
Fall Prone	U	2.00
Favored Status	R	7.00
Fickle Finger Of Fate	C	0.25
Fifteen Minutes of Fame	R	5.00
File Transfer	U	1.00
Financial Shenanigans	C	0.30
First Aid Kit	C	0.25
Flak Plating	C	0.30
Flow of Acid	R	4.00
Fly	U	1.00
Forced March	U	1.00
Forgotten Orders	C	0.30
Foxhole	U	1.00
Framed!	U	1.00
Free Marine	C	0.25
Freelancer	C	0.30
Fukido	U	1.30
Fukimura No. 12 Kamikaze	R	5.00
Fury of the Clansmen	R	4.00
Gale Force Winds	R	4.00
Gaze	R	4.00
Gehenna Puker	R	5.00
Get Me Out Of Here!	C	0.30
Gift of Fate	U	1.00
Golden Lion	C	0.25
Greater Domination	R	4.00
Greater Hypnosis	R	4.00
Greater Telepathy	R	4.00
Grenade Launcher	R	5.00
Gun Running	C	0.30

Card name	Rarity	Price
Hand of Death	U	1.50
Hatamoto	C	0.25
Heavy Fog	C	0.25
Heimburg	U	1.50
Heretic	C	0.25
Hero Worship	R	7.00
Hidden In The Shadows	C	0.25
Hit Them Where It Hurts	U	1.50
HMG MK. XIXB Charger	R	5.00
Honorary Baptism	U	1.00
Hussar	C	0.25
Hypnosis	C	0.25
Illusion	U	1.50
Immaculate Fury	R	4.00
Imperial Doomlord	R	5.00
Imperial Southpaw	R	4.00
Improve Self	U	1.00
Inconspicuous	U	1.30
Indigestion	U	1.50
Infantry	C	0.25
Infection	U	1.50
Infiltration	R	4.00
Influence	U	1.00
Inhuman Practices	C	0.30
Initiative	C	0.25
Inner Strength	C	0.30
Inquisitor	C	0.25
Inquisitor Majoris	R	5.00
Insane Dance	U	1.50
Insider Trading	C	0.30
Inspired	C	0.10
Insubordination	U	1.00
Internal Affairs Crackdown	R	4.00
Invoke Frenzy	R	4.00
Invoke Pain	U	1.00
Invulnerability	U	1.00
Item Vision	U	1.00
Jammed!	C	0.30
Joy of Victory	C	0.25
Keeper of The Art	R	4.00
Kinetic Empathy	U	1.00
Knighthood	U	1.00
Kratach	U	1.50
L&A Plasma Carbine	U	1.30
Lack Of Resources	C	0.30
Legionnaire of Semai	C	0.25
Levitation	U	1.00
Longshore	U	1.50
Lost Paperwork	U	1.00
Lucky Shot	C	0.25

RARITY KEY C = Common U = Uncommon R = Rare VR = Very Rare UR = Ultra Rare F = Foil card X = Fixed/standard in all decks

Card name	Rarity	Price
Luna	U	1.50
Making An Example	C	0.30
Malfunction!	C	0.25
Manifest Destiny	R	5.00
Manipulative Empathy	U	1.00
Marcus The Heretic [23]	R	9.00
Martial Training	R	4.00
Martian Banshee	C	0.25
Matter Transfer	C	0.30
Max Steiner	R	5.00
Mental Constitution	U	1.00
Mental Shield	C	0.30
Mentalism Empathy	C	0.30
Mercurian Guardsman	C	0.30
Metal Detector [24]	C	0.30
Mind Melt	U	1.50
Miscommunication	U	1.00
Missionary	C	0.30
Mitch Hunter	R	5.00
Monetary Discrepancies	R	7.00
Mortificator	C	0.25
Mortis Sword	U	1.00
Motion Detector	C	0.30
Mystic [25]	U	1.00
Mystical Training	R	4.00
Narrow Escape!	U	1.50
Necromutant	C	0.25
Necromutant Frenzy	U	1.50
Necrovisual Link	R	5.00
Negative Karma	R	4.00
Nepharite of Algeroth	R	5.00
Nepharite of Demnogonis	R	5.00
Nepharite of Ilian [26]	R	5.00
Nepharite of Muawijhe	R	5.00
Nepharite Of Semai	R	5.00
Nepharite Warlord	U	2.50
Nicholai	U	2.50
Nimrod Autocannon	R	5.00
Noted Efficiency	U	1.00

Card name	Rarity	Price
Open Auction	C	0.30
Palisade	C	0.30
Personal Anti-Personnel Mines [27]	R	5.00
Personnel Budget	C	0.30
Personnel Shortage	C	0.30
Phantasm	U	1.00
Planning Ahead	U	1.50
Planning Commission	U	1.50
Portable Force Shield	R	5.00
Portal of Dark Healing	R	4.00
Portal of Undeath	R	5.00
Portents of Victory [28]	U	1.00
Positive Karma	U	1.00
Possess	R	4.00
Powerful Blow	C	0.25
Premonition	U	1.50
Premonition Empathy	U	1.00
Pretorian Stalker	R	5.00
Primal Scream	R	7.00
Prove Your Valor	R	4.00
Psycho-Scanner [29]	R	4.00
Punisher Blade	U	1.00
Punisher Handgun	U	1.00
Purple Shark	R	4.00
Ragathol	U	1.00
Rams Air Cavalry	U	1.30
Razide	R	4.00
Recalled	R	5.00
Recollection	C	0.30
Red Tape [30]	R	7.00
Reinforcements	U	1.50
Repentance	R	4.00
Reputation	R	5.00
Retraining	U	1.50
Revelation	U	1.50
Reversal of Fortune	R	5.00
Revisor	C	0.25
Sabotage!	R	4.00

Card name	Rarity	Price
Sacred Warrior [31]	C	0.25
Sacrifice Of Nathaniel	C	0.30
Sacrifice Of The Master	U	1.50
Samurai	C	0.25
San Dorado	U	1.50
Scalper	U	1.00
Scarce Ammunition	U	1.50
Screaming Legionnaire	C	0.25
Scythe of Semai	R	4.00
Sea Lion [32]	C	0.25
Sean Gallagher	R	4.00
Secret Headquarters	R	4.00
Secret Mission	R	5.00
Self-Sacrifice	R	7.00
Sgt. McBride	U	1.50
Share The Wealth	C	0.30
Sharpshooter	R	4.00
Sherman .74 Model 13 Bolter	U	1.30
Shrieketh [33]	R	4.00
Shroud	R	4.00
Silent Auction	C	0.30
Sleep	R	4.00
SMG MK. III Interceptor	U	1.30
Smoke Bomb	R	1.30
Snub The Cardinal	R	4.00
Solace	R	7.00
Special Commendation	U	1.00
Speed [34]	U	1.00
Spoke In The Cog	U	1.00
Spy in The Ranks	R	4.00
Stigmata	R	5.00
Strategic Restructuring	U	1.50
Strength In Numbers	C	0.30
Strengthen Your Resolve	C	0.30
Suicide Mission	R	4.00
Suicide Warhead	U	1.50
Sunset Striker [35]	C	0.25
Surprise Attack	U	1.00

Card name	Rarity	Price
Surprise Invasion!	U	1.00
Sworn Vengeance	U	1.50
Symmetry Drain	C	0.30
T-32 "Wolfclaw" JBT	R	5.00
Tactical Advantage	U	1.00
Tainted Conjurer	U	1.50
Tainted!	R	4.00
Tatsuo [36]	R	4.00
Telepathic Message	U	1.00
Telepathy	C	0.25
Templar	U	1.50
The Cathedral	U	1.50
The Darkness Flows	C	0.30
The Great Darkness Is Displeased	C	0.30
The HQ	U	1.50
Time Death	R	5.00
Time Rot [37]	R	4.00
Total Carnage	C	0.30
Traitor Discovered	R	5.00
Trench	C	0.30
Trencher	C	0.25
True Gate	R	4.00
Undead Legionnaire	C	0.25
Undercover Agents	R	4.00
Valerie Duval	R	4.00
Valkyrie [38]	C	0.25
Vassht	U	1.30
Venusian Ranger	C	0.25
Violator Sword	U	1.30
Weapons Manifest	R	7.00
Well-rounded Squad	R	4.00
What Is Thy Bidding?	C	0.30
Whispers of Heresy	R	5.00
Wind of Insanity	U	1.00
Wolfbane Light Cavalry [39]	U	1.30
Yojimbo	R	4.00
Young Guard	C	0.25
Zenithian Soulslayer	U	1.50

Doomtrooper • Inquisition

Target Games AB/Heartbreaker Hobbies • Released **May 1995**
175 cards in set • **IDENTIFIER: Gold "IS" figure at lower right**

• Booster packs contain 8 cards; booster displays contain 60 boosters

   Doomtrooper is known as the "Techno-Fantasy Card Game" because it has a "magical" fantasy element, the Art and the Dark Symmetry. These mystic forces are at the command of the Brotherhood and the Dark Legion, each of which is led by the Cardinal and the Dark Apostles respectively.

   Inquisition adds a large number of Art and Dark Symmetry cards to the *Doomtrooper* game, as well as a new class of cards: Relics. Relics are devices that depend on the Art or the Dark Symmetry to grant power. The five Dark Apostles also appear in this set, as does their master, **That Which is Not to Be Named**, a real game-breaker of a card (especially in combination with **Desperate Times**), which turns all Dark Legion attacks into killing rather than wounding attacks.

   Altogether, a powerful expansion that continues a strong CCG line. — *James A. Mishler*

You will need **20** nine-pocket pages to store this set. (10 doubled up)

Set (175 cards)	80.00
Booster Display Box	60.00
Booster Pack	1.20

Card name	Rarity	Price
AC-41 "Purifier" [1]	U1	2.00
AG-17 "Panzerknacker"	U1	2.00
Age Of Catastrophe	U1	2.00
Algeroth Cultist	C1	0.25
Algeroth Apostle Of War	U1	2.00

Card name	Rarity	Price
Annihilation	U1	2.00
Antiquarian	C3	0.20
Apostate	U2	0.50
Archer Sniper Rifle [2]	U2	1.50
Archetypal Timepiece	U1	2.00
Arctic Wave	C1	0.25
Armor Of The True Assassin	U1	2.00
Armor Of Unholiness	U1	2.00
Attack Prediction	C1	0.25
Attraction	C2	0.25

Card name	Rarity	Price
Avenger Sword	C1	0.25
Azogar	C1	0.25
Barbarous Power [3]	C2	0.25
Bauhaus Bully	U1	2.00
Behest	C2	0.25
Black Bullets	U2	0.50
Bodyguard	C2	0.25
Bolster Your Forces	C2	0.25
Book Of Law	U2	0.50
Bringer Of Light	U1	2.00

Card name	Rarity	Price
Callistonian Conqueror	U2	0.50
Canyle [4]	C2	0.25
Cardinal Durand	U1	2.00
Cardinal's Bank	U1	2.00
Castigator Battlespear	C2	0.25
Chain Bayonet	U1	2.00
Charge	C3	0.20
Coagulant Autoinjector	C1	0.25
Codex Of Concealed Perception	U1	2.00

RARITY KEY C3 = Most Common C2 = Common C1 = Least Common U2 = Less Uncommon U1 = More Uncommon R = Rare

Card name	Rarity	Price
☐ Combat Coordinator	U1	2.00
☐ Commendation	C1	0.25
5		
☐ Curse Of Algeroth	C2	0.25
☐ Dai-Sho Of The Ancient Emperors	U1	2.00
☐ Dark Huntsman	U2	0.50
☐ Dark Summoning	U2	0.50
☐ Declaration Of Corporate Dissension	C1	0.25
☐ Decoration	C1	0.25
☐ Demnogonis Cultist	C1	0.25
☐ Demnogonis The Befouler	U1	2.00
☐ Desperate Times	U1	2.00
6		
☐ Dispose	C1	0.25
☐ Distracted	C3	0.20
☐ Doctor Diana	C2	0.25
☐ Double Duty	U1	2.00
☐ DPAT-9 "Deuce"	U1	2.00
☐ Duty Roster	C3	0.20
☐ Elemental Alteration	C2	0.25
☐ Eminent Summoner	C1	0.25
☐ Enlarge	C1	0.25
7		
☐ Envision	C1	0.25
☐ Equilibrium	C1	0.25
☐ Eradicator Deathdroid	U1	2.00
☐ Essential Summons	C1	0.25
☐ Eternal Curse	U2	0.50
☐ Evil Eye	C1	0.25
☐ Exorcise Injuries	C1	0.25
☐ Exorcist Glove	U1	2.00
☐ Factory	C2	0.25
8		
☐ Ferocity	C3	0.20
☐ Field Repair Kit	C1	0.25
☐ Fist Of Fury	C1	0.25
☐ Forgery	U2	0.50
☐ Fragment Of The True Chip	U1	2.00

Card name	Rarity	Price
☐ Golem Of Darkness	U2	0.50
☐ Greater Divination	C1	0.25
☐ Greater Manipulation	U1	2.00
☐ Grizzly Battle Tank	U1	2.00
9		
☐ Gusts Of Hesitation	C2	0.25
☐ Heist	U2	0.50
☐ Hellblaster	U1	2.00
☐ Hellhound Necrotank	U1	2.00
☐ Hidden Cache	C2	0.25
☐ Hideout	C2	0.25
☐ Icarus Jet Fighter	U2	0.50
☐ Ilian Cultist	C1	0.25
☐ Ilian Temple Sentinel	C1	0.25
10		
☐ Ilian Mistress Of The Void	U1	2.00
☐ Improved Kratach	U2	0.50
☐ Industrial Complex	U2	0.50
☐ Inquisitor Battle Dress	C2	0.25
☐ Krynston's Skull	U1	2.00
☐ Laser Sight	C3	0.20
☐ Loot And Pillage	U1	2.00
☐ Loot The Dead	C1	0.25
☐ Mask Of The Vestals	U1	2.00
11		
☐ Mentor	C1	0.25
☐ Mission Statement	U1	2.00
☐ Monstrous Power	C1	0.25
☐ Mortal Wound	U1	2.00
☐ Mortification	C1	0.50
☐ Muawijhe Cultist	C1	0.25
☐ Muawijhe Lord Of Visions	U1	2.00
☐ Mystic Battle Dress	C2	0.25
☐ Nathaniel's Opportunity	U2	0.50
12		
☐ Nazgaroth	U1	2.00
☐ Necrobionics	C1	0.25
☐ Necromakina	U1	2.00
☐ Necromower	U2	0.50
☐ Nimrod MK 1	U1	2.00

Card name	Rarity	Price
☐ Noted Collector	C3	0.20
☐ Orb of the Smaller Servants	U1	2.00
☐ Pacifism	C1	0.25
13		
☐ Plagiarize	C1	0.25
☐ Plague Bearer	C1	0.25
☐ Plague Gun	U1	2.00
☐ Power Stabilizer	C1	0.25
☐ Preferred Spell	C2	0.25
☐ Press	C1	0.25
☐ Punisher Combo	C1	0.25
☐ Reassignment	U1	2.00
☐ Recognition	C1	0.25
☐ Reliquary	U1	2.00
14		
☐ Renegade Apostate	U2	0.50
☐ Scion Of Ilian	U2	0.50
☐ Scroll Of Unholy Invocation	U1	2.00
☐ Semai Cultist	C1	0.25
☐ Semai Lord Of Spite	U1	2.00
☐ Sewers	C1	0.25
☐ Shadow Walker	C2	0.25
☐ Shriek	C2	0.25
☐ Skepticism	U1	2.00
15		
☐ Smell Of War	C1	0.25
☐ Snipers!	U1	2.00
☐ SR MK. XII "Assailant"	U1	2.00
☐ SSW4200P	U1	2.00
☐ Storm Of Chaos	U2	0.50
☐ Subversive Agent	U2	0.50
☐ Summon Defense	C1	0.25
☐ Summon Hero	U2	0.50
☐ Summon Item	C1	0.25
16		
☐ Summon Relic	C1	0.25
☐ Summon Spell	C2	0.25
☐ Summon Trooper	C2	0.25
☐ Summoning Empathy	C2	0.25
☐ Supply Line Severed	C1	0.25

Card name	Rarity	Price
☐ Taxation	U1	2.00
☐ Tekron	U2	0.50
☐ Thadeus's Pallet	C3	0.20
☐ That Which is Not to be Named	U1	2.00
17		
☐ The Black Gate	U1	2.00
☐ The Burroughs Cathedral	U1	2.00
☐ The Falcon Of Pilgrims	U1	2.00
☐ The First Directorate	U1	2.00
☐ The Fourth Directorate	U1	2.00
☐ The Fukido Cathedral	U1	2.00
☐ The Gibson Cathedral	U1	2.00
☐ The Heimburg Cathedral	U1	2.00
☐ The Liber Hereticus	U1	2.00
18		
☐ The Longshore Cathedral	U1	2.00
☐ The San Dorado Cathedral	U1	2.00
☐ The Second Directorate	U1	2.00
☐ The Shillelagh	U1	2.00
☐ The Stone Archives	U1	2.00
☐ The Third Directorate	U1	2.00
☐ The Volksburg Cathedral	U1	2.00
☐ Tight Formation	C3	0.20
☐ Tithe	C1	0.25
19		
☐ Transfiguration	C2	0.25
☐ Transmutation	C1	0.25
☐ Ungodly Power	U1	2.00
☐ Unholy Eye	U1	2.00
☐ Unholy Power	U2	0.50
☐ Vac Engineer	C2	0.25
☐ Valpurgius	U1	2.00
☐ Vault Of Unholy Restoration	U1	2.00
☐ Venusian Marshal	U2	0.50
20		
☐ Vince Diamond	U1	2.00
☐ Wave Of Righteousness	U2	0.50
☐ Wrath Of Algeroth	U1	2.00
☐ Zenithian Slaughtermaster	C1	0.20

Doomtrooper • *Warzone*

Target Games AB/Heartbreaker Hobbies • Released **August 1995**
131 cards in set • **IDENTIFIER: Gold "Z" at lower right**

• Booster packs contain 8 cards; booster displays contain 60 boosters

In the Solar System of the *Mutant Chronicles* setting, Warzones are areas where the conflict with the Dark Legion and the battles between the Corporations continue unabated. In addition to many new cards that support the common company warrior, *Warzone* introduces the Warzones to *Doomtrooper* game play.

Warzones are played into a players' Squad or Kohort; they are usable by the Defender in a battle, and can give bonuses and/or penalties to Fight, Shoot, Armor, and Value during a battle. Some Warzones give additional benefits in the text of the card, accruing to specific Doomtrooper affiliations, the Brotherhood or the Dark Legion.

Warzone adds a strategic feel to the tactical nature of the *Doomtrooper* CCG. — **James A. Mishler**

You will need **15** nine-pocket pages to store this set. (8 doubled up)

BANNER BEARER

STANDARD BEARER. This warrior inspires his comrades. All Imperial warriors in your Squad, except this Banner Bearer, gain +2 to A while this warrior is present. The Banner Bearer will not affect its own ratings, but others may.

Set (131 cards)		60.00
Booster Display Box		60.00
Booster Pack		1.20

Card name	Rarity	Price
1		
☐ Aide-De-Camp	C3	0.15
☐ Air Assault	U2	2.30
☐ Airbrush/M516S Shotgun	C2	0.20
☐ Amnesty	U2	2.50
☐ Anti-Tank Minefield	U1	4.30
☐ Artillery Support	U2	2.40
☐ Assault Engineer	U2	2.50
☐ Asteroid Settlement	C2	0.20
☐ Backfire	U1	4.50

Card name	Rarity	Price
2		
☐ Banner Bearer	C3	0.15
☐ Barrage Balloons	U2	2.40
☐ Battle Functionary	C1	0.30
☐ Bauhaus Cop	C3	0.15
☐ Bio-Giant	U1	4.30
☐ Black Widow	U2	2.40
☐ Brain Strain	U2	2.40
☐ Brass Apocalypt	C1	0.30
☐ Bushi	C3	0.15
3		
☐ Capitaine	C1	0.30
☐ Captain	C1	0.30
☐ Charles Sykes	U1	4.60

Card name	Rarity	Price
☐ Citadel Sanctum	U2	2.50
☐ Clan Membership	C2	0.20
☐ Cleansing Flame	U2	2.40
☐ Close Air Support	U2	2.40
☐ Clumsiness	C2	0.20
☐ Code Of Honor	C2	0.20
4		
☐ Combat Overseer	C3	0.15
☐ Command Helmet	C1	0.30
☐ Commander Chieftain	C1	0.30
☐ Commando Raid	C2	0.20
☐ Crater Of Anatholia	C2	0.20
☐ Crusader SP Rocket Launcher	U2	2.60

Card name	Rarity	Price
☐ Cyberopolis	U2	2.30
☐ Cyril Dent	U1	4.30
☐ Death Angel	U2	2.40
5		
☐ Death Row	U2	2.30
☐ Destroyer	U2	2.50
☐ Dragonfish	U2	2.40
☐ Ejection Seat	C2	0.20
☐ Elite Trooper	U2	2.50
☐ Eonian Justifier	U1	3.80
☐ Escape!	C2	0.20
☐ Eva Valmonte	C2	0.20
☐ Excrutiating Power Flow	U2	2.40

RARITY KEY C3 = Most Common C2 = Common C1 = Least Common U2 = Less Uncommon U1 = More Uncommon R = Rare

Card name	Rarity	Price
6		
☐ Faulty Supplies	U2	2.40
☐ Field Marshal Johnstone	U1	4.00
☐ Fizzle	C2	0.20
☐ Flight Commander	C1	0.30
☐ Fruits Of War	U2	2.40
☐ General Michael Kell	U1	4.40
☐ Giacchio Forza 750	U2	2.40
☐ Grand Assault	U2	2.40
☐ Grand Tactician	C3	0.15
7		
☐ Graveton Archipelago	C2	0.20
☐ Great Grey	U2	2.50
☐ Great Rust Desert	C2	0.20
☐ Grim Reaper	U2	2.50
☐ GT Offroad B52	U2	2.40
☐ Hagelsturm/5516D Shotgun	C2	0.20
☐ Helstrom Mountains	C2	0.30
☐ Hero Award	U2	2.40
☐ Home Turf Asteroid Belt	U2	2.40
8		
☐ Home Turf Mars	U2	2.40
☐ Home Turf Mercury	U2	2.40
☐ Home Turf Venus	U2	2.40

Card name	Rarity	Price
☐ Honor Award	C2	0.20
☐ Immaculate Spawn	C2	0.20
☐ Infested Asteroid	C2	0.20
☐ Jet Pack	C2	0.20
☐ Jito	C3	0.15
☐ Karnophage	C2	0.20
9		
☐ Klein Helitek Dragonfly	U2	2.40
☐ Kommandant	C1	0.30
☐ Lamb For The Slaughter	U1	4.50
☐ Lancelot Light Freighter	U1	4.30
☐ Lord Nozaki	U1	4.50
☐ Mandible/SA-SG 7200 Shotgun	C2	0.20
☐ McCraig Line	C2	0.20
☐ Mercurian Diamond Caverns	C2	0.30
☐ Mercurian Maculator	C2	0.20
10		
☐ Meta Cannon	U1	2.80
☐ Minefield	U2	2.50
☐ Misfire	C2	0.20
☐ Mishimese Dragonbike	C2	0.20
☐ Natural Disaster	U2	2.50
☐ No-Man's Land	C2	0.30

Card name	Rarity	Price
☐ Paparazzo	C3	0.15
☐ Pegasus Scout Bike	U2	2.40
☐ Phobos & Deimos	C2	0.20
11		
☐ Point Guard	C2	0.20
☐ President Charles W. Colding	U1	4.50
☐ Pressing Matters	U1	4.60
☐ Prison Camp	C2	0.20
☐ Programmed	U1	4.60
☐ Rattlesnake	U2	2.40
☐ Reaper Of Souls	U2	2.40
☐ Rear Guard	C2	0.20
☐ Reaver Troop Carrier	U2	2.40
12		
☐ Recruitment	U2	2.50
☐ Sacred Outpost	U2	2.60
☐ Scheduled Briefings	U2	2.50
☐ Scout Bat	C2	0.20
☐ Secret Assassin	U2	2.50
☐ Self-Destruct Programming	U2	2.50
☐ Sergeant	C3	0.15
☐ Shell Shocked	C2	0.20
☐ Shelter Of The Crowd	U1	4.50

Card name	Rarity	Price
13		
☐ Shinrikyo Underworld	C2	0.30
☐ Shugo	C1	0.30
☐ Special Forces Training	U2	2.50
☐ Squadron Commander	C3	0.15
☐ Staff Gen. Constance Romanov	U1	4.50
☐ Strategic Bombing	U1	4.60
☐ Subterfuge	U1	4.30
☐ Sudden Death	U1	4.50
☐ Suicide Attack	U2	2.50
14		
☐ Supreme Necromagus	U2	2.50
☐ Ta6500 Cybermech	U2	2.50
☐ Tactical Computer	C1	0.30
☐ Technomancer	U2	2.50
☐ The Nineteenth Executive	U1	4.50
☐ The Unofficial Doctrine	C2	0.20
☐ Tormentor Incinerator	C2	0.20
☐ Transfer	U2	2.50
☐ Turn Of Events	U2	2.50
15		
☐ Unholy Carronade	U2	2.50
☐ Venom Bat	C2	0.20
☐ Venusian Jungle	C2	0.20
☐ Victoria	C2	0.20
☐ War Medic	C3	0.15

Doomtrooper • Mortificator

Target Games AB/Heartbreaker Hobbies • Released October 1995

122 cards in set

• Booster packs contain 8 cards; booster displays contain 60 boosters

Mortificator centers on boosting the power of the Brotherhood, the mystical organization that eternally is at odds with the Dark Legion. Mortificators are the assassins of the Brotherhood; this expansion gives them various Poisons that may be used in their battles. Mortificators may, in general, attack anyone, regardless of affiliations, and thus are very potent Doomtrooper cards.

Unfortunately, there is only one Mortificator available in the set (**Crenshaw the Redeemer**), and as he is a Personality, only one Mortificator can be in play in any one game, severely limiting the usefulness of the Mortificator only cards! **Nicolai**, a Promo Personality card, is considered a Mortificator, but that only brings the number of Mortificators to two. A slight but meaningful error in expansion design. — *James A. Mishler*

Set (122 cards)	**65.00**
Booster Display Box	**60.00**
Booster Pack	**2.00**

Card name	Rarity	Price
1		
☐ Admonish Resistance	C2	0.30
☐ Air-To-Ground Missile	C2	0.30
☐ Amnesia	U2	2.30
☐ And Stay Dead!	U1	5.30
☐ Antidote	C3	0.15
☐ Armor-Piercing Ammo	U2	2.80
☐ Autogyro	C2	0.30
☐ Back Door	C2	0.20
☐ Battle Cry	C2	0.20
2		
☐ Bauhaus Security Guard	C2	0.45
☐ Bite The Dust	U2	2.30
☐ Black Venom	U2	1.80
☐ Blasting Away	C2	0.20
☐ Blessed Blood	C3	0.15
☐ Blessed By Apostle	C2	0.20
☐ Bluff	C2	0.20
☐ Booby Trap	U2	2.30
☐ Bribery	U2	2.30
3		
☐ Burglary	U2	2.30
☐ Cardinal's Blood	C2	0.30
☐ Carnage	U1	5.30
☐ Censer Drops	C2	0.30
☐ Certified Operator	C2	0.30
☐ Club Arkadin	C2	0.30
☐ Concealed Weapon	C2	0.20
☐ Cornered	U2	2.30
☐ Crenshaw The Redeemer	U2	4.30

Card name	Rarity	Price
4		
☐ Currency Exchange	C2	0.30
☐ Cursed Artifact	C2	0.20
☐ Day Of Mourning	C2	0.20
☐ Dead Zone	C2	0.20
☐ Deal With It	U1	5.30
☐ Death Maze	C2	0.20
☐ Defensive Barrier	C2	0.20
☐ Deja Vu	C2	0.20
☐ Don't Call Again!	U2	2.30
5		
☐ Dwindling Faith	C2	0.20
☐ Eat This!	U2	2.30
☐ Economic Breakdown	U2	2.30
☐ Embassy	C2	0.20
☐ Entitlement	C2	0.20
☐ Erwin Stahler	C2	0.45
☐ Falling Market	U2	2.30
☐ Fill 'Em Up	C2	0.30
☐ Foreseeing Talisman	U2	2.00
6		
☐ Ghost In The Machine	U2	2.30
☐ Golgotha Unleashed	U2	4.30
☐ Golgotha's Citadel	U2	2.30
☐ Gung Ho	U2	2.30
☐ Hasty Getaway	U1	5.30
☐ Hidden	C2	0.20
☐ Holy Protector	C2	0.20
☐ Illumination	U2	2.30
☐ Inconvenient Phone Call	C2	0.30
7		
☐ Inferior Technology	U2	2.30
☐ Informants	C2	0.30
☐ Into The Dark	C2	0.20
☐ "It Shall Be Done, Excellency"	U2	2.30

Card name	Rarity	Price
☐ Jake Kramer	U2	3.80
☐ Joker!	U1	10.25
☐ Life Insurance	C2	0.30
☐ Lifeguard Armor	U2	2.80
☐ Listen Up!	C2	0.30
8		
☐ Living On The Edge	U2	2.30
☐ Local Thug	C2	0.60
☐ Lotus Blossom	U2	2.80
☐ Luna Memorial Hospital	C2	0.30
☐ Master Of Disguise	U2	2.30
☐ Mercenary	U2	5.30
☐ Metropolitan Prophet	U2	3.80
☐ Mindslayer	U2	2.30
☐ Moral Decay	U2	2.30
9		
☐ No Loose Ends	C3	0.15
☐ Oh Yeah?!	U2	2.30
☐ Pandora's Box	C3	0.15
☐ Panic Button	C2	0.30
☐ Platinum Dream	U2	2.30
☐ Play It Again	U2	2.30
☐ Pound Of Flesh	U1	5.30
☐ Powerful Command	U2	2.30
☐ Punch Drunk	C2	0.30
10		
☐ Pursuit	C2	0.30
☐ Rage	C2	0.30
☐ Reactive Armor Plates	C2	0.30
☐ Reflection	C2	0.30
☐ Replicant Lab	U2	2.30
☐ Repudiate	U2	2.30
☐ Rising Market	U2	2.30
☐ Robbed Blind	U2	2.30
☐ Russian Roulette	C2	0.20

Card name	Rarity	Price
11		
☐ Sachs 9000gl	C2	0.30
☐ Secret	U2	0.80
☐ Shore Leave	C2	0.20
☐ Smoke Screen	C2	0.30
☐ Solidarity	U2	2.30
☐ Special Orders	U2	0.45
☐ Spiraling Death	U2	2.30
☐ Spirit Of Nathaniel	U2	5.30
☐ Stun Grenade	U2	2.30
12		
☐ Superior Quality	U2	2.30
☐ Suppressing Fire	U2	2.30
☐ Surface-To-Air Missile	C2	0.30
☐ Surveillance Ship	U2	2.30
☐ Switched Labels	U2	2.30
☐ Symmetry Flow	U2	2.80
☐ Temporary Insanity	U2	2.30
☐ Terrorist Attack	C2	0.30
☐ The Curator's Gift	C3	0.15
13		
☐ The Stahler Palace	U2	2.80
☐ Think Again	U2	2.30
☐ Throwing It All Away	U2	2.30
☐ To Be Or Not To Be	C2	0.30
☐ Trail Of Evidence	C2	0.20
☐ Training	C2	0.20
☐ Trust In The Arms	U2	2.30
☐ Try And Stop Me!	U2	2.30
☐ Untouchable	U2	2.30
14		
☐ Wanna Play?	U1	5.30
☐ Watch Tower	C2	0.30
☐ Watchful Eye	U2	2.30
☐ What Have We Here?	U2	2.30
☐ Wolfe	U2	4.80

RARITY KEY C3 = Most Common C2 = Common C1 = Least Common U2 = Less Uncommon U1 = More Uncommon R = Rare

Doomtrooper • *Golgotha*

Target Games AB/Heartbreaker Hobbies • Released **April 1996**

80 cards in set plus **11** Info cards

- Booster packs contain 15 cards plus one Info card; booster displays contain 20 boosters

    Golgotha doubled the number of cards in *Doomtrooper* expansion boosters to 15 cards and one Info card. Two of the Info cards in *Golgotha* were Rules cards that changed the prior rules for using Relics and Warzones, while the third Rule card included the rules for using Alliances cards, introduced in this expansion. *Golgotha* has some hideously powerful cards, including the aforementioned Alliances cards, which give a player a serious edge over opponents that do not have *Golgotha* cards.

    Fortunately, the more broken cards are limited to one in play at a time or even one per deck, slightly balancing the effects of this powerful expansion. — *James A. Mishler*

> You will need
> **9**
> nine-pocket pages to store this set.
> (5 doubled up)

Set (80 cards)		50.00
Booster Display Box		40.00
Booster Pack		1.70

Card name	Rarity	Price
☐ Armory	C1	0.50
☐ Arms Convoy	C1	0.50
☐ Atilla III	C1	1.50
☐ Attrition	C1	0.50
☐ Backlash	C2	0.25
☐ Banishment	C1	1.50
☐ Bank Of Bauhaus	C1	0.50
☐ Barracks	C1	0.50
☐ Bauhaus	C2	0.25
☐ Behemoth Armor	C1	1.50
☐ Callistonian Sundancer	C2	0.25
☐ Capitol	C2	0.25
☐ Carcass Suit	C1	0.50
☐ Cartel Enforcement	C2	0.25
☐ Change In Momentum	C1	0.50
☐ Changeling Power	C1	1.50
☐ Chris Jackson	C2	0.25

Card name	Rarity	Price
☐ Cliffhanger	C1	0.50
☐ Close But No Cigar	C1	0.50
☐ Close Call!	C1	0.50
☐ Combat Fatigue	C1	1.50
☐ Coral Beach	C2	0.25
☐ Cybertronic	C2	0.25
☐ Desert Scorpion	C2	0.25
☐ Doomsday Proclaimer	C2	0.25
☐ Double Time	C2	0.25
☐ Economic Collapse	C1	1.50
☐ Equal Rights	C2	0.25
☐ Extortion	C1	1.50
☐ Festering Wounds	C1	0.50
☐ Foolœs Gold	C1	0.50
☐ Fortify Warzone	C1	0.50
☐ Fury Elite Guard	C2	0.25
☐ Golgotha Mistress of Symmetry	C1	2.50
☐ Golgotha's Mirror	C1	1.00
☐ Honor The Emperor	C1	0.50
☐ Hostile Takeover	C2	0.25

Card name	Rarity	Price
☐ Impale	C1	1.50
☐ Imperial	C2	0.25
☐ Infantry Sniper	C1	1.50
☐ Infrared Goggles	C2	0.25
☐ Inquisition	C1	0.50
☐ Inquisitor Simon	C2	0.25
☐ Lack Of Faith	C1	0.50
☐ Last Ritesman	C2	0.25
☐ Leashed	C1	0.50
☐ Leveled Field	C1	0.50
☐ Limited Resources	C2	0.25
☐ Martyr	C1	1.50
☐ Mishima	C2	0.25
☐ Missing In Action	C1	0.50
☐ Mutiny	C2	0.25
☐ Nothing Is Sacred	C1	1.50
☐ Out Of Fuel	C1	0.50
☐ Pretorian Behemoth	C2	0.25
☐ Rescue Mission	C2	0.25
☐ Saladin	C1	0.50
☐ Scrambling Device	C1	0.50

Card name	Rarity	Price
☐ Second Thoughts	C1	0.50
☐ Sergeant Carter	C1	1.50
☐ Shinobi	C1	1.50
☐ Stolen Paperwork	C1	0.50
☐ Surplus	C2	0.25
☐ Symmetry Failure	C1	0.50
☐ Tax Refund	C1	0.50
☐ Territorial Advantage	C2	0.25
☐ The Brotherhood	C2	0.25
☐ The Dark Legion	C2	0.25
☐ The First Amendment	C2	0.25
☐ Timothy Macguire	C1	1.50
☐ Toshiro	C2	0.25
☐ Total Eclipse	C1	1.50
☐ Touched By The Light	C1	0.50
☐ Troop Transfer	C1	0.50
☐ Truce	C1	1.50
☐ Tucked Away	C1	0.50
☐ Undying Loyalty	C1	0.50
☐ Wartime Retribution	C1	0.50
☐ Yahoo!	C1	1.50
☐ Yuichiro	C2	0.25

Doomtrooper • *Apocalypse*

Target Games AB/Heartbreaker Hobbies • Released **September 1996**

80 cards in set plus **10** Info cards

- Booster packs contain 15 cards plus one Info card; booster displays contain 36 boosters

    Apocalypse is a mixed bag of new rules and new cards. It adds Ki Powers to the game, special abilities that can be used by Mishima affiliated Doomtroopers. *Apocalypse* adds the concept of Annihilating a card (removing it from the game) and adds a Post-Play icon to the card design. There are also several clarifications regarding timing, which warriors can attack other warriors, and vehicle use. The set includes a good mix of cards, including an additional Mortificator and several Dark Legion Relics.

    However, the new Ki Powers were little consolation for the fact that *Apocalypse* was the overall weakest of the expansions for *Doomtrooper*. — *James A. Mishler*

> You will need
> **9**
> nine-pocket pages to store this set.
> (5 doubled up)

Set (80 cards)		50.00
Booster Display Box		40.00
Booster Pack		1.70

Card name	Rarity	Price
☐ A Nasty Surprise	C1	0.50
☐ A Second Chance	C1	0.50
☐ Adamantium Will	C1	0.50
☐ Administrative Crackdown	C1	0.50
☐ Adrenaline Implants	C1	1.50
☐ Andrew Drougan	C2	0.25
☐ Anti-Personnel Grenade	C1	0.50
☐ Aura Of Mystical Resistance	C1	0.50
☐ Battlefield Chaos	C2	0.25
☐ Board Room	C1	0.50
☐ Boot Camp	C2	0.25
☐ Brainwave Bomb	C1	0.50
☐ Brother Claudius	C1	0.50
☐ Brother Stern	C2	0.25
☐ Colonel Maxwell	C1	2.50
☐ Cryotech Chamber	C1	1.50
☐ Dark Mystic	C2	0.25

Card name	Rarity	Price
☐ Demon Hunter	C2	0.25
☐ Dire Portents	C1	0.50
☐ Discreet Meeting Room	C1	0.50
☐ Elemental Master	C1	0.50
☐ Epidermal Plates	C1	0.50
☐ Escape Hatch	C2	0.25
☐ Eye Of Algeroth	C1	0.50
☐ Factory Retrofit	C1	1.50
☐ Fortified Entrenchment	C2	0.25
☐ Freedom Brigadeer	C2	0.25
☐ Freelancer Patriarch	C2	0.25
☐ Good Luck Charm	C1	1.50
☐ Graveyard	C2	0.25
☐ Grey Mystic	C2	0.25
☐ Guard Station	C1	0.50
☐ Hands Of Stone	C1	1.50
☐ Hardened Fist	C2	0.25
☐ Inner Shame	C2	0.25
☐ Innocent Bauble	C1	0.50
☐ Kadaver	C2	0.25
☐ Kanji's Lucky Sense	C1	0.50

Card name	Rarity	Price
☐ Keitoku Asano	C1	0.50
☐ Ki Self Healing	C1	0.50
☐ Ki Teleportation	C1	0.50
☐ Kritana	C2	0.25
☐ Maledrach	C1	0.50
☐ Mishimese Ceremonial Blade	C1	0.50
☐ Museum	C2	0.25
☐ Nicola Brannaghan	C1	0.50
☐ Nomura's Quickened Step	C1	0.50
☐ Paladine's Favor	C1	0.50
☐ Pass The Buck	C1	0.50
☐ Perimeter Alarm	C1	0.50
☐ Promoted	C2	0.25
☐ Protective Wall	C1	1.50
☐ Red Guard Legionnaire	C2	0.25
☐ Samurai Armor	C2	1.00
☐ Sanctuary	C1	1.50
☐ Shadow Master	C2	1.50
☐ Shadow Walk	C1	0.50
☐ Shogun	C2	0.25
☐ Soul Well	C1	0.50

Card name	Rarity	Price
☐ Summon Warzone	C1	0.50
☐ Supreme Concentration	C1	1.50
☐ Surveillance Bug	C2	0.25
☐ Symmetry Stone	C1	0.50
☐ Targeting Installation	C2	0.25
☐ The Chameleon's Skin	C1	0.50
☐ The Cobra's Venomous Strike	C1	1.50
☐ The Crow's Piercing Glance	C1	0.50
☐ The Mongoose's Artful Dodge	C1	0.50
☐ The Monkey's Foot	C1	0.50
☐ Toronaga's Raging Might	C1	1.50
☐ Total War!	C1	1.50
☐ Triangulating Scope	C2	0.25
☐ Visionary Crystal	C1	0.50
☐ Weapon Link	C2	0.25
☐ Weapons Expert	C1	1.50
☐ White Mystic	C2	0.25
☐ Wolfbane Honor Guard	C2	0.25
☐ Working On The Sly	C1	0.50
☐ Yomura's Amulet	C2	0.25
☐ Yorama's Deflecting Hands	C1	1.50

RARITY KEY C3 = Most Common **C2** = Common **C1** = Least Common **U2** = Less Uncommon **U1** = More Uncommon **R** = Rare

Doomtrooper • *Paradise Lost*

Manufacturer • Released **1997**
124 cards in set • **IDENTIFIER: Mutant skull at lower right**

- Booster packs contain 15 cards plus 1 Info card;
- Booster displays contain 36 boosters

Paradise Lost takes the action in *Doomtrooper* from the other planets of the Solar System back to the cradle of Humanity. A ruined, wasted, Dark Symmetry-dominated Earth, a dark planet of barbarians, mutant beasts and lost technologies... a Dark Eden. Related thematically with the **Dark Eden** CCG, the *Paradise Lost* expansion adds the battlefields of Earth to the *Doomtrooper* game system. A new Area is added to game play, similar to the Squad and the Kohort, called the Outpost. The Outpost is the location on Earth where players have their warriors do battle. Unlike Squads and Kohorts, from which any warrior may attack another warrior, a warrior in the Outpost can only attack warriors in an opponent's Outpost. A warrior may be moved from Squad or Kohort to the Outpost using one Action, except for Tribal Warriors, which must remain on Earth in the Outpost.

Four new factions are introduced in *Paradise Lost*, the four great tribes of ruined Europe. The Sons of Rasputin, the Templars, Crescentia, and the Lutheran Triad all vie for dominance in Dark Eden, loosely allying with or warring with the forces of the Cartel and the Brotherhood while locked in eternal battle with one another. The Outpost may only contain cards from one Tribe at a time, and may only hold Doomtroopers or Dark Legion warriors, never both at the same time. Tribal Warriors have Beasts to assist them, as other warriors have Vehicles. The most powerful Relics in Doomtrooper appear in *Paradise Lost*, the four Key-Code Skulls, which, when combined in the hands of a single warrior, may be used to kill all warriors in the Squad, Outpost, or Kohort of a single player (scoring points for kills)!

Paradise Lost was the swan song for the *Doomtrooper* game. A planned new edition of *Doomtrooper* was not released, nor was the planned new edition expansion, **Ragnarok**. Target Games AB and its U.S. affiliate, Heartbreaker Hobbies, both left the game business several years later. — ***James A. Mishler***

Doomtrooper lives on

As mentioned previously, *Doomtrooper* still has a following on the web, led by *Doomtrooper* designer Bryan Winter. You can find out more about *Doomtrooper* and its web-based afterlife at Doomtrooper Central: *www.thewinternet.com/games/doomtrooper/*

> You will need **14** nine-pocket pages to store this set. (7 doubled up)

Set (124 cards)	75.00
Booster Display Box	70.00
Booster Pack	2.00

Card name	Rarity	Price
1		
Advanced Security System	C3	0.20
Anti-Toxin	C2	0.30
Asian Key-Code Skull	U1	3.30
Battle Madness	C1	0.60
Behold The Future Possibilities	C1	0.60
Blitztank	U2	3.30
Bloody Coup	U1	0.40
Body Armor	C3	0.80
Brotherbound Sergeant	C1	0.20
2		
Brotherbound Trooper	C3	0.70
Brotherhood Archives	U3	1.00
Burning Lungs	U3	0.80
Captured!	U3	0.80
Cavalier	C2	0.30
Central Europe	C1	0.60
Colonel Harding	U1	3.30
Corarius Transport	U1	2.30
Corsair	C1	0.80
3		
Cossack	C1	0.80
Cossack Kommendant	C1	1.10
Cossack Scout	C2	0.30
Crenshaw - Island Team Member	U1	3.30
Crescentian Twotusk	U2	0.80
Curbed	U3	0.80
Eastern Europe	C1	0.60
Eclipse Mammoth	C1	0.45
Emissaries	C3	0.20
4		
Equine	C3	0.20

Card name	Rarity	Price
European Key-Code Skull	U1	3.30
Flammen Soldat	U2	1.30
Fusilier	C1	1.10
Gang Up!	U2	0.80
Garbage Dump	C3	0.20
Gendarme	C3	0.20
Gendarme Bestal	U1	3.50
Get Off That Rock	C3	0.20
5		
Gomorrian Emasculator	U2	1.00
Grave Robbers	U2	0.80
Greymourn Trenchartillery	U2	1.00
Grimgrind Airvessel	U2	0.80
Grinder - Island Team Member	U1	3.80
Gunfighter	U3	0.80
Heavy Cavalier	U3	0.90
High Seer Castor	U2	1.00
Higher Value On Life	C2	0.30
6		
Holy Urox	U2	1.00
Horde Centurion	U2	1.30
Horde Trooper	C3	0.20
Indigo - Island Team Member	U1	3.30
Inoculations	C2	0.30
Ironshark	U3	0.80
Jaeger Commando	U1	3.30
Jihad Infantry Trooper	C1	0.80
Loyal To The Legion	U3	0.80
7		
Lurker	C1	0.60
Lutheran Disciple	C3	0.20
Lutheran Sergeant	U2	1.30
Manhunt	U2	1.30
Marine Serett	U2	0.80
Martyr	U2	1.30

Card name	Rarity	Price
Master Valpurgius	U1	3.80
Mastodont	C1	0.45
Mastodont Handler	C2	0.30
8		
Mitch Hunter - Island Team Member	U1	3.80
Mutated Strain	U3	0.80
Nassal	C3	0.20
Navigational Error	U1	3.30
Noble Beast	C2	0.60
North American Key-Code Skull	U1	3.30
Northwestern Europe	C1	0.60
Off To The Butcher	C2	0.20
Our Enemy's Weakness Is Exposed	C1	0.80
9		
Our True Enemy Is Revealed	C1	0.80
Our Will Is Beyond Measure	C1	0.80
Palanquin Airvessel	C1	0.60
Parasitic Stupor	U3	0.80
Patriarch	C2	0.30
Phische	C3	0.20
Pillaged Munitions	U1	3.30
Planetary Bombing	U3	1.30
Power Induction	C3	0.20
10		
Predatorian	C2	0.20
Prisoner Work Camp	C1	0.60
Private Collector	U2	1.30
Prophet	C2	0.30
Prophetic Vision	C2	0.20
Rampage!	U3	0.80
Raze The Land	U1	3.30
Razor Wire Fence	U3	0.80
Red Plague	U3	0.80

Card name	Rarity	Price
11		
Redeployment	C1	0.60
Redirect	C1	0.60
Requisition	U3	0.80
Rivetbull	C1	0.60
Rustlers!	U2	0.80
Sacred Tear	U2	1.00
Schwerwaffe Soldat	C2	0.30
Scout Cavalier	C1	0.80
Shock Soldat	U2	1.00
12		
Skull-Seeker	U3	1.30
Soldat	C3	0.20
Soldat Kommendant	U1	3.80
South American Key-Code Skull	U1	3.30
Southern Europe	C1	0.60
Summit Meeting	U1	3.80
Support Artillery Ox	C1	0.80
Tailwave	U1	3.80
Templar Legionnaire	C3	0.20
13		
Templar Marine	U3	1.00
The Calling	C2	0.80
The Conviction	C1	0.80
The Defiance	C1	0.60
The Howling Is Upon Us	C1	0.80
The Protection	C1	0.80
The Sacrifice	C1	0.80
Tight Grip	C3	0.20
Torrent Battle Wagon	C2	0.20
14		
Tusked Serett	C1	0.60
Urban Tactics	C1	0.60
V-3	U3	0.80
Veiled Dart	U2	1.00
Verounist Stingray	U3	0.80
Withering Death	U3	0.80
Zhurgon	U1	3.80

Dragonball Z

Score (a division of Playoff Corp.) • First set, **Saiyan Saga**, released **June 2000**
250 cards in set • **IDENTIFIER:** 🁢 symbol at lower left corner

- Starter decks contain 54 cards; starter displays contain 10 starters
- Booster packs contain 9 cards; booster displays contain 36 boosters

The **Dragonball Z** card game is based upon the worldwide hit anime (cartoon) of the same name, which chronicles the exploits of Son Goku and his friends and family as they deal with various threats to themselves and to Earth in general. The *Dragonball* set was the most popular part of **Ani-Mayhem**, and in 2000 it got a CCG all its own.

The CCG allows players to do battle as one of the many hero or villain personalities from the series. Battles are conducted using various physical and energy attacks as well as non-combat cards. Both heroes and villains are also able to use other "good" or "bad" guys from the series as allies. The game offers three different ways to win: You can run your opponent out of cards by damaging them with attacks; you can collect all seven Dragon Balls; or you can evolve into the most powerful character.

Card-wise, *Dragonball Z* offers some of the best and worst premium cards ever. The "high-tech" foil cards available in every starter deck are incredible, one of the better premiums of any CCG. Unfortunately, the other foils are among the worst premiums ever. The gold color makes them difficult to read, and handling them causes scratches.

Dragonball was an early entry in the influx of new CCGs into the market following the monster hit *Pokémon* (forgive the pun). Such times are usually challenging for any new game, but *Dragonball Z*, with its strong license, did well for itself, becoming the top-selling new CCG in 2000. A second set, **Frieza Saga**, was released in October, and **Trunk Saga** was planned for early 2001. — *Orren McKay*

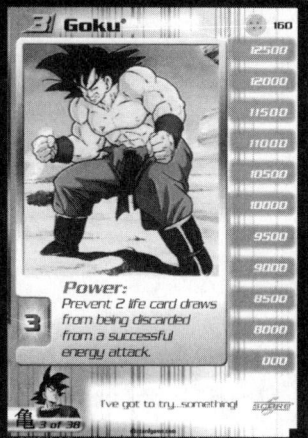

Concept	●●●○○
Gameplay	●●●○○
Card art	●●●○○
Player pool	●●●○○

Set (250 cards)	260.00	*You will need* **28** *nine-pocket pages to store this set. (14 doubled up)*
Foil set	925.00	
Starter Display Box	115.00	
Booster Display Box	100.00	
Starter Deck	11.50	
Booster Pack	3.40	

REGULAR	#	Card name	Rarity	FOIL
☐ 3.50	191	A Beginner's Heart is Dedicated	R	8.00 ☐
☐ 4.00	229	Ally Wins!	R	8.00 ☐
☐ 1.00	156	Ally's Sacrifice	U	3.00 ☐
☐ 3.80	224	Baba Witch Viewing Drill	R	8.00 ☐
☐ 3.90	225	Baba's Energy Blast	R	8.50 ☐
☐ 3.90	204	Battle Pausing	R	8.00 ☐
☐ 1.00	135	Black Arm Bar Drill	U	3.00 ☐
☐ 1.00	72	Black Axe Heel Kick	U	3.00 ☐
☐ 1.00	71	Black Back Kick	U	3.00 ☐
☐ 1.00	131	Black Bear Hug Drill	U	3.00 ☐
☐ 1.00	152	Black Defender Drill	U	3.00 ☐
☐ 1.00	67	Black Elbow Strike	U	3.00 ☐
☐ 1.00	65	Black Fore Fist Punch	U	3.00 ☐
☐ 1.00	136	Black Free-Style Drill	U	3.00 ☐
☐ 1.00	68	Black Front Kick	U	3.00 ☐
☐ 1.00	74	Black Jump Turn Kick	U	3.00 ☐
☐ 1.00	66	Black Knife Hand Strike	U	3.00 ☐
☐ 1.00	143	Black Physical Drill	U	3.00 ☐
☐ 1.00	73	Black Rear Spin Kick	U	3.00 ☐
☐ 3.90	235	Black Shadow Drill	R	8.50 ☐
☐ 1.00	69	Black Side Kick	U	3.00 ☐
☐ 1.00	147	Black Striking Drill	U	3.00 ☐
☐ 1.00	127	Black Takedown Drill	U	3.00 ☐
☐ 1.00	70	Black Turning Kick	U	3.00 ☐
☐ 1.00	99	Blazing Anger!	U	3.00 ☐
☐ 0.25	59	Blue Big Outside Drop	C	1.20 ☐
☐ 1.00	63	Blue Big Whirl Throw	U	3.00 ☐
☐ 1.00	61	Blue Body Drop Throw	U	3.00 ☐
☐ 1.00	145	Blue Breakfall Drill	U	3.00 ☐
☐ 1.00	138	Blue Cradle Drill	U	3.00 ☐
☐ 1.00	129	Blue Deceiving Drill	U	3.00 ☐
☐ 1.00	141	Blue Enemies Drill	U	3.00 ☐
☐ 0.25	11	Blue Forward Foot Sweep	C	1.20 ☐

REGULAR	#	Card name	Rarity	FOIL
☐ 1.00	64	Blue Ground Holding	U	3.00 ☐
☐ 0.25	12	Blue Hip Spring Throw	C	1.20 ☐
☐ 1.00	62	Blue Inner Leg Throw	U	3.00 ☐
☐ 3.90	233	Blue Life Defense Drill	R	8.60 ☐
☐ 1.00	150	Blue Neck Restraint Drill	U	3.00 ☐
☐ 1.00	125	Blue Off-Balancing Opponent Drill	U	3.00 ☐
☐ 0.25	60	Blue One Arm Shoulder Throw	C	1.40 ☐
☐ 1.00	133	Blue Reversal Drill	U	3.00 ☐
☐ 0.25	13	Blue Round Throw	C	1.20 ☐
☐ 0.25	14	Blue Shoulder Wheel	C	1.40 ☐
☐ 3.60	209	Broken Scouter	R	8.50 ☐
☐ 1.00	87	Bulma (level 1)	U	3.00 ☐
☐ 3.80	222	Bulma Finds a Dragon Ball	R	8.50 ☐
☐ 3.60	223	Bulma Finds a Drill	R	8.50 ☐
☐ 0.25	23	Burning Rage!	C	1.40 ☐
☐ 1.00	86	Chi-Chi (level 1)	U	3.00 ☐
☐ 1.00	104	Chiaotzu (level 1)	U	3.00 ☐
☐ 1.00	105	Chiaotzu (level 2)	U	3.00 ☐
☐ 3.20	230	Chiaotzu's Drill	R	8.50 ☐
☐ 1.00	123	Chiaotzu's Energy Manipulation	U	3.00 ☐
	250	Chiaotzu's Physical Defense	URF	25.00 ☐
☐ 3.90	200	Cutting the Tail	R	8.50 ☐
☐ 1.00	89	Dream Chamber Training	U	3.00 ☐
☐ 3.90	199	Dream Fighting	R	8.50 ☐
☐ 3.90	242	Dream Machine Battle	R	8.50 ☐
☐ 0.25	15	Earth Dragon Ball 1	C	1.40 ☐
☐ 0.25	16	Earth Dragon Ball 2	C	1.40 ☐
☐ 1.00	75	Earth Dragon Ball 3	U	3.00 ☐
☐ 1.00	76	Earth Dragon Ball 4	U	3.00 ☐
☐ 1.00	77	Earth Dragon Ball 5	U	3.00 ☐
☐ 4.00	186	Earth Dragon Ball 6	R	9.00 ☐
☐ 4.00	187	Earth Dragon Ball 7	R	9.90 ☐
☐ 4.00	188	Earth Dragon Ball Capture	R	8.50 ☐
☐ 4.00	189	Earth Dragon Ball Combat	R	8.50 ☐
☐ 3.90	190	Enraged!	R	8.50 ☐

Dragonball foils

Some *Dragonball Z* cards have foil and regular versions; some just one or the other. That's how they're listed.

REGULAR	#	Card name	Rarity	FOIL
☐ 1.00	157	Eyes of the Dragon	U	3.00 ☐
☐ 0.25	30	"Fall 7 times, get up 8 times."	C	1.20 ☐
☐ 0.25	31	Fortify Your Spirit	C	1.20 ☐
☐ 1.00	164	Gohan (level 1)	X	
	181	Gohan (level 1HT)	XF	4.00 ☐
☐ 1.00	165	Gohan (level 2)	X	
☐ 1.00	166	Gohan (level 3)	X	
☐ 1.00	111	Gohan's Energy Defense	U	3.00 ☐
☐ 3.60	214	Gohan's Father Save	R	8.50 ☐
☐ 0.25	26	Gohan's Physical Attack	C	1.20 ☐
☐ 1.00	158	Goku (level 1)	X	
	179	Goku (level 1HT)	XF	4.00 ☐
☐ 1.00	159	Goku (level 2)	X	
☐ 1.00	160	Goku (level 3)	X	
☐ 0.25	46	Goku Anger Attack	C	1.20 ☐
☐ 0.25	44	Goku Body Throw!	C	1.20 ☐
☐ 1.00	153	Goku Energy Blast!	U	3.00 ☐
☐ 1.00	101	Goku Honor Duel!	U	3.00 ☐
☐ 3.90	237	Goku's Capturing Drill	R	8.50 ☐
☐ 1.00	108	Goku's Energy Defense	U	3.00 ☐
☐ 3.90	202	Goku's Lucky Break	R	8.50 ☐
☐ 3.90	231	Goku's Mixing Drill	R	8.00 ☐
☐ 0.25	25	Goku's Physical Attack	C	1.30 ☐
	248	Goku's Plan	URF	21.50 ☐
☐ 0.25	24	Goku's Surprise Attack	C	1.20 ☐
☐ 0.25	48	Goku's Touch	C	1.20 ☐
	247	Goku's Truce	URF	22.50 ☐
☐ 4.00	205	Grabbing the Tail	R	8.00 ☐
☐ 4.00	195	Hero Advantage	R	8.00 ☐
☐ 0.25	17	Hidden Power Level	C	1.30 ☐
☐ 0.25	33	It's the Little Things That Matter	C	1.20 ☐
☐ 1.00	79	King Kai Training	U	3.00 ☐
☐ 1.00	88	King Kai Uniform	U	3.00 ☐
☐ 3.80	238	King Kai's Calming	R	8.00 ☐
☐ 1.00	167	Krillin (level 1)	X	
		Krillin (level 1HT)	XF	4.50 ☐
☐ 1.00	168	Krillin (level 2)	X	
☐ 1.00	169	Krillin (level 3)	X	
☐ 4.00	215	Krillin's Drill	R	8.50 ☐
☐ 1.00	113	Krillin's Energy Attack	U	3.00 ☐
☐ 4.00	216	Krillin's Energy Disk	R	8.00 ☐

RARITY KEY C = Common U = Uncommon R = Rare VR = Very Rare UR = Ultra Rare F = Foil card X = Fixed/standard in all decks

REGULAR	#	Card name	Rarity	FOIL
1.00	112	Krillin's Physical Defense	U	3.00
	249	Medic Kit	URF	17.50
1.00	149	Meditation Drill	U	3.00
1.00	90	Mother's Touch	U	3.00
1.00	176	Nappa (level 1)	X	
	185	Nappa (level 1HT)	XF	4.50
1.00	177	Nappa (level 2)	X	
1.00	178	Nappa (level 3)	X	
3.90	206	Nappa's Blinding Flare	R	8.00
1.00	120	Nappa's Energy Aura	U	3.00
1.00	121	Nappa's Physical Resistance	U	3.00
0.25	5	Orange Arm Bar	C	1.20
1.00	146	Orange Body Shifting Drill	U	3.00
1.00	142	Orange Energy Drill	U	3.00
3.90	234	Orange Focusing Drill	R	8.00
0.25	51	Orange Hip Throw	C	1.20
0.25	53	Orange Holding After Takedown	C	1.20
1.00	151	Orange Joint Restraint Drill	U	3.00
0.25	4	Orange Leg Sweep	C	1.20
1.00	126	Orange Lifting Drill	U	3.00
0.25	52	Orange Neck Restraints	C	1.20
1.00	134	Orange Off-Balancing Drill	U	3.00
0.25	2	Orange One Knuckle Punch	C	1.20
0.25	50	Orange Shoulder Throw	C	1.20
1.00	137	Orange Spontaneous Drill	U	3.00
0.25	1	Orange Standing Fist Punch	C	1.20
1.00	130	Orange Tripping Drill	U	3.00
0.25	3	Orange Two Knuckle Punch	C	1.20
0.25	49	Orange Wrist Flex Takedown	C	1.20
1.00	161	Piccolo (level 1)	X	
	180	Piccolo (level 1HT)	XF	3.40
1.00	162	Piccolo (level 2)	X	
1.00	163	Piccolo (level 3)	X	
1.00	155	Piccolo Defense Drill	U	3.00
1.00	103	Piccolo Honor Duel!	U	3.00
1.00	154	Piccolo Sidestep!	U	3.00
1.00	109	Piccolo's Energy Attack	U	3.00
3.90	212	Piccolo's Flight	R	8.00
1.00	110	Piccolo's Physical Defense	U	3.00
3.80	213	Plant Two Saibaimen	R	8.00
3.90	207	Power Gifting	R	8.00
1.00	97	Power Up More!	U	3.00
1.00	98	Power Up the Most!	U	3.00
0.25	22	Power Up!	C	1.20
1.00	170	Raditz (level 1)	X	
	183	Raditz (level 1HT)	XF	4.50
1.00	171	Raditz (level 2)	X	
1.00	172	Raditz (level 3)	X	

REGULAR	#	Card name	Rarity	FOIL
3.90	219	Raditz Energy Burst	R	8.00
1.00	117	Raditz Energy Wall	U	3.00
3.90	210	Raditz Flying Kick	R	8.00
1.00	102	Raditz Honor Duel!	U	3.00
1.00	118	Raditz Physical Defense	U	3.00
0.25	47	Raditz Total Defense	C	1.20
0.25	58	Red Back Kick	C	1.20
1.00	144	Red Coordination Drill	U	3.00
0.25	10	Red Elbow Strike	C	1.20
0.25	55	Red Front Kick	C	1.20
1.00	128	Red Knee Pick Drill	U	3.00
0.25	54	Red Knee Strike	C	1.20
0.25	8	Red Knife Hand	C	1.20
4.00	232	Red Life Attack Drill	R	8.00
0.25	6	Red Lunge Punch	C	1.20
0.25	9	Red Palm Heel Strike	C	1.20
1.00	124	Red Penetrating Defense Drill	U	3.00
1.00	148	Red Pressure-Point Drill	U	3.00
1.00	140	Red Reading Drill	U	3.00
0.25	7	Red Reverse Punch	C	1.20
1.00	132	Red Rolling Drill	U	3.00
0.25	57	Red Round Kick	C	1.20
0.25	56	Red Side Kick	C	1.20
1.00	139	Red Wrist Control Drill	U	3.00
3.90	193	Respect the Spirit	R	8.00
4.00	217	Ribs Broken	R	8.00
1.00	78	Roshi Training	U	3.00
4.00	239	Roshi's Calming	R	8.50
4.00	243	Saibaimen (level 1)	R	8.00
4.00	244	Saibaimen (level 2)	R	8.00
4.00	245	Saibaimen (level 3)	R	8.00
4.00	246	Saibaimen (level 4)	R	8.00
4.00	198	Saiyan Appraisal Maneuver	R	8.50
0.25	18	Saiyan Arm Throw	C	1.20
1.00	81	Saiyan Armor	U	3.00
4.00	197	Saiyan Battle Terms	R	8.00
0.25	45	Saiyan City Destruction	C	1.20
1.00	95	Saiyan Energy Aura	U	3.00
1.00	94	Saiyan Energy Blast	U	3.00
1.00	92	Saiyan Energy Defense	U	3.00
1.00	91	Saiyan Energy Throw	U	3.00
0.25	19	Saiyan Full Spin Kick	C	1.20
4.00	196	Saiyan Honor Quest	R	8.00
1.00	93	Saiyan Mental Energy Attack	U	3.00
0.25	21	Saiyan Neck Hold	C	1.20
4.00	236	Saiyan Power Drill	R	8.00
0.25	20	Saiyan Pressure Punch	C	1.20
1.00	96	Saiyan Sweeping Defense	U	3.00

REGULAR	#	Card name	Rarity	FOIL
1.00	80	Saiyan Training	U	3.00
4.00	203	Saiyan Truce Card	R	8.00
0.25	43	Senzu Bean	C	1.20
0.25	39	Straining Ankle Smash Move	C	1.20
0.25	38	Straining Arm Drag Move	C	1.20
0.25	40	Straining Energy Defense Move	C	1.20
0.25	36	Straining Fake Left Move	C	1.20
0.25	41	Straining Head Lock Move	C	1.20
0.25	34	Straining Off-Balancing Move	C	1.20
0.25	35	Straining Penetrating Attack Move	C	1.20
0.25	42	Straining Rolling Escape Move	C	1.20
0.25	37	Straining Tripping Move	C	1.20
4.00	192	Teaching the Unteachable Forces Observation	R	8.50
3.90	208	Terrible Wounds	R	8.00
4.00	201	The Tail Grows Back	R	8.00
0.25	32	The Untroubled Mind is Focused	C	1.20
1.00	82	Tien (level 1)	U	3.00
1.00	83	Tien (level 2)	U	3.00
4.00	211	Tien Mind Reading Trick	R	8.00
1.00	114	Tien's Energy Defense	U	3.00
0.25	27	Tien's Physical Attack	C	1.20
3.90	226	T-Rex Defense	R	8.50
3.90	227	T-Rex Offense	R	8.50
3.90	218	Unexpected Allies	R	8.00
4.00	194	Unselfish Behavior is Best	R	8.00
1.00	173	Vegeta (level 1)	X	
	184	Vegeta (level 1HT)	XF	3.90
1.00	174	Vegeta (level 2)	X	
1.00	175	Vegeta (level 3)	X	
4.00	241	Vegeta's Dragon Ball Capture	R	8.00
1.00	119	Vegeta's Energy Blast	U	3.00
0.25	28	Vegeta's Physical Stance	C	1.20
4.00	228	Vegeta's Plans	R	8.50
4.00	221	Vegeta's Quickness Drill	R	8.00
3.80	220	Vegeta's Stance	R	8.50
1.00	100	Vegeta's Surprise Defense	U	3.00
4.00	240	Vegeta's Trick	R	8.00
1.00	106	Yajirobe (level 1)	U	3.00
1.00	107	Yajirobe (level 2)	U	3.00
1.00	122	Yajirobe's Energy Attack	U	3.00
0.25	29	Yajirobe's Physical Attack	C	1.20
1.00	84	Yamcha (level 1)	U	3.00
1.00	85	Yamcha (level 2)	U	3.00
1.00	115	Yamcha's Energy Attack	U	3.00
1.00	116	Yamcha's Physical Defense	U	3.00

Dragonball Z • Promos

Score (a division of Playoff Corp.)

Promo cards for *Dragonball Z* appeared in *Scrye* and were given away at Burger King. **Trunks Saga** preview cards were available in **Frieza Saga** packs.

REGULAR	#	Card name	Set	FOIL
6.00	BK5	Frieza's Spirit	BurgKng	
6.70	BK6	Super Saiyan Goku's Power	BurgKng	
6.00	BK7	Vegeta's Smirk	BurgKng	
6.50	P1	Goku (level 4)	Saiyan	20.25
5.80	P2	Piccolo (level 4)	Saiyan	17.75
5.00	P3	Vegeta (level 4)	Saiyan	20.00
6.50	P4	Raditz (level 4)	Saiyan	20.00
8.50	P5	Gohan (level 4)	Saiyan	20.00
5.90	P6	Krillin (level 4)	Saiyan	16.25
5.00	P7	Nappa (level 4)	Saiyan	18.00
13.50	P4	error dupe of P1	Saiyan	
11.00	115	error dupe of P7	Saiyan	
7.00	P1	King Cold Smiles	Frieza	
7.00	P2	The Luck of Trunks	Frieza	

REGULAR	#	Card name	Set	FOIL
8.00	P3	Frieza's Luck	Frieza	
8.00	P4	Frieza's Rage	Frieza	
7.00	P5	Hero Anger	Frieza	
7.00	P6	Trunks did What?	Frieza	
7.00	P7	The Talking Ends Here!	Frieza	
7.00	P8	Good Advice	Frieza	
7.00	P9	Just Kidding	Frieza	
7.00	P10	"No, really?"	Frieza	
0.50	Pre1	The Talking Ends Here!	Fr-TrnksC	1.40
0.50	Pre2	Just Kidding	Fr-TrnksC	1.40
1.10	Pre3	"No, Really Drill?"	Fr-TrnksU	3.80
1.10	Pre4	Good Advice	Fr-TrnksU	3.80
4.00	Pre5	The Luck of Trunks	Fr-TrnksR	10.00
4.00	Pre6	Trunks did What?	Fr-TrnksR	10.00

REGULAR	#	Card name	Set	FOIL
6.00	BK1	Goku's Attack	BurgKng	
6.00	BK2	Gohan's Anger	BurgKng	
6.00	BK3	Krillin's Trick	BurgKng	
6.00	BK4	Piccolo's Revenge	BurgKng	

RARITY KEY C = Common U = Uncommon R = Rare VR = Very Rare UR = Ultra Rare F = Foil card X = Fixed/standard in all decks

Dragonball Z • *Frieza Saga*

Score (a division of Playoff Corp.) • Released **October 2000**

125 cards in set • **IDENTIFIER:** ⬡ symbol at lower left corner

- Booster packs contain 9 cards
- Booster displays contain 36 boosters

Several months after the successful initial release, Score advanced the *Dragonball Z* story with *Frieza Saga*, a booster packs-only expansion.

Where *Saiyan Saga* focused on physical combat, *Frieza Saga* pays more attention to enhancing energy combat. New allies for players appear in several cards each, including Frieza, Guldo, Jeice, Dodora, Dende, Chiatzu, and Captain Ginyu. Score hoped to inspire new themed decks featuring the unique powers of Guldo, Namcha, Tien, Nail, and Yajirobe.

The *Saiyan Saga* release also features brighter foil designs than found in the previous release. In advance of this release, Score developed a tournament kit for retailers featuring holographic foil cards for all participants and special orange warrior swords for winners.

With *Frieza Saga*, **Dragonball Z** became the longest-running game to come out from Score's parent company, Playoff Corp. It had previously released one-shot CCGs **One-on-One Hockey Challenge** and **Hyborian Gates** (through its now-defunct Cardz label). — *John Jackson Miller*

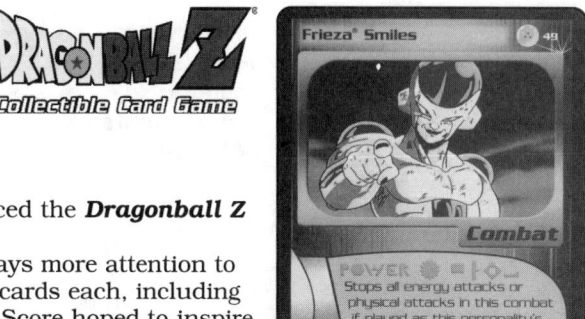

Look closely
The **Dragonball Z** CCG should not be confused with the **Dragonball Z** expansion to **Ani-Mayhem**.

Set (125 cards)	150.00
Foil Set	762.50
Booster Display Box	100.00
Booster Pack	3.50

You will need 14 nine-pocket pages to store this set. (7 doubled up)

	REGULAR #	Card name	Rarity	FOIL
☐ 0.25	26	A Hospital Stay	C	1.70 ☐
☐ 0.25	36	Alien Anger!	C	1.70 ☐
☐ 1.00	84	Black Driving Leg Thrust	U	3.90 ☐
☐ 1.00	72	Black Energy Stamina Drill	U	3.90 ☐
☐ 1.00	80	Black Erasing Drill	U	3.90 ☐
☐ 1.00	83	Black Right Cross	U	3.90 ☐
☐ 1.00	68	Black Stamina Drill	U	3.90 ☐
☐ 1.00	82	Black Standing Position	U	3.90 ☐
☐ 4.00	112	Black Swift Elbow Strike	R	11.00 ☐
☐ 1.00	70	Blue Allies Drill	U	3.90 ☐
☐ 0.25	7	Blue Energy Implosion	C	1.70 ☐
☐ 4.00	99	Blue Energy Outburst	R	11.00 ☐
☐ 4.00	98	Blue Jolting Shoulder Wheel	R	10.00 ☐
☐ 1.00	66	Blue Mental Drill	U	3.90 ☐
☐ 1.00	42	Bulma (level 2)	U	3.90 ☐
☐ 4.00	120	Bulma's Scouter	R	10.00 ☐
☐ 1.00	50	Captain Ginyu Poses	U	3.90 ☐
☐ 1.00	74	Captain Ginyu Reversal Drill	U	3.90 ☐
☐ 1.00	43	Chiaotzu (level 3)	U	3.90 ☐
☐ 1.00	64	Chiaotzu's Glaring Power	U	3.90 ☐
☐ 1.00	41	Chi-Chi (level 2)	U	3.90 ☐
☐ 1.00	77	Dende Healing Drill	U	3.90 ☐
☐ 1.00	48	Dende the Unlikely Hero (level 1)	U	3.90 ☐
☐ 4.00	105	Dende's Help	R	10.00 ☐
☐ 1.00	38	Dodoria (level 1)	U	3.90 ☐
☐ 1.00	53	Dodoria Boom	U	3.90 ☐
☐ 0.25	31	Dodoria Energy Attack	C	2.00 ☐
☐ 0.25	32	Dodoria Flames of Fury	C	2.00 ☐
☐ 1.00	87	Earth Dragon Ball Capture	U	3.80 ☐
☐ 0.25	13	Empowerment!	C	2.00 ☐
☐ 4.20	122	Focusing Is Everything	R	10.50 ☐
☐ 1.00	49	Frieza Smiles	U	3.90 ☐
	124	Frieza the Master	URF	47.50 ☐
☐ 1.00	60	Frieza's Blasting Wave	U	3.90 ☐
☐ 1.00	79	Frieza's Influencing Drill	U	3.90 ☐
☐ 5.00	95	Gohan (level 4)	R	10.00 ☐
☐ 1.00	78	Gohan Anger Drill	U	3.90 ☐
☐ 1.00	56	Gohan's Anger Blast	U	3.90 ☐

	Card name		Type	Rarity	Price
☐ 0.25	15	Gohan's Erupting Strike		C	1.60 ☐
☐ 4.10	114	Gohan's Stomp		R	10.50 ☐
☐ 5.70	93	Goku On Namek (level 4)		R	11.50 ☐
	125	Goku the Super Saiyan (level 4)		URF	50.00 ☐
☐ 0.25	14	Goku's Destroying Force		C	1.60 ☐
☐ 1.00	54	Goku's Energy Absorption		U	3.90 ☐
☐ 4.00	116	Goku's Quickness		R	10.00 ☐
☐ 0.25	29	Goku's Sudden Outburst		C	1.60 ☐
☐ 5.00	106	Goku's Super Saiyan Blast!		R	11.00 ☐
☐ 1.00	45	Guldo (level 1)		U	3.90 ☐
☐ 1.00	46	Guldo (level 2)		U	3.90 ☐
☐ 1.00	47	Guldo (level 3)		U	3.90 ☐
☐ 1.00	55	Guldo's Time Drill		U	3.90 ☐
☐ 1.00	88	Hero Enraged!		U	3.90 ☐
☐ 4.10	101	Hero Teamwork Drill		R	10.50 ☐
☐ 4.00	103	Human Technology		R	10.00 ☐
☐ 1.00	37	Jeice (level 1)		U	3.90 ☐
☐ 1.00	52	Jeice Comet Attack		U	3.90 ☐
☐ 1.00	51	Jeice Shouts		U	3.90 ☐
☐ 0.25	33	Jeice Spiral Flash		C	1.60 ☐
☐ 1.00	75	Jeice's Style Drill		U	3.90 ☐
☐ 4.00	100	Kami as your ally		R	10.50 ☐
☐ 4.00	113	Kami Fades		R	10.00 ☐
☐ 6.00	90	Krillin On Namek (level 4)		R	12.00 ☐
☐ 1.00	57	Krillin's Anger Blast		U	3.90 ☐
☐ 1.00	81	Krillin's Power Block		U	3.90 ☐
☐ 4.00	111	Krillin's Power Tap		R	11.00 ☐
☐ 4.20	119	Mommy's Coming Dear		R	10.00 ☐
☐ 5.00	117	Nail Inspired (level 2)		R	10.00 ☐
☐ 5.00	96	Nail The Namekian (level 1)		R	12.00 ☐
☐ 5.00	110	Nail the Namekian Hero (level 2)		R	12.00 ☐
☐ 4.70	91	Nappa Restored (level 4)		R	10.00 ☐
☐ 1.00	62	Nappa's Visionary Attack		U	3.90 ☐
☐ 1.00	67	Orange Destruction Drill		U	3.90 ☐
☐ 0.25	2	Orange Energy Manipulation		C	1.60 ☐
☐ 0.25	28	Orange Fist Detonation		C	1.60 ☐
☐ 1.00	71	Orange Leg Drill		U	3.90 ☐
☐ 0.25	1	Orange Lightning Strike		C	1.60 ☐
☐ 0.25	3	Orange Power Attack		C	1.60 ☐
☐ 0.25	27	Orange Wrist Motion		C	1.60 ☐
☐ 5.70	94	Piccolo (level 4)		R	11.50 ☐
☐ 4.00	115	Piccolo's Stomp		R	10.50 ☐
☐ 4.00	107	Piccolo's Wisdom		R	10.00 ☐
☐ 4.20	104	Power		R	11.25 ☐

	Card name		Type	Rarity	Price
☐ 0.25	19	Powerful Followers		C	1.70 ☐
☐ 5.70	92	Raditz Restored (level 4)		R	10.00 ☐
☐ 0.25	8	Recoome Energy Throw		C	1.70 ☐
☐ 1.00	65	Red Energy Defense Drill		U	3.90 ☐
☐ 0.25	5	Red Energy Disk		C	1.60 ☐
☐ 0.25	6	Red Energy Disk Blasting		C	1.60 ☐
☐ 0.25	4	Red Energy Reverse		C	1.60 ☐
☐ 4.00	123	Red Foot Jolt		R	10.00 ☐
☐ 1.00	73	Red Implosion Drill		U	3.90 ☐
☐ 1.00	69	Red Phasing Drill		U	4.20 ☐
☐ 0.25	10	Saiyan Concussion Punch		C	1.70 ☐
☐ 0.25	12	Saiyan Energy Focus		C	1.70 ☐
☐ 0.25	34	Saiyan Energy Spike		C	1.70 ☐
☐ 0.25	35	Saiyan Focusing Power		C	1.70 ☐
☐ 0.25	9	Saiyan Jolting Kick		C	1.70 ☐
☐ 0.25	11	Saiyan Neck Strike		C	1.70 ☐
☐ 0.25	18	Saiyan Thought Blast		C	1.70 ☐
☐ 0.25	24	Straining Back Striking Move		C	1.70 ☐
☐ 0.25	21	Straining Blasting Move		C	1.70 ☐
☐ 0.25	23	Straining Defense Move		C	1.70 ☐
☐ 0.25	22	Straining Energy Move		C	1.70 ☐
☐ 0.25	20	Straining Floating Attack Move		C	1.70 ☐
☐ 4.00	97	Straining Force Positioning Move		R	10.50 ☐
☐ 0.25	25	Straining Lightning Strike Move		C	1.70 ☐
☐ 1.00	86	Straining Neck Move		U	3.90 ☐
☐ 1.00	85	Straining Outburst Move		U	3.90 ☐
☐ 4.00	118	The Plan		R	10.50 ☐
☐ 4.00	121	This Too Shall Pass		R	10.50 ☐
☐ 1.00	39	Tien (level 3)		U	3.90 ☐
☐ 0.25	16	Tien's Jolting Aura		C	1.70 ☐
☐ 1.00	58	Tien's Power Burst		U	3.90 ☐
☐ 0.25	30	Time's a Warrior's Tool		C	1.70 ☐
☐ 1.00	76	Vegeta Getting Bashed Drill		U	3.90 ☐
☐ 5.00	89	Vegeta On Namek (level 4)		R	10.00 ☐
☐ 1.00	61	Vegeta's Anger Stash		U	3.90 ☐
☐ 0.25	17	Vegeta's Jolting Slash		C	1.70 ☐
☐ 4.00	109	Villain's Sacrifice		R	12.00 ☐
☐ 4.20	102	Villain's Teamwork Drill		R	11.50 ☐
☐ 1.00	44	Yajirobe the Hero (level 3)		U	3.90 ☐
☐ 1.00	63	Yajirobe's Gifting Drill		U	3.90 ☐
☐ 1.00	40	Yamcha (level 3)		U	3.90 ☐
☐ 4.00	108	Yamcha's Good Wishes		R	10.00 ☐
☐ 1.00	59	Yamcha's Skillful Defense		U	3.90 ☐

RARITY KEY C = Common U = Uncommon R = Rare VR = Very Rare UR = Ultra Rare F = Foil card X = Fixed/standard in all decks

Dredd

Round Table Productions imported in the U.S. by **Pinnacle Entertainment Group**
First set, *Limited Edition*, released in the U.S. **August 2000**
300 cards in set

- Starter "patrol" decks contain 60 cards; starter displays contain 10 starters
- Booster packs contain 11 cards; booster displays contain 36 boosters

Designed by **Robin Elliot, Simon Lucas,** and **Jeremy Norton**

Based on the comic-book adventures of Judge Dredd, **Dredd** is set in Mega City One, the vast metropolis that spans the eastern coast of the United States in the middle of the Third Millennium. Players take the part of senior Judges commanding a squad of junior Judges through the crime-ridden blocks of the future.

A player wins by collecting 20 Prestige points or five Commendations or containing all four Dark Judges. A player can also lose the game if all his Judges are discarded or "wasted" (i.e., killed), if he is ever required to draw a card from his deck and cannot, or if his whole team of junior Judges is suspended due to Demerits.

A player starts the game with up to five Judges with a combined total Experience of no more than 40, as well as a hand of seven cards (decks must have a minimum of 40 cards, no maximum). **Dredd** is played in a sequence of four Phases that make up a single Turn. Each Phase has one to five Rounds during which each player will get a chance to play cards. Each Turn is run by the Duty Judge, which is the player that starts the Turn with the most Prestige (each starting junior Judge is worth a number of Prestige). The Duty Judge manages each Round of each Phase.

While **Dredd** catches the flavor of the Judge Dredd comics, it also unfortunately catches too much of the flavor of *NYPD Blue, Law & Order,* or any one of a half-dozen cop shows. The subject matter could have received far more exciting treatment; as it stands, some Judge Dredd fans will find it to be an interesting game, but others will find it Guilty of Inciting Boredom. — *James A. Mishler*

Concept	●●●○○
Gameplay	●●●●○○
Card art	●●○○○
Player pool	●●○○○

Set (300 cards)	127.00
Starter Display Box	75.00
Booster Display Box	87.00
Starter Deck	9.30
Booster Pack	2.80

You will need **34** nine-pocket pages to store this set. (17 doubled up)

PROMO CARDS

Card name	Type	Price
☐ Get Mean	promo	2.00
☐ Hold It Creep	promo	2.00

Card name	Type	Rarity	Price
1			
☐ A Cry for Help	Incident	R	2.50
☐ A Disturbing Vision	Incident	C	0.20
☐ A Time of Crisis	Event	R	2.50
☐ Abandoned Subway Station	Scene	C	0.20
☐ Abdicate Responsibility	Incident	C	0.20
☐ Above And Beyond	Event	R	2.50
☐ Aggro Dome	Scene	V	0.40
☐ Ambush	Incident	R	2.50
☐ Anonymous Tip off	Incident	C	0.20
2			
☐ Apocalypse War Remembered	Event	R	2.50
☐ Armed Robbery	Crime	C	0.20
☐ Arson	Crime	C	0.20
☐ Assault	Crime	V	0.40
☐ Awaiting Developments	Incident	R	2.50
☐ Bad Attitude	Incident	C	0.20
☐ Baptism Of Fire	Event	R	2.50
☐ Batgliders	Resource	U	0.70
☐ Benji Doonan	Perp	U	0.70
3			
☐ Bike Cannon	Incident	U	0.70
☐ Binoculars	Resource	C	0.20
☐ Birdie Lie Detector	Resource	U	0.70
☐ Blackmail	Crime	C	0.20
☐ Block Mania	Event	R	2.50
☐ Block War	Crime	C	0.20
☐ Body Sharking	Crime	C	0.20
☐ Botanic Gardens	Scene	C	0.20

Card name	Type	Rarity	Price
☐ Burden Of Responsibility	Incident	C	0.20
4			
☐ Captain Skank	Perp	V	0.40
☐ Case Closed	Incident	R	2.50
☐ Central Park	Scene	C	0.20
☐ Change Of Priorities	Incident	U	0.70
☐ Citi-Def Squad	Perp	U	0.70
☐ Cling Net	Resource	C	0.20
☐ Cloning Experiment	Incident	R	2.50
☐ Commanding Presence	Incident	C	0.20
☐ Concentrated Aggression	Resource	C	0.20
5			
☐ Confession	Incident	U	0.70
☐ Contract Murder	Crime	C	0.20
☐ Cool Under Fire	Incident	C	0.20
☐ Cover All Exits	Incident	C	0.20
☐ Crimeblitz	Event	U	0.70
☐ Crimewave	Incident	R	2.50
☐ Crisis of Confidence	Incident	R	2.50
☐ Cry Of the Werewolf	Event	R	2.50
☐ Cyril J. Ratfinkle	Perp	U	0.70
6			
☐ Death	Perp	U	0.70
☐ Deja Vu	Resource	R	2.50
☐ Denise Delacroix	Perp	U	0.70
☐ Disgrace To the Uniform	Incident	R	2.50
☐ Disintegrater	Incident	R	2.50
☐ Disorderly Behaviour	Crime	C	0.20
☐ Disregarding Authority	Incident	C	0.20
☐ Disused Warehouse	Scene	C	0.20
☐ Dr. James Julius Gold	Perp	U	0.70
7			
☐ Dream Palace	Scene	C	0.20
☐ Dredd's Comportment	Resource	R	3.80
☐ Droidnapping	Crime	C	0.20
☐ Dubious Accolade	Incident	R	2.50
☐ Edwin The Confessor	Perp	R	4.50
☐ Emergency Med Pack	Resource	C	0.20
☐ Evaluating All Options	Incident	C	0.20
☐ Exemplary Cadet Record	Incident	U	0.70
☐ Exo Men	Perp	V	0.40

Card name	Type	Rarity	Price
8			
☐ Extreme Prejudice	Event	R	2.50
☐ F. Loyd Mazny Complex	Scene	C	0.20
☐ Fear	Perp	R	4.50
☐ Feeling Lucky	Incident	C	0.20
☐ Fellow Judge	Incident	R	4.50
☐ Fire	Perp	R	2.50
☐ Firm Grasp of the Law	Resource	R	2.50
☐ Forced Confession	Incident	R	2.50
☐ Forensic Squad	Resource	R	3.50
9			
☐ Foresight	Resource	R	3.50
☐ Forever Towers	Scene	V	0.40
☐ Freeze Lawbreaker	Incident	R	4.50
☐ Future Shock Syndrome	Incident	R	4.50
☐ Gila Munja Assassin	Perp	R	4.50
☐ Glitzy Pullhouse Nightclub	Scene	C	0.20
☐ Going It Alone	Incident	U	0.70
☐ Good Connections	Incident	C	0.20
☐ Gunrunning	Crime	C	0.20
10			
☐ Heat Seeker Rounds	Resource	R	2.50
☐ Hellfire Club	Perp	V	0.40
☐ Hidden Talents	Incident	R	2.50
☐ Hideout	Incident	U	0.70
☐ Hi-Ex Rounds	Resource	R	2.50
☐ High Speed Chase	Incident	R	2.50
☐ Hunk Smythe	Perp	U	0.70
☐ H-Wagon	Resource	U	0.70
☐ I Am the Law	Incident	U	0.70
11			
☐ I Know My Duty	Incident	C	0.20
☐ Illegal Assembly	Crime	V	0.40
☐ Illegal Boing	Crime	C	0.20
☐ Impersonating A Judge	Crime	C	0.20
☐ In My Sights	Incident	R	2.50
☐ Inadmissable Evidence	Incident	R	2.50
☐ Increased Accountability	Incident	C	0.20
☐ Increased Awareness	Resource	R	2.50
☐ Iron Discipline	Resource	C	0.20

RARITY KEY **C** = Common **U** = Uncommon **R** = Rare **F** = Foil card **V** = Vital

Card name	Type	Rarity	Price
12			
☐ Iso Cube Breakout	Incident	C	0.20
☐ Judge Adams	Judge	U	0.70
☐ Judge Agee	Judge	V	0.40
☐ Judge Anderson	Judge	R	6.00
☐ Judge Bram	Judge	V	0.40
☐ Judge Castillo	Judge	U	0.70
☐ Judge Churchill	Judge	U	0.70
☐ Judge Cicero	Judge	V	0.40
☐ Judge Cole	Judge	U	0.70
13			
☐ Judge Corey	Judge	U	0.70
☐ Judge Dawson	Judge	V	0.40
☐ Judge Degaulle	Judge	R	5.50
☐ Judge Dekker	Judge	R	5.50
☐ Judge Diablo	Judge	V	0.40
☐ Judge Dredd	Judge	V	0.50
☐ Judge Ecks	Judge	U	0.70
☐ Judge Edwards	Judge	U	0.70
☐ Judge Egmont	Judge	U	0.70
14			
☐ Judge Garcia	Judge	U	0.70
☐ Judge Geller	Judge	R	5.50
☐ Judge Giant	Judge	V	0.40
☐ Judge Goon	Judge	R	5.50
☐ Judge Harrison	Judge	V	0.40
☐ Judge Hershey	Judge	R	5.50
☐ Judge Holme	Judge	V	0.40
☐ Judge Janus	Judge	U	0.70
☐ Judge Jordan	Judge	U	0.70
15			
☐ Judge Karyn	Judge	R	5.50
☐ Judge Kazinski	Judge	V	0.40
☐ Judge Kennedy	Judge	V	0.40
☐ Judge Korkoran	Judge	U	0.70
☐ Judge Lincoln	Judge	V	0.40
☐ Judge March	Judge	V	0.40
☐ Judge Mccall	Judge	V	0.40
☐ Judge Morphy	Judge	R	5.50
☐ Judge Murder	Crime	C	0.20
16			
☐ Judge Ocks	Judge	V	0.40
☐ Judge Omar	Judge	R	5.50
☐ Judge Perrier	Judge	U	0.70
☐ Judge Petersen	Judge	U	0.70
☐ Judge Phillips	Judge	U	0.70
☐ Judge Powell	Judge	V	0.40
☐ Judge Rashid	Judge	U	0.70
☐ Judge Rheiner	Judge	U	0.70
☐ Judge Rosenberg	Judge	U	0.70
17			
☐ Judge Shenker	Judge	R	5.50
☐ Judge Souster	Judge	U	0.70
☐ Judge Sutton	Judge	V	0.40
☐ Judge Tokuda	Judge	U	0.70
☐ Judge Vega	Judge	V	0.40
☐ Judge Warren	Judge	V	0.40
☐ Judge Young	Judge	V	0.40
☐ Judge's Daystick	Resource	C	0.20
☐ Junior	Perp	R	4.50
18			
☐ Justice Dept PR Team	Resource	R	2.50
☐ Juve Uprising	Event	R	3.50
☐ Kevin O'Neill	Perp	U	0.70
☐ Kidnapping	Crime	V	0.40
☐ Laser Cannon	Incident	U	0.70
☐ Latent Psi	Event	R	3.50
☐ Lawmaster Self Destruct	Incident	C	0.20
☐ Lawrod Rifle	Resource	R	2.50
☐ League Of Fatties	Perp	V	0.40
19			
☐ Leroy Tamerlain	Perp	U	0.70
☐ Let's Rock	Incident	U	0.70
☐ Link	Perp	V	0.40
☐ List Of Suspects	Incident	R	2.50

Card name	Type	Rarity	Price
☐ Loonies	Perp	V	0.40
☐ Losing Support	Incident	U	0.70
☐ Lucky Shot	Incident	C	0.20
☐ Manta Prowl Tank	Resource	R	2.50
☐ Manta Strike	Incident	R	2.50
20			
☐ Mantis Syndicate	Perp	V	0.40
☐ Mapping the Mind	Resource	R	3.50
☐ Marksmanship	Resource	R	3.50
☐ Marlon Shakespeare	Perp	V	0.40
☐ Mass Breakout	Incident	R	3.50
☐ Mass Murder	Crime	V	0.40
☐ Max Normal	Incident	R	2.50
☐ MCBS Newscast	Incident	U	0.70
☐ Mean Machine	Perp	R	3.50
21			
☐ Med Centre	Scene	C	0.20
☐ Med Squad	Resource	R	2.50
☐ Mega City 5000	Event	R	4.80
☐ Mega City's Finest	Event	U	0.70
☐ Mega Mall	Scene	V	0.40
☐ Megway Sliproad	Scene	U	0.70
☐ Memorial Promenade	Scene	C	0.20
☐ Merc Ramsey	Perp	U	0.70
☐ Messing With Your Mind	Incident	R	3.50
22			
☐ Mortis	Perp	R	4.50
☐ Mr. Nobody	Perp	U	0.70
☐ Murder	Crime	V	0.40
☐ Museum Of 20th Century	Scene	U	0.70
☐ Natural Born Killer	Incident	R	2.50
☐ Neon Knights	Perp	U	0.70
☐ New Legal Interpretations	Incident	C	0.20
☐ No Way Judge	Incident	C	0.20
☐ Orlok	Perp	R	3.50
23			
☐ Otto Sump's Ugly Clinic	Scene	U	0.70
☐ Pa	Perp	R	4.50
☐ Paperwork	Incident	C	0.20
☐ Pat Wagon	Resource	C	0.20
☐ Pattern Of Behaviour	Incident	U	0.70
☐ Pedway	Scene	C	0.20
☐ Perilous Gantry	Scene	V	0.40
☐ Political Ambitions	Event	R	3.50
☐ Poor Filing	Incident	C	0.20
24			
☐ Possession of Comics	Crime	C	0.20
☐ Possession of Explosives	Crime	C	0.20
☐ Possession of Firearms	Crime	C	0.20
☐ Pressure Pad Trap	Incident	U	0.70
☐ Problem Block	Incident	C	0.20
☐ Professional Rivalry	Incident	R	4.50
☐ Psi Judge	Resource	U	0.70
☐ Psionic Amplifier	Incident	R	4.50
☐ Psychic Duelling	Resource	R	4.50
25			
☐ Psychic Strike	Incident	R	4.50
☐ Psychological Profiling	Event	R	4.50
☐ Puglies	Perp	R	3.50
☐ Quick Thinking	Incident	C	0.20
☐ Rad Pit	Scene	C	0.20
☐ Rathole Eatery	Scene	C	0.20
☐ Reckless Gambit	Incident	R	3.50
☐ Red Light Gang	Perp	V	0.40
☐ Reliable Informant	Incident	R	2.50
26			
☐ Reliving the Past	Incident	R	2.50
☐ Rex Peters	Perp	U	0.70
☐ Rex Squeers	Perp	U	0.70
☐ Rico Dredd	Perp	R	5.80
☐ Ricochet Rounds	Resource	R	2.50
☐ Rigid Self Control	Resource	C	0.20
☐ Robosurgeon	Perp	U	0.70
☐ Robot Repair Centre	Scene	C	0.20
☐ Rogue Lawmaster	Perp	R	2.50

Card name	Type	Rarity	Price
27			
☐ Running Out Of Options	Incident	U	0.70
☐ Scarface Joe Levine	Perp	V	0.40
☐ Scrawling	Crime	C	0.20
☐ Secondment	Incident	R	2.50
☐ Sector House Haunting	Event	R	2.50
☐ Sedgewick & Partners	Incident	R	3.50
☐ Shaky Pete Coco	Perp	U	0.70
☐ Shuggy Hall	Scene	U	0.70
☐ Sid Skid	Perp	V	0.40
28			
☐ SJS Emergency Powers	Incident	R	2.50
☐ SJS Scrutiny	Incident	U	0.70
☐ SJS Team	Resource	R	3.50
☐ Sky Rail Platform	Scene	C	0.20
☐ Slick Willy	Perp	U	0.70
☐ Smokatorium	Scene	C	0.20
☐ Spacer	Perp	V	0.40
☐ Spikes' Harvey Rotten	Perp	U	0.70
☐ Spirit of Co-operation	Event	R	2.50
29			
☐ Spit Gun	Incident	R	4.50
☐ Spot Check	Incident	C	0.20
☐ Statue of Judgement	Scene	V	0.40
☐ Statue of Liberty	Scene	V	0.40
☐ Street Judge Patrol	Resource	R	3.50
☐ Stumm Cannon	Resource	U	0.70
☐ Stump Gun	Incident	C	0.20
☐ Suicide Box	Incident	R	2.50
☐ Superior Firepower	Incident	C	0.20
30			
☐ Supreme Sacrifice	Incident	R	3.50
☐ Tactical Thinking	Resource	R	2.50
☐ Taking Cover	Incident	C	0.20
☐ Tapping	Crime	V	0.40
☐ Tek Field Test	Resource	R	2.50
☐ Tek Judge	Resource	U	0.70
☐ Temporary Assignment	Incident	R	2.50
☐ The Benefit of Experience	Resource	R	2.50
☐ The Bugglys	Perp	U	0.70
31			
☐ The Coming Darkness	Event	R	2.50
☐ The Executioner	Perp	U	0.70
☐ The Fink	Perp	U	0.70
☐ The Jong Family	Perp	V	0.40
☐ The Long Walk	Event	U	0.70
☐ The New You	Scene	C	0.20
☐ The Phantom	Perp	V	0.40
☐ The Rabbit Hutch	Scene	V	0.40
☐ The Respect of Your Peers	Incident	C	0.20
32			
☐ The White Cliffs Of Dover	Scene	C	0.20
☐ Thorough Investigation	Incident	U	0.70
☐ Threatening Behaviour	Crime	C	0.20
☐ To Cage The Beast	Event	U	0.70
☐ Total Amateur	Incident	C	0.20
☐ Traffic Duty	Incident	R	2.50
☐ Troggies	Perp	U	0.70
☐ Tween Block Plaza	Scene	V	0.40
☐ Umpty Bagging	Crime	V	0.40
33			
☐ Un-American Graffiti	Event	R	2.50
☐ Unauthorised Mental Scan	Incident	C	0.20
☐ Under Pressure	Incident	C	0.20
☐ Vandalism	Crime	V	0.40
☐ Vindicated	Incident	R	2.50
☐ Voice Print	Incident	U	0.70
☐ Wally Squad Report	Incident	R	2.50
☐ Warning Shot	Incident	C	0.20
☐ Whitey U	Perp	U	0.70
34			
☐ You Won't Take Me Alive	Incident	R	2.50
☐ Zoom-Tube Station	Scene	C	0.20
☐ Zoot Smiley	Perp	U	0.70

RARITY KEY C = Common U = Uncommon R = Rare F = Foil card V = Vital

Dune

Wizards of the Coast (Five Rings)/Last Unicorn Games • First set, *Eye of the Storm*, released **October 1997**
301 cards in set • **IDENTIFIER: Card reads © 1997**

- Starter decks contain 60 cards; starter displays contain 12 starters
- Booster packs contain 15 cards; booster displays contain 36 boosters

Dune is based, no surprise here, on Frank Herbert's epic series, and the mechanics reflect the books' complexity.

Players represent the heads of minor Houses aspiring to become a Great House and join the Landsraad. A player begins the game with a homeworld card (one of six major sponsoring powers), the Dune card Subdued (facedown), and two decks: An Imperial Deck (10+cards), which contains powerful, but unique cards; and a House Deck (40+ cards), which contains weaker, but non-unique cards. To win (and become a Great House), a player must have 10 Favor and 10 Spice (melange).

The player may play House cards simply by paying the cost on the card, but Imperial cards must be Petitioned, via an auction. If the player wins, the Imperial card enters play, but if the opponent wins, he pays the difference between the bid and starting cost of the card and the card, does not enter play. An interesting twist is that a player may play cards facedown and out of game, accruing one Solaris (money) per turn, allowing players to purchase expensive cards over time.

There are four types of combat: Arbitration (political), Battle (mass combat), Intrigue, and Duels. The first two can gain a player Favor, the last two, Solaris, although permanent loss to your opponent is rare. Spice is gained from card effects either directly, or by acquiring it from the Guild Horde, which begins with eight Spice.

The game is a good simulation of the series, being complex and rather slow-moving. The player must wade through many unfamiliar terms, and, without a thorough knowledge of the books, it is difficult to understand, let alone get into, the game.

Last Unicorn Games, better known for its *Star Trek Role-Playing Game*, was purchased by Wizards of the Coast in the spring of 2000, giving fans hope that the *Dune* CCG would find a new life at Wizards of the Coast. But Decipher took away the *Star Trek* license in a coup announced that August at Gen Con, and, in December, Wizards' owner Hasbro laid off all but one member of the Last Unicorn team and closed the offices. — *Michael Greenholdt*

Concept	●●○○○
Gameplay	●●●○○
Card art	●●●○○
Player pool	●○○○○

Set (301 cards)	136.00
Starter Display Box	79.50
Booster Display Box	80.00
Starter Deck	8.50
Booster Pack	2.60

You will need 34 nine-pocket pages to store this set. (17 doubled up)

Card name	Type	Rarity	Price
Aborted Raid	Tactic	U	0.45
Accomplished Blademaster	Enhncmt	U	0.45
Act of Cowardice	Venture	U	0.45
Albrecht Nim	Ally	R	2.00
Alliance Negotiations	Event	C	0.10
Ambitious Enterprise	Tactic	C	0.10
Arclight Assault	Venture	C	0.10
Armistice Treaty	Event	U	0.45
Arms Training	Enhncmt	C	0.10
Arrakeen	Fief	X	0.25
Assassin Cohort	Personnel	C	0.15
Assembly of Lords	Event	R	4.00
Atreides Battalion	Personnel	U	0.45
Atreides Propagandist	Aide	R	2.00
Back to the Wall	Tactic	R	3.50
Badge of the Lion	Enhncmt	U	0.45
Baliset	Equipment	C	0.15
Baron Vladimir Harkonnen	Ally	X	1.30
Battle Captive	Tactic	R	3.90
Battle Fatalities	Tactic	R	2.50
Bene Tleilax Accord	Charter	R	1.50
Best Blade	Venture	C	0.10
Betrayal	Venture	R	2.50
Blade Parry	Tactic	R	3.40
Blinding Defense	Tactic	C	0.10
Bodies in the Well	Tactic	R	3.00
Brilliant Rhetoric	Tactic	U	0.45

Card name	Type	Rarity	Price
Buyout Agreement	Tactic	R	3.50
Caladan	Fief	X	1.00
Caladanan Exports	Charter	X	1.00
Carryall	Equipment	C	0.10
Carthag	Fief	X	0.25
Chani	Ally	X	1.30
Chaumurky	Venture	R	3.40
CHOAM Delegate	Aide	C	0.10
CHOAM Directorship	Charter	R	1.40
CHOAM Dividends	Event	C	0.10
CHOAM Insolvency	Event	R	3.30
CHOAM League	Personnel	C	0.10
CHOAM Recess	Event	U	0.45
CHOAM Restructuring	Event	U	0.45
Claim Initiative	Tactic	C	0.10
Coins under the Table	Venture	C	0.10
Collusion	Tactic	R	3.00
Column of Smoke	Tactic	C	0.10
Command Center	Enhncmt	C	0.15
Commander Aramsham	Ally	X	1.30
Compel Surrender	Venture	R	3.00
Coriolis Storm	Event	C	0.10
Count Hasimir Fenring	Ally	X	1.30
Covert Venture	Tactic	R	2.80
Crysknife	Equipment	R	2.30
Desert-Rigged Ornithopter	Equipment	C	0.15
Device Malfunction	Tactic	C	0.10
Diplomacy	Enhncmt	C	0.10
Diplomatic Initiative	Tactic	U	0.45
Doctor Kynes	Ally	R	1.50
Dorvin Saeth	Ally	X	1.30
Dr. Wellington Yueh	Ally	R	1.50
Dueling Honors	Tactic	U	0.45

Card name	Type	Rarity	Price
Duke Leto Atreides	Ally	X	2.00
Duncan Idaho	Ally	R	1.50
Dune	Fief	X	0.25
Dune Charter Renewal	Event	R	4.00
Dune Smuggler	Aide	C	0.15
Early Procurement	Tactic	R	3.00
Ecological Testing Site	Enhncmt	U	0.60
Emperor's Outrage	Event	U	0.45
Engineering Corps	Personnel	R	3.00
Exchange Proxy	Venture	C	0.10
Exchange Seat	Charter	R	1.40
Exchange Suspension	Tactic	R	3.00
Exchange Violation	Tactic	R	3.00
Expeditionary Invasion	Venture	R	3.30
False Allegations	Tactic	C	0.10
False Diversion	Tactic	C	0.10
Famous Battle Account	Tactic	U	0.45
Fanaticism	Tactic	C	0.10
Feigned Unreadiness	Tactic	C	0.10
Feyd Rautha	Ally	X	1.30
Financial Reward	Tactic	U	0.45
Flip-Dart	Equipment	R	3.00
Focused Gambit	Tactic	C	0.10
Fold-Space Complications	Tactic	R	3.80
Forbidden Match	Venture	C	0.10
Forbidden Zone	Fief	X	1.00
Formal Discharge	Venture	C	0.10
Formal Impressment	Tactic	R	3.00
Formidable Patron	Enhncmt	C	0.15
Fremen Battalion	Personnel	U	0.45
Fremen Naib	Aide	R	3.30
Full Reverend Mother	Enhncmt	R	4.00
Gaius Helen Mohiam	Ally	X	1.30

Card name	Type	Rarity	Price
Garrison	Enhncmt	C	0.10
Gauvir Mucca	Ally	X	1.30
Giedi Prime	Fief	X	1.00
Glossu Rabban	Ally	X	1.30
Gom Jabbar	Equipment	R	3.10
Guard Commander	Aide	C	0.10
Guild Entourage	Personnel	U	0.45
Guild Heighliner	Equipment	R	3.90
Guild Navigator	Aide	R	4.00
Guild Stockpiling	Event	U	0.45
Guild Surplus	Event	U	0.45
Gurney Halleck	Ally	X	1.30
Hand of God	Enhncmt	C	0.15
Harkonnen Battalion	Personnel	U	0.45
Harkonnen Industries	Charter	X	1.00
Harkonnen Slavemaster	Aide	R	2.60
Harvesting Contract	Charter	R	1.40
Heat Sickness	Enhncmt	U	0.45
Heir Designate	Enhncmt	R	3.50
Hereditary Claim	Enhncmt	C	0.15
Hidden Reserves	Tactic	R	4.00
High Steersman	Enhncmt	R	4.00
Historic Acquisition	Venture	R	3.80
Hoarding Tithe	Event	U	0.45
Holding Tithes	Event	C	0.10
Hostage Option	Tactic	R	3.00
House Agent	Aide	C	0.10
House Assassin	Aide	U	0.45
House Atomics	Venture	R	4.00
House Battalion	Personnel	C	0.10
House Mentat	Aide	U	0.45
House Physician	Aide	C	0.10
House Shield Generator	Equipment	R	3.00
House Swordmaster	Aide	U	0.45
House Turmoil	Event	R	3.00
Hunter Seeker	Equipment	U	0.45
Iakin Nefud	Ally	R	1.50
Imperial Basin	Fief	X	0.25
Imperial Codex	Tactic	R	3.50
Imperial Conditioning	Enhncmt	U	0.45
Imperial Courtiers	Personnel	R	3.10
Imperial Favor	Event	C	0.10
Imperial Fete	Event	R	4.00
Imperial Intervention	Tactic	C	0.10
Imperial Recess	Tactic	U	0.45
Imperial Reprimand	Event	C	0.15
Imperial Revenues	Charter	X	1.00
Imperial Seal	Enhncmt	R	3.30
Imperial Suk School Profits	Charter	R	1.40
Implicate Traitor	Venture	C	0.10
Industrial Sabotage	Venture	U	0.45
Inert Poison	Tactic	R	4.00
Informal Induction	Venture	U	0.45
Intelligence Espionage	Tactic	C	0.10
Interests of Detente	Tactic	R	3.30
Invocation of Caste	Tactic	U	0.45
Irulan's Peace	Event	U	0.45
Jamis, Fremen Warrior	Ally	X	1.30
Jareh Benquait	Ally	R	1.30
Juice of Sapho	Enhncmt	C	0.15
Kaitain	Fief	X	1.00
Kindjal	Equipment	C	0.10
Knife Switch	Tactic	U	0.45
Knife Tip Shatters	Tactic	C	0.10
Korba	Ally	R	1.50
Lady Jessica	Ally	X	1.30
Lady Margot	Ally	X	1.30
Landsraad Coalition	Personnel	C	0.10
Landsraad Emissary	Aide	U	0.45
Landsraad Inquest	Event	U	0.45
Landsraad Summit	Event	R	3.00
Lasgun Rifle	Equipment	R	3.60
Levenbreche	Aide	R	2.40
Liquidation Measures	Venture	R	4.00
Liscia Theirese	Ally	R	1.50
Litany Against Fear	Venture	U	0.45
Long, Cold Night	Tactic	U	0.45
Low Morale	Tactic	C	0.10
Machines from Ix	Charter	R	1.40
Magnanimous Appeal	Tactic	U	0.45
Maker Hooks	Equipment	R	3.40
Marshalling of the Troops	Tactic	U	0.45
Master of Assassins	Enhncmt	U	0.45
Maula Pistol	Equipment	C	0.15
Mentat Analysis	Enhncmt	U	0.25
Mentat Precision	Tactic	U	0.45
Military Appropriations	Charter	R	2.50
Military Transport	Event	C	0.15
Missionaria Protectiva	Personnel	U	0.20
Moonlit Fray	Tactic	U	0.45
Naib's Countenance	Enhncmt	R	2.80
Oberon	Ally	X	2.00
Oil Lense Binoculars	Equipment	C	0.15
Order of the Sword	Enhncmt	U	0.45
Palace Keep	Enhncmt	U	0.45
Paul Atreides	Ally	X	1.30
Peer of the Realm	Enhncmt	U	0.50
Perilous Terrain	Tactic	U	0.45
Personal Shield	Equipment	C	0.10
Petitioning Delays	Event	C	0.10
Petitioning Savvy	Tactic	R	3.00
Petitioning Tithe	Tactic	R	3.50
Philanthropy Drive	Event	R	3.50
Piter de Vries	Ally	R	1.50
Pogrom	Venture	C	0.10
Poison Gas Tooth	Enhncmt	R	4.00
Poison Snooper	Equipment	C	0.15
Poisoned Blade	Tactic	R	3.80
Policy of Oppression	Venture	C	0.10
Powerful Ally	Tactic	U	0.45
Pre-Emptive Strike	Tactic	U	0.25
Predawn Ritual	Tactic	C	0.20
Prescience	Enhncmt	U	0.45
Prescience Shielding	Enhncmt	R	4.00
Prescience Trance	Venture	U	0.45
Princess Irulan	Ally	X	1.30
Priority Matter	Tactic	C	0.10
Proces Verbal	Venture	U	0.45
Production Bonus	Event	R	3.50
Production Setbacks	Tactic	C	0.10
Prophetic Vision	Venture	R	3.00
Provoke Insurgency	Venture	C	0.10
Public Defamation	Tactic	C	0.10
Quality Inspection	Tactic	R	3.50
Rachag Stimulants	Tactic	C	0.10
Recruitment Drive	Venture	C	0.10
Renegade Sister	Aide	R	3.50
Residual Poison	Enhncmt	R	3.50
Return to the Floor	Venture	C	0.10
Sabotage Device	Equipment	U	0.45
Salvaging Operation	Venture	R	3.00
Sand Scrub	Venture	U	0.45
Sandworm	Event	C	0.15
Sardaukar Battalion	Personnel	U	0.45
Scuttled Negotiation	Tactic	R	3.50
Secret Allegiance	Enhncmt	U	0.45
Secund-Elect	Tactic	U	0.45
Security Sweep	Tactic	C	0.10
Seismic Probes	Equipment	R	3.40
Shaddam IV	Ally	X	1.30
Sharing of Inner Lives	Venture	R	3.50
Shield Failure	Tactic	C	0.10
Shield Fighting	Enhncmt	U	0.45
Shigawire Bonds	Enhncmt	R	4.00
Sietch Community	Enhncmt	U	0.50
Silo Destruction	Venture	R	3.80
Sister Ramallo	Ally	R	1.50
Sisterhood Covenant	Charter	X	1.00
Slip-Tip	Equipment	U	0.45
Slow Attack	Tactic	C	0.10
Smuggler Activity	Event	U	0.45
Smuggler Bribes	Charter	R	1.40
Spacing Industries	Charter	R	1.30
Spice Addiction	Enhncmt	R	4.50
Spice Blow	Event	C	0.10
Spice Harvester	Equipment	C	0.10
Spice Mining Inspection	Event	R	4.00
Spice Trance	Venture	U	0.45
Spotter Control	Charter	R	1.40
Sterling Reputation	Tactic	U	0.45
Stilgar	Ally	X	1.30
Storm Hazard	Tactic	C	0.10
Stranglehold	Venture	U	0.40
Stunner	Equipment	U	0.45
Subterfuge	Enhncmt	C	0.10
Subvert Arrangement	Venture	U	0.60
Supply Tampering	Tactic	R	3.50
Surgical Strike	Venture	U	0.45
Surprise Assault	Tactic	U	0.45
Suspensor Technologies	Charter	R	1.40
Symbol of Authority	Equipment	R	3.60
Terrain Advantage	Tactic	R	3.50
Terrorism	Venture	U	0.45
The Minor Erg	Fief	X	0.25
The Open Bled	Fief	X	0.25
The Shadout Mapes	Ally	R	1.50
Thopter Outpost	Enhncmt	C	0.10
Thufir Hawat	Ally	R	1.50
Thumper	Equipment	R	2.60
Tiger Cunning	Tactic	U	0.45
Timed Drug	Enhncmt	R	4.00
Traverse Fold-Space	Venture	R	4.50
Trespass Accord	Charter	X	1.00
Truth Sayer	Enhncmt	R	3.80
Truth Saying	Venture	R	3.50
Tupile	Fief	X	1.00
Twilight Assault	Venture	C	0.10
Unforseen Difficulties	Tactic	U	0.45
Unprecedented Intercession	Venture	R	3.50
Usurp Holding	Venture	C	0.10
Valor	Enhncmt	C	0.10
Vanish without Trace	Tactic	U	0.45
Vendetta	Venture	R	3.00
Venomous Faith	Tactic	U	0.45
Voice Command	Venture	U	0.45
Waking Dream Premonition	Venture	U	0.45
Wallach IX	Fief	X	1.00
Water Rationing	Venture	C	0.15
Water Riot	Event	R	3.00
Weapon Misfire	Tactic	C	0.10
Weather Control	Charter	X	1.00
Weirding Combat	Enhncmt	U	0.45
Weirding Talent	Enhncmt	U	0.45
Weirding Way	Venture	U	0.45
Well-Placed Bribes	Tactic	C	0.10
Windtrap	Enhncmt	C	0.15
Windtrap Technologies	Charter	R	1.40
Witness Testimonial	Tactic	U	0.45

RARITY KEY C = Common U = Uncommon R = Rare VR = Very Rare UR = Ultra Rare F = Foil card X = Fixed/standard in all decks

Dune • Judge of the Change 1

Wizards of the Coast (Five Rings)/Last Unicorn Games
Released **February 1998**
61 cards in set • **IDENTIFIER: "Illus © 1998"**

- Booster packs contain 15 cards; booster displays contain 48 boosters
- Combo displays contain 36 boosters and 12 **Eye of the Storm** starters

Released using an "episode" format similar to Five Rings' Rolling Thunder, **Judge of Change** continues the story line from the first *Dune* novel. The three 61-card expansions actually form one normal-size expansion.

Each *Judge of the Change* release features a new Sponsor, all of them related to the blue-collar aspects of Dune. **Episode 1** introduces the Dune Smugglers, **Episode 2** the Spice Miner's Guild, and **Episode 3** the Water Seller's Union.

This set was released in booster packs only, but **Eye of the Storm** starter decks were offered in "combo" display packs with *Judge* boosters. — **Michael Greenholdt**

Set (61 cards)	77.00
Combo Display Box	65.00
Booster Display Box	70.00
Booster Pack	2.70

You will need **7** nine-pocket pages to store this set. (4 doubled up)

Card name	Type	Rarity	Price
Ancestral Provenance	Tactic	U	0.50
Arbiter Authority	Decree	R	2.30
Arbiter Proclamation	Tactic	C	0.15
Atreides House Guard	Personnel	U	0.50
Atreides Occupation	Event	U	0.50
Baraka	Aide	U	0.50
Casting Nets	Tactic	C	0.15
Certificate of Allegiance	Tactic	U	0.50
Change of Fief	Event	U	0.50
CHOAM Contract	Charter	R	2.30
Communinet Transmitter	Equipment	C	0.15
Conversion Contracts	Charter	X	1.50
Directed Retreat	Tactic	C	0.15
Dump Box Deployment	Venture	U	0.50
Dune Men	Personnel	C	0.15
Emperor's Truthsayer	Decree	R	2.30
Festival of the Harvest	Event	U	0.50

Card name	Type	Rarity	Price
Fremen Sietch Reserves	Personnel	U	0.50
Guild Spokesman	Aide	U	0.50
Harvester Pad	Enhancemt	U	0.50
Harvesting Summit	Event	X	1.50
Hebe	Ally	R	2.30
His Majesty's Fief	Decree	R	2.30
House Frigate	Equipment	U	0.50
Imperial Servant	Enhancemt	R	2.50
Intelligence Report	Tactic	R	2.30
Judge of the Change	Decree	X	3.00
Justice of the Great	Enhancemt	C	0.15
Learning of the Wise	Enhancemt	C	0.15
Lt. Aneirin	Ally	X	2.00
Matter of Kanly	Venture	U	0.50
Mess'r Coss	Ally	X	2.00
Omri B'rrican	Ally	X	2.00
Pardee	Ally	X	2.00
Pillar of Fire	Tactic	U	0.50
Plasteel Industries	Charter	R	2.30
Prana-Bindu Suspension	Tactic	R	3.50
Prayers of the Righteous	Enhancemt	C	0.15
Pyon Elder	Aide	C	0.15

Card name	Type	Rarity	Price
Pyon Labor Force	Personnel	C	0.15
Pyon Village	Enhancemt	C	0.15
Razzia	Venture	U	0.50
Sandmaster	Aide	U	0.50
Schlag Hide Exports	Charter	R	2.00
Shield Wall Bases	Charter	X	1.50
Silo Pillaging Spice Raid	Tactic	C	0.15
Siridar Tithes	Charter	R	2.30
Sister Baruna	Ally	R	2.80
Spice Dogs	Personnel	C	0.15
Spice Driver Spice	Aide	U	0.50
Spice Infusion	Enhancemt	R	2.00
Spotter Flight	Venture	U	0.50
Straight-Line Computation	Tactic	C	0.15
The Great Flat	Fief	X	1.00
The Shield Wall	Fief	X	1.00
Tivor Manx	Ally	X	2.00
Ultra-Fast Coagulation	Enhancemt	R	3.00
Valor of the Brave	Enhancemt	C	0.15
Vessel of Karama	Venture	U	0.50
Whale Fur Industries	Charter	R	2.50
Wormsign	Event	U	0.50

Dune • Judge of the Change 2

Wizards of the Coast (Five Rings)/Last Unicorn • Released **April 1998** • **61** cards in set

- Booster packs contain 15 cards; booster displays contain 48 boosters
- Combo displays contain 36 boosters and 12 **Eye of the Storm** starters

Set (61 cards)	77.00
Combo Display Box	65.00
Booster Display Box	70.00
Booster Pack	2.70

You will need **7** nine-pocket pages to store this set. (4 doubled up)

Card name	Type	Rarity	Price
Amtal Accord	Venture	U	0.50
Arrakeen Patriarch	Aide	C	0.15
Arrakeen Water Facilities	Charter	X	1.50
Arsunt	Fief	X	1.00
Assassin's Honor	Tactic	C	0.15
Atreides Sector-Guard	Aide	U	0.50
Botanical Testing Grant	Charter	R	2.30
Carthag Engineering	Charter	R	2.30
Cesar "La" Layre	Ally	R	2.30
Contract Negotiations	Event	U	0.50
Culmination of Dark Things	Event	U	0.50
Cutteray	Equipment	U	0.50
Emrys Jago	Ally	R	2.50
Fakhir Zirut	Ally	X	2.00
Fortune of Al-Lat	Venture	U	0.50
Glacier Mining Operation	Charter	X	1.50
Glacier Refinery	Enhancemt	U	0.50

Card name	Type	Rarity	Price
Governor of Arrakis	Decree	X	3.00
Guild Bank Arbiter	Decree	R	2.30
Guild Bank Representative	Enhancemt	R	2.30
Guild Shuttle	Equipment	R	3.00
Harkonnen Sleeper	Aide	U	0.50
Harkonnen Sleeper Troop	Personnel	U	0.50
Ice Riggers	Personnel	C	0.15
Infraction of the Change	Tactic	R	2.30
Ionesco Valdeshar	Ally	X	2.00
Kanly Omissia	Enhancemt	R	2.50
Kulon Husbandry	Charter	R	2.00
Lida Banfi	Ally	X	2.00
Lingar Bewt	Ally	X	2.00
Mantene Principia	Tactic	C	0.15
Mark of the Drowned Man	Venture	U	0.50
Noble Born	Enhancemt	C	0.15
Northern Polar Sink	Fief	X	1.00
Period of Truce	Event	U	0.50
Petitioning Coup	Tactic	U	0.50
Petitioning Retribution	Event	U	0.50
Prana-Bindu Conditioning	Enhancemt	C	0.15
Precept of Istislah	Venture	U	0.50

Card name	Type	Rarity	Price
Rapier	Equipment	C	0.15
Ritual Combat	Tactic	R	2.30
Scars of Remembrance	Tactic	C	0.15
Semuta Addiction	Enhancemt	C	0.15
Shifting Tides	Tactic	U	0.50
Siridar Governorship	Charter	R	2.30
Soaks	Personnel	C	0.15
Sponsored Funding	Charter	R	2.30
Stillsuit	Equipment	C	0.15
Strategic Positioning	Tactic	C	0.15
Strategy Delegation	Personnel	C	0.15
Support of the Houses	Tactic	U	0.50
Tithing Clemency	Decree	R	2.30
Turn of Events	Venture	U	0.50
Unreckoned Numbers	Enhancemt	C	0.15
Water Despot	Decree	R	2.30
Water Marshal	Aide	U	0.50
Water Peddler	Aide	U	0.50
Water Shortage	Event	X	1.50
Water Tribute	Tactic	C	0.15
Weirding Embassy	Personnel	U	0.50
Zenzi Bewt	Ally	X	2.00

RARITY KEY **C** = Common **U** = Uncommon **R** = Rare **VR** = Very Rare **UR** = Ultra Rare **F** = Foil card **X** = Fixed/standard in all decks

Dune • Judge of the Change 3

Wizards of the Coast (Five Rings)/Last Unicorn • Released **June 1998** • **61** cards in set

- Booster packs contain 15 cards; booster displays contain 48 boosters
- Combo displays contain 36 boosters and 12 **Eye of the Storm** starters

Set (61 cards)	77.00	**You will need 7** nine-pocket pages to store this set. (4 doubled up)
Combo Display Box	65.00	
Booster Display Box	70.00	
Booster Pack	2.70	

Card name	Type	Rarity	Price
1			
Advance Team Reports	Tactic	C	0.15
Alliance Review Board	Charter	R	2.30
Approximation Analysis	Venture	U	0.50
Assembly Chairmanship	Charter	R	2.30
Attack Sinister	Tactic	C	0.15
Broken Arrangement	Tactic	U	0.50
Carthag Privateer	Aide	C	0.15
Commandeer Transport	Venture	U	0.50
Command Of the Padishah	Venture	U	0.50
2			
Desert Hawk	Aide	U	0.50
Diplomatic Settlement	Tactic	C	0.15
El-Sayal Rain of Sand	Event	U	0.50
Elacca Languor	Enhancemt	C	0.15
Esmar Tuek	Ally	X	2.00
Eyes of Ibad	Venture	U	0.50
False Wall South	Fief	X	1.00
Feige Treazal	Ally	X	2.00

Card name	Type	Rarity	Price
Free Trader Scout	Aide	U	0.50
3			
Ghost Caravan	Event	X	1.50
Grumman Fiat	Tactic	U	0.50
Guild Spy Ring	Personnel	U	0.50
Hagga Basin	Fief	X	1.00
Honorarium Familia	Enhancemt	C	0.15
House Subfief	Decree	R	2.30
Imperial Entourage	Personnel	U	0.50
Irrevocable Directorship	Decree	R	2.30
Kaldo Radij	Ally	R	3.00
4			
Mahdi	Enhancemt	R	3.00
Muddled Vision	Tactic	R	2.30
Name of the Great Mother	Tactic	U	0.50
Otheym	Ally	R	2.30
Padishah Lapdog	Aide	U	0.50
Passage Within	Venture	U	0.50
Pre-Spice Mass	Event	U	0.50
Private Consortium	Enhancemt	C	0.15
Proctor of Spies	Aide	U	0.50
5			
Production Quota	Event	U	0.50
Protracted Duration	Tactic	C	0.15
Pru-Door Scenario	Tactic	C	0.15

Card name	Type	Rarity	Price
Pundi Rice Market	Charter	R	1.90
Pyretic Conscience	Enhancemt	C	0.15
Quasi-Fief	Decree	X	1.50
Remy Egusku	Ally	X	2.00
Shadow Partnership	Charter	R	2.30
Shari-A Projects	Charter	R	2.30
6			
Smuggler Band	Personnel	C	0.15
Smuggler Battalion	Personnel	C	0.15
Smuggler Frigate	Equipment	R	3.30
Smuggler's Ambassador	Decree	R	2.30
Smuggling Revenues	Charter	X	1.50
Sonar Probe	Equipment	C	0.15
"Soo Soo" Nejhre	Ally	X	2.00
Staban Tuek	Ally	X	2.00
The Voice	Enhancemt	U	0.50
7			
Trafficking Partnership	Charter	X	1.50
Troop Carrier	Equipment	C	0.15
Umma	Enhancemt	R	3.00
Undermine Support	Tactic	R	2.30
Vanguard Battalion	Personnel	C	0.15
Wake Shot	Equipment	U	0.50
War of Assassins	Event	U	0.50

Dune • Thunder at Twilight 1

Wizards of the Coast (Five Rings)/Last Unicorn • Released **August 1998**

61 cards in set • **IDENTIFIER: "TaT" on card bottom**

- Booster packs contain 15 cards; booster displays contain 48 boosters
- Combo displays contain 36 boosters and 12 **Eye of the Storm** starters

Each of the three **Thunder at Twilight** mini-expansions upgraded one of the Great House Sponsor powers. **Thunder at Twilight 1** revamped House Atreides, giving the starting homeworld an advantage on Dune and increasing the power of the House's Allies.

Thunder at Twilight 2 deals with the Harkonnens, who move their headquarters to Dune, and adjusts the powers of their Allies. — **Michael Greenholdt**

Set (61 cards)	77.00	**You will need 7** nine-pocket pages to store this set. (4 doubled up)
Combo Display Box	65.00	
Booster Display Box	70.00	
Booster Pack	2.70	

Card name	Type	Rarity	Price
1			
Ancestral Provenance	Tactic	U	0.50'
Advance Base	Enhancemt	C	0.10
Arakeen Richece	Personnel	C	0.10
Atreides Brigade	Personnel	C	0.10
Backstabbing	Tactic	C	0.10
Battle-Rigged Thopter	Equipment	C	0.10
Benefice of Allegiance	Event	X	1.00
Bill of Particulars	Enhancemt	U	0.25
Black Market Enterprise	Charter	R	5.00
Capt. Trumane	Aide	R	1.50
2			
Dharva Glynn, Miner's Guild Counsel	Aide	X	1.50
Directorship Kickbacks	Charter	R	3.00
Distrans Message	Tactic	U	0.25
Drag-Line Outfit	Equipment	C	0.10
Ducal Signet Ring	Decree	R	2.00
Ducal Tithes	Charter	X	1.00
Duchy of Arrakis	Fief	X	2.00
Duke Leto Atreides	Ally	X	3.00
Duncan Idaho	Ally	R	2.00

Card name	Type	Rarity	Price
3			
Expert Command	Enhancemt	C	0.10
Fabled Crysknife	Equipment	U	0.25
Fencing Operation	Venture	R	5.00
Focus Awareness	Venture	U	0.25
Fog of Battle	Tactic	C	0.10
Grant Furlough	Venture	U	0.25
Gurney Halleck, Troubador-Warrior	Ally	X	2.00
Harvesting Oufit	Personnel	U	0.25
Honor Guard	Personnel	U	0.25
4			
Incite Hysteria	Tactic	C	0.10
Insert Watchers	Venture	R	1.50
Instrument of the Guild	Decree	R	2.00
Lady Jessica, Concubine of Duke Leto	Ally	X	2.50
Landsraad Spokesman	Enhancemt	R	1.50
Lighter Pilot	Aide	U	0.25
Lt. Fedor, Field Commander	Aide	R	1.50
Master of Arms, Guard Commander	Aide	C	0.10
Melee Training	Enhancemt	C	0.10
5			
Mobilization of the Tribes	Event	U	0.25
Open Battle	Venture	U	0.25
Paul Atreides, Son of Duke Leto	Ally	X	5.00

Card name	Type	Rarity	Price
Political Blackmail	Venture	U	0.25
Political Broadsiding	Tactic	C	0.10
Prevail in Kanly	Venture	R	3.00
Propaganda Corps	Personnel	C	0.10
Regional Assignment	Venture	U	0.25
Resurrect Alliance	Venture	R	3.00
6			
Revolt of the Dew Gatherers	Event	U	0.25
Sack of the Guild Bank	Event	U	0.25
Scorn of the Landsraad	Event	U	0.25
Shadowed Place	Enhancemt	R	2.00
Shaitan's Bargain	Tactic	U	0.25
Sister of the Azhar	Aide	U	0.25
Splintered Rock	Fief	X	1.00
Stake Reputation	Tactic	U	0.25
Storm Damage	Enhancemt	U	0.25
7			
Supply Routing	Tactic	C	0.10
Surpass Mining Quota	Venture	R	1.50
Tame Arrakis	Venture	X	1.00
Thopter Piloting	Enhancemt	C	0.10
Thufir Hawat, Master of Assassins	Ally	R	2.00
Unfulfill'd Plans	Tactic	U	0.25
Water Magnate	Decree	R	2.00

RARITY KEY C = Common U = Uncommon R = Rare VR = Very Rare UR = Ultra Rare F = Foil card X = Fixed/standard in all decks

Dune • Thunder at Twilight 2

Wizards of the Coast (Five Rings)/Last Unicorn • Released **September 1998** • **59** cards in set

- Booster packs contain 15 cards; booster displays contain 48 boosters
- Combo displays contain 36 boosters and 12 **Eye of the Storm** starters

Set (61 cards)	72.00
Combo Display Box	65.00
Booster Display Box	70.00
Booster Pack	2.70

You will need **7** nine-pocket pages to store this set. (4 doubled up)

Card name	Rarity	Price
Amtal Accord	U	0.50
Abduct Heir	R	2.00
Baron Vladimir Harkonnen	X	3.00
Baronial Tithes	X	1.00
Battle Company	C	0.10
Beyond the Faufreluches	R	1.50
Breeding Program	R	1.50
Cannon Artillery	C	0.10
Challenge by Combat	R	2.50
CHOAM Complot	C	0.10
Contract Audits	U	0.30
Counter Conspiracy	U	0.30
Czigo	R	2.00
Deep Training	C	0.10
Demolition Corps	C	0.10
Dew Harvesting	R	2.00
Disguised Sardaukar	C	0.10

Card name	Rarity	Price
Disguising Uniform	U	0.30
Dishonorable Knifework	U	0.30
Dr. Yueh, The Traitor	X	2.00
Dune Regency - Harkonnen	X	2.00
Exploit CHOAM Channels	U	0.30
Fall of a Great Rival	X	1.00
Fremen Band	R	3.00
Fremen Marauder	U	0.30
Gang Assailants	C	0.10
Glossu Rabban, Regent of Arrakis	X	1.00
Gross Soliciting	U	0.30
Guild Bank	U	0.30
Hazard Rates	U	0.30
Hellhounds	C	0.10
House Armory	U	0.30
Hydraulic Initiative Corps	U	0.30
Immobilize Urban Center	R	1.50
Imperial Suk	C	0.10
Jarmush	R	2.00
Lt. Kinet	R	2.00
Maneuver Pawn	U	0.30

Card name	Rarity	Price
Manual of the Friendly Desert	C	0.10
Medical Tampering	U	0.30
Mockery of CHOAM	U	0.30
Overwhelming Affluence	C	0.10
Piter de Vries	R	3.00
Political Combine	C	0.10
Political Conniving	C	0.10
Regent-Siridar	X	1.00
Scavenging Warfare	U	0.30
School Injunction	C	0.10
Schooled Adept	R	1.50
Scout 'Thopter	C	0.10
Seat of Governance	R	2.00
Shelter the Lisan Al-Gaib	R	2.00
Smuggling Compact	U	0.30
Styros	X	1.00
Suborn Suk	R	2.50
Tahaddi Al-Burhan	U	0.30
Thunder At Twilight	X	2.00
Tsimpo	X	1.00
Umman Kudu	X	1.00
Weather Scanner	U	0.30

Dune • Thunder at Twilight 3

Wizards of the Coast (Five Rings)/Last Unicorn • Released **October 1998** • **58** cards in set

- Booster packs contain 15 cards; booster displays contain 48 boosters
- Combo displays contain 36 boosters and 12 **Eye of the Storm** starters

The third of the three mini-expansion concerns House Carrino. Unlike Atreides and Harkonnen, Carrino stays off-world, taking up residence at Sardaukar. This homeworld allows the Corrino player to bring in one Corrino allegiance troop for free each turn. This house also does well in the Allies department, especially in defense and Arbitration.

Thunder at Twilight also introduces two new card types, Program Ventures and Nexus Events. Program Ventures are deployed at the beginning of the game and are revealed once the deployment conditions are met, giving the player some kind of bonus. Nexus Events are played like normal Events but have a continuing effect on the game, persisting for a number of turns equal to the Solaris needed to play them.

A further expansion, **Second Moon Rising**, never came out. — **Michael Greenholdt**

Set (58 cards)	68.00
Combo Display Box	62.00
Booster Display Box	68.00
Booster Pack	2.70

You will need **7** nine-pocket pages to store this set. (4 doubled up)

Card name	Rarity	Price
Assailant's Calling Card	C	0.10
Assertion of Mining Rights	U	0.30
Blood Feuding	U	0.30
Byzantine Corruption	R	1.50
CHOAM Company Flag	R	2.00
Cielago Distrans	C	0.10
Commander Aramsham	X	2.00
Corrupt Water Official	U	0.30
Culmination of Training	U	0.30
Division Leader	C	0.10
Dominate the Assembly	R	3.00
Dr Kynes	X	2.00
Emperor Shaddam IV	X	3.00
Emperor's Proxy	X	2.00
Enlist Survivor	U	0.30
Evangelina	R	2.00

Card name	Rarity	Price
Folk of Grabban and Pan	C	0.10
Gaius Helen Mohiam	X	2.00
Genetic Factor	U	0.30
Grant Quarter	C	0.10
Guild Security Division	U	0.30
High College	R	1.50
House Courier	C	0.10
Imperial Agents	C	0.10
Inititive Coup	R	3.00
Jarah Benquait	X	2.00
Kardif	R	2.00
Landing Field	C	0.10
Lasgun Turret	R	2.00
Letter of Credit	U	0.30
Lisan Al-Giab	R	3.00
Lost in the Desert	R	1.50
Lt. Erta	R	2.00
Marduk	R	2.50
PreOrdained Sequence	U	0.30
Program of Extermination	U	0.30
Relinquish Claim	C	0.10

Card name	Rarity	Price
Remain Invisible	R	1.50
Right of the Farfreluches	X	1.00
Sabotage	C	0.10
Salsa Secundus	X	1.00
Sarduakar Drop-Battalion	C	0.10
Sarduakar Mystique	U	0.30
Silo Trust Management	R	2.50
Skirmishing Spoils	R	1.50
Smuggler Underground	U	0.30
Spice Stockpiling	R	3.00
Sterilization Proceedings	U	0.30
The Assassins Handbook	C	0.10
The Broken Land	X	1.00
Transfer Orders	C	0.10
Traverse the Alam Al-Mithal	U	0.30
Troop Crusher	C	0.10
Truthtrance Inquest	U	0.30
Unleashed Horror	U	0.30
Usurp CHOAM Directorship	X	1.00
Watchdog	U	0.30
Witching Power	U	0.30

RARITY KEY   **C** = Common   **U** = Uncommon   **R** = Rare   **VR** = Very Rare   **UR** = Ultra Rare   **F** = Foil card   **X** = Fixed/standard in all decks

Eagles

Columbia Games • First set, **Waterloo**, released **December 1995**

300 cards in set • **600** variant versions

• Starter decks contain 60 cards; starter displays contain 12 starters

Designed by **Tom Dalgliesh**

   Eagles returns gaming to its long-lost roots: Napoleonic war gaming. *Eagles* deals specifically with the battles of the Hundred Days, Napoleon's last hurrah.

   The game contains rules for four battles, Ligny, Quatre Bras, Wavre, and the pivotal Waterloo, along with rules for running a campaign game based on all four battles. Like **Dixie**, Columbia's other CCG, *Eagles* brings history and gaming together in a very playable game that even those unaware of the history can enjoy.

   The *Eagles* game system is essentially a refined version of *Dixie* (refer to that listing) with a few notable changes. Most importantly, unlike *Dixie*, only one enemy position must be occupied to win the game. The Morale system is more defined, and is distinct from the Combat Value of the individual unit. Infantry also takes full advantage of Napoleonic tactics, adding rules for Line, Column, and Square formations.

   Also, the rules for Generals have been expanded from the *Dixie* system. Overall, the rules for *Eagles* are more complete and comprehensive that the early rules for *Dixie*, a factor which lends a more satisfying level of strategy to *Eagles* play than experienced in *Dixie* (**Gettysburg** showed no small influence from the developments in *Eagles*).

   Where *Dixie* had no rarities, *Eagles* had rarities than didn't matter. Every *Eagles* card was printed in three versions, a Gold, Silver, and Bronze, referring to the ink color in the box at the upper-left hand corner of the card. The manufacturer goes to great lengths to reassure players that the colors make no difference in gameplay, leading one to wonder why they bothered at all. So it's really just the 1995 equivalent of **Magic** foils, although the size of the set is such that if any obsessive player wants them all he'll need a whopping *900 cards!* (But full sets are still available from Columbia, so it's not quite as daunting a task as it sounds. Storing them is.)

   While the subject matter holds an honored position in the annals of adventure gaming, it unfortunately had limited appeal in the modern CCG market. *Eagles* also apparently had limited appeal to *grognards* (veteran gamers) — not a high enough lead factor, one might assume. A shame, for *Eagles* is an excellent way to introduce younger gamers to the joys of Napoleonic wargaming. — *James A. Mishler*

Concept	●●●●○
Gameplay	●●●●○
Card art	●●●○○
Player pool	●○○○○

British 23rd Foot (Royal Welsh Fuzileers)

Gold Set (300 cards)	300.00
Silver Set (300 cards)	150.00
Bronze Set (300 cards)	40.00
Starter Display Box	95.00
Starter Deck	8.00

You will need **34** nine-pocket pages to store one set. *(17 doubled up)*

You will need **100** nine-pocket pages to store all three sets. *(50 doubled up)*

G	S	B	#	CARD NAME	ARMY	TYPE	GOLD PRICE	SILVR PRICE	BRNZ PRICE
☐	☐	☐	1	L'Empereur Napoléon	French	General	2.00	1.00	0.50
☐	☐	☐	2	"Maréchal Soult, Duc de Dalmatia"	French	General	2.00	1.00	0.50
☐	☐	☐	3	Comte Drouot	French	General	2.00	1.00	0.50
☐	☐	☐	4	1e Grenadiers (Vieille Garde)	French	Infantry	2.00	1.00	0.50
☐	☐	☐	5	3e Grenadiers (Moyenne Garde)	French	Infantry	2.00	1.00	0.50
☐	☐	☐	6	1e Chasseurs (Vieille Garde)	French	Infantry	2.00	1.00	0.50
☐	☐	☐	7	3e Chasseurs (Moyenne Garde)	French	Infantry	2.00	1.00	0.50
☐	☐	☐	8	1e Tirailleurs (Jeune Garde)	French	Infantry	2.00	1.00	0.50
☐	☐	☐	9	1e Voltigeurs (Jeune Garde)	French	Infantry	2.00	1.00	0.50
☐	☐	☐	10	Dragons de L'Impératrice	French	Cavalry	2.00	1.00	0.50
☐	☐	☐	11	Lanciers Rouges	French	Cavalry	2.00	1.00	0.50
☐	☐	☐	12	Artillerie à pied (12p)	French	Artillery	2.00	1.00	0.50
☐	☐	☐	13	Artillerie à pied (12p)	French	Artillery	2.00	1.00	0.50
☐	☐	☐	14	Artillerie à pied (6p)	French	Artillery	2.00	1.00	0.50
☐	☐	☐	15	Artillerie à pied (6p)	French	Artillery	2.00	1.00	0.50
☐	☐	☐	16	Artillerie à cheval (6p)	French	Artillery	2.00	1.00	0.50
☐	☐	☐	17	Artillerie à cheval (6p)	French	Artillery	2.00	1.00	0.50
☐	☐	☐	18	"Mouton, Comte de Lobau"	French	General	2.00	1.00	0.50
☐	☐	☐	19	11e Régiment de Ligne	French	Infantry	2.00	1.00	0.50
☐	☐	☐	20	84e Régiment de Ligne	French	Infantry	2.00	1.00	0.50
☐	☐	☐	21	5e Régiment Léger	French	Infantry	2.00	1.00	0.50
☐	☐	☐	22	107e Régiment de Ligne	French	Infantry	2.00	1.00	0.50
☐	☐	☐	23	8e Régiment Léger	French	Infantry	2.00	1.00	0.50
☐	☐	☐	24	75e Régiment de Ligne	French	Infantry	2.00	1.00	0.50
☐	☐	☐	25	Artillerie à pied (6p)	French	Artillery	2.00	1.00	0.50
☐	☐	☐	26	Artillerie à pied (6p)	French	Artillery	2.00	1.00	0.50
☐	☐	☐	27	Maréchal Ney	French	General	2.00	1.00	0.50
☐	☐	☐	28	Comte d'Erlon	French	General	2.00	1.00	0.50
☐	☐	☐	29	54e Régiment de Ligne	French	Infantry	2.00	1.00	0.50
☐	☐	☐	30	105e Régiment de Ligne	French	Infantry	2.00	1.00	0.50
☐	☐	☐	31	13e Régiment Léger	French	Infantry	2.00	1.00	0.50
☐	☐	☐	32	51e Régiment de Ligne	French	Infantry	2.00	1.00	0.50
☐	☐	☐	33	46e Régiment de Ligne	French	Infantry	2.00	1.00	0.50
☐	☐	☐	34	25e Régiment de Ligne	French	Infantry	2.00	1.00	0.50
☐	☐	☐	35	8e Régiment de Ligne	French	Infantry	2.00	1.00	0.50
☐	☐	☐	36	95e Régiment de Ligne	French	Infantry	2.00	1.00	0.50
☐	☐	☐	37	7e Hussards	French	Cavalry	2.00	1.00	0.50
☐	☐	☐	38	Artillerie à pied (12p)	French	Artillery	2.00	1.00	0.50
☐	☐	☐	39	Artillerie à pied (6p)	French	Artillery	2.00	1.00	0.50
☐	☐	☐	40	Comte Reille	French	General	2.00	1.00	0.50
☐	☐	☐	41	61e Régiment de Ligne	French	Infantry	2.00	1.00	0.50
☐	☐	☐	42	108e Régiment de Ligne	French	Infantry	2.00	1.00	0.50
☐	☐	☐	43	1e Régiment Léger	French	Infantry	2.00	1.00	0.50
☐	☐	☐	44	1e Régiment de Ligne	French	Infantry	2.00	1.00	0.50
☐	☐	☐	45	11e Régiment Léger	French	Infantry	2.00	1.00	0.50
☐	☐	☐	46	12e Régiment Léger	French	Infantry	2.00	1.00	0.50
☐	☐	☐	47	93e Régiment de Ligne	French	Infantry	2.00	1.00	0.50
☐	☐	☐	48	100e Régiment de Ligne	French	Infantry	2.00	1.00	0.50

RARITY KEY   **B** = Bronze (Common)   **S** = Silver (Uncommon)   **G** = Gold (Rare)

G S B	#	CARD NAME	ARMY	TYPE	GOLD PRICE	SILVR PRICE	BRNZ PRICE
☐☐☐	49	6e Lanciers	French	Cavalry	2.00	1.00	0.50
☐☐☐	50	Artillerie à pied (6p)	French	Artillery	2.00	1.00	0.50
☐☐☐	51	Artillerie à pied (6p)	French	Artillery	2.00	1.00	0.50
☐☐☐	52	Maréchal Grouchy	French	General	2.00	1.00	0.50
☐☐☐	53	Comte Vandamme	French	General	2.00	1.00	0.50
☐☐☐	54	23e Régiment de Ligne	French	Infantry	2.00	1.00	0.50
☐☐☐	55	37e Régiment de Ligne	French	Infantry	2.00	1.00	0.50
☐☐☐	56	34e Régiment de Ligne	French	Infantry	2.00	1.00	0.50
☐☐☐	57	2e Suisse	French	Infantry	2.00	1.00	0.50
☐☐☐	58	12e Régiment de Ligne	French	Infantry	2.00	1.00	0.50
☐☐☐	59	33e Régiment de Ligne	French	Infantry	2.00	1.00	0.50
☐☐☐	60	9e Chasseurs à cheval	French	Cavalry	2.00	1.00	0.50
☐☐☐	61	Artillerie à pied (12p)	French	Artillery	2.00	1.00	0.50
☐☐☐	62	Artillerie à pied (6p)	French	Artillery	2.00	1.00	0.50
☐☐☐	63	Comte Gérard (W)	French	General	2.00	1.00	0.50
☐☐☐	64	30e Régiment de Ligne	French	Infantry	2.00	1.00	0.50
☐☐☐	65	63e Régiment de Ligne	French	Infantry	2.00	1.00	0.50
☐☐☐	66	59e Régiment de Ligne	French	Infantry	2.00	1.00	0.50
☐☐☐	67	48e Régiment de Ligne	French	Infantry	2.00	1.00	0.50
☐☐☐	68	111e Régiment de Ligne	French	Infantry	2.00	1.00	0.50
☐☐☐	69	50e Régiment de Ligne	French	Infantry	2.00	1.00	0.50
☐☐☐	70	6e Hussards	French	Cavalry	2.00	1.00	0.50
☐☐☐	71	Artillerie à pied (6p)	French	Artillery	2.00	1.00	0.50
☐☐☐	72	Artillerie à pied (6p)	French	Artillery	2.00	1.00	0.50
☐☐☐	73	Comte Exelmans	French	General	2.00	1.00	0.50
☐☐☐	74	1e Hussards	French	Cavalry	2.00	1.00	0.50
☐☐☐	75	1e Lanciers	French	Cavalry	2.00	1.00	0.50
☐☐☐	76	5e Dragons	French	Cavalry	2.00	1.00	0.50
☐☐☐	77	4e Dragons	French	Cavalry	2.00	1.00	0.50
☐☐☐	78	Artillerie à cheval (6p)	French	Artillery	2.00	1.00	0.50
☐☐☐	79	Artillerie à cheval (6p)	French	Artillery	2.00	1.00	0.50
☐☐☐	80	Kellermann, Comte de Valmy	French	General	2.00	1.00	0.50
☐☐☐	81	2e Dragons	French	Cavalry	2.00	1.00	0.50
☐☐☐	82	2e Carabiniers	French	Cavalry	2.00	1.00	0.50
☐☐☐	83	1e Cuirassiers	French	Cavalry	2.00	1.00	0.50
☐☐☐	84	5e Cuirassiers	French	Cavalry	2.00	1.00	0.50
☐☐☐	85	Artillerie à cheval (6p)	French	Artillery	2.00	1.00	0.50
☐☐☐	86	Artillerie à cheval (6p)	French	Artillery	2.00	1.00	0.50
☐☐☐	87	Bossu Wood	French	Terrain	2.00	1.00	0.50
☐☐☐	88	Gemioncourt	French	Terrain	2.00	1.00	0.50
☐☐☐	89	Malerne Pond	French	Terrain	2.00	1.00	0.50
☐☐☐	90	Plancenoit	French	Terrain	2.00	1.00	0.50
☐☐☐	91	La Belle Alliance	French	Terrain	2.00	1.00	0.50
☐☐☐	92	Mon Plaisir	French	Terrain	2.00	1.00	0.50
☐☐☐	93	Ammo Depletion	French	Special	2.00	1.00	0.50
☐☐☐	94	Bayonet Charge	French	Special	2.00	1.00	0.50
☐☐☐	95	Rally	French	Special	2.00	1.00	0.50
☐☐☐	96	Double Grape	French	Special	2.00	1.00	0.50
☐☐☐	97	Ricochet Fire	French	Special	2.00	1.00	0.50
☐☐☐	98	Howitzer Fire	French	Special	2.00	1.00	0.50
☐☐☐	99	Fatigue	French	Special	2.00	1.00	0.50
☐☐☐	100	Panic	French	Special	2.00	1.00	0.50
☐☐☐	101	Battle Confusion	French	Special	2.00	1.00	0.50
☐☐☐	102	Battle Smoke	French	Special	2.00	1.00	0.50
☐☐☐	103	Lost Order	French	Special	2.00	1.00	0.50
☐☐☐	104	Late Reserves	French	Special	2.00	1.00	0.50
☐☐☐	105	Friendly Fire	French	Special	2.00	1.00	0.50
☐☐☐	106	Defection	French	Special	2.00	1.00	0.50
☐☐☐	107	Vive L'Empereur	French	Special	2.00	1.00	0.50
☐☐☐	108	Sappeurs	French	Special	2.00	1.00	0.50
☐☐☐	109	Grand Battery	French	Special	2.00	1.00	0.50
☐☐☐	110	Grand Charge	French	Special	2.00	1.00	0.50
☐☐☐	111	Duke of Wellington	AngDtch	General	2.00	1.00	0.50
☐☐☐	112	Willem, Prins van Oranje	AngDtch	General	2.00	1.00	0.50
☐☐☐	113	MG George Cook	AngDtch	General	2.00	1.00	0.50
☐☐☐	114	British 1st Foot Guards	AngDtch	Infantry	2.00	1.00	0.50
☐☐☐	115	British Coldstream Guards	AngDtch	Infantry	2.00	1.00	0.50
☐☐☐	116	KGL Horse Artillery (9p)	AngDtch	Artillery	2.00	1.00	0.50
☐☐☐	117	LG Karl von Alten	AngDtch	General	2.00	1.00	0.50
☐☐☐	118	British 73rd Foot	AngDtch	Infantry	2.00	1.00	0.50
☐☐☐	119	KGL 8th Line	AngDtch	Infantry	2.00	1.00	0.50
☐☐☐	120	Hannover Grubenhagen Infanterie	AngDtch	Infantry	2.00	1.00	0.50
☐☐☐	121	Nassau 1ste Infanterie	AngDtch	Infantry	2.00	1.00	0.50
☐☐☐	122	KGL Foot Artillery (9p)	AngDtch	Artillery	2.00	1.00	0.50
☐☐☐	123	LG Baron Perponcher-Sedlnitzky	AngDtch	General	2.00	1.00	0.50
☐☐☐	124	Nederlandse 27de Jager	AngDtch	Infantry	2.00	1.00	0.50
☐☐☐	125	Nassau 2de Infanterie 5C	AngDtch	Infantry	2.00	1.00	0.50
☐☐☐	126	Nederlandse Artillerie (6p)	AngDtch	Artillery	2.00	1.00	0.50
☐☐☐	127	LG Baron Chassé	AngDtch	General	2.00	1.00	0.50
☐☐☐	128	Nederlandsee Militie	AngDtch	Infantry	2.00	1.00	0.50
☐☐☐	129	Nederlandse 12de Infanterie	AngDtch	Infantry	2.00	1.00	0.50
☐☐☐	130	Artillerie à pied Belge (6p)	AngDtch	Artillery	2.00	1.00	0.50
☐☐☐	131	LG Lord Hill	AngDtch	General	2.00	1.00	0.50
☐☐☐	132	LG Sir Henry Clinton	AngDtch	General	2.00	1.00	0.50
☐☐☐	133	British 52nd Light (Oxfords)	AngDtch	Infantry	2.00	1.00	0.50
☐☐☐	134	KGL 1st Line	AngDtch	Infantry	2.00	1.00	0.50
☐☐☐	135	Hannover Osnabrück Landwehr	AngDtch	Infantry	2.00	1.00	0.50
☐☐☐	136	Royal Foot Artillery (9p)	AngDtch	Artillery	2.00	1.00	0.50
☐☐☐	137	British 23rd Foot (Royal Welsh)	AngDtch	Infantry	2.00	1.00	0.50
☐☐☐	138	British 54th (West Norfolk) Foot	AngDtch	Infantry	2.00	1.00	0.50
☐☐☐	139	Hannover Lauenberg Infanterie	AngDtch	Infantry	2.00	1.00	0.50
☐☐☐	140	Hannover Fußbatterie (6p)	AngDtch	Artillery	2.00	1.00	0.50
☐☐☐	141	LG Sir Charles Coleville	AngDtch	General	2.00	1.00	0.50
☐☐☐	142	Nederlandse 5de Oost-Indische	AngDtch	Infantry	2.00	1.00	0.50
☐☐☐	143	Nederlandse 15de Militie	AngDtch	Infantry	2.00	1.00	0.50
☐☐☐	144	1e Ligne Belge	AngDtch	Infantry	2.00	1.00	0.50
☐☐☐	145	Nederlandse Voet Artillerie (6p)	AngDtch	Artillery	2.00	1.00	0.50
☐☐☐	146	LG Sir Thomas Picton	AngDtch	General	2.00	1.00	0.50
☐☐☐	147	British 95th Rifles	AngDtch	Infantry	2.00	1.00	0.50
☐☐☐	148	British 42nd Foot (Black Watch)	AngDtch	Infantry	2.00	1.00	0.50
☐☐☐	149	Hannover Giffhorn Landwehr	AngDtch	Infantry	2.00	1.00	0.50
☐☐☐	150	Royal Foot Artillery (9p)	AngDtch	Artillery	2.00	1.00	0.50
☐☐☐	151	British 27th Foot (Inniskillings)	AngDtch	Infantry	2.00	1.00	0.50
☐☐☐	152	Hannover Verden Landwehr	AngDtch	Infantry	2.00	1.00	0.50
☐☐☐	153	Royal Foot Artillery (9p)	AngDtch	Artillery	2.00	1.00	0.50
☐☐☐	154	Herzog von Braunschweig	AngDtch	General	2.00	1.00	0.50
☐☐☐	155	Braunschweiger Avantgarde	AngDtch	Infantry	2.00	1.00	0.50
☐☐☐	156	Braunschweiger Leicht-Infanterie	AngDtch	Infantry	2.00	1.00	0.50
☐☐☐	157	Braunschweiger Linien-Infanterie	AngDtch	Infantry	2.00	1.00	0.50
☐☐☐	158	Braunschweiger Husaren	AngDtch	Cavalry	2.00	1.00	0.50
☐☐☐	159	Braunschweiger Fußbatterie (6p)	AngDtch	Artillery	2.00	1.00	0.50
☐☐☐	160	LG Paget, Earl of Uxbridge	AngDtch	General	2.00	1.00	0.50
☐☐☐	161	British 1st Life Guards	AngDtch	Cavalry	2.00	1.00	0.50
☐☐☐	162	British 2nd Dragoons (Scots Greys)	AngDtch	Cavalry	2.00	1.00	0.50
☐☐☐	163	KGL 1st Light Dragoons	AngDtch	Cavalry	2.00	1.00	0.50
☐☐☐	164	British 16th (Queen's) Dragoons	AngDtch	Cavalry	2.00	1.00	0.50
☐☐☐	165	British 7th (Queen's Own) Hussars	AngDtch	Cavalry	2.00	1.00	0.50
☐☐☐	166	KGL 1st Hussars	AngDtch	Cavalry	2.00	1.00	0.50
☐☐☐	167	British 13th Light Dragoons	AngDtch	Cavalry	2.00	1.00	0.50
☐☐☐	168	Hannover, Cumberland Husaren	AngDtch	Cavalry	2.00	1.00	0.50

After-market prices

You may notice that all **Eagles** cards have the same after-market price. That is, in part, because there are no rarities within the set and because every card in the set is still available for direct-order from the manufacturer, Columbia Games, both as singles and as sets. The three columns in our **Eagles** list indicate prices on the Bronze set, the Silver set, and the Gold set.

The same after-market factors apply to Columbia's Civil War CCG **Dixie** and its expansions, **Shiloh** and **Gettysburg**. Those games, however, do *not* have Gold, Silver, and Bronze versions of cards.

RARITY KEY B = Bronze (Common) S = Silver (Uncommon) G = Gold (Rare)

G	S	B	#	CARD NAME	ARMY	TYPE	GOLD PRICE	SILVR PRICE	BRNZ PRICE
☐	☐	☐	169	Nederlandse 1ste Karabiniers	AngDtch	Cavalry	2.00	1.00	0.50
☐	☐	☐	170	5e Dragons Belge	AngDtch	Cavalry	2.00	1.00	0.50
☐	☐	☐	171	Nederlandse 6de Huzaren	AngDtch	Cavalry	2.00	1.00	0.50
☐	☐	☐	172	Royal Horse Artillery (Howitzers)	AngDtch	Artillery	2.00	1.00	0.50
☐	☐	☐	173	Royal Horse Artillery (9p)	AngDtch	Artillery	2.00	1.00	0.50
☐	☐	☐	174	La Haie Sainte	AngDtch	Terrain	2.00	1.00	0.50
☐	☐	☐	175	Mont St. Jean	AngDtch	Terrain	2.00	1.00	0.50
☐	☐	☐	176	Hougoumont	AngDtch	Terrain	2.00	1.00	0.50
☐	☐	☐	177	Braine L'Alleud	AngDtch	Terrain	2.00	1.00	0.50
☐	☐	☐	178	Papelotte	AngDtch	Terrain	2.00	1.00	0.50
☐	☐	☐	179	Ohain Ridge	AngDtch	Terrain	2.00	1.00	0.50
☐	☐	☐	180	Bossu Wood	AngDtch	Terrain	2.00	1.00	0.50
☐	☐	☐	181	Quatre Bras	AngDtch	Terrain	2.00	1.00	0.50
☐	☐	☐	182	Cherry Woods	AngDtch	Terrain	2.00	1.00	0.50
☐	☐	☐	183	Ammo Depletion	AngDtch	Special	2.00	1.00	0.50
☐	☐	☐	184	Bayonet Charge	AngDtch	Special	2.00	1.00	0.50
☐	☐	☐	185	Rally	AngDtch	Special	2.00	1.00	0.50
☐	☐	☐	186	Double Grape	AngDtch	Special	2.00	1.00	0.50
☐	☐	☐	187	Ricochet Fire	AngDtch	Special	2.00	1.00	0.50
☐	☐	☐	188	Howitzer Fire	AngDtch	Special	2.00	1.00	0.50
☐	☐	☐	189	Fatigue	AngDtch	Special	2.00	1.00	0.50
☐	☐	☐	190	Panic	AngDtch	Special	2.00	1.00	0.50
☐	☐	☐	191	Battle Confusion	AngDtch	Special	2.00	1.00	0.50
☐	☐	☐	192	Battle Smoke	AngDtch	Special	2.00	1.00	0.50
☐	☐	☐	193	Lost Order	AngDtch	Special	2.00	1.00	0.50
☐	☐	☐	194	Late Reserves	AngDtch	Special	2.00	1.00	0.50
☐	☐	☐	195	Friendly Fire	AngDtch	Special	2.00	1.00	0.50
☐	☐	☐	196	Emergency Prone	AngDtch	Special	2.00	1.00	0.50
☐	☐	☐	197	Reverse Slope	AngDtch	Special	2.00	1.00	0.50
☐	☐	☐	198	The Colours	AngDtch	Special	2.00	1.00	0.50
☐	☐	☐	199	Congreve Rockets	AngDtch	Special	2.00	1.00	0.50
☐	☐	☐	200	Shrapnel	AngDtch	Special	2.00	1.00	0.50
☐	☐	☐	201	Feldmarschall von Blücher	Prussian	General	2.00	1.00	0.50
☐	☐	☐	202	Generalleutnant von Gneisenau	Prussian	General	2.00	1.00	0.50
☐	☐	☐	203	Generalleutnant von Zieten II	Prussian	General	2.00	1.00	0.50
☐	☐	☐	204	12. (2. Brandenburger) Infanterie	Prussian	Infantry	2.00	1.00	0.50
☐	☐	☐	205	24. (4. Brandenburger) Infanterie	Prussian	Infantry	2.00	1.00	0.50
☐	☐	☐	206	1. Westfälische Landwehr	Prussian	Infantry	2.00	1.00	0.50
☐	☐	☐	207	6. (1. Westpreussische) Infanterie	Prussian	Infantry	2.00	1.00	0.50
☐	☐	☐	208	28. (1. Bergische) Infanterie	Prussian	Infantry	2.00	1.00	0.50
☐	☐	☐	209	2. Westfälische Landwehr	Prussian	Infantry	2.00	1.00	0.50
☐	☐	☐	210	7. (2. Westpreussische) Infanterie	Prussian	Infantry	2.00	1.00	0.50
☐	☐	☐	211	29. (2. Bergische) Infanterie	Prussian	Infantry	2.00	1.00	0.50
☐	☐	☐	212	3. Westfälische Landwehr	Prussian	Infantry	2.00	1.00	0.50
☐	☐	☐	213	19. (7. Reserve) Infanterie	Prussian	Infantry	2.00	1.00	0.50
☐	☐	☐	214	4. Westfälische Landwehr	Prussian	Infantry	2.00	1.00	0.50
☐	☐	☐	215	5. (Brandenburger) Dragoner	Prussian	Cavalry	2.00	1.00	0.50
☐	☐	☐	216	6. (Lützower) Ulanen	Prussian	Cavalry	2.00	1.00	0.50
☐	☐	☐	217	Fußbatterie (12p)	Prussian	Artillery	2.00	1.00	0.50
☐	☐	☐	218	Fußbatterie (6p)	Prussian	Artillery	2.00	1.00	0.50
☐	☐	☐	219	Fußbatterie (6p)	Prussian	Artillery	2.00	1.00	0.50
☐	☐	☐	220	Berittene Batterie (6p)	Prussian	Artillery	2.00	1.00	0.50
☐	☐	☐	221	Generalmajor von Pirch	Prussian	General	2.00	1.00	0.50
☐	☐	☐	222	2. (1. Pommersche) Infanterie	Prussian	Infantry	2.00	1.00	0.50
☐	☐	☐	223	25. (Lützower) Infanterie	Prussian	Infantry	2.00	1.00	0.50
☐	☐	☐	224	5. Westfälische Landwehr	Prussian	Infantry	2.00	1.00	0.50
☐	☐	☐	225	9. (1. Kollberger) Infanterie	Prussian	Infantry	2.00	1.00	0.50
☐	☐	☐	226	26. (1. Elbische) Infanterie	Prussian	Infantry	2.00	1.00	0.50*
☐	☐	☐	227	1. Elbische Landwehr	Prussian	Infantry	2.00	1.00	0.50
☐	☐	☐	228	14. (2. Reserve) Infanterie	Prussian	Infantry	2.00	1.00	0.50
☐	☐	☐	229	22. (10. Reserve) Infanterie	Prussian	Infantry	2.00	1.00	0.50
☐	☐	☐	230	2. Elbische Landwehr	Prussian	Infantry	2.00	1.00	0.50
☐	☐	☐	231	21. (9. Reserve) Infanterie	Prussian	Infantry	2.00	1.00	0.50
☐	☐	☐	232	23. (11. Reserve) Infanterie	Prussian	Infantry	2.00	1.00	0.50
☐	☐	☐	233	3. Elbische Landwehr	Prussian	Infantry	2.00	1.00	0.50
☐	☐	☐	234	1. (Königin) Dragoner	Prussian	Cavalry	2.00	1.00	0.50
☐	☐	☐	235	3. (Brandenburger) Husaren	Prussian	Cavalry	2.00	1.00	0.50
☐	☐	☐	236	4. Kurmärkische Lw Kavallerie	Prussian	Cavalry	2.00	1.00	0.50
☐	☐	☐	237	11. Husaren	Prussian	Cavalry	2.00	1.00	0.50
☐	☐	☐	238	Fußbatterie (12p)	Prussian	Artillery	2.00	1.00	0.50
☐	☐	☐	239	Fußbatterie (6p)	Prussian	Artillery	2.00	1.00	0.50
☐	☐	☐	240	Fußbatterie (6p)	Prussian	Artillery	2.00	1.00	0.50
☐	☐	☐	241	Berittene Batterie (6p)	Prussian	Artillery	2.00	1.00	0.50
☐	☐	☐	242	Generalleutnant von Thielmann 0/1	Prussian	General	2.00	1.00	0.50
☐	☐	☐	243	8. (Leib-) Infanterie (Jäger)	Prussian	Infantry	2.00	1.00	0.50
☐	☐	☐	244	30. Infanterie	Prussian	Infantry	2.00	1.00	0.50
☐	☐	☐	245	1. Kurmärkische Landwehr	Prussian	Infantry	2.00	1.00	0.50
☐	☐	☐	246	27. Infanterie	Prussian	Infantry	2.00	1.00	0.50
☐	☐	☐	247	2. Kurmärkische Landwehr	Prussian	Infantry	2.00	1.00	0.50
☐	☐	☐	248	3. Kurmärkische Landwehr	Prussian	Infantry	2.00	1.00	0.50
☐	☐	☐	249	4. Kurmärkische Landwehr	Prussian	Infantry	2.00	1.00	0.50
☐	☐	☐	250	31. Infanterie	Prussian	Infantry	2.00	1.00	0.50
☐	☐	☐	251	5. Kurmärkische Landwehr	Prussian	Infantry	2.00	1.00	0.50
☐	☐	☐	252	6. Kurmärkische Landwehr	Prussian	Infantry	2.00	1.00	0.50
☐	☐	☐	253	7. Ulanen	Prussian	Cavalry	2.00	1.00	0.50
☐	☐	☐	254	7. Dragoner	Prussian	Cavalry	2.00	1.00	0.50
☐	☐	☐	255	6. Kurmärkische Lw Kavallerie	Prussian	Cavalry	2.00	1.00	0.50
☐	☐	☐	256	Fußbatterie (6p)	Prussian	Artillery	2.00	1.00	0.50
☐	☐	☐	257	Fußbatterie (6p)	Prussian	Artillery	2.00	1.00	0.50
☐	☐	☐	258	Berittene Batterie (6p)	Prussian	Artillery	2.00	1.00	0.50
☐	☐	☐	259	Graf Bülow von Dennewitz	Prussian	General	2.00	1.00	0.50
☐	☐	☐	260	10. (1. Schlesische) Infanterie	Prussian	Infantry	2.00	1.00	0.50
☐	☐	☐	261	2. Neumärkische Landwehr	Prussian	Infantry	2.00	1.00	0.50
☐	☐	☐	262	3. Neumärkische Landwehr	Prussian	Infantry	2.00	1.00	0.50
☐	☐	☐	263	11. (2. Schlesische) Infanterie	Prussian	Infantry	2.00	1.00	0.50
☐	☐	☐	264	1. Pommersche Landwehr	Prussian	Infantry	2.00	1.00	0.50
☐	☐	☐	265	2. Pommersche Landwehr	Prussian	Infantry	2.00	1.00	0.50
☐	☐	☐	266	18. (6. Reserve) Infanterie	Prussian	Infantry	2.00	1.00	0.50
☐	☐	☐	267	3. Schlesische Landwehr 2D	Prussian	Infantry	2.00	1.00	0.50
☐	☐	☐	268	4. Schlesische Landwehr 2D	Prussian	Infantry	2.00	1.00	0.50
☐	☐	☐	269	15. (3. Reserve) Infanterie	Prussian	Infantry	2.00	1.00	0.50
☐	☐	☐	270	1. Schlesische Landwehr 2D	Prussian	Infantry	2.00	1.00	0.50
☐	☐	☐	271	2. Schlesische Landwehr 2D	Prussian	Infantry	2.00	1.00	0.50
☐	☐	☐	272	1. (Westpreussische) Ulanen	Prussian	Cavalry	2.00	1.00	0.50
☐	☐	☐	273	8. Husaren 1B	Prussian	Cavalry	2.00	1.00	0.50
☐	☐	☐	274	1. Neumärkische Lw Kavallerie	Prussian	Cavalry	2.00	1.00	0.50
☐	☐	☐	275	2. Schlesische Lw Kavallerie 2D	Prussian	Cavalry	2.00	1.00	0.50
☐	☐	☐	276	Fußbatterie (12p)	Prussian	Artillery	2.00	1.00	0.50
☐	☐	☐	277	Fußbatterie (6p)	Prussian	Artillery	2.00	1.00	0.50
☐	☐	☐	278	Fußbatterie (6p)	Prussian	Artillery	2.00	1.00	0.50
☐	☐	☐	279	Berittene Batterie (6p)	Prussian	Artillery	2.00	1.00	0.50
☐	☐	☐	280	Sombreffe	Prussian	Terrain	2.00	1.00	0.50
☐	☐	☐	281	Ligny Brook	Prussian	Terrain	2.00	1.00	0.50
☐	☐	☐	282	Ligny	Prussian	Terrain	2.00	1.00	0.50
☐	☐	☐	283	Bussy Hill	Prussian	Terrain	2.00	1.00	0.50
☐	☐	☐	284	Ligny Brook	Prussian	Terrain	2.00	1.00	0.50
☐	☐	☐	285	St. Amand	Prussian	Terrain	2.00	1.00	0.50
☐	☐	☐	286	River Dyle	Prussian	Terrain	2.00	1.00	0.50
☐	☐	☐	287	Wavre	Prussian	Terrain	2.00	1.00	0.50
☐	☐	☐	288	Limale Bridge	Prussian	Terrain	2.00	1.00	0.50
☐	☐	☐	289	Ammo Depletion	Prussian	Special	2.00	1.00	0.50
☐	☐	☐	290	Bayonet Charge	Prussian	Special	2.00	1.00	0.50
☐	☐	☐	291	Double Grape	Prussian	Special	2.00	1.00	0.50
☐	☐	☐	292	Rally	Prussian	Special	2.00	1.00	0.50
☐	☐	☐	293	Howitzer Fire	Prussian	Special	2.00	1.00	0.50
☐	☐	☐	294	Fatigue	Prussian	Special	2.00	1.00	0.50
☐	☐	☐	295	Battle Confusion	Prussian	Special	2.00	1.00	0.50
☐	☐	☐	296	Battle Smoke	Prussian	Special	2.00	1.00	0.50
☐	☐	☐	297	Lost Order	Prussian	Special	2.00	1.00	0.50
☐	☐	☐	298	Friendly Fire	Prussian	Special	2.00	1.00	0.50
☐	☐	☐	299	Vorwarts!	Prussian	Special	2.00	1.00	0.50
☐	☐	☐	300	No Quarter	Prussian	Special	2.00	1.00	0.50

RARITY KEY **B** = Bronze (Common)   **S** = Silver (Uncommon)   **G** = Gold (Rare)

Echelons of Fire

Medallion Simulations • First set, *First Edition*, released **May 1995**
At least **70** cards in set • **IDENTIFIER: Modern military images; dark tan borders**

- Starter decks contain 65 cards; starter displays contain 10 starters
- Booster packs contain 15 cards; booster displays contain 36 boosters

Echelons of Fire depicts a sudden warming of the Cold War between the U.S. and the U.S.S.R. and stands as a faithful recreation of military combat. Of course, in achieving that, the game design became hellishly complex. If you've enjoyed miniatures combat games, with modifiers for different aspects of a battle, this is the game for you.

In *Fire*, players use aircraft, anti-aircraft guns, amphibious vehicles, tanks, minefields, engineers, and about a dozen other special cards and abilities. Players first have to build a battlefield: Each starter comes with five Terrain cards, each with a modifier regarding specific types of Combatants. (Tanks don't do well in towns, but soldiers do.) Each turn, players draw a card, play a Supply card (either ammo or fuel), and brings troops, vehicles and Support cards (guns, gear) into play face down. Supply points limit the amont of equipment you can have in play. When you're feeling tough, you can flip some guys over and send them marching through a specific Terrain using a Manuever card. The combat plays out quite a bit like **Magic: The Gathering**, but, with all of the other special cards and abilities, the game does have a great deal of depth.

If it seems complicated, it's because it's trying to accurately represent something that really is that complex. In the end, it appealed mostly to miniatures and war buffs. — *Richard Weld*

Concept	●●●○○
Gameplay	●●○○○
Card art	●●○○○
Player pool	○○○○○

Set (70 known cards)	72.00
Starter Display Box	63.00
Booster Display Box	58.00
Starter Deck	7.00
Booster Pack	2.00

You will need **9** nine-pocket pages to store this set. (5 doubled up)

Card name	Rarity	Price
Air-Dropped Supplies	VR	3.00
Ambush	VR	3.00
Anti-Personnel Mines	R	2.00
Anti-Tank Mines	R	2.00
Artillery Strike [1 Medium Mortar]	R	2.00
Bridge [Stone]	U	0.50
Bridge [Wood]	U	0.50
City #1 [At sunset]	U	0.50
City #2 [On waterfront]	U	0.50
City #3 [Rooftops]	U	0.50
City #4 [Stores]	U	0.50
Clear Skies	VR	3.00
Delaying Action	R	2.00
Dense Fog	R	2.00
Foxhole	R	2.00
Foxholes	VR	3.00
Grenades [Fragmentation]	U	0.50
Grenades [Smoke]	U	0.50

Card name	Rarity	Price
Heavy Snow	VR	3.00
Hills	U	0.50
Hull Down	VR	3.00
Left Flanking	C	0.10
Medic Team	R	2.00
N.D.G. Fire Team	C	0.10
N.D.G. Fire Team [Engineers]	VR	3.00
N.D.G. Fire Team [Reconnaissance]	R	2.00
N.D.G. Light S.A.M.	VR	3.00
N.D.G. Sergeant	C	0.10
N.D.G. Sniper	VR	3.00
Open	U	0.50
Radio Net	VR	3.00
Recon	U	0.50
Right Flanking	C	0.10
Sand Bagged Position	R	2.00
Soviet (N.D.G) 82mm	R	2.00
Soviet (N.D.G) RPG-7	U	0.50
Soviet (N.D.G) T-72	VR	3.00
Soviet (N.D.G) T-80	VR	3.00
Soviet (N.D.G.) BMP	R	2.00
Soviet (N.D.G.) BRDM	R	2.00
Soviet (N.D.G.) Hind	VR	3.00
Soviet (N.D.G.) PKM	U	0.50
Soviet (N.D.G.) PT-76	R	2.00
Soviet (N.D.G.) Sagger	U	0.50

Card name	Rarity	Price
Soviet Special Forces	VR	3.00
Supply [Ammunition]	C	0.10
Supply [Fuel]	C	0.10
Thrust	C	0.10
Town #1 [Wooded]	C	0.10
Town #2 [Snowy]	C	0.10
U.S. A-10 Thunderbolt	VR	3.00
U.S. AH-64 Apache	VR	3.00
U.S. Aid Station	VR	3.00
U.S. Dragon	U	0.50
U.S. Fire Team	C	0.10
U.S. Fire Team [Airborne]	VR	3.00
U.S. Fire Team [Engineers]	VR	3.00
U.S. Fire Team [Reconnaissance]	R	2.00
U.S. Humm-V L.M.G.	R	2.00
U.S. Humm-V TOW	R	2.00
U.S. Light S.A.M.	VR	3.00
U.S. M-1 Abrams	VR	3.00
U.S. M-16/M-203	U	0.50
U.S. M-2 Bradley	R	2.00
U.S. M-60 L.M.G.	U	0.50
U.S. M-728 C.E.V.	VR	3.00
U.S. M.G. Team	R	2.00
U.S. Sergeant	C	0.10
Wireless Radio	R	2.00
Woods	C	0.10

Echelons of Fire • 2nd Edition

Medallion Simulations • Released **October 1995**

At least **95** cards in set • **IDENTIFIER: Modern military images; light tan borders**

- Starter decks contain 65 cards; starter displays contain 10 starters
- Booster packs contain 15 cards; booster displays contain 36 boosters

New cards appear for British and Serbian forces in **Echelons of Fire 2nd Edition.** There are minor text changes on other cards, and the borders on the card faces are lighter than for **1st Edition.** This is another situation where the manufacturer's card list was incomplete; our list has every card we've been able to find. — *John Jackson Miller*

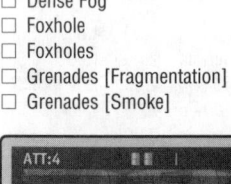

You will need **11** nine-pocket pages to store this set. (6 doubled up)

Set (95 cards)	65.00
Starter Display Box	60.00
Booster Display Box	50.00
Starter Deck	6.50
Booster Pack	1.50

Card name	Rarity	Price
500 Pounders	R	1.50
Air Strike	VR	2.50
Air-Dropped Supplies	VR	2.50
Ambush	VR	2.50
Anti-Personnel Mines	R	1.50

RARITY KEY   **C** = Common   **U** = Uncommon   **R** = Rare   **VR** = Very Rare   **UR** = Ultra Rare   **F** = Foil card   **X** = Fixed/standard in all decks

Card name	Rarity	Price
☐ Anti-Tank Mines	R	1.50
☐ Artillery Strike [1 Heavy Mortar]	R	1.50
☐ Bridge [Stone]	U	0.25
☐ Bridge [Wood]	U	0.25
[2]		
☐ City #1 [At sunset]	U	0.25
☐ City #2 [On waterfront]	U	0.25
☐ City #3 [Rooftops]	U	0.25
☐ City #4 [Stores]	U	0.25
☐ Clear Skies	VR	2.50
☐ Delaying Action	R	1.50
☐ Dense Fog	R	1.50
☐ Foxhole	R	1.50
☐ Foxholes	VR	2.50
[3]		
☐ Grenades [Fragmentation]	U	0.25
☐ Grenades [Smoke]	U	0.25
☐ Heavy Snow	VR	2.50
☐ Hills	U	0.25
☐ Hull Down	VR	2.50
☐ Left Flanking	C	0.05
☐ Medic Team	R	1.50
☐ N.D.G. Fire Team	C	0.05
☐ N.D.G. Fire Team [Engineers]	VR	2.50
[4]		
☐ N.D.G. Fire Team [Reconnaissance]	R	1.50
☐ N.D.G. Light S.A.M.	VR	2.50
☐ N.D.G. Sergeant	C	0.05
☐ N.D.G. Sniper	VR	2.50
☐ Open	U	0.25
☐ Radio Net	VR	2.50
☐ Recon	U	0.25
☐ Right Flanking	C	0.05

Card name	Rarity	Price
☐ River	C	0.05
[5]		
☐ Sand Bagged Position	R	1.50
☐ Serb Fire Team	VR	2.50
☐ Soviet (N.D.G) 120mm	VR	2.50
☐ Soviet (N.D.G) 82mm	R	1.50
☐ Soviet (N.D.G) RPG-7	U	0.25
☐ Soviet (N.D.G) T-72	VR	2.50
☐ Soviet (N.D.G) T-80	VR	2.50
☐ Soviet (N.D.G) BMP	R	1.50
☐ Soviet (N.D.G) BRDM	R	1.50
[6]		
☐ Soviet (N.D.G) BRDM-1	VR	2.50
☐ Soviet (N.D.G) Hind	VR	2.50
☐ Soviet (N.D.G) PKM	U	0.25
☐ Soviet (N.D.G) PT-76	R	1.50
☐ Soviet (N.D.G) Sagger	U	0.25
☐ Soviet (Serb) T-54	R	1.50
☐ Soviet (Serb) T-62	R	1.50
☐ Soviet (Serb) ZSU-57/2	VR	2.50
☐ Soviet AA-7	VR	2.50
[7]		
☐ Soviet MIG-29 Fulcrum	VR	2.50
☐ Soviet Special Forces	VR	2.50
☐ Soviet SU-25 Frogfoot	VR	2.50
☐ Supply [Ammunition]	C	0.05
☐ Supply [Fuel 2x]	VR	2.50
☐ Supply [Fuel]	C	0.05
☐ Thrust	C	0.05
☐ Town #1 [Wooded]	C	0.05
☐ Town #2 [Snowy]	C	0.05
[8]		
☐ U.K. Fire Team	R	1.50
☐ U.K. L.M.G.	U	0.25

Card name	Rarity	Price
☐ U.K. Sergeant	R	1.50
☐ U.K. Warrior	R	1.50
☐ U.S. 2nd Lieutenant	VR	2.50
☐ U.S. A-10 Thunderbolt	VR	2.50
☐ U.S. AH-64 Apache	VR	2.50
☐ U.S. Aid Station	VR	2.50
☐ U.S. Dragon	U	0.25
[9]		
☐ U.S. F-15 Eagle	VR	2.50
☐ U.S. Fire Team	C	0.05
☐ U.S. Fire Team [Air Mobile]	VR	2.50
☐ U.S. Fire Team [Airborne]	VR	2.50
☐ U.S. Fire Team [Engineers]	VR	2.50
☐ U.S. Fire Team [Reconnaissance]	R	1.50
☐ U.S. Humm-V L.M.G.	R	1.50
☐ U.S. Humm-V TOW	R	1.50
☐ U.S. Light S.A.M.	VR	2.50
[10]		
☐ U.S. M-1 Abrams	VR	2.50
☐ U.S. M-16/M-203	U	0.25
☐ U.S. M-2 Bradley	R	1.50
☐ U.S. M-60 L.M.G.	U	0.25
☐ U.S. M-728 C.E.V.	VR	2.50
☐ U.S. M.G. Team	R	1.50
☐ U.S. Maverick	VR	2.50
☐ U.S. MK-19 40mm	R	1.50
☐ U.S. Sergeant	C	0.05
[11]		
☐ U.S. Sidewinder	VR	2.50
☐ U.S. Sparrow	VR	2.50
☐ U.S. UH-60 Blackhawk	VR	2.50
☐ Wireless Radio	R	1.50
☐ Woods	C	0.05

Echelons of Fury

Medallion Simulations • Released May 1995

At least **62** cards in set • **IDENTIFIER: WWII images; dark tan borders**

- Starter decks contain 65 cards; starter displays contain 10 starters
- Booster packs contain 15 cards; booster displays contain 36 boosters

Designed by **Scot D. Hunt**

Echelons of Fury uses the same "Tactical Command Series" gaming system as *Echelons of Fire*, and it is for most purposes the same game. But simulating World War II combat rather than modern combat, there are obviously some changes. No helicopter combat here, and the factions are Americans and German rather than American and Soviet.

As with *Echelons of Fire*, all of the cards are realistically painted in shades of brown and green camouflage, which often makes the tiny black print hard to read. But they do have a great layout for statistics across the top line, title along the side, and special abilities in a box off to the lower-right side. The look of these cards is bland but appropriate to the feel of the game.

Like *Fire*, *Echelons of Fury* would appeal to anyone who is a war buff or a miniatures buff (preferably both). The almost insane amounts of detail definitely stress realism: The Tactical Command Series games allow for many weird abilities and, as such, are hard to pick up. The dense rulebook isn't easy to wade through, either. Deck-tuning is mandatory, as well: My first *Echelons of Fire* starter deck had three bombs to attach to planes but no planes to attach them to. — *Richard Weld*

Scrye Notes: *The manufacturer's published card lists for both **Echelons** games has proven incomplete. We found a few dozen unannounced cards in **2nd Edition Fire** and caution that the set numbers we're giving for each **Echelons** set may not be final. If you find any that we haven't, drop us a line.*

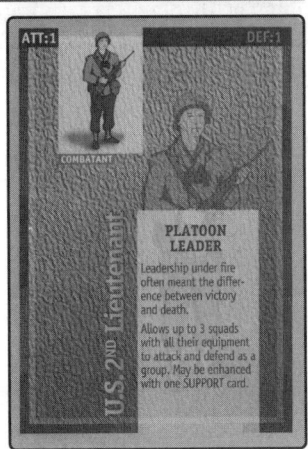

Concept	●●●○○
Gameplay	●●○○○
Card art	●●○○○
Player pool	○○○○○

Set (62 known cards)	69.00
Starter Display Box	61.50
Booster Display Box	57.00
Starter Deck	7.50
Booster Pack	2.00

You will need **7** nine-pocket pages to store this set. (4 doubled up)

Card name	Rarity	Price
[1]		
☐ Air-Dropped Supplies	VR	3.00
☐ Ambush	R	2.00
☐ Anti-Personnel Mines	R	2.00
☐ Anti-Tank Mines	R	2.00

Card name	Rarity	Price
☐ Artillery Strike [1 Medium Mortar]	R	2.00
☐ Bridge - Stone	U	0.50
☐ Bridge - Wood	U	0.50
☐ City #1 [At Sunset]	U	0.50
☐ City #2 [On waterfront]	U	0.50

RARITY KEY C = Common U = Uncommon R = Rare VR = Very Rare UR = Ultra Rare F = Foil card X = Fixed/standard in all decks

Card name	Rarity	Price
☐ City #3 [Rooftops]	U	0.50
☐ City #4 [Stores]	U	0.50
☐ Clear Skies	VR	3.00
☐ Delaying Action	R	2.00
☐ Dense Fog	R	2.00
☐ Foxhole	R	2.00
☐ Foxholes	VR	3.00
☐ French Squad [Partisans]	VR	3.00
☐ German 88mm Gun	VR	3.00
☐ German Hetzer	VR	3.00
☐ German Ju-87 Stuka	VR	3.00
☐ German Lieutenant [Platoon Leader]	C	0.10
☐ German Me-109	VR	3.00
☐ German MG-34	R	2.00
☐ German MG-42	U	0.50
☐ German Panzerfaust	U	0.50
☐ German Pz-III	VR	3.00
☐ German Sdk-251	R	2.00

Card name	Rarity	Price
☐ German Squad [Engineers]	R	2.00
☐ German Squad [Regulars]	C	0.10
☐ German Squad [Waffen SS]	VR	3.00
☐ Grenades [Fragmentation]	U	0.50
☐ Grenades [Smoke]	U	0.50
☐ Heavy Snow	VR	3.00
☐ Hills	U	0.50
☐ Hull Down	VR	3.00
☐ Left Flanking	C	0.10
☐ Medic Team	R	2.00
☐ Open	U	0.50
☐ Radio Net	VR	3.00
☐ Recon	U	0.50
☐ Right Flanking	C	0.10
☐ Sandbagged Position	R	2.00
☐ Supply [Ammunition]	C	0.10
☐ Supply [Fuel]	C	0.10
☐ Thrust	C	0.10

Card name	Rarity	Price
☐ Town [Wooded]	C	0.10
☐ U.S. .30 Cal. LMG	U	0.50
☐ "U.S. 2.36"" Bazooka"	U	0.50
☐ U.S. 2nd Lieutenant [Platoon Leader]	C	0.10
☐ U.S. 57mm Gun	R	2.00
☐ U.S. 81mm Mortar	R	2.00
☐ U.S. Autorifleman	R	2.00
☐ U.S. M-3 Halftrack	R	2.00
☐ U.S. M-4 Sherman	VR	3.00
☐ U.S. M-5 Stuart	R	2.00
☐ U.S. P-47 Thunderbolt	VR	3.00
☐ U.S. P-51 Mustang	VR	3.00
☐ U.S. Squad [Airborne]	VR	3.00
☐ U.S. Squad [Engineers]	R	2.00
☐ U.S. Squad [Regulars]	C	0.10
☐ Wireless Radio	R	2.00
☐ Woods	C	0.10

Echelons of Fury • 2nd Edition

Medallion Simulations • Released October 1995

At least **94** cards in set • **IDENTIFIER: Light tan border**

- Starter decks contain 65 cards; starter displays contain 10 starters
- Booster packs contain 15 cards; booster displays contain 36 boosters

Minor changes appear with **Echelons of Fury: 2nd Edition** cards; some of the "time-less" card faces, such as Terrain and Supply, are the same as in **Echelons of Fire: 2nd Edition.**

As noted under **Echelons of Fury: 1st Edition**, several cards not on the publisher's prerelease card list appeared in *Echelons of Fire 2nd Edition*, and we would presume that some some made their way into *Echelons of Fury 2nd Edition*, as well.

Where we found cards with no publisher-announced rarity, we used cards with known rarities to figure out where the Very Rare and Rare "slots" were in the booster packs, to come up with an approximated rarity. — **John Jackson Miller**

Set (94 known cards)	63.00
Starter Display Box	60.00
Booster Display Box	50.00
Starter Deck	6.50
Booster Pack	1.50

You will need **11** nine-pocket pages to store this set. (6 doubled up)

Card name	Rarity	Price
☐ Air-Dropped Supplies	VR	3.00
☐ 500 Pounders	R	1.50
☐ Air Strike	R	1.50
☐ Air-Dropped Supplies	VR	2.50
☐ Ambush	R	1.50
☐ Anti-Personnel Mines	R	1.50
☐ Anti-Tank Mines	R	1.50
☐ Artillery Strike [1 Heavy Mortar]	R	1.50
☐ Artillery Strike [Starshell]	R	1.50
☐ Bridge - Stone	U	0.25

Card name	Rarity	Price
☐ Bridge - Wood	U	0.25
☐ British Achilles	VR	2.50
☐ British Bren	U	0.25
☐ British Leader	R	1.50
☐ British Mosquito	VR	2.50
☐ British Piat	U	0.25
☐ British Spitfire	VR	2.50
☐ British Squad	R	1.50
☐ Brothel	VR	2.50
☐ Camouflage	R	1.50
☐ City #1 [At Sunset]	U	0.25
☐ City #2 [On waterfront]	U	0.25
☐ City #3 [Rooftops]	U	0.25
☐ City #4 [Stores]	U	0.25
☐ Clear Skies	VR	2.50
☐ Delaying Action	R	1.50
☐ Dense Fog	R	1.50
☐ Flamenwerfer	VR	2.50
☐ Foxhole	R	1.50
☐ Foxholes	VR	2.50
☐ German 88mm Gun	VR	2.50
☐ German FW-190	VR	2.50
☐ German Lieutenant [Armor Leader]	VR	2.50
☐ German Lieutenant [Platoon Leader]	C	0.05
☐ German Me-109	VR	2.50
☐ German MG-34	R	1.50
☐ German MG-42	U	0.25
☐ German Panther	VR	2.50
☐ German Panzerfaust	U	0.25

Card name	Rarity	Price
☐ German Panzershreck	U	0.25
☐ German Pz-IV F2	R	1.50
☐ German Sdk-251	R	1.50
☐ German Squad [Hitlerjugend SS]	VR	2.50
☐ German Squad [Regulars]	C	0.05
☐ German SS Armor Leader	VR	2.50
☐ German STG-III	R	1.50
☐ German Storch	VR	2.50
☐ German Tiger I	VR	2.50
☐ German Tiger II	VR	2.50
☐ Grenades [Fragmentation]	U	0.25
☐ Grenades [Smoke]	U	0.25
☐ Heavy Rain	VR	2.50
☐ Heavy Snow	VR	2.50
☐ Hills	U	0.25
☐ Hull Down	VR	2.50
☐ Left Flanking	C	0.05
☐ Light Rain	R	1.50
☐ Medic Team	R	1.50
☐ Night	R	1.50
☐ Open	U	0.25
☐ Radio Net	VR	2.50
☐ Recon	U	0.25
☐ Right Flanking	C	0.05
☐ River	U	0.25
☐ Roadblock	R	1.50
☐ Sandbagged Position	R	1.50
☐ Supply [Ammunition]	C	0.05
☐ Supply [Fuel 2x]	VR	2.50
☐ Supply [Fuel]	C	0.05

Collector alert

"There were a number of 'bonus' displays for **Echelons** that went out with large numbers of rare cards in them. In these, the variety is somewhat reduced, but the payoff with rare cards is tremendous. Unlike with fantasy card games, in **Echelons** the objective is to get duplicate cards, thereby building a unit which has the consistency and integrity to get the job done."

— **Scot D. Hunt,**
Medallion Simulations

RARITY KEY C = Common U = Uncommon R = Rare VR = Very Rare UR = Ultra Rare F = Foil card X = Fixed/standard in all decks

Card name	Rarity	Price		Card name	Rarity	Price		Card name	Rarity	Price
☐ Thrust	C	0.05		☐ U.S. 57mm Gun	R	1.50		☐ U.S. M-8 Greyhound	R	1.50
☐ Town [Snowy]	C	0.05		☐ U.S. 81mm Mortar	R	1.50		☐ U.S. P-47 Thunderbolt	VR	2.50
☐ Town [Wooded]	C	0.05		☐ U.S. Autorifleman	R	1.50		☐ U.S. P-51 Mustang	VR	2.50
☐ U.S. .30 Cal. LMG	U	0.25		☐ U.S. Douglas C-47	VR	2.50		☐ U.S. Squad [Airborne]	VR	2.50
9				10				11		
☐ U.S. .50 Cal.	R	1.50		☐ U.S. M-26 Pershing	UR	3.00		☐ U.S. Squad [Regulars]	C	0.05
☐ U.S. 1st Lieutenant [Airborne Leader]	VR	2.50		☐ U.S. M-3 Halftrack	R	1.50		☐ Veteran Pilot	VR	2.50
☐ "U.S. 2.36"" Bazooka"	U	0.25		☐ U.S. M-4 Sherman	VR	2.50		☐ Wireless Radio	R	1.50
☐ U.S. 2nd Lieutenant [Armor Leader]	VR	2.50		☐ U.S. M-5 Stuart	R	1.50		☐ Woods	C	0.05
☐ U.S. 2nd Lieutenant [Platoon Leader]	C	0.05		☐ U.S. M-7 Priest	VR	2.50				

Echelons of Fury • *Pacific Campaign*

Medallion Simulations • Released **December 1995**

At least **96** cards in set • **IDENTIFIER: Japanese WWII images; light tan border**

- Starter decks contain 65 cards; starter displays contain 10 starters
- Booster packs contain 15 cards; booster displays contain 36 boosters

Pacific Campaign adapts *Echelons of Fury* to the war versus Japan, with cards geared toward island war. Freighters supply the Allied player, who must get landing craft loaded and onto shore under the watchful eyes aboard Allied destroyers. The Japanese player counters with dive bombers, bunkers, caves, and booby traps.

Pacific Campaign was both the first expansion for either *Echelons* game and the last release in the Tactical Combat Series. In late 1995, Medallion Simulations announced plans for a further *Echelons of Fury* expansion (one covering the Russian front) and an *Echelons of Fire* expansion positing a modern-day war versus North Korea. They never came to pass. The unrelated **Ruinsworld**, which shipped the same month as *Pacific Campaign*, rounds out Medallion's CCG offerings.— *John Jackson Miller*

Above: Card art only

Set (96 known cards)	**67.00**
Starter Display Box	**55.00**
Booster Display Box	**58.00**
Starter Deck	**5.75**
Booster Pack	**2.25**

You will need **11** nine-pocket pages to store this set. (6 doubled up)

Card name	Type	Rarity	Price
1			
☐ "Air-Dropped Supplies, Supplies"		VR	2.00
☐ "Ambush, Tactical Manuever"		R	1.00
☐ Ammunition		C	0.10
☐ Anti-Personnel Mines		R	1.00
☐ Anti-Tank Mines		R	1.00
☐ ANZAC Bren Gun			0.20
☐ ANZAC Flamethrower			0.20
☐ ANZAC Lieutenant			0.20
☐ ANZAC Piat		U	0.25
2			
☐ ANZAC Sherman Crab			0.20
☐ ANZAC Squad			0.20
☐ Artillery Strike [1 Heavy Mortar]		R	1.00
☐ Artillery Strike [1 Medium Mortar]		R	1.00
☐ Artillery Strike [Shore Bombardment]		R	1.00
☐ Artillery Strike [Starshell]		R	1.00
☐ Australian Coastwatcher			0.20
☐ Beach - Lagoon			0.20
☐ Beach - Open and Exposed			0.20
3			
☐ Beach - Poor Visibility			0.20
☐ Booby Trap			0.20
☐ Camouflage		R	1.00
☐ Caves			0.20
☐ Day			0.20
☐ Dense Jungle			0.20
☐ Double Fuel		VR	2.00
☐ Fuel		C	0.10
☐ Grenades [Fragmentation]		U	0.25
4			
☐ Grenades [Smoke Grenades]		U	0.25
☐ Guadacanal			0.20
☐ Hills - Jungle Hills [blue]			0.20
☐ Hills - Jungle Hills [red]			0.20

Card name	Type	Rarity	Price
☐ "Hull Down, Emplacement"		VR	2.00
☐ Iwo Jima			0.20
☐ Japanese 1st Lieutenant			0.20
☐ Japanese 2nd Lieutenant			0.20
☐ Japanese 60mm			0.20
5			
☐ Japanese 75mm			0.20
☐ Japanese 81mm			0.20
☐ Japanese A6M2			0.20
☐ "Japanese D3A ""Val"""			0.20
☐ Japanese MG Position			0.20
☐ Japanese Model 99 7.7mm			0.20
☐ Japanese Pill Box			0.20
☐ Japanese Sand Bagged Position		R	1.00
☐ Japanese Sniper			0.20
6			
☐ Japanese Squad			0.20
☐ Japanese Squad			0.20
☐ Japanese Tunneling			0.20
☐ Japanese Type 95 Ha-Go			0.20
☐ Japanese Type 97 Te-Ke			0.20
☐ Left Flanking		C	0.10
☐ Light Jungle			0.20
☐ Medic Team		R	1.00
☐ Medium Jungle			0.20
7			
☐ Monsoon			0.20
☐ Mt. Suribachi			0.20
☐ Native Guide			0.20
☐ New Guinea			0.20
☐ Night		VR	2.00
☐ Open (Grassy)			0.20
☐ Open (Rocky)		U	0.25
☐ "Rain, Weather"		VR	2.00
☐ "Recon, Reconnaissance"		U	0.25
8			
☐ Right Flanking		C	0.10
☐ River		U	0.25
☐ Saipan			0.20
☐ Shellhole			0.20
☐ Tarawa			0.20

Card name	Type	Rarity	Price
☐ Thrust		C	0.10
☐ U.S. .30 Cal. LMG		U	0.25
☐ U.S. 1st Lieutenant		VR	2.00
☐ "U.S. 2.36"" Bazooka"		U	0.25
9			
☐ U.S. 2nd Lieutenant		U	0.25
☐ U.S. 75mm M3			0.20
☐ U.S. 81mm Mortar		R	1.00
☐ U.S. Autorifleman		R	1.00
☐ U.S. F4U-1 Corsair			0.20
☐ U.S. F4U-1D Corsair			0.20
☐ U.S. F6F-3 Hellcat			0.20
☐ U.S. Freighter [Fleet Supply Ship]			0.20
☐ "U.S. Freighter, Supply Ship (#1) [5 Fuel]"			0.20
10			
☐ "U.S. Freighter, Supply Ship (#2) [4 Fuel]"			0.20
☐ "U.S. Freighter, Supply Ship (#3)"			0.20
☐ U.S. LCM			0.20
☐ U.S. LCP			0.20
☐ U.S. LVT(A)-4 Amtrak			0.20
☐ U.S. LVT-2			0.20
☐ U.S. M-5A1 Stuart		R	1.00
☐ U.S. M-8 Howitzer			0.20
☐ U.S. Marine BAR			0.20
11			
☐ U.S. Napalm			0.20
☐ U.S. Squad [Marines]			0.20
☐ U.S. Squad [Regulars]		C	0.10
☐ U.S.S. Johnston Class			0.20
☐ Veteran Pilot		VR	2.00
☐ Wireless Radio		R	1.00

RARITY KEY **C** = Common   **U** = Uncommon   **R** = Rare   **VR** = Very Rare   **UR** = Ultra Rare   **F** = Foil card   **X** = Fixed/standard in all decks

Fantasy Adventures

Mayfair Games • Released June 1996

450 cards in set

- Starter decks contain 100 cards, a rulebook, a help book, and two six-sided dice
- Starter displays contain 6 decks
- Booster packs contain 15 cards; booster displays contain 36 packs

Designed by Bill Fawcett and Tom Smith

Based on Mayfair's excellent non-collectible card game *Encounters*, **Fantasy Adventures** adapts the classic to a collectible format.

The game shares elements with both CCGs and with role-playing games, both in game design and game play. Every game consists of four Game Turns, each having a number of Player Turns equal to the number of players in the game. The player with the most Gold Piece Value in undefeated Heroes and assigned Items at the end of Game Turn Four wins the game. Players also lose if all their Heroes are defeated at the end of any one Player Turn.

Players have two decks in Fantasy Adventures, a Hero Deck and an Encounter Deck. The Hero Deck contains the Heroes that the player will send on adventures, while the Encounter Deck contains the Monsters and Traps the player will set against the Heroes of opposing players, as well as the Spells and Items that he will assign to his own Heroes. Each player begins the game with ten cards from each deck. A player builds an adventuring party of eight Heroes (discarding the extra two) and assigns up to three Items from his Encounter hand to his heroes. Players roll to determine who starts the game as the Monster Player (MP); then, everyone draws their Encounter hand up to ten cards (twelve in the case of the MP).

The MP puts together Encounters for as many of the opponents as he chooses. Encounters consist of Traps and Monsters. The MP plays the Encounters in the order of her choice, with each players' Encounter being finished before moving to the next. The target players' Heroes must first resolve any Traps in the encounter; some Heroes are better at traps than others. After all Traps are resolved, Surprise and Melee Combat are determined. Combat consists of each Hero and opposing Monster rolling a die, adding their basic Melee value and any modifiers, and comparing totals. Highest total wins. Special Actions are then determined, (Some Heroes and Monsters have special abilities.) Once all Monsters have been defeated, a victorious player can add as many Items from his hand to his party as he wishes. If a party Retreats, only one item may be added. Play then passes to the next player.

The original *Encounters* was a nice beer-and-pretzels card game, while the expanded version in *Fantasy Adventures* tried to present itself as something more. It never had the chance to evolve beyond its humble origins, becoming, instead, "Mayfair's other CCG besides **Sim City**." It might have been better if released as an expanded edition of *Encounters* rather than a full-fledged CCG. Announced **Wheel of Time** and **World of Aden** expansions were dropped, and it quickly fell into obscurity. — *James A. Mishler*

Concept	●●○○○
Gameplay	●●●○○
Card art	●●○○○
Player pool	○○○○○

Set (450 cards)	97.75
Starter Display Box	45.00
Booster Display Box	52.00
Starter Deck	10.00
Booster Pack	2.00

You will need 50 nine-pocket pages to store this set. (25 doubled up)

PROMO CARDS

Card name			Rarity	Price
☐ Lord Delos			promo	1.50
☐ Mrem			promo	1.50
☐ Nyean Assassins			promo	1.50
☐ Sarah's Sister			promo	1.50
☐ Sylvan Haunts			promo	1.50
☐ Volan Lyre			promo	1.50

Card name	Class	Type	Rarity	Price
☐ Abare Flameweaver	Water	Hero	UR	2.00
☐ Abishai	Air	Hero	UR	2.00
☐ Abyss Demon	Earth	Monster	UR	2.00
☐ Aegelen Warrior	Air	Monster	U	0.25
☐ Aelia	Fire	Hero	UR	2.00
☐ Aelic Darklord	Water	Monster	R	1.00
☐ Aereite	Air	Monster	C	0.10

Card name	Class	Type	Rarity	Price
☐ Aesette Darklord	Air	Monster	R	1.00
☐ Airwaves	Air	Spell	VC	0.05
☐ Akhabbu	Air	Hero	R	1.00
☐ Akhenaton	Air	Hero	UR	2.00
☐ Alaric	Fire	Hero	UR	2.00
☐ Aleators	Air	Monster	R	1.00
☐ Aleista Amyntas	Fire	Hero	UR	2.00
☐ Amber Pendant		Item	U	0.25
☐ Amenemhat	Air	Hero	UR	2.00
☐ Amenosphynx	Air	Monster	U	0.25
☐ Andre de Montbard	Earth	Hero	UR	2.00
☐ Ankh of Ptah		Item	U	0.25
☐ Arcson Gilmaster	Water	Hero	UR	2.00
☐ Arelae Fiend	Fire	Monster	U	0.25
☐ Arentha Aronica	Fire	Hero	UR	2.00
☐ Armor of Reversal		Item	UR	2.00
☐ Arnold de Farges	Earth	Hero	UR	2.00
☐ Arpentix	Air	Monster	X	0.50
☐ Artus Ceelark	Water	Hero	UR	2.00
☐ Artusean Merfolk	Water	Monster	R	1.00
☐ Asa Rex	Air	Hero	UR	2.00
☐ Ashur bel kala	Air	Hero	R	1.00

Card name	Class	Type	Rarity	Price
☐ Asirius Nanteus	Fire	Hero	UR	2.00
☐ Askelon	Air	Hero	R	1.00
☐ Astral Wolves	Air	Monster	U	0.25
☐ Astrid Bernrobber	Water	Hero	C	0.10
☐ Athailiah	Air	Hero	R	1.00
☐ Auvergne	Fire	Hero	R	1.00
☐ Auxiliary	Fire	Hero	X	0.50
☐ Axe of Doom		Item	R	1.00
☐ Baal	Air	Monster	UR	2.00
☐ Back from the Light	Air	Spell	U	0.25
☐ Baene Demon	Water	Monster	R	1.00
☐ Balien of Ibein	Earth	Hero	UR	2.00
☐ Balti	Fire	Hero	UR	2.00
☐ Bane Blade		Item	R	1.00
☐ Barbonne de Fayel	Earth	Hero	R	1.00
☐ Barenau	Fire	Hero	UR	2.00
☐ Barician Assassin	Air	Monster	C	0.10
☐ Belgae	Fire	Hero	U	0.25
☐ Benaiah ben Jehoida	Air	Hero	UR	2.00
☐ Bernae of Clairvaux	Earth	Hero	R	1.00
☐ Berserker	Water	Spell	U	0.25
☐ Betrayal Scroll		Item	U	0.25

RARITY KEY **VC** = Very Common **C** = Common **U** = Uncommon **R** = Rare **UR** = Ultra Rare **X** = Fixed/standard in all decks

Card name	Class	Type	Rarity	Price
Biban el Moluk	Air	Hero	UR	2.00
Bieceph	Earth	Monster	U	0.25
Bjorn Windstalker	Water	Hero	UR	2.00
7				
Blaseus	Fire	Hero	R	1.00
Blasphemy	Air	Spell	R	1.00
Blaze Commander	Fire	Hero	UR	2.00
Bribe	Fire	Spell	U	0.25
Brom Demian	Air	Monster	U	0.25
Brom Golem	Fire	Monster	UR	2.00
Brom Nomads	Earth	Monster	X	0.50
Brom Wolves	Fire	Monster	X	0.50
Bromalopes	Earth	Monster	R	1.00
8				
Bromian Assassin	Earth	Monster	C	0.10
Bromian Beastlord	Earth	Monster	C	0.10
Bromian Darklord	Earth	Monster	R	1.00
Bromian Great Bow		Item	R	1.00
Bromian Guard	Fire	Monster	C	0.10
Bromian Man Beast	Fire	Monster	U	0.25
Bromian Wyrm	Fire	Monster	C	0.10
Bromic Demon	Earth	Monster	UR	2.00
Bructeri	Fire	Hero	UR	2.00
9				
Burchard of Sion	Earth	Hero	UR	2.00
Byron	Fire	Hero	X	0.50
Caedicius	Fire	Hero	UR	2.00
Caeleteph	Earth	Monster	X	0.50
Calpurn Piso	Fire	Hero	UR	2.00
Captain's Sword		Item	U	0.25
Celestine	Earth	Hero	C	0.10
Celian Scaleshield	Water	Hero	UR	2.00
Celor Orka	Water	Monster	U	0.25
10				
Cerelopes	Air	Monster	VC	0.05
Cerise	Earth	Hero	UR	2.00
Cesorlain	Water	Monster	UR	2.00
Chainmail Coat		Item	VC	0.05
Changeling's Scroll		Item	R	1.00
Chatti Caecina	Fire	Hero	UR	2.00
Cloud Dragon	Air	Monster	UR	2.00
Cloud Wizard	Air	Hero	X	0.50
Cobra Rex	Earth	Monster	C	0.10
11				
Companion	Air	Hero	X	0.50
Constantius	Air	Hero	UR	2.00
Corenmege	Fire	Monster	R	1.00
Countess de Champag	Air	Hero	UR	2.00
Courage	Water	Spell	R	1.00
Crag Windonei	Fire	Monster	R	1.00
Crest of Brom		Item	UR	2.00
Cross Current	Water	Spell	U	0.25
Crystal Dwarves	Earth	Hero	UR	2.00
12				
Crystal Scarab		Item	U	0.25
Cursed Ones	Fire	Monster	R	1.00
Cyral Harbeast	Earth	Monster	C	0.10
Dailette	Earth	Monster	X	0.50
Dark Stalker	Water	Monster	C	0.10
Deanna de Jenine	Earth	Hero	UR	2.00
Death	Air	Monster	UR	2.00
Death Wish	Fire	Spell	U	0.25
Deception Trap		Trap	VC	0.05
13				
Deir el Bahri	Air	Hero	UR	2.00
Devonian Darklord	Fire	Monster	R	1.00
Diamond Ring		Item	U	0.25
Dicorpia	Earth	Monster	UR	2.00
Doom Gate	Water	Spell	U	0.25
Dragonette	Air	Monster	X	0.50
Drake Frohbohsen	Water	Hero	R	1.00
Druid	Earth	Hero	X	0.50
Dwarven Battle Axe		Item	U	0.25
14				
Dwarven Crossbow		Item	U	0.25
Dwarven Mace		Item	VC	0.05
Dwarven Morningstar		Item	U	0.25
Dwarven Shield		Item	VC	0.05
Dwarven Sword		Item	R	1.00
Dwarven Trap		Trap	VC	0.05
Dynoid	Fire	Monster	U	0.25
Earth Shield	Earth	Spell	VC	0.05
Eikran	Air	Monster	X	0.50
15				
Elven Bow		Item	U	0.25
Elven Harp		Item	U	0.25
Enchanted Flock	Earth	Spell	U	0.25
Enchanted Mace		Item	VC	0.05
Enchantment Trap		Trap	R	1.00
Enemy Within	Water	Spell	C	0.10
Enroa de Ensigne	Earth	Hero	UR	2.00
Erin Bencon	Air	Hero	UR	2.00
Familiar	Earth	Spell	VC	0.05
16				
Far Hunter	Air	Monster	R	1.00
Farsight	Earth	Spell	U	0.25
Fastfire	Fire	Spell	VC	0.05
Fate's Hand Pendant		Item	R	1.00
Fayenna	Earth	Monster	C	0.10
Felker Wraith	Air	Monster	R	1.00
Ferric Darklord	Water	Monster	R	1.00
Ferric Demon	Water	Monster	UR	2.00
Fire Elemental	Fire	Monster	R	1.00
17				
Fire Shield	Fire	Spell	VC	0.05
Fire Wall	Fire	Spell	VC	0.05
Fireball	Fire	Spell	U	0.25
Fireball Scroll		Item	U	0.25
Flame Barrier	Fire	Spell	C	0.10
Flame Commander	Fire	Hero	R	1.00
Flame Trap		Trap	U	0.25
Flame Wizards	Fire	Hero	X	0.50
Flameblade	Fire	Spell	VC	0.05
18				
Flight	Air	Spell	VC	0.05
Fog	Water	Spell	VC	0.05
Forest Dragon	Earth	Monster	R	1.00
Forest Guardian	Earth	Monster	C	0.10
Forest Sergas	Earth	Monster	U	0.25
Forstchen Schwarzmont	Earth	Hero	R	1.00
Frendelsette Tucerette	Air	Hero	UR	2.00
Gargoyles	Earth	Monster	U	0.25
Gauls	Fire	Hero	X	0.50
19				
Gean de Chartes	Earth	Hero	UR	2.00
Gerdheim Wavewarrior	Water	Hero	UR	2.00
Gideon	Air	Hero	UR	2.00
Goedfrey de Bouillon	Earth	Hero	UR	2.00
Golden Dragon	Fire	Monster	UR	2.00
Golden Pendant		Item	R	1.00
Gorm Helm		Item	R	1.00
Gorm Oath Sworn	Water	Monster	U	0.25
Gorm Scarab		Item	R	1.00
20				
Gorm Tiger	Earth	Monster	C	0.10
Gorm Water Dogs	Fire	Monster	X	0.50
Gorm's Armor		Item	R	1.00
Gorm's Sword		Item	R	1.00
Gormian Airholm	Earth	Monster	U	0.25
Gormian Assassin	Fire	Monster	X	0.50
Gormian Centaurs	Water	Monster	C	0.10
Gormian Enchanter	Fire	Monster	R	1.00
Gormian Sethrek	Fire	Monster	R	1.00
21				
Gormian Sliloth	Fire	Monster	R	1.00
Gormian Termoids	Water	Monster	X	0.50
Gormish Guardians	Earth	Monster	C	0.10
Gormish Horde	Earth	Monster	C	0.10
Gorneden	Fire	Monster	U	0.25
Greater Grevent	Water	Monster	R	1.00
Green Wand		Item	U	0.25
Gremlin	Fire	Monster	X	0.50
Grendelar Hessette	Water	Hero	UR	2.00
22				
Greptoid Riders	Fire	Monster	X	0.50
Gryphynes	Earth	Monster	U	0.25
Guermo de Chartes	Earth	Hero	R	1.00
Guilette de Marest	Earth	Hero	UR	2.00
Gustav Jonson	Water	Hero	UR	2.00
Hakessian Darklord	Earth	Monster	R	1.00
Hammits	Fire	Monster	X	0.50
Hargavian Giant	Water	Monster	U	0.25
Harmony	Earth	Spell	C	0.10
23				
Hastus Gonalius	Fire	Hero	UR	2.00
Hatshepsut	Air	Hero	UR	2.00
Hawara	Air	Hero	UR	2.00
Heal	Earth	Spell	VC	0.05
Healer's Trap		Trap	U	0.25
Healing Airs	Air	Spell	VC	0.05
Healing Scroll		Item	VC	0.05
Heatwave	Fire	Spell	U	0.25
Hedge Wizard	Earth	Hero	X	0.50
24				
Helm of Bast		Item	UR	2.00
Helm of Slaying		Item	R	1.00
Hezekiah	Air	Hero	UR	2.00
Hierogryph	Air	Monster	U	0.25
Hierophant	Water	Hero	X	0.50
High Priestess	Air	Hero	X	0.50
Holy Armor		Item	U	0.25
Honi Frey of Oaksten	Water	Hero	UR	2.00
Hoplite	Air	Hero	X	0.50
25				
Horn of Far Warning		Item	U	0.25
Horned Method	Earth	Monster	U	0.25
Howler	Fire	Monster	VC	0.05
Hugh de Payens	Earth	Hero	UR	2.00
Ian Stronghand	Water	Hero	UR	2.00
Illusion Trap		Trap	VC	0.05
Ingmare Nordskold	Water	Hero	R	1.00
Ingrid	Water	Hero	UR	2.00
Isin Lara	Air	Hero	UR	2.00
26				
Jacque de Marest	Earth	Hero	UR	2.00
Jacque de Molay	Earth	Hero	UR	2.00
Janya Maitzfrend	Water	Hero	R	1.00
Jean de Marest	Earth	Hero	R	1.00
Jodian Assassin	Earth	Monster	C	0.10
Jodian Darklord	Air	Monster	R	1.00
Jodian Lich	Air	Monster	U	0.25
Jodian Lucre	Air	Monster	R	1.00
Jodian Shremp	Air	Monster	X	0.50
27				
Jorge Olaf	Water	Hero	UR	2.00
Josiah ben Claigus	Air	Hero	UR	2.00
Judith de Hurst	Earth	Hero	UR	2.00
Jugurtha	Fire	Hero	UR	2.00
Julia Antogenes	Air	Hero	R	1.00
Karl QueenHerald	Water	Hero	UR	2.00
Karotid	Air	Monster	X	0.50
Kerak le Feve	Earth	Hero	UR	2.00
Kerillian Darklord	Fire	Monster	R	1.00
28				
Ki's Victory Armor		Item	UR	2.00
Kite Shield		Item	U	0.25
Kitren	Fire	Monster	C	0.10
Kremsur	Fire	Monster	C	0.10
Lara Farseeker	Air	Hero	U	0.25
Leather Armor		Item	VC	0.05
Legionnaire	Fire	Hero	X	0.50
Leigh Griffinbane	Water	Hero	R	1.00
Lesser Devil	Air	Monster	C	0.10
29				
Lightning Blade		Item	VC	0.05

RARITY KEY VC = Very Common C = Common U = Uncommon R = Rare UR = Ultra Rare X = Fixed/standard in all decks

Card name	Class	Type	Rarity	Price
Limassol	Air	Hero	R	1.00
Liots	Earth	Monster	C	0.10
Living Art Trap		Trap	C	0.10
Lizcanths	Earth	Monster	X	0.50
Lorea	Water	Monster	U	0.25
Lucky Charm		Item	R	1.00
Lunar Curse	Air	Spell	U	0.25
Lurkers	Water	Monster	U	0.25
30				
Macaabes	Air	Hero	X	0.50
Magic Trap		Trap	VC	0.05
Magical Dart Scroll		Item	VC	0.05
Malinx	Earth	Monster	R	1.00
Malthian Darklord	Earth	Monster	R	1.00
Man at Arms	Earth	Hero	X	0.50
Marcus Civilus	Fire	Hero	UR	2.00
Margoids	Water	Monster	U	0.25
31				
Marine	Water	Hero	X	0.50
Mask of Gorm		Item	UR	2.00
Mask of Ra		Item	R	1.00
Mask of Tristan		Item	R	1.00
Mate	Water	Hero	X	0.50
Meille Caithwarren	Water	Hero	UR	2.00
Melnearean Demon	Earth	Monster	R	1.00
Merbethian Shaman	Fire	Monster	C	0.10
Merharpies	Water	Monster	U	0.25
Merlion Darklord	Water	Monster	R	1.00
32				
Merloit	Water	Monster	X	0.50
Merlords	Water	Monster	R	1.00
Merzellan Darklord	Fire	Monster	R	1.00
Metellus Gabenius	Fire	Hero	R	1.00
Millan the Scott	Earth	Hero	UR	2.00
Mindwall	Water	Spell	VC	0.05
Misdirection	Water	Spell	VC	0.05
Mist Trap		Trap	VC	0.05
Mountain Sylph	Air	Monster	X	0.50
33				
Mummy	Air	Monster	U	0.25
Muratus	Fire	Hero	UR	2.00
Mystic Dart	Earth	Spell	VC	0.05
Nalsurus Beast	Earth	Monster	C	0.10
Narbo	Fire	Hero	C	0.10
Narsurs	Fire	Monster	C	0.10
Natural Cure	Earth	Spell	C	0.10
Night Piper	Earth	Monster	VC	0.05
Nixals	Water	Monster	C	0.10
34				
Nyean Demon	Fire	Monster	R	1.00
Nyean Helm		Item	R	1.00
Octoon Darklords	Earth	Monster	R	1.00
Omri Telemachus	Air	Hero	UR	2.00
Oracle	Fire	Hero	X	0.50
Orb of Gorm		Item	U	0.25
Orb of Orlow		Item	R	1.00
Orcans	Water	Monster	R	1.00
Orgoplais	Air	Monster	R	1.00
35				
Orlettes	Water	Monster	X	0.50
Orlow's Infernal Ring		Item	VC	0.05
Orlow's Shelter		Item	U	0.25
Orphalian Merfolk	Water	Monster	R	1.00
Orsus	Earth	Monster	U	0.25
Ortheons	Water	Monster	X	0.50
Pedro de Montaigu	Earth	Hero	UR	2.00
Pegasus	Air	Monster	C	0.10
Pendant of Pits		Item	U	0.25

Card name	Class	Type	Rarity	Price
36				
Pernasips	Water	Monster	R	1.00
Phoenix	Fire	Monster	R	1.00
Phonien Alens	Fire	Monster	U	0.25
Pianki	Air	Hero	C	0.10
Pier Hidgell	Water	Hero	UR	2.00
Pilot	Water	Hero	X	0.50
Pit Trap		Trap	C	0.10
Pitroons	Water	Monster	U	0.25
Plate Armor		Item	VC	0.05
37				
Plegeron	Air	Monster	U	0.25
Poul Ander	Water	Hero	U	0.25
Praetorian	Fire	Hero	X	0.50
Premonition	Fire	Spell	U	0.25
Ranger	Earth	Hero	X	0.50
Rayner	Fire	Hero	UR	2.00
Resurrect	Earth	Spell	U	0.25
Rexin Darklord	Air	Monster	R	1.00
Ring of Bast		Item	UR	2.00
38				
Ring of Control		Item	R	1.00
Ring of Gorm		Item	U	0.25
Ring of Mastery		Item	X	0.50
Ring of Power		Item	U	0.25
Ring of Scrying		Item	U	0.25
Ring of Speed		Item	UR	2.00
Ring of Wings		Item	U	0.25
River Snake	Water	Monster	X	0.50
Robinia Baleiu	Fire	Hero	UR	2.00
39				
Rope Trick	Air	Spell	U	0.25
Ruad de Isle	Earth	Hero	UR	2.00
Ruby Ring		Item	U	0.25
Sacrifice	Earth	Spell	R	1.00
Safita	Earth	Hero	UR	2.00
Sailor	Water	Hero	X	0.50
Salamander	Fire	Monster	R	1.00
Sapphire Ring		Item	R	1.00
Saving Scroll		Item	U	0.25
40				
Scarlet Scarab		Item	U	0.25
Schlein Assassin	Fire	Monster	U	0.25
Schleing	Earth	Monster	X	0.50
Scimitar		Item	U	0.25
Screamer	Air	Monster	U	0.25
Scroll of Blessing		Item	VC	0.05
Scroll of Knowledge		Item	U	0.25
Scroll of Safety		Item	U	0.25
Sea Dragon	Water	Monster	R	1.00
41				
Seagren Heartwer	Water	Hero	UR	2.00
Second Chance	Water	Spell	U	0.25
Selenkin	Water	Monster	R	1.00
Self Control	Water	Spell	VC	0.05
Selkies	Water	Monster	R	1.00
Senlings	Water	Monster	C	0.10
Serenger	Fire	Monster	C	0.10
Sergeant	Earth	Hero	X	0.50
Serpethian Darklord	Water	Monster	R	1.00
42				
Shade	Air	Monster	R	1.00
Shadow	Water	Monster	U	0.25
Shamblea	Air	Monster	U	0.25
Shared Blessing	Air	Spell	U	0.25
Short Bow		Item	VC	0.05
Skryling's Helm		Item	R	1.00
Skulker	Air	Monster	X	0.50
Skull Dragon	Water	Monster	R	1.00
Slieths	Earth	Monster	U	0.25
43				
Smoke Screen	Fire	Spell	C	0.10
Snyth	Water	Monster	R	1.00
Soothing	Earth	Spell	VC	0.05
Sorrow	Water	Spell	C	0.10

Card name	Class	Type	Rarity	Price
Sparks	Fire	Spell	VC	0.05
Spearman	Air	Hero	X	0.50
Spider Magnus	Water	Monster	UR	2.00
Spirit Lightning	Air	Spell	VC	0.05
Spirit Stealer	Water	Monster	R	1.00
44				
Splash Sprites	Water	Monster	X	0.50
Spryads	Earth	Monster	C	0.10
Squire	Earth	Hero	X	0.50
Staff of Banishing		Item	R	1.00
Staff of Fireballs		Item	VC	0.05
Staff of Healing		Item	VC	0.05
Staff of Might		Item	U	0.25
Staff of Protection		Item	U	0.25
Stanwin	Water	Hero	UR	2.00
45				
Storm Shield	Air	Spell	VC	0.05
Succulante	Air	Monster	C	0.10
Sudia Albani	Fire	Hero	UR	2.00
Summon Aide	Earth	Spell	U	0.25
Summon Aide Scroll		Item	U	0.25
Summon Creature	Fire	Spell	VC	0.05
Summoning Trap		Trap	U	0.25
Sun Blade		Item	VC	0.05
Sun Hawk	Earth	Monster	U	0.25
46				
Sun Shield		Item	U	0.25
Sunburst	Air	Spell	C	0.10
Sunken Treasure	Water	Spell	U	0.25
Sus Wavewalker	Water	Hero	UR	2.00
Sword of Right		Item	VC	0.05
Syon Gryphon	Fire	Monster	C	0.10
T-Rex	Earth	Monster	R	1.00
Tangle Trap		Trap	VC	0.05
Taramsets	Water	Monster	R	1.00
47				
Target Shield		Item	VC	0.05
Teleport Trap		Trap	U	0.25
Teuten Darklord	Fire	Monster	R	1.00
The Flowing	Water	Spell	U	0.25
The Four Powers	Earth	Spell	VC	0.05
Theodora	Earth	Hero	UR	2.00
Thomas Berard	Earth	Hero	UR	2.00
Time Warp Scroll		Item	U	0.25
Timeshift	Water	Spell	VC	0.05
48				
Tortesque	Fire	Monster	R	1.00
Tower Snake	Earth	Monster	U	0.25
Trapestry	Air	Spell	C	0.10
True Gryphons	Earth	Monster	U	0.25
Turning	Air	Spell	VC	0.05
Undead Legion	Air	Monster	R	1.00
Undeath	Air	Monster	UR	2.00
Unicorn	Earth	Monster	R	1.00
Vangereen	Air	Monster	UR	2.00
49				
Viro Demon	Water	Monster	C	0.10
Vita Alver	Water	Hero	UR	2.00
Vol Haverson	Water	Hero	UR	2.00
Vomisa ben Isaac	Fire	Hero	C	0.10
Vultegon	Air	Monster	U	0.25
War Hawks	Earth	Monster	R	1.00
Water Trap		Trap	U	0.25
Wave Wizard	Water	Hero	X	0.50
Web	Water	Spell	VC	0.05
50				
Werewolf	Earth	Monster	C	0.10
Wieston Sheitwraith	Water	Hero	R	1.00
Wind Trap		Trap	U	0.25
Windforce	Air	Spell	C	0.10
Windlord	Air	Monster	R	1.00
Windonei	Air	Monster	C	0.10
Wizard's Staff		Item	U	0.25
Wizardry Scroll		Item	R	1.00
Zanthor	Fire	Monster	C	0.10

Latest game prices

Current prices for the in-demand cards from "living" CCGs (those still being supported with new releases) can be found in each issue of *Scrye*.

RARITY KEY VC = Very Common C = Common U = Uncommon R = Rare UR = Ultra Rare X = Fixed/standard in all decks

Fastbreak

Wildstorm • First set, *One-on-One Basketball*, released **August 1996**

303 cards plus **2** promos in set

Concept	●●●○○
Gameplay	●●●○○
Card art	●●○○○
Player pool	○○○○○

- Starter decks contain 60 cards; starter displays contain 12 starters
- Booster packs contain 12 cards; booster displays contain 36 boosters

Fastbreak takes a humorous approach to pro basketball, with such cards as **Kill the Mascot** and more fouls than one can count.

Two five-man teams line up a card's length apart. A basketball token, provided, is placed between the two centers. Players then visualize a 5x5 grid in which the teams move. Instead of moving player cards, the ball moves up columns and across rows. A Dribble card is played when moving the ball down court, and can be resisted with a Grab card. Passes are resisted with Steals, and Shoot cards are resisted with Blocks. There are also Wild cards which provide effects outside of moving the ball. Play continues to any agreed upon number of points.

The art is cartoony, but characters and images occur on multiple cards, building a consistent theme. The card design makes it easy to understand, and the best traits of this game are its humor and the realism. Unfortunately, *Fastbreak* caught on about as well as any sports CCG without a professional sports license has — which is to say it never made it to the postseason. — *Richard Weld*

You will need **34** nine-pocket pages to store this set. (17 doubled up)

Set (303 cards)		63.00
Starter Display Box		49.00
Booster Display Box		52.00
Starter Deck		5.00
Booster Pack		1.00

Promo Cards

Card name	Rarity	Price
☐ Bust the Backboard	Pr	1.50
☐ Trample	Pr	1.50

Card name	Rarity	Price
☐ A Little Shove	C	0.05
☐ A Not-So-Little Shove	C	0.05
☐ Aaron "Money" Brooks	R	1.00
☐ Abe Stass	X	0.20
☐ Aggressive Move	C	0.05
☐ Air Ball!	U	0.35
☐ Air Horn	U	0.35
☐ Albert "Agreeable Al" Madison	X	0.20
☐ Alley Oop!	U	0.35
☐ Amazing Defense	U	0.35
☐ Announcer Snaps	R	1.00
☐ Anthony "Duke" Softway	X	0.20
☐ Antonio Baka-Guy	R	1.00
☐ Arctic Alexander Koi	R	1.00
☐ Arik "The Lion" Maurois	X	0.20
☐ Attack the Ball	C	0.05
☐ Backdoor Layup	C	0.05
☐ Backdoor Pass	C	0.05
☐ Bad Bart Zuckerman	U	0.35
☐ Bad Call	R	1.00
☐ Bam!	U	0.35
☐ Bat Away	C	0.05
☐ Bear Hug	C	0.05
☐ Behind-the-Back Pass	C	0.05
☐ Bench Glue	R	1.00
☐ Bert Geiger "Counter"	X	0.20
☐ Between the Legs	C	0.05
☐ Bobbled Pass	C	0.05
☐ Bobby Burket	C	0.05
☐ Body Contact	C	0.05
☐ Bottoms, Baby!	U	0.35
☐ Bounce Pass	C	0.05
☐ Bram "The Count" Dawkins	X	0.20
☐ Break Free	U	0.35
☐ Break Loose	U	0.35
☐ Bribe Player	R	1.00
☐ Bribe Ref	R	1.00
☐ Brick	C	0.05
☐ Brick Bradley	C	0.05
☐ Bullet	C	0.05

Card name	Rarity	Price
☐ Bump and Grab	C	0.05
☐ Chanting Fans	U	0.35
☐ Charge!	C	0.05
☐ Cheerleaders	U	0.35
☐ Chest Pass	C	0.05
☐ Chet Miles	X	0.20
☐ Chris Pitzer	U	0.35
☐ Coast to Coast	C	0.05
☐ Concentration	U	0.35
☐ Continuation	U	0.35
☐ Corey "The Flea" Salko	Ch	2.00
☐ Crowd Riot	R	1.00
☐ Cut the Lights	U	0.35
☐ Dale Sample	X	0.20
☐ Daniel "Alamo" Crockett	X	0.20
☐ Daryl "No Stress" Wessner	Ch	2.00
☐ Dave "The Kid" McCann	Ch	2.00
☐ Dead Ball	R	1.00
☐ Devon "The Mouth" Haskins	R	1.00
☐ Dish	C	0.05
☐ Dish Out	C	0.05
☐ Donte Moulton	Ch	2.00
☐ Double Pump	C	0.05
☐ Draw Charge	C	0.05
☐ Drive the Lane	C	0.05
☐ Dustin "Thor" Kelley	X	0.20
☐ Eugene Schmidt	X	0.20
☐ Fadeaway Jumper	C	0.05
☐ Fast Break	C	0.05
☐ Feral Kerwyn Faust	U	0.35
☐ Find the Open Man	C	0.05
☐ Finger Roll	C	0.05
☐ Flash Bulbs	U	0.35
☐ Foot Block	C	0.05
☐ Force Double Dribble	C	0.05
☐ Force Out	C	0.05
☐ Force Travel	C	0.05
☐ Freaky Fergus Williams	X	0.20
☐ Fred "Moon" Mullin	R	1.00
☐ Freddie Fraser	X	0.20
☐ From Out of Nowhere!	U	0.35
☐ Gahiji "The Hunter" Eduvala	X	0.20
☐ Gambling Spectators	U	0.35
☐ Garth Neal	X	0.20
☐ Get Back!	U	0.35
☐ Give and Go	C	0.05
☐ Goaltending	R	1.00
☐ Goggles Murphy	C	0.05
☐ Good "D"	C	0.05
☐ Good Rhythm	U	0.35
☐ Goonie Smith	X	0.20

Card name	Rarity	Price
☐ Grab It!	R	1.00
☐ Grab the Ball	C	0.05
☐ Great Inbounds Pass	C	0.05
☐ Great Plan	R	1.00
☐ Hack	C	0.05
☐ Haglev "The Viking" Petterson	X	0.20
☐ Hand Check	C	0.05
☐ Handoff	C	0.05
☐ Hands in the Face	C	0.05
☐ Hands Like Glue	U	0.35
☐ Hands Up!	C	0.05
☐ Harass	R	1.00
☐ Head Fake	C	0.05
☐ Head-Bounce Pass	C	0.05
☐ Heckling Fan	U	0.35
☐ Helga Mishkov	C	0.05
☐ Hit the Boards	R	1.00
☐ Hook Shot	C	0.05
☐ Hoop Him!	R	1.00
☐ Hot from 3-Point Land!	U	0.35
☐ Hugh Jeego	C	0.05
☐ I Don't Think So!	R	1.00
☐ Ibrahim Mpalesu	C	0.05
☐ Ice Patch	R	1.00
☐ In the Zone	U	0.35
☐ In Your Face!	U	0.35
☐ Incredible "D"	C	0.05
☐ Inspirational Speech	R	1.00
☐ Inspired Coaching	R	1.00
☐ Intentional Foul	U	0.35
☐ Interception!	U	0.35
☐ It's Outta Here!	U	0.35
☐ Ivan Dawson	C	0.05
☐ Jam	C	0.05
☐ Jeff "Blanky" Blankenhorn	U	0.35
☐ Jeremy "Whiz Kid" Singer	Ch	2.00
☐ Jerome Starr	X	0.20
☐ Jethro McCoy	C	0.05
☐ Jimmy "Butta" Buck	R	1.00
☐ Jimmy Jelks	R	1.00
☐ John Shlump	U	0.35
☐ John Uhrich	X	0.20
☐ Joseph Deo	C	0.05
☐ Juke	C	0.05
☐ Jump Shot	C	0.05
☐ Jumping Jacks	C	0.05
☐ Kalomo Johnson	C	0.05
☐ Karim Bull	X	0.20
☐ Kill the Mascot!	U	0.35
☐ Kimball "The Lid" Edson	X	0.20
☐ Kiss the Glass	C	0.05

Card name	Rarity	Price
☐ Knock 'em Down	U	0.35
☐ Knock Away	C	0.05
☐ Kris "The Knife" Oprisko	R	1.00
☐ Kurt "Stony" Steiner	X	0.20
☐ Laurie Mackenzie	U	0.35
☐ Layup	C	0.05
☐ Legendary Coaching	U	0.35
☐ Leslie Childs	X	0.20
☐ Lob	C	0.05
☐ Look, Up in the Sky!	U	0.35
☐ Lothar Held	X	0.20
☐ Mad Mike Geisler	X	0.20
☐ Magnetized Ball	R	1.00
☐ Make Your Own Luck	R	1.00
☐ Marshall King	C	0.05
☐ Marvelous Defense	U	0.35
☐ Mascot Attacks!	R	1.00
☐ Mascot Subs In	U	0.35
☐ Matt Forbeck	X	0.20
☐ Max "The Head" Lewitt	X	0.20
☐ Meleke Kalamua	X	0.20
☐ Mikhail "Little Bear" Pushkin	C	0.05
☐ Monster Block	U	0.35
☐ Monster Dunk	U	0.35
☐ Montel "The Master" Turner	R	1.00
☐ Move the Ball	C	0.05
☐ Mykl "Lucky 7" Albano	Ch	2.00
☐ Myron "The Butcher" Simpson	U	0.35
☐ Mysterious Malik Israel	R	1.00
☐ New Hairdo	U	0.35
☐ Nik "The Accountant" Kolinsky	Ch	2.00
☐ No-Look Pass	U	0.35
☐ Noah Aigg	X	0.20
☐ Nuthin' But Net	U	0.35
☐ One-on-One	C	0.05
☐ Organ Music	U	0.35
☐ Orlando Rust	X	0.20
☐ Over the Back	C	0.05
☐ Overhead Pass	C	0.05
☐ Pat Faesslar	R	1.00
☐ Paul Duffy	X	0.20
☐ Pekka Mekkenin	R	1.00
☐ Perimeter Defense	U	0.35
☐ Phil "The Chief" Mancuso	X	0.20
☐ Pick & Roll	C	0.05
☐ Pick Fight!	R	1.00
☐ Pick His Pocket	U	0.35
☐ Play With Pain	R	1.00
☐ Poke in the Eye	C	0.05
☐ Pop a Trey	C	0.05

Card name	Rarity	Price	Card name	Rarity	Price	Card name	Rarity	Price	Card name	Rarity	Price
Pop It Back Out	C	0.05	Shango "The Goat" Levallier	C	0.05	Sucker Punch	R	1.00	Tony "The Hawk" Ravenelli	C	0.05
Product Endorsement	R	1.00	Shoe Contract	U	0.35	Superb Defense	U	0.35	Top of the Key	C	0.05
Protect the Ball	U	0.35	Short Shot Clock	U	0.35	Superstar Status	R	1.00	Toss	C	0.05
Putback	C	0.05	Shot Clock Magic	U	0.35	Swat!	U	0.35	Touch Pass	U	0.35
Qua'il Abubakker	U	0.35	Shove and Take	U	0.35	Sweat Slick	R	1.00	Tough "D"	C	0.05
Railroad	U	0.35	Show Character	R	1.00	Swervyn Mervyn	X	0.20	Trap	C	0.05
Rainbow	U	0.35	Sidearm Pass	C	0.05	Swish!	U	0.35	Trifecta	U	0.35
Razzle Dazzle	U	0.35	Sixto Velasquez	X	0.20	Tap Away	C	0.05	Trip	C	0.05
Reach Around	C	0.05	Slam Dunk!	U	0.35	Tap In	C	0.05	TV Timeout	R	1.00
Reach In	C	0.05	Slap the Ball Free	C	0.05	Technical Foul	U	0.35	Two-on-One	U	0.35
Rejected!	C	0.05	Slop	C	0.05	Terrence Hollywood	R	1.00	Two-on-Two Pass	U	0.35
Rexford "Ital" Anselm	X	0.20	Smack It Loose	C	0.05	The Men in Black	R	1.00	"Ugly" Ion Grotescu	C	0.05
Rick "Loco" Loiko	R	1.00	Smack!	C	0.05	The Wave	U	0.35	Vernell Butterfield	R	1.00
Riki Shriver	X	0.20	Snag Pass	C	0.05	Theo Pong	X	0.20	W. Harold Les	U	0.35
Rocket	U	0.35	Snatch Pass	C	0.05	Three Seconds	U	0.35	Warner Jones	C	0.05
Roger "Ro-bot" Bot	R	1.00	Snowball Fight	R	1.00	Three-on-One	U	0.35	Wesley Taitt	U	0.35
Rogue Laser Show	R	1.00	Spacey Shavon Lewis	U	0.35	Three-on-Three	U	0.35	Who's Got the Ball?	R	1.00
Ronnell "Dude" Childs	R	1.00	Spaulding Sangwich	C	0.05	Three-on-Two	U	0.35	Wild Pass	C	0.05
Russell "Sticks" Hoffman	X	0.20	Spike the Water	R	1.00	Three-Point Play	U	0.35	Windmilling	U	0.35
Sammy "Senior Sam" Humphries	C	0.05	Spin	C	0.05	Throw a Chair	R	1.00	Winston Carver	X	0.20
Scoreboard Controls	R	1.00	Spring-Loaded Shoes	U	0.35	Throw Elbow	C	0.05	Woody Bang	X	0.20
Scottie Finn	X	0.20	Stanley Lee	X	0.20	Throw Knee	C	0.05	Work Free	C	0.05
Screen Play	C	0.05	Stefan "Psycho" Hampton	X	0.20	Tie Down	C	0.05	Work Loose	C	0.05
Sean Ang	X	0.20	Stickum	U	0.35	Tim "Trey" Mitsky	U	0.35	Work the Perimeter	U	0.35
Sean Gender	X	0.20	Sticky Fingers	U	0.35	Tip Play	C	0.05	Wrestling Match	C	0.05
Second Wind	R	1.00	Strong Defense	C	0.05	Tipped It	C	0.05	Wrist Slap	C	0.05
Set Shot	C	0.05	Stuff	C	0.05	Tipped Pass	C	0.05	Yuri "Big Bear" Tretyak	Ch	2.00
			Stutter Step	C	0.05	Tobias "The Gimp" Queck	X	0.20	Zebra Jam!	R	1.00

Flights of Fantasy

Concept	●○○○○
Gameplay	○◐○○○
Card art	●●●●○
Player pool	○○○○○

Destini Productions • Released **September 1994** • **118** cards in set
• Booster packs contain 10 cards; booster displays contain 50 packs

Flights of Fantasy is only a CCG in such a *broad* definition of the term that it is *not* generally credited as being the second one following *Magic*. But given the explosive demand in those earliest days of the CCG craze, it's easy to understand why someone would think of adding a (very minor!) game element to what is really a card art set.

Flights features the work of Ed Beard, Jr., a popular artist in gaming. (He did the cover for *Scrye* #1!) Card backs, read sequentially, tell short stories relating to the art.

That's fine, but the "game" looks grafted on. Players pit cards of story characters against each other. Near the copyright text (and in a scarcely larger font), cards note an attribute for each. Players roll dice and note that character's score. Repeat 29 times, then add to see who wins. That's about it. If you like doing your taxes, this is for you.

Beard's art is wonderful, but people looking for a *game* should save their dollars and play Serial Number Poker with them. It's cheaper and there's less math. — *John Jackson Miller*

You will need **14** nine-pocket pages to store this set. (7 doubled up)

Set (118 cards)	45.00
Booster Display Box	25.00
Booster Pack	1.00

Promo cards

Card name	Price
Flights of Fantasy	4.50
Mystical Scroll of Infinite Knowledge	4.50
Vile of Blood	4.50
Well of Endurance	4.50

Card name	Rarity	Price	Card name	Rarity	Price	Card name	Rarity	Price	Card name	Rarity	Price	Card name	Rarity	Price
Ace Fighter	C	0.10	Chansi	C	0.10	General Lugeron	C	0.10	Mirror	C	0.10	Scalovates	C	0.10
Acheron 3010	C	0.10	Clive Shulte	C	0.10	Gorgon	C	0.10	Mithraic	C	0.10	Scarecrow	C	0.10
Agromex	C	0.10	Complete Puzzle of 9 Dragons	R	0.80	Grave Diggers	C	0.10	Moon Dragoness	R	0.80	Scintillating Dragoness	R	0.80
Alexandrian	C	0.10	Crows	C	0.10	Grotts	C	0.10	Nazi Soldier	C	0.10	Scutisorex	C	0.10
Alien Billiards	UR	1.50	Crylys	C	0.10	Guardian of the Universe	C	0.10	Neutron Dragoness	R	0.80	Shaman	C	0.10
Alpha-Z	C	0.10	Cryos	C	0.10	Isogoniks	C	0.10	Nosferatu	C	0.10	Slade	C	0.10
Andric	C	0.10	Darnaylia	C	0.10	Jester	C	0.10	Nyctea	C	0.10	Solar Dragoness	R	0.80
Anguian	C	0.10	Demons	C	0.10	Kakahri	C	0.10	Ocxolytes	C	0.10	Stone Guardian	C	0.10
Arch Angel	C	0.10	Dotrene	C	0.10	Keitsektok	C	0.10	Ogress	C	0.10	Terrasesis	C	0.10
Artimedos	C	0.10	Dr. M. E. Phistopheles	C	0.10	Kelly D. Grassette Beard	UR	1.50	Pollux	C	0.10	Teufel	C	0.10
Artist Bio	UR	1.50	Dragon Automaton	R	0.80	Kestrelin	C	0.10	Pollux Sculpture	UR	1.50	Teufel	R	0.80
Bohg	C	0.10	Drogah	C	0.10	Khnemu	C	0.10	Power Incarnate	C	0.10	The Cosmic Cleansing	UR	1.50
Castor	C	0.10	Druid Forest	C	0.10	King Ogdin Loven	C	0.10	Pycesus	C	0.10	The Harvest	UR	1.50
Cat Beast	C	0.10	Dryxtar	C	0.10	Knight Specter	R	0.80	Pyro Revolt	C	0.10	"The Social Gathering"	UR	1.50
Cephalodine	C	0.10	Encladus	C	0.10	Komodo	C	0.10	Quark Dragoness	R	0.80	The Swan	UR	1.50
Chacmagyes	C	0.10	Ergloph	C	0.10	Kryophoros	C	0.10	Racniz	C	0.10	Tri-lateral Textangula	R	0.80
			Ether Dragoness	R	0.80	Krystalin	C	0.10	Radiation Dragoness	R	0.80	Urutu	C	0.10
			Father Tonoff	C	0.10	Leo LeGrande'	C	0.10	Rakshasa	C	0.10	Virago	C	0.10
			Flights of Fantasy Wizard	R	0.80	Lostomatid	C	0.10	Rodeka	C	0.10	Volcano	C	0.10
			"FoF" Collage	UR	1.50	Lunar Worm	C	0.10	Rule Card A	R	0.80	Vulture	C	0.10
			Forest	C	0.10	M-6 Annihilator	C	0.10	Rule Card B	R	0.80	Walker	C	0.10
			Friar Matthew	C	0.10	M-6 Sentry	C	0.10	Rule Card C	R	0.80	Walking Dead	C	0.10
			Ganesa	C	0.10	Madame Marishka	C	0.10	Sacred Relic	C	0.10	White Dove	C	0.10
			Gargoyle	C	0.10	Medepoch	C	0.10	Saji	C	0.10	Winter Play	UR	1.50
			Geisha	UR	1.50	Megohm	C	0.10	Sarka	C	0.10	Wolf	C	0.10
						Mind Control Beast	UR	1.50	Saurian	C	0.10			

RARITY KEY C = Common U = Uncommon R = Rare UR = Ultra Rare Ch = Chase card X = Fixed/standard in all decks

Galactic Empires

Companion Games • First set, *Alpha*, Released **September 1994**
89 cards in set • **IDENTIFIER: Plastic coated; edges are rough with perforation marks**

• Starter decks contain 50 cards
• Booster packs contain 10 cards

One of the "class of '94," *Galactic Empires* was based on Companion Games' unauthorized releases for Task Force's *Star Fleet Battles* game. For a CCG that never reached beyond a niche audience, *Galactic Empires* generated many large expansions — and more promo cards than any other CCG in history. By the time the final release rolled around in 1997, players had nearly 3,500 *Galactic Empires* cards to choose from!

Although *Galactic Empires* has many different card types, the primary types are ships and terrain. Unlike many CCGs, the limiting factor on getting cards in play is the number of card plays, rather than resources. A player can play three cards in a turn, regardless of type.

To win, a player must put 25 points of damage into the opponent's Headquarters sector. Ships guard this Headquarters sector, while the terrain gives a player the resources to engage the ships, so that they can fire. A ship protects the sector even if the player lacks the resources to engage the ship. The basic aim is to destroy an opponent's ships, either by fire or by card play, and expose the Headquarters sector to fire.

The *Alpha* release was noted for its complicated rules for both deck construction and play, for not having enough cards to make the complexity work, and for an offer of $1,000 to the winner of the Origins and Gen Con tournaments.

The *Alpha* cards were plastic coated and wore well, the best that could be said of this release. — *Michael Greenholdt*

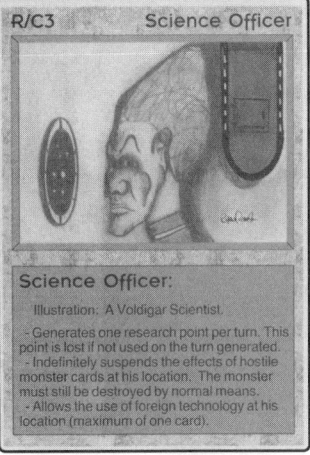

R/C3	Science Officer

Science Officer:

Illustration: A Voldigar Scientist.

- Generates one research point per turn. This point is lost if not used on the turn generated.
- Indefinitely suspends the effects of hostile monster cards at his location. The monster must still be destroyed by normal means.
- Allows the use of foreign technology at his location (maximum of one card).

Concept	●●●●○
Gameplay	●●○○○
Card art	●●○○○
Player pool	○○○○○

Set (89 cards)	33.00
Starter Display Box	20.00
Booster Display Box	22.00
Starter Deck	5.00
Booster Pack	1.00

You will need 10 nine-pocket pages to store this set. (5 doubled up)

Card name	Type	Rarity	Price
Aldibrik Munitions Plant	T4	C	0.20
Argo	T7	R	2.40
Argonian Battlecruiser [Star Left]	S7	R	2.40
Argonian Battlecruiser [Star Rt.]	S7	R	2.40
Argonian Destroyer	S4	C	0.20
Argonian Frigate [Shadow Left]	S3	C	0.20
Argonian Frigate [Shadow Right]	S3	C	0.20
Argonian Light Cruiser	S5	C	0.20
Argonian Strobe	E7	R	2.40
Argonian Typhoon Heavy Cruiser	S6	C	0.20
Asteroid Field	T6	U	0.60
Base Station	B4	C	0.20
Benakis Asteroid Belt	T3	C	0.20
Biruk's Comet	T2	C	0.20
Black Hole	T6	R	2.40
Boarding Party [Corp Humans]	C1	C	0.20
Bolaar IV	T4	C	0.20
Bolaar Light Pirate Raider	S3	U	0.60
Breakdown	O1	C	0.20
Breakdown	O5	R	2.40
Bribe Pirate	O8	R	2.40
Candor II	T5	R	2.40
Captain (Mazgar)	C6	R	2.40
Cargo	E1	C	0.20
Cramannerak	T5	C	0.20
Defensive Satellites [Planet Left]	B2	R	2.40
Defensive Satellites [Planet Right]	B2	R	2.40
Deflection Xfer Device (Bolaar BKG)	E6	R	2.40
Doctor [Krebiz]	R/C2	C	0.20
Engineer [Indirigan - Shoulders]	C3	C	0.20
Fighter	R/E5	R	2.40
Fighter Pilot	C4	R	2.40
Fleet Freighter [Front Left]	S1	C	0.20
Fleet Freighter [Front Right]	S1	C	0.20

Card name	Type	Rarity	Price
Fleet Tug	S2	C	0.20
Forced Retreat	O5	R	2.40
Forced Retreat	O3	C	0.20
Heavy Phaser Refit	E4	R	2.40
Heavy Shield Refit	E3	R	2.40
Illness	O2	R	2.40
Indig's Comet	T4	R	2.40
Injury	O4	U	0.60
Invinco Guardian	M6	R	2.40
Ion Storm	H2	C	0.20
Ion Storm	H5	R	2.40
Kalin's Small Red Nebula	T2	C	0.20
Krebiz Battle Capsule	S2	U	0.60
Krebiz Claw Hvy Cruiser [Small Planet]	S5	C	0.20
Krebiz Clipper Frigate [Front Left]	S2	C	0.20
Krebiz Clipper Frigate [Front Right]	S2	C	0.20
Krebiz Heavy Capsule	S2	C	0.20
Krebiz Light Capsule	S1	VC	0.10
Krebiz Mandible Cruiser [No Planet]	S4	C	0.20
Krebiz Medium Capsule	S1	C	0.20
Krebiz Pincer Destroyer	S3	C	0.20
Krebiz Pseudo Capsule	E1	U	0.60
Large Asteroid	T1	C	0.20
Large Phaser Eel	M5	R	2.40
Marine [Corporate Human]	R/C4	R	2.40
Moon	T3	U	0.60
Nebula - Homecloud	T5	R	2.40
Nova [Effect Left]	H4	R	2.40
Nova [Effect Right]	H4	R	2.40
Phaser Refit	E2	C	0.20
Planet Gouge	M2	U	0.60
Planetary Shield	B1	C	0.20
Plasma Field	T/H2	C	0.20
Probe	E1	C	0.20

Card name	Type	Rarity	Price
Pulsar	H3	C	0.20
Repair Delivery	R/O4	R	2.40
Scandig	T8	R	2.40
Science Officer [Voldigar]	R/C3	C	0.20
Shield Fiend	M3	R	2.40
Shield Refit	E1	C	0.20
Shuttlecraft [Front Left]	R/E3	C	0.20
Shuttlecraft [Front Right]	R/E3	C	0.20
Small Moon	T1	C	0.20
Small Phaser Eel	M1	VC	0.10
Space Dragon	M4	C	0.20
Space Station	B3	R	2.40
Surprise Attack	O7	R	2.40
Time Warp	H1	C	0.20
Tractor Beam	R/E2	C	0.20
Transporter	R/E2	VC	0.10
Type II Supernova	H6	R	2.40
Vektrea Prime	T5	C	0.20
Vektrean Mercenaries Light Cruiser	S4	R	2.40
Vorn Ringed Gas Giant [Probe Telem]	T6	R	2.40
Weapons Officer	C5	R	2.40

Card types

In *Galactic Empires*, the letter is a generic indicator (C=crew, S=ship, etc.). The number indicates the card's strength.

RARITY KEY **VC** = Very Common **C** = Common **U** = Uncommon **R** = Rare **VR** = Very Rare **F** = Foil card **X** = Fixed/standard in all decks

SCRYE Collectible Card Game Checklist and Price Guide • **159**

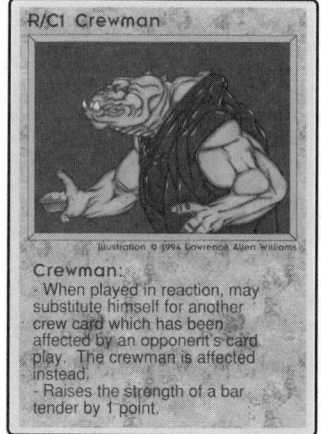

Galactic Empires • Beta

Companion Games • Released **October 1994**

90 cards in set • **IDENTIFIER: Plastic-coated with no perforation marks**

• Starter decks contain 50 cards • Booster packs contain 10 cards

Galactic Empires: Beta is essentially a second printing of **Alpha**. They're cut better than the *Alpha* cards, and that's the main distinguishing factor. A few cards also have different artwork. — *Michael Greenholdt*

Set (90 cards)	27.00	
Starter Display Box	17.00	
Booster Display Box	17.00	
Starter Deck	5.00	
Booster Pack	1.00	

You will need **10** nine-pocket pages to store this set. (5 doubled up)

Card name	Type	Rarity	Price
☐ Aldibrik Munitions Plant	T4	C	0.15
☐ Argo	T7	R	2.40
☐ Argonian Battlecruiser [Star Left]	S7	R	2.40
☐ Argonian Destroyer	S4	C	0.15
☐ Argonian Frigate [Shadow Left]	S3	C	0.15
☐ Argonian Light Cruiser	S5	C	0.15
☐ Argonian Strobe	E7	R	2.40
☐ Argonian Typhoon Heavy Cruiser	S6	C	0.15
☐ Asteroid Field	T6	U	0.50
☐ Base Station	B4	C	0.15
☐ Benakis Asteroid Belt	T3	C	0.15
☐ Biruk's Comet	T2	C	0.15
☐ Black Hole	T6	C	0.15
☐ Boarding Party [Corp Humans]	C1	C	0.15
☐ Bolaar IV	T4	C	0.15
☐ Bolaar Light Pirate Raider	S3	U	0.50
☐ Breakdown	O1	C	0.15
☐ Breakdown	O5	R	2.40
☐ Bribe Pirate	O6	R	2.40
☐ Candor II	T5	R	2.40

Card name	Type	Rarity	Price
☐ Captain (Mazgar)	C6	R	2.40
☐ Cargo	E1	C	0.15
☐ Communications Officer [Voldigar]	C4	R	2.40
☐ Cramannerak	T5	C	0.15
☐ Defensive Satellites [Planet Left]	B2	R	2.40
☐ Defensive Satellites [Planet Right]	B2	R	2.40
☐ Deflection Xfer Device (Bolaar BKG)	E6	R	2.40
☐ Doctor [Krebiz]	R/C2	C	0.15
☐ Engineer [Indirigan - No Shoulders]	C3	C	0.15
☐ Fighter	R/E5	R	2.40
☐ Fighter Pilot	C4	R	2.40
☐ Fleet Freighter [Front Left]	S1	C	0.15
☐ Fleet Freighter [Front Right]	S1	C	0.15
☐ Fleet Tug	S2	C	0.15
☐ Forced Retreat	O5	R	2.40
☐ Forced Retreat	O3	C	0.15
☐ Heavy Phaser Refit	E4	R	2.40
☐ Heavy Shield Refit	E3	R	2.40
☐ Illness	O2	R	2.40
☐ Injury	O4	R	2.40
☐ Invinco Guardian	M6	R	2.40
☐ Ion Storm	H2	C	0.15
☐ Ion Storm	H5	R	2.40
☐ Kalin's Small Red Nebula	T2	C	0.15
☐ Krebiz Battle Capsule	S2	U	0.50
☐ Krebiz Claw Hvy Cruiser[Dust Trails]	S5	C	0.15
☐ Krebiz Clipper Frigate [Front Left]	S2	C	0.15
☐ Krebiz Clipper Frigate [Front Right]	S2	C	0.15
☐ Krebiz Heavy Capsule	S2	C	0.15
☐ Krebiz Light Capsule	S1	VC	0.10
☐ Krebiz Mandible Lt Cruiser [Blue Pnt]	S4	U	0.50
☐ Krebiz Medium Capsule	S1	C	0.15
☐ Krebiz Pincer Destroyer	S3	C	0.15
☐ Krebiz Pseudo Capsule	E1	U	0.50
☐ Krebiz Sabot Sequencer	E6	R	2.40

Card name	Type	Rarity	Price
☐ Large Asteroid	T1	C	0.15
☐ Large Phaser Eel	M5	U	0.50
☐ Marine [Corporate Human]	R/C4	R	2.40
☐ Moon	T3	U	0.50
☐ Nebula - Homecloud	T5	R	2.40
☐ Nova [Effect Left]	H4	R	2.40
☐ Nova [Effect Right]	H4	R	2.40
☐ Phaser Refit	E2	C	0.15
☐ Planet Gouge	M2	C	0.15
☐ Planetary Shield	B1	C	0.15
☐ Plasma Field	T/H2	U	0.50
☐ Point Symbols		U	0.50
☐ Probe	E1	C	0.15
☐ Pulsar	H3	C	0.15
☐ Repair Delivery	R/O4	R	2.40
☐ Scandig	T8	R	2.40
☐ Science Officer [Indirigan]	R/C1	C	0.15
☐ Shield Fiend	M3	VC	0.10
☐ Shield Refit	E1	C	0.15
☐ Shuttlecraft [Front Left]	R/E3	C	0.15
☐ Shuttlecraft [Front Right]	R/E3	C	0.15
☐ Small Moon	T1	C	0.15
☐ Small Phaser Eel	M1	C	0.15
☐ Sochess Comet	T6	R	2.40
☐ Space Dragon	M4	U	0.50
☐ Space Station	B3	R	2.40
☐ Surprise Attack	O7	R	2.40
☐ Time Warp	H1	C	0.15
☐ Tractor Beam	R/E2	C	0.15
☐ Transporter	R/E2	VC	0.10
☐ Type II Supernova	H6	R	2.40
☐ Vektrea Prime	T5	C	0.15
☐ Vektrean Mercenaries Light Cruiser	S4	R	2.40
☐ Vorn Ringed Gas Giant	T6	R	2.40
☐ Weapons Officer [Scorpead]	C5	R	2.40

Galactic Empires • Primary

Companion Games • Released **December 1994**

444 cards in set • **IDENTIFIER: Only set on cardstock with 1994 trademarks**

• Starter decks contain 50 cards

• Booster packs contain 10 cards

Galactic Empires: Primary was the release that made the game. A set with more than 400 cards finally allowed the deck construction rules to work.

Each deck had to have eight different card types, with at least one card of each strength value (1 through 10) and a minimum of five cards. With these restrictions, it had been very difficult to create a deck measurably different from other decks with the **Alpha** and **Beta** editions.

Primary cards are printed on regular card stock, as are all subsequent releases. — *Michael Greenholdt*

Set (444 cards)	42.00	
Starter Display Box	24.00	
Booster Display Box	14.00	
Starter Deck	5.00	
Booster Pack	1.00	

You will need **50** nine-pocket pages to store this set. (25 doubled up)

Card name	Type	Rarity	Price
☐ Academy	B7	VR	3.00
☐ Accelerated Timeline	L9	VR	3.00
☐ Administrative Facility	B5	R	2.50
☐ Admiral	C9	VR	3.00
☐ Advanced Preparedness	R/L8	VR	3.00
☐ Akru Supernova	H10	UR	4.00
☐ Aldibrik Munitions Plant	T4	R	2.50

Card name	Type	Rarity	Price
☐ Alien Abduction	O6	VR	3.00
☐ Alien Artifact	L7	VR	3.00
☐ Alien Love Interest	R/O8	R	2.50
☐ Alien Parasites	M3	U	0.80
☐ Alliance Treaty	O9	VR	3.00
☐ Ambassador	C5	VR	3.00
☐ Ancient Molting	A5	VR	3.00

RARITY KEY VC = Very Common C = Common U = Uncommon R = Rare VR = Very Rare F = Foil card X = Fixed/standard in all decks

160 • SCRYE Collectible Card Game Checklist and Price Guide

Card name	Type	Rarity	Price
Ancient Spacefarer	C6	VR	3.00
Anomaly Portal	R/L7	VR	3.00
Anti-Tractor	R/E4	U	0.80
Antimatter Mine	E5	VR	3.00
3			
Antimatter Singularity	H7	VR	3.00
Argo	T7	VR	3.00
Argonian Assault Carrier	S4	U	0.80
Argonian Battlecruiser [Star Rt.]	S7	R	2.50
Argonian Battleship	S9	VR	3.00
Argonian Command Cruiser	S6	R	2.50
Argonian Cruiser	S4	U	0.80
Argonian Destroyer	S4	C	0.10
Argonian Dreadnought	S8	VR	3.00
4			
Argonian Escort	S2	C	0.10
Argonian Frigate [Shadow Left]	S3	C	0.10
Argonian Heavy Carrier	S7	R	2.50
Argonian Light Cruiser	S5	C	0.10
Argonian Minesweeper	S4	U	0.80
Argonian Science Vessel	S3	C	0.10
Argonian Strobe	E7	VR	3.00
Argonian Typhoon Heavy Cruiser	S6	U	0.80
Armory Moon	T3	VC	0.05
5			
Assassin	C8	VR	3.00
Asteroid Field	T6	R	2.50
Astromorph	M5	R	2.50
Automaton	A3	R	2.50
Bar Tender	R/C1	R	2.50
Base Commander	C6	VR	3.00
Base Station	B4	R	2.50
Battlestation	B6	R	2.50
Benakis Asteroid Belt	T3	C	0.10
6			
Biruk's Comet	T2	VC	0.05
Black Hole	T6	VR	3.00
Boarding Party	C7	VR	3.00
Boarding Party [Corp Humans]	C1	VC	0.05
Boarding Party [Corporate S Team]	C4	R	2.50
Bolaar Battlecruiser	S6	R	2.50
Bolaar Cargo Express	S4	R	2.50
Bolaar Dreadnought	S7	VR	3.00
Bolaar IV	T4	U	0.80
7			
Bolaar Light Pirate Raider	S3	U	0.80
Bolaar Medium Raider	S3	U	0.80
Bolaar Phaser Capacitors	E8	VR	3.00
Bolaar Stealth Raider	S4	U	0.80
Bolaar Ultra Light Raider	S2	U	0.80
Bounty Hunter	C4	U	0.80
Breakdown	O1	C	0.10
Breakdown	O5	VR	3.00
Bribe Pirate	O6	R	2.50
8			
Broken Supply Lines	O6	R	2.50
Bureaucracy	O3	R	2.50
Candor II	T5	U	0.80
Capital Revitalization	O7	VR	3.00
Capsule Engine Pack	E1	U	0.80
Captain (Mazgar)	C6	R	2.50
Captain's Bluff	R/A6	VR	3.00
Captured Satellite	T1	C	0.10
Cargo	E1	C	0.10
9			
Cargo [Indirigan Packs]	E3	U	0.80
Civilian Captain	C2	C	0.10
Clone	C6	VR	3.00
Comet Dragoness	D4	U	0.80
Comet Impact	O2	R	2.50
Commando	R/C6	R	2.50
Commerce Moon	T2	U	0.80
Commercial Outpost	B1	C	0.10
Commodore	C8	VR	3.00
10			
Communications Officer	C5	U	0.80
Computer Virus	O8	VR	3.00
Confidential First Chief Executive Deputy Assistant to the...	C1	U	0.80
Corporate Battlecruiser	S7	R	2.50
Corporate Battleship	S9	VR	3.00
Corporate Command Cruiser	S7	R	2.50
Corporate Destroyer	S3	C	0.10
Corporate Dreadnought	S8	VR	3.00
Corporate Escort	S2	C	0.10
11			
Corporate Frigate	S2	C	0.10
Corporate Heavy Cruiser	S6	U	0.80
Corporate Homeworld	T9	VR	3.00
Corporate Light Cruiser	S4	C	0.10
Corporate Minesweeper	S4	U	0.80
Corporate Scout Cruiser	S5	C	0.10
Corrupt Politician	C4	U	0.80
Cosmic Rays	H4	R	2.50
Crab Pulsar	H6	R	2.50
12			
Cramannerak	T5	U	0.80
Crewman	R/C1	VC	0.05
Cursed Alien Artifact	L4	U	0.80
Damage Control Team	R/C6	R	2.50
Dark Dragoness	D3	R	2.50
Defense Grid	E5	VR	3.00
Defensive Electronic Warfare	R/O3	U	0.80
Defensive Override	R/L5	R	2.50
Defensive Satellites [Planet Left]	B2	C	0.10
13			
Defensive Satellites [Planet Right]	B2	C	0.10
Deflection Xfer Device (Bolaar BKG)	E6	VR	3.00
Deinos Nameh - Dragon King	D10	UR	4.00
Demigod Diversion	R/L8	VR	3.00
Derelict Spacecraft	O5	U	0.80
Dimensional Portal	H9	VR	3.00
Distress Beacon	R/L6	VR	3.00
Distribution Node	E1	C	0.10
Distribution Nodes	E5	U	0.80
14			
Distribution Nodes	E9	VR	3.00
Divergent Anomaly	H1	C	0.10
Doctor [Argonian]	R/C7	R	2.50
Doctor [Krebiz]	R/C2	C	0.10
Doctor [Krebiz] - Misprint	R/C7	C	0.10
Dragon Automaton [Ability BKG]	A9	VR	3.00
Dragon Cave	T5	R	2.50
Dragon Coupling	O5	VR	3.00
Dragon Hatchling	D1	U	0.80
15			
Dragon Hatchling	D2	R	2.50
Dragon Hole	T3	U	0.80
Dragon Lair	T8	VR	3.00
Dragon Lair	T9	VR	3.00
Draxos III - Dragon Queen	D10	UR	4.00
Dust Cloud	H1	C	0.10
Early Warning Beacon	O3	C	0.10
Economic Crises	O8	VR	3.00
EM Burst	H5	U	0.80
16			
Emer. Damage Control [Equip Bkg]	R/O8	VR	3.00
Emergency Capsule Separation	R/O6	R	2.50
Emergency Power	R/E3	R	2.50
Energy Flux Mode Enhancement	E8	VR	3.00
Engine Synchronization	E3	C	0.10
Engineer [Indirigan - No Shoulders]	C3	R	2.50
Ensign	C2	C	0.10
Eon Molting	A7	VR	3.00
Escape Pod	E1	C	0.10
17			
Ether Dragoness	D9	VR	3.00
Evasive Maneuvers	R/O5	R	2.50
Expeditious Reserves	L7	VR	3.00
False Intelligence Report	O7	R	2.50
False Mine	R/E1	U	0.80
Fatal Horror	M8	VR	3.00
Fighter	R/E5	R	2.50
Fighter Garrison	B2	U	0.80
Fighter Pilot	C4	VR	3.00
18			
Fleet Freighter [Front Left]	S1	C	0.10
Fleet Freighter [Front Right]	S1	C	0.10
Fleet Tug	S2	R	2.50
Forced Retreat	O5	R	2.50
Forced Retreat	O3	C	0.10
Forced Retreat	O7	VR	3.00
Fuser	E8	VR	3.00
Fuser Mechanism	E1	VC	0.05
Garbage Scow	S6	U	0.80
19			
General	C8	VR	3.00
Gold Vein	O2	U	0.80
Gorgochok System	T6	VR	3.00
GP Chamber	R/E2	U	0.80
Gravity Pocket	H8	VR	3.00
Gravity Wave	H2	C	0.10
Greater Automaton	A5	VR	3.00
Hand Held Weapon	A2	U	0.80
Hangar Bay	E4	VR	3.00
20			
Harvesters	M4	VR	3.00
Hcsuar - Drahcir System	T5	VC	0.05
Heavy Fighter	R/E7	VR	3.00
Heavy Phaser Refit	E4	U	0.80
Heavy Shield Refit	E3	R	2.50
Heavy Shuttlecraft	R/E4	U	0.80
Heavy Weapon Refit	E3	U	0.80
Heavy Weapon Refit	E6	R	2.50
Heavy Weapons Backfire	R/L5	R	2.50
21			
Helmsman	C2	C	0.10
Hot Nobelium	A4	R	2.50
Huge Phaser Eel	M9	VR	3.00
Hull Rotation	R/E4	U	0.80
Hydrogen Dragoness	D5	R	2.50
Illness	O1	C	0.10
Illness	O5	U	0.80
Illness	O9	VR	3.00
Independent Freighter	S2	U	0.80
22			
Independent Pirate Ship	S3	U	0.80
Independent Pirate Ship	S4	R	2.50
Independent Pirate Ship	S7	VR	3.00
Independent Tug	S3	VR	3.00
Indirigan Battlecruiser	S8	VR	3.00
Indirigan Battleship	S10	UR	4.00
Indirigan Chieftain	C9	VR	3.00
Indirigan Destroyer	S5	U	0.80
Indirigan Dreadnought	S9	VR	3.00
23			
Indirigan Escort	S3	C	0.10
Indirigan Female	C1	R	2.50
Indirigan Frigate	S4	VC	0.05
Indirigan Heavy Carrier	S8	VR	3.00
Indirigan Heavy Cruiser	S7	VR	3.00
Indirigan Light Carrier	S3	C	0.10
Indirigan Light Cruiser	S6	R	2.50
Indirigan Medium Cruiser	S6	R	2.50
Information Leak	O4	U	0.80
24			
Injury	O2	C	0.10
Injury	O6	U	0.80
Insanity	O5	R	2.50
Insanity	O9	VR	3.00
Interplanetary Conflict	O7	VR	3.00
Invinco Guardian	M3	C	0.10
Invinco Guardian	M6	R	2.50
Ion Storm	H2	C	0.10
Ion Storm	H5	R	2.50
25			
Ionized Particle Field	T2	C	0.10
Jnaphahr	T5	U	0.80
Juggernaut	M7	VR	3.00
Kalin's Small Red Nebula	T2	VC	0.05
Kraken	M9	VR	3.00
Krebiz Armor	E1	C	0.10
Krebiz Armor	E2	U	0.80
Krebiz Armor	E3	R	2.50
Krebiz Battle Capsule	S2	R	2.50
26			
Krebiz Carrier Capsule	S2	U	0.80
Krebiz Claw Hvy Cruiser [Dust Trails]	S5	C	0.10
Krebiz Clipper Frigate [Front Left]	S2	C	0.10
Krebiz Clipper Frigate [Front Right]	S2	U	0.80

RARITY KEY   VC = Very Common   C = Common   U = Uncommon   R = Rare   VR = Very Rare   F = Foil card   X = Fixed/standard in all decks

Card name	Type	Rarity	Price
Krebiz Command Capsule	S2	R	2.50
Krebiz Dreadnought Capsule	S3	VR	3.00
Krebiz Escort Capsule	S1	U	0.80
Krebiz Heavy Capsule	S2	C	0.10
Krebiz Kraken Dreadnought	S6	R	2.50
Krebiz Light Capsule	S1	C	0.10
Krebiz Light Carrier Capsule	S1	U	0.80
Krebiz Mandible Cruiser [Blue Planet]	S4	C	0.10
Krebiz Medium Capsule	S1	C	0.10
Krebiz Minesweeper Capsule	S1	U	0.80
Krebiz Pincer Destroyer	S3	C	0.10
Krebiz Pseudo Capsule	E1	U	0.80
Krebiz Science Capsule	S1	U	0.80
Krebiz Scout Capsule	S2	U	0.80
Krebizar	T7	VR	3.00
Labor Strikes	O6	VR	3.00
Laboratory	E2	C	0.10
Large Asteroid	T1	C	0.10
Large Mine Field	H6	VR	3.00
Large Phaser Eel	M5	R	2.50
Lesser Automaton	A1	U	0.80
Local Police Ship	S4	R	2.50
Lost Fleet	L9	VR	3.00
Love Interest	O4	C	0.10
Luck Demon	R/M9	VR	3.00
Lucky Crew Action	R/L1	VC	0.05
Lucky Maneuver	R/L6	VR	3.00
Lucky Shield Repair	L4	R	2.50
Lucky Targeting	L3	U	0.80
Luxury Liner	S6	VR	3.00
Maelstrom	H7	VR	3.00
Malpractice	R/L2	C	0.10
Marauder	C9	VR	3.00
Marine [Corporate Human]	R/C4	U	0.80
Mechad Battlecruiser	S6	R	2.50
Mechad Battleship	S8	VR	3.00
Mechad Command Cruiser	S6	R	2.50
Mechad Destroyer	S3	C	0.10
Mechad Dreadnought	S7	VR	3.00
Mechad Escort	S2	C	0.10
Mechad Frigate	S2	C	0.10
Mechad Heavy Cruiser	S5	C	0.10
Mechad Light Cruiser	S4	C	0.10
Mechad Medium Cruiser	S4	U	0.80
Mechad Overlord	C8	VR	3.00
Mechad Scout Cruiser	S4	U	0.80
Mechad System	T8	VR	3.00
Mercenary	C2	C	0.10
Mercenary	C6	R	2.50
Meteor Shower	H2	U	0.80
Millennia Molting	A1	U	0.80
Mind Control Beast	M6	VR	3.00
Mine Rack	E7	VR	3.00
Miscommunications	R/L4	VR	3.00
Monster Healing	R/L4	R	2.50
Monster Overstrike	R/L4	VR	3.00
Moon	T3	C	0.10
Moon Dragoness	D8	VR	3.00
Multi-Purpose Phasers	R/E4	R	2.50
Mutineer	R/C5	VR	3.00
Mystic Wanderer	C7	VR	3.00
Natural Disaster	O2	U	0.80
Navigational Error	L4	VR	3.00
Navigator	C4	R	2.50
Nebula - Homecloud	T5	VR	3.00
Nebula Dragon	D9	VR	3.00
Neutron Dragoness	D7	VR	3.00
Nova [Effect Left]	H4	U	0.80
Nova [Effect Right]	H4	U	0.80
Nuclear Mine	E2	C	0.10
Nurse	C3	U	0.80
Occumbus	M5	R	2.50

Card name	Type	Rarity	Price
Offensive Electronic Warfare	O3	C	0.10
Offensive/Defensive Elec. War.	R/O3	U	0.80
Omniscience	A6	VR	3.00
Oort Dragoness	D2	U	0.80
Operations Officer	C6	R	2.50
Ordinance Officer	C2	U	0.80
Ore Carrier	S5	R	2.50
Ore Moon	T3	C	0.10
Personal Corvette	E9	R	3.00
Phaser Malfunction	R/L2	VR	3.00
Phaser Refit	E2	C	0.10
Phaser Refit [Shield Refit Art]	E2	C	0.10
Pirate Activity	O5	U	0.80
Pirate Captain	C4	R	2.50
Pirate's Cache	L3	U	0.80
Plague	O8	VR	3.00
Planet Gouge	M2	U	0.80
Planetary Destruction - The Destruction of Argon VIII	O10	UR	4.00
Planetary Leader	R/C6	VR	3.00
Planetary Phaser Base	B4	U	0.80
Planetary Revolt	O8	VR	3.00
Planetary Shield	B1	C	0.10
Plasma Field	T/H2	C	0.10
Podekkur Prime	T4	U	0.80
Point Symbols		VC	0.05
Political Upheaval	O5	VR	3.00
Power Generation Platform	B3	R	2.50
Power Leech	M5	R	2.50
Primordial Warrior	C10	UR	4.00
Probe	E1	C	0.10
Pulsar	H3	C	0.10
Quark Dragoness	D3	R	2.50
Quartermaster	C5	VR	3.00
Quasar	H3	R	2.50
Rabuff Locttoor	T4	C	0.10
Radiation Dragoness	D4	VR	3.00
Radioactive Dust Cloud	H3	U	0.80
Rear Admiral	C8	R	2.50
Repair Bay	E6	VR	3.00
Repair Delivery	R/O4	VR	3.00
Repair Malfunction	R/L3	R	2.50
Repair Station	B3	U	0.80
Repulsion Beam	E2	VR	3.00
Research Base	B4	U	0.80
Research Defiler	M1	R	2.50
Reserve Commodore	C7	VR	3.00
Reserve Power	E3	R	2.50
Reserve Power	E6	VR	3.00
Sabot Sequencer	E6	VR	3.00
Saboteur	C7	R	2.50
Scandig	T8	VR	3.00
Scentari Snails	M6	VR	3.00
Scholar	C10	UR	4.00
Science Officer [Bolaar]	R/C6	R	2.50
Scientific Breakthrough	R/O7	VR	3.00
Scintillating Dragoness	D1	U	0.80
Security Officer	R/C4	U	0.80
Seductress	M6	VR	3.00
Self Destruction	O8	VR	3.00
Serious Hull Breach	O2	R	2.50
Shadow	M3	U	0.80
Shield Fiend	M3	VC	0.05
Shield Refit	E1	U	0.80
Ship Collector	M8	VR	3.00
Ship Mimic	M5	VR	3.00
Shipyard	B8	VR	3.00
Shroud	E9	VR	3.00
Shuttle Bomb	E4	U	0.80
Shuttle Eater	M6	VR	3.00
Shuttle Malfunction	R/L4	U	0.80
Shuttlecraft [Front Left]	R/E3	C	0.10

Card name	Type	Rarity	Price
Shuttlecraft [Front Right]	R/E3	C	0.10
Sigry III	T3	U	0.80
Siobhan 7	T4	VC	0.05
Sirens	M4	U	0.80
Slick Bargainer	A2	VR	3.00
Small Mine Field	H3	R	2.50
Small Moon	T1	C	0.10
Small Phaser Eel	M1	C	0.10
Snare Vines	M2	U	0.80
Sochess Comet	T6	R	2.50
Solar Dragoness	R/D6	VR	3.00
Space Debris	O2	U	0.80
Space Dragon	M4	U	0.80
Space Station	B3	U	0.80
Space Vertigo	M2	VC	0.05
Space Yacht	S2	U	0.80
Spacetacean	M4	R	2.50
Spiritual Leader	C4	R	2.50
Spy	R/C6	R	2.50
Spy Technician	R/C5	VR	3.00
Squadron Commander	C6	VR	3.00
Star	T5	R	2.50
Starbase	B9	VR	3.00
Stellar Map	E4	VR	3.00
Subspace Stabilizer	E10	UR	4.00
Suicide Squad	C5	R	2.50
Sun Spot	R/O1	U	0.80
Super - Massive Star	T10	UR	4.00
Super Computer	E6	R	2.50
Surface Dragoness	D8	VR	3.00
Surface Monster	M5	R	2.50
Surprise Attack	O7	VR	3.00
Tactical Retreat	R/O5	R	2.50
Targeting Error	R/L8	VR	3.00
Technician	C3	C	0.10
Technological Breakthrough	O8	VR	3.00
Telepath	R/C6	VR	3.00
Temporal Space Rift	H5	VR	3.00
Terraforming	O5	VR	3.00
Time Warp	H1	VR	3.00
Tractor Beam	R/E2	R	2.50
Tram Refit	E4	U	0.80
Transporter	R/E2	VC	0.05
Transporter Malfunction	R/L3	U	0.80
Transporter [Neuclear Mine - bottom]	R/E2	C	0.10
Tri-lateral Textangula	M7	VR	3.00
Tri-Millennia Molting	A3	R	2.50
Tuforeous Dead Zone	H9	VR	3.00
Twin Planets - Verkirsh I & II	T5	R	2.50
Type II Supernova	H6	VR	3.00
Unlucky Targeting	R/L3	R	2.50
Unsuccessful Minesweeping (Void)	L4	U	0.80
Vektrea Prime	T5	R	2.50
Vektrean Asteroid Outpost (Void)	T5	R	2.50
Vektrean Asteroid Starbase (Void)	T9	VR	3.00
Vektrean Mercenaries Battlecruiser	S6	VR	3.00
Vektrean Mercenaries Destroyer	S3	U	0.80
Vektrean Mercenaries Frigate	S2	U	0.80
Vektrean Mercenaries Heavy Cruiser	S5	U	0.80
Vektrean Mercenaries Light Cruiser	S4	U	0.80
Visilikiiy's Eye	M6	R	2.50
Void Dragoness	D5	VR	3.00
Volatile Cargo	E5	VR	3.00
Vorn Ringed Gas Giant	T6	VR	3.00
Wandering Desire	O3	R	2.50
Wandering Desire	O5	R	2.50
War Veteran	C4	UR	4.00
Warp Engine Breech	L2	R	2.50
Warp Field Destabilization Gun	E6	VR	3.00
Warp Funnel	H4	U	0.80
Weapons Officer	C5	R	2.50
Zarom	M5	R	2.50

RARITY KEY **VC** = Very Common **C** = Common **U** = Uncommon **R** = Rare **VR** = Very Rare **F** = Foil card **X** = Fixed/standard in all decks

162 • *SCRYE Collectible Card Game Checklist and Price Guide*

Galactic Empires • Universe

Companion Games • Released **November 1995**

565 cards in set • **IDENTIFIER: Sharper colors than in previous releases**

- Starter decks contain 10 cards; starter displays contain 6 starters
- Booster packs contain 14 cards; booster displays contain 36 boosters

This enormous release was the fourth base set for *Galactic Empires* put out in a little over a year. *Universe Edition* added more than 100 cards from the *New Empires*, *Time Gates*, and *Powers of the Mind* expansions, including one of the new races, the Tufor, to the set released in the *Primary* edition. — *Michael Greenholdt*

SCRYE NOTES: *As you may have noticed, it's practically impossible to tell between some individual* **Galactic Empires** *releases, sometimes even with the help of a card list. The tipoffs, where they exist, are often the result of an error by the manufacturer rather than design. Needless to say, we consider the decision by Companion Games not to label a dozen expansions within a 3,500-card game to be gratuitously irritating.*

Set (565 cards)	45.00	**You will need**
Starter Display Box	20.00	**63** nine-pocket pages to store this set. (32 doubled up)
Booster Display Box	24.00	
Starter Deck	5.00	
Booster Pack	1.00	

Card name	Type	Rarity	Price
Academy	B7	VR	2.50
Accelerated Aging	O6	R	2.40
Accelerated Timeline	L9	VR	2.50
Ace Fighter Pilot	C6	R	2.40
Administrative Facility	B5	R	2.40
Administrator	R/C6	U	0.80
Admiral	C9	VR	2.50
Advanced Preparedness	R/L8	VR	2.50
Aldibrik Munitions Plant	T4	R	2.40
Alfven Wave	H6	R	2.40
Alien Artifact	L7	R	2.40
Alien Love Interest	R/O8	R	2.40
Alien Parasites	M3	U	0.80
Alliance Treaty	O9	VR	2.50
Ambassador	C5	VR	2.50
Anarchist	A5	VR	2.50
Ancient Molting	A5	VR	3.00
Ancient Ruins	B2	C	0.20
Ancient Spacefarer	C6	VR	2.50
Android	C7	R	2.40
Anomaly Portal	R/L7	VR	2.50
Antimatter Mine	E5	VR	2.50
Apollo Body	T1	VC	0.05
Argo	T7	VR	2.50
Argonian Assault Carrier	S4	R	2.40
Argonian Battlecruiser [Star Rt.]	S7	VR	2.50
Argonian Battleship	S9	VR	2.50
Argonian Command Cruiser	S6	VR	2.50
Argonian Cruiser	S4	R	2.40
Argonian Destroyer	S4	R	2.40
Argonian Dreadnought	S8	VR	2.50
Argonian Escort	S2	R	2.40
Argonian Frigate [Shadow Left]	S3	U	0.80
Argonian Heavy Carrier	S7	VR	2.50
Argonian Heavy Cruiser	S5	VR	2.50
Argonian Light Cruiser	S5	R	2.40
Argonian Minesweeper	S4	VR	2.50
Argonian Sector HQ	-	VR	2.50
Argonian Strobe	E7	VR	2.50
Armory Moon	T3	VC	0.05
Artifact - Galactic Prism	L8	VR	2.50
Artifact - Krebiz Monolith	L6	VR	2.50
Artificial Landmass	A10	UR	5.00
Artificial Satellite	T2	U	0.80
Assassin	C8	VR	2.50
Assault Fighter	R/E8	VR	2.50

Card name	Type	Rarity	Price
Asteroid Field	T6	R	2.40
Asteroid Shield	R/T2	R	2.40
Astral Dragoness	D6	VR	2.50
Astromorph	M5	R	2.40
Aurora Borealis	A5	R	2.40
Aurora Effect	L3	VR	2.50
Automaton	A3	R	2.40
Bar Tender	R/C1	R	2.40
Base Commander	C6	VR	2.50
Base Station	B4	R	2.40
Battle Suit	A5	U	0.80
Battlestation	B6	R	2.40
Benakis Asteroid Belt	T3	C	0.20
Biruk's Comet	T2	VC	0.05
Black Hole	T6	R	2.40
Boarding Party	C3	U	0.80
Boarding Party	C7	VR	2.50
Boarding Party [Corp Humans]	C1	C	0.20
Boarding Party [Corporate S Team]	C4	R	2.40
Bolaar IV	T4	U	0.80
Bounty Hunter	C4	U	0.80
Breached City	R/O6	R	2.40
Broken Supply Lines	O6	R	2.40
Brown Dwarf	T3	U	0.80
Bureaucracy	O3	U	0.80
Bureaucrat	C6	U	0.80
Candor II	T5	U	0.80
Capital Revitalization	O7	VR	2.50
Captain	C5	U	0.80
Captain's Bluff	R/A6	VR	2.50
Captured Satellite	T1	C	0.20
Cargo	E1	C	0.20
Central Galactic Bank	B7	VR	2.50
CEO	C8	VR	2.50
CFO	C6	R	2.40
Citadel	R/B8	VR	2.50
Clone	C6	VR	2.50
Clydon Battle Craft	R/S2	VR	2.50
Clydon Carrier Craft	R/S2	U	0.80
Clydon Heavy Star Cruiser	S5	VR	2.50
Clydon Light Star Cruiser	S3	R	2.40
Clydon Man-O-War	S6	VR	2.50
Clydon Medium Star Cruiser	S4	VR	2.50
Clydon Mine Craft	R/S1	U	0.80
Clydon Science Craft	R/S1	R	2.40
Clydon Sector HQ	-	VR	2.50
Clydon Ultra-Light Cruiser	S2	U	0.80
Clydon War Craft	R/S1	R	2.40
Clydon War Cruiser	S5	R	2.40
Comet Impact	O2	R	2.40
Commando	R/C6	R	2.40
Commodore	C8	VR	2.50
Computer Virus	O8	VR	2.50

Card name	Type	Rarity	Price
Confidential Coordinating First Chief Executive Deputy Assistant to the…	C1	U	0.80
Corporate Battlecruiser	S7	VR	2.50
Corporate Battleship	S9	VR	2.50
Corporate Command Cruiser	S7	VR	2.50
Corporate Destroyer	S3	U	0.80
Corporate Dreadnought	S8	VR	2.50
Corporate Escort	S2	U	0.80
Corporate Frigate	S2	U	0.80
Corporate Heavy Cruiser	S6	VR	2.50
Corporate Homeworld	T9	VR	2.50
Corporate Light Cruiser	S4	R	2.40
Corporate Minesweeper	S4	R	2.40
Corporate Scout Cruiser	S5	R	2.40
Corporate Sector HQ	-	VR	2.50
Corrupt Politician	C4	U	0.80
Cosmic Cyclone	H6	VR	2.50
Cosmic Rays	H4	R	2.40
Crab Pulsar	H6	R	2.40
Cramannerak	T5	U	0.80
Crewman	R/C1	C	0.20
Criminal Judge	C7	VR	2.50
Crinkled Timeline	R/O3	U	0.80
Crystal Planet	T3	C	0.20
Cursed Alien Artifact	L4	U	0.80
Cyber Disturbance	H3	U	0.80
Cyber Mage	C4	R	2.40
Cyber Mites	M7	R	2.40
Cyber-Programmer	C2	C	0.20
Damage Control Team	R/C6	R	2.40
Data Bank	B5	R	2.40
Defense Grid	E5	VR	2.50
Defensive Electronic Warfare	R/O3	U	0.80
Defensive Override	R/L5	R	2.40
Defensive Satellites [Planet Right]	B2	C	0.20
Demigod Diversion	R/L8	VR	2.50
Dependency World	T5	R	2.40
Dimensional Portal	H9	VR	2.50
Discovery of Discoveries	O9	VR	2.50
Distant Sun	T4	C	0.20
Distortion Generator	R/E6	U	0.80
Distortion Pocket	H7	VR	2.50
Distress Beacon	R/L6	R	2.40
Distribution Node	E1	R	2.40
Distribution Nodes	E5	U	0.80
Distribution Nodes	E9	VR	2.50
Divergence of Psy	H1	U	0.80
Divergent Anomaly	H1	C	0.20
Doctor [Argonian]	R/C7	R	2.40
Double Agent	A6	R	2.40
Dragon Automaton [Dragon Bkg.]	A9	VR	2.50
Dragon Cave	T5	R	2.40

RARITY KEY **VC** = Very Common **C** = Common **U** = Uncommon **R** = Rare **VR** = Very Rare **F** = Foil card **X** = Fixed/standard in all decks

Card name	Type	Rarity	Price
Dragon Egg	T3	C	0.20
Dragon Hole	T3	U	0.80
Dragon Lair	T8	VR	2.50
Dragon Lair	T9	VR	2.50
Dragon Sector HQ	-	VR	2.50
Duo-Brain	A8	VR	2.50
Dust Cloud	H1	C	0.20
Economic Crises	O8	VR	2.50
EM Burst	H5	U	0.80
Emer. Damage Control	R/O8	VR	2.50
Emergency Power	R/E3	R	2.40
Emergency Rescue Ship	S5	R	2.40
Energy Flux Mode Enhancement	E8	VR	2.50
Engineer	C2	U	0.80
Ensign	C2	U	0.80
Entertaining Pastime	O4	R	2.40
Eon Molting	A7	VR	2.50
Escape Pod	E1	C	0.20
Escaped Prisoner	C3	U	0.80
Ether Dragoness	D9	VR	2.50
Evasive Maneuvers	R/O5	R	2.40
Evil Temple	B6	VR	2.50
Expeditious Reserves	L7	VR	2.50
Explosive Mine	E1	C	0.20
Explosive Ore Carrier	S10	UR	5.00
False Distress Call	O4	U	0.80
False Intelligence Report	O7	R	2.40
False Mine	R/E1	U	0.80
Fighter	R/E5	R	2.40
Fighter Garrison	B2	U	0.80
Fleet Freighter [Front Left]	S1	C	0.20
Fleet Tug	S2	R	2.40
Flood	O4	C	0.20
Forced Retreat	O4	U	0.80
Forming System	T4	C	0.20
Frayed Time Spindle	L8	VR	2.50
Gaia Planet	T4	R	2.40
Galactic Armageddon	L10	UR	5.00
Garbage Scow	S6	U	0.80
Gas Giant	T9	VR	2.50
General	C8	VR	2.50
Golbular Cluster	T6	R	2.40
Gold Vein	O2	C	0.20
Gorgochok System	T6	VR	2.50
Gravity Pocket	H4	U	0.80
Gravity Pocket	H8	VR	3.00
Gravity Wave	H2	C	0.20
Greater Automaton	A5	VR	2.50
Hand Held Weapon	A2	U	0.80
Harvesters	M4	VR	2.50
Hcsuar - Drahcir System	T5	VC	0.05
Heavy Fighter	R/E7	VR	2.50
Heavy Phaser Refit	E4	U	0.80
Heavy Planetary Shield	B3	U	0.80
Heavy Shield Refit	E3	R	2.40
Heavy Shuttlecraft	R/E4	U	0.80
Heavy Weapon Refit	E6	R	2.40
Heavy Weapon Refit	E3	U	0.80
Heavy Weapons Backfire	R/L5	R	2.40
Helmsman	C2	C	0.20
Hologram	R/E9	VR	2.50
Hospital	B6	R	2.40
Hot Nobelium	A4	R	2.40
Huge Invinco Guardian	M9	VR	2.50
Hull Rotation	R/E4	VR	2.50
Hydrogen Dragoness	D5	VR	2.50
Hypercube	E10	UR	5.00
Ice Moon	T3	C	0.20
Illness	O1	C	0.20
Illness	O9	VR	2.50
Illness - Aldibrik Ailment	O3	U	0.80
Independent Freighter	S2	U	0.80
Independent Pirate Ship	S4	R	2.40
Independent Tug	S3	VR	2.50
Indirigan Destroyer	S5	U	0.80
Indirigan Female	C1	R	2.40
Indirigan Light Cruiser	S6	R	2.40
Infestation Inhibitor	A1	U	0.80
Informant	R/C1	R	2.40
Information Leak	O4	U	0.80
Insanity	O5	R	2.40
Insanity	O9	VR	2.50
Instant Reaction	R/O3	U	0.80
Intercept Action	R/O1	U	0.80
Intergalactic Void	T10	UR	5.00
Interplanetary Conflict	O7	VR	2.50
Interstellar Plasma	R/H7	R	2.40
Invinco Guardian	M3	C	0.20
Ion Storm	H2	C	0.20
Ion Storm	H5	R	2.40
Ionized Particle Field	T2	C	0.20
Juggernaut	M7	VR	2.50
Kraken	M9	VR	2.50
Krebiz Armor	E1	R	2.40
Krebiz Armor	E3	R	2.40
Krebiz Battlecruiser (Claw/Battle)	S7	VR	2.50
Krebiz Battleship (Kraken/Dread)	S9	VR	2.50
Krebiz Command Ship (Mandib/Cmd)	S6	R	2.40
Krebiz Escort Ship (Clip/Escort)	S3	R	2.40
Krebiz Hvy Carrier (Kraken/Carrier)	S8	VR	2.50
Krebiz Hvy Cruiser (Mandible/Hvy)	S6	VR	2.50
Krebiz Lt Carrier (Pincer/Lt Carr)	S4	U	0.80
Krebiz Minesweeper (Clip/Mineswp)	S3	R	2.40
Krebiz Scout Ship (Pincer/Scout)	S5	U	0.80
Krebiz Sector HQ	-	VR	2.50
Krebizar	T7	VR	2.50
Labor Strikes	O6	VR	2.50
Landing Officer	A3	U	0.80
Large Asteroid	T1	C	0.20
Large Mine Field	H6	R	2.40
Legendary Officer	C10	UR	5.00
Lesser Automaton	A1	U	0.80
Lieutenant	C4	U	0.80
Local Police Ship	S4	R	2.40
Logic	A2	C	0.20
Lost Fleet	L9	VR	2.50
Luck Demon	R/M9	VR	2.50
Lucky Crew Action	R/L1	C	0.20
Lucky Maneuver	R/L6	VR	2.50
Lucky Shield Repair	L4	R	2.40
Luxury Liner	S6	VR	2.50
Maelstrom	H7	VR	2.50
Manufacturing Plant	B8	VR	2.50
Marauder	C9	VR	2.50
Marine [Corporate Human]	R/C4	U	0.80
Mechad Battlecruiser	S6	VR	2.50
Mechad Battleship	S8	VR	2.50
Mechad Command Cruiser	S6	VR	2.50
Mechad Destroyer	S3	U	0.80
Mechad Dreadnought	S7	VR	2.50
Mechad Escort	S2	R	2.40
Mechad Heavy Cruiser	S5	R	2.40
Mechad Medium Cruiser	S4	R	2.40
Mechad Minesweeper	S5	R	2.40
Mechad Network Interface	E8	VR	2.50
Mechad Scout Cruiser	S4	R	2.40
Mechad Sector HQ	-	VR	2.50
Mechad System	T8	VR	2.50
Mental Anguish	A6	R	2.40
Mental Inspiration	A5	U	0.80
Mercenary	C2	C	0.20
Mercenary	C6	R	2.40
Meteor Shower	H2	U	0.80
Military Outpost	B1	C	0.20
Mind Control Beast	M6	VR	2.50
Mind Guard	R/A4	U	0.80
Mind Mold Symbionts	A5	R	2.40
Mind Turning	R/O8	VR	2.50
Mine Rack	E7	VR	2.50
Miscommunications	R/L4	VR	2.50
Miscreant	A7	VR	2.50
Modified Timeline	L8	VR	2.50
Monster Healing	R/L4	R	2.40
Monster Overstrike	R/L4	VR	2.50
Moon	T3	C	0.20
Moon Dragoness	D8	VR	2.50
Mutineer	R/C5	VR	2.50
Mystic Wanderer	C7	VR	2.50
Natural Disaster	O2	U	0.80
Navigational Error	L4	VR	2.50
Navigator	C4	R	2.40
Nebula - Homecloud	T5	VR	2.50
Nebula Dragon	D9	VR	2.50
Neutrino Dragoness	D6	VR	2.50
Neutron Dragoness	D7	VR	2.50
Nuclear Mine	E2	C	0.20
Nurse	C3	U	0.80
Occumbus	M5	R	2.40
Offensive Electronic Warfare	O3	C	0.20
Offensive/Defensive Elec. War.	R/O3	U	0.80
Omniscience	A6	VR	2.50
Oort Cloud	T2	U	0.80
Oort Dragoness	D2	VR	2.50
Operations Officer	C6	R	2.40
Ordinance Officer	C2	U	0.80
Ore Carrier	S5	R	2.40
Out of Season	R/O7	U	0.80
P. O. T. Battlecruiser	S7	VR	2.50
P. O. T. Battleship	S9	VR	2.50
P. O. T. Destroyer	S4	U	0.80
P. O. T. Dreadnought	S8	VR	2.50
P. O. T. Escort	S2	R	2.40
P. O. T. Fighter Carrier	S6	VR	2.50
P. O. T. Frigate	S3	U	0.80
P. O. T. Hy Cruiser	S5	VR	2.50
P. O. T. Lt Cruiser	S5	VR	2.50
P. O. T. Minesweeper	S4	R	2.40
P. O. T. Science Cutter	S3	R	2.40
P. O. T. Scout Cruiser	S5	R	2.40
P. O. T. Sector HQ	-	VR	2.50
Penal Colony	B5	R	2.40
Personal Base	B1	U	0.80
Phase Rats	M3	C	0.20
Phaser Magnifier Refit	E7	VR	2.50
Phaser Malfunction	R/L2	U	0.80
Phaser Refit	E2	C	0.20
Pirate System	T5	R	2.40
Pirate's Cache	L3	U	0.80
Plague	O8	VR	2.50
Planet Gouge	M2	C	0.20
Planetary Leader	R/C6	R	2.40
Planetary Phaser Base	B4	U	0.80
Planetary Revolt	O8	VR	2.50
Planetary Shield	B1	C	0.20
Planetary Storm	T1	U	0.80
Planetary Transportation	E5	C	0.20
Plasma Dragoness	D3	VR	2.50

RARITY KEY VC = Very Common   C = Common   U = Uncommon   R = Rare   VR = Very Rare   F = Foil card   X = Fixed/standard in all decks

Card name	Type	Rarity	Price
Plasma Field	T/H2	C	0.20
Plasmatic Nebula	T8	VR	2.50
Podekkur Prime	T4	C	0.20
41			
Police Cutter	S2	U	0.80
Political Clout	O6	R	2.40
Political Upheaval	O5	VR	2.50
Populated Moon	T2	C	0.20
Power Generation Platform	B3	R	2.40
Probe	E1	C	0.20
Prophet	C6	R	2.40
Protostar	T3	C	0.20
Pulsar	H3	VC	0.05
42			
Quantum Black Hole	T7	VC	0.05
Quantum Occurrence	O7	R	2.40
Quark	H8	VR	2.50
Quark Dragoness	D3	VR	2.50
Quartermaster	C5	VR	2.50
Quasar	H3	R	2.40
Rabuff Locttoor	T4	C	0.20
Radiation Dragoness	D4	VR	2.50
Radioactive Dust Cloud	H3	U	0.80
43			
Rear Admiral	C8	VR	2.50
Redgelon	M8	VR	2.50
Refueler	S4	R	2.40
Repair Base	B9	VR	2.50
Repair Delivery	R/O4	VR	2.50
Repair Malfunction	R/L3	R	2.40
Repair Moon	T3	C	0.20
Repair Skid	B3	U	0.80
Repulsion Beam	E2	VR	2.50
44			
Rescue Attempt	G3	VC	0.05
Research Base	B4	U	0.80
Research Defiler	M1	R	2.40
Research Developer	C7	VR	2.50
Reserve Power	E3	R	2.40
Ring System	T5	R	2.40
Rogue Couple	C6	R	2.40
Rom's Periodic Comet	T3	C	0.20
Sabot Sequencer	E6	VR	2.50
45			
Saboteur	C7	R	2.40
Safe Haven	A7	VR	2.50
Scandig	T8	VR	2.50
Scandig Blob	M3	U	0.80
Science Officer	R/C4	C	0.20
Science Officer [Bolaar]	R/C6	R	2.40
Scientif. Enhanced Tectonic Plate	L4	U	0.80
Scientific Breakthrough	R/O7	VR	2.50
Scintillating Dragoness	D1	R	2.40
46			
Scorpead Battlecruiser	S7	VR	2.50
Scorpead Battleship	S9	VR	2.50
Scorpead Command Cruiser	S6	VR	2.50
Scorpead Destroyer	S3	U	0.80
Scorpead Dreadnought	S8	VR	2.50
Scorpead Escort	S2	U	0.80
Scorpead Heavy Cruiser	S6	VR	2.50
Scorpead Light Cruiser	S5	R	2.40
Scorpead Lore	T7	VR	2.50
47			
Scorpead Minesweeper	S4	R	2.40
Scorpead Science Ship	S4	U	0.80
Scorpead Scout Cruiser	S5	R	2.40
Scorpead Sector HQ	-	VR	2.50
Security Officer	R/C4	U	0.80
Seductress	M6	R	2.40
Self Destruction	O8	VR	2.50
Sensor Planet	T7	VR	2.50
Serious Hull Breach	O2	R	2.40
48			
Sextaraan Web Crawlers	R/M1	C	0.20
Shadow	M3	U	0.80
Shield Fiend	M3	VC	0.05
Shield Refit	E1	U	0.80
Ship Collector	M8	VR	2.50
Ship Collision	O9	R	2.40
Ship from the Future	R/S1	U	0.80
Ship Mimic	M5	VR	2.50
Shipping Delays [part 2]	R/O2	R	2.40
49			
Shipyard	B8	VR	2.50
Shuttle Bomb	E4	U	0.80
Shuttle Malfunction	R/L4	U	0.80
Shuttlecraft [Front Right]	R/E3	C	0.20
Sigry III	T3	U	0.80
Slick Bargainer	A2	VR	2.50
Small Mine Field	H3	U	0.80
Small Moon	T1	C	0.20
Small Phaser Eel	M1	C	0.20
50			
Snare Vines	M2	C	0.20
Sochess Comet	T6	R	2.40
Solar Dragoness	R/D6	VR	2.50
Solitude	G4	C	0.20
Space Dragon	M4	U	0.80
Space Station	B3	U	0.80
Space Vertigo	R/M3	C	0.20
Space Yacht	S2	U	0.80
Spacetacean	M4	R	2.40
51			
Spiritual Guidance	A8	U	0.80
Spiritual Leader	C4	R	2.40
Spiritual Leader	C10	UR	5.00
Spiritual Leader	C8	VR	2.50
Spiritual Temple	B4	C	0.20
Spy	R/C6	R	2.40
Squadron Commander	C6	R	2.40
Star	T5	R	2.40
Starbase	B9	VR	2.50
52			
Starving Artist	R/C1	VR	2.50
Stasis Mine	E6	VR	2.50
Stealth Fighter	R/E3	U	0.80
Stellar Map	E4	VR	2.50
Strategy	A1	C	0.20
Struc. (no R)		U	0.80
Structural Degeneration	O8	VR	2.50
Suicide Squad	C5	R	2.40
Sun Spot	R/O1	U	0.80
53			
Super Computer	E6	R	2.40
Supernova Remnant	T4	U	0.80
Supersonic Flow	H2	C	0.20
Surprise Attack	O7	VR	2.50
Survey Mission	G2	C	0.20
Survey Shuttle	E4	U	0.80
Suspended Animation	R/L9	VR	2.50
Sysop	C1	R	2.40
System - Penteir	T5	R	2.40
54			
Tactical Fighter	R/E6	VR	2.50
Tactical Officer	C7	VR	2.50
Tactical Retreat	R/O5	R	2.40
Tactician	C6	R	2.40
Targeting Error	R/L8	VR	2.50
Tarragym Effect	O8	R	2.40
Teamster	C4	C	0.20
Technological Breakthrough	O8	VR	2.50
Tectonic Burrower	M5	U	0.80
55			
Telepath	R/C6	VR	2.50
Temporal Correction	R/L7	R	2.40
Temporal Mechanic	C4	VR	2.50
Temporal Shuttle	E7	U	0.80
Temporal Transporter	R/E3	U	0.80
Terraforming	O5	VR	2.50
Terrain Attack Shuttle	R/E1	U	0.80
Time Discrepancy	R/O8	U	0.80
Time Dragoness	D8	VR	2.50
56			
Time Intrusion	H9	VR	2.50
Time Keeper	M10	UR	5.00
Time Keeper	R/M4	U	0.80
Time Lore	R/A8	VR	2.50
Time Manipulation	G1	C	0.20
Time Merchant	C5	VR	2.50
Time Thief	M6	R	2.40
Time Tornado	H7	R	2.40
Time Typhoon	R/H7	VR	2.50
57			
Time Warp	H10	UR	5.00
Time Warp	H1	VR	2.50
Time Wave	H9	VR	2.50
Toxic Waste Spill	O10	UR	5.00
Tractor Beam	R/E2	R	2.40
Tram Refit	E2	C	0.20
Tram Refit	E4	U	0.80
Transporter	R/E2	C	0.20
Transporter Malfunction	R/L3	U	0.80
58			
Transporter Mine	R/E4	U	0.80
Tri-lateral Textangula	M7	VR	2.50
Tri-Millennia Molting	A3	R	2.40
Trophy Hunter	R/C4	U	0.80
Tufor Battleship	S9	VR	2.50
Tufor Command Launch	S6	VR	2.50
Tufor Cutter	S3	U	0.80
Tufor Destroyer	S4	R	2.40
Tufor Dreadnought	S8	VR	2.50
59			
Tufor Escort	S2	R	2.40
Tufor Fighter Carrier	S6	VR	2.50
Tufor Heavy Cruiser	S5	VR	2.50
Tufor Light Cruiser	S4	R	2.40
Tufor Lt Fighter Carrier[no ftrs]	S3	R	2.40
Tufor Mine Cruiser	S6	VR	2.50
Tufor Mine Platform	B3	C	0.20
Tufor Research Scout	S4	R	2.40
Tufor Sector HQ	-	VR	2.50
60			
Tufor War Cruiser	S7	VR	2.50
Tuforeous Dead Zone	H9	VR	2.50
Twin Planets - Verkirsh I & II	T5	R	2.40
Twist of Fate	R/L8	VR	2.50
Type II Supernova	H6	VR	2.50
Undead Dragoness	D8	VR	2.50
Undiscovered System	T7	VR	2.50
Unlucky Targeting	R/L3	R	2.40
Unsuccessful Minesweeping (Rev.)	R/L4	U	0.80
61			
Vacation Planet	T3	R	2.40
Vektrea Prime	T5	R	2.40
Vektrean Asteroid Outpost (Rev.)	T/B5	R	2.40
Vektrean Asteroid Starbase (Rev.)	T/B9	VR	2.50
Vektrean Mercenaries Battlecruiser	S6	VR	2.50
Vektrean Mercenaries Destroyer	S3	U	0.80
Vektrean Mercenaries Dreadnought	S7	VR	2.50
Vektrean Mercenaries Frigate	S2	C	0.20
62			
Vektrean Mercenaries Heavy Cruiser	S5	U	0.80
Vektrean Mercenaries Light Cruiser	S4	U	0.80
Vektrean Mercenaries Spy Cruiser	S6	R	2.40
Vektrean Sector HQ	-	VR	2.50
Visilikiiy's Eye	M6	R	2.40
Void Angel	M6	R	2.40
Void Dragoness	D5	VR	2.50
Volatile Terrain	R/O5	VC	0.05
Vorn Ringed Gas Giant	T6	VR	2.50
63			
Vymezies Matter	M4	U	0.80
Wandering Desire	O3	R	2.40
Warp Engine Breech	L2	R	2.40
Warp Field Destabilization Gun	E6	VR	2.50
Warp Funnel	H4	U	0.80
Weapons Officer	C5	U	0.80
Zambarez	T5	U	0.80
Zarom	M5	R	2.40

RARITY KEY VC = Very Common C = Common U = Uncommon R = Rare VR = Very Rare F = Foil card X = Fixed/standard in all decks

Galactic Empires • New Empires

B10 ●●●★★ ◇◇◇◇◇◇◇★
Tufor Operations Base   ✛

Illustration © 1995 Randy Richards' Rook
- May only be used in Tufor decks.
■■■: Thunderbolt Devastators
✛✛✛✛✛✛✛✛✛✛: Phasers

Companion Games • Released **April 1995**
209 cards in set • **IDENTIFIER: None; most, but not all © 1995**

NEW EMPIRES

- Starter decks contain 50 cards; starter displays contain 12 starters
- Booster packs contain 12 cards; booster displays contain 36 boosters

The first "true" expansion in the **Galactic Empires** series, **New Empires**, introduced four new major races (Clydon, P.O.T., Scorpead, and Tufor) and many of the staple crew cards (cards representing personnel that have a continuing effect) and ability cards (cards that affect or augment crew).

This expansion also began the explosive increase in available terrain cards, cards that soon overshadowed the terrain found in the base sets. — *Michael Greenholdt*

You will need **24** nine-pocket pages to store this set. (12 doubled up)

Set (209 cards)	35.00
Starter Display Box	29.00
Booster Display Box	32.00
Starter Deck	5.00
Booster Pack	1.00

Card name	Rarity	Price
1		
Accidental Evolution	VR	3.50
Ace Fighter Pilot	R	2.50
Administrator	U	0.60
Agro Moon	C	0.10
Alfven Wave	R	2.50
Anarchist	R	2.50
Ancient Ruins	C	0.10
Android	R	2.50
Artifact - Dragon Gem of Protection	R	2.50
2		
Artifact - Galactic Prism	VR	3.50
Artifact - Krebiz Monolith	VR	3.50
Artifact - Star Gate	VR	3.50
Artifact - War Medal of Yorl	U	0.60
Assault Fighter	VR	3.50
Assault Rifle	U	0.60
Astral Dragoness	VR	3.50
Aurora Effect	VR	3.50
Avatar	URF	5.00
3		
Battle Suit	U	0.60
Bionic Enhancement	C	0.10
Blayok Protostar	C	0.10
Bolaar Heavy Cargo Express	VR	3.50
Bosheegh	C	0.10
Bureaucrat	U	0.60
Captured Moon	C	0.10
Cerebral Void	U	0.60
Civilian Transporter	C	0.10
4		
Cloning Device	VR	3.50
Clydon Battle Craft	VR	3.50
Clydon Carrier Craft	U	0.60
Clydon Energy Armor	U	0.60
Clydon Heavy Star Cruiser	VR	3.50
Clydon Light Star Cruiser	R	2.50
Clydon Man-O-War	VR	3.50
Clydon Medium Star Cruiser	VR	3.50
Clydon Mine Craft	U	0.60
5		
Clydon Science Craft	R	2.50
Clydon Scout Craft	U	0.60
Clydon Super-Massive Planet	URF	5.00
Clydon Ultra-Light Cruiser	U	0.60
Clydon War Craft	R	2.50
Clydon War Cruiser	R	2.50
Command Disjunction	U	0.60
Cosmic Cyclone	VR	3.50

Card name	Rarity	Price
6		
Cyber Disturbance	U	0.60
Cyber Mage	R	2.50
Cyber Mage	VR	3.50
Cyber Mites	R	2.50
Cyber-Programmer	C	0.10
Cyborg Death	VR	3.50
Defense Grid	VR	3.50
Demolition Expertise	U	0.60
Dependency World	R	2.50
Deviant	U	0.60
7		
Devolution	R	2.50
Distortion Pocket	VR	3.50
Double Agent	R	2.50
Duo-Brain	VR	3.50
Emergency Rescue Ship	R	2.50
Energy Moon	C	0.10
Escaped Prisoner	U	0.60
Evil Temple	VR	3.50
Explosive Mine	C	0.10
8		
False Distress Call	U	0.60
Femerazi	U	0.60
Gas Giant	VR	3.50
Genetic Mutation	C	0.10
Gravity Pocket	U	0.60
Green Fighter Pilot	C	0.10
Heavy Planetary Shield	U	0.60
Hologram	VR	3.50
Hospital	R	2.50
9		
Illness - Aldibrik Ailment	U	0.60
Illness - Space Deterioration	U	0.60
Independant Pirate Cruiser	U	0.60
Intelligence Officer	U	0.60
Interstellar Plasma	R	2.50
Intoxication	U	0.60
Legendary Pirate Captain	URF	5.00
Lieutenant	U	0.60
Logic	C	0.10
10		
Lucky Mine Explosion	C	0.10
Magnetic Cloud	C	0.10
Magus Dragoness	U	0.60
Manufacturing Plant	VR	3.50
Master Spy	VR	3.50
Mechad Network Interface	VR	3.50
Media Personality	C	0.10
Medical Scanner	C	0.10
Mental Anguish	R	2.50
11		
Mind Mold Symbionts	R	2.50
Mine Deployment System	VR	3.50
Miscreant	VR	3.50
Monster Defense System	U	0.60
Nagiridni Pirate Cruiser (Indir)	VR	3.50
Nagiridni Pirate Destroyer (Indir)	R	2.50
Nagiridni Pirate Scout (Indir)	U	0.60
Neutrino Dragoness	VR	3.50

Card name	Rarity	Price
12		
Obelisk System	C	0.10
Orbital Decay	U	0.60
P. O. T. Armed Launch	C	0.10
P. O. T. Battlecruiser	VR	3.50
P. O. T. Battleship	VR	3.50
P. O. T. Command Cruiser (Void)	R	2.50
P. O. T. Destroyer	U	0.60
P. O. T. Dreadnought	VR	3.50
P. O. T. Escort	R	2.50
P. O. T. Fighter Carrier	VR	3.50
13		
P. O. T. Frigate	U	0.60
P. O. T. Hy Cruiser	VR	3.50
P. O. T. Lt Cruiser	VR	3.50
P. O. T. Medium Cruiser	R	2.50
P. O. T. Minesweeper	R	2.50
P. O. T. Science Cutter	R	2.50
P. O. T. Scout Cruiser	R	2.50
Parallel Universe	C	0.10
Penal Colony	R	2.50
14		
Phantom	U	0.60
Phase Dragoness	R	2.50
Phase Rats	C	0.10
Phaser Fighter	U	0.60
Phaser Magnifier Refit	VR	3.50
Pirate System	R	2.50
Plasma Dragoness	VR	3.50
Plasmatic Nebula	VR	3.50
Political Clout	R	2.50
15		
Prophet	R	2.50
Protion	R	2.50
Radial Dish	C	0.10
Rat Infestation	C	0.10
Redgelon	VR	3.50
Refueler	R	2.50
Repair Base	VR	3.50
Research Developer	VR	3.50
Robotic Crew	C	0.10
16		
Rom's Periodic Comet	C	0.10
Scandig Blob	U	0.60
Science Officer	C	0.10
Scorpead Battlecruiser	VR	3.50
Scorpead Battleship	VR	3.50
Scorpead Command Cruiser	VR	3.50
Scorpead Destroyer	U	0.60
Scorpead Dreadnought	VR	3.50
Scorpead Escort	U	0.60
17		
Scorpead Frigate	U	0.60
Scorpead Heavy Cruiser	VR	3.50
Scorpead Light Cruiser	R	2.50
Scorpead Lore	VR	3.50
Scorpead Minesweeper	R	2.50
Scorpead Science Ship	R	2.50
Scorpead Scout Cruiser	R	2.50
Sensor Planet	VR	3.50
Sextaraan Web Crawlers	C	0.10

Card name	Rarity	Price
18		
Ship Collision	R	2.50
Skull Reaper	VR	3.50
Skullets	U	0.60
Slave Trader	VR	3.50
Spiritual Leader	VR	3.50
Spiritual Temple	U	0.60
Star Quake	U	0.60
Stasis Mine	VR	3.50
Strategy	C	0.10
19		
Structural Degeneration	VR	3.50
Super Tanker	VR	3.50
Supersonic Flow	C	0.10
Supreme Leader	URF	5.00
Symnergenic Cloud	R	2.50
Sysop	R	2.50
System - Penteir	R	2.50
Tactical Fighter	VR	3.50
Tactical Officer	VR	3.50
20		
Tactician	R	2.50
Tarragym Effect	R	2.50
Teamster	C	0.10
Techno - Sorcerer Base	URF	5.00
Tectonic Burrower	U	0.60
The Soulless	U	0.60
Time Portal	URF	5.00
Transport Shuttle	C	0.10
Transporter Mine	U	0.60
21		
Tufor Battleship	VR	3.50
Tufor Command Launch	VR	3.50
Tufor Cutter	U	0.60
Tufor Destroyer	R	2.50
Tufor Dreadnought	VR	3.50
Tufor Escort	R	2.50
Tufor Fighter Carrier	VR	3.50
Tufor Heavy Cruiser	VR	3.50
Tufor Light Cruiser	R	2.50
22		
Tufor Lt Fighter Carrier	C	0.10
Tufor Mine Cruiser	VR	3.50
Tufor Mine Layer	R	2.50
Tufor Operations Base	URF	5.00
Tufor Research Scout	R	2.50
Tufor Science Platform	U	0.60
Tufor War Cruiser	VR	3.50
Undead Dragoness	VR	3.50
Vacation Planet	R	2.50
23		
Vektrean Mercenaries Dreadnought	VR	3.50
Void Angel	R	2.50
Vortex Dragoness	VR	3.50
Vymezies Blaze	R	2.50
Vymezies Matter	U	0.60
Vymezies Particle	C	0.10
Warning Buoy	R	2.50
Yorl the Forsaken	URF	5.00
Zaggoth Guardian	URF	5.00
24		
Zaggoth Mordeth	URF	5.00
Zambarez	U	0.60

RARITY KEY C = Common ■ U = Uncommon ■ R = Rare ■ VR = Very Rare ■ UR = Ultra Rare ■ F = Foil card ■ X = Fixed/standard in all decks

166 • *SCRYE Collectible Card Game Checklist and Price Guide*

Galactic Empires • Powers of the Mind

Companion Games • Released **July 1995**

152 cards in set • IDENTIFIER: None; all © 1995 on face

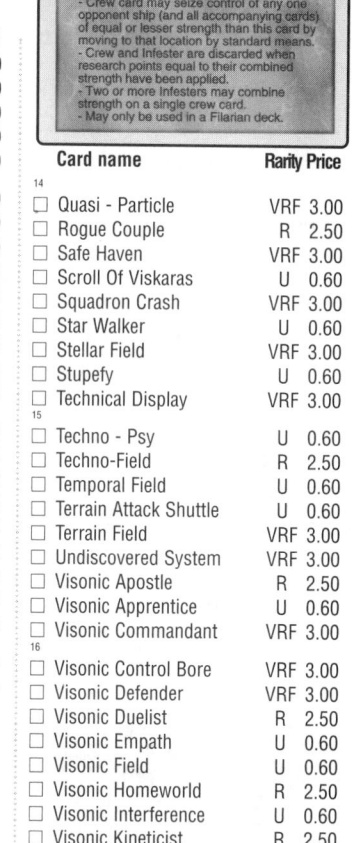

A7 Filarian Infester

Illustration © 1995 Melissa Benson

Filarian Infester:
- Played on your own crew card.
- Crew card may seize control of any one opponent ship (and all accompanying cards) of equal or lesser strength than this card by moving to that location by standard means.
- Crew and Infester are discarded when research points equal to their combined strength have been applied.
- Two or more Infesters may combine strength on a single crew card.
- May only be used in a Filarian deck.

• Booster packs contain 12 cards; booster displays (5,500 produced) contain 36 boosters

Powers of the Mind introduced Psionic powers to **Galactic Empires** and includes two new races that rely on psionic characters instead of ships to guard their empires.

While these races never became popular, and so never accumulated much of a win-loss record, when added in as minor race allies to the other more standard races, they produced a substantial impact on the game. — *Michael Greenholdt*

You will need **17** nine-pocket pages to store this set. (8 doubled up)

Card name	Rarity	Price
Set (152 cards)		29.00
Booster Display Box		23.00
Booster Pack		1.00

Card name	Rarity	Price
Arduous Study	R	2.50
Artifact - Scepter of Time	VRF	3.00
Asteroid Shield	R	2.50
Atmospheric Evasion	U	0.60
Breached City	R	2.50
Central Galactic Bank	VRF	3.00
CEO	VRF	3.00
CFO	R	2.50
Chakan; The Forever Man	URF	5.00
Citadel	VRF	3.00
Comet Control	U	0.60
Corporeal Defender	VRF	3.00
Corporeal Field	U	0.60
Corporeal Traveler (anti Psy)	R	2.50
Cosmic String	R	2.50
Cyber Mage Implant	R	2.50
Data Bank	R	2.50
Derranged Psy	U	0.60
Desolation	U	0.60
Discovery of Discoveries	VRF	3.00
Divergence of Psy	U	0.60
Dragon Harness	R	2.50
Dragon Muzzle	R	2.50
Electro-Field	U	0.60
Energy Storage Facility	VRF	3.00
Entertaining Pastime	R	2.50
Evolving Terrain	VRF	3.00
Exploration Mission	VRF	3.00
Field of Channeling	R	2.50
Field of Chaos	R	2.50
Field of Death	VRF	3.00
Field of Matter	R	2.50
Field of Minor Wilding	U	0.60
Field of Power	U	0.60
Field of Viscaras	R	2.50
Field Transferal (Psy)	VRF	3.00

Card name	Rarity	Price
Fighter Support	U	0.60
Filarian Infester	U	0.60
Filarian Infester	R	2.50
Filarian Infester	R	2.50
Filarian Infester	VRF	3.00
Filarian Infester	VRF	3.00
Filarian Mind Lord	R	2.50
Healing Field	VRF	3.00
Huge Invinco Guardian	VRF	3.00
Hypnotic Trance	VRF	3.00
Illness - Psychic Burnout	VRF	3.00
Impending Chaos	U	0.60
Infestation Inhibitor	U	0.60
Informant	R	2.50
Inoperative Gravity	R	2.50
Interstellar Field	VRF	3.00
Lesser Healing Field	U	0.60
Material Evil	R	2.50
Mental Inspiration	U	0.60
Mind Field	VRF	3.00
Mind Guard	U	0.60
Mind Shield	U	0.60
Mind Turning	U	0.60
Mind Turning	R	2.50
Mind Turning	VRF	3.00
Minor Terrain Field	R	2.50
Opposite Extension	U	0.60
Parasitic Augmentation	R	2.50
Parasitic Dispersion	R	2.50
Personal Base	U	0.60
Personal Cruiser	U	0.60
Planet Govessera	VRF	3.00
Plasma Vortex	U	0.60
Political Intrigue	URF	5.00
Projected Infestation	R	2.50
Psionic Enhancement	R	2.50
Psionic Soothing	R	2.50
Psy Control Base	VRF	3.00
Psy Disease (anti Psy)	U	0.60
Psy Dragoness	U	0.60

Card name	Rarity	Price
Psy Entrantrix	VRF	3.00
Psy Healer	U	0.60
Psy Marine	VRF	3.00
Psy Meditation Base	VRF	3.00
Psy Moon	U	0.60
Psy Mutation (anti Psy)	U	0.60
Psy Outpost	U	0.60
Psy Pyramid	R	2.50
Psy Relay	R	2.50
Psy Responder	R	2.50
Psy Seduction	R	2.50
Psy Training	R	2.50
Psy Training Site	R	2.50
Psyber Mage	R	2.50
Psybot	U	0.60
Psybot	VRF	3.00
Psycanti Apostle	R	2.50
Psycanti Apprentice	U	0.60
Psycanti Commandant	VRF	3.00
Psycanti Conflagration	VRF	3.00
Psycanti Deception	U	0.60
Psycanti Defender	VRF	3.00
Psycanti Duelist	R	2.50
Psycanti Empath	U	0.60
Psycanti Field	U	0.60
Psycanti Kineticist	R	2.50
Psycanti Master	URF	5.00
Psycanti Muse	U	0.60
Psycanti Occultist	R	2.50
Psycanti Paladin	VRF	3.00
Psycanti Plane Enhancement	VRF	3.00
Psycanti Planetesimal	R	2.50
Psycanti Pledge	U	0.60
Psycanti Practitioner	U	0.60
Psycanti Projection Station	R	2.50
Psycanti Sub - Master	VRF	3.00
Psychotic Sludge	U	0.60
Psychotic Sludge (anti Psy)	R	2.50
Psyvis System	VRF	3.00
Quantum Decay	VRF	3.00
Quark	VRF	3.00

Card name	Rarity	Price
Quasi - Particle	VRF	3.00
Rogue Couple	R	2.50
Safe Haven	VRF	3.00
Scroll Of Viskaras	U	0.60
Squadron Crash	VRF	3.00
Star Walker	U	0.60
Stellar Field	VRF	3.00
Stupefy	U	0.60
Technical Display	VRF	3.00
Techno - Psy	U	0.60
Techno-Field	R	2.50
Temporal Field	U	0.60
Terrain Attack Shuttle	U	0.60
Terrain Field	VRF	3.00
Undiscovered System	VRF	3.00
Visonic Apostle	R	2.50
Visonic Apprentice	U	0.60
Visonic Commandant	VRF	3.00
Visonic Control Bore	VRF	3.00
Visonic Defender	VRF	3.00
Visonic Duelist	R	2.50
Visonic Empath	U	0.60
Visonic Field	U	0.60
Visonic Homeworld	R	2.50
Visonic Interference	U	0.60
Visonic Kineticist	R	2.50
Visonic Master	URF	5.00
Visonic Muse	U	0.60
Visonic Occultist	R	2.50
Visonic Paladin	VRF	3.00
Visonic Pledge	U	0.60
Visonic Practitioner	U	0.60
Visonic Sub - Master	VRF	3.00
Visonicuins	R	2.50
Warehouse	VRF	3.00

Galactic Empires • Time Gates

Companion Games • Released **August 1995**

157 cards in set • IDENTIFIER: None; all © 1995 on face

M6 Time Thief

Illustration © 1995 Lubov

Time Thief:
- Played on a stack of cards.
- Each turn, owner of the affected stack must use a card play to move the time thief to a stack in another fleet (except the time thief player's fleet) or discard one card (not a card play) played to or against any part of that stack.
- Discarded when a card of greater strength is discarded from the affected stack in response to this card.

• Booster packs contain 12 cards; booster displays (5,500 produced) contain 36 boosters

Time Gates introduced the Time Origin, a second, separate playing area. Some cards in this supplement went to the Time Origin when destroyed in the main play area. Although few cards in the Time Origin could cross over to the main area, fire from the main area could affect the Time Origin. Many of the cards in Time Gates shared a temporal motif, including Time Knights, a crew type that included many powerful, continuing effects. — *Michael Greenholdt*

You will need **18** nine-pocket pages to store this set. (9 doubled up)

Card name	Rarity	Price
Set (157 cards)		25.00
Booster Display Box		20.00
Booster Pack		1.00

Card name	Rarity	Price
Accelerated Aging	R	2.50
Accelerated Burn	U	0.60
Ante Accelerator	VRF	3.30
Anti - Time Mine Field	R	2.50

Card name	Rarity	Price
Anti-Time Exchange	R	2.50
Artifact - Timeglass	VRF	3.30
Aurora Borealis	R	2.50
Base Relocation	U	0.60
Base Thrusters	R	2.50

RARITY KEY C = Common U = Uncommon R = Rare VR = Very Rare UR = Ultra Rare F = Foil card X = Fixed/standard in all decks

SCRYE Collectible Card Game Checklist and Price Guide • **167**

Card name	Rarity	Price
2		
Catastrophic Repetition	VRF	3.30
Cessation of Engagement	U	0.60
Cessation of Events	U	0.60
Cessation of Fire	VRF	3.30
Cessation of Production	R	2.50
Cessation of Time	R	2.50
Continuum Disorder	R	2.50
Crew Capture	R	2.50
Criminal Judge	VRF	3.30
3		
Crinkled Timeline	U	0.60
Cryogenic Convict	U	0.60
Cybercyst	U	0.60
Cybersist	U	0.60
Discard Delay	U	0.60
Discard Equivalency	VRF	3.30
Discard Exchange	U	0.60
Distortion Generator	U	0.60
Dream State	U	0.60
4		
Dyson Sphere	URF	5.00
Early Shipment	U	0.60
Entity Swap	R	2.50
Father of Time	URF	5.00
Flood	R	2.50
Frayed Time Spindle	VRF	3.30
Future Ship	VRF	3.30
Future Transmission	U	0.60
Galacticnet	R	2.50
5		
Headquarters Overhaul	VRF	3.30
Instant Reaction	U	0.60
Intercept Action	U	0.60
Invasion Force	U	0.60
Janitor	R	2.50
Lost In Space	U	0.60
Mirror Skinned Phaser Eel	U	0.60
Modified Timeline	VRF	3.30
Monster Halt	R	2.50
6		
Out of Phase World	R	2.50

Card name	Rarity	Price
Out of Season	U	0.60
Past Transmission	U	0.60
Phaser Distorter	VRF	3.30
Premonition	U	0.60
Quantum Occurrence	R	2.50
Repair Supply Base	VRF	3.30
Repeat Fire	VRF	3.30
Research Mandator	U	0.60
7		
Reserve Call Up	VRF	3.30
Resource Theft	R	2.50
Sequential Continuum	U	0.60
Ship from the Future	U	0.60
Shipping Delays - 1	R	2.50
Shipping Delays - 2	R	2.50
Shipping Delays - 3	R	2.50
Shipping Delays - 4	R	2.50
Shipping Delays - 5	R	2.50
8		
Shipping Delays - 6	R	2.50
Shipping Delays - 7	R	2.50
Shipping Delays - 8	R	2.50
Space - Time Diversion	U	0.60
Shipping Delays - 9	R	2.50
Shipping Delays - 10	R	2.50
Space-Time Portal	R	2.50
Star Well	VRF	3.30
Starburst Accelerator	VRF	3.30
9		
Stasis Canister	U	0.60
Stellar Gas Cloud	R	2.50
Suark Beast	U	0.60
Suark Breed (C1)	U	0.60
Suark Breed (C2)	U	0.60
Suark Breed (C3)	R	2.50
Suark Breed (C4)	R	2.50
Suark Breed (C5)	R	2.50
Suark Breed (C6)	VRF	3.30
10		
Suspended Animation	VRF	3.30
Temporal Comprehension	R	2.50

Card name	Rarity	Price
Temporal Correction	R	2.50
Temporal Engineer	VRF	3.30
Temporal Fighter	U	0.60
Temporal Ion Storm	R	2.50
Temporal Loophole	R	2.50
Temporal Mechanic	VRF	3.30
Temporal Shifter	U	0.60
11		
Temporal Shuttle	U	0.60
Temporal Snake	U	0.60
Temporal Snake	R	2.50
Temporal Snake	VRF	3.30
Temporal Transporter	U	0.60
Temporal Transporter	VRF	3.30
Time Assault Team	R	2.50
Time Capsule	U	0.60
Time Capsule	R	2.50
12		
Time Capsule	VRF	3.30
Time Compression	U	0.60
Time Discrepancy	U	0.60
Time Dragoness	R	2.50
Time Enclave	U	0.60
Time Enclave	R	2.50
Time Evacuation	R	2.50
Time Exchange	U	0.60
Time Expansion	U	0.60
13		
Time Fiend	R	2.50
Time Gap Generator	R	2.50
Time Gate	U	0.60
Time Guardian	R	2.50
Time Intrusion	VRF	3.30
Time Jump	R	2.50
Time Keeper	U	0.60
Time Knight	URF	5.00
Time Knight	VRF	3.30
14		
Time Knight	VRF	3.30
Time Knight	VRF	3.30
Time Knight	VRF	3.30

Card name	Rarity	Price
Time Knight	VRF	3.30
Time Knight	VRF	3.30
Time Knight	VRF	3.30
Time Knight	VRF	3.30
Time Knight	VRF	3.30
Time Lore	VRF	3.30
15		
Time Machine	VRF	3.30
Time Merchant	VRF	3.30
Time Screen	R	2.50
Time Shield	VRF	3.30
Time Ship	U	0.60
Time Ship	R	2.50
Time Ship	VRF	3.30
Time Skip	U	0.60
Time Switch	U	0.60
16		
Time Thief	R	2.50
Time Tornado	R	2.50
Time Trap	U	0.60
Time Typhoon	VRF	3.30
Time Wave	U	0.60
Time Wave	R	2.50
Time Wave	VRF	3.30
Timeline Alteration	VRF	3.30
Timeline Reversal	URF	5.00
17		
Tranoan Battlecruiser	VRF	3.30
Tranoan Destroyer	VRF	3.30
Tranoan Dreadnought	VRF	3.30
Tranoan Frigate	VRF	3.30
Tranoan Time Cruiser	VRF	3.30
Tranoan Time Ship	VRF	3.30
Trophy Hunter	U	0.60
Twist of Fate	VRF	3.30
Unlucky Crew Action	U	0.60
18		
Vacuum Effect	VRF	3.30
Veterinarian	R	2.50
Well of Time	VRF	3.30
Wreckage Survivors	R	2.50

S8 ■■ ◆◆◆◆
Ship of the Ancients

Illustration © 1995 Mark Poole

Ship of the Ancients:
The lost empire known as the 'Ancients' would occasionally appear to aid one of the empires. They were highly advanced. May use foreign or exclusive technology or crew.

++++++++: Phasers

Galactic Empires • *Advanced Technologies*

Companion Games • Released **November 1995**

152 cards in set • **IDENTIFIER: None; all © 1995 on faces**

GALACTIC EMPIRES

• Booster packs contain 12 cards; booster displays (4,500 produced) contain 36 boosters

As implied by the name, ***Advanced Technologies*** introduced many new concepts, especially in equipment (cards that modified ships, crew, or bases), ships, and bases. Each of the original races gains a new super-heavy ship as well as a light ship type, the patrol ship, which returns to the owning player's hand when destroyed. — *Michael Greenholdt*

You will need **17** nine-pocket pages to store this set. (9 doubled up)

Set (152 cards)	**24.00**
Booster Display Box	**18.00**
Booster Pack	**1.00**

Card name	Rarity	Price
1		
Alien Technology Expert	U	0.50
Ammo Reserve	VR	2.90
Anti-Starcraft	U	0.60
Argonian Flagship	UR	6.50
Argonian Patrol Ship	U	0.50
Argonian Spy Ship	R	2.40
Argonian Troop Ship	U	0.50
Armor System Refit	U	0.50
Armor System Refit (Leopan)	R	2.40
2		
Armory Base	VR	2.90

Card name	Rarity	Price
Automation	VR	2.90
Base Relocation Tug	U	0.50
Battery	U	0.50
Battle Sled	R	2.40
Blood Clydon	R	2.40
Bolaar Boarding Cruiser	R	2.40
Bolaar Negotiator	VR	2.90
Bolaar Patrol Ship	U	0.50
3		
Bolaar Spy Scout	U	0.50
Border Post	R	2.40
Border Station	VR	2.90
Cloning Device	VR	2.90
Clydon Boarding Warcraft	R	2.40
Clydon Energy Armor	U	0.50
Clydon Spy Warcraft	U	0.50
Clydon Troop Warcraft	U	0.50
Command & Control Center	R	2.40
4		
Corporate Carrier	U	0.50
Corporate Flagship	UR	6.50

Card name	Rarity	Price
Corporate Influence	R	2.40
Corporate Patrol Scout	U	0.50
Corporate Patrol Ship	R	2.40
Corporate Spy Ship	R	2.40
Corporate Troop Ship	U	0.50
Cosmic Cataclysm	VR	2.90
Deck Crew	R	2.40
5		
Demobilization	VR	2.90
Distortion Cannon Failure	R	2.40
Distortion Cannon Refit	R	2.40
Dragon Saddle	VR	2.90
Drone Clydon	U	0.50
Energy Flux	VR	2.90
Equipment Malfunction	VR	2.90
Espionage Satellite	U	0.50
EWACS Shuttlecraft	VR	2.90
6		
Fighter Defense System	VR	2.90
Fighter Installation	U	0.50
Formation Lights	R	2.40

Card name	Rarity	Price
Freighter Station	U	0.50
Fuser	VR	2.90
Fusion Mine	VR	2.90
Gaseous Degeneration	R	2.40
Guardian Field	R	2.40
Heavy Patrol Capsule Refit	VR	2.90
7		
Heavy Weapons Platform	R	2.40
Hyperspace Detonator Refit	R	2.40
Hyperspace Vortex	R	2.40
Hyperspace Vortex	U	0.50
Il'ith I'karnas	VR	2.90
Imperial Clydon	VR	2.90
Improved Automaton	R	2.40
Indirigan Supercarrier (Invincible Loner tribe)	UR	6.50
Intergalactic Grave Robbers	VR	2.90
8		
Invasion	R	2.40
Krebiz Cargo Capsule	U	0.50
Krebiz Dreadnought Carrier	VR	2.90

RARITY KEY C = Common U = Uncommon R = Rare VR = Very Rare UR = Ultra Rare F = Foil card X = Fixed/standard in all decks

168 • *SCRYE Collectible Card Game Checklist and Price Guide*

Card name	Rarity	Price
☐ Krebiz King Kraken	VR	2.90
☐ Landing Signal Officer	U	0.50
☐ Light Battle Sled	U	0.50
☐ Mechad Infiltration Unit	U	0.50
☐ Mechad Juggernaut	VR	2.90
☐ Mechad Patrol Scout	U	0.50
[9]		
☐ Mechad Patrol Ship	U	0.50
☐ Mechad Patrol Ship Leader	R	2.40
☐ Mechad Patrol Support Ship	R	2.40
☐ Mechanization	U	0.50
☐ Merchant Ship	VR	2.90
☐ Military Police	VR	2.90
☐ Mine Defenses	VR	2.90
☐ Mine Deployment Failure	VR	2.90
☐ Mining Expedition	U	0.50
[10]		
☐ Minor Luck Demon	R	2.40
☐ Monster Defense System (Rev.)	R	2.40
☐ Munition Processing Ship	U	0.50
☐ Murphy's Law	VR	2.90
☐ Officer's Saber	R	2.40
☐ Oscillating Transporter	R	2.40
☐ P.O.T. Command Cruiser (Rev.)	R	2.40
☐ P.O.T. Flagship	UR	6.50

Card name	Rarity	Price
☐ P.O.T. Lt Cruiser-Centaurian	R	2.40
[11]		
☐ P.O.T. Patrol Launch	U	0.50
☐ P.O.T. Spy Cutter	U	0.50
☐ P.O.T. Star Cruiser - Peladine	R	2.40
☐ P.O.T. Star Destroyer - Tequan	U	0.50
☐ P.O.T. Star Frigate - Tequan	U	0.50
☐ P.O.T. Troop Transport	U	0.50
☐ Patrol Capsule Refit	U	0.50
☐ Patrol Scout Refit	R	2.40
☐ Patrol Ship	U	0.50
[12]		
☐ Patrol Ship Courier	VR	2.90
☐ Patrol Ship Support Base	U	0.50
☐ Patrol Ship Tender	U	0.50
☐ Plasma Stream Accelerator	VR	2.90
☐ Position	U	0.50
☐ Power Generation Complex	R	2.40
☐ Projection Station [Equipment Bkg.]	U	0.50
☐ Protection Field	VR	2.90
☐ Pseudo Capsule	U	0.50
[13]		
☐ Red Tape	R	2.40
☐ Repair Tug	R	2.40

Card name	Rarity	Price
☐ Research Field	U	0.50
☐ Salvage Ship	R	2.40
☐ Scorpead Battle Carrier	VR	2.90
☐ Scorpead Patrol Ship	U	0.50
☐ Scorpead Spy Ship	R	2.40
☐ Scorpead Troop Ship	R	2.40
☐ Shield Penetration Failure	R	2.40
[14]		
☐ Shield Penetration Refit	VR	2.90
☐ Shield Resonance Wave	VR	2.90
☐ Ship of the Ancients	R	2.40
☐ Ship Upgrade	R	2.40
☐ Ship Upgrade	U	0.50
☐ Shuttle Malfunction	VR	2.90
☐ Solitary Station	U	0.50
☐ Space Remora	R	2.40
☐ Space Remora	U	0.50
[15]		
☐ Space Remora	VR	2.90
☐ Strobe Malfunction	R	2.40
☐ Targeting Systems	UR	6.50
☐ Thick Shelled Crab	U	0.50
☐ Time Alteration Device	VR	2.90
☐ Tour Guide	C	0.25
☐ Tractor Beam	VR	2.90

Card name	Rarity	Price
☐ Transporter Malfunction	VR	2.90
☐ Tufor Flagship	UR	6.50
[16]		
☐ Tufor Mine Accelerator	VR	2.90
☐ Tufor Mine Patrol Ship	U	0.50
☐ Tufor Patrol Scout	U	0.50
☐ Tufor Patrol Ship	R	2.40
☐ Tufor Spy Ship	R	2.40
☐ Tufor Troop Ship	U	0.50
☐ Unit Overhaul	VR	2.90
☐ Vacater Battle Cruiser (Indirigan)	VR	2.90
☐ Vacater Dreadnought (Indirigan)	VR	2.90
[17]		
☐ Vacater Heavy Cruiser (Indirigan)	VR	2.90
☐ Variable Plasma Overload	VR	2.90
☐ Variable Plasma Refit	VR	2.90
☐ Vektrean Asteroid Station [Gen BKG] B	VR	2.90
☐ Vektrean Command Override	VR	2.90
☐ Vektrean Leadership	R	2.40
☐ Vektrean Loyalty	VR	2.90
☐ Vektrean Patrol Ship	U	0.50

Galactic Empires • Piracy

Companion Games • Released March 1996
205 cards in set • IDENTIFIER: © 1996 on some faces

• Booster packs contain 6 cards; booster displays contain 36 boosters

Sold in tiny six-card packs, the **Piracy** expansion has a pirate motif, in the same way **Time Gates** has a time motif. Two new races are included, the Corporate Pirates and the Leopan. In addition, the two pirate fleets introduced in **Primary Edition**, the Bolaar and the Vektreans, are expanded and filled out.

The pirate fleets' main claim to fame was the ability to steal resources from their opponents' terrain. — **Michael Greenholdt**

Set (205 cards)		29.00
Booster Display Box		21.00
Booster Pack		1.00

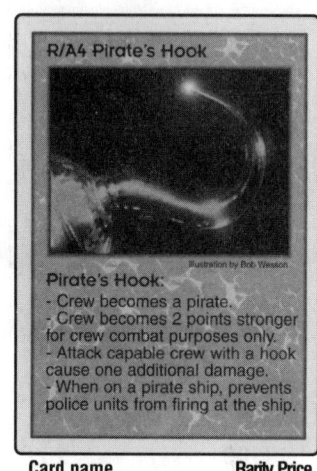

R/A4 Pirate's Hook
Illustration by Bob Wasson

Pirate's Hook:
- Crew becomes a pirate.
- Crew becomes 2 points stronger for crew combat purposes only.
- Attack capable crew with a hook cause one additional damage.
- When on a pirate ship, prevents police units from firing at the ship.

You will need **23** nine-pocket pages to store this set. (12 doubled up)

Card name	Rarity	Price
[1]		
☐ Archeology	VR	3.00
☐ Archeology Ship	U	0.80
☐ Armor System Failure	VR	3.00
☐ Asteroids	U	0.80
☐ Avian Dragon	U	0.80
☐ Blockade	VR	3.00
☐ Bolaar Battlecruiser	VR	3.00
☐ Bolaar Cargo Express	U	0.80
☐ Bolaar Dreadnought	VR	3.00
[2]		
☐ Bolaar Flagship	VR	3.00
☐ Bolaar Heavy Cargo Express	VR	3.00
☐ Bolaar Light Pirate Raider	U	0.80
☐ Bolaar Medium Raider	U	0.80
☐ Bolaar Patrol Ship	U	0.80
☐ Bolaar Sector HQ	VR	3.00
☐ Bolaar Stealth Raider	U	0.80
☐ Bolaar Ultra-Light Raider	U	0.80
☐ Buccaneer	VR	3.00
[3]		
☐ Burrowing Dragoness	U	0.80
☐ Camouflage World	VR	3.00
☐ Cargo Hold	U	0.80
☐ Celestial Comet	U	0.80
☐ Change Of Identity	U	0.80
☐ Civil War	VR	3.00
☐ Civilian Captain	U	0.80
☐ Clan Boss	VR	3.00
☐ Corporate Pirate Assault Cruiser	VR	3.00
[4]		
☐ Corporate Pirate Battlecruiser	VR	3.00
☐ Corporate Pirate Enforcer	VR	3.00

Card name	Rarity	Price
☐ Corporate Pirate Heavy Cruiser	U	0.80
☐ Corporate Pirate Landing Cruiser	U	0.80
☐ Corporate Pirate Light Cruiser	U	0.80
☐ Corporate Pirate Light Enforcer	U	0.80
☐ Corporate Pirate Patrol Scout	U	0.80
☐ Corporate Pirate Patrol Ship	U	0.80
[5]		
☐ Corporate Pirate Raider	U	0.80
☐ Corporate Pirate Spy Ship	U	0.80
☐ Corporate Pirate Stealth Cruiser	VR	3.00
☐ Corporate Pirate Stealth Destroyer	U	0.80
☐ Corporate Pirate Tug	U	0.80
☐ Covert Operations	U	0.80
☐ Creature From the Black Hole	VR	3.00
☐ Cyber Dragoness	VR	3.00
☐ Defended Territory	VR	3.00
☐ Defensive Mine Field	VR	3.00
[6]		
☐ Deflection/Transfer Device - Bolaar	VR	3.00
☐ Deflection/Transfer Device - Clydon	VR	3.00
☐ Degeneration Device	VR	3.00
☐ Dimensional Dementia	U	0.80
☐ Docking Ring	UR	7.00
☐ Dragon Eggs	VR	3.00
☐ Dragon Lair	VR	3.00
☐ Dragon Rider	VR	3.00
☐ Dual Launch Tubes	U	0.80
[7]		
☐ Early Warning	U	0.80
☐ Early Warning	U	0.80
☐ Electronic Warfare Base	U	0.80
☐ Energy Dragoness	VR	3.00
☐ Espionage Training	VR	3.00

Card name	Rarity	Price
☐ Filarian Overlord	VR	3.00
☐ Forgotten Planet	U	0.80
☐ Forgotten Ruins	U	0.80
☐ Formation Maneuver	VR	3.00
[8]		
☐ Funeral Cruiser	VR	3.00
☐ Gaia Separation	U	0.80
☐ Galactic Cataclysm	UR	7.00
☐ General Quarters	UR	7.00
☐ Ghost Fleet	VR	3.00
☐ Gohest's Pirate Ship	UR	7.00
☐ Gohest's Rescue Launch	U	0.80
☐ Gravitational Pull	VR	3.00
☐ Gravity Well	U	0.80
[9]		
☐ Gunnery Station	VR	3.00
☐ Hasty Retreat	U	0.80
☐ Holographic Simulator	VR	3.00
☐ Hostile Terrain	U	0.80
☐ Ice Age	U	0.80
☐ Illegal Cargo	U	0.80
☐ Independent Pirate Ship	U	0.80
☐ Independent Pirate Ship	VR	3.00
☐ Infiltration Array	VR	3.00
[10]		
☐ Leopan Battlecruiser	VR	3.00
☐ Leopan Carrier Cruiser	U	0.80
☐ Leopan Command Cruiser	VR	3.00
☐ Leopan Destroyer	U	0.80
☐ Leopan Heavy Cruiser	U	0.80
☐ Leopan Heavy War Cruiser	VR	3.00
☐ Leopan Light Cruiser	U	0.80
☐ Leopan Minesweeper	U	0.80
[11]		
☐ Leopan Patrol Ship	U	0.80
☐ Leopan Raiding Captain	U	0.80
☐ Leopan Raiding Party	U	0.80

Card name	Rarity	Price
☐ Leopan Raiding Party	VR	3.00
☐ Leopan Scout Frigate	U	0.80
☐ Leopan Sector HQ	VR	3.00
☐ Leopan Stealth Raiding Ship	VR	3.00
☐ Leopan Stealth Satellite	U	0.80
☐ Leopan Troop Ship	U	0.80
[12]		
☐ Leopan War Cruiser	VR	3.00
☐ Lost Pirate Ship	VR	3.00
☐ Main Bridge	U	0.80
☐ Major Religious Installation	VR	3.00
☐ Master Pirate	U	0.80
☐ Microscopic Black Hole	U	0.80
☐ Mind Programmer	U	0.80
☐ Mind Programmer	VR	3.00
☐ Minor Religious Installation	U	0.80
☐ Moon - Oversized Moon	U	0.80
[13]		
☐ Moon - Storage Moon	U	0.80
☐ Moon - Tranoan Moon	U	0.80
☐ Multi-Purpose Phasers - Bolaar	VR	3.00
☐ Multi-Purpose Phasers - Indirigan	VR	3.00
☐ Nagiridni Pirate Battlecruiser	VR	3.00
☐ Nagiridni Pirate Cruiser	VR	3.00
☐ Nagiridni Pirate Destroyer	U	0.80
☐ Navigational Error	VR	3.00
☐ Nebula - Dragon Nebula	VR	3.00
[14]		
☐ Nebula - Leopan Nebula	VR	3.00

RARITY KEY C = Common U = Uncommon R = Rare VR = Very Rare UR = Ultra Rare F = Foil card X = Fixed/standard in all decks

Card name	Rarity	Price		Card name	Rarity	Price		Card name	Rarity	Price		Card name	Rarity	Price
Not-So-Supreme Leader	VR	3.00		Planet - Nrutas	U	0.80	[19]	Shroud Web Device	U	0.80		Terradeforming	VR	3.00
Orbital Engineer	VR	3.00		Planet - Shrouded Planet	VR	3.00		Slave Trader	VR	3.00		Time Defiler	VR	3.00
Peace Mission	VR	3.00		Planet - Virgin Planet	VR	3.00		Small Moon - Corporate Moon	U	0.80		Tomb Of The Far Side Pharaoh	VR	3.00
Phaser Resonator	VR	3.00		Planet - Water World	VR	3.00		Small Moon - Hidden Moon	U	0.80		Toroidal Black Hole	VR	3.00
Pirate Activity	U	0.80	[17]	Planet Of Ill Repute	U	0.80		Social Combat	U	0.80		Trade Ship	VR	3.00
Pirate Alcove	VR	3.00		Planet- Atoll	U	0.80		Solar Winds	U	0.80		Tranoan Homeworld	VR	3.00
Pirate Captain	VR	3.00		Planetary Raid	VR	3.00		Space Illness	U	0.80		Transporter Chief	U	0.80
Pirate Currency	U	0.80		Police Cruiser	VR	3.00		Spiritual Ascension	U	0.80	[22]	Travel Agency	U	0.80
[15]				Police Headquarters	U	0.80		Spy	U	0.80		Undercover Agent	U	0.80
Pirate Engineer	U	0.80		Power Outage	U	0.80	[20]	Star	U	0.80		Urbanization	U	0.80
Pirate Fighter	U	0.80		Privateer	UR	7.00		Stolen Technology	U	0.80		Utopia	VR	3.00
Pirate Nebula	U	0.80		Projection Station	VR	3.00		Surface Dragoness	VR	3.00		Vektrean Asteroid Satellite	U	0.80
Pirate Outpost	U	0.80		Raiding Fleet	U	0.80		System - Indirigan Former				Vektrean Asteroid Station	VR	3.00
Pirate Raid	U	0.80	[18]	Raiding Mission	U	0.80		Homeworld	VR	3.00		Vicious Six Command Cruiser	VR	3.00
Pirate Wench	VR	3.00		Reinvestment	VR	3.00		System - Moon System	U	0.80		Vicious Six Destroyer - Left	VR	3.00
Pirate's Cache	U	0.80		Renegade Ship	VR	3.00		System Degeneration	VR	3.00		Vicious Six Destroyer - Right	VR	3.00
Pirate's Hook	VR	3.00		Rogue Cop	U	0.80		Tax Collector	U	0.80	[23]			
Pirate's Horde	VR	3.00		Rogue Dragoness	U	0.80		Technological Breakthrough	VR	3.00		Vicious Six Dreadnought	VR	3.00
[16]				Sargassos	U	0.80		Tectonic Marauder	VR	3.00		Vicious Six Fleet Survey Cruiser	VR	3.00
Pirate's Parrot	VR	3.00		Shinnicera	VR	3.00	[21]					Vicious Six Heavy Cruiser	VR	3.00
Planescape	U	0.80		Shroud	VR	3.00		Temporal Conscience	VR	3.00		Walk The Plank	VR	3.00
Planet - Bolaar II	VR	3.00		Shroud Web	VR	3.00		Temporal Repetition	U	0.80		Wandering Desire	U	0.80
Planet - Massive Ore Planet	VR	3.00										Warp Field	U	0.80
Planet - Muckstra	U	0.80										White Nobelium	VR	3.00

Galactic Empires • *Comedy Club*

Companion Games • Released **August 1996**
102 cards in set • **IDENTIFIER: None**

GALACTIC EMPIRES

You will need
12
nine-pocket pages to store this set.
(6 doubled up)

• Starter displays contain 12 boosters

By far the smallest and silliest of the *Galactic Empires* expansions, *Comedy Club* nevertheless contains some powerful and important cards.

The tongue-in-cheek and strange card titles (and powers) put off many collectors in a game that, until this release, had been a very serious presentation. Still, there's something to be said for an expansion that contains **Buffy the Time Knight Slayer**, years before the TV show revived the film character. — *Michael Greenholdt*

Set (102 cards)	26.00
Starter Display Box	23.00
Starter Pack	1.00

SCRYE NOTES: *Many of these cards have multiple versions; there is no effect on play.*

Card name	Rarity	Price		Card name	Rarity	Price		Card name	Rarity	Price
[1]				Donut Shop	U	0.50		Mime Pajamas	U	0.50		Space Penguin	U	0.50
8-Ball	U	0.50		Eat at Joe's (1 of 4 quotes)	U	0.50		Mime Protection Chamber	U	0.50		Space Penguin	U	0.50
Ace of Clubs	U	0.50		Either Dragoness	U	0.50		Mime Rack	U	0.50	[10]			
Admiral's Rear (1 of 4 quotes)	U	0.50		Face Paint	U	0.50	[7]	Molecular Transporter	U	0.50		Speaking Part (1 of 4 quotes)	U	0.50
And Now For Something				Fast Food Franchise (1 of				Money Hungry Weasels	U	0.50		Steak Sauce (1 of 4 quotes)	U	0.50
Completely Different	UR	4.00		4 quotes)	U	0.50		Night Club Comedian	U	0.50		Super Model	U	0.50
Arduous Study (1 of 4 quotes)	U	0.50	[4]	Garbage Planet	U	0.50		Night Club Comedian	UR	4.00		The Comedy Club on the		
Barmaid (1 of 4 quotes)	U	0.50		Gentlealien's Club (1 of 4 quotes)	U	0.50		Night Club Comedian (1 of				Far Side of the Galaxy	UR	4.00
Bob's Used Spaceship Lot	U	0.50		Groupie	U	0.50		4 quotes)	U	0.50		The Club	U	0.50
Bouncer Training Club	U	0.50		Heckler	U	0.50		Pizza Delivery Alien (1 of 4				The Club	C	0.10
Buffy the Time Knight Slayer				Holographic Mime	U	0.50		quotes)	U	0.50		The Commodores	U	0.50
(1 of 4 quotes)	U	0.50		Home Base	U	0.50		Planet - Earth	U	0.50		The Ensign in the Red Shirt	U	0.50
[2]				In Phase World	U	0.50		Planet - Mime Homeworld	U	0.50		The Old Switcheroo	U	0.50
Call it Good	U	0.50		Kenobi	U	0.50	[8]	Poker Night	U	0.50	[11]			
Captain's Bluff (1 of 4 quotes)	U	0.50		Kitty Cat Club (1 of 4 quotes)	U	0.50		Protest Ship	U	0.50		Time Accelerant (1 of 3		
Casino	U	0.50	[5]	Kung Fu Dragon	U	0.50		Psychiatric Ward (1 of 4 quotes)	U	0.50		quotes)	U	0.50
Comet - Out of Control Comet	U	0.50		Lead Balloon Factory	U	0.50		Road Sign	U	0.50		Time Gait	U	0.50
Comet Control	U	0.50		Lobster Boat	U	0.50		Road Sign	U	0.50		Time Hiccup	U	0.50
Chakan's Hat	U	0.50		Lobster Market	U	0.50		Rock Lobster	U	0.50		Twist of Fate II	U	0.50
Cinema	U	0.50		Lobster Nebula	U	0.50		Rubber Ball Planet	U	0.50		Unlucky Mime Explosion (1		
Clown Car (1 of 4 quotes)	U	0.50		Lucky Mime Explosion (1				Sabot Tour	U	0.50		of 4 quotes)	U	0.50
Clown College (1 of 4 quotes)	U	0.50		of 4 quotes)	U	0.50		Sahnadrrei's Weapon Shop	U	0.50		Used Spaceship Dealer -		
[3]				Mad Scientiist	U	0.50		Sales Representative	U	0.50		A.K.A. Bob (1 of 4 quotes)	U	0.50
Coffee House (1 of 4 quotes)	U	0.50		Master Mime	UR	4.00	[9]	Salt Water World	U	0.50		Vektrean Asteroid Outhouse	U	0.50
Comedy Club Sector HQ	U	0.50		Mime	U	0.50		Shameless Argonian				Wanna-be Game Designer	U	0.50
Defensive Satellites	U	0.50	[6]	Mime	U	0.50		Sunbathing Nude	U	0.50		Warp Funnel Cakes	U	0.50
Derelict Fighter	C	0.10		Mime	U	0.50		Ship From The Present	U	0.50	[12]			
				Mime	U	0.50		Shuttlebus	U	0.50		We Have Special Plans for		
				Mime Control Beast	U	0.50		Sign Post (1 of 4 quotes)	U	0.50		this Card	U	0.50
				Mime Intrusion (1 of 4 quotes)	U	0.50		Soft Chewy Center of the Planet	U	0.50		What's This Button For?		
				Mime Knight	U	0.50		Space Penguin	U	0.50		(1 of 4 quotes)	U	0.50
												You Missed Me By That		
												Much	U	0.50

RARITY KEY C = Common U = Uncommon R = Rare VR = Very Rare UR = Ultra Rare F = Foil card X = Fixed/standard in all decks

170 • SCRYE Collectible Card Game Checklist and Price Guide

Galactic Empires • *Persona*

Companion Games • Released **November 1996**
205 cards in set • **IDENTIFIER: None**

• Booster displays contain 96 boosters

In **Galactic Empires**, the term Persona extends to any cards with the trait, not just crew cards. A Persona card is unique; no other player can have one in play when such a card is already in play. They can be quite powerful and lend themselves to game-breaking combinations.

In addition to focusing on such cards, the **Persona** expansion also introduces Nobility crew cards, crew cards that produce resources like terrain. — *Michael Greenholdt*

> You will need
> **23**
> nine-pocket pages to store this set.
> (12 doubled up)

Set (205 cards)	**27.00**
Booster Display Box	**20.00**
Booster Pack	**1.00**

Card name	Rarity	Price
1		
Adamantine Hull - Sound Construction	VR	2.00
Advanced Specimen	U	0.80
Alien Love	U	0.80
Allizdog	U	0.80
Amphibian Desire	U	0.80
Ancient Control Network	U	0.80
Ancient Studies	U	0.80
Ancient's Library	VR	2.00
Ancients Portal	VR	2.00
2		
Antimatter Equivalent	VR	2.00
Aqaaran Disjunction	U	0.80
Aqaaran Fighter	U	0.80
Aqaaran Holy Day	U	0.80
Argonian Heavy Gale Fighter	U	0.80
Artifact - Empire Constitution	VR	2.00
Artifact - Spiritual Symbol	U	0.80
Artifact - Time Knight's Scepter	VR	2.00
Ascension	U	0.80
3		
Assault Tank	VR	2.00
Battlesled	VR	2.00
Bodyguard	U	0.80
Bolaar Fighter	U	0.80
Boomerang Racks	U	0.80
Boring Probe	U	0.80
Breeder	VR	2.00
Chef	U	0.80
Chief Engineer	VR	2.00
4		
City of Forever	U	0.80
Clydon Fighter	U	0.80
Clydon Flagship	VR	2.00
Clydon Heavy Warcraft	VR	2.00
Clydon Imperial General	VR	2.00
Clydon System	VR	2.00
Coffee Break	U	0.80
Communications Supervisor	VR	2.00
Construction Team	U	0.80
5		
Cook	U	0.80
Corporate Employee	U	0.80
Corporate Fighter	U	0.80
Corporate Gold Card	U	0.80
Cryptologist	U	0.80
Crystalline Detection Manifestation	U	0.80
Cybernetic Engineer	VR	2.00
Dark Circuitry	UR	5.00
Defensive Aircraft	U	0.80
6		
Drag Racing	U	0.80
Dragon Sun	U	0.80
Electronic Warfare Specialist	VR	2.00
Emergency Maintenance Team	U	0.80

Card name	Rarity	Price
Endri K'tal	VR	2.00
Espionage	VR	2.00
Explorer	VR	2.00
Filarian Moon - Infested Moon	VR	2.00
Filarian Needle Fighter	U	0.80
7		
Fireman Suit Malfunction	U	0.80
First Sergeant	VR	2.00
Flight Attendant	U	0.80
Flight Deck Supervisor	VR	2.00
Floating City	U	0.80
Fluctuating Stasis Mine	U	0.80
Free Trade Zone	U	0.80
Galactic Credit Bureau	VR	2.00
Galactic Depression	VR	2.00
8		
Galactic Parcel Ship	U	0.80
Garbage Man	U	0.80
Genetic Variant	VR	2.00
Gorilla Warfare Specialists	U	0.80
Grand Chieftain - Marchias	VR	2.00
Grand Time Keeper - Sir Thomas Seth	VR	2.00
Htim'	VR	2.00
Hydroponic Technician	U	0.80
Illness - Space Sickness	U	0.80
9		
I'm a Persona	U	0.80
Indirigan Chieftain - Licifrous	VR	2.00
Indirigan Chieftain - Lone Wolf	VR	2.00
Indirigan Chieftain - Murinca	VR	2.00
Indirigan Chieftain - Noaha	VR	2.00
Indirigan Chieftain - Urvill	VR	2.00
Indirigan Female	VR	2.00
Indirigan Gypsy Fighter	U	0.80
Indirigan Tattoo	VR	2.00
10		
Infinite Potential	U	0.80
Installation Field	U	0.80
Instant Reaction Persona	U	0.80
Insurrection	U	0.80
Intergalactic Transgate	VR	2.00
Ixubermorth Citadel	VR	2.00
Jungle Love	U	0.80
Jungle Moths	U	0.80
J'xar Heavy Carrier	VR	2.00
11		
J'xar High Guard - J'x Yr'llite	VR	2.00
J'xar Jump Fighter	U	0.80
Krebiz Homeland	VR	2.00
Leopan Fighter	U	0.80
Leopan Technologist	VR	2.00
Logistics Officer	VR	2.00
Lone Wolf Battlecruiser	VR	2.00
Lone Wolf Command Cruiser	U	0.80
Lone Wolf Destroyer	U	0.80
12		
Lone Wolf Dreadnought	VR	2.00
Lone Wolf Police Cruiser	VR	2.00
Luck Guy	U	0.80
Lunar Eclipse	U	0.80

Card name	Rarity	Price
Mad Chemist	U	0.80
Mainframe System - Desiree	VR	2.00
Marine Major	VR	2.00
Master Navigator	VR	2.00
Metamorphosis	U	0.80
13		
Methane Atmosphere	U	0.80
Millionaire	VR	2.00
Mind Thief	VR	2.00
Moon - Scorpead Dominated Moon	VR	2.00
Negotiator	U	0.80
Noble Jester	U	0.80
Noble Countess	VR	2.00
Noble Duke	U	0.80
Noble Earl	VR	2.00
14		
Noble Knight	VR	2.00
Noble Knight Templar	VR	2.00
Noble Laird	VR	2.00
Noble Mar grave	VR	2.00
Noble Marquis	VR	2.00
Noble Robber Baron	VR	2.00
Noble Scout	U	0.80
Noble Sovereign	VR	2.00
Noble Squire	U	0.80
15		
Noble Thaine	VR	2.00
Noble Viscount	VR	2.00
Nuclear Incident	U	0.80
Offspring	U	0.80
Overwatch Dragon	U	0.80
Parasite Torpedoes	VR	2.00
Party Animals	U	0.80
Peace Treaty	U	0.80
Pendulum Defect	VR	2.00
16		
Pendulum Effect	U	0.80
Perfect Specimen	VR	2.00
Perpetual Motion Machine	VR	2.00
Perseverance	U	0.80
Phaser Targeting Refit	VR	2.00
Pioneer	VR	2.00
Planet - J'xar Transgalactic	VR	2.00
Planet - Leopan Operations Planet	VR	2.00
Planet - Mechad Planet - Arretia	VR	2.00
17		
Planet - P.O.T. Element Capital	VR	2.00
Planet - Vektrea Minor	U	0.80
Planet - Zedan Regional Colony	VR	2.00
Planet Gouge	U	0.80
Planet - Nagir XII	U	0.80
Planetoid-Argonian Fighter Pl.	VR	2.00
Plasma Phasers	U	0.80
Prehistoric Space Beast	VR	2.00
Psycanti Fighter	U	0.80
18		
Quicksand	VR	2.00
Radioactive Being	U	0.80

Card name	Rarity	Price
Rebel Leader	UR	5.00
Reestablish Territory	U	0.80
Refuge - Aqaaran Aquatic Refuge	VR	2.00
Renegade Science Officer	VR	2.00
Repair Asteroid	VR	2.00
Research Dragoness	U	0.80
Research Mandator	VR	2.00
19		
Research Probe	U	0.80
Reserve Cruiser	VR	2.00
Reserve Lock	U	0.80
Resources Management - Personnel Department	U	0.80
Riot	U	0.80
Royal Indirigan Tattoo	VR	2.00
Salvage Mission	UR	5.00
Sa'meh E'no	VR	2.00
Secret Agent Alien	VR	2.00
20		
Senior Admiral	VR	2.00
Senior Helmsman	VR	2.00
Skeleton Crew	U	0.80
Solar Eclipse	VR	2.00
Sound Construction	VR	2.00
Speedy Delivery Alien	U	0.80
Street People	U	0.80
Suicide Mission	U	0.80
Surface Probe	VR	2.00
21		
System - Bolaar Covert System	VR	2.00
System - Corporate System	VR	2.00
System - Tufor System	VR	2.00
System - Vektrea System	VR	2.00
Tecnopilot	U	0.80
Teleportation Station	U	0.80
Terask	U	0.80
Terrestrial Overgrowth	U	0.80
Theme Park (Comedy Club)	VR	2.00
22		
Time Monarch	VR	2.00
Tranoan Fighter	U	0.80
Tranquilizer Mount	U	0.80
Troop Freighter	VR	2.00
Tufor Fighter	U	0.80
Vektrean Asteroid Flagstar	UR	5.00
Vektrean Fighter	U	0.80
Veterans of Galactic Wars Hall	U	0.80
Visionary	U	0.80
23		
Visonic Fighter	U	0.80
War Prophet	UR	5.00
Warcraft Coordinator	VR	2.00
Weapons Security	U	0.80
World Collector	VR	2.00
Zedan Chief Assassin	VR	2.00
Zedan Fighter	U	0.80

RARITY KEY C = Common   U = Uncommon   **R** = Rare   **VR** = Very Rare   **UR** = Ultra Rare   **F** = Foil card   **X** = Fixed/standard in all decks

Galactic Empires • Invaders (also known as "X")

Companion Games • Released January 1997

246 cards in set • **IDENTIFIER: None; see below**

• Booster packs contain 5 cards; displays contain 96 boosters

GALACTIC EMPIRES

You will need **28** nine-pocket pages to store this set. (14 doubled up)

Invaders covers fleets from outside the galaxy. Six more races are added, and several older races get heavy and specialty ships, bringing the total to 19 races plus the two psionic races. Two years in, the designers were starting to show the strain of making the races different. — *Michael Greenholdt*

SCRYE NOTES: *This is the "mystery" set, in more ways than one: Packs have no set name but feature a giant "X." (This was the 10th "series" release by Companion's count.) • Some cards (like the one at left) are oriented upside-down when you look at them next to earlier cards — "up" has the white ship on top of the flip side, so you can tell looking at cards in an opponent's hand that he's got cards from this set! • And players were also expected to build this 246-card set from packs which contained **only five cards,** the stingiest packs we've found for any CCG, before or since!*

A6 Senior Officer Training

Illustration © 1996 Aaron Williams

Officer Training: ●● ·XX

Provides the following to the crew's location:
- 2 less supply needed to engage.
- 2 less damage each opponent volley.

Set (246 cards)	31.00
Booster Display Box	20.00
Booster Pack	1.00

Card name	Rarity	Price
1		
Andromeda Beast	U	0.50
Andromeda Bound Battlecruiser	U	0.50
Andromeda Bound Command Cruiser	U	0.50
Andromeda Bound Freighter	U	0.50
Andromeda Bound Heavy Freighter	U	0.50
Andromeda Bound Munitions Cruiser	U	0.50
Andromeda Bound Survey Cruiser	U	0.50
Aqaaran Battlecraft	VR	3.00
Aqaaran Battlepost	VR	3.00
2		
Aqaaran Carrier Craft	U	0.50
Aqaaran Dreadnought Craft	VR	3.00
Aqaaran Fighter Base	U	0.50
Aqaaran Flagship	UR	6.00
Aqaaran Star Base	VR	3.00
Aqaaran Sun Base	UR	6.00
Argonian Defender	U	0.50
Barren Moon	U	0.50
Base Engineer	U	0.50
3		
Base Responder	VR	3.00
Battalisk	VR	3.00
Biodome	U	0.50
Boarding Beast	U	0.50
Bolaar Pirate Base	VR	3.00
Cadet	U	0.50
Castle Rognar	VR	3.00
Cloning Station	U	0.50
Clydon Warcraft Base	U	0.50
4		
Clydon Warcraft Dock	U	0.50
Colony Ship	VR	3.00
Colony Ship	VR	3.00
Command Craft (Aqaaran)	VR	3.00
Command Post (Aqaaran)	VR	3.00
Converted Freighter	U	0.50
Corporate Defender Base	VR	3.00
Corporate Economic Base	VR	3.00
Crash Maneuver	U	0.50
5		
Dark Mountain	VR	3.00
Dark Mountain	VR	3.00
Defender Base	VR	3.00
Defender Craft (Aqaaran)	VR	3.00
Demotion	U	0.50
Destroyer (Aqaaran)	VR	3.00
Eclipse Position	VR	3.00
Eclipse Position	VR	3.00
Emergency Evacuation	UR	6.00
6		
Energy Panels	U	0.50

Card name	Rarity	Price
Extreme Conflict	UR	6.00
Fighter Combat	U	0.50
Fire Breathing	U	0.50
Fleet Maneuver	U	0.50
Flight Craft (Aqaaran)	U	0.50
Flight School	U	0.50
Gauntlet of Time	VR	3.00
Geko Gnats	VR	3.00
7		
Geko Gnats	VR	3.00
Gekonauak Apprentice	R	2.40
Gekonauak Commander	VR	3.00
Gekonauak Hornet (2 versions)	VR	3.00
Gekonauak Kamikaze	U	0.50
Gekonauak King	VR	3.00
Gekonauak Needle	R	2.40
Gekonauak Queen	VR	3.00
Gekonauak Samurai	VR	3.00
8		
Gekonauak Shogun Warrior	VR	3.00
Gekonauak Soldier	U	0.50
Gekonauak Stinger	U	0.50
Gekonauak Subwarrior	R	2.40
Gekonauak Swarmer	U	0.50
Gekonauak Trainee	R	2.40
Gekonauak Warrior	VR	3.00
Gekonauak Wasp	R	2.40
Gekonauak Worker	VR	3.00
9		
Global Lava	U	0.50
Globule	VR	3.00
Hazard Transceiver	U	0.50
Heavy Craft (Aqaaran)	VR	3.00
Heavy Defender Base	VR	3.00
Holdfast Ship (Aqaaran)	VR	3.00
Hostile Environment Automaton	U	0.50
Insanity - Hallucinatory Space	VR	3.00
Insanity - Space Hallucination	VR	3.00
10		
Intergalactic Terrorist	U	0.50
Isolated Base	U	0.50
J'xar Armed Jumpship	R	2.40
J'xar Assault Cruiser	R	2.40
J'xar Battlecruiser	VR	3.00
J'xar Battleship	VR	3.00
J'xar Command Cruiser	VR	3.00
J'xar Dreadnought	VR	3.00
J'xar Flagship	UR	6.00
11		
J'xar Gravidic Engineer	VR	3.00
J'xar Heavy Cruiser	R	2.40
J'xar Heavy Jumpship	U	0.50
J'xar Jump Base	U	0.50
J'xar Jump Launcher	C	0.15
J'xar Light Cruiser	C	0.15
J'xar Medium Jumpship	R	2.40
J'xar Minesweeper Jumpship	U	0.50
J'xar Science Cruiser	U	0.50

Card name	Rarity	Price
12		
J'xar Scout	U	0.50
J'xar Troop	U	0.50
Krebiz Capsule Base	VR	3.00
Krebiz Heavy Defender	VR	3.00
Krebiz Krill-F Fighter	U	0.50
Krebiz Light Defender	VR	3.00
Lagrange Point	VR	3.00
Large Patrol Orgonism	U	0.50
Leisure Station	U	0.50
13		
Leopan Battleship	U	0.50
Leopan Capture Mission	U	0.50
Leopan Dreadnought	U	0.50
Leopan Raiding Pilot	VR	3.00
Leopan Raiding Pilot	VR	3.00
Leopan Troop Ship	U	0.50
Light Craft (Aqaaran)	VR	3.00
Mechad Core Fighter	VR	3.00
Mechad Power Base	U	0.50
14		
Mechad Virus Fighter	U	0.50
Mining Drone	U	0.50
Moon - Dimensional Moon	U	0.50
Moon - Gekonauak Moon	VR	3.00
Moon - Tiny Moon	VR	3.00
Moon - Treglean Moon	U	0.50
Mystic	VR	3.00
Mystic	VR	3.00
Observation Window	U	0.50
15		
Officer Training	VR	3.00
Orbital Mine	U	0.50
Ore Shuttle	U	0.50
Orgon Attacher	R	2.40
Orgon Blob	VR	3.00
Orgon Consumer	VR	3.00
Orgon Emalgemate	U	0.50
Orgon Engulfer	VR	3.00
Orgon Groth	R	2.40
16		
Orgon Mire	R	2.40
Orgon Seed	U	0.50
Orgon Separator	VR	3.00
Orgon Slag	R	2.40
Orgon Slath	R	2.40
Orgon Slime	VR	3.00
Orgon Sludge	R	2.40
Orgon Sprig	U	0.50
Orgon Straith	VR	3.00
17		
Orgonic Frenzy	U	0.50
Orgonism	R	2.40
Orion Nebula	U	0.50
Outpost Craft (Aqaaran)	VR	3.00
P.O.T. Centaurian Base	VR	3.00
P.O.T. Tequan Base	VR	3.00
Parallel Timesight	VR	3.00
Patrol Craft (Aqaaran)	VR	3.00

Card name	Rarity	Price
Patrol Orgonism	R	2.40
18		
Penal Correction Station	U	0.50
Personal Fighter	U	0.50
Personal Transportation	VR	3.00
Personal Transportation	VR	3.00
Phaser Bolt System	VR	3.00
Planet - Conquered Planet	VR	3.00
Planet - Gekonauak Outpost	VR	3.00
Planet - Treglean Outpost	U	0.50
Planet - ZDI Random Colony	VR	3.00
19		
Planet Rise	U	0.50
Primitive Society	U	0.50
Prisoners	U	0.50
Producer (Aqaaran)	VR	3.00
Quantum Flare	U	0.50
Rescue Specialist	U	0.50
Satellite D/R System	U	0.50
Scorpead Stinger Fighter	VR	3.00
Scout Patrol Craft (Aqaaran)	VR	3.00
20		
Secret Service Alien	U	0.50
Senior Officer Training	VR	3.00
Sensor Mine	U	0.50
Sneak Attack	VR	3.00
Sneak Attack	VR	3.00
Solar Corona (2 versions)	VR	3.00
Solar Disk	U	0.50
Solar Flare	U	0.50
Soldier of Fortune	U	0.50
21		
Space-Time Rift	VR	3.00
Space-Time Rift	VR	3.00
Spatial Disjunction	U	0.50
Spiritual Familiar	VR	3.00
Spontaneous Explosion	U	0.50
Star Spindle	VR	3.00
Star Spindle	VR	3.00
Starship Insurance	VR	3.00
Starship Insurance	VR	3.00
22		
Strafing Attack	U	0.50
Sublight Debris	VR	3.00
Sublight Debris	VR	3.00
Submarine (Aqaaran)	VR	3.00
Submersible (Aqaaran)	VR	3.00
Sun - Craft Site	VR	3.00
Surface Craft (Aqaaran)	VR	3.00
Surface Explosions	VR	3.00
Surface Vortex	U	0.50
23		
Surprise Maneuver	U	0.50
Survivalist	U	0.50
Target Acquisition Link (2 versions)	VR	3.00
Tavern	U	0.50
Technical Readout (2 versions)	VR	3.00
Temporary Insanity	VR	3.00

RARITY KEY C = Common U = Uncommon R = Rare VR = Very Rare UR = Ultra Rare F = Foil card X = Fixed/standard in all decks

Card name	Rarity	Price
☐ Temporary Insanity 2	VR	3.00
☐ Thermographic Display (2 versions)	VR	3.00
☐ Tight Maneuver	U	0.50
[24]		
☐ Timeless City	U	0.50
☐ Tranoan Time Bomb	VR	3.00
☐ Tranquility	U	0.50
☐ Transgate Stabilizers	VR	3.00
☐ Transgate Stabilizers	VR	3.00
☐ Traveler	U	0.50
☐ Treglean Carrier	U	0.50
☐ Treglean Destroyer	U	0.50

Card name	Rarity	Price
☐ Treglean Dreadnought	VR	3.00
[25]		
☐ Treglean Fleet Coordinator	VR	3.00
☐ Treglean Light Cruiser	U	0.50
☐ Vacation	U	0.50
☐ Vacation Planet - Golf World	U	0.50
☐ Vektrean Asteroid Freighter	U	0.50
☐ War Effort	U	0.50
☐ Water Tanker (Aqaaran)	VR	3.00
☐ Weather Satellite	U	0.50
☐ Zedan Battlecruiser	VR	3.00

Card name	Rarity	Price
[26]		
☐ Zedan Battleship	VR	3.00
☐ Zedan Carrier	U	0.50
☐ Zedan Command Cruiser	VR	3.00
☐ Zedan Destroyer	U	0.50
☐ Zedan Dreadnought	VR	3.00
☐ Zedan Escort	U	0.50
☐ Zedan Flagship	UR	6.00
☐ Zedan Heavy Destroyer	R	2.40
☐ Zedan Infiltrator	VR	3.00
[27]		
☐ Zedan Invasion Base	U	0.50

Card name	Rarity	Price
☐ Zedan Light Cruiser	R	2.40
☐ Zedan Light Scout	U	0.50
☐ Zedan Minesweeper	U	0.50
☐ Zedan Patrol Scout	U	0.50
☐ Zedan Patrol Ship	VR	3.00
☐ Zedan Patrol Ship Tender	R	2.40
☐ Zedan Shifter	VR	3.00
☐ Zedan Spy Cruiser	VR	3.00
[28]		
☐ Zedan Survey Cruiser	U	0.50
☐ Zedan Troop Ship	U	0.50
☐ Zedan War Cruiser	R	2.40

Galactic Empires • Allied Forces

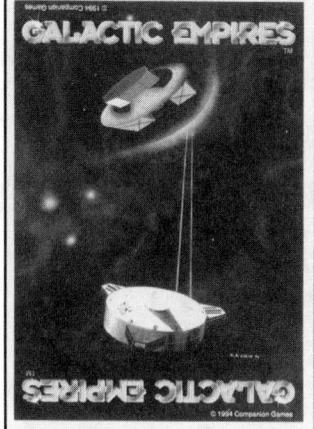

Companion Games • Released April 1997
145 cards in set • **IDENTIFIER: None**
• Starter displays come in 4-deck and 12-deck configurations

The last **Galactic Empires** expansion released before Companion Games' bankruptcy, **Allied Forces** is unusually ship-heavy, since, in addition to the eight races added to the game, the expansion adds ships to most of the other previous races.

Even with this massive addition, there were still 20 more races in the works. Two more expansions, **Realms of the Ancients** and **Cyberspace**, were announced but never released. As of this writing, a few websites devoted to the game remain. — **Michael Greenholdt**

> You will need **17** nine-pocket pages to store this set. (9 doubled up)

	Price
Set (145 cards)	24.00
Starter (12) Display Box	19.00
Booster Pack	1.00

Card name	Rarity	Price
[1]		
☐ Andromeda Beast	U	0.50
☐ Armed Tug	R	2.40
☐ Asteroid-Massive Asteroid	R	2.40
☐ Aux. Shields & Positron Emitter	VR	3.00
☐ Binary Star	R	2.40
☐ Bolaar Battleship	VR	3.00
☐ Bolaar Command Cruiser	VR	3.00
☐ Corporate Pirate Assault Destroyer	VR	3.00
☐ Corporate Pirate Stealth Raider	VR	3.00
☐ Developed Outpost	R	2.40
[2]		
☐ Drone Bombardment Cruiser	VR	3.00
☐ Drone Command Ship	R	2.40
☐ Drone Converter	R	2.40
☐ Drone Deflector Cruiser	VR	3.00
☐ Drone Escort	VR	3.00
☐ Drone Heavy Bombardier	VR	3.00
☐ Drone Heavy Deflector	VR	3.00
☐ Drone Heavy Escort	VR	3.00
☐ Drone Ore Freighter	VR	3.00
[3]		
☐ Drone Patrol Support Ship	R	2.40
☐ Drone Sector HQ	VR	3.00
☐ Drone War Freighter	VR	3.00
☐ Dust Belt	R	2.40
☐ Emergency Rescue Ship	VR	3.00
☐ Erodi Battlecruiser	VR	3.00
☐ Erodi Command Cruiser	R	2.40
☐ Erodi Destabilized Zone	R	2.40
☐ Erodi Heavy Cruiser	VR	3.00
[4]		
☐ Erodi Heavy War Cruiser	VR	3.00
☐ Erodi Light Cruiser	VR	3.00
☐ Erodi Light Nova Cruiser	VR	3.00
☐ Erodi Light War Cruiser	VR	3.00
☐ Erodi Science Craft	R	2.40
☐ Erodi Scout Destroyer	R	2.40

Card name	Rarity	Price
☐ Erodi Sector HQ	VR	3.00
☐ Event Horizon	R	2.40
☐ Fictitious Ship	R	2.40
[5]		
☐ Fleet Disjunction	VR	3.00
☐ Heavy War Cruiser	VR	3.00
☐ Independent Pirate Raider	VR	3.00
☐ Independent Trader	VR	3.00
☐ Ion and Nova Cannon Rules	VR	3.00
☐ Ion Storm-Positron Storm	VR	3.00
☐ Ionized Particle Field	R	2.40
☐ Ionized Phaser Eel	VR	3.00
☐ Ionized Phaser Eel	VR	3.00
[6]		
☐ Leopan Heavy Patrol Ship	VR	3.00
☐ Leopan Patrol Support Ship	VR	3.00
☐ Liege-Noble Liege	R	2.40
☐ Luxury Gig	VR	3.00
☐ Maeuvering Thruster Rules	VR	3.00
☐ Nebula-Tarra'ki Homecloud Expanse	R	2.40
☐ Neutron Star	R	2.40
☐ Noble Fighter	R	2.40
☐ Noble Sector HQ - Noble Amassed Fleet	VR	3.00
[7]		
☐ Noble Sector HQ-Noble Reclaimed Space	VR	3.00
☐ Pakta'don Battlecruiser	R	2.40
☐ Pakta'don Command Ship	R	2.40
☐ Pakta'don Destroyer	VR	3.00
☐ Pakta'don Escort	VR	3.00
☐ Pakta'don Frigate	VR	3.00
☐ Pakta'don Heavy Cruiser	VR	3.00
☐ Pakta'don Light Cruiser	VR	3.00
☐ Pakta'don Minesweeper	R	2.40
[8]		
☐ Pakta'don Plasmatic Cloud	R	2.40
☐ Pakta'don Sector HQ	VR	3.00
☐ Pakta'don Spy Cruiser	R	2.40
☐ Pakta'don Troop Ship	VR	3.00
☐ Paraloid Armed Craft	R	2.40
☐ Paraloid Heavy Storm Cruiser	R	2.40
☐ Paraloid Light Storm Cruiser	R	2.40

Card name	Rarity	Price
☐ Paraloid Man-at-Arms	R	2.40
☐ Paraloid Medium Star Cruiser	R	2.40
[9]		
☐ Paraloid Munition Craft	R	2.40
☐ Paraloid Patrol Cruiser	R	2.40
☐ Paraloid Rules	VR	3.00
☐ Paraloid Scout Craft	R	2.40
☐ Paraloid Sector HQ	VR	3.00
☐ Paraloid Troop Craft	R	2.40
☐ Phaser Overload Device	VR	3.00
☐ Planet-Shon-ti Swarm Homeground	R	2.40
☐ Planet-Trochilidae Homeworld	R	2.40
[10]		
☐ Planetary Debris	R	2.40
☐ Planetary Shield - Ecosphere	R	2.40
☐ Plasmatic Pulse Device	VR	3.00
☐ Pocket Supernova	VR	3.00
☐ Pulse Phaser Rules	VR	3.00
☐ Shield Synchronizer	R	2.40
☐ Shon-ti Attrition Cruiser	VR	3.00
☐ Shon-ti Battlecruiser	R	2.40
☐ Shon-ti Command Cruiser	VR	3.00
[11]		
☐ Shon-ti Defender Cruiser	R	2.40
☐ Shon-ti Escort	VR	3.00
☐ Shon-ti Frigate	VR	3.00
☐ Shon-ti Heavy Cruiser	R	2.40
☐ Shon-ti Heavy Destroyer	VR	3.00
☐ Shon-ti Light Cruiser	VR	3.00
☐ Shon-ti Patrol Ship	VR	3.00
☐ Shon-ti Sector HQ	VR	3.00
☐ Special Ship System Rules	VR	3.00
[12]		
☐ Star Cluster	R	2.40
☐ Swarm Bolt Accelerator	R	2.40
☐ Swarm Bolt Rules	VR	3.00
☐ Tarra'ki Attrition Destroyer	VR	3.00
☐ Tarra'ki Attrition Frigate	VR	3.00
☐ Tarra'ki Command Cruiser	R	2.40
☐ Tarra'ki Escort	R	2.40
☐ Tarra'ki Heavy Escort	VR	3.00
☐ Tarra'ki Heavy War Cruiser	VR	3.00
[13]		
☐ Tarra'ki Light Carrier	R	2.40

Card name	Rarity	Price
☐ Tarra'ki Medium Cruiser	VR	3.00
☐ Tarra'ki Scout	VR	3.00
☐ Tarra'ki Sector HQ	VR	3.00
☐ Tarra'ki Spy Destroyer	VR	3.00
☐ Tarra'ki War Destroyer	VR	3.00
☐ Trade Ship	VR	3.00
☐ Tramp Freigher	R	2.40
☐ Treglean Attrition Destroyer	VR	3.00
[14]		
☐ Treglean Attrition Frigate	VR	3.00
☐ Treglean Command Cruiser	R	2.40
☐ Treglean Escort	VR	3.00
☐ Treglean Heavy Cruiser	VR	3.00
☐ Treglean Heavy Scout	VR	3.00
☐ Treglean Minesweeper	R	2.40
☐ Treglean Police Cruiser	VR	3.00
☐ Treglean Police Ship	VR	3.00
☐ Treglean Science Vessel	VR	3.00
[15]		
☐ Treglean Sector HQ - Treglean Headquarters	VR	3.00
☐ Treglean War Cruiser	R	2.40
☐ Trochilidae Battlecruiser	VR	3.00
☐ Trochilidae Command Ship	R	2.40
☐ Trochilidae Escort	VR	3.00
☐ Trochilidae Heavy Cruiser	VR	3.00
☐ Trochilidae Heavy Escort	VR	3.00
☐ Trochilidae Heavy Troop Ship	R	2.40
☐ Trochilidae Light Cruiser	VR	3.00
[16]		
☐ Trochilidae Medium Cruiser	VR	3.00
☐ Trochilidae Minesweeper	VR	3.00
☐ Trochilidae Scout Cruiser	R	2.40
☐ Trochilidae Sector HQ	VR	3.00
☐ Trochilidae Sector HQ (a Leopan ally)	R	2.40
☐ Trochilidae Swift Destroyer	VR	3.00
☐ Troop Ship	VR	3.00
☐ Twin Moons	R	2.40
[17]		
☐ War Ship	VR	3.00
☐ Weapon Group Rules	VR	3.00

RARITY KEY C = Common U = Uncommon R = Rare VR = Very Rare UR = Ultra Rare F = Foil card X = Fixed/standard in all decks

Galactic Empires • Promos and premiums

Companion Games • 353 cards known to exist

GALACTIC EMPIRES

How does a game like **Galactic Empires** get more than 350 promo cards? Many of them aren't, *really*. Sure, Companion inserted cards in many magazines and gave many away at conventions, and we've tried to note the sources for each such card below. But most were produced for special orders — stores or individuals would design a card and pay a fee, and get a few hundred copies of the card in return.

Modern CCG makers considering a similar tactic should dial up Companion Games and ask whether it saved the company. — *John Jackson Miller*

Q10 Empires In Conflict

Played on 2 opponent fleets
- All ships in those fleets can only fire at other affected fleet
- Lasts for one complete turn and is then discarded.

SCRYE

Illustration © 1994 Melissa Benson

You will need 40 nine-pocket pages to store this set. (20 doubled up)

Card name	Type	Price
Access Field (Anthony Medici)	T/F2	3.50
Adaptive Programming	R/A3	6.80
Aerospace Procurement Officer	C3	6.80
Aesthetic Balance	G8	6.80
Aesthetic Beast	M5	6.80
Aesthetic Carrier	S7	6.80
Aesthetic Creature	M1	6.80
Aesthetic Cruiser	S/G6	6.80
Aesthetic Escort	S2	6.80
Aesthetic Express	S4	6.80
Aesthetic Fiend	R/M7	6.80
Aesthetic Fighter	R/E5	6.80
Aesthetic Marine Recruit Depot	T8	6.80
Aesthetic Monster	M3	6.80
Aesthetic Twin	T5	6.80
Aestheticism	A1	6.80
Altered Timeline (Wargames West)	L8	3.50
Alternate Universe	T3	6.80
Andy Warphole	C10	6.80
Angel's Treasure (Anthony Medici)	T10	3.50
Anthony Medici	S5	6.80
Archeologist (Berkeley Games Dist)	C5	3.50
Art Critic	S7	6.80
Art Patrol Aesthetic	S1	6.80
Artifact - Collector (Toy Collector)	L7	6.80
Artifact - Galactic Paintbrush	L5	6.80
Artifact Critic	R/M6	6.80
Asteroid Field (Anthony Medici)	T8	3.50
Astromorph (Anthony Medici)	M7	3.50
Auer's Isotope	H6	6.80
Avarian Mechanic	R/C4	6.80
Bart Abels	S5	6.80
Battle Advisor (1 In 8 Tactics)	C10	3.50
Battle Bird	E2	6.80
Battle Bird	E4	6.80
Battle Bird	E5	6.80
Battle Bird	E6	6.80
Black Market	L6	3.50
Bolaar Pirate Raider (retail mail orders)	S5	10.00
Bolaar Pirate Raider Leader	S6	6.80
Brood Dragoness	D6	6.80
Cargo Transporter	R/E5	6.80
CCR	S5	6.80
Chronos (Cards Un-Ltd)	T8	3.50
Cleansing Ammunition	E6	6.80
Cleansing Device	E8	6.80
Collateral Damage (John Perreault)	R/O3	6.80
Collect Things	G7	6.80
Collector's Artifact (Wizard's Orb)	L1	6.80
Collector's Box	I4	6.80
Collector's Flagship	S7	6.80
Collector's Library	B7	6.80

Card name	Type	Price
Collector's Storage Case	E7	6.80
Collector's World (Cards4U Inc)	T7	3.50
Color Blind Painter	M7	6.80
Comet - Moore's Comet	T3	6.80
Comic Plus	S5	6.80
Comicology	S5	6.80
Command Central (Anthony Medici)	T6	3.50
Communications Training (Ventura Magazine)	A5	3.50
Companion Games Flagship	S6	3.50
Control Matrix (Play Mat)	E6	3.50
Convoy Escort (Diamond)	R/O4	3.50
Cosmic Cataclysm	H10	6.80
Council of Six Battlecruiser	S8	6.80
Council of Six Battleship	S10	6.80
Council of Six Command Cruiser	S7	6.80
Council of Six Command Destroyer	S5	6.80
Council of Six Diplomatic Cruiser	S7	6.80
Council of Six Dreadnought	S9	6.80
Council of Six Escort	S3	6.80
Council of Six Heavy War Cruiser	S7	6.80
Council of Six Homeworld	T8	6.80
Council of Six Medium Cruiser	S6	6.80
Council of Six Patrol Ship	S2	6.80
Council of Six Scout	S4	6.80
Council of Six Super Heavy Cruiser	S7	6.80
Covert GSS (Anthony Medici)	S3	3.50
Crater Dragoness	D7	6.80
Custom Planet (Aviary)	T7	6.80
Custom Planet (Pastimes)	T3	6.80
Custom Planet (Pastimes)	T7	6.80
Custom System (Junkyard)	T5	6.80
Cyber Beast (Dractus)	M3	3.50
Dark Hand Patrol Fighter (Bill Murray)	E1	6.80
Deans Drake	D2	6.80
Deleter	S9	6.80
Divergent Anomaly (Anthony Medici)	H3	3.50
DNA (Andrew & Paul)	S5	6.80
Dog House	B5	6.80
Dog Pound (Wardogs)	T3	3.50
DOK's	T4	3.50
Draconic Collector	D7	6.80
Dragon Lair (Anthony Medici)	T6	3.50
Dragon Marksman	A6	6.80
Dragon Nest (Elmer Lyons)	T5	6.80
Dragon Nest (Elmer Lyons)	T7	6.80
Dragon Rider	S5	6.80
Emergency Fire Cruiser	S5	6.80
Emergency Medical Technician (Cantrip #1)	R/A3	3.50
Emergency Shields	R/E1	6.80
Empires In Conflict (Scrye #7 - 1/10)	O10	3.50
Empires In Conflict (Scrye #7 - 9/10)	O6	3.50
Engineering Corps (Shadis #18.5 - June)	R/C4	3.50
Enhanced Robotics	A5	6.80
Entrepreneur (Combo #5 - June)	C2	6.80
Espionage Platform	B2	3.50
Exogeologist (Cantrip #2)	R/C5	3.50
Expanding Universe	T1	6.80

Card name	Type	Price
Explosive Asteroid (David Van Cleef)	T3	6.80
Extreme Phaser Refit	E7	6.80
Eyrie	B5	6.80
Fantasy System (Anthony Medici)	T7	3.50
Filarian Breeding Ground (Anthony Medici)	T5	3.50
Forsaken Planet (Anthony Medici)	T6	3.50
Frat House	B3	6.80
Freak Occurance	O5	6.80
Freelance Purist	C8	3.50
Galactic Convention (Gen Con 95)	O5	3.50
Galactic Trade World (Dan Gosselin)	T5	3.50
Game Supply Ship (FPG Inc.)	S5	6.80
Game Supply Ship (Starbase One)	S5	6.80
Game Supply Smuggler	S6	6.80
Games Import	S5	6.80
Gamesmasters	S5	6.80
Garshain Battlecruiser	S8	6.80
Garshain Battleship	S10	6.80
Garshain Command Cruiser	S7	6.80
Garshain Command Destroyer	S5	6.80
Garshain Dreadnought Carrier	S9	6.80
Garshain Escort	S3	6.80
Garshain Frigate	S4	6.80
Garshain Heavy Carrier	S7	6.80
Garshain Medium Carrier	S6	6.80
Garshain Patrol Ship	S2	6.80
Garshain System	T8	6.80
George Brown	S5	6.80
Giant Battle Bird	E8	6.80
Gopin's Grenadiers	S5	6.80
Gray Death Batlecruiser	S8	6.80
Gray Death Battle Barge	S7	6.80
Gray Death Battleship	S10	6.80
Gray Death Boarding Ship	R/S4	6.80
Gray Death Carrier	S6	6.80
Gray Death Command Cruiser	S7	6.80
Gray Death Command Destroyer	S5	6.80
Gray Death Dreadnought	S9	6.80
Gray Death Escort	S3	6.80
Gray Death Patrol Ship	S2	6.80
Growing Economy (GI newsletter)	B5	10.00
GS Carrier (David Van Cleef)	S5	3.50
GSS (Anthony Medici)		3.50
GSS (Bart Abels - Logo)	S5	3.50
GSS (Bart Abels)		3.50
GSS (CCR)		3.50
GSS (Chessex)	S5	3.50
GSS (Comic Plus)		3.50
GSS (Comicology)		3.50
GSS (Companion Games)	S5	3.50
GSS (DNA - Andrew & Paul)		3.50
GSS (Gamesmasters)		3.50
GSS (George Brown)		3.50
GSS (Gopin's Grenadiers Distributing)	S5	3.50
GSS (Gopin's Grenadiers)		3.50
GSS (Grosnor Sportscards Inc)	S5	3.50
GSS (Loren Crabb)		3.50
GSS (Multigenre Inc)	S5	3.50

Card name	Type	Price
GSS (Name Here (Sample))	S5	3.50
GSS (Neal Feldman)		3.50
GSS (New York Hall Of Science)		3.50
GSS (Nick Sauer)		3.50
GSS (Patricia Bieksha)		3.50
GSS (PBM Express)	S5	3.50
GSS (Platinum Brothers)	S5	3.50
GSS (Rodney Johnson)		3.50
GSS (Vincent Bieksha)		3.50
GSS (War Dogs)		3.50
GSS - Alternative Cards	S10	6.80
Hairy Tarantula	M8	6.80
Heavy Artillery	A10	6.80
Hedge Maze	T5	6.80
Helix Crystal	T1	6.80
HQ Repair Team	C5	6.80
Ice Dragoness (GI #4)	D7	3.50
IGMC Replenishment Ship - Albert Sidaras	S5	6.80
Indirigan Chieftain - Council of Six - Neah	C9	6.80
Indirigan Chieftain - Council of Six - Nohs	C9	6.80
Indirigan Chieftain - Garshain	C9	6.80
Indirigan Chieftain - Gray Death	C9	6.80
Indirigan Chieftain - Infected	R/C9	6.80
Indirigan Chieftain - Violator	C7	6.80
Indirigan Sub-chieftain - Meerkats	C5	6.80
Infected Carrier	S6	6.80
Infected Dread Savior	S10	6.80
Infected Escort	S3	6.80
Infected Heavy Carrier	S8	6.80
Infected Heavy Cruiser	S7	6.80
Infected Light Cruiser	S5	6.80
Infected Patrol Ship	S2	6.80
Infected Super Heavy Cruiser	S9	6.80
Infected Tug	S4	6.80
Infected World	T8	6.80
Infiltrator Satellite (Anthony Medici)	T1	3.50
Intergalactic T-shirt Trader	S5	6.80
Intrepid Wanderer	S10	6.80
Intruder Alert System (Ventura 2)	R/E2	3.50
Jozef (Cards Un-Ltd)	T7	3.50
Katryn (Cards Un-Ltd)	T6	3.50
Ko's Nebula	R/H7	6.80
Lexis Prime	T6	6.80
Long Range Transporters	Q5	6.80
Loppy's Parking Garage	T2	6.80
Loren Crabb	S5	6.80
Mad Jack's Hole (Anthony Medici)	T5	3.50
Mannstein System - George Stewart	T5	6.80
Marine-NCO	R/C5	6.80
Mathematical Ship	S5	6.80
Mayfair System	T10	3.50
Medici's Comet (Anthony Medici)	T3	3.50
Meerkats Command Destroyer	S5	6.80
Meerkats Dreadnought	S9	6.80
Meerkats Heavy Escort	S5	6.80
Meerkats Patrol Ship	S2	6.80
Megasonic Phase Distorter	E7	3.50
Military Reservations	R/O3	6.80
Military Reservations	R/O6	6.80
Mint Card Bar & Grill	I5	6.80
Moon - Espionage Moon	T3	6.80
Moon - Garden Moon	T2	6.80
Mutiny Ship (Cards III. #18 (June)	O4	3.50
Nagiridni Boarding Cruiser	S6	6.80
Nagiridni Destroyer	S3	6.80
Nagiridni Mine Cruiser	S7	6.80
Nagiridni Pirate Cruiser	S7	6.80

Card name	Type	Price
Nagiridni Pirate Outpost	T1	6.80
Nagiridni Salvage Tug	S4	6.80
Neal Feldman	S5	6.80
Network Repeater (Dan St. Jean)	T5	3.50
Neumannia (Anthony Medici)	T8	3.50
New Albion (S & A Games)	T6	3.50
New York Hall of Science	S5	6.80
Nick Sauer	S5	6.80
Opportunistic Rogue (Cantrip #3)	C1	3.50
Paint Job	E1	6.80
Paradise Aesthetic	T3	6.80
Paradise Planet (GRS)	T5	3.50
Parallel Universe	T2	6.80
Paranoid Planet (Anthony Medici)	T8	3.50
Partial Regeneration - Dan Gosselin	R/O2	6.80
Patrice (Cards Un-Ltd)	T5	3.50
Patricia Bieksha	S5	6.80
Patrol Dragoness (Magic Cards)	D4	3.50
Patrol Ship Factory (GF #3)	Q1	3.50
PBM Express	T5	3.50
Personal World (Anthony Medici)	T7	3.50
Phillipavis	T7	6.80
Phillipo's Moon - Custom Phillipo's Moon	T4	6.80
Phillipo's World (Harry Phillipo)	T6	6.80
Pilot Background (Pyramid Sep 95)	A3	3.50
Planet (Anthony Medici)	T4	3.50
Planet (Gopin's Grenadiers Distributing)	T3	3.50
Planet (Jenkintown)	T5	3.50
Planet (Neal Feldman)	T8	3.50
Planet - Custom Art Supply Depot	T4	6.80
Planet - Custom Junkyard	T3	6.80
Planet - Custom Military Reservation	T5	6.80
Planet - Custom Planet	T9	6.80
Planet - Custom Planet ('Devastated World')	T7	6.80
Planet - Custom Planet ('Museum World')	T7	6.80
Planet - Custom Planet ('Pastime Planet')	T6	6.80
Planet - Custom Planet (PBM Express)	T5	6.80
Planet - Planet of the Chaos Lords	T4	6.80
Planetary Shield	B3	6.80
Planetary Shield	R/B2	6.80
Planetary Shield (George Stewart)	B9	6.80
Portrait Artiste	C1	6.80
Positron Field (Anthony Medici)	T/F5	3.50
Primal Planet (Anthony Medici)	T5	3.50
Propagationist Patrol Ship	S2	6.80
Psy Temple (Berkley South)	B6	3.50
Psychotic Commandant	P6	6.80
Rodney Johnson	S5	6.80
Scholar's Retreat (Anthony Medici)	T6	3.50
Science Academy (Anthony Medici)	B7	3.50
Science Academy (Anthony Medici)	B10	3.50
Science Academy (Hobby Games)	B6	3.50
Scientific Knowledge (Ventura Magazine)	A2	3.50
Sculpting Dragoness	D7	6.80
Sculptor	S3	6.80
Secret Research Base	B3	6.80
Security Background (Chessex)	A6	3.50
Ship Of The Ancients (GI #3)	S8	3.50
Shuttle Bay Explosion (Collect! June)	L6	3.50
Silver Eagle Wargame Supplies	T7	3.50
Sleeping Dragoness (Mint Card Co)	D5	3.50
Small Planet - Reactionary World	T4	6.80
Smuggler's Haven (Anthony Medici)	T7	3.50
Space Vista Aesthetic	T3	6.80
Spacer's Retirement Home	B6	6.80
Spatial Manipulation	G1	6.80
Spy Central (Anthony Medici)	T9	3.50

Card name	Type	Price
Star (Anthony Medici)	T7	3.50
Star - Antimatter Star	T3	6.80
Star - Massive Red Giant	T9	6.80
Star Dance	H9	6.80
Statistician	C5	6.80
Stefania (Cards Un-Ltd)	T10	3.50
Storm World	T5	3.50
Subspace Compression (Alan Gopin)	H6	6.80
Sudden Migration	O5	6.80
Super Genius	C4	6.80
Super Genius	C6	6.80
Surrealia	T5	6.80
System - Custom System ('Collector's System')	T7	6.80
Taxi Shuttle	R/E6	6.80
Temporal Dragoness	D5/5	6.80
Tending Dragoness	D1	6.80
The Collector	C7	6.80
The House of Cards	B5	6.80
Time Trap	R/H2	6.80
Time Traveling Arms Dealer (Conjure #4 - 1/8)	C10	3.50
Time Traveling Arms Dealer (Conjure #4 - 7/8)	C3	3.50
Time Tremor (GF #4)	H7	3.50
Tourist Ship	S4	6.80
Tranoan Command Cruiser (Anthony Medici)	S6/4	3.50
Tranoan Patrol Ship (Anthony Medici)	S1/9	3.50
Tranoan Satellite (Anthony Medici)	T3/7	3.50
Unfortunate Accident	L7	6.80
Union Hall	B4	6.80
Unstable Planet (Anthony Medici)	T9	3.50
Urban Influence (GF #2)	A10	3.50
Vektrean Asteroid Carrier (Mint Card Co.)	T/B7	3.50
Vincent Bieksha	S5	6.80
Vinciennes (Cards Un-Ltd)	T9	3.50
Vinciennes Battlecruiser	S8	6.80
Vinciennes Battleship	S10	6.80
Vinciennes Command Cruiser	S7	6.80
Vinciennes Command Escort	S3	6.80
Vinciennes Dreadnought	S9	6.80
Vinciennes Heavy Escort	S6	6.80
Vinciennes Patrol Ship	S2	6.80
Violator's Pirate	S7	6.80
Violator's Pirate	S8	6.80
Violator's Pirate	S9	6.80
War Dog	C5	6.80
War Dogs	S5	6.80
War Veteran (Nationals)	C10	3.50
War Veteran (Sanctioned Tournament)	C4	3.50
Website	T6	6.80
White Dwarf (CG Staff)	T4	3.50
White Ship	S3	3.50
Wizard's Familiar	M3	6.80
Wizard's Ring	A5	6.80

Identifying sets

Adding to the difficulty in determining which **Galactic Empires** card goes with which release, every single card back says "©1994 Companion Games" whether the card came out that year or not.

Rely more on the copyright date on the card's face, when it appears there — which it doesn't always…

RARITY KEY **C** = Common **U** = Uncommon **R** = Rare **VR** = Very Rare **UR** = Ultra Rare **F** = Foil card **X** = Fixed/standard in all decks

Gridiron Fantasy Football

Precedence in partnership with **Upper Deck**

Inaugural Hobby Edition and *Inaugural Retail Edition* released **August 1995**

357 cards in set • **IDENTIFIER: Hobby, Retail cards same; 50 cards unique to each set**
- Starter decks contain 65 cards; starter displays contain 10 starters
- Booster packs contain 14 cards; booster displays contain 36 boosters

Designed by **Paul W. Brown III, David Hewitt,** and **John Myler**

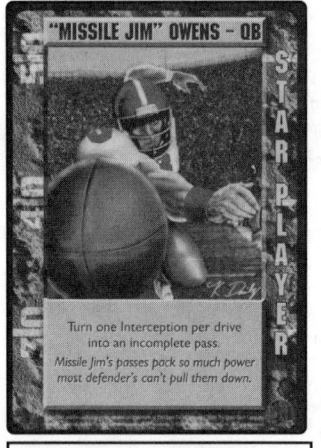

"MISSILE JIM" OWENS – QB

STAR PLAYER

Turn one Interception per drive into an incomplete pass.

Missile Jim's passes pack so much power most defender's can't pull them down.

The first sport-based CCG on the market, **Gridiron Fantasy Football** is set in the weird and violent football league of the near future. With no official license (Donruss released its NFL CCG, **Red Zone**, two months later), *Gridiron* compensates by adding some pro wrestling themes (XFL, ayone?), depicting a football game along with dark, nasty, and villainous activities behind the scenes. *Gridiron* earns its "fantasy" title by adding oddities from shotgun-toting running backs to alien abductions of opposing coaches.

Gameplay is simple: Each player has five unique Team cards, which can include one Coach, one Franchise, and up to three Star Players, Traditions, Formations, or Assets. Each player builds an Offensive and Defensive Playbook from cards of the appropriate types, and each has Offensive and Defensive Action Decks. Games consist of 10 drives.

The parody failed to grab true football fans, while the CCG didn't meet expectations of non-fans simply looking for a good CCG. Sportscard firm Upper Deck delivered sales to the mass market, but it wasn't enough to get *Gridiron* another set of downs. The 1996 expansions *Championship, Traditions,* and *Blacklist* never came out. — *James A. Mishler*

SCRYE NOTES: As with **Fastbreak**, some characters are friends of the designers. "Missile Jim" Owens, at left, is based on the ad rep at the time for **Comics & Games Retailer** magazine.

Concept	●●●○○
Gameplay	●●○○○
Card art	●●○○○
Player pool	○○○○○

Set (357 cards)	43.00
Starter Display Box	16.00
Booster Display Box	20.00
Starter Deck	5.00
Booster Pack	1.00

You will need 40 nine-pocket pages to store this set. (20 doubled up)

Champions (tournament sponsors and winners)

☐ Tradition		Pr	3.00
☐ E.M.T.	Off Action	Pr	2.00
☐ Medevac Assault	Def Actn	Pr	2.00

Card name	Type	Rarity	Price
☐ 5th Down	Def Actn	R	0.75
☐ 20 Man Brawl	Run Def	U	0.25
☐ .22 Defense (Hobby only)	Pass Def	R	1.50
☐ 110 Percent	Def Actn	C	0.05
☐ Adapt and Overcome (Hobby only)	Def Actn	R	1.50
☐ Adaptable Defense	Run Def	C	0.05
☐ Adaptable Offense	Off Actn	U	0.25
☐ Adaptable Team	Tradition	R	0.75
☐ Adrenaline Rush	Off Actn	C	0.05
☐ Aerial Bombardment	Off Actn	R	0.75
☐ Antonio Mason (SS)	Def Star	U	0.25
☐ Apply Your Strengths	Off Actn	U	0.25
☐ Attrition Offense	Off Run	U	0.25
☐ Awesome Cheerleaders	Asset	R	0.75
☐ Back Against the Wall	Def Actn	C	0.05
☐ Bad Attitude	Off Actn	C	0.05
☐ Bad Spot	Def Actn	C	0.05
☐ Balanced Defense	Run Def	C	0.05
☐ Ball Control Offense	Off Actn	U	0.25
☐ Ball-Breaker (Hobby only)	Def Actn	R	1.50
☐ Barons	Franchise	R	0.75
☐ Battle Cry	Run Def	R	0.75
☐ Big Play Defense (Retail only)	Def Actn	Ch	5.00
☐ Blackmail (Hobby only)	Asset	R	1.50
☐ Blimp Disaster (Hobby only)	Def Actn	Ch	5.00
☐ Blitzkrieg	Off Actn	R	0.75
☐ Blizzard (Retail only)	Off Actn	R	1.25
☐ Blocked Kick	Def Actn	C	0.05
☐ Bored Fans (Retail only)	Def Actn	R	1.25
☐ Breakthrough	Def Actn	U	0.25
☐ Bribe the Ref	Off Actn	C	0.05
☐ Bring In the Big Guns	Def Actn	U	0.25
☐ Broken Defense	Off Actn	R	0.75
☐ Brushed Aside	Off Actn	C	0.05

Card name	Type	Rarity	Price
☐ Burn Twice as Bright	Def Actn	R	0.75
☐ Burns Half As Long	Off Actn	R	0.75
☐ Burst of Speed	Off Actn	C	0.05
☐ By the Book (Retail only)	Def Actn	R	1.25
☐ Captive Cheerleaders (Hobby only)	Off Pass	R	1.50
☐ Carlton Davis (WR)	Off Star	U	0.25
☐ Carpe Futbol	Pass Def	R	0.75
☐ Catapult Play (Hobby only)	Off Run	R	1.50
☐ Celebrity Appearance (Hobby only)	Off Actn	R	1.50
☐ Chain Lightning (Hobby only)	Off Run	R	1.50
☐ Cheerleader Distraction (Hobby only)	Def Actn	R	1.50
☐ Chester Knight (DT)	Def Star	R	0.75
☐ Chris Ferguson (K)	Off Star	R	0.75
☐ Clean-Cut Reputation (Retail only)	Asset	Ch	5.00
☐ Clear the Benches (Hobby only)	Def Actn	R	1.50
☐ Close the Option (Retail only)	Pass Def	R	1.25
☐ Close-Up (Retail only)	Off Actn	R	1.25
☐ Coach David Hughes	Coach	R	0.75
☐ Coach Jake Everheart	Coach	U	0.25
☐ Coach Jon Miller	Coach	U	0.25
☐ Coach Mark McKenna	Coach	R	0.75
☐ Coach Nate Washington	Coach	U	0.25
☐ Coach Pol Braun	Coach	R	0.75
☐ Coach Ralph Siegel	Coach	R	0.75
☐ Coach Randal Sackles	Coach	C	0.05
☐ Coach Stan Zylstra	Coach	U	0.25
☐ Code of Honor	Tradition	R	0.75
☐ Come-From-Behind Winners	Tradition	U	0.25
☐ Concealed Punch	Def Actn	C	0.05
☐ Conservative Offense	Off Actn	C	0.05
☐ Corporate Sponsors	Asset	C	0.05
☐ Crossing Pattern	Off Pass	C	0.05
☐ Crossing the "T" (Retail only)	Pass Def	R	1.25
☐ Crowd Noise (Hobby only)	Off Actn	R	1.50
☐ Crush the Enemy	Def Actn	R	0.75
☐ Crush the Pocket	Pass Def	U	0.25
☐ Crushing Impact	Def Actn	C	0.05
☐ Crushing Impact (error, 4 penalty chance)	Def Actn	C	0.05
☐ Curl	Off Pass	C	0.05
☐ Cursed Play (Hobby only)	Def Actn	R	1.50
☐ Cutting Corners	Run Def	U	0.25
☐ Dame Fortune	Def Actn	U	0.25
☐ Darryl Rice (HB)	Off Star	U	0.25
☐ Deep Defense	Pass Def	U	0.25
☐ Defective Ball (Retail only)	Def Actn	R	1.25
☐ Delay of Game	Def Actn	U	0.25
☐ Delay the Inevitable	Def Actn	R	0.75

Card name	Type	Rarity	Price
☐ Demoralized	Def Actn	C	0.05
☐ Determined Line	Tradition	R	0.75
☐ Diehard Fans	Asset	U	0.25
☐ Disputed Call	Def Actn	C	0.05
☐ Dive	Off Run	C	0.05
☐ Dodge and Weave	Off Actn	C	0.05
☐ Dodge Out of Bounds	Off Actn	C	0.05
☐ Dogpile Defense	Run Def	U	0.25
☐ Don't Fear the Reaper	Off Actn	C	0.05
☐ Double Coverage	Pass Def	U	0.25
☐ Double Dealing (Hobby only)	Off Actn	R	1.50
☐ Down and Out	Off Pass	C	0.05
☐ Downfield Substitution (Retail only)	Off Pass	Ch	5.00
☐ Downpour (Retail only)	Def Actn	R	1.25
☐ Drastic Measures (Hobby only)	Off Actn	Ch	5.00
☐ Draw	Off Run	U	0.25
☐ Dwight Teague (G)	Off Star	U	0.25
☐ Eagle-Eyed Ref	Def Actn	U	0.25
☐ Edward Usher (DE)	Def Star	R	0.75
☐ Elbow Smash (Hobby only)	Def Actn	R	1.50
☐ Eldon Van Patton (LB)	Def Star	U	0.25
☐ Elite Secondary	Tradition	C	0.05
☐ Erroneous Flag	Def Actn	R	0.75
☐ Establish the Pass	Off Pass	U	0.25
☐ Establish the Run	Off Run	U	0.25
☐ Exhaustion	Off Actn	C	0.05
☐ Experimental Technology (Hobby only)	Asset	Ch	5.00
☐ Facemasking	Def Actn	C	0.05
☐ Falling Star	Off Pass	R	0.75
☐ Fan Protest (Retail only)	Def Actn	R	1.25
☐ Fan Reception	Off Actn	U	0.25
☐ Fans Storm the Field (Retail only)	Def Actn	R	1.25
☐ Favorite Trick (Hobby only)	Off Actn	R	1.50
☐ Femme Fatal (Hobby only)	Pass Def	Ch	5.00
☐ Field Awareness	Off Actn	C	0.05
☐ Final Surge	Off Actn	U	0.25
☐ Fireworks Misfire (Hobby only)	Off Actn	R	1.50
☐ Flag	Off Pass	U	0.25
☐ Flair	Off Pass	C	0.05
☐ Flea Flicker	Off Pass	R	0.75
☐ Flood the Line	Run Def	U	0.25
☐ Flush the Quarterback	Def Actn	C	0.05
☐ Flying Wedge (Retail only)	Off Run	R	1.25
☐ Fog (Retail only)	Off Actn	R	1.25
☐ Food Poisoning (Retail only)	Off Actn	R	1.25
☐ Football Voodoo (Hobby only)	Tradition	Ch	5.00

RARITY KEY **C** = Common **U** = Uncommon **R** = Rare **VR** = Very Rare **Ch** = Chase **F** = Foil card **X** = Fixed/standard in all decks

Card name	Type	Rarity	Price
Footrace	Off Actn	C	0.05
For the Good of the Team	Def Actn	R	0.75
Forcing the Turnover (Retail only)	Tradition	Ch	5.00
Friendly Reminder	Def Actn	R	0.75
"Friends" in the Stands	Asset	U	0.25
Frontal Assault (Hobby only)	Off Actn	R	1.50
Fugitives	Franchise	R	0.75
Fumblerooski	Off Run	R	0.75
Gamble	Off Actn	U	0.25
Gaston Forrester (DE)	Def Star	C	0.05
George Smalley (FB)	Off Star	U	0.25
Giveaway/Takeaway	Tradition	R	0.75
God On Your Side	Def Actn	U	0.25
Good Hustle	Def Actn	C	0.05
Good Karma	Off Actn	U	0.25
Good Sportsmanship (Retail only)	Def Actn	R	1.25
Good Timing (Hobby only)	Def Actn	R	1.50
Gopher Holes (Hobby only)	Off Actn	R	1.50
Greased Pigskin (Hobby only)	Run Def	R	1.50
Griffons	Franchise	R	0.75
Gust of Wind (Retail only)	Def Actn	R	1.25
Hail Mary	Off Pass	R	0.75
Hailstorm (Retail only)	Def Actn	R	1.25
Hangover (Retail only)	Def Actn	R	1.25
He Could Go All The Way	Off Actn	R	0.75
Heat Wave (Retail only)	Off Actn	R	1.25
HelmetCam (Retail only)	Off Actn	R	1.25
Hold the Line	Run Def	C	0.05
Holding	Off Actn	C	0.05
Hometown Referee	Asset	R	0.75
Hostile Press (Retail only)	Off Actn	R	1.25
Hurry the QB	Pass Def	R	0.75
Hurry-Up Offense	Off Actn	R	0.75
I - Formation	Formation	C	0.05
I Got It!	Def Actn	U	0.25
Ice Bowl (Retail only)	Off Actn	R	1.25
In the Clear	Off Actn	R	0.75
In the Line of Fire	Off Actn	C	0.05
In The Zone	Off Actn	U	0.25
Inadvertent Whistle (Retail only)	Off Actn	R	1.25
Insect Swarm (Retail only)	Def Actn	R	1.25
Instant Replay (Retail only)	Off Actn	Ch	5.00
Intimidation	Def Actn	C	0.05
Jesters	Franchise	C	0.05
Jump the Gun	Def Actn	C	0.05
Keep Your Eye on the Ball	Def Actn	R	0.75
Ken Fuji (C)	Off Star	U	0.25
Ken Holder (SS)	Def Star	U	0.25
Key on the Halfback	Run Def	C	0.05
Kick Return	Def Actn	U	0.25
Killer Weightroom	Asset	U	0.25
Know the Enemy (Hobby only)	Off Actn	R	1.50
Kristopher Quinn (T)	Off Star	U	0.25
Kurt Harley (CB)	Def Star	R	0.75
Late Hit	Def Actn	C	0.05
Lawrence Kinkaid (FB)	Off Star	R	0.75
Linebacker Anchor	Pass Def	U	0.25
Linebacker Assist	Def Actn	U	0.25
Linebacker Blitz	Pass Def	C	0.05
Linebacker in Position	Run Def	U	0.25
Linebackers Forward	Formation	C	0.05
Liquid Heat (Hobby only)	Run Def	Ch	5.00
Llamas	Franchise	C	0.05
Long Range Field Goal	Off Actn	U	0.25
Loose Ball	Off Actn	U	0.25
Lorenzo Denver (QB)	Off Star	U	0.25
Lost in the Sun (Retail only)	Def Actn	R	1.25
Low Flying Blimp	Off Actn	R	0.75
Lucky (Retail only)	Tradition	Ch	5.00
Lucky Socks (Hobby only)	Asset	Ch	5.00
Lurking Doom	Off Actn	R	0.75
Man to Man	Pass Def	C	0.05
Man-to-Man Defense	Formation	C	0.05
Marshals	Franchise	R	0.75
Martial Arts Training	Asset	R	0.75
Mascot Hostage (Hobby only)	Pass Def	R	1.50
Mascot K.O. (Retail only)	Off Run	R	1.25
Maximum Momentum	Off Actn	C	0.05
Meat Grinder	Off Actn	C	0.05
Mental Matchup	Off Actn	R	0.75
Merciless	Tradition	R	0.75
Military Track Coach	Asset	R	0.75
Milton Tanner (QB)	Off Star	U	0.25
"Missile" Jim Owens (QB)	Off Star	C	0.05
Mississippi Mud (Retail only)	Def Actn	R	1.25
Mixed Defense	Pass Def	R	0.75
Mixed Signals (Retail only)	Off Actn	R	1.25
Mobile Fieldgoals (Hobby only)	Asset	R	1.50
New Age Girlfriends	Tradition	U	0.25
Nickel Defense	Formation	C	0.05
Nightmare	Def Actn	C	0.05
No Resistance	Off Actn	U	0.25
No-Huddle Offense (Retail only)	Off Actn	R	1.25
Not This Time	Def Actn	R	0.75
Off-Tackle	Off Run	C	0.05
Offensive Interference	Off Actn	C	0.05
Onside Kick	Off Actn	C	0.05
Option Pass (Retail only)	Off Pass	R	1.25
Option Run	Off Run	U	0.25
Other Priorities	Off Actn	R	0.75
Out of Bounds	Def Actn	C	0.05
Outside Blitz	Pass Def	C	0.05
Paul Swanhart (WR)	Off Star	U	0.25
Paying the Price	Off Actn	C	0.05
Penetrate the Line	Def Actn	R	0.75
Pickoff Artists	Tradition	U	0.25
Piledrivers	Franchise	R	0.75
Play Clean (Retail only)	Off Actn	R	1.25
Play It Safe	Off Actn	U	0.25
Play On	Off Actn	U	0.25
Play to the Crowd	Off Pass	R	0.75
Plow Them Under	Def Actn	C	0.05
Pointing Fingers (Hobby only)	Def Actn	R	1.50
Post	Off Pass	R	0.75
Power Dive	Off Run	U	0.25
Power Outage (Retail only)	Def Actn	R	1.25
Power Sweep	Off Run	U	0.25
Pressure's High	Def Actn	C	0.05
Prevent Defense	Pass Def	R	0.75
Product Endorsement	Off Pass	C	0.05
QB Sneak	Off Run	C	0.05
Quick Hands	Pass Def	R	0.75
Quick Hands	Def Actn	R	0.75
Quick Pass	Off Pass	C	0.05
Quick Reflexes (Hobby only)	Def Actn	R	1.50
Raising the Stakes (Hobby only)	Def Actn	R	1.50
Rally (Retail only)	Off Actn	Ch	5.00
Ravens	Franchise	R	0.75
Receiver Corps	Tradition	R	0.75
Redzone "D"	Tradition	U	0.25
Ref on the Ball	Off Actn	U	0.25
Referee "Conference" (Retail only)	Off Actn	R	1.25
Regimentals	Franchise	R	0.75
Rene Scoffield (CB)	Def Star	U	0.25
Reno Sanders (HB)	Off Star	U	0.25
Reversal of Fortune (Hobby only)	Off Actn	R	1.50
Reverse	Off Run	U	0.25
Rick Barringer (FS)	Def Star	U	0.25
"Right Place, Right Time"	Def Actn	R	0.75
Riot in the Stands (Hobby only)	Off Actn	R	1.50
Rise to the Challenge	Off Actn	C	0.05
Rolling Thunder (Hobby only)	Off Actn	R	1.50
Rose Colored Glasses (Retail only)	Run Def	R	1.25
Rosin	Off Actn	C	0.05
Rough Customers	Tradition	R	0.75
Roughing the Passer	Def Actn	C	0.05
Rubin Levine (FS)	Def Star	U	0.25
Sack Celebration (Retail only)	Def Actn	R	1.25
Safety Stop	Run Def	U	0.25
Santos Gil (LB)	Def Star	U	0.25
Scoreboard Commandos (Hobby only)	Asset	R	1.50
Screen	Off Pass	U	0.25
Second Wind	Def Actn	C	0.05
Secret Weapon	Def Actn	R	0.75
Shady Assistant	Asset	U	0.25
Shake Up the QB	Def Actn	R	0.75
Shane Bennett (TE)	Off Star	U	0.25
Shotgun Formation	Formation	C	0.05
Shoving	Def Actn	C	0.05
Sideline Smash	Off Actn	C	0.05
Sidelines	Off Actn	C	0.05
Slant	Off Pass	U	0.25
Sleet (Retail only)	Off Actn	R	1.25
Smokescreen (Hobby only)	Off Actn	R	1.50
Smothering Backfield	Def Actn	R	0.75
Snag the Ball (Retail only)	Run Def	R	1.25
Solid Coverage (Hobby only)	Def Actn	R	1.50
Solid Impact	Def Actn	C	0.05
Solid Zone	Pass Def	C	0.05
Spearing	Off Actn	C	0.05
Spiked Drinks (Hobby only)	Pass Def	R	1.50
Split-Back Formation	Formation	C	0.05
Spontaneous Human Combustion (Hobby only)	Def Actn	Ch	5.00
Sports "Medicine"	Off Actn	C	0.05
Star Ancestor (Retail only)	Def Actn	Ch	5.00
Star Power	Def Actn	U	0.25
Statue of Liberty (Retail only)	Off Run	R	1.25
Stay In Bounds	Run Def	U	0.25
Stolen Playbook (Hobby only)	Def Actn	R	1.50
Stretch the Resources	Run Def	U	0.25
Strong Running Game	Tradition	R	0.75
Stuffed	Def Actn	C	0.05
Suck It In (Hobby only)	Off Actn	R	1.50
Sun Desert Stadium (Retail only)	Asset	R	1.25
Superstar	Off Actn	U	0.25
Sweep	Off Run	C	0.05
T. C. Kraver (Kick Returns)	Off Star	U	0.25
Take Out the Ref (Hobby only)	Off Pass	R	1.50
Team Psychic (Hobby only)	Def Actn	R	1.50
Team Sawbones	Asset	R	0.75
Ten Man Wall	Run Def	U	0.25
Teradome (Retail only)	Asset	R	1.25
Test of Strength	Off Actn	C	0.05
The Boot	Off Actn	U	0.25
The Stars Are Right (Retail only)	Off Actn	R	1.25
The Wave	Off Actn	U	0.25
The Will To Win	Off Actn	C	0.05
They're Everywhere	Def Actn	R	0.75
Third and Inches	Def Actn	U	0.25
Thoroughbreds	Franchise	R	0.75
Three and Out	Def Actn	U	0.25
Tight Coverage	Pass Def	R	0.75
Tip Your Hand	Def Actn	R	0.75
Tobias Richards (QB)	Off Star	R	0.75
Topsy-Turvey (Hobby only)	Off Actn	R	1.50
Tough Home Turf	Asset	R	0.75
Trap	Off Run	U	0.25
Trash Talking	Off Actn	U	0.25
Tripping	Def Actn	C	0.05
Twelfth Man	Def Actn	R	0.75
Twist of Fate	Off Actn	R	0.75
Two Tight Ends	Formation	C	0.05
Ty Richter (LB)	Def Star	R	0.75
UFO Abduction (Hobby only)	Off Run	Ch	5.00
Unshakable (Retail only)	Tradition	Ch	5.00
Unstoppable	Off Actn	R	0.75
Using the Options	Tradition	R	0.75
Vigilante Fans	Off Actn	R	0.75
Volleyball Pass	Off Pass	U	0.25
Vow of Celibacy (Hobby only)	Tradition	Ch	5.00
Wall of Stone	Tradition	U	0.25
War of Attrition	Def Actn	R	0.75
Wear Them Out	Def Actn	C	0.05
Well-Drilled Team	Off Actn	R	0.75
Where'd He Go?	Off Actn	R	0.75
Wind At Your Back (Hobby only)	Off Actn	R	1.50
Winds of Change (Hobby only)	Def Actn	R	1.50
Wrong Way (Retail only)	Def Actn	Ch	5.00
You Can Run But You Can't Hide	Def Actn	C	0.05
Zone Defense	Formation	C	0.05

RARITY KEY C = Common U = Uncommon R = Rare VR = Very Rare Ch = Chase F = Foil card X = Fixed/standard in all decks

Guardians

FPG (Friedlander Publishing Group) • First set, *Limited*, released **September 1995**
279 cards in set • **IDENTIFIER: Small blue dot on bottom after copyright notice**
• Starter decks contain 60 cards; starter displays contain 10 decks
• Booster packs contain 14 cards; booster displays contain 36 packs
Designed by **Keith "Keith" Parkinson** and **Luke "Luke" Peterschmidt**

Guardians claims to be a game based upon the "true past," when powerful beings called Vierkun Guardians fought each other over the destiny of reality — using Babes, Beer, and Gold. And little things called Schnee, with lots of fur and big fangs. And Supermodels. We can't forget the Supermodels. Needless to say, the game doesn't take itself (or anything it touches on) terribly seriously.

The game system itself is, however, pretty good. Each player starts with three location cards (their "strongholds") and between the players rest six empty spaces — conquer all six to win. Players do this by assembling an army of creatures, placing them under a mystical shield, and sending them off onto the board. When your army meets an opposing army, you fight. Combat is awfully quick and decisive. You can also win by destroying five of your opponent's shields (*i.e.* wipe out his entire army five times). Or, if you can make it across the board and attack his three stronghold cards, you might be able to take them out. Or, if you are really foolish, there are rules for attacking a Guardian. A great initiative system adds to the fast-paced nature of this game. Strategy comes in when you have to decide where to place your armies, whom to put in which army and how to resolve combats. Also, unlike many games with a great combat system, this one has spells you can cast at your opponent.

While not a hit, *Guardians* was admired for its art. (Its manufacturer, FPG, was then one of the leading makers of "art" trading cards, and many cards in the CCG were from artists who had done sets for FPG, including Brom and Don Maitz.) The card art was chosen to look inspiring, mythical, and humorous. The **Ploogak the Conqueror** card may be a giant frog in candy-striped tights, but he *is* a fearsome critter. The statistics on the cards are easy to make out, and there are only a couple of them, so the art is extra-large on many of the cards. — *Richard Weld*

You will need
31
nine-pocket
pages to store
this set.
(16 doubled up)

Concept	●●●○○
Gameplay	●●●○○
Card art	●●●●●
Player pool	○○○○○

Set (279 cards)	50.00
Starter Display Box	20.00
Booster Display Box	15.00
Starter Deck	3.00
Booster Pack	1.50

Card name	Rarity	Price
Agent of Shadow	R1	1.50
Amber Well	C1	0.10
Amulet of Flying	U1	0.25
Ancient Ogre	R2	1.50
Angel	C1	0.10
Annihilator Cloud	U2	0.25
Anvil of Heaviness	C1	0.10
Archangel Magnus	R1	1.50
Archangel Odessa	R1	1.50
Archer	C2	0.10
Arms of the Earth	R2	1.50
Axeman	U2	0.25
Baal-a-Gog	U1	0.25
Babe Hound	C1	0.10
Babes	C2	0.10
Baleful Eye	C1	0.10
Bantam Drake	U1	0.25
Bealzebub	R1	1.50

Card names

Some *Guardians* cards have only generic names, but some have very different abilities.

Here, we've listed them by the image and point value (Standard Bearer Ox (19)) or artist name (Shield Brom's Dragon).

Card name	Rarity	Price
Beer	C2	0.10
Big Groaning Cankerd	U1	0.25
Black Lung	C1	0.10
Black Unicorn	R2	1.50
Blackthwaite Jumpers	U1	0.25
Bold Mold	U1	0.25
Bone Shambler	R2	1.50
Brap Back Goblins	U1	0.25
Brown Back Goblins	C1	0.10
Bruce the Goose	R1	1.50
Bulbous Clamjack	C1	0.10
Bungee Bony Ridged	U1	0.25
Burrowing Barg	C2	0.10
Captain	C1	0.10
Captain Red Nose	R2	1.50
Carreg Amroth (C) Stronghold	SP	0.80
Carreg Amroth (L) Stronghold	SP	0.80
Carreg Amroth (R) Stronghold	SP	0.80
Cave Giant	C1	0.10
Cherub	R2	1.50
Cleric	U1	0.25
Control Destiny	U1	0.25
Corporal	C1	0.10
Corruption Stream	R2	1.50
Cow	R2	1.50
Crook End Snoot	C1	0.10
Crook End Snooter	U1	0.25
Crystal Flash	R2	1.50
Cyclops	C1	0.10
Darkness Elemental	R2	1.50
Death	R2	1.50
Demon Horde of Kabod	U1	0.25
Desert Giant	C1	0.10
Detect Life Force	C1	0.10
Devil Dog	C1	0.10

Card name	Rarity	Price
Devil Hedgehog	C1	0.10
Dispel Magic	C2	0.10
Djinn	U1	0.25
Doomwing	U1	0.25
Dragon Wing Lord	R1	1.50
Dreaded Doom Dog	C1	0.10
Drooling Clamjack	C1	0.10
Dry Heaps	SP	0.80
Earth Elemental	C1	0.10
Earth Mother	R2	1.50
Elder Cave Giant	U2	0.25
Embryonic Witch	U2	0.25
Energy Eater	C1	0.10
Energy Leach	R2	1.50
Energy Toad	U1	0.25
Energy Well	R3	1.50
Eternal Witch Lord	R2	1.50
Eye of Long Spying	C1	0.10
Eye of Missile Mayhem	R2	1.50
Female Pixie	U1	0.25
Female Titan	C1	0.10
Finn-Swamp King	R2	1.50
Fire Elemental	R2	1.50
Fire Walker	C1	0.10
Flame Cannon	R1	1.50
Floyd the Flying Pig	U2	0.25
Force Barrier	R2	1.50
Gaar-Influencer of the Masses	R1	1.50
Giant Penguin	C1	0.10
Gn'Obby Gnomes	U1	0.25
Gn'Olegable Gnomes	R2	1.50
Gn'Omish Gnomes	C1	0.10
Gold	C2	0.10
Goldthwaite Jumpers	U2	0.25
Gorgal Skag	C1	0.10
Grand Avatar	R1	1.50

Card name	Rarity	Price
Grand Phooba Schnee	R1	1.50
Great Fanged Ogre	U1	0.25
Greater Air Elemental	U1	0.25
Greater Energy Elemental	R1	1.50
Greedy Fiend	U2	0.25
Grilbus	C1	0.10
Grim Skull	R3	1.50
Gringe Commander	R2	1.50
Groupie	U1	0.25
Gunner	C1	0.10
Haba Naba Daba	R3	1.50
Haba Naba Kaba	C1	0.10
Hair-de-hobbins	C1	0.10
Hammer of Doom	R2	1.50
Harkin-Spreader of the Wealth	R2	1.50
Heels of Speed	U2	0.25
Helm of the Brotherhood	R2	1.50
Holy Grail	R2	1.50
Horse	C1	0.10
Huge Rock Giant	U2	0.25
Humungus Fungus	R1	1.50
Ice Elemental	C1	0.10
Ice Ogre	C1	0.10
Ice Spirit	C1	0.10
Ice Storm	C1	0.10
Idiot	R2	1.50
Idiot Fiend	U1	0.25
Iron Crag Bagglers	C1	0.10
Iron Crag Bogüglers	C1	0.10
Iron Crag Bugglers	C1	0.10
Iron Lord	U1	0.25
Jibber	C1	0.10
Khnumian Stronghold (C)	SP	0.80
Khnumian Stronghold (L)	SP	0.80
Khnumian Stronghold (R)	SP	0.80
Kikijub	U1	0.25

RARITY KEY **C** = Common **U** = Uncommon **R** = Rare **#** = Sublevel of rarity: lower numbers are rarer **SP**: Special (basic or "lands")

178 • SCRYE Collectible Card Game Checklist and Price Guide

Card name	Rarity	Price
King of Mystfall	R2	1.50
Labyrinth of Spires	SP	0.80
Lake Serpent	R2	1.50
Lancer	U1	0.25
Large Idol	U1	0.25
Lawyer	R1	1.50
Leprechaun	C1	0.10
Light Elemental	R2	1.50
Lorg Mole	U1	0.25
Mad Fiend	U2	0.25
Magic Feedback	U1	0.25
Magma Elemental	C1	0.10
Major Party Animal	U1	0.25
Make Juice	C2	0.10
Male Pixie	C1	0.10
Male Titan	U2	0.25
Marshal	U1	0.25
Master Gunner	U1	0.25
Merchant	U1	0.25
Minataur	C1	0.10
Mist Veiler	R2	1.50
Monolith of Power	U1	0.25
Moon Spirit	U1	0.25
Mountains	SP	0.80
Mud Elemental	C1	0.10
Mule	C1	0.10
Na 'Boob	R2	1.50
Old Mold	C1	0.10
Old Nick	R1	1.50
Paladin	R2	1.50
Party Animal	R2	1.50
"Pauly, Official Parrot"	R2	1.50
Pepe's Slow Down	U2	0.25
Pesky Varmit	C1	0.10
Phantom Stalker	R2	1.50
Pig Dog	U1	0.25
Pink Flamingos	R1	1.50
Ploogak the Conqueror	R2	1.50
Polar Ice Ogre	U1	0.25
Potion of Movement Essence	U2	0.25
Power Lunch	C2	0.10
Primordial Goo	C1	0.10
Rain Spirit	U2	0.25
Rak Nam-Leader of the Mighty	SP	0.80
Reverend Smilin' Jack	R2	1.50
Rik' Sook	R2	1.50
Rivers and Lakes	SP	0.80

Card name	Rarity	Price
Rock Giant	C1	0.10
Rock Lord	U1	0.25
Rock Rat	R2	1.50
Rock Spirit	C1	0.10
Rocks of Skull Cracking	C1	0.10
Rooster	C2	0.10
Rot Rat	C1	0.10
Rouge Specter	U1	0.25
Roving Force Inferno	R1	1.50
Sabu Amantek (C)	SP	0.80
Sabu Amantek (L)	SP	0.80
Sabu Amantek (R)	SP	0.80
Sacrificial Alter	R2	1.50
Sand Lord	C1	0.10
Schneeble	U1	0.25
Seer	C2	0.10
Shadow of Ashes	R2	1.50
Shadow Spy	U1	0.25
Shadow Warrior	R2	1.50
Shield Brom's Angelic	SP	0.80
Shield Brom's Demonic	SP	0.80
Shield Brom's Dragon	SP	0.80
Shield Brom's Skull	SP	0.80
Shield Maitz's Dark	SP	0.80
Shield Maitz's Lightning	SP	0.80
Shield Ploog's Chicken	SP	0.80
Shield Ploog's Ox	SP	0.80
Shield Warhola's Snakes	SP	0.80
Siin-Stealer of the Power	SP	0.80
Skeletal Minion	C1	0.10
Slag Bunny	U1	0.25
Sleeping Spirit	C1	0.10
Slippery Slime	R2	1.50
Sloarch	U1	0.25
Smoke Spirit	U1	0.25
Snibs Bony Ridged	U1	0.25
Snogwart	C1	0.10
Snow Daughters	C1	0.10
Sorcerer	R3	1.50
Speckled Clamjack	C1	0.10
Sphinx	U1	0.25
Spirit of the Forge	R2	1.50
Spirit of the Hunt	R1	1.50
St. Ballantine's Evocation	C1	0.10
Stinking Spirit	U1	0.25
Stndrd Bearer Angelic (13)	R2	1.50
Stndrd Bearer Angelic (19)	U1	0.25
Stndrd Bearer Chicken (12)	U1	0.25

Card name	Rarity	Price
Stndrd Bearer Chicken (5)	U1	0.25
Stndrd Bearer Dark (14)	U1	0.25
Stndrd Bearer Dark (16)	R2	1.50
Stndrd Bearer Demonic (19)	R2	1.50
Stndrd Bearer Demonic (4)	U1	0.25
Stndrd Bearer Dragon (15)	U1	0.25
Stndrd Bearer Dragon (19)	R2	1.50
Stndrd Bearer Lightning (14)	R2	1.50
Stndrd Bearer Lightning (4)	U1	0.25
Stndrd Bearer Ox (19)	R2	1.50
Stndrd Bearer Ox (5)	U1	0.25
Stndrd Bearer Skull (16)	U1	0.25
Stndrd Bearer Skull (21)	R2	1.50
Stndrd Bearer Snake (17)	R2	1.50
Stndrd Bearer Snake (6)	U1	0.25
Succubus	U1	0.25
Summon Gravity Well	C1	0.10
Summons Gate	R2	1.50
Sun Spirits	C2	0.10
Super Model	U1	0.25
Swamp	SP	0.80
Swordsman	C2	0.10
Tangle Web	U1	0.25
Teleport Tower	U1	0.25
Tes Let-Leader with Foresight	SP	0.80
Thackle	C1	0.10
Thak-Steady Hand	R2	1.50
Thunder Hawk	R2	1.50
Tiny Flying Fungus	C1	0.10
Tookle-Leader of the Many	R2	1.50

Card name	Rarity	Price
Trumpeter	U1	0.25
Ugly Wart Fiend	U2	0.25
Valkyrie Spirit	R2	1.50
Vampire	C1	0.10
Vampire Hunters	C1	0.10
Vampire Lord	R2	1.50
Vapor Elemental	U1	0.25
Varmit Archers	C1	0.10
Visionary	C2	0.10
Vitales Dark Cloud	U1	0.25
Wailing Specter	U1	0.25
Warrior Spirit	U1	0.25
Watcher	U1	0.25
Water Nymph	C2	0.10
Water Spout	C1	0.10
Whispering Spirits	C1	0.10
White Unicorn	R1	1.50
Wild Nymph	C1	0.10
Will'o the Wisp	U1	0.25
Wind Spirit	C1	0.10
Winterseed's Maiden	R2	1.50
Winterseed's Mistress	U1	0.25
Wood Nymph	C1	0.10
Wood Spirit	C1	0.10
Woods	SP	0.80
Wraith	R2	1.50
Yandrax	U1	0.25
Yard Rat	U2	0.25
Zombie	U1	0.25

Guardians • Dagger Isle

FPG (Friedlander Publishing Group) • Released **November 1995**

120 cards in set • **IDENTIFIER: Dagger (†) at bottom by copyright line**

- Booster packs contain 14 cards; booster displays contain 36 boosters

Subtitled the "Western Expansion," **Guardians: Dagger Isle** adds everyone's favorite party animals to the wacky Guardians mix: Pirates! There are also Spirits, Undead, Angels, Devils, Evil Twins, Wanderers, Giants, Slag Beasts, and Barnyard Animals to go around (though how a **Buzzard** qualifies as a Barnyard Animal is beyond us).

An interesting aside: Much of the art from the *Guardians* game was later resurrected in the *Stratego Legends* board game by Avalon Hill. — *James A. Mishler*

You will need **14** nine-pocket pages to store this set. (7 doubled up)

Santa's Beer Sled

Play as a Command Card. Opponent must show you all cards in his/her combat hand which can be bribed by Beer. Choose one and consider that card to be bribed.

Spell   13

Artwork © 1995 Semenik ♦ GUARDIANS™ is a trademark of FPG, Inc.

Set (120 cards)	40.00
Booster Display Box	15.00
Booster Pack	1.50

Card name	Rarity	Price
Angel of Death	C1	5.30
Arcane Infusion	C1	0.60
Argammond's Vision	C3	0.20

Card name	Rarity	Price
Arwyddyn	C4	0.20
Assassin of Shadow	C2	0.90
Barrow Wight	C3	0.20
Bone Fright	R3	1.00
Brom's Angelic	C1	0.20
Brom's Demonic	C1	0.80
Brom's Dragon	C1	0.80

Card name	Rarity	Price
Brom's Goblin	C1	0.80
Brom's Goblin	R3	1.30
Brom's Goblin	C4	0.20
Brom's Goblin 2	R2	1.50
Brom's Skull	C1	0.80
Buster Scrimbo	C3	0.20
Buzzard	C4	0.20
Cabin Boy	C4	0.20

Card name	Rarity	Price
Cactus McFingers	C2	0.20
Captain Hannibal Hawks	R2	1.40
Captain Red Noseoid	C2	0.20
Caring Guy	C4	0.20

RARITY KEY C = Common   U = Uncommon   R = Rare   # = Sublevel of rarity: lower numbers are rarer   **SP: Special (basic or "lands")**

Card name	Rarity	Price
Castellan Keir	C1	0.20
Champs the Wonder dog	R1	7.00
Channeling Flux	C4	0.20
Chephros	C3	0.20
Crash	C3	0.20
Curse of the Betrayed	C3	0.20
Cuthbert the Resurrector	R4	1.00
Dagger Isle Stronghold (C)	R3	1.40
Dagger Isle Stronghold (L)	R3	1.40
Dagger Isle Stronghold (R)	R3	1.40
Druk	C3	0.20
Dust Geyser	C1	2.60
Eagle-Eye McFinny	R3	1.40
"Elandar, Mighty Wizard"	R1	7.00
Essence of Babeatude	C2	0.60
Famine	R2	5.30
Fangris the Hunter	C4	0.20
Farmer Brown	R1	4.50
First Mate Muldoon	C2	0.20
Flame Geyser	C3	0.20
Giant Aunts	C2	0.20
Grahzue - Lover of Vice	R3	1.10
Great Ba'te	C1	3.60
Great Black Ri'shar	R3	1.40
Great Horned Troll	R3	1.00
Green Missy	C4	0.20
Groatie	R4	0.90
Grotto Troll	C3	0.20
Gumbo Jake	C2	0.20
Hackthorn Strangler	C2	0.20
"Hal, A Tosis Dragon"	R2	1.60
Hand of Chronos	R2	4.00
Heisenburg's missiles	C3	0.20
Holy Avenger	R2	1.50
Hook Toed Gnasher	C2	0.20
Howl of the Dead	C1	4.60
Howling Reaver	C2	0.20
"Jambo Slick, Smuggler"	C1	0.60
Jamchops The Trader	C3	0.20
Jonstollo the Seeker	C4	0.20
Kasmir's Blitz	C3	0.20
Kazrian Squawker	C4	0.20
Knife of Shadow	C4	0.20
Koset of the Light	C3	0.20
Land Drake	R3	1.40
Lizard Skin Lynn	C4	0.20
Lowland Troll	C2	0.80
Lying Scum	C4	0.20
Magnate Justice	C4	0.20
Maitz Dark	C1	0.20
Maitz Lightning	C1	0.20
Manly Guy	C1	0.70
Monolith of Chaos	C2	0.20
Necromancer	R2	1.50
Old Gumper	C4	0.20
"Ongo, Air Traffic Controller"	R3	1.10
Oppressed Slaves	C2	0.20
P'Tal - Keeper of the Balance	R2	1.40
Peace	C1	3.10
Pestilence	R1	4.30
Petrified Heart	C3	0.20
Phase Assassin	R3	1.00
Pirate Double Cross	C4	0.20
Pirate Log Platform	R3	1.30
Pirate Raiding Party	C3	0.20
Ploog's Chicken	C1	0.80
Ploog's Ox	C1	0.80
Ranged Attack Platform	R3	1.30
Razor Shiefa	C4	0.20
Razor Sliph	R3	1.00
Reverend Smilin' Jackoid	C2	0.20
Roaming Steam Geyser	R3	5.00
Rotten Guy	C2	0.20
Santa's Beer Sled	C2	0.20
Schneebolt	C2	0.20
Scurvy Dog	R3	1.00
Seraphim	C3	0.20
Shadrune	R3	1.00
Slimwit Man	R2	1.30
Sooooooul Mirror	R2	5.30
Spectre's Ward	C3	0.20
Spikey Crenalations	R2	1.50
Spirit Guide	C3	0.20
Starling Dodd Boys	C3	0.20
Summon Dimensional Fire Well	R2	3.80
Summon Loghammer's Sapper	R3	5.00
Supermodeloid	C2	0.80
The Black Eye	R3	1.10
The Great Balderoon	C1	0.70
Valley Troll	C4	0.20
Vensuni inferno Swarm	R1	5.50
Voodoo Wizard	C4	0.60
War	C4	0.20
Warhola's Snakes	C1	0.20
Warwick's Aura	C2	0.70
Weasly Guy	C3	0.80
Work Crew	R3	1.00
Yap Attack	C2	0.20

Guardians • Drifter's Nexus

FPG (Friedlander Publishing Group) • Released **April 1996**

124 cards in set • **IDENTIFIER: Infinity symbol (∞) at bottom by copyright line**

• Booster packs contain 8 cards; booster displays contain 60 boosters

Billed as an "Even More Western *Guardians* Expansion," *Drifter's Nexus* brings a touch of the Old West to the Guardians lineup... a touched touch, that is. Cards such as **Captain South America**, **Chickenhead McCracken**, and **Lizards on the Toast** added even more weirdness to a game that was already several light years past left field.

The gooftude even extends to the booster box, which has a "Scratch and Sniff" spot on the bottom — or it would if FPG could afford it. "You cannot possibly imagine the cost of producing a real Scratch and Sniff sticker," the box reads. "Please feel free to smell the box anyhow and imagine the odor of your choice." — *James A. Mishler*

You will need **14** nine-pocket pages to store this set. (7 doubled up)

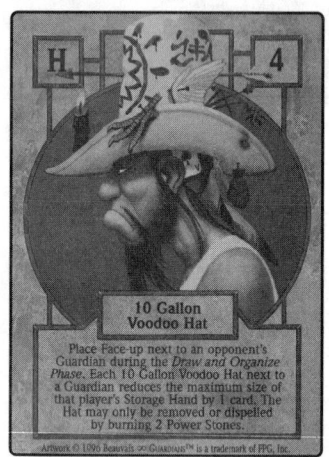

10 Gallon Voodoo Hat

Place Face-up next to an opponent's Guardian during the *Draw and Organize Phase*. Each 10 Gallon Voodoo Hat next to a Guardian reduces the maximum size of that player's Storage Hand by 1 card. The Hat may only be removed or dispelled by burning 2 Power Stones.

Artwork © 1996 Beanvex ∞∞ GUARDIAN™ is a trademark of FPG, Inc.

Set (124 cards)	40.00
Booster Display Box	15.00
Booster Pack	1.50

Card name	Rarity	Price
10 Gallon Voodoo Hat	U3	1.60
Al' Jabah	U1	0.90
Alarm Bells	U3	0.90
Altar of Takuli	C4	0.20
Angel of Righteousness	C1	0.20
Annoying Gnats in the Hood	C4	0.20
"Arnath, Lord of the Skies"	U1	1.40
"Baezhu, Overlord of Twisted Ways"	C4	0.20
Bagpipes of Fear	U3	1.00
Barnacle Bazulee'	R4	2.10
Black Locust	R1	8.50
"Bob, Snapping Gob"	R4	1.90
"Bruno Smashmouth, Union Boss"	C1	0.20
"Buzz, Vampire Mosquito"	U3	1.10
Caddy	C1	0.20
Captain South America	R1	11.00
Carrag the Black	R2	5.30
Chickenhead McCracken	U1	1.10
Clamjack Bomber	C3	0.20
"Crackhatch, at Large"	U1	1.40
Cratur Hobbs	U2	0.90
Dead-Eye McGrue	U3	0.90
Delilah Rangoon	C1	0.30
Demorgan the Inciter	R2	5.30
Disc of Slin	C3	0.20
Disgruntled Postal Worker	U2	1.60
Drifter's Nexus Stronghold (L)	R3	3.00
Drifter's Nexus Stronghold (C)	R3	2.00
Drifter's Nexus Stronghold (R)	R3	2.00
"Eats, Cockroach King"	U2	0.90
Etherwave Magna Lock	U1	1.40
"Garuda Kahn, First Disciple"	R4	2.10
Gateway to Mystfall	R1	7.00
Giant Babe	C1	0.30
Giant Shaman	R3	3.30
"Gnorg, Overlord of the Swamps"	U2	0.60
Goat	U3	0.60
Golden Fleecer	U3	1.40
Golfer	U2	1.40
Gopher	U4	1.10
Grunwald the Usurper	R4	1.90
Handles O'Rourke	R1	8.80
Head of Gudea	R4	1.90
Hostage Crisis	U2	0.90
Icky Bugs	C3	0.20
Initiate of Entropy	U4	1.10
Iron Crag Brew Mountain	C2	0.20
"Ix, Overlord of the Waters"	C3	0.20
Jalupee Lobo	U4	0.90
Karnis the Transcender	U2	1.00
Little Voodoo Hat	R1	7.00
Lizards on the Toast	R3	3.30
Longshot Louie	U3	1.10
Maitz Hotel	C1	0.10
Master Tactician	C1	0.20
Medallion of Skyphos	U2	1.40
Medicine Man	C3	0.20
"Mendu Sada, the Havoc"	R4	1.90
Mighty Tiki God	U4	0.60
Ministry of Tax Collection	R1	7.00
"Mu Kir' Agavati, Second Disciple"	U3	0.90
"Nob, Rapacious Gob"	R4	1.90
Orella of the Mist	R2	5.30
Oscar the Wonder Chimp	R1	7.00
"Phil, Bar Fly"	C2	0.20
Planes of Entropy	C1	0.20
Press Leak	U4	1.10
Prince of the Lost	C2	0.20
Professor Heisenberg	R2	5.30
Pulse Wave	C4	0.20
Ragmort's Engineers	U2	1.10
Randy Creek Regulars	R1	7.00
Red Master of Shadow	C3	0.20
"Rey, Overlord of Trees"	C1	0.20
River Giant	C3	0.20
Rock of Far Rolling	C4	0.20
Rosetta Stone	R1	7.30
Saboteurs	C3	0.20
Sarcophogus of Haidra	C4	0.20
Secret Catacombs	R3	2.00
Sewage Back Up	U1	1.10
Shadow Strike	C2	0.20
Shield-Skeleton 14	C4	0.20
Shield-Skeleton 16	C4	0.20
Shield-Skeleton 3	C4	0.20
Shield-Skeleton 7	C4	0.20
Shield/Terrain	U3	0.90
"Shin Chio, Third Disciple"	R2	6.80
Shroud of Grahzue	R2	5.30
"Sikura, Preceptor of Prophets"	R2	6.80
Slatch Willer	C3	0.20
"Slor, Overlord of the Wastes"	U4	0.90

RARITY KEY   C = Common   U = Uncommon   R = Rare   VR = Very Rare   UR = Ultra Rare   F = Foil card   X = Fixed/standard in all decks

180 • *SCRYE Collectible Card Game Checklist and Price Guide*

Card name	Rarity	Price		Card name	Rarity	Price		Card name	Rarity	Price		Card name	Rarity	Price
☐ Small Mox	C1	0.20		☐ The Amazing Cider-Man	U1	0.25		☐ "Urufa, Queen of Goblins"	R4	2.30		☐ Wheel of Law	U4	1.10
☐ Soggybottom Gertz	R3	3.30		☐ The Hollens Grove	C2	0.20		☐ "Vek' Nedra, Master of Disciples"	R2	6.80		☐ Wizard's Tower	U2	0.90
☐ Spirit Mountain	C2	0.20		☐ The Maitz Motel	C2	0.20		☐ Vesuvious Rex	R3	2.50		☐ Woodland Troll	C4	0.20
☐ Standard Bearer-Skeleton	U1	1.40		☐ The S.S. House of Babes	C2	0.20		☐ Vikia Tso'Shan'Lu	R3	4.30		☐ Woolverine	C4	0.20
☐ Standard Bearer-Skeleton	R2	5.50		☐ Thief of Shadow	U4	1.00		☐ Voodoo Hat	R2	5.30		☐ "Xaz, Thief of Twilight"	R4	2.40
☐ Standard of the Elements	U1	1.40		☐ Tiger Baloo	C4	0.20		☐ Warwick's Banishment	U1	1.50		☐ "You can't see me, I'm a Vampire"	U4	0.90
☐ Summon Entropy Storm	R3	3.00		☐ Tree Ogre	C2	0.20		☐ Whalebone Rick	U4	0.90		☐ "Zelda, Bag Lady Bug"	C2	0.20
☐ Tablet of Ancathus	R1	7.00		☐ "Uras, Overlord of the Mountains"	C3	0.20						☐ "Zob, Gurgling Gob"	R4	2.30
☐ Tanniker Smith	C1	0.20												

Guardians • Necropolis Park

FPG (Friedlander Publishing Group) • Released **August 1996**

103 cards in set • **IDENTIFIER: Omega (Ω) at bottom by copyright line**

• Booster packs contain 8 cards; booster displays contain 60 boosters

You will need **12** nine-pocket pages to store this set. (6 doubled up)

What do you get when your cross Ancient Egyptians (mostly dead ones), dinosaurs (mostly live ones), lots of beer, a couple babes, and lots of dead cats? We don't know, either, but we think it would look a lot like the *Necropolis Park* expansion for *Guardians*.

The expansion that "went so far west it came back out of the east," *Necropolis Park* was supposed to be followed in 1997 by the expansion *Seven Seas* and a *Metallic* (presumably holofoil) version. But hobbled by a declining market for its main staple, entertainment cards, the failure of its other CCG, *Dark Age*, and the less-than-hoped for response to *Guardians*, FPG left the business. "Silly" games didn't exactly leave the hobby — see *Magic: Unglued, Monty Python*, and *Austin Powers* — but *Guardians'* serious commitment to absurdity may top them all. — *James A. Mishler*

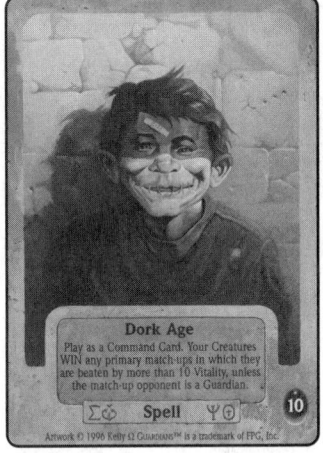

Dork Age
Play as a Command Card. Your Creatures WIN any primary match-ups in which they are beaten by more than 10 Vitality, unless the match-up opponent is a Guardian.
Spell
Artwork © 1996 Kelly 42 Guardians™ is a trademark of FPG, Inc.

Set (103 cards)		**30.00**
Booster Display Box		**15.00**
Booster Pack		**1.50**

Card name	Rarity	Price		Card name	Rarity	Price		Card name	Rarity	Price		Card name	Rarity	Price
☐ "40,000 Useless War Hammers"	R	5.60		☐ "Imhotep, Visier of Djoser"	R	6.60		☐ Scarab of Bounty	C	0.20		☐ Squibby	R	5.40
☐ Ancient Tome of Dispensation	C	0.20		☐ Iron Force of Sethos	C	0.20		☐ "Sebek, Queen of Magicians"	R	5.60		☐ Standard Bearer-Drum	U	5.10
☐ Ankh	C	0.20		☐ "Ishtar, Queen of the Heaps"	R	6.60		☐ Secauris	C	0.20		☐ Standard Bearer-Drum 25	R	5.10
☐ Ba Choomba	C	0.20		☐ Jimandu	C	0.20		☐ "Shackzu, Field Marshal"	R	5.60		☐ "Tavinmoor, First Called"	R	3.60
☐ Barrow Downs	C	0.20		☐ "Jinshade, Second Called"	R	6.90		☐ Shadow Bank Job	C	0.20		☐ The Minx	C	0.20
☐ "Bellaret, Third Called"	R	5.60		☐ Joomjaba	U	0.60		☐ Shadow Beer Heist	R	5.60		☐ The Ol' Switcheroo	C	0.20
☐ Blue Mountain Leechfoot	R	5.60		☐ Judge Dredge	U	0.60		☐ Shadow Panty Raid	C	0.20		☐ "Theib, Master of Scribes"	C	0.20
☐ "Buffy, Evil Hornbag"	U	0.60		☐ Jungle	C	0.20		☐ "Shield, Drum 15"	U	0.60		☐ Tiny Whining Cankerd	C	0.20
☐ Chant of Osirans	C	0.20		☐ "K'Hutek, Protector of the Fallen"	C	0.30		☐ "Shield, Drum 5"	U	0.60		☐ Tomb of the Bulzuru	C	0.20
☐ Chief Lector Priest of Sethos	C	0.20		☐ "Kurgan, Blademaster of the Exiled"	C	0.20		☐ "Shield, Drum Terrain"	U	0.60		☐ Total Chaos	R	5.60
☐ "Dachas, Supreme Leader"	R	5.60		☐ Limited Big Time Rebate	C	0.20		☐ Silver Server	C	0.20		☐ U.R. First	C	0.20
☐ Dead Cats	C	0.20		☐ Lotus Flower Water Garden	C	0.20		☐ Slackback Chak	C	0.20		☐ Vestibule of Kabod	U	0.60
☐ Death Pit of Djoser	C	0.20		☐ "Lucinda, Evil Hornbag"	R	5.60		☐ Slim Jab	C	0.20		☐ Voodoo Hat Rack	C	0.20
☐ Doogop the Greedy	C	0.20		☐ Mayor McEvil	C	0.20		☐ Snale Pit	C	0.60		☐ "Wanda, Evil Hornbag"	R	5.60
☐ Dork Age	U	0.60		☐ Mayor McFood	R	5.60		☐ Sneaky Varmint	C	0.20		☐ Warwick's Conversion	C	0.20
☐ Drizzle Bone the Hack	C	0.20		☐ Mayor McGreed	C	0.20								
☐ Eater of the Dead	C	0.20		☐ McHooter's Distraction	R	5.60								
☐ "Eisnmir, Master of Possessions"	C	0.30		☐ Mocodabi	C	0.20								
☐ Evil Baron Stoner	C	0.20		☐ "Moheidra, Mistress of Souls"	C	0.20								
☐ Exploding Tweezle	R	1.30		☐ Morb's Revenge	C	0.20								
☐ Fan Bearer	C	0.30		☐ Mummy	C	0.20								
☐ Fatback Chak	U	0.60		☐ Necropolis Park (L)	U	0.60								
☐ Festus	C	0.20		☐ Necropolis Park (C)	U	0.60								
☐ Footlocker of Conflagration	U	0.90		☐ Necropolis Park (R)	U	0.60								
☐ "Gehrund, Field Marshal"	R	5.60		☐ Noknaga	C	0.20								
☐ "Geldspar, Court Magician"	C	0.20		☐ Nubian Slave Girl	C	0.30								
☐ Gift of Isis	C	0.20		☐ Obelisk of Bablos	C	0.20								
☐ Gift of Osirus	C	0.20		☐ Odious Clamjack	C	0.20								
☐ Gorcoo	C	0.20		☐ Pharaoh Djoser	C	0.20								
☐ Greenback Chak	C	0.20		☐ Plague Walker	C	0.20								
☐ Guardian Angel	U	0.90		☐ Priest of Horus	R	5.60								
☐ "Heliopolis, Temple of Re"	C	0.20		☐ Priest of Sethos	R	5.60								
☐ High Priest of Sethos	C	0.20		☐ Priestess of Isis	C	0.20								
☐ High Priestess of Isis	U	0.90		☐ "Rachur, Field Marshal"	R	6.90								
☐ Humahuma	C	0.20		☐ Rocks at Rhuadan	C	0.20								
				☐ Rye Beaner	R	5.60								
				☐ Sales Weasel	C	0.20								
				☐ Scamp Jones	U	0.60								

Guardians • Promos

FPG (Friedlander Publishing Group)

IDENTIFIER: Black dot by copyright

Two of the *Guardians* promotional cards are simply cards from the *Limited* set. **Leprechaun** appeared in *Scrye* #11 (Dec. 1995), and **Hair-de-hobbins** appeared in *Scrye* #13 (Mar. 1996).

Both of those feature the blue dots consistent with *Limited* edition cards. Not so for a "true" promo card, the **Cheesy Con Souvenir Twizzle**, which FPG gave out at conventions. It's got a black dot, and we presume that's the promotional symbol — we *think*.

That's because we've also turned up several copies of **Druk**, a common from *Guardians: Dagger Isle*, which does not have the standard dagger symbol and instead has a black dot. Our assumption is that it's either a misprint or a promotional early version from before *Dagger Isle* was released.

Either way, a common is still a common and is worth about as much.

☐ Cheesy Con Souvenir Twizzle	Promo	5.00
☐ Druk (black dot)	?	0.20

Hercules

Wizards of the Coast • First set, *The Legendary Journeys*, released **July 1998**

180 cards in set

- Starter decks contain 40 cards and two large rules sheets
- Starter displays contain 18 starters, three each of six different theme decks
- Boosters contain 12 cards; booster displays contain 45 boosters

Designed by **Charlie Catinus, Mike Davis, Skaff Elias, Richard Garfield, Joe Grace, Jim Lin,** and **Joel Mick**

Based on the syndicated TV series of the same name, ***Hercules: The Legendary Journeys*** is the third and last game released using the ARC System. *Hercules* is compatible with ***Xena: Warrior Princess*** and **C•23**, the first two ARC System releases.

Hercules finds the hero and his companions are the good guys doing battle against evil warlords, horrible monsters, and wrathful gods. The *Hercules* game system accurately captures the feel of the TV series, though the campiness of the series is downplayed in favor of rock'em sock'em action.

The ARC System is a simplified Deckmaster system, similar in many respects to ***Magic: The Gathering***. There are four different types of cards in the ARC System: Resource, Character, Combat, and Action cards. "Tapping" is a core game mechanism in the ARC System, as it is in Deckmaster. Unlike *Magic*, however, there are only three different "colors" in *Hercules*, Red "Urban/Monetary Resources" (locations such as **Treasure Trove** and **Warlord Camp**), Green "Rural/Supplies Resources" (**Wedding Feast** and **Hidden Clearing**) and Blue "Mystic/Magical Resources" (**Gates to the Underworld** and **Altar to Hera**). Resources are played and then tapped to bring Characters into play or to play Combat or Action cards. Character, Combat, and Action cards each are of a single color; at least one of the resources tapped to use a card must be of the same color as that card.

Characters attack an opponent; the opponent may defend with Characters, Combat, or Action cards (unlike Deckmaster, defending Characters tap). If an attacking Character is unblocked, it will deal damage directly to the opponent's deck; one card discarded for every point of damage. A player who loses all cards loses the game.

The spinoff *Xena* had surpassed the *Hercules* TV series in popularity by this time, and of the ARC games only *Xena* got an expansion set. *Hercules* was a labor to sell, and unsold packs wound up lining the stables of King Augeas. — *James A. Mishler*

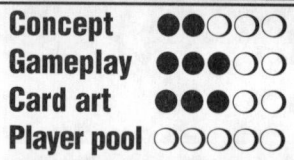

Concept	●●○○○
Gameplay	●●●○○
Card art	●●●○○
Player pool	○○○○○

Set (180 cards)	72.00
Starter Display Box	30.00
Booster Display Box	60.00
Starter Deck	7.50
Booster Pack	2.50

You will need 20 nine-pocket pages to store this set. *(10 doubled up)*

#	Card Name	Color	Type	Rar	Price
73	48 Sons of Martinus	Blue	Char	C	0.25
79	Adolescent Dragon	Blue	Char	C	0.25
2	Aid from Iolaus	Green	Act	C	0.30
117	Altar to Hera	Blue	Res	X	0.30
155	Ambitious Warlord	Red	Char	U	1.00
75	Ancient Mummy	Blue	Char	C	0.25
10	Angry Villager	Green	Char	C	0.25
63	Answered Prayers	Blue	Act	C	0.25
81	Antaeus Guards the Way	Blue	Cbt	C	0.25
106	Aphrodite	Blue	Char	R	4.00
66	Aphrodite's Wiles	Blue	Act	C	0.25
134	Archer Squad	Red	Char	C	0.25
127	Archery Contest	Red	Act	C	0.25
112	Ares	Blue	Char	R	7.50
94	Ares's Automaton	Blue	Char	U	1.00
77	Ares's Mesomorphs	Blue	Char	C	0.25
90	Ares's Wagon	Blue	Char	U	0.90
17	Argonaut	Green	Char	C	0.25
99	Artemis's Blessing	Blue	Act	R	3.00
45	Atalanta	Green	Char	R	3.50
101	Athena's Plan	Blue	Act	R	2.50
174	"Autolycus, King of Thieves"	Red	Char	R	4.00
20	Banding Together	Green	Cbt	C	0.25
177	Bath House	Red	Res	X	0.30
5	Beautiful Princess	Green	Char	C	0.25
93	Blind Prophet	Blue	Char	U	0.90
85	Blind Prophet's Curse	Blue	Act	U	1.00
84	Blind Prophet's Vision	Blue	Act	U	0.90

#	Card Name	Color	Type	Rar	Price
143	Broken Truce	Red	Act	U	0.90
116	Burial Chamber	Blue	Res	X	0.30
38	Burn the Building	Green	Cbt	U	1.00
80	Captured by Hera	Blue	Cbt	C	0.25
98	Captured by the Gods	Blue	Cbt	U	0.90
165	Catapult Attack	Red	Act	R	3.00
157	Caught by Iolaus	Red	Cbt	U	0.90
159	Celebration	Red	Act	R	3.00
126	Centaur Attack	Red	Act	C	0.25
173	Centaur Mentor	Red	Char	R	3.00
65	Charon's Fare	Blue	Act	C	0.25
11	Clumsy Giant	Green	Char	C	0.25
8	Crafty Hunter	Green	Char	C	0.25
105	Cross-Time Adventure	Blue	Act	R	3.00
15	Cyclops	Green	Char	C	0.25
26	Dance Instructor	Green	Char	U	0.90
179	Dance Studio	Red	Res	X	0.30
131	Dangerous Warrior	Red	Char	C	0.25
150	Daughters of Thespius	Red	Char	U	0.90
91	Delphian Oracle	Blue	Char	U	0.90
100	Demeter's Curse	Blue	Act	R	3.00
37	Destructiveness	Green	Cbt	U	0.90
151	Devious Schemers	Red	Char	U	0.90
82	Difficult Choice	Blue	Act	U	0.90
67	Divine Healing	Blue	Act	C	0.25
97	Divine Intervention	Blue	Cbt	U	0.90
114	Divine Justice	Blue	Cbt	R	3.00
36	Do The Twanky Twiddle!	Green	Cbt	U	0.90
108	Drunken Satyrs	Blue	Char	R	3.00
47	Eastern Acrobat	Green	Char	R	3.00
171	Eastern Trainer	Red	Char	R	2.80
152	Elite Archers	Red	Char	U	0.90
170	Elite Forces	Red	Char	R	2.00
22	Entangled	Green	Act	U	0.90
86	Eternal Winter	Blue	Act	U	1.00

#	Card Name	Color	Type	Rar	Price
28	Exotic Dancer	Green	Char	U	0.90
121	Fair Trial	Red	Act	C	0.30
169	Falafel	Red	Char	R	3.00
23	Festival	Green	Act	U	1.00
60	Festival Grounds	Green	Res	X	0.45
12	Forest Raider	Green	Char	C	0.25
148	Fortunes of War	Red	Act	U	1.00
120	Gates to the Underworld	Blue	Res	X	0.45
83	Ghostly Informant	Blue	Act	U	1.00
74	Giant Eel	Blue	Char	C	0.30
132	Gladiator Slave	Red	Char	C	0.25
107	Golden Hind	Blue	Char	R	3.00
142	Good Lawyer	Red	Act	U	1.00
111	Graegus	Blue	Char	R	3.50
139	Greedy Warlord	Red	Char	C	0.30
46	Guardian Minotaurs	Green	Char	R	3.00
110	Hades	Blue	Char	R	3.00
59	Hall of the Golden Fleece	Green	Res	X	0.45
122	Hangman's Justice	Red	Act	C	0.25
40	"Help Us, Hercules!"	Green	Act	R	3.00
95	Hera's Enforcer	Blue	Char	U	1.00
78	Hera's Executioners	Blue	Char	C	0.30
96	Hera's Hydra	Blue	Char	U	1.00
102	Hera's Transformation	Blue	Act	R	3.00
54	Herc Helps Out	Green	Cbt	R	3.00
19	Herculean Effort	Green	Cbt	C	0.30
50	Hercules	Green	Char	R	9.50
124	Hercules Bowls 'Em Over	Red	Act	C	0.30
161	Hercules Cracks Some Heads	Red	Act	R	3.00
33	Hercules Leads the Way	Green	Cbt	U	1.00
162	Hercules Strikes	Red	Act	R	3.00
21	Hercules Trains the Villagers	Green	Cbt	C	0.35
175	Hercules's Backhand	Red	Cbt	R	3.00
34	Heroic Sacrifice	Green	Cbt	U	1.00

#	Card Name	Color	Type	Rar	Price
☐ 115	"Hey, Boys!"	Blue	Cbt	R	3.00
☐ 58	Hidden Clearing	Green	Res	X	0.45
☐ 136	Hired Centaur Archers	Red	Char	C	0.25
☐ 153	Hired Centaur Crosbow Archers	Red	Char	U	1.00
☐ 130	Hired Warrior	Red	Char	C	0.30
☐ 55	Hit 'Em While They're Down	Green	Cbt	R	3.00
☐ 30	Hunting Party	Green	Char	U	1.00
☐ 52	I Hate Hera!	Green	Cbt	R	3.00
☐ 53	I Hate Warlords!	Green	Cbt	R	3.50
☐ 35	Individual Effort	Green	Cbt	U	1.00
☐ 141	Insight	Red	Cbt	C	0.30
☐ 167	Inspirational Leader	Red	Char	R	2.80
☐ 49	Iolaus	Green	Char	R	3.50
☐ 129	Ironhead Warrior	Red	Char	C	0.30
☐ 71	Living Dead	Blue	Char	C	0.25
☐ 118	Magical Cave	Blue	Res	X	0.30
☐ 89	Mandrake	Blue	Char	U	0.90
☐ 29	Manure Farmers	Green	Char	U	0.90
☐ 48	Martial Arts Mistress	Green	Char	R	3.00
☐ 146	Massage Break	Red	Act	U	1.00
☐ 43	Master Tactician	Green	Char	R	2.50
☐ 166	Military King	Red	Char	R	3.00
☐ 42	Military Leader	Green	Char	R	3.00
☐ 135	Minor Warlord	Red	Char	C	0.30
☐ 64	Nemesis Strikes!	Blue	Act	C	0.25
☐ 9	Overworked Mother	Green	Char	C	0.25
☐ 62	Path Not Taken	Blue	Act	C	0.25
☐ 41	Pie-Eating Contest	Green	Act	R	3.00

#	Card Name	Color	Type	Rar	Price
☐ 149	Pillage the Village	Red	Act	U	1.00
☐ 72	Possessed Virgins	Blue	Char	C	0.30
☐ 138	Pretender to the Throne	Red	Char	C	0.25
☐ 76	Priest of Dionysus	Blue	Char	C	0.25
☐ 18	Primord	Green	Char	C	0.25
☐ 144	Pyro's Flame	Red	Act	U	1.00
☐ 6	Questing Farmer	Green	Char	C	0.25
☐ 163	Reckless Warlords	Red	Act	R	3.00
☐ 14	Resourceful Villagers	Green	Char	C	0.25
☐ 164	Royal Decree	Red	Act	R	3.00
☐ 128	Royal Guards	Red	Char	C	0.25
☐ 168	Salmoneus	Red	Char	R	5.00
☐ 125	Salmoneus Sells Your House	Red	Act	C	0.25
☐ 123	Salmoneus's Self-Actualization Seminar	Red	Act	C	0.30
☐ 57	Satyr Hollow	Green	Res	X	0.30
☐ 44	Satyr Instructor	Green	Char	R	2.50
☐ 7	Satyr Wannabes	Green	Char	C	0.25
☐ 3	Send 'Em Flying	Green	Act	C	0.25
☐ 69	Servants of Hera	Blue	Char	C	0.25
☐ 92	Servants of the Fates	Blue	Char	U	0.80
☐ 88	She-Demon Strikes!	Blue	Act	U	1.00
☐ 70	Soldier of Hades	Blue	Char	C	0.25
☐ 156	Sound the Charge	Red	Cbt	U	0.90
☐ 4	Spoiled Princess	Green	Char	C	0.25
☐ 25	Struggling Farmers	Green	Char	U	0.90
☐ 103	Summoned Aid	Blue	Act	R	3.00
☐ 104	Swallowed by a Sea Serpent	Blue	Act	R	3.00

#	Card Name	Color	Type	Rar	Price
☐ 61	Sword of Veracity	Blue	Act	C	0.25
☐ 68	Temple Protector	Blue	Char	C	0.25
☐ 109	The Blue Priest	Blue	Char	R	3.00
☐ 160	The Daughters of Thespius Are Coming!	Red	Act	R	3.00
☐ 147	Tides of Battle	Red	Act	U	1.00
☐ 51	To the Last Breath	Green	Cbt	R	3.00
☐ 180	Town Square	Red	Res	X	0.30
☐ 133	Trapped Entryways	Red	Char	C	0.25
☐ 13	Traveling Boxer	Green	Char	C	0.25
☐ 137	Treacherous Warrior	Red	Char	C	0.25
☐ 178	Treasure Trove	Red	Res	X	0.30
☐ 158	Tricked by Autolycus	Red	Cbt	U	0.90
☐ 87	Trip Across the Styx	Blue	Act	U	1.00
☐ 1	Underworld Rescue	Green	Act	C	0.25
☐ 39	Unexpected Help	Green	Act	R	3.00
☐ 31	Unruly Mob	Green	Char	U	1.00
☐ 24	Vengeful Amazon	Green	Char	U	0.90
☐ 140	Vengeful Warlord	Red	Char	C	0.25
☐ 172	Walking War Machine	Red	Char	R	3.00
☐ 27	Wandering Healer	Green	Char	U	0.90
☐ 16	Wandering Tribe	Green	Char	C	0.25
☐ 154	War Machine	Red	Char	U	1.00
☐ 176	Warlord Camp	Red	Res	X	0.30
☐ 32	Warrior Tribe	Green	Char	U	1.00
☐ 56	Wedding Feast	Green	Res	X	0.30
☐ 119	Wedding Temple	Blue	Res	X	0.30
☐ 145	Whim of the Queen	Red	Act	U	0.90
☐ 113	Zeus	Blue	Char	R	7.50

Heresy

Last Unicorn Games • First set, *Kingdom Come*, released **September 1995**
374 cards in set

- Starter decks contain 60 cards; starter displays contain 12 decks
- Booster packs contain 15 cards; booster displays contain 36 packs

In **Heresy**, angels and demons banished to Earth try to find a way to get home. Players take the role of leader of some of these outcasts, and, through battle, they hope to gain enough "Tau" energy to reopen the gateway home. Oddly enough, though, the only way to store and handle this spiritual force is using the Internet. So, by training flunkies to write HTML code, players develop Web pages in which to store all of this energy. Angels and demons have infested the Internet to build a gateway to Heaven? This game pegs the needle on the Weird-O-Meter.

Heresy plays easily and has a familiar system. Characters come in seven different Convictions, each with a Call Value that players generate by Opening their Domains. With each Character having an Attack and Defense expressed as X/Y, the game mechanics here are, for all intents and purposes, **Magic: The Gathering**. Differences do show up, but not that many. The most important one is that players actually control two chunks of real estate: the Real World and the Matrix (a few years before the movie, even!). Each game turn goes like this: untap, flip over face-down cards, pay upkeep, play one land in the Real World, play one land in the Matrix, tap lands to cast Miracles, tap lands to summon Characters, move Characters from one land to another, attack, store Tau, activate the gateway, and win the game.

The oversized card art is well done, and the cards are easy to read. The gameplay itself is *so* similar to **Magic**, though, it's a wonder Last Unicorn never heard about it. (Then, again, Wizards of the Coast *did* buy the company in 1999 and shut the office down in 2000...) The over-sized cards were not endearing to either retailers or players, and the seven-color scheme made it so difficult to build an effective deck that many didn't bother. An expansion for August 1996, **Project Demiurge**, was cancelled.

It has, however, a small but dedicated following — on the Internet. — *Richard Weld*

Concept	●●●○○
Gameplay	●●●○○
Card art	●●●●○
Player pool	●○○○○

Set (374 cards)	37.00	You will need
Starter Display Box	18.00	**42** six-pocket pages to store this set. (21 doubled up)
Booster Display Box	20.00	
Starter Deck	5.00	
Booster Pack	1.00	

☐ Card name	Type	Rarity	Price
☐ Abbadona	Host	U	0.60
☐ Abdiel	Host	U	0.90
☐ Access Denied	Miracle	C	0.15
☐ Adetum	Miracle	C	0.15
☐ Affirmation	Miracle	C	0.15
☐ Albertus Magnus	Heathen	R	2.80
☐ Alchemic Citadel	Aleph	U	0.80

☐ Card name	Type	Rarity	Price
☐ Anakim	Host	C	0.15
☐ Anathema	Miracle	C	0.50
☐ Ankh of the Necropolis	Aleph	U	0.80
☐ Apollyon	Host	R	2.80
☐ Arakab	Host	U	0.80
☐ Archon	Enhancmt	U	0.90
☐ Arctic Razor I	Location	U	0.90

RARITY KEY C = Common **U** = Uncommon **R** = Rare **VR** = Very Rare **UR** = Ultra Rare **F** = Foil card **X** = Fixed/standard in all decks

Card name	Type	Rarity	Price
Arena	Location	R	2.80
Ariadne	Enhancmt	C	0.15
Arioch	Host	U	0.90
Arizona Free Zone	Location	R	4.00
Ark of the Covenant	Aleph	R	3.00
Arthur Glaston	Heathen	R	3.00
Ashmedai	Host	R	2.80
Asser Criel	Aleph	U	0.80
Astaroth	Host	R	4.00
Atrophy	Enhancmt	U	0.80
Aureum Vellus	Aleph	R	2.50
Avarice	Enhancmt	C	0.15
Awakened	Heathen	R	4.00
Azrael	Host	C	0.15
Bael	Host	R	2.80
Balance of the Qaddisin	Aleph	R	4.00
Balberith	Host	C	0.15
Banish	Enhancmt	C	0.15
Basilica Philosophica	Aleph	R	4.00
Beelzebul	Host	R	3.50
Beleth	Host	U	0.80
Belial	Host	C	0.15
Belphegor	Host	C	0.15
Betrayal	Miracle	R	3.00
Blind Faith	Enhancmt	U	0.80
Body Thief	Cel Power	U	0.80
Book of the Angel Raziel	Aleph	R	2.50
Bookworm V.1	Cel Power	C	0.15
Boomerang	Miracle	C	0.15
Boon of Vassago	Miracle	C	0.15
Bordeaux-Barcelona Sprawl	Location	R	4.00
Breach	Enhancmt	U	0.90
Byblos	Location	U	0.80
Cacophonites	Heathen	C	0.15
Caim	Host	U	0.40
Caliel	Host	U	0.80
Camiel, Chief of Aeons	Host	U	0.80
Carnivean	Host	U	0.90
Cassiel	Host	U	0.80
Castrum	Miracle	C	0.15
Charity	Enhancmt	C	0.15
Charon	Heathen	R	4.00
Chief of the Apostates	Enhancmt	R	2.80
Chief of the Destroyers	Enhancmt	R	2.80
Chief of the Planets	Enhancmt	R	2.80
Chief of the Punishers	Enhancmt	R	2.80
Chosen One	Enhancmt	C	0.15
Chromeopaths	Heathen	C	0.15
City of Metal	Location	R	4.00
Cloak	Miracle	C	0.15
Congo Depth Preserve	Location	L	0.05
Conventicle of the Chalice	Heathen	U	0.80
Corporate AI	Heathen	R	3.00
Corporate Arcology	Location	L	0.05
Corpsemen	Heathen	C	0.15
Cosmic Furnace	Aleph	U	0.90
Crown of Solomon	Aleph	U	0.90
Cup of Oblivion	Aleph	U	0.90
CURE	Miracle	R	2.50
Cyberdeck	Enhancmt	C	0.15
Cyberzealot	Heathen	C	0.15
Demagogue	Heathen	U	0.60
Denounce	Enhancmt	R	4.00
Derdekea	Host	U	0.80
Desert Perimeter	Location	U	0.60
Diadem of Anu	Aleph	R	4.00
Dies Irae (The Day of Wrath)	Cel Power	R	3.50
Divinopolis	Location	R	2.50
Doppleganger	Heathen	R	3.00
Drain	Miracle	C	0.15
Dubiel	Host	U	0.80
Emerald Tablet	Aleph	R	3.00
Encrypt	Miracle	U	0.90
Enlightenment	Enhancmt	R	2.50
Envy	Enhancmt	C	0.15
Ephemerae	Host	C	0.15
Epiphany	Miracle	C	0.15
Ethnarch	Enhancmt	U	0.90
Euroreach	Location	L	0.05
Exael	Host	U	0.60
Excalibur Corporation	Heathen	R	3.00
Excalibur Megatrust	Location	R	3.00
Exodus	Cel Power	R	4.00
Eye and the Wind	Miracle	C	0.15
Faith	Enhancmt	C	0.15
False Messiah	Heathen	U	0.80
False Prophet	Heathen	C	0.15
Fanatics	Heathen	U	0.80
Federal Core	Location	R	4.00
Fellowship of Cybermystic Consciousness	Heathen	C	0.15
Ferrymen	Heathen	U	0.90
Firestorm	Cel Power	C	0.15
First Church of Eugenics Ascendant	Heathen	C	0.15
Fixer	Heathen	C	0.15
Flatline	Miracle	U	0.80
Focalor	Host	U	0.80
Followers of the New Kingdom	Heathen	C	0.15
Force Majeure	Enhancmt	C	0.15
Fortitude	Enhancmt	C	0.15
Fractal Heresy	Heathen	R	2.80
Free City	Location	L	0.05
Gabriel, Chief of Angels	Host	R	3.30
Gabrielites	Heathen	C	0.15
Gaians	Heathen	C	0.15
Gamaliel	Host	C	0.15
Geasa	Miracle	C	0.15
Ghost in the Machine	Enhancmt	C	0.15
Gluttony	Enhancmt	C	0.50
Golab	Host	R	3.00
Golem	Miracle	C	0.15
Government Geodesic	Location	U	0.60
Governor of the Zodiac	Enhancmt	R	2.50
Great Crusade	Cel Power	R	3.50
Great Pack	Aleph	R	2.80
Grift	Miracle	R	4.00
Grigori	Host	C	0.15
Hadraniel	Host	U	0.90
Haniel, Chief of Principalities	Host	U	0.60
Harbinger	Enhancmt	C	0.15
Harbonah	Host	C	0.15
Hard Corps	Heathen	C	0.15
Harlequin	Enhancmt	U	0.80
Harrowing	Cel Power	R	3.30
Hate	Enhancmt	C	0.15
Haven	Enhancmt	R	3.00
Headhunter	Enhancmt	C	0.15
Heliopolis	Location	U	1.00
Helix	Miracle	C	0.15
Hemah	Host	U	0.60
Hermeticum	Heathen	U	0.80
Hermit	Heathen	R	4.00
Holy Grail	Aleph	R	4.00
Hope	Enhancmt	C	0.15
Horn of Reckoning	Aleph	U	0.60
Houri	Host	C	0.15
Iblis	Host	C	0.15
Imprisonment	Enhancmt	U	0.60
Imram	Enhancmt	R	3.00
Incubi	Host	C	0.15
Industrial Underground	Location	U	0.60
Infernus	Heathen	R	2.50
Intercept	Miracle	U	0.90
Interdict	Miracle	U	0.60
Invocation	Miracle	C	0.15
Invulnerable	Enhancmt	U	0.80
Ionian Column	Heathen	U	0.90
Israfel	Host	U	0.80
Ithuriel	Host	C	0.15
Jihad	Enhancmt	R	3.00
Judgment	Cel Power	R	3.50
Juggler	Heathen	C	0.15
Jurors	Heathen	U	0.80
Justice	Enhancmt	C	0.15
Kabael	Host	U	0.90
Karoz	Host	C	0.15
Kiev Grid	Location	L	0.05
Kushiel	Host	U	1.00
Lauviah	Host	C	0.15
Lawless Mercantile Center	Location	U	0.80
Lazarus Project	Cel Power	U	0.80
Lehiah	Host	U	0.60
Leonardo DaVinci	Heathen	C	0.15
Lilith	Host	R	4.00
Living Breach	Enhancmt	R	4.00
London Dome	Location	R	3.50
Looking Glass	Miracle	R	4.00
Los	Host	C	0.15
Lurk	Miracle	U	0.80
Lust	Enhancmt	C	0.15
Mage	Heathen	R	4.00
Malik	Host	C	0.15
Mammon	Host	U	0.80
Manichaeans	Heathen	C	0.15
Mansemat	Host	C	0.15

Heresy tips

"**Heresy** has a generous discard rule. You can get rid of your whole hand without penalty each and every turn if you wish. Greedy players will capitalize on this and gobble through their decks, searching for the best cards they can get. Unfortunately, players who chew through their decks too quickly will be sweating bullets when they come to their last few cards without a sufficient amount of Tau to activate a gate.

"Hey, they don't call greed a deadly sin for nothing!"

— *Matt Sturm, Scrye #11 (Dec 95)*

RARITY KEY C = Common   U = Uncommon   R = Rare   VR = Very Rare   UR = Ultra Rare   F = Foil card   X = Fixed/standard in all decks

Card name	Type	Rarity	Price
Marchosias	Host	U	0.80
Martial Law	Enhancmt	U	0.80
Martyr	Heathen	C	0.15
Maskweavers	Heathen	U	0.90
32			
Megacity Core	Location	U	0.80
Melchisedec	Host	C	0.15
Memory Cache	Enhancmt	C	0.15
Memunim	Host	C	0.15
Mephistophiel	Host	U	0.80
Michael, Chief of Archangels	Host	R	3.50
33			
Michaelines	Heathen	U	1.00
Minion	Enhancmt	U	0.80
Mistress of the Four Seasons	Enhancmt	R	4.00
Mole	Enhancmt	U	0.90
Moloch	Host	U	0.80
Mulciber	Host	C	0.15
34			
Murmur	Host	C	0.15
Namaah	Host	C	0.15
Nanael	Host	C	0.15
Nathanael	Host	R	2.50
Nergal	Host	C	0.15
Netlink	Enhancmt	C	0.15
35			
Netwalking	Enhancmt	U	0.60
Neuroplug	Enhancmt	C	0.15
New Templars	Heathen	U	0.80
Nile Shard	Location	L	0.05
Ocean Military Sphere	Location	U	0.80
Old World City	Location	L	0.05
36			
One of the Lost	Enhancmt	R	3.00
Ophaniel, Chief of Cherubim	Host	R	2.80
Optical Server Hub	Enhancmt	R	4.00
Oracle	Heathen	R	3.00
Orbital Strike Platform	Enhancmt	C	0.15
Orphic Egg	Heathen	U	0.60
37			
Osaka Expanse	Location	L	0.05
Outland Tunnels	Location	L	0.05
Outmodes	Heathen	C	0.15
Paimon	Host	U	0.80
Parashim	Host	C	0.15
Patron	Enhancmt	C	0.15
38			
Pax Sanctorum	Enhancmt	R	4.00
Pestilence	Cel Power	U	0.80
Phantom Box	Heathen	R	2.50
Phanuel	Host	C	0.15
Phorlakh	Host	U	0.60
Pillar of Fire	Enhancmt	C	0.15
39			
Populeum	Enhancmt	U	0.60
Possibility Rakers	Heathen	U	0.60
Pride	Enhancmt	C	0.15
Prince of the Four Altitudes	Enhancmt	R	3.30
Prometheus Project	Cel Power	U	1.00
Prophecy	Miracle	R	4.00
40			
Proxy	Miracle	R	3.00
Prudence	Enhancmt	C	0.15
Puffer	Heathen	C	0.15
Purgatory V	Location	U	1.00
Pursan	Host	C	0.15
Pythagoreans	Heathen	R	4.00
41			
Rabdos	Host	C	0.15
Raguel	Host	C	0.15
Raphael, Chief of Authorities	Host	C	0.15
Raphaelites	Heathen	U	0.90
Rapture	Enhancmt	C	0.50
Rashiel	Host	C	0.15
42			
Raum	Host	U	0.90
Raziel	Host	U	0.80
Reaper	Enhancmt	U	0.60
Recompile	Miracle	U	1.00
Redemption	Cel Power	R	3.80
Remiel	Host	C	0.15
43			
Remote Biodome	Location	L	0.05
Renegade	Miracle	R	3.00
Renunciation	Enhancmt	U	0.80
Repair	Cel Power	U	0.80
Replication	Cel Power	U	0.60
Research Arcology	Location	U	0.50
44			
Resounding	Cel Power	R	4.00
Resurrection	Cel Power	U	0.80
Revelation	Cel Power	R	4.00
Revoke	Miracle	U	0.80
Rhasis	Heathen	R	3.00
Rimmon	Host	R	2.90
45			
Rimspace	Location	L	0.05
Rio Net	Location	L	0.05
Rodolphine Tables	Aleph	U	0.60
Rodolphines	Heathen	C	0.15
Rogue	Heathen	U	0.80
Rogue Maelstrom	Cel Power	R	4.00
46			
Ruler of the 28 Mansions of the Moon	Enhancmt	R	3.30
Sabrael	Host	C	0.15
Salvation	Cel Power	R	4.00
Sammael	Host	R	4.00
Sandalphon, Chief of Seraphim	Host	R	3.30
Sarim	Enhancmt	C	0.15
47			
Scylla	Miracle	R	3.00
Scythe of Saturn	Aleph	U	1.00
Seafloor Metroplex	Location	L	0.05
Seal of Solomon	Aleph	R	4.00
Sentinel	Enhancmt	C	0.15
Shift	Enhancmt	U	0.90
48			
Silat	Host	C	0.15
Simulacrum	Heathen	U	0.80
Sisters of the Rood	Heathen	R	2.90
Sithriel	Host	C	0.15
Skinner Box	Enhancmt	C	0.15
Sloth	Enhancmt	C	0.15
49			
Soldiers of Gaia	Heathen	U	0.60
Solomon	Heathen	R	4.00
Soulless	Heathen	R	3.00
Sovereign	Enhancmt	C	0.15
St. Crispin's Day	Enhancmt	R	2.90
Stim Puppets	Heathen	C	0.15
50			
Stirring Oration	Miracle	C	0.15
Subterfuge	Miracle	U	1.00
Suture	Enhancmt	U	0.60
Sword of Abdiel	Aleph	R	3.00
Sybil	Heathen	U	0.60
Tacouin	Host	C	0.15
51			
Taliesin	Heathen	R	3.00
Tartaruchi	Host	C	0.15
Temperance	Enhancmt	C	0.15
Tempest	Cel Power	R	4.00
Terethel	Host	U	0.80
Terror	Cel Power	U	0.60
52			
Thausael	Host	R	4.00
The Black Angel	Host	C	0.15
The Clavicule	Aleph	U	0.60
The Damnation	Location	R	2.80
The Iron Maiden	Heathen	R	4.00
The Rim	Location	R	3.30
53			
Theft	Cel Power	U	0.90
Theurgicum	Heathen	U	0.60
Thread	Cel Power	R	4.00
Tir fo Thuinn, Land under the Waves	Location	R	2.00
Titania Perimeter	Location	U	0.80
Towers of Ur	Location	R	2.80
54			
Travelling	Enhancmt	R	4.00
True Messiah, The Lamb	Heathen	R	3.00
True Messiah, The Lion	Heathen	R	3.00
True Name	Enhancmt	R	3.50
True Prophet	Heathen	U	0.60
True Word	Miracle	R	3.00
55			
Tsunami	Cel Power	R	2.50
Turmoil	Miracle	C	0.15
Tutankhamen	Enhancmt	R	2.50
Unchallengeable	Enhancmt	R	3.40
Uncle Jack	Heathen	U	0.80
Unseen Aid	Enhancmt	R	2.50
56			
Uplink	Enhancmt	C	0.15
Urban Defense Grid	Enhancmt	C	0.15
Urban Sprawl	Location	L	0.05
Uriel	Host	U	0.80
Usiel	Host	R	3.00
Valens	Heathen	R	4.00
57			
Vatican Arcology	Location	R	2.90
Vault	Enhancmt	R	2.80
Vedic Datacache	Location	U	0.80
Veil	Miracle	U	0.80
Verchiel	Host	U	0.60
Vessel Of Hauras	Aleph	U	0.90
58			
Vevaliah	Host	C	0.15
Virtual Cross	Enhancmt	R	3.00
Virtual Dead	Heathen	R	3.50
Virtual Messiah	Heathen	U	1.00
Vivisection	Miracle	C	0.15
Vual	Host	U	0.80
59			
Wailing Ones	Heathen	R	4.00
Wall	Host	U	0.80
Warden of the Elements	Enhancmt	R	3.00
Warden of the Seven Celestial Halls	Enhancmt	R	4.00
Weaver	Heathen	R	2.60
Web	Enhancmt	C	0.15
60			
Wild Hunt	Heathen	R	4.00
Wipe	Cel Power	C	0.15
Word of the Irin	Aleph	U	0.60
World Tree	Aleph	R	4.00
Wotan's Hall	Location	R	4.00
Wraith V. 6.6	Enhancmt	R	2.60
61			
Wrap-Around	Enhancmt	C	0.15
Wrath	Enhancmt	U	0.60
Xaphan	Host	U	0.80
Zadkiel, Chief of Dominions	Host	U	1.00
Zaphkiel, Chief of Thrones	Host	C	0.15
Zoners	Heathen	C	0.15
Zophiel	Host	R	3.00
Zurich Metabank	Location	U	1.10

Tip to future designers

If you're looking to create the next great CCG, history has a tip: cards sell better when they're playing-card size. **Sim City** and **Heresy** both broke the mold but couldn't retrain enough buyers in their habits.

It is by no means an impossible task, but only a *very* strong game will succeeds with the deck stacked against it from the outset.

RARITY KEY C = Common U = Uncommon R = Rare VR = Very Rare UR = Ultra Rare F = Foil card X = Fixed/standard in all decks

Highlander

Highlander was part of the "Swordmaster" system, a line not unlike the Deckmaster System. It was also the only game in the system.

- Starter decks contain 52 cards; starter displays contain 12 starters
- Booster packs contain 15 cards; booster displays contain 36 boosters

Based on the movies and TV series of the same name, the ***Highlander*** CCG likewise chronicles the exploits of various Immortals, hardy individuals who constantly battle each other to determine who will be the last survivor: "There can be only one."

These confrontations primarily take the form of sword fights, since an Immortal can only be killed by decapitation, and this is the aspect the CCG concentrates on. Each player selects an Immortal Persona and attempts to defeat an opponent through the use of various attacks, blocks, and dodges. In addition to the simple attacks and defenses, location, event, object, and situation cards based upon events from the movies and series are also employed. ***Series Edition***, as the name implies, covers elements from the *Highlander* TV series, and serves as a base set for the game.

Highlander has a number of things that distinguish it from other games. One is the concept of "rips," cards that are *torn in half* to use. It was common for players to collect rips from various people who "ripped" on them, often having them signed or having the ripper write some type of special message. Ripping on someone in a tournament was a very important and often difficult choice, as rips were not replaced and no new rips could be added to one's deck until the tournament ended.

Another innovative concept was the idea of "ability." *Highlander* didn't have the standard life total of many games; it had ability, which usually started at 15. The added twist was that this ability was also your hand size. As damage was taken, your maximum hand size shrank. This meant that, once damage started being dealt, it was very easy for the trend to continue, as your hand kept getting smaller.

Finally, *Highlander* had the Head Shot, simulating the only way to kill an Immortal. A number of cards existed to implement this, and it was viewed as a stylish way to win. It also had an impact on tournaments — which were double elimination, unless someone took your head. If this occurred, then you were eliminated from the tournament.

Popular for a while, *Highlander*'s decline was greatly accelerated by the delays that plagued its manufacturer. — **Orren McKay**

Concept	●●●○○
Gameplay	●●●●○
Card art	●○○○○
Player pool	●●○○○

Set (165 cards)	150.00
Starter Display Box	75.00
Booster Display Box	65.00
Starter Deck	10.00
Booster Pack	3.00

You will need **19** nine-pocket pages to store this set. (10 doubled up)

Card name	Type	Rarity	Price
[1]			
☐ Alan Baines	Event	R	4.00
☐ Amanda	Persona	R	10.00
☐ Amanda: Back Away	Dodge	U	1.00
☐ Amanda: Continuity	Situation	U	1.00
☐ Amanda: Distract	Dodge	R	5.00
☐ Amanda: Jump	Dodge	U	1.00
☐ Amanda: Left Side Step	Dodge	U	1.00
☐ Amanda: Master's Advice	Situation	R	5.00
☐ Amanda: Master's Attack	Attack	R	8.00
[2]			
☐ Amanda: Right Side Step	Dodge	U	1.00
☐ Amanda: Seduce	Event	R	5.00
☐ Amanda: Steal	Event	U	1.00
☐ Amanda: Surprise Attack	Event	R	5.00
☐ Angry Mob	Event	C	0.35
☐ Avery Hoskins	Situation	R	3.00
☐ Carl	Situation	R	3.00
☐ Caught in the Act	Event	U	1.00
☐ Challenge	Event	C	0.35
[3]			
☐ Charlie	Event	R	3.00
☐ Connor MacLeod	Persona	R	15.00
☐ Connor MacLeod: Back Away	Dodge	U	1.00
☐ Connor MacLeod: Combination	Event	U	1.00
☐ Connor MacLeod: Continuity	Situation	U	1.00

Card name	Type	Rarity	Price
☐ Connor MacLeod: Disarm	Event	U	1.00
☐ Connor MacLeod: Dodge	Dodge	U	1.00
☐ Connor MacLeod: Extra Shot	Event	U	1.00
☐ Connor MacLeod: Power Blow	Event	U	1.00
[4]			
☐ Counterfeit: Abduction	Plot	C	0.35
☐ Counterfeit: Betrayal	Plot	C	0.35
☐ Counterfeit: Plastic Surgery	Plot	C	0.35
☐ Darius	Event	R	30.00
☐ Darkness: Lights Out	Plot	C	0.35
☐ Darkness: The Bait	Plot	C	0.35
☐ Darkness: The Trap	Plot	C	0.35
☐ Duncan MacLeod	Persona	R	15.00
☐ Duncan MacLeod: Back Away	Dodge	U	1.00
[5]			
☐ Duncan MacLeod: Battle Rage	Event	R	6.00
☐ Duncan MacLeod: Combination	Event	U	1.00
☐ Duncan MacLeod: Continuity	Situation	U	1.00
☐ Duncan MacLeod: Disarm	Event	U	1.00
☐ Duncan MacLeod: Dodge	Dodge	U	1.00
☐ Duncan MacLeod: Extra Shot	Event	U	1.00
☐ Duncan MacLeod: Flashback	Situation	U	1.00
☐ Duncan MacLeod: Inspiration	Event	R	6.00
☐ Duncan MacLeod: Jump	Dodge	U	1.00
[6]			
☐ Duncan MacLeod: Master's Advice	Situation	R	6.00
☐ Duncan MacLeod: Master's Attack	Attack	R	10.00
☐ Duncan MacLeod: Master's Dodge	Dodge	R	10.00
☐ Duncan MacLeod: Power Blow	Event	U	1.00
☐ Duncan MacLeod: Trip	Event	U	1.00
☐ Elizabeth Vaughn	Event	C	0.35
☐ Extra Weapon	Object	C	0.35
☐ Feint	Event	C	0.35

Card name	Type	Rarity	Price
[7]			
☐ Fortune Teller	Event	R	3.00
☐ Gypsy	Event	C	0.35
☐ Gypsy Lover	Situation	C	0.35
☐ Head Shot	Event	C	0.35
☐ Heroic Deed	Event	R	4.00
☐ Holy Ground (4 Card)	Event	C	0.35
☐ Holy Ground (Forfeit)	Event	C	0.35
☐ Interference	Event	C	0.35
☐ Investigation	Event	C	0.35
☐ Left Guard	Block	C	0.35
[8]			
☐ Linda Plager	Event	R	4.00
☐ Lower Center Attack	Attack	C	0.35
☐ Lower Center Block	Block	C	0.35
☐ Lower Left Attack	Attack	C	0.35
☐ Lower Left Block	Block	C	0.35
☐ Lower Right Attack	Attack	C	0.35
☐ Lower Right Block	Block	C	0.35
☐ Luther	Persona	R	10.00
☐ Luther: Back Away	Dodge	U	1.00
[9]			
☐ Luther: Combination	Event	U	1.00
☐ Luther: Continuity	Situation	U	1.00
☐ Luther: Disappear	Event	R	5.00
☐ Luther: Disarm	Event	U	1.00
☐ Luther: Dodge	Dodge	U	1.00
☐ Luther: Intimidate	Event	R	5.00
☐ Luther: Power Blow	Event	U	1.00
☐ Luther: Taunt	Event	R	5.00
☐ Luther: Trip	Event	U	1.00
[10]			
☐ Master	Situation	R	3.00
☐ Maurice	Event	R	4.00

RARITY KEY C = Common **U** = Uncommon **R** = Rare **VR** = Very Rare **UR** = Ultra Rare **F** = Foil card **X** = Fixed/standard in all decks

Card name	Type	Rarity	Price
☐ Middle Left Attack	Attack	C	0.35
☐ Middle Right Attack	Attack	C	0.35
☐ Misfortune	Event	C	0.35
☐ Mugging	Event	C	0.35
☐ Narrow Escape	Event	C	0.35
☐ Nefertiri	Persona	R	10.00
☐ Nefertiri: Back Away	Dodge	U	1.00
11			
☐ Nefertiri: Battle Rage	Event	U	1.00
☐ Nefertiri: Combination	Event	U	1.00
☐ Nefertiri: Continuity	Situation	U	1.00
☐ Nefertiri: Desperation	Event	R	5.00
☐ Nefertiri: Disarm	Event	U	1.00
☐ Nefertiri: Dodge	Dodge	U	1.00
☐ Nefertiri: Extra Shot	Event	U	1.00
☐ Nefertiri: Power Blow	Event	U	1.00
☐ Nefertiri: Seduce	Event	R	5.00
12			
☐ Nefertiri: Trip	Event	U	1.00
☐ Pedestrian (No Attacks)	Situation	C	0.35
☐ Pedestrian (Ped-5)	Situation	C	0.35
☐ Police (Prevent Damage)	Event	C	0.35
☐ Police (Remove Situation)	Event	C	0.35
☐ Quality Blade	Object	C	0.35
☐ Recover Weapon	Event	C	0.35
☐ Renee Delaney	Event	R	4.00
☐ Reporter	Event	C	0.35
13			
☐ Richie Ryan	Persona	R	10.00
☐ Richie Ryan: Back Away	Dodge	U	1.00

Card name	Type	Rarity	Price
☐ Richie Ryan: Battle Rage	Event	R	5.00
☐ Richie Ryan: Combination	Event	U	1.00
☐ Richie Ryan: Continuity	Situation	U	1.00
☐ Richie Ryan: Dodge	Dodge	U	1.00
☐ Richie Ryan: Extra Shot	Event	U	1.00
☐ Richie Ryan: Luck	Event	R	5.00
☐ Richie Ryan: Master's Advice	Situation	R	5.00
14			
☐ Richie Ryan: Master's Trick	Block	R	6.00
☐ Richie Ryan: Power Blow	Event	U	1.00
☐ Richie Ryan: Trip	Event	U	1.00
☐ Right Guard	Block	C	0.35
☐ Scorn	Situation	R	4.00
☐ Sea Witch: Hook	Plot	C	0.35
☐ Sea Witch: Line	Plot	C	0.35
☐ Sea Witch: Sinker	Plot	C	0.35
☐ Segur	Event	R	3.00
15			
☐ Slan Quince	Persona	R	10.00
☐ Slan Quince: Back Away	Dodge	U	1.00
☐ Slan Quince: Berserk	Event	R	6.00
☐ Slan Quince: Intimidate	Event	R	6.00
☐ Slan Quince: Run Through	Event	R	7.00
☐ Slan Quince: Shooting Blade	Attack	R	5.00
☐ Stamina	Event	C	0.35
☐ Street Punk	Event	U	1.00
☐ Tessa	Situation	R	3.00
16			
☐ Thrust	Attack	C	0.35
☐ Underworld Contact	Event	R	4.00
☐ Unexpected Assistance	Event	R	3.00

Card name	Type	Rarity	Price
☐ Unholy Alliance: Alliance	Plot	C	0.35
☐ Unholy Alliance: Ambush	Plot	C	0.35
☐ Unholy Alliance: Discovery	Plot	C	0.35
☐ Upper Center Attack	Attack	C	0.35
☐ Upper Center Block	Block	C	0.35
☐ Upper Left Attack	Attack	C	0.35
17			
☐ Upper Left Block	Block	C	0.35
☐ Upper Right Attack	Attack	C	0.35
☐ Upper Right Block	Block	C	0.35
☐ Watcher (Counter)	Situation	R	4.00
☐ Watcher (Fair Fight)	Situation	C	0.35
☐ Watcher (Treatment)	Event	U	1.00
☐ Watcher: Hunter (2 Damage)	Event	C	0.35
☐ Watcher: Hunter (Discard Dodge)	Event	C	0.35
☐ Watcher: Hunter (Sniper)	Event	R	3.00
18			
☐ Xavier St. Cloud	Persona	R	10.00
☐ Xavier St. Cloud: Alliance	Event	R	5.00
☐ Xavier St. Cloud: Back Away	Dodge	U	1.00
☐ Xavier St. Cloud: Disarm	Event	U	1.00
☐ Xavier St. Cloud: Dodge	Dodge	U	1.00
☐ Xavier St. Cloud: Forethought	Situation	R	5.00
☐ Xavier St. Cloud: Hook	Event	U	1.00
☐ Xavier St. Cloud: Plan Ahead	Situation	R	5.00
☐ Xavier St. Cloud: Poison Gas	Situation	R	5.00
19			
☐ Xavier St. Cloud: Power Blow	Event	U	1.00
☐ Xavier St. Cloud: Stalk	Attack	R	5.00
☐ Xavier St. Cloud: Trip	Event	U	1.00

Highlander • Movie Edition

Thunder Castle Games • Released August 1996

302 cards in set • **IDENTIFIER: Cards © Davis-Panzer Productions**

- Starter decks contain 55 cards; starter displays contain 12 starters
- Booster packs contain 15 cards; booster displays contain 28 boosters

Movie Edition, surprisingly enough, focuses on the characters and events from the *Highlander* movies. This set provides a number of staple cards; the most difficult of these to find is **Focus**, which allows a player to cancel the effect of a situation. This was vital in avoiding some very unpleasant outcomes. It was allegedly an uncommon card, but from our experiences, this simply could not have been the case.

Aside from **Focus**, *Movie Edition* did little to shake up the **Highlander** CCG environment beyond providing a few more tournament-caliber cards.— ***Orren McKay***

SCRYE NOTES: *According to gamer legend, if you stare carefully at a stack of* **Highlander: Movie Edition** *cards while shuffling them, you will see a better movie than* **Highlander 2: The Quickening.** *We haven't wanted to try.*

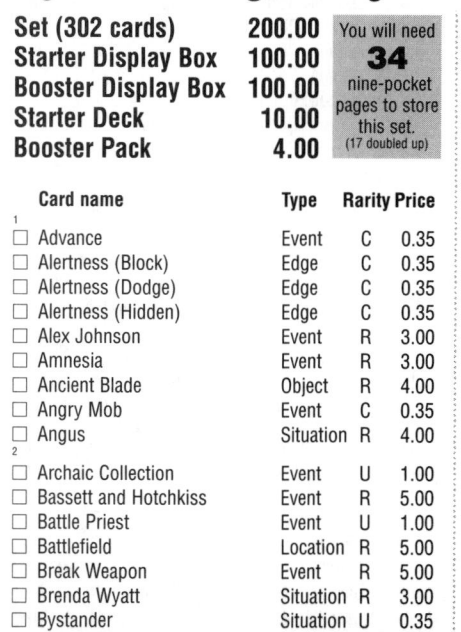

Kiss Your Butt Goodbye

EVENT
All players must discard all dodges in their hands. If a player does not discard any dodges, he takes 2 damage.
© Davis-Panzer Productions

	Price	You will need
Set (302 cards)	200.00	**34** nine-pocket pages to store this set. (17 doubled up)
Starter Display Box	100.00	
Booster Display Box	100.00	
Starter Deck	10.00	
Booster Pack	4.00	

Card name	Type	Rarity	Price
1			
☐ Advance	Event	C	0.35
☐ Alertness (Block)	Edge	C	0.35
☐ Alertness (Dodge)	Edge	C	0.35
☐ Alertness (Hidden)	Edge	C	0.35
☐ Alex Johnson	Event	R	3.00
☐ Amnesia	Event	R	3.00
☐ Ancient Blade	Object	R	4.00
☐ Angry Mob	Event	C	0.35
☐ Angus	Situation	R	4.00
2			
☐ Archaic Collection	Event	U	1.00
☐ Bassett and Hotchkiss	Event	R	5.00
☐ Battle Priest	Event	U	1.00
☐ Battlefield	Location	R	5.00
☐ Break Weapon	Event	R	5.00
☐ Brenda Wyatt	Situation	R	3.00
☐ Bystander	Situation	U	0.35

Card name	Type	Rarity	Price
☐ Bystander	Event	C	1.00
☐ Candy	Event	R	6.00
3			
☐ Careful Planning	Edge	C	0.35
☐ Cat and Mouse (Attack)	Situation	U	1.00
☐ Cat and Mouse (Defense)	Situation	U	1.00
☐ Cat and Mouse (Endurance)	Situation	U	1.00
☐ Catwalk	Location	R	4.00
☐ Caught in the Act	Event	U	1.00
☐ Cave-In	Event	U	1.00
☐ Challenge	Event	C	0.35
☐ Collapse	Event	U	1.00
4			
☐ Connor MacLeod	Pregame	UR	30.00
☐ Connor MacLeod	Persona	R	15.00
☐ Connor MacLeod: Back Away	Dodge	U	1.00
☐ Connor MacLeod: Battle Rage	Event	R	6.00
☐ Connor MacLeod: Combination	Event	U	1.00
☐ Connor MacLeod: Continuity	Situation	U	1.00
☐ Connor MacLeod: Dodge	Dodge	U	1.00
☐ Connor MacLeod: Duck	Dodge	U	1.00
☐ Connor MacLeod: Extra Shot	Event	U	1.00
5			
☐ Connor MacLeod: Flashback	Event	R	6.00
☐ Connor MacLeod: Master's Advice	Situation	R	6.00

Card name	Type	Rarity	Price
☐ Connor MacLeod: Master's Attack	Attack	R	10.00
☐ Connor MacLeod: Master's Block	Block	R	10.00
☐ Connor MacLeod: Master's Disarm	Event	R	10.00
☐ Connor MacLeod: Master's Dodge	Dodge	R	10.00
☐ Connor MacLeod: Master's Lunge	Attack	R	10.00
☐ Connor MacLeod: Power Blow	Event	U	1.00
☐ Connor MacLeod: Slash (LL to UR)	Attack	R	4.00
6			
☐ Connor MacLeod: Slash (UL to LR)	Attack	R	4.00
☐ Connor MacLeod: Trip	Event	U	1.00
☐ Courage (Attack)	Edge	U	1.00
☐ Courage (Defense)	Edge	U	1.00
☐ Cursed	Situation	C	0.35
☐ Dangerous Ground	Event	U	1.00
☐ David Blake	Event	R	3.00
☐ Dead End Alley	Location	R	4.00
☐ Desert	Location	R	5.00
7			
☐ Destruction: Defeat	Situation	U	1.00
☐ Destruction: Duel	Situation	U	1.00
☐ Destruction: Tonight You Sleep In Hell!	Event	U	1.00
☐ Dirty Trick: Kick	Attack	C	0.35
☐ Dirty Trick: Pummel	Attack	C	0.35
☐ Dirty Trick: Shove	Attack	C	0.35

RARITY KEY	C = Common	U = Uncommon	R = Rare	VR = Very Rare	UR = Ultra Rare	F = Foil card	X = Fixed/standard in all decks

Card name	Type	Rarity	Price
☐ Disarm	Event	U	1.00
☐ Discard Weapon	Event	U	1.00
☐ Disgruntled Mortal	Event	R	4.00
☐ Distraction	Event	C	0.35
☐ Dr. Alan Neyman	Event	R	4.00
☐ Dr. Sonny Jackson	Event	R	3.00
☐ Dugal MacLeod	Situation	R	5.00
☐ Dust Cloud	Event	U	1.00
☐ Excessive Force	Edge	U	1.00
☐ Explosion	Event	U	1.00
☐ Extra Weapon	Object	C	0.35
☐ Factory	Location	R	4.00
☐ Feint (Hidden)	Edge	U	1.00
☐ Feint (Retrieve Attack)	Event	C	0.35
☐ Focus	Edge	U	1.00
☐ Focused Block (UC)	Block	C	0.35
☐ Focused Block (UL)	Block	C	0.35
☐ Focused Block (UR)	Block	C	0.35
☐ Garfield	Situation	R	4.00
☐ General Katana	Pregame	UR	25.00
☐ General Katana	Persona	R	10.00
☐ General Katana: Back Away	Dodge	U	1.00
☐ General Katana: Combination	Event	U	1.00
☐ General Katana: Do It Yourself	Event	R	5.00
☐ General Katana: Dodge	Dodge	U	1.00
☐ General Katana: Extra Shot	Event	U	1.00
☐ General Katana: Intimidate	Event	R	5.00
☐ General Katana: Master's Attack	Attack	R	7.00
☐ General Katana: Master's Block	Block	R	7.00
☐ General Katana: Power Blow	Event	U	1.00
☐ General Katana: Run-Away Train	Event	R	5.00
☐ General Katana: Taunt	Event	R	5.00
☐ General Katana: Toadies	Event	R	5.00
☐ General Katana: Trip	Event	U	1.00
☐ Generic Immortal	Persona	U	1.00
☐ Get Away From It All	Event	C	0.35
☐ Head Hunter: Arrest	Event	U	1.00
☐ Head Hunter: Clues	Situation	U	1.00
☐ Head Hunter: Research	Situation	U	1.00
☐ Head Shot	Event	C	0.35
☐ Heather	Situation	R	3.00
☐ Hidden Shrine	Event	U	1.00
☐ Higher Ground	Situation	C	0.35
☐ Holy Ground	Event	C	0.35
☐ Holy Ground	Location	C	0.35
☐ Honed Weapon	Event	R	3.00
☐ Honor Bound	Situation	U	1.00
☐ Improvised Weapon	Attack	U	1.00
☐ Improvised Weapon	Object	R	5.00
☐ Incompetence	Event	U	1.00
☐ Influence	Event	C	0.35
☐ Interference	Event	C	0.35
☐ Investigation	Event	C	0.35
☐ Iron Will	Edge	C	0.35
☐ Jack Donovan	Situation	R	3.00
☐ John MacLeod	Event	R	3.00
☐ Joy Ride: Dead End	Event	U	1.00
☐ Joy Ride: Speed	Situation	U	1.00
☐ Joy Ride: Take the Wheel	Situation	U	1.00
☐ Kate	Event	U	1.00
☐ Khabul Khan	Pregame	UR	25.00
☐ Khabul Khan	Persona	R	10.00
☐ Khan: Armor (Breastplate)	Object	R	5.00
☐ Khan: Armor (Greaves)	Object	R	5.00
☐ Khan: Armor (Helmet)	Object	R	5.00
☐ Khan: Back Away	Dodge	U	1.00
☐ Khan: Battle Rage	Event	R	8.00
☐ Khan: Combination	Event	U	1.00
☐ Khan: Continuity	Situation	U	1.00

Card name	Type	Rarity	Price
☐ Khan: Dodge	Dodge	U	1.00
☐ Khan: Extra Shot	Event	U	1.00
☐ Khan: Flashback	Event	R	5.00
☐ Khan: Power Blow	Event	U	1.00
☐ Khan: Trip	Event	U	1.00
☐ Kirk Matunas	Event	R	3.00
☐ Kiss Your Butt Goodbye	Event	R	4.00
☐ Lean and Mean	Edge	U	1.00
☐ Left Guard	Block	C	0.35
☐ Lost Love	Event	R	3.00
☐ Louise Marcus	Situation	R	4.00
☐ Lower Center Attack 1	Attack	X	0.35
☐ Lower Center Attack 2	Attack	X	0.35
☐ Lower Center Attack 3	Attack	X	0.35
☐ Lower Center Block 1	Block	X	0.35
☐ Lower Center Block 2	Block	X	0.35
☐ Lower Center Block 3	Block	X	0.35
☐ Lower Guard	Block	C	0.35
☐ Lower Left Attack 1	Attack	X	0.35
☐ Lower Left Attack 2	Attack	X	0.35
☐ Lower Left Attack 3	Attack	X	0.35
☐ Lower Left Block 1	Block	X	0.35
☐ Lower Left Block 2	Block	X	0.35
☐ Lower Left Block 3	Block	X	0.35
☐ Lower Right Attack 1	Attack	X	0.35
☐ Lower Right Attack 2	Attack	X	0.35
☐ Lower Right Attack 3	Attack	X	0.35
☐ Lower Right Block 1	Block	X	0.35
☐ Lower Right Block 2	Block	X	0.35
☐ Lower Right Block 3	Block	X	0.35
☐ Lt. Frank Moran	Event	R	3.00
☐ Master's Advance	Situation	R	8.00
☐ Master's Domain	Event	R	7.00
☐ Master's Endurance	Situation	R	3.00
☐ Master's Stance	Situation	R	3.00
☐ Master's Stratagem	Situation	R	3.00
☐ Middle Left Attack 1	Attack	X	0.35
☐ Middle Left Attack 2	Attack	X	0.35
☐ Middle Left Attack 3	Attack	X	0.35
☐ Middle Right Attack 1	Attack	X	0.35
☐ Middle Right Attack 2	Attack	X	0.35
☐ Middle Right Attack 3	Attack	X	0.35
☐ Mishap	Event	U	1.00
☐ Mountain Cave	Location	R	6.00
☐ Nakano	Pregame	UR	25.00
☐ Nakano	Persona	R	10.00
☐ Nakano: Back Away	Dodge	U	1.00
☐ Nakano: Combination	Event	U	1.00
☐ Nakano: Continuity	Situation	U	1.00
☐ Nakano: Dodge	Dodge	U	1.00
☐ Nakano: Duck	Dodge	U	1.00
☐ Nakano: Flashback	Event	R	5.00
☐ Nakano: Master's Disarm	Event	R	5.00
☐ Nakano: Master's Maneuver	Situation	R	5.00
☐ Nakano: Mirror Image	Situation	R	5.00
☐ Nakano: Power Blow	Event	U	1.00
☐ Nakano: Shadow of the Mind	Situation	R	5.00
☐ Nakano: Swords to Snakes	Situation	R	5.00
☐ Nakano: Trip	Event	U	1.00
☐ Narrow Escape	Event	U	1.00
☐ Nemesis: Fade Away	Situation	U	1.00
☐ Nemesis: Fatigue	Situation	U	1.00
☐ Nemesis: Mistrust	Situation	U	1.00
☐ Nemesis: Psychosis	Situation	U	1.00
☐ Nemesis: Self-Betrayal	Situation	U	1.00
☐ Nemesis: Subdued	Situation	U	1.00
☐ Parking Garage	Location	R	4.00
☐ Parry (Left Side)	Block	C	0.35
☐ Parry (Right Side)	Block	C	0.35
☐ Parrying Blade	Object	R	4.00

Card name	Type	Rarity	Price
☐ Patience	Edge	U	1.00
☐ Pedestrian (Hidden)	Situation	C	0.35
☐ Pedestrian (No Attacks)	Situation	C	0.35
☐ Pierre Bouchet	Event	R	4.00
☐ Pistol (LC)	Attack	R	4.00
☐ Pistol (MC)	Attack	R	4.00
☐ Pistol (UC)	Attack	R	4.00
☐ Police (Prevent Damage)	Event	C	0.35
☐ Police (Remove Situation)	Event	C	0.35
☐ "Practice, Practice, Practice"	Edge	C	0.35
☐ Psyche	Event	R	4.00
☐ Quality Blade	Object	X	0.35
☐ Rachel Ellenstein	Situation	R	3.00
☐ Reconnaissance	Edge	U	1.00
☐ Recover Weapon	Event	C	0.35
☐ Right Guard	Block	C	0.35
☐ Riposte (MC)	Attack	C	0.35
☐ Riposte (UC)	Attack	C	0.35
☐ Riposte (UL)	Attack	C	0.35
☐ Riposte (UR)	Attack	C	0.35
☐ Rooftop	Location	R	3.00
☐ Ruins	Location	R	6.00
☐ Rush	Event	U	1.00
☐ Sacrifice	Situation	R	4.00
☐ Schemer	Edge	R	4.00
☐ Scorn	Situation	R	3.00
☐ Second Wind	Event	R	3.00
☐ Selective Memory	Edge	U	1.00
☐ Simple Mind	Situation	R	4.00
☐ Skylight	Event	U	1.00
☐ Slash (Horizontal)	Attack	U	1.00
☐ Slash (Vertical)	Attack	U	1.00
☐ Slippery Footing	Event	U	1.00
☐ Spinning Attack (ML)	Attack	C	0.35
☐ Spinning Attack (MR)	Attack	C	0.35
☐ Spinning Attack (UL)	Attack	C	0.35
☐ Spinning Attack (UR)	Attack	C	0.35
☐ Stamina	Event	C	0.35
☐ Street Punk	Event	U	1.00
☐ Stumble	Event	C	0.35
☐ Stunning Blow (UC)	Attack	U	1.00
☐ Stunning Blow (UL)	Attack	U	1.00
☐ Stunning Blow (UR)	Attack	U	1.00
☐ Sunda Kastagir	Pregame	UR	25.00
☐ Sunda Kastagir	Persona	R	10.00
☐ Sunda Kastagir: Back Away	Dodge	U	1.00
☐ Sunda Kastagir: Boom Boom	Event	R	5.00
☐ Sunda Kastagir: Charm	Event	R	5.00
☐ Sunda Kastagir: Combination	Event	U	1.00
☐ Sunda Kastagir: Continuity	Situation	U	1.00
☐ Sunda Kastagir: Dodge	Dodge	U	1.00
☐ Sunda Kastagir: Extra Shot	Event	U	1.00
☐ Sunda Kastagir: Flashback	Event	R	5.00
☐ Sunda Kastagir: Master's Attack	Attack	R	8.00
☐ Sunda Kastagir: Master's Guard	Block	R	8.00
☐ Sunda Kastagir: Power Blow	Event	U	1.00
☐ Sunda Kastagir: Trip	Event	U	1.00
☐ The Kurgan	Pregame	UR	30.00
☐ The Kurgan	Persona	R	20.00
☐ The Kurgan: Back Away	Dodge	U	1.00
☐ The Kurgan: Bloodlust	Event	R	10.00
☐ The Kurgan: Combination	Event	U	1.00
☐ The Kurgan: Continuity	Situation	U	1.00
☐ The Kurgan: Disguise	Situation	R	8.00
☐ The Kurgan: Extra Shot	Event	U	1.00
☐ The Kurgan: Flashback	Event	R	5.00
☐ The Kurgan: Follow-Up	Event	R	5.00
☐ The Kurgan: Hammer Blow	Event	R	6.00
☐ The Kurgan: Master's Disarm	Event	R	8.00
☐ The Kurgan: Power Blow	Event	U	1.00

RARITY KEY C = Common U = Uncommon R = Rare VR = Very Rare UR = Ultra Rare F = Foil card X = Fixed/standard in all decks

Card name	Type	Rarity	Price
☐ The Kurgan: Run Through	Event	R	8.00
☐ The Kurgan: Scare	Event	R	5.00
☐ The Kurgan: Taunt	Event	R	4.00
☐ The Kurgan: Trip	Event	U	1.00
☐ Thief	Event	C	0.35
☐ Thrust 1	Attack	X	0.35
☐ Thrust 2	Attack	X	0.35
☐ Thrust 3	Attack	X	0.35
☐ Tight Squeeze	Situation	U	1.00
☐ TSC Troopers	Event	U	1.00
☐ Twist of Fate	Event	U	1.00

Card name	Type	Rarity	Price
☐ Unexpected Assistance	Event	R	5.00
☐ Upper Center Attack 1	Attack	X	0.35
☐ Upper Center Attack 2	Attack	X	0.35
☐ Upper Center Attack 3	Attack	X	0.35
☐ Upper Center Block 1	Block	X	0.35
☐ Upper Center Block 2	Block	X	0.35
☐ Upper Center Block 3	Block	X	0.35
☐ Upper Guard	Block	C	0.35
☐ Upper Hand	Event	R	4.00
☐ Upper Left Attack 1	Attack	X	0.35
☐ Upper Left Attack 2	Attack	X	0.35

Card name	Type	Rarity	Price
☐ Upper Left Attack 3	Attack	X	0.35
☐ Upper Left Block 1	Block	X	0.35
☐ Upper Left Block 2	Block	X	0.35
☐ Upper Left Block 3	Block	X	0.35
☐ Upper Right Attack 1	Attack	X	0.35
☐ Upper Right Attack 2	Attack	X	0.35
☐ Upper Right Attack 3	Attack	X	0.35
☐ Upper Right Block 1	Block	X	0.35
☐ Upper Right Block 2	Block	X	0.35
☐ Upper Right Block 3	Block	X	0.35
☐ Weapon Bind	Edge	U	1.00

Highlander • *Watcher's Chronicle*

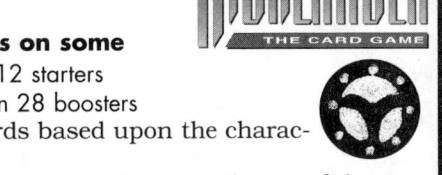

Thunder Castle Games • Released **February 1998**

113 cards in set • **IDENTIFIER:** © Gaumont; symbols on some

- Starter decks contain 52 cards; starter displays contain 12 starters
- Booster packs contain 15 cards; booster displays contain 28 boosters

   The Watcher's Chronicle adds more persona cards based upon the characters from the *Highlander* TV series.

   The most sought-after card from this set was the pre-game **Darius**, easily one of the most expensive and hardest to find cards in *Highlander*. It was not uncommon for it to sell for more than $100. This set also had +1 ability cards for its personas and the personas from *Series Edition*. — *Orren McKay*

Set (113 cards)	150.00
Booster Display Box	75.00
Booster Pack	3.00

You will need 13 nine-pocket pages to store this set. (7 doubled up)

Card name	Type	Rarity	Price
☐ Advance Warning	Situation	C	0.30
☐ Amanda	Pregame	UR	20.00
☐ Amanda: Acrobat	Edge	R	5.00
☐ Amanda: Master Thief	Edge	R	3.80
☐ Annie Devlin	Persona	R	8.00
☐ Annie Devlin	Pregame	UR	10.75
☐ Annie Devlin: Back Away	Dodge	U	6.80
☐ Annie Devlin: Battle Rage	Event	R	3.80
☐ Annie Devlin: Combination	Event	R	5.00
☐ Annie Devlin: Continuity	Situation	U	0.90
☐ Annie Devlin: Duck	Dodge	U	1.80
☐ Annie Devlin: Escape	Situation	R	3.80
☐ Annie Devlin: Evade (Left)	Dodge	U	0.60
☐ Annie Devlin: Evade (Right)	Dodge	U	1.00
☐ Annie Devlin: Extra Shot	Event	U	1.00
☐ Annie Devlin: Flashback	Situation	R	3.80
☐ Annie Devlin: Master's Attack	Attack	R	3.80
☐ Annie Devlin: Run Through	Event	R	3.80
☐ Annie Devlin: Trip	Event	U	1.00
☐ Cat and Mouse (Attack)	Plot	C	0.30
☐ Cat and Mouse (Draw)	Plot	C	1.40
☐ Circular Parry (LL)	Block	U	0.60
☐ Circular Parry (LR)	Block	U	0.90
☐ Circular Parry (UL)	Block	U	0.90
☐ Circular Parry (UR)	Block	U	1.80
☐ Code Red	Event	C	0.30
☐ Connor MacLeod	Pregame	UR	30.00
☐ Darius	Pregame	UR	30.00
☐ Dojo	Situation	C	0.30
☐ Donna Ondrejka	Event	R	3.00
☐ Dr. Anne Lindsay	Situation	C	0.70
☐ Duncan MacLeod	Pregame	UR	30.00
☐ Duncan MacLeod: Duck	Dodge	R	5.00
☐ Duncan MacLeod: Master's Block	Block	R	8.00
☐ Duncan MacLeod: Slash (UL-LR)	Attack	R	6.00

Card name	Type	Rarity	Price
☐ Duncan MacLeod: Slash (UR-LL)	Attack	R	6.00
☐ Flashing Blade	Edge	C	0.30
☐ Flurry Strike (MC)	Attack	C	0.30
☐ Flurry Strike (ML)	Attack	C	0.30
☐ Flurry Strike (MR)	Attack	C	0.70
☐ Hideo Koto	Situation	C	0.30
☐ Hugh Fitzcairn	Persona	R	6.30
☐ Hugh Fitzcairn	Pregame	UR	10.25
☐ Hugh Fitzcairn: Back Away	Dodge	U	1.00
☐ Hugh Fitzcairn: Charm	Event	R	5.00
☐ Hugh Fitzcairn: Combination	Event	U	1.00
☐ Hugh Fitzcairn: Continuity	Situation	U	1.00
☐ Hugh Fitzcairn: Evade (Left)	Dodge	U	1.00
☐ Hugh Fitzcairn: Evade (Right)	Dodge	U	1.00
☐ Hugh Fitzcairn: Fast Talk	Event	R	3.80
☐ Hugh Fitzcairn: Flashback	Situation	R	3.80
☐ Hugh Fitzcairn: Master's Block	Block	R	4.80
☐ Hugh Fitzcairn: Seduce	Event	R	6.00
☐ Hugh Fitzcairn: Trip	Event	U	1.00
☐ Immortal Wound	Situation	C	0.30
☐ Impressive Move	Event	C	0.30
☐ James Horton	Situation	C	0.30
☐ James Horton	Pregame	R	7.00
☐ Joe Dawson	Situation	C	3.20
☐ Joe Dawson	Pregame	R	4.10
☐ Kalas	Persona	R	8.00
☐ Kalas	Pregame	UR	10.50
☐ Kalas: Back Away	Dodge	U	1.00
☐ Kalas: Combination	Event	U	0.90
☐ Kalas: Continuity	Situation	U	1.80
☐ Kalas: Extra Shot	Event	U	0.60
☐ Kalas: Flashback	Event	R	3.80
☐ Kalas: Forgery	Event	R	5.00
☐ Kalas: Intimidate	Event	R	3.80
☐ Kalas: Master's Advice	Situation	R	3.80
☐ Kalas: Power Blow	Event	U	0.60
☐ Kalas: Song of the Executioner (Jealousy)	Plot	U	1.80
☐ Kalas: Song of the Executioner (Malice)	Plot	U	1.80
☐ Kalas: Song of the Executioner (Protege)	Plot	U	0.60

Card name	Type	Rarity	Price
☐ Kalas: Stalk	SpAttack	R	3.80
☐ Kalas: Trip	Event	U	1.00
☐ Kern	Persona	R	8.00
☐ Kern	Pregame	UR	11.25
☐ Kern: Back Away	Dodge	U	1.80
☐ Kern: Bowie Knife	Object	R	3.80
☐ Kern: Flashback	Event	R	3.00
☐ Kern: Hogg	Object	R	5.00
☐ Kern: Power Blow	Event	U	0.60
☐ Kern: Rage	Event	R	3.80
☐ Kern: Trip	Event	U	1.00
☐ Lighthouse	Location	R	3.30
☐ Lunge	Edge	U	1.00
☐ Luther	Pregame	UR	20.00
☐ Luther: Endure Pain	Edge	R	3.80
☐ Master Swordsman	Att/Def		8.00
☐ Nefertiri	Pregame	UR	20.00
☐ Nefertiri: Temptress	Event	R	3.80
☐ Nefertiri: Vengeance	Event	R	3.80
☐ Nemesis: Compromise	Situation	C	0.35
☐ Nemesis: Falsetto	Situation	U	1.00
☐ Nemesis: Fooled Again	Situation	C	0.35
☐ Nemesis: Overbearing	Situation	U	1.00
☐ Plot Twist	Edge	U	0.60
☐ Richie Ryan	Pregame	UR	20.00
☐ Richie Ryan: Quick Learner	Event	R	3.80
☐ Signorina Arianna	Situation	C	0.30
☐ Slan Quince	Pregame	UR	20.00
☐ Slan Quince: The Cat	Situation	R	5.00
☐ Watcher Database	Object	C	0.30
☐ Watcher Involvement	Situation	R	2.80
☐ Watcher Regional HQ	Location	R	3.30
☐ Watcher Revealed	Edge	C	0.30
☐ Watcher Tribunal	Event	C	0.30
☐ Watcher's Chronicle	Object	R	2.40
☐ Watcher's Oath	Situation	R	2.80
☐ Watcher: Agents Threatened	Event	C	0.30
☐ Xavier St. Cloud	Pregame	UR	20.00
☐ Xavier St. Cloud: Hidden Explosives	Event	R	5.00

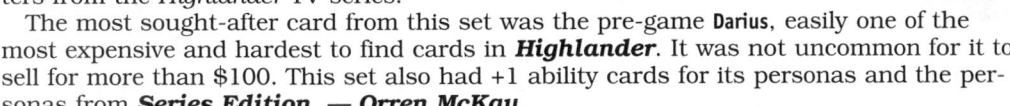

RARITY KEY **C** = Common **U** = Uncommon **R** = Rare **VR** = Very Rare **UR** = Ultra Rare **F** = Foil card **X** = Fixed/standard in all decks

Highlander • The Gathering

Thunder Castle Games • Released **June 1998**

110 cards in set • **IDENTIFIER:** © Davis/Panzer Productions

- Starter decks contain 55 cards; starter displays contain 12 starters
- Booster packs contain 15 cards; booster displays contain 28 boosters

The Gathering (where have we heard that name on a CCG before?) is an unexciting **Highlander** set, recycling **Movie Edition** cards and adding a few new personas, some new cards for previous sets' personas, and a few cards to fix some overpowered deck strategies.

The only truly interesting trait of this set is that it adds two Ramirez (the character in the Highlander movies played by Sean Connery) premium cards to the game. Unfortunately, since these cards were Ramirez-specific and there was no Ramirez persona, the only persona able to use them was Richie Ryan, due to his ability to use one card from other Immortals. — *Orren McKay*

Set (110 cards)	100.00	
Starter Display Box	80.00	
Booster Display Box	65.00	
Starter Deck	10.00	
Booster Pack	3.00	

You will need **13** *nine-pocket pages to store this set. (7 doubled up)*

Card name	Type	Rarity	Price
Asgard	Situation	C	0.35
Bait and Switch	Edge	C	0.35
Brawler	Edge	U	1.00
Breakout	Event	U	1.00
Clan Priest	Event	R	4.00
Conjure	Event	C	0.35
Connor MacLeod (Master)	Pregame	UR	30.00
Connor MacLeod: Solitude	Situation	R	5.00
Connor MacLeod: Spirit of the Stag	Situation	R	5.00
Corda and Reno	Persona	R	10.00
Corda and Reno (Master)	Pregame	UR	25.00
Corda and Reno: Back Away	Dodge	U	1.00
Corda and Reno: Casual Killer	Situation	R	3.00
Corda and Reno: Death From Above	Event	R	3.00
Corda and Reno: Flying Machine (Hover Board)	Object	R	5.00
Corda and Reno: Flying Machine (Wings)	Object	R	5.00
Corda and Reno: Grapple	Situation	R	3.00
Corda and Reno: Maniacal Laugh (May not attack)	Event	R	4.00
Corda and Reno: Maniacal Laugh (Must attack)	Event	R	4.00
Corda and Reno: Power Blow	Event	U	1.00
Corda and Reno: The Equalizer	Object	R	4.00
Cover (Left/Right)	Situation	C	0.35
Cover (Right/Left)	Situation	C	0.35
Desecration	Event	U	1.00
Destruction	Event	U	1.00
Detective Walter Bedsoe	Edge	R	3.00
Discipline (Attack)	Edge	C	0.35
Discipline (Special)	Edge	C	0.35
"Do as I Say, Woman!"	Event	R	3.00
General Katana (Master)	Pregame	UR	25.00
Head Hunter	Event	U	1.00
Iman Fasil	Persona	R	10.00
Iman Fasil (+1 Ability)	Pregame	UR	25.00
Iman Fasil: Back Away	Dodge	U	1.00
Iman Fasil: Backflip	Dodge	R	5.00
Iman Fasil: Continuity	Situation	U	1.00
Iman Fasil: Duck	Dodge	U	1.00

Card name	Type	Rarity	Price
Iman Fasil: Fleche	Edge	R	4.00
Iman Fasil: Left Side Step	Dodge	U	1.00
Iman Fasil: Lunge	Attack	R	4.00
Iman Fasil: Master's Disarm	Event	R	8.00
Iman Fasil: Master's Lunge	Attack	R	8.00
Iman Fasil: Power Blow	Event	U	1.00
Iman Fasil: Ride Side Step	Dodge	U	1.00
Kane	Persona	R	10.00
Kane: Back Away	Dodge	U	1.00
Kane: Diviniation	Event	R	4.00
Kane: Ephemeral Wound	Event	R	4.00
Kane: Fury	Event	R	8.00
Kane: Open Mind	Event	R	4.00
Kane: Power Blow	Event	U	1.00
Kane: Shapeshift	Event	R	6.00
Kane: Taunt	Event	R	4.00
Kane: Teleport	Situation	R	6.00
Kane: Trip	Event	U	1.00
Kastagir (Master)	Pregame	UR	25.00
Kastagir: Blood Brothers	Edge	R	4.00
Kastagir: Master's Guard	Block	R	4.00
Khan (Master)	Pregame	UR	25.00
Khan: Armorer	Edge	R	4.00
Khan: Forged Armor	Object	R	4.00
Khan: Plunder	Situation	R	4.00
Kurgan: Master of the Hunt	Situation	R	4.00
Kurgan: Master's Head Shot	Attack	R	8.00
Kurgan: Skull Helmet	Object	R	8.00
Laundry Room	Location	R	3.00
Lean and Mean	Edge	C	0.35
Lt. John Stenn	Situation	R	3.00
MacLeod Bagpipes	Object	R	3.00
Master's Sanctuary	Situation	R	3.00
Memories (Edge)	Edge	C	0.35
Memories (Special)	Edge	C	0.35
Mental Ward	Location	R	3.00
Nakano: Weapon's Training	Situation	R	3.00
Nakano: You've Already Lost	Edge	R	3.00
Nemesis: Disillusioned - Kane	Situation	U	1.00

Card name	Type	Rarity	Price
Nemesis: Fit Of Depression - Iman Fasil	Situation	U	1.00
Nemesis: Grounded! - Corda and Reno	Situation	U	1.00
Nemesis: Surrender - Yung Dol Kim	Situation	U	1.00
Precinct	Edge	C	0.35
Ramirez: Experience Counts	Situation	UR	25.00
Ramirez: Master's Advantage	Situation	UR	25.00
Remembrance	Situation	R	3.00
Riposte (LC)	Attack	C	0.35
Riposte (LL)	Attack	C	0.35
Riposte (LR)	Attack	C	0.35
Riposte (ML)	Attack	C	0.35
Riposte (MR)	Attack	C	0.35
Security Guard (Object)	Situation	C	0.35
Security Guard (Situation)	Situation	C	0.35
Sheathe Weapon	Edge	C	0.35
Slash (Left)	Attack	C	0.35
Slash (Lower)	Attack	C	0.35
Slash (Right)	Attack	C	0.35
Slash (Upper)	Attack	C	0.35
Spiritual Center	Location	R	3.00
Steamed	Event	U	1.00
The Kurgan (Master)	Pregame	UR	30.00
The Sorceror Nakano (Master)	Pregame	UR	25.00
Trench Coat	Object	C	0.35
Yung Dol Kim	Persona	R	10.00
Yung Dol Kim (Master)	Pregame	UR	25.00
Yung Dol Kim: Back Away	Dodge	U	1.00
Yung Dol Kim: Continuity	Situation	U	1.00
Yung Dol Kim: Cutting Room Floor	Event	R	4.00
Yung Dol Kim: Frenzy	Situation	R	5.00
Yung Dol Kim: Master's Attack	Attack	R	8.00
Yung Dol Kim: Power Blow	Event	U	1.00
Yung Dol Kim: Run Away	Situation	R	4.00
Yung Dol Kim: Trip	Event	U	1.00

RARITY KEY   **C** = Common   **U** = Uncommon   **R** = Rare   **VR** = Very Rare   **UR** = Ultra Rare   **F** = Foil card   **X** = Fixed/standard in all decks

Highlander • *Arms & Tactics*

Thunder Castle Games • Released **November 1998**

219 cards in set • IDENTIFIER: © Gaumont; round symbols on bottom

- Starter decks contain 55 cards; starter displays contain 12 starters
- Booster packs contain 15 cards; booster displays contain 28 boosters

Arms and Tactics changed the face of *Highlander*, introducing the concept of weapons. Until *A&T*, everyone was simply assumed to use a generic sword. Now it became possible to use various types of swords, such as rapiers or katanas, or even a war axe or shield. These new weapons also have special abilities.

A&T also introduces crystals, which allow players to violate a basic rule of deck construction. Each *Highlander* deck is required to contain one of each of the nine basic attacks and six basic blocks, but players are allowed to replace one of these basic cards for each crystal they have.

Two popular new pre-game cards are added: **Remove 5** and **Break Glass**. **Remove 5** allows a player to remove five cards from his deck from the game. While this may seem foolish, it actually isn't. *Highlander* didn't allow for sideboarding in tournaments, and it was possible for one's hand to become locked with useless or unplayable cards. **Remove 5** allows potentially useless cards to be removed from one's deck after the strategy of your opponent became known. **Break Glass** is simply a low-powered rip. Still, the fact that it was usable once per game instead of once per tournament and not destroyed by use made it invaluable. — *Orren McKay*

You will need **25** nine-pocket pages to store this set. (13 doubled up)

Set (219 cards)	150.00
Starter Display Box	80.00
Booster Display Box	65.00
Starter Deck	10.00
Booster Pack	3.00

Card name	Rarity	Price
Alertness (Block)	U	1.00
Alertness (Dodge)	U	1.00
Alertness (Hidden)	U	11.00
Amanda: Femme Fatale	U	1.00
Amanda: Mistaken Identity	R	4.00
Annie Devlin: Eye for an Eye	U	1.00
Annie Devlin: Flashing Blade	R	3.00
Arms and Tactics (Break Glass)	UR	25.00
Arms and Tactics (Remove 5 Cards)	UR	25.00
Bad Luck (3 Card)	C	0.35
Bad Luck (Discard)	C	0.35
Big and Bad	U	1.00
Broad Bladed Spear	R	10.00
Broad Bladed Spear: Impale	R	5.00
Broad Bladed Spear: Quality Blade	U	1.00
Broad Bladed Spear: Spinning Block (Left)	C	0.35
Broad Bladed Spear: Spinning Block (Right)	C	0.35
Broad Bladed Spear: Spinning Block (Upper)	C	0.35
Ceirdwyn	R	10.00
Ceirdwyn	UR	25.00
Ceirdwyn: Alaine	U	1.00
Ceirdwyn: Back Away	U	1.00
Ceirdwyn: Battle Rage	U	1.00
Ceirdwyn: Callum	R	4.00
Ceirdwyn: Continuity	U	1.00
Ceirdwyn: Evade (Left)	C	0.35
Ceirdwyn: Evade (Right)	C	0.35
Ceirdwyn: Flashback	U	1.00
Ceirdwyn: Jakob	U	1.00
Ceirdwyn: Master's Attack	R	8.00
Ceirdwyn: Master's Dodge	R	4.00
Ceirdwyn: Myra	U	1.00
Ceirdwyn: Neva	R	4.00
Ceirdwyn: Power Blow	U	1.00

Card name	Rarity	Price
Ceirdwyn: Retribution	R	4.00
Ceirdwyn: Trip	U	1.00
Change of Fortune	C	0.35
Claymore	R	10.00
Claymore: Cleave (Center)	C	0.35
Claymore: Cleave (Middle)	C	0.35
Claymore: Hammer Blow	U	1.00
Claymore: Quality Blade	U	1.00
Claymore: Reach	R	5.00
Concentration	R	3.00
Concentration	R	3.00
Crystal #1	UR	25.00
Crystal #2	UR	25.00
Crystal #3	UR	25.00
Cull the Weak (1)	C	0.35
Cull the Weak (2)	C	0.35
Cull the Weak (3)	C	0.35
Defensive Stance	C	0.35
Diane Terrin	R	4.00
Dirty Trick (Choke)	R	8.00
Dirty Trick (Head Butt)	C	0.35
Dirty Trick (Tackle)	C	0.35
Disarm (Block)	C	0.35
Double Eagle	R	3.00
Dueling Grounds	R	3.00
Duelist (1)	C	0.35
Duelist (2)	C	0.35
Duelist (3)	C	0.35
Duncan MacLeod: Master of Disguise	U	1.00
Duncan MacLeod: T-Bird	U	1.00
Encumbered	U	1.00
Extra Weapon	C	0.35
Focus (Opponent's Turn)	R	4.00
Focus (Opponent's Turn)	U	1.00
Foresight	U	1.00
Generic Immortal (A&D)	R	8.00
Generic Immortal (Jr)	R	8.00
Generic Immortal (Res)	R	8.00
Generic Immortal (WoC)	R	8.00
Gladius	R	10.00
Gladius: Deflect (UL)	C	0.35
Gladius: Deflect (UR)	C	0.35
Gladius: Quality Blade	U	1.00
Gladius: Stab (ML)	U	1.00
Gladius: Stab (MR)	U	1.00

Card name	Rarity	Price
Gladius: Twist	R	5.00
Gypsy Camp	R	3.00
Gypsy's Curse	U	1.00
Head Shot	C	0.35
Holy Ground (Look)	C	0.35
Impulse	U	1.00
In Cold Blood	U	1.00
Iron Will (±1)	C	0.35
Joe's	R	4.00
Kalas: Insurance (3 Card)	R	5.00
Kalas: Insurance (You Discard)	R	5.00
Kalas: Master's Block	R	5.00
Kanis	R	10.00
Kanis	UR	25.00
Kanis: Back Away	U	1.00
Kanis: Evade (Left)	C	0.35
Kanis: Evade (Right)	C	0.35
Kanis: Flashback	U	1.00
Kanis: Hound (Cornwall)	R	5.00
Kanis: Hound (Hampton)	R	5.00
Kanis: Hound (Lancaster)	R	5.00
Kanis: Leader of the Pack	R	5.00
Kanis: Master of the Hunt	R	5.00
Kanis: Master's Maneuver	R	5.00
Kanis: Power Blow	U	1.00
Kanis: Purebreed	U	1.00
Kanwulf	R	10.00
Kanwulf	UR	25.00
Kanwulf: Back Away	U	1.00
Kanwulf: Battle Rage	R	5.00
Kanwulf: Combination	U	1.00
Kanwulf: Continuity	U	1.00
Kanwulf: Evade (Left)	C	0.35
Kanwulf: Evade (Right)	C	0.35
Kanwulf: Extra Shot	U	1.00
Kanwulf: Flashback	U	1.00
Kanwulf: Master's Advice	R	5.00
Kanwulf: Sacrifice	R	5.00
Kanwulf: Trip	U	1.00
Katana Sword	R	10.00
Katana Sword: Lightning Reflexes	R	5.00
Katana Sword: Lightning Strike (block)	U	1.00
Katana Sword: Lightning Strike (dodge)	U	1.00

Card name	Rarity	Price
Katana Sword: Quality Blade	U	1.00
Kern: Calm Before the Storm	R	3.00
Kern: Musket	R	3.00
Left Guard	C	0.35
Lower Guard	C	0.35
Luther: Incense of Pain	R	4.00
Luther: Master's Attack	R	8.00
Martin Hyde	R	10.00
Martin Hyde	UR	25.00
Martin Hyde: Back Away	U	1.00
Martin Hyde: Combination	U	1.00
Martin Hyde: Continuity	U	1.00
Martin Hyde: Evade (Left)	C	0.35
Martin Hyde: Evade (Right)	C	0.35
Martin Hyde: Extra shot	U	1.00
Martin Hyde: Hunter	U	1.00
Martin Hyde: Intimidate	R	4.00
Martin Hyde: Master's Block	R	5.00
Martin Hyde: Master's Trick	R	4.00
Martin Hyde: Stalk	R	4.00
Martin Hyde: Weapon Bind	R	4.00
Matthew McCormick	U	1.00
Misfortune	C	0.35
Narrow Escape (Avoid)	C	0.35
Nefertiri: Have a Good Life	R	4.00
Nemesis (Ceirdwyn)	U	1.00
Nemesis (Kanis)	U	1.00
Nemesis (Kanwulf)	U	1.00
Nemesis (Martin Hyde)	U	1.00
Nemesis (Paul Kinman)	U	1.00
Parrying Blade	R	10.00
Parrying Blade: Dual Attack (LL, UR)	R	5.00
Parrying Blade: Dual Attack (UL, LR)	R	5.00
Parrying Blade: Surprise Strike (ML)	C	0.35
Parrying Blade: Surprise Strike (MR)	C	0.35
Parrying Blade: Trap	R	5.00
Paul Kinman	R	10.00
Paul Kinman	UR	25.00
Paul Kinman: 9mm	R	4.00
Paul Kinman: Back Away	U	1.00
Paul Kinman: Combination	U	1.00
Paul Kinman: Continuity	U	1.00

RARITY KEY C = Common U = Uncommon R = Rare VR = Very Rare UR = Ultra Rare F = Foil card X = Fixed/standard in all decks

Card name	Rarity	Price
☐ Paul Kinman: Contract Killer	R	4.00
☐ Paul Kinman: Deceiver	U	1.00
☐ Paul Kinman: Reload	U	1.00
☐ Paul Kinman: Side Step (Left)	U	1.00
☐ Paul Kinman: Side Step (Right)	U	1.00
☐ Paul Kinman: Taunt	R	4.00
☐ Paul Kinman: Trip	U	1.00
20		
☐ Police (Damage)	C	0.35
☐ Police (Situation)	C	0.35
☐ Rail Yard	R	3.00
☐ Rapier	R	10.00
☐ Rapier: Bleeding Wound	U	1.00
☐ Rapier: Quality Blade	U	1.00
☐ Rapier: Slice (UL, MC)	C	0.35

Card name	Rarity	Price
☐ Rapier: Slice (UR, MC)	C	0.35
☐ Reconnaissance	U	1.00
21		
☐ Richie Ryan: Master's Attack	R	10.00
☐ Right Guard	C	0.35
☐ Ring of Fire	R	4.00
☐ Rules of the Game A	U	1.00
☐ Rules of the Game E	U	1.00
☐ Rules of the Game R	U	1.00
☐ Run For Your Life	C	0.35
☐ Saber	R	10.00
☐ Saber: Guard (UL)	U	1.00
22		
☐ Saber: Guard (UR)	U	1.00
☐ Saber: Quality Blade	U	1.00
☐ Saber: Slash (Left)	C	0.35

Card name	Rarity	Price
☐ Saber: Slash (Right)	R	5.00
☐ Saber: Slash (Upper)	C	0.35
☐ Shield	R	10.00
☐ Shield: Under Cover	R	5.00
☐ Shifting Sands	U	1.00
23		
☐ Slan Quince: Brute	U	1.00
☐ Slan Quince: Mask	U	1.00
☐ Slash (Center)	C	0.35
☐ Slash (Middle)	C	0.35
☐ Slaughter House	R	4.00
☐ Sources Revealed	U	1.00
☐ Sulphur Plant	R	3.00
☐ Swashbuckler	R	3.00
☐ The Bigger They Are..	U	1.00

Card name	Rarity	Price
☐ The Circle	R	4.00
24		
☐ The Gathering	R	5.00
☐ Theatre	R	4.00
☐ There Can Be Only One B	R	5.00
☐ There Can Be Only One D	R	5.00
☐ Up And At Them	C	0.35
☐ Upper Guard	C	0.35
☐ Vice Grip	U	1.00
☐ War Axe	R	10.00
☐ War Axe: Attack Weapon	U	1.00
25		
☐ War Axe: Quality Blade	U	1.00
☐ War Axe: Throw	R	5.00
☐ Xavier St. Cloud: Loot	R	4.00

SITUATION: PLOT
Reunion: When this card enters play search through your Endurance for any one Always Go With The Winner, reveal it to your opponent and place it into your hand. Reshuffle your Endurance.

© Gaumont Television

Highlander • *Four Horsemen*

Thunder Castle Games • Released **March 1999**

105 cards in set • **IDENTIFIER:** © Gaumont; round symbols at lower right

- Booster packs contain 12 cards; booster displays contain 28 boosters

After the upheaval caused by **Arms and Tactics**, the **Four Horsemen** expansion seems a bit tame. It continued much of what *Arms & Tactics* started, adding three more crystals, three additional pre-game premiums, and more personas. — *Orren McKay*

Set (105 cards)	100.00
Booster Display Box	65.00
Booster Pack	3.00

You will need **12** nine-pocket pages to store this set. (6 doubled up)

Card name	Type	Rarity	Price
1			
☐ A&T (Continue)	Pregame	UR	25.00
☐ A&T (Head Shot)	Pregame	UR	25.00
☐ A&T (Keep)	Pregame	UR	25.00
☐ Advance Warning	Situation	C	0.35
☐ All Out Defense	Situation	U	1.00
☐ Always Go With The Winner (Reunion)	Plot	C	0.35
☐ Always Go With The Winner (Secret All.)	Plot	C	0.35
☐ Amanda: Low Blow	Attack	R	5.00
☐ Back Away	Dodge	U	1.00
2			
☐ Back Away	Dodge	U	1.00
☐ Back Away	Dodge	U	1.00
☐ Back Away	Dodge	U	1.00
☐ Balladeer	Situation	R	4.00
☐ Blatant Clue	Object	R	4.00
☐ Block and Strike	Att-Def	C	0.35
☐ Carolyn Marsh	Event	C	0.35
☐ Caspian	Persona	R	10.00
☐ Caspian (+1)	Pregame	UR	25.00
3			
☐ Cassandra	Persona	R	10.00
☐ Cassandra (+1)	Pregame	UR	25.00
☐ Child's Mind	Situation	R	3.00
☐ Close Quarters	Situation	C	0.35
☐ Combination	Event	U	1.00
☐ Combination	Event	U	1.00
☐ Comes A Horsemen	Attack	R	4.00
☐ Crystal (Clio)	Pregame	UR	25.00
☐ Crystal (Erato)	Pregame	UR	25.00
4			
☐ Crystal (Melpomene)	Pregame	UR	25.00
☐ Depravity	Situation	R	4.00

Card name	Type	Rarity	Price
☐ Dodge	Dodge	U	1.00
☐ Dodge	Dodge	U	1.00
☐ Dodge	Dodge	U	1.00
☐ Duck	Dodge	U	1.00
☐ Duende	Situation	R	3.00
☐ Enchanted Voice (evt)	Event	U	1.00
☐ Enchanted Voice (sit)	Situation	U	1.00
5			
☐ End Of Time	Situation	R	8.00
☐ Extra Shot	Event	U	1.00
☐ Famine	Situation	R	8.00
☐ Flamboyant Attack (obj)	EDG	C	0.35
☐ Flamboyant Attack (sit)	EDG	C	0.35
☐ Flashback	Event	U	1.00
☐ Flashback	Event	U	1.00
☐ Flashback	Event	U	1.00
☐ For the Departed	Event	U	1.00
6			
☐ Foresight	Situation	R	6.00
☐ Illusion	Event	R	4.00
☐ Impressive Move	Event	R	3.00
☐ Kern: Relentless	Event	R	4.00
☐ Kronos	Persona	R	10.00
☐ Kronos (+1)	Pregame	UR	25.00
☐ Luther: Malicious Grin	Event	R	6.00
☐ Master Head Shot	Event	R	10.00
☐ Master's Attack	Attack	R	4.00
7			
☐ Master's Attack (left)	Attack	R	4.00
☐ Master's Attack (right)	Attack	R	4.00
☐ Master's Block	EDG	R	4.00
☐ Master's Block	Block	R	4.00
☐ Master's Dodge	Dodge	R	4.00
☐ Master's Proficiency	Situation	R	4.00
☐ Monkey	Situation	C	0.35
☐ Nemesie (Committed)	Situation	U	1.00
☐ Nemesis (1000 Regrets)	Situation	U	1.00
8			
☐ Nemesis (Dark Secret)	Situation	U	1.00
☐ Nemesis (Dim Witted)	Situation	U	1.00
☐ Nemesis (You're Hist-discard)	Situation	R	3.00
☐ Nemesis (You're Hist-draw)	Situation	U	1.00
☐ On Your Knees	Event	R	3.00
☐ Overextended Att (each)	Attack	C	0.35
☐ Pagliaccio	Situation	R	3.00
☐ Peeping Tom	Situation	R	3.00
☐ Persistence	Event	R	3.00
9			
☐ Precognition	Event	R	4.00
☐ Prime Block	Block	R	4.00

Card name	Type	Rarity	Price
☐ Protected Resources	Situation	R	3.00
☐ Rhesus Virus	Object	U	1.00
☐ Run Through	Event	R	5.00
☐ Sadistic Pleasure	Situation	R	3.00
☐ Safe House	Situation	R	3.00
☐ Season Six	Event	R	5.00
☐ See No Evil	Situation	R	3.00
10			
☐ Seer	Situation	R	3.00
☐ Silas	Persona	R	10.00
☐ Silas (+1)	Pregame	UR	25.00
☐ Skinning Knife	Object	R	4.00
☐ Submarine Base	Location	R	3.00
☐ Taunt	Event	R	4.00
☐ The Apocalypse	Event	R	7.00
☐ The Bronze Age	Location	R	3.00
☐ The Game (att)	Situation	C	0.35
11			
☐ The Game (def)	Situation	C	0.35
☐ The Vampire	Plot	R	4.00
☐ Thrown Dagger	Attack	R	4.00
☐ Trench Coat	Object	C	0.35
☐ Trip	Event	U	1.00
☐ Trip	Event	U	1.00
☐ Trip	Event	U	1.00
☐ Unforseen Event	Event	R	3.00
☐ Vindication	Situation	R	3.00
12			
☐ War Paint	Situation	C	0.35
☐ Weapon Master	Situation	R	3.00
☐ Weighted Blade	Object	R	3.00
☐ Well Prepared Defense	Event	U	1.00
☐ Xavier: Master Tactician	Situation	R	3.00
☐ Yuk-Hsui Chun	Situation	R	3.00

RARITY KEY C = Common   U = Uncommon   R = Rare   VR = Very Rare   UR = Ultra Rare   F = Foil card   X = Fixed/standard in all decks

Highlander • The Methos Collection

Thunder Castle Games

50 cards in set

The Methos persona, hands down the most powerful in the game, was *only* available in the tin set, **The Methos Collection**.

Methos was the reason for the introduction of different types of **Highlander** tournaments. Type A tournaments allowed any *Highlander* cards, while Type B tournaments prohibited the use of **Collection** cards (*Methos* and **Duncan**) and Quickenings.

Another interesting fact about this collection was that only buying one collection did not provide enough cards to effectively play Methos. Two collections were required to field a deck. — *Orren McKay*

The Methos Collection	62.50

Cards unique to the set:

Card name	Price		Card name	Price
[1] ☐ Adam Pierson	3.30		☐ Methos: Flashback	3.30
☐ Methos	3.30		☐ Methos: Immortal Research	3.30
☐ Methos (Premium #1)	3.30		☐ Methos: Live Forever	3.30
☐ Methos (Premium #2)	3.30		☐ Methos: Master's Wisdom	3.30
☐ Methos (Quickening)	3.30		☐ Methos: Methos?	3.30
☐ Methos: A Master's Focus	3.30		☐ Methos: Power Blow	3.30
☐ Methos: Back Away	3.30		[3] ☐ Methos: Secret Identity	3.30
☐ Methos: Combination	3.30		☐ Methos: Superior Tactics	3.30
☐ Methos: Continuity	3.30		☐ Methos: The Gift	3.30
[2] ☐ Methos: Dawn of Time	3.30		☐ Methos: Trip	3.30
☐ Methos: Dodge	3.30		☐ Treachery	3.30
☐ Methos: Extra Shot	3.30			

Highlander • Quickenings

Thunder Castle Games

Quickening cards were awarded to **Highlander** tournament winners. These cards duplicate all or part of a specific Immortal's persona Ability. They can be included in the six pre-game cards allowed to enhance various deck strategies.

Quickenings can also be dangerous to play in tournaments. As part of the *Highlander* mythos, if an Immortal loses his head, his opponent gains his power. This was reflected in the game by making any Quickenings played with in tournaments a forced "ante": If you lost your head in a tournament, and were playing with Quickenings, your opponent won them. Most players obeyed a gentleman's agreement to trade any Quickenings won in this fashion back after the game. Nevertheless, it did provide an added thrill to playing with them in tournaments.

The major drawback to Quickenings was that, in order to receive them for winning a tournament, the tournament results had to be submitted to the manufacturer, Thunder Castle Games, which would then mail the cards to the winner. Some players back then perceived a breakdown in customer service: Some hardcore *Highlander* players said it was not uncommon for it to take three to six months and a number of long-distance phone calls to finally receive the Quickenings they were owed. — *Orren McKay*

Card name	Price		Card name	Price
[1] ☐ Quickening (3 or 5 Card Exertions)	6.00		☐ Quickening (Extra Weapon)	6.00
☐ Quickening (Additional Point of Damage)	6.00		☐ Quickening (Look at Hidden Attacks)	6.00
☐ Quickening (Attack Areas Blocked)	6.00		☐ Quickening (Make Power Blows)	6.00
☐ Quickening (Attacks as Blocks)	6.00		☐ Quickening (Master Cards)	6.00
☐ Quickening (Block Power Blows)	6.00		☐ Quickening (No Special/Hidden Attack)	6.00
☐ Quickening (Discard to Endurance)	6.00		☐ Quickening (Remove Situations)	6.00
☐ Quickening (Draw to Ability)	6.00		☐ Quickening (Successful Block/Hidden Attack)	6.00
☐ Quickening (Duplicate Event)	6.00		☐ Quickening (Top Card of Endurance)	6.00
☐ Quickening (Exert One at a Time)	6.00		[3] ☐ Quickening (Twice Number of Plots)	6.00
[2] ☐ Quickening (Exhaustion 3 Ability)	6.00		☐ Quickening (Use non-Reserved Cards)	6.00

Highlander • Promos

Thunder Castle Games

38 known cards

Highlander has a large number of promotional cards. Many of these cards were only given out once, in specific magazines, by certain game distributors, or at conventions. If you didn't happen to attend the specific con, or missed buying the magazine, the only way to get these cards was to trade for them. There was even a promo card that was only available by getting it personally from the president of Thunder Castle Games, Mike Sager. Cards are, indeed, named after their source: **Scrye** appeared in *Scrye* #13 (Mar 96).

Promo cards were vital to every deck. Players who owned **The Nexus** always included it. Plus, certain deck types required promos like **Chessex** or **Safe Haven** (situation) to function. This made getting into *Highlander* and building decks exceedingly difficult on new players, since trading was the only way to get most of the promo cards they had missed by not starting earlier. — *Orren McKay*

Card name	Set	Price		Card name	Set	Price		Card name	Set	Price
[1] ☐ Adventures Distributing		2.50		☐ Dragon		2.50		☐ Safe Haven		2.50
☐ Ancestral Blade		2.50		☐ Feedback Card	Movie	2.50		☐ Scrye		2.50
☐ Asgard		2.50		☐ Flashback		2.50		[4] ☐ Sovereign Media		2.50
☐ Berkeley Game Distributors		2.50		☐ Forged Steel		2.50		☐ The Armory		2.50
☐ Chessex		2.50		☐ Greenfield Hobby		2.50		☐ The Eyes Have It 1 (Peeping Tom)		2.50
☐ Collect		2.50		☐ Illusory Terrain		2.50		☐ The Eyes Have It 2 (In Your Sights)		2.50
☐ Conjure		2.50		[3] ☐ Inquest		2.50		☐ The Eyes Have It 3		2.50
☐ Customer Feedback	Watch	2.50		☐ Lurker		2.50		☐ Thunder Castle Games (Angus MacLeod)		2.50
☐ Darius		2.50		☐ Master		2.50		☐ Thunder Castle Games (Connor MacLeod)		2.50
[2] ☐ Delusions		2.50		☐ Master Race		2.50		☐ Thunder Castle Games (Lt. Frank Moran)		2.50
☐ Director's Cut		2.50		☐ NEXUS		2.50		☐ Wargames West		2.50
☐ Divine Intervention		2.50		☐ NEXUS Sign Up Card	Movie	2.50		[5] ☐ Watcher Field Agents		2.50
				☐ Pyramid		2.50		☐ Worm		2.50

RARITY KEY C = Common U = Uncommon R = Rare **VR** = Very Rare **UR** = Ultra Rare **F** = Foil card **X** = Fixed/standard in all decks

Hyborian Gates

Cardz (a division of **Playoff Corp.**) • Released **July 1995**
451 cards in set

- Starter decks contain 55 cards; starter displays contain 6 two-deck starters
- Booster packs contain 15 cards; booster displays contain 36 boosters

Weeks before its competitor, FPG, leapt into the 1995 CCG clut with **Guardians**, art-card maker Cardz released its own CCG showcasing the art of Boris Vallejo and Julie Bell, even flying game reviewers in to meet the artists.

In **Hyborian Gates**, Earth is the battleground for a cross-dimensional war. Eons ago, Hyboria, Gaea, Osiris, Chaos, Asgard, and Atlantis waged a war across several dimensions, ours among them. Then they left. Humans still have dim racial memories of these wars and preserved them as legends. In truth, the wars still rage on.

In the game, players build a gameboard layout of six cards, one for each dimension; the goal of the game is to control all six. Players then play a gate card on the dimension to which it corresponds, allowing them to send Trooper cards there. If enemy troops are found there, combat follows. The mechanics of the game are simple: A trooper has a home dimension, an attack value, and a defense value. You can also attach technology, vehicles, or companions that will add to the trooper's numbers. In combat, the attacker declares his champion, the defender declares his, and then combat rounds begin.

Rounds follow a simple pattern: The defender may draw three cards (or to a max hand size of seven); the attacker may play a combat card face down; the defender may play one face up; a mage card permits the playing of a spell; and the round resolves by comparing scores. In case of a draw, another round begins. It is possible for a battle to never resolve, causing the whole game to be stuck in a draw! The mechanics of moving to a dimension are smoother: A gate can transport a person to a dimension, and a gate powered by a pyramid may transport two. By adding more pyramids, players can overload the gate and destroy it, adding some deep strategies to an otherwise pointless game.

Combining clear card design and large type with gorgeous art by Boris Vallejo and Julie Bell would normally make a CCG a winner, but in *Hyborian Gates* the paintings are cropped horribly, and at least a dozen paintings are split up into two to four cards, completely destroying the look of them. Some art choices were likewise foolish: Using a 1970s book cover showing kids in bellbottoms for the card **Mentalists of Tunetha** was sinful.

With the exception of poor art choices and an incomplete combat system, the game wasn't all that bad, but Vallejo fans found themselves better served with his non-CCG card releases. A 1996 expansion, **Gatemasters**, never happened. — *Richard Weld*

Concept	●●●○○	
Gameplay	●●○○○	
Card art	●●○○○	
Player pool	●●○○○	

Cardz also has produced CCGs under the Playoff label (**One on One Hockey**) and the Score label (**Dragonball Z**).

You will need **51** nine-pocket pages to store this set. (26 doubled up)

Set (451 cards)	84.00
Starter Display Box	25.00
Booster Display Box	24.00
Starter Deck	3.50
Booster Pack	1.00

Card name	Rarity	Price
1		
☐ A Vampire Moon	C	0.10
☐ Absorption	R	1.00
☐ Action Mistress	U	0.20
☐ Adeluvians	R	1.50
☐ Agrelius	UR	3.00
☐ Agrippa's Curse	R	2.00
☐ Alasandra	UR	3.00
☐ Alien Logic	C	0.10
☐ Amazons of Troy	C	0.10
2		
☐ Amber Tide	UR	2.00
☐ Amber Watcher	C	0.10
☐ Amunet's Gate	G	0.10
☐ Ancient Gate	UR	15.00
☐ Angel in Glass	U	0.20
☐ Angel Storm	UR	6.00
☐ Anger of the Gods	UR	2.00
☐ Annwn's Gate	G	0.10
☐ Antarea	R	1.50
3		
☐ Anubis' Gate	G	0.10
☐ Apollo's Gate	G	0.10
☐ Aquanian	R	2.00
☐ Archeens	UR	3.00
☐ Archeons	U	0.20

Card name	Rarity	Price
☐ Arnth	R	2.00
☐ Art Imitates Life	C	0.10
☐ Atlun	UR	3.00
☐ Attack!	R	1.00
4		
☐ Atum's Gate	G	0.10
☐ Awesome Strength	UR	2.00
☐ Axes of Horleen	R	1.00
☐ Baath	R	1.00
☐ Bar Folk	R	1.00
☐ Battler	R	1.50
☐ Beast of Temple Doom	C	0.10
☐ Bengali	R	1.50
☐ Beserker	U	0.20
5		
☐ Black Gambit One	UR	2.00
☐ Black Planet	UR	3.00
☐ Bladed Couple	U	0.20
☐ Blaster	UR	3.00
☐ Blaze	R	1.00
☐ Blaze Goddess	C	0.10
☐ Boon Companions	C	0.10
☐ Bor's Gate	G	0.10
☐ Brak the Brave	U	0.20
6		
☐ Bright Speedster	UR	2.00
☐ Brigit's Gate	G	0.10
☐ Bringers of Light	C	0.10
☐ Brothers to the Sword	C	0.10
☐ Bugle of the Vortex	C	0.10

Card name	Rarity	Price
☐ Can't Happen	R	2.00
☐ Castle Rising	R	1.50
☐ Castle Standish	C	0.10
☐ Cat Quickness	C	0.10
7		
☐ Centaurin	UR	2.50
☐ Cerberus' Gate	G	0.10
☐ Changeling	R	1.50
☐ Char Dragon	C	0.10
☐ Chargest	R	1.00
☐ Charta Harpy	U	0.20
☐ Chimaera's Gate	G	0.10
☐ Chrome Jaws	C	0.10
☐ Claws of Victory	R	1.00
8		
☐ Clear Reign	R	1.00
☐ Cleito's Gate	G	0.10
☐ Cloak Master	U	0.20
☐ Condoon	UR	2.50
☐ Corbin	U	0.20
☐ Crimson Force	U	0.20
☐ Crimson Ice	U	0.20
☐ Crimson Spheres of Valor	C	0.10
☐ Crimson Tide	R	1.50
9		
☐ Crom Cruach's Gate	G	0.10
☐ Cronus' Gate	G	0.10
☐ Dagda's Gate	G	0.10
☐ Dark Challenger	U	0.20
☐ Dark Drifter	UR	3.00

Card name	Rarity	Price
☐ Dark Lightning	R	2.00
☐ Dawn Retreat	R	1.00
☐ Dazzler	UR	3.00
☐ Death Mists	UR	3.00
10		
☐ Death Rider	R	1.50
☐ Death Sentinel	C	0.10
☐ Death Taster	UR	2.50
☐ Death's Sister	UR	2.00
☐ Deceiver	U	0.20
☐ Del Sin	R	1.00
☐ Demeter's Gate	G	0.10
☐ Dinos of the Mount	C	0.10
☐ Djin	UR	3.00
11		
☐ Doom Suit	C	0.10
☐ Doris' Gate	G	0.10
☐ Dragon Helper	U	0.20
☐ Dragon Knight	R	1.00
☐ Dragon of the Veil	UR	2.00
☐ Dragon Rage	UR	3.00
☐ Dragon Rider	U	0.20
☐ Dragon Riders of Ott	R	1.50
☐ Dragon Slayer	UR	2.50
12		
☐ Dream Team	C	0.10
☐ Dream Warriors	U	0.20
☐ Drop Troops of Zen	C	0.10
☐ Earth Riser	UR	2.00
☐ Earth Walking	U	0.20
☐ Easy Rider	UR	2.00

Card name	Rarity	Price
☐ Ebony Darkness	UR	2.50
☐ Ebony Death Watcher	U	0.20
☐ Electra	UR	2.50
13		
☐ Elf Action	U	0.20
☐ Emerald Force	R	1.00
☐ Emerald Ice	UR	2.00
☐ Emerald Slayer	C	0.10
☐ Emerald Tide	U	0.20
☐ Emerald Titan	R	1.50
☐ Encapsulation	R	1.00
☐ Energy Fields	C	0.10
☐ Energy Mountain	U	0.20
14		
☐ Europa's Gate	G	0.10
☐ Fallen	C	0.10
☐ Fangs	C	0.10
☐ Far Eyed Soarer	C	0.10
☐ Feathered Mistress	C	0.10
☐ Feline	U	0.20
☐ Feline Fems of Nerth	C	0.10
☐ Final Spear	C	0.10
☐ Flame Thrower	UR	3.00
15		
☐ Flortian	R	1.00
☐ Flutter Twins	UR	3.00
☐ Flyers of the Vortex	C	0.10
☐ Forcien	R	1.00
☐ Formulators	UR	3.00
☐ Fregja's Gate	G	0.10

RARITY KEY **C** = Common **U** = Uncommon **R** = Rare **VR** = Very Rare **UR** = Ultra Rare **F** = Foil card **X** = Fixed/standard in all decks

Card name	Rarity	Price
Galaxy Lightning Corp	UR	3.00
Garm's Gate	G	0.10
Gate Cruiser	UR	2.50
16		
Gate Ship	UR	3.00
Georgian Avian	C	0.10
Gigavolts	C	0.10
Glitz	U	0.20
Goblin	U	0.20
Gold Ice	U	0.20
Good Prospects	U	0.20
Gorgat	R	2.00
17		
Gorgons' Gate	G	0.10
Green Dragon of Thuu	U	0.20
Grendel's Gate	G	0.10
Grow-alt	UR	2.50
Gruug	UR	3.00
Guardian of the Mists	C	0.10
Hade's Gate	G	0.10
Hathor's Gate	G	0.10
Hel's Gate	G	0.10
18		
Helios	R	1.00
Hera's Blade	R	2.00
Hera's Gate	G	0.10
Hespera's Gate	G	0.10
Hestia's Gate	G	0.10
Himself	R	2.00
Honor's Hope	UR	3.00
Horse Allies	C	0.10
Horus' Gate	G	0.10
Hyde	UR	3.00
19		
Ice Nightwing	C	0.10
Icon Warrior	UR	3.00
Illusion Maker	R	2.00
Immuna	R	2.00
Imps of Neff	R	2.00
Interested Cats	R	2.00
Io's Gate	G	0.10
Ivory Ice	U	0.20
Ivory Lady	UR	3.00
20		
Jaded Couple	UR	3.00
Jump	UR	3.00
Just A Dragon	C	0.10
Just A Man	C	0.10
Kai-Louw	C	0.10
Kargars	R	2.00
Kargon Ranger	U	0.20
King Tuan	UR	3.00
Kingdom Breaker	UR	3.00
21		
Knights of Time	C	0.10
Kraken's Gate	G	0.10
Kufu's Blessing	C	0.10
Lady of Ice	C	0.10
Land's Guardian	C	0.10
Last Bridge Holder	UR	3.00
Last Defenders	U	0.20
Last Minotaur	U	0.20
Laz Couple	UR	3.00
22		
Lesser Ebony Guardian	R	2.00
Lesser Siren	U	0.20
Leveler	U	0.20
Leviathan of Taz	C	0.10
Lifters	C	0.10
Light Bringers	U	0.20
Light of Day	U	0.20

Card name	Rarity	Price
Light Storm	U	0.20
Light's Godling	UR	3.00
23		
Lightning Daughter	R	2.00
Lightning Dragon	UR	3.00
Lightning Fist	UR	3.00
Lightning Master	UR	3.00
Lightning Sifter	UR	3.00
Lightning Striker	R	2.00
Lightning Thrower	UR	3.00
Lights Lady	U	0.20
Little Fiend	R	2.00
24		
Lizardeen Specialist	UR	3.00
Loki's Gate	G	0.10
Lone Guardian	UR	3.00
Lost in Thought	U	0.20
Lugh's Gate	G	0.10
Major Players	C	0.10
Mark in Defense	UR	3.00
Mawling	R	2.00
Mentalists of Tunetha	C	0.10
25		
Mer-Cees	U	0.20
Mer-done	R	2.00
Mer-Lass	C	0.10
Mer-She	R	2.00
Mer-Tians	U	0.20
Merlina	U	0.20
Midnight Web Spinner	C	0.10
Mind Jewel	C	0.10
Minor Black Grunnel	C	0.10
26		
Minor Bold Ones	U	0.20
Minor Char Beast	U	0.20
Minor Raider	UR	3.00
Mist Dwellers	R	2.00
Mist Dwellers of Surn	R	2.00
Mistress of Horse	C	0.10
Misty City	U	0.20
Mix Master	UR	3.00
Modern Man	C	0.10
27		
Monarch Bat	C	0.10
Monster Confusion	U	0.20
Monster Friendship	U	0.20
Monster Willow	C	0.10
Moon Dance	C	0.10
Moon Rider	U	0.20
Morpheus Calls	R	2.00
Mountain Challenge	U	0.20
Mountain Monster	C	0.10
28		
Mountain Protection	U	0.20
Mountain Support	U	0.20
Mutating	R	2.00
Nature's Call	R	2.00
Nebula Cruiser	C	0.10
Nereus' Gate	G	0.10
Nevik	R	2.00
New Ark	U	0.20
New Growth	UR	3.00
29		
New Life	R	2.00
Night Lightning	UR	3.00
Night's Cloak	UR	3.00
Night's Teacher	UR	3.00
Nile's Gift	C	0.10
Niut's Gate	G	0.10
Noah's Way	U	0.20

Card name	Rarity	Price
Nomad	UR	3.00
Not Likely	R	2.00
30		
Not Today	R	2.00
Oceanus' Gate	G	0.10
Odin's Gate	G	0.10
Offering	R	2.00
Olympus Beckons	R	2.00
Osiran Safety	U	0.20
Painted Woman	U	0.20
Path's Handmaiden	U	0.20
Pazuzu's Gate	G	0.10
31		
Peace Bringer	R	2.00
Peace Peak	U	0.20
Peaceful Intent	U	0.20
Peek Twins	U	0.20
Pistoleer	C	0.10
Pontus' Gate	G	0.10
Power Blade Master	U	0.20
Power of the Mountain	R	2.00
Powered Gateway	R	2.00
32		
Protected	R	2.00
Protectors	U	0.20
Ptah's Gate	G	0.10
Quatzalatzan	U	0.20
Quest for Truth	C	0.10
Quick Star	C	0.10
Quickbeam	R	2.00
Quickening Mist	UR	3.00
Re's Gate	G	0.10
33		
Recovery	R	2.00
Red Assassin	UR	3.00
Red Blade	C	0.10
Red Field of Force	C	0.10
Red Ghosts of Time	C	0.10
Red Rob	U	0.20
Red Slayer	C	0.10
Red Titan	U	0.20
Reever	R	2.00
34		
Reptile Mistress	C	0.10
Rest Stop	UR	2.00
Restless	R	1.00
Rider	R	1.50
Rok the Relentless	R	2.00
Romulus	U	0.20
Roon	R	1.50
Royal Ice	U	0.20
Royal Inspection	R	1.00
35		
Rulers of Anselon	UR	2.50
Rumblers	UR	2.00
Running For Your Life	U	0.20
Salazia	U	0.20
Salezians	U	0.20
Sanshall	R	1.00
Saucer of Yeanol	C	0.10
Saurian Rider	UR	3.50
Scorpion's Sting	R	2.00
36		
Scylla's Gate	G	0.10
Sea Challenger	C	0.10
Seket	UR	2.00
Sekmet's Gate	G	0.10
Senella	U	0.20
Serfs of Nod	C	0.10
Serpent City	U	0.20
Serpent Warriors	U	0.20

Card name	Rarity	Price
Shadow Creature	UR	3.00
37		
She Terror	UR	2.00
She Who Watches	UR	2.00
Shejun	UR	2.00
Shield Man	UR	2.00
Ship of Boris	C	0.10
Ship of the Ages	C	0.10
Ships of the Night	C	0.10
Shrieken	R	1.50
Shu's Gate	G	0.10
38		
Sigmund	R	1.00
Silencers	C	0.10
Simmer	R	1.00
Simple Sphere	UR	3.00
Sinder	UR	2.50
Skull Ship	R	1.50
Sky City of Zen	C	0.10
Sky Mistress	U	0.20
Sky Slasher	UR	2.00
39		
Sky Technician	UR	2.00
Slave Freer	UR	2.00
Snake Minions	UR	2.50
Snow Cats	UR	2.00
Solidity	UR	2.00
Spirit Gunner	UR	2.00
Star Warrior	C	0.10
Starship of Thang	C	0.10
Stone Dragon	U	0.20
40		
Strength Bonus	U	0.20
Styx's Gate	G	0.10
Summoned Aggressor	UR	3.00
Summoner	U	0.20
Supplicant	UR	2.50
Surge Protector	C	0.10
Surprise Attack	R	1.00
Sword of Protection	R	1.50
Swords Woman	C	0.10
41		
Tainted Merchant	UR	2.50
Tamer	R	1.50
Tandaleea	U	0.20
Tanian	UR	3.00
Tareel	U	0.20
Tarn Women	U	0.20
Tarnish	R	1.00
Task Master	UR	2.50
Tav Mists	U	0.20
42		
Tellat	R	1.50
Terzan	U	0.20
Testing	R	1.00
The Archer of Fletchen	C	0.10
The Axer	C	0.10
The Bladesman	C	0.10
The Call	R	2.00
The Crimson Courser	C	0.10
The Dancing Pair	C	0.10
43		
The Enchanted Falls	U	0.20
The Firbolg's Gate	G	0.10
The Fire Axeman	C	0.10
The Friend	C	0.10
The Hydra's Gate	G	0.10
The Man	R	2.00
The Mysts	R	2.00
The Norns' Gate	G	0.10

Card name	Rarity	Price
The Pond of Peace	U	0.20
44		
The Power Within	C	0.10
The Red Seeress	C	0.10
The Resistors	U	0.20
The Rider	U	0.20
The Russels	R	1.00
The Telden	U	0.10
The Wall	R	1.00
The White Lady	C	0.10
Thief in the Night	UR	2.00
45		
Thoth's Gate	G	0.10
Threes	UR	2.00
Titan Flames	R	1.00
Tomaniee	U	0.20
Tomorrows City	UR	3.00
Ton	C	0.10
Transformation	UR	3.00
Transport Bot	C	0.10
Treen	U	0.20
46		
Tronst	R	1.00
Troubled Centaurian	U	0.20
Tun	R	1.00
Twister	R	1.50
Typhon's Gate	G	0.10
Typhus	UR	3.00
Ultimate Battle	U	0.20
Uncaring Fiend	R	1.50
Unicorn of Zen	C	0.10
47		
Universal Trooper	UR	3.00
Utter Distraction	C	0.10
Vanessa	UR	3.00
Vanhelephant	R	1.50
Victor's Wish	C	0.10
Victoria Companion	G	0.10
Victory	R	1.50
Victory's Grasp	UR	2.50
Viking Gods	C	0.10
48		
Vortex Dish	U	0.20
Vortex Quake	C	0.10
Vortex Walker	U	0.20
Warden's Castle	C	0.10
Watcher	UR	3.00
Wax and Wane	R	1.00
Weapons Masters	C	0.10
Weapons of Semaj	R	2.00
Weapons of Thor	U	0.20
49		
Weapons of Yanny	U	0.20
Were-Lion	C	0.10
White Grasp	R	2.00
White Magic Vessel of Doos	C	0.10
White Rider	U	0.20
Winged Piercer	R	2.00
Winged Warrior	R	2.00
Wingling	R	2.00
Winning	UR	3.00
50		
Wolves of Garthank	U	0.20
World Essence	U	0.20
Wren	U	0.20
Wrestlers	UR	2.00
Xerecles	R	1.00
Xermies	R	1.50
Zaben Tat	U	0.20
Zagreus' Gate	G	0.10
Zapper	R	1.50
51		
Zeus' Gate	G	0.10

RARITY KEY **C** = Common **U** = Uncommon **R** = Rare **VR** = Very Rare **UR** = Ultra Rare **F** = Foil card **X** = Fixed/standard in all decks

SCRYE Collectible Card Game Checklist and Price Guide • **195**

Illuminati: New World Order

Steve Jackson Games • First set, **Limited**, released **December 1994**

409 cards in set • **IDENTIFIER: Card name NOT in italics; type is gold**

• Starter sets contain two 55-card decks and rulebook; starter displays contain 6 sets
• Booster packs contain 15 cards; booster displays contain 36 boosters

Designed by **Steve Jackson**

Looking at the exploding collectible card game phenomenon and trying to figure out how to participate, it was an easy decision for Steve Jackson to adapt his already successful *Illuminati* card game (inspired by the *Illuminatus!* trilogy of conspiracy novels of Robert Anton Wilson and Robert Shea) to collectible play. The result was the company's biggest-selling game for several years.

Illuminati: New World Order plays similarly to its predecessor. Each player is an Illuminatus, one of the secret societies trying to control the world through clandestine control of its important organizations and personalities. These group cards, ranging from the **FBI** and the **CIA** to **Girlie Magazines**, **Las Vegas**, and **Al Gore**, are captured and added to a power structure that each player builds in front of him. Players win by building a power structure of a predetermined size (based on number of players) or fulfilling a special victory condition unique to their Illuminati group or by fulfilling a special victory condition on a Goal card.

Play is complicated by hundreds of plot cards that allow everything from deck manipulation to large bonuses on specific attacks, defense against specific attacks, and more. "New World Order" cards even change rules of the game and remain in play until forced out by a replacement NWO card or some other combination of cards and abilities. In addition to the wackiness of the plot cards, every group card also has some special ability that affects the game. Keeping track of all the modifiers and how all the special rule-breakers interact gets awfully complicated at times but is part of the demented fun.

The graphic design of the cards is excellent, and the art is different from any other CCG. The art for *INWO* (as it came to be called) looks more like political cartooning than anything else, emphasizing icons and simple line art (colored after the fact by computer) rather than the fine-art approach of *Magic: The Gathering* and other CCGs of the time. At least one buyer bought the cards just to read the jokes.

Veteran gamers invariably compared the CCG version to the original 1980s game, some finding the CCG adaptation didn't play quite as naturally. But *INWO* still spawned two expansions and a book, and, after the initial CCG boom passed, Jackson brought the original non-collectible (but itself thrice-expanded) *Illuminati* back to press with the glossy new cards. (Of course, then *that* got an expansion, *Illuminati Y2K*. A non-collectible collectible card conspiracy? Hmmm...) — **Scott D. Haring**

Orbital Mind Control Lasers

By using the Lasers' action, you may add, remove, or reverse an alignment of any group in play. You may do this at any time except during a privileged attack. The change lasts only for the rest of the current player's turn.

Unique Gadget   ACTION

Card shown from *Unlimited Edition*

Concept	●●●○○
Gameplay	●●●○○
Card art	●●●●○
Player pool	●○○○○

Buy the box

Hidden humor can be found on the starter and booster display boxes for *Illuminati: New World Order.*

"Put the box down, human," is one of a number of subliminal directives to be found on the packaging...

LIMITED Set (409 cards)	124.00
Starter Display Box	32.00
Booster Display Box	37.00
Starter Deck	7.00
Booster Pack	1.80
UNLIMITED Set (409 cards)	107.50
Starter Display Box	29.00
Booster Display Box	35.00
Starter Deck	6.00
Booster Pack	1.50

Illuminati: New World Order • Unlimited

Steve Jackson Games • Released **March 1995**

409 cards in set • **IDENTIFIER: Card name in italics; type is pink or blue**

• Starter sets contain two 55-card decks and rulebook; starter displays contain 6 sets
• Booster packs contain 15 cards; booster displays contain 36 boosters

With the **Limited Edition** of **Illuminati: New World Order** selling out quickly, Steve Jackson Games rushed an **Unlimited Edition** into print in early 1995.

It is identical to the *Limited Edition* in all but cosmetic ways. The color scheme of the face was changed. The *Unlimited Edition* uses pink (for groups) and blue (for plots) card title type, instead of gold, and the type is italic. The card backs were unchanged, so cards from both editions could be used in the same deck. — **Scott D. Haring**

LIMITED Card Name		Type	Rarity	UNLIMITED
[1]				
☐ 5.00	18 1/2-Minute Gap	Plot	R	3.40 ☐
☐ 1.50	A Thousand Points of Light	PNWO	U	1.00 ☐
☐ 0.15	A.M.A.	Grp.	C	0.10 ☐
☐ 2.00	Adepts of Hermes	Ill.	I	1.80 ☐
☐ 0.10	Agent in Place	Plot	C	0.10 ☐
☐ 2.00	Air Magic	Plot	U	1.30 ☐
☐ 0.15	Al Gore	Per.	C	0.10 ☐
☐ 0.10	Albino Alligators	Plot	C	0.10 ☐
☐ 0.10	Alternate Goals	Plot	C	0.10 ☐

LIMITED Card Name		Type	Rarity	UNLIMITED
[2]				
☐ 0.10	American Autoduel Association	Grp.	C	0.10 ☐
☐ 5.00	An Offer You Can't Refuse	Plot	R	3.40 ☐
☐ 0.10	And STAY Dead!	Plot	C	0.10 ☐
☐ 0.25	Angel's Feather	Res.	C	0.15 ☐
☐ 6.00	Angst	Plot	R	3.90 ☐
☐ 5.00	Annual Convention	Plot	R	3.40 ☐
☐ 0.10	Anti-Nuclear Activists	Grp.	C	0.10 ☐
☐ 5.00	Antiwar Activists	Grp.	R	3.40 ☐
☐ 0.10	Are We Having Fun Yet?	Plot	C	0.10 ☐
[3]				
☐ 6.50	Ark of the Covenant	Res.	R	4.10 ☐
☐ 0.10	Assertiveness Training	Plot	C	0.10 ☐
☐ 0.10	Atomic Monster	Dis.	C	0.10 ☐
☐ 2.00	B.A.T.F.	Grp.	U	1.30 ☐
☐ 0.10	Backlash	Plot	C	0.10 ☐

LIMITED Card Name		Type	Rarity	UNLIMITED
☐ 1.50	Bank Merger	Plot	U	1.00 ☐
☐ 5.50	Bank of England	Grp.	R	3.60 ☐
☐ 2.50	Bavarian Illuminati	Ill.	I	2.00 ☐
☐ 0.10	Benefit Concert	Plot	C	0.10 ☐
[4]				
☐ 2.00	Bermuda Triangle	Ill.	I	1.80 ☐
☐ 0.10	Big Media	Grp.	C	0.10 ☐
☐ 0.25	Bigfoot	Res.	C	0.15 ☐
☐ 0.10	Bigger Business	PNWO	U	0.30 ☐
☐ 0.15	Bill Clinton	Per.	C	0.10 ☐
☐ 0.10	Bimbo at Eleven	Plot	C	0.10 ☐
☐ 0.10	Bjorne	Per.	C	0.10 ☐
☐ 0.15	Black Activists	Grp.	C	0.10 ☐
☐ 2.00	Blitzkrieg	Plot	R	1.90 ☐
[5]				
☐ 0.10	Blood, Toil, Tears and Sweat	Plot	C	0.10 ☐

You will need 46 nine-pocket pages to store this set. (23 doubled up)

RARITY KEY   **C** = Common   **U** = Uncommon   **R** = Rare   **VR** = Very Rare   **UR** = Ultra Rare   **F** = Foil card   **X** = Fixed/standard in all decks

196 • SCRYE Collectible Card Game Checklist and Price Guide

LIMITED Card Name	Type	Rarity	UNLIMITED
6.00 Bodyguard	Plot	R	3.90
3.00 Book of Kells	Res.	U	1.80
2.00 Botched Contact	Plot	U	1.30
0.10 Boy Sprouts	Grp.	C	0.10
0.10 Brazil	Plc.	C	0.10
2.00 Bribery	Plot	U	1.30
5.00 C.I.A.	Grp.	R	3.40
0.10 Cable TV	Grp.	C	0.10
0.10 California	Plc.	C	0.10
5.50 Canada	Plc.	R	3.60
0.10 Car Bomb	Ass.	C	0.10
5.00 Cattle Mutilators	Grp.	R	3.40
1.80 Celebrity Spokesman	Plot	U	1.10
1.50 Censorship	Plot	U	1.00
0.10 Center for Disease Control	Plc.	U	0.30
0.25 Center for Weird Studies	Res.	C	0.15
4.00 CFL-AIO	Grp.	R	2.90
0.10 Charismatic Leader	Plot	C	0.10
0.10 Chicken in Every POT	PNWO	C	0.10
5.00 China	Plc.	R	3.40
2.00 Church of Elvis	Grp.	U	1.30
0.10 Citizenship Award	Plot	C	0.10
0.25 Clipper Chip	Res.	C	0.15
1.50 Clone	Plot	U	1.00
0.25 Clone Arrangers	Grp.	C	0.15
0.10 Cold Fusion	Plot	C	0.10
1.80 Combined Disasters	Plot	U	1.10
1.80 Comic Books	Grp.	U	1.10
2.00 Commitment	Plot	U	1.30
5.00 Computer Security	Plot	R	3.40
2.00 Computer Virus	Plot	U	1.30
1.50 Congressional Wives	Grp.	U	1.00
0.25 Conspiracy Theorists	Grp.	C	0.15
4.50 Corruption	Plot	R	3.10
5.00 Count Dracula	Per.	R	3.40
4.80 Counter-Revolution	Plot	R	3.30
2.00 Counterspell	Plot	U	1.30
5.00 Cover of Darkness	Plot	R	3.40
5.50 Cover-Up	Plot	R	3.60
1.50 Criminal Overlords	PlGol	U	1.00
0.10 Crop Circles	Plot	C	0.10
5.00 Crystal Skull	Res.	R	3.40
0.10 Currency Speculation	Plot	C	0.10
6.00 Cyborg Soldiers	Res.	R	3.90
0.10 Cycle Gangs	Grp.	C	0.10
0.15 Dan Quayle	Per.	C	0.10
4.80 Deasil Engine	Plot	R	3.30
2.50 Death Mask	Res.	U	1.50
0.10 Deep Agent	Plot	C	0.10
1.80 Democrats	Grp.	U	1.10
0.10 Dentists	Grp.	C	0.10
2.00 Deprogrammers	Grp.	U	1.30
0.10 Dictatorship	Plot	C	0.10
1.50 Dinosaur Park	Plc.	U	1.00
2.00 Discordian Society	Ill.	I	1.80
2.00 Dollars for Decency	Plot	U	1.30
2.00 Don't Forget to Smash the State	PNWO	C	1.00
0.10 Double-Cross	Plot	C	0.10
0.10 Druids	Grp.	C	0.10
0.10 Early Warning	Plot	C	0.10
0.10 Earth Magic	Plot	C	0.10
0.10 Earthquake	Dis.	C	0.10
0.25 Earthquake Projector	Res.	C	0.15
5.30 Eat The Rich!	Plot	R	3.50
0.10 Eco-Guerrillas	Grp.	C	0.10
5.50 EFF	Grp.	R	3.60
6.00 Elders of Zion	Grp.	R	3.90
3.00 Eliza	Res.	U	1.80
10.00 Elvis	Per.	R	5.90
6.00 Embezzlement	Plot	R	3.90
0.10 Emergency Powers	Plot	C	0.10
0.10 Empty Vee	Grp.	C	0.10
4.00 Energy Crisis	PNWO	R	2.90
0.10 England	Plc.	C	0.10
0.10 Epidemic	Dis.	C	0.10
4.00 Evil Geniuses for a Better Tomorrow	Grp.	R	2.90
0.10 Exposed!	Plot	C	0.10
0.10 F.B.I.	Grp.	C	0.10
6.00 Faction Fight	Plot	R	3.90
0.10 Fast Food Chains	Grp.	C	0.10
2.00 Fear and Loathing	PNWO	U	1.30
1.80 Federal Reserve	Grp.	U	1.10
1.50 Feminists	Grp.	U	1.00
1.80 Fidel Castro	Per.	U	1.10
0.15 Fiendish Fluoridators	Grp.	C	0.10
5.00 Finland	Plc.	R	3.40
0.15 Flat Earthers	Grp.	C	0.10
1.80 Flower Power	Plot	U	1.10
0.25 Flying Saucer	Res.	C	0.15
0.10 Fnord Motor Company	Grp.	C	0.10
0.25 Fnord!	Plot	C	0.15
1.50 Foiled!	Plot	U	1.00
1.80 Forgery	Plot	U	1.10
0.25 France	Plc.	C	0.15
0.25 Fraternal Orders	Grp.	C	0.15
0.10 Fratricide	PlGol	C	0.10
1.80 Freaking the Mundanes	Plot	U	1.10
6.00 Fred Birch Society	Grp.	R	3.90
1.50 Full Moon	Plot	U	1.00
0.10 Fundie Money	Plot	C	0.10
1.50 Gang War	Plot	U	1.00
1.50 Gay Activists	Grp.	U	1.00
0.25 George Bush	Per.	C	0.15
0.10 George the Janitor	Plot	C	0.10
5.00 Germany	Plc.	R	3.40
1.50 Giant Kudzu	Dis.	U	1.00
0.25 Girlie Magazines	Grp.	C	0.15
2.50 Gnomes of Zurich	Ill.	I	2.00
5.00 Goldfish Fanciers	Grp.	R	3.40
0.25 Good Polls	Plot	C	0.15
0.10 Gordo Remora	Per.	C	0.10
0.10 Grassroots Support	Plot	C	0.10
4.50 Gremlins	Plot	R	3.10
2.00 Gun Control	PNWO	U	1.30
0.10 Gun Lobby	Grp.	C	0.10
1.80 Hackers	Grp.	U	1.10
0.10 Hail Eris!	PlGol	C	0.10
0.25 Hallucinations	Res.	C	0.15
0.25 Hammer of Thor	Res.	C	0.15
0.10 Harmonica Virgins	Plot	C	0.10
0.10 Hat Trick	Plot	C	0.10
0.10 Hawaii	Plc.	C	0.10
2.30 Head in a Jar	Plot	U	1.40
6.00 Hex	Plot	R	3.90
3.00 Hidden City	Res.	U	1.80
5.50 Hidden Influence	Plot	R	3.60
0.25 Hillary Clinton	Per.	C	0.15
0.10 Hit and Run	Ass.	C	0.10
7.50 Hitler's Brain	Res.	R	4.60
1.50 Hoax!	Plot	U	1.00
1.80 Hollywood	Plc.	U	1.10
0.10 Hurricane	Dis.	C	0.10
2.50 I Lied	Plot	U	1.50
2.50 I.R.S.	Grp.	U	1.50
0.15 Imelda Marcos	Per.	C	0.10
6.00 Immortality Serum	Res.	R	3.90
0.10 Imposter	Plot	C	0.10
0.10 Infobahn	Plot	C	0.10
0.10 Intellectuals	Grp.	C	0.10
0.10 Interference	Plot	C	0.10
0.10 International Cocaine Smugglers	Grp.	C	0.10
6.00 International Communist Conspiracy	Grp.	R	3.90
2.00 International Weather Organization	Grp.	U	1.30
6.00 Israel	Plc.	R	3.90
5.00 Italy	Plc.	R	3.40
0.10 Jake Day	Plot	C	0.10
0.10 Japan	Plc.	C	0.10
0.10 Jihad	Plot	C	0.10
6.00 Jimmy Hoffa	Per.	R	3.90
0.10 Joggers	Grp.	C	0.10
1.80 Junk Mail	Grp.	U	1.10
0.25 Just Say No	Plot	C	0.15
0.10 Ketchup Is A Vegetable	Plot	C	0.10
5.00 Kill For Peace!	PlGol	R	3.40
0.10 Kinder and Gentler	Plot	C	0.10
0.10 KKK	Grp.	C	0.10
2.00 L-4 Society	Grp.	U	1.30
0.10 Las Vegas	Plc.	C	0.10
2.00 Law and Order	PNWO	U	1.30
0.10 Lawyers	Grp.	C	0.10
1.50 Let Them Eat Cake!	PlGol	U	1.00
0.10 Let's Get Organized	Plot	C	0.10
1.50 Let's Get REALLY Organized	Plot	U	1.00
6.00 Let's You and Him Fight	Plot	R	3.90
0.10 Liberal Agenda	Plot	C	0.10
5.00 Libertarians	Grp.	R	3.40
5.00 Liquor Companies	Grp.	R	3.40
0.10 Loan Sharks	Grp.	C	0.10
1.80 Local Police Departments	Grp.	U	1.10
0.25 Loch Ness Monster	Res.	C	0.15
6.00 Logic Bomb	Plot	R	3.90
0.10 Madison Avenue	Grp.	C	0.10
2.00 Manuel Noriega	Per.	U	1.30
0.10 March on Washington	Plot	C	0.10
1.50 Margaret Thatcher	Per.	U	1.00
1.80 Market Manipulation	Plot	U	1.10
0.25 Martial Law	Plot	C	0.15
0.25 Martyrs	Plot	C	0.15
5.00 Mass Murder	Plot	R	3.40
0.25 Media Blitz	Plot	C	0.15
5.50 Media Connections	Plot	R	3.60
0.25 Media Sensation	Per.	C	0.15
0.25 Mercenaries	Res.	C	0.15
6.00 Messiah	Plot	R	3.90
1.80 Meteor Strike	Dis.	U	1.10
1.80 MI-5	Grp.	U	1.10
0.25 Midas Mill	Res.	C	0.15
0.10 Military-Industrial Complex	PNWO	C	0.10
0.25 Miracle Diet Plan	Plot	C	0.15
5.50 Mistaken Identity	Plot	R	3.60
0.10 Mob Influence	Plot	C	0.10
0.10 Monopoly	Plot	C	0.10
0.10 Moonbase	Plc.	C	0.10
0.10 Moonies	Grp.	C	0.10
0.10 Moral Minority	Grp.	C	0.10
6.00 Mossad	Grp.	R	3.90
0.10 Mothers' March	Plot	C	0.10
2.30 Multinational Oil Corporations	Grp.	U	1.40
2.50 Murphy's Law	Plot	U	1.50
0.10 Mutual Betrayal	Plot	C	0.10
4.00 N.S.A.	Grp.	R	2.90
4.50 Nancy Reagan	Per.	R	3.10
1.50 NASA	Grp.	U	1.00
0.10 Nationalization	Plot	C	0.10
5.00 NATO	Grp.	R	3.40
3.00 Necronomicon	Res.	U	1.80
0.10 Nephews of God	Grp.	C	0.10
0.10 Never Surrender	Plot	C	0.10
0.10 New Blood	Plot	C	0.10
1.80 New Federal Budget	Plot	U	1.10
1.80 New York	Plc.	U	1.10
5.50 Nice Idea. It's Mine Now.	Plot	R	3.60
0.10 Ninjas	Grp.	C	0.10

RARITY KEY C = Common U = Uncommon R = Rare VR = Very Rare UR = Ultra Rare F = Foil card X = Fixed/standard in all decks

LIMITED Card Name	Type	Rarity	UNLIMITED
0.10 Nobel Peace Prize	Plot	C	0.10
0.10 Nuclear Accident	Dis.	C	0.10
29			
0.10 Nuclear Power Companies	Grp.	C	0.10
1.50 Offshore Banks		U	1.00
2.00 Ollie North	Per.	U	1.30
0.10 OPEC	Grp.	C	0.10
5.50 Opportunity Knocks	Plot	R	3.60
2.00 Orbit One	Plc.	U	1.30
0.25 Orbital Mind Control Lasers	Res.	C	0.15
0.10 Paranoids	Grp.	C	0.10
0.10 Payoff	Plot	C	0.10
30			
0.10 Peace In Our Time	PNWO	C	0.10
0.10 Pentagon	Plc.	C	0.10
8.00 Perpetual Motion Machine	Res.	R	4.90
1.50 Phone Company	Grp.	U	1.00
0.10 Phone Phreaks	Grp.	C	0.10
5.50 Plague of Demons	Dis.	R	3.60
1.80 Pledge Drive	Plot	U	1.10
0.10 Poison	Ass.	C	0.10
2.00 Political Correctness	PNWO	U	1.30
31			
5.00 Pollsters	Grp.	R	3.40
0.10 Post Office	Grp.	C	0.10
0.10 Power Corrupts	Plot	C	0.10
2.00 Power for Its Own Sake	PlGol	R	1.90
0.10 Power Grab	Plot	C	0.10
1.50 Power to the People	PlGol	U	1.00
1.50 Prince Charles	Per.	U	1.00
1.50 Princess Di	Per.	U	1.00
0.25 Principia Discordia	Res.	C	0.15
32			
0.10 Privatization	Plot	C	0.10
0.10 Privileged Attack	Plot	C	0.10
1.80 Professional Sports	Grp.	U	1.10
1.80 Psychiatrists	Grp.	U	1.10
0.10 Pulitzer Prize	Plot	C	0.10
0.10 Punk Rockers	Grp.	C	0.10
0.10 Purge	Plot	C	0.10
1.50 Rain of Frogs	Dis.	U	1.00
5.00 Reach Out . . .	Plot	R	3.40
33			
0.10 Read My Lips	Plot	C	0.10
0.10 Recording Industry	Grp.	C	0.10
5.00 Red Cross	Grp.	R	3.40
1.80 Red Scare	Plot	U	1.10
2.00 Reformed Church of Satan	Grp.	U	1.30
0.10 Religious Reich	Grp.	C	0.10
1.80 Reload!	Plot	U	1.10
0.10 Reorganization	Plot	C	0.10

LIMITED Card Name	Type	Rarity	UNLIMITED
1.80 Republicans	Grp.	U	1.10
34			
5.00 Resistance Is Useless!	Plot	R	3.40
2.00 Revolution!	Plot	U	1.30
5.00 Rewriting History	Plot	R	3.40
5.00 Rifkinites	Grp.	R	3.40
1.50 Robot Sea Monsters	Grp.	U	1.00
0.25 Rogue Boomer	Res.	C	0.15
0.10 Ronald Reagan	Per.	C	0.10
0.10 Rosicrucians	Grp.	C	0.10
5.00 Ross Perot	Per.	R	3.40
35			
0.10 Russia	Plc.	C	0.10
5.00 S.M.O.F.	Grp.	R	3.40
5.00 Sabotage	Plot	R	3.40
0.10 Saddam Hussein	Per.	C	0.10
1.50 Saturday Morning Cartoons	Grp.	U	1.00
0.10 Save the Whales	Plot	C	0.10
2.00 Savings & Loan Scam	Plot	U	1.30
5.00 Savings and Loans	Grp.	R	3.40
5.50 Scandal	Plot	R	3.60
36			
0.10 Science Fiction Fans	Grp.	C	0.10
5.00 Secret Service	Grp.	R	3.40
2.00 Secrets Man Was Not Meant to Know	Plot	U	1.30
1.50 Secular Humanists	Grp.	U	1.00
2.50 Seize The Time!	Plot	U	1.50
0.10 Self-Esteem	Plot	C	0.10
0.10 Semiconscious Liberation Army	Grp.	C	0.10
5.00 Senate Investigating Committee	Plot	R	3.40
37			
2.50 Servants of Cthulhu	Ill.	I	2.00
2.00 Shangri-La	Ill.	I	1.80
7.00 Shroud of Turin	Res.	R	4.40
2.00 Silicon Valley	Plc.	U	1.30
0.10 Slush Fund	Plot	C	0.10
1.80 Sniper	Ass.	U	1.10
0.10 Society for Creative Anarchism	Grp.	C	0.10
0.10 Solidarity	PNWO	C	0.10
7.50 Soulburner	Res.	R	4.60
38			
4.50 South American Nazis	Grp.	R	3.10
6.00 Spasm of Violence	Plot	R	3.90
0.10 Spear of Longinus	Res.	C	0.10
0.10 Stealing the Plans	Plot	C	0.10
0.10 Stock Split	Plot	C	0.10
0.10 Stonehenge	Plc.	C	0.10

LIMITED Card Name	Type	Rarity	UNLIMITED
0.10 Straighten Up	Plot	C	0.10
4.50 Subliminals	Grp.	R	3.10
1.80 Sucked Dry and Cast Aside!	Plot	U	1.10
39			
2.50 Suicide Squad	Res.	U	1.50
6.00 Supreme Court	Grp.	R	3.90
0.10 Survivalists	Grp.	C	0.10
1.50 Sweeping Reforms	Plot	U	1.00
0.10 Sweepstakes Prize	Plot	C	0.10
0.10 Swiss Bank Account	Plot	C	0.10
0.10 Switzerland	Plc.	C	0.10
1.50 Tabloids	Grp.	U	1.00
0.10 Talisman of Ahrimanes	Plot	C	0.10
2.50 Tax Breaks	Plot	U	1.50
40			
6.00 Tax Reform	PNWO	R	3.90
0.10 Telephone Psychics	Grp.	C	0.10
0.10 Templars	Grp.	C	0.10
0.10 Terrorist Nuke	Plot	C	0.10
5.00 Texas	Plc.	R	3.40
0.10 The Auditor from Hell	Plot	C	0.10
0.10 The Big Score	Plot	C	0.10
6.00 The Big Sellout	Plot	R	3.90
0.25 The Bronze Head	Res.	C	0.15
41			
0.10 The Corporate Masters	PlGol	C	0.10
5.50 The First Thing We Do, Let's Kill All The Lawyers	Plot	R	3.60
0.25 The Frog God	Res.	C	0.15
0.10 The Hand of Madness	PlGol	C	0.10
6.00 The Holy Grail	Res.	R	3.90
2.00 The Internet Worm	Plot	U	1.30
3.00 The Library at Alexandria	Res.	U	1.80
6.00 The Mafia	Grp.	R	3.90
5.50 The Men in Black	Grp.	R	3.60
42			
2.50 The Network	Ill.	I	2.00
5.00 The Oregon Crud	Dis.	R	3.40
0.10 The Second Bullet	Plot	C	0.10
5.00 The Stars Are Right	Plot	R	3.40
6.00 The Weak Link	Plot	R	3.90
0.10 The Weird Turn Pro	Plot	C	0.10
0.10 Tidal Wave	Dis.	C	0.10
6.00 Time Warp	Plot	R	3.90
0.10 Tobacco Companies	Grp.	C	0.10
43			
0.25 Tornado	Dis.	C	0.15
0.25 Trekkies	Grp.	C	0.15
5.50 Triliberal Commission	Grp.	R	3.60
0.25 TV Preachers	Grp.	C	0.15
2.00 UFOs	Ill.	I	1.80
5.50 Underground Newspapers	Grp.	R	3.60
0.25 United Nations	Grp.	C	0.15
5.00 Unlucky 13	Plot	R	3.40
5.00 Unmasked!	Plot	R	3.40
44			
2.00 Up Against the Wall!	PlGol	R	1.90
0.25 Upheaval!	Plot	C	0.15
0.10 Urban Gangs	Grp.	C	0.10
0.10 Vampires	Grp.	C	0.10
0.10 Vatican City	Plc.	C	0.10
0.10 Video Games	Grp.	C	0.10
1.50 Volcano	Dis.	U	1.00
0.10 Volunteer Aid	Plot	C	0.10
0.10 Voodoo Economics	Plot	C	0.10
45			
1.80 Voudonistas	Grp.	U	1.10
0.10 Vultures	Plot	C	0.10
0.10 W.I.T.C.H.	Grp.	C	0.10
0.10 Wall Street	Grp.	C	0.10
3.00 Warehouse 23	Res.	U	1.80
0.10 Wargamers	Grp.	C	0.10
2.50 Weather Satellite	Res.	U	1.50
2.00 Whispering Campaign	Plot	C	0.15
6.00 Withering Curse	Ass.	R	3.90
46			
5.00 World Cup Victory	Plot	R	3.40
0.10 World Hunger	PNWO	C	0.10
6.00 World War 3	PNWO	R	3.90
0.25 Xanadu	Res.	C	0.15

RARITY KEY   **C** = Common   **U** = Uncommon   **R** = Rare   **VR** = Very Rare   **UR** = Ultra Rare   **F** = Foil card   **X** = Fixed/standard in all decks

Illuminati: New World Order • Assassins

Steve Jackson Games • Released **August 1995**

123 cards in set • **IDENTIFIER: None; has Limited Edition design**

• Booster packs contain 8 cards; booster displays contain 60 boosters

The **Assassins** supplement for **Illuminati: New World Order** introduced a tenth Illuminati group, **The Society of Assassins**, new rules for neutralizing groups by freezing all cards of a particular type or paralyzing a specific card or even "zapping" an Illuminati directly, plus a bunch of new group and plot cards to further complicate the mayhem.

Assassins cards have the same backs as all other *INWO* cards. Their faces use the same graphic design as the *Limited Edition.* — *Scott D. Haring*

Set (123 cards)	46.00
Booster Display Box	23.00
Booster Pack	1.30

You will need **14** nine-pocket pages to store this set. *(7 doubled up)*

Card name	Type	Rarity	Price
A Brief Attack of Conscience	PlZap	C	0.10
Al Amarja	Place	R	2.50
Alien Abduction	Plot	R	2.50
Anarchists Unite!	PlZap	C	0.10
Antitrust Legislation	NWO Yel	R	2.00
Anything Worth Doing Is Worth Overdoing	PlZap	C	0.10
Apathy	NWO Red	R	2.50
Arms Dealers	Organztn	R	4.30
Australia	Place	R	3.00
Australian Rules	NWO Red	C	0.10
Back to the Drawing Board	PlZap	U	0.40
Back to the Salt Mines	Plot	U	0.40
Backfire	PlFrz	U	0.40
Backmasquerade	Plot	C	0.10
Bait and Switch	PlZap	C	0.10
Bar Codes	Plot	U	0.40
Beach Party	Plot	C	0.10
Bite the Wax Tadpole	PlFrz	C	0.10
Black Helicopters	Resource	U	0.40
Blinded by Science	Goal	C	0.10
Blivit	Resource	U	0.40
Brushfire War	PlZap	C	0.10
Cat Juggling	PlParal	C	0.10
Cease-Fire	Plot	C	0.10
Chain Letter	PlParal	C	0.10
Church of Violentology	Organztn	R	4.30
Contract on America	PlParal	C	0.10
Copy Shops	Organztn	U	0.40
Crackdown on Crime	PlParal	C	0.10
Crusade	Plot	C	0.10
Day Care Centers	Organztn	U	0.40
Death To All Fanatics	PlParal	C	0.10
Defection	Plot	C	0.10
Dittoheads	Organztn	U	0.40
Dolphins	Plot	C	0.10
Don't Rock The Boat	PlZap	C	0.10
Don't Touch That Dial!	Plot	U	0.40
Drought	Disaster	R	2.00
Drug Companies	Organztn	UR	6.00
Earth First!	Goal	R	2.50
End of the World	NWO Yel	C	0.10
Enough is Enough	PlParal	C	0.10
EPA	Organztn	U	0.40
Every Year is Worse	PlParal	C	0.10
Exorcism	Plot	C	0.10
Family Values	PlZap	C	0.10
Fickle Finger of Fate	PlZap	U	0.40
Five-Year Plan	PlFrz	U	0.40
Flesh-Eating Bacteria	Disaster	UR	7.00
Floating Point Error	PlFrz	U	0.40
Frankenfood	Plot	C	0.10

Card name	Type	Rarity	Price
General Disorder	Persnlty	R	2.80
Global Warming	NWO Blue	C	0.10
Go Fish	Plot	U	0.40
"Go, Lemmings, Go!"	Plot	UR	5.00
Grave Robbers	Plot	R	2.50
Hubble Trouble	PlFrz	C	0.10
Illuminati University	Place	UR	10.00
Interesting Times	NWO Blue	R	2.50
Junk Bonds	PlFrz	C	0.10
Killer Satellite	Resource	U	0.40
Lab Explosion	PlZap	C	0.10
Lama Ramadingdong	Persnlty	U	0.40
Lenin's Body	Resource	U	0.40
Let the Sunshine In	PlFrz	C	0.10
Lyndon LaRouche	Persnlty	R	3.00
May Day	Plot	C	0.10
Metric System	PlParal	C	0.10
Militia	Organztn	UR	6.00
My Karma Ran Over Your Dogma	PlZap	C	0.10
Near Miss	Plot	C	0.10
Nevermore!	Plot	U	0.40
Newt Gingrich	Persnlty	R	3.00
No Beer!	Disaster	UR	5.00
Nutrition Nazis	Organztn	R	4.30
Oil Spill	Disaster	R	2.50
Orgone Grinder	Resource	U	0.40
Pale People In Black	Organztn	R	4.30
Partition	Plot	C	0.10
Pave the Earth!	PlFrz	U	0.40
Pizza for the Secret Meeting	Plot	C	0.10
Population Reduction	Goal	R	2.50
Power Satellite	Resource	U	0.40
Recycling Centers	Organztn	U	0.40
Regi$tered Trademark	Plot	R	2.50
Reverse Whammy	Plot	C	0.10
School Prayer	PlFrz	C	0.10
Science Alarmists	Organztn	R	4.30
Screaming Meme	Resource	R	2.50
Secret Master	Plot	UR	5.00

Card name	Type	Rarity	Price
Security Leak	PlZap	U	0.40
Shock Jocks	Organztn	R	4.30
Society of Assassins	Illuminati	U	0.40
Sorry, Wrong Number	PlZap	U	0.40
Spontaneous Combustion	Assntn	UR	5.00
Spy Satellite	Resource	R	2.00
State Lotteries	Organztn	U	0.40
Sudden European Vacation	Plot	R	2.00
Sufficiently Advanced Technology	Plot	C	0.10
Supernova	Plot	C	0.10
Supreme Court Nomination	Plot	U	0.40
Swingers	Organztn	R	4.30
Take The Money And Run	PlZap	C	0.10
TANSTAAFL	PlZap	C	0.10
Teddy Kennedy	Persnlty	U	0.40
Teflon Coating	Plot	C	0.10
The Big Prawn	Resource	R	2.50
The Green Party	Organztn	U	0.40
The Irish Flu	Plot	UR	5.00
The Magic Goes Away	NWO Red	R	2.50
The Meek Shall Inherit	PlZap	C	0.10
The Thule Group	Organztn	UR	6.00
This Was Only A Test	Plot	C	0.10
Truck Bomb	Plot	U	0.40
Vile Secretions	PlParal	U	0.40
Visualize Whirled Peas	NWO Yel	R	2.50
Vladimir Zhirinovsky	Persnlty	U	0.40
Waiting Period	PlParal	C	0.10
Watermelons	NWO Blue	R	2.50
Whistle Blowers	PlParal	C	0.10
Witch Hunt	Plot	C	0.10
X-Ray Specs	Resource	R	2.50
You Are What You Eat	Plot	C	0.10

Illuminati: New World Order • Blank Cards

Steve Jackson Games

Released **July 1995** • **50** special cards in set • **IDENTIFIER: Oh, please...**

• Booster packs contain 20 cards; booster displays contain 28 packs

Another quickie marketing idea to capitalize on the success of **Illuminati: New World Order**, the **Blank Cards** are just that: blank cards, half with the plot back and half with the group back. Many players were having fun inventing their own cards (several websites dedicated to new *INWO* cards still flourish today), and the *Blank Cards* were created for them. Each pack had a cover card with one of 50 silly ideas of things to do with the cards, like: "Employ as a talisman to ward off giant crawdads," or, "Tape them together into a giant pyramid and fly it like a kite. When the sky darkens, wait for further instructions." — *Scott D. Haring*

Display Box	10.00	Single Pack	0.50

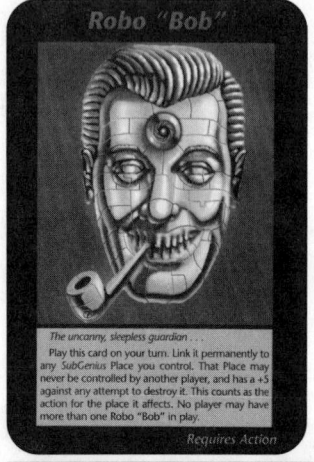

Robo "Bob"

The uncanny, sleepless guardian . . .
Play this card on your turn. Link it permanently to any SubGenius Place you control. That Place may never be controlled by another player, and has a +5 against any attempt to destroy it. This counts as the action for the place it affects. No player may have more than one Robo "Bob" in play.

Requires Action

Illuminati: New World Order • SubGenius

Steve Jackson Games • Released **1998**
100 card set • **IDENTIFIER: Black backgrounds on card faces; names in italics**
Designed by **Steve Jackson** and **Lynette R.F. Cowper**

SubGenius is a stand-alone supplement for **Illuminati: New World Order** — it can be played by itself, or the cards can be mixed into a traditional *INWO* game.

The Church of the SubGenius is a real organization, a pseudo-religion and pop cultural movement that spends most of its time satirizing religions and pop cultural movements, including itself. (Its central figure, J.R. "Bob" Dobbs, appears often in this set.) The standalone game is for two to four players and plays most like a **One With Everything** game, with all the group cards coming from a central deck and captured from a central uncontrolled pile.

SubGenius makes a strange game even stranger. This set also features the weirdest, most mind-bending art ever seen on any CCG card. Many devotees of the Church of the SubGenius have, apparently, powerful computers with graphics programs, tremendous creativity, and way too much free time. These artists have traded their strange SubGenius-themed creations over the Internet for years, and Steve Jackson Games used the best ones (and their creators) for the bizarre art in this set.

INWO SubGenius card backs are identical to all other INWO cards. The faces use the same graphic design as the Factory Set. — **Scott D. Haring**

The non-CCG

The similar cards from the non-CCG *Illuminati: Deluxe* can be differentiated by their card backs, which don't say **New World Order**.

SubGenius Case	20.00
SubGenius Box	5.00

Card name	Type	Price
1		
☐ 13013	Plot	0.50
☐ Advanced Supersonic Aluminum Nazi Hell Creatures from Beneath the Hollow Earth	Group	5.00
☐ Anti-Slack	Plot	0.50
☐ Arise!	Goal	0.50
☐ Attitude Mutation	Plot	0.50
☐ "Bobbies"	Group	3.00
☐ Brag of the SubGenius	Goal	0.50
☐ Bulldada	Plot	0.50
☐ Cast Out False Prophets!	Goal	0.50
2		
☐ Church of Middle America	Group	3.00
☐ Church of the SubGenius	Illuminati	1.80
☐ Church of the SubGenius	Illuminati	1.80

Illuminati: New World Order • Promo Cards

Steve Jackson Games

Three of the earliest magazine promos, **The Great Pyramid** and **Pyramid Marketing Schemes** from *Pyramid* magazine and **Trading Card Games** from *Duelist*, had the Limited Edition design and were reprinted in **One With Everything** — but not **Unlimited Edition**.

As one might expect, the alignment for **Trading Card Games** is "Weird."

Card name	Type	Price
☐ Convenience Stores		3.00
☐ Pyramid Marketing Schemes	Group	2.00
☐ Strange Bedfellows		2.00
☐ The Great Pyramid	Place	2.00
☐ Trading Card Games	Group	3.50

You will need **12** nine-pocket pages to store this set. (6 doubled up)

Card name	Type	Price
☐ Church of the SubGenius	Illuminati	1.80
☐ Church of the SubGenius	Illuminati	1.80
☐ Citizens for Normalcy	Group	3.00
☐ Comet Hail-Bob	Plot	0.50
☐ Connie Dobbs	Personality	0.50
☐ Corrective Phrenologists	Group	3.00
3		
☐ Dallas Catacombs	Place	0.50
☐ Decency is OK!	Plot	0.50
☐ Devival	Plot	0.50
☐ Divine Mail Order	Group	3.00
☐ Dobbstown	Place	0.50
☐ Dokstok	Place	0.50
☐ Dr. K'Taden Legume	Personality	0.50
☐ Drs. for "Bob"	Group Dirt	2.50
☐ Eternal Salvation or Triple your Money Back	Plot	0.50
4		
☐ Excremeditation	Plot	0.50
☐ Fake Healing	Plot	0.50
☐ False Overman	Plot	0.50
☐ False Prophets	Group	3.00
☐ False Slack	Plot	0.50
☐ 'Frop Farm	Place	0.50
☐ Give Me Slack, Or Give Me Food	Plot	0.50
☐ Glorps	Group	3.00
☐ Good Sex for Mutants Dating League	Group	2.50
5		
☐ Head Launching	Plot	0.25
☐ Inherently Bogus	Plot	0.50
☐ Janor Device	Resource	0.35
☐ Jesus B.	Persnlty	0.50
☐ JHVH-1	Plot	0.50
☐ Kill "Bob!"	Plot	0.50
☐ League for Obvious Decency	Group	2.50
☐ Local Clenches	Group	3.00
☐ Luck Plane	Plot	0.50
6		
☐ Martyr Meter	Resource	0.35
☐ Mediocretinism	Plot	0.25
☐ Miraculous Manifestation	Plot	0.50
☐ More Slack	Plot	0.50
☐ MWOWM	Group	3.00
☐ Nental Ife	Plot	0.50
☐ NHGH	Persnlty	0.50
☐ "Official, all Inclusive, Divine Excuse"	Plot	0.50
☐ . . . Or Kill Me!	Plot	0.50
7		
☐ OverMan	Plot	0.50

Card name	Type	Price
☐ OverMan Philo Drummond	Personlity	0.50
☐ Phlegm Elementals	Group	3.00
☐ Pinks	Group	3.00
☐ Psychic Pstench	Plot	0.50
☐ Rain of Prairie Squid	Plot	0.50
☐ Random Jesii	Plot	0.50
☐ Rant!	Plot	0.50
☐ Repent!	Plot	0.50
8		
☐ Reverend Ivan Stang	Personality	0.50
☐ Robo "Bob"	Plot	0.50
☐ Rogue SubGenii	Group	3.00
☐ S.C.A.M	Plot	0.25
☐ S.L.A.K.	Group	2.50
☐ S.P.U.T.U.M.	Group	2.50
☐ Sacred Jests	Plot	0.50
☐ Sacred Stencil	Resource	0.35
☐ Saucer Landing Strip	Place	0.50
9		
☐ Schizm	Plot	0.50
☐ Science Cannot Remove the Terror of the Gods!	Goal	0.50
☐ Secret FisTemple	Group	3.00
☐ Shordurpersav	Plot	0.50
☐ Slackfusion	Plot	0.25
☐ Smite Them All!	Plot	0.50
☐ Speakers in Tongues	Group	3.00
☐ St. Janor Hypercleats	Personality	0.50
☐ Stark Fist of Removal	Plot	0.50
10		
☐ SubGenius FisTemples	Group	4.00
☐ Sultan of Slack	Plot	0.50
☐ Tape Runs Out...	Plot	0.25
☐ The 13th Apostle	Plot	0.50
☐ The Anti"Bob"	Goal	0.50
☐ The Hour of Slack	Group	3.00
☐ The Prescriptures	Resource	0.35
☐ The Saint of Sales	Plot	0.50
☐ The True Pipe	Resource	0.35
11		
☐ The World Ends Tomorrow and You May Die!	Plot	0.50
☐ They May Be Pink...	Plot	0.25
☐ Three-Fisted Tales of "Bob"	Resource	0.80
☐ Time Control	Plot	0.50
☐ www.subgenius.com	Group	4.00
☐ X-Day	Plot	0.50
☐ Xists	Group	3.00
☐ Yacatisma	Plot	0.50
☐ Yetis	Group	3.80
12		
☐ You'd Pay to Know What You Really Think!	Plot	0.50

RARITY KEY **C** = Common **U** = Uncommon **R** = Rare **VR** = Very Rare **UR** = Ultra Rare **F** = Foil card **X** = Fixed/standard in all decks

Imajica (Also known as *Clive Barker's Imajica*)

HarperPrism • Released **August 1997**

330 cards in set plus **6** promo cards

- Starter decks contain two 60-card decks; starter displays contain 6 decks
- Booster packs contain 15 cards; booster displays contain 36 packs

Book publisher HarperCollins found out about CCGs in a profitable way: It was the initial publisher of the ***Magic: The Gathering*** novels, which many people bought just to rip out the back page and send in for a *Magic* promo card. Wizards of the Coast later took its book publishing rights back, but HarperCollins remembered the profits well enough to release its own CCG based on the work of one of its authors, Clive Barker.

In ***Imajica***, Earth is one of the five Dominions, realities one can travel to and from. As one of the few who know this, the player's goal is to build power by having his Allies seize control of one site in each of the five Dominions.

Players begin by placing Site cards for each of the five realms in the common playing area. Each turn, players draw two cards and play a couple of Ally cards. Allies have three statistics: Strength (for combat), Magic (for seizing sites) and Prime (how hard they are to sway to one side; players may play 7 Prime worth of characters every turn). Allies enter play in one of the three areas on the player's side of the board, the Reserve. They can't do anything there but they are also safe from attacks.

Once Allies are moved into the Active area, they can attack, be attacked, or attempt to seize a site. Seizing a site is a simple mechanic, but it can be hard to pull off. Players check the Site's resistance level and then send a group of people who have at least that much Magic to attempt the seizure. The opponent may send a group to oppose them, and, if they have more magic, everyone goes home. If an opponent sends a group, he may play Influence cards, a special type of card that only works in this phase. These can really mess you up. Of course, there are also cards called Paths that get played on the Site to make the seizure either more difficult or easier (depending upon who played them). Once a site it seized, it leaves the center of the board and slides over to the winning player's Stage area, where he must keep cards there to defend it. If one of those cards is lost, the site goes back to the center of the table. Getting out lots of people is a big part of the strategy.

The cards are pseudo-gothic and disturbing, done very well. Card layout is clear, with card type, alignment, name, uniqueness, home dimension, gender, strength, magic, prime and special abilities all clearly marked and easy to discern. The rulebook, on the other hand, is tough to crack, but it does include tables for all of the important phases and steps. *Imajica*'s mechanics are well-designed, intuitive, and fun, but there are too many card types with limitations on when they can be played.

This is a small problem, easily fixed by tuning one's deck, but it is something to be aware of. Not enough people were apparently aware of *Imajica*, however, and it vanished without a single expansion. — *Richard Weld*

Concept	●●●●○
Gameplay	●●●○○
Card art	●●●○○
Player pool	○○○○○

Patently unique

When Wizards of the Coast asked for royalties from other CCG manufacturers after its trading-card game patent went through, ***Imajica***'s HarperPrism was the only company that publicly agreed to pay up.

You will need 37 nine-pocket pages to store this set. *(18 doubled up)*

Set (330 cards)	45.00
Starter Display Box	17.00
Booster Display Box	20.00
Starter Deck	5.00
Booster Pack	1.00

Promo cards

Clive Barker	10.00
Emsphet Iisau	2.00
Foek Foek	2.00
Lost Soul	2.00
Marios Kascarika	2.00
Pullusic	5.00

Card name	Rarity	Price
[1]		
52nd and Madison	C	0.05
Abelove	U	0.25
Actor Chappie	C	0.05
Alice Tyrwhitt	C	0.05
Alvus Nadir	C	0.05
Amnesia	R	2.00
Ana	R	2.00
Anarchy	U	0.25
Angels	C	0.05
[2]		
Animi Adfectus	U	0.75

Card name	Rarity	Price
Anniversary of the Reconciliation	R	2.00
Aping	U	0.50
Arae 'ke' gei	R	2.00
Arson	C	0.05
Azzimulto	C	0.05
Bastion of the Banu	C	0.05
Beatrix	U	0.75
Bem	R	2.00
[3]		
Blessing of Hapexamendios	U	0.75
Blind	R	2.00
Blue Egg	R	3.00
Blue Eye	R	2.00
Boston Bowl	C	0.05
Breach of Contract	C	0.05
Bunyan Blew	R	3.00
Bureau of Justice	C	0.05
Caelum	R	2.00
[4]		
Call to Arms	U	0.75
Call to the Dead	U	0.75
Carol	C	0.05
Celestine	R	2.00
Chamber of the Goddesses	U	0.50

Card name	Rarity	Price
Chant - the Facilitator	R	2.00
Chant's Letter	C	0.05
Charlie Estabrook	C	0.05
Charlotte Feaver	U	0.50
[5]		
Charon Memorial	R	2.00
Ched Lo Ched the Flowering Place	C	0.05
Chester Klein	C	0.05
Chicka Jackeen (Lucius Cobbitt)	R	2.00
Christos	R	3.00
City of the Unbeheld	R	2.00
Clara Leash	U	0.75
Clem	U	0.50
Clerkenwell	U	0.25
[6]		
Coaxial Tasko - the Wretched	C	0.05
Concupiscentia	C	0.05
Confession	U	0.50
Consequences	U	0.50
Cornered	C	0.05
Cosacosa	C	0.05
Covent Garden	R	3.00
Cradle of Chzercemit	R	2.00

Card name	Rarity	Price
Cradle Parasite	U	0.75
[7]		
Crucifix	R	2.00
Culus 'su' erai	C	0.05
Darkness in a deeper dark	U	0.75
Dearther Encampment	R	3.00
Deliquium Kesparate	U	0.50
Destiny	C	0.05
Dies Natalis Solis Invictus	C	0.05
Digressio	C	0.05
Discipline	C	0.05
[8]		
Doeki	C	0.05
Dottle	R	3.00
Doubling	U	0.75
Doxios	U	0.50
Dreadlocks	C	0.05
Duncan Skeet	C	0.05
Dux Demesne	U	0.25
Effatoi	U	0.25
Efreet Splendid	C	0.05
[9]		
Eloign Splendid	U	0.75
Emblem Splendid	C	0.05
Emotion: Bliss	U	0.75
Emotion: Fear	C	0.05

RARITY KEY **C** = Common **U** = Uncommon **R** = Rare **VR** = Very Rare **UR** = Ultra Rare **F** = Foil card **X** = Fixed/standard in all decks

Card name	Rarity	Price
Emotion: Frenzy	C	0.05
Emotion: Guilt	C	0.05
Emotion: Hate	U	0.50
Emotion: Loneliness	C	0.05
Emotion: Lust	U	0.50
10		
Emotion: Tranquility	U	0.75
Erasure	R	2.00
Esmond Bloom Godolphin	U	0.75
Espionage	U	0.50
Eurhetemec Chianculi	U	0.25
Eurhetemec Kesparate	C	0.05
Eurhetemec Ruins	C	0.05
Express	U	0.25
Failed Reconciliation	R	2.00
11		
False Prophet	C	0.05
Famous Last Words	C	0.05
Father Athanasius	R	2.00
Feit	C	0.05
Feit of Holding	C	0.05
Flaute	C	0.05
Floccus Dado	C	0.05
Flores Roxborough	C	0.05
Flute's Visions	U	0.75
12		
Fragments of Light	C	0.05
Friendly Wager	R	2.00
Gamut Street #28	R	2.00
Gaud Maybellome's Encyclopedia of Heavenly Signs	U	0.25
Geiss the Witherer	U	0.75
Geist	R	3.00
Gek-a-gek	U	0.75
General Mattalaus	R	2.00
General Racidio	R	2.00
13		
General Rosengarten	R	2.00
Gentle - John Furie Zacharias	R	2.00
Gentle's Map	U	0.50
Geoffrey Light	C	0.05
Gideon	U	0.75
Giles Bloxham	U	0.50
Glyph	R	2.00
Go Back!	C	0.05
God of Forgers	U	0.50
14		
Goddess' Cell	R	3.00
Goetic Kicaranki Nun	U	0.75
Gossip	C	0.05
Graveolents	C	0.05
Guardian Angel	R	3.00
Hairstone Banty	U	0.25
Hakaridek	U	0.50
Hampstead Heath	C	0.05
Hapexamendios' Cleansing Fire	R	2.00
15		
Happi	C	0.05
Harsh Terrain	C	0.05
Hebbert Peccable	R	2.00

Card name	Rarity	Price
Henry Holland	R	2.00
Heratae Hammeryock	R	2.00
Hezoir	C	0.05
Hidden Shadows	U	0.75
High Holborn	U	0.75
High Pass of Jokalaylau	R	3.00
16		
Hills of the Conscious Cloud	R	2.00
Hittehitte	R	2.00
Hoi-polloi Peccable	U	0.75
Hologram	C	0.05
Homeland	C	0.05
Hoopreo	C	0.05
Horace Tyrwhitt	U	0.75
Horsebone	C	0.05
Hubert Shales - the Sloth	U	0.75
17		
Hugger-Mussus	R	2.00
Huzzah Aping	R	2.00
Huzzah Odell	U	0.75
Iahmandhas	U	0.75
Inanitas	C	0.05
Ipse	C	0.05
Irish	C	0.05
Isaac Abelove - Lawyer	U	0.75
Isthmus Oculi	U	0.75
18		
Izaak	C	0.05
Jassick	R	2.00
Jokalaylau	R	2.00
Joshua Godolphin	R	2.00
Judith Odell	R	2.00
Kenny Soames	C	0.05
Kething's cul de sac	R	2.00
Kill yourself soon	C	0.05
Klupo	U	0.50
19		
Kopje Cor	U	0.75
Kreauchee	C	0.05
Kurganaal	U	0.75
Kuthuss	C	0.05
Kuttner Dowd	R	2.00
Kwem	C	0.05
L'Himby	R	2.00
Lace Gate	C	0.05
Larumday Splendid	R	2.00
20		
Lenten Way	R	2.00
Letters of Faith	C	0.05
Lewis Leader - Lawyer	U	0.75
Liberatore	C	0.05
Like the back of my hand	U	0.25
Likerish Street	C	0.05
Lionel Wakeman	U	0.75
Little Ease	U	0.75
Loitus Hammeryock	U	0.75
21		
Lotti Yap	C	0.05
Lu 'chur' chem	U	0.25
M'amoite	U	0.25
Mai-kZÿ	U	0.25
Maison de SantZÿ	U	0.25
Make the many one	C	0.05
Malbaker's Numbubo	C	0.05
Manhattan	R	2.00
Marlin	U	0.25
22		
Matthias McGann	U	0.50
May everything be as it seems	C	0.05
Meditation Room	C	0.05
Memory	C	0.05
Mercy	R	2.00
Merrow Ti Ti	C	0.05
Misplaced Stones	R	2.00
Mites	U	0.75

Card name	Rarity	Price
Monday	U	0.50
23		
Mount of Lipper Bayak	U	0.25
Nathanial Godolphin	U	0.25
Nikaetomaas	R	2.00
Nisi Nirvana	R	2.00
Nullianac	R	2.00
Ode to Sartori	U	0.50
Oke T'Noon Kesparate	C	0.05
Oliver McGann	U	0.50
Omootajive	C	0.05
24		
Oscar Esmond Godolphin	U	0.50
Out of site out of mind	U	0.75
Oxford	U	0.75
Palace	R	2.00
Paramarola	C	0.05
Patashoqua	R	2.00
Patashoquan Highway	U	0.50
Peace	R	3.00
Peccable's House	R	4.00
25		
Peripeteria	U	0.75
Piccadilly Station	U	0.75
Pie 'oh' pah	R	2.00
Pinguis	R	2.00
Pivot Fragments	R	3.00
Pivot Tower	R	2.00
Pivotal Voices	R	2.00
Pluthero Quexos' 1st Law of Drama	C	0.05
Pneuma	C	0.05
26		
Poems to Union	R	2.00
Pontiff Farrow	U	0.50
Possession	U	0.50
Prayer Book	C	0.05
Prediction	C	0.05
Pregnancy	C	0.05
Preparations	U	0.50
Prisoners of Hapexamendios	U	0.75
Prophetic Paintings	C	0.05
27		
Public Executions	R	2.00
Purge of the Tabula Rasa	R	2.00
Quaisoir	R	2.00
Realm of Hapexamendios	R	2.00
Renunciance	R	2.00
Resurrection	R	2.00
Retribution	C	0.05
Ring of Stones	R	2.00
Ritual	C	0.05
28		
Rivalry	C	0.05
River Advena	R	2.00
River Fefer	C	0.05
River Noy	U	0.50
River Ovum	C	0.05
Rivers in Reverse	U	0.75
Rout	C	0.05
Roxborough Tower	R	2.00
Roxborough's Letter	U	0.50
29		
Ruukassh!	R	2.00
Sacrifice	U	0.75
Saint Martin in the Fields	C	0.05
Saints Creaze and Evendown	R	2.00
Sanctum	R	2.00
Sartori	R	2.00
Scintillants	R	2.00
Scopique	R	2.00
Scoriae Kesparate	U	0.50
30		
Second Thoughts	R	4.00
Seidux	U	0.50

Card name	Rarity	Price
Severed Alliance	U	0.75
Shiverick Square	C	0.05
Silken Sword	R	2.00
Simone	C	0.05
Sister	C	0.05
Slew	C	0.05
Sorcery	U	0.75
31		
South Bank	C	0.05
Spina Tor	C	0.05
Squalling	C	0.05
St. Bartholomew's Fair	R	2.00
Statue of the Etook Ha'chiit	R	2.00
Streatham	U	0.50
Sublime	R	2.00
Substitution	R	2.00
Succulent Rock	R	2.00
32		
Summon Nullianac	U	0.75
Swamps of Loquiot	U	0.75
Sway-worker	U	0.50
Synod	R	3.00
Tabula Rasan Library	R	2.00
Tartarus	R	2.00
Tauro Splith	R	2.00
Taxation Court	C	0.05
Taylor Briggs	U	0.50
33		
Thank you and goodnight	C	0.05
The Bazaar	U	0.75
The Future was a Woman	U	0.50
The Retreat	R	3.00
The Righteous	R	2.00
Thes 'reh' ot - Lawyer	U	0.50
Thomas Roxborough	U	0.50
Tick Raw the Evocator	R	2.00
Tin of Colors	U	0.75
34		
TishalullZÿ	C	0.05
Tolland	C	0.05
Tombs of the Vehement Loki Lobb	C	0.05
Tour	R	2.00
Transport	R	3.00
Tree of Immoralities	U	0.75
Uma Umagammagi	U	0.75
Uma's Temple	C	0.05
Unanswered Prayers	C	0.05
35		
Undone	R	2.00
Uredo	R	3.00
Uter Musky	R	2.00
Vanaeph	U	0.75
Vanessa	U	0.25
Verdette Street	U	0.25
Viaticum Kesparate	R	2.00
Vigor N'Ashap - Oethac	U	0.75
Virilus	U	0.25
36		
Voider	U	0.50
Vuvaku	R	2.00
Wake of Hapexamendios	R	2.00
We are what we are	C	0.05
We do as we do	R	2.00
Wheym	C	0.05
Whim of Hapexamendios	R	2.00
Wrath of Hapexamendios	R	2.00
Yark Lazarevich	U	0.50
37		
Yeaty	C	0.05
Yoke	U	0.75
Yzordderrex	R	2.00
Yzordderrexian War Machine	R	2.00
Zarzi	C	0.05
Zenetics	U	0.50

Illustrious Imajica

Illustrators whose works can be found on *Imajica* cards include H.R. Giger, Tom Baxa, Eric Dinyer, Jeff Laubenstein, Carl Lundgren, Ted McKeever, and even Clive Barker himself.

RARITY KEY C = Common U = Uncommon R = Rare VR = Very Rare UR = Ultra Rare F = Foil card X = Fixed/standard in all decks

James Bond 007

Heartbreaker/Target Games AB • First set, *Goldeneye*, released **November 1995**

207 cards in set

• Starter decks contain 60 cards and rules; starter displays contain 10 starters
• Booster packs contain 15 cards; booster displays contain 60 boosters

One of several new CCGs released by Heartbreaker in late 1995, *James Bond 007* is about, well, James Bond, aka Agent 007. Got it? OK. The release, in support of the first Brosnan Bond flick, *GoldenEye*, includes material from every past film (including *Thunderball*, which even Victory Games couldn't do with its 1980s role-playing game).

As in every Bond movie, the goal is to complete missions and score points. Players pose as Directors of the British Secret Service (choose your own letter) and play James Bonds, Allies, and Q equipment for these folks to use. That's right: *Bonds*. There are a dozen different "aspects" of 007, each with different skills. One of each can be in play. Players also deploy Missions, Villains, Obstacles, Locations and Henchmen for opponents to fight. If possible, players must start a new Plot stack each turn; if they have a Plot card from the same movie as a Plot stack, they may add the new one as a subplot to the prior card, making the mission more difficult. As each Plot requires different skills, players pick a Bond who can do them to send across. Bond, his equipment, and his allies must have all the right skills, and their statistics must exceed those required for the mission. If you defeat all of the cards, you score the points. That's the basis, but there is more to it: If you have a villain or henchman in play, you can sic them on your opponent's Bonds.

Sadly, the combat system is pointless. If a henchman with a combat value of 10 attacks a Bond who has a 6, Bond is wounded. When he is wounded again, he dies. But, if Bond plays a card to raise his combat value to 11, the henchman just goes home annoyed. Bond can't kill a henchman unless he can complete the mission the henchman is attached to.

The cards are clear, easy to read, and simple to use. The skills are represented by a set of icons. If a card one wants to play on a Bond requires a skill, the skill is printed in red. If it grants a skill, the icon is blue — very neat.

The set was small, however, and the starter decks were a bit too random for good gameplay. A supplement, *Villians and Women*, was announced for 1996 but never made it. — *Richard Weld*

You will need **23** nine-pocket pages to store this set. (12 doubled up)

Concept	●●●○○
Gameplay	●●●○○
Card art	●●●○○
Player pool	○○○○○

Set (207 cards)	**38.00**
Starter Display Box	**20.00**
Booster Display Box	**20.00**
Starter Deck	**5.00**
Booster Pack	**1.00**

Card name	Rarity	Price
A Brand New Toy	U	0.30
A Gentleman's Duties	U	0.30
A Giant Step For Mankind	U	0.30
A Helping Hand	C	0.10
Acrostar Mini-Jet	U	0.30
Alec Trevelyan (006)	Ch	5.00
All Part Of My Plan	R	1.00
Ambush!	C	0.10
Aris Kristatos	U	0.30
Assaulted	C	0.10
"Aston Martin "Volante"	Ch	4.00
Aston Martin DB-5	R	1.00
Atlantis	R	1.00
Auric Goldfinger	U	0.30
Avenge Felix Leiter	U	0.30
Bar	U	0.30
Baron Samedi	U	0.30
Bell Jet Pack	U	0.30
Blofeld	R	2.00
Blofeld's Assassin	R	0.30
Blow From Above	U	0.30
Bond Theme Music	R	2.00
Boris Grishenko	C	0.10
Brad Whitaker	R	1.00
Bridge Out!	C	0.10

Card name	Rarity	Price
Bring in the Cavalry	U	0.30
Brutal Force	R	1.00
Bull's-Eye	C	0.10
Bungie Jump	C	0.10
Buzz-Saw Yo-Yo	C	0.10
Caged	C	0.10
Carnival In Rio	R	1.00
Cat And Mouse	R	1.00
Club Card	C	0.10
Colonel Rosa Klebb's Shoe Knife	U	0.30
Concealed Knife Belt	C	0.10
Connections	Ch	4.00
Counterintelligence	U	0.30
Crab Key	R	1.00
Customs Officials	R	1.00
Daily Workout	U	0.30
Deadly Attack	R	1.00
Destroy Cocaine Factory	R	1.00
Destroy Laser Satellite	U	0.30
Dismantle Nuclear Bombs	R	1.00
Domino	R	2.00
Double Agent	U	0.30
Doubly Prepared	R	1.00
Dr. Kananga	C	0.10
Dr. No	U	0.30
Dr. No's Dragon Tank	U	0.30
Electrocuted	R	1.00
Emilio Largo	R	2.00
Equalize	R	1.00
Ernst Stavro Blofeld	Ch	5.00
Escape Route	R	1.00

Card name	Rarity	Price
Explosive Pen	U	0.30
Faux Pas	C	0.10
Felix Leiter	C	0.10
Fifth Gear	C	0.10
Find Goldeneye	C	0.10
Fiona Volpe	R	2.00
Fire From The Sky	C	0.10
Firefight	U	0.30
Focused	U	0.30
Fort Knox	C	0.10
Francisco Scaramanga	C	0.10
Franz Sanchez	R	2.00
Friends In High Places	C	0.10
Garrote	C	0.10
General Orlov	R	2.00
General Ourumov	C	0.10
Gobinda	C	0.10
Helga Brandt	U	0.30

Card name	Rarity	Price
Heller	R	2.00
Hidden Agenda	R	1.00
High Stakes	U	0.30
Honey Rider	U	0.30
Horrible Weather	R	1.00
How Rude!	R	1.00
Hugo Drax	U	0.30
Improved Gondola	U	0.30
Incredible Escape!	R	1.00
Indiscretion	R	1.00
Information Center	C	0.10
Jack Wade	C	0.10
Jaws	U	0.30
J.I.M. Diving Equipment	R	1.00
Kara Milovy	R	2.00
Kissy	R	2.00
Leadership	Ch	4.00
License To Kill	R	3.00

Licensed to ill?

Bond films are a punster's playground, but the minimalist flavor text on the Bond cards verges on the cloying. Samples of Brosnan (and the occasional Sean Connery):

"Hard at work on Her Majesty's Secret Service."

"Sending postcards from Russia with love."

"Revealed for your eyes only."

"Things that would scare the living daylights out of lesser men don't faze Bond."

"You've got to to think fast when you only live twice!"

And the Carly Simon double-header: "Nobody does it better" and "Baby, you're the best!"

RARITY KEY C = Common   U = Uncommon   R = Rare   VR = Very Rare   UR = Ultra Rare   F = Foil card   X = Fixed/standard in all decks

Card name	Rarity	Price
Little Nellie	R	1.00
Live Twice	U	0.30
Lotus Esprit Submarine Car	R	1.00
Lupe Lamora	U	0.30
M	U	0.30
M Is Displeased	R	1.00
Magda	U	0.30
[12]		
Main Strike Mine	U	0.30
Major Anya Amasova	C	0.10
Malfunction	R	1.00
Martial Training	U	0.30
Mary Goodnight	U	0.30
Max Zorin	C	0.10
May Day	C	0.10
Melina Havelock	R	2.00
Milton Krest	U	0.30
[13]		
Miss Caruso	U	0.30
Miss Moneypenny	C	0.10
Modified BMW	U	0.30
Monte Carlo Casino	C	0.10
Naomi	R	2.00
Natayla Simonova	C	0.10
Necros	U	0.30
Octopus	C	0.10
Octopussy	R	3.00
[14]		
Oddjob	U	0.30
Omega Laser Watch	C	0.10
"One Step Forward, Two Steps Back"	Ch	4.00
Ousted	U	0.30
Out Of The Blue	C	0.10

Card name	Rarity	Price
Overheated	C	0.10
Pam Bouvier	Ch	5.00
Paula Caplan	R	2.00
Prevent Conventional War	U	0.30
[15]		
Prevent Extermination of Agents	C	0.10
Prevent Nerve Gas Attack	R	1.00
Prevent Nuclear Launch	U	0.30
Prevent World War Three	C	0.10
Prince Kamal Khan	C	0.10
Professor Dent	R	2.00
Pussy Galore	U	0.30
Q	C	0.10
Quarrel	R	1.00
[16]		
Quick Thinking	C	0.10
Rapier Wit	U	0.30
Reassignment	R	1.00
Red Grant	R	2.00
Retribution	R	1.00
Retrieve Decoding Machine	U	0.30
Retrieve The A.T.A.C.	C	0.10
Retrieve the Solex Agitator	C	0.10
Rosa Klebb's Shoe Knife	C	0.10
[17]		
Save Gold Reserve	Ch	4.00
Save Silicon Valley	R	1.00
Scuba Gear	C	0.10
Setup	U	0.30
Shark-Infested Waters	R	1.00
Sheriff J. W. Pepper	U	0.30
Silence is Golden	U	0.30
Snappy One-Liner	U	0.30

Card name	Rarity	Price
Snowstorm	U	0.30
[18]		
Solitaire	R	2.00
Soviet War Room	Ch	4.00
Soviet Weapons Research Center	R	1.00
Space Station	U	0.30
S.P.E.C.T.R.E. Consortium	U	0.30
S.P.E.C.T.R.E. Headquarters	R	3.00
S.P.E.C.T.R.E. Is Unprepared	U	0.30
S.P.E.C.T.R.E. Island	C	0.10
Speedboat	C	0.10
[19]		
St. Petersburg	U	0.30
Stacey Sutton	U	0.30
Sticky Situation	C	0.10
Stop Heroin Flow to the U.S.	R	1.00
Strict Rules Of Golf	R	1.00
Submachine Gun	U	0.30
Supertanker Liparus	C	0.10
Swoosh!	U	0.30
Take Down	R	1.00
[20]		
Tatiana Romanova	U	0.30
Tee Hee	C	0.10
The Daredevil	C	0.10
The Disco Volante	U	0.30
The Inventive Champion	C	0.10
The Legend	Ch	5.00
The Man Behind The Scenes	C	0.10
The Man For The Job	C	0.10
The Marksman	C	0.10

Card name	Rarity	Price
[21]		
The Navy Hero	C	0.10
The Perfect Companion	U	0.30
The Protector	R	2.00
The Secret Agent	C	0.10
The Silent Visitor	C	0.10
The Specialist	C	0.10
The Warrior	C	0.10
This Never Happened to the Other Fellow	R	1.00
Tiffany Case	U	0.30
[22]		
Time Bomb	U	0.30
Tricky Situation	R	1.00
Uncontrolled Aircraft	C	0.10
Underwater Vehicle	C	0.10
Valentin Zukovsky	R	2.00
Venice	U	0.30
Vodka Martini	U	0.30
Volcano Rocket Base	C	0.10
Walther PPK With Silencer	C	0.10
[23]		
We Have All The Time In The World	R	1.00
Weapon Jam	C	0.10
Wet Suit	C	0.10
Wild Goose Chase	R	1.00
Winning Smile	R	1.00
Xenia Onatopp	C	0.10
Your Worst Nightmare	U	0.30
Zora & Vida	U	0.30
Zorin's Blimp	C	0.10

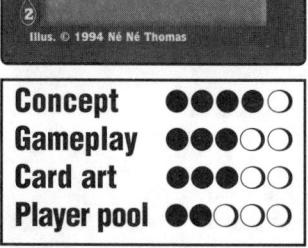

.44 Magnum
Weapon, Gun.
2R each strike, with an optional maneuver each combat.
[2]
Illus. © 1994 Né Né Thomas

Jyhad

Wizards of the Coast, based on a license from **White Wolf** • Released **September 1994**

438 cards in set

- Starter decks contain 76 cards; starter displays contain 10 starters
- Booster packs contain 19 cards; booster displays contain 36 boosters

Inspired by and licensing the White Wolf story-telling game ***Vampire: The Masquerade, Jyhad*** was Wizards of the Coast's second CCG and the third proper CCG to reach the market. Booster packs contain a whopping 19 cards, which would *not* be a harbinger of card-counts to come.

In *Jyhad*, players take the part of ancient vampires who fight wars through their minion vampires and other dupes. Each player starts with two decks, a minion deck that contains all of the player's vampires (Kindred), and a play deck that contains the rest of the player's cards. Each player starts the game with 30 Blood Points and loses when he or she has zero Blood Points remaining. The last player left standing wins. This can be tricky since a player must expend Blood Points out of the pool to bring vampire minions into play. There are seven clans of Vampires, each with their specialties among the vampiric powers, called Disciplines. By themselves, the Disciplines have no game effects, but allow the player to play certain cards at a greater or lesser effect, depending on how well the vampire has mastered the requisite Discipline.

Designed as a multi-player game, *Jyhad* devotes a lot of cards and rules to re-creating the politics among the Kindred. This can make for long sessions, especially in large games.

Concerns over offending Arab-American sensibilities — plus a desire to more closely identify with the source game — led to the rerelease of *Jyhad* as ***Vampire: The Eternal Struggle*** the next year. — **Michael Greenholdt**

Concept	●●●●○
Gameplay	●●●○○
Card art	●●●○○
Player pool	●●○○○

Set (438 cards)	175.00
Starter Display Box	40.00
Booster Display Box	48.00
Starter Deck	4.00
Booster Pack	0.50

You will need **49** nine-pocket pages to store this set. (25 doubled up)

Card name	Type	Rarity	Price
[1]			
.44 Magnum	Eq	C	0.20
Aaron's Feeding Razor	Eq	R	3.50

Card name	Type	Rarity	Price
Academic Hunting Grounds	Uq loc	U	1.30
Aching Beauty	-	U	0.90
Acrobatics	Co	C	0.20
Adrianne	V	V	0.40
Agrippina	V	V	0.40
Aid from Bats	Co	C	0.20
Al's Army Apparatus	UqLoc	R	3.50
[2]			
Aleph	V	V	0.40
Amaranth	Co	U	0.70

Card name	Type	Rarity	Price
Anarch Revolt	-	U	0.90
Anarch Troublemaker	Uq	R	2.70
Anastasia Grey	V	V	0.40
Ancient Influence	PoA	C	0.20
Ancilla Empowerment	PoA	C	0.20
Andreas - Bard of Crete	V	V	0.40
Angel	V	V	0.40
[3]			
Angus - The Unruled	V	V	0.40
Animalism	Sk	C	0.20

RARITY KEY C = Common   U = Uncommon   R = Rare   VR = Very Rare   UR = Ultra Rare   F = Foil card   V = Vampire deck

Card name	Type	Rarity	Price		Card name	Type	Rarity	Price		Card name	Type	Rarity	Price
Anneke	V	V	0.40		**11**					Fragment of the Book of Nod	Uq	R	4.50
Anson	V	V	0.40		Conservative Agitation	PoA	C	0.20		Freak Drive	AcM	R	4.00
Anvil	V	V	0.40		Courtland Leighton	V	V	0.40		**19**			
Appolonius	V	V	0.40		Crusher	V	V	0.40		Frenzy	Oot	C	0.20
Arcane Library	UqLoc	R	3.30		Cryptic Mission	Ac	C	0.20		Game of Malkav	-	U	0.80
Archon	PoA	V	0.90		Cryptic Rider	AcMod	U	0.70		Gangrel De-evolution	-	U	0.90
Arms Dealer	AI	U	0.90		Cultivated Blood Shortage	-	U	0.80		Gangrel Justicar	PoA	R	2.80
4					Cunctator Motion	PoA	R	2.50		Ghoul Escort	Re	R	3.50
Army of Rats	Ac	C	0.20		Curse of Nitocris	Uq	R	3.00		Ghoul Retainer	Re	R	2.50
Arson	Ac	C	0.20		Dancin' Dana	V	V	0.40		Giant's Blood	-	R	3.30
Art Museum	UqLoc	R	4.30		**12**					Gideon Fontaine	V	V	0.40
Ascendance	-	C	0.20		Dawn Operation	AcM	U	0.70		Gilbert Duane	V	V	0.40
Assault Rifle	Eq	U	0.90		Day Operation	AcM	R	2.30		**20**			
Astrid Thomas	V	V	0.40		Dead-end Alley	Co	C	0.20		Gird Minions	-	C	0.20
Asylum Hunting Ground	UqLoc	U	0.90		Deal with the Devil	-	C	0.20		Gitane St. Claire	V	V	0.40
Aura Reading	Co	U	0.70		Deer Rifle	Eq	C	0.20		Giuliano Vincenzi	V	V	0.40
5					Deflection	ReA	C	0.20		Glaser Rounds	Co	U	0.80
Auspex	Sk	C	0.20		Delaying Tactics	ReA	U	0.90		Gleam of Red Eyes	Co	C	0.20
Autarkis Persecution	PoA	C	0.20		Delilah Easton	V	V	0.40		Golconda - Inner Peace	-	R	2.80
Backways	UqLoc	U	0.90		Demetrius Slater	V	V	0.40		Govern the Unaligned	Ac	C	0.20
Badger	V	V	0.40		**13**					Grave Robbing	Ac	U	0.90
Basilia	V	V	0.40		Democritus	V	V	0.40		Grenade	Eq	U	0.80
Bastard Sword	Eq	U	0.80		Didi Meyers	V	V	0.40		**21**			
Bear Paw	V	V	0.40		Dieter Kleist	V	V	0.40		Grendel - The Worm Eaten	V	V	0.40
Behind You	Co	R	4.00		Dimple	V	V	0.40		Growing Fury	Co	C	0.20
Betrayer	-	R	4.50		Disarming Presence	AcM	U	0.80		Gunther - Beast Lord	V	V	0.40
Bewitching Oration	AcM	C	0.20		Disguised Weapon	Co	C	0.20		Gypsies	AI	U	0.90
6					Disputed Territory	PoA	C	0.20		Hasina Kesi	V	V	0.40
Bianca	V	V	0.40		Distraction	Ac	R	3.30		Haven Uncovered	-	C	0.20
Black Cat	V	V	0.40		Dodge	Co	C	0.20		Hawg	Eq	C	0.20
Blood Bond	Ac	U	0.70		**14**					Heather Florent-The Opportunist	V	V	0.40
Blood Doll	Ma	C	0.30		Dollface	V	V	0.40		Hector Sosa	V	V	0.40
Blood Fury	Co	C	0.20		Domain Challenge	PoA	C	0.20		**22**			
Blood Puppy	Uq	R	3.30		Dominate	Sk	C	0.20		Helena Casimir	V	V	0.40
Blood Rage	Co	C	0.20		Don Cruez - The Idealist	V	V	0.40		Hell Hound	AI	R	3.50
Bloodhunt	Ac	U	0.80		Dorian Strack	V	V	0.40		Hidden Lurker	Ac	C	0.20
Blur	Co	C	0.20		Dr. Jest	V	V	0.40		High Stakes	PoA	R	3.30
7					Dr. John Casey	V	V	0.40		Homunculus	Re	U	0.80
Body of Sun	Co	R	3.50		Dragon Breath Rounds	Co	U	0.90		Hostile Take Over	-	R	4.00
Bomb	Eq	U	0.90		Drain Essence	Co	U	0.80		Ignatius	V	V	0.40
Bonding	AcM	C	0.20		**15**					Igo - The Hungry	V	V	0.40
Boxed In	Co	C	0.20		Dramatic Upheaval	PoA	V	0.60		Illegal Search and Seizure	-	C	0.20
Brainwash	-	C	0.20		Drawing Out the Beast	Co	C	0.20		**23**			
Brazil	V	V	0.40		Dre - Leader of the Cold Dawn	V	V	0.40		Immortal Grapple	Co	R	3.50
Bribes	AcM	C	0.20		Dread Gaze	ReA	C	0.20		Indomitability	Co	C	0.20
Brujah Frenzy	oot	U	0.90		Duck	V	V	0.40		Infernal Pursuit	Co	U	0.60
Brujah Justicar	PoA	R	3.00		Eagle's Sight	ReA	U	0.70		Information Highvay	UqLoc	U	1.00
8					Earth Control	AcM	C	0.20		IR Goggles	Eq	U	0.80
Business Pressure	AcM	R	1.30		Earth Meld	Co	C	0.20		Ivory Bow	Eq	R	2.80
Bum's Rush	Ac	C	0.30		Ebanezer Roush	V	V	0.40		J.S. Simmons Esq.	Re:Uq	R	2.70
Burst of Sunlight	Co	R	3.50		**16**					Jackie Therman	Re:Uq	R	2.90
Camarilla Exemplary	PoA	C	0.20		Eco Terrorists	Uq loc	R	3.50		Jazz Wentworth	V	V	0.40
Camille Devereux	V	V	0.40		Effective Management	-	C	0.20		**24**			
Canine Horde	Co	C	0.20		Elder Kindred Network	ReA	U	0.80		Jing Wei	V	V	0.40
Cardano	V	V	0.40		Elder Library	Uq loc	C	0.30		Justine - Elder of Dallas	V	V	0.40
Cassandra - Magus Prime	V	V	0.50		Elliot Sinclair-Virtuoso Thespian	V	V	0.40		Kallista - Master Sculptor	V	V	0.40
Cat Burglary	Ac	R	3.30		Elysium: The Arboretum	UqLoc	U	0.90		Kindred Intelligence	Ac	R	2.80
9					Emerson Bridges	VE-Pn	V	0.40		Kindred Restructure	PoA	V	0.90
Cat's Guidance	ReA	C	0.20		Enchant Kindred	Ac	C	0.20		Kindred Segregation	PoA	V	0.90
Cauldron of Blood	Co	C	0.20		Enhanced Senses	ReA	C	0.20		Kindred Society Games	-	R	3.00
Celerity	Sk	C	0.20		**17**					Kine Dominance	Ac	R	2.80
Chainsaw	Eq	U	0.70		Entrancement	Ac	R	4.30		Kine Resources Contested	PoA	C	0.20
Change of Target	AcM	U	0.80		Faceless Night	AcM	C	0.20		**25**			
Chantry	UqLoc	U	0.90		Fake Out	Co	C	0.20		Koko	V	V	0.40
Charming Lobby	Ac	U	0.80		Fame	-	U	0.90		KRCG News Radio	UqLoc	U	0.90
Charnas the Imp	Re	R	3.00		Far Mastery	Ac	R	2.90		Laptop Computer	Eq	C	0.20
Chester DuBois	V	V	0.40		Fast Hands	Co	U	0.80		Lazarus	V	V	0.40
10					Fast Reaction	ReA	C	0.20		Legal Manipulations	Ac	C	0.20
Claws of the Dead	Co	C	0.20		Felicia Mostrom	V	V	0.40		Letter from Vienna	-	U	0.90
Cloak the Gathering	AcM	C	0.20		Fists of Death	Co	R	2.80		Lextalionis	V	V	0.80
Colin Flynn	V	V	0.40		**18**					Life Boon	Oot	U	0.70
Computer Hacking	Ac	C	0.35		Flak Jacket	Eq	C	0.20		Lost in Crowds	AcM	C	0.20
Concealed Weapon	Co	C	0.20		Flame Thrower	Eq	U	1.60		**26**			
Conditioning	AcM	C	0.20		Flash	Co	C	0.20		Loyal Street Gang	AI	U	0.90
Conquer the Beast	Co	R	2.80		Flesh of Marble	Co	R	2.90		Lucia Pacciola	V	V	0.40
Consanguineous Boon	PoA	C	0.20		Form of Mist	Co	U	0.70		Lucian	V	V	0.40
Consanguineous Condemnation	PoA	C	0.20		Form of the Ghost	Co	C	0.20		Lucky Blow	Co	C	0.20
					Fortitude	Sk	C	0.20		Lucretia - Cess Queen	V	V	0.40

RARITY KEY C = Common   U = Uncommon   R = Rare   VR = Very Rare   UR = Ultra Rare   F = Foil card   X = Fixed/standard in all decks

Card name	Type	Rarity	Price
Lupo	V	V	0.40
Lydia Van Cuelen	V	V	0.40
Madness Network	Uq	R	3.30
Magic of the Smith	Ac	R	2.80

27

Card name	Type	Rarity	Price
Majesty	Co	C	0.20
Major Boon	Oot	U	0.80
Malkavian Dementia	Ma	U	0.70
Malkavian Justicar	PoA	R	3.00
Malkavian Prank	-	R	3.00
Malkavian Time Auction	-	R	2.90
Manstopper Rounds	Co	U	0.70
Mariel - Lady Thunder	V	V	0.40
Marty Lechtansi	V	V	0.40

28

Card name	Type	Rarity	Price
Masika	V	V	0.40
"Mask of 1,000 faces"	AcM	U	0.80
Masquerade Endangered	Oot	U	0.80
Masquerade Enforcement	V	V	0.80
Melissa Barton	V	V	0.40
Merill Molitor	V	V	0.40
Metro Underground	UqLoc	U	0.90
Mighty Grapple	Co	C	0.20
Milicent Smith-Pur Vamp Hunter	Uq	R	2.50

29

Card name	Type	Rarity	Price
Minion Tap	-	C	0.20
Minor Boon	Oot	U	0.90
Miranda Sanova	V	V	0.40
Misdirection	-	C	0.20
Mob Connections	Uq	U	0.90
Monocle of Clarity	Eq	R	2.50
Movement of the Mind	Co	C	0.20
Movement of the Slow Body	Ac	U	0.60
Mr. Winthrop	Re:Uq	R	2.90

30

Card name	Type	Rarity	Price
Muddled Vampire Hunter	Al	U	0.90
Murder of Crows	Re	R	2.80
Natasha Volfchek	V	V	0.40
Navar McClaren	V	V	0.40
Night Moves	Ac	U	0.80
Nik	V	V	0.40
Nimble Feet	Co	C	0.20
Normal	V	V	0.40
Nosferatu Justicar	PoA	R	2.90

31

Card name	Type	Rarity	Price
Nosfreatu Putresence	Co	U	0.90
Obedience	ReA	U	0.80
Obfuscate	Sk	C	0.20
Open Grate	Co	C	0.20
Outcast mage	Al	U	0.90
Owl Companion	Re	U	0.90
Ozmo	V	V	0.40
Parity Shift	PoA	V	0.80
Patagia - Flaps Allowing Limited Flight	Ac	R	2.30

32

Card name	Type	Rarity	Price
Peace Treaty	PoA	C	0.20
Police Department	UqLoc	U	0.90
Political Ally	Al:Uq	R	3.80
Political Backlash	ReA	C	0.20
Political Flux	PoA	C	0.20
Potence	Sk	C	0.20
Powerbase: Chicago	UqLoc	U	1.30
"Powerbase: Washington, D.C."	UqLoc	U	1.30
Praxis Seizure:Atlanta	PoA	R	3.50

33

Card name	Type	Rarity	Price
Praxis Seizure:Boston	PoA	R	3.80
Praxis Seizure:Chicago	PoA	R	3.50
Praxis Seizure:Cleveland	PoA	R	3.50
Praxis Seizure:Dallas	PoA	R	3.50
Praxis Seizure:Houstan	PoA	R	3.50
Praxis Seizure:Miami	PoA	R	3.50
Praxis Seizure:Seattle	PoA	R	3.50
Praxis Seizure:Washington DC	PoA	R	4.00
Praxis: Solomon	PoA	V	0.50

34

Card name	Type	Rarity	Price
Presence	Sk	C	0.20

Card name	Type	Rarity	Price
Protean	Sk	C	0.20
Protracted Investment	-	C	0.20
Psyche	Co	U	0.70
(Physchic) Psychic Projection	Ac	R	3.00
Psychic Veil	Ac	R	2.30
Pulled Fangs	Co	R	3.80
Pulling Strings	ReA	U	0.70
Pulse of the Canaille	Ac	U	0.80

35

Card name	Type	Rarity	Price
Quinton McDonnell	V	V	0.40
Rake	V	V	0.40
Ramiel Dupre	V	V	0.40
Rampage	Ac	U	0.60
Rapid Healing	Ac	C	0.20
Rat's Warning	ReA	C	0.20
Raven Spy	Re	U	0.70
Read Intentions	Co	C	0.20
Regaining the Upper Hand	PoA	C	0.20

36

Card name	Type	Rarity	Price
Renegade Garou	Al	R	2.80
Resplendent Protector	Re	R	2.30
Restoration	Ac	C	0.20
Reversal of Fortunes	PoA	V	0.70
Ricki Van Demsy	V	V	0.40
Ritual Challenge	Ac	R	3.10
Ritual of the Bitter Rose	Co/ReA	R	2.90
Roland Bishop	V	V	0.40
Roland Loussarian	V	V	0.40

37

Card name	Type	Rarity	Price
Roman Alexander	V	V	0.40
Roreca Quaid	V	V	0.40
Rotschreck	Oot	U	0.80
Rowan Ring	Eq:Uq	R	2.80
Roxanne-Rectrix of the13th floor	V	V	0.40
RPG Launcher	Eq	R	2.40
Rufina Soledad	V	V	0.40
Rumors of Gehenna	PoA	R	3.00
Sabbat Threat	PoA	V	0.60

38

Card name	Type	Rarity	Price
Sabine Lafitte	V	V	0.40
Sammy	V	V	0.40
Sarah Cobbler	V	V	0.40
Saturday Night Special	Eq	C	0.20
Sawed-off Shotgun	Eq	C	0.20
Scorn of Adonis	AcM	U	0.80
Sebastian Marley	V	V	0.40
Seduction	AcM	C	0.20
Selma - The Repugnant	V	V	0.40

39

Card name	Type	Rarity	Price
Sengir Dagger	Eq	R	2.80
Shattering Blow	Co	C	0.20
Sheldon - Lord of the Clog	V	V	0.40
Short Term Investment	-	C	0.20
Sideslip	Co	C	0.20
Sir Walter Nash	V	V	0.40
Skin of Night	Co	U	0.90
Skin of Rock	Co	C	0.20
Skin of Steel	Co	C	0.20

40

Card name	Type	Rarity	Price
Slum Hunting ground	UqLoc	U	1.10
Smiling Jack the Anarch	Uq	R	3.30
Smudge - The Ignored	V	V	0.40
Social Charm	Ac	C	0.20
Society Hunting Ground	UqLoc	U	0.90
Society of Leopold	Uq	R	2.50
Soul Gem of Etrius	Eq:Uq	R	3.30
Sport Bike	Eq:vcl	U	0.80
Spying Mission	AcM	U	0.80

41

Card name	Type	Rarity	Price
Stake	Eq	U	0.90
Storm Sewers	UqLoc	U	0.90
Submachine Gun	Eq	U	0.70
Succubus Club	UqLoc	R	2.80
Sudden Reversal	Oot	U	0.80
Surprise Influence	ReA	C	0.20
Sylvester Simms	V	V	0.40
Talbot's Chainsaw	Eq	R	3.50

Card name	Type	Rarity	Price
Tasha Morgan (a)	Re	R	2.90

42

Card name	Type	Rarity	Price
Tasha Morgan (b)	Re	R	3.90
Taste of Vitae	Co	U	0.70
Tatiana Romanov	V	V	0.40
Telepathic Vote Counting	AcM	R	2.20
Telepathic Counter	ReA	C	0.20
Telepathic Misdirection	ReA	C	0.25
Temptation of Greater Power	-	R	2.80
Thadius Zho (Mage)	Al	R	3.00

43

Card name	Type	Rarity	Price
Thaumaturgy	sk	C	0.20
The 1st Tradition:Masquerade	PoA	R	1.50
The Second Tradition: Domain	ReA	U	0.70
The Third Tradition: Progeny	Ac	U	0.80
The 4th Tradition:The Accounting	Ac	U	0.80
The Fifth Tradition: Hospitality	Ac	U	0.70
The Sixth Tradition: Destruction	Ac	U	0.80
The Barrens	UqLoc	C	0.20
The Embrace	Ac	R	3.90
The Knights	Al:Uq	R	3.30

44

Card name	Type	Rarity	Price
The Labyrinth	UqLoc	U	0.90
The Rack	UqLoc	U	0.90
The Slashers	Al	R	3.30
The Spawning Pool	UqLoc	R	3.50
The Spirit's Touch	ReA	C	0.20
Theft of Vitae	Co	C	0.20
Thomas Thorne	V	V	0.40
Threats	AcM	C	0.20
Thrown Gate	Co	C	0.20

45

Card name	Type	Rarity	Price
Thrown Sewer Lid	Co	C	0.20
Tiberius - Scandalmonger	V	V	0.40
Timothy Crowley	VE-Pn	V	0.40
Toreador Justicar	PoA	R	3.30
Torn Signpost	Co	U	0.50
Tragic Love Affair	-	U	0.80
Trap	Co	C	0.20
Tremere Justicar	PoA	R	3.30
Tura Vaughn	V	V	0.40

46

Card name	Type	Rarity	Price
Tusk - Talebearer	V	V	0.40
Ulugh Beg - The Watcher	V	V	0.40
Uma Hatch	V	V	0.40
Undead Persistence	Co	U	0.70
Undead Strength	Co	C	0.20
Unflinching Persistence	Co	C	0.20
Unnatural Disaster	-	C	0.20
Uptown Hunting Ground	UqLoc	U	0.90
Uriah Winter	V	V	0.40

47

Card name	Type	Rarity	Price
Vampiric Speed	Co	C	0.20
Vampiric Disease	-	R	1.20
Vanish from Mind's Eye	Co	C	0.20
Vast Wealth	-	U	0.90
Ventrue Headquarters	UqLoc	U	0.90
Ventrue Justicar	PoA	R	3.00
Violette Prentiss	V	V	0.40
Vliam Andor	V	V	0.40
Voter Captivation	AcM	U	0.70

48

Card name	Type	Rarity	Price
Vulnerability	-	U	0.80
Wake with Evenings Freshness	ReA	C	0.20
Walk of Flame	Co	U	0.70
Warzone Hunting Ground	UqLoc	U	0.90
Weather Control	Co	U	0.70
Well-aimed Car	Co	U	0.80
Wolf Claws	Co	C	0.20
Wolf Companion	Re	U	0.70
Wynn	V	V	0.40

49

Card name	Type	Rarity	Price
XTC Laced Blood	Oot	R	2.90
Yuri - The Talon	V	V	0.40
Zack North	V	V	0.40
Zebulon	V	V	0.40
Zip Gun	Co	U	0.70
Zoo Hunting Ground	UqLoc	U	0.90

RARITY KEY C = Common U = Uncommon R = Rare VR = Very Rare UR = Ultra Rare F = Foil card X = Fixed/standard in all decks

Killer Instinct

Topps • Released **June 1996**

342 cards in set, plus **6** promo cards

- Starter decks contain 60 cards; starter displays contain 12 starters
- Booster packs contain 12 cards; booster displays contain 24 boosters

Quick — what was Nintendo's first CCG experience? If you said **Pokémon**, you're off by a few years (and a few genres). When all the sportscard mainstays were leaping into the CCG realm, one of the best-known, Topps, became one of the latest to take the plunge, releasing **Killer Instinct**, based on the Nintendo combat action video game.

In the far future, Ultratech, a massive corporation, has seized control of the Earth. By holding tournaments of martial skill, they hope to keep the masses entertained and pacified. As Shadow Corporations, players hope to overthrow Ultratech for their own ends by recruiting fighters and winning the tournament.

To this end, players have three card types: Effects, Moves, and Arenas. Effects can be played throughout the game, have instantaneous effects, and are pretty dull. A player builds a fighter by stacking 7 Move cards, including a Special Move specific to that combatant. Each turn, players draw two cards, outfit their fighters with more Moves, or play a new Special Move for a different fighter and start training him. If either player has more than one fighter, players bid for the right to choose the matchup. Many cards have point values. By placing some face down, players hope to come out ahead and have their giants stomp the opponent's shrimps.

Players choose an Arena card, listing a place and a special effect, in which to fight. The opponent can play Arena cards from the same place, but which have different special effects. These have point values, and winning the fight lets a player score them.

In the innovative combat system, each player picks up his fighter, looks at the Moves, picks seven, and places them in any order. Then, players show their first Moves. On top of each move is a red splotch of blood and a number. If your number lines up with your opponent's splotch, you hit him and do that much damage. On either side of each card is an icon which is either a fist or a foot and which is either red, yellow, or white. If you hit and then play a card whose left-hand icon matches the right-hand icon on the prior move, you've played a combo and do extra damage. After seven moves, the match is ended. Points are scored, and the turn sequence starts anew. When one player has won three matches, the game is over. Count up the points scored to see who has won.

Many cards are well done, but a lot are ugly low-resolution screen captures from the video game. Layout, though, is fantastic, and the combat system is fast, tight, and original: one of the best quick-combat systems around. The only problem is that players need to be able to get through their decks faster. After losing a fight, you must discard one move from your current fighter, and, if you go below seven, he is no longer eligible to fight. So, if you don't have a Move to give him waiting in your hand, he can't fight the next round. Pass for three rounds and you forfeit the game. You will rarely be able to field a second fighter, because you will be too busy stocking up your current man. There just weren't enough Moves in the starters.

In the end, *Killer Instinct* didn't have enough moves for 1996's consolidatiing CCG market, and left the ring without a single expansion. — *Richard Weld*

Famous Last Words!

COMBAT EFFECT
Recite a cool and appropriate line immediately after defeating an opponent for an additional Pick.
"Yeah, eat it!"

Concept	●●●○○
Gameplay	●●●○○
Card art	●●○○○
Player pool	○○○○○

Killer reverb

Killer Instinct's sales may still resonate with Topps, which didn't join other sportscard makers in leaping back into the market after **Pokémon**. Having achieved success with its 1999 non-CCG Pokémon cards, Topps reportedly designed a CCG for **The Blair Witch Project** but didn't release it for fear of a **Killer Instinct** repeat.

> You will need **38** nine-pocket pages to store this set. (19 doubled up)

Set (342 cards)	**34.00**
Starter Display Box	**15.00**
Booster Display Box	**18.00**
Starter Deck	**4.00**
Booster Pack	**1.00**

Promo cards

Card name	Rarity	Price
BZZRAK	pr	0.75
Feel The Power	pr	0.75
Fireball	pr	0.75
Rule the World	pr	0.75
Stomp	pr	0.75
Techno-Mage	pr	0.75

Card name	Rarity	Price
Acid Spit [1]	R	1.00
Air Box Sabotage	U	0.25
Aliens Are People Too	R	1.00
America's Favorite	R	1.00
Artificial Intelligence	C	0.10
Assassin	R	1.00
Auto-Systems	C	0.10
Avalanche Slide	R	1.00

Card name	Rarity	Price
Awesome Combo [2]	C	0.10
Awesome Victory	C	0.10
B. Orchid	R	1.50
B.O.P. Raid	U	0.25
B.O.P. Revelation	U	0.25
B.O.P. Triumphant	U	0.25
Bad Press	U	0.25
Bask	U	0.25
Bat Attack	C	0.10
Baton Crunch [3]	R	1.00
Battle Cry	C	0.10
Beta Testing Complete	R	1.00
Betting Syndicate	R	1.00
Bite of the Werewolf	R	1.00
Black Ice	U	0.25
Blaster Combo	C	0.10
Blazing Sun	C	0.10
Blocked Kick	C	0.10
Blocked Punch	C	0.10
Blocked Special [4]	C	0.10
Blood Bath	C	0.10

Card name	Rarity	Price
Blood Frenzy	U	0.25
Boiling Lava	C	0.10
Boneshaker	U	0.25
Boom Box	R	1.00
Bribe	R	1.00
Brutal Combo	C	0.10
Buuuurp	R	1.00
Camera Slam (Combo) [5]	R	1.00
Camera Slam (Sabrewulf)	R	1.00
Car Bomb	U	0.25
Cheerleaders	R	1.00
Chief Thunder	R	1.50
Cinder	R	1.50
Cinder Fights Dirty	U	0.25
Cinder Turns up the Heat	R	1.00
Cinder's Escape [6]	R	1.00
Claw Stab	R	1.00
Claws of the Tiger	C	0.10
Clone	R	1.00
Cold Shoulder	U	0.25
Combo Breaker (Cinder)	C	0.10

Card name	Rarity	Price
Combo Breaker (Combo)	C	0.10
Combo Breaker (Fulgore)	C	0.10
Combo Breaker (Glacius)	C	0.10
Combo Breaker (Jago)	C	0.10
Combo Breaker (Orchid) [7]	C	0.10
Combo Breaker (Riptor)	C	0.10
Combo Breaker (Sabrewulf)	C	0.10
Combo Breaker (Spinal)	C	0.10
Combo Breaker (Thunder)	C	0.10
Combo King	U	0.25
Computer Raid	U	0.25
Corp Infiltration	U	0.25
Corp Penetration	U	0.25
Corporate Espionage [8]	U	0.25
Corporate Raid	R	1.00
Crumbling Bridge	R	1.00
Cyberdash	U	0.25
Cyclone	U	0.25
Danger	C	0.10
Dash	U	0.25
Death From Below	R	1.00

RARITY KEY C = Common   **U** = Uncommon   **R** = Rare   **VR** = Very Rare   **UR** = Ultra Rare   **F** = Foil card   **X** = Fixed/standard in all decks

Card name	Rarity	Price
☐ Death's A Beach	R	1.00
9		
☐ Denizens of Darkness	R	1.00
☐ DNA Mutation	R	1.00
☐ Dragon Breath	U	0.25
☐ Drive On	U	0.25
☐ Dummy Corp	R	1.00
☐ Eagle Avenged	U	0.25
☐ Eavesdropper	U	0.25
☐ Eerie Aura	U	0.25
☐ Efficiency Expert	R	1.00
10		
☐ Elixir of Life	C	0.10
☐ Endokuken	C	0.10
☐ Even Up	U	0.25
☐ Exploitation	C	0.10
☐ Eye of the Tiger	U	0.25
☐ Eyedol	R	1.50
☐ Eyedol Takes a Fall	R	1.00
☐ Eyelaser	U	0.25
☐ Fame and Fortune	R	1.00
11		
☐ Famous Last Words	C	0.10
☐ Fight On	C	0.10
☐ Fire and Ice	R	1.00
☐ Fire Cat	U	0.25
☐ Fireflash	U	0.25
☐ Firestorm	R	1.00
☐ Flaming Bat	C	0.10
☐ Flaming Venom	C	0.10
☐ Flickering Shadows	U	0.25
12		
☐ Flik Flak	U	0.25
☐ Foiled	C	0.10
☐ Freeze Out	C	0.10
☐ Frog Morph	R	1.00
☐ Fulgore	R	1.50
☐ Full Moon Rage	U	0.25
☐ Gene Thieves	U	0.25
☐ Glacius	R	1.50
☐ Glass Jaw	C	0.10
13		
☐ Groin Pull	U	0.25
☐ Grudge Match	U	0.25
☐ Gut Boiler	R	1.00
☐ Hacker	R	1.50
☐ Haymaker	R	1.00
☐ Head Cannon	R	1.00
☐ Heartburn	R	1.00
☐ Heat Stroke	R	1.00
☐ Heatfist	U	0.25
14		
☐ Heatsink	U	0.25
☐ Heavy Bag	R	1.00
☐ High Block	C2	0.05
☐ High Fierce Kick	C2	0.05
☐ High Fierce Punch	C2	0.05
☐ High Medium Kick	C2	0.05
☐ High Medium Punch	C2	0.05
☐ High Quick Kick	C2	0.05
☐ High Quick Punch	C2	0.05
15		
☐ Holding Corp	R	1.00
☐ Home Turf	C	0.10
☐ Hostile Takeover	R	1.00
☐ Howl	U	0.25
☐ Humiliation (Cinder)	R	1.00
☐ Humiliation (Combo)	R	1.00
☐ Humiliation (Fulgore)	R	1.00
☐ Humiliation (Glacius)	R	1.00
☐ Humiliation (Jago)	R	1.00
16		
☐ Humiliation (Orchid)	R	1.00
☐ Humiliation (Spinal)	R	1.00
☐ Humiliation (Thunder)	R	1.00
☐ Hyper Combo	C	0.10
☐ Ice Armor	R	1.00
☐ Ice Injection	R	1.00

Card name	Rarity	Price
☐ Ice Lance	U	0.25
☐ Ice Pool	R	1.00
☐ Ichi-Ni-San	U	0.25
17		
☐ Icy Surface	R	1.00
☐ Idea Men	R	1.00
☐ Incineration	R	1.00
☐ Inferno	C	0.10
☐ Inside Bet	R	1.00
☐ Inspiration	U	0.25
☐ Jago	R	1.50
☐ Jago's Quest	U	0.25
☐ Jeering Mob	C	0.10
18		
☐ Jump Rake	U	0.25
☐ Jumping Fierce Kick	C2	0.05
☐ Jumping Fierce Punch	C2	0.05
☐ Jumping Fire Breath	U	0.25
☐ Jumping Medium Kick	C2	0.05
☐ Jumping Medium Punch	C2	0.05
☐ Jumping Quick Kick	C2	0.05
☐ Jumping Quick Punch	C2	0.05
☐ Jumping Retreat	C2	0.05
19		
☐ Kamikaze Katanas	R	1.00
☐ Kick It	C	0.10
☐ Kidnapped	U	0.25
☐ Killer Combo	C	0.10
☐ KILR Highlights	R	1.00
☐ KILR-TV	R	1.00
☐ King Combo	C	0.10
☐ Knee KO	U	0.25
☐ Lasaken	C	0.10
20		
☐ Laser Batons	R	1.00
☐ Laser Blade	U	0.25
☐ Laserstorm	C	0.10
☐ Legions of the Doomed	R	1.00
☐ Lethal Blow	U	0.25
☐ Lights Out	R	1.00
☐ Liquidize	U	0.25
☐ Long Range	R	1.00
☐ Low Block	C2	0.05
21		
☐ Low Fierce Kick	C2	0.05
☐ Low Fierce Punch	C2	0.05
☐ Low Medium Kick	C2	0.05
☐ Low Medium Punch	C2	0.05
☐ Low Quick Kick	C2	0.05
☐ Low Quick Punch	C2	0.05
☐ Lucky Dodge	U	0.25
☐ Master Combo	C	0.10
☐ Meat Cleaver	R	1.00
22		
☐ Meat Puppets	C	0.10
☐ Media Blitz	U	0.25
☐ Media Hound	U	0.25
☐ Megaglitch	U	0.25
☐ Meltdown	R	1.00
☐ Mercy	U	0.25
☐ Micro-Fusion Chip	U	0.25
☐ Micro-Mimic V2.0	U	0.25
☐ Mirage	U	0.25
23		
☐ Mole	R	1.00
☐ Monster Combo	C	0.10
☐ Negotiations are Closed	C	0.10
☐ Network	R	1.00
☐ Niguu Giri	U	0.25
☐ Out of the Shadows	U	0.25
☐ Overextended Attack	U	0.25
☐ Paparazzi	U	0.25
☐ Paper Pagoda	U	0.25
24		
☐ Peek-A-Boo	R	1.00
☐ Perilous Leap	U	0.25
☐ Phoenix	C	0.10

Card name	Rarity	Price
☐ Plasma-Port	U	0.25
☐ Plasmaslice	U	0.25
☐ Power Devour	U	0.25
☐ Power Surge	U	0.25
☐ Powerline	C	0.10
☐ PR Manager	R	1.00
25		
☐ Prometheus Ambulance		
Service	R	1.00
☐ Promoter	R	1.00
☐ Protest	U	0.25
☐ Public Sympathy	C	0.10
☐ Punching Bag	U	0.25
☐ Ratings Sweep	C	0.10
☐ Recycle	R	1.00
☐ Reflect	U	0.25
☐ Reverse Jump Rake	U	0.25
26		
☐ Reverse Sabrespin	U	0.25
☐ Reverse Triplax	U	0.25
☐ Riptor	R	1.50
☐ Riptor Rage	U	0.25
☐ Rise from the Ashes	C	0.10
☐ Ritual Of Sammamish	U	0.25
☐ Rollercoaster	U	0.25
☐ Saboteur	R	1.00
☐ Sabrecut	U	0.25
27		
☐ Sabrepounce	U	0.25
☐ Sabreroll	U	0.25
☐ Sabrespin	U	0.25
☐ Sabrewulf	R	1.50
☐ Sacrifice	R	1.00
☐ Sammamish	U	0.25
☐ Sandstorm	R	1.00
☐ Scalp 'Em	R	1.00
☐ Scaly Hide	C	0.10
28		
☐ Scandal	R	1.00
☐ Scorcher	C	0.10
☐ Searing Skull	C	0.10
☐ Second Chance	U	0.25
☐ Second Wind	C	0.10
☐ Sell-Out	U	0.25
☐ Shadow CEO	R	1.00
☐ Shadow Espionage	R	1.00
☐ Shadow Spies	U	0.25
29		
☐ Shadow Strike	U	0.25
☐ Shaky Bridge	U	0.25
☐ Shield Spike	R	1.00
☐ Shockwave	C	0.10
☐ Side Bet	U	0.25
☐ Silencer	R	1.00
☐ Skele-Slide	U	0.25
☐ Skeleport	U	0.25
☐ Slippery Surface	U	0.25
30		
☐ Snow Meld	C	0.10
☐ Soulsword	U	0.25
☐ Spinal	R	1.50
☐ Spinal's Chilling Cackle	U	0.25
☐ Spinal: The Movie	U	0.25
☐ Spinfist	U	0.25
☐ Spirit Hatchets	R	1.00
☐ Spirit of the Tiger	R	1.00
☐ Spirit Slash	R	1.00
31		
☐ Spoils of Victory	U	0.25
☐ Stall	U	0.25
☐ Stunned	C	0.10
☐ Summon Chevy	R	1.00
☐ Summon Chi	C	0.10
☐ Super Combo	C	0.10
☐ Super Gene Pool	U	0.25
☐ Super Searing Skull	U	0.25

Card name	Rarity	Price
☐ Supernatural Energy	C	0.10
32		
☐ Supernova	U	0.25
☐ Supreme Victory	C	0.10
☐ Sword of Doom	R	1.00
☐ Sword Sweep	U	0.25
☐ System Shock	U	0.25
☐ T.K.O.	U	0.25
☐ Tail Spike	R	1.00
☐ Tailflip	U	0.25
☐ Talk the Talk	C	0.10
33		
☐ Team Up	U	0.25
☐ Teleport Device	U	0.25
☐ Terminal Velocity	R	1.00
☐ Terrible Talons	R	1.00
☐ The Agony of the Feet	R	1.00
☐ The Beast Emerges	R	1.00
☐ The Big Fall	C	0.10
☐ The Claw	R	1.00
☐ The Commish	U	0.25
34		
☐ The Crowd Goes Wild	U	0.25
☐ The Cure	R	1.00
☐ The Deal	R	1.00
☐ The Death of Orchid	U	0.25
☐ The Mangler	R	1.50
☐ The Manual of Arms	R	1.00
☐ The Monster Confirmed	R	1.00
☐ The Scent of Fear	U	0.25
☐ The Tiger's Claws	R	1.00
35		
☐ The Trashman Cometh	R	1.00
☐ The Wager	R	1.00
☐ Thunder Hatchets	R	1.00
☐ Tiebreaker	C	0.10
☐ Tiger Fury	U	0.25
☐ Tiger's Claws	R	1.00
☐ Time Out	U	0.25
☐ TJ Combo	R	1.00
☐ TJ's Crib	C	0.10
36		
☐ TJ's Homeboys	U	0.25
☐ TJ's Title Restored	R	1.00
☐ Tomahawk	U	0.25
☐ Trailblazer	U	0.25
☐ Trial Of The Century	U	0.25
☐ Trip	C	0.10
☐ Triplax	U	0.25
☐ Triple Combo	C	0.10
☐ Turbo Laser	R	1.00
37		
☐ Ultra Combo	C	0.10
☐ Ultratech Raid	C	0.10
☐ Ultratech Revealed	R	1.00
☐ Vengeance	R	1.00
☐ Vid-Screens	C	0.10
☐ Vital Blow	C	0.10
☐ Wait For It	R	1.00
☐ Weak Spot (High Fierce)	C	0.10
☐ Weak Spot (High		
Medium)	U	0.25
38		
☐ Weak Spot (High Quick)	R	1.00
☐ Weak Spot (Jumping		
Fierce)	C	0.10
☐ Weak Spot (Jumping		
Medium)	U	0.25
☐ Weak Spot (Jumping		
Quick)	R	1.00
☐ Weak Spot (Low Fierce)	C	0.10
☐ Weak Spot (Low Medium)	U	0.25
☐ Weak Spot (Low Quick)	R	1.00
☐ Who?	U	0.25
☐ Wind Kick	U	0.25

RARITY KEY C = Common   **U** = Uncommon   **R** = Rare   **VR** = Very Rare   **UR** = Ultra Rare   **F** = Foil card   **X** = Fixed/standard in all decks

Kult

Target Games AB/Heartbreaker • First set, *Limited Edition*, released **November 1995**
262 cards in set • **IDENTIFIER: Narrow font used for artist names**

- Starter decks contain 60 cards; starter displays contain 10 starters
- Booster packs contain 15 cards; booster displays contain 36 boosters

Designed by **Bryan Winter**

Kult was one of three (!) CCGs released by Target in the United States in November 1995, along with *James Bond 007* and *The Crow*. And while the *The Crow* may be a morose chronicle about a dead guy, it's positively light and carefree compared with *Kult*.

The universe of *Kult* is an abandoned prison, built by an absent god whose crazy disciples now delight in ruining the lives of its mortal inhabitants. Then we have the bad guys (!), demons battling for control of the universe.

Each player focuses his deck on one of the Major Arcana cards (crazy disciples or demons) and builds a "conspiracy" around it — a pattern of cards in the shape of a pentagram, no less. With inhuman servants surrounding the Arcana card, players use their human cards in a different area to enthrall the general population. Counters keep track of these sad souls, as humans convey their worship first to the inhuman servants, and then to the demon or crazed disciple Arcana card. The number of thralls in the common area up for grabs is such that only one player can win, so players must fight for them.

Gameplay isn't bad, but it means having to look at the cards. And such cards! There's one called **Gory** (and it is) but others are worse, like **Open Artery**, **Putrefy Other's Body**, **Skin Trade**, **Under the Skin**, and **Torn Asunder**. We prefer the card **Run, You Fool, Run!**, which is good advice for prospective buyers. Our first two reviewers for *Kult*, neither easily offended, were too sickened by the content and artwork to write. So it fell to yours truly (who, as a reader of independent comics in the 1990s, presumably has a tougher stomach) to find the bottom line: *Kult* nearly singlehandedly undoes all the work professionals in the gaming industry have done to debunk the popular misconception that games are filled with Satanic and violent overtones. In a word, *yecch*.

Kult somehow spun off one expansion before sinking into the depths. We include the list here for when the subpeona comes. — *John Jackson Miller*

PAWN OF DREAMS. The Muckraker's base CV is doubled when in combat with a LICTOR, RAZIDE or CREATURE.

You will need **30** nine-pocket pages to store this set. (15 doubled up)

Concept	⬤⬤⬤⬤⬤
Gameplay	⬤⬤⬤◯◯
Card art	◯◯◯◯◯
Player pool	◯◯◯◯◯

Set (262 cards)	36.00
Starter Display Box	12.00
Booster Display Box	16.00
Starter Deck	4.50
Booster Pack	1.00

Card name	Rarity	Price
[1]		
☐ 22/24 Rue de Sevigne	U	0.25
☐ 44 Ladbrooke Hill	U	0.25
☐ Ability To Dupe	C	0.05
☐ Ace in the Hole	U	0.25
☐ Admiral Lyle P. Crowley	U	0.25
☐ Adnan Kazour	U	0.25
☐ Aggression	C	0.05
☐ Agitator	C	0.05
☐ Alter Your Body	C	0.05
[2]		
☐ Andrea Bergstrom	U	0.25
☐ Anselm Hoder	U	0.25
☐ Antagonism	U	0.25
☐ Anton Pradwyck	U	0.25
☐ Anton Teptov	U	0.25
☐ Artist	C	0.05
☐ Asteroth Stirs	U	0.25
☐ Automatic Rifle	U	0.25
☐ Avenger	C	0.05
[3]		
☐ Avenging Angel	U	0.25
☐ Azaqui	U	0.25
☐ Baal Reshef-Lord of Pestilence	U	0.25
☐ Beirut Hilton	U	0.25
☐ Bernauer Krankenhaus	U	0.25
☐ Binah	M	0.75
☐ Black Guardsman	C	0.05
☐ Blood Angel	C	0.05
☐ Blood Venue	C	0.05
[4]		

Card name	Rarity	Price
☐ Bloodthirst	U	0.25
☐ Blue-Collar Worker	C	0.05
☐ Born Again	C	0.05
☐ Bulletproof Vest	C	0.05
☐ Burnt-Out Occultist	C	0.05
☐ Business Executive	C	0.05
☐ Camera	U	0.25
☐ Cardinal Giorgio Biotti	U	0.25
☐ Carrier of Pestilence	C	0.05
[5]		
☐ Chagidiel	M	0.75
☐ Chesed	M	0.75
☐ Child of Chagidiel	C	0.05
☐ Chokmah	M	0.75
☐ Cleansing	U	0.25
☐ Cleaving	C	0.05
☐ Coatlicue- Goddess Of Chaos	U	0.25
☐ Company Careerist	C	0.05
☐ Conjurer	C	0.05
[6]		
☐ Contort Other	U	0.25
☐ Crossbreed	U	0.25
☐ Curse	C	0.05
☐ Djeraba	U	0.25
☐ Don Michael Cimarro	U	0.25
☐ Dr. Mortimer Blanco	U	0.25
☐ Dream Walk	C	0.05
☐ Dream World	C	0.05
☐ Drifter	C	0.05
[7]		
☐ Drug Addict	C	0.05
☐ Drug Dealer	C	0.05
☐ Dupont Circle	U	0.25
☐ Eraser	U	0.25
☐ Excrucy	C	0.05
☐ Executioner	C	0.05
☐ Eye For An Eye	C	0.05
☐ Factuary	C	0.05

Card name	Rarity	Price
☐ Faith Shortcut	C	0.05
[8]		
☐ Family Secret	U	0.25
☐ Fast Reactions	C	0.05
☐ Femme Fatale	C	0.05
☐ Fettered	U	0.25
☐ Fetus Alteration	U	0.25
☐ Fight Fire with Fire	C	0.05
☐ Find Object	C	0.05
☐ Fly in the Ointment	C	0.05
☐ Gamaliel	M	0.75
[9]		
☐ Gamichicoth	M	0.75
☐ Gang Member	C	0.05
☐ Garden of the White Dragon	U	0.25
☐ Geburah	M	0.75
☐ General Hu	U	0.25
☐ General Juan Martinez	U	0.25
☐ Golab	M	0.75
☐ Gory	C	0.05
☐ Grand Master Marcus	U	0.25
[10]		
☐ Grenade	U	0.25
☐ Guilty!	C	0.05
☐ Hades Walk	C	0.05
☐ Handgun	C	0.05
☐ Hareb-Serap	M	0.75
☐ Harrington's District	U	0.25
☐ Haunted	C	0.05
☐ Hauptquartier Argente	U	0.25
☐ Haury	C	0.05
[11]		
☐ Hayworth Emergency Aid	U	0.25
☐ Heralds of Death	C	0.05
☐ Hod	M	0.75
☐ Hole in the Sky	U	0.25
☐ Hooked Up	C	0.05

Card name	Rarity	Price
☐ Huang Li-Pao	U	0.25
☐ Hunger Spirit	U	0.25
☐ Hunting Instinct	C	0.05
☐ Impaled	C	0.05
[12]		
☐ Incinerator	U	0.25
☐ Inferno	U	0.25
☐ Insane Killer	U	0.25
☐ Jelena Kalenko	U	0.25
☐ Jonathan Hayworth	U	0.25
☐ Journalist	C	0.05
☐ Just in Time	C	0.05
☐ Kali Durga Temple Servant	C	0.05
☐ Karma	C	0.05
[13]		
☐ Kether	M	0.75
☐ Kingpin	C	0.05
☐ Knight of Light	C	0.05
☐ Ktonor	U	0.25
☐ Lack of Faith	C	0.05
☐ Le Marquis	C	0.05
☐ Leash of Believers	C	0.05
☐ Leonard Sakhil	U	0.25
☐ Lictor	C	0.05
[14]		
☐ Longfeather's Purgatory	U	0.25
☐ Los Renuncios Mission	U	0.25
☐ Luigi Cantorre	U	0.25
☐ Mad Scientist	C	0.05
☐ Madness Walk	C	0.05
☐ Malice	C	0.05
☐ Malkuth	M	0.75
☐ Maniphestos	C	0.05
☐ Manipulate Death	C	0.05
[15]		
☐ Manipulate Dream	C	0.05

Card name	Rarity	Price
☐ Manipulate Passion	C	0.05
☐ Manipulate Senses	C	0.05
☐ Maoro Nakemi	U	0.25
☐ Marbas-Lord of Pain	U	0.25
☐ Maria Feodorova	U	0.25
☐ Mass Suggestion	C	0.05
☐ Meat Hook	C	0.05
☐ Misguidance	U	0.25
[16]		
☐ Mislead	C	0.05
☐ Molest Soul	U	0.25
☐ Morbid Experiments	C	0.05
☐ Morgue	U	0.25
☐ Muckraker	C	0.05
☐ Musician	C	0.05
☐ Nachtkinder	C	0.05
☐ Nahemoth	M	0.75
☐ Natural Weapon	U	0.25
[17]		
☐ Neonate	U	0.25
☐ Nepharite	U	0.25
☐ Netzach	M	0.75
☐ New Age Pagan	C	0.05
☐ No Man's Land	U	0.25
☐ "No Pain, No Gain"	C	0.05
☐ Nywere	U	0.25
☐ O Luong	C	0.05
☐ Oaxici	C	0.05
[18]		
☐ Occult Experience	C	0.05
☐ Open Artery	C	0.05
☐ Out of Control	C	0.05
☐ Outcast	C	0.05
☐ Pact with Dark Power	U	0.25
☐ Parthenogenesis	C	0.05
☐ Pearls for the Swines	C	0.05
☐ Perpetuity	C	0.05
☐ Petty Criminal	C	0.05

Card Checklist (continued)

Card name	Rarity	Price
[19]		
Pierre Lombard	U	0.25
Plague	U	0.25
Plainclothes Cop	C	0.05
Population Explosion	U	0.25
Possessed	U	0.25
Power Failure	C	0.05
Priest	C	0.05
Prince Rainer Von Habsburg	U	0.25
[20]		
Private Investigator	C	0.05
Professional	C	0.05
Prostitute	C	0.05
Protective Skin	U	0.25
Psychotherapy	U	0.25
Purgatory	U	0.25
Purgatov	U	0.25
Purge Power	U	0.25
Purified	C	0.05
Putrefy Other's Body	C	0.05
[21]		
Rage Of The Masses	C	0.05
Razide	C	0.05

Card name	Rarity	Price
Redemption	C	0.05
Regeneration	C	0.05
Relocate	U	0.25
Researcher	C	0.05
"Run, You Fool, Run!"	C	0.05
Sabbath	U	0.25
Sadomasochist	U	0.25
[22]		
Samael	M	0.75
Samuel Harrington	U	0.25
Sanatorium	C	0.05
Sand Rider	U	0.25
Sathariel	M	0.75
Scalpel	C	0.05
Secret Agent	C	0.05
Sell Your Soul	C	0.05
Seraphim	U	0.25
[23]		
Servailant	U	0.25
Siamese Twin	C	0.05
Skin Trade	U	0.25
Slaves Of Pain	C	0.05
Soldier	C	0.05
Sorry	C	0.05

Card name	Rarity	Price
Spineless	U	0.25
Strapped	C	0.05
Student	C	0.05
[24]		
Sub-Machine Gun	U	0.25
Symbol Bondage	C	0.05
Takeo Oshima	U	0.25
Teacher	C	0.05
Telekinesis	C	0.05
Temple of Kali Durga	U	0.25
Temporary Insanity	U	0.25
Thaumiel	M	0.75
The Bergstrom Institute	U	0.25
[25]		
The Borderland	U	0.25
The Cathedral	U	0.25
The City of the Dead	C	0.05
The Cross	U	0.25
The Cube	U	0.25
The Guardian	U	0.25
The Hatching Chambers	U	0.25
The Hunting Grounds	U	0.25
The Inner Labyrinth	U	0.25

Card name	Rarity	Price
[26]		
The Labyrinth	U	0.25
The Living City	C	0.05
"The Lord Gives, The Lord Takes"	U	0.25
The Machine City	U	0.25
The Maze	C	0.05
The Mirror Halls	C	0.05
The Nakamura Building	U	0.25
The Ruins	U	0.25
The Tormented Army	C	0.05
[27]		
The Underground	C	0.05
The Voice of the Blood	U	0.25
The Void	U	0.25
Time and Spacewalk	C	0.05
Tiphany Reeder	U	0.25
Tiphareth	M	0.75
Togarini	M	0.75
Tomb Bondage	U	0.25
Torn Asunder	U	0.25

Card name	Rarity	Price
[28]		
Tracking Device	C	0.05
True Vision	U	0.25
Two is More than One	U	0.25
U.S.S. Reliant	U	0.25
Uncontrolled Shape Change	U	0.25
Under The Skin	U	0.25
Undertaker	U	0.25
Unholy Hunger	C	0.05
Unhuman Appearance	U	0.25
[29]		
Ushers	C	0.05
Vacuum	U	0.25
Veteran	C	0.05
Victim of Crime	C	0.05
Voice of Pain	C	0.05
Vortex	U	0.25
War Hound	C	0.05
Yesod	M	0.75
Yoshiko Nakamura	U	0.25
[30]		
Youth Prison 315	U	0.25

BURIED ALIVE

INFLUENCE A BEING IN ANY MYSTIC CROSS. Then remove this card from the game. Stick the affected Being FACE-UP into its owners Draw pile, about half-way down (discard Being's attachments). When the Being is drawn it is immediately discarded and the player must skip his or her NEXT FULL turn.

Kult • Inferno

Target Games AB/Heartbreaker • Released **July 1997**

125 cards in set • **IDENTIFIER: Wider font used for artist names**

• Booster packs contain 15 cards; booster displays contain 36 boosters

The *Inferno* expansion serves to actually darken the world of *Kult*, if that's possible. Well, maybe it is. **Fetish**, which depicts a man licking a high-heeled shoe, is relatively tame, but they get worse from there. **Beget** depicts imprisoned nude pregnant women, delivering for the cause. **Near-Death Experience** is hardly just that, if you ask the woman on the card being devoured by a demon. **Slaughterhouse 5** depicts people hanging around, if you know what we mean. It is, in short, the grossest expansion to the grossest CCG ever.

"Just looking at *Kult* can turn your eyeballs inside out and make you want to run your soul through the washing machine," said one reviewer. That might normally still attract the curious, but don't bother. There are more stylish and simply better horror CCGs about.

Gamers, this is the kind of CCG that could've gotten us all on *Dateline NBC*. Thank your own personal deities that it didn't — and that it's gone. — *John Jackson Miller*

You will need **14** nine-pocket pages to store this set. (7 doubled up)

	Price
Set (125 cards)	32.00
Booster Display Box	15.00
Booster Pack	1.00

Card name	Price
[1]	
911	0.50
Aborted	0.50
Adobi	0.50
Agentii	0.50
Al Quatil	0.50
Anthony Barkley	0.50
Astral Projection	0.50
Asylum	0.50
Azghoul	0.50
[2]	
Banishment	0.50
Banquet	0.50
Baptism	0.50
Beget	0.50
Below Zero	0.50
Berkfield's Boarding School	0.50
Blaspheme	0.50
Blood Is Thicker Than Water	0.50
Boiler Room	0.50
[3]	
Book Burning	0.50
Buried Alive	0.50
Cadaver	0.50

Card name	Price
Cane	0.50
Carcass	0.50
Cataclysm	0.50
Cemetery	0.50
Ceremony	0.50
Chainsaw	0.50
[4]	
Circus	0.50
Clergy	0.50
Cold-Hearted	0.50
"Cormayas, Arizona"	0.50
Crop	0.50
Crucify	0.50
Curfew	0.50
Damon Blackraven	0.50
Diabolism	0.50
[5]	
Dr. Crane	0.50
Exorcism	0.50
Eye Of The Tornado	0.50
Fetish	0.50
Freakshow	0.50
Grand Master Holmstraum	0.50
Gunnar	0.50
Headless	0.50
Helen Badou	0.50
[6]	
Heller	0.50
High-Strung	0.50

Card name	Price
Imposter	0.50
Incubation Halls	0.50
Ioannes	0.50
Iron Maiden	0.50
Jason Lacrosse	0.50
Kiss Of Death	0.50
[7]	
Limbo	0.50
Living Dead	0.50
Lord Of The Insects	0.50
Magical Door	0.50
Malachi	0.50
Marcus Abernathy	0.50
Marked For Life	0.50
Mask	0.50
Mass Grave	0.50
Master Of Reality	0.50
[8]	
Matador	0.50
Meeting With The Self	0.50
Meltdown	0.50
Mesmerize	0.50
Messiah	0.50
Metamorph	0.50
Narcissism	0.50
Near-Death Experience	0.50
Nocturne	0.50
[9]	
Oedipus Complex	0.50
Omen	0.50

Card name	Price
Organ Donor	0.50
Orphanage	0.50
Past Midnight	0.50
Personal Hell	0.50
Perversion	0.50
Pier 38	0.50
Proto-Techrone	0.50
[10]	
Razor	0.50
Rebecca Shaeffer	0.50
Religious Path	0.50
Sacred Soil	0.50
Sadist	0.50
Sandburn Prison	0.50
Shredded	0.50
Six Feet Under	0.50
Slate	0.50
[11]	
Slaughterhouse 5	0.50
Sperm Bank	0.50
Spontaneous Combustion	0.50
Squeezed	0.50
Stained	0.50
Stone To Flesh	0.50
Stranger Aeons	0.50
Stretched	0.50
Suicidal	0.50
[12]	
Tanned	0.50

Card name	Price
Tell-Tale Heart	0.50
The Authorities	0.50
The Bazaar	0.50
The Blind One	0.50
The Cable Way	0.50
The Centrifuge Halls	0.50
The Clockworks	0.50
The Dog	0.50
[13]	
The Eternal Circle	0.50
The Face Mancusi	0.50
The Fool	0.50
The Forgotten Man	0.50
The Hanging	0.50
The Isle Of Dogs	0.50
The Libraries	0.50
The Memory Banks	0.50
The Primal Sea	0.50
[14]	
Under The Bed	0.50
Under The Oak	0.50
Videodrome	0.50
Vivarium	0.50
Watchwork	0.50
Weeder	0.50
Wolf In Lamb's Clothing	0.50
Wrapped Around My Finger	0.50

RARITY KEY C = Common U = Uncommon R = Rare VR = Very Rare UR = Ultra Rare F = Foil card X = Fixed/standard in all decks

Last Crusade

Designed by **Pinnacle Entertainment Group**, originally released by **Chameleon Eclectic**
Released **December 1995**, rereleased by Pinnacle **November 2000**
300 cards in set

- Starter decks contain 60 cards; starter displays contain 10 decks
- Booster packs contain 12 cards; booster displays contain 36 packs

Designed by **John Hopler**

It's World War II and the ground war is on in Europe — in the CCG world, anyway. The second WWII CCG in six months (after **Echelons of Fury**), **Last Crusade** arms players with troops, tanks, and planes and sends them after the enemy headquarters.

Each player picks a side and uses a 54-cards deck plus 6 terrain cards. A 3x3 grid is set up as the battlefield, with the HQs on opposite sides, just off the field. Players also choose their starting troops. The Germans get more points to spend on troops than the Americans, but the Americans get reinforced more quickly.

Players start by playing, face-down, units into their HQ: tanks, soldiers, and planes. Then players fly their planes around the board and position them to spy on cards or drop bombs. During this phase, an opponent may shoot at them if the plane passes an anti-aircraft gun. (Remember, cards are face down.) Planes can "recon" facedown troops in a terrain they are adjacent to and then may drop their bombs, if they have them. Finally, it's time to move ground troops, inching across the board until the foe is met.

Terrain modifies the outcome of ground battles. In cities, tanks are at a disadvantage, but in the clear fields, they can run infantry down. Each card has four statistics, determining its attacks against infantry, armor, and airplanes, as well as their resiliency. The goal, of course, is to eventually capture the enemy HQ, and, once that's done, even if an opponent has cards left on the board, the game is over. Players add up the Supply costs of everything killed, plus a bonus for capturing the HQ, and the higher total wins. It is possible to capture the HQ and still lose the game: No Pyrrhic victories here.

It's a good simulation, with legible cards and stock WWII photos for art. Units which have statistics stenciled in transparent text behind their names can be hard to read, but, since you can usually tell which cards are planes and tanks, it isn't too big a deal.

Last Crusade went away early on but is available again from its designer, Pinnacle, which has announced it's working on a **Russian Front** expansion. — **Richard Weld**

Monty Throws a Fit

Play on enemy Headquarters
Inadequate port facilities caused Montgomery and Patton to compete for available supplies. Enemy is -1 die supply/turn and may not perform assaults. Indefinite. Unique.

Concept	●●●●○
Gameplay	●●●●○
Card art	●●●○○
Player pool	●○○○○

Cards are sorted here by their numbers and not by their unit names, which can be confusing to alphabetize.

Set (300 cards)	63.00	You will need
Starter Display Box	32.00	**34**
Booster Display Box	38.75	nine-pocket pages to store this set.
Starter Deck	6.40	(17 doubled up)
Booster Pack	1.40	

#	Card name	Type	Rarity	Price
☐ [W010]	Light Woods	Terrain	C	0.15
☐ [W011]	Light Woods	Terrain	C	0.15
☐ [W012]	Town	Terrain	C	0.15
☐ [W013]	City	Terrain	C	0.15
☐ [W014]	Clear	Terrain	C	0.15
☐ [W015]	Clear	Terrain	C	0.15
☐ [W016]	Clear	Terrain	C	0.15
☐ [W017]	Clear	Terrain	C	0.15
☐ [W018]	Bocage	Terrain	C	0.15
☐ [W019]	Bocage	Terrain	C	0.15
☐ W020	Bridge	Terrain	C	0.15
☐ W021	Village	Terrain	C	0.15
☐ W022	Light Woods	Terrain	C	0.15
☐ W023	Village	Terrain	C	0.15
☐ W024	Heavy Forest	Terrain	C	0.15
☐ W025	Hills	Terrain	C	0.15
☐ W026	Hills	Terrain	C	0.15
☐ W027	Hills	Terrain	C	0.15
☐ W028	Swamp	Terrain	C	0.15
☐ W029	Heavy Forest	Terrain	C	0.15
☐ W100	Green Infantry	American	C	0.15
☐ W101	57mm AT Gun	American	C	0.15
☐ W102	M10 Wolverine	American	C	0.15
☐ W103	Platoon Leader	American	C	0.15
☐ W104	Veteran Troops	American	C	0.15
☐ W105	Cargo Truck	American	C	0.15

#	Card name	Type	Rarity	Price
☐ W106	Patrol Captured	American	C	0.15
☐ W107	Engineers	American	C	0.15
☐ W108	Green Infantry	American	C	0.15
☐ W109	37mm AT Gun	American	C	0.15
☐ W110	Green Infantry	American	C	0.15
☐ W111	60mm Mortar	American	C	0.15
☐ W112	Camo Netting	American	C	0.15
☐ W113	Smokescreen	American	C	0.15
☐ W114	Veteran Troops	American	C	0.15
☐ W115	M3 Halftrack	American	C	0.15
☐ W116	MG Crew	American	C	0.15
☐ W117	M18 Hellcat	American	C	0.15
☐ W118	M8 Greyhound	American	C	0.15
☐ W119	Sniper	American	C	0.15
☐ W120	Rifle Platoon	American	C	0.15
☐ W121	81mm Mortar	American	C	0.15
☐ W122	Recon	American	C	0.15
☐ W123	Covered Approach	American	C	0.25
☐ W124	Airborne Platoon	American	C	0.15
☐ W125	M3 Stuart	American	C	0.15
☐ W126	Bazooka Team	American	C	0.15
☐ W127	Fuel Shortage	American	C	0.15
☐ W128	Rifle Platoon	American	C	0.15
☐ W129	Jeep Recon Unit	American	C	0.15
☐ W130	Rifle Platoon	American	C	0.15
☐ W131	75mm Howitzer	American	C	0.15
☐ W132	40mm AA Gun	American	C	0.15
☐ W133	Hull Down	American	C	0.15
☐ W134	Airborne Platoon	American	C	0.15
☐ W135	M4 Sherman	American	C	0.15
☐ W136	Barbed Wire	American	C	0.15
☐ W137	M4A3E8	American	C	0.15
☐ W138	P-51 Mustang	American	C	0.15

#	Card name	Type	Rarity	Price
☐ W139	Order Confusion	American	C	0.15
☐ W150	8cm Mortar	German	C	0.15
☐ W151	Veteran Infantry	German	C	0.15
☐ W152	2cm Flakvierling	German	C	0.15
☐ W153	Recon	German	C	0.15
☐ W154	Supplies	German	C	0.15
☐ W155	Panzer Grenadiers	German	C	0.15
☐ W156	3.7cm Flak 43	German	C	0.15
☐ W157	Patrol Captured	German	C	0.15
☐ W158	Order Confusion	German	C	0.15
☐ W159	Rifle Platoon	German	C	0.15
☐ W160	75mm Howitzer	German	C	0.15
☐ W161	Green Infantry	German	C	0.15
☐ W162	Jagdpanzer IV	German	C	0.15
☐ W163	Engineers	German	C	0.15
☐ W164	Sniper	German	C	0.15
☐ W165	Panzer Grenadiers	German	C	0.15
☐ W166	Panzer Mk IV	German	C	0.15
☐ W167	MG Crew	German	C	0.15
☐ W168	AP Minefield	German	C	0.15
☐ W169	Veteran Infantry	German	C	0.15
☐ [W170]	Covered Approach	German	C	0.25
☐ [W171]	Green Infantry	German	C	0.15
☐ [W172]	Pak 38 AT Gun	German	C	0.15
☐ [W173]	Battalion Staff	German	C	0.15
☐ [W174]	Platoon Leader	German	C	0.15
☐ [W175]	Volks Grenadiers	German	C	0.15
☐ [W176]	Panzer Mk IVH	German	C	0.15
☐ [W177]	Panzerfausts	German	C	0.15
☐ [W178]	AT Minefield	German	C	0.15
☐ [W179]	Cargo Truck	German	C	0.15
☐ [W180]	Hull Down	German	C	0.15
☐ [W181]	Rifle Platoon	German	C	0.15

RARITY KEY C = Common U = Uncommon R = Rare VR = Very Rare UR = Ultra Rare F = Foil card X = Fixed/standard in all decks

#	Card name	Type	Rarity	Price	#	Card name	Type	Rarity	Price	#	Card name	Type	Rarity	Price
☐ [W182]	5cm Mortar	German	C	0.15	19					☐ W332	Proximity Shells	American	R	1.40
☐ [W183]	Puma	German	C	0.15	☐ W262	15cm Rockets	German	U	0.40	☐ W333	Partisan Activity	American	R	1.40
☐ [W184]	Smokescreen	German	C	0.15	☐ W263	Arty Ammo Dump	German	U	0.60	27				
☐ [W185]	Conscripts	German	C	0.25	☐ W264	Wurfrahmen 40	German	U	0.40	☐ W334	Alertness	American	R	1.40
☐ [W186]	Stug III	German	C	0.15	☐ W265	Cloudy	German	U	0.40	☐ W335	B-26 Marauder	American	R	1.40
☐ [W187]	Barbed Wire	German	C	0.15	☐ W266	Hetzer	German	U	0.40	☐ W336	Time on Target	American	R	1.40
☐ [W188]	Mixed Minefield	German	C	0.15	☐ W267	Reinforcements	German	U	0.40	☐ W337	Divisional Reserve	American	R	2.40
12					☐ W268	Pillbox	German	U	0.40	☐ W338	Medal of Honor	American	R	1.40
☐ [W189]	Camouflage	German	C	0.15	☐ W269	Prepared Position	German	U	0.40	☐ W339	Tanker Ace	American	R	1.40
☐ [W200]	Troop Convoy	American	U	0.40	☐ W270	88mm AA/AT	German	U	0.60	☐ W340	"7.2" Rockets	American	R	1.40
☐ [W201]	Supply Cache	American	U	0.40	20					☐ W341	George Patton	American	R	2.40
☐ [W202]	Traffic Jam	American	U	0.40	☐ W271	Wirblewind	German	U	0.40	☐ W342	Manpower Shortage	American	R	1.40
☐ [W203]	Cloudy	American	U	0.40	☐ W272	Ostwind	German	U	0.40	28				
☐ [W204]	AvGas Shortage	American	U	0.40	☐ W273	SdKfz 233	German	U	0.40	☐ W343	Armorer's Miracle	American	R	1.40
☐ [W205]	105mm Howitzer	American	U	0.40	☐ W274	Panther	German	U	0.60	☐ W344	Ditched Aircraft	American	R	1.40
☐ [W206]	ARV	American	U	0.40	☐ W275	Luftwaffe Purge	German	U	0.40	☐ W345	Flying Fortress	American	R	1.40
☐ [W207]	Arty Preplan	American	U	0.40	☐ W276	Wires Cut	German	U	0.40	☐ W346	Field Hospital	American	R	2.40
13					☐ W277	Command Hit	German	U	0.40	☐ W347	Sabotaged Ammo	American	R	1.40
☐ [W208]	Mixed Minefield	American	U	0.40	☐ W278	Traffic Jam	German	U	0.40	☐ W348	Air Ace	American	R	1.40
☐ [W209]	Supplies	American	U	0.40	☐ W279	SNAFU	German	U	0.40	☐ W349	90mm AA/AT	American	R	1.90
☐ W210	"3" AT Gun	American	U	0.40	21					☐ W350	15cm Gun	German	R	1.40
☐ W211	Night Infiltration	American	U	0.40	☐ [W280]	Nashorn	German	U	0.40	☐ W351	Monty Throws a Fit	German	R	2.40
☐ W212	SNAFU	American	U	0.40	☐ [W281]	Brumbar	German	U	0.40	29				
☐ W213	Reinforcements	American	U	0.40	☐ [W282]	SdKfz 251	German	U	0.40	☐ W352	Overextended	German	R	1.40
☐ W214	Arty Ammo Dump	American	U	0.60	☐ [W283]	Night Infiltration	German	U	0.40	☐ W353	Railway Gun	German	R	1.40
☐ W215	"4.5" Rockets	American	U	0.40	☐ [W284]	Bergepanzer	German	U	0.40	☐ W354	28cm Rockets	German	R	1.40
☐ W216	Drop Tanks	American	U	0.40	☐ [W285]	Gun Tubes Worn	German	U	0.40	☐ W355	Ju-88	German	R	1.40
14					☐ [W286]	Sarge is Hit!	German	U	0.40	☐ W356	Erwin Rommel	German	R	1.40
☐ W217	Surprise Attack	American	U	0.40	☐ [W287]	Arty Preplan	German	U	0.40	☐ W357	Supply Strike	German	R	1.40
☐ W218	HVAP	American	U	0.40	☐ [W288]	Surprise Attack	German	U	0.40	☐ W358	Ditched Aircraft	German	R	1.40
☐ W219	Rag-Tag Circus	American	U	0.40	22					☐ W359	Crash Landing	German	R	1.40
☐ W220	"4.2" Mortar	American	U	0.40	☐ [W289]	Trenchfoot	German	U	0.40	☐ W360	King Tiger	German	R	1.40
☐ W221	L-4 Grasshopper	American	U	0.40	☐ [W290]	Storch	German	U	0.40	30				
☐ W222	Medics	American	U	0.40	☐ [W291]	Tiger	German	U	1.10	☐ W361	Divisional Reserve	German	R	2.40
☐ W223	Battalion Staff	American	U	0.40	☐ [W292]	Supply Cache	German	U	0.40	☐ W362	Scramble	German	R	1.40
☐ W224	Espionage	American	U	0.40	☐ [W293]	Baseplate	German	U	0.60	☐ W363	Hummel	German	R	1.40
☐ W225	Rockets	American	U	0.40	☐ [W294]	Bombs	German	U	0.40	☐ W364	Sturmtiger	German	R	1.40
15					☐ [W295]	Lurkers & Shirkers	German	U	0.40	☐ W365	Cloudbank	German	R	1.40
☐ W226	Air Offensive	American	U	0.40	☐ [W296]	SdKfz 251	German	U	0.40	☐ W366	Heavy Fog	German	R	1.40
☐ W227	Wires Cut	American	U	0.40	☐ [W297]	Arty Ammo Out	German	U	0.60	☐ W367	Bad Weather	German	R	1.40
☐ W228	Trenchfoot	American	U	0.40	23					☐ W368	Demolition	German	R	1.40
☐ W229	Flamethrower	American	U	0.40	☐ [W298]	Fortified Building	German	U	0.40	☐ W369	Espionage	German	R	1.40
☐ W230	M4 Halftrack	American	U	0.40	☐ [W299]	Medics	German	U	0.40	31				
☐ W231	P-47 Thunderbolt	American	U	0.40	☐ [W300]	M12 King Kong	American	R	2.40	☐ W370	Fw 190-A8	German	R	1.40
☐ W232	Gun Tubes Worn	American	U	0.40	☐ [W301]	B-24 Liberator	American	R	1.40	☐ W371	Ferry	German	R	1.40
☐ W233	AP Minefield	American	U	0.40	☐ [W302]	Forward Observer	American	R	1.40	☐ W372	Pontoon Bridge	German	R	1.40
☐ W234	Ultra	American	U	0.40	☐ [W303]	Pontoon Bridge	American	R	1.40	☐ W373	Jagdpanther	German	R	1.40
16					☐ [W304]	Assault Boats	American	R	1.40	☐ W374	Jagdtiger	German	R	1.40
☐ W235	105mm M4	American	U	0.40	☐ [W305]	M26 Pershing	American	R	2.40	☐ W375	Drop Tanks	German	R	1.40
☐ W236	Mistaken ID	American	U	0.40	☐ [W306]	Omar Bradley	American	R	1.40	☐ W376	Field Hospital	German	R	2.40
☐ W237	Sabotage	American	U	0.40	24					☐ W377	Bergetiger	German	R	2.40
☐ W238	Arty Ammo Out	American	U	0.60	☐ [W307]	Critical Sector	American	R	1.40	☐ W378	Sniper Rearguard	German	R	1.40
☐ W239	M3 Halftrack	American	U	0.40	☐ [W308]	Crash Landing	American	R	1.40	32				
☐ W240	M7 Priest	American	U	0.40	☐ [W309]	Scramble	American	R	1.40	☐ W379	Blown Dam	German	R	1.40
☐ W241	Bombs	American	U	0.40	☐ W310	Calliope	American	R	1.40	☐ [W380]	Bf-110	German	R	1.40
☐ W242	Sarge is Hit!	American	U	0.40	☐ W311	Rangers	American	R	1.40	☐ [W381]	Dragon's Teeth	German	R	1.40
☐ W243	AT Minefield	American	U	0.40	☐ W312	Company CO	American	R	1.40	☐ [W382]	Railhead	German	R	2.40
17					☐ W313	DUKW	American	R	1.40	☐ [W383]	Fw 190-D	German	R	1.40
☐ W244	Hedgecutter	American	U	0.40	☐ W314	Conscripts Desert	American	R	1.40	☐ [W384]	Bf-109	German	R	1.40
☐ W245	M24 Chaffee	American	U	0.40	☐ W315	P-38 Lightning	American	R	1.40	☐ [W385]	Alertness	German	R	1.40
☐ W246	Bad Coordinates	American	U	0.40	25					☐ [W386]	Forward Observer	German	R	1.40
☐ W247	Command Hit	American	U	0.40	☐ W316	Heavy Fog	American	R	1.40	☐ [W387]	Company CO	German	R	1.40
☐ W248	Russian Offensive	American	U	0.40	☐ W317	Der Führer Sleeps	American	R	1.40	33				
☐ W249	Flank Attack	American	U	0.40	☐ W318	Airborne Drop	American	R	1.40	☐ [W388]	Waffen SS	German	R	1.40
☐ W250	Marder III	German	U	0.40	☐ W319	Assassination Plot	American	R	1.40	☐ [W389]	Iron Cross	German	R	1.40
☐ W251	Motorcycle Troops	German	U	0.40	☐ W320	155mm Gun	American	R	1.40	☐ [W390]	Ambush	German	R	1.40
☐ W252	Pak 40 75mm AT	German	U	0.40	☐ W321	Ambush	American	R	1.40	☐ [W391]	Mop Up	German	R	1.40
18					☐ W322	Cloud Bank	American	R	1.40	☐ [W392]	Armorer's Miracle	German	R	1.40
☐ W253	Pak 43 88mm AT	German	U	0.40	☐ W323	Railhead	American	R	1.40	☐ [W393]	Ju-87 Stuka	German	R	1.40
☐ W254	10cm Mortar	German	U	0.40	☐ W324	Hitler Commands	American	R	1.40	☐ [W394]	Me-262	German	R	1.40
☐ W255	Mistaken ID	German	U	0.40	26					☐ [W395]	Kampfgruppen	German	R	1.40
☐ W256	HVAP	German	U	0.40	☐ W325	A-20 Havoc	American	R	1.40	☐ [W396]	Critical Sector	German	R	1.40
☐ W257	Flamethrower	German	U	0.40	☐ W326	Bad Weather	American	R	1.40	34				
☐ W258	Flank Attack	German	U	0.40	☐ W327	No Retreat	American	R	1.40	☐ [W397]	Channel Storm	German	R	2.40
☐ W259	Bad Coordinates	German	U	0.40	☐ W328	Roadblock	American	R	1.40	☐ [W398]	Panzer Ace	German	R	1.40
☐ W260	Wespe	German	U	0.40	☐ W329	M36 Jackson	American	R	2.40	☐ [W399]	Air Ace	German	R	1.40
☐ W261	10.5cm Howitzer	German	U	0.40	☐ W330	240mm Gun	American	R	1.90					
					☐ W331	Supply Strike	American	R	1.40					

RARITY KEY C = Common U = Uncommon R = Rare VR = Very Rare UR = Ultra Rare F = Foil card X = Fixed/standard in all decks

Legend of the Burning Sands

Wizards of the Coast (Five Rings Division) • *Episode 1: Shadow of the Tyrant*, released **July 1998**
156 cards in set • **IDENTIFIER: No symbol next to copyright at lower right**

You will need **18** nine-pocket pages to store this set. (9 doubled up)

- Starter decks contain 60 cards; starter displays contain 12 starters
- Booster packs contain 11 cards; booster displays contain 48 boosters

Call it **Legend of the Five Rings** West. Or rather, Middle East. In 1998, Five Rings Publishing decided to expand the world of Rokugan by telling the tales of Medinat al-Salaam, the City of a Thousand Stories.

Factions battle for control of the city, their primary weapon: precious water. Water and copper are played as permanents like Heroes, Followers, Holdings, and Items, as well as more ephemeral cards, such as Actions and Spells. Factions can raid to steal Water, battle to destroy sections of the city, or challenge heroes to a duel. All cards have a Fate value, which is used as the randomizer in all actions. A player wins by eliminating his opponent's water supplies or by bringing in to play various Story cards to create an enduring legend in the City of a Thousand Stories. The beginning factions include the Assassins, led by the classic **Old Man of the Mountain**; the Moto, the Unicorn Clan from *Legend of the Five Rings*; and the Senpet, Egyptian-style imperialsts from the west.

Episode 2: Secrets and Lies introduces the Ashalan, a group of mystic Immortals, and the Qabal, a powerful conspiracy of sorcerers, while *Episode 3: Black Hand, Black Heart* introduced the Ebonites, an order of crusaders, and the Jackals, an order of thieves and rogues.

Legend of the Burning Sands caught the flavor of the mythical middle east better than *Magic: The Gathering*'s *Arabian Nights* set, and gained a small and staunch following. Too small, however, to maintain the production of the game. *Legend of the Burning Sands* ended with the release of the what was intended to be the new basic set (*Awakenings*) set, the same year the game premiered. — *James Mishler*

Concept	●●●●○
Gameplay	●●●○○
Card art	●●●●○
Player pool	●○○○○

Set (156 cards)	74.00		
Starter Display Box	58.00		
Booster Display Box	63.00		
Starter Deck	7.00		
Booster Pack	2.00		

Card name	Type	Rar	Price
A Commander'sCourage	Actn	C	0.15
A Dying Sahir's Tale	Story	U	0.50
A Handful of Sand	Actn	R	4.00
A Vision of Doom	Actn	C	0.15
Abd al-Zhayn	Hero	R	4.00
Abresax	Hero	R	4.00
Adnan	Hero	C	0.15
Advanced Scout	Follo	C	0.15
al-Hazaad	Hero	C	0.15
Al-Zhayn's Trained Peacocks	Follo	C	0.15
Alim's Charm of Protection	Actn	U	0.50
Ambush	Actn	R	4.00
Ancestral Sword of the Kirin	Item	X	3.00
Archers	Follo	C	0.15
Argoun	Hero	C	0.15
Army of Ghuls	Actn	R	1.50
Asori	Hero	U	0.50
Attack at Dawn	Actn	R	6.00
Auction Block	Holdg	U	0.50
Bad Dates	Actn	U	0.50
Badr al Din's Chains of Binding	Actn	R	1.50
Baha al Din's Brass Lamp	Actn	U	0.50
Bekhten	Hero	C	0.15
Belly Dancer	Holdg	C	0.15
Belly of the Desert	Actn	C	0.15
Blind Luck	Actn	U	0.50
Blood Oath	Actn	U	0.50
Bonepicker	Hero	C	0.15
Book of the Dead	Item	X	3.00
Broken Weapon	Actn	U	0.50
Burning Oil	Holdg	C	0.15
Camel	Item	C	0.15
Ceremony of the Hidden Heart	Actn	R	1.50
Chandra	Hero	C	0.15
City Guard	Follo	U	0.50

Card name	Type	Rar	Price
Contest of Wills	Actn	U	0.50
Copper Mine	Holdg	C	0.15
Crossbow	Item	U	0.50
Curse of the Rot Within	Spell	U	0.50
Den of Iniquity	Holdg	U	0.50
Desert Spring	Actn	C	0.15
Desert Warriors	Follo	U	0.50
Desperate Reserves	Actn	U	0.50
Dhul Fiqar Knife	Item	C	0.15
Divided We Fall	Actn	C	0.15
Divination	Actn	U	0.50
Diving through the Crowd	Actn	R	2.50
Doctor	Holdg	R	4.00
Dream Magic	Spell	R	2.50
Dust to Dust	Spell	U	0.50
Elephant	Follo	U	4.00
Eyeslicer	Hero	C	0.15
Faida	Hero	R	2.50
Faith	Actn	U	0.50
Fatima	Hero	U	0.50
Flying Carpet	Item	R	1.50
Gaheris	Hero	R	6.00
Ghiyath	Hero	R	2.50
Haggling	Actn	U	0.50
Harem	Holdg	C	0.15
Harik's Ruby	Spell	R	5.00
Haroun	Hero	R	3.00
Heavy Cavalry	Follo	R	4.00
Hensatti	Hero	R	5.00
Hisham's Healing Shop	Actn	R	2.50
Indira	Hero	R	2.50
Janan Barakah	Hero	R	2.50
Jangir	Hero	U	0.50
Jewel of the Desert	City	X	1.50
Jinn of a Thousand Midnights	Spell	C	0.15
Jinn of Decay	Spell	U	0.50
Jinn of Desire	Spell	U	0.50
Jinn of the New Moon	Spell	R	4.00
Kabdar Fassal	Hero	U	0.50
Kara	Hero	R	4.00
Keseth	Hero	C	0.50
Khadi Justice	Actn	R	2.50
Khaidu	Hero	C	0.15

Card name	Type	Rar	Price
Khitai	Hero	R	3.00
Kiyoshi	Hero	U	0.50
Knife Fight	Actn	U	0.50
Know Your Weakness	Actn	U	0.50
Lands of the Scarab	City	U	0.50
Let Him Bleed	Actn	U	0.50
Library	Holdg	R	3.00
Lost to the Sands	Actn	C	0.15
Lurking Shadows	Actn	R	3.00
Marishka	Hero	C	0.15
Martyr	Actn	U	0.50
Mendi-Duad	Hero	U	0.50
Monkey Man	Hero	U	0.50
Moonless Night	Actn	U	0.50
Moto Steeds	Follo	U	0.50
Nekhebet	Hero	R	3.00
Nepherus	Hero	U	0.50
Nim	Hero	R	2.00
No Escape	Actn	C	0.15
Nowhere to Run	Actn	C	0.15
Old Man of the Mountain	Hero	R	6.00
One Dinari	Actn	C	0.15
One Water	Actn	C	0.15
Position is Power	Actn	U	0.50
Qer Apet	Hero	C	0.15
Qolat Assassin	Actn	R	4.00
Qolat Master	Actn	R	6.00
Ramontet	Hero	U	0.50
Roc	Hero	R	2.50
Sabina	Hero	C	0.15
Sabotage	Actn	C	0.15
Safiyya's Sweetwater	Holdg	R	5.00
Sandstorm	Actn	C	0.15
Secret Well	City	R	5.00
Seduction	Actn	U	0.50
Senpet Garrison	City	R	5.00
Shadows Within the Walls	City	R	5.00
Shala	Hero	U	0.50
Shalimar	Hero	U	0.50
Shielded Armor	Item	C	0.15
Shu-kai	Hero	U	0.50
Sound Planning	Actn	C	0.15
Spices	Holdg	C	0.15
Sudden Strike	Actn	R	5.00

Card name	Type	Rar	Price
Sun's Anger	Actn	R	3.00
Swift Revenge	Actn	U	0.50
Takiyah	Hero	U	0.50
The Arrow's Bite	Actn	R	2.00
The Empire of the Scarab	Stghld	X	3.00
The Eye of Night	Hero	R	4.00
The Fields of Rolling Grain	City	R	3.00
The Heart of the Common Man	Actn	C	0.15
The Hidden Keep of the Assassins	Stghld	X	3.00
The Merchant Quarter	City	R	5.00
The Moto Oasis	Stghld	X	3.00
The Prophet's Wall	Holdg	C	0.15
The River Quarter	City	R	5.00
The Sultan's Tithe	Actn	R	2.50
The Tale of Selqet's Capture	Story	U	0.50
The Tale of the Last Raid	Story	U	0.50
The Tale of the Moto and the Scarab	Story	U	0.50
The Tale of the Stolen Heart	Story	U	0.50
The Weight of Dreams	Actn	C	0.15
The Wicked Moon	Item	X	3.00
Thieves Quarter	City	U	0.50
Trade Route	Holdg	C	0.15
Trials of Desperation	Actn	C	0.15
Umar's Mirror	Actn	R	1.50
Voice of the Ten Thousand Gods	Actn	C	0.15
Watchtower	Holdg	U	0.50
Water From a Mirage	Actn	R	1.50
Wheat Fields	Holdg	C	0.15
Wijdan's Fabulous Carpet Shop	Holdg	R	2.00
Wisdom of the Stars	Actn	C	0.15
With My Brother Beside Me	Actn	C	0.15
With the Sun At Our Back	Actn	R	2.50
Yesugai	Hero	C	0.15
Yodaitai Legions	Follo	U	0.50

RARITY KEY C = Common **U** = Uncommon **R** = Rare **VR** = Very Rare **UR** = Ultra Rare **F** = Foil card **X** = Fixed/standard in all decks

Legend of the Burning Sands •
Episode 2: Secrets and Lies

Wizards of the Coast (Five Rings Division) • Released **August 1998**

104 cards in set • **IDENTIFIER: Cross (✠) symbol next to copyright at lower right**

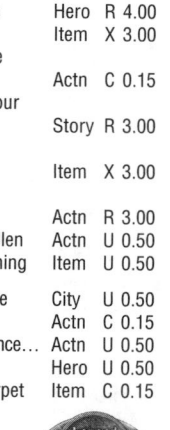

You will need **12** nine-pocket pages to store this set. (6 doubled up)

- Starter decks contain 60 cards; starter displays contain 12 starters
- Booster packs contain 11 cards; Booster displays contain 48 boosters

Set (104 cards)	65.00
Starter Display Box	58.00
Booster Display Box	63.00
Starter Deck	7.00
Booster Pack	2.00

Card name	Type	Rar	Price
A Sahir's Doom	Actn	U	0.50
Across the Desert at Midnight	Actn	R	3.00
Adil	Hero	C	0.15
Afshan Jarr	Hero	C	0.15
Afshin	Spell	R	4.00
Al-Balah	Holdg	U	0.50
Allies in the Crowd	Actn	C	0.15
Althira	Hero	R	2.00
Amru	Hero	R	4.00
Anbari Khalil	Hero	R	5.00
Ashim's Rainbow Shield	Spell	U	0.50
Atep	Hero	C	0.15
Baha al-Din	Holdg	R	4.00
Bandits	Follo	R	3.00
Barda the Hawk	Hero	C	0.15
Bazaar	Holdg	U	0.50

Card name	Type	Rar	Price
Black Steel Sword	Item	R	3.00
Blacksmith	Holdg	U	0.50
Bodyguard	Follo	R	4.00
Book of Nine Hundred and Ninety-Nine Pages	Spell	R	4.00
Crysteel Sword	Item	C	0.15
Dark Alley	Actn	C	0.15
Dawuud	Hero	U	0.50
Dena	Hero	C	0.15
Dharr's Vow	Actn	C	0.15
Duel of Wits	Actn	U	0.50
Duqaq's School of Astronomy	City	U	0.50
Eunuchs	Follo	C	0.15
Eyla the Protector	Hero	C	0.15
Glass Blower	Holdg	R	3.00
Golem	Hero	R	4.00
Gullet	Hero	U	0.50
Hakhim's Seal	Spell	U	0.50
Heart of the Beast	Spell	C	0.15
Hekau	Hero	R	5.00
Hojyn	Hero	C	0.15
Jackal Ambush	Actn	R	3.00
Jamilah	Hero	C	0.15
Jenna's Shop of Wonders	Holdg	C	0.15
Jinn of Infinite Eyes	Spell	R	3.00
Julianna Barakah	Hero	U	0.50
Kai	Spell	C	0.15
Kalesha Sesh	Hero	R	3.00
Kara's Last Stand	Actn	U	0.50
Katani	Hero	R	3.00
Kurrat al-Ayn	Hero	R	2.50

Card name	Type	Rar	Price
Lakeisha's Sky Raiders	Follo	U	0.50
Lammassar	Hero	U	0.50
Light Cavalry	Follo	C	0.15
Lizard of Water and Fire	Follo	R	3.00
Manala Shessim	Hero	C	0.15
Matsu Gohei	Hero	R	3.00
Mind Control	Spell	U	0.50
Mirali	Hero	U	0.50
Moto Marik	Hero	R	3.00
Muhad'di	Holdg	U	0.50
Mulah's Coffee House	Holdg	U	0.50
Nizam	Hero	C	0.15
Ntzoke's Amulet of Night	Item	C	0.15
Offensive Terrain	Actn	C	0.15
Patience	Actn	U	0.50
Poison	Actn	R	3.00
Praying at the Wall	Actn	U	0.50
Qabal Strnghld	Stghld	X	2.50
R'adijr, the Thunderfoot	Hero	U	0.50
Rahjid	Hero	R	3.00
Run for your Life	Actn	C	0.15
Samarhad	Hero	U	0.50
San'a	Hero	R	4.00
Sewer Expedition	Actn	C	0.15
Sewer Ghuls	Follo	U	0.50
Shadow Ambush	Actn	U	0.50
Shosuro Hametsu	Hero	R	3.00
Slaves of the Senpet Temple	Actn	U	0.50
Small Betrayals	Actn	U	0.50
Small Well	Holdg	C	0.15
Spearmen	Follo	C	0.15

Card name	Type	Rar	Price
Spirit Blade	Spell	R	3.00
Spy	Actn	C	0.15
Stand Together	Actn	C	0.15
Strange Bedfellows	Actn	C	0.15
Tabari	Hero	U	0.50
Tahir	Spell	R	5.00
Taja's Lesson	Actn	R	3.00
Tarya	Hero	C	0.15
Tasir	Hero	R	4.00
The Blood of a Jinn	Actn	C	0.15
The Blood of the Prophet	Actn	U	0.50
The Caliph	Hero	R	4.00
The City of the Seventh Star	Stghld	X	2.50
The Fist of the Scarab	Actn	U	0.50
The Grey Woman	Hero	R	4.00
The Khadja	Item	X	3.00
The Sahir and the Goddess	Actn	C	0.15
The Tale of the Four Goddesses	Story	R	3.00
The Three-Sided Seal of Sul	Item	X	3.00
The Wrath of the Black Stone	Actn	R	3.00
To Avenge the Fallen	Actn	U	0.50
Tome of Summoning	Item	U	0.50
Underground Lake	City	U	0.50
Visions of Solace	Actn	C	0.15
We Have One Chance…	Actn	U	0.50
Zenaida	Hero	U	0.50
Zinan's Flying Carpet	Item	C	0.15

Legend of the Burning Sands •
Episode 3: Black Hand, Black Heart

Wizards of the Coast (Five Rings Division) • Released **September 1998**

106 cards in set • **IDENTIFIER: Star (✦) symbol next to copyright at lower right**

You will need **12** nine-pocket pages to store this set. (6 doubled up)

- Starter decks contain 60 cards; starter displays contain 12 starters
- Booster packs contain 11 cards; Booster displays contain 48 boosters

Set (106 cards)	65.00
Starter Display Box	58.00
Booster Display Box	63.00
Starter Deck	7.00
Booster Pack	2.00

Card name	Type	Rar	Price
A Dangerous Gift	Actn	R	2.50
Asadhel Jumah	Hero	U	0.50
Ashalla	Hero	C	0.15
Balance	Hero	R	2.50
Bayushi Tangen	Hero	R	2.50

Card name	Type	Rar	Price
Beasts Below	Follo	C	0.15
Blessing of a Thousand Dreams	Actn	U	0.50
Blessing of Lady Sun's Mercy	Actn	R	2.50
Brotherhood of the Black Hand	Follo	R	2.50
Burning Marketplace	Holdg	U	0.50
Chandar	Hero	R	2.50
Chandra	Hero	R	2.50
Curse of Lost Youth	Spell	U	0.50
Defending the Innocent	Actn	U	0.50
Dhar-Hama	Actn	R	2.50
Dry Well	Actn	R	2.50
Ebonite Temple of the Black Stone	Stghld	X	2.50
Eclipse	Actn	C	0.15
Enala	Hero	R	3.50
Enigma	Hero	C	0.15
Fatima	Hero	U	0.50
Feast for the Ghuls	Actn	R	2.50

Card name	Type	Rar	Price
Felah Hassan	Hero	C	0.15
Genocide	Actn	U	0.50
Gold Merchant	Holdg	C	0.15
Goods From the East	Actn	C	0.15
Haythum Za'nul	Hero	C	0.15
Hekau Captured	Actn	R	2.50
Hitomi Tashima	Hero	R	2.50
Hole in the Sky	Actn	U	0.50
Jackal City of Bones	Stghld	X	2.50
Jangir	Hero	R	2.50
Jangir	Hero	R	2.50
Jinn of Reflection	Spell	R	2.50
Jinn Retainer	Follo	U	0.50
Jubal the Knife	Hero	C	0.15
Judgement	Hero	R	2.50
Kalib al Asim	Hero	U	0.50
Kiyoshi	Hero	R	2.50
Labib al Hatim	Hero	R	2.50
Lady Sun's Temple	Holdg	U	0.50
Leap of Faith	Actn	R	2.50
Madness	Actn	C	0.15

Card name	Type	Rar	Price
Matishiya	Hero	C	0.15
Meeting Your Destiny	Actn	U	0.50
Moving the Constellations	Actn	C	0.15
Mubarak	Holdg	R	3.50
Nagah Abominations	Follo	U	0.50
Night of the Burning Sky	Actn	U	0.50
Night of the Seven Stars	Actn	C	0.15
Nim Visits the Stranger	Actn	U	0.50
No Way Out	Actn	C	0.15
Noble House of al-Haffit	Holdg	R	3.50
Pashal	Hero	C	0.15
Plague of Cobras	Actn	C	0.15
Political Manuever	Actn	C	0.15
Public Execution Grounds	Holdg	U	0.50
Qer Apet	Hero	U	0.50
Raising the Dead	Actn	C	0.15

RARITY KEY	C = Common U = Uncommon R = Rare VR = Very Rare UR = Ultra Rare F = Foil card X = Fixed/standard in all decks

Card name	Type	Rar	Price
☐ Ramontet	Hero	U	0.50
☐ Ramontet	Hero	U	0.50
☐ Redemption's Court	Actn	U	0.50
☐ Rogue's Fortune	Actn	U	0.50

8

Card name	Type	Rar	Price
☐ Rohshem	Hero	C	0.15
☐ Scimitar	Item	C	0.15
☐ Searching the Streets	Actn	R	2.50
☐ Seff Seven-Fingers	Hero	C	0.15
☐ Shadow Horde	Follo	C	0.15
☐ Shard of the Ancients	Item	X	2.50
☐ Sibirah	Hero	C	0.15
☐ Silver Merchant	Holdg	U	0.50
☐ Stealing From the Dead	Actn	R	2.50

9

Card name	Type	Rar	Price
☐ Stealing Horses	Actn	U	0.50
☐ Taking You With Me	Actn	R	2.50
☐ Templar Master of Stars	Hero	U	0.50
☐ Test of the Stone	Actn	U	0.50
☐ The Circle of Three	Holdg	R	2.50
☐ The City of Bronze	Actn	C	0.15
☐ The City of Orphans	Holdg	R	2.50
☐ The Ferryman	Hero	C	0.15
☐ The Great Hunt	Actn	C	0.15

10

Card name	Type	Rar	Price
☐ The House of the Heavens	Holdg	C	0.15
☐ The Kindness of Strangers	Actn	R	2.50

Card name	Type	Rar	Price
☐ The Last Oasis	Actn	R	3.50
☐ The Maze	City	R	2.50
☐ The Moto Attack	Actn	U	0.50
☐ The Nightmare Devourer	Spell	C	0.10
☐ The Obsidian Mirror	Item	R	2.50
☐ The Sewers	City	U	0.50
☐ The Soul of the Slayer	Item	X	2.50

11

Card name	Type	Rar	Price
☐ The Star's Blessing	Spell	U	0.50
☐ The Tale of Selqet and the Eye of Night	Story	R	2.50
☐ The Twins Jana	Hero	U	0.50
☐ The White Palm	Actn	C	0.15

Card name	Type	Rar	Price
☐ The Wrath of the Khadi	Actn	R	2.50
☐ Thugs	Follo	C	0.15
☐ Traitorous Advisor	Holdg	U	0.50
☐ True Name	Actn	U	0.50
☐ Wardah the Urchin-Mistress	Hero	C	0.15

12

Card name	Type	Rar	Price
☐ We Must Prepare	Actn	U	0.50
☐ What Remains	Actn	U	0.50
☐ Words of Glass	Item	R	2.50
☐ Words of Sand	Item	U	0.50
☐ Yaminah	Hero	C	0.15
☐ Yodajin Templar	Hero	U	0.50
☐ You Don't Get Away That Easy	Actn	R	2.50

Legend of the Burning Sands • Awakenings

Wizards of the Coast (Five Rings Division) • Released **September 1998**

464 cards in set • **IDENTIFIER: Crescent (○) symbol next to copyright**

- Starter decks contain 60 cards; starter displays contain 12 starters
- Booster packs contain 11 cards; Booster displays contain 48 boosters

You will need **44** nine-pocket pages to store this set. (22 doubled up)

Awakenings relaunched *Legend of the Burning Sands* with a greatley expanded set, intended to allow new players to join in with advanced players and their decks.

Awakenings introduces five new factions, the Celestial Alliance (Jinns), the Houses of Dahab (the Kolat for Legend of the Five Rings), the Ivory Kingdoms (raiding Hindu-style warlords), the Ra'Shari (a mysterious organization of wandering mystics), and the Yodatai (Greco-Roman-style conquerors).

This set was the end of the story for *Burning Sands*, at least for now. — *James Mishler*

Set (464 cards)	**96.00**
Starter Display Box	**65.00**
Booster Display Box	**63.00**
Starter Deck	**7.00**
Booster Pack	**2.00**

1

Card name	Type	Rar	Price
☐ A Better World	Actn	R	4.00
☐ A Call to Arms	Actn	C	0.10
☐ A Coming Storm	Actn	C	0.10
☐ A Commander's Courage	Actn	X	5.00
☐ A Hole In the World	Holdg	C	0.10
☐ A Moment's Hesitation	Actn	C	0.10
☐ A Vision of Doom	Actn	X	5.00
☐ Abd al-Zhayn	Hero	X	5.00
☐ Abdul-Rafi's	Holdg	U	0.50

2

Card name	Type	Rar	Price
☐ Across the Desert at Midnight	Actn	X	5.00
☐ Adil	Hero	X	5.00
☐ Adira	Hero	U	0.50
☐ Adnan	Hero	X	5.00
☐ Adnan the Long-Winded	Hero	U	0.50
☐ Adrianna	Hero	R	4.00
☐ Advanced Scout	Follo	X	5.00
☐ Afshan Jarr	Hero	X	5.00
☐ Ajbar ibn Kaleel	Spell	R	3.50

3

Card name	Type	Rar	Price
☐ Akhad ibd Kaleel	Hero	X	5.00
☐ al Amaq	Spell	R	3.00
☐ al Ashwa!	Actn	U	0.50
☐ Al'a the Siege-Master	Hero	U	0.50
☐ al-Hazaad	Hero	X	5.00
☐ al-Zhayn's Trained Peacocks	Follo	X	5.00
☐ Alakrai	Spell	U	0.50
☐ Alhena	Hero	C	0.10
☐ Amahla	Hero	X	5.00

4

Card name	Type	Rar	Price
☐ Amber	Hero	C	0.10
☐ An Avatar Enraged	Actn	U	0.50
☐ Ancient Pillars of Qaharaba	City	R	4.00
☐ Argoun	Hero	X	5.00
☐ Asadhel Jumah	Hero	X	5.00
☐ Ashalla	Hero	X	5.00
☐ Asifet of the Fleet	Spell	R	3.00
☐ Asori	Hero	X	5.00
☐ Assassin Gathering Well	Actn	U	0.50

5

Card name	Type	Rar	Price
☐ Auction Block	Holdg	X	5.00
☐ Augury	Actn	R	4.00
☐ Aurelian	Hero	R	4.00
☐ Avitus	Hero	U	0.50
☐ Away With You!	Actn	U	0.50
☐ Ayna, a Jinn of Qanon	Spell	C	0.10
☐ Bad Dates	Actn	X	5.00
☐ Badr al-din	Hero	U	0.50
☐ Baha al Din's Brass Lamp	Actn	X	5.00

6

Card name	Type	Rar	Price
☐ Bakiza	Hero	C	0.10
☐ Balak the Hanif	Hero	U	0.50
☐ Baqiri	Hero	C	0.10
☐ Barda the Hawk	Hero	X	5.00
☐ Barricade Shield	Item	U	0.50
☐ Bazaar	Holdg	X	5.00
☐ Beda 'al Sin	Hero	R	4.00
☐ Bedayah	Item	X	5.00
☐ Bekhten	Hero	X	5.00

7

Card name	Type	Rar	Price
☐ Belly Dancer	Holdg	X	5.00
☐ Bitter Shadows	Actn	C	0.10
☐ Black Earth	Actn	C	0.10
☐ Blacksmith	Holdg	X	5.00
☐ Blade of the Depths	Item	C	0.10
☐ Blessing of the Prophet	Actn	R	4.00
☐ Blighted Fields	Spell	U	0.50
☐ Blinded by Fate	Spell	R	4.00
☐ Blockade	Actn	C	0.10

8

Card name	Type	Rar	Price
☐ Blood Calls For Blood	Actn	R	4.00
☐ Blood Money	Actn	U	0.50
☐ Blood Oath	Actn	X	5.00
☐ Blood of the Caliph	Item	X	5.00
☐ Bonepicker	Hero	X	5.00
☐ Borrowed Time	Actn	R	4.00
☐ Buried Alive	Actn	U	0.50
☐ Burning Oil	Holdg	X	5.00
☐ By Force of Will Alone	Actn	U	0.50

9

Card name	Type	Rar	Price
☐ By My Blood	Actn	C	0.10
☐ By Order of the Caliph	Actn	C	0.10
☐ By Royal Edict	Actn	U	0.50
☐ Camel	Item	X	5.00
☐ Captured!	Actn	C	0.10
☐ Casualties of Fate	Actn	R	4.00
☐ Cat of Many Tongues	Item	X	5.00
☐ Catapult Crew	Follo	R	4.00
☐ Ceremony of the Black Heart	Spell	U	0.50

10

Card name	Type	Rar	Price
☐ Chandra	Hero	X	5.00
☐ Charity	Actn	U	0.50
☐ City Gates	Holdg	U	0.50
☐ City Guard	Follo	X	5.00
☐ City in Flames	Actn	R	4.00
☐ Conquest	Panth	R	5.00
☐ Contest of Wills	Actn	X	5.00
☐ Convening the Twelve	Actn	C	0.10
☐ Copper Mine	Holdg	X	5.00

11

Card name	Type	Rar	Price
☐ Counter Attack	Actn	C	0.10
☐ Crossbow	Item	X	5.00
☐ Crysalis	Spell	R	4.00
☐ Crysteel Sword	Item	X	5.00
☐ Curse of Eternal Beauty	Spell	C	0.10
☐ Curse of Lost Youth	Spell	X	5.00
☐ Curse of the Rot Within	Spell	X	5.00
☐ Dahab Translator	Follo	R	4.00
☐ Daiyra	Hero	R	4.00

12

Card name	Type	Rar	Price
☐ Dangerous Manuevers	Actn	U	0.50
☐ Dark Disgrace	Actn	C	0.10
☐ Dark Journey Home	Story	R	3.00
☐ Dawn	Hero	U	0.50
☐ Dawuud	Hero	X	5.00
☐ Death by Scarab	Actn	R	4.00
☐ Death of a Butcher	Actn	R	4.00
☐ Dehydration	Actn	U	0.50
☐ Den of Iniquity	Holdg	X	5.00

13

Card name	Type	Rar	Price
☐ Desert Ambush	Actn	U	0.50
☐ Desert Outpost	City	U	0.50
☐ Desert Spring	Actn	X	5.00
☐ Desert Warriors	Follo	X	5.00
☐ Desperate Prayer	Actn	U	0.50
☐ Desperate Reserves	Actn	X	5.00
☐ Dharr	Hero	C	0.10
☐ Dhul Figar Knife	Item	X	5.00
☐ Discorporation	Spell	R	4.00

14

Card name	Type	Rar	Price
☐ Diversion	Actn	C	0.10
☐ Divided We Fall	Actn	X	5.00
☐ Divination	Actn	X	5.00
☐ Doomed City of Laramun	Stghld	X	5.00
☐ Doppelgangers	Follo	R	4.00
☐ Drunken Stupor	Actn	C	0.10
☐ Duel of Wits	Actn	X	5.00
☐ Duqaq's School of Astronomy	City	X	5.00

Card name	Type	Rar	Price
☐ Dust to Dust	Spell	X	5.00

15

Card name	Type	Rar	Price
☐ Ebonite Temple of the Black Stone	Stghld	X	5.00
☐ Eda Ishan	Hero	C	0.10
☐ Effendi	Hero	U	0.50
☐ Elite Sentries	Follo	R	4.00
☐ Emiral	Hero	R	3.00
☐ Enemy of My Enemy	Actn	U	0.50
☐ Every Man's Army	Actn	C	0.10
☐ Eyeslicer	Hero	X	5.00
☐ Eyla the Protector	Hero	X	5.00

16

Card name	Type	Rar	Price
☐ Face of a Child	Actn	C	0.10
☐ Faith	Actn	X	5.00
☐ Fatima	Hero	X	5.00
☐ Fazil	Hero	X	5.00
☐ Felah Hassan	Hero	X	5.00
☐ Ferran	Hero	U	0.50
☐ Festival Grounds	Holdg	C	0.10
☐ Forbidden	Actn	R	4.00
☐ Forget	Spell	U	0.50

17

Card name	Type	Rar	Price
☐ Forgiveness	Actn	U	0.50
☐ Gaijin Broadsword	Item	C	0.10
☐ Galerius	Hero	U	0.50
☐ Galon Trillius	Hero	C	0.10
☐ Gash	Hero	U	0.50
☐ Gathriq	Spell	U	0.50
☐ Gazing Into the Rift	Actn	R	4.00
☐ Giya	Hero	U	0.50
☐ Glass Eye of Qaliq	Item	R	3.00

18

Card name	Type	Rar	Price
☐ Gold Merchant	Holdg	X	5.00
☐ Goods From the East	Actn	X	5.00
☐ Guardian of the Rift	Actn	U	0.50
☐ Guerilla Tactics	Actn	C	0.10
☐ Gullet	Hero	X	5.00
☐ Haja the Twice-Born	Hero	X	5.00
☐ Hanif Escapees	Actn	U	0.50
☐ Harem	Holdg	X	5.00
☐ Haroun	Hero	R	4.00

19

Card name	Type	Rar	Price
☐ Heart of the Beast	Spell	X	5.00
☐ Heartless Moon	Actn	C	0.10
☐ Hearts of the Khadi	Actn	C	0.10
☐ Hidden Shame	Actn	C	0.10
☐ Hila	Hero	C	0.10

RARITY KEY C = Common U = Uncommon R = Rare VR = Very Rare UR = Ultra Rare F = Foil card X = Fixed/standard in all decks

Card name	Type	Rar	Price
Hojyn	Hero	X	5.00
Hole In the Sky	Actn	X	5.00
Immortal Council	Actn	U	0.50
Immortality's End	Actn	C	0.10
20			
Inhuman Condition	Actn	C	0.10
Inner Doubt	Actn	C	0.10
Interrogation	Actn	C	0.10
Israk ibn Kaleel	Hero	U	0.50
Ivory Boxes	Actn	C	0.10
Ivory Market	Holdg	C	0.10
J'li'lu's Fire	Actn	R	4.00
Jackal City of Bones	Stghld	X	5.00
Jackals' Hall of Souls	Holdg	C	0.10
21			
Jamilah	Hero	X	5.00
Jandaq Slave Caverns	Holdg	U	0.50
Jangir	Hero	X	5.00
Jaqhabet	Hero	C	0.10
Jenna's Shop of Wonders	Holdg	X	5.00
Jewel of the Desert	City	X	5.00
Jeweled Monkey	Item	R	4.00
Jinn Horde	Follo	R	4.00
Jinn of a Thousand Midnights	Spell	X	5.00
22			
Jinn of Decay	Spell	X	5.00
Jinn of Desire	Spell	X	5.00
Jinn of Destruction	Spell	X	5.00
Jinn of Virtue	Hero	C	0.10
Jinn Retainer	Follo	X	5.00
Journal of a Madman	Item	X	5.00
Jubla the Knife	Hero	X	5.00
Just Business	Actn	C	0.10
Kabdar Fassal	Hero	X	5.00
23			
Kai	Spell	X	4.00
Kali-Ma	Hero	R	4.00
Kali-Ma Idol	Item	X	5.00
Kara	Hero	R	4.00
Kara's Training	Actn	R	4.00
Kasib al Atif	Hero	R	4.00
Katarine of the Sheel	Hero	R	4.00
Keeper of the Marble Flame	Spell	C	0.10
Kepsat	Hero	U	0.50
24			
Keseth	Hero	X	4.00
Khadi Command	Actn	U	0.50
Khadi Overlord	Actn	R	4.00
Khaidu	Hero	X	5.00
Kiyoshi	Hero	X	5.00
Knife Fight	Actn	X	5.00
Know Your Weakness	Actn	X	5.00
Knowledge	Item	X	5.00
Kosus of Byrnia	Hero	R	5.00
25			
Kumpal	Hero	U	0.50
Kyurhi the Wanderer	Hero	C	0.10
Lady Sun's Wrath	Spell	C	0.10
Lammassar	Hero	X	5.00
Laqsha	Hero	U	0.50
Let Him Bleed	Actn	X	5.00
Let None Interfere	Actn	R	4.00
Library	Holdg	X	5.00
Lost to the Sands	Actn	X	5.00
26			
Love of Siblings	Actn	U	0.50
Lurza	Hero	R	4.00
Malakai	Hero	C	0.10
Manala Shessim	Hero	X	5.00
Manhunt	Actn	U	0.50
Marayid	Hero	R	4.00
Marishla	Hero	X	5.00
Masters of the Blood Red Tiger	Follo	R	4.00
Maymun	Hero	X	5.00
27			
Meeting Your Destiny	Actn	X	5.00
Melinda	Hero	C	0.10
Mendi-Duad	Hero	X	5.00
Merchant Caravan	Follo	C	0.10
Message from the Dead	Actn	U	0.50
Milk of the Scorpion	Actn	R	4.00

Card name	Type	Rar	Price
Mind Control	Spell	X	4.00
Mirali	Hero	X	5.00
Mohandis the Enchanter	Hero	U	0.50
28			
Monkey Man	Hero	X	5.00
Monkey Man Exp	Hero	R	4.00
Moto Steeds	Follo	X	5.00
Mulah's Coffee House	Holdg	X	5.00
Mummified Jinn Skull	Item	X	5.00
Narrow Escape!	Actn	U	0.50
Nedif Yamen	Hero	C	0.10
Nefir	Hero	C	0.10
Nehayah	Item	X	5.00
29			
Nepherus	Hero	X	5.00
Nepherus	Hero	R	4.00
Nessid	Follo	U	0.50
Never Look Back	Actn	C	0.10
New Allies	Actn	R	4.00
New Beginnings	Actn	R	4.00
Nim	Hero	R	4.00
Nizam	Hero	X	5.00
No Escape	Actn	X	5.00
30			
Nursed Back to Health	Actn	C	0.10
Octavius	Hero	C	0.10
Old Friends	Actn	R	4.00
Olive Groves of Menhir	Holdg	C	0.10
Omal	Hero	U	0.50
Onaja	Actn	U	0.50
One Dinari	Actn	X	5.00
One Water	Actn	X	5.00
Pashal	Hero	X	5.00
31			
Peddler's Row	Holdg	U	0.50
Phyrrus	Hero	U	0.50
Plague of Cobras	Actn	X	5.00
Poisoning the Well	Actn	C	0.10
Political Maneuver	Actn	X	5.00
Portals of Delight and Fancy	Holdg	C	0.10
Precious Cargo	Actn	U	0.50
Promise of the Young Ones	Actn	U	0.50
Public Execution Grounds	Holdg	X	5.00
32			
Puja the Believer	Hero	C	0.10
Punjat	Hero	R	4.00
Purity of Conquest	Actn	C	0.10
Qabal Stghld	Stghld	X	5.00
Qaliraq's Mystical Lute	Item	R	3.00
Qamus	Hero	C	0.10
Qasbah	Holdg	U	0.50
Qashima	Hero	R	4.00
Qer Apet	Hero	X	5.00
33			
Qolat Machinations	Actn	C	0.10
Quick Justice	Actn	R	4.00
Ra'Shari Caravan	Stghld	X	5.00
Ra'Shari Dancers	Follo	U	0.50
Ra'Shari Mystics	Follo	C	0.10
Rabah al Gazi	Hero	C	0.10
Raghib	Hero	C	0.10
Rahmid	Hero	U	0.50
Raising the Dead	Actn	X	5.00
34			
Ramonet	Hero	X	5.00
Rampart	Holdg	C	0.10
Raniyah	Hero	R	4.00
Ratib al 'Ideem	Hero	C	0.10
Raya	Hero	R	4.00
Razed University	Holdg	R	4.00
Re the Keeper	Panth	R	5.00
Retribution	Actn	R	4.00
Rite of Assassination	Actn	R	4.00
35			
Ritual of Binding	Spell	C	0.10
Ritual of the Awakening	Spell	R	4.00
Rogue Assassins	Follo	U	0.50
Rogue's Fortune	Actn	X	5.00
Rohshem	Hero	X	5.00
Ropp 'Cht 'Cht	Hero	R	3.00
Routed	Actn	X	5.00
Ruminations	Actn	C	0.10
Sabina	Hero	X	5.00

Card name	Type	Rar	Price
36			
Sadjem	Hero	R	4.00
Samand the Quick	Hero	U	0.50
Samarhad	Hero	X	5.00
Sanctuary	Holdg	C	0.10
Saqr al Fediq	Holdg	R	3.00
Sarna	Hero	C	0.10
Secret Passage	Actn	C	0.10
Seff Seven Fingers	Hero	X	5.00
Seff Seven Fingers Exp	Hero	R	4.00
37			
Sehai the Healer	Hero	U	0.50
Senpet Trackers	Follo	R	5.00
Sentinel Point	Holdg	R	3.00
Sha-gir	Hero	U	0.50
Shadow Ambush	Actn	R	4.00
Shagala the Damned	Hero	C	0.10
Shala	Hero	X	5.00
Shalimar	Hero	X	5.00
Shalimar Exp	Hero	R	4.00
38			
Shielded Armor	Item	X	5.00
Shipwreck!	Actn	U	0.50
Shiva the Destroyer	Panth	R	5.00
Shosuro Tage	Hero	R	4.00
Show of Force	Actn	U	0.50
Shu-kai	Hero	X	5.00
Sibirah	Hero	X	5.00
Silver Merchant	Holdg	X	5.00
Small Well	Holdg	X	5.00
39			
Soraph	Hero	U	0.50
Soul Stealing	Spell	C	0.10
Sound Planning	Actn	X	5.00
Spearmen	Follo	X	5.00
Spices	Holdg	X	5.00
Spirit-Keep of the Yodatai	Stghld	X	5.00
Spiritforge	Item	X	5.00
Staff of Sumarkhan	Item	C	0.10
Stairs of Samarrat	Holdg	C	0.10
40			
Steed of the Goddess	Item	X	5.00
Strange Bedfellows	Actn	X	5.00
Sustain Life	Spell	C	0.10
Sylmun	Hero	R	4.00
Tabari	Hero	X	5.00
Takiyah	Hero	X	5.00
Tareekh Farenkha	Hero	C	0.10
Tarya	Hero	X	5.00
Temple of Kali-Ma	Stghld	X	5.00
41			
Tempting Death	Actn	U	0.50
Tent City of the Yodatai	City	R	4.00
The Askaree	Follo	R	4.00
The Black Heart	Item	R	4.00
The Blood of a Jinn	Actn	X	5.00
The Blood-Sworn	Follo	U	0.50
The Celestial Alliance	Stghld	X	5.00
The City of Bronze	Actn	X	5.00
The City of the Seventh Star	Stghld	X	5.00
42			
The Cleansing	Actn	U	0.50
The Crossroads	Spell	U	0.50
The Crystal Hourglass	Item	X	5.00
The Cursed	Follo	U	0.50
The Eleventh Tribe	City	X	5.00
The Empire of the Senpet	Stghld	X	5.00
The End of Oppression	Actn	U	0.50
The Face of Evil	Actn	U	0.50
The Fallen Star	Item	R	5.00
43			
The Ferryman	Hero	X	5.00
The Final Sacrifice	Actn	R	4.00
The Final Strike	Actn	R	4.00
The Goddess Ascendant	Actn	X	5.00
The Goddess Enraged	Actn	U	0.50
The Goddess Reborn	Actn	U	0.50
The Goddess Unleashed	Actn	C	0.10
The Halls of Reflection	City	U	0.50
The Heart of the Common Man	Actn	X	5.00
44			
The Hidden Keep of the Assassins	Stghld	X	5.00

Card name	Type	Rar	Price
The House of the Heavens	Holdg	X	5.00
The Jinn of Eternal Beauty	Hero	U	0.50
The Last Days	Actn	C	0.10
The Last Stop	City	R	5.00
The Living Memory	Hero	R	4.00
The Long Silence	Actn	C	0.10
The Lure of Kaleel	Panth	R	5.00
The Ma'ghul	Hero	U	0.50
45			
The Mark of Kali	Actn	R	4.00
The Mighty and Merciless Sea	Panth	R	5.00
The Modari	Follo	C	0.10
The Moto Oasis	Stghld	X	5.00
The Pale Moon's Glare	Actn	C	0.10
The Parapets	Holdg	U	0.50
The Qadaam	Follo	C	0.10
The Rod of Dahab	Item	X	5.00
The Royal Throne	Holdg	R	4.00
46			
The Scale Man	Holdg	C	0.10
The Seed of Qanon	Spell	U	0.50
The Senpet Phalanx	Follo	U	0.50
The Sewers	City	X	5.00
The Silver Tongue	Hero	U	0.50
The Tale of the Fourth Avatar 1	Story	R	3.00
The Tale of the Fourth Avatar 2	Story	R	3.00
The Tear of Heaven	Item	X	5.00
The Thoroughfare	City	R	4.00
47			
The Twins Janan	Hero	X	5.00
The Weight of Dreams	Actn	X	5.00
The Will of Shilah	Panth	R	5.00
The Wounded Man	Hero	R	4.00
Thieves Quarters	City	X	5.00
Thugs	Follo	X	5.00
Tiger Companions	Follo	U	0.50
Tomb Raiding	Actn	R	4.00
Toth the Trickster	Panth	R	5.00
48			
Trade Embargo	Actn	U	0.50
Trade Route	Holdg	X	5.00
Truth	Hero	C	0.10
Truth of the Prophecy	Actn	U	0.50
Twilight Terrors	Actn	R	4.00
Ulterior Motive	Actn	U	0.50
Unbound	Actn	U	0.50
Unexpected Rescue	Actn	X	5.00
Valeria	Hero	U	0.50
49			
Vendetta	Story	U	0.50
Vengeance	Hero	C	0.10
Vespa	Hero	C	0.10
Victim of the East	Hero	C	0.10
Vishnu the Preserver	Panth	R	5.00
Visions of Solace	Actn	X	5.00
Visions of the End	Actn	U	0.50
Voice of the Star	Actn	X	5.00
Voice of the Ten Thousand Gods	Actn	X	5.00
50			
Wagi al Musakin	Hero	C	0.10
Wajh	Actn	U	0.50
Waking the Beast	Actn	C	0.10
War in the Streets	Actn	C	0.10
Watchtower	Holdg	X	5.00
Water Bags	Actn	U	0.50
Wheat Fields	Holdg	X	5.00
Wisdom of the Stars	Actn	X	5.00
With My Brother Beside Me	Actn	X	5.00
51			
Withdrawal	Actn	U	0.50
Withheld Fury	Actn	C	0.10
Worth of the Dead	Actn	C	0.10
Yaminah	Hero	X	5.00
Yesugai	Hero	X	5.00
Yodajin Templar	Hero	X	5.00
Yodatai Heavy Cavalry	Follo	R	4.00
Yodatai Legions	Follo	X	5.00
Yodatai Medium Infantry	Follo	U	0.50
52			
Yodatai Scouts	Follo	C	0.10
Young Love	Actn	C	0.10
Yuna	Hero	C	0.10
Zenaida	Hero	X	5.00
Zinan's Flying Carpet	Item	X	5.00

RARITY KEY C = Common U = Uncommon R = Rare VR = Very Rare UR = Ultra Rare F = Foil card X = Fixed/standard in all decks

Legend of the Five Rings

Alderac Entertainment Group • First set, *Imperial Edition*, released **November 1995**
303 cards in set • **IDENTIFIER: Cards © 1995; marbled black border w. red/gold ribbon**

- Starter decks contain 60 cards; starter displays contain 10 starters
- Booster packs contain 15 cards; booster displays contain 36 boosters

Lead designer **David Williams**; original co-designers, **Ryan Dancey** and **Matt Wilson**

Legend of the Five Rings (*L5R*) is not only one of the few games from the "class of '95" still in publication today, but it continues to have a devoted player base — no matter who's publishing it. Alderac moved it to its Five Rings label, which it then sold to Wizards of the Coast, which put the game up for sale in December 2000. Doubtless, those players will continue to seek it out whatever the label reads.

The CCG is set in a feudal Japan-like setting and showcases several unusual game mechanics. Each player plays with two decks, the Dynasty deck and the Fate deck. The Dynasty deck includes personalities (characters that are the core of the game), holdings (which produce gold to purchase cards and other continuing effects), and events (which have a one-time, but often major, effect on the game). Instead of a hand of cards, however, Dynasty cards are placed facedown, one in each of a player's four provinces. At the beginning of a player's turn, the cards are turned face up, so both players can see them. A player can purchase a Dynasty card with the gold from his or her Stronghold (a free starting card that gives the player some gold production and defines the attributes of the player's clan) or with gold-producing holdings.

The Fate deck operates like a conventional deck. Players have a concealed hand and draw a card at the end of their turn. Fate cards include followers, which increase a personality's unit's combat force, action cards that have varying game effects, item cards that directly affect a personality, and spells that only shujenga (spell casters) can use.

Legend of the Five Rings has two types of combat: battles, which target provinces and use personalities' and followers' military force; and duels, which are one-on-one combats fought between personalities using their chi rating. Duels can be fought during battles.

Significant to *Legend of the Five Rings* are the different types of victories a player can achieve. A player can win through a military victory by destroying all of an opponent's provinces. If a player accumulates 40 or more family honor, he or she scores an honor victory. A player gains an enlightenment victory if he or she can bring all five elemental ring cards (hence the name of the game) into play. If a player's family honor falls to -20 or less, that player loses. These multiple paths to victory give the game tremendous scope. There are many decks that win without ever attacking the opposing deck.

Imperial Edition was a solid base set, and many of the cards introduced are still important five years later. Of special note are the clan swords that increase a character's force and chi by one each for each personality of the appropriate clan the player controls. They are among the most expensive cards in the game. — *Michael Greenholdt*

Concept	●●●●○
Gameplay	●●●●○
Card art	●●●○○
Player pool	●●●●○

Logo logic

The logo for *Legends of the Five Rings* has evolved over the years. In 2000, Wizards of the Coast had to delete the five rings from the logo after the International Olympic Committee cried foul.

You will need **34** nine-pocket pages to store this set. (17 doubled up)

Set (303 cards)			322.50
Starter Display Box			200.00
Booster Display Box			212.50
Starter Deck			21.00
Booster Pack			5.50

Card name	Type	Rarity	Price
☐ Agasha Tamori	Pers	C	0.15
☐ Air Dragon	Pers	R	7.00
☐ Akodo Kage	Pers	U	1.00
☐ Akodo Toturi	Pers	R	5.00
☐ Alhundro Cornejo	Pers	U	1.00
☐ Alliance	Event	U	1.00
☐ Ambush	Actn	R	6.00
☐ Ancestral Sword of the Crab	Item	X	25.00
☐ Ancestral Sword of the Crane	Item	X	30.00
☐ Ancestral Sword of the Dragon	Item	X	35.00
☐ Ancestral Sword of the Lion	Item	X	35.00

Card name	Type	Rarity	Price
☐ Ancestral Sword of the Phoenix	Item	X	35.00
☐ Ancestral Sword of the Unicorn	Item	X	35.00
☐ Animate Dead	Spell	U	1.00
☐ Apprentice	Follo	R	5.00
☐ Archers	Follo	C	0.15
☐ Armour of Sun-Tao	Item	U	1.50
☐ Armour of the Golden Samurai	Item	U	1.50
☐ Asahina Tamako	Pers	U	1.00
☐ Asahina Tomo	Pers	C	0.15
☐ Asako Yasu	Pers	R	5.00
☐ Avoid Fate	Actn	R	12.00
☐ Barbican	Holdg	U	1.00
☐ Battering Ram Crew	Follo	U	1.00
☐ Bayushi Kachiko	Pers	R	6.00
☐ Bayushi Togai	Pers	R	5.00
☐ Be Prepared to Dig Two Graves	Actn	R	4.00
☐ Biting Steel	Spell	C	0.15
☐ Black Smith	Holdg	C	0.15

Card name	Type	Rarity	Price
☐ Blackmail	Actn	R	5.00
☐ Blazing Arrows	Actn	U	1.00
☐ Block Supply Lines	Actn	C	0.15
☐ Blood Sword	Item	C	0.15
☐ Bloom of the White Orchid	Event	R	4.60
☐ Bon Festival	Event	U	1.00
☐ Bountiful Harvest	Actn	R	5.00
☐ Breach of Etiquette	Actn	U	2.00
☐ Break Morale	Actn	C	0.15
☐ Brilliant Victory	Actn	C	0.15
☐ Call Upon The Wind	Spell	C	0.15
☐ Careful Planning	Actn	C	0.15
☐ Castle of Water	Spell	C	0.15
☐ Celestial Alignment	Event	R	4.50
☐ Charge	Actn	C	0.15
☐ Chrysanthemum Festival	Event	R	5.30
☐ Climbing Gear	Item	U	1.00
☐ Cloak of Night	Spell	R	4.00
☐ Contentious Terrain	Actn	C	0.15
☐ Copper Mine	Holdg	C	0.15

Card name	Type	Rarity	Price
☐ Counterattack	Actn	U	2.00
☐ Counterspell	Spell	U	1.20
☐ Crystal Katana	Item	U	0.15
☐ Daidoji Uji	Pers	C	0.15
☐ Dance Troupe	Holdg	U	1.00
☐ Dead Walk The Earth	Event	R	4.80
☐ Deadly Ground	Actn	C	0.15
☐ Deafening War Drums of Fu Leng	Item	R	5.00
☐ Debt of Honor	Actn	R	4.00
☐ Diamond Mine	Holdg	U	1.30
☐ Dispersive Terrain	Actn	C	0.15
☐ Doji Hoturi	Pers	R	6.00
☐ Doji Yosai	Pers	C	0.10
☐ Dragon Helm	Item	U	1.00
☐ Dragon of Fire	Pers	R	8.00
☐ Earth Dragon	Pers	R	7.80
☐ Earthquake	Spell	U	1.30
☐ Egg of P'an Ku	Actn	R	10.00
☐ Elemental Ward	Spell	U	1.00
☐ Emergence of the Tortoise	Event	R	5.00

RARITY KEY C = Common U = Uncommon R = Rare VR = Very Rare UR = Ultra Rare F = Foil card X = Fixed/standard in all decks

Card name	Type	Rarity	Price
Emperor's Peace	Event	U	1.00
Encircled Terrain	Actn	C	0.15
Energy Transference	Spell	C	0.15
9			
Entrapping Terrain	Actn	C	0.15
Evil Feeds Upon Itself	Event	U	1.30
Evil Portents	Actn	R	4.00
Explosives	Actn	U	1.30
Famous Poet	Holdg	C	0.15
Fan of Command	Item	R	5.00
Fantastic Gardens	Holdg	U	0.90
Feign Death	Actn	R	6.00
Feint	Actn	R	5.00
10			
Fire Breather	Follo	R	4.60
Fires of Purity	Spell	U	1.00
Fist of Osano-Wo	Spell	R	5.00
Flight of Dragons	Actn	U	1.00
Focus	Actn	R	10.00
Forest	Holdg	C	0.15
Forgotten Tomb	Holdg	R	5.00
Fort On A Hill	Holdg	R	5.00
Foxwife	Follo	R	5.00
11			
Frenzy	Actn	U	1.00
Fury of Osano Wo	Spell	C	0.10
Gaijin Mercenaries	Follo	R	4.50
Geisha Assassin	Actn	R	5.00
Ginawa	Pers	C	0.15
Glimpse of the Unicorn	Event	U	0.90
Go Master	Holdg	C	0.15
Goblin Chuckers	Follo	C	0.15
Goblin Mob	Follo	C	0.15
12			
Goblin Warmonger	Pers	C	0.15
Gold Mine	Holdg	C	0.15
Greater Mujina	Follo	U	1.00
Hawk Riders	Follo	R	5.00
Hawks and Falcons	Holdg	C	0.15
Heart of the Inferno	Spell	R	5.00
Heavy Cavalry	Follo	U	1.10
Heavy Infantry	Follo	U	1.10
Heichi Chokei	Pers	C	0.15
13			
Hida Amoro	Pers	U	1.00
Hida Kisada	Pers	R	6.00
Hida Sukune	Pers	C	0.15
Hida Tampako	Pers	C	0.15
Hida Tsuru	Pers	U	1.00
Hida Yakamo	Pers	R	5.00
Hida Yakamo (Crab Clan Oni)	Pers	R	8.30
Hisa	Pers	C	0.10
Honorable Seppuku	Actn	C	0.15
14			
Horiuchi Shoan	Pers	C	0.15
Hurricane	Event	U	1.00
Iaijitsu Challenge	Actn	C	0.15
Iaijitsu Duel	Actn	C	0.15
Ide Tadaji	Pers	R	5.00
Ikoma Ujiaki	Pers	R	5.00
Immortal Steel	Spell	R	5.00
Imperial Acrobats	Holdg	R	5.00
Imperial Gift	Event	R	6.00
15			
Imperial Quest	Event	R	5.00
Inheritance	Event	R	10.50
Intersecting Highways	Actn	C	0.15
Investigation	Actn	R	5.00
Iris Festival	Event	R	5.00
Iron Mine	Holdg	C	0.15
Isawa Kaede	Pers	U	1.00
Isawa Tadaka	Pers	U	1.00
Isawa Tomo	Pers	U	1.00
16			
Isawa Tsuke	Pers	R	6.00
Isawa Uona	Pers	C	0.15
Iuchi Daiyu	Pers	U	0.90
Iuchi Karasu	Pers	U	1.00
Iuchi Takaai	Pers	R	5.00
Jade Bow	Item	C	0.20
Jade Hand	Item	R	5.00
Jade Works	Holdg	C	0.15
Kakita Toshimoko	Pers	R	5.00
17			
Kakita Yinobu	Pers	U	1.00
Kakita Yoshi	Pers	R	5.00
Kakita Yuri	Pers	U	0.90
Kharmic Strike	Actn	U	2.00
Ki-Rin	Pers	R	5.00
Kitsu Toju	Pers	C	0.15
Kitsuki Yasu	Pers	R	5.00
Kolat Assassin	Actn	U	1.80
Kolat Infiltrator	Actn	U	1.00
18			
Kolat Master	Actn	R	7.00
Kolat Servant	Pers	U	1.00
Kuni Yori	Pers	U	1.00
Kyoso no Oni	Pers	U	1.00
Legendary Victory	Actn	U	1.00
Lesser Mujina	Follo	C	0.15
Light Cavalry	Follo	C	0.15
Light Infantry	Follo	C	0.15
Look into the Void	Spell	C	0.15
19			
Market Place	Holdg	C	0.15
Marries a Barbarian	Actn	U	1.00
Marsh Troll	Follo	U	1.20
Martyr	Actn	U	1.00
Mask of the Oni	Item	U	1.00
Master of the Tea Ceremony	Holdg	R	5.00
Master Smith	Holdg	U	1.00
Matsu Agetoki	Pers	U	1.50
Matsu Gohei	Pers	C	0.15
20			
Matsu Hiroru	Pers	U	1.00
Matsu Imura	Pers	U	1.00
Matsu Tsuko	Pers	R	5.00
Matsu Yojo	Pers	C	0.15
Meditation	Actn	C	0.15
Medium Cavalry	Follo	C	0.15
Medium Infantry	Follo	C	0.15
Mercy	Actn	R	4.50
Mirumoto Daini	Pers	C	0.15
21			
MIrumoto Hitomi	Pers	C	0.15
Mirumoto Sukune	Pers	U	1.00
Mists of Illusion	Spell	U	1.00
Miya Yoto	Pers	U	1.00
Moat	Holdg	C	0.15
Morito	Pers	C	0.15
Morito Tokei	Pers	C	0.15
Moshi Wakiza	Pers	C	0.15
Moto Tsume	Pers	U	1.00
22			
Naga Bowmen	Follo	U	1.20
Naga Bushi	Follo	C	0.15
Naga Shugenja	Pers	C	0.15
Naga Spearmen	Follo	U	1.20
Naga Warlord	Pers	C	0.15
Naginata	Item	C	0.15
Naka Kuro	Pers	R	5.00
Necromancer	Pers	U	1.30
Night Medallion	Item	R	5.00
23			
Ninja Genin	Follo	U	1.00
Ninja Shapeshifter	Pers	U	2.00
Ninja Spy	Pers	C	0.15
Ninja Stronghold	Holdg	R	5.00
Ninja Thief	Actn	U	1.50
Oath of Fealty	Actn	C	0.15
Occult Murders	Event	U	0.90
Occupied Terrain	Actn	C	0.15
Ogre Bushi	Pers	U	1.50
24			
Oni no Akuma	Pers	R	5.00
Oni no Shikibu	Pers	U	1.00
Oni no Tsuburu	Pers	U	1.00
Oracle of Earth	Holdg	R	5.00
Oracle of Fire	Holdg	R	5.00
Oracle of Water	Holdg	R	5.00
Oracle of Wind	Holdg	R	5.00
Otaku Kamoko	Pers	C	0.15
Outflank	Actn	C	0.15
25			
Pearl Divers	Holdg	C	0.15
Peasant Revolt	Event	U	1.00
Personal Champion	Follo	R	5.00
Plague	Event	U	1.20
Poisoned Weapon	Actn	R	5.80
Port	Holdg	C	0.15
Proposal of Peace	Event	R	4.00
Rally Troops	Actn	C	0.20
Rallying Cry	Actn	C	0.25
26			
Ratling Bushi	Follo	U	1.00
Ratling Pack	Follo	C	0.15
Reflective Pool	Spell	R	5.00
Refuse Advantage	Actn	R	5.00
Remorseful Seppuku	Actn	C	0.20
Resist Magic	Actn	R	4.00
Retired General	Holdg	C	0.15
Retreat	Actn	U	1.00
Ring of Air	Actn	U	1.50
27			
Ring of Earth	Actn	U	1.50
Ring of Fire	Actn	U	1.50
Ring of the Void	Actn	U	1.50
Ring of Water	Actn	U	1.50
Rise of the Phoenix	Event	R	5.00
Sacrificial Altar	Holdg	U	1.00
Sake Works	Holdg	U	0.90
Samurai Cavalry	Follo	R	5.00
Samurai Warriors	Follo	R	5.00
28			
Sanctified Temple	Holdg	C	0.15
Sanzo	Pers	C	0.15
School of Wizardry	Holdg	R	12.00
Scout	Follo	C	0.15
Scribe	Follo	R	5.00
Secrets on the Wind	Spell	U	1.00
Shadow Samurai	Follo	R	4.80
Shady Dealings	Actn	U	1.00
Shame	Actn	U	1.30
29			
Shiba Katsuda	Pers	C	0.15
Shiba Tsukune	Pers	C	0.15
Shiba Ujimitsu	Pers	R	6.00
Shinjo Hanari	Pers	U	1.30
Shinjo Yasamura	Pers	C	0.15
Shinjo Yokatsu	Pers	R	5.00
Shuriken of Serpents	Item	C	0.15
Shuten Doji	Pers	U	1.00
Silver Mine	Holdg	C	0.15
30			
Skeletal Troops	Follo	C	0.15
Small Farm	Holdg	C	0.20
Sneak Attack	Actn	R	5.00
Solar Eclipse	Event	R	5.00
Spearmen	Follo	C	0.15
Spirit Guide	Follo	R	5.00
Stables	Holdg	C	0.15
Star of Laramun	Item	U	1.50
Strength of Purity	Actn	U	2.00
31			
Summon Faeries	Spell	C	0.15
Summon Swamp Spirits	Spell	U	1.00
Summon Undead Champion	Spell	R	5.00
Superior Tactics	Actn	C	0.15
Temple of the Ancestors	Holdg	U	1.00
Terrible Standard of Fu'Leng	Item	R	5.00
Test of Honor	Actn	R	6.80
Test of Stone	Event	U	1.00
Test of the Emerald Champion	Event	R	5.00
32			
The Demon Bride of Fu Leng	Pers	R	5.00
Togashi Hoshi	Pers	R	5.50
Togashi Mitsu	Pers	U	1.00
Togashi Yokuni	Pers	R	6.00
Togashi Yoshi	Pers	U	1.00
Toku	Pers	C	0.15
Torrential Rain	Spell	R	5.00
Touch of Death	Spell	R	6.00
Trade Route	Holdg	U	1.00
33			
Traversable Terrain	Actn	C	0.15
Unexpected Allies	Event	U	0.90
Unscalable Walls	Holdg	C	0.15
Void Dragon	Pers	R	7.50
Walking the Way	Spell	U	1.80
Water Dragon	Pers	R	7.00
Way of Deception	Actn	U	1.00
Wind Born Speed	Spell	C	0.20
Winds of Change	Spell	U	0.80
34			
Wings of Fire	Spell	C	0.20
Wyrm Riders	Follo	U	1.00
Yasuki Taka	Pers	C	0.20
Yogo Junzo	Pers	R	5.60
Yotsu Seiki	Pers	C	0.10
Zombie Troops	Follo	U	1.00

RARITY KEY C = Common U = Uncommon R = Rare VR = Very Rare UR = Ultra Rare F = Foil card X = Fixed/standard in all decks

Legend of the Five Rings • *Emerald Edition*

Five Rings Publishing • Released **June 1996**

312 cards in set • **IDENTIFIER: Cards © 1996; marbled black border**

You will need **34** nine-pocket pages to store this set. (17 doubled up)

- Starter decks contain 60 cards; starter displays contain 12 starters
- Booster packs contain 11 cards; booster displays contain 36 boosters

Emerald Edition re-released the basic set, with clan armor cards replacing the clan swords. The clan armor cards, while good, are not considered as powerful as the clan swords, but this was, nonetheless, the set that put *Legend of the Five Rings* on the map. Ten thousand starter decks were given away at GenCon 1996.

From the start, the designers made it clear that the storyline associated with the game would be an important influence on the cards and expansions released. Each new expansion would be influenced by the results of large tournaments held in the prior six months or year. There came to be a role-playing aspect to *L5R*, as players identified with their chosen clans: Crab, Crane, Dragon, Lion, Phoenix, or Unicorn.

The Crab clan features a lot of warrior personalities, with an emphasis on fortifications. The Crab stronghold allows the Crab to increase the toughness of a province. Honor gain is the forte of the Crane clan. Their personalities tend toward political abilities and dueling. The Crane stronghold can be bowed (turned) to gain honor. The Dragon clan has a powerful mix of samurai and shugenja. As they lose provinces, the remainder gain strength. Military science is the specialty of the Lion clan. Their stronghold gives them a bonus in attacking. The Phoenix is blessed with many shugenja, and the stronghold produces extra gold when purchasing shugenja or spells. Cavalry is the strength of the Unicorns, allowing them to out-maneuver their opponents. — *Michael Greenholdt*

Set (312 cards)	250.00
Starter Display Box	96.00
Booster Display Box	102.50
Starter Deck	10.50
Booster Pack	3.30

Card name	Type	Rarity	Price
1			
☐ Agasha Tamori	Pers	C	0.20
☐ Air Dragon	Pers	R	5.00
☐ Akodo Kage	Pers	U	0.70
☐ Akodo Toturi	Pers	R	4.50
☐ Alhundro Cornejo	Pers	U	0.60
☐ Alliance	Event	U	0.80
☐ Ambush	Actn	R	7.50
☐ Ancestral Armor of the Crab	Item	R	7.00
☐ Ancestral Armor of the Crane	Item	R	7.00
2			
☐ Ancestral Armor of the Dragon	Item	R	5.50
☐ Ancestral Armor of the Lion	Item	R	5.50
☐ Ancestral Armor of the Phoenix	Item	R	5.30
☐ Ancestral Armor of the Unicorn	Item	R	7.00
☐ Animate Dead	Spell	U	0.80
☐ Apprentice	Follo	R	3.00
☐ Archers	Follo	C	0.20
☐ Armour of Sun-Tao	Item	U	0.50
☐ Armour of the Golden Samurai	Item	U	0.05
3			
☐ Asahina Tamako	Pers	U	0.60
☐ Asahina Tomo	Pers	C	0.20
☐ Asako Yasu	Pers	R	3.00
☐ Avoid Fate	Actn	R	14.00
☐ Barbican	Holdg	U	0.80
☐ Battering Ram Crew	Follo	U	0.70
☐ Bayushi Kachiko	Pers	R	6.00
☐ Bayushi Togai	Pers	R	3.80
☐ Be Prepared to Dig Two Graves	Actn	R	3.10
4			
☐ Biting Steel	Spell	C	0.20
☐ Black Smith	Holdg	C	0.20
☐ Blackmail	Actn	R	3.00

Card name	Type	Rarity	Price
☐ Blazing Arrows	Actn	U	0.70
☐ Block Supply Lines	Actn	C	0.20
☐ Blood Sword	Item	C	0.20
☐ Bloom of the White Orchid	Event	R	3.10
☐ Bon Festival	Event	U	0.80
☐ Bountiful Harvest	Actn	R	4.30
5			
☐ Breach of Etiquette	Actn	U	1.30
☐ Break Morale	Actn	C	0.20
☐ Brilliant Victory	Actn	C	0.20
☐ Call Upon The Wind	Spell	C	0.20
☐ Careful Planning	Actn	C	0.20
☐ Castle of Water	Spell	C	0.20
☐ Celestial Alignment	Event	R	3.10
☐ Charge	Actn	C	0.20
☐ Chrysanthemum Festival	Event	R	3.00
6			
☐ Climbing Gear	Item	U	0.80
☐ Cloak of Night	Spell	R	2.80
☐ Contentious Terrain	Actn	C	0.20
☐ Copper Mine	Holdg	C	0.20
☐ Counterattack	Actn	U	2.00
☐ Counterspell	Spell	C	0.70
☐ Crystal Katana	Item	U	0.80
☐ Daidoji Uji	Pers	C	0.20
☐ Dance Troupe	Holdg	U	0.70
7			
☐ Dead Walk The Earth	Event	R	3.10
☐ Deadly Ground	Actn	C	0.20
☐ Deafening War Drums of Fu'Leng	Item	R	3.00
☐ Debt of Honor	Actn	R	2.90
☐ Diamond Mine	Holdg	U	0.70
☐ Dispersive Terrain	Actn	C	0.20
☐ Doji Hoturi	Pers	R	5.00
☐ Doji Yosai	Pers	C	0.20
☐ Dragon Helm	Item	U	0.80
8			
☐ Dragon of Fire	Pers	R	5.00
☐ Earth Dragon	Pers	R	5.00
☐ Earthquake	Spell	U	0.70
☐ Egg of P'an Ku	Actn	R	9.00
☐ Elemental Ward	Spell	U	0.80
☐ Emergence of the Tortoise	Event	R	3.10
☐ Emperor's Peace	Event	U	0.70

Card name	Type	Rarity	Price
☐ Encircled Terrain	Actn	C	0.20
☐ Energy Transference	Spell	C	0.20
9			
☐ Entrapping Terrain	Actn	C	0.20
☐ Evil Feeds Upon Itself	Event	U	0.80
☐ Evil Portents	Actn	R	13.00
☐ Explosives	Actn	U	1.00
☐ Famous Poet	Holdg	C	0.20
☐ Fan of Command	Item	R	4.00
☐ Fantastic Gardens	Holdg	U	0.50
☐ Feign Death	Actn	R	6.00
☐ Feint	Actn	R	2.90
10			
☐ Fire Breather	Follo	R	3.00
☐ Fires of Purity	Spell	U	0.80
☐ Fist of Osano Wo	Spell	R	5.00
☐ Flight of Dragons	Actn	U	0.70
☐ Focus	Actn	R	13.00
☐ Forest	Holdg	C	0.20
☐ Forgotten Tomb	Holdg	R	3.00
☐ Fort On A Hill	Holdg	R	2.80
☐ Foxwife	Follo	R	3.00
11			
☐ Frenzy	Actn	U	0.70
☐ Fury of Osano Wo	Spell	C	0.20
☐ Gaijin Mercenaries	Follo	R	2.50
☐ Geisha Assassin	Actn	R	4.00
☐ Ginawa	Pers	C	0.20
☐ Glimpse of the Unicorn	Event	U	0.80
☐ Go Master	Holdg	C	0.20
☐ Goblin Chuckers	Follo	C	0.20
☐ Goblin Mob	Follo	C	0.20
12			
☐ Goblin Warmonger	Pers	C	0.20
☐ Gold Mine	Holdg	C	0.20
☐ Greater Mujina	Follo	U	0.70
☐ Hawk Riders	Follo	R	3.20
☐ Hawks and Falcons	Holdg	C	0.20
☐ Heart of the Inferno	Spell	R	2.70
☐ Heavy Cavalry	Follo	U	1.00
☐ Heavy Infantry	Follo	U	0.80
☐ Heichi Chokei	Pers	C	0.20
13			
☐ Hida Amoro	Pers	U	0.80
☐ Hida Kisada	Pers	R	4.00
☐ Hida Sukune	Pers	U	0.80
☐ Hida Tampako	Pers	C	0.20
☐ Hida Tsuru	Pers	U	0.70

Card name	Type	Rarity	Price
☐ Hida Yakamo	Pers	R	3.30
☐ Hida Yakamo	Pers	R	7.00
☐ Hisa	Pers	C	0.20
☐ Honorable Seppuku	Actn	C	0.20
14			
☐ Horiuchi Shoan	Pers	C	0.20
☐ Hurricane	Event	U	0.80
☐ Iaijitsu Challenge	Actn	C	0.20
☐ Iaijitsu Duel	Actn	C	0.20
☐ Ide Tadaji	Pers	R	2.50
☐ Ikoma Ujiaki	Pers	R	3.80
☐ Immortal Steel	Spell	R	4.00
☐ Imperial Acrobats	Holdg	R	2.80
☐ Imperial Gift	Event	R	8.00
15			
☐ Imperial Quest	Event	R	3.10
☐ Inheritance	Event	R	21.00
☐ Intersecting Highways	Actn	C	0.20
☐ Investigation	Actn	R	4.00
☐ Iris Festival	Event	R	4.00
☐ Iron Mine	Holdg	C	0.20
☐ Isawa Kaede	Pers	U	0.80
☐ Isawa Tadaka	Pers	U	0.80
☐ Isawa Tomo	Pers	U	0.70
16			
☐ Isawa Tsuke	Pers	R	5.00
☐ Isawa Uona	Pers	C	0.20
☐ Iuchi Daiyu	Pers	U	0.80
☐ Iuchi Karasu	Pers	U	0.80
☐ Iuchi Takaai	Pers	R	3.10
☐ Jade Bow	Item	C	0.20
☐ Jade Hand	Item	R	5.00
☐ Jade Works	Holdg	C	0.20
☐ Kakita Toshimoko	Pers	R	3.00
17			
☐ Kakita Yinobu	Pers	U	0.50
☐ Kakita Yoshi	Pers	R	3.30
☐ Kakita Yuri	Pers	U	0.70
☐ Kharmic Strike	Actn	R	1.00
☐ Ki-Rin	Pers	R	5.00
☐ Kitsu Motso	Pers	R	3.30
☐ Kitsu Toju	Pers	C	0.20
☐ Kitsuki Yasu	Pers	R	3.50
☐ Kolat Assassin	Actn	U	1.00
18			
☐ Kolat Infiltrator	Actn	U	0.50
☐ Kolat Master	Actn	R	7.00
☐ Kolat Servant	Pers	U	0.90
☐ Kuni Yori	Pers	U	0.70

RARITY KEY C = Common U = Uncommon R = Rare VR = Very Rare UR = Ultra Rare F = Foil card X = Fixed/standard in all decks

Card name	Type	Rarity	Price
Kyoso no Oni	Pers	U	0.80
Legendary Victory	Actn	U	0.80
Lesser Mujina	Follo	C	0.20
Light Cavalry	Follo	C	0.20
Light Infantry	Follo	C	0.20
Look into the Void	Spell	C	0.20
Market Place	Holdg	C	0.20
Marries a Barbarian	Actn	U	0.90
Marsh Troll	Follo	U	0.80
Martyr	Actn	U	0.60
Mask of the Oni	Item	U	0.80
Master of the Tea Ceremony	Holdg	R	4.80
Master Smith	Holdg	U	0.80
Matsu Agetoki	Pers	U	0.80
Matsu Gohei	Pers	C	0.20
Matsu Hiroru	Pers	U	1.00
Matsu Imura	Pers	U	0.50
Matsu Tsuko	Pers	R	4.00
Matsu Yojo	Pers	C	0.20
Meditation	Actn	C	0.20
Medium Cavalry	Follo	C	0.20
Medium Infantry	Follo	C	0.20
Mercy	Actn	R	3.00
Mirumoto Daini	Pers	C	0.20
MIrumoto Hitomi	Pers	C	0.20
Mirumoto Sukune	Pers	U	0.70
Mists of Illusion	Spell	U	0.20
Miya Yoto	Pers	U	0.80
Moat	Holdg	C	0.20
Morito	Pers	C	0.20
Morito Tokei	Pers	C	0.20
Moshi Wakiza	Pers	C	0.20
Moto Tsume	Pers	U	0.70
Naga Abominination	Pers	R	5.00
Naga Bowmen	Follo	U	0.80
Naga Bushi	Follo	C	0.20
Naga Shugenja	Pers	C	0.20
Naga Spearmen	Follo	U	0.80
Naga Warlord	Pers	C	0.20
Naginata	Item	C	0.20
Naka Kuro	Pers	R	3.60
Necromancer	Pers	U	0.90
Night Medallion	Item	R	4.50
Ninja Genin	Follo	U	0.80
Ninja Shapeshifter	Pers	U	1.80
Ninja Spy	Pers	C	0.20
Ninja Stronghold	Holdg	R	8.00
Ninja Thief	Actn	U	0.50
Oath of Fealty	Actn	C	0.20
Occult Murders	Event	U	0.80
Occupied Terrain	Actn	C	0.20
Ogre Bushi	Pers	U	0.80
Oni no Akuma	Pers	R	2.80
Oni no Shikibu	Pers	U	0.80
Oni no Tsuburu	Pers	U	0.80
Oracle of Earth	Holdg	R	4.80
Oracle of Fire	Holdg	R	4.80
Oracle of Water	Holdg	R	4.80
Oracle of Wind	Holdg	R	4.80
Otaku Kamoko	Pers	C	0.20
Outflank	Actn	C	0.20
Pearl Divers	Holdg	C	0.20
Peasant Revolt	Event	U	0.80
Personal Champion	Follo	R	3.00
Plague	Event	U	0.80
Poisoned Weapon	Actn	R	7.00
Port	Holdg	C	0.20
Proposal of Peace	Event	R	3.00
Rally Troops	Actn	C	0.20
Rallying Cry	Actn	C	0.25
Ratling Bushi	Follo	U	0.70
Ratling Pack	Follo	C	0.20
Reflective Pool	Spell	R	3.00
Refuse Advantage	Actn	R	2.50
Remorseful Seppuku	Actn	C	0.20
Resist Magic	Actn	R	3.00
Retired General	Holdg	C	0.20
Retreat	Actn	U	0.80
Ring of Air	Actn	U	0.60
Ring of Earth	Actn	U	0.90
Ring of Fire	Actn	U	0.60
Ring of the Void	Actn	U	0.70
Ring of Water	Actn	U	0.60
Rise of the Phoenix	Event	R	3.20
Sacrificial Altar	Holdg	U	0.80
Sake Works	Holdg	U	0.80
Samurai Cavalry	Follo	R	3.00
Samurai Warriors	Follo	R	4.00
Sanctified Temple	Holdg	C	0.20
Sanzo	Pers	C	0.20
School of Wizardry	Holdg	R	14.00
Scout	Follo	C	0.20
Scribe	Follo	R	5.00
Secrets on the Wind	Spell	U	0.80
Shadow Samurai	Follo	R	3.00
Shady Dealings	Actn	U	0.80
Shame	Actn	U	0.90
Shiba Katsuda	Pers	C	0.20
Shiba Tsukune	Pers	C	0.20
Shiba Ujimitsu	Pers	R	5.00
Shinjo Hanari	Pers	U	0.70
Shinjo Yasamura	Pers	C	0.20
Shinjo Yokatsu	Pers	R	3.80
Shosuro Hametsu	Pers	R	3.00
Shuriken of Serpents	Item	C	0.20
Shuten Doji	Pers	U	1.00
Silver Mine	Holdg	C	0.20
Skeletal Troops	Follo	C	0.20
Small Farm	Holdg	C	0.20
Sneak Attack	Actn	R	11.00
Solar Eclipse	Event	R	3.40
Spearmen	Follo	C	0.20
Spirit Guide	Follo	R	5.00
Stables	Holdg	C	0.20
Star of Laramun	Item	U	1.00
Strength of Purity	Actn	U	1.50
Summon Faeries	Spell	C	0.20
Summon Swamp Spirits	Spell	U	0.70
Summon Undead Champion	Spell	R	4.50
Superior Tactics	Actn	C	0.20
Temple of the Ancestors	Holdg	U	0.80
Terrible Standard of Fu'Leng	Item	R	3.30
Test of Honor	Actn	R	9.50
Test of Stone	Event	U	0.50
Test of the Emerald Champion	Event	R	3.60
The Demon Bride of Fu Leng	Pers	R	2.50
Togashi Hoshi	Pers	R	3.80
Togashi Mitsu	Pers	U	0.80
Togashi Yokuni	Pers	R	3.80
Togashi Yoshi	Pers	U	1.50
Toku	Pers	C	0.20
Torrential Rain	Spell	R	3.30
Touch of Death	Spell	R	4.10
Trade Route	Holdg	U	1.00
Traversable Terrain	Actn	C	0.20
Unexpected Allies	Event	U	0.80
Unscalable Walls	Holdg	U	0.80
Void Dragon	Pers	R	3.80
Walking the Way	Spell	U	3.50
Water Dragon	Pers	R	3.00
Way of Deception	Actn	U	0.80
Wind Born Speed	Spell	C	0.20
Winds of Change	Spell	U	0.80
Wings of Fire	Spell	C	0.20
Wyrm Riders	Follo	U	0.70
Yasuki Taka	Pers	C	0.20
Yogo Junzo	Pers	R	3.10
Yotsu Seiki	Pers	C	0.20
Zombie Troops	Follo	U	0.70

Shinjo Yasamura
Unicorn Clan Samurai • Cavalry
Open: Once per turn, he can give one Follower in this unit the Cavalry trait until the end of the turn.
"I saw him there with the golden horizon behind him, and I knew our armies would suffer a terrible fate that day."

Legend of the Five Rings • Obsidian Edition

Five Rings Publishing • Released June 1997

310 cards in set • IDENTIFIER: Black border w/fine brown lines OBSIDIAN EDITION

- Starter decks contain 60 cards; starter displays contain 12 starters
- Booster packs contain 15 cards; booster displays contain 36 boosters

In the third base set, we learn that the Emperor's wife, Bayushi Kachiko, has been poisoning her husband in revenge for the destruction of her clan, so weakening him that he was susceptible to the Dark Lord Fu Leng's possession. Her feelings of guilt are to play a pivotal role in events to come.

There were few cards added or omitted in *Obsidian Edition*, as compared to *Emerald*. The major change was the substitution of the ancestral standard cards for the clan armor cards. The ancestral standards give a bonus to followers attached to the personality and a penalty to opposing personalities of the same clan. By and large, the standards are considered less useful than the clan armor cards. — *Michael Greenholdt*

You will need **35** nine-pocket pages to store this set. (18 doubled up)

Set (310 cards)	225.00
Starter Display Box	66.00
Booster Display Box	80.00
Starter Deck	9.00
Booster Pack	2.50

Card name	Type	Rarity	Price
Agasha Tamori	Pers	C	0.20
Air Dragon	Pers	R	5.60
Akodo Kage	Pers	U	0.70
Akodo Toturi	Pers	R	4.00
Aljundro Cornejo	Pers	U	0.50
Alliance	Event	U	0.70
Ambush	Actn	R	5.00
Ancestral Standard of the Crab Clan	Item	X	3.80
Ancestral Standard of the Crane Clan	Item	X	3.80
Ancestral Standard of the Dragon Clan	Item	X	3.80
Ancestral Standard of the Lion Clan	Item	X	3.80
Ancestral Standard of the Phoenix Clan	Item	X	3.50
Ancestral Standard of the Unicorn Clan	Item	X	3.50
Animate the Dead	Spell	U	0.70
Apprentice	Follo	R	4.00
Archers	Follo	C	0.20
Armour of Sun Tao	Item	U	0.60
Armour of the Golden Samurai	Item	U	0.60
Asahina Tamako	Pers	U	0.50
Asahina Tomo	Pers	C	0.20
Asako Yasu	Pers	R	4.90
Avoid Fate	Actn	R	5.60
Barbican	Holdg	U	0.70
Battering Ram Crew	Follo	U	0.50
Bayushi Kachiko	Pers	R	6.00
Bayushi Togai	Pers	R	3.60
Be Prepared to Dig Two Graves	Actn	R	3.20
Biting Steel	Spell	C	0.20
Blackmail	Actn	R	3.40
Blacksmiths	Holdg	C	0.20
Blazing Arrows	Actn	C	0.50
Block Supply Lines	Actn	C	0.20
Blood Sword	Item	C	0.20
Bloom of the White Orchid	Event	R	3.00
Bon Festival	Event	U	0.60
Bountiful Harvest	Actn	R	4.50
Breach of Etiquette	Actn	U	1.00
Break Morale	Actn	C	0.20
Brilliant Victory	Actn	C	0.20
Call Upon The Wind	Spell	C	0.20

RARITY KEY C = Common U = Uncommon R = Rare VR = Very Rare UR = Ultra Rare F = Foil card X = Fixed/standard in all decks

Card name	Type	Rarity	Price
Careful Planning	Actn	C	0.20
Castle of Water	Spell	C	0.20
Celestial Alignment	Event	R	3.00
Charge	Actn	C	0.20
Chrysanthemum Festival	Event	R	5.00
Climbing Gear	Item	U	0.80
Cloak of Night	Spell	R	3.00
Contentious Terrain	Actn	C	0.20
Copper Mine	Holdg	C	0.20
Counterattack	Actn	U	1.20
Counterspell	Spell	U	0.50
Crystal Katana	Item	C	0.20
Daidoji Uji	Pers	C	0.20
Dance Troupe	Holdg	U	0.50
Dead Walk The Earth	Event	R	3.00
Deadly Ground	Actn	C	0.20
Deafening War Drums of Fu Leng	Item	R	3.00
Debt of Honor	Actn	R	3.00
Demon Bride of Fu Leng	Pers	R	4.00
Diamond Mine	Holdg	U	0.50
Dispersive Terrain	Actn	C	0.20
Doji Hoturi	Pers	R	5.00
Doji Yosai	Pers	C	0.20
Dragon Helm	Item	U	0.80
Dragon of Fire	Pers	R	5.60
Earth Dragon	Pers	R	5.80
Earthquake	Spell	U	0.50
Egg of Pan Ku	Actn	R	8.00
Elemental Ward	Spell	U	0.50
Emergence of the Tortoise	Event	R	3.10
Emperor's Peace	Event	U	0.60
Encircled Terrain	Actn	C	0.20
Energy Transference	Spell	C	0.20
Entrapping Terrain	Actn	C	0.20
Evil Feeds Upon Itself	Event	U	0.80
Evil Portents	Actn	R	5.50
Explosives	Actn	U	1.00
Famous Poet	Holdg	R	3.00
Fan of Command	Item	R	4.00
Fantastic Gardens	Holdg	U	0.50
Feign Death	Actn	R	5.00
Feint	Actn	R	3.00
Fire Breather	Follo	R	3.10
Fires of Purity	Spell	U	0.60
Fist of Osano Wo	Spell	R	4.60
Flight of Dragons	Actn	U	0.60
Focus	Actn	R	7.20
Forest	Holdg	C	0.20
Forgotten Tomb	Holdg	R	3.20
Fort On A Hill	Holdg	R	3.00
Foxwife	Follo	R	3.50
Frenzy	Actn	U	1.00
Fury of Osano-Wo	Spell	C	0.15
Gaijin Mercenaries	Follo	R	2.60
Geisha Assassin	Actn	R	4.10
Ginawa	Pers	C	0.20
Glimpse of the Unicorn	Event	U	0.80
Go Master	Holdg	C	0.20
Goblin Chuckers	Follo	C	0.20
Goblin Mob	Follo	C	0.20
Goblin Warmonger	Pers	C	0.20
Gold Mine	Holdg	C	0.20
Greater Mujina	Follo	U	0.70
Hawk Riders	Follo	R	3.20
Hawks and Falcons	Holdg	C	0.20
Heart of the Inferno	Spell	R	3.00
Heavy Cavalry	Follo	U	0.80
Heavy Infantry	Follo	U	0.80
Heichi Chokei	Pers	C	0.20
Hida Amoro	Pers	U	0.80
Hida Kisada	Pers	R	4.40
Hida Sukune	Pers	C	0.20
Hida Tampako	Pers	C	0.20
Hida Tsuru	Pers	U	0.70
Hida Yakamo	Pers	R	5.00
Hida Yakamo (Crab Clan Oni)	Pers	R	6.00
Honorable Seppuku	Actn	C	0.20
Horiuchi Shoan	Pers	C	0.20
Hurricane	Event	U	0.60
Iaijutsu Challenge	Actn	C	0.20
Iaijutsu Duel	Actn	C	0.20
Ide Tadaji	Pers	R	2.50
Ikoma Ujiaki	Pers	R	4.00
Immortal Steel	Spell	R	3.50
Imperial Acrobats	Holdg	R	3.60
Imperial Gift	Event	R	5.30
Imperial Quest	Event	R	5.00
Inheritance	Event	R	12.00
Intersecting Highways	Actn	C	0.20
Investigation	Actn	R	4.00
Iris Festival	Event	R	4.00
Iron Mine	Holdg	C	0.20
Isawa Kaede	Pers	U	0.60
Isawa Tadaka	Pers	U	0.80
Isawa Tomo	Pers	U	0.50
Isawa Tsuke	Pers	R	5.00
Isawa Uona	Pers	C	0.20
Iuchi Daiyu	Pers	U	0.50
Iuchi Karasu	Pers	U	0.60
Iuchi Takaai	Pers	R	3.00
Jade Bow	Item	C	0.20
Jade Hand	Item	R	5.00
Jade Works	Holdg	C	0.20
Kakita Toshimoko	Pers	R	5.50
Kakita Yinobu	Pers	U	0.50
Kakita Yoshi	Pers	R	4.00
Kakita Yuri	Pers	U	0.50
Kharmic Strike	Actn	U	0.90
Ki-Rin	Pers	R	5.00
Kitsu Motso	Pers	R	3.30
Kitsu Toju	Pers	C	0.20
Kitsuki Yasu	Pers	R	4.30
Kolat Assassin	Actn	U	1.00
Kolat Infiltrator	Actn	U	0.50
Kolat Master	Actn	R	7.00
Kolat Servant	Pers	C	0.90
Kuni Yori	Pers	U	0.50
Kyoso no Oni	Pers	U	0.80
Legendary Victory	Actn	U	0.70
Lesser Mujina	Follo	C	0.20
Light Cavalry	Follo	C	0.20
Light Infantry	Follo	C	0.20
Look into the Void	Spell	C	0.20
Market Place	Holdg	C	0.20
Marries a Barbarian	Actn	U	0.70
Marsh Troll	Follo	U	0.70
Martyr	Actn	U	0.70
Mask of the Oni	Item	U	0.60
Master of the Tea Ceremony	Holdg	R	4.20
Master Smith	Holdg	U	0.80
Matsu Agetoki	Pers	U	0.70
Matsu Gohei	Pers	C	0.20
Matsu Hiroru	Pers	C	0.70
Matsu Imura	Pers	U	0.60
Matsu Tsuko	Pers	R	5.00
Matsu Yojo	Pers	C	0.20
Meditation	Actn	C	0.20
Medium Cavalry	Follo	C	0.20
Medium Infantry	Follo	C	0.20
Mercy	Actn	R	3.30
Mirumoto Daini	Pers	C	0.20
MIrumoto Hitomi	Pers	C	0.20
Mirumoto Sukune	Pers	U	0.50
Mists of Illusion	Spell	U	0.50
Miya Yoto	Pers	U	0.50
Moat	Holdg	C	0.20
Morito	Pers	C	0.20
Morito Tokei	Pers	C	0.20
Moshi Wakiza	Pers	C	0.20
Moto Tsume	Pers	U	0.70
Naga Bowmen	Follo	U	0.80
Naga Bushi	Follo	C	0.20
Naga Shugenja	Pers	C	0.20
Naga Spearmen	Follo	U	0.60
Naga Warlord	Pers		
Naginata	Item	C	0.20
Naka Kuro	Pers	R	4.50
Necromancer	Pers	U	0.70
Night Medallion	Item	R	4.00
Ninja Genin	Follo	U	0.70
Ninja Shapeshifter	Pers	U	1.40
Ninja Spy	Pers	C	0.20
Ninja Stronghold	Holdg	R	6.00
Ninja Thief	Actn	U	0.50
Oath of Fealty	Actn	C	0.20
Occult Murders	Event	U	0.60
Occupied Terrain	Actn	C	0.20
Ogre Bushi	Pers	U	0.50
Oni no Akuma	Pers	R	4.20
Oni no Shikibu	Pers	U	0.50
Oni no Tsuburu	Pers	U	0.60
Oracle of Earth	Holdg	R	4.00
Oracle of Fire	Holdg	R	4.40
Oracle of Water	Holdg	R	4.80
Oracle of Wind	Holdg	R	4.10
Otaku Kamoko	Pers	C	0.20
Outflank	Actn	C	0.20
Pearl Divers	Holdg	C	0.20
Peasant Revolt	Event	U	0.60
Personal Champion	Follo	R	3.00
Plague	Event	U	0.60
Poisoned Weapon	Actn	R	4.50
Port	Holdg	C	0.20
Proposal of Peace	Event	R	3.20
Rally Troops	Actn	C	0.20
Rallying Cry	Actn	C	0.15
Ratling Bushi	Follo	U	0.70
Ratling Pack	Follo	C	0.20
Reflective Pool	Spell	R	3.00
Refuse Advantage	Actn	R	2.90
Remorseful Seppuku	Actn	C	0.20
Resist Magic	Actn	R	3.10
Retired General	Holdg	C	0.20
Retreat	Actn	U	0.70
Ring of Air	Actn	U	0.70
Ring of Earth	Actn	U	1.00
Ring of Fire	Actn	U	0.60
Ring of the Void	Actn	U	1.00
Ring of Water	Actn	U	0.70
Rise of the Phoenix	Event	R	3.10
Sacrificial Altar	Holdg	U	0.60
Sake Works	Holdg	U	0.60
Samurai Cavalry	Follo	R	4.00
Samurai Warriors	Follo	R	4.50
Sanctified Temple	Holdg	C	0.20
Sanzo	Pers	C	0.20
School of Wizardry	Holdg	R	7.00
Scout	Follo	C	0.20
Scribe	Follo	R	5.00
Secrets on the Wind	Spell	U	0.80
Shadow Samurai	Follo	R	3.60
Shady Dealings	Actn	U	0.80
Shame	Actn	U	0.80
Shiba Katsuda	Pers	C	0.20
Shiba Tsukune	Pers	C	0.20
Shiba Ujimitsu	Pers	R	5.00
Shinjo Hanari	Pers	U	0.50
Shinjo Yasamura	Pers	C	0.20
Shinjo Yokatsu	Pers	R	4.00
Shosuro Hametsu	Pers	R	3.10
Shuriken of Serpents	Item	C	0.20
Shuten Doji	Pers	U	0.90
Silver Mine	Holdg	C	0.20
Skeletal Troops	Follo	C	0.20
Small Farm	Holdg	C	0.20
Sneak Attack	Actn	R	6.00
Solar Eclipse	Event	R	3.00
Spearmen	Follo	C	0.20
Spirit Guide	Follo	R	4.50
Stables	Holdg	C	0.20
Star of Laramun	Item	U	0.90
Strength of Purity	Actn	U	1.30
Summon Faeries	Spell	C	0.20
Summon Swamp Spirits	Spell	U	0.50
Summon Undead Champion	Spell	R	5.00
Superior Tactics	Actn	C	0.20
Temple of the Ancestors	Holdg	U	0.50
Terrible Standard of Fu Leng	Item	R	4.00
Test of Honor	Actn	R	5.30
Test of Stone	Event	U	0.50
Test of the Emerald Champion	Event	R	3.80
The Ancestral House of the Lion	Strgld	X	1.00
The Esteemed House of the Crane	Strgld	X	1.00
The Mountain Keep of Dragon	Strgld	X	1.00
The Provincial Estate of the Unicorn	Strgld	X	1.00
The Sacred Temple of the Phoenix	Strgld	X	1.00
The War Fortress of the Crab	Strgld	X	1.00
Togashi Hoshi	Pers	R	5.00
Togashi Mitsu	Pers	U	0.70
Togashi Yokuni	Pers	R	5.70
Togashi Yoshi	Pers	U	0.80
Toku	Pers	C	0.20
Torrential Rain	Spell	R	4.00
Touch of Death	Spell	R	5.60
Trade Route	Holdg	U	1.00
Traversable Terrain	Actn	C	0.20
Unexpected Allies	Event	U	0.70
Unscalable Walls	Holdg	C	0.20
Void Dragon	Pers	R	6.50
Walking the Way	Spell	U	1.80
Water Dragon	Pers	R	5.80
Way of Deception	Actn	U	0.70
Wind Born Speed	Spell	C	0.20
Winds of Change	Spell	U	0.60
Wings of Fire	Spell	U	0.20
Wyrm Riders	Follo	U	0.60
Yasuki Taka	Pers	C	0.20
Yogo Junzo	Pers	R	4.00
Yotsu Seiki	Pers	C	0.20
Zombie Troops	Follo	U	0.50

RARITY KEY C = Common U = Uncommon R = Rare VR = Very Rare UR = Ultra Rare F = Foil card X = Fixed/standard in all decks

Legend of the Five Rings • Jade Edition

Wizards of the Coast (Five Rings Division) • Released **March 1998**

334 cards in set • **IDENTIFIER: Black borders with jade swirls**

- Starter decks contain 60 cards; starter displays contain 12 starters
- Booster packs contain 15 cards; booster displays contain 36 boosters

After the defeat of Fu Leng, the ronin Toturi, once the most honored general in the empire, ascends the throne. The land is still in turmoil when the new emperor disappears.

The ***Jade Edition*** base set ushered in a new format for tournaments, the Jade-extended (only personalities, events and spells from the *Jade* set and later are legal, but all other cards are allowed) and strict Jade (only cards published in the *Jade* set or later may be used). These restrictions were made to reflect the changes in the ***Legend of the Five Rings*** world and force players to accommodate the storyline changes made in the game. In keeping with this change, the Jade set differed from previous base sets, incorporating many of the cards from previous expansions while eliminating others. The ancestral standard cards were replaced by the clan charters, issued by Toturi at the beginning of his reign. The charters are gold-producing holdings that are cheap to bring out but can only pay for the specific clan's personalities. — *Michael Greenholdt*

You will need **38** nine-pocket pages to store this set. (19 doubled up)

Set (334 cards)	195.00
Starter Display Box	60.00
Booster Display Box	67.00
Starter Deck	7.00
Booster Pack	2.50

Card name	Type	Rarity	Price
1			
☐ A Glimpse of Soul's Shadow	Kiho	U	0.80
☐ A Moment of Truth	Actn	R	3.00
☐ Accessible Terrain	Actn	C	0.10
☐ Agasha Gennai	Pers	C	0.35
☐ Agasha Tamori	Pers	C	0.15
☐ Alliance	Event	U	0.50
☐ Along the Coast at Midnight	Actn	R	3.00
☐ Ambush	Actn	R	5.50
☐ Ancestral Guidance	Kiho	R	3.00
2			
☐ Archers	Follo	C	0.10
☐ Architects of the Wall	Event	R	3.00
☐ Armor of Osano-Wo	Item	R	1.50
☐ Armour of Sun-Tao	Item	U	0.50
☐ Armour of the Golden Samurai	Item	R	1.50
☐ Arrows from the Woods	Actn	C	0.10
☐ Asahina Tamako	Pers	U	0.50
☐ Ashamana	Pers	C	0.15
☐ Ashigaru	Follo	C	0.10
3			
☐ Avoid Fate	Actn	R	14.00
☐ Balash	Pers	C	0.15
☐ Barbican	Holdg	U	0.80
☐ Basecamp	Holdg	C	0.15
☐ Battering Ram Crew	Follo	R	1.50
☐ Bayushi Aramoro	Pers	U	0.50
☐ Bayushi Yokuan	Pers	R	2.30
☐ Biting Steel	Spell	U	0.50
☐ Black Market	Holdg	C	0.15
4			
☐ Black Smith	Holdg	C	0.15
☐ Block Supply Lines	Actn	C	0.10
☐ Blood Sword	Item	U	0.50
☐ Bountiful Harvest	Actn	R	3.00
☐ Breach of Etiquette	Actn	U	1.00
☐ Bridged Pass	Holdg	U	0.50
☐ Brilliant Victory	Actn	C	0.10
☐ Bushi Dojo	Holdg	U	0.50
☐ Careful Planning	Actn	C	0.10
5			
☐ Catching the Wind's Favor	Kiho	C	0.10
☐ Charge	Actn	C	0.15
☐ Charter of the Crab Clan	Item	X	4.00
☐ Charter of the Crane Clan	Item	X	4.00

Card name	Type	Rarity	Price
☐ Charter of the Dragon Clan	Item	X	4.00
☐ Charter of the Lion Clan	Item	X	4.00
☐ Charter of the Mantis Clan	Item	X	4.00
☐ Charter of the Phoenix Clan	Item	X	4.00
☐ Charter of the Scorpion Clan	Item	X	4.00
6			
☐ Charter of the Unicorn Clan	Item	X	4.00
☐ Charter of Toturi's Army	Item	X	4.00
☐ Chrysanthemum Festival	Event	R	3.00
☐ Clan Heartland	Regn	R	3.00
☐ Climbing Gear	Item	U	0.50
☐ Confusion at Court	Actn	C	0.20
☐ Contentious Terrain	Actn	C	0.10
☐ Copper Mine	Holdg	C	0.15
☐ Corrupt Geisha House	Holdg	C	0.25
7			
☐ Corrupt Iron Mines	Holdg	C	0.25
☐ Corrupt Silver Mines	Holdg	C	0.25
☐ Corruption of the Harmonies	Event	U	0.50
☐ Counterattack	Actn	U	2.00
☐ Crossroads	Regn	C	0.15
☐ Crushing Attack	Actn	R	2.00
☐ Daidoji Sembi	Pers	C	0.35
☐ Daidoji Uji	Pers	R	3.00
☐ Daisho Technique	Actn	U	0.60
8			
☐ Deadly Ground	Actn	C	0.10
☐ Defend Your Honor	Actn	U	0.60
☐ Defenders of the Realm	Actn	U	0.80
☐ Diamond Mine	Holdg	U	0.50
☐ Dispersive Terrain	Actn	C	0.30
☐ Diversionary Tactics	Actn	C	0.30
☐ Doji Chomei	Pers	U	0.50
☐ Doji Kuwanan	Pers	R	3.00
☐ Doji Reju	Pers	C	0.20
9			
☐ Doji Shizue	Pers	C	0.35
☐ Double Chi	Kiho	C	0.15
☐ Elite Heavy Infantry	Follo	R	1.50
☐ Elite Light Infantry	Follo	U	0.50
☐ Elite Medium Infantry	Follo	U	0.50
☐ Emperor's Peace	Event	U	0.50
☐ Enlightenment	Actn	U	0.60
☐ Enough Talk	Actn	R	1.50
☐ Entrapping Terrain	Actn	C	0.30
10			
☐ Evil Feeds Upon Itself	Event	U	0.50

Card name	Type	Rarity	Price
☐ Explosives	Actn	R	3.00
☐ Fan of Command	Item	R	3.00
☐ Fantastic Gardens	Holdg	U	0.50
☐ Farmlands	Regn	C	0.15
☐ Fist of the Earth	Kiho	C	0.10
☐ Flatlands	Regn	C	0.15
☐ Focus	Actn	R	11.00
☐ Forest	Holdg	C	0.15
11			
☐ Fortified Coast	Regn	U	0.50
☐ Freezing the Lifeblood	Kiho	U	0.60
☐ Frenzy	Actn	U	0.90
☐ Fury of the Earth	Kiho	C	0.10
☐ Gambling House	Holdg	U	0.50
☐ Garrison	Holdg	U	0.50
☐ Geisha Assassin	Actn	R	3.00
☐ Geisha House	Holdg	C	0.15
☐ Gift of the Wind	Kiho	C	0.10
12			
☐ Ginawa	Pers	R	3.00
☐ Glimpse of the Unicorn	Event	U	0.50
☐ Go Master	Holdg	C	0.15
☐ Goblin Mob	Follo	C	0.05
☐ Goblin Warmonger	Pers	C	0.15
☐ Gold Mine	Holdg	C	0.15
☐ Hawks and Falcons	Holdg	C	0.15
☐ He's Mine	Actn	C	0.50
☐ Heavy Cavalry	Follo	U	0.50
13			
☐ Heavy Infantry	Follo	U	0.35
☐ Heichi Chokei	Pers	C	0.30
☐ Hida O-Ushi	Pers	R	3.00
☐ Hida Tadashiro	Pers	C	0.15
☐ Hida Unari	Pers	U	0.50
☐ Hida Yakamo	Pers	R	3.00
☐ Higher Ground	Actn	U	0.50
☐ Hiruma Yoshi	Pers	C	0.15
☐ Hitomi	Pers	R	5.00
14			
☐ Hitomi Kokujin	Pers	R	2.00
☐ Hizuka	Pers	C	0.35
☐ Hoseki	Pers	U	0.50
☐ Hurricane	Event	U	0.50
☐ Iaijitsu Challenge	Actn	C	0.35
☐ Iaijitsu Duel	Actn	C	0.35
☐ Ikoma Kaoku	Pers	U	0.50
☐ Ikoma Ryozo	Pers	U	0.80
☐ Ikoma Tsanuri	Pers	R	5.00
15			
☐ Imperial Gift	Event	R	6.00
☐ Imperial Honor Guard	Follo	R	0.05
☐ Imperial Palace Guard	Follo	R	0.05
☐ Inaccessible Regn	Regn	U	0.50
☐ Inheritance	Event	R	19.00

Card name	Type	Rarity	Price
☐ Investigation	Actn	R	3.00
☐ Iris Festival	Event	R	4.00
☐ Iron Mine	Holdg	C	0.35
☐ Isawa Norikazu	Pers	R	3.00
16			
☐ Isawa Osugi	Pers	U	0.50
☐ Isha	Pers	U	0.50
☐ Island Wharf	Holdg	C	0.35
☐ Iuchi Karasu	Pers	U	0.50
☐ Iuchi Katta	Pers	U	0.50
☐ Jade Bow	Item	C	0.10
☐ Jade Works	Holdg	C	0.35
☐ Kage	Pers	R	3.00
☐ Kaiu Suman	Pers	U	0.50
17			
☐ Kakita Yoshi	Pers	R	2.30
☐ Kappuksu	Pers	U	0.50
☐ Kaze-Do	Kiho	C	0.10
☐ Kenku Teacher	Follo	U	0.50
☐ Kharmic Strike	Actn	U	0.60
☐ Kitsu Motso	Pers	R	1.50
☐ Kitsu Okura	Pers	C	0.35
☐ Kitsuki Yasu	Pers	R	3.00
☐ Kolat Assassin	Actn	U	0.80
18			
☐ Kolat Interference	Actn	R	2.00
☐ Kolat Master	Actn	R	5.00
☐ Komaro	Pers	C	0.15
☐ Kuni Yori	Pers	R	3.00
☐ Kyoso no Oni	Pers	R	3.00
☐ Led From the True Path	Kiho	R	2.30
☐ "Lies, Lies, Lies ..."	Actn	R	3.00
☐ Light Cavalry	Follo	C	0.10
☐ Light Infantry	Follo	C	0.15
19			
☐ Mantis Budoka	Follo	R	2.00
☐ Mantis Bushi	Follo	R	3.00
☐ Market Place	Holdg	C	0.35
☐ Marries a Barbarian	Actn	U	0.50
☐ Master of the Rolling River	Kiho	U	0.50
☐ Master Smith	Holdg	U	0.50
☐ Matsu Agetoki	Pers	R	0.60
☐ Matsu Goemon	Pers	C	0.60
☐ Matsu Hiroru	Pers	R	2.30
20			
☐ Matsu Seijuro	Pers	U	0.50
☐ Medium Cavalry	Follo	C	2.60
☐ Medium Infantry	Follo	C	0.10
☐ Mirumoto Daini	Pers	R	2.00
☐ Mirumoto Sukune	Pers	U	0.50
☐ Mirumoto Taki	Pers	C	0.35
☐ Mitsu (exp)	Pers	R	3.00
☐ Moshi Wakiza (exp)	Pers	R	3.00

RARITY KEY C = Common   U = Uncommon   R = Rare   VR = Very Rare   UR = Ultra Rare   F = Foil card   X = Fixed/standard in all decks

Card name	Type	Rarity	Price
Mountain Pass	Regn	C	0.15
21			
Mounts	Follo	U	0.50
Mukami	Pers	C	0.15
Naga Bowmen	Follo	U	0.80
Naga Bushi	Follo	C	0.30
Naga Guard	Follo	C	0.30
Naga Spearmen	Follo	U	0.50
Naginata	Item	C	0.10
Naka Kuro	Pers	R	4.00
Narrow Ground	Actn	C	0.30
22			
Night Medallion	Item	R	3.00
Ninja Genin	Follo	R	0.80
Ninja Kidnapper	Actn	R	3.00
Ninja Shapeshifter	Pers	U	1.00
Ninja Spy	Pers	C	0.15
Ninja Thief	Actn	U	0.80
No-Dachi	Item	C	0.10
Oath of Fealty	Actn	C	0.30
Occult Murders	Event	U	0.50
23			
Ogre Bushi	Pers	U	0.50
Ogre Warriors	Follo	R	4.00
One with the Elements	Kiho	U	0.50
Oni no Akuma	Pers	R	3.00
Oracle of Earth	Holdg	R	3.00
Oracle of Fire	Holdg	R	3.00
Oracle of Void	Holdg	R	3.00
Oracle of Water	Holdg	R	3.00
Oracle of Wind	Holdg	R	3.00
24			
Otaku Baiken	Pers	C	0.15
Otaku Kamoko	Pers	R	5.00
Outflank	Actn	C	0.30
Pearl Bed	Holdg	C	0.35
Pearl Divers	Holdg	U	0.50
Peasant Revolt	Event	U	0.50
Piercing the Soul	Kiho	U	0.50
Pitch and Fire	Holdg	C	0.35
Plains above Evil	Regn	U	0.50
25			
Poisoned Weapon	Actn	R	6.00
Port	Holdg	C	0.35
Prayer Shrines	Holdg	C	0.35
Proposal of Peace	Event	R	4.00
Qamar	Pers	R	4.00

Card name	Type	Rarity	Price
Radakast	Pers	U	0.50
Rallying Cry	Actn	U	0.60
Ratling Bushi	Follo	U	0.80
Ratling Constricts	Follo	C	2.80
26			
Ratling Pack	Follo	C	0.30
Refugees	Actn	C	0.60
Remorseful Seppuku	Actn	U	0.50
Resist Magic	Actn	R	2.80
Retired General	Holdg	U	0.50
Retreat	Actn	R	2.30
Ring of Air	Actn	U	0.80
Ring of Earth	Actn	U	0.80
Ring of Fire	Actn	U	0.80
27			
Ring of the Void	Actn	U	0.90
Ring of Water	Actn	U	0.80
Rise of the Phoenix	Event	R	3.00
"Rise, Brother"	Actn	R	2.00
River Delta	Regn	U	0.50
Ryosei	Pers	C	0.15
Samurai Cavalry	Follo	R	2.50
Samurai Warriors	Follo	R	2.80
Sanctified Temple	Holdg	C	0.60
28			
Sanzo	Pers	C	0.15
School of Wizardry	Holdg	R	9.00
Scout	Follo	C	0.30
Secrets on the Wind	Spell	R	1.80
Shahadet	Pers	R	3.30
Shalasha	Pers	C	0.15
Shame	Actn	U	0.50
Shashakar	Pers	R	3.00
Shiba Norikazu	Pers	R	2.00
29			
Shiba Tsukune	Pers	R	4.00
Shield Wall	Follo	U	0.80
Shinjo Morito	Pers	R	3.00
Shinjo Sanetama	Pers	C	0.35
Shinjo Shirasu	Pers	C	0.35
Shinjo Yokatsu	Pers	R	3.00
Shuriken of Serpents	Item	U	0.50
Silver Mine	Holdg	C	0.15
Skeletal Troops	Follo	C	0.30
30			
Small Farm	Holdg	C	0.35
Sneak Attack	Actn	R	6.00

Card name	Type	Rarity	Price
Spearmen	Follo	C	0.30
Spirit Guide	Follo	R	4.00
Stables	Holdg	C	0.15
Star of Laramun	Item	R	3.00
Stifling Wind	Spell	U	0.50
Street to Street	Actn	U	0.80
Strength of my Ancestors	Kiho	C	0.30
31			
Strength of Purity	Actn	U	1.00
Strike with No-Thought	Actn	R	2.00
Suana	Pers	U	0.50
Superior Tactics	Actn	C	0.30
Swamp Spirits	Follo	C	0.30
Swamplands	Regn	C	0.35
Takuan	Pers	R	3.00
Test of Honor	Actn	R	7.00
Test of Might	Actn	C	0.15
32			
Test of the Emerald Champion	Event	R	2.80
Tetsubo	Item	C	0.10
The Ancestral House of the Lion	Stghld	X	0.50
The Brotherhood of the Shensei	Stghld	X	0.50
The Code of Bushido	Actn	R	3.00
The Esteemed House of the Crane	Stghld	X	0.50
The Final Breath	Actn	U	0.50
The Fires that Cleanse	Spell	R	3.00
The Great Walls of Kaiu	Stghld	X	0.50
33			
The Hidden Temple of the Naga	Stghld	X	0.50
The Mountain Keep of Dragon	Stghld	X	0.50
The Provincial Estate of Unicorn	Stghld	X	0.50
The Purity of Shinsei	Kiho	R	3.00
The Ruines of Isawa Castle	Stghld	X	0.50
The Shadow Stronghold of Bayushi	Stghld	X	0.50
The Shadowlands Horde	Stghld	X	0.50

Card name	Type	Rarity	Price
The Sight of Death	Kiho	U	0.50
The Soul Goes Forth	Kiho	U	0.50
34			
The Tao of the Naga	Event	R	3.00
The Touch of Amaterasu	Kiho	R	3.00
The Wrath of Osano-Wo	Kiho	C	0.60
The Yoritomo Alliance	Stghld	X	0.50
Togashi Hoshi	Pers	R	3.50
Togashi Mitsu	Pers	X	0.50
Togashi Yoshi	Pers	R	2.00
Toku	Pers	U	0.50
Toturi's Army	Stghld	X	0.50
35			
Touch of Death	Spell	R	4.00
Touching the Soul	Kiho	U	0.80
Traversable Terrain	Actn	C	0.10
Treacherous Terrain	Actn	C	0.30
Treaty with the Naga	Item	X	4.00
Tsuruchi	Pers	U	0.50
Turtle's Shell	Actn	R	3.00
Unattuned	Kiho	R	2.30
Unexpected Allies	Event	U	0.50
36			
Unscalable Walls	Holdg	C	0.15
Void Strike	Kiho	U	0.80
Vows of the Brotherhood	Item	X	4.00
Wakizashi	Item	C	0.30
Walking the Way	Spell	R	4.00
Way of Deception	Actn	R	3.00
Wounded in Battle	Actn	U	0.80
Writings of Kuni Yori	Item	X	4.00
Yasuki Nokatsu	Pers	C	0.15
37			
Yasuki Taka	Pers	U	0.50
Yodin	Pers	R	4.00
Yoritomo	Pers	R	4.00
Yoritomo Kamoto	Pers	R	4.00
Yoritomo Kanbe	Pers	U	0.50
Yoritomo Masasue	Pers	U	0.50
Yoritomo Takuni	Pers	C	0.15
Yoritomo Tsuyu	Pers	U	0.50
Yoshi	Pers	U	0.50
38			
Zombie Troops	Follo	U	0.50

Legend of the Five Rings • *Pearl Edition*

Wizards of the Coast (Five Rings Division) • Released **1999**

365 cards in set • **IDENTIFIER: Black borders with purple whorls**

- Starter decks contain 60 cards; starter displays contain 12 starters
- Booster packs contain 15 cards; booster displays contain 36 boosters

In the fifth basic set, the story of Toturi and the ninja continues. Toturi is acting strangely, and his commands are tearing the empire apart.

Pearl Edition followed *Jade Edition*'s lead and cards found in this basic set were all Jade-legal. This set was also the first to introduce the new card designs.

There were quite a few changes from *Jade* to *Pearl*, with some personalities being reprinted as experienced, and some Fate cards being included from intervening sets. The biggest change was the substitution of family weapons, such as the **Isawa Naginata** and the **Mirumoto Wakazashi**, for the Clan Charters. — *Michael Greenholdt*

You will need **41** nine-pocket pages to store this set. (21 doubled up)

Set (365 cards)	193.00
Starter Display Box	50.00
Booster Display Box	58.00
Starter Deck	9.90
Booster Pack	2.60

Card name	Type	Rarity	Price
1			
A Glimpse of Soul's Shadow	Kiho	U	0.60
A Moment of Truth	Actn	R	3.00

Card name	Type	Rarity	Price
Accessible Terrain	Actn	C	0.15
Agasha Gennai	Pers	C	0.20
Agasha Tamori	Pers	C	0.20
Alliance	Event	U	0.40
Along the Coast at Midnight	Actn	R	4.00
Ambush	Actn	R	3.50
Ancestral Guidance	Kiho	R	2.50
2			
Another Time	Actn	X	2.00
Archers	Follo	C	0.15

Card name	Type	Rarity	Price
Architects of the Wall	Event	R	2.50
Armor of Osano-Wo	Item	R	1.80
Arrows from the Woods	Actn	C	0.15
Asahina Tamako	Pers	U	0.50
Ashamana	Pers	C	0.20
Ashigaru	Follo	C	0.15
Avoid Fate	Actn	R	11.50
3			
Balash	Pers	C	0.20
Barbican	Holdg	U	0.40

Card name	Type	Rarity	Price
Basecamp	Holdg	C	0.20
Battering Ram Crew	Follo	R	1.80
Bayushi Aramoro	Pers	U	0.50
Bayushi Yokuan	Pers	R	2.50
Biting Steel	Spell	U	0.25
Black Market	Holdg	C	0.20
Blacksmiths	Holdg	C	0.20
4			
Block Supply Lines	Actn	C	0.15
Blood Sword	Item	U	0.40
Bo Stick	Item	X	2.00

Card name	Type	Rarity	Price
Bountiful Harvest	Actn	R	2.50
Breach of Etiquette	Actn	U	0.80
Bridged Pass	Holdg	U	0.40
Brilliant Victory	Actn	C	0.15
Bushi Dojo	Holdg	U	0.50
Careful Planning	Actn	C	0.15
5			
Catching the Wind's Favor	Kiho	C	0.15
Charge	Actn	C	0.20
Chrysanthemum Festival	Event	R	2.50
Clan Heartland	Regn	R	3.00
Climbing Gear	Item	U	0.40
Confusion at Court	Actn	C	0.25
Contentious Terrain	Actn	C	0.15
Coordinated Fire	Actn	X	2.00
Copper Mine	Holdg	C	0.20
6			
Cornered	Actn	X	2.00
Corrupt Geisha House	Holdg	X	0.50
Corrupted Iron Mine	Holdg	X	0.50
Corrupted Silver Mine	Holdg	X	0.50
Corruption of the Harmonies	Event	U	0.40
Counterattack	Actn	U	1.00
Crossroads	Regn	C	0.20
Crushing Attack	Actn	R	2.50
Daidoji Sembi	Pers	C	0.20
7			
Daidoji Uji	Pers	R	2.50
Daidoji Uji (exp)	Pers	R	3.00
Daisho Technique	Actn	U	0.50
Deadly Ground	Actn	C	0.15
Defend Your Honor	Actn	U	0.50
Defenders of the Realm	Actn	U	0.50
Diamond Mine	Holdg	U	0.50
Dispersive Terrain	Actn	C	0.15
Diversionary Tactics	Actn	C	0.15
8			
Doji Chomei	Pers	U	0.50
Doji Kuwanan	Pers	R	2.50
Doji Kuwanan (exp)	Pers	R	3.00
Doji Reju	Pers	C	0.25
Doji Shizue	Pers	C	0.20
Double Chi	Kiho	C	0.20
Earthquake	Spell	X	2.00
Elite Heavy Infantry	Follo	R	1.80
Elite Light Infantry	Follo	U	0.50
9			
Elite Medium Infantry	Follo	U	0.50
Emperor's Peace	Event	U	0.40
Encircled Terrain	Actn	X	1.00
Enlightenment	Actn	U	0.50
Enough Talk	Actn	R	1.80
Entrapping Terrain	Actn	C	0.15
Evil Feeds Upon Itself	Event	U	0.40
Explosives	Actn	R	2.50
Fan of Command	Item	R	2.80
10			
Fantastic Gardens	Holdg	U	0.50
Farmlands	Regn	C	0.20
Fist of the Earth	Kiho	C	0.15
Flatlands	Regn	C	0.20
Focus	Actn	R	11.50
Forest	Holdg	C	0.20
Fortified Coast	Regn	U	0.25
Freezing the Lifeblood	Kiho	U	0.50
Frenzy	Actn	U	0.50
11			
Fury of the Earth	Kiho	C	0.15
Gambling House	Holdg	U	0.50
Garrison	Holdg	U	0.40
Geisha Assassin	Actn	R	2.50
Geisha House	Holdg	C	0.20
Gift of the Wind	Kiho	C	0.15
Ginawa	Pers	R	2.50
Ginawa (exp)	Pers	X	3.00
Glimpse of the Unicorn	Event	U	0.40
12			
Go Master	Holdg	C	0.20
Goblin Sneaks	Follo	X	2.00
Goblin Wizard	Pers	X	2.00
Gold Mine	Holdg	C	0.20
Hawks and Falcons	Holdg	C	0.20
He's Mine	Actn	C	0.40
Heavy Cavalry	Follo	U	0.50
Heavy Infantry	Follo	U	0.35
Heichi Chokei	Pers	C	0.15
13			
Hida O-Ushi	Pers	R	2.50
Hida Tadashiro	Pers	U	0.20
Hida Unari	Pers	U	0.50
Hida Yakamo	Pers	R	3.50
Higher Ground	Actn	U	0.40
Hiruma Yoshi	Pers	C	0.20
Hitomi	Pers	R	5.00
Hitomi Kokujin	Pers	R	2.00
Hizuka	Pers	C	0.20
14			
Hoseki	Pers	U	0.40
Hurricane	Event	U	0.40
Iaijitsu Challenge	Actn	C	0.20
Iaijitsu Duel	Actn	C	0.20
Ikoma Kaoku	Pers	U	0.40
Ikoma Ryozo	Pers	U	0.40
Ikoma Tsanuri	Pers	R	3.50
Imperial Gift	Event	R	5.50
Imperial Honor Guard	Follo	C	0.15
15			
Imperial Palace Guard	Follo	C	0.15
Inaccessible Regn	Regn	U	0.25
Inheritance	Event	R	12.00
Inner Fire	Actn	X	2.00
Investigation	Actn	R	2.50
Iris Festival	Event	R	3.80
Iron Mine	Holdg	C	0.20
Isawa Norikazu	Pers	R	4.80
Isawa Osugi	Pers	U	0.40
16			
Isha	Pers	U	0.40
Isha	Pers	U	0.50
Isha (exp)	Pers	X	2.00
Island Wharf	Holdg	C	0.20
Iuchi Karasu	Pers	U	0.40
Iuchi Karasu (exp)	Pers	R	2.00
Iuchi Katta	Pers	U	0.50
Jade Bow	Item	C	0.15
Jade Works	Holdg	C	0.20
17			
Kage	Pers	R	3.00
Kaiu Suman	Pers	U	0.50
Kakita Yoshi	Pers	R	2.50
Kappuksu	Pers	U	0.50
Kaze- Do	Kiho	C	0.15
Kenku Teacher	Follo	U	0.40
Kharmic Strike	Actn	U	0.60
Kitsu Motso	Pers	X	1.00
Kitsu Okura	Pers	C	0.20
18			
Kitsuki Yasu	Pers	R	2.30
Kolat Assassin	Actn	U	0.50
Kolat Interference	Actn	R	2.00
Kolat Master	Actn	R	5.30
Komaro	Pers	C	0.20
Kuni Yori	Pers	X	1.00
Kuni Yori (exp)	Pers	R	2.30
Kyoso no Oni	Pers	U	0.50
Led From the True Path	Kiho	R	2.50
19			
"Lies, Lies, Lies"	Actn	R	2.30
Light Cavalry	Follo	C	0.15
Light Infantry	Follo	C	0.15
Mantis Budoka	Follo	R	2.00
Mantis Bushi	Follo	R	2.80
Marketplace	Holdg	C	0.20
Marries a Barbarian	Actn	U	0.40
Master of Rolling River	Kiho	U	0.50
Master Smith	Holdg	U	0.40
20			
Matsu Agetoki	Pers	U	0.60
Matsu Agetoki (exp)	Pers	R	3.00
Matsu Goemon	Pers	C	0.20
Matsu Hiroru	Pers	R	2.00
Matsu Seijuro	Pers	U	0.40
Matsu Turi	Pers	X	1.00
Medium Cavalry	Follo	C	2.60
Medium Infantry	Follo	C	0.15
Mirumoto Daini	Pers	R	2.00
21			
Mirumoto Daini (exp)	Pers	R	3.00
Mirumoto Sukune	Pers	U	0.50
Mirumoto Taki	Pers	C	0.20
Mitsu	Pers	R	2.50
Morito	Pers	R	3.00
Moshi Wakiza	Pers	R	2.50
Moshi Wakiza (exp)	Pers	R	3.00
Moto Sada	Pers	X	2.00
Mountain Pass	Regn	C	0.20
22			
Mounts	Follo	U	0.50
Mukami	Pers	U	0.50
Naga Bowmen	Follo	U	0.50
Naga Bushi	Follo	C	0.15
Naga Guard	Follo	C	0.15
Naga Shugenja	Pers	X	1.00
Naga Spearmen	Follo	U	0.50
Naga Warlord	Pers	X	1.00
Naginata	Item	C	0.15
23			
Naka Kuro	Pers	R	2.00
Narrow Ground	Actn	C	0.15
Nemesis	Actn	X	2.00
Night Battle	Actn	X	2.00
Night Medallion	Item	R	2.00
Ninja Genin	Follo	C	0.15
Ninja Kidnapper	Actn	R	2.30
Ninja Shapeshifter	Pers	U	0.80
Ninja Spy	Pers	C	0.20
24			
Ninja Thief	Actn	U	0.50
No-Dachi	Item	C	0.15
Oath of Fealty	Actn	C	0.15
Occult Murders	Event	U	0.40
Ogre Bushi	Pers	U	0.50
Ogre Warriors	Follo	R	3.50
One with the Elements	Kiho	U	0.50
Oni no Akuma	Pers	R	2.50
Oni no Ogulu	Pers	X	2.00
25			
Oracle of Earth	Holdg	R	2.00
Oracle of Fire	Holdg	R	2.30
Oracle of Void	Holdg	R	3.00
Oracle of Water	Holdg	R	2.30
Oracle of Wind	Holdg	R	2.00
Otaku Baiken	Pers	C	0.20
Otaku Kamoko	Pers	R	4.50
Otaku Kamoko (exp)	Pers	R	5.00
Outflank	Actn	C	0.15
26			
Pearl Bed	Holdg	C	0.20
Pearl Divers	Holdg	U	0.50
Peasant Levies	Follo	X	2.00
Peasant Revolt	Event	U	0.40
Piercing the Soul	Kiho	U	0.50
Pitch and Fire	Holdg	C	0.20
Plains above Evil	Regn	C	0.25
Poisoned Weapon	Actn	R	6.00
Port	Holdg	C	0.20
27			
Prayer Shrines	Holdg	C	0.20
Proposal of Peace	Event	R	2.50
Qamar	Pers	R	4.00
Radakast	Pers	U	0.40
Rallying Cry	Actn	U	0.50
Ratling Bushi	Follo	U	0.50
Ratling Constrips	Follo	C	2.60
Ratling Pack	Follo	C	0.15
Refugees	Actn	C	0.20
28			
Remorseful Seppuku	Actn	U	0.40
Resist Magic	Actn	R	2.30
Retired General	Holdg	U	0.40
Retreat	Actn	R	2.50
Ring of Air	Actn	U	0.50
Ring of Earth	Actn	U	0.50
Ring of Fire	Actn	U	0.50
Ring of the Void	Actn	U	0.50
Ring of Water	Actn	U	0.50
29			
Rise of the Phoenix	Event	R	1.80
"Rise, Brother"	Actn	R	2.00
River Delta	Regn	U	0.25
Ryokan's Sword	Item	X	2.50
Ryosei	Pers	C	0.20
Samurai Cavalry	Follo	C	2.50
Samurai Warriors	Follo	R	2.50
Sanctified Temple	Holdg	C	0.20
Sanzo	Pers	C	0.20
30			
School of Wizardry	Holdg	R	7.00
Scout	Follo	C	0.15
Secrets on the Wind	Spell	R	2.00
Shahadet	Pers	R	3.50
Shalasha	Pers	C	0.20
Shame	Actn	U	0.50
Shashakar	Pers	R	3.00
Shiba Tsukune	Pers	R	3.50
Shiba Tsukune (exp)	Pers	R	4.00
31			
Shield Wall	Follo	U	0.50
Shinjo Morito	Pers	R	3.00
Shinjo Sanetama	Pers	C	0.20
Shinjo Shirasu	Pers	C	0.20
Shinjo Yokatsu	Pers	R	2.00
Shuriken of Serpents	Item	U	0.40
Silver Mine	Holdg	C	0.20
Skeletal Troops	Follo	C	0.15
Small Farm	Holdg	C	0.20
32			
Sneak Attack	Actn	R	5.50
Spearmen	Follo	C	0.15
Spirit Guide	Follo	R	3.80
Stables	Holdg	C	0.20
Stand Against the Waves	Actn	X	2.00
Stand Firm	Actn	X	2.00
Stifling Wind	Spell	U	0.40
Street to Street	Actn	U	0.60
Strength of my Ancestors	Kiho	C	0.15
33			
Strength of Purity	Actn	U	0.80
Strike with No-Thought	Actn	R	2.30
Suana	Pers	U	0.40
Superior Tactics	Actn	C	0.15
Swamp Spirits	Follo	C	0.15
Swamplands	Regn	C	0.20
Takuan	Pers	R	3.00
Test of Honor	Actn	R	8.00
Test of Might	Actn	C	0.20
34			
Test of the Emerald Champion	Event	R	1.80
Tetsubo	Item	C	0.15
Tetsuya's Bo Staff	Item	X	3.00
The Ancient Halls of the Lion	Stghld	X	2.50
The Armour of Sun-Tao	Item	U	0.40

RARITY KEY C = Common   U = Uncommon   R = Rare   VR = Very Rare   UR = Ultra Rare   F = Foil card   X = Fixed/standard in all decks

Card name	Type	Rarity	Price
The Armour of the Golden Samurai	Item	R	1.80
The Brotherhood of Shinsei	Stghld	X	2.50
The Code of Bushido	Actn	R	2.50
The Daidoji Yari	Item	X	3.00
[35]			
The Esteemed House of the Crane	Stghld	X	2.50
The Final Breath	Actn	U	0.40
The Fires that Cleanse	Spell	R	2.00
The Great Walls of Kaiu	Stghld	X	2.50
The Hidden Temples of the Naga	Stghld	X	2.50
The Hiruma Tetsubo	Item	X	3.50
The Ikoma Tessen	Item	X	3.50
The Isawa Naginata	Item	X	3.50
The Isha's Yumi	Item	X	3.50
[36]			
The Kitsune Nagamaki	Item	X	3.50

Card name	Type	Rarity	Price
The Lost Ono of Osano-Wo	Item	X	3.50
The Mirumoto Wakizashi	Item	X	3.50
The Mountain Keep of the Dragon	Stghld	X	2.50
The Otaku Nageyari	Item	X	3.50
The Provincial Estate of the Unicorn	Stghld	X	2.50
The Purity of Shinsei	Kiho	R	2.50
The Ruins of Isawa Castle	Stghld	X	2.50
The Shadow Stronghold of the Bayushi	Stghld	X	2.50
[37]			
The Shadowlands Horde	Stghld	X	2.50
The Sight of Death	Kiho	U	0.50
The Soul Goes Forth	Kiho	U	0.50
The Star of Laramun	Item	R	2.50
The Tao of the Naga	Event	R	3.00

Card name	Type	Rarity	Price
The Turtle's Shell	Actn	R	2.00
The Wrath of Osano-Wo	Kiho	U	0.50
The Yogo's Jitte	Item	X	3.50
The Yoritomo Alliance	Stghld	X	2.50
[38]			
There is No Hope	Event	X	2.00
Togashi Hoshi	Pers	R	2.80
Togashi Mitsu	Pers	U	0.40
Toku	Pers	U	0.40
Toku (exp)	Pers	R	3.00
Torturi's Daisho	Item	R	3.00
Toturi's Army	Stghld	X	2.50
Touch of Amaterasu	Kiho	R	2.50
Touch of Death	Spell	R	4.00
[39]			
Touching the Soul	Kiho	U	0.50
Traversable Terrain	Actn	C	0.15
Treacherous Terrain	Actn	C	0.15
Tsuruchi	Pers	U	0.40
Unattuned	Kiho	R	2.50

Card name	Type	Rarity	Price
Unexpected Allies	Event	U	0.40
Unscalable Walls	Holdg	C	0.20
Void Strike	Kiho	U	0.60
Wakizashi	Item	C	0.15
[40]			
Walking the Way	Spell	R	3.50
Way of Deception	Actn	R	2.30
Wounded in Battle	Actn	U	0.50
Yasuki Nokatsu	Pers	C	0.20
Yasuki Taka	Pers	U	0.40
Yodin	Pers	R	3.00
Yoritomo	Pers	R	4.50
Yoritomo Kamoto	Pers	R	3.50
Yoritomo Kanbe	Pers	U	0.40
[41]			
Yoritomo Masasue	Pers	U	0.40
Yoritomo Takuni	Pers	U	0.20
Yoritomo Tsuyu	Pers	U	0.40
Yoshi	Pers	U	0.40
Zombie Troops	Follo	U	0.50

Legend of the Five Rings • Shadowlands

Alderac Entertainment Group • Released **April 1996**

156 cards in set • **IDENTIFIER: Purple/green borders**

- Starter decks contain 60 cards; starter displays contain 12 starters
- Booster packs contain 15 cards; booster displays contain 36 boosters

The evil enemies of Rokugan (the fantasy land in which *Legend of the Five Rings* is set) appear in considerable numbers in the first expansion. Oni (demons) abound, as do the Naga, the snake people who are the sworn enemies of the Shadowland creatures. Many cards affecting Shadowlands cards, both positively and negatively, make their appearance.

Two new clans are also introduced. The Naga are non-humans dedicated to opposing the Shadowlands. The Naga cannot win via honor, but are immune to fear effects and can produce a follower token each turn from the Stronghold. The devious Scorpion clan's provinces are harder to destroy and they do not lose when their honor drops to -20, although, like the Naga, they cannot win an honor victory. — *Michael Greenholdt*

You will need **18** nine-pocket pages to store this set. (9 doubled up)

Set (156 cards)	132.50
Starter Display Box	90.00
Booster Display Box	80.50
Starter Deck	8.50
Booster Pack	2.50

Card name	Type	Rarity	Price
[1]			
A Gift Of Honor	Actn	R	4.50
A Stout Heart	Actn	U	1.00
Accessible Terrain	Actn	C	0.20
Ancient Spear of the Naga	Item	X	5.00
Another Time	Actn	C	0.25
Arrows from the Woods	Actn	C	0.20
Ashigaru	Follo	C	0.20
Ashlim	Pers	U	1.00
Balash	Pers	C	0.20
[2]			
Bayushi Aramoro	Pers	U	1.00
Bayushi Goshiu	Pers	U	1.00
Bayushi Hisa	Pers	C	0.20
Bayushi Kyoto	Pers	R	4.50
Bayushi Supai	Follo	R	4.30
Bayushi Tomaru	Pers	C	0.25
Blood of Midnight	Spell	C	0.20
Call To Arms	Actn	U	1.00
Change of Loyalty	Actn	R	5.00
[3]			
Confusion at Court	Actn	C	0.25
Contemplate the Void	Spell	C	0.20
Corrupted Ground	Actn	C	0.25
Corrupted Iron Mine	Holdg	C	0.20
Court Jester	Actn	U	1.00
Crystal Arrow	Item	C	0.20
Dark Divination	Spell	R	4.50

Card name	Type	Rarity	Price
Dark Oracle of Air	Holdg	R	5.00
Dark Oracle of Earth	Holdg	R	5.00
[4]			
Dark Oracle of Fire	Holdg	R	5.00
Dark Oracle of Water	Holdg	R	5.00
Darkness feeds	Actn	R	5.00
Dashmar	Pers	R	5.00
Defend your Honor	Actn	C	0.25
Desperate Measures	Event	U	1.00
Doji Hoturi	Pers	R	6.00
Doji House Guard	Follo	U	1.00
Doom of the Crab	Event	U	1.00
[5]			
Doom of the Crane	Event	U	1.00
Doom of the Dragon	Event	U	1.00
Doom of the Lion	Event	U	1.00
Doom of the Naga	Event	U	1.00
Doom of the Phoenix	Event	U	1.00
Doom of the Scorpion	Event	U	1.00
Doom of the Unicorn	Event	U	1.00
Earthworks	Holdg	C	0.20
Enough Talk!	Actn	U	1.00
[6]			
Evil Ward	Spell	U	1.00
False Alliance	Actn	R	4.30
Final Charge	Actn	R	4.30
Force of Will	Spell	C	0.25
Forced March	Actn	U	1.00
Gambling House	Holdg	C	0.20
Garegosu no Bakemono	Follo	R	5.00
Geisha House	Holdg	C	0.20
Goblin Shaman	Pers	C	0.25
[7]			
Gust of wind	Spell	U	1.00
Han-kyu	Item	U	1.00
He's Mine	Actn	C	0.20
Hida House Guard	Follo	U	1.00

Card name	Type	Rarity	Price
Hida O-Ushi	Pers	R	5.00
Hiruma Kage	Pers	U	1.00
His Most Favored	Actn	R	5.00
Ikiryo	Follo	C	0.20
Ikoma Kaoku	Pers	U	1.00
[8]			
Impassable Terrain	Actn	C	0.25
Imperial Levying	Event	R	4.00
Isawa Tadaka	Pers	R	5.00
Isha	Pers	R	4.00
Jade Arrow	Item	U	1.00
Jade Goblet	Item	U	1.00
Kakita Torikago	Pers	C	0.25
Kakita Yogoso	Pers	C	0.25
Kitsu Motso	Pers	R	4.80
[9]			
Kolat Oyabun	Holdg	U	1.00
Kumo	Pers	C	0.20
Levy Troops	Actn	U	1.00
Mamoru	Pers	U	1.00
Mantis Bushi	Follo	R	5.00
Mara	Pers	U	1.00
Matsu Chokoku	Pers	C	0.25
Matsu House Guard	Follo	U	1.00
Minor Oni Servant	Follo	R	5.00
[10]			
Mirumoto Hitomi	Pers	U	1.00
Mirumoto House Guard	Follo	U	1.00
Mirumoto Taki	Pers	C	0.25
Mountain Goblin	Pers	C	0.20
Nageteppo	Item	U	1.00
New Year's Celebration	Event	R	4.30
Obsidian Hand	Item	R	5.00
Obsidian Mirror	Item	R	4.80
Oni no Ogon	Pers	U	1.00
[11]			
Oni no Sanru	Pers	U	1.00

Card name	Type	Rarity	Price
Oni no Titsu	Pers	R	4.80
Otaku Kamoko	Pers	U	1.00
Otaku Kojiro	Pers	R	5.00
Pearl Bed	Holdg	C	0.20
Pennaggolan	Pers	C	0.20
Plague Zombies	Follo	C	0.25
Plea of the Peasants	Actn	U	1.00
Porcelain Mask of Fu Leng	Item	R	5.00
[12]			
Qamar	Pers	C	0.25
Rampant Plague	Event	R	5.00
Ratling Conscripts	Follo	C	0.20
Ratling Scavenger	Pers	C	0.25
Ratling Thief	Pers	U	1.00
Setsuban Festival	Event	R	4.50
Shabura	Pers	U	1.00
Shadow Madness	Actn	U	1.00
[13]			
Shadowlands Madmen	Follo	R	4.00
Shadowlands Sickness	Actn	U	1.00
Shagara	Pers	C	0.25
Shapeshifting	Spell	R	4.50
Shiba House Guard	Follo	U	1.00
Shiba Tetsu	Pers	C	0.25
Shinjo House Guard	Follo	U	1.00
Shinjo Tsuburo	Pers	C	0.20
Shosuro Hametsu	Pers	X	3.20
Shosuro Taberu	Pers	U	1.00
[14]			
Shosuro Tage	Pers	R	4.80
Skeletal Archers	Follo	C	0.25
Soshi Bantaro	Pers	C	0.25
Stale Wind	Spell	U	1.00
Stalemated Terrain	Actn	C	0.10
Strike at the Tail	Actn	R	4.50
Suspended Terrain	Actn	C	0.20

RARITY KEY C = Common U = Uncommon R = Rare VR = Very Rare UR = Ultra Rare F = Foil card X = Fixed/standard in all decks

Card name	Type	Rarity	Price
Sympathetic Energies	Spell	C	0.25
Temple of Bishamon	Holdg	C	0.20
Terrible Standard of Fu Leng	Item	R	4.80
Test of Might	Actn	C	0.25
Tetsubo	Item	C	0.25
The Broken Sword of the Scorpion	Item	X	5.00
The Code of Bushido	Actn	U	1.00
The Falling Darkness	Event	R	4.30
The Festering Pit of Fu Leng	Holdg	R	5.80
The Fire from Within	Spell	U	1.00
The Hidden Temples of the Naga	Stghld	X	4.00
The Hooded Ronin	Pers	R	5.00
The Laughing Monk	Pers	C	0.25
The Nameless One	Pers	U	1.00
The Rising Sun	Event	R	4.50
The Ruined Fortress of the Scorpion	Stghld	X	4.00
The Turtle's Shell	Actn	U	1.00
Threat of War	Actn	R	4.30
Thunder Dragon	Pers	R	6.00
Togashi Gaijutsu	Pers	R	5.00
Tomb of Jade	Spell	C	0.25
Touch of Despair	Spell	R	4.50
Touch of Fu Leng	Spell	R	4.50
Twist of Fate	Actn	R	4.50
Utter Defeat	Actn	R	5.00
Wakizashi	Item	C	0.20
Warhorses	Item	C	0.20
When Darkness Draws Near	Actn	R	4.30
Winning Kachiko's Favor	Actn	R	5.00
Wounded in Battle	Actn	C	0.20
Yasuki Nokatsu	Pers	C	0.20
Yukki No Onna	Pers	C	0.20

Black Market

Lose 3 Honor. All Trade Routes in play produce 2 less gold. All Ports in play produce 1 less gold.

Bow and lose 1 Honor to produce 2 gold. If Black Market is controlled by a Crane player, Black Market produces 3 gold when bowed.

Legend of the Five Rings • Forbidden Knowledge

Five Rings Publishing • Released **August 1996**

150 cards in set • **IDENTIFIER: Rust-colored borders**

• Booster packs contain 11 cards; booster displays contain 36 boosters

In the **Legend of the Five Rings** storyline, the forces of darkness continue to put pressure on the fractured clans of Rokugan. **Forbidden Knowledge** released many Black Scrolls, evil spells connected to the prophecy of the rise of the Dark Lord, Fu Leng. The Black Scrolls tended to have powerful game effects, but usually with a price, such as slowly killing the shugenja casting the spell. The Scrolls lend themselves to powerful combinations.

A new type of Dynasty card was introduced in Forbidden Knowledge, the region. A region card was attached to the province it appeared and has some continuing game effect, usually modest in scope. In addition, many more Oni and Naga appeared. — *Michael Greenholdt*

You will need **17** nine-pocket pages to store this set. (9 doubled up)

Set (150 cards)	125.00
Booster Display Box	71.00
Booster Pack	2.50

Card name	Type	Rarity	Price
A Black Scroll is Opened	Event	U	0.80
A Terrible Oath	Spell	R	4.00
Akiyoshi	Pers	C	0.15
Akodo Godaigo	Pers	R	4.00
An Untold Cost	Event	R	4.00
Armor of Earth	Item	R	4.50
Artificer	Holdg	C	0.15
Asako Oyo	Pers	U	0.80
Bandit Hideout	Holdg	C	0.15
Bayushi Baku	Pers	U	1.00
Bayushi Shoju	Pers	R	4.30
Beiden Pass	Regn	U	1.00
Black Market	Holdg	C	0.15
Black Wind from the Soul	Spell	R	4.00
Bog Hag	Pers	C	0.15
Brash Hero	Actn	C	0.15
Bribery	Actn	U	0.80
Bushi Dojo	Holdg	C	0.15
Calling the Elements	Spell	C	0.15
Chasing the Wind	Actn	R	3.80
Courage of the Seven Thunders	Spell	U	0.80
Crossroads	Regn	C	0.15
Crushing Attack	Actn	U	1.00
Dairya	Pers	R	5.00
Dark Daughter of Fu Leng	Pers	R	3.80
Dealing With Shadows	Event	U	1.00
Delicate Calculations	Actn	C	0.15
Disharmony	Actn	C	0.15
Diversionary Tactics	Actn	C	0.15
Doji Kuwanan	Pers	C	0.15
Dragon Sword is Broken	Event	U	1.00
Dripping Poison	Item	U	1.00
Enlightenment	Actn	C	0.15
Family Loyalty	Actn	R	3.80
Farmlands	Regn	C	0.15
Fearful Populace	Actn	U	1.00
Flatlands	Regn	C	0.15
Fu Leng's Steeds	Actn	U	1.00
Fusaki	Pers	C	0.15
Garrote	Item	U	1.00
Goblin Berserkers	Follo	C	0.15
Gunsen of Water	Item	R	4.00
Hazardous Ground	Actn	C	0.15
Higher Ground	Actn	C	0.15
Ide Daikoku	Pers	R	4.00
Ikoma Tsanuri	Pers	U	1.00
Ikoma Ujiaki	Pers	R	4.00
Imperial Funeral	Event	U	0.80
Isawa Natsune	Pers	C	0.15
Isawa Uona	Pers	R	4.50
Jadestrike	Spell	C	0.15
Kaiu Kenru	Pers	C	0.15
Kaiu Suman	Pers	U	1.00
Kakita Foruku	Pers	U	1.00
Kakita Toshimoko	Pers	R	5.00
Katana of Fire	Item	R	4.50
Kemmei	Pers	C	0.15
Kolat Saboteur	Actn	R	4.00
Kolat Whisperer	Pers	R	4.00
Kotaro	Follo	R	4.00
Kuni Wastelands	Regn	R	4.50
Kuni Yori	Pers	R	4.70
Lesser Oni	Follo	C	0.35
Mantis Budoka	Follo	U	0.80
Mantis Samurai	Follo	U	1.00
Matsu Toshiro	Pers	C	0.15
Mempo of the Void	Item	R	4.50
Merchant Caravan	Holdg	C	0.35
Mirumoto Daini	Pers	R	5.00
Mountain Pass	Regn	C	0.15
Moving the Shadow	Actn	C	0.15
Nemesis	Actn	U	0.80
Ningyo	Holdg	C	0.15
Ninja Kidnapper	Actn	U	1.00
No-dachi	Item	C	0.15
Not this Day!	Event	U	1.00
Ogre Warriors	Follo	R	4.00
Oni no Akeru	Pers	U	1.00
Oni no Jimen	Pers	U	1.00
Oni no Kaze	Pers	U	1.00
Oni no Mizu	Pers	U	1.00
Oni no Seiryoku	Pers	U	1.00
Oni no Taki-Bi	Pers	U	1.00
Passing on the Soul	Actn	U	0.80
Pearl of Wisdom	Event	R	3.80
Personal Standard	Item	C	0.15
Pikemen	Follo	C	0.15
Plains of Otosan Uchi	Regn	R	4.50
Purity of the Seven Thunders	Spell	R	4.00
Qarash	Pers	U	0.90
Ramash	Pers	C	0.15
Reserve Movement	Actn	U	0.80
Return of the Fallen Lord	Spell	R	4.00
Reversal of Fortunes	Spell	U	0.90
Ride Until Dawn	Actn	R	3.80
Scorn	Actn	C	0.15
Seikua	Pers	C	0.15
Seize the Day	Event	R	3.80
Shahadet	Pers	R	4.00
Sharing the Strength of Many	Spell	C	0.15
Shield Wall	Follo	U	1.00
Shinjo Mosaku	Pers	U	1.00
Shinjo Sadato	Pers	C	0.15
Spoils of War	Actn	R	4.00
Strength of the Earth	Event	U	0.80
Strike At The Roots	Spell	C	0.15
Strike with No-Thought	Actn	U	1.00
Swamplands	Regn	C	0.15
The Ancestral Sword of Hantei	Item	R	7.00
The Arrow Knows the Way	Actn	R	5.00
The Battlements of Matsu Castle	Holdg	R	4.10
The Coward's Way	Actn	U	1.00
The Doji Plains	Regn	U	1.00
The Elements' Fury	Spell	U	1.00
The Emerald Armor	Item	R	4.50
The Eye of Shorihotsu	Item	U	1.00
The Final Breath	Actn	C	0.15
The Fires that Cleanse	Spell	U	1.00
The First Shout	Actn	C	0.35
The Gates of Hida Castle	Holdg	R	4.00
The Imperial Standard	Item	R	4.50
The Iron Citadel	Spell	R	4.00
The Isawa Woodlands	Regn	U	0.90
The Kaiu Walls	Regn	U	1.00
The Kakita Pallisades	Holdg	R	3.60
The Path to Inner Peace	Spell	C	0.15
The People's Expense	Actn	C	0.15
The Price of War	Event	U	0.80
The Ruined Keep of Fu Leng	Regn	R	3.80
The Second Shout	Actn	C	0.25
The Shinjo Parade Grounds	Holdg	R	4.00
The Third Shout	Actn	U	1.00
The Tides of Battle	Actn	R	3.80
The Togashi Bastion	Holdg	R	4.00
The Towers of Isawa Castle	Holdg	R	4.00
The Walking Horror of Fu Leng	Spell	R	4.10
The Wasting Disease	Spell	R	5.50
Those Who Stand Alone	Actn	C	0.15
Togashi Mikoto	Pers	C	0.15
Togashi Rinjin	Pers	U	1.00
Tsuruchi	Pers	C	0.15
Unfettered Attack	Actn	U	1.00
Virtues of Command	Actn	U	0.80
Wheel of Fate	Spell	U	0.80
Whispering Winds	Spell	C	0.15
Wind-Borne Slumbers	Spell	U	0.90
Yari of Air	Item	R	4.00
Your life is mine	Actn	R	3.80
Yugo Asami	Pers	C	0.15
Yugo Junzo	Pers	R	4.00

RARITY KEY C = Common U = Uncommon R = Rare VR = Very Rare UR = Ultra Rare F = Foil card X = Fixed/standard in all decks

Legend of the Five Rings • Anvil of Despair

Five Rings Publishing • Released **November 1996**

152 cards in set • **IDENTIFIER: Cards have steely blue borders**

- Starter decks contain 60 cards; starter displays contain 12 starters
- Booster packs contain 11 cards; booster displays contain 46 boosters

You will need **17** nine-pocket pages to store this set. (9 doubled up)

As the eleventh Black Scroll is unsealed, the Dark Lord, Fu Leng, is released and possesses the last emperor. The clans find themselves oathbound to an evil madman. Anvil of Despair introduced two new strongholds, neither of them clans in the full sense of the word, although Toturi's Army operates as one.

Toturi's Army is a collection of vagabond warriors brought together by Toturi, a former Lion clan samurai. A Toturi player can more easily bring into play unaligned and Toturi's Army personalities, since honor requirements are ignored, but cannot have more than two Shadowland cards in his or her deck. The Shadowlands gain a champion (Yogo Junzo) and a stronghold, Yogo Junzo's Army. Shadowlands personalities are immune to fear and ignore honor gains and losses. While not a powerful stronghold, it does allow free play of the Shadowlands creatures.

Two cards of special note in this expansion were To Do What We Must and Kakita Shinjin. These cards are the basis for a deck type called the Exploding Crane Deck. To Do What We Must is a Fate action card that allows the player to destroy one of his or her personalities in battle in order to destroy an opposing unit with a Force equal to or less than the personality's Force plus personal honor. Crane personalities receive a bonus. Kakita Shinjin, a Crane personality, can bow when one of the player's personalities is destroyed to receive honor equal to the personality's personal honor. With this combination, a Crane player could destroy a powerful opposing unit and gain honor doing it, speeding the deck toward an honor victory. — *Michael Greenholdt*

Set (152 cards)			125.00
Starter Display Box			82.00
Booster Display Box			80.00
Starter Deck			8.00
Booster Pack			2.00

Card name	Type	Rarity	Price
A Hidden Fortress	Holdg	U	1.00
A Moment of Truth	Actn	R	4.00
A Prophecy fulfilled	Spell	R	5.00
A Thunder's Sacrifice	Spell	R	5.00
Agasha Koishi	Pers	C	0.20
Akodo Kage	Pers	R	5.00
Ancestral Shrines of Otosan Uchi	Holdg	C	0.20
Ancient Librarian	Pers	U	1.00
Arrival of the Emerald Champion	Actn	R	5.00
As the Shadow Falls	Actn	U	1.00
At the Last Moment	Actn	C	0.20
Basecamp	Holdg	C	0.20
Battlefield of Shallow Graves	Actn	C	0.25
Bayushi Kachiko	Pers	R	6.00
Bayushi Tangan	Pers	C	0.20
Benevolent Protection of Shinsei	Spell	C	0.20
Blood Oath	Actn	C	0.20
Bo Stick	Item	C	0.20
Candle of the Void	Item	U	1.00
Cornered	Actn	C	0.20
Corrupted Energies	Actn	U	1.00
Corrupted Silver Mine	Holdg	C	0.25
Corruption of the Harmonies	Actn	U	1.00
Cremation	Actn	U	1.00
Daidoji Sembi	Pers	C	0.20
Daidoji Uji	Pers	R	5.00
Daisho Technique	Actn	C	0.20
Defender from Beyond	Spell	U	1.00
Disarmament	Actn	C	0.20
Disfavored	Actn	R	5.00

Card name	Type	Rarity	Price
Disrupted Resources	Actn	R	5.00
Doom of Fu Leng	Spell	R	4.50
Drum of Water	Item	U	1.00
Duty to the Clan	Actn	U	1.00
Duty to the Empire	Actn	R	4.80
Elemental Vortex	Follo	U	1.00
Emperor's Protection	Actn	U	1.00
Essence of Fire	Spell	C	0.20
Essence of the Void	Spell	C	0.20
Essence of Water	Spell	C	0.20
Fields of the Asahina Temple	Regn	C	0.20
Fight to the Setting Sun	Actn	C	0.20
Forests of Shinomen	Regn	C	0.20
Fortified Coast	Regn	U	1.00
Fu Leng's Horde	Actn	R	5.00
Garden of Purification	Holdg	C	0.20
Golden Obi of the Sun Goddess	Item	R	5.00
Hammer of Earth	Item	U	1.00
Hida Unari	Pers	C	0.20
Hida Yakamo	Pers	R	5.00
Hirariko	Pers	U	1.00
Hoseki	Pers	U	1.00
Hototogitsu	Actn	U	1.00
Ikoma Kimura	Pers	C	0.20
Imperial Honor Guard	Follo	U	1.00
Imperial Taxation	Actn	U	1.00
Inaccessible Regn	Regn	U	1.00
Isawa Osugi	Pers	U	1.00
Isawa Tsuke	Pers	R	5.00
Kaiu Pass	Regn	U	1.00
Kaiu Utsu	Pers	U	1.00
Kakita Shijin	Pers	U	1.00
Kamoto	Pers	C	0.20
Kisada's Blockade	Actn	R	5.00
Kolat Infomation Peddler	Pers	C	0.25
Kolat Instigator	Actn	R	5.00
Kolat Interference	Actn	U	1.00
Kusatte Iru	Pers	R	4.50
Kyojin	Pers	U	1.00
"Lies, Lies, Lies …"	Actn	U	1.00

Card name	Type	Rarity	Price
Mantle of Fire	Item	U	1.00
Matsu Seijuro	Pers	U	1.00
Mikaru	Pers	C	0.20
Mikio	Pers	R	5.00
Minor Shugenja	Follo	C	0.20
Monsoon	Actn	U	1.00
Mountain of the Thunders	Regn	R	5.00
Naga Guard	Follo	C	0.20
Night Battle	Actn	C	0.25
Oni no Tadaka	Pers	C	0.20
Otaku Baiken	Pers	C	0.20
Peasant Defense	Actn	C	0.20
Pitch and Fire	Holdg	C	0.20
Plague Infested Region	Regn	U	1.00
Plague Skulls	Item	R	5.00
Political Dissent	Actn	R	5.00
Possession	Spell	R	5.00
Prophecy of the Hero	Spell	R	5.00
Qakar	Pers	U	1.00
Radakast	Pers	C	0.20
Ratling Conjuror	Pers	C	0.20
Refugees	Actn	C	0.30
Retirement	Actn	U	1.00
Return of Fu Leng	Actn	R	5.00
"Rise, Brother"	Actn	U	1.00
River Regn	Regn	C	0.20
Scorched Earth	Regn	C	0.20
Shallow Victory	Actn	R	5.00
Shashakar	Pers	R	5.00
Shinjo Morito	Pers	R	4.50
Shinjo Yasoma	Pers	U	1.00
Shiryo no Akodo	Follo	R	5.00
Shiryo no Bayushi	Follo	R	5.00
Shiryo no Hiruma	Follo	R	4.80
Shiryo no Isawa	Follo	R	4.80
Shiryo no Kakita	Follo	R	5.00
Shiryo no Shinjo	Follo	R	4.50
Shiryo no Togashi	Follo	R	5.00
Slander	Actn	U	1.00
Spiritual Presence	Spell	C	0.20

Card name	Type	Rarity	Price
Stall until Sunrise	Actn	C	0.20
Stealing the Soul	Spell	U	1.00
Stifling Wind	Spell	C	0.20
Strategic Victory	Actn	U	1.00
Summon Nightstalker	Spell	U	1.00
Suzume Mukashino	Pers	C	0.20
Takuan	Pers	R	4.80
Tapestry of Air	Item	U	1.00
Tessen	Item	C	0.20
The Blood Feud	Actn	R	5.00
The Bronze Gong of the Hantei	Holdg	R	4.70
The Celestial Pattern	Actn	U	1.00
The Darkest Day	Actn	U	1.00
The Face of Fear	Actn	C	0.20
The Perfect Gift	Actn	R	4.50
The Tao of the Naga	Actn	R	5.00
The Way of Air	Actn	U	1.00
The Way of Earth	Actn	U	1.00
The Way of Fire	Actn	U	1.00
The Way of Water	Actn	U	1.00
There Is No Hope	Actn	R	4.80
To Avenge Our Ancestors	Actn	R	4.50
To Do What We Must	Actn	U	1.00
To the Last Man	Actn	R	4.80
Togashi Kokujin	Pers	R	4.80
Togashi Yama	Pers	U	1.00
Togashi Yokuni	Pers	R	5.00
Tomb of Iushiban	Holdg	R	4.50
Torturous Terrain	Actn	C	0.20
Toturi	Pers	R	5.40
Trading Grounds	Holdg	C	0.20
Training grounds	Regn	C	0.20
Traveling Poet	Follo	C	0.20
Treacherous Terrain	Actn	C	0.20
Tsukuro	Pers	R	5.00
Valley of Shadow	Regn	R	5.00
Watchtower	Holdg	C	0.20
Wetlands Regn	Regn	C	0.20
Yodin	Pers	R	5.00
Yogo Ichiba	Pers	U	1.00

RARITY KEY C = Common   U = Uncommon   R = Rare   VR = Very Rare   UR = Ultra Rare   F = Foil card   X = Fixed/standard in all decks

SCRYE Collectible Card Game Checklist and Price Guide • **227**

Nobuo
3   4
0   1
Mantis Clan Shugenja
Whenever Nobuo bows to produce a spell,
the spell is destroyed.

Legend of the Five Rings •
Crimson & Jade

Five Rings Publishing • Released **March 1997**

161 cards in set • **IDENTIFIER: Cards © 1997, have jade borders**

- Starter decks contain 60 cards; starter displays contain 12 starters
- Booster packs contain 11 cards; booster displays contain 46 boosters

As the war in Rokugan is joined in earnest, the monks of Shinsei are forced into the conflict, when Yogo Junzo attacks their temples to prevent an ancient prophecy from being fulfilled. The Crane clan funds an alliance of smaller clans to increase the armed opposition to the Shadowlands. These events are reflected in **Crimson & Jade** as two new Strongholds are released.

The **Brotherhood of Shinsei** allows the Monk player to bow the stronghold whenever he or she meets one of the conditions to play a ring card and retrieve the ring card from the Fate deck. This gives the Brotherhood a tremendous advantage when attempting an enlightenment victory. **Yoritomo's Alliance** allows the player to trade honor for gold when bowing the stronghold for gold, an ability that can greatly speed up a Yoritomo deck.

A new type of Fate action card was introduced in *Crimson & Jade*, the kiho. Kiho are like spells but usually cost no gold and are usable once. For the most part, they reproduce spell effects and can be cast only by monks and shugenja. — *Michael Greenholdt*

You will need
18
nine-pocket pages to store this set.
(9 doubled up)

Set (161 cards)	122.50
Starter Display Box	130.00
Booster Display Box	140.00
Starter Deck	12.00
Booster Pack	3.00

Card name	Type	Rarity	Price
1			
A Glimpse of the Soul's Shadow	Actn	C	0.25
A Samurai's Fury	Actn	R	5.00
A Spirit of Water	Actn	C	0.10
Agasha Heizo	Pers	C	0.20
Along the Coast at Midnight	Actn	R	5.00
An Oni's Fury	Actn	U	1.00
Ancestral Guidance	Actn	R	5.00
Ancestral Weapons of the Mantis	Item	X	5.00
Antidote	Item	U	1.00
2			
Architects of the Great Wall	Event	R	5.00
Are You With Me?	Event	U	1.00
Armor of the Shadow Warrior	Item	R	5.00
Armory	Holdg	C	0.25
Asahina Tomo	Pers	R	5.00
Ashamana	Pers	C	0.20
Bad Kharma	Actn	R	5.00
Bandit Gang	Follo	C	0.25
3			
Barbarian Horde	Actn	R	4.50
Bayushi Tasu	Pers	U	1.00
Borderland	Regn	U	1.00
Breaking Blow	Actn	U	1.00
Bridged Pass	Holdg	C	0.20
Brotherhood of Shinsei	Stghld	X	1.00
Brothers of Thunder	Follo	U	1.00
Carrier Pigeon	Actn	C	0.25
Catching the Wind's Favor	Actn	C	0.20
Chime of Harmony	Item	C	0.20
4			
Chinoko	Pers	U	1.30
Clan Banner	Item	R	5.00
Clan Heartland	Regn	R	5.00
Corrupted Copper Mine	Holdg	C	0.25
Counterfeit	Actn	U	1.00
Courier	Follo	C	0.20
Cowardice	Actn	U	1.00
Dance of the Elements	Actn	U	1.00
Deploy Reserves	Actn	U	1.00
5			
Disrupt the Aura	Spell	C	0.20
Divine the Future	Spell	U	1.00
Doji Reju	Pers	C	0.25

Card name	Type	Rarity	Price
Double Chi	Actn	C	0.20
Dragon's Teeth	Holdg	C	0.20
Engineering Crew	Holdg	C	0.25
Extortion	Actn	R	5.00
Fiery Wrath	Spell	R	4.80
Fight for My Favor	Actn	U	1.00
6			
Fist of the Earth	Actn	C	0.20
Forced Alliance	Actn	R	5.00
Forest of Thorns	Holdg	U	1.00
Fresh Horses	Actn	U	1.00
Genzo	Pers	R	4.50
Gift of the Wind	Actn	C	0.20
Ginawa	Pers	R	5.30
Hida Yakamo	Pers	R	6.00
Hiruma Yoshi	Pers	C	0.20
7			
Historian	Holdg	C	0.25
Hitoshi	Pers	C	0.25
Hyobe	Pers	U	1.00
Ikoma Ryozo	Pers	C	0.20
Incense of Concentration	Item	U	1.00
Inner Fire	Actn	U	1.00
Isawa Norikazu	Pers	R	5.00
Isawa Tomo	Pers	U	1.00
Island Wharf	Holdg	C	0.20
8			
Iuchi Daiyu	Pers	R	5.00
Kado	Pers	C	0.25
Kakita Ichiro	Pers	U	1.00
Kanbe	Pers	C	0.20
Kenku	Follo	U	1.00
Kenku Teacher	Follo	C	0.20
Kenshin's Helm	Item	U	1.00
Kitsu Motso	Pers	R	5.00
Know Your Enemy	Actn	R	5.00
9			
Koichi	Pers	C	0.20
Kolat Bodyguard	Follo	U	1.00
Kolat's Favor	Item	U	1.00
Light of the Sun Goddess	Event	U	1.00
Lost Valley	Regn	C	0.20
Mantis Clan Shugenja	Follo	U	1.00
Masasue	Pers	C	0.20
Master of the Rolling River	Actn	U	1.00

Card name	Type	Rarity	Price
Matsu Goemon	Pers	C	0.20
10			
Mine Riots	Event	U	1.00
Moto Sada	Pers	C	0.25
Moto Tsume	Pers	R	5.00
Mounts	Follo	C	0.20
Mukami	Pers	C	0.20
Naming the True Evil	Event	R	5.00
Narrow Ground	Actn	C	0.20
New Taxes	Event	U	1.00
Night of a Thousand Fires	Actn	U	1.00
11			
Nobuo	Pers	U	1.00
Norio	Pers	C	0.25
Ogre Outlaw	Pers	U	1.50
One Koku	Actn	C	0.25
Oni no Chi	Pers	U	1.00
Oni no Genso	Pers	C	0.25
Oni warding	Spell	R	4.50
Orochi	Pers	R	5.30
Osano-Wo's Breath	Spell	U	1.00
12			
Pearl-Encrusted Staff	Item	R	5.00
Peasant Levies	Follo	C	0.25
Prayer Shrines	Holdg	C	0.20
Robes of Shinsei	Item	U	1.00
Ryosei	Pers	C	0.20
Secluded Ravine	Regn	C	0.25
Severed from the Emperor	Event	R	5.00
Shabura	Pers	R	5.00
Shadow of the Dark God	Event	U	1.00
13			
Shalasha	Pers	U	1.00
Shiba Shingo	Pers	C	0.20
Shinjo Rojin	Pers	C	0.25
Shinjo Tashima	Pers	U	1.00
Shinsei's Shrine	Regn	R	5.00
Shiryo no Agasha	Follo	R	5.00
Shiryo no Doji	Follo	R	5.00
Shiryo no Hida	Follo	R	4.80
Shiryo no Matsu	Follo	R	5.00
14			
Shiryo no Otaku	Follo	R	5.00
Shiryo no Shiba	Follo	R	5.00
Shiryo no Shosuro	Follo	R	5.00
Shosuro Sadato	Pers	C	0.20
Soshi Bantaro	Pers	R	4.50

Card name	Type	Rarity	Price
Stand Against the Waves	Actn	C	0.25
Stand Firm	Actn	C	0.20
Strength of My Ancestors	Actn	C	0.20
Strike of Flowing Water	Actn	C	0.25
15			
Suana	Pers	U	1.00
Summons from Beyond	Event	U	1.00
Sunken City	Regn	R	5.00
Superior Strategist	Actn	R	5.00
Takao	Pers	U	1.00
Takuni	Pers	C	0.20
Taro	Pers	C	0.20
Temple of Osano-Wo	Regn	X	4.00
Tetsuya	Pers	R	5.00
16			
The Battle at Isawa Palace	Event	U	1.00
The Death of Tsuko	Event	R	5.00
The fault is mine.	Actn	C	0.20
The Great Bear	Holdg	R	5.00
The Hooded Ronin	Pers	R	6.00
The Purity of Shinsei	Actn	R	5.00
The Touch of Shinsei	Actn	R	5.00
The Wrath of Osano-wo	Actn	C	0.20
The Yasuki Estates	Regn	C	0.20
17			
Togashi Jodome	Pers	U	1.00
Togashi Mitsu	Pers	R	5.00
Tokiuji	Pers	C	0.25
Toturi's Fan	Item	R	4.50
Tradeposts of the Mantis	Regn	C	0.20
Tsunami	Event	U	1.00
Tsuo	Pers	C	0.25
Tunnel System	Holdg	C	0.25
Visage of the Void	Item	U	1.00
18			
Void Strike	Actn	U	1.00
Winter Warfare	Event	R	6.00
Wisdom the Wind Brings	Actn	U	1.00
Yasuki Kojiro	Pers	U	1.00
Yoritomo	Pers	R	6.00
Yoritomo's Alliance	Stghld	X	5.00
You Walk With Evil	Actn	R	5.00
Yugoro	Pers	R	5.00

RARITY KEY   **C** = Common   **U** = Uncommon   **R** = Rare   **VR** = Very Rare   **UR** = Ultra Rare   **F** = Foil card   **X** = Fixed/standard in all decks

Legend of the Five Rings •
Time of the Void

Wizards of the Coast (Five Rings Division) • Released **August 1997**
229 cards in set • **IDENTIFIER: Black borders with brown accents**

- Starter decks contain 60 cards; starter displays contain 12 starters
- Booster packs contain 11 cards; booster displays contain 46 boosters

By **Time of the Void**, the events in the prophecies of Uikku have come to pass. The seven Thunders, who in ages past imprisoned the Dark Lord with the Black Scrolls, have been reborn to oppose him again. Disturbingly, the prophecies are silent on the outcome.

In the set, the Crab, Crane, Dragon, Phoenix, Scorpion, and Unicorn clans each receive a Thunder personality. The seventh Thunder is the rogue Lion, **Toturi**. Two clans, the Crab and the Phoenix, split, as some members went over to the Shadowlands. This is reflected by the two new strongholds in *Time of the Void*. The Crab stronghold, the **Great Walls of Kaiu**, reduces the cost of fortifications and forbids the Crab from using Shadowlands cards. The **Ruins of Isawa Castle** allows the Phoenix player to bow the stronghold to retrieve a kiho from his or her deck. — *Michael Greenholdt*

You will need **26** nine-pocket pages to store this set. (13 doubled up)

Set (229 cards)	125.00
Starter Display Box	227.00
Booster Display Box	135.00
Starter Deck	9.00
Booster Pack	3.20

Card name	Type	Rarity	Price
A Good Day to Die	Actn	U	1.00
A Moment of Clarity	Actn	U	1.00
A Moment of Truth	Actn	R	4.10
A Soul of Thunder	Event	U	1.00
A Test of Courage	Actn	C	0.25
Agasha Gennai	Pers	C	0.20
Agasha Tunnels	Regn	U	1.25
Akiyoshi	Pers	U	1.00
Akodo Tactical School	Holdg	R	5.00
Al-Hazaad	Pers	U	1.00
Al-Rashid	Pers	C	0.20
An Exhibition	Actn	C	0.25
Ancestral Standard of the Scorpion	Item	R	5.00
Ancient Armor of The Qamar	Item	R	5.50
As Far as the Eye Can See	Regn	R	5.00
Asako Ishio	Pers	U	1.00
Asako Togama	Pers	C	0.25
Ashan	Pers	C	0.25
Augury	Spell	R	5.00
Battle Standard of the Mantis	Item	R	5.00
Battle Standard of the Naga	Item	R	5.00
Battle Standard of the Shinsei	Item	R	5.00
Bayushi Goshiu	Pers	R	5.00
Bayushi Hisa	Pers	U	1.00
Bayushi Kachiko	Pers	R	6.50
Bayushi Marumo	Pers	C	0.20
Bend Like a Reed	Actn	C	0.25
Berserkers	Follo	C	0.25
Bonds of Darkness	Event	R	5.00
Burning Your Essence	Actn	R	5.00
Chi Strike	Actn	R	5.00
Concealed Weapon	Actn	R	5.00
Contested Ground	Actn	C	0.20
Coordinated Fire	Actn	C	0.20
Corrupt Geisha House	Holdg	C	0.25
Corrupt Gold Mines	Holdg	C	0.25
Corrupt Stables	Holdg	C	0.25

Card name	Type	Rarity	Price
Corrupted Regn	Regn	C	0.25
Counting the Lost	Actn	U	1.00
Crystal Gate	Holdg	C	0.20
Curse of the Jackal	Spell	C	0.25
Dark Lord's Favor	Actn	C	0.25
Dashmar	Pers	U	1.00
Depth of the Void	Spell	U	1.00
Destiny Has No Secrets	Actn	C	0.25
Disenlightenment	Actn	R	4.50
Distractions of the Flesh	Actn	C	0.25
Doji Chomei	Pers	C	0.20
Doji Hoturi	Pers	R	7.00
Doji Kuwanan	Pers	U	1.00
Doji Shizue	Pers	C	0.20
Doji Yosai	Pers	R	4.90
Elite Heavy Infantry	Follo	U	1.00
Elite Light Infantry	Follo	C	0.25
Elite Medium Infantry	Follo	C	0.25
Enlistment	Event	U	1.50
Eshru	Pers	C	0.20
Essence of Air	Spell	U	1.00
Essence of Earth	Spell	U	1.00
Factionism	Event	R	5.00
Familiar Surroundings	Actn	C	0.25
Fatal Mistake	Actn	R	4.80
Festival of Long Sticks	Event	R	5.00
Final Stand	Actn	R	5.00
Flight of Doves	Spell	U	1.00
Flying Carpet	Item	R	5.00
Fog	Actn	C	0.25
For the Empire!	Actn	U	1.00
Forgiveness	Kiho	C	0.25
Gaijin Merchant	Follo	U	0.90
Gekkai	Pers	U	1.00
Goblin Madcaps	Follo	C	0.25
Goblin Sneaks	Follo	C	0.25
Goblin War Standard	Item	C	0.20
Goblin wizard	Pers	C	0.25
Harima	Pers	U	1.00
Heavy Mounted Infantry	Follo	U	1.00
Hida Amoro	Pers	U	1.00
Hida O-Ushi	Pers	R	3.50
Hida Tadashiro	Pers	C	0.20
Hida War College	Holdg	R	5.00
Hida Yakamo	Pers	X	2.50
Hizuka	Pers	C	0.20
Horde of Fu Leng	Follo	C	0.25
Horsebowmen	Follo	C	0.25

Card name	Type	Rarity	Price
I Believed in You …	Actn	C	0.25
Ikoma Tsanuri	Pers	R	5.00
In Time of War	Event	U	1.00
Isawa Suma	Pers	C	0.20
Isawa Tadaka	Pers	X	3.00
Isawa Uona	Pers	U	1.40
Isha	Pers	R	4.00
Iuchi Karasu	Pers	U	1.00
Izaku Library	Holdg	C	0.25
Jade Dragon	Pers	R	5.00
Jujitsu Duel	Actn	U	1.00
Junzo's Battle Standard	Item	R	5.00
Kage	Pers	R	5.00
Kakita Kenjutsu School	Holdg	R	5.00
Kakita Yoshi	Pers	U	1.10
Kappuksu	Pers	U	1.00
Kaze-do	Kiho	C	0.20
Kitsu Okura	Pers	C	0.20
Kitsu Toju	Pers	U	1.00
Know the School	Actn	C	0.25
Kolat Spy	Actn	C	0.25
Komaro	Pers	C	0.20
Kuni Sensin	Pers	C	0.20
Kyujutsu	Actn	C	0.25
Lady Kitsune	Pers	C	0.20
Legions of Fu Leng	Spell	C	0.25
Lessons from the Past	Actn	C	0.25
Light Mounted Infantry	Follo	C	0.20
Matsu Agetoki	Pers	R	4.00
Matsu Gohei	Pers	U	1.00
Matsu Hiroru	Pers	R	5.00
Matsu Turi	Pers	C	0.20
Mighty Protection	Spell	R	5.00
Mikio	Pers	U	1.00
Mirumoto Hitomi	Pers	R	6.00
Mirumoto Yukihira	Pers	U	1.00
Moshi Wakiza	Pers	U	1.00
Mounted Spearmen	Follo	C	0.20
Mujina Chieftain	Pers	C	0.20
Mujina Miners	Holdg	U	1.00
Mystical Terrain	Spell	C	0.25
Necromancer	Pers	R	5.00
Ninja Stalkers	Follo	U	1.00
Nogoten's Bow	Item	U	0.40
Obsidian Blade	Item	C	0.20
Offer of Fealty	Actn	C	0.20
One with the Elements	Kiho	C	0.25
Oni no Ianwa	Pers	R	5.00
Oni no Pekkle	Pers	C	0.25

Card name	Type	Rarity	Price
Oni no Ugulu	Pers	C	0.25
Oracle of the Void	Holdg	R	4.50
Otaku Kamoko	Pers	R	7.00
Plans within Plans	Actn	U	1.00
Qamar	Pers	R	5.00
Radakast	Pers	U	1.00
Rebuilding the Kaiu Walls	Event	U	1.00
Regions of Rokugan	Event	U	1.00
"Rest, My Brother"	Kiho	U	1.00
River Delta	Regn	U	1.00
Ruins of the Isawa Library	Holdg	R	5.00
Ryokan's Sword	Item	C	0.25
Sailors	Follo	C	0.25
Salute of the Samurai	Actn	R	5.00
Sanctified Ground	Regn	C	0.20
Seikua	Pers	R	5.00
Shahadet's Legion	Follo	R	4.00
Shiba Tsukune	Pers	R	5.00
Shinjo Hanari	Pers	R	5.00
Shinjo Riding Stables	Holdg	R	5.00
Shinjo Sanetama	Pers	C	0.20
Shinjo Shirasu	Pers	C	0.20
Shinjo Yasamura	Pers	U	1.00
Shinobi	Actn	U	1.00
Shiryo no Asahina	Follo	R	4.50
Shiryo no Asako	Follo	R	4.50
Shiryo no Ide	Follo	R	4.50
Shiryo no Ikoma	Follo	R	4.50
Shiryo no Kaiu	Follo	R	4.50
Shiryo no Mirumoto	Follo	R	4.50
Shiryo no Yogo	Follo	R	4.50
Shiryo no Yoritomo	Follo	R	4.80
Shosuro Hametsu	Pers	U	1.00
Stance of the Mountain	Actn	C	0.20
Strength of Osano-Wo	Spell	C	0.20
Strength of the Dark One	Spell	U	1.00
Strike Without Striking	Actn	U	1.00
Surrender	Actn	U	1.00
Swamp Goblins	Follo	C	0.25
Sysh	Pers	C	0.20
Taquar	Pers	C	0.20
Teeth of the Serpent	Event	U	1.00
The Ancestral Home of the Lion	Stghld	U	1.00
The Brotherhood of the Shinsei	Stghld	U	1.00

RARITY KEY C = Common U = Uncommon R = Rare VR = Very Rare UR = Ultra Rare F = Foil card X = Fixed/standard in all decks

SCRYE Collectible Card Game Checklist and Price Guide • **229**

Card name	Type	Rarity	Price
The Darkest Magics	Event	R	5.00
The Enlightened Ruler	Event	R	5.00

[21]

Card name	Type	Rarity	Price
The Esteemed House of the Crane	Stghld	U	1.00
The Great Walls of Kaiu	Stghld	X	1.00
The Heavy Shadow of Fear	Event	U	1.00
The Hero's Triumph	Event	U	1.00
The Hidden Heart of Iuchiban	Holdg	R	5.00
The Hidden Temple of the Naga	Stghld	U	1.00
The Light of Amaterasu	Spell	C	0.20
The Longest Night	Event	R	5.00
The Mountain Keep of Dragon	Stghld	U	1.00

[22]

Card name	Type	Rarity	Price
The Path of Wisdom	Actn	R	5.00
The Phoenix is Reborn	Spell	U	1.00
The Plains of Amaterasu	Regn	U	1.00
The Provincial Estate of Unicorn	Stghld	U	1.00
The Ruined Fortress of the Scorpion	Stghld	U	1.00
The Ruins of Isawa Castle	Stghld	X	1.00
The Sacred Temple of the Phoenix	Stghld	U	1.00
The Scorpion's Sting	Actn	R	5.00
The Sight of Death	Kiho	U	1.00

[23]

Card name	Type	Rarity	Price
The Time is Now	Actn	R	5.00
The Touch of Amaterasu	Kiho	U	1.00

Card name	Type	Rarity	Price
The Twelfth Black Scroll	Item	R	5.50
The Twelve Ronin	Follo	R	5.00
The War Fortress of the Crab	Stghld	U	1.00
The Yoritomo Alliance	Stghld	U	1.00
To Save an Empire	Event	R	5.00
Today We Die	Actn	R	5.00
Togashi Kama	Pers	C	0.20

[24]

Card name	Type	Rarity	Price
Togashi Testing Ground	Holdg	R	5.00
Togashi Yokuni	Pers	R	5.00
Togashi Yoshi	Pers	U	1.00
Toku	Pers	U	1.00
Toturi	Pers	R	7.00
Toturi's Army	Stghld	U	1.00
Toturi's Battle Standard	Item	R	5.00
Toturi's Last Stand	Event	R	5.00

Card name	Type	Rarity	Price
Toturi's Tactics	Actn	R	5.00

[25]

Card name	Type	Rarity	Price
Troops from the Woods	Actn	C	0.25
Tsuyu	Pers	C	0.20
Unattuned	Kiho	U	1.00
Untrustworthy	Actn	U	1.00
Warrior Monks	Follo	U	1.00
Wedge	Actn	R	6.50
Yasuki Taka	Pers	U	1.00
Yodin	Pers	R	5.00
Yogo Junzo's Army	Stghld	U	1.00

[26]

Card name	Type	Rarity	Price
Yogo Oshio	Pers	C	0.20
Yoritomo	Pers	R	7.00
Yoritomo's Armor	Item	R	5.00
Your Last Mistake	Actn	U	1.00

Legend of the Five Rings •
Scorpion Clan Coup: Episode 1

Wizards of the Coast (Five Rings Division) • Released **November 1997**

53 cards in set • **IDENTIFIER: Black borders with red cracks**

- Starter decks contain 60 cards; combo displays contain 24 boosters and 6 starters
- Booster packs contain 11 cards; booster displays contain 46 boosters

The **Scorpion Clan Coup** sets are a prequel to the Clan Wars saga. When the Scorpion clan discovers the prophecies of Uikku, it attempts to overthrow the emperor and seize control of the empire to forestall the prophecies. Many personalities found in the Clan Wars are seen here as "inexperienced" versions.

A new way of winning is introduced. **The 38th Hantei Falls** allows a player to win, if he can play the four wall of Otosan Uchi (unique fortifications) before the event has resolved. Cards to control how events resolve are mandatory in a deck looking for this kind of victory.

A new Scorpion stronghold, **The Shadow Stronghold of the Bayushi**, is included, reflecting the trusted position they held as the emperor's secret police. At the cost of one honor, the Scorpion player can look at an opponent's Fate hand. — *Michael Greenholdt*

You will need **6** nine-pocket pages to store this set. (3 doubled up)

Set (53 cards)	37.00
Combo Display Box	25.00
Booster Display Box	34.00
Starter Deck	6.50
Booster Pack	1.40

[1]

Card name	Type	Rarity	Price
A Samurai Never Stands Alone	Actn	C	0.20
Agasha's Illusion	Spell	R	2.00
Ancestral Sword of the Scorpion	Item	U	2.00
Armor of Osano-Wo	Item	C	0.20
Arrival of the Unicorns	Actn	C	0.10
Bayushi Dozan	Pers	C	0.15
Bayushi Kachiko (Inexp)	Pers	R	2.50
Bayushi Shoju (Inexp)	Pers	X	2.00
Bayushi Yokuan	Pers	R	2.00

[2]

Card name	Type	Rarity	Price
Behind Night's Shadow	Actn	R	1.50
Cavalry Raiders	Follo	C	0.15
Daikua	Pers	C	0.15
Divinity Pool	Holdg	C	0.15
East Wall of Otosan Uchi	Holdg	R	2.50
Flood	Spell	C	0.15
Freezing Lifeblood	Kiho	C	0.10
Garrison	Holdg	C	0.15
Hantei the 38th	Pers	R	2.50

[3]

Card name	Type	Rarity	Price
Hatsuko	Pers	C	0.10
Hiruma's Last Breath	Spell	R	1.50
Imperial Palace Guard	Follo	R	1.80
Isawa Tomo's Portal	Regn	C	0.80
Ishikawa	Pers	R	2.00
Iuchi Katta	Pers	C	0.15

Card name	Type	Rarity	Price
Jurojin's Touch	Kiho	C	0.15
Lieutenant Morito	Follo	R	1.30
Lions Attack the Crane	Event	R	2.00

[4]

Card name	Type	Rarity	Price
Musubi	Actn	C	1.00
Plains Above Evil	Regn	C	0.20
Political Distraction	Actn	C	0.20
Political Mistake	Actn	R	2.00
Robbing the Dead	Actn	C	0.15
Sanado	Pers	R	1.00
Shinjo Yokatsu	Pers	R	2.10
Shioda	Pers	C	0.15
Shosuro Ikawa	Pers	C	0.15

[5]

Card name	Type	Rarity	Price
Soshi Taoshi	Pers	R	2.00
Soshi Ujemi	Follo	R	1.90
South Wall of Otosan Uchi	Holdg	R	2.50

Card name	Type	Rarity	Price
Storehouses	Holdg	C	0.15
Streets of Otosan Uchi	Regn	C	0.15
The 38th Hantei Falls	Event	R	2.20
The Endless Well	Kiho	R	1.60
The Exalted Ugu	Pers	C	0.10
The First Scroll is Opened	Event	R	1.70

[6]

Card name	Type	Rarity	Price
The Secret Entrance	Actn	C	0.10
The Shadow Stronghold of the Bayushi	Stghld	X	1.30
The Soul Goes Forth	Kiho	C	0.15
The Unclean Cut	Actn	C	0.10
Through the Waterways	Actn	R	2.00
Toturi is Drugged	Actn	R	2.00
War Wagon	Item	C	0.20
Yogo Shidachi	Pers	C	0.15

Legend of the Five Rings
• Scorpion Clan Coup: Episode 2

Wizards of the Coast (Five Rings Division) • Released **November 1997**

50 cards in set • **IDENTIFIER: Black borders with red cracks**

- Starter decks contain 60 cards; combo displays contain 24 boosters and 6 starters
- Booster packs contain 11 cards; booster displays contain 46 boosters

Bayushi Shoju, the daimyo (lord) of the Scorpion clan, has taken the throne, but the remaining clans are mustering to defeat the usurper. The remaining two walls of Otosan Uchi were released in this expansion, completing the set of cards needed for the new victory conditions. — *Michael Greenholdt*

You will need **6** nine-pocket pages to store this set. (3 doubled up)

Set (50 cards)	35.00	Starter Deck	6.50	
Combo Display Box	25.00	Booster Pack	1.40	
Booster Display Box	34.00			

Card name	Type	Rarity	Price
A Vision of Truth	Actn	R	1.80
Agasha Nabe	Pers	C	0.10

RARITY KEY C = Common U = Uncommon R = Rare VR = Very Rare UR = Ultra Rare F = Foil card X = Fixed/standard in all decks

Card name	Type	Rarity	Price
Arrival of the Unicorns	Actn	C	0.10
Asahina Uojin	Pers	C	0.20
Bayushi Dairu	Pers	R	1.50
Bayushi House Guard	Follo	R	1.50
Bayushi Kyono	Pers	C	0.15
Bayushi Yojiro	Pers	C	0.10
Defenders of the Realm	Actn	C	0.20

2

Card name	Type	Rarity	Price
Disloyalty	Actn	C	0.20
Doji Satsume	Pers	R	2.00
Fury of the Earth	Kiho	C	0.10
Gift of Fealty	Actn	R	1.50
Hasagawa	Pers	C	0.15
Hida Matyu	Pers	C	0.15

Card name	Type	Rarity	Price
Hojatsu's Blade	Item	C	0.20
Iaijutsu Art	Actn	C	0.20
Isawa Sze	Pers	R	1.50

3

Card name	Type	Rarity	Price
Kappa	Pers	C	0.10
Kuroshin's Prayer	Spell	R	1.50
Led From the True Path	Kiho	R	1.50
Lieutenant Daini	Follo	R	1.50
Lieutenant Uji	Follo	R	1.50
Matsu Hokitare	Pers	C	0.15
Matsu Tsuko	Pers	R	1.70
Monk Advisors	Follo	C	0.15
My Enemy's Weakness	Event	R	1.60

4

Card name	Type	Rarity	Price
Ninja Shapeshifter	Pers	R	1.50

Card name	Type	Rarity	Price
North Wall of Otosan Uchi	Holding	R	2.00
One Man's Honor	Event	R	1.80
Piercing the Soul	Kiho	C	0.20
Plains of Fast Troubles	Regn	C	0.20
Ranbe	Pers	R	1.80
Rearguard	Actn	C	0.15
Shazaar	Pers	C	0.10
Shinjo Goshi	Pers	R	1.00

5

Card name	Type	Rarity	Price
Shoju's Armor	Item	R	1.80
Soshi's Curse	Spell	C	0.20
The Dragon Pearl	Item	R	2.50
The Face of My Enemy	Actn	R	2.00
The Fair Voice of Lies	Event	R	1.90

Card name	Type	Rarity	Price
The Karmic Wheel Spins	Event	R	1.80
The Moment Before the Strike	Actn	C	0.15
The Purity of Kitsu	Spell	R	1.80
The Ruby of Iuchiban	Item	R	1.80

6

Card name	Type	Rarity	Price
The True Lands	Kiho	R	1.30
Touching the Soul	Kiho	C	0.20
Trading Port	Holdg	C	0.10
West Wall of Otosan Uchi	Holdg	R	2.00
When Men Stand Divided	Actn	C	0.15

Legend of the Five Rings • Scorpion Clan Coup: Episode 3

Wizards of the Coast (Five Rings Division) • Released **November 1997**

52 cards in set • **IDENTIFIER: Black borders with red cracks**

- Starter decks contain 60 cards; combo displays contain 24 boosters and 6 starters
- Booster packs contain 11 cards; booster displays contain 46 boosters

As the siege of the Imperial capitol reaches its climax, the (so far) neutral Crab clan arrives. Although wooed by the Scorpions, the Crabs do not support the coup, and the imperial city is retaken. The Scorpion clan is hunted down by the Crane clan, and the 39th Hantei emperor ascends the throne. Ironically, it is this emperor that is fated to fulfill the Uikku prophecies. This expansion marked the official end of the Clan War saga, having detailed how the Clan War started. — *Michael Greenholdt*

You will need **6** nine-pocket pages to store this set. (3 doubled up)

Set (52 cards)	36.00
Combo Display Box	25.00
Booster Display Box	34.00
Starter Deck	6.50
Booster Pack	1.40

1

Card name	Type	Rarity	Price
A Final Duel	Event	R	1.10
A Greater Destiny	Actn	R	1.40
Acolyte Kaede	Follo	R	1.20
Agasha Mumoko	Pers	C	0.20
Agasha's Mirror	Item	C	0.15
Akodo Hari	Pers	C	0.15
Akodo Ikawa	Pers	C	0.15
Akodo Matoko	Pers	C	0.80
Akodo Toturi	Pers	X	1.50

2

Card name	Type	Rarity	Price
All Distances are One	Spell	C	0.20
Asashina's Breath	Spell	R	1.40
Bayushi's Labyrinth	Holdg	R	1.40
Fires of Retribution	Actn	C	0.20
Give Me Your Hand	Event	R	1.40
Heartbeat Drummers	Holdg	C	0.15
Hida Kisada	Pers	R	2.10
Hiruma Osuno	Pers	C	0.20
Isawa Ujina	Pers	R	1.80

3

Card name	Type	Rarity	Price
Isawa's Helm	Item	R	2.00
Jitte	Item	C	0.20
Kaiu Castle	Regn	R	1.50
Kyudo	Actn	C	0.20
Lieutenant Sukune	Follo	R	1.50
Lieutenant Tsanuri	Follo	R	1.40

Card name	Type	Rarity	Price
Mirror Image	Spell	C	0.20
Mirumoto Satsu	Pers	R	1.70
Obi of Protection	Item	R	1.60

4

Card name	Type	Rarity	Price
Plains of the Emerald Champion	Regn	C	0.20
Quarry	Holdg	C	0.20
Shiba Kyo	Pers	C	0.20
Street to Street	Actn	C	0.20
Streets of Otosan Uchi	Regn	C	0.15
Subversion	Actn	R	1.00
Sunabe	Pers	C	0.20
Suru's Mempo	Item	R	1.50
Swamp Spirits	Follo	C	0.15

5

Card name	Type	Rarity	Price
Tell the Tale	Actn	C	0.15
The Ancient Halls of the Akodo	Stghld	X	1.00

Card name	Type	Rarity	Price
The Courage of Osano-Wo	Event	R	1.80
The Crab Arrive	Actn	C	0.15
The Fog of War	Actn	C	0.20
The Fortune's Wisdom	Kiho	C	0.20
The Hub Villages	Regn	C	0.20
The Master Painter	Holdg	R	1.50
The People's Champion	Actn	R	1.40

6

Card name	Type	Rarity	Price
The Shiba Fortification	Holdg	R	1.50
The Soul of Akodo	Actn	R	1.50
The Soul of Shiba	Spell	R	1.70
The Temples of Shinsei	Regn	R	1.30
The World Stood Still	Event	R	1.50
Whispers of the Land	Spell	C	0.15
Yazaki	Pers	C	0.15

Legend of the Five Rings • The Hidden Emperor: Episode 1

Wizards of the Coast (Five Rings Division) • Released **June 1998**

52 cards in set • **IDENTIFIER: Dark vertical wood-grain borders**

- Starter decks contain 60 cards; combo displays contain 36 boosters and 6 starters
- Booster packs contain 8 cards; booster displays contain 72 boosters

Two years after taking the throne, Toturi I disappears, throwing the empire into turmoil. The Naga, once allied to the Crab clan, abandon them and begin attacking the Dragon clan, while the other clans jockey for position.

Cards in this expansion closely follow the storyline, including the event **Storming Mirumoto Mountain** and the region **Hiruma Castle**, which the Crab clan has taken with the Naga's help.

The Hidden Emperor expansions were part of an experimental release system, Rolling Thunder. About 50 cards, one third the size of a normal expansion, were released monthly for six months. In theory, it allowed a collector to spread out the expense. In practice, it was not well received, since it made collecting full sets difficult. — *Michael Greenholdt*

You will need **6** nine-pocket pages to store this set. (3 doubled up)

Set (52 cards)	69.50
Combo Display Box	62.50
Booster Display Box	67.50
Starter Deck	8.10
Booster Pack	1.80

1

Card name	Type	Rarity	Price
A Time for Mortal Men	Actn	C	0.20
Aiki Tactics	Actn	R	3.00
Blackened Sky	Actn	U	1.80
Broken Guard	Actn	R	2.50
Chasing Osano-Wo	Kiho	C	0.20

Card name	Type	Rarity	Price
Concealed Archers	Actn	C	0.20
Cricket	Item	C	0.20
Dai-Kyu of Anekkusai	Item	U	0.50
Daidoji Rekai	Pers	C	0.20

2

Card name	Type	Rarity	Price
Damesh	Pers	C	0.20

Card name	Type	Rarity	Price
Day and Night	Actn	R	2.50
Elite Spearmen	Follo	C	0.20
Flanking Maneuver	Actn	C	0.20
Flee the Darkness	Kiho	U	1.30
Fu Leng's Skull	Holdg	R	2.50
Grove of the Five Masters	Holdg	U	0.60

RARITY KEY C = Common   U = Uncommon   R = Rare   VR = Very Rare   UR = Ultra Rare   F = Foil card   X = Fixed/standard in all decks

Card name	Type	Rarity	Price		Card name	Type	Rarity	Price		Card name	Type	Rarity	Price		Card name	Type	Rarity	Price
☐ Hasame	Pers	C	0.20		☐ Master's Tactics	Actn	R	2.50		☐ Ralish	Pers	C	0.20		☐ Takuan	Pers	R	2.50
☐ Haunted Lands	Regn	C	0.20		☐ Mizu-do	Kiho	C	0.20		☐ Rebuilding the Empire	Event	U	0.80		☐ The Hidden Emperor	Event	R	4.50
☐ Heart of the Shinomen Forest	Stghld	X	2.50		☐ Mukami	Pers	U	0.80		☐ Scouting Team	Follo	C	0.20		☐ The Hiruma Dojo	Holdg	C	0.60
☐ Hiruma Castle	Regn	U	0.80		☐ Naga Apprentice	Follo	U	1.00		☐ Selection of the Chancellor	Event	U	0.80		☐ The Jade Throne	Item	R	3.00
☐ Ikudaiu	Pers	C	0.20		☐ Naga Storm Mirumoto Mountain	Event	U	0.80		☐ Shahadet	Pers	X	3.80		☐ The Mountains Below Kyuden Hitomi	Regn	C	0.20
☐ Imperial Legion	Follo	U	1.00		☐ Naka Kuro	Pers	R	4.50		☐ Shinjo Yokatsu	Pers	R	3.80		☐ The People's Hero	Actn	C	0.20
☐ Journey to the Burning Sands	Actn	U	0.80		☐ Open Fields	Actn	C	0.20		☐ Shiryo no Hoturi	Follo	R	2.50		☐ The Scorpion Children	Holdg	C	0.20
☐ Kakita Yoshi	Pers	R	2.50		☐ Otaku Tetsuko	Pers	C	0.20		☐ Shiryo no Tsuko	Follo	R	3.30		☐ Tidal Land Bridge	Regn	R	2.50
☐ Kyoso no Oni	Pers	R	2.50		☐ Otomo Banu	Pers	U	0.80		☐ Show Me Your Stance	Actn	U	0.80					
					☐ Political Marriage	Actn	U	0.80										

Legend of the Five Rings •
The Hidden Emperor: Episode 2
Wizards of the Coast (Five Rings Division) • Released **July 1998**
52 cards in set • **IDENTIFIER: Dark vertical wood-grain borders**

You will need **6** nine-pocket pages to store this set. (3 doubled up)

Set (52 cards)	69.00
Combo Display Box	62.50
Booster Display Box	67.50
Starter Deck	8.10
Booster Pack	1.80

- Starter decks contain 60 cards; combo displays contain 36 boosters and 6 starters
- Booster packs contain 8 cards; booster displays contain 72 boosters

The elected chancellor Takuan manages to hold the empire together and prevent open warfare from breaking out, although the Naga are continuing their attack on the Dragon clan. The death of the Emerald Champion has spread doubt throughout the empire, and the move by the clans to occupy the throne begins in the shadows.

Cards released in **Hidden Emperor 2** continued to reflect the storyline. A new stronghold for the Dragon clan was released, **Kyuden Hitomi**. The stronghold allows the player to place five cards from his or her Fate deck in reserve. The player can bow the stronghold to take a card instead of drawing from the Fate Deck. — **Michael Greenholdt**

Card name	Type	Rarity	Price
☐ Ancestral Duty	Event	R	3.30
☐ Betrayal	Actn	U	0.80
☐ Chitatchikkan	Follo	U	1.00
☐ Daidoji Tsumerai	Pers	C	0.20
☐ Deadly Message	Actn	U	0.80
☐ Double Agent	Actn	R	2.50
☐ Doubt	Actn	R	2.50
☐ Drawing Fire	Actn	C	0.20
☐ Flooded Pass	Actn	C	0.20
☐ Ginawa	Pers	R	2.50
☐ Hitomi (Exp 3)	Pers	X	6.00
☐ Hitomi Akuai	Pers	C	0.20
☐ Hitomi Tashima	Pers	U	0.80
☐ Hitsu-do	Actn	C	0.20
☐ Imperial Ambassadorship	Event	R	2.50
☐ Iuchi Shahai	Pers	C	0.20
☐ Kirazo	Pers	C	0.25

Card name	Type	Rarity	Price		Card name	Type	Rarity	Price		Card name	Type	Rarity	Price
☐ Ki–Rin's Shrine	Holdg	R	2.50		☐ Root the Mountain	Actn	C	0.20		☐ Tattooing Chamber	Holdg	R	3.00
☐ Kisada's Funeral	Event	U	1.50		☐ Ryoko Owari	Regn	R	2.50		☐ Tchickchuk	Pers	C	0.20
☐ Kitsune Diro	Pers	C	0.20		☐ Shinjo's Breath	Actn	U	1.50		☐ The Bayushi Provinces	Regn	C	0.20
☐ Kyuden Hitomi	Stghld	X	2.50		☐ Shinsei's Fan	Item	C	0.20		☐ The Daini	Pers	R	2.50
☐ Meishodo Amulet	Item	C	0.20		☐ Shireikan	Follo	U	0.80		☐ The Dragon's Heart	Actn	R	3.00
☐ Mystic Ground	Regn	C	0.20		☐ Shiryo no Tadaka	Follo	R	3.80		☐ The Search Begins	Event	U	1.00
☐ Ninja Mystic	Pers	R	3.00		☐ Shosuro Nishiko	Pers	U	0.80		☐ The Shinjo Stockades	Holdg	C	0.20
☐ Norikazu's Ravings	Event	U	0.80		☐ Slap the Wave	Actn	R	2.50		☐ The Song of Blood	Actn	C	0.25
☐ Palisades	Holdg	C	0.20		☐ Sting of the Wasp	Actn	C	0.20		☐ Token of Jade	Item	C	0.20
☐ Purging the House	Actn	R	2.50		☐ Suspicions	Event	U	0.80		☐ Veil of Shadows	Actn	U	0.80
☐ Rise Again!	Actn	U	0.80		☐ The Tattered Ear Tribe	Follo	C	0.20		☐ Writ of the Magistrate	Item	U	1.00
					☐ Tattooed Men	Follo	R	5.00		☐ Yoritomo Hogosha	Pers	U	0.80

Legend of the Five Rings •
The Hidden Emperor: Episode 3
Wizards of the Coast (Five Rings Division) • Released **August 1998**
52 cards in set • **IDENTIFIER: Dark vertical wood-grain borders**

You will need **6** nine-pocket pages to store this set. (3 doubled up)

Set (52 cards)	69.00
Combo Display Box	62.50
Booster Display Box	67.50
Starter Deck	8.10
Booster Pack	1.80

- Starter decks contain 60 cards; combo displays contain 36 boosters and 6 starters
- Booster packs contain 8 cards; booster displays contain 72 boosters

It's been four months since Toturi disappeared, and the strain on the empire is starting to show. While open warfare is still the exception, it's only a matter of time before hostilities begin. The monks of Rokugan once again enter secular affairs, reflected by their new stronghold, **The House of Tao**. The player begins with an elemental ring in play but must discard all rings if the player plays a Shadowlands card. — **Michael Greenholdt**

Card name	Type	Rarity	Price
☐ Abandoning the Fortunes	Event	C	0.50
☐ Aramoro	Pers	C	0.80
☐ Ascension of the Mantis	Event	R	4.00
☐ Banish all Shadows	Actn	R	5.50
☐ Empty Words	Actn	C	0.50
☐ Enlightened Tutor	Follo	C	0.50
☐ Face of Ninube	Actn	C	0.20
☐ Fields of the Morning Sun	Regn	C	0.20
☐ Finding the Balance	Event	R	2.50
☐ Fortified Infantry	Follo	C	0.20
☐ Grasp the Earth Dragon	Actn	R	2.50
☐ Hitomi Kazaq	Pers	C	0.20
☐ Hitomi Kokujin	Pers	R	3.00
☐ Hold This Ground	Actn	C	0.20

Card name	Type	Rarity	Price		Card name	Type	Rarity	Price		Card name	Type	Rarity	Price
☐ Hoshi Eisai	Pers	C	0.20		☐ Not While I Breathe	Actn	C	0.50		☐ The Dark Sanctuary	Holdg	R	2.50
☐ Hoshi Masaru	Pers	C	0.20		☐ Otaku Meadows	Regn	C	0.20		☐ The Efforts of the Clan	Actn	R	2.50
☐ Ikoma Ryozo	Pers	R	2.50		☐ Restoring the Doji Treasury	Event	C	0.80		☐ The Grey Crane	Pers	R	3.00
☐ Kamoko's Charge	Actn	C	0.80		☐ Retired Wasp General	Holdg	C	0.20		☐ The House of Tao	Stghld	X	2.50
☐ Kobune Crew	Follo	C	0.50		☐ River Bridge of Kaiu	Holdg	C	0.20		☐ The New Way	Item	C	0.20
☐ Kuni Utagu	Pers	C	0.20		☐ Ryoku	Actn	C	0.50		☐ The Touch of the Lands	Actn	C	0.20
☐ Kuni Yori	Pers	R	4.30		☐ Sacrifices for Our Future	Event	C	0.80		☐ Togashi Hoshi	Pers	X	4.80
☐ Let Your Spirit Guide You	Actn	R	4.00		☐ Seppun Kossori	Pers	C	0.20		☐ Torii Shrine	Holdg	C	0.50
☐ Mercy Shrouds the Earth	Actn	C	0.25		☐ Shiryo no Kisada	Follo	R	2.50		☐ Trusted Council	Actn	C	0.80
☐ Monastery	Holdg	R	4.50		☐ Stand or Run	Actn	C	0.50		☐ Tsuchi-do	Actn	C	0.20
☐ Moto Soro	Pers	C	0.80		☐ Suzume Yugoki	Pers	C	0.50		☐ Tsuruchi's Arrow	Item	R	3.50
☐ Move to the Bushes	Actn	R	2.50		☐ Takao's Jingasa	Item	C	0.20		☐ Umi Amaterasu	Regn	C	0.20
☐ Mushin	Actn	C	0.20							☐ Where Shinsei Stood	Actn	C	0.20

RARITY KEY C = Common U = Uncommon R = Rare VR = Very Rare UR = Ultra Rare F = Foil card X = Fixed/standard in all decks

Legend of the Five Rings •
The Hidden Emperor: Episode 4
Wizards of the Coast (Five Rings Division) • Released **September 1998**

52 cards in set • **IDENTIFIER: Dark vertical wood-grain borders**

- Starter decks contain 60 cards; combo displays contain 36 boosters and 6 starters
- Booster packs contain 8 cards; booster displays contain 72 boosters

A year of chaos has passed since Toturi disappeared and open war now rages. The Lion clan marches on the Crab while proposing peace. The Unicorn clan has assumed police authority over the empire, killing those they deem traitors, while the newly risen Mantis clan war with the Cranes. The Chancellor holds the Imperial court, but the slightest sign of weakness could cause the collapse of the court.

Reflecting its newly acquired police powers, the Unicorn clan gains a new stronghold, **The Otaku Palaces**. Magistrates can join the clan for one less gold and once per turn, the Unicorn player can straighten all of the cards in a cavalry unit when attacked. This is looked on as the best Unicorn stronghold in the game. — *Michael Greenholdt*

> **You will need**
> **6**
> nine-pocket pages to store this set.
> (3 doubled up)

Set (52 cards)		**69.00**
Combo Display Box		**49.00**
Booster Display Box		**50.00**
Starter Deck		**8.10**
Booster Pack		**1.80**

Card name	Type	Rarity	Price
☐ A Dark Foretelling	Event	R	2.50
☐ Akodo Hall of Ancestors	Holdg	R	2.50
☐ Arrows from the Ranks	Actn	C	0.20
☐ Asako Hosigeru	Pers	C	0.20
☐ Bayushi Technique	Actn	U	1.00
☐ Desperate Wager	Actn	R	2.50
☐ Die Tsuchi	Item	C	0.20
☐ Doji Shizue	Pers	R	3.00
☐ Doom of the Brotherhood	Event	U	1.00

Card name	Type	Rarity	Price
☐ Festival of the River of Stars	Event	R	2.50
☐ Flattery	Actn	C	0.20
☐ Funeral Pyre	Holdg	C	0.20
☐ Goblin War Truck	Item	U	1.00
☐ Goldsmith	Holdg	C	0.20
☐ Hida Yasamura	Pers	R	2.50
☐ Hitomi Technique	Actn	U	1.00
☐ Ide Ashijun	Pers	C	0.20
☐ Itako	Pers	U	1.00
☐ Kitsuki Evidence	Actn	C	0.20
☐ Kitsuki Kaagi	Pers	U	1.50
☐ Kitsuki Kaagi's Journal	Item	U	1.00
☐ Kolat Geisha	Follo	C	0.20
☐ Lay of the Land	Actn	R	2.50
☐ Lessons from Kuro	Item	R	2.50

Card name	Type	Rarity	Price
☐ Malekish	Pers	C	0.25
☐ Matsu Ketsui	Pers	R	2.50
☐ Mujina Tricks	Actn	C	0.20
☐ Ninja Saboteur	Follo	R	2.50
☐ Noble Sacrifice	Actn	R	3.00
☐ Oni no Gekido	Pers	U	1.50
☐ Otaku Kamoko	Pers	X	4.80
☐ Otaku Xieng Chi	Pers	U	1.00
☐ Philosopher	Holdg	C	0.20
☐ Plains of Foul Tears	Regn	C	0.20
☐ Refuge of the Three Sisters	Regn	U	1.00
☐ Ronin Dojo	Holdg	C	0.20
☐ Ryosei	Pers	U	1.00
☐ Shinjo Groomsman	Holdg	R	3.00
☐ Shinjo Technique	Actn	U	1.00

Card name	Type	Rarity	Price
☐ Shinjo Tsuburo	Pers	R	2.50
☐ Shiryo no Moto	Follo	R	2.50
☐ Takuan Technique	Actn	U	1.00
☐ The Boundless Depths of Water	Kiho	U	1.50
☐ The Great Feast	Event	U	1.50
☐ The Iuchi Plains	Regn	C	0.20
☐ The Kami Watch Over Me	Spell	U	1.50
☐ The Naga Akasha	Actn	R	2.50
☐ The Otaku Palaces	Stghld	X	1.50
☐ The Power of Incompleteness	Kiho	C	0.20
☐ The Price of Failure	Actn	C	0.20
☐ Walk Through the Mountains	Kiho	C	0.20
☐ War Dogs	Follo	R	3.50

Legend of the Five Rings •
The Hidden Emperor: Episode 5
Wizards of the Coast (Five Rings Division) • Released **November 1998**

52 cards in set • **IDENTIFIER: Dark vertical wood-grain borders**

- Starter decks contain 60 cards; combo displays contain 36 boosters and 6 starters
- Booster packs contain 8 cards; booster displays contain 72 boosters

Chaos mounts as the great clans move to secure their interests, threatened by the vacant throne. Unnoticed, two people begin their quest to find the emperor. A new champion arises in the Dragon clan, Hitomi, who calls for peace and extends a message of goodwill to all those who would join her in a quest for enlightenment.

The Mantis, whose leader Yoritomo is making a bid for the throne, receive a new stronghold, **Kyuden Yoritomo**. The stronghold counts as a port, but is not affected by cards affecting ports. Several holdings and other cards are modified by the number of ports in play and the stronghold has an unprecedented province strength of 8, but that's about it. — *Michael Greenholdt*

> **You will need**
> **6**
> nine-pocket pages to store this set.
> (3 doubled up)

Set (52 cards)		**69.00**
Combo Display Box		**49.00**
Booster Display Box		**50.00**
Starter Deck		**8.10**
Booster Pack		**1.80**

Card name	Type	Rarity	Price
☐ A Stone Circle	Holdg	C	0.20
☐ Akodo Dagger	Item	R	4.00
☐ Basher's Club	Item	U	0.80
☐ Battle Hardened	Actn	R	2.50
☐ Bayushi Aramasu	Pers	U	1.30
☐ Bayushi Yojiro	Pers	U	0.80
☐ Blade of Secrets	Item	R	2.50
☐ Corrupted Jade Sliver	Item	U	0.80
☐ Doom of Toturi	Event	R	2.50

Card name	Type	Rarity	Price
☐ Drawing Out the Darkness	Actn	U	0.80
☐ Facing Your Devils	Actn	C	0.20
☐ Flaming Ground	Holdg	U	0.80
☐ Hida Technique	Actn	U	1.00
☐ Hitomi Kobai	Pers	R	5.00
☐ Holy Home Village	Regn	C	0.25
☐ Imperial Edicts	Actn	C	0.20
☐ Island Barricades	Holdg	U	0.80
☐ Island of Silk	Regn	R	3.50
☐ Iuchi Karasu	Pers	U	0.80
☐ Jama Suru	Pers	C	0.20
☐ Kouta	Pers	C	0.20
☐ Kuni Mokuma's Guide	Item	R	3.50
☐ Kyuden Yoritomo	Stghld	X	3.00
☐ Large Farm	Holdg	C	0.60

Card name	Type	Rarity	Price
☐ March of the Alliance	Event	R	2.50
☐ Matsu Hiroru	Pers	R	2.50
☐ Matsu Turi	Pers	U	0.80
☐ Naga Pearl Guardian	Follo	C	0.20
☐ "One Life, One Destiny"	Actn	R	3.50
☐ Out of the Shadows	Actn	C	0.20
☐ Ratling Hordes	Actn	C	0.20
☐ Ratling Villages	Regn	C	0.20
☐ Salt the Earth	Actn	C	0.20
☐ Sanzo (exp)	Pers	R	3.50
☐ Shiba Technique	Actn	U	1.00
☐ Shiryo no Nodatai	Follo	R	2.50
☐ Shiryo no Osano-Wo	Follo	R	2.50
☐ Shrine of Osano-Wo	Holdg	R	4.30

Card name	Type	Rarity	Price
☐ Silk Works	Holdg	C	0.25
☐ Takao	Pers	U	0.80
☐ Take the Initiative	Actn	C	0.20
☐ The Great Silence	Actn	U	1.00
☐ The Otaku Stables Burn	Event	R	2.50
☐ The Way of Death	Actn	U	1.00
☐ Unrequited Love	Actn	C	0.20
☐ Wasp Archers	Follo	R	4.50
☐ When Dark Winds Howl	Event	U	0.80
☐ Yoritomo (exp 2)	Pers	X	5.30
☐ Yoritomo Nodoteki	Pers	C	0.20
☐ Yoritomo Technique	Actn	U	1.00
☐ Yoritomo Yukue	Pers	R	2.50
☐ Zokujin	Follo	C	0.20

RARITY KEY C = Common U = Uncommon R = Rare VR = Very Rare UR = Ultra Rare F = Foil card X = Fixed/standard in all decks

Legend of the Five Rings •
The Hidden Emperor: Episode 6

Wizards of the Coast (Five Rings Division) • Released **December 1998**

52 cards in set • **IDENTIFIER: Dark vertical wood-grain borders**

Set (52 cards)	69.00
Combo Display Box	49.00
Booster Display Box	50.00
Starter Deck	8.10
Booster Pack	1.80

• Starter decks contain 60 cards; combo displays contain 36 boosters and 6 starters
• Booster packs contain 8 cards; booster displays contain 72 boosters

It has been a year and a half since the emperor disappeared, and six months since Yoritomo took Beiden Pass and fortified it. The Crane and Unicorn have allied in a desperate bid to oust Yoritomo from his fortress. Daidoji Uji, the leader of the Crane's Daidoji family, has split from the clan and has marched north to stop Mantis troops from allying with the Lion, leading the Crane to the brink of a civil war.

To reflect the possible split in the Crane clan, the Crane received a new stronghold, **The Iron Fortress of the Daidoji**. The honor requirement for Daidoji personalities is ignored, but any non-samurai or shugenja cost three more gold. The stronghold also allows the Crane player to duel an opposing personality in battle by bowing the stronghold. — *Michael Greenholdt*

Card name	Type	Rarity	Price
1			
☐ Ancestral Duty	Event	R	3.30
☐ 700 Soldier Plain	Regn	U	0.80
☐ A Pure Stroke	Actn	R	3.50
☐ Battle Maidens	Follo	C	0.20
☐ Big Stink	Regn	U	0.80
☐ Blackened Claws	Item	C	0.20
☐ Chi Projection	Actn	C	0.20
☐ Cleansing Bell	Holdg	C	0.20
☐ Coordinated Strike	Actn	R	3.50
☐ Cultists	Follo	C	0.20
2			
☐ Daidoji Karasu	Pers	R	3.50
☐ Daidoji Osen	Pers	C	0.20
☐ Death of the Ki-Rin	Event	R	2.50
☐ Dharma Technique	Actn	U	1.00
☐ Doji Kuwanan	Pers	X	5.00
☐ Doom of the Alliance	Event	U	0.80
☐ Eshru	Pers	R	2.50
☐ Haunted	Follo	U	1.00
☐ Hida O Ushi	Pers	R	4.30

Card name	Type	Rarity	Price
3			
☐ Hitomi Reju	Pers	U	0.90
☐ Hoshi Wayan	Pers	C	0.20
☐ Ikoma Technique	Actn	U	1.00
☐ Isawa Norikazu	Pers	R	3.50
☐ Kachiko's Fan	Item	U	0.80
☐ Kakita Ariteko	Pers	C	0.20
☐ Kakita Technique	Actn	U	1.00
☐ Kansen	Follo	U	1.00
☐ Legacy of the Dark One	Actn	U	1.00
4			
☐ Makashi	Pers	U	1.00
☐ Makoto	Actn	R	2.50

Card name	Type	Rarity	Price
☐ Oni No Akuma	Pers	U	0.80
☐ Otaku Steed	Item	C	0.20
☐ Prophet's Tower	Holdg	U	0.80
☐ Ratling Nest	Holdg	C	0.20
☐ Ratling Spy	Actn	C	0.20
☐ Shiryo no Tetsuya	Follo	R	2.50
☐ Shosuro Chian	Pers	C	0.20
5			
☐ Silk Farm	Holdg	C	0.20
☐ Speak with the Voices of the Dead	Actn	R	2.50
☐ Storms of War	Actn	C	0.20
☐ Teach the Mountain	Actn	R	3.30
☐ The Iron Cranes	Actn	C	0.20

Card name	Type	Rarity	Price
☐ The Iron Fortress of the Daidoji	Stghld	X	3.00
☐ The Silk Road	Regn	C	0.20
☐ Togashi's Daisho	Item	R	4.00
☐ Tohaku	Pers	C	0.15
6			
☐ Trapping Tactics	Actn	C	0.20
☐ Tutor	Holdg	R	3.50
☐ Unrelenting Terror	Actn	R	2.50
☐ Valley of the Two Generals	Regn	C	2.50
☐ War in the Shadowlands	Event	R	2.50
☐ Way of Shadow	Actn	U	1.00
☐ Wisdom Gained	Event	U	0.80

Legend of the Five Rings •
The Dark Journey Home

Wizards of the Coast (Five Rings Division) • Released **January 1999**

154 cards in set • **IDENTIFIER: Dark vertical wood-grain borders**

• Starter decks contain 60 cards; starter displays contain 12 starters
• Booster packs contain 8 cards; booster displays contain 72 boosters

As winter falls, the news of Toturi's return rocks the empire. The Mantis have been driven northward and now make a bid for the empty lands of the Phoenix clan. The Agasha family of the Dragons oppose the Mantis, as the Agasha are torn between loyalty to Hitomi and fear of her "new beginning." The Crane clan's division continues as the Daidoji family wars against the new Emerald Champion, while the rest of the clan continue to hound the Mantis.

With *Dark Journey Home*, Five Rings resumed the normal expansion pattern and abandoned the Rolling Thunder system. Three new strongholds are included. The Phoenix's **Eternal Halls of the Shiba** makes all human shugenja in the player's deck aligned to the Phoenix clan and allows the Phoenix player to return a cast Kiho to his or her hand by discarding a card. The Phoenix would dominate the tournament scene for some time after this release, and so the stronghold received errata.

The legendary Ninja made its debut as a major power in *Dark Journey Home* with a stronghold, **The Dark Path of Shadow**. Non-personality ninja cards, such as followers, cost two less gold and the Ninja can send all attackers home if its total chi is less than 10. There had been ninja cards and personalities since the **Imperial Edition**, but now they had a home.

The Palace of Otosan-Uchi was the new stronghold for Toturi's Army, and reflected their new position as an Imperial force. Imperial cards cost two less gold, and once per turn, the Toturi player could attach a follower reducing the cost by the personality's Force. In addition, the player started with the Imperial Favor. — *Michael Greenholdt*

Set (154 cards)	115.00
Starter Display Box	59.50
Booster Display Box	64.00
Starter Deck	7.00
Booster Pack	1.50

Card name	Type	Rarity	Price
1			
☐ A Dark Moment	Actn	C	0.25
☐ A Glimpse Beyond	Actn	R	5.00
☐ A Kolat Revealed	Event	U	1.00
☐ Agasha Gennai	Pers	R	5.00
☐ Agasha Kusabi	Pers	U	1.00
☐ Aka Mizu-umi	Regn	U	1.00
☐ Ambition	Item	R	5.00
☐ Arrow of the Four Winds	Actn	R	4.50
☐ Arrowroot Tattoo	Actn	U	1.00
2			
☐ Asahina Dorai	Pers	C	0.25
☐ Ashigaru Archers	Follo	C	0.25
☐ Ashigaru Spearmen	Follo	C	0.25
☐ Assassins	Holdg	C	0.25

Card name	Type	Rarity	Price
☐ Balash	Pers	U	1.00
☐ Battlements	Holdg	C	0.25
☐ Bayushi Areru	Pers	U	1.00
☐ Bells of the Dead	Regn	C	0.25
☐ Black Finger River	Regn	C	0.25
3			
☐ Blessings of Isawa	Event	U	1.00
☐ Blood Arrows of Yajinden	Item	C	0.25

Card name	Type	Rarity	Price
☐ Bonsai Garden	Holdg	C	0.25
☐ Centipede Tattoo	Actn	U	1.00
☐ Chochu	Pers	C	0.25
☐ Clay Horse	Item	C	0.25
☐ Contemplation	Actn	C	0.25
☐ Contested Holdg	Actn	R	5.00
☐ Crane Tattoo	Actn	U	1.00

Card name	Type	Rarity	Price
4			
☐ Creating the Monkey Clan	Event	U	1.00
☐ Crystal Nagamaki	Item	U	1.00
☐ Daidoji Rekai	Pers	R	5.00
☐ Dangai	Pers	C	0.25
☐ "Deeds, not Words"	Actn	U	1.00
☐ Disgraced	Actn	U	1.00

RARITY KEY C = Common U = Uncommon R = Rare VR = Very Rare UR = Ultra Rare F = Foil card X = Fixed/standard in all decks

234 • *SCRYE Collectible Card Game Checklist and Price Guide*

Card name	Type	Rarity	Price
Disobedience	Actn	R	5.00
Dragon Tattoo	Actn	U	1.00
Dragon's Tail Star	Event	U	1.00
Dragonfly Tattoo	Actn	U	1.00
Emergence of the Masters	Spell	C	0.25
Eternal Halls of the Shiba	Stghld	X	3.00
Falling Star Strike	Kiho	C	0.25
Final Haiku	Actn	R	5.00
Firebird Falls	Regn	R	5.00
Full Moon Tattoo	Actn	U	1.00
Glimpse of Kage	Event	U	1.00
Goju Adorai	Pers	X	5.00
Golden Sun Plain	Regn	R	5.00
Heavy Ground	Actn	C	0.25
Held Terrain	Actn	R	4.50
Heroic Opportunities	Actn	R	5.00
Hida Rohiteki	Pers	C	0.25
Hidden Blade	Actn	R	5.00
Hiruma Osuno	Pers	R	5.00
Hitomi Dajan	Pers	C	0.25
Hitomi Iyojin	Pers	U	1.00
Hitomi Juppun	Pers	U	1.00
Hitomi Nakuso	Pers	U	1.00
Hoshi Maseru	Pers	U	1.00
Hunted	Actn	U	1.00
Ikoma Gunjin	Pers	U	1.00
Isawa Hochiu	Pers	U	1.00
Isawa Kaede	Pers	R	5.00
Isawa Taeruko	Pers	C	0.25
Kage	Pers	R	5.50
Kharma	Actn	U	1.00

Card name	Type	Rarity	Price
Kitsu Sanako	Pers	U	1.00
Kitsuki Iyekao	Holdg	U	1.00
Kitsuki's Coin	Item	R	5.00
Kolat Agent	Holdg	C	0.30
Kolat Recruiter	Actn	R	5.00
Let Him Escape	Actn	R	5.00
Lion Tattoo	Actn	U	1.00
Lion's Pride	Follo	R	5.00
Lord Moon's Blood	Item	R	5.00
Loss of face	Actn	C	0.30
Magic Mud	Actn	U	1.00
Maho-Tsukai	Follo	R	4.50
Mamoru	Pers	U	1.00
Mantis House Guard	Follo	U	1.00
Mantle of the Jade Champion	Item	R	5.00
Master of Destiny	Kiho	R	5.00
Matsu Toki	Pers	U	1.00
Moshi Hito	Pers	C	0.25
Moto Amadare	Pers	C	0.25
Moto Fanatics	Follo	U	1.00
Mountain Tattoo	Actn	U	1.00
Nightmares of Iuchiban	Actn	R	5.00
Ninja Infiltrator	Pers	R	5.00
Ninja Questioner	Pers	U	1.00
Ninja Shadowalker	Pers	C	0.25
Ninja Tricks	Actn	U	1.00
Ninube Ogoku	Pers	C	0.25
Osari Plains	Regn	C	0.25
Phoenix Tattoo	Actn	U	1.00
Pillaging	Actn	C	0.25
Plain of Desperate Evil	Spell	U	1.00

Card name	Type	Rarity	Price
Poison Dartgun	Item	C	0.25
Pride	Actn	C	0.25
Proud Words	Actn	C	0.25
Purity of Spirit	Kiho	C	0.25
Ratling Scout	Follo	C	0.25
Rebuilding the Temples	Event	R	4.50
Retired Advisor	Holdg	R	4.50
Rise from the Ashes	Spell	U	1.00
River of the Dark Moon	Holdg	R	4.50
River of the Last Stand	Regn	R	4.50
Ropp'tch'tch	Pers	R	5.00
Seppun Toshiken	Pers	R	5.00
Shadow Brand	Actn	C	0.25
Shadowlands Contagion	Actn	R	4.50
Shadowlands Marsh	Regn	U	1.00
Shiba Gensui	Pers	C	0.25
Shiba Tetsu	Pers	U	1.00
Shiba Tsukune	Pers	X	4.00
Shinko Kamiko	Pers	R	5.00
Shiryo no Goju	Follo	R	5.00
Shiryo no Kuni	Follo	R	5.00
Shiryo no Yurei	Follo	R	5.00
Shosuro	Pers	R	5.00
Shotai	Pers	R	5.00
Siege	Actn	C	0.30
Slidge	Pers	C	0.25
Smoke and Mirrors	Actn	U	1.00
Stagnation	Kiho	C	0.25
Stand Together	Actn	R	4.50
Steep Terrain	Actn	C	0.25
Strike of Silent Waters	Kiho	U	1.00
Tattooed	Actn	U	1.00
Tausha	Pers	C	0.25

Card name	Type	Rarity	Price
Test of the Jade Champion	Event	R	4.50
The Agasha Join the Phoenix	Event	R	4.50
The Agasha Libraries	Holdg	C	0.25
The Age of Man	Event	U	1.00
The Daimyo's Command	Actn	R	4.50
The Dark Path of Shadow	Stghld	X	1.50
The Edge of the Shinomen Forest	Holdg	C	0.25
The Palace of Otosan Uchi	Stghld	X	1.50
The Path Not Taken	Kiho	R	4.50
The Wave Men	Event	R	4.50
Threat	Actn	C	0.25
Tiger Tattoo	Actn	U	1.00
Toku	Pers	R	5.00
Toritaka Genzo	Pers	R	5.00
Toturi the First	Pers	X	4.00
Toturi's Return	Event	U	1.00
Touch the Lands	Kiho	C	0.25
Treacherous Pass	Regn	C	0.25
Tsuruchi	Pers	R	5.00
Twilight Mountains	Regn	R	4.50
Twisting Ravine	Actn	C	0.30
Tzurui	Pers	U	1.00
Virtuous Heart	Spell	C	0.25
Warstained Fields	Regn	C	0.25
Winds and Fortunes	Actn	U	1.00
Yotsu Seou	Pers	C	0.25

Legend of the Five Rings • Honor Bound

Wizards of the Coast (Five Rings Division) • Released **June 1999**

173 cards in set • **IDENTIFIER: Black borders with dark red whorls**

> You will need
> **20**
> nine-pocket pages to store this set.
> (10 doubled up)

- Starter decks contain 60 cards; starter displays contain 12 starters
- Booster packs contain 11 cards; booster displays contain 48 boosters

The shadow that has fallen over Toturi continues to plague him and the empire. Shadowland armies strike against the Lion and Crab in an attempt to enter the empire, the Crane civil war goes on, and shadows that kill the dead roam the land.

Three new strongholds were released in **Honor Bound**. **Sepulcher of Bone** is a new Shadowland stronghold that makes undead decks more powerful. **The Towers of the Yogo** allow the Scorpion player to bow a personality in battle to bow an opposing personality or follower. **The Citadel of the Hiruma** allows the Crab to double a personality's force when defending, although the personality dies at the end of the turn.

A new way of winning is also introduced with the **Master of Five** event. If a player has the five elemental oracles (air, earth, fire, water and void) when this event resolves, the player wins. Thereafter, any player who takes one of each of the five elemental actions in his or her turn wins at the beginning of that player's next turn. Master of Five brought the number of different victory conditions up to eight.

This set also introduces a new type of card, the sensei. A player may start with one sensei card in play before the game begins. They give the player an advantage and/or modify the player's stronghold. — *Michael Greenholdt*

Set (173 cards)	**110.00**
Combo Display Box	**72.00**
Booster Display Box	**75.75**
Starter Deck	**8.10**
Booster Pack	**2.20**

Card name	Type	Rarity	Price
A New Teacher	Actn	R	4.50
Abresax	Pers	R	5.00
Akodo's Leadership	Holdg	R	4.80
Amnesia	Spell	U	1.00
An Empty Victory	Event	R	4.50

Card name	Type	Rarity	Price
Ancient Sage	Holdg	C	0.25
Asako Provinces	Regn	C	0.25
Awakening Shakoki Dogu	Actn	C	0.25
Bandit Attack	Actn	C	0.25
Bandit Raids	Event	U	1.00
Barricades	Holdg	C	0.25
Bayushi Eiyo	Pers	C	0.25
Bayushi Goshiu (exp2)	Pers	R	5.00
Bayushi Hisa (exp2)	Pers	R	5.00
Bayushi Kachiko (exp3)	Pers	X	5.00

Card name	Type	Rarity	Price
Benefices of the Emperor	Event	R	4.50
Black Pearl	Item	R	5.00
Bleeding the Elements	Actn	U	1.00
Blessing upon the Lands	Kiho	C	0.25
Bloodstrike	Kiho	R	5.00
Builders	Holdg	C	0.25
Burn It Down	Actn	C	0.25
Command Staff	Follo	U	1.00
Curse of the Rot Within	Item	C	0.25
Daidoji Kedamono	Pers	C	0.25

Card name	Type	Rarity	Price
Dairya (exp2)	Pers	R	5.50
Dark Bargains	Actn	U	1.00
Darkness Beyond Darkness	Actn	U	1.00
Dashmar (exp2)	Pers	R	5.00
Deep Forest	Holdg	U	1.00
Doji Adoka	Pers	C	0.25
Dragon's Claw Katana	Item	U	1.00
Elite Pikeman	Follo	C	0.25
Energy Terrain	Actn	C	0.25
Face of the Nameless	Actn	R	4.50

RARITY KEY C = Common   U = Uncommon   R = Rare   VR = Very Rare   UR = Ultra Rare   F = Foil card   X = Fixed/standard in all decks

SCRYE Collectible Card Game Checklist and Price Guide • **235**

Card name	Type	Rarity	Price
Famine	Event	U	1.00
5			
Fear's Bane	Spell	C	0.25
Feydn Rafiq	Pers	C	0.25
Firestorm Legion	Follo	R	4.50
Flameseeker	Pers	C	0.25
Flashing Blades	Actn	U	1.00
Force of Honor	Actn	C	0.25
Forest Fire	Actn	C	0.25
Forgotten Lesson	Actn	R	4.50
Fortress of the Dragonfly	Holdg	C	0.25
6			
Ghedai	Pers	C	0.25
Gift of the Maker	Spell	U	1.00
Gohei's Daisho	Item	R	5.00
Goju Stalkers	Follo	U	1.00
Hasame (exp)	Pers	R	5.00
Hassuk's Golden Bow	Item	C	0.25
Hida O-Ushi (exp3)	Pers	X	3.50
High Morale	Actn	C	0.25
Hiruma Yugure	Pers	C	0.25
7			
Hiruma Zunguri	Pers	C	0.25
Hitomi Kagetora	Pers	U	1.00
Hitomi's Defeat	Kiho	U	1.00
Hizuka (exp)	Pers	R	5.00
Hojyn	Pers	U	1.00
Hoshi Wayan (exp)	Pers	R	5.00
Hoshi's Challenge	Event	U	1.00
Ikoma Ken'o	Pers	U	1.00
Isawa Norikazu (exp2)	Pers	R	5.00
8			
Isawa Tanayama (exp2)	Pers	R	5.00
Iuchi Shahai (exp)	Pers	R	5.00
Kabuki Theater Troupe	Holdg	U	1.00
Kaede Snsei	Snsei	R	5.50
Kaimetsu-Uo's Ono	Item	C	0.25
Kakita Kaiten	Pers	U	1.00
Kakita's "The Sword"	Holdg	R	5.00
Kenshinzen	Follo	R	4.50
Kisada Sensei	Snsei	U	1.00
9			

Card name	Type	Rarity	Price
Kitsu Osen (exp Daidoji Osen)	Pers	R	5.00
Kolat Apprentice	Follo	R	5.00
Kolat Duplicate	Event	R	4.50
Kuni Yasashii	Pers	C	0.25
Kuni Yori (exp3)	Pers	X	5.00
Lord Moon's Bones	Item	R	5.00
Lord Moon's Smile	Spell	R	4.50
Low Morale	Actn	C	0.25
Mantis Fleet	Item	C	0.25
10			
Master of Bushido	Holdg	U	1.00
Matsu Morishigi	Pers	C	0.25
Mercenaries	Follo	C	0.25
Mirumoto Uso	Pers	C	0.25
Mirumoto's "Niten"	Item	U	1.00
Moment of Brilliance	Actn	U	1.00
Monopoly	Event	U	1.00
Monsoon Season	Event	U	1.00
11			
Moto Tsume (exp2)	Pers	R	6.00
Moto Yesugai	Pers	U	1.00
Mountains of the Phoenix	Actn	C	0.25
Ninja Mimic	Pers	U	1.00
Ninja Mystic (exp2)	Pers	R	5.00
Nishiko	Pers	R	5.00
Nunchaku	Item	U	1.00
Oh-chi'chek	Follo	C	0.25
Okura is Released	Actn	U	1.00
One Life, One Action	Actn	C	0.25
12			
Oni no Okura	Pers	U	1.00
Oseuth	Pers	U	1.00
Otomo Yayu	Pers	C	0.25
Palace of the Emerald Champion	Regn	R	4.50
Pincer Attack	Actn	C	0.25
Porthungluin	Pers	U	1.00
Pressure	Actn	C	0.25
Return of the Kami	Event	R	5.00

Card name	Type	Rarity	Price
Rik'tik'tichek	Pers	U	1.00
13			
Rodrigo	Pers	C	0.25
Rugged Ground	Actn	C	0.25
Sabotage	Actn	U	1.00
Saigorei	Pers	U	1.00
Seppun Nakao	Pers	U	1.00
Sepulcher of Bone	Stghld	X	2.00
Shiba Ningen	Pers	U	1.00
Shiba Raigen	Pers	C	0.25
Shinjo's Judgment	Actn	R	4.50
14			
Shoju Sensei	Snsei	R	5.00
Shosuro Taberu (exp)	Pers	R	5.00
Shosuro Taushui	Pers	C	0.25
Shurin Storms	Kiho	R	4.50
Silence	Pers	U	1.00
Silent War	Actn	U	1.00
Slaughter of the Imperial Court	Event	R	4.50
Soshi Jujun	Pers	C	0.25
Soshi Tomyako	Pers	C	0.30
15			
Souls of the Betrayed	Actn	R	4.50
Stain upon the Soul	Kiho	U	1.00
Stars Scatter	Kiho	U	1.00
Stress	Actn	U	1.00
Sword of the Emerald Champion	Item	R	5.00
Swordmaster	Actn	C	0.25
Temple of Blood	Holdg	C	0.25
Temple to Shinsei	Holdg	U	1.00
The Citadel of the Hiruma	Stghld	X	2.00
16			
The Emperor's Lands	Regn	U	1.00
The Emperor's Left Hand	Actn	U	1.00
The Emperor's Right Hand	Actn	U	1.00
The Empty Pyre	Actn	U	1.00

Card name	Type	Rarity	Price
The Enemy of My Enemy	Event	U	1.00
The False Tao	Item	R	5.00
The Head of My Enemy	Actn	R	4.50
The Kaiu Forge	Holdg	U	1.00
The Master of Five	Event	R	4.50
17			
The Towers of the Yogo	Stghld	X	2.50
The Unquiet Grave of Hida Amoro	Regn	C	0.25
The Wind's Truth	Kiho	C	0.25
Thy Master's Will	Spell	R	4.50
Tiger's Teeth	Actn	U	1.00
Torn from the Past	Event	U	1.00
Toshimoko Sensei	Snsei	R	5.00
Toturi Sensei	Snsei	R	5.00
Treachery and Deceit	Actn	R	5.00
18			
Trenches	Holdg	C	0.25
Tribute to Your House	Actn	R	4.50
Uji Snsei	Snsei	U	1.00
Uragirimono	Pers	C	0.25
Victory at Hiruma Castle	Actn	R	4.50
Volcano	Regn	R	4.50
Volturnum	Regn	R	4.50
Way of the Void	Actn	R	5.00
Whispers of Twilight	Spell	C	0.25
19			
Whistling Arrows	Actn	U	1.00
Wide Terrain	Actn	U	1.00
Will of the Emperor	Actn	U	1.00
Within Your Soul	Kiho	U	1.00
Yakamo's Funeral	Event	R	4.50
Yokatsu Sensei	Snsei	R	5.00
Yokuni Sensei	Snsei	U	1.00
Yoritomo Denkyu	Pers	C	0.25
Yoritomo Komori	Pers	U	1.00
20			
Yoritomo Masasue	Pers	R	5.00
Yoshun	Pers	C	0.25

Kukanchi

Legend of the Five Rings • Ambition's Debt

Wizards of the Coast (Five Rings Division) • Released **November 1999**

181 cards in set • **IDENTIFIER: Dark borders with barely visible whorls; no © date**

- Starter decks contain 60 cards; starter displays contain 12 starters
- Booster packs contain 11 cards; booster displays contain 48 boosters

Powerful magic forces are at work. The imperial capitol is besieged by several of the clans, while Toturi I is a pawn of the ninja, the agents of the Shadow. Another secret organization, the Kolat, plot the destruction of all of those involved.

Many of the Fate cards in this expansion deal with dueling or special Ninja actions. Another method of winning is introduced with the event **Death of Onnotangu**, which indicates that if a player has **The Obsidian Hand**, **Lord Moon's Blood**, and **Lord Moon's Bones** attached to any version of Mirumoto Hitomi, the player wins.

Three new strongholds are released as well. **The Kitsu Tombs** allow a Lion player to ignore negative effects from playing oni by bowing a shugenja. **The New Akasha** allows the Naga to bring Crab personalities into play for two less gold and give a force and chi bonus to Crab and Naga personalities when an army contains both types. **The Spawning Ground** is the new Shadowlands stronghold, which gives a force and chi bonus to all of the player's goblins, ogres, oni, and trolls. — *Michael Greenholdt*

You will need **21** nine-pocket pages to store this set. (11 doubled up)

Set (181 cards)	150.00
Combo Display Box	90.00
Booster Display Box	93.50
Starter Deck	9.00
Booster Pack	2.50

Card name	Type	Rarity	Price
1			
27 Days of Darkness	Event	U	1.00
A Chance Meeting	Actn	U	1.00
A Plague of Locusts	Event	U	1.00
Akodo Fields	Regn	U	1.00
Armorer	Holdg	C	0.25

Card name	Type	Rarity	Price
Asahina Dorai	Pers	R	4.00
Asahina Tsukiyoka	Pers	C	0.20
Ashigaru Levies	Actn	C	0.20
Ashlim	Pers	R	4.00
2			
Assault on Otosan Uchi	Event	U	1.00
At'tok'tuk Sen	Snsei	R	4.00
Baby Ki-Rin	Item	R	4.00

Card name	Type	Rarity	Price
Bad Health	Actn	U	1.00
Bakeneko	Pers	C	0.25
Barracks	Holdg	C	0.25
Bayushi Aramasu	Pers	R	5.00
Bayushi Urei	Pers	C	0.20
Be the Mountain	Kiho	C	0.25
3			
Bitter Destiny	Event	R	4.00

Card name	Type	Rarity	Price
Bloodspeaker's Deal	Actn	U	1.00
Bokken	Item	C	0.25
Botsumoku	Pers	C	0.20
Calm Winds	Event	U	1.00
Carpenter Pass	Regn	U	1.00
Celestial Gift	Spell	U	1.00
Concede Defeat	Actn	C	0.20

RARITY KEY **C** = Common **U** = Uncommon **R** = Rare **VR** = Very Rare **UR** = Ultra Rare **F** = Foil card **X** = Fixed/standard in all decks

Card name	Type	Rarity	Price
☐ Costly Alliance	Actn	C	0.25
☐ Critical Duel	Actn	C	0.20
☐ Dangerous Terrain	Actn	C	0.25
☐ Dark Energies	Actn	R	4.00
☐ Darkness Within	Actn	C	0.25
☐ Dead Eyes	Actn	U	1.00
☐ Death of Onnotangu	Event	R	4.00
☐ Declaration of War	Event	U	1.00
☐ Defensible Position	Actn	C	0.20
☐ Den of Spies	Holdg	U	1.00
☐ Deny the Emperor	Actn	R	4.00
☐ Dirty Politics	Actn	R	4.00
☐ Dragon's Strength	Event	U	1.00
☐ Dying Effort	Actn	R	4.00
☐ Entrench	Actn	U	1.00
☐ Exile's Road	Regn	R	4.00
☐ Fallen Lion Fortress	Event	R	4.00
☐ Family Shrine	Holdg	C	0.25
☐ Finding the Harmony	Kiho	U	1.00
☐ Footsteps of Madness	Actn	R	4.00
☐ Forethought	Actn	R	4.00
☐ Forgotten Lands	Regn	R	4.00
☐ Fortune's Turn	Spell	C	0.25
☐ "Forward, March!"	Actn	C	0.25
☐ Goju Utsuei	Pers	C	0.25
☐ Greensnake	Follo	C	0.25
☐ Gyosho	Pers	U	1.00
☐ Hate's Heart	Kiho	R	4.00
☐ Hida Amoro	Pers	R	5.00
☐ Hida Yakamo	Pers	X	4.10
☐ Hirariko	Pers	R	4.00
☐ Hiruma Snsei	Snsei	R	4.00
☐ Honor's Cost	Actn	U	1.00
☐ "Honor, Bah!"	Actn	R	4.00
☐ Hoshi Kumonosu	Pers	C	0.25
☐ Ichiro Kihongo	Pers	U	1.00
☐ Ikoma Ryozo	Pers	X	3.60
☐ Ikoma Snsei	Snsei	U	1.00
☐ Ikoma Tsanuri	Pers	R	5.00
☐ Ikoma Yosei	Pers	U	1.00
☐ Ikudaiu	Pers	R	4.00
☐ Imperial Highway	Regn	C	0.25
☐ Imperial Summons	Actn	C	0.25
☐ In Search of Future	Actn	C	0.20
☐ Infantry Square	Actn	C	0.25
☐ Isawa Kaede	Pers	R	4.00
☐ Isawa Mitori	Pers	U	1.00
☐ Issut	Pers	C	0.20

Card name	Type	Rarity	Price
☐ Judgment of Toshiken	Actn	U	1.00
☐ Kage	Pers	R	6.00
☐ Kage Sen	Snsei	U	1.00
☐ Kakita Aihara	Pers	U	1.00
☐ Kakita Teacher	Actn	U	1.00
☐ Kitsune Diro	Pers	R	5.00
☐ Kolat Bookkeeping	Actn	U	1.00
☐ Kukanchi	Pers	C	0.20
☐ Kuro Snsei	Snsei	R	4.00
☐ Kuro's Fire	Spell	R	4.00
☐ Large Shrine	Holdg	C	0.25
☐ Lookout Mountain	Regn	C	0.25
☐ Mantis Marine Troops	Follo	R	4.00
☐ Matsu Daoquan	Pers	C	0.25
☐ Matsu Mori	Pers	C	0.20
☐ Moetechi	Pers	C	0.20
☐ Morikage	Regn	R	4.00
☐ Moto Soro	Pers	R	4.00
☐ Naga Spies	Follo	U	1.00
☐ Nio Snsei	Snsei	R	5.00
☐ Norikazu Snsei	Snsei	R	4.00
☐ Nue	Pers	C	0.20
☐ Oath of Courage	Actn	U	1.00
☐ Obake	Follo	U	1.00
☐ Olyah	Pers	U	1.00
☐ Ono	Item	U	1.00
☐ Orschat	Pers	C	0.20
☐ Otomo Shishi	Pers	C	0.25
☐ Overconfidence	Actn	C	0.20
☐ Oyuchi	Pers	U	1.00
☐ Parade Ground Practice	Actn	C	0.25
☐ Poisoned	Actn	C	0.25
☐ Poisoned Honor	Actn	C	0.25
☐ Ratling Archers	Follo	U	1.00
☐ Ravine	Actn	C	0.20
☐ Recovering the True Tao	Event	U	1.00
☐ Roshungi	Pers	U	1.00
☐ Ruantek	Pers	C	0.25
☐ Savaged Fields	Regn	U	1.00
☐ Scorpion Courtiers	Follo	R	4.00
☐ Seppun Mashita	Pers	C	0.20
☐ Shadow Beast	Pers	C	0.20
☐ Shakoki Dogu	Item	R	4.00
☐ Shiba Kyukyo	Pers	C	0.20
☐ Shiba Odoshi	Pers	U	1.00
☐ Shinjo Shono	Pers	C	0.20
☐ Shipyard	Holdg	C	0.25
☐ Shiryo no Kaze	Follo	R	4.00
☐ Shiryo no Takuan	Follo	R	4.00

Card name	Type	Rarity	Price
☐ Shiryo no Yasuki	Follo	R	4.00
☐ Shiyokai	Pers	U	1.00
☐ Shooting Star Strike	Kiho	U	1.00
☐ Shosuro Dojo	Holdg	R	4.00
☐ Shosuro Yudoka	Pers	U	1.00
☐ Shugenja Students	Follo	U	1.00
☐ Sorrow's Path	Regn	C	0.25
☐ Storm of Arrows	Actn	C	0.25
☐ Strong Words	Actn	U	1.00
☐ Suana	Pers	R	4.00
☐ Summoning the Moon	Actn	R	4.00
☐ Tactical Maneuvers	Actn	U	1.00
☐ Tangen's Lies	Holdg	R	4.00
☐ Temple Guard	Follo	U	1.00
☐ The Damned	Follo	C	0.25
☐ The Gates to Jigoku	Regn	R	4.00
☐ The Guardian of Rift	Holdg	R	4.00
☐ The Ikoma Histories	Holdg	U	1.00
☐ The Kitsu Tombs	Stghld	X	3.00
☐ The Legion of 2,000	Follo	R	4.00
☐ The New Akasha	Stghld	X	3.00
☐ The Path of Akodo	Holdg	U	1.00
☐ The Prophecies	Actn	R	4.00
☐ The River around Hill	Kiho	C	0.25
☐ The Spawning Ground	Stghld	X	3.00
☐ The Sun in Shadow	Actn	U	1.00
☐ The Swifter Arrow	Actn	U	1.00
☐ The Way of the Zokujin	Actn	C	0.25
☐ Three Star Sky	Actn	C	0.25

Card name	Type	Rarity	Price
☐ Togashi Hoshi	Pers	R	5.00
☐ Togashi Shinseken	Pers	U	1.00
☐ Tohaku	Pers	R	4.00
☐ Toichi	Pers	U	1.00
☐ Tonbo Toryu	Pers	C	0.20
☐ Toturi's Treatise	Item	U	1.00
☐ Touching the Void	Actn	U	1.00
☐ Troll Raiders	Event	U	1.00
☐ Tsuruchi's Legion	Follo	R	4.00
☐ Undead Cavalry	Follo	C	0.25
☐ Unmaker's Shadow	Event	R	4.00
☐ Unsure	Actn	C	0.25
☐ Void's Path	Spell	R	4.00
☐ War Weary	Event	U	1.00
☐ Woodland Reserves	Actn	C	0.20
☐ Yabanjin Horsemen	Follo	C	0.25
☐ Yasuki Nokatsu	Pers	R	4.00
☐ Yasuki Taka	Pers	R	5.00
☐ Yodin Snsei	Snsei	R	4.00
☐ Yokai no Junzo	Follo	X	3.00
☐ Yokatsu	Pers	R	5.00
☐ Yori Snsei	Snsei	R	4.00
☐ Yoritomo Chujitsu	Pers	U	1.00
☐ Yoritomo Furikae	Pers	C	0.20
☐ Yoritomo Sen	Snsei	U	1.00
☐ Yoshi	Pers	R	5.00
☐ Yoshi Snsei	Snsei	U	1.00
☐ Yoshi's Last Stand	Regn	C	0.25
☐ Yosuchi	Pers	C	0.20

Identifying *Legend* sets

Look at a pile of **Legend of the Five Rings** cards from different sets and you may think there's no way to tell which card's from which set. Not so, although the card identifier the manufacturer chose is so subtle as to be nearly useless.

Hold a **Legend of the Five Rings** card face up under a light. Check the card border — the actual black outline circling the entire card. It's dark, but it probably has blotches or streaks.

That's the identifier. Cards with green spots that look like water damage are from **Fire and Shadow**, *etc.*

On second thought, you may be better off just looking them up on our list...

RARITY KEY **C** = Common **U** = Uncommon **R** = Rare **VR** = Very Rare **UR** = Ultra Rare **F** = Foil card **X** = Fixed/standard in all decks

Legend of the Five Rings • Fire & Shadow

Wizards of the Coast (Five Rings Division) • Released **March 2000**

187 cards in set • **IDENTIFIER: Black with dark green whorls**

- Starter decks contain 60 cards; starter displays contain 12 starters
- Booster packs contain 11 cards; booster displays contain 48 boosters

The dead are returning to the land of the living while the elements go mad in Rokugan. The emperor is dying in the ruins of the palace, all the while the Shadow within him growing. With the Jade Throne empty, the clans battle for it.

Three new strongholds are included. **The Dragon's Iron Mountain** negates attacking cavalry's maneuver advantage. **Kyuden Kitsune** is a stronghold for the Fox clan allowing the player to purchase Fox cards for two less gold and to count non-Mantis Yoritomo's Alliance personalities as part of the Fox clan. **The Temple of the Crow** allows a player to discard his or her current sensei card to bring in a new one from the deck. — *Michael Greenholdt*

> You will need **21** nine-pocket pages to store this set. (11 doubled up)

	Price
Set (187 cards)	145.00
Combo Display Box	90.00
Booster Display Box	100.00
Starter Deck	9.00
Booster Pack	2.80

Card name	Type	Rarity	Price
Agasha Fujita	Pers	U	1.00
Akui Cliffs	Regn	C	0.15
Ambush Strategist	Follo	C	0.15
Ancestors Possess the Living	Actn	R	4.00
Asako Kaushen	Pers	U	1.00
Asako Sagoten	Pers	C	0.15
Ascendance	Actn	R	4.00
Ashalan Sandsmith	Holdg	C	0.15
Assuming the Championship	Actn	R	4.00
Balyezn Rafiq	Pers	U	1.00
Bayushi Aramasu (Exp 2)	Pers	R	5.00
Bayushi Aramoro (Exp 2)	Pers	R	5.00
Bayushi Muraisan	Pers	C	0.15
Blade of Kaiu	Item	U	1.00
Blood and Darkness	Spell	R	4.00
Bloodstained Rage	Actn	C	0.15
Bridge to Jigoku	Regn	R	4.00
Burden of the Word	Item	R	4.00
Campsite	Regn	U	1.00
Capturing the Soul	Spell	R	4.00
Chasing the Shadow	Actn	R	4.00
Come One at a Time	Actn	C	0.15
Command of the Kami	Actn	U	1.00
Corrupted Dojo	Holdg	C	0.15
Crab Cavalry	Follo	R	4.00
Crisis in Command	Actn	C	0.15
Cross-Clan Wedding	Event	R	4.00
Crow Tattoo	Actn	U	1.00
Dakosho	Pers	C	0.15
Dangerous Choices	Actn	R	4.00
Dark Energies Run Red	Event	U	1.00
Decoy	Follo	R	4.00
Defeat the Reserves	Actn	C	0.15
Den of Mujina	Holdg	U	1.00
Divided Loyalties	Actn	R	4.00
Djahab	Pers	U	1.00
Doji Chomei (Exp) (Crane)	Pers	R	5.00
Doji Chomei (Exp) (Yoritomi)	Pers	R	4.50
Doji Jiro	Pers	C	0.15
Elemental Attunement	Actn	R	4.00
Emerald Magistrates	Follo	R	4.00

Card name	Type	Rarity	Price
Emissary of the Ivory Kingdoms	Event	U	1.00
Eternal Darkness	Spell	U	1.00
Far from the Empire	Event	R	5.50
Fate's Merciful Hand	Kiho	U	1.00
Fearful Presence	Actn	U	1.00
Fearsome Strength	Actn	U	1.00
Feeding on Flesh	Kiho	R	4.00
Fields of the Dead	Regn	C	0.15
Final Words	Event	R	4.00
Gift of the Emperor Victory	Actn	R	5.00
Grandfather's Jaw	Item	C	0.15
Hanoshi	Pers	C	0.15
Hantei Sensei	Sensei	U	1.00
Harsh Lessons	Actn	C	0.15
Heart of the Damned	Kiho	C	0.15
Heimin Village	Regn	U	1.00
Hida Nezu	Pers	U	1.00
Hida Rohiteki (Exp)	Pers	R	5.00
Hidden from the Empire	Actn	C	0.15
Hitomi Bujun (Exp)	Pers	R	5.00
Honorable Sacrifice	Event	U	1.00
House of Contracts	Holdg	C	0.15
Hsi Tsu	Pers	C	0.15
Hummingbird Tattoo	Actn	U	1.00
Hurricane Initiates	Follo	C	0.15
Ide Buodin	Pers	C	0.15
Ikoma Gunjin (Exp)	Pers	R	5.00
Imperial Surveyor	Holdg	C	0.15
Iron Mountain	Stghld	X	0.50
Isawa Toiko	Pers	C	0.15
Jian	Pers	U	1.00
Journey to Otosan Uchi	Actn	C	0.15
Kachiko Calls to Thunder	Event	U	1.00
Kachiko's Promises	Event	R	4.50
Kaiu Endo	Pers	C	0.15
Kaiu Siege Engine	Follo	C	0.15
Kakita Ichiro (Exp)	Pers	R	4.50
Kitsu	Pers	R	5.50
Kitsu Gongsun	Pers	U	1.00
Kitsu Huiyuan	Pers	R	4.50
Kitsu Snsei	Snsei	R	5.00
Kitsuki Mizuochi	Pers	U	1.00
Kitsune Shudo	Pers	C	0.15
Kitsune Tsuke	Pers	C	0.15
Know the Evil	Kiho	U	1.00
Kolat Assistance	Actn	R	4.50
Kumo (Exp)	Pers	R	4.50
Kyuden Kitsune	Stghld	X	0.50
Last Refuge	Actn	U	1.00
Last Words	Actn	C	0.15

Card name	Type	Rarity	Price
Mack'uk	Pers	C	0.15
Maintain Balance	Kiho	C	0.15
Mantis Isles	Regn	U	1.00
Mara (Exp)	Pers	R	4.50
Masamune Katana	Item	C	0.15
Matsu Suhada	Pers	C	0.15
Mine Cave-In	Event	U	1.00
Mirumoto Songui	Pers	C	0.15
Mirumoto Sukune (Exp)	Pers	X	0.50
Mirumoto Watanubo	Pers	U	1.00
Mirumoto Yuyake	Pers	C	0.15
Mismanaged Troops	Actn	U	1.00
Miya Yuritogen	Pers	U	1.00
Miya's Sasumata	Spell	R	4.50
Mohai	Pers	U	1.00
Moto Notu	Pers	R	4.50
Moto Toyotomi	Pers	U	1.00
My Life for Yours	Actn	U	1.00
Never Yield	Actn	U	1.00
New Beginnings	Actn	U	1.00
Ninja Shadow-Walker (Exp)	Pers	R	5.00
Ninja-to	Item	R	4.50
Of One Mind	Actn	U	1.00
One Last Battle	Actn	R	4.50
Oni no Megada	Follo	C	0.15
Oni no Okura (Exp)	Pers	R	4.50
Oracle of Thunder	Holdg	R	4.50
Oskuda	Pers	U	1.00
Otaku Xieng Chi (Exp)	Pers	R	4.50
Owned	Actn	U	1.00
Pearl Magic	Kiho	C	0.15
Pestilence	Actn	C	0.15
Pitfall	Holdg	C	0.15
Primal Rage	Actn	U	1.00
Proud Heritage	Kiho	C	0.15
Provision Storehouse	Holdg	C	0.15
Purusha	Pers	C	0.15
Ratling Youth	Follo	U	1.00
Relief	Actn	C	0.15
Remember What You Have Seen	Actn	C	0.15
Remember Your Oath	Actn	R	4.50
Return of Myth	Event	U	1.00
Return of the True Champion	Event	U	1.00
Rights of the Challenged	Actn	C	0.15
Road of Dust	Regn	U	1.00
Run for Your Life	Actn	C	0.15
Ryosei (Exp 2)	Pers	X	0.50
Ryoshun's First Gift	Spell	U	1.00
Sanctified Blade	Item	U	1.00
Sanjuro	Pers	C	0.15
Satsume Snsei	Snsei	U	1.00

Card name	Type	Rarity	Price
Scrolls of Norikazu	Item	R	4.50
Seppun Snsei	Snsei	U	1.00
Seppun Toshiken (Exp)	Pers	R	4.50
Sharpest Blade	Actn	R	4.50
Shasyahkar	Pers	R	4.50
Shi-Khan Wastes	Regn	U	1.00
Shiba Gensui (Exp)	Pers	R	4.50
Shifting Ground	Actn	U	1.00
Shinobi Corruption	Spell	U	1.00
Shipping Lanes	Holdg	C	0.15
Shokansuru	Holdg	U	1.00
Shosuro Technique	Actn	R	5.00
Shrine of the Dragon Champion	Holdg	C	0.15
Single Combat	Actn	C	0.15
Skeletal Elite	Follo	R	4.50
Skirmisher's Pike	Item	C	0.15
Slaughter of the Land	Actn	U	1.00
Sleeping Lake	Regn	R	4.50
Soul's Sacrifice	Actn	U	1.00
Spectral Guide	Follo	U	1.00
Spirit of the Bright Eye	Actn	U	1.00
Spreading the Shadow	Actn	U	1.00
Stepping between the Cracks	Kiho	R	4.50
Sword of the Sun	Item	R	4.50
Taka Snsei	Snsei	R	4.00
Takao (Exp 2)	Pers	X	2.30
Tattoo of the Night Sky	Actn	U	1.00
Tax Collector	Holdg	C	0.10
Temple of Divine Influence	Holdg	R	4.50
Temples of the Crow	Stghld	X	0.50
The Dark Moto Snsei	Snsei	R	4.50
Third Mask of Iuchiban	Item	R	4.50
Togashi Jodome (Exp) (Dragon)	Pers	R	4.50
Togashi Jodome (Exp) (Monk)	Pers	R	4.50
Toritaka Kitao	Pers	C	0.15
Tricked	Actn	C	0.20
Triumphant Victory	Event	R	4.50
Tsuruchi (Exp 2)	Pers	R	5.00
Ujina Tomo	Pers	C	0.15
Venerable Stature	Actn	C	0.15
White Shore Plain	Actn	U	1.00
Yabanjin Sorcerer	Follo	U	1.00
Yoritomo Okan	Pers	U	1.00
Yoritomo Refuses the Throne	Event	U	1.00
Yotsu Sabieru	Pers	U	1.00

RARITY KEY C = Common U = Uncommon R = Rare VR = Very Rare UR = Ultra Rare F = Foil card X = Fixed/standard in all decks

Legend of the Five Rings •
Soul of the Empire

Wizards of the Coast (Five Rings division) • Released **July 2000**

187 cards in set • **IDENTIFIER: Dark green whorls in border, lighter than** *Fire and Shadow*

- Starter decks contain 60 cards; starter displays contain 12 starters
- Booster packs contain 11 cards; booster displays contain 48 boosters

   The armies of Rokugan march on the shadowed city of Volturnum to defeat Goju, the Shadow, and seal the gates to the lands of the dead. Dead heroes join the battle, including Toturi, who has been purified of the Shadow's taint by death.

   Soul sees the return of Dragons (the beasts, not the clan) to the Jade environment, as well as token cards, used to mark the gain of followers from various cards. The new stronghold **Kosaten Shiro** allows the Crane player to purchase gold- and honor-producing holdings for one less gold, allowing the Cranes to bring in one gold holding for free. — *Michael Greenholdt*

You will need **21** nine-pocket pages to store this set. *(11 doubled up)*

Set (187 cards)		**142.00**
Starter Display Box		**95.00**
Booster Display Box		**100.00**
Starter Deck		**8.80**
Booster Pack		**2.80**

Card name	Type	Rarity	Price
Air Dragon Exp.	Pers	R	4.00
Amoro's Honor	Kiho	U	0.50
Armor of the Ebony Samurai	Item	U	0.50
Armor of the Monkey Clan	Item	U	0.50
Armor of the Twilight Mountains	Item	C	0.10
Armored Steeds	Follo	C	0.25
Asahina Archers	Follo	R	4.00
Ashida	Pers	C	0.10
Bayushi Aramoro Exp. 2 Aramoro	Pers	R	4.00
Bayushi Goshiu Exp. 3	Pers	R	5.00
Bayushi Hisa Exp. 3	Pers	U	0.50
Bayushi Ikita	Pers	C	0.10
Bayushi Meharu	Pers	C	0.10
Bhakarash	Pers	C	0.10
Bide Your Time	Actn	C	0.10
Blessing of the Celestial Heavens	Actn	C	0.10
Blood Rite	Spell	R	4.00
Bloodstained Forest	Spell	U	0.50
Bokatu	Pers	C	0.10
Brothers in Blood	Kiho	R	4.00
Burning the Ashes	Spell	C	0.10
Cavalry Screen	Actn	C	0.10
Chains of Jigoku	Spell	U	0.50
City of Empty Dreams	Actn	C	0.10
City of Living Flames	Actn	C	0.10
City of Loyalty	Actn	C	0.10
City of Tears	Actn	C	0.10
City of White Clouds	Actn	C	0.10
Cornering Maneuver	Actn	C	0.10
Daidoji Rekai Exp. 2	Pers	R	4.00
Daidoji Technique	Actn	U	0.50
Dairya Exp. 3	Pers	R	4.00
Dark Plains	Regn	U	0.50
Deadly Fright	Actn	C	0.10
Death-Seeker Technique	Actn	U	0.50
Defenders of the Wall	Follo	R	3.50
Devastation	Actn	C	0.10
Doji Benku	Pers	C	0.10
Doji Kuwanan Exp. 3	Pers	X	2.00
Draft Notice	Item	U	0.50
Dragon of Fire Exp.	Pers	R	4.00
Dragon's Tooth	Item	R	4.00
Earth Dragon Exp.	Pers	R	4.00
Elder Goju	Pers	C	0.10
Empty Crevasse	Hold	C	0.10
Eyes Shall Not See	Spell	C	0.10
Fearful Soul	Actn	C	0.10
Fields of Courage	Regn	U	0.50
Fields of the Moon	Regn	U	0.50
Firefly Tattoo	Actn	U	0.50
For My Clan	Actn	U	0.50
Fortified Ground	Actn	U	0.50
From Broken Ground	Kiho	C	0.10
Fulfilling My Duty	Actn	C	0.10
Fully Armed	Actn	C	0.10
Ginawa Exp. 3	Pers	R	4.50
Glory Grounds	Regn	C	0.10
Goju Adorai Exp.	Pers	R	4.00
Half-Beat Strike	Actn	R	4.00
Heavy Barde	Item	R	3.50
Hida Tsuru Exp.	Pers	R	4.00
Hiruma Abun	Pers	C	0.10
Hitomi Iyojin Exp.	Pers	R	4.00
Hoshi Eisai Exp.	Pers	U	0.50
Hoshi Sensei	Sensei	R	4.00
Hoshi Wayan Exp. 2	Pers	R	4.00
Hoturi Sensei	Sensei	R	4.00
Hurlspit Goblins	Follo	U	0.50
Ide Tadaji Exp.	Pers	U	0.50
Imperial Wedding	Event	U	0.50
Increased Production	Actn	C	0.10
Into the Heavens	Event	U	0.50
Iron Mountain	Stghld	X	2.00
Isawa Tomo Exp. 2	Pers	U	0.50
Jal-Pur Raiders	Follo	U	0.50
Jama Suru Exp.	Pers	U	0.50
Kaede's Tears	Kiho	R	3.50
Kage Exp. 5	Pers	R	4.50
Kakita Kyruko	Pers	C	0.10
Kakita Yoshi Exp. 3	Pers	U	0.50
Karmic Link	Kiho	U	0.50
Katana of the Twilight Mountains	Item	C	0.10
Keda	Pers	C	0.10
Kingdom of Ghosts	Actn	C	0.10
Kitsu Motso Exp. 2	Pers	R	4.00
Kolat Chambers	Hold	U	0.50
Kolat Courtiers	Event	U	0.50
Kosaten Shiro	Stghld	X	2.00
Kyoso no Oni Exp. 2	Pers	R	4.00
Kyuden Kitsune	Stghld	X	2.00
Lessons of Honor	Actn	U	0.50
Lost Souls	Follo	R	3.50
Magistrate's Blade	Item	R	4.00
Master Courtier	Hold	U	0.80
Mat'tck	Pers	C	0.10
Matsu Agetoki Exp. 2	Pers	R	4.00
Matsu Domotai	Pers	C	0.10
Mirumoto Taki Exp.	Pers	U	0.50
Moon and Sun	Event	U	0.50
Moto Chargers	Follo	C	0.10
Moto Gaheris Exp.	Pers	X	2.00
Moto Tsugi	Pers	C	0.10
Mukami Exp. 2	Pers	R	4.00
Naga Vipers	Follo	U	0.50
Naka Kuro Exp. 2	Pers	R	4.00
Nature Provides	Kiho	C	0.10
Ninja Mystic Exp. 3	Pers	R	4.00
Ninja Shadow-Walker Exp.	Pers	U	0.50
Nori Farm	Hold	C	0.10
Norikesh	Pers	C	0.10
Northern Provinces of the Moto	Stghld	X	2.00
O-Ushi Sensei	Sensei	R	4.00
O-Ushi's Hammer	Item	R	4.00
Oni no Byoki	Follo	U	0.50
Oni no Gorusei	Pers	C	0.10
Oni no Okura Exp. 2	Pers	U	0.50
Oni Podling	Follo	R	3.50
Orochi Tattoo	Actn	U	0.50
Otaku Kamoko Exp. 4	Pers	R	4.00
Otaku Sahijir	Pers	C	0.10
Otomo Sensei	Sensei	R	4.00
Otomo Towers	Regn	U	0.50
Overwhelm	Actn	C	0.20
Passage of Time	Actn	U	0.80
Past Glories	Spell	U	0.50
Political Favors	Hold	C	0.10
Public Ridicule	Event	U	0.50
Question without an Answer	Kiho	R	4.00
Rank Hath Privilege	Actn	R	3.50
Rebirth of the Dark Daughter	Actn	U	0.50
Regional Travel Papers	Item	C	0.10
Restoring the Age of Myth	Spell	U	0.50
Return of Thunder	Event	U	0.50
Riding Yari	Item	U	0.50
Ruined Earth	Spell	R	3.50
Ryoshun's Last Words	Kiho	C	0.10
Seppun Toshiken Exp. 2	Pers	R	4.50
Shadow Assassins	Follo	C	0.10
Shadowed Wastes	Actn	U	0.50
Shiba Kiku	Pers	C	0.10
Shiba Tsukune Exp. 3	Pers	R	4.00
Shinjo Hanari Exp. 2	Pers	R	4.00
Shirasu Sensei	Sensei	R	4.00
Shiryo no Chiroku	Follo	R	4.00
Shiryo no Gohei	Follo	R	4.00
Shiryo no Hantei	Follo	R	4.00
Shiryo no Kunliu	Follo	R	4.00
Shrine of the Dead	Holdg	C	0.10
Shrines of the Emperor	Holdg	U	0.50
Sniping	Actn	U	0.80
Something Worth Dying For	Actn	U	0.50
Son of the Clan	Actn	C	0.10
Soul of the Empire	Event	U	0.50
Spy Network	Hold	C	0.10
Steel and Iron	Actn	R	5.00
Strike from Behind	Actn	R	3.50
Suana Exp. 2	Pers	R	4.00
Swamp Marsh	Actn	U	0.80
Temples of the Crow	Stghld	X	2.00
Temples of the New Tao	Regn	C	0.10
Tetsuya Sensei	Sensei	R	4.00
The Emperor Returns	Actn	U	0.50
The Grey Crane Exp. 3	Pers	R	4.00
The Sun Returns	Actn	R	4.50
Thunder Dragon Exp.	Pers	R	4.00
Time of Destiny	Actn	U	0.50
Togashi Mitsu Exp. 2	Pers	R	4.00
Togashi Senai	Pers	C	0.10
Toku Exp. 3	Pers	U	0.50
Toritaka Mariko	Pers	C	0.10
Toturi the First Exp. 4	Pers	X	2.00
Traveling Caravan	Hold	C	0.10
Tsunami Legion	Follo	U	0.50
Vigilant Keep of the Monkey	Stghld	X	2.00
Void Dragon Exp.	Pers	R	4.50
Void Guard	Follo	U	0.50
Water Dragon Exp.	Pers	R	4.00
When Spirits Walked	Event	U	0.50
Where the Sun Walked	Actn	R	4.00
Winter Court	Event	U	0.50
Yaro	Pers	C	0.10
Yasuki Nokatsu Exp. 2	Pers	R	4.00
Yodin Sensei	Sensei	R	4.00
Yoritomo Exp. 3	Pers	R	4.00
Yoritomo Furikae Exp.	Pers	U	0.50
Yotsu Shoku	Pers	C	0.10
Z'orr'tek	Pers	C	0.10

RARITY KEY C = Common U = Uncommon R = Rare VR = Very Rare UR = Ultra Rare F = Foil card X = Fixed/standard in all decks

Legend of the Five Rings • *Spirit Wars*

Wizards of the Coast (Five Rings division) • Released **November 2000**
197 cards in set • **IDENTIFIER: Red ovals in border, artist names on bottom**

- Starter decks contain 60 cards; starter displays contain 12 starters
- Booster packs contain 11 cards; booster displays contain 48 boosters

This is an unusual expansion in that it bridges the storyline from the **Hidden Emperor** series to the announced **Gold Edition** storyline. While many of the cards will be Gold-legal, the Spirit stronghold will not, as the Gold timeline takes place some 30 years later, and the Spirit Wars have long since resolved.

Three strongholds are included. **The Shrine of the Spirits** is the most interesting, as it starts with six provinces, but has a zero province strength. — *Michael Greenholdt*

SCRYE NOTES: *Due to a misprint,* Devastation of Beiden Pass *was printed both as a Rare and as a Common.*

You will need **22** nine-pocket pages to store this set. (11 doubled up)

	Price
Set (197 cards)	140.00
Starter Display Box	96.00
Booster Display Box	100.00
Starter Deck	8.80
Booster Pack	2.80

Card name	Type	Rarity	Price
1			
Akodo Ginawa Exp. 4 Ginawa	Pers	R	4.00
Akodo Ijiasu	Pers	U	0.50
Akodo Quehao	Pers	R	3.00
Akodo Sensei	Sensei	U	0.80
Amaterasu's Furnace	Regn	U	0.50
Ancestral Dictate	Action	U	0.50
Ancestral Protection	Action	R	3.00
Ancient Knowledge	Kiho	U	0.50
Arriving at the Imperial Gates	Action	U	0.50
2			
Asako Misao	Pers	U	0.50
Asako Riders	Follo	R	3.00
Back Banner	Item	C	0.15
Battle at White Shore Plain	Action	U	0.50
Battle of Drowned Honor	Action	C	0.15
Battle of Quiet Winds	Action	C	0.15
Battle of Shallow Waters	Action	C	0.15
Bayushi Baku Exp.	Pers	R	4.50
Bayushi Paneki	Pers	C	0.15
3			
Bayushi Yojiro Exp. 2	Pers	R	3.00
Beginning and End	Kiho	R	3.00
Birth of the Anvil	Event	R	3.00
Birth of the Sword	Event	R	3.00
Birth of the Wolf	Event	R	3.00
Bitter	Item	R	3.50
Bronze Lantern	Item	R	3.00
Call the Spirit	Spell	R	3.00
Chou-Sin	Pers	C	0.15
4			
Clay Soldiers	Follo	C	0.15
Cliffs of Golden Tears	Regn	U	0.50
Crab Tattoo	Action	R	3.00
Cursed Ground	Regn	U	0.50
Daidoji Hachi	Pers	C	0.15
Dark Secrets	Action	C	0.15
Devastation of Beiden Pass	Spell	C+R*	0.20
Doji Kurohito	Pers	U	0.50
Doji Meihu	Pers	U	0.50
5			
Doji Reju Exp. 2 Hitomi Reju	Pers	R	4.00
Dragon Dancers	Holdg	C	0.15
Earthquake at Otosan Uchi	Event	R	3.00
East Wall of Otosan Uchi	Holdg	R	3.50

Card name	Type	Rarity	Price
Emperor's Favor	Event	R	3.50
Emperor's Under-Hand	Holdg	R	3.50
Empress's Guard	Follo	R	3.50
Fall of the Alliance	Event	R	3.00
Fall on Your Knees	Action	R	3.00
6			
Fallen Ground	Action	U	0.50
Fallen Legion	Follo	U	0.50
Fields of Darkness	Regn	C	0.15
Fields of the Sun	Regn	R	3.00
Giuniko	Pers	C	0.15
Great Crater	Regn	R	3.00
Guard the House	Action	C	0.15
Hantei XVI	Pers	X	2.00
Hesitation	Action	U	0.50
7			
Hida Hio	Pers	C	0.15
Hida Kuon	Pers	C	0.15
Hida Kuroda	Pers	C	0.15
Hida Sukune Exp. 2	Pers	R	3.00
Hida Tsuneo	Pers	R	3.50
Hitomi's Glare	Kiho	R	3.00
Honorable	Item	R	3.50
Ide Gokun	Pers	U	0.50
Ikoma Tsai	Pers	C	0.15
8			
Imperial Census	Event	R	3.00
Infantry Charge	Action	C	0.15
Inkyo	Follo	C	0.15
Intelligence Agent	Holdg	U	0.50
Interruption	Action	U	0.50
Iron Mempo	Item	C	0.15
Isawa Metigaru	Pers	C	0.15
Isawa Nakamuro	Pers	C	0.15
Kaiu Sensei	Sensei	R	3.50
9			
Kakita Kaiten Exp.	Pers	R	3.00
Kamoko's Constellation	Event	R	3.50
Kitsu Dejiko	Pers	C	0.15
Kitsune	Pers	C	0.15
Knowing Lands and Giving Trees	Regn	U	0.50
Kohuri	Pers	C	0.15
Kuni Utagu Exp.	Pers	R	3.00
Lady of the Forest Sensei	Sensei	U	0.80
Lalesha	Pers	C	0.15
10			
Last Gift	Action	C	0.15
Lay the Blame	Action	C	0.15
Let the Spirit Move You	Kiho	C	0.15
Lsinyuan	Pers	C	0.15
Luring Tactics	Action	U	0.50
Mara's Farewell	Action	C	0.15
Master Smith Ascends	Spell	C	0.15
Mirumoto Ukira	Pers	C	0.15
Mirumoto Uso Exp.	Pers	R	1.60
11			
Miya Dosonu	Pers	U	2.80
Miya Sensei	Sensei	U	1.80
Miya Yemi	Pers	U	2.30
Mizuichi	Pers	C	0.35

Card name	Type	Rarity	Price
Mokoto	Pers	U	0.50
Morito Exp. 2 Shinjo Morito	Pers	R	3.00
Mortal Flesh	Kiho	U	0.50
Moshi Shanegon	Pers	U	0.50
Moto Hideyo	Pers	C	0.15
12			
Moto Technique	Action	R	3.00
Moto Vordu	Pers	C	0.15
Moving the Wind	Kiho	U	0.50
Nage-yari	Item	C	0.15
New Kimono	Item	C	0.15
Nightmare	Action	U	0.50
Noble Halls of the Akodo	Spell	X	0.80
Noekam	Pers	U	0.50
North Wall of Otosan Uchi	Holdg	R	3.50
13			
Obsidian Statues	Regn	R	3.00
Old Debts	Follo	C	0.15
Oni no Fushiki	Pers	C	0.15
Oni no Yamaso	Holdg	C	0.15
Oni Spawn	Follo	C	0.15
Otomo Dsichi	Pers	R	4.00
Otomo Hoketuhime	Pers	C	0.15
Personal Sacrifice	Action	C	0.15
Poorly Placed Garden	Holdg	C	0.15
14			
Quiet Tombs	Regn	C	0.15
Ratling Scroungers	Follo	R	3.50
Return for Training	Action	U	0.50
Revealing the Bastard	Event	R	3.50
Revering the Past	Event	R	4.50
Right to Rule	Event	R	3.50
Roshungi Exp.	Pers	R	3.00
Ruin and Devastation	Spell	U	0.50
Saigorei Exp.	Pers	R	3.00
15			
Scaring the Masses	Action	U	0.50
Scholarship	Action	C	0.15
Shasyahkar Exp.	Pers	R	3.00
Shaunasea	Pers	U	0.50
Shiba Aikune	Pers	C	0.15
Shiba Ningen Exp.	Pers	R	3.50
Shinjo Shono Exp.	Pers	R	3.00
Shiryo no Ch'i	Follo	R	3.00
Shiryo no Hotei	Follo	R	3.00
16			
Shiryo no Nyoko	Follo	R	3.50
Shiryo no Rohata	Follo	R	3.00
Shiryo no Shoju	Follo	R	3.50
Shiryo no Taisa	Follo	R	3.50
Shiryo no Ujik-hai	Follo	R	3.50
Shosuro Chian Exp.	Pers	R	3.00
Shrine of the Evening Star	Holdg	R	3.00
Shrine of the Spirits	Spell	X	0.80
Shuriken	Item	C	0.15
17			
Sign of Weakness	Action	U	0.50
Signal Corps	Follo	U	0.50
Simple Huts	Holdg	C	0.15

Card name	Type	Rarity	Price
Snow Crane Tattoo	Action	R	3.50
Sodegarami	Item	C	0.15
Soshi Angai	Pers	U	0.50
Soul Sword	Spell	C	0.15
South Wall of Otosan Uchi	Holdg	R	3.50
Spirit Bells	Holdg	U	0.50
18			
Spirit Hounds	Follo	C	0.15
Star-Filled Steel	Spell	U	0.50
Sumai Match	Event	R	3.50
Suzume Roshi	Pers	C	0.15
Suzume Sensei	Sensei	U	0.80
Taikon	Pers	U	0.50
Tamori Chosai	Pers	C	0.15
Tamori Shaitung	Pers	U	0.50
Temptation	Action	C	0.15
19			
Te'tik'kir	Pers	C	0.15
Three-Stone River	Action	U	0.50
Through the Flames	Action	C	0.15
Togashi Mio	Pers	C	0.15
Torii Arch	Holdg	C	0.15
Torii Tattoo	Action	C	0.15
Towers of the Asako	Spell	X	0.80
Treaty	Item	U	0.50
Tsi Yoji	Pers	U	0.50
20			
Tsuko Sensei	Sensei	X	1.50
Tsuko's Heart	Follo	U	0.50
Tsuruchi Okame	Pers	C	0.15
Turn of Fate	Spell	U	0.50
Uidori	Pers	U	0.50
Undead Legion	Follo	U	0.50
Uona Sensei	Sensei	X	1.50
Usagi Gohei	Pers	U	0.50
Utaku Yu-Pan	Pers	U	0.50
21			
Wall of Bones	Holdg	C	0.15
War Paints	Kiho	R	3.50
Warriors of the Great Climb	Follo	U	0.50
Wasp Sensei	Sensei	U	0.80
Weapons Cache	Action	C	0.15
West Wall of Otosan Uchi	Holdg	R	3.50
Where Tsanuri Fell	Action	R	3.00
Witch Hunt	Action	U	0.50
Witch Hunter's Accusation	Action	U	0.50
22			
Wutho	Pers	U	0.50
Yakamo's Smile	Kiho	R	3.00
Yeiseo	Pers	C	0.15
Yoee'trr	Pers	U	0.50
Yokai no Mizushai	Follo	R	3.00
Yoritomo Aramasu Exp. 3 Bayushi Aramasu	Pers	R	3.50
Yoritomo Kitao	Pers	C	0.15
Yoritomo Yukue Exp.	Pers	R	3.50

RARITY KEY **C** = Common • **U** = Uncommon • **R** = Rare • **VR** = Very Rare • **UR** = Ultra Rare • **F** = Foil card • **X** = Fixed/standard in all decks

Towers of the Asako

5 / 3 / 6

Reaction: When an action targets one of your Shugenja Personalities, bow the Towers of the Asako to cancel it.

Reaction: When an action targets one of your Samurai, bow one of your Shugenja Personalities to cancel it.

Illus. Ginny McKee ©2000 Wizards. All rights reserved.

Legend of the Five Rings • Promos and specials
Alderac/Five Rings/Wizards of the Coast

Preview deck (85 cards)   97.50

Many special cards are available for *Legends of the Five Rings*. In the list below, cards marked **"F"** under **Kind** are foil cards from the Clan Wars foil series. Cards marked **"MB"** are "Mon-backed," having their clan symbols on their backs instead of the game logo.

Most cards below are marked with the initials of the sets they're associated with; all can be found on previous pages except for Imperial (here abbreviated **"IMP"**, which are cards which were available from the Imperial Assembly organization.

> You will need
> **21**
> nine-pocket pages to store this set.
> (11 doubled up)

Promos and specials

Card name	Set	Kind	Price
A Stout Heart	HB	F	2.50
A Time of Legends			3.00
Ancestral Home of the Lion			3.00
Annexation			6.00
Another Time	HB	F	2.50
As The Shadow Falls	AD	F	2.00
Asahina Tomo	HB	F	2.50
Ashlim	AD	F	2.00
Bad Karma	AD	F	9.50
Bayushi Dozan	HB	F	2.50
Beiden Pass	AD	F	2.00
Bend Like a Reed	FS	F	3.00
Blood of Midnight	FS	F	3.00
Bonds of Darkness	FS	F	3.50
Bridged Pass	AD	F	2.00
Brotherhood of Shinsei	CJ	MB	3.00
Brothers of Thunder	FS	F	2.00
Burning Your Essence	FS	F	9.00
Chi Strike	AD	F	3.00
Corrupt Gold Mines	AD	F	3.00
Corrupted Ground	FS	F	2.00
Court Jester	HB	F	2.50
Disenlightenment	FS	F	3.00
Disfavored	AD	F	2.00
Disharmony	AD	F	2.00
Doom of the Dark Lord			4.00
Dragon Sword is Broken	AD	F	2.00

Legend of the Five Rings • Heroes of Rokugan

These 27 cards were available in a binder from the Imperial Assembly organization.

Set (27 cards)   190.00

	Price
Anvil of Despair	5.00
Atarasi's Armor	5.00
Celestial Dragon	12.75
Cherry Blossom Festival	4.10
Goju Yume	9.00
Gusai	6.10
Hida Osano-Wo	5.00
Isawa Ijime	5.00
Judgement	10.50
Kakita Rensei	10.00
Land of the Dead	5.20
Matsu Hitomi	15.00
Mirumoto Tokeru	6.80
Miya Mashigai	5.00
One Virtue and Seventy Faults	3.00
Otaku Shiko	7.80
Qatol	10.50
Revealing the Ancient Wisdom	5.00
Rezan	5.30
Seppun Murayasu	4.10
Shinsei's Riddle	4.30
Shosuro Furuyari	5.00
Someisa	5.00
Spirit Legion	5.00
The First Oni	7.80
Warrens of the Nezumi	10.00
Yasuki Kaneko	5.30

Card name	Set	Kind	Price
Dragon's Teeth	HB	F	2.50
Duty of the Magistrate			3.00
Eternal Halls of the Shiba	DJH	MB	2.00
Exile			5.00
Extortion	HB	F	2.50
False Alliance	HB	F	2.50
Familiar Surroundings	HB	F	2.50
Fatal Mistake	AD	F	2.00
Fight for the Dawn			4.30
Force of Will	HB	F	2.50
Forward Patrol			5.00
Fu Leng's Steeds	FS	F	2.00
Fu Leng's Victory			4.50
Goblin Beserkers	AD	F	2.00
Goblin War Standard	FS	F	3.00
Goblin Wizard	AD	F	2.00
Heart of the Shinomen Forest	HE	MB	2.50
Hida Sukune			7.50
Hida Sukune	AD	F	2.00
Hida Tsuru	HB	F	2.50
Horsebowmen	HB	F	2.50
Imperial Ambassador			15.00
Imperial Favor (Token)			1.50
Inner Fire	AD	F	2.00
Junzo's Army	AOD	MB	3.00
Kachiko's Kiss			6.50
Kakita Ichiro	AD	F	2.00
Kemmei	FS	F	3.00
Koichi	FS	F	2.00
Kyuden Hitomi	HE	MB	2.50
Kyuden Yoritomo	HE	MB	2.50
Legion of Two Thousand foil-stamped			5.00
Lessons from the Past	AD	F	2.00
Master of the Tea Ceremony	FS	F	3.00
Master Painter	HB	F	2.50
Matsu Toshiro	HB	F	2.50
Matsu Turi			2.50
Mountain of the Seven Thunders	FS	F	3.00
Naga Abominination			8.00
Night Battle	FS	F	3.00
Ningyo	AD	F	2.00
Oni no Kamu	FS	F	4.50
Otomo Sorai			5.00
Peasant Levies	FS	F	3.00
Pikemen	AD	F	2.00
Plague Zombies	AD	F	2.00
Plains of the Emerald Champion	AD	F	2.00
Plans Within Plans	HB	F	3.00
Political Distraction	AD	F	2.00
Prophecies of Uikku			3.00
Ranbe	FS	F	3.00
Robes of Shinsei	FS	F	3.00
Sake Works	AD	F	2.00
Sanctified Ground	HB	F	2.50
Scrye			4.50
Secluded Ravine	FS	F	3.00
Seer			8.00
Seikua			5.00
Seppun Baka			5.00

Card name	Set	Kind	Price
Setsuban Festival	HB	F	2.50
Shabura	FS	F	3.00
Shadowlands Madmen	FS	F	3.00
Shadowlands Sickness	HB	F	2.50
Shagara	FS	F	3.00
Shahadet's Legion	FS	F	2.00
Shiba Katsuda	FS	F	2.00
Shiba Kyo	HB	F	2.50
Shiba Shingo	HB	F	2.50
Shinjo Sadato	FS	F	3.00
Shioda	FS	F	3.00
Skeletal Archers	HB	F	2.50
Soshi Taoshi	AD	F	2.00
Stance of the Mountain	HB	F	2.50
Stand Firm	AD	F	2.00
Stifling Wind	FS	F	2.00
Sunken City	FS	F	3.50
Suspended Terrain	AD	F	2.00
Sympathetic Energies	AD	F	2.00
Tao of the Shinsei			5.00
Tattoo Madness			10.00
The Ancestral Home of the Lion	Imp	MB	3.50
The Ancestral Home of the Lion	Eml	MB	2.00
The Ancestral House of the Lion	Jad	MB	1.50
The Ancient Halls of the Lion	Prl	MB	1.50
The Arrow Knows the Way	AD	F	5.00
The Brotherhood of Shinsei	Prl	MB	1.50
The Brotherhood of the Shensei	Jad	MB	1.50
The Celestial Pattern	FS	F	3.00
The Dark Path of Shadow	DJH	MB	2.00
The Esteemed House of the Crane	Imp	MB	3.50
The Esteemed House of the Crane	Emr	MB	2.00
The Esteemed House of the Crane	Jad	MB	1.50
The Esteemed House of the Crane	Prl	MB	1.50
The Face of Fear	FS	F	3.00
The Fair Voice of Lies	HB	F	2.50
The False Hoturi			5.50
The Farther you Fall			8.00
The Festering Pit of Fu Leng	AD	F	8.00
The Final Breath	HB	F	2.50
The Fire from Within	AD	F	2.00
The First Scroll is Opened	HB	F	2.50
The Great Walls of Kaiu	Jad	MB	2.00
The Great Walls of Kaiu	Prl	MB	1.50
The Hidden Temple of the Naga	Jad	MB	2.00
The Hidden Temples of the Naga	SL	MB	3.00
The Hidden Temples of the Naga	Prl	MB	1.50
The House of Tao	HE	MB	1.50
The Iron Fortress of the Daidoji	HE	MB	1.50

Card name	Set	Kind	Price
The Kaiu Walls	HB	F	2.50
The Monstrous War Machine of Fu Leng			3.50
The Mountain Keep of Dragon	Jad	MB	1.50
The Mountain Keep of the Dragon	Imp	MB	3.50
The Mountain Keep of the Dragon	Emr	MB	2.00
The Mountain Keep of the Dragon	Prl	MB	1.50
The Otaku Palaces	HE	MB	1.50
The Palace of Otosan Uchi	DJH	MB	2.00
The Price of War	FS	F	3.00
The Prophesies of Uikku			3.00
The Provincial Estate of the Unicorn	Imp	MB	3.50
The Provincial Estate of the Unicorn	Emr	MB	2.00
The Provincial Estate of the Unicorn	Prl	MB	1.50
The Provincial Estate of Unicorn	Jad	MB	1.50
The Ruined Fortress of the Scorpion	SL	MB	3.00
The Ruins of Isawa Castle	Jad	MB	2.00
The Ruins of Isawa Castle	Prl	MB	1.50
The Sacred Temple of the Phoenix	Imp	MB	3.50
The Sacred Temple of the Phoenix	Emr	MB	2.00
The Shadow Stronghold of Bayushi	Jad	MB	2.00
The Shadow Stronghold of the Bayushi	Prl	MB	1.50
The Shadowlands Horde	Jad	MB	2.00
The Shadowlands Horde	Prl	MB	1.50
The Tao of Shinsei			5.00
The Twelve Ronin	FS	F	3.00
The War Fortress of the Crab	Imp	MB	3.50
The War Fortress of the Crab	Emr	MB	2.00
The Yoritomo Alliance	Jad	MB	2.00
The Yoritomo Alliance	Prl	MB	1.50
Time of the Void			6.50
To Avenge Our Ancestors	AD	F	2.00
Togashi Jodome	AD	F	2.00
Tomb of Iuchiban	HB	F	2.50
Tomb of Jade	HB	F	2.50
Toturi is Drugged	HB	F	3.00
Toturi's Army	AOD	MB	6.00
Toturi's Army	Jad	MB	2.00
Toturi's Army	Prl	MB	1.50
Trade Route	FS	F	3.00
Trading Grounds	AD	F	2.00
Troops from the Woods	AD	F	2.00
Tunnel System	HB	F	2.50
War in the Heavens			2.00
Warrior Monks	FS	F	3.50
Wetlands	HB	F	2.50
Yogo Shidachi	HB	F	2.50
Yoritomo's Alliance	CJ	MB	3.00

Trading Card Game

Looney Tunes

Wizards of the Coast • Released **October 2000**

210 cards in set

- Starter decks contain 50 cards; starter displays contain 6 starters
- Booster packs contain 15 cards; booster displays contain 36 boosters

Designed by **James Ernest**

Concept	●●●○○
Gameplay	●●●○○
Card art	●●●○○
Player pool	●○○○○

Based on the famous cartoons, **Looney Tunes** cards depict characters from Bugs Bunny and Daffy Duck to lesser-known characters such as Nasty Canasta and Giovanni Jones. The game, as befits a James Ernest design, is fun and deceptively simple. Two or more players share a Movie deck, from which four scenes from famous Looney Tunes cartoons are set out in a Storyboard. Players then attempt to "steal" scenes by playing Actors whose values are lower than or equal to, but not over, the scene in question. Different card colors also affect scene stealing. Special Effect cards and additional Scenes played from a player's Personal deck can also be used to change the rules and cause merry havoc with the game. Just as in the cartoons…

Unfortunately, *Looney Tunes* as a collectible card game was DOA, intended as it was as a one-time, holiday-season release. It does, however, make a nice root-beer-and-pretzels card game for young game players. — *James Mishler*

You will need **24** nine-pocket pages to store this set. (12 doubled up)

Set (210 cards)	100.00
Starter Display Box	81.00
Booster Display Box	78.75
Starter Deck	10.25
Booster Pack	3.00

Card name	Type	Rarity	Price
1			
☐ 14-Carrot Rabbit	Scene	X	0.25
☐ A Hare Grows in Manhattan	Scene	X	0.25
☐ Abominable Snowman	Actor	R	3.00
☐ Abominable Snowstorm	SpEff	R	3.00
☐ Abracadabra	SpEff	U	0.50
☐ Acme Bat-Man's Outfit	SpEff	R	3.00
☐ A-lad-in His Lamp (4)	Scene	C	0.15
☐ A-lad-in His Lamp (5)	Scene	X	0.25
☐ Ali-Baba Bunny (2)	Scene	X	0.25
2			
☐ Ali-Baba Bunny (9)	Scene	U	0.50
☐ Aludium Q-36 Explosive Space Modulator	SpEff	U	0.50
☐ Anvil	SpEff	U	0.50
☐ Baby-Buggy Bunny	Scene	X	0.25
☐ Baby-Faced Finster	Actor	C	0.15
☐ Backgrounds, Please!	SpEff	R	3.00
☐ Ballot-Box Bunny	Scene	X	0.25
☐ Baseball Bugs	Scene	U	0.50
☐ Baton Bunny	Scene	X	0.25
3			
☐ Beaky Buzzard	Actor	R	3.00
☐ Beep, Beep	Scene	X	0.25
☐ Big Cannon	SpEff	U	0.50
☐ Big-House Bunny	Scene	X	0.25
☐ Bigger Cannon	SpEff	R	3.00
☐ Birds Anonymous (3)	Scene	C	0.15
☐ Birds Anonymous (7)	Scene	X	0.25
☐ Birthday Cake	SpEff	R	3.00
☐ Box-Office Bunny	Scene	X	0.25
4			
☐ Broomstick Bunny	Scene	X	0.25
☐ Bugs Bunny (3)	Actor	C	0.15
☐ Bugs Bunny (9)	Actor	R	3.00
☐ Bugs Bunny as Female Hunter	Actor	U	0.50
☐ Bugs Bunny, Cowboy	Actor	R	3.00
☐ Bugs Bunny Dressed as Daffy	Actor	R	3.00

Card name	Type	Rarity	Price
☐ Bugs Bunny in Bag-Dad	Actor	C	0.15
☐ Bugs Bunny, Leopold	Actor	P	5.00
☐ Bugs Bunny, Matador	Actor	U	0.50
5			
☐ Bugs Bunny, Rabbit of Seville	Actor	U	0.50
☐ Bully for Bugs	Scene	X	0.25
☐ Bye-Bye, Bluebeard	Scene	X	0.25
☐ Captain Hareblower	Scene	C	0.15
☐ Casting Call	SpEff	U	0.50
☐ Change of Scenery	SpEff	U	0.50
☐ Claude Cat	Actor	U	0.50
☐ Creative Digging	SpEff	U	0.50
☐ Daffy Duck (2)	Actor	U	0.50
6			
☐ Daffy Duck (4)	Actor	C	0.15
☐ Daffy Duck (7)	Actor	U	0.50
☐ Daffy Duck Dressed as Bugs	Actor	C	0.15
☐ Daffy Duck, Duck Dodgers (6)	Actor	R	3.00
☐ Daffy Duck, Duck Dodgers (7)	Actor	P	5.00
☐ Daffy Duck Hunt (2)	Scene	C	0.15
☐ Daffy Duck Hunt (3)	Scene	X	0.25
☐ Daffy Duck, The Scarlet Pumpernickel	Actor	C	0.15
☐ Defying Gravity	SpEff	R	3.00
7			
☐ Dehydrated Martian	SpEff	R	3.00
☐ Devil-May-Hare	Scene	X	0.25
☐ Disintegrating Pistol	SpEff	U	0.50
☐ Dog-Pounded (6)	Scene	X	0.25
☐ Dog-Pounded (8)	Scene	C	0.15
☐ Don't Give Up the Sheep (1)	Scene	X	0.25
☐ Don't Give Up the Sheep (4)	Scene	C	0.15
☐ Dripalong Daffy	Scene	X	0.25
☐ Duck Dodgers in the 24th and a Half Century	Scene	X	0.25
8			
☐ Duck Season	SpEff	R	3.00
☐ Duck! Rabbit! Duck!	Scene	X	0.25
☐ EGAD!	SpEff	U	0.50
☐ Elmer Fudd (3)	Actor	R	3.00
☐ Elmer Fudd (4)	Actor	C	0.15
☐ Elmer Fudd (5)	Actor	C	0.15
☐ Elmer Fudd, Rabbit of Seville	Actor	U	0.50
☐ Elmer Fudd, Siegfried	Actor	P	5.00
☐ Emily and Agatha	Actor	C	0.15
9			
☐ Fair-Haired Hare	Scene	X	0.25
☐ Falling Hare	Scene	X	0.25

Card name	Type	Rarity	Price
☐ Fast and Furry-ous (4, 112/160)Scene		C	0.15
☐ Fast and Furry-ous (4, 24/50)	Scene	X	0.25
☐ Ferocious Lion	SpEff	U	0.50
☐ Fire-Sneezing Dragon	Actor	C	0.15
☐ Fleet-Foot Jet-Propelled Tennis Shoes	SpEff	R	3.00
☐ Foghorn Leghorn (5)	Actor	C	0.15
☐ Foghorn Leghorn (6)	Actor	R	3.00
10			
☐ For Scent-imental Reasons (6)	Scene	X	0.25
☐ For Scent-imental Reasons (8)	Scene	U	0.50
☐ From A to Z-Z-Z-Z	Scene	X	0.25
☐ Giovanni Jones	Actor	C	0.15
☐ Goofy Gophers	Actor	R	3.00
☐ Gossamer	Actor	R	3.00
☐ Granny (5)	Actor	C	0.15
☐ Granny (6)	Actor	U	0.50
☐ Granny (7)	Actor	R	3.00
11			
☐ Hair-Raising Hare	Scene	C	0.15
☐ Hassan	Actor	R	3.00
☐ Heroic Lighting	SpEff	R	3.00
☐ High-Diving Hare	Scene	X	0.25
☐ Highway Robbery	SpEff	R	3.00
☐ Hippety Hopper	Actor	C	0.15
☐ Hocus Pocus	SpEff	R	3.00
☐ Holdup	SpEff	R	3.00
☐ Hopalong Casualty	Scene	X	0.25
12			
☐ Hubie and Bertie	Actor	U	0.50
☐ Hypnotism	SpEff	U	0.50
☐ I Haven't Got a Hat	Scene	X	0.25
☐ Jackrabbit and the Beanstalk	Scene	X	0.25
☐ Jose and Manuel	Actor	U	0.50
☐ Jumpin' Jupiter	Scene	C	0.15
☐ Last-Minute Shuffle	SpEff	U	0.50
☐ Left Turn at Albuquerque	SpEff	R	3.00
☐ Little Boy Boo	Scene	X	0.25
13			
☐ Little Red Riding Rabbit	Scene	X	0.25
☐ Long-Haired Hare	Scene	X	0.25
☐ Magic Lamp	SpEff	R	3.00
☐ Marc Antony	Actor	R	3.00
☐ Marvin the Martian (1)	Actor	R	3.00
☐ Marvin the Martian (2)	Actor	U	0.50
☐ Marvin the Martian (3)	Actor	P	5.00
☐ Maw, Paw, and Junior	Actor	C	0.15
☐ Mechanical Decoy	SpEff	U	0.50

Card name	Type	Rarity	Price
14			
☐ Michigan J. Frog	Actor	R	3.00
☐ Mouse-Wreckers (4)	Scene	X	0.25
☐ Mouse-Wreckers (9)	Scene	U	0.50
☐ Nasty Canasta	Actor	C	0.15
☐ Neanderthal Rabbit	Actor	C	0.15
☐ Of Course You Realize, This Means War.	SpEff	R	3.00
☐ Old Grey Hare	Scene	X	0.25
☐ One Froggy Evening	Scene	X	0.25
☐ Operation: Rabbit	Scene	X	0.25
15			
☐ Pablo and Fernando	Actor	U	0.50
☐ Pepé Le Pew (7)	Actor	U	0.50
☐ Pepé Le Pew Dressed as Valentino	Actor	R	3.00
☐ Play It Again, Doc	SpEff	U	0.50
☐ Porky Pig (2)	Actor	U	0.50
☐ Porky Pig (3)	Actor	C	0.15
☐ Porky Pig (4)	Actor	C	0.15
☐ Porky Pig (5)	Actor	U	0.50
☐ Porky Pig, Friar Tuck	Actor	R	3.00
16			
☐ Porky's Hare Hunt	Scene	X	0.25
☐ Pronoun Trouble	SpEff	R	3.00
☐ Quick Thinking	SpEff	U	0.50
☐ Rabbit Fire (3)	Scene	C	0.15
☐ Rabbit Fire (7)	Scene	X	0.25
☐ Rabbit Hood	Scene	X	0.25
☐ Rabbit of Seville (1)	Scene	X	0.25
☐ Rabbit of Seville (2)	Scene	C	0.15
☐ Rabbit Punch	Scene	X	0.25
17			
☐ Rabbit Season	SpEff	R	3.00
☐ Rabbit Seasoning	Scene	X	0.25
☐ Ralph Phillips	Actor	C	0.15
☐ Ralph Wolf	Actor	U	0.50
☐ Rehydrated Martian	Actor	C	0.15
☐ Roadrunner (4)	Actor	R	3.00
☐ Roadrunner (5, 5/160)	Actor	P	5.00
☐ Roadrunner (5, 87/160)	Actor	C	0.15
☐ Roadrunner (7)	Actor	U	0.50
18			
☐ Robin-Hood Daffy	Scene	C	0.15
☐ Robot Watchdog	SpEff	R	3.00
☐ Roll Call	SpEff	R	3.00
☐ Sam Sheepdog	Actor	U	0.50
☐ Shamus O'Toole	Actor	R	3.00
☐ Sheriff of Nottingham	Actor	C	0.15
☐ Showbiz Bugs	Scene	U	0.50
☐ Skating Penguin	Actor	R	3.00
☐ Smokey	Actor	U	0.50
19			
☐ Sneak Preview	SpEff	R	3.00

RARITY KEY C = Common   U = Uncommon   R = Rare   VR = Very Rare   UR = Ultra Rare   F = Foil card   X = Fixed/standard in all decks

Card name	Type	Rarity	Price
☐ Special Delivery	SpEff	R	3.00
☐ Speedy Gonzales (8)	Actor	R	3.00
☐ Spike and Chester	Actor	U	0.50
☐ Stork	Actor	R	3.00
☐ Suit of Armor	SpEff	U	0.50
☐ Sylvester (2)	Actor	U	0.50
☐ Sylvester (3)	Actor	C	0.15
☐ Sylvester (4)	Actor	U	0.50
☐ Sylvester (5)	Actor	C	0.15
☐ Sylvester (6, 6/160)	Actor	P	5.00
☐ Sylvester (6, 91/160)	Actor	C	0.15
☐ Tasmanian Devil (2)	Actor	R	3.00
☐ Tasmanian Devil (8, 33/160)	Actor	R	3.00

Card name	Type	Rarity	Price
☐ Tasmanian Devil (8, 7/160)	Actor	P	5.00
☐ The Scarlet Pumpernickel (4)	Scene	C	0.15
☐ The Scarlet Pumpernickel (5)	Scene	X	0.25
☐ Transylvania 6-5000	Scene	X	0.25
☐ Trusty Quarterstaff	SpEff	U	0.50
☐ Tweety (4)	Actor	U	0.50
☐ Tweety (5)	Actor	C	0.15
☐ Tweety (6)	Actor	C	0.15
☐ Tweety (7)	Actor	P	5.00
☐ Tweety (8)	Actor	U	0.50
☐ Tweety's SOS	Scene	X	0.25

Card name	Type	Rarity	Price
☐ Water, Water, Every Hare (8)	Scene	X	0.25
☐ Water, Water, Every Hare (9)	Scene	C	0.15
☐ What's Opera, Doc? (5)	Scene	C	0.15
☐ What's Opera, Doc? (9)	Scene	X	0.25
☐ What's Up, Doc?	Scene	X	0.25
☐ Whoa Be Gone	Scene	X	0.25
☐ Widow Hen	Actor	R	3.00
☐ Wile E. Coyote (1)	Actor	P	5.00
☐ Wile E. Coyote (2)	Actor	U	0.50
☐ Wile E. Coyote (3)	Actor	C	0.15
☐ Wile E. Coyote (4)	Actor	C	0.15
☐ Wile E. Coyote (5)	Actor	R	3.00

Card name	Type	Rarity	Price
☐ Witch Hazel (2)	Actor	R	3.00
☐ Witch Hazel (3)	Actor	C	0.15
☐ Witch Hazel (4)	Actor	C	0.15
☐ Witch Hazel's Cauldron	SpEff	R	3.00
☐ Yosemite Sam (1)	Actor	C	0.15
☐ Yosemite Sam (2)	Actor	P	5.00
☐ Yosemite Sam (6)	Actor	U	0.50
☐ Yosemite Sam, Black Knight	Actor	R	3.00
☐ Yosemite Sam, Hunting	Actor	C	0.15
☐ Yosemite Sam, Sam Shultz	Actor	U	0.50
☐ Yosemite Sam, Von Schamm	Actor	C	0.15

Lost Colony (a.k.a. *Lost Colony Showdown*)

Pinnacle Entertainment Group • First set, *Fear the Reapers*, released 2000

114 cards in set

- Starter decks contain 65 cards; starter displays contain 6 starters
- Booster packs contain 30 cards; booster displays contain 10 boosters

Designed by **Shane Lacy Hensley** and **John Hopler**

Lost Colony takes the horror-western genre of *Deadlands* to the Final Frontier. Humans arrive on the planet Banshee and try to conquer it from the less-advanced native species. But the Tunnel back to Earth collapses, and the colonists are trapped.

Three factions battle for supremacy: the Reapers (with their native allies), UN EXFOR, and the Rangers. The game is won when a player controls all four of the opponent's home areas until the beginning of the next turn. Location cards generate credits to purchase cards. Troops and Heroes attack each other across a "No Man's Land."

Combat is simple. Players target troops against one another, defender going first. Random values are generated by pulling a card. If the value of the card is less than or equal to the card's attack value, the attack succeeds. Damage is cumulative on a troop card, when damage exceeds toughness the card is discarded. Troops can use gear, weapons, transport, and in some cases, mystic powers to increase their ability to attack. — *James Mishler*

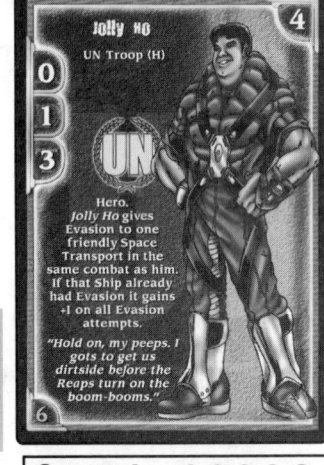

You will need **13** nine-pocket pages to store this set. (7 doubled up)

Set (114 cards)	75.00		
Starter Display Box	55.00		
Booster Display Box	55.00		
Starter Deck	8.00		
Booster Pack	4.90		

Card name	Type	Rarity	Price
☐ Algae Farm	Loc	C	0.10
☐ Ambush	Act	C	0.10
☐ Anouk Archer	Trp	C	0.10
☐ Anouk Shaman	Trp	C	0.10
☐ Anouk Warrior	Trp	C	0.10
☐ Assault Rifle	Gear	U	0.50
☐ Assault Vest	Gear	C	0.10
☐ Astrophobia	Act	R	3.00
☐ Atax	Gear	C	0.10
☐ Azeel Plainsriders	Trp	U	0.50
☐ Banshee's Pain	MPwr	R	3.00
☐ Bionoculars	Gear	C	0.10
☐ Blood Brothers	Act	C	0.10
☐ Blood Juice	Gear	R	3.50
☐ Bloodthirsty	Act	C	0.10
☐ Bug Farm	Loc	C	0.10
☐ Butterfingers	Act	C	0.10
☐ Captain Norton	Hero	F	0.35
☐ Caravan	Adv	C	0.10
☐ Chanouk	Trp	U	0.50
☐ Colonists	Trp	C	0.10
☐ Colt Peacemaker	Gear	F	0.35
☐ Com-unit	Gear	U	0.50
☐ Commando SMG	Gear	C	0.10
☐ Company Colors	Gear	F	0.35

Card name	Type	Rarity	Price
☐ Compo Armor	Gear	U	0.50
☐ Converted Freighter	Trp	U	0.80
☐ Corporal	Trp	U	0.80
☐ Dave Ross	Hero	F	1.40
☐ Death's Head Saloon	Loc	F	1.40
☐ Debbi Dallas	Hero	F	2.10
☐ Die	SPwr	R	3.00
☐ Digger Ambush	Act	R	3.00
☐ Diggers	Adv	U	0.50
☐ Dirt Bike	Gear	C	0.10
☐ Dogfight	Adv	U	0.50
☐ Domburg	Loc	VR	7.50
☐ Druitt's Station	Loc	U	0.50
☐ Duck and Cover	Act	U	0.50
☐ Engine Trouble	Act	VR	7.50
☐ Extreme Paranoia	Act	R	3.00
☐ First Aid Kit	Gear	C	0.20
☐ Flaming Mos	Loc	F	0.35
☐ Frag Grenade	Gear	R	3.00
☐ Ghost Rock Mine	Loc	C	0.10
☐ Goliath's Belt	Loc	U	0.50
☐ Gorgon APC	Trp	R	3.50
☐ Green Dragon	Trp	R	4.00
☐ Green Lightning	SPwr	R	3.50
☐ Gunfighter	Trp	C	0.10
☐ Hangin' Tree	Adv	U	0.50
☐ Havoc Missle	Gear	U	0.50
☐ Hero	Adv	F	0.35
☐ Hired Gun	Trp	C	0.10
☐ Hoss	Trp	R	3.50
☐ Hot Loads	Gear	C	0.10
☐ I Am The Law!	Act	U	0.60

Card name	Type	Rarity	Price
☐ Invigorate	MPwr	U	0.50
☐ Iridium Mine	Loc	U	0.50
☐ Jolly Ho	Hero	R	3.50
☐ Kreech's Skull	Gear	R	3.00
☐ Kryll	Hero	F	0.35
☐ Laser Scope	Gear	U	0.50
☐ Lasseter	Hero	R	3.00
☐ Last Stand	Loc	F	0.35
☐ Life	MPwr	U	0.50
☐ Lumber Camp	Loc	U	0.50
☐ Mercs	Trp	VR	7.50
☐ Nicolai	Hero	F	0.35
☐ Night Watch	Trp	U	0.50
☐ Nurse	Trp	C	0.20
☐ Oasis	Loc	C	0.10
☐ Officer's Pistol	Gear	C	0.10
☐ Parting Shot	Act	U	0.50
☐ Peace In Our Time	Adv	C	0.10
☐ Point Defense	Gear	U	0.50
☐ Poisoned Water Hole	Adv	U	0.50
☐ Private	Trp	U	0.60
☐ Puppet	SPwr	R	3.00
☐ Ranger HQ	Loc	F	0.35
☐ Razorwings	Adv	U	0.50
☐ Reaper Scavs	Trp	U	0.60
☐ Redbeard	Adv	R	3.00
☐ Reserve Tanks	Gear	R	3.00
☐ Rex	Adv	R	3.00
☐ Right Cross	Act	C	0.10
☐ Showdown	Adv	U	0.50
☐ Skaak	Hero	F	0.35
☐ Skeleton Crew	Adv	U	0.50

Concept	●●●○○		
Gameplay	●●●○○		
Card art	●●●○○		
Player pool	●○○○○		

Card name	Type	Rarity	Price
☐ Smoke Grenade	Gear	C	0.20
☐ Sneak Attack	Act	R	3.00
☐ Speedster	Trp	C	0.10
☐ Spook Juice	Gear	R	3.00
☐ Sticky Bugs	Adv	U	0.50
☐ Takala War Party	Adv	U	0.50
☐ Tamarin	Hero	R	3.50
☐ Tanis Mine	Loc	U	0.50
☐ Tech Sergeant Hendricks	Hero	F	0.35
☐ Technophobia	Act	R	3.00
☐ Teeth	Adv	U	0.50
☐ Temptaion Militia	Trp	U	0.50
☐ The Bunker	Loc	F	0.35
☐ The Kid	Hero	R	3.50
☐ The Only Good Anouk...	Act	R	3.00
☐ The Willies	Act	R	3.00
☐ Trawler	Loc	C	0.10
☐ Trophy	Adv	F	0.35
☐ Ultralight	Gear	C	0.10
☐ UNS Foster	Loc	F	0.35
☐ Vaccine	Adv	VR	10.00
☐ Wasted Youth	Act	C	0.10
☐ Weak Spot	Act	C	0.10
☐ Wolverine	Hero	R	3.00
☐ Worldstorm	Adv	F	0.35

JOLLY HO • 4 • UN Troop (H) • 0 1 3 • UN • Hero. *Jolly Ho* gives Evasion to one friendly Space Transport in the same combat as him. If that Ship already had Evasion it gains +1 on all Evasion attempts. "Hold on, my peeps. I gots to get us dirtside before the Reaps turn on the boom-booms." • 6

RARITY KEY C = Common U = Uncommon R = Rare VR = Very Rare UR = Ultra Rare F = Foil card X = Fixed/standard in all decks

Magi Nation

Interactive Imagination • First set, *Duel*, released **October 2000**
190 cards in set

DUEL ™

Concept	●●●●○
Gameplay	●●●●○
Card art	●●●●○
Player pool	●●●○○

- Starter decks contain 40 cards; starter displays contain 10 starters
- Booster packs contain 11 cards; booster displays contain 36 boosters

Magi-Nation melds a novel, simple, and elegant game system with a strong setting and wonderful anime style art.

The world consists of five regions, Arderial (air), Orothe (water), Underneath (earth), Cald (fire), and Naroom (forests) — and Magi from each battle for dominance.

Each player has three Magi, each attuned to a single region. Only one is in play at a time. Each Magi has energy points to spend on creatures, spells, and relics. Energy is transferred from the Magi to the summoned creature. Spells and relics produce various effects, from further energy transferral to special combat abilities. Most creatures also have a special power. Creatures attack each other, reducing their respective energy levels. A Magi may be attacked directly when he has no creatures remaining for defense. A Magi that has no creatures and no personal energy is defeated. Defeat all three of an opponent's Magi to win.

Magi-Nation started slowly but began picking up steam at the beginning of 2001. A tournament series and Gameboy cartridge are planned. — *James Mishler*

You will need **22** nine-pocket pages to store this set. (11 doubled up)

Set (190 cards)	**152.50**
Starter Display Box	**100.00**
Booster Display Box	**91.50**
Starter Deck	**10.00**
Booster Pack	**3.00**

Card name	Type	Rarity	Price
Abaquist	Orothe	U2	0.50
Adis	Ardl	U1	1.00
Agovo	Under	U2	0.50
Alaban	Ardl	U2	0.80
Amulet of Ombor	Under	R1	4.00
Ancestral Flute	Univ	U2	0.50
Arboll	Nar	C2	0.25
Arbollit	Cald	C2	0.25
Arderial's Crown	Ardl	R1	3.80
Ashgar	Cald	R1	4.00
Ayebaw	Ardl	R2	4.00
Balamant	Nar	R2	4.00
Balamant Pup	Nar	U2	0.80
Baloo Root	Univ	C2	0.25
Barak	Cald	R1	4.00
Bhatar	Nar	R1	3.50
Bisiwog	Under	C2	0.25
Blu	Orothe	R1	4.00
Book of Ages	Univ	U2	0.80
Book of Life	Nar	R1	4.00
Bottomless Pit	Under	U2	0.80
Brub	Under	C2	0.25
Burrow	Under	C2	0.25
Bwill	Orothe	C2	0.25
Carillion	Nar	C2	0.25
Carnivorous Cave	Under	C2	0.25
Cave Hyren	Under	R2	4.00
Cave In	Under	R1	4.00
Cave Rudwot	Under	C2	0.25
Channeler's Gloves	Univ	U1	0.50
Cloud Narth	Ardl	C2	0.25
Cloud Sceptre	Ardl	U1	1.00
Colossus	Univ	U1	0.80
Coral Hyren	Orothe	R2	4.00
Corf	Orothe	C2	0.25
Corf Pearl	Orothe	U1	0.50
Crystal Arboll	Under	C2	0.25
Cyclone Vashp	Ardl	R2	4.00
Deep Hyren	Orothe	R2	4.00
Digging Goggles	Under	U2	0.80
Diobor	Cald	C2	0.25
Drakan	Cald	U1	0.80
Dream Balm	Univ	C2	0.25
Ebylon	Orothe	U1	0.80

Card name	Type	Rarity	Price
Eclipse	Ardl	R2	4.00
Eebit	Nar	U2	1.00
Energy Band	Nar	R2	4.00
Enrich	Under	U1	0.80
Entangle	Orothe	R2	4.00
Epik	Ardl	U2	0.80
Evu	Nar	R1	4.00
Eye of the Storm	Ardl	U2	0.80
Fire Chogo	Cald	C2	0.25
Fire Flow	Cald	C2	0.25
Fire Grag	Cald	U2	0.50
Fireball	Cald	C2	0.25
Flame Control	Cald	R1	4.00
Flame Geyser	Cald	U2	0.80
Flame Hyren	Cald	R2	3.80
Flood of Energy	Nar	R2	4.00
Fog Bank	Ardl	U1	0.80
Fossik	Under	U1	0.80
Furok	Nar	C2	0.25
Gar	Cald	U1	0.80
Giant Carillion	Nar	U1	0.80
Giant Korrit	Under	R2	3.00
Giant Parathin	Orothe	R1	4.00
Giant Parmalag	Under	R2	4.00
Giant Vulbor	Under	U1	0.50
Gloves of Crystal	Under	R1	3.20
Gogor	Under	U1	0.80
Gorgle's Ring	Cald	R2	3.00
Greater Vaal	Cald	R1	4.00
Grega	Cald	U1	0.80
Ground Breaker	Under	U2	0.80
Grow	Nar	C2	0.25
Gruk	Under	U1	1.00
Gum-Gum	Under	C2	0.25
Heat Lens	Cald	R1	4.00
Hood of Hiding	Nar	U2	0.80
Hubdra's Spear	Orothe	R1	4.00
Hyren's Call	Nar	R1	4.00
Implosion	Orothe	C2	0.25
Jaela	Ardl	R1	4.00
Karak	Orothe	U2	0.80
Kelthet	Cald	C2	0.25
Korrit	Under	U1	0.50
Lasada	Ardl	U1	1.00
Lava Aq	Cald	U2	0.80
Lava Arboll	Cald	U2	0.50
Lava Balamant	Cald	U1	0.50
Leaf Hyren	Nar	C2	0.25

Card name	Type	Rarity	Price
Lightning	Ardl	C2	0.25
Lightning Hyren	Ardl	C2	0.25
Lovian	Ardl	R2	4.00
Magam	Cald	R1	4.00
Magma Armor	Cald	C2	0.25
Magma Hyren	Cald	R1	4.00
Mask of Abwyn	Ardl	U2	0.50
Megathan	Orothe	R1	4.00
Mirror Pendant	Univ	U1	0.50
Mobis	Orothe	R1	4.00
Motash	Under	R1	4.00
Motash's Staff	Under	R2	4.00
Mushroom Hyren	Under	U2	0.80
Nimbulo	Ardl	R1	4.00
O'Qua	Orothe	R1	4.00
Ora	Ardl	R1	4.00
Orathan	Orothe	R2	4.00
Orathan Flyer	Ardl	R1	4.00
Orish	Ardl	R1	4.00
Orlon	Orothe	U1	0.60
Ormagon	Under	R1	4.00
Orothean Belt	Orothe	U1	0.80
Orothean Gloves	Orothe	R1	4.00
Orothean Goggles	Orothe	U2	0.80
Orpus	Orothe	C2	0.25
Orthea	Orothe	U1	0.80
Orwin	Nar	R1	4.00
Orwin's Gaze	Nar	U1	1.00
Orwin's Staff	Nar	R1	3.50
Pack Korrit	Under	C2	0.25
Paralit	Orothe	U2	0.50
Parmalag	Under	C2	0.25
Pharan	Ardl	C2	0.25
Platheus	Orothe	R2	4.00
Plith	Nar	C2	0.25
Poad	Nar	U1	0.80
Pruitt	Nar	U1	0.80
Quor	Cald	C2	0.25
Quor Pup	Cald	U2	0.50
Raxis	Cald	R2	4.00
Relic Mirror	Univ	U2	1.00
Relic Stalker	Univ	C2	0.25
Ring of Secrets	Univ	U1	0.50
Robe of Vines	Nar	U1	0.80
Robes of the Ages	Univ	U2	0.80
Rod of Coals	Cald	R2	3.30
Rudwot	Nar	U1	0.80
Sap of Life	Nar	R2	4.00
Scroll of Fire	Cald	R1	4.00

Card name	Type	Rarity	Price
Sea Barl	Orothe	C2	0.25
Shimmer	Ardl	U1	0.50
Shockwave	Ardl	U2	0.80
Shooting Star	Ardl	C2	0.25
Sinder	Cald	U1	1.00
Sphor	Orothe	C2	0.25
Spirit of the Flame	Cald	R2	3.00
Staff of Hyren	Univ	C2	0.25
Staff of Korrits	Under	R2	3.00
Stagadan	Nar	R2	4.00
Storm Cloud	Ardl	R2	3.50
Storm Ring	Ardl	R1	3.80
Stradus	Ardl	U1	1.00
Strag	Under	U1	1.00
Submerge	Orothe	C2	0.25
Syphon Stone	Univ	C2	0.25
Syphon Vortex	Cald	U1	0.50
Tap Roots	Nar	C2	0.25
Thermal Blast	Cald	C2	0.25
Thunder Hyren	Ardl	R1	4.00
Thunder Vashp	Ardl	C2	0.25
Thunderquake	Under	R1	4.00
Tidal Wave	Orothe	U1	0.80
Timber Hyren	Nar	R1	3.50
Trug	Under	R1	4.00
Tryn	Nar	U1	1.00
Twee	Nar	R2	3.50
Typhoon	Orothe	R2	4.00
Ulk	Under	R1	3.50
Undertow	Orothe	U2	0.50
Updraft	Ardl	C2	0.25
Vaal	Cald	R2	4.00
Valkan	Cald	U1	1.00
Vellup	Ardl	R2	4.00
Vinoc	Nar	C2	0.25
Vortex of Knowledge	Nar	U2	0.50
Vulbor	Under	R2	4.00
Warrior's Boots	Univ	U1	0.50
Water of Life	Univ	U2	0.50
Weebo	Nar	C2	0.25
Wellisk	Orothe	C2	0.25
Wellisk Pup	Orothe	C2	0.25
Wence	Nar	R1	4.00
Whall	Orothe	U1	1.00
Will of Orothe	Orothe	R1	4.00
Xyx	Ardl	C2	0.25
Xyx Elder	Ardl	U1	0.50
Xyx Minor	Ardl	C2	0.25
Yaki	Nar	U1	1.00

RARITY KEY C = Common U = Uncommon R = Rare VR = Very Rare UR = Ultra Rare F = Foil card X = Fixed/standard in all decks

Magic: The Gathering

Wizards of the Coast • First set, *Alpha*, general release **August 1993**
290 cards plus **5** variants in set • **IDENTIFIER: Rounder edges; black borders**
• Starter decks contain 60 cards; starter displays contain 10 starters
• Booster packs contain 15 cards; booster displays contain 36 boosters
Designed by **Richard Garfield**

Richard Garfield and Wizards of the Coast turned the gaming industry on its ear with the introduction of *Magic: the Gathering* at Origins during the summer of 1993. The first "collectible card game" (CCG), *Magic* was designed to be portable, customizable, and loads of fun. Appealing to fantasy role-players, board gamers, and collectors alike, *Magic*'s success spawned numerous CCG's in the years that followed. While many of these failed to catch on, there were enough success stories to carve a new niche in the gaming community for collectible card games.

One of the game's most distinguishing themes is the designation of five colors of *Magic* spells, with almost all of the cards divided among them. Each color has themes that the designers have tried to follow for cards in each base set and expansion. Red is the color of fire, earth, war and chaos; Black is the color of evil, undeath, and corruption; Blue is the color of water, air, trickery and mind control; White is the color of good, law, order, and purity; Green is the color of nature, growth, and life. There are also cards designated as artifacts, considered "colorless," and can be used in any color deck.

Besides spell cards, there are also land cards that are generally used as resources to enable players to cast their spells. Lands produce an imaginary currency called "mana" that players use to cast their spells. There are five "basic" lands that each give different colored mana: mountains for red mana, swamps for black mana, islands for blue mana, plains for white mana, and forests for green mana.

Another feature of the game was that each card should "break the rules" and that the way the card interacted in the game would be presented on the card itself. This allowed each player, with knowledge of just the basic rules, to sit down with someone who is playing a deck made up of completely different cards and still be able to play a game of *Magic* without constantly consulting a rule book.

Magic was also originally an "ante" game, in which duels were played for a card anted as a prize. This was usually donea by flipping over the top card of each player's deck before the game and putting it aside for the winner of the match. However, as the game grew more popular, and desired cards became harder to find, many people did not want to risk losing their prized cards and stopped playing for ante. Wizards of the Coast eventually discontinued printing ante-related cards and banned these cards in tournament play, and the "ante rule" was finally phased out of the game.

Magic's explosive growth in popularity exceeded everyone's wildest imaginations. Players can find decks and booster packs of the game in convenient stores, bookstores, and hobby stores around the globe. The *Magic* Grand Prix and Pro Tours, with stops the world over, have been so successful that there are now people who can make a living playing the game. The curious can even tune into professional matches aired on ESPN2. With a loyal and growing fan base, and solid support from Wizards of the Coast, *Magic* sets the standard for all current and future CCGs.

About *Alpha*: After its debut at Origins in July of 1993, *Magic: the Gathering* was released to the gaming world on Aug. 5, 1993. The "Alpha" edition (the name doesn't appear on the boxes) consisted of 295 cards with a print run of 2.6 million. — *Bennie Smith*

Concept	●●●●●
Gameplay	●●●●●
Card art	●●●○○
Player pool	●●●●●

You will need **33** nine-pocket pages to store this set. (17 doubled up)

The *Alpha* Unholy Strength (top) had a pentacle which was dropped by *Fourth Edition*, leading to what became known as the "Michael Jackson" card.

	Price
Set (290 cards + 5 variants)	**4,250.00**
Starter Display Box	**2,762.50**
Booster Display Box	**3,962.50**
Starter Deck	**287.50**
Booster Pack	**180.00**

Card name	Color	Type	Rarity	Price
☐ Air Elemental	Blue	Sum	U	2.90
☐ Ancestral Recall	Blue	Ins	R	200.00
☐ Animate Artifact	Blue	EArt	U	2.00
☐ Animate Dead	Black	EDCr	U	3.00
☐ Animate Wall	White	EWa	R	8.00
☐ Ankh of Mishra	Artifact	C	R	10.00
☐ Armageddon	White	Sor	R	45.00
☐ Aspect of Wolf	Green	ECr	R	10.00
☐ Bad Moon	Black	E	R	25.00
☐ Badlands[2]	Blk/Rd	DL	R	50.00
☐ Balance	White	Sor	R	30.00

Card name	Color	Type	Rarity	Price
☐ Basalt Monolith	Artifact	M	U	5.00
☐ Bayou	Blk/Gr	DL	R	49.50
☐ Benalish Hero	White	Sum	C	1.00
☐ Berserk	Green	Ins	U	40.00
☐ Birds of Paradise	Green	Sum	R	50.00
☐ Black Knight	Black	Sum	U	8.00
☐ Black Lotus	Artifact	M	R	437.50
☐ Black Vise[3]	Artifact	C	U	8.00
☐ Black Ward	White	ECr	U	2.00
☐ Blaze of Glory	White	Ins	R	35.00
☐ Blessing	White	ECr	R	12.00
☐ Blue Elemental Blast	Blue	Int	C	1.00
☐ Blue Ward	White	ECr	U	2.00
☐ Bog Wraith	Black	Sum	U	2.50
☐ Braingeyser	Blue	Sor	R	25.00
☐ Burrowing	Red	ECr	U	2.00
☐ Camouflage[4]	Green	Ins	U	8.50

Card name	Color	Type	Rarity	Price
☐ Castle	White	E	U	2.00
☐ Celestial Prism	Artifact	M	U	2.60
☐ Channel	Green	Sor	U	3.00
☐ Chaos Orb	Artifact	M	R	80.00
☐ Chaoslace	Red	Int	R	8.00
☐ Circle of Protection: Blue	White	E	C	1.00
☐ Circle of Protection: Green	White	E	C	1.00
☐ Circle of Protection: Red	White	E	C	1.80
☐ Circle of Protection: White[5]	White	E	C	1.00
☐ Clockwork Beast	Artifact	Cr	R	8.00
☐ Clone	Blue	Sum	U	10.00
☐ Cockatrice	Green	Sum	R	15.00
☐ Consecrate Land	White	EL	U	9.00
☐ Conservator	Artifact	M	U	2.00
☐ Contract from Below	Black	Sor	R	10.00
☐ Control Magic	Blue	ECr	U	6.00
☐ Conversion	White	E	U	2.30

RARITY KEY						**CARD TYPES: See page 246**
C = Common	**U** = Uncommon	**R** = Rare	**VR** = Very Rare	**UR** = Ultra Rare	**F** = Foil card	

Card name	Color	Type	Rarity	Price
6				
☐ Copper Tablet	Artifact	C	U	9.00
☐ Copy Artifact	Blue	E	R	22.00
☐ Counterspell	Blue	Int	U	15.00
☐ Craw Wurm	Green	Sum	C	1.00
☐ Creature Bond	Blue	ECr	C	1.00
☐ Crusade	White	E	R	26.75
☐ Crystal Rod	Artifact	P		2.00
☐ Cursed Land	Black	EL	U	2.00
☐ Cyclopean Tomb	Artifact	M	R	55.00
7				
☐ Dark Ritual	Black	Int	C	5.00
☐ Darkpact	Black	Sor	R	8.00
☐ Death Ward	White	Ins	C	1.00
☐ Deathgrip	Black	E	U	2.30
☐ Deathlace	Black	Int	R	6.00
☐ Demonic Attorney	Black	Sor	R	10.00
☐ Demonic Hordes	Black	Sum	R	25.00
☐ Demonic Tutor	Black	Sor	U	20.00
☐ Dingus Egg	Artifact	C	R	10.00
8				
☐ Disenchant	White	Ins	C	4.50
☐ Disintegrate	Red	Sor	C	3.00
☐ Disrupting Scepter	Artifact	M	R	22.50
☐ Dragon Whelp	Red	Sum	U	4.40
☐ Drain Life	Black	Sor	C	2.00
☐ Drain Power	Blue	Sor	R	10.00
☐ Drudge Skeletons	Black	Sum	C	1.00
☐ Dwarven Demolition Team	Red	Sum	U	6.00
☐ Dwarven Warriors	Red	Sum	C	1.00
9				
☐ Earth Elemental	Red	Sum	U	2.80
☐ Earthbind	Red	ECr	C	1.00
☐ Earthquake	Red	Sor	R	19.00
☐ Elvish Archers	Green	Sum	R	15.00
☐ Evil Presence	Black	EL	U	2.30
☐ False Orders	Red	Ins	C	2.00
☐ Farmstead	White	E	R	10.00
☐ Fastbond	Green	E	R	15.00
☐ Fear	Black	ECr	C	1.00
10				
☐ Feedback	Blue	EE	U	2.00
☐ Fire Elemental	Red	Sum	U	2.30
☐ Fireball	Red	Sor	C	5.00
☐ Firebreathing	Red	ECr	C	1.00

Card name	Color	Type	Rarity	Price
☐ Flashfires	Red	Sor	U	2.50
☐ Flight	Blue	ECr	C	1.00
☐ Fog	Green	Ins	C	1.00
☐ Force of Nature	Green	Sum	R	30.00
☐ Forcefield	Artifact	P	R	106.75
11				
☐ Forest (ver. 1)	Green	L	C	1.00
☐ Forest (ver. 2)	Green	L	C	1.00
☐ Fork	Red	Int	R	40.00
☐ Frozen Shade	Black	Sum	C	1.00
☐ Fungusaur	Green	Sum	R	12.00
☐ Gaea's Liege	Green	Sum	R	14.50
☐ Gauntlet of Might	Artifact	C	R	100.00
☐ Giant Growth	Green	Ins	C	3.00
☐ Giant Spider	Green	Sum	C	1.00
12				
☐ Glasses of Urza	Artifact	M	U	2.30
☐ Gloom	Black	E	U	3.00
☐ Goblin Balloon Brigade	Red	Sum	C	3.00
☐ Goblin King	Red	Sum	R	18.00
☐ Granite Gargoyle	Red	Sum	R	15.00
☐ Gray Ogre	Red	Sum	C	1.00
☐ Green Ward	White	E	U	2.00
☐ Grizzly Bears	Green	Sum	C	1.00
☐ Guardian Angel	White	Ins	C	1.00
13				
☐ Healing Salve	White	Ins	C	1.00
☐ Helm of Chatzuk	Artifact	M	R	8.50
☐ Hill Giant	Red	Sum	C	1.00
☐ Holy Armor	White	ECr	C	1.00
☐ Holy Strength	White	ECr	C	1.00
☐ Howl from Beyond	Black	Ins	C	1.00
☐ Howling Mine	Artifact	C	R	27.00
☐ Hurloon Minotaur	Red	Sum	C	1.00
☐ Hurricane	Green	Sor	U	4.00
14				
☐ Hypnotic Specter	Black	Sum	U	18.00
☐ Ice Storm	Green	Sor	U	22.00
☐ Icy Manipulator	Artifact	M	U	39.00
☐ Illusionary Mask	Artifact	P	R	36.50
☐ Instill Energy	Green	ECr	U	2.80
☐ Invisibility	Blue	ECr	C	2.50
☐ Iron Star	Artifact	P	U	2.00
☐ Ironclaw Orcs	Red	Sum	C	1.00
☐ Ironroot Treefolk	Green	Sum	C	1.00
15				
☐ Island (ver. 1)	Blue	L	C	1.00
☐ Island (ver. 2)	Blue	L	C	1.00
☐ Island Sanctuary	White	E	R	15.00
☐ Ivory Cup	Artifact	P	U	2.00
☐ Jade Monolith	Artifact	P	R	10.00
☐ Jade Statue	Artifact	M	U	12.00
☐ Jayemdae Tome	Artifact	M	R	25.00
☐ Juggernaut	Artifact	ACr	U	10.00
☐ Jump	Blue	Ins	C	1.00
16				
☐ Karma	White	E	U	3.00
☐ Keldon Warlord	Red	Sum	U	3.00
☐ Kormus Bell	Artifact	C	R	8.00
☐ Kudzu	Green	EL	R	10.00
☐ Lance	White	ECr	U	2.50
☐ Ley Druid	Green	Sum	U	2.80
☐ Library of Leng	Artifact	C	U	2.50
☐ Lich	Black	E	R	48.00
☐ Lifeforce	Green	E	U	2.80
17				
☐ Lifelace	Green	Int	R	7.00
☐ Lifetap	Blue	E	U	2.10
☐ Lightning Bolt	Red	Ins	C	9.00
☐ Living Artifact	Green	EArt	R	9.50
☐ Living Lands	Green	EL	R	8.50
☐ Living Wall	Artifact	ACr	U	3.00
☐ Llanowar Elves	Green	Sum	C	2.80
☐ Lord of Atlantis	Blue	Sum	R	22.00
☐ Lord of the Pit	Black	Sum	R	24.25
18				
☐ Lure	Green	ECr	U	2.30

Card name	Color	Type	Rarity	Price
☐ Magical Hack	Blue	Int	R	9.00
☐ Mahamoti Djinn	Blue	Sum	R	25.00
☐ Mana Flare	Red	E	R	19.00
☐ Mana Short	Blue	Ins	R	14.00
☐ Mana Vault	Artifact	M	R	20.00
☐ Manabarbs	Red	E	R	10.00
☐ Meekstone	Artifact	C	R	10.00
☐ Merfolk of the Pearl Trident	Blue	Sum	C	1.00
19				
☐ Mesa Pegasus	White	Sum	C	1.00
☐ Mind Twist	Black	Sor	R	11.00
☐ Mons's Goblin Raiders	Red	Sum	C	1.00
☐ Mountain (ver. 1)	Red	L	C	1.00
☐ Mountain (ver. 2)	Red	L	C	1.00
☐ Mox Emerald	Artifact	M	R	200.00
☐ Mox Jet	Artifact	M	R	200.00
☐ Mox Pearl	Artifact	M	R	200.00
☐ Mox Ruby	Artifact	M	R	200.00
20				
☐ Mox Sapphire	Artifact	M	R	200.00
☐ Natural Selection	Green	Ins	R	30.00
☐ Nether Shadow	Black	Sum	R	15.00
☐ Nettling Imp	Black	Sum	U	3.00
☐ Nevinyrral's Disk	Artifact	M	R	42.50
☐ Nightmare	Black	Sum	R	25.00
☐ Northern Paladin	White	Sum	R	15.00
☐ Obsianus Golem	Artifact	ACr	U	2.00
☐ Orcish Artillery	Red	Sum	U	3.00
21				
☐ Orcish Oriflamme	Red	E	U	6.50
☐ Paralyze	Black	ECr	C	1.00
☐ Pearled Unicorn	White	Sum	C	1.00
☐ Personal Incarnation	White	Sum	R	12.00
☐ Pestilence	Black	E	C	1.00
☐ Phantasmal Forces	Blue	Sum	U	3.00
☐ Phantasmal Terrain	Blue	Sum	C	1.00
☐ Phantom Monster	Blue	Sum	U	3.00
☐ Pirate Ship	Blue	Sum	R	10.00
22				
☐ Plague Rats	Black	Sum	C	1.00
☐ Plains (ver. 1)	White	L	C	1.00
☐ Plains (ver. 2)	White	L	C	1.00
☐ Plateau	Rd/Wh	DL	R	50.00
☐ Power Leak	Blue	EE	C	1.00
☐ Power Sink	Blue	Int	C	1.10
☐ Power Surge	Red	E	R	11.00
☐ Prodigal Sorcerer	Blue	Sum	C	2.00
☐ Psionic Blast	Blue	Ins	U	25.00
23				
☐ Psychic Venom	Blue	EL	C	1.00
☐ Purelace	White	Int	R	6.50
☐ Raging River	Red	E	R	40.00
☐ Raise Dead	Black	Sor	C	1.00
☐ Red Elemental Blast	Red	Ins	C	1.00
☐ Red Ward	White	ECr	U	2.00
☐ Regeneration	Green	ECr	C	1.00
☐ Regrowth	Green	Sor	U	11.00
☐ Resurrection	White	Sor	U	2.80
24				
☐ Reverse Damage	White	Ins	R	12.00
☐ Righteousness	White	Ins	R	10.00
☐ Roc of Kher Ridges	Red	Sum	R	15.00
☐ Rock Hydra	Red	Sum	R	20.00
☐ Rod of Ruin	Artifact	M	U	2.50
☐ Royal Assassin	Black	Sum	R	30.00
☐ Sacrifice	Black	Int	U	2.30
☐ Samite Healer	White	Sum	C	1.00
☐ Savannah	Gr/Wh	DL	R	50.00
25				
☐ Savannah Lions	White	Sum	R	22.00
☐ Scathe Zombies	Black	Sum	C	1.00
☐ Scavenging Ghoul	Black	Sum	U	2.00
☐ Scrubland	Blk/Wh	DL	R	47.50
☐ Scryb Sprites	Green	Sum	C	1.00
☐ Sea Serpent	Blue	Sum	C	1.00
☐ Sedge Troll	Red	Sum	R	15.00
☐ Sengir Vampire	Black	Sum	U	15.00

Magic card type key

Art:	Artifact
ACr:	Artifact Creature
C:	Continuous Artifact
Cr:	Creature
DL:	Dual Land
E:	Enchantment
EArt:	Enchant Artifact
EArtCr:	Enchant Artifact Creature
ECr:	Enchant Creature
EE:	Enchant Enchantment
EL:	Enchant Land
EW:	Enchant World
EWall:	Enchant Wall
Ins:	Instant
Int:	Interrupt
L:	Land
LL:	Legendary Land
M:	Mono Artifact
P:	Poly Artifact
SmL:	Summon Legend
Sor:	Sorcery
Sum:	Summon
PC:	Pre-Constructed Deck

RARITY KEY C = Common U = Uncommon R = Rare VR = Very Rare UR = Ultra Rare F = Foil card X = Fixed/standard in all decks

Card name	Color	Type	Rarity	Price
☐ Serra Angel	White	Sum	U	25.00
26				
☐ Shanodin Dryads	Green	Sum	C	1.00
☐ Shatter	Red	Ins	C	1.00
☐ Shivan Dragon	Red	Sum	R	52.50
☐ Simulacrum	Black	Ins	U	2.00
☐ Sinkhole	Black	Sor	C	15.00
☐ Siren's Call	Blue	Ins	U	2.30
☐ Sleight of Mind	Blue	Int	R	10.00
☐ Smoke	Red	E	R	10.00
☐ Sol Ring	Artifact	M	U	20.00
27				
☐ Soul Net	Artifact	P	U	2.00
☐ Spell Blast	Blue	Int	C	1.00
☐ Stasis	Blue	E	R	15.00
☐ Steal Artifact	Blue	EArt	U	3.00
☐ Stone Giant	Red	Sum	U	2.00
☐ Stone Rain	Red	Sor	C	1.10
☐ Stream of Life	Green	Sor	C	1.00
☐ Sunglasses of Urza	Artifact	C	R	10.50
☐ Swamp (ver. 1)	Black	L	C	1.00
28				
☐ Swamp (ver. 2)	Black	L	C	1.00
☐ Swords to Plowshares	White	Ins	U	10.00
☐ Taiga	Gr/Rd	DL	R	55.00
☐ Terror	Black	Ins	C	1.30
☐ The Hive	Artifact	M	R	9.00

Card name	Color	Type	Rarity	Price
☐ Thicket Basilisk	Green	Sum	U	2.80
☐ Thoughtlace	Blue	Int	R	8.00
☐ Throne of Bone	Artifact	P	U	2.30
☐ Timber Wolves	Green	Sum	R	10.00
29				
☐ Time Vault	Artifact	M	R	75.00
☐ Time Walk	Blue	Sor	R	225.00
☐ Timetwister	Blue	Sor	R	160.00
☐ Tranquility	Green	Sor	C	1.00
☐ Tropical Island	Blk/Gr	DL	R	45.00
☐ Tsunami	Green	Sor	U	2.80
☐ Tundra	Blu/Wh	DL	R	50.00
☐ Tunnel	Red	Ins	U	2.30
☐ Twiddle	Blue	Ins	C	1.80
30				
☐ Two-Headed Giant	Red	Sum	R	45.00
☐ Underground Sea	Blk/Blu	DL	R	50.00
☐ Unholy Strength	Black	ECr	C	1.00
☐ Unsummon	Blue	Ins	C	1.00
☐ Uthden Troll	Red	Sum	U	3.00
☐ Verduran Enchantress	Green	Sum	R	15.00
☐ Vesuvan Doppelganger	Blue	Sum	R	45.00
☐ Veteran Bodyguard	White	Sum	R	18.00
☐ Volcanic Eruption	Blue	Sor	R	10.00
31				
☐ Wall of Air	Blue	Sum	U	2.80
☐ Wall of Bone	Black	Sum	U	2.00

Card name	Color	Type	Rarity	Price
☐ Wall of Brambles	Green	Sum	U	2.30
☐ Wall of Fire	Red	Sum	U	2.30
☐ Wall of Ice	Green	Sum	U	2.30
☐ Wall of Stone	Red	Sum	U	2.00
☐ Wall of Swords	White	Sum	U	2.50
☐ Wall of Water	Blue	Sum	U	2.00
☐ Wall of Wood	Green	Sum	C	1.00
32				
☐ Wanderlust	Green	ECr	U	2.30
☐ War Mammoth	Green	Sum	C	1.00
☐ Warp Artifact	Black	EArt	R	8.00
☐ Water Elemental	Blue	Sum	U	2.80
☐ Weakness	Black	ECr	C	1.00
☐ Web	Green	ECr	R	8.00
☐ Wheel of Fortune	Red	Sor	R	35.00
☐ White Knight	White	Sum	U	7.00
☐ White Ward	White	ECr	U	2.00
33				
☐ Wild Growth	Green	EL	C	1.00
☐ Will-O'-The-Wisp	Black	Sum	R	15.00
☐ Winter Orb	Artifact	C	R	23.00
☐ Wooden Sphere	Artifact	P	R	2.00
☐ Word of Command	Black	Ins	R	50.00
☐ Wrath of God	White	Sor	R	45.00
☐ Zombie Master	Black	Sum	R	13.50

Magic: The Gathering • Beta

Wizards of the Coast • Released **October 1993**

302 cards in set • **IDENTIFIER: Less rounded edges; black borders**

- Starter decks contain 60 cards; starter displays contain 10 starters
- Booster packs contain 15 cards; booster displays contain 36 boosters

For the **Beta** edition, corrections to a few cards were made and a few cards were added to bring the mix up to 302 cards. *Beta* had a print run of 7.3 million cards, and these black-bordered editions quickly sold out.

Rules clarifications were added to the Beta rulebooks, and a story by Richard Garfield was removed. *Beta* display boxes have UPC codes on them; **Alpha**'s don't.

These early **Magic: The Gathering** cards featured some of the game's most powerful and sought-after cards; **Black Lotus**, the Moxen, **Ancestral Recall**, **Timetwister**, and **Time Walk** are now called the "Power Nine," spells that were often thrown in any deck to make it just plain better that those who didn't have these cards. — *Bennie Smith*

You will need 34 nine-pocket pages to store each set. (17 doubled up)

Magic: The Gathering • Unlimited

Wizards of the Coast • Released **December 1993**

302 cards in set • **IDENTIFIER: White borders; double frame on card faces; darker colors**

- Starter decks contain 60 cards; starter displays contain 10 starters
- Booster packs contain 15 cards; booster displays contain 36 boosters

When **Beta** sold out quickly, a 35 million card white-bordered version was released as the "Unlimited" edition. Errors appeared in the set, however, and led to the release of **Revised** months later. — *Bennie Smith*

Megabucks

It's here in **Magic: Beta** that you'll find the most expensive CCG card around — **Black Lotus**, at $462.50. And the **Beta** set, at $5,150, is the most expensive item available in gaming.

Unlimited card shown below.

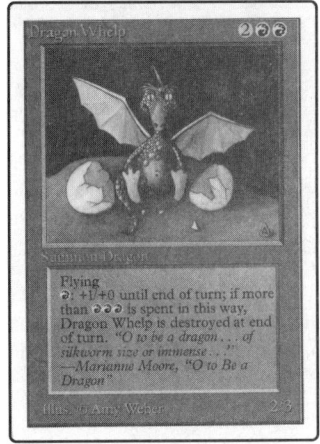

BETA

Set (292 cards + 10 variants)	5,150.00
Starter Display Box	2,700.00
Booster Display Box	3,700.00
Starter Deck	302.50
Booster Pack	130.00

UNLIMITED

Set (292 cards + 10 variants)	2,450.00
Starter Display Box	2,150.00
Booster Display Box	2,850.00
Starter Deck	225.00
Booster Pack	100.00

BET price	Card name	Color	Type	Rar	UNL price
1					1
☐ 3.00	Air Elemental	Blue	Sum	U	1.00 ☐
☐ 190.00	Ancestral Recall	Blue	Ins	R	150.00 ☐
☐ 2.00	Animate Artifact	Blue	EArt	U	1.00 ☐
☐ 2.80	Animate Dead	Black	EDCr	U	1.00 ☐
☐ 8.00	Animate Wall	White	EWa	R	5.00 ☐
☐ 10.50	Ankh of Mishra	Artifact	C	R	5.00 ☐
☐ 40.00	Armageddon	White	Sor	R	9.50 ☐
☐ 10.00	Aspect of Wolf	Green	ECr	R	5.50 ☐
☐ 27.50	Bad Moon	Black	E	R	8.00 ☐
2					2
☐ 50.00	Badlands	Blk/Rd	DL	R	17.50 ☐
☐ 32.50	Balance	White	Sor	R	6.00 ☐
☐ 4.00	Basalt Monolith	Artifact	M	U	2.00 ☐
☐ 50.00	Bayou	Blk/Gr	DL	R	16.50 ☐
☐ 1.00	Benalish Hero	White	Sum	C	0.50 ☐
☐ 40.00	Berserk	Green	Ins	U	31.00 ☐

BET price	Card name	Color	Type	Rar	UNL price
☐ 45.00	Birds of Paradise	Green	Sum	R	12.00 ☐
☐ 9.00	Black Knight	Black	Sum	U	2.00 ☐
☐ 462.50	Black Lotus	Artifact	M	R	300.00 ☐
3					3
☐ 9.00	Black Vise	Artifact	C	U	1.80 ☐
☐ 2.00	Black Ward	White	ECr	U	1.00 ☐
☐ 45.00	Blaze of Glory	White	Ins	R	26.50 ☐
☐ 12.00	Blessing	White	ECr	R	5.00 ☐
☐ 1.00	Blue Elemental Blast	Blue	Int	C	0.50 ☐
☐ 2.00	Blue Ward	White	ECr	U	1.00 ☐
☐ 2.00	Bog Wraith	Black	Sum	U	1.00 ☐
☐ 25.00	Braingeyser	Blue	Sor	R	11.00 ☐
☐ 2.00	Burrowing	Red	ECr	U	1.00 ☐
4					4
☐ 8.00	Camouflage	Green	Ins	U	5.00 ☐
☐ 2.00	Castle	White	E	U	1.00 ☐
☐ 2.00	Celestial Prism	Artifact	M	U	1.00 ☐

RARITY KEY C = Common U = Uncommon R = Rare VR = Very Rare UR = Ultra Rare F = Foil card X = Fixed/standard in all decks

BET price	Card name	Color	Type	Rar	UNL price
3.00	Channel	Green	Sor	U	1.00
80.00	Chaos Orb	Artifact	M	R	65.00
7.00	Chaoslace	Red	Int	R	4.50
1.00	Circle of Protection: Black	White	E	C	0.50
1.00	Circle of Protection: Blue	White	E	C	0.50
1.00	Circle of Protection: Green	White	E	C	0.50
1.30	Circle of Protection: Red	White	E	C	0.50
1.00	Circle of Protection: White	White	E	C	0.50
10.00	Clockwork Beast	Artifact	Cr	R	5.00
10.00	Clone	Blue	Sum	U	5.00
13.00	Cockatrice	Green	Sum	R	5.00
12.00	Consecrate Land	White	EL	U	7.00
2.00	Conservator	Artifact	M	U	1.00
9.00	Contract from Below	Black	Sor	R	5.00
8.00	Control Magic	Blue	ECr	U	2.00
2.00	Conversion	White	E	U	1.00
8.00	Copper Tablet	Artifact	C	U	4.00
23.50	Copy Artifact	Blue	E	R	7.50
15.00	Counterspell	Blue	Int	U	1.50
1.00	Craw Wurm	Green	Sum	C	0.50
1.00	Creature Bond	Blue	ECr	C	0.50
30.00	Crusade	White	E	R	9.00
2.00	Crystal Rod	Artifact	P	U	1.00
2.00	Cursed Land	Black	EL	U	1.00
57.50	Cyclopean Tomb	Artifact	M	R	38.50
5.00	Dark Ritual	Black	Int	C	0.50
8.00	Darkpact	Black	Sor	R	4.00
1.00	Death Ward	White	Ins	C	0.50
2.00	Deathgrip	Black	E	U	1.00
7.00	Deathlace	Black	Int	R	3.50
10.00	Demonic Attorney	Black	Sor	R	5.00
25.00	Demonic Hordes	Black	Sum	R	13.25
25.00	Demonic Tutor	Black	Sor	U	6.00
9.50	Dingus Egg	Artifact	C	R	5.00
5.00	Disenchant	White	Ins	C	0.50
2.50	Disintegrate	Red	Sor	C	0.50
25.00	Disrupting Scepter	Artifact	M	R	5.00
4.30	Dragon Whelp	Red	Sum	U	2.00
3.00	Drain Life	Black	Sor	C	0.50
10.00	Drain Power	Blue	Sor	R	5.00
1.00	Drudge Skeletons	Black	Sum	C	0.50
8.00	Dwarven Demolition Team	Red	Sum	U	6.00
1.00	Dwarven Warriors	Red	Sum	C	0.50
2.00	Earth Elemental	Red	Sum	U	1.00
1.00	Earthbind	Red	ECr	C	0.50
25.00	Earthquake	Red	Sor	R	5.50
19.00	Elvish Archers	Green	Sum	R	5.50
2.00	Evil Presence	Black	EL	U	1.00
3.00	False Orders	Red	Ins	C	1.00
9.00	Farmstead	White	E	R	5.00
19.00	Fastbond	Green	E	R	6.00
1.00	Fear	Black	ECr	C	0.50
2.00	Feedback	Blue	EE	U	1.00
2.00	Fire Elemental	Red	Sum	U	1.00
5.00	Fireball	Red	Sor	C	0.50
1.00	Firebreathing	Red	ECr	C	0.50
3.00	Flashfires	Red	Sor	U	1.00
1.00	Flight	Blue	ECr	C	0.50
1.00	Fog	Green	Ins	C	0.50
25.00	Force of Nature	Green	Sum	R	9.00
115.00	Forcefield	Artifact	P	R	75.00
1.00	Forest (ver. 1)	Green	L	C	0.25
1.00	Forest (ver. 2)	Green	L	C	0.25
1.00	Forest (ver. 3)	Green	L	C	0.25
42.50	Fork	Red	Int	R	18.00
1.00	Frozen Shade	Black	Sum	C	0.50
12.00	Fungusaur	Green	Sum	R	5.00
15.00	Gaea's Liege	Green	Sum	R	7.00
110.00	Gauntlet of Might	Artifact	C	R	80.00
3.00	Giant Growth	Green	Ins	C	0.50
1.00	Giant Spider	Green	Sum	C	0.50
2.00	Glasses of Urza	Artifact	M	U	1.00
3.50	Gloom	Black	E	U	1.00
2.90	Goblin Balloon Brigade	Red	Sum	U	1.00
19.50	Goblin King	Red	Sum	R	7.80
17.50	Granite Gargoyle	Red	Sum	R	9.00
1.00	Gray Ogre	Red	Sum	C	0.50
2.00	Green Ward	White	E	U	1.00
1.00	Grizzly Bears	Green	Sum	C	0.50
1.00	Guardian Angel	White	Ins	C	0.50
1.00	Healing Salve	White	Ins	C	0.50
9.50	Helm of Chatzuk	Artifact	M	R	4.00
1.00	Hill Giant	Red	Sum	C	0.50
1.00	Holy Armor	White	ECr	C	0.50
1.00	Holy Strength	White	ECr	C	0.50
1.00	Howl from Beyond	Black	Ins	C	0.50
28.00	Howling Mine	Artifact	C	R	10.00
1.00	Hurloon Minotaur	Red	Sum	C	0.50
4.50	Hurricane	Green	Sor	U	1.00
15.00	Hypnotic Specter	Black	Sum	R	3.50
24.00	Ice Storm	Green	Sor	U	15.50
40.00	Icy Manipulator	Artifact	M	R	25.00
45.00	Illusionary Mask	Artifact	P	R	30.00
3.00	Instill Energy	Green	ECr	U	1.00
3.00	Invisibility	Blue	ECr	C	1.00
2.00	Iron Star	Artifact	P	U	1.00
1.00	Ironclaw Orcs	Red	Sum	C	0.50
1.00	Ironroot Treefolk	Green	Sum	C	0.50
1.30	Island (ver. 1)	Blue	L	C	0.25
1.30	Island (ver. 2)	Blue	L	C	0.25
1.30	Island (ver. 3)	Blue	L	C	0.25
8.00	Island Sanctuary	White	E	R	5.00
2.00	Ivory Cup	Artifact	P	U	1.00
10.00	Jade Monolith	Artifact	P	R	2.00
15.00	Jade Statue	Artifact	M	U	7.00
30.00	Jayemdae Tome	Artifact	M	R	5.00
10.00	Juggernaut	Artifact	ACr	U	4.00
1.00	Jump	Blue	Ins	C	0.50
3.50	Karma	White	E	U	1.00
3.30	Keldon Warlord	Red	Sum	U	1.00
10.00	Kormus Bell	Artifact	C	R	5.00
9.00	Kudzu	Green	EL	R	5.00
2.00	Lance	White	ECr	U	1.00
2.00	Ley Druid	Green	Sum	U	1.00
2.50	Library of Leng	Artifact	C	U	1.00
45.00	Lich	Black	E	R	38.00
2.50	Lifeforce	Green	E	U	1.00
6.50	Lifelace	Green	Int	R	3.00
2.00	Lifetap	Blue	E	U	1.00
10.00	Lightning Bolt	Red	Ins	C	1.00
9.00	Living Artifact	Green	EArt	R	5.00
10.00	Living Lands	Green	EL	R	5.00
3.00	Living Wall	Artifact	ACr	U	1.00
3.50	Llanowar Elves	Green	Sum	C	0.50
20.00	Lord of Atlantis	Blue	Sum	R	7.50
25.00	Lord of the Pit	Black	Sum	R	10.00
2.00	Lure	Green	ECr	U	1.00
11.00	Magical Hack	Blue	Int	R	5.00
25.00	Mahamoti Djinn	Blue	Sum	R	9.00
23.00	Mana Flare	Red	E	R	7.30
15.00	Mana Short	Blue	Ins	R	6.00
23.75	Mana Vault	Artifact	M	R	6.00
12.00	Manabarbs	Red	E	R	5.00
17.50	Meekstone	Artifact	C	R	6.50
1.00	Merfolk of the Pearl Trident	Blue	Sum	C	0.50
1.00	Mesa Pegasus	White	Sum	C	0.50
15.00	Mind Twist	Black	Sor	R	6.50
1.00	Mons's Goblin Raiders	Red	Sum	C	0.50
1.00	Mountain (ver. 1)	Red	L	C	0.25
1.00	Mountain (ver. 2)	Red	L	C	0.25
1.00	Mountain (ver. 3)	Red	L	C	0.25
212.50	Mox Emerald	Artifact	M	R	150.00
215.00	Mox Jet	Artifact	M	R	160.00
217.50	Mox Pearl	Artifact	M	R	165.00
217.50	Mox Ruby	Artifact	M	R	165.00
225.00	Mox Sapphire	Artifact	M	R	175.00
29.50	Natural Selection	Green	Ins	R	28.00
12.00	Nether Shadow	Black	Sum	R	5.00
4.00	Nettling Imp	Black	Sum	U	2.00
50.00	Nevinyrral's Disk	Artifact	M	R	10.00
27.50	Nightmare	Black	Sum	R	8.00
15.00	Northern Paladin	White	Sum	R	7.00
2.00	Obsianus Golem	Artifact	ACr	U	1.00
2.50	Orcish Artillery	Red	Sum	U	1.00
3.00	Orcish Oriflamme	Red	E	U	1.00
1.00	Paralyze	Black	ECr	C	0.50
1.00	Pearled Unicorn	White	Sum	C	0.50
15.00	Personal Incarnation	White	Sum	R	6.00
1.00	Pestilence	Black	E	C	0.50
2.00	Phantasmal Forces	Blue	Sum	U	1.00
1.00	Phantasmal Terrain	Blue	Sum	C	0.50
2.00	Phantom Monster	Blue	Sum	U	1.00
10.00	Pirate Ship	Blue	Sum	R	5.00
1.00	Plague Rats	Black	Sum	C	0.50
1.00	Plains (ver. 1)	White	L	C	0.25
1.00	Plains (ver. 2)	White	L	C	0.25
1.00	Plains (ver. 3)	White	L	C	0.25
50.00	Plateau	Rd/Wh	DL	R	20.00
1.00	Power Leak	Blue	EE	C	0.50
1.80	Power Sink	Blue	Int	C	0.50
10.00	Power Surge	Red	E	R	5.00
2.00	Prodigal Sorcerer	Blue	Sum	C	0.50
30.00	Psionic Blast	Blue	Ins	U	25.00
1.00	Psychic Venom	Blue	EL	C	0.50
5.00	Purelace	White	Int	R	3.00
40.00	Raging River	Red	E	R	35.00
1.00	Raise Dead	Black	Sor	C	0.50
1.00	Red Elemental Blast	Red	Ins	C	0.50
2.00	Red Ward	White	ECr	U	1.00
1.00	Regeneration	Green	ECr	C	0.50
12.00	Regrowth	Green	Sor	R	0.80
3.00	Resurrection	White	Sor	U	1.00
15.00	Reverse Damage	White	Ins	R	7.00
14.00	Righteousness	White	Ins	R	6.00
15.00	Roc of Kher Ridges	Red	Sum	R	8.00
20.00	Rock Hydra	Red	Sum	R	12.50
3.00	Rod of Ruin	Artifact	M	U	5.00
35.00	Royal Assassin	Black	Sum	R	15.00
2.00	Sacrifice	Black	Int	R	1.00
1.00	Samite Healer	White	Sum	C	0.50
52.50	Savannah	Grn/Wh	DL	R	18.50
25.00	Savannah Lions	White	Sum	R	7.00
1.00	Scathe Zombies	Black	Sum	C	0.50
2.00	Scavenging Ghoul	Black	Sum	U	1.00
50.00	Scrubland	Blk/Wh	DL	R	18.00
1.00	Scryb Sprites	Green	Sum	C	0.50
1.00	Sea Serpent	Blue	Sum	C	0.50
14.00	Sedge Troll	Red	Sum	R	7.00
19.00	Sengir Vampire	Black	Sum	U	5.00

RARITY KEY C = Common U = Uncommon R = Rare VR = Very Rare UR = Ultra Rare F = Foil card **CARD TYPES: See page 246**

BET price	Card name	Color	Type	Rar	UNL price
30.00	Serra Angel	White	Sum	U	6.00
1.00	Shanodin Dryads	Green	Sum	C	0.50
1.00	Shatter	Red	Ins	C	0.50
55.00	Shivan Dragon	Red	Sum	R	17.00
2.00	Simulacrum	Black	Ins	U	1.00
17.50	Sinkhole	Black	Sor	C	10.00
2.00	Siren's Call	Blue	Ins	U	1.00
10.00	Sleight of Mind	Blue	Int	R	5.00
9.30	Smoke	Red	E	R	5.00
25.00	Sol Ring	Artifact	M	U	4.00
2.00	Soul Net	Artifact	P	U	1.00
1.00	Spell Blast	Blue	Int	C	0.50
20.00	Stasis	Blue	E	R	6.00
2.50	Steal Artifact	Blue	EArt	U	1.00
2.00	Stone Giant	Red	Sum	U	1.00
2.00	Stone Rain	Red	Sor	C	0.50
1.00	Stream of Life	Green	Sor	C	0.50
10.00	Sunglasses of Urza	Artifact C		R	4.00
1.00	Swamp (ver. 1)	Black	L	C	0.25
1.00	Swamp (ver. 2)	Black	L	C	0.25
1.00	Swamp (ver. 3)	Black	L	C	0.25
17.50	Swords to Plowshares	White	Ins	U	2.00
55.00	Taiga	Grn/Rd	DL	R	18.50
2.00	Terror	Black	Ins	C	0.50

BET price	Card name	Color	Type	Rar	UNL price
10.00	The Hive	Artifact M		R	5.00
3.00	Thicket Basilisk	Green	Sum	U	1.00
5.00	Thoughtlace	Blue	Int	R	3.00
2.00	Throne of Bone	Artifact P		U	1.00
9.00	Timber Wolves	Green	Sum	R	5.00
70.00	Time Vault	Artifact M		R	51.00
250.00	Time Walk	Blue	Sor	R	175.00
177.50	Timetwister	Blue	Sor	R	145.00
1.00	Tranquility	Green	Sor	C	0.50
50.00	Tropical Island	Blk/Gr	DL	R	20.00
2.50	Tsunami	Green	Sor	U	1.00
55.00	Tundra	Blu/Wh	DL	R	20.00
2.00	Tunnel	Red	Ins	U	1.00
1.00	Twiddle	Blue	Ins	C	0.50
50.00	Two-Headed Giant	Red	Sum	R	38.00
50.00	Underground Sea	Blk/Blu	DL	R	18.50
1.50	Unholy Strength	Black	ECr	C	0.50
1.00	Unsummon	Blue	Ins	C	0.50
2.50	Uthden Troll	Red	Sum	U	1.00
14.00	Verduran Enchantress	Grn	Sum	R	5.50
35.00	Vesuvan Doppelganger	Blue	Sum	R	18.00
20.00	Veteran Bodyguard	White	Sum	R	8.00
10.00	Volcanic Eruption	Blue	Sor	R	5.00
55.00	Volcanic Island	Blu/Rd	DL	R	18.50

BET price	Card name	Color	Type	Rar	UNL price
2.50	Wall of Air	Blue	Sum	U	1.00
2.00	Wall of Bone	Black	Sum	U	1.00
2.00	Wall of Brambles	Green	Sum	U	1.00
2.00	Wall of Fire	Red	Sum	U	1.00
2.00	Wall of Ice	Green	Sum	U	1.00
2.00	Wall of Stone	Red	Sum	U	1.00
2.50	Wall of Swords	White	Sum	U	1.00
2.00	Wall of Water	Blue	Sum	U	1.00
1.00	Wall of Wood	Green	Sum	C	0.50
2.00	Wanderlust	Green	ECr	U	1.00
1.00	War Mammoth	Green	Sum	C	0.50
8.30	Warp Artifact	Black	EArt	R	5.00
2.00	Water Elemental	Blue	Sum	U	1.00
1.00	Weakness	Black	ECr	C	0.50
8.00	Web	Green	ECr	R	4.00
35.00	Wheel of Fortune	Red	Sor	R	12.00
10.00	White Knight	White	Sum	R	2.00
2.00	White Ward	White	ECr	U	1.00
1.50	Wild Growth	Green	EL	C	0.50
21.00	Will-O'-The-Wisp	Black	Sum	R	7.80
27.50	Winter Orb	Artifact C		R	7.00
2.00	Wooden Sphere	Artifact P		U	1.00
50.00	Word of Command	Black	Ins	R	39.00
50.00	Wrath of God	White	Sor	R	10.00
11.00	Zombie Master	Black	Sum	R	7.00

Magic: The Gathering • Revised

MAGIC The Gathering

Wizards of the Coast • Released April 1994

306 cards in set • **IDENTIFIER: White border, single frame on card face; "washy" colors**

- Starter decks contain 60 cards; starter displays contain 10 starters
- Booster packs contain 15 cards; booster displays contain 36 boosters

The **Revised** edition of the basic set was released in April 1994 and included 306 cards. Many of the first editions' overly powerful cards were removed, and cards from the first two **Magic** expansions, **Arabian Nights** and **Antiquities**, were added to the mix. Mainstays such as **Millstone, Dancing Scimitar, Ivory Tower, Erg Raiders, Sorceress Queen, Atog**, and **Desert Twister** made this transition to the base set.

Players who enjoyed the raw power of **Alpha/Beta/Unlimited** were generally disappointed to see so many of their favorite high-octane cards leave, to be replaced by relatively weaker cards. *Revised* did reprint the popular "dual lands" (lands that could produce either of two different colored mana) and also cleaned up several rules and graphical oversights from the previous basic set. — *Bennie Smith*

You will need **34** nine-pocket pages to store this set. (17 doubled up)

Library of Leng — Artifact. You must skip the discard phase of your turn. If a card forces you to discard, you may choose to discard to top of your library rather than to graveyard. If discard is random, you may look at card before deciding where to discard it. Illus. © Daniel Gelon

Set (296 cards + 10 variants)		**274.00**
Starter Display Box		**275.50**
Booster Display Box		**340.50**
Starter Deck		**34.00**
Booster Pack		**10.00**

Card name	Color	Type	Rarity	Price
Air Elemental	Blue	Int	U	1.00
Aladdin's Lamp	Artifact	Art	R	3.00
Aladdin's Ring	Artifact	Art	R	3.00
Animate Artifact	Blue	EArt	U	1.00
Animate Dead	Black	ECr	U	1.00
Animate Wall	White	EWa	R	3.00
Ankh of Mishra	Artifact	Art	R	4.00
Armageddon	White	Sor	R	6.00
Armageddon Clock	Artifact	Art	R	3.00
Aspect of Wolf	Green	ECr	R	3.00
Atog	Red	Sum	C	0.25
Bad Moon	Black	E	R	6.00
Badlands	Blk/Rd	DL	R	13.00
Balance	White	Sor	R	4.80
Basalt Monolith	Artifact	Art	U	1.00
Bayou	Blk/Gr	DL	R	12.75
Benalish Hero	White	Sum	C	0.20
Birds of Paradise	Green	Sum	R	8.00
Black Knight	Black	Sum	U	1.00

Card name	Color	Type	Rarity	Price
Black Vise	Artifact	Art	U	1.00
Black Ward	White	ECr	U	0.70
Blessing	White	ECr	R	4.00
Blue Elemental Blast	Blue	Int	C	0.20
Blue Ward	White	ECr	U	0.90
Bog Wraith	Black	Sum	U	1.00
Bottle of Suleiman	Artifact	Art	R	3.00
Braingeyser	Blue	Sor	R	7.00
Brass Man	Artifact	ACr	U	1.00
Burrowing	Red	ECr	U	0.90
Castle	White	E	U	0.90
Celestial Prism	Artifact	Art	U	1.00
Channel	Green	Sor	U	1.00
Chaoslace	Red	Int	R	2.30
Circle of Protection: Black	White	E	C	0.20
Circle of Protection: Blue	White	E	C	0.15
Circle of Protection: Green	White	E	C	0.20
Circle of Protection: Red	White	E	C	0.15
Circle of Protection: White	White	E	C	0.20
Clockwork Beast	Artifact	ACr	R	3.50
Clone	Blue	Sum	R	3.00
Cockatrice	Green	Sum	R	4.00
Conservator	Artifact	Art	U	1.00
Contract from Below	Black	Sor	R	3.50
Control Magic	Blue	ECr	U	1.00

Card name	Color	Type	Rarity	Price
Conversion	White	E	U	1.00
Copy Artifact	Blue	E	R	5.50
Counterspell	Blue	Int	U	1.00
Craw Wurm	Green	Sum	C	0.20
Creature Bond	Blue	ECr	C	0.20
Crumble	Green	Ins	U	1.00
Crusade	White	E	R	5.00
Crystal Rod	Artifact	Art	U	1.00
Cursed Land	Black	EL	U	1.00
Dancing Scimitar	Artifact	ACr	R	3.30
Dark Ritual	Black	Int	C	0.25
Darkpact	Black	Sor	R	3.00
Death Ward	White	Ins	C	0.20
Deathgrip	Black	E	U	1.00
Deathlace	Black	Int	R	3.00
Demonic Attorney	Black	Sor	R	4.00
Demonic Hordes	Black	Sum	R	7.50
Demonic Tutor	Black	Sor	U	3.50
Desert Twister	Green	Sor	U	1.00
Dingus Egg	Artifact	Art	R	3.20
Disenchant	White	Ins	C	0.20
Disintegrate	Red	Sor	C	0.25
Disrupting Scepter	Artifact	Art	R	3.00
Dragon Engine	Artifact	ACr	R	2.80
Dragon Whelp	Red	Sum	U	1.00

RARITY KEY C = Common U = Uncommon R = Rare VR = Very Rare UR = Ultra Rare F = Foil card **CARD TYPES: See page 246**

Card name	Color	Type	Rarity	Price
Drain Life	Black	Sor	C	0.25
Drain Power	Blue	Sor	R	3.00
Drudge Skeletons	Black	Sum	C	0.20
9				
Dwarven Warriors	Red	Sum	C	0.20
Dwarven Weaponsmith	Red	Sum	U	1.00
Earth Elemental	Red	Sum	U	1.00
Earthbind	Red	ECr	C	0.25
Earthquake	Red	Sor	R	4.00
Ebony Horse	Artifact	Art	R	3.00
El -Hajjaj	Black	Sum	R	3.50
Elvish Archers	Green	Sum	R	3.00
Energy Flux	Blue	E	U	1.00
10				
Erg Raiders	Black	Sum	C	0.20
Evil Presence	Black	EL	U	0.90
Eye for an Eye	White	Ins	R	3.50
Farmstead	White	EL	R	4.30
Fastbond	Green	E	R	5.00
Fear	Black	ECr	C	0.20
Feedback	Blue	EE	U	1.00
Fire Elemental	Red	Sum	U	1.00
Fireball	Red	Sor	C	0.25
11				
Firebreathing	Red	ECr	C	0.15
Flashfires	Red	Sor	U	1.00
Flight	Blue	ECr	C	0.20
Flying Carpet	Artifact	Art	R	3.00
Fog	Green	Ins	C	0.20
Force of Nature	Green	Sum	R	6.30
Forest (ver. 1)	Green	L	C	0.10
Forest (ver. 2)	Green	L	C	0.10
Forest (ver. 3)	Green	L	C	0.10
12				
Fork	Red	Int	R	15.00
Frozen Shade	Black	Sum	C	0.20
Fungusaur	Green	Sum	R	4.00
Gaea's Liege	Green	Sum	R	5.00
Giant Growth	Green	Ins	C	0.20
Giant Spider	Green	Sum	C	0.15
Glasses of Urza	Artifact	Art	U	1.00
Gloom	Black	E	U	1.00
Goblin Balloon Brigade	Red	Sum	U	1.00
13				
Goblin King	Red	Sum	R	5.20
Granite Gargoyle	Red	Sum	R	5.00
Gray Ogre	Red	Sum	C	0.20
Green Ward	White	ECr	U	1.00
Grizzly Bears	Green	Sum	C	0.20
Guardian Angel	White	Ins	C	0.25
Healing Salve	White	Ins	C	0.20
Helm of Chatzuk	Artifact	Art	R	3.00
Hill Giant	Red	Sum	C	0.20
14				
Holy Armor	White	ECr	C	0.20
Holy Strength	White	ECr	C	0.20
Howl from Beyond	Black	Ins	C	0.20
Howling Mine	Artifact	Art	R	6.00
Hurkyl's Recall	Blue	Ins	R	3.00
Hurloon Minotaur	Red	Sum	C	0.20
Hurricane	Green	Sor	U	1.00
Hypnotic Specter	Black	Sum	U	2.00
Instill Energy	Green	ECr	U	1.00
15				
Iron Star	Artifact	Art	U	1.00
Ironroot Treefolk	Green	Sum	C	0.20
Island (ver. 1)	Blue	L	C	0.15
Island (ver. 2)	Blue	L	C	0.15
Island (ver. 3)	Blue	L	C	0.15
Island Fish Jasconius	Blue	Sum	R	3.00
Island Sanctuary	White	E	R	4.00
Ivory Cup	Artifact	Art	U	0.90
Ivory Tower	Artifact	Art	R	5.00
16				
Jade Monolith	Artifact	Art	R	3.00
Jandor's Ring	Artifact	Art	R	4.00
Jandor's Saddlebags	Artifact	Art	R	3.00
Jayemdae Tome	Artifact	Art	R	4.00
Juggernaut	Artifact	ACr	U	1.00
Jump	Blue	Ins	C	0.20
Karma	White	E	U	1.00
Keldon Warlord	Red	Sum	U	1.00
Kird Ape	Red	Sum	C	0.30
17				
Kormus Bell	Artifact	Art	R	3.00
Kudzu	Green	EL	R	4.00
Lance	White	ECr	U	1.00
Ley Druid	Green	Sum	U	0.90
Library of Leng	Artifact	Art	U	1.00
Lifeforce	Green	E	U	1.00
Lifelace	Green	Int	R	2.00
Lifetap	Blue	E	U	1.00
Lightning Bolt	Red	Ins	C	0.50
18				
Living Artifact	Green	EArt	R	3.00
Living Lands	Green	E	R	4.00
Living Wall	Artifact	Art	U	1.00
Llanowar Elves	Green	Sum	C	0.25
Lord of Atlantis	Blue	Sum	R	4.80
Lord of the Pit	Black	Sum	R	6.00
Lure	Green	ECr	U	1.00
Magical Hack	Blue	Int	R	4.00
Magnetic Mountain	Red	E	R	3.00
19				
Mahamoti Djinn	Blue	Sum	R	6.00
Mana Flare	Red	E	R	5.00
Mana Short	Blue	Ins	R	4.00
Mana Vault	Artifact	Art	R	4.00
Manabarbs	Red	E	R	4.00
Meekstone	Artifact	Art	R	4.00
Merfolk of the Pearl Trident	Blue	Sum	C	0.20
Mesa Pegasus	White	Sum	C	0.20
Mijae Djinn	Red	Sum	R	4.00
20				
Millstone	Artifact	Art	R	5.00
Mind Twist	Black	Sor	R	5.00
Mishra's War Machine	Artifact	ACr	R	3.00
Mons's Goblin Raiders	Red	Sum	C	0.20
Mountain (ver. 1)	Red	L	C	0.10
Mountain (ver. 2)	Red	L	C	0.10
Mountain (ver. 3)	Red	L	C	0.10
Nether Shadow	Black	Sum	R	4.00
Nettling Imp	Black	Sum	U	1.00
21				
Nevinyrral's Disk	Artifact	Art	R	6.40
Nightmare	Black	Sum	R	6.00
Northern Paladin	White	Sum	R	4.50
Obsianus Golem	Artifact	ACr	U	1.00
Onulet	Artifact	ACr	R	2.40
Orcish Artillery	Red	Sum	U	1.00
Orcish Oriflamme	Red	E	U	1.00
Ornithopter	Artifact	ACr	U	1.00
Paralyze	Black	ECr	C	0.20
22				
Pearled Unicorn	White	Sum	C	0.20
Personal Incarnation	White	Sum	R	4.00
Pestilence	Black	E	C	0.20
Phantasmal Forces	Blue	Sum	U	1.00
Phantasmal Terrain	Blue	EL	C	0.20
Phantom Monster	Blue	Sum	U	1.00
Pirate Ship	Blue	Sum	R	3.00
Plague Rats	Black	Sum	C	0.20
Plains (ver. 1)	White	L	C	0.10
23				
Plains (ver. 2)	White	L	C	0.10
Plains (ver. 3)	White	L	C	0.10
Plateau	Rd/Wh	DL	R	13.25
Power Leak	Blue	EE	C	0.20
Power Sink	Blue	Int	C	0.25
Power Surge	Red	E	R	3.30
Primal Clay	Artifact	ACr	R	3.00
Prodigal Sorcerer	Blue	Sum	C	0.20
Psychic Venom	Blue	EL	C	0.20
24				
Purelace	White	Int	R	2.00
Raise Dead	Black	Sor	C	0.20
Reconstruction	Blue	Sor	C	0.25
Red Elemental Blast	Red	Int	C	0.20
Red Ward	White	ECr	U	0.70
Regeneration	Green	ECr	C	0.20
Regrowth	Green	Sor	U	1.00
Resurrection	White	Sor	U	1.00
Reverse Damage	White	Ins	R	4.80
25				
Reverse Polarity	White	Ins	U	1.00
Righteousness	White	Ins	R	4.00
Roc of Kher Ridges	Red	Sum	R	5.00
Rock Hydra	Red	Sum	R	7.00
Rocket Launcher	Artifact	Art	R	4.00
Rod of Ruin	Artifact	Art	U	1.00
Royal Assassin	Black	Sum	R	11.00
Sacrifice	Black	Int	U	1.00
Samite Healer	White	Sum	C	0.20
26				
Savannah	Gr/Wh	DL	R	13.00
Savannah Lions	White	Sum	R	5.00
Scathe Zombies	Black	Sum	C	0.20
Scavenging Ghoul	Black	Sum	U	1.00
Scrubland	Blk/Wh	DL	R	12.75
Scryb Sprites	Green	Sum	C	0.20
Sea Serpent	Blue	Sum	C	0.20
Sedge Troll	Red	Sum	R	5.00
Sengir Vampire	Black	Sum	U	3.00
27				
Serendib Efreet	Blue	Sum	R	6.00
Serra Angel	White	Sum	U	4.50
Shanodin Dryads	Green	Sum	C	0.20
Shatter	Red	Ins	C	0.20
Shatterstorm	Red	Sor	U	1.00
Shivan Dragon	Red	Sum	R	12.75
Simulacrum	Black	Ins	U	1.00
Siren's Call	Blue	Ins	U	1.00
Sleight of Mind	Blue	Int	R	3.00
28				
Smoke	Red	E	R	3.80
Sol Ring	Artifact	Art	U	1.00
Sorceress Queen	Black	Sum	R	4.50
Soul Net	Artifact	Art	U	0.90
Spell Blast	Blue	Int	C	0.20
Stasis	Blue	E	R	4.00
Steal Artifact	Blue	EArt	U	1.00
Stone Giant	Red	Sum	U	1.00
Stone Rain	Red	Sor	C	0.20
29				
Stream of Life	Green	Sor	C	0.20
Sunglasses of Urza	Artifact	Art	R	3.00
Swamp (ver. 1)	Black	L	C	0.15
Swamp (ver. 2)	Black	L	C	0.15
Swamp (ver. 3)	Black	L	C	0.15
Swords to Plowshares	White	Ins	U	1.00
Taiga	Rd/Gr	DL	R	13.25
Terror	Black	Ins	C	0.20
The Hive	Artifact	Art	R	4.00
30				
The Rack	Artifact	Art	U	1.00
Thicket Basilisk	Green	Sum	U	1.00
Thoughtlace	Blue	Int	R	2.00
Throne of Bone	Artifact	Art	U	0.90
Timber Wolves	Green	Sum	R	3.00
Titania's Song	Green	E	R	3.00
Tranquility	Green	Sor	C	0.20

RARITY KEY C = Common   U = Uncommon   R = Rare   VR = Very Rare   UR = Ultra Rare   F = Foil card   **CARD TYPES: See page 246**

Card name	Color	Type	Rarity	Price
☐ Tropical Island	Blu/Gr	DL	R	13.25
☐ Tsunami	Green	Sor	U	1.00
31				
☐ Tundra	Blu/Wh	DL	R	13.50
☐ Tunnel	Red	Ins	U	1.00
☐ Underground Sea	Blk/Blu	DL	R	12.75
☐ Unholy Strength	Black	ECr	C	0.20
☐ Unstable Mutation	Blue	ECr	C	0.20
☐ Unsummon	Blue	Ins	C	0.20
☐ Uthden Troll	Red	Sum	U	1.00
☐ Verduran Enchantress	Green	Sum	R	4.00
☐ Vesuvan Doppelganger	Blue	Sum	R	15.50
32				
☐ Veteran Bodyguard	White	Sum	R	6.00

Card name	Color	Type	Rarity	Price
☐ Volcanic Eruption	Blue	Sor	R	3.00
☐ Volcanic Island	Blu/Rd	DL	R	13.25
☐ Wall of Air	Blue	Sum	U	1.00
☐ Wall of Bone	Black	Sum	U	1.00
☐ Wall of Brambles	Green	Sum	U	1.00
☐ Wall of Fire	Red	Sum	U	1.00
☐ Wall of Ice	Green	Sum	U	1.00
☐ Wall of Stone	Red	Sum	U	1.00
33				
☐ Wall of Swords	White	Sum	U	1.00
☐ Wall of Water	Blue	Sum	U	1.00
☐ Wall of Wood	Green	Sum	C	0.15
☐ Wanderlust	Green	ECr	U	1.00
☐ War Mammoth	Green	Sum	C	0.20

Card name	Color	Type	Rarity	Price
☐ Warp Artifact	Black	EArt	R	3.00
☐ Water Elemental	Blue	Sum	U	1.00
☐ Weakness	Black	ECr	C	0.20
☐ Web	Green	ECr	R	3.00
34				
☐ Wheel of Fortune	Red	Sor	R	8.00
☐ White Knight	White	Sum	U	1.00
☐ White Ward	White	ECr	U	1.00
☐ Wild Growth	Green	EL	C	0.20
☐ Will-O'-The-Wisp	Black	Sum	R	5.00
☐ Winter Orb	Artifact	Art	R	5.00
☐ Wooden Sphere	Artifact	Art	U	1.00
☐ Wrath of God	White	Sor	R	6.80
☐ Zombie Master	Black	Sum	R	3.80

Magic: The Gathering • Fourth Edition
Wizards of the Coast • Released April 1995
368 cards plus **10** variants • **IDENTIFIER: White border, double frame; © 1995 on bottom**

- Starter decks contain 60 cards; starter displays contain 10 starters
- Booster packs contain 15 cards; booster displays contain 36 boosters

As **Magic** grew in popularity and was exposed to a larger pool of players, Wizards of the Coast was able to evaluate the game as never before and better determine which card designs were unbalanced. With this and a desire to add new dynamics to the game, in April 1995, Wizards released the **Fourth Edition** of the basic **Magic** set, dropping 51 cards from **Revised** and adding 122 cards from previous expansions, bringing the base set total to a whopping 378 cards.

Gone were such favorites as **Sol Ring, Demonic Tutor, Fastbond, Regrowth, Fork, Wheel of Fortune, Serendib Efreet**, and all the dual lands. However, Wizards did bring back many good cards from expansions, including **Sylvan Library, Fellwar Stone, Mishra's Factory, Strip Mine, Ball Lightning, Time Elemental**, and **Land Tax**. This basic set lasted two years, producing a stable set of cards for players to build decks from. — **Bennie Smith**

You will need **42** nine-pocket pages to store this set. (21 doubled up)

Set (368 cards + 10 variants)			195.00
Starter Display Box			100.00
Booster Display Box			117.50
Starter Deck			11.00
Booster Pack			4.00
Gift set			25.00

Card name	Color	Type	Rarity	Price
1				
☐ Abomination	Black	Sum	U	1.00
☐ Air Elemental	Blue	Int	U	1.00
☐ Alabaster Potion	White	Ins	C	0.20
☐ Aladdin's Lamp	Artifact	M	R	3.00
☐ Aladdin's Ring	Artifact	M	R	3.00
☐ Ali Baba	Red	Sum	U	1.00
☐ Amrou Kithkin	White	Sum	C	0.20
☐ Amulet of Kroog	Artifact	Art	C	0.20
☐ Angry Mob	White	Sum	U	1.00
2				
☐ Animate Artifact	Blue	EArt	U	1.00
☐ Animate Dead	Black	ECr	U	1.00
☐ Animate Wall	White	EWall	R	3.00
☐ Ankh of Mishra	Artifact	C	R	3.50
☐ Apprentice Wizard	Blue	Sum	C	0.25
☐ Armageddon	White	Sor	R	7.00
☐ Armageddon Clock	Artifact	C	R	3.00
☐ Ashes to Ashes	Black	Sor	U	1.00
☐ Ashnod's Battle Gear	Artifact	M	U	1.00
3				
☐ Aspect of Wolf	Green	ECr	R	3.00
☐ Backfire	Blue	ECr	U	1.00
☐ Bad Moon	Black	E	R	6.00
☐ Balance	White	Sor	R	5.00
☐ Ball Lightning	Red	Sum	R	10.00
☐ Battering Ram	Artifact	ACr	C	0.20
☐ Benalish Hero	White	Sum	C	0.20
☐ Bird Maiden	Red	Sum	C	0.20
☐ Birds of Paradise	Green	Sum	R	8.00
4				
☐ Black Knight	Black	Sum	U	1.00
☐ Black Mana Battery	Artifact	A	R	3.00

Card name	Color	Type	Rarity	Price
☐ Black Vise	Artifact	C	U	1.00
☐ Black Ward	White	ECr	U	0.50
☐ Blessing	White	ECr	R	4.00
☐ Blight	Black	EL	U	1.00
☐ Blood Lust	Red	Ins	C	0.20
☐ Blue Elemental Blast	Blue	Int	C	0.20
☐ Blue Mana Battery	Artifact	A	R	3.00
5				
☐ Blue Ward	White	ECr	U	0.50
☐ Bog Imp	Black	Sum	C	0.20
☐ Bog Wraith	Black	Sum	U	1.00
☐ Bottle of Suleiman	Artifact	M	R	3.00
☐ Brainwash	White	ECr	C	0.20
☐ Brass Man	Artifact	ACr	U	0.80
☐ Bronze Tablet	Artifact	M	R	3.00
☐ Brothers of Fire	Red	Sum	C	0.25
6				
☐ Burrowing	Red	ECr	U	0.70
☐ Carnivorous Plant	Green	Sum	C	0.20
☐ Carrion Ants	Black	Sum	U	1.00
☐ Castle	White	E	U	0.70
☐ Cave People	Red	Sum	U	0.80
☐ Celestial Prism	Artifact	M	U	1.00
☐ Channel	Green	Sor	U	1.00
☐ Chaoslace	Red	Int	R	3.00
☐ Circle of Protection: Artifacts	White	E	U	1.00
☐ Circle of Protection: Black	White	E	C	0.20
7				
☐ Circle of Protection: Blue	White	E	C	0.20
☐ Circle of Protection: Green	White	E	C	0.20
☐ Circle of Protection: Red	White	E	C	0.20
☐ Circle of Protection: White	White	E	C	0.25
☐ Clay Statue	Artifact	ACr	C	0.20
☐ Clockwork Avian	Artifact	ACr	R	3.00
☐ Clockwork Beast	Artifact	ACr	R	3.00
☐ Cockatrice	Green	Sum	R	4.00
☐ Colossus of Sardia	Artifact	ACr	R	6.00
8				
☐ Conservator	Artifact	M	U	1.00
☐ Control Magic	Blue	ECr	U	1.00

Card name	Color	Type	Rarity	Price
☐ Conversion	White	E	U	1.00
☐ Coral Helm	Artifact	P	R	3.00
☐ Cosmic Horror	Black	Sum	R	4.00
☐ Counterspell	Blue	Int	U	1.00
☐ Craw Wurm	Green	Sum	C	0.20
☐ Creature Bond	Blue	ECr	C	0.20
☐ Crimson Manticore	Red	Sum	R	3.00
9				
☐ Crumble	Green	Ins	U	0.80
☐ Crusade	White	E	R	5.00
☐ Crystal Rod	Artifact	P	U	0.80
☐ Cursed Land	Black	EL	U	0.80
☐ Cursed Rack	Artifact	C	U	1.00
☐ Cyclopean Mummy	Black	Sum	C	0.20
☐ Dancing Scimitar	Artifact	ACr	R	3.00
☐ Dark Ritual	Black	Int	C	0.25
☐ Death Ward	White	Ins	C	0.20
10				
☐ Deathgrip	Black	E	U	0.80
☐ Deathlace	Black	Int	R	2.00
☐ Desert Twister	Green	Sor	U	1.00
☐ Detonate	Red	Sor	U	0.80
☐ Diabolic Machine	Artifact	ACr	U	0.70
☐ Dingus Egg	Artifact	C	R	3.00
☐ Disenchant	White	Ins	C	0.25
☐ Disintegrate	Red	Sor	C	0.25
☐ Disrupting Scepter	Artifact	M	R	3.00
11				
☐ Divine Transformation	White	ECr	U	1.00
☐ Dragon Engine	Artifact	ACr	R	2.00
☐ Dragon Whelp	Red	Sum	U	1.00
☐ Drain Life	Black	Sor	C	0.25
☐ Drain Power	Blue	Sor	R	4.00
☐ Drudge Skeletons	Black	Sum	C	0.20
☐ Durkwood Boars	Green	Sum	C	0.20
☐ Dwarven Warriors	Red	Sum	C	0.20
☐ Earth Elemental	Red	Sum	U	0.80
12				
☐ Earthquake	Red	Sor	R	4.00
☐ Ebony Horse	Artifact	M	R	3.00
☐ Elder Land Wurm	White	Sum	R	3.00

Card name	Color	Type	Rarity	Price
El -Hajjaj	Black	Sum	R	4.00
Elven Riders	Green	Sum	U	1.00
Elvish Archers	Green	Sum	R	3.50
Energy Flux	Blue	E	U	1.00
Energy Tap	Blue	Sor	C	0.25
Erg Raiders	Black	Sum	C	0.20

13

Card name	Color	Type	Rarity	Price
Erosion	Blue	ELnd	C	0.20
Eternal Warrior	Red	ECr	C	0.20
Evil Presence	Black	ELnd	U	0.50
Eye for an Eye	White	Ins	R	3.00
Fear	Black	ECr	C	0.20
Feedback	Blue	EE	U	0.80
Fellwar Stone	Artifact	Art	U	1.00
Fire Elemental	Red	Sum	U	0.80
Fireball	Red	Sor	C	0.25

14

Card name	Color	Type	Rarity	Price
Firebreathing	Red	ECr	C	0.20
Fissure	Red	Ins	C	0.25
Flashfires	Red	Sor	U	0.80
Flight	Blue	ECr	C	0.20
Flood	Blue	E	C	0.20
Flying Carpet	Artifact	M	R	3.00
Fog	Green	Ins	C	0.20
Force of Nature	Green	Sum	R	6.00
Forest (ver. 1)	Green	Lnd	C	0.10

15

Card name	Color	Type	Rarity	Price
Forest (ver. 2)	Green	Lnd	C	0.10
Forest (ver. 3)	Green	Lnd	C	0.10
Fortified Area	White	E	C	0.20
Frozen Shade	Black	Sum	C	0.20
Fungusaur	Green	Sum	R	3.00
Gaea's Liege	Green	Sum	R	5.00
Gaseous Form	Blue	ECr	C	0.20
Ghost Ship	Blue	Sum	U	0.70
Giant Growth	Green	Ins	C	0.25

16

Card name	Color	Type	Rarity	Price
Giant Spider	Green	Sum	C	0.20
Giant Strength	Red	ECr	C	0.20
Giant Tortoise	Blue	Sum	C	0.20
Glasses of Urza	Artifact	M	U	0.70
Gloom	Black	E	U	1.00
Goblin Balloon Brigade	Red	Sum	U	1.00
Goblin King	Red	Sum	R	5.00
Goblin Rock Sled	Red	Sum	C	0.20
Grapeshot Catapult	Artifact	ACr	C	0.20

17

Card name	Color	Type	Rarity	Price
Gray Ogre	Red	Sum	C	0.20
Greed	Black	E	R	3.00
Green Mana Battery	Artifact	Art	R	3.00
Green Ward	White	ECr	U	0.70
Grizzly Bears	Green	Sum	C	0.20
Healing Salve	White	Ins	C	0.20
Helm of Chatzuk	Artifact	M	R	3.00
Hill Giant	Red	Sum	C	0.20
Holy Armor	White	ECr	C	0.20

18

Card name	Color	Type	Rarity	Price
Holy Strength	White	ECr	C	0.20
Howl from Beyond	Black	Ins	C	0.25
Howling Mine	Artifact	C	R	6.00
Hurkyl's Recall	Blue	Ins	R	3.00
Hurloon Minotaur	Red	Sum	C	0.20
Hurr Jackal	Red	Sum	R	3.00
Hurricane	Green	Sor	U	1.00
Hypnotic Specter	Black	Sum	U	2.00
Immolation	Red	ECr	C	0.20

19

Card name	Color	Type	Rarity	Price
Inferno	Red	Ins	R	4.00
Instill Energy	Green	ECr	U	1.00
Iron Star	Red	Sum	C	0.25
Ironclaw Orcs	Artifact	P	C	0.20
Ironroot Treefolk	Green	Sum	C	0.20
Island (ver. 1)	Blue	Lnd	C	0.10
Island (ver. 2)	Blue	Lnd	C	0.10
Island (ver. 3)	Blue	Lnd	C	0.10
Island Fish Jasconius	Blue	Sum	R	3.00

20

Card name	Color	Type	Rarity	Price
Island Sanctuary	White	E	R	4.00

Card name	Color	Type	Rarity	Price
Ivory Cup	Artifact	P	U	1.00
Ivory Tower	Artifact	C	R	5.00
Jade Monolith	Artifact	P	R	3.00
Jandor's Saddlebags	Artifact	M	R	3.00
Jayemdae Tome	Artifact	M	R	4.00
Jump	Blue	Ins	C	0.20
Junun Efreet	Black	Sum	U	1.00
Karma	White	E	U	1.00

21

Card name	Color	Type	Rarity	Price
Keldon Warlord	Red	Sum	U	1.00
Killer Bees	Green	Sum	U	1.00
Kismet	White	E	U	1.00
Kormus Bell	Artifact	C	R	4.00
Land Leeches	Green	Sum	C	0.20
Land Tax	White	E	R	5.00
Leviathan	Blue	Sum	R	5.00
Ley Druid	Green	Sum	U	0.50
Library of Leng	Artifact	C	U	1.00

22

Card name	Color	Type	Rarity	Price
Lifeforce	Green	E	U	0.80
Lifelace	Green	Int	R	3.00
Lifetap	Blue	E	U	0.50
Lightning Bolt	Red	Ins	C	0.50
Living Artifact	Green	EArt	R	3.00
Living Lands	Green	E	R	3.00
Llanowar Elves	Green	Sum	C	0.25
Lord of Atlantis	Blue	Sum	R	4.50
Lord of the Pit	Black	Sum	R	6.00

23

Card name	Color	Type	Rarity	Price
Lost Soul	Black	Sum	C	0.25
Lure	Green	ECr	U	0.80
Magical Hack	Blue	Int	R	3.50
Magnetic Mountain	Red	E	R	3.00
Mahamoti Djinn	Blue	Sum	R	6.00
Mana Clash	Red	Sor	R	3.00
Mana Flare	Red	E	R	5.00
Mana Short	Blue	Ins	R	4.00
Mana Vault	Artifact	M	R	4.00

24

Card name	Color	Type	Rarity	Price
Manabarbs	Red	E	R	3.00
Marsh Gas	Black	Ins	C	0.20
Marsh Viper	Green	Sum	C	0.20
Meekstone	Artifact	C	R	3.00
Merfolk of the Pearl Trident	Blue	Sum	C	0.20
Mesa Pegasus	White	Sum	C	0.20
Millstone	Artifact	M	R	5.00
Mind Bomb	Blue	Sor	U	0.80
Mind Twist	Black	Sor	R	4.00

25

Card name	Color	Type	Rarity	Price
Mishra's Factory (Fall)	Land	Lnd	U	2.50
Mishra's War Machine	Artifact	ACr	R	3.00
Mons's Goblin Raiders	Red	Sum	C	0.20
Morale	White	Ins	C	0.20
Mountain (ver. 1)	Red	Lnd	C	0.10
Mountain (ver. 2)	Red	Lnd	C	0.10
Mountain (ver. 3)	Red	Lnd	C	0.10
Murk Dwellers	Black	Sum	C	0.20
Nafs Asp	Green	Sum	C	0.20

26

Card name	Color	Type	Rarity	Price
Nether Shadow	Black	Sum	R	4.00
Nevinyrral's Disk	Artifact	M	R	6.00
Nightmare	Black	Sum	R	6.00
Northern Paladin	White	Sum	R	4.00
Oasis	Land	Lnd	U	1.00
Obsianus Golem	Artifact	ACr	U	1.00
Onulet	Artifact	ACr	R	3.00
Orcish Artillery	Red	Sum	U	0.80
Orcish Oriflamme	Red	E	U	0.80

27

Card name	Color	Type	Rarity	Price
Ornithopter	Artifact	ACr	U	0.50
Osai Vultures	White	Sum	U	0.50
Paralyze	Black	ECr	C	0.20
Pearled Unicorn	White	Sum	C	0.20
Personal Incarnation	White	Sum	R	4.00
Pestilence	Black	E	C	0.25
Phantasmal Forces	Blue	Sum	U	0.80
Phantasmal Terrain	Blue	ELnd	C	0.20

Card name	Color	Type	Rarity	Price
Phantom Monster	Blue	Sum	U	0.80

28

Card name	Color	Type	Rarity	Price
Piety	White	Ins	C	0.20
Pikemen	White	Sum	C	0.20
Pirate Ship	Blue	Sum	R	3.00
Pit Scorpion	Black	Sum	C	0.20
Plague Rats	Black	Sum	C	0.20
Plains (ver. 1)	White	Lnd	C	0.10
Plains (ver. 2)	White	Lnd	C	0.10
Plains (ver. 3)	White	Lnd	C	0.10
Power Leak	Blue	EE	C	0.20

29

Card name	Color	Type	Rarity	Price
Power Sink	Blue	Int	C	0.25
Power Surge	Red	E	R	3.50
Pradesh Gypsies	Green	Sum	C	0.20
Primal Clay	Artifact	ACr	R	3.00
Prodigal Sorcerer	Blue	Sum	C	0.20
Psionic Entity	Blue	Sum	R	3.00
Psychic Venom	Blue	ELnd	C	0.20
Purelace	White	Int	R	2.00
Pyrotechnics	Red	Sor	U	1.00

30

Card name	Color	Type	Rarity	Price
Radjan Spirit	Green	Sum	U	0.80
Rag Man	Black	Sum	R	3.00
Raise Dead	Black	Sor	C	0.20
Rebirth	Green	Sor	R	3.00
Red Elemental Blast	Red	Int	C	0.20
Red Mana Battery	Artifact	Art	R	3.00
Red Ward	White	ECr	U	0.50
Regeneration	Green	ECr	C	0.20
Relic Bind	Blue	EArt	R	3.00

31

Card name	Color	Type	Rarity	Price
Reverse Damage	White	Ins	R	4.00
Righteousness	White	Ins	R	4.00
Rod of Ruin	Artifact	M	U	1.00
Royal Assassin	Black	Sum	R	10.00
Samite Healer	White	Sum	C	0.20
Sandstorm	Green	Ins	C	0.20
Savannah Lions	White	Sum	R	5.00
Scathe Zombies	Black	Sum	C	0.20
Scavenging Ghoul	Black	Sum	U	1.00

32

Card name	Color	Type	Rarity	Price
Scryb Sprites	Green	Sum	C	0.20
Sea Serpent	Blue	Sum	C	0.20
Seeker	White	ECr	C	0.20
Segovian Leviathan	Blue	Sum	U	0.80
Sengir Vampire	Black	Sum	U	4.00
Serra Angel	White	Sum	U	5.00
Shanodin Dryads	Green	Sum	C	0.20
Shapeshifter	Artifact	ACr	U	1.00
Shatter	Red	Ins	C	0.20

33

Card name	Color	Type	Rarity	Price
Shivan Dragon	Red	Sum	R	15.00
Simulacrum	Black	Ins	U	1.00
Sindbad	Blue	Sum	U	1.00
Siren's Call	Blue	Ins	U	0.70
Sisters of the Flame	Red	Sum	C	0.20
Sleight of Mind	Blue	Int	R	3.00
Smoke	Red	E	R	3.00
Sorceress Queen	Black	Sum	R	5.00
Soul Net	Artifact	P	U	0.80

34

Card name	Color	Type	Rarity	Price
Spell Blast	Blue	Int	C	0.20
Spirit Link	White	ECr	U	1.50
Spirit Shackle	Black	ECr	U	0.80
Stasis	Blue	E	R	5.00
Steal Artifact	Blue	EArt	U	0.80
Stone Giant	Red	Sum	U	0.80
Stone Rain	Red	Sor	C	0.20
Stream of Life	Green	Sor	C	0.20
Strip Mine [horizon, uneven terraces]	Land	Lnd	U	2.00

35

Card name	Color	Type	Rarity	Price
Sunglasses of Urza	Artifact	C	R	3.00
Sunken City	Blue	E	C	0.20
Swamp (ver. 1)	Black	Lnd	C	0.10
Swamp (ver. 2)	Black	Lnd	C	0.10
Swamp (ver. 3)	Black	Lnd	C	0.10

Card name	Color	Type	Rarity	Price
Swords to Plowshares	White	Ins	U	1.00
Sylvan Library	Green	E	R	5.00
Tawnos's Wand	Artifact	M	U	0.70
Tawnos's Weaponry	Artifact	M	U	0.80
36				
Tempest Efreet	Red	Sum	R	3.00
Terror	Black	Ins	C	0.20
Tetravus	Artifact	ACr	R	3.00
The Brute	Red	ECr	C	0.20
The Hive	Artifact	M	R	3.00
The Rack	Artifact	C	U	1.00
Thicket Basilisk	Green	Sum	U	1.00
Thoughtlace	Blue	Int	R	2.00
Throne of Bone	Artifact	P	U	0.80
37				
Timber Wolves	Green	Sum	R	3.00
Time Elemental	Blue	Sum	R	5.00
Titania's Song	Green	E	R	3.00
Tranquility	Green	Sor	C	0.20
Triskelion	Artifact	ACr	R	4.00
Tsunami	Green	Sor	U	0.80
Tundra Wolves	White	Sum	C	0.20
Tunnel	Red	Ins	U	0.70
Twiddle	Blue	Ins	C	0.20

Card name	Color	Type	Rarity	Price
38				
Uncle Istvan	Black	Sum	U	1.00
Unholy Strength	Black	ECr	C	0.20
Unstable Mutation	Blue	ECr	C	0.20
Unsummon	Blue	Ins	C	0.20
Untamed Wilds	Green	Sor	U	0.80
Urza's Avenger	Artifact	ACr	R	3.00
Uthden Troll	Red	Sum	U	1.00
Vampire Bats	Black	Sum	C	0.20
Venom	Green	ECr	C	0.20
39				
Verduran Enchantress	Green	Sum	R	4.00
Visions	White	Sor	U	1.00
Volcanic Eruption	Blue	Sor	R	3.00
Wall of Air	Blue	Sum	U	0.50
Wall of Bone	Black	Sum	U	0.50
Wall of Brambles	Green	Sum	U	0.50
Wall of Dust	Red	Sum	U	0.70
Wall of Fire	Red	Sum	U	0.50
Wall of Ice	Green	Sum	U	0.50
40				
Wall of Spears	Artifact	ACr	C	0.20
Wall of Stone	Red	Sum	U	0.50
Wall of Swords	White	Sum	U	0.70
Wall of Water	Blue	Sum	U	0.50

Card name	Color	Type	Rarity	Price
Wall of Wood	Green	Sum	C	0.20
Wanderlust	Green	ECr	U	0.80
War Mammoth	Green	Sum	C	0.20
Warp Artifact	Black	EArt	R	3.00
Water Elemental	Blue	Sum	U	0.80
41				
Weakness	Black	ECr	C	0.20
Web	Green	ECr	R	3.00
Whirling Dervish	Green	Sum	U	1.00
White Knight	White	Sum	U	1.00
White Mana Battery	Artifact	Art	R	3.00
White Ward	White	ECr	U	0.50
Wild Growth	Green	ELnd	C	0.20
Will-O-The-Wisp	Black	Sum	R	5.00
Winds of Change	Red	Sor	R	4.00
42				
Winter Blast	Green	Sor	U	1.00
Winter Orb	Artifact	C	R	5.00
Wooden Sphere	Artifact	P	U	0.70
Word of Binding	Black	Sor	U	0.50
Wrath of God	White	Sor	R	7.00
Xenic Poltergeist	Black	Sum	R	3.00
Yotian Soldier	Artifact	ACr	C	0.20
Zephyr Falcon	Blue	Sum	C	0.20
Zombie Master	Black	Sum	R	4.00

Magic: The Gathering • Fifth Edition

Wizards of the Coast • Released March 1997

434 cards plus **15** variants in set • **IDENTIFIER: White border; © 1997**

- Starter decks contain 60 cards; starter displays contain 10 starters
- Booster packs contain 15 cards; booster displays contain 36 boosters

March 1997 brought the largest **Magic** basic set of all at a monstrous 429 cards.

Despite the large selection of cards in **Fifth Edition**, many of the favorite base set cards from the past two years got the axe, with the removal of **Black Vise, Ivory Tower, Hypnotic Specter, Mind Twist, Sengir Vampire, Channel, Mishra's Factory, Strip Mine, Lightning Bolt, Control Magic, Mahamoti Djinn, Balance, Land Tax, Serra Angel,** and **Swords to Plowshares**.

With a few exceptions such as **Necropotence, Incinerate,** and the **Ice Age** painlands, the cards added to the set did little to fill the vacuum left behind. This created a lackluster base set with little in the way of playable cards and started a sad trend towards base sets generally being overshadowed by the more powerful expansion sets and ignored by the players. — **Bennie Smith**

Air Elemental

Flying

These spirits of the air are winsome and wild and cannot be truly contained. Only marginally intelligent, they often substitute whimsy for strategy, delighting in mischief and mayhem.

4/4

You will need **50** nine-pocket pages to store this set. (25 doubled up)

Set (434 cards + 15 variants)		199.00
Starter Display Box		99.50
Booster Display Box		99.00
Starter Deck		10.00
Booster Pack		3.00

Card name	Set	Color	Type	Rarity	Price
1					
Abbey Gargoyles	HM	White	Sum	U	0.80
Abyssal Specter	IA	Black	Sum	U	1.00
Adarkar Wastes	IA	Land	L	R	5.00
Aether Storm	HM	Blue	E	U	0.80
Air Elemental	A	Blue	Sum	U	0.90
Akron Legionnaire	LG	White	Sum	R	3.00
Alabaster Potion	LG	White	Ins	C	0.20
Aladdin's Ring	AN	Artifact	M	R	3.00
Ambush Party	HM	Red	Sum	C	0.20
2					
Amulet of Kroog	AQ	Artifact	M	C	0.20
Angry Mob	DK	White	Sum	U	1.00
An-Havva Constable	HM	Green	Sum	R	2.50
Animate Dead	A	Black	EDCr	U	1.00
Animate Wall	A	White	EWa	R	3.00
Ankh of Mishra	A	Artifact	C	R	3.80
Anti-Magic Aura	LG	Blue	ECr	U	0.80
Arenson's Aura	IA	White	E	U	0.50
Armageddon	A	White	Sor	R	7.00
3					
Armor of Faith	IA	White	ECr	C	0.20
Ashes to Ashes	DK	Black	Sor	U	0.80

Card name	Set	Color	Type	Rarity	Price
Ashnod's Altar	AQ	Artifact	P	U	0.90
Ashnod's Transmogrant	AQ	Artifact	M	C	0.25
Aspect of Wolf	A	Green	ECr	R	3.00
Atog	AQ	Red	Sum	U	0.50
Aurochs	IA	Green	Sum	C	0.25
Aysen Bureaucrats	HM	White	Sum	C	0.20
Azure Drake	LG	Blue	Sum	U	0.50
4					
Bad Moon	A	Black	E	R	5.50
Ball Lightning	DK	Red	Sum	R	9.00
Barbed Sextant	IA	Artifact	Art	C	0.20
Barl's Cage	DK	Artifact	Art	R	3.00
Battering Ram	AQ	Artifact	ACr	C	0.20
Benalish Hero	A	White	Sum	C	0.20
Binding Grasp	IA	Blue	ECr	U	1.00
Bird Maiden	AN	Red	Sum	C	0.20
Birds of Paradise	A	Green	Sum	R	6.70
5					
Black Knight	A	Black	Sum	U	1.00
Blessed Wine	IA	White	Ins	C	0.20
Blight	LG	Black	EL	U	0.90
Blinking Spirit	IA	White	Sum	R	5.00
Blood Lust	LG	Red	Ins	C	0.20
Bog Imp	DK	Black	Sum	C	0.20
Bog Rats	DK	Black	Sum	C	0.20
Bog Wraith	A	Black	Sum	U	0.80
Boomerang	LG	Blue	Ins	C	0.20
6					
Bottle of Suleiman	AN	Artifact	M	R	3.00
Bottomless Vault	FE	Land	L		R	3.00

Card name	Set	Color	Type	Rarity	Price
Brainstorm	IA	Blue	Ins	C	0.20
Brainwash	DK	White	ECr	C	0.20
Brassclaw Orcs	FE	Red	Sum	C	0.20
Breeding Pit	FE	Black	E	U	1.00
Broken Visage	HM	Black	Ins	R	3.00
Brothers of Fire	DK	Red	Sum	C	0.20
Brushland	IA	Land	L	R	5.00
7					
Carapace	HM	Green	ECr	C	0.20
Caribou Range	IA	White	EL	R	4.00
Carrion Ants	LG	Black	Sum	U	1.00
Castle	A	White	E	C	0.50
Cat Warriors	LG	Green	Sum	C	0.15
Cave People	DK	Red	Sum	U	0.60
Chub Toad	IA	Green	Sum	C	0.20
Circle of Protection: Artifacts	AQ	White	E	U	1.00
Circle of Protection: Black	B	White	E	C	0.15
8					
Circle of Protection: Blue	A	White	E	C	0.15
Circle of Protection: Green	A	White	E	C	0.20
Circle of Protection: Red	A	White	E	C	0.15
Circle of Protection: White	A	White	E	C	0.20
City of Brass	AN	Land	L	R	7.00

RARITY KEY C = Common U = Uncommon R = Rare VR = Very Rare UR = Ultra Rare F = Foil card **CARD TYPES: See page 246**

SCRYE Collectible Card Game Checklist and Price Guide • **253**

Card name	Set	Color	Type	Rarity	Price
Clay Statue	AQ	Artifact	ACr	C	0.20
Cloak of Confusion	IA	Black	ECr	C	0.20
Clockwork Beast	A	Artifact	Cr	R	4.00
Clockwork Steed	HM	Artifact	ACr	U	0.70
Cockatrice	A	Green	Sum	R	4.00
Colossus of Sardia	AQ	Artifact	ACr	R	5.00
Conquer	IA	Red	EL	U	0.80
Coral Helm	AQ	Artifact	P	R	3.00
Counterspell	A	Blue	Int	C	0.25
Craw Giant	LG	Green	Sum	U	0.90
Craw Wurm	A	Green	Sum	C	0.20
Crimson Manticore	LG	Red	Sum	R	3.00
Crown of the Ages	IA	Artifact	Art	R	3.00
Crumble	AQ	Green	Ins	U	0.50
Crusade	A	White	E	R	5.90
Crystal Rod	A	Artifact	P	U	0.50
Cursed Land	A	Black	EL	U	0.50
Dance of Many	DK	Blue	E	R	3.00
Dancing Scimitar	AN	Artifact	ACr	R	3.00
Dandân	AN	Blue	Sum	C	0.25
Dark Maze	HM	Blue	Sum	C	0.20
Dark Ritual	A	Black	Int	C	0.20
D'Avenant Archer	LG	White	Sum	C	0.20
Death Speakers	HM	White	Sum	C	0.20
Death Ward	A	White	Ins	C	0.15
Deathgrip	A	Black	E	U	0.80
Deflection	IA	Blue	Int	R	5.50
Derelor	FE	Black	Sum	R	4.00
Desert Twister	AN	Green	Sor	U	1.00
Detonate	AQ	Red	Sor	U	0.80
Diabolic Machine	DK	Artifact	Art	U	0.50
Dingus Egg	A	Artifact	C	R	3.00
Disenchant	A	White	Ins	C	0.25
Disintegrate	A	Red	Sor	C	0.25
Disrupting Scepter	A	Artifact	M	R	3.00
Divine Offering	LG	White	Ins	C	0.15
Divine Transformation	LG	White	ECr	U	1.00
Dragon Engine	AQ	Artifact	ACr	R	3.00
Drain Life	A	Black	Sor	C	0.25
Drain Power	A	Blue	Sor	R	3.00
Drudge Skeletons	A	Black	Sum	C	0.15
Durkwood Boars	LG	Green	Sum	C	0.15
Dust to Dust	DK	White	Sor	U	0.80
Dwarven Catapult	FE	Red	Ins	U	0.50
Dwarven Hold	FE	Land	L	R	3.00
Dwarven Ruins	FE	Land	L	U	0.60
Dwarven Soldier	FE	Red	Sum	C	0.20
Dwarven Warriors	A	Red	Sum	C	0.15
Earthquake	A	Red	Sor	R	5.00
Ebon Stronghold	FE	Land	L	U	0.60
Elder Druid	IA	Green	Sum	R	4.00
Elkin Bottle	IA	Artifact	Art	R	3.00
Elven Riders	LG	Green	Sum	U	0.80
Elvish Archers	A	Green	Sum	R	4.00
Energy Flux	AQ	Blue	E	U	0.50
Enervate	IA	Blue	Ins	C	0.20
Erg Raiders	AN	Black	Sum	C	0.25
Errantry	IA	Red	ECr	C	0.20
Eternal Warrior	LG	Red	ECr	C	0.15
Evil Eye of Orms-by-Gore	LG	Black	Sum	U	1.00
Evil Presence	A	Black	EL	U	0.50
Eye for an Eye	AN	White	Ins	R	3.00
Fallen Angel	LG	Black	Sum	U	1.00
Fear	A	Black	ECr	C	0.15
Feedback	A	Blue	EE	U	0.50
Feldon's Cane	AQ	Artifact	M	U	1.00
Fellwar Stone	DK	Artifact	Art	U	1.00
Feroz's Ban	HM	Artifact	Art	R	3.00
Fire Drake	DK	Red	Sum	U	0.60
Fireball	A	Red	Sor	C	0.25
Firebreathing	A	Red	ECr	C	0.20
Flame Spirit	IA	Red	Sum	U	0.50
Flare	IA	Red	Ins	C	0.20
Flashfires	A	Red	Sor	U	0.80
Flight	A	Blue	ECr	C	0.15
Flood	DK	Blue	E	C	0.15
Flying Carpet	AN	Artifact	M	R	3.00
Fog	A	Green	Ins	C	0.20
Force of Nature	A	Green	Sum	R	6.00
Force Spike	LG	Blue	Int	C	0.25
Forest (ver. 1)	A	Land	L	L	0.10
Forest (ver. 2)	A	Land	L	L	0.10
Forest (ver. 3)	A	Land	L	L	0.10
Forest (ver. 4)	A	Land	L	L	0.10
Forget	HM	Blue	Sor	R	3.00
Fountain of Youth	DK	Artifact	Art	U	0.80
Foxfire	IA	Green	Ins	C	0.20
Frozen Shade	A	Black	Sum	C	0.20
Funeral March	HM	Black	ECr	C	0.15
Fungusaur	A	Green	Sum	R	3.00
Fyndhorn Elder	IA	Green	Sum	U	1.00
Game of Chaos	IA	Red	Sor	R	3.00
Gaseous Form	LG	Blue	ECr	C	0.20
Gauntlets of Chaos	LG	Artifact	A	R	3.50
Ghazbán Ogre	AN	Green	Sum	C	0.20
Giant Growth	A	Green	Ins	C	0.25
Giant Spider	A	Green	Sum	C	0.15
Giant Strength	LG	Red	ECr	C	0.20
Glacial Wall	IA	Blue	Sum	U	0.50
Glasses of Urza	A	Artifact	M	U	0.50
Gloom	A	Black	E	U	1.00
Goblin Digging Team	DK	Red	Sum	C	0.20
Goblin Hero	DK	Red	Sum	C	0.15
Goblin King	A	Red	Sum	R	5.00
Goblin War Drums	FE	Red	E	C	0.20
Goblin Warrens	FE	Red	E	R	3.00
Grapeshot Catapult	AQ	Artifact	ACr	C	0.15
Greater Realm of Preservation	LG	White	E	U	1.00
Greater Werewolf	HM	Black	Sum	U	0.50
Grizzly Bears	A	Green	Sum	C	0.15
Havenwood Battleground	FE	Land	L	U	0.60
Heal	IA	White	Ins	C	0.20
Healing Salve	A	White	Ins	C	0.15
Hecatomb	IA	Black	E	R	5.00
Helm of Chatzuk	A	Artifact	M	R	3.00
Hill Giant	A	Red	Sum	C	0.15
Hipparion	IA	White	Sum	C	0.20
Hollow Trees	FE	Land	L	R	3.00
Holy Strength	A	White	ECr	C	0.15
Homarid Warrior	FE	Blue	Sum	C	0.20
Howl from Beyond	A	Black	Ins	C	0.25
Howling Mine	A	Artifact	C	R	5.80
Hungry Mist	HM	Green	Sum	C	0.20
Hurkyl's Recall	AQ	Blue	Ins	R	3.00
Hurloon Minotaur	A	Red	Sum	C	0.15
Hurricane	A	Green	Sor	U	1.00
Hydroblast	IA	Blue	Int	U	0.80
Icatian Phalanx	FE	White	Sum	U	0.50
Icatian Scout	FE	White	Sum	C	0.20
Icatian Store	FE	Land	L	R	3.00
Icatian Town	FE	White	Sor	R	3.00
Ice Floe	IA	Land	L	U	1.00
Imposing Visage	IA	Red	ECr	C	0.20
Incinerate	IA	Red	Ins	C	0.25
Inferno	DK	Red	Ins	R	4.00
Infinite Hourglass	IA	Artifact	Art	R	3.00
Initiates of the Ebon Hand	FE	Black	Sum	C	0.20
Instill Energy	A	Green	ECr	U	0.80
Iron Star	A	Artifact	P	U	0.50
Ironclaw Curse	HM	Red	ECr	R	3.00
Ironclaw Orcs	A	Red	Sum	C	0.15
Ironroot Treefolk	A	Green	Sum	C	0.15
Island (ver. 1)	A	Land	L	L	0.10
Island (ver. 2)	A	Land	L	L	0.10
Island (ver. 3)	A	Land	L	L	0.10
Island (ver. 4)	A	Land	L	L	0.10
Island Sanctuary	A	White	E	R	4.00
Ivory Cup	A	Artifact	P	U	0.90
Ivory Guardians	LG	White	Sum	U	0.50
Jade Monolith	A	Artifact	P	R	3.00
Jalum Tome	AQ	Artifact	M	R	3.00
Jandor's Saddlebags	AN	Artifact	M	R	3.00
Jayemdae Tome	A	Artifact	M	R	3.50
Jester's Cap	IA	Artifact	Art	R	10.00
Johtull Wurm	IA	Green	Sum	U	0.80
Jokulhaups	IA	Red	Sor	R	6.00
Joven's Tools	HM	Artifact	Art	U	0.80
Justice	IA	White	E	U	1.00
Juxtapose	LG	Blue	Sor	R	3.50
Karma	A	White	E	U	1.00
Karplusan Forest	IA	Land	L	R	5.00
Keldon Warlord	A	Red	Sum	U	1.00
Killer Bees	LG	Green	Sum	U	1.00
Kismet	LG	White	E	U	1.00
Kjeldoran Dead	IA	Black	Sum	C	0.20
Kjeldoran Royal Guard	IA	White	Sum	R	3.00
Kjeldoran Skycaptain	IA	White	Sum	U	0.80
Knight of Stromgald	IA	Black	Sum	U	1.00
Krovikan Fetish	IA	Black	ECr	C	0.20
Krovikan Sorcerer	IA	Blue	Sum	C	0.20
Labyrinth Minotaur	HM	Blue	Sum	C	0.20
Leshrac's Rite	IA	Black	ECr	U	0.50
Leviathan	DK	Blue	Sum	R	4.00
Ley Druid	A	Green	Sum	C	0.20
Lhurgoyf	IA	Green	Sum	R	5.50
Library of Leng	A	Artifact	C	U	1.00
Lifeforce	A	Green	E	U	0.80
Lifetap	A	Blue	E	U	
Living Artifact	A	Green	EArt	R	3.00
Living Lands	A	Green	EL	R	3.00
Llanowar Elves	A	Green	Sum	C	0.25
Lord of Atlantis	A	Blue	Sum	R	4.50

Reprint key

The source sets for cards in *Fifth* and *Sixth Edition* are noted by the following abbreviations:

4E:	Fourth Edition	HM:	Homelands
5E:	Fifth Edition	IA:	Ice Age
A:	Alpha	LG:	Legends
AN:	Arabian Nights	M:	Mirage
AQ:	Antiquities	S:	Stronghold
B:	Beta	T:	Tempest
DK:	The Dark	US:	Urza's Saga
EX:	Exodus	V:	Visions
FE:	Fallen Empires	WL:	Weatherlight

RARITY KEY C = Common U = Uncommon R = Rare VR = Very Rare UR = Ultra Rare F = Foil card   **CARD TYPES: See page 246**

Card name	Set	Color	Type	Rarity	Price
Lord of the Pit	A	Black	Sum	R	6.00
Lost Soul	LG	Black	Sum	C	0.20
29					
Lure	A	Green	ECr	U	0.50
Magical Hack	A	Blue	Int	R	4.00
Magus of the Unseen	IA	Blue	Sum	R	3.00
Mana Clash	DK	Red	Sor	R	3.00
Mana Flare	A	Red	E	R	5.00
Mana Vault	A	Artifact	M	R	4.00
Manabarbs	A	Red	E	R	3.00
Marsh Viper	DK	Green	Sum	C	0.20
Meekstone	A	Artifact	C	R	3.30
30					
Memory Lapse	HM	Blue	Int	C	0.15
Merfolk of the Pearl Trident	A	Blue	Sum	C	0.20
Mesa Falcon	HM	White	Sum	C	0.20
Mesa Pegasus	A	White	Sum	C	0.15
Millstone	AQ	Artifact	M	R	5.00
Mind Bomb	DK	Blue	Sor	U	0.50
Mind Ravel	IA	Black	Sor	C	0.20
Mind Warp	IA	Black	Sor	U	0.90
Mindstab Thrull	FE	Black	Sum	C	0.20
31					
Mole Worms	IA	Black	Sum	U	0.50
Mons's Goblin Raiders	A	Red	Sum	C	0.20
Mountain (ver. 1)	A	Land	L	L	0.10
Mountain (ver. 2)	A	Land	L	L	0.10
Mountain (ver. 3)	A	Land	L	L	0.10
Mountain (ver. 4)	A	Land	L	L	0.10
Mountain Goat	IA	Red	Sum	C	0.15
Murk Dwellers	DK	Black	Sum	C	0.20
Nature's Lore	IA	Green	Sor	C	0.15
32					
Necrite	FE	Black	Sum	C	0.20
Necropotence	IA	Black	E	R	6.00
Nether Shadow	A	Black	Sum	R	4.00
Nevinyrral's Disk	A	Artifact	M	R	7.00
Nightmare	A	Black	Sum	R	5.50
Obelisk of Undoing	AQ	Artifact	M	R	3.00
Orcish Artillery	A	Red	Sum	U	0.80
Orcish Captain	FE	Red	Sum	U	0.50
Orcish Conscripts	IA	Red	Sum	C	0.20
33					
Orcish Farmer	IA	Red	Sum	C	0.20
Orcish Oriflamme	A	Red	E	U	0.50
Orcish Squatters	IA	Red	Sum	R	4.00
Order of the Sacred Torch	IA	White	Sum	R	4.00
Order of the White Shield	IA	White	Sum	U	1.00
Orgg	FE	Red	Sum	R	3.00
Ornithopter	AQ	Artifact	ACr	U	0.50
Panic	IA	Red	Ins	C	0.20
Paralyze	A	Black	ECr	C	0.25
34					
Pearled Unicorn	A	White	Sum	C	0.15
Pentagram of the Ages	IA	Artifact	Art	R	3.00
Personal Incarnation	A	White	Sum	R	4.00
Pestilence	A	Black	E	C	0.25
Phantasmal Forces	A	Blue	Sum	U	0.50
Phantasmal Terrain	A	Blue	Sum	C	0.15
Phantom Monster	A	Blue	Sum	U	0.80
Pikemen	DK	White	Sum	C	0.25
Pirate Ship	A	Blue	Sum	R	3.00
35					
Pit Scorpion	LG	Black	Sum	C	0.20
Plague Rats	A	Black	Sum	C	0.15
Plains (ver. 1)	A	Land	L	L	0.10
Plains (ver. 2)	A	Land	L	L	0.10
Plains (ver. 3)	A	Land	L	L	0.10
Plains (ver. 4)	A	Land	L	L	0.10
Portent	IA	Blue	Sor	C	0.20
Power Sink	A	Blue	Int	U	0.50
Pox	IA	Black	Sor	R	4.00
36					
Pradesh Gypsies	LG	Green	Sum	C	0.15
Primal Clay	AQ	Artifact	ACr	R	3.00
Primal Order	HM	Green	E	R	3.00
Primordial Ooze	LG	Red	Sum	U	0.50
Prismatic Ward	IA	White	Ecr	C	0.20
Prodigal Sorcerer	A	Blue	Sum	C	0.20
Psychic Venom	A	Blue	EL	C	0.20
Pyroblast	IA	Red	Int	U	1.00
Pyrotechnics	LG	Red	Sor	U	1.00
37					
Rabid Wombat	LG	Green	Sum	U	1.00
Radjan Spirit	LG	Green	Sum	U	0.60
Rag Man	DK	Black	Sum	R	3.00
Raise Dead	A	Black	Sor	C	0.15
Ray of Command	IA	Blue	Ins	C	0.25
Recall	LG	Blue	Sor	R	3.50
Reef Pirates	HM	Blue	Sum	C	0.20
Regeneration	A	Green	ECr	C	0.20
Remove Soul	LG	Blue	Int	C	0.20
38					
Repentant Blacksmith	AN	White	Sum	C	0.25
Reverse Damage	A	White	Ins	R	4.00
Righteousness	A	White	Ins	R	4.00
Rod of Ruin	A	Artifact	M	U	0.50
Ruins of Trokair	FE	Land	L	U	0.60
Sabretooth Tiger	IA	Red	Sum	C	0.20
Sacred Boon	IA	White	Ins	U	0.50
Samite Healer	A	White	Sum	C	0.15
Sand Silos	FE	Land	L	R	3.00
39					
Scaled Wurm	IA	Green	Sum	C	0.20
Scathe Zombies	A	Black	Sum	C	0.15
Scavenger Folk	DK	Green	Sum	C	0.15
Scryb Sprites	A	Green	Sum	C	0.20
Sea Serpent	A	Blue	Sum	C	0.20
Sea Spirit	IA	Blue	Sum	U	0.50
Sea Sprite	HM	Blue	Sum	U	0.50
Seasinger	FE	Blue	Sum	U	1.00
Segovian Leviathan	LG	Blue	Sum	U	0.60
40					
Sengir Autocrat	HM	Black	Sum	R	3.00
Seraph	IA	White	Sum	R	5.00
Serpent Generator	LG	Artifact	A	R	4.00
Serra Bestiary	HM	White	ECr	U	0.50
Serra Paladin	HM	White	Sum	U	0.50
Shanodin Dryads	A	Green	Sum	C	0.15
Shapeshifter	AQ	Artifact	ACr	U	1.00
Shatter	A	Red	Ins	C	0.20
Shatterstorm	AQ	Red	Sor	U	1.00
41					
Shield Bearer	IA	White	Sum	C	0.20
Shield Wall	LG	White	Ins	C	0.15
Shivan Dragon	A	Red	Sum	R	12.00
Shrink	HM	Green	Ins	C	0.20
Sibilant Spirit	IA	Blue	Sum	R	4.00
Skull Catapult	IA	Artifact	Art	U	0.50
Sleight of Mind	A	Blue	Int	R	3.50
Smoke	A	Red	E	R	3.00
Sorceress Queen	AN	Black	Sum	R	4.00
42					
Soul Barrier	IA	Blue	E	C	0.15
Soul Net	A	Artifact	P	U	0.50
Spell Blast	A	Blue	Int	C	0.25
Spirit Link	LG	White	ECr	U	1.00
Stampede	IA	Green	Ins	R	3.00
Stasis	A	Blue	E	R	4.00
Steal Artifact	A	Blue	EArt	U	0.60
Stone Giant	A	Red	Sum	U	0.50
Stone Rain	A	Red	Sor	C	0.20
43					
Stone Spirit	IA	Red	Sum	U	0.50
Stream of Life	A	Green	Sor	C	0.15
Stromgald Cabal	IA	Black	Sum	R	3.00
Sulfurous Springs	IA	Land	L	R	5.00
Svyelunite Temple	FE	Land	L	U	0.60
Swamp (ver. 1)	A	Land	L	L	0.10
Swamp (ver. 2)	A	Land	L	L	0.10
Swamp (ver. 3)	A	Land	L	L	0.10
Swamp (ver. 4)	A	Land	L	L	0.10
44					
Sylvan Library	LG	Green	E	R	5.00
Tarpan	IA	Green	Sum	C	0.20
Tawnos's Weaponry	AQ	Artifact	M	U	0.80
Terror	A	Black	Ins	C	0.20
The Brute	LG	Red	ECr	C	0.20
The Hive	A	Artifact	M	R	3.30
The Wretched	LG	Black	Sum	R	4.00
Thicket Basilisk	A	Green	Sum	U	0.90
Throne of Bone	A	Artifact	P	U	0.60
45					
Thrull Retainer	FE	Black	ECr	C	0.50
Time Bomb	IA	Artifact	Art	R	4.00
Time Elemental	LG	Blue	Sum	R	5.00
Titania's Song	AQ	Green	E	R	3.00
Torture	HM	Black	ECr	C	0.20
Touch of Death	IA	Black	Sor	C	0.20
Tranquility	A	Green	Sor	C	0.20
Truce	HM	White	Ins	R	3.00
Tsunami	A	Green	Sor	C	0.50
46					
Tundra Wolves	LG	White	Sum	C	0.20
Twiddle	A	Blue	Ins	C	0.25
Underground River	IA	Land	L	R	5.00
Unholy Strength	A	Black	ECr	C	0.20
Unstable Mutation	AN	Blue	ECR	C	0.20
Unsummon	A	Blue	Ins	C	0.20
Untamed Wilds	LG	Green	Sor	U	0.50
Updraft	IA	Blue	Ins	C	0.15
Urza's Avenger	AQ	Artifact	ACr	R	3.00
47					
Urza's Bauble	IA	Artifact	Art	U	1.00
Urza's Mine	AQ	Land	L	C	0.25
Urza's Power Plant	AQ	Land	L	C	0.25
Urza's Tower	AQ	Land	L	C	0.25
Vampire Bats	LG	Black	Sum	C	0.20
Venom	DK	Green	ECr	C	0.20
Verduran Enchantress	A	Green	Sum	R	4.00
Vodalian Soldiers	FE	Blue	Sum	C	0.20
Wall of Air	A	Blue	Sum	U	0.50
48					
Wall of Bone	A	Black	Sum	U	0.50
Wall of Brambles	A	Green	Sum	U	0.50
Wall of Fire	A	Red	Sum	U	0.50
Wall of Spears	AQ	Artifact	ACr	C	0.15
Wall of Stone	A	Red	Sum	U	0.50
Wall of Swords	A	White	Sum	U	0.50
Wanderlust	A	Green	ECr	U	0.60
War Mammoth	A	Green	Sum	C	0.20
Warp Artifact	A	Black	EArt	R	3.00
49					
Weakness	A	Black	ECr	C	0.20
Whirling Dervish	LG	Green	Sum	U	1.00
White Knight	A	White	Sum	U	1.00
Wild Growth	A	Green	EL	C	0.15
Wind Spirit	IA	Blue	Sum	U	0.80
Winds of Change	LG	Red	Sor	R	3.00
Winter Blast	LG	Green	Sor	U	0.80
Winter Orb	A	Artifact	C	R	5.00
Wolverine Pack	LG	Green	Sum	U	0.50
50					
Wooden Sphere	A	Artifact	P	U	0.50
Word of Blasting	IA	Red	Ins	U	0.80
Wrath of God	A	White	Sor	R	7.00
Wyluli Wolf	AN	Green	Sum	R	3.00
Xenic Poltergeist	AQ	Black	Sum	R	3.00
Zephyr Falcon	LG	Blue	Sum	C	0.15
Zombie Master	A	Black	Sum	R	3.00
Zur's Weirding	IA	Blue	E	R	4.00

RARITY KEY C = Common U = Uncommon R = Rare VR = Very Rare UR = Ultra Rare F = Foil card CARD TYPES: See page 246

Magic: The Gathering • Classic (a.k.a. Sixth Edition)

Wizards of the Coast • Released **April 1999**

335 cards plus **15** variants in set • **IDENTIFIER: Six (VI) symbol on cards**

- Starter decks contain 75 cards; starter displays contain 12 starters
- Booster packs contain 15cards; booster displays contain 36 boosters

Released in 1999, what would have been the Sixth Edition of **Magic** was named **Classic** and was designed as a stepping stone for a starter-level player to make the jump from **Portal** to advanced **Magic** play.

The basic set includes only 350 cards, with many of the signature **Ice Age**-block cards like **Necropotence, Jester's Cap, Pyro** and **Hydroblasts**, and **Lhurgoyf** removed in favor of **Mirage**-block cards like **Necrosavant**, the *Mirage/Visions* Tutors, and **Hammer of Bogardan**. Green gets a bumper crop of good utility cards reprinted with **Creeping Mold, River Boa,** and **Uktabi Orangutan**, but this is balanced out by the extremely powerful green hoser **Perish**.

Many cards that had been in the base set since **Alpha** fell victim to Wizards' desire to make a simpler base set. The removal of first strike and trample creature abilities meant no more **White** or **Black Knights**, and a fond farewell to the big monsters **Lord of the Pit** and **Force of Nature**. Inexplicably, another veteran of all the previous base sets and a poster-child for the game, **Shivan Dragon**, was also cut from the lineup. The base-set card pool continued to pale in comparison to the expansion sets.

Classic also brought sweeping rules changes, geared toward simplifying and streamlining rules that had grown complex and confusing. A card type, "interrupts," vanished by becoming instants. The changes turned the game on its head and caused heartache and confusion for long-time players who were used to the complex rules. However, the rules were simpler for new players and were a step in the right direction for the game. *Seventh Edition* has been announced for April 2001. — *Bennie Smith*

You will need **39** nine-pocket pages to store this set. (20 doubled up)

Rarities can be found in the color of the expansion symbol (see list at bottom).

	Price
Set (335 cards + 15 variants)	175.00
Starter Display Box	95.00
Booster Display Box	80.00
Starter Deck	10.00
Booster Pack	3.00

Card name	Set	Color	Type	Rarity	Price
Abbey Gargoyles	HM	White	Sum	U	0.80
Abduction	WL	Blue	ECr	U	1.00
Abyssal Hunter	M	Black	Sum	R	4.00
Abyssal Specter	IA	Black	Sum	U	1.00
Adarkar Wastes	IA	Land	L	R	5.00
Æther Flash	WL	Red	E	U	1.00
Agonizing Memories	WL	Black	Sor	U	1.00
Air Elemental	A	Blue	Sum	U	1.00
Aladdin's Ring	AN	Artifact	M	R	3.00
Amber Prison	M	Artifact	A	R	4.00
Anaba Bodyguard	HL	Red	Sum	C	0.20
Anaba Shaman	HL	Red	Sum	C	0.20
Ancestral Memories	M	Blue	Sor	R	4.00
Animate Wall	A	White	EWa	R	3.00
Ankh of Mishra	A	Artifact	C	R	4.00
Archangel	V	White	Sum	R	6.00
Ardent Militia	WL	White	Sum	U	0.80
Armageddon	A	White	Sor	R	6.30
Armored Pegasus	T	White	Sum	C	0.20
Ashen Powder	M	Black	Sor	R	4.00
Ashnod's Altar	AQ	Artifact	P	U	0.60
Balduvian Barbarians	IA	Red	Sum	C	0.20
Balduvian Horde	All	Red	Sum	R	9.50
Birds of Paradise	A	Green	Sum	R	6.70
Blaze	P	Red	Sor	U	1.00
Blight	LG	Black	EL	U	1.00
Blighted Shaman	M	Black	Sum	U	1.00
Blood Pet	T	Black	Sum	C	0.20
Bog Imp	DK	Black	Sum	C	0.20
Bog Rats	DK	Black	Sum	C	0.20
Bog Wraith	A	Black	Sum	U	0.80
Boil	T	Red	Ins	U	1.00
Boomerang	LG	Blue	Ins	C	0.20
Bottle of Suleiman	AN	Artifact	M	R	3.00

Card name	Set	Color	Type	Rarity	Price
Browse	All	Blue	E	U	1.00
Brushland	IA	Land	L	R	4.50
Burrowing	A/4	Red	ECr	U	0.50
Call of the Wild	W	Green	E	R	4.00
Castle	A	White	E	U	0.50
Cat Warriors	LG	Green	Sum	C	0.20
Celestial Dawn	M	White	E	R	5.00
Charcoal Diamond	M	Artifact	A	U	1.00
Chill	T	Blue	E	U	1.00
Circle of Protection: Black	B	White	E	C	0.20
Circle of Protection: Blue	A	White	E	C	0.20
Circle of Protection: Green	A	White	E	C	0.20
Circle of Protection: Red	A	White	E	C	0.20
Circle of Protection: White	A	White	E	C	0.20
City of Brass	AN	Land	L	R	6.80
Coercion	T	Black	Sor	C	0.20
Conquer	IA	Red	EL	U	0.80
Counterspell	A	Blue	Int	C	0.25
Creeping Mold	V	Green	Sor	U	1.00
Crimson Hellkite	M	Red	Sum	R	6.30
Crusade	A	White	E	R	5.00
Crystal Rod	A	Artifact	P	U	0.80
Crystal Vein	M	Land	L	U	1.00
Cursed Totem	M	Artifact	A	R	5.00
Dancing Scimitar	AN	Artifact	ACr	R	3.00
Daraja Griffin	V	White	Sum	U	0.90
Daring Apprentice	M	Blue	Sum	R	3.50
D'Avenant Archer	LG	White	Sum	C	0.20
Deflection	IA	Blue	Int	R	5.00
Dense Foliage	WL	Green	E	R	4.00
Derelor	FE	Black	Sum	R	4.00
Desertion	V	Blue	Int	R	5.00
Diminishing Returns	All	Blue	Sor	R	4.00
Dingus Egg	A	Artifact	C	R	3.50
Disenchant	A	White	Ins	C	0.20

Card name	Set	Color	Type	Rarity	Price
Disrupting Scepter	A	Artifact	M	R	4.00
Divine Transformation	LG	White	ECr	U	1.00
Doomsday	WL	Black	Sor	R	4.50
Dragon Engine	AQ	Artifact	ACr	R	3.00
Dragon Mask	V	Artifact	A	U	1.00
Dread of Night	T	Black	E	U	1.00
Dream Cache	T	Blue	Sor	C	0.20
Drudge Skeletons	A	Black	Sum	C	0.20
Dry Spell	HL	Black	Sor	C	0.20
Dwarven Ruins	FE	Land	L	U	0.60
Early Harvest	M	Green	Ins	R	3.50
Earthquake	A	Red	Sor	R	5.00
Ebon Stronghold	FE	Land	L	U	0.60
Ekundu Griffin	M	White	Sum	C	0.20
Elder Druid	IA	Green	Sum	R	4.00
Elven Cache	V	Green	Sor	C	0.20
Elven Riders	LG	Green	Sum	U	0.80
Elvish Archers	A	Green	Sum	R	4.00
Enfeeblement	M	Black	ECr	C	0.20
Enlightened Tutor	M	White	Ins	U	1.00
Ethereal Champion	M	White	Sum	R	4.00
Evil Eye of Orms-by-Gore	LG	Black	Sum	U	1.00
Exile	All	White	Ins	R	5.00
Fallen Angel	LG	Black	Sum	R	3.00
Fallow Earth	M	Green	Sor	U	0.80
Familiar Ground	WL	Green	E	U	1.00
Fatal Blow	WL	Black	Ins	C	0.20
Fear	A	Black	ECr	C	0.20
Feast of the Unicorn	HL	Black	ECr	C	0.20
Femeref Archers	M	Green	Sum	U	1.00
Feral Shadow	M	Black	Sum	C	0.20
Fervor	WL	Red	E	R	3.80
Final Fortune	M	Red	Ins	R	5.00
Fire Diamond	M	Artifact	A	U	1.00
Fire Elemental	A/4	Red	Sum	U	0.60
Firebreathing	A	Red	ECr	C	0.20
Fit of Rage	WL	Red	Sor	C	0.20
Flame Spirit	IA	Red	Sum	C	0.20
Flash	M	Blue	Ins	R	3.30
Flashfires	A	Red	Sor	U	0.50

RARITY KEY C = Common (black symbol) U = Uncommon (silver symbol) R = Rare (gold symbol) **CARD TYPES: See page 246**

Card name	Set	Color	Type	Rarity	Price
☐ Flight	A	Blue	ECr	C	0.20
☐ Flying Carpet	AN	Artifact	M	R	3.00
☐ Fog	A	Green	Ins	C	0.20
☐ Fog Elemental	WL	Blue	Sum	C	0.20
☐ Forbidden Crypt	M	Black	E	R	4.00
☐ Forest (ver. 1)	A	Land	L	L	0.10
☐ Forest (ver. 2)	A	Land	L	L	0.10
☐ Forest (ver. 3)	A	Land	L	L	0.10
☐ Forest (ver. 4)	A	Land	L	L	0.10
14					
☐ Forget	HM	Blue	Sor	R	3.00
☐ Fountain of Youth	DK	Artifact	Art	U	0.80
☐ Fyndhorn Brownie	IA	Green	Sum	C	0.20
☐ Fyndhorn Elder	IA	Green	Sum	U	1.00
☐ Gaseous Form	LG	Blue	ECr	C	0.20
☐ Giant Growth	A	Green	Ins	C	0.20
☐ Giant Spider	A	Green	Sum	C	0.20
☐ Giant Strength	LG	Red	ECr	C	0.20
☐ Glacial Wall	IA	Blue	Sum	U	0.80
15					
☐ Glasses of Urza	A	Artifact	M	U	0.50
☐ Goblin Digging Team	DK	Red	Sum	C	0.20
☐ Goblin Elite Infantry	M	Red	Sum	C	0.20
☐ Goblin Hero	DK	Red	Sum	C	0.20
☐ Goblin King	A	Red	Sum	R	5.00
☐ Goblin Recruiter	V	Red	Sum	U	1.00
☐ Goblin Warrens	FE	Red	E	R	3.00
☐ Gorilla Chieftain	A	Green	Sum	C	0.20
☐ Gravebane Zombie	M	Black	Sum	U	0.80
16					
☐ Gravedigger	T	Black	Sum	C	0.20
☐ Greed	L/4	Black	E	R	3.00
☐ Grinning Totem	M	Artifact	A	U	7.50
☐ Grizzly Bears	A	Green	Sum	C	0.20
☐ Hammer of Bogardan	M	Red	Sor	R	10.00
☐ Harmattan Efreet	M	Blue	Sum	U	0.60
☐ *	FE	Land	L	U	0.60
☐ Healing Salve	A	White	Ins	C	0.20
☐ Heavy Ballista	WL	White	Sum	U	0.80
17					
☐ Hecatomb	IA	Black	E	R	5.00
☐ Hero's Resolve	T	White	ECr	C	0.20
☐ Hidden Horror	WL	Black	Sum	U	1.00
☐ Horned Turtle	T	Blue	Sum	C	0.20
☐ Howl from Beyond	A	Black	Ins	C	0.20
☐ Howling Mine	A	Artifact	C	R	5.00
☐ Hulking Cyclops	V	Red	Sum	U	1.00
☐ Hurricane	A	Green	Sor	R	3.00
☐ Icatian Town	FE	White	Sor	R	3.50
18					
☐ Illicit Auction	M	Red	Sor	R	3.50
☐ Infantry Veteran	V	White	Sum	C	0.20
☐ Infernal Contract	M	Black	Sor	R	4.00
☐ Inferno	DK	Red	Ins	R	4.00
☐ Insight	T	Blue	E	U	0.80
☐ Inspiration	V	Blue	Ins	C	0.20
☐ Iron Star	A	Artifact	P	U	0.50
☐ Island (ver. 1)	A	Land	L	L	0.10
☐ Island (ver. 2)	A	Land	L	L	0.10
19					
☐ Island (ver. 3)	A	Land	L	L	0.10
☐ Island (ver. 4)	A	Land	L	L	0.10
☐ Ivory Cup	A	Artifact	P	U	0.60
☐ Jade Monolith	A	Artifact	P	R	3.00
☐ Jalum Tome	AQ	Artifact	M	R	3.00
☐ Jayemdae Tome	A	Artifact	M	R	3.00
☐ Jokulhaups	IA	Red	Sor	R	5.00
☐ Juxtapose	LG	Blue	Sor	R	3.50
☐ Karplusan Forest	IA	Land	L	R	4.80
20					
☐ Kismet	LG	White	E	U	1.00
☐ Kjeldoran Dead	IA	Black	Sum	C	0.20
☐ Kjeldoran Royal Guard	IA	White	Sum	R	4.00
☐ Lead Golem	M	Artifact	ACr	U	0.60

Card name	Set	Color	Type	Rarity	Price
☐ Leshrac's Rite	IA	Black	ECr	U	0.50
☐ Library of Lat-Nam	All	Blue	Sor	R	4.50
☐ Light of Day	T	White	E	U	1.00
☐ Lightning Blast	T	Red	Ins	C	0.20
☐ Living Lands	A	Green	EL	R	3.00
21					
☐ Llanowar Elves	A	Green	Sum	C	0.20
☐ Longbow Archer	V	White	Sum	U	1.00
☐ Lord of Atlantis	A	Blue	Sum	R	4.00
☐ Lost Soul	LG	Black	Sum	C	0.20
☐ Lure	A	Green	ECr	U	0.50
☐ Mana Prism	M	Artifact	A	U	0.80
☐ Mana Short	A/4	Blue	Ins	R	4.50
☐ Manabarbs	A	Red	E	R	4.00
☐ Marble Diamond	M	Artifact	A	U	1.00
22					
☐ Maro	M	Green	Sum	R	5.50
☐ Meekstone	A	Artifact	C	R	3.00
☐ Memory Lapse	HM	Blue	Int	C	0.20
☐ Merfolk of the Pearl Trident	A	Blue	Sum	C	0.20
☐ Mesa Falcon	HM	White	Sum	C	0.20
☐ Millstone	AQ	Artifact	M	R	4.50
☐ Mind Warp	IA	Black	Sor	U	0.80
☐ Mischievous Poltergeist	WL	Black	Sum	U	0.80
☐ Moss Diamond	M	Artifact	A	U	1.00
23					
☐ Mountain (ver. 1)	A	Land	L	L	0.10
☐ Mountain (ver. 2)	A	Land	L	L	0.10
☐ Mountain (ver. 3)	A	Land	L	L	0.10
☐ Mountain (ver. 4)	A	Land	L	L	0.10
☐ Mountain Goat	IA	Red	Sum	C	0.20
☐ Mystic Compass	All	Artifact	A	U	1.00
☐ Mystical Tutor	M	Blue	Ins	U	1.00
☐ Nature's Resurgence	WL	Green	Sor	R	4.00
☐ Necrosavant	V	Black	Sum	R	4.00
24					
☐ Nightmare	A	Black	Sum	R	5.00
☐ Obsianus Golem	A/4	Artifact	ACr	U	1.00
☐ Orcish Artillery	A	Red	Sum	U	0.50
☐ Orcish Oriflamme	A	Red	E	U	0.50
☐ Order of the Sacred Torch	IA	White	Sum	R	4.00
☐ Ornithopter	AQ	Artifact	ACr	U	0.50
☐ Pacifism	US	White	ECr	C	0.20
☐ Painful Memories	M	Black	Sor	C	0.20
☐ Panther Warriors	V	Green	Sum	C	0.20
25					
☐ Patagia Golem	M	Artifact	ACr	U	0.80
☐ Pearl Dragon	M	White	Sum	R	5.00
☐ Pentagram of the Ages	IA	Artifact	Art	R	3.00
☐ Perish	T	Black	Sor	U	1.00
☐ Pestilence	A	Black	E	U	0.50
☐ Phantasmal Terrain	A	Blue	Sum	C	0.20
☐ Phantom Warrior	WL	Blue	Sum	U	1.00
☐ Phyrexian Vault	M	Artifact	A	U	0.60
☐ Pillage	All	Red	Sor	U	1.00
26					
☐ Plains (ver. 1)	A	Land	L	L	0.10
☐ Plains (ver. 2)	A	Land	L	L	0.10
☐ Plains (ver. 3)	A	Land	L	L	0.10
☐ Plains (ver. 4)	A	Land	L	L	0.10
☐ Polymorph	M	Blue	Sor	R	4.00
☐ Power Sink	A	Blue	Int	U	0.50
☐ Pradesh Gypsies	LG	Green	Sum	C	0.20
☐ Primal Clay	AQ	Artifact	ACr	R	3.00
☐ Prodigal Sorcerer	A	Blue	Sum	C	0.20
27					
☐ Prosperity	V	Blue	Sor	U	1.00
☐ Psychic Transfer	M	Blue	Sor	R	4.00
☐ Psychic Venom	A	Blue	EL	C	0.20
☐ Pyrotechnics	LG	Red	Sor	C	0.25
☐ Python	V	Black	Sum	C	0.20
☐ Radjan Spirit	LG	Green	Sum	U	0.60
☐ Rag Man	DK	Black	Sum	R	3.00

Card name	Set	Color	Type	Rarity	Price
☐ Raging Goblin	Ex	Red	Sum	C	0.20
☐ Raise Dead	A	Black	Sor	C	0.20
28					
☐ Rampant Growth	M	Green	Sor	C	0.20
☐ Razortooth Rats	WL	Black	Sum	C	0.20
☐ Recall	LG	Blue	Sor	R	3.50
☐ Reckless Embermage	M	Red	Sum	R	4.00
☐ Redwood Treefolk	WL	Green	Sum	C	0.20
☐ Regal Unicorn	P	White	Sum	C	0.20
☐ Regeneration	A	Green	ECr	C	0.20
☐ Relearn	WL	Blue	Sor	U	0.80
☐ Relentless Assault	V	Red	Sor	R	7.50
29					
☐ Remedy	V	White	Ins	C	0.20
☐ Remove Soul	LG	Blue	Int	C	0.20
☐ Reprisal	A	White	Ins	U	0.80
☐ Resistance Fighter	V	White	Sum	C	0.20
☐ Reverse Damage	A	White	Ins	R	4.00
☐ River Boa	V	Green	Sum	U	1.00
☐ Rod of Ruin	A	Artifact	M	U	0.50
☐ Rowen	V	Green	E	R	4.00
☐ Ruins of Trokair	FE	Land	L	U	0.60
30					
☐ Sabretooth Tiger	IA	Red	Sum	C	0.20
☐ Sage Owl	WL	Blue	Sum	C	0.20
☐ Samite Healer	A	White	Sum	C	0.20
☐ Scaled Wurm	IA	Green	Sum	C	0.20
☐ Scathe Zombies	A	Black	Sum	C	0.20
☐ Sea Monster	T	Blue	Sum	C	0.20
☐ Segovian Leviathan	LG	Blue	Sum	U	0.60
☐ Sengir Autocrat	HM	Black	Sum	R	3.70
☐ Serenity	WL	White	E	R	4.00
31					
☐ Serra's Blessing	WL	White	E	U	1.00
☐ Shanodin Dryads	A	Green	Sum	C	0.20
☐ Shatter	A	Red	Ins	C	0.20
☐ Shatterstorm	AQ	Red	Sor	R	3.00
☐ Shock	S	Red	Ins	C	0.25
☐ Sibilant Spirit	IA	Blue	Sum	R	4.00
☐ Skull Catapult	IA	Artifact	A	U	0.80
☐ Sky Diamond	M	Artifact	A	U	1.00
☐ Snake Basket	V	Artifact	A	R	5.00
32					
☐ Soldevi Sage	All	Blue	Sum	U	0.60
☐ Soul Net	A	Artifact	P	U	0.50
☐ Spell Blast	A	Blue	Int	C	0.20
☐ Spirit Link	LG	White	ECr	U	1.00
☐ Spitting Drake	V	Red	Sum	U	1.00
☐ Spitting Earth	P	Red	Sor	C	0.20
☐ Stalking Tiger	M	Green	Sum	C	0.20
☐ Standing Troops	Ex	White	Sum	C	0.20
☐ Staunch Defenders	T	White	Sum	U	0.90
33					
☐ Stone Rain	A	Red	Sor	C	0.20
☐ Storm Cauldron	A	Artifact	A	R	4.50
☐ Storm Crow	A	Blue	Sum	C	0.20
☐ Strands of Night	WL	Black	E	U	0.80
☐ Stream of Life	A	Green	Sor	C	0.20
☐ Stromgald Cabal	IA	Black	Sum	R	3.50
☐ Stupor	M	Black	Sor	U	1.00
☐ Sulfurous Springs	IA	Land	L	R	5.00
☐ Summer Bloom	V	Green	Sor	U	1.00
34					
☐ Sunweb	M	White	Sum	R	3.00
☐ Svyelunite Temple	FE	Land	L	U	0.60
☐ Swamp (ver. 1)	A	Land	L	L	0.10
☐ Swamp (ver. 2)	A	Land	L	L	0.10
☐ Swamp (ver. 3)	A	Land	L	L	0.10
☐ Swamp (ver. 4)	A	Land	L	L	0.10
☐ Syphon Soul	L	Black	Sor	C	0.20
☐ Talruum Minotaur	M	Red	Sum	C	0.20
☐ Tariff	WL	White	Sor	R	3.30
35					
☐ Teferi's Puzzle Box	V	Artifact	A	R	4.00
☐ Terror	A	Black	Ins	C	0.25

RARITY KEY C = Common (black symbol) U = Uncommon (silver symbol) R = Rare (gold symbol) **CARD TYPES: See page 246**

Card name	Set	Color	Type	Rarity	Price
☐ The Hive	A	Artifact	M	R	4.00
☐ Thicket Basilisk	A	Green	Sum	U	0.90
☐ Throne of Bone	A	Artifact	P	U	0.60
☐ Tidal Surge	S	Blue	Sor	C	0.20
☐ Trained Armodon	T	Green	Sum	C	0.20
☐ Tranquil Grove	WL	Green	E	R	4.00
☐ Tranquility [36]	A	Green	Sor	C	0.20
☐ Tremor	V	Red	Sor	C	0.20
☐ Tundra Wolves	LG	White	Sum	C	0.20
☐ Uktabi Orangutan	V	Green	Sum	U	1.00
☐ Uktabi Wildcats	M	Green	Sum	R	4.00
☐ Underground River	IA	Land	L	R	4.50
☐ Unseen Walker	M	Green	Sum	U	0.80
☐ Unsummon	A	Blue	Ins	C	0.20
☐ Untamed Wilds	LG	Green	Sor	U	0.60

Card name	Set	Color	Type	Rarity	Price
☐ Unyaro Griffin [37]	M	White	Sum	U	0.80
☐ Vampiric Tutor	V	Black	Ins	R	8.00
☐ Venerable Monk	S	White	Sum	C	0.20
☐ Verduran Enchantress	A	Green	Sum	R	4.00
☐ Vertigo	IA	Red	Ins	U	0.90
☐ Viashino Warrior	M	Red	Sum	C	0.20
☐ Vitalize	WL	Green	Ins	C	0.20
☐ Vodalian Soldiers	FE	Blue	Sum	C	0.20
☐ Volcanic Dragon	M	Red	Sum	R	6.00
☐ Volcanic Geyser [38]	M	Red	Ins	U	1.00
☐ Waiting in the Weeds	M	Green	Sor	R	4.00
☐ Wall of Air	A	Blue	Sum	U	0.50
☐ Wall of Fire	A	Red	Sum	U	0.50
☐ Wall of Swords	A	White	Sum	U	0.60

Card name	Set	Color	Type	Rarity	Price
☐ Wand of Denial	V	Artifact	A	R	4.00
☐ Warmth	T	White	E	U	1.00
☐ Warrior's Honor	V	White	Ins	C	0.20
☐ Warthog	V	Green	Sum	U	0.80
☐ Wild Growth [39]	A	Green	EL	C	0.20
☐ Wind Drake	T	Blue	Sum	C	0.20
☐ Wind Spirit	IA	Blue	Sum	U	0.80
☐ Wooden Sphere	A	Artifact	P	U	0.50
☐ Worldly Tutor	M	Green	Ins	U	1.00
☐ Wrath of God	A	White	Sor	R	6.80
☐ Wyluli Wolf	AN	Green	Sum	R	3.80
☐ Zombie Master	A	Black	Sum	R	4.00
☐ Zur's Weirding	IA	Blue	E	R	4.00

Magic: The Gathering • Arabian Nights

Wizards of the Coast • Released December 1993

92 cards in set • **IDENTIFIER: Scimitar symbol on cards**

• Booster packs contain 9 cards; booster displays contain 36 boosters

Released five months after the release of the basic game, **Arabian Nights** is the first expansion set for **Magic: the Gathering**. A small expansion of only 92 cards (5 million printed in all), the set is heavily influenced by the classic Middle Eastern "1001 Nights" collection of stories and features such familiar figures as Aladdin, Sinbad, and Ali Baba.

Many of the efreets and djinns are highly playable, being relatively cheap to cast, with drawbacks that are negligible. **Juzam Djinn, Ehrnam Djinn**, and **Serendib Efreet** have been popular creature cards featured in top decks over the years. **Library of Alexandria**, which allows a player to draw a card if he has seven in his hand, became a powerful addition to decks and is often the tenth card added after the "Power Nine." **City of Brass** cards have been vital components to multicolor decks since their release, especially with their addition to the basic set. — **Bennie Smith and Joshua C.H. Claytor**

Set (78 cards plus 14 variants) 900.00
Booster Display Box 4,500.00
Booster Pack 100.00

You will need **11** nine-pocket pages to store this set. (6 doubled up)

Card name	Color	Type	Rarity	Price
☐ Air Elemental [1]	Blue	Sum	U	2.90
☐ Abu Ja'far	White	Sum	U3	4.00
☐ Aladdin	Red	Sum	U2	9.00
☐ Aladdin's Lamp	Artifact	M	U2	5.00
☐ Aladdin's Ring	Artifact	M	U2	5.00
☐ Ali Baba	Red	Sum	U3	3.00
☐ Ali from Cairo	Red	Sum	U2	75.00
☐ Army of Allah (a)	White	Sum	C1	5.00
☐ Army of Allah (b)	White	Ins	C3	5.00
☐ Bazaar of Baghdad [2]	Land	L	U3	18.00
☐ Bird Maiden (a)	Red	Sum	C2	1.60
☐ Bird Maiden (b)	Red	Sum	C2	1.50
☐ Bottle of Suleiman	Artifact	M	U2	4.00
☐ Brass Man	Artifact	ACr	U3	3.00
☐ Camel	White	Sum	C5	2.00
☐ City in a Bottle	Artifact	C	U2	18.00
☐ City of Brass	Land	L	U3	25.00
☐ Cuombajj Witches	Black	Sum	C4	1.00
☐ Cyclone [3]	Green	E	U3	4.00
☐ Dancing Scimitar	Artifact	ACr	U2	4.00
☐ Dandan	Blue	Sum	C4	1.00
☐ Desert	Land	L	C11	3.70
☐ Desert Nomads	Red	Sum	C4	2.00
☐ Desert Twister	Green	Sor	U3	4.00
☐ Diamond Valley	Land	L	U2	60.00
☐ Drop of Honey	Green	E	U2	40.00
☐ Ebony Horse	Artifact	M	U2	4.00

Card name	Type		Rarity	Price
☐ Elephant Graveyard [4]	Land	L	U2	30.00
☐ El-Hajjaj	Black	Sum	U2	5.00
☐ Erg Raiders (a)	Black	Sum	C2	1.00
☐ Erg Raiders (b)	Black	Sum	C3	1.00
☐ Erhnam Djinn	Green	Sum	U2	27.00
☐ Eye for an Eye	White	Ins	U3	5.00
☐ Fishliver Oil (a)	Blue	ECr	C1	1.00
☐ Fishliver Oil (b)	Blue	ECr	C3	1.00
☐ Flying Carpet	Artifact	M	U3	4.00
☐ Flying Men [5]	Blue	Sum	C5	5.00
☐ Ghazban Ogre	Green	Sum	C4	1.00
☐ Giant Tortoise (a)	Blue	Sum	C1	1.00
☐ Giant Tortoise (b)	Blue	Sum	C3	1.00
☐ Guardian Beast	Black	Sum	U2	65.00
☐ Hasran Ogress (a)	Black	Sum	C2	1.00
☐ Hasran Ogress (b)	Black	Sum	C3	1.00
☐ Hurr Jackal	Red	Sum	C4	1.50
☐ Ifh-Biff Efreet	Green	Sum	U2	30.00
☐ Island Fish Jasconius [6]	Blue	Sum	U2	5.00
☐ Island of Wak-Wak	Land	L	U2	40.00
☐ Jandor's Ring	Artifact	M	U2	5.00
☐ Jandor's Saddlebags	Artifact	M	U2	4.50
☐ Jeweled Bird	Artifact	M	U2	4.00
☐ Jihad	White	E	U2	40.00
☐ Junun Efreet	Black	Sum	U2	10.00
☐ Juzam Djinn	Black	Sum	U2	180.00
☐ Khabal Ghoul	Black	Sum	U3	40.00
☐ King Suleiman [7]	White	Sum	U2	20.00
☐ Kird Ape	Red	Sum	C5	3.00
☐ Library of Alexandria	Land	L	U3	100.00
☐ Magnetic Mountain	Red	E	U3	4.00
☐ Merchant Ship	Blue	Sum	U3	5.00
☐ Metamorphosis	Green	Sor	C4	1.00

Card name	Type		Rarity	Price
☐ Mijae Djinn	Red	Sum	U2	6.00
☐ Moorish Cavalry (a)	White	Sum	C1	3.00
☐ Moorish Cavalry (b)	White	Sum	C4	3.00
☐ Mountain [8]	Land	L	C1	6.00
☐ Nafs Asp (a)	Green	Sum	C2	1.00
☐ Nafs Asp (b)	Green	Sum	C3	1.00
☐ Oasis	Land	L	U4	3.00
☐ Old Man of the Sea	Blue	Sum	U2	34.00
☐ Oubliette (a)	Black	E	C2	4.00
☐ Oubliette (b)	Black	E	C2	4.00
☐ Piety (a)	White	Ins	U2	1.00
☐ Piety (b)	White	Ins	U2	1.00
☐ Pyramids [9]	Artifact	P	U2	20.00
☐ Repentant Blacksmith	White	Sum	U2	3.00
☐ Ring of Ma'ruf	Artifact	M	U3	35.00
☐ Rukh Egg (a)	Red	Sum	C1	11.00
☐ Rukh Egg (b)	Red	Sum	C3	11.00
☐ Sandals of Abdallah	Artifact	M	U3	5.00
☐ Sandstorm	Green	Ins	C4	1.00
☐ Serendib Djinn	Blue	Sum	U2	25.00
☐ Serendib Efreet	Blue	Sum	U2	25.00
☐ Shahrazad [10]	White	Sor	U2	25.00
☐ Sindbad	Blue	Sum	U3	4.00
☐ Singing Tree	Green	Sum	U2	35.00
☐ Sorceress Queen	Black	Sum	U3	10.00
☐ Stone-Throwing Devils (a)	Black	Sum	C1	5.00
☐ Stone-Throwing Devils (b)	Black	Sum	C3	5.00
☐ Unstable Mutation	Blue	ECr	C5	1.00
☐ War Elephant (a)	White	Sum	C1	1.70
☐ War Elephant (b)	White	Sum	C3	1.70
☐ Wyluli Wolf (a) [11]	Green	Sum	C1	4.30
☐ Wyluli Wolf (b)	Green	Sum	C4	4.30
☐ Ydwen Efreet	Red	Sum	U2	10.00

RARITY KEY C = Common U = Uncommon R = Rare VR = Very Rare #: Times card appears on press sheet; lower numbers are rarer

Magic: The Gathering • Antiquities

Wizards of the Coast • Released **March 1994**

92 cards plus **15** variants • **IDENTIFIER: Anvil symbol; black border**

• Booster packs contain 8 cards; booster displays contain 60 boosters

Cards in the artifact-heavy set ***Antiquities*** depict The Brothers War, a battle between Urza and Mishra for the rule of Terisiare. As opposed to the literary theme of ***Arabian Nights***, this original storyline developed into the setting for the ***Magic*** universe

Many cards in this set became popular. **Mishra's Factory**, a land good for either colorless mana or powering an "assembly worker" creature, later became the basis for the "man-lands" in **Urza's Legacy**. Four versions appear, depicting the seasons. **Ivory Tower**, rewards large hands with life points. As many slightly different versions exist for **Strip Mine**, a card popular in land-destruction decks. **Millstone**, which forces an opponent to discard cards from his library, quickly became a tournament staple.

Look for the card **Atog**, which eventually inspired a whole cycle of different colored **Atogs** that crossed several expansions.

Poor collation on this set resulted in Wizards of the Coast offering to buy back significant numbers of ***Antiquities*** cards from customers. We doubt anyone sent in a **Candelabra of Tawnos**, which untapped as many lands as the player could afford and remains the most expensive card in the set. — ***Bennie Smith & Joshua C.H. Claytor***

Set (91 cards plus				
15 variants)	275.00			
Booster Display Box	900.00			
Booster Pack	20.00			

You will need 12 nine-pocket pages to store this set. (6 doubled up)

Card name	Color	Type	Rarity	Price
□ Amulet of Kroog	Artifact	M	C	0.50
□ Argivian Archaeologist	White	Sum	R	35.50
□ Argivian Blacksmith	White	Sum	U	1.00
□ Argothian Pixies	Green	Sum	C	0.50
□ Argothian Treefolk	Green	Sum	C	0.50
□ Armageddon Clock	Artifact	C	R	5.00
□ Artifact Blast	Red	Int	C	0.50
□ Artifact Possession	Black	EArt	C	0.50
□ Artifact Ward	White	ECr	C	0.50
□ Ashnod's Altar	Artifact	P	U	1.00
□ Ashnod's Battle Gear	Artifact	M	U	1.00
□ Ashnod's Transmogrant	Artifact	M	U	1.00
□ Atog	Red	Sum	C	0.50
□ Battering Ram	Artifact	ACr	C	0.50
□ Bronze Tablet	Artifact	M	R	6.80
□ Candelabra of Tawnos	Artifact	M	R	41.00
□ Circle of Protection: Artifacts	White	E	U	3.00
□ Citanul Druid	Green	Sum	U	2.00
□ Clay Statue	Artifact	ACr	C	0.50
□ Clockwork Avian	Artifact	ACr	R	6.50
□ Colossus of Sardia	Artifact	ACr	R	11.00
□ Coral Helm	Artifact	P	R	5.00
□ Crumble	Green	Ins	C	0.50
□ Cursed Rack	Artifact	C	C	1.30
□ Damping Field	White	E	U	2.00
□ Detonate	Red	Sor	U	2.00
□ Drafna's Restoration	Blue	Sor	C	0.50
□ Dragon Engine	Artifact	ACr	C	0.50
□ Dwarven Weaponsmith	Red	Sum	U	1.00
□ Energy Flux	Blue	E	U	2.00
□ Feldon's Cane	Artifact	M	U	5.80
□ Gaea's Avenger	Green	Sum	R	12.00
□ Gate to Phyrexia	Black	E	U	2.00
□ Goblin Artisans	Red	Sum	U	1.00
□ Golgothian Sylex	Artifact	M	R	6.00
□ Grapeshot Catapult	Artifact	ACr	C	0.50
□ Haunting Wind	Black	E	U	2.00
□ Hurkyl's Recall	Blue	Ins	R	4.00
□ Ivory Tower	Artifact	C	U	7.00
□ Jalum Tome	Artifact	M	R	5.00
□ Martyrs of Korlis	White	Sum	U	3.00
□ Mightstone	Artifact	C	U	3.00

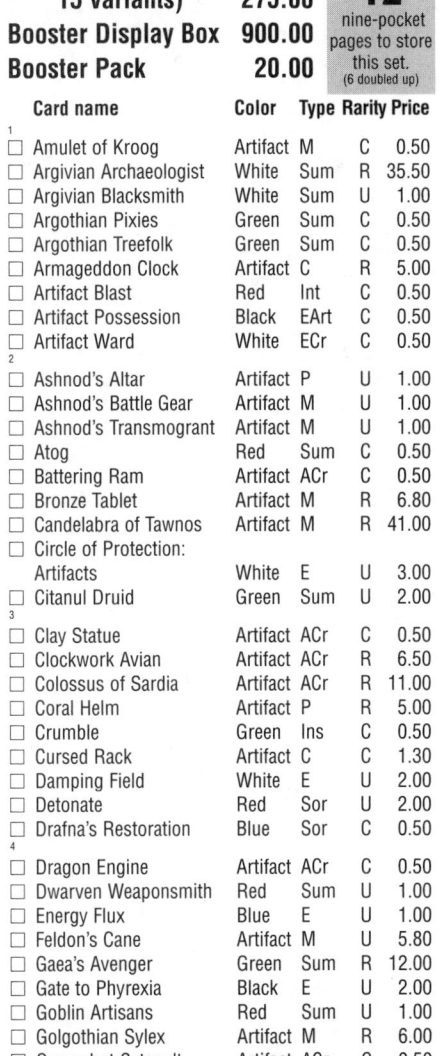

Card name	Color	Type	Rarity	Price
□ Millstone	Artifact	M	U	6.00
□ Mishra's Factory (fall)	Land	L	C	9.50
□ Mishra's Factory (spring)	Land	L	U	9.50
□ Mishra's Factory (summer)	Land	L	U	10.00
□ Mishra's Factory (winter)	Land	L	R	11.50
□ Mishra's War Machine	Artifact	ACr	R	5.00
□ Mishra's Workshop	Land	L	R	27.00
□ Obelisk of Undoing	Artifact	M	R	5.00
□ Onulet	Artifact	ACr	U	1.00
□ Orcish Mechanics	Red	Sum	C	0.50
□ Ornithopter	Artifact	ACr	C	0.50
□ Phyrexian Gremlins	Black	Sum	C	0.50
□ Power Artifact	Blue	EArt	U	3.00
□ Powerleech	Green	E	U	2.00
□ Priest of Yawgmoth	Black	Sum	C	0.50
□ Primal Clay	Artifact	ACr	U	1.50
□ Rakalite	Artifact	P	U	1.30
□ Reconstruction	Blue	Sor	C	0.50
□ Reverse Polarity	White	Ins	C	0.50
□ Rocket Launcher	Artifact	P	U	3.00
□ Sage of Lat-Nam	Blue	Sum	C	0.50
□ Shapeshifter	Artifact	ACr	R	5.50
□ Shatterstorm	Red	Sor	R	4.00
□ Staff of Zegon	Artifact	M	C	0.50
□ Strip Mine (no sky)	Land	L	C	8.00
□ Strip Mine (no sky, tower)	Land	L	U	8.00
□ Strip Mine (sky, even steps)	Land	L	U	8.00
□ Strip Mine (sky, uneven steps)	Land	L	U	8.00
□ Su-Chi	Artifact	ACr	U	5.00

Card name	Color	Type	Rarity	Price
□ Tablet of Epityr	Artifact	P	C	0.50
□ Tawnos's Coffin	Artifact	M	R	20.00
□ Tawnos's Wand	Artifact	M	U	1.30
□ Tawnos's Weaponry	Artifact	M	U	1.30
□ Tetravus	Artifact	ACr	R	7.00
□ The Rack	Artifact	C	U	1.50
□ Titania's Song	Green	E	U	2.00
□ Transmute Artifact	Blue	Sor	U	2.00
□ Triskelion	Artifact	ACr	R	7.00
□ Urza's Avenger	Artifact	ACr	R	8.00
□ Urza's Chalice	Artifact	P	C	0.50
□ Urza's Mine (sphere)	Land	L	C	0.50
□ Urza's Mine (mouth)	Land	L	C	0.50
□ Urza's Mine (pulley)	Land	L	C	0.50
□ Urza's Mine (tower)	Land	L	C	0.50
□ Urza's Miter	Artifact	P	R	5.50
□ Urza's Power Plant (bug)	Land	L	C	0.50
□ Urza's Power Plant (columns)	Land	L	C	0.50
□ Urza's Power Plant (sphere)	Land	L	C	0.50
□ Urza's Power Plant (rock)	Land	L	C	0.50
□ Urza's Tower (forest)	Land	L	C	0.50
□ Urza's Tower (mountains)	Land	L	C	0.50
□ Urza's Tower (plains)	Land	L	C	0.50
□ Urza's Tower (shore)	Land	L	C	0.50
□ Wall of Spears	Artifact	ACr	U	1.00
□ Weakstone	Artifact	C	U	2.00
□ Xenic Poltergeist	Black	Sum	U	2.00
□ Yawgmoth Demon	Black	Sum	R	8.50
□ Yotian Soldier	Artifact	ACr	C	0.50

Magic: The Gathering • Collector's Edition

Wizards of the Coast • Released **December 1993**

363 cards in set

IDENTIFIER: Corners squared; gold border on back

Early in the craze, Wizards produced 17,000 boxed sets featuring ***Magic*** cards as trading cards (with square corners, thereby unplayable). Most sets were sold in North America, while 3,500 of the total were sold overseas and labelled as such.

Set (Domestic, opened)	187.50
Set (Domestic, unopened)	250.00
Set (International, opened)	200.00
Set (International, unopened)	280.00

RARITY KEY C = Common **U** = Uncommon **R** = Rare **VR** = Very Rare **UR** = Ultra Rare **F** = Foil card **CARD TYPES: See page 246**

Illus. © 1994 Christopher Rush

Magic: The Gathering • Legends

Wizards of the Coast • Released **June 1994**

310 cards in set • **IDENTIFIER: Column symbol; black border**

• Booster packs contain 15 cards; booster displays contain 36 boosters

Wizards of the Coast whipped the initial **Magic** frenzy to its absolute height with **Legends**, a mammoth 310-card expansion set including some of the most powerful cards ever printed. Some still regard it as the best expansion set for any CCG ever.

With its larger booster packs, *Legends* was intended to be a "stand-alone" set, but few players limited themselves to just using cards from *Legends*. The vast majority quickly incorporated the best cards into decks mixed with the rest of the *Magic* card pool. And the "best" cards were numerous. **Mana Drain**, **The Abyss**, **Moat**, and **Mirror Universe** are the cream of this crop. *Legends* also introduces a bevy of new game mechanics: The creature ability Rampage, Legendary lands and creatures, multi-color "gold cards" and Enchant Worlds all add fresh twists to the game.

It's also with *Legends* that Wizards of the Coast's supply problems hit their "legendary" crisis proportions. *Magic*'s popularity had grown beyond anyone's anticipation, and the 35-million card print-run was gone in an instant, as *Legends* packs flew off the shelves at whatever price retailers gave them. Which was often quite a bit, since retailers tended to get one box of *Legends* for every 10 ordered, and were *buying* boxes for as much as $400 each by October. ***Bennie Smith & Joshua C.H. Claytor***

Set (310 cards)	875.00		
Booster Display Box	1,100.00		
Booster Pack	40.00		

You will need 35 nine-pocket pages to store this set. (18 doubled up)

Card name	Color	Type	Rarity	Price
Amulet of Kroog	Artifact M		C	0.50
Ærathi Berserker	Red	Sum	U	3.00
Abomination	Black	Sum	U	2.30
Acid Rain	Blue	Sor	R	22.00
Active Volcano	Red	Ins	C	1.00
Adun Oakenshield	Multi	SmL	R	10.00
Adventurer's Guildhouse	Land	L	U	2.00
Aisling Leprechaun	Green	Sum	C	0.90
Akron Legionnaire	White	Sum	R	8.00
Al-abara's Carpet	Artifact A		R	10.00
Alabaster Potion	White	Ins	C	0.70
Alchor's Tomb	Artifact A		R	11.00
All Hallow's Eve	Black	Sor	R	35.00
Amrou Kithkin	White	Sum	C	0.90
Angelic Voices	White	E	R	10.00
Angus Mackenzie	Multi	SmL	R	12.00
Anti-Magic Aura	Blue	ECr	C	1.00
Arboria	Green	EW	U	3.50
Arcades Sabboth	Multi	Sum	R	15.00
Arena of the Ancients	Artifact A		R	8.00
Avoid Fate	Green	Int	C	1.00

Card name	Color	Type	Rarity	Price
Axelrod Gunnarson	Multi	SmL	R	10.00
Ayesha Tanaka	Multi	SmL	R	8.00
Azure Drake	Blue	Sum	U	2.00
Backdraft	Red	Ins	U	3.00
Backfire	Blue	ECr	U	2.30
Barbary Apes	Green	Sum	C	0.90
Barktooth Warbeard	Multi	SmL	U	3.00
Bartel Runeaxe	Multi	SmL	R	13.00
Beasts of Bogardan	Red	Sum	U	2.80
Black Mana Battery	Artifact A		U	4.00
Blazing Effigy	Red	Sum	C	0.90
Blight	Black	EL	U	3.00
Blood Lust	Red	Ins	U	3.50
Blue Mana Battery	Artifact A		U	4.00
Boomerang	Blue	Ins	C	0.90
Boris Devilboon	Multi	SmL	R	11.00
Brine Hag	Blue	Sum	U	3.00
Bronze Horse	Artifact ACr		R	8.00
Carrion Ants	Black	Sum	R	10.00
Cat Warriors	Green	Sum	C	0.90
Cathedral of Serra	Land	L	U	2.50
Caverns of Despair	Red	EW	R	8.00
Chain Lightning	Red	Sor	C	3.00
Chains of Mephistopheles	Black	E	R	20.00
Chromium	Multi	SmL	R	15.00
Cleanse	White	Sor	R	17.00
Clergy of the Holy Nimbus	White	Sum	C	1.00
Cocoon	Green	ECr	U	2.50
Concordant Crossroads	Green	EW	R	8.00
Cosmic Horror	Black	Sum	R	9.00
Craw Giant	Green	Sum	U	4.00
Crevasse	Red	E	U	3.00
Crimson Kobolds	Red	Sum	C	1.00
Crimson Manticore	Red	Sum	R	7.00
Crookshank Kobolds	Red	Sum	C	1.00
Cyclopean Mummy	Black	Sum	C	0.70
D'Avenant Archer	White	Sum	C	0.90
Dakkon Blackblade	Multi	SmL	R	13.00
Darkness	Black	Ins	C	1.00
Deadfall	Green	E	U	2.50
Demonic Torment	Black	ECr	U	3.00
Devouring Deep	Blue	Sum	C	0.90
Disharmony	Red	Ins	R	9.00
Divine Intervention	White	E	R	10.00
Divine Offering	White	Ins	C	0.90

Card name	Color	Type	Rarity	Price
Divine Transformation	White	ECr	R	9.00
Dream Coat	Blue	ECr	U	3.00
Durkwood Boars	Green	Sum	C	0.90
Dwarven Song	Red	Ins	U	3.00
Elder Land Wurm	White	Sum	R	10.00
Elder Spawn	Blue	Sum	R	10.00
Elven Riders	Green	Sum	R	7.00
Emerald Dragonfly	Green	Sum	C	0.90
Enchanted Being	White	Sum	C	0.90
Enchantment Alteration	Blue	Ins	C	1.00
Energy Tap	Blue	Sor	C	0.90
Equinox	White	EL	C	1.00
Eternal Warrior	Red	ECr	U	2.00
Eureka	Green	Sor	R	35.00
Evil Eye of Orms-By-Gore	Black	Sum	U	3.00
Fallen Angel	Black	Sum	U	6.00
Falling Star	Red	Sor	R	15.00
Feint	Red	Ins	C	0.90
Field of Dreams	Blue	EW	R	15.00
Fire Sprites	Green	Sum	C	0.90
Firestorm Phoenix	Red	Sum	R	25.00
Flash Counter	Blue	Int	C	1.00
Flash Flood	Blue	Ins	C	0.90
Floral Spuzzem	Green	Sum	U	3.00
Force Spike	Blue	Int	C	1.00
Forethought Amulet	Artifact A		R	13.00
Fortified Area	White	E	U	2.50
Frost Giant	Red	Sum	U	3.00
Gabriel Angelfire	Multi	SmL	R	10.00
Gaseous Form	Blue	ECr	C	0.90
Gauntlets of Chaos	Artifact A		R	10.00
Ghosts of the Damned	Black	Sum	C	1.00
Giant Slug	Black	Sum	C	0.90
Giant Strength	Red	ECr	C	0.90
Giant Turtle	Green	Sum	C	0.90
Glyph of Delusion	Blue	Ins	C	1.00
Glyph of Destruction	Red	Ins	C	0.90
Glyph of Doom	Black	Ins	C	1.00
Glyph of Life	White	Ins	C	0.90
Glyph of Reincarnation	Green	Ins	C	0.90
Gosta Dirk	Multi	SmL	R	10.00
Gravity Sphere	Red	EW	R	25.00
Great Defender	White	Ins	U	3.00
Great Wall	White	E	U	3.00

Half *Legends*

For part of the production run of *Legends*, the uncommon cards were divided up between different lots of booster boxes such that it was impossible to get them all from one box.

As it did with *Antiquities*, Wizards of the Coast instituted a return program whereby players could return uncommons from one set for uncommons from the other. It's safe to assume it's no longer in service, so if you're ponying up a grand for a display box, be prepared that you might not get all the uncommons (that is, presuming you dare to open it)!

RARITY KEY C = Common • U = Uncommon • R = Rare • **VR** = Very Rare • **UR** = Ultra Rare • **F** = Foil card • **CARD TYPES: See page 246**

Card name	Color	Type	Rarity	Price
Greater Realm of Preservation	White	E	U	6.00
Greed	Black	E	R	7.50
Green Mana Battery	Artifact	A	U	4.00
Gwendlyn Di Corci	Multi	SmL	R	15.00
Halfdane	Multi	SmL	R	13.00
Hammerheim	Land	LL	U	3.50
Hazezon Tamar	Multi	SmL	R	15.00
Headless Horseman	Black	Sum	C	1.00
Heaven's Gate	White	Ins	U	3.00
Hell Swarm	Black	Ins	C	0.90
Hell's Caretaker	Black	Sum	R	14.00
Hellfire	Black	Sor	R	20.00
Holy Day	White	Ins	C	0.90
Horn of Deafening	Artifact	A	R	8.00
Hornet Cobra	Green	Sum	C	0.90
Horror of Horrors	Black	E	U	3.00
Hunding Gjornersen	Multi	SmL	U	3.00
Hyperion Blacksmith	Red	Sum	U	3.00
Ichneumon Druid	Green	Sum	U	3.00
Immolation	Red	ECr	C	0.90
Imprison	Black	ECr	R	12.00
In the Eye of Chaos	Blue	EW	R	15.00
Indestructible Aura	White	Ins	C	1.00
Infernal Medusa	Black	Sum	U	3.50
Infinite Authority	White	ECr	R	13.50
Invoke Prejudice	Blue	E	R	12.00
Ivory Guardians	White	Sum	U	3.00
Jacques le Vert	Multi	SmL	R	13.00
Jasmine Boreal	Multi	SmL	U	3.00
Jedit Ojanen	Multi	SmL	U	3.00
Jerrard of the Closed Fist	Multi	SmL	U	3.00
Johan	Multi	SmL	R	12.00
Jovial Evil	Black	Sor	R	17.50
Juxtapose	Blue	Sor	R	9.00
Karakas	Land	LL	U	4.00
Kasimir the Lone Wolf	Multi	SmL	U	3.00
Keepers of the Faith	White	Sum	C	0.90
Kei Takahashi	Multi	SmL	R	9.00
Killer Bees	Green	Sum	R	15.00
Kismet	White	E	U	3.80
Knowledge Vault	Artifact	A	R	12.00
Kobold Drill Sergeant	Red	Sum	U	6.00
Kobold Overlord	Red	Sum	R	15.00
Kobold Taskmaster	Red	Sum	U	6.00
Kobolds of Kher Keep	Red	Sum	C	1.00
Kry Shield	Artifact	A	U	3.00
Lady Caleria	Multi	SmL	R	12.00
Lady Evangela	Multi	SmL	R	11.00
Lady Orca	Multi	SmL	U	3.00
Land Equilibrium	Blue	E	R	15.00
Land Tax	White	E	U	7.00
Land's Edge	Red	EW	R	10.00
Lesser Werewolf	Black	Sum	U	3.00
Life Chisel	Artifact	A	U	4.00
Life Matrix	Artifact	A	R	12.00
Lifeblood	White	E	R	12.00
Living Plane	Green	EW	R	21.00
Livonya Silone	Multi	SmL	R	15.00
Lord Magnus	Multi	SmL	U	3.00
Lost Soul	Black	Sum	C	1.00
Mana Drain	Blue	Int	U	45.00
Mana Matrix	Artifact	A	R	11.00
Marble Priest	Artifact	ACr	U	3.00
Marhault Elsdragon	Multi	SmL	U	3.00
Master of the Hunt	Green	Sum	R	25.00
Mirror Universe	Artifact	A	R	75.00
Moat	White	E	R	52.50
Mold Demon	Black	Sum	R	9.00
Moss Monster	Green	Sum	C	0.90
Mountain Stronghold	Land	L	U	2.50
Mountain Yeti	Red	Sum	U	2.50
Nebuchadnezzar	Multi	SmL	R	12.00
Nether Void	Black	EW	R	40.00
Nicol Bolas	Multi	SmL	R	18.00
North Star	Artifact	A	R	14.00
Nova Pentacle	Artifact	A	R	15.00
Osai Vultures	White	Sum	C	0.90
Palladia-Mors	Multi	SmL	R	16.00
Part Water	Blue	Sor	U	3.00
Pavel Maliki	Multi	SmL	U	3.00
Pendelhaven	Land	LL	U	3.80
Petra Sphinx	White	Sum	R	9.00
Pit Scorpion	Black	Sum	C	0.90
Pixie Queen	Green	Sum	R	12.00
Planar Gate	Artifact	A	R	15.00
Pradesh Gypsies	Green	Sum	U	1.50
Presence of the Master	White	E	U	4.50
Primordial Ooze	Red	Sum	U	2.00
Princess Lucrezia	Multi	SmL	U	3.50
Psionic Entity	Blue	Sum	R	10.00
Psychic Purge	Blue	Sor	C	1.00
Puppet Master	Blue	ECr	U	3.00
Pyrotechnics	Red	Sor	C	1.00
Quagmire	Black	E	U	3.00
Quarum Trench Gnomes	Red	Sum	R	12.00
Rabid Wombat	Green	Sum	U	3.00
Radjan Spirit	Green	Sum	U	2.50
Raging Bull	Red	Sum	C	0.90
Ragnar	Multi	SmL	R	11.00
Ramirez DePietro	Multi	SmL	U	3.50
Ramses Overdark	Multi	SmL	R	12.00
Rapid Fire	White	Ins	R	10.00
Rasputin Dreamweaver	Multi	SmL	R	13.00
Rebirth	Green	Sor	R	8.00
Recall	Blue	Sor	R	13.00
Red Mana Battery	Artifact	A	U	4.00
Reincarnation	Green	Ins	U	3.00
Relic Barrier	Artifact	A	U	5.00
Relic Bind	Blue	EA	U	3.00
Remove Enchantments	White	Ins	C	1.00
Remove Soul	Blue	Int	C	0.90
Reset	Blue	Int	U	8.00
Revelation	Green	EW	R	10.00
Reverberation	Blue	Ins	R	15.00
Righteous Avengers	White	Sum	U	3.00
Ring of Immortals	Artifact	A	R	14.50
Riven Turnbull	Multi	SmL	U	3.00
Rohgahh of Kher Keep	Multi	SmL	R	15.00
Rubinia Soulsinger	Multi	SmL	R	11.00
Rust	Green	Int	C	0.90
Sea King's Blessing	Blue	Ins	U	3.00
Seafarer's Quay	Land	L	U	2.00
Seeker	White	ECr	U	2.80
Segovian Leviathan	Blue	Sum	U	2.50
Sentinel	Artifact	ACr	R	8.00
Serpent Generator	Artifact	A	R	12.00
Shelkin Brownie	Green	Sum	C	0.90
Shield Wall	White	Ins	U	2.80
Shimian Night Stalker	Black	Sum	U	3.00
Silhouette	Blue	Ins	U	3.00
Sir Shandlar of Eberyn	Multi	SmL	U	3.00
Sivitri Scarzam	Multi	SmL	U	3.00
Sol'kanar the Swamp King	Multi	SmL	R	16.00
Spectral Cloak	Blue	ECr	U	8.00
Spinal Villian	Red	Sum	R	16.00
Spirit Link	White	ECr	U	5.50
Spirit Shackle	Black	ECr	C	0.90
Spiritual Sanctuary	White	E	R	10.00
Stangg	Multi	SmL	R	10.00
Storm Seeker	Green	Ins	U	5.00
Storm World	Red	EW	R	12.50
Subdue	Green	Ins	C	1.00
Sunastian Falconer	Multi	SmL	U	3.00
Sword of the Ages	Artifact	A	R	30.00
Sylvan Library	Green	E	U	6.80
Sylvan Paradise	Green	Ins	U	3.00
Syphon Soul	Black	Sor	C	1.00
Takklemaggot	Black	ECr	U	2.00
Telekinesis	Blue	Ins	R	10.00
Teleport	Blue	Ins	R	8.00
Tempest Efreet	Red	Sum	R	8.00
Tetsuo Umezawa	Multi	SmL	R	14.00
The Abyss	Black	EW	R	65.00
The Brute	Red	ECr	C	0.90
The Lady of the Mountain	Multi	SmL	U	3.00
The Tabernacle at Pendrell Vale	Land	LL	R	25.00
The Wretched	Black	Sum	R	17.00
Thunder Spirit	White	Sum	R	28.00
Time Elemental	Blue	Sum	R	15.00
Tobias Andrion	Multi	SmL	U	3.00
Tolaria	Land	LL	U	3.80
Tor Wauki	Multi	SmL	U	3.00
Torsten Von Ursus	Multi	SmL	U	3.00
Touch of Darkness	Black	Ins	U	3.00
Transmutation	Black	Ins	C	1.00
Triassic Egg	Artifact	A	R	8.00
Tuknir Deathlock	Multi	SmL	R	10.00
Tundra Wolves	White	Sum	C	0.90
Typhoon	Green	Sor	R	12.00
Undertow	Blue	E	U	3.00
Underworld Dreams	Black	E	U	26.00
Unholy Citadel	Land	L	U	2.00
Untamed Wilds	Green	Sor	U	3.00
Urborg	Land	LL	U	3.50
Ur-Drago	Multi	SmL	R	10.00
Vaevictis Asmadi	Multi	SmL	R	15.00
Vampire Bats	Black	Sum	C	0.90
Venarian Gold	Blue	ECr	C	1.00
Visions	White	Sor	U	3.00
Voodoo Doll	Artifact	A	R	8.00
Walking Dead	Black	Sum	C	0.90
Wall of Caltrops	White	Sum	C	1.00
Wall of Dust	Red	Sum	U	3.00
Wall of Earth	Red	Sum	C	0.90
Wall of Heat	Red	Sum	C	0.90
Wall of Light	White	Sum	U	3.00
Wall of Opposition	Red	Sum	R	8.00
Wall of Putrid Flesh	Black	Sum	U	3.00
Wall of Shadows	Black	Sum	C	0.90
Wall of Tombstones	Black	Sum	C	3.00
Wall of Vapor	Blue	Sum	C	0.90
Wall of Wonder	Blue	Sum	U	2.50
Whirling Dervish	Green	Sum	U	4.50
White Mana Battery	Artifact	A	U	4.00
Willow Satyr	Green	Sum	R	12.50
Winds of Change	Red	Sor	U	3.50
Winter Blast	Green	Sor	R	8.50
Wolverine Pack	Green	Sum	C	0.90
Wood Elemental	Green	Sum	R	11.50
Xira Arien	Multi	SmL	R	10.00
Zephyr Falcon	Blue	Sum	C	0.90

RARITY KEY   C = Common   U = Uncommon   R = Rare   VR = Very Rare   UR = Ultra Rare   F = Foil card   CARD TYPES: See page 246

Preacher

Summon Preacher

2: Gain control of one of opponent's creatures.
Opponent chooses which target creature you
control. If Preacher becomes untapped, you lose
control of this creature; you may choose not to
untap Preacher as normal during your untap
phase. You also lose control of the creature if
Preacher leaves play or at end of game.

Illus. ©1994 Quinton Hoover   1/1

Magic: The Gathering • The Dark

Wizards of the Coast • Released **August 1994**

119 cards in set • **IDENTIFIER: Crescent moon symbol; black border**

• Booster packs contain 8 cards; booster displays contain 60 boosters

Culminating a full year of rapid set releases since *Magic*'s debut, the 119-card set **The Dark** could not help but disappoint in the wake of the size, power, and innovation of **Legends**. But it was only minor disappointment, as this set focusing on (what else?) the darker side of *Magic* added some new wrinkles. Many *Dark* cards damage not only the opponent, but the card's controller as well.

A few standouts are included, such as **Maze of Ith**, a land with the power to untap creatures; **Ball Lightning**, a 6/1 creature with Trample that's immune to summoning sickness; and the non-basic land hoser **Blood Moon**.

The Dark also adds a new win condition with the introduction of poisonous creatures. Players receive poison counters if they take damage from a poisonous creature; if at any time a player gets 10 poison counters, he loses the game.

With a print run of 62 million cards, higher than the much larger *Legends* set, *The Dark* still managed to sell out. Time saw the market take this into consideration, and sets of *The Dark* rarely sold for more than $200 even during the initial boom. They're down to an average of a dollar a card now. — **Bennie Smith & Joshua C.H. Claytor**

Set (119 cards)	120.00
Booster Display Box	300.00
Booster Pack	6.50

You will need **14** nine-pocket pages to store this set. (7 doubled up)

Card name	Color	Type	Rarity	Price
1				
☐ Amulet of Kroog	Artifact	M	C	0.50
☐ Amnesia	Blue	Sor	U2	2.00
☐ Angry Mob	White	Sum	U2	1.50
☐ Apprentice Wizard	Blue	Sum	U1	2.10
☐ Ashes to Ashes	Black	Sor	C3	0.25
☐ Ball Lightning	Red	Sum	U1	12.00
☐ Banshee	Black	Sum	U2	1.00
☐ Barl's Cage	Artifact	Art	U1	3.50
☐ Blood Moon	Red	E	U1	5.00
☐ Blood of the Martyr	White	Ins	U2	1.30
2				
☐ Bog Imp	Black	Sum	C3	0.15
☐ Bog Rats	Black	Sum	C3	0.15
☐ Bone Flute	Artifact	Art	U2	1.00
☐ Book of Rass	Artifact	Art	U2	1.00
☐ Brainwash	White	ECr	C3	0.15
☐ Brothers of Fire	Red	Sum	U2	0.80
☐ Carnivorous Plant	Green	Sum	C3	0.15
☐ Cave People	Red	Sum	U2	1.00
☐ City of Shadows	Land	L	U1	5.00
3				
☐ Cleansing	White	Sor	U1	4.00
☐ Coal Golem	Artifact	Art	U2	1.00
☐ Curse Artifact	Black	EArt	U2	1.00
☐ Dance of Many	Blue	E	U1	4.00
☐ Dark Heart of the Wood	Multi	Sum	C3	0.25
☐ Dark Sphere	Artifact	Art	U2	2.00

Card name	Color	Type	Rarity	Price
☐ Deep Water	Blue	E	C3	0.15
☐ Diabolic Machine	Artifact	Art	U2	1.00
☐ Drowned	Blue	Sum	C3	0.15
4				
☐ Dust to Dust	White	Sor	C3	0.15
☐ Eater of the Dead	Black	Sum	U2	1.00
☐ Electric Eel	Blue	Sum	U2	1.00
☐ Elves of Deep Shadow	Green	Sum	U2	2.00
☐ Erosion	Blue	EL	C3	0.15
☐ Eternal Flame	Red	Sor	U1	3.50
☐ Exorcist	White	Sum	U1	5.00
☐ Fasting	White	E	U2	1.00
☐ Fellwar Stone	Artifact	Art	U2	2.50
5				
☐ Festival	White	Ins	C3	0.15
☐ Fire and Brimstone	White	Ins	U2	1.00
☐ Fire Drake	Red	Sum	U2	1.30
☐ Fissure	Red	Ins	C3	0.15
☐ Flood	Blue	E	U2	1.00
☐ Fountain of Youth	Artifact	Art	U2	1.00
☐ Frankenstein's Monster	Black	Sum	U1	6.00
☐ Gaea's Touch	Green	E	C3	0.25
☐ Ghost Ship	Blue	Sum	C3	0.15
6				
☐ Giant Shark	Blue	Sum	C3	0.15
☐ Goblin Caves	Red	EL	C3	0.15
☐ Goblin Digging Team	Red	Sum	C3	0.15
☐ Goblin Hero	Red	Sum	C3	0.15
☐ Goblin Rock Sled	Red	Sum	C3	0.15
☐ Goblin Shrine	Red	EL	C3	0.15
☐ Goblin Wizard	Red	Sum	U1	4.50
☐ Goblins of the Flarg	Red	Sum	C3	0.15
☐ Grave Robbers	Black	Sum	U1	4.00
7				
☐ Hidden Path	Green	E	U1	3.80
☐ Holy Light	White	Ins	C3	0.15
☐ Inferno	Red	Ins	U1	4.80
☐ Inquisition	Black	Sor	C3	0.15
☐ Knights of Thorn	White	Sum	U1	5.00
☐ Land Leeches	Green	Sum	C3	0.15
☐ Leviathan	Blue	Sum	U1	5.50
☐ Living Armor	Artifact	Art	U2	1.00
☐ Lurker	Green	Sum	U1	4.00
8				
☐ Mana Clash	Red	Sor	U1	3.50
☐ Mana Vortex	Blue	E	U1	4.50
☐ Marsh Gas	Black	Ins	C3	0.15
☐ Marsh Goblins	Multi	Sum	C3	0.25
☐ Marsh Viper	Green	Sum	C3	0.15
☐ Martyr's Cry	White	Sor	U1	4.00
☐ Maze of Ith	Land	L	C1	10.00
☐ Merfolk Assassin	Blue	Sum	U2	3.50
☐ Mind Bomb	Blue	Sor	U1	2.50

Card name	Color	Type	Rarity	Price
9				
☐ Miracle Worker	White	Sum	C3	0.15
☐ Morale	White	Ins	C3	0.15
☐ Murk Dwellers	Black	Sum	C3	0.15
☐ Nameless Race	Black	Sum	U1	4.00
☐ Necropolis	Artifact	Art	U2	1.70
☐ Niall Silvain	Green	Sum	U1	3.00
☐ Orc General	Red	Sum	U2	1.30
☐ People of the Woods	Green	Sum	U2	1.30
☐ Pikemen	White	Sum	C3	0.15
10				
☐ Preacher	White	Sum	U1	10.50
☐ Psychic Allergy	Blue	E	U1	4.00
☐ Rag Man	Black	Sum	U1	5.00
☐ Reflecting Mirror	Artifact	Art	U2	2.00
☐ Riptide	Blue	Ins	C3	0.15
☐ Runesword	Artifact	Art	U2	1.00
☐ Safe Haven	Land	L	U1	4.00
☐ Savaen Elves	Green	Sum	C3	0.25
☐ Scarecrow	Artifact	Art	U2	2.00
11				
☐ Scarwood Bandits	Green	Sum	U1	3.00
☐ Scarwood Goblins	Multi	Sum	C3	0.25
☐ Scarwood Hag	Green	Sum	U2	1.30
☐ Scavenger Folk	Green	Sum	C3	0.15
☐ Season of the Witch	Black	E	U1	4.00
☐ Sisters of the Flame	Red	Sum	U2	1.00
☐ Skull of Orm	Artifact	Art	U2	3.00
☐ Sorrow's Path	Land	L	U1	3.00
☐ Spitting Slug	Green	Sum	U2	1.00
12				
☐ Squire	White	Sum	C3	0.15
☐ Standing Stones	Artifact	Art	U2	1.30
☐ Stone Calendar	Artifact	Art	U1	4.50
☐ Sunken City	Blue	E	C3	0.15
☐ Tangle Kelp	Blue	ECr	U2	1.00
☐ The Fallen	Black	Sum	U1	1.00
☐ Tivadar's Crusade	White	Sor	U2	1.00
☐ Tormod's Crypt	Artifact	Art	U2	1.00
☐ Tower of Coireall	Artifact	Art	U2	1.00
13				
☐ Tracker	Green	Sum	U1	5.00
☐ Uncle Istvan	Black	Sum	U2	1.30
☐ Venom	Green	ECr	C3	0.15
☐ Wand of Ith	Artifact	Art	U2	2.30
☐ War Barge	Artifact	Art	U2	2.00
☐ Water Wurm	Blue	Sum	C3	0.15
☐ Whippoorwill	Green	Sum	U2	1.50
☐ Witch Hunter	White	Sum	U1	4.00
☐ Word of Binding	Black	Sor	C3	0.15
14				
☐ Worms of the Earth	Black	E	U1	3.00
☐ Wormwood Treefolk	Green	Sum	U1	3.50

RARITY KEY C = Common   **U** = Uncommon   **R** = Rare   **VR** = Very Rare   **#:** Times card appears on press sheet; lower numbers are rarer

Magic: The Gathering • *Fallen Empires*

Wizards of the Coast • Released **November 1995**

102 cards plus **85** variants in set • **IDENTIFIER: Crown symbol; black borders**

• Booster packs contain 8 cards; booster displays contain 60 boosters

Fallen Empires — what an ironically appropriate name.

This was the release when Wizards of the Coast would finally get *Magic* production up to speed to fill orders, shipping in several waves of more than a quarter of a *billion* cards — or over half a million boxes. It was also the release which would *really* break *Magic* out of the hobby into the mass market, with thousands of boxes available through computer stores and other mall outlets. (Wizards of the Coast had pledged in *Scrye* #4 that it would only sell *Revised,* and not any black-bordered releases, to mass-market stores, but a number of chains set up accounts with hobby distributors and got *Fallen Empires* anyway.) Stakes were enormous, so much so that Wizards warned that it would hold its distributor and retail customers to pay for whatever they ordered.

Unfortunately, *Fallen Empires* hit the hobby with a big wet thud.

Part of the problem was that where *Legends* is packed with interesting cards and *The Dark* has a few favorites, *Fallen Empires* is a yawn-inducing lot of low-powered "theme" creatures. In an attempt to make creature decks popular, Wizards populated the set with saprolings, thrulls, thallids, and merfolk, many needing multiple taps (registered by counters, not included) to do anything interesting. The set holds some value for casual gamers, but there is a noticeable lack of quality cards for the serious *Magic* player — and despite some positive initial reactions, players soon began to turn on it. With the exception of **Hymn to Torach, Order of Leitbur, Order of the Ebon Hand, Aeolipile**, and the infamous **High Tide**, *Fallen Empires* is filled with sub-par cards which few players ran in their decks. Add to this that Decipher picked the same month to launch **Star Trek**, and you've got $87 *Fallen Empires* boxes going for less than half that within six months.

The failure of a single expansion to enhance gameplay might seem to make little difference today, but expectations for the set were *so* high, that its every problem echoed throughout the hobby. Retailers unable to meet demand on previous releases had over-ordered *Fallen Empires*, sometimes recklessly. (One game retailer accustomed to receiving only 10% of his *Magic* orders bet against another allocation by ordering 10 times what he needed — in his case, 550 display boxes. *Every one* shipped, at a loss to him of tens of thousands of dollars.) A lackluster set — now available at discount from mass-market competitors — was a good candidate to sit on the shelf forever.

Despite its initial warning, Wizards of the Coast went back to the table with hobby distributors, accepting less in payment and even returns in some cases — and it slowed down its rapid expansion schedule so that players and collectors could better keep up with the card releases. But while players may casually debate whether *Fallen Empires* or *Homelands* deserves the title of "worst expansion ever," for some unlucky people, *Fallen Empires* was "game over" for their businesses. — ***John Jackson Miller & Bennie Smith***

From the crash...

"Wizards of the Coast seems to have fallen and it can't get up. Sales of **Fallen Empires** are steady, but most of the buyers are new **Magic** players (who think it's the Basic Set), whereas some of the older players say the only value of the cards is nutritional.

"It has become 'hip' to put down **Fallen Empires** around here..."

— **Mark Cooper and Jeremy Shaffner**, *Premier Comics & Games, Merrillville, Ind.*, *writing in* **Scrye** #6 *(Apr 94)*

Set (102 cards plus 85 variants)				
Set (102 cards plus 85 variants)	**50.00**			
Booster Display Box	**65.00**			
Booster Pack	**1.40**			

You will need **21** nine-pocket pages to store this set. (11 doubled up)

Card name	Color	Type	Rarity	Price
1				
☐ Aeolipile	Artifact	Art	U1	2.00
☐ Armor Thrull (ver. 1)	Black	Sum	C1	0.25
☐ Armor Thrull (ver. 2)	Black	Sum	C1	0.25
☐ Armor Thrull (ver. 3)	Black	Sum	C1	0.25
☐ Armor Thrull (ver. 4)	Black	Sum	C1	0.25
☐ Balm of Restoration	Artifact	Art	U1	1.50
☐ Basal Thrull (ver. 1)	Black	Sum	C1	0.20
☐ Basal Thrull (ver. 2)	Black	Sum	C1	0.20
☐ Basal Thrull (ver. 3)	Black	Sum	C1	0.20
2				
☐ Basal Thrull (ver. 4)	Black	Sum	C1	0.20
☐ Bottomless Vault	Land	L	U1	2.00
☐ Brassclaw Orcs (ver. 1)	Red	Sum	C1	0.20
☐ Brassclaw Orcs (ver. 2)	Red	Sum	C1	0.20
☐ Brassclaw Orcs (ver. 3)	Red	Sum	C1	0.20
☐ Brassclaw Orcs (ver. 4)	Red	Sum	C1	0.20
☐ Breeding Pit	Black	E	U3	1.50
☐ Combat Medic (ver. 1)	White	Sum	C1	0.20
☐ Combat Medic (ver. 2)	White	Sum	C1	0.20
3				

Card name	Color	Type	Rarity	Price
☐ Combat Medic (ver. 3)	White	Sum	C1	0.20
☐ Combat Medic (ver. 4)	White	Sum	C1	0.20
☐ Conch Horn	Artifact	Art	U1	2.00
☐ Deep Spawn	Blue	Sum	U3	0.50
☐ Delif's Cone	Artifact	Art	C1	0.25
☐ Delif's Cube	Artifact	Art	U1	2.00
☐ Derelor	Black	Sum	U1	2.50
☐ Draconian Cylix	Artifact	Art	U1	2.00
☐ Dwarven Armorer	Red	Sum	U1	2.00
4				
☐ Dwarven Catapult	Red	Ins	U3	0.50
☐ Dwarven Hold	Land	L	U1	3.00
☐ Dwarven Lieutenant	Red	Sum	U3	0.50
☐ Dwarven Ruins	Land	L	U2	1.00
☐ Dwarven Soldier (ver. 1)	Red	Sum	C1	0.20
☐ Dwarven Soldier (ver. 2)	Red	Sum	C1	0.20
☐ Dwarven Soldier (ver. 3)	Red	Sum	C1	0.20
☐ Ebon Praetor	Black	Sum	U1	2.50
☐ Ebon Stronghold	Land	L	U2	1.00
5				
☐ Elven Fortress (ver. 1)	Green	E	C1	0.20
☐ Elven Fortress (ver. 2)	Green	E	C1	0.20
☐ Elven Fortress (ver. 3)	Green	E	C1	0.20
☐ Elven Fortress (ver. 4)	Green	E	C1	0.20
☐ Elven Lyre	Artifact	Art	U1	2.00
☐ Elvish Farmer	Green	Sum	U1	2.00
☐ Elvish Hunter (ver. 1)	Green	Sum	C1	0.20

Card name	Color	Type	Rarity	Price
☐ Elvish Hunter (ver. 2)	Green	Sum	C1	0.20
☐ Elvish Hunter (ver. 3)	Green	Sum	C1	0.20
6				
☐ Elvish Scout (ver. 1)	Green	Sum	C1	0.20
☐ Elvish Scout (ver. 2)	Green	Sum	C1	0.20
☐ Elvish Scout (ver. 3)	Green	Sum	C1	0.20
☐ Farrel's Mantle	White	ECr	U3	0.50
☐ Farrel's Zealot (ver. 1)	White	Sum	C1	0.20
☐ Farrel's Zealot (ver. 2)	White	Sum	C1	0.20
☐ Farrel's Zealot (ver. 3)	White	Sum	C1	0.20
☐ Farrelite Priest	White	Sum	U3	0.50
☐ Feral Thallid	Green	Sum	U3	0.50
7				
☐ Fungal Bloom	Green	E	U1	2.00
☐ Goblin Chirurgeon (ver. 1)	Red	Sum	C1	0.20
☐ Goblin Chirurgeon (ver. 2)	Red	Sum	C1	0.20
☐ Goblin Chirurgeon (ver. 3)	Red	Sum	C1	0.20
☐ Goblin Flotilla	Red	Sum	U1	2.00
☐ Goblin Grenade (ver. 1)	Red	Sor	C1	0.25
☐ Goblin Grenade (ver. 2)	Red	Sor	C1	0.25
☐ Goblin Grenade (ver. 3)	Red	Sor	C1	0.25
☐ Goblin Kites	Red	E	U3	0.50
8				
☐ Goblin War Drums (ver. 1)	Red	E	C1	0.20
☐ Goblin War Drums (ver. 2)	Red	E	C1	0.20
☐ Goblin War Drums (ver. 3)	Red	E	C1	0.20
☐ Goblin War Drums (ver. 4)	Red	E	C1	0.20

RARITY KEY   C = Common   **U** = Uncommon   **R** = Rare   **VR** = Very Rare   **#:** Times card appears on press sheet; lower numbers are rarer

Card name	Color	Type	Rarity	Price
Goblin Warrens	Red	E	U1	3.00
Hand of Justice	White	Sum	U1	4.00
Havenwood Battleground	Land	L	U2	1.00
Heroism	White	E	U3	0.50
High Tide (ver. 1)	Blue	Ins	C1	0.25
9				
High Tide (ver. 2)	Blue	Ins	C1	0.25
High Tide (ver. 3)	Blue	Ins	C1	0.25
Hollow Trees	Land	L	U1	2.00
Homarid (ver. 1)	Blue	Sum	C1	0.20
Homarid (ver. 2)	Blue	Sum	C1	0.20
Homarid (ver. 3)	Blue	Sum	C1	0.20
Homarid (ver. 4)	Blue	Sum	C1	0.20
Homarid Shaman	Blue	Sum	U1	2.00
Homarid Spawning Bed	Blue	E	U3	0.50
10				
Homarid Warrior (ver. 1)	Blue	Sum	C1	0.25
Homarid Warrior (ver. 2)	Blue	Sum	C1	0.25
Homarid Warrior (ver. 3)	Blue	Sum	C1	0.25
Hymn to Tourach (ver. 1)	Black	Sor	C1	0.25
Hymn to Tourach (ver. 2)	Black	Sor	C1	0.25
Hymn to Tourach (ver. 3)	Black	Sor	C1	0.25
Hymn to Tourach (ver. 4)	Black	Sor	C1	0.25
Icatian Infantry (ver. 1)	White	Sum	C1	0.20
Icatian Infantry (ver. 2)	White	Sum	C1	0.20
11				
Icatian Infantry (ver. 3)	White	Sum	C1	0.20
Icatian Infantry (ver. 4)	White	Sum	C1	0.20
Icatian Javelineers (ver. 1)	White	Sum	C1	0.20
Icatian Javelineers (ver. 2)	White	Sum	C1	0.20
Icatian Javelineers (ver. 3)	White	Sum	C1	0.20
Icatian Lieutenant	White	Sum	U1	2.00
Icatian Moneychanger (ver. 1)	White	Sum	C1	0.20
Icatian Moneychanger (ver. 2)	White	Sum	C1	0.20
Icatian Moneychanger (ver. 3)	White	Sum	C1	0.20
12				
Icatian Phalanx	White	Sum	U3	0.80
Icatian Priest	White	Sum	U3	0.50
Icatian Scout (ver. 1)	White	Sum	U3	0.50
Icatian Scout (ver. 2)	White	Sum	U3	0.50
Icatian Scout (ver. 3)	White	Sum	U3	0.50
Icatian Scout (ver. 4)	White	Sum	U3	0.50
Icatian Skirmishers	White	Sum	U1	2.00
Icatian Store	Land	L	U1	2.00

Card name	Color	Type	Rarity	Price
Icatian Town	White	Sor	U1	3.00
13				
Implements of Sacrifice	Artifact	Art	U1	2.00
Initiates of the Ebon Hand (ver. 1)	Black	Sum	C1	0.25
Initiates of the Ebon Hand (ver. 2)	Black	Sum	C1	0.25
Initiates of the Ebon Hand (ver. 3)	Black	Sum	C1	0.25
Merseine (ver. 1)	Blue	ECr	C1	0.20
Merseine (ver. 2)	Blue	ECr	C1	0.20
Merseine (ver. 3)	Blue	ECr	C1	0.20
Merseine (ver. 4)	Blue	ECr	C1	0.20
Mindstab Thrull (ver. 1)	Black	Sum	C1	0.20
14				
Mindstab Thrull (ver. 2)	Black	Sum	C1	0.20
Mindstab Thrull (ver. 3)	Black	Sum	C1	0.20
Necrite (ver. 1)	Black	Sum	C1	0.20
Necrite (ver. 2)	Black	Sum	C1	0.20
Necrite (ver. 3)	Black	Sum	C1	0.20
Night Soil (ver. 1)	Green	E	C1	0.25
Night Soil (ver. 2)	Green	E	C1	0.25
Night Soil (ver. 3)	Green	E	C1	0.25
Orcish Captain	Red	Sum	U3	0.50
15				
Orcish Spy (ver. 1)	Red	Sum	C1	0.20
Orcish Spy (ver. 2)	Red	Sum	C1	0.20
Orcish Spy (ver. 3)	Red	Sum	C1	0.20
Orcish Veteran (ver. 1)	Red	Sum	C1	0.20
Orcish Veteran (ver. 2)	Red	Sum	C1	0.20
Orcish Veteran (ver. 3)	Red	Sum	C1	0.20
Orcish Veteran (ver. 4)	Red	Sum	C1	0.20
Order of Leitbur (ver. 1)	White	Sum	C1	0.25
Order of Leitbur (ver. 2)	White	Sum	C1	0.25
16				
Order of Leitbur (ver. 3)	White	Sum	C1	0.25
Order of the Ebon Hand (ver. 1)	Black	Sum	C1	0.25
Order of the Ebon Hand (ver. 2)	Black	Sum	C1	0.25
Order of the Ebon Hand (ver. 3)	Black	Sum	C1	0.25
Orgg	Red	Sum	U1	2.50
Raiding Party	Red	E	U3	0.80
Rainbow Vale	Land	L	U1	3.00
Ring of Renewal	Artifact	Art	U1	2.00
River Merfolk	Blue	Sum	U1	3.00

Card name	Color	Type	Rarity	Price
17				
Ruins of Trokair	Land	L	U2	0.70
Sand Silos	Land	L	U1	2.00
Seasinger	Blue	Sum	U3	1.00
Soul Exchange	Black	Sor	U3	0.50
Spirit Shield	Artifact	Art	U1	2.00
Spore Cloud (ver. 1)	Green	Ins	C1	0.20
Spore Cloud (ver. 2)	Green	Ins	C1	0.20
Spore Cloud (ver. 3)	Green	Ins	C1	0.20
Spore Flower	Green	Sum	U3	0.80
18				
Svyelunite Priest	Blue	Sum	U3	0.50
Svyelunite Temple	Land	L	U2	1.00
Thallid (ver. 1)	Green	Sum	C1	0.25
Thallid (ver. 2)	Green	Sum	C1	0.25
Thallid (ver. 3)	Green	Sum	C1	0.25
Thallid (ver. 4)	Green	Sum	C1	0.25
Thallid Devourer	Green	Sum	U3	0.50
Thelon's Chant	Green	E	U3	0.80
Thelon's Curse	Green	E	U1	2.00
19				
Thelonite Druid	Green	Sum	U3	0.80
Thelonite Monk	Green	Sum	U1	2.00
Thorn Thallid (ver. 1)	Green	Sum	C1	0.20
Thorn Thallid (ver. 2)	Green	Sum	C1	0.20
Thorn Thallid (ver. 3)	Green	Sum	C1	0.20
Thorn Thallid (ver. 4)	Green	Sum	C1	0.20
Thrull Champion	Black	Sum	U1	3.00
Thrull Retainer	Black	ECr	U3	0.50
Thrull Wizard	Black	Sum	U3	0.50
20				
Tidal Flats (ver. 1)	Blue	E	C1	0.25
Tidal Flats (ver. 2)	Blue	E	C1	0.25
Tidal Flats (ver. 3)	Blue	E	C1	0.25
Tidal Influence	Blue	E	U3	0.50
Tourach's Chant	Black	E	U3	0.80
Tourach's Gate	Black	EL	U1	2.00
Vodalian Knights	Blue	Sum	U1	3.00
Vodalian Mage (ver. 1)	Blue	Sum	C1	0.20
Vodalian Mage (ver. 2)	Blue	Sum	C1	0.20
21				
Vodalian Mage (ver. 3)	Blue	Sum	C1	0.20
Vodalian Soldiers (ver. 1)	Blue	Sum	C1	0.20
Vodalian Soldiers (ver. 2)	Blue	Sum	C1	0.20
Vodalian Soldiers (ver. 3)	Blue	Sum	C1	0.20
Vodalian Soldiers (ver. 4)	Blue	Sum	C1	0.20
Vodalian War Machine	Blue	Sum	U1	2.00
Zelyon Sword	Artifact	Art	U1	2.00

Hecatomb

Enchantment

When Hecatomb comes into play, sacrifice four creatures.
0: Tap target swamp you control to have Hecatomb deal 1 damage to target creature or player.

Illus. NeNe Thomas

Magic: The Gathering • *Ice Age*

Wizards of the Coast • Released **June 1995**

373 cards plus **10** variants in set • **IDENTIFIER: Snowflake symbol; black border**

- Starter decks contain 60 cards; starter displays contain 10 starters
- Booster packs contain 15 cards; booster displays contain 36 boosters

After the frantic pace of expansion releases in 1994, anticipation was high for *Ice Age*, the first *Magic* set in eight months. As the first true stand-alone expansion — designed to be playable without any cards from the base set — *Ice Age* was the basis for a block tournament format, the first of many block formats to come.

Ice Age includes "snow-covered" lands, acting as normal basic lands but interacting with other cards that key on snow-covered lands. *Ice Age* also introduces a new mechanic called "cumulative upkeep," which makes the cost of keeping the card in play more and more costly each upkeep. *Ice Age* also includes popular, powerful cards such as **Jester's Cap, Zuran Orb, Demonic Consultation, Pox, Lhurgoyf, Jokulhaups, Enduring Renewal**, and **Stormbind**.

At the time, a strange little card called **Necropotence** was mostly ignored by the *Magic* community, but this powerful enchantment that trades life for cards soon proved to be the best card-drawing engine in the history of the game. *Fallen Empires* had brought **Hymn** and **Order** cards to the environment and these, combined with **Necropotence**, heralded the dark time of the "Necro" deck. For a long while, in a tournament, players were either playing Necro or anti-Necro. — ***Bennie Smith & Orren McKay***

	Price
Set (373 cards plus 10 variants)	200.00
Starter Display Box	100.00
Booster Display Box	122.50
Starter Deck	11.00
Booster Pack	4.00

You will need **43** nine-pocket pages to store this set. (22 doubled up)

Card name	Color	Type	Rarity	Price
1				
Abyssal Specter	Black	Sum	U	1.00
Adarkar Sentinel	Artifact	ACr	U	1.00
Adarkar Unicorn	White	Sum	C	0.25
Adarkar Wastes	Land	L	R	5.00
Aegis of the Meek	Artifact	Art	R	3.00

RARITY KEY C = Common U = Uncommon R = Rare VR = Very Rare #: Times card appears on press sheet; lower numbers are rarer

Card name	Color	Type	Rarity	Price
Aggression	Red	ECr	U	1.00
Altar of Bone	Multi	Sor	R	3.00
Amulet of Quoz	Artifact	Art	R	3.00
Anarchy	Red	Sor	U	1.00
2				
Arctic Foxes	White	Sum	C	0.25
Arcum's Sleigh	Artifact	Art	U	1.00
Arcum's Weathervane	Artifact	Art	U	1.00
Arcum's Whistle	Artifact	Art	U	1.00
Arenson's Aura	White	E	C	0.25
Armor of Faith	White	ECr	C	0.25
Arnjlot's Ascent	Blue	E	C	0.25
Ashen Ghoul	Black	Sum	U	1.00
Aurochs	Green	Sum	C	0.25
3				
Avalanche	Red	Sor	U	1.00
Balduvian Barbarians	Red	Sum	C	0.25
Balduvian Bears	Green	Sum	C	0.25
Balduvian Conjurer	Blue	Sum	U	1.00
Balduvian Hydra	Red	Sum	R	4.00
Balduvian Shaman	Blue	Sum	C	0.25
Barbarian Guides	Red	Sum	C	0.25
Barbed Sextant	Artifact	Art	C	0.25
Baton of Morale	Artifact	Art	U	1.00
4				
Battle Cry	White	Ins	U	1.00
Battle Frenzy	Red	Ins	C	0.25
Binding Grasp	Blue	ECr	U	1.00
Black Scarab	White	ECr	U	1.00
Blessed Wine	White	Ins	C	0.25
Blinking Spirit	White	Sum	R	6.30
Blizzard	Green	E	R	3.00
Blue Scarab	White	ECr	U	1.00
Bone Shaman	Red	Sum	C	0.25
5				
Brainstorm	Blue	Ins	C	0.25
Brand of Ill Omen	Red	ECr	R	3.00
Breath of Dreams	Blue	E	U	1.00
Brine Shaman	Black	Sum	C	0.25
Brown Ouphe	Green	Sum	C	0.25
Brushland	Land	L	R	5.00
Burnt Offering	Black	Int	C	0.25
Call to Arms	White	E	R	4.00
Caribou Range	White	EL	R	4.00
6				
Celestial Sword	Artifact	Art	R	3.00
Centaur Archer	Multi	Sum	U	1.00
Chaos Lord	Red	Sum	R	4.00
Chaos Moon	Red	E	R	4.00
Chromatic Armor	Multi	ECr	R	3.00
Chub Toad	Green	Sum	C	0.25
Circle of Protection: Black	White	E	C	0.25
Circle of Protection: Blue	White	E	C	0.25
Circle of Protection: Green	White	E	C	0.25
7				
Circle of Protection: Red	White	E	C	0.25
Circle of Protection: White	White	E	C	0.25
Clairvoyance	Blue	Ins	C	0.25
Cloak of Confusion	Black	ECr	C	0.25
Cold Snap	White	E	U	1.00
Conquer	Red	EL	U	1.00
Cooperation	White	ECr	C	0.25
Counterspell	Blue	Int	C	0.25
Crown of the Ages	Artifact	Art	R	4.00
8				
Curse of Marit Lage	Red	E	R	3.00
Dance of the Dead	Black	EDCr	U	1.00
Dark Banishing	Black	Ins	C	0.25
Dark Ritual	Black	Int	C	0.25
Death Ward	White	Ins	C	0.25
Deflection	Blue	Int	R	8.00
Demonic Consultation	Black	Ins	U	1.00

Card name	Color	Type	Rarity	Price
Despotic Scepter	Artifact	Art	R	4.00
Diabolic Vision	Multi	Sor	U	1.00
9				
Dire Wolves	Green	Sum	C	0.25
Disenchant	White	Ins	C	0.25
Dread Wight	Black	Sum	R	3.00
Dreams of the Dead	Blue	E	U	1.00
Drift of the Dead	Black	Sum	U	1.00
Drought	White	E	U	1.00
Dwarven Armory	Red	E	R	3.00
Earthlink	Multi	R	R	3.00
Earthlore	Green	EL	C	0.25
10				
Elder Druid	Green	Sum	R	4.00
Elemental Augury	Multi	E	R	3.30
Elkin Bottle	Artifact	Art	R	3.00
Elvish Healer	White	Sum	C	0.25
Enduring Renewal	White	E	R	5.30
Energy Storm	White	E	R	3.30
Enervate	Blue	Ins	C	0.25
Errant Minion	Blue	ECr	C	0.25
Errantry	Red	ECr	C	0.25
11				
Essence Filter	Green	Sor	C	0.25
Essence Flare	Blue	ECr	C	0.25
Essence Vortex	Multi	Ins	U	1.00
Fanatical Fever	Green	Ins	U	1.00
Fear	Black	ECr	C	0.25
Fiery Justice	Multi	Sor	R	3.00
Fire Covenant	Multi	Ins	U	1.00
Flame Spirit	Red	Sum	U	1.00
Flare	Red	Ins	C	0.25
12				
Flooded Woodlands	Multi	E	R	3.00
Flow of Maggots	Black	Sum	R	3.00
Folk of the Pines	Green	Sum	C	0.25
Forbidden Lore	Green	EL	R	3.50
Force Void	Blue	Int	U	1.00
Forest (ver. 1)	Land	L	C	0.25
Forest (ver. 2)	Land	L	C	0.25
Forest (ver. 3)	Land	L	C	0.25
Forgotten Lore	Green	Sor	U	1.00
13				
Formation	White	Ins	R	3.00
Foul Familiar	Black	Sum	C	0.25
Foxfire	Green	Ins	C	0.25
Freyalise Supplicant	Green	Sum	U	1.00
Freyalise's Charm	Green	E	U	1.00
Freyalise's Winds	Green	E	R	3.00
Fumarole	Multi	Sor	U	1.00
Fylgja	White	ECr	C	0.25
Fyndhorn Bow	Artifact	Art	U	1.00
14				
Fyndhorn Brownie	Green	Sum	C	0.25
Fyndhorn Elder	Green	Sum	U	1.00
Fyndhorn Elves	Green	Sum	C	0.25
Fyndhorn Pollen	Green	E	R	3.00
Game of Chaos	Red	Sor	R	3.30
Gangrenous Zombies	Black	Sum	C	0.25
Gaze of Pain	Black	Sor	C	0.25
General Jarkeld	White	SmL	R	4.00
Ghostly Flame	Multi	E	R	3.00
15				
Giant Growth	Green	Ins	C	0.25
Giant Trap Door Spider	Multi	SmL	U	1.00
Glacial Chasm	Land	L	U	1.00
Glacial Crevasses	Red	E	R	3.00
Glacial Wall	Blue	Sum	U	1.00
Glaciers	Multi	E	R	3.50
Goblin Lyre	Artifact	Art	R	3.00
Goblin Mutant	Red	Sum	U	1.00
Goblin Sappers	Red	Sum	C	0.25
16				
Goblin Ski Patrol	Red	Sum	C	0.25
Goblin Snowman	Red	Sum	U	1.00
Gorilla Pack	Green	Sum	C	0.25
Gravebind	Black	Ins	R	3.00
Green Scarab	White	ECr	U	1.00

Card name	Color	Type	Rarity	Price
Grizzled Wolverine	Red	Sum	C	0.25
Hallowed Ground	White	E	U	1.00
Halls of Mist	Land	L	R	3.00
17				
Heal	White	Ins	C	0.25
Hecatomb	Black	E	R	5.30
Hematite Talisman	Artifact	Art	U	1.00
Hipparion	White	Sum	U	1.00
Hoar Shade	Black	Sum	C	0.25
Hot Springs	Green	EL	R	3.00
Howl from Beyond	Black	Ins	C	0.25
Hurricane	Green	Sor	U	1.00
Hyalopterous Lemure	Black	Sum	U	1.00
Hydroblast	Blue	Int	C	0.25
18				
Hymn of Rebirth	Multi	Sor	U	1.00
Ice Cauldron	Artifact	Art	R	4.00
Ice Floe	Land	L	U	1.00
Iceberg	Blue	E	U	1.00
Icequake	Black	Sor	U	1.00
Icy Manipulator	Artifact	Art	U	6.50
Icy Prison	Blue	E	R	3.00
Illusionary Forces	Blue	Sum	C	0.25
Illusionary Presence	Blue	Sum	R	3.00
19				
Illusionary Terrain	Blue	E	U	1.00
Illusionary Wall	Blue	Sum	C	0.25
Illusions of Grandeur	Blue	E	R	4.00
Imposing Visage	Red	ECr	C	0.25
Incinerate	Red	Ins	C	0.25
Infernal Darkness	Black	E	R	4.00
Infernal Denizen	Black	Sum	R	3.00
Infinite Hourglass	Artifact	Art	R	3.50
Infuse	Blue	Ins	C	0.25
20				
Island (ver. 1)	Land	L	C	0.25
Island (ver. 2)	Land	L	C	0.25
Island (ver. 3)	Land	L	C	0.25
Jester's Cap	Artifact	Art	R	12.50
Jester's Mask	Artifact	Art	R	7.00
Jeweled Amulet	Artifact	Art	U	1.00
Johtull Wurm	Green	Sum	U	1.00
Jokulhaups	Red	Sor	R	6.00
Juniper Order Druid	Green	Sum	C	0.25
21				
Justice	White	E	U	1.00
Karplusan Forest	Land	L	R	5.00
Karplusan Giant	Red	Sum	U	1.00
Karplusan Yeti	Red	Sum	R	4.00
Kelsinko Ranger	White	Sum	C	0.25
Kjeldoran Dead	Black	Sum	C	0.25
Kjeldoran Elite Guard	White	Sum	U	1.00
Kjeldoran Frostbeast	Multi	Sum	U	1.00
Kjeldoran Guard	White	Sum	C	0.25
22				
Kjeldoran Knight	White	Sum	R	4.00
Kjeldoran Phalanx	White	Sum	R	3.00
Kjeldoran Royal Guard	White	Sum	R	3.00
Kjeldoran Skycaptain	White	Sum	U	1.00
Kjeldoran Skyknight	White	Sum	C	0.25
Kjeldoran Warrior	White	Sum	C	0.25
Knight of Stromgald	Black	Sum	U	1.00
Krovikan Elementalist	Black	Sum	U	1.00
Krovikan Fetish	Black	ECr	C	0.25
23				
Krovikan Sorcerer	Blue	Sum	C	0.25
Krovikan Vampire	Black	Sum	U	1.00
Land Cap	Land	L	R	3.00
Lapis Lazuli Talisman	Artifact	Art	U	1.00
Lava Burst	Red	Sor	C	0.25
Lava Tubes	Land	L	R	3.00
Legions of Lim-Dul	Black	Sum	C	0.25
Leshrac's Rite	Black	ECr	U	1.00
Leshrac's Sigil	Black	E	U	1.00
24				
Lhurgoyf	Green	Sum	R	6.00
Lightning Blow	White	Ins	R	3.00
Lim-Dul's Cohort	Black	Sum	C	0.25

RARITY KEY C = Common U = Uncommon R = Rare VR = Very Rare UR = Ultra Rare F = Foil card CARD TYPES: See page 246

Card name	Color	Type	Rarity	Price
Lim-Dul's Hex	Black	E	U	1.00
Lost Order of Jarkeld	White	Sum	R	3.00
Lure	Green	ECr	U	1.00
Maddening Wind	Green	ECr	U	1.00
Magus of the Unseen	Blue	Sum	R	3.00
Malachite Talisman	Artifact	Art	U	1.00
Marton Stromgald	Red	SmL	R	5.00
Melee	Red	Ins	U	1.00
Melting	Red	E	U	1.00
Mercenaries	White	Sum	R	4.00
Merieke Ri Berit	Multi	SmL	R	3.30
Mesmeric Trance	Blue	E	R	3.00
Meteor Shower	Red	Sor	C	0.25
Mind Ravel	Black	Sor	C	0.25
Mind Warp	Black	Sor	U	1.00
Mind Whip	Black	ECr	R	3.00
Minion of Leshrac	Black	Sum	R	5.00
Minion of Tevesh Szat	Black	Sum	R	4.50
Mistfolk	Blue	Sum	C	0.25
Mole Worms	Black	Sum	U	1.00
Monsoon	Multi	E	R	3.00
Moor Fiend	Black	Sum	C	0.25
Mountain (ver. 1)	Land	L	C	0.25
Mountain (ver. 2)	Land	L	C	0.25
Mountain (ver. 3)	Land	L	C	0.25
Mountain Goat	Red	Sum	C	0.25
Mountain Titan	Multi	Sum	R	3.50
Mudslide	Red	E	R	3.00
Musician	Blue	Sum	R	3.00
Mystic Might	Blue	EL	R	3.00
Mystic Remora	Blue	E	C	0.25
Nacre Talisman	Artifact	Art	U	1.00
Naked Singularity	Artifact	Art	R	4.00
Nature's Lore	Green	Sor	U	1.00
Necropotence	Black	E	R	7.00
Norritt	Black	Sum	C	0.25
Oath of Lim-Dul	Black	E	R	4.00
Onyx Talisman	Artifact	Art	U	1.00
Orcish Cannoneers	Red	Sum	U	1.00
Orcish Conscripts	Red	Sum	C	0.25
Orcish Farmer	Red	Sum	C	0.25
Orcish Healer	Red	Sum	U	1.00
Orcish Librarian	Red	Sum	R	3.00
Orcish Lumberjack	Red	Sum	C	0.25
Orcish Squatters	Red	Sum	R	4.00
Order of the Sacred Torch	White	Sum	R	4.00
Order of the White Shield	White	Sum	U	1.00
Pale Bears	Green	Sum	R	3.00
Panic	Red	Ins	C	0.25
Pentagram of the Ages	Artifact	Art	R	5.00
Pestilence Rats	Black	Sum	C	0.25

Card name	Color	Type	Rarity	Price
Phantasmal Mount	Blue	Sum	U	1.00
Pit Trap	Artifact	Art	U	1.00
Plains (ver. 1)	Land	L	C	0.25
Plains (ver. 2)	Land	L	C	0.25
Plains (ver. 3)	Land	L	C	0.25
Polar Kraken	Blue	Sum	R	5.30
Portent	Blue	Sor	C	0.25
Power Sink	Blue	Int	C	0.25
Pox	Black	Sor	R	5.00
Prismatic Ward	White	ECr	C	0.25
Pygmy Allosaurus	Green	Sum	R	3.00
Pyknite	Green	Sum	C	0.25
Pyroblast	Red	Int	C	0.25
Pyroclasm	Red	Sor	U	1.00
Rally	White	Ins	C	0.25
Ray of Command	Blue	Ins	C	0.25
Ray of Erasure	Blue	Ins	C	0.25
Reality Twist	Blue	E	R	4.00
Reclamation	Multi	E	R	3.00
Red Scarab	White	ECr	U	1.00
Regeneration	Green	ECr	C	0.25
Rime Dryad	Green	Sum	C	0.25
Ritual of Subdual	Green	E	R	3.50
River Delta	Land	L	R	4.00
Runed Arch	Artifact	Art	R	3.50
Sabretooth Tiger	Red	Sum	C	0.25
Sacred Boon	White	Ins	U	1.00
Scaled Wurm	Green	Sum	C	0.25
Sea Spirit	Blue	Sum	U	1.00
Seizures	Black	ECr	C	0.25
Seraph	White	Sum	R	6.00
Shambling Strider	Green	Sum	C	0.25
Shatter	Red	Ins	C	0.25
Shield Bearer	White	Sum	C	0.25
Shield of the Ages	Artifact	Art	U	1.00
Shyft	Blue	Sum	R	3.00
Sibilant Spirit	Blue	Sum	R	5.00
Silver Erne	Blue	Sum	U	1.00
Skeleton Ship	Multi	SmL	R	4.00
Skull Catapult	Artifact	Art	U	1.00
Sleight of Mind	Blue	Int	U	1.00
Snow Devil	Blue	ECr	C	0.25
Snow Fortress	Artifact	ACr	R	3.00
Snow Hound	White	Sum	U	1.00
Snowblind	Green	ECr	R	3.00
Snow-Covered Forest	Land	L	C	0.25
Snow-Covered Island	Land	L	C	0.25
Snow-Covered Mountain	Land	L	C	0.25
Snow-Covered Plains	Land	L	C	0.25
Snow-Covered Swamp	Land	L	C	0.25
Snowfall	Blue	E	C	0.25

Card name	Color	Type	Rarity	Price
Soldevi Golem	Artifact	ACr	R	4.00
Soldevi Machinist	Blue	Sum	U	1.00
Soldevi Simulacrum	Artifact	ACr	U	1.00
Songs of the Damned	Black	Int	C	0.25
Soul Barrier	Blue	E	U	1.00
Soul Burn	Black	Sor	C	0.25
Soul Kiss	Black	ECr	C	0.25
Spectral Shield	Multi	ECr	U	1.00
Spoils of Evil	Black	Int	R	3.00
Spoils of War	Black	Sor	R	3.00
Staff of the Ages	Artifact	Art	R	4.00
Stampede	Green	Ins	R	4.00
Stench of Evil	Black	Sor	U	1.00
Stone Rain	Red	Sor	C	0.25
Stone Spirit	Red	Sum	U	1.00
Stonehands	Red	ECr	C	0.25
Storm Spirit	Multi	Sum	R	4.00
Stormbind	Multi	E	R	5.00
Stromgald Cabal	Black	Sum	R	4.00
Stunted Growth	Green	Sor	R	4.00
Sulfurous Springs	Land	L	R	5.00
Sunstone	Artifact	Art	U	1.00
Swamp (ver. 1)	Land	L	C	0.25
Swamp (ver. 2)	Land	L	C	0.25
Swamp (ver. 3)	Land	L	C	0.25
Swords to Plowshares	White	Ins	U	1.00
Tarpan	Green	Sum	C	0.25
Thermokarst	Green	Sor	U	1.00
Thoughtleech	Green	E	U	1.00
Thunder Wall	Blue	Sum	U	1.00
Timberline Ridge	Land	L	R	3.00
Time Bomb	Artifact	Art	R	4.00
Tinder Wall	Green	Sum	C	0.25
Tor Giant	Red	Sum	C	0.25
Total War	Red	E	R	3.00
Touch of Death	Black	Sor	C	0.25
Touch of Vitae	Green	Ins	U	1.00
Trailblazer	Green	Ins	R	3.00
Underground River	Land	L	R	5.00
Updraft	Blue	Ins	U	1.00
Urza's Bauble	Artifact	Art	U	1.00
Veldt	Land	L	R	3.00
Venomous Breath	Green	Ins	U	1.00
Vertigo	Red	Ins	U	1.00
Vexing Arcanix	Artifact	Art	R	5.00
Vibrating Sphere	Artifact	Art	R	3.00
Walking Wall	Artifact	ACr	U	1.00
Wall of Lava	Red	Sum	U	1.00
Wall of Pine Needles	Green	Sum	U	1.00
Wall of Shields	Artifact	ACr	U	1.00
War Chariot	Artifact	Art	U	1.00
Warning	White	Ins	C	0.25
Whalebone Glider	Artifact	Art	U	1.00
White Scarab	White	ECr	U	1.00
Whiteout	Green	Ins	U	1.00
Wiitigo	Green	Sum	R	4.00
Wild Growth	Green	EL	C	0.25
Wind Spirit	Blue	Sum	U	1.00
Wings of Aesthir	Multi	ECr	U	1.00
Winter's Chill	Blue	Ins	R	4.00
Withering Wisps	Black	E	U	1.00
Woolly Mammoths	Green	Sum	C	0.25
Woolly Spider	Green	Sum	C	0.25
Word of Blasting	Red	Ins	U	1.00
Word of Undoing	Blue	Ins	C	0.25
Wrath of Marit Lage	Blue	E	R	3.50
Yavimaya Gnats	Green	Sum	U	1.00
Zuran Enchanter	Blue	Sum	C	0.25
Zuran Orb	Artifact	Art	U	1.50
Zuran Spellcaster	Blue	Sum	C	0.25
Zur's Weirding	Blue	E	R	4.00

RARITY KEY C = Common U = Uncommon R = Rare VR = Very Rare UR = Ultra Rare F = Foil card **CARD TYPES: See page 246**

Magic: The Gathering • Chronicles

Wizards of the Coast • Released September 1995

125 cards plus 9 variants in set • IDENTIFIER: Expansion symbols, but white borders

• Booster packs contain 12 cards; booster displays contain 45 boosters

Be careful what you wish for, CCG players. *Magic* fans who'd missed out on cards from earlier, short-run expansions demanded this set, which provided "Unlimited" or playable white-bordered versions of select expansion cards — complete with the original expansion symbol. But many cards reprinted in *Chronicles* saw the prices for their original versions drop — making them unpopular with retailers.

The presence of the expansion symbols may lead newer collectors today to think they've got the originals. Always check those borders... — *John Jackson Miller*

Set (125 cards plus 9 variants)		97.50
Booster Display Box		112.00
Booster Pack		3.00

You will need 14 nine-pocket pages to store this set (7 doubled up)

Card name	Set	Color	Type	Rarity	Price
Abu Jafar	AN	White	Sum	U3	1.00
Active Volcano	LE	Red	Ins	C3	0.15
Akron Legionnaire	LE	White	Sum	U1	2.00
Aladdin	AN	Red	Sum	U1	2.80
Angelic Voices	LE	White	Enc	U1	4.00
Arcades Sabboth	LE	Multi	SmL	U1	5.00
Arena of the Ancients	LE	Artifact	Art	U1	3.00
Argothian Pixies	AQ	Green	Sum	C3	0.15
Ashnod's Altar	AQ	Artifact	Art	C2	0.25
Ashnod's Transmogrant	AQ	Artifact	Art	C2	0.25
Axelrod Gunnarson	LE	Multi	SmL	U1	3.00
Ayesha Tanaka	LE	Multi	SmL	U1	2.50
Azure Drake	LE	Blue	Sum	U3	0.80
Banshee	DK	Black	Sum	U3	0.80
Barl's Cage	DK	Artifact	Art	U1	2.00
Beasts of Bogardan	LE	Red	Sum	U3	1.00
Blood Moon	DK	Red	E	U1	4.00
Blood of the Martyr	DK	White	Ins	U3	1.00
Bog Rats	DK	Black	Sum	C3	0.15
Book of Rass	DK	Artifact	Art	U1	1.50
Boomerang	LE	Blue	Ins	C3	0.15
Bronze Horse	LE	Artifact	ACr	U1	2.00
Cat Warriors	LE	Green	Sum	C3	0.15
Chromium	LE	Multi	SmL	U1	5.00
City of Brass	AN	Land	L	U1	7.50
Cocoon	LE	Green	ECr	U3	1.00
Concordant Crossroads	LE	Green	EW	U1	3.50
Craw Giant	LE	Green	Sum	U1	1.00
Cuombajj Witches	AN	Black	Sum	C3	0.15
Cyclone	AN	Green	E	U1	2.00
Dakkon Blackblade	LE	Multi	SmL	U1	4.00
Dance of Many	DK	Blue	E	U1	3.00
Dandan	AN	Blue	ECr	C3	0.25
D'Avenant Archer	LE	White	Sum	C3	0.15
Divine Offering	LE	White	Ins	C3	0.15
Emerald Dragonfly	LE	Green	Sum	C3	0.15
Enchantment Alteration	LE	Blue	Ins	U3	0.80
Erhnam Djinn	AN	Green	Sum	U3	4.00
Fallen Angel	LE	Black	Sum	U1	1.00
Feldon's Cane	AQ	Artifact	Art	C2	0.50
Fire Drake	DK	Red	Sum	U3	1.00
Fishliver Oil	AN	Blue	ECr	C3	0.15
Flash Flood	LE	Blue	Ins	C3	0.15
Fountain of Youth	DK	Artifact	Art	C2	0.25
Gabriel Angelfire	LE	Multi	SmL	U1	3.00
Gauntlets of Chaos	LE	Artifact	Art	U1	3.00
Ghazban Ogre	AN	Green	Sum	C3	0.15
Giant Slug	LE	Black	Sum	U3	0.15
Goblin Artisans	AQ	Red	Sum	U3	1.00
Goblin Digging Team	DK	Red	Sum	C3	0.15
Goblin Shrine	DK	Red	ELnd	C3	0.15
Goblins of the Flarg	DK	Red	Sum	C3	0.15
Hasran Ogress	AN	Black	Sum	C3	0.15

Card name	Set	Color	Type	Rarity	Price
Hell's Caretaker	LE	Black	Sum	U1	5.00
Horn of Deafening	LE	Artifact	Art	U1	2.50
Indestructible Aura	LE	White	Ins	C3	0.15
Ivory Guardians	LE	White	Sum	U3	1.00
Jalum Tome	AQ	Artifact	Art	U1	3.00
Jeweled Bird	AN	Artifact	Art	U1	2.00
Johan	LE	Multi	SmL	U1	4.00
Juxtapose	LE	Blue	Sor	U1	3.00
Keepers of the Faith	LE	White	Sum	C3	0.15
Kei Takahashi	LE	Multi	SmL	C1	0.25
Land's Edge	LE	Red	EW	U1	4.00
Living Armor	DK	Artifact	Art	C2	0.15
Marhault Elsdragon	LE	Multi	SmL	C1	0.25
Metamorphosis	AN	Green	Ins	C3	0.15
Mountain Yeti	LE	Red	Sum	C3	0.20
Nebuchadnezzer	LE	Multi	SmL	U1	4.00
Nicol Bolas	LE	Multi	SmL	U1	5.00
Obelisk of Undoing	AQ	Artifact	Art	U1	3.00
Palladia-Mors	LE	Multi	SmL	U1	5.00
Petra Sphinx	LE	White	Sum	U1	3.00
Primordial Ooze	LE	Red	Sum	U3	1.00
Puppet Master	LE	Blue	ECr	U3	1.00
Rabid Wombat	LE	Green	Sum	U1	1.00
Rakalite	AQ	Artifact	Art	U1	2.00
Recall	LE	Blue	Sor	U3	1.80
Remove Soul	LE	Blue	Int	C3	0.15
Repentant Blacksmith	AN	White	Sum	C3	0.25
Revelation	LE	Green	EW	U1	3.00
Rubinia Soulsinger	LE	Multi	SmL	U1	4.00
Runesword	DK	Artifact	Art	C2	0.25
Safe Haven	DK	Land	L	U1	2.50
Scavenger Folk	DK	Green	Sum	C3	0.15
Sentinel	LE	Artifact	ACr	U1	3.00
Serpent Generator	LE	Artifact	Art	U1	4.00
Shield Wall	LE	White	Ins	U3	0.80
Shimian Nightstalker	LE	Black	Sum	U3	0.50
Sivitri Scarzam	LE	Multi	SmL	C1	0.25
Sol'Kanar the Swamp King	LE	Multi	SmL	U1	5.00
Stangg	LE	Multi	SmL	U1	4.00
Storm Seeker	LE	Green	Ins	U3	2.00

Card name	Set	Color	Type	Rarity	Price
Takklemaggot	LE	Blue	ECr	U3	1.00
Teleport	LE	Blue	Ins	U1	3.00
The Fallen	DK	Black	Sum	U3	1.00
The Wretched	LE	Black	Sum	U1	5.00
Tobias Andrion	LE	Multi	SmL	C1	0.25
Tor Wauki	LE	Multi	SmL	C1	0.25
Tormod's Crypt	DK	Artifact	Art	C2	0.25
Transmutation	LE	Black	Ins	C3	0.15
Triassic Egg	LE	Artifact	Art	U1	3.00
Urza's Mine (sphere)	LE	Land	L	C1	0.25
Urza's Mine (mouth)	LE	Land	L	C1	0.25
Urza's Mine (pulley)	LE	Land	L	C1	0.25
Urza's Mine (tower)	AQ	Land	L	C1	0.25
Urza's Powerplant (bug)	AQ	Land	L	C1	0.25
Urza's Powerplant (columns)	AQ	Land	L	C1	0.25
Urza's Powerplant (rock)	AQ	Land	L	C1	0.25
Urza's Powerplant (sphere)	AQ	Land	L	C1	0.25
Urza's Tower (forest)	AQ	Land	L	C1	0.25
Urza's Tower (mountains)	AQ	Land	L	C1	0.25
Urza's Tower (plains)	AQ	Land	L	C1	0.25
Urza's Tower (shore)	AQ	Land	L	C1	0.25
Vaevictis Asmadi	LE	Multi	SmL	U1	5.00
Voodoo Doll	LE	Artifact	Art	U1	3.00
Wall of Heat	LE	Red	Sum	C3	0.15
Wall of Opposition	LE	Red	Sum	U3	1.00
Wall of Shadows	LE	Black	Sum	C3	0.10
Wall of Vapor	LE	Blue	Sum	C3	0.15
Wall of Wonder	LE	Blue	Sum	U3	1.00
War Elephant	AN	White	Sum	C3	0.15
Witch Hunter	DK	White	Sum	U3	1.00
Xira Arien	LE	Multi	SmL	U1	4.00
Yawgmoth Demon	AQ	Black	Sum	U1	3.00

Magic: The Gathering • Pro Tour Collector Set Inaugural Edition (aka New York Pro Tour set)

Wizards of the Coast • Released September 1996

112 cards in set plus reference cards, rulebooks

Following the institution of the *Magic* professional tournament system, Wizards of the Coast commemorated the initial event by reprinting its eight top decks in a special set. Card backs are different, borders are gold, and a replica of the player's signature appears on each.

NY Pro-Tour Set (unopened)	112.50
NY Pro-Tour Set (opened)	72.50

RARITY KEY **C** = Common **U** = Uncommon **R** = Rare **VR** = Very Rare **#:** Cards with lower numbers are rarer than ones with high numbers

Magic: The Gathering • Homelands

Wizards of the Coast • Released **January 1996**

115 cards plus **25** variants in set • **IDENTIFIER: World symbol; black borders**

• Booster packs contain 8 cards; booster displays contain 60 boosters

    Magic's seventh expansion develops some of the backstory on cards from the basic set, focusing on Serra and Sengir (from **Serra Angel** and **Sengir Vampire**). While the storyline is interesting, the cards themselves are weak or too expensive to play and **Homelands** is considered by many to be the worst expansion ever.

    While *Homelands* has no thematic tie to **Ice Age**, it was considered for tournament purposes part of the Ice Age "block" of expansions along with Alliances — although saying that it was considered for tournaments at all may be an overstatement. The few playable cards to come from this set include **Autumn Willow**, **Serrated Arrows**, **Spectral Bears**, and **Merchant Scroll**, and **Baron Sengir**, and **Eron the Relentless** occasionally showed up in decks, but nearly all of the rest of the set was considered so bad it was not even fit for casual play. Even collectors had little fun with *Homelands*, since variant cards were all by the same artist!

    Wizards *gave away* display boxes of *Homelands* at summer conventions, and buried the idea of 8-card pack expansions for good. — **Bennie Smith & Orren McKay**

You will need 16 nine-pocket pages to store this set. (8 doubled up)

Set (115 cards plus 25 variants)	50.00
Booster Display Box	65.00
Booster Pack	1.80

Card name	Color	Type	Rarity	Price
Abbey Gargoyles	White	Sum	U3	1.00
Abbey Matron (ver. 1)	White	Sum	C2	0.20
Abbey Matron (ver. 2)	White	Sum	C2	0.20
Aether Storm	Blue	E	U3	1.00
Aliban's Tower (ver. 1)	Red	Ins	C2	0.20
Aliban's Tower (ver. 2)	Red	Ins	C2	0.20
Ambush	Red	Ins	C1	0.20
Ambush Party (ver. 1)	Red	Sum	C2	0.20
Ambush Party (ver. 2)	Red	Sum	C2	0.20
Anaba Ancestor	Red	Sum	U1	2.50
Anaba Bodyguard (ver. 1)	Red	Sum	C2	0.25
Anaba Bodyguard (ver. 2)	Red	Sum	C2	0.25
Anaba Shaman (ver. 1)	Red	Sum	C2	0.25
Anaba Shaman (ver. 2)	Red	Sum	C2	0.25
Anaba Spirit Crafter	Red	Sum	U1	2.50
An-Havva Constable	Green	Sum	U1	2.00
An-Havva Inn	Green	Sor	U3	1.00
An-Havva Township	Land	L	U3	1.00
An-Zerrin Ruins	Red	E	U1	2.00
Apocalypse Chime	Artifact	Art	U1	2.00
Autumn Willow	Green	SmL	U1	5.00
Aysen Abbey	Land	L	U3	1.00
Aysen Bureaucrats (ver. 1)	White	Sum	C2	0.20
Aysen Bureaucrats (ver. 2)	White	Sum	C2	0.20
Aysen Crusader	White	Sum	U1	2.50
Aysen Highway	White	E	U1	2.50
Baki's Curse	Blue	Sor	U1	2.00
Baron Sengir	Black	SmL	U1	6.00
Beast Walkers	White	Sum	U1	2.00
Black Carriage	Black	Sum	U1	2.00
Broken Visage	Black	Ins	U1	2.00
Carapace (ver. 1)	Green	ECr	C2	0.20
Carapace (ver. 2)	Green	ECr	C2	0.20
Castle Sengir	Land	L	U3	1.00
Cemetery Gate (ver. 1)	Black	Sum	C2	0.20
Cemetery Gate (ver. 2)	Black	Sum	C2	0.20
Chain Stasis	Blue	Ins	U1	2.50
Chandler	Red	SmL	C1	0.25
Clockwork Gnomes	Artifact	ACr	C1	0.25
Clockwork Steed	Artifact	ACr	C1	0.25
Clockwork Swarm	Artifact	ACr	C1	0.25
Coral Reef	Blue	E	C1	0.25

Card name	Color	Type	Rarity	Price
Dark Maze (ver. 1)	Blue	Sum	C2	0.20
Dark Maze (ver. 2)	Blue	Sum	C2	0.20
Daughter of Autumn	Green	SmL	U1	2.80
Death Speakers	White	Sum	U3	1.00
Didgeridoo	Artifact	Art	U1	2.50
Drudge Spell	Black	E	U3	0.50
Dry Spell (ver. 1)	Black	Sor	C2	0.20
Dry Spell (ver. 2)	Black	Sor	C2	0.20
Dwarven Pony	Red	Sum	U1	2.00
Dwarven Sea Clan	Red	Sum	U1	2.00
Dwarven Trader (ver. 1)	Red	Sum	C2	0.20
Dwarven Trader (ver. 2)	Red	Sum	C2	0.20
Ebony Rhino	Artifact	ACr	C1	0.25
Eron the Relentless	Red	SmL	U3	1.00
Evaporate	Red	Sor	U3	0.80
Faerie Noble	Green	Sum	U1	2.50
Feast of the Unicorn (ver. 1)	Black	ECr	C2	0.20
Feast of the Unicorn (ver. 2)	Black	ECr	C2	0.20
Feroz's Ban	Artifact	Art	U1	2.50
Folk of An-Havva (ver. 1)	Green	Sum	C2	0.20
Folk of An-Havva (ver. 2)	Green	Sum	C2	0.20
Forget	Blue	Sor	U1	2.00
Funeral March	Black	ECr	C1	0.25
Ghost Hounds	Black	Sum	U3	0.90
Giant Albatross (ver. 1)	Blue	Sum	C2	0.20
Giant Albatross (ver. 2)	Blue	Sum	C2	0.20
Giant Oyster	Blue	Sum	U3	1.00
Grandmother Sengir	Black	SmL	U1	2.00
Greater Werewolf	Black	Sum	C1	0.25
Hazduhr the Abbot	White	SmL	U1	2.00
Headstone	Black	Ins	C1	0.25
Heart Wolf	Red	Sum	U1	2.00
Hungry Mist (ver. 1)	Green	Sum	C2	0.20
Hungry Mist (ver. 2)	Green	Sum	C2	0.20
Ihsan's Shade	Black	SmL	U3	1.30
Irini Sengir	Black	SmL	U1	1.00
Ironclaw Curse	Red	ECr	U1	2.00
Jinx	Blue	Ins	C1	0.25
Joven	Red	SmL	C1	0.25
Joven's Ferrets	Green	Sum	C1	0.25
Joven's Tools	Artifact	Art	U3	1.00
Koskun Falls	Black	EW	U1	2.00
Koskun Keep	Land	L	U3	0.90
Labyrinth Minotaur (ver. 1)	Blue	Sum	C2	0.20
Labyrinth Minotaur (ver. 2)	Blue	Sum	C2	0.20
Leaping Lizard	Green	Sum	C1	0.25
Leeches	White	Sor	U1	2.00
Mammoth Harness	Green	ECr	U1	2.00

Card name	Color	Type	Rarity	Price
Marjhan	Blue	Sum	U1	2.50
Memory Lapse (ver. 1)	Blue	Int	C2	0.25
Memory Lapse (ver. 2)	Blue	Int	C2	0.25
Merchant Scroll	Blue	Sor	C1	0.25
Mesa Falcon (ver. 1)	White	Sum	C2	0.20
Mesa Falcon (ver. 2)	White	Sum	C2	0.20
Mystic Decree	Blue	EW	U1	3.00
Narwhal	Blue	Sum	U1	2.00
Orcish Mine	Red	EL	U3	0.80
Primal Order	Green	E	U1	4.00
Prophecy	White	Sor	C1	0.25
Rashka the Slayer	White	SmL	U3	0.90
Reef Pirates (ver. 1)	Blue	Sum	C2	0.20
Reef Pirates (ver. 2)	Blue	Sum	C2	0.20
Renewal	Green	Sor	C1	0.25
Retribution	Red	Sor	U3	0.80
"Reveka, Wizard Savant"	Blue	SmL	U1	2.50
Root Spider	Green	Sum	U3	1.00
Roots	Green	ECr	U3	0.80
Roterothopter	Artifact	ACr	C1	0.25
Rysorian Badger	Green	Sum	U1	2.00
Samite Alchemist (ver. 1)	White	Sum	C2	0.20
Samite Alchemist (ver. 2)	White	Sum	C2	0.20
Sea Sprite	Blue	Sum	U3	1.00
Sea Troll	Blue	Sum	U3	0.80
Sengir Autocrat	Black	Sum	U1	3.50
Sengir Bats (ver. 1)	Black	Sum	C2	0.20
Sengir Bats (ver. 2)	Black	Sum	C2	0.20
Serra Aviary	White	EW	U1	3.00
Serra Bestiary	White	ECr	C1	0.25
Serra Inquisitors	White	Sum	U3	0.90
Serra Paladin	White	Sum	C1	0.25
Serrated Arrows	Artifact	Art	C1	0.25
Shrink (ver. 1)	Green	Ins	C2	0.20
Shrink (ver. 2)	Green	Ins	C2	0.20
Soraya the Falconer	White	SmL	U1	2.00
Spectral Bears	Green	Sum	U3	1.00
Timmerian Fiends	Black	Sum	U1	1.80
Torture (ver. 1)	Black	ECr	C2	0.20
Torture (ver. 2)	Black	ECr	C2	0.20
Trade Caravan (ver. 1)	White	Sum	C2	0.20
Trade Caravan (ver. 2)	White	Sum	C2	0.20
Truce	White	Ins	U1	2.00
Veldrane of Sengir	Black	SmL	U1	2.30
Wall of Kelp	Blue	Sum	U1	2.00
Willow Faerie (ver. 1)	Green	Sum	C2	0.20
Willow Faerie (ver. 2)	Green	Sum	C2	0.20
Willow Priestess	Green	Sum	U1	3.00
Winter Sky	Red	Sor	U3	3.00
Wizards' School	Land	L	U3	1.00

RARITY KEY C = Common   U = Uncommon   R = Rare   VR = Very Rare   #: Cards with lower numbers are rarer than ones with high numbers

268 • SCRYE Collectible Card Game Checklist and Price Guide

Magic: The Gathering • Alliances

Wizards of the Coast • Released **June 1996**

144 cards plus **55** variants in set • **IDENTIFIER: Pennant symbol; black borders**

• Booster packs contain 12 cards; booster displays contain 45 boosters

What better to follow a wretched expansion with than a great one?

Alliances, the first expansion set not printed at Carta Mundi and the first designed as an addition to an existing expansion, includes mechanics from *Ice Age* and follows the same storyline, It introduces "pitch spells," cards with alternative casting costs, which involve removing a same-colored spell in hand from the game instead of paying mana to cast it. **Contagion**, **Bounty of the Hunt**, **Pyrokinesis**, and especially **Force of Will** were immediate pitch-spell hits. (The white pitch spell, **Scars of the Veteran**, never really caught on.)

Alliances also has extremely powerful lands such as **Kjeldoran Outpost**, **Lake of the Dead**, and **Thawing Glaciers**, which in particular greatly aided the creation of three-, four- and five-color decks. Other notable cards include **Krovikan Horror**, **Gorilla Shaman**, **Pillage**, **Arcane Denial**, **Browse**, **Exile**, and **Lim-Dul's Vault**.

The one letdown from the set was **Balduvian Horde**, which before *Alliance*'s release was said to be a new red **Juzam Djinn** but was instead a feeble, barely playable substitute. But with plenty of good, playable cards and exciting new game mechanics, *Alliances* is considered one of the best expansions of all time. It certainly gave a shot in the arm to the CCG industry, which had suffered a rotten year. — ***Bennie Smith & Orren McKay***

Set (144 cards plus 55 variants)	120.00
Booster Display Box	140.00
Booster Pack	5.00

You will need 23 nine-pocket pages to store this set. (12 doubled up)

Card name	Color	Type	Rarity	Price
1				
Aesthir Glider (ver. 1)	Artifact	ACr	C1	0.20
Aesthir Glider (ver. 2)	Artifact	ACr	C1	0.20
Agent of Stromgald (ver. 1)	Red	Sum	C1	0.20
Agent of Stromgald (ver. 2)	Red	Sum	C1	0.20
Arcane Denial (ver. 1)	Blue	Int	C1	0.20
Arcane Denial (ver. 2)	Blue	Int	C1	0.20
Ashnod's Cylix	Artifact	Art	R2	3.00
Astrolabe (ver. 1)	Artifact	Art	C1	0.20
Astrolabe (ver. 2)	Artifact	Art	C1	0.20
2				
Awesome Presence (ver. 1)	Blue	ECr	C1	0.20
Awesome Presence (ver. 2)	Blue	ECr	C1	0.20
Balduvian Dead	Black	Sum	U2	1.00
Balduvian Horde	Red	Sum	R2	12.00
Balduvian Trading Post	Land	L	R2	5.00
Balduvian War-Makers (ver. 1)	Red	Sum	C1	0.20
Balduvian War-Makers (ver. 2)	Red	Sum	C1	0.20
Benthic Explorers (ver. 1)	Blue	Sum	C1	0.20
Benthic Explorers (ver. 2)	Blue	Sum	C1	0.20
3				
Bestial Fury (ver. 1)	Red	ECr	C1	0.20
Bestial Fury (ver. 2)	Red	ECr	C2	0.20
Bounty of the Hunt	Green	Ins	U2	1.00
Browse	Blue	E	U2	1.00
Burnout	Red	Int	U2	1.00
Carrier Pigeons (ver. 1)	White	Sum	C1	0.20
Carrier Pigeons (ver. 2)	White	Sum	C1	0.20
Casting of Bones (ver. 1)	Black	ECr	C1	0.20
Casting of Bones (ver. 2)	Black	ECr	C1	0.20
4				
Chaos Harlequin	Red	Sum	R2	3.00
Contagion	Black	Ins	U2	1.00
Deadly Insect (ver. 1)	Green	Sum	U3	1.00
Deadly Insect (ver. 2)	Green	Sum	U3	1.00
Death Spark	Red	Ins	U2	1.00
Diminishing Returns	Blue	Sor	R2	5.00
Diseased Vermin	Black	Sum	U2	1.00
Dystopia	Black	E	R2	4.00
Elvish Bard	Green	Sum	U2	1.00
5				
Elvish Ranger (ver. 1)	Green	Sum	C1	0.20
Elvish Ranger (ver. 2)	Green	Sum	C1	0.20
Elvish Spirit Guide	Green	Sum	U2	1.00
Energy Arc	Multi	Ins	U2	1.00

Card name	Color	Type	Rarity	Price
Enslaved Scout (ver. 1)	Red	Sum	C1	0.20
Enslaved Scout (ver. 2)	Red	Sum	C1	0.20
Errand of Duty (ver. 1)	White	Ins	C1	0.20
Errand of Duty (ver. 2)	White	Ins	C1	0.20
Exile	White	Ins	R2	5.50
6				
False Demise (ver. 1)	Blue	ECr	U3	1.00
False Demise (ver. 2)	Blue	ECr	U3	1.00
Fatal Lore	Black	Sor	R2	3.50
Feast or Famine (ver. 1)	Black	Ins	U3	1.00
Feast or Famine (ver. 2)	Black	Ins	U3	1.00
Fevered Strength (ver. 1)	Black	Ins	C1	0.20
Fevered Strength (ver. 2)	Black	Ins	C2	0.20
Floodwater Dam	Artifact	Art	R2	3.00
Force of Will	Blue	Int	U2	3.00
7				
Foresight (ver. 1)	Blue	Sor	C1	0.20
Foresight (ver. 2)	Blue	Sor	C1	0.20
Fyndhorn Druid (ver. 1)	Green	Sum	C1	0.20
Fyndhorn Druid (ver. 2)	Green	Sum	C1	0.20
Gargantuan Gorilla	Green	Sum	R2	4.50
Gift of the Woods (ver. 1)	Green	ECr	C1	0.20
Gift of the Woods (ver. 2)	Green	ECr	C1	0.20
Gorilla Berserkers (ver. 1)	Green	Sum	C1	0.20
Gorilla Berserkers (ver. 2)	Green	Sum	C2	0.20
8				
Gorilla Chieftan (ver. 1)	Green	Sum	C1	0.20
Gorilla Chieftan (ver. 2)	Green	Sum	C1	0.20
Gorilla Shaman (ver. 1)	Red	Sum	U3	1.00
Gorilla Shaman (ver. 2)	Red	Sum	U3	1.00
Gorilla War Cry (ver. 1)	Red	Ins	C1	0.20
Gorilla War Cry (ver. 2)	Red	Ins	C2	0.20
Guerilla Tactics (ver. 1)	Red	Ins	C1	0.20
Guerilla Tactics (ver. 2)	Red	Ins	C2	0.20
Gustha's Scepter	Artifact	Art	R2	4.00
9				
Hail Storm	Green	Ins	U2	1.00
Heart of Yavimaya	Land	L	R2	5.00
Helm of Obedience	Artifact	Art	R2	8.00
Inheritance	White	E	U2	1.00
Insidious Bookworms (ver. 1)	Black	Sum	C1	0.20
Insidious Bookworms (ver. 2)	Black	Sum	C1	0.20
Ivory Gargoyle	White	Sum	R2	5.50
Juniper Order Advocate	White	Sum	U2	1.00
Kaysa	Green	Sum	R2	5.00
10				
Keeper of Tresserhorn	Black	Sum	R2	5.00
Kjeldoran Escort (ver. 1)	White	Sum	C1	0.20
Kjeldoran Escort (ver. 2)	White	Sum	C2	0.20
Kjeldoran Home Guard	White	Sum	U2	1.00

Card name	Color	Type	Rarity	Price
Kjeldoran Outpost	Land	L	R2	9.00
Kjeldoran Pride (ver. 1)	White	ECr	C1	0.20
Kjeldoran Pride (ver. 2)	White	ECr	C1	0.20
Krovikan Horror	Black	Sum	R2	4.00
Krovikan Plague	Black	ECr	U2	1.00
11				
Lake of the Dead	Land	L	R2	10.00
Lat-Nam's Legacy (ver. 1)	Blue	Ins	C1	0.20
Lat-Nam's Legacy (ver. 2)	Blue	Ins	C1	0.20
Library of Lat-Nam	Blue	Sor	R2	4.00
Lim-Dul's High Guard (ver. 1)	Black	Sum	C1	0.20
Lim-Dul's High Guard (ver. 2)	Black	Sum	C1	0.20
Lim-Dul's Paladin	Multi	Sum	U2	1.00
Lim-Dul's Vault	Multi	Ins	U2	1.00
Lodestone Bauble	Artifact	Art	R2	4.00
12				
Lord of Tresserhorn	Multi	SmL	R2	6.00
Martyrdom (ver. 1)	White	Ins	C1	0.20
Martyrdom (ver. 2)	White	Ins	C1	0.20
Misfortune	Multi	Sor	R2	4.00
Mishra's Groundbreaker	Artifact	Art	U2	1.00
Misinformation	Black	Ins	U2	1.00
Mystic Compass	Artifact	Art	U2	1.00
Nature's Blessing	Multi	E	U2	1.00
Nature's Chosen	Green	ECr	U2	1.00
13				
Nature's Wrath	Green	E	R2	4.00
Noble Steeds (ver. 1)	White	E	C1	0.20
Noble Steeds (ver. 2)	White	E	C1	0.20
Omen of Fire	Red	Ins	R2	3.50
Phantasmal Fiend (ver. 1)	Black	Sum	C1	0.20
Phantasmal Fiend (ver. 2)	Black	Sum	C1	0.20
Phantasmal Sphere	Blue	Sum	R2	3.00
Phelddagrif	Multi	SmL	R2	4.00
Phyrexian Boon (ver. 1)	Black	ECr	C1	0.20
14				
Phyrexian Boon (ver. 2)	Black	ECr	C1	0.20
Phyrexian Devourer	Artifact	ACr	R2	3.00
Phyrexian Portal	Artifact	Art	R2	4.00
Phyrexian War Beast (ver. 1)	Artifact	ACr	C1	0.20
Phyrexian War Beast (ver. 2)	Artifact	ACr	C1	0.20
Pillage	Red	Sor	U2	2.00
Primitive Justice	Red	Sor	U2	1.00
Pyrokinesis	Red	Ins	U2	1.00
Reinforcements (ver. 1)	White	Ins	C1	0.20
15				
Reinforcements (ver. 2)	White	Ins	C1	0.20
Reprisal (ver. 1)	White	Ins	U3	1.00

Magic: The Gathering • *Mirage*

Wizards of the Coast • Released **October 1996**

335 cards plus **15** variants in set • **IDENTIFIER: Palm tree symbol; black borders**

- Starter decks contain 60 cards; booster displays contain 12 boosters
- Booster packs contain 15 cards; booster displays contain 36 boosters

Released in the fall of 1996, ***Mirage*** was the largest non-basic set produced up to that time at 350 cards. Designed as another stand-alone like ***Ice Age***, but with a tropical theme, it also introduced ***Magic***'s ***Fifth Edition*** rule changes.

Mirage brings several new, well-designed game mechanics such as flanking and phasing, and new twists to cards such as creature enchantments that can be cast as instants. This set also features charms for each color, giving the controller three different options to play with.

Notable cards from the set include the Guildmages of each color (especially Granger and Shadow), Jolrael's Centaurs, Wall of Roots, Dwarven Miner, Hammer of Bogardan, Sacred Mesa, Cadaverous Bloom, Frenetic Efreet, and "fetch lands," played as a uncounterable way for fetching dual lands. — ***Bennie Smith & Joshua C.H. Claytor***

Set (335 cards plus 15 variants)	160.00
Starter Display Box	95.00
Booster Display Box	90.00
Starter Deck	10.00
Booster Pack	3.30

You will need **39** nine-pocket pages to store this set. (19 doubled up)

RARITY KEY **C** = Common **U** = Uncommon **R** = Rare **VR** = Very Rare **#:** Cards with lower numbers are rarer than ones with high numbers

Card name	Color	Type	Rarity	Price	Card name	Color	Type	Rarity	Price	Card name	Color	Type	Rarity	Price
☐ Decomposition	Green	ECr	U	1.00	☐ Harbor Guardian	Multi	Sum	U	0.80	☐ Painful Memories	Black	Sor	U	1.00
☐ Delirium	Multi	Ins	U	1.00	☐ Harmattan Efreet	Blue	Sum	U	1.00	☐ Patagia Golem	Artifact	ACr	U	0.80
☐ Dirtwater Wraith	Black	Sum	C	0.25	☐ Haunting Apparition	Multi	Sum	U	0.90	☐ Paupers' Cage	Artifact	A	R	3.00
☐ Discordant Spirit	Multi	Sum	R	3.50	☐ Hazerider Drake	Multi	Sum	U	1.00	☐ Pearl Dragon	White	Sum	R	5.10
9					☐ Healing Salve	White	Ins	C	0.25	☐ Phyrexian Dreadnought	Artifact	ACr	R	6.80
☐ Disempower	White	Ins	C	0.25	☐ Hivis of the Scale	Red	SmL	R	4.00	☐ Phyrexian Purge	Multi	Sor	R	3.30
☐ Disenchant	White	Ins	C	0.25	17					☐ Phyrexian Tribute	Black	Sor	R	3.00
☐ Dissipate	Blue	Int	U	1.00	☐ Horrible Hordes	Artifact	ACr	U	1.00	☐ Phyrexian Vault	Artifact	A	U	0.80
☐ Divine Offering	White	Ins	C	0.25	☐ Igneous Golem	Artifact	ACr	U	1.00	25				
☐ Divine Retribution	White	Ins	R	3.00	☐ Illicit Auction	Red	Sor	R	4.00	☐ Plains (ver. 1)	Land	L	C	0.15
☐ Drain Life	Black	Sor	C	0.20	☐ Illumination	White	Int	U	1.00	☐ Plains (ver. 2)	Land	L	C	0.15
☐ Dread Specter	Black	Sum	U	1.00	☐ Incinerate	Red	Ins	C	0.25	☐ Plains (ver. 3)	Land	L	C	0.15
☐ Dream Cache	Blue	Sor	C	0.25	☐ Infernal Contract	Black	Sor	R	5.00	☐ Plains (ver. 4)	Land	L	C	0.15
☐ Dream Fighter	Blue	Sum	C	0.25	☐ Iron Tusk Elephant	White	Sum	U	0.90	☐ Political Trickery	Blue	Sor	R	3.00
10					☐ Island (ver. 1)	Land	L	C	0.15	☐ Polymorph	Blue	Sor	R	4.00
☐ Dwarven Miner	Red	Sum	U	1.00	☐ Island (ver. 2)	Land	L	C	0.15	☐ Power Sink	Blue	Int	C	0.25
☐ Dwarven Nomad	Red	Sum	C	0.25	18					☐ Preferred Selection	Green	E	R	4.00
☐ Early Harvest	Green	Ins	R	3.00	☐ Island (ver. 3)	Land	L	C	0.15	☐ Prismatic Boon	Multi	Ins	U	1.00
☐ Ebony Charm	Black	Ins	C	0.25	☐ Island (ver. 4)	Land	L	C	0.15	26				
☐ Ekundu Griffin	White	Sum	C	0.25	☐ Ivory Charm	White	Ins	C	0.25	☐ Prismatic Circle	White	E	C	0.25
☐ Ekundu Cyclops	Red	Sum	C	0.25	☐ Jabari's Influence	White	Ins	R	3.00	☐ Prismatic Lace	Blue	Ins	R	3.00
☐ Elixir of Vitality	Artifact	A	U	0.90	☐ Jolrael's Centaur	Green	Sum	C	0.25	☐ Psychic Transfer	Blue	Sor	R	3.00
☐ Emberwilde Caliph	Multi	Sum	R	3.00	☐ Jolt	Blue	Ins	C	0.25	☐ Purgatory	Multi	E	R	4.00
☐ Emberwilde Djinn	Red	Sum	R	3.30	☐ Jungle Patrol	Green	Sum	R	3.00	☐ Purraj of Urborg	Black	SmL	R	3.50
11					☐ Jungle Troll	Multi	Sum	U	1.00	☐ Pyric Salamander	Red	Sum	C	0.25
☐ Energy Bolt	Multi	Sor	R	3.00	☐ Jungle Wurm	Green	Sum	C	0.25	☐ Quirion Elves	Green	Sum	C	0.25
☐ Energy Vortex	Blue	E	R	3.00	19					☐ Radiant Essence	Multi	Sum	U	1.00
☐ Enfeeblement	Black	ECr	C	0.25	☐ Kaervek's Hex	Black	Sor	U	0.80	☐ Raging Spirit	Red	Sum	C	0.25
☐ Enlightened Tutor	White	Ins	U	1.30	☐ Kaervek's Purge	Multi	Sor	U	1.00	27				
☐ Ersatz Gnomes	Artifact	ACr	U	0.80	☐ Kaervek's Torch	Red	Sor	C	0.25	☐ Rampant Growth	Green	Sor	C	0.25
☐ Ether Well	Blue	Ins	U	1.00	☐ Karoo Meerkat	Green	Sum	U	1.00	☐ Rashida Scalebane	White	SmL	R	4.00
☐ Ethereal Champion	White	Sum	R	3.00	☐ Kukemssa Pirates	Blue	Sum	R	3.00	☐ Ravenous Vampire	Black	Sum	U	1.00
☐ Fallow Earth	Green	Sor	U	0.80	☐ Kukemssa Serpent	Blue	Sum	C	0.25	☐ Ray of Command	Blue	Ins	C	0.25
☐ Favorable Destiny	White	ECr	U	1.00	☐ Lead Golem	Artifact	ACr	U	1.00	☐ Razor Pendulum	Artifact	A	R	3.00
12					☐ Leering Gargoyle	Multi	Sum	R	3.00	☐ Reality Ripple	Blue	Ins	C	0.25
☐ Femeref Archers	Green	Sum	U	1.00	☐ Lightning Reflexes	Red	ECr	C	0.25	☐ Reckless Embermage	Red	Sum	R	3.00
☐ Femeref Healer	White	Sum	C	0.25	20					☐ Reflect Damage	Multi	Ins	R	4.00
☐ Femeref Knight	White	Sum	C	0.25	☐ Lion's Eye Diamond	Artifact	A	R	4.00	☐ Regeneration	Green	ECr	C	0.25
☐ Femeref Scouts	White	Sum	C	0.25	☐ Locust Swarm	Green	Sum	U	1.00	28				
☐ Feral Shadow	Black	Sum	C	0.25	☐ Lure of Prey	Green	Ins	R	3.00	☐ Reign of Chaos	Red	Sor	U	1.00
☐ Fetid Horror	Black	Sum	C	0.25	☐ Malignant Growth	Multi	E	R	3.00	☐ Reign of Terror	Black	Sor	U	0.80
☐ Final Fortune	Red	Ins	R	5.00	☐ Mana Prism	Artifact	A	U	1.00	☐ Reparations	Multi	E	R	4.00
☐ Fire Diamond	Artifact	A	U	1.00	☐ Mangara's Blessing	White	Ins	U	1.00	☐ Restless Dead	Black	Sum	C	0.25
☐ Firebreathing	Red	ECr	C	0.25	☐ Mangara's Equity	White	E	U	1.00	☐ Ritual of Steel	White	ECr	C	0.25
13					☐ Mangara's Tome	Artifact	A	R	3.50	☐ Rock Basilisk	Multi	Sum	R	4.00
☐ Flame Elemental	Red	Sum	U	1.00	☐ Marble Diamond	Artifact	A	U	1.00	☐ Rocky Tar Pit	Land	L	U	0.90
☐ Flare	Red	Ins	C	0.25	21					☐ Roots of Life	Green	E	U	1.00
☐ Flash	Blue	Ins	R	3.00	☐ Maro	Green	Sum	R	5.00	☐ Sabertooth Cobra	Green	Sum	C	0.25
☐ Flood Plain	Land	L	U	1.00	☐ Meddle	Blue	Int	U	1.00	29				
☐ Floodgate	Blue	Sum	U	0.80	☐ Melesse Spirit	White	Sum	U	1.00	☐ Sacred Mesa	White	E	R	6.00
☐ Fog	Green	Ins	C	0.25	☐ Memory Lapse	Blue	Int	C	0.20	☐ Sand Golem	Artifact	ACr	U	0.90
☐ Foratog	Green	Sum	U	1.00	☐ Merfolk Raiders	Blue	Sum	C	0.25	☐ Sandbar Crocodile	Blue	Sum	C	0.25
☐ Forbidden Crypt	Black	E	R	4.00	☐ Merfolk Seer	Blue	Sum	C	0.25	☐ Sandstorm	Green	Ins	C	0.20
☐ Forest (ver. 1)	Land	L	C	0.15	☐ Mind Bend	Blue	Ins	U	1.00	☐ Sapphire Charm	Blue	Ins	C	0.25
14					☐ Mind Harness	Blue	ECr	U	1.00	☐ Savage Twister	Multi	Sor	U	1.00
☐ Forest (ver. 2)	Land	L	C	0.15	☐ Mindbender Spores	Green	Sum	R	3.00	☐ Sawback Manticore	Multi	Sum	R	4.00
☐ Forest (ver. 3)	Land	L	C	0.15	22					☐ Sea Scryer	Blue	Sum	C	0.25
☐ Forest (ver. 4)	Land	L	C	0.15	☐ Mire Shade	Black	Sum	U	0.90	☐ Sealed Fate	Multi	Sor	U	1.00
☐ Forsaken Wastes	Black	EW	R	5.00	☐ Miser's Cage	Artifact	A	R	3.00	30				
☐ Frenetic Efreet	Multi	Sum	R	4.00	☐ Mist Dragon	Blue	Sum	R	5.60	☐ Searing Spear Askari	Red	Sum	C	0.25
☐ Giant Mantis	Green	Sum	C	0.25	☐ Moss Diamond	Artifact	A	U	1.00	☐ Seedling Charm	Green	Ins	C	0.25
☐ Gibbering Hyenas	Green	Sum	C	0.25	☐ Mountain (ver. 1)	Land	L	C	0.10	☐ Seeds of Innocence	Green	Sor	R	3.00
☐ Goblin Elite Infantry	Red	Sum	C	0.25	☐ Mountain (ver. 2)	Land	L	C	0.10	☐ Serene Heart	Green	Ins	C	0.25
☐ Goblin Scouts	Red	Sor	U	1.00	☐ Mountain (ver. 3)	Land	L	C	0.10	☐ Sewer Rats	Black	Sum	C	0.15
15					☐ Mountain (ver. 4)	Land	L	C	0.10	☐ Shadow Guildmage	Black	Sum	C	0.20
☐ Goblin Soothsayer	Red	Sum	U	1.00	☐ Mountain Valley	Land	L	U	1.00	☐ Shadowbane	White	Ins	U	1.00
☐ Goblin Tinkerer	Red	Sum	C	0.25	23					☐ Shallow Grave	Black	Ins	R	4.00
☐ Granger Guildmage	Green	Sum	C	0.20	☐ Mtenda Griffin	White	Sum	U	1.00	☐ Shaper Guildmage	Blue	Sum	C	0.25
☐ Grasslands	Land	L	U	0.90	☐ Mtenda Herder	White	Sum	C	0.25	31				
☐ Grave Servitude	Black	ECr	C	0.25	☐ Mtenda Lion	Green	Sum	C	0.20	☐ "Shauku, Endbringer"	Black	SmL	R	3.00
☐ Gravebane Zombie	Black	Sum	C	0.20	☐ Mystical Tutor	Blue	Ins	U	1.00	☐ Shauku's Minion	Multi	SmM	U	1.00
☐ Grim Feast	Multi	E	R	3.50	☐ Natural Balance	Green	Sor	R	4.50	☐ Shimmer	Blue	E	R	3.00
☐ Grinning Totem	Artifact	A	R	7.80	☐ Nettletooth Djinn	Green	Sum	C	0.25	☐ Sidar Jabari	White	SmL	R	3.50
☐ "Hakim, Loreweaver"	Blue	SmL	R	4.00	☐ Noble Elephant	White	Sum	C	0.25	☐ Sirocco	Red	Ins	U	1.00
16					☐ Nocturnal Raid	Black	Ins	U	0.80	☐ Skulking Ghost	Black	Sum	C	0.20
☐ Hall of Gemstone	Green	EW	R	4.00	☐ Null Chamber	White	EW	R	4.00	☐ Sky Diamond	Artifact	A	U	1.00
☐ Hammer of Bogardan	Red	Sor	R	13.00	24					☐ Soar	Blue	ECr	C	0.25
☐ Harbinger of Night	Black	Sum	R	4.00	☐ Pacifism	White	ECr	C	0.25					

RARITY KEY C = Common U = Uncommon R = Rare VR = Very Rare UR = Ultra Rare F = Foil card **CARD TYPES:** See page 246

SCRYE Collectible Card Game Checklist and Price Guide • **271**

Card name	Color	Type	Rarity	Price
☐ Soul Echo	White	E	R	3.50
☐ Soul Rend	Black	Ins	U	1.00
☐ Soulshriek	Black	Ins	C	0.25
☐ Spatial Binding	Multi	E	U	1.00
☐ Spectral Guardian	White	Sum	R	3.00
☐ Spirit of the Night	Black	SmL	R	7.80
☐ Spitting Earth	Red	Sor	C	0.25
☐ Stalking Tiger	Green	Sum	C	0.25
☐ Stone Rain	Red	Sor	C	0.20
☐ Stupor	Black	Sor	U	1.00
☐ Subterranean Spirit	Red	Sum	R	3.00
☐ Sunweb	White	Sum	R	3.50
☐ Superior Numbers	Green	Sor	U	0.90
☐ Suq'Ata Firewalker	Blue	Sum	U	1.00
☐ Swamp (ver. 1)	Land	L	C	0.15
☐ Swamp (ver. 2)	Land	L	C	0.15
☐ Swamp (ver. 3)	Land	L	C	0.15
☐ Swamp (ver. 4)	Land	L	C	0.15
☐ Tainted Specter	Black	Sum	R	3.00
☐ Talruum Minotaur	Red	Sum	C	0.25
☐ Taniwha	Blue	SmL	R	4.00
☐ Teeka's Dragon	Artifact	ACr	R	6.00
☐ Teferi's Curse	Blue	EP	C	0.25
☐ Teferi's Drake	Blue	Sum	C	0.25
☐ Teferi's Imp	Blue	Sum	R	3.00
☐ Teferi's Isle	Land	LL	R	3.00
☐ Telim'Tor	Red	SmL	R	3.30
☐ Telim'Tor's Darts	Artifact	A	U	1.00
☐ Telim'Tor's Edict	Red	Ins	R	3.00
☐ Teremko Griffin	White	Sum	C	0.25
☐ Thirst	Blue	ECr	C	0.25
☐ Tidal Wave	Blue	Ins	U	1.00
☐ Tombstone Stairwell	Black	EW	R	4.00
☐ Torrent of Lava	Red	Sor	R	3.00
☐ Tranquil Domain	Green	Ins	C	0.25
☐ Tropical Storm	Green	Sor	U	1.00
☐ Uktabi Faerie	Green	Sum	C	0.25
☐ Uktabi Wildcats	Green	Sum	R	4.00
☐ Unerring Sling	Artifact	A	U	1.00
☐ Unfulfilled Desires	Multi	E	R	3.00
☐ Unseen Walker	Green	Sum	U	1.00
☐ Unyaro Bee Sting	Green	Sor	U	1.00
☐ Unyaro Griffin	White	Sum	U	1.00
☐ Urborg Panther	Black	Sum	C	0.25
☐ Vaporous Djinn	Blue	Sum	U	1.00
☐ Ventifact Bottle	Artifact	A	R	3.00
☐ Viashino Warrior	Red	Sum	C	0.25
☐ Vigilant Martyr	White	Sum	U	1.00
☐ Village Elder	Green	Sum	C	0.25
☐ Vitalizing Cascade	Multi	Ins	U	1.00
☐ Volcanic Dragon	Red	Sum	R	6.00
☐ Volcanic Geyser	Red	Ins	U	1.00
☐ Waiting in the Weeds	Green	Sor	R	3.80
☐ Wall of Corpses	Black	Sum	C	0.25
☐ Wall of Resistance	White	Sum	C	0.15
☐ Wall of Roots	Green	Sum	C	0.25
☐ Ward of Lights	White	ECr	C	0.25
☐ Warping Wurm	Multi	Sum	R	3.00
☐ Wave Elemental	Blue	Sum	U	0.80
☐ Wellspring	Multi	EL	R	3.00
☐ Wild Elephant	Green	Sum	C	0.25
☐ Wildfire Emissary	Red	Sum	U	1.00
☐ Windreaper Falcon	Multi	Sum	U	1.00
☐ Withering Boon	Black	Int	U	1.00
☐ Worldly Tutor	Green	Ins	U	1.00
☐ Yare	White	Ins	R	3.00
☐ Zebra Unicorn	Multi	Sum	U	1.00
☐ Zhalfirin Commander	White	Sum	U	0.90
☐ Zhalfirin Knight	White	Sum	C	0.25
☐ Zirilan of the Claw	Red	SmL	R	4.00
☐ Zombie Mob	Black	Sum	U	0.80
☐ "Zuberi, Golden Feather"	White	SmL	R	4.00

Kookus — 3●● — Summon Djinn — Trample — During your upkeep, if you do not control at least one Keeper of Kookus, Kookus deals 3 damage to you and attacks this turn if able. ●: +1/+0 until end of turn — Illus. Scott Hampton — 3/5

Magic: The Gathering • Visions

Wizards of the Coast • Released **February 1997**

167 cards in set • IDENTIFIER: 'V' symbol; black borders

• Booster packs contain 15 cards; booster displays contain 36 boosters

    Visions, the first expansion to **Mirage** (and the "Mirage block" for tournaments), builds on the new mechanics of phasing and flanking. But *Visions* is most noteworthy for the introduction of creatures with "coming-into-play" effects that proved to be very popular.

    Nekrataal, **Man o' War**, and **Uktabi Orangutan** all provide useful card advantage effects, especially when combined with the "bounce back to your hand" themes also found in *Visions*. Other stand-outs include **Vampiric Tutor**, **Funeral**, **Emerald Charms**, **Creeping Mold**, **Quirion Ranger**, **River Boa**, **Quicksand**, **Undiscovered Paradise**, **Impulse**, **Tithe**, and **Squandered Resources**.

    Extremely well designed and chock-full of playable cards, *Visions* is considered one of the best *Magic* expansion sets of all time. — *Bennie Smith*

You will need 19 nine-pocket pages to store this set. (10 doubled up)

Set (167 cards)	150.00
Booster Display Box	125.00
Booster Pack	4.00

Card name	Color	Type	Rarity	Price
☐ Aku Djinn	Black	Sum	R	3.80
☐ Anvil of Bogardan	Artifact	Art	R	4.00
☐ Archangel	White	Sum	R	6.00
☐ Army Ants	Multi	Sum	U	1.00
☐ Betrayal	Blue	ECr	C	0.25

Card name	Color	Type	Rarity	Price
☐ Blanket of Night	Black	E	U	1.00
☐ Bogardan Phoenix	Red	Sum	R	4.00
☐ Brass-Talon Chimera	Artifact	ACr	U	0.60
☐ Breathstealer's Crypt	Multi	E	R	3.80
☐ Breezekeeper	Blue	Sum	C	0.25
☐ Brood of Cockroaches	Black	Sum	U	0.90
☐ Bull Elephant	Green	Sum	C	0.25
☐ Chronatog	Blue	Sum	R	4.00
☐ City of Solitude	Green	E	R	7.00
☐ Cloud Elemental	Blue	Sum	C	0.25
☐ Coercion	Black	Sor	C	0.25
☐ Coral Atoll	Land	L	U	0.80
☐ Corrosion	Multi	E	R	3.00
☐ Creeping Mold	Green	Sor	U	1.00
☐ Crypt Rats	Black	Sum	C	0.25
☐ Daraja Griffin	White	Sum	U	1.00
☐ Dark Privilege	Black	ECr	C	0.25
☐ Death Watch	Black	Ecr	C	0.25
☐ Desertion	Blue	Int	R	5.00
☐ Desolation	Black	E	U	1.00
☐ Diamond Kaleidoscope	Artifact	Art	R	4.00
☐ Dormant Volcano	Land	L	U	0.80
☐ Dragon Mask	Artifact	Art	U	1.00
☐ Dream Tides	Blue	E	U	1.00
☐ Dwarven Vigilantes	Red	Sum	C	0.25
☐ Elephant Grass	Green	E	U	0.80
☐ Elkin Liar	Red	EW	R	3.00
☐ Elven Cache	Green	Sor	C	0.25
☐ Emerald Charm	Green	Ins	C	0.25
☐ Equipoise	White	E	R	4.00
☐ Everglades	Land	L	U	0.80
☐ Eye of Singularity	White	EW	R	4.00
☐ Fallen Askari	Black	Sum	C	0.25
☐ Femeref Enchantress	Multi	Sum	R	3.00
☐ Feral Instinct	Green	Ins	C	0.25
☐ Fireblast	Red	Ins	C	0.25
☐ Firestorm Hellkite	Multi	Sum	R	6.00
☐ Flooded Shoreline	Blue	E	R	3.00
☐ Forbidden Ritual	Black	Sor	R	3.30
☐ Foreshadow	Blue	Ins	U	1.00
☐ Freewind Falcon	White	Sum	C	0.25
☐ Funeral Charm	Black	Ins	C	0.25

RARITY KEY C = Common U = Uncommon R = Rare VR = Very Rare UR = Ultra Rare F = Foil card **CARD TYPES: See page 246**

272 • SCRYE Collectible Card Game Checklist and Price Guide

Card name	Color	Type	Rarity	Price
☐ Giant Caterpillar	Green	Sum	C	0.25
☐ Goblin Recruiter	Red	Sum	U	1.00
☐ Goblin Swine-Rider	Red	Sum	C	0.25
☐ Gossamer Chains	White	E	C	0.25
☐ Griffin Canyon	Land	L	R	4.00
☐ Guiding Spirit	Multi	Sum	R	3.30
☐ Hearth Charm	Red	Ins	C	0.25

7

Card name	Color	Type	Rarity	Price
☐ Heat Wave	Red	E	U	1.00
☐ Helm of Awakening	Artifact	Art	U	1.00
☐ Honorable Passage	White	Ins	U	1.00
☐ Hope Charm	White	Ins	C	0.25
☐ Hulking Cyclops	Red	Sum	U	1.00
☐ Impulse	Blue	Ins	C	0.20
☐ Infantry Veteran	White	Sum	C	0.25
☐ Infernal Harvest	Black	Sor	C	0.25
☐ Inspiration	Blue	Ins	C	0.25

8

Card name	Color	Type	Rarity	Price
☐ Iron-Heart Chimera	Artifact	ACr	U	1.00
☐ Jamuraan Lion	White	Sum	C	0.25
☐ Juju Bubble	Artifact	A	U	1.00
☐ Jungle Basin	Land	L	U	1.00
☐ Kaervek's Spite	Black	Ins	R	4.00
☐ Karoo	Land	L	U	1.00
☐ Katabatic Winds	Green	E	R	3.00
☐ Keeper of Kookus	Red	Sum	C	0.25
☐ King Cheetah	Green	Sum	C	0.25

9

Card name	Color	Type	Rarity	Price
☐ Knight of the Mists	Blue	Sum	C	0.20
☐ Knight of Valor	White	Sum	C	0.20
☐ Kookus	Red	Sum	R	4.00
☐ Kyscu Drake	Green	Sum	U	1.00
☐ Lead-Belly Chimera	Artifact	ACr	U	1.00
☐ Lichenthrope	Green	Sum	R	3.00
☐ Lightning Cloud	Red	E	R	4.00
☐ Longbow Archer	White	Sum	U	1.00
☐ Magma Mine	Artifact	A	R	3.50

10

Card name	Color	Type	Rarity	Price
☐ Man-o'-War	Blue	Sum	C	0.20
☐ Matopi Golem	Artifact	ACr	U	0.80
☐ Miraculous Recovery	White	Ins	U	0.80
☐ Mob Mentality	Red	ECr	U	1.00
☐ Mortal Wound	Green	ECr	C	0.25
☐ Mundungu	Multi	Sum	U	1.00

Card name	Color	Type	Rarity	Price
☐ Mystic Veil	Blue	ECr	C	0.25
☐ Natural Order	Green	Sor	R	4.00
☐ Necromancy	Black	E	U	1.00

11

Card name	Color	Type	Rarity	Price
☐ Necrosavant	Black	Sum	R	4.00
☐ Nekrataal	Black	Sum	U	1.00
☐ Ogre Enforcer	Red	Sum	R	4.00
☐ Ovinomancer	Blue	Sum	U	1.00
☐ Panther Warriors	Green	Sum	C	0.25
☐ Parapet	White	E	C	0.20
☐ Peace Talks	White	Sor	U	1.00
☐ Phyrexian Marauder	Artifact	ACr	R	4.00
☐ Phyrexian Walker	Artifact	ACr	C	0.25

12

Card name	Color	Type	Rarity	Price
☐ Pillar Tombs of Aku	Black	EW	R	4.50
☐ Prosperity	Blue	Sor	U	1.00
☐ Pygmy Hippo	Multi	Sum	R	3.50
☐ Python	Black	Sum	C	0.25
☐ Quicksand	Land	L	U	1.00
☐ Quirion Druid	Green	Sum	R	4.00
☐ Quirion Ranger	Green	Sum	C	0.20
☐ Raging Gorilla	Red	Sum	C	0.25
☐ Rainbow Efreet	Blue	Sum	R	5.00

13

Card name	Color	Type	Rarity	Price
☐ Relentless Assault	Red	Sor	R	8.00
☐ Relic Ward	White	E	U	1.00
☐ Remedy	White	Ins	C	0.25
☐ Resistance Fighter	White	Sum	C	0.25
☐ Retribution of the Meek	White	Sor	R	4.00
☐ Righteous Aura	White	E	C	0.25
☐ Righteous War	Multi	E	R	4.00
☐ River Boa	Green	Sum	C	0.25
☐ Rock Slide	Red	Ins	C	0.25

14

Card name	Color	Type	Rarity	Price
☐ Rowen	Green	E	R	3.00
☐ Sands of Time	Artifact	A	R	4.00
☐ Scalebane's Elite	Multi	Sum	U	1.00
☐ Shimmering Efreet	Blue	Sum	U	1.00
☐ Shrieking Drake	Blue	Sum	C	0.25
☐ Simoon	Multi	Ins	U	1.00
☐ Sisay's Ring	Artifact	A	C	0.25
☐ Snake Basket	Artifact	A	R	5.50
☐ Solfatara	Red	Ins	C	0.25

15

Card name	Color	Type	Rarity	Price
☐ Song of Blood	Red	Sor	C	0.25

Card name	Color	Type	Rarity	Price
☐ Spider Climb	Green	ECr	C	0.25
☐ Spitting Drake	Red	Sum	U	1.00
☐ Squandered Resources	Multi	E	R	5.00
☐ Stampeding Wildebeests	Green	Sum	U	1.00
☐ Suleiman's Legacy	Multi	E	R	4.00
☐ Summer Bloom	Green	Sor	U	1.00
☐ Sun Clasp	White	ECr	C	0.25
☐ Suq'Ata Assassin	Black	Sum	U	1.00

16

Card name	Color	Type	Rarity	Price
☐ Suq'Ata Lancer	Red	Sum	C	0.25
☐ Talruum Champion	Red	Sum	C	0.25
☐ Talruum Piper	Red	Sum	U	1.00
☐ Tar Pit Warrior	Black	Sum	C	0.25
☐ Teferi's Honor Guard	White	Sum	U	1.00
☐ Teferi's Puzzle Box	Artifact	A	R	4.00
☐ Teferi's Realm	Blue	EW	R	3.00
☐ Tempest Drake	Multi	Sum	U	1.00
☐ Three Wishes	Blue	Ins	R	3.00

17

Card name	Color	Type	Rarity	Price
☐ Time and Tide	Blue	Ins	U	1.00
☐ Tin-Wing Chimera	Artifact	ACr	U	1.00
☐ Tithe	White	Ins	R	5.00
☐ Tremor	Red	Sor	C	0.25
☐ Triangle of War	Artifact	A	R	3.00
☐ Uktabi Orangutan	Green	Sum	U	1.00
☐ Undiscovered Paradise	Land	L	R	8.00
☐ Undo	Blue	Sor	C	0.25
☐ Urborg Mindsucker	Black	Sum	C	0.25

18

Card name	Color	Type	Rarity	Price
☐ Vampiric Tutor	Black	Ins	R	10.00
☐ Vampirism	Black	ECr	U	0.90
☐ Vanishing	Blue	ECr	C	0.25
☐ Viashino Sandstalker	Red	Sum	U	1.00
☐ Viashivan Dragon	Multi	Sum	R	7.00
☐ Vision Charm	Blue	Ins	C	0.25
☐ Wake of Vultures	Black	Sum	C	0.25
☐ Wand of Denial	Artifact	A	R	4.00
☐ Warrior's Honor	White	Ins	C	0.25

19

Card name	Color	Type	Rarity	Price
☐ Warthog	Green	Sum	C	0.20
☐ Waterspout Djinn	Blue	Sum	U	1.00
☐ Wicked Reward	Black	Ins	C	0.25
☐ Wind Shear	Green	Ins	U	1.00
☐ Zhalfirin Crusader	White	Sum	R	4.00

Magic: The Gathering • *Weatherlight*

Wizards of the Coast • Released **June 1997**

167 cards in set • **IDENTIFIER: Open book symbol; black borders**

• Booster packs contain 15 cards; booster displays contain 36 boosters

Rounding out the **Mirage** block, **Weatherlight** was not nearly as well received as **Visions** — in part, perhaps, because it got less powerful as time went on.

At the time of release, the wording of **Abeyance** made the card a powerhouse, sending many players scrambling to get their tournament-limit four copies. **Abeyance** was effectively a white cantrip "timewalk," taking away the ability for an opponent to play spells during one turn. Wizards of the Coast eventually realized its mistake, but instead of changing the way the card worked, it changed the rules on drawing mana from land to make **Abeyance** much less powerful.

Notable cards from *Weatherlight* include **Steel Golem, Spinning Darkness, Gaea's Blessing, Rogue Elephant, Gemstone Mine, Ouphidian, Aura of Silence,** and **Gerrard's Wisdom.** — *Bennie Smith*

You will need **19** nine-pocket pages to store this set. (10 doubled up)

Lotus Vale

Land

When Lotus Vale comes into play, sacrifice two untapped lands or bury Lotus Vale.
✪: Add three mana of any one color to your mana pool.
At what price beauty?

Weatherlight

Set (167 cards)	110.00
Booster Display Box	90.00
Booster Pack	3.30

Card name	Color	Type	Rarity	Price
☐ Abduction	Blue	ECr	U	1.00
☐ Abeyance	White	Ins	R	7.50
☐ Abjure	Blue	Int	C	0.25
☐ Aboroth	Green	Sum	R	5.00
☐ Abyssal Gatekeeper	Black	Sum	C	0.25
☐ AEther Flash	Red	E	U	1.00
☐ Agonizing Memories	Black	Sor	U	0.50

1

Card name	Color	Type	Rarity	Price
☐ Alabaster Dragon	White	Sum	R	5.00
☐ Alms	White	E	C	0.25

2

Card name	Color	Type	Rarity	Price
☐ Ancestral Knowledge	Blue	E	R	4.00
☐ Angelic Renewal	White	E	C	0.25
☐ Apathy	Blue	ECr	C	0.25
☐ Arctic Wolves	Green	Sum	U	0.50
☐ Ardent Militia	White	Sum	C	0.25
☐ Argivian Find	White	Ins	U	1.00
☐ Argivian Restoration	Blue	Sor	U	0.50
☐ Aura of Silence	White	E	U	1.00
☐ Avizoa	Blue	Sum	R	4.00

Card name	Color	Type	Rarity	Price
3				
☐ Bösium Strip	Artifact	Art	R	5.00
☐ Barishi	Green	Sum	U	1.00
☐ Barrow Ghoul	Black	Sum	C	0.25
☐ Benalish Infantry	White	Sum	C	0.25
☐ Benalish Knight	White	Sum	C	0.25

Card name	Color	Type	Rarity	Price
☐ Benalish Missionary	White	Sum	C	0.25
☐ Betrothed of Fire	Red	ECr	C	0.25
☐ Bloodrock Cyclops	Red	Sum	C	0.25
☐ Blossoming Wreath	Green	Ins	C	0.20
☐ Bogardan Firefiend	Red	Sum	C	0.25
☐ Boiling Blood	Red	Ins	C	0.25
☐ Bone Dancer	Black	Sum	R	4.00
☐ Briar Shield	Green	ECr	C	0.25
☐ Bubble Matrix	Artifact	Art	R	5.00
☐ Buried Alive	Black	Sor	U	1.00
☐ Call of the Wild	Green	E	R	4.00
☐ Chimeric Sphere	Artifact	Art	U	0.50
☐ Choking Vines	Green	Ins	C	0.25
☐ Cinder Giant	Red	Sum	U	0.50
☐ Cinder Wall	Red	Sum	C	0.25
☐ Circling Vultures	Black	Sum	U	0.50
☐ Cloud Djinn	Blue	Sum	U	0.80
☐ Coils of the Medusa	Black	ECr	C	0.25
☐ Cone of Flame	Red	Sor	U	1.00
☐ Debt of Loyalty	White	Ins	R	4.00
☐ Dense Foliage	Green	E	R	4.00
☐ Desperate Gambit	Red	Ins	U	0.80
☐ Dingus Staff	Artifact	Art	U	1.00
☐ Disrupt	Blue	Int	C	0.25
☐ Doomsday	Black	Sor	R	4.50
☐ Downdraft	Green	E	U	0.50
☐ Duskrider Falcon	White	Sum	C	0.20
☐ Dwarven Berserker	Red	Sum	C	0.25
☐ Dwarven Thaumaturgist	Red	Sum	R	4.00
☐ Empyrial Armor	White	ECr	C	0.25
☐ Ertai's Familiar	Blue	Sum	R	3.00
☐ Fallow Wurm	Green	Sum	U	1.00
☐ Familiar Ground	Green	E	U	1.00
☐ Fatal Blow	Black	Ins	C	0.25
☐ Fervor	Red	E	R	4.00
☐ Festering Evil	Black	E	U	0.50
☐ Fire Whip	Red	Ecr	C	0.25
☐ Firestorm	Red	Ins	R	5.00
☐ Fit of Rage	Red	Sor	C	0.25
☐ Fledgling Djinn	Black	Sum	C	0.25
☐ Flux	Blue	Sor	C	0.25
☐ Fog Elemental	Blue	Sum	C	0.25
☐ Foriysian Brigade	White	Sum	U	0.50
☐ Fungus Elemental	Green	Sum	R	3.00
☐ Gaea's Blessing	Green	Sor	U	1.00
☐ Gallowbraid	Black	Sum	R	4.00
☐ Gemstone Mine	Land	Lnd	U	2.00
☐ Gerrard's Wisdom	White	Sor	U	1.00
☐ Goblin Bomb	Red	E	R	5.00
☐ Goblin Grenadiers	Red	Sum	U	0.50
☐ Goblin Vandal	Red	Sum	C	0.25
☐ Guided Strike	White	Ins	C	0.25
☐ Harvest Wurm	Green	Sum	C	0.25
☐ Haunting Misery	Black	Sor	C	0.25
☐ Heart of Bogardan	Red	E	R	4.00
☐ Heat Stroke	Red	E	R	4.00
☐ Heavy Ballista	White	Sum	C	0.20
☐ Hidden Horror	Black	Sum	U	1.00
☐ Hurloon Shaman	Red	Sum	U	0.50
☐ Infernal Tribute	Black	E	R	4.00
☐ Inner Sanctum	White	E	R	4.00
☐ Jabari's Banner	Artifact	Art	U	0.50
☐ Jangling Automaton	Artifact	ACr	C	0.25
☐ Kithkin Armor	White	ECr	C	0.25
☐ Lava Hounds	Red	Sum	U	0.50
☐ Lava Storm	Red	Ins	C	0.25
☐ Liege of the Hollows	Green	Sum	R	3.00
☐ Llanowar Behemoth	Green	Sum	U	1.00
☐ Llanowar Druid	Green	Sum	C	0.25
☐ Llanowar Sentinel	Green	Sum	C	0.25
☐ Lotus Vale	Land	Lnd	R	8.00
☐ Mana Chains	Blue	ECr	C	0.25
☐ Mana Web	Artifact	Art	R	4.00
☐ Manta Ray	Blue	Sum	C	0.25
☐ Maraxus of Keld	Red	Sum	R	5.00
☐ Master of Arms	White	Sum	U	0.50
☐ Merfolk Traders	Blue	Sum	C	0.25
☐ Mind Stone	Artifact	Art	C	0.25
☐ Mischievous Poltergeist	Black	Sum	U	0.50
☐ Mistmoon Griffin	White	Sum	U	1.00
☐ Morinfen	Black	Sum	R	4.00
☐ Mwonvuli Ooze	Green	Sum	R	3.00
☐ Nature's Kiss	Green	ECr	C	0.25
☐ Nature's Resurgence	Green	Sor	R	4.00
☐ Necratog	Black	Sum	U	1.00
☐ Noble Benefactor	Blue	Sum	U	0.80
☐ Null Rod	Artifact	Art	R	4.00
☐ Odylic Wraith	Black	Sum	U	0.50
☐ Ophidian	Blue	Sum	C	0.25
☐ Orcish Settlers	Red	Sum	U	1.00
☐ Paradigm Shift	Blue	Sor	R	3.50
☐ Peacekeeper	White	Sum	R	5.00
☐ Pendrell Mists	Blue	E	R	4.00
☐ Phantom Warrior	Blue	Sum	U	1.00
☐ Phantom Wings	Blue	ECr	C	0.25
☐ Phyrexian Furnace	Artifact	Art	U	0.50
☐ Psychic Vortex	Blue	E	R	3.00
☐ Razortooth Rats	Black	Sum	C	0.25
☐ Redwood Treefolk	Green	Sum	C	0.25
☐ Relearn	Blue	Sor	U	1.00
☐ Revered Unicorn	White	Sum	U	0.50
☐ Roc Hatchling	Red	Sum	U	1.00
☐ Rogue Elephant	Green	Sum	C	0.25
☐ Sage Owl	Blue	Sum	C	0.25
☐ Sawtooth Ogre	Red	Sum	C	0.25
☐ Scorched Ruins	Land	Lnd	R	5.00
☐ Serenity	White	E	R	4.00
☐ Serra's Blessing	White	E	U	1.00
☐ Serrated Biskelion	Artifact	ACr	U	1.00
☐ Shadow Rider	Black	Sum	C	0.25
☐ Shattered Crypt	Black	Sor	C	0.25
☐ Soul Shepherd	White	Sum	C	0.25
☐ Southern Paladin	White	Sum	R	4.00
☐ Spinning Darkness	Black	Ins	C	0.25
☐ Steel Golem	Artifact	ACr	U	1.00
☐ Strands of Night	Black	E	U	0.50
☐ Straw Golem	Artifact	ACr	U	0.50
☐ Striped Bears	Green	Sum	C	0.25
☐ Sylvan Hierophant	Green	Sum	U	1.00
☐ Tariff	White	Sor	R	4.00
☐ Teferi's Veil	Blue	E	U	0.80
☐ Tendrils of Despair	Black	Sor	C	0.25
☐ Thran Forge	Artifact	Art	U	0.50
☐ Thran Tome	Artifact	Art	R	3.00
☐ Thunderbolt	Red	Ins	C	0.25
☐ Thundermare	Red	Sum	R	7.00
☐ Timid Drake	Blue	Sum	U	0.50
☐ Tolarian Drake	Blue	Sum	C	0.25
☐ Tolarian Entrancer	Blue	Sum	R	4.00
☐ Tolarian Serpent	Blue	Sum	R	4.00
☐ Touchstone	Artifact	Art	U	1.00
☐ Tranquil Grove	Green	E	R	4.00
☐ Uktabi Efreet	Green	Sum	C	0.25
☐ Urborg Justice	Black	Ins	R	4.00
☐ Urborg Stalker	Black	Sum	R	3.50
☐ Veteran Explorer	Green	Sum	U	0.50
☐ Vitalize	Green	Ins	C	0.25
☐ Vodalian Illusionist	Blue	Sum	U	0.80
☐ Volunteer Reserves	White	Sum	U	0.50
☐ Wave of Terror	Black	E	R	3.00
☐ Well of Knowledge	Artifact	Art	R	4.50
☐ Winding Canyons	Land	Lnd	R	5.00
☐ Xanthic Statue	Artifact	Art	R	5.00
☐ Zombie Scavengers	Black	Sum	C	0.25

RARITY KEY C = Common U = Uncommon R = Rare VR = Very Rare UR = Ultra Rare F = Foil card **CARD TYPES: See page 246**

274 • SCRYE Collectible Card Game Checklist and Price Guide

Magic: The Gathering • *Tempest*

Wizards of the Coast • Released **October 1997**

335 cards and **15** variants in set • **IDENTIFIER: Cloud symbol; black borders**

- Starter decks contain 70 cards; starter displays contain 12 starters
- Booster packs contain 15 cards; booster displays contain 36 boosters
- Preconstructed decks include **Slivers**, **Deep Freeze**, **Flames of Rath**, and **Swarm**

The Rath Cycle begins with **Tempest**, as does the tradition of offering preconstructed decks. *Tempest* introduces amazingly powerful and original mechanics such as **Buyback** and **Shadow**, and a unique new creature type in Slivers, monsters that share their special abilities with other Slivers in play.

With *Tempest*, quick, aggressive decks gained an edge on control decks, featuring cards like **Cursed Scroll**, **Jackal Pup**, **Soltari Priests** and **Monks**, and **Eladamri's Vineyard**. Expensive spells had to dramatically impact the game, either winning outright or significantly controlling the board; cards like **Living Death** fit the bill. Other standout cards include **Scroll Rack**, **Corpse Dance**, **Scragnoth**, **Verdant Force**, **Wasteland**, **Mogg Fanatic**, **Capsize**, **Tradewind Rider**, and **Whispers of the Muse**, which made *Tempest* a big hit for *Magic* players. — ***Bennie Smith***

Earthcraft

1(G)

Enchantment

Tap an untapped creature you control:
Untap target basic land.

*"The land gives up little, but we are
masters of persuasion."*
—Eladamri, Lord of Leaves

Illus. Randy Gallegos
©1997 Wizards of the Coast, Inc.

Set (335 cards plus 15 variants)	225.00	
Starter Display Box	105.00	
Booster Display Box	100.00	
Starter Deck	10.50	
Booster Pack	3.40	

You will need 39 nine-pocket pages to store this set. (20 doubled up)

PC = In preconstructed decks; card is therefore more common than others of its rarity

Card name	Color	Type	Rarity	PC	Price
Abduction	Blue	ECr	U	PC	1.00
Abandon Hope	Black	Sor	U		1.00
Advance Scout	White	Sum	C		0.25
Aftershock	Red	Sor	C	PC	0.25
Altar of Dementia	Artifact	Art	R		5.00
Aluren	Green	E	R	PC	5.00
Ancient Runes	Red	E	U		0.50
Ancient Tomb	Land	Lnd	U		0.80
Angelic Protector	White	Sum	U		0.90
Anoint	White	Ins	C	PC	0.25
Apes of Rath	Green	Sum	U		0.60
Apocalypse	Red	Sor	R		5.00
Armor Sliver	White	Sum	U		0.90
Armored Pegasus	White	Sum	C		0.25
Auratog	White	Sum	R		4.00
Avenging Angel	White	Sum	R	PC	5.00
Barbed Sliver	Red	Sum	U		1.00
Bayou Dragonfly	Green	Sum	C	PC	0.25
Bellowing Fiend	Black	Sum	R		3.80
Benthic Behemoth	Blue	Sum	R		4.50
Blood Frenzy	Red	Ins	C	PC	0.25
Blood Pet	Black	Sum	C		0.25
Boil	Red	Ins	U		1.00
Booby Trap	Artifact	Art	R		5.00
Bottle Gnomes	Artifact	ArtCr	U		1.00
Bounty Hunter	Black	Sum	R		5.00
Broken Fall	Green	E	C		0.25
Caldera Lake	Land	Lnd	R		5.00
Canopy Spider	Green	Sum	C	PC	0.25
Canyon Drake	Red	Sum	R		3.50
Canyon Wildcat	Red	Sum	C		0.25
Capsize	Blue	Ins	C	PC	0.25
Carrionette	Black	Sum	R		3.80
Chaotic Goo	Red	Sum	R		3.30
Charging Rhino	Green	Sum	U		0.90
Chill	Blue	E	U		1.00
Choke	Green	E	U		1.00
Circle of Protection: Black	White	E	C		0.25
Circle of Protection: Blue	White	E	C		0.25

Card name	Color	Type	Rarity	PC	Price
Circle of Protection: Green	White	E	C		0.25
Circle of Protection: Red	White	E	C		0.25
Circle of Protection: Shadow	White	E	C		0.25
Circle of Protection: White	White	E	C		0.25
Clergy en-Vec	White	Sum	C		0.25
Clot Sliver	Black	Sum	C	PC	0.25
Cloudchaser Eagle	White	Sum	C	PC	0.25
Coercion	Black	Sor	C	PC	0.25
Coffin Queen	Black	Sum	R		5.00
Coiled Tinviper	Artifact	ArtCr	C	PC	0.25
Cold Storage	Artifact	Art	R		4.00
Commander Greven il-Vec	Black	Sum	R		6.50
Corpse Dance	Black	Ins	R		5.00
Counterspell	Blue	Int	C	PC	0.25
Crazed Armodon	Green	Sum	R		3.00
Crown of Flames	Red	ECr	C		0.25
Cursed Scroll	Artifact	Art	R		18.00
Dark Banishing	Black	Ins	C	PC	0.25
Dark Ritual	Black	MS	C	PC	0.25
Darkling Stalker	Black	Sum	C	PC	0.25
Dauthi Embrace	Black	E	U		0.80
Dauthi Ghoul	Black	Sum	U		0.60
Dauthi Horror	Black	Sum	C	PC	0.25
Dauthi Marauder	Black	Sum	C		0.25
Dauthi Mercenary	Black	Sum	U		0.60
Dauthi Mindripper	Black	Sum	U	PC	1.00
Dauthi Slayer	Black	Sum	C	PC	0.25
Deadshot	Red	Sor	R		3.00
Death Pits of Rath	Black	E	R		4.50
Diabolic Edict	Black	Ins	C	PC	0.25
Dirtcowl Wurm	Green	Sum	R		5.00
Disenchant	White	Ins	C	PC	0.25
Dismiss	Blue	Int	U	PC	1.00
Disturbed Burial	Black	Sor	C		0.25
Dracoplasm	Multi	Sum	R		5.00
Dread of Night	Black	E	U		1.00
Dream Cache	Blue	Sor	C	PC	0.25
Dregs of Sorrow	Black	Sor	R		4.00
Duplicity	Blue	E	R		4.50
Earthcraft	Green	E	R		5.00
Echo Chamber	Artifact	Art	R		4.50
Eladamri's Vineyard	Green	E	R		6.00
"Eladamri, Lord of Leaves"	Green	Sum	R		6.00
Elite Javelineer	White	Sum	C		0.25
Elven Warhounds	Green	Sum	R	PC	4.00
Elvish Fury	Green	Ins	C	PC	0.25
Emerald Medallion	Artifact	Art	R		4.00
Emmessi Tome	Artifact	Art	R	PC	3.50

Card name	Color	Type	Rarity	PC	Price
Endless Scream	Black	ECr	C	PC	0.25
Energizer	Artifact	ArtCr	R		4.00
Enfeeblement	Black	ECr	C	PC	0.25
Enraging Licid	Red	Sum	U		0.50
Ertai's Meddling	Blue	Int	R	PC	4.00
Escaped Shapeshifter	Blue	Sum	R		4.00
Essence Bottle	Artifact	Art	U	PC	0.80
Evincar's Justice	Black	Sor	C		0.25
Excavator	Artifact	Art	U		0.50
Extinction	Black	Sor	R	PC	4.00
Fevered Convulsions	Black	E	R	PC	4.00
Field of Souls	White	E	R		4.50
Fighting Drake	Blue	Sum	U		0.50
Firefly	Red	Sum	U	PC	0.50
Fireslinger	Red	Sum	C	PC	0.25
Flailing Drake	Green	Sum	U		0.50
Flickering Ward	White	ECr	U	PC	1.00
Flowstone Giant	Red	Sum	C	PC	0.25
Flowstone Salamander	Red	Sum	U	PC	1.00
Flowstone Sculpture	Artifact	ArtCr	R		4.00
Flowstone Wyvern	Red	Sum	R		4.50
Fool's Tome	Artifact	Art	R		3.50
Forest (ver. 1)	Land	Lnd	C	PC	0.25
Forest (ver. 2)	Land	Lnd	C	PC	0.25
Forest (ver. 3)	Land	Lnd	C	PC	0.25
Forest (ver. 4)	Land	Lnd	C	PC	0.25
Frog Tongue	Green	ECr	C		0.25
Fugitive Druid	Green	Sum	R		4.00
Furnace of Rath	Red	E	R	PC	6.00
Fylamarid	Blue	Sum	U		0.90
Gallantry	White	Ins	U		1.00
Gaseous Form	Blue	ECr	C	PC	0.25
Gerrard's Battle Cry	White	E	R		4.50
Ghost Town	Land	Lnd	U		0.80
Giant Crab	Blue	Sum	C		0.25
Giant Strength	Red	ECr	C		0.25
Goblin Bombardment	Red	E	U	PC	1.00
Gravedigger	Black	Sum	C	PC	0.25
Grindstone	Artifact	Art	R		5.80
Hand to Hand	Red	E	R		4.00
Hanna's Custody	White	E	R		5.00
Harrow	Green	Ins	U		1.00
Havoc	Red	E	U		1.00
Heart Sliver	Red	Sum	C		0.25
Heartwood Dryad	Green	Sum	C		0.25
Heartwood Giant	Green	Sum	R		4.00
Heartwood Treefolk	Green	Sum	U		0.50
Helm of Possession	Artifact	Art	R		5.00
Hero's Resolve	White	ECr	C		0.25
Horned Sliver	Green	Sum	U		1.00
Horned Turtle	Blue	Sum	C	PC	0.25

Card name	Color	Type	Rarity	PC	Price
☐ Humility	White	E	R		5.30
☐ Imps' Taunt	Black	Ins	U		0.50
☐ Insight	Blue	E	U		0.60
☐ Interdict	Blue	Int	U		1.00
☐ Intuition	Blue	Ins	R		5.00
☐ Invulnerability	White	Ins	U	PC	0.90
17					
☐ Island (ver. 1)	Land	Lnd	C	PC	0.25
☐ Island (ver. 2)	Land	Lnd	C	PC	0.25
☐ Island (ver. 3)	Land	Lnd	C	PC	0.25
☐ Island (ver. 4)	Land	Lnd	C	PC	0.25
☐ Jackal Pup	Red	Sum	U		0.80
☐ Jet Medallion	Artifact	Art	R		5.00
☐ Jinxed Idol	Artifact	Art	R		4.00
☐ Kezzerdrix	Black	Sum	R		4.00
☐ Kindle	Red	Ins	C	PC	0.25
18					
☐ Knight of Dawn	White	Sum	U	PC	1.00
☐ Knight of Dusk	Black	Sum	U		1.00
☐ Krakilin	Green	Sum	U	PC	1.00
☐ Leeching Licid	Black	Sum	U		1.00
☐ Legacy's Allure	Blue	E	U	PC	0.80
☐ Legerdemain	Blue	Sor	U		0.80
☐ Light of Day	White	E	U		1.00
☐ Lightning Blast	Red	Ins	C	PC	0.25
☐ Lightning Elemental	Red	Sum	C	PC	0.25
19					
☐ Living Death	Black	Sor	R		8.00
☐ Lobotomy	Multi	Sor	U	PC	1.00
☐ Lotus Petal	Artifact	Art	C		0.25
☐ Lowland Giant	Red	Sum	C		0.25
☐ Maddening Imp	Black	Sum	R		3.50
☐ Magmasaur	Red	Sum	R	PC	3.00
☐ Magnetic Web	Artifact	Art	R		4.00
☐ Mana Severance	Blue	Sor	R		4.50
☐ Manakin	Artifact	ArtCr	C		0.25
20					
☐ Manta Riders	Blue	Sum	C	PC	0.25
☐ Marble Titan	White	Sum	R		4.00
☐ Marsh Lurker	Black	Sum	C		0.25
☐ Master Decoy	White	Sum	C	PC	0.25
☐ Mawcor	Blue	Sum	R		3.50
☐ Maze of Shadows	Land	Lnd	U	PC	1.00
☐ Meditate	Blue	Ins	R		6.00
☐ Metallic Sliver	Artifact	ArtCr	C	PC	0.25
☐ Mindwhip Sliver	Black	Sum	U	PC	0.60
21					
☐ Minion of the Wastes	Black	Sum	R		5.00
☐ Mirri's Guile	Green	E	R		4.50
☐ Mnemonic Sliver	Blue	Sum	U	PC	0.90
☐ Mogg Cannon	Artifact	Art	U		0.90
☐ Mogg Conscripts	Red	Sum	C		0.25
☐ Mogg Fanatic	Red	Sum	C	PC	0.25
☐ Mogg Hollows	Land	Lnd	U		1.00
☐ Mogg Raider	Red	Sum	C		0.25
☐ Mogg Squad	Red	Sum	U		0.80
22					
☐ Mongrel Pack	Green	Sum	R		4.00
☐ Mountain (ver. 1)	Land	Lnd	C	PC	0.25
☐ Mountain (ver. 2)	Land	Lnd	C	PC	0.25
☐ Mountain (ver. 3)	Land	Lnd	C	PC	0.25
☐ Mountain (ver. 4)	Land	Lnd	C	PC	0.25
☐ Mounted Archers	White	Sum	C		0.25
☐ Muscle Sliver	Green	Sum	C	PC	0.25
☐ Natural Spring	Green	Sor	C		0.25
☐ Nature's Revolt	Green	E	R		4.50
23					
☐ Needle Storm	Green	Sor	U	PC	0.90
☐ No Quarter	Red	E	R		3.50
☐ Nurturing Licid	Green	Sum	U		0.50
☐ Opportunist	Red	Sum	U		0.50
☐ Oracle en-Vec	White	Sum	R		4.00
☐ "Orim, Samite Healer"	White	Sum	R		4.00
☐ Orim's Prayer	White	E	U		1.00
☐ Overrun	Green	Sor	U	PC	1.00
☐ Pacifism	White	ECr	C	PC	0.25
24					
☐ Pallimud	Red	Sum	R		4.00
☐ Patchwork Gnomes	Artifact	ArtCr	U		0.50
☐ Pearl Medallion	Artifact	Art	R		5.00
☐ Pegasus Refuge	White	E	R		3.30
☐ Perish	Black	Sor	U		1.00
☐ Phyrexian Grimoire	Artifact	Art	R		3.50
☐ Phyrexian Hulk	Artifact	ArtCr	U		0.50
☐ Phyrexian Splicer	Artifact	Art	U		0.80
☐ Pincher Beetles	Green	Sum	C	PC	0.25
25					
☐ Pine Barrens	Land	Lnd	R		4.80
☐ Pit Imp	Black	Sum	C	PC	0.25
☐ Plains (ver. 1)	Land	Lnd	C	PC	0.25
☐ Plains (ver. 2)	Land	Lnd	C	PC	0.25
☐ Plains (ver. 3)	Land	Lnd	C	PC	0.25
☐ Plains (ver. 4)	Land	Lnd	C	PC	0.25
☐ Power Sink	Blue	Int	C	PC	0.25
☐ Precognition	Blue	E	R	PC	4.00
☐ Propaganda	Blue	E	U	PC	1.00
26					
☐ Puppet Strings	Artifact	Art	U	PC	1.00
☐ Quickening Licid	White	Sum	U		0.50
☐ Rain of Tears	Black	Sor	U	PC	1.00
☐ Rampant Growth	Green	Sor	C	PC	0.25
☐ Ranger en-Vec	Multi	Sum	U	PC	0.60
☐ Rathi Dragon	Red	Sum	R		8.00
☐ Rats of Rath	Black	Sum	C		0.25
☐ Reality Anchor	Green	Ins	C		0.25
☐ Reanimate	Black	Sor	U		0.90
27					
☐ Reap	Green	Ins	U		0.50
☐ Reckless Spite	Black	Ins	U		0.60
☐ Recycle	Green	E	R	PC	5.00
☐ Reflecting Pool	Land	Lnd	R		10.00
☐ Renegade Warlord	Red	Sum	U		1.00
☐ Repentance	White	Sor	U	PC	1.00
☐ Respite	Green	Ins	C		0.25
☐ Rolling Thunder	Red	Sor	C	PC	0.25
☐ Root Maze	Green	E	R		4.00
28					
☐ Rootbreaker Wurm	Green	Sum	C		0.25
☐ Rootwalla	Green	Sum	C	PC	0.25
☐ Rootwater Depths	Land	Lnd	U	PC	1.00
☐ Rootwater Diver	Blue	Sum	U		0.60
☐ Rootwater Hunter	Blue	Sum	U		0.60
☐ Rootwater Matriarch	Blue	Sum	R		4.00
☐ Rootwater Shaman	Blue	Sum	R		3.50
☐ Ruby Medallion	Artifact	Art	R		5.00
☐ Sacred Guide	White	Sum	R		4.00
29					
☐ Sadistic Glee	Black	ECr	C		0.25
☐ Safeguard	White	E	R		4.00
☐ Salt Flats	Land	Lnd	R		5.00
☐ Sandstone Warrior	Red	Sum	C	PC	0.25
☐ Sapphire Medallion	Artifact	Art	R		5.50
☐ Sarcomancy	Black	E	R		5.00
☐ Scabland	Land	Lnd	R		5.00
☐ Scalding Tongs	Artifact	Art	R		5.00
☐ Scorched Earth	Red	Sor	R		4.00
30					
☐ Scragnoth	Green	Sum	U		1.00
☐ Screeching Harpy	Black	Sum	U	PC	0.50
☐ Scroll Rack	Artifact	Art	R		6.00
☐ Sea Monster	Blue	Sum	C		0.25
☐ Searing Touch	Red	Ins	U	PC	0.90
☐ Seeker of Skybreak	Green	Sum	C		0.25
☐ Segmented Wurm	Multi	Sum	U		0.80
☐ "Selenia, Dark Angel"	Multi	Sum	R		5.00
☐ Serene Offering	White	Ins	U		1.00
31					
☐ Servant of Volrath	Black	Sum	C		0.25
☐ Shadow Rift	Blue	Ins	C		0.25
☐ Shadowstorm	Red	Sor	U		0.80
☐ Shatter	Red	Ins	C	PC	0.25
☐ Shimmering Wings	Blue	ECr	C		0.25
☐ Shocker	Red	Sum	R		5.00
☐ Sky Spirit	Multi	Sum	U		0.90
☐ Skyshroud Condor	Blue	Sum	U		0.50
☐ Skyshroud Elf	Green	Sum	C	PC	0.25
32					
☐ Skyshroud Forest	Land	Lnd	R		5.00
☐ Skyshroud Ranger	Green	Sum	C		0.25
☐ Skyshroud Troll	Green	Sum	C		0.25
☐ Skyshroud Vampire	Black	Sum	U	PC	1.00
☐ Soltari Crusader	White	Sum	U	PC	0.80
☐ Soltari Emissary	White	Sum	R		4.00
☐ Soltari Foot Soldier	White	Sum	C	PC	0.25
☐ Soltari Guerrillas	Multi	Sum	R	PC	4.00
☐ Soltari Lancer	White	Sum	C	PC	0.25
33					
☐ Soltari Monk	White	Sum	U		1.00
☐ Soltari Priest	White	Sum	U		1.00
☐ Soltari Trooper	White	Sum	C	PC	0.25
☐ Souldrinker	Black	Sum	U		0.60
☐ Spell Blast	Blue	Int	C	PC	0.25
☐ Spike Drone	Green	Sum	C	PC	0.25
☐ Spinal Graft	Black	ECr	C		0.25
☐ Spirit Mirror	White	E	R		4.50
☐ Spontaneous Combustion	Multi	Ins	U		0.80
34					
☐ Squee's Toy	Artifact	Art	C	PC	0.25
☐ Stalking Stones	Land	Lnd	U		1.00
☐ Starke of Rath	Red	Sum	R		4.00
☐ Static Orb	Artifact	Art	R		4.00
☐ Staunch Defenders	White	Sum	U		0.80
☐ Steal Enchantment	Blue	EE	U		0.90
☐ Stinging Licid	Blue	Sum	U		0.60
☐ Stone Rain	Red	Sor	C	PC	0.25
☐ Storm Front	Green	E	U		0.50
35					
☐ Stun	Red	Ins	C		0.25
☐ Sudden Impact	Red	Ins	U		1.00
☐ Swamp (ver. 1)	Land	Lnd	C	PC	0.25
☐ Swamp (ver. 2)	Land	Lnd	C	PC	0.25
☐ Swamp (ver. 3)	Land	Lnd	C	PC	0.25
☐ Swamp (ver. 4)	Land	Lnd	C	PC	0.25
☐ Tahngarth's Rage	Red	ECr	U		0.50
☐ Talon Sliver	White	Sum	C		0.25
☐ Telethopter	Artifact	ArtCr	U		0.50
36					
☐ Thalakos Dreamsower	Blue	Sum	U		0.50
☐ Thalakos Lowlands	Land	Lnd	U		1.00
☐ Thalakos Mistfolk	Blue	Sum	U		0.25
☐ Thalakos Seer	Blue	Sum	U		0.25
☐ Thalakos Sentry	Blue	Sum	U		0.25
☐ Thumbscrews	Artifact	Art	R		5.00
☐ Time Ebb	Blue	Sor	C	PC	0.25
☐ Time Warp	Blue	Sor	R		11.00
☐ Tooth and Claw	Red	E	R		3.00
37					
☐ Torture Chamber	Artifact	Art	R		4.00
☐ Tradewind Rider	Blue	Sum	R		13.25
☐ Trained Armodon	Green	Sum	C	PC	0.25
☐ Tranquility	Green	Sor	C	PC	0.25
☐ Trumpeting Armodon	Green	Sum	U		0.50
☐ Twitch	Blue	Ins	C		0.25
☐ Unstable Shapeshifter	Blue	Sum	R		4.50
☐ Vec Townships	Land	Lnd	U	PC	1.00
☐ Verdant Force	Green	Sum	R		7.00
38					
☐ Verdigris	Green	Ins	U		0.80
☐ Vhati il-Dal	Multi	Sum	R		4.00
☐ Volrath's Curse	Blue	ECr	C		0.25
☐ Wall of Diffusion	Red	Sum	C		0.25
☐ Warmth	White	E	U		0.80
☐ Wasteland	Land	Lnd	U		1.00
☐ Watchdog	Artifact	ArtCr	U		0.50
☐ Whim of Volrath	Blue	Ins	R		4.00
☐ Whispers of the Muse	Blue	Ins	U	PC	1.00
39					
☐ Wild Wurm	Red	Sum	U	PC	1.00
☐ Wind Dancer	Blue	Sum	U		0.50
☐ Wind Drake	Blue	Sum	C	PC	0.25
☐ Winds of Rath	White	Sor	R		5.00
☐ Winged Sliver	Blue	Sum	C	PC	0.25
☐ Winter's Grasp	Green	Sor	U		1.00
☐ Wood Sage	Multi	Sum	R		4.00
☐ Worthy Cause	White	Ins	U		1.00

RARITY KEY **C** = Common **U** = Uncommon **R** = Rare **F** = Foil **PC** = In preconstructed decks **CARD TYPES: See page 246**

276 • SCRYE Collectible Card Game Checklist and Price Guide

Magic: The Gathering • Stronghold

Wizards of the Coast • Released **March 1998**

143 cards in set • **IDENTIFIER: Door with portcullis symbol; black borders**

- Starter decks contain 60 cards; starter displays contain 12 starters
- Booster packs contain 15 cards; booster displays contain 36 boosters
- Preconstructed decks include **Call of the Kor**, **The Spikes**, **Migraine**, and **Sparkler**

As part two of the Rath Cycle, **Stronghold** started another practice that Wizards of the Coast continues to this day. Beginning with *Stronghold*, the second and third small expansion sets also came with preconstructed or "theme" decks.

Including more Shadows, buyback spells, and multicolor Slivers, *Stronghold* built on *Tempest*'s success and added twists. A cycle of playable walls, the popular **Spike Feeder**, and a new creature type for white decks, the **en-Kor**, made *Stronghold* another hit. Other notable cards include **Mox Diamond**, **Awakening**, **Shard Phoenix**, and **Dream Halls**. — *Bennie Smith*

SCRYE NOTES: *Beginning with **Portal** and continuing through **Stronghold**, Wizards offered boosters and starters in "blister packs," packages for placement on pegs in mass-market stores. It later went to "J-pegs" — not computer files, but rather stick-on hooks.*

Set (143 cards)	142.50
Starter Display Box	90.00
Booster Display Box	99.00
Starter Deck	9.00
Booster Pack	3.00

You will need 16 nine-pocket pages to store this set. (8 doubled up)

Card name	Color	Type	Rarity	PC	Price
Abduction	Blue	ECr	U	PC	1.00
Acidic Sliver	Multi	Sum	U		1.00
Amok	Red	E	R		3.00
Awakening	Green	E	R		5.00
Bandage	White	Ins	C		0.25
Bottomless Pit	Black	E	U	PC	1.00
Brush With Death	Black	Sor	C		0.25
Bullwhip	Artifact	Art	U		1.00
Burgeoning	Green	E	R		4.00
Calming Licid	White	Sum	U		0.50
Cannibalize	Black	Sor	C		0.25
Carnassid	Green	Sum	R		4.00
Change of Heart	White	Ins	C		0.25
Cloud Spirit	Blue	Sum	C	PC	0.25
Constant Mists	Green	Ins	U		1.00
Contemplation	White	E	U		1.00
Contempt	Blue	EArtCr	C	PC	0.25
Conviction	White	EArtCr	C		0.25
Convulsing Licid	Red	Sum	U		1.00
Corrupting Licid	Black	Sum	U		1.00
Craven Giant	Red	Sum	C		0.25
Crossbow Ambush	Green	Ins	C		0.25
Crovax the Cursed	Black	SumL	R		5.00
Crystalline Sliver	Multi	Sum	U		1.00
Dauthi Trapper	Black	Sum	U		1.00
Death Stroke	Black	Sor	C	PC	0.25
Dream Halls	Blue	E	R		4.00
Dream Prowler	Blue	Sum	C		0.25
Duct Crawler	Red	Sum	C		0.25
Dungeon Shade	Black	Sum	C		0.25
Elven Rite	Green	Sor	U	PC	1.00
Endangered Armodon	Green	Sum	C		0.25
Ensnaring Bridge	Artifact	Art	R	PC	5.00
Evacuation	Blue	Ins	R	PC	4.00
Fanning the Flames	Red	Sor	U	PC	1.00
Flame Wave	Red	Sor	U		1.00
Fling	Red	Ins	C		0.25
Flowstone Blade	Red	EArtCr	C	PC	0.25
Flowstone Hellion	Red	Sum	U		1.00
Flowstone Mauler	Red	Sum	R		4.00
Flowstone Shambler	Red	Sum	C		0.25
Foul Imp	Black	Sum	C	PC	0.25
Furnace Spirit	Red	Sum	C		0.25
Gliding Licid	Blue	Sum	U		1.00

Card name	Color	Type	Rarity	PC	Price
Grave Pact	Black	E	R		5.00
Hammerhead Shark	Blue	Sum	C		0.25
Heartstone	Artifact	Art	U	PC	1.00
Heat of Battle	Red	E	U		1.00
Hermit Druid	Green	Sum	R	PC	4.00
Hesitation	Blue	E	U		1.00
Hibernation Sliver	Multi	Sum	U		1.00
Hidden Retreat	White	E	R		4.00
Honor Guard	White	Sum	C		0.25
Horn of Greed	Artifact	Art	R		4.00
Hornet Cannon	Artifact	Art	U	PC	1.00
Intruder Alarm	Blue	E	R	PC	4.00
Invasion Plans	Red	E	R		4.00
Jinxed Ring	Artifact	Art	R		4.00
Lab Rats	Black	Sor	C	PC	0.25
Lancers en-Kor	White	Sum	C	PC	1.00
Leap	Blue	Ins	C		0.25
Lowland Basilisk	Green	Sum	C	PC	0.25
Mana Leak	Blue	Int	C	PC	0.25
Mask of the Mimic	Blue	Ins	U		1.00
Megrim	Black	E	U	PC	1.00
Mind Games	Blue	Ins	C	PC	0.25
Mind Peel	Black	Sor	U	PC	1.00
Mindwarper	Black	Sum	R	PC	3.00
Mob Justice	Red	Sor	C		0.25
Mogg Bombers	Red	Sum	C		0.25
Mogg Flunkies	Red	Sum	C		0.25
Mogg Infestation	Red	Sor	R		4.00
Mogg Maniac	Red	Sum	U		1.00
Morgue Thrull	Black	Sum	C		0.25
Mortuary	Black	E	R		5.00
Mox Diamond	Artifact	Art	R		15.00
Mulch	Green	Sor	C		0.25
Nomads en-Kor	White	Sum	C	PC	0.25
Overgrowth	Green	EL	C		0.25
Portcullis	Artifact	Art	R	PC	4.00
Primal Rage	Green	E	U		1.00
Provoke	Green	Ins	C		0.25
Pursuit of Knowledge	White	E	R		6.00
Rabid Rats	Black	Sum	C	PC	0.25
Ransack	Blue	Sor	U	PC	1.00
Rebound	Blue	Int	U		1.00
Reins of Power	Blue	Ins	R	PC	4.00
Revenant	Black	Sum	R		4.00
Rolling Stones	White	E	R		4.00
Ruination	Red	Sor	R		4.00
Sacred Ground	White	E	R		4.00
Samite Blessing	White	EArtCr	C		0.25
Scapegoat	White	Ins	U		1.00
Seething Anger	Red	Sor	C		0.25

Card name	Color	Type	Rarity	PC	Price
Serpent Warrior	Black	Sum	C		0.25
Shaman en-Kor	White	Sum	R	PC	4.00
Shard Phoenix	Red	Sum	R		5.00
Shifting Wall	Artifact	ArtCr	U		1.00
Shock	Red	Ins	C	PC	0.25
Sift	Blue	Sor	C		0.25
Silver Wyvern	Blue	Sum	R		4.00
Skeleton Scavengers	Black	Sum	R	PC	4.00
Skyshroud Archer	Green	Sum	C		0.25
Skyshroud Falcon	White	Sum	C		0.25
Skyshroud Troopers	Green	Sum	C		0.25
Sliver Queen	Multi	Sum	R		10.00
Smite	White	Ins	C	PC	0.25
Soltari Champion	White	Sum	R	PC	4.00
Spike Breeder	Green	Sum	R	PC	4.00
Spike Colony	Green	Sum	C	PC	0.25
Spike Feeder	Green	Sum	U	PC	1.00
Spike Soldier	Green	Sum	U	PC	1.00
Spike Worker	Green	Sum	C	PC	0.25
Spindrift Drake	Blue	Sum	C		0.25
Spined Sliver	Multi	Sum	U		1.00
Spined Wurm	Green	Sum	C		0.25
Spirit en-Kor	White	Sum	C	PC	0.25
Spitting Hydra	Red	Sum	R		4.00
Stronghold Assassin	Black	Sum	R		4.00
Stronghold Taskmaster	Black	Sum	U		1.00
Sword of the Chosen	Artifact	LArt	R		3.00
Temper	White	Ins	U	PC	1.00
Tempting Licid	Green	Sum	U	PC	1.00
Thalakos Deceiver	Blue	Sum	R		4.00
Tidal Surge	Blue	Sor	C		0.25
Tidal Warrior	Blue	Sum	C		0.25
Torment	Black	EArtCr	C		0.25
Tortured Existence	Black	E	C		0.25
Venerable Monk	White	Sum	C		0.25
Verdant Touch	Green	Sor	R	PC	3.00
Victual Sliver	Multi	Sum	U		1.00
Volrath's Gardens	Green	E	R		4.00
Volrath's Laboratory	Artifact	Art	R		4.00
Volrath's Shapeshifter	Blue	Sum	R		4.00
Volrath's Stronghold	Land	Lnd	R		6.50
Walking Dream	Blue	Sum	U		1.00
Wall of Blossoms	Green	Sum	U		1.00
Wall of Essence	White	Sum	U		1.00
Wall of Razors	Red	Sum	U	PC	1.00
Wall of Souls	Black	Sum	U		1.00
Wall of Tears	Blue	Sum	U		1.00
Warrior Angel	White	Sum	R		5.00
Warrior en-Kor	White	Sum	U	PC	1.00
Youthful Knight	White	Sum	C		0.25

RARITY KEY C = Common U = Uncommon R = Rare F = Foil PC = In preconstructed decks   **CARD TYPES: See page 246**

Null Brooch

4

Artifact

2, ◊, Discard your hand: Counter target noncreature spell. Play this ability as an interrupt.

Give away everything so others have nothing.
—Brooch inscription

Illus. DiTerlizzi

Magic: The Gathering • *Exodus*

Wizards of the Coast • Released **June 1998**

143 cards in set • IDENTIFIER: Bridge symbol; black borders

- Starter decks contain 60 cards; starter displays contain 12 starters
- Booster packs contain 15 cards; booster displays contain 36 boosters
- Preconstructed decks include **Widowmaker**, **Groundbreaker**, **Dominator**, and **White Heat**

Exodus introduces a few notable changes to the look of *Magic* cards designed to help collectors. Card rarity is now identified by the color of the expansion symbol: black for common, silver for uncommon, and gold for rare. The size of each set is now noted at the bottom of each card, as well as the number of the card in the set.

Exodus continues most of the *Tempest* themes (except for the curious exclusion of Slivers), and also brings a cycle of Keeper and Oath cards. *Exodus* introduces two key cards to a powerful new deck type with **Survival of the Fittest** and **Recurring Nightmare**. "Rec-Sur" decks combine searching for utility creatures with recursion to control the board and dominate the game. This set was filled with extremely playable cards such as Oath of Ghouls, Hatred, Oath of Druids, Mirri, Spike Weaver, Price of Progress, Forbid, Mind Over Matter, Paladin en-Vec, Soul Warden, Cataclysm, Shattering Pulse, and Allay. — *Bennie Smith*

EXODUS

Set (143 cards)	137.50	
Starter Display Box	90.00	
Booster Display Box	93.25	
Starter Deck	9.30	
Booster Pack	3.30	

You will need 16 nine-pocket pages to store this set. *(8 doubled up)*

Card#	Card name	Color	Type	Rarity	PC	Price
27	AEther Tide	Blue	Sor	C		0.20
1	Allay	White	Ins	C		0.20
79	Anarchist	Red	Sum	C	PC	0.20
2	Angelic Blessing	White	Sor	C		0.20
105	Avenging Druid	Green	Sum	C		0.20
106	Bequeathal	Green	ECr	C		0.20
53	Carnophage	Black	Sum	C		0.25
107	Cartographer	Green	Sum	U		0.80
54	Cat Burglar	Black	Sum	C		0.20
3	Cataclysm	White	Sor	R		7.30
4	Charging Paladin	White	Sum	C		0.20
80	Cinder Crawler	Red	Sum	C		0.20
143	City of Traitors	Land	Lnd	R		4.00
131	Coat of Arms	Artifact	Art	R		7.80
5	Convalescence	White	E	R		4.00
108	Crashing Boars	Green	Sum	U		0.80
55	Culling the Weak	Black	MS	C		0.25
28	Cunning	Blue	ECr	C		0.20
29	Curiosity	Blue	ECr	U		1.00
56	Cursed Flesh	Black	ECr	C		0.20
57	Dauthi Cutthroat	Black	Sum	U		1.00
58	Dauthi Jackal	Black	Sum	C	PC	0.20
59	Dauthi Warlord	Black	Sum	U		1.00
60	Death's Duet	Black	Sor	C		0.20
81	Dizzying Gaze	Red	ECr	C		0.20
30	Dominating Licid	Blue	Sum	R	PC	4.00
109	Elven Palisade	Green	E	U		1.00
110	Elvish Berserker	Green	Sum	C		0.20
61	Entropic Specter	Black	Sum	R		3.00
31	Ephemeron	Blue	Sum	R		4.00
32	Equilibrium	Blue	E	R	PC	4.50
132	Erratic Portal	Artifact	Art	R	PC	4.00
33	"Ertai, Wizard Adept"	Blue	Sum	R		7.00
6	Exalted Dragon	White	Sum	R		5.00
34	Fade Away	Blue	Sor	C	PC	0.20
82	Fighting Chance	Red	Ins	R		3.00
83	Flowstone Flood	Red	Sor	U	PC	1.00
35	Forbid	Blue	Int	U	PC	1.00
62	Fugue	Black	Sor	U		1.00
84	Furnace Brood	Red	Sum	U		1.00
63	Grollub	Black	Sum	C		0.20
64	Hatred	Black	Ins	R		6.30
7	High Ground	White	E	U		1.00

Card#	Card name	Color	Type	Rarity	PC	Price
111	Jackalope Herd	Green	Sum	C		0.20
112	Keeper of the Beasts	Green	Sum	U		1.00
65	Keeper of the Dead	Black	Sum	U		1.00
85	Keeper of the Flame	Red	Sum	U		1.00
8	Keeper of the Light	White	Sum	U		1.00
36	Keeper of the Mind	Blue	Sum	U	PC	1.00
37	Killer Whale	Blue	Sum	U	PC	1.00
9	Kor Chant	White	Ins	C		0.20
10	Limited Resources	White	E	R	PC	5.00
86	Mage il-Vec	Red	Sum	C		0.20
38	Mana Breach	Blue	E	U		1.00
113	Manabond	Green	E	R		4.00
87	Maniacal Rage	Red	ECr	C		0.20
133	Medicine Bag	Artifact	Art	U		0.80
134	Memory Crystal	Artifact	Art	R		4.50
39	Merfolk Looter	Blue	Sum	C	PC	0.20
66	Mind Maggots	Black	Sum	U	PC	1.00
40	Mind Over Matter	Blue	E	R		5.00
135	Mindless Automaton	Artifact	Art	R	PC	3.00
41	Mirozel	Blue	Sum	U	PC	1.00
114	"Mirri, Cat Warrior"	Green	Sum	R		5.00
88	Mogg Assassin	Red	Sum	U		0.80
89	Monstrous Hound	Red	Sum	R	PC	3.00
67	Nausea	Black	Sor	C	PC	0.20
68	Necrologia	Black	Ins	U		1.00
136	Null Brooch	Artifact	Art	R	PC	5.00
115	Oath of Druids	Green	E	R		6.00
69	Oath of Ghouls	Black	E	R		4.00
11	Oath of Lieges	White	E	R		4.00
90	Oath of Mages	Red	E	R		3.00
42	Oath of Scholars	Blue	E	R	PC	4.00
91	Ogre Shaman	Red	Sum	R		3.00
92	Onslaught	Red	E	C	PC	0.20
12	Paladin en-Vec	White	Sum	R	PC	7.00
93	Pandemonium	Red	E	R		6.00
94	Paroxysm	Red	ECr	U		1.00
13	Peace of Mind	White	E	U		1.00
14	Pegasus Stampede	White	Sor	U	PC	0.80
15	Penance	White	E	U		1.00
70	Pit Spawn	Black	Sum	R		5.00
71	Plaguebearer	Black	Sum	R		4.00
116	Plated Rootwalla	Green	Sum	C		0.20
117	Predatory Hunger	Green	ECr	C		0.20
95	Price of Progress	Red	Ins	U		1.00
118	Pygmy Troll	Green	Sum	C		0.20
119	Rabid Wolverines	Green	Sum	C		0.20
96	Raging Goblin	Red	Sum	C		0.25
97	Ravenous Baboons	Red	Sum	R		3.00
16	Reaping the Rewards	White	Ins	C		0.20
98	Reckless Ogre	Red	Sum	C		0.20
120	Reclaim	Green	Ins	C		0.20
17	Reconnaissance	White	E	U	PC	1.00

Card#	Card name	Color	Type	Rarity	PC	Price
72	Recurring Nightmare	Black	E	R		6.00
121	Resuscitate	Green	Ins	U		0.80
43	Robe of Mirrors	Blue	ECr	C		0.25
122	Rootwater Alligator	Green	Sum	C		0.20
44	Rootwater Mystic	Blue	Sum	C		0.20
99	Sabertooth Wyvern	Red	Sum	U		0.80
100	Scalding Salamander	Red	Sum	U	PC	1.00
73	Scare Tactics	Black	Ins	C		0.20
45	School of Piranha	Blue	Sum	C		0.20
46	Scrivener	Blue	Sum	U		0.80
101	Seismic Assault	Red	E	R		5.00
18	Shackles	White	ECr	C	PC	0.20
102	Shattering Pulse	Red	Ins	C	PC	0.20
19	Shield Mate	White	Sum	C		0.20
137	Skyshaper	Artifact	Art	U		0.80
123	Skyshroud Elite	Green	Sum	U		1.00
124	Skyshroud War Beast	Green	Sum	R		3.50
74	Slaughter	Black	Ins	U		1.00
125	Song of Serenity	Green	E	U		1.00
103	Sonic Burst	Red	Ins	C	PC	0.25
20	Soltari Visionary	White	Sum	C	PC	0.20
21	Soul Warden	White	Sum	C		0.25
138	Spellbook	Artifact	Art	U		1.00
104	Spellshock	Red	E	U		0.80
139	Sphere of Resistance	Artifact	Art	R		4.00
75	Spike Cannibal	Black	Sum	U		1.00
126	Spike Hatcher	Green		R		4.00
127	Spike Rogue	Green	Sum	U		0.80
128	Spike Weaver	Green	Sum	R		5.00
22	Standing Troops	White	Sum	C		0.20
129	Survival of the Fittest	Green	E	R		6.00
47	Thalakos Drifters	Blue	Sum	R		4.00
48	Thalakos Scout	Blue	Sum	C	PC	0.20
49	Theft of Dreams	Blue	Sor	C		0.20
140	Thopter Squadron	Artifact	Art	R	PC	3.00
76	Thrull Surgeon	Black	Sum	C	PC	0.20
141	Transmogrifying Licid	Artifact	Art	U		1.00
23	Treasure Hunter	White	Sum	U		0.80
50	Treasure Trove	Blue	E	U	PC	1.00
77	Vampire Hounds	Black	Sum	C	PC	0.20
78	Volrath's Dungeon	Black	E	R	PC	4.00
24	Wall of Nets	White	Sum	R	PC	3.50
51	Wayward Soul	Blue	Sum	C	PC	0.25
25	Welkin Hawk	White	Sum	C	PC	0.20
52	Whiptongue Frog	Blue	Sum	C		0.20
130	Wood Elves	Green	Sum	C		0.20
142	Workhorse	Artifact	Art	R		3.00
26	Zealots en-Dal	White	Sum	U		1.00

RARITY KEY C = Common (black symbol) • U = Uncommon (silver symbol) • R = Rare (gold symbol) • PC = In preconstructed decks

Magic: The Gathering • Urza's Saga

Wizards of the Coast • Released **October 1998**

335 cards and **15** variants in set • **IDENTIFIER: Gears symbol; black borders**

- Tournament decks contain 75 cards, theme decks 60; starter displays contain 12 starters
- Booster packs contain 15 cards; booster displays contain 36 boosters
- Preconstructed decks include **Sleeper**[1], **Special Delivery**[2], **The Plague**[3], and **Tombstone**[4]

The surprisingly potent **Urza's Saga** brought several new game mechanics. While some were only occasionally seen, Echo proved popular, enabling players to get powerful creatures into play earlier by paying the casting cost over two turns. The most powerful mechanic added is blue's "free" spells, which allow the caster to untap lands equal to the casting cost of the spell upon resolution. When partnered with graveyard manipulation from the Rath block, particularly **Recurring Nightmare** and **Survival of the Fittest**, one could generate a recursive engine that proved abusive. Wizards of the Coast soon issued errata on these free spells so that they would only untap lands if played from the hand.

Urza's Saga has a wealth of overpowered cards. Many have found their way onto banned and restricted lists for various tournament formats, including cards such as **Yawgmoth's Will**, **Tolarian Academy**, **Time Spiral**, and **Windfall**. Other standout cards from the set include **Duress**, **Albino Troll**, **Pouncing Jaguar**, **Gaea's Cradle**, **Sneak Attack**, **Wildfire**, **Stroke of Genius**, and **Worship**. Arguably the best creature ever printed, **Morphling** also debuted in *Saga*.

The power in *Saga* led to "Combo Winter," a time reminiscent of the old "Necro" days. Tournament games were determined simply by who got their combo into action first, and games in this period seldom went past the third or fourth turn. For many players, this was not an enjoyable time to be playing **Magic**, explaining why Wizards reacted with its bannings. — **Bennie Smith & Orren McKay**

*Numbers below 'PC' here refer to which preconstructed deck the card appears in. Decks 1-4 are listed above; 5-8 appear with **Urza's Legacy**.*

Set (335 cards plus				
15 variants)	210.00			
Starter Display Box	130.00			
Booster Display Box	119.50			
Starter Deck	10.00			
Booster Pack	3.40			

You will need **39** nine-pocket pages to store this set. (20 doubled up)

Card#	Card name	Color	Type	Rarity	PC	Price
	1 Absolute Grace	White	E	U		1.00
	2 Absolute Law	White	E	U		1.00
	229 Abundance	Green	E	R		5.00
	115 Abyssal Horror	Black	Sum	R	4	3.50
	58 Academy Researchers	Blue	Sum	U		1.00
	172 Acidic Soil	Red	Sor	U		1.00
	230 Acridian	Green	Sum	C	2,8	0.25
	231 Albino Troll	Green	Sum	U		1.00
	232 Anaconda	Green	Sum	U	2	0.80
	3 Angelic Chorus	White	E	R		5.00
	4 Angelic Page	White	Sum	C	1	0.25
	59 Annul	Blue	Int	C		0.25
	173 Antagonism	Red	E	R		3.00
	174 Arc Lightning	Red	Sor	C	2,6	0.25
	60 Arcane Laboratory	Blue	E	U		1.00
	233 Argothian Elder	Green	Sum	U		0.90
	234 Argothian Enchantress	Green	Sum	R		5.50
	235 Argothian Swine	Green	Sum	C	5	0.25
	236 Argothian Wurm	Green	Sum	R	2	5.00
	61 Attunement	Blue	E	R		4.00
	62 Back to Basics	Blue	E	R		4.40
	63 "Barrin, Master Wizard"	Blue	SmL	R		4.00
	286 Barrin's Codex	Artifact A		R	1	3.50
	175 Bedlam	Red	E	R		3.50
	116 Befoul	Black	Sor	C	3	0.25
	117 Bereavement	Black	E	U		1.00
	237 Blanchwood Armor	Green	E Cr	U		1.00
	238 Blanchwood Treefolk	Green	Sum	C		0.25
	319 Blasted Landscape	Land	L	U		1.00
	118 Blood Vassal	Black	Sum	C	3	0.25
	119 Bog Raiders	Black	Sum	C		0.25
	176 Brand	Red	Ins	R		3.00
	177 Bravado	Red	E Cr	C		0.25
	120 Breach	Black	Ins	C		0.25
	5 Brilliant Halo	White	E Cr	C	1	0.25
	239 Bull Hippo	Green	Sum	U	2	0.80

Card name	Type		Rarity		Price
178 Bulwark	Red	E	R		3.80
121 Cackling Fiend	Black	Sum	C		0.25
240 Carpet of Flowers	Green	E	U		1.00
122 Carrion Beetles	Black	Sum	C		0.25
64 Catalog	Blue	Ins	C	4,7	0.25
6 Catastrophe	White	Sor	R		6.00
287 Cathodion	Artifact A	Cr	U		1.00
241 Cave Tiger	Green	Sum	C		0.25
242 Child of Gaea	Green	Sum	R		6.00
288 Chimeric Staff	Artifact A		R		5.00
243 Citanul Centaurs	Green	Sum	R		5.00
289 Citanul Flute	Artifact A		R		4.00
244 Citanul Hierophants	Green	Sum	R		4.00
290 Claws of Gix	Artifact A		U		1.00
7 Clear	White	Ins	U	1	0.80
65 Cloak of Mists	Blue	E Cr	C		0.25
66 Confiscate	Blue	EP	U	4,8	1.00
8 Congregate	White	Ins	C		0.25
123 Contamination	Black	E	R		4.50
291 Copper Gnomes	Artifact A	Cr	R		3.00
67 Coral Merfolk	Blue	Sum	C		0.25
124 Corrupt	Black	Sor	C	3,6	0.25
245 Cradle Guard	Green	Sum	U	2,5	1.00
179 Crater Hellion	Red	Sum	R		5.80
125 Crazed Skirge	Black	Sum	U		1.00
246 Crosswinds	Green	E	U	5	1.00
292 Crystal Chimes	Artifact A		U		1.00
68 Curfew	Blue	Ins	C		0.25
126 Dark Hatchling	Black	Sum	R		3.80
127 Dark Ritual	Black	MS	C		0.25
128 Darkest Hour	Black	E	R		4.00
9 Defensive Formation	White	E	U		1.00
129 Despondency	Black	E Cr	U	4	0.90
180 Destructive Urge	Red	E Cr	U		1.00
130 Diabolic Servitude	Black	E	U	4	0.90
10 Disciple of Grace	White	Sum	C	1,3	0.25
11 Disciple of Law	White	Sum	C	1	0.25
131 Discordant Dirge	Black	E	R		3.30
12 Disenchant	White	Ins	C	1,3,5,7	0.25
181 Disorder	Red	Sor	U		1.00
69 Disruptive Student	Blue	Sum	C		0.25
70 Douse	Blue	E	U		0.90
293 Dragon Blood	Artifact A		U	1,7	0.90
71 Drifting Djinn	Blue	Sum	R		4.00
320 Drifting Meadow	Land	L	C	3-5,7	0.25

Card name	Type		Rarity		Price
182 Dromosaur	Red	Sum	C		0.25
132 Duress	Black	Sor	C		0.25
133 Eastern Paladin	Black	Sum	R		4.30
183 Electryte	Red	Sum	R		4.00
13 Elite Archers	White	Sum	R		3.60
247 Elvish Herder	Green	Sum	C	5	0.25
248 Elvish Lyrist	Green	Sum	C		0.25
72 Enchantment Alteration	Blue	Ins	U		1.00
249 Endless Wurm	Green	Sum	R		5.00
294 Endoskeleton	Artifact A		U	1	0.80
73 Energy Field	Blue	E	R		5.00
74 Exhaustion	Blue	Sor	U	8	1.00
134 Exhume	Black	Sor	C	4	0.25
250 Exploration	Green	E	R		5.00
135 Expunge	Black	Ins	C	3,4,6	0.25
14 Faith Healer	White	Sum	R		4.00
184 Falter	Red	Ins	C		0.25
185 Fault Line	Red	Ins	R		4.30
251 Fecundity	Green	E	U		0.80
252 Fertile Ground	Green	EL	C		0.25
186 Fiery Mantle	Red	E Cr	C	2	0.25
187 Fire Ants	Red	Sum	U		0.80
136 Flesh Reaver	Black	sum	U	3	0.90
295 Fluctuator	Artifact A		R		4.00
75 Fog Bank	Blue	Sum	U	7	1.00
Forest (ver. 1)	Land	L	L		0.10
Forest (ver. 2)	Land	L	L		0.10
Forest (ver. 3)	Land	L	L		0.10
Forest (ver. 4)	Land	L	L		0.10
253 Fortitude	Green	E Cr	C		0.25
254 Gaea's Bounty	Green	Sor	C	5	0.25
321 Gaea's Cradle	Land	LL	R		10.00
255 Gaea's Embrace	Green	E Cr	U	5	1.00
188 Gamble	Red	Sor	R		4.50
76 Gilded Drake	Blue	Sum	R		4.00
15 Glorious Anthem	White	E	R		6.00
189 Goblin Cadets	Red	Sum	U		0.80
190 Goblin Lackey	Red	Sum	U		1.00
191 Goblin Matron	Red	Sum	C		0.25
192 Goblin Offensive	Red	Sor	U		1.00
193 Goblin Patrol	Red	Sum	C	2	0.25
194 Goblin Raider	Red	Sum	C		0.25
195 Goblin Spelunkers	Red	Sum	C		0.25
196 Goblin War Buggy	Red	Sum	C	2	0.25
256 Gorilla Warrior	Green	Sum	C		0.25

Card name	Color	Type	Rarity	PC	Price
☐ 296 Grafted Skullcap	Artifact	A	R		3.50
☐ 77 Great Whale	Blue	Sum	R		5.00
☐ 257 Greater Good	Green	E	R		4.00
☐ 258 Greener Pastures	Green	E	R		4.00
☐ 197 Guma	Red	Sum	U		0.90
☐ 259 Hawkeater Moth	Green	Sum	U		1.00
☐ 198 Headlong Rush	Red	Ins	C	6	0.25
☐ 16 Healing Salve	White	Ins	C		0.25
☐ 199 Heat Ray	Red	Ins	C	2,6	0.25
☐ 17 Herald of Serra	White	Sum	R		5.00
☐ 78 Hermetic Study	Blue	E 5	C		0.25
☐ 79 Hibernation	Blue	Ins	U		1.00
☐ 260 Hidden Ancients	Green	E	U	2	1.00
☐ 261 Hidden Guerrillas	Green	E	U		1.00
☐ 262 Hidden Herd	Green	E	R		3.00
☐ 263 Hidden Predators	Green	E	C		3.00
☐ 264 Hidden Spider	Green	E	C	2	0.25
☐ 265 Hidden Stag	Green	E	R		3.00
☐ 137 Hollow Dogs	Black	Sum	C		0.25
☐ 297 Hopping Automaton	Artifact	A Cr	U		1.00
☐ 80 Horseshoe Crab	Blue	Sum	C		0.25
☐ 18 Humble	White	Ins	U	1,35	1.00
☐ 266 Hush	Green	Sor	C	2,8	0.25
☐ 138 Ill-Gotten Gains	Black	Sor	R		3.50
☐ 81 Imaginary Pet	Blue	Sum	R		4.00
☐ 19 Intrepid Hero	White	Sum	R		4.00
☐ Island (ver. 1)	Land	L	L		0.10
☐ Island (ver. 2)	Land	L	L		0.10
☐ Island (ver. 3)	Land	L	L		0.10
☐ Island (ver. 4)	Land	L	L		0.10
☐ 200 Jagged Lightning	Red	Sor	U	2	1.00
☐ 298 "Karn, Silver Golem"	Artifact	A Cr	R		5.50
☐ 82 Launch	Blue	E 5	C		0.25
☐ 201 Lay Waste	Red	Sor	C		0.25
☐ 299 Lifeline	Artifact	A	R		6.00
☐ 202 Lightning Dragon	Red	Sum	R		7.50
☐ 83 Lilting Refrain	Blue	E	U		1.00
☐ 84 Lingering Mirage	Blue	EL	U		0.80
☐ 139 Looming Shade	Black	Sum	C	6	0.25
☐ 300 Lotus Blossom	Artifact	A	R		5.00
☐ 267 Lull	Green	Ins	C		0.25
☐ 140 Lurking Evil	Black	E	R		3.50
☐ 141 Mana Leech	Black	Sum	U		0.80
☐ 203 Meltdown	Red	Sor	U		1.00
☐ 301 Metrognome	Artifact	A	R		4.00
☐ 268 Midsummer Revel	Green	E	R		4.00
☐ 302 Mishra's Helix	Artifact	A	R		5.00
☐ 303 Mobile Fort	Artifact	A Cr	U	7	0.90
☐ 20 Monk Idealist	White	Sum	U	1	0.80
☐ 21 Monk Realist	White	Sum	C	1	0.25
☐ 85 Morphling	Blue	Sum	R		7.50
☐ 343 Mountain (ver. 1)	Land	L	L		0.10
☐ 343 Mountain (ver. 2)	Land	L	L		0.10
☐ 343 Mountain (ver. 3)	Land	L	L		0.10
☐ 343 Mountain (ver. 4)	Land	L	L		0.10
☐ 142 No Rest for the Wicked	Black	E	U		1.00
☐ 304 Noetic Scales	Artifact	A	R		4.00
☐ 204 Okk	Red	Sum	R		3.00
☐ 22 Opal Acrolith	White	E	U	3	1.00
☐ 23 Opal Archangel	White	E	R		4.30
☐ 24 Opal Caryatid	White	E	C	1	0.25
☐ 25 Opal Gargoyle	White	E	C	1	0.25
☐ 26 Opal Titan	White	E	R	1	3.00
☐ 143 Oppression	Black	E	R		4.00
☐ 144 Order of Yawgmoth	Black	Sum	U		1.00
☐ 205 Outmaneuver	Red	Ins	U		1.00
☐ 27 Pacifism	White	E Cr	C	1,5,7	0.25
☐ 145 Parasitic Bond	Black	E Cr	U		1.00
☐ 28 Pariah	White	E Cr	R	3	5.00
☐ 29 Path of Peace	White	Sor	C	7	0.25
☐ 30 Pegasus Charger	White	Sum	C	1	0.25
☐ 86 Pendrell Drake	Blue	Sum	C	4	0.25
☐ 87 Pendrell Flux	Blue	E Cr	C		0.25
☐ 88 Peregrine Drake	Blue	Sum	U	8	1.00
☐ 146 Persecute	Black	Sor	R		5.80
☐ 147 Pestilence	Black	E	C	3	0.25
☐ 306 Phyrexian Colossus	Artifact	A Cr	R		5.00
☐ 148 Phyrexian Ghoul	Black	Sum	C	4	0.25
☐ 306 Phyrexian Processor	Artifact	A	R		6.00
☐ 322 Phyrexian Tower	Land	LL	R		4.50
☐ 307 Pit Trap	Artifact	A	U		1.00
☐ Plains (ver. 1)	Land	L	L		0.10
☐ Plains (ver. 2)	Land	L	L		0.10
☐ Plains (ver. 3)	Land	L	L		0.10
☐ Plains (ver. 4)	Land	L	L		0.10
☐ 31 Planar Birth	White	Sor	R		4.00
☐ 149 Planar Void	Black	E	U		1.00
☐ 323 Polluted Mire	Land	L	C	3-4,6	0.25
☐ 269 Pouncing Jaguar	Green	Sum	C	2	0.25
☐ 89 Power Sink	Blue	Int	C	4,7	0.25
☐ 90 Power Taint	Blue	EE	C		0.25
☐ 32 Presence of the Master	White	E	U		1.00
☐ 150 Priest of Gix	Black	Sum	U		1.00
☐ 270 Priest of Titania	Green	Sum	C		0.25
☐ 308 Purging Scythe	Artifact	A	R		4.00
☐ 151 Rain of Filth	Black	Ins	U		1.00
☐ 206 Rain of Salt	Red	Sor	U		1.00
☐ 152 Ravenous Skirge	Black	Sum	C		0.25
☐ 207 Raze	Red	Sor	C		0.25
☐ 91 Recantation	Blue	E	R		3.80
☐ 153 Reclusive Wight	Black	Sum	U		0.90
☐ 33 Redeem	White	Ins	U		1.00
☐ 208 Reflexes	Red	E Cr	C		0.25
☐ 271 Rejuvenate	Green	Sor	C		0.25
☐ 34 Remembrance	White	E	R		3.80
☐ 324 Remote Isle	Land	L	C	4,7-8	0.25
☐ 154 Reprocess	Black	Sor	R		4.00
☐ 92 Rescind	Blue	Ins	C	4	0.25
☐ 272 Retaliation	Green	E	U		1.00
☐ 209 Retromancer	Red	Sum	C		0.25
☐ 93 Rewind	Blue	Int	C	8	0.25
☐ 210 Rumbling Crescendo	Red	E	R		3.80
☐ 35 Rune of Protection: Artifacts	White	E	U		1.00
☐ 36 Rune of Protection: Black	White	E	C	3	0.25
☐ 37 Rune of Protection: Blue	White	E	C		0.25
☐ 38 Rune of Protection: Green	White	E	C		0.25
☐ 39 Rune of Protection: Lands	White	E	R		2.80
☐ 40 Rune of Protection: Red	White	E	C		0.25
☐ 41 Rune of Protection: White	White	E	C		0.25
☐ 42 Sanctum Custodian	White	Sum	C	1,7	0.25
☐ 43 Sanctum Guardian	White	Sum	U	3	0.90
☐ 94 Sandbar Merfolk	Blue	Sum	C	4	0.25
☐ 95 Sandbar Serpent	Blue	Sum	U	4	0.80
☐ 155 Sanguine Guard	Black	Sum	U		1.00
☐ 211 Scald	Red	E	U		1.00
☐ 212 Scoria Wurm	Red	Sum	R		4.00
☐ 213 Scrap	Red	Ins	C	2	0.25
☐ 44 Seasoned Marshal	White	Sum	U		1.00
☐ 45 Serra Avatar	White	Sum	R		10.00
☐ 46 Serra Zealot	White	Sum	C		0.25
☐ 47 Serra's Embrace	White	E Cr	U	1	1.00
☐ 48 Serra's Hymn	White	E	U		1.00
☐ 49 Serra's Liturgy	White	E	R		3.00
☐ 325 Serra's Sanctum	Land	LL	R		4.00
☐ 50 Shimmering Barrier	White	Sum	U		0.80
☐ 216 Shiv's Embrace	Red	E Cr	U	2	1.00
☐ 326 Shivan Gorge	Land	LL	R		5.00
☐ 214 Shivan Hellkite	Red	Sum	R		5.30
☐ 215 Shivan Raptor	Red	Sum	U	2	1.00
☐ 96 Show and Tell	Blue	Sor	R		5.00
☐ 217 Shower of Sparks	Red	Ins	C	2	0.25
☐ 156 Sicken	Black	E Cr	C	3,4	0.25
☐ 51 Silent Attendant	White	Sum	C	3	0.25
☐ 157 Skirge Familiar	Black	Sum	U		0.80
☐ 158 Skittering Skirge	Black	Sum	C		0.25
☐ 159 Sleeper Agent	Black	Sum	R		3.50
☐ 327 Slippery Karst	Land	L	C	2,8	0.25
☐ 309 Smokestack	Artifact	A	R		5.00
☐ 328 Smoldering Crater	Land	L	C	2,6	0.25
☐ 218 Sneak Attack	Red	E	R		7.30
☐ 97 Somnophore	Blue	Sum	R	4	4.00
☐ 52 Songstitcher	White	Sum	U	1	0.80
☐ 53 Soul Sculptor	White	Sum	R		4.00
☐ 160 Spined Fluke	Black	Sum	C		1.00
☐ 98 Spire Owl	Blue	Sum	C		0.25
☐ 273 Sporogenesis	Green	E	R		4.00
☐ 274 Spreading Algae	Green	EL	U		1.00
☐ 219 Steam Blast	Red	Sor	U		1.00
☐ 99 Stern Proctor	Blue	Sum	U	4	0.90
☐ 100 Stroke of Genius	Blue	Ins	R		10.50
☐ 220 Sulfuric Vapors	Red	E	R		4.00
☐ 101 Sunder	Blue	Ins	R		4.50
☐ 339 Swamp (ver. 1)	Land	L	L		0.10
☐ 339 Swamp (ver. 2)	Land	L	L		0.10
☐ 339 Swamp (ver. 3)	Land	L	L		0.10
☐ 339 Swamp (ver. 4)	Land	L	L		0.10
☐ 275 Symbiosis	Green	Ins	C	2,5	0.25
☐ 161 Tainted AEther	Black	E	R		4.00
☐ 102 Telepathy	Blue	E	U		0.90
☐ 310 Temporal Aperture	Artifact	A	R		5.00
☐ 329 Thran Quarry	Land	L	R		8.00
☐ 311 Thran Turbine	Artifact	A	U	2	1.00
☐ 221 Thundering Giant	Red	Sum	U	2	1.00
☐ 103 Time Spiral	Blue	Sor	R		10.00
☐ 276 Titania's Boon	Green	Sor	U		1.00
☐ 277 Titania's Chosen	Green	Sum	U		1.00
☐ 330 Tolarian Academy	Land	LL	R		6.00
☐ 104 Tolarian Winds	Blue	Ins	C		0.25
☐ 222 Torch Song	Red	E	U	2	1.00
☐ 278 Treefolk Seedlings	Green	Sum	U		1.00
☐ 279 Treetop Rangers	Green	Sum	C		0.25
☐ 105 Turnabout	Blue	Ins	U	4	1.00
☐ 312 Umbilicus	Artifact	A	R		4.00
☐ 162 Unnerve	Black	Sor	U		0.25
☐ 163 Unworthy Dead	Black	Sum	C	3	0.25
☐ 313 Urza's Armor	Artifact	A	U	3	1.00
☐ 164 Vampiric Embrace	Black	E Cr	U		1.00
☐ 165 Vebulid	Black	Sum	R		3.00
☐ 106 Veil of Birds	Blue	E	C		0.25
☐ 107 Veiled Apparition	Blue	E	U		0.90
☐ 108 Veiled Crocodile	Blue	E	R		3.00
☐ 109 Veiled Sentry	Blue	E	U		1.00
☐ 110 Veiled Serpent	Blue	E	C		0.25
☐ 280 Venomous Fangs	Green	E Cr	C		0.25
☐ 281 Vernal Bloom	Green	E	R		3.80
☐ 223 Viashino Outrider	Red	Sum	C		0.25
☐ 224 Viashino Runner	Red	Sum	C	6	0.25
☐ 225 Viashino Sandswimmer	Red	Sum	R		3.50
☐ 226 Viashino Weaponsmith	Red	Sum	C		0.25
☐ 166 Victimize	Black	Sor	U	4	1.00
☐ 167 Vile Requiem	Black	E	U		1.00
☐ 54 Voice of Grace	White	Sum	U	1	1.00
☐ 55 Voice of Law	White	Sum	U	1	1.00
☐ 314 Voltaic Key	Artifact	A	U		1.00
☐ 227 Vug Lizard	Red	Sum	U		1.00
☐ 315 Wall of Junk	Artifact	A Cr	U	3	0.80
☐ 282 War Dance	Green	E	U		1.00
☐ 56 Waylay	White	Ins	U	1	1.00
☐ 168 Western Paladin	Black	Sum	R		4.00
☐ 316 Whetstone	Artifact	A	R		3.50

Card name	Color	Type	Rarity	PC	Price
☐ 283 Whirlwind	Green	Sor	R		3.60
☐ 284 Wild Dogs	Green	Sum	C	2	0.25
☐ 228 Wildfire	Red	Sor	R	2	5.00
☐ 111 Windfall	Blue	Sor	U		1.00
☐ 285 Winding Wurm	Green	Sum	C		0.25

Card name	Color	Type	Rarity	PC	Price
☐ 317 Wirecat	Artifact	A Cr	U		0.90
39					
☐ 169 Witch Engine	Black	Sum	R		3.50
☐ 112 Wizard Mentor	Blue	Sum	C	4	0.25
☐ 318 Worn Powerstone	Artifact	A			1.00
☐ 57 Worship	White	E	R	3	7.00

Card name	Color	Type	Rarity	PC	Price
☐ 170 Yawgmoth's Edict	Black	E	U		1.00
☐ 171 Yawgmoth's Will	Black	Sor	R		8.00
☐ 113 Zephid	Blue	Sum	R		4.00
☐ 114 Zephid's Embrace	Blue	E Cr	U	8	1.00

Magic: The Gathering • Unglued

Wizards of the Coast • Released **August 1998**

94 cards in set • **IDENTIFIER: Broken egg symbol; black borders**

• Booster packs contain 10 cards; booster displays contain 48 boosters

Others had produced parody **Magic** cards, but these are the only "official" ones. Full of silly cards with contradictory or meaningless effects, **Unglued** rewarded longtime players by poking fun at some of the foibles of the game — and of gamers.

Bureaucracy has lots of small print; **B.F.M. (Big Furry Monster)** is so big he needs two cards; **Mesa Chicken** forces players to act, well, like chickens. **Chaos Confetti** sent up the (possible apocryphal) story of the player who tore up an expensive **Chaos Orb** in order to whack more cards.

Putting the cards in numerical order, you'll find a secret message from Wizards of the Coast on the card bottoms. It involves wombats. — *John Jackson Miller*

Set (94 cards)	75.00
Booster Display Box	76.50
Booster Pack	2.00

You will need 11 nine-pocket pages to store this set. (6 doubled up)

Card name	Color	Type	Rarity	Price
[1]				
☐ Ashnod's Coupon	Artifact	Art	R	3.00
☐ B.F.M. (Big Furry Monster)-L	Black	Sum	R	6.00
☐ B.F.M. (Big Furry Monster)-R	Black	Sum	R	6.00
☐ Blacker Lotus	Artifact	Art	R	5.00
☐ Bronze Calendar	Artifact	Art	U	0.50
☐ Bureaucracy	Blue	E	R	2.00
☐ Burning Cinder Fury of Crimson Chaos Fire	Red	E	R	3.00
☐ Cardboard Carapace	Green	ECr	R	4.00
☐ Censorship	Blue	E	U	0.50
[2]				
☐ Chaos Confetti	Artifact	Art	C	0.25
☐ Charm School	White	EPla	U	0.50
☐ Checks and Balances	Blue	E	U	0.50
☐ Chicken a la King	Blue	Sum	R	3.00
☐ Chicken Egg	Red	Sum	C	0.20
☐ Clam Session	Blue	Sum	C	0.20
☐ Clam-I-Am	Blue	Sum	C	0.20
☐ Clambassadors	Blue	Sum	C	0.20
☐ Clay Pigeon	Artifact	ACr	U	0.50
[3]				
☐ Common Courtesy	Blue	E	U	0.50
☐ Deadhead	Black	Sum	C	0.20
☐ Denied!	Blue	Int	C	0.20
☐ Double Cross	Black	Sor	C	0.20
☐ Double Deal	Red	Sor	C	0.20
☐ Double Dip	White	Ins	C	0.20
☐ Double Play	Green	Sor	C	0.20
☐ Double Take	Blue	Ins	C	0.20
☐ Elvish Impersonators	Green	Sum	C	0.20
[4]				
☐ Flock of Rabid Sheep	Green	Sor	U	0.50
☐ Forest	Green	L	C	0.25
☐ Fowl Play	Blue	ECr	C	0.20
☐ Free-for-All	Blue	E	R	3.00
☐ Free-Range Chicken	Green	Sum	C	0.20
☐ Gerrymandering	Green	Sor	U	0.50
☐ Get a Life	White	Ins	U	0.50
☐ Ghazban Ogress	Green	Sum	C	0.20
☐ Giant Fan	Artifact	Art	R	3.00
[5]				
☐ Goblin	Red	Tok	U	0.50
☐ Goblin Bookie	Red	Sum	C	0.20

Card name	Color	Type	Rarity	Price
☐ Goblin Bowling Team	Red	Sum	C	0.25
☐ Goblin Tutor	Red	Ins	U	0.50
☐ Growth Spurt	Green	Ins	C	0.20
☐ Gus	Green	Sum	C	0.25
☐ Handcuffs	Black	E	U	0.50
☐ Hungry Hungry Heifer	Green	Sum	U	0.50
☐ Hurloon Wrangler	Red	Sum	C	0.25
[6]				
☐ "I'm Rubber, You're Glue"	White	E	R	3.00
☐ Incoming!	Green	Sor	R	3.00
☐ Infernal Spawn of Evil	Black	Sum	R	5.00
☐ Island	Blue	L	C	0.25
☐ Jack-in-the-Mox	Artifact	Art	R	4.00
☐ Jalum Grifter	Red	SmL	R	3.00
☐ Jester's Sombrero	Artifact	Art	R	3.00
☐ Jumbo Imp	Black	Sum	U	0.50
☐ Knight of the Hokey Pokey	White	Sum	C	0.20
[7]				
☐ Krazy Kow	Red	Sum	C	0.25
☐ Landfill	Red	Sor	R	3.00
☐ Lexivore	White	Sum	U	0.50
☐ "Look at Me, I'm the DCI"	White	Sor	R	3.00
☐ Mesa Chicken	White	Sum	C	0.25
☐ "Mine, mine, mine!"	Green	E	R	3.00
☐ Mirror Mirror	Artifact	Art	R	5.00
☐ Miss Demeanor	White	Sum	U	0.50
☐ Mountain	Red	L	C	0.50
[8]				
☐ Once More with Feeling	White	Sor	R	3.00
☐ Organ Harvest	Black	Sor	C	0.25
☐ Ow	Black	E	R	3.00
☐ Paper Tiger	Artifact	ACr	C	0.25

Card name	Color	Type	Rarity	Price
☐ Pegasus	White	Tok	U	0.50
☐ Plains	White	L	C	0.25
☐ Poultrygeist	Black	Sum	C	0.25
☐ Prismatic Wardrobe	White	Sor	C	0.25
☐ Psychic Network	Blue	E	R	2.50
[9]				
☐ Ricochet	Red	E	U	0.50
☐ Rock Lobster	Artifact	ACr	C	0.20
☐ Scissors Lizard	Artifact	ACr	C	0.25
☐ Sex Appeal	White	Ins	C	0.25
☐ Sheep	Green	Tok	U	0.50
☐ Soldier	White	Tok	U	0.80
☐ Sorry	Blue	E	U	0.50
☐ Spark Fiend	Red	Sum	R	2.50
☐ Spatula of the Ages	Artifact	Art	U	0.50
[10]				
☐ Squirrel	Green	Tok	U	0.80
☐ Squirrel Farm	Green	E	R	4.00
☐ "Strategy, Schmategy"	Red	Sor	R	3.00
☐ Swamp	Black	L	C	0.50
☐ Team Spirit	Green	Ins	C	0.25
☐ Temp of the Damned	Black	Sum	C	0.25
☐ The Cheese Stands Alone	White	E	R	3.00
☐ The Ultimate Nightmare of Wizards of the Coast® Customer Service	Blue	Sor	U	0.50
☐ "Timmy, Power Gamer"	Green	SmL	R	3.00
[11]				
☐ Urza's Contact Lenses	Artifact	Art	U	0.50
☐ Urza's Science Fair Project	Artifact	ACr	U	0.50
☐ Volrath's Motion Sensor	Black	EPla	U	0.50
☐ Zombie	Black	Tok	U	0.50

Magic: The Gathering • Anthologies

Wizards of the Coast • Released **November 1998**

120 cards plus book in card storage box

Anthologies celebrated five years of **Magic** with two preconstructed decks featuring cards from every expansion up to **Urza's Saga**. Token cards from **Unglued** (such as the one at right) were also included, as was a tiny 64-page book covering the history of the game and organized play.

The box, when emptied, can hold 350 cards in standard-sized sleeves.

Anthologies box	**25.00**

Magic: The Gathering • *Urza's Legacy*

Wizards of the Coast • Released **March 1999**

143 cards and **143** foil cards in set • **IDENTIFIER: Hammer symbol; black borders**

- Starter decks contain 60 cards; starter displays contain 12 starters
- Booster packs contain 15 cards; booster displays contain 36 boosters
- Preconstructed decks include **Crusher**[5], **Phyrexian Assault**[6], **Radiant's Revenge**[7], and **Time Drain**[8]

After the wealth of powerful cards from *Urza's Saga*, players could hardly wait to see what was next. Wizards had a surprise for them in *Urza's Legacy* with the introduction of premium foil versions of the cards, inserted in random booster packs. These playable cards proved to be a big hit with collectors and players both.

More powerful new cards arrive in *Legacy*, with **Grim Monolith, Phyrexian Plaguelord, Crop Rotation, Deranged Hermit, Rancor, Faerie Conclave, Treetop Village, Avalanche Riders, Palinchron, Tinker,** and **Mother of Runes** all quickly finding homes in new decks.

Memory Jar proved to be *too* good, another mistake that was added to banned and restricted lists for tournament play. — *Bennie Smith*

URZA'S LEGACY

Set, no foils (143 cards)	140.00
Foil set (143 cards)	797.50
Starter Display Box	105.00
Booster Display Box	118.75
Starter Deck	10.00
Booster Pack	3.50

You will need **16** *nine-pocket pages to store this set. (8 doubled up)*

REGPRICE	#	Card Name	Color	Rarity	PC	FOILPRICE	
0.25	73	About Face	Red	C		3.50	
0.25	1	Angelic Curator	White	C		3.50	
0.80	121	Angel's Trumpet	Artifact	U		7.00	
3.50	25	Anthroplasm	Blue	R	8	20.00	
4.00	26	Archivist	Blue	R	8	20.00	
0.25	27	Aura Flux	Blue	C		3.50	
1.00	74	Avalanche Riders	Red	U	6	8.00	
4.00	122	Beast of Burden	Artifact	R		18.00	
4.00	2	Blessed Reversal	White	R		20.00	

[2]

REGPRICE	#	Card Name	Color	Rarity	PC	FOILPRICE	
0.90	97	Bloated Toad	Green	U	8	7.00	
1.00	49	Bone Shredder	Black	U	6	7.50	
0.25	28	Bouncing Beebles	Blue	C		3.50	
3.50	50	Brink of Madness	Black	R		20.00	
0.25	3	Burst of Energy	White	C		3.50	
0.25	4	Cessation	White	C		3.50	
0.25	29	Cloud of Faeries	Blue	C	8	3.50	
4.00	123	Crawlspace	Artifact	R		20.00	
0.25	98	Crop Rotation	Green	C		4.00	

[3]

REGPRICE	#	Card Name	Color	Rarity	PC	FOILPRICE	
4.00	124	Damping Engine	Artifact	R		20.00	
0.90	99	Darkwatch Elves	Green	U	8	7.00	
0.25	75	Defender of Chaos	Red	C	6	3.50	
0.25	5	Defender of Law	White	C		3.50	
5.00	125	Defense Grid	Artifact	R		20.00	
5.00	100	Defense of the Heart	Green	R	5	20.00	
4.00	30	Delusions of Mediocrity	Blue	R		20.00	
6.00	101	Deranged Hermit	Green	R		20.00	

[4]

REGPRICE	#	Card Name	Color	Rarity	PC	FOILPRICE	
0.25	6	Devout Harpist	White	C		3.50	
1.00	51	Engineered Plague	Black	U	6	7.00	
0.25	7	Erase	White	C	5,7	3.50	
3.80	52	Eviscerator	Black	R		20.00	
0.25	8	Expendable Troops	White	C		3.50	
1.00	139	Faerie Conclave	Land	U	8	7.50	
4.00	31	Fleeting Image	Blue	R		20.00	
0.25	53	Fog of Gnats	Black	C	6	3.50	
1.00	140	Forbidding Watchtower	Land	U		7.00	
0.25	32	Frantic Search	Blue	C	8	3.50	

[5]

REGPRICE	#	Card Name	Color	Rarity	PC	FOILPRICE	
1.00	102	Gang of Elk	Green	U	5	7.00	
1.00	141	Ghitu Encampment	Land	U	6	7.50	
0.90	76	Ghitu Fire-Eater	Red	U		7.00	

REGPRICE	#	Card Name	Color	Rarity	PC	FOILPRICE	
0.25	77	Ghitu Slinger	Red	C	6	3.50	
0.90	78	Ghitu War Cry	Red	U		7.00	
0.25	54	Giant Cockroach	Black	C	6	3.50	
0.25	79	Goblin Medics	Red	C	6	3.50	
4.00	80	Goblin Welder	Red	R		20.00	
0.25	81	Granite Grip	Red	C		3.50	

[6]

REGPRICE	#	Card Name	Color	Rarity	PC	FOILPRICE	
5.80	126	Grim Monolith	Artifact	R		20.00	
0.90	103	Harmonic Convergence	Green	U		7.00	
4.00	104	Hidden Gibbons	Green	R		20.00	
0.90	9	Hope and Glory	White	U		7.00	
4.00	82	Impending Disaster	Red	R		20.00	
0.25	33	Intervene	Blue	C	8	3.50	
4.00	127	Iron Maiden	Artifact	R		20.00	
0.25	10	Iron Will	White	C		3.50	
0.90	128	Jhoira's Toolbox	Artifact	U		7.00	

[7]

REGPRICE	#	Card Name	Color	Rarity	PC	FOILPRICE	
3.80	11	Karmic Guide	White	R		20.00	
0.90	34	King Crab	Blue	U		7.00	
1.00	12	Knighthood	White	U		7.00	
1.00	83	Last-Ditch Effort	Red	U		7.00	
0.25	84	Lava Axe	Red	C		3.50	
1.00	35	Levitation	Blue	U		7.00	
0.90	105	Lone Wolf	Green	U	5	7.00	
3.50	55	Lurking Skirge	Black	R		20.00	
0.90	13	Martyr's Cause	White	U		7.00	

[8]

REGPRICE	#	Card Name	Color	Rarity	PC	FOILPRICE	
3.50	129	Memory Jar	Artifact	R		20.00	
6.00	106	Might of Oaks	Green	R		20.00	
0.25	36	Miscalculation	Blue	C	7,8	4.00	
4.00	85	Molten Hydra	Red	R	6	20.00	
1.00	14	Mother of Runes	White	U	5,7	8.00	
7.00	107	Multani, Maro-Sorcerer	Green	R		20.00	
0.25	108	Multani's Acolyte	Green	C		3.50	
1.00	109	Multani's Presence	Green	U		7.00	
5.00	56	No Mercy	Black	R		20.00	

[9]

REGPRICE	#	Card Name	Color	Rarity	PC	FOILPRICE	
3.50	15	Opal Avenger	White	R		20.00	
0.25	16	Opal Champion	White	C	7	3.50	
1.00	37	Opportunity	Blue	U	7,8	7.00	
0.25	57	Ostracize	Black	C		3.50	
5.00	38	Palinchron	Blue	R		20.00	
0.25	86	Parch	Red	C		4.00	
0.90	17	Peace and Quiet	White	U		7.00	
0.25	58	Phyrexian Broodlings	Black	C	6	3.50	
0.25	59	Phyrexian Debaser	Black	C	6	3.50	

[10]

REGPRICE	#	Card Name	Color	Rarity	PC	FOILPRICE	
0.90	60	Phyrexian Defiler	Black	U	6	7.00	
0.25	61	Phyrexian Denouncer	Black	C	6	3.50	
4.00	62	Phyrexian Plaguelord	Black	R	6	20.00	
1.00	63	Phyrexian Reclamation	Black	U	6	7.00	
0.25	64	Plague Beetle	Black	C		3.50	
5.00	18	Planar Collapse	White	R		20.00	
4.00	19	Purify	White	R		20.00	
0.25	87	Pygmy Pyrosaur	Red	C		3.50	
5.00	88	Pyromancy	Red	R		20.00	

[11]

REGPRICE	#	Card Name	Color	Rarity	PC	FOILPRICE	
5.00	130	Quicksilver Amulet	Artifact	R		20.00	
1.00	89	Rack and Ruin	Red	U		7.00	
6.00	20	Radiant, Archangel	White	R		20.00	
1.00	21	Radiant's Dragoons	White	U	7	7.50	
0.25	22	Radiant's Judgment	White	C	5,7	3.50	
0.25	110	Rancor	Green	C	5	4.00	
0.90	65	Rank and File	Black	U		7.00	
1.00	39	Raven Familiar	Blue	U	7	7.00	
0.90	40	Rebuild	Blue	U		7.00	

[12]

REGPRICE	#	Card Name	Color	Rarity	PC	FOILPRICE	
0.25	111	Repopulate	Green	C		3.50	
6.30	131	Ring of Gix	Artifact	R	7	20.00	
3.30	90	Rivalry	Red	R		20.00	
3.00	132	Scrapheap	Artifact	R		20.00	
5.00	41	Second Chance	Blue	R		20.00	
5.50	91	Shivan Phoenix	Red	R		20.00	
0.25	66	Sick and Tired	Black	C		3.50	
0.25	112	Silk Net	Green	C	5	3.50	
0.25	113	Simian Grunts	Green	C	5,8	4.00	

[13]

REGPRICE	#	Card Name	Color	Rarity	PC	FOILPRICE	
0.25	67	Sleeper's Guile	Black	C		3.50	
0.25	42	Slow Motion	Blue	C		3.50	
0.25	92	Sluggishness	Red	C		3.50	
0.25	43	Snap	Blue	C	8	3.50	
1.00	142	Spawning Pool	Land	U	6	7.50	
4.00	68	Subversion	Black	R		20.00	
1.00	23	Sustainer of the Realm	White	U	7	7.00	
0.25	69	Swat	Black	C		3.50	
0.90	70	Tethered Skirge	Black	U	6	7.00	

[14]

REGPRICE	#	Card Name	Color	Rarity	PC	FOILPRICE	
0.25	44	Thornwind Faeries	Blue	C	7,8	3.50	
5.00	133	Thran Lens	Artifact	R		20.00	
1.00	134	Thran War Machine	Artifact	U	8	7.00	
3.50	135	Thran Weaponry	Artifact	R		20.00	
1.00	136	Ticking Gnomes	Artifact	U	5,7	7.00	
0.90	45	Tinker	Blue	U		8.00	
0.25	24	Tragic Poet	White	C		3.50	
1.00	71	Treacherous Link	Black	U	6	7.00	
0.25	114	Treefolk Mystic	Green	C		3.50	

[15]

REGPRICE	#	Card Name	Color	Rarity	PC	FOILPRICE	
1.00	143	Treetop Village	Land	U	5,8	8.00	
0.25	72	Unearth	Black	C		3.50	
4.00	137	Urza's Blueprints	Artifact	R	7	20.00	
0.25	93	Viashino Bey	Red	C		3.50	
1.00	94	Viashino Cutthroat	Red	U	6	7.00	
1.00	95	Viashino Heretic	Red	U	6	7.00	
0.25	96	Viashino Sandscout	Red	C		3.50	
0.25	46	Vigilant Drake	Blue	C	7	3.50	
0.90	47	Walking Sponge	Blue	U	8	7.00	

[16]

REGPRICE	#	Card Name	Color	Rarity	PC	FOILPRICE	
0.25	115	Weatherseed Elf	Green	C		3.50	
0.25	48	Weatherseed Faeries	Blue	C		3.50	
5.10	116	Weatherseed Treefolk	Green	R	5,8	20.00	
4.00	138	Wheel of Torture	Artifact	R		20.00	
0.90	117	Wing Snare	Green	U	5	7.00	
0.25	118	Yavimaya Granger	Green	C	5	3.50	
0.25	119	Yavimaya Scion	Green	C	5	3.50	
0.25	120	Yavimaya Wurm	Green	C	5	3.50	

RARITY KEY **C** = Common (black symbol) **U** = Uncommon (silver symbol) **R** = Rare (gold symbol) **#** = In preconstructed deck

Magic: The Gathering • *Urza's Destiny*

Wizards of the Coast • Released **June 1999**

143 cards and **143** foil cards in set • **IDENTIFIER: Flask symbol; black borders**

- Starter decks contain 60 cards; starter displays contain 12 starters
- Booster packs contain 15 cards; booster displays contain 36 boosters
- Preconstructed decks include **Assassin, Battle Surge, Enchanter,** and **Fiendish Nature**

There was no way that Wizards could keep the pace of powerful cards introduced in the first two sets of the Urza's block, right? ***Urza's Destiny*** proved otherwise.

Destiny cards walked the fine line of being almost too good, with **Masticore, Powder Keg, Phyrexian Negator, Plow Under, Rofellos, Yavimaya Elder, Opposition,** and **Treachery** adding muscle to many decks. **Masticore** made things dangerous for "weenie" decks, as even the larger creatures feared it if enough mana was to be had. The set also provides powerful new cards to fuel combo decks, such as **Opalescence, Replenish, Yawgmoth's Bargain, Donate,** and **Academy Rector.**

On the whole, the Urza's block of cards were just too powerful. Some long-time players left ***Magic***, disgusted at games that were over too soon. — ***Bennie Smith & Orren McKay***

Set, no foils (143 cards)	125.00
Foil set (143 cards)	775.50
Starter Display Box	100.00
Booster Display Box	104.00
Starter Deck	10.00
Booster Pack	3.30

You will need **16** nine-pocket pages to store this set. (8 doubled up)

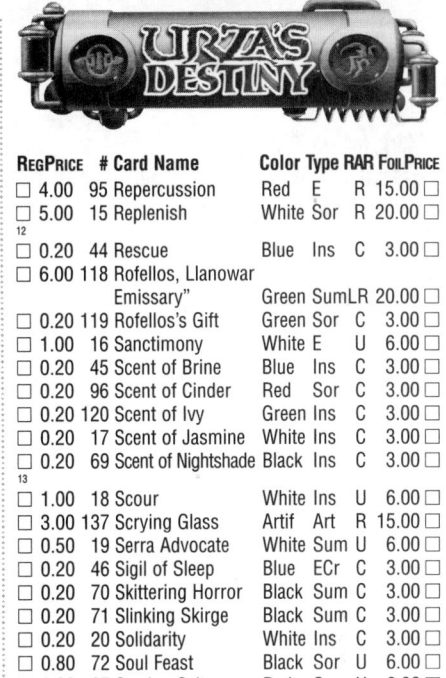

REGPRICE	#	Card Name	Color	Type	RAR	FOILPRICE
5.00	1	Academy Rector	White	Sum	R	20.00
1.00	76	Æther Sting	Red	E	U	6.00
5.00	101	Ancient Silverback	Green	Sum	R	15.50
3.00	51	Apprentice Necromancer	Black	Sum	R	15.00
1.00	2	Archery Training	White	ECr	U	6.00
4.00	52	Attrition	Black	E	R	15.00
4.00	26	Aura Thief	Blue	Sum	R	15.00
4.00	27	Blizzard Elemental	Blue	Sum	R	17.50
4.00	77	Bloodshot Cyclops	Red	Sum	R	15.00
3.00	53	Body Snatcher	Black	Sum	R	15.00
0.50	126	Braidwood Cup	Artif	Art	U	6.00
0.50	127	Braidwood Sextant	Artif	Art	U	6.00
0.50	128	Brass Secretary	Artif	ArtCr	U	6.00
0.50	28	Brine Seer	Blue	Sum	U	6.00
0.20	29	Bubbling Beebles	Blue	Sum	C	3.00
0.50	54	Bubbling Muck	Black	Sor	C	3.00
1.00	129	Caltrops	Artif	Art	U	6.00
0.20	3	Capashen Knight	White	Sum	C	3.00
0.20	4	Capashen Standard	White	ECr	C	3.00
0.20	5	Capashen Templar	White	Sum	C	3.00
3.00	55	Carnival of Souls	Black	E	R	15.00
0.20	56	Chime of Night	Black	ECr	C	3.00
0.50	78	Cinder Seer	Red	Sum	U	6.00
0.20	79	Colos Yearling	Red	Sum	C	3.00
1.00	102	Compost	Green	E	U	6.00
6.00	80	Covetous Dragon	Red	Sum	R	20.00
0.50	30	Disappear	Blue	ECr	U	6.00
0.20	57	Disease Carriers	Black	Sum	C	3.00
3.50	31	Donate	Blue	Sor	R	20.00
0.20	58	Dying Wail	Black	ECr	C	3.00
0.20	103	Elvish Lookout	Green	Sum	C	3.00
6.00	104	Elvish Piper	Green	Sum	R	20.00
5.00	105	Emperor Crocodile	Green	Sum	R	17.50
0.50	59	Encroach	Black	Sor	U	6.00
1.00	60	Eradicate	Black	Sor	U	6.00
0.50	130	Extruder	Artif	ArtCr	U	6.00
5.00	6	False Prophet	White	Sum	R	19.00
0.20	32	Fatigue	Blue	Sor	C	3.00
0.20	7	Fend Off	White	Ins	C	3.00
0.50	61	Festering Wound	Black	ECr	U	6.00
0.20	8	Field Surgeon	White	Sum	C	3.00
0.20	81	Flame Jet	Red	Sor	C	3.00
0.20	33	Fledgling Osprey	Blue	Sum	C	3.00
3.00	9	Flicker	White	Sor	R	15.00
0.80	131	Fodder Cannon	Artif	Art	U	6.00

REGPRICE	#	Card Name	Color	Type	RAR	FOILPRICE
0.80	106	Gamekeeper	Green	Sum	U	6.00
1.00	82	Goblin Berserker	Red	Sum	U	6.00
3.00	83	Goblin Festival	Red	E	R	15.00
0.20	84	Goblin Gardener	Red	Sum	C	3.00
4.00	85	Goblin Marshal	Red	Sum	R	18.00
0.20	86	Goblin Masons	Red	Sum	C	3.00
0.20	107	Goliath Beetle	Green	Sum	C	3.00
0.20	108	Heart Warden	Green	Sum	C	3.00
0.20	87	Hulking Ogre	Red	Sum	C	3.00
1.00	109	Hunting Moa	Green	Sum	U	6.00
0.20	34	Illuminated Wings	Blue	ECr	C	3.00
3.00	88	Impatience	Red	E	R	15.00
1.00	89	Incendiary	Red	ECr	U	6.00
0.50	35	Iridescent Drake	Blue	Sum	U	6.00
0.80	110	Ivy Seer	Green	Sum	U	6.00
1.00	10	Jasmine Seer	White	Sum	U	6.00
3.00	132	Junk Diver	Artif	ArtCr	R	15.00
1.00	90	Keldon Champion	Red	Sum	U	6.00
0.20	91	Keldon Vandals	Red	Sum	C	3.00
0.20	36	Kingfisher	Blue	Sum	C	3.00
1.00	92	Landslide	Red	Sor	U	6.00
0.80	62	Lurking Jackals	Black	E	U	6.00
0.20	111	Magnify	Green	Ins	C	3.00
0.50	133	Mantis Engine	Artif	ArtCr	U	6.00
0.50	93	Mark of Fury	Red	ECr	C	3.00
0.20	112	Marker Beetles	Green	Sum	C	3.00
0.20	11	Mask of Law and Grace	White	ECr	C	3.00
4.00	12	Master Healer	White	Sum	R	15.00
10.00	134	Masticore	Artif	ArtCr	R	24.50
0.25	37	Mental Discipline	Blue	E	C	3.00
4.00	135	Metalworker	Artif	ArtCr	R	17.50
0.50	38	Metathran Elite	Blue	Sum	U	6.00
0.20	39	Metathran Soldier	Blue	Sum	C	3.00
0.50	113	Momentum	Green	ECr	U	6.00
0.20	114	Multani's Decree	Green	Sor	C	3.00
0.80	63	Nightshade Seer	Black	Sum	U	6.00
5.00	13	Opalescence	White	E	R	18.00
5.00	40	Opposition	Blue	E	R	17.50
4.00	115	Pattern of Rebirth	Green	ECr	R	15.00
0.20	64	Phyrexian Monitor	Black	Sum	C	3.00
5.00	65	Phyrexian Negator	Black	Sum	R	20.00
0.50	66	Plague Dogs	Black	Sum	U	6.00
0.20	116	Plated Spider	Green	Sum	C	3.00
5.00	117	Plow Under	Green	Sor	R	15.00
5.50	136	Powder Keg	Artif	Art	R	20.00
1.00	41	Private Research	Blue	ECr	U	6.00
1.00	42	Quash	Blue	Ins	U	6.00
4.00	67	Rapid Decay	Black	Ins	R	15.00
0.20	68	Ravenous Rats	Black	Sum	C	3.00
4.00	43	Rayne, Academy Chancellor	Blue	SumLR		15.50
0.20	94	Reckless Abandon	Red	Sor	C	3.00
0.20	14	Reliquary Monk	White	Sum	C	3.00

REGPRICE	#	Card Name	Color	Type	RAR	FOILPRICE
4.00	95	Repercussion	Red	E	R	15.00
5.00	15	Replenish	White	Sor	R	20.00
0.20	44	Rescue	Blue	Ins	C	3.00
6.00	118	Rofellos, Llanowar Emissary"	Green	SumLR		20.00
0.20	119	Rofellos's Gift	Green	Sor	U	3.00
1.00	16	Sanctimony	White	E	U	6.00
0.20	45	Scent of Brine	Blue	Ins	C	3.00
0.20	96	Scent of Cinder	Red	Sor	C	3.00
0.20	120	Scent of Ivy	Green	Ins	C	3.00
0.20	17	Scent of Jasmine	White	Ins	C	3.00
0.20	69	Scent of Nightshade	Black	Ins	C	3.00
1.00	18	Scour	White	Ins	U	6.00
3.00	137	Scrying Glass	Artif	Art	R	15.00
0.50	19	Serra Advocate	White	Sum	U	6.00
0.20	46	Sigil of Sleep	Blue	ECr	C	3.00
0.20	70	Skittering Horror	Black	Sum	C	3.00
0.20	71	Slinking Skirge	Black	Sum	C	3.00
0.20	20	Solidarity	White	Ins	U	6.00
0.80	72	Soul Feast	Black	Sor	U	6.00
1.00	97	Sowing Salt	Red	Sor	U	6.00
1.00	121	Splinter	Green	Sor	U	6.00
0.20	73	Squirming Mass	Black	Sum	C	3.00
4.00	138	Storage Matrix	Artif	Art	R	15.50
0.20	122	Taunting Elf	Green	Sum	C	3.00
0.20	47	Telepathic Spies	Blue	Sum	C	3.00
5.00	48	Temporal Adept	Blue	Sum	R	15.75
4.00	21	Tethered Griffin	White	Sum	R	15.00
1.00	49	Thieving Magpie	Blue	Sum	U	6.00
6.00	123	Thorn Elemental	Green	Sum	R	20.00
1.00	139	Thran Dynamo	Artif	Art	U	6.00
1.00	140	Thran Foundry	Artif	Art	U	6.00
4.30	141	Thran Golem	Artif	ArtCr	R	17.50
0.20	22	Tormented Angel	White	Sum	C	3.00
5.50	50	Treachery	Blue	ECr	R	20.00
0.20	98	Trumpet Blast	Red	Ins	C	3.00
0.20	74	Twisted Experiment	Black	ECr	C	3.00
4.00	142	Urza's Incubator	Artif	Art	R	15.00
0.50	23	Voice of Duty	White	Sum	U	6.00
0.50	24	Voice of Reason	White	Sum	U	6.00
5.00	99	Wake of Destruction	Red	Sor	R	15.50
0.20	25	Wall of Glare	White	Sum	C	3.00
0.20	100	Wild Colos	Red	Sum	C	3.00
0.20	124	Yavimaya Elder	Green	Sum	C	3.00
1.00	125	Yavimaya Enchantress	Green	Sum	U	6.00
5.00	143	Yavimaya Hollow	Land	LL	R	20.00
8.00	75	Yawgmoth's Bargain	Black	E	R	21.50

Magic: The Gathering • Mercadian Masques

Wizards of the Coast • Released **October 1999**

335 cards and **335** foil cards in set • **IDENTIFIER: Mask symbol; black borders**

- Tournament decks contain 75 cards, theme decks 60; starter displays contain 12 starters
- Booster packs contain 15 cards; booster displays contain 36 boosters
- Pre-constructed decks include **Deepwood Menace**, **Disruptor**, **Rebel's Call**, and **Tidal Mastery**

Mercadian Masques kicks off the Masques block with such new mechanics as alternative casting cost spells, Spellshapers, Rebels, and Mercenaries with recruiters to search them out. While the power level is downright anemic when compared to the full-blooded cards in the Urza block, there are still plenty of good cards in the set, including **Nether Spirit**, **Thrashing Wumpus**, **Unmask**, **Hunted Wumpus**, **Dust Bowl**, **Rishadan Port**, **Squee**, **Two-Headed Dragon**, **Misdirection**, **Thwart**, **Ivory Mask**, **Devout Witness**, and **Story Circle**.

Where *Masques* truly shines (along with the sets that follow) is as a well-balanced set for limited play, whether it's sealed-deck or draft. — *Bennie Smith*

You will need **39** nine-pocket pages to store this set. (20 doubled up)

Set, no foils (335 cards + 15 variants)	242.50
Foil set (335 cards + 15 variants)	1,430.00
Starter Display Box	100.00
Booster Display Box	95.00
Tournament Deck	10.00
Pre-constructed Deck	10.00
Booster Pack	3.30

REGPRICE	#	Card Name	Color	Type	RAR	FOILPRICE
5.00	1	Academy Rector	White	Sum	R	20.00
3.50	58	Aerial Caravan	Blue	Cr	R	15.00
1.00	1	Afterlife	White	Ins	U	5.00
0.25	2	Alabaster Wall	White	Cr	C	3.00
0.25	115	Alley Grifters	Black	Cr	C	3.00
0.25	229	Ancestral Mask	Green	ECr	C	3.00
4.00	3	Armistice	White	E	R	15.00
1.00	172	Arms Dealer	Red	Cr	U	6.00
1.00	4	Arrest	White	ECr	U	5.50
4.00	286	Assembly Hall	Artif	Art	R	15.00
1.00	5	Ballista Squad	White	Cr	U	5.50
0.25	59	Balloon Peddler	Blue	Cr	C	3.00
1.00	287	Barbed Wire	Artif	Art	U	5.50
5.00	288	Bargaining Table	Artif	Art	R	15.00
0.25	173	Battle Rampart	Red	Cr	C	3.00
4.00	174	Battle Squadron	Red	Cr	R	15.00
4.00	230	Bifurcate	Green	Sor	R	16.00
4.00	116	Black Market	Black	E	R	15.00
0.25	175	Blaster Mage	Red	Cr	C	3.00
0.25	60	Blockade Runner	Blue	Cr	C	3.00
3.00	176	Blood Hound	Red	Cr	R	15.00
5.00	177	Blood Oath	Red	Ins	R	15.00
1.00	231	Boa Constrictor	Green	Cr	U	5.00
0.25	117	Bog Smugglers	Black	Cr	C	3.00
0.25	118	Bog Witch	Black	Cr	C	3.00
0.25	61	Brainstorm	Blue	Ins	C	3.00
4.00	178	Brawl	Red	Ins	R	15.00
1.00	232	Briar Patch	Green	E	U	5.50
6.00	62	Bribery	Blue	Sor	R	18.00
0.25	63	Buoyancy	Blue	ECr	C	3.00
1.00	119	Cackling Witch	Black	Cr	U	5.00
4.50	233	Caller of the Hunt	Green	Cr	R	15.00
0.25	120	Cateran Brute	Black	Cr	C	3.00
1.00	121	Cateran Enforcer	Black	Cr	U	5.50
1.00	122	Cateran Kidnappers	Black	Cr	U	5.50
5.00	123	Cateran Overlord	Black	Cr	R	20.00
0.25	124	Cateran Persuader	Black	Cr	C	3.00
5.00	125	Cateran Slaver	Black	Cr	R	15.50
1.00	126	Cateran Summons	Black	Sor	U	5.50
1.00	234	Caustic Wasps	Green	Cr	U	5.00
0.25	179	Cave Sense	Red	ECr	C	3.00
5.00	180	Cave-In	Red	Sor	R	17.00
0.25	181	Cavern Crawler	Red	Cr	C	3.00
0.25	182	Ceremonial Guard	Red	Cr	C	3.00
1.00	64	Chambered Nautilus	Blue	Cr	U	5.00
1.00	65	Chameleon Spirit	Blue	Cr	U	5.50
5.00	66	Charisma	Blue	ECr	R	18.00
0.25	6	Charm Peddler	White	Cr	C	3.00
1.00	7	Charmed Griffin	White	Cr	U	5.00
4.00	8	Cho-Arrim Alchemist	White	Cr	R	15.00
4.00	9	Cho-Arrim Bruiser	White	Cr	R	15.00
1.00	10	Cho-Arrim Legate	White	Cr	U	5.00
5.00	11	Cho-Manno, Revolutionary	White	Cr	R	18.00
0.25	12	Cho-Manno's Blessing	White	ECr	C	3.00
1.00	183	Cinder Elemental	Red	Cr	U	5.50
5.00	235	Clear the Land	Green	Sor	R	15.50
1.00	184	Close Quarters	Red	E	U	5.00
0.25	67	Cloud Sprite	Blue	Cr	C	3.00
1.00	68	Coastal Piracy	Blue	E	U	5.50
5.00	236	Collective Unconscious	Green	Sor	R	16.00
4.00	13	Common Cause	White	E	R	15.00
4.00	127	Conspiracy	Black	E	R	15.00
4.00	14	Cornered Market	White	E	R	15.00
4.00	128	Corrupt Official	Black	Cr	R	15.00
0.25	69	Counterspell	Blue	Ins	C	4.00
4.00	70	Cowardice	Blue	E	R	15.00
4.00	15	Crackdown	White	E	R	15.00
3.00	185	Crag Saurian	Red	Cr	R	15.00
0.25	186	Crash	Red	Ins	C	3.00
1.00	289	Credit Voucher	Artif	Art	U	5.50
1.00	290	Crenellated Wall	Artif	Art	U	5.50
4.00	291	Crooked Scales	Artif	Art	R	15.00
0.25	16	Crossbow Infantry	White	Cr	C	3.00
5.00	292	Crumbling Sanctuary	Artif	Art	R	20.00
1.00	71	Customs Depot	Blue	E	U	5.00
0.25	129	Dark Ritual	Black	Ins	C	4.00
0.25	72	Darting Merfolk	Blue	Cr	C	3.00
5.00	237	Dawnstrider	Green	Cr	R	18.00
0.25	238	Deadly Insect	Green	Cr	C	3.00
1.00	130	Deathgazer	Black	Cr	U	5.00
0.25	239	Deepwood Drummer	Green	Cr	C	3.00
4.00	240	Deepwood Elder	Green	Cr	R	15.00
0.25	131	Deepwood Ghoul	Black	Cr	C	3.00
1.00	132	Deepwood Legate	Black	Cr	U	5.00
1.00	241	Deepwood Tantiv	Green	Cr	U	5.00
0.25	242	Deepwood Wolverine	Green	Cr	C	3.00
0.25	73	Dehydration	Blue	ECr	C	3.00
5.00	133	Delraich	Black	Cr	R	20.00
1.00	243	Desert Twister	Green	Sor	U	6.00
0.25	17	Devout Witness	White	Cr	C	3.00
1.00	74	Diplomatic Escort	Blue	Cr	U	5.50
0.25	75	Diplomatic Immunity	Blue	ECr	C	3.00
0.25	18	Disenchant	White	Ins	C	3.00
4.00	293	Distorting Lens	Artif	Art	R	18.00
0.25	76	Drake Hatchling	Blue	Cr	C	3.00
7.00	316	Dust Bowl	Land	L	R	20.00
4.00	77	Embargo	Blue	E	R	15.00
1.00	78	Energy Flux	Blue	E	U	5.00
1.00	134	Enslaved Horror	Black	Cr	U	5.00
4.00	244	Erithizon	Green	Cr	R	15.00
4.00	135	Extortion	Black	Sor	R	15.00
4.00	79	Extravagant Spirit	Blue	Cr	R	15.50
4.00	294	Eye of Ramos	Artif	Art	R	16.00
1.00	80	False Demise	Blue	ECr	U	5.50
0.25	245	Ferocity	Green	ECr	C	3.00
3.00	187	Flailing Manticore	Red	Cr	R	15.00
1.00	188	Flailing Ogre	Red	Cr	U	5.00
0.25	189	Flailing Soldier	Red	Cr	C	3.00
0.25	190	Flaming Sword	Red	ECr	C	3.00
4.00	246	Food Chain	Green	E	R	16.00
5.00	236	Forced March	Black	Sor	R	18.00
0.10	347	Forest (ver. 1)	Land	L	L	3.00
0.10	347	Forest (ver. 2)	Land	L	L	3.00
0.10	347	Forest (ver. 3)	Land	L	L	3.00
0.10	347	Forest (ver. 4)	Land	L	L	3.00
4.00	247	Foster	Green	E	R	15.00
1.00	317	Fountain of Cho	Land	L	U	6.00
4.50	19	Fountain Watch	White	Cr	R	16.00
0.25	20	Fresh Volunteers	White	Cr	C	3.00
0.25	191	Furious Assault	Red	E	C	3.00
4.00	248	Game Preserve	Green	E	R	15.00
4.00	295	General's Regalia	Artif	Art	R	15.00
0.25	192	Gerrard's Irregulars	Red	Cr	C	3.00
1.00	137	Ghoul's Feast	Black	Ins	U	5.00
0.25	249	Giant Caterpillar	Green	Cr	C	3.00
1.00	81	Glowing Anemone	Blue	Cr	U	5.00
1.00	250	Groundskeeper	Green	Cr	U	5.50
0.25	82	Gush	Blue	Ins	C	3.00
1.00	193	Hammer Mage	Red	Cr	U	5.50
1.00	138	Haunted Crossroads	Black	E	U	6.00
4.00	296	Heart of Ramos	Artif	Art	R	15.00
1.00	297	Henge Guardian	Artif	ACr	U	5.00
1.00	318	Henge of Ramos	Land	L	U	5.50
0.25	319	Hickory Woodlot	Land	L	L	3.00
5.00	320	High Market	Land	L	R	18.00
1.00	83	High Seas	Blue	E	U	5.50
0.25	139	Highway Robber	Black	Cr	C	3.00
1.00	194	Hired Giant	Red	Cr	U	5.00
5.00	21	Honor the Fallen	White	Ins	R	15.50
0.25	84	Hoodwink	Blue	Ins	C	3.00
4.00	298	Horn of Plenty	Artif	Art	R	15.00
4.00	299	Horn of Ramos	Artif	Art	R	16.00
0.25	251	Horned Troll	Green	Cr	C	3.00

RARITY KEY C = Common (black symbol)   U = Uncommon (silver symbol)   R = Rare (gold symbol)   **CARD TYPES:** See page 246

RegPrice	#	Card Name	Color	Type	RAR	FoilPrice
0.25	252	Howling Wolf	Green	Cr	C	3.00
1.00	253	Hunted Wumpus	Green	Cr	U	6.00
1.00	22	Ignoble Soldier	White	Cr	U	6.00
1.00	85	Indentured Djinn	Blue	Cr	U	6.00
3.00	140	Instigator	Black	Cr	R	15.00
0.25	141	Insubordination	Black	Ecr	C	3.00
1.00	142	Intimidation	Black	E	U	5.50
0.25	254	Invigorate	Green	Ins	C	3.00
0.25	23	Inviolability	White	ECr	C	3.00
1.00	300	Iron Lance	Artif	Art	U	5.00
0.10	335	Island (ver. 1)	Land	L	L	3.00
0.10	335	Island (ver. 2)	Land	L	L	3.00
0.10	335	Island (ver. 3)	Land	L	L	3.00
0.10	335	Island (ver. 4)	Land	L	L	3.00
5.30	24	Ivory Mask	White	E	R	18.00
1.00	301	Jeweled Torque	Artif	Art	U	5.50
5.00	25	Jhovall Queen	White	Cr	R	16.00
1.00	26	Jhovall Rider	White	Cr	U	5.50
3.00	86	Karn's Touch	Blue	Ins	R	15.00
0.25	195	Kris Mage	Red	Cr	C	3.00
4.00	302	Kyren Archive	Artif	Art	R	15.00
0.25	196	Kyren Glider	Red	Cr	C	3.00
1.00	197	Kyren Legate	Red	Cr	U	5.00
1.00	198	Kyren Negotiations	Red	E	U	5.50
0.25	199	Kyren Sniper	Red	Cr	C	3.00
4.00	303	Kyren Toy	Artif	Art	R	15.00
0.25	255	Land Grant	Green	Sor	C	3.00
1.00	143	Larceny	Black	E	U	5.50
1.00	27	Last Breath	White	Ins	U	5.00
4.00	200	Lava Runner	Red	Cr	R	16.00
1.00	256	Ley Line	Green	E	U	5.50
4.00	144	Liability	Black	E	R	15.00
0.25	201	Lightning Hounds	Red	Cr	C	3.00
4.00	202	Lithophage	Red	Cr	R	17.00
1.00	257	Lumbering Satyr	Green	Cr	U	5.50
0.25	203	Lunge	Red	Ins	C	3.00
1.00	258	Lure	Green	ECr	U	5.50
0.25	145	Maggot Therapy	Black	Ecr	C	3.00
5.00	304	Magistrate's Scepter	Artif	Art	R	15.00
1.00	204	Magistrate's Veto	Red	E	U	5.50
5.00	259	Megatherium	Green	Cr	R	16.00
4.00	305	Mercadian Atlas	Artif	Art	R	15.00
1.00	321	Mercadian Bazaar	Land	L	U	5.50
3.00	306	Mercadian Lift	Artif	Art	R	15.00
1.00	205	Mercadia's Downfall	Red	Ins	U	5.50
4.00	146	Midnight Ritual	Black	Sor	R	15.00
6.00	87	Misdirection	Blue	Ins	R	20.00
0.25	147	Misshapen Fiend	Black	Cr	C	3.00
0.25	88	Misstep	Blue	Sor	C	3.00
1.00	148	Molting Harpy	Black	Cr	U	5.00
0.25	28	Moment of Silence	White	Ins	C	3.00
4.00	307	Monkey Cage	Artif	Art	R	18.00
1.00	29	Moonlit Wake	White	E	U	6.00
0.10	343	Mountain (ver. 1)	Land	L	L	3.00
0.10	343	Mountain (ver. 2)	Land	L	L	3.00
0.10	343	Mountain (ver. 3)	Land	L	L	3.00
0.10	343	Mountain (ver. 4)	Land	L	L	3.00
0.25	30	Muzzle	White	ECr	C	3.00
4.00	260	Natural Affinity	Green	Ins	R	16.00
4.50	149	Nether Spirit	Black	Cr	R	18.00
0.25	31	Nightwind Glider	White	Cr	C	3.00
1.00	32	Noble Purpose	White	E	U	5.50
5.00	150	Notorious Assassin	Black	Cr	R	15.00
1.00	206	Ogre Taskmaster	Red	Cr	U	5.00
0.25	33	Orim's Cure	White	Ins	C	3.00
5.00	89	Overtaker	Blue	Cr	R	15.00
1.00	308	Panacea	Artif	Art	U	5.00
4.00	261	Pangosaur	Green	Cr	R	15.00
0.25	322	Peat Bog	Land	L	C	3.00
0.25	34	Pious Warrior	White	Cr	C	3.00
0.10	331	Plains (ver. 1)	Land	L	L	3.00
0.10	331	Plains (ver. 2)	Land	L	L	3.00
0.10	331	Plains (ver. 3)	Land	L	L	3.00
0.10	331	Plains (ver. 4)	Land	L	L	3.00
0.25	90	Port Inspector	Blue	Cr	C	3.00
5.00	309	Power Matrix	Artif	Art	R	16.00
1.00	151	Pretender's Claim	Black	ECr	U	5.00
1.00	152	Primeval Shambler	Black	Cr	U	5.00
4.00	310	Puffer Extract	Artif	Art	U	5.50
4.00	207	Pulverize	Red	Sor	R	15.00
4.00	208	Puppet's Verdict	Red	Ins	R	15.00
1.00	153	Putrefaction	Black	E	U	5.00
1.00	154	Quagmire Lamprey	Black	Cr	U	5.00
1.00	155	Rain of Tears	Black	Sor	U	5.50
1.00	35	Ramosian Captain	White	Cr	U	5.50
1.00	36	Ramosian Commander	White	Cr	U	5.00
0.25	37	Ramosian Lieutenant	White	Cr	C	3.00
0.25	38	Ramosian Rally	White	Ins	C	3.00
0.25	39	Ramosian Sergeant	White	Cr	C	3.00
4.00	40	Ramosian Sky Marshal .	White	Cr	R	15.00
0.25	156	Rampart Crawler	Black	Cr	C	3.00
4.00	41	Rappelling Scouts	White	Cr	R	15.50
0.25	323	Remote Farm	Land	L	C	3.00
1.00	42	Renounce	White	Ins	U	5.50
0.25	43	Revered Elder	White	Cr	C	3.00
4.00	44	Reverent Mantra	White	Ins	R	15.00
1.00	262	Revive	Green	Sor	U	5.50
1.00	45	Righteous Aura	White	E	U	5.00
1.00	46	Righteous Indignation	White	E	U	5.00
0.25	91	Rishadan Airship	Blue	Cr	C	3.00
3.00	92	Rishadan Brigand	Blue	Cr	R	15.00
0.25	93	Rishadan Cutpurse	Blue	Cr	C	3.00
1.00	94	Rishadan Footpad	Blue	Cr	U	5.00
4.00	311	Rishadan Pawnshop	Artif	Art	R	15.00
15.00	324	Rishadan Port	Land	L	R	25.00
1.00	209	Robber Fly	Red	Cr	U	5.00
1.00	210	Rock Badger	Red	Cr	U	5.00
0.25	157	Rouse	Black	Ins	C	3.00
0.25	263	Rushwood Dryad	Green	Cr	C	3.00
6.00	264	Rushwood Elemental	Green	Cr	R	17.00
1.00	325	Rushwood Grove	Land	L	U	5.50
0.25	265	Rushwood Herbalist	Green	Cr	C	3.00
1.00	266	Rushwood Legate	Green	Cr	U	5.00
1.00	267	Saber Ants	Green	Cr	U	5.50
0.25	268	Sacred Prey	Green	Cr	C	3.00
1.00	95	Sailmonger	Blue	Cr	U	5.00
3.00	96	Sand Squid	Blue	Cr	R	15.00
0.25	326	Sandstone Needle	Land	L	C	3.00
3.00	97	Saprazzan Bailiff	Blue	Cr	R	15.00
1.00	98	Saprazzan Breaker	Blue	Cr	U	5.00
1.00	327	Saprazzan Cove	Land	L	U	5.50
4.00	99	Saprazzan Heir	Blue	Cr	R	15.00
1.00	100	Saprazzan Legate	Blue	Cr	U	5.50
0.25	101	Saprazzan Outrigger	Blue	Cr	C	3.00
0.25	102	Saprazzan Raider	Blue	Cr	C	3.00
0.25	328	Saprazzan Skerry	Land	L	C	3.00
1.00	158	Scandalmonger	Black	Cr	U	5.00
4.00	47	Security Detail	White	E	R	15.00
5.00	211	Seismic Mage	Red	Cr	R	15.00
0.25	159	Sever Soul	Black	Sor	C	3.00
0.25	212	Shock Troops	Red	Cr	C	3.00
1.00	103	Shoving Match	Blue	Ins	U	5.00
4.00	160	Silent Assassin	Black	Cr	R	15.00
0.25	269	Silverglade Elemental	Green	Cr	C	3.00
1.00	270	Silverglade Pathfinder	Green	Cr	U	5.50
0.25	213	Sizzle	Red	Sor	C	3.00
0.25	161	Skulking Fugitive	Black	Cr	C	3.00
4.00	312	Skull of Ramos	Artif	Art	R	16.00
1.00	271	Snake Pit	Green	E	U	5.50
0.25	272	Snorting Gahr	Green	Cr	C	3.00
0.25	162	Snuff Out	Black	Ins	C	3.00
0.25	48	Soothing Balm	White	Ins	C	3.00
1.00	104	Soothsaying	Blue	E	U	5.50
0.25	163	Soul Channeling	Black	ECr	C	3.00
0.25	164	Specter's Wail	Black	Sor	C	3.00
0.25	273	Spidersilk Armor	Green	E	C	3.00
4.00	49	Spiritual Focus	White	E	R	15.00
5.00	274	Spontaneous Generation	Green	Sor	R	16.00
0.25	275	Squall	Green	Sor	C	3.00
1.00	276	Squallmonger	Green	Cr	U	5.50
8.00	214	Squee, Goblin Nabob	Red	Cr	R	20.00
4.00	105	Squeeze	Blue	E	R	15.00
1.00	277	Stamina	Green	ECr	U	5.00
4.00	106	Statecraft	Blue	E	R	15.00
0.25	50	Steadfast Guard	White	Cr	C	3.00
0.25	107	Stinging Barrier	Blue	Cr	C	3.00
0.25	215	Stone Rain	Red	Sor	C	3.00
1.00	51	Story Circle	White	E	U	6.00
1.00	165	Strongarm Thug	Black	Cr	U	5.00
1.00	329	Subterranean Hangar	Land	L	U	5.50
1.00	278	Sustenance	Green	E	U	5.00
0.10	339	Swamp (ver. 1)	Land	L	L	3.00
0.10	339	Swamp (ver. 2)	Land	L	L	3.00
0.10	339	Swamp (ver. 3)	Land	L	L	3.00
0.10	339	Swamp (ver. 4)	Land	L	L	3.00
0.25	52	Task Force	White	Cr	C	3.00
5.00	216	Tectonic Break	Red	Sor	R	18.00
4.00	217	Territorial Dispute	Red	E	R	15.00
0.25	53	Thermal Glider	White	Cr	C	3.00
4.00	218	Thieves' Auction	Red	Sor	R	15.00
5.00	166	Thrashing Wumpus	Black	Cr	R	18.00
0.25	219	Thunderclap	Red	Ins	C	3.00
1.00	108	Thwart	Blue	Ins	U	6.00
0.25	109	Tidal Bore	Blue	Ins	C	3.00
5.00	110	Tidal Kraken	Blue	Cr	R	18.00
0.25	279	Tiger Claws	Green	ECr	C	3.00
1.00	111	Timid Drake	Blue	Cr	U	5.00
1.00		Tonic Peddler	White	Cr	U	5.50
4.00	313	Tooth of Ramos	Artif	Art	R	16.00
4.00	330	Tower of the Magistrate	Land	L	R	15.50
1.00	314	Toymaker	Artif	ACr	U	5.00
5.00	112	Trade Routes	Blue	E	R	15.00
0.25	280	Tranquility	Green	Sor	C	3.00
1.00	55	Trap Runner	White	Cr	U	5.50
0.25	220	Tremor	Red	Sor	C	3.00
8.00	221	Two-Headed Dragon	Red	Cr	R	20.00
0.25	167	Undertaker	Black	Cr	C	3.00
5.00	168	Unmask	Black	Sor	R	20.00
4.00	169	Unnatural Hunger	Black	ECr	R	15.00
1.00	222	Uphill Battle	Red	E	U	5.50
0.25	170	Vendetta	Black	Ins	C	3.00
1.00	281	Venomous Breath	Green	Ins	U	5.00
0.25	282	Venomous Dragonfly	Green	Cr	C	3.00
4.00	283	Vernal Equinox	Green	E	R	15.00
5.00	284	Vine Dryad	Green	Cr	R	16.00
0.25	285	Vine Trellis	Green	Cr	C	3.00
1.00	223	Volcanic Wind	Red	Sor	U	5.00
1.00	171	Wall of Distortion	Black	Cr	U	5.00
1.00	224	War Cadence	Red	E	U	5.50
1.00	113	War Tax	Blue	E	U	5.50
1.00	225	Warmonger	Red	Cr	U	5.00
1.00	226	Warpath	Red	Ins	U	5.00
0.25	114	Waterfront Bouncer	Blue	Cr	C	3.00
5.00	56	Wave of Reckoning	White	Sor	R	18.00
0.25	227	Wild Jhovall	Red	Cr	C	3.00
1.00	57	Wishmonger	White	Cr	U	5.00
1.00	228	Word of Blasting	Red	Ins	U	5.00
4.00	315	Worry Beads	Artif	Art	R	15.00

RARITY KEY C = Common (black symbol)   U = Uncommon (silver symbol)   R = Rare (gold symbol)   **CARD TYPES:** See page 246

Kill Switch

3

Artifact

2, ⊕: Tap all other artifacts. They don't untap during their controllers' untap steps as long as Kill Switch remains tapped.

Success is largely a matter of knowing which lever to pull.

Illus. Brian Snöddy
©1993-2000 Wizards of the Coast, Inc. 133/143

Magic: The Gathering • Nemesis

Wizards of the Coast • Released **February 2000**

143 cards and **143** foil cards in set • **IDENTIFIER: Halberd (axe) symbol; black borders**

- Starter decks contain 60 cards; starter displays contain 12 starters
- Booster packs contain 15 cards; booster displays contain 36 boosters
- Pre-constructed decks include **Breakdown, Eruption, Mercenaries,** and **Replicator**

   Nemesis, the first follow-up expansion to **Mercadian Masques**, introduces the Fading mechanic, a new spin on cumulative upkeep. While these cards are temporary in nature, they generally have a profound impact on the game while they're in play. Fading cards like **Tanglewire, Blastoderm, Saproling Burst, Jolting Merfolk, Parallax Tide,** and **Parallax Wave** all made an impact on the constructed-deck **Magic** scene.

   Other noteworthy cards from **Nemesis** include **Death Pit Offering, Massacre, Reverent Silence, Kor-Haven, Rath's Edge, Rootwater Thief, Rising Waters, Blinding Angel, Lin Sivvi,** and **Seal of Cleansing. — Bennie Smith**

NEMESIS

You will need **16** nine-pocket pages to store this set. (8 doubled up)

Set, no foils (143 cards)	140.50
Foil set (143 foil cards)	875.00
Starter Display Box	96.00
Booster Display Box	90.00
Pre-constructed Starter Deck	10.00
Booster Pack	3.30

REGPRICE	#	Card Name	Color	Rarity	FOILPRICE
0.20	26	Accumulated Knowledge	Blue	C	3.00
4.00	27	Aether Barrier	Blue	R	15.00
0.20	28	Air Bladder	Blue	C	3.00
1.00	76	Ancient Hydra	Red	U	6.00
1.00	1	Angelic Favor	White	U	6.00
1.00	101	Animate Land	Green	U	6.00
1.00	77	Arc Mage	Red	U	6.00
5.50	51	Ascendant Evincar	Black	R	15.00
4.00	2	Avenger en-Dal	White	R	15.00
1.00	52	Battlefield Percher	Black	U	6.00
1.00	126	Belbe's Armor	Artifact	U	6.00
0.20	53	Belbe's Percher	Black	C	3.00
4.00	127	Belbe's Portal	Artifact	R	15.00
0.25	102	Blastoderm	Green	C	3.00
6.00	3	Blinding Angel	White	R	19.00
0.20	78	Bola Warrior	Red	C	3.00
1.00	54	Carrion Wall	Black	U	6.00
1.00	4	Chieftain en-Dal	White	U	6.00
0.20	29	Cloudskate	Blue	C	3.00
1.00	103	Coiling Woodworm	Green	U	6.00
4.00	128	Complex Automaton	Artifact	R	15.00
1.00	55	Dark Triumph	Black	U	6.50
0.20	30	Daze	Blue	C	3.00
5.00	56	Death Pit Offering	Black	R	15.00
0.20	5	Defender en-Vec	White	C	3.00
0.20	6	Defiant Falcon	White	C	3.00
1.00	7	Defiant Vanguard	White	U	6.00
4.00	57	Divining Witch	Black	R	15.00
1.00	31	Dominate	Blue	U	6.00
0.20	79	Downhill Charge	Red	C	3.00
1.00	32	Ensnare	Blue	U	6.00
4.00	129	Eye of Yawgmoth	Artifact	R	15.00
0.20	8	Fanatical Devotion	White	C	3.00
0.25	80	Flame Rift	Red	C	3.00
1.00	130	Flint Golem	Artifact	U	6.00
0.80	131	Flowstone Armor	Artifact	U	6.00
0.20	81	Flowstone Crusher	Red	C	3.00
5.00	82	Flowstone Overseer	Red	R	15.00

REGPRICE	#	Card Name	Color	Rarity	FOILPRICE
4.00	83	Flowstone Slide	Red	R	15.00
0.20	84	Flowstone Strike	Red	C	3.00
1.00	85	Flowstone Surge	Red	U	6.00
0.80	132	Flowstone Thopter	Artifact	U	6.00
0.20	86	Flowstone Wall	Red	C	3.00
0.20	104	Fog Patch	Green	C	3.00
0.20	105	Harvest Mage	Green	C	3.00
0.20	33	Infiltrate	Blue	C	3.00
1.00	34	Jolting Merfolk	Blue	U	6.00
5.00	133	Kill Switch	Artifact	R	15.00
5.00	141	Kor Haven	Land	R	16.50
0.20	87	Laccolith Grunt	Red	C	3.00
0.20	88	Laccolith Rig	Red	C	3.00
5.00	89	Laccolith Titan	Red	R	15.00
1.00	90	Laccolith Warrior	Red	U	6.00
0.20	91	Laccolith Whelp	Red	C	3.00
0.20	9	Lashknife	White	C	3.00
0.20	10	Lawbringer	White	C	3.00
0.20	11	Lightbringer	White	C	3.00
7.00	12	Lin Sivvi, Defiant Hero	White	R	19.00
4.00	92	Mana Cache	Red	R	15.00
1.00	58	Massacre	Black	U	6.50
1.00	59	Mind Slash	Black	U	6.00
0.20	60	Mind Swords	Black	C	3.00
1.00	93	Mogg Alarm	Red	U	6.00
1.00	94	Mogg Salvage	Red	U	6.00
0.20	95	Mogg Toady	Red	C	3.00
4.00	96	Moggcatcher	Red	R	15.00
0.20	106	Mossdog	Green	C	3.00
4.00	61	Murderous Betrayal	Black	R	15.00
1.00	107	Nesting Wurm	Green	U	6.00
0.20	13	Netter en-Dal	White	C	3.00
1.00	14	Noble Stand	White	U	6.00
0.20	15	Off Balance	White	C	3.00
4.00	16	Oracle's Attendants	White	R	15.00
0.20	35	Oraxid	Blue	C	3.00
4.00	108	Overlaid Terrain	Green	R	15.00
4.00	109	Pack Hunt	Green	R	15.00
4.00	36	Pale Moon	Blue	R	15.00
0.20	62	Parallax Dementia	Black	C	3.00
4.00	134	Parallax Inhibitor	Artifact	R	15.00
5.00	63	Parallax Nexus	Black	R	15.00
5.30	37	Parallax Tide	Blue	R	16.50
6.00	17	Parallax Wave	White	R	18.00
0.20	64	Phyrexian Driver	Black	C	3.00
1.00	65	Phyrexian Prowler	Black	U	6.00
0.20	66	Plague Witch	Black	C	3.00
5.50	135	"Predator, Flagship"	Artifact	R	16.50
1.00	136	Rackling	Artifact	U	6.00
5.00	67	Rathi Assassin	Black	R	15.00
1.00	68	Rathi Fiend	Black	U	6.00
0.20	69	Rathi Intimidator	Black	C	3.00
4.00	142	Rath's Edge	Land	R	15.00

REGPRICE	#	Card Name	Color	Rarity	FOILPRICE
1.00	110	Refreshing Rain	Green	U	6.00
1.00	137	Rejuvenation Chamber	Artifact	U	6.00
0.20	111	Reverent Silence	Green	C	3.00
5.30	112	Rhox	Green	R	16.50
5.00	38	Rising Waters	Blue	R	16.50
0.20	39	Rootwater Commando	Blue	C	3.00
7.00	40	Rootwater Thief	Blue	R	16.50
1.00	97	Rupture	Red	U	6.00
1.00	138	Rusting Golem	Artifact	U	6.00
5.00	113	Saproling Burst	Green	R	16.50
5.00	114	Saproling Cluster	Green	R	15.00
4.00	41	Seahunter	Blue	R	15.00
0.20	18	Seal of Cleansing	White	C	3.00
0.20	70	Seal of Doom	Black	C	3.00
0.25	98	Seal of Fire	Red	C	3.00
0.20	42	Seal of Removal	Blue	C	3.00
0.25	115	Seal of Strength	Green	C	3.00
3.50	99	Shrieking Mogg	Red	R	15.00
0.20	19	Silkenfist Fighter	White	C	3.00
1.00	20	Silkenfist Order	White	U	6.00
1.00	21	Sivvi's Ruse	White	U	6.00
3.50	22	Sivvi's Valor	White	R	15.00
4.00	116	Skyshroud Behemoth	Green	R	15.00
0.20	117	Skyshroud Claim	Green	C	3.00
0.20	118	Skyshroud Cutter	Green	C	3.00
5.00	119	Skyshroud Poacher	Green	R	15.00
0.20	120	Skyshroud Ridgeback	Green	C	3.00
0.20	121	Skyshroud Sentinel	Green	C	3.00
4.00	43	Sliptide Serpent	Blue	R	15.00
0.20	44	Sneaky Homunculus	Blue	C	3.00
0.20	71	Spineless Thug	Black	C	3.00
5.00	23	Spiritual Asylum	White	R	15.00
0.20	72	Spiteful Bully	Black	C	3.00
1.00	122	Stampede Driver	Green	U	6.00
1.00	45	Stronghold Biologist	Blue	U	6.50
0.20	73	Stronghold Discipline	Black	C	3.00
4.00	100	Stronghold Gambit	Red	R	14.50
1.00	46	Stronghold Machinist	Blue	U	6.00
1.00	47	Stronghold Zeppelin	Blue	U	6.00
1.00	48	Submerge	Blue	U	6.00
7.00	139	Tangle Wire	Artifact	R	19.00
1.00	143	Terrain Generator	Land	U	6.00
0.20	24	Topple	White	C	3.00
0.20	123	Treetop Bracers	Green	C	3.00
0.20	49	Trickster Mage	Blue	C	3.00
0.20	74	Vicious Hunger	Black	C	3.00
1.00	140	Viseling	Artifact	U	6.00
1.00	25	Voice of Truth	White	U	6.00
6.00	75	Volrath the Fallen	Black	R	16.50
0.20	50	Wandering Eye	Blue	C	3.00
1.00	124	Wild Mammoth	Green	U	6.00
1.00	125	Woodripper	Green	U	6.00

RARITY KEY C = Common (black symbol)   U = Uncommon (silver symbol)   R = Rare (gold symbol)   **CARD TYPES: See page 246**

Magic: The Gathering • Prophecy

Wizards of the Coast • Released **June 2000**

143 cards and **143** foil cards in set • **IDENTIFIER: Crystal symbol; black borders**

- Starter decks contain 60 cards; starter displays contain 12 starters
- Booster packs contain 15 cards; booster displays contain 36 boosters
- Pre-constructed decks include **Distress**, **Pummel**, **Slither**, and **Turnaround**

The last expansion to the Masques block, *Prophecy* features "Rhystic" spells which grow more powerful if an opponent does not pay a designated cost. However, cards so dependent on an opponent's actions proved not to be very appealing to most players.

Prophecy also adds cycles of cards for all colors, such as Legendary Spellshapers, Avatars, and Winds. Too expensive for constructed *Magic* play, these powerful cards proved to be popular for the casual gamer. *Prophecy* does bring a few constructed gems with cards like **Chimeric Idol**, **Rebel Informer**, **Spitting Spider**, **Foil**, and **Spiketail Hatchling**.

With perhaps the weakest selection of tournament cards since *Homelands*, *Prophecy* is generally regarded as a fun, less competitive-oriented set. — *Bennie Smith*

Set, no foils (143 cards)	150.000	
Foil set (143 foil cards)	765.00	
Starter Display Box	109.00	
Booster Display Box	95.00	
Pre-constructed Starter Deck	10.00	
Booster Pack	3.30	

You will need 16 nine-pocket pages to store this set. (8 doubled up)

RegPrice	#	Card Name	Color	Type	RAR	FoilPrice
0.80	1	Abolish	White	Ins	U	5.00
0.20	55	Agent of Shauku	Black	Cr	C	2.00
4.50	28	Alexi, Zephyr Mage	Blue	Cr	R	15.00
0.20	29	Alexi's Cloak	Blue	E	C	2.00
0.20	2	Aura Fracture	White	E	C	2.00
5.80	82	Avatar of Fury	Red	Cr	R	18.00
5.00	3	Avatar of Hope	White	Cr	R	15.00
5.30	109	Avatar of Might	Green	Cr	R	15.00
5.80	30	Avatar of Will	Blue	Cr	R	15.00
7.00	56	Avatar of Woe	Black	Cr	R	20.00
1.00	83	Barbed Field	Red	E	U	5.00
4.00	4	Blessed Wind	White	Sor	R	13.50
3.50	57	Bog Elemental	Black	Cr	R	13.00
0.25	58	Bog Glider	Black	Cr	C	2.00
0.20	84	Branded Brawlers	Red	Cr	C	2.00
1.00	85	Brutal Suppression	Red	E	U	5.00
0.20	110	Calming Verse	Green	Sor	C	2.00
4.00	5	Celestial Convergence	White	E	R	12.00
0.90	59	Chilling Apparition	Black	Cr	U	5.00
1.00	136	Chimeric Idol	Artif	Art	U	6.00
1.00	86	Citadel of Pain	Red	E	U	5.00
0.20	31	Coastal Hornclaw	Blue	Cr	C	2.00
3.40	60	Coffin Puppets	Black	Cr	R	13.50
4.30	137	Copper-Leaf Angel	Artif	Cr	R	15.00
1.00	111	Darba	Green	Cr	U	5.00
0.20	61	Death Charmer	Black	Cr	C	2.00
5.00	32	Denying Wind	Blue	Sor	R	13.50
0.20	62	Despoil	Black	Sor	C	2.00
0.20	87	Devastate	Red	Sor	C	2.00
0.20	6	Diving Griffin	White	Cr	C	2.00
4.30	112	Dual Nature	Green	E	R	13.50
4.00	113	Elephant Resurgence	Green	Sor	R	13.50
0.80	63	Endbringer's Revel	Black	E	U	5.00
0.80	7	Entangler	White	E	U	5.00
0.90	33	Excavation	Blue	E	U	5.00
0.20	8	Excise	White	Ins	C	2.00
0.20	88	Fault Riders	Red	Cr	C	2.00
0.20	64	Fen Stalker	Black	Cr	C	2.00
3.30	89	Fickle Efreet	Red	Cr	R	13.50
0.80	90	Flameshot	Red	Sor	U	5.00
0.20	65	Flay	Black	Sor	C	2.00
0.80	9	Flowering Field	White	E	U	5.00
1.00	34	Foil	Blue	Ins	U	6.00
4.00	114	Forgotten Harvest	Green	E	R	13.50

RegPrice	#	Card Name	Color	Type	RAR	FoilPrice
0.90	10	Glittering Lion	White	Cr	U	5.00
0.20	11	Glittering Lynx	White	Cr	C	2.00
5.00	66	Greel, Mind Raker	Black	Cr	R	15.00
0.20	67	Greel's Caress	Black	E	C	2.00
0.20	35	Gulf Squid	Blue	Cr	C	2.00
0.20	36	Hazy Homunculus	Blue	Cr	C	2.00
4.00	37	Heightened Awareness	Blue	E	R	15.00
0.80	138	Hollow Warrior	Artif	Cr	U	5.00
4.00	68	Infernal Genesis	Black	E	R	13.50
0.20	91	Inflame	Red	Ins	C	2.00
4.00	12	Jeweled Spirit	White	Cr	R	15.00
5.00	115	Jolrael, Empress of Beasts	Green	Cr	R	15.00
0.20	116	Jolrael's Favor	Green	E	C	2.00
0.80	92	Keldon Arsonist	Red	Cr	U	5.00
4.00	139	Keldon Battlewagon	Artif	Cr	R	15.00
0.20	93	Keldon Berserker	Red	Cr	C	2.00
4.00	94	Keldon Firebombers	Red	Cr	R	15.00
5.00	95	Latulla, Keldon Overseer	Red	Cr	R	15.00
0.20	96	Latulla's Orders	Red	E	C	2.00
0.90	97	Lesser Gargadon	Red	Cr	U	5.00
1.00	117	Living Terrain	Green	E	U	5.00
6.00	13	Mageta, the Lion	White	Cr	R	20.00
0.20	14	Mageta's Boon	White	Ecr	C	2.00
1.00	38	Mana Vapors	Blue	Sor	U	5.00
0.20	118	Marsh Boa	Green	Cr	C	2.00
5.00	15	Mercenary Informer	White	Cr	R	15.00
0.20	16	Mine Bearer	White	Cr	C	2.00
0.80	17	Mirror Strike	White	Ins	U	5.00
4.50	119	Mungha Wurm	Green	Cr	R	15.00
0.80	69	Nakaya Shade	Black	Cr	U	5.00
0.80	70	Noxious Field	Black	E	U	5.00
0.80	71	Outbreak	Black	Sor	U	5.00
4.00	39	Overburden	Blue	E	R	13.50
0.20	98	Panic Attack	Red	Sor	C	2.00
1.00	72	Pit Raptor	Black	Cr	U	5.00
0.20	73	Plague Fiend	Black	Cr	C	2.00
5.00	74	Plague Wind	Black	Sor	R	15.00
4.00	40	Psychic Theft	Blue	Sor	R	13.50
0.20	120	Pygmy Razorback	Green	Cr	C	2.00
0.50	41	Quicksilver Wall	Blue	Cr	U	5.00
4.80	75	Rebel Informer	Black	Cr	R	15.00
0.20	42	Rethink	Blue	Ins	C	2.00
1.00	18	Reveille Squad	White	Cr	U	5.00
1.00	142	Rhystic Cave	Land	Lnd	U	5.00
0.20	19	Rhystic Circle	White	E	C	2.00
0.20	43	Rhystic Deluge	Blue	E	C	2.00
0.25	99	Rhystic Lightning	Red	Ins	C	2.50
1.00	44	Rhystic Scrying	Blue	Sor	U	5.00
0.20	20	Rhystic Shield	White	Ins	C	2.00
0.20	45	Rhystic Study	Blue	E	C	2.00
1.00	76	Rhystic Syphon	Black	Sor	U	5.00

RegPrice	#	Card Name	Color	Type	RAR	FoilPrice
5.00	77	Rhystic Tutor	Black	Sor	R	16.50
0.20	121	Rib Cage Spider	Green	Cr	C	2.00
0.20	46	Ribbon Snake	Blue	Cr	C	2.00
0.20	100	Ridgeline Rager	Red	Cr	C	2.00
1.00	122	Root Cage	Green	E	U	5.00
3.80	21	Samite Sanctuary	White	E	R	13.50
0.80	101	Scoria Cat	Red	Cr	U	5.00
4.40	102	Search for Survivors	Red	Sor	R	13.50
5.00	103	Searing Wind	Red	Ins	R	14.50
4.00	22	Sheltering Prayers	White	E	R	14.50
0.80	23	Shield Dancer	White	Cr	U	5.00
4.00	47	Shrouded Serpent	Blue	Cr	R	15.00
0.20	123	Silt Crawler	Green	Cr	C	2.50
0.80	124	Snag	Green	Ins	U	5.00
0.20	24	Soul Charmer	White	Cr	C	2.00
0.20	78	Soul Strings	Black	Sor	C	2.00
1.00	48	Spiketail Drake	Blue	Cr	U	5.00
0.20	49	Spiketail Hatchling	Blue	Cr	C	2.50
0.80	125	Spitting Spider	Green	Cr	U	5.00
0.20	126	Spore Frog	Green	Cr	C	3.00
0.20	104	Spur Grappler	Red	Cr	C	2.50
5.00	127	Squirrel Wrangler	Green	Cr	R	16.50
0.20	79	Steal Strength	Black	Ins	C	2.00
0.20	50	Stormwatch Eagle	Blue	Cr	C	2.00
0.80	51	Sunken Field	Blue	E	U	5.00
0.80	25	Sword Dancer	White	Cr	U	5.00
4.00	105	Task Mage Assembly	Red	E	R	15.00
0.20	128	Thresher Beast	Green	Cr	C	2.00
0.20	129	Thrive	Green	Sor	C	2.00
0.20	26	Trenching Steed	White	Cr	C	2.00
0.20	27	Troubled Healer	White	Cr	C	2.00
4.30	52	Troublesome Spirit	Blue	Cr	R	15.00
0.80	130	Verdant Field	Green	E	U	5.00
4.10	106	Veteran Brawlers	Red	Cr	R	15.00
0.20	131	Vintara Elephant	Green	Cr	C	2.00
0.90	132	Vintara Snapper	Green	Cr	U	5.00
5.00	133	Vitalizing Wind	Green	Ins	R	15.00
0.80	80	Wall of Vipers	Black	Cr	U	5.00
4.00	140	Well of Discovery	Artif	Art	R	13.50
0.80	141	Well of Life	Artif	Art	U	5.00
0.80	107	Whip Sergeant	Red	Cr	U	5.00
0.20	81	Whipstitched Zombie	Black	Cr	C	2.00
0.80	134	Wild Might	Green	Ins	C	2.50
0.80	53	Windscouter	Blue	Cr	U	5.00
1.00	135	Wing Storm	Green	Sor	U	5.00
4.00	143	Wintermoon Mesa	Land	Lnd	R	14.50
0.20	54	Withdraw	Blue	Ins	C	2.50
0.20	108	Zerapa Minotaur	Red	Cr	C	2.00

RARITY KEY C = Common (black symbol) U = Uncommon (silver symbol) R = Rare (gold symbol) **CARD TYPES: See page 246**

Magic: The Gathering • Invasion

Wizards of the Coast • Released October 2000

350 cards and **350** foil cards in set • **IDENTIFIER:** "Coalition" symbol; black borders

- Tournament decks contain 75 cards, theme decks 60; starter displays contain 12 starters
- Booster packs contain 15 cards; booster displays contain 36 boosters
- Pre-constructed decks include **Blowout**, **Dismissal**, **Heavy Duty**, and **Spectrum**

In **Invasion**, Wizards focuses on multi-color decks. More than a quarter of the cards are multi-color "gold" cards, and many of the single-color cards interact with other colors.

In a new mechanic, an additional "kicker" cost (sometimes of another color) may be paid when the spell is played to boost the effect of the card. "Split" cards, actually two different-colored spells printed on the same card, allow the caster to choose which spell to use. These new mechanics produced a set full of flexibility and utility, with plenty of room for varying deck designs. Other interesting features include sorceries that can be played as instants for an additional mana cost, "domain" cards that become more powerful for each basic land type you control, and five new Dragon Legends.

Standout cards include **Fires of Yavimaya, Urza's Rage, Absorb, Route,** and **Fact or Fiction.** — *Bennie Smith*

You will need
39 nine-pocket pages to store this set.
(20 doubled up)

Set, no foils (350 cards + 15 variants)	300.00
Foil set (350 foil cards)	723.00
Starter Display Box	108.00
Booster Display Box	90.00
Tournament Deck	10.00
Pre-constructed Starter Deck	10.00
Booster Pack	3.30

RegPrice	#	Card Name	Color	Type	RAR	FoilPrice
6.00	226	Absorb	Multi	Ins	R	25.00
1.00	91	Addle	Black	Sor	U	6.00
5.00	227	Æther Rift	Multi	E	R	20.00
0.25	181	Aggressive Urge	Green	Ins	C	3.00
0.25	92	Agonizing Demise	Black	Ins	C	3.00
4.00	1	Alabaster Leech	White	Cr	R	20.00
1.00	297	Alloy Golem	Artif	Art	U	6.00
0.25	136	Ancient Kavu	Red	Cr	C	3.00
0.25	319	Ancient Spring	Land	Lnd	C	3.00
4.00	93	Andradite Leech	Black	Cr	R	20.00
1.00	2	Angel of Mercy	White	Cr	U	6.00
1.00	228	Angelic Shield	Multi	E	U	6.00
1.00	94	Annihilate	Black	Ins	U	6.00
1.00	320	Archaeological Dig	Land	Lnd	U	6.00
0.25	3	Ardent Soldier	White	Cr	C	3.00
0.25	229	Armadillo Cloak	Multi	E	C	3.00
4.00	230	Armored Guardian	Multi	Cr	R	20.00
5.00	231	Artif Mutation	Multi	Ins	R	20.00
1.00	295	Assault/Battery	Rd/Gr	Sor	U	6.00
5.00	4	Atalya, Samite Master	White	Cr	R	20.00
5.00	232	Aura Mutation	Multi	Ins	R	20.00
1.00	233	Aura Shards	Multi	E	U	6.00
1.00	234	Backlash	Multi	Ins	U	6.00
4.00	235	Barrin's Spite	Multi	Sor	R	20.00
0.25	46	Barrin's Unmaking	Blue	Ins	C	3.00
1.00	5	Benalish Emissary	White	Cr	U	6.00
1.00	6	Benalish Heralds	White	Cr	U	6.00
0.25	7	Benalish Lancer	White	Cr	C	3.00
0.25	8	Benalish Trapper	White	Cr	C	3.00
4.00	137	Bend or Break	Red	Sor	R	20.00
4.00	182	Bind	Green	Ins	R	20.00
5.50	236	Blazing Specter	Multi	Cr	R	22.50
5.00	47	Blind Seer	Blue	Cr	R	20.00
1.00	9	Blinding Light	White	Sor	U	6.00
1.00	298	Bloodstone Cameo	Artif	Art	U	6.00
5.00	183	Blurred Mongoose	Green	Cr	R	20.00
0.25	95	Bog Initiate	Black	Cr	C	3.00

RegPrice	#	Card Name	Color	Type	RAR	FoilPrice
4.00	48	Breaking Wave	Blue	Sor	R	20.00
1.00	138	Breath of Darigaaz	Red	Sor	U	6.00
4.00	139	Callous Giant	Red	Cr	R	20.00
1.00	184	Canopy Surge	Green	Sor	U	6.00
0.25	10	Capashen Unicorn	White	Cr	C	3.00
5.00	237	Captain Sisay	Multi	Cr	R	20.00
1.00	238	Cauldron Dance	Multi	Ins	U	6.00
1.00	239	Charging Troll	Multi	Cr	U	7.00
1.00	299	Chromatic Sphere	Artif	Art	U	6.00
1.00	240	Cinder Shade	Multi	Cr	U	6.00
5.00	241	Coalition Victory	Multi	Sor	R	25.00
2.00	321	Coastal Tower	Land	Lnd	U	9.00
4.00	141	Collapsing Borders	Red	E	R	20.00
4.00	49	Collective Restraint	Blue	E	R	20.00
1.00	96	Cremate	Black	Ins	U	6.00
0.25	11	Crimson Acolyte	White	Cr	C	3.00
6.00	242	Crosis, the Purger	Multi	Cr	R	27.50
1.00	300	Crosis's Attendant	Artif	Art	U	6.00
0.25	142	Crown of Flames	Red	E	C	3.00
5.00	12	Crusading Knight	White	Cr	R	20.00
5.00	97	Crypt Angel	Black	Cr	R	20.00
4.00	50	Crystal Spray	Blue	Ins	R	20.00
0.25	98	Cursed Flesh	Black	E	C	3.00
7.00	243	Darigaaz, the Igniter	Multi	Cr	R	25.00
1.00	301	Darigaaz's Attendant	Artif	Art	U	6.00
5.00	13	Death or Glory	White	Sor	R	20.00
1.00	99	Defiling Tears	Black	Ins	U	6.00
4.50	100	Desperate Research	Black	Sor	R	20.00
5.00	101	Devouring Strossus	Black	Cr	R	20.00
0.25	14	Dismantling Blow	White	Ins	C	3.00
1.00	51	Disrupt	Blue	Ins	U	7.00
5.00	52	Distorting Wake	Blue	Sor	R	20.00
4.00	15	Divine Presence	White	E	R	20.00
5.00	102	Do or Die	Black	Sor	R	20.00
1.00	302	Drake-Skull Cameo	Artif	Art	U	6.00
0.25	53	Dream Thrush	Blue	Cr	C	3.00
1.00	103	Dredge	Black	Ins	U	6.00
6.00	244	Dromar, the Banisher	Multi	Cr	R	27.50
1.00	303	Dromar's Attendant	Artif	Art	U	6.00
5.00	245	Dueling Grounds	Multi	E	R	20.00
0.25	104	Duskwalker	Black	Cr	C	3.00
2.00	322	Elfhame Palace	Land	Lnd	U	9.00
1.00	185	Elfhame Sanctuary	Green	E	U	6.00
5.00	186	Elvish Champion	Green	Cr	R	22.50
5.00	54	Empress Galina	Blue	Cr	R	20.00
1.00	55	Essence Leak	Blue	E	U	6.00
0.25	56	Exclude	Blue	Ins	C	3.00
0.25	105	Exotic Curse	Black	E	C	3.00
0.25	187	Explosive Growth	Green	Ins	C	3.00
1.00	57	Fact or Fiction	Blue	Ins	U	7.00
0.25	58	Faerie Squadron	Blue	Cr	C	3.00
0.25	188	Fertile Ground	Green	E	C	3.00

RegPrice	#	Card Name	Color	Type	RAR	FoilPrice
5.00	16	Fight or Flight	White	E	R	20.00
1.00	143	Firebrand Ranger	Red	Cr	U	6.00
1.00	246	Fires of Yavimaya	Multi	E	U	7.00
0.25	106	Firescreamer	Black	Cr	C	3.00
0.15	323	Forest (ver. 1)	Land	Lnd	L	3.00
0.15	323	Forest (ver. 2)	Land	Lnd	L	3.00
0.15	323	Forest (ver. 3)	Land	Lnd	L	3.00
0.15	323	Forest (ver. 4)	Land	Lnd	L	3.00
0.25	247	Frenzied Tilling	Multi	Sor	C	3.00
0.25	248	Galina's Knight	Multi	Cr	C	3.00
0.25	327	Geothermal Crevice	Land	Lnd	C	3.00
5.00	144	Ghitu Fire	Red	Sor	R	20.00
0.25	17	Glimmering Angel	White	Cr	C	3.00
5.00	18	Global Ruin	White	Sor	R	20.00
1.00	145	Goblin Spy	Red	Cr	U	6.00
1.00	107	Goham Djinn	Black	Cr	U	6.00
1.00	146	Halam Djinn	Red	Cr	U	6.00
5.00	249	Hanna, Ship's Navigator	Multi	Cr	R	20.00
0.25	189	Harrow	Green	Ins	C	3.00
5.00	19	Harsh Judgment	White	E	R	20.00
1.00	108	Hate Weaver	Black	Cr	U	6.00
1.00	250	Heroes' Reunion	Multi	Ins	U	6.00
0.25	20	Holy Day	White	Ins	C	3.00
0.25	147	Hooded Kavu	Red	Cr	C	3.00
1.00	251	Horned Cheetah	Multi	Cr	U	6.00
1.00	252	Hunting Kavu	Multi	Cr	U	6.00
0.25	109	Hypnotic Cloud	Black	Sor	C	3.00
0.25	328	Irrigation Ditch	Land	Lnd	C	3.00
0.15	329	Island (ver. 1)	Land	Lnd	L	3.00
0.15	329	Island (ver. 2)	Land	Lnd	L	3.00
0.15	329	Island (ver. 3)	Land	Lnd	L	3.00
0.15	329	Island (ver. 4)	Land	Lnd	L	3.00
5.00	190	Jade Leech	Green	Cr	R	22.50
5.00	304	Juntu Stakes	Artif	Art	R	20.00
4.50	253	Kangee, Aerie Keeper	Multi	Cr	R	20.00
0.25	148	Kavu Aggressor	Red	Cr	C	3.00
1.00	191	Kavu Chameleon	Green	Cr	U	6.00
0.25	192	Kavu Climber	Green	Cr	C	3.00
4.00	193	Kavu Lair	Green	E	R	20.00
5.00	149	Kavu Monarch	Red	Cr	R	20.00
1.00	150	Kavu Runner	Red	Cr	U	6.00
0.25	151	Kavu Scout	Red	Cr	C	3.00
6.00	194	Kavu Titan	Green	Cr	R	20.00
4.00	333	Keldon Necropolis	Land	Lnd	R	20.00
1.00	21	Liberate	White	Ins	U	6.00
1.00	152	Lightning Dart	Red	Ins	U	6.00
0.25	195	Llanowar Cavalry	Green	Cr	C	3.00
0.25	196	Llanowar Elite	Green	Cr	C	3.00
0.25	254	Llanowar Knight	Multi	Cr	C	3.00
0.25	197	Llanowar Vanguard	Green	Cr	C	3.00
4.00	153	Loafing Giant	Red	Cr	R	17.50

RARITY KEY C = Common (black symbol) U = Uncommon (silver symbol) R = Rare (gold symbol) **CARD TYPES: See page 246**

Crosis, the Purger — 3UBR

Creature — Dragon Legend

Flying

Whenever Crosis, the Purger deals combat damage to a player, you may pay 2B. If you do, choose a color. That player reveals his or her hand and discards all cards of that color from it.

Illus. Pete Venters

6/6

RegPrice	#	Card Name	Color	Type	RAR	FoilPrice
1.00	255	Lobotomy	Multi	Sor	U	7.00
5.00	305	Lotus Guardian	Artif	Art	R	20.00
5.00	154	Mages' Contest	Red	Ins	R	20.00
5.00	59	Mana Maze	Blue	E	R	20.00
0.25	155	Maniacal Rage	Red	E	C	3.00
1.00	60	Manipulate Fate	Blue	Sor	U	6.00
5.00	110	Marauding Knight	Black	Cr	R	20.00
5.00	61	Metathran Aerostat	Blue	E	R	20.00
1.00	62	Metathran Transport	Blue	Cr	U	6.00
0.25	63	Metathran Zombie	Blue	Cr	C	3.00
5.00	256	Meteor Storm	Multi	E	R	20.00
1.00	198	Might Weaver	Green	Cr	U	6.00
6.00	199	Molimo, Maro-Sorcerer	Green	Cr	R	20.00
0.15	334	Mountain (ver. 1)	Land	Lnd	L	3.00
0.15	334	Mountain (ver. 2)	Land	Lnd	L	3.00
0.15	334	Mountain (ver. 3)	Land	Lnd	L	3.00
0.15	334	Mountain (ver. 4)	Land	Lnd	L	3.00
0.25	111	Mourning	Black	E	C	3.00
0.25	112	Nightscape Apprentice	Black	Cr	C	3.00
4.00	113	Nightscape Master	Black	Cr	R	20.00
5.00	257	Noble Panther	Multi	Cr	R	20.00
0.25	200	Nomadic Elf	Green	Cr	C	3.00
6.00	156	Obliterate	Red	Sor	R	22.50
0.25	22	Obsidian Acolyte	White	Cr	C	3.00
0.25	64	Opt	Blue	Ins	C	3.00
1.00	258	Ordered Migration	Multi	Sor	U	6.00
0.25	23	Orim's Touch	White	Ins	C	3.00
5.00	259	Overabundance	Multi	E	R	20.00
0.25	157	Overload	Red	Ins	C	3.00
1.00	294	Pain/Suffering	Blk/Rd	Sor	U	7.00
0.25	65	Phantasmal Terrain	Blue	E	C	3.00
4.00	306	Phyrexian Altar	Artif	Art	R	20.00
0.25	114	Phyrexian Battleflies	Black	Cr	C	3.00
4.00	115	Phyrexian Delver	Black	Cr	R	20.00
5.00	116	Phyrexian Infiltrator	Black	Cr	R	20.00
5.00	307	Phyrexian Lens	Artif	Art	R	20.00
0.25	117	Phyrexian Reaper	Black	Cr	C	3.00
0.25	118	Phyrexian Slayer	Black	Cr	C	3.00
0.25	201	Pincer Spider	Green	Cr	C	3.00
1.00	119	Plague Spitter	Black	Cr	U	6.00
0.25	260	Plague Spores	Multi	Sor	C	3.00
0.15	338	Plains (ver. 1)	Land	Lnd	L	3.00
0.15	338	Plains (ver. 2)	Land	Lnd	L	3.00
0.15	338	Plains (ver. 3)	Land	Lnd	L	3.00
0.15	338	Plains (ver. 4)	Land	Lnd	L	3.00
5.00	308	Planar Portal	Artif	Art	R	20.00
1.00	24	Pledge of Loyalty	White	E	U	6.00
0.25	158	Pouncing Kavu	Red	Cr	C	3.00
1.00	309	Power Armor	Artif	Art	U	6.00
0.25	25	Prison Barricade	White	Cr	C	3.00
0.25	66	Probe	Blue	Sor	C	3.00
0.25	67	Prohibit	Blue	Ins	C	3.00
0.25	26	Protective Sphere	White	E	C	3.00
4.00	68	Psychic Battle	Blue	E	R	20.00
1.00	202	Pulse of Llanowar	Green	E	U	7.00
4.00	27	Pure Reflection	White	E	R	20.00
5.00	261	Pyre Zombie	Multi	Cr	R	22.50
0.25	203	Quirion Elves	Green	Cr	C	3.00
0.25	204	Quirion Sentinel	Green	Cr	C	3.00
0.25	205	Quirion Trailblazer	Green	Cr	C	3.00
1.00	159	Rage Weaver	Red	Cr	U	6.00
4.00	262	Raging Kavu	Multi	Cr	R	20.00
1.00	69	Rainbow Crow	Blue	Cr	U	6.00
0.25	28	Rampant Elephant	White	Cr	C	3.00
0.25	120	Ravenous Rats	Black	Cr	C	3.00
0.25	29	Razorfoot Griffin	White	Cr	C	3.00
4.00	263	Reckless Assault	Multi	E	R	20.00
1.00	121	Reckless Spite	Black	Ins	U	6.00
0.25	264	Recoil	Multi	Ins	C	3.00
0.25	122	Recover	Black	Sor	C	3.00
0.25	70	Repulse	Blue	Ins	C	3.00
5.00	206	Restock	Green	Sor	R	20.00
0.25	30	Restrain	White	Ins	C	3.00
0.25	31	Reviving Dose	White	Ins	C	3.00
1.00	265	Reviving Vapors	Multi	Ins	U	6.00
1.00	32	Rewards of Diversity	White	E	U	6.00
6.00	33	Reya Dawnbringer	White	Cr	R	20.00
1.00	266	Riptide Crab	Multi	Cr	U	6.00
1.00	310	Rith's Attendant	Artif	Art	U	7.00
6.50	267	Rith, the Awakener	Multi	Cr	R	20.00
0.25	160	Rogue Kavu	Red	Cr	C	3.00
1.00	207	Rooting Kavu	Green	Cr	U	6.00
5.00	34	Rout	White	Sor	R	22.50
4.00	161	Ruby Leech	Red	Cr	R	20.00
1.00	35	Ruham Djinn	White	Cr	U	6.00
5.00	268	Sabertooth Nishoba	Multi	Cr	R	20.00
2.00	342	Salt Marsh	Land	Lnd	U	9.00
1.00	269	Samite Archer	Multi	Cr	U	6.00
1.00	36	Samite Ministration	White	Ins	U	6.00
4.00	71	Sapphire Leech	Blue	Cr	R	20.00
5.00	208	Saproling Infestation	Green	E	R	20.00
5.00	209	Saproling Symbiosis	Green	Sor	R	20.00
0.25	162	Savage Offensive	Red	Sor	C	3.00
0.25	163	Scarred Puma	Red	Cr	C	3.00
0.25	123	Scavenged Weaponry	Black	E	C	3.00
0.25	164	Scorching Lava	Red	Ins	C	3.00
1.00	210	Scouting Trek	Green	Sor	U	6.00
1.00	165	Searing Rays	Red	Sor	U	6.00
1.00	311	Seashell Cameo	Artif	Art	U	6.00
1.00	270	Seer's Vision	Multi	E	U	6.00
0.25	211	Serpentine Kavu	Green	Cr	C	3.00
0.25	37	Shackles	White	E	C	3.00
0.25	72	Shimmering Wings	Blue	E	C	3.00
1.00	166	Shivan Emissary	Red	Cr	U	6.00
1.00	167	Shivan Harvest	Red	Sor	U	6.00
2.00	343	Shivan Oasis	Land	Lnd	U	9.00
0.25	271	Shivan Zombie	Multi	Cr	C	3.00
0.25	73	Shoreline Raider	Blue	Cr	C	3.00
1.00	272	Simoon	Multi	Ins	U	6.00
1.00	168	Skittish Kavu	Red	Cr	U	6.00
7.00	169	Skizzik	Red	Cr	R	22.50
1.00	74	Sky Weaver	Blue	Cr	U	6.00
1.00	273	Sleeper's Robe	Multi	E	U	6.00
0.25	170	Slimy Kavu	Red	Cr	C	3.00
1.00	274	Slinking Serpent	Multi	Cr	U	6.00
1.00	275	Smoldering Tar	Multi	E	U	6.00
0.25	124	Soul Burn	Black	Sor	C	3.00
1.00	312	Sparring Golem	Artif	Art	U	6.00
4.00	276	Spinal Embrace	Multi	Ins	R	20.00
5.00	38	Spirit of Resistance	White	E	R	20.00
1.00	39	Spirit Weaver	White	Cr	U	6.00
1.00	293	Spite/Malice	Blu/Bk	Ins	U	7.00
4.00	125	Spreading Plague	Black	E	R	20.00
5.00	277	Stalking Assassin	Multi	Cr	R	20.00
4.00	171	Stand or Fall	Red	E	R	20.00
1.00	292	Stand/Deliver	Wh/Blu	Ins	U	6.00
1.00	278	Sterling Grove	Multi	E	U	6.00
0.25	75	Stormscape Apprentice	Blue	Cr	C	3.00
4.00	76	Stormscape Master	Blue	Cr	R	20.00
0.25	40	Strength of Unity	White	E	U	6.00
0.25	172	Stun	Red	Ins	C	3.00
1.00	212	Sulam Djinn	Green	Cr	U	6.00
0.25	344	Sulfur Vent	Land	Lnd	C	3.00
0.25	41	Sunscape Apprentice	White	Cr	C	3.00
4.00	42	Sunscape Master	White	Cr	R	20.00
0.10	345	Swamp (ver. 1)	Land	Lnd	L	3.00
0.10	345	Swamp (ver. 2)	Land	Lnd	L	3.00
0.10	345	Swamp (ver. 3)	Land	Lnd	L	3.00
0.10	345	Swamp (ver. 4)	Land	Lnd	L	3.00
1.00	77	Sway of Illusion	Blue	Ins	U	6.00
0.25	126	Tainted Well	Black	E	C	3.00
1.00	213	Tangle	Green	Ins	U	6.00
5.00	173	Tectonic Instability	Red	E	R	20.00
1.00	43	Teferi's Care	White	E	U	6.00
5.00	279	Teferi's Moat	Multi	E	R	20.00
5.00	78	Teferi's Response	Blue	Ins	R	20.00
5.00	313	Tek	Artif	Art	R	20.00
4.50	79	Temporal Distortion	Blue	E	R	20.00
5.00	214	Thicket Elemental	Green	Cr	R	20.00
0.25	215	Thornscape Apprentice	Green	Cr	C	3.00
4.00	216	Thornscape Master	Green	Cr	R	20.00
0.25	174	Thunderscape Apprentice	Red	Cr	C	3.00
4.00	175	Thunderscape Master	Red	Cr	R	20.00
0.25	80	Tidal Visionary	Blue	Cr	C	3.00
1.00	314	Tigereye Cameo	Artif	Art	U	6.00
0.25	349	Tinder Farm	Land	Lnd	C	3.00
1.00	81	Tolarian Emissary	Blue	Cr	U	6.00
0.25	82	Tower Drake	Blue	Cr	C	3.00
0.25	217	Tranquility	Green	Sor	C	3.00
0.25	83	Traveler's Cloak	Blue	E	C	3.00
1.00	218	Treefolk Healer	Green	Cr	U	6.00
1.00	127	Trench Wurm	Black	Cr	U	6.00
6.00	280	Treva, the Renewer	Multi	Cr	R	22.50
1.00	315	Treva's Attendant	Artif	Art	U	6.00
0.25	176	Tribal Flames	Red	Sor	C	3.00
1.00	316	Troll-Horn Cameo	Artif	Art	U	6.00
5.00	281	Tsabo Tavoc	Multi	Cr	R	20.00
5.00	128	Tsabo's Assassin	Black	Cr	R	20.00
5.00	129	Tsabo's Decree	Black	Ins	R	20.00
6.00	317	Tsabo's Web	Artif	Art	R	20.00
0.25	177	Turf Wound	Red	Ins	C	3.00
5.00	130	Twilight's Call	Black	Sor	R	20.00
6.00	282	Undermine	Multi	Ins	R	25.00
1.00	283	Urborg Drake	Multi	Cr	U	6.00
1.00	131	Urborg Emissary	Black	Cr	U	6.00
0.25	132	Urborg Phantom	Black	Cr	C	3.00
1.00	133	Urborg Shambler	Black	Cr	U	6.00
0.25	134	Urborg Skeleton	Black	Cr	C	3.00
2.00	350	Urborg Volcano	Land	Lnd	U	9.00
4.00	318	Urza's Filter	Artif	Art	R	20.00
6.00	178	Urza's Rage	Red	Ins	R	22.50
8.00	219	Utopia Tree	Green	Cr	R	22.50
6.00	220	Verdeloth the Ancient	Green	Cr	R	20.00
1.00	221	Verduran Emissary	Green	Cr	U	6.00
0.25	179	Viashino Grappler	Red	Cr	C	3.00
1.00	284	Vicious Kavu	Multi	Cr	U	6.00
0.25	222	Vigorous Charge	Green	Ins	C	3.00
5.00	285	Vile Consumption	Multi	E	R	20.00
1.00	84	Vodalian Hypnotist	Blue	Cr	U	6.00
0.25	85	Vodalian Merchant	Blue	Cr	C	3.00
0.25	86	Vodalian Serpent	Blue	Cr	C	3.00
0.25	286	Vodalian Zombie	Multi	Cr	C	3.00
5.00	287	Void	Multi	Sor	R	22.50
1.00	288	Voracious Cobra	Multi	Cr	U	6.00
1.00	223	Wallop	Green	Sor	U	6.00
0.25	224	Wandering Stream	Green	Sor	C	3.00
1.00	87	Wash Out	Blue	Sor	U	6.00
1.00	296	Wax/Wane	Gr/Wh	Ins	U	7.00
1.00	44	Wayfaring Giant	White	Cr	U	6.00
4.00	88	Well-Laid Plans	Blue	E	R	20.00
0.25	225	Whip Silk	Green	E	C	3.00
0.25	289	Wings of Hope	Multi	E	C	3.00
4.00	45	Winnow	White	Ins	R	20.00
0.25	89	Worldly Counsel	Blue	Ins	C	3.00
0.25	290	Yavimaya Barbarian	Multi	Cr	C	3.00
1.00	291	Yavimaya Kavu	Multi	Cr	U	6.00
5.00	135	Yawgmoth's Agenda	Black	E	R	20.00
1.00	90	Zanam Djinn	Blue	Cr	U	6.00
0.25	180	Zap	Red	Ins	C	3.00

RARITY KEY C = Common (black symbol)   U = Uncommon (silver symbol)   R = Rare (gold symbol)   **CARD TYPES: See page 246**

Lord of the Undead ①☿☿

Creature — Lord

All Zombies get +1/+1.
1 ☿, ☿: Return target Zombie card from your graveyard to your hand.

"I confer with Death itself. What could you possibly do to injure me?"
—Lord Dralnu

Illus. Brom
©1993-2001 Wizards of the Coast, Inc. 44/143   2/2

Magic: The Gathering • *Planeshift*

Wizards of the Coast • Released **February 2001**

143 cards and **143** foil cards in set • **IDENTIFIER: Galaxy symbol; black borders**

- Starter decks contain 60 cards; starter displays contain 12 starters
- Booster packs contain 15 cards; booster displays contain 36 boosters
- Pre-constructed decks include **Barrage**, **Comeback**, **Domain**, and **Scout**

Planeshift, the first expansion in the *Invasion* block, builds on the themes of that earlier set including "domain" cards and beefed-up kicker spells.

A new mechanic is introduced called "gating," wherein the spell requires the return of a "permanent" to the caster's hand when played. Many of these spells produce powerful effects for very little mana.

The gold rush also continued with plenty of multicolor cards, many of them quite playable. Cards that shine in *Planeshift* include **Meddling Mage**, the cycle of Battlemages, **Phyrexian Scuta**, **Eladamri's Call**, **Fleetfoot Panther**, and **Questing Phelddagrif**. — *Bennie Smith*

PLANESHIFT

You will need **16** nine-pocket pages to store this set. (8 doubled up)

Too new for pricing!
See current issues of SCRYE for the latest after-market prices!

Reg #	Card Name	Color	Type	Rarity	Foil
20	Allied Strategies	Blue	Sor	U	
77	Alpha Kavu	Green	Cr	U	
78	Amphibious Kavu	Green	Cr	C	
96	Ancient Spider	Multi	Cr	R	
21	Arctic Merfolk	Blue	Cr	C	
1	Aura Blast	White	Ins	C	
2	Aurora Griffin	White	Cr	C	
39	Bog Down	Black	Sor	C	
58	Caldera Kavu	Red	Cr	C	
97	Cavern Harpy	Multi	Cr	C	
98	Cloud Cover	Multi	E	R	
22	Confound	Blue	Ins	C	
136	Crosis's Catacombs	Land	Lnd	U	
99	Crosis's Charm	Multi	Ins	U	
137	Darigaaz's Caldera	Land	Lnd	U	
100	Darigaaz's Charm	Multi	Ins	U	
101	Daring Leap	Multi	Ins	U	
40	Dark Suspicions	Black	E	R	
59	Deadapult	Red	E	R	
41	Death Bomb	Black	Ins	C	
102	Destructive Flow	Multi	E	R	
42	Diabolic Intent	Black	Sor	R	
3	Disciple of Kangee	White	Cr	C	
4	Dominaria's Judgment	White	Ins	R	
103	Doomsday Specter	Multi	Cr	R	
131	Draco	Artif	ArtCr	R	
104	Dralnu's Crusade	Multi	E	R	
23	Dralnu's Pet	Blue	Cr	R	
138	Dromar's Cavern	Land	Lnd	U	
105	Dromar's Charm	Multi	Ins	U	
106	Eladamri's Call	Multi	Ins	U	
24	Ertai's Trickery	Blue	Ins	U	
107	Ertai, the Corrupted	Multi	Cr	R	
25	Escape Routes	Blue		C	
43	Exotic Disease	Black	Sor	U	
79	Falling Timber	Green	Ins	C	

Reg #	Card Name	Color	Type	Rarity	Foil
60	Flametongue Kavu	Red	Cr	U	
108	Fleetfoot Panther	Multi	Cr	U	
139	Forsaken City	Land	Lnd	R	
80	Gaea's Herald	Green	Cr	R	
81	Gaea's Might	Green	Ins	C	
26	Gainsay	Blue	Ins	U	
109	Gerrard's Command	Multi	Ins	C	
61	Goblin Game	Red	Sor	R	
5	Guard Dogs	White	Cr	U	
6	Heroic Defiance	White	E Cr	C	
7	Hobble	White	E Cr	C	
8	Honorable Scout	White	Cr	C	
110	Horned Kavu	Multi	Cr	C	
111	Hull Breach	Multi	Sor	C	
27	Hunting Drake	Blue	Cr	C	
62	Implode	Red	Sor	U	
63	Insolence	Red	E Cr	C	
64	Kavu Recluse	Red	Cr	C	
65	Keldon Mantle	Red	E Cr	C	
112	Keldon Twilight	Multi	E	R	
9	Lashknife Barrier	White	E	U	
113	Lava Zombie	Multi	Cr	C	
44	Lord of the Undead	Black	Cr	R	
45	Maggot Carrier	Black	Cr	C	
66	Magma Burst	Red	Ins	C	
82	Magnigoth Treefolk	Green	Cr	R	
114	Malicious Advice	Multi	Ins	C	
132	Mana Cylix	Artif	Art	U	
10	March of Souls	White	Sor	R	
115	Marsh Crocodile	Multi	Cr	U	
116	Meddling Mage	Multi	Cr	R	
140	Meteor Crater	Land	Lnd	R	
67	Mire Kavu	Red	Cr	C	
83	Mirrorwood Treefolk	Green	Cr	U	
68	Mogg Jailer	Red	Cr	U	
69	Mogg Sentry	Red	Cr	R	
46	Morgue Toad	Black	Cr	C	
84	Multani's Harmony	Green	E Cr	U	
117	Natural Emergence	Multi	E	R	
85	Nemata, Grove Guardian	Green	Cr	R	
47	Nightscape Battlemage	Black	Cr	U	
48	Nightscape Familiar	Black	Cr	C	
49	Noxious Vapors	Black	Sor	U	
11	Orim's Chant	White	Ins	R	
50	Phyrexian Bloodstock	Black	Cr	C	
51	Phyrexian Scuta	Black	Cr	R	
118	Phyrexian Tyranny	Multi	E	R	
28	Planar Overlay	Blue	Sor	R	
86	Planeswalker's Favor	Green	E	R	
70	Planeswalker's Fury	Red	E	R	
12	Planeswalker's Mirth	White	E	R	
29	Planeswalker's Mischief	Blue	E	R	
52	Planeswalker's Scorn	Black	E	R	
13	Pollen Remedy	White	Ins	C	

Reg #	Card Name	Color	Type	Rarity	Foil
87	Primal Growth	Green	Sor	C	
88	Pygmy Kavu	Green	Cr	C	
119	Questing Phelddagrif	Multi	Cr	R	
89	Quirion Dryad	Green	Cr	R	
90	Quirion Explorer	Green	Cr	C	
120	Radiant Kavu	Multi	Cr	R	
121	Razing Snidd	Multi	Cr	U	
122	Rith's Charm	Multi	Ins	U	
141	Rith's Grove	Land	Lnd	U	
91	Root Greevil	Green	Cr	C	
30	Rushing River	Blue	Ins	C	
14	Samite Elder	White	Cr	R	
15	Samite Pilgrim	White	Cr	C	
123	Sawtooth Loon	Multi	Cr	U	
31	Sea Snidd	Blue	Cr	C	
32	Shifting Sky	Blue	E	U	
124	Shivan Wurm	Multi	Cr	R	
53	Shriek of Dread	Black	Ins	C	
125	Silver Drake	Multi	Cr	C	
71	Singe	Red	Ins	C	
54	Sinister Strength	Black	E Cr	C	
33	Sisay's Ingenuity	Blue	E Cr	C	
133	Skyship Weatherlight	Artif	Art	R	
92	Skyshroud Blessing	Green	Ins	U	
55	Slay	Black	Ins	U	
34	Sleeping Potion	Blue	E Cr	C	
72	Slingshot Goblin	Red	Cr	C	
126	Sparkcaster	Multi	Cr	U	
134	Star Compass	Artif	Art	U	
127	Steel Leaf Paladin	Multi	Cr	C	
93	Stone Kavu	Green	Cr	C	
35	Stormscape Battlemage	Blue	Cr	U	
36	Stormscape Familiar	Blue	Cr	C	
73	Strafe	Red	Sor	U	
135	Stratadon	Artif	ArtCr	U	
37	Sunken Hope	Blue	E	R	
16	Sunscape Battlemage	White	Cr	U	
17	Sunscape Familiar	White	Cr	C	
18	Surprise Deployment	White	Ins	U	
74	Tahngarth, Talruum Hero	Red	Cr	R	
142	Terminal Moraine	Land	Lnd	U	
128	Terminate	Multi	Ins	C	
94	Thornscape Battlemage	Green	Cr	U	
95	Thornscape Familiar	Green	Cr	U	
75	Thunderscape Battlemage	Red	Cr	U	
76	Thunderscape Familiar	Red	Cr	C	
129	Treva's Charm	Multi	Ins	U	
143	Treva's Ruins	Land	Lnd	U	
130	Urza's Guilt	Multi	Sor	R	
19	Voice of All	White	Cr	U	
56	Volcano Imp	Black	Cr	C	
57	Warped Devotion	Black	E	U	
38	Waterspout Elemental	Blue	Cr	R	

RARITY KEY C = Common (black symbol) U = Uncommon (silver symbol) R = Rare (gold symbol) **CARD TYPES: See page 246**

Magic: The Gathering • Portal

Wizards of the Coast • Released **June 1997**

200 cards and **22** variants in set • **IDENTIFIER: Circular symbol, © 1997**

- Starters contain two 35-card decks, playmats, and booster pack; starter displays contain 12 starters
- Booster packs contain 15 cards; booster displays contain 36 boosters

Wizards of the Coast released **Portal** as an introductory **Magic** set for non-gamers-greatly simplifying the rules and reducing the number of card types to three: Land, Summon Creature, and Sorcery cards. The starter set comes with two 35-card pre-constructed decks, a booster pack, two playmats, a play guide, and a rulebook. The playmat lays the basics of the game out for a player to view while playing, including which cards go where, where to place the deck and discard pile, a life total bar, and a list of the most basic rules.

The decks are constructed in a specific order; players do not shuffle before they begin their first game. The play guide outlines for the players exactly what they will do during the first five rounds of their game, from what cards are drawn to what cards to play, how they attack and who will defend. It's an excellent introduction for a complete novice, as it gives the player a feel for the game's action.

The cards themselves are distinct from other *Magic* cards in that they have special symbols to help players identify the offense and defense values of the creatures. Cards also explain the specifics of the play and do not rely on simply listing an ability name. The card art is little different, including some pieces of questionable content for an introductory set designed for young players. — *James Mishler*

Set (200 cards + 22 variants)	125.00
Starter Display Box	90.00
Booster Display Box	87.50
Starter Deck	9.00
Booster Pack	3.00
Portal Gift Set	15.00

You will need 25 nine-pocket pages to store this set. (13 doubled up)

Card name	Color	Type	Rarity	Price
1				
☐ Alabaster Dragon	White	Sum	R	6.00
☐ Alluring Scent	Green	Sor	R	2.00
☐ Anaconda (ver. 1)	Green	Sum	U	0.50
☐ Anaconda (ver. 2)	Green	Sum	U	0.50
☐ Ancestral Memories	Blue	Sor	R	3.00
☐ Angelic Blessing	White	Sor	C	0.10
☐ Archangel	White	Sum	R	8.50
☐ Ardent Militia	White	Sum	U	0.50
☐ Armageddon	White	Sor	R	10.00
2				
☐ Armored Pegasus	White	Sum	C	0.10
☐ Arrogant Vampire	Black	Sum	U	0.50
☐ Assassin's Blade	Black	Sor	U	0.50
☐ Balance of Power	Blue	Sor	R	3.50
☐ Baleful Stare	Blue	Sor	U	0.50
☐ Bee Sting	Green	Sor	U	0.50
☐ Blaze (ver. 1)	Red	Sor	U	0.50
☐ Blaze (ver. 2)	Red	Sor	U	0.50
☐ Blessed Reversal	White	Sor	R	3.00
3				
☐ Blinding Light	White	Sor	R	2.30
☐ Bog Imp	Black	Sum	C	0.10
☐ Bog Raiders	Black	Sum	C	0.10
☐ Bog Wraith	Black	Sum	U	0.50
☐ Boiling Seas	Red	Sor	U	0.50
☐ Border Guard	White	Sum	C	0.10
☐ Breath of Life	White	Sor	C	0.10
☐ Bull Hippo	Green	Sum	U	0.50
☐ Burning Cloak	Red	Sor	C	0.10
4				
☐ Capricious Sorcerer	Blue	Sum	R	2.00
☐ Charging Bandits	Black	Sum	U	0.50
☐ Charging Paladin	White	Sum	U	0.50
☐ Charging Rhino	Green	Sum	R	2.00
☐ Cloak of Feathers	Blue	Sor	C	0.10
☐ Cloud Dragon	Blue	Sum	R	4.00
☐ Cloud Pirates	Blue	Sum	C	0.10
☐ Cloud Spirit	Blue	Sum	U	0.50
☐ Command of Unsummoning	Blue	Sor	U	0.50
5				
☐ Coral Eel	Blue	Sum	C	0.10
☐ Craven Giant	Red	Sum	C	0.10

Card name	Color	Type	Rarity	Price
☐ Craven Knight	Black	Sum	C	0.10
☐ Cruel Bargain	Black	Sor	R	3.00
☐ Cruel Fate	Blue	Sor	R	3.00
☐ Cruel Tutor	Black	Sor	R	3.00
☐ Deep Wood	Green	Sor	U	0.50
☐ Deep-Sea Serpent	Blue	Sum	U	0.50
☐ Defiant Stand	White	Sor	U	0.50
6				
☐ Déjà Vu	Blue	Sor	C	0.10
☐ Desert Drake	Red	Sum	U	0.50
☐ Devastation	Red	Sor	R	4.00
☐ Devoted Hero	White	Sum	C	0.10
☐ Djinn of the Lamp	Blue	Sum	R	4.50
☐ Dread Charge	Black	Sor	R	3.50
☐ Dread Reaper	Black	Sum	R	3.00
☐ Dry Spell	Black	Sor	U	0.30
☐ Earthquake	Red	Sor	R	5.00
7				
☐ Ebon Dragon	Black	Sum	R	5.00
☐ Elite Cat Warrior (ver. 1)	Green	Sum	C	0.15
☐ Elite Cat Warrior (ver. 2)	Green	Sum	C	0.15
☐ Elven Cache	Green	Sor	C	0.10
☐ Elvish Ranger	Green	Sum	C	0.10
☐ Endless Cockroaches	Black	Sum	R	3.00
☐ Exhaustion	Blue	Sor	R	3.00
☐ False Peace	White	Sor	C	0.10
☐ Feral Shadow	Black	Sum	C	0.10
8				
☐ Final Strike	Black	Sor	R	3.00
☐ Fire Dragon	Red	Sum	R	5.00
☐ Fire Imp	Red	Sum	U	0.50
☐ Fire Snake	Red	Sum	C	0.10
☐ Fire Tempest	Red	Sor	R	3.00
☐ Flashfires	Red	Sor	U	0.50

Card name	Color	Type	Rarity	Price
☐ Fleet-Footed Monk	White	Sum	C	0.10
☐ Flux	Blue	Sor	U	0.50
☐ Foot Soldiers	White	Sum	C	0.10
9				
☐ Forest (ver. 1)	Land	Lnd	L	0.25
☐ Forest (ver. 2)	Land	Lnd	L	0.25
☐ Forest (ver. 3)	Land	Lnd	L	0.20
☐ Forest (ver. 4)	Land	Lnd	L	0.20
☐ Forked Lightning	Red	Sor	R	3.00
☐ Fruition	Green	Sor	C	0.10
☐ Giant Octopus	Blue	Sum	C	0.10
☐ Giant Spider	Green	Sum	C	0.10
☐ Gifts of Estates	White	Sor	R	2.50
10				
☐ Goblin Bully	Red	Sum	C	0.10
☐ Gorilla Warrior	Green	Sum	C	0.10
☐ Gravedigger	Black	Sum	U	0.50
☐ Grizzly Bears	Green	Sum	C	0.10
☐ Hand of Death (ver. 1)	Black	Sor	C	0.15
☐ Hand of Death (ver. 2)	Black	Sor	C	0.15
☐ Harsh Justice	White	Sor	R	3.00
☐ Highland Giant	Red	Sum	C	0.10
☐ Hill Giant	Red	Sum	C	0.10
11				
☐ Horned Turtle	Blue	Sum	C	0.10
☐ Howling Fury	Black	Sor	C	0.10
☐ Hulking Cyclops	Red	Sum	U	0.50
☐ Hulking Goblin	Red	Sum	C	0.10
☐ Hurricane	Green	Sor	R	1.50
☐ Ingenious Thief	Blue	Sum	U	0.50
☐ Island (ver. 1)	Land	Lnd	L	0.25
☐ Island (ver. 2)	Land	Lnd	L	0.25
☐ Island (ver. 3)	Land	Lnd	L	0.10
12				
☐ Island (ver. 4)	Land	Lnd	L	0.10

RARITY KEY C = Common U = Uncommon R = Rare L = Land UR = Ultra Rare F = Foil card **CARD TYPES: See page 246**

Card name	Color	Type	Rarity	Price
Jungle Lion	Green	Sum	C	0.10
Keen-Eyed Archers	White	Sum	C	0.10
King's Assassin	Black	Sum	R	6.00
Knight Errant	White	Sum	C	0.10
Last Chance	Red	Sor	R	3.50
Lava Axe	Red	Sor	C	0.10
Lava Flow	Red	Sor	U	0.50
Lizard Warrior	Red	Sum	C	0.10
Man-o'-War	Blue	Sum	U	0.80
Mercenary Knight	Black	Sum	R	3.00
Merfolk of the Pearl Trident	Blue	Sum	C	0.10
Mind Knives	Black	Sor	C	0.10
Mind Rot	Black	Sor	C	0.10
Minotaur Warrior	Red	Sum	C	0.10
Mobilize	Green	Sor	C	0.10
Monstrous Growth (ver. 1)	Green	Sor	C	0.15
Monstrous Growth (ver. 2)	Green	Sor	C	0.15
Moon Sprite	Green	Sum	U	0.50
Mountain (ver. 1)	Land	Lnd	L	0.25
Mountain (ver. 2)	Land	Lnd	L	0.20
Mountain (ver. 3)	Land	Lnd	L	0.10
Mountain (ver. 4)	Land	Lnd	L	0.10
Mountain Goat	Red	Sum	U	0.50
Muck Rats	Black	Sum	C	0.10
Mystic Denial	Blue	Sor	U	1.00
Natural Order	Green	Sor	R	4.00
Natural Spring	Green	Sor	U	0.50
Nature's Cloak	Green	Sor	R	3.00
Nature's Lore	Green	Sor	C	0.10
Nature's Ruin	Black	Sor	U	1.00
Needle Storm	Green	Sor	U	1.00
Noxious Toad	Black	Sum	U	0.50
Omen	Blue	Sor	C	0.10
Owl Familiar	Blue	Sum	C	0.10
Panther Warriors	Green	Sum	C	0.10
Path of Peace	White	Sor	C	0.10
Personal Tutor	Blue	Sor	U	0.80
Phantom Warrior	Blue	Sum	R	2.00
Pillaging Horde	Red	Sum	R	7.00
Plains (ver. 1)	Land	Lnd	L	0.25
Plains (ver. 2)	Land	Lnd	L	0.25
Plains (ver. 3)	Land	Lnd	L	0.20
Plains (ver. 4)	Land	Lnd	L	0.10
Plant Elemental	Green	Sum	U	0.50
Primeval Force	Green	Sum	R	3.00
Prosperity	Blue	Sor	R	2.50
Pyroclasm	Red	Sor	R	2.50
Python	Black	Sum	C	0.10
Raging Cougar	Red	Sum	C	0.10
Raging Goblin (ver. 1)	Red	Sum	C	0.25
Raging Goblin (ver. 2)	Red	Sum	C	0.25
Raging Minotaur	Red	Sum	C	0.10
Rain of Salt	Red	Sor	U	0.70
Rain of Tears	Black	Sor	U	1.00
Raise Dead	Black	Sor	C	0.10
Redwood Treefolk	Green	Sum	C	0.10
Regal Unicorn	White	Sum	C	0.10
Renewing Dawn	White	Sor	U	0.50
Rowan Treefolk	Green	Sum	C	0.10
Sacred Knight	White	Sum	C	0.10
Sacred Nectar	White	Sor	C	0.10
Scorching Spear	Red	Sor	C	0.10
Scorching Winds	Red	Sor	U	0.50
Seasoned Marshal	White	Sum	U	0.50
Serpent Assassin	Black	Sum	R	4.00
Serpent Warrior	Black	Sum	C	0.10
Skeletal Crocodile	Black	Sum	C	0.10
Skeletal Snake	Black	Sum	C	0.10
Snapping Drake	Blue	Sum	C	0.10
Sorcerous Sight	Blue	Sor	C	0.10
Soul Shred	Black	Sor	C	0.10
Spined Wurm	Green	Sum	C	0.10
Spiritual Guardian	White	Sum	R	3.00
Spitting Earth	Red	Sor	C	0.15
Spotted Griffin	White	Sum	C	0.10
Stalking Tiger	Green	Sum	C	0.10
Starlight	White	Sor	U	0.50
Starlit Angel	White	Sum	U	0.50
Steadfastness	White	Sor	C	0.10
Stern Marshal	White	Sum	R	2.50
Stone Rain	Red	Sor	C	0.10
Storm Crow	Blue	Sum	C	0.10
Summer Bloom	Green	Sor	R	2.00
Swamp (ver. 1)	Land	Lnd	L	0.25
Swamp (ver. 2)	Land	Lnd	L	0.20
Swamp (ver. 3)	Land	Lnd	L	0.10
Swamp (ver. 4)	Land	Lnd	L	0.10
Sylvan Tutor	Green	Sor	R	3.00
Symbol of Unsummoning	Blue	Sor	C	0.10
Taunt	Blue	Sor	R	2.00
Temporary Truce	White	Sor	R	2.30
Theft of Dreams	Blue	Sor	U	0.50
Thing from the Deep	Blue	Sum	R	3.00
Thundering Wurm	Green	Sum	R	3.00
Thundermare	Red	Sum	R	7.80
Tidal Surge	Blue	Sor	C	0.10
Time Ebb	Blue	Sor	C	0.10
Touch of Brilliance	Blue	Sor	C	0.10
Treetop Defense	Green	Sor	R	3.00
Undying Beast	Black	Sum	C	0.10
Untamed Wilds	Green	Sor	U	0.50
Valorous Charge	White	Sor	U	0.50
Vampiric Feast	Black	Sum	U	0.50
Vampiric Touch	Black	Sor	C	0.10
Venerable Monk	White	Sum	U	0.30
Vengeance	White	Sor	U	0.50
Virtue's Ruin	Black	Sor	U	1.00
Volcanic Dragon	Red	Sum	R	7.20
Volcanic Hammer	Red	Sor	C	0.25
Wall of Granite	Red	Sum	U	0.50
Wall of Swords	White	Sum	U	0.50
Warrior's Charge (ver. 1)	White	Sor	C	0.15
Warrior's Charge (ver. 2)	White	Sor	C	0.15
Whiptail Wurm	Green	Sum	U	0.50
Wicked Pact	Black	Sor	R	3.00
Willow Dryad	Green	Sum	C	0.10
Wind Drake	Blue	Sum	C	0.10
Winds of Change	Red	Sor	R	3.00
Winter's Grasp	Green	Sor	U	0.70
Withering Gaze	Blue	Sor	U	0.50
Wood Elves	Green	Sum	R	2.50
Wrath of God	White	Sor	R	9.70

Dakmor Bat ⓑⓑ
Creature — Bat ⊘
Flying
The bat thrives on what underestimates it.
Illus. Una Fricker. 1/10

Magic: The Gathering • Portal Second Age

Wizards of the Coast • Released **June 1998**

155 cards, **10** variants in set • **IDENTIFIER: Circular symbol © 1998**

- Starter decks contain 40 cards; starter displays contain 15 starters
- Booster packs contain 10 cards; booster displays contain 36 boosters

This set continues the tradition of the original **Portal** set, and offers a general story background to tie together the cards, as was being done with the standard **Magic** sets.

Portal Second Age card art seems to have been crafted to be been friendlier to new-comers. It was the last true "Portal" set available in the United States, as the next intro-ductory set offered was a 1999 **Starter** repackaging of **Classic**. — *James Mishler*

PORTAL SECOND AGE

You will need **19** nine-pocket pages to store this set. (10 doubled up)

Set (155 cards + 10 variants)	150.00
Starter Display Box	35.00
Booster Display Box	90.00
Starter Deck	4.00
Booster Pack	2.50
Portal Second Age Gift Set	13.00

Card name	Color	Type	Rarity	Price
Abyssal Nightstalker	Black	Sum	U	0.45
Air Elemental	Blue	Sum	U	0.45
Alaborn Cavalier	White	Sum	U	0.45
Alaborn Grenadier	White	Sum	C	0.10
Alaborn Musketeer	White	Sum	C	0.10
Alaborn Trooper	White	Sum	C	0.10
Alaborn Veteran	White	Sum	R	2.80
Alaborn Zealot	White	Sum	U	0.45
Alluring Scent	Green	Sor	R	2.00
Ancient Craving	Black	Sor	R	3.50
Angel of Fury	White	Sum	R	3.50
Angel of Mercy	White	Sum	U	0.45
Angelic Blessing	White	Sor	C	0.10
Angelic Wall	White	Sum	C	0.10
Apprentice Sorcerer	Blue	Sum	U	0.45
Archangel	White	Sum	R	5.00
Armageddon	White	Sor	R	6.40
Armored Galleon	Blue	Sum	U	0.45
Armored Griffin	White	Sum	U	0.45
Barbtooth Wurm	Green	Sum	C	0.10
Bargain	White	Sor	U	0.45
Bear Cub	Green	Sum	C	0.10
Bee Sting	Green	Sor	U	0.45
Blaze	Red	Sor	U	0.45
Bloodcurdling Scream	Black	Sor	U	0.45
Breath of Life	White	Sor	C	0.10
Brimstone Dragon	Red	Sum	R	4.80
Brutal Nightstalker	Black	Sum	U	0.45
Chorus of Woe	Black	Sor	C	0.10
Coastal Wizard	Blue	Sum	U	3.00
Coercion	Black	Sor	U	0.40
Cruel Edict	Black	Sor	C	0.10
Cunning Giant	Red	Sum	R	2.10
Dakmor Bat	Black	Sum	C	0.10
Dakmor Plague	Black	Sor	U	0.25
Dakmor Scorpion	Black	Sum	C	0.10
Dakmor Sorceress	Black	Sum	R	1.00
Dark Offering	Black	Sor	U	0.60

RARITY KEY C = Common U = Uncommon R = Rare L = Land UR = Ultra Rare 'F = Foil card **CARD TYPES: See page 246**

Card name	Color	Type	Rarity	Price
Deathcoil Wurm	Green	Sum	R	1.00
Deep Wood	Green	Sor	U	1.00
Déjà Vu	Blue	Sor	C	0.10
Denizen of the Deep	Blue	Sum	R	4.50
Earthquake	Red	Sor	R	2.80
Exhaustion	Blue	Sor	R	3.00
Extinguish	Blue	Sor	C	0.10
Eye Spy	Blue	Sor	U	0.45
False Summoning	Blue	Sor	C	0.10
Festival of Trokin	White	Sor	C	0.10
Forest (ver. 1)	Land	Lnd	L	0.15
Forest (ver. 2)	Land	Lnd	L	0.15
Forest (ver. 3)	Land	Lnd	L	0.15
Foul Spirit	Black	Sum	U	0.35
Goblin Cavaliers	Red	Sum	C	0.10
Goblin Firestarter	Red	Sum	U	0.45
Goblin General	Red	Sum	R	3.00
Goblin Glider	Red	Sum	C	0.10
Goblin Lore	Red	Sor	U	0.45
Goblin Matron	Red	Sum	U	0.45
Goblin Mountaineer	Red	Sum	C	0.10
Goblin Piker	Red	Sum	C	0.10
Goblin Raider	Red	Sum	C	0.10
Goblin War Cry	Red	Sor	U	0.45
Goblin War Strike	Red	Sor	C	0.10
Golden Bear	Green	Sum	C	0.10
Hand of Death	Black	Sor	C	0.10
Harmony of Nature	Green	Sor	U	0.45
Hidden Horror	Black	Sum	R	3.00
Hurricane	Green	Sor	R	2.50
Ironhoof Ox	Green	Sum	U	0.45
Island (ver. 1)	Land	Lnd	L	0.15
Island (ver. 2)	Land	Lnd	L	0.15
Island (ver. 3)	Land	Lnd	L	0.15
Jagged Lightning	Red	Sor	U	0.45
Just Fate	White	Sor	R	1.00
Kiss of Death	Black	Sor	U	0.45
Lava Axe	Red	Sor	C	0.10
Lone Wolf	Green	Sum	U	0.45
Lurking Nightstalker	Black	Sum	C	0.10
Lynx	Green	Sum	C	0.10
Magma Giant	Red	Sum	R	3.50
Mind Rot	Black	Sor	C	0.10
Moaning Spirit	Black	Sum	C	0.10
Monstrous Growth	Green	Sor	C	0.10
Mountain (ver. 1)	Land	Lnd	L	0.15
Mountain (ver. 2)	Land	Lnd	L	0.15
Mountain (ver. 3)	Land	Lnd	L	0.15
Muck Rats	Black	Sum	C	0.10
Mystic Denial	Blue	Sor	U	0.45
Natural Spring	Green	Sor	C	0.10
Nature's Lore	Green	Sor	C	0.10
Nightstalker Engine	Black	Sum	R	1.00
Norwood Archers	Green	Sum	C	0.10
Norwood Priestess	Green	Sum	R	3.00
Norwood Ranger	Green	Sum	C	0.10
Norwood Riders	Green	Sum	C	0.10
Norwood Warrior	Green	Sum	C	0.10
Obsidian Giant	Red	Sum	U	0.45
Ogre Arsonist	Red	Sum	U	0.45
Ogre Berserker	Red	Sum	C	0.10
Ogre Taskmaster	Red	Sum	U	0.45
Ogre Warrior	Red	Sum	C	0.10
Path of Peace	White	Sor	C	0.10
Piracy	Blue	Sor	R	3.00
Plains (ver. 1)	Land	Lnd	L	0.15
Plains (ver. 2)	Land	Lnd	L	0.15
Plains (ver. 3)	Land	Lnd	L	0.15
Plated Wurm	Green	Sum	C	0.10
Predatory Nightstalker	Black	Sum	U	0.45
Prowling Nightstalker	Black	Sum	C	0.10
Raging Goblin	Red	Sum	C	0.10
Raiding Nightstalker	Black	Sum	C	0.10
Rain of Daggers	Black	Sor	R	3.00
Raise Dead	Black	Sor	C	0.10
Rally the Troops	White	Sor	U	0.45
Ravenous Rats	Black	Sum	C	0.10
Razorclaw Bear	Green	Sum	R	3.00
Relentless Assault	Red	Sor	R	4.00
Remove	Blue	Sor	U	0.45
Renewing Touch	Green	Sor	U	0.45
Return of the Nightstalkers	Black	Sor	R	4.00
Righteous Charge	White	Sor	C	0.10
Righteous Fury	White	Sor	R	3.30
River Bear	Green	Sum	U	0.45
Salvage	Green	Sor	C	0.10
Screeching Drake	Blue	Sum	C	0.10
Sea Drake	Blue	Sum	U	0.45
Sleight of Hand	Blue	Sor	C	0.10
Spitting Earth	Red	Sor	C	0.10
Steam Catapult	White	Sum	R	2.80
Steam Frigate	Blue	Sum	U	0.45
Stone Rain	Red	Sor	C	0.10
Swamp (ver. 1)	Land	Lnd	L	0.15
Swamp (ver. 2)	Land	Lnd	L	0.15
Swamp (ver. 3)	Land	Lnd	L	0.15
Swarm of Rats	Black	Sum	C	0.10
Sylvan Basilisk	Green	Sum	R	3.00
Sylvan Yeti	Green	Sum	R	4.00
Talas	Blue	Sum	R	1.50
Talas Air Ship	Blue	Sum	C	0.10
Talas Explorer	Blue	Sum	C	0.10
Talas Merchant	Blue	Sum	C	0.10
Talas Scout	Blue	Sum	C	0.10
Talas Warrior	Blue	Sum	R	1.00
Temple Acolyte	White	Sum	C	0.10
Temple Elder	White	Sum	U	0.45
Temporal Manipulation	Blue	Sor	R	3.00
Theft of Dreams	Blue	Sor	U	0.45
Tidal Surge	Blue	Sor	C	0.10
Time Ebb	Blue	Sor	C	0.10
Touch of Brilliance	Blue	Sor	C	0.10
Town Sentry	White	Sum	C	0.10
Tree Monkey	Green	Sum	C	0.10
Tremor	Red	Sor	C	0.10
Trokin High Guard	White	Sum	C	0.10
Undo	Blue	Sor	U	0.40
Untamed Wilds	Green	Sor	U	0.45
Vampiric Spirit	Black	Sum	R	4.00
Vengeance	White	Sor	U	0.45
Volcanic Hammer	Red	Sor	C	0.10
Volunteer Militia	White	Sum	C	0.10
Warrior's Stand	White	Sor	U	0.45
Wild Griffin	White	Sum	C	0.10
Wild Ox	Green	Sum	U	0.45
Wildfire	Red	Sor	R	4.30
Wind Sail	Blue	Sor	C	0.10

Magic: The Gathering • Portal: Three Kingdoms

Wizards of the Coast • Released **June 1999**

170 cards and **10** variants in set • **IDENTIFIER: Three horizontal marks**

- Starter decks contain 70 cards; starter displays contain 12 starters
- Booster packs contain 15 cards; booster displays contain 36 boosters

Combining Chinese history with mythology, the "Three Kingdoms" era stirs Chinese imaginations much as the Arthurian mythos does for Western imaginations. The rich historical background was often the subject of other games, most notably a series of Nintendo and computer games in the mid-'80s, and just begged to be used in a trading-card game format.

Wizards of the Coast answered the call, offering *Portal: Three Kingdoms* it not only in China and Japan but also as an introductory set in English in Australia — thus barely making our cut as a CCG originally published in English! — *James Mishler*

You will need **25** nine-pocket pages to store this set. (13 doubled up)

Zodiac Dog 2◊
Creature — Dog
Mountainwalk (If defending player has a mountain in play, Zodiac Dog can't be blocked.)
"...Jiang Wei alone still strove with might and main / Nine times more he fought the north—in vain...."
Illus. Qi Baocheng
2/120

Set (170 cards + 10 variants)	162.50
Starter Display Box	105.00
Booster Display Box	125.00
Starter Deck	10.00
Booster Pack	3.00

Card name	Color	Rarity	Price
Alert Shu Infantry	White	U	0.70
Ambition's Cost	Black	R	2.00
Balance of Power	Blue	R	2.00
Barbarian General	Red	U	0.60
Barbarian Horde	Red	C	0.15
Blaze	Red	U	0.45
Borrowing 100,000 Arrows	Blue	U	0.45
Borrowing the East Wind	Green	R	2.00
Brilliant Plan	Blue	U	0.60
Broken Dam	Blue	C	0.15
Burning Fields	Red	C	0.15
Burning of Xinye	Red	R	2.00
Cao Cao, Lord of Wei	Black	R	3.00
Cao Ren, Wei Commander"	Black	R	3.00
Capture of Jingzhou	Blue	R	2.00
Champion's Victory	Blue	U	0.40
Coercion	Black	U	0.45
Control of the Court	Red	U	0.45
Corrupt Court Official	Black	U	0.40
Corrupt Eunuchs	Red	U	0.45
Council of Advisors	Blue	U	0.60
Counterintelligence	Blue	U	0.40
Cunning Advisor	Black	U	0.45
Deception	Black	C	0.15
Desert Sandstorm	Red	C	0.15
Desperate Charge	Black	U	0.60
Diaochan, Artful Beauty	Red	R	3.00
Dong Zhou, the Tyrant	Red	R	3.00
Eightfold Maze	White	R	2.00
Empty City Ruse	White	U	0.45
Eunuchs' Intrigues	Red	U	0.45
Exhaustion	Blue	R	2.00
Extinguish	Blue	C	0.15

RARITY KEY C = Common U = Uncommon R = Rare L = Land UR = Ultra Rare F = Foil card **CARD TYPES: See page 246**

Card name	Color	Rarity	Price
False Defeat	White	C	0.15
False Mourning	Green	U	0.45
Famine	Black	U	0.45
5			
Fire Ambush	Red	C	0.15
Fire Bowman	Red	U	0.45
Flanking Troops	White	U	0.40
Forced Retreat	Blue	C	0.15
Forest (ver. 1)	Land	C	0.15
Forest (ver. 2)	Land	C	0.15
Forest (ver. 3)	Land	C	0.15
Forest Bear	Green	C	0.15
Ghostly Visit	Black	C	0.15
6			
Guan Yu, Sainted Warrior	White	R	3.00
Guan Yu's 1,000-Li March	White	R	2.00
Heavy Fog	Green	U	0.60
Hua Tuo, Honored Physician	Green	R	3.00
Huang Zhong, Shu General	White	R	3.00
Hunting Cheetah	Green	U	0.45
Imperial Edict	Black	C	0.15
Imperial Recruiter	Red	U	0.45
Imperial Seal	Black	R	2.00
7			
Independent Troops	Red	C	0.15
Island (ver. 1)	Land	C	0.15
Island (ver. 2)	Land	C	0.15
Island (ver. 3)	Land	C	0.15
Kongming, "Sleeping Dragon"	White	R	3.00
Kongming's Contraptions	White	R	2.00
Lady Sun	Blue	R	3.00
Lady Zhurong, Warrior Queen	Green	R	3.00
Liu Bei, Lord of Shu	White	R	3.00
8			
Lone Wolf	Green	U	0.40
Loyal Retainers	White	U	0.45
Lu Bu, Master-at-Arms	Red	R	3.00
Lu Meng, Wu General	Blue	R	3.00
Lu Su, Wu Advisor	Blue	R	3.00

Card name	Color	Rarity	Price
Lu Xun, Scholar General	Blue	R	3.00
Ma Chao, Western Warrior	Red	R	3.00
Marshaling the Troops	Green	R	2.00
Meng Huo, Barbarian King	Green	R	3.00
9			
Meng Huo's Horde	Green	C	0.15
Misfortune's Gain	White	C	0.15
Mountain (ver. 1)	Land	C	0.15
Mountain (ver. 2)	Land	C	0.15
Mountain (ver. 3)	Land	C	0.15
Mountain Bandit	Red	C	0.15
Mystic Denial	Blue	U	0.40
Overwhelming Forces	Black	R	2.00
Pang Tong, "Young Phoenix"	White	R	3.00
10			
Peach Garden Oath	White	U	0.45
Plains (ver. 1)	Land	C	0.15
Plains (ver. 2)	Land	C	0.15
Plains (ver. 3)	Land	C	0.15
Poison Arrow	Black	U	0.45
Preemptive Strike	Blue	C	0.15
Rally the Troops	White	U	0.70
Ravages of War	White	R	2.00
Ravaging Horde	Red	U	0.45
11			
Red Cliffs Armada	Blue	U	0.45
Relentless Assault	Red	R	2.00
Renegade Troops	Red	U	0.60
Return to Battle	Black	C	0.15
Riding Red Hare	White	C	0.15
Riding the Dilu Horse	Green	R	2.00
Rockslide Ambush	Red	U	0.60
Rolling Earthquake	Red	R	2.00
Sage's Knowledge	Blue	C	0.15
12			
Shu Cavalry	White	C	0.15
Shu Defender	White	C	0.15
Shu Elite Companions	White	U	0.70
Shu Elite Infantry	White	C	0.15
Shu Farmer	White	C	0.15
Shu Foot Soldiers	White	C	0.15
Shu General	White	U	0.45

Card name	Color	Rarity	Price
Shu Grain Caravan	White	C	0.15
Shu Soldier-Farmers	White	U	0.45
13			
Sima Yi, Wei Field Marshal	Black	R	3.00
Slashing Tiger	Green	R	2.00
Southern Elephant	Green	C	0.15
Spoils of Victory	Green	U	0.50
Spring of Eternal Peace	Green	C	0.15
Stalking Tiger	Green	C	0.15
Stolen Grain	Black	U	0.45
Stone Catapult	Black	R	2.00
Stone Rain	Red	C	0.15
14			
Strategic Planning	Blue	U	0.50
Straw Soldiers	Blue	C	0.15
Sun Ce, Young Conqueror	Blue	R	3.00
Sun Quan, Lord of Wu	Blue	R	3.00
Swamp (ver. 1)	Land	C	0.15
Swamp (ver. 2)	Land	C	0.15
Swamp (ver. 3)	Land	C	0.15
Taoist Hermit	Green	U	0.40
Taoist Mystic	Green	R	2.00
15			
Taunting Challenge	Green	R	2.00
Three Visits	Green	C	0.15
Trained Cheetah	Green	U	0.45
Trained Jackal	Green	C	0.15
Trip Wire	Green	U	0.60
Vengeance	White	U	0.45
Virtuous Charge	White	C	0.15
Volunteer Militia	White	C	0.15
Warrior's Oath	Red	R	2.00
16			
Warrior's Stand	White	U	0.40
Wei Ambush Force	Black	C	0.15
Wei Assassins	Black	U	0.45
Wei Elite Companions	Black	U	0.45
Wei Infantry	Black	C	0.15
Wei Night Raiders	Black	U	0.45
Wei Scout	Black	C	0.15
Wei Strike Force	Black	C	0.15
Wielding the Green Dragon	Green	C	0.15
17			
Wolf Pack	Green	R	2.00

Card name	Color	Rarity	Price
Wu Admiral	Blue	U	0.45
Wu Elite Cavalry	Blue	C	0.15
Wu Infantry	Blue	C	0.15
Wu Light Cavalry	Blue	C	0.15
Wu Longbowman	Blue	U	0.60
Wu Scout	Blue	C	0.15
Wu Spy	Blue	U	0.60
Wu Warship	Blue	C	0.15
18			
Xiahou Dun, the One-Eyed	Black	R	3.00
Xun Yu, Wei Advisor	Black	R	3.00
Yellow Scarves Cavalry	Red	C	0.15
Yellow Scarves General	Red	R	2.00
Yellow Scarves Troops	Red	C	0.15
Young Wei Recruit	Black	C	0.15
Yuan Shao, the Indecisive	Red	R	3.00
Yuan Shao's Infantry	Red	U	0.40
Zhang Fei, Fierce Warrior	White	R	3.00
19			
Zhang He, Wei General	Black	R	3.00
Zhang Liao, Hero of Hefei	Black	R	3.00
Zhao Zilong, Tiger General	White	R	3.00
Zhou Yu, Chief Commander	Blue	R	3.00
Zhuge Jin, Wu Strategist	Blue	R	3.00
Zodiac Dog	Red	C	0.15
Zodiac Dragon	Red	R	4.00
Zodiac Goat	Red	C	0.15
Zodiac Horse	Green	U	0.45
20			
Zodiac Monkey	Green	C	0.15
Zodiac Ox	Green	U	0.60
Zodiac Pig	Black	C	0.45
Zodiac Rabbit	Green	C	0.15
Zodiac Rat	Black	C	0.15
Zodiac Rooster	Green	C	0.15
Zodiac Snake	Black	C	0.15
Zodiac Tiger	Green	U	0.45
Zuo Ci, the Mocking Sage	Green	R	3.00

Magic: The Gathering • *Vanguard*

Wizards of the Coast

4 waves of **8** cards • **IDENTIFIER: Cards are 3.5" by 5"**

You've seen their names, now use them in games. Characters for such mainstays as Urza and Mishra got giant cards in this series of promos and gift sets, usable in *Magic* variants.

Vanguard Set	11.00
Ertai	2.00
Gerrard	2.00
Karn	2.50
Maraxus	2.00
Mirri	2.00
Sisay	2.00
Squee	2.00
Tahngarth	2.00

Vanguard 2 Set	11.00
Barrin	2.00
Crovax	2.00
Greven il-Vec	2.00
Hanna	2.00
Orim	2.00
Selenia	2.00
Starke	2.00
Volrath	2.00

Vanguard 3 Set	11.00
Eladamri	2.00
Lyna	2.00
Multani	2.00
Oracle	2.00
Rofellos	2.00
Sidar Kondo	2.00
Silver Queen, Brood Mother	2.00
Takara	2.00

Vanguard 4 Set	24.00
Ashnod	3.00
Gix	2.50
Mishra	3.00
Serra	3.00
Tawnos	3.00
Titania	3.00
Urza	3.00
Xantcha	3.00

Magic: The Gathering • *Beatdown*

Wizards of the Coast

Released **October 2000**

122 cards in set plus 2 20-sided dice

• **IDENTIFIER: Spiked club symbol**

Battle Royale for two, *Beatdown* featues two 61-card prebuilt decks (including two exclusive foil cards). The "spindown life counters" inside are actually customized 20-sided dice.

With this set's marketing, Wizards of the Coast somehow got its "expert" player base confused with pro wrestling fans. *Beatdown*'s box label is surprisingly coarse, encouraging players to "open up sum whup-ass" with this "bad-ass set." So much for our next argument that games don't glorify violence... — *John Jackson Miller*

Beatdown Box Set		20.50
Erhnam Djinn	F	7.50
Sengir Vampire	F	7.50

Magic: The Gathering • Arena & DCI
Wizards of the Coast
IDENTIFIER: Arena symbol (at right)

Beginnning with events in 10 U.S. cities Aug. 2, 1996, Wizards of the Coast's Arena tournament program made a number of variant cards available to participants.

Unless your name is Tom Chanpheng, you won't be checking the box for **1996 World Champion**. Only one copy of the card was ever made!

Card name	Variant	Foil?	Price
☐ Disenchant	Arena		20.00
☐ Fireball	Arena		14.50
☐ Forest	Arena		4.00
☐ Island	Arena		4.00
☐ Mountain	Arena		4.00
☐ Plain	Arena		4.00
☐ Swamp	Arena		4.00
☐ Counterspell	DCI		15.00
☐ Crusade	DCI	F	100.00
☐ Giant Growth	DCI	F	17.00
☐ Incinerate	DCI		12.50
☐ 1996 World Champion	DCI		

Magic: The Gathering • 6" x 9"
Wizards of the Coast • 38 cards • IDENTIFIER: Cards are 6" by 9"

Some cards were so big on the tournament scene they couldn't get any bigger, so Wizards of the Coast blew them up. **Black Lotus** and **Chaos Orb** cards became more available (if just as unusable in real play) in these giant promos.

The **6x9 Aswan Jaguar** is the only one of the so-called **Astral Set** of Microprose promo cards that ever actually appeared. The other 11 were "virtual" cards.

	Price			Price
[1] ☐ 6x9 Aswan Jaguar (Microprose)	5.00		☐ 6x9 Jester's Cap (White-border)	5.00
☐ 6x9 Autumn Willow	6.50		☐ 6x9 Juzam Djinn	10.00
☐ 6x9 Balance	7.00		☐ 6x9 Karplusan Forest	5.00
☐ 6x9 Balduvian Hordes	8.00		☐ 6x9 Lhurgoyf	7.50
☐ 6x9 Black Knight	6.50		☐ 6x9 Library of Alexandria	10.00
☐ 6x9 Black Lotus	10.00		☐ 6x9 Mirror Universe	8.50
☐ 6x9 Blinking Spirit	7.00		☐ 6x9 Mountain	5.00
☐ 6x9 Chaos Orb	8.00		☐ 6x9 Necropotence	8.50
☐ 6x9 City of Brass	8.00	[4]	☐ 6x9 Nether Shadow	6.50
[2] ☐ 6x9 Deflection	6.00		☐ 6x9 Personal Incarnation	6.00
☐ 6x9 Earthquake	7.00		☐ 6x9 Plains	5.00
☐ 6x9 Erhnam Djinn	7.00		☐ 6x9 Serra Angel (Guay)	7.50
☐ 6x9 Fallen Angel	6.50		☐ 6x9 Serra Angel (Shuler)	7.00
☐ 6x9 Forest	5.00		☐ 6x9 Shivan Dragon	10.00
☐ 6x9 Guardian Beast	8.00		☐ 6x9 Sol'kanar the Swamp King	6.00
☐ 6x9 Hurloon Minotaur	5.00		☐ 6x9 Swamp	5.00
☐ 6x9 Icy Manipulator	8.00		☐ 6x9 Vesuvan Doppelganger	8.00
[3] ☐ 6x9 Island	5.00	[5]	☐ 6x9 Wheel of Fortune	8.00
☐ 6x9 Ivory Tower	6.00		☐ 6x9 Zuran Orb	7.00

Magic: The Gathering • Promo cards

It may not seem that **Magic** needed much promotion in the beginning, but Wizards of the Coast did it anyway. Those that appear below are mostly special cards or versions that can be differentiated from those that were later sold in the expansion sets. The preview **Avatar of Hope**, for example, is a special foil version of the card that later appeared in **Prophecy** that can be distinguished from the later regular foil version.

"Novel" cards were part of HarperPrism's redemption program. Its *Magic* novels had coupons that could be ripped out and mailed in for cards like **Arena**. (A pen is the card symbol.) During the craze, a number of players bought the books without even reading them just to get the coupons — and vandalism of books on the shelves was commonplace. Still, the sales convinced HarperPrism to get into the CCG business itself with **Imajica**.

Many cards available in magazines were the same ones that appeared in sets and aren't listed here. *Scrye* #4.4 (Nov 97) even had a **Vanguard** card, **Ertai**. The biggest magazine promotion, for **Ice Age**, involved 10 or so magazines including *Scrye* and *Comics Buyer's Guide*. Some of the other magazines aren't around any more, but the all the **Norritts** — the card common to all the magazines — certainly are. — **John Jackson Miller**

Card name	Source	Foil?	Price
[1] ☐ Arena	Novel		7.00
☐ Avatar of Hope	Prophecy	F	12.00
☐ Balduvian Horde		F	15.00
☐ Beast of Burden	Urza's Legacy	F	5.00
☐ Chill		F	8.00
☐ Dirtcowl Wurm	Tempest	F	11.00
☐ Duress		F	15.00
☐ Enlightened Tutor		F	17.00
☐ False Prophet	Urza's Destiny	F	4.00
[2] ☐ Forest (U.S.)		F	4.50
☐ Gaea's Cradle		F	75.00
☐ Giant Badger	Novel		5.00
☐ Island (U.S.)		F	5.00
☐ Karn, Silver Golem		F	10.00
☐ Lightning Bolt		F	57.50
☐ Lightning Dragon	Urza's Saga	F	18.50
☐ Lightning Hounds		F	2.00

Card name	Source	Foil?	Price
☐ Longbow Archer		F	14.50
[3] ☐ Mana Crypt	Novel		15.00
☐ Mind Warp		F	8.00
☐ Monstrous Hound	Exodus	F	3.50
☐ Mountains (U.S.)		F	4.50
☐ Nalathni Dragon	DragonCon		6.00
☐ Overtaker	Mercadian	F	12.00
☐ Pillage		F	17.50
☐ Plains (U.S.)		F	4.50
[4] ☐ Pouncing Jaguar		F	9.00
☐ Prodigal Sorcerer		F	10.00
☐ Raging Kavu	Invasion	F	6.00
☐ Rathi Assassin	Nemesis	F	4.00
☐ Revenant Stronghold		F	10.00
☐ Rewind		F	9.00
☐ Rhox		F	7.50
☐ River Boa		F	25.00
☐ Serra Angel		F	100.00
☐ Serra Avatar		F	62.50
[5] ☐ Sewers of Estark	Novel		5.00
☐ Shock		F	25.00
☐ Skittering Skirge		F	8.00
☐ Stone Rain		F	24.00

Card name	Source	Foil?	Price
☐ Stroke of Genius		F	47.50
☐ Swamp (U.S.)		F	5.00
☐ Terror		F	11.00
☐ Thran Quarry		F	15.00
☐ Uktabi Orangutan		F	12.50
[6] ☐ Vampiric Tutor		F	95.00
☐ Volcanic Geyser		F	10.00
☐ Warmonger		F	2.00
☐ Windseeker Centaur	Novel		5.00

Magic: The Gathering • Starter 2000
Box set with CD-ROM 9.50

Error *Magic* cards ○

There's more about oddball misprint cards (and why we don't provide prices for them) in the introduction to this book, but there are some interesting **Magic** ones.

There are several pre-production errors — wrong copyrights and symbols. The weirdest, though, is a printing error: Several cards for **Fallen Empires** left Carta Mundi with the backs for another game entirely, **Wyvern**!

RARITY KEY C = Common U = Uncommon R = Rare VR = Very Rare UR = Ultra Rare F = Foil card X = Fixed/standard in all decks

SCRYE Collectible Card Game Checklist and Price Guide • **295**

Middle-earth

Iron Crown Enterprises • First set, ***The Wizards Limited***, released **December 1995**

484 cards in set • **IDENTIFIER: Black borders**

- Starter decks contain 15 cards; starter displays contain 36 starters
- Booster packs contain 76 cards; booster displays contain 10 boosters

Designed by **Coleman Charlton** and **Mike Reynolds**

Concept	●●●●○
Gameplay	●●●●○
Card art	●●●●○
Player pool	●●○○○

Based on the legendary *Lord of the Rings* series of books by J.R.R. Tolkien, the **Middle-earth: The Wizards Collectible Card Game** appealed to virtually every CCG fan familiar with the books. The game itself is probably one of the most complex CCGs in existence, but that didn't deter many die-hard Middle-earth fans.

There are four basic types of cards: characters, resources, hazards, and sites. Sites form their own deck, which is unshuffled; players simply announce that they are traveling to a site and play the proper card. The other three types are shuffled together into a deck, except for the starting company of characters. Players start with a company of characters, which may include such luminaries as **Aragorn**, **Bilbo**, or **Gimli**. Wizards (such as **Gandalf** and **Saruman**) are extremely powerful characters who come out later in the game and who also carry a great risk: if they are killed, their owners lose the game (though later rule changes made you only lose points for getting your wizard killed).

The companies travel around Middle-earth using the site cards, and on the way, opponents can play hazard cards (representing creatures, natural blockades and other such obstacles). Players can play resources to overcome these trials. A pair of six-sided dice are needed to resolve combat as well as in a few other situations (such as corruption checks, which can force your characters to depart your party when they succumb to various means of corruption, much like the One Ring corrupted Boromir in the books).

When you arrive at a site, you can usually play items, factions and other cards (all a subset of resources) that grant you Marshalling Points (MP's). The game is usually won by the player with the most MP's after play decks have been exhausted a certain number of times. It is also possible, though extremely difficult, to win the game as in the books: locate the One Ring and throw it into Mount Doom.

The game works well in either a two-player or multi-player format, and the artwork is excellent. Iron Crown produced fine strategy guides for each set, up until The White Hand. Each had several chapters on how to best use the themes of the set, and provided every card image in the set. Each image was accompanied by a paragraph of lore and a paragraph of strategy.

The game was popular for about three years, but increasing rules complexity and the lack of timely expansions were its downfall. Iron Crown went out of business in 2000, and the CCG license has been picked up by Decipher, which plans to make its own original CCG based on the movies coming out in 2001. — ***Jason Winter***

Limited and *Unlimited* cards have no identifying runes. Other sets have small runes (some barely visible at all) in the second small octagon from the bottom.

Middle-earth • *Unlimited*

Iron Crown Enterprises • Released **April 1996**

484 cards in set • **IDENTIFIER: Blue borders**

- Starter decks contain 15 cards; starter displays contain 36 starters
- Booster packs contain 76 cards; booster displays contain 10 boosters

Errata and minor changes to wording were the only gameplay differences between **Unlimited** and **Limited** set. The garish blue borders were met with skepticism among art-conscious gamers. A **Second Edition** of *Unlimited* was announced, but we are unaware of any differences in the sets or in price — if it was ever released. — ***Jason Winter***

You will need **54** nine-pocket pages to store **each set**. (27 doubled up)

LIMITED

Set (484 cards)	290.00
Starter Display Box	107.50
Booster Display Box	122.50
Starter Deck	13.75
Booster Pack	4.00

UNLIMITED

Set (484 cards)	182.50
Starter Display Box	50.00
Booster Display Box	49.00
Starter Deck	7.00
Booster Pack	2.10

LIMITED	Card name	Type	Rarity	UNLTD
☐ 0.25	A Chance Meeting	Resource	C	0.15 ☐
☐ 0.25	A Friend or Three	Resource	C2	0.15 ☐
☐ 0.25	Abductor	Hazard	C	0.15 ☐
☐ 1.30	Adrazar	Character	X	0.35 ☐
☐ 10.00	Adûnaphel	Hazard	R	6.00 ☐
☐ 8.00	Agburanar	Hazard	R	5.50 ☐
☐ 9.00	Akhôrahil	Hazard	R	8.50 ☐
☐ 1.00	Alatar	Character	X	0.80 ☐
☐ 1.50	Align Palantír	Resource	U	0.80 ☐
☐ 0.25	Ambusher	Hazard	C	0.15 ☐
☐ 0.30	Amon Hen	Site	C	0.35 ☐
☐ 1.30	Anborn	Character	U	0.80 ☐
☐ 0.25	Andrast	Region	C	0.15 ☐
☐ 0.25	Andrast Coast	Region	C	0.15 ☐
☐ 0.30	Anduin River	Resource	C2	0.15 ☐
☐ 0.25	Anduin Vales	Region	C2	0.15 ☐
☐ 5.50	Andúril, the Flame of the West	Resource	R	3.50 ☐

LIMITED	Card name	Type	Rarity	UNLTD
☐ 0.25	Anfalas	Region	C2	0.15 ☐
☐ 0.30	Angmar	Region	C	0.15 ☐
☐ 1.00	Annalena	Character	X	0.35 ☐
☐ 0.30	Anórien	Region	C2	0.15 ☐
☐ 1.50	Aragorn II	Character	X	1.00 ☐
☐ 1.50	Arinmîr	Character	U	0.80 ☐
☐ 6.50	Army of the Dead	Resource	R	3.00 ☐
☐ 0.25	Arouse Denizens	Hazard	C2	0.15 ☐
☐ 0.25	Arouse Minions	Hazard	C2	0.15 ☐
☐ 0.25	Arthedain	Region	C2	0.15 ☐
☐ 6.00	Arwen	Character	R	3.00 ☐
☐ 0.25	Ash Mountains	Resource	C	0.15 ☐
☐ 8.00	Assassin	Hazard	R	5.00 ☐
☐ 1.30	Athelas	Resource	U	0.80 ☐
☐ 0.25	Awaken Denizens	Hazard	C2	0.15 ☐
☐ 0.25	Awaken Minions	Hazard	C2	0.15 ☐

RARITY KEY C2 = Most Common C = Common U = Uncommon R = Rare UR = Ultra Rare X = Fixed/standard in all decks

Limited	Card name	Type	Rarity	Unltd
1.50	Awaken the Earth's Fire	Hazard	U	0.80
1.00	Bag End	Site	X	0.35
1.80	Balin	Character	U	0.80
11.00	Balrog of Moria	Hazard	R	5.00
1.00	Bandit Lair	Site	X	0.35
8.00	Bane of the Ithil-stone	Hazard	R	4.50
7.30	Barad-dûr	Site	R	4.00
1.00	Bard Bowman	Character	X	0.35
1.50	Barliman Butterbur	Character	U	0.80
1.30	Barrow-downs	Site	X	0.35
1.40	Barrow-wight	Hazard	U	0.80
0.25	Bay of Belfalas	Region	C	0.15
0.25	Beautiful Gold Ring	Resource	C2	0.15
0.25	Belfalas	Region	C	0.15
1.30	Beorn	Character	X	0.35
1.30	Beorn's House	Site	X	0.35
1.00	Beornings	Resource	X	0.35
1.30	Beregond	Character	X	0.35
1.80	Beretar	Character	U	0.80
1.80	Bergil	Character	U	0.80
1.50	"Bert" (Bûrat)	Hazard	U	0.80
0.35	Bifur	Character	C	0.15
15.00	Bilbo	Character	R	8.00
1.50	Bill the Pony	Resource	U	0.80
0.25	Block	Resource	C	0.15
0.35	Blue Mountain Dwarf-hold	Site	C	0.15
1.30	Blue Mountain Dwarves	Resource	U	0.80
0.35	Bofur	Character	C	0.15
1.80	Bombur	Character	U	0.80
1.30	Book of Mazarbul	Resource	U	0.80
1.00	Boromir II	Character	X	0.35
1.30	Bree	Site	X	0.35
1.30	Bridge	Resource	U	0.80
0.25	Brigands	Hazard	C2	0.15
0.25	Brown Lands	Region	C	0.15
0.25	Call of Home	Hazard	C2	0.15
1.30	Call of the Sea	Hazard	U	0.80
0.30	Cameth Brin	Site	C	0.15
0.25	Cardolan	Region	C2	0.15
4.70	Carn Dûm	Site	R	2.50
0.25	Cave-drake	Hazard	C2	0.15
1.50	Caves of Úlund	Site	U	0.80
1.50	Celeborn	Character	X	0.35
0.25	Choking Shadows	Hazard	C	0.15
8.00	Círdan	Character	R	6.00
5.00	Cirith Ungol	Site	R	2.00
4.00	Clear Skies	Resource	R	1.80
6.00	Clouds	Hazard	R	2.50
0.30	Concealment	Resource	C	0.15
0.25	Corpse-candle	Hazard	C	0.15
1.50	Corsairs of Umbar	Hazard	U	0.80
1.50	Cracks of Doom	Resource	U	0.80
0.25	Crebain	Hazard	C	0.15
6.40	Daelomin	Hazard	R	5.50
0.25	Dagger of Westernesse	Resource	C2	0.15
0.30	Dagorlad	Region	C	0.15
8.00	Dáin II	Character	R	4.50
1.50	Damrod	Character	U	0.80
1.50	Dancing Spire	Site	U	0.80
0.25	Dark Quarrels	Resource	C2	0.15
1.50	Dead Marshes	Site	U	0.80
6.10	Denethor II	Character	R	3.50
0.25	Despair of the Heart	Hazard	C	0.15
1.50	Dimrill Dale	Site	U	0.80
0.25	Dodge	Resource	C	0.15
0.30	Dol Amroth	Site	C	0.15
6.00	Dol Guldur	Site	R	4.00
0.90	Doors of Night	Hazard	X	0.35
1.80	Dori	Character	U	0.80
0.25	Dorwinion	Region	C	0.15
1.30	Dragon's Desolation	Hazard	U	1.00
0.30	Dreams of Lore	Resource	C2	0.15
1.30	Drowning Seas	Hazard	U	0.80
0.30	Drúadan Forest	Site	C	0.15
6.50	Dunharrow	Site	R	3.00
0.25	Dunland	Region	C	0.15
1.00	Dunlendings	Resource	X	0.35
1.30	Dunnish Clan-hold	Site	X	0.35
1.50	Durin's Axe	Resource	U	0.80
0.35	Dwalin	Character	C	0.15
9.50	Dwar of Waw	Hazard	R	5.50
6.50	Dwarven Ring of Barin's Tribe	Resource	R	3.50
6.00	Dwarven Ring of Bávor's Tribe	Resource	R	4.00
7.00	Dwarven Ring of Drúin's Tribe	Resource	R	3.50
7.50	Dwarven Ring of Durin's Tribe	Resource	R	3.50
6.50	Dwarven Ring of Dwálin's Tribe	Resource	R	3.50
1.30	Dwarven Ring of Thélor's Tribe	Resource	U	0.80
1.30	Dwarven Ring of Thrár's Tribe	Resource	U	0.80
6.00	Eagle-mounts	Resource	R	3.00
0.30	Eagles' Eyrie	Site	C	0.15
1.50	Earth of Galadriel's Orchard	Resource	U	0.80
4.50	Easterling Camp	Site	R	3.00
5.00	Easterlings	Resource	R	3.00
0.30	Edhellond	Site	C	0.15
1.50	Edoras	Site	X	0.35
7.00	Elf-song	Resource	R	6.00
0.25	Elf-stone	Resource	C2	0.15
1.50	Elladan	Character	X	1.00
1.30	Elrohir	Character	X	1.00
10.00	Elrond	Character	R	8.00
0.25	Elven Cloak	Resource	C2	0.15
0.25	Elven Shores	Region	C	0.15
5.50	Elves of Lindon	Resource	R	3.00
0.25	Enedhwaith	Region	C	0.15
1.40	Ent-draughts	Resource	U	0.80
1.00	Ents of Fangorn	Resource	X	0.35
1.50	Eomer	Character	U	0.80
1.50	Eowyn	Character	U	0.80
0.25	Eriadoran Coast	Region	C	0.15
1.30	Erkenbrand	Character	X	0.35
0.25	Escape	Resource	C	0.15
0.30	Ettenmoors	Site	C	0.15
9.30	Eye of Sauron	Hazard	R	6.00
0.25	Fair Gold Ring	Resource	C2	0.15
4.50	Fair Sailing	Resource	R	3.00
0.25	Fair Travels in Border-lands	Resource	C	0.15
6.00	Fair Travels in Dark-domains	Resource	R	4.00
6.00	Fair Travels in Free-domains	Resource	R	4.00
0.25	Fair Travels in Shadow-lands	Resource	C	0.15
0.25	Fair Travels in Wilderness	Resource	C	0.15
0.25	Fangorn	Region	C	0.15
1.00	Faramir	Resource	X	0.25
0.30	Far-sight	Character	C	0.35
6.00	Favor of the Valar	Resource	R	3.00
9.00	Fell Beast	Hazard	R	7.00
5.50	Fell Turtle	Hazard	R	4.00
0.25	Fell Winter	Hazard	C	0.15
0.25	Fellowship	Resource	C2	0.15
1.50	Fíli	Character	U	0.80
1.50	Fog	Resource	U	0.80
0.25	Ford	Resource	C	0.15
0.30	Forlong	Character	C	0.15
0.25	Forochel	Region	C	0.15
0.25	Foul Fumes	Hazard	C	0.15
13.00	Frodo	Character	R	8.00
9.80	Galadriel	Character	R	7.50
4.50	Galva	Character	R	3.00
1.50	Gamling the Old	Character	U	0.80
1.50	Gandalf	Character	X	1.50
0.25	Gap of Isen	Region	C2	0.15
0.90	Gates of Morning	Resource	X	0.35
1.50	Ghân-buri-Ghân	Character	U	0.80
0.25	Ghosts	Hazard	C	0.15
0.25	Ghouls	Hazard	C	0.15
0.25	Giant	Hazard	C2	0.15
0.25	Giant Spiders	Hazard	C2	0.15
1.30	Gildor Inglorion	Character	X	0.35
1.80	Gimli	Character	X	1.00
0.30	Gladden Fields	Site	C	0.15
1.50	Glamdring	Resource	U	1.00
1.50	Glittering Caves	Site	U	0.80
1.50	Glóin	Character	U	0.80
0.25	Gloom	Hazard	C	0.15
1.30	Glorfindel II	Character	X	0.35
1.00	Goblin-gate	Site	X	0.35
1.50	Goldberry	Resource	U	0.80
1.80	Gollum	Resource	U	1.00
7.50	Gollum's Fate	Resource	R	4.00
0.25	Gorgoroth	Region	C	0.15
6.50	Great Ship	Resource	R	4.00
0.25	Great-road	Resource	C	0.15
1.50	Great-shield of Rohan	Resource	U	0.80
0.25	Greed	Hazard	C	0.15
0.30	Grey Havens	Site	C	0.15
0.25	Grey Mountain Narrows	Region	C	0.15
0.25	Gundabad	Region	C	0.15
6.00	Gwaihir	Resource	R	3.00
1.50	Halbarad	Character	U	0.80
7.00	Haldalam	Character	R	3.00
1.50	Haldir	Character	U	0.80
0.25	Halfling Stealth	Resource	C2	0.15
0.25	Halfling Strength	Resource	C2	0.15
0.25	Half-trolls of Far Harad	Hazard	C	0.15
0.35	Háma	Character	C	0.15
0.25	Harondor	Region	C	0.15
0.25	Hauberk of Bright Mail	Resource	C	0.15
0.25	Healing Herbs	Resource	C2	0.15
0.25	Heart of Mirkwood	Region	C	0.15
1.30	Henneth Annûn	Site	X	0.35
6.50	Hiding	Resource	R	4.00
0.25	High Pass	Region	C2	0.15
1.50	Hillmen	Resource	U	0.80
1.50	Himring	Site	U	0.80
9.00	Hoarmûrath of Dír	Hazard	R	5.00
8.50	Hobbits	Resource	R	5.00
0.25	Hollin	Region	C2	0.15
0.30	Horn of Anor	Resource	C	0.15
0.25	Horse Plains	Region	C	0.15
0.25	Horses	Resource	C	0.15
0.25	Huorn	Hazard	C	0.15
0.25	Imlad Morgul	Region	C	0.15
1.50	Imrahil	Character	U	0.80
8.00	Indûr Dawndeath	Hazard	R	6.00

RARITY KEY C2 = Most Common C = Common U = Uncommon R = Rare UR = Ultra Rare X = Fixed/standard in all decks

Limited	Card name	Type	Rarity	Unltd
1.50	Irerock	Site	U	0.80
1.00	Iron Hill Dwarf-hold	Site	X	0.35
1.00	Iron Hill Dwarves	Resource	X	0.35
0.25	Iron Hills	Region	C	0.15
1.00	Isengard	Site	X	0.35
7.00	Isles of the Dead that Live	Site	R	3.00
0.25	Ithilien	Region	C	0.15
11.50	Khamûl the Easterling	Hazard	R	9.00
0.30	Khand	Region	C	0.15
1.00	Kili	Character	X	0.80
0.30	Kindling of the Spirit	Resource	C	0.15
1.50	Knights of Dol Amroth	Resource	U	0.80
0.30	Lake-town	Site	C	0.15
0.25	Lamedon	Region	C	0.15
1.30	Lapse of Will	Resource	U	0.80
1.30	Leaflock	Resource	U	0.80
0.25	Lebennin	Region	C2	0.15
1.50	Legolas	Character	U	0.80
1.50	Lesser Ring	Resource	U	0.80
7.50	Leucaruth	Hazard	R	6.00
0.25	Lindon	Region	C2	0.15
0.25	Lond Galen	Site	C	0.15
0.25	Long Winter	Hazard	C	0.15
0.30	Lordly Presence	Resource	C2	0.15
0.30	Lórien	Site	C	0.15
0.30	Lossadan Cairn	Site	C	0.15
0.30	Lossadan Camp	Site	C	0.15
1.50	Lossoth	Resource	U	0.80
5.00	Lost at Sea	Hazard	R	3.00
0.25	Lost in Border-lands	Hazard	C	0.15
5.50	Lost in Dark-domains	Hazard	R	3.00
0.25	Lost in Free-domains	Hazard	C	0.15
0.25	Lost in Shadow-lands	Hazard	C	0.15
0.25	Lost in the Wilderness	Hazard	C	0.15
6.00	Lucky Search	Resource	R	4.00
0.25	Lucky Strike	Resource	C	0.15
1.40	Lure of Creation	Hazard	U	0.80
0.25	Lure of Expedience	Hazard	C	0.15
0.25	Lure of Nature	Hazard	C2	0.15
5.00	Lure of Power	Hazard	R	4.00
0.25	Lure of the Senses	Hazard	C	0.15
1.50	Mablung	Character	U	0.80
1.50	Magic Ring of Courage	Resource	U	0.80
1.50	Magic Ring of Lore	Resource	U	0.80
1.50	Magic Ring of Nature	Resource	U	0.80
1.50	Magic Ring of Stealth	Resource	U	0.80
1.50	Magic Ring of Words	Resource	U	0.80
1.30	Men of Anfalas	Resource	U	0.80
1.00	Men of Anórien	Resource	X	0.35
1.40	Men of Dorwinion	Resource	U	0.80
1.40	Men of Lamedon	Resource	U	0.80
1.40	Men of Lebennin	Resource	U	0.80
1.40	Men of Northern Rhovanion	Resource	U	0.80
1.50	Merry	Character	U	0.80
6.00	Minas Morgul	Site	R	3.00
1.00	Minas Tirith	Site	X	0.35
1.50	Minions Stir	Hazard	U	0.80
1.50	Mirror of Galadriel	Resource	U	0.80
0.25	Miruvor	Resource	C	0.15
0.25	Misty Mountains	Resource	C2	0.15
1.50	Moon	Resource	U	0.80
8.00	Morannon	Resource	R	4.00
8.00	Morgul Night	Hazard	R	6.00
8.00	Morgul-horse	Hazard	R	4.00
7.00	Morgul-knife	Hazard	R	4.00
1.00	Moria	Site	X	0.35
1.50	Mount Doom	Site	U	0.80
1.00	Mount Gram	Site	X	0.35
1.50	Mount Gundabad	Site	U	0.80
0.25	Mountains of Shadow	Resource	C	0.15
9.00	Mouth of Sauron	Hazard	R	8.00
0.25	Mouths of the Anduin	Region	C	0.15
5.50	Múmak (Oliphant)	Hazard	R	3.00
0.30	Muster	Resource	C	0.15
0.25	Muster Disperses	Hazard	C	0.15
1.50	Narsil	Resource	U	1.00
7.00	Narya	Resource	R	4.00
7.50	Nenya	Resource	R	4.00
0.25	New Friendship	Resource	C	0.15
1.50	New Moon	Hazard	U	0.80
0.25	Night	Hazard	C	0.15
0.30	Nori	Character	C	0.15
0.25	Northern Rhovanion	Region	C2	0.15
0.25	Númeriador	Region	C	0.15
0.25	Nurn	Region	C	0.15
1.50	Oin	Character	U	0.80
0.30	Old Forest	Site	C	0.15
0.25	Old Friendship	Resource	C	0.15
1.50	Old Man Willow	Hazard	U	0.80
0.25	Old Pûkel Gap	Region	C	0.15
0.25	Old Pûkel-land	Region	C	0.15
0.25	Old Road	Resource	C2	0.15
1.50	Olog-hai (Trolls)	Hazard	U	0.80
0.25	Orc-guard	Hazard	C	0.15
1.40	Orc-lieutenant	Hazard	U	0.80
0.25	Orc-patrol	Hazard	C2	0.15
0.25	Orc-raiders	Hazard	C2	0.15
1.30	Orcrist	Resource	U	0.80
0.25	Orc-warband	Hazard	C	0.15
0.25	Orc-warriors	Hazard	C2	0.15
0.25	Orc-watch	Hazard	C	0.15
0.30	Ori	Character	C	0.15
0.30	Orophin	Character	C	0.15
1.50	Ost-in-Edhil	Site	U	0.80
5.00	Palantír of Amon Sûl	Resource	R	3.50
5.50	Palantír of Annúminas	Resource	R	3.50
1.50	Palantír of Elostirion	Resource	U	0.80
1.30	Palantír of Minas Tirith	Resource	U	0.80
1.30	Palantír of Orthanc	Resource	U	0.80
6.00	Palantír of Osgiliath	Resource	R	4.00
1.00	Pallando	Character	X	1.00
5.50	Paths of the Dead	Resource	R	3.00
1.30	Peath	Character	X	0.35
0.30	Pelargir	Site	C	0.15
0.25	Persuasive Words	Resource	C	0.15
1.40	Pick-pocket	Hazard	U	0.80
1.50	Pippin	Character	U	0.80
1.40	Plague of Wights	Hazard	U	0.80
0.25	Potion of Prowess	Resource	C	0.15
1.40	Praise to Elbereth	Resource	U	0.80
0.25	Precious Gold Ring	Resource	C2	0.15
5.50	Pûkel-men	Hazard	R	2.00
1.50	Quickbeam	Resource	U	0.80
1.50	Quiet Lands	Resource	U	0.80
1.00	Radagast	Character	X	0.80
1.00	Rangers of Ithilien	Resource	X	0.35
1.00	Rangers of the North	Resource	X	0.35
1.30	Red Arrow	Resource	U	0.80
1.30	Red Book of Westmarch	Resource	U	0.80
0.25	Redhorn Gate	Region	C2	0.15
0.25	Reforging	Resource	C	0.15
8.50	Ren the Unclean	Hazard	R	6.50
0.25	Rescue Prisoners	Resource	C2	0.15
7.00	Return of the King	Resource	R	3.00
1.00	Rhosgobel	Site	X	0.35
0.25	Rhudaur	Region	C2	0.15
1.00	Riders of Rohan	Resource	X	0.35
1.50	Ringlore	Resource	U	0.80
0.25	Risky Blow	Resource	C	0.15
0.30	Rivendell	Site	C	0.15
0.25	River	Hazard	C2	0.15
5.50	Roäc the Raven	Resource	R	3.00
1.00	Robin Smallburrow	Character	X	0.35
5.50	Rogrog	Hazard	R	3.00
0.25	Rohan	Region	C2	0.15
1.00	Ruined Signal Tower	Site	X	0.35
7.00	Sacrifice of Form	Resource	R	4.00
1.80	Sam Gamgee	Character	U	0.80
1.30	Sapling of the White Tree	Resource	U	0.80
0.30	Sarn Goriwing	Site	C	0.15
1.50	Saruman	Character	X	1.00
1.30	Scroll of Isildur	Resource	U	0.80
6.50	Secret Entrance	Resource	R	3.50
0.25	Secret Passage	Resource	C	0.15
6.80	Shadowfax	Resource	R	4.00
9.50	Shelob	Hazard	R	4.50
7.00	Shelob's Lair	Site	R	4.00
0.25	Shield of Iron-bound Ash	Resource	C2	0.15
0.30	Shrel-Kain	Site	C	0.15
8.00	Siege	Hazard	R	5.00
6.00	Silent Watcher	Hazard	R	4.00
4.50	Skinbark	Resource	R	3.00
0.25	Slayer	Hazard	C	0.15
12.50	Smaug	Hazard	R	8.00
5.00	Snowstorm	Hazard	R	3.30
0.25	Southern Mirkwood	Region	C2	0.15
0.30	Southern Rhovanion	Region	C	0.15
6.00	Southron Oasis	Site	R	3.00
5.00	Southrons	Resource	R	3.00
1.50	Star-glass	Resource	U	0.80
1.50	Stars	Resource	U	0.80
0.30	Stealth	Resource	C	0.15
1.50	Sting	Resource	U	0.80
6.00	Stone of Erech	Resource	R	3.00
5.50	Stone-circle	Site	R	3.00
4.50	Storms of Ossë	Hazard	R	3.00
1.40	Sun	Resource	U	0.80
0.25	Sword of Gondolin	Resource	C2	0.15
0.25	Tempering Friendship	Resource	C2	0.15
0.35	Test of Form	Resource	C2	0.15
0.25	Test of Lore	Resource	C2	0.15
7.50	The Arkenstone	Resource	R	4.00
7.00	The Balance of Things	Hazard	R	3.00
1.30	The Burden of Time	Hazard	U	0.80
1.50	The Cock Crows	Resource	U	0.80
1.50	The Evenstar	Resource	U	0.80
1.50	The Great Eagles	Resource	U	0.80
5.50	The Great Goblin	Hazard	R	3.00
1.00	The Lonely Mountain	Site	X	0.35
6.50	The Mithril-coat	Resource	R	3.00
8.50	The Nazgûl are Abroad	Hazard	R	6.00
1.40	The Old Thrush	Resource	U	1.00
32.00	The One Ring	Resource	R	20.00
8.30	The Pale Sword	Hazard	R	3.00
8.00	The Precious	Hazard	R	4.00
1.50	The Ring's Betrayal	Hazard	U	0.80
0.25	The Shire	Region	C	0.15
5.50	The Stones	Site	R	3.00
1.50	The White Towers	Site	U	0.80
7.00	The White Tree	Resource	R	3.00
10.00	The Will of Sauron	Hazard	R	7.00
6.80	The Will of the Ring	Hazard	R	3.00
0.90	The Wind Throne	Site	X	0.35
1.50	Théoden	Character	X	1.00
7.80	Thief	Hazard	R	3.00
8.00	Thorin II	Character	R	3.30
0.25	Thorough Search	Resource	C	0.15
1.30	Thranduil	Character	X	0.35
1.30	Thranduil's Halls	Site	X	0.35
6.00	Tolfalas	Site	R	3.00

RARITY KEY C2 = Most Common   C = Common   U = Uncommon   R = Rare   UR = Ultra Rare   X = Fixed/standard in all decks

Limited	Card name	Type	Rarity	Unltd
☐ 1.50	"Tom" (Tûma)	Hazard	U	0.80 ☐
☐ 8.00	Tom Bombadil	Resource	R	4.00 ☐
☐ 0.25	Tookish Blood	Hazard	C	0.15 ☐
☐ 1.50	Torque of Hues	Resource	U	0.80 ☐
☐ 1.00	Tower Guard of Minas Tirith	Resource	X	0.35 ☐
☐ 8.00	Traitor	Hazard	R	4.00 ☐
☐ 1.50	Treebeard	Resource	U	0.80 ☐
☐ 6.00	True Fána	Resource	R	4.00 ☐
☐ 0.25	Twilight	Hazard	C2	0.15 ☐
☐ 0.25	Udûn	Region	C	0.15 ☐
☐ 1.40	Use Palantír	Resource	U	0.80 ☐
☐ 9.50	Uvatha the Horseman	Hazard	R	6.50 ☐
☐ 6.50	Vale of Erech	Site	R	4.00 ☐
☐ 0.25	Vanishment	Resource	C	0.15 ☐
☐ 5.00	Variag Camp	Site	R	3.00 ☐
☐ 6.00	Variags of Khand	Resource	R	3.00 ☐
☐ 7.50	Vilya	Resource	R	5.50 ☐
☐ 0.30	Vôteli	Character	C	0.15 ☐
☐ 4.50	Vygavril	Character	R	3.00 ☐
☐ 1.50	Wacho	Character	U	0.80 ☐
☐ 1.30	Wake of War	Hazard	U	0.80 ☐
☐ 0.25	Wargs	Hazard	C2	0.15 ☐
☐ 1.50	Watcher in the Water	Hazard	U	0.80 ☐
☐ 0.25	Weariness of the Heart	Hazard	C2	0.15 ☐
☐ 0.90	Weathertop	Site	X	0.35 ☐
☐ 1.30	Wellinghall	Site	X	0.35 ☐
☐ 0.25	Western Mirkwood	Region	C	0.15 ☐
☐ 0.25	White Mountains	Resource	C	0.15 ☐
☐ 1.50	"William" (Wûluag)	Hazard	U	0.80 ☐
☐ 10.50	Witch-king of Angmar	Hazard	R	6.80 ☐
☐ 0.25	Withered Heath	Region	C	0.15 ☐
☐ 6.30	Wizard's Fire	Resource	R	3.00 ☐
☐ 1.50	Wizard's Flame	Resource	U	0.80 ☐
☐ 1.50	Wizard's Laughter	Resource	U	0.80 ☐
☐ 7.00	Wizard's Ring	Resource	R	5.00 ☐
☐ 1.50	Wizard's River-horses	Resource	U	0.80 ☐
☐ 0.25	Wizard's Test	Resource	C	0.15 ☐
☐ 4.30	Wizard's Voice	Resource	R	3.00 ☐
☐ 0.25	Wold & Foothills	Region	C2	0.15 ☐
☐ 0.25	Wolves	Hazard	C2	0.15 ☐
☐ 1.00	Wood-elves	Resource	X	0.35 ☐
☐ 0.25	Woodland Realm	Region	C2	0.15 ☐
☐ 1.50	Woodmen	Resource	U	0.80 ☐
☐ 0.30	Woodmen-town	Site	C	0.15 ☐
☐ 6.50	Words of Power and Terror	Hazard	R	3.00 ☐
☐ 0.30	Wose Passage-hold	Site	C	0.15 ☐
☐ 5.00	Woses of Old Pûkel-land	Resource	R	3.00 ☐
☐ 1.30	Woses of the Drúadan Forest	Resource	U	0.80 ☐

Middle-earth • The Dragons

Iron Crown Enterprises • Released **June 1996**

180 cards in set • **IDENTIFIER: Faint rune at lower right, looks like a bent 'F'**

• Booster packs contain 15 cards; booster displays contain 36 boosters

The first expansion set for **Middle-earth**, **The Dragons** obviously focuses on the big flying lizards of Middle-earth, such as Smaug and such lesser-known dragons as Itangast and Bairanax. Many of the new cards, hazard and resource, deal with dragons, fighting dragons, avoiding dragons, and finding dragons' treasures.

The set includes several solid cards, most notably the **Emerald of the Mariner**, one of the few items that can make corruption checks easier, rather than harder. The dragon hazard cards themselves come in three forms: the dragon, the dragon "at home" and the dragon "ahunt," all with slightly different effects but all still carrying the dragon label, making them more valuable cards. — **Jason Winter**

FAST ASLEEP

SHORT-EVENT

+3 to one burglary attempt. Alternatively, -2 to the prowess of one automatic-attack.

"There he lay, a vast red-golden dragon, fast asleep; a thrumming came from his jaws and nostrils, and wreaths of smoke, but his fires were low in slumber." —Hob

ART BY DENIZO CHIACCHIERA

©1996 Tolkien Enterprises

Set (180 cards)	145.00
Booster Display Box	60.00
Booster Pack	2.10

You will need 20 nine-pocket pages to store this set. (10 doubled up)

Card name	Type	Rarity	Price
☐ A Short Rest	Resource	C2	0.25
☐ Adamant Helmet	Resource	C2	0.25
☐ Agburanar Ahunt	Hazard	U2	1.00
☐ Agburanar at Home	Hazard	R3	3.00
☐ Alert the Folk	Resource	U2	1.00
☐ And Forth He Hastened	Resource	C2	0.25
☐ Arrows Shorn of Ebony	Resource	U2	1.00
☐ Bairanax	Hazard	R2	5.00
☐ Bairanax Ahunt	Hazard	U2	1.00
☐ Bairanax at Home	Hazard	R3	3.50
☐ Belegaer	Resource	C1	0.25
☐ Black Breath	Hazard	R2	3.00
☐ Bounty of the Hoard	Resource	C2	0.25
☐ Bow of Dragon-horn	Resource	U2	1.00
☐ Brand	Character	U2	1.00
☐ Buhr Widu	Site	U2	1.00
☐ Burglary	Resource	C2	0.25
☐ Carrion Birds	Hazard	C2	0.25
☐ Cave Worm	Hazard	C1	0.25
☐ Cloudless Day	Resource	U2	1.00
☐ Cram	Resource	C2	0.25
☐ Cruel Caradhras	Hazard	U2	1.00
☐ Daelomin Ahunt	Hazard	U2	1.00
☐ Daelomin at Home	Hazard	R3	3.00
☐ Dale	Site	U2	1.00
☐ Deftness of Agility	Hazard	R3	2.50
☐ Dire Wolves	Hazard	C2	0.25
☐ Dragon's Blood	Hazard	C2	0.35
☐ Dragon's Breath	Hazard	U2	1.00
☐ Dragon's Curse	Hazard	C1	0.25
☐ Dragon's Hunger	Resource	R3	2.50
☐ Dragon's Terror	Hazard	U2	1.00
☐ Dragon-feuds	Resource	U2	1.00
☐ Dragon-lore	Resource	U2	1.00
☐ Dragon-sickness	Hazard	C2	0.25
☐ Dunlending Raiders	Hazard	C1	0.25
☐ Dwarven Hoard	Resource	C2	0.25
☐ Eärcaraxë	Hazard	R2	6.00
☐ Eärcaraxë Ahunt	Hazard	U2	1.00
☐ Eärcaraxë at Home	Hazard	R3	3.00
☐ Echo of All Joy	Resource	U2	1.00
☐ Elf-path	Resource	C2	0.25
☐ Emerald of Doriath	Resource	U2	1.00
☐ Emerald of the Mariner	Resource	R2	8.00
☐ Enruned Shield	Resource	U2	1.00
☐ Exile of Solitude	Hazard	R3	2.00
☐ Fast Asleep	Resource	C2	0.25
☐ Fever of Unrest	Hazard	R3	3.00
☐ Flatter a Foe	Resource	C1	0.25
☐ Foolish Words	Hazard	C2	0.25
☐ Forod	Resource	C1	0.25
☐ Fram Framson	Character	R2	6.00
☐ Framsburg	Site	U2	1.00
☐ Frenzy of Madness	Hazard	R3	3.00
☐ From the Pits of Angband	Hazard	U2	1.00
☐ Galdor	Character	U2	1.00
☐ Gift of Comprehension	Resource	C1	0.25
☐ Gold Belt of Lórien	Resource	U2	1.00
☐ Gold Hill	Site	U2	1.00
☐ Gondmaeglom	Site	U2	1.00
☐ Gothmog	Hazard	R2	5.00
☐ Habergeon of Silver	Resource	C2	0.25
☐ Half an Eye Open	Hazard	C1	0.25
☐ Harad	Resource	C1	0.25
☐ Helm of Her Secrecy	Resource	R2	5.00
☐ "Here, There, or Yonder"	Resource	U2	1.00
☐ Hey! come merry dol!	Resource	C2	0.25
☐ Hobgoblins	Hazard	C2	0.25
☐ Host of Bats	Hazard	U2	1.00
☐ Houses of Healing	Resource	C2	0.25
☐ Ice-drake	Hazard	C1	0.25
☐ Icy Touch	Hazard	C2	0.25
☐ Incite Denizens	Hazard	C2	0.25
☐ Incite Minions	Hazard	C2	0.25
☐ Ioreth	Character	U2	1.00
☐ Isle of the Ulond	Site	U2	1.00
☐ Itangast	Hazard	R2	7.00
☐ Itangast Ahunt	Hazard	U2	1.00
☐ Itangast at Home	Hazard	R3	3.00
☐ King under the Mountain	Resource	R2	6.00
☐ Known to an Ounce	Hazard	R2	5.00
☐ Land-drake	Hazard	C2	0.25
☐ Left Behind	Hazard	U2	1.00
☐ Legendary Hoard	Resource	R2	5.00
☐ Lesser Spiders	Hazard	C2	0.25
☐ Leucaruth Ahunt	Hazard	U2	1.00
☐ Leucaruth at Home	Hazard	R3	2.50
☐ Light-drake	Hazard	C2	0.25
☐ Look More Closely Later	Resource	C1	0.25
☐ Lore of the Ages	Resource	C2	0.25
☐ Magical Harp	Resource	U2	1.00
☐ Many Foes He Fought	Resource	C2	0.25
☐ Many Sorrows Befall	Hazard	R2	4.00
☐ Many Turns and Doublings	Resource	C2	0.25
☐ Map to Mithril	Resource	U2	1.00
☐ Marsh-drake	Hazard	C2	0.25
☐ Marvels Told	Resource	C2	0.25
☐ Master of Esgaroth	Resource	C2	0.25
☐ Master of Wood, Water, or Hill	Resource	C2	0.25

RARITY KEY C = Common   U = Uncommon   R = Rare   # = Cards with lower numbers are rarer   X = Fixed/standard in all decks

Card name	Type	Rarity	Price
12			
☐ Mathom Lore	Resource	R2	6.00
☐ Memories Stolen	Hazard	R2	4.00
☐ Men of Dale	Resource	U2	1.00
☐ Men of Lake-town	Resource	U2	1.00
☐ More Sense Than You	Resource	C2	0.25
☐ Morgul-rats	Hazard	R3	2.50
☐ Necklace of Silver and Pearls	Resource	C1	0.25
☐ Nenseldë the Wingild	Resource	R2	4.00
☐ No Escape from My Magic	Hazard	R2	5.00
13			
☐ Noose of the Sea	Hazard	U2	1.00
☐ Not at Home	Resource	C2	0.25
☐ Ovir Hollow	Site	U2	1.00
☐ Parsimony of Seclusion	Hazard	R3	2.50
☐ Passion of Wrath	Hazard	R3	2.50
☐ Peril Returned	Hazard	C2	0.25
☐ Pledge of Conduct	Resource	C2	0.25
☐ Prowess of Age	Hazard	R3	3.00
☐ Prowess of Might	Hazard	R3	3.00
14			
☐ Rain-drake	Hazard	C2	0.25
☐ Refuge	Resource	C2	0.25
☐ Returned Exiles	Resource	R2	6.00
☐ Rhûn	Resource	C1	0.25
☐ Riddling Talk	Resource	U2	1.00
☐ Rumor of Wealth	Hazard	U2	1.00
☐ Sand-drake	Hazard	U2	1.00
☐ Sated Beast	Resource	U2	1.00
☐ Scabbard of Chalcedony	Resource	C2	0.25

Card name	Type	Rarity	Price
15			
☐ Scatha	Hazard	R2	8.00
☐ Scatha Ahunt	Hazard	U2	1.00
☐ Scatha at Home	Hazard	R3	2.50
☐ Scorba	Hazard	R2	8.00
☐ Scorba Ahunt	Hazard	U2	1.00
☐ Scorba at Home	Hazard	R3	3.00
☐ Sea Serpent	Hazard	C1	0.25
☐ Searching Eye	Hazard	C2	0.25
☐ Secret News	Resource	C2	0.25
16			
☐ Shadow of Mordor	Hazard	R2	8.00
☐ Skin-changer	Resource	R2	8.00
☐ Sleepless Malice	Hazard	U2	1.00
☐ Smaug Ahunt	Hazard	U2	1.00
☐ Smaug at Home	Hazard	R3	2.50
☐ Song of the Lady	Hazard	R2	4.00
☐ Staff Asunder	Resource	R2	3.00
☐ Star of High Hope	Resource	U2	1.00
☐ Stormcrow	Hazard	C2	0.35
17			
☐ Subtlety of Guile	Hazard	R3	2.00
☐ Tales of the Hunt	Resource	C2	0.25
☐ Tharbad	Site	U2	1.00
☐ The Riddle Game	Resource	R2	3.00
☐ Thráin II	Character	R2	8.00
☐ Three Golden Hairs	Resource	U2	1.00
☐ Thrór's Map	Resource	U2	1.00
☐ Thunder's Companion	Hazard	C2	0.25
☐ Times Are Evil	Hazard	U2	1.00

Card name	Type	Rarity	Price
18			
☐ Trickery	Resource	C2	0.25
☐ True Cold-drake	Hazard	C1	0.25
☐ True Fire-drake	Hazard	C1	0.25
☐ Twice-baked Cakes	Resource	C1	0.25
☐ Valiant Sword	Resource	C2	0.25
☐ Vanish in Sunlight!	Resource	U2	1.00
☐ Velocity of Haste	Hazard	R3	4.00
☐ Warm Now Be Heart and Limb	Resource	C2	0.25
☐ Washed and Refreshed	Resource	C2	0.25
19			
☐ Waybread	Resource	U3	1.00
☐ Were-worm	Hazard	R2	6.00
☐ When I Know Anything	Resource	C2	0.25
☐ Wielded Twice	Resource	C2	0.25
☐ Wild Fell Beast	Hazard	R2	8.00
☐ Winds of Wrath	Hazard	R2	4.00
☐ Winged Cold-drake	Hazard	U2	1.00
☐ Winged Fire-drake	Hazard	U2	1.00
☐ Wit	Resource	U2	1.00
20			
☐ Withered Lands	Hazard	C1	0.25
☐ Wizard Uncloaked	Resource	U2	1.00
☐ Wizards's Staff	Resource	U2	1.00
☐ Wolf-riders	Hazard	C2	0.25
☐ Wondrous Maps	Resource	C1	0.35
☐ Worm's Stench	Hazard	U2	1.00
☐ Wormsbane	Resource	R2	5.00
☐ Worn and Famished	Hazard	C2	0.25
☐ Zarak Dûm	Site	U2	1.00

Middle-earth • Dark Minions

Iron Crown Enterprises • Released **November 1996**

180 cards in set • **IDENTIFIER: Faint rune at lower right, looks like an angular 'B'**

• Booster packs contain 15 cards; booster displays contain 36 boosters

This set's primary contribution to the game is agent cards, which represent evil minions a player can move around Middle-earth, separate from his party, to disrupt or attack an opponent. Because the agents are played face-down and move secretly, an opponent can never be sure of their location. Despite their power, the complexity of the mechanics for moving and attacking deterred many from their use.

Dark Minions also introduces Under-deeps sites, sites located beneath the surface of Middle-earth with their own rules for movement. Creatures and hazards located at such sites tend to be nastier than their surface counterparts, but the rewards (the ability to play multiple high-MP cards) can be great.

Because most of the agents were characters culled from sources other than the four books in the series, *Minions* lacked for true "main characters" and general power cards, though several useful utility cards come from the set. — *Jason Winter*

Set (180 cards)	150.00		
Booster Display Box	60.00		
Booster Pack	2.60		

You will need **20** nine-pocket pages to store this set. (10 doubled up)

Card name	Type	Rarity	Price
1			
☐ Aiglos	Item	R2	8.00
☐ An Article Missing	Hazard	U2	0.90
☐ An Unexpected Outpost	Hazard	C2	0.25
☐ An Unexpected Party	Resource	R3	4.50
☐ Anarin	Minion	U2	0.90
☐ Ancient Stair	Resource	U2	0.90
☐ Angmar Arises	Hazard	U2	0.25
☐ Armory	Resource	U2	0.90
☐ Await the Advent of Allies	Resource	U2	0.90
2			
☐ Aware of their Ways	Hazard	U2	0.90
☐ Baduila	Minion	R2	5.30
☐ Balance Between Powers	Resource	R3	3.30
☐ Barrow-blade	Resource	C2	0.25
☐ Bill Ferny	Minion	C1	0.25
☐ Bring Our Curses Home	Hazard	R3	2.00
☐ Bûthrakaur the Green	Creature	R2	5.50

Card name	Type	Rarity	Price
☐ Chance of Being Lost	Hazard	U2	0.90
☐ Chill Douser	Creature	U2	0.90
3			
☐ Choice of Lúthien	Resource	R2	5.50
☐ Crown of Flowers	Resource	C2	0.30
☐ Cunning Foes	Hazard	C2	0.25
☐ Cup of Farewell	Resource	U2	0.90
☐ Dark Numbers	Resource	U2	0.60
☐ Dâsakûn	Minion	C2	0.30
☐ Deallus	Minion	C1	0.25
☐ Doubled Vigilance	Hazard	C2	0.25
☐ Dragon-helm	Item	R2	5.50
4			
☐ Drór	Minion	C1	0.25
☐ Drums	Hazard	U2	0.90
☐ Durin's Bane	Creature	R2	8.50
☐ Dwarven Light-stone	Item	U2	0.90
☐ Earth-tremors	Hazard	U2	0.90
☐ Elerína	Minion	R2	6.00
☐ Elwen	Minion	U2	0.90
☐ Endless Whispers	Hazard	U2	0.90
☐ Enduring Tales	Resource	C2	0.25
5			
☐ Eun	Minion	C1	0.30
☐ Exhalation of Decay	Hazard	C2	0.25
☐ Eyes of Mandos	Resource	R3	4.00

Card name	Type	Rarity	Price
☐ Eyes of the Shadow	Hazard	U2	0.90
☐ Face out of Sight	Resource	C1	0.25
☐ Faces of the Dead	Hazard	C2	0.25
☐ Fate of the Ithil-stone	Resource	R2	5.50
☐ Fifteen Birds in Five Firtrees	Resource	R3	3.60
☐ Fireworks	Resource	C2	0.25
6			
☐ Firiel	Minion	R2	5.00
☐ First of the Order	Resource	R3	3.10
☐ Flies and Spiders	Hazard	C1	0.25
☐ Foes Shall Fall	Hazard	U2	0.90
☐ Folco Boffin	Character	U2	0.90
☐ Forewarned Is Forearmed	Resource	C2	0.25
☐ Forgotten Scrolls	Item	C2	0.25
☐ Fori the Beardless	Minion	U2	0.90
☐ Free to Choose	Resource	C2	0.25
7			
☐ Gems of Arda	Item	R3	3.50
☐ Gergeli	Minion	C1	0.30
☐ Gisulf	Minion	C1	0.30
☐ Gnaw with Words	Hazard	C2	0.25
☐ Golodhros	Minion	R2	6.30
☐ Good Sense Revolts	Hazard	C2	0.25
☐ Great Need or Purpose	Hazard	U2	0.90
☐ Great Secrets Buried There	Hazard	U2	0.90

RARITY KEY   C = Common   **U** = Uncommon   **R** = Rare   **#** = Cards with lower numbers are rarer   **X** = Fixed/standard in all decks

Card name	Type	Rarity	Price
☐ Hall of Fire	Resource	C2	0.25
8			
☐ Haudh-in-Gwanûr	Site	U2	0.90
☐ Healing of Nimrodel	Resource	C2	0.25
☐ Helms of Iron	Hazard	U2	0.90
☐ Herb-lore	Resource	R3	3.00
☐ Here Is a Snake!	Resource	C2	0.25
☐ Herion	Minion	C1	0.30
☐ Hermit's Hill	Site	U2	0.90
☐ Hidden Knife	Resource	C1	0.25
☐ Hobbit-lore	Resource	R3	3.50
9			
☐ "Horns, Horns, Horns"	Resource	C1	0.30
☐ Hour of Need	Resource	R3	3.00
☐ Hundreds of Butterflies	Resource	C2	0.25
☐ I Know Much about You	Resource	C2	0.25
☐ In Darkness Bind Them	Hazard	C2	0.25
☐ In Great Wrath	Hazard	U2	0.90
☐ In the Heart of his Realm	Hazard	R3	2.50
☐ Inner Cunning	Hazard	C2	0.25
☐ Into Dark Tunnels	Resource	C1	0.25
10			
☐ Into the Smoking Cone	Resource	R2	5.50
☐ Ivic	Minion	U2	0.90
☐ Jûoma	Minion	U2	0.90
☐ Knowledge of the Enemy	Resource	U3	0.90
☐ Leaf Brooch	Item	C2	0.25
☐ Leamon	Minion	C1	0.30
☐ Like the Crash of Battering-rams	Hazard	R3	3.10
☐ Lindion the Oronín	Ally	U2	0.90
☐ Little Snuffler	Creature	U2	0.90
11			
☐ Lobelia Sackville Baggins	Hazard	U2	0.90
☐ Long Dark Reach	Hazard	R3	3.40
☐ Lost Tome	Item	C2	0.25
☐ Mallorn	Resource	R2	7.00
☐ Memories Recalled	Resource	C2	0.25
☐ Mistress Lobelia	Ally	U2	0.90
☐ Mithril	Item	R2	7.00
☐ Mordor in Arms	Hazard	U2	0.90
☐ More Alert than Most	Resource	C2	0.25
12			
☐ My Precious	Hazard	R2	5.00
☐ Nameless Thing	Creature	U2	0.90

Card name	Type	Rarity	Price
☐ Necklace of Girion	Item	R2	3.50
☐ Neither so Ancient Nor so Potent	Hazard	U2	0.90
☐ Never Seen Him	Hazard	C2	0.25
☐ Nimloth	Minion	C1	0.25
☐ No Waiting to Wonder	Resource	C2	0.25
☐ No Way Forward	Hazard	C2	0.25
☐ Noble Hound	Ally	C2	0.25
13			
☐ Nobody's Friend	Hazard	C2	0.25
☐ Noldo-lantern	Item	U2	0.90
☐ Ôm-buri-Ôm	Minion	U2	0.90
☐ Ordered to Kill	Resource	R3	3.00
☐ Out of the Black Sky	Hazard	R3	3.10
☐ Pale Dream-maker	Hazard	R3	2.00
☐ Palm to Palm	Resource	C2	0.25
☐ Pass the Doors of Dol Guldur	Resource	R2	5.50
☐ Phial of Galadriel	Item	R2	6.00
14			
☐ Pierced by Many Wounds	Hazard	C2	0.25
☐ Pôn-ora-Pôn	Minion	U2	0.60
☐ Râisha	Minion	U2	0.90
☐ Rank upon Rank	Hazard	C2	0.25
☐ Reaching Shadow	Hazard	C2	0.25
☐ Rebuild the Town	Resource	C2	0.25
☐ Redoubled Force	Hazard	C2	0.25
☐ Reluctant Final Parting	Hazard	U2	0.90
☐ Revealed to all Watchers	Hazard	R2	5.00
15			
☐ Saw Further and Deeper	Resource	C2	0.25
☐ Scimitars of Steel	Hazard	U2	0.60
☐ Secret Ways	Resource	C2	0.25
☐ Seek without Success	Hazard	C2	0.25
☐ Seized by Terror	Hazard	C2	0.25
☐ Sentinels of Númenor	Resource	U2	0.60
☐ Shadow out of the Dark	Creature	R2	4.50
☐ Smoke Rings	Resource	C2	0.25
☐ Spells of the Barrow-wights	Hazard	U2	0.50
16			
☐ Spider of the Môrlat	Creature	C1	0.45
☐ Stirring Bones	Creature	R2	6.00
☐ Sudden Fury	Hazard	C2	0.25
☐ Súrion	Minion	C2	0.30
☐ Taladhan	Minion	R2	6.00
☐ The Black Enemy's Wrath	Hazard	R3	3.00

Card name	Type	Rarity	Price
☐ The Dwarves Are upon You!	Resource	U2	0.90
☐ The Gem-deeps	Site	U2	0.90
☐ The Grimburgoth	Minion	R2	6.00
17			
☐ The Hunt	Resource	R3	3.30
☐ The Iron-deeps	Site	R2	5.50
☐ The Moon Is Dead	Hazard	C2	0.25
☐ The Pûkel-deeps	Site	U2	0.90
☐ The Reach of Ulmo	Hazard	U2	0.90
☐ The Sulfur-deeps	Site	R2	5.00
☐ The Under-courts	Site	R2	5.00
☐ The Under-galleries	Site	R2	5.50
☐ The Under-gates	Site	U2	0.90
18			
☐ The Under-grottos	Site	U2	0.90
☐ The Under-leas	Site	U2	0.90
☐ The Under-vaults	Site	U2	0.90
☐ The Way is Shut	Hazard	U2	0.90
☐ The Windlord Found Me	Resource	U2	0.90
☐ To Get You Away	Hazard	R3	2.50
☐ To the Uttermost Foundations	Resource	U2	0.90
☐ Token of Goodwill	Resource	R3	2.50
☐ Tribal Banner	Hazard	C2	0.25
19			
☐ Tribal Totem	Hazard	R3	3.00
☐ Troll-purse	Hazard	U2	0.90
☐ Twisted Tales	Hazard	U2	0.90
☐ Two or Three Tribes Present	Hazard	C2	0.25
☐ Umagaur the Pale	Creature	R2	5.50
☐ Urlurtsu Nurn	Site	U2	0.90
☐ Vein of Arda	Resource	C1	0.25
☐ Waylaid, Wounded, and Orc-dragged	Hazard	U2	0.90
☐ When You Know More	Resource	C2	0.25
20			
☐ Which Might Be Lies	Hazard	C2	0.25
☐ Will not Come Down	Hazard	U2	0.90
☐ Wisp of Pale Sheen	Creature	C1	0.25
☐ Withdrawn to Mordor	Resource	C1	0.25
☐ Woffung	Minion	C1	0.30
☐ Wormtongue	Minion	R2	6.30
☐ Wound of Long Burden	Hazard	C2	0.25
☐ Wraith-lord	Hazard	R2	8.00
☐ Your Welcome Is Doubtful	Hazard	U2	0.90

Middle-earth • The Lidless Eye

Iron Crown Enterprises • Released May 1997

417 cards in set • **IDENTIFIER: VERY faint rune at lower right, looks like a bent 'H'**

- Starter decks contain 75 cards; starter displays contain 10 starters
- Booster packs contain 15 cards; booster displays contain 36 boosters

This stand-alone set adds a new play option: Instead of assuming the persona of one of the Wizards, a player can become a Ringwraith in the service of Sauron. The object of the game is still basically the same: attain Marshalling Points by obtaining items, factions, and so on, or, instead of destroying the One Ring, take it back to Sauron in Barad-dur. New rules, as well as a whole new set of resources and sites, became necessary.

The most significant rule change is how hazards attack the evil parties. The term "detainment" was created to indicate that an attack would only tap characters, rather than wound or kill them. The logic is that a band of orcs would clearly try to kill a Wizard and his party but might be more lenient to a Ringwraith and his minions. Similarly, new hazards are issued, representing such "good" creatures as elves and dwarves, that attack minion parties but only detain hero parties.

It was easy to play hero decks against minion decks, or any other combination of minion versus hero. But, one disadvantage to this system is that players often had to bring two hazard mixes to tournaments, since hazards that were good against heroes were rarely good against minions and vice versa. Overall, despite the complexities (especially when trying to figure out if an attack would or would not be detainment), the set was well-received and injected some welcome variety into the game. — *Jason Winter*

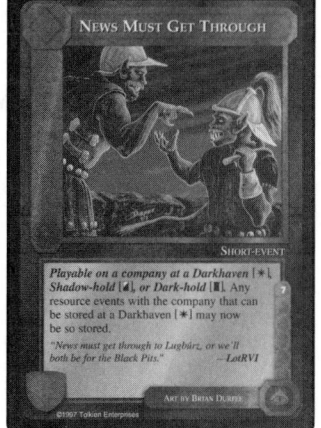

Set (417 cards)	275.00		
Starter Display Box	88.50		
Booster Display Box	84.50		
Starter Deck	10.50		
Booster Pack	3.00		

You will need **47** nine-pocket pages to store this set. (24 doubled up)

Card name	Type	Rarity	Price
1			
☐ A Little Gold Ring	Resource	C	0.20
☐ A Malady Without Healing	Resource	R	5.00
☐ A Nice Place to Hide	Resource	C	0.20
☐ Adunaphel the Ringwraith	Character	X	0.50

Card name	Type	Rarity	Price
☐ Adunaphel Unleashed	Resource	R	4.80
☐ Agburanar Roused	Resource	R	5.50
☐ Akhorahil the Ringwraith	Character	X	0.50

RARITY KEY C = Common U = Uncommon R = Rare # = Cards with lower numbers are rarer X = Fixed/standard in all decks

Card name	Type	Rarity	Price
☐ Akhorahil Unleashed	Resource	R	4.50
☐ All Thought Bent Upon It	Resource	U	0.80
2			
☐ Ambusher	Hazard	C	0.20
☐ Amon Hen	Site	U	0.80
☐ An Untimely Whisper	Resource	U	0.70
☐ Arouse Defenders	Hazard	C	0.20
☐ Arouse Denizens	Hazard	C	0.20
☐ Arthadan Rangers	Hazard	U	0.80
☐ Asternak	Character	X	0.50
☐ Awaiting the Call	Resource	U	0.50
☐ Awaken Defenders	Hazard	C	0.20
3			
☐ Awaken Denizens	Hazard	C	0.20
☐ Back to the Fray	Resource	U	0.90
☐ Bade to Rule	Resource	C	0.20
☐ Bag End	Site	U	0.90
☐ Balchoth	Faction	R	4.00
☐ Bandit Lair	Site	U	0.80
☐ Barad-Dur	Site	X	0.80
☐ Barrow-Downs	Site	X	0.80
☐ Barrow-Wight	Hazard	U	0.80
4			
☐ Belegorn	Character	U	0.50
☐ Beorn's House	Site	U	0.80
☐ Beorning Toll	Hazard	R	5.00
☐ Beornings	Faction	R	4.30
☐ Binding-ring	Resource	R	4.50
☐ Bitter Cold	Resource	R	4.00
☐ Black Mace	Resource	U	1.00
☐ Black Rain	Resource	R	4.80
☐ Black Rider	Resource	C	0.25
5			
☐ Black Trolls	Resource	U	0.70
☐ Black-Hide Shield	Resource	C	0.20
☐ Black-Mail Coat	Resource	C	0.20
☐ Blackbole	Resource	R	4.50
☐ Blazon of the Eye	Resource	C	0.20
☐ Blow Turned	Resource	C	0.20
☐ Blue Mountain Dwarf-hold	Site	R	4.00
☐ Bold Thrust	Resource	C	0.20
☐ Bree	Site	U	0.80
6			
☐ Brigands	Hazard	C	0.20
☐ Bright Gold Ring	Resource	U	0.80
☐ Broad-Headed Spear	Resource	C	0.20
☐ Broin	Character	R	4.50
☐ Buhr Widu	Site	X	0.50
☐ Burning Rick, Cot, and Tree	Resource	U	0.80
☐ By the Ringwraith's Word	Resource	C	0.20
☐ Calendal	Character	R	6.00
☐ Call of Home	Hazard	C	0.20
7			
☐ Cameth Brin	Site	U	0.80
☐ Carambor	Character	R	5.00
☐ Carn Dum	Site	C/X	0.20
☐ Catch an Elusive Scent	Resource	U	0.80
☐ Cave Worm	Hazard	C	0.35
☐ Cave-Drake	Hazard	C	0.20
☐ Caves of Ulund	Site	X	0.80
☐ Chill Them with Fear	Hazard	R	4.80
☐ Cirith Gorgor	Site	U	0.80
8			
☐ Cirith Ungol	Site	U	0.80
☐ Ciryaher	Character	U	0.50
☐ Come By Night Upon Them	Resource	R	4.50
☐ Corpse-Candle	Hazard	C	0.20
☐ Covetous Thoughts	Hazard	U	0.80
☐ Crack in the Wall	Resource	U	0.80
☐ Crooked Promptings	Resource	C	0.20
☐ Dale	Site	X	0.60
☐ Darkness Under Tree	Hazard	R	3.50
9			
☐ Dead Marshes	Site	U	0.80
☐ Deeper Shadows	Resource	U	0.80
☐ Despair of the Heart	Hazard	C	0.20
☐ Dimrill Dale	Site	U	0.80
☐ Dire Wolves	Hazard	C	0.20

Card name	Type	Rarity	Price
☐ Diversion	Resource	C	0.20
☐ Dogrib	Character	U	0.50
☐ Dol Amroth	Site	R	4.00
☐ Dol Guldur	Site	C/X	0.20
10			
☐ Doors of Night	Hazard	C	0.20
☐ Dorelas	Character	U	0.50
☐ Down Down to Goblin-Town	Resource	U	0.80
☐ Druadan Forest	Site	U	0.80
☐ Dunharrow	Site	U	0.80
☐ Dunlending Spy	Character	U	0.70
☐ Dunlendings	Faction	R	3.50
☐ Dunnish Clan-Hold	Site	U	0.80
☐ Dwar the Ringwraith	Character	X	0.50
11			
☐ Dwar Unleashed	Resource	R	4.00
☐ Dwarven Ring of Barin's Tribe	Resource	R	5.00
☐ Dwarven Ring of Bavor's Tribe	Resource	R	5.00
☐ Dwarven Ring of Druin's Tribe	Resource	R	5.00
☐ Dwarven Ring of Durin's Tribe	Resource	R	5.00
☐ Dwarven Ring of Dwalin's Tribe	Resource	R	5.00
☐ Easterling Camp	Site	X	0.60
☐ Easterlings	Resource	X	0.80
☐ Edoras	Site	X	0.80
12			
☐ Elf-lord Revealed in Wrath	Hazard	R	6.50
☐ Elves Upon Erantry	Hazard	C	0.20
☐ Ent in Search of Entwives	Hazard	U	0.80
☐ Eradan	Character	U	0.80
☐ Ettenmoors	Site	X	0.60
☐ Fell Rider	Resource	C	0.20
☐ Fell Winter	Hazard	C	0.20
☐ Focus Palantir	Resource	U	0.80
☐ Foolish Words	Hazard	C	0.20
13			
☐ Forced March	Resource	C	0.20
☐ Foul Trophies	Resource	R	4.00
☐ Foul-Smelling Paste	Resource	C	0.20
☐ Freeze the Flesh	Resource	R	4.50
☐ Geann a-Lisch	Site	C/X	0.20
☐ Ghosts	Hazard	C	0.20
☐ Ghouls	Hazard	C	0.20
☐ Giant	Hazard	C	0.20
☐ Giant Spiders	Hazard	C	0.20
14			
☐ Gifts as Given of Old	Resource	C	0.20
☐ Gladden Fields	Site	U	0.80
☐ Gleaming Gold Ring	Resource	C	0.20
☐ Glittering Caves	Site	U	0.90
☐ Gobel Mirlond	Site	U	0.80
☐ Goblin-Gate	Site	X	0.60
☐ Goblins of Goblin-Gate	Resource	X	0.50
☐ Gold Chains in the Wind	Resource	R	5.00
☐ Gold Ring that Sauron Fancies	Resource	C	0.20
15			
☐ Gondmaeglom	Site	X	0.80
☐ Gondorian Rangers	Hazard	C	0.20
☐ Gorbag	Character	X	0.90
☐ Greed	Hazard	C	0.20
☐ Grey Mountain Goblins	Resource	X	0.80
☐ Grishnakh	Character	X	0.90
☐ Gulla	Character	R	4.50
☐ Hador	Character	U	0.80
☐ Half-Trolls	Resource	U	0.80
16			
☐ Haud-in-Gwanur	Site	X	0.80
☐ Heedless Revelry	Hazard	R	4.50
☐ Hendolen	Character	R	3.50
☐ Henneth Annun	Site	U	0.80
☐ Heralded Lord	Resource	U	0.80
☐ Hermit's Hill	Site	U	0.80
☐ Hidden Ways	Resource	C	0.20
☐ Hide in Dark Places	Resource	U	0.70
☐ High Helm	Resource	U	0.80
17			
☐ Hill Trolls	Resource	R	5.00
☐ Hillmen	Resource	R	4.30
☐ Hoarmurath the Ringwraith	Character	X	0.50

Card name	Type	Rarity	Price
☐ Hoarmurath Unleashed	Resource	R	4.30
☐ Hobgoblins	Hazard	C	0.20
☐ Honey on the Tongue	Resource	R	4.00
☐ Horse-Lords	Hazard	C	0.20
☐ Horseman in the Night	Character	C	0.20
☐ Huron	Hazard	C	0.20
18			
☐ I'll be at Your Heels	Resource	C	0.20
☐ I'll Report You	Resource	C	0.25
☐ Ice-orcs	Resource	R	4.50
☐ In the Name of Mordor	Resource	U	0.80
☐ Incite Defenders	Hazard	C	0.20
☐ Incite Denizens	Hazard	C	0.20
☐ Indur the Ringwraith	Character	X	0.50
☐ Indur Unleashed	Resource	R	4.50
☐ Iron Hill Dwarf-hold	Site	R	4.50
19			
☐ Iron Road	Resource	U	0.80
☐ Isengard	Site	U	0.80
☐ Jerrek	Character	X	0.80
☐ Khamul the Ringwraith	Character	X	0.50
☐ Khamul Unleashed	Resource	R	4.00
☐ Kill All But NOT the Halflings	Resource	R	5.00
☐ Lagduf	Character	U	0.80
☐ Lake-Town	Site	U	0.80
☐ Land-Drake	Hazard	C	0.20
20			
☐ Landroval	Hazard	R	5.00
☐ Last Child of Ungoliant	Resource	R	5.00
☐ Lawless Men	Hazard	C	0.20
☐ Layos	Character	X	0.80
☐ Leg It Double Quick	Resource	R	4.00
☐ Lesser Spiders	Hazard	C	0.20
☐ Lieutenant of Angmar	Character	R	7.00
☐ Lieutenant of Dol Guldur	Character	R	7.00
☐ Lieutenant of Morgul	Character	R	7.50
21			
☐ Lond Galen	Site	U	0.80
☐ Long Winter	Hazard	C	0.20
☐ Lossadan Cairn	Site	U	0.80
☐ Lossadan Camp	Site	U	0.80
☐ Lost in Border-Lands	Hazard	C	0.20
☐ Lost in Free-Domains	Hazard	C	0.20
☐ Lost in Shadow-Lands	Hazard	C	0.20
☐ Lost in Wilderness	Hazard	C	0.20
☐ Luitprand	Character	X	0.80
22			
☐ Lure of Expedience	Hazard	C	0.20
☐ Lure of Nature	Hazard	C	0.20
☐ Lure of the Senses	Hazard	C	0.20
☐ Magic Ring of Delusion	Resource	U	0.90
☐ Magic Ring of Enigma	Resource	U/X	0.80
☐ Magic Ring of Fury	Resource	U/X	0.80
☐ Magic Ring of Guile	Resource	U/X	0.80
☐ Magic Ring of Lies	Resource	U/X	0.80
☐ Magic Ring of Savagery	Resource	U/X	0.80
23			
☐ Magic Ring of Shadows	Resource	U	0.90
☐ Magic Ring of Weals	Resource	U	0.90
☐ Marsh-Drake	Hazard	C	0.20
☐ Men of Dorwinion	Resource	X	0.80
☐ Messenger of Mordor	Resource	R	5.00
☐ Minas Morgul	Site	C/X	0.20
☐ Minas Tirith	Site	X	0.80
☐ Minions Stir	Hazard	U	0.80
☐ Minor Ring	Resource	C	0.20
24			
☐ Misty Mountain Wargs	Resource	U	0.90
☐ Morgul-blade	Resource	R	4.50
☐ Moria	Site	X	0.80
☐ Motionless Among the Slain	Resource	R	4.30
☐ Mount Doom	Site	U	0.80
☐ Mount Gram	Site	U	0.80
☐ Mount Gundabad	Site	X	0.80
☐ Muster Disperses	Hazard	C	0.20
☐ Muzgash	Character	X	0.80
25			
☐ Nain	Site	R	3.00

RARITY KEY **C** = Common   **U** = Uncommon   **R** = Rare   **#** = Cards with lower numbers are rarer   **X** = Fixed/standard in all decks

Card name	Type	Rarity	Price
Nevido Smod	Character	X	2.10
News Must Get Through	Character	X	0.50
News of Doom	Resource	R	3.50
News of the Shire	Hazard	R	4.00
No More Nonsense	Resource	R	4.00
No News of Our Riding	Resource	R	3.00
Not Slay Needlessly	Resource	U	0.80
Nothing to Eat or Drink	Resource	U	0.80
Nurniag Camp	Hazard	C	0.30
Nurniags	Resource	U	0.80
Odoacer	Character	X	0.80
Old Cache	Resource	C	0.20
Old Prejudice	Resource	R	4.00
Old Troll	Character	U	0.80
One Dear to You	Resource	R	4.30
Orc Brawler	Character	C	0.20
Orc Captain	Character	U/X	0.50
Orc Chieftain	Character	U/X	0.50
Orc Quarrels	Resource	C	0.20
Orc Sniffler	Character	C	0.20
Orc Stealth	Resource	U	0.80
Orc Tracker	Character	C/X	0.20
Orc Veteran	Character	C/X	0.20
Orc-Draughts	Resource	C	0.20
Orc-Liquor	Resource	C	0.20
Orc-mounts	Resource	R	4.30
Orc-Raiders	Hazard	C	0.20
Orc-Warband	Hazard	C	0.20
Orc-Watch	Hazard	C	0.20
Orcs of Angmar	Resource	U	0.80
Orcs of Gorgoroth	Resource	U	0.80
Orcs of Gundabad	Resource	X	0.90
Orcs of Mirkwood	Resource	X	0.80
Orcs of Moria	Resource	X	0.90
Orcs of the Ash Mountains	Resource	U	0.80
Orcs of the Ephel Duath	Resource	U	0.90
Orcs of the Red Eye	Resource	U	0.80
Orcs of the Udun	Resource	U	0.90
Ost-in-Edhil	Site	U	0.80
Ostisen	Character	X	0.80
Palantir of Amon Sul	Resource	R	5.00
Palantir of Annúminas	Resource	R	5.00
Palantir of Elostirion	Resource	R	5.00
Palantir of Minas Tirith	Resource	U	1.00
Palantir of Orthanc	Resource	U	1.00
Palantir of Osgiliath	Resource	R	4.80
Paltry Ring	Resource	C	0.20
Pelargir	Site	U	0.80
Perfect Gold Ring	Resource	R	5.00
Pirates	Hazard	R	4.50
Plague	Hazard	R	3.00
Plague of Wights	Hazard	U	0.90
Poison	Resource	R	3.80
Poisonous Despair	Resource	U	0.80
Pon Opar	Character	X	0.90
Radgug	Character	U	0.80
Raider-Hold	Site	U	0.80
Rats!	Hazard	U	0.50
Ready to His Will	Resource	R	5.30
Rebel-Talk	Hazard	C	0.20
Red Book of Westmarch	Resource	U	0.80
Remnants of Old Robberies	Resource	R	4.50
Ren the Ringwraith	Character	X	0.50
Ren Unleashed	Resource	R	4.50
River	Hazard	C	0.20
Ruined Signal Tower	Site	U	0.80
Rumor of the One	Resource	R	4.50
Ruse	Resource	R	5.00
Sable Shield	Resource	U	0.90
Sarn Goriwing	Site	X	0.80
Saw-Toothed Blade	Resource	C	0.20

Card name	Type	Rarity	Price
Scatha Roused	Resource	R	5.50
Scorba Roused	Resource	R	6.50
Scroll of Isildur	Resource	U	1.00
Searching Eye	Hazard	C	0.20
Secrets of Their Forging	Resource	U	1.00
Seize Prisoners	Resource	C	0.20
Sellswords Between Characters	Hazard	C	0.20
Shadow-Cloak	Resource	U	0.80
Shagrat	Character	X	0.90
Shamas	Character	R	4.50
Shelob's Lair	Site	U	0.80
Shrel-Kain	Site	X	0.80
Shut Yer Mouth	Hazard	U	0.80
Skies of Fire	Resource	C	0.20
Slayer	Hazard	C	0.25
Smart and Secret	Resource	C	0.20
Smaug Roused	Resource	R	6.80
Smoke on the Wind	Resource	R	4.50
Snaga	Character	R	4.80
Snaga-Hai	Resource	C	0.20
Sneakin'	Resource	R	4.80
So You've Come Back	Hazard	U	0.80
Some Secret Art of Flame	Resource	R	4.50
Something Has Slipped	Hazard	R	4.00
Sons of Kings	Hazard	C	0.20
Southron Oasis	Site	X	0.60
Southrons	Resource	X	0.80
Spying out the Land	Resource	R	4.30
Stabbed Him in His Sleep	Resource	C	0.20
Stay Her Appetite	Hazard	R	4.00
Stench of Mordor	Hazard	U	0.80
Stinker	Resource	U	0.90
Stirring Bones	Hazard	C	0.20
Stone Trolls	Resource	U	0.80
Stone-Circle	Site	U	0.80
Strange Rations	Resource	C	0.20
Sudden Call	Resource	C/X	0.20
Swag	Resource	U	0.80
Swarm of Bats	Resource	C	0.20
Swift Strokes	Resource	U	0.80
Tarcil	Character	R	4.80
Test of Fire	Resource	C	0.20
Tharbad	Site	U	0.80
That Ain't No Secret	Resource	C	0.20
That's Been Heard Before Tonight	Resource	C	0.20
The Border-Watch	Hazard	C	0.20
The Iron Crown	Resource	R	7.80
The Least of Gold Rings	Resource	C	0.20
The Lidless Eye	Resource	R	11.00
The Lonely Mountain	Site	X	0.80
The Mithril-coat	Resource	R	6.00
The Mouth	Character	R	8.00
The Names Among Them	Resource	C/X	0.20
The One Ring	Resource	R	22.50
The Oracle's Ring	Resource	R	5.50
The Reviled Ring	Resource	R	5.00
The Ring Leaves It's Mark	Resource	C	0.20
The Ring Will Have But One Master	Hazard	R	6.00
The Roving Eye	Hazard	R	5.00
The Stones	Site	R	4.50
The Warding Ring	Resource	R	5.00
The Warg-king	Resource	R	4.00
The Water's Tithe	Resource	U	1.00
The White Towers	Site	U	0.80
The Wind Throne	Site	X	0.80
The Witch-King	Character	X	0.90
The Witch-king Unleashed	Resource	R	5.00
The Worthy Hills	Site	R	4.00

Card name	Type	Rarity	Price
They Ride Together	Resource	R	4.50
Thing Stolen	Resource	U	0.80
Thranduil's Folk	Hazard	R	4.50
Thranduil's Halls	Site	X	0.80
Threats	Resource	R	4.30
Threlin	Character	R	5.30
Thrice Outnumbered	Hazard	U	0.80
Thunder's Companion	Hazard	C	0.20
Tidings of Bold Spies	Hazard	C	0.20
Tidings of Death	Resource	R	4.50
Tidings of Doubt and Danger	Hazard	U	0.80
To Satisfy the Questioner	Resource	C	0.20
Trifling Ring	Resource	C	0.20
Troll Lout	Character	C	0.20
Troll-Chief	Character	U/X	0.50
Tros Hesnef	Character	U	0.80
True Fire-Drake	Hazard	C	0.20
Twilight	Hazard	C	0.20
Two-headed Troll	Resource	R	6.00
Uchel	Character	U	0.70
Ufthak	Character	R	5.50
Ulkaur the Tongueless	Character	R	5.50
Umbarean Corsairs	Resource	U	0.80
Under His Blow	Resource	C	0.20
Ungol-Orcs	Resource	U	1.00
Urlurtsu Nurn	Site	R	4.00
Uruk-hai	Resource	R	4.30
Uruk-lieutenant	Hazard	R	5.40
Uvatha the Ringwraith	Character	X	0.50
Uvatha Unleashed	Resource	R	4.50
Vale of Erech	Site	X	0.60
Variag Camp	Site	X	0.60
Variags of Khand	Resource	X	0.80
Veils Flung Away	Hazard	U	0.80
Veils of Shadow	Resource	R	4.50
Voices of Malice	Resource	C	0.20
Waiting Shadow	Hazard	R	5.00
Wake of War	Hazard	C	0.20
Wandering Eldar	Hazard	R	4.30
War-Warg	Resource	C	0.20
War-Wolf	Resource	C	0.20
Wargs	Hazard	C	0.20
Wargs of the Forochel	Resource	R	4.80
Watcher in the Water	Hazard	U	0.80
We Have Come to Kill	Resource	R	4.50
Weariness of the Heart	Hazard	C	0.20
Webs of Fear and Treachery	Hazard	R	4.00
Weigh All Things to a Nicety	Resource	C	0.20
Where There's a Whip	Resource	R	5.00
While the Yellow Face Sleeps	Resource	R	4.50
Whip	Resource	U	0.80
White Mountain Wolves	Resource	R	4.50
Wild Trolls	Hazard	C	0.20
Wisdom to Wield	Resource	U	0.80
Woodmen	Resource	X	0.80
Woodmen-Town	Site	X	0.60
Words of Menace and Deceit	Resource	R	4.80
Wose Passage-Hold	Site	U	0.80
Woses of the Eryn Vorn	Resource	R	3.80
Wrath of the West	Hazard	U	0.80

Middle-earth • Special sets

Middle-earth Gift Set	37.50
Middle-earth: The Wizards Starter Set	13.50
Middle-earth Challenge Deck	8.50

RARITY KEY C = Common U = Uncommon R = Rare # = Cards with lower numbers are rarer X = Fixed/standard in all decks

Middle-earth • Against the Shadow

Iron Crown Enterprises • Released **August 1997**

170 cards in set • **IDENTIFIER: Faint rune '<' at lower right**

• Booster packs contain 15 cards; booster displays contain 36 boosters

The fourth expansion for **Middle-earth, Against the Shadow** focuses mainly on interaction between hero and minion parties. Because of the infrequency of such encounters, the set was not particularly well-received. It contained a mix of hero and minion resources, but the most interesting cards are the hazards designed to represent major hero characters, like the Nazgul hazards in the original set. — **Jason Winter**

Set (170 cards)		102.50
Booster Display Box		90.00
Booster Pack		3.00

You will need **19** nine-pocket pages to store this set. (10 doubled up)

Card name	Type	Rarity	Price
A Lie in Your Eyes	Event	R2	2.80
Above the Abyss	Event	C3	0.20
Alatar the Hunter	Creature	R2	2.30
All the Bells Ringing	Event	U3	0.90
Alliance of Free Peoples	Event	R2	3.00
Alone and Unadvised	Event	C3	0.20
Ancient Black Axe	Item	R2	3.00
Angmarim	Faction	R2	3.00
Angmarim	Faction	R1	3.00
Asdraigs	Faction	U2	1.00
Bairanax Roused	Faction	R1	7.00
Biter and Beater!	Event	C2	0.25
Black Horse	Ally	C3	0.30
Black Numenoreans	Faction	U2	1.00
Bow of the Galadhrim	Item	U2	1.00
Burat ("Bert")	Minion	U2	1.00
Cirith Gorgor	Site	R2	2.80
Come at Need	Event	C2	0.25
Corsairs of Rhûn	Faction	U2	1.00
Creature of an Older World	Ally	R2	3.30
Daelomin Roused	Faction	R1	7.00
Dancing Spire	Site	U2	1.00
Dark Tryst	Event	C3	0.20
Driven By a Madness	Event	U3	0.90
Drughu	Event	U3	0.90
Durin's Folk	Creature	C3	0.20
Dwarven Ring of Thelor's Tribe	Item	U2	1.00
Dwarven Ring of Thrar's Tribe	Item	U2	1.00
Dwarven Travelers	Creature	C3	0.20
Eagles' Eyrie	Site	U2	1.00
Eärcaraxë Roused	Faction	R1	8.50
Early Harvest	Event	C2	0.25
Edhellond	Site	R2	2.90
Enchanted Stream	Event	C3	0.20
Enchantments of Surpassing Excellence	Event	C3	0.30
Eye Never Sleeping	Event	U3	0.90
Faithless Steward	Event	R2	2.50
Far Below the Deepest Delvings	Event	U3	0.90
Farmer Maggot	Event	R1	4.00
Fealty Under Trial	Event	C2	0.25
FEAR! FIRE! FOES!	Event	C3	0.30
Framsburg	Site	R2	3.00
Full of Froth and Rage	Event	C2	0.25
Galadhrim	Creature	C2	0.25
Gandalf the Wanderer	Creature	R2	4.50
Geann a-Lisch	Site	U2	1.00
Gobel Mírlond	Site	U2	1.00
Goblin Earth-plumb	Item	C2	0.25
Gold Hill	Site	U2	1.00

Card name	Type	Rarity	Price
Great Bats	Ally	C3	0.20
Great Lord of Goblin-gate	Ally	R2	3.00
Grey Havens	Site	R2	3.00
Hail of Darts	Event	R2	3.50
Haradrim	Faction	R2	3.00
Haradrim	Faction	U2	1.00
Helm of Fear	Item	U2	1.00
Himring	Site	U2	1.00
Hoard Well-searched	Event	C2	0.25
Hold Rebuilt and Repaired	Event	C2	0.25
Hounds of Sauron	Event	R2	3.00
Irerock	Site	U2	1.00
Iron Shield of Old	Item	C2	0.25
Isle of the Ulond	Site	U2	1.00
Isles of the Dead that Live	Site	U2	1.00
Itangast Roused	Faction	R1	7.00
Ithil-stone	Item	R1	5.00
Jewel of Beleriand	Item	C2	0.25
Join With That Power	Event	C3	0.20
Knights of the Prince	Creature	R2	2.60
Lady of the Golden Wood	Creature	R2	3.30
Legendary Stair	Event	C2	0.25
Leucaruth Roused	Faction	R1	10.00
Lord of the Carrock	Creature	R2	3.30
Lord of the Haven	Creature	R2	3.00
Lorien	Site	R2	3.00
Master of the House	Creature	R2	3.00
Mauhur	Minion	R2	3.00
Mionid	Minion	U2	1.00
Morgul-orcs	Faction	R2	2.50
Mount Slain	Event	R2	2.50
Near to Hear a Whisper	Event	R2	2.50
Necklace of Girion	Item	R2	3.00
No Strangers at this Time	Event	C3	0.20
Nuriags	Faction	U2	1.00
Nurniag Camp	Site	U2	1.00
Nurniags	Faction	R1	7.00
Old Forest	Site	U2	1.00
Old Treasure	Item	C2	0.25
One Foe to Breed a War	Event	R2	3.00
Orc-mail	Event	R2	2.50
Orcs of Dol Guldur	Faction	R2	3.00
Orders from Lugbûrz	Event	U3	0.90
Our Own Wolves	Event	R2	2.80
Ovir Hollow	Site	U2	1.00
Padding Feet	Event	R2	2.60
Pallando the Soul-keeper	Creature	R2	3.50
Perchen	Minion	U2	1.00
Petty-dwarves	Faction	R2	2.50
Petty-dwarves	Faction	R2	2.80
Pilfer Anything Unwatched	Event	U2	1.00
Power Against the Shadow	Event	C3	0.20
Power Built by Waiting	Event	C3	0.20
Powers too Dark and Terrible	Event	R2	3.00
Radagast the Tamer	Creature	R2	3.00
Raider-hold	Site	U2	1.00
Records Unread	Item	C2	0.25
Regiment of Black Crows	Ally	C3	0.20
Returned Beyond All Hope	Event	C2	0.25
Rhosgobel	Site	R2	3.00

Card name	Type	Rarity	Price
Ride Against the Enemy	Event	C3	0.20
Riven Gate	Event	R2	3.00
Rivendell	Site	R2	3.00
Sack Over the Head	Event	U3	0.90
Safe from the Shadow	Event	C2	0.25
Saruman the Wise	Creature	R2	3.80
Secret Book	Item	C2	0.25
Short Legs are Slow	Event	U3	0.90
Slip Treacherously	Event	C3	0.20
Spies Feared	Event	R2	2.50
Steeds	Event	R2	2.50
Steward's Guard	Creature	C2	0.25
Stout Men of Gondor	Creature	C3	0.20
Summons from Long Sleep	Event	C2	0.25
The Ash Mountain Deeps	Event	C2	0.25
The Balrog	Ally	R2	5.50
The Dark Power	Event	U3	0.90
The Gem-deeps	Site	R2	3.00
The Great Eye	Event	R2	3.00
The Iron-deeps	Site	R2	3.00
The Misty Mountain Deeps	Event	C2	0.25
The Mountains of Shadow Deeps	Event	C2	0.25
The Pukel-deeps	Site	R2	2.60
The Sulfur-deeps	Site	U2	1.00
The Sun Unveiled	Event	C3	0.20
The Tormented Earth	Event	U3	0.90
The Undeeps of Anduin	Event	C2	0.25
The Under-courts	Site	U2	1.00
The Under-galleries	Site	U2	1.00
The Under-gates	Site	U2	1.00
The Under-grottos	Site	U2	1.00
The Under-leas	Site	U2	1.00
The Under-roads	Event	C2	0.25
The Under-vaults	Site	U2	1.00
The White Mountains Cavern-ways	Event	C2	0.25
The Worthy Hills	Site	U2	1.00
Thong of Fire	Item	R2	3.00
Thrall-ring	Item	R2	3.00
Thror's Map	Item	U2	1.00
Tokens to Show	Event	C2	0.25
Tolfalas	Site	U2	1.00
Tower Raided	Event	R2	2.80
Treason the Greatest Foe	Event	R2	2.80
Tribute Garnered	Event	C2	0.25
Trolls from the Mountains	Creature	C2	0.25
Troth-ring	Item	R2	3.00
Trouble on All Borders	Event	C2	0.25
Tuma ("Tom")	Minion	U2	1.00
Turning Hope into Despair	Event	C3	0.20
Unhappy Blows	Event	R2	2.90
Use Your Legs	Event	R2	2.80
Usriev of Treachery	Item	C3	0.20
Wain-easterlings	Faction	U2	1.00
Wain-easterlings	Faction	U2	1.00
Weathertop	Site	U2	1.00
Well-preserved	Event	U3	0.90
Wellinghall	Site	U2	1.00
Will Shaken	Event	R2	2.80
World Gnawed by the Nameless	Event	R2	2.80
Woses of the Eryn Vorn	Faction	U2	1.00
Wuluag ("William")	Minion	U2	1.00

Middle-earth • *The White Hand*

Iron Crown Enterprises • Released **November 1997**

122 cards in set

• Booster packs contain 12 cards; booster displays contain 36 boosters

The White Hand introduces another option for play: Fallen-wizards. Each of the original five wizards receives an alternate persona card, representing that wizard had he given up the fight against Sauron. A new subset of resources, stage resources, were introduced specifically for Fallen-wizards, which offered various benefits and "stage points," a measure of how far a wizard had fallen into madness.

While providing for interesting gameplay, the addition of Fallen-wizards added to the already burgeoning complexity of the game and required a few more specialized hazards for play against Fallen-wizards. Some players were beginning to get turned off to the complexity, and to the general lack of recognizable material. The mere concept of Gandalf as a "Fallen-wizard" was a deterrent to many. — *Jason Winter*

Set (122 cards)	87.50	**You will need**
Booster Display Box	97.00	**14** nine-pocket pages to store this set. (7 doubled up)
Booster Pack	3.00	

Card name	Type	Rarity	Price
1			
A Merrier World	Resource	C3	0.20
A New Ringlord	Resource	R3	4.00
A Panoply of Wings	Resource	C3	0.20
A Strident Spawn	Resource	U3	0.60
Alatar	Character	C4	0.20
An Untimely Brood	Resource	C3	0.20
Arcane School	Resource	R3	2.50
Await the Onset	Resource	R2	3.30
Bad Company	Resource	C3	0.20
2			
Beasts of the Wood	Resource	C3	0.20
Blasting Fire	Resource	C4	0.20
Blind to All Else	Resource	C3	0.20
Blind to the West	Hazard	C4	0.20
Bow of Alatar	Resource	R2	4.50
Cast from the Order	Hazard	R2	3.80
Chambers in the Royal Court	Resource	U3	0.60
Counterfeit	Resource	R3	3.00
Crept Along Cleverly	Resource	C4	0.20
3			
Cruel Claw Perceived	Hazard	R3	2.10
Deep Mines	Site	C3	0.20
Delver's Harvest	Resource	U3	0.60
Doeth (Durthak)	Character	R2	4.40
Double-dealing	Resource	C4	0.20
Earth-eater	Resource	R3	2.60
Echoes of the Song	Hazard	C4	0.20
Euog (Ulzog)	Character	R2	4.30
Flotsam and Jetsam	Hazard	R3	2.60
4			
Fool's Bane	Hazard	U3	0.60
Fortress of the Towers	Resource	U3	0.60
Foul Tooth Unsheathed	Hazard	C3	0.20
Friend of Secret Things	Resource	U3	0.60
Gandalf	Character	C4	0.20
Gandalf's Friend	Resource	U3	0.60
Gatherer of Loyalties	Resource	C3	0.25
Girdle of Radagast	Resource	R2	4.60
Give Welcome to the Unexpected	Resource	R2	3.40
5			
Glove of Radagast	Resource	R2	3.60
Gnawed Ways	Resource	R3	2.60
Goblin-faces	Hazard	R3	2.60
Govern the Storms	Resource	R3	2.90
Great Patron	Resource	C3	0.25
Great Ruse	Resource	U3	0.60
Greater Half-orcs	Resource	R3	2.60
Grey Embassy	Resource	U3	0.60
Guarded Haven	Resource	U3	0.60
6			
Half-orcs	Resource	U3	0.60
Heart Grown Cold	Hazard	U3	0.60
Hidden Haven	Resource	C4	0.20

Card name	Type	Rarity	Price
Huntsman's Garb	Resource	U3	0.60
Ill-favoured Fellow	Character	C3	0.20
In the Grip of Ambition	Hazard	C3	0.20
Inner Rot	Hazard	R3	2.60
Ire of the East	Hazard	C4	0.20
Isengard	Site	C3	0.20
7			
Join the Hunt	Resource	U3	0.60
Keys of Orthanc	Resource	R2	3.90
Keys to the White Towers	Resource	R2	3.70
Legacy of Smiths	Resource	C3	0.25
Liquid Fire	Resource	R3	2.60
Longing for the West	Hazard	U3	0.60
Lugdush	Character	U3	0.60
Man of Skill	Resource	U3	0.60
Many-coloured Robes	Resource	U3	0.60
8			
Mask Torn	Hazard	R3	2.80
Master of Shapes	Resource	U3	0.60
Mechanical Bow	Resource	C4	0.20
Mischief in a Mean Way	Resource	R3	2.80
Nature's Revenge	Hazard	R3	2.60
Never Refuse	Resource	U3	0.60
Noble Steed	Resource	C4	0.20
Open to the Summons	Resource	U3	0.60
Oromë's Warders	Resource	R2	3.40
9			
Pallando	Character	C4	0.20
Pallando's Apprentice	Resource	U3	0.60
Pallando's Hood	Resource	U3	0.60
Piercing All Shadows	Resource	U3	0.60
Plotting Ruin	Resource	C3	0.20
Pocketed Robes	Resource	U3	0.60
Poison of his Voice	Resource	U3	0.60
Power Relinquished to Artifice	Hazard	R3	2.50
Promptings of Wisdom	Resource	U3	0.60
10			
Prophet of Doom	Resource	R2	3.80
Radagast	Character	C4	0.20
Radagast's Black Bird	Resource	U3	0.60
Rhosgobel	Site	C3	0.20

Card name	Type	Rarity	Price
Ring of Fire	Resource	R2	4.40
Rolled down to the Sea	Hazard	R2	3.70
Saruman	Character	C4	0.20
Saruman's Machinery	Resource	R3	3.00
Saruman's Ring	Resource	R2	4.50
11			
Shameful Deeds	Resource	U3	0.60
Shifter of Hues	Resource	R3	2.50
Sly Southerner	Character	C3	0.25
Sojourn in Shadows	Resource	R3	2.50
Something Else at Work	Hazard	R3	2.60
Spells Born of Discord	Resource	U3	0.60
Squint-eyed Brute	Character	C3	0.25
Squire of the Hunt	Resource	U3	0.60
Stave of Pallando	Resource	R2	3.80
12			
The Black Council	Resource	R3	2.80
The Fiery Blade	Resource	R3	2.80
The Forge-master	Resource	U3	0.60
The Fortress of Isen	Resource	U3	0.60
The Great Hunt	Resource	R2	4.00
The Grey Hat	Resource	U3	0.90
The White Council	Resource	R3	2.60
The White Hand	Resource	R2	5.50
The White Towers	Site	C4	0.20
13			
The White Wizard	Resource	R2	4.50
Thrall of the Voice	Resource	C4	0.20
Truths of Doom	Resource	U3	0.60
Uglæk	Character	R2	4.30
Vile Fumes	Resource	U4	0.50
War-forges	Resource	U3	0.60
White Light Broken	Resource	U3	0.60
Whole Villages Roused	Hazard	R3	2.50
Wild Horses	Resource	R3	2.50
14			
Wild Hounds	Resource	U3	0.60
Will You Not Come Down?	Hazard	U3	0.60
Winged Change-master	Resource	R3	2.80
Wizard's Myrmidon	Resource	C3	0.20
Wizard's Trove	Resource	R3	2.80

Middle-earth • *Promo cards*

Iron Crown distributed a healthy number of promotional cards for Middle-earth, many in magazines. **Neeker-Breekers** appeared in *Scrye* #12 (Jan 96), **Fury of the Iron Crown** appeared in *Scrye* #14 (May 1996), and **Deadly Dart** appeared in *Scrye* 4.2 (Jun 97).

The Iron Crown cards were a nice little in-joke for those who paid attention to manufacturer names.

Card name	Set	Price
1		
Angmar Arises		1.50
Bill Ferny		2.50
Black Arrow	Wizards	4.50
Deadly Dart		2.50
Fatty Bolger		2.50
Fury of the Iron Crown	Wizards	4.00
Ireful Flames	Dragons	2.50

Card name	Set	Price
More Alert Than Most		2.50
Neeker Breekers	Wizards	2.30
2		
Never Seen Him		1.50
Storm Crow		1.50
The Arkenstone		1.50
The Iron Crown	Wizards	4.00

RARITY KEY **C** = Common **U** = Uncommon **R** = Rare **VR** = Very Rare **UR** = Ultra Rare **F** = Foil card **X** = Fixed/standard in all decks

Middle-earth • The Balrog

Iron Crown Enterprises • Released **September 1998**

104 cards in set • **IDENTIFIER: Faint rune at lower right; looks like backwards 'R'**

• Available in two 132-card fixed starters, **The Shadow-deeps** and **Balrog's Host**

The last set for **Middle-earth** was released almost a full year after **The White Hand**, and interest in the game had nearly died off completely. **The Balrog** was packaged in two separate pre-constructed decks which contained all cards in the set. No booster packs were issued.

With *The Balrog*, players can take yet another persona, that of the evil Balrog, a fallen maia, similar to Sauron, who also seeks dominance over Middle-earth. The Balrog generally resides in the Under-deeps (and uses different site cards for the Under-deeps than a minion player) and has several Balrog-specific resource cards. Other than that, a Balrog player typically uses minion resources and plays similar to a Ringwraith, albeit with a somewhat different feel.

By this point, all the different options had diluted the game and even hardcore players were having a difficult time maintaining interest, especially with the delay between sets. Iron Crown announced a **Dwarf Lords** expansion for 1999, but it never came out.

Middle-earth CCG profits, it turned out, had to go to retire the game company's other non-CCG debts piled up in the previous decade — so the company wasn't well armed for the CCG slowdown in the late 1990s. When Iron Crown filed Chapter 11 in August 1999, its president, Pete Fenlon, said he pinned future hopes on the *Lord of the Rings* movies, then projected to hit screens in late 2000. As always with Hollywood, the pictures didn't make that schedule, and at Gen Con 2000 Decipher announced it had won the CCG rights. Iron Crown officially closed its doors at the end of 2000, destroying all unsold CCG product. — *Jason Winter & John Jackson Miller*

Set (104 cards)	42.50
Starter Display Box	94.00
Starter Deck	16.00

You will need 12 nine-pocket pages to store this set. (6 doubled up)

Note: As this expansion was released in two fixed 132-card starters, rarities here refer to how many copies of the card appear in the two boxes. There is no chance involved in finding any given card.

Card name	Type	Rarity	Price
A Few Recruits	Faction	C	0.10
A More Evil Hour	Event	R	1.40
Ancient Deep-hold	Site	U	0.50
Ancient Secrets	Event	C	0.10
Angband Revisited	Event	C	0.10
Azog	Character	U	0.50
Barad-Dur	Site	U	0.50
Beorning Skin-changers	Creature	U	0.60
Black Vapour	Event	U	0.50
Bolg	Character	U	0.50
Breach the Hold	Event	U	0.50
Buthrakaur	Character	R	1.90
Carn Dum	Site	U	0.50
Carrion Feeders	Creature	C	0.20
Cave Troll	Ally	C	0.20
Caverns Unchoked	Event	C	0.10
Challenge the Power	Event	R	1.90
Cirith Gorgor	Site	U	0.50
Cirith Ungol	Site	U	0.50
Cloaked by Darkness	Event	U	0.50
Crept Along Carefully	Event	U	0.50
Crooked-Legged Orc	Character	C	0.10
Crowned with Storm	Event	R	1.40
Darkness Made by Malice	Event	U	0.60
Darkness Wielded	Event	R	1.40
Descent through Fire	Event	R	2.00
Desire All for Thy Belly	Event	R	2.00

Card name	Type	Rarity	Price
Diminish and Depart	Event	R	2.00
Dol Guldur	Site	C	0.10
Eddy in Fate's Tide	Event	R	1.40
Elven Rope	Item	U	0.60
Evil Things Lingering	Ally	R	1.40
Flame of Udun	Event	C	0.10
Fled into Darkness	Event	R	1.40
Foe Dismayed	Event	C	0.10
Gangways over the Fire	Event	U	0.50
Glance of Arien	Event	R	1.40
Going Ever Under Dark	Event	U	0.50
Great Army of the North	Event	R	2.00
Great Fissure	Event	C	0.10
Great Shadow	Event	C	0.10
Great Troll	Ally	U	0.60
Grond	Event	R	1.40
Heart of Dark Fire	Event	R	1.40
Hill-troll	Character	C	0.10
Imprisoned and Mocked	Event	R	1.40
Invade Their Domain	Event	R	1.40
Long Greivous Siege	Event	R	2.00
Longbottom Leaf	Event	C	0.20
Lord and Usurper	Event	R	1.40
Maker's Map	Event	U	0.50
Memories of Old Torture	Event	R	1.40
Minas Morgul	Site	U	0.50
Mine or No One's	Event	R	1.40
Monstrosity of Diverse Shape	Event	R	1.40
Moria	Site	C	0.10
Mountain-maggot (#2)	Character	C	0.10
Nasty Slimy Thing	Ally	R	1.90
No Better Use	Event	R	1.40
Obey Him or Die	Event	C	0.10
Olog Warlords	Creature	U	0.50
Orders from the Great Demon	Event	C	0.10
Out He Sprang	Event	C	0.10
People Diminished	Event	R	1.40
Press-Gang	Event	R	1.40
Prone to Violence	Event	R	1.40

Card name	Type	Rarity	Price
Remains of Thangorodrim	Site	U	0.50
Roam the Waste	Event	U	0.50
Roots of the Earth	Event	C	0.10
Rumours of Rings	Event	U	0.60
Sauron	Event	U	0.60
Scourge of Fire	Event	R	1.40
Shelob's Brood	Creature	C	0.20
Show Things Unbidden	Event	R	1.40
Spawn of Ungoliant	Event	R	1.40
Stabbing Tongue of Fire	Item	R	2.40
Strangling Coils	Event	C	0.10
Strider	Character	R	7.50
Tempest of Fire	Event	U	0.50
Terror Heralds Doom	Event	U	0.50
The Balrog	Character	C	0.10
The Drowning-deeps	Site	U	0.50
The Gem-deeps	Site	C	0.10
The Iron-deeps	Site	C	0.10
The Pukel-deeps	Site	C	0.10
The Reek	Event	R	1.40
The Rusted-deeps	Site	U	0.50
The Sulfur-deeps	Site	C	0.10
The Sun Shone Fiercely	Event	U	0.50
The Under-courts	Site	U	0.50
The Under-galleries	Site	U	0.50
The Under-gates	Site	C	0.10
The Under-grottos	Site	C	0.10
The Under-leas	Site	C	0.10
The Under-vaults	Site	C	0.10
The Wind-deeps	Site	C	0.10
To Fealty Sworn	Event	R	2.00
Umagaur	Character	R	4.40
Unabated in Malice	Event	R	1.40
Ungoliant's Foul Issue	Event	R	1.40
Ungoliant's Progeny	Event	R	1.40
Vanguard of Might	Event	R	1.40
Whip of Many Thongs	Item	R	2.40
Whispers of Rings	Event	U	0.60

MLB Showdown

Wizards of the Coast • First set, **2000 Edition**, released **April 2000**

512 cards plus **62** premiums in set

- Starter decks contain 64 cards, playmat, and 20-sided die
- Booster packs contain 9 cards; Booster displays contain 36 boosters

Lead designer, **Tom Wylie**

MLB Showdown, a mass-market-targeted CCG based on Major League Baseball, using real-life players, represents Wizards of the Coast's first foray into sports games. Not coincidentally, it became the first sports CCG to find any measure of success.

Each player has a point value, and teams must consist of 5,000 points worth of players. Like other tabletop baseball games, such as *Strat-O-Matic*, players roll a die to determine whether the pitcher's or batter's card is consulted for the result of each individual at-bat. Since pitchers' cards have mostly outs and batters' cards have mostly hits and walks, players want to get the results on their cards. Odds of getting a result on a player's card are determined by the Control rating of the pitcher and the On-Base rating of the batter. After the proper card is determined, another die is rolled, and a chart on the card is consulted to find if the result is an strikeout, walk, single, home run, *etc.*

Players also have a 40- or 60-card strategy deck, which is usually divided into three types of cards: red cards help offense, blue cards help defense/pitching, and white cards are utility cards, playable on offense or defense. Each card clearly states when it can be played ("Play with a runner on first," etc.) so timing issues are virtually non-existent.

Given how large baseball-card sets are, it should come as little surprise that this became the largest basic set for any CCG to date. As with regular baseball cards, the cards of popular players, such as Mark McGwire and Ken Griffey Jr. skyrocketed in value. Special premium cards were made available to retailers. Wizards made a point of promoting *Showdown* directly to the fans, giving away starter decks in baseball parks.

Showdown is a decent simulation whose simplicity is a benefit to baseball fans who may be intimidated by the complexity of a *Strat-O-Matic*-type game. In addition to 2000's **Pennant Run** set, Wizards of the Coast plans to release at least one new set a year with updated players, using the most recent year's statistics (players in the original set were based on 1999 statistics). — *Jason Winter*

You will need **58** nine-pocket pages to store this set. (29 doubled up)

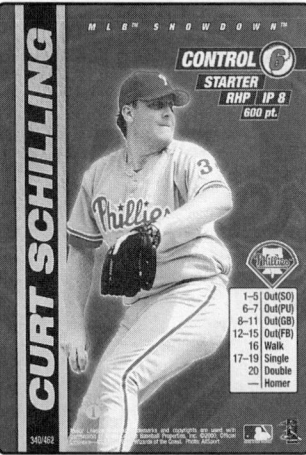

Concept	●●●●○	
Gameplay	●●●○○	
Card art	●●●○○	
Player pool	●●●○○	

Set (512 cards plus			
62 premiums)			437.50
Starter Display Box			92.50
Booster Display Box			100.00
Starter Deck			10.00
Booster Pack			3.40

# Card name	Team	Type	Price
1 Garret Anderson	ANA	Pl	1.00
2 Tim Belcher	ANA	Pl	1.00
3 Gary DiSarcina	ANA	Pl	1.00
4 Darin Erstad	ANA	Pl	1.00
5 Chuck Finley	ANA	Pr	8.00
6 Troy Glaus	ANA	Pl	1.00
7 Todd Greene	ANA	Pl	1.00
8 Jeff Huson	ANA	Pl	1.00
9 Orlando Palmeiro	ANA	Pl	1.00
10 Troy Percival	ANA	Pl	1.00
11 Mark Petkovsek	ANA	Pl	1.00
12 Tim Salmon	ANA	Pl	1.00
13 Steve Sparks	ANA	Pl	1.00
14 Mo Vaughn	ANA	Pl	1.00
15 Matt Walbeck	ANA	Pl	1.00
16 Jay Bell	ARI	Pr	7.00
17 Andy Benes	ARI	Pl	1.00
18 Omar Daal	ARI	Pl	1.00
19 Steve Finley	ARI	Pl	1.00
20 Andy Fox	ARI	Pl	1.00
21 Hanley Frias	ARI	Pl	1.00
22 Bernard Gilkey	ARI	Pl	1.00
23 Luis Gonzalez	ARI	Pr	8.00
24 Randy Johnson	ARI	Pr	20.00
25 Travis Lee	ARI	Pl	1.00
26 Matt Mantei	ARI	Pl	1.00
27 Dan Plesac	ARI	Pl	1.00
28 Kelly Stinnett	ARI	Pl	1.00
29 Greg Swindell	ARI	Pl	1.00
30 Matt Williams	ARI	Pr	8.00
31 Tony Womack	ARI	Pl	1.00

# Card name	Team	Type	Price
32 Bret Boone	ATL	Pl	1.00
33 Tom Glavine	ATL	Pl	1.00
34 Jose Hernandez	ATL	Pl	1.00
35 Brian Hunter	ATL	Pl	1.00
36 Andruw Jones	ATL	Pl	1.00
37 Chipper Jones	ATL	Pr	15.00
38 Brian Jordan	ATL	Pl	1.00
39 Ryan Klesko	ATL	Pl	1.00
40 Keith Lockhart	ATL	Pl	1.00
41 Greg Maddux	ATL	Pr	7.00
42 Kevin Millwood	ATL	Pr	8.50
43 Eddie Perez	ATL	Pl	1.00
44 Mike Remlinger	ATL	Pl	1.00
45 John Rocker	ATL	Pl	1.00
46 John Smoltz	ATL	Pl	1.00
47 Walt Weiss	ATL	Pl	1.00
48 Gerald Williams	ATL	Pl	1.00
49 Rich Amaral	BAL	Pl	1.00
50 Brady Anderson	BAL	Pl	1.00
51 Albert Belle	BAL	Pl	1.00
52 Mike Bordick	BAL	Pl	1.00
53 Jeff Conine	BAL	Pl	1.00
54 Delino DeShields	BAL	Pl	1.00
55 Scott Erickson	BAL	Pl	1.00
56 Charles Johnson	BAL	Pl	1.00
57 Mike Mussina	BAL	Pl	1.00
58 Jesse Orosco	BAL	Pl	1.00
59 Sidney Ponson	BAL	Pl	1.00
60 Jeff Reboulet	BAL	Pl	1.00
61 "Cal Ripken, Jr."	BAL	Pr	15.00
62 B. J. Surhoff	BAL	Pl	1.00
63 Mike Timlin	BAL	Pl	1.00
64 Rod Beck	BOS	Pl	1.00
65 Damon Buford	BOS	Pl	1.00
66 Rheal Cormier	BOS	Pl	1.00
67 Nomar Garciaparra	BOS	Pr	15.00
68 Butch Huskey	BOS	Pl	1.00
69 Darren Lewis	BOS	Pl	1.00
70 Derek Lowe	BOS	Pl	1.00

# Card name	Team	Type	Price
71 Pedro Martinez	BOS	Pr	18.00
72 Trot Nixon	BOS	Pl	1.00
73 Jose Offerman	BOS	Pl	1.00
74 Troy O'Leary	BOS	Pl	1.00
75 Mark Portugal	BOS	Pl	1.00
76 Pat Rapp	BOS	Pl	1.00
77 Mike Stanley	BOS	Pl	1.00
78 John Valentin	BOS	Pl	1.00
79 Jason Varitek	BOS	Pl	1.00
80 Tim Wakefield	BOS	Pl	1.00
81 Rick Aguilera	CHC	Pl	1.00
82 Jeff Blauser	CHC	Pl	1.00
83 Kyle Farnsworth	CHC	Pl	1.00
84 Gary Gaetti	CHC	Pl	1.00
85 Mark Grace	CHC	Pl	1.00
86 Lance Johnson	CHC	Pl	1.00
87 Jon Lieber	CHC	Pl	1.00
88 Mickey Morandini	CHC	Pl	1.00
89 Jose Nieves	CHC	Pl	1.00
90 Jeff Reed	CHC	Pl	1.00
91 Henry Rodriguez	CHC	Pl	1.00
92 Scott Sanders	CHC	Pl	1.00
93 Benito Santiago	CHC	Pl	1.00
94 Sammy Sosa	CHC	Pr	25.00
95 Steve Trachsel	CHC	Pl	1.00
96 James Baldwin	CHW	Pl	1.00
97 Mike Caruso	CHW	Pl	1.00
98 Ray Durham	CHW	Pl	1.00
99 Brook Fordyce	CHW	Pl	1.00
100 Bob Howry	CHW	Pl	1.00
101 Paul Konerko	CHW	Pl	1.00
102 Carlos Lee	CHW	Pl	1.00
103 Greg Norton	CHW	Pl	1.00
104 Magglio Ordonez	CHW	Pl	1.00
105 Jim Parque	CHW	Pl	1.00
106 Bill Simas	CHW	Pl	1.00
107 Chris Singleton	CHW	Pl	1.00
108 Mike Sirotka	CHW	Pl	1.00
109 Frank Thomas	CHW	Pr	10.00

# Card name	Team	Type	Price
110 Craig Wilson	CHW	Pl	1.00
111 Aaron Boone	CIN	Pl	1.00
112 Mike Cameron	CIN	Pl	1.00
113 Sean Casey	CIN	Pr	9.00
114 Danny Graves	CIN	Pl	1.00
115 Pete Harnisch	CIN	Pl	1.00
116 Barry Larkin	CIN	Pr	10.00
117 Pokey Reese	CIN	Pl	1.00
118 Scott Sullivan	CIN	Pl	1.00
119 Eddie Taubensee	CIN	Pl	1.00
120 Brett Tomko	CIN	Pl	1.00
121 Michael Tucker	CIN	Pl	1.00
122 Greg Vaughn	CIN	Pl	1.00
123 Ron Villone	CIN	Pl	1.00
124 Scott Williamson	CIN	Pr	8.00
125 Dmitri Young	CIN	Pl	1.00
126 Roberto Alomar	CLE	Pr	9.00
127 Harold Baines	CLE	Pl	1.00
128 Dave Burba	CLE	Pl	1.00
129 Bartolo Colon	CLE	Pl	1.00
130 Einar Diaz	CLE	Pl	1.00
131 Travis Fryman	CLE	Pl	1.00
132 Mike Jackson	CLE	Pl	1.00
133 David Justice	CLE	Pl	1.00
134 Kenny Lofton	CLE	Pr	10.00
135 Charles Nagy	CLE	Pl	1.00
136 Manny Ramirez	CLE	Pr	9.00
137 Richie Sexson	CLE	Pl	1.00
138 Paul Shuey	CLE	Pl	1.00
139 Jim Thome	CLE	Pr	8.00
140 Omar Vizquel	CLE	Pl	1.00
141 Enrique Wilson	CLE	Pl	1.00
142 Kurt Abbott	COL	Pl	1.00
143 Pedro Astacio	COL	Pl	1.00
144 Jeff Barry	COL	Pl	1.00
145 Dante Bichette	COL	Pl	1.00
146 Henry Blanco	COL	Pl	1.00
147 Brian Bohanon	COL	Pl	1.00
148 Vinny Castilla	COL	Pl	1.00

RARITY KEY C = Common U = Uncommon R = Rare VR = Very Rare UR = Ultra Rare F = Foil card X = Fixed/standard in all decks

SCRYE Collectible Card Game Checklist and Price Guide • 307

# Card name	Team	Type	Price
☐149 Jerry Dipoto	COL	Pl	1.00
☐150 Todd Helton	COL	Pl	1.00
☐151 Darryl Kile	COL	Pl	1.00
☐152 Curtis Leskanic	COL	Pl	1.00
☐153 Neifi Perez	COL	Pl	1.00
18			
☐154 Terry Shumpert	COL	Pl	1.00
☐155 Dave Veres	COL	Pl	1.00
☐156 Larry Walker	COL	Pr	10.00
☐157 Brad Ausmus	DET	Pl	1.00
☐158 Frank Catalanotto	DET	Pl	1.00
☐159 Tony Clark	DET	Pl	1.00
☐160 Deivi Cruz	DET	Pl	1.00
☐161 Damion Easley	DET	Pl	1.00
☐162 Juan Encarnacion	DET	Pl	1.00
19			
☐163 Karim Garcia	DET	Pl	1.00
☐164 Bobby Higginson	DET	Pl	1.00
☐165 Todd Jones	DET	Pl	1.00
☐166 Gabe Kapler	DET	Pl	1.00
☐167 Dave Mlicki	DET	Pl	1.00
☐168 Brian Moehler	DET	Pl	1.00
☐169 C. J. Nitkowski	DET	Pl	1.00
☐170 Dean Palmer	DET	Pr	8.00
☐171 Jeff Weaver	DET	Pl	1.00
20			
☐172 Antonio Alfonseca	FLA	Pl	1.00
☐173 Bruce Aven	FLA	Pl	1.00
☐174 Dave Berg	FLA	Pl	1.00
☐175 Luis Castillo	FLA	Pr	8.00
☐176 Ryan Dempster	FLA	Pl	1.00
☐177 Brian Edmondson	FLA	Pl	1.00
☐178 Alex Gonzalez	FLA	Pl	1.00
☐179 Mark Kotsay	FLA	Pl	1.00
☐180 Derrek Lee	FLA	Pl	1.00
21			
☐181 Braden Looper	FLA	Pl	1.00
☐182 Mike Lowell	FLA	Pl	1.00
☐183 Brian Meadows	FLA	Pl	1.00
☐184 Mike Redmond	FLA	Pl	1.00
☐185 Dennis Springer	FLA	Pl	1.00
☐186 Preston Wilson	FLA	Pl	1.00
☐187 Jeff Bagwell	HOU	Pr	10.00
☐188 Derek Bell	HOU	Pl	1.00
☐189 Craig Biggio	HOU	Pl	1.00
22			
☐190 Tim Bogar	HOU	Pl	1.00
☐191 Ken Caminiti	HOU	Pl	1.00
☐192 Scott Elarton	HOU	Pl	1.00
☐193 Tony Eusebio	HOU	Pl	1.00
☐194 Carl Everett	HOU	Pr	9.00
☐195 Mike Hampton	HOU	Pr	10.00
☐196 Richard Hidalgo	HOU	Pl	1.00
☐197 Stan Javier	HOU	Pl	1.00
☐198 Jose Lima	HOU	Pl	1.00
23			
☐199 Jay Powell	HOU	Pl	1.00
☐200 Shane Reynolds	HOU	Pl	1.00
☐201 Bill Spiers	HOU	Pl	1.00
☐202 Billy Wagner	HOU	Pr	10.00
☐203 Carlos Beltran	KAN	Pr	8.00
☐204 Johnny Damon	KAN	Pl	1.00
☐205 Jermaine Dye	KAN	Pl	1.00
☐206 Carlos Febles	KAN	Pl	1.00
☐207 Jeremy Giambi	KAN	Pl	1.00
24			
☐208 Chad Kreuter	KAN	Pl	1.00
☐209 Jeff Montgomery	KAN	Pl	1.00
☐210 Joe Randa	KAN	Pl	1.00
☐211 Jose Rosado	KAN	Pl	1.00
☐212 Rey Sanchez	KAN	Pl	1.00
☐213 Scott Service	KAN	Pl	1.00
☐214 Tim Spehr	KAN	Pl	1.00
☐215 Jeff Suppan	KAN	Pl	1.00
☐216 Mike Sweeney	KAN	Pl	1.00
25			
☐217 Jay Witasick	KAN	Pl	1.00
☐218 Adrian Beltre	LOS	Pl	1.00
☐219 Pedro Borbon	LOS	Pl	1.00
☐220 Kevin Brown	LOS	Pr	10.00
☐221 Mark Grudzielanek	LOS	Pl	1.00
☐222 Dave Hansen	LOS	Pl	1.00
☐223 Todd Hundley	LOS	Pl	1.00
☐224 Eric Karros	LOS	Pl	1.00
☐225 Raul Mondesi	LOS	Pl	1.00
26			
☐226 Chan Ho Park	LOS	Pl	1.00

# Card name	Team	Type	Price
☐227 Jeff Shaw	LOS	Pl	1.00
☐228 Gary Sheffield	LOS	Pr	9.00
☐229 Ismael Valdes	LOS	Pl	1.00
☐230 Jose Vizcaino	LOS	Pl	1.00
☐231 Devon White	LOS	Pl	1.00
☐232 Eric Young	LOS	Pl	1.00
☐233 Ron Belliard	MIL	Pl	1.00
☐234 Sean Berry	MIL	Pl	1.00
27			
☐235 Jeromy Burnitz	MIL	Pr	8.00
☐236 Jeff Cirillo	MIL	Pl	1.00
☐237 Marquis Grissom	MIL	Pl	1.00
☐238 Geoff Jenkins	MIL	Pl	1.00
☐239 Scott Karl	MIL	Pl	1.00
☐240 Mark Loretta	MIL	Pl	1.00
☐241 Mike Myers	MIL	Pl	1.00
☐242 David Nilsson	MIL	Pr	9.00
☐243 Hideo Nomo	MIL	Pl	1.00
28			
☐244 Alex Ochoa	MIL	Pl	1.00
☐245 Jose Valentin	MIL	Pl	1.00
☐246 Bob Wickman	MIL	Pl	1.00
☐247 Steve Woodard	MIL	Pl	1.00
☐248 Chad Allen	MIN	Pl	1.00
☐249 Ron Coomer	MIN	Pl	1.00
☐250 Cristian Guzman	MIN	Pl	1.00
☐251 Denny Hocking	MIN	Pl	1.00
☐252 Torii Hunter	MIN	Pl	1.00
29			
☐253 Corey Koskie	MIN	Pl	1.00
☐254 Matt Lawton	MIN	Pl	1.00
☐255 Joe Mays	MIN	Pl	1.00
☐256 Doug Mientkiewicz	MIN	Pl	1.00
☐257 Eric Milton	MIN	Pl	1.00
☐258 Brad Radke	MIN	Pr	8.00
☐259 Terry Steinbach	MIN	Pl	1.00
☐260 Mike Trombley	MIN	Pl	1.00
☐261 Todd Walker	MIN	Pl	1.00
30			
☐262 Bob Wells	MIN	Pl	1.00
☐263 Shane Andrews	MON	Pl	1.00
☐264 Michael Barrett	MON	Pl	1.00
☐265 Orlando Cabrera	MON	Pl	1.00
☐266 Brad Fullmer	MON	Pl	1.00
☐267 Vladimir Guerrero	MON	Pr	10.00
☐268 Wilton Guerrero	MON	Pl	1.00
☐269 Dustin Hermanson	MON	Pl	1.00
☐270 Steve Kline	MON	Pl	1.00
31			
☐271 Manny Martinez	MON	Pl	1.00
☐272 Mike Thurman	MON	Pl	1.00
☐273 Ugueth Urbina	MON	Pl	1.00
☐274 Javier Vazquez	MON	Pl	1.00
☐275 Jose Vidro	MON	Pl	1.00
☐276 Rondell White	MON	Pl	1.00
☐277 Chris Widger	MON	Pl	1.00
☐278 Edgardo Alfonzo	NYM	Pr	10.00
☐279 Armando Benitez	NYM	Pl	1.00
32			
☐280 Roger Cedeno	NYM	Pl	1.00
☐281 Dennis Cook	NYM	Pl	1.00
☐282 Shawon Dunston	NYM	Pl	1.00
☐283 Matt Franco	NYM	Pl	1.00
☐284 Darryl Hamilton	NYM	Pl	1.00
☐285 Rickey Henderson	NYM	Pr	9.00
☐286 Orel Hershiser	NYM	Pl	1.00
☐287 Al Leiter	NYM	Pl	1.00
☐288 John Olerud	NYM	Pl	1.00
33			
☐289 Rey Ordonez	NYM	Pl	1.00
☐290 Mike Piazza	NYM	Pr	13.00
☐291 Kenny Rogers	NYM	Pl	1.00
☐292 Robin Ventura	NYM	Pl	1.00
☐293 Turk Wendell	NYM	Pl	1.00
☐294 Masato Yoshii	NYM	Pl	1.00
☐295 Scott Brosius	NYY	Pl	1.00
☐296 Roger Clemens	NYY	Pr	10.00
☐297 David Cone	NYY	Pr	6.00
34			
☐298 Chad Curtis	NYY	Pl	1.00
☐299 Chili Davis	NYY	Pl	1.00
☐300 Orlando Hernandez	NYY	Pl	1.00
☐301 Derek Jeter	NYY	Pr	15.00
☐302 Chuck Knoblauch	NYY	Pl	1.00
☐303 Ricky Ledee	NYY	Pl	1.00
☐304 Tino Martinez	NYY	Pl	1.00
☐305 Ramiro Mendoza	NYY	Pl	1.00

# Card name	Team	Type	Price
☐306 Paul O'Neill	NYY	Pl	1.00
35			
☐307 Andy Pettitte	NYY	Pl	1.00
☐308 Jorge Posada	NYY	Pl	1.00
☐309 Mariano Rivera	NYY	Pr	10.00
☐310 Mike Stanton	NYY	Pl	1.00
☐311 Bernie Williams	NYY	Pr	10.00
☐312 Kevin Appier	OAK	Pl	1.00
☐313 Eric Chavez	OAK	Pl	1.00
☐314 Ryan Christenson	OAK	Pl	1.00
☐315 Jason Giambi	OAK	Pr	8.00
36			
☐316 Ben Grieve	OAK	Pl	1.00
☐317 Buddy Groom	OAK	Pl	1.00
☐318 Gil Heredia	OAK	Pl	1.00
☐319 A. J. Hinch	OAK	Pl	1.00
☐320 John Jaha	OAK	Pl	1.00
☐321 Doug Jones	OAK	Pl	1.00
☐322 Omar Olivares	OAK	Pl	1.00
☐323 Tony Phillips	OAK	Pl	1.00
☐324 Matt Stairs	OAK	Pl	1.00
37			
☐325 Miguel Tejada	OAK	Pl	1.00
☐326 Randy Velarde	OAK	Pr	9.00
☐327 Bobby Abreu	PHI	Pr	8.00
☐328 Marlon Anderson	PHI	Pl	1.00
☐329 Alex Arias	PHI	Pl	1.00
☐330 Rico Brogna	PHI	Pl	1.00
☐331 Paul Byrd	PHI	Pl	1.00
☐332 Ron Gant	PHI	Pl	1.00
☐333 Doug Glanville	PHI	Pl	1.00
38			
☐334 Wayne Gomes	PHI	Pl	1.00
☐335 Kevin Jordan	PHI	Pl	1.00
☐336 Mike Lieberthal	PHI	Pl	1.00
☐337 Steve Montgomery	PHI	Pl	1.00
☐338 Chad Ogea	PHI	Pl	1.00
☐339 Scott Rolen	PHI	Pl	1.00
☐340 Curt Schilling	PHI	Pr	10.00
☐341 Kevin Sefcik	PHI	Pl	1.00
☐342 Mike Benjamin	PIT	Pl	1.00
39			
☐343 Kris Benson	PIT	Pl	1.00
☐344 Adrian Brown	PIT	Pl	1.00
☐345 Brant Brown	PIT	Pl	1.00
☐346 Brad Clontz	PIT	Pl	1.00
☐347 Brian Giles	PIT	Pr	9.00
☐348 Jason Kendall	PIT	Pr	10.00
☐349 Al Martin	PIT	Pl	1.00
☐350 Warren Morris	PIT	Pl	1.00
☐351 Todd Ritchie	PIT	Pl	1.00
40			
☐352 Scott Sauerbeck	PIT	Pl	1.00
☐353 Jason Schmidt	PIT	Pl	1.00
☐354 Ed Sprague	PIT	Pl	1.00
☐355 Mike Williams	PIT	Pl	1.00
☐356 Kevin Young	PIT	Pl	1.00
☐357 Andy Ashby	SAD	Pl	1.00
☐358 Ben Davis	SAD	Pl	1.00
☐359 Tony Gwynn	SAD	Pr	10.00
☐360 Sterling Hitchcock	SAD	Pl	1.00
41			
☐361 Trevor Hoffman	SAD	Pr	8.00
☐362 Damian Jackson	SAD	Pl	1.00
☐363 Wally Joyner	SAD	Pl	1.00
☐364 Phil Nevin	SAD	Pl	1.00
☐365 Eric Owens	SAD	Pl	1.00
☐366 Ruben Rivera	SAD	Pl	1.00
☐367 Reggie Sanders	SAD	Pl	1.00
☐368 John Vander Wal	SAD	Pl	1.00
☐369 Quilvio Veras	SAD	Pl	1.00
42			
☐370 Matt Whisenant	SAD	Pl	1.00
☐371 Woody Williams	SAD	Pl	1.00
☐372 Rich Aurilia	SAF	Pl	1.00
☐373 Marvin Benard	SAF	Pl	1.00
☐374 Barry Bonds	SAF	Pr	13.00
☐375 Ellis Burks	SAF	Pl	1.00
☐376 Alan Embree	SAF	Pl	1.00
☐377 Shawn Estes	SAF	Pl	1.00
☐378 John Johnstone	SAF	Pl	1.00
43			
☐379 Jeff Kent	SAF	Pl	1.00
☐380 Brent Mayne	SAF	Pl	1.00
☐381 Bill Mueller	SAF	Pl	1.00
☐382 Robb Nen	SAF	Pl	1.00
☐383 Russ Ortiz	SAF	Pl	1.00
☐384 Kirk Rueter	SAF	Pl	1.00

# Card name	Team	Type	Price
☐385 F. P. Santangelo	SAF	Pl	1.00
☐386 J. T. Snow	SAF	Pl	1.00
☐387 David Bell	SEA	Pl	1.00
44			
☐388 Jay Buhner	SEA	Pl	1.00
☐389 Russ Davis	SEA	Pl	1.00
☐390 Freddy Garcia	SEA	Pl	1.00
☐391 "Ken Griffey, Jr."	SEA	Pr	35.00
☐392 John Halama	SEA	Pl	1.00
☐393 Brian L. Hunter	SEA	Pl	1.00
☐394 Raul Ibanez	SEA	Pl	1.00
☐395 Tom Lampkin	SEA	Pl	1.00
☐396 Edgar Martinez	SEA	Pr	10.00
45			
☐397 Jose Mesa	SEA	Pl	1.00
☐398 Jamie Moyer	SEA	Pl	1.00
☐399 Jose Paniagua	SEA	Pl	1.00
☐400 Alex Rodriguez	SEA	Pr	20.00
☐401 Dan Wilson	SEA	Pl	1.00
☐402 Manny Aybar	STL	Pl	1.00
☐403 Ricky Bottalico	STL	Pl	1.00
☐404 Kent Bottenfield	STL	Pl	1.00
☐405 Darren Bragg	STL	Pl	1.00
46			
☐406 Alberto Castillo	STL	Pl	1.00
☐407 J. D. Drew	STL	Pl	1.00
☐408 Jose Jimenez	STL	Pl	1.00
☐409 Ray Lankford	STL	Pl	1.00
☐410 Joe McEwing	STL	Pl	1.00
☐411 Willie McGee	STL	Pl	1.00
☐412 Mark Mcgwire	STL	Pr	35.00
☐413 Darren Oliver	STL	Pl	1.00
☐414 Lance Painter	STL	Pl	1.00
47			
☐415 Edgar Renteria	STL	Pl	1.00
☐416 Fernando Tatis	STL	Pr	10.00
☐417 Wilson Alvarez	TAM	Pl	1.00
☐418 Rolando Arrojo	TAM	Pl	1.00
☐419 Wade Boggs	TAM	Pl	1.00
☐420 Miguel Cairo	TAM	Pl	1.00
☐421 Jose Canseco	TAM	Pr	8.00
☐422 John Flaherty	TAM	Pl	1.00
☐423 Roberto Hernandez	TAM	Pl	1.00
48			
☐424 Dave Martinez	TAM	Pl	1.00
☐425 Fred McGriff	TAM	Pl	1.00
☐426 Paul Sorrento	TAM	Pl	1.00
☐427 Kevin Stocker	TAM	Pl	1.00
☐428 Bubba Trammell	TAM	Pl	1.00
☐429 Rick White	TAM	Pl	1.00
☐430 Randy Winn	TAM	Pl	1.00
☐431 Bobby Witt	TAM	Pl	1.00
☐432 Royce Clayton	TEX	Pl	1.00
49			
☐433 Tim Crabtree	TEX	Pl	1.00
☐434 Juan Gonzalez	TEX	Pl	1.00
☐435 Tom Goodwin	TEX	Pl	1.00
☐436 Rusty Greer	TEX	Pl	1.00
☐437 Rick Helling	TEX	Pl	1.00
☐438 Mark McLemore	TEX	Pl	1.00
☐439 Mike Morgan	TEX	Pl	1.00
☐440 Rafael Palmeiro	TEX	Pr	10.00
☐441 Ivan Rodriguez	TEX	Pr	10.00
50			
☐442 Aaron Sele	TEX	Pl	1.00
☐443 Lee Stevens	TEX	Pl	1.00
☐444 Mike Venafro	TEX	Pl	1.00
☐445 John Wetteland	TEX	Pl	1.00
☐446 Todd Zeile	TEX	Pl	1.00
☐447 Jeff Zimmerman	TEX	Pr	8.00
☐448 Tony Batista	TOR	Pl	1.00
☐449 Homer Bush	TOR	Pl	1.00
☐450 Jose Cruz, Jr.	TOR	Pl	1.00
51			
☐451 Carlos Delgado	TOR	Pl	1.00
☐452 Kelvim Escobar	TOR	Pl	1.00
☐453 Tony Fernandez	TOR	Pr	7.50
☐454 Darrin Fletcher	TOR	Pl	1.00
☐455 Shawn Green	TOR	Pr	8.00
☐456 Pat Hentgen	TOR	Pl	1.00
☐457 Billy Koch	TOR	Pl	1.00
☐458 Graeme Lloyd	TOR	Pl	1.00
☐459 Brian McRae	TOR	Pl	1.00
52			
☐460 David Segui	TOR	Pl	1.00
☐461 Shannon Stewart	TOR	Pl	1.00
☐462 David Wells	TOR	Pl	1.00

RARITY KEY **C** = Common **U** = Uncommon **R** = Rare **VR** = Very Rare **UR** = Ultra Rare **F** = Foil card **X** = Fixed/standard in all decks

# Card name	Team	Type	Price
☐S01 Bad Call		Strat	0.50
☐S02 Big Inning		Strat	0.50
☐S03 Bobbled in the Outfield		Strat	0.50
☐S04 Clutch Hitting		Strat	0.50
☐S05 Do or Die		Strat	0.50
☐S06 Down the Middle		Strat	0.50
53			
☐S07 Ducks on the Pond		Strat	0.50
☐S08 Favorable Matchup		Strat	0.50
☐S09 Free Steal		Strat	0.50
☐S10 Get Under It		Strat	0.50
☐S11 Great Lead		Strat	0.50
☐S12 Hard Slide		Strat	0.50
☐S13 High Fives		Strat	0.50
☐S14 Last Chance		Strat	0.50

# Card name	Team	Type	Price
☐S15 Long Single		Strat	0.50
54			
☐S16 Out of Gas		Strat	0.50
☐S17 Out of Position		Strat	0.50
☐S18 Pl the Percentages		Strat	0.50
☐S19 Rally Cap		Strat	0.50
☐S20 Rattled		Strat	0.50
☐S21 Runner Not Held		Strat	0.50
☐S22 Slow Roller		Strat	0.50
☐S23 Stick a Fork in Him		Strat	0.50
☐S24 Swing for the Fences		Strat	0.50
55			
☐S25 To the Warning Track		Strat	0.50
☐S26 Whiplash		Strat	0.50
☐S27 Wide Throw		Strat	0.50
☐S28 Wild Pitch		Strat	0.50

# Card name	Team	Type	Price
☐S29 By the Book		Strat	0.50
☐S30 Dominating		Strat	0.50
☐S31 Full Windup		Strat	0.50
☐S32 Good Fielding		Strat	0.50
☐S33 Gun 'Em Down!		Strat	0.50
56			
☐S34 He's Got a Gun		Strat	0.50
☐S35 In the Groove		Strat	0.50
☐S36 In the Zone		Strat	0.50
☐S37 Infield In		Strat	0.50
☐S38 Intimidation		Strat	0.50
☐S39 Just over the Wall		Strat	0.50
☐S40 Knock the Ball Down		Strat	0.50
☐S41 Lefty Specialist		Strat	0.50
☐S42 Nerves of Steel		Strat	0.50

# Card name	Team	Type	Price
57			
☐S43 Nothing but Heat		Strat	0.50
☐S44 Pitchout		Strat	0.50
☐S45 Pumped Up		Strat	0.50
☐S46 Quick Pitch		Strat	0.50
☐S47 Rally Killer		Strat	0.50
☐S48 Short Fly		Strat	0.50
☐S49 Three Up, Three Down		Strat	0.50
☐S50 Trick Pitch		Strat	0.50
☐S51 Belt-High		Strat	0.50
58			
☐S52 Change in Strategy		Strat	0.50
☐S53 Grounder to Second		Strat	0.50
☐S54 StealingSignals		Strat	0.50
☐S55 Swing at Anything		Strat	0.50

MLB Showdown • Pennant Run

Wizards of the Coast • Released **September 2000**

175 cards plus 20 premiums • **IDENTIFIER: Pennant symbol on cards**

• Booster packs contain 9 cards; booster displays contain 36 boosters

The first expansion set for **MLB Showdown** includes several player cards not included in the first set, as well as players that changed teams in the 1999-2000 off-season.

Many of the "new" players were ones who had been injured for most of 1999, and so their cards reflected statistics from 1998 and 1999. Others were rookies whose cards were created using their minor league stats, adjusted for major league play. Players with new teams had their stats adjusted for their new home park — as an example, the **Darryl Kile** who pitched in Colorado in the original set was much worse than the St. Louis version of **Darryl Kile** in *Pennant Run*. The set also includes 25 new strategy cards. — *Jason Winter*

You will need
20
nine-pocket pages to store this set.
(10 doubled up)

Set (175 cards plus 20 premiums)			387.50
Booster Display Box			**87.00**
Booster Pack			**3.10**

# Card name	Team	Type	Price
1			
☐ 1 Kent Bottenfield	ANA	Pl	0.50
☐ 2 Ken Hill	ANA	Pl	0.50
☐ 3 Adam Kennedy	ANA	Pl	0.50
☐ 4 Ben Molina	ANA	Pl	0.50
☐ 5 Scott Spiezio	ANA	Pl	0.50
☐ 6 Brian Anderson	ARI	Pl	0.50
☐ 7 Erubiel Durazo	ARI	Pr	6.00
☐ 8 Armando Reynoso	ARI	Pl	0.50
☐ 9 Russ Springer	ARI	Pl	0.50
2			
☐ 10 Todd Stottlemyre	ARI	Pl	0.50
☐ 11 Tony Womack	ARI	Pl	0.50
☐ 12 Andres Galarraga	ATL	Pr	7.00
☐ 13 Javy Lopez	ATL	Pr	7.00
☐ 14 Kevin McGlinchy	ATL	Pl	0.50
☐ 15 Terry Mulholland	ATL	Pl	1.00
☐ 16 Reggie Sanders	ATL	Pl	0.50
☐ 17 Harold Baines	BAL	Pl	0.50
☐ 18 Will Clark	BAL	Pl	0.80
3			
☐ 19 Mike Trombley	BAL	Pl	0.50
☐ 20 Manny Alexander	BOS	Pl	0.80
☐ 21 Carl Everett	BOS	Pr	6.00
☐ 22 Ramon Martinez	BOS	Pr	7.00
☐ 23 Bret Saberhagen	BOS	Pl	0.50
☐ 24 John Wasdin	BOS	Pl	0.50
☐ 25 Joe Girardi	CHC	Pl	0.50
☐ 26 Ricky Gutierrez	CHC	Pl	0.50
☐ 27 Glenallen Hill	CHC	Pl	0.50
4			
☐ 28 Kevin Tapani	CHC	Pl	0.50
☐ 29 Kerry Wood	CHC	Pr	7.00
☐ 30 Eric Young	CHC	Pl	0.50
☐ 31 Keith Foulke	CHW	Pr	6.00
☐ 32 Mark L. Johnson	CHW	Pl	0.80
☐ 33 Sean Lowe	CHW	Pl	0.50
☐ 34 Jose Valentin	CHW	Pl	0.50
☐ 35 Dante Bichette	CIN	Pl	0.50
☐ 36 Ken Griffey, Jr.	CIN	Pr	25.00
5			
☐ 37 Denny Neagle	CIN	Pl	0.50
☐ 38 Steve Parris	CIN	Pl	0.80
☐ 39 Dennys Reyes	CIN	Pl	0.50
☐ 40 Sandy Alomar, Jr.	CLE	Pl	0.50
☐ 41 Chuck Finley	CLE	Pr	7.00

# Card name	Team	Type	Price
☐ 42 Steve Karsay	CLE	Pl	0.50
☐ 43 Steve Reed	CLE	Pl	0.50
☐ 44 Jaret Wright	CLE	Pl	0.50
☐ 45 Jeff Cirillo	COL	Pl	0.50
6			
☐ 46 Tom Goodwin	COL	Pl	0.80
☐ 47 Jeffrey Hammonds	COL	Pl	0.50
☐ 48 Mike Lansing	COL	Pl	0.50
☐ 49 Aaron Ledesma	COL	Pl	0.50
☐ 50 Brent Mayne	COL	Pl	0.50
☐ 51 Doug Brocail	DET	Pl	0.50
☐ 52 Robert Fick	DET	Pl	0.80
☐ 53 Juan Gonzalez	DET	Pl	0.50
☐ 54 Hideo Nomo	DET	Pl	0.50
7			
☐ 55 Luis Polonia	DET	Pl	0.50
☐ 56 Brant Brown	FLA	Pl	0.50
☐ 57 Alex Fernandez	FLA	Pl	0.50
☐ 58 Cliff Floyd	FLA	Pl	0.50
☐ 59 Dan Miceli	FLA	Pl	0.50
☐ 60 Vladimir Nunez	FLA	Pl	0.50
☐ 61 Moises Alou	HOU	Pr	6.00
☐ 62 Roger Cedeno	HOU	Pr	6.00
☐ 63 Octavio Dotel	HOU	Pl	0.50
8			
☐ 64 Mitch Meluskey	HOU	Pl	0.50
☐ 65 Daryle Ward	HOU	Pl	0.50
☐ 66 Mark Quinn	KAN	Pr	7.00
☐ 67 Brad Rigby	KAN	Pl	0.50
☐ 68 Blake Stein	KAN	Pl	0.50
☐ 69 Mac Suzuki	KAN	Pl	0.50
☐ 70 Terry Adams	LOS	Pl	0.50
☐ 71 Darren Dreifort	LOS	Pl	0.80
☐ 72 Kevin Elster	LOS	Pl	0.50
9			
☐ 73 Shawn Green	LOS	Pr	7.00
☐ 74 Todd Hollandsworth	LOS	Pl	0.50
☐ 75 Gregg Olson	LOS	Pl	0.80
☐ 76 Kevin Barker	MIL	Pl	0.80
☐ 77 Jose Hernandez	MIL	Pl	0.80
☐ 78 Dave Weathers	MIL	Pl	0.80
☐ 79 Hector Carrasco	MIN	Pl	1.00
☐ 80 Eddie Guardado	MIN	Pl	0.80
☐ 81 Jacque Jones	MIN	Pl	0.80
10			
☐ 82 David Ortiz	MIN	Pl	1.00
☐ 83 Peter Bergeron	MON	Pl	0.50
☐ 84 Hideki Irabu	MON	Pl	0.50
☐ 85 Lee Stevens	MON	Pl	0.50
☐ 86 Anthony Telford	MON	Pl	0.50
☐ 87 Derek Bell	NYM	Pl	0.50

# Card name	Team	Type	Price
☐ 88 John Franco	NYM	Pl	0.50
☐ 89 Mike Hampton	NYM	Pr	6.00
☐ 90 Bobby J. Jones	NYM	Pl	0.50
11			
☐ 91 Todd Pratt	NYM	Pl	0.50
☐ 92 Todd Zeile	NYM	Pl	0.50
☐ 93 Jason Grimsley	NYY	Pl	0.50
☐ 94 Roberto Kelly	NYY	Pl	0.50
☐ 95 Jim Leyritz	NYY	Pl	0.50
☐ 96 Ramiro Mendoza	NYY	Pl	0.50
☐ 97 Rich Becker	OAK	Pl	0.50
☐ 98 Ramon Hernandez	OAK	Pl	0.50
☐ 99 Tim Hudson	OAK	Pr	5.00
12			
☐ 100 Jason Isringhausen	OAK	Pl	0.80
☐ 101 Mike Magnante	OAK	Pl	0.50
☐ 102 Olmedo Saenz	OAK	Pl	0.50
☐ 103 Mickey Morandini	PHI	Pl	0.50
☐ 104 Robert Person	PHI	Pl	0.50
☐ 105 Desi Relaford	PHI	Pl	0.50
☐ 106 Jason Christiansen	PIT	Pl	0.50
☐ 107 Wil Cordero	PIT	Pl	0.50
☐ 108 Francisco Cordova	PIT	Pl	0.50
13			
☐ 109 Chad Hermansen	PIT	Pl	0.50
☐ 110 Pat Meares	PIT	Pl	1.00
☐ 111 Aramis Ramirez	PIT	Pl	0.50
☐ 112 Bret Boone	SAD	Pl	0.50
☐ 113 Matt Clement	SAD	Pl	1.00
☐ 114 Carlos Hernandez	SAD	Pl	0.50
☐ 115 Ryan Klesko	SAD	Pl	0.50
☐ 116 Dave Magadan	SAD	Pl	0.50
☐ 117 Al Martin	SAD	Pl	0.50
14			
☐ 118 Bobby Estalella	SAF	Pl	0.80
☐ 119 Livan Hernandez	SAF	Pl	0.50
☐ 120 Doug Mirabelli	SAF	Pl	0.50
☐ 121 Joe Nathan	SAF	Pl	0.50
☐ 122 Mike Cameron	SEA	Pl	0.50
☐ 123 Mark McLemore	SEA	Pl	0.50
☐ 124 Gil Meche	SEA	Pl	0.50
☐ 125 John Olerud	SEA	Pl	0.50
☐ 126 Arthur Rhodes	SEA	Pl	0.50
15			
☐ 127 Aaron Sele	SEA	Pr	6.00
☐ 128 Jim Edmonds	STL	Pr	6.00
☐ 129 Pat Hentgen	STL	Pl	0.50
☐ 130 Darryl Kile	STL	Pl	0.50
☐ 131 Eli Marrero	STL	Pl	1.00
☐ 132 Dave Veres	STL	Pl	1.00
☐ 133 Fernando Vina	STL	Pl	1.00

# Card name	Team	Type	Price
☐ 134 Vinny Castilla	TAM	Pl	1.00
☐ 135 Juan Guzman	TAM	Pl	1.00
16			
☐ 136 Ryan Rupe	TAM	Pl	1.00
☐ 137 Greg Vaughn	TAM	Pr	6.00
☐ 138 Gerald Williams	TAM	Pl	1.00
☐ 139 Esteban Yan	TAM	Pl	1.00
☐ 140 Tom Evans	TEX	Pl	1.00
☐ 141 Gabe Kapler	TEX	Pl	1.00
☐ 142 Ruben Mateo	TEX	Pr	7.00
☐ 143 Kenny Rogers	TEX	Pl	1.00
☐ 144 David Segui	TEX	Pl	1.00
17			
☐ 145 Tony Batista	TOR	Pl	1.00
☐ 146 Chris Carpenter	TOR	Pl	1.00
☐ 147 Brad Fullmer	TOR	Pl	1.00
☐ 148 Alex Gonzalez	TOR	Pl	1.00
☐ 149 Roy Halladay	TOR	Pl	1.00
☐ 150 Raul Mondesi	TOR	Pr	7.00
☐ S1 Afterburners		Strat	0.35
☐ S2 Change Sides		Strat	0.35
☐ S3 Patience is a Virtue		Strat	0.35
18			
☐ S4 Payoff Pitch		Strat	0.35
☐ S5 Pointers		Strat	0.35
☐ S6 Professional Baserunner		Strat	0.35
☐ S7 Professional Hitter		Strat	0.35
☐ S8 Protect the Runner		Strat	0.35
☐ S9 Rough Outing		Strat	0.35
☐ S10 Shelled		Strat	0.35
☐ S11 Take What's Given		Strat	0.35
☐ S12 Tricky Hop		Strat	0.35
19			
☐ S13 Aggressive Coaching		Strat	0.35
☐ S14 Cut Off in the Gap		Strat	0.35
☐ S15 Great Start		Strat	0.35
☐ S16 Insult to Injury		Strat	0.35
☐ S17 Job Well Done		Strat	0.35
☐ S18 Low and Away		Strat	0.35
☐ S19 Outfield In		Strat	0.35
☐ S20 Put Out the Fire		Strat	0.35
☐ S21 Rotation Pl		Strat	0.35
20			
☐ S22 Swiss Army Closer		Strat	0.35
☐ S23 Whoops!		Strat	0.35
☐ S24 Pep Talk		Strat	0.35
☐ S25 Revenue Sharing		Strat	0.35

RARITY KEY C = Common U = Uncommon R = Rare VR = Very Rare UR = Ultra Rare F = Foil card X = Fixed/standard in all decks

Monster Rancher

Artbox • Released June 2000

99 cards plus **33** premium cards in set

- Introductory two-player starters contain two 30-card decks; two-player displays contain 6 decks
- Starter decks contain 60 cards; starter displays contain 8 decks
- Booster packs contain 11 cards; booster displays contain 36 packs

Designed by **Matt Forbeck**

Monster Rancher is the third in the line of "kids with trained battle monsters" games, following **Pokémon** and **Digi-Battle**. Based on the television series of the same name, *Monster Rancher* has the most complex game system of the three, and, while it's superior to that of *Digibattle* and *Pokémon*, it is also not as easy to grasp as *Pokémon*.

There are five card types: monster cards, training cards, event cards, battle cards, and attachment cards. Monsters have four abilities: power, intelligence, speed, and defense. They are given loyalty through the course of the game and they also have a life value. Training cards improve these abilities and are necessary to give the monster access to its more powerful attacks. The objective of the game is to win three fame counters by defeating an opponent's monster in a battle.

Monsters face off in an arena made up of five spaces. Card icons that a player has in hand determine a monster's movement in the arena. Monsters can charge, retreat, hold, or shove the opposing monster, provided the appropriate card is in hand. Each attack has a certain range at which it may be used, as well as a damage modifier. When an attack is made, the appropriate ability, plus any bonuses from training, is added to the pull value of a card chosen from a player's hand. This value is compared to the target monster's defense, plus bonuses, plus a pull number. Any value above defense is multiplied by the attack's damage rating. When a monster takes as much or more damage than it has life, it is knocked out. If a monster takes more damage than it has life, it might be injured and not usable until it is healed through an event or an attachment.

Poor marketing and distribution prevented Artbox from taking advantage of the *brief* popularity advantage *Monster Rancher* had over *Pokémon*. That, combined with more complex (if superior) rules, kept *Monster Rancher* from breaking out. A planned expansion set has, as of press time, been placed on "indefinite hold." — **James A. Mishler**

Concept	●●●○○
Gameplay	●●●○○
Card art	●●●○○
Player pool	○○○○○

Set (132 cards)	185.00
Starter Display Box	90.00
Booster Display Box	90.00
2-player Starter	9.00
Starter Deck	10.00
Booster Pack	3.00

#	Card name	Rarity	Price
78	A Hard Knock Life	U	0.80
1	Abacus	U	0.80
2	Alan	F	8.50
2	Alan	R	4.00
17	Bad Food	U	0.80
18	Bad Monster	F	8.50
18	Bad Monster	R	3.50
28	Battle Maker	F	8.50
28	Battle Maker	R	3.50
30	Big Blue	U	0.80
3	Big Meal	C	0.25
31	Black Dino	U	0.80
32	Blue Hare	U	0.80
79	Brilliant Idea	C	0.25
29	Call to Battle	U	0.80
33	Captain Black Dino	F	8.50
33	Captain Black Dino	R	3.50
34	Captain Clay	F	8.50
34	Captain Clay	R	3.50
35	Captain Dino	F	8.50
35	Captain Dino	R	3.50
36	Captain Evil Hare	F	8.50
36	Captain Evil Hare	R	3.50
37	Captain Jell	F	8.50
37	Captain Jell	R	3.50
38	Captain Kuro	F	8.50
38	Captain Kuro	R	3.50

#	Card name	Rarity	Price
39	Captain Weeds	F	8.50
39	Captain Weeds	R	3.50
40	Captain Zuum	F	8.50
40	Captain Zuum	R	3.50
4	Cards	F	8.50
4	Cards	R	3.50
41	Clay	C	0.25
80	Clever Dodge	U	0.90
5	Cup of Water	C	0.25
42	Daton	U	0.80
43	Datonare	U	0.80
44	Dino	C	0.25
6	Disguise	U	0.80
81	Doing Awesome	U	0.90
45	Dragon	U	0.80
19	Earthquake!	F	8.50
19	Earthquake!	R	3.50
20	Errantry	U	0.80
46	Evil Hare	F	8.50
46	Evil Hare	R	3.50
47	Falcon	F	8.50
47	Falcon	R	3.50
82	Feel the Power	U	0.80
83	Feeling Good	C	0.25
84	Feeling Great	C	0.25
21	Flash Flood	F	8.50
21	Flash Flood	R	3.50
7	Flowers	F	8.50
7	Flowers	R	3.50
85	Friends for Life	C	0.25
48	Gali	F	8.50
48	Gali	R	3.50
49	Gangster	F	8.50
49	Gangster	R	3.50
8	Genki	C	0.25

#	Card name	Rarity	Price
50	Golem	C	0.25
51	Gooji	F	8.50
51	Gooji	R	3.50
52	Grey Wolf	F	8.50
52	Grey Wolf	R	3.50
86	Hard as Nails	U	0.90
53	Hare	C	0.25
54	Hare Hound	U	0.80
55	Henger	C	0.30
9	Holly	C	0.25
56	Horn	F	8.50
56	Horn	R	3.50
25	I'm Calling You Out!	F	8.50
25	I'm Calling You Out!	R	3.50
57	Jell	C	0.25
58	Joker	F	8.50
58	Joker	R	3.50
59	Kuro	U	0.90
87	Life in the Fast Lane	C	0.25
88	Living Smart	U	0.80
89	Make Friends	C	0.25
10	Medicine	U	0.90
60	Mocchi	C	0.25
11	Money	U	0.80
61	Monol	F	8.50
61	Monol	R	3.50
12	Mystery Disc	F	8.50
12	Mystery Disc	R	3.50
62	Naga	F	8.50
62	Naga	R	3.50
13	Net	U	0.90
90	Outta the Way!	C	0.25
26	Pick on a Rookie	F	8.50
26	Pick on a Rookie	R	3.50
63	Pink Suezo	C	0.25

#	Card name	Rarity	Price
64	Pixie	C	0.25
91	Power Move	U	0.80
92	Power Up	C	0.25
22	R & R	C	0.25
93	Race to the Finish	C	0.25
16	Rainy Day	C	0.25
65	Red Eye	C	0.25
66	Red Worm	F	8.50
66	Red Worm	R	3.50
14	Roller Blades	C	0.25
23	Sale	F	8.50
23	Sale	R	3.50
67	Sandy	U	0.80
68	Seed Sister	F	8.50
68	Seed Sister	R	3.50
94	Smart Move	U	0.80
95	Speed Demon	C	0.25
69	Spot Dino	C	0.25
96	Strong Block	U	0.80
97	Study Hard	C	0.25
70	Suezo	C	0.25
71	Tecno Dragon	F	8.50
71	Tecno Dragon	R	3.50
27	The Big Smackdown	U	0.90
98	Think Fast	U	0.80
72	Tiger	C	0.25
99	Toughen Up	C	0.25
15	Trap	C	0.25
73	Usaba	F	8.50
73	Usaba	R	3.50
74	Weeds	U	0.80
24	Whoops!	U	0.80
75	Worm	U	0.80
76	Zilla	U	0.90
77	Zuum	C	0.25

RARITY KEY						
C = Common	**U** = Uncommon	**R** = Rare	**VR** = Very Rare	**UR** = Ultra Rare	**F** = Foil card	**X** = Fixed/standard in all decks

Monty Python and the Holy Grail

(Also known as *Mønti Pythøn ik den Hølie Gräilen*)

Kenzer & Company • Released **June 1996**

"**514** cards in set..." ("**314** sir!") "Right, **314** cards in set"

- Starter decks contain 60 cards; starter displays contain 12 decks
- Booster packs contain 15 cards; booster displays contain 36 packs

Designed by **Brian Jelke**, **Steve Johansson**, **David Kenzer**, **Adam Niepomnik**, and **Mark Schultz**

If you haven't seen *Monty Python and the Holy Grail*, go out now, get a copy, and watch it. I'll wait right here for you. I would suggest the widescreen version, DVD if you have one. Thank you for your cooperation. If you have seen the movie, please continue... Here, now, I told you, if you haven't seen the movie, go see it right away. Stop reading this. You can't read the rest of this until you've seen the movie. It's right there in the fine print at the start of the book, so don't complain to me. All right, be that way, but I warned you!

The **Monty Python** CCG is based upon the five-time Huascar-nominated movie *[The Bolivian Film Academy's Huascar is the second-most prestigious South American film award, second only to the Chilean Golden Llama. – ed.]*. The game system was developed by blind, deaf, and chaste monks over a period of almost fifteen years. The rulebook was printed using ink milked from the finest Indonesian squids and printed on paper recycled exclusively from the linen of mummified pharaohs of the 13th Dynasty. Each card was lovingly hand-crafted by Swedish moose-herders in the off season, using only the finest hand-dyed llama skin leather, and then painted by Bolivian llama ranchers at no less than 5,000 feet above sea level. Each starter deck box was carved from Heart-of-Redwood, while each booster pack was extruded from gold filigree salvaged from the *H.M.S. Titanic*.

The game system itself is a perfect example of the baroque style, most commonly found during the height of the reign of King Henry VIII, when it was used to determine the order of succession. The players face off, shake hands, exchange pleasantries, and commence playing. Each player builds a representative board of England out of 12 cards from his own deck, face down (note that the map follows pre-Edwardian borders in general but does include the Welsh March). Each player provides two cards to build Avalon, the island that falls between the two Englands, and the ultimate goal of the players.

Each player then places one Knight and one Page to carry his coconuts (usually **Arthur** and **Pansy**, though the Queen Mum is fond of starting off with **Lancelot** and **Concorde**). This "Round Table" then adventures through the map of England, encountering other Knights (which can be invited to join the Round Table), Castles, Villages, and Perils, such as the **Vicious Chicken of Bristol**, a **Horde of Young Virgins**, or **Frenchmen**. A player's Knights will do battle with these opponents using their combat prowess or their mighty wits. Each player may play cards into their opponent's England in order to slow him down. Once the knights are in Avalon, they may search for the Holy Grail.

The first player to find it wins *huge* tracts of land... — **James Mishler**

SCRYE NOTES: *Seriously, the 1975* **Holy Grail** *film has been happily quoted (some would say run into the ground) by gamers for years, explaining how it came to be the subject of a game. The CCG attracted a small cult following of gamers, and is still actively supported by Kenzer, better known for its* **Knights of the Dinner Table** *comic book.*

Concept	●●●○○
Gameplay	●●●○○
Card art	●●○○○
Player pool	●○○○○

A Witch

"Well, she turned me into a newt. - A newt? - I got better."

Adversary. Combat 2. *Witch* turns one knight into a newt for a grail number draw of turns. *Witch* chooses the knight.

or: +1 to a village event draw

design © 1996 Kenzer & Co. All Rights Reserved   still © MPFC Ltd.   304

Promos from *Knights of the Dinner Table*

What? No Sara? No Bob? Well, no Bob is OK, we guess...

☐ Sir B.A. Felton		2.00
☐ Sir Brian Van Hoose		2.00
☐ Sir Dave Bozwell		2.00

Set (314 cards)	**118.50**	You will need
Starter Display Box	**131.50**	**35** nine-pocket pages to store this set. (18 doubled up)
Booster Display Box	**104.50**	
Starter Deck	**9.20**	
Booster Pack	**2.70**	

# Card name	Type	Rarity	Price
☐ 1 Castle Abblasore	Castle	R	3.00
☐ 2 Advancing Behavior	Taunt	C/X1	0.15
☐ 3 African Swallow Steals Coconuts	Event	R	3.00
☐ 4 Ain't Heard Nothing	Taunt	U	0.50
☐ 5 Sir Allardin o' The Isles	Knight	R	3.00
☐ 6 Allo	Event	R	3.00
☐ 7 Already Got One	Event	R	3.00
☐ 8 Anarcho-Syndicalist Commune	Village	C/X1	0.15
☐ 9 Sir Andred	Advrsy	R	3.00
☐ 10 Angelic Influence	Event	R	3.00
☐ 11 Angry Mob	Advrsy	C	0.15
☐ 12 Castle Anthrax	Castle	C/X2	0.10
☐ 13 Arcane Writing	Item	U	0.50

# Card name	Type	Rarity	Price
☐ 14 Archibald The Page	Page	C/X2	0.10
☐ 15 Arrested	Event	R	1.30
☐ 16 Castle Arrrghhh	Castle	C/X2	0.10
☐ 17 Arthur, King of the Britons 1	Knight	X1	0.25
☐ 18 Arthur, King of the Britons 2	Knight	X1	0.25
☐ 19 Arthur, King of the Britons 3	Knight	X1	0.25
☐ 20 Arthur, King of the Britons 4	Knight	X1	0.25
☐ 21 Averting Eyes	Event	R	3.00
☐ 22 Baden Hill	Land	C/X2	0.10
☐ 23 Sir Balin	Knight	C	0.15
☐ 24 Banana-Shaped	Event	U	0.25
☐ 25 Castle Bealevale	Castle	U	0.50
☐ 26 Castle Bedegraine	Castle	U	0.50
☐ 27 Sir Bedevere	Knight	X1	0.25
☐ 28 Bedivere's Village	Village	C/X1	0.15
☐ 29 Kingdom Of Benwick	Land	U	0.50
☐ 30 Big Beds	Event	R	3.00
☐ 31 A Bit Longer	Event	R	3.00
☐ 32 Black Forest	Land	C/X2	0.10
☐ 33 Bloodletting	Event	U	0.50
☐ 34 Blow My Nose	Taunt	C	0.15
☐ 35 Castle Bodium	Castle	U	0.25

# Card name	Type	Rarity	Price
☐ 36 Boil Your Bottom	Taunt	U	0.25
☐ 37 Book Of Armaments	Item	U	0.50
☐ 38 Sir Bors	Knight	C/X2	0.10
☐ 39 Brain Of A Duck	Taunt	U	0.25
☐ 40 Castle Brangoris	Castle	C	0.15
☐ 41 Brave Sir Robin Song, vs. I	Song	C/X1	0.50
☐ 42 Brave Sir Robin Song, vs. II	Song	U	0.50
☐ 43 Brave Sir Robin Song, vs. III	Song	R	1.00
☐ 44 Brave Sir Robin Song, vs. IV	Song	C/X1	0.50
☐ 45 Brave Sir Robin Song, vs. V	Song	R	1.00
☐ 46 Bri The Page	Page	C/X1	0.15
☐ 47 Bride's Father	Persona	U	0.25
☐ 48 Bridge Of Death	Land	C	0.15
☐ 49 Bridgekeeper	Advrsy	U	0.50
☐ 50 Bring Out Your Dead	Event	C	0.15
☐ 51 Brother Maynard	Persona	C	0.15
☐ 52 Brother Maynard's Roommate	Persona	U	0.50
☐ 53 Burn Her Anyway	Event	R	3.00
☐ 54 Cave Of Caerbannog	Land	C/X2	0.10
☐ 55 Camelot	Castle	C/X2	0.10
☐ 56 Land Of Camelot	Land	C/X2	0.10

RARITY KEY **C** = Common **U** = Uncommon **R** = Rare **VR** = Very Rare **X1** = In fixed deck #1 **X2** = In fixed deck #2

#	Card name	Type	Rarity	Price
☐ 57	Castle Carbonek	Castle	U	0.25
☐ 58	Cartoonist Dies	Event	R	3.00
☐ 59	Castle Guards	Advrsy	C/X2	0.10
☐ 60	Castle Guards	Advrsy	C/X1	0.80
☐ 61	Castle Guards	Advrsy	U	0.50
☐ 62	Catapult	Item	U	0.50
☐ 63	Forest Of Certain Death	Land	C/X2	0.10
☐ 64	Charge	Event	U	0.25
☐ 65	Charles The Page	Page	C/X2	0.10
☐ 66	Chauncey The Page	Page	C/X1	0.15
☐ 67	Chicken	Taunt	U	0.50
☐ 68	Church Influence	Event	R	3.00
☐ 69	Concorde	Page	C/X3	0.10
☐ 70	Confusion	Event	U	0.50
☐ 71	Land Of Cornwall	Land	C	0.15
☐ 72	Cry Of Distress	Event	U	0.25
☐ 73	Sir Damas	Advrsy	R	3.00
☐ 74	Dancing Knight	Knight	C	0.15
☐ 75	The Dark Forest Of Ewing	Land	C/X2	0.10
☐ 76	Dead Collector	Persona	R	3.00
☐ 77	Debate	Event	R	3.00
☐ 78	Delay Taunt	Event	R	3.00
☐ 79	Dennis	Advrsy	U	0.50
☐ 80	Depart A Lot	Taunt	U	0.25
☐ 81	Detraction	Taunt	U	0.50
☐ 82	Dingo	Advrsy	C	0.15
☐ 83	Direct Attack	Event	R	3.00
☐ 84	Doctors?	Event	C	0.15
☐ 85	Don't Frighten Us	Taunt	U	0.50
☐ 86	Dragon Of Angnor	Advrsy	U	0.50
☐ 87	Dragon Ship	Item	U	0.50
☐ 88	Dramatic Escape	Event	R	3.00
☐ 89	Draw	Event	U	0.25
☐ 90	Dumb Idea	Event	U	0.50
☐ 91	Eccentric Performance	Event	U	0.25
☐ 92	Sir Ector	Knight	C/X2	0.10
☐ 93	Edward The Knight Perilous	Advrsy	U	0.50
☐ 94	Electric Donkey	Taunt	C/X1	0.15
☐ 95	Emperor	Event	U	0.25
☐ 96	English Types	Taunt	U	0.25
☐ 97	Enlightenment	Event	R	3.00
☐ 98	Excalibur	Item	R	5.50
☐ 99	Expulsion	Event	C	0.15
☐ 100	Extra Coconuts	Item	U	0.50
☐ 101	Fallen To His Death	Event	U	0.25
☐ 102	Famous Historian	Persona	C/X1	0.15
☐ 103	Farcical Aquatic Ceremony	Taunt	C/X2	0.10
☐ 104	Farm Animals	Event	U	0.25
☐ 105	Flesh Wound	Event	C	0.15
☐ 106	Foul Weather	Event	R	3.00
☐ 107	Free For All	Event	R	3.00
☐ 108	French Fellows	Advrsy	U	0.50
☐ 109	French Taunter	Advrsy	U	0.50
☐ 110	Frenchman	Advrsy	C/X1	0.15
☐ 111	Friendly Castle	Event	C	0.80
☐ 112	Sir Gaheris	Knight	R	3.50
☐ 113	Sir Galahad (The Pure)	Knight	X1	0.25
☐ 114	Sir Gareth Of Orkney	Knight	U	0.25
☐ 115	Sir Garlon (The Invisible Knight)	Advrsy	U	0.50
☐ 116	Sir Gawain	Knight	C/X2	0.10
☐ 117	Generic Castle	Castle	U	0.50
☐ 118	Generic Knight	Knight	U	0.50
☐ 119	Generic Land	Land	U	0.25
☐ 120	Generic Page	Page	C/X1	0.15
☐ 121	Generic Peril	Advrsy	U	0.50
☐ 122	Generic Village	Village	U	0.25
☐ 123	Get On With It	Event	C	0.15
☐ 124	Get Slop Poured On You	Event	C	0.15
☐ 125	Gimpy The Page	Page	C/X2	0.10
☐ 126	God	Event	R	3.00
☐ 127	Land Of Gore	Land	U	0.50
☐ 128	Gorge Of Eternal Peril	Land	U	0.25
☐ 129	Gorilla	Advrsy	R	3.00
☐ 130	Grail-Shaped Beacon	Event	R	3.00
☐ 131	Green Knight	Advrsy	R	3.00
☐ 132	Groin Hit	Event	U	0.50
☐ 133	Groveling	Event	R	3.00
☐ 134	Castle Of Guy De Loimbard	Castle	C/X2	0.10
☐ 135	Harmless Bunny	Event	R	3.00
☐ 136	Sir Helius	Advrsy	R	3.00
☐ 137	Help From Beyond	Event	R	3.00
☐ 138	Prince Herbert	Persona	U	0.50
☐ 139	Historian's Wife	Persona	R	3.00
☐ 140	Hoard Of Young Virgins	Advrsy	U	0.50
☐ 141	The Holy Grail	Item	R	5.50
☐ 142	The Holy Hand Grenade of Antioch	Item	R	5.50
☐ 143	Holy Men	Event	R	3.00
☐ 144	Hue The Knight Perilous	Advrsy	C	0.15
☐ 145	Humphrey The Page	Page	C/X2	0.10
☐ 146	I'M Not Dead Yet	Event	R	0.60
☐ 147	Ian The Page	Page	C/X1	0.80
☐ 148	Idiom	Event	U	0.50
☐ 149	Impaled	Event	R	3.00
☐ 150	Impass	Event	U	0.50
☐ 151	Impostor	Event	C	0.15
☐ 152	Imprisoned	Event	U	0.50
☐ 153	Inferior	Event	U	0.25
☐ 154	Inferiority	Taunt	U	0.25
☐ 155	Infighting	Event	R	3.00
☐ 156	Injustice	Event	R	3.00
☐ 157	Intermission	Event	R	3.00
☐ 158	Castle Jagent	Castle	R	3.00
☐ 159	Jimmy The Page	Page	R	4.30
☐ 160	Sir Kay	Knight	R	3.00
☐ 161	Killer Rabbit	Advrsy	R	4.30
☐ 162	Knights Of The Round Table Song, vs. I	Song	C/X1	0.80
☐ 163	Knights Of The Round Table Song, vs. II	Song	U	0.50
☐ 164	Knights Of The Round Table Song, vs. III	Song	C	0.50
☐ 165	Knights Who Say Ni	Advrsy	U	0.50
☐ 166	Knock It Off	Event	U	0.50
☐ 167	La Vache	Event	R	3.00
☐ 168	Lady Of The Lake	Event	U	0.50
☐ 169	Lancelot	Knight	X1	0.25
☐ 170	Last Chance	Event	R	3.00
☐ 171	Left Behind	Event	R	3.00
☐ 172	Legendary Black Beast	Advrsy	U	0.50
☐ 173	Let's Be Nice To Him	Event	R	3.00
☐ 174	Lie	Event	R	3.00
☐ 175	Sir Lionel	Knight	R	3.00
☐ 176	Land Of Listenoise	Land	R	3.00
☐ 177	The Land of Logres	Land	C	0.15
☐ 178	Land Of Lothian	Land	R	3.00
☐ 179	Lucky Shot	Event	U	0.50
☐ 180	Mack The Page	Page	R	3.00
☐ 181	Maggy The Page	Page	C/X1	0.15
☐ 182	Castle Magouns	Castle	U	0.25
☐ 183	Major Taunt	Taunt	R	3.00
☐ 184	Major Taunt	Taunt	R	3.00
☐ 185	Major Taunt	Taunt	R	3.00
☐ 186	Major Taunt	Taunt	R	3.00
☐ 187	Village Of Malehaut	Village	R	3.00
☐ 188	Kingdom Of Mercia	Land	R	3.00
☐ 189	Message	Event	C	0.15
☐ 190	A Mistake	Event	U	0.50
☐ 191	Model	Event	U	0.25
☐ 192	Monks1	Advrsy	R	3.00
☐ 193	Monks2	Persona	U	0.50
☐ 194	Morgan Le Fay	Advrsy	R	3.00
☐ 195	Much Rejoicing	Event	C	0.80
☐ 196	Frozen Land Of Nador	Land	C	0.15
☐ 197	Sir Naram	Knight	R	3.00
☐ 198	Nasty Ways	Event	U	0.25
☐ 199	Nathan The Page	Page	C	0.15
☐ 200	A Newt?	Event	C	0.15
☐ 201	Forest Of Ni	Land	U	0.50
☐ 202	Nigel The Page	Page	C/X2	0.10
☐ 203	Northumbria	Land	U	0.50
☐ 204	Not-So-Legendary Black Beast	Advrsy	R	3.00
☐ 205	Nothing	Event	R	3.00
☐ 206	Obnoxious Minstrel	Persona	C/X1	0.15
☐ 207	Old Crone	Advrsy	C	0.15
☐ 208	Olfin Bedwere II Of Rheged	Advrsy	U	0.50
☐ 209	Outrageous Accent	Taunt	U	0.50
☐ 210	Patsy 1	Page	X1	0.25
☐ 211	Patsy 2	Page	X1	0.25
☐ 212	Patsy 3	Page	X1	0.25
☐ 213	Patsy 4	Page	X1	0.25
☐ 214	Sir Pellinore	Knight	U	0.50
☐ 215	Sir Percivale	Knight	R	3.50
☐ 216	Sir Perimones (The Red Knight)	Knight	C	0.15
☐ 217	Sir Persante (The Blue Knight)	Knight	R	3.00
☐ 218	Sir Phelot	Advrsy	R	3.00
☐ 219	Doctor Piglet	Persona	U	0.50
☐ 220	Sir Pinell	Advrsy	R	3.00
☐ 221	Plague	Event	R	3.00
☐ 222	Plague-Ridden Village	Village	C/X2	0.10
☐ 223	A Plan	Event	R	3.00
☐ 224	Police	Advrsy	U	0.50
☐ 225	Positive Id	Event	U	0.50
☐ 226	Prince Herbert Song	Song	R	1.00
☐ 227	Private Parts	Taunt	U	0.25
☐ 228	Questions Three: Air Speed Velocity	Question	R	1.00
☐ 229	Questions Three: Assyria	Question	U	0.50
☐ 230	Questions Three: Cleese	Question	C	0.50
☐ 231	Questions Three: Dead Collector	Question	R	1.00
☐ 232	Questions Three: Dennis	Question	R	1.00
☐ 233	Questions Three: Feast	Question	U	0.50
☐ 234	Questions Three: Fire Tricks	Question	R	1.00
☐ 235	Questions Three: First Knight	Question	R	1.00
☐ 236	Questions Three: Floats	Question	U	0.50
☐ 237	Questions Three: Gilliam	Question	C	0.50
☐ 238	Questions Three: Jones	Question	C/X1	0.50
☐ 239	Questions Three: King Arthur	Question	C	0.50
☐ 240	Questions Three: Palin	Question	C	0.50
☐ 241	Questions Three: Penalty	Question	C/X1	0.50
☐ 242	Questions Three: Scene 24	Question	U	0.50
☐ 243	Questions Three: Unladen Swallow	Question	C	0.50
☐ 244	Questions Three: Writers	Question	C/X1	0.50
☐ 245	Questionsthree: Idle	Question	C/X1	0.50
☐ 246	Remain Gone	Taunt	U	0.50
☐ 247	Repression	Event	C	0.15
☐ 248	Kingdom Of Rheged	Land	C	0.15
☐ 249	Brave Sir Robin	Knight	X1	0.25
☐ 250	Roger The Shrubber	Persona	R	3.00
☐ 251	Rope	Item	C	0.15
☐ 252	Ruined Village	Village	C	0.15
☐ 253	Run Away	Event	U	0.50
☐ 254	Sank Into The Swamp	Event	U	0.25
☐ 255	Science	Event	U	0.50
☐ 256	Scottland	Land	U	0.50
☐ 257	A Scratch	Event	C	0.15
☐ 258	Scribe	Persona	R	3.00
☐ 259	Scroll Of Sacred Words: Nee-Wom	Item	R	3.00
☐ 260	Scroll Of Sacred Words: Ni	Item	C	0.25
☐ 261	Scroll Of Sacred Words: Peng	Item	U	0.50
☐ 262	Sea Of Fate	Land	R	3.00
☐ 263	Seasons	Event	U	0.50
☐ 264	Second Time	Event	R	3.00
☐ 265	Secret Word	Event	R	3.00
☐ 266	Seeking	Event	R	3.00
☐ 267	Shrubbery	Item	U	0.50
☐ 268	A Silly Place	Event	C	0.15
☐ 269	Sir Not Appearing In This Film	Knight	C	0.15
☐ 270	Sir Paste Your Picture Here	Knight	C/X2	0.10
☐ 271	Sir Pram A Lot	Knight	U	0.50
☐ 272	Sir Robin's Minstrels	Persona	C/X2	0.10
☐ 273	Slaying Of The Historian	Event	R	1.30

RARITY KEY C = Common **U** = Uncommon **R** = Rare **VR** = Very Rare **X1** = In fixed deck #1 **X2** = In fixed deck #2

# Card name	Type	Rarity	Price
☐ 274 The Spanish Inquisition	Advrsy	R	3.00
☐ 275 A Spanking	Event	R	3.00
☐ 276 Stone Dead	Event	R	3.00
☐ 277 Kingdom Of Strangore	Land	R	3.00
☐ 278 Strength	Event	U	0.50
☐ 279 Castle Surhaute	Castle	R	3.00
32			
☐ 280 Swamp Castle	Castle	C/X2	0.10
☐ 281 Swamp Land	Land	U	0.50
☐ 282 Tall Tower	Castle	C/X1	0.15
☐ 283 Tantrist O' The White	Knight	R	3.00
☐ 284 Tea & Biscuits	Event	R	3.00
☐ 285 Three-Headed Knight	Advrsy	C/X2	0.10
☐ 286 Tintagel Castle	Castle	U	0.25
☐ 287 Transgression	Event	U	0.50

# Card name	Type	Rarity	Price
☐ 288 Sir Tristram	Knight	R	1.00
33			
☐ 289 Unclog My Nose	Taunt	C	0.15
☐ 290 Castle Vagon	Castle	R	3.00
☐ 291 Very Dull	Event	R	3.00
☐ 292 Vicious Chicken Of Bristol	Advrsy	C/X2	0.10
☐ 293 Vital Clue	Item	R	3.00
☐ 294 Vote	Event	U	0.50
☐ 295 War	Event	U	0.25
☐ 296 Wedding Guests	Persona	C	0.15
☐ 297 Wedding Party	Event	R	3.00
34			
☐ 298 Land Of Wessex	Land	U	0.50
☐ 299 Who Sent You?	Event	U	0.25
☐ 300 William The Page	Page	C/X2	0.10

# Card name	Type	Rarity	Price
☐ 301 Doctor Winston	Persona	R	1.50
☐ 302 Sir Wisshard	Knight	U	0.25
☐ 303 Witch Burning	Event	U	0.50
☐ 304 A Witch	Advrsy	C/X2	0.10
☐ 305 Wooden Badger	Event	R	3.00
☐ 306 Write Your Own Adversary	Advrsy	C	0.15
35			
☐ 307 Write Your Own Castle	Castle	C	0.15
☐ 308 Write Your Own Event	Event	C	0.15
☐ 309 Write Your Own Item	Item	C	0.15
☐ 310 Write Your Own Knight	Knight	C	0.15
☐ 311 Write Your Own Land	Land	C	0.15
☐ 312 Write Your Own Taunt	Taunt	C	0.15
☐ 313 Write Your Own Village	Village	C	0.80
☐ 314 Zoot	Advrsy	C/X2	0.10

Monty Python and the Holy Grail •
Taunt You a Second Time

Kenzer & Co. • Released **August 2000** • **158** cards in set
• Starter decks contain 60 cards; there are no starter displays

Je ne sais pas si je veux faire ceci. Ce sont tous les Anglais-types. Comment on indique-t-il le "cirque de vol encore"? Rien, ils sont ici!

"'Allo! Silly card-game playing types! I yam 'ere to eentroduce jou to ze gratest card-game on ze mar-ket, ze wondairful Monty Python et ze... mmm... 'ow do you zay eet again? Aha! *Mais naturellement!* **Monty Python's Flying Vole et ze Holy Grail.** *Non? Que voulez-vous dire, pas 'campagnol'?*"

A, certainement, langage idiot qu'ils ont, et il?

"'Allo again! Eet ees seemple, card-shuffling so-called card-game playing types! Zaire ees more of *me* een ze expansion, et eet 'as ze Knnnniggets zat say, 'Ni,' et le sorcier Tim, et le Black Knnnnigget, et much more."

Maintenant, allez-vous-en ou je vous raille une deuxième fois!

"What, jou are steel 'ere? *Heure de se débarasser de ce type. Cherchez la vache!*"

BWOINGGG! "Mooooooooo!" — **Jåms Mishlér**

You will need
18
nine-pocket pages to store this set.
(9 doubled up)

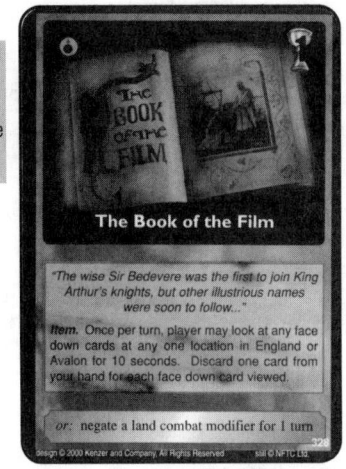

The Book of the Film

"The wise Sir Bedevere was the first to join King Arthur's knights, but other illustrious names were soon to follow..."

Item. Once per turn, player may look at any face down cards at any one location in England or Avalon for 10 seconds. Discard one card from your hand for each face down card viewed.

or: negate a land combat modifier for 1 turn

Set (158 cards)	53.75
Starter Deck	**9.00**

# Card name	Type	Rarity	Price
1			
☐ 315 142 Mexican Whooping Llamas	Advrsy	R	1.00
☐ 316 1st Soldier	Advrsy	C/X1	0.05
☐ 317 2nd Soldier	Advrsy	R	1.00
☐ 318 Acne	Taunt	U	0.25
☐ 319 African Swallow	Advrsy	R	1.00
☐ 320 Anarcho-Syndicalist Commune	Land	R	1.00
☐ 321 Appy the Page	Page	R	1.00
☐ 322 Autonomous Collective	Village	C/X1	0.05
☐ 323 Avalon	Land	R	1.00
2			
☐ 324 Be Quiet	Taunt	R	1.00
☐ 325 Begorrah	Taunt	C	0.05
☐ 326 Black Knight	Advrsy	C/X2	0.15
☐ 327 Bloody Hell	Event	U	0.25
☐ 328 The Book of the Film	Item	C/X2	0.05
☐ 329 Bow and Arrow	Item	R	1.00
☐ 330 Sir Bruce	knight	C/X2	0.05
☐ 331 Buggering Off	Event	X1	0.05
☐ 332 But Father	Taunt	X1	0.05
3			
☐ 333 Cap of Idiocy	Item	X1	0.05
☐ 334 Cart Master	Persona	X1	0.05
☐ 335 Cartoon Forest	Land	R	1.00
☐ 336 Dead Person	Persona	C/X2	0.05
☐ 337 Sir Clarke	Knight	C	0.05
☐ 338 Confused Guard	Advrsy	U	0.25
☐ 339 Crapper	Advrsy	U	0.25
☐ 340 Creek Fiend	Advrsy	U	0.25
☐ 341 Dagger	Item	X1	0.05
4			
☐ 342 Delirious	Event	C/X1	0.05
☐ 343 Dennis' Mother	Advrsy	U	0.25
☐ 344 Disbelief	Event	R	1.00
☐ 345 Don't be Afraid of Him	Event	R	1.00
☐ 346 Dress Her Up	Event	C/X2	0.05
☐ 347 Dressed as a witch	Event	U	0.25
☐ 348 Duck	Advrsy	C	0.05
☐ 349 Earthquake	Event	U	0.25
☐ 350 English Knights	Taunt	U	0.25

# Card name	Type	Rarity	Price
5			
☐ 351 Enough Music	Event	U	0.25
☐ 352 Evil Cat beater	Advrsy	C/X2	0.05
☐ 353 Executive Officer	Advrsy	U	0.25
☐ 354 False Count	Event	C	0.05
☐ 355 Fanfare	Event	C/X1	0.05
☐ 356 Fart	Taunt	U	0.25
☐ 357 Faulty Coconuts	Item	R	1.00
☐ 358 Ferocious Taunt	Taunt	C/X1	0.05
☐ 359 Flower Vase	tItem	R	1.00
6			
☐ 360 Food trough Wiper	Taunt	C/X1	0.05
☐ 361 Fooling Anyone	Event	U	0.25
☐ 362 Fooling Yourself	Event	C	0.05
☐ 363 Foul and Cruel	Taunt	U	0.25
☐ 364 Friendly Guard	Persona	C	0.05
☐ 365 Galahad's Shield	Item	C	0.05
☐ 366 Git	Taunt	U	0.25
☐ 367 Glass of Water	Item	R	1.00
☐ 368 Got One	Event	C/X2	0.05
7			
☐ 369 Great Find	Event	C/X2	0.05
☐ 370 Sir Gringamore	Advrsy	C/X2	0.05
☐ 371 Guy De Loimbard	Advrsy	U	0.50
☐ 372 A Happy Occasion	Event	R	1.00
☐ 373 Head Off	Event	C/X2	0.05
☐ 374 A Herring	Item	C/X1	0.05
☐ 375 Hiccups	Event	U	0.25
☐ 376 Hidden Knowledge	Event	U	0.25
☐ 377 Highlands	Land	C/X2	0.05
8			
☐ 378 Holiday in Sweden	Event	U	0.25
☐ 379 I got Better	Event	C/X2	0.05
☐ 380 Interspace Toothbrush	Item	C/X1	0.05
☐ 381 Join My Court	Event	U	0.25
☐ 382 King of Swamp Castle	Persona	R	1.50
☐ 383 Knighting	Event	C/X3	0.05
☐ 384 Knights Who Til Recently Said Ni	Advrsy	U	0.50
☐ 385 Lancelot's Shield	Item	C	0.05
☐ 386 Lightning	Page	U	0.25
9			
☐ 387 A Looney	Taunt	R	1.00
☐ 388 Lucky John	Page	C	0.05

# Card name	Type	Rarity	Price
☐ 389 Mace	Item	C/X2	0.05
☐ 390 Major Taunt 1 (No chance...)	Taunt	R	1.00
☐ 391 Major Taunt 2	Taunt	R	1.00
☐ 392 Mallet to the Head	Event	R	1.00
☐ 393 Marriage	Event	U	0.25
☐ 394 Mayhem	Event	U	0.25
☐ 395 Men of Valor	Event	U	0.25
10			
☐ 396 Midget	Advrsy	C	0.05
☐ 397 Mightiest Tree In the Forest	Land	R	1.00
☐ 398 Migration	Event	C	0.05
☐ 399 Moistened Bint	Advrsy	U	0.25
☐ 400 Moose	Advrsy	U	0.25
☐ 401 Moose Bite	Event	U	0.25
☐ 402 More than Reasonable	Event	R	1.00
☐ 403 Mr. Newt	Persona	U	0.30
☐ 404 Mud	Item	U	0.25
11			
☐ 405 No Chance	Taunt	U	0.25
☐ 406 No Class	Event	C/X2	0.05
☐ 407 No More	Taunt	U	0.25
☐ 408 No Problems	Event	C/X1	0.05
☐ 409 Nobility	Event	U	0.25
☐ 410 Non-Migratory	Event	U	0.25
☐ 411 Not Quite So Brave	Event	R	1.00
☐ 412 A Note	Item	R	1.00
☐ 413 Notlob	Village	C	0.05
12			
☐ 414 Nursery	Land	U	0.25
☐ 415 Oh Dear	Event	U	0.25
☐ 416 Old Man from Scene 24	Persona	C/X1	0.05
☐ 417 Outrageous Accent	Event	C/X2	0.05
☐ 418 Packy the Page	Page	U	0.25
☐ 419 Passing Ruffians	Advrsy	C	0.05
☐ 420 Penguin of Bristol	Advrsy	R	1.00
☐ 421 Pissing off Home	Taunt	R	1.00
☐ 422 Pointless Land	Land	U	0.25
13			
☐ 423 Princess Lucky	Persona	U	0.25
☐ 424 Pyrotechnics	Event	C/X1	0.05
☐ 425 Questions Three: Drag	Q3	C	0.05
☐ 426 Questions Three: Favorite Color	Q3	R	1.00
☐ 427 Questions Three: Latin Chant	Q3	X1	0.05

RARITY KEY C = Common U = Uncommon R = Rare VR = Very Rare X1 = In fixed deck #1 X2 = In fixed deck #2

#	Card name	Type	Rarity	Price
☐ 428	Questions Three: What Year	Q3	U	0.25
☐ 429	Rake	Item	U	0.25
☐ 430	Ralph the Wonder Llama	Advrsy	C/X2	0.05
☐ 431	Ratification	Event	U	0.25
☐ 432	The Robinson	Advrsy	U	0.25
☐ 433	Rude Gesture	Taunt	U	0.25
☐ 434	Scale	Item	C/X1	0.05
☐ 435	Separate Ways	Event	U	0.25
☐ 436	Sequined Vest	Item	U	0.25
☐ 437	Sheep's Bladder	Item	C	0.05
☐ 438	Silence	Event	C	0.05
☐ 439	Silly Request	Taunt	C/X2	0.05
☐ 440	Single handed	Event	R	1.00
☐ 441	Sir Robin's Shield	Item	U	0.25
☐ 442	Slink	Event	U	0.25

#	Card name	Type	Rarity	Price
☐ 443	Soiled my Armor	Event	R	1.00
☐ 444	Soothsayer	Advrsy	R	1.00
☐ 445	Special Guest	Event	R	1.00
☐ 446	Splash	Event	U	0.25
☐ 447	Staff of Fire	Item	R	1.00
☐ 448	Strand of Creeper	Item	C/X2	0.05
☐ 449	Sweden	Land	R	1.00
☐ 450	Sword of Parrying	Item	R	1.00
☐ 451	Tim the Enchanter	Persona	R	2.00
☐ 452	Tiny Brain	Taunt	U	0.25
☐ 453	Too Perilous	Event	R	1.00
☐ 454	Torture Rack	Item	U	0.25
☐ 455	A Treat	Event	R	1.00
☐ 456	Trojan Rabbit	Item	R	1.50
☐ 457	Un Cadeau	Event	R	1.00

#	Card name	Type	Rarity	Price
☐ 458	Invisible Card	Item	C	0.05
☐ 459	Severed Head	Event	C/X2	0.05
☐ 460	Wazzed Stiff	Event	R	1.00
☐ 461	Wedding Groomsmen	Advrsy	C/X1	0.05
☐ 462	Weight Ratios	Event	U	0.25
☐ 463	Well I'm Awfully Sorry	Event	R	1.00
☐ 464	Where are Your Manners	Event	U	0.25
☐ 465	Whoa there	Event	C	0.05
☐ 466	Wicked Cat Beater	Advrsy	U	0.25
☐ 467	Window Dresser	Taunt	U	0.25
☐ 468	Witchcraft	Event	U	0.25
☐ 469	With a Herring	Taunt	R	1.00
☐ 470	Write Yer Own	Page	R	1.00
☐ 471	You Make Me Sad	Event	R	1.00
☐ 472	Your Mother	Taunt	R	1.00

Mortal Kombat

Brady Games • Released January 1996 • 300 cards in set

- Starter decks contain 60 cards; starter displays contain 12 starters
- Booster packs contain 15 cards; booster displays contain 36 boosters

A battle brews between the warriors of Outworld and the defenders of Earth. If the Earthlings don't win in martial arts combat, an army will overrun the Earth. No pressure.

Based on the arcade game, **Mortal Kombat** introduced several elements not seen elsewhere in CCGs. Each player chooses one character to play and loads a deck with attacks, defenses, Kombos, and special cards for that character. The player with initiative may make attacks until the opposing player blocks or evades one of them. Then, both players draw cards and the opponent fights back. This simulates the video game, where one player can pound the buttons a nanosecond before his opponent and keep hitting, while the other player stands there and takes it.

Simple, but there are amazing twists. Rules exist for ranged combat: A character can fight hand-to-hand, in close combat, or a few feet back, throwing stuff. Moving around adds yet more depth. A player can wind up behind his opponent, which can be interesting, if confusing. Another feature movement adds is the chance for a big brawl. There are 20 character cards, so, if you were to use a large playing surface with a grid pattern, you could, in, in theory play out the whole tournament of *Mortal Kombat* in one day. The rules for a two-player game are good, but the brawl rules are a stroke of genius. It's practically a miniatures warfare system.

The starters are thoroughly random, which is a bit of a disappointment, since it means buyers get a lot of specials for characters they don't have. (There *is* a rules-fix for this.)

Mortal Kombat was from Brady Games, which published an early unauthorized strategy guide for **Magic**. But *Mortal Kombat* hit the market when the glut was worst and the customers were few, so you need a guide to find someone who sold much of it. — ***Richard Weld***

Concept	●●●○○
Gameplay	●●●○○
Card art	●●○○○
Player pool	○○○○○

SPECIAL EFFECT

SPIRIT OF THE DRAGON
Special Effect

Kombatant gains +2 Speed and +3 Strength for 1action, non-accumulative.

Set (300 cards)	**72.25**
Starter Display Box	**27.50**
Booster Display Box	**31.00**
Starter Deck	**5.80**
Booster Pack	**1.40**

You will need **34** nine-pocket pages to store this set. (300 doubled up)

Card name	Type	Rarity	Price
☐ 2-Hit Kombo (1 basic/1 special)	Kombo	C	0.05
☐ 2-Hit Kombo (2 basic)	Kombo	C	0.05
☐ 2-hit Kombo (2 special)	Kombo	C	0.05
☐ 3-Hit Kombo (1 basic/2 special)	Kombo	U	0.30
☐ 3-Hit Kombo (2 basic/1 special)	Kombo	U	0.30
☐ 3-Hit Kombo (3 basic)	Kombo	U	0.30
☐ 4-Hit Kombo (1 basic/3 special)	Kombo	R	2.00
☐ 4-Hit Kombo (3 basic/1 special)	Kombo	R	2.00
☐ All Out Block	Defense	R	2.00
☐ Ankle Kick	Attack	C	0.05
☐ Baraka	Char	U	0.30
☐ Baraka: Babality	FinMov	U	0.30
☐ Baraka: Backhand Punch	SpMov	C	0.05
☐ Baraka: Blade Fury	SpMov	R	2.00
☐ Baraka: Blade Rush	SpMov	U	0.30

Card name	Type	Rarity	Price
☐ Baraka: Blade Swipe	SpMov	C	0.05
☐ Baraka: Decapitation	Fatality	U	0.30
☐ Baraka: Double Kick	SpMov	R	2.00
☐ Baraka: Gift Box	Friend	U	0.30
☐ Baraka: High Spark Toss	SpMov	U	0.30
☐ Baraka: Spark Toss	SpMov	C	0.05
☐ Body Kick	Attack	C	0.05
☐ Body Punch	Attack	C	0.05
☐ Breakout	Defens	R	2.00
☐ Chi Power: Healing	SpEff	U	0.30
☐ Chi Power: Shout	SpEff	C	0.05
☐ Chi Power: Speed	SpEff	C	0.05
☐ Confusion	SpEff	C	0.05
☐ Control Breathing	SpEff	U	0.30
☐ Copy Move	SpEff	U	0.30
☐ Cornered	SpEff	U	0.30
☐ Crouch	Defens	C	0.05
☐ Crouch Kick	Attack	C	0.05
☐ Crouch Punch	Attack	C	0.05
☐ Crouched Block	Defens	C	0.05
☐ Deep Concentration	SpEff	U	0.30
☐ Desperation	SpEff	C	0.05
☐ Dirty Trick	SpEff	C	0.05
☐ Disrupt Chi Power	SpEff	C	0.05
☐ Dodge	Defens	R	2.00
☐ Doubt	SpEff	U	0.30
☐ Escape	SpEff	C	0.05

Card name	Type	Rarity	Price
☐ Feint	SpEff	R	2.00
☐ Flip	Defens	C	0.05
☐ Frenzy	SpEff	U	0.30
☐ Goro	Char	R	2.00
☐ Goro: Babality	FinMov	R	2.00
☐ Goro: Double Uppercut	SpMov	R	2.00
☐ Goro: Drawn & Quartered	Fatality	R	2.00
☐ Goro: Fireball Punch	SpMov	R	0.30
☐ Goro: Four Handed Pound	SpMov	R	2.00
☐ Goro: Grab And Squeeze	SpMov	U	0.30
☐ Goro: Overhead Toss	SpMov	R	2.00
☐ Goro: Patty Cake	Friend	R	2.00
☐ Goro: Push	SpMov	U	0.30
☐ Goro: Stomp	SpMov	R	2.00
☐ Head Kick	Attack	C	0.05
☐ Head Punch	Attack	C	0.05
☐ High Block	Defens	C	0.05
☐ High Power Block	Defens	U	0.30
☐ Hop Kick	Attack	U	0.30
☐ Hop Punch	Attack	U	0.30
☐ Inner Strength	SpEff	R	2.00
☐ Instinct	SpEff	R	2.00
☐ Jade	Char	R	2.00
☐ Jade: Air Attack	SpMov	U	0.30
☐ Jade: Babality	FinMov	R	2.00
☐ Jade: Elbow Punch	SpMov	C	0.05
☐ Jade: Fan Lift	SpMov	R	2.50
☐ Jade: Fan Swipe	SpMov	C	0.05

RARITY KEY C = Common U = Uncommon R = Rare VR = Very Rare UR = Ultra Rare F = Foil card X = Fixed/standard in all decks

Card name	Type	Rarity	Price
☐ Jade: Fan Throw	SpMov	U	0.30
☐ Jade: Jade Dragon	Friend	R	2.00
9			
☐ Jade: Jaded	Fatality	R	2.00
☐ Jade: Phantasmal Defens	SpMov	R	2.00
☐ Jade: Whirlwind Toss	SpMov	R	2.00
☐ Jax	Char	U	0.30
☐ Jax: Babality	FinMov	U	0.30
☐ Jax: Back Breaker	SpMov	U	0.30
☐ Jax: Energy Wave	SpMov	U	0.30
☐ Jax: Gotcha Grab	SpMov	R	2.00
☐ Jax: Ground Smash	SpMov	U	0.30
10			
☐ Jax: Head Crusher	Fatality	U	0.30
☐ Jax: Overhead Hammer	SpMov	U	0.30
☐ Jax: Paper Dolls	Friend	U	0.30
☐ Jax: Quadruple Slam	SpMov	R	2.00
☐ Jax: Take Down	SpMov	C	0.05
☐ Johnny Cage	Char	C	0.05
☐ Johnny Cage: Autograph	Friend	C	0.05
☐ Johnny Cage: Babality	FinMov	C	0.05
☐ Johnny Cage: Drop Kick	SpMov	U	0.30
11			
☐ Johnny Cage: Green Bolt	SpMov	C	0.05
☐ Johnny Cage: Groin Punch	SpMov	R	3.00
☐ Johnny Cage: High Green Bolt	SpMov	C	0.05
☐ Johnny Cage: Shadow Kick	SpMov	U	0.30
☐ Johnny Cage: Shadow Uppercut	SpMov	R	2.00
☐ Johnny Cage: Stomach Jab	SpMov	C	0.05
☐ Johnny Cage: Uppercut Decapitation	Fatality	C	0.05
☐ Jump	Defens	C	0.05
☐ Jump Kick	Attack	C	0.05
12			
☐ Jump Kick Backward	Attack	C	0.05
☐ Jump Punch	Attack	C	0.05
☐ Jump Punch Backward	Attack	C	0.05
☐ Kahn's Throne	SpEff	U	0.30
☐ Kano	Char	C	0.05
☐ Kano: Babality	FinMov	C	0.05
☐ Kano: Cannonball	SpMov	U	0.30
☐ Kano: Cooking With Kano	Friend	C	0.05
☐ Kano: Double Knife Slash	SpMov	C	0.05
13			
☐ Kano: Eye Gouge	SpMov	R	2.00
☐ Kano: Headbutt	SpMov	U	0.30
☐ Kano: Heart Rip	Fatality	C	0.05
☐ Kano: Knife Toss	SpMov	C	0.05
☐ Kano: Palm Strike	SpMov	C	0.05
☐ Kano: Speed Roundhouse	SpMov	R	2.00
☐ Kintaro	Char	R	3.00
☐ Kintaro: Aerial Stomp	SpMov	R	2.00
☐ Kintaro: Babality	FinMov	R	2.00
14			
☐ Kintaro: Body Crush	SpMov	U	0.30
☐ Kintaro: Body Slam	SpMov	R	2.00
☐ Kintaro: Fireball Spit	SpMov	C	0.05
☐ Kintaro: Four Handed Slam	SpMov	R	3.00
☐ Kintaro: Power Uppercut	SpMov	R	2.00
☐ Kintaro: Shadow Warriors	Friend	R	2.00
☐ Kintaro: Torso Tear	Fatality	R	2.00
☐ Kintaro: Underhand Toss	SpMov	R	3.00
☐ Kitana	Char	U	0.30
15			
☐ Kitana: Air Attack	SpMov	U	0.30
☐ Kitana: Babality	FinMov	U	0.30
☐ Kitana: Birthday Cake	Friend	U	0.30
☐ Kitana: Double Fan Swipe	SpMov	R	2.00
☐ Kitana: Elbow Punch	SpMov	C	0.05
☐ Kitana: Eye Rake	SpMov	U	0.30
☐ Kitana: Fan Lift	SpMov	R	2.50
☐ Kitana: Fan Swipe	SpMov	C	0.05
☐ Kitana: Fan Throw	SpMov	U	0.30
16			
☐ Kitana: Kiss of Death	Fatality	U	0.30
☐ Knee Kick	Attack	C	0.05
☐ Kung Lao	Char	U	0.30
☐ Kung Lao: Aerial Kick	SpMov	R	2.00
☐ Kung Lao: Babality	FinMov	U	0.30
☐ Kung Lao: Ground Teleport	SpMov	U	0.30
☐ Kung Lao: Hat Reflect	SpMov	R	2.00
☐ Kung Lao: Hat Slice	Fatality	U	0.30
☐ Kung Lao: Hat Swipe	SpMov	C	0.05
17			
☐ Kung Lao: Hat Throw	SpMov	U	0.30
☐ Kung Lao: Headbutt	SpMov	U	0.30

Card name	Type	Rarity	Price
☐ Kung Lao: Magic Rabbit	Friend	U	0.30
☐ Kung Lao: Whirlwind Spin	SpMov	U	0.30
☐ Level the Playing Field	SpEff	U	0.30
☐ Liu Kang	Char	C	0.05
☐ Liu Kang: Babality	FinMov	C	0.05
☐ Liu Kang: Bicycle Kick	SpMov	R	2.00
☐ Liu Kang: Disco Boogie	Friend	C	0.05
18			
☐ Liu Kang: Dragon Bite	Fatality	C	0.05
☐ Liu Kang: Dragon Fire	SpMov	U	0.25
☐ Liu Kang: Feint Kick	SpMov	U	0.30
☐ Liu Kang: Flying Kick	SpMov	C	0.05
☐ Liu Kang: Forearm Punch	SpMov	C	0.05
☐ Liu Kang: Jumping Dragon Fireball	SpMov	C	0.05
☐ Liu Kang: Repeating Kick	SpMov	U	0.30
☐ Low Block	Defens	C	0.05
☐ Low Power Block	Defens	U	0.30
19			
☐ Mid Block	Defens	C	0.05
☐ Mid Power Block	Defens	U	0.30
☐ Mileena	Char	U	0.30
☐ Mileena: Babality	FinMov	U	0.30
☐ Mileena: Elbow Punch	SpMov	C	0.05
☐ Mileena: Flower Power	Friend	U	0.30
☐ Mileena: Ground Roll	SpMov	U	0.30
☐ Mileena: Man Eater	Fatality	U	0.30
☐ Mileena: Sai Lunge	SpMov	U	0.30
20			
☐ Mileena: Sai Throw	SpMov	C	0.05
☐ Mileena: Teleport	SpMov	U	0.30
☐ Mileena: Teleport Kick	SpMov	R	2.00
☐ Mileena: Throat Strike	SpMov	R	2.00
☐ Muscle Spasm	SpEff	C	0.05
☐ Noob Saibot	Char	R	2.00
☐ Noob Saibot: Babality	FinMov	R	2.00
☐ Noob Saibot: Backhand Punch	SpMov	U	0.30
☐ Noob Saibot: Dark Attack	SpMov	R	2.00
21			
☐ Noob Saibot: Fast Strike	SpMov	R	2.00
☐ Noob Saibot: Harpoon	SpMov	R	2.00
☐ Noob Saibot: Shadow Cloak	SpMov	R	2.00
☐ Noob Saibot: Shadow Phase	SpMov	U	0.30
☐ Noob Saibot: Shadow Spirits	Fatality	R	2.00
☐ Noob Saibot: Slide Kick	SpMov	U	0.30
☐ Noob Saibot: Will You Be My ...	Friend	R	2.00
☐ Planned Attack	SpEff	U	0.30
☐ Rayden	Char	C	0.05
22			
☐ Rayden's Fury	SpEff	U	0.30
☐ Rayden: Babality	FinMov	C	0.05
☐ Rayden: Blinding Attack	SpMov	R	2.00
☐ Rayden: Body Launch Torpedo	SpMov	U	0.30
☐ Rayden: Electrocution	SpMov	R	2.00
☐ Rayden: Kid Thunder	Friend	C	0.05
☐ Rayden: Lightning Throw	SpMov	U	0.30
☐ Rayden: Mini Uppercut	SpMov	C	0.05
☐ Rayden: Shock Therapy	Fatality	C	0.05
23			
☐ Rayden: Teleport	SpMov	U	0.30
☐ Rayden: Thunder Strike	SpMov	R	2.00
☐ Reptile	Char	U	0.30
☐ Reptile: Acid Spit	SpMov	U	0.30
☐ Reptile: Babality	FinMov	U	0.30
☐ Reptile: Backhand Punch	SpMov	C	0.05
☐ Reptile: Forceball	SpMov	U	0.30
☐ Reptile: Invisibility	SpMov	R	2.00
☐ Reptile: Lizard Lunch	Fatality	U	0.30
24			
☐ Reptile: Poison Claws	SpMov	U	0.30
☐ Reptile: Reptile Doll	Friend	U	0.30
☐ Reptile: Slide Kick	SpMov	U	0.30
☐ Reptile: Tongue Strike	SpMov	R	2.00
☐ Reset Round	SpEff	R	2.00
☐ Retreat	Defens	R	2.00
☐ Reverse Kick	Attack	C	0.05
☐ Reverse Punch	Attack	C	0.05
☐ Roll To Your Feet	SpEff	C	0.05
25			
☐ Roundhouse Kick	Attack	C	0.05
☐ Scorpion	Char	C	0.05
☐ Scorpion: Air Throw	SpMov	U	0.30
☐ Scorpion: Babality	FinMov	C	0.05
☐ Scorpion: Backhand Punch	SpMov	C	0.05
☐ Scorpion: Decoy	SpMov	R	2.00
☐ Scorpion: Harpoon Spear	SpMov	U	0.30

Card name	Type	Rarity	Price
☐ Scorpion: Hellfire Strike	SpMov	R	2.00
☐ Scorpion: Leg Grab	SpMov	C	0.05
26			
☐ Scorpion: Scorpion Doll	Friend	C	0.05
☐ Scorpion: Teleport Punch	SpMov	U	0.30
☐ Scorpion: Toasty	Fatality	C	0.05
☐ Shang Tsung	Char	R	2.00
☐ Shang Tsung: Babality	FinMov	R	2.00
☐ Shang Tsung: Double Skull Launch	SpMov	U	0.30
☐ Shang Tsung: Levitate	SpMov	U	0.30
☐ Shang Tsung: Life Drain	SpMov	R	2.00
☐ Shang Tsung: Morph	SpMov	C	0.05
27			
☐ Shang Tsung: Rainbow	Friend	R	2.00
☐ Shang Tsung: Skull Launch	SpMov	C	0.05
☐ Shang Tsung: Soul Stealer	Fatality	R	2.00
☐ Shang Tsung: Triple Skull Launch	SpMov	R	2.00
☐ Shao Kahn	Char	R	2.00
☐ Shao Kahn: Babality	FinMov	R	2.00
☐ Shao Kahn: Dance of Death	Friend	R	2.00
☐ Shao Kahn: Lightning Charge	SpMov	R	2.00
☐ Shao Kahn: Lightning Spear	SpMov	R	2.00
28			
☐ Shao Kahn: Neck Breaker	Fatality	R	2.00
☐ Shao Kahn: Plane Shift	SpMov	R	2.00
☐ Shao Kahn: Right Hook	SpMov	R	2.00
☐ Shao Kahn: Shoulder Charge	SpMov	R	2.00
☐ Shao Kahn: Spirit Hold	SpMov	R	2.00
☐ Shao Kahn: Taunt	SpMov	U	0.30
☐ Sheer Will	SpEff	U	0.30
☐ Sidestep	Defens	U	0.30
☐ Smoke	Char	R	2.00
29			
☐ Smoke: Babality	FinMov	R	2.00
☐ Smoke: Backhand Punch	SpMov	C	0.05
☐ Smoke: Harpoon Air Grab	SpMov	R	2.00
☐ Smoke: Harpoon Throw	SpMov	U	0.30
☐ Smoke: Slde Kick	SpMov	R	2.00
☐ Smoke: Smoke	SpMov	U	0.30
☐ Smoke: Smoke Dodge	SpMov	R	2.00
☐ Smoke: Smoke Inhalation	Fatality	R	2.00
☐ Smoke: Smoke Rings	Friend	R	2.00
30			
☐ Smoke: Smoke Screen	SpMov	R	2.00
☐ Sonya Blade	Char	C	0.05
☐ Sonya Blade: Arm Lock Takedown	SpMov	R	2.00
☐ Sonya Blade: Babality	FinMov	C	0.05
☐ Sonya Blade: Clothes Line	SpMov	U	0.30
☐ Sonya Blade: Forearm Smash	SpMov	C	0.05
☐ Sonya Blade: Good Sport Medal	Friend	C	0.05
☐ Sonya Blade: Kiss of Death	Fatality	C	0.05
☐ Sonya Blade: Leg Scissors	SpMov	U	0.30
31			
☐ Sonya Blade: Reverse Throw	SpMov	R	2.00
☐ Sonya Blade: Ring Wave	SpMov	C	0.05
☐ Sonya Blade: Square Wave Flight	SpMov	U	0.30
☐ Spin	SpEff	C	0.05
☐ Spirit of the Dragon	SpEff	R	2.00
☐ Steal Move	SpEff	R	2.00
☐ Strategy	SpEff	R	2.00
☐ Stumble	SpEff	C	0.05
☐ Sub Zero	Char	C	0.05
32			
☐ Sub Zero: Babality	FinMov	C	0.05
☐ Sub Zero: Backhand Punch	SpMov	C	0.05
☐ Sub Zero: Deep Freeze	Fatality	C	0.05
☐ Sub Zero: Frost Bite	SpMov	U	0.30
☐ Sub Zero: Ground Freeze	SpMov	U	0.30
☐ Sub Zero: Ice Shards	SpMov	R	2.00
☐ Sub Zero: Iceball	SpMov	U	0.30
☐ Sub Zero: Shoulder Dash	SpMov	R	2.00
☐ Sub Zero: Slide Kick	SpMov	U	0.30
33			
☐ Sub Zero: Sub-Zero Doll	Fatality	C	0.05
☐ Sweep Kick	Attack	C	0.05
☐ Taunt	SpEff	R	2.00
☐ Telegraphing the Blow	SpEff	R	2.00
☐ The Gods of Fate	SpEff	R	2.00
☐ Throw	Attack	C	0.05
☐ Touch of Death	SpEff	R	2.00
☐ Tranquility	SpEff	C	0.05
☐ Trapped	SpEff	U	0.30
34			
☐ Ultimate Kombo	Kombo	R	2.00
☐ Uppercut	Attack	C	0.05
☐ Vendetta	SpEff	U	0.30

RARITY KEY C = Common U = Uncommon R = Rare VR = Very Rare UR = Ultra Rare F = Foil card X = Fixed/standard in all decks

Mythos

Chaosium • First set, *Limited Edition*, released **March 1996**
216 cards in set • **IDENTIFIER: Cards are © 1996**
• Starter decks contain 60 cards; starter displays contain 10 starters
• There are no "Limited Edition" booster packs
Designed by **Charlie Krank**

Concept	●●●○○
Gameplay	●●●○○
Card art	●●●○○
Player pool	○○○○○

The **Mythos** CCG, like Chaosium's earlier **Call of Cthulhu** role-playing game, is based on the writings of H.P. Lovecraft and other horror authors who followed in his footsteps.

Players of *Mythos* take the part of an investigator in the world of the Cthulhu Mythos, where they discover the horrible secrets behind the true history of our world. Each player takes his investigator on an adventure, discovering secrets, finding and using mystical items, exploring exotic locations, and generally trying to avoid going insane.

Each player uses a deck of 60 cards containing adventures, allies, artifacts, events, locations, monsters, spells, and tomes. An adventure card has a series of goals that must be met during play, fulfilled from within a player's own deck. A player is really playing against his own deck, rather than directly against opponents, except when an opponent uses monstrous threats to stop him from fulfilling his goals. A game immediately ends when one of the investigators completes his adventure. The player who has the greatest total adventure points and remaining sanity points is the winner.

Fans of *Call of Cthulhu* were quick to either condemn the game as a poor cousin or praise it as a CCG finally worth playing. There has been a small following, but, while the game is still available in general circulation, for the most part it never really caught on. Today it sleeps alongside Great Cthulhu in Sunken R'lyeh, dreaming of the day that the stars will be right… — *James Mishler*

"Wilbur had with him the priceless but imperfect copy of Dr. Dee's English version which his grandfather bequeathed him…"
— H.P. Lovecraft, "The Dunwich Horror"

Set (216 cards)	157.50
Starter Display Box	40.50
Starter Deck	6.50

You will need 24 nine-pocket pages to store this set. (12 doubled up)

Promo cards

Card name	Type		Price
☐ Create Your Own Adventure	Adventure		0.60
☐ Howard Lovecraft	Ally		1.20

Card name	Type	Rarity	Price
☐ 197 E. Pickman Street	Location	C	0.25
☐ A Heroic Rescue	Adventure	U	0.80
☐ Abigail Winthrop Marsh	Ally	C	0.25
☐ Adventurous Dilettante	Investigator	I	1.50
☐ Albert N. Wilmarth	Ally	U	0.80
☐ Albert Shiny	Ally	R	3.00
☐ Ammi Pierce	Ally	C	0.20
☐ Ammi Pierce's Tottering Cottage	Location	C	0.20
☐ Amnesia	Event	C	0.25
☐ An Unexpected Calamity	Event	U	0.90
☐ Ann White	Ally	C	0.20
☐ Arkham Historical Society	Location	C	0.25
☐ Arkham Rare Books & Maps	Location	R	2.80
☐ Arkham Sanitarium	Location	U	0.80
☐ Arthur Munroe	Ally	C	0.20
☐ Asenath Waite Derby	Ally	R	2.50
☐ Assembly Hall	Location	C	0.20
☐ Asylum for the Deranged	Location	U	0.80
☐ Aylesbury	Location	C	0.20
☐ Bacteriophobia	Event	C	0.20
☐ Barnabas Marsh	Ally	R	2.50
☐ Barrier of Naach-Tith	Spell	C	0.20
☐ Beatrice is Released from the Attic	Event	R	3.00
☐ Black Binding	Spell	U	0.80
☐ Bolton	Location	C	0.25
☐ Book of Dzyan (English)	Tome	C	0.25
☐ Brilliant Egyptian Archaeologist	Investigator	I	1.50
☐ Brown University John Hay Library	Location	C	0.25
☐ Call of Cthulhu	Tome	C	0.25
☐ Capable Graduate Student	Investigator	I	1.50
☐ Car	Event	C	0.30
☐ Catastrophic Failure	Event	C	0.20
☐ Chant of Thoth	Spell	U	0.80

Card name	Type	Rarity	Price
☐ Chapman Farmhouse	Location	R	2.50
☐ Charles Dexter Ward	Ally	U	0.80
☐ Children Have Nightmares	Event	U	0.80
☐ Chime of Tezchaptl	Artifact	R	3.00
☐ Christchurch Cemetery (Arkham)	Location	R	2.50
☐ Christchurch Cemetery (Innsmouth)	Location	R	2.60
☐ Church of Starry Wisdom	Location	U	0.80
☐ Circles of Thaol	Spell	C	0.25
☐ Claustrophobia	Event	C	0.25
☐ Cleric of Fading Faith	Investigator	I	1.50
☐ Cloud Memory	Spell	C	0.25
☐ Colour Out of Space	Monster	C	0.25
☐ Conanicut Island Private Hospital	Location	U	0.80
☐ Controversial French Mystic	Investigator	I	1.50
☐ Crawford Tillinghast	Ally	U	0.80
☐ Crowninshield House	Location	C	0.25
☐ Cthaat Aquadingen	Tome	R	3.00
☐ Cultes Des Goules	Tome	C	0.25
☐ Curse of the Rat-Thing	Spell	C	0.25
☐ Dawn of a New Day	Event	C	0.25
☐ Deep One	Monster	C	0.25
☐ Demophobia	Event	C	0.25
☐ Dendrophobia	Event	R	2.50
☐ Direct Sunlight	Event	U	0.80
☐ Discover Secret Cache	Event	U	0.80
☐ Dr. Marinus Bicknell Willett	Ally	C	0.20
☐ Drought	Event	U	0.80
☐ Dynamite	Artifact	C	0.25
☐ Earnest Reporter	Investigator	I	1.50
☐ Earthquake!	Event	U	0.80
☐ Eclipse of the Sun	Event	R	2.50
☐ Edward Pickman Derby	Ally	R	2.50
☐ Elder Things	Monster	R	2.90
☐ Elephant Gun	Artifact	U	0.80
☐ Enchanted Cane	Artifact	R	3.00
☐ Eosophobia	Event	C	0.20
☐ Ephraim Waite	Ally	R	2.50
☐ Esoteric Order of Dagon	Location	R	3.50
☐ Exuberant Boston Flapper	Investigator	I	1.50
☐ Faith Baptist Church	Location	C	0.20
☐ Father Dagon	Monster	U	0.80
☐ Fire Vampires	Monster	C	0.25
☐ First Baptist Church	Location	C	0.25

Card name	Type	Rarity	Price
☐ Flee to Special Room	Event	C	0.25
☐ Flying Polyp	Monster	R	3.00
☐ Formless Spawn	Monster	C	0.25
☐ Full Moon	Event	U	0.80
☐ George Birch	Ally	C	0.20
☐ Ghasts	Monster	C	0.20
☐ Ghatanathoa	Monster	U	0.80
☐ Ghoul	Monster	C	0.20
☐ Giant Albino Penguins	Monster	C	0.20
☐ Gnoph-Keh	Monster	R	4.00
☐ Golden Eye Society	Location	U	0.80
☐ Goody Fowler's Ghost	Monster	C	0.25
☐ Grizzled Boston Detective	Investigator	I	1.50
☐ Hands of Colubra	Spell	C	0.20
☐ Hangman's Hill	Location	R	2.50
☐ Hardened Chicago Gangster	Investigator	I	1.50
☐ Harney Reginald Opens Fire	Event	C	0.25
☐ Harvey Walters	Ally	C	0.20
☐ Haunted French Sculptor	Investigator	I	1.50
☐ Home of Laban Shrewsbury	Location	R	2.50
☐ Hound of the Tindalos	Event	U	0.80
☐ Hurricane	Event	U	0.80
☐ Hydrophobia	Event	U	0.80
☐ Iatrophobia	Event	R	3.00
☐ In the Nick of Time	Event	U	0.80
☐ Influenza	Event	C	0.25
☐ Innsmouth Courier	Location	C	0.20
☐ Inquisitive Chinese Intellectual	Investigator	I	1.50
☐ Instability in the Mythos (Car)	Event	C	0.25
☐ Instability in the Mythos (Door)	Event	C	0.25
☐ Ithaqua	Monster	C	0.20
☐ Jeremiah Brewster	Ally	C	0.25
☐ Jewelry of the Deep Ones	Artifact	U	0.80
☐ K.J. Hooper	Ally	C	0.25
☐ Keenness of Two Alike	Spell	R	2.80
☐ King in Yellow (English)	Tome	C	0.20
☐ King in Yellow (French)	Tome	R	2.60
☐ Knee-Deep in Doom	Adventure	C	0.20
☐ Mad German Inventor	Investigator	I	1.50
☐ Marsh Refining Co.	Location	U	0.80
☐ Martense Kin	Monster	C	0.20
☐ Martense Mansion	Location	R	2.60
☐ Massachusetts State Hospital	Location	U	0.80
☐ Mercy Dexter	Ally	C	0.20

RARITY KEY C = Common U = Uncommon R = Rare I = Investigator card F = Foil card X = Fixed/standard in all decks

Card name	Type	Rarity	Price
Mi-Go	Monster	C	0.25
Mi-Go Braincase	Artifact	R	3.00
Mist Projector	Artifact	R	3.10
Monophobia	Event	C	0.25
Morose Veteran of the Great War	Investigator	I	1.50
Mother Hydra	Monster	U	0.80
15			
Nahum Gardner	Ally	C	0.20
Nahum Gardner's Place	Location	U	0.80
Nameless Cults, Bridewell Edition	Tome	C	0.25
Necronomicon, Dee Ed.	Tome	C	0.20
New Moon	Event	U	0.80
Nightgaunts	Monster	C	0.25
North Burial Ground	Location	C	0.25
Nyarlathotep	Monster	R	3.40
Nyhargo Dirge	Spell	C	0.20
16			
Obsessive/Compulsive	Event	R	2.50
Old Arkham Cemetery	Location	C	0.25
On The Edge	Adventure	R	2.70
One Dark and Stormy Night	Adventure	C	0.20
Pack of Rat Things	Monster	C	0.20
Paracelsus' Sword	Artifact	U	0.80
Peck Valley Cemetery	Location	R	2.60
Pipes of Madness	Spell	U	0.80
Police investigation	Event	C	0.25
17			
Ponape Scripture, Hoag Ms.	Tome	C	0.20
Potter's Field	Location	C	0.20
Powerful Storms	Event	C	0.20
Pragmatic Hobo	Investigator	I	1.50
Proud Prussian Submariner	Investigator	I	1.50
Randolph Carter	Ally	R	2.60
Raymond Legrasse	Ally	C	0.25
Respected New England Doctor	Investigator	I	1.50

Card name	Type	Rarity	Price
18			
Rhabdophobia	Event	U	0.80
Rhan Tegoth	Monster	C	0.25
Rhoby Harris	Ally	R	2.50
Ring of Eibon	Artifact	R	2.90
Robert Blake's Study	Location	C	0.25
Robert Harrison Blake	Ally	R	2.50
Robert Marsh	Ally	U	0.80
Scotophobia	Event	C	0.25
Seal of Isis	Artifact	C	0.25
Sefton Asylum	Location	U	0.80
19			
Serpent People	Monster	C	0.25
Seven Cryptical Books of H'san (English)	Tome	U	0.80
Shantaks	Monster	C	0.25
Shining Trapezohedron	Artifact	U	0.80
Shoggoth	Monster	U	0.80
Shotgun	Artifact	C	0.25
Shrivelling	Spell	C	0.20
Sign of Eibon	Spell	C	0.20
Sign of Kish	Spell	U	0.80
20			
Skeletons	Monster	C	0.25
South Woods Memorial Cemetery	Location	C	0.20
Sphere of Nath	Artifact	R	2.50
St. John's Churchyard	Location	R	2.50
Staid University Professor	Investigator	I	1.50
Stand Against the Order	Adventure	R	2.90
Star Stone of Mnar	Artifact	U	0.80
Tempest Mountain	Location	C	0.25
The Arkham Advertiser	Location	C	0.20
21			
The Birds and the Byakhees	Adventure	R	2.60
The Brazen Head	Artifact	U	0.80
The Curious Parcel	Adventure	C	0.20

Card name	Type	Rarity	Price
The Great Epidemic	Adventure	R	3.00
The House on Olney Court	Location	R	2.90
The Innsmouth Look	Event	R	3.00
The Interesting Shop	Adventure	C	0.20
The Lonely House in the Woods	Location	R	2.50
The Lowell Street Cafe	Location	C	0.20
22			
The Marsh Mansion	Location	R	3.00
The Outsider	Adventure	R	2.50
The Shunned House	Location	R	2.90
The Theron-Marks Society	Adventure	U	0.80
The Ultra-Violet	Artifact	R	3.00
The Unfortunate Nephew	Investigator	I	1.50
The Unnamable House	Location	U	0.80
The Waite House	Location	C	0.25
Thieves in your Attic	Event	C	0.25
23			
Thurston's Tavern	Location	C	0.20
Tommygun	Artifact	C	0.20
Townsfolk Riot	Event	U	0.80
Train	Event	C	0.25
Triskaidekaphobia	Event	R	2.50
Typhoid	Event	U	0.70
Unaussprechlichen Kulten	Tome	C	0.25
Vampire	Monster	U	0.80
Voorish Sign	Spell	R	2.50
24			
Waning Moon	Event	C	0.20
Ward Mansion	Location	U	0.80
Wave of Oblivion	Spell	R	2.50
Waxing Moon	Event	C	0.20
Wrack	Spell	C	0.20
Yithian Mental Contact	Event	U	0.90
Your First Big Story	Adventure	C	0.20
Zadok Allen	Ally	C	0.20
Zombies	Monster	C	0.25

Mythos • The Expeditions of Miskatonic University

Chaosium• Released **March 1996**

67 new cards in set **IDENTIFIER: Cards are © 1996**

• Booster packs contain 13 cards, booster displays contain 36 packs

The first **Mythos** booster set, which released at the same time as the **Limited** starter set, expands the world of *Mythos* by including locations from Europe, such as Stonehenge, the British Museum, and the Catacombs of Rome.

It includes such allies as the infamous Whateleys and the literary master Lord Dunsany. It also includes mystical tomes found in the library of Miskatonic University, as well as professors and students from that infamous school. — *James Mishler*

Set (67 cards)	78.50
Booster Display Box	43.50
Booster Pack	2.30

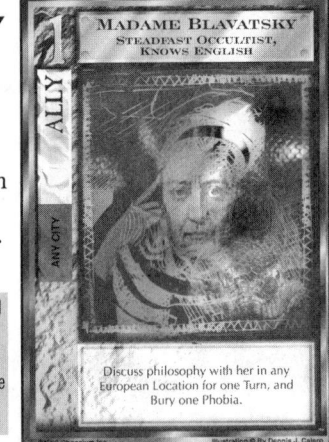

MADAME BLAVATSKY
STEADFAST OCCULTIST,
KNOWS ENGLISH

ALLY

ANY CITY

Discuss philosophy with her in any European Location for one Turn, and Bury one Phobia.

You will need
24
nine-pocket pages to store this set.
(12 doubled up)

Card name	Type	Rarity	Price
1			
A Day In The Life of a Miskatonic University Student	Adventure	C	0.25
Angles of Tagh Clatur	Spell	C	0.25
Arthur Jermyn	Ally	C	0.25
Bibliothèque Nationale	Location	C	0.25
Bishop's Brook Bridge	Location	C	0.25
British Museum	Location	C	0.25
Capt. Edward Norrys	Ally	C	0.25
Capt. Karl Heinrich	Ally	C	0.25
Catacombs of Rome	Location	C	0.25
2			
Chateau Des Fausses Flames	Location	R	3.00
Closed-Cockpit Monoplane	Event	U	1.00
Cold Spring Glen	Location	U	0.80
Congregational Church	Location	R	2.80
De Vermiis Mysteriis	Tome	R	3.00
Dennys Barry	Ally	C	0.25
Devil's Hopyard	Location	U	0.80
Dirigible	Event	C	0.25
Dominate	Spell	C	0.25
3			
Dr. Allen Halsey	Ally	U	0.80
Eltdown Shards, Winters-Hall Ed.	Tome	C	0.25
Erich Zann	Ally	R	3.00
Eusapia Paladino	Ally	R	3.00

Card name	Type	Rarity	Price
Exham Priory	Location	C	0.25
Henry Armitage	Ally	U	0.80
Herbert West	Ally	C	0.30
Huntingdon Asylum for Lunatics	Location	U	1.00
Il Mondo Occulto	Location	R	2.90
4			
Jermyn House	Location	R	2.80
Knight's Head inn	Location	C	0.25
La Mole Antonelliana	Location	C	0.25
Lavinia Whateley	Ally	C	0.25
Liber Ivonis	Tome	C	0.25
Lord Edward Dunsany	Ally	R	3.00
Lost in the Catacombs	Adventure	C	0.25
Madame Blavatsky	Ally	R	3.00
Mauretania	Event	U	0.80
5			
Miskatonic U. Medical School	Location	U	0.80
Miskatonic U. Memorial Hall	Location	C	0.25
Miskatonic U. Orne Library	Location	C	0.25
Miskatonic U. Science Annex	Location	R	2.90
Nameless Cults, Golden Goblin Edition	Tome	C	0.25
Nathaniel Wingate Peaslee	Ally	C	0.25
Necronomicon (Greek)	Tome	C	0.25
Necronomicon (Latin)	Tome	U	1.20
Old Man Whateley	Ally	R	3.10
6			
Old Mill Ruins	Location	C	0.25
Osborn's General Store	Location	C	0.25

Card name	Type	Rarity	Price
Prof. Wingate Peaslee	Ally	R	2.70
Remote Whateley Farmhouse	Location	C	0.25
Sentinel Hill	Location	U	0.80
Seth Bishop Ruins	Location	R	3.20
Son of Yog-Sothoth	Monster	U	0.80
Stonehenge	Location	C	0.25
The Auction	Adventure	U	0.80
7			
The Auction House	Location	C	0.25
The Catacombs Beneath Paris	Location	U	0.80
The Dunwich Horror	Adventure	R	3.00
The Expedition	Adventure	U	0.80
The Highland Loch	Location	C	0.25
The Necropolis	Location	R	2.80
The Office of Dr. Freud	Location	U	1.00
The Secret of Power and Glory Is Yours	Adventure	U	0.80
The Unspeakable Oath	Adventure	R	3.00
8			
Titanic	Event	R	2.50
Typhoon	Event	C	0.25
Wilbur Whateley	Ally	U	0.80
Zachariah Whateley	Ally	C	0.25

RARITY KEY C = Common U = Uncommon R = Rare I = Investigator card F = Foil card X = Fixed/standard in all decks

Mythos • *Cthulhu Rising*

Chaosium • Released **April 1996**

67 cards in set **IDENTIFIER: Cards are © 1996**

• Booster packs contain 13 cards, booster displays contain 36 packs

The second **Mythos** set explores the Pacific, under which sleeps Cthulhu, the core entity of the mythos. **Cthulhu Rising** brings a slew of island locations into play, spells and tomes (including the **Book of Eibon**), and Dread **Cthulhu** himself. The set is more useful in concert with the ships found in the first set, as the islands are mostly accessible only by sea. (Two additional travel by sea options, **Tramp Steamer** and **U-Boat**, appear in this set). — *James Mishler*

CTHULHU
ISLAND, WAXING MOON
MONSTER
GREAT OLD ONE

"In his house at R'lyeh dead Cthulhu waits dreaming"
—H.P. Lovecraft, "The Call of Cthulhu"
All Monsters may join.
No Investigator may gain Sanity.

You will need 8 nine-pocket pages to store this set. (4 doubled up)

Set (67 cards)	76.50
Booster Display Box	42.50
Booster Pack	2.30

Card name	Type	Rarity	Price
Abhoth	Monster	U	0.80
Aldebaran Moves in the Sky	Event	C	0.25
Arthur Machen	Ally	C	0.20
Assault on Y'ha-Nthlei	Adventure	R	2.30
Astrophobia	Event	R	2.10
Bal Sagoth	Location	R	2.20
Become Spectral Hunter	Spell	R	2.60
Body Warping of Gorgoroth	Spell	R	2.30
Book of Dzyan (Atlantean)	Tome	U	0.80
Book of Eibon (Atlantean)	Tome	C	0.20
Book of Eibon (Hyperborean)	Tome	U	0.80
Byakhee	Monster	C	0.20
Call Power of Nyambe	Spell	R	2.40
Celeano	Location	U	0.80
Create Time Warp	Spell	R	2.80
Cthulhu	Monster	U	0.80
Devil Reef	Location	C	0.20

Card name	Type	Rarity	Price
Devolution	Spell	C	0.20
Dimensional Shambler	Monster	C	0.25
Disk of the Hyades	Artifact	C	0.20
Diving Suit	Artifact	C	0.20
Dread Curse of Azathoth	Spell	R	2.70
Easter Island	Location	C	0.25
Edgar Allen Poe	Ally	C	0.20
Elder Sign	Spell	C	0.20
Eltdown Shards (Glyphs)	Tome	C	0.20
Fly	Spell	C	0.20
George Gammell Angel	Ally	C	0.20
Harvard University Houghton Library of Rare Books	Location	U	0.80
Hastur	Monster	R	3.00
Kiss of Dagon	Spell	C	0.20
Lost Temple of Atlantis	Location	U	0.70
Mao Ceremony	Spell	R	2.00
Mist of R'lyeh	Spell	C	0.20
One of the Circle	Adventure	U	0.80
Orne Formulae & Diagrams	Artifact	R	2.50
Otaheite	Location	C	0.20
Ponape	Location	C	0.25
Ponape Scripture (Glyphs)	Tome	C	0.25
Powder of Ibn Ghazi	Spell	C	0.20
R'lyeh	Location	U	0.80
R'lyeh Disk, Left Fragment	Artifact	U	0.70

Card name	Type	Rarity	Price
R'lyeh Disk, Right Fragment	Artifact	U	0.70
R'lyeh Disk, Top Fragment	Artifact	U	0.70
R'lyeh Text (Atlantean)	Tome	C	0.20
Radiance of Alsophocus	Spell	C	0.20
Retoka	Location	C	0.20
Robert W. Chambers	Ally	C	0.20
Sarnath Sigil	Spell	C	0.20
Schizophrenia	Event	C	0.20
Seaplane	Event	R	2.70
Song of Hastur	Spell	R	2.40
Soul Singing	Spell	C	0.25
Space Mead	Artifact	U	0.70
Star Spawn of Cthulhu	Monster	C	0.25
Steal Life	Spell	R	2.30
The Cruise	Adventure	U	0.70
The Royal Geographic Society	Adventure	U	0.70
The Strange Case of Charles Fort	Adventure	R	2.10
The Temple	Adventure	U	0.70
Thirty-Five Abominable Adulations of the Bloated One	Spell	R	2.70
Tramp Steamer	Event	C	0.20
U-Boat	Event	U	0.80
Voola Ritual	Spell	C	0.20
Wakalea	Ally	C	0.20
William Channing Webb	Ally	C	0.20
Y'ha-Nthlei	Location	R	2.40

Mythos • *Legend of the Necronomicon*

Chaosium • Released **May 1996**

67 cards in set • **IDENTIFIER: Cards are © 1996**

• Booster packs contain 13 cards, booster displays contain 36 packs

The third and final of the booster-only sets, **Legend** brings investigators to the Middle East, where they can visit the Sphinx with T.E. Lawrence, or explore the Valley of the Kings with **Richard Upton Pickman** after a Surprise Meeting. Several cards in this set allow characters from the Past to join an investigator as an ally, allowing interesting combinations and abilities. — *James Mishler*

ABDUL ALHAZRAD
CORRUPT CULTIST, KNOWS ARABIC & HYPERBOREAN
ALLY
MIDDLE EAST PAST

He penned the famous couplet:
"That is not dead which can eternal lie,
And with strange aeons even death may die."
Can know any two Spells. Bury Spells in your Story Deck after they are cast.

You will need 8 nine-pocket pages to store this set. (4 doubled up)

Set (67 cards)	73.50
Booster Display Box	38.25
Booster Pack	2.20

Card name	Type	Rarity	Price
Abdul Alhazrad	Ally	U	0.80
Acrophobia	Event	C	0.20
Ahmed	Ally	C	0.20
Akhenaten's Tomb	Location	R	2.70
Al-Azhar University	Location	R	2.50
Alexandria Museum of Antiquities	Location	C	0.20
Book of Eibon (English)	Tome	C	0.20
Boston Globe	Location	C	0.20
Brotherhood of the Black Pharaoh	Adventure	R	2.40
Brown Jenkin	Ally	R	3.00
Cairo Qahwa	Location	C	0.25
Camel	Event	C	0.20

Card name	Type	Rarity	Price
Carl Stanford	Ally	R	2.90
City Morgue	Location	C	0.20
Command the Dead	Spell	C	0.25
Consume Likeness	Spell	R	2.70
Copp's Hill Burying Ground	Location	R	2.50
Create Bad Corpse Dust	Spell	C	0.20
Create Gate	Spell	C	0.25
Dhole	Monster	C	0.20
Eibon's Wheel of Mist	Spell	R	2.70
Faraz Najir	Ally	C	0.20
Great Temple at Karnak	Location	R	2.80
Grecian Lekythos	Artifact	C	0.20
Grivas Old and New Books	Location	C	0.20
Hospital for the Insane	Location	U	0.80
Ibrahim Amin	Ally	C	0.20
John Scott	Ally	U	0.80
Joseph Curwen	Ally	R	2.60
Kalil Kareem	Ally	C	0.20
Keziah Mason	Ally	R	3.00
Kitab Al Azif (Arabic)	Tome	U	0.80
Lamp of Alhazrad	Artifact	U	0.80
Livre d'Ivon	Tome	U	0.80

Card name	Type	Rarity	Price
Make Money Fast!	Adventure	U	0.70
Mosque of Amr	Location	C	0.20
Mosque of Ibn Tulun	Location	U	0.80
Mummy	Monster	C	0.20
Olaus Wormius	Ally	U	0.80
Orne's Black	Spell	C	0.20
Pickman's Apartment	Location	R	2.80
R'lyeh Text (Chinese)	Tome	R	2.60
Remortification	Spell	R	2.50
Resurrection	Spell	C	0.25
Richard Upton Pickman	Ally	C	0.20
Sand Dwellers	Monster	C	0.20
Save The World!	Adventure	C	0.20
Secrets of the Silver Twilight	Adventure	U	0.70
Seeking Everlasting Life 1	Adventure	U	0.70
Seeking Everlasting Life 2	Adventure	U	0.70
Seven Cryptical Books of H'san (Chinese)	Tome	R	2.70
Sign of Barzai	Spell	C	0.20
Silver Twilight Lodge	Location	U	0.80
Simon Orne	Ally	R	2.80

RARITY KEY **C** = Common **U** = Uncommon **R** = Rare **I** = Investigator card **F** = Foil card **X** = Fixed/standard in all decks

Card name	Type	Rarity	Price
Societe Royale de Geographie D'Egypte	Location	C	0.20
Summon Great Cthulhu	Adventure	R	2.80
Surprise Meeting	Event	C	0.25
T.E. Lawrence	Ally	U	0.80

Card name	Type	Rarity	Price
The Chosen of Bast	Monster	C	0.20
The Docks	Location	C	0.25
The Muski	Location	C	0.20
The Sphinx	Location	C	0.20
The Sun Worshipper	Adventure	U	0.70

Card name	Type	Rarity	Price
Thomas F. Malone	Ally	C	0.20
Tomb of the Prophet Daniel	Location	R	2.40
Tree of Sayede Mandura	Location	C	0.20
Valley of the Kings	Location	U	0.80

Mythos • Dreamlands Limited

Chaosium • Released **January 1997**

210 cards in set • **IDENTIFIER: Cards © 1997**

- Starter decks contain 60 cards, booster displays contain 10 decks
- Booster packs contain 13 cards, booster displays contain 36 packs

This set provides the **Mythos** game a new starting point: a setting in the Dreamlands, as outlined in Lovecraft's novel, *Dream Quest of Unknown Kadath*, among other stories. Players journey to **Sarkomand** in the North, or to the **Harbor of Celephais**. Or retreat to **Serranian** to quell their nightmares or **The Marketplace of Ulthar** to seek out artifacts of dream.

To fans of *Unknown Kadath* the set is a rich presentation of things glimpsed at in story, while it also adds interesting twists and turns to the game. — *James Mishler*

Set (210 cards)	97.50
Starter Display Box	35.25
Booster Display Box	37.50
Starter Deck	7.80
Booster Pack	2.30

You will need 24 nine-pocket pages to store this set. (12 doubled up)

Card name	Type	Rarity	Price
A Lender Be	Adventure	C	0.15
A Midsummer Night's Dream	Adventure	R	1.90
Accouterments of Heroes	Artifact	U	0.60
Algol	Event	C	0.15
Anathema	Spell	U	0.60
Angry Zoogs	Event	C	0.15
Armed and Clueless	Adventure	R	1.90
Atal the High Priest	Ally	U	0.60
Barrier of Seol Seril	Spell	C	0.15
Barzai the Wise	Ally	R	2.00
Basalt Pillars of the West	Location	C	0.15
Basil Elton	Ally	C	0.15
Basilisk	Monster	R	2.00
Batophobia	Event	C	0.15
Battle Axe	Artifact	R	1.90
Being of Ib	Monster	C	0.15
Betrayal	Event	R	1.90
Beyond Your Wildest Dreams	Adventure	C	0.15
Black Galley	Event	R	2.50
Blizzard	Event	C	0.15
Bokrug	Monster	C	0.15
Book of Beautiful Devices	Tome	C	0.15
Bored Housewife	Investigator	I	1.30
Buopoth	Monster	C	0.15
Carter's Clock	Artifact	R	2.00
Carter's Quest	Adventure	R	1.90
Castle of the Great Ones on Kadath	Location	R	2.00
Cat from Saturn	Monster	C	0.15
Cats of Ulthar	Event	U	0.60
Cavern of Flame	Location	U	0.60
Channel Prophecy	Spell	U	0.60
Chorazin	Monster	R	1.90
City of Gugs	Location	C	0.15
Come Sail Away	Adventure	C	0.15
Command Lamp-Eft	Spell	C	0.15
Concentric Rings of the Worm	Spell	C	0.15
Cornwall-by-the-Sea	Location	R	1.90
Crag of Ghouls	Location	U	0.60
Crystal Sword	Artifact	C	0.15
Crystal World	Spell	R	1.90
Cultus Maleficarum	Tome	R	2.00
Days of Wine and Roses	Adventure	R	1.90
Deflection	Spell	U	0.60
Dhole	Monster	R	1.90
Doomed if You Do	Adventure	C	0.15
Dream Sending of Glaaki	Spell	R	2.00
Elephant Caravan	Event	C	0.15

Card name	Type	Rarity	Price
Embody Charnal Odor of Xura	Spell	C	0.15
Enthusiastic Chorus Girl	Investigator	I	1.30
Equilateral Screen	Spell	U	0.60
Ettienne-Laurent de Marigny	Ally	R	1.90
Even Stranger Case of Charles Fort	Adventure	R	1.90
Evening	Event	U	0.50
Exploited Coal Miner	Investigator	I	1.30
Falsely Imprisoned Convict	Investigator	I	1.30
Far Side of the Moon	Location	C	0.15
Fireworm of Parg	Monster	U	0.60
Four-Armed is Forewarned	Adventure	C	0.15
Gate of Deeper Slumber	Location	R	1.90
Ghasts	Monster	C	0.15
Ghost-Being of Ib	Ally	U	0.60
Ghoul	Monster	C	0.15
Gnor	Monster	C	0.15
Great Abyss	Location	C	0.15
Great Library of the Dreamlands	Location	C	0.15
Great Library of the Dreamlands	Location	R	1.90
Great Library of the Dreamlands	Location	C	0.15
Great Library of the Dreamlands	Location	U	0.90
Green Mist of Doom	Spell	C	0.15
Guardians of the Great Ones	Event	U	0.50
Gug	Monster	C	0.15
Haragrim	Ally	R	1.90
Harbor of the Black Galley	Location	C	0.15
Hesper Payne	Ally	R	2.00
Hester Payne's House	Location	C	0.15
Highway Robbery	Event	U	0.60
Homeless Waif	Investigator	I	1.30
Howard Lovecraft	Ally	C	0.15
Ibbix the Harbormaster	Ally	R	1.90
Idol of Bokrug	Artifact	C	0.15
If I Ran the Zoog	Adventure	U	0.60
Ilarnek	Location	C	0.15
Iranon the Explorer	Ally	C	0.15
Ironmind	Spell	R	1.90
King Kuranes	Ally	C	0.15
Kranon	Ally	C	0.15
Kuranes' Manor-House	Location	R	1.90
Lassitude of Phein	Spell	C	0.15
Leng Spider	Monster	R	3.00
Lesser Shantak	Monster	C	0.15
Lin Carter	Ally	U	0.60
Lunar Eclipse	Event	C	0.15
Lute of Oonai	Artifact	U	0.50
Lyric Poet	Investigator	I	1.30
Magic Spear	Artifact	U	0.60
Man of Leng	Monster	U	0.60
Merchant of Ill Repute	Ally	U	0.50
Minion of Karakal	Monster	U	0.50
Monolith of Ib	Artifact	C	0.15
Monstres and Their Kynde	Tome	C	0.15

Card name	Type	Rarity	Price
Moon Quest	Adventure	U	0.60
Moon-Beast	Monster	C	0.15
Mt. Ngranek	Location	C	0.15
Mysteries of Thalarion	Spell	C	0.15
Nasht & Kaman-Thah	Ally	C	0.15
Nightgaunts	Monster	C	0.15
Nightmare	Event	U	0.60
Nodens	Monster	U	0.60
North Point Lighthouse	Location	C	0.15
Old Brick Powderhouse	Location	C	0.15
Overworked Telephone Operator	Investigator	I	1.30
Papyrus of Ilarnek	Tome	C	0.15
Peaks of Thok	Location	U	0.60
Perchance	Adventure	C	0.15
Petition of Menes	Spell	C	0.15
Phobophobia	Event	U	0.60
Plateau of Leng	Location	C	0.15
Pnakotic Manuscripts	Tome	U	0.60
Polaris	Event	R	1.90
Processional Boulevard	Location	R	1.90
Rain of Fish	Event	U	0.50
Randolph Carter	Ally	C	0.15
Richard Upton Pickman	Ally	C	0.15
Rude Awakening	Event	R	1.90
Sarkomand	Location	C	0.15
Serranian	Location	C	0.15
Shantaks	Monster	C	0.15
Ship of Clouds	Event	C	0.15
Shipwreck	Event	R	1.90
Sky Galleon	Event	C	0.15
Splendid Cathuria	Location	U	0.60
Strange Humanoid Encounter	Event	R	1.90
Street of Tears	Location	C	0.15
Sun Spots	Event	C	0.15
Swarm of Insects	Event	U	0.60
Tachyphobia	Event	C	0.15
Taran-Ish	Ally	C	0.15
Tcho-Tcho People	Monster	U	0.60
Temple of the Elder Ones	Location	C	0.15
Temple of the Great Ones	Location	C	0.15
Thag Weed	Artifact	C	0.15
Thaumaturgical Prodigies in the New England Canaan	Tome	U	0.60
Thaumaturgical Prodigies in the New-English Canaan	Tome	C	0.15
The Art of Magic	Adventure	U	0.60
The Awful Doom of Cerrit	Spell	R	2.00
The Beast in the Cataract	Event	R	1.90
The Book of the Black Stones	Tome	R	1.90
The Bridge over the River Skai	Location	R	1.90

RARITY KEY **C** = Common **U** = Uncommon **R** = Rare **I** = Investigator card **F** = Foil card **X** = Fixed/standard in all decks

Card name	Type	Rarity	Price
The Captain of the White Ship	Ally	C	0.15
The Cat Chieftain	Ally	C	0.15
The Causeway and Father Neptune	Location	R	1.90
The Children Have Sweet Dreams	Event	R	2.00
The Cliffs of Glass	Location	R	1.90
The Enchanted Stone	Location	C	0.15
The Enchanted Wood	Location	C	0.15
The Gate of Oneirology	Spell	C	0.15
The Gathering	Adventure	C	0.15
The Great Bazaar	Location	C	0.15
The Great Menagerie	Adventure	C	0.15
The Harbor of Celephais	Location	C	0.15
The Hero's Journey	Adventure	U	0.50
The Hovel of the Cat Haters	Location	C	0.15
The Hunter	Ally	U	0.60
The King of Ilek-Vad	Ally	U	0.60
The Labyrinths of the Gnorri	Location	C	0.15
The Market-Place	Location	C	0.15
The Meow Ceremony	Adventure	C	0.15
The Merchant's Quarter	Location	R	1.90
The Nameless Lake	Location	R	2.00

Card name	Type	Rarity	Price
The Necronomicon, Dreamlands Edition	Tome	U	0.50
The Old Woman of the Enchanted Wood	Ally	U	0.60
The Onyx Temple	Location	U	0.50
The Opal Throne	Location	C	0.15
The Palace of Seventy Delights	Location	R	1.90
The Ravening Madness	Spell	R	2.00
The Rope & Anchor Tavern	Location	U	0.60
The Ruins of Ib	Location	C	0.15
The Ruins of Sarnath	Location	C	0.15
The Silver Key	Artifact	C	0.15
The Snake-Den	Location	C	0.15
The Sorcerer's Apprentice	Adventure	R	1.90
The Stars are Right	Event	U	0.60
The Strange High House in the Mist	Location	C	0.15
The Street of Pillars	Location	C	0.15
The Tall Lighthouse	Location	R	1.90
The Temple of Bokrug	Location	U	0.60
The Temple of Loveliness at Kiran	Location	U	0.60
The Turquoise Temple of Nath-Horthath	Location	U	0.60

Card name	Type	Rarity	Price
The Voynich Manuscript	Tome	R	1.90
The White Ship	Event	U	0.60
The White Whale Inn	Location	C	0.15
The Zoog Chieftain	Ally	C	0.15
Throth's Stalwart	Spell	R	1.90
Tower of Koth	Location	C	0.15
Tukor	Ally	C	0.15
Twister	Event	C	0.15
Unacknowledged Author	Investigator	I	1.30
Utopian Socialist	Investigator	I	1.30
Vale of Pnoth	Location	R	1.90
Vaults of Zin	Location	C	0.15
Voonith	Monster	U	0.60
Vortex of Far Journeying	Spell	U	0.60
Wandering Peddler	Ally	U	0.60
War Horse	Artifact	R	1.90
Whirligig	Spell	R	1.90
Widowed Seamstress	Investigator	I	1.30
Wine of Pnoth	Artifact	C	0.15
Yak	Event	U	0.60
Zebra	Event	C	0.15
Zenig of Aphorat	Artifact	U	0.60

Mythos • New Aeon (also known as Mythos Now)

Chaosium • Released November 1997 • 205 cards in set

- Starter decks contain 60 cards, starter displays contain 10 decks
- Booster packs contain 13 cards, booster displays contain 36 packs

This set restarted the **Mythos** game in the current era of the Great Conspiracy, centered around the alien Grays, Men in Black, and modern interpretations of the Cthulhu mythos. This added interesting new cards, especially "artifacts" like the Tactical Nuclear Device.

This second shift to a new starter set within the same year may have done *Mythos* in. There are still staunch players of the game, but there have not been any sets released since 1997. Chaosium also had the rights to the CCG version of the computer game *Doom*, but, perhaps gunshy after *Mythos*, it never released anything. — **James Mishler**

Set (210 cards)	92.75
Starter Display Box	40.25
Booster Display Box	42.75
Starter Deck	6.50
Booster Pack	2.10

Card name	Type	Rarity	Price
747	Event	C	0.20
Acid Rain	Event	C	0.15
Alex Cordry	Ally	R	1.90
Alien Abduction	Event	C	0.15
An Unexpected Calamity	Event	R	1.90
Anti-Gravity Harness	Artifact	C	0.20
Area 51	Location	C	0.15
Artist Colony	Location	U	0.60
Ashes, Ashes, Azathoth	Adventure	U	0.60
Azathoth	Monster	R	2.50
Azathoth And Others	Tome	U	0.60
B-Movie Script	Tome	C	0.20
Bank Vault	Artifact	C	0.15
Bibliophobia	Event	R	1.90
Billington's Woods	Location	C	0.15
Black Belt	Artifact	R	1.90
Blackout	Event	C	0.20
Bless	Spell	R	1.90
Blink of an Eye	Event	C	0.15
Brother of the Yellow Sign	Ally	C	0.15
Bulletproof Vest	Artifact	R	1.90
Call the Unnamed One	Spell	C	0.20
Camp Bright Star	Adventure	C	0.20
Carlyle House Museum	Location	C	0.15
Chainsaw	Artifact	C	0.15
Chakota Beast	Monster	U	0.60
Chaosium	Location	C	0.20
Chronoportation	Spell	C	0.15
Chrysler Building	Location	R	1.90
Cité Tatoue	Location	U	0.60
Cloning Chamber	Artifact	R	2.00
Colosseum	Location	C	0.15
Colour Out Of Space	Monster	R	2.30
Create Stasis	Spell	U	0.60

Card name	Type	Rarity	Price
Crop Circles	Event	U	0.45
Cthulhu For President	Event	U	0.60
Cthulhu Statuette	Artifact	C	0.15
Cykranosh	Location	R	1.90
Dark Horse	Adventure	U	0.60
Darkness of the Void	Spell	R	1.90
Dawn Biozyme Research Lab	Location	C	0.20
Day the Sun Stood Still	Adventure	C	0.20
Daybreak	Event	C	0.20
DBZ Spacelab	Location	C	0.60
Deliverance	Adventure	C	0.15
"Delta Green, Alpha Squad"	Ally	R	1.90
Diabolical Cultist/Obsequious Televangelist	Investigator	C	0.10
Different Worlds	Adventure	C	0.20
Dimensional Shambler	Monster	U	0.40
Disturbing Portrait	Artifact	C	0.15
Dr. Carl Jung	Ally	R	2.50
Dr. Carlos MacDonald	Ally	U	0.60
Dr. MacDonald's House	Location	U	0.50
Ebola Virus	Event	U	0.60
Eiffel Tower	Location	C	0.15
Emergency Medical Equipment	Artifact	U	0.60
Enthrall Victims	Spell	U	0.60
European Space Agency	Location	C	0.20
Evoke Doppleganger	Spell	R	1.90
Exorcism	Spell	U	0.60
False Dawn	Event	C	0.15
First National Grocery	Location	R	1.90
Fish-Head Rock	Location	R	1.90
Flesh Ward	Spell	U	0.60
Fractal Creatures	Monster	R	2.00
Fragmentation Grenade	Artifact	C	0.15
Frivolous Lawsuit	Event	R	1.90
G.G. D'Arn	Ally	R	1.90

Card name	Type	Rarity	Price
Gilman House Hotel	Location	U	0.60
Giovanni Angellis	Ally	C	0.15
Giulio Cesare Hotel	Location	C	0.15
Going Postal	Event	C	0.15
Government Quarantine	Event	U	0.60
Grasp Of Cthulhu	Spell	R	1.90
Greenwich Village	Location	C	0.20
Greys	Monster	C	0.20
Halitosiphobia	Event	R	1.90
Harbor Place Hotel	Location	R	1.90
Haz-Mat Team	Ally	C	0.15
Helicopter	Event	R	1.90
Henri Zann	Ally	R	1.90
High Priest of Elvis	Ally	R	1.90
Hitch A Ride	Event	C	0.20
Hitman from Medellin	Event	R	1.90
Hound of Tindalos	Monster	C	0.15
Howard Lovecraft	Ally	C	0.20
Hydrophilia	Event	C	0.15
Ill Omen	Event	R	1.90
Insidious Ululation of the Invisible Supplicants	Spell	U	0.60
INTERPOL Headquarters, Italy	Location	C	0.15
IRS Auditor	Event	U	0.60
Its Full Of Stars!	Event	R	1.90
J. Edgar Hoover Building	Location	C	0.20
Joe Schienfeld	Ally	R	1.90
Johnny Booger	Ally	C	0.15
Ju-Ju House	Location	C	0.20
Kennedy Space Center	Location	C	0.20
Laptop Computer	Artifact	C	0.20
Larva of the Other Gods, First Stage	Monster	U	0.60
Larva Of The Other Gods, Second Stage	Monster	U	0.60

RARITY KEY C = Common U = Uncommon R = Rare I = Investigator card F = Foil card X = Fixed/standard in all decks

Card name	Type	Rarity	Price
Lascaux Caves	Location	C	0.15
Lefferts Corners	Location	C	0.20
Look to the Future	Adventure	C	0.15
Louvre	Location	C	0.20
Lovecraft's Grave	Location	U	0.60
M16 Assault Rifle	Artifact	C	0.20
Maison Nationale De Santé	Location	U	0.60
Make Them Pay!	Adventure	C	0.20
[13] Maple Hill	Location	C	0.20
Massa Di Requiem Per Shuggay	Tome	C	0.15
McCarty's News Stand	Location	U	0.60
Mechanophobia	Event	C	0.20
Media Hyperbole	Event	U	0.60
Men in Black	Monster	C	0.20
Mental Suggestion	Spell	C	0.15
Mi-Go	Monster	C	0.15
Monatomic Translocation	Spell	C	0.20
[14] Motion Sickness	Event	R	1.90
Mr. Shiny's Burger Palace	Location	C	0.20
Mugging	Event	C	0.15
Museo del Palazzo Venezia	Location	C	0.15
Napoleon Whateley	Ally	C	0.20
Nemesis	Event	C	0.20
Night at the Opera	Adventure	C	0.15
Nikola Tesla	Ally	C	0.20
[15] Notre Dame	Location	U	0.60
Nuclear Winter	Event	R	1.90
Obed Marsh Memorial	Location	U	0.60
Obsessed Federal Agent/ Obsessed Agent in a Mi-Go Braincase	Investigator	C	0.10
One Small Step	Adventure	U	0.60
Operation Nemesis	Adventure	C	0.20
Out Of My Mind	Adventure	R	1.90
Outbreak	Adventure	U	0.60
Ozzy Orne	Ally	C	0.20
Pallid Programmer/ Deep-One Hybrid	Investigator	C	0.10

Card name	Type	Rarity	Price
[16] Patricia Bridgitte Jodoin	Ally	C	0.20
Pentagon	Location	C	0.20
Plan 9	Adventure	U	0.60
Plastic Explosive	Artifact	R	1.90
Police Investigation	Event	C	0.15
Poltergeist	Event	C	0.20
Porta Portese	Location	C	0.20
Portophilia	Event	C	0.20
[17] Professor L.N. Isinwyll	Ally	C	0.20
"Promises, Promises"	Adventure	C	0.15
Prophecies of Nostradamus	Tome	U	0.60
Radiation Suit	Artifact	R	1.90
Regalia of the Outer Gods	Artifact	R	1.90
Reverend Baxter Lully	Ally	C	0.20
Robert Bloch	Ally	U	0.60
Rue D'Auseil	Location	R	1.90
Ruined Top-Secret Warehouse	Location	C	0.20
[18] Sandy Petersen	Ally	C	0.20
Second Psychiatric Hospital	Location	U	0.60
Serial Killer	Event	C	0.15
Serpent People	Monster	C	0.20
Servants of the Silver Twilight	Monster	C	0.20
Shaggai Mental Possession	Spell	U	0.60
Shariil Sophast	Ally	R	1.90
Shoggoth Lord	Monster	R	3.00
Shub-Niggurath	Monster	U	0.60
Shuttle Icarus	Event	U	0.60
[19] Sirius	Event	C	0.15
Skeptical Pathologist/ Grinning Ghoul	Investigator	C	0.10
Smithsonian Institution	Location	C	0.20
Smugglers Tunnels	Location	C	0.15
Song of the Stellar Larvae	Spell	U	0.60
Space Suit	Artifact	R	1.90
Star Vampire	Monster	R	2.30
Stealth Fighter	Artifact	R	2.00
Tactical Nuclear Bomb	Artifact	U	0.60

Card name	Type	Rarity	Price
[20] Tank	Artifact	U	0.60
Taser	Artifact	C	0.20
Television	Event	C	0.15
Temple to Aesthog	Location	C	0.20
Temporal Lash	Spell	R	1.90
Terrorist Strike	Event	R	1.90
Thaasophobia	Event	C	0.15
The Internet	Tome	C	0.20
The Mall	Location	C	0.20
[21] The Vatican	Location	U	0.60
Time Flux	Event	U	0.60
Time Machine	Artifact	C	0.15
Today's Tabloid Headlines	Adventure	U	0.45
Toodee-6	Ally	U	0.60
Trigger-Happy Mercenary/ Sardonic Serpentman	Investigator	C	0.10
Tsathoggua	Monster	R	2.50
Turquoise Skyhawk	Ally	U	0.60
Tycho Base	Location	U	0.60
[22] U.S. Coastguard Station	Location	C	0.20
UFO	Event	U	0.45
Unexpected Eclipse	Event	C	0.20
United Nations	Location	C	0.20
Werewolf	Monster	U	0.60
Whispers Pulp Magazine Collection	Tome	C	0.15
With Neighbors Like These...	Adventure	C	0.15
Wreck of the Hellene	Location	C	0.20
Yithian Psychic Possession	Event	R	1.90
[23] Yog Sothoth	Monster	R	3.50
Yucca Mountain Project	Location	R	1.90
Yuggoth	Location	R	1.90
Yuggoth Attacks!	Adventure	R	1.90
Zanthu Tablets	Tome	C	0.20
Zanthu Tablets: A Conjectural Translation	Tome	C	0.15
Zombies	Monster	C	0.15

Mythos • Standard Edition

Chaosium • Released 1996 • 97 unique cards in set

- Two player starter decks contain 104 cards, starter displays contain 6 decks
This two-player set is completely compatible with the rest of the *Mythos* line. The **Standard** set concentrates on New England, the backyard of genre founder H.P. Lovecraft. It's designed to make it easy for new players and non-Cthulhu fans to start playing. — *James Mishler*

You will need **11** nine-pocket pages to store this set. (6 doubled up)

Starter 2-player Deck 9.30

Card name	Type	Price
[1]		
.30/'06 Bolt-Action Rifle	Artif	0.10
.32 Revolver	Artif	0.10
Agoraphobia	Event	0.10
Alone in the World	Advntr	0.10
Ambush	Event	0.10
American Museum of Natural History	Locat	0.10
Arkham Gazette	Locat	0.10
Arkham Horror	Advntr	0.10
Arkham Mystical Supply	Locat	0.10
[2]		
Arkham Police Station	Locat	0.10
Bellevue Hospital	Locat	0.10
Blasphemous Obeisance	Spell	0.10
Boston & Maine Train Station	Locat	0.10
Car (2 versions)	Event	0.10
Cast-Iron Skillet	Artif	0.10
Caverns Beneath the Old Church	Locat	0.10
Central Hill	Locat	0.10
Chelsea Book Shop	Locat	0.10
[3]		
Command of the Bloody Tongue	Spell	0.10
Congregational Hospital	Locat	0.10
Cthulhu Rising	Event	0.10
Dark Young	Monst	0.10

Card name	Type	Price
Dawn of the Solstice	Event	0.10
Deep One	Monst	0.10
Downpour	Event	0.10
Dr. Allen	Ally	0.10
Dr. Hammond's Nerve and Brain Tablets	Artif	0.10
[4]		
Dust of Suleiman	Spell	0.10
Dysentery	Event	0.10
Efficiophobia	Event	0.10
Enchanted Knife	Artif	0.10
Essex Institute	Locat	0.10
Evening	Event	0.10
Faithful Hounds	Artif	0.10
Frank Belknap Long	Ally	0.10
Gomes	Ally	0.10
[5]		
Governmental Cover-Up	Event	0.10
Granny Orne	Ally	0.10
Granny Orne's House	Locat	0.10
Harry Houdini	Ally	0.20
Henry Wentworth Akeley	Ally	0.10
High Noon	Event	0.10
Howard Lovecraft	Ally	0.20
Hunting Horror	Monst	0.10
Hutchison Cipher	Tome	0.10
[6]		
Insect from Shaggai	Monst	0.10
King's Church Cemetary	Locat	0.10
Laban Shrewsbury	Ally	0.10

Card name	Type	Price
Letter From a Friend	Tome	0.10
Lightning Gun	Artif	0.10
Lonely Akeley Farmhouse	Locat	0.10
Luther Harden	Ally	0.10
Martin's Beach	Locat	0.10
Mi-Go	Monst	0.10
[7]		
Midnight	Event	0.10
Miskatonic University Commons	Locat	0.10
Miss Anna Tilton	Ally	0.10
Miss Greene's Home	Locat	0.10
Mrs. Sonia Lovecraft	Ally	0.10
N'Gah-Kthun	Monst	0.10
N'Kai	Locat	0.10
Namquite Point	Locat	0.10
Newburyport Historical Society	Locat	0.10
[8]		
Newburyport Public Library	Locat	0.10
Old Congregational Church	Locat	0.10
Penn Central Train Station	Locat	0.10
Petrify	Spell	0.10
Portaphobia	Event	0.10
Providence Historical Society	Locat	0.10
Questionable Judgement	Advntr	0.10
Ray Stuckey	Ally	0.10
Red Hook	Locat	0.10

Card name	Type	Price
[9]		
Revelations of Glaaki	Tome	0.10
Samuel Winsor	Ally	0.10
Searching for Laban Shrewsbury	Advntr	0.10
Servant of Glaaki	Monst	0.10
Servitor of the Outer Gods	Monst	0.10
Seventh House on the Left	Locat	0.10
Speech Machine	Artif	0.10
Squire Sawyer Whateley	Ally	0.10
Succumb to Temptation	Event	0.10
[10]		
The Athenaeum	Locat	0.10
The Forgotten Crypt	Locat	0.10
The House on Water Street	Locat	0.10
The Martin's Beach Monster	Monst	0.10
The Mystery at Martin's Beach	Advntr	0.10
The Old Gibbett	Locat	0.10
The Price	Advntr	0.10
The Terrible Old Man	Ally	0.10
The Two Scepters	Artif	0.10
[11]		
Tiara of Opulent Fantasy	Artif	0.10
Train (2 versions)	Event	0.10
Tulzscha	Monst	0.10
Two Cities and a Tale	Advntr	0.10
Waterbury State Hospital	Locat	0.10
Whispers in Darkness	Advntr	0.10
Yithian	Monst	0.10

RARITY KEY C = Common U = Uncommon R = Rare I = Investigator card F = Foil card X = Fixed/standard in all decks

Netrunner

Wizards of the Coast • First set, *Limited*, released **April 1996**
374 cards in set • **IDENTIFIER: "V. 1.0" appears on cards**

- Starters contain two 60-card decks, 60-page full-color rulebook; starter displays contain 6 starters
- Boosters contain 15 cards; booster displays contain 36 boosters

Designed by **Richard Garfield**

> You will need
> **42**
> nine-pocket pages to store this set.
> (21 doubled up)

This Deckmaster game brought R. Talsorian's *Cyberpunk* role-playing game to a CCG. Dark and gritty, the future is home to Corporations controlling the world, with data as the commodity. Battling them are Runners, elite hackers working to "liberate" the Corp's vital information, either for profit or for kicks.

With an asymmetric gameplay element giving the Corp and Runners almost entirely different styles of play, ***Netrunner*** moves away from phase-based turns to an action-based turn structure. Both players have a set number of actions to use during a turn and they can be used with few restrictions. This means that cards and other resources are not as difficult to come by and the real strategy comes from knowing how best to use this freedom. With such flexibility, each game will be different from the last after even the first turn. Another feature is that the Corp plays its cards face-down, leading to a very strong element of bluffing and double-guessing in the game.

This two-player game consists of both sides trying to score seven agenda points. The Corporation must protect its Agendas in data forts using defensive measures, called Ice, or by discouraging the Runner through Ambush cards. The Runner essentially needs nothing to steal the seven points from the Corp, but can augment his abilities with programs, hardware, and other resources. These can help to break through the Ice, prevent damage, or provide income. But, it's not uncommon for the Corp to destroy the Runner's tech, and even the Runner. If the Runner is flatlined (*i.e.*, killed), the Corp scores a victory.

To help score the Agendas, the Corp can spend over the odds to play a card that adds several advancement counters in a single action. This allows it to be scored within a turn, minimizing the amount of time the agenda is in a potentially unsecure data fort. This technique of "Fast Advancement" is a popular strategy and can be used alongside other, secondary tactics. Also available to the Corp is "Tag'n'Bag," whereby the Corp is intent on flatlining the Runner. The extreme case of Tag'n'Bag is to approximate the Runner's general location and accelerate a large meteorite into that area.

Since the Corp's actions tend to dictate gameplay, Runner strategies are harder to define. Two general ones are "Multiple Access," where the Runner focuses on a central data fort and accesses several cards on each run to improve the odds of snatching something, and "Sabotage" decks, which aim to deprive the Corp of bits and cards while destroying the installed cards to prevent the Corp from being able to achieve its goals.

Netrunner received critical acclaim for its design and gameplay and it remains one of the better two-player CCGs. However, the perceived expense of the starter deck (despite containing two 60-card decks) put some players off. The optimistically large print run was perhaps *Netrunner*'s undoing, with sales never seeming to meet expectations. Even so, *Netrunner* generated, for a time, a dedicated fan-base around the world. — *Philip Harvey*

Concept	●●●●○
Gameplay	●●●●○
Card art	●●●○○
Player pool	●○○○○

Set (374 cards)	168.25
Starter Display Box	65.00
Booster Display Box	55.00
Starter Deck	10.50
Booster Pack	2.00

Card name	Side	Type	Rarity	Price
Aardvark	Corp	Upgrd	R	4.00
Access through Alpha	Run	Res	R	4.50
Access to Arasaka	Run	Res	V	0.60
Access to Kiribati	Run	Res	V	0.60
Accounts Receivable	Corp	Op	C	0.10
ACME Savings and Loan	Corp	Node	U	0.50
Afreet	Run	Prog	U	0.50
AI Boon	Run	Prog	R	4.50
AI Chief Financial Officer	Corp	Agnda	R	4.50
All-Nighter	Run	Prep	C	0.10
Annual Reviews	Corp	Op	U	0.50
Anonymous Tip	Run	Prep	R	4.00
Antiquated Interface Routines	Corp	Upgrd	U	0.50
Arasaka Owns You	Run	Prep	R	4.50
Arasaka Portable Prototype	Run	Hard	R	4.50
"Armadillo" Armored Road Home	Run	Hard	U	0.50
Armored Fridge	Run	Hard	U	0.50
Artemis 2020	Run	Hard	U	0.50
Artificial Security Directors	Corp	Agnda	R	4.50
Asp	Corp	Ice	C	0.10
Audit of Call Records	Corp	Op	C	0.10
Aujourd' Oni	Run	Res	R	4.50
Back Door to Hilliard	Run	Res	C	0.10

Card name	Side	Type	Rarity	Price
Back Door to Orbital Air	Run	Res	V	0.60
Baedeker's Net Map	Run	Prog	C	0.10
Bakdoor™	Run	Prog	U	0.50
Ball and Chain	Corp	Ice	U	0.50
Banpei	Corp	Ice	C	0.10
Bartmoss Memorial Icebreaker	Run	Prog	R	5.00
BBS Whispering Campaign	Corp	Node	U	0.25
Bioweapons Engineering	Corp	Agnda	R	4.50
Bizarre Encryption Scheme	Corp	Upgrd	U	0.50
Black Dahlia	Run	Prog	V	0.60
Black Ice Quality Assurance	Corp	Agnda	R	4.50
Blink	Run	Prog	U	0.50
Blood Cat	Corp	Node	R	4.50
Boardwalk	Run	Prog	U	0.50
Bodyweight™ Data Crèche	Run	Hard	R	4.50
Bodyweight™ Synthetic Blood	Run	Prep	U	0.80
Bolter Cluster	Corp	Ice	C	0.10
Braindance Campaign	Corp	Node	C	0.25
Broker	Run	Res	C	0.10
Butcher Boy	Run	Prog	U	0.50
Canis Major	Corp	Ice	U	0.50
Canis Minor	Corp	Ice	U	0.50
Cascade	Run	Prog	U	0.50
Cerberus	Corp	Ice	C	0.10

Card name	Side	Type	Rarity	Price
Chance Observation	Corp	Op	C	0.10
Chester Mix	Corp	Upgrd	R	4.00
Chicago Branch	Corp	Node	U	0.50
Chimera	Corp	Upgrd	R	4.00
Cinderella	Corp	Ice	U	0.50
City Surveillance	Corp	Node	R	3.50
Cloak	Run	Prog	C	0.10
Closed Accounts	Corp	Op	U	0.50
Clown	Run	Prog	C	0.25
Cockroach	Run	Prog	U	0.50
Code Corpse	Corp	Ice	U	0.50
Code Viral Cache	Run	Res	R	4.00
Codecracker	Run	Prog	V	0.60
Codeslinger	Run	Prog	V	0.60
Core Command: Jettison Ice	Run	Prep	U	0.50
Corolla Speed Chip	Run	Hard	C	0.10
Corporate Ally	Run	Res	R	4.50
Corporate Boon	Corp	Agnda	V	0.60
Corporate Coup	Corp	Agnda	V	0.60
Corporate Detective Agency	Corp	Op	U	0.50
Corporate Downsizing	Corp	Agnda	V	0.60
Corporate Negotiating Center	Corp	Node	R	4.00
Corporate Retreat	Corp	Agnda	V	0.60
Corporate War	Corp	Agnda	V	0.60

RARITY KEY C = Common U = Uncommon R = Rare V = Very Rare UR = Ultra Rare F = Foil card X = Fixed/standard in all decks

322 • *SCRYE Collectible Card Game Checklist and Price Guide*

Card name	Side	Type	Rarity	Price
Corprunner's Shattered Remains	Corp	Node	U	0.50
Cortical Scanner	Corp	Ice	R	4.50
Cortical Scrub	Corp	Ice	C	0.10
Cowboy Sysop	Corp	Node	U	0.50
Crash Everett, Inventive Fixer	Run	Res	U	0.50
Crybaby	Corp	Upgrd	R	3.50
Crystal Palace Station Grid	Corp	Upgrd	U	0.50
Crystal Wall	Corp	Ice	C	0.10
Custodial Position	Run	Prep	C	0.10
Cyfermaster™	Run	Prog	V	0.60
D'Arc Knight	Corp	Ice	C	0.10
Danshi's Second ID	Run	Res	U	0.50
Data Darts	Corp	Ice	U	0.50
Data Fort Reclamation	Corp	Agnda	V	0.60
Data Masons	Corp	Node	R	4.50
Data Naga	Corp	Ice	U	0.50
Data Raven	Corp	Ice	U	0.50
Data Wall	Corp	Ice	C	0.10
Data Wall 2.0	Corp	Ice	C	0.10
Databroker	Run	Res	U	0.50
Datapool® by Zetatech	Corp	Op	U	0.50
Day Shift	Corp	Op	U	0.50
Deal with Militech	Run	Prep	R	4.50
Dedicated Response Team	Corp	Upgrd	U	0.50
Deep Thought	Run	Prog	R	4.00
Dept. of Truth Enhancement	Corp	Node	U	0.50
Dermatech Bodyplating	Run	Hard	U	0.50
Desperate Competitor	Run	Prep	R	4.00
Detroit Police Contract	Corp	Agnda	V	0.60
Dieter Esslin	Corp	Upgrd	R	3.50
Diplomatic Immunity	Run	Res	R	4.50
Disinfectant, Inc.	Corp	Node	R	4.00
Dogcatcher	Run	Prog	U	0.50
Dr. Dreff	Corp	Upgrd	U	0.50
"Drifter" Mobile Environment	Run	Hard	U	0.50
Dropp™	Run	Prog	U	0.50
Dupré	Run	Prog	R	4.50
Dwarf	Run	Prog	C	0.10
Edgerunner, Inc., Temps	Corp	Op	U	0.50
Edited Shipping Manifests	Run	Prep	C	0.10
Efficiency Experts	Corp	Op	C	0.10
Emergency Self-Construct	Run	Prog	R	4.00
Employee Empowerment	Corp	Agnda	V	0.60
Encoder, Inc.	Corp	Node	R	4.50
Encryption Breakthrough	Corp	Agnda	R	4.50
Endless Corridor	Corp	Ice	R	4.00
ESA Contract	Corp	Node	U	0.50
Euromarket Consortium	Corp	Node	U	0.50
Evil Twin	Run	Prog	R	4.50
Executive Extraction	Corp	Agnda	R	4.50
Executive Wiretaps	Run	Prep	C	0.10
Experimental AI	Corp	Node	U	0.50
Expert Schedule Analyzer	Run	Prog	U	0.50
Fait Accompli	Run	Prog	U	0.50
Fall Guy	Run	Res	V	0.60
False Echo	Run	Prog	R	4.50
Falsified-Transactions Expert	Corp	Op	R	4.50
Fang	Corp	Ice	C	0.10
Fang 2.0	Corp	Ice	C	0.10
Fatal Attractor	Corp	Ice	R	4.50
Fetch 4.0.1	Corp	Ice	C	0.10
Field Reporter for Ice and Data	Run	Res	R	4.50
Filter	Corp	Ice	C	0.10
Fire Wall	Corp	Ice	C	0.10
Flak	Run	Prog	U	0.50
Floating Runner BBS	Run	Res	U	0.50
Force Shield	Run	Prog	C	0.10
Forged Activation Orders	Run	Prep	R	4.50
Forgotten Backup Chip	Run	Prep	C	0.10
Fortress Architects	Corp	Node	R	4.50
Fortress Respecification	Run	Prep	R	4.50
Fragmentation Storm	Corp	Ice	U	0.50

Card name	Side	Type	Rarity	Price
Full Body Conversion	Run	Hard	R	4.50
Genetics-Visionary Acquisition	Corp	Agnda	R	4.00
Gideon's Pawnshop	Run	Prep	C	0.10
"Green Knight" Surge Buffers	Run	Hard	C	0.10
Gremlins	Run	Prog	U	0.50
Grubb	Run	Prog	U	0.50
Hacker Tracker Central	Corp	Node	U	0.50
Hammer	Run	Prog	V	0.60
Haunting Inquisition	Corp	Ice	R	4.50
Hell's Run	Run	Res	U	0.50
Holovid Campaign	Corp	Node	C	0.25
Homewrecker™	Corp	Ice	C	0.10
Hostile Takeover	Corp	Agnda	V	0.60
Hot Tip for WNS	Run	Prep	R	4.00
HQ Interface	Run	Hard	C	0.10
Hunt Club BBS	Run	Prep	C	0.10
Hunter	Corp	Ice	U	0.50
I Got a Rock	Corp	Node	R	4.50
I Spy	Run	Prog	U	0.50
Ice and Data's Guide to the Net	Run	Prep	U	0.50
Ice Pick Willie	Corp	Ice	C	0.10
Ice Transmutation	Corp	Agnda	V	0.50
If You Want It Done Right...	Run	Prep	C	0.10
Imp	Run	Prog	U	0.60
Incubator	Run	Prog	R	4.00
Information Laundering	Corp	Node	U	0.50
Inside Job	Run	Prep	U	0.60
Investment Firm	Corp	Node	U	0.50
Invisibility	Run	Prog	C	0.10
Jack 'n' Joe	Run	Prep	C	0.10
Jack Attack	Corp	Ice	U	0.50
Jackhammer	Run	Prog	V	0.80
Japanese Water Torture	Run	Prog	R	4.00
Jenny Jett	Corp	Upgrd	R	4.00
Jerusalem City Grid	Corp	Upgrd	R	4.00
Joan of Arc	Run	Prog	R	4.50
Junkyard BBS	Run	Res	U	0.60
Karl de Veres, Corporate Stooge	Run	Res	U	0.50
Keeper	Corp	Ice	C	0.10
Kilroy Was Here	Run	Prep	U	0.50
Krash	Run	Prog	U	0.50
Krumz	Corp	Node	R	4.00
Laser Wire	Corp	Ice	R	4.50
Leland, Corporate Bodyguard	Run	Res	C	0.10
Liche	Corp	Ice	U	0.50
Lifesaver™ Nanosurgeons	Run	Hard	R	4.00
Livewire's Contacts	Run	Prep	C	0.10
Loan from Chiba	Run	Res	U	0.60
Loony Goon	Run	Prog	V	0.60
Ludicrine™ Booster Drug	Run	Prog	U	0.60
Main-Office Relocation	Corp	Agnda	V	0.50
Management Shake-Up	Corp	Op	C	0.10
Mantis, Fixer-at-Large	Run	Prep	C	0.10
Marine Arcology	Corp	Agnda	V	0.60
Mastiff	Corp	Ice	U	0.50
Mazer	Corp	Ice	U	0.50
Microtech 'Trode Set	Run	Hard	R	4.50
Microtech AI Interface	Run	Prog	R	4.50
Microtech Backup Drive	Run	Hard	C	0.10
Militech MRAM Chip	Run	Hard	C	0.10
misc.for-sale	Run	Prep	R	4.00
MIT West Tier	Run	Prep	R	4.50
Mouse	Run	Prog	U	0.50
MRAM Chip	Run	Hard	U	0.60
Mystery Box	Run	Prog	R	4.00
N.E.T.O.	Run	Res	R	4.00
Namatoki Plaza	Corp	Upgrd	U	0.50
Nasuko Cycle	Run	Hard	V	0.60
Nerve Labyrinth	Corp	Ice	R	4.50
Netspace Inverter	Run	Prog	R	4.50
Netwatch Credit Voucher	Corp	Op	C	0.10
Netwatch Operations Office	Corp	Agnda	V	0.60

Card name	Side	Type	Rarity	Price
Neural Blade	Corp	Ice	C	0.10
Nevinyrral	Corp	Node	R	4.00
New Blood	Corp	Op	R	4.00
New Galveston City Grid	Corp	Upgrd	R	4.00
Newsgroup Filter	Run	Prog	U	0.50
Newsgroup Taunting	Corp	Node	U	0.60
Night Shift	Corp	Op	C	0.10
Nomad Allies	Run	Res	V	0.60
Off-Site Backups	Corp	Op	U	0.50
Olivia Salazar	Corp	Upgrd	U	0.50
Omni Kismet, Ph.D.	Corp	Upgrd	R	4.00
Omniscience Foundation	Corp	Node	U	0.50
On-Call Solo Team	Corp	Agnda	V	0.60
Open-Ended® Milage Program	Run	Prep	C	0.10
Organ Donor	Run	Prep	R	4.00
Overtime Incentives	Corp	Op	U	0.50
Pacifica Regional AI	Corp	Node	R	4.50
Pandora's Deck	Run	Hard	U	0.50
Paris City Grid	Corp	Upgrd	U	0.50
Parraline 5750	Run	Hard	C	0.10
Pattel's Virus	Run	Prog	U	0.50
pi in the 'Face	Corp	Ice	C	0.10
Pile Driver	Run	Prog	V	0.60
PK-6089a	Run	Hard	C	0.10
Planning Consultants	Corp	Op	C	0.10
Playful AI	Run	Prep	R	4.50
Pocket Virtual Reality	Corp	Ice	U	0.50
Political Coup	Corp	Agnda	V	0.60
Political Overthrow	Corp	Agnda	R	4.50
Poltergeist	Run	Prog	R	4.50
Polymer Breakthrough	Corp	Agnda	V	0.60
Power Grid Overload	Corp	Op	U	0.50
Pox	Corp	Op	U	0.50
Preying Mantis	Run	Res	R	4.50
Priority Requisition	Corp	Agnda	V	0.60
Priority Wreck	Run	Prep	R	4.50
Private Cybernet Police	Corp	Agnda	V	0.60
Private LDL Access	Run	Prep	U	0.50
Project Babylon	Corp	Agnda	V	0.60
Project Consultants	Corp	Op	U	0.50
Punitive Counterstrike	Corp	Op	U	0.50
Quandary	Corp	Ice	C	0.10
Quest for Cattekin	Run	Res	R	3.50
R&D Interface	Run	Hard	C	0.10
R&D-Protocol Files	Run	Prog	U	0.50
Rabbit	Run	Prog	U	0.50
Raffles	Run	Prog	V	0.60
Ramming Piston	Run	Prog	V	0.60
Raptor	Run	Prog	V	0.60
Raven Microcyb Eagle	Run	Hard	C	0.10
Raven Microcyb Owl	Run	Hard	C	0.10
Razor Wire	Corp	Ice	R	4.50
Record Reconstructor	Run	Hard	R	4.00
Red Herrings	Corp	Upgrd	U	0.50
Reflector	Run	Prog	R	4.50
Reinforced Wall	Corp	Ice	R	4.50
Remote Facility	Corp	Node	U	0.50
Replicator	Run	Prog	U	0.50
Rescheduler	Corp	Node	U	0.50
Restrictive Net Zoning	Run	Res	U	0.60
Rex	Corp	Ice	C	0.10
Rigged Investments	Run	Res	C	0.10
Rio De Janeiro City Grid	Corp	Upgrd	U	0.50
Rock Is Strong	Corp	Ice	U	0.50
Rockerboy Promotion	Corp	Node	C	0.10
Romp through HQ	Run	Prep	U	0.50
Ronin Around	Run	Res	R	4.50
Roving Submarine	Corp	Upgrd	R	4.50
Rustbelt HQ Branch	Corp	Node	U	0.50
Scatter Shot	Run	Prog	R	4.00
Schlaghund	Corp	Node	R	4.50
Scorched Earth	Corp	Op	U	0.60
Score!	Run	Prep	C	0.10

RARITY KEY **C** = Common **U** = Uncommon **R** = Rare **V** = Very Rare **UR** = Ultra Rare **F** = Foil card **X** = Fixed/standard in all decks

Card name	Side	Type	Rarity	Price
33				
Scramble	Corp	Ice	C	0.10
Security Code WORM Chip	Run	Prep	U	0.60
Security Net Optimization	Corp	Agnda	V	0.60
Security Purge	Corp	Agnda	R	4.00
SeeYa	Run	Prog	C	0.10
Self-Modifying Code	Run	Prog	R	4.00
Sentinels Prime	Corp	Ice	U	0.50
Setup!	Corp	Node	C	0.10
Shaka	Run	Prog	V	0.60
34				
Shield	Run	Prog	C	0.10
Shock.r	Corp	Ice	U	0.50
Short-Term Contract	Run	Res	C	0.10
Shotgun Wire	Corp	Ice	R	4.50
Shredder Uplink Protocol	Run	Prog	U	0.50
Signpost	Run	Prog	U	0.50
Silicon Saloon Franchise	Run	Res	R	4.50
Silver Lining Recovery Protocol	Corp	Op	R	4.50
Singapore City Grid	Corp	Upgrd	R	3.50
35				
Skälderviken SA Beta Test Site	Corp	Node	R	4.50
Skivviss	Run	Prog	U	0.50
Sleeper	Corp	Ice	C	0.20
Smarteye	Run	Prog	C	0.20
Smith's Pawnshop	Run	Res	U	0.50
Sneak Preview	Run	Prep	R	4.50
Snowball	Run	Prog	R	3.50
Social Engineering	Run	Prep	U	0.50
Solo Squad	Corp	Node	U	0.50
36				
South African Mining Corp	Corp	Node	U	0.50
Speed Trap	Run	Prog	U	0.50

Card name	Side	Type	Rarity	Price
Spinn® Public Relations	Corp	Node	C	0.10
Startup Immolator	Run	Prog	U	0.50
Strike Force Kali	Corp	Agnda	R	4.50
Stumble through Wilderspace	Run	Prep	U	4.50
Submarine Uplink	Run	Res	U	0.50
Subsidiary Branch	Corp	Agnda	V	0.60
Succubus	Run	Prog	R	4.00
37				
Superior Net Barriers	Corp	Agnda	R	4.50
Synchronized Attack on HQ	Run	Prep	R	4.50
Systematic Layoffs	Corp	Op	C	0.10
Team Restructuring	Corp	Op	U	0.60
Technician Lover	Run	Res	U	0.50
Techtronica™ Utility Suit	Run	Hard	U	0.50
Temple Microcode Outlet	Run	Prep	C	0.10
Terrorist Reprisal	Run	Prep	R	4.50
Tesseract Fort Construction	Corp	Upgrd	R	4.50
38				
The Shell Traders	Run	Res	R	5.00
The Short Circuit	Run	Res	C	0.10
The Springboard	Run	Res	C	0.10
Tinweasel	Run	Prog	V	0.60
TKO 2.0	Corp	Ice	C	0.10
Tokyo-Chiba Infighting	Corp	Upgrd	R	4.00
Too Many Doors	Corp	Ice	R	4.50
Top Runners' Conference	Run	Res	R	4.50
Total Genetic Retrofit	Run	Prep	R	4.00
39				
TRAP!	Corp	Node	U	0.60
Trauma Team™	Run	Res	U	0.50
Triggerman	Corp	Ice	C	0.10
Trojan Horse	Corp	Op	C	0.10

Card name	Side	Type	Rarity	Price
Turbeau Delacroix	Corp	Upgrd	U	0.50
Tutor	Corp	Ice	R	4.00
Twenty-Four-Hour Surveillance	Corp	Upgrd	R	4.50
Tycho Extension	Corp	Agnda	V	0.50
Tycho Mem Chip	Run	Hard	C	0.10
40				
Umbrella Policy	Run	Res	U	0.50
Urban Renewal	Corp	Op	C	0.10
Vacant Soulkiller	Corp	Node	U	0.50
Vacuum Link	Corp	Ice	R	4.50
Valu-Pak Software Bundle	Run	Prep	U	0.60
Vapor Ops	Corp	Node	U	0.50
Vewy Vewy Quiet	Run	Prog	C	0.10
Viral 15	Corp	Ice	U	0.50
Virizz	Corp	Ice	U	0.50
41				
Virus Test Site	Corp	Node	U	0.50
Wall of Ice	Corp	Ice	R	4.50
Wall of Static	Corp	Ice	C	0.10
Washington, D.C., City Grid	Corp	Upgrd	R	4.00
Weather-to-Finance Pipe	Run	Prep	U	0.50
Wild Card	Run	Prog	V	0.60
Wilson, Weeflerunner Apprentice	Run	Res	U	0.50
Wizard's Book	Run	Prog	V	0.50
Worm	Run	Prog	V	0.50
42				
WuTech Mem Chip	Run	Hard	C	0.10
Zetatech Mem Chip	Run	Hard	C	0.10
Zetatech Software Installer	Run	Prog	U	0.60
Zombie	Corp	Ice	C	0.10
ZZ22 Speed Chip	Run	Hard	C	0.10

Raymond Ellison — 0

Upgrade-Sysop
Install Raymond Ellison only in a subsidiary data fort.

🗘: Remove any number of advancement counters from cards installed in this data fort. Gain ❷ for each advancement counter removed. Use this ability only during a run. At the end of the run, return to the bank any of the bits gained that you did not spend.

Illus. Phil Hale

Netrunner • *Proteus*

Wizards of the Coast • Released **September 1996**

154 cards in set • **IDENTIFIER: "V. 2.0" appears on cards**

• Boosters contain 15 cards; booster displays contain 36 boosters

   Proteus gives the Corp transmutating Ice, which changes type, and the runner receives the tech to allow Icebreakers to Morph against the Ice anticipated on a run. With Hidden Resources, the Runner can give the Corp a taste of its own medicine by playing cards face-down. The Runner also gets a new victory condition where if the Corp ever has seven Bad Publicity counters, it loses the game instantly.

   Along with mutating Ice the Corp has some other nifty tricks. Sysops like **Lisa Blight** allow Ice subroutines to be repeated, making life difficult for the Runner, and **Manhunt** is the Tag n' Bag card of choice, as it has the possiblity of getting six tags on the Runner in one action. Ironically, now is the time that some Runners stop worrying about being tagged, as **Drone for a Day**, combined with damage prevention from *Limited*, can be used to good effect as a new bit engine. Along with the help of some strong viruses the Runner gains some powerful abilities to help herself or cripple the Corp.

   Proteus introduced some good new concepts to the main *Netrunner* set that changed the way the game was played. Despite the unfortunate inclusion of some cards that discourage player interaction, the meta-game became more important, and this was the set that offered Corporations the chance of World Domination. — *Philip Harvey*

Set (154 cards)	69.50
Booster Display Box	39.75
Booster Pack	2.10

You will need 18 nine-pocket pages to store this set. (9 doubled up)

Card name	Side	Type	Rarity	Price
1				
AI Board Member	Corp	Agenda	R	4.00
All-Hands	Run	Prep	C	0.15
Armageddon	Run	Prog	R	3.00
Back Door to Netwatch	Run	Res	R	3.00
Back Door to Rivals	Run	Res	C	0.15
Bargain with Viacox	Run	Res	R	3.00
Bel-Digmo Antibody	Corp	Node	U	0.30
Big Frackin' Gun	Run	Prog	C	0.15
Black Widow	Run	Prog	U	0.30
2				
Blackmail	Run	Prep	R	3.00
Bolt-Hole	Run	Res	C	0.15
Boring Bit	Run	Prog	C	0.15
Brain Wash	Corp	Ice	C	0.15

Card name	Side	Type	Rarity	Price
Bug Zapper	Corp	Ice	U	0.30
Bulldozer	Run	Prog	U	0.30
Caryatid	Corp	Ice	U	0.30
Charity Takeover	Corp	Agenda	C	0.15
Chiba Bank Account	Run	Res	C	0.15
3				
Chihuahua	Corp	Ice	C	0.15
Colonel Failure	Corp	Ice	R	4.00
Corporate Guard Temps	Corp	Op	U	0.30
Corporate Headhunters	Corp	Agenda	C	0.15
Corrosion	Run	Prog	C	0.15
Cortical Cybermodem	Run	Hard	C	0.15
Cortical Stimulators	Run	Hard	C	0.15
Coyote	Corp	Ice	C	0.15
Credit Blocks	Corp	Ice	C	0.15
4				
Credit Consolidation	Corp	Op	C	0.15
Credit Subversion	Run	Res	U	0.30
Cruising for Netwatch	Run	Prep	C	0.15
Crumble	Run	Prog	U	0.30
Cybertech Think Tank	Corp	Node	R	3.00

Card name	Side	Type	Rarity	Price
Data Sifters	Corp	Op	C	0.15
Datacomb	Corp	Ice	C	0.15
Death from Above	Run	Res	R	3.00
Death Yo-Yo	Corp	Ice	C	0.15
5				
Decoy Signal	Run	Prep	C	0.15
Demolition Run	Run	Prep	U	0.30
Department of Misinformation	Corp	Node	R	3.00
Digiconda	Corp	Ice	U	0.30
Disgruntled Ice Technician	Run	Prep	U	0.30
Disintegrator	Run	Prog	U	0.30
Dog Pile	Corp	Ice	U	0.30
Doppleganger Antibody	Corp	Node	C	0.15
Drone for a Day	Run	Prep	C	0.15
6				
Emergency Rig	Corp	Op	U	0.30
Enterprise Inc. Shields	Run	Prog	C	0.15
Eurocorpse Spin Chip	Run	Hard	U	0.30
Executive Boot Camp	Corp	Node	R	3.00
Expendable Family Member	Run	Res	C	0.15
Faked Hit	Run	Prep	U	0.30

Card name	Side	Type	Rarity	Price
Fetal AI	Corp	Agenda	R	4.00
Food Fight	Corp	Ice	C	0.15
Forward's Legacy	Run	Prog	U	0.30
7				
Frame-Up	Run	Prep	R	4.00
Fubar	Run	Prog	U	0.30
Galatea	Corp	Ice	C	0.15
Garbage In	Run	Prog	U	0.30
Gatekeeper	Corp	Ice	C	0.15
Get Ready to Rumble	Run	Res	U	0.30
Government Contract	Corp	Node	C	0.15
Herman Revista	Corp	Upgrd	U	0.30
Highlighter	Run	Prog	U	0.30
8				
Hijack	Run	Prep	R	3.00
Homing Missile	Corp	Ice	U	0.30
HQ Mole	Run	Res	C	0.15
Hunting Pack	Corp	Ice	U	0.30
Ice and Data Special Report	Run	Prep	C	0.15
Iceberg	Corp	Ice	R	3.00
Identity Donor	Run	Prep	R	4.00
LDL Traffic Analyzers	Corp	Node	R	3.00
Lesley Major	Corp	Upgrd	R	3.00
9				
Lesser Arcana	Corp	Ice	C	0.15
Liberated Savings Account	Run	Res	C	0.15
Lisa Blyte	Corp	Upgrd	R	3.00
Live News Feed	Run	Prep	R	3.00
Locker	Run	Res	R	3.00
Lockjaw	Run	Prog	C	0.15
Lucidrine Drip Feed	Run	Hard	R	3.00
Manhunt	Corp	Op	C	0.15
Marcel DeSoleil	Corp	Upgrd	R	3.00
10				
Marionette	Corp	Ice	C	0.15
Marked Accounts	Corp	Agenda	C	0.15
Mastermind	Corp	Ice	U	0.30
Mercenary Subcontract	Run	Res	U	0.30
Minotaur	Corp	Ice	U	0.30

Card name	Side	Type	Rarity	Price
Misleading Access Menus	Corp	Ice	C	0.15
Mobile Barricade	Corp	Ice	R	3.00
Morphing Tool	Run	Prog	U	0.30
Networked Center	Corp	Upgrd	R	3.00
11				
Obfuscated Fortress	Corp	Upgrd	R	4.00
On the Fast Track	Run	Prep	U	0.30
Panic Button	Corp	Upgrd	U	0.30
Pattel Antibody	Corp	Node	U	0.30
Pavit Bharat	Corp	Upgrd	R	4.00
Pirate Broadcast	Run	Prep	R	3.00
Please Don't Choke Anyone	Corp	Agenda	R	3.00
Poisoned Water Supply	Run	Prep	R	3.00
Prearranged Drop	Run	Prep	R	3.00
12				
Precision Bribery	Run	Res	U	0.30
Project Venice	Corp	Agenda	C	0.15
Project Zurich	Corp	Agenda	C	0.15
"Promises, Promises"	Run	Prep	R	3.00
R&D Mole	Run	Res	C	0.15
Rasmin Bridger	Corp	Upgrd	U	0.30
Raymond Ellison	Corp	Upgrd	U	0.30
Reconnaissance	Run	Prep	C	0.15
Redecorator	Run	Prog	C	0.15
13				
Remote Detonator	Run	Prep	U	0.30
Rent-to-Own Contract	Corp	Op	U	0.30
Research Bunker	Corp	Upgrd	R	3.00
Riddler	Corp	Ice	C	0.15
Roadblock	Corp	Ice	R	3.00
Runner Sensei	Run	Res	C	0.15
Rush Hour	Run	Prep	C	0.15
Sandstorm	Corp	Ice	C	0.15
Scaffolding	Corp	Ice	C	0.15
14				
Scaldan	Run	Prog	R	4.50
Schlaghund Pointers	Corp	Op	U	0.30
Senatorial Field Trip	Run	Prep	R	3.00
Simon Francisco	Corp	Upgrd	U	0.30

Card name	Side	Type	Rarity	Price
Simulacrum	Run	Res	R	3.00
Siren	Corp	Node	U	0.30
Skeleton Passkeys	Run	Prog	C	0.15
Skullcap	Run	Prog	C	0.15
Snowbank	Corp	Ice	C	0.15
15				
Sphinx 2006	Corp	Ice	U	0.30
Stakeout	Run	Prep	C	0.15
Stereogram Antibody	Corp	Node	R	4.00
Streetware Distributor	Run	Res	C	0.15
Subliminal Corruption	Run	Prep	U	0.30
Sumo 2008	Corp	Ice	U	0.30
Sunburst Cranial Interface	Run	Hard	C	0.15
Swiss Bank Account	Run	Res	C	0.15
Syd Meyer Superstores	Corp	Node	C	0.15
16				
Taxman	Run	Prog	U	0.30
Test Spin	Run	Prep	R	3.00
The Deck	Run	Hard	R	4.00
The Personal Touch	Run	Prep	C	0.15
Time to Collect	Run	Res	R	3.00
Toughonium Wall	Corp	Ice	R	3.00
Tumblers	Corp	Ice	C	0.15
Twisty Passages	Corp	Ice	C	0.15
Underworld Mole	Corp	Op	C	0.15
17				
Vienna 22	Run	Prog	U	0.30
Viral Breeding Ground	Corp	Agenda	C	0.15
Viral Pipeline	Run	Prog	R	4.00
Walking Wall	Corp	Ice	C	0.15
Washed-Up Solo Construct	Corp	Ice	C	0.15
Weapons Depot	Corp	Upgrd	R	5.00
Weefle Initiation	Run	Prep	C	0.15
Wired Switchboard	Run	Res	C	0.15
World Domination	Corp	Agenda	R	6.00
18				
Wrecking Ball	Run	Prog	C	0.15

Netrunner • Classic

Wizards of the Coast • Released **November 1999**
52 new cards in set • **IDENTIFIER: "V. 2.1" appears on cards**

• Boosters contain 15 cards; booster displays contain 24 boosters

After three years, the second expansion finally appeared. With 52 new cards taken from previously unreleased sets, **Classic** looked set to inject new life into the game.

Classic introduces "double" cards that are more powerful than normal versions, but take an extra action to play, giving decks the chance to be more compact at the expense of greater complexity. A new piece of Ice is introduced that can move between data forts as often as it can be paid for, offering the Corp superior security. Stealth becomes a stronger element, as Sleepy Ice and some Upgrades punish the Noisy Runners.

This small expansion did as much as it could, but marketing was a problem. The "Classic" name plus booster artwork similar to the basic set gave many the impression that the set was not new, contributing to its failure to sell. — **Philip Harvey**

Vintage Camaro

Hardware-Vehicle

0, Forgo your next action: Avoid receiving a tag.

"I'm not firing a LAW at that! It's a classic!"

Illus. Romas

v2.1 © 1996–1999 WotC

Set (52 new cards)	48.50
Starter Display Box	36.50
Booster Display Box	38.75
Starter Deck	9.50
Booster Pack	2.10

You will need **6** nine-pocket pages to store this set. (3 doubled up)

Card name	Side	Type	Rarity	Price
1				
Badtimes	Corp	Op	C	0.10
Baskerville	Corp	Ice	U	0.25
Bolter Swarm	Corp	Ice	C	0.10
Boostergang Connections	Run	Prep	U	0.25
Brain Drain	Corp	Ice	U	0.25
Corporate Shuffle	Corp	Op	C	0.10
Corruption	Run	Prep	U	0.25
Crash Space	Run	Res	U	0.25
Data Fort Remapping	Corp	Agenda	C	0.10
2				
Deadeye	Corp	Ice	C	0.10
Do the 'Drine™	Run	Prep	U	0.25
Dumpster	Corp	Ice	U	0.25
Early Worm	Run	Prog	C	0.10

Card name	Side	Type	Rarity	Price
Elena Laskova	Run	Res	U	0.25
Entrapment	Corp	Ice	C	0.10
Executive File Clerk	Run	Res	C	0.10
Finders Keepers	Run	Prep	C	0.10
Glacier	Corp	Ice	U	0.25
3				
Gypsy™ Schedule Analyzer	Run	Prep	U	0.25
Imperial Guard	Corp	Ice	C	0.10
Indiscriminate Response Team	Corp	Node	U	0.25
Library Search	Run	Prep	C	0.10
Little Black Box	Run	Hard	U	0.25
London City Grid	Corp	Upgrd	U	0.25
Matador	Run	Prog	C	0.10
Meat Upgrade	Run	Prep	U	0.25
MS-todon	Run	Prog	C	0.10
4				
Networking	Run	Prep	C	0.10
Omnitech "Spinal Tap" Cybermodem	Run	Hard	U	0.25
Omnitech Wet Drive	Run	Hard	U	0.25
Panzer Run	Run	Prep	C	0.10
Psychic Friend	Run	Prog	C	0.10

Card name	Side	Type	Rarity	Price
Puzzle	Corp	Ice	C	0.10
Reclamation Project	Corp	Op	U	0.25
Rent-I-Con	Run	Prog	U	0.25
Running Interference	Run	Prep	U	0.25
5				
Sandbox Dig	Run	Res	C	0.10
Satellite Monitors	Corp	Node	C	0.10
Schematics Search Engine	Run	Prog	U	0.25
Self-Destruct	Corp	Upgrd	C	0.10
Shock Treatment	Corp	Upgrd	U	0.25
Sterdroid	Corp	Upgrd	C	0.10
Strategic Planning Group	Corp	Node	U	0.25
Street Enforcer	Corp	Upgrd	U	0.25
Superglue	Run	Prog	C	0.10
6				
Superserum	Corp	Agenda	U	0.25
Theorem Proof	Corp	Agenda	U	0.25
Trapdoor	Corp	Ice	U	0.25
Unlisted Research Lab	Corp	Agenda	C	0.10
Vintage Camaro	Run	Hard	C	0.10
Vortex	Corp	Ice	C	0.10
Zetatech Portastation	Run	Hard	C	0.10

RARITY KEY C = Common U = Uncommon R = Rare V = Very Rare UR = Ultra Rare F = Foil card X = Fixed/standard in all decks

On the Edge

Atlas Games/Trident • First release, Limited, released **October 1994**

269 cards in set • **IDENTIFIER: No copyright; titles have brown type**

- Starter decks contain 60 cards; starter displays contain 10 starters
- Booster packs contain 10 cards; booster displays contain 60 boosters

Following the success of **Magic: The Gathering**, Atlas Games released a CCG based on its role-playing game, *Over the Edge*. Both games are based on a fictional island in the Mediterranean called Al Amarja, where numerous conspiracies, aliens, and plots to take over the world reside. (Say the name quickly and find that it's "All A Mirage.") **On the Edge** focuses on players' personal conspiracy attempts to control the island, and from there, the world.

Influence is gained by generating "pull," which is also used to bring cards into play. Manipulation of resources is vitally important. Also, since losing a character with pull reduces one's influence, protecting those characters is as important as using them to further a victory condition. *On the Edge* introduces a system of "rank and file," wherein players play their characters into three rows and any number of columns. Opponents could only attack the front-most character in a given column, making short-term defense simple but long-term defense difficult.

Before the first expansion, most decks consisted of the D'Aubainnes, the rulers of the island, and the Pharaohs, who were an ancient race of superhumans. The former were powerful because of their large pull values and inherent structure of defense. The latter were popular because of their immunity to attack, and their potent attack strategy using such cards as **Anti-Matter Grenade**.

On the Edge got caught up in the flood of games released during 1994 and 1995, and had trouble staying on the surface. It also competed for "intellectual space" with the later-released (but ironically already established) CCG **Illuminati**. The game developed a cult following , but the two expansions announced for 1996, **Wetworks** and **Chaos Plague**, were never released. — *Brian Kallenbach*

Concept	●●●○○
Gameplay	●●●○○
Card art	●●○○○
Player pool	●○○○○

On the Edge • Unlimited Edition

Atlas Games/Trident • Released **December 1994**

269 cards in set • **IDENTIFIER: No copyright; titles have yellow type**

The **Unlimited Edition** was simply a reprint of the **Limited** when the first run ran out. There were minor changes to the rulebook, and minor changes to some of the resource cards. The play style remained essentially the same, with players modifying their decks a little better to counter the D'Aubainne and Pharaoh decks.

The Glugs gained a popular deck archetype, due to the **Copper Dagger**'s high pull capability, as well as its anti-Pharaoh effect. — *Brian Kallenbach*

LIMITED EDITION

Set (269 cards)	67.50
Starter Display Box	27.25
Booster Display Box	32.00
Starter Deck	5.30
Booster Pack	1.10

You will need **30** nine-pocket pages to store this set. (15 doubled up)

UNLIMITED EDITION

Set (269 cards)	52.75
Starter Display Box	23.00
Booster Display Box	25.50
Starter Deck	5.00
Booster Pack	1.00

You will need **30** nine-pocket pages to store this set. (15 doubled up)

	Card name	Type	Rarity	Price
1				
☐ 0.60	88 Abanobi Famani	U	0.50 ☐
☐ 2.00	159 Abdullah Mustafa	R	1.50 ☐
☐ 0.60	145 Abel Ludo	U	0.50 ☐
☐ 0.60	86 Adelina Escobar	U	0.50 ☐
☐ 0.20	157 Akio Morimoto	C	0.10 ☐
☐ 0.60	85 Akorra Encombi	U	0.50 ☐

	Card name	Type	Rarity	Price
☐ 0.20	12 Al Amarjan Friends	C	0.10 ☐
☐ 0.60	204 Aleksandr Rominosky	U	0.50 ☐
☐ 0.20	252 Ali Twine	C	0.10 ☐
2				
☐ 0.60	18 Amok	U	0.50 ☐
☐ 0.20	260 Andrea Vernon	C	0.10 ☐
☐ 0.60	197 Angela Reyes	U	0.50 ☐
☐ 0.60	19 Anti-Matter Grenade	U	0.50 ☐
☐ 2.00	109 Anwar Hallajin	R	1.50 ☐
☐ 0.60	20 Aries Ambush	U	0.50 ☐
☐ 0.60	21 Armada	U	0.50 ☐
☐ 0.20	175 Arthur Pendrick	C	0.10 ☐
☐ 0.20	148 Arwa Marabu	C	0.10 ☐
3				
☐ 2.00	194 Asha Rayhar	R	1.50 ☐
☐ 0.60	23 Astral Doorway	U	0.50 ☐
☐ 0.20	24 Astral Flux	C	0.10 ☐
☐ 2.00	25 Astral Interference	R	1.50 ☐
☐ 2.00	26 Astral Mimicry	R	1.50 ☐
☐ 2.00	27 Astral Negatrons	R	1.50 ☐
☐ 0.20	28 Astral Wisdom	C	0.10 ☐
☐ 2.00	29 Atavism: Ninja	R	1.50 ☐
☐ 2.00	30 Aura of Evil	R	1.50 ☐
4				
☐ 0.20	43 Aurora Bolt	C	0.10 ☐
☐ 2.00	40 Avan Bloodlord	R	1.50 ☐
☐ 0.20	31 Bad Luck	C	0.10 ☐
☐ 0.20	112 Barber Hammock	C	0.10 ☐
☐ 2.00	32 Battle Bike	R	1.50 ☐

	Card name	Type	Rarity	Price
☐ 0.60	33 Beginner's Luck	U	0.50 ☐
☐ 0.60	35 Bellow	U	0.50 ☐
☐ 0.60	91 Ben Feather-on-Wind	U	0.50 ☐
☐ 2.00	36 Bestial Rampage	R	1.50 ☐
5				
☐ 2.00	37 Betelguesan	R	1.50 ☐
☐ 0.20	38 Bitter & Herb	C	0.10 ☐
☐ 0.20	39 Blackmail	C	0.10 ☐
☐ 0.60	41 Bloodlust	U	0.50 ☐
☐ 2.00	42 Body Double	R	1.50 ☐
☐ 0.20	45 Break-Bones	C	0.10 ☐
☐ 0.20	46 Breakage	C	0.10 ☐
☐ 0.60	48 Bull-Beater	U	0.50 ☐
☐ 0.60	223 Burford J. Slystick	U	0.50 ☐
6				
☐ 0.60	49 Bystander Effect	U	0.50 ☐
☐ 2.00	54 Charisma	R	1.50 ☐
☐ 0.20	200 Cherri Robinson	C	0.10 ☐
☐ 2.00	68 Cheryl D'Aubainne	R	1.50 ☐
☐ 0.20	55 Chikutorpl	C	0.10 ☐
☐ 0.60	57 Cloak Ambush	U	0.50 ☐
☐ 0.60	58 Cloak Hit	U	0.50 ☐
☐ 2.00	245 Clyde Throckmorton	R	1.50 ☐
☐ 0.20	60 Concealable Weaponry	C	0.10 ☐
7				
☐ 2.00	69 Constance D'Aubainne	R	1.50 ☐
☐ 0.20	61 Contacts in the Art Scene	C	0.10 ☐
☐ 2.00	62 Copper Dagger	R	1.50 ☐
☐ 2.00	63 Coral Entity	R	1.50 ☐

RARITY KEY C = Common U = Uncommon R = Rare VR = Very Rare UR = Ultra Rare F = Foil card X = Fixed/standard in all decks

		Card name	Type	Rarity	Price
☐ 0.60	64	Counter-Intelligence		U	0.50 ☐
☐ 0.20	65	Crystal Trap		C	0.10 ☐
☐ 2.00	66	Cut-Ups Machine		R	1.50 ☐
☐ 0.20	67	Cyanide Capsule		C	0.10 ☐
☐ 2.00	80	Cyril Doros		R	1.50 ☐
8					
☐ 2.00	13	Dalal Allar		R	1.50 ☐
☐ 0.20	73	Dark Aura Ring		C	0.10 ☐
☐ 2.00	74	Deadly Inspiration		R	1.50 ☐
☐ 2.00	107	Deborah Grierson		R	1.50 ☐
☐ 0.60	75	Deportation Investigation		U	0.50 ☐
☐ 2.00	22	Dev Ashana		R	1.50 ☐
☐ 0.20	189	Dinesh Rajpal		C	0.10 ☐
☐ 0.60	77	Disinformation		U	0.50 ☐
☐ 2.00	78	Disintegrator Ray		R	1.50 ☐
9					
☐ 0.20	259	Dmitri Vatsavos		C	0.10 ☐
☐ 0.20	79	DNA Difficulties		C	0.10 ☐
☐ 0.20	206	Don Rozo		C	0.10 ☐
☐ 0.60	170	Dr. Furchtegott Nusbaum		U	0.50 ☐
☐ 0.60	156	Dr. Paulo Montserrat		U	0.50 ☐
☐ 0.20	81	Dumb Luck		C	0.10 ☐
☐ 0.20	82	Duro-Trench		C	0.10 ☐
☐ 2.00	83	ELF Wave Generator		R	1.50 ☐
☐ 2.00	225	Eliza Smith		R	1.50 ☐
10					
☐ 0.20	84	Empty		C	0.10 ☐
☐ 2.00	108	Erik Gudne		R	1.50 ☐
☐ 0.60	150	Fabrissa Melors		U	0.50 ☐
☐ 2.00	17	Fahd Amaq		R	1.50 ☐
☐ 0.60	202	Fernando Rodriguez		U	0.50 ☐
☐ 0.20	104	Frank Germaine		C	0.10 ☐
☐ 0.20	93	Friends in Arms Barrio		C	0.10 ☐
☐ 0.20	94	Friends in Broken Wings Barrio		C	0.10 ☐
☐ 0.20	95	Friends in Flowers Barrio		C	0.10 ☐
11					
☐ 0.20	96	Friends in Four Points Barrio		C	0.10 ☐
☐ 0.20	97	Friends in Golden Barrio		C	0.10 ☐
☐ 0.20	98	Friends in Great Men Barrio		C	0.10 ☐
☐ 0.20	99	Friends in Sunken Barrio		C	0.10 ☐
☐ 0.20	100	Frogbreath		C	0.10 ☐
☐ 0.60	101	Fury		U	0.50 ☐
☐ 0.60	102	Gang A-Gley		U	0.50 ☐
☐ 0.60	50	Gemma Candiru		U	0.50 ☐
☐ 2.00	103	Genetic Prejudice		R	1.50 ☐
12					
☐ 2.00	139	George Lazarus		R	1.50 ☐
☐ 0.60	16	Ghadir Allemi		U	0.50 ☐
☐ 0.20	146	Giovanni Mancini		C	0.10 ☐
☐ 0.60	221	Giuseppe Sizo		U	0.50 ☐
☐ 2.00	2	Gladsteins' Secret		R	1.50 ☐
☐ 2.00	3	Glorious Lords' Secret		R	1.50 ☐
☐ 2.00	4	Glugs' Secret		R	1.50 ☐
☐ 0.20	105	Good Luck		C	0.10 ☐
☐ 2.00	106	Gremlins		R	1.50 ☐
13					
☐ 0.60	261	Guglielmo Vigneto		U	0.50 ☐
☐ 2.00	114	Hank Henderson		R	1.50 ☐
☐ 0.20	133	Hans Knudson		C	0.10 ☐
☐ 2.00	89	Harry Fang		R	1.50 ☐
☐ 2.00	217	Havani Shagasemi		R	1.50 ☐
☐ 2.00	5	Hermetics' Secret		R	1.50 ☐
☐ 0.60	116	Hidden Gear		U	0.50 ☐
☐ 0.60	266	Holly Winter		U	0.50 ☐
☐ 0.60	118	Hostage		U	0.50 ☐
14					
☐ 0.20	119	Hostility Channeler		C	0.10 ☐
☐ 0.20	120	Hostility Detector		C	0.10 ☐
☐ 2.00	121	Human Ch'i Gun		R	1.50 ☐
☐ 0.20	122	Hypno-Disc		C	0.10 ☐
☐ 0.60	124	Immunity		U	0.50 ☐
☐ 0.60	125	Inspiration		U	0.50 ☐
☐ 0.60	126	Intelligence Contacts		U	0.50 ☐
☐ 2.00	127	International Influence		R	1.50 ☐
☐ 0.20	123	Isa Ifaq		C	0.10 ☐
15					
☐ 0.20	201	J.S. Rocket		C	0.10 ☐
☐ 0.60	187	Jack Rack		U	0.50 ☐
☐ 2.00	11	Jagannath Adhi		R	1.50 ☐
☐ 0.20	51	James R. Cartwright		C	0.10 ☐
☐ 2.00	70	Jean-Christophe D'Aubainne		R	1.50 ☐
☐ 0.20	72	Joana d'Fabelle		C	0.10 ☐
☐ 0.60	134	Joey Ko		U	0.50 ☐
☐ 0.60	130	Johnny Kazoo		U	0.50 ☐
☐ 0.60	190	Jonny Rama		U	0.50 ☐
16					
☐ 0.60	211	Juana Salvador		U	0.50 ☐
☐ 0.60	34	Julio Beitleiro		U	0.50 ☐
☐ 2.00	163	Kamorro N'Duban		R	1.50 ☐
☐ 2.00	228	Karla Sommers		R	1.50 ☐
☐ 2.00	129	Karmic Assassin		R	1.50 ☐
☐ 2.00	131	Kergillian Implant		R	1.50 ☐
☐ 2.00	6	Kergillian' Secret		R	1.50 ☐
☐ 0.60	132	Kidnap		U	0.50 ☐
☐ 0.20	117	Kunigunde Himmelsbach		C	0.10 ☐
17					
☐ 2.00	136	Latent Hero		R	1.50 ☐
☐ 2.00	137	Latent Psychic Attack		R	1.50 ☐
☐ 2.00	138	Latent Strength		R	1.50 ☐
☐ 0.60	140	Lee G'won Foo		U	0.50 ☐
☐ 0.20	113	Leif Hardarson		C	0.10 ☐
☐ 2.00	141	Ley Line Nexus		R	1.50 ☐
☐ 0.60	229	Linda Sourinen		U	0.50 ☐
☐ 0.60	47	Lino Briazzi		U	0.50 ☐
☐ 0.20	142	Loot		C	0.10 ☐
18					
☐ 0.60	143	Lope		U	0.50 ☐
☐ 0.20	90	Lou Farazzi		C	0.10 ☐
☐ 0.60	144	Loyalty Conditioning		U	0.50 ☐
☐ 0.20	240	Malak Suzier		C	0.10 ☐
☐ 2.00	128	Mamduh Jalla		R	1.50 ☐
☐ 0.20	147	Mantra		C	0.10 ☐
☐ 2.00	87	Manuela Eselbrust		R	1.50 ☐
☐ 0.60	171	Marla Oceana		U	0.50 ☐
☐ 2.00	205	Mars Royale		R	1.50 ☐
19					
☐ 0.60	173	Martin Oumage		U	0.50 ☐
☐ 2.00	269	Mary Zule		R	1.50 ☐
☐ 2.00	15	Mattias Allemande		R	1.50 ☐
☐ 0.60	56	Mihaly Cieznick		U	0.50 ☐
☐ 0.60	44	Mikhail Borisov		U	0.50 ☐
☐ 0.60	151	Military Contacts		U	0.50 ☐
☐ 2.00	152	Mind Control Messages		R	1.50 ☐
☐ 0.60	153	Mole		U	0.50 ☐
☐ 2.00	154	Molly, Queen Mother of Baboons		R	1.50 ☐
20					
☐ 2.00	155	Money Talks		R	1.50 ☐
☐ 2.00	71	Monique D'Aubainne		R	1.50 ☐
☐ 0.60	92	Mugly Flats		U	0.50 ☐
☐ 0.60	158	Multi-Dimension		U	0.50 ☐
☐ 0.60	160	Mutant Ambush		U	0.50 ☐
☐ 0.60	161	Mutant Sympathies		U	0.50 ☐
☐ 0.60	162	Mutation		U	0.50 ☐
☐ 2.00	164	Nachtmeister		R	1.50 ☐
☐ 2.00	165	Nano-Tech Medical Machines		R	1.50 ☐
21					
☐ 0.20	166	Negative Energy		C	0.10 ☐
☐ 2.00	167	Neuro-Star		R	1.50 ☐
☐ 2.00	168	New Blood		R	1.50 ☐
☐ 2.00	169	Number Three		R	1.50 ☐
☐ 0.20	172	Oppenheimer Contacts		C	0.10 ☐
☐ 0.20	174	Patrol Baboon		C	0.10 ☐
☐ 0.20	227	Peer Solgerkvist		C	0.10 ☐
☐ 2.00	7	Pharoahs' Secret		R	1.50 ☐
☐ 0.20	207	Pietro Ruffo		C	0.10 ☐
22					
☐ 0.20	176	Pistol-Grip Chainsaw		C	0.10 ☐
☐ 0.20	177	Polymer Clothing		C	0.10 ☐
☐ 2.00	178	Portable Sub-Sonics		R	1.50 ☐
☐ 2.00	179	Portia		R	1.50 ☐
☐ 0.60	180	Possession		U	0.50 ☐
☐ 2.00	218	Prem K. Sharma		R	1.50 ☐
☐ 2.00	181	Psi Gun		R	1.50 ☐
☐ 0.20	182	Psychic Flux		C	0.10 ☐
☐ 0.20	183	Psychic Sensitivity		C	0.10 ☐
23					
☐ 2.00	184	Psychic Singularity		R	1.50 ☐
☐ 0.60	185	Psychic Virus		U	0.50 ☐
☐ 0.20	186	Psychovore		C	0.10 ☐
☐ 2.00	188	Radio Laser Satellite		R	1.50 ☐
☐ 2.00	191	Rampage		R	1.50 ☐
☐ 0.60	203	Randy Rogers		U	0.50 ☐
☐ 0.20	192	Ransom		C	0.10 ☐
☐ 2.00	193	Ravage		R	1.50 ☐
☐ 0.20	231	Raw Steamer		C	0.10 ☐
24					
☐ 2.00	195	Red Orca		R	1.50 ☐
☐ 0.20	196	Reek Rend		C	0.10 ☐
☐ 0.20	52	Ricardo Cerdo		C	0.10 ☐
☐ 2.00	149	Ricardo Martinez		R	1.50 ☐
☐ 0.60	135	Rigor Kwasek		U	0.50 ☐
☐ 2.00	199	Riots		R	1.50 ☐
☐ 0.60	198	Robert Richardson		U	0.50 ☐
☐ 0.60	53	Roger Chalk		U	0.50 ☐
☐ 0.60	209	Sabotage		U	0.50 ☐
25					
☐ 2.00	210	SACQ		R	1.50 ☐
☐ 0.20	256	Sally Undokku		C	0.10 ☐
☐ 0.60	115	Saxolf Hermann		U	0.50 ☐
☐ 0.20	212	Seamless Shirt		C	0.10 ☐
☐ 0.60	213	Seklut Poison		U	0.50 ☐
☐ 0.60	214	Self-Actualizer		U	0.50 ☐
☐ 0.20	216	Sensitivity		C	0.10 ☐
☐ 2.00	219	Shreds		R	1.50 ☐
☐ 0.20	76	Silver Detti		C	0.10 ☐
26					
☐ 2.00	220	Simon Xin		R	1.50 ☐
☐ 2.00	59	Sir Arthur Compton		R	1.50 ☐
☐ 0.20	222	Slag		C	0.10 ☐
☐ 0.60	224	Smear Campaign		U	0.50 ☐
☐ 0.20	226	Sneak		C	0.10 ☐
☐ 2.00	230	Status Quo		R	1.50 ☐
☐ 2.00	251	Stefano Turolli		R	1.50 ☐
☐ 0.60	233	Stinger Mark V		U	0.50 ☐
☐ 0.60	234	Stun Gas		U	0.50 ☐
27					
☐ 2.00	235	Stun Ray		R	1.50 ☐
☐ 0.60	236	Stun Ring		U	0.50 ☐
☐ 0.60	237	Sub-Sonics		U	0.50 ☐
☐ 2.00	14	Sunshine Allarha		R	1.50 ☐
☐ 0.60	239	Super-Vitamin Diet		U	0.50 ☐
☐ 2.00	241	Switch-Flipping		R	1.50 ☐
☐ 2.00	238	Takeshi Sumanoto		R	1.50 ☐
☐ 0.60	243	Terrors		U	0.50 ☐
☐ 2.00	10	The Dirt on Dr. Nusbaum		R	1.50 ☐
28					
☐ 2.00	1	The Dirt on Her Exaltedness Monique D'Aubainne, Historic Liberator and Current Shepherdess of Al Amarja		R	1.50 ☐
☐ 2.00	242	The Terminal		R	1.50 ☐
☐ 0.60	208	Thor Runestone		U	0.50 ☐
☐ 2.00	244	Throckmorton Device		R	1.50 ☐
☐ 0.60	246	Total Taxi		U	0.50 ☐
☐ 0.60	247	Trade Contacts in the Edge		U	0.50 ☐
☐ 0.60	248	Trident Morale		U	0.50 ☐
☐ 2.00	8	Tridents' Secret		R	1.50 ☐
☐ 2.00	249	Trugga		R	1.50 ☐
29					
☐ 0.60	250	Tulpa		U	0.50 ☐
☐ 2.00	9	Tulpas' Secret		R	1.50 ☐
☐ 0.20	111	Twilight Hammer		C	0.10 ☐
☐ 2.00	110	Umar Halleen		R	1.50 ☐
☐ 2.00	253	UN Forces		R	1.50 ☐
☐ 0.60	254	Unanticipated Influence		U	0.50 ☐
☐ 2.00	255	Underground Trident HQ		R	1.50 ☐
☐ 0.20	257	Unexpected Difficulties		C	0.10 ☐
☐ 2.00	215	Veronica Sellers		R	1.50 ☐
30					
☐ 0.20	258	Vibe Valiant		C	0.10 ☐
☐ 0.60	262	Ward Against Enemies		U	0.50 ☐
☐ 0.20	263	Weegzon		C	0.10 ☐
☐ 0.20	264	Weird Radiation		C	0.10 ☐
☐ 0.60	265	Wheel of Fortune		U	0.50 ☐
☐ 0.60	232	Wheeler Stein		U	0.50 ☐
☐ 0.60	267	Wiretap		U	0.50 ☐
☐ 0.20	268	Zipper		C	0.10 ☐

RARITY KEY C = Common **U** = Uncommon **R** = Rare **VR** = Very Rare **UR** = Ultra Rare **F** = Foil card **X** = Fixed/standard in all decks

Zipper — Street Scum — **0**

Art by Cheryl Mandus

Human, Low-Life

3
1

He's the kind of guy who might mug an unsuspecting tourist in a dark alley.

268

On the Edge • *Standard*

Atlas Games/Trident • Released **March 1995**

270 cards in set • **IDENTIFIER: No ©; titles have yellow type**

• Starter decks contain 60 cards; starter displays contain 10 starters
• Booster packs contain 10 cards; booster displays contain 60 boosters

   Standard was the same set as before with yellow type instead of brown for the titles, and with a 270th card, **Resounding Bell**. Due to the ultra-rare nature of **Resounding Bell**, it quickly became the game's hottest card to get, and, despite its lackluster gameplay, it commanded a high price in trading and on singles markets. Today, it's worth a couple of bucks. — **Brian Kallenbach**

Set (270 cards)	**55.00**
Starter Display Box	**21.00**
Booster Display Box	**23.75**
Starter Deck	**5.00**
Booster Pack	**1.00**

#	Card Name	Rarity	Price
1			
88	Abanobi Famani	U	0.50
159	Abdullah Mustafa	R	1.50
145	Abel Ludo	U	0.50
86	Adelina Escobar	U	0.50
157	Akio Morimoto	C	0.10
85	Akorra Encombi	U	0.50
12	Al Amarjan Friends	C	0.10
204	Aleksandr Rominosky	U	0.50
252	Ali Twine	C	0.10
2			
18	Amok	U	0.50
260	Andrea Vernon	C	0.10
197	Angela Reyes	R	1.50
19	Anti-Matter Grenade	U	0.50
109	Anwar Hallajin	R	1.50
20	Aries Ambush	U	0.50
21	Armada	U	0.50
175	Arthur Pendrick	C	0.10
148	Arwa Marabu	C	0.10
3			
194	Asha Rayhar	R	1.50
23	Astral Doorway	U	0.50
24	Astral Flux	C	0.10
25	Astral Interference	R	1.50
26	Astral Mimicry	R	1.50
27	Astral Negatrons	R	1.50
28	Astral Wisdom	C	0.10
29	Atavism: Ninja	R	1.50
30	Aura of Evil	R	1.50
4			
43	Aurora Bolt	C	0.10
40	Avan Bloodlord	R	1.50
31	Bad Luck	C	0.10
112	Barber Hammock	C	0.10
32	Battle Bike	R	1.50
33	Beginner's Luck	U	0.50
35	Bellow	U	0.50
91	Ben Feather-on-Wind	U	0.50
36	Bestial Rampage	R	1.50
5			
37	Betelguesan	R	1.50
38	Bitter & Herb	C	0.10
39	Blackmail	C	0.10
41	Bloodlust	U	0.50

#	Card Name	Rarity	Price
42	Body Double	R	1.50
45	Break-Bones	C	0.10
46	Breakage	C	0.10
48	Bull-Beater	U	0.50
223	Burford J. Slystick	U	0.50
6			
49	Bystander Effect	U	0.50
54	Charisma	R	1.50
200	Cherri Robinson	C	0.10
68	Cheryl D'Aubainne	R	1.50
55	Chikutorpl	C	0.10
57	Cloak Ambush	U	0.50
58	Cloak Hit	U	0.50
245	Clyde Throckmorton	R	1.50
60	Concealable Weaponry	C	0.10
7			
69	Constance D'Aubainne	R	1.50
61	Contacts in the Art Scene	C	0.10
62	Copper Dagger	R	1.50
63	Coral Entity	R	1.50
64	Counter-Intelligence	U	0.50
65	Crystal Trap	C	0.10
66	Cut-Ups Machine	R	1.50
67	Cyanide Capsule	C	0.10
80	Cyril Doros	R	1.50
8			
13	Dalal Allar	R	1.50
73	Dark Aura Ring	C	0.10
74	Deadly Inspiration	R	1.50
107	Deborah Grierson	R	1.50
75	Deportation Investigation	U	0.50
22	Dev Ashana	R	1.50
189	Dinesh Rajpal	C	0.10
77	Disinformation	U	0.50
78	Disintegrator Ray	R	1.50
9			
259	Dmitri Vatsavos	C	0.10
79	DNA Difficulties	C	0.10
206	Don Rozo	C	0.10
170	Dr. Furchtegott Nusbaum	U	0.50
156	Dr. Paulo Montserrat	U	0.50
81	Dumb Luck	C	0.10
82	Duro-Trench	C	0.10
83	ELF Wave Generator	R	1.50
225	Eliza Smith	R	1.50
10			
84	Empty	C	0.10
108	Erik Gudne	R	1.50
150	Fabrissa Melors	U	0.50
17	Fahd Amaq	R	1.50
202	Fernando Rodriguez	C	0.10
104	Frank Germaine	C	0.10
93	Friends in Arms Barrio	C	0.10
94	Friends in Broken Wings Barrio	C	0.10
95	Friends in Flowers Barrio	C	0.10
11			
96	Friends in Four Points Barrio	C	0.10

#	Card Name	Rarity	Price
97	Friends in Golden Barrio	C	0.10
98	Friends in Great Men Barrio	C	0.10
99	Friends in Sunken Barrio	C	0.10
100	Frogbreath	C	0.10
101	Fury	U	0.50
102	Gang A-Gley	U	0.50
50	Gemma Candiru	U	0.50
103	Genetic Prejudice	R	1.50
12			
139	George Lazarus	R	1.50
16	Ghadir Allemi	U	0.50
146	Giovanni Mancini	C	0.10
221	Giuseppe Sizo	U	0.50
2	Gladsteins' Secret	R	1.50
3	Glorious Lords' Secret	R	1.50
4	Glugs' Secret	R	1.50
105	Good Luck	C	0.10
106	Gremlins	R	1.50
13			
261	Guglielmo Vigneto	U	0.50
114	Hank Henderson	R	1.50
133	Hans Knudson	C	0.10
89	Harry Fang	R	1.50
217	Havani Shagasemi	R	1.50
5	Hermetics' Secret	R	1.50
116	Hidden Gear	U	0.50
266	Holly Winter	U	0.50
118	Hostage	U	0.50
14			
119	Hostility Channeler	C	0.10
120	Hostility Detector	C	0.10
121	Human Ch'i Gun	R	1.50
122	Hypno-Disc	C	0.10
124	Immunity	U	0.50
125	Inspiration	U	0.50
126	Intelligence Contacts	U	0.50
127	International Influence	R	1.50
123	Isa Ifaq	C	0.10
15			
201	J.S. Rocket	C	0.10
187	Jack Rack	U	0.50
11	Jagannath Adhi	R	1.50
51	James R. Cartwright	C	0.10
70	Jean-Christophe D'Aubainne	R	1.50
72	Joana d'Fabelle	C	0.10
134	Joey Ko	U	0.50
130	Johnny Kazoo	U	0.50
190	Jonny Rama	U	0.50
16			
211	Juana Salvador	U	0.50
34	Julio Beitleiro	U	0.50
163	Kamorro N'Duban	R	1.50
228	Karla Sommers	R	1.50
129	Karmic Assassin	R	1.50
131	Kergillian Implant	R	1.50
6	Kergillian' Secret	R	1.50
132	Kidnap	U	0.50
117	Kunigunde Himmelsbach	C	0.10
17			
136	Latent Hero	R	1.50
137	Latent Psychic Attack	R	1.50

#	Card Name	Rarity	Price
138	Latent Strength	R	1.50
140	Lee G'won Foo	U	0.50
113	Leif Hardarson	R	1.50
141	Ley Line Nexus	R	1.50
229	Linda Sourinen	U	0.50
47	Lino Briazzi	U	0.50
142	Loot	C	0.10
18			
143	Lope	U	0.50
90	Lou Farazzi	C	0.10
144	Loyalty Conditioning	U	0.50
240	Malak Suzier	C	0.10
128	Mamduh Jalla	R	1.50
147	Mantra	C	0.10
87	Manuela Eselbrust	R	1.50
171	Marla Oceana	R	1.50
205	Mars Royale	R	1.50
19			
173	Martin Oumage	U	0.50
269	Mary Zule	R	1.50
15	Mattias Allemande	R	1.50
56	Mihaly Cieznick	U	0.50
44	Mikhail Borisov	U	0.50
151	Military Contacts	U	0.50
152	Mind Control Messages	R	1.50
153	Mole	U	0.50
154	Molly, Queen Mother of Baboons	R	1.50
20			
155	Money Talks	R	1.50
71	Monique D'Aubainne	R	1.50
92	Mugly Flats	U	0.50
158	Multi-Dimension	U	0.50
160	Mutant Ambush	U	0.50
161	Mutant Sympathies	U	0.50
162	Mutation	U	0.50
164	Nachtmeister	R	1.50
165	Nano-Tech Medical Machines	R	1.50
21			
166	Negative Energy	C	0.10
167	Neuro-Star	R	1.50
168	New Blood	R	1.50
169	Number Three	R	1.50
172	Oppenheimer Contacts	C	0.10
174	Patrol Baboon	C	0.10
227	Peer Solgerkvist	C	0.10
7	Pharoahs' Secret	R	1.50
207	Pietro Ruffo	C	0.10
22			
176	Pistol-Grip Chainsaw	C	0.10
177	Polymer Clothing	C	0.10
178	Portable Sub-Sonics	R	1.50
179	Portia	R	1.50
180	Possession	U	0.50
218	Prem K. Sharma	R	1.50
181	Psi Gun	R	1.50
182	Psychic Flux	C	0.10
183	Psychic Sensitivity	C	0.10
23			
184	Psychic Singularity	R	1.50
185	Psychic Virus	U	0.50
186	Psychovore	C	0.10

RARITY KEY **C** = Common **U** = Uncommon **R** = Rare **VR** = Very Rare **UR** = Ultra Rare **F** = Foil card **X** = Fixed/standard in all decks

#	Card Name	Rarity	Price
188	Radio Laser Satellite	R	1.50
191	Rampage	R	1.50
203	Randy Rogers	U	0.50
192	Ransom	C	0.10
193	Ravage	R	1.50
231	Raw Steamer	C	0.10
195	Red Orca	R	1.50
196	Reek Rend	C	0.10
270	Resounding Bell	R	2.30
52	Ricardo Cerdo	C	0.10
149	Ricardo Martinez	R	1.50
135	Rigor Kwasek	U	0.50
199	Riots	R	1.50
198	Robert Richardson	U	0.50
53	Roger Chalk	U	0.50
209	Sabotage	U	0.50
210	SACQ	R	1.50
256	Sally Undokku	C	0.10

#	Card Name	Rarity	Price
115	Saxolf Hermann	U	0.50
212	Seamless Shirt	C	0.10
213	Seklut Poison	U	0.50
214	Self-Actualizer	U	0.50
216	Sensitivity	C	0.10
219	Shreds	R	1.50
76	Silver Detti	C	0.10
220	Simon Xin	R	1.50
59	Sir Arthur Compton	R	1.50
222	Slag	C	0.10
224	Smear Campaign	U	0.50
226	Sneak	C	0.10
230	Status Quo	R	1.50
251	Stefano Turolli	R	1.50
233	Stinger Mark V	U	0.50
234	Stun Gas	U	0.50
235	Stun Ray	R	1.50
236	Stun Ring	U	0.50

#	Card Name	Rarity	Price
237	Sub-Sonics	U	0.50
14	Sunshine Allarha	R	1.50
239	Super-Vitamin Diet	U	0.50
241	Switch-Flipping	R	1.50
238	Takeshi Sumanoto	R	1.50
243	Terrors	U	0.50
10	The Dirt on Dr. Nusbaum	R	1.50
1	The Dirt on Her Exaltedness, Monique D'Aubainne, Historic Liberator and Current Shepherdess of Al Amarja	R	1.50
242	The Terminal	R	1.50
208	Thor Runestone	U	0.50
244	Throckmorton Device	R	1.50
246	Total Taxi	U	0.50
247	Trade Contacts in the Edge	U	0.50
248	Trident Morale	U	0.50
8	Tridents' Secret	R	1.50

#	Card Name	Rarity	Price
249	Trugga	R	1.50
250	Tulpa	U	0.50
9	Tulpas' Secret	R	1.50
111	Twilight Hammer	C	0.10
110	Umar Halleen	R	1.50
253	UN Forces	R	1.50
254	Unanticipated Influence	U	0.50
255	Underground Trident HQ	R	1.50
257	Unexpected Difficulties	C	0.10
215	Veronica Sellers	R	1.50
258	Vibe Valiant	C	0.10
262	Ward Against Enemies	U	0.50
263	Weegzon	C	0.10
264	Weird Radiation	U	0.50
265	Wheel of Fortune	U	0.50
232	Wheeler Stein	U	0.50
267	Wiretap	U	0.50
268	Zipper	C	0.10

On the Edge • *The Cut-Ups Project*

Atlas Games/Trident • Released **February 1995**

90 cards in set • IDENTIFIER: 'C' next to card number

- Booster packs contain 10 cards; booster displays contain 60 boosters

   On the Edge's first expansion (don't let the letter fool you) marked perhaps the most radical expansion to come out for a CCG at the time. The set focuses on the battle between the forces of control and chaos on the island, but with a slight twist. Instead of the norm, the forces of chaos lead a valiant struggle to slow the advance of various evil plots on the island. As a result, the CCG gained quite a few strange new cards.

   The first are environmentals, which completely change the victory conditions of the game. The new conditions range from spelling words with card titles to having as many different cards by different artists as possible. Also, in **Copyright Violation**, *Cut-Ups* features the only card which specifically allow you to play a card from another CCG.

   Decks at this time featured the new Victory Changing Environmentals, due to the fact that they could cancel out the influence-heavy decks, as well as the **TIE Fighter** from the *Star Wars* CCG, due to how well it combined with **Copyright Violation**. Another potent card from the set, **Rain of Walrus**, introduced a heavy character-removal element to a lot of decks. — *Brian Kallenbach*

> You will need **18** nine-pocket pages to store this set. (9 doubled up)

		Rarity	Price
Set (90 cards)			**43.25**
Booster Display Box			**24.00**
Booster Pack			**1.00**

#	Card Name	Rarity	Price
C53	Abbas Nadjafi	C	0.10
C51	Akio Morimoto	U	0.50
C83	Anatoly Taghel	U	0.50
C6	Andalusia Dog	U	0.50
C89	Anoop Varma	U	0.50
C31	Antenella Falchi	C	0.10
C50	Apocalypse Moorhouse	U	0.50
C41	Audrey Itsulaaq	C	0.10
C7	Blatant Scam	U	0.50
C12	Brownshirt	C	0.10
C66	C.A. Radford	U	0.50
C67	C.A. Radford	U	0.50
C68	C.A. Radford	C	0.10
C69	C.A. Radford	U	0.50
C70	C.A. Radford	C	0.10
C13	Censorship Flap	U	0.50
C15	Chaos Chancer	C	0.10
C16	Charm Bracelet	U	0.50
C17	Cheap Baboon Trick	U	0.50
C76	Claude-Lucien Rouvier	C	0.10
C8	Claus Brinker	C	0.10
C20	Closet Surrealists	C	0.10
C21	Coatless Code	U	0.50
C22	Copyright Violation	U	0.50
C24	Cut-Ups Method	U	0.50
C25	Death Car	U	0.50

#	Card Name	Rarity	Price
C26	Deep Pockets	U	0.50
C27	Deific Aura	U	0.50
C30	Duped and Narcotized Masses	C	0.10
C19	Dzamilla Chielminski	C	0.10
C58	Emer O'Tillery	C	0.10
C42	Emmanuelle Karmitz	U	0.50
C36	Eunice Rae Hopner	U	0.50
C46	Evan MacDonald	C	0.10
C65	Excel Quitlong	U	0.50
C29	Eyeballs Drillbit	U	0.50
C32	Fall of the Wall	U	0.50
C33	Fractal Infection	C	0.10
C34	Funkasite	U	0.50
C35	Giblets Granberry	U	0.50
C37	Horrors Count	C	0.10
C38	Ideological Polarization	U	0.50
C90	Isil Ziya	C	0.10
C9	Jacob Brinker	U	0.50
C10	Jeroen Brinker	U	0.50
C40	John Isidor	C	0.10
C44	Koanhead	U	0.50
C55	Kofi Ogunlala	U	0.50
C45	Life Imitates Art	U	0.50
C82	Malak Suzier	U	0.50
C57	Mary Olekobaai	U	0.50
C5	Matti Aaltonen	C	0.10
C47	Message to Space	U	0.50
C39	Michiko Ishii	U	0.50
C48	Mircea	U	0.50

#	Card Name	Rarity	Price
C52	Mrs. Brinker	U	0.50
C54	Newtonian Slam	C	0.10
C56	Oil Pan Annie	C	0.10
C88	Olimpia Urgeghe	U	0.50
C49	Oliver de Moleron	U	0.50
C59	Paralytic Bananna	U	0.50
C11	Pere Brinker	U	0.50
C60	Personnel Copier	U	0.50
C61	Pocket Panic Button	U	0.50
C62	Protoplankton	C	0.10
C63	Pythagorean Convulsion	U	0.50
C64	Quantum Squeezer	U	0.50
C71	Rain of Walrus	U	0.50
C72	Really Quite Angry Kid	C	0.10
C73	Recursive Time Loop	U	0.50
C74	Rex	U	0.50
C75	Rising Fanaticism	C	0.10
C23	Robert "Doc" Cross	C	0.10

#	Card Name	Rarity	Price
C77	Sacrifical Bloodbath	U	0.50
C2	Secret of the Cut-Ups	U	0.50
C80	Serhiy Stech	U	0.50
C78	Stairway to Nowhere	C	0.10
C79	Stasis Accumulator	U	0.50
C81	Sub-Random Subversion	C	0.10
C14	The Centipede	C	0.10
C1	The Deal With Sub-Randomness	U	0.50
C28	The Dimension of Gnerust	C	0.10
C3	The Truth About Chaos	U	0.50
C4	The Truth About Control Addiction	U	0.50
C84	Tiffany Trilobite	U	0.50
C85	Unattainable Desire	C	0.10
C86	Undeserved Power	U	0.50
C87	Unified Conspiracy Theory	C	0.10
C43	William Kear	U	0.50
C18	Yuzhou Chen	U	0.50

Symbolism

Don't be fooled by the identifying symbols with *On the Edge* expansions — the letters are not in alphabetical order, as you might suspect. "A" is for *Arcana*, actually the last set; "C" for *Cut-Ups Project*, the first. We've yet to figure out why *Shadows* is labeled "D" — unless it's a reference to the expansion's logo, where the "D" is larger than the other letters.

Perhaps it's a conspiracy...

RARITY KEY C = Common U = Uncommon R = Rare VR = Very Rare UR = Ultra Rare F = Foil card X = Fixed/standard in all decks

On the Edge • Shadows

Atlas Games/Trident • Released **May 1995**

117 cards in set • **IDENTIFIER: 'D' next to card number**

• Booster packs contain 10 cards; booster displays contain 60 boosters

    On the Edge's second expansion marked a step forward in the overall storyline on the island. Monique D'Aubainne died and was reanimated to retain her hold on the island, as little-known pest exterminator Clyde Throckmorton begins to realize his true destiny as ruler of the world. Honest.

    The D'Aubainne deck came back with a vengeance at this time, due to the fact that Monique gained the Astral trait, making her a little bit easier to buy. However, due to the prominence of Cut-Ups decks, Control Koanhead decks, Throckmorton Machine decks, and Baboon decks, no deck had real control over the tournament scene. — *Brian Kallenbach*

> You will need
> **13**
> nine-pocket pages to store this set.
> (7 doubled up)

Set (117 cards)		41.00
Booster Display Box		23.50
Booster Pack		1.00

#	Card Name	Rarity	Price
☐D1	About the Low-Lifes	U	0.50
☐D19	Ace J. Cirrus	C	0.10
☐D68	Ajay Obalago	U	0.50
☐D9	Alicia Andromeda	C	0.10
☐D6	All-Fours	U	0.50
☐D79	Alonzo Rubio	U	0.50
☐D14	Andrew Banks	U	0.50
☐D89	Aniela Stansky	U	0.50
☐D10	Annie the Rib	C	0.10
☐D55	Anya Huesco	U	0.50
☐D11	Astral Tempest	C	0.10
☐D12	Atavism: Priestess of Mu	U	0.50
☐D56	Azza Jami	U	0.50
☐D48	Barber Hammock	U	0.50
☐D81	Benjamin Sells	C	0.10
☐D36	Betty Frenum	U	0.50
☐D16	Bolstered Heart	U	0.50
☐D18	Bums' Rush	C	0.10
☐D99	Clyde Throckmorton	U	0.50
☐D52	Consuela Herrera	U	0.50
☐D20	Contacts in the CPC	C	0.10
☐D93	Cooper Syme	C	0.10
☐D22	Crackdown	U	0.50
☐D2	Crime & Punishment	U	0.50
☐D24	De-Individuator	U	0.50

#	Card Name	Rarity	Price
☐D25	Dead, Dead, Dead	C	0.10
☐D100	Dolores Titania	U	0.50
☐D17	Dr. Renee Boneau	U	0.50
☐D47	Eddie Haggle	U	0.50
☐D27	Eel	U	0.50
☐D28	El Zod 7	C	0.10
☐D75	Elizabeth Pock	U	0.50
☐D29	Facelessness	C	0.10
☐D95	Fea Terronez	U	0.50
☐D33	Fishwipe	C	0.10
☐D34	Flux	U	0.50
☐D35	Formless	U	0.50
☐D62	Freddie Manger	U	0.50
☐D37	Friends in Justice Barrio	C	0.10
☐D38	Friends Under the Street	C	0.10
☐D83	Gayth Silver	C	0.10
☐D7	Ghadir Allemi	U	0.50
☐D61	Giovanni Mancini	U	0.50
☐D73	Giurgiu Otinka	U	0.50
☐D108	Great White	U	0.50
☐D63	Gregory Mantle	U	0.50
☐D44	Gum It Up	C	0.10
☐D46	Hack-Master	C	0.10
☐D49	Hand Out to the Lost	C	0.10
☐D77	Hank Ramas	C	0.10
☐D50	Heating Up	U	0.50
☐D53	Honor Among Thieves	C	0.10
☐D54	Howdah	U	0.50
☐D51	Jerry Heckle	U	0.50
☐D43	Jill Grunder	U	0.50

#	Card Name	Rarity	Price
☐D21	Jorge Corriendo	U	0.50
☐D41	Julie Grouse	U	0.50
☐D64	Kalev Maran	U	0.50
☐D57	Knobs	C	0.10
☐D58	Kwik Klinik	U	0.50
☐D116	Laura Zoom	U	0.50
☐D59	LeThuy Injection	C	0.10
☐D71	Lissy Omgek	U	0.50
☐D76	Lujayn Qufra	U	0.50
☐D8	Lyubov Anatova	U	0.50
☐D117	M'ay Zung	U	0.50
☐D113	Margarita Yelmo	U	0.50
☐D30	May Ferendi	U	0.50
☐D39	Miriam Galaxy	C	0.10
☐D23	Monique D'Aubainne	U	0.50
☐D5	Monty Albion	U	0.50
☐D67	Moonsilk	U	0.50
☐D3	Mr. LeThuy's Secret	U	0.50
☐D60	Mr. Tramh LeThuy	U	0.50
☐D80	Norton Rumple	C	0.10
☐D115	Oma Zero	U	0.50
☐D114	Omni Yushka	C	0.10
☐D72	Orders From Tomorrow	C	0.10
☐D32	Otto Finkelstein	U	0.50
☐D74	Otz	U	0.50
☐D40	Pepper Grange	C	0.10
☐D109	Rhonda Widdershins	C	0.10
☐D65	Rita Milagro	U	0.50
☐D15	Rixa Bekker	U	0.50
☐D92	Robert Stop	C	0.10
☐D94	Rod "Scabs" Tar	C	0.10

#	Card Name	Rarity	Price
☐D69	Rodney Odge	C	0.10
☐D45	Roman Gundle	U	0.50
☐D31	Roz Fernseh	U	0.50
☐D112	Sandy Yama	C	0.10
☐D70	Seiji Ogata	U	0.50
☐D82	Shake 'Em Out	C	0.10
☐D106	Simon Wallop	C	0.10
☐D84	Slaughter	U	0.50
☐D85	Sludge	C	0.10
☐D86	Smack Back Attack	C	0.10
☐D87	Spike	C	0.10
☐D88	Squeaks	U	0.50
☐D90	Startle	C	0.10
☐D91	Starwalk	C	0.10
☐D26	T. Joe Dreck	U	0.50
☐D105	Tanja Voss	U	0.50
☐D4	The Net's Secret	U	0.50
☐D96	"The Radiator"	U	0.50
☐D97	The Skids	C	0.10
☐D98	The Squeeze	C	0.10
☐D42	Thunder Gruen	U	0.50
☐D13	Tommy Bakka	U	0.50
☐D101	Touchy Explosives	C	0.10
☐D102	Underworld Contacts	C	0.10
☐D103	Vibro Blaster	C	0.10
☐D66	Vincent Moire	C	0.10
☐D104	Vortex	U	0.50
☐D107	Walter Was	U	0.50
☐D78	Wanda Rod	U	0.50
☐D110	Wrench	C	0.10
☐D111	Xotok	U	0.50

On the Edge • Arcana

Atlas Games • Released **August 1995**

117 cards in set • **IDENTIFIER: 'A' next to card number**

• Booster packs contain 10 cards; booster displays contain 60 boosters

    Arcana focuses primarily on the two major forms of "magic" on the island: Psychic, which manifested as telepathy, telekinesis, and the like, and Astral, which used the more traditional methods of casting spells and invoking runes.

    The expansion released a couple of updates to previous factions, but focused on newer ones based around Psychic and Astral cards. The most significant cards in the set were the new **Monique D'Aubainne**, and Ur-Master, which created a "mini-Pharaoh" out of any personality. — *Brian Kallenbach*

    SCRYE NOTES: *Four "chase cards" were inserted into the display boxes themselves, at the rate of two per box. Eleven cards (noted with *) also have variant art or background colors.*

> You will need
> **18**
> nine-pocket pages to store this set.
> (9 doubled up)

Set (117 cards)		55.25
Booster Display Box		25.50
Booster Pack		1.00

#	Card Name	Rarity	Price
☐A53	Adrian Fig	U	0.50
☐A147	Alisher Usman*	U	0.50

#	Card Name	Rarity	Price
☐A11	Alter-Edge	U	0.50
☐A39	Anastasia Crowely	U	0.50
☐A40	Anastasia Crowely	U	0.50
☐A76	Andrej Kawierna	U	0.50
☐A99	Anima Nee-Owoo	C	0.10
☐A15	Anubis Scrolls	U	0.50
☐A16	Astral Egg	U	0.50
☐A17	Astral Refractor	C	0.10

#	Card Name	Rarity	Price
☐A18	Atavism: Necromancer	U	0.50
☐A19	Atavism: Priestess of Thoth	U	0.50
☐A73	Athena Iakatos	U	0.50
☐A1	Atlanteans' Secret	U	0.50
☐A20	Bad Vibes	U	0.50
☐A22	Bast	U	0.50
☐A23	Belakarkov	C	0.10

#	Card Name	Rarity	Price
☐A26	Big Mitts	U	0.50
☐A81	Billy Kwei	U	0.50
☐A105	Bjorn Nkwera	C	0.10
☐A27	Blind Spot	C	0.10
☐A121	Blush Quay	C	0.10
☐A28	Book of Malahel	U	0.50
☐A29	Book of Putrescences	U	0.50
☐A30	Broadcast	U	0.50
☐A21	Bruce Barret	C	0.10

RARITY KEY C = Common   U = Uncommon   R = Rare   Ch = Chase card   UR = Ultra Rare   F = Foil card   X = Fixed/standard in all decks

#	Card Name	Rarity	Price
A31	Bubbles	U	0.50
A72	Bulk Hertzog	U	0.50
A32	Canopic Jar	U	0.50
A33	Carcinogenia	U	0.50
A34	Cat's Feet	C	0.10
A35	Charismatic Resevoir	C	0.10
A36	Chateau Melmoth	C	0.10
A94	Cheb Mehenni	C	0.10
Ch4	Chris Robinson	Ch	3.50
A37	CPC Crackdown	U	0.50
A38	CPC Headquarters	U	0.50
A98	Damayanti Narasimhaiah	C	0.10
A42	Dark Secrets of Arthur Compton	C	0.10
A43	Delicatessen	U	0.50
A44	Devourer	U	0.50
A89	Djibril Maougal	C	0.10
A77	Donna Khalifah	C	0.10
A46	Doubting Thomas	C	0.10
A111	Dr. Jamaranathy Panil	C	0.10
A148	Dr. Maria Valdez	U	0.50
A104	Dumiso Nkomo*	U	0.50
A114	Eileen Pitchford	C	0.10
A149	Ellen Wu	U	0.50
A79	Eugene Krebbs	C	0.10
A50	Execration	U	0.50
A51	Exorcism	U	0.50
A100	Farah Nekhbet	U	0.50
A82	Fava Lahkdar	C	0.10
A56	Flooding Nile	U	0.50
A124	Fob Saline	C	0.10
A57	Forked Tongue	U	0.50
A58	Friends in Science Barrio	C	0.10
A59	Gherwalbus	C	0.10
A117	Gilbert Portwine	C	0.10
A150	Ginger Yang	C	0.10
A61	Gnaoul	U	0.50
Ch3	Grim Linden	Ch	3.50
A130	Hanni Shahal	C	0.10
A66	Harem Conspiracy	U	0.50
A67	Harmattan	U	0.50
A69	Head on the Door	C	0.10
A70	Healing Statue	U	0.50
A122	Horus Redwell	U	0.50
A54	Ingred Fjernsen	U	0.50
A74	Iron Skin	C	0.10
A135	Isabel Soyinka	C	0.10
A152	Isis Zaman	U	0.50
A113	Islam Petri	U	0.50
Ch1	Janis	Ch	3.50
A134	Jersey Smith	U	0.50
A131	Josephina Shoukry	U	0.50
A139	Judy Swelter	U	0.50
A75	Kamikaze	U	0.50
A140	Kate Taylor	C	0.10
A78	Kiyoteru Wakai	C	0.10
A80	Kunimatsu Kozo	C	0.10
A106	Leila Noureddin	U	0.50
A83	Lightning Strike	C	0.10
A52	Lou Farazi	U	0.50
A84	Love Philtre	C	0.10
A85	Ma'at	U	0.50
A138	Madeline Svora*	C	0.10
A86	Magic Mural	U	0.50
A88	Mammon	U	0.50
A96	Marilyn Munyaradzi*	C	0.10
A90	Marlowe Reading Room	U	0.50
A93	Media Skepticism	U	0.50
A12	Melinda Amduat*	U	0.50
A48	Mesut Economou	C	0.10
A87	Michelle Malafi	C	0.10
A95	Misdirection	C	0.10
A41	Monique D'Aubaine	U	0.50
A97	Myriad	C	0.10
A68	Nawal Al-Haz	C	0.10
A101	Nekromuzzle	C	0.10
A103	Nickels	C	0.10
A115	Nicolae Plesu	C	0.10
A102	Nicolai Nemeth	C	0.10
A55	Nicolas Flamel	U	0.50
A63	Notify Grout	C	0.10
A112	Paranormal Unity Theory	U	0.50
A14	Peach Angelic	C	0.10
A116	Poltergeist	C	0.10
A133	Pressure Sly*	C	0.10
A118	Psi Cat*	C	0.10
A119	Psychic Anomaly	U	0.50
A120	Psychic Time Bomb	C	0.10
A153	Qubilah Zeroual	U	0.50
A145	Raul Trevino	C	0.10
A91	Ricardo Martinez	U	0.50
A123	Ring of Gyges	U	0.50
A60	Rosa Ghitoni	C	0.10
A47	Ross Dowden	C	0.10
A13	Ruth Anati	C	0.10
A64	Saeb Hanoun	C	0.10
A49	Sani Enahoro	C	0.10
A125	Scarab	C	0.10
A126	Secret Temple of Thoth	U	0.50
A127	Sephira	U	0.50
A128	Seven Oils	C	0.10
A129	Shadrach*	U	0.50
Ch2	Signe Lathiere	Ch	3.50
A92	Sister Mary Evangeline	C	0.10
A132	Slipper	U	0.50
A136	Spackle	C	0.10
A137	Spaulding Manuscript	U	0.50
A24	Stas Bendick	C	0.10
A144	Steno Topic	C	0.10
A62	Suvadra GoldStone	C	0.10
A6	Tablets of Kish	U	0.50
A45	Tanja Djilas	U	0.50
A141	Telekinetic Punch	U	0.50
A2	The Cabal's Story	C	0.10
A65	The Harayelicon	U	0.50
A3	The Magic Circle's Secret	U	0.50
A4	The Purpose of the Neutralizers	U	0.50
A5	The Secret of the Saou	U	0.50
A7	The Theory Behind Astral Powers	U	0.50
A8	The Theory Behind Psychic Powers	U	0.50
A9	The Truth About Necromancy	U	0.50
A142	Throttle	U	0.50
A25	Tomek Bereszowsky	C	0.10
A143	Topaz Tidore*	U	0.50
A71	Triple Henderson	C	0.10
A108	Umberto Palladino	U	0.50
A109	Umberto Palladino	U	0.50
A110	Umberto Palladino	U	0.50
A146	Ur-Master	U	0.50
A10	Vera Afanasyevna*	U	0.50
A151	Yashga	C	0.10
A107	Yvonne Pacheco	C	0.10

On the Edge • Promos and specials

#	Card name	Price
S1	Astral Wisdom	2.40
S12	Bavarian Illuminati	2.50
S20	C. A. Radford	2.00
S13	Closet Surrealists	2.50
S14	Deep Pockets	2.50
S15	Desperate Ritual	2.00
S3	Dmitri Vatsavos	2.50
S23	Helene Clark	2.00
S22	Isil Ziya	2.00
S6	Kamorro N'Duban	2.30
S5	Kergillian Implant	2.50
S10	Linda Sourinen	2.00
S8	Lope	2.60
S17	Mary Olekobaai	2.00
S16	Message to Space	2.00
S9	Nachtmeister	2.00
S18	Personnel Copier	2.00
S19	Quantum Flux	2.00
S21	Rain of Walrus	3.00
S4	Red Orca	2.30
S2	Saleem Helicopter	2.50
S7	Scythian Ring	2.50
S24	Sekhem	2.00
S11	Throckmorton Domination	2.80

One-on-One Hockey Challenge • Premiere

Playoff • Released **September 1995**

330 cards in set

- Starter decks contain 50 cards and dice; starter displays contain 8 starters
- Booster packs contain 12 cards; booster displays contain 36 boosters

Both interesting and true to the sport, *One on One Hockey Challenge* from Playoff allows players to compete a game in the National Hockey League.

Each player chooses six cards to represent his team by position – a center, two defensemen, a right wing, a left wing, and a goalie — and lays them out in the play area. The goal is, obviously, to get the puck, skate your team forward, and shoot for a goal. When a player can attempt a shot, custom six-sided dice, with two blank sides, are used to get a Shoot stat. The goalie's Block statistic is consulted to see if a shot is scored.

Players use the three cards in their hand to get into position to shoot. The cards allow you to Skate a player forward to take a shot, Shoot, Pass, or Steal.

Cards are basically attractive, although it may be hard to find a full set as many of the rares appeared only in the starters. The game does a good job of simulating hockey, and knowledge of the NHL definitely helps get a solid team together.

Produced by sportscard-maker Playoff mostly for the mass market, *One-on-One* was the first sports-related CCG to hit the stands. Few hobby retailers rarely stocked it, and in some places it went quickly to the penalty — er, discount box. — ***Richard Weld***

★ Add +1 to a SKATE action.

HOCKEY ONE on ONE CHALLENGE

PATRICK ROY
Montreal
G 33 55
© 1995 Playoff Corporation Printed in U.S.A. © NHL

Concept	●●●○○
Gameplay	●●●●○
Card art	●●●○○
Player pool	○○○○○

Set (330 cards)	326.75
Starter Display Box	42.00
Booster Display Box	48.00
Starter Deck	8.80
Booster Pack	2.30

You will need **13** nine-pocket pages to store this set. (7 doubled up)

#	Card name	Rarity	Price
1	Guy Hebert	C	0.15
2	Paul Kariya	C	1.00
3	Mike Sillinger	C	0.15
4	Oleg Tverdovsky	C	0.15
5	Ray Bourque	C	0.50
6	Alexei Kasatanov	C	0.15
7	Blaine Lacher	C	0.15
8	Cam Neeley	C	0.15
9	Adam Oates	C	0.15
10	Kevin Stevens	C	0.15
11	Donald Audett	C	0.15
12	Dominik Hasek	C	0.15

RARITY KEY C = Common U = Uncommon R = Rare Ch = Chase card UR = Ultra Rare F = Foil card X = Fixed/standard in all decks

#	Card name	Rarity	Price
13	Pat LaFountaine	C	0.15
14	Alexei Zhitnik	C	0.15
15	Steve Chiasson	C	0.15
16	Theoren Fleury	C	0.15
17	Phil Housley	C	0.15
18	Joe Nieuwendyk	C	0.15
3			
19	Gary Roberts	C	0.15
20	German Titov	C	0.15
21	Ed Belfour	C	1.00
22	Chris Chelios	C	0.15
23	Bernie Nicholls	C	0.15
24	Jeremy Roenick	C	0.50
25	Peter Forsberg	C	0.50
26	Sylvain Lefebvre	C	0.15
27	Owen Nolan	C	0.15
4			
28	Joe Sakic	C	0.50
29	Jocelyn Thibault	C	0.15
30	Dave Gagner	C	0.15
31	Mike Modano	C	0.15
32	Andy Moog	C	0.15
33	Paul Coffey	C	0.15
34	Sergei Federov	C	1.00
35	Keith Primeau	C	0.15
36	Ray Sheppard	C	0.15
5			
37	Jason Amott	C	0.15
38	David Oliver	C	0.15
39	Mike Stapleton	C	0.15
40	Jesse Belanger	C	0.15
41	Paul Laus	C	0.15
42	Rob Niedermayer	C	0.15
43	Brian Skrudland	C	0.15
44	John Vanbiesbruck	C	0.15
45	Sean Burke	C	0.15
6			
46	Andrew Cassels	C	0.15
47	Brendan Shanahan	C	1.00
48	Rob Blake	C	0.15
49	Tony Granato	C	0.15
50	Wayne Gretzky	C	1.50
51	Marty McSorley	C	0.15
52	Jamie Storr	C	0.15
53	Vincent Damphousse	C	0.15
54	Mark Racchi	C	0.15
7			
55	Patrick Roy	C	1.00
56	Pierre Turgeon	C	0.15
57	Matrin Brodeur	C	0.15
58	Bill Guerin	C	0.15
59	Scott Niedermayer	C	0.15
60	Stephane Richer	C	0.15
61	Scott Stevens	C	0.15
62	Patrick Flatley	C	0.15
63	Brett Lindros	C	0.15
8			
64	Mathieu Schneider	C	0.15
65	Kirk Muller	C	0.15
66	Adam Graves	C	0.15
67	Alexei Kovalev	C	0.15
68	Brian Leetch	C	0.15
69	Mike Richter	C	0.15
70	Pat Verbeek	C	0.15
71	Luc Robitaille	C	0.15
72	Radek Bonk	C	0.15
9			
73	Alexandre Daigle	C	0.15
74	Alexei Yashin	C	0.15
75	Eric Desjardins	C	0.15
76	Eric Lindros	C	1.00
77	Ron Francis	C	0.15
78	Jaromir Jagr	C	1.00
79	Mario Lemieux	C	1.00
80	Ken Wregget	C	0.15
81	Francois Leroux	C	0.15
10			
82	Pat Falloon	C	0.15
83	Jeff Friesen	C	0.15
84	Arturs Irbe	C	0.15
85	Igor Larionov	C	0.15
86	Shayne Corson	C	0.15
87	Geoff Courtnall	C	0.15
88	Steve Duchesne	C	0.15
89	Brett Hull	C	0.50
90	Al Macinnis	C	1.00
11			
91	Brian Bellows	C	0.15
92	Chris Gratton	C	0.15
93	Dave Andreychuk	C	0.15
94	Tie Domi	C	0.15
95	Mike Gartner	C	0.15
96	Doug Gilmour	C	0.15
97	Larry Murphy	C	0.15
98	Felix Potvin	C	0.50
99	Mats Sundin	C	0.15
12			
100	Pavel Bure	C	0.15
101	Kirk Mclean	C	0.15
102	Alexander Mogilny	C	0.15
103	Christian Ruuttu	C	0.15
104	Jim Carey	C	0.15
105	Joe Juneau	C	0.15
106	Jason Allison	C	0.15
107	Teppo Numminen	C	0.15
108	Teemu Selanne	C	0.15
13			
109	Keith Tkachuk	C	0.15
110	Alexei Zhamnov	C	0.15
111	Patrick Camback	U	0.80
112	Bobby Dollas	U	0.80
113	Guy Hebert	U	0.80
114	Paul Kariya	U	1.80
115	Shaun Van Allen	U	0.80
116	Ray Bourque	U	0.80
117	Mariusz Czerkawski	U	0.80
14			
118	Todd Elik	U	0.80
119	Blaine Lacher	U	0.80
120	Cam Neely	U	0.80
121	Adam Oates	U	0.80
122	Dave Reid	U	0.80
123	Kevin Stevens	U	0.80
124	Garry Galley	U	0.80
125	Dominik Hasek	U	0.80
126	Brian Holzinger	U	0.80
15			
127	Pat LaFountaine	U	0.80
128	Mike Peca	U	0.80
129	Phil Housley	U	0.80
130	Paul Kruse	U	0.80
131	Ronnie Stem	U	0.80
132	Zarley Zalapski	U	0.80
133	Patrick Poulin	U	0.80
134	Bob Probert	U	0.80
135	Jeremy Roenick	U	1.80
16			
136	Adam Deadmarsh	U	0.80
137	Peter Forsberg	U	0.80
138	Andrei Kovalenko	U	0.80
139	Joe Sakic	U	0.80
140	Derian Hatcher	U	0.80
141	Grant Ledyard	U	0.80
142	Mike Modano	U	0.80
143	Paul Coffey	U	0.80
144	Sergei Federov	U	1.80
17			
145	Vladimi Konstantinov	U	0.80
146	Nicklas Lidstrom	U	0.80
147	Steve Yzerman	U	0.80
148	Igor Kravchuk	U	0.80
149	Kirk Maltby	U	0.80
150	Boris Mironov	U	0.80
151	Bill Ranford	U	0.80
152	Stu Barnes	U	0.80
153	Jesse Belanger	U	0.80
18			
154	Scott Mellanby	U	0.80
155	Adam Burt	U	0.80
156	Steve Rice	U	0.80
157	Brendan Shanahan	U	2.80
158	Glen Wesley	U	0.80
159	Wayne Gretzky	U	2.80
160	Daryl Sydor	U	0.80
161	Rick Tocchet	U	0.80
162	Brenoit Brunet	U	0.80
19			
163	J. J. Daigneault	U	0.80
164	Saku Kolvu	U	0.80
165	Lyle Odelein	U	0.80
166	Patrick Roy	U	2.30
167	Scott Stevens	U	0.80
168	Valerie Zelepukin	U	0.80
169	Steve Thomas	U	0.80
170	Dennis Vaske	U	0.80
171	Brett Lindros	U	0.80
20			
172	Zigmund Palffy	U	0.80
173	Ray Ferraro	U	0.80
174	Brian Leetch	U	0.80
175	Mark Messier	U	1.80
176	Ulf Samuelsson	U	0.80
177	Don Beaupre	U	0.80
178	Alexandre Daigle	U	0.80
179	Steve Larouche	U	0.80
180	Scott Levins	U	0.80
21			
181	Ron Hextall	U	0.80
182	Eric Lindros	U	2.30
183	Mikael Renburg	U	0.80
184	Kjell Samuelsson	U	0.80
185	Jaromir jagr	U	1.80
186	Mario Lemieux	U	1.80
187	Sergei Zubov	U	0.80
188	Bryan Smolinski	U	0.80
189	Dmitri Mironov	U	0.80
22			
190	Ulf Dahlen	U	0.80
191	Arturs Irbe	U	0.80
192	Craig Janney	U	0.80
193	Sandis Ozolinsh	U	0.80
194	Jon Casey	U	0.80
195	Brett Hull	U	1.80
196	Esa Tikkanen	U	0.80
197	Brian Bradley	U	0.80
198	Daren Puppa	U	0.80
23			
199	Alexander Selivanov	U	0.80
200	Rob Zamuner	U	0.80
201	Ken Baumgartner	U	0.80
202	Doug Gilmour	U	0.80
203	Kenny Jonsson	U	0.80
204	Felix Potvin	U	1.30
205	Randy Wood	U	0.80
206	Jeff Brown	U	0.80
207	Pavel Bure	U	0.80
24			
208	Trevor Linden	U	0.80
209	Alexander Mogilny	U	0.80
210	Roman Oksiuta	U	0.80
211	Cliff Ronning	U	0.80
212	Peter Bondra	U	0.80
213	Jim Carey	U	0.80
214	Pat Peake	U	0.80
215	Mike Tinordi	U	0.80
216	Mike Eastwood	U	0.80
25			
217	Nelson Emerson	U	0.80
218	Dave manson	U	0.80
219	Teemu Selanne	U	0.80
220	Keith Tkachuk	U	0.80
221	Bob Corkum	R	2.00
222	Peter Douris	R	2.00
223	Paul Kariya	R	17.50
224	Todd Krygier	R	2.00
225	Mike Sillinger	R	2.00
26			
226	Ray Bourque	R	2.50
227	Fred Knipscheer	R	2.00
228	Cam Neely	R	2.50
229	Adam Oates	R	2.50
230	Jason Dawe	R	2.50
231	Yuri Khmyley	R	2.00
232	Bob Sweeney	R	2.00
233	Trevor Kidd	R	2.50
234	Eric Daze	R	2.00
27			
235	Tony Amonte	R	2.50
236	Jeremy Roenick	R	10.00
237	Denis Savard	R	2.00
238	Gary Suter	R	2.50
239	Peter Forsberg	R	10.50
240	Curtis Leschyshyn	R	2.00
241	Owen Nolan	R	2.50
242	Joe Sakic	R	10.50
243	Veleri Kamensky	R	2.00
28			
244	Claude Lemieux	R	2.00
245	Bob Bassen	R	2.00
246	Shane Churla	R	2.00
247	Todd harvey	R	2.00
248	Kevin Hatcher	R	2.00
249	Richard Matvichuk	R	2.00
250	Mike Modano	R	2.00
251	Dino Ciccarelli	R	2.00
252	Paul Coffey	R	7.00
29			
253	Sergei Federov	R	21.00
254	Vyacheslav Kozlov	R	2.00
255	Mike vernon	R	2.00
256	Jason Bonsignore	R	2.00
257	Dean McAmmond	R	2.00
258	Bill Ranford	R	2.50
259	Doug Weight	R	2.00
260	Bob Kudelski	R	2.00
261	Dave Lowry	R	2.00
30			
262	Gord Murphy	R	2.00
263	Rob Niedermayer	R	2.00
264	Frantisek Kucera	R	2.00
265	Paul Ranheim	R	2.00
266	Geoff Sanderson	R	2.00
267	Darren Turcotte	R	2.00
268	Pat Conacher	R	2.00
269	Wayne Gretzky	R	60.00
270	Kelly Hrudey	R	2.00
31			
271	Jari Kurri	R	2.00
272	Patrice Briseboise	R	2.00
273	Vladimir Malakhov	R	2.00
274	Patrick Roy	R	37.50
275	Martin Brodeur	R	10.50
276	Neal Broten	R	2.00
277	Sergei Brylin	R	3.00
278	John MacLean	R	2.00
279	Wendel Clark	R	2.00
32			
280	Travis Green	R	2.00
281	Scott Lechance	R	2.00
282	Tommy Salo	R	2.00
283	Brian Leetch	R	2.50
284	Mark Messier	R	11.00
285	Sergei Nemchinov	R	2.00
286	Luc Robitaille	R	5.00
287	Sean Hill	R	2.00
288	Jim Paek	R	2.00
33			
289	Martin Straka	R	2.00
290	Sylvain Turgeon	R	2.00
291	Rob BrindAmour	R	2.50
292	Kevin Haller	R	2.00
293	John LeClair	R	2.00
294	Eric Lindros	R	38.00
295	John Otto	R	2.00
296	Chris Therien	R	2.00
297	Jaromir Jagr	R	29.00
34			
298	Mario Lemieux	R	39.00
299	Glen Murray	R	2.00
300	Petr Nedved	R	2.00
301	Jamie Baker	R	2.00
302	Arturs Irbe	R	2.00
303	Jayson More	R	2.00
304	Ray Whitney	R	2.00
305	Geoff Courtnall	R	2.50
306	Dale Hawerchuk	R	2.00
35			
307	Brett Hull	R	16.50
308	Ian Laperriere	R	2.00
309	Chris Pronger	R	34.50
310	Roman Hamrilk	R	2.00
311	Petr Klima	R	2.00
312	John Tucker	R	2.00
313	Paul Ysebaert	R	2.00
314	Ken Baumgartner	R	2.00
315	Doug Gilmour	R	7.00
36			
316	Pavel Bure	R	11.00
317	Brett Hedican	R	2.00
318	Alexandre Moligny	R	7.00
319	Mike Ridley	R	2.00
320	Peter Bondra	R	2.00
321	Sylvain Cote	R	2.00
322	Dale Hunter	R	2.00
323	Keith Jones	R	2.00
324	Kelly Miller	R	2.00
37			
325	Tim Cheveldae	R	2.00
326	Dallas Drake	R	2.00
327	Igor Korolev	R	2.00
328	Teppo Numminen	R	2.00
329	Teemu Selanne	R	14.00
330	Alexei Zhamnov	R	4.80

RARITY KEY C = Common U = Uncommon R = Rare VR = Very Rare UR = Ultra Rare F = Foil card X = Fixed/standard in all decks

OverPower (a.k.a. *Marvel OverPower, DC...*, etc.)

Fleer/Skybox • First release, *Marvel Limited*, released **August 1995**
346 cards in set • **IDENTIFIER: Bright yellow background; character names in italics**

- Starter decks contain 55 cards; starter displays contain 8 starters
- Booster packs contain 9 cards; booster displays contain 36 boosters

Magic excited comics fans just as much as gamers. *Magic* was being sold in comics shops as early as 1993, and since the speculative boom in comics had peaked in 1993, *Magic* helped keep a *lot* of those stores open in 1994. For their part, many comics fans had always wanted to role-play existing comics characters — but options were limited. The oldest game in the hobby, *Champions*, didn't have a license from either Marvel and DC — and TSR's and Mayfair's games for those companies only hooked a fraction of their comics readers. *Magic* gave comics readers dreams of a future Deckmaster engine allowing Marvel, DC, and other publishers' characters to coexist and compete.

Enter Marvel Entertainment, which had recently bought trading-card companies Fleer and SkyBox and which had been doing big business in comics trading cards before the peak. Doing its own CCG seemed a way to liven things up, and *OverPower* was born.

In *OverPower* (originally, it was only ***Marvel*** *OverPower*) players do battle using teams of heroes, all with values for three traits: Energy, Fighting, and Strength. Players can defeat a character by landing 20 points of damage or doing damage against all three traits. Mission cards for the set are on trading-card stock with square corners.

A game for CCG beginners, ***OverPower*** was heavily promoted by Marvel in its comics. It was expanded to cover DC heroes, although players were sorry to find that the two versions, maybe for licensing reasons, had different card backs and couldn't be integrated. (Opaque-backed sleeves solved the problem, but it was seen as a serious miscue.)

Suffering from the *enormous* debt piled up by its majority owner in his drive to turn it into a "mini-Disney," Marvel sought bankruptcy protection in late 1996 and sold off Fleer/Skybox a while later. *OverPower* was transferred to Marvel's interactive division, but by then the thrill was gone. A few hardcore players remain. — *John Jackson Miller*

Concept	●●●●○
Gameplay	●●●○○
Card art	●●●○○
Player pool	●○○○○

Set (346 cards)	**67.50**
Starter Display Box	**15.00**
Booster Display Box	**20.00**
Starter Deck	**5.00**
Booster Pack	**1.30**

You will need **39** nine-pocket pages to store this set. (20 doubled up)

Card name	Type	Rarity	Price
[1]			
☐ Age of Apocalypse 1	Miss	U	0.50
☐ Age of Apocalypse 2	Miss	U	0.50
☐ Age of Apocalypse 3	Miss	U	1.00
☐ Age of Apocalypse 4	Miss	U	0.50
☐ Age of Apocalypse 5	Miss	U	0.50
☐ Age of Apocalypse 6	Miss	U	0.50
☐ Age of Apocalypse 7	Miss	U	0.50
☐ Alien Technology	Univ	C	0.10
☐ Annihilation Affair 1	Miss	U	0.50
[2]			
☐ Annihilation Affair 2	Miss	U	0.50
☐ Annihilation Affair 3	Miss	U	0.50
☐ Annihilation Affair 4	Miss	U	0.50
☐ Annihilation Affair 5	Miss	U	0.50
☐ Annihilation Affair 6	Miss	U	0.50
☐ Annihilation Affair 7	Miss	U	0.50
☐ Apocalypse	Char	R	3.00
☐ Apocalypse: Enhance Strength	Spec	U	0.50
☐ Apocalypse: Genetic Engineering	Spec	U	0.50
[3]			
☐ Apocalypse: Mega Morph	Spec	R	2.00
☐ Apocalypse: Shape Shift	Spec	C	0.35
☐ Apocalypse: Survival of the Fittest	Spec	U	0.50
☐ Beast	Char	U	0.50
☐ Beast: Analyze	Spec	C	0.10
☐ Beast: Animal Dexterity	Spec	C	0.10
☐ Beast: Beastial Brawn	Spec	C	0.10
☐ Beast: Biochemist	Spec	U	0.50
☐ Beast: Drop Kick	Spec	U	0.50
[4]			
☐ Bishop	Char	C	0.10
☐ Bishop: Absorb Energy	Spec	C	0.10
☐ Bishop: Draw Enemy Fire	Spec	C	0.10
☐ Bishop: Plasma Gun	Spec	U	0.50

Card name	Type	Rarity	Price
☐ Bishop: Spectrum Blast	Spec	R	2.50
☐ Bishop: XSE Tactics	Spec	C	0.10
☐ Booster Shot	Univ	C	0.10
☐ Cable	Char	R	3.30
☐ Cable: Battle Tactics	Spec	U	0.50
[5]			
☐ Cable: Bionic Eye	Spec	U	0.50
☐ Cable: Bodyslide	Spec	C	0.10
☐ Cable: Cover Fire	Spec	U	0.50
☐ Cable: Custom Firearms	Spec	U	0.50
☐ Captain America	Char	R	3.50
☐ Captain America: Avenger	Spec	U	0.50
☐ Captain America: Mighty Shield	Spec	U	0.50
☐ Captain America: Ricochet Shield	Spec	U	0.50
☐ Captain America: Stars and Stripes	Spec	U	0.50
[6]			
☐ Captain America: Super Soldier	Spec	U	0.50
☐ Carnage	Char	C	0.10
☐ Carnage: Blade Hand	Spec	C	0.10
☐ Carnage: Climb	Spec	C	0.10
☐ Carnage: Insane Rage	Spec	C	0.10
☐ Carnage: Ruthless	Spec	R	2.00
☐ Carnage: Symbiotic Web	Spec	R	2.30
☐ Chain	Univ	C	0.10
☐ City Bus	Univ	U	0.40
[7]			
☐ Colossus	Char	U	0.50
☐ Colossus: Fastball Special	Spec	U	0.50
☐ Colossus: Haymaker	Spec	C	0.10
☐ Colossus: Metal Barrier	Spec	C	0.10
☐ Colossus: Skin of Steel	Spec	U	0.50
☐ Colossus: Smash Object	Spec	C	0.10
☐ Crossbow	Univ	U	0.40
☐ Cyclops	Char	C	0.10
☐ Cyclops: Fearless Leader	Spec	C	0.10
[8]			
☐ Cyclops: Ground Blast	Spec	R	2.00
☐ Cyclops: Optic Obliteration	Spec	C	0.10
☐ Cyclops: Visual Sweep	Spec	C	0.10
☐ Cyclops: Wide Beam	Spec	C	0.10
☐ Deadpool	Char	C	0.10
☐ Deadpool: Assassin	Spec	R	2.00

Card name	Type	Rarity	Price
☐ Deadpool: High Threshold of Pain	Spec	R	2.80
☐ Deadpool: Killing Machine	Spec	C	0.10
☐ Deadpool: Regeneration	Spec	C	0.10
[9]			
☐ Deadpool: Super Spy	Spec	C	0.10
☐ Divine Intervention	Univ	C	0.10
☐ Doctor Doom	Char	C	0.10
☐ Doctor Doom: Concussion Beams	Spec	C	0.10
☐ Doctor Doom: Energy Dampening Field	Spec	C	0.10
☐ Doctor Doom: Super Genius	Spec	R	3.00
☐ Doctor Doom: Time Machine	Spec	C	0.25
☐ Doctor Doom: Villainous Plot	Spec	R	2.00
☐ Doctor Octopus	Char	C	0.10
[10]			
☐ Doctor Octopus: Criminal Mastermind	Spec	C	0.10
☐ Doctor Octopus: Evasive Action	Spec	U	0.50
☐ Doctor Octopus: Grasping Tentacles	Spec	R	2.00
☐ Doctor Octopus: Multi-Armed Menace	Spec	C	0.10
☐ Doctor Octopus: Villainous Shield	Spec	C	0.10
☐ Dumpster	Univ	U	0.40
☐ Elektra	Char	R	3.30
☐ Elektra: Anticipate	Spec	U	0.50
☐ Elektra: Martial Artist	Spec	R	2.00
[11]			
☐ Elektra: Ninja Master	Spec	U	0.50
☐ Elektra: Resurrection	Spec	U	0.50
☐ Elektra: Sai	Spec	U	0.50
☐ EM Force Lines	Univ	U	0.40
☐ Energy 1	Pwr	C	0.10
☐ Energy 2	Pwr	C	0.10
☐ Energy 3	Pwr	C	0.10
☐ Energy 4	Pwr	C	0.10
☐ Energy 5	Pwr	C	0.10
[12]			
☐ Energy 6	Pwr	C	0.10
☐ Energy 7	Pwr	U	0.25
☐ Energy 8	Pwr	R	1.30
☐ Energy Booster	Univ	C	0.10
☐ Energy Enhancer	Univ	U	0.40

RARITY KEY C = Common U = Uncommon R = Rare VR = Very Rare UR = Ultra Rare F = Foil card X = Fixed/standard in all decks

Card name	Type	Rarity	Price
☐ Energy Maximizer	Univ	C	0.10
☐ Fatal Attractions 1	Miss	C	0.10
☐ Fatal Attractions 2	Miss	C	0.10
☐ Fatal Attractions 3	Miss	C	0.10
13			
☐ Fatal Attractions 4	Miss	C	0.10
☐ Fatal Attractions 5	Miss	C	0.10
☐ Fatal Attractions 6	Miss	C	0.10
☐ Fatal Attractions 7	Miss	C	0.10
☐ Fighting 1	Pwr	C	0.10
☐ Fighting 2	Pwr	C	0.10
☐ Fighting 3	Pwr	C	0.10
☐ Fighting 4	Pwr	C	0.10
☐ Fighting 5	Pwr	C	0.10
14			
☐ Fighting 6	Pwr	C	0.10
☐ Fighting 7	Pwr	U	0.25
☐ Fighting 8	Pwr	R	1.30
☐ Gambit	Char	C	0.10
☐ Gambit: 52 Card Pickup	Spec	C	0.10
☐ Gambit: Charge Object	Spec	C	0.10
☐ Gambit: Charm	Spec	R	2.00
☐ Gambit: Intercept Object	Spec	C	0.10
☐ Gambit: Staff Attack	Spec	U	0.50
15			
☐ Generator	Univ	C	0.10
☐ Girder	Univ	C	0.10
☐ Hand Grenade	Univ	C	0.10
☐ Hobgoblin	Char	C	0.10
☐ Hobgoblin: Concussion Grenade	Spec	C	0.10
☐ Hobgoblin: Goblin Glider	Spec	U	0.50
☐ Hobgoblin: Pumpkin Bomb	Spec	C	0.10
☐ Hobgoblin: Razor Bats	Spec	C	0.10
☐ Hobgoblin: Stun Gas	Spec	R	2.00
16			
☐ Hot Dog Cart	Univ	C	0.10
☐ Hulk	Char	U	0.50
☐ Hulk: Enraged	Spec	R	4.50
☐ Hulk: Green Goliath	Spec	U	0.50
☐ Hulk: Hulk Smash	Spec	C	0.10
☐ Hulk: Intimidate	Spec	R	2.00
☐ Hulk: Shrug Off	Spec	C	0.10
☐ Human Torch	Char	R	3.50
☐ Human Torch: Fire Shield	Spec	U	0.50
17			
☐ Human Torch: Fire Storm	Spec	C	0.10
☐ Human Torch: Inferno	Spec	U	0.50
☐ Human Torch: Nova Burst	Spec	R	2.30
☐ Human Torch: Searing Heat	Spec	U	0.50
☐ Hunk of Asphalt	Univ	C	0.10
☐ Infestation Incident 1	Miss	U	0.50
☐ Infestation Incident 2	Miss	U	0.50
☐ Infestation Incident 3	Miss	U	0.50
☐ Infestation Incident 4	Miss	U	0.50
18			
☐ Infestation Incident 5	Miss	U	0.50
☐ Infestation Incident 6	Miss	U	0.50
☐ Infestation Incident 7	Miss	U	0.50
☐ Infinity Gauntlet 1	Miss	C	0.10
☐ Infinity Gauntlet 2	Miss	C	0.10
☐ Infinity Gauntlet 3	Miss	C	0.10
☐ Infinity Gauntlet 4	Miss	C	0.10
☐ Infinity Gauntlet 5	Miss	C	0.10
☐ Infinity Gauntlet 6	Miss	C	0.10
19			
☐ Infinity Gauntlet 7	Miss	C	0.10
☐ Invisible Woman	Char	R	3.50
☐ Invisible Woman: Bubble Shield	Spec	U	0.50
☐ Invisible Woman: Force Field	Spec	U	0.50
☐ Invisible Woman: Invisibility	Spec	U	0.50
☐ Invisible Woman: Invisible Ram	Spec	R	2.00
☐ Invisible Woman: Unseen Assailant	Spec	U	0.50
☐ Iron Man	Char	R	3.50
☐ Iron Man: Concealed Arsenal	Spec	U	0.50
20			
☐ Iron Man: Heat Seeking Missile	Spec	R	2.50
☐ Iron Man: In the Line of Fire	Spec	U	0.50
☐ Iron Man: Radar Warning	Spec	U	0.50

Card name	Type	Rarity	Price
☐ Iron Man: Tactical Computer	Spec	R	2.50
☐ Jean Grey	Char	C	0.10
☐ Jean Grey: Mental Deflection	Spec	C	0.10
☐ Jean Grey: Mind Over Matter	Spec	U	0.50
☐ Jean Grey: Mind Scan	Spec	C	0.10
☐ Jean Grey: Telekinesis	Spec	C	0.10
21			
☐ Jean Grey: Telepathic Unity	Spec	R	2.00
☐ Jubilee	Char	C	0.10
☐ Jubilee: Blinding Flare	Spec	C	0.10
☐ Jubilee: Distracting Burst	Spec	C	0.10
☐ Jubilee: Fireworks	Spec	C	0.10
☐ Jubilee: Plasmoid Flash	Spec	R	2.00
☐ Jubilee: Spectrum Tease	Spec	C	0.10
☐ Lamp Post	Univ	C	0.10
☐ Laser Pistol	Univ	U	0.40
22			
☐ Machine Gun	Univ	C	0.10
☐ Magneto	Char	R	3.50
☐ Magneto: Evil Genius	Spec	U	0.50
☐ Magneto: Gravity Alteration	Spec	U	0.50
☐ Magneto: Magnetic Shield	Spec	U	0.50
☐ Magneto: Paralyze Opponent	Spec	R	2.00
☐ Magneto: Repel Object	Spec	U	0.50
☐ Manhole Cover	Univ	C	0.10
☐ Maximum Carnage 1	Miss	C	0.10
23			
☐ Maximum Carnage 2	Miss	C	0.10
☐ Maximum Carnage 3	Miss	C	0.10
☐ Maximum Carnage 4	Miss	C	0.10
☐ Maximum Carnage 5	Miss	C	0.10
☐ Maximum Carnage 6	Miss	C	0.10
☐ Maximum Carnage 7	Miss	C	0.10
☐ Mr. Fantastic	Char	R	3.50
☐ Mr. Fantastic: Ingenuity	Spec	C	0.10
☐ Mr. Fantastic: Protect Teammate	Spec	U	0.50
24			
☐ Mr. Fantastic: Python Hold	Spec	U	0.50
☐ Mr. Fantastic: Stretch Attack	Spec	U	0.50
☐ Mr. Fantastic: Team Leader	Spec	U	0.50
☐ Multipower 1	Pwr	C	0.10
☐ Multipower 2	Pwr	C	0.10
☐ Multipower 3	Pwr	C	0.10
☐ Multipower 4	Pwr	C	0.25
☐ Mystique	Char	R	3.00
☐ Mystique: Commando Raid	Spec	U	0.50
25			
☐ Mystique: Cool Under Fire	Spec	U	0.50
☐ Mystique: Illusion of Ally	Spec	U	0.50
☐ Mystique: Infiltration	Spec	C	0.10
☐ Mystique: Surprise Attack	Spec	R	2.00
☐ Omega Red	Char	U	0.50
☐ Omega Red: Carbonadium Coils	Spec	C	0.10
☐ Omega Red: Drain Lifeforce	Spec	C	0.10
☐ Omega Red: KGB Training	Spec	C	0.10
☐ Omega Red: Sacrificial Lamb	Spec	C	0.10
26			
☐ Omega Red: Tendril Tactics	Spec	R	2.00
☐ Power Cosmic	Univ	C	0.10
☐ Power Lines	Univ	C	0.10
☐ Professor X	Char	C	0.10
☐ Professor X: Cerebro	Spec	C	0.10
☐ Professor X: Psionic Hold	Spec	R	2.00
☐ Professor X: Psychic Scan	Spec	C	0.10
☐ Professor X: Telepathic Coordination	Spec	R	2.00
☐ Professor X: X-Men Founder	Spec	C	0.10
27			
☐ Psylocke	Char	R	3.00
☐ Psylocke: Combat Prowess	Spec	U	0.50
☐ Psylocke: Mental Hold	Spec	R	2.00
☐ Psylocke: Psi Fighting	Spec	U	0.50
☐ Psylocke: Psychic Knife	Spec	R	3.00
☐ Psylocke: Thought Probe	Spec	U	0.50
☐ Punisher	Char	U	0.50
☐ Punisher: Full Auto	Spec	C	0.10
☐ Punisher: Secret Weapon	Spec	R	2.00
28			
☐ Punisher: Smoke Screen	Spec	C	0.10

Card name	Type	Rarity	Price
☐ Punisher: Sniper	Spec	C	0.10
☐ Punisher: Vendetta	Spec	R	2.80
☐ Rhino	Char	C	0.10
☐ Rhino: Bowl Over	Spec	C	0.10
☐ Rhino: Pinball Blow	Spec	C	0.10
☐ Rhino: Rhino Charge	Spec	C	0.10
☐ Rhino: Rhino Hide	Spec	U	0.50
☐ Rhino: Romp n' Stomp	Spec	C	0.10
29			
☐ Rocket Launcher	Univ	C	0.10
☐ Rogue	Char	C	0.10
☐ Rogue: Intercept Attack	Spec	C	0.10
☐ Rogue: Mutagenic Drain	Spec	R	2.00
☐ Rogue: Power Transfer	Spec	C	0.10
☐ Rogue: Sky Soar	Spec	C	0.10
☐ Rogue: Super Strength	Spec	U	0.50
☐ Sabretooth	Char	C	0.10
☐ Sabretooth: Blood Hunt	Spec	R	2.80
30			
☐ Sabretooth: Bloodlust	Spec	C	0.10
☐ Sabretooth: Danger Scent	Spec	C	0.10
☐ Sabretooth: Healing Factor	Spec	C	0.10
☐ Sabretooth: Wildcat Attack	Spec	C	0.10
☐ Silver Surfer	Char	U	0.50
☐ Silver Surfer: Cosmic Healing	Spec	C	0.10
☐ Silver Surfer: Energy Protection	Spec	C	0.10
☐ Silver Surfer: Force Shield	Spec	C	0.10
☐ Silver Surfer: Power Cosmic	Spec	R	3.00
31			
☐ Silver Surfer: Rearrange Matter	Spec	C	0.10
☐ Spider-Man	Char	R	6.50
☐ Spider-Man: Arachnid Agility	Spec	U	0.50
☐ Spider-Man: Spider Sense	Spec	U	0.50
☐ Spider-Man: Wall Crawl	Spec	C	0.10
☐ Spider-Man: Web	Spec	R	2.50
☐ Spider-Man: Web Shield	Spec	U	0.50
☐ Spider-Woman	Char	C	0.10
☐ Spider-Woman: Arachnophobia	Spec	C	0.10
32			
☐ Spider-Woman: Psi-Web	Spec	R	2.50
☐ Spider-Woman: Spider Attack	Spec	C	0.10
☐ Spider-Woman: Spider Strength	Spec	C	0.10
☐ Spider-Woman: Web Lines	Spec	C	0.10
☐ Storm	Char	C	0.10
☐ Storm: Chain Lightning	Spec	C	0.10
☐ Storm: Emotional Outburst	Spec	R	3.00
☐ Storm: Flight	Spec	C	0.10
☐ Storm: Hurricane Winds	Spec	C	0.10
33			
☐ Storm: Summon Elemental Power	Spec	R	2.00
☐ Strength 1	Pwr	C	0.10
☐ Strength 2	Pwr	C	0.10
☐ Strength 3	Pwr	C	0.10
☐ Strength 4	Pwr	C	0.10
☐ Strength 5	Pwr	C	0.10
☐ Strength 6	Pwr	C	0.10
☐ Strength 7	Pwr	U	0.50
☐ Strength 8	Pwr	R	2.30
34			
☐ Sword	Univ	C	0.10
☐ Taxi Cab	Univ	C	0.10
☐ Teamwork (6 Energy to Use)	Univ	C	0.10
☐ Teamwork (6 Fighting to Use)	Univ	C	0.10
☐ Teamwork (6 Strength to Use)	Univ	C	0.10
☐ Teamwork (7 Energy to Use)	Univ	R	2.00
☐ Teamwork (7 Fighting to Use)	Univ	R	2.00
☐ Teamwork (7 Strength to Use)	Univ	R	2.00
☐ Teamwork (8 Energy to Use)	Univ	R	2.00
35			
☐ Teamwork (8 Fighting to Use)	Univ	R	2.00
☐ Teamwork (8 Strength to Use)	Univ	R	2.00
☐ Thing	Char	C	0.10
☐ Thing: Bear Hug	Spec	C	0.10
☐ Thing: Clobberin' Time	Spec	R	3.00
☐ Thing: Revoltin' Development	Spec	R	2.50
☐ Thing: Rock Skin	Spec	C	0.10
☐ Thing: Temper Tantrum	Spec	C	0.10

Card name	Type	Rarity	Price
Thor	Char	C	0.10
Thor: God of Thunder	Spec	C	0.10
Thor: Mjolnir Speaks	Spec	U	0.50
Thor: Mystic Uru Metal	Spec	C	0.10
Thor: Power of Asgard	Spec	R	2.50
Thor: Protect Teammate	Spec	C	0.10
Throwing Blades	Univ	C	0.10
Training (E & F, 5 or less, +3)	Univ	C	0.10
Training (E & F, 5 or less, +4)	Univ	C	0.10
Training (E & S, 5 or less, +3)	Univ	C	0.10
Training (E & S, 5 or less, +4)	Univ	C	0.10

Card name	Type	Rarity	Price
Training (F & S, 5 or less, +3)	Univ	C	0.10
Training (F & S, 5 or less, +4)	Univ	C	0.10
Tree	Univ	C	0.10
Venom	Char	R	3.00
Venom: Alien Webbing	Spec	C	0.10
Venom: Creepy Crawler	Spec	U	0.50
Venom: Panic Attack	Spec	R	2.00
Venom: Rampage	Spec	U	0.50
Venom: Symbiotic Snare	Spec	R	2.30
War Machine	Char	C	0.10
War Machine: Battle Computer	Spec	R	2.50

Card name	Type	Rarity	Price
War Machine: Energy Shield	Spec	C	0.10
War Machine: Guided Missile	Spec	C	0.10
War Machine: Hidden Weapon	Spec	C	0.10
War Machine: Unleash Arsenal	Spec	U	0.50
Wolverine	Char	R	5.30
Wolverine: Berserk Attack	Spec	U	0.50
Wolverine: Fighting Instinct	Spec	C	0.10
Wolverine: Heal	Spec	U	0.50
Wolverine: Snikt!	Spec	U	0.50
Wolverine: Wounded Animal	Spec	R	6.30

OverPower • Power Surge

Fleer/Skybox • Released January 1996

269 cards in set

IDENTIFIER: Darker yellow background; character names in bigger, serif font

• Booster packs contain 9 cards; booster displays contain 36 boosters

In what would be considered today a huge boosters-only expansion, Fleer gave the Marvel game such characters as the legendary **Silver Surfer**, the slinky **Black Cat**, and the why-did-anyone-ever-read-this-guy's-comics **Ghost Rider**.

Character cards, for the most part, are bumped up to a higher level of rarity. A number of the "essential" cards from *Limited* — trait cards and item cards — turn up again here, often at different rarity levels than they had in *Limited*. — ***John Jackson Miller***

Set (269 cards)	30.50
Booster Display Box	25.00
Booster Pack	2.00

You will need 30 nine-pocket pages to store this set. (15 doubled up)

Card name	Type	Rarity	Price
Alien Technology	Univ	U	0.40
Apocalypse: Instant Evolution	Spec	U	0.50
Banshee	Char	VR	3.30
Banshee: Interpol Training	Spec	U	0.50
Banshee: Luck O' the Irish	Spec	VR	2.80
Banshee: Shatter Shriek	Spec	VR	2.80
Banshee: Sonic Glide	Spec	VR	2.80
Banshee: Super Scream	Spec	VR	4.00
Banshee: Vocal Hypnosis	Spec	VR	2.80
Beast: Acrobatics	Spec	U	0.50
Bishop: Body Armor	Spec	U	0.50
Black Cat	Char	R	1.80
Black Cat: Bad Luck	Spec	VR	2.80
Black Cat: Cat Burglar	Spec	VR	2.80
Black Cat: Cat Fight	Spec	U	0.50
Black Cat: Femme Fatale	Spec	VR	3.80
Black Cat: Kiss of Death	Spec	VR	3.30
Black Cat: Nine Lives	Spec	U	0.50
Blob	Char	VR	2.80
Blob: Absorb Impact	Spec	U	0.80
Blob: Blubber Block	Spec	VR	2.80
Blob: Bottomless Belly	Spec	VR	2.80
Blob: Heavy Hitter	Spec	R	1.30
Blob: Immovable Object	Spec	U	0.50
Blob: Sumo Slam	Spec	VR	3.80
Booster Shot	Univ	C	0.10
Cable: Really Big Gun	Spec	R	2.50
Captain America: Inspiration	Spec	U	0.50
Carnage: Alien Healing	Spec	R	1.00
Chain	Univ	U	0.40
City Bus	Univ	R	2.00
Colossus: Iron Curtain	Spec	R	1.00
Cyclops: Remove Visor	Spec	VR	3.30
Daredevil	Char	VR	3.30
Daredevil: Agility	Spec	VR	2.80
Daredevil: Alertness	Spec	U	0.80
Daredevil: Billy Club	Spec	VR	4.00
Daredevil: Blind Man's Bluff	Spec	U	0.80

Card name	Type	Rarity	Price
Daredevil: Hypersenses	Spec	VR	2.80
Daredevil: Man Without Fear	Spec	VR	2.80
Deadpool: Bushwack	Spec	U	0.80
Divine Intervention	Univ	C	0.10
Doctor Doom: Expendable Ally	Spec	U	0.50
Doctor Octopus: Master Inventor	Spec	VR	2.80
Doctor Strange	Char	VR	2.80
Doctor Strange: Crimson Bands of Cyttorak	Spec	VR	3.50
Doctor Strange: Eldritch Blasts	Spec	U	0.50
Doctor Strange: Eye of Agamotto	Spec	VR	2.80
Doctor Strange: Mists of Morpheus	Spec	R	1.80
Doctor Strange: Necromancy	Spec	VR	3.30
Doctor Strange: Sorcerer Supreme	Spec	VR	2.80
Domino	Char	VR	2.80
Domino: Double Down	Spec	U	0.50
Domino: Fall into Place	Spec	R	1.00
Domino: Lady Luck	Spec	VR	2.80
Domino: Shrapnel Bomb	Spec	VR	3.50
Domino: Six Pack Attack	Spec	U	0.50
Domino: Tripwire	Spec	VR	2.80
Dumpster	Univ	C	0.10
Elektra: Shuriken	Spec	U	0.60
EM Force Lines	Univ	R	0.90
Energy 1	Pwr	C	0.10
Energy 2	Pwr	C	0.10
Energy 3	Pwr	C	0.10
Energy 4	Pwr	C	0.10
Energy 5	Pwr	C	0.10
Energy 6	Pwr	C	0.10
Energy 7	Pwr	C	0.40
Energy 8	Pwr	C	0.80
Energy Booster	Univ	C	0.10
Energy Enhancer	Univ	U	0.80
Energy Maximizer	Univ	U	0.40
Fighting 1	Pwr	C	0.10
Fighting 2	Pwr	C	0.10
Fighting 3	Pwr	C	0.10
Fighting 4	Pwr	C	0.10
Fighting 5	Pwr	C	0.10
Fighting 6	Pwr	C	0.10
Fighting 7	Pwr	U	0.80
Fighting 8	Pwr	U	0.60
Gambit: Ace in the Hole	Spec	R	1.30

Card name	Type	Rarity	Price
Generator	Univ	C	0.10
Ghost Rider	Char	R	1.80
Ghost Rider: Bat out of Hell	Spec	VR	2.80
Ghost Rider: Demon Chain	Spec	U	0.50
Ghost Rider: Fire and Brimstone	Spec	U	0.50
Ghost Rider: Hell on Wheels	Spec	VR	4.00
Ghost Rider: Penance Stare	Spec	VR	2.80
Ghost Rider: Spirit of Vengeance	Spec	VR	3.30
Girder	Univ	C	0.10
Hand Grenade	Univ	U	0.40
Hobgoblin: Secret Pouches	Spec	VR	2.80
Hot Dog Cart	Univ	C	0.10
Hulk: Power Leap	Spec	R	4.50
Human Torch: Flame On	Spec	R	1.00
Hunk of Asphalt	Univ	C	0.10
Iceman	Char	VR	2.80
Iceman: Blood Chill	Spec	VR	3.80
Iceman: Frostbite	Spec	R	1.00
Iceman: Hail Storm	Spec	U	0.50
Iceman: Ice Armor	Spec	VR	2.80
Iceman: Snow Blind	Spec	R	1.00
Iceman: Sub-Zero	Spec	VR	3.00
Invisible Woman: Invisible Saboteur	Spec	U	0.50
Iron Man: Industrial Waste	Spec	R	2.50
Jean Grey: Mutant Motivation	Spec	U	0.50
Jubilee: Prismatic Flare	Spec	VR	3.80
Juggernaut	Char	VR	2.80
Juggernaut: Battering Ram	Spec	VR	4.00
Juggernaut: Head Butt	Spec	U	0.80
Juggernaut: Ignore Blow	Spec	R	1.00
Juggernaut: Raze	Spec	U	0.80
Juggernaut: Smash Incoming Object	Spec	VR	2.80
Juggernaut: Unstoppable Force	Spec	VR	2.80
Lamp Post	Univ	U	0.80
Laser Pistol	Univ	R	0.90
Longshot	Char	VR	2.80
Longshot: Four-Fingered Fury	Spec	VR	2.80
Longshot: Freedom Fighter	Spec	U	0.50
Longshot: Hollow Bones	Spec	VR	2.80
Longshot: Lucky Bounce	Spec	VR	2.80

RARITY KEY C = Common U = Uncommon R = Rare VR = Very Rare UR = Ultra Rare F = Foil card X = Fixed/standard in all decks

Card name	Type	Rarity	Price
Longshot: One In A Million	Spec	VR	2.80
Longshot: Roll With The Punches	Spec	R	1.00
Machine Gun	Univ	R	0.90
Magneto: Power Flux	Spec	R	1.80
Mandarin	Char	VR	3.30
Mandarin: Arch Villain	Spec	VR	2.80
Mandarin: Disintegrate	Spec	VR	2.80
Mandarin: Electromagnetic Shield	Spec	U	0.50
Mandarin: Mastermind	Spec	VR	2.80
Mandarin: Mind Control	Spec	VR	2.90
Mandarin: Vortex Beam	Spec	R	1.80
Manhole Cover	Univ	U	0.80
Mojo	Char	VR	2.80
Mojo: Bodyguard	Spec	VR	3.00
Mojo: It's A Rap	Spec	U	0.50
Mojo: Prime Time	Spec	VR	3.30
Mojo: Rewrite Script	Spec	VR	2.80
Mojo: Spineless Plot	Spec	VR	2.80
Mojo: Supreme Edits	Spec	R	1.00
Mr. Fantastic: Object Bounce	Spec	U	0.50
Mr. Sinister	Char	VR	2.80
Mr. Sinister: Backstab	Spec	R	1.80
Mr. Sinister: Hidden Agenda	Spec	VR	2.80
Mr. Sinister: Inside Information	Spec	R	2.50
Mr. Sinister: Malleable Maneuver	Spec	VR	2.80
Mr. Sinister: Merciless Mutant	Spec	U	0.50
Mr. Sinister: Power Scheme	Spec	R	1.30
Multipower 1	Pwr	C	0.10
Multipower 2	Pwr	U	0.80
Multipower 3	Pwr	R	1.30
Multipower 4	Pwr	VR	1.80
Mysterio	Char	VR	2.80
Mysterio: Alter Perception	Spec	VR	3.30
Mysterio: Hollywood Horror	Spec	VR	2.80
Mysterio: Mist And Mirrors	Spec	U	0.50
Mysterio: Now You See It …	Spec	VR	3.50
Mysterio: Poison Props	Spec	VR	2.80
Mysterio: Stuntman	Spec	VR	3.00
Mystique: Mistaken Identity	Spec	R	1.30
Namor	Char	R	1.80

Card name	Type	Rarity	Price
Namor: Atlantis Attacks	Spec	U	0.50
Namor: Bounty Of The Sea	Spec	VR	3.50
Namor: Imperious Rex	Spec	VR	4.00
Namor: Land, Sea, And Air	Spec	VR	2.80
Namor: Watery Grave	Spec	VR	2.80
Namor: Winged Feet	Spec	U	0.50
Omega Red: Secrete Pheromones	Spec	VR	3.50
Power Cosmic	Univ	U	0.40
Power Lines	Univ	U	0.40
Professor X: Read Mind	Spec	R	1.30
Psylocke: Illusion	Spec	U	0.80
Punisher: Flame Thrower	Spec	R	1.00
Rhino: Scare Tactics	Spec	R	1.00
Rocket Launcher	Univ	C	0.10
Rogue: Mutant Missile	Spec	R	2.00
Sabretooth: Rabid Beast	Spec	U	0.50
Scarlet Spider	Char	VR	3.30
Scarlet Spider: Arachnid Gizmos	Spec	R	1.30
Scarlet Spider: Hidden Pouches	Spec	VR	2.80
Scarlet Spider: Impact Webbing	Spec	VR	3.30
Scarlet Spider: New Warrior	Spec	U	0.50
Scarlet Spider: Spider Web	Spec	VR	2.80
Scarlet Spider: Sticky Fingers	Spec	VR	3.00
Scarlet Witch	Char	VR	2.80
Scarlet Witch: Change Outcome	Spec	VR	2.80
Scarlet Witch: Hex Power	Spec	VR	4.00
Scarlet Witch: Mutant Magic	Spec	R	1.00
Scarlet Witch: Sorceress Slam	Spec	R	1.80
Scarlet Witch: Spell Of Destruction	Spec	U	0.50
Scarlet Witch: Spontaneous Combustion	Spec	VR	2.90
Separation Anxiety 1	Miss	C	0.10
Separation Anxiety 2	Miss	C	0.10
Separation Anxiety 3	Miss	C	0.10
Separation Anxiety 4	Miss	C	0.10
Separation Anxiety 5	Miss	C	0.10
Separation Anxiety 6	Miss	C	0.10
Separation Anxiety 7	Miss	C	0.10
She Hulk	Char	R	1.50

Card name	Type	Rarity	Price
She Hulk: Elbow Grease	Spec	VR	2.80
She Hulk: Emerald Allure	Spec	U	0.50
She Hulk: Gamma Girl	Spec	R	2.50
She Hulk: Power Proxy	Spec	U	0.50
She Hulk: She-Hulk Smash	Spec	VR	2.80
She Hulk: Vitamin "G"	Spec	R	1.00
Silver Sable	Char	VR	2.80
Silver Sable: Chia	Spec	U	0.60
Silver Sable: Hidden Weapon	Spec	VR	3.00
Silver Sable: Katana	Spec	R	1.00
Silver Sable: Kevlar	Spec	VR	2.80
Silver Sable: Leadership	Spec	U	0.60
Silver Sable: One With The Sword	Spec	R	1.00
Silver Surfer: Double Power Blast	Spec	R	1.00
Sins of the Future 1	Miss	C	0.10
Sins of the Future 2	Miss	C	0.10
Sins of the Future 3	Miss	C	0.10
Sins of the Future 4	Miss	C	0.10
Sins of the Future 5	Miss	C	0.10
Sins of the Future 6	Miss	C	0.10
Sins of the Future 7	Miss	C	0.10
Spider-Man: Taunt	Spec	R	1.00
Spider-Woman: Psionic Attack	Spec	R	2.00
Storm: Weather Manipulation	Spec	R	1.00
Strength 1	Pwr	C	0.10
Strength 2	Pwr	C	0.10
Strength 3	Pwr	C	0.10
Strength 4	Pwr	C	0.10
Strength 5	Pwr	C	0.10
Strength 6	Pwr	C	0.10
Strength 7	Pwr	U	0.60
Strength 8	Pwr	U	0.60
Strong Guy	Char	VR	2.80
Strong Guy: Fit Of Laughter	Spec	R	1.00
Strong Guy: Kinetic Absorption	Spec	U	0.50
Strong Guy: Knuckle Sandwich	Spec	U	0.50
Strong Guy: Mighty Mutant	Spec	VR	2.80
Strong Guy: Pile It On	Spec	VR	3.00
Strong Guy: Rock & Roll	Spec	VR	2.80
Super Skrull	Char	VR	2.80
Super Skrull: Alien Fire	Spec	R	2.50
Super Skrull: Fists of Stone	Spec	VR	2.00
Super Skrull: Flexible Form	Spec	VR	2.80
Super Skrull: Imitation	Spec	VR	2.80
Super Skrull: Invisible Invasion	Spec	R	2.00
Super Skrull: Skrull And Crossbones	Spec	VR	2.80
Sword	Univ	U	0.40
Taxi Cab	Univ	R	2.00
Teamwork (6 Energy to Use)	Univ	R	1.30
Teamwork (6 Fighting to Use)	Univ	R	1.30
Teamwork (6 Strength to Use)	Univ	U	0.80
Teamwork (7 Energy to Use)	Univ	U	0.90
Teamwork (7 Fighting to Use)	Univ	R	1.30
Teamwork (7 Strength to Use)	Univ	R	1.10
Teamwork (8 Energy to Use)	Univ	R	1.30
Teamwork (8 Fighting to Use)	Univ	R	1.30
Teamwork (8 Strength to Use)	Univ	R	1.10
Thing: Brute Force	Spec	U	0.50
Thor: Airborne Avenger	Spec	U	0.80
Throwing Blades	Univ	C	0.10
Training (E & F, 5 or less, +3)	Univ	U	0.80
Training (E & F, 5 or less, +4)	Univ	R	0.90
Training (E & S, 5 or less, +3)	Univ	U	0.60
Training (E & S, 5 or less, +4)	Univ	R	0.90
Training (F & S, 5 or less, +3)	Univ	U	0.80
Training (F & S, 5 or less, +4)	Univ	R	1.30
Tree	Univ	U	0.50
Venom: Alien Symbiote	Spec	R	1.00
War Machine: Shield Teammate	Spec	U	0.60
Wolverine: Rage	Spec	U	0.50

OverPower • Promo cards

Card name	Price
Any Character: Arkham Asylum	3.00
Any Character: Deal with the Devil	6.00
Any Character: Justice League	3.00
Any Character: The Bat Cave	3.00
Any Character: The Fortress of Solitude	3.00
Any Character: Urban Hunters	3.00
Any Hero: Alien Symbiote	4.00
Any Hero: Confusion	4.50
Any Hero: Death from Above	3.50
Any Hero: Gamma Terror	3.50
Any Hero: God of Mischief	3.50
Any Hero: Guardian Angel	3.50
Any Hero: Savage Land	4.50
Any Hero: Unlucky at Love	3.50
Any Hero: Web-Headed Wizard	4.00
Assault On Onslaught: Do Or Die!	3.00
Assault On Onslaught: Fighting Spirit Lives!	3.00

Card name	Price
Assault On Onslaught: Helping Hands	3.00
Assault On Onslaught: On The Move	3.00
Assault On Onslaught: Spy Discovered!	3.00
Assault On Onslaught 1	2.50
Assault On Onslaught 2	2.50
Assault On Onslaught 3	2.50
Assault On Onslaught 4	2.50
Assault On Onslaught 5	2.50
Assault On Onslaught 6	2.50
Assault On Onslaught 7	2.50
Beyonder	3.00
Captain Universe	2.50
Carnage: Combat Chaos	4.00
Daemonite Voodoo	3.00
Dark Beast	3.00
Doppelganger	3.50
Doctor Octopus: Killer Crush	4.00
Future Backlash	3.00
Galactus	3.00
Hobgoblin: Frightening Visage	4.00
Holocaust	4.50
Holocaust: Apocalyptic Minion	2.50
Holocaust: Consume Lifeforce	2.50

Card name	Price
Holocaust: Death Cannon	2.50
Holocaust: Devastate	2.50
Holocaust: Impervious Crystal	2.50
Holocaust: Otherwordly Evil	2.50
Mysterio Misdirection	4.00
Onslaught	4.50
Onslaught: Baptism Of Fire	3.50
Onslaught: Dark Enigma	2.50
Onslaught: Merciless Conqueror	2.50
Onslaught: Mutant Gestalt	2.50
Onslaught: Psychic Absorption	2.50
Onslaught: Raw Power	3.50
Post	3.50
Post: Gather Info	2.50
Post: Herald Of Onslaught	2.50
Post: Lethal Tester	2.50
Post: Obfuscate	2.50
Post: Protective Plates	2.50
Post: Strategic Assault	2.50
Rhino: Stampede	4.00
Scarlet Spider: Scarlet Savior	4.00
Spider Man: Over the Edge	4.00
Team X	3.00
Venom	4.00
Wynonna Earp	3.00

RARITY KEY C = Common U = Uncommon R = Rare VR = Very Rare UR = Ultra Rare F = Foil card X = Fixed/standard in all decks

OverPower • Mission Control

Fleer/Skybox • Released **April 1996**

At least **146** cards in set • **IDENTIFIER: Circuit board background; © 1996**

• Booster packs contain 9 cards; booster displays contain 36 boosters

Mission and event cards are this set's major contribution; a square-cornered mission card appears in every booster pack. **Mission Control** commemorates both well-remembered Marvel storylines, such as the classic "Dark Phoenix" saga, as well as its later crossover "events," such as the painful "Maxiumum Carnage." — **John Jackson Miller**

SCRYE NOTES: *We've found four different Adam Warlock cards in **Mission Control** packs that aren't part of the "official" list. They're listed at the end, below.*

Set (146 cards)	26.50
Booster Display Box	13.50
Booster Pack	1.00

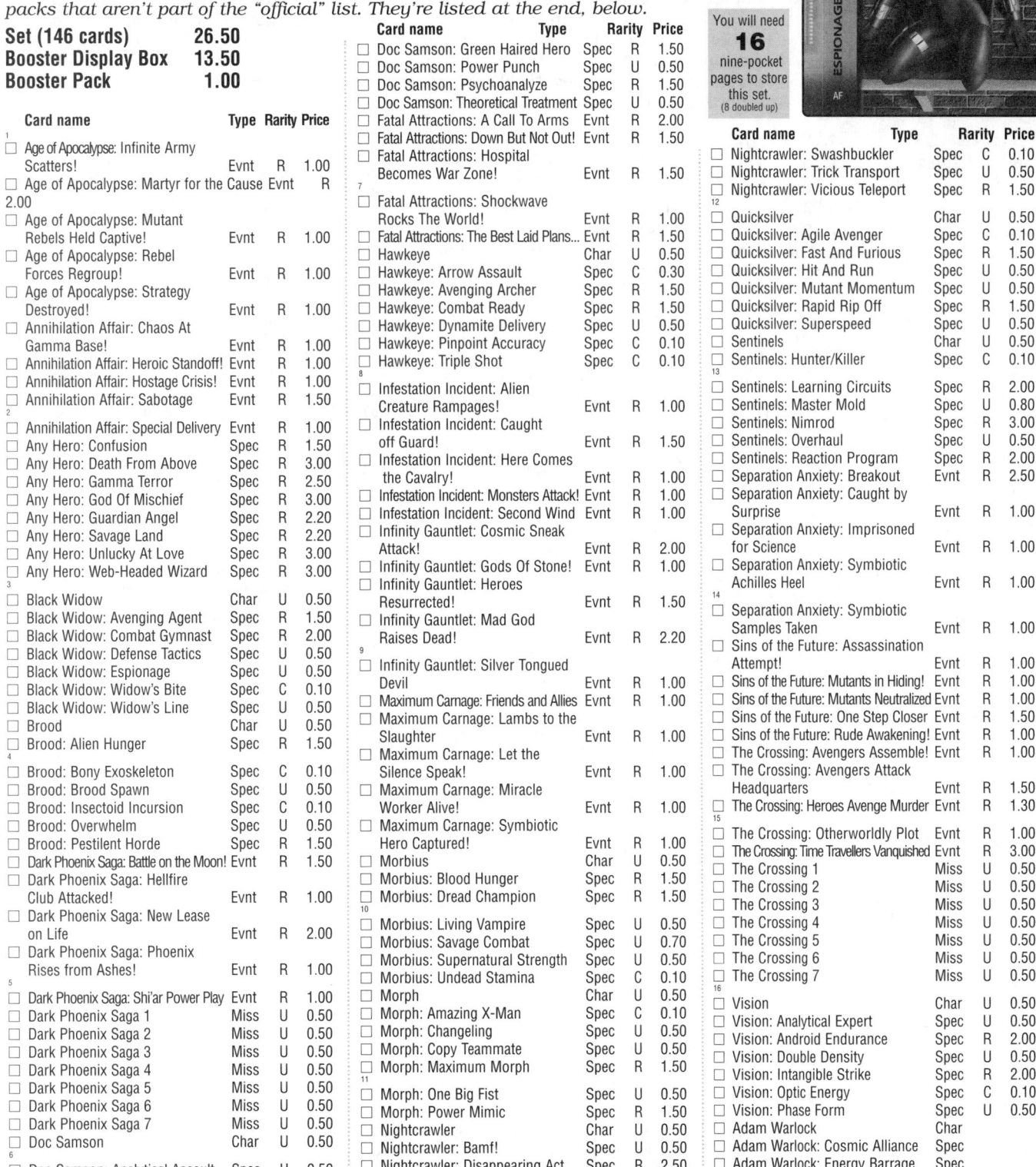

You will need **16** *nine-pocket pages to store this set. (8 doubled up)*

Card name	Type	Rarity	Price
☐ Age of Apocalypse: Infinite Army Scatters!	Evnt	R	1.00
☐ Age of Apocalypse: Martyr for the Cause	Evnt	R	2.00
☐ Age of Apocalypse: Mutant Rebels Held Captive!	Evnt	R	1.00
☐ Age of Apocalypse: Rebel Forces Regroup!	Evnt	R	1.00
☐ Age of Apocalypse: Strategy Destroyed!	Evnt	R	1.00
☐ Annihilation Affair: Chaos At Gamma Base!	Evnt	R	1.00
☐ Annihilation Affair: Heroic Standoff!	Evnt	R	1.00
☐ Annihilation Affair: Hostage Crisis!	Evnt	R	1.00
☐ Annihilation Affair: Sabotage	Evnt	R	1.50
☐ Annihilation Affair: Special Delivery	Evnt	R	1.00
☐ Any Hero: Confusion	Spec	R	1.50
☐ Any Hero: Death From Above	Spec	R	3.00
☐ Any Hero: Gamma Terror	Spec	R	2.50
☐ Any Hero: God Of Mischief	Spec	R	3.00
☐ Any Hero: Guardian Angel	Spec	R	2.20
☐ Any Hero: Savage Land	Spec	R	2.20
☐ Any Hero: Unlucky At Love	Spec	R	3.00
☐ Any Hero: Web-Headed Wizard	Spec	R	3.00
☐ Black Widow	Char	U	0.50
☐ Black Widow: Avenging Agent	Spec	R	1.50
☐ Black Widow: Combat Gymnast	Spec	R	2.00
☐ Black Widow: Defense Tactics	Spec	U	0.50
☐ Black Widow: Espionage	Spec	U	0.50
☐ Black Widow: Widow's Bite	Spec	C	0.10
☐ Black Widow: Widow's Line	Spec	U	0.50
☐ Brood	Char	U	0.50
☐ Brood: Alien Hunger	Spec	R	1.50
☐ Brood: Bony Exoskeleton	Spec	C	0.10
☐ Brood: Brood Spawn	Spec	U	0.50
☐ Brood: Insectoid Incursion	Spec	C	0.10
☐ Brood: Overwhelm	Spec	U	0.50
☐ Brood: Pestilent Horde	Spec	R	1.50
☐ Dark Phoenix Saga: Battle on the Moon!	Evnt	R	1.50
☐ Dark Phoenix Saga: Hellfire Club Attacked!	Evnt	R	1.00
☐ Dark Phoenix Saga: New Lease on Life	Evnt	R	2.00
☐ Dark Phoenix Saga: Phoenix Rises from Ashes!	Evnt	R	1.00
☐ Dark Phoenix Saga: Shi'ar Power Play	Evnt	R	1.00
☐ Dark Phoenix Saga 1	Miss	U	0.50
☐ Dark Phoenix Saga 2	Miss	U	0.50
☐ Dark Phoenix Saga 3	Miss	U	0.50
☐ Dark Phoenix Saga 4	Miss	U	0.50
☐ Dark Phoenix Saga 5	Miss	U	0.50
☐ Dark Phoenix Saga 6	Miss	U	0.50
☐ Dark Phoenix Saga 7	Miss	U	0.50
☐ Doc Samson	Char	U	0.50
☐ Doc Samson: Analytical Assault	Spec	U	0.50
☐ Doc Samson: Gamma Muscle	Spec	C	0.10

Card name	Type	Rarity	Price
☐ Doc Samson: Green Haired Hero	Spec	R	1.50
☐ Doc Samson: Power Punch	Spec	U	0.50
☐ Doc Samson: Psychoanalyze	Spec	R	1.50
☐ Doc Samson: Theoretical Treatment	Spec	U	0.50
☐ Fatal Attractions: A Call To Arms	Evnt	R	2.00
☐ Fatal Attractions: Down But Not Out!	Evnt	R	1.50
☐ Fatal Attractions: Hospital Becomes War Zone!	Evnt	R	1.50
☐ Fatal Attractions: Shockwave Rocks The World!	Evnt	R	1.00
☐ Fatal Attractions: The Best Laid Plans...	Evnt	R	1.50
☐ Hawkeye	Char	U	0.50
☐ Hawkeye: Arrow Assault	Spec	C	0.30
☐ Hawkeye: Avenging Archer	Spec	R	1.50
☐ Hawkeye: Combat Ready	Spec	R	1.50
☐ Hawkeye: Dynamite Delivery	Spec	U	0.50
☐ Hawkeye: Pinpoint Accuracy	Spec	C	0.10
☐ Hawkeye: Triple Shot	Spec	C	0.10
☐ Infestation Incident: Alien Creature Rampages!	Evnt	R	1.00
☐ Infestation Incident: Caught off Guard!	Evnt	R	1.50
☐ Infestation Incident: Here Comes the Cavalry!	Evnt	R	1.00
☐ Infestation Incident: Monsters Attack!	Evnt	R	1.00
☐ Infestation Incident: Second Wind	Evnt	R	1.00
☐ Infinity Gauntlet: Cosmic Sneak Attack!	Evnt	R	2.00
☐ Infinity Gauntlet: Gods Of Stone!	Evnt	R	1.00
☐ Infinity Gauntlet: Heroes Resurrected!	Evnt	R	1.50
☐ Infinity Gauntlet: Mad God Raises Dead!	Evnt	R	2.20
☐ Infinity Gauntlet: Silver Tongued Devil	Evnt	R	1.00
☐ Maximum Carnage: Friends and Allies	Evnt	R	1.00
☐ Maximum Carnage: Lambs to the Slaughter	Evnt	R	1.00
☐ Maximum Carnage: Let the Silence Speak!	Evnt	R	1.00
☐ Maximum Carnage: Miracle Worker Alive!	Evnt	R	1.00
☐ Maximum Carnage: Symbiotic Hero Captured!	Evnt	R	1.00
☐ Morbius	Char	U	0.50
☐ Morbius: Blood Hunger	Spec	R	1.50
☐ Morbius: Dread Champion	Spec	R	1.50
☐ Morbius: Living Vampire	Spec	U	0.50
☐ Morbius: Savage Combat	Spec	U	0.70
☐ Morbius: Supernatural Strength	Spec	U	0.50
☐ Morbius: Undead Stamina	Spec	C	0.10
☐ Morph	Char	U	0.50
☐ Morph: Amazing X-Man	Spec	C	0.10
☐ Morph: Changeling	Spec	U	0.50
☐ Morph: Copy Teammate	Spec	U	0.50
☐ Morph: Maximum Morph	Spec	R	1.50
☐ Morph: One Big Fist	Spec	U	0.50
☐ Morph: Power Mimic	Spec	R	1.50
☐ Nightcrawler	Char	U	0.50
☐ Nightcrawler: Bamf!	Spec	U	0.50
☐ Nightcrawler: Disappearing Act	Spec	R	2.50
☐ Nightcrawler: Prehensile Tail	Spec	C	0.10

Card name	Type	Rarity	Price
☐ Nightcrawler: Swashbuckler	Spec	C	0.10
☐ Nightcrawler: Trick Transport	Spec	U	0.50
☐ Nightcrawler: Vicious Teleport	Spec	R	1.50
☐ Quicksilver	Char	U	0.50
☐ Quicksilver: Agile Avenger	Spec	C	0.10
☐ Quicksilver: Fast And Furious	Spec	R	1.50
☐ Quicksilver: Hit And Run	Spec	U	0.50
☐ Quicksilver: Mutant Momentum	Spec	U	0.50
☐ Quicksilver: Rapid Rip Off	Spec	R	1.50
☐ Quicksilver: Superspeed	Spec	U	0.50
☐ Sentinels	Char	U	0.50
☐ Sentinels: Hunter/Killer	Spec	C	0.10
☐ Sentinels: Learning Circuits	Spec	R	2.00
☐ Sentinels: Master Mold	Spec	U	0.80
☐ Sentinels: Nimrod	Spec	R	3.00
☐ Sentinels: Overhaul	Spec	U	0.50
☐ Sentinels: Reaction Program	Spec	R	2.00
☐ Separation Anxiety: Breakout	Evnt	R	2.50
☐ Separation Anxiety: Caught by Surprise	Evnt	R	1.00
☐ Separation Anxiety: Imprisoned for Science	Evnt	R	1.00
☐ Separation Anxiety: Symbiotic Achilles Heel	Evnt	R	1.00
☐ Separation Anxiety: Symbiotic Samples Taken	Evnt	R	1.00
☐ Sins of the Future: Assassination Attempt!	Evnt	R	1.00
☐ Sins of the Future: Mutants in Hiding!	Evnt	R	1.00
☐ Sins of the Future: Mutants Neutralized	Evnt	R	1.00
☐ Sins of the Future: One Step Closer	Evnt	R	1.50
☐ Sins of the Future: Rude Awakening!	Evnt	R	1.00
☐ The Crossing: Avengers Assemble!	Evnt	R	1.00
☐ The Crossing: Avengers Attack Headquarters	Evnt	R	1.50
☐ The Crossing: Heroes Avenge Murder	Evnt	R	1.30
☐ The Crossing: Otherworldly Plot	Evnt	R	1.00
☐ The Crossing: Time Travellers Vanquished	Evnt	R	3.00
☐ The Crossing 1	Miss	U	0.50
☐ The Crossing 2	Miss	U	0.50
☐ The Crossing 3	Miss	U	0.50
☐ The Crossing 4	Miss	U	0.50
☐ The Crossing 5	Miss	U	0.50
☐ The Crossing 6	Miss	U	0.50
☐ The Crossing 7	Miss	U	0.50
☐ Vision	Char	U	0.50
☐ Vision: Analytical Expert	Spec	U	0.50
☐ Vision: Android Endurance	Spec	R	2.00
☐ Vision: Double Density	Spec	U	0.50
☐ Vision: Intangible Strike	Spec	R	2.00
☐ Vision: Optic Energy	Spec	C	0.10
☐ Vision: Phase Form	Spec	U	0.50
☐ Adam Warlock	Char		
☐ Adam Warlock: Cosmic Alliance	Spec		
☐ Adam Warlock: Energy Barrage	Spec		
☐ Adam Warlock: Soul Gem	Spec		

RARITY KEY C = Common U = Uncommon R = Rare VR = Very Rare UR = Ultra Rare F = Foil card X = Fixed/standard in all decks

OverPower • DC (a.k.a. *Batman/Superman*)

Fleer/Skybox • Released **October 1996**
334 cards in set • **IDENTIFIER:** © 1996

- Starter decks contain 69 cards; starter displays contain 12 starters
- Booster packs contain 9 cards; booster displays contain 36 boosters

Similar to its Marvel counterpart in all but mythos, **DC OverPower** uses characters from Marvel's "distinguished competition," DC Comics. Card backs are different, but play is identical — and enhanced, as the DC version adds a fourth trait, Intellect.

The addition of the new cards and fourth trait much enlivened play, and players (with opaque-backed card sleeves) used DC and Marvel cards interchangeably, enjoying the thought of super-hero teams combining Spider-Man, Batman, Hulk, and Superman.

The box label actually reads "DC Batman Superman," perhaps as an aid to the mass-market buyer. As Marvel and DC had found out in publicizing their "DC vs. Marvel" crossover in early 1996, few "civilians" know which characters belong to which company.

— *John Jackson Miller & Orren McKay*

Set (334 cards)	61.00
Starter Display Box	21.25
Booster Display Box	17.50
Starter Deck	5.00
Booster Pack	1.30

You will need 38 nine-pocket pages to store this set. (19 doubled up)

Card name	Type	Rarity	Price
1			
Ally (5 Energy or Less)	Univ	C	0.10
Ally (5 Fighting or Less)	Univ	U	0.50
Ally (5 Intellect or Less)	Univ	U	0.50
Ally (5 Strength or Less)	Univ	U	0.50
Ally (6 Energy or More)	Univ	C	0.10
Ally (6 Intellect or More)	Univ	C	0.10
Ally (7 Energy or More)	Univ	C	0.10
Ally (7 Fighting or More)	Univ	C	0.10
Ally (7 Intellect or More)	Univ	C	0.10
2			
Ally (7 Strength or More)	Univ	C	0.10
Azrael	Char	VR	5.00
Azrael: Avenging Angel	Spec	U	0.50
Azrael: Battle Armor	Spec	C	0.10
Azrael: Divine Inspiration	Spec	R	2.00
Azrael: Flaming Sword	Spec	R	2.00
Azrael: The System	Spec	VR	4.80
Bane	Char	VR	5.00
Bane: Enhanced Physique	Spec	R	2.00
3			
Bane: Feral Rage	Spec	U	0.50
Bane: Intimidation	Spec	U	0.50
Bane: Vengeance Of Bane	Spec	R	2.30
Bane: Venom Injection	Spec	VR	5.00
Basic (6 Energy to Use +1)	Univ	C	0.10
Basic (6 Energy to Use +2)	Univ	C	0.10
Basic (6 Energy to Use +3)	Univ	U	0.50
Basic (6 Fighting to Use +1)	Univ	C	0.10
Basic (6 Fighting to Use +2)	Univ	C	0.10
4			
Basic (6 Fighting to Use +3)	Univ	U	0.50
Basic (6 Intellect to Use +1)	Univ	C	0.10
Basic (6 Intellect to Use +2)	Univ	C	0.10
Basic (6 Intellect to Use +3)	Univ	U	0.50
Basic (6 Strength to Use +1)	Univ	C	0.10
Basic (6 Strength to Use +2)	Univ	C	0.10
Basic (6 Strength to Use +3)	Univ	U	0.50
Basic (7 Energy to Use +1)	Univ	C	0.10
Basic (7 Energy to Use +2)	Univ	C	0.10
5			
Basic (7 Energy to Use +3)	Univ	U	0.50
Basic (7 Fighting to Use +1)	Univ	C	0.10
Basic (7 Fighting to Use +2)	Univ	C	0.10
Basic (7 Fighting to Use +3)	Univ	U	0.50
Basic (7 Intellect to Use +1)	Univ	C	0.10
Basic (7 Intellect to Use +2)	Univ	C	0.10
Basic (7 Intellect to Use +3)	Univ	U	0.50
Basic (7 Strength to Use +1)	Univ	C	0.10
Basic (7 Strength to Use +2)	Univ	C	0.10
6			
Basic (7 Strength to Use +3)	Univ	U	0.50

Card name	Type	Rarity	Price
Basic (8 Energy to Use +1)	Univ	C	0.10
Basic (8 Energy to Use +2)	Univ	C	0.10
Basic (8 Energy to Use +3)	Univ	U	0.60
Basic (8 Fighting to Use +1)	Univ	C	0.10
Basic (8 Fighting to Use +2)	Univ	C	0.10
Basic (8 Fighting to Use +3)	Univ	U	0.60
Basic (8 Intellect to Use +1)	Univ	C	0.10
Basic (8 Intellect to Use +2)	Univ	C	0.10
7			
Basic (8 Intellect to Use +3)	Univ	U	0.60
Basic (8 Strength to Use +1)	Univ	C	0.10
Basic (8 Strength to Use +2)	Univ	C	0.10
Basic (8 Strength to Use +3)	Univ	U	0.60
Batman	Char	R	5.00
Batman: Batarang	Spec	U	0.50
Batman: Magnesium Flare	Spec	U	0.50
Batman: Martial Arts Expert	Spec	VR	5.00
Batman: Master Detective	Spec	R	2.80
8			
Batman: Olympic Level Athlete	Spec	R	2.00
Brainiac	Char	VR	5.50
Brainiac: Force Field	Spec	R	2.30
Brainiac: Force Of Mind	Spec	C	0.10
Brainiac: Lord Of Warworld	Spec	R	2.30
Brainiac: Mental Control	Spec	VR	4.50
Brainiac: Mental Illusions	Spec	U	0.50
Catwoman	Char	R	2.30
Catwoman: Cat-Like Reflexes	Spec	U	0.50
9			
Catwoman: Cunning Thief	Spec	VR	5.00
Catwoman: Nine Lives	Spec	U	0.50
Catwoman: Razor Sharp Claws	Spec	R	2.30
Catwoman: Whip Strike	Spec	R	2.00
Comm Gordon And The GCPD	Char	U	0.80
Comm Gordon And The GCPD: Reinforcements	Spec	U	0.80
Comm Gordon And The GCPD: Riot Gear	Spec	R	2.00
Comm Gordon And The GCPD: Sting Operation	Spec	VR	5.00
Comm Gordon And The GCPD: Swat Team	Spec	VR	4.50
10			
Comm Gordon And The GCPD: Tear Gas Guns	Spec	R	2.00
Cyborg	Char	R	2.30
Cyborg: Cold-Blooded Killer	Spec	R	2.00
Cyborg: Doom From Above	Spec	VR	4.50
Cyborg: Laser Vision	Spec	U	0.50
Cyborg: Mechanical Metamorph	Spec	VR	5.00
Cyborg: Regeneration	Spec	R	2.00
Doomsday	Char	VR	5.00
Doomsday: Bony Protrusions	Spec	R	2.30
11			
Doomsday: Irresistible Force	Spec	R	2.00
Doomsday: Out For Blood	Spec	U	0.50
Doomsday: Tough Hide	Spec	C	0.10
Doomsday: Unearthly Strength	Spec	VR	4.50

Card name	Type	Rarity	Price
Energy 1	Pwr	C	0.10
Energy 2	Pwr	C	0.10
Energy 3	Pwr	C	0.10
Energy 4	Pwr	C	0.10
Energy 5	Pwr	U	0.50
12			
Energy 6	Pwr	U	0.50
Energy 7	Pwr	R	3.50
Energy 8	Pwr	VR	4.00
Eradicator	Char	U	0.80
Eradicator: Airborne Assault	Spec	U	0.50
Eradicator: Energy Blast	Spec	R	2.00
Eradicator: Power Punch	Spec	VR	5.00
Eradicator: Self Healing	Spec	R	2.00
Eradicator: Vengeful Protector	Spec	C	0.10
13			
Eye Of The Storm 1	Miss	C	0.10
Eye Of The Storm 2	Miss	C	0.10
Eye Of The Storm 3	Miss	C	0.10
Eye Of The Storm 4	Miss	C	0.10
Eye Of The Storm 5	Miss	C	0.10
Eye Of The Storm 6	Miss	C	0.10
Eye Of The Storm 7	Miss	C	0.10
Eye Of The Storm File 061906.01	Evnt	C	0.10
Eye Of The Storm File 061906.02	Evnt	C	0.10
14			
Eye Of The Storm File 061906.05	Evnt	C	0.10
Eye Of The Storm File 061906.08	Evnt	C	0.10
Eye Of The Storm File 061906.10	Evnt	C	0.10
Fighting 1	Pwr	C	0.10
Fighting 2	Pwr	C	0.10
Fighting 3	Pwr	C	0.10
Fighting 4	Pwr	C	0.10
Fighting 5	Pwr	U	0.50
Fighting 6	Pwr	U	0.50
15			
Fighting 7	Pwr	R	3.00
Fighting 8	Pwr	VR	4.00
Hazard	Char	U	0.80
Hazard: Cutting Laser	Spec	R	2.00
Hazard: Cybernetic Strength	Spec	R	2.00
Hazard: Flight Pack	Spec	C	0.10
Hazard: Split	Spec	U	0.50
Hazard: Telekinetic Fist	Spec	VR	5.00
Huntress	Char	R	2.30
16			
Huntress: Crossbow	Spec	U	0.60
Huntress: Expert Tracker	Spec	R	2.50
Huntress: Sneak Attack	Spec	VR	4.80
Huntress: Throwing Knives	Spec	U	0.50
Huntress: Trained Gymnast	Spec	R	2.30
Intellect 1	Pwr	C	0.10
Intellect 2	Pwr	C	0.10
Intellect 3	Pwr	C	0.10
Intellect 4	Pwr	C	0.10
17			
Intellect 5	Pwr	U	0.50
Intellect 6	Pwr	U	0.50

RARITY KEY C = Common U = Uncommon R = Rare VR = Very Rare UR = Ultra Rare F = Foil card X = Fixed/standard in all decks

Card name	Type	Rarity	Price
☐ Intellect 7	Pwr	R	3.00
☐ Intellect 8	Pwr	VR	4.00
☐ Into The Depths 1	Miss	C	0.10
☐ Into The Depths 2	Miss	C	0.10
☐ Into The Depths 3	Miss	C	0.10
☐ Into The Depths 4	Miss	C	0.10
☐ Into The Depths 5	Miss	C	0.10

18

Card name	Type	Rarity	Price
☐ Into The Depths 6	Miss	C	0.10
☐ Into The Depths 7	Miss	C	0.10
☐ Into The Depths File 271266.02	Evnt	C	0.10
☐ Into The Depths File 271266.04	Evnt	C	0.10
☐ Into The Depths File 271266.07	Evnt	C	0.10
☐ Into The Depths File 271266.09	Evnt	C	0.10
☐ Into The Depths File 271266.10	Evnt	C	0.10
☐ Joker	Char	R	3.00
☐ Joker: Acid Spray Flower	Spec	R	2.00

19

Card name	Type	Rarity	Price
☐ Joker: Double Cross	Spec	U	0.50
☐ Joker: High Voltage Joy Buzzer	Spec	R	2.00
☐ Joker: Joker Venom	Spec	VR	5.00
☐ Joker: Maniacal Genius	Spec	C	0.10
☐ Killer Croc	Char	U	0.80
☐ Killer Croc: Brute Force	Spec	R	2.00
☐ Killer Croc: Rampage	Spec	U	0.50
☐ Killer Croc: Scaly Skin	Spec	U	0.50
☐ Killer Croc: Slippery Escape	Spec	R	2.00

20

Card name	Type	Rarity	Price
☐ Killer Croc: Wrestling Hold	Spec	VR	5.00
☐ Knockout	Char	U	0.80
☐ Knockout: Female Fury	Spec	U	0.50
☐ Knockout: Hot Tempered	Spec	R	2.00
☐ Knockout: Killer Physique	Spec	U	0.50
☐ Knockout: Mighty Blow	Spec	R	2.30
☐ Knockout: Picking A Fight	Spec	VR	5.00
☐ Lex Luthor	Char	U	0.80
☐ Lex Luthor: Global Resources	Spec	R	2.00

21

Card name	Type	Rarity	Price
☐ Lex Luthor: Power Hungry	Spec	C	0.10
☐ Lex Luthor: Prototype Blaster	Spec	R	2.30
☐ Lex Luthor: Ruthless Adversary	Spec	VR	5.00
☐ Lex Luthor: Skilled Martial Artist	Spec	U	0.50
☐ Metallo	Char	U	0.80
☐ Metallo: Damage Control	Spec	R	2.00
☐ Metallo: Eye Beams	Spec	VR	5.00
☐ Metallo: Mechanical Juggernaut	Spec	VR	4.50
☐ Metallo: Servo-Assisted Strength	Spec	C	0.10

22

Card name	Type	Rarity	Price
☐ Metallo: Walking Arsenal	Spec	U	0.50
☐ Metropolis SCU	Char	U	0.80
☐ Metropolis SCU: Battlesuit Brigade	Spec	R	2.00
☐ Metropolis SCU: Heavy Artillery	Spec	VR	4.80
☐ Metropolis SCU: Paramilitary Training	Spec	C	0.10
☐ Metropolis SCU: Sniper Fire	Spec	R	2.30
☐ Metropolis SCU: Stun Guns	Spec	U	0.50
☐ Might Over Mind 1	Miss	C	0.10
☐ Might Over Mind 2	Miss	C	0.10

23

Card name	Type	Rarity	Price
☐ Might Over Mind 3	Miss	C	0.10
☐ Might Over Mind 4	Miss	C	0.10
☐ Might Over Mind 5	Miss	C	0.10
☐ Might Over Mind 6	Miss	C	0.10
☐ Might Over Mind 7	Miss	C	0.10
☐ Might Over Mind File 179603.01	Evnt	C	0.10
☐ Might Over Mind File 179603.04	Evnt	C	0.10
☐ Might Over Mind File 179603.06	Evnt	C	0.10
☐ Might Over Mind File 179603.08	Evnt	C	0.10

24

Card name	Type	Rarity	Price
☐ Might Over Mind File 179603.11	Evnt	C	0.10
☐ Multipower 1	Pwr	U	0.50
☐ Multipower 2	Pwr	R	2.00
☐ Multipower 3	Pwr	VR	3.50
☐ Multipower 4	Pwr	VR	4.00
☐ Nightwing	Char	R	3.00
☐ Nightwing: Circus Acrobat	Spec	R	2.00

Card name	Type	Rarity	Price
☐ Nightwing: Escrima Sticks	Spec	U	0.50
☐ Nightwing: Expert Sleuth	Spec	U	0.50

25

Card name	Type	Rarity	Price
☐ Nightwing: Glider Wings	Spec	C	0.10
☐ Nightwing: Titans Founder	Spec	R	2.00
☐ Parasite	Char	U	0.80
☐ Parasite: Cellular Reconstruction	Spec	VR	4.50
☐ Parasite: Kinetic Absorption	Spec	U	0.50
☐ Parasite: Power Theft	Spec	R	2.30
☐ Parasite: Sucking The City Dry	Spec	U	0.50
☐ Parasite: Vitality Drain	Spec	R	2.00
☐ Penguin	Char	R	2.30

26

Card name	Type	Rarity	Price
☐ Penguin: Birds Of Prey	Spec	U	0.50
☐ Penguin: Feathery Distraction	Spec	VR	5.00
☐ Penguin: Flame Thrower Umbrella	Spec	U	0.50
☐ Penguin: Master Planner	Spec	R	2.00
☐ Penguin: Smoke Umbrella	Spec	R	2.00
☐ Poison Ivy	Char	R	2.30
☐ Poison Ivy: Master Manipulator	Spec	R	2.00
☐ Poison Ivy: Poison Kiss	Spec	VR	4.80
☐ Poison Ivy: Seductress	Spec	C	0.10

27

Card name	Type	Rarity	Price
☐ Poison Ivy: Strangle Vines	Spec	VR	4.80
☐ Poison Ivy: Venus Flytrap	Spec	U	0.50
☐ Ra's Al Ghul	Char	R	2.30
☐ Ra's Al Ghul: Demon's Head	Spec	U	0.50
☐ Ra's Al Ghul: Lazarus Pit	Spec	VR	4.50
☐ Ra's Al Ghul: Master Swordsman	Spec	U	0.50
☐ Ra's Al Ghul: Megalomaniac	Spec	R	2.80
☐ Ra's Al Ghul: Talia	Spec	R	3.00
☐ Race Against Crime 1	Miss	C	0.10

28

Card name	Type	Rarity	Price
☐ Race Against Crime 2	Miss	C	0.10
☐ Race Against Crime 3	Miss	C	0.10
☐ Race Against Crime 4	Miss	C	0.10
☐ Race Against Crime 5	Miss	C	0.10
☐ Race Against Crime 6	Miss	C	0.10
☐ Race Against Crime 7	Miss	C	0.10
☐ Race Against Crime File 661216.01	Evnt	C	0.10
☐ Race Against Crime File 661216.04	Evnt	C	0.10
☐ Race Against Crime File 661216.06	Evnt	C	0.10

29

Card name	Type	Rarity	Price
☐ Race Against Crime File 661216.09	Evnt	C	0.10
☐ Race Against Crime File 661216.10	Evnt	C	0.10
☐ Riddler	Char	R	2.30
☐ Riddler: Colt Revolver	Spec	U	0.50
☐ Riddler: Death Trap	Spec	R	2.30
☐ Riddler: Dirty Cheat	Spec	U	0.50
☐ Riddler: Master Of Misdirection	Spec	VR	4.50
☐ Riddler: Query And Echo	Spec	R	2.30
☐ Robin	Char	U	0.80

30

Card name	Type	Rarity	Price
☐ Robin: Bo Staff	Spec	R	2.00
☐ Robin: Expert Training	Spec	C	0.10
☐ Robin: Insignia Dart	Spec	R	2.00
☐ Robin: Loyal Partner	Spec	U	0.50
☐ Robin: Quick Thinking	Spec	VR	4.80
☐ Steel	Char	R	2.30
☐ Steel: Boot Jets	Spec	R	2.00
☐ Steel: Exo-Skeleton	Spec	U	0.50
☐ Steel: Hammer	Spec	VR	5.00

31

Card name	Type	Rarity	Price
☐ Steel: Human Shield	Spec	U	0.50
☐ Steel: Rivet Gun	Spec	R	2.00
☐ Strength 1	Pwr	C	0.10
☐ Strength 2	Pwr	C	0.10
☐ Strength 3	Pwr	C	0.10
☐ Strength 4	Pwr	C	0.10
☐ Strength 5	Pwr	U	0.50
☐ Strength 6	Pwr	U	0.50
☐ Strength 7	Pwr	R	3.00

32

Card name	Type	Rarity	Price
☐ Strength 8	Pwr	VR	4.00
☐ Superboy	Char	R	2.30
☐ Superboy: Cool Shades	Spec	R	2.00
☐ Superboy: Dubbilex	Spec	VR	4.80
☐ Superboy: Kid Of Steel	Spec	U	0.50
☐ Superboy: Tactile Telekinesis	Spec	R	2.00
☐ Superboy: Up, Up, And Away	Spec	U	0.50
☐ Supergirl	Char	R	2.30
☐ Supergirl: Cloaking Shield	Spec	R	2.00

33

Card name	Type	Rarity	Price
☐ Supergirl: Levitation	Spec	U	0.50
☐ Supergirl: Psychokinetic Bolt	Spec	U	0.50
☐ Supergirl: Shapeshift	Spec	VR	4.50
☐ Supergirl: Telekinetic Shield	Spec	R	2.00
☐ Superman	Char	R	3.00
☐ Superman: Defying Earth's Gravity	Spec	U	0.50
☐ Superman: Earth's Greatest Hero	Spec	R	2.00
☐ Superman: Heat Vision	Spec	U	0.50
☐ Superman: Last Son Of Krypton	Spec	VR	5.00

34

Card name	Type	Rarity	Price
☐ Superman: Man Of Steel	Spec	R	2.00
☐ Teamwork (6 Energy to Use)	Univ	U	0.50
☐ Teamwork (6 Fighting to Use)	Univ	U	0.50
☐ Teamwork (6 Intellect to Use)	Univ	U	0.50
☐ Teamwork (6 Strength to Use)	Univ	U	0.50
☐ Teamwork (7 Energy to Use)	Univ	R	2.00
☐ Teamwork (7 Fighting to Use)	Univ	R	2.30
☐ Teamwork (7 Intellect to Use)	Univ	R	2.00
☐ Teamwork (7 Strength to Use)	Univ	R	2.30

35

Card name	Type	Rarity	Price
☐ Teamwork (8 Energy to Use)	Univ	U	0.50
☐ Teamwork (8 Fighting to Use)	Univ	U	0.50
☐ Teamwork (8 Intellect to Use)	Univ	U	0.50
☐ Teamwork (8 Strength to Use)	Univ	U	0.50
☐ Thorn	Char	U	0.80
☐ Thorn: Barbed Lash	Spec	R	2.00
☐ Thorn: Battle Instinct	Spec	R	2.00
☐ Thorn: Combat Daggers	Spec	U	0.50
☐ Thorn: Explosive Charge	Spec	VR	4.50

36

Card name	Type	Rarity	Price
☐ Thorn: Street Fighter	Spec	C	0.10
☐ Training (5 E/F or Less +3)	Univ	C	0.10
☐ Training (5 E/F or Less +4)	Univ	U	0.50
☐ Training (5 E/I or Less +3)	Univ	C	0.10
☐ Training (5 E/I or Less +4)	Univ	U	0.50
☐ Training (5 E/S or Less +3)	Univ	C	0.10
☐ Training (5 E/S or Less +4)	Univ	U	0.50
☐ Training (5 F/I or Less +3)	Univ	C	0.10
☐ Training (5 F/I or Less +4)	Univ	U	0.50

37

Card name	Type	Rarity	Price
☐ Training (5 F/S or Less +3)	Univ	C	0.10
☐ Training (5 F/S or Less +4)	Univ	U	0.50
☐ Training (5 S/I or Less +3)	Univ	C	0.10
☐ Training (5 S/I or Less +4)	Univ	U	0.50
☐ Two-Face	Char	R	2.30
☐ Two-Face: .45 Automatic	Spec	R	2.30
☐ Two-Face: Criminal Mastermind	Spec	U	0.80
☐ Two-Face: Double Trouble	Spec	R	2.00
☐ Two-Face: Flip Of The Coin	Spec	U	0.50

38

Card name	Type	Rarity	Price
☐ Two-Face: Tommy Gun	Spec	VR	4.50

Marvel versus DC

"After *DC OverPower*, with its fourth trait, Intellect, hit the scene, many new strategies and a slew of dream-team decks came out of nowhere.

"Unfortunately, this set made the three-trait Marvel cards look feeble by comparison!"

— *Richard Weld*,
*writing in Scrye 8.2
(Feb/Mar 2001)*

RARITY KEY C = Common U = Uncommon R = Rare VR = Very Rare UR = Ultra Rare F = Foil card X = Fixed/standard in all decks

OverPower • IQ (a.k.a. Marvel IQ)

Fleer/SkyBox • Released **February 1997**

279 cards in set • **IDENTIFIER: Lighter yellow background; IQ symbols**

• Booster packs contain 15 cards; booster displays contain 36 boosters

Players generally consider **IQ** to be *the* **OverPower** expansion. With this set, cards in the Marvel game receive the fourth trait, Intelligence, which debuted in **DC OverPower**.

In addition to adding new heroes to the game, *IQ* also contains updated hero cards adding the intelligence trait to the characters released in the three preceding sets. *IQ* also contains additional Special cards for the reprinted heroes. — **Orren McKay**

You will need **31** nine-pocket pages to store this set. (16 doubled up)

Set (279 cards)	77.50
Booster Display Box	47.75
Booster Pack	2.80

Card name	Type	Rarity	Price
Ally (6 Fighting to Use)	Univ	U	0.50
Ally (6 Strength to Use)	Univ	U	0.50
Ally (8 Energy to Use)	Univ	C	0.20
Ally (8 Fighting to Use)	Univ	C	0.20
Ally (8 Intellect to Use)	Univ	C	0.20
Ally (8 Strength to Use)	Univ	C	0.20
Any Hero: Alien Symbiote	Spec	R	3.00
Any Hero: Power Leech	Spec	VR	7.00
Apocalypse	Char	VR	5.50
Apocalypse: Ageless Evil	Spec	U	0.50
Apocalypse: Techno-Virus	Spec	VR	5.30
Banshee	Char	R	2.00
Banshee: Cassidy Keep	Spec	U	0.50
Beast	Char	R	2.00
Beast: Ambidexterity	Spec	U	0.50
Beast: Brilliant Deduction	Spec	U	0.50
Bishop	Char	R	5.00
Bishop: Paramilitary Skill	Spec	C	0.20
Bishop: Temporal Anomaly	Spec	VR	4.30
Black Cat	Char	R	2.00
Black Cat: Feline Fortune	Spec	C	0.20
Black Cat: Feline Fury	Spec	U	0.50
Black Widow	Char	R	2.00
Black Widow: Champion	Spec	U	0.50
Black Widow: KGB Intelligence	Spec	U	0.80
Blob	Char	R	2.00
Blob: Flabby Fighter	Spec	VR	3.80
Brood	Char	R	2.00
Brood: Plan Of Conquest	Spec	C	0.20
Brood: Power Hungry Monsters	Spec	VR	3.80
Cable	Char	VR	7.50
Cable: Askani'son	Spec	VR	4.80
Captain America	Char	R	9.00
Captain America: Sentinel Of Liberty	Spec	VR	5.30
Carnage	Char	R	2.00
Carnage: Anarchy	Spec	VR	4.50
Carnage: Destructive Mind	Spec	U	0.50
Colossus	Char	R	2.00
Colossus: Mighty Metal	Spec	C	0.20
Colossus: Organic Steel	Spec	U	0.50
Cyclops	Char	R	2.00
Cyclops: Battle Savvy	Spec	U	0.50
Cyclops: X-Men Strategy	Spec	U	0.50
Daredevil	Char	R	2.00
Daredevil: Blind Justice	Spec	U	0.50
Daredevil: Radar Combat	Spec	C	0.20
Deadpool	Char	R	2.00
Deadpool: Distracting Chatter	Spec	U	0.50

Card name	Type	Rarity	Price
Deadpool: Don't Lose Your Head!	Spec	VR	6.50
Doc Samson	Char	R	2.00
Doc Samson: Cautious Advisor	Spec	U	0.50
Doc Samson: Head Shrinker	Spec	U	0.80
Doctor Doom	Char	VR	7.00
Doctor Doom: Diplomatic Immunity	Spec	VR	5.30
Doctor Doom: Doombots	Spec	VR	5.30
Doctor Octopus	Char	R	2.00
Doctor Octopus: Big Plans	Spec	U	0.80
Doctor Strange	Char	R	5.00
Doctor Strange: Catastrophe Magic	Spec	U	0.50
Doctor Strange: Defender	Spec	VR	5.30
Domino	Char	R	2.00
Domino: Battle Medic	Spec	U	0.50
Domino: Dumb Luck	Spec	U	0.80
Elektra	Char	R	2.00
Elektra: Infiltration	Spec	U	0.50
Elektra: Ninja Trap	Spec	VR	4.80
Forge	Char	R	5.00
Forge: Cherokee Magic	Spec	VR	4.80
Forge: Cybernetic Limbs	Spec	C	0.20
Forge: Footsoldier Training	Spec	C	0.20
Forge: The Maker	Spec	C	0.20
Forge: The Neutralizer	Spec	C	0.20
Gambit	Char	R	2.00
Gambit: Kinetic Detonation	Spec	U	0.80
Gambit: Sinister Connection	Spec	U	0.50
Ghost Rider	Char	R	5.00
Ghost Rider: Skeletal Summoning	Spec	U	0.50
Ghost Rider: Spiritual Duality	Spec	C	0.20
Green Goblin	Char	U	0.80
Green Goblin: Explosive Pumpkins	Spec	U	0.80
Green Goblin: Flying Platform	Spec	C	0.20
Green Goblin: Gauntlet Blasters	Spec	C	0.20
Green Goblin: Goblin Legacy	Spec	VR	4.80
Green Goblin: Murderous Ploy	Spec	U	0.50
Hawkeye	Char	R	2.00
Hawkeye: Field Dressing	Spec	U	0.50
Hawkeye: Quiver Of Arrows	Spec	U	0.50
Henry Pym	Char	R	5.00
Henry Pym: Ant-Man	Spec	C	0.20
Henry Pym: Giant-Man	Spec	C	0.25
Henry Pym: Goliath	Spec	C	0.20
Henry Pym: Medical Knowledge	Spec	U	0.50
Henry Pym: Yellowjacket	Spec	C	0.20
Hobgoblin	Char	U	0.80
Hobgoblin: Cybernetic Upgrade	Spec	U	0.80
Hobgoblin: Goblin Cache	Spec	U	0.50
Holocaust: Horrifying Image	Spec	C	0.25
Hulk	Char	R	5.00
Hulk: Gamma Transfusion	Spec	VR	4.80
Human Torch	Char	R	2.00
Human Torch: Fire Cage	Spec	U	0.80
Human Torch: Hot Head	Spec	U	0.50
Iceman	Char	R	2.00
Iceman: Ice Tactics	Spec	C	0.20
Intellect 1	Pwr	C	0.20
Intellect 2	Pwr	C	0.20

Card name	Type	Rarity	Price
Intellect 3	Pwr	C	0.20
Intellect 4	Pwr	C	0.20
Intellect 5	Pwr	C	0.20
Intellect 6	Pwr	C	0.25
Intellect 7	Pwr	U	1.00
Intellect 8	Pwr	R	4.50
Invisible Woman	Char	R	2.00
Invisible Woman: Protective Wall	Spec	U	0.80
Invisible Woman: Team Coordination	Spec	U	0.50
Iron Man	Char	VR	8.00
Iron Man: Stealth Armor	Spec	C	0.20
Iron Man: Weapons Inventor	Spec	U	0.50
Jean Grey	Char	R	2.00
Jean Grey: Phoenix Effect	Spec	U	0.80
Jean Grey: Psychic Soothing	Spec	U	0.50
Jubilee	Char	R	2.00
Jubilee: Troublemaker	Spec	U	0.50
Jubilee: Wisecrack	Spec	U	0.50
Juggernaut	Char	R	5.00
Juggernaut: Magic Helm	Spec	C	0.20
Kingpin	Char	R	5.00
Kingpin: Business Savvy	Spec	U	0.50
Kingpin: Crime Magnate	Spec	VR	3.80
Kingpin: Sumo Knowledge	Spec	VR	5.30
Kingpin: Underworld Henchmen	Spec	C	0.20
Kingpin: Walking Stick	Spec	C	0.20
Longshot	Char	R	2.00
Longshot: Fortunate Accident	Spec	U	0.50
Longshot: Purity Of Thought	Spec	VR	4.80
Magneto	Char	R	5.00
Magneto: Magnetic Devastation	Spec	C	0.25
Magneto: Master Of Magnetism	Spec	VR	5.30
Mandarin	Char	R	2.00
Mandarin: Energy Void	Spec	VR	3.80
Mandarin: Master Tactician	Spec	U	0.50
Mister Fantastic	Char	VR	8.00
Mister Fantastic: Fantastic Mind	Spec	U	1.00
Mister Fantastic: Inventive Genius	Spec	U	0.50
Mister Sinister	Char	VR	7.50
Mister Sinister: Cloning Process	Spec	VR	4.30
Mister Sinister: Marauder	Spec	VR	5.50
Mojo	Char	U	0.80
Mojo: Caught On Film	Spec	U	0.50
Mojo: Director's Cut	Spec	U	0.50
Morbius	Char	R	2.00
Morbius: Induce Panic	Spec	U	0.50
Morbius: Shadowy Escape	Spec	C	0.20
Morph	Char	R	2.00
Morph: Ridiculous Behavior	Spec	C	0.20
Morph: Substitute Death	Spec	VR	4.30
Multipower 1	Pwr	C	0.25
Multipower 2	Pwr	C	0.25
Multipower 3	Pwr	U	1.00
Multipower 4	Pwr	R	4.00
Mysterio	Char	U	1.00
Mysterio: Holographic Decoy	Spec	C	0.20
Mysterio: Mysteryvision	Spec	U	0.50
Mystique	Char	U	0.80

Card name	Type	Rarity	Price
Mystique: Fatal Marksman	Spec	U	0.50
Mystique: Government Agent	Spec	U	0.50
Namor	Char	R	2.00
Namor: Neptune's Armor	Spec	U	0.50
Namor: Sub-Mariner	Spec	VR	5.30
Nick Fury	Char	R	5.00
Nick Fury: Agent of S.H.I.E.L.D.	Spec	C	0.20
Nick Fury: Battle Strategy	Spec	VR	4.50
Nick Fury: Howling Commando	Spec	U	0.50
Nick Fury: Infinity Formula	Spec	U	0.50
Nick Fury: War Hero	Spec	C	0.20
Nightcrawler	Char	R	2.00
Nightcrawler: Acrobatic Precision	Spec	C	0.20
Nightcrawler: Power 'Port	Spec	VR	4.80
Omega Red	Char	R	5.00
Omega Red: Carbonadium Synthesizer	Spec	VR	5.30
Omega Red: Twin Tentacles	Spec	C	0.20
Onslaught: Cannon Fodder	Spec	VR	6.00
Post: Covert Manipulations	Spec	U	1.00
Professor X	Char	R	5.00
Professor X: Mindwipe	Spec	VR	5.50
Professor X: Psychic Shield	Spec	U	0.50
Psylocke	Char	R	2.00
Psylocke: Crimson Dawn	Spec	VR	4.80
Psylocke: Lady Mandarin	Spec	C	0.20
Punisher	Char	R	2.00
Punisher: Dodge	Spec	U	0.50
Punisher: Outwit	Spec	U	0.50
Quicksilver	Char	R	5.00
Quicksilver: High Speed Impact	Spec	VR	4.80
Quicksilver: Rapid-Fire Punches	Spec	C	0.20
Red Skull	Char	R	5.00
Red Skull: Cosmic Cube	Spec	VR	4.30
Red Skull: Depraved Evil	Spec	U	0.50
Red Skull: Dust Of Death	Spec	U	1.00
Red Skull: Evil Super Soldier	Spec	VR	4.80
Red Skull: Master Racist	Spec	U	0.50
Rhino	Char	R	2.00
Rhino: Animal Stamina	Spec	C	0.20
Rogue	Char	R	5.00
Rogue: Combination Punch	Spec	C	0.20
Rogue: Southern Belle	Spec	C	0.20
Sabretooth	Char	R	5.00
Sabretooth: Dangerous Mind	Spec	C	0.20
Sabretooth: Government Operative	Spec	U	0.50
Scarlet Spider	Char	R	5.00
Scarlet Spider: Clonal Confusion	Spec	C	0.20
Scarlet Witch	Char	R	5.00
Scarlet Witch: Improbability Hex	Spec	U	0.50
Scarlet Witch: Witchcraft	Spec	C	0.20
Sentinels	Char	R	5.00
Sentinels: Mutant Countermeasures	Spec	C	0.20
Sentinels: Robot Mentality	Spec	C	0.20
Shadowcat	Char	U	1.00
Shadowcat: Computer Genius	Spec	C	0.20
Shadowcat: Electronic Scramble	Spec	U	0.50
Shadowcat: Ghostly Phase	Spec	U	0.50
Shadowcat: Pryde And Wisdom	Spec	C	0.20
Shadowcat: Soulsword	Spec	C	0.25
She Hulk	Char	R	5.00
She Hulk: Brains & Brawn	Spec	C	0.20
She Hulk: Public Defender	Spec	C	0.20
Silver Sable	Char	U	0.80
Silver Sable: Battle Plans	Spec	C	0.20
Silver Sable: Sandman	Spec	C	0.20
Silver Surfer	Char	R	5.00
Silver Surfer: Cosmic Awareness	Spec	C	0.20
Spider-Man	Char	VR	10.50
Spider-Man: Clonal Confusion	Spec	C	0.20
Spider-Man: Science Whiz	Spec	C	0.20
Spider-Woman	Char	U	0.80
Spider-Woman: Force Works	Spec	C	0.20
Spider-Woman: Rescue Operation	Spec	C	0.20
Storm	Char	R	2.00
Storm: Morlock Combat	Spec	C	0.20
Storm: X-Men Leader	Spec	C	0.20
Strong Guy	Char	R	4.00
Strong Guy: Bodyguard	Spec	C	0.20
Strong Guy: Simple Strategy	Spec	C	0.20
Super Skrull	Char	R	5.00
Super Skrull: Alien Methods	Spec	C	0.20
Super Skrull: Fantastic Enemy	Spec	C	0.25
Teamwork (6 Fighting to Use)	Univ	C	0.25
Teamwork (6 Intellect to Use)	Univ	C	0.25
Teamwork (7 Energy to Use)	Univ	C	0.25
Teamwork (7 Intellect to Use)	Univ	C	0.25
Teamwork (7 Strength to Use)	Univ	C	0.25
Teamwork (8 Energy to Use F/I)	Univ	C	0.25
Teamwork (8 Energy to Use S/I)	Univ	C	0.25
Teamwork (8 Fighting to Use E/I)	Univ	C	0.25
Teamwork (8 Fighting to Use S/I)	Univ	C	0.25
Teamwork (8 Intellect to Use F/S)	Univ	C	0.25
Teamwork (8 Strength to Use E/I)	Univ	C	0.25
Thing	Char	R	5.00
Thing: Bucket O' Shame	Spec	U	0.50
Thor	Char	VR	7.50
Thor: Gift Of The Gods	Spec	C	0.25
Thor: Viking Pyre	Spec	VR	5.30
Venom	Char	R	5.00
Venom: Eddie Brock: Reporter	Spec	C	0.30
Venom: Healing Bond	Spec	U	0.50
Vision	Char	R	5.00
Vision: Android Avenger	Spec	C	0.20
Vision: Calculated Attack	Spec	C	0.20
War Machine	Char	R	5.00
War Machine: War Drone	Spec	U	0.50
White Queen	Char	R	5.00
White Queen: Cold-Hearted Enemy	Spec	C	0.20
White Queen: Hellfire Leader	Spec	C	0.20
White Queen: Mental Override	Spec	C	0.20
White Queen: Mutant Headmistress	Spec	C	0.20
White Queen: Telepathic Manipulator	Spec	VR	5.30
Wolverine	Char	R	9.00
Wolverine: Canucklehead	Spec	VR	5.30
Wolverine: Savage Regression	Spec	U	0.50

OverPower • Justice League (a.k.a. JLA)

Fleer/Skybox • Released **February 1997**

197 cards in set • **IDENTIFIER: JLA symbol appears on cards; © 1997**

• Booster packs contain 15 cards; booster displays contain 36 boosters

"Well-timed" is an apropriate description for the only expansion for **OverPower**'s DC Comics line. Up and down in popularity for years since its creation in November 1960, the Justice League of America became cool again with the late 1996 release of the relaunched *JLA* comics series by Grant Morrison. (As such, many refer to this set as "JLA" — and while it does appear on the cards, *Justice League* appears on the packs.)

Whatever you call it, characters from that super-hero organization make the CCG scene in this expansion. — **John Jackson Miller**

You will need **22** nine-pocket pages to store this set. (11 doubled up)

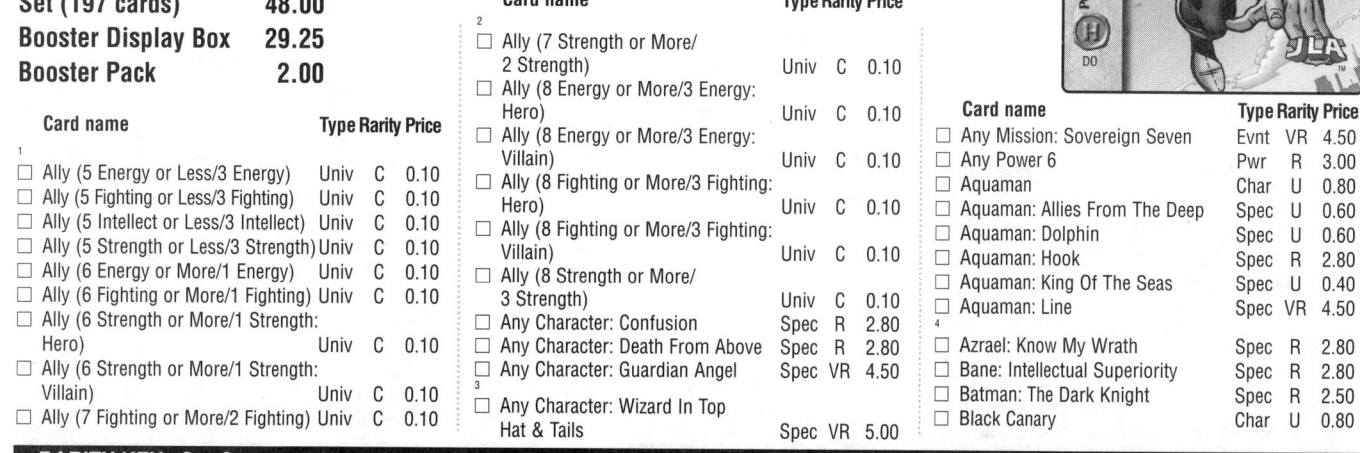

	Price
Set (197 cards)	48.00
Booster Display Box	29.25
Booster Pack	2.00

Card name	Type	Rarity	Price
Ally (5 Energy or Less/3 Energy)	Univ	C	0.10
Ally (5 Fighting or Less/3 Fighting)	Univ	C	0.10
Ally (5 Intellect or Less/3 Intellect)	Univ	C	0.10
Ally (5 Strength or Less/3 Strength)	Univ	C	0.10
Ally (6 Energy or More/1 Energy)	Univ	C	0.10
Ally (6 Fighting or More/1 Fighting)	Univ	C	0.10
Ally (6 Strength or More/1 Strength: Hero)	Univ	C	0.10
Ally (6 Strength or More/1 Strength: Villain)	Univ	C	0.10
Ally (7 Fighting or More/2 Fighting)	Univ	C	0.10
Ally (7 Strength or More/2 Strength)	Univ	C	0.10
Ally (8 Energy or More/3 Energy: Hero)	Univ	C	0.10
Ally (8 Energy or More/3 Energy: Villain)	Univ	C	0.10
Ally (8 Fighting or More/3 Fighting: Hero)	Univ	C	0.10
Ally (8 Fighting or More/3 Fighting: Villain)	Univ	C	0.10
Ally (8 Strength or More/3 Strength)	Univ	C	0.10
Any Character: Confusion	Spec	R	2.80
Any Character: Death From Above	Spec	R	2.80
Any Character: Guardian Angel	Spec	VR	4.50
Any Character: Wizard In Top Hat & Tails	Spec	VR	5.00

Card name	Type	Rarity	Price
Any Mission: Sovereign Seven	Evnt	VR	4.50
Any Power 6	Pwr	R	3.00
Aquaman	Char	U	0.80
Aquaman: Allies From The Deep	Spec	U	0.60
Aquaman: Dolphin	Spec	U	0.60
Aquaman: Hook	Spec	R	2.80
Aquaman: King Of The Seas	Spec	U	0.40
Aquaman: Line	Spec	VR	4.50
Azrael: Know My Wrath	Spec	R	2.80
Bane: Intellectual Superiority	Spec	R	2.80
Batman: The Dark Knight	Spec	R	2.50
Black Canary	Char	U	0.80

RARITY KEY C = Common   U = Uncommon   R = Rare   VR = Very Rare   UR = Ultra Rare   F = Foil card   X = Fixed/standard in all decks

SCRYE Collectible Card Game Checklist and Price Guide • 341

Card name	Type	Rarity	Price
Black Canary: Bird Of Prey	Spec	C	0.10
Black Canary: Opening Flower Discipline	Spec	U	0.60
Black Canary: Street Smarts	Spec	VR	4.00
Black Canary: The Oracle Connection	Spec	U	0.60
Black Canary: Working Clothes	Spec	C	0.10
Blue Beetle	Char	C	0.10
Blue Beetle: Airgun	Spec	U	0.60
Blue Beetle: Bwah-Ha-Ha-Ha!	Spec	U	0.80
Blue Beetle: Frictionless Foam	Spec	R	1.90
Blue Beetle: Quick Wits	Spec	U	0.60
Blue Beetle: The Bug	Spec	U	0.60
Booster Gold	Char	C	0.10
Booster Gold: Energy Absorption Field	Spec	VR	4.50
Booster Gold: Gauntlet Energy Blast	Spec	C	0.10
Booster Gold: Midas Mode	Spec	U	0.60
Booster Gold: Quarterback Sneak	Spec	U	0.80
Booster Gold: Skeets	Spec	U	0.60
Brainiac: Brain Drain	Spec	R	3.00
Captain Atom	Char	R	2.80
Captain Atom: Anti-Gravity Field	Spec	VR	4.50
Captain Atom: Atomic Bolt	Spec	VR	4.50
Captain Atom: Atomic Punch	Spec	C	0.10
Captain Atom: Quantum Jump	Spec	VR	4.50
Captain Atom: Skin Alloy	Spec	U	0.60
Captain Marvel	Char	U	0.80
Captain Marvel: Power of Zeus	Spec	U	0.60
Captain Marvel: Speed of Mercury	Spec	VR	4.50
Captain Marvel: Stamina of Atlas	Spec	VR	4.50
Captain Marvel: Strength of Hercules	Spec	U	0.80
Captain Marvel: The Marvel Family	Spec	R	2.80
Catwoman: Prowling By Night	Spec	R	2.50
Comm Gordon And The GCPD: TheBat Signal	Spec	R	2.50
Cyborg: Interstellar Menace	Spec	R	2.50
Darkseid	Char	R	3.50
Darkseid: Desaad	Spec	U	0.60
Darkseid: Granny Goodness	Spec	U	0.60
Darkseid: Kalibak	Spec	U	0.80
Darkseid: Lord Of Apokolips	Spec	VR	4.50
Darkseid: Omega Effect	Spec	VR	4.50
Doctor Polaris	Char	C	0.10
Doctor Polaris: Black Hole Force Beam	Spec	VR	4.50
Doctor Polaris: Force Of Nature	Spec	U	0.60
Doctor Polaris: Magnetic Energy Bolt	Spec	C	0.10
Doctor Polaris: Magnetic Sphere	Spec	U	0.60
Doctor Polaris: Make The Blood Boil	Spec	VR	4.50
Doomsday: Engine Of Destruction	Spec	R	2.50
Double Shot (6E/6F to Use: Intellect)	Tac	C	0.10
Double Shot (6E/6S to Use: Energy)	Tac	C	0.10
Double Shot (6F/6E to Use: Fighting)	Tac	C	0.10
Double Shot (6F/6E to Use: Strength)	Tac	C	0.10
Double Shot (6F/6S to Use: Intellect)	Tac	C	0.10
Double Shot (6I/6E to Use: Strength)	Tac	C	0.10
Double Shot (6I/6F to Use: Intellect)	Tac	C	0.10
Double Shot (6I/6F to Use: Strength)	Tac	C	0.10
Double Shot (6I/6S to Use: Fighting)	Tac	C	0.10
Double Shot (6S/6E to Use: Fighting)	Tac	C	0.10
Double Shot (6S/6E to Use: Intellect)	Tac	C	0.10
Double Shot (6S/6F to Use: Energy)	Tac	C	0.10
Double Shot (6S/6I to Use: Fighting)	Tac	C	0.10
Double Shot (6S/6I to Use: Strength)	Tac	C	0.10
Eradicator: A Lasting Impression	Spec	R	1.90
Green Arrow	Char	U	0.80
Green Arrow: Aikido Strike	Spec	C	0.10
Green Arrow: Eddie Fyers	Spec	U	0.60
Green Arrow: Kyudo Discipline	Spec	VR	4.50
Green Arrow: The Emerald Archer	Spec	VR	4.50
Green Arrow: The Longbow Hunter	Spec	U	0.60
Green Lantern	Char	U	0.80
Green Lantern: Goin' Ballistic	Spec	C	0.10
Green Lantern: Gotcha!	Spec	U	0.60
Green Lantern: Let's Get Medieval!	Spec	VR	4.50
Green Lantern: Power of Imagingation	Spec	VR	4.50
Green Lantern: This Is A Gun	Spec	U	0.80
Hawkman	Char	U	0.80
Hawkman: Cestus Glove	Spec	VR	4.50
Hawkman: Katar Blade	Spec	VR	4.50
Hawkman: Mace	Spec	U	0.80
Hawkman: Thanagarian Blaster	Spec	C	0.10
Hawkman: The Winged Warrior	Spec	VR	4.50
Hazard: Cyber-Jacked	Spec	U	0.80
Huntress: Thrill Of The Hunt	Spec	R	2.80
Joker: Keys To The Kingdom	Spec	R	2.50
Killer Croc: Dumb Luck	Spec	R	2.00
"Knockout: 8, 9, 10, You're Out!"	Spec	R	2.50
Lex Luthor: Art Of The Deal	Spec	R	3.00
Martian Manhunter	Char	U	0.80
Martian Manhunter: Alien Physique	Spec	VR	4.50
Martian Manhunter: Malleable Form	Spec	U	0.60
Martian Manhunter: Martian Strength	Spec	R	2.50
Martian Manhunter: Martian Vision	Spec	VR	4.50
Martian Manhunter: Telepathic Probe	Spec	U	0.60
Metallo: I'll Be Back!	Spec	R	2.50
Metropolis SCU: Courage Under Fire	Spec	R	2.50
Mister Miracle	Char	U	0.80
Mister Miracle: Aero Disks	Spec	VR	4.50
Mister Miracle: Big Barda	Spec	U	0.60
Mister Miracle: Mother Box	Spec	VR	4.50
Mister Miracle: Oberon	Spec	U	0.60
Mister Miracle: Super-Escape Artist	Spec	C	0.10
Neron	Char	R	3.00
Neron: Lord Of The Underworld	Spec	VR	4.50
Neron: Necromantic Blast	Spec	U	0.80
Neron: Seduction Of The Innocent	Spec	U	0.60
Neron: Your Heart's Desire	Spec	VR	4.50
Neron: Your Soul Is Mine!	Spec	U	0.80
Nightwing: Ties That Bind	Spec	R	2.50
Orion	Char	R	3.00
Orion: Astro-Glider	Spec	U	0.80
Orion: Boom Tube	Spec	U	0.80
Orion: Consult The Source	Spec	VR	4.50
Orion: Mother Box	Spec	VR	4.50
Orion: Source Of The Beast	Spec	C	0.10
Parallax	Char	R	3.50
Parallax: Beware My Power	Spec	VR	4.50
Parallax: Heroic Redemption	Spec	U	0.60
Parallax: In Blackest Night	Spec	U	0.60
Parallax: In Brightest Day	Spec	C	0.10
Parallax: Zero Hour	Spec	VR	4.50
Parasite: Doc Parasite	Spec	R	2.50
Poison Ivy: Blowing You A Kiss	Spec	R	2.50
Ra's Al Ghul: The Clench	Spec	R	2.50
Robin: Surfing The Net	Spec	R	3.00
Steel: Night Vision Goggles	Spec	R	2.50
Superboy: The Ravers	Spec	R	2.50
Supergirl: Girl Of Steel	Spec	R	3.00
Superman: The Man Beyond Tomorrow	Spec	R	3.00
The Brave And The Bold: Aquaman vs. Deep Six	Evnt	C	0.10
The Brave And The Bold: Batman vs. Kanto	Evnt	C	0.10
The Brave And The Bold: Blue Beetle vs. Glorious Godfrey	Evnt	C	0.10
The Brave And The Bold: Darkseid's Elite	Evnt	C	0.10
The Brave And The Bold: Green Arrow, Black Canary, Amazing Grace	Evnt	C	0.10
The Brave And The Bold 1	Miss	C	0.10
The Brave And The Bold 2	Miss	C	0.10
The Brave And The Bold 3	Miss	C	0.10
The Brave And The Bold 4	Miss	C	0.10
The Brave And The Bold 5	Miss	C	0.10
The Brave And The Bold 6	Miss	C	0.10
The Brave And The Bold 7	Miss	C	0.10
The Flash	Char	C	0.10
The Flash: 1-2 (Thousand) Punch	Spec	C	0.10
The Flash: Reap The Whirlwind	Spec	U	0.60
The Flash: Speed-Lending	Spec	U	0.80
The Flash: Tapping The Speed Force	Spec	VR	4.50
The Flash: The Fastest Man Alive	Spec	U	0.60
The Penguin: Gotham's Emperor Penguin	Spec	R	2.80
The Ray	Char	R	3.80
The Ray: Blinded By The Light	Spec	VR	5.00
The Ray: Energy Shield	Spec	U	0.60
The Ray: In A Blaze Of Power	Spec	VR	5.00
The Ray: Light Constructs	Spec	U	0.80
The Ray: Speed Of Light	Spec	C	0.10
The Riddler: Prince Of Puzzles	Spec	R	2.50
The Trickster	Char	R	2.80
The Trickster: Bait And Switch	Spec	U	0.60
The Trickster: Clean Getaway	Spec	U	0.60
The Trickster: Don't Mind Me	Spec	C	0.10
The Trickster: Smooth Talker	Spec	VR	4.50
The Trickster: The Shell Game	Spec	VR	4.50
Thorn: Tell Me What You Know	Spec	R	2.50
Two-Face: Law And Disorder	Spec	VR	3.30
Wonder Woman	Char	R	3.00
Wonder Woman: Amazon Might	Spec	VR	4.50
Wonder Woman: Blessed By The Gods	Spec	VR	4.50
Wonder Woman: Bullets & Bracelets	Spec	C	0.10
Wonder Woman: Gift Of Flight	Spec	U	0.80
Wonder Woman: Lasso Of Truth	Spec	VR	4.50

Snub of the gods

You can get a **Captain Marvel** card for **Strength of Hercules**, **Stamina of Atlas**, **Power of Zeus**, and **Speed of Mercury**, but nothing for "Wisdom of Solomon" or "Courage of Achilles."

Can you say, "HAZM"?

In the CCG, that's all you can say...

RARITY KEY C = Common U = Uncommon R = Rare VR = Very Rare UR = Ultra Rare F = Foil card X = Fixed/standard in all decks

OverPower • Monumental

Fleer/SkyBox • Released **May 1997**

289 cards in set • **IDENTIFIER: Backgrounds have brick pattern**

- Starter decks contain 65 cards; starter displays contain 12 starters
- Booster packs contain 15 cards; booster displays contain 36 boosters

The first starter/booster Marvel set since **Limited**, **Monumental** adds a number of new characters to the mix. It also introduces location cards, which allow teams of certain heroes to gain special benefits. — *Orren McKay*

SCRYE NOTES: *The four Adam Warlock cards in* **Monumental** *are* **not** *the four we mentioned as being surprise additions to to* **Mission Control**. *They have different card art and backgrounds (but the same statistics).*

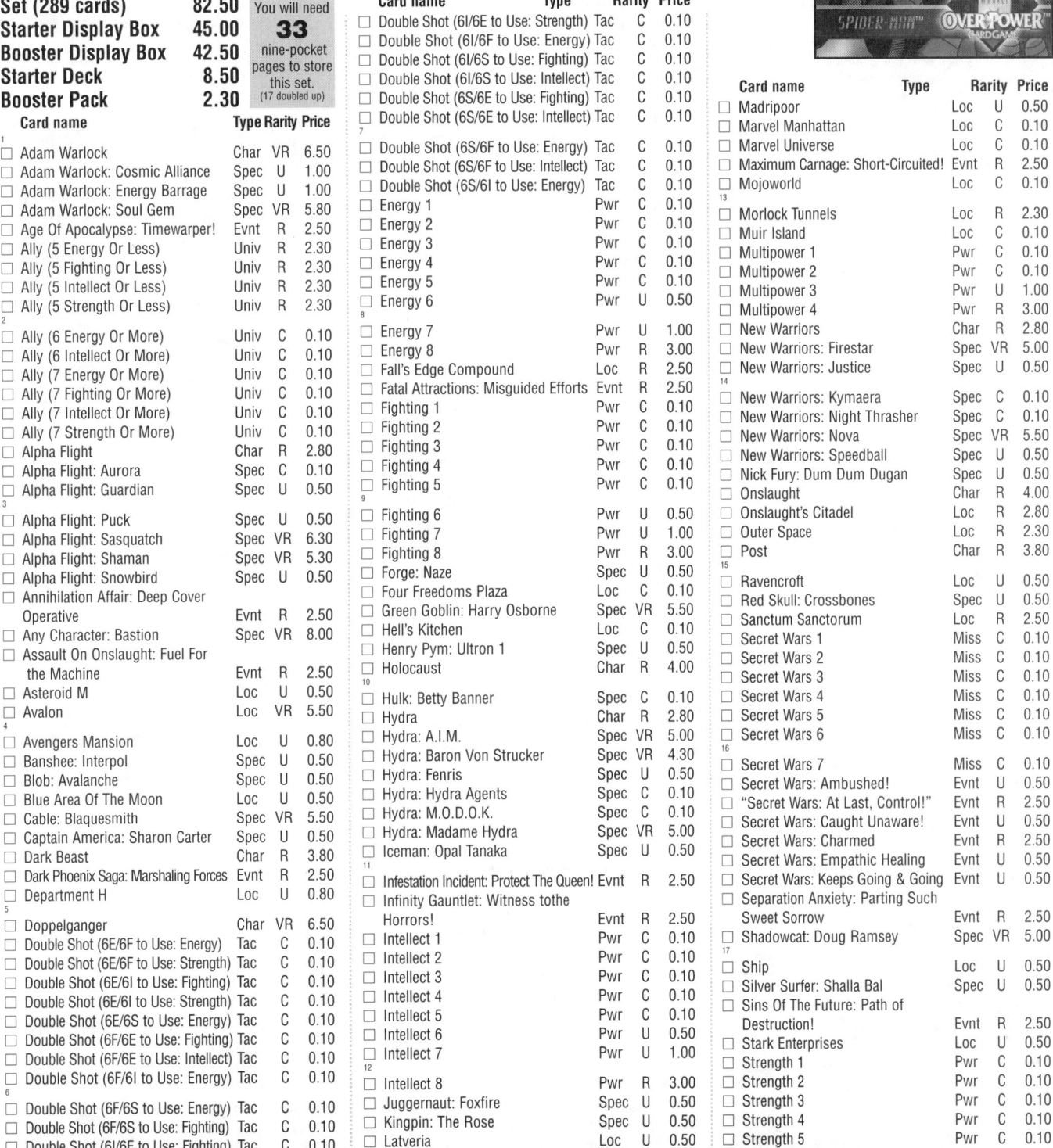

Set (289 cards)	82.50
Starter Display Box	45.00
Booster Display Box	42.50
Starter Deck	8.50
Booster Pack	2.30

You will need 33 nine-pocket pages to store this set. (17 doubled up)

Card name	Type	Rarity	Price
1			
Adam Warlock	Char	VR	6.50
Adam Warlock: Cosmic Alliance	Spec	U	1.00
Adam Warlock: Energy Barrage	Spec	U	1.00
Adam Warlock: Soul Gem	Spec	VR	5.80
Age Of Apocalypse: Timewarper!	Evnt	R	2.50
Ally (5 Energy Or Less)	Univ	R	2.30
Ally (5 Fighting Or Less)	Univ	R	2.30
Ally (5 Intellect Or Less)	Univ	R	2.30
Ally (5 Strength Or Less)	Univ	R	2.30
2			
Ally (6 Energy Or More)	Univ	C	0.10
Ally (6 Intellect Or More)	Univ	C	0.10
Ally (7 Energy Or More)	Univ	C	0.10
Ally (7 Fighting Or More)	Univ	C	0.10
Ally (7 Intellect Or More)	Univ	C	0.10
Ally (7 Strength Or More)	Univ	C	0.10
Alpha Flight	Char	R	2.80
Alpha Flight: Aurora	Spec	C	0.10
Alpha Flight: Guardian	Spec	U	0.50
3			
Alpha Flight: Puck	Spec	U	0.50
Alpha Flight: Sasquatch	Spec	VR	6.30
Alpha Flight: Shaman	Spec	VR	5.30
Alpha Flight: Snowbird	Spec	U	0.50
Annihilation Affair: Deep Cover Operative	Evnt	R	2.50
Any Character: Bastion	Spec	VR	8.00
Assault On Onslaught: Fuel For the Machine	Evnt	R	2.50
Asteroid M	Loc	U	0.50
Avalon	Loc	VR	5.50
4			
Avengers Mansion	Loc	U	0.80
Banshee: Interpol	Spec	U	0.50
Blob: Avalanche	Spec	U	0.50
Blue Area Of The Moon	Loc	U	0.50
Cable: Blaquesmith	Spec	VR	5.50
Captain America: Sharon Carter	Spec	U	0.50
Dark Beast	Char	R	3.80
Dark Phoenix Saga: Marshaling Forces	Evnt	R	2.50
Department H	Loc	U	0.80
5			
Doppelganger	Char	VR	6.50
Double Shot (6E/6F to Use: Energy)	Tac	C	0.10
Double Shot (6E/6F to Use: Strength)	Tac	C	0.10
Double Shot (6E/6I to Use: Fighting)	Tac	C	0.10
Double Shot (6E/6I to Use: Strength)	Tac	C	0.10
Double Shot (6E/6S to Use: Energy)	Tac	C	0.10
Double Shot (6F/6E to Use: Fighting)	Tac	C	0.10
Double Shot (6F/6E to Use: Intellect)	Tac	C	0.10
Double Shot (6F/6I to Use: Energy)	Tac	C	0.10
6			
Double Shot (6F/6S to Use: Energy)	Tac	C	0.10
Double Shot (6F/6S to Use: Fighting)	Tac	C	0.10
Double Shot (6I/6E to Use: Fighting)	Tac	C	0.10

Card name	Type	Rarity	Price
Double Shot (6I/6E to Use: Strength)	Tac	C	0.10
Double Shot (6I/6F to Use: Energy)	Tac	C	0.10
Double Shot (6I/6S to Use: Fighting)	Tac	C	0.10
Double Shot (6I/6S to Use: Intellect)	Tac	C	0.10
Double Shot (6S/6E to Use: Fighting)	Tac	C	0.10
Double Shot (6S/6E to Use: Intellect)	Tac	C	0.10
7			
Double Shot (6S/6F to Use: Energy)	Tac	C	0.10
Double Shot (6S/6F to Use: Intellect)	Tac	C	0.10
Double Shot (6S/6I to Use: Energy)	Tac	C	0.10
Energy 1	Pwr	C	0.10
Energy 2	Pwr	C	0.10
Energy 3	Pwr	C	0.10
Energy 4	Pwr	C	0.10
Energy 5	Pwr	C	0.10
Energy 6	Pwr	U	0.50
8			
Energy 7	Pwr	U	1.00
Energy 8	Pwr	R	3.00
Fall's Edge Compound	Loc	R	2.50
Fatal Attractions: Misguided Efforts	Evnt	R	2.50
Fighting 1	Pwr	C	0.10
Fighting 2	Pwr	C	0.10
Fighting 3	Pwr	C	0.10
Fighting 4	Pwr	C	0.10
Fighting 5	Pwr	C	0.10
9			
Fighting 6	Pwr	U	0.50
Fighting 7	Pwr	U	1.00
Fighting 8	Pwr	R	3.00
Forge: Naze	Spec	U	0.50
Four Freedoms Plaza	Loc	C	0.10
Green Goblin: Harry Osborne	Spec	VR	5.50
Hell's Kitchen	Loc	C	0.10
Henry Pym: Ultron 1	Spec	U	0.50
Holocaust	Char	R	4.00
10			
Hulk: Betty Banner	Spec	C	0.10
Hydra	Char	R	2.80
Hydra: A.I.M.	Spec	VR	5.00
Hydra: Baron Von Strucker	Spec	VR	4.30
Hydra: Fenris	Spec	U	0.50
Hydra: Hydra Agents	Spec	C	0.10
Hydra: M.O.D.O.K.	Spec	C	0.10
Hydra: Madame Hydra	Spec	VR	5.00
Iceman: Opal Tanaka	Spec	U	0.50
11			
Infestation Incident: Protect The Queen!	Evnt	R	2.50
Infinity Gauntlet: Witness to the Horrors!	Evnt	R	2.50
Intellect 1	Pwr	C	0.10
Intellect 2	Pwr	C	0.10
Intellect 3	Pwr	C	0.10
Intellect 4	Pwr	C	0.10
Intellect 5	Pwr	C	0.10
Intellect 6	Pwr	U	0.50
Intellect 7	Pwr	U	1.00
12			
Intellect 8	Pwr	R	3.00
Juggernaut: Foxfire	Spec	U	0.50
Kingpin: The Rose	Spec	U	0.50
Latveria	Loc	U	0.50

Card name	Type	Rarity	Price
Madripoor	Loc	U	0.50
Marvel Manhattan	Loc	C	0.10
Marvel Universe	Loc	C	0.10
Maximum Carnage: Short-Circuited!	Evnt	R	2.50
Mojoworld	Loc	C	0.10
13			
Morlock Tunnels	Loc	R	2.30
Muir Island	Loc	C	0.10
Multipower 1	Pwr	C	0.10
Multipower 2	Pwr	C	0.10
Multipower 3	Pwr	U	1.00
Multipower 4	Pwr	R	3.00
New Warriors	Char	R	2.80
New Warriors: Firestar	Spec	VR	5.00
New Warriors: Justice	Spec	U	0.50
14			
New Warriors: Kymaera	Spec	C	0.10
New Warriors: Night Thrasher	Spec	C	0.10
New Warriors: Nova	Spec	VR	5.50
New Warriors: Speedball	Spec	U	0.50
Nick Fury: Dum Dum Dugan	Spec	U	0.50
Onslaught	Char	R	4.00
Onslaught's Citadel	Loc	R	2.80
Outer Space	Loc	R	2.30
Post	Char	R	3.80
15			
Ravencroft	Loc	U	0.50
Red Skull: Crossbones	Spec	U	0.50
Sanctum Sanctorum	Loc	R	2.50
Secret Wars 1	Miss	C	0.10
Secret Wars 2	Miss	C	0.10
Secret Wars 3	Miss	C	0.10
Secret Wars 4	Miss	C	0.10
Secret Wars 5	Miss	C	0.10
Secret Wars 6	Miss	C	0.10
16			
Secret Wars 7	Miss	C	0.10
Secret Wars: Ambushed!	Evnt	U	0.50
"Secret Wars: At Last, Control!"	Evnt	R	2.50
Secret Wars: Caught Unaware!	Evnt	U	0.50
Secret Wars: Charmed	Evnt	R	2.50
Secret Wars: Empathic Healing	Evnt	U	0.50
Secret Wars: Keeps Going & Going	Evnt	U	0.50
Separation Anxiety: Parting Such Sweet Sorrow	Evnt	R	2.50
Shadowcat: Doug Ramsey	Spec	VR	5.00
17			
Ship	Loc	U	0.50
Silver Surfer: Shalla Bal	Spec	U	0.50
Sins Of The Future: Path of Destruction!	Evnt	R	2.50
Stark Enterprises	Loc	U	0.50
Strength 1	Pwr	C	0.10
Strength 2	Pwr	C	0.10
Strength 3	Pwr	C	0.10
Strength 4	Pwr	C	0.10
Strength 5	Pwr	C	0.10

RARITY KEY C = Common U = Uncommon R = Rare VR = Very Rare UR = Ultra Rare F = Foil card X = Fixed/standard in all decks

Card name	Type	Rarity	Price
18			
Strength 6	Pwr	U	0.50
Strength 7	Pwr	U	1.00
Strength 8	Pwr	R	3.00
Teamwork (6 Energy to Use F/I)	Univ	C	0.10
Teamwork (6 Energy to Use S/I)	Univ	C	0.10
Teamwork (6 Fighting to Use E/I)	Univ	C	0.10
Teamwork (6 Intellect to Use E/F)	Univ	C	0.10
Teamwork (6 Intellect to Use F/S)	Univ	C	0.10
Teamwork (6 Strength to Use E/I)	Univ	C	0.10
19			
Teamwork (6 Strength to Use F/I)	Univ	C	0.10
Teamwork (7 Energy to Use S/I)	Univ	C	0.10
Teamwork (7 Fighting to Use E/I)	Univ	C	0.10
Teamwork (7 Fighting to Use S/I)	Univ	C	0.10
Teamwork (7 Intellect to Use E/F)	Univ	C	0.10
Teamwork (7 Intellect to Use E/S)	Univ	C	0.10
Teamwork (7 Strength to Use E/I)	Univ	C	0.10
Teamwork (8 Intellect to Use E/F)	Univ	C	0.10
Teamwork (8 Intellect to Use E/S)	Univ	C	0.10
20			
Teamwork (8 Strength to Use F/I)	Univ	C	0.10
The Acolytes	Char	R	2.50
The Acolytes: Exodus	Spec	U	1.00
The Acolytes: Fabian Cortez	Spec	VR	4.00
The Acolytes: Rusty Collins	Spec	U	0.80
The Acolytes: Senyaka	Spec	VR	4.50
The Acolytes: Skids	Spec	U	0.50
The Acolytes: Unuscione	Spec	U	0.50
The Coming of Galactus 1	Miss	C	0.10
21			
The Coming of Galactus 2	Miss	C	0.10
The Coming of Galactus 3	Miss	C	0.10
The Coming of Galactus 4	Miss	C	0.10
The Coming of Galactus 5	Miss	C	0.10
The Coming of Galactus 6	Miss	C	0.10
The Coming of Galactus 7	Miss	C	0.10
The Coming of Galactus: Coordinated Effort	Evnt	U	0.50
The Coming of Galactus: Desperate Gamble	Evnt	R	2.50
The Coming of Galactus: Everyone Has A Part To Play	Evnt	U	0.50
22			
The Coming of Galactus: Galactic Busy Work	Evnt	U	0.50
The Coming of Galactus: Herald Betrays Galactus	Evnt	R	2.80
The Coming of Galactus: Heroic Effort	Evnt	U	0.50
The Concrete Jungle	Loc	U	0.50
The Crossing: Rebirth!	Evnt	R	2.50
The Daily Bugle	Loc	R	2.30

Card name	Type	Rarity	Price
The Danger Room	Loc	U	0.80
The Enforcers	Char	R	2.50
The Enforcers: Fancy Dan	Spec	U	0.50
23			
The Enforcers: Hammer Harrison	Spec	C	0.10
The Enforcers: Montana	Spec	U	0.50
The Enforcers: Mr. Big	Spec	VR	5.00
The Enforcers: Ox	Spec	U	0.80
The Enforcers: Snake Marston	Spec	U	0.50
The Hand	Char	VR	5.00
The Hand: Dissolving Corpses	Spec	VR	4.50
The Hand: Kirigi	Spec	U	0.50
The Hand: Lord Daito	Spec	U	0.50
24			
The Hand: Ninja	Spec	U	0.80
The Hand: Shinobi Shaw	Spec	VR	4.50
The Hand: Snakeroot	Spec	U	0.80
The Helicarrier	Loc	U	0.50
The Hellfire Club	Char	R	3.00
The Hellfire Club: Hellfire Soldiers	Spec	C	0.10
The Hellfire Club: Madelyne Pryor	Spec	VR	5.50
The Hellfire Club: Sebastian Shaw	Spec	U	0.50
The Hellfire Club: Selene	Spec	VR	5.50
25			
The Hellfire Club: Tessa	Spec	VR	5.00
The Hellfire Club: Trevor Fitzroy	Spec	U	0.50
The Inhumans	Char	R	2.80
The Inhumans: Black Bolt	Spec	VR	6.30
The Inhumans: Gorgon	Spec	VR	4.30
The Inhumans: Karnak	Spec	U	0.80
The Inhumans: Lockjaw	Spec	U	0.50
The Inhumans: Medusa	Spec	VR	4.50
The Inhumans: Triton	Spec	U	0.50
26			
The Kree	Char	R	2.80
The Kree: Colonel Yon-Rogg	Spec	VR	5.00
The Kree: Interstellar Empire	Spec	U	1.00
The Kree: Prime Minister Zarek	Spec	U	0.50
The Kree: Ronan The Accuser	Spec	VR	6.00
The Kree: Sentry	Spec	VR	5.00
The Kree: Supreme Intelligence	Spec	U	0.50
The Marauders	Char	R	2.80
The Marauders: Arc Light	Spec	U	0.80
27			
The Marauders: Blockbuster	Spec	U	0.80
The Marauders: Harpoon	Spec	VR	5.00
The Marauders: Malice	Spec	VR	6.00
The Marauders: Scalphunter	Spec	U	0.50
The Marauders: Vertigo	Spec	U	0.50
The Morlocks	Char	VR	5.50
The Morlocks: Caliban	Spec	VR	5.50
The Morlocks: Callisto	Spec	U	0.50

Card name	Type	Rarity	Price
The Morlocks: Erg	Spec	U	0.80
28			
The Morlocks: Masque	Spec	VR	5.50
The Morlocks: Sunder	Spec	C	0.10
The Morlocks: Tar Baby	Spec	U	0.50
The Outback	Loc	U	0.50
The Reavers	Char	R	2.80
The Reavers: Bone Breaker	Spec	U	0.80
The Reavers: Cyborgs	Spec	C	0.10
The Reavers: Deathstrike	Spec	VR	6.00
The Reavers: Donald Pierce	Spec	U	0.50
29			
The Reavers: Pretty Boy	Spec	VR	4.30
The Reavers: Skull Buster	Spec	VR	5.30
The Savage Land	Loc	R	2.30
The Serpent Society	Char	R	2.80
The Serpent Society: Anaconda	Spec	VR	5.00
The Serpent Society: Asp	Spec	VR	5.50
The Serpent Society: Cobra	Spec	U	0.80
The Serpent Society: Death Adder	Spec	U	0.50
The Serpent Society: Diamondback	Spec	C	0.10
30			
The Serpent Society: Sidewinder	Spec	U	0.50
The Shi'ar	Char	R	2.80
The Shi'ar: D'ken	Spec	U	0.50
The Shi'ar: Deathbird	Spec	C	0.10
The Shi'ar: Gladiator	Spec	VR	6.00
The Shi'ar: Lillandra	Spec	U	0.50
The Shi'ar: M'krann Crystal	Spec	VR	5.00
The Shi'ar: Warstar	Spec	VR	4.50
The Starjammers	Char	R	2.80
31			
The Starjammers: Binary	Spec	VR	6.30
The Starjammers: Ch'od	Spec	U	0.50
The Starjammers: Corsair	Spec	U	0.50
The Starjammers: Hepzibah	Spec	C	0.10
The Starjammers: Keeyah	Spec	U	0.50
The Starjammers: Raza	Spec	VR	6.30
The Vault	Loc	U	0.50
Thing: Aunt Petunia	Spec	U	0.50
War Machine: Pepper Potts	Spec	VR	4.80
32			
White Queen: The Hellions	Spec	VR	5.00
Wundagore Mountain	Loc	U	0.50
X-Babies	Char	R	3.50
X-Babies: Li'l Colossus	Spec	U	1.00
X-Babies: Li'l Cyclops	Spec	VR	5.00
X-Babies: Li'l Dazzler	Spec	U	1.00
X-Babies: Li'l Longshot	Spec	U	1.00
X-Babies: Li'l Rogue	Spec	VR	5.00
X-Babies: Li'l Wolvie	Spec	U	1.00
33			
X-Mansion	Loc	U	0.50

OverPower • Marvel Classic

Fleer/SkyBox • Released **September 1997**

289 cards in set • **IDENTIFIER: Red backgrounds**

- Starter decks contain 65 cards; starter displays contain 12 starters
- Booster packs contain 15 cards; booster displays contain 36 boosters

Classic introduces Artifacts, special tactics cards based upon powerful items from the comic books such as **The Infinity Gauntlet** and **The Super Soldier Serum**. There are also more characters, although with such big names as **Deathlok**, **Dazzler**, and **Absorbing Man**, Fleer was quickly running out of material. (Note that Marvel's Captain Marvel shows up here as **Captain Marvell**, perhaps to prevent confusion with the DC version.)

This was the last set to come from Fleer/Skybox. On Jan. 28, 1998, responsibility for **OverPower** production and support shifted to Marvel Interactive, a division that Marvel *wasn't* selling off in its bankruptcy sale. — **John Jackson Miller & Orren McKay**

Set (215 cards)	82.50
Starter Display Box	42.50
Booster Display Box	40.00
Starter Deck	7.80
Booster Pack	2.30

You will need **24** nine-pocket pages to store this set. (12 doubled up)

Card name	Type	Rarity	Price
1			
Absorbing Man	Char	R	3.50
Absorbing Man: Absorb Properties	Spec	R	3.50
Absorbing Man: Crusher Creel	Spec	C	0.15
Absorbing Man: Molecular Mimic	Spec	U	0.60
Absorbing Man: Rebuild Form	Spec	U	0.60
Absorbing Man: Titania	Spec	C	0.15

Card name	Type	Rarity	Price
Absorbing Man: Wrecking Ball	Spec	C	0.15
Adam Warlock: The Infinity Watch	Spec	C	0.15
Age Of Apocalypse	Loc	R	3.50
2			
Alpha Flight: Murmur	Spec	U	0.60
Angel: Horseman Of Apocalypse	Char	C	0.15

RARITY KEY **C** = Common **U** = Uncommon **R** = Rare **VR** = Very Rare **UR** = Ultra Rare **F** = Foil card **X** = Fixed/standard in all decks

Card name	Type	Rarity	Price
☐ Any Character: New Universe	Spec	VR	6.50
☐ Any Mission: To Save The World!	Evnt	R	3.00
☐ Any Power 7	Pwr	U	0.80
☐ Artifact: Adamantium Tentacles	Tac	R	4.00
☐ Artifact: Pym Particles	Tac	C	0.15
☐ Artifact: The Book Of The Darkhold	Tac	R	4.00
☐ Artifact: The Cosmic Control Rod	Tac	R	4.00
☐ Artifact: The Infinity Gauntlet	Tac	VR	8.00
☐ Artifact: The Serpent Crown	Tac	R	4.00
☐ Artifact: The Super Soldier Serum	Tac	R	4.00
☐ Artifact: The Ultimate Nullifier	Tac	R	4.00
☐ Baron Mordo	Char	R	3.50
☐ Baron Mordo: Bargain Lifeforce	Spec	U	0.60
☐ Baron Mordo: Demonic Summons	Spec	R	3.50
☐ Baron Mordo: Illusion Casting	Spec	U	0.60
☐ Baron Mordo: Jealous Disciple	Spec	C	0.15
☐ Baron Mordo: Mystical Menace	Spec	C	0.15
☐ Baron Mordo: Spell Of Silence	Spec	C	0.15
☐ Beta Ray Bill	Char	C	0.15
☐ Black Panther	Char	R	4.00
☐ Black Panther: African Monarch	Spec	C	0.15
☐ Black Panther: Agile Warrior	Spec	U	0.80
☐ Black Panther: Black Panther Power	Spec	R	4.00
☐ Black Panther: Heart Shaped Herb	Spec	C	0.15
☐ Black Panther: Jungle Savvy	Spec	C	0.15
☐ Black Panther: Wakandan Technology	Spec	U	0.60
☐ Bullseye	Char	R	3.50
☐ Bullseye: Assassin For Hire	Spec	U	0.60
☐ Bullseye: Carefree Killer	Spec	C	0.15
☐ Bullseye: Everything's A Weapon!	Spec	R	3.00
☐ Bullseye: Murderer	Spec	C	0.15
☐ Bullseye: Precision Shot	Spec	C	0.15
☐ Bullseye: Relentless Assault	Spec	U	0.80
☐ Captain Mar-Vell	Char	U	0.80
☐ Captain Mar-Vell: Cosmic Awareness	Spec	C	0.15
☐ Captain Mar-Vell: Kree Stratagem	Spec	C	0.15
☐ Captain Mar-Vell: Nega-Bands	Spec	U	0.60
☐ Captain Mar-Vell: Protector of the Universe	Spec	C	0.15
☐ Captain Mar-Vell: Rick Jones	Spec	R	3.50
☐ Captain Mar-Vell: Universal Alignment	Spec	R	3.00
☐ Dazzler	Char	U	0.80
☐ Dazzler: Absorb Sound	Spec	R	3.00
☐ Dazzler: Disco Diva	Spec	C	0.15
☐ Dazzler: Focus Energy	Spec	R	3.00
☐ Dazzler: Longshot Love	Spec	U	0.80
☐ Dazzler: Mojoworld Rebel	Spec	C	0.15
☐ Dazzler: Roller Queen	Spec	C	0.15
☐ Deathlok	Char	U	0.80
☐ Deathlok: Cybercorpse	Spec	C	0.15
☐ Deathlok: Internal 'Puter	Spec	C	0.15
☐ Deathlok: John "Siege" Kelly	Spec	R	3.50
☐ Deathlok: Luther Manning	Spec	R	4.00
☐ Deathlok: Michael Collins	Spec	R	3.00
☐ Deathlok: Really Strong Laser	Spec	C	0.15
☐ Doctor Doom: 2099	Char	R	4.00
☐ Double Shot (6E/6F To Use: Intellect)	Tac	C	0.15
☐ Double Shot (6E/6I To Use: Energy)	Tac	C	0.15
☐ Double Shot (6E/6S To Use: Fighting)	Tac	C	0.15
☐ Double Shot (6E/6S To Use: Intellect)	Tac	C	0.15
☐ Double Shot (6F/6E To Use: Strength)	Tac	C	0.15
☐ Double Shot (6F/6I To Use: Fighting)	Tac	C	0.15
☐ Double Shot (6F/6I To Use: Strength)	Tac	C	0.15
☐ Double Shot (6F/6S To Use: Intellect)	Tac	C	0.15
☐ Double Shot (6I/6E To Use: Intellect)	Tac	C	0.15
☐ Double Shot (6I/6F To Use: Intellect)	Tac	C	0.15
☐ Double Shot (6I/6F To Use: Strength)	Tac	C	0.15
☐ Double Shot (6I/6S To Use: Energy)	Tac	C	0.15
☐ Double Shot (6S/6E To Use: Strength)	Tac	C	0.15
☐ Double Shot (6S/6F To Use: Strength)	Tac	C	0.15

Card name	Type	Rarity	Price
☐ Double Shot (6S/6I To Use: Fighting)	Tac	C	0.15
☐ Double Shot (6S/6I To Use: Strength)	Tac	C	0.15
☐ Dracula	Char	R	3.50
☐ Dracula: Children Of The Night	Spec	C	0.15
☐ Dracula: Deny Victory	Spec	C	0.15
☐ Dracula: Lifeblood	Spec	U	0.80
☐ Dracula: Lord Of The Vampires	Spec	R	3.00
☐ Dracula: Mesmerize	Spec	C	0.15
☐ Dracula: Summon Thunder	Spec	U	0.80
☐ Falcon	Char	U	0.80
☐ Falcon: Aerial Maneuvers	Spec	C	0.15
☐ Falcon: Flyby	Spec	C	0.15
☐ Falcon: Mechanical Wings	Spec	U	0.40
☐ Falcon: Power Dive	Spec	VR	5.00
☐ Falcon: Redwing	Spec	R	3.50
☐ Falcon: Snap Wilson	Spec	C	0.15
☐ Forge: Spiritual Purging	Spec	R	4.00
☐ Gamma Base	Loc	C	0.15
☐ Green Goblin: Revelations	Spec	U	0.60
☐ Havok	Char	U	0.80
☐ Havok: Annihilate	Spec	R	3.50
☐ Havok: Cosmic Battery	Spec	C	0.15
☐ Havok: Geo-Knowledge	Spec	U	0.60
☐ Havok: Plasma Flare	Spec	C	0.15
☐ Havok: Sibling Rivalry	Spec	C	0.15
☐ Havok: The Brotherhood	Spec	R	3.00
☐ Henry Pym: Founding Avenger	Spec	C	0.15
☐ Heroes For Hire	Char	R	6.00
☐ Heroes For Hire: Hercules	Spec	C	0.15
☐ Heroes For Hire: Iron Fist	Spec	R	3.50
☐ Heroes For Hire: Power Man	Spec	U	0.60
☐ Heroes For Hire: The Black Knight	Spec	C	0.15
☐ Heroes For Hire: The Hulk	Spec	U	0.60
☐ Heroes For Hire: White Tiger	Spec	C	0.15
☐ Holocaust: Nemesis	Spec	C	0.15
☐ Hulk: Mr. Fix-It	Char	R	4.00
☐ Human Torch: Invaders	Char	U	0.80
☐ Hydra: Fortunato	Spec	R	4.00
☐ Invisible Woman: Malice	Char	U	0.80
☐ Iron Man: Original Armor	Char	C	0.15
☐ Ka-Zar	Char	U	0.80
☐ Ka-Zar: Jungle Savvy	Spec	C	0.15
☐ Ka-Zar: King Of The Savage Land	Spec	R	3.50
☐ Ka-Zar: Lord Kevin Plunder	Spec	U	0.60
☐ Ka-Zar: Primitive Arsenal	Spec	R	4.00
☐ Ka-Zar: Shanna The She-Devil	Spec	C	0.15
☐ Ka-Zar: Zabu	Spec	C	0.15
☐ Kingpin: Asian Connections	Spec	R	3.50
☐ Leader	Char	U	0.80
☐ Leader: Freehold	Spec	C	0.15
☐ Leader: Green 'N Mean	Spec	C	0.15
☐ Leader: Omnibus	Spec	R	3.00
☐ Leader: Techno-Arsenal	Spec	U	0.60
☐ Leader: The Regeneration Crystal	Spec	R	3.00
☐ Leader: Twisted Mentality	Spec	C	0.15
☐ Maggot	Char	R	5.00
☐ Maggot: Awesome Aussie	Spec	C	0.15
☐ Maggot: Slugfest	Spec	R	3.50
☐ Maggot: Tunnel Worms	Spec	U	0.80
☐ Marrow	Char	R	5.00
☐ Marrow: Bone Snap	Spec	C	0.15
☐ Marrow: Doubleheart	Spec	U	0.60
☐ Marrow: Morlock History	Spec	R	3.50
☐ Mole Man	Char	U	0.80
☐ Mole Man: Energy Staff	Spec	U	0.60
☐ Mole Man: Monster Island	Spec	VR	6.00
☐ Mole Man: Social Outcast	Spec	C	0.15
☐ Mole Man: Strategic Tunneling	Spec	C	0.15
☐ Mole Man: The Mole Men	Spec	C	0.15
☐ Mole Man: Uproot Earth	Spec	R	3.50

Card name	Type	Rarity	Price
☐ New Warriors: Turbo	Spec	C	0.15
☐ Nick Fury: LMD	Spec	U	0.60
☐ Onslaught: Dark Thoughts	Spec	C	0.15
☐ Post: Mysterious Past	Spec	C	0.15
☐ Psycho-Man	Char	U	0.80
☐ Psycho-Man: Doubt	Spec	R	4.00
☐ Psycho-Man: Emotion Box	Spec	C	0.15
☐ Psycho-Man: Fear	Spec	U	0.60
☐ Psycho-Man: Hate	Spec	C	0.15
☐ Psycho-Man: Malice	Spec	R	3.00
☐ Psycho-Man: Microverse Menace	Spec	C	0.15
☐ Puppet Master	Char	U	0.80
☐ Puppet Master: Alicia Masters	Spec	C	0.15
☐ Puppet Master: Automatons	Spec	U	0.80
☐ Puppet Master: Criminal Mastermind	Spec	C	0.15
☐ Puppet Master: Liddleville	Spec	R	3.00
☐ Puppet Master: Mental Domination	Spec	R	3.00
☐ Puppet Master: Mystic Clay	Spec	C	0.15
☐ Red Skull: The Scourge	Spec	C	0.15
☐ Reyes	Char	R	3.50
☐ Reyes: Force Projection	Spec	R	3.00
☐ Reyes: Medical Background	Spec	C	0.15
☐ Reyes: Reluctant Hero	Spec	U	0.60
☐ Scorpion	Char	U	0.80
☐ Scorpion: Acid Spray	Spec	C	0.15
☐ Scorpion: Arachnid Strength	Spec	C	0.15
☐ Scorpion: Mac Gargan: Private Eye	Spec	R	3.00
☐ Scorpion: Savage Insanity	Spec	C	0.15
☐ Scorpion: Scorpion Sting	Spec	U	0.80
☐ Scorpion: The Jameson Connection	Spec	R	3.00
☐ Shadowcat: Cat Claws	Spec	C	0.15
☐ Shadowcat: Age Of Apocalypse	Char	VR	6.00
☐ Shang Chi: Master Of Kung Fu	Char	U	0.80
☐ Shang Chi: Master Of Kung Fu: Fu Manchu	Spec	R	3.00
☐ Shang Chi: Master Of Kung Fu: Kung Fu Secrets	Spec	C	0.15
☐ Shang Chi: Master Of Kung Fu: Meditative Focus	Spec	R	3.50
☐ Shang Chi: Master Of Kung Fu: Mi-6	Spec	C	0.15
☐ Shang Chi: Master Of Kung Fu: Sudden Strike	Spec	C	0.15
☐ Shang Chi: Master Of Kung Fu: The Elixir Vitae	Spec	U	0.60
☐ Spider-Man: Symbiotic Costume	Char	R	6.00
☐ Superpatriot	Char	U	0.80
☐ The Acolytes: Amelia Voght	Spec	U	0.60
☐ The Big Apple	Loc	C	0.15
☐ The Enforcers: The Eel	Spec	U	0.40
☐ The Hand: Erynys	Spec	C	0.15
☐ The Hellfire Club: Emma Frost	Spec	C	0.15
☐ The Inhumans: Maximus The Mad	Spec	C	0.15
☐ The Kree: Dr. Minerva	Spec	U	0.60
☐ The Marauders: Riptide	Spec	U	0.60
☐ The Morlocks: Leech	Spec	C	0.15
☐ The Reavers: Gateway	Spec	R	3.50
☐ The Serpent Society: Fer-De-Lance	Spec	C	0.15
☐ The Sewer	Loc	C	0.15
☐ The Shi'ar: Nightside	Spec	C	0.15
☐ The Starjammers: Professor X	Spec	R	3.00
☐ Thunderbolts	Char	U	0.80
☐ Thunderbolts: Atlas	Spec	C	0.15
☐ Thunderbolts: Citizen V	Spec	R	3.50
☐ Thunderbolts: M.A.C.H.1	Spec	C	0.15
☐ Thunderbolts: Meteorite	Spec	R	3.00
☐ Thunderbolts: Songbird	Spec	C	0.15
☐ Thunderbolts: Techno	Spec	C	0.15
☐ Wakanda	Loc	R	3.50
☐ White Queen: Corporate Cutthroat	Spec	C	0.15
☐ X-Babies: Li'l Iceman	Spec	C	0.15

RARITY KEY C = Common U = Uncommon R = Rare VR = Very Rare UR = Ultra Rare F = Foil card X = Fixed/standard in all decks

OverPower • Image

Marvel Interactive/Wildstorm • Released **September 1998**

217 cards in set • **IDENTIFIER: Green card backs**

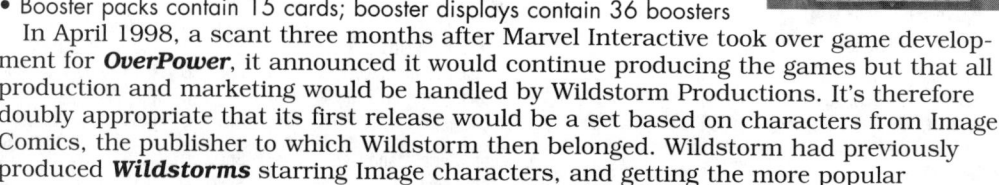

- Starter decks contain 60 cards; starter displays contain 12 starters
- Booster packs contain 15 cards; booster displays contain 36 boosters

In April 1998, a scant three months after Marvel Interactive took over game development for **OverPower**, it announced it would continue producing the games but that all production and marketing would be handled by Wildstorm Productions. It's therefore doubly appropriate that its first release would be a set based on characters from Image Comics, the publisher to which Wildstorm then belonged. Wildstorm had previously produced **Wildstorms** starring Image characters, and getting the more popular **OverPower** game basically reassured the end of *Wildstorms*.

Image cards were theoretically compatible with other *OverPower* cards, but they came with yet a third different card back. Wildstorm placed its mission cards on regular cardstock, unlike Fleer/SkyBox's heavier trading cards. — ***John Jackson Miller***

Set (217 cards)	96.25	
Starter Display Box	57.00	**You will need 25** nine-pocket pages to store this set. (13 doubled up)
Booster Display Box	55.00	
Starter Deck	8.20	
Booster Pack	2.10	

Card name	Type	Rarity	Price
1			
☐ Ally (5 Energy or Less)	Univ	C	0.10
☐ Ally (5 Fighting or Less)	Univ	C	0.10
☐ Ally (5 Intellect or Less)	Univ	C	0.10
☐ Ally (5 Strength or Less)	Univ	C	0.10
☐ Ally (6 Energy or More)	Univ	C	0.10
☐ Ally (6 Fighting or More)	Univ	C	0.10
☐ Ally (6 Intellect or More)	Univ	C	0.10
☐ Ally (6 Strength or More)	Univ	C	0.10
☐ Any Character: Flight	Spec	R	3.00
2			
☐ Any Character: Massive Muscles	Spec	R	3.30
☐ Any Character: Super Speed	Spec	R	3.50
☐ Any Power 8	Pwr	VR	3.80
☐ Artifact: Linkstone	Tac	VR	5.50
☐ Artifact: Myrlu Symbiote	Tac	VR	5.50
☐ Artifact: Shadowhelmet	Tac	VR	5.50
☐ Artifact: The Witchblade	Tac	R	2.80
☐ Backlash	Char	C	0.10
☐ Backlash: Altered Physiology	Spec	C	0.10
3			
☐ Backlash: Combat Agility	Spec	U	0.60
☐ Backlash: Government Trooper	Spec	U	0.60
☐ Backlash: Mist Body	Spec	R	3.30
☐ Backlash: Psi-Whips	Spec	R	3.50
☐ Backlash: Team 7	Spec	U	0.70
☐ Basic (Any Power 6 to Use +2)	Univ	VR	5.00
☐ Brass: Armored Powerhouse	Spec	R	3.30
☐ Brass: Computer Tracking	Spec	U	0.70
☐ Brass: Weapons Array	Spec	R	3.30
4			
☐ Coda Island	Loc	U	0.70
☐ Curse	Char	C	0.10
☐ Curse: Appendage Of Death	Spec	R	3.00
☐ Curse: Brutal Disection	Spec	R	2.50
☐ Curse: Exoskeleton	Spec	C	0.10
☐ Curse: Religious Zeal	Spec	U	0.70
☐ Curse: Techno-Life	Spec	C	0.10
☐ Curse: Wrist Rockets	Spec	C	0.10
☐ Energy 1	Pwr	C	0.10
5			
☐ Energy 2	Pwr	C	0.10
☐ Energy 3	Pwr	C	0.10
☐ Energy 4	Pwr	C	0.10
☐ Energy 5	Pwr	C	0.10
☐ Energy 6	Pwr	C	0.10
☐ Energy 7	Pwr	C	0.10
☐ Energy 8	Pwr	C	0.10
☐ Fairchild	Char	R	4.80
☐ Fairchild: Fist Full Of Danger	Spec	U	0.70
6			
☐ Fairchild: Gen-Active	Spec	C	0.10

Card name	Type	Rarity	Price
☐ Fairchild: Impenetrable	Spec	R	3.80
☐ Fairchild: Level Headed Leader	Spec	U	0.70
☐ Fairchild: Pure Muscle	Spec	U	0.70
☐ Fairchild: Super Smarts	Spec	R	3.30
☐ Fighting 1	Pwr	C	0.10
☐ Fighting 2	Pwr	C	0.10
☐ Fighting 3	Pwr	C	0.10
☐ Fighting 4	Pwr	C	0.10
7			
☐ Fighting 5	Pwr	C	0.10
☐ Fighting 6	Pwr	C	0.10
☐ Fighting 7	Pwr	C	0.10
☐ Fighting 8	Pwr	C	0.10
☐ Grifter	Char	R	5.00
☐ Grifter: Bullseye Shot	Spec	R	2.80
☐ Grifter: Coda Training	Spec	U	0.70
☐ Grifter: Nerves Of Steel	Spec	R	2.50
☐ Grifter: Smart-Ass	Spec	U	0.70
8			
☐ Grifter: Team 7	Spec	U	0.70
☐ Grifter: WildC.A.T.	Spec	C	0.10
☐ Grunge	Char	U	0.70
☐ Grunge: Danger Seeker	Spec	R	2.80
☐ Grunge: Dense	Spec	U	0.70
☐ Grunge: Gen-Active	Spec	U	0.70
☐ Grunge: Lover Boy	Spec	C	0.10
☐ Grunge: Martial Arts Training	Spec	C	0.10
☐ Grunge: Molecular Assimilation	Spec	R	2.80
9			
☐ Intellect 1	Pwr	C	0.10
☐ Intellect 2	Pwr	C	0.10
☐ Intellect 3	Pwr	C	0.10
☐ Intellect 4	Pwr	C	0.10
☐ Intellect 5	Pwr	C	0.10
☐ Intellect 6	Pwr	C	0.10
☐ Intellect 7	Pwr	C	0.10
☐ Intellect 8	Pwr	C	0.10
☐ Killrazor	Char	C	0.10
10			
☐ Killrazor: Biomorphic Blades	Spec	U	0.70
☐ Killrazor: Deadly Mutation	Spec	C	0.10
☐ Killrazor: Inner Peace	Spec	R	2.50
☐ Killrazor: Outer Fury	Spec	R	3.00
☐ Killrazor: Strykeforce	Spec	C	0.10
☐ Killrazor: Will Power	Spec	C	0.10
☐ Malebolgia	Char	VR	10.25
☐ Malebolgia: Demonic Magick	Spec	C	0.10
☐ Malebolgia: Hellbent	Spec	U	0.70
11			
☐ Malebolgia: Infernal Pact	Spec	U	0.70
☐ Malebolgia: Master Of The Darklands	Spec	R	4.00
☐ Malebolgia: Reign Of Fire	Spec	U	0.70
☐ Malebolgia: Signed In Blood	Spec	R	4.30
☐ Multipower 1	Pwr	C	0.10
☐ Multipower 2	Pwr	C	0.10
☐ Multipower 3	Pwr	C	0.10
☐ Multipower 4	Pwr	C	0.10
☐ Multipower 5	Pwr	VR	3.80

Card name	Type	Rarity	Price
12			
☐ New York City	Loc	C	0.10
☐ Omniverse	Loc	U	0.70
☐ Overkill	Char	U	0.70
☐ Overkill: Armor	Spec	U	0.70
☐ Overkill: Contract Hit	Spec	R	3.50
☐ Overkill: Cyborg	Spec	U	0.70
☐ Overkill: High Caliber	Spec	U	0.70
☐ Overkill: Mob Connections	Spec	C	0.10
☐ Overkill: One Man Army	Spec	R	2.80
13			
☐ Ripclaw	Char	R	4.30
☐ Ripclaw: Animal Rage	Spec	C	0.10
☐ Ripclaw: Cyberforce	Spec	C	0.10
☐ Ripclaw: Mechanical Mutant	Spec	U	0.70
☐ Ripclaw: Native Magic	Spec	R	3.50
☐ Ripclaw: Pacifist Heart	Spec	R	3.80
☐ Ripclaw: Rip And Tear	Spec	U	0.70
☐ Savage Dragon	Char	R	5.30
☐ Savage Dragon: Amazing Recovery	Spec	U	0.70
14			
☐ Savage Dragon: Bullet Proof	Spec	C	0.10
☐ Savage Dragon: Chicago PD	Spec	C	0.10
☐ Savage Dragon: Dragon Brawl	Spec	U	0.70
☐ Savage Dragon: Freak Force	Spec	C	0.10
☐ Savage Dragon: Savage Strength	Spec	R	3.00
☐ Shadowhawk	Char	U	0.90
☐ Shadowhawk: Back Snap	Spec	R	3.50
☐ Shadowhawk: Battle Armor	Spec	C	0.10
☐ Shadowhawk: Brutal Revenge	Spec	R	3.50
15			
☐ Shadowhawk: Hospitalize	Spec	C	0.10
☐ Shadowhawk: Night Prowler	Spec	U	0.70
☐ Shadowhawk: Urban Predator	Spec	U	0.70
☐ Shattered Image: Cyberforce vs. Giger	Evnt	U	0.60
☐ Shattered Image: Entropy Field	Evnt	R	3.50
☐ Shattered Image: Gen¹³ vs. The Regulators	Evnt	U	0.60
☐ Shattered Image: Mighty Men to the Rescue	Evnt	U	0.60
☐ Shattered Image: Spawn Spys	Evnt	U	0.60
☐ Shattered Image: Witchblade on the Scene	Evnt	R	3.50
16			
☐ Shattered Image 1	Miss	U	0.60
☐ Shattered Image 2	Miss	U	0.60
☐ Shattered Image 3	Miss	U	0.60
☐ Shattered Image 4	Miss	R	2.50
☐ Shattered Image 5	Miss	U	0.60
☐ Shattered Image 6	Miss	U	0.60
☐ Shattered Image 7	Miss	U	0.60
☐ Spawn	Char	R	6.80
☐ Spawn: CIA Training	Spec	C	0.10
17			
☐ Spawn: Heavy Weapons	Spec	C	0.10
☐ Spawn: Living Costume	Spec	R	3.00
☐ Spawn: Magickal Chains	Spec	C	0.10
☐ Spawn: Preternatural Powers	Spec	U	0.70

RARITY KEY C = Common   U = Uncommon   R = Rare   VR = Very Rare   UR = Ultra Rare   F = Foil card   X = Fixed/standard in all decks

Card name	Type	Rarity	Price
☐ Spawn: Protector Of The Innocent	Spec	U	0.70
☐ Spawn's Alley	Loc	U	1.00
☐ Strength 1	Pwr	C	0.10
☐ Strength 2	Pwr	C	0.10
☐ Strength 3	Pwr	C	0.10
[18]			
☐ Strength 4	Pwr	C	0.10
☐ Strength 5	Pwr	C	0.10
☐ Strength 6	Pwr	C	0.10
☐ Strength 7	Pwr	C	0.10
☐ Strength 8	Pwr	C	0.10
☐ Stryker	Char	C	0.10
☐ Stryker: Armed And Dangerous	Spec	R	3.00
☐ Stryker: Cyberforce Leader	Spec	C	0.10
☐ Stryker: Digital Imaging	Spec	U	0.70
[19]			
☐ Stryker: Mutant Cyborg	Spec	U	0.70
☐ Stryker: Serious Arsenal	Spec	R	3.80
☐ Stryker: Tough As Nails	Spec	U	0.70
☐ Teamwork (6 Energy to Use)	Univ	C	0.10
☐ Teamwork (6 Fighting to Use)	Univ	C	0.10
☐ Teamwork (6 Intellect to Use)	Univ	C	0.10
☐ Teamwork (6 Strength to Use)	Univ	C	0.10
☐ The Darkness	Char	R	7.00
☐ The Darkness: Demigod of the Dark	Spec	R	2.80
[20]			
☐ The Darkness: Killing Touch	Spec	R	3.50

Card name	Type	Rarity	Price
☐ The Darkness: Lifelike Exoskin	Spec	U	0.70
☐ The Darkness: Night Flight	Spec	U	0.70
☐ The Darkness: Restore Health	Spec	C	0.10
☐ The Darkness: Shadow Motion	Spec	C	0.10
☐ Tiffany	Char	R	4.50
☐ Tiffany: Costume Ribbons	Spec	C	0.10
☐ Tiffany: Crusade	Spec	R	3.00
☐ Tiffany: Heavenly Agent	Spec	R	3.00
[21]			
☐ Tiffany: Holy Order	Spec	U	0.70
☐ Tiffany: Lance	Spec	U	0.70
☐ Tiffany: Magickal Hunter	Spec	C	0.10
☐ Velocity	Char	U	0.70
☐ Velocity: Cyberforce	Spec	C	0.10
☐ Velocity: High Speed Reflexes	Spec	C	0.10
☐ Velocity: Internal Hardware	Spec	R	3.50
☐ Velocity: Protective Skin	Spec	U	0.70
☐ Velocity: Quick Thinking	Spec	R	3.00
[22]			
☐ Velocity: Speedthrough	Spec	R	2.80
☐ Violator	Char	R	5.80
☐ Violator: Clown Morph	Spec	U	0.70
☐ Violator: Connive	Spec	C	0.10
☐ Violator: Darkland's Army	Spec	VR	5.80
☐ Violator: Demonic Powers	Spec	C	0.10

Card name	Type	Rarity	Price
☐ Violator: Devil's Advocate	Spec	C	0.10
☐ Violator: Heart Attack	Spec	R	3.30
☐ Voodoo: Dangerous Dancer	Spec	R	3.00
[23]			
☐ Voodoo: True Vision	Spec	R	3.00
☐ Voodoo: WildC.A.T.	Spec	U	0.70
☐ Witchblade	Char	R	7.80
☐ Witchblade: Biomech Tendrils	Spec	U	0.70
☐ Witchblade: Energy Wrath	Spec	R	4.50
☐ Witchblade: Forensic Science	Spec	U	0.70
☐ Witchblade: NYPD Instinct	Spec	C	0.10
☐ Witchblade: Protective Drive	Spec	C	0.10
☐ Witchblade: The Chosen	Spec	VR	7.00
[24]			
☐ Wynonna Earp: Famous Lineage	Spec	U	0.70
☐ Wynonna Earp: Shootout	Spec	R	3.50
☐ Wynonna Earp: Smoking Guns	Spec	R	4.30
☐ Zealot	Char	R	4.50
☐ Zealot: Clef Blade	Spec	U	0.70
☐ Zealot: Coda Discipline	Spec	C	0.10
☐ Zealot: Kherubim	Spec	R	2.50
☐ Zealot: Sister's Support	Spec	U	0.70
☐ Zealot: Warrior Soul	Spec	VR	5.80
[25]			
☐ Zealot: WildC.A.T.	Spec	U	0.70

OverPower • X-Men

Marvel Interactive/Wildstorm • Released December 1998

217 cards in set • **IDENTIFIER: 'X' pattern in card backgrounds**

• Booster packs contain 15 cards; booster displays contain 36 boosters

Despite what the name suggests, the **X-Men** expansion is a bit light on actual X-Men. It adds a few of those less popular X-Men that had been overlooked in previous expansions, but contains a good deal of non-X-Men and clone characters for existing X-Men.

There's no little bit of irony associated with this set. Remember that Marvel, which had previously done a role-playing game with TSR, chose in 1995 to do its own CCG rather than do a game with an establshed company like Wizards of the Coast. By 1998, Marvel was doing a role-playing game again — with Wizards of the Coast, which had since bought TSR out. And Marvel's next CCG release after this one would be from Wizards of the Coast — coincidentally, **X-Men** again.

And many familiar with the Coke/Pepsi relationship between Marvel and DC thought DC would never let Marvel use DC characters in a CCG. Not only did it, but by this last **OverPower** release, Marvel's partner Wildstorm had been bought by DC in the fall of 1998! The release date above is an estimate — *OverPower* had all but dropped off the radar by this point — but *X-Men OverPower* packs have all three publishers' names as producers: Marvel, DC, and Wildstorm! — ***John Jackson Miller & Orren McKay***

You will need **23** nine-pocket pages to store this set. (12 doubled up)

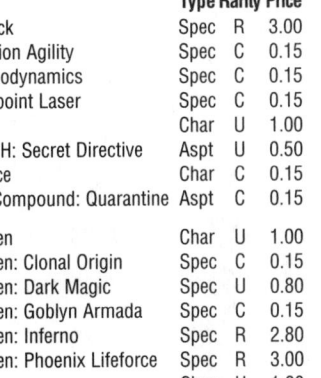

Set (217 cards)	78.75
Booster Display Box	52.00
Booster Pack	2.00

Card name	Type	Rarity	Price
[1]			
☐ Ally (5 Energy or Less)	Univ	C	0.10
☐ Age Of Apocalypse: Historical Twist	Aspt	R	3.30
☐ "Ally: Amos ""Fred"" Duncan"	Univ	C	0.15
☐ Ally: Chief Authier	Univ	C	0.15
☐ Ally: Lila Cheney	Univ	C	0.15
☐ Ally: Trish Trilby	Univ	C	0.15
☐ Alpha Flight: Vindicator	Spec	C	0.15
☐ Angel: The Fallen	Char	C	0.15
☐ Angel: The Fallen: Neuro-Toxin	Spec	U	0.40
☐ Any Character: Devourer Of Worlds	Spec	R	5.50
[2]			
☐ Any Homebase: A-Next	Aspt	R	5.30
☐ Artifact: Adamantium	Tac	U	1.00
☐ Artifact: Image Inducer	Tac	C	0.15
☐ Artifact: M'krann Fragment	Tac	R	2.80
☐ Artifact: The Siege Perilous	Tac	U	1.00
☐ Asteroid 'M': Orbital Hideout	Aspt	U	0.50
☐ Avalon: Mutant Refuge	Aspt	R	3.50

Card name	Type	Rarity	Price
☐ Bastion	Char	U	1.00
☐ Beast: The Brute	Char	U	1.00
[3]			
☐ Callisto	Char	C	0.15
☐ Cape Citadel	Loc	U	0.80
☐ Cape Citadel: The Benassi Rocket	Aspt	R	3.80
☐ Captain Britain	Char	U	1.00
☐ Captain Britain: Battleworthy	Spec	C	0.15
☐ Captain Britain: Physics Genius	Spec	U	0.40
☐ Captain Britain: Prodigious Strength	Spec	R	2.00
☐ Captain Britain: Super Endurance	Spec	R	3.30
☐ Captain Britain: Supersonic	Spec	U	1.00
[4]			
☐ Cerebro	Char	R	4.00
☐ Cerebro: Catalogue	Spec	U	0.80
☐ Cerebro: Computer Origin	Spec	R	2.80
☐ Cerebro: Mutant Seeker	Spec	C	0.15
☐ Cerebro: Sentinel Evolution	Spec	C	0.15
☐ Cerebro: The Founder	Spec	C	0.15
☐ Colossus: Age Of Apocalypse	Char	U	1.00
☐ Crux	Char	C	0.15
☐ Crux: Coldforce	Spec	C	0.15
[5]			
☐ Crux: Heatforce	Spec	C	0.15

Card name	Type	Rarity	Price
☐ Crux: Payback	Spec	R	3.00
☐ Crux: Precision Agility	Spec	C	0.15
☐ Crux: Thermodynamics	Spec	C	0.15
☐ Dazzler: Pinpoint Laser	Spec	C	0.15
☐ Deathbird	Char	U	1.00
☐ Department H: Secret Directive	Aspt	U	0.50
☐ Donald Pierce	Char	C	0.15
☐ Fall's Edge Compound: Quarantine	Aspt	C	0.15
[6]			
☐ Goblyn Queen	Char	U	1.00
☐ Goblyn Queen: Clonal Origin	Spec	C	0.15
☐ Goblyn Queen: Dark Magic	Spec	U	0.80
☐ Goblyn Queen: Goblyn Armada	Spec	C	0.15
☐ Goblyn Queen: Inferno	Spec	R	2.80
☐ Goblyn Queen: Phoenix Lifeforce	Spec	R	3.00
☐ Grey King	Char	U	1.00
☐ Grey King: Analytical Genius	Spec	C	0.15
☐ Grey King: Carrier Wave	Spec	C	0.15
[7]			
☐ Grey King: Leader	Spec	C	0.15
☐ Grey King: Psychic Neutralizer	Spec	U	0.80
☐ Grey King: TK Beam	Spec	R	3.30
☐ Havok: Mutant X	Spec	C	0.15
☐ Havok: Mutant X	Char	U	0.40

Card name	Type	Rarity	Price
Iceman: The Ice-Man	Char	U	1.00
Jean Grey: Dark Phoenix	Char	R	5.80
Krakoa	Loc	C	0.15
Krakoa: The Living Island	Aspt	C	0.15
8			
Landau, Luckman & Lake	Loc	C	0.15
Landau, Luckman & Lake: Warp Chamber	Aspt	R	3.50
Landslide	Char	C	0.15
Landslide: Appetite for Destruction	Spec	C	0.15
Landslide: Big Bully	Spec	U	0.80
Landslide: Massive Speed	Spec	C	0.15
Landslide: Short Fuse	Spec	R	3.00
Landslide: Wallop	Spec	C	0.15
Madripoor: Underworld Center	Aspt	C	0.15
9			
Maggot: Intestinal Fortitude	Spec	R	3.50
Marrow: Battlebones	Spec	C	0.15
Marvel Manhattan: Excelsior!	Aspt	C	0.15
Marvel Universe: Excelsior!	Aspt	C	0.15
Maverick	Char	R	4.00
Maverick: Combat Armor	Spec	C	0.15
Maverick: Freelance Spy	Spec	R	3.50
Maverick: Kinetic Absorption	Spec	C	0.15
Maverick: Legacy Regression	Spec	C	0.15
10			
Maverick: Power Channel	Spec	U	0.80
Mercury	Char	U	1.00
Mercury: Combat Experience	Spec	U	0.80
Mercury: Mercenary Code	Spec	C	0.15
Mercury: Mercuric Blades	Spec	C	0.15
Mercury: Metallic Control	Spec	C	0.15
Mercury: Soldier-Of-Fortune	Spec	R	3.50
Mojoworld: Tv Dimension	Aspt	U	0.50
Morlock Tunnels: Hidden World	Aspt	U	0.50
11			
Muir Island: Genetic Research	Aspt	U	0.50
Multiple Man	Char	C	0.15
Multiple Man: Duplicate Self	Spec	C	0.15
Multiple Man: Legacy Survivor	Spec	R	3.00
Multiple Man: Multiply and Conquer	Spec	R	3.00
Multiple Man: Outnumber	Spec	C	0.15
Multiple Man: Team Madrox	Spec	C	0.15
Namor: Sub-Mariner	Char	R	4.00
Onslaught's Citadel: Electromagnetic Pulse	Aspt	C	0.15
12			
Outback: Pirate Technology	Aspt	U	0.50
Phoenix	Char	U	1.00
Phoenix: Askani Founder	Spec	R	3.00
Phoenix: Child Of The Future	Spec	R	3.00
Phoenix: Manifest Phoenix	Spec	R	3.30
Phoenix: Mutant Hound	Spec	C	0.15
Phoenix: Telepathic Power	Spec	C	0.15
Polaris	Char	U	1.00

Card name	Type	Rarity	Price
Polaris: Energy Warp	Spec	C	0.15
13			
Polaris: Ensnare	Spec	U	0.50
Polaris: Magnetic Field	Spec	C	0.15
Polaris: Manipulate Magnetism	Spec	C	0.15
Polaris: Reverse Polarity	Spec	C	0.15
Princess Bar	Loc	C	0.15
Princess Bar: Identity Swap	Aspt	C	0.15
Psylocke: Betsy Braddock	Char	C	0.15
Rapture	Char	U	1.00
Rapture: Avian Mutation	Spec	C	0.15
14			
Rapture: Flightpath	Spec	C	0.15
Rapture: Mercy Killing	Spec	R	3.00
Rapture: Psychic Sword	Spec	C	0.15
Rapture: Release Soul	Spec	C	0.15
Reyes: Triage	Spec	C	0.15
Rogue: Brotherhood of Evil Mutants	Char	C	0.15
Sabra	Char	U	1.00
Sabra: Bladefire	Spec	R	2.50
Sabra: High Durability	Spec	R	2.30
15			
Sabra: Lethal Agent	Spec	R	2.80
Sabra: Mossad	Spec	U	0.80
Sabra: Mutant Musculature	Spec	C	0.15
Shadow King	Char	U	1.00
Shadow King: Astral Lifeform	Spec	C	0.15
Shadow King: Possess Others	Spec	R	3.50
Shadow King: Psi-Screen	Spec	C	0.15
Shadow King: Telepathic Manipulation	Spec	C	0.15
Shadow King: Twist Desire	Spec	R	2.80
16			
Ship: Celestial Origin	Aspt	U	0.50
Spider-Girl	Char	C	0.15
Spider-Girl: Clever Fighter	Spec	C	0.15
Spider-Girl: Mayday	Spec	R	3.50
Spider-Girl: Spider Mobility	Spec	C	0.15
Spider-Girl: Wall Walker	Spec	R	3.00
Spider-Girl: Web Action	Spec	U	0.80
Storm: Bloodstorm	Char	U	1.00
Storm: Neutralized	Char	C	0.15
17			
Sunfire	Char	U	1.00
Sunfire: Atomic Flame	Spec	R	3.00
Sunfire: Ionize Matter	Spec	C	0.15
Sunfire: Nationalist Zeal	Spec	C	0.15
Sunfire: Radiate Heat	Spec	R	3.00
Sunfire: Solar Flare	Spec	C	0.15
Taskmaster	Char	U	1.00
Taskmaster: Photographic Reflexes	Spec	R	3.00
Taskmaster: Replica Shield	Spec	C	0.15
18			
Taskmaster: Spy Camera	Spec	R	2.80
Taskmaster: Trained Lackeys	Spec	C	0.15

Card name	Type	Rarity	Price
Taskmaster: Weapons Master	Spec	C	0.15
The Acolytes: Frenzy	Spec	C	0.15
The Danger Room: Holographic Attackers R	Aspt	R	4.00
The Hellfire Club: Von Roehm	Spec	R	3.80
The Marauders: Prism	Spec	C	0.15
The Morlocks: Run From Slaughter	Spec	C	0.15
19			
The Reavers: Cybernetic Rebirth	Spec	U	0.40
The Shi'ar: Fang	Spec	C	0.15
The Starjammers: Majestrix Lilandra	Spec	C	0.15
Thunderbird	Char	U	1.00
Thunderbird: Apache Warrior	Spec	C	0.15
Thunderbird: Cellular Density	Spec	C	0.15
Thunderbird: Keen Senses	Spec	C	0.15
Thunderbird: Powerhouse	Spec	C	0.15
Thunderbird: Ultimate Sacrifice	Spec	R	3.50
Typhoid Mary	Char	U	1.00
20			
Typhoid Mary: Assassinate	Spec	C	0.15
Typhoid Mary: Bloody Mary	Spec	R	3.50
Typhoid Mary: Dressed To Kill	Spec	R	3.50
Typhoid Mary: Fractured Personality	Spec	C	0.15
Typhoid Mary: Sociopath	Spec	C	0.15
Wolverine: Weapon X	Char	R	6.30
Wundagore Mountain: The Knights Of Wundagore	Aspt	C	0.15
X-Babies: Li'l Phoenix	Spec	C	0.15
X-Man	Char	R	6.30
21			
X-Man: Apocalyptic Survival	Spec	C	0.15
X-Man: Illusory Reality	Spec	R	3.00
X-Man: Sinister Creation	Spec	C	0.15
X-Man: Street Prophet	Spec	U	0.80
X-Man: Ultimate Potential	Spec	R	3.30
X-Mansion: Mutant Schooling	Aspt	U	0.50
X-Men: Original Team	Char	C	0.15
X-Men: Original Team: Angel	Spec	U	0.40
X-Men: Original Team: Beast	Spec	C	0.15
22			
X-Men: Original Team: Cyclops	Spec	C	0.15
X-Men: Original Team: Iceman	Spec	R	2.00
X-Men: Original Team: Marvel Girl	Spec	U	1.00
X-World	Loc	U	0.80
X-World: Parallel Dimension	Aspt	U	0.50
Xaos	Char	U	1.00
Xaos: Autistic Withdrawal	Spec	C	0.15
Xaos: Chaos Burst	Spec	U	0.80
Xaos: Fractal Plasma	Spec	C	0.15
23			
Xaos: Protective Instinct	Spec	C	0.15
Xaos: The Evil Eye	Spec	C	0.15

Pez

U.S. Games Systems • Released June 2000
204 cards in set

- Starter decks contain 120 cards and booster pack
- Booster packs contain 9 cards

What a strange way for a CCG manufacter to follow up **Wyvern**.

The premise of **Pez**, released by U.S. Game Systems in the initial boom of CCGs following **Pokémon**, is that players are trying to collect Pez dispensers. (Which presumes, of course, that you're familiar with the concept. For our overseas readers yet to get this advance in confectionary technology, Pez dispensers distribute little candy wafers from the necks of plastic toy characters. Got it? Good.) The first to collect 25 points worth of Pez dispensers wins.

Believe it or not, **Pez** is easy to learn, fast, fun, and just as addictive as the little candies that inspire it. There are two decks of cards, Flavors and Dispensers. Flavor cards say **Grape**, **Orange**, **Strawberry**, or **Lemon**. Each Dispenser card has a point value, a number of Flavor cards needed to play to score those points and, for a select few, special abilities.

You will need
23
nine-pocket
pages to store
this set.
(12 doubled up)

RARITY KEY C = Common U = Uncommon R = Rare VR = Very Rare UR = Ultra Rare F = Foil card X = Fixed/standard in all decks

348 • SCRYE Collectible Card Game Checklist and Price Guide

For example, a Dispenser may say Orange, Orange, Grape, Lemon and be worth eight points. Those Flavor cards must be played into the dispenser in that order.

Between players sit four face-up Dispenser cards. First, players draw their five-card hands, play out the first four Dispensers, and determine who goes first. Each player may take two actions and draw two cards. There are three actions. A player can move a Dispenser card from the middle into his collection by playing the first Flavor card on it. If the Dispenser card starts with two of the same Flavor, a player may play both of them as one action. The second action is adding one Flavor card to a Dispenser already in a collection, slowly filling it up and hoping to score points. The last action is playing Flavor cards to remove a Flavor of the same type from an opponent's Dispenser.

While immediately the butt of jokes in the gaming hobby for coming so far out of left field, the game is surprisingly fast and fun, involving a fair combination of luck and strategy. *Pez* cards have a weird mix of happy cartoon art and creepy retro-'50s dispensers, but are easy to read. Other than a couple of ultra-rares, *Pez* is a small enough set to be collected fairly easily. It comes in fixed starters (including a booster so there's some variety) and industry-standard boosters. No candy, though… — *Richard Weld*

	Rating
Concept	●●○○○
Gameplay	●●●○○
Card art	●●●○○
Player pool	●○○○○

Set (204 cards)	91.75
Starter Display Box	22.25
Booster Display Box	26.00
Starter Deck	5.00
Booster Pack	1.50

# Card Name	Type	Rarity	Price
39 Air Spirit	Disp	R	1.50
45 Air Spirit	Disp	R	1.50
171 Angel	Disp	U	0.25
177 Angel	Disp	U	0.25
145 Astronaut	Disp	R	1.50
169 Astronaut	Disp	R	1.50
12 Baseball Glove	Disp	U	0.25
25 Baseball Glove	Disp	U	0.25
74 Big Top Elephant	Disp	R	1.50
104 Big Top Elephant	Disp	R	1.50
62 Boy PEZ Pal	Disp	C	0.10
112 Boy PEZ Pal	Disp	C	0.10
182 Boy with Cap	Disp	U	0.25
189 Boy with Cap	Disp	U	0.25
174 Bride	Disp	R	1.50
180 Bride	Disp	R	1.50
75 Brown Bear	Disp	C	0.10
91 Brown Bear	Disp	C	0.10
32 Bubbleman	Disp	C	0.10
156 Bunny	Disp	C	0.10
166 Bunny	Disp	C	0.10
86 Cat with Derby	Disp	U	0.25
105 Cat with Derby	Disp	U	0.25
65 Chick with Hat	Disp	C	0.10
94 Chick with Hat	Disp	C	0.10
79 Chick without Hat	Disp	R	1.50
100 Chick without Hat	Disp	R	1.50
135 Circus Elephant	Disp	U	0.25
157 Circus Elephant	Disp	U	0.25
183 Clown with Collar	Disp	U	0.25
190 Clown with Collar	Disp	U	0.25
6 Coach Whistle	Disp	C	0.10
122 Cockatoo	Disp	U	0.25
186 Cockatoo	Disp	U	0.25
67 Cow	Disp	U	0.25
83 Cow	Disp	U	0.25
63 Cowboy	Disp	R	1.50
115 Cowboy	Disp	R	1.50
16 Crazy Fruit Orange	Disp	U	0.25
36 Crazy Fruit Orange	Disp	U	0.25
143 Crazy Fruit Pear	Disp	R	1.50
154 Crazy Fruit Pear	Disp	R	1.50
131 Crazy Fruit Pineapple	Disp	R	1.50
163 Crazy Fruit Pineapple	Disp	R	1.50
72 Crocodile	Disp	U	0.25
124 Crocodile	Disp	U	0.25

# Card Name	Type	Rarity	Price
54 Diabolic	Disp	R	1.50
58 Diabolic	Disp	R	1.50
11 Diecut Easter Bunny	Disp	R	1.50
66 Diecut Easter Bunny	Disp	R	1.50
132 Doctor	Disp	R	1.50
141 Doctor	Disp	R	1.50
130 Dog Whistle	Disp	C	0.10
164 Dog Whistle	Disp	C	0.10
103 Donkey Whistle	Disp	C	0.10
38 Duck with Flower	Disp	U	0.25
55 Duck with Flower	Disp	U	0.25
128 Easter Bunny	Disp	C	0.10
111 Elephant	Disp	C	0.10
162 Elephant	Disp	C	0.10
9 Engineer	Disp	R	1.50
35 Engineer	Disp	R	1.50
170 Fireman	Disp	U	0.25
176 Fireman	Disp	U	0.25
150 Fly-Saur	Disp	C	0.10
125 Fly-Saur	Disp	C	0.10
90 Football Player	Disp	R	1.50
195 Football Player	Disp	R	1.50
134 Frog Whistle	Disp	C	0.10
144 Frog Whistle	Disp	C	0.10
69 Giraffe	Disp	R	1.50
97 Giraffe	Disp	R	1.50
76 Girl PEZ Pal	Disp	C	0.10
93 Girl PEZ Pal	Disp	C	0.10
85 Gorilla	Disp	U	0.25
106 Gorilla	Disp	U	0.25
Grape	Flav	X	0.05
187 Groom	Disp	R	1.50
193 Groom	Disp	R	1.50
7 Happy Henry	Disp	C	0.10
167 Happy Henry	Disp	C	0.10
49 He-Saur	Disp	C	0.10
136 He-Saur	Disp	C	0.10
199 He-Saur	Disp	UR	5.50
200 He-Saur	Disp	UR	5.50
78 Hippo	Disp	C	0.10
87 Hippo	Disp	C	0.10
19 I-Saur	Disp	C	0.10
146 I-Saur	Disp	C	0.10
60 Ice Bear	Disp	C	0.10
110 Ice Bear	Disp	C	0.10
29 Knight	Disp	U	0.25
44 Knight	Disp	U	0.25
13 Koala Whistle	Disp	U	0.25
26 Koala Whistle	Disp	U	0.25
129 Lamb	Disp	C	0.10
153 Lamb	Disp	C	0.10
Lemon	Flav	X	0.05
98 Lil Lion	Disp	U	0.25

# Card Name	Type	Rarity	Price
116 Lil Lion	Disp	U	0.25
59 Long-Face Clown	Disp	R	1.50
109 Long-Face Clown	Disp	R	1.50
173 Maharajah	Disp	U	0.25
191 Maharajah	Disp	U	0.25
3 Mimic the Monkey	Disp	U	0.25
33 Mimic the Monkey	Disp	U	0.25
96 Monkey Sailor	Disp	U	0.25
121 Monkey Sailor	Disp	U	0.25
27 Mr. Ugly	Disp	U	0.25
41 Mr. Ugly	Disp	U	0.25
51 Naughty Neil	Disp	C	0.10
114 Naughty Neil	Disp	C	0.10
152 Nurse	Disp	R	1.50
165 Nurse	Disp	R	1.50
4 Octopus	Disp	U	0.25
34 Octopus	Disp	U	0.25
40 One-Eyed Monster	Disp	U	0.25
57 One-Eyed Monster	Disp	U	0.25
Orange	Flav	X	0.05
84 Panther	Disp	R	1.50
120 Panther	Disp	R	1.50
52 Parrot Whistle	Disp	C	0.10
161 Parrot Whistle	Disp	C	0.10
48 Penguin Whistle	Disp	C	0.10
196 Penguin Whistle	Disp	C	0.10
5 Peter PEZ	Disp	C	0.10
31 Peter PEZ	Disp	C	0.10
77 Pig Whistle	Disp	U	0.25
113 Pig Whistle	Disp	U	0.25
178 Pilot	Disp	R	1.50
185 Pilot	Disp	R	1.50
172 Pirate	Disp	U	0.25
184 Pirate	Disp	U	0.25
61 Policeman	Disp	U	0.25
92 Policeman	Disp	U	0.25
10 Pony-Go-Round	Disp	U	0.25
23 Pony-Go-Round	Disp	U	0.25
2 Psychedelic Eye	Disp	R	1.50
15 Psychedelic Eye	Disp	R	1.50
28 Psychedelic Eye	Disp	R	1.50
42 Psychedelic Eye	Disp	R	1.50
133 Psychedelic Flower	Disp	R	1.50
168 Psychedelic Flower	Disp	R	1.50
21 Pumpkin	Disp	C	0.10
81 Pumpkin	Disp	C	0.10
71 Raven	Disp	U	0.25
82 Raven	Disp	U	0.25
126 Red-Face Panda	Disp	R	1.50
137 Red-Face Panda	Disp	R	1.50
188 Ringmaster	Disp	R	1.50
194 Ringmaster	Disp	R	1.50

# Card Name	Type	Rarity	Price
1 Roar the Lion	Disp	U	0.25
14 Roar the Lion	Disp	U	0.25
8 Rooster	Disp	U	0.25
43 Rooster	Disp	U	0.25
99 Safari Crocodile	Disp	C	0.10
102 Safari Crocodile	Disp	C	0.10
140 Safari Hippo	Disp	C	0.10
155 Safari Hippo	Disp	C	0.10
73 Safari Lion	Disp	C	0.10
117 Safari Lion	Disp	C	0.10
20 Sailor	Disp	R	1.50
50 Sailor	Disp	R	1.50
68 Santa	Disp	C	0.10
101 Santa	Disp	C	0.10
30 Scarewolf	Disp	R	1.50
56 Scarewolf	Disp	R	1.50
107 She-Saur	Disp	C	0.10
158 She-Saur	Disp	C	0.10
179 Sheik	Disp	U	0.25
192 Sheik	Disp	U	0.25
175 Sheriff	Disp	R	1.50
181 Sheriff	Disp	R	1.50
53 Skull	Disp	C	0.10
70 Skull	Disp	C	0.10
22 Slimy Sid	Disp	C	0.10
149 Slimy Sid	Disp	C	0.10
80 Snowman	Disp	C	0.10
119 Snowman	Disp	C	0.10
197 Space Trooper	Disp	UR	5.50
198 Space Trooper	Disp	UR	5.50
18 Spook	Disp	R	1.50
37 Spook	Disp	R	1.50
Strawberry	Flav	X	0.05
46 Valentine Heart	Disp	R	1.50
139 Valentine Heart	Disp	C	0.10
24 Vamp	Disp	R	1.50
89 Vamp	Disp	R	1.50
142 Vintage Bunny	Disp	R	1.50
151 Vintage Bunny	Disp	R	1.50
95 Vintage Cow	Disp	U	0.25
118 Vintage Cow	Disp	U	0.25
127 Vintage Pumpkin	Disp	U	0.25
138 Vintage Pumpkin	Disp	U	0.25
88 Vintage Santa	Disp	R	1.50
123 Vintage Santa	Disp	R	1.50
17 Witch	Disp	C	0.10
47 Witch	Disp	C	0.10
148 Yappy Dog	Disp	U	0.25
160 Yappy Dog	Disp	U	0.25
147 Yellow-Face Panda	Disp	R	1.50
159 Yellow-Face Panda	Disp	R	1.50
64 Zombie	Disp	R	1.50
108 Zombie	Disp	R	1.50

RARITY KEY C = Common   U = Uncommon   R = Rare   VR = Very Rare   UR = Ultra Rare   F = Foil card   X = Fixed/standard in all decks

Pokémon

Wizards of the Coast • First U.S. set, **1st Edition**, released **January 1999**
102 cards in set • **IDENTIFIER: Circular edition 1 symbol**

• Booster packs contain 11 cards; booster displays contain 36 boosters

The **Pokémon Trading Card Game** is for the most part, a translation into English of the Japanese **Pocket Monsters** CCG, based upon the popular Nintendo Game Boy game and anime (Japanese cartoon) of the same name.

Pokémon was designed to be a game for the 7-12 age range — when Wizards of the Coast solicited it in late 1998, few hobby shops, with their older clienteles, wanted it at all! As such, the rules are simple and easy to learn. In the game, each player assumes the role of a trainer of Pokémon, or Pocket Monsters, and selects several to do battle with those of other trainers. Each player assembles a deck of exactly 60 cards with no more than four of any single card except basic energy.

Play begins with each player drawing a hand of seven cards. Both players then place one or more "Basic" Pokémon face down upon the table. One of these is the "active" Pokémon and any additional Basic Pokémon, up to five, are placed on the "Bench." Both players then set aside six "prize" cards. One prize card is drawn every time an opponent's Pokémon is defeated. When all six prizes are drawn, that player wins. A player also wins if his opponent has no basic Pokémon in play or runs out of cards.

On a player's turn, he draws a card and can play cards from his hand, including new Basic Pokémon or trainer cards. A player can also evolve the Pokémon already in play into more powerful Pokémon. Finally, a player may attack with active Pokémon, usually dealing damage to the opponent's active Pokémon, and play passes to the opponent.

Pokémon was intended to be a starter game to get players into CCGs, and it was hoped that these new players would eventually provide much-needed replacements for players of the more advanced CCGs who had moved on. What Wizards of the Coast got was something far greater than *anyone* could have imagined — a big piece of the youth pop-cultural fad of the year. Beanie Babies, Mighty Morphin' Power Rangers, Teenage Mutant Ninja Turtles: All had their day on *every* kid's want list, and it happened that when Pokémon's turn came, CCG cards were the most affordable way for kids to buy in.

And buy they did. In the summer of 1999, *Pokémon* became the first and only CCG to outsell **Magic: the Gathering**. It also did the impossible, bringing CCGs out of the hobby shops and firmly into the mainstream. At the height of its popularity, there were pieces on the local news and references to it in network sitcoms and even late night TV. Large department chains such as Wal-Mart and Toys 'R' Us started selling everything Pokémon, and, helped by a feature film, it dominated the 1999 Christmas season.

Wizards wasn't prepared for the demand — and game retailers, who'd passed on the kiddie game when it was first offered — grew furious when they couldn't get more. Since it had never been *meant* for the hobby, most of it was headed to the mass market, causing resentment toward Wizards among game retailers. Wizards exacerbated the situation when, in May 1999, it bought the Game Keeper chain of mall stores, causing retailers to allege preferential treatment in the availability of *Pokémon* to these stores. Game shops felt even further from the center of this brave new world when the boom caught the attention of Wall Street. On Sept. 9, 1999, Hasbro, which had earlier purchased game industry icon Avalon Hill, bought Wizards of the Coast for $325 million. But game stores still did well for themselves, collectively splitting at least $100 million in 1999 from *Pokémon* sales alone — if the cards all sold at suggested retail price, which very few did!

Worrisome was that perhaps more than half the buyers weren't playing the CCG at all, but simply trading the cards. Wizards and retailers worked hard to set up tournaments to encourage play. But as usual with fads, a backlash occured. *Pokémon* "the craze" seemed to end around the April 2000 release of *Team Rocket*. It remains popular with its player base, but the days of Pokékids busting down the door are past.

But it must be acknowledged that *Pokémon* gave the CCG world a giant shot of adrenaline. The newfound interest drove many companies to pursue the audience, and a tremendous wave of CCGs followed in 2000, including **Digi-Battle, Dragonball Z, Sailor Moon**, and many more. — **Orren McKay and John Jackson Miller**

Pokémon • Unlimited

Wizards of the Coast • Released **January 1999**
101 cards in set • **IDENTIFIER: No symbol on card**

• Preconstructed 'theme' starter decks contain 60 cards; starter displays contain 8 starters
• Booster packs contain 11 cards; booster displays contain 36 boosters
• Theme decks include **Blackout, Brushfire, Overgrowth**, and **Zap!**

The **Unlimited** set is identical to **1st Edition** except for the absence of the *1st Edition* symbol from cards and the absence of the holofoil **Machamp** from the set.

The holofoil Charizard *became, for a good while,* **Pokémon**'s *answer to* **Magic**'s Black Lotus *in terms of popularity with CCG speculators.*

Concept	●●●●○
Gameplay	●●●●○
Card art	●●●○○
Player pool	●●●●●

Lotto Pokémon

Some parents didn't know **Pokémon** was a game at all and failed to grasp the concept of card rarities — becoming angry when they found they couldn't just buy a complete set. Wizards even had to fight a class-action suit claiming that random card packs represented an illegal lottery. The suit failed: As long as the manufacturer contends that their cards are only worth suggested retail, it's in no danger. ABC's John Stossel reported on the case on **20/20** as an example of "lawyers gone wild."

Given that parental mood, it's surprising Decipher came out with its own Pokémon scratch-off cards (similar to *Battlecards*) in late 1999. "Scratchees" had a brief appearance in stores.

RARITY KEY **C** = Common **U** = Uncommon **R** = Rare **E** =Energy **F** = Foil card **X** = Fixed/standard in all decks

Pokémon • Base Set 2

Wizards of the Coast • Released **February 2000**

130 cards in set • **IDENTIFIER: Pokéball in a '2' on card**

- Preconstructed 'theme' starter decks contain 60 cards; starter displays contain 8 starters
- Booster packs contain 11 cards; booster displays contain 36 boosters
- Theme decks include **Grass Chopper, Lightning Bug, Psych Out,** and **Hot Water**

    Base Set 2 re-releases the original set in an edition that includes some cards from the **Jungle** expansion. Wizards of the Coast got to add a number of features which probably would've helped back during the initial release: a CD-ROM in one set and a CD-ROM and video in another helped buyers learn the game.

    Disappointment invariably arose from some younger customers who couldn't understand that their *Base Set 2* **Charizard** wasn't the one everyone was paying big money for. All it was was playable, so one might consider that *Base Set 2* really helped the kid players and served to winnow out the kid speculators. — ***John Jackson Miller***

You will need **15** *nine-pocket pages to store this set. (8 doubled up)*

RARITY KEY C = Common   U = Uncommon   R = Rare   E = Energy   F = Foil card   X = Fixed/standard in all decks

Card name	Type	Rarity	Price
☐ Exeggcute	Grass	C	0.25
☐ Exeggutor	Grass	U	1.00
☐ Farfetch'd	Colorless	U	1.00
☐ Fearow	Colorless	U	1.00
5			
☐ Fighting Energy	Energy	E	0.25
☐ Fire Energy	Energy	E	0.25
☐ Full Heal	Trainer	U	1.00
☐ Gastly	Psychic	C	0.25
☐ Goldeen	Water	C	0.25
☐ Grass Energy	Energy	E	0.25
☐ Growlithe	Fire	U	1.00
☐ Gust of Wind	Trainer	C	0.25
☐ Gyarados	Grass	F	8.50
6			
☐ Haunter	Psychic	U	1.00
☐ Hitmonchan	Fighting	F	8.50
☐ Imposter Professor Oak	Trainer	R	2.90
☐ Item Finder	Trainer	R	2.70
☐ Ivysaur	Grass	U	1.00
☐ Jigglypuff	Colorless	C	0.25
☐ Jynx	Psychic	U	1.00
☐ Kadabra	Psychic	U	1.00
☐ Kakuna	Grass	U	1.00
7			
☐ Kangaskhan	Colorless	R	4.00
☐ Lass	Trainer	R	2.90

Card name	Type	Rarity	Price
☐ Lightning Energy	Energy	E	0.25
☐ Likitung	Colorless	U	1.00
☐ Machoke	Fighting	U	1.00
☐ Machop	Fighting	U	0.25
☐ Magikarp	Water	U	1.00
☐ Magmar	Fire	U	1.00
☐ Magnemite	Lightning	C	0.25
8			
☐ Magneton	Lightning	F	7.80
☐ Maintenance	Trainer	U	1.00
☐ Marowak	Fighting	U	1.00
☐ Meowth	Colorless	C	0.25
☐ Metapod	Grass	C	0.25
☐ Mewtwo	Psychic	F	9.00
☐ Mr. Mime	Psychic	R	5.00
☐ Nidoking	Grass	F	10.00
☐ Nidoqueen	Grass	F	9.50
9			
☐ Nidoran (female)	Grass	C	0.25
☐ Nidoran (male)	Grass	C	0.25
☐ Nidorina	Grass	U	1.00
☐ Nidorino	Grass	U	1.00
☐ Ninetales	Fire	F	7.50
☐ Onix	Fighting	C	0.25
☐ Paras	Grass	C	0.25
☐ Parasect	Grass	U	1.00
☐ Persian	Colorless	U	1.00

Card name	Type	Rarity	Price
10			
☐ Pidgeot	Colorless	F	9.00
☐ Pidgeotto	Colorless	R	3.80
☐ Pidgey	Colorless	C	0.25
☐ Pikachu	Lightning	C	0.25
☐ Pinsir	Grass	R	4.00
☐ PlusPower	Trainer	U	1.00
☐ Poké Ball	Trainer	C	0.25
☐ Pokédex	Trainer	U	1.00
☐ Pokémon Breeder	Trainer	R	2.40
11			
☐ Pokémon Center	Trainer	U	1.00
☐ Pokémon Trader	Trainer	R	2.90
☐ Poliwag	Water	C	0.25
☐ Poliwhirl	Water	U	1.00
☐ Poliwrath	Water	F	9.50
☐ Potion	Trainer	C	0.25
☐ Professor Oak	Trainer	U	1.00
☐ Psychic Energy	Energy	E	0.25
☐ Raichu	Lightning	F	10.00
12			
☐ Raticate	Colorless	U	1.00
☐ Rattata	Colorless	C	0.25
☐ Rhydon	Fighting	U	1.00
☐ Rhyhorn	Fighting	U	0.25
☐ Sandshrew	Fighting	C	0.25
☐ Scoop Up	Trainer	R	2.40
☐ Scyther	Grass	F	10.00

Card name	Type	Rarity	Price
☐ Seaking	Water	U	1.00
☐ Seel	Water	U	1.00
13			
☐ Snorlax	Colorless	R	4.00
☐ Spearow	Colorless	C	0.25
☐ Squirtle	Water	C	0.25
☐ Starmie	Water	C	0.25
☐ Staryu	Water	C	0.25
☐ Super Energy Removal	Trainer	R	3.80
☐ Super Potion	Trainer	U	1.00
☐ Switch	Trainer	C	0.25
☐ Tangela	Grass	C	0.25
14			
☐ Tauros	Colorless	U	1.00
☐ Venomoth	Grass	R	3.00
☐ Venonat	Grass	C	0.25
☐ Venusaur	Grass	F	12.00
☐ Victreebel	Grass	R	4.00
☐ Voltorb	Lightning	C	0.25
☐ Vulpix	Fire	C	0.25
☐ Wartortle	Water	U	1.00
☐ Water Energy	Energy	E	0.25
15			
☐ Weedle	Grass	C	0.25
☐ Weepinbell	Grass	U	1.00
☐ Wigglytuff	Colorless	F	10.00
☐ Zapdos	Lightning	F	9.50

Flareon — Stage 1 — Evolves from Eevee — Put Flareon on the Basic Pokémon — 70 HP — Flame Pokémon. Length: 2' 11", Weight: 55 lbs. — Quick Attack: Flip a coin. If heads, this attack does 10 damage plus 20 more damage; if tails, this attack does 10 damage. 10+ — Flamethrower: Discard 1 Energy card attached to Flareon in order to use this attack. 60 — When storing thermal energy in its body, its temperature could soar to over 1600 degrees. LV.28 #136 — 3/64

Pokémon • Jungle 1st and Unlimited

Wizards of the Coast • Released July 1999

64 cards in set • **IDENTIFIER: Flower symbol on Unlimited**
- Theme decks (**Power Reserve, Water Blast**) contain 60 cards; theme displays contain 8 decks
- Booster packs contain 9 cards; booster displays contain 36 boosters

Jungle, the first expansion for **Pokémon**, hit when supply was scarcest and was a resounding success for both collectors and players alike. Because most of the cards were previously announced in the Japanese **Pocket Monsters**, the element of surprise was gone, but collectors still liked it because it added Pokémon absent from the base set.

Players liked it because it added some of the most influential cards in the game, **Wigglytuff** and **Scyther**. **Wigglytuff** had a big impact on the metagame as this archetype (focusing on getting a Turn 2 **Wiggly** to do 60 damage) became very prevalent at the West Coast Super Trainer Showdown. **Scyther** became an important element in **Wigglytuff** and Haymaker decks (decks that use "Big Basic Pokemon," or BBP's for quick beatdown) as **Scyther** would play the role of versatile Pokémon, taking the damage when necessary, resisting other decks that used **Hitmonchan**. — *Ka-Lok Fung*

JUNGLE 1ST EDITION
Set (64 cards)	280.00
Booster Display Box	279.50
Booster Pack	9.00

JUNGLE UNLIMITED
Set (64 cards)	170.00
Starter Display Box	108.00
Booster Display Box	135.00
Two-player set	15.00
Pre-constructed deck	14.00
Booster Pack	4.00

> You will need **8** nine-pocket pages to store this set. (4 doubled up)

1ST EDIT.	Card name	Type		Rarity	UNLIMITED
1					
☐ 0.45	Bellsprout	Grass	C	0.25	☐
☐ 1.00	Butterfree	Grass	U	1.00	☐
☐ 14.50	Clefable	Colorless	F	12.00	☐
☐ 6.00	Clefable	Colorless	R	5.00	☐
☐ 0.50	Cubone	Fighting	C	0.25	☐
☐ 1.00	Dodrio	Colorless	U	1.00	☐
☐ 0.50	Eevee	Colorless	C	0.25	☐
☐ 13.00	Electrode	Lightning	F	10.00	☐
☐ 5.40	Electrode	Lightning	R	4.70	☐
2					
☐ 0.50	Exeggcute	Grass	C	0.25	☐
☐ 1.00	Exeggutor	Grass	U	1.00	☐
☐ 1.00	Fearow	Colorless	U	1.00	☐
☐ 15.00	Flareon	Fire	F	12.00	☐

1ST EDIT.	Card name	Type		Rarity	UNLIMITED
☐ 7.80	Flareon	Fire	R	6.00	☐
☐ 1.00	Gloom	Grass	U	1.00	☐
☐ 0.50	Goldeen	Water	C	0.25	☐
☐ 0.50	Jigglypuff	Colorless	C	0.25	☐
☐ 15.00	Jolteon	Lightning	F	12.75	☐
3					
☐ 7.80	Jolteon	Lightning	R	6.00	☐
☐ 14.75	Kangaskhan	Colorless	F	10.00	☐
☐ 6.80	Kangaskhan	Colorless	R	5.00	☐
☐ 1.00	Lickitung	Colorless	U	1.00	☐
☐ 0.45	Mankey	Fighting	C	0.25	☐
☐ 1.00	Marowak	Fighting	U	1.00	☐
☐ 0.50	Meowth	Colorless	C	0.25	☐
☐ 16.00	Mr. Mime	Psychic	F	12.50	☐
☐ 7.00	Mr. Mime	Psychic	R	6.00	☐
4					
☐ 15.00	Nidoqueen	Grass	F	12.00	☐
☐ 6.00	Nidoqueen	Grass	R	5.00	☐
☐ 0.50	Nidoran (F)	Grass	C	0.25	☐
☐ 1.00	Nidorina	Grass	U	1.00	☐
☐ 0.50	Oddish	Grass	C	0.25	☐
☐ 0.45	Paras	Grass	C	0.25	☐
☐ 1.00	Parasect	Grass	U	1.00	☐
☐ 1.00	Persian	Colorless	U	1.00	☐
☐ 13.00	Pidgeot	Colorless	F	12.00	☐
5					
☐ 6.00	Pidgeot	Colorless	R	5.00	☐
☐ 0.50	Pikachu	Lightning	C	0.25	☐

1ST EDIT.	Card name	Type		Rarity	UNLIMITED
☐ 15.00	Pinsir	Grass	F	10.75	☐
☐ 5.40	Pinsir	Grass	R	5.00	☐
☐ 0.50	Poké Ball	Trainer	C	0.25	☐
☐ 1.00	Primeape	Fighting	U	1.00	☐
☐ 1.00	Rapidash	Fire	U	1.00	☐
☐ 1.00	Rhydon	Fighting	U	1.00	☐
☐ 0.50	Rhyhorn	Fighting	C	0.25	☐
6					
☐ 16.00	Scyther	Grass	F	12.25	☐
☐ 6.00	Scyther	Grass	R	6.00	☐
☐ 1.00	Seaking	Water	U	1.00	☐
☐ 15.00	Snorlax	Colorless	F	12.00	☐
☐ 6.00	Snorlax	Colorless	R	5.50	☐
☐ 0.45	Spearow	Colorless	C	0.25	☐
☐ 1.00	Tauros	Colorless	U	1.00	☐
☐ 14.00	Vaporeon	Water	F	10.00	☐
☐ 6.80	Vaporeon	Water	R	5.00	☐
7					
☐ 14.00	Venomoth	Grass	F	12.00	☐
☐ 6.00	Venomoth	Grass	R	5.00	☐
☐ 0.50	Venonat	Grass	C	0.25	☐
☐ 13.00	Victreebel	Grass	F	11.00	☐
☐ 6.00	Victreebel	Grass	R	5.00	☐
☐ 14.75	Vileplume	Grass	F	10.00	☐
☐ 6.00	Vileplume	Grass	R	5.00	☐
☐ 1.00	Weepinbell	Grass	U	1.00	☐
8					
☐ 15.00	Wigglytuff	Colorless	F	12.00	☐
☐ 7.00	Wigglytuff	Colorless	R	5.00	☐

RARITY KEY C = Common U = Uncommon R = Rare E = Energy F = Foil card X = Fixed/standard in all decks

Pokémon • Fossil 1st and Unlimited

Wizards of the Coast • Released **November 1999**

64 cards in set • **IDENTIFIER: Bony foot symbol on *Unlimited***

- Theme decks (**Bodyguard, Lockdown**) contain 60 cards; theme displays contain 8 decks
- Booster packs contain 9 cards; booster displays contain 36 boosters

Fossil was the first expansion to differ from its Japanese counterpart: Wizards of the Coast left Mew out of this set. This card was later released as a promo given out by card shops and various retailers. But since the main terror from Japanese *Fossil* was Mew, U.S. *Fossil* caused nothing close to the upheaval players had expected.

Aerodactyl was expected to be the other big threat with its ability to prevent evolution. It did make the occasional appearance in decks, but did little to change the environment overall. *Fossil*'s lackluster assortment of trainers further lessened its impact. It provided some new playable Pokémon like Lapras and Ditto, but it did little else.

Fossil was released at the height of the Poké-frenzy in the mass market. In game shops, *Pokémon* was still prized, but pro players looked more for Japanese cards. — ***Orren McKay***

FOSSIL 1ST EDITION

Set (64 cards)	337.50
Booster Display Box	244.50
Booster Pack	7.00

FOSSIL UNLIMITED

Set (64 cards)	177.50
Starter Display Box	92.00
Booster Display Box	130.00
Pre-constructed deck	10.50
Booster Pack	4.00

> You will need **7** nine-pocket pages to store this set. (3 doubled up)

1ST EDIT.	Card name	Type	Rarity	UNLIMITED
☐ 15.00	Aerodactyl	Fighting	F	12.00 ☐
☐ 6.00	Aerodactyl	Fighting	R	5.50 ☐
☐ 1.00	Arbok	Grass	U	1.00 ☐
☐ 15.00	Articuno	Water	F	12.00 ☐
☐ 6.50	Articuno	Water	R	5.00 ☐
☐ 1.00	Cloyster	Water	U	1.00 ☐
☐ 15.00	Ditto	Colorless	F	12.00 ☐
☐ 7.00	Ditto	Colorless	R	5.00 ☐
☐ 15.75	Dragonite	Colorless	F	13.00 ☐
☐ 7.00	Dragonite	Colorless	R	5.00 ☐
☐ 0.35	Ekans	Grass	C	0.25 ☐
☐ 0.35	Energy Search	Trainer	C	0.25 ☐

1ST EDIT.	Card name	Type	Rarity	UNLIMITED
☐ 0.35	Gambler	Trainer	C	0.25 ☐
☐ 1.00	Gastly	Psychic	U	1.00 ☐
☐ 15.00	Gengar	Psychic	F	12.00 ☐
☐ 6.30	Gengar	Psychic	R	5.00 ☐
☐ 0.35	Geodude	Fighting	C	0.25 ☐
☐ 1.00	Golbat	Grass	U	1.00 ☐
☐ 1.00	Golduck	Water	U	1.00 ☐
☐ 1.00	Golem	Fighting	U	1.00 ☐
☐ 1.00	Graveler	Fighting	U	1.00 ☐
☐ 0.35	Grimer	Grass	C	0.25 ☐
☐ 13.00	Haunter	Psychic	F	10.00 ☐
☐ 6.00	Haunter	Psychic	R	4.50 ☐
☐ 14.00	Hitmonlee	Fighting	F	12.00 ☐
☐ 6.00	Hitmonlee	Fighting	R	5.00 ☐
☐ 0.35	Horsea	Water	C	0.25 ☐
☐ 12.00	Hypno	Psychic	F	10.00 ☐
☐ 6.00	Hypno	Psychic	R	5.00 ☐
☐ 0.35	Kabuto	Fighting	C	0.25 ☐
☐ 14.00	Kabutops	Fighting	F	12.00 ☐
☐ 6.00	Kabutops	Fighting	R	5.00 ☐
☐ 1.00	Kingler	Water	U	1.00 ☐
☐ 0.35	Krabby	Water	C	0.25 ☐
☐ 11.00	Lapras	Water	F	10.00 ☐
☐ 5.50	Lapras	Water	R	5.00 ☐
☐ 1.00	Magmar	Fire	U	1.00 ☐

1ST EDIT.	Card name	Type	Rarity	UNLIMITED
☐ 11.00	Magneton	Lightning	F	10.00 ☐
☐ 5.50	Magneton	Lightning	R	5.00 ☐
☐ 14.00	Moltres	Fire	F	12.00 ☐
☐ 7.00	Moltres	Fire	R	5.00 ☐
☐ 1.00	Mr. Fuji	Trainer	U	1.00 ☐
☐ 10.00	Muk	Grass	F	10.00 ☐
☐ 5.50	Muk	Grass	R	5.00 ☐
☐ 0.35	Mysterious Fossil	Trainer	C	0.25 ☐
☐ 0.35	Omanyte	Water	C	0.25 ☐
☐ 1.00	Omastar	Water	U	1.00 ☐
☐ 0.35	Psyduck	Water	C	0.25 ☐
☐ 14.00	Raichu	Lightning	F	13.00 ☐
☐ 6.00	Raichu	Lightning	R	5.50 ☐
☐ 0.35	Recycle	Trainer	C	0.25 ☐
☐ 1.00	Sandslash	Fighting	U	1.00 ☐
☐ 1.00	Seadra	Water	U	1.00 ☐
☐ 0.35	Shellder	Water	C	0.25 ☐
☐ 1.00	Slowbro	Psychic	U	1.00 ☐
☐ 0.35	Slowpoke	Psychic	C	0.25 ☐
☐ 0.50	Tentacool	Water	C	0.25 ☐
☐ 1.00	Tentacruel	Water	U	1.00 ☐
☐ 1.00	Weezing	Grass	U	1.00 ☐
☐ 14.00	Zapdos	Lightning	F	12.00 ☐
☐ 6.50	Zapdos	Lightning	R	6.00 ☐
☐ 0.35	Zubat	Grass	C	0.25 ☐

Pokémon • Team Rocket 1st and Unlimited

Wizards of the Coast • Released **April 2000**

83 cards in set • **IDENTIFIER: 'R' symbol on *Unlimited***

- Theme decks (**Devastation, Trouble**) contain 60 cards; theme displays contain 8 decks
- Booster packs contain 9 cards; booster displays contain 36 boosters

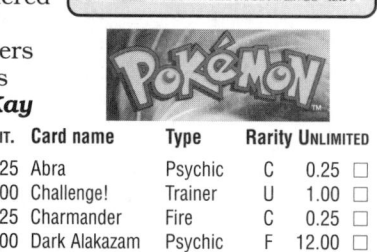

Team Rocket expansion also differed from its Japanese counterpart, but by an addition, not an omission. Dark Raichu, numbered "83 of 82," was highly sought after by collectors but was only mediocre in play. *Team Rocket* also adds "dark" versions of many of the Pokémon from previous sets. These also did little to affect the tournament environment. The best, Dark Charizard, was more playable than his "light" counterpart, but was still difficult to play because he was a Stage 2 Pokemon with only 80 HP.

Energy cards are the most exciting addition. Rainbow Energy provides any type of energy, greatly helping in the building of decks with three or more energy types. The Full Heal and Potion Energy cards both had special effects; Full Heal removed Poison, Sleep, Confusion, and Paralysis, and Potion healed one damage counter. Nothing in *Team Rocket* was considered game-breaking, but it did have a number of cards that made appearances in decks.

Team Rocket was the first ***Pokémon*** expansion that was reasonably easy for retailers to keep in stock. This was a big indication that the *Pokémon* fever had broken. Packs were still selling reasonably well, but singles had slowed dramatically. — ***Orren McKay***

TEAM ROCKET 1ST EDITION

Set (83 cards)	262.50
Booster Display Box	177.50
Pre-constructed deck	11.25
Booster Pack	5.00

TEAM ROCKET UNLIMITED

Set (83 cards)	280.00
Booster Display Box	118.50
Pre-constructed deck	10.00
Booster Pack	3.50

> You will need **10** nine-pocket pages to store this set. (5 doubled up)

1ST EDIT.	Card name	Type	Rarity	UNLIMITED
☐ 0.25	Abra	Psychic	C	0.25 ☐
☐ 1.00	Challenge!	Trainer	U	1.00 ☐
☐ 0.25	Charmander	Fire	C	0.25 ☐
☐ 15.00	Dark Alakazam	Psychic	F	12.00 ☐
☐ 6.00	Dark Alakazam	Psychic	R	5.00 ☐

1ST EDIT.	Card name	Type	Rarity	UNLIMITED
11.75	Dark Arbok	Grass	F	10.00
5.00	Dark Arbok	Grass	R	5.00
20.00	Dark Blastoise	Water	F	17.25
10.00	Dark Blastoise	Water	R	6.10
2				
40.00	Dark Charizard	Fire	F	30.00
12.00	Dark Charizard	Fire	R	8.30
1.00	Dark Charmeleon	Fire	U	1.00
1.00	Dark Dragonair	Colorless	U	1.00
16.00	Dark Dragonite	Colorless	F	12.00
6.00	Dark Dragonite	Colorless	R	5.00
11.75	Dark Dugtrio	Fighting	F	9.50
5.00	Dark Dugtrio	Fighting	R	4.00
1.00	Dark Electrode	Lightning	U	1.00
3				
1.00	Dark Flareon	Fire	U	1.00
1.00	Dark Gloom	Grass	U	1.00
12.00	Dark Golbat	Grass	F	9.90
5.00	Dark Golbat	Grass	R	4.00
1.00	Dark Golduck	Water	U	1.00
12.00	Dark Gyarados	Water	F	10.00
5.90	Dark Gyarados	Water	R	5.00
11.50	Dark Hypno	Psychic	F	9.50
5.00	Dark Hypno	Psychic	R	4.00
4				
1.00	Dark Jolteon	Lightning	U	1.00
1.00	Dark Kadabra	Psychic	U	1.00
12.00	Dark Machamp	Fighting	F	8.50
5.00	Dark Machamp	Fighting	R	4.00
1.00	Dark Machoke	Fighting	U	1.00
10.00	Dark Magneton	Lightning	F	8.40

1ST EDIT.	Card name	Type	Rarity	UNLIMITED
5.00	Dark Magneton	Lightning	R	4.00
1.00	Dark Muk	Grass	U	1.00
1.00	Dark Persian	Colorless	U	1.00
5				
1.00	Dark Primeape	Fighting	U	1.00
30.00	Dark Raichu	Lightning	F	20.00
1.00	Dark Rapidash	Fire	U	1.00
0.25	Dark Raticate	Colorless	C	0.25
12.00	Dark Slowbro	Psychic	F	10.00
5.00	Dark Slowbro	Psychic	R	4.00
1.00	Dark Vaporeon	Water	U	1.00
12.00	Dark Vileplume	Grass	F	12.00
5.70	Dark Vileplume	Grass	R	5.00
6				
1.00	Dark Wartortle	Water	U	1.00
11.00	Dark Weezing	Grass	F	8.00
5.00	Dark Weezing	Grass	R	4.00
1.00	Digger	Trainer	U	1.00
0.25	Diglett	Fighting	C	0.25
0.25	Dratini	Colorless	C	0.25
0.25	Drowzee	Psychic	C	0.25
0.25	Eevee	Colorless	C	0.25
0.25	Ekans	Grass	C	0.25
7				
1.00	Full Heal Energy	Energy	U	1.00
0.30	Goop Gas Attack	Trainer	C	0.25
0.25	Grimer	Grass	C	0.25
15.00	Here Comes Team Rocket!	Trainer	F	11.25
6.00	Here Comes Team Rocket!	Trainer	R	5.00

1ST EDIT.	Card name	Type	Rarity	UNLIMITED
1.00	Imposter Oak's Revenge	Trainer	U	1.00
0.25	Koffing	Grass	C	0.25
0.25	Machop	Fighting	C	0.25
1.00	Magikarp	Water	U	1.00
8				
0.25	Magnemite	Lightning	C	0.25
0.25	Mankey	Fighting	C	0.25
0.25	Meowth	Colorless	C	0.25
1.00	Nightly Garbage Run	Trainer	U	1.00
0.25	Oddish	Grass	C	0.25
0.25	Ponyta	Fire	C	0.25
1.00	Porygon	Colorless	U	1.00
1.00	Potion Energy	Energy	U	1.00
0.25	Psyduck	Water	C	0.25
9				
15.00	Rainbow Energy	Energy	F	12.00
6.50	Rainbow Energy	Energy	R	5.00
0.25	Rattata	Colorless	C	0.25
12.00	Rocket's Sneak Attack	Trainer	F	9.00
5.00	Rocket's Sneak Attack	Trainer	R	3.80
1.00	Sleep!	Trainer	U	1.00
0.25	Slowpoke	Psychic	C	0.25
0.25	Squirtle	Water	C	0.25
1.00	The Boss's Way	Trainer	U	1.00
10				
0.25	Voltorb	Lightning	C	0.25
0.25	Zubat	Grass	C	0.25

TRAINER
Narrow Gym — Stadium Card

Pokémon • Gym Heroes 1st and Unlimited

Wizards of the Coast • Released August 2000

132 cards in set • **IDENTIFIER: Light stadium symbol on *Unlimited***

- Theme decks (**Brock, Erika, Lt. Surge,** and **Misty**) contain 60 cards; theme displays contain 8 decks
- Booster packs contain 9 cards; booster displays contain 36 boosters

The first part of the two-part Gym expansion, *Gym Heroes* surprised the *Pokémon* CCG community in the extent to which composition did not strictly follow its counterpart in Japanese *Pocket Monsters*. Previewed at the West Coast Super Trainer Showdown, *Heroes* lacked the "oomph" it was expected to have on the metagame, mainly due the fact that some of the better Gym cards would appear in *Gym Challenge*.

However, there are still a few good cards in the set. Some of the best-known are **Rocket's Hitmonchan, Rocket's Scyther, The Rocket's Trap,** and **No Removal Gym**. The two Pokémon started to appear in some decks and changed the metagame into one in which status effect became a bit more popular. **The Rocket's Trap** led to the development of the Trapper branch of Haymaker decks, combining **Impostor Oak's Revenge** with **The Rocket's Trap** to eliminate an opponent's hand. Finally, **No Removal Gym** made **Energy Removal** extremely costly.

All in all, *Gym Heroes* was a fairly good set but its brother, *Challenge*, would outshine and outclass it easily. — *Ka-Lok Fung*

GYM HEROES 1ST EDITION

Set (132 cards)	225.00
Booster Display Box	113.50
Booster Pack	4.00

GYM HEROES UNLIMITED

Set (132 cards)	175.00
Starter Display Box	70.00
Booster Display Box	86.00
Pre-constructed deck	10.00
Booster Pack	4.00

You will need **15** nine-pocket pages to store this set. (8 doubled up)

1ST EDIT.	Card name	Type	Rarity	UNLIMITED
1				
0.25	Blaine's Charmander	Fire	C	0.25
0.25	Blaine's Gamble	Trainer	C	0.25
0.25	Blaine's Growlithe (Lvl. 15)	Fire	C	0.25

1ST EDIT.	Card name	Type	Rarity	UNLIMITED
1.00	Blaine's Growlithe (Lvl. 17)	Fire	U	1.00
1.00	Blaine's Kangaskhan	Colorless	U	1.00
1.00	Blaine's Last Resort	Trainer	U	1.00
1.00	Blaine's Magmar	Fire	U	1.00
12.00	Blaine's Moltres	Fire	F	11.75
0.25	Blaine's Ponyta	Fire	C	0.25
2				
5.00	Blaine's Quiz #1	Trainer	R	5.00
0.25	Blaine's Tauros	Colorless	C	0.25
0.25	Blaine's Vulpix	Fire	C	0.25
9.90	Brock	Trainer	F	8.00
5.00	Brock	Trainer	R	5.00
0.25	Brock's Geodude (Lvl. 13)	Fighting	C	0.25
1.00	Brock's Geodude (Lvl. 17)	Fighting	U	1.00
1.00	Brock's Golbat	Grass	U	1.00
5.00	Brock's Golem	Fighting	R	5.00
3				
1.00	Brock's Graveler	Fighting	U	1.00

1ST EDIT.	Card name	Type	Rarity	UNLIMITED
1.00	Brock's Lickitung	Colorless	U	1.00
0.25	Brock's Mankey (Lvl. 10)	Fighting	C	0.25
0.25	Brock's Mankey (Lvl. 12)	Fighting	C	0.25
5.00	Brock's Onix (Lvl. 30)	Fighting	R	5.00
0.25	Brock's Onix (Lvl. 41)	Fighting	C	0.25
12.00	Brock's Rhydon	Fighting	F	9.90
5.00	Brock's Rhyhorn (Lvl. 25)	Fighting	R	5.00
0.25	Brock's Rhyhorn (Lvl. 29)	Fighting	C	0.25
4				
0.25	Brock's Sandshrew (Lvl. 13)	Fighting	C	0.25
0.25	Brock's Sandshrew (Lvl. 20)	Fighting	C	0.25
5.00	Brock's Sandslash	Fighting	R	5.00

RARITY KEY C = Common   U = Uncommon   R = Rare   E = Energy   F = Foil card   X = Fixed/standard in all decks

Card name	Type	Rarity	Price
1.00 Brock's Training Method	Trainer	U	1.00
0.25 Brock's Vulpix	Fire	C	0.25
0.25 Brock's Zubat (Lvl. 11)	Grass	C	0.25
5.00 Brock's Zubat (Lvl. 5)	Grass	R	5.00
1.00 Celadon City Gym	SSS	U	1.00
1.00 Cerulean City Gym	SSS	U	1.00
5.00 Charity	Trainer	R	4.50
0.25 Energy Flow	Trainer	C	0.25
9.90 Erika	Trainer	F	8.00
5.00 Erika	Trainer	R	5.00
0.25 Erika's Bellsprout (Lvl. 12)	Grass	C	0.25
0.25 Erika's Bellsprout (Lvl. 15)	Grass	C	0.25
10.00 Erika's Clefable	Colorless	F	9.00
5.00 Erika's Clefairy	Colorless	R	5.00
12.00 Erika's Dragonair	Colorless	F	11.00
1.00 Erika's Dratini	Colorless	U	1.00
0.25 Erika's Exeggcute (Lvl. 12)	Grass	C	0.25
1.00 Erika's Exeggcute (Lvl. 15)	Grass	U	1.00
1.00 Erika's Exeggutor	Grass	U	1.00
1.00 Erika's Gloom (Lvl. 24)	Grass	U	1.00
1.00 Erika's Gloom (Lvl. 28)	Grass	U	1.00
1.00 Erika's Maids	Trainer	U	1.00
1.00 Erika's Oddish (Lvl. 12)	Grass	U	1.00
0.25 Erika's Oddish (Lvl. 15)	Grass	C	0.25
1.00 Erika's Perfume	Trainer	U	0.80
0.25 Erika's Tangela	Grass	C	0.25
5.00 Erika's Victreebel	Grass	R	5.00
10.00 Erika's Vileplume	Grass	F	10.00
1.00 Erika's Weepinbell (Lvl. 26)	Grass	U	1.00
1.00 Erika's Weepinbell (Lvl. 30)	Grass	U	1.00
0.25 Fighting Energy	Energy	C	0.25

Card name	Type	Rarity	Price
0.25 Fire Energy	Energy	C	0.25
1.00 Good Manners	Trainer	U	1.00
0.25 Grass Energy	Energy	C	0.25
0.25 Lightning Energy	Energy	C	0.25
9.90 Lt. Surge	Trainer	F	8.00
5.00 Lt. Surge	Trainer	R	5.50
5.00 Lt. Surge's Electabuzz (Lvl. 22)	Lightning	R	5.80
12.00 Lt. Surge's Electabuzz (Lvl. 28)	Lightning	F	12.00
11.00 Lt. Surge's Fearow	Colorless	F	9.90
1.00 Lt. Surge's Magnemite (Lvl. 10)	Lightning	U	1.00
0.25 Lt. Surge's Magnemite (Lvl. 12)	Lightning	C	0.25
10.00 Lt. Surge's Magneton	Lightning	F	9.00
0.25 Lt. Surge's Pikachu	Lightning	C	0.25
5.00 Lt. Surge's Raichu	Lightning	R	5.50
1.00 Lt. Surge's Raticate	Colorless	U	1.00
0.25 Lt. Surge's Rattata	Colorless	C	0.25
0.25 Lt. Surge's Spearow (Lvl. 17)	Colorless	C	0.25
1.00 Lt. Surge's Spearow (Lvl. 8)	Colorless	U	1.00
1.00 Lt. Surge's Treaty	Trainer	U	1.00
0.25 Lt. Surge's Voltorb	Lightning	C	0.25
1.00 Minion of Team Rocket	Trainer	U	1.00
9.90 Misty	Trainer	F	8.00
5.00 Misty	Trainer	R	5.00
5.00 Misty's Cloyster	Water	R	5.00
0.25 Misty's Duel	Trainer	C	0.25
0.25 Misty's Goldeen (Lvl. 10)	Water	C	0.25
5.00 Misty's Goldeen (Lvl. 8)	Water	R	5.00
0.25 Misty's Horsea	Water	C	0.25
0.25 Misty's Poliwag	Water	C	0.25
1.00 Misty's Poliwhirl	Water	U	1.00
5.00 Misty's Poliwrath	Water	R	5.00
1.00 Misty's Psyduck	Water	U	1.00
12.00 Misty's Seadra	Water	F	10.00

Card name	Type	Rarity	Price
1.00 Misty's Seaking	Water	U	1.00
0.25 Misty's Seel	Water	C	0.25
0.25 Misty's Shellder	Water	C	0.25
1.00 Misty's Starmie	Water	U	1.00
0.25 Misty's Staryu	Water	C	0.25
5.00 Misty's Tentacool (Lvl. 12)	Water	R	5.00
1.00 Misty's Tentacool (Lvl. 16)	Water	U	1.00
10.00 Misty's Tentacruel	Water	F	9.90
1.00 Misty's Wrath	Trainer	U	1.00
0.25 Narrow Gym	Trainer	C	0.25
5.00 No Removal Gym	Trainer	R	6.00
1.00 Pewter City Gym	Trainer	U	1.00
0.25 Psychic Energy	Energy	C	0.25
1.00 Recall	Trainer	U	1.00
12.00 Rocket's Hitmonchan	Fighting	F	11.00
12.00 Rocket's Moltres	Fire	F	11.00
12.00 Rocket's Scyther	Grass	F	11.00
5.00 Rocket's Snorlax	Colorless	R	5.00
0.25 Sabrina's Abra	Psychic	C	0.25
0.25 Sabrina's Drowzee	Psychic	C	0.25
1.00 Sabrina's ESP	Trainer	U	1.00
0.25 Sabrina's Gastly	Psychic	C	0.25
0.25 Sabrina's Gaze	Trainer	C	0.25
12.00 Sabrina's Gengar	Psychic	F	10.00
1.00 Sabrina's Haunter	Psychic	U	1.00
1.00 Sabrina's Jynx	Psychic	U	1.00
0.25 Sabrina's Mr. Mime	Psychic	C	0.25
1.00 Sabrina's Slowbro	Psychic	U	1.00
0.25 Sabrina's Slowpoke	Psychic	C	0.25
5.00 Sabrina's Venomoth	Grass	R	5.00
0.25 Sabrina's Venonat	Grass	C	0.25
1.00 Secret Mission	Trainer	U	1.00
5.00 The Rocket's Training Gym	Trainer	R	5.00
10.00 The Rocket's Trap	Trainer	F	9.90
1.00 Tickling Machine	Trainer	U	1.00
0.25 Trash Exchange	Trainer	C	0.25
1.00 Vermilion City Gym	Trainer	U	1.00
0.25 Water Energy	Energy	C	0.25

Pokémon • Gym Challenge 1st and Unlimited

Wizards of the Coast • Released October 2000

132 cards in set • IDENTIFIER: Dark stadium symbol on *Unlimited*

- Theme decks (**Blaine, Giovanni, Koga, Sabrina**) contain 60 cards; theme displays contain 8 decks
- Booster packs contain 9 cards; booster displays contain 36 boosters

The second release inspired by the Japanese *Gym Leaders* set, *Gym Challenge* is best remembered for its cards that contain a variety of interesting game mechanics. **Koga's Pidgey** is one, with an attack that brings out another Pokémon. **Sabrina's Alakazam**'s Pokémon Power, Psylink, has very interesting ramifications for the metagame. And **Rocket's Zapdos** is the "Big Basic Pokémon" that makes the Trapper deck complete. **Rocket's Mewtwo** and **Sabrina's Kadabra** are also great cards from this set. — *Ka-Lok Fung*

GYM CHALLENGE 1ST EDITION

Set (132 cards)	437.50
Booster Display Box	121.75
Booster Pack	4.00

GYM CHALLENGE UNLIMITED

Set (132 cards)	370.00
Starter Display Box	75.00
Booster Display Box	90.00
Pre-constructed deck	10.00
Booster Pack	3.30

You will need **15** nine-pocket pages to store this set. (8 doubled up)

1ST EDIT. Card name	Type	Rarity	UNLIMITED
12.00 Blaine	Trainer	F	8.00
5.00 Blaine	Trainer	R	5.00

Card name	Type	Rarity	Price
12.00 Blaine's Arcanine	Fire	F	11.00
21.00 Blaine's Charizard	Fire	F	19.00
0.25 Blaine's Charmander	Fire	C	0.25
1.00 Blaine's Charmeleon	Fire	U	1.00
1.00 Blaine's Dodrio	Colorless	U	1.00
0.25 Blaine's Doduo	Colorless	C	0.25
0.25 Blaine's Growlithe	Fire	C	0.25
0.25 Blaine's Mankey	Fighting	C	0.25
5.00 Blaine's Ninetails	Fire	R	5.00
0.25 Blaine's Ponyta	Fire	C	0.25
1.00 Blaine's Quiz #2	Trainer	U	1.00
1.00 Blaine's Quiz #3	Trainer	U	1.00
1.00 Blaine's Rapidash	Fire	U	1.00
0.25 Blaine's Rhyhorn	Fighting	C	0.25
0.25 Blaine's Vulpix	Fire	C	0.25

Card name	Type	Rarity	Price
0.25 Brock's Diglett	Fighting	C	0.25
5.00 Brock's Dugtrio	Fighting	R	4.60
0.25 Brock's Geodude	Fighting	C	0.25
1.00 Brock's Graveler	Fighting	U	1.00
12.00 Brock's Ninetails	Fire	F	11.00
1.00 Brock's Primape	Fighting	U	1.00
5.00 Brock's Protection	Trainer	R	4.30
1.00 Brock's Sandslash	Fighting	U	1.00
1.00 Brock's Vulpix	Fire	U	1.00
5.00 Chaos Gym	Trainer	R	4.30

Brock's Ninetales 70 HP

STAGE 2 — Evolves from Brock's Vulpix — Put Brock's Ninetales on the Basic Pokémon

Fox Pokémon. Length: 3' 7", Weight: 44 lbs.

Pokémon Power: Shapeshift Once during your turn (before your attack), you may attach an Evolution card from your hand to Brock's Ninetales. (This doesn't count as evolving Brock's Ninetales.) Treat Brock's Ninetales as if it were that Pokémon instead. It can't evolve, devolve, or use the Pokémon Power of that Pokémon. During your turn, you may discard the Evolution card attached to Brock's Ninetales. If Brock's Ninetales is Asleep, Confused or Paralyzed. When Brock's Ninetales becomes Asleep, Confused or Paralyzed, discard all Evolution cards attached to it.

		Will-o'-the-wisp	30
weakness	resistance	retreat cost	

RARITY KEY C = Common   U = Uncommon   R = Rare   E = Energy   F = Foil card   X = Fixed/standard in all decks

Card name	Type	Rarity	Price
1.00 Cinnabar City Gym	Trainer	U	1.00
1.00 Erika's Bellsprout	Grass	U	1.00
1.00 Erika's Bulbasaur	Lightning	U	1.00
1.00 Erika's Clefairy	Colorless	U	1.00
1.00 Erika's Ivysaur	Grass	U	1.00
0.25 Erika's Jigglypuff	Colorless	C	0.25
4.00 Erika's Kindness	Trainer	R	4.00
0.25 Erika's Oddish	Grass	C	0.25
0.25 Erika's Paras	Grass	C	0.25

5
Card name	Type	Rarity	Price
13.50 Erika's Venusaur	Grass	F	12.00
0.25 Fervor	Trainer	C	0.25
0.25 Fighting Energy	Energy	C	0.25
0.25 Fire Energy	Energy	C	0.25
1.00 Fuchsia City Gym	Trainer	U	1.00
12.00 Giovanni	Trainer	F	8.00
5.00 Giovanni	Trainer	R	4.50
12.00 Giovanni's Gyarados	Water	F	12.00
4.50 Giovanni's Last Resort	Trainer	R	4.00

6
Card name	Type	Rarity	Price
12.00 Giovanni's Machamp	Fighting	F	12.00
1.00 Giovanni's Machoke	Fighting	U	1.00
0.25 Giovanni's Machop	Fighting	C	0.25
0.25 Giovanni's Magikarp	Water	C	0.25
0.25 Giovanni's Meowth	Colorless	C	0.25
1.00 Giovanni's Meowth	Colorless	U	1.00
12.50 Giovanni's Nidoking	Grass	F	12.00
5.00 Giovanni's Nidoqueen	Grass	R	5.00
0.25 Giovanni's Nidoran (female)	Grass	C	0.25

7
Card name	Type	Rarity	Price
0.25 Giovanni's Nidoran (male)	Grass	C	0.25
1.00 Giovanni's Nidorina	Grass	U	1.00
1.00 Giovanni's Nidorino	Grass	U	1.00
12.00 Giovanni's Persian	Colorless	F	12.00
5.50 Giovanni's Pinsir	Grass	R	5.00
0.25 Grass Energy	Energy	C	0.25
12.00 Koga	Trainer	F	10.00

Card name	Type	Rarity	Price
5.00 Koga	Trainer	R	5.00
5.00 Koga's Arbok	Grass	R	4.80

8
Card name	Type	Rarity	Price
12.00 Koga's Beedrill	Grass	F	12.00
12.00 Koga's Ditto	Colorless	F	12.00
0.25 Koga's Ekans	Grass	C	0.25
1.00 Koga's Golbat	Grass	U	1.00
0.25 Koga's Grimer	Grass	C	0.25
1.00 Koga's Kakuna	Grass	U	1.00
0.25 Koga's Koffing	Grass	C	0.25
1.00 Koga's Koffing	Grass	U	1.00
5.00 Koga's Muk	Grass	R	5.00

9
Card name	Type	Rarity	Price
1.00 Koga's Ninja Trick	Trainer	U	1.00
5.00 Koga's Pidgeotto	Colorless	R	5.00
0.25 Koga's Pidgey	Colorless	C	0.25
1.00 Koga's Pidgey	Colorless	U	1.00
0.25 Koga's Tangela	Grass	C	0.25
0.25 Koga's Weedle	Grass	C	0.25
1.00 Koga's Weezing	Grass	U	1.00
0.25 Koga's Zubat	Grass	C	0.25
0.25 Lightning Energy	Energy	C	0.25

10
Card name	Type	Rarity	Price
1.00 Lt. Surge's Electrode	Lightning	U	1.00
1.00 Lt. Surge's Evee	Colorless	U	1.00
5.50 Lt. Surge's Jolteon	Lightning	R	5.00
0.25 Lt. Surge's Pikachu	Lightning	C	0.25
14.00 Lt. Surge's Raichu	Lightning	F	12.00
1.00 Lt. Surge's Raticate	Colorless	U	1.00
0.25 Lt. Surge's Rattata	Colorless	C	0.25
5.00 Lt. Surge's Secret Plan	Trainer	R	4.00
0.25 Lt. Surge's Voltorb	Lightning	C	0.25

11
Card name	Type	Rarity	Price
1.00 Master Ball	Trainer	U	1.00
1.00 Max Revive	Trainer	U	1.00
1.00 Misty's Dewgong	Water	U	1.00
12.00 Misty's Golduck	Water	F	12.00
12.00 Misty's Gyarados	Water	F	12.00
0.25 Misty's Horsea	Water	C	0.25
0.25 Misty's Magikarp	Water	C	0.25
0.25 Misty's Poliwag	Water	C	0.25

Card name	Type	Rarity	Price
0.25 Misty's Psyduck	Water	C	0.25

12
Card name	Type	Rarity	Price
0.25 Misty's Seel	Water	C	0.25
0.25 Misty's Staryu	Water	C	0.25
1.00 Misty's Tears	Trainer	U	1.00
4.00 Misty's Wish	Trainer	R	3.90
0.25 Psychic Energy	Energy	C	0.25
5.00 Resistance Gym	Trainer	R	4.00
14.00 Rocket's Mewtwo	Psychic	F	12.00
1.00 Rocket's Minefield Gym	Trainer	U	1.00
1.00 Rocket's Secret Experiment	Trainer	U	1.00

13
Card name	Type	Rarity	Price
14.00 Rocket's Zapdos	Lightning	F	12.00
12.00 Sabrina	Trainer	F	8.00
5.50 Sabrina	Trainer	R	4.50
0.25 Sabrina's Abra Lv. 12	Psychic	C	0.25
0.25 Sabrina's Abra Lv. 18	Psychic	C	0.25
12.00 Sabrina's Alakazam	Psychic	F	12.00
0.25 Sabrina's Drowzee	Psychic	C	0.25
0.25 Sabrina's Gastly Lv. 10	Psychic	C	0.25

14
Card name	Type	Rarity	Price
0.25 Sabrina's Gastly Lv. 9	Psychic	C	0.25
6.00 Sabrina's Gengar	Psychic	R	5.00
6.00 Sabrina's Golduck	Water	R	5.00
1.00 Sabrina's Haunter	Psychic	U	1.00
1.00 Sabrina's Hypno	Psychic	U	1.00
1.00 Sabrina's Jynx	Psychic	U	1.00
1.00 Sabrina's Kadabra	Psychic	U	1.00
1.00 Sabrina's Mr. Mime	Psychic	U	1.00
0.25 Sabrina's Porygon	Colorless	C	0.25
1.00 Sabrina's Psychic Control	Trainer	U	1.00

15
Card name	Type	Rarity	Price
0.25 Sabrina's Psyduck	Water	C	0.25
1.00 Saffron City Gym	Trainer	U	1.00
0.25 Transparent Walls	Trainer	C	0.25
1.00 Viridian City Gym	Trainer	U	1.00
0.25 Warp Point	Trainer	C	0.25
0.25 Water Energy	Energy	C	0.25

Electabuzz 70 HP — Basic Pokémon
Electric Pokémon. Length: 3' 7", Weight: 66 lbs.
Punch 20
Swift 30 — This attack's damage isn't affected by Weakness, Resistance, Pokémon Powers, or any other effects on the Defending Pokémon.

Pokémon • **Neo Genesis** 1st and Unlimited

Wizards of the Coast • Released **December 2000**

111 cards in set • **IDENTIFIER: Two star symbols on Unlimited**

- Theme decks (**Cold Fusion, Hot Foot**) contain 60 cards; theme displays contain 8 decks
- Booster packs contain 9 cards; booster displays contain 36 boosters

Neo Genesis was something of a surprise. Not the set itself, necessarily, but that Wizards of the Coast got it out in 2000 at all. The licensing process with Nintendo was so arduous that the Japanese **Pocket Monsters** game had, by early 2000, developed a lead of nearly a year over Wizards of the Coast's U.S. expansions. This couldn't help but dull the excitement among U.S. players, since *Scrye* magazine was translating the Japanese cards as soon as they became available in order to tip off players as to what might be coming. It was a unique dilemma for a CCG designer to be in: The world knows what to expect from your set before you even begin working on it!

Neo, **Neo 2**, and **Neo 3** had been the big news from the *Pocket Monsters* world in 2000, and few even by **Gym Challenge** expected Wizards could get a *Neo* release out during the year. To its credit, Wizards got *Neo Genesis* out just under the wire. Now U.S. and Japanese Pokémon games were at least on Neo sets at the same time. Lugia became the prize of the U.S. set.

Around the time of *Genesis'* release, Wizards' parent Hasbro suffered stock pains and enforced cutbacks at Wizards of the Coast. While the game remains popular, as of press time, no new **Pokémon** sets were on the schedule. — *John Jackson Miller*

NEO GENESIS 1ST EDITION
Set (132 cards) 465.50
Booster Display Box 85.00
Booster Pack 4.00

NEO GENESIS UNLIMITED
Set (132 cards) 379.50
Starter Display Box 75.00
Booster Display Box 90.00
Pre-constructed deck 15.25
Booster Pack 3.30

You will need **13** nine-pocket pages to store this set. (6 doubled up)

1ST EDIT. Card name	Type	Rarity	UNLIMITED
1			
1.00 Aipom	Colorless	U	0.80
10.00 Ampharos	Water	F	9.00
5.00 Arcade Game	Trainer	R	3.00
1.00 Ariados	Grass	U	1.00
10.00 Azumarill	Water	F	9.00
1.00 Bayleef Lv. 22	Grass	U	1.00

1ST EDIT. Card name	Type	Rarity	UNLIMITED
1.00 Bayleef Lv. 39	Grass	U	1.00
12.00 Bellossom	Grass	F	9.00
0.25 Berry	Trainer	C	0.30
2			
1.00 Bill's Teleporter	Trainer	U	1.00
1.00 Card-Flip Game	Trainer	U	1.00
0.25 Chikorita Lv. 12	Grass	C	0.30
0.25 Chikorita Lv. 19	Grass	C	0.30

RARITY KEY C = Common U = Uncommon R = Rare E = Energy F = Foil card X = Fixed/standard in all decks

Card name	Type	Rarity	Price		Card name	Type	Rarity	Price		Card name	Type	Rarity	Price
☐ 0.25 Chinchou	Lightning	C	0.30 ☐		☐ 1.00 Lanturn	Lightning	U	1.00 ☐		☐ 1.00 Quilava Lv. 35	Fire	U	1.00 ☐
☐ 1.00 Clefairy	Colorless	U	1.00 ☐		☐ 1.00 Ledian	Grass	U	1.00 ☐		☐ 5.00 Recycle Energy	Energy	R	3.50 ☐
☐ 5.00 Cleffa	Colorless	R	4.00 ☐		☐ 0.25 Ledyba	Grass	C	0.30 ☐		[10]			
☐ 1.00 Croconaw Lv. 34	Water	U	1.00 ☐		☐ 0.25 Lightning Energy	Energy	E	0.25 ☐		☐ 1.00 Seadra	Water	U	1.00 ☐
☐ 1.00 Croconaw Lv. 41	Water	U	1.00 ☐		☐ 17.50 Lugia	Colorless	F	15.00 ☐		☐ 0.50 Sentret	Colorless	C	0.30 ☐
[3]					☐ 6.00 Magby	Fire	R	4.00 ☐		☐ 0.50 Shuckle	Grass	C	0.30 ☐
☐ 0.25 Cyndaquil Lv. 14	Fire	C	0.30 ☐		☐ 1.00 Magmar	Fire	U	1.00 ☐		☐ 10.00 Skarmory	Grass	F	9.00 ☐
☐ 0.25 Cyndaquil Lv. 21	Fire	C	0.30 ☐		☐ 0.25 Mantine	Water	C	0.30 ☐		☐ 1.00 Skiploom	Grass	U	1.00 ☐
☐ 5.00 Darkness Energy	Energy	R	5.00 ☐		[7]					☐ 12.00 Slowking	Psychic	F	9.00 ☐
☐ 5.00 Donphan	Fighting	R	3.00 ☐		☐ 0.25 Mareep	Lightning	C	0.30 ☐		☐ 0.25 Slowpoke	Psychic	C	0.30 ☐
☐ 0.25 Double Gust	Trainer	C	0.30 ☐		☐ 0.25 Marill	Water	C	0.30 ☐		☐ 5.00 Sneasel	Dark	R	5.00 ☐
☐ 5.00 Ecogym	Trainer	R	3.50 ☐		☐ 5.00 Mary	Trainer	R	3.00 ☐		☐ 0.25 Snubbull	Colorless	C	0.30 ☐
☐ 1.00 Electabuzz	Lightning	U	1.00 ☐		☐ 10.00 Meganium Lv. 54	Grass	F	10.00 ☐		[11]			
☐ 5.00 Elekid	Lightning	R	5.00 ☐		☐ 11.00 Meganium Lv. 57	Grass	F	10.00 ☐		☐ 0.25 Spinarak	Grass	C	0.30 ☐
☐ 5.00 Energy Charge	Trainer	R	3.00 ☐		☐ 10.00 Metal Energy	Energy	F	9.00 ☐		☐ 1.00 Sprout Tower	Trainer	U	1.00 ☐
[4]					☐ 1.00 Miltank	Colorless	U	1.00 ☐		☐ 0.25 Stantler	Colorless	C	0.30 ☐
☐ 12.00 Feraligatr Lv. 56	Water	F	11.00 ☐		☐ 1.00 Miracle Berry	Trainer	U	1.00 ☐		☐ 11.00 Steelix	Metal	F	10.00 ☐
☐ 12.00 Feraligatr Lv. 69	Water	F	11.00 ☐		☐ 0.25 Moo-Moo Milk	Trainer	C	0.30 ☐		☐ 0.25 Sudowoodo	Fighting	C	0.30 ☐
☐ 0.25 Fighting Energy	Energy	E	0.25 ☐		[8]					☐ 1.00 Sunflora	Grass	U	1.00 ☐
☐ 0.25 Fire Energy	Energy	E	0.25 ☐		☐ 5.00 Murkrow	Dark	R	3.00 ☐		☐ 0.25 Sunkern	Grass	C	0.30 ☐
☐ 1.00 Flaaffy	Lightning	U	1.00 ☐		☐ 0.25 Natu	Psychic	C	0.30 ☐		☐ 5.00 Super Energy Retrieval	Trainer	R	4.00 ☐
☐ 5.00 Focus Band	Trainer	R	3.00 ☐		☐ 1.00 New Pokédex	Trainer	U	1.00 ☐		☐ 0.25 Super Rod	Trainer	C	0.30 ☐
☐ 1.00 Furret	Colorless	U	1.00 ☐		☐ 1.00 Noctowl	Colorless	U	1.00 ☐		[12]			
☐ 0.25 Girafarig	Psychic	C	0.30 ☐		☐ 0.25 Oddish	Grass	C	0.30 ☐		☐ 1.00 Super Scoop Up	Trainer	U	1.00 ☐
☐ 0.25 Gligar	Fighting	C	0.30 ☐		☐ 0.25 Onix	Fighting	C	0.30 ☐		☐ 0.25 Swinub	Water	C	0.30 ☐
[5]					☐ 1.00 Phanpy	Fighting	U	1.00 ☐		☐ 5.00 Time Capsule	Trainer	R	3.00 ☐
☐ 1.00 Gloom	Grass	U	1.00 ☐		☐ 15.00 Pichu	Lightning	F	14.00 ☐		☐ 1.00 Togepi	Colorless	U	1.00 ☐
☐ 1.00 Gold Berry	Trainer	U	1.00 ☐		☐ 0.50 Pikachu	Lightning	C	0.30 ☐		☐ 14.00 Togetic	Colorless	F	14.00 ☐
☐ 1.00 Granbull	Colorless	U	1.00 ☐		[9]					☐ 0.25 Totodile Lv. 20	Water	C	0.30 ☐
☐ 0.25 Grass Energy	Energy	E	0.25 ☐		☐ 1.00 Piloswine	Water	U	1.00 ☐		☐ 0.25 Totodile Lv. 8	Water	C	0.30 ☐
☐ 12.00 Heracross	Grass	F	9.00 ☐		☐ 5.00 PokéGear	Trainer	R	3.00 ☐		☐ 15.00 Typhlosion Lv. 55	Fire	F	12.00 ☐
☐ 0.25 Hoothoot	Colorless	C	0.30 ☐		☐ 0.25 Pokémon March	Trainer	C	0.30 ☐		☐ 12.50 Typhlosion Lv. 57	Fire	F	12.00 ☐
☐ 0.25 Hopip	Grass	C	0.30 ☐		☐ 1.00 Professor Elm	Trainer	U	1.00 ☐		[13]			
☐ 0.25 Horsea	Water	C	0.30 ☐		☐ 0.25 Psychic Energy	Energy	E	0.25 ☐		☐ 0.25 Water Energy	Energy	E	0.25 ☐
☐ 10.00 Jumpluff	Grass	F	9.00 ☐		☐ 1.00 Quagsire	Water	U	1.00 ☐		☐ 0.25 Wooper	Metal	C	0.30 ☐
[6]					☐ 1.00 Quilava Lv. 28	Fire	U	1.00 ☐		☐ 1.00 Xatu	Psychic	U	1.00 ☐
☐ 10.00 Kingdra	Water	F	9.00 ☐										

Pokémon • Promos

Wizards of the Coast

IDENTIFIER: Black star symbol on most

Wizards of the Coast's promotional card program for its *Pokémon* CCG is one of the bettter organized efforts to come along. Black stars with numbers helped players associate promo cards with specific sources.

Celebrated promo releases include those at movie theaters for the *Pokémon: The First Movie* and *Pokémon: The Movie 2000*. Cards in video boxes, video game boxes, and magazines led people to buy some of those items just for the cards. And Burger King's decision to run a *Pokémon* CCG promotion must have gotten someone a raise, as it went over so well that Burger King organized *Pokémon* "trading nights." — ***John Jackson Miller***

Card name	Foil?	Price
[1]		
☐ Aerodactyl (Fossil) [Stamped Prerelease]		15.00
☐ Ancient Mew [Pokémon Movie 2000]	F	7.60
☐ Clefable (Jungle) [Stamped Prerelease]		19.00
☐ Kabuto (Fossil) [gold stamped]		5.00
☐ Meowth [gold-bordered]		5.30
☐ Misty's Seadra [Stamped Prerelease]		6.00
☐ Pikachu (stamped with E3)		11.00
☐ Pikachu (stamped with foil shooting star)		8.00
☐ Pikachu (colossal card)		5.00
[2]		
☐ Black Star #1: Pikachu [Pokémon League]		7.00
☐ Black Star #2: Electabuzz [1st Pokémon movie]		6.00
☐ Black Star #3: Mewtwo [1st Pokémon movie]		7.50
☐ Black Star #4: Pikachu [1st Pokémon movie]		6.00
☐ Black Star #5: Dragonite [1st Pokémon movie]		6.00

Card name	Foil?	Price
☐ Black Star #6: Arcanine [Pokémon League]		6.00
☐ Black Star #7: Jigglypuff [Atlantic Records]		12.00
☐ Black Star #8: Mew [Pokémon League]		3.00
☐ Black Star #9: Mew holofoil	F	15.00
[3]		
☐ Black Star #10: Meowth [Nintendo Power]	F	15.00
☐ Black Star #11: Eevee [Pokémon League]		4.50
☐ Black Star #12: Mewtwo [Nintendo Power]		28.00
☐ Black Star #13: Venusaur [Nintendo Player's Guide]		15.00
☐ Black Star #14: Mewtwo [movie videotape]		5.00
☐ Black Star #15: Cool Porygon [N64]	F	32.00
☐ Black Star #16: Computer Error [Pokémon League]		2.00
☐ Black Star #17: Dark Persian	F	10.00
☐ Black Star #18: Team Rocket's Meowth		4.00
[4]		
☐ Black Star #19: Sabrina's Abra		6.00

You will need 4 nine-pocket pages to store this set. (2 doubled up)

Card name	Foil?	Price
☐ Black Star #20: Psyduck		7.00
☐ Black Star #21: Moltres [Pokémon Movie 2000]		6.00
☐ Black Star #22: Articuno [Pokémon Movie 2000]		6.00
☐ Black Star #23: Zapdos [Pokémon Movie 2000]		6.00

Read more about it

For more information about *Pokémon* strategies, look for our book ***Scrye Presents The Ultimate Pokémon Price and Player's Guide***, in stores now.

And you can always find translations for the latest Japanese sets in current issues of ***Scrye***.

RARITY KEY	C = Common	U = Uncommon	R = Rare	E = Energy	F = Foil card	X = Fixed/standard in all decks

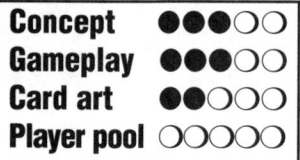

PowerCardz

Caliber Game Systems • First set, *First Strike*, released **July 1995**

300 cards in set • **IDENTIFIER: Different backs from *Spawn* set**

• Starter decks contain 50 cards; starter displays contain 12 starters

• Booster packs contain 15 cards; booster displays contain 36 boosters

Concept	●●●○○
Gameplay	●●●○○
Card art	●●○○○
Player pool	○○○○○

What was the first super-hero CCG to adapt an existing comics universe (instead of the made-up one of *Super Deck*)? *OverPower* is a good guess, but *PowerCardz* actually beats it by a few weeks. Knight Press, an indie comics publisher, had set a few issues in its Sky Universe — and in 1995 took an interest in CCGs. The Knight team had a fantasy CCG called *Realms Arcana* nearly into production — promo cards were released — when the chance came to develop a CCG for Caliber Press, which had picked up the Sky comics line. And Caliber and Knight associate Beau Smith worked for Spawn creator Todd McFarlane, explaining the high-profile nature of the second *PowerCardz* release. Mystery solved!

The game itself is good, but not terribly exciting. Every turn, each player slaps down a character and declares attacks on opposing characters. It's sort of a super-hero pyramid scheme. A player starts with one hero on Turn 1 and on Turn 2 plays another. Each character has several attacks and a few defenses. Play starts with the character with the highest speed stat attacking an opposing character, and slower characters' attacks follow. As characters are knocked out, they lose their chance to act. A player out of characters loses.

The cards look intimidating, with tiny words and numbers, but the design for the basic set is clear, with only three background colors. The tuck-boxes for booster packs, unique in the CCG world, give the packaging a rather low-tech look.

Soon Image did its own CCGs through Wildstorm, and without Spawn's name *PowerCardz* vanished. Caliber planned more CCGs, but the only one announced, *Daemonstorm*, never came out. — *Richard Weld & John Jackson Miller*

You will need **34** nine-pocket pages to store this set. (17 doubled up)

Set (300 cards)	84.65
Starter Display Box	22.50
Booster Display Box	26.00
Starter Deck	5.50
Booster Pack	1.00

#	Card name	Rarity	Price
1			
203	Abduct City Official	C	0.05
204	Abduct President	C	0.05
187	Act of Terrorism	C	0.05
21	Adriana Kessler	C	0.05
16	Agent Parsons	C	0.05
140	Ally	U	0.25
164	Ambush!	U	0.25
19	Angel Shadow	C	0.05
281	Aquarius	C	0.05
2			
95	Arcane Powers	U	0.25
150	Arch-Nemesis	U	0.25
291	Aries	C	0.05
139	Arsenal	R	1.00
276	Atomic Sub	C	0.05
157	Aura of Fear	U	0.25
61	Automatic Dodge	C	0.05
200	Bank Robbery	C	0.05
8	Barricade	R	1.00
3			
102	Battle Armor	U	0.25
274	Beacon (Golden Age)	C	0.05
279	Beacon (Silver Age)	C	0.05
181	Beck	U	0.25
85	Berserk!	U	0.25
192	Berzerker	U	0.25
62	Big Gun	C	0.05
194	Blind Elimination	R	1.00
270	Blitz (Golden Age)	C	0.05
4			
275	Blitz (Silver Age)	C	0.05
36	Bobtail	C	0.05
11	Brightblade	U	0.25
32	Bronze Blade	C	0.05
81	Bullseye!	U	0.25
45	Byre	C	0.05
27	Caijun	C	0.05
189	Call Enhancement	UR	1.50
172	Call Hero	R	1.00
5			
197	Call Tech Force	R	1.00
180	Call Villain	R	1.00
285	Cancer	C	0.05
282	Capricorn	C	0.05
296	Catalyst	UR	1.50

#	Card name	Rarity	Price
246	Caul	U	0.25
255	Chariot	U	0.25
217	Charon	R	1.00
224	Cheops	U	0.25
6			
47	CHESS Unit	C	0.05
4	Christiana Blood	C	0.05
184	Computer Virus	C	0.05
73	Cops	C	0.05
127	Corporation	UR	1.50
67	Counter Enhancement	C	0.05
205	Create Mass Hysteria	C	0.05
74	Cyber Appendage	U	0.25
88	Cybercycle	C	0.05
7			
25	Cybertek	U	0.25
90	Damsel in Distress	C	0.05
122	Dark Enchantresses	R	1.00
199	Dark Flaxen	UR	2.00
156	Dazed	U	0.25
261	Death	U	0.25
134	Debriefing	UR	1.50
94	Deck Soldiers	U	0.25
120	Demonicus	C	0.05
8			
244	Dense Woodland	C	0.05
209	Destroy City	C	0.05
263	Devil	U	0.25
228	Diabla	R	1.00
169	Disarm	U	0.25
185	Discover Identity	R	1.00
210	Dominate Country	C	0.05
40	Dominion	U	0.25
227	Domino	R	1.00
9			
196	Doppleganger	UR	2.00
50	Double Cross	C	0.05
167	Double Team!	U	0.25
236	Dr. Spencer	C	0.05
243	Earthquake	R	1.00
295	Electric Blue	U	0.25
252	Emperor	U	0.25
251	Empress	U	0.25
162	Enfeeble	U	0.25
10			
132	Enhance Enhancement	UR	1.50

#	Card name	Rarity	Price
153	Enraged	R	1.00
163	Ensnare	U	0.25
75	Fast Attack	C	0.05
101	Fatal Strike	U	0.25
193	Fatigue	R	1.00
110	Fightmaster	C	0.05
144	Flare	U	0.25
191	Flash Bomb	R	1.00
11			
198	Flaxen	UR	3.50
293	Fleetwing	R	1.00
248	Fool	U	0.25
76	Force Field	C	0.05
142	Force of Will	C	0.05
168	Forestall	C	0.05
151	Former Friends	U	0.25
258	Fortune	U	0.25
114	Frank Dietrich	C	0.05
12			
34	Frenzy	U	0.25
245	Frozen Tundra	C	0.05
214	Fuego	C	0.05
211	Fusion	R	1.00
175	G.I.	C	0.05
49	Garrick	C	0.05
286	Gemini	C	0.05
143	Ghostly Guardian	U	0.25
77	Glancing Blow	C	0.05
13			
218	Gnome	U	0.25
212	Gossamer	C	0.05
84	Great Luck	U	0.25
124	Grimbludd	C	0.05
118	Gurk	C	0.05
17	Haggard	C	0.05
260	Hang Man	C	0.05
137	Hard Target	U	0.25
207	Harm Innocent People	C	0.05
14			
136	Haymaker	U	0.25
128	Headquarters	UR	1.50
300	Hellgirl	UR	1.50
257	Hermit	U	0.25
253	Hierophant	U	0.25
250	High Priestess	UR	1.50
22	Hope LeBeck	C	0.05

#	Card name	Rarity	Price
70	Hostage	C	0.05
38	Huntarr	C	0.05
15			
234	Hunter Seeker	C	0.05
173	Indigo	C	0.05
125	Infernus	C	0.05
68	Informant	U	0.25
78	Ion Tank	U	0.25
171	Ivory	C	0.05
235	Jammin'	C	0.05
28	Jewel	C	0.05
201	Jewelry Heist	C	0.05
16			
46	John Hollister	C	0.05
268	Judgement	R	1.00
256	Justice	U	0.25
298	Kabuki	UR	3.50
107	Kalleth	C	0.05
48	Katharsys	R	1.00
31	Khamal Khan	C	0.05
299	King Zombie	U	0.25
121	Klaash	R	1.00
17			
278	Knight Watchman	C	0.05
220	Komodo	U	0.25
287	Leo	C	0.05
289	Libra	C	0.05
63	Lightning Reflexes	C	0.05
55	Lilith	U	0.25
23	Litlit	C	0.05
231	Lotus	U	0.25
254	Lovers	U	0.25
18			
54	Magaira	U	0.25
131	Magical Dweomer	UR	1.50
249	Magician	R	1.00
123	Magistrate	C	0.05
106	Mama Callie	R	1.00
160	Manifest Power	U	0.25
29	Marhawk	C	0.05
37	Marta	UR	1.50
146	Massive Speed	R	1.00
19			
148	Massive Spirit	C	0.05
145	Massive Strength	R	1.00
147	Massive Will	C	0.05
237	Masterspy	C	0.05
72	Med-Lab	U	0.25

#	Card name	Rarity	Price
202	Media Blitz	C	0.05
52	Merlin	UR	1.50
18	Midnight Montana	C	0.05
183	Mike	U	0.25
20			
104	Mila-Police	U	0.25
226	Mime	U	0.25
159	Mimic Device	U	0.25
86	Mind Control	U	0.25
129	Mind Shield	UR	1.50
267	Moon	U	0.25
213	Mother Russia	R	1.00
280	Mr. Mask	C	0.05
91	Mysterious Ally	U	0.25
21			
87	Mystic Claw	U	0.25
89	N.I.K.E.	U	0.25
103	Natural Disaster	U	0.25
117	Necrose	C	0.05
82	Neutralize	U	0.25
182	Nightlinger	U	0.25
230	Oba	U	0.25
53	One Eyed Jack	C	0.05
241	Open Sea	R	1.00
22			
240	Outer Space	R	1.00
221	Outrider	C	0.05
58	Pando	C	0.05
13	Pandora	U	0.25
155	Paralysis	C	0.05
80	Partner	U	0.25
174	Peacekeeper	UR	2.00
133	Peculiar Terrain	UR	1.50
64	Persistance	C	0.05
23			
116	Pierre Tepes	C	0.05
113	Pioneer	C	0.05
290	Pisces	C	0.05
51	Portyl	U	0.25
149	Power Booster	R	1.00
223	Procyon	U	0.25
141	Psychic Probe	U	0.25
15	Race Danger	C	0.05
35	Ragtag	C	0.05
24			
166	Raid Headquarters	R	1.00
60	Rave	C	0.05
98	Rebirth!	U	0.25

RARITY KEY C = Common U = Uncommon R = Rare VR = Very Rare UR = Ultra Rare F = Foil card X = Fixed/standard in all decks

#	Card name	Rarity	Price
170	Reflect Attack	C	0.05
83	Rejuvenate	C	0.05
111	Retro	C	0.05
138	Return Fire	U	0.25
41	Rhianna	U	0.25
56	Robespierre	U	0.25
92	Saboteur	U	0.25
283	Sagitarius	C	0.05
59	Saki	C	0.05
44	Samuroid	U	0.25
292	Scorpio	C	0.05
177	Scythe	C	0.05
2	Seeker	UR	2.00
26	Selene LeBeck	C	0.05
93	Sensei	U	0.25
229	Sentinel	U	0.25
112	Seraph	C	0.05
12	Shalimar	U	0.25
216	Shamal	C	0.05

#	Card name	Rarity	Price
14	Shepherd	U	0.25
10	Shrike	U	0.25
69	Sidekick	R	1.00
195	Sight Elimination	UR	1.50
233	Sir Steel	U	0.25
20	Skorch	C	0.05
190	Smokescreen	U	0.25
161	Sonic Gun	U	0.25
42	Soul Breed	C	0.05
9	Soulfire	R	1.00
225	Sputnik	C	0.05
105	Spy	C	0.05
265	Star	U	0.25
206	Steal Major Satellite	C	0.05
178	Steal Technology	C	0.05
186	Stop Volcano	U	0.25
119	Straight Jacket	R	1.00
259	Strength	U	0.25
266	Sun	U	0.25

#	Card name	Rarity	Price
3	Superior	UR	1.50
33	T-Rex	C	0.05
165	Takeover Corporation	R	1.00
208	Takeover Network	C	0.05
5	Tamara Rose	C	0.05
219	Tank	R	1.00
179	Tap Magical Source	C	0.05
284	Taurus	C	0.05
99	Team Support	R	1.00
30	Tek Knight	U	0.25
7	Temblor	U	0.25
262	Temperance	U	0.25
1	Tempered Steele	UR	1.50
39	The Eel	C	0.05
71	Thugs	C	0.05
273	Thunder Girl	C	0.05
238	Thundershower	R	1.00
57	Tig	C	0.05

#	Card name	Rarity	Price
176	Tigercat	C	0.05
239	Tight Quarters	R	1.00
154	Time Bomb	U	0.25
97	Time Lord Defender	R	1.00
65	Time Shard I	U	0.25
66	Time Shard II	U	0.25
96	Time Ship	R	1.00
6	Time Stepper	R	1.00
100	Time Storm	R	1.00
135	Time-Stone	UR	1.50
232	Tokamak	U	0.25
264	Tower	U	0.25
43	Trimalion	C	0.05
242	Typhoon	R	1.00
272	Ultiman (Golden Age)	C	0.05
277	Ultiman (Silver Age)	C	0.05
152	Ultimate Faith	U	0.25

#	Card name	Rarity	Price
130	Ultra-force Field	UR	1.50
294	Umbra	U	0.25
79	Uneasy Truce	U	0.25
24	Vanessa	C	0.05
271	Venus	C	0.05
158	Vigilance	C	0.05
288	Virgo	C	0.05
247	Volcanic Upheaval	C	0.05
109	Vortex	C	0.05
215	Wall	C	0.05
222	Warhead	C	0.05
126	Warlace	C	0.05
108	Warloch	C	0.05
297	Wispmaid	U	0.25
115	Witchfire	C	0.05
269	World	R	1.00
188	Wyvern	U	0.25

PowerCardz • Spawn

Caliber Game Systems • Released September 1995

190 cards in set • **IDENTIFIER: Different card backs**

- Starter decks contain 50 cards; starter displays contain 12 starters
- Booster packs contain 15 cards; booster displays contain 36 boosters

The **Spawn** expansion adds characters from Todd McFarlane's *Spawn* comics setting to *PowerCardz*. It marks the first CCG appearance of Spawn characters, which would later appear in the Image Comics editions of the **Wildstorms** and **OverPower**.

The color backgrounds of the cards are changed, with red for Evil, blue for Good, gold for neutral, and green for enhancements. There are problems with the collation in this set, with multiple boosters in the same display having the exact same card mix. — *Richard Weld*

You will need **22** nine-pocket pages to store this set. (11 doubled up)

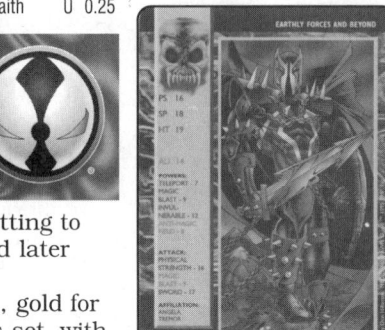

Set (190 cards)	73.00
Starter Display Box	21.00
Booster Display Box	23.00
Starter Deck	5.00
Booster Pack	1.00

#	Card name	Rarity	Price
79	Abduct Wanda	U	0.50
22	Admonisher	C	0.10
15	Al Simmons	U	0.50
26	Anahita	U	0.70
2	Angela	R	3.00
76	Angela's Lance	U	0.80
147	Angelic Ribbons	R	1.60
23	Angelic Servitors	U	0.50
33	Anti-Spawn	C	0.10
114	Arsenal	R	1.40
169	Assassination Attempt	C	0.10
78	Assault Terry	U	0.50
92	Automatic Dodge	C	0.10
127	Berserk!	U	0.70
94	Big Gun	C	0.10
41	Billy Kincaid	C	0.10
157	Bless	C	0.10
176	Blinding Flash	U	0.50
149	Blood Scrying	R	1.40
108	Boomer	U	0.50
44	Brains	C	0.10
125	Bullseye!	U	0.80
52	Bums	C	0.10
34	Byron	C	0.10
53	C.I.A. Contact	C	0.10
150	Call Phlebiac	R	1.40
56	Callindra	C	0.10
145	Cape Attack!	R	1.60
143	Chain Frenzy!	R	1.60
185	Chief Banks	U	0.50
4	Clown	U	0.50
11	Commando Spawn	U	1.30
160	Company Crossover	R	1.60

#	Card name	Rarity	Price
42	Concerned Citizens	C	0.10
141	Cosmic Angela	UR	6.80
117	Count Cagliostro	UR	5.00
96	Counter Enhancement	U	0.50
45	Counter Maneuver	C	0.10
109	Cthugan Metabuse	U	0.50
39	Curse	C	0.10
158	Curse	C	0.10
188	Cut-Throat	R	2.60
103	Dark Broody Guy	C	0.10
187	Dark Kincaid	U	0.80
68	Darklands	U	0.50
132	Dazed	U	0.50
86	Demon Horde	U	0.70
167	Destroy Building	C	0.10
134	Disarm	U	0.50
180	Discover Armory	U	0.80
146	Divine Intervention	R	1.60
62	Drone Angels	C	0.10
51	Elemental Fire	C	0.10
67	Elysium	U	0.50
190	Fairchild	R	2.00
120	Fast Attack	C	0.10
128	Final Strike	U	0.70
152	First Impression	C	0.10
121	Force Field	C	0.10
133	Forestall	C	0.10
102	Future Spawn	UR	7.50
32	Gabrielle	UR	5.00
14	Giant Spawn	C	0.10
122	Glancing Blow	C	0.10
63	Grandma Blake	C	0.10
189	Grifter	R	2.00
115	Guardian	R	1.90
61	Guardian Angel	C	0.10
119	Hand of Malebolgia	C	0.10
130	Hard Target	C	0.10
28	Harry Houdini	UR	6.00
129	Haymaker	U	0.70

#	Card name	Rarity	Price
181	Hell Corsairs	C	0.10
43	Hell Creature	C	0.10
154	Holy Light	C	0.10
148	Hunting License	R	1.00
112	Ice Shrimp	U	0.50
159	Image Crossover	R	1.60
155	Innocent Bystanders	C	0.10
163	Invade Darklands	C	0.10
164	Invade Earth	C	0.10
162	Invade Elysium	R	1.60
36	James	C	0.10
118	Jason Wynn	UR	5.00
184	John Sansker	R	1.00
77	Kidnap Cyan	U	0.50
186	Krazed Klansmen	U	0.50
25	Kuan Yin	U	0.50
91	Lightning Reflexes	C	0.10
47	Link	C	0.10
73	MacNeil & Volokhov	R	1.60
88	Mafia Hitmen	R	1.40
175	Massive Aura	C	0.10
173	Massive Speed	R	2.10
172	Massive Strength	R	2.10
174	Massive Will	C	0.10
64	Media Contact	C	0.10
60	Medieval Spawn	UR	7.50
70	Medieval Spawn	R	3.30
80	Medieval Spawn	U	1.30
90	Medieval Spawn	U	1.00
100	Medieval Spawn	C	0.10
110	Medieval Spawn	C	0.10
113	Meta Squid	C	0.10
55	Metatron	R	1.60
82	Monster Rig	U	0.80
101	Mutant Spawn	R	3.00
75	Myrlu Bond	R	1.60
136	Mystical Armor	UR	5.00
135	Mystical Sword	R	1.60
89	Nacreous Containment	C	0.10

#	Card name	Rarity	Price
87	Necro Plasm	C	0.10
93	Neutralize	C	0.10
13	Ninja Spawn	UR	8.80
168	Organized Crime	C	0.10
5	Overkill	C	0.10
124	Partner	U	0.50
95	Persistence	C	0.10
151	Phlebiac Taunt	R	1.40
12	Pilot Spawn	U	1.30
65	Police Contact	U	0.40
182	Power Booster	R	1.90
171	Power Drain	U	0.50
74	Prime Monad	R	1.40
177	Protected Senses	C	0.10
183	Rafael	R	1.60
97	Rebirth!	R	1.60
38	Redeemer	UR	5.00
126	Rejuvenate	C	0.10
131	Return Fire	U	0.70
81	Robot Duplicate	U	0.50
105	Rogue Angel	C	0.10
104	Rogue Myrlu	U	0.50
8	Sam Burke	U	0.40
49	Sandalphon Dragon	UR	5.00
27	Saranyu	U	0.50
153	Shadow of Evil	C	0.10
71	Shadowlands	U	0.50
140	Sibling Rivalry	C	0.10
66	Simmonsville	U	0.50
46	Smokey	C	0.10
57	Smut	U	0.50
142	Soul Gourmet	U	0.50
111	Soul Scalper	U	0.50
24	Soul Trapper	U	0.70
1	Spawn	UR	7.50
10	Spawn	R	5.00
20	Spawn	U	1.00
30	Spawn	U	1.30
40	Spawn	C	0.10

#	Card name	Rarity	Price
50	Spawn	C	0.10
84	Spawn Air Cycle	R	1.60
138	Spawn Alley	U	0.50
99	Spawn Battle Horse	UR	6.30
72	Spawn Mobile	C	0.10
144	Spawn Unmasked	R	2.60
54	Stasis Field	UR	5.00
139	Street Tank	U	0.80
31	Surielle	U	0.80
179	Tactical Nuke	U	0.80
161	Takeover Bowery	R	1.40
170	Takeover Satellite	C	0.10
98	Team Support	UR	5.00
178	Terran Affairs Contact	U	0.50
6	Terry Fitzgerald	C	0.10
37	The Creep Gang	C	0.10
85	The Flux	R	1.40
156	The Fuzz	C	0.10
35	The Nerd Gang	C	0.10
69	The Overlap	U	0.50
106	Thugs	C	0.10
58	Ticki Tacki	U	0.50
48	Tony Twist	U	0.50
166	Torment the Living	C	0.10
29	Tremor	R	1.00
9	Twitch	U	0.40
123	Uneasy Truce	U	0.50
16	Vacillator	UR	5.00
19	Vandalizer	U	0.50
17	Vaporizer	UR	5.00
107	Vertebreaker	UR	5.00
18	Victimizer	UR	5.00
21	Villifier	UR	5.00
116	Vindicator	U	0.50
3	Violator	U	1.00
83	Violator Chopper	UR	5.00
59	Wampyr	C	0.10
7	Wanda Blake	U	0.50
137	Warrior Angels	C	0.10
165	Wreak Havoc	C	0.10

Quest for the Grail

Horizon Games/Stone Ring • First set, **Preview Edition**, released **August 1995**
125 cards in set • **IDENTIFIER: Narrow gray borders**
• Starter decks contain 60 cards
Designed by **Ian Hense**, **David F. Nalle**, **Paul Reeves**, and **Richard Trainham**

Before the release of **Monty Python and The Holy Grail** CCG, that vessel found its way into a more serious CCG. The funny one was more successful.

Players in **Quest for the Grail** partially re-enact the Arthurian myth cycle by forming a round table of Knights who, through various Quests, gain enough Valor to seek the Grail. Each player has a 40-card Court deck and a 10-card Quest deck. The player draws a card from his Court deck, after which he may play a Domain from his hand in the Build Phase; warriors (including Knights and Kings) in the Deployment Phase; and Companions (such as Enchanters, Ladies, and Minstrels) in the Assignment Phase. The player pays upkeep for his warriors with Power generated by his Domains; any warrior whose upkeep is not paid is discarded.

The meat of the turn is the Challenge Phase, during which each warrior may spend his action going on a Quest, issuing a challenge, or Questing for the Grail. All Quests in play are open to be met by the warriors of any player. Each Quest challenges a warrior in various ways, usually in combat. In combat each participant rolls two six-sided dice against his Prowess score; if the result is less than or equal to Prowess, the target is hit and takes damage is against its Endurance. Combat continues until one or both combatants are wounded beyond Endurance, upon which they die. Combat is simultaneous.

When a warrior defeats a Quest he may take its Valor in points; once a Knight has 12 or more Valor, he may Quest for the Grail by successfully completing three Quests in a row without his Valor falling below 12. The first player to have a Knight successfully Quest for the Grail wins; there are also other alternate victory conditions.

The only two editions were the special **Preview Edition** and very limited **Limited Edition**, both with small print runs and poor distribution. This is a shame, since the system, while clunky at times, showed potential for growth, and the cards, while not of the highest quality, did capture the feel of the Arthurian legend. — **James Mishler**

> You will need **14** nine-pocket pages to store this set. (7 doubled up)

Rating	
Concept	●●●○○
Gameplay	●●●●○
Card art	●●○○○
Player pool	○○○○○

	Price
Set (125 cards)	48.00
Starter Deck	8.00

Card name	Type	Rarity	Price
1			
Assassin	Warrior	R	1.50
Axe of Cleaving	Reward	C	0.20
Binding	Spell	C	0.20
Black Knight	Quest	C	0.20
Blatant Beast	Quest	C	0.20
Blight	Spell	R	1.50
Brigand Knight	Quest	C	0.20
Britain (Ver. 1)	Domain	C	0.20
Britain (Ver. 2)	Domain	C	0.20
2			
Britain (Ver. 3)	Domain	C	0.20
Chimera	Quest	R	2.00
Cloak of Silence	Reward	U	0.60
Combat Experience (A)	Reward	R	1.50
Combat Experience (B)	Reward	R	1.50
Concentration (A)	Combat	C	0.20
Concentration (B)	Combat	C	0.20
Cornwall (Ver. 1)	Domain	C	0.20
Cornwall (Ver. 2)	Domain	C	0.20
3			
Cornwall (Ver. 3)	Domain	C	0.20
Counterspell	Spell	U	0.60
Cunning Blade	Spell	C	0.20
Dark Alliance	Spell	R	1.50
Defamation	Event	U	0.60
Demoiselle Blanchefleur	Cmpnion	U	0.60
Demoiselle Sans Nom	Cmpnion	C	0.20
Dispossession	Event	C	0.20
Enchanted Sleep	Spell	R	1.50
4			
Ensorceled Wood	Quest	R	1.50
Enthrall	Spell	R	1.50
Exile	Event	R	1.50
Flail	Reward	C	0.20
Fury (A)	Combat	C	0.20

Card name	Type	Rarity	Price
Fury (B)	Combat	C	0.20
Giant	Quest	U	0.60
Giant of Arroy	Quest	C	0.20
Gift of Three Mothers	Spell	U	0.60
5			
Goblin	Quest	U	0.60
Grail Maidens	Event	R	1.50
Great Serpent of Gore	Quest	R	2.00
Great Worm	Quest	C	0.20
Green Knight	Quest	R	2.00
Healing Prayer	Event	C	0.20
Holy Aid	Spell	U	0.60
Insult to a Lady	Event	U	0.60
King Arthur of South Wales	King	R	5.00
6			
King Berrant of the Hundred Knights	King	U	0.60
King Leodegrance of Britain	King	R	2.00
King Ryence of North Wales	King	R	2.00
King Uther Pendragon of Logres	King	R	3.00
Knight Errant	Knight	C	0.20
Knight of the Black Lands	Quest	R	2.00
Lady Belle Isoult	Cmpnion	R	1.50
Lady Croisette	Cmpnion	U	0.60
Lady Enid	Cmpnion	U	0.60
7			
Lady Lesolie of the Fountain	Cmpnion	U	0.60
Lady Lynette	Cmpnion	R	1.50
Lady Vivian	Cmpnion	R	1.50
Lady Ygraine	Cmpnion	U	0.60
Lady Yvette	Cmpnion	R	1.50
Lesser Worm of the Mount	Quest	C	0.20

Card name	Type	Rarity	Price
Man at Arms (A)	Warrior	C	0.20
Man at Arms (B)	Warrior	U	0.60
Master Ralph the Merchant	Event	R	1.50
8			
Nightmare Fiend	Quest	C	0.20
North Wales (Ver. 1)	Domain	C	0.20
North Wales (Ver. 2)	Domain	C	0.20
North Wales (Ver. 3)	Domain	C	0.20
Ogre	Quest	C	0.20
Page	Cmpnion	U	0.60
Perilous Garde	Quest	R	2.00
Plague	Event	R	1.50
Platemail	Reward	C	0.20
9			
Queen of the Wastelands	Cmpnion	U	0.60
Recognition of Worth	Event	U	0.60
Red Ettin	Quest	R	1.50
Revenant	Spell	U	0.60
Righteousness	Combat	C	0.20
Robber Knight	Knight	U	0.60
Sacred Vigil	Event	C	0.20
Saxon King	King	U	0.60
Saxon Raider	Quest	C	0.20
10			
Saxon Thane	Warrior	U	0.60
Serpent of Moray	Quest	U	0.60
Shield of Valor	Reward	U	0.60
Siege Perilous	Reward	R	2.00
Sir Bors de Ganis of Gaul	Knight	R	2.00
Sir Gawaine of Orkney	Knight	R	3.00
Sir Kay	Knight	R	2.00
Sir Lamorack of Gales	Knight	R	2.00
Sir Lavaine of Corbin	Knight	R	2.00
11			
Sir Lionel of Britain	Knight	R	2.00
Sir Mador de la Porte	Knight	R	2.00
Sir Mordred	Knight	R	3.00

Card name	Type	Rarity	Price
Sir Palamydes the Saracen	Knight	R	2.00
Sir Pellias	Knight	U	0.60
Sir Percevant	Knight	U	0.60
Sir Percival of Gales	Knight	R	2.00
Sir Sagramore le Desirous	Knight	U	0.60
Sir Tristram of Lyonesse	Knight	R	3.00
12			
Sir Ulfias	Knight	R	2.00
South Wales (Ver. 1)	Domain	C	0.20
South Wales (Ver. 2)	Domain	C	0.20
South Wales (Ver. 3)	Domain	C	0.20
Spear of Longinus	Reward	R	2.00
Spear of Ysbaddi	Reward	C	0.20
Spirit Guardian	Spell	R	1.50
Squire (A)	Warrior	C	0.20
Squire (B)	Warrior	U	0.60
13			
Submission	Event	R	1.50
Summer Solstice	Event	R	1.50
The Dolorous Blade	Reward	U	0.60
The Round Table	Reward	R	3.00
Unicorn	Quest	R	2.50
Vision of Death	Spell	C	0.20
Vision of the Grail	Event	U	0.60
Vow of Chastity	Vow	U	0.60
Vow of Obedience	Vow	U	0.60
14			
Vow of Poverty	Vow	U	0.60
Wastelands (Ver. 1)	Domain	U	0.60
Wastelands (Ver. 2)	Domain	U	0.60
Welsh Archer	Cmpnion	U	0.60
White Knight	Quest	U	0.60
Winter Solstice	Event	R	1.50
Wyrm of Corbin	Quest	U	0.60
Yelande the Silent Maiden	Cmpnion	U	0.60

RARITY KEY C = Common U = Uncommon R = Rare VR = Very Rare UR = Ultra Rare F = Foil card X = Fixed/standard in all decks

Quest for the Grail • Limited

Stone Ring • Released **December 1995**
280 cards in set • **IDENTIFIER: Broader borders**

- Starter decks contain 56 cards; starter displays contain 10 starters
- Booster packs contain 14 cards; booster displays contain 40 boosters

The **Limited Edition** set of **Quest for the Grail** more than doubled the number of cards in the game. Card borders changed from silver and gold to red. Also, the game company that produced it went through a name change.

Most game players couldn't get into the game, appreciating neither the classical style of the art nor the indirectly competitive style of the game. The random element of combat was also a turnoff for many used to the more certain strategies of absolute values. Expansions **Knights of the Isles** and **Saga of the Volsungs** never came out. — *James Mishler*

> You will need
> **32**
> nine-pocket pages to store this set.
> (16 doubled up)

Black Knight

PRO 6	Quest Knight	STR 5
END 7	*The fourth, who always rideth arm'd in black, a huge man-beast of boundless savagery.* -Gareth and Lynette, Tennyson	2

©1995 Stone Ring Games

Set (280 cards)		87.50
Starter Display Box		23.00
Booster Display Box		27.00
Starter Deck		5.00
Booster Pack		1.00

Promo cards

Card name	Type	Price
☐ Giant's Horde	Quest	2.50
☐ Phantom Host	Quest	2.50
☐ Wyrm of the Crags	Creature	4.00

Card name	Type	Rarity	Price
☐ Afanc	Quest	C	0.10
☐ Armor of Righteousness	Reward	U	1.00
☐ Assassin	Warrior	R	2.00
☐ Astalot	Domain	R	2.00
☐ Axe of Cleaving	Reward	C	0.05
☐ Beaumains' Blessing	Event	U	0.50
☐ Black Knight	Quest	C	0.05
☐ Blessed Scabbard	Reward	R	2.00
☐ Blessed Sword	Reward	R	2.00
☐ Blight	Spell	R	2.00
☐ Boreyne	Quest	C	0.10
☐ Brigand Knight	Quest	C	0.05
☐ Britain	Domain	C	0.05
☐ Britain	Domain	C	0.05
☐ Britain	Domain	C	0.05
☐ Britomart of Norgalis	Knight	R	3.00
☐ Brittany	Domain	C	0.05
☐ Brittany	Domain	C	0.05
☐ Brittany	Domain	C	0.05
☐ Cambria	Domain	C	0.05
☐ Cambria	Domain	C	0.05
☐ Cambria	Domain	C	0.05
☐ Camelot	Domain	R	4.00
☐ Cancellation	Event	C	0.05
☐ Chainmail	Reward	C	0.05
☐ Challenge of Sovreignty	Event	R	2.00
☐ Chevron Shield	Reward	C	0.05
☐ Chimera	Quest	U	1.50
☐ Cloak of Silence	Reward	U	0.50
☐ Combat Experience	Reward	U	0.50
☐ Combat Experience	Reward	U	0.50
☐ Combat Experience	Reward	U	0.50
☐ Concentration	Combat	C	0.05
☐ Cornwall	Domain	C	0.05
☐ Cornwall	Domain	C	0.05
☐ Cornwall	Domain	C	0.05
☐ Counterspell	Spell	U	0.50
☐ Curse of Epona	Event	R	2.00
☐ Dagger	Reward	C	0.05
☐ Dark Alliance	Spell	U	0.50
☐ Dastardly Blow	Combat	C	0.05

Card name	Type	Rarity	Price
☐ Defamation	Event	U	0.50
☐ Demoiselle Blanchefleur	Cmpnion	U	0.25
☐ Demoiselle Sans Nom	Cmpnion	C	0.10
☐ Desperate Lunge	Combat	C	0.05
☐ Dispossession	Event	U	0.25
☐ Dodge	Combat	C	0.05
☐ Dolorous Blade	Reward	R	3.00
☐ Dolorous Blow	Spell	R	2.00
☐ Drought	Event	U	0.50
☐ Enchanted Sleep	Spell	U	0.25
☐ Ensorceled Wood	Quest	R	2.00
☐ Enthrall	Spell	R	2.00
☐ Eternal Brand	Spell	C	0.10
☐ Excalibur	Reward	R	5.00
☐ Exile	Event	U	0.50
☐ Faerie Ring	Quest	U	1.00
☐ Fall of Lyonesse	Event	R	3.00
☐ Famine	Event	U	0.50
☐ Feint	Combat	C	0.05
☐ Floating Sword	Quest	C	0.05
☐ Flood	Event	R	2.00
☐ Forest Broceliande	Domain	U	0.50
☐ Fury	Combat	C	0.05
☐ Gaul	Domain	C	0.05
☐ Gaul	Domain	C	0.05
☐ Gaul	Domain	C	0.05
☐ Gealt	Warrior	C	0.05
☐ Giant of Arroy	Quest	C	0.10
☐ Giant of Canbenet	Quest	C	0.10
☐ Giant of the Wold	Quest	C	0.05
☐ Gift of Three Mothers	Spell	U	0.50
☐ Goblin	Quest	C	0.05
☐ Gomeret	Domain	U	0.50
☐ Gomeret	Domain	U	0.50
☐ Grail Maidens	Event	R	2.00
☐ Great Serpent of Gore	Quest	U	1.50
☐ Great Wyrm	Quest	U	1.50
☐ Green Knight	Quest	R	2.00
☐ Griffon	Quest	C	0.05
☐ Healing Draught	Spell	U	1.00
☐ Healing Prayer	Event	C	0.05
☐ Hermit of the Forest	Cmpnion	C	0.10
☐ Hippogriff	Quest	U	1.50
☐ Holy Grace	Spell	C	0.05
☐ Holy Relic	Reward	R	3.00
☐ Hounds of Gwyn	Event	U	0.25
☐ Imprisonment	Event	U	0.25
☐ Kernion	Quest	C	0.05
☐ King Aguysans of Cambria	King	U	0.50
☐ King Arthur of South Wales	King	R	5.00
☐ King Ban of Gomeret	King	R	2.00
☐ King Berrant	King	U	0.50

Card name	Type	Rarity	Price
☐ King Bors of Gaul	King	R	2.00
☐ King Brandegoris of Strangore	King	R	2.00
☐ King Howell of Brittany	King	R	2.00
☐ King Leodegrance of Britain	King	U	1.00
☐ King Mark of Cornwall	King	R	2.00
☐ King Meliadus of Lyonesse	King	R	2.00
☐ King Mordaunt of North Umber	King	R	2.00
☐ King Pellinore of Listinoise	King	U	1.00
☐ King Roaz the Reaver	King	R	2.00
☐ King Ryence of North Wales	King	R	2.00
☐ King Urien of Rheged	King	R	2.00
☐ King Uther Pendragon	King	R	5.00
☐ Knight Errant	Knight	C	0.05
☐ Knight of the Black Lands	Quest	R	3.00
☐ Knight of the Sparrow-Hawk	Quest	C	0.05
☐ Lady Belle Isoult	Cmpnion	R	2.00
☐ Lady Croisette	Cmpnion	U	0.50
☐ Lady Elose	Cmpnion	U	0.25
☐ Lady Elouise the Fair	Cmpnion	U	0.50
☐ Lady Enid	Cmpnion	U	0.50
☐ Lady Layonesse	Cmpnion	U	0.25
☐ Lady Lesolie of the Fountain	Cmpnion	U	0.50
☐ Lady Moeya of Brittany	Cmpnion	U	0.50
☐ Lady Nymue	Cmpnion	R	3.00
☐ Lady of the Lake	Cmpnion	R	3.00
☐ Lady Ragnell the Foul	Cmpnion	R	2.00
☐ Lady Vivian	Cmpnion	R	2.00
☐ Lady Ygraine	Cmpnion	U	0.25
☐ Lady Yvaine	Cmpnion	U	0.50
☐ Lady Yvette	Cmpnion	R	2.00
☐ Lance	Reward	C	0.05
☐ Lesser Wyrm of the Mount	Quest	C	0.05
☐ Listinoise	Domain	U	0.50
☐ Listinoise	Domain	U	0.50
☐ Love Philtre	Spell	C	0.10
☐ Lyonesse	Domain	U	1.00
☐ Lyonesse	Domain	U	1.00
☐ Madness	Spell	R	2.00
☐ Man at Arms	Warrior	C	0.05
☐ Master at Arms	Warrior	U	0.25
☐ Master Ralph the Merchant	Event	R	2.00
☐ Merlin	Cmpnion	R	5.00
☐ Minstrel	Cmpnion	U	0.50
☐ Mirror of Shalott	Quest	R	2.00

Card name	Type	Rarity	Price
☐ Mordant Wyrm	Quest	C	0.05
☐ Nightmare Fiend	Quest	C	0.10
☐ North Humber	Domain	C	0.05
☐ North Humber	Domain	C	0.05
☐ North Humber	Domain	C	0.05
☐ North Wales	Domain	C	0.05
☐ North Wales	Domain	C	0.05
☐ North Wales	Domain	C	0.05
☐ Ogre	Quest	C	0.10
☐ Page	Cmpnion	C	0.05
☐ Palfrey	Reward	C	0.05
☐ Parry	Combat	C	0.05
☐ Pas des Armes	Event	R	2.00
☐ Perilous Blade	Reward	R	2.00
☐ Perilous Garde	Quest	R	2.00
☐ Phantom Path	Spell	U	0.25
☐ Phoenix	Quest	C	0.05
☐ Plague	Event	R	2.00
☐ Platemail	Reward	C	0.05
☐ Power of the Grail	Event	R	3.00
☐ Prophecy	Spell	C	0.05
☐ Queen Elizabeth of Lyonesse	Cmpnion	R	3.00
☐ Queen Guinevere	Cmpnion	R	5.00
☐ Queen Helen of Gomeret	Cmpnion	U	0.25
☐ Queen Morgana le Fay	Cmpnion	R	5.00
☐ Queen of the Wastelands	Cmpnion	U	0.50
☐ Quest for the White Hart	Quest	R	2.00
☐ Questing Beast	Quest	C	0.05
☐ Recognition of Worth	Event	U	0.25
☐ Red Dragon	Quest	C	0.05
☐ Red Ettin	Quest	U	0.25
☐ Red Knight	Quest	C	0.05
☐ Revenant	Spell	U	0.50
☐ Rheged	Domain	C	0.05
☐ Rheged	Domain	C	0.05
☐ Righteousness	Combat	C	0.05
☐ River Horse of Avon	Reward	U	1.00
☐ Robber Knight	Knight	C	0.05
☐ Round Table	Reward	R	3.00
☐ Royal Lineage	Event	R	2.00
☐ Sacred Veil	Reward	U	0.50
☐ Sacred Vigil	Event	C	0.10
☐ Satyr	Quest	R	2.00
☐ Saxon King	King	U	0.50
☐ Saxon Thane	Warrior	C	0.05
☐ Sea Maid	Quest	U	1.00
☐ Sea Witch	Quest	C	0.05
☐ Sergeant at Arms	Warrior	U	0.50
☐ Serpent of Moray	Quest	C	0.05

RARITY KEY C = Common U = Uncommon R = Rare VR = Very Rare UR = Ultra Rare F = Foil card X = Fixed/standard in all decks

SCRYE Collectible Card Game Checklist and Price Guide • **361**

Card name	Type	Rarity	Price
☐ Shield of Valor	Reward	R	2.00
☐ Shieldbearer	Cmpnion	C	0.05
☐ Siege Perilous	Reward	R	2.00

22

Card name	Type	Rarity	Price
☐ Sir Accalon of Gaul	Knight	U	0.50
☐ Sir Balan	Knight	U	0.50
☐ Sir Balin le Sauvage	Knight	U	0.50
☐ Sir Bedivere the Cup Bearer	Knight	R	2.00
☐ Sir Blamore of Gaul	Knight	C	0.05
☐ Sir Blyant of Gales	Knight	C	0.05
☐ Sir Borre	Knight	R	2.00
☐ Sir Bors de Ganis of Gaul	Knight	R	2.00

23

Card name	Type	Rarity	Price
☐ Sir Colgrance of Gore	Knight	U	0.50
☐ Sir Cylhwych	Knight	U	0.50
☐ Sir Dagonet the Fool	Knight	R	2.00
☐ Sir Domas de Noir	Knight	U	0.50
☐ Sir Ector de Maris	Knight	U	0.50
☐ Sir Engamore	Knight	U	0.25
☐ Sir Ewaine de Blanchemains	Knight	U	0.50
☐ Sir Galahad	Knight	R	4.00
☐ Sir Gawaine of Orkney	Knight	R	3.00
☐ Sir Geraint	Knight	R	2.00

24

Card name	Type	Rarity	Price
☐ Sir Gotegrim of Britain	Knight	C	0.05
☐ Sir Griflet le Fise			

Card name	Type	Rarity	Price
de Dieu	Knight	U	0.50
☐ Sir Kay	Knight	R	3.00
☐ Sir Lamorak of Gales	Knight	R	2.00
☐ Sir Lancelot of the Lake	Knight	R	5.00
☐ Sir Lavaine of Corbin	Knight	U	0.50
☐ Sir Lionel of Britain	Knight	U	0.25
☐ Sir Lucian the Butler	Knight	U	0.50
☐ Sir Mador de la Porte	Knight	R	2.00

25

Card name	Type	Rarity	Price
☐ Sir Mordred	Knight	R	4.00
☐ Sir Nasciens	Knight	R	2.00
☐ Sir Palamydes the Saracen	Knight	U	0.50
☐ Sir Pellias	Knight	U	0.50
☐ Sir Percevant	Knight	R	2.00
☐ Sir Percival of Gales	Knight	R	2.00
☐ Sir Pinal	Knight	R	2.00
☐ Sir Sagramore le Desirous	Knight	R	2.00
☐ Sir Tristram of Lyonesse	Knight	R	3.00

26

Card name	Type	Rarity	Price
☐ Sir Turquine	Knight	R	2.00
☐ Sir Ulfias	Knight	U	0.25
☐ Sir Wigalois	Knight	R	2.00
☐ South Wales	Domain	C	0.05
☐ South Wales	Domain	C	0.05

Card name	Type	Rarity	Price
☐ South Wales	Domain	C	0.05
☐ Spear of Longinus	Reward	R	2.00
☐ Spectral Mount	Quest	U	0.50
☐ Spirit Guardian	Spell	U	0.25

27

Card name	Type	Rarity	Price
☐ Spirit Guide	Spell	C	0.10
☐ Squire	Warrior	C	0.05
☐ Storm Season	Event	U	0.50
☐ Strangore	Domain	C	0.05
☐ Strangore	Domain	C	0.05
☐ Subdue Beast	Spell	U	0.50
☐ Submission	Event	R	2.00
☐ Sword in the Stone	Quest	R	3.50
☐ Swordbearer	Cmpnion	C	0.05

28

Card name	Type	Rarity	Price
☐ The Blessed Spear	Reward	R	2.50
☐ Time of Darkness	Event	R	2.00
☐ Time of Glory	Event	R	2.00
☐ Toast of Honor	Quest	R	2.00
☐ Touch of Wayland	Spell	R	2.00
☐ Tourney	Event	U	0.50
☐ Unicorn	Quest	R	3.00
☐ Usurpation	Event	R	2.00
☐ Vision of Death	Spell	C	0.05

29

Card name	Type	Rarity	Price
☐ Vision of the Grail	Event	R	3.00
☐ Vital Blow	Combat	C	0.05
☐ Vow of Atonement	Vow	U	0.50
☐ Vow of Chastity	Vow	C	0.05

Card name	Type	Rarity	Price
☐ Vow of Obedience	Vow	C	0.05
☐ Vow of Poverty	Vow	C	0.05
☐ Vow of Silence	Vow	U	0.50
☐ Vow of Vengeance	Vow	U	0.50
☐ Vow of Vigelence	Vow	U	0.25

30

Card name	Type	Rarity	Price
☐ War Chariot	Reward	R	2.00
☐ War Pig of Gales	Cmpnion	R	2.00
☐ Warhawk	Cmpnion	C	0.05
☐ Warhorse	Reward	U	1.00
☐ Wastelands	Domain	U	0.50
☐ Wastelands	Domain	U	0.50
☐ Weakness	Combat	C	0.05
☐ Welsh Archer	Cmpnion	U	0.25
☐ Wild Boar of Listinoise	Quest	C	0.05

31

Card name	Type	Rarity	Price
☐ Winds of Boreas	Event	U	0.25
☐ Winged Horror	Quest	U	0.50
☐ Wings of Blaeduth	Reward	R	2.00
☐ Witch of the Woods	Cmpnion	U	0.25
☐ Wizard's Glamour	Spell	C	0.05
☐ Wolf	Quest	C	0.05
☐ Wraith	Quest	U	0.25
☐ Wyrm of Corbin	Quest	C	0.05
☐ Yelande the Silent Maiden	Cmpnion	U	1.00

32

Card name	Type	Rarity	Price
☐ Yeoman	Warrior	C	0.05

BONUS

153

Skillful Driving
When you are on the same track space as an opponent, add 1 track space for each match. This track space only.
Driver Bonus: Can be used for 2 track spaces.

RACE ACTION

Racing Challenge

Upper Deck • Released **August 2000**

227 cards and **90** metallic cards in set

- Starter decks contain 60 cards, car tokens, and playmat; starter displays contain 10 starters
- Booster packs contain 9 cards; booster displays contain 24 boosters

Sportscard manufacturer Upper Deck continued its 2000 re-entry into the CCG field with an easy-to-learn game based on the NASCAR auto racing license.

Players lay out a racetrack mat with 16 blanks to be filled with track cards. Players take turns playing Track cards out of their decks, starting at the beginning of the course and working their way around. Track cards have three icons on them: Tires, Engine, and Skill. These icons appear in one of five colors: red, yellow, blue, black, and green. Matching these icons is a major portion of the game.

Once the track is built, each player places a car token at the starting line and reveals his Driver card. Once a driver is selected, an Engine card, a Skill card, and two sets of Tires are selected. Gas tank markers are set to 22 gallons, three Race Action cards are drawn, and the race begins. With each turn, the car moves one space forward, and, by matching the Tire, Engine, and Skill icons on the track and car, you can move further ahead. Of course, players must take into account the amount of gas used and pit stops.

The core set has four starters and many "metal" chase cards, making it difficult to build a set — but tuning your deck here provides a *massive* advantage. The art is of professional quality, but you can occasionally see where more than one card was cut from the same action shot. The mechanics (no pun intended) of **Racing Challenge** are good, but you may feel more warmly about it as a board game than a CCG.

Racing cards are a hard enough sell to sports fans, and the track record of racing card games since *Mille Bornes* isn't much better. Upper Deck no longer has the license. — *Richard Weld*

Rating					
Concept	●	●	○	○	○
Gameplay	●	●	●	○	○
Card art	●	●	○	○	○
Player pool	●	●	○	○	○

Set (227 regular cards)	97.25
Starter Display Box	85.00
Booster Display Box	65.00
Starter Deck	8.00
Booster Pack	2.00

You will need 26 nine-pocket pages to store this set. (13 doubled up)

Reg Price	#	Card name	Type	Rarity	Metal
☐ 3.50	141	Accident: Gordon	Actn	R	8.00 ☐
☐ 0.20	178	Accident: Labonte	Actn	X	
☐ 0.20	119	Accident: Martin	Actn	X	
☐ 0.20	102	Bite: Earnhardt, Jr.	Actn	X	
☐ 0.60	94	Bite: Jarrett	Actn	U	3.00 ☐
☐ 0.20	177	Bite: Labonte	Actn	X	
☐ 0.10	168	Bite: Stewart	Actn	C	0.70 ☐

Reg Price	#	Card name	Type	Rarity	Metal
☐ 3.00	185	Black Flag: Labonte	Actn	R	7.50 ☐
☐ 0.20	148	Black Flag: Wallace	Actn	X	
[2]					
☐ 6.30	06R	Blown Motor: Earnhardt, Jr.	Actn	UR	
☐ 0.20	8	Bobby Labonte	Drvr	X	
☐ 5.50	16	Bobby Labonte	Drvr	R	10.00 ☐
☐ 3.00	96	Bump: Jarrett	Actn	R	7.50 ☐
☐ 0.05	120	Bump: Martin	Actn	C	0.70 ☐
☐ 0.60	170	Bump: Stewart	Actn	U	3.00 ☐
☐ 0.20	50	Checkered Flag: red/red/blue	Trck	X	
☐ 0.20	32	Checkered Flag: red/red/red	Trck	X	
☐ 0.20	188	Compression Ratio: Earnhardt	Actn	X	

Reg Price	#	Card name	Type	Rarity	Metal
[3]					
☐ 0.20	68	Compression Ratio: Earnhardt	Actn	X	
☐ 0.20	98	Compression Ratio: Earnhardt, Jr.	Actn	X	
☐ 0.20	128	Compression Ratio: Gordon	Actn	X	
☐ 0.20	83	Compression Ratio: Jarrett	Actn	X	
☐ 0.20	173	Compression Ratio: Labonte	Actn	X	
☐ 0.20	113	Compression Ratio: Martin	Actn	X	
☐ 0.20	158	Compression Ratio: Stewart	Actn	X	

RARITY KEY C = Common   U = Uncommon   R = Rare   VR = Very Rare   UR = Ultra Rare   F = Foil card   X = Fixed/standard in all decks

REG PRICE	#	Card name	Type	Rarity	METAL
0.20	143	Compression Ratio: Wallace	Actn	X	
0.20	88	Congestion: Jarrett	Actn	X	
0.20	164	Congestion: Stewart	Actn	X	
0.60	155	Congestion: Wallace	Actn	U	3.00
0.20	1	Dale Earnhardt	Drvr	X	
15.50	9	Dale Earnhardt	Drvr	R	20.00
0.20	3	Dale Earnhardt, Jr.	Drvr	X	
8.00	11	Dale Earnhardt, Jr.	Drvr	R	12.50
0.20	2	Dale Jarrett	Drvr	X	
8.00	10	Dale Jarrett	Drvr	R	12.50
0.20	133	Damaged Wheelwell: Gordon	Actn	X	
0.20	179	Damaged Wheelwell: Labonte	Actn	X	
3.50	156	Damaged Wheelwell: Wallace	Actn	R	8.00
0.20	69	Dialed In: Earnhardt	Actn	X	
0.20	99	Dialed In: Earnhardt, Jr.	Actn	X	
0.20	129	Dialed In: Gordon	Actn	X	
0.20	84	Dialed In: Jarrett	Actn	X	
0.20	174	Dialed In: Labonte	Actn	X	
0.20	114	Dialed In: Martin	Actn	X	
0.20	159	Dialed In: Stewart	Actn	X	
0.20	144	Dialed In: Wallace	Actn	X	
0.05	76	Dirty Air: Earnhardt	Actn	C	0.70
0.05	166	Dirty Air: Stewart	Actn	C	0.70
0.05	150	Dirty Air: Wallace	Actn	C	0.70
0.20	71	Downforce: Earnhardt	Actn	X	
0.20	101	Downforce: Earnhardt, Jr.	Actn	X	
0.20	131	Downforce: Gordon	Actn	X	
0.20	86	Downforce: Jarrett	Actn	X	
0.20	189	Downforce: Jarrett	Actn	X	
0.20	176	Downforce: Labonte	Actn	X	
0.20	116	Downforce: Martin	Actn	X	
0.20	161	Downforce: Stewart	Actn	X	
0.20	146	Downforce: Wallace	Actn	X	
0.60	78	Drafting: Earnhardt	Actn	U	3.00
0.10	138	Drafting: Gordon	Actn	C	0.70
0.20	87	Drafting: Jarrett	Actn	X	
0.60	169	Drafting: Stewart	Actn	U	3.00
40.00	05D	Earnhardt: Variant Photo	Drvr	UR	
27.50	06D	Earnhardt, Jr.: Variant Photo	Drvr	UR	
0.50	23	Engine: black	Engn	U	3.00
0.50	22	Engine: blue	Engn	U	3.00
0.50	26	Engine: green	Engn	U	3.00
0.50	24	Engine: red	Engn	U	3.00
0.50	25	Engine: yellow	Engn	U	3.00
2.50	97	Equalize: Jarrett	Actn	R	7.00
0.05	121	Equalize: Martin	Actn	C	0.70
2.50	171	Equalize: Stewart	Actn	R	7.00
0.60	79	Fast Crew: Earnhardt	Actn	U	3.00
0.60	139	Fast Crew: Gordon	Actn	U	3.00
0.60	183	Fast Crew: Labonte	Actn	U	3.00
0.20	117	Fast Crew: Martin	Actn	X	
6.30	01R	Fast Groove: Wallace	Actn	UR	
6.30	02R	Flat Out: Jarrett	Actn	UR	
4.00	112	Flat Spotted: Earnhardt, Jr.	Actn	R	8.50
0.20	134	Flat Spotted: Gordon	Actn	X	
6.30	09R	Flat Tire	Actn	UR	
6.30	12R	Fuel Efficiency	Actn	UR	
6.30	03R	Fuel Efficiency: Martin	Actn	UR	
40.00	08D	Gordon: Variant Photo	Drvr	UR	
6.30	11R	Green Flag	Actn	UR	
6.30	05R	Green Flag: Earnhardt	Actn	UR	
4.50	80	Groove: Earnhardt	Actn	R	9.00
0.20	132	Groove: Gordon	Actn	X	
0.60	124	Groove: Martin	Actn	U	3.00
0.60	109	In the Chute: Earnhardt, Jr.	Actn	U	3.00
0.60	93	In the Chute: Jarrett	Actn	U	3.00
0.20	147	In the Chute: Wallace	Actn	X	
27.50	02D	Jarrett: Variant Photo	Drvr	UR	
0.20	5	Jeff Gordon	Drvr	X	
15.50	13	Jeff Gordon	Drvr	R	20.00
27.50	04D	Labonte: Variant Photo	Drvr	UR	
4.50	81	Loose Engine Parts: Earnhardt	Actn	R	9.00
0.20	192	Loose Engine Parts: Gordon	Actn	X	
0.05	91	Loose Engine Parts: Jarrett	Actn	C	0.70
0.05	122	Loose Engine Parts: Martin	Actn	C	0.70
6.30	07R	Loose Stuff: Stewart	Actn	UR	
0.05	92	Lug Nuts Not Tightened: Jarrett	Actn	C	0.70
0.05	182	Lug Nuts Not Tightened: Labonte	Actn	C	0.70
2.50	127	Lug Nuts Not Tightened: Martin	Actn	R	7.00
2.50	172	Lug Nuts Not Tightened: Stewart	Actn	R	7.00
0.05	180	Marbles: Labonte	Actn	C	0.70
0.20	149	Marbles: Wallace	Actn	X	
0.20	4	Mark Martin	Drvr	X	
8.00	12	Mark Martin	Drvr	R	12.50
27.50	03D	Martin: Variant Photo	Drvr	UR	
0.20	103	No Daylight: Earnhardt, Jr.	Actn	X	
4.50	142	No Daylight: Gordon	Actn	R	9.00
2.50	187	No Daylight: Labonte	Actn	R	7.00
3.50	110	Oil Slick: Earnhardt, Jr.	Actn	R	8.00
0.05	89	Oil Slick: Jarrett	Actn	C	0.70
2.50	186	Oil Slick: Labonte	Actn	R	7.00
0.20	193	Oil Slick: Wallace	Actn	X	
4.50	82	Pit Fire: Earnhardt	Actn	R	9.00
0.05	135	Pit Fire: Gordon	Actn	C	0.70
0.20	196	Pit Fire: Wallace	Actn	X	
0.05	74	Push: Earnhardt	Actn	C	0.70
0.05	151	Push: Wallace	Actn	C	0.70
0.20	73	Red Flag: Earnhardt	Actn	X	
0.20	191	Red Flag: Martin	Actn	X	
0.20	163	Red Flag: Stewart	Actn	X	
0.05	104	Restrictor Plate: Earnhardt, Jr.	Actn	C	0.70
0.05	167	Restrictor Plate: Stewart	Actn	C	0.70
0.20	6	Rusty Wallace	Drvr	X	
8.00	14	Rusty Wallace	Drvr	R	12.50
3.50	111	Serious Bump: Earnhardt, Jr.	Actn	R	8.00
0.05	90	Serious Bump: Jarrett	Actn	C	0.70
0.05	181	Serious Bump: Labonte	Actn	C	0.70
0.50	28	Skill: black	Skll	U	3.00
0.50	27	Skill: blue	Skll	U	3.00
0.50	31	Skill: green	Skll	U	3.00
0.50	29	Skill: red	Skll	U	3.00
0.50	30	Skill: yellow	Skll	U	3.00
0.60	108	Skillful Driving: Earnhardt, Jr.	Actn	U	3.00
3.00	184	Skillful Driving: Labonte	Actn	R	7.50
0.20	162	Skillful Driving: Stewart	Actn	X	
0.10	153	Skillful Driving: Wallace	Actn	C	0.70
0.05	136	Slick: Gordon	Actn	C	0.70
3.00	125	Slick: Martin	Actn	R	7.50
0.20	194	Slick: Stewart	Actn	X	
0.05	165	Slick: Stewart	Actn	C	0.70
0.20	72	Slingshot: Earnhardt	Actn	X	
0.60	123	Slingshot: Martin	Actn	U	3.00
0.60	154	Slingshot: Wallace	Actn	U	3.00
0.05	75	Smashed Quarterpanel: Earnhardt	Actn	C	0.70
0.05	105	Smashed Quarterpanel: Earnhardt, Jr.	Actn	C	0.70
0.20	195	Smashed Quarterpanel: Labonte	Actn	X	
3.00	126	Smashed Quarterpanel: Martin	Actn	R	7.50
6.30	10R	Speeding in Pit Road	Actn	UR	
27.50	07D	Stewart: Variant Photo	Drvr	UR	
0.20	70	Stickers: Earnhardt	Actn	X	
0.20	100	Stickers: Earnhardt, Jr.	Actn	X	
0.20	190	Stickers: Earnhardt, Jr.	Actn	X	
0.20	130	Stickers: Gordon	Actn	X	
0.20	85	Stickers: Jarrett	Actn	X	
0.20	175	Stickers: Labonte	Actn	X	
0.20	115	Stickers: Martin	Actn	X	
0.20	160	Stickers: Stewart	Actn	X	
0.20	145	Stickers: Wallace	Actn	X	
0.05	77	Stop and Go: Earnhardt	Actn	C	0.70
0.05	137	Stop and Go: Gordon	Actn	C	0.70
0.20	197	Stop and Go: Stewart	Actn	X	
6.30	04R	Stroking: Labonte	Actn	UR	
6.30	08R	Tight: Gordon	Actn	UR	
0.50	18	Tire: black	Tire	U	3.00
6.50	05T	Tire: black, blue: Earnhardt	Tire	UR	
6.50	07T	Tire: black, green: Stewart	Tire	UR	
6.50	06T	Tire: black, yellow: Earnhardt, Jr.	Tire	UR	
0.50	17	Tire: blue	Tire	U	3.00
6.50	09T	Tire: blue, green	Tire	UR	
6.50	08T	Tire: blue, yellow: Gordon	Tire	UR	
0.50	21	Tire: green	Tire	U	3.00
0.50	19	Tire: red	Tire	U	3.00
6.50	01T	Tire: red, black: Wallace	Tire	UR	
6.50	02T	Tire: red, blue: Jarrett	Tire	UR	
6.50	04T	Tire: red, green: Labonte	Tire	UR	
6.50	03T	Tire: red, yellow: Martin	Tire	UR	
0.50	20	Tire: yellow	Tire	U	3.00
6.50	10T	Tire: yellow, green	Tire	UR	
0.20	7	Tony Stewart	Drvr	X	
8.00	15	Tony Stewart	Drvr	R	12.50
0.05	107	Too Many Men Over Wall: Earnhardt, Jr.	Actn	C	0.70
3.00	157	Too Many Men Over Wall: Wallace	Actn	R	7.50
0.20	51	Track: black/black/yellow	Trck	X	
0.20	58	Track: black/blue/green	Trck	X	
0.20	59	Track: black/green/blue	Trck	X	
0.20	34	Track: black/red/black	Trck	X	
0.20	40	Track: black/red/yellow	Trck	X	
0.20	41	Track: black/yellow/red	Trck	X	
0.20	52	Track: blue/black/black	Trck	X	
0.20	55	Track: blue/black/blue	Trck	X	
0.20	44	Track: blue/black/green	Trck	X	
0.20	37	Track: blue/blue/blue	Trck	X	
0.20	45	Track: blue/green/black	Trck	X	
0.20	61	Track: blue/red/yellow	Trck	X	
0.20	62	Track: blue/yellow/red	Trck	X	
0.20	48	Track: green/black/blue	Trck	X	
0.20	66	Track: green/blue/yellow	Trck	X	
0.20	42	Track: green/green/black	Trck	X	
0.20	65	Track: green/red/black	Trck	X	
0.20	60	Track: green/yellow/green	Trck	X	
0.20	49	Track: green/yellow/red	Trck	X	
0.20	35	Track: red/black/green	Trck	X	
0.20	53	Track: red/blue/black	Trck	X	
0.20	67	Track: red/blue/red	Trck	X	
0.20	43	Track: red/green/green	Trck	X	
0.20	54	Track: red/green/yellow	Trck	X	
0.20	36	Track: red/yellow/blue	Trck	X	
0.20	57	Track: red/yellow/yellow	Trck	X	
0.20	46	Track: yellow/black/red	Trck	X	
0.20	64	Track: yellow/blue/black	Trck	X	
0.20	38	Track: yellow/blue/blue	Trck	X	
0.20	47	Track: yellow/green/blue	Trck	X	
0.20	39	Track: yellow/green/yellow	Trck	X	
0.20	63	Track: yellow/red/green	Trck	X	
0.20	33	Track: yellow/red/red	Trck	X	
0.20	56	Track: yellow/yellow/blue	Trck	X	
0.05	106	Track Debris: Earnhardt, Jr.	Actn	C	0.70
0.05	152	Track Debris: Wallace	Actn	C	0.70
27.50	01D	Wallace: Variant Photo	Drvr	UR	
0.60	140	Yellow Flag: Gordon	Actn	U	3.00
3.00	95	Yellow Flag: Jarrett	Actn	R	7.50
0.20	118	Yellow Flag: Martin	Actn	X	

RARITY KEY C = Common U = Uncommon R = Rare VR = Very Rare UR = Ultra Rare F = Foil card X = Fixed/standard in all decks

Rage

White Wolf • First set, *Limited*, released **May 1995**

321 cards in set • **IDENTIFIER: Seal; four slashes at upper left**

Concept	●●●●○
Gameplay	●●●○○
Card art	●●●○○
Player pool	●○○○○

- Starter decks contain 60 cards; starter displays contain 10 starters
- Double-deck starters contain 120 cards; displays contain 6 starters
- Booster packs contain 12 cards; booster displays contain 24 boosters

Adapted from White Wolf's role-playing game *Werewolf: The Apocalypse*, **Rage** pits two or more packs of werewolves against each other in a fight for supremacy, in an I-go-you-go combat game.

To win, a player must eliminate opposing cards whose victory points equal or exceed a predetermined amount. Every werewolf (garou) has a Renown rating which yields a like amount of victory points. Each player starts with a pack of werewolves whose total Renown are equal to the victory threshold.

Each player has two decks, a Sept deck, which is made up of allies, equipment, and Gifts (spell-like abilities), and a combat deck, which is only used when resolving combats. Garou cards are double-sided and only turn into their fighting form (crinos, a kind of giant wolf man) after taking damage. No new werewolves come into play, and if you lose your last garou, you are eliminated from the game.

Rage gave White Wolf, which had earlier licensed *Vampire* CCG rights to Wizards of the Coast, the chance to do a CCG all its own. Unfortunately, it also meant taking on all the risks, too, and *Rage* suffered during the CCG slowdown of 1996-1997. In 1998, White Wolf outsourced production and distribution of the game — to Wizards of the Coast's Five Rings Division. — ***Michael Greenholdt***

LIMITED

Set (321 cards)	75.00
Starter Display Box	42.00
Booster Display Box	36.00
Starter Deck	7.50
Booster Pack	2.10

UNLIMITED

Set (321 cards)	68.00
Starter Display Box	37.00
Booster Display Box	32.00
Starter Deck	5.00
Booster Pack	2.00

You will need **36** nine-pocket pages to store this set. (18 doubled up)

Rage • Unlimited

White Wolf • Released **1996**

321 cards in set • **IDENTIFIER: No shiny seal; four slashes at upper left**

- Starter decks contain 60 cards; starter displays contain 10 starters
- Booster packs contain 12 cards; booster displays contain 24 boosters

LIMITED	Card name	Rarity	UNLIMITED
0.20	.38 Special	C	0.15
0.60	9mm Semi-Auto Pistol	U	0.80
1.50	Alaskan Wolf Hunt	R	1.50
14.00	Alexandru ThunderRage	UR	5.00
2.00	Alias	R	1.50
1.80	Allamande Ratkin	R	1.50
0.25	Allison Kachina	U	1.50
0.20	Amari Howls-from-Soul	C	0.15
0.25	Anna Eyes of the Sun	U	1.40
1.80	Anna Kliminski	R	1.60
0.25	Antonine Teardrop	U	1.40
0.20	Attacking the Wyrm	C	0.15
0.60	Aura of Confidence	U	0.80
1.80	Aurgra Gurahl	R	1.60
0.60	Awe	U	0.80
1.80	Balor's Gaze	R	1.50
0.20	Banana Split	C	0.15
0.25	Bane Arrow	U	0.80
0.20	Battle Song	C	0.45
0.25	Beastmind	U	0.80
0.20	Bite	C	0.15

Promos

Card name	Price	Card name	Price
Arkady	5.00	Plaintif Jassling	3.00
Battle Fervor	5.00	Pure Breede	3.00
Bryony McLeod	5.00	Rite: Victory Party	3.00
Eye of Luna	3.00	Shadow Walker	3.00
Get Medieval	8.50	Sower of Thunder	5.00
Glass Elemental	3.00	Venerable Cactus Spirit	3.00
Hunger of the Kindred	3.00	Wanchese's Bow	3.00
Keiser	3.00	Wolf Home	3.00

LIMITED	Card name	Rarity	UNLIMITED
0.25	Black Spiral Dancer	U	0.80
0.20	Bladetooth	C	0.15
0.20	Blissful Ignorance	C	0.15
0.20	Block	C	0.15
0.25	Block and Strike	U	0.80
1.80	Blood-on-the-Wind	R	1.50
0.20	Body Blow	C	0.15
1.50	Body Wrack	R	1.50
1.50	Bones of Shakir Hind	R	1.50
1.50	Bottlecap of Shakey Mac	R	1.80
0.20	Broken Limb	C	0.20
1.80	Bron Mac Fionn	R	1.80
0.25	Buggerhead	U	1.40
0.25	Bum Rush	U	0.80
0.20	Burrow	C	0.15
0.60	Caern Building	U	0.80
1.50	Calling a Champion	R	0.90
0.25	Camouflage	U	1.40
0.25	Careful Strike	U	1.40
0.90	Carla Grimsson	U	1.40
0.20	Carleson Ruah	C	0.15
0.60	Catfeet	U	0.80
0.25	Cernonous	U	1.40
0.90	Charging Bull	U	1.60
0.25	Chimera	U	0.80
1.50	Circular Attack	R	1.50
1.50	Close the Bawn	R	1.50
0.25	Cockroach	U	0.80
0.25	Command Spirit	U	0.80
1.50	Coup De Grace	R	1.80
0.20	Crescent Moon	C	0.15
0.20	Crick Rumwrangler	C	0.15
1.50	Critical Blow	R	0.90
0.25	Curse of Hatred	U	0.80
1.50	Deranged Mokole	R	1.50
0.20	Dharma Bum	C	0.15
0.20	Diem	C	0.15
0.25	Disarm	U	0.80

LIMITED	Card name	Rarity	UNLIMITED
1.50	Disembowelment	R	1.50
0.60	Distractions	U	0.80
0.20	Dodge	C	0.15
1.50	Drunken Revelry	R	1.50
0.25	Dry Gulch	U	0.80
0.20	Eater-of-Bears	C	0.15
0.20	Edgewalker	C	0.15
0.25	Elder Stone	U	1.40
1.80	Elder Vampire	R	1.80
2.00	Entrail Rend	R	1.50
0.25	Entrapment	U	0.80
1.50	Evade and Strike	R	0.90
0.20	Evan Heals-the-Past	C	0.15
1.80	Evasion	R	1.00
0.20	Exorcism	C	0.15
0.25	Eye of the Cobra	U	1.40
0.25	Eyes Gouged	U	0.80
0.20	Eyes-of-Frost	C	0.15
1.50	Faerie Kin	R	1.50
0.60	Falcon	U	0.80
2.00	Fang Dagger	R	1.00
0.20	Fang Jumper	C	0.15
1.80	Fang Necklace of Fenris	R	0.90
1.80	Fast Strike	R	1.50
1.50	Feather of the Phoenix	R	1.50
0.60	Feint	U	0.80
0.60	Fenris	U	0.80
1.50	Fenris' Bite	R	1.50
0.20	Flak Jacket	C	0.15
0.60	Flame Spirit	U	0.80
0.20	Flesh Wound	C	0.15
1.50	Flower of Aphrodite	R	1.50
0.20	Fomori (Rage 2)	C	0.15
0.20	Fomori (Rage 3)	C	0.15
2.50	Forceful Wind	R	0.90
0.25	Frenzy	U	1.40
0.20	Full Moon	C	0.15
0.60	Fur Gnarl	U	0.80

RARITY KEY C = Common U = Uncommon R = Rare VR = Very Rare UR = Ultra Rare F = Foil card X = Fixed/standard in all decks

Limited	Card name	Rarity	Unlimited
0.20	Furmling	C	0.15
0.20	Gaffling Pest	C	0.15
12			
2.00	Gaia's Vengeance	R	2.00
1.80	Gangrel Ally	R	1.80
1.50	Garbage Food Poisoning	R	0.90
0.20	Gathering for the Departed	C	0.15
0.90	Geas	U	1.40
0.25	Gere Hunts-the Hunters	U	1.40
0.20	Gesar	C	0.15
0.20	Gibbous Moon	C	0.15
0.20	Gift of the Porcupine	C	0.15
13			
0.20	Glancing Blow	C	0.15
1.50	Glib Tongue	R	1.50
1.80	Golgol Fangs-First	R	1.80
0.25	Goll Mac Mourna	U	1.40
2.00	Grand Klaive	R	1.80
0.25	Grandfather Thunder	U	0.80
0.20	Grazing Wound	C	0.15
1.80	Greater Banishment	R	1.80
0.25	Grek Twice-Tongue	U	1.40
14			
0.25	Greyfist	U	1.40
0.25	Griffin	U	0.80
1.50	Grimfang	R	1.80
0.25	Growls-at-Moon	U	1.40
1.80	Guides-to-Truth	R	1.50
20.00	Gunnar Draugrbane	UR	5.00
0.20	Half Moon	C	0.15
1.50	Harano Gloom	R	1.80
0.25	Head Wound	U	1.40
15			
0.25	Heart of Fury	U	0.80
0.20	Hogling	C	0.15
0.20	Howard Koar	C	0.15
0.25	Hunting Party	U	0.80
0.25	Icy Chill of Despair	U	0.80
2.00	Impergium	R	1.50
1.50	Inbred Disorder	R	0.90
1.50	Incarna Sigil	R	1.50
0.20	Insightful Eyes	C	0.15
16			
0.20	Ivan Korda	C	0.15
14.00	Jack Debiltongue	UR	10.00
0.20	Jackal's Curse	C	0.15
0.20	Jacky Gecko	C	0.20
0.25	Jam Technology	U	0.80
1.50	Journey Onward	R	0.90
1.50	Journey to the East	R	0.90
0.20	Jubati	C	0.15
1.50	Julisha of the Thousand Masks	R	1.80
17			
1.50	Justice Under Gaia	R	0.90
14.00	Kelly Still Waters	UR	10.00
1.50	Kinfolk - Enviomental Activist	R	1.50
1.80	Kinfolk - Small Town Cop	R	1.50
1.50	Kinfolk - Soldier of Fortune	R	1.80
1.50	Kinfolk - TV Reporter	R	1.50
1.80	Kinfolk - Veterinarian	R	1.00
20.00	Klaital Stargazer	UR	5.00
1.80	Klaive	R	1.50
18			
0.20	Kneecapper	C	0.15
1.50	Knife Wind	R	1.80
0.25	Lamurun	U	1.60
1.80	Leadership Challenge	R	0.90
1.50	Legendary Leadership	R	0.90
0.20	Lesser Banishment	C	0.15
14.00	Leukippes	UR	5.00
14.00	Lone Wolf Lupo	UR	5.00
1.40	Lord Albrecht	U	1.40
19			
1.50	Lost Calling	R	0.90
1.50	Lucky Blow	R	1.50
0.25	Luna's Armor	U	0.80
1.80	Luna's Links	R	1.50
2.00	Lunar Eclipse	R	1.80
1.80	Mamu	R	1.80
1.80	Mangle	R	1.50
0.25	Mari Cabrah	U	1.40
1.80	Massive Wound	R	0.90
20			
2.30	Master of the Pack	R	1.80

Limited	Card name	Rarity	Unlimited
1.60	Matriarch Mourning	R	1.80
0.25	Merciful Blow	U	0.80
0.60	Messenger's Fortitude	U	0.80
0.60	Might of Thor	U	0.80
0.20	Mindspeak	C	0.15
1.50	Mokole Hide	R	1.50
0.25	Moon Bridge Escape	U	0.80
1.50	Moon Sign	R	1.50
21			
0.20	Morgan the Unworthy	C	0.15
1.80	Morihei High-Mountain	R	1.80
1.50	Mother Larissa	R	1.80
0.20	Mother's Touch	C	0.15
0.20	Natasha Moon Chaser	C	0.15
0.25	Naturae Boon	U	0.80
0.25	Nephthys Mu'at	U	1.40
0.25	Nerve Cluster	U	0.80
0.20	New Moon	C	0.15
22			
0.25	No Escape	U	0.80
0.20	No'iri'n Ni' Dhonaill	C	0.15
0.25	Odor of Skunk	U	0.80
0.20	Off-Balance Attack	C	0.15
17.00	Oisin Mac Gaelach	UR	5.00
12.00	Old Red Eagle	UR	10.00
0.25	Old Storm-Chaser	U	1.60
14.00	Old Wolf of the Woods	UR	5.00
0.60	Organ Puncture	U	0.80
23			
0.20	Overextended Attack	C	0.15
0.25	Owl	U	0.80
0.25	Pack Defense	U	0.80
0.20	Passer	C	0.15
1.50	Peace of Nature	R	1.80
1.80	Pearl River	R	1.80
0.25	Pegasus	U	0.80
0.25	Pentex Forestry Team	U	0.80
1.50	Pentex Refinery	R	2.00
24			
0.20	Persuasion	C	0.15
1.80	Portable Computer	R	1.80
1.50	Praise the Malformed	R	0.90
2.00	Progenitor Mage	R	1.80
0.25	Pumpkin Man	U	0.80
0.20	Questor Treetalker	C	0.15
0.25	Quoting the Litany	U	1.40
1.50	Ragnarok	R	0.90
0.20	Rainpuddle	C	0.15
25			
0.60	Rat	U	0.80
0.25	Razor Claws	U	0.80
0.20	Reclaiming the Stolen	C	0.15
1.40	Remove Gaia's Blessing	U	1.40
0.60	Rend and Tear	U	0.80
0.20	Rite of Glory	C	0.15
1.50	Rite of Investiture	R	1.80
0.20	Rite of Passage	C	0.15
0.20	Rite of Wisdom	C	0.15
26			
0.25	Rite of Wounding	U	0.80
0.20	Ritual Challenge	C	0.15
0.25	Roar of Storms	U	1.40
1.50	Roger Daly	R	1.80
0.25	Roll Over	U	0.80
0.20	Roshen One-Arm	C	0.15
0.60	Run Like Hell	U	0.80
0.20	Running Creek	C	0.15
1.80	Samuel Haight	R	1.50
27			
1.50	Sands of Sleep	R	1.50
0.25	Satire Song	U	0.80
0.20	Saving Face	C	0.15
0.20	Scar Throat Leech-Killer	C	0.15
0.20	Scourging the Wyrm	C	0.15
1.50	Scouting Mission	R	0.90
0.25	Scratches-at-Fleas	U	1.40
0.60	Scream of Gaia	U	0.80
0.20	Serenity	C	0.15
28			
1.80	Shakar	R	0.90
0.20	Shapeshift	C	0.15
0.60	Shieldmate	U	0.80
20.00	Shogeka Hunter Moon	UR	5.00
1.80	Shotgun	R	2.00

Limited	Card name	Rarity	Unlimited
0.25	Shroud	U	0.80
14.00	Shu Horus	UR	5.00
29			
1.80	Silhouette	R	1.50
1.50	Silver Ammo	R	1.50
1.60	Silver Claws	R	1.00
0.20	Silver Record	C	0.15
0.20	Simon Gentle	C	0.15
0.20	Sings-for-the-Beast	C	0.15
1.40	Sister Judith Paws-of-Light	U	1.40
2.00	Skindancer	R	1.00
0.25	Sneak Attack	U	1.40
0.20	Sofya Softkiller	C	0.15
0.20	Solid Blow	C	0.15
30			
0.25	Son-of-Moonlight	U	1.40
0.25	Song Chiang	U	1.40
0.60	Song of Rage	U	0.80
1.50	Song of the Great Beast	R	1.80
2.00	Spear of Deceit	R	1.50
1.80	Spine Crushed	R	1.50
1.50	Spirit Drain	R	1.50
0.25	Spirit of the Fray	U	0.80
0.20	Spotlight	C	0.15
31			
0.25	Stag	U	0.80
0.20	Stands-Like-Mountain	C	1.10
0.20	Staredown	C	0.15
0.20	Sticky Paws	C	0.15
0.20	Stinging Wound	C	0.15
0.25	Stone of Scorn	U	0.80
1.50	Surprise Ally	R	1.50
1.80	Surprise Attack	R	0.90
1.80	Survivor	R	1.50
32			
0.20	Susan Anthony	C	0.20
0.20	Swipe	C	0.15
0.20	Syntax	C	0.15
0.60	Take the True Form	U	0.80
1.50	Taking the Death Blow	R	1.50
0.20	Tanzut	C	0.15
0.25	Taunt	U	0.80
0.25	Teeth-of-Titanium	U	1.40
0.25	Telling Blow	U	0.80
33			
1.50	The Piper	R	1.50
0.25	The Stolen Wolf	U	0.80
0.25	Thomas Kachina	C	0.20
0.25	Thunder Tiger	U	1.40
0.20	Tim Rowantree	C	0.15
0.25	Trackless Waste	U	0.80
0.20	Tribal Alliance	C	0.15
1.80	Tribal War	R	1.80
0.60	True Fear	U	0.80
34			
0.25	True Silverheels	U	1.40
0.60	Uktena	U	0.80
1.50	Uktena Wyrmfoe	R	2.00
1.50	Umbral Escape	R	1.50
0.20	Umbral Quest	C	0.15
0.25	Unicorn	U	0.80
0.20	Victory Party	C	0.15
0.20	Virus-to-Wyrm	C	0.15
0.25	Vital Blow	U	0.80
35			
0.20	Volcheka Ibarruri	C	0.15
1.50	Walks-with-Might	R	1.80
1.50	War Paint of Wahya Ohni	R	1.50
0.60	Wendigo	U	0.80
1.40	Whelp Body	U	1.40
0.20	Wind-Across-the-Hills	C	0.15
0.20	Winter Wolf	C	0.15
1.60	Wisdom of the Seer	R	1.80
0.20	Wolf Kinfolk	C	0.15
36			
0.20	Wolf Spirit	C	0.15
1.50	Wyrm Skin	R	1.50
1.50	Wyrm Slayer, Ronin Garou	R	1.80
1.50	Wyrm Taint	R	1.50
14.00	Yuri Tvarovitch	UR	5.00
0.25	Zachary Ellison	U	1.40

RARITY KEY C = Common U = Uncommon R = Rare VR = Very Rare UR = Ultra Rare F = Foil card X = Fixed/standard in all decks

Rage • The Umbra

White Wolf • Released **September 1995**

95 cards in set • **IDENTIFIER: Two curved lines at upper left**

Set (95 cards)		62.00
Booster Display Box		34.00
Booster Pack		2.00

• Booster packs contain 15 cards; booster displays contain 24 boosters

    Umbra introduces three new card types, Caerns, Quests, and Realms, as well as the Umbra, the spirit world, to which all werewolves can travel. The Umbra can be a place of refuge or danger, depending on the spirits encountered. — **Michael Greenholdt**

Card name	Rarity	Price
Allies Gateway	R	2.00
Amanda Withers-in-Sun	U	0.50
Banishment by the Council	R	2.00
Battleground	UR	10.00
Bjorn Blood-from-Stone	U	0.50
Born to Nature	C	0.15
Bunyip Spirit	C	0.25
Caern of Awakening	R	2.00
Caern of Bygone Visions	R	2.00
Caern of Ichiyo Modoribashi	R	2.00
Caern of the Bloodfist	R	2.00
Caern of the Crescent Moon	R	2.00
Caern of the Painted Sands	R	2.00
Caern of the Snow Leopard	R	2.00
Caern of the Tri-Spiral	R	2.00
Caern of the Waking Dream	R	2.00
Caern of the Weeping Daughter	R	2.00
Caern of the Western Eye	R	2.00
Cassandra Shadow-watcher	U	1.00
Childling	U	0.50
Close Gauntlet	C	0.25
Council for Universal Trade	R	2.00
Deep Journey	C	0.15
Dr. Stephen "Mindbender" Garrison	U	0.50

Card name	Rarity	Price
Drattosi	C	0.15
Dreamspeaker Mage	R	3.00
Engling	C	0.15
Faerie Armor	R	2.30
Fast Shift	R	2.00
Fireclaw	U	0.50
Flux	UR	10.00
Gateway of the Hyena	C	0.15
Gauntlet Flux (+1)	C	0.15
Gauntlet Flux (+2)	C	0.15
Gauntlet Flux (-1)	C	0.15
Gauntlet Flux (-2)	C	0.15
Glass Elemental	C	0.15
Guardian Spider	C	0.15
Heart of Midnight	R	2.80
Hyperion	U	0.80
Jackal's Quest	U	0.80
Jannok	C	0.15
Jennifer Moon-Wizened	U	0.50
Ka Spirit	U	0.80
Kinfolk: Shaman	C	0.25
Laughs-at-Death	R	2.30
Legendary	UR	10.00

Card name	Rarity	Price
Memory Ribbon	C	0.25
Moon Bridge Assault	U	0.50
Moon Bridge Attack	U	0.50
Morozhki	C	0.25
Nadia Wyrmfoe	U	0.50
Naomi	U	0.50
Nexus Crawler	R	2.30
Night Master	R	2.00
Nightmare Coin	U	0.50
Nocturna	U	0.50
Opening the Moon Bridges	C	0.25
Opening the Silver Window	R	2.00
Pack Reprimand	U	0.50
Pangaea	UR	10.00
Parting the Velvet Curtain	C	0.15
Pattern Spider	C	0.15
Petrov Tzarovitch	R	2.30
Phantasmi	C	0.15
Phoebe	U	0.80
Power of the Ways	C	0.15
Purity of Spirit	C	0.15
Quest of Spirit	C	0.15
Quest of Valor	U	0.50
Redirected Attack	U	0.50

Card name	Rarity	Price
Reject	U	0.50
Rite of Binding	U	0.50
Rite of Claiming	U	0.50
Rite of Realm Binding	R	2.00
Rite of Return	R	2.00
Runs-without-Pack	U	0.50
Sap Spirit	R	2.00
Scent of Distinction	C	0.15
Seeks-the-Truth	U	0.50
Sees-through-Stars	U	0.50
Serpentine	C	0.15
Shakey Mac	U	0.50
Step Sideways	U	0.50
Stormcrow	R	2.00
Stuck Sideways	R	2.00
Summer Country	UR	10.00
Umbral Flurry	C	0.15
Umbral Wave	U	0.80
Wahya-Ohni	U	0.50
Wheel of Ptah	R	2.00
World of Human	C	0.15
Wyldling	C	0.15
Wyldstone	C	0.25
Wyldstorm	R	2.50

Rage • The Wyrm

White Wolf • Released **December 1995**

186 cards in set • **IDENTIFIER: Swirl at upper left**

• Booster packs contain 15 cards; booster displays contain 24 boosters

    The Wyrm allows players to create decks using the "bad guys" of the werewolf universe. The major factions are the 7th Generation (occultist conspirators), Black Spiral Dancers (werewolves gone bad) and Pentex (the main werewolf enemy). A new card, the Victim, is also introduced. — **Michael Greenholdt**

Set (186 cards)		64.50
Booster Display Box		36.00
Booster Pack		2.00

Card name	Rarity	Price
A Bus Full of People	C	0.15
Air of Authority	U	1.10
Airt Gateway	C	0.15
Airt Mastery	U	0.60
Allies Below	U	0.60
Allonzo Montoya	R	2.50
Amelia	R	2.00
Angus, The White Howler	R	1.50
Ass Whuppin' Lynch Mob	C	0.15
Avenging Wraith	R	2.00
Balefire	U	0.50
Bane Moonbridge	U	0.60
Bane Sword	R	1.50
Battle Quest	U	1.30
Beast-of-War	U	0.90
Beat Cop	C	0.15

Card name	Rarity	Price
Beat Unmerciful	U	1.10
Bitch Slap	C	0.15
Blood Dagger	C	0.15
Blossum	C	0.15
Bob Goldstein, Ace Reporter	R	2.00
Breath of the Defiled	R	2.00
Bully's Quest	C	0.15
Business Merger	U	0.50
Caern of Rytthiku	R	3.00
Caern of the Blood God	R	3.00
Caern of the Unwashed Child	R	2.00
Cannibal Slug	C	0.15
Cellular Phone	U	1.30
Chainsaw	R	2.00
Chirox The Unfeeling	U	1.10
Churjuroc's Tusk	UR	13.50
Congressional Hearing	R	1.50
Consumption of Gaia	C	0.10
Corinna	C	0.15
Corporate Acquisition	U	0.50
Corporate Credit Card	R	2.00
Corporate Security	C	0.15
Corporate Take-over	R	1.50
Corrupting Presence	C	0.15
Count Vladimir Rustovich	UR	20.00
Cult Leader	R	2.00
Cultist	C	0.15

Card name	Rarity	Price
Curb Stomp	C	0.15
Defiler	U	0.90
Dis-Arm	R	2.00
Dr. Mordecai's Home Chemistry Set	R	1.00
Dr. Spencer	C	1.10
Ear Lober	C	0.15
Eater-of-Souls	U	0.90
Enticer	R	2.50
Environmental Action	U	1.10
Every Day is Halloween	U	0.50
Experimental Fomori	U	0.50
Family of Five	C	0.15
Family Pet	C	0.15
Fangthane Bloodjaw	C	0.15
FBI Agent	U	0.50
FBI Investigation	R	2.00
Fetal Position	U	0.50
Fomori Dock Worker	C	0.15
Fool's Quest	R	2.00
Fooled You!	U	1.40
Friends In High Places	U	0.90
G'lough, "Dance of Corruption"	R	2.00
Gang Beating	U	0.90
Garou Kinfolk	U	0.50
Gates of Malfeas	R	1.50

Card name	Rarity	Price
Glade Child	U	0.80
Gooshy Gooze	U	1.30
Greenpeace Assault Team	R	1.50
Grudge Match	U	0.60
Hamstringed	C	0.15
Happy Tourists	R	1.50
Heart Breaker	R	1.50
High School Athlete	C	0.15
Honest Senator	U	0.20
Horns of the Impaler	U	0.50
Hunts-at-Night	U	0.80
Incarna Avatar	R	2.00
Infectious Touch	U	0.50
Jack-O-Lantern	U	0.50
Jane Thurber	C	0.15
Johnathon Roark	C	0.15
Johnson P. Donovan	C	0.15
Kills-the-Weak	U	0.50
Kirijama, "The Hidden Foe"	R	2.00
Kiss of the Wyrm	R	2.00
Kitalid the Deceiver	C	0.15
Lander's Nylon Stocking	R	2.00
Latonia The Temptress	U	0.80
Lion's Pelt	U	0.60
Little Petey	C	0.15
Longtooth soulkiller	R	1.50
Lord of the Realm	R	2.00

RARITY KEY C = Common U = Uncommon R = Rare VR = Very Rare UR = Ultra Rare F = Foil card X = Fixed/standard in all decks

Card name	Rarity	Price
Lorenz Winkler	U	0.50
Lost Cub	U	0.50
Lotus	C	0.15
Mad Scientist	U	0.50
[12] Mage of the Celestial Chorus	R	2.00
Mage's Talisman	R	2.50
Mailman	C	0.15
Malfeas	UR	12.00
Man In Black	R	1.50
Martyr's Quest	R	2.00
Mass Pollution	C	0.15
Maxmillian	C	0.15
Meat Puppet	U	0.20
[13] Miles Kent	C	0.15
Mockmaw	UR	15.00
Mockmaw's Battle Axe	R	1.50
Morgan	R	1.50
Movie Star	R	2.00
Mr. Iguana	U	0.80
Neighborhood Watch Group	C	0.15
Newspaper Vendor	C	0.15
Oil of Corruption	U	0.80
[14] Old One-Eye	C	0.15

Card name	Rarity	Price
Pentex Executive & Limousine	R	1.50
Pipe Bomb	R	1.50
Playground Full of Kids	C	0.15
Priest	U	0.80
Psychotic Hallucinations	R	2.00
Psychotic Stalker	R	1.50
Punitive Damages	C	0.15
Ragnor The Terror	C	0.15
[15] Reckless Stunt	R	1.50
Reckless Swing	C	0.15
Red Alert	U	1.00
Red Hot Baby Powder	U	0.50
Red-Headed Stepchild	R	1.50
Reinvesting Profits	R	1.50
Renegade Werewolf Hunter	U	0.80
Rent Assunder	R	2.00
Rite of Summoning	C	0.45
[16] Rite of the Black Spiral	U	0.80
Rite of the Pentarch	R	1.00
Ritual of the Dark Spiral	R	1.50
Roar of the Wyrm	U	0.90
Ronin Garou	R	3.00
Savage Fury	C	0.15

Card name	Rarity	Price
Septum Crushed	C	0.15
Serpent's Quest	C	0.15
Shoragg	C	0.15
[17] Sidhe Knight	R	1.50
Skin of the Hellbound	U	1.80
Snickers	U	0.80
Spiritual Revelation	R	2.00
Splinter the Weakened Mind	U	1.30
Stench of Death	C	0.15
Street Bum	C	0.15
Subjugation of Gaia	U	1.00
Submachine Gun	R	1.50
[18] Suffering Bastard	U	0.50
Survival Nut	U	0.80
Survival of the Fittest	C	0.15
Swat Officer	U	0.50
Sybil	U	0.80
T.F. MacNeil	R	1.50
Taste of Pain	C	0.15
Tear Gas Cannister	U	0.50
Technician #7	C	0.15
[19] Telemarketing Campaign	U	1.30
The Bat	R	2.00

Card name	Rarity	Price
The General	R	2.00
There You Are!	C	0.15
Toga of Dionysius	U	1.00
Toga Party	C	0.15
Totem Form	R	2.00
Touch of the Eel	U	0.50
Trinity Hive Caern	UR	12.00
[20] Tsannik	R	1.80
Typhoon The Unpure	C	0.15
Uncle Freddy	C	0.15
Unlucky Lune	C	0.15
Urban Renewal	C	0.15
Vampire Blood	R	2.50
Vigilante	U	0.50
Voice of Reason	U	0.50
Voragg The Unbound	C	0.15
[21] Wailer	C	0.15
Wandering Gaffling	C	0.15
War Knife of Benning Simon	R	2.00
Whip of the Wicked	R	2.00
Wyrm Hide	C	0.15
Zhyzhak	UR	15.00

Rage • The War of the Amazon

White Wolf • Released **April 1996**

140 cards in set • **IDENTIFIER: Slashes and swirl at upper left**
• Booster packs contain 15 cards; booster displays contain 24 boosters

Centered on one of the last pristine areas on Earth, the Amazon Basin, this release introduces new, alternate victory conditions. Instead of gaining victory points for destroying opposing cards, victory can only be gained by winning Battlefield cards, either saving or destroying the rainforest, depending on your deck's allegiance. — *Michael Greenholdt*

You will need **16** nine-pocket pages to store this set. (8 doubled up)

Set (140 cards)		57.50
Booster Display Box		35.00
Booster Pack		2.00

Card name	Rarity	Price
[1] Alestro	U	0.80
Amazon Warriors	U	1.00
Ambush	U	1.80
Anaconda Gafflings	C	0.20
Atahualpa, Blood of the Incas	R	1.50
Athena	U	0.80
Avahuasca	C	0.20
Bane Infestation	C	0.15
Barnaby Shadrack	R	1.50
[2] Battle Fervor	R	1.50
Battle of Screaming Mud	R	1.00
Battle of Vista Cataract	U	0.60
Bellow	C	0.15
Bivouac	C	0.20
Black Claw	R	1.30
Board of Directors	U	1.00
Border Territory Skirmish	C	0.20
Brazilian Bureaucrat	U	0.90
[3] Breath of Fire	R	1.30
Candomble Witch Doctor	R	1.40
Cataclysm	R	2.00
Cityboy Kinfolk	C	0.15
Clever Diversion	U	1.00
Conquistador's Sword	UR	16.00
Den of Rorth, Son of Bast	U	0.60
Distracting Spirits	C	0.20
Dorado Realm	UR	21.00
[4] Dr. Pearvos Smythe, the Hunter	C	0.20
Dragon	U	0.80
Dragon's Breath	U	0.80
Ectoplasmic Extrusion	U	0.80
El Dorado	UR	18.50
El Guapo	R	1.50
Environmental Action Group	U	0.80

Card name	Rarity	Price
Ewaipanoma	C	0.15
Excitable Good Ol' Boy	U	0.80
[5] Experimental Cybernetics	U	0.80
Eyes of Hate	U	0.80
Fancy Footwork	R	1.40
Fangs-Through-Eye	C	0.20
Feather Mound Skirmish	U	0.60
Feline Grace	C	0.15
Fetish Sundering	U	1.00
Fool's Gold	U	1.30
Forestry Development	C	0.15
[6] Forestry Outpost Raid	C	0.20
Fortuna	R	2.00
Frenar	C	0.15
Gaia's Breath	U	0.80
Gaia's Will Corrupted	R	1.50
Ghost Raptor Attack	U	1.00
Ghost Raptor Membership	U	0.80
Granola Pete	C	0.15
Grrash tak'hyrrr	U	0.60
[7] Guidance From Below	U	0.90
Hapless Villagers	C	0.20
Heavy Machine Gun	U	0.80
Hell's Hand Hive	R	1.80
Hellhole Assault	U	0.60
Hidden Supplies	C	0.20
Hollow Heart Caern	U	0.80
Iron Will	U	1.00
Jaguar	U	0.80
[8] Joseph Herlech	UR	13.50
Juicy Johnes	C	0.20
Juki, Sun Halo	C	0.15
Kiss of Life	U	1.00
Leap of the Kangaroo	C	0.20
Legal Chicanery	R	1.30
Liberal Pop Singer	R	1.50
Lord of the Battlefield	C	0.20
Lord of the Jungle	U	0.90

Card name	Rarity	Price
[9] Lost in the Jungle	R	1.40
Lost Map	U	0.80
Machete	C	0.20
Maim	U	0.90
Mantle of El Dorado	R	3.00
Markhat	U	0.80
Misfit Fomori	C	0.20
Mists of Vengeance	U	0.80
Monsoon	C	0.20
[10] Nerve Agent	U	0.80
Night Terror	U	0.80
Nuclear Sauna	U	0.80
Operation Blight	U	1.00
Orville	R	1.30
Outcast Bastet	R	1.50
Panthesilea	C	0.15
Pentex Headquarters	R	1.00
Pentex Patrol	C	0.20
[11] Pentex Strip Miners	C	0.20
Pentex Supply Lines	U	0.80
Prentice Turner	U	0.80
Ranch Apocalypse	R	1.00
Reinforcements	U	0.80
Rends-the-Innocent	U	0.80
Rescue Mission	U	0.80
Retaking the Field	C	0.20
Ribs Crushed	U	0.90
[12] Ring of Fire	C	0.20
Ritual of the Dark Spiral	R	1.50
Riverbank Enfilade	U	0.60
Roars Like Thunder	U	0.80
Rocket Launcher	R	1.50
Routing Deforestation	C	0.20
Rytti, Horned Thunder	C	0.20
Sept of Gold	UR	18.50
Shriek	C	0.15
[13] Shroud of the Jungle	R	1.40
Sky River Caern	R	2.00

Card name	Rarity	Price
Spiral Boomerang	U	1.00
Spirit Backlash	R	1.50
Spirit of the Tiger	C	0.15
Spirit Tiger	U	0.90
Stand Like A Fool	R	1.30
Suicide Fomori Team	R	1.30
Superior Tactics	C	0.20
[14] Supply Station Raid	U	0.60
Surveillance Foray	U	0.60
Svajda	C	0.15
Swift Reconnaissance	R	1.80
Tamara Lovegrove	C	0.20
Temple Ruins Ambush	C	0.15
The Cleaner	U	0.90
Throat Bare	C	0.15
Tourist Litterbug Lout	C	0.20
[15] Tracer Rounds	C	0.20
Tremere Warlock	R	1.50
Tribal Warriors	C	0.15
Tribal Wisdom	U	0.80
Unbound Bane	C	0.20
Unseelie Troll	U	0.80
Urban Clash	U	1.00
Village Annexation	C	0.20
Visit from White Father	U	2.00
[16] Walking Between Worlds	U	0.80
War Council	U	0.80
War of Attrition	U	0.60
Warehouse Brawl	U	1.00
Wild Animals	U	0.80

RARITY KEY C = Common U = Uncommon R = Rare VR = Very Rare UR = Ultra Rare F = Foil card X = Fixed/standard in all decks

Rage • Legacy of the Tribes

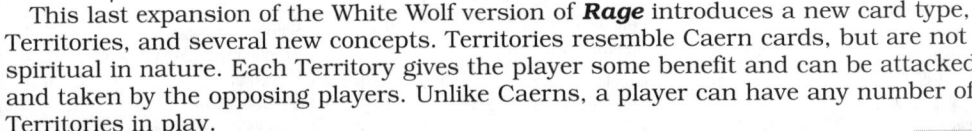

White Wolf • Released **October 1996**

215 cards in set • **IDENTIFIER: Three slashes over two**

• Booster packs contain 12 cards; booster displays contain 24 boosters

This last expansion of the White Wolf version of **Rage** introduces a new card type, Territories, and several new concepts. Territories resemble Caern cards, but are not spiritual in nature. Each Territory gives the player some benefit and can be attacked and taken by the opposing players. Unlike Caerns, a player can have any number of Territories in play.

In addition, some character cards have Rivalries with other characters. Rivals will not serve in the same pack. Some characters introduced in previous releases received new, updated cards. The updated characters could not serve in the same pack as their older incarnation, being the same person. — **Michael Greenholdt**

You will need **24** nine-pocket pages to store this set. (12 doubled up)

Set (215 cards)	62.00
Booster Display Box	35.00
Booster Pack	2.00

Card name	Rarity	Price
Abandoned Shed	C	0.15
Aegis	R	2.00
Aeneid Fomori	U	1.30
Akashic Brother	R	2.50
Allya Sun-Follower	U	1.50
Ancestral Burial Mounds	R	2.00
Anubis Stone	R	3.00
Attunement	U	1.50
Aurora Jaggling	U	1.50
Austere Temple	R	3.00
Balance of Gaia	U	1.30
Balkan Fief	R	1.30
Bawn	U	1.50
Bawn Guardian	C	0.15
Bear	U	1.30
Bestowing the Boon	C	0.15
Beta Status	C	0.15
Black Dog Game Factory	C	0.15
Blightscape	U	1.30
Brave New World	U	1.50
Brutal Kick	U	1.30
Bull	U	1.30
Bureaucratic Blueprints	C	0.15
Caias Katyrev	C	0.15
Call of the Wyrm	C	0.15
Camp Farris	R	2.00
Cesare Sodalis	C	0.15
Chantry	U	1.30
Chaser-After	U	1.30
Checking the Classifieds	U	1.50
Chronicle of the Black Labyrinth	U	1.50
Cleft in Twain	R	3.50
Concertina Wire	C	0.15
Connections	R	2.00
Conrad Walks-the-Line	U	1.30
Corcoran Mac Andrews	C	0.15
Corrupt Kinfolk	C	0.15
Crookpaw	U	1.30
Cynic's Quest	U	1.30
Cyran Far-Traveler	R	3.80
Danica Rimbaud	U	1.30
Dark Moon's Femur	R	3.00
Dead Zone	U	1.30
Death Rattle	U	1.50
Detective Jourgensen	R	2.00
Discredited Lineage	R	2.00
Doc Chaney's Power Goggles	C	0.15
Don Campisi	U	1.50
Dreams-of-Wonder	C	0.15
Dreamweaver Kitsune	U	1.50

Card name	Rarity	Price
Drunken Vandals	C	0.15
Evan Heals-The-Past	U	1.30
Fatal Flaw	C	0.15
Firebomb	U	2.00
Firebrand	U	1.30
Fist of the Comet	C	0.15
Flamethrower	U	3.00
Flying Tiger	U	2.00
Foreclosure	R	2.00
Fox Frenzy	C	0.15
Fractured Nephandus	U	1.50
Frankweiler Sword	R	3.50
Freide Counts-The-Scalps	C	0.15
Gaia's Favored Messenger	U	1.50
Gaia's Grace	C	0.15
Get Medieval	C	0.05
Ghost Lance	C	0.15
Giant Dogs Besiege City!	R	2.00
Gloom At Midnight	UR	5.00
Grand Restructuring	U	1.00
Grandfather Bannion	R	2.50
Griffin Avatar	U	1.50
Grimm Brings-Blood	U	1.30
Gungnir	R	3.00
Harmon Truefriend	R	3.00
Head or Gut?	U	1.30
Hereditary Castle	R	2.00
Hidden Lair	U	1.50
Higher Calling	C	0.15
Homestead	U	1.30
Howls Like Thunder	R	3.00
Iglanotti The Wise	U	1.50
Improvised Weapon	U	2.00
Invocation of Hakaken	C	0.15
Invoke Harano	U	1.50
Janus	C	0.15
Jason O'Kelly	U	1.50
John Hidden-Moon	R	3.00
Jorge Bolivar	UR	15.00
Joseph Roars-as-Bull	R	3.00
Kelly Brounard	C	0.15
Kids Love Arson	U	2.00
Kinfolk Den	C	0.15
King Albrecht	R	3.50
Kiss of Helios	R	2.50
Kithain Freehold	U	1.30
Lend a Hand	U	2.00
Longwalker's Glade	R	2.00
Manling Pendant	U	1.50
Mantis Form	U	1.50
Margrave Konietzko	R	4.00
Mari Cabrah	R	3.00
Markus Rage-Like-Fire	R	2.50
Medicine Bag	U	2.00
Melody Truthsinger	C	0.15

Card name	Rarity	Price
Mizrait	C	0.15
Modi Votishal	UR	17.50
Monster Joe's Truck-n-Tow	R	2.00
Moon Sister Cult	U	1.50
Nacho Snax	C	0.15
National Park	C	0.15
Nemesis	C	0.15
Nwinda Moonsilver	UR	17.50
Omens Foretold	C	0.15
Open Wounds	U	1.30
Orb of The Umbra	R	3.00
Pandora's Box	R	3.00
Passive Aggression	R	3.00
Patagia	U	1.50
Pentex First Team 43	U	2.00
Pervis and Pig-Fed	U	1.30
Phoebe's Veil	U	2.00
Phreak	C	0.15
Pietr Windstride	U	1.30
Pine Cone	R	1.00
Pine Dagger	U	2.00
Poignant Parable	C	0.15
Police Precinct	C	0.15
Pup Pid	U	1.00
Quest For Dominance	C	0.15
Questor	R	3.00
Rampage	C	0.15
Realm Key	C	0.15
Redemption	U	1.30
Renew the Cycle	U	1.50
Renown Admonishment	U	1.00
Resource Appropriation	C	0.15
Revilement	R	3.00
Rezoning Committee	C	0.15
Rheya Wrath-of-Heaven	UR	5.00
Rilkean Heart	U	1.30
Riposte	U	1.30
Rite of Chiminage	C	0.15
Rite of Renunciation	R	2.00
Rite of Scarification	U	1.50
Rite of Talisman Dedication	C	0.05
Rival's Quest	C	0.15
Roofwalker	R	3.00
Root Beer Charlie	C	0.15
Runs-to-the-Sunset	U	1.50
Sabbat Fiend	R	3.50
Samedi Wretch	U	1.50
Sariya Travels-The-Plains	U	1.30
Scarecrow	U	1.50
Scent of Sweet Honey	C	0.15
Scooterfangs	U	1.30
Scourge-of-Men	U	1.30
Security System	U	1.50
Sees-Past-Lies	C	0.15
Self-Serving Giovanni	U	1.50

Card name	Rarity	Price
Sept of the Five Winds	R	2.00
Serene Wilderness	R	2.00
Shattering the Binding Fetters	C	0.15
Shield of Gaia	U	1.30
Siberakh Relation	U	1.50
Skull Pig	C	0.15
Slash and Burn	C	0.15
Son of Tyre	U	1.30
Spirit Circle	R	3.00
Spirit Drum of Calm-Thunder	U	1.50
Sports Car	C	0.15
St. Vincent's Cathedral	U	1.30
Stalks Death	R	3.50
Stanislav Prochnow	C	0.15
Stonehenge	R	2.00
Strange Rain	U	1.30
Suburban High School Kid	C	0.15
Surly Redcap	U	1.50
Tabula Rasa	R	3.00
Tambertail's heart	R	4.00
Tech Speak	U	1.30
Th' M'Gregors	C	0.15
The Black Room	R	2.00
The Calyx	R	2.00
The Docks	U	1.30
The Litany's Guidance	R	3.00
The Naysayer's Hovel	U	1.30
The Pit	R	1.50
The Silver Crown	R	3.00
The Under-Barrows	C	0.15
The Vigil Forsaken	U	1.30
The Wolves are out there	U	1.50
Thunder's Gauntlet	R	4.00
Tibetan Monastery	R	2.00
Tracker-By-Moonlight	R	3.00
Twice Born	U	2.00
Twilight Operative	U	2.00
Ultimate Argument of Logic	U	1.50
Unwitting Ghoul	C	0.15
Vagabond Skindancer	U	1.50
Verbena Mage	R	2.00
Voracious Spectre	C	0.15
War Lodge	R	3.00
Wasp Talons	U	1.30
Water Spirit	U	1.30
Wearing the Bear Shirt	U	1.30
Weasel	U	1.30
Weaver's Quest	C	0.15
Web Drive Interface	R	3.00
Wildkin Kami	R	3.00
William Wallace's Bones	R	3.00
Windchaser	C	0.15
Yunwi Amai'yine'hi	U	1.30
Zlogar The Unrepentant	C	0.15
Zmei	R	4.50

RARITY KEY C = Common   U = Uncommon   R = Rare   VR = Very Rare   UR = Ultra Rare   F = Foil card   X = Fixed/standard in all decks

Rage • Across Las Vegas: Phase 1 (a.k.a. *Snake Eyes*)

Wizards of the Coast (Five Rings)/White Wolf • Released **August 1998**

104 cards in set • **IDENTIFIER: Card type appears in frame**

- Starter decks contain 60 cards; combo displays contain 6 starters and 24 boosters
- Booster packs contain 8 cards; booster displays contain 24 boosters

Not long after the seeming demise of **Rage**, Wizards of the Coast revived it as **Rage Across Las Vegas**. The game mechanics were *considerably* revised for this series of releases, so much so that earlier cards are not entirely compatible. The changes toned down the destructiveness of combat and increased the thought required of players. — *Michael Greenholdt*

You will need **12** nine-pocket pages to store this set. (6 doubled up)

CHILL OF EARLY FROST

Requires: Wendigo.

All Garou in Homid form (and human Allies) in your pack and in one other target pack take 2 wounds. Place characters killed from the target pack in your victory pile. If any of your characters are killed, remove them from play.

	Price
Set (104 cards)	60.00
Combo Display Box	45.00
Booster Display Box	39.00
Starter Deck	8.00
Booster Pack	2.00

Card name	Rarity	Price
A Blur of Motion	C1	1.50
A Little Bit of This	C1	1.50
All-Out Assault!	X	1.30
Bane Crow	F	12.00
Big Honkin' Club	X	1.30
Blur of the Milky Eye	C1	3.00
Bob and Weave	C1	1.50
Body Shift	X	1.00
Burrow	C1	1.50
Call Out the Cannibal	C1	1.90
Camouflage	C1	2.30
Cat Feet	C1	2.30
Cautious Defiance	C2	0.20
Chameleon Spirit	C2	0.20
Chill of Early Frost	C1	1.50
Counting Coup	X	1.30
Crush	X	1.30
Curse of Hatred	C1	3.00
Dishin' Up the Combo!	C1	1.90
Ditch Fight	C1	1.50
Drain Fury	C1	1.50
Dreams-of-Wonder	C1	3.00
Dust Spirit	C1	1.50

Card name	Rarity	Price
Eilif the White	C1	3.00
Evan's Move	C1	1.50
Fenris	C1	2.30
Fenris' Bite	C1	2.30
Feral Lobotomy	C2	0.20
Fetal Position	C1	1.50
Fight On!	C1	1.50
Follow Through	C1	1.50
Friede Counts-the-Scalps	X	1.50
Get of Fenris	X	1.00
Gillian Fangs-First	C1	3.80
Glib Tongue	C1	3.00
Gnosis Blade	C1	1.10
Great Old Oak Spirit	C1	1.50
Greet the Sun	C1	1.90
Halt the Coward's Flight	C1	2.30
Head Butt!	X	1.30
Healing Period	C2	0.20
Hide-of-Iron	C1	3.00
Hogling	X	1.00
Hunts-The-Wounded	C2	0.20
Kara Quick-to-Steal	X	1.50
Knee to the Head	C2	0.20
Lay Down the Law	C2	0.20
Leeds Quick-to-Anger	C1	3.80
Marko Mudspeaker	C1	3.00
Marta Laughs-at-Fear	C1	3.80
Might of Thor	C1	2.30
Naturae Boon	X	1.00

Card name	Rarity	Price
Painful Block	C2	0.20
Pounce	C1	1.50
Primal Combat	C1	1.50
Quick Slash	C1	1.50
Resist Pain	C1	2.30
Revere the Litany	C1	1.90
Rite of Pack Praise	C1	1.90
Rite of the Questing Stone	C1	1.90
Roll with the Blow	C2	0.20
Roundhouse	X	1.00
Rronuhn	F	12.00
Sanctuary Chimes	C2	0.20
Scent-of-Blood	C1	3.00
Sense Guilt	C2	0.20
Sidestep	C1	1.50
Silver Record	X	1.30
Sings-with-Eagles	X	2.00
Sky Running	C1	2.30
Slurs-the-Truth	C2	0.20
Snarl of the Predator	C1	2.30
Soft Brain	X	1.50
Song of Rage	C1	2.30
Speaks-of-Fire	C1	3.00
Speed of the Wild	C1	1.90
Spirit Ward	C1	2.30
Sprints-with-the-Wind	C1	3.40
Stalling for Time	C2	0.20
Stand Down	C1	1.50
Steel Arm to the Chest	X	1.30

Card name	Rarity	Price
Stillwater Packmother	C1	3.00
Strength of Will	C2	0.20
Strike and Fade	C1	1.50
Strip of Standing	C1	1.90
Swipe	X	1.30
Talks-to-Spirits	X	1.50
The Blessing of Freya	C2	0.20
The Falling Touch	C1	2.30
The Pelt of Peace	C1	3.00
Throwin' Garbage	C2	0.20
Thumb Lock	C2	0.20
Thunderwyrm	C2	0.20
Torvald the Unstoppable	X	1.50
True Fear	C1	2.30
Twist Knife	C2	0.20
War Paint	X	1.00
Weak Arm	C1	2.30
Well-Planned Counter	X	1.30
Wendigo	C1	2.30
Wendigo	X	1.00
Wendigo Scream	C1	2.30
Whelp Body	C1	2.30
Wisdom of the Ancient Ways	C2	0.20

Rage • Across Las Vegas: Phase 2

Wizards of the Coast (Five Rings)/White Wolf • Released **September 1998**

103 cards in set • **IDENTIFIER: Card type appears in frame**

- Starter decks contain 60 cards; combo displays contain 6 starters and 24 boosters
- Booster packs contain 8 cards; booster displays contain 24 boosters

You will need **12** nine-pocket pages to store this set. (6 doubled up)

GREKKO GOODHEART

Bone Gnawer • Ahroun • Metis • Male

RAGE 8
GNOSIS 3
HEALTH 9

Grekko cannot regenerate. Wounds can never be removed from him, even by card effects.

	Price
Set (103 cards)	58.00
Combo Display Box	30.00
Booster Display Box	27.00
Starter Deck	6.50
Booster Pack	1.80

Card name	Rarity	Price
Bartender at the Ragnarok	C1	1.00
Beg	C1	0.90
Binary Thinking	C2	0.20
Bleeding Geckal	C1	0.80
Block and Roll	C1	0.80
Bodyguard	C1	0.80
Bone Breaker	X	1.50

Card name	Rarity	Price
Bone Gnawers	X	1.00
Bone Gnawers Tattoo	C1	0.80
Bookta Banjabo	C1	0.80
Call of the Wyld	C1	0.80
Callous Polluter	C1	0.80
Chomp!	X	1.30
Crick Rumwrangler	C1	0.80
Curse of the Back Alleys	C1	0.80
Deep Understanding	C1	0.80
Dionysis' Reversion	C1	0.80
Disquiet	C1	0.80
Disruptor	C1	0.80
Duck Killer Blow	C2	0.20
Feline Pounce	C1	0.80
Fierce Rest	C1	0.80
Fireclaw	C1	0.80
Furmling	C2	0.20
Gaia's Vengeance	C1	0.80
Get of Fenris Tattoo	C1	0.80
Gift of the Termite	C1	0.80
Gluttony	C1	0.80
Gnaw at the Wound	X	1.30
Go for the Throat!	C1	0.80
Gordon Goffe	X	1.50

Card name	Rarity	Price
Grekko Goodheart	C1	0.80
Griffin	C1	0.80
Guide the Swarm	C2	0.20
Heal the Spirit	C2	0.20
Healing Dance	C1	0.80
Hopeless Flailing	C1	0.80
Howls-Like-Thunder	X	1.50
Hunts-by-Neon	X	1.50
Hunts-for-Blood	C1	0.80
Hyena Spirit	C2	0.20
Inquire of Gaia	C1	0.80
Julio Achilli	X	1.50
Kangaroo Leap	C1	0.80
Karen Shack-Burner	C1	0.80
Lunchtime!	C1	0.80
Lupine Fury!	C1	0.80
Mace	C1	0.80
Marta's Compass	C1	0.80
Mayor of Las Vegas	F	9.50
Moe Stimple	C1	0.80
Monica McGivern	C1	0.80
Odious Aroma	C1	0.80
Personal Trainers	C2	0.20
Pimp Slap	C1	0.80

Card name	Rarity	Price
Pipe Bomb	C1	0.80
Proving Ground	C1	0.80
Quicksand	C1	0.80
Ragnarok Employees	X	1.30
Rat	C1	0.80
Rat Spirit	C1	0.80
Rat's Dagger	X	1.30
Recycle	C1	0.80
Red Talon Tattoo	C1	0.80
Red Talons	X	1.00
Rend	C1	0.80
Rings of Thimmel	C1	0.80
Rite of Binding Sustenance	C1	0.80
Rite of Keres	C1	0.80
Rite of the Cotton Hollows	C1	0.80
Roach Spirit	C1	0.80
Robert Maurer	C1	0.80
Root Beer Charlie	C1	0.80
Runs-In-The-Lead	C1	0.80
Scornful Laugh	X	1.30
Scour the Dregs	C1	0.80
Scrying Set	C2	0.20
Sewer Lid Shield	C1	0.80
Sig Royfried	C1	0.80

RARITY KEY **C** = Common **U** = Uncommon **R** = Rare **F** = Foil **#** = Lower numbers are rarer **X** = Fixed/standard in all decks

SCRYE Collectible Card Game Checklist and Price Guide • 369

Card name	Rarity	Price	Card name	Rarity	Price	Card name	Rarity	Price	Card name	Rarity	Price
☐ Sight from Beyond	C1	0.80	☐ Strength of Purpose	C2	0.20	☐ Tribal War	C2	0.20	☐ We Hunt in the Shadows	C1	1.10
☐ Silver Claws	C1	0.80	☐ Survivor	C1	0.80	☐ Trips-the-Cautious	C1	1.40	☐ Wendigo Tattoo	C1	1.10
☐ Speed	C2	0.20	☐ Talkin' Trash!	C2	0.20	☐ Trixie Hill	F	9.50	☐ Whack Upside t'Head	X	1.30
☐ Stance of the Viper	C1	0.80	☐ The Drinking Song	C1	0.80	☐ Trusts-in-Fury	X	1.50	☐ Wicked Counter	C1	1.00
☐ Steel-Toed Boots	C1	0.80	☐ Thieving Talons of the Magpie	C2	0.20	☐ Vengeful Strike	C1	1.00	☐ Wolf Spirit	C1	1.00
☐ Straight Punch	C1	0.80	☐ Tony "Ham" Borgia	C1	0.80	☐ Walks-in-Shadows	C1	1.60	☐ Yuletide Rite	C1	1.00

RUMORS OF TROUBLE

Long Event

Requires: Silent Strider or Philodox.

Prey get the starting initiative in combats this turn.

"Thank you all for coming to hear me out. I bring you grave news, brought me by the heart of Fellwar the Cursed and the eyes of a Bastet..." –Natasha Moon Chaser

Rage • *Across Las Vegas: Phase 3*

Wizards of the Coast (Five Rings)/White Wolf • Released **October 1998**

94 cards in set • **IDENTIFIER: Card type appears in frame**

- Starter decks contain 60 cards; combo displays contain 6 starters and 24 boosters
- Booster packs contain 8 cards; booster displays contain 24 boosters

You will need
11
nine-pocket pages to store this set.
(6 doubled up)

	Price		Card name	Rarity	Price	Card name	Rarity	Price	Card name	Rarity	Price
Set (94 cards)	**58.00**		☐ Conflict of Interest	C1	1.10	☐ Kidney Punch	C2	0.20	☐ Slick Tongue	C2	0.20
Combo Display Box	**30.00**		☐ Corinna	C1	1.00	☐ Killian Quicktalker	X	1.30	☐ Smooth Talkin'	X	0.80
Booster Display Box	**27.00**		☐ D'siah	C1	1.10	☐ Let Us Speak of Peace	C1	0.90	☐ Song of Intuition	C2	0.20
Starter Deck	**6.50**		☐ Dark Tidings	C2	0.20	☐ Lost in the Woods	C1	0.90	☐ Spirit Whistle	C2	0.20
Booster Pack	**1.80**		☐ Defiler	C1	1.30	☐ Mask of Imitation	C1	1.10	☐ "Stings, Don't It?"	C2	0.20
Card name	Rarity	Price	☐ Devin Silent Walker	C1	1.50	☐ Massive Mold Spirit	C1	0.90	☐ Stipple the Unclean	C1	1.60
☐ 9mm Semi-Automatic	C1	1.10	☐ Disarming Knowledge	C2	0.20	☐ Minke	F	9.00	☐ Stomp	C1	1.00
☐ An Eye for an Eye	C2	0.20	☐ Don't Even Try	C2	0.20	☐ Moon Sign	C1	1.10	☐ Stop Yanking My Chain!	X	0.80
☐ Beast Mind	C1	1.00	☐ Dorik Kirdor	C1	1.60	☐ Mother Blackfang	C1	1.60	☐ Storm Crow Spirit	C2	0.20
☐ Boris	C1	1.50	☐ Dugal Steady-Hand	C1	1.40	☐ Nadia Wyrmfoe	C1	1.50	☐ Streetwise	C2	0.20
☐ Brackt	C1	1.50	☐ EAC Committee Chair	C1	1.10	☐ Nasty Neck Kick	C1	0.90	☐ Strip of Confidence	C1	0.90
☐ Call for Power	C2	0.20	☐ Elemental Gift	C1	1.10	☐ Natasha Moon Chaser	X	1.30	☐ Superior Position	X	0.90
☐ Clap of Thunder	C1	0.90	☐ Even the Field	C2	0.20	☐ Observe Trends	C1	0.90	☐ Talk of Peace	C1	1.10
☐ Clarissa Smoothtongue	C1	1.40	☐ Eyepoke	C2	0.20	☐ Owl	C1	1.00	☐ Talk to Sleep	C1	1.00
☐ Clean Slate	C1	0.90	☐ Fellwar the Cursed	C1	1.40	☐ Painful Insult	X	1.10	☐ Tara Spiritrunner	X	1.30
☐ Close to the Surface	F	9.00	☐ Fishbone Walker	C1	1.40	☐ Paints-Your-Nightmares	X	1.30	☐ The Hand that Feeds Me	C1	0.90
			☐ Flip	C2	0.20	☐ Paralyzing Stare	C1	1.00	☐ Thick Pelt	C1	1.10
			☐ Fool's Luck	C1	1.10	☐ Reading the Soul	C2	0.20	☐ Tongues	C2	0.20
			☐ Grandfather Thunder	C1	0.90	☐ Rite of Contrition	C2	0.20	☐ Touch of Death	C1	1.10
			☐ Greet the Moon	C1	0.90	☐ Rite of Ostracism	C2	0.20	☐ Trade Favors	C1	0.90
			☐ Gut That Wyrm!	C1	1.00	☐ Rob the Power of the Wyrm	C1	1.00	☐ Travelling Spirit	C2	0.20
			☐ Gutbuster	C1	1.00	☐ Rumors of Trouble	C2	0.20	☐ Tribal Peace	C1	1.00
			☐ Hide from View	X	0.80	☐ Shadow Lords	X	0.80	☐ Trick Talk	X	0.90
			☐ Hunting Party	C1	0.90	☐ Shadow Lords Tattoo	C1	1.10	☐ Truth-Seeker	X	1.30
			☐ In Your Face!	X	0.80	☐ Shadows by the Firelight	C1	1.10	☐ Wakshaani	C2	0.20
			☐ Inclusion	C1	1.10	☐ Shall We Dance?	C2	0.20	☐ Well Prepared	C1	0.90
			☐ Inspiration	C1	1.30	☐ Silent Strider Tattoo	C1	1.10	☐ Wyrm Hunt	C1	1.00
			☐ K'to the Oracle	C1	1.40	☐ Silent Striders	X	0.80	☐ Zin-Shaar	X	1.30

PUXATAWNY PAT

Human • Gambler • Male • Unique

RAGE 5
GNOSIS 2
HEALTH 4

At the start of the Main Phase, all players must "call" or "fold." All players who call reveal their hands. The player revealing the highest total of Gnosis costs and Renown puts the top card of his Sept deck into his Victory Pile, where it is worth 1 Renown.

Rage • *Across Las Vegas: Phase 4*

Wizards of the Coast (Five Rings)/White Wolf • Released **November 1998**

95 cards in set • **IDENTIFIER: Card type appears in frame**

- Starter decks contain 60 cards; combo displays contain 6 starters and 24 boosters
- Booster packs contain 8 cards; booster displays contain 24 boosters

Due to a collation error, **Halo of the Sun** and **Regal Bearing** only appear in the starter decks.

You will need
11
nine-pocket pages to store this set.
(6 doubled up)

	Price		Card name	Rarity	Price	Card name	Rarity	Price	Card name	Rarity	Price
Set (95 cards)	**58.00**		☐ Bone Gnawers	C1	0.50	☐ Gather Goods	C1	0.50	☐ Philodox	X	0.80
Combo Display Box	**30.00**		☐ Bonehead Maneuver	C1	0.50	☐ Get of Fenris	C1	0.50	☐ Protect the Wild	C1	0.50
Booster Display Box	**27.00**		☐ Bridge Walker	C1	0.50	☐ Get Rite of Passage	C1	0.50	☐ Puxatawny Pat	F	9.00
Starter Deck	**6.50**		☐ Caterwaul	C1	0.50	☐ Goading Your Enemy	C1	0.50	☐ Rally to the Cause	C2	0.10
Booster Pack	**1.80**		☐ Channel Spirit	C2	0.10	☐ Grand Convocation	C1	0.50	☐ Red Talons	C1	0.50
Card name	Rarity	Price	☐ Chant of the Run	C1	0.50	☐ Halo of the Sun	C1	0.50	☐ Regal Bearing	X	0.80
☐ Balance Man and Beast	X	0.80	☐ Chastity Bidwell	C2	0.10	☐ Helen Ogelthorp	C1	0.50	☐ Regroup	C1	0.50
☐ Balance of Power	C2	0.10	☐ Confusion of Principles	C1	0.50	☐ Hero's Stand	C1	0.50	☐ Reverence for the Judge	C1	0.50
☐ Bane Host Mother	C1	0.50	☐ Control the Agenda	C1	0.50	☐ Hunt Blessing	C1	0.50	☐ Rite for the Dead	C2	0.10
☐ Bane of Doom	C1	0.50	☐ Cornered Rat	C1	0.50	☐ Imitation	C1	0.50	☐ Rite of Accord	C1	0.50
☐ Berton	X	0.80	☐ Corrupted Blight Child	C1	0.50	☐ Inge Torsdatter	X	0.80	☐ Rite of Reconciliation	C2	0.10
☐ Bison Spirit	C1	0.50	☐ Death Kiss	C2	0.10	☐ Kari Fishmarm	X	0.80	☐ Rite of Renunication	C1	0.50
☐ Black Beak	C1	0.50	☐ Defiance of Gaia	C1	0.50	☐ Kicks-at-the-Mirror	C1	0.50	☐ Rite of Summoning	C1	0.50
			☐ Distractions	X	0.80	☐ Little Hans	C1	0.50	☐ Rite of the Fetish	C2	0.10
			☐ Equal Honor	C1	0.50	☐ Lolita	C1	0.50	☐ Rite of the Time Tunnel	C1	0.50
			☐ Eye Gouge	C2	0.10	☐ Lummox	X	0.80	☐ Scalp Hunt	C1	0.50
			☐ Fast Face Kick	C1	0.50	☐ Moonshine Windfall	C1	0.50	☐ Sense the Unnatural	C1	0.50
			☐ Feminine Wiles	C2	0.10	☐ Mutt	X	0.80	☐ Shadow Lords	C1	0.50
			☐ Fineous Dougan	C1	0.50	☐ Old Oak	C1	0.50	☐ Sheriff Thompson	C1	0.50
			☐ Five Bears	C2	0.10	☐ Pathetic Sniveling	C2	0.10	☐ Silent Striders	C1	0.50
			☐ Gaia's Guidance	C1	0.50	☐ Persistant Howls	C2	0.10	☐ Sings-of-Gaia	X	0.80
			☐ Galliard	X	0.80	☐ Peter Finnegan	C1	0.50	☐ Sister Agnes	C1	0.50

RARITY KEY **C** = Common   **U** = Uncommon   **R** = Rare   **UR** = Ultra Rare   **#** = Lower numbers are rarer   **X** = Fixed/standard in all decks

Card name	Rarity	Price		Card name	Rarity	Price		Card name	Rarity	Price		Card name	Rarity	Price
☐ Smoke Dancer	C1	0.50		☐ Staredown	C1	0.50		☐ Tornado River	C1	0.50		[11] ☐ Voice of Passion	C1	0.50
☐ Speed Kills	C1	0.50		☐ Steals-the-Wind	C1	0.50		☐ Totem Gift	C1	0.50		☐ Wanted Dead or Alive	C1	0.50
☐ Spirit of the Vulture	C1	0.50		[10] ☐ Stressful Events	C2	0.10		☐ Umbral Cleansing	C2	0.10		☐ War Song	C1	0.50
☐ Spirit Smack	C2	0.10		☐ Tally Rand	C1	0.50		☐ Umbral Slash	C1	0.50		☐ Wendigo	C1	0.50
☐ Spirits' Aide	C2	0.10		☐ Three Amigos	C1	0.50		☐ Umbral Song	C2	0.10		☐ Y'Broke Mah Leg!	C1	0.50
☐ Spite and Malice	C2	0.10						☐ Vision Doll	F	9.00				

Rage • Across Las Vegas: Phase 5

Wizards of the Coast (Five Rings)/White Wolf • Released **December 1998**

88 cards in set • **IDENTIFIER: Card type appears in frame**

- Starter decks contain 60 cards; combo displays contain 6 starters and 24 boosters
- Booster packs contain 8 cards; booster displays contain 24 boosters

You will need **10** nine-pocket pages to store this set. (5 doubled up)

Set (88 cards)	**58.00**
Combo Display Box	**30.00**
Booster Display Box	**27.00**
Starter Deck	**6.50**
Booster Pack	**1.80**

[1] Card name	Rarity	Price
☐ A Tear for the Prey	C2	0.10
☐ Amazon's Labrys	C1	0.50
☐ Annie Quickhand	C2	0.10
☐ Bad Mojo	C1	0.50
☐ Bag of Tricks	C1	0.50
☐ Betty Crumbine	X	0.80
☐ Bill Clanton	X	0.80
☐ Bitch Slap	C1	0.50
☐ Black Furies	X	0.80
[2] ☐ Blazing Eyes	C2	0.10
☐ Block and Stirke	C2	0.10
☐ Blue Moon	F	9.00
☐ Bonehead	C1	0.50
☐ Bourbon Betty	C1	0.50
☐ Calm Foe's Rage	C1	0.50
☐ Carried on the Wind	C1	0.50
☐ Challenge the Leader	C1	0.50
☐ Cheap Shot	C2	0.10
[3] ☐ Children of Gaia	X	0.80
☐ Clarissa Fillmore	C1	0.50

Card name	Rarity	Price
☐ Dangerous Dame	C2	0.10
☐ Doing Gaia's Work	C2	0.10
☐ Dove Spirit	C1	0.50
☐ Fetish Doll	C1	0.50
☐ Finds-the-Way	C1	0.50
☐ Flames of Hestia	C2	0.10
☐ Force of Wills	C2	0.10
[4] ☐ Fox Spirit	C2	0.10
☐ Gaia's Ghost Shirt	C1	0.50
☐ Gaia's Strength	C1	0.50
☐ Grandmother's Touch	C2	0.10
☐ Greta von Karpen	C1	0.50
☐ Hail the Sun	C1	0.50
☐ Healing Sleep	C1	0.50
☐ Heart of Fury	C2	0.10
☐ Hope Bidwell	C1	0.50
[5] ☐ I'll Kill You!	C1	0.50
☐ Influence of Fear	C1	0.50
☐ Janus the Beast	X	0.80
☐ Kaspiri	C1	0.50
☐ Kathy Williams	C2	0.10
☐ Knocker	C2	0.10
☐ Lash of the Furies	X	0.80
☐ Matthem Poison-to-Peace	C1	0.50
☐ Merciful Offerings	C1	0.50
[6] ☐ Midnight Raid	C1	0.50

Card name	Rarity	Price
☐ Mind Eater	C1	0.50
☐ Mold the Spirit	C2	0.10
☐ Moon Daughter's Gift	C1	0.50
☐ Mrs. Florence	C1	0.50
☐ One Mean Hombre	C2	0.10
☐ Open Moon Bridges	C1	0.50
☐ Peaceful Solutions	X	0.80
☐ Pegasus	C1	0.50
[7] ☐ Play Against the Fury	C1	0.50
☐ Proud Defense	C1	0.50
☐ Rite of Gaian Blood	C1	0.50
☐ Rite of Pure Breeding	C2	0.10
☐ Rite of Resolution	C2	0.10
☐ Rite of Teaching	C2	0.10
☐ Rite of the Parted Veil	C1	0.50
☐ Scout	C1	0.50
☐ Set 'Em Up...	C2	0.10
[8] ☐ Shared Blood	C1	0.50
☐ Sharp Ears	X	0.80
☐ Simon Peacemaker	X	0.80
☐ Sister McGuire	C2	0.10
☐ Sleeping Brook	C1	0.50
☐ Song of the Seasons	C2	0.10
☐ Spellbinding Oration	C1	0.50
☐ Spider's Song	C1	0.50
☐ Spirit Friend	C1	0.50
[9] ☐ Spirit of Hate	C1	0.50

KNOCKER

Spirit • Fae

RAGE 7
GNOSIS 5
HEALTH 4

Requires: Children of Gaia or cohorts.
Knocker regenerates all wounds after any combat in the Umbra.
You must discard Knocker and the top three cards of your Sept deck if the Umbra level reaches 4 or 5.

Card name	Rarity	Price
☐ Strength from Pain	C1	0.50
☐ Strike of Lightning	C1	0.50
☐ Surprise Lunge	C2	0.10
☐ The Moot is Moot	C2	0.10
☐ The Trodden Track	C2	0.10
☐ Thick Hide Jack	X	0.80
☐ Total Disregard	C1	0.50
[10] ☐ Touch of the Muse	C1	0.50
☐ Trust of Gaia	C1	0.50
☐ Umbra-La	C1	0.50
☐ Umbral Heave	C1	0.50
☐ Unicorn	C1	0.50
☐ Walks-Between-Worlds	X	0.80
☐ Wyrm Cutting	C1	0.50
☐ Wyrm Wind	F	9.00

Rage • Across Las Vegas: Phase 6

Wizards of the Coast (Five Rings)/White Wolf • Released **January 1999**

88 cards in set • **IDENTIFIER: Card type appears in frame**

- Starter decks contain 60 cards; combo displays contain 6 starters and 24 boosters
- Booster packs contain 8 cards; booster displays contain 24 boosters

You will need **10** nine-pocket pages to store this set. (5 doubled up)

Set (88 cards)	**58.00**
Combo Display Box	**30.00**
Booster Display Box	**27.00**
Starter Deck	**6.50**
Booster Pack	**1.80**

[1] Card name	Rarity	Price
☐ Arthur Getty	C1	0.60
☐ Bane Flies	F	10.25
☐ Bane Spider	C2	0.15
☐ Boomer	C1	0.60
☐ Boot Hill	C1	0.60
☐ Boots of Justice	C1	0.60
☐ Bottle Nose Bob's Gang	C1	0.60
☐ Call for Health	C2	0.15
☐ Call of the Wyrm	C1	0.60
[2] ☐ Collar the Mongrel	C1	0.60
☐ Commanding Voice	X	0.80
☐ Construction Site	C2	0.15
☐ Death Valley	C2	0.15
☐ Delilah Morden	C1	0.60
☐ Delilah Morden	C1	0.60
☐ Deputy Dan Coleman	C2	0.15
☐ Eagle Headdress	C1	0.60
☐ Engineer	C2	0.15

[3] Card name	Rarity	Price
☐ Facing the Final Journey	C1	0.60
☐ Failing Spirit	C1	0.60
☐ Feast Upon Snake's Wisdom	C1	0.60
☐ Fire -in-Desert	C1	0.60
☐ Flame Spirit	C1	0.60
☐ Four Corners	C2	0.15
☐ Grand Canyon	C1	0.60
☐ Gray Coat	C1	0.60
☐ Griff Murphy	C1	0.60
[4] ☐ Guinevere	X	0.80
☐ Hangin' Posse	C1	0.60
☐ Hawk Spirit	C1	0.60
☐ High Squeal	F	10.25
☐ Honorary Pack Member	C2	0.15
☐ Hoofpaw	C1	0.60
☐ Igauna Moonrunner	X	0.80
☐ Instant Replay	C2	0.15
☐ Iron Mark	C1	0.60
☐ Iron Riders	X	0.80
☐ It's Too Late	C1	0.60
☐ Jackal's Whisper	C1	0.60
☐ ...Knock 'Em Down	C1	0.60
☐ Lead by Example	C2	0.15
☐ Long Finger	C2	0.15

Card name	Rarity	Price
☐ Madness	C1	0.60
☐ Minor Banishment	C1	0.60
☐ Monkey King	C1	0.60
[6] ☐ Monument Park	C1	0.60
☐ Morning Dew	X	0.80
☐ Morning Hawk	C1	0.60
☐ Mortimer Jones	X	0.80
☐ Naomi	X	0.80
☐ Navajo Burial Grounds	C2	0.15
☐ Pandora's Box	C1	0.60
☐ Payin' for a Ride	C2	0.15
☐ Poltergeist	C2	0.15
[7] ☐ Purifier of Souls	C1	0.60
☐ Push Sideways	C2	0.15
☐ Rage from Spirit's Pain	X	0.80
☐ Rattler's Bite	C1	0.60
☐ Release Spirit	C2	0.15
☐ Rite of Passage	C1	0.60
☐ Run for Ground	C2	0.15
☐ S & P Railroad	C1	0.60
☐ Seam Between Worlds	C2	0.15
[8] ☐ Shroud	C1	0.60
☐ Sneaky Pete	C2	0.15
☐ Spirit Block	C2	0.15

CONSTRUCTION SITE

Tech

RAGE 5
GNOSIS 1
HEALTH 3

Neutral: The Umbra moves up 1 point during the Start of Turn Phase.
Controller: If you reclaim the Construction Site, move the Umbra down 1 level.

Card name	Rarity	Price
☐ Spirit Knowledge	C1	0.60
☐ Spirit Lash	C1	0.60
☐ Spirit of the Bird	C1	0.60
☐ Spirit of the Fray	C1	0.60
☐ Spirit Punch	C2	0.15
☐ Spirit Wall	C1	0.60
[9] ☐ Spirit Wrack	C1	0.60
☐ Spirit's Wisdom	C1	0.60
☐ Stoking Fury's Furnace	C1	0.60
☐ Strength of Steam	C1	0.60
☐ Taking the Brunt	C1	0.60
☐ The Meeting	C1	0.60
☐ Too Fast for You?	C2	0.15
☐ Tribal Cooperation	C1	0.60

Card name	Rarity	Price		Card name	Rarity	Price		Card name	Rarity	Price		Card name	Rarity	Price
☐ Uktena	C1	0.60		☐ Umbral Escape	C2	0.15		☐ Umbral Stop	C2	0.15		☐ Walks-with-Wisdom	C1	0.60
☐ Uktena	X	0.80		☐ Umbral Paradise	C1	0.60		☐ Umbral Victory Dance	C1	0.60		☐ You Failed Gaia	C1	0.60

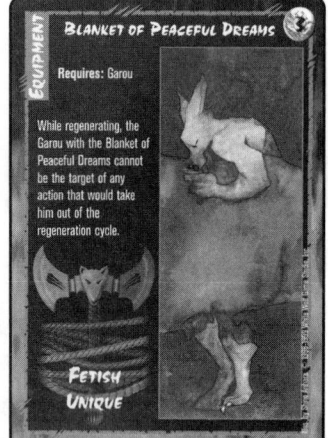

EQUIPMENT

BLANKET OF PEACEFUL DREAMS

Requires: Garou

While regenerating, the Garou with the Blanket of Peaceful Dreams cannot be the target of any action that would take him out of the regeneration cycle.

FETISH
UNIQUE

Rage • *Across Las Vegas: Equinox*
Wizards of the Coast (Five Rings)/White Wolf • Released **March 1999**
230s cards in set • **IDENTIFIER: Card type appears in frame**

- Starter decks contain 60 cards; combo displays contain 6 starters and 24 boosters
- Booster packs contain 8 cards; booster displays contain 24 boosters

You will need **26** nine-pocket pages to store this set. (13 doubled up)

Set (230 cards)	**73.50**
Combo Display Box	**30.00**
Booster Display Box	**27.00**
Starter Deck	**6.50**
Booster Pack	**1.80**

Card name	Rarity	Price
☐ Acid Bane	R	2.00
☐ Adapt	U	0.75
☐ Ahroun	X	1.00
☐ Alexandra Rasputin	R	2.00
☐ Arm Block	C	0.15
☐ Ashen Taylor	F	6.75
☐ Awe	C	0.15
☐ Backhand	C	0.15
☐ Backpedal	U	0.75
☐ Balance	U	0.75
☐ Balefire Elemental	C	0.15
☐ Balor's Gaze	U	0.75
☐ Banana Split	R	2.00
☐ Bandit Blackmane	X	1.00
☐ Bane of Pain	U	0.75
☐ Banshee	C	0.15
☐ Bear Hug	C	0.15
☐ Big 'Ol 2 x 4	C	0.15
☐ Big Tony Casaldi	U	0.75
☐ Black Furies Tattoo	C	0.15
☐ Black Spiral Soldier	C	0.15
☐ Blanket of Peaceful Dreams	U	0.75
☐ Blissful Ignorance	R	2.00
☐ Blood Lust	C	0.15
☐ Blood of Kings	U	0.75
☐ Box the Ears	C	0.15
☐ Brian the Iceman	U	0.75
☐ Call Before the Storm	U	0.75
☐ Call to Glory	U	0.75
☐ Cheap Kitchen Knife	C	0.15
☐ Children of Gaia Tattoo	C	0.15
☐ Chimera	C	0.15
☐ Choose Your Side	U	0.75
☐ Cindermane	R	2.00
☐ Cindy Paradise	R	2.00
☐ Clarence Darius	X	1.00
☐ Claws-of-Clay	R	2.00
☐ Cleaning up the 'Rok	C	0.15
☐ Closing the Moon Bridges	C	0.15
☐ Cobra Spirit	U	0.75
☐ Command	X	1.00
☐ Corcoran Smithy	R	2.00
☐ Crazy Gregor	R	2.00
☐ Cries-of-death	R	2.00

Card name	Rarity	Price
☐ Cub's Roar	C	0.15
☐ Culling thenclean	U	0.75
☐ Cunning Koan	C	0.15
☐ Daniel Coleman	F	6.75
☐ Danny O'Doul	R	2.00
☐ Dark Times Ahead	U	0.75
☐ Darmoth Moorswalker	R	2.00
☐ Death Dust	U	0.75
☐ Deceptive Strike	U	0.75
☐ Defensive Posture	U	0.75
☐ Deflect the Blow	C	0.15
☐ Directing the Soul	C	0.15
☐ Disco Suit	U	0.75
☐ Douglas MacDougal	R	2.00
☐ Dr. Lydia Tsien	R	2.00
☐ Dreams of the Past	C	0.15
☐ Duck	U	0.75
☐ Eat This!	C	0.15
☐ Elvis Impersonator	C	0.15
☐ Eye of the Falcon	U	0.75
☐ Eyes-of-Crystal	R	2.00
☐ Faerie Fyre	C	0.15
☐ Faerie Kin	U	0.75
☐ Falcon	C	0.15
☐ Falcon Arrows	U	0.75
☐ Fang of the Far-Sighted	R	2.00
☐ Feng Shui	U	0.75
☐ Fiana Tattoo	C	0.15
☐ Fianna	X	1.00
☐ Fight with the Wind	C	0.15
☐ Fighting Dirty	C	0.15
☐ Finger Snap	C	0.15
☐ Fire Fist	R	2.00
☐ Focus Your Rage	U	0.75
☐ Forceful Wind	C	0.15
☐ Formal Challenge	C	0.15
☐ Gaia's Best	C	0.15
☐ Going Underground	C	0.15
☐ Gremlins	C	0.15
☐ Gut Like a Fish	U	0.75
☐ Haymaker	C	0.15
☐ Honor for the Tribe	C	0.15
☐ Hunts-without-Lobes	R	2.00
☐ Impromptu Concolation	X	1.00
☐ Inner Light	U	0.75
☐ Inner Strength	U	0.75
☐ Instinctive Backlash	U	0.75
☐ Iron Willpower	U	0.75
☐ Ivor Brice	R	2.00
☐ Jackie Keaton	R	2.00
☐ Joseph Sandstone	R	2.00
☐ Justin Spirit-Friend	R	2.00
☐ Kathy Williams	F	6.75
☐ Kayla the Singer	R	2.00
☐ Kidneys of Steel	C	0.15
☐ Kimmie the Blackjack Dealer	R	2.00
☐ King of the Clurichaun	U	0.75
☐ Klaive of Yuri Tvarivitch	R	2.00
☐ Knockback	C	0.15
☐ Knot of Protection	U	0.75
☐ Knowledge of the Wind	C	0.15

Card name	Rarity	Price
☐ Lady Canvas	R	2.00
☐ Laugh at Pain	U	0.75
☐ Laura FaeQueen	R	2.00
☐ Laying the Guilt	R	2.00
☐ Leader of the Pack	R	2.00
☐ Learn from Experience	U	0.75
☐ Learning the Trade	C	0.15
☐ Luigi "Wise Guy" Tuscano	U	0.75
☐ Luna's Avenger	U	0.75
☐ Luna's Bullets	U	0.75
☐ Metis to Society	U	0.75
☐ Mick Buffet	U	0.75
☐ Mind Block	U	0.75
☐ Mist Man	C	0.15
☐ Mob Enforcer	C	0.15
☐ Molotov Cocktail	C	0.15
☐ Mychal	U	0.75
☐ Neon Elemental	C	0.15
☐ Nicah Sunset	R	2.00
☐ Nicolas Lonewalker	R	2.00
☐ Nicole Vanhausen	R	2.00
☐ Nuthin' Special	C	0.15
☐ Ol' Lady Woodford	R	2.00
☐ Om	C	0.15
☐ Om Chakala Phat	U	0.75
☐ One-Armed Bandit	R	2.00
☐ Onset of Harano	R	2.00
☐ Passive Aggression	U	0.75
☐ Pattern of Theft	U	0.75
☐ Paws of the Newborn Cub	U	0.75
☐ Phantasm	R	2.00
☐ Pipes of Terror	U	0.75
☐ Police Crackdown	U	0.75
☐ Preternatural Awareness	X	1.00
☐ Protectors of the Weak	C	0.15
☐ Puma Angryheart	R	2.00
☐ Questioning	U	0.75
☐ Quick Jaw	R	2.00
☐ Ragabash	X	1.00
☐ Raindancer	R	2.00
☐ Rake the Eyes	C	0.15
☐ Randy on the Run	R	2.00
☐ Reason	C	0.15
☐ Rebecca Johnson	X	1.00
☐ Regis Wallace	X	1.00
☐ Respect for the Downtrodden	U	0.75
☐ Rite of Leadership	C	0.15
☐ Rite of the Opened Sky	C	0.15
☐ Rite of the Stolen Wolf	R	2.00
☐ Rommel's Scepter	U	0.75
☐ Ruins of the Hotel Lazon	R	2.00
☐ Samhain	U	0.75
☐ Sarah Parker	R	2.00
☐ Secret of Gaia	U	0.75
☐ Sees-by-Stars	R	2.00
☐ Sees-Your-Heart	X	1.00
☐ Sergei the Executioner	F	6.75
☐ Sheryl	F	6.75
☐ Shootin' Craps	R	2.00
☐ Silence the Doubter	U	0.75
☐ Silent Stan	R	2.00
☐ Silver Fang Tattoo	C	0.15

Card name	Rarity	Price
☐ Silver Fangs	X	1.00
☐ Sings-for-the-Beast	R	2.00
☐ Skull Pig	C	0.15
☐ Sleep of the Hero	U	0.75
☐ Speed-of-the-Wind	R	2.00
☐ Spinning Block	U	0.75
☐ Spirit of Chance	R	2.00
☐ Spirit of the Lake	U	0.75
☐ Spirit of Thunder	C	0.15
☐ Spirit Vessel	R	2.00
☐ St. Mary's Orphanage	R	2.00
☐ Stag	C	0.15
☐ Standing Together	C	0.15
☐ Stargazer Tattoo	C	0.15
☐ Stargazers	X	1.00
☐ Steel Jaw	U	0.75
☐ Steven Altmeyer	U	0.75
☐ Stumpy McGee	R	2.00
☐ Surface Attunement	U	0.75
☐ Sword of William Wallace	R	2.00
☐ Take the Pain	U	0.75
☐ Talons of the Falcon	U	0.75
☐ Tamara Leeches-for-Pawns	R	2.00
☐ Tara Malesbane	R	2.00
☐ Taste for Blood	C	0.15
☐ Taylor Spirit-Friend	R	2.00
☐ The Dean Micheals	R	2.00
☐ The Lightning Spear	U	0.75
☐ The Ragnarok Casino	R	2.00
☐ Theurge	X	1.00
☐ Thomas Reichal	R	2.00
☐ Tina Clear-Skull	R	2.00
☐ Tire Iron	U	0.75
☐ Toad Spirit	C	0.15
☐ Toe Stomp	C	0.15
☐ Torc of Wisdom	U	0.75
☐ Trackers-by-Moonlight	X	1.00
☐ Two Tails	R	2.00
☐ Uktena Tattoo	C	0.15
☐ Ulf Hammarskald	R	2.00
☐ Umbral Manipulation	C	0.15
☐ Unbalance	R	2.00
☐ Uncluttered Mind	U	0.75
☐ Uncontrollable Fury	R	2.00
☐ Unicorn's Milk	C	0.15
☐ Vegas Showgirls	C	0.15
☐ Velocitor	R	2.00
☐ Verbena Druid	U	0.75
☐ Victim of the Wyrm	R	2.00
☐ Victoria Anne	X	1.00
☐ Vinny Vincent	R	2.00
☐ Virus-to-Wyrm	R	2.00
☐ Wallace's Battle Standard	U	0.75
☐ War Whiskey	C	0.15
☐ Whispering Wind	R	2.00
☐ Wilhelm Nighthunter	X	1.00
☐ Wisdom of the Seer	U	0.75
☐ Wisdom of the Spirits	U	0.75
☐ Words-of-Fury	R	2.00
☐ Wrath of Gaia	C	0.15
☐ Wyrm Vitalizer	C	0.15
☐ Xavier Wyrmslayer	X	1.00
☐ You're so Predictable	C	0.15

RARITY KEY C = Common U = Uncommon R = Rare F = Foil # = Lower numbers are rarer X = Fixed/standard in all decks

Red Zone

Donruss/NXT Games • First set, *Premiere*, released **October 1995**
336 cards in set • **IDENTIFIER: No "95" symbol on cards**

You will need **38** nine-pocket pages to store this set. (19 doubled up)

- Starter decks contain 80 cards and playmat; starter displays contain 10 starters
- Booster packs contain 12 cards; booster displays contain 36 boosters

Donruss, one of the sportscard manufacturers duking it out in the mid-1990s, hit the market in 1995 with the first CCG with a National Football League license: ***Red Zone.***

Players draft teams by taking turns picking their favorite cards out of their decks — the only restriction being that they can't use someone that their opponent already has in play. That's where the simplicity ends. For the kickoff, one player flips the top card of his deck and reads the K value in yards. The other player flips the top card of his deck and reads the KR value. Calculate where the ball is for the first play using the formula K-20+Kr = Ball. Then comes the first play. Players put an offensive or defensive play card face-down on the table. Players reveal these cards and then flip a card off their decks. The flipped card tells the player what color their play was.

Players then compare their color and play (for example, Green Fullback Drive or Yellow Stunt Defense) against one of the two three-page charts included in the game to get a yardage number. That's how many yards the ball moves forward. The basic rules take up the first 12 pages of the rulebook. After that come 32 more pages explaining what results with a letter code (DL, LB, OL, RB, WR, F, Long, INC, INT, DB, DL*, LB*, or QB). Using each and every one of these codes allows players to simulate interceptions, tackles, fumbles, and injuries, just like a real game of professional football.

This game is for stats-obsessed football junkies, players of *Strat-o-Matic Football* and *Statis-Pro Football*. That's not necessarily the same group as CCG fans, as Donruss found out; the game is *so* complex and involves *so* much table-checking that there isn't much room for excitement. (The game actually plays pretty close to real-time NFL football — but how many people want to play a CCG that lasts more than an hour?)

Red Zone survived to get an expansion set, which is more than its sister baseball game, ***Top of the Order*** did. The NXT design team began the ***X-Files*** CCG project at Donruss, which moved to USPC when Donruss got out of the act. **— Richard Weld**

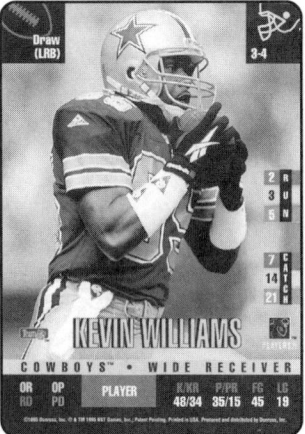

Concept	●●●○○
Gameplay	●●○○○
Card art	●●●○○
Player pool	○○○○○

Set (336 cards)			257.00
Starter Display Box			46.00
Booster Display Box			50.00
Double Deck			12.00
Starter Deck			8.00
Booster Pack			2.00

Promos

Card name	Team	Rarity	Price
☐ Super Bowl XXX Deion Sanders			7.50

Card name	Team	Rarity	Price
1			
☐ Adams, Sam	Sea	C	0.20
☐ Aikman, Troy	Dal	R	7.50
☐ Alexander, Derrick	Cle	U	0.70
☐ Alexander, Elijah	Den	U	0.70
☐ Allen, Marcus	KC	U	0.70
☐ Anders, Kimble	KC	R	1.50
☐ Anderson, Eddie	Oak	VC	0.15
☐ Anderson, Richie	NYJ	C	0.20
☐ Armstrong, Bruce	NE	C	0.20
2			
☐ Atwater, Steve	Den	C	0.20
☐ Bailey, Johnny	StL	C	0.70
☐ Ball, Jerry	Oak	C	0.20
☐ Ballard, Howard	Sea	R	1.50
☐ Banks, Carl	Cle	C	0.20
☐ Bankston, Michael	Ari	U	0.70
☐ Barker, Roy	Min	C	0.20
☐ Barnett, Fred	Phi	U	0.70
☐ Barrow, Micheal	Hou	U	0.70
3			
☐ Baxter, Brad	NYJ	VC	0.15
☐ Bennett, Cornelius	Buf	R	1.50
☐ Bennett, Edgar	GrB	R	1.50
☐ Bennett, Tony	Ind	R	1.50
☐ Bernstine, Rod	Den	R	1.50
☐ Biekert, Greg	Oak	U	0.70
☐ Bishop, Blaine	Hou	C	0.20
☐ Blackmon, Robert	Sea	VC	0.15
☐ Blackshear, Jeff	Sea	C	0.20

Card name	Team	Rarity	Price
4			
☐ Blades, Bennie	Det	U	0.70
☐ Blades, Brian	Sea	U	0.70
☐ Bledsoe, Drew	NE	U	1.50
☐ Bono, Steve	KC	C	0.20
☐ Bowens, Tim	Mia	C	0.20
☐ Brim, Mike	Cin	C	0.20
☐ Brisby, Vincent	NE	C	0.20
☐ Brock, Stan	SD	U	0.70
☐ Brooks, Michael	NYG	C	0.20
5			
☐ Brooks, Reggie	Was	VC	0.15
☐ Brown, Chad	Pit	R	1.50
☐ Brown, Dave	NYG	C	0.20
☐ Brown, Derek	NO	U	0.70
☐ Brown, Gary	Hou	U	0.70
☐ Brown, J.B.	Mia	C	0.20
☐ Brown, Larry	Dal	U	0.70
☐ Brown, Lomas	Det	R	1.50
☐ Brown, Tim	Oak	R	1.50
6			
☐ Brown, Vincent	NE	C	0.20
☐ Bruce, Isaac	StL	C	0.20
☐ Buchanan, Ray	Ind	R	1.50
☐ Buck, Vince	NO	C	0.20
☐ Burnett, Rob	Cle	R	1.50
☐ Butler, Leroy	GrB	C	0.20
☐ Byars, Keith	Mia	U	0.70
☐ Byner, Earnest	Cle	U	0.70
☐ Cain, Joe	Chi	C	0.20
7			
☐ Calloway, Chris	NYG	U	0.70
☐ Campbell, Jeseae	NYG	C	0.20
☐ Carrier, Mark	Chi	U	0.70
☐ Carter, Cris	Min	VC	0.15
☐ Carter, Dale	KC	C	0.20
☐ Carter, Tom	Was	C	0.20
☐ Casillas, Tony	NYJ	C	0.20
☐ Centers, Larry	Ari	C	0.70
☐ Childresea, Ray	Hou	U	0.70

Card name	Team	Rarity	Price
8			
☐ Coates, Ben	NE	R	1.50
☐ Coleman, Ben	Ari	VC	0.15
☐ Collins, Mark	KC	C	0.20
☐ Conlan, Shane	StL	C	0.20
☐ Conway, Curtis	Chi	C	0.20
☐ Copeland, Ruseaell	Buf	C	0.20
☐ Coryatt, Quentin	Ind	C	0.20
☐ Cox, Bryan	Mia	U	0.70
☐ Crockett, Ray	Den	U	0.70
9			
☐ Crosea, Jeff	Mia	U	0.70
☐ Cunningham, Ed	Ari	C	0.20
☐ Cunningham, Randall	Phi	U	1.50
☐ Curry, Eric	TB	VC	0.15
☐ Daniel, Eugene	Ind	C	0.20
☐ Davidson, Kenny	Hou	C	0.20
☐ Davis, Eric	SF	U	0.70
☐ Davis, Willie	KC	U	0.70
☐ Dawkins, Sean	Ind	C	0.20
10			
☐ Dawson, Dermontti	Pit	C	0.20
☐ Dawson, Lake	KC	C	0.20
☐ Del Rio, Jack	Min	R	1.50
☐ Dilfer, Trent	TB	U	0.70
☐ Dishman, Cris	Hou	R	1.50
☐ Doleman, Chris	Atl	U	0.70
☐ Dombrowski, Jim	NO	C	0.20
☐ Drayton, Troy	StL	C	0.20
☐ Dronett, Shane	Den	C	0.20
11			
☐ Duffy, Roger	NYJ	U	0.70
☐ Early, Quinn	NO	C	0.20
☐ Edwards, Dixon	Dal	C	0.20
☐ Ellard, Henry	Was	R	1.50
☐ Elliott, John	NYG	C	0.20
☐ Elway, John	Den	R	2.50
☐ Emanuel, Bert	Atl	U	0.70
☐ Esiason, Boomer	NYJ	C	0.20
☐ Everett, Jim	NO	U	0.70

Card name	Team	Rarity	Price
12			
☐ Everett, Thomas	TB	VC	0.15
☐ Everitt, Steve	Cle	C	0.20
☐ Faulk, Marshall	Ind	R	1.50
☐ Fina, John	Buf	R	1.50
☐ Fletcher, Simon	Den	U	0.70
☐ Floyd, William	SF	U	0.70
☐ Fontenot, Albert	Chi	C	0.20
☐ Fortin, Roman	Atl	C	0.20
☐ Fredrickson, Rob	Oak	C	0.20
13			
☐ Fryar, Irving	Mia	R	1.50
☐ Fuller, William	Phi	R	1.50
☐ Galbreath, Harry	GrB	C	0.20
☐ Gardner, Carwell	Buf	C	0.20
☐ Garner, Charlie	Phi	C	0.70
☐ Gash, Sam	NE	C	0.20
☐ George, Jeff	Atl	R	1.50
☐ Gilbert, Sean	StL	C	0.20
☐ Glenn, Aaron	NYJ	C	0.20
14			
☐ Goeas, Leo	StL	C	0.20
☐ Graham, Jeff	Chi	C	0.20
☐ Green, Darrell	Was	R	1.50
☐ Greene, Kevin	Pit	R	1.50
☐ Gruber, Paul	TB	C	0.20
☐ Grunhard, Tim	KC	C	0.20
☐ Guyton, Myron	NE	C	0.20
☐ Habib, Brian	Den	C	0.20
☐ Haley, Charles	Dal	R	1.50
15			
☐ Hall, Courtney	SD	U	0.70
☐ Hamilton, Keith	NYG	VC	0.15
☐ Hampton, Rodney	NYG	C	0.20
☐ Hanks, Merton	SF	R	1.50
☐ Harbaugh, Jim	Ind	U	0.70
☐ Harmon, Ronnie	SD	U	0.70
☐ Harper, Dwayne	SD	C	0.20
☐ Harris, Jackie	TB	C	0.20
☐ Harris, Raymont	Chi	C	0.20

RARITY KEY **VC** = Very Common **C** = Common **U** = Uncommon **R** = Rare **VR** = Very Rare **F** = Foil card **X** = Fixed/standard in all decks

Card name	Team	Rarity	Price
16			
Harrison, Nolan	Oak	U	0.70
Harrison, Rodney	SD	C	0.20
Harvey, Ken	Was	R	1.50
Hawkins, Courtney	TB	C	0.20
Haynes, Michael	NO	U	0.70
Hearst, Garrison	Ari	U	0.70
Hebron, Vaughn	Phi	C	0.20
Heck, Andy	Chi	U	0.70
Heller, Ron	Mia	U	0.70
17			
Herrod, Jeff	Ind	C	0.20
Hester, Jeseaie	StL	U	0.70
Heyward, Craig	Atl	C	0.20
Hill, Eric	Ari	U	0.70
Hill, Greg	KC	C	0.20
Hinton, Chris	Min	C	0.20
Hoard, Leroy	Cle	R	1.50
Holmes, Lester	Phi	U	0.70
Hopkins, Brad	Hou	R	1.50
18			
Hostetler, Jeff	Oak	C	0.20
Houston, Bobby	NYJ	C	0.20
Humphries, Stan	SD	C	0.20
Hurst, Maurice	NE	R	1.50
Irvin, Michael	Dal	R	1.50
Ismail, Qadry	Min	U	0.70
Ismail, Raghib	Oak	R	2.50
Jackson, Greg	Phi	R	1.50
Jackson, Michael	Cle	C	0.20
19			
Jamison, George	KC	C	0.20
Jefferson, Shawn	SD	U	0.70
Jeffires, Haywood	Hou	C	0.20
Jenkins, James	Was	VC	0.15
Johnson, Charles	Pit	U	0.70
Johnson, D.J.	Atl	R	1.50
Johnson, Mike	Det	C	0.20
Johnson, Pepper	Cle	U	0.70
Johnson, Tim	Was	C	0.20
20			
Johnston, Daryl	Dal	C	0.20
Jones, Brent	SF	U	0.70
Jones, Clarence	StL	U	0.70
Jones, Henry	Buf	C	0.20
Jones, Mike	NE	C	0.20
Jones, Sean	GrB	R	1.50
Jones, Tony	Cle	U	0.70
Kelly, Jim	Buf	R	1.50
Kennedy, Cortez	Sea	C	0.20
21			
Kirby, Terry	Mia	R	1.50
Koonce, George	GrB	C	0.20
Kramer, Erik	Chi	C	0.20
Kratch, Bob	NE	VC	0.15
Lachey, Jim	Was	U	0.70

Card name	Team	Rarity	Price
Lake, Carnell	Pit	U	0.70
Langham, Antonio	Cle	U	0.70
Lee, Amp	Min	U	0.70
Lee, Shawn	SD	U	0.70
22			
Lett, Leon	Dal	U	0.70
Lewis, Mo	NYJ	R	1.50
Lloyd, Greg	Pit	R	1.50
Lowdermilk, Kirk	Ind	C	0.20
Lyght, Todd	StL	U	0.70
Lynch, Lorenzo	Ari	C	0.20
Maddox, Mark	Buf	VC	0.15
Malamala, Siupeli	NYJ	C	0.20
Marino, Dan	Mia	R	2.50
23			
Martin, Tony	SD	U	0.70
Martin, Wayne	NO	R	1.50
Marts, Lonnie	TB	C	0.20
Maseaey, Robert	Det	C	0.20
Mathis, Terance	Atl	R	1.50
Matthews, Clay	Atl	VC	0.15
Mayberry, Tony	TB	C	0.20
Mayhew, Martin	TB	C	0.20
Mcdaniel, Ed	Min	U	0.70
24			
Mcdaniel, Randall	Min	C	0.20
Mcdaniel, Terry	Oak	R	1.50
Mcdonald, Tim	SF	C	0.20
Mcduffie, O.J.	Mia	U	0.70
Mcgee, Tony	Cin	C	0.20
Mcglockton, Chester	Oak	R	1.50
Means, Natrone	SD	R	1.50
Mickell, Darren	KC	C	0.20
Milburn, Glyn	Den	U	0.70
25			
Miller, Anthony	Den	R	1.50
Miller, Chris	StL	C	0.20
Miller, Corey	NYG	C	0.20
Mims, Chris	SD	R	1.50
Mirer, Rick	Sea	U	0.70
Mitchell, Brian	Was	U	0.70
Mitchell, Johnny	NYJ	C	0.20
Mitchell, Scott	Det	VC	0.15
Moon, Warren	Min	R	2.50
26			
Moore, Herman	Det	R	1.50
Morgan, Anthony	GrB	C	0.20
Mosebar, Don	Oak	U	0.70
Neal, Lorenzo	NO	VC	0.15
Newton, Nate	Dal	U	0.70
Nickerson, Hardy	TB	C	0.20
Norton, Ken	SF	R	1.50
Novacek, Jay	Dal	R	1.50
O'Donnell, Neil	Pit	C	0.20
27			
O'Neal, Leslie	SD	R	1.50

Card name	Team	Rarity	Price
Parker, Glenn	Buf	U	0.70
Parmalee, Bernie	Mia	C	0.20
Perriman, Brett	Det	U	0.70
Pickens, Carl	Cin	U	0.70
Pleasant, Anthony	Cle	VC	0.15
Plummer, Gary	SF	C	0.20
Pritchard, Mike	Den	C	0.20
Randle, John	Min	R	1.50
28			
Reed, Andre	Buf	R	1.50
Reed, Jake	Min	C	0.20
Rhett, Errict	TB	C	0.20
Rice, Jerry	SF	R	5.00
Riesenberg, Doug	NYG	C	0.20
Roaf, William	NO	R	1.50
Robinson, Eddie	Hou	C	0.20
Robinson, Eugene	Sea	C	0.20
Romanowski, Bill	Phi	C	0.20
29			
Rosea, Kevin	Atl	C	0.20
Rucker, Keith	Cin	C	0.20
Ruettgers, Ken	GrB	C	0.20
Sanders, Barry	Det	R	1.50
Scott, Darnay	Cin	R	1.50
Scroggins, Tracy	Det	C	0.20
Seals, Ray	Pit	C	0.20
Searcy, Leon	Pit	R	1.50
Seau, Junior	SD	R	1.50
30			
Seay, Mark	SD	C	0.20
Sharpe, Shannon	Den	U	0.70
Sherrard, Mike	NYG	U	0.70
Shields, Will	KC	C	0.20
Shuler, Heath	Was	U	0.70
Simien, Tracy	KC	VC	0.15
Simmons, Clyde	Ari	C	0.20
Singleton, Chris	Mia	C	0.20
Siragusa, Tony	Ind	C	0.20
31			
Slade, Chris	NE	R	1.50
Smith, Al	Hou	C	0.20
Smith, Anthony	Oak	U	0.70
Smith, Bruce	Buf	R	1.50
Smith, Darrin	Dal	U	0.70
Smith, Irv	NO	C	0.20
Smith, Kevin	Dal	U	0.70
Smith, Neil	KC	R	1.50
Smith, Robert	Min	C	0.20
32			
Smith, Thomas	Buf	C	0.20
Smith, Vinson	Chi	U	0.70
Sparks, Phillippi	NYG	U	0.70
Spencer, Jimmy	NO	C	0.20
Spielman, Chris	Det	U	0.70
Steuseaie, Todd	Min	C	0.20
Strahan, Michael	NYG	C	0.20

Card name	Team	Rarity	Price
Strickland, Fred	GrB	C	0.20
Stubblefield, Dana	SF	R	1.50
33			
Swann, Eric	Ari	U	0.70
Swayne, Harry	SD	C	0.20
Taylor, John	SF	R	1.50
Teague, George	GrB	U	0.70
Testaverde, Vinny	Cle	VC	0.15
Thigpen, Yancey	Pit	C	0.20
Thomas, William	Phi	R	1.50
Tillman, Lewis	Chi	C	0.20
Tolbert, Tony	Dal	C	0.20
34			
Tubbs, Winfred	NO	C	0.20
Tuggle, Jeseaie	Atl	C	0.20
Tuinei, Mark	Dal	R	1.50
Turnbull, Renaldo	NO	R	1.50
Turner, Eric	Cle	R	1.50
Turner, Floyd	Ind	VC	0.15
Vardell, Tommy	Cle	U	0.70
Vincent, Troy	Mia	R	1.50
Wallace, Steve	SF	R	1.50
35			
Walsh, Steve	Chi	U	0.70
Warren, Chris	Sea	R	1.50
Washington, Dewayne	Min	C	0.20
Webb, Richmond	Mia	C	0.20
White, Reggie	GrB	R	5.00
Whitfield, Bob	Atl	R	1.50
Widell, Doug	Det	R	1.50
Wilkinson, Dan	Cin	C	0.20
Williams, Aeneas	Ari	R	1.50
36			
Williams, Bernard	Phi	U	0.70
Williams, Calvin	Phi	C	0.20
Williams, Darryl	Cin	C	0.20
Williams, David	Hou	R	1.50
Williams, Harvey	Oak	C	0.20
Williams, James	Chi	C	0.20
Williams, John L.	Pit	C	0.20
Williams, Kevin	Dal	C	0.20
Wisniewski, Steve	Oak	C	0.20
37			
Wolford, Will	Ind	R	1.50
Wooden, Terry	Sea	R	1.50
Woods, Tony	Was	C	0.20
Woodson, Darren	Dal	U	0.70
Woodson, Rod	Pit	R	1.50
Woolford, Donnell	Chi	R	1.50
Wright, Toby	StL	C	0.20
Young, Bryant	SF	C	0.20
Young, Robert	StL	C	0.20
38			
Young, Steve	SF	R	2.50
Zimmerman, Gary	Den	C	0.20
Zordich, Michael	Phi	R	1.50

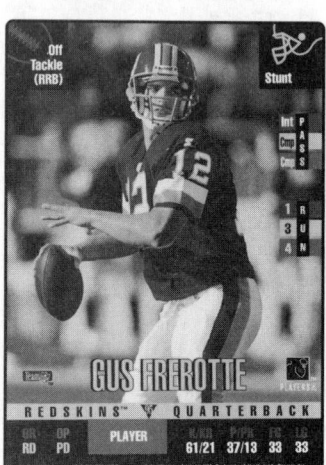

Red Zone • 1995 Expansion Teams

RED ZONE

Donruss/NXT Games • Released **Dec 1995**

98 cards in set • **IDENTIFIER: "95" symbol on cards**

• Booster packs contain 12 cards; booster displays contain 36 boosters

The only expansion released for **Red Zone** focuses on cards for the expansion teams, the Carolina Panthers and the Jacksonville Jaguars. The set includes fan favorites **Brett Favre, Deion Sanders,** and **Emmitt Smith. — *James Mishler***

You will need **11** nine-pocket pages to store this set. (6 doubled up)

Set (98 cards)		68.00
Booster Display Box		45.00
Booster Pack		2.00

Card name	Team	Rarity	Price
1			
Allen, Terry	Was	R	2.00
Andy, Harmon	Phi	U	0.70
Bates, Mario	NO	C	0.20
Bettis, Jerome	StL	U	0.70
Bieniemy, Eric	Cin	U	0.70

Card name	Team	Rarity	Price
Birden, J.J.	Atl	C	0.20
Blake, Jeff	Cin	U	0.70
Boselli, Tony	Jax	C	0.20
Brockemeyer, Blake	Car	C	0.20
2			
Brooks, Bill	Buf	C	0.20
Brooks, Robert	GrB	C	0.20
Brunell, Mark	Jax	C	0.20
Carrier, Mark	Car	R	2.00
Carter, Ki Jana	Cin	R	2.00

Card name	Team	Rarity	Price
Cash, Keith	KC	C	0.20
Chandler, Chris	Hou	C	0.20
Chrebet, Wayne	NYJ	C	0.20
Clark, Vinnie	Jax	R	2.00
3			
Collins, Kerry	Car	U	0.70
Davis, Terrell	Den	U	0.70
Don, Davey	Jax	C	0.20
Dunbar, Vaughn	Jax	C	0.20
Ellison, James	TB	C	0.20

RARITY KEY VC = Very Common   **C** = Common   **U** = Uncommon   **R** = Rare   **VR** = Very Rare   **F** = Foil card   **X** = Fixed/standard in all decks

374 • *SCRYE Collectible Card Game Checklist and Price Guide*

Card name	Team	Rarity	Price
Favre, Brett	GrB	VR	10.00
Ferrotte, Gus	Was	C	0.20
Fox, Mike	Car	C	0.20
Francis, James	Cin	U	0.70

4

Card name	Team	Rarity	Price
Galloway, Joey	Sea	R	2.00
Gardner, Moe	Atl	C	0.20
Gibson, Dennis	Cha	C	0.20
Goganious, Keith	Jax	C	0.20
Graham, Derrick	Car	U	0.70
Green, Eric	Mia	R	2.00
Griffith, Howard	Car	C	0.20
Hansen, Phil	Buf	C	0.20
Harper, Alvin	TB	VR	5.00

5

Card name	Team	Rarity	Price
Holmes, Darrick	Buf	U	0.70
Howard, Desmond	Jax	R	2.00
Jackson, Willie	Jax	C	0.20
Jenkins, Carlos	StL	C	0.20
Joyner, Seth	Ari	R	2.00
Kaufman, Napoleon	Oak	U	0.70

Card name	Team	Rarity	Price
Kordell, Stewart	Pit	VR	5.00
Kozerski, Bruce	Cin	C	0.20
Krieg, Dave	Ari	C	0.20

6

Card name	Team	Rarity	Price
Lageman, Jeff	Jax	U	0.70
Lathon, Lamar	Car	U	0.70
Levens, Dorsey	GrB	C	0.20
Loville, Derek	SF	U	0.70
Mamula, Mike	Phi	C	0.20
Mark, Chmura	GrB	C	0.20
Martin, Curtis	NE	C	0.20
Mcdowell, Bubba	Car	C	0.20
Meggett, Dave	NE	C	0.20

7

Card name	Team	Rarity	Price
Metcalf, Eric	Atl	U	0.70
Metzelaars, Pete	Car	C	0.20
Mills, Sam	Car	C	0.20
Mincy, Charles	Min	C	0.20
Moore, Derrick	Car	C	0.20
Moore, Rob	Ari	C	0.20
Morris, Bam	Pit	U	0.70

Card name	Team	Rarity	Price
Moss, Winton	Sea	C	0.20
Patton, Marvcus	Was	C	0.20

8

Card name	Team	Rarity	Price
Paup, Bryce	Buf	VR	5.00
Pegram, Eric	Pit	C	0.20
Perry, Michael Dean	Den	U	0.70
Porter, Rufus	NO	C	0.20
Potts, Roosevelt	Ind	R	2.00
Rison, Andre	Cle	R	2.00
Rivers, Ron	Det	C	0.20
Roberts, Tim	NE	C	0.20
Salaam, Rashaan	Chi	R	2.00

9

Card name	Team	Rarity	Price
Sanders, Chris	Hou	U	0.70
Sanders, Deion	Dal	VR	10.00
Sanders, Frank	Ari	R	2.00
Sapolu, Jesse	SF	U	0.70
Sapp, Warren	TB	C	0.20
Sargent, Kevin	Cin	R	2.00
Scott, Todd	NYJ	C	0.20
Simmons, Ed	Was	C	0.20

Card name	Team	Rarity	Price
Smith, Emmitt	Dal	VR	10.00

10

Card name	Team	Rarity	Price
Smith, Rod	Car	C	0.20
Smith, Steve	Sea	U	0.70
Steed, Joel	Pit	C	0.20
Stewart, James	Jax	C	0.20
Swilling, Pat	Oak	U	0.70
Thomas, Henry	Det	R	2.00
Thomas, Rodney	Hou	C	0.20
Tovar, Steve	Cin	C	0.20
Washington, Marvin	NYJ	C	0.20

11

Card name	Team	Rarity	Price
Washington, Mickey	Jax	C	0.20
Watters, Ricky	Phi	VR	5.00
Westbrook, Michael	Was	U	0.70
Wheatley, Tyrone	NYG	U	0.70
Widell, Dave	Jax	C	0.20
Williams, Gerald	Car	C	0.20
Williams, James	Jax	C	0.20
Zorich, Chris	Chi	C	0.20

Redemption

Cactus Game Design • First set, *Limited*, released **July 1995**; *Unlimited*, **November 1995**
162 cards in set • **IDENTIFIER:** © by artist name in *Limited*; by company in *Unlimited*
- Starters decks contain 100 cards; *Limited* displays contain **A**, **B** starters; *Unlimited* has **C**, **D**
- Boosters packs contain 8 cards; booster displays contain 45 boosters

Designed by **Rob Anderson**

Whereas the magical and occult elements of *Magic: The Gathering* never received nearly the criticism that *Dungeons & Dragons* had before, a case could still be made for a niche market for "family-friendly" CCGs. Rob Anderson's Cactus Design Group sought to fill this niche with *Redemption*, a CCG with a Christian perspective.

The game consists of Heroes and Evil Characters battling each other. The goal of the game is for the Heroes to save the "Lost Souls" while the Evil Characters try to foil these attempts. Along the way, there are various "helper" cards that one can use on both sides to enhance a Hero's ability to rescue a Lost Soul or for an Evil Character to prevent the rescue. Some of these enhancement cards include dominant cards (cards that have an instantaneous effect on the game) and cards that set aside or heal characters. Turns consist of drawing of cards, playing Heroes and Evil Characters, and recovery attempts. Whoever rescues all of the opponent's Lost Souls first is declared the winner.

Redemption stood in opposition to games with occult themes and gave retailers something to offer parents disturbed by other offerings. (It's notable that the object of the *Kult* CCG is almost the direct opposite of *Redemption!*) *Redemption* received good press in places where gaming traditionally had not gotten favorable treatment, such as on *The 700 Club*. But, while it sold well through alternative channels such as Christian bookstores, *Redemption* was never a widespread hit in the hobby market — not because of its themes, but its play. Released in an era when complex CCGs were the norm instead of the exception, its relative simplicity kept hard-core gamers away. — *Ka-Lok Fung*

3/3 Obedience of Noah

Thus did Noah; according to all that God commanded him, so did he.
Genesis 6:2

SCRYE 8 Illus. © Michael Carroll

Scrye promo variant of Limited card above

Concept	●●●●○
Gameplay	●●●○○
Card art	●●○○○
Player pool	●●○○○

You will need **21** nine-pocket pages to store the larger set. *(11 doubled up)*

Redemption • Second Edition

Cactus Game Design • *Second Edition* cards released **September 2000** • **189** cards in set

Just as *Unlimited* had added 'C' and 'D' starters and a few new cards to the base set in 1995, *Second Edition* adds several more, replacing the 'C' and 'D' starters from *Unlimited*. There are no *Second Edition* booster packs as of press time.

LIMITED

Set (162 cards)	56.50
Starter Display Box	40.00
Booster Display Box	45.00
Starter Deck	8.00
Booster Pack	2.00

UNLIMITED/SECOND EDITION

Set (189 cards)	50.00
Starter Display Box	38.00
Booster Display Box	42.00
Starter Deck	7.50
Booster Pack	1.50

Promo cards

Burial	2.00
Lost Soul (Ezekiel 36:19)	2.50
Meditation	2.00
Plague of Flies	2.00
Shoes of Peace	2.00
Stillness	2.00

LIMITED	Card name	Rarity	2ND EDIT
1.50	Aaron's Rod	R	1.00
1.50	Abaddon the Destroyer	R	1.00
1.50	Abandonment	R	1.00
0.50	Abel	X	0.50
	Abihu	U	0.25
0.25	Adino	U	0.25
0.25	Ahab	U	0.25

LIMITED	Card name	Rarity	2ND EDIT
0.10	Alertness	C	0.05
	Ancient Evil	X	0.50
0.10	Angel Food	C	0.05
1.00	Angel of the Lord	X	0.75
0.25	Antidote	U	0.25
0.25	Asahel	U	0.25
1.50	Authority of Christ	R	1.00
0.10	Axe	C	0.05
1.50	Balm of Gilead	R	1.00
0.10	Banner	C	0.05
0.10	Banner of Love	C	0.05
	Banner of Truth	X	0.50
	Baptism	X	0.50

LIMITED	Card name	Rarity	2ND EDIT
0.25	Barnabas	U	0.25
0.10	Battle Axe	C	0.05
	Bear	X	0.50
2.00	Beast from the Earth	R	1.50
2.00	Beast from the Sea	R	1.50
0.10	Boils	C	0.05
0.25	Bow and Arrow	U	0.25
0.10	Bow and Arrow	C	0.05
2.00	Brass Serpent	R	1.50
0.10	Bravery of David	C	0.05
1.50	Bread of Life	R	1.00
0.50	Breastplate of Righteousness	X	0.50
0.10	Buckler	C	0.05

RARITY KEY **C** = Common **U** = Uncommon **R** = Rare **VR** = Very Rare **UR** = Ultra Rare **F** = Foil card **X** = Fixed/standard in all decks

Limited	Card name	Rarity	2nd Edit
	Burning Censer	X	0.50
1.50	Cage	R	1.00
1.50	Chains	R	1.00
0.10	Chariots of Iron	C	0.05
0.10	Chariots of the Sun	C	0.05
1.50	Chastisement of the Lord	R	1.00
0.50	Christian Martyr	X	0.50
0.25	Christian Soldier	U	0.25
1.50	Clemency of David	R	1.00
0.10	Coat of Mail	C	0.05
0.10	Commitment of Paul	C	0.05
1.50	Compassion of Jeremiah	R	1.00
0.25	Cornelius	U	0.25
0.25	Courage	U	0.25
0.10	Courage of Esther	C	0.05
1.50	Cruelty	R	1.00
1.50	Darkness	R	1.00
0.25	David's Sling	U	0.25
0.25	David's Staff	U	0.25
0.25	Deborah	U	0.25
0.10	Dedication of Samuel	C	0.05
1.50	Delilah	R	1.50
0.10	Determination of Nehemiah	C	0.05
1.50	Devotion of Ruth	R	1.00
0.10	Discord	C	0.05
0.25	Doeg	U	0.25
0.10	Ehud's Dagger	C	0.05
0.10	Endurance	C	0.05
	Ephah	X	0.50
0.25	Esther	U	0.25
0.10	Evil	C	0.05
	Evil Armor	X	0.50
	Evil Fire	X	0.50
	Evil Spawn	X	0.50
1.50	Ezekiel's Stick	R	1.00
0.25	Faith	U	0.25
0.10	Faith of Abraham	C	0.05
0.25	Faithful Servant	U	0.25
0.10	Faithfulness of Luke	C	0.05
0.25	False Shepherds	U	0.25

Limited	Card name	Rarity	2nd Edit
0.25	False Teachers	U	0.25
0.10	Fearlessness of Joshua	C	0.05
0.10	Fiery Darts	C	0.05
0.10	Five Smooth Stones	C	0.05
0.10	Forcefulness of Isaiah	C	0.05
	Foreign Enemy	X	0.50
0.10	Forgiveness of Joseph	C	0.05
1.50	Frog Demons	R	1.00
0.10	Gentleness	C	0.05
0.25	Gideon	U	0.25
3.00	Goliath	R	2.00
0.10	Goliath's Spear	C	0.05
0.10	Goodness	C	0.05
0.10	Grief	C	0.05
0.25	Haman	U	0.25
0.25	Hannah	U	0.25
0.10	Hard Hearted Religious Leaders	C	0.05
1.50	Hate	R	1.00
1.50	Healing	R	1.00
0.25	Helmet of Brass	U	0.25
0.50	Helmet of Salvation	X	0.50
0.25	Herodias	U	0.25
	Holy of Holies	X	0.50
0.10	Hope	C	0.05
0.10	Humility of Moses	C	0.05
0.25	Hushai	U	0.25
0.25	Jaazaniah	U	0.25
	Jacob	X	0.75
0.25	Jezebel	U	0.25
1.50	Joab	R	1.00
0.25	Jonathon	U	0.25
0.10	Joy	C	0.05
0.25	Judas Iscariot	U	0.25
1.50	Kindness	R	1.00
	King's Sword	X	0.50
	Lamb's Righteousness	X	0.50
0.10	Lance	C	0.05
1.50	Leaves for Healing	R	1.00
1.50	Locusts from the Pit	R	1.00
0.10	Long-Suffering of John	C	0.05
0.50	Lost Soul (Ephesians 5:14)	X	0.50

Limited	Card name	Rarity	2nd Edit
0.50	Lost Soul (Ezekiel 34:12)	X	0.50
0.50	Lost Soul (I Kings 17:12)	X	0.50
0.50	Lost Soul (II Timothy 2:26)	X	0.50
0.50	Lost Soul (II Timothy 3:6-7)	X	0.50
1.50	Lost Soul (Isaiah 42:7)	R	1.00
0.50	Lost Soul (Job 33:27-28)	X	0.50
1.50	Lost Soul (Luke 13:25)	R	1.00
0.50	Lost Soul (Luke 15:6)	X	0.50
1.50	Lost Soul (Proverbs 22:14)	R	1.00
0.10	Love	C	0.05
0.10	Loyalty of Jonathon	C	0.05
0.25	Mark	U	0.25
5.00	Mary	R	4.00
1.50	Meekness of Isaac	R	1.00
0.10	Mercy of James	C	0.05
0.25	Mighty Warrior	U	0.25
0.25	Miriam	U	0.25
1.50	Net	R	1.00
1.50	Obedience of Noah	R	1.00
0.25	Ointment	U	0.25
0.25	Othniel	U	0.25
0.10	Patience	C	0.05
1.50	Patience of Job	R	1.00
1.50	Peace	R	1.00
0.25	Pharaoh	U	0.25
0.50	Pillar of a Cloud	X	0.50
0.10	Poison	C	0.05
	Poison of Dragons	X	0.50
	Power of the Cross	X	0.50
1.50	Prayer and Fasting	R	1.00
	Priestly Breastpalte	X	0.50
0.10	Purity of Enoch	C	0.05
1.50	Rage	R	1.00

Limited	Card name	Rarity	2nd Edit
0.25	Rebekah	U	0.25
2.50	Red Dragon	R	1.50
1.50	Repentance	R	1.00
0.10	Rod of Iron	C	0.05
	Roman Prison	X	0.50
0.25	Ruth	U	0.25
0.25	Salome	U	0.25
	Samaria	X	0.50
5.00	Samson	R	2.50
0.25	Samuel	U	0.25
	Search	X	0.50
0.25	Shamgar	U	0.25
0.50	Shield of Faith	X	0.50
0.25	Shimei	U	0.25
0.25	Silas	U	0.25
	Sinful Army	X	0.50
	Sinful Kingdom	X	0.50
1.50	Sleep	R	1.00
1.50	Snare	R	1.00
1.00	Son of God	X	0.75
1.50	Sound the Alarm	R	1.00
1.50	Speed	R	1.00
0.10	Steadfastness of Peter	C	0.05
1.50	Stocks	R	1.00
0.10	Stone of Thebez	C	0.05
0.25	Stone Throwers	U	0.25
0.10	Strength	C	0.05
	Strong Demon	X	0.50
1.50	Submissiveness of Mary	R	1.00
	Swift Horses	X	0.50
0.50	Sword of the Spirit	X	0.50
0.25	Task Master	U	0.25
	Tears for a Friend	X	0.50
0.25	Temperance	U	0.25
	The Body of Christ	X	0.50
0.10	Treachery	C	0.05
0.10	Truthfulness of Nathan	C	0.05
0.25	Uriah	U	0.25
1.50	Vain Philosophy	R	1.00
1.50	Whore of Babylon	R	1.00
1.50	Wildness	R	1.00
0.25	Wisdom	U	0.25

Molten Calf Worship

Set Evil Character aside for 5 turns, Character returns with abilities increased 4/8.

And he received them at their hand, and fashioned it with a graving tool, after he had made it a molten calf: and they said, These be thy gods, O Israel, which brought thee up out of the land of Egypt. Exodus 32: 4

Illus. Michael Ulrich
© Cactus Game Design, Inc.

Set (106 cards)	**42.00**
Booster Display Box	**35.00**
Booster Pack	**1.75**

Redemption • The Prophets

Cactus Game Design • Released **July 1996**

106 cards in set • **IDENTIFIER: None; © by company name**

You will need **12** nine-pocket pages to store this set. (6 doubled up)

• Booster packs contain 8 cards; booster displays contain 45 boosters

The first expansion for **Redemption**, **The Prophets** adds more cards based on bibilical figures. The Prophets, while adding to the card pool, has few uniquely powerful cards and its impact on the metagame was limited. — *Ka-Lok Fung*

Card name	Rarity	Price
Agabus	U	0.25
Ahaziah	U	0.25
Amos	U	0.25
Anna	C	0.10
Arrow of Deliverance	C	0.10
Ashtoreth Worship (Boulden)	C	0.10
Ashtoreth Worship (Hodgson)	C	0.10
Astrologers	U	0.25
Baal Worship	C	0.10
Bad Figs	C	0.10
Baggage	R	1.00
Balaam	U	0.25
Belshazzar	C	0.10
Chaldeans	U	0.25
Charred Vine	R	1.00
Confusion	R	1.00
Covenant with Death	C	0.10
Cup of Wrath	R	1.00
Damsel wit Spirit of Divination	U	0.25
Daniel	U	0.25
Den of Robbers	R	1.00

Card name	Rarity	Price
Drawn Sword	C	0.10
Dungeon of Malchiah	R	1.00
Elisha	U	0.25
Elisha's Bones	R	1.00
Enchanter	U	0.25
Ezekiel	U	0.50
False Dreams	R	1.00
False Peace	R	1.00
False Prophesy	R	1.00
False Prophets	R	1.00
False Wisdom	C	0.10
Filthy Garments	U	0.25
First Figs	C	0.10
Floating Ax Head	C	0.10
Forest Fire	U	0.25
Four Horns	U	0.25
Furnace of God's Wrath	R	1.00

Card name	Rarity	Price
Gad	U	0.25
Goat with Horn	C	0.10
Golden Lampstand	C	0.10
Great Image	R	1.00
Habakkuk	U	0.25
Hammer of God	C	0.10
Highway	U	0.25
Hinds' Feet	C	0.10
Hosea	U	0.25
Hulda	U	0.25
Hunger	R	1.00
Ignorance	U	0.25
Image of Jealousy	C	0.10
Iron Pan	U	0.25
Isaiah	U	0.25
Jeremiah	U	0.25
John	U	0.25

Card name	Rarity	Price		Card name	Rarity	Price		Card name	Rarity	Price		Card name	Rarity	Price
☐ John the Baptist	U	0.50		☐ Mountain of God	C	0.10		[10] ☐ Simeon	U	0.25		☐ Users of Curious Arts	U	0.25
☐ Jonah	U	0.50		☐ Nebuchadnezzar	U	0.50		☐ Stone Cut with out Hands	U	0.25		☐ Vain Vision	U	0.25
☐ Large Tree	R	1.00		☐ Paintings of Abominations	U	0.25		☐ Strange Vine	C	0.10		☐ Valley of Dry Bones	R	1.00
☐ Lies	U	0.25		☐ Paul's Girdle	C	0.10		☐ Sun Worship	R	1.00		☐ Wall of Fire	U	0.50
☐ Lion Dwelling with the Calf	R	1.00		[9] ☐ Philip's Daughters	C	0.10		☐ The Branch	U	0.25		☐ Weeping for Tammuz	C	0.10
☐ Live Coal	C	0.10		☐ Potter and the Clay	U	0.25		☐ The False Prophet	R	1.00		☐ Wheel within a Wheel	R	1.00
☐ Malachi	U	0.25		☐ Prince of Persia	R	1.00		☐ The Flying Scroll	C	0.10		[12] ☐ Witch of Endor	R	2.00
☐ Manasseh	U	0.25		☐ Prophets of Baal	U	0.25		☐ The Girdle	C	0.10		☐ Wizards	U	0.50
[8] ☐ Manasseh's Altar	C	0.10		☐ Prophets of Samaria	U	0.25		☐ The Vineyard	R	1.00		☐ Woman in the Ephah	C	0.10
☐ Measuring Line	C	0.10		☐ Ram with Two Horns	R	1.00		[11] ☐ The Watchman	U	0.25		☐ Workers with Familiar Spirits	U	0.25
☐ Molech Worship	R	1.00		☐ Razor	C	0.10		☐ Torn Mantle	R	1.00		☐ Yoke of Iron	R	1.00
☐ Molten Calf Worship	U	0.25		☐ River Flowing from Temple	R	1.00		☐ Two Olive Branches	R	1.00		☐ Zechariah	C	0.10
☐ Moses	R	2.00		☐ Shemaiah	U	0.25						☐ Zephaniah	C	0.10

Redemption • Women of the Bible

Cactus Game Design • Released July 1997

82 cards in set • **IDENTIFIER: None; © by company name**

- Booster packs contain 8 cards; booster displays contain 45 boosters

Women of the Bible, as the name indicates, consists mainly of cards with references to Biblical women. However, **Women of the Bible** is best remembered for being the first expansion to introduce a new game mechanic: the usage of site cards.

The addition of the site mechanic added an interesting strategy element to **Redemption**'s metagame as both an offense and defensive tool. Now, a Lost Soul would be confined to a specific territory. Now, players had to come armed with their own site cards to rescue Lost Souls or face being repelled in every attempt. An offensive and defensive tool, Lost Souls became an important part of *Redemption*.

Women is unique in that it was the only *Redemption* expansion with no card rarity. This was great for players and collectors, but it probably was an economic mistake, since demand for cards in this set is much reduced. — *Ka-Lok Fung*

You will need **10** nine-pocket pages to store this set. (5 doubled up)

Set (82 cards)	37.00
Booster Display Box	30.00
Booster Pack	1.75

Card name	Price
[1] ☐ A Look Back	0.25
☐ Abigail	0.25
☐ Assyria	0.25
☐ Athaliah	0.25
☐ Babylon	0.25
☐ Bathsheba	0.50
☐ Bravery of Priscilla	0.25
☐ Carelessness	0.25
☐ Children	0.25
[2] ☐ Claudia	0.25
☐ Coat of Many Colors	1.00
☐ Counsel of Abigail	0.25
☐ Dance of Death	0.25

Card name	Price
☐ Deceit of Sapphira	0.25
☐ Destruction of Athaliah	0.25
☐ Drawn Water	0.25
☐ Egypt	0.25
☐ Elisabeth	0.25
[3] ☐ Eve	2.00
☐ Lost Soul (Ezekiel 13:18)	0.25
☐ Falling Away	0.25
☐ Foolish Advice	0.25
☐ Foolishness of Five Virgins	0.25
☐ Forbidden Fruit	0.50
☐ Gomer	0.25
☐ Great Faith	0.25
☐ Halah	0.25
[4] ☐ Herod's Dungeon	0.25
☐ Hospitality of Martha	0.25
☐ Idle Gossip	0.25

Card name	Price
☐ Jael	0.25
☐ Jael's Nail	0.25
☐ Jairus' Daughter	0.25
☐ Jeremiah 7:18	0.25
☐ Joanna	0.25
☐ Job's Wife	0.25
[5] ☐ Jochebed	0.25
☐ King's Daughter	0.25
☐ Kir	0.25
☐ Lamentation of Rachel	0.25
☐ Lamenting for Jepthah's Daughter	0.25
☐ Laughter	0.25
☐ Leah	0.25
☐ Lion's Den	0.25
☐ Lot's Daughters	0.25
[6] ☐ Lot's Wife	0.50

Card name	Price
☐ Love for Rachel	0.25
☐ Lydia	0.25
☐ Martha	0.25
☐ Mary Magdalene	1.00
☐ Mary of Bethany	1.00
☐ Media	0.25
☐ Michal	0.25
☐ Midwives	0.25
[7] ☐ Naomi	0.25
☐ New Jerusalem	0.50
☐ New Jerusalem (site)	0.50
☐ Pharaoh's Daughter	0.25
☐ Pharaoh's Prison	0.25
☐ Piety of Mary	0.25
☐ Pit of Dothan	0.25
☐ Potiphar's Wife	0.25
☐ Praises	0.25
[8] ☐ Prison	0.25

Card name	Price
☐ Prison of Asa	0.25
☐ Proverbs 7:27	0.25
☐ Queen of Sheba	0.50
☐ Rachel	0.25
☐ Rahab	0.25
☐ Reach of Desperation	0.25
☐ Rhoda's Gladness	0.25
☐ Rizpah's Sackcloth	0.25
[9] ☐ Sapphira	0.25
☐ Sarah	0.25
☐ Scarlet Line	0.25
☐ Scorn of Michal	0.25
☐ Silly Women	0.25
☐ Sorrow of Mary	0.25
☐ Temptation	0.25
☐ Treachery of Jezebel	0.25
☐ Woman of Thebez	0.25
[10] ☐ Women as Snares	0.25

Redemption • The Warriors

Cactus Game Design • Released June 1999

171 cards in set • **IDENTIFIER: None; © by company name**

- Booster packs contain 10 cards

The best-selling **Redemption** expansion on the Christian specialty market, **Warriors** is known for the addition of the Artifact game mechanic and the introduction of a new brigade for the Heroes. Artifacts have important game-changing effects. Although a player can have as many Artifacts (represented by the Grail icon) as he wants on the table, only one artifact can be active at any given time. As for the new Silver brigade, players may choose Heroes and Evil Characters from a variety of brigades for use in decks. The Silver brigade is primarily made of angels and its enhancement cards deal with angels.

Warriors was well received by the dedicated fan base of Redemptioners. Collectors' tastes were even satisfied due to inclusion of ultra-rares in this expansion. *Redemption* is still actively supported by Cactus, which plans **The Apostles** for June 2001. — *Ka-Lok Fung*

You will need **19** nine-pocket pages to store this set. (10 doubled up)

Set (171 cards)	51.00
Booster Display Box	40.00
Booster Pack	2.25

Card name	Rarity	Price		Card name	Rarity	Price		Card name	Rarity	Price
[1] ☐ Abishai	C	0.10		☐ Abner's Spear	C	0.10		☐ Ahithophel	U	0.25
☐ Abizer	U	0.25		☐ Absalom	U	0.25		☐ Angel at Jerusalem	C	0.10
				☐ Adino's Spear	C	0.10		☐ Angel at Shur	C	0.10

RARITY KEY C = Common U = Uncommon R = Rare VR = Very Rare UR = Ultra Rare F = Foil card X = Fixed/standard in all decks

Card name	Rarity	Price
Angel at the Tomb	C	0.10
Angel Chariots	U	0.25
Angel in the Path	U	0.25
Angel with the Secret Name	C	0.10
Answered Prayer	U	0.25
Ark of the Covenant	UR	5.00
Armorbearer	U	0.25
Babylon the Great	C	0.10
Bad Figs	C	0.10
Battle Axe	C	0.10
Battle Prayer	C	0.10
Beast from the Earth	U	0.50
Beast from the Sea	R	1.50
Belt of Truth	UR	2.50
Benaiah	R	1.00
Blood of the Lamb	R	1.00
Boils	C	0.10
Bow & Arrow	R	1.00
Bow and Arrow	C	0.10
Breastplate of Righteousness	UR	2.50
Buckler	C	0.10
Captain of the Host	R	1.50
Chariot of Fire	U	0.50
Cherubim	C	0.10
Coat of Mail	C	0.10
Courage	U	0.25
Crown of Thorns	U	0.25
Cruelty	C	0.10
Darkness	U	0.25
Dart	C	0.10
David	R	2.00
David	R	2.00
David's Harp	U	0.25
Death & Hades	R	1.00
Desecration of the Graves	C	0.10
Devourer	R	1.00
Dragon Raid	U	0.25
Edge of the Sword	C	0.10
Ehud's Dagger	R	1.00
Eleazar	C	0.10
Elhanan	R	1.00

Card name	Rarity	Price
Elijah's Mantle	U	0.25
Evil Angel	U	0.25
Evil Spirit	R	1.00
Evil Strength	C	0.10
Faith as Children	C	0.10
Fallen Angel	U	0.25
Fallen Warrior	C	0.10
Fiery Serpents	C	0.10
Five Smooth Stones	R	1.00
Flaming Sword	U	0.50
Flight	U	0.25
Fortify Site	U	0.25
Fortress of Antonia	C	0.10
Frog Demons	C	0.10
Gabriel	U	0.50
Gathering of Angels	C	0.10
Glittering Spear	C	0.10
Glittering Sword	R	1.00
Goliath's Spear	C	0.10
Goshen	U	0.25
Guards	U	0.25
Harvest Time	UR	2.50
Helez	C	0.10
Helmet of Brass	C	0.10
Helmet of Salvation	UR	2.50
Holy Grail	R	2.00
Ira	R	1.00
Ishbibenob	U	0.25
Ittai	C	0.10
Jashobeam	C	0.10
Jashobeam's Spear	C	0.10
King of Tyrus	UR	2.50
King Saul	R	1.50
King Saul	U	0.50
Kingdoms of the World	U	0.25
Lahmi	U	0.25
Lamhi's Spear	C	0.10
Land Made Waste	C	0.10
Leprosy	C	0.10
Locust from the Pit	C	0.10
Lost Soul (Psalm 1:4)	U	0.25

Card name	Rarity	Price
Lost Soul (Ezekiel 31:14)	C	0.10
Lost Soul (Ezekiel 34:16)	C	0.10
Lost Soul (Jeremiah 50:6)	C	0.10
Lost Soul (Luke 19:10)	C	0.10
Lying in Wait	U	0.25
Mace	U	0.25
Maharai	U	0.25
Mask of Arrogance	R	1.00
Mask of Fear	R	1.00
Mask of Pride	R	1.00
Mask of Self-Glorification	R	1.00
Mask of Vanity	C	0.10
Mask of Worldliness	R	1.00
Michael	UR	5.00
Might of Angels	R	1.00
Mist	U	0.25
Mocking Soldier	C	0.10
Moses	R	3.00
New Jerusalem	UR	3.00
Ointment	C	0.10
Pestilence	R	1.00
Pillar of Fire	UR	3.00
Poison	C	0.10
Potter's Field	U	0.25
Prince Jonathan	U	0.25
Prince of Greece	R	1.00
Prince of this World	R	1.00
Prince of Tyrus	U	0.25
Profanation	C	0.10
Protection of Angels	U	0.25
Put to Flight	R	1.00
Raising of the Saints	U	0.25
Ram's Horn	U	0.25
Red Dragon	U	0.50
Redemption	C	0.10
Resurrection	C	0.10
Rod of Iron	U	0.25
Saint of Virtue	U	0.25
Saph	R	1.00
Saul's Javelin	C	0.10

Card name	Rarity	Price
Saul's Spear	C	0.10
Seige	R	1.00
Seraphim [Isaiah 6:2]	C	0.10
Seraphim [Isaiah 6:6]	C	0.10
Shadow of Death	U	0.25
Shamhuth	R	1.00
Shammah	C	0.10
Shield of Faith	UR	2.50
Sibbechai	U	0.25
Simeon	U	0.25
Sling	C	0.10
Sodom	C	0.10
Spear of Joshua	C	0.10
Stirring the Water	C	0.10
Sword	C	0.10
Sword of the Lord	R	1.00
Sword of Vengence	U	0.25
Table's of the Law	U	0.25
The Book of Life	R	1.00
The Fifth Trumpet	U	0.25
The First Seal	R	1.00
The First Trumpet	U	0.25
The Fourth Trumpet	U	0.25
The Golden Censer	U	0.25
The Long Day	R	1.00
The Number of the Beast	U	0.25
The Second Seal	R	1.00
The Second Trumpet	U	0.25
The Seventh Trumpet	U	0.25
The Sixth Trumpet	U	0.25
The Strong Angel	R	1.00
The Third Seal	C	0.10
The Third Trumpet	U	0.25
Tormentors	C	0.10
Tower	R	1.00
Viper Bite	C	0.10
Wall of Water	C	0.10
Warrior in Training	U	0.25
Witch of Endor	C	0.10
Words of Encouragement	R	1.00
Wrath of Satan	R	1.00

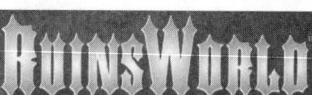

Ruinsworld

Medallion Simulations • Released **December 1995**

199 cards in set

You will need **23** nine-pocket pages to store this set. (12 doubled up)

Concept	●●○○○
Gameplay	●●●○○
Card art	●●●○○
Player pool	○○○○○

Lesser Elemental

• Starter decks contain 65 cards • Booster packs contain 15 cards

Following its entry into the CCG field with the wargames **Echelons of Fire** and **Echelons of Fury**, Medallion Simulations took on adapting role-playing games to CCGs with **RuinsWorld**.

Similar to the **Fantasy Adventures** from Mayfair Games and *Dragon Storm*, Black Dragon Press's later and more successful release which wasn't strictly speaking a CCG, *Ruinsworld* gives each player a Character for adventuring. By contrast with *Dragon Storm*, where players use cards from the same pool face-up to serve, essentially, as markers on a character sheet, *Ruinsworld* players each bring their own multiple decks to the table. Players equipping their characters with items from their Marketplace decks, encounter creatures from their Journey Decks, and battle for treasure found in their play decks. If this sounds like **Banemaster** without one player being the bad guy, it is. It's even possible to play *Ruinsworld* solo against your own stacked deck.

The system and generic game world did not fire the imagination of players, and it had an *extremely* brief appearance in stores. The cards shown in this book were obtained from Australia after much searching. We hope we saved you a trip. — **James Mishler**

	Price
Set (199 cards)	35.00
Starter Deck	5.00
Booster Pack	1.00

Card name	Rar	Price
2 Handed Battle Axe	R	2.00
2 Handed Sword	U	0.50

Card name	Rar	Price
Astral Deamon	U	0.25
Astral Enlightenment	R	1.00
Attack 3	VC	0.05
Attack 4	VC	0.05
Attack 5	VC	0.05
Attack 6	VC	0.05
Attack 7	VC	0.05

Card name	Rar	Price
Attack/Initiative 3	C	0.10
Attack/Initiative 4	VC	0.05
Attack/Initiative 5	VC	0.05
Attack/Initiative 6	VC	0.05
Attack/Initiative 7	C	0.10
Backpack	C	0.10
Band of Gypsies	U	0.25

Card name	Rar	Price
Bardin	R	1.00
Barding	R	1.50
Behemoth	U	0.50
Book Fiend	VC	0.05
Bore Worms	U	0.25
Bounty	R	1.00

Card name	Rar	Price
Bridge Out	R	1.00
Brigandine	U	0.25
Capital	U	0.25
Caravan Duty	R	1.00
Cart	U	0.25
Castle	U	0.25

RARITY KEY VC = Very Common **C** = Common **U** = Uncommon **R** = Rare **VR** = Very Rare **F** = Foil card **X** = Fixed/standard in all decks

Card name	Rar	Price
Cave Dweller	U	0.25
Cave Slug	R	1.00
Chainmail	R	1.50
City	U	0.25
Club	R	1.00
Club	R	1.00
Coastline	VC	0.05
Crossbow	U	0.25
5		
Crossing	C	0.10
Crypt Thing	U	0.25
Dagger	C	0.10
Darian	R	1.00
Dead End	C	0.10
Defense 4	VC	0.05
Defense 5	VC	0.05
Defense 6	VC	0.05
Defense 7	VC	0.05
6		
Defense 8	VC	0.05
Defense Rune	R	1.00
Defense/Initiative 4	VC	0.05
Defense/Initiative 5	C	0.10
Defense/Initiative 6	VC	0.05
Defense/Initiative 7	VC	0.05
Defense/Initiative 8	VC	0.05
Deliver Message	R	1.00
7		
Diplomacy 1	VC	0.05
Diplomacy 10	VC	0.05
Diplomacy 2	U	0.25
Diplomacy 8	U	0.25
Diplomacy 9	C	0.10
Draktar	U	0.25
Druidic Grove	U	0.25
Dungeon Entrance	C	0.10
Dust Storm	R	1.00
Dwarf Cleric	R	1.50
8		
Dwarf Cleric	R	1.50
Dwarf Rogue	R	1.50
Dwarf Stronghold	C	0.10
Dwarf Warrior	R	1.50
Dwarf Wizard	R	1.50
Earthquake	U	0.25
Eclipse	R	1.00
Elf Cleric	R	1.50
Elf Warrior	R	1.50
9		
Elf Wizard	R	1.50
Elven Glade	R	1.00
Faerie	C	0.10
Festival	R	1.00
Find Lost Artifact	R	1.00
Fire Drake	C	0.25
Flail	U	0.25
Flee 1	C	0.10
Flee 10	U	0.25
10		
Flee 2	C	0.10
Flee 9	C	0.10
Flee 9	VC	0.05
Flesh Golem	U	0.25
Forrests	VC	0.05
Full Moon	U	0.25
Giant Spider	R	1.00
Gloves of The Rogue	U	0.25
Gnasher	U	0.25
11		
Gnashru Daemon	VC	0.05
Goblin	R	1.00
Great Axe	U	0.50
Great Red Dragon	U	0.75
Greater Devil	C	0.10
Gregor's Dagger	R	1.00
Hall of Heroes	R	1.00
Hamlet	U	0.25
Hand Axe	C	0.10
12		
Heal Rune	U	0.25
Helm of Wit	R	1.00
Horn of Sounding	R	1.00
Human Cleric	R	1.50
Human Rogue	R	1.50
Initiative Rune	R	2.00
Invisibility Rune	R	2.00
Keep	C	0.10
13		
Ketric	R	1.00
Kings' Patrol	C	0.10
Krelites	U	0.25
Large Horde	U	0.25
Large Shield	C	0.10
Leather Armor	U	0.25
Left Angle	C	0.10
Lesser Elemental	R	2.00
Liche Lord	U	0.25
14		
Lizard Man	VC	0.05
Long Bow	C	0.10
Long Bow	R	1.00
Long Sword	U	0.25
Long Sword	U	0.25
Long Sword	R	1.00
Long Sword	R	1.00
Mace	C	0.10
Maelik Zar	U	0.25
Magic 2 Handed Sword	U	0.75
15		
Magic Arrow	R	2.00
Magic Brigandine	R	2.00
Magic Leather Armor	U	0.50
Magic Platemail	R	2.00
Magic Studded Leather	R	2.00
Malkazarr	R	1.00
Marauders	U	0.25
Medusa	U	0.50
Minotaur	C	0.25
16		
Missile Rune	R	1.50
Morning Star	R	1.00
Mountains	VC	0.05
Mud	U	0.25
Neanderthal	R	1.00
Ogre	C	0.25
Oil	C	0.10
Oil Lantern	C	0.10
Orc Raiders	U	0.25
17		
Pegasus	C	0.25
Plains	VC	0.05
Plate Armor	U	0.50
Platemail	C	0.10
Quicksand	U	0.25
Recover Stolen Items	U	0.25
Renewal	R	1.00
Rescue Maiden	R	1.00
Riding Horse	C	0.10
18		
Right Angle	C	0.10
Ring of Protection	U	0.50
Ring of Quicksilver	R	1.50
Ring of Strength	R	1.50
Rogue Equipment	C	0.10
Rolling Hills	VC	0.05
Shadow Warrior	C	0.10
Shantrel	R	1.00
Shield of Defense	R	2.00
19		
Short Bow	C	0.10
Short Bow	R	1.00
Short Sword	U	0.25
Short Sword	U	0.25
Slave Traders	C	0.10
Small Horde	R	1.00
Small Shield	C	0.10
Staff of Foresite	U	0.25
Straight	C	0.10
20		
Studded Leather	R	1.00
Summer Solstice	R	1.00
Survival Gear	U	0.25
Swamp	VC	0.05
Swampling	VC	0.05
T-Section	U	0.25
Teleport Rune	R	1.00
Tomb Guardian	U	0.25
Torch	C	0.10
21		
Torrential Downpour	R	1.00
Torture Chamber	U	0.25
Town	C	0.10
Town Under Siege	R	1.00
Traveling Merchant	C	0.10
Troll	VC	0.05
Village	U	0.25
Vorac	R	1.00
Wagon	C	0.10
22		
Warhammer	U	0.25
Warhorse	U	0.25
Warlord Stronghold	U	0.25
Wererat	U	0.25
Werewolf	R	2.00
Wizard Lord Keep	C	0.10
Wizard Tower	R	1.00
Zaric	R	1.00
Zombie	C	0.10
23		
Zombie Warrior	U	0.25

Sailor Moon

Dart Flipcards • First set, *Premiere*, released **July 2000**

160 cards in set

Concept	●●●●○
Gameplay	●●●○○
Card art	●●●●●○
Player pool	●●●○○

- Starter decks contain 60 cards; starter displays contain 6 starters
- Booster packs contain 11 cards; booster displays contain 36 boosters

An early entry in the post-*Pokémon* anime CCG boom, **Sailor Moon** is based on the popular Japanese animated series about five girls who transform into the Sailor Scouts to battle evil. The game owes many of its mechanics to the *Sailor Moon* role-playing game published by Guardians of Order, which consulted on the project. The *Sailor Moon* anime series contains five blocks of episodes, of which the CCG covers the first two.

Some of the basics of *Sailor Moon* resemble *Pokémon*. Each player starts with one Sailor Scout/Knight and one monster card in play. The player can add energy cards to a Sailor Scout or monster to enable more potent attacks. To win, a player must destroy enough victory points' worth of an opponent's monsters to meet the agreed-upon Level (4, 5, or 6, depending on game length). The Scouts/Knights start at Level 1 but can be replaced by higher-level versions of the same character, with an increase in power and health.

There are some major differences, though. The biggest is that a player cannot attack another player's Scout/Knight. A player can choose to attack monsters, who attack back, but the monsters never initiate combat. Also, the game uses Jan-Ken-Pon, essentially rock-paper-scissors, as a randomizer. Several powers and abilities call for the player to win one or more contests to activate the effect. — **Michael Greenholdt**

Set (160 cards)		190.00
Starter Display Box		80.00
Booster Display Box		95.00
Two-player Starter		10.00
Starter Deck		10.00
Booster Pack		3.00

*You will need **18** nine-pocket pages to store this set. (9 doubled up)*

#	Card name	Type	Rar	Price
140	Alan	Vlln	R	4.00
25	Amphibia	Mon	C	0.25
84	Andrew Furuhata	Per	U	0.60
33	Animal Instinct	Mon	C	0.25
141	Ann	Vlln	R	4.00
82	Artemis	Per	U	0.80
144	Avery	Vlln	R	4.00
31	Avocado	Mon	C	0.25
61	Baamu	Mon	U	0.60
53	Baby-Sitting	Evnt	C	0.25
15	Bakene	Mon	C	0.25
143	Bertie	Vlln	R	4.00
7	Black Widow	Mon	C	0.25
11	Bobo the Vulture	Mon	C	0.25
1	Body Power	Pwr	C	0.25
12	Bumboo	Mon	C	0.25
89	Cardian Flute	Item	U	0.60
142	Catzi	Vlln	R	3.50
40	Chad Kumada	Per	C	0.25
57	Combat Training	Evnt	C	0.25
94	Confusion	Evnt	U	0.60
43	Costume	Item	C	0.25
54	Cram School	Evnt	C	0.25
49	Damage Transfer	Evnt	C	0.25
92	Dark Crystal Wedge	Item	U	0.60
91	Dark Fruit	Item	U	0.60
66	Derela/Kyameran	Mon	U	0.60

SAILOR MOON

SAILOR MOON — SAILOR SCOUT — LEVEL 3 — 90 HEALTH

	Moon Tiara Magic	30
	Moon Healing Activation	40
	Cosmic Moon Power	50
	Moon Scepter Elimination	90

Favorite color: white Favorite Food: ice cream
Strengths: crying, loyalty Weaknesses: lateness, school

132 / 160

RARITY KEY **VC** = Very Common **C** = Common **U** = Uncommon **R** = Rare **VR** = Very Rare **F** = Foil card **X** = Fixed/standard in all decks

# Card name	Type	Rar	Price
4			
☐ 51 Detention	Evnt	C	0.25
☐ 96 Discovery!	Evnt	U	0.80
☐ 70 Doom & Gloom Girls	Mon	U	0.60
☐ 34 Doom & Gloom Guys	Mon	C	0.25
☐ 35 Dragon/Timewarp Genie	Mon	C	0.25
☐ 147 Emerald	VIln	R	3.50
☐ 139 Evil Prince Darien	VIln	R	5.00
☐ 60 Fail a Test	Evnt	C	0.25
☐ 21 Faraion	Mon	C	0.25
5			
☐ 93 FM No.10	Evnt	U	0.60
☐ 28 Four Face	Mon	C	0.25
☐ 18 Fro/Blizzard	Mon	C	0.25
☐ 29 Frosty/Hypnotica	Mon	C	0.25
☐ 10 Game Machine Man	Mon	C	0.25
☐ 50 Good Night's Rest	Evnt	C	0.25
☐ 39 Grandpa Hino	Per	C	0.25
☐ 101 Green Yoma from London	Evnt	U	0.60
☐ 32 Grim Man	Mon	C	0.25
6			
☐ 102 Hidden	Evnt	U	0.60
☐ 62 Iguaala	Mon	U	0.60
☐ 124 Imperium Silver Crystal	Item	R	4.00
☐ 80 Injector	Mon	U	0.60
☐ 75 Insectia	Mon	U	0.60
☐ 119 Jedite	VIln	U	1.00
☐ 76 Jellax/Droido	Mon	U	0.60
☐ 67 Jumo	Mon	U	0.60
☐ 47 Knight Armor	Item	C	0.25
7			
☐ 5 Kyurene/Garoben	Mon	C	0.25
☐ 8 Leo the Lion	Mon	C	0.25
☐ 131 Lose Powers	Evnt	R	3.10
☐ 46 Love Letter	Item	C	0.25
☐ 36 Luna	Per	C	0.25
☐ 90 Luna Ball	Item	U	0.80
☐ 87 Luna Pen	Item	U	1.00
☐ 42 Lunch!	Item	C	0.25

# Card name	Type	Rar	Price
8			
☐ 138 Malachite	VIln	R	5.00
☐ 78 Marzipan	Mon	U	0.60
☐ 38 Melvin Gurio	Per	C	0.25
☐ 98 Memories of the Past	Evnt	U	0.80
☐ 2 Mind Power	Pwr	C	0.25
☐ 44 Mini-Computer & VR Goggles	Item	C	0.25
☐ 73 Minotaur	Mon	U	0.60
☐ 81 Mistrust	Mon	U	0.60
☐ 16 Mitsuaami	Mon	C	0.25
☐ 37 Molly Osaka	Per	C	0.25
9			
☐ 123 Moon Star Locket	Item	R	3.00
☐ 112 Moonlight Knight: Level 1	Kngt	U	0.60
☐ 26 Mophead	Mon	C	0.25
☐ 103 More Dark Power	Evnt	U	0.80
☐ 4 Morga/Kigaan	Mon	C	0.25
☐ 83 Ms. Haruna	Per	U	0.60
☐ 20 Mud Minion Horde	Mon	C	0.25
☐ 22 Nacrid	Mon	C	0.25
☐ 126 Negamoon Bomb	Item	R	3.10
10			
☐ 105 Negative Energy Shield	Evnt	U	0.80
☐ 88 Negaverse Crystal	Item	U	0.60
☐ 48 Negaverse Sword	Item	C	0.25
☐ 137 Nephlite	VIln	R	5.00
☐ 69 Ninjana	Mon	U	0.60
☐ 104 Not So Tough	Evnt	U	0.60
☐ 45 Ofuda Scroll	Item	C	0.25
☐ 127 On the Ball	Evnt	R	4.00
☐ 129 Overpowering Attack	Evnt	R	4.00
11			
☐ 19 Papion	Mon	C	0.25
☐ 65 Petasos/Gemini Warriors	Mon	U	0.60
☐ 27 Pierrot	Mon	C	0.25
☐ 122 Pocket Communicator	Item	R	3.00
☐ 17 Polite Society	Mon	C	0.25

# Card name	Type	Rar	Price
☐ 68 Pox	Mon	U	0.60
☐ 113 Prince Darien: Level 1	Kngt	U	0.60
☐ 149 Prince Diamond	VIln	R	4.50
☐ 145 Prizma	VIln	R	3.50
12			
☐ 158 Queen Beryl	VIln	F	17.25
☐ 23 Racy	Mon	C	0.25
☐ 63 Ramwoir/Dream Dolly	Mon	U	0.60
☐ 56 Rats!	Evnt	C	0.25
☐ 97 Redistribute Power	Evnt	U	0.60
☐ 79 Regalia	Mon	U	0.60
☐ 100 Regeneration	Evnt	U	0.60
☐ 99 Resignation	Evnt	U	0.80
☐ 77 Rhonda	Mon	U	0.60
13			
☐ 121 Rini	Per	R	4.00
☐ 146 Rubeus	VIln	R	3.50
☐ 58 Run Away!	Evnt	C	0.25
☐ 109 Sailor Jupiter: Level 1	Sail	U	1.00
☐ 117 Sailor Jupiter: Level 2	Sail	U	1.00
☐ 135 Sailor Jupiter: Level 3	Sail	R	5.00
☐ 155 Sailor Jupiter: Level 4	Sail	F	14.50
☐ 108 Sailor Mars: Level 1	Sail	U	1.00
☐ 116 Sailor Mars: Level 2	Sail	U	1.00
14			
☐ 134 Sailor Mars: Level 3	Sail	R	6.00
☐ 154 Sailor Mars: Level 4	Sail	F	14.50
☐ 107 Sailor Mercury: Level 1	Sail	U	1.00
☐ 115 Sailor Mercury: Level 2	Sail	U	1.00
☐ 133 Sailor Mercury: Level 3	Sail	R	5.00
☐ 153 Sailor Mercury: Level 4	Sail	F	14.50
☐ 106 Sailor Moon: Level 1	Sail	U	1.00
☐ 114 Sailor Moon: Level 2	Sail	U	1.00

# Card name	Type	Rar	Price
☐ 132 Sailor Moon: Level 3	Sail	R	7.00
15			
☐ 152 Sailor Moon: Level 4	Sail	F	20.00
☐ 151 Sailor Pluto	Evnt	F	20.00
☐ 110 Sailor Venus: Level 1	Sail	U	1.00
☐ 118 Sailor Venus: Level 2	Sail	U	1.00
☐ 136 Sailor Venus: Level 3	Sail	R	5.00
☐ 156 Sailor Venus: Level 4	Sail	F	14.50
☐ 86 Sammy Tsukino	Per	U	0.60
☐ 148 Sapphire	VIln	R	4.30
☐ 130 Self-Sacrifice	Evnt	R	3.10
16			
☐ 85 Serena's Parents	Per	U	0.60
☐ 74 Skulker	Mon	U	0.60
☐ 3 Soul Power	Pwr	C	0.25
☐ 125 Spaceship	Item	R	3.10
☐ 52 Split Attack	Evnt	C	0.25
☐ 128 Strength of the Fallen	Evnt	R	4.00
☐ 55 Taunt	Evnt	C	0.25
☐ 14 Techniclon	Mon	C	0.25
☐ 95 Temple Blessing	Evnt	U	0.60
17			
☐ 64 Tensie/Akan	Mon	U	0.60
☐ 160 The Negaforce	VIln	F	16.50
☐ 41 The Tree of Life	Per	C	0.25
☐ 30 Thunderclap	Mon	C	0.25
☐ 6 Titus	Mon	C	0.25
☐ 111 Tuxedo Mask: Level 1	Kngt	U	1.00
☐ 157 Tuxedo Mask: Level 2	Kngt	F	17.75
☐ 72 Vampeal	Mon	U	0.60
☐ 13 Veena/Misha & Janelle	Mon	C	0.25
18			
☐ 24 Vulturos	Mon	C	0.25
☐ 71 Water Sprite	Mon	U	0.60
☐ 59 What's That?	Evnt	C	0.25
☐ 150 Wicked Lady	VIln	R	5.00
☐ 159 Wiseman	VIln	F	15.50
☐ 9 Yasha/Plant Sisters	Mon	C	0.25
☐ 120 Zoycite	VIln	U	0.80

Scooby-Doo!

Journeyman Press • Released **August 2000**

219 cards in set

- Starter decks contain 120 cards; starter displays contain 12 starters
- Booster packs contain 12 cards; booster displays contain 36 boosters

In what is essentially a re-tooled version of the **X-Files** CCG produced years before by the same design team, the **Scooby-Doo!** Expandable Card Game allows players to pose as the cowardly mutt, Shaggy, and the rest of the gang in solving mysteries.

Players take turns investigating locations and finding clues, while opponents play cards to block. Each player gets one copy of each of the five Mystery Inc. members, each of which has a once-per-game special ability. In addition, 15 Clue cards, which show title shot screens of different episodes, are used to solve a mystery.

Scooby-Doo! poses a number of collecting challenges, but a complete set should be achievable with some work. First, there are foil chase cards of the Mystery Inc. crew, about two per booster box. Then, there are the pop-up versions of these five characters. Each starter comes with one at random, so you either have to trade for the ones you need or just keep buying starters. They may also fall as inserts in packs.

Art is taken directly from Hanna-Barbara footage, and the cards are easy to read. It's a bit long for an entry-level game, falling into the zone between quick and dirty CCGs, like **Pez**, and great tactical CCGs, like **Legend of the Five Rings**. — *Richard Weld*

Concept	●●●○○
Gameplay	●●●○○
Card art	●●●○○
Player pool	●●○○○

Play this card during your Villain phase to use Scooby-Doo as a +2 Fright Level Monster for the rest of the turn. Return Scooby-Doo to his original Location at the end of the turn.

You will need **25** nine-pocket pages to store this set. (13 doubled up)

Set (219 cards)	185.00
Starter Display Box	85.00
Booster Display Box	85.00
Starter Deck	9.50
Booster Pack	3.00

Card name	Type	Rarity	Price
1			
☐ 2000 Year-Old Mummy	Mnst	R	7.00
☐ A Clue for Scooby-Doo	Clue	X	0.60
☐ A Gaggle of Galloping Ghosts	Clue	X	0.60
☐ A Night of Fright is No Delight	Clue	X	0.60
☐ A. Fong, Oriental Art Dealer	Frnd	U	0.80

RARITY KEY C = Common U = Uncommon R = Rare VR = Very Rare UR = Ultra Rare F = Foil card X = Fixed/standard in all decks

Card name	Type	Rarity	Price
"After all, what could be in the pantry?"	Evnt	C	0.25
Alligator	Mnst	C	0.25
Automatic Pogo Stick	Item	C	0.25
"Back from his watery grave."	Evnt	U	0.80
Bank Guard	Frnd	C	0.25
Bat	Mnst	C	0.25
Bedlam in the Big Top	Clue	X	0.60
Biplane	Item	U	0.80
Biplane Crash	Evnt	C	0.25
Black Knight	Mnst	C	0.25
Brave Shaggy	Evnt	U	0.80
Buffet Table at 3:00	Evnt	R	3.50
Captain Cutler's Seaweed-Covered Ghost	Mnst	U	0.80
Chandelier	Item	U	0.80
Chicken Coop	Loc	C	0.25
Chinese Zombies	Mnst	C	0.25
Clown's Rubber Ladder	Item	U	0.80
"C'mon you scaredy cats!"	Evnt	C	0.25
Costume Tent	Loc	C	0.25
"Count me out!"	Evnt	R	3.50
Crystal Ball	Item	C	0.25
Curio Shop	Loc	C	0.25
Curio Shop Proprietor	Frnd	C	0.25
Daphne	Char	X	2.10
Dead End	Item	C	0.25
Decoy for a Dognapper	Clue	X	0.60
Dining Room	Evnt	C	0.25
Dodgem Car	Item	U	0.80
Dognapper	Mnst	R	7.00
"Don't ever let us do that again."	Evnt	R	3.50
"Don't look now but company's coming"	Evnt	C	0.25
Dracula	Mnst	C	0.25
Drawbridge	Item	U	0.80
Dungeon	Loc	U	0.80
Dynamite	Item	R	3.50
Ebenezer Sharpe	Frnd	C	0.25
Egg Beater	Item	C	0.25
Elephant	Item	C	0.25
Evil Teddy Bear	Item	C	0.25
Eyes in the Cave	Evnt	C	0.25
Finding a Bone	Evnt	C	0.25
"First get rid of that ridiculous paper hat."	Evnt	U	0.80
Floor Grate	Item	C	0.25
Flying Monster	Evnt	R	3.50
Fortune Teller	Frnd	U	0.80
Foul Play in Funland	Clue	X	0.60
Franken Castle	Loc	C	0.25
Frankenstein's Monster	Mnst	C	0.25
Fred	Char	X	2.10
"Freddy, where are you?"	Evnt	C	0.25
Fu Leng Chi	Frnd	U	0.80
Funhouse Mirror	Item	U	0.80
Funland	Loc	C	0.25
Ghost Clown	Mnst	R	7.00
Ghost of Zhen Tuo	Mnst	U	0.80
Ghost Ship	Loc	C	0.25
Ghost Soup	Evnt	U	0.80
Ghost Sword	Item	C	0.25
Giant Electromagnet	Item	R	3.50
Giant Steamer Trunk	Item	U	0.80
Girl Dog Puppet	Item	U	0.80
"Give me that you mutt!"	Evnt	R	3.50
Go Away Ghost Ship	Clue	X	0.60
Graveyard of Ships	Loc	C	0.25
Gypsy Wagon	Loc	C	0.25
"Ha-Ha! Rou rissed re!"	Evnt	U	0.80
Hall of Mirrors	Loc	C	0.25
Handkerchief	Item	C	0.25
Haunted House Hang-Up	Clue	X	0.60
Hay Baler	Evnt	C	0.25
Hermit of the Hill cave	Loc	U	0.80
"He's fast!"	Evnt	R	3.50
"He's taking a ride on the ferris wheel."	Evnt	U	0.80
"Hey Shaggy, I see you found us!"	Evnt	C	0.25
Hollowed-Out Log	Item	U	0.80
Horse and Buggy	Item	C	0.25
Hot Dog Stand	Evnt	C	0.25
"I forgot Scooby!"	Evnt	R	3.50
"I have a hunch."	Evnt	U	0.80
"I just lost my appetite."	Evnt	C	0.25
"I ron't ree ranything."	Evnt	R	3.50
"I'll make him pay for what he did to my hair."	Evnt	C	0.25
"I'll Save you Scooby!"	Evnt	C	0.25
"It didn't stop him!"	Evnt	C	0.25
"It's only a power failure."	Evnt	U	0.80
"It's sure dark out."	Evnt	R	3.50
"I've seen this before."	Evnt	R	3.50
Jack in the Box	Item	C	0.25
Jeepers It's the Creeper	Clue	X	0.60
Jeweler's Glasses	Item	U	0.80
Johnny the Puppet	Item	C	0.25
Ladder	Item	C	0.25
Lasso	Item	R	3.50
Laundry	Loc	U	0.80
"Leave it to Daphne to pick the wrong door."	Evnt	R	3.50
"Let's Keep Watch From Here."	Evnt	R	3.50
"Let's vote on it, mystery or pizza pie."	Evnt	C	0.25
Lighthouse	Loc	U	0.80
"Like, I don't think he believes us!"	Evnt	R	3.50
Liverwurst	Item	C	0.25
Log Chute	Item	C	0.25
Long Twisting Stairs	Item	C	0.25
Love Boat	Item	C	0.25
Mad Scientist Rumpus Room	Loc	C	0.25
"Man, this is like dark in this tunnel."	Evnt	R	3.50
"Man's best friend is a mouse."	Evnt	R	3.50
Mask of Zhen Tuo	Item	R	3.50
Max the Midget	Frnd	C	0.25
Mine Your Own Business	Clue	X	0.60
Miner 49'er	Mnst	C	0.25
Monkeys Are Funny	Evnt	R	3.50
Monster Decoy	Item	C	0.25
Mr. Barnstorm	Frnd	R	4.00
Mr. C.L. Magnus	Frnd	C	0.25
Mr. Carswell	Frnd	U	0.80
Mr. Greenway	Frnd	C	0.25
Mr. Jenkins	Frnd	C	0.25
Mr. Leech	Frnd	C	0.25
Mr. Wickles	Frnd	C	0.25
Mrs. Cutler	Frnd	C	0.25
Museum	Loc	C	0.25
Museum Rear Entrance	Loc	U	0.80
Mystery Machine	Item	R	3.50
Mystery Mask Mix-Up	Clue	X	0.60
No Rhent!?!	Evnt	U	0.80
Open the Shade	Evnt	C	0.25
Paper Pirate Hat	Item	U	0.80
Phone Booth	Item	R	3.50
Pile of Dead Fish	Item	U	0.80
Plunger Arrows	Item	C	0.25
Pop	Frnd	C	0.25
Prompter's Box	Item	C	0.25
Pulling the Shade	Evnt	C	0.25
Red Beard's Cabin	Loc	U	0.80
Relic Room	Loc	C	0.25
Rope and Plank Bridge	Item	C	0.25
Samson the Strongman	Frnd	C	0.25
Sarah Jenkins	Frnd	R	4.00
Saw Mill	Loc	C	0.25
Scooby-Doo	Char	X	2.10
"Scooby-Doo and a mummy, too"	Clue	X	0.60
Scooby-Doo Lays an Egg	Evnt	U	0.80
"Scooby-Doo says the coast is clear."	Evnt	R	3.50
"Scooby Snacks, boxes of 'em!"	Evnt	U	0.80
Secret Cove	Loc	C	0.25
Shadow Phantom	Mnst	C	0.25
Shaggy	Char	X	2.10
"Shaggy, do you have my extra glasses?"	Evnt	C	0.25
"Shaggy is a ghost!"	Evnt	R	3.50
"Show him the clue Shaggy."	Evnt	R	3.50
Skeleton Head	Item	C	0.25
Snow Ghost	Mnst	U	0.80
"So they think they've escaped me."	Evnt	R	3.50
"Soap, I hardly use it myself."	Evnt	C	0.25
Speed Boat	Item	C	0.25
Stage	Loc	C	0.25
"Stop it! Stop it! I can't stand it!"	Evnt	R	3.50
Strange Cave	Loc	C	0.25
Suit of Armor	Item	C	0.25
Sunken Ship	Loc	C	0.25
Surfboard	Item	C	0.25
Tapestry	Item	C	0.25
Temple in the Hills	Loc	C	0.25
"That's just how I planned it."	Evnt	R	3.50
That's Snow Ghost	Clue	X	0.60
The Backstage Rage	Clue	X	0.60
The Barn	Loc	C	0.25
The Big Top	Loc	C	0.25
The Butler	Frnd	U	0.80
The Creeper	Mnst	U	0.80
The Crypt	Loc	U	0.80
The Flying Mystery Machine	Evnt	R	3.50
The Library	Evnt	C	0.25
"The lights are going off all over."	Evnt	R	3.50
The Menagerie	Loc	U	0.80
The Mystery Machine Breaks Down	Evnt	U	0.80
The Plank	Item	R	3.50
Theater	Loc	C	0.25
"There goes our only clue."	Evnt	R	3.50
"There were two of me?"	Evnt	R	3.50
"There's no one else on this island."	Evnt	C	0.25
"There's nothing to be afraid of."	Evnt	U	0.80
"This is the first time I've wanted to leave Funland."	Evnt	R	3.50
"This is your last warning."	Evnt	R	3.50
"Time for a little ventriloquism."	Evnt	U	0.80
Torture Chamber	Loc	C	0.25
Train Coming	Evnt	R	3.50
Tubs of Dry Ice	Item	C	0.25
Tunnel of Love	Loc	U	0.80
"Uh oh, We lost Shaggy!"	Evnt	R	3.50
Underwater Passage	Item	C	0.25
Velma	Char	X	2.10
Velma Loses Her Glasses	Evnt	R	3.50
Violin-Case Room	Loc	U	0.80
"Watch the pretty coin of gold"	Evnt	R	3.50
"We can't go back, Scooby."	Evnt	C	0.25
"We can't go home now."	Evnt	U	0.80
"We didn't get a chance to look for clues."	Evnt	R	3.50
We Got 'Em!	Evnt	C	0.25
"We got Shaggy and Scooby."	Evnt	U	0.80
"We got ask you the same question."	Evnt	R	3.50
"Well, it got away."	Evnt	U	0.80
"We've been cut in half"	Evnt	R	3.50
What a Night for a Knight	Clue	X	0.60
"What you can't see can't hurt you."	Evnt	R	3.50
When Stuffed Animals Attack	Evnt	R	3.50
"Witchcraft made easy"	Item	C	0.25
Wolf's End Lodge	Loc	C	0.25
Wolfman	Mnst	C	0.25
Yacht	Item	C	0.25
"You can run the fastest if he's there."	Evnt	R	3.50
"You know the signal, don't you Scoob?"	Evnt	R	3.50
"You'd make a good monster, Scoob!"	Evnt	C	0.25
"Yum, yum, yum and a Liverwurst Ala-Mode."	Evnt	R	3.50

RARITY KEY C = Common U = Uncommon R = Rare VR = Very Rare UR = Ultra Rare F = Foil card X = Fixed/standard in all decks

Shadowfist

Daedalus • First set, *Limited*, released **June 1995**

323 cards in set • **IDENTIFIER: Foil symbol appears at upper right of face;** © **1995**

- Starter decks contain 60 cards; starter displays contain 12 starters
- Booster packs contain 12 cards; booster displays contain 36 boosters

Based on Hong Kong action movies, ***Shadowfist*** pits five factions from different times against each other. The Dragons, mostly from our time, fight to preserve the *status quo*. The Ascended, animals given human form, control the present-day world. The Guiding Hand, 19th century martial artists, seek to impose order. The Eaters of the Lotus are sorcerers and demons from ancient China. The Architects of the Flesh are a totalitarian society from the future who have melded magic and science.

The mechanics reflect the frenetic pace of the films. Each player may play one Feng Shui site per turn, with the victory going to the first player to play six sites. The catch is that a player can *never* play the sixth site; he must take it from an opponent. Since victory is instantaneous, the game is a constant back and forth of attacks. The sites are also the primary source of a player's resources to pay for cards, including new sites.

Unlike many CCGs, characters may be attacked, just as sites can. Also, aside from running an opponent out of cards, there is no way to make him lose. If you destroy or capture all an opponent's sites, he can simply play another site. Because of this, passive strategies do not fare well in *Shadowfist*. Since tapped characters can still defend sites, there is usually no reason not to attack in a two-player game.

Like its namesake's son, Daedalus fell from the gaming sky, leaving Z-Man Games to resurrect *Shadowfist* in 2000. — ***Michael Greenholdt***

Inner Sanctum

1 | 11

Feng Shui Site
Once Inner Sanctum has been revealed, you may not place new feng shui sites into its column. Too great a chi flow can be as hazardous as too little.

Artwork © 1995
Jeff Menges

Shadowfist • Standard

Daedalus • Released **October 1995**

323 cards in set • **IDENTIFIER: No foil symbol; card is** © **1995**

Standard is identical to ***Limited*** but for the planned exclusion of eight unique characters from Standard. *Planned*, because a few (marked below with asterisks) were accidentally printed and have since become sought-after cards. Dropping characters may have been the start of a move to a storyline-driven game à la ***Legend of the Five Rings***.

Concept	●●●●○		
Gameplay	●●●●○		
Card art	●●●●○		
Player pool	●●●○○		

LIMITED

Set (323 cards)	155.00
Starter Display Box	43.00
Booster Display Box	48.00
Starter Deck	9.00
Booster Pack	2.50

You will need **36** *nine-pocket pages to store this set. (18 doubled up)*

STANDARD

Set (323 cards)	127.50
Starter Display Box	36.50
Booster Display Box	41.50
Starter Deck	7.50
Booster Pack	2.30

You will need **36** *nine-pocket pages to store this set. (18 doubled up)*

LIMITED	Card name	Rarity	STANDARD
☐ 0.70	$10,000 Man	U	0.40 ☐
☐ 0.20	Abominable Lab	C	0.15 ☐
☐ 0.20	Abominable Wave	C	0.15 ☐
☐ 4.00	Abysmal Daughter	R	4.60 ☐
☐ 0.20	Abysmal Horror	C	0.15 ☐
☐ 0.80	Abysmal Spirit	U	0.50 ☐
☐ 11.75	Adrienne Hart *	R/UR	11.75 ☐
☐ 0.50	Alabaster Javelin	U	0.40 ☐
☐ 0.20	Alchemist's Lair	C	0.15 ☐
☐ 0.10	Alpha Beast	VC	0.05 ☐
☐ 0.50	Amulet of the Turtle	U	0.40 ☐
☐ 0.05	Ancestral Tomb	VC	0.05 ☐
☐ 0.20	Ancient Grove	C	0.15 ☐
☐ 0.05	Ancient Temple	VC	0.05 ☐
☐ 1.00	Arcanotechnician	U	0.60 ☐
☐ 0.50	Arcanowave Pulse	U	0.40 ☐
☐ 0.80	Arcanowave Reinforcer	U	0.50 ☐
☐ 0.80	Arcanowave Researcher	U	0.40 ☐
☐ 0.25	Armored in Life	C	0.30 ☐
☐ 0.50	Array of Stunts	U	0.40 ☐
☐ 4.00	Assassins in Love	R	4.10 ☐
☐ 0.80	Attack Helicopter	U	0.50 ☐

LIMITED	Card name	Rarity	STANDARD
☐ 0.05	Auspicious Termites	VC	0.05 ☐
☐ 0.05	Average Joe	VC	0.05 ☐
☐ 0.15	Back for Seconds	C	0.15 ☐
☐ 0.50	Bag Full of Guns	U	0.50 ☐
☐ 4.00	Banish	R	4.90 ☐
☐ 3.50	Baptism of Fire	R	2.60 ☐
☐ 4.50	Battlechimp Potemkin	R	3.90 ☐
☐ 0.20	Beneficial Realignment	C	0.15 ☐
☐ 5.00	Big Brother Tsien	R	4.40 ☐
☐ 0.80	Big Bruiser	U	0.40 ☐
☐ 0.70	Bite of the Jellyfish	U	0.40 ☐
☐ 1.00	Blade Palm	U	0.60 ☐
☐ 0.05	Blessed Orchard	VC	0.05 ☐
☐ 0.15	Booby Trap	C	0.15 ☐
☐ 3.50	Brain Bug EQ3200	R	2.60 ☐
☐ 0.50	Brain Eater	U	0.40 ☐
☐ 4.00	Bull Market	R	4.10 ☐
☐ 0.20	Buro Assassin	C	0.15 ☐
☐ 0.50	Buro Official	U	0.40 ☐
☐ 0.20	Cabinet Minister	C	0.15 ☐
☐ 4.00	Capoeira Master	R	3.90 ☐
☐ 0.05	Cave Network	VC	0.05 ☐
☐ 0.50	Cellular Reinvigoration	U	0.40 ☐
☐ 0.80	Chains of Bone	U	0.40 ☐
☐ 0.50	Charmed Life	U	0.40 ☐
☐ 5.00	Chin Ken	R	2.90 ☐
☐ 0.20	Chinese Doctor	C	0.30 ☐
☐ 0.50	Chromosome Screamer	U	0.40 ☐
☐ 0.80	Church Official	U	0.40 ☐
☐ 3.00	City Square	R	2.90 ☐
☐ 0.50	Claw of the Tiger	U	0.40 ☐
☐ 0.20	Code Red	C	0.15 ☐
☐ 1.00	Combat Aircar	U	0.50 ☐
☐ 0.50	Confucian Sage	U	0.40 ☐
☐ 0.20	Confucian Stability	C	0.15 ☐
☐ 0.70	Contract of the Fox	U	0.40 ☐
☐ 0.20	Covert Operation	C	0.15 ☐
☐ 0.70	Cry of the Forgotten Ancestor	U	0.40 ☐

LIMITED	Card name	Rarity	STANDARD
☐ 0.80	Curtain of Fullness	U	0.40 ☐
☐ 0.20	Dance of the Centipede	C	0.15 ☐
☐ 4.00	Dangerous Experiment	R	2.90 ☐
☐ 0.20	Dawn of the Righteous	C	0.15 ☐
☐ 5.00	Death Touch	R	3.10 ☐
☐ 0.20	Deathtrap	C	0.15 ☐
☐ 5.00	Desdemona Deathangel	R	4.10 ☐
☐ 0.50	Difficulty at the Beginning	U	0.40 ☐
☐ 0.50	Dim Mak	U	0.40 ☐
☐ 0.50	Disintegrator Ray	U	0.40 ☐
☐ 0.20	DNA Mage	C	0.30 ☐
☐ 5.00	Dr. April Mucosa	R	4.60 ☐
☐ 7.00	Draco	R	6.40 ☐
☐ 0.50	Dragon Adept	U	0.50 ☐
☐ 0.20	Dragon Fighter	C	0.15 ☐
☐ 5.00	Dragon Mountain	R	3.90 ☐
☐ 3.00	Drug Lab	R	3.60 ☐
☐ 0.20	Dump Warrior	C	0.15 ☐
☐ 0.20	Edge Warrior	C	0.15 ☐
☐ 4.00	Elderly Monk	R	3.90 ☐
☐ 0.10	Eunuch Underling	VC	0.05 ☐
☐ 0.10	Everyday Hero	VC	0.05 ☐
☐ 6.00	Evil Twin	R	4.60 ☐
☐ 0.20	Expendable Unit	C	0.15 ☐
☐ 0.80	Explosives	U	0.60 ☐
☐ 0.20	Faked Death	C	0.15 ☐
☐ 0.20	Family Estate	C	0.15 ☐
☐ 0.05	Family Home	VC	0.05 ☐
☐ 0.05	Family Restaurant	VC	0.05 ☐
☐ 5.00	Feast of Souls	R	3.10 ☐
☐ 0.20	Final Brawl	C	0.30 ☐
☐ 0.80	Fire in the Lake	U	0.50 ☐
☐ 0.80	Fist of the Bear	U	0.40 ☐
☐ 4.00	Fists of Legend	R	4.40 ☐
☐ 5.00	Floating Fortress	R	4.10 ☐
☐ 0.80	Flood on the Mountain	U	0.50 ☐
☐ 3.50	Flying Guillotine	U	2.60 ☐
☐ 6.00	Fong Sai Yuk	R	4.10 ☐

RARITY KEY VC = Very Common C = Common U = Uncommon R = Rare UR = Ultra Rare F = Foil card X = Fixed/standard in all

LIMITED	Card name	Rarity	STANDARD
0.80	Fortune of the Turtle	U	0.40
4.00	Fox Pass	R	4.10
0.10	Friends of the Dragon	VC	0.05
0.80	Fusion Rifle	U	0.40
1.00	Fusion Tank	U	0.60
0.20	Gadgeteer	C	0.15
7.00	Gao Zhang	R	6.40
0.20	Gardener	C	0.15
4.50	Ghostly Seducer	R	3.10
0.80	Gnarled Horror	U	0.50
0.80	Gnarled Marauder	U	0.50
0.10	Golden Candle Society	VC	0.05
0.15	Golden Comeback	C	0.30
0.50	Green Monk	U	0.40
0.80	Grenade Launcher	U	0.50
0.05	Grove of Willows	VC	0.05
0.20	Gruff Lieutenant	C	0.15
0.05	Hallowed Earth	VC	0.05
0.20	Hands Without Shadow	C	0.15
0.20	Havoc Suit	C	0.15
0.20	Healing Earth	C	0.15
0.20	Helix Chewer	C	0.15
0.20	Helix Rethread	C	0.15
0.80	Heroic Conversion	U	0.60
0.80	Hill of the Turtle	U	0.40
7.00	Homo Omega	R	6.40
0.20	Hopping Vampire	C	0.15
0.80	Hostile Takeover	U	0.40
0.20	House on the Hill	C	0.15
4.00	I Ching	R	2.60
13.50	Iala Mané *	R/UR	11.75
0.20	Ice Warriors	C	0.15
0.30	Illusory Bridge	C	0.15
4.00	Imperial Boon	R	3.60
1.30	Imperial Guard	U	0.40
0.30	Imprisoned	C	0.30
0.20	Inauspicious Reburial	C	0.15
0.20	Inexorable Corruption	C	0.15
0.50	Infernal Plague	U	0.40
0.25	Infernal Temple	C	0.15
0.10	Inner Sanctum	VC	0.05
0.10	Instrument of the Hand	VC	0.05
1.00	Into the Light	U	0.60
0.20	Iron and Silk	C	0.15
15.00	Jack Donovan *	R/UR	11.75
0.05	Jagged Cliffs	VC	0.05
6.00	Johann Bonengel	R	4.90
5.00	Johnny Tso	R	3.90
11.00	Jueding Shelun *	R/UR	9.60
5.00	Kan Li	R	4.40
6.00	Kar Fai	R	3.90
0.25	Killing Rain	C	0.30
7.00	King of the Thunder Pagoda	R	6.40
5.00	Kinoshita House	R	5.10
0.80	Kun Kan	U	0.50
1.00	Larcenous Mist	U	0.40
0.20	Last Outpost	C	0.15
3.50	Last Stand	R	4.40
0.05	Lily Pond	VC	0.05
0.10	Liquidators	VC	0.05
4.00	Luis Camacho	R	3.60
11.00	Mad Dog McCroun *	R/UR	10.50
0.20	Marked For Death	C	0.15
0.05	Marsh	VC	0.05
0.80	Masked Avenger	U	0.40
0.50	Maverick Cop	U	0.40
0.20	Midnight Whisperer	C	0.15
1.30	Might of the Elephant	U	0.60
0.50	Military Commandant	U	0.40
0.20	Mole Network	C	0.15
0.50	Monkey King	U	0.40
0.50	Monster Hunter	U	0.40
0.05	Mooks	VC	0.05
6.00	Mother of Corruption	R	6.40
0.20	Motorcycle	C	0.15
0.05	Mountain Retreat	VC	0.05
3.00	Mourning Tree	R	4.10
4.00	Mr. X	R	4.90
0.50	Muckraking Journalist	U	0.40
0.50	Mutoid	U	0.40
0.20	Mysterious Return	C	0.15
0.50	Mysterious Stranger	U	0.40
0.15	Natural Order	C	0.15
0.25	Nerve Gas	C	0.30
0.20	Netherworld Passageway	C	0.15
2.00	Neutron Bomb	U	0.60
4.00	Nine Cuts	R	4.10
10.25	Nirmal Yadav *	R/UR	9.80
0.80	"Now You've Made Us Mad"	U	0.40
0.80	Old Hermit	U	0.40
5.50	Old Master	R	2.40
1.00	One Hundred Names	U	0.40
0.80	Onslaught of the Turtle	U	0.40
0.20	Operation Killdeer	C	0.15
0.50	Orange Monk	U	0.40
0.25	Orbital Laser Strike	C	0.30
5.00	Oscar Balbuena	R	4.60
0.80	Paper Trail	U	0.40
3.00	Philippe Benoit	R	4.90
0.50	Poison Needles	U	0.40
0.50	Police State	U	0.40
3.00	Police Station	R	2.60
0.50	Political Lock	U	0.40
0.50	Positive Chi	U	0.40
4.00	Power of the Great	R	3.10
5.00	Probability Manipulator	R	4.10
0.80	Progress of the Mouse	U	0.50
5.00	Prototype X	R	3.90
0.80	Proving Ground	U	0.50
0.10	PubOrd Officer	VC	0.05
0.20	PubOrd Raid	C	0.15
0.20	PubOrd Sniper	C	0.15
0.10	PubOrd Squad	VC	0.05
4.00	Quai Li	R	3.10
6.00	Quan Lo	R	3.90
6.00	Queen of the Ice Pagoda	R	6.40
0.20	Really Big Gun	C	0.15
0.20	Realpolitik	C	0.15
5.00	Redeemed Assassin	R	4.60
1.00	Reinvigoration Process	U	0.50
0.50	Return to the Center	U	0.40
0.20	Righteous One	C	0.15
0.20	Rigorous Discipline	C	0.15
0.10	Ring Fighter	VC	0.05
5.00	Roar of the Beast	R	4.10
0.50	Robot Arm	U	0.40
0.80	Robust Feng Shui	U	0.60
0.05	Sacred Ground	VC	0.05
5.00	Sacred Heart Hospital	R	4.10
4.00	Safehouse	R	4.10
0.80	Salvage	U	0.60
0.50	Satellite Surveillance	U	0.40
0.80	Scroll of Incantation	U	0.50
4.00	Seal of the Wheel	R	4.10
4.00	Secret Headquarters	R	4.90
0.20	Secret Laboratory	C	0.15
0.20	Security	C	0.15
0.50	Seed of the New Flesh	U	0.50
0.20	Shadow Creeper	C	0.15
8.00	Shadowfist	R	5.40
0.10	Shadowy Horror	VC	0.05
0.35	Shadowy Mentor	C	0.30
5.00	Shamanistic Lieutenant	R	4.60
1.00	Shaolin Master	U	0.40
0.10	Shaolin Monk	VC	0.05
0.20	Shaolin Sanctuary	C	0.15
0.20	Shaolin Warrior	C	0.15
0.20	Shattering Fire	C	0.15
0.50	Shattering Jade	U	0.40
5.00	Shell of the Tortoise	R	3.10
5.00	Shifting Loyalties	R	4.90
0.50	Shifting Tao	U	0.40
6.00	Shih Ho Kuai	R	4.10
0.50	Silver Band	U	0.40
5.00	Silver Fist	R	4.40
0.10	Sinister Priest	VC	0.05
5.00	Snake Man	R	3.10
4.00	Soul Maze	R	4.10
1.00	Soul of the Shark	U	0.50
0.20	Speed Boat	C	0.15
0.80	Sphere of Defilement	U	0.50
3.50	Spirit Frenzy	R	3.60
0.20	Sports Car	C	0.15
0.70	State of Emergency	U	0.60
0.80	Sting of the Scorpion	U	0.40
0.05	Stone Garden	VC	0.05
4.00	Strike Force	R	4.10
0.10	Student of the Bear	VC	0.05
0.80	Subterfuge	U	0.40
2.50	Suicide Mission	R	2.40
8.80	Sun Chen *	R/UR	10.25
1.00	Super Soldier	U	0.40
0.20	Superior Technology	C	0.15
0.10	Swat Team	VC	0.05
0.20	Swiss Banker	C	0.15
0.20	Sword of Biting	C	0.15
0.10	Swordsman	VC	0.05
6.00	Tactical Team	R	4.10
5.00	Tatsuya Yanai	R	4.10
0.10	Test Subjects	VC	0.05
3.00	The Crucible	R	4.40
0.20	The Demon Within	C	0.15
1.00	The General	U	0.60
3.00	The Hanging Coffins	R	2.60
0.50	The Hungry	U	0.40
0.10	The Pledged	VC	0.05
1.00	The Rackets	U	0.40
1.00	The Reconstructed	U	0.40
4.00	The Red Lantern Tavern	R	4.10
5.00	The Unspoken Name	R	4.90
5.00	Theft of Fortune	R	3.10
14.25	Thing With 1000 Tongues*	R/UR	11.50
0.10	Thorns of the Lotus	VC	0.05
0.50	Throwing Star	U	0.40
0.20	Thunder Knights	C	0.15
0.50	Thunder on the Mountain	U	0.40
0.80	Thunder on Thunder	U	0.40
0.70	Tomb of the Beast	U	0.40
5.00	Tomb Spirit	R	3.90
0.80	Tooth of the Snake	U	0.40
0.20	Tortured Memories	C	0.15
0.30	Trade Center	C	0.30
0.20	Training Sequence	C	0.15
5.00	Tranquil Persuader	R	4.10
3.50	Turtle Beach	R	3.10
3.00	Ultimate Mastery	R	4.40
0.50	Undercover	U	0.40
0.70	Undercover Cop	U	0.40
0.80	Vampiric Touch	U	0.50
0.10	Vassals of the Lotus	VC	0.05
0.50	Veiling of the Light	U	0.40
0.20	Victory for the Underdog	C	0.15
0.80	Vivisector	U	0.60
4.00	Vladimir Kovalov	R	3.90
1.80	Walker of the Purple Twilight	U	0.50
0.20	Walking Corpses	C	0.15
3.00	Water Sword	R	4.40
4.00	Web of the Spider	R	4.10
0.20	Whirlwind Strike	C	0.15
0.20	White Disciple	C	0.15
6.00	White Ninja	R	6.60
0.80	Wind Across Heaven	U	0.50
0.80	Wind on the Mountain	U	0.60
6.00	Wong Fei Hong	R	4.10
7.00	Zheng Yi Quan	R	6.40

RARITY KEY VC = Very Common C = Common U = Uncommon R = Rare UR = Ultra Rare F = Foil card X = Fixed/standard in all

Homo Omega

10

Buro Cyborg
Unique. **Toughness: 2.** Once during each Main Shot, you may return a **Weapon** State on this card to its owner's hand :: Play a **Weapon** State with a different title on this card at –X cost. X= the cost of the returned State.

Artwork © 2000
Mark Tedin

1 1 1 1 ✱ 6   1 ✱ ✱ ✱

Shadowfist • *Year of the Dragon*

Z-Man Games • Released **August 2000**

110 cards in set • **IDENTIFIER:** © 2000

• Starter decks contain 50 cards; starter displays contain 10 starters

In 1996, Daedalus ceased publishing ***Shadowfist***. Three years later, Zev Schlasinger's Z-Man Games announced that it would resume publication and support of the game. Rather then re-issue any of the old works, Z-Man released what amounts to a new basic set in ***Year of the Dragon***, made up of five 50-card starter card decks, one for each of the original main factions. We're listing it here as a basic set, before the expansions.

The decks mainly contain previously released cards with a few new cards in each starter deck. The decks themselves are pre-constructed and play well out of the box. *Year of the Dragon* is well-suited for sealed-deck tournaments and helping new players get into the game, but the decision not to reprint the bulk of the previous cards in one expansion may create a chasm between the old guard and new players. — *Michael Greenholdt*

You will need **13** nine-pocket pages to store this set. (7 doubled up)

Set (110 cards)		50.00
Starter Display Box		80.00
Starter Deck		9.00

Card name	Rarity	Price
Abominable Lab	X	0.50
Abysmal Absorber	X	0.50
Amulet of the Turtle	X	0.50
Arcanowave Reinforcer	X	0.50
Birdhouse Cafe	X	0.50
Blade Palm	X	0.50
Blessed Orchard	X	0.50
Blood of the Valiant	X	0.50
Blue Monk	X	0.50
Bronze Sentinel	X	0.50
Bull Market	X	0.50
Buro Godhammer	X	0.50
Cave Network	X	0.50
CDCA Scientist	X	0.50
CHAR	X	0.50
City Park	X	0.50
City Square	X	0.50
Claw of the Dragon	X	0.50
Confucian Stability	X	0.50
Covert Operation	X	0.50
Curio Shop	X	0.50
Dangerous Experiment	X	0.50
Dirk Wisely's Gambit	X	0.50
Discerning Fire	X	0.50
Draco	X	0.50

Card name	Rarity	Price
Eunuch Underling	X	0.50
Evil Twin	X	0.50
Explosives	X	0.50
Family Estate	X	0.50
Festival Circle	X	0.50
Field of Tentacles	X	0.50
Final Brawl	X	0.50
Floating Restaurant	X	0.50
Four Burning Fists	X	0.50
Fox Pass	X	0.50
Friends of the Dragon	X	0.50
Gambling House	X	0.50
Gardener	X	0.50
Glimpse of the Abyss	X	0.50
Golden Candle Society	X	0.50
Golden Comeback	X	0.50
Hacker	X	0.50
Hands Without Shadow	X	0.50
Helix Chewer	X	0.50
Helix Rethread	X	0.50
Homo Omega	X	0.50
House on the Hill	X	0.50
Inexorable Corruption	X	0.50
Infernal Temple	X	0.50
Inner Sanctum	X	0.50
Iron and Silk	X	0.50
Jade Valley	X	0.50
Jagged Cliffs	X	0.50
Jane Q. Public	X	0.50

Card name	Rarity	Price
Kinoshita House	X	0.50
Kun Kan	X	0.50
Kung Fu Student	X	0.50
Little Jim	X	0.50
Maverick Cop	X	0.50
Mole Network	X	0.50
Nerve Gas	X	0.50
Netherworld Vet	X	0.50
Neutron Bomb	X	0.50
Nine Dragon Temple	X	0.50
Operation Killdeer	X	0.50
Paper Trail	X	0.50
Perpetual Motion Machine	X	0.50
Plasma Trooper	X	0.50
Pocket Demon	X	0.50
Prototype X	X	0.50
PubOrd Officer	X	0.50
Pump-Action Shotgun	X	0.50
Rat Fink	X	0.50
Red Monk	X	0.50
Redeemed Gunman	X	0.50
Righteous Fist	X	0.50
Rigorous Discipline	X	0.50
Robot Arm	X	0.50
Sacred Heart Hospital	X	0.50
Sam Mallory	X	0.50
Satellite Intelligence	X	0.50
Secret Headquarters	X	0.50

Card name	Rarity	Price
Shadowfist	X	0.50
Shadowy Mentor	X	0.50
Shan Tsu	X	0.50
Shaolin Sanctuary	X	0.50
Shattering Fire	X	0.50
Shield of Pure Soul	X	0.50
Sinister Priest	X	0.50
Sting of the Scorpion	X	0.50
Stone Garden	X	0.50
Student of the Bear	X	0.50
Student of the Shark	X	0.50
Suicide Mission	X	0.50
Surprise, Surprise	X	0.50
Test Subjects	X	0.50
The Hungry	X	0.50
The Iron Monkey	X	0.50
The Pledged	X	0.50
Thing with a Thousand Tongues	X	0.50
Ting Ting	X	0.50
Tortured Memories	X	0.50
Tricia Kwok	X	0.50
Turtle Beach	X	0.50
Vassals of the Lotus	X	0.50
Violet Meditation	X	0.50
Vivisector	X	0.50
Walking Corpses	X	0.50
White Disciple	X	0.50
Wong Fei Hong	X	0.50

CHAR

6

BuroMil Cyborg
Damage CHAR inflicts in combat is reduced as his Fighting score decreases but cannot be reduced or redirected by any other means. CHAR takes no damage from Fire cards.

Artwork © 1995
Richard Kane Ferguson

1 ✱ 4   1 ✱

Shadowfist • *Netherworld*

Daedalus • Released **August 1995**

134 cards in set • **IDENTIFIER: Artist name in larger type;** © 1995

• Booster packs contain 12 cards; booster displays contain 36 boosters

This expansion rounds out two minor groups introduced in the ***Limited/Standard Editions*** such that they became viable major factions.

The Jammers come from the same future as the Architects of the Flesh, and are their sworn enemies. The Jammers use Tech to great effect, and many of their best characters are cyborg monkeys. Like the Dragons, they are more interested in stopping the world domination of the other factions than ruling the world themselves.

The Four Monarchs are ancient elemental powers, exiled to the Netherworld by the Ascended. Each of the Monarchs is associated with an element, and, as a group, the Monarchs have powerful magical abilities. — *Michael Greenholdt*

You will need **15** nine-pocket pages to store this set. (8 doubled up)

Set (134 cards)		87.75
Booster Display Box		35.00
Booster Pack		2.00

Card name	Rarity	Price
Abysmal Absorber	U	0.80
Abysmal Deceiver	U	1.30

Card name	Rarity	Price
Abysmal Prince	U	0.80
Agony Grenade	U	0.70
Ancestral Sanctuary	U	0.50
Avenging Thunder	U	0.70
Bao Chou	R	4.00
Biomass Reprocessing Center	U	0.70

Card name	Rarity	Price
Blade Freak	U	0.70
Blanket of Darkness	R	4.00
Brain Fire	C	0.20
Brain Sucker	C	0.20
Bronze Sentinel	C	0.15
"Burn, Baby, Burn!"	U	0.80

Card name	Rarity	Price
Butterfly Knight	C	0.15
Capture Squad	U	0.70
CHAR	U	1.50
Chi Sucker	C	0.20
Chimp Shack	C	0.20
Claws of Darkness	U	0.80

RARITY KEY	C = Common	U = Uncommon	R = Rare	VR = Very Rare	UR = Ultra Rare	F = Foil card	X = Fixed/standard in all decks

Card name	Rarity	Price
Counterfeit Heart	R	3.80
Dark Traveler	C	0.20
Darkness Pagoda	R	3.50
Darkness Priestess	C	0.20
Death Shadow	R	4.50
Death-O-Rama	C	0.20
Demolitions Expert	C	0.20
Desire Manipulator	U	0.90
Discerning Fire	C	0.20
Doomed Lackey	C	0.20
Elevator to the Netherworld	R	4.50
Enchanted Sword	U	0.70
Entropy Is Your Friend	U	1.00
Eugene Fo	R	4.30
Festival Circle	C	0.15
Field of Tentacles	C	0.20
Fire and Darkness Pavilion	R	4.50
Fire Assassin	U	1.00
Fire Martyr	U	0.50
Fire Pagoda	R	4.50
Fire Warriors	C	0.20
Flying Bladder	U	0.80
Flying Crescent	U	1.00
Flying Kick	C	0.10
Fortress of Shadow	C	0.20
Foul Hatchling	C	0.10
Furious George	R	3.80
Garden of Bronze	C	0.20
Gearhead	U	0.50

Card name	Rarity	Price
Ghost Assassin	U	1.00
Gnarled Attuner	R	4.80
Gorilla Warfare	R	3.50
Green Senshi Chamber	R	4.00
Grenade Posse	C	0.20
Guiyu Zui	R	4.50
Gunrunner	U	1.00
Heat of Battle	C	0.20
House of Mirrors	C	0.20
Ice Courtier	U	1.00
Ice Diadem	U	1.00
Ice Falcons	C	0.20
Ice Healer	C	0.20
Ice Pagoda	R	4.80
Ice Shards	R	5.00
Ice Tiger	C	0.20
IKTV Rebroadcast Link	U	1.30
Jamal Hopkins	R	3.80
Jason X	R	4.50
Jimmy Wai	R	4.00
Jueding Bao-Fude	R	5.00
Kiii-YAAAH!	C	0.20
King of the Fire Pagoda	R	6.00
Locksley Station	R	4.00
Lord Shi	R	5.00
Mad Bomber	C	0.20
Marisol	R	4.30
Mark of Fire	C	0.20
Molten Heart	R	3.50

Card name	Rarity	Price
Monkey House	U	0.50
Necromantic Conspiracy	U	1.00
Netherworld Return	U	0.50
Netherworld Vet	C	0.10
New Manifesto	C	0.15
Operation Green Strike	U	1.00
Orange Senshi Chamber	R	3.50
Orango Tank	R	4.50
Perpetual Motion Machine	C	0.25
Pinball Hall	C	0.20
Pocket Demon	C	0.25
Queen of the Darkness Pagoda	R	7.00
Rah Rah Rasputine	R	5.00
RedGlare Chapel	R	4.00
Repulsor Beams	U	0.80
Resistance Squad	C	0.20
Reverend RedGlare	R	4.50
Ring of Gates	C	0.15
Rust Garden	C	0.15
Serena Ku	R	4.00
Sergeant Blightman	R	3.80
Shield of Pure Soul	U	0.80
Shields of Darkness	U	0.80
Shinobu Yashida	R	4.00
Sibling Rivalry	U	0.50
Soul Diver	C	0.20
Soul of the Dragon	U	1.30
Storm of the Just	C	0.20

Card name	Rarity	Price
Sucker Rounds	U	0.50
Sung Hi	R	5.00
Surprise, Surprise	C	0.20
Tanbi Guiawu	R	4.50
The Displaced	C	0.20
The Faceless	C	0.20
The Fox Outfoxed	U	1.00
The Golden Gunman	R	4.50
The Losers	C	0.10
The Prof	R	5.50
Thunder Pagoda	R	4.00
Thunder Squire	C	0.10
Thunder Sword	R	4.30
Tick... Tick... Tick...	U	0.80
Ting Ting	R	8.50
Triumvirate Dealmaker	U	1.00
Tunnel Ganger	C	0.20
Undercover Agent	C	0.20
Violet Meditation	C	0.20
Violet Monk	U	0.50
Wall of a Thousand Eyes	C	0.20
Whirlpool of Blood	C	0.20
White Senshi Chamber	R	4.00
Wu Ta-Hsi	R	4.50
Xiu Xie Jiang	R	5.00
Yellow Monk	U	0.50
Yellow Senshi Chamber	R	4.00
Ze Botelho	R	5.00

Shadowfist • Flashpoint

Daedalus • Released **March 1996**

145 cards in set • IDENTIFIER: © 1996

- Booster packs contain 8 cards; booster displays contain 30 boosters

Although considered the weaker of the two expansions Daedalus put out, **Flashpoint** introduced many cards that became stock cards in decks.

Most of the Feng Shui sites have some type of power or ability, a trend that started in **Netherworld**. A new type of non-Feng Shui site, the Battle site, is introduced. These sites were to have an important impact on the game. — **Michael Greenholdt**

You will need **17** nine-pocket pages to store this set. (9 doubled up)

	Price
Set (145 cards)	72.00
Booster Display Box	80.00
Booster Pack	9.00

Card name	Rarity	Price
Alchemist's Lair	C	0.15
Anomaly Spirit	U	0.80
Arcanoseed	U	0.80
Arcanostriker	U	0.80
Arcanotank	U	0.80
Arcanotower 2056	R	4.90
Arcanotower Now	R	4.90
Arcanoworms	U	0.80
Art of War	U	0.80
Bad Colonel	U	0.80
Birdhouse Cafe	C	0.15
Blood of the Valiant	C	0.15
Bloody Horde	C	0.15
Both Guns Blazing	C	0.15
Buro GodHammer	C	0.15
BuroMil Elite	C	0.15
BuroMil Grunt	C	0.15
BuroMil Ninja	C	0.15
Bzzzzzt!	U	0.80
Carnival of Carnage	C	0.15
CAT Tactics	U	0.80
Cheap Punks	C	0.15
Chimpanzer	C	0.15
City Park	C	0.15
Claw of Fury	C	0.15

Card name	Rarity	Price
Claw of the Dragon	C	0.15
Coffee-Stained Cop	U	0.80
Colonel Griffith	R	4.90
Comrades in Arms	C	0.15
Cop on Vacation	U	0.80
Creche of the New Flesh	C	0.15
Curio Shop	C	0.15
Cyclone of Knives	U	0.80
Dallas Rocket	C	0.15
Dark's Soft Whisper	U	0.80
Destroyer	U	0.80
Dirk Wisely's Gambit	C	0.15
Disinformation Packet	U	0.80
Doomsday Device	U	0.80
Drop Troopers	U	0.80
Drunken Stance	C	0.15
Dunwa Saleem	R	4.90
Encephalon Screamer	C	0.15
Ex-Commando	C	0.15
Fighting Spirit	C	0.15
Fire Sled	C	0.15
Flying Windmill Kick	C	0.15
Fortuitous Chi	C	0.15
Forty-Story Inferno	U	0.80
Genghis X	R	4.90
Gibbering Horror	U	0.80
Glimpse of the Abyss	U	0.80
Gonzo Journalist	C	0.15
Gorilla Fighter	U	0.80

Card name	Rarity	Price
Grease Monkey	U	0.80
Hacker	C	0.15
Heart of the Rainforest	C	0.15
Hidden Sanctuary	C	0.15
Home Front, The	U	0.80
Homemade Tank	C	0.15
Hosed	U	0.80
Hover Tank	C	0.15
In Your Face Again	C	0.15
Invincible Chi	U	0.80
Jane Q. Public	C	0.15
Joey Paz	R	4.40
Johnny Badhair	R	4.40
Just a Rat	U	0.80
Just Another Consumer	C	0.15
Kar Fai's Crib	R	4.40
Killing Ground	C	0.15
Kung Fu Student	C	0.15
Laughter of the Wind	U	0.80
Leatherback	U	0.80
Let's Book!	U	0.80
Little Jim	R	4.40
Lodge Politics	C	0.15
MegaTank	U	0.80
Melissa Aguelera	R	4.40
Memory Reprocessing	U	0.80
Mirror Dancer	U	0.80
Monkeywrenching	C	0.15

Card name	Rarity	Price
Mountain Warrior	C	0.15
Mr. Big	R	3.80
Napalm Sunrise	C	0.15
Night Market	C	0.15
Nuked	C	0.15
Old Hermit's Gambit	C	0.15
Open Season	U	0.80
Orange Meditation	C	0.15
Paradox Cube	U	0.80
Peacock Summit	C	0.15
Plasma Trooper	C	0.15
Pod Trooper	C	0.15
Portal in Tower Square	U	0.80
Portal Jockey	C	0.15
Pump-Action Shotgun	C	0.15
Purist	U	0.80
Purist Sorceror	U	0.80
Rain of Fury	U	0.60
Rainforest Grove	C	0.15
Rainforest River	U	0.80
Rainforest Temple	C	0.15
Red Monk	U	0.80
Redeemed Gunman	C	0.15
Registry of the Damned	U	0.80
Resistance is Futile	U	0.80
Rhys Engel	R	5.30
Righteous Fist	C	0.15
Rocket Scientist	C	0.15
Sam Mallory	R	3.80

RARITY KEY C = Common U = Uncommon R = Rare VR = Very Rare UR = Ultra Rare F = Foil card X = Fixed/standard in all decks

Card name	Rarity	Price		Card name	Rarity	Price		Card name	Rarity	Price		Card name	Rarity	Price
☐ Sampan Village	C	0.15		☐ Sniper Nest	C	0.15		☐ Ting Ting's Gambit	C	0.15		☐ Virtuous Hood	U	0.80
☐ Satellite Intelligence	U	0.80		☐ Spawn of the New Flesh	U	0.80		☐ Too Much Monkey				☐ Wandering Monk	U	0.80
☐ Scorched Earth	U	0.50		☐ Spirit Pole	U	0.80		Business	C	0.15		☐ We Know Where You Live	U	0.80
☐ Scrappy Kid	U	0.80		☐ Stolen Police Car	C	0.15		☐ Total War	U	0.80		☐ Who's The Big Man Now?!	C	0.15
☐ Shan Tsu	R	4.40		☐ Student of the Shark	C	0.15		☐ Trust Me, I've Got A Plan	C	0.15		☐ Wing of the Crane	U	0.80
☐ Shaolin Surprise	C	0.15		☐ Stunt Man	C	0.15		☐ Turtle Island	C	0.15		☐ Xiaoyang Yun	R	4.10
[14]				[15]				☐ Underground, The	U	0.80		☐ Yakuza Enforcer	C	0.15
☐ Silver Jet	R	4.40		☐ Supercomputer	U	0.80		[16]				[17]		
☐ Slo Mo Vengance	C	0.15		☐ Tank Warfare	U	0.80		☐ Underworld Presence	U	0.80		☐ Year of the Rat	U	0.80
☐ Smart Missile	C	0.15		☐ Thunder Champion	U	0.80		☐ Vile Prodigy	C	0.15				

Seven Evils

10

Demon Lord

Unique. Unturns when any opponent turns a Feng Shui Site. Toast a Character you control to give Seven Evils **Independent** until the end of the turn.

Artwork © 2000
Stephen Snyder

✪✪✪ 6

Shadowfist • *Throne War*

Z-Man Games • Released **August 2000**
80 cards in set • **IDENTIFIER:** © 2000

• Starter decks contain 50 cards; starter displays contain 10 starters

    Throne War, Z-Man Games' first booster expansion set for ***Shadowfist***, is set in China in 69 A.D., the time of the Eaters of the Lotus. The current emperor, a pawn of the Lotus, is dying, and the stage is set for the other factions, especially the Guiding Hand, to alter history. Naturally, *Throne War* focuses on the Guiding Hand and the Eaters of the Lotus. The Jammers receive several useful cards, as well.

    Although other factions receive short shrift, announced expansions look to even things up. Z-Man Games reprinted several useful cards from the previous sets in *Throne War*, something that will probably continue in future releases. — **Michael Greenholdt**

Set (80 cards)		90.00
Starter Display Box		65.00
Starter Deck		2.70

Promo cards

☐ Once and Future Champion	pr	2.00
☐ Open a Can of Whupass	pr	2.00
☐ White Ninja	pr	2.00

Card name	Rarity	Price
[1]		
☐ Andrea Van de Graaf	R	4.00
☐ Apes of Wrath	U	0.50
☐ Ba-BOOM!	R	4.00
☐ Bandit Chief	U	0.50
☐ Bandit Hideout	U	0.50
☐ Black Flag Rebels	C	0.10
☐ Blade of Darkness	U	0.80
☐ Blue Monk	U	0.50
☐ Cave of a Thousand Banners	U	0.50
[2]		
☐ Competitive Intelligence	C	0.10
☐ Darkness Adept	U	0.50
☐ Darkness Priestess	C	0.10

Card name	Rarity	Price		Card name	Rarity	Price		Card name	Rarity	Price
☐ Demon Emperor	R	3.00		☐ Infernal Pact	U	0.50		☐ Sinister Accusations	U	0.50
☐ Desolate Ridge	U	0.50		[5]				☐ Smiling Heaven Lake	C	0.10
☐ Die!!	U	0.50		☐ Jui Szu	R	3.00		☐ Sword of the Dragon King	U	0.50
☐ Discerning Fire	C	0.10		☐ Just Another Consumer	C	0.10		☐ Temple of the Angry Spirits	U	0.50
☐ Dr. Celeste Carter	R	3.00		☐ Kar Fai	R	4.00		☐ The Blue Cardinal's Guards	U	0.50
☐ Dr. John Haynes	R	3.00		☐ Leung Mui	R	4.00		[8]		
[3]				☐ Mad Monk	R	3.00		☐ The Dragon Throne	U	0.50
☐ Eagle Mountain	C	0.10		☐ Möbius Gardens	C	0.10		☐ The Emperor	R	4.00
☐ Earth Poisoner	C	0.10		☐ Napalm Addict	U	0.80		☐ The Monkey Who Would		
☐ Eater of Fortune	U	0.50		☐ Obsidian Eye	U	0.80		Be King	R	3.00
☐ Elite Guards	C	0.10		☐ Oliver Chen	R	3.00		☐ Time Bandits	U	0.50
☐ Evil Twin	U	0.50		[6]				☐ Titanium Johnson	R	4.00
☐ Farseeing Rice Grains	C	0.10		☐ Palace Guards	C	0.10		☐ True Son of Heaven	R	4.00
☐ Festival of Giants	C	0.10		☐ Payback Time	U	0.50		☐ Twin Thunder Kick	U	0.50
☐ Final Sacrifice	C	0.10		☐ Peasant Uprising	C	0.10		☐ Two Hundred Knives of Pain	U	0.50
☐ Flying Sleeves	C	0.10		☐ Petroglyphs	C	0.10		☐ Ulterior Motives	C	0.10
[4]				☐ Pocket Demon	C	0.10		[9]		
☐ Flying Sword Stance	C	0.10		☐ Puzzle Garden	C	0.10		☐ Underworld Tracker	U	0.50
☐ For China!	U	0.50		☐ Rebel Camp	U	0.50		☐ Violet Meditation	C	0.10
☐ Gao Zhang	R	4.00		☐ Resistance Squad	C	0.10		☐ Wandering Teacher	U	0.80
☐ Grizzly Pass	C	0.10		☐ Righteous Protector	C	0.10		☐ Weird Science	U	0.50
☐ Hall of Brilliance	R	3.00		[7]				☐ Whirlpool of Blood	C	0.10
☐ Hsiung-nu Mercenaries	C	0.10		☐ Scrounging	C	0.10		☐ Who Wants Some?	U	0.50
☐ Imperial Palace	R	4.00		☐ Seven Evils	R	4.00		☐ Who's the Monkey Now?	U	0.80
☐ Inauspicious Return	C	0.10		☐ Shattering Fire	C	0.10		☐ Xin Kai Sheng	R	4.00
				☐ Shi Zi Hui	R	4.00				

STOMPER • GANGER

7

✊ 2

6/7
(A1)

Troll Runner. Stamina
"Howza 'bout you and me wrassle?"

© 1997 FASA. All Rights Reserved. Illustration: Paul Bonner.

Shadowrun

FASA • First set, **Limited**, released **August 1997**
352 cards in set • **IDENTIFIER: No "U" in lower left corner**

• Starter decks contain 70 cards; starter displays contain 12 starters

• Booster packs contain 15 cards; booster displays contain 36 boosters

    Having licensed the CCG rights for its most popular property, ***Battletech***, to Wizards of the Coast, FASA determined to produce on its own the ***Shadowrun*** CCG, based on its top-selling Cyberpunk role-playing game of the same name.

    Set in the Seattle of 2058, *Shadowrun* finds that cybernetic technology has advanced to the point that users can transcend human limitations. At the same time, magic has returned to the world, and various non-human races have returned. National governments have faded away, and the world is run by large corporations. Shadowrunners are individuals who operate outside the system, in the pay of, or fighting, the large corporations.

    The CCG itself is set up much like a role-playing game. The goal is to gain Reputation Points equal to an agreed-upon limit by capturing Objective cards. The Objectives are defended by Challenge cards, which any player can play on any Objective (or his own Runners) which represent foes, traps, and obstacles.

RARITY KEY   **C** = Common   **U** = Uncommon   **R** = Rare   **VR** = Very Rare   **UR** = Ultra Rare   **F** = Foil card   **X** = Fixed/standard in all decks

Players spend Nuyen (new yen, get it?) to purchase Runners, the characters on their teams. They may also purchase gear, spells and/or spirits. Each player starts with an income of 4 Nuyen per turn. When ready, players can send their Runners against an Objective, trying to overcome the Challenges protecting it and gain the Reputation points for the Objective.

Some players found that, in actual play, a number of aspects of the game (including a complete card type or two) were irrelevant to most victory strategies. And, without Wizards of the Coast's marketing oomph, *Shadrowrun* didn't make it into as many stores as *BattleTech* had. So *Shadowrun* ran long enough to receive one expansion, **Underworld**. The only one announced for 1998, **Corp War**, never came out.

In January 2001, FASA announced it would wind down operations after nearly two decades in gaming. *Shadowrun* and *Battletech* gaming system rights were licensed to FASA alum Jordan Weisman, who had just hit it big with the collectible miniatures game **Mage Knight Rebellion**. — *Michael Greenholdt & John Jackson Miller*

Concept	●●●○○
Gameplay	●●●○○
Card art	●●●○○
Player pool	●○○○○

Set (352 cards)	162.50
Starter Display Box	70.00
Booster Display Box	75.00
Starter Deck	9.00
Booster Pack	3.00

You will need **40** nine-pocket pages to store this set. (20 doubled up)

Promo cards

Card name	Type	Price
Adam Bomb • Legendary Rocker	Runner	5.00
Flatline • Street Samurai	Runner	5.00
Foxy Roxy • Legendary Flirt	Runner	5.00
Fuchi Industries	Location	5.00
Hatchetman 2057 • Cyborg	Runner	5.00
Maglock Passkey	Gear	5.00
Nerps!	Special	5.00

Card name	Type	Rarity	Price
Abducted!	Special	R	4.00
Ajax • Rigger	Runner	C	0.10
All or Nothing	Stinger	R	4.00
Ally Spirit	Gear	C	0.10
Amazonian Hunt	Objective	U	0.80
Ambidextrous	Special	R	4.00
Ambush	Challenge	U	0.50
Ambushed En Route	Challenge	C	0.10
Ancients' Turf	Challenge	U	0.80
Anti-Astral Barrier	Challenge	R	4.00
Archie McDeven • Detective	Runner	R	4.50
Ares Macrotechnology	Location	R	4.00
Ares Predator	Gear	C	0.10
Armor Skin	Gear	U	0.50
Armor Spell	Gear	U	0.50
Armored Vest	Gear	C	0.10
Armor-piercing Ammo	Gear	R	4.00
Assassination	Objective	C	0.10
Astral Sense	Gear	C	0.10
Astral Sentry	Challenge	U	0.50
Automated Patrol Vehicle	Gear	U	0.80
Aztechnology	Location	R	4.00
Bad Lunch	Special	C	0.10
Bad Reputation	Stinger	U	0.80
Bam-Bam • Street Samurai	Runner	R	5.50
Bar Fight	Special	U	1.00
Barney Phyffe	Challenge	R	4.00
Basilisk	Challenge	C	0.10
Beretta	Gear	U	0.50
Black Hammer	Gear	C	0.10
Blazing Guns	Stinger	U	0.50
Blindsided	Stinger	R	4.50
Block Party	Special	U	0.50
Bolt of Power	Gear	C	0.10
Booby Trap	Challenge	C	0.10
Bounty Hunter	Contact	C	0.10
Brain Freeze	Stinger	R	4.00
Browse	Gear	C	0.10

Card name	Type	Rarity	Price
Bugged Deck	Special	U	0.50
Bulldog Van	Gear	U	0.50
Bullet Barrier	Gear	R	4.50
Caesar • Decker	Runner	R	4.00
Cake Walk	Objective	U	0.50
Camo	Gear	R	4.00
Cannonball • Mercenary	Runner	C	0.10
Caves of Halferville	Location	C	0.10
Cermak Blast	Objective	C	0.10
Ceska VZ/120	Gear	C	0.10
Change of Plans	Stinger	U	0.50
Cherry Bomb • Mercenary	Runner	U	0.80
Chipjack 1	Gear	C	0.10
Chipjack 2	Gear	U	0.50
Chipjack 3	Gear	R	5.00
Chomps-2000 Guard Dog	Challenge	U	0.80
Chop Shop	Location	U	0.50
City Spirit	Gear	U	0.50
Cleanse the Hive	Objective	R	4.50
Club Vortex	Location	U	0.80
Clutch • Rigger	Runner	R	4.50
Corporate Secretary	Contact	C	0.10
Corpselight	Challenge	C	0.10
Cortex Bomb	Gear	R	4.00
Courier Run	Objective	C	0.10
Cover Up	Special	U	0.50
Cowards	Stinger	R	4.00
Crash	Gear	R	4.00
Crawler Patrol Drone	Gear	C	0.10
Critter Hunt	Objective	C	0.10
Crossfire	Objective	U	1.00
Custom System	Challenge	R	4.00
Cyberarm	Gear	C	0.10
Cyber-Psychosis	Special	R	4.00
Da' Profezzur • Street Samurai	Persnl	R	4.50
Dante • Street Mage	Runner	C	0.10
D-day • Ganger	Runner	C	0.10
Decker Coffeehouse	Location	U	0.50
Defiance Shotgun	Gear	U	0.50
Defiance Taser	Gear	R	4.00
Deja Vu	Stinger	C	0.10
Dermal Plating	Gear	U	1.00
Desert Hit	Objective	U	0.50
Detect Enemy	Gear	C	0.10
Dirk Montgomery • Detective	Persnl	R	5.00
Distraction	Stinger	R	4.00
Doberman Patrol Vehicle	Gear	R	4.00
Doc Wagon (Gold)	Gear	U	0.80
Doc Wagon (Platinum)	Gear	R	5.00
Dodger • Decker	Persnl	R	4.50
Domino • Street Samurai	Runner	U	0.50
Double Jeopardy!	Challenge	U	0.50
Dr. Apocalypse • Combat Mage	Runner	R	4.00

Card name	Type	Rarity	Price
Dragon Hunt	Objective	R	4.50
Drake • Mercenary	Runner	R	4.50
Drive-By	Special	U	1.00
Dunkelzahn's Black Book	Objective	R	4.50
Eco-War!	Objective	U	0.50
Electrified Fence	Challenge	C	0.10
Elemental	Gear	C	0.10
Elite Security Guards	Challenge	U	0.50
Elite Security Mage	Challenge	R	4.00
Elven Hitman	Contact	C	0.10
Evaluate	Gear	C	0.10
Even Steven	Special	U	0.50
Explosive Rounds	Gear	C	0.10
Extended Clip	Gear	U	0.50
Extraction	Objective	C	0.10
Eyekiller	Challenge	U	0.50
Fairlight Excalibur	Gear	R	4.00
False Mentor	Stinger	R	6.00
Fastjack • Decker	Persnl	R	5.00
Feeding Ghouls	Challenge	C	0.10
Fireball	Gear	U	0.80
Flechette Rounds	Gear	U	0.50
Flock of Geese	Challenge	R	4.50
FN Mag-5	Gear	U	0.50
FNHAR	Gear	U	0.50
Foretelling	Gear	U	0.50
Fort Knocks	Objective	C	0.10
Free Spirit	Challenge	U	0.50
Fringe Surgeon	Contact	U	0.50
Fuchi Cyber-6	Gear	R	5.50
Fugitive Run	Objective	U	0.50
Fusion Gate	Challenge	U	0.50
Fusion Run	Objective	U	0.50
Gang War	Objective	C	0.10
Ganger Leader	Contact	U	0.50
Ghost Who Walks • Street Samurai	Persnl	R	5.00
Glitz • Rocker	Runner	C	0.10
Gore Tusk • Street Samurai	Runner	C	0.10
Grandfather Bones • Shaman	Runner	C	0.10
Greater Elemental	Gear	R	5.50
Green Apple Quicksteps	Stinger	C	0.20
Grizzly • Mercenary	Runner	R	5.00
Guardian Dracoform	Challenge	R	5.50
Guardian Earth Elemental	Challenge	R	5.00
Guardian Fire Elemental	Challenge	R	5.00
Gut Check!	Challenge	C	0.10
Gutter Rat • Street Shaman	Runner	R	4.00
Gyro Stabilizer	Gear	R	4.00
Halloweener Hell	Challenge	U	0.80
Hand Razors	Gear	C	0.10
Harlequin's Game	Objective	C	0.10
Harley Scorpion	Gear	U	0.50
Hatchetman • Street Samurai	Runner	C	0.10
Haunted High Rise	Objective	C	0.10

RARITY KEY C = Common   U = Uncommon   R = Rare   VR = Very Rare   UR = Ultra Rare   F = Foil card   X = Fixed/standard in all decks

SCRYE Collectible Card Game Checklist and Price Guide • **387**

Card name	Type	Rarity	Price
Hawkwind • Shaman	Runner	U	0.50
Heal	Gear	U	0.80
Heavy Armor (Full)	Gear	R	5.00
Heavy Armor (Partial)	Gear	R	4.50
Heavy Sentry Gun	Challenge	R	4.00
Hellblast	Gear	R	4.00
Hellhound	Challenge	R	4.00
Hellish Traffic	Challenge	C	0.10
18			
Hermetic Library	Location	U	0.50
Highbrow • Mage	Runner	R	5.00
Highway Showdown	Challenge	R	4.50
Hit and Run	Challenge	C	0.10
HK227	Gear	U	0.50
Hog	Gear	C	0.10
Hollywood • Decker	Runner	C	0.10
Humanis Policlub Ganger	Contact	R	4.00
Hunter Drone	Gear	C	0.10
19			
Hunting Gargoyle	Challenge	U	0.80
Ice Queen • Decker	Runner	R	6.00
Impossible Mission	Objective	R	4.00
Incubus	Challenge	R	4.50
Infected Chrome	Special	U	0.50
Ingram Valiant	Gear	U	0.50
Integrated Control Center	Challenge	U	0.50
Invisibility	Gear	C	0.10
Iron Mike • Mercenary	Runner	R	5.00
20			
Jack Hammer • Rigger	Runner	C	0.10
Jack Skater • Street Samurai	Persnl	R	5.00
Jackyl • Burned-out-Mage	Runner	C	0.10
Just a Rumor	Stinger	R	4.00
Kamikaze Run	Objective	R	4.00
Katana	Gear	C	0.10
Kham • Mercenary	Persnl	R	4.50
Killer Drone	Challenge	R	5.00
Knight Errant Guards	Challenge	U	0.50
21			
Knock-Knock	Special	R	4.80
Knuckles • Bodyguard	Runner	U	0.50
Kraker-Jack • Decker	Runner	U	0.50
Kromagnus • Rocker	Runner	C	0.10
Laser Scope	Gear	U	0.50
Lined Coat	Gear	U	0.50
Loaded Dice	Stinger	C	0.10
Lofwyr's Schemes	Stinger	R	4.00
Lone Star Patrol	Challenge	C	0.10
22			
Lord Torgo • Ganger Leader	Persnl	R	6.00
Luck o' the Irish	Stinger	C	0.10
Lucky Wabbit's Foot	Gear	R	5.00
Macabre • Street Samurai	Runner	U	0.50
Mafia Goons	Challenge	U	0.50
Mage Strike Force	Challenge	U	0.80
Maglocks	Challenge	C	0.10
Major Drain	Stinger	R	4.50
Manticore	Challenge	U	0.80
23			
Marek • Combat Mage	Runner	R	5.00
Matrix Crash	Special	R	4.00
Media Chick	Contact	C	0.10
Microskimmer	Gear	U	0.50
Milk Run	Objective	C	0.10
Mine Field	Challenge	C	0.10
Mob War!	Objective	C	0.10
Monofilament Whip	Gear	R	4.30
Moon Shadow • Shaman	Runner	R	4.50
24			
Moonlighting	Stinger	C	0.10
Motion Detectors	Challenge	R	4.00
Mr. Black	Contact	C	0.50
Mr. Johnson	Contact	C	0.10
Muscle Replacement	Gear	U	0.80
Nature Spirit	Gear	U	0.50
Nets	Challenge	C	0.10
Nightshade • Street Mage	Runner	C	0.10

Card name	Type	Rarity	Price
25			
No Way Out	Stinger	U	0.50
Operation Cottonmouth	Objective	C	0.10
Operation Up and Over	Objective	U	0.50
Orion • Street Mage	Runner	C	0.10
Panther Assault Cannon	Gear	R	5.00
Pappy • Street Shaman	Runner	R	4.50
Poison Gas Trap	Challenge	U	0.50
PRC-44B Yellowjacket	Gear	R	4.50
Protect and Defend	Objective	C	0.10
Ragnarock-Concert of the Century	Objective	U	0.50
26			
Rampaging Mutant	Special	U	0.80
Ranger Arms SM-3	Gear	R	4.80
Ranger X	Gear	U	0.50
Ravage • Street Samurai	Persnl	R	5.00
Razor Heads Turf	Challenge	U	0.50
Razorback • Street Samurai	Runner	U	0.50
Reaper • Mercenary	Runner	U	0.50
Red Alert	Special	R	4.00
Red Widow • Street Samurai	Runner	U	0.80
27			
Redirect Datatrail	Gear	R	4.00
Redline • Ganger	Runner	C	0.10
Reinforcements	Stinger	U	0.50
Remington 750	Gear	R	5.00
Renraku	Location	R	4.00
Retinal Scanner	Challenge	C	0.10
Ricochet	Stinger	U	0.50
Riots	Special	U	0.80
Ripper • Rocker	Runner	R	5.00
28			
Roadrash • Rigger	Runner	C	0.10
Robo-Plant Revolt!	Objective	C	0.10
Room 5B78	Objective	R	4.00
Roto-Drone	Gear	C	0.10
Rough Night	Stinger	U	0.50
Ruger Super Warhawk	Gear	U	0.50
Rus on Retainer	Challenge	R	4.00
Rush Job	Special	R	4.00
Sabotaged Controls	Challenge	U	0.50
29			
Saeder-Krupp	Location	R	5.00
Sally Tsung • Mage	Persnl	R	4.50
Sam the Sleuth • Detective	Runner	U	0.80
Scarecrow • Street Mage	Runner	U	0.50
Scatter • Rat Shaman	Persnl	R	4.50
Scorpio • Bodyguard	Runner	R	5.00
Security Camera	Challenge	C	0.10
Security Consultant	Challenge	U	0.80
Security Decker	Challenge	R	4.00
30			
Security Drone	Challenge	C	0.10
Security Guards	Challenge	C	0.10
Security Rigger	Challenge	R	4.00
Sentry Gun	Challenge	C	0.10
Shade • Street Shaman	Runner	C	0.10
Shadowland	Location	R	4.50
Shadowplay	Objective	C	0.10
Shasta • Mage	Runner	C	0.10
Shellshock • Mercenary	Runner	C	0.10
31			
Shopping Cart Lady	Contact	U	0.50
Silencer	Gear	C	0.10
Sim Sensation	Challenge	U	0.50
Site of Power	Objective	C	0.10
Skag • Street Shaman	Runner	R	4.50
Skidz • Rigger	Runner	U	0.50
Skillsoft: Athletics	Gear	R	4.50
Skillsoft: Demolitions	Gear	R	4.50
Skillsoft: Firearms	Gear	C	0.10
32			
Skillsoft: Gunnery	Gear	U	0.50
Skillsoft: Melee	Gear	C	0.10
Skillsoft: Piloting	Gear	R	4.50
Skillsoft: Social	Gear	U	0.50

Card name	Type	Rarity	Price
Skillsoft: Stealth	Gear	R	5.00
Skillsoft: Technical	Gear	U	0.50
Skwaaaaaark! • Cyborg	Runner	R	6.00
Sleaze	Gear	U	0.50
Sleep	Gear	U	0.50
33			
Smartgun Link	Gear	R	4.50
Sniper Roost	Location	R	4.50
Sony CTY-360	Gear	C	0.10
Squatter	Contact	R	4.00
Static • Wiz Kid Decker	Runner	U	0.90
Steal Wiz Softs	Objective	C	0.10
Steamroller	Gear	U	0.80
Steppin' Wulf Ambush	Challenge	R	4.80
Sticky Fingers	Gear	R	4.50
34			
Stilleto • Ganger	Runner	U	0.50
Stim Patch	Gear	C	0.10
Stomper • Ganger	Runner	C	0.10
Street Scum	Challenge	C	0.10
Streetline Special	Gear	C	0.10
Stun Gloves	Gear	R	4.00
Sucker Run	Objective	C	0.10
Sudden Goblinization	Stinger	R	5.00
Suicide Run	Stinger	R	4.00
35			
Swarm of Drones	Challenge	U	0.50
Syn • Ganger	Runner	C	0.10
Tactics: Converge	Stinger	U	0.50
Tactics: Scatter	Stinger	U	0.50
Talismonger	Contact	U	0.50
Tempest • Combat Mage	Runner	R	5.00
The Big Chase!	Challenge	R	4.50
The Fat Man	Contact	R	4.00
The Festerin' Tusk	Location	R	4.00
36			
The Funhouse	Challenge	U	0.50
The Hideaway	Location	R	4.00
The Iron Lung	Location	C	0.10
The Mole • Decker	Runner	U	0.50
The Ork Underground	Location	U	0.50
The Preacher • Street Mage	Runner	U	0.50
The Warehouse	Location	C	0.10
The Z-Zone	Location	R	5.00
Thrash • Rocker	Runner	C	0.10
37			
Tiki Head Enigma	Objective	C	0.10
Time-Delayed Bomb	Challenge	R	4.50
Tin Man • Cyborg	Runner	R	5.00
Tinkerbell • Rigger	Runner	U	0.50
Tiny • Decker	Runner	R	5.00
Tir Tairngire	Location	C	0.10
Titan • Street Shaman	Runner	R	5.00
Toxic Spirit	Challenge	U	0.50
Troll Bouncer	Contact	U	0.50
38			
Turbo • Ganger	Runner	C	0.10
Uncle Joe • Burned-out-Mage	Runner	U	0.80
Urban Brawl	Objective	U	0.80
Uzi III	Gear	C	0.10
Vindicator Minigun	Gear	C	0.10
Viper • Ganger	Runner	U	0.50
Voiceprint ID Scanner	Challenge	C	0.10
Walther Palm Pistol	Gear	U	0.50
Wanted	Special	U	0.50
39			
Watcher Spirit	Gear	C	0.10
Wetwork	Objective	C	0.10
Wheeler • Rigger	Persnl	R	5.00
Whoops!	Stinger	U	0.50
Wild Goose Chase	Stinger	U	0.80
Wired Reflexes	Gear	R	4.50
Wishbone • Shaman	Runner	U	0.50
Yak Attack!	Challenge	C	0.10
Yamaha Rapier	Gear	C	0.10
40			
Yoshimo Chang	Contact	R	4.50

RARITY KEY **C** = Common **U** = Uncommon **R** = Rare **VR** = Very Rare **UR** = Ultra Rare **F** = Foil card **X** = Fixed/standard in all decks

Shadowrun • Underworld

FASA • Released **March 1998**
140 cards in set • **IDENTIFIER: 'U' in lower left corner**
• Booster packs contain 15 cards; booster displays contain 36 boosters

Underworld, the only expansion released for **Shadowrun** CCG, concentrates on such criminal organizations as the Yakuza, Mafia and Lone Star and also such individual gangs as the Halloweeners and Ancients. Demonstrating one benefit from having both lines under one roof, many of the elements came from recent source books from the role-playing game,

More spells, spirits, and drones are added to the game in this expansion. While some of the new cards are only really useful if incorporated into a certain kind of "themed" deck, most integrate well with cards from the first set, **Limited**. There are several anti-runner cards that target "muscle" (big character) decks and bring the game back into balance. — **Michael Greenholdt**

Set (140 cards)	80.00		
Booster Display Box	42.50		
Booster Pack	2.50		

You will need 16 nine-pocket pages to store this set. (8 doubled up)

Promo cards

Card name	Type		Price
Genetics Lab	Location		3.50
King Of The Hill	Objective		4.00
The Skills To Pay The Bills	Special		3.50

Card name	Type	Rarity	Price
1			
911	Stinger	C	0.10
Acid Mist	Gear	R	3.50
Ancients	Special	C	0.10
Arson	Special	C	0.10
Backdoor	Stinger	R	4.00
Banzai • Yakuza Thug	Runner	U	0.50
Baseball Bat	Gear	C	0.10
Bear Totem	Special	U	0.50
Better Offer	Special	R	3.00
2			
Bio-Lab Raid	Objective	C	0.10
Black Credstick	Gear	R	4.00
Bowzer • Mafia Thug	Runner	U	0.50
Brain Fart	Special	U	0.50
Cement Shoes	Special	R	3.50
Coffin Hotel	Location	R	4.00
Combat Fetishes	Gear	C	0.10
Conflicting Loyalties	Special	C	0.10
Copycat Syndrome	Special	C	0.10
3			
Crime Wave	Objective	U	0.50
Dante's Inferno	Location	C	0.10
Dazzle	Gear	C	0.10
Dirty Cop	Special	C	0.10
Duncan • Lone Star Beat Cop	Runner	U	0.50
Enviro Bodysuit	Gear	C	0.10
Fixed-Fire Cannons	Gear	C	0.10
Forced Attrition	Stinger	C	0.10
Friend Of A Friend	Stinger	U	0.50
4			
Genetic Monstrosity	Challenge	C	0.10
Gizmo • Ganger	Runner	C	0.10
Halloweeners	Special	U	0.50
Handcuffs	Gear	U	0.50
Heckler Spirit	Gear	R	4.30
Hell House	Objective	U	0.50
Holmes • Detective	Runner	R	4.00
Humanis Policlub Rally	Objective	U	0.50
Humbug • Ganger	Runner	R	4.00
5			
In The Spotlight	Stinger	C	0.10
In-Fighting	Special	C	0.10
Innocent Bystander	Stinger	U	0.50
Intimidation	Stinger	U	0.50

Card name	Type	Rarity	Price
Ivan • Lone Star Riot Cop	Runner	R	4.50
Jade • Yakuza Agent	Runner	U	0.50
Jinx	Gear	U	0.50
Jinx Spirit	Gear	U	0.50
Kilroy Wuz Here!	Stinger	C	0.10
6			
Last Stand	Stinger	R	3.50
Leader Of The Pack	Special	R	3.80
Leo's Pawn Shop	Location	C	0.10
Loki • Mafia Thug	Runner	U	0.50
Lone Star Beat Cops	Challenge	C	0.10
Lone Star Crowd Control	Challenge	C	0.10
Lone Star Drone	Gear	C	0.10
Lone Star HQ	Location	C	0.10
Lone Star K9 Unit	Challenge	U	0.50
7			
Lone Star Lock-Up	Location	C	0.10
Lone Star Sergeant	Contact	R	4.00
Lone Star Snitch	Contact	C	0.10
Lone Star Surveillance	Special	C	0.10
Lone Star Tracker Drone	Challenge	U	0.50
Lone Star Undercover	Stinger	R	3.80
Long Arm Of The Law	Special	U	0.50
Longhorn • Mercenary	Runner	R	5.00
Louie Da' Bruiser • Mafia Thug	Runner	R	4.00
8			
Lurker • Ganger Mage	Runner	C	0.10
M11 Tommygun	Gear	C	0.10
Mafia Interests	Challenge	C	0.10
Meet The Family	Challenge	U	0.50
Mendez • Lone Star Cop	Runner	C	0.10
Metahuman Prejudice	Stinger	R	3.50
Moment of Clarity	Stinger	R	4.00
Mugsy • Mafia Thug	Runner	C	0.10
Mystic Testing Grounds	Objective	C	0.10
9			
Ninja Guard	Contact	R	4.00
Nosferatu Den	Objective	U	0.50
Odysseus • Street Samurai	Runner	U	0.50
One Of The Family	Special	C	0.10
Outstanding Performance	Stinger	U	0.50
Overseas Interests	Objective	C	0.10
Owl Totem	Special	C	0.10
Poison	Gear	U	0.50
Poor Craftsmanship	Special	U	0.50
10			
Pressure Plates	Challenge	C	0.10
Protective Spirit	Gear	C	0.10
Punch Drunk	Special	C	0.10
Ram Spell	Gear	C	0.10
Rat Totem	Special	C	0.10
Razor Heads	Special	C	0.10
Retirement	Special	C	0.10
Riot Foam	Stinger	C	0.10
Ro-Jin • Yakuza Bodyguard	Runner	R	4.50

Card name	Type	Rarity	Price
11			
Robo-Doc	Gear	C	0.10
Sancho • Ganger	Runner	U	0.50
Scatterbrain Raid	Challenge	U	0.50
Scatterbrains	Special	U	0.50
Secret Agenda	Stinger	R	3.50
Seppuku	Stinger	U	0.50
Shady Manager	Contact	U	0.50
Shakedown	Stinger	U	0.50
Shipyard Showdown	Objective	C	0.10
12			
Shriek 1000	Gear	U	0.50
Shuriken	Gear	C	0.10
Sisko • Lone Star Detective	Runner	C	0.10
Skitz • Ganger	Runner	U	0.50
Snake Totem	Special	R	4.00
Some Things Never Change	Stinger	C	0.25
Special Delivery	Special	U	0.50
Spell Lock	Gear	R	3.50
Spreading The Disease	Special	U	0.50
13			
Stand Aside!	Stinger	C	0.10
State Of Confusion	Stinger	R	3.80
Street Kid	Contact	U	0.50
Street Violence	Special	U	0.50
Street Wars	Objective	C	0.10
Stripdown	Stinger	C	0.10
Suicidal Tendencies	Special	C	0.10
Switchblade	Gear	R	4.50
Tenaka • Yakuza Agent	Runner	C	0.10
14			
Test of Honor	Special	U	0.50
The Big Break	Special	U	0.50
The Big Rig	Gear	C	0.10
The Black Market	Location	U	0.50
The Brain	Gear	C	0.10
The Docks	Location	U	0.50
The Doomsday Device	Objective	R	5.00
The Eternal Vow	Special	C	0.10
The Ghost Dance	Objective	C	0.10
15			
The Initiation	Objective	R	4.00
The Price Of Fame	Special	U	0.50
The Vault	Objective	C	0.10
Tommygun • Mafia Thug	Runner	C	0.10
Trogs	Special	R	3.50
Turf War	Objective	C	0.10
Unstable Ally	Special	U	0.50
Wake The Dead	Objective	C	0.10
Widow's Trap	Challenge	R	4.00
16			
Wildfire • Lone Star Combat Mage	Runner	R	5.50
Wind Spirit	Gear	C	0.10
Yakuza Assassin	Challenge	R	4.00
Yakuza Hit Squad	Challenge	U	0.50
Yakuza Street Thugs	Challenge	C	0.10

RARITY KEY **C** = Common **U** = Uncommon **R** = Rare **VR** = Very Rare **UR** = Ultra Rare **F** = Foil card **X** = Fixed/standard in all decks

SimCity

Mayfair Games • First set, *Limited*, released **May 1995**
518 cards in set • **IDENTIFIER: No symbol**
- Starter decks contain 120 cards; starter displays contain 12 starters
- Booster packs contain 15 cards; booster displays contain 36 boosters

Designed by **Darwin Bromley**

	Concept	●○○○○
	Gameplay	●●●●○
	Card art	●●●○○
	Player pool	●○○○○

You will need **58** nine-pocket pages to store this set. (29 doubled up)

Inspired by the Maxis computer game, the **SimCity** CCG involves building a generic city from the ground up. Followed by expansions using real sites from real cities, *SimCity* heralded a game world where, one day, sights from your own hometown might turn up in a CCG deck.

Each player places a card, representing one city block. Players start with Village cards (terrain, farms, housing) and eventually work their way up to Metropolis cards. Each time a card is placed, the player gains an amount of money. The first player to reach the preset limit, usually $250, wins.

Based, as it was, on a solitaire computer game, the *SimCity* CCG is one of the lowest-conflict CCGs, as the aim of each player is to add to the city. The only attack cards are natural disasters, which can wipe out whole city blocks. Many of the City and Metropolis cards are double-length, a unusual feature in the CCG world shared only by **Heresy**.

While an interesting game, the concept would have been better suited to a standard card game, rather than a CCG. Initial curiosity was restoked with releases based on real cities, and a huge number of promo cards immortalized companies and faces from the gaming industry. (Game designer Darwin Bromley appears at left.) But *SimCity* stopped halfway through an ambitious slate of city releases: Sets for **Hollywood**, **Paris**, **Toronto**, and **Denver** were announced for 1997 but never came out. — *Michael Greenholdt*

Set (518 cards)	**181.30**
Starter Display Box	**43.00**
Booster Display Box	**50.00**
Starter Deck	**8.00**
Booster Pack	**2.00**

Card name	Type	Rarity	Price
1			
19 Puddingham Ct.	Resd	U	0.25
50's Joint	Com	R	1.00
69 S. Downey Circle	Resd	C	0.10
101 Pleasant Av.	Resd	C	0.10
209 N. Timber St.	Resd	C	0.10
211 E. Main St.	Resd	C	0.10
212 Bethany Blvd.	Resd	U	0.25
473 Queensway Ct.	Resd	C	0.10
723 W. Ninth St.	Resd	C	0.10
2			
857 Jefferson Ave.	Resd	C	0.10
1011 Kenneth Av.	Resd	U	0.25
1306 Hunt Club Dr.	Resd	U	0.25
1850 W. Byron	Resd	U	0.25
1942 Willard St.	Resd	C	0.10
2124 Wiltshire Blvd.	Resd	C	0.10
4046 N. Campbell	Resd	C	0.10
4629 Cornelia St.	Resd	U	0.25
Abandoned Industry	Inds	R	1.00
3			
Abandoned Store	Com	R	1.00
Accountant	Com	U	0.25
Acropolis	Spcl	UR	3.00
Administrative Centery	CSrv	U	0.25
Air Force Academy	Spcl	UR	2.00
Air Force Base	Spcl	UR	2.00
Air Freight Company	Com	UR	2.00
Airline Ticket Center	CSrv	UR	2.00
Alamo	Spcl	UR	3.00
4			
Alcatraz Island	Spcl	UR	3.00
Animation Studio	Inds	UR	2.00
Apartment Building	Resd	U	0.25

Card name	Type	Rarity	Price
Apartment Building	Resd	U	0.25
Apothecary	Com	R	1.00
Appliance Superstore	Com	UR	2.00
Aquarium	CSrv	R	1.00
Art Center	Com	U	0.25
Art Institute	CSrv	UR	2.00
5			
Art Museum	CSrv	UR	2.00
Art Museum	CSrv	UR	2.00
Asphalt Plant	Inds	UR	2.00
Auto Mall	Com	UR	2.00
Auto Repair Shop	Com	C	0.10
Automobile Manufacturer	Inds	UR	2.00
Ayers Rock	Spcl	UR	3.00
Bakery	Com	C	0.10
Ball Park	Com	R	1.00
6			
Bank	Com	R	1.00
Barber Shop	Com	R	1.00
Barn	Agri	C	0.10
Barn	Agri	C	0.10
Barn	Agri	C	0.10
Barn	Agri	C	0.10
Barrens	Undv	C	0.10
Basilica of Guadelupe	Resd	UR	3.00
Battery Park	CSrv	UR	2.00
7			
Beach Coastline	Undv	U	0.25
Beach Resort	Com	UR	2.00
Bed & Breakfast	Com	C	0.10
Bensenville Fire Station	CSrv	C	0.10
Blacksmith	Inds	R	1.00
Boat Builder	Inds	R	1.00
Boat Rental	Com	R	1.00
Book Distribution Center	Inds	UR	2.00
Book Store	Com	C	0.10
8			
Botanical Gardens	Resd	UR	2.00
Box Maker	Inds	U	0.25
Brewery	Inds	U	0.25
Brickmaker	Inds	R	1.00

Card name	Type	Rarity	Price
Bridge	Undv	R	1.00
Bridge	Undv	U	0.25
Bridge	Undv	U	0.25
Bridge	Undv	U	0.25
Broadway	Com	UR	2.00
9			
Bus Barn	CSrv	U	0.25
Bus Terminal	CSrv	R	1.00
Caesar's Palace Hotel & Casino	Com	UR	2.50
Candy Factory	Inds	R	1.00
Candy Store	Com	R	1.00
Car Wash	Com	U	0.25
Career Training Center	Inds	R	1.00
Carta Mundi	Inds	R	1.00
Casino	Com	R	1.00
10			
Castle	Resd	UR	2.00
Catholic Church	Resd	U	0.25
Cavern	Undv	R	1.00
Cemetery	Spcl	R	1.00
Central Park	CSrv	UR	2.50
Chicago Fire Station	CSrv	C	0.10
Children's Museum	CSrv	UR	2.00
Christian Church	Resd	U	0.25
Cineplex	Com	UR	2.00
11			
City Council Chairman	Mayr	U	0.25
City Hall	Spcl	R	1.00
City Park	CSrv	R	1.00
Civic Theatre	Com	R	1.00
Cliff Dwelling	Undv	UR	2.00
Club House	Resd	R	1.00
Coal-Burning Power Plant	Inds	C	0.10
Coal-Burning Power Plant	Inds	C	0.10
Coal-Burning Power Plant	Inds	C	0.10
12			
Coastline	Undv	U	0.25
College	CSrv	C	0.10
Colonial Gentry Home	Resd	C	0.10

Card name	Type	Rarity	Price
Colonial Home	Resd	C	0.10
Colonial Servants' Quarters	Resd	C	0.10
Colosseum	Spcl	UR	2.00
Comisky Park Stadium	Com	UR	3.00
Com Relocation	Dis	R	1.00
Community Center	CSrv	U	0.25
13			
Computer Manufacturer	Inds	UR	2.00
Concert Arena	Com	UR	2.00
Concrete Firm	Inds	R	1.00
Concrete Plant	Inds	U	0.25
Condo	Resd	U	0.25
Condominium	Resd	R	1.00
Construction Firm	Inds	U	0.25
Container Dock	Inds	UR	2.00
Control Tower	CSrv	R	1.00
14			
Contruction Site	Spcl	UR	2.00
Convention Center	Com	UR	2.00
Cook County Police Station	CSrv	U	0.25
Co-op	Resd	UR	2.00
Cooper	Inds	R	1.00
Corporate Headquarters	Com	UR	2.00
Corporate Office	Com	R	1.00
Corrupt Council Member: (Agri)	Cncl	R	1.00
Corrupt Council Member: (CSrv)	Cncl	R	1.00
15			
Corrupt Council Member: (Inds)	Cncl	R	1.00
Corrupt Council Member: (Resd)	Cncl	R	1.00
Corrupt Council Member: (Spcl)	Cncl	R	1.00
Corrupt Council Member: (Com)	Cncl	R	1.00
Council Member: (CSrv)	Cncl	U	0.25

RARITY KEY   **C** = Common   **U** = Uncommon   **R** = Rare   **VR** = Very Rare   **UR** = Ultra Rare   **F** = Foil card   **X** = Fixed/standard in all decks

Card name	Type	Rarity	Price
Council Member: (Com)	Cncl	U	0.25
Council Member: (Inds)	Cncl	U	0.25
Council Member: (Resd)	Cncl	U	0.25
Council Member: (Spcl)	Cncl	U	0.25
16			
Council Member (man w/glasses)	Cncl	C	0.10
Council Member (man w/out glasses)	Cncl	C	0.10
Council Member (woman w/necklace)	Cncl	C	0.10
Council Member (woman w/out necklace)	Cncl	C	0.10
Council Member: (Agri)	Cncl	U	0.25
Country Schoolhouse	Resd	R	1.00
County Courthouse	Spcl	U	0.25
Cracker Tower	Inds	U	0.25
Crime Wave	Dis	U	0.25
17			
Criminal Courthouse	Spcl	U	0.25
Cruise Line Dock	Com	UR	2.00
Currency Exchange	Com	R	1.00
Dairy	Inds	UR	2.00
Dairy Barn	Agri	C	0.10
Dairy Farm	Agri	C	0.10
Dairy Farm	Agri	C	0.10
Dentist's Office	Com	R	1.00
Department Store	Com	C	0.10
18			
Desert Research Center	CSrv	UR	2.00
Diamond Head	Undv	UR	2.50
District Courthouse	Spcl	UR	2.00
District Post Office	CSrv	UR	2.00
Domed Stadium	CSrv	UR	2.00
Domed Stadium	Com	UR	2.00
Dormitory	Resd	C	0.10
Doughnut Shop	Com	R	1.00
Drilling Rig	Inds	UR	2.00
19			
Drive In Theatre	Com	R	1.00
Drought	Dis	U	0.25
Drug Store	Com	C	0.10
Dry Cleaners	Com	C	0.10
Du Page Police Station	CSrv	C	0.10
Duplex	Resd	U	0.25
Election	Dis	U	0.25
Electrician	Com	U	0.25
Electronics Manufacturer	Inds	U	0.25
20			
Emissions Testing Facility	CSrv	R	1.00
Episcopal Church	Resd	U	0.25
Excalibur Hotel & Casino	Com	UR	2.50
Express Delivery Company	Com	UR	2.00
Factory	Inds	R	1.00
Fairgrounds	Spcl	UR	2.00
Farm	Agri	C	0.10
Farm Implement Manufacturer	Inds	UR	2.00
21			
Farmhouse	Agri	C	0.10
Farmhouse	Agri	C	0.10
Farmhouse	Agri	C	0.10
Farming Conglomerate	Agri	UR	2.00
Fast Food Restaurant	Com	C	0.10
Field	Agri	C	0.10
Field	Agri	C	0.10
Field	Agri	C	0.10
Field	Agri	C	0.10
Fire Station 52 & 65	CSrv	C	0.10
22			
Fire Station Headquarters	CSrv	UR	2.00

Card name	Type	Rarity	Price
Fire!	Dis	U	0.25
Flinders St. Station	Com	UR	2.00
Flood	Dis	U	0.25
Florist	Com	U	0.25
Fondue Restaurant	Com	C	0.10
Food Distributor	Inds	U	0.25
Food Packaging Plant	Inds	U	0.25
Forbidden City	CSrv	UR	3.00
23			
Forest	Undv	C	0.10
Forest	Undv	C	0.10
Forest	Undv	C	0.10
Forest	Undv	C	0.10
Forest	Undv	C	0.10
Forest	Undv	C	0.10
Forest Preserve	Undv	R	1.00
Fountain	Spcl	UR	2.00
Fraternity House	Resd	C	0.10
24			
Freight Yard	Inds	UR	2.00
Funeral Parlor	Com	U	0.25
Garden Shop	Com	R	1.00
Gas Station	Com	C	0.10
Gas Station	Com	C	0.10
General Store	Com	C	0.10
Ghost Removal Service	Com	UR	2.50
Golden Gate Bridge	Undv	UR	3.00
Golf Course	CSrv	UR	2.00
25			
Government Reform	Dis	R	1.00
Governor	Mayr	R	1.00
Grade School	Resd	C	0.10
Graduate School	CSrv	R	1.00
Grain Elevator	Agri	U	0.25
Grand Canyon	Undv	UR	3.00
Gravel Supplier	Inds	C	0.10
Great Pyramids	Spcl	UR	3.00
Great Wall of China	Spcl	UR	3.00
26			
Greek Orthodox Church	Resd	U	0.25
Grocery Store	Com	C	0.10
Groundskeeper's House	Resd	R	1.00
Guardhouse	CSrv	R	1.00
Gym	CSrv	U	0.25
Hangar	CSrv	R	1.00
Hardware Store	Com	U	0.25
Haunted House	Resd	R	1.00
Health Spa	Resd	UR	2.00
27			
Helipad	CSrv	R	1.00
High School	Resd	C	0.10
High-Rise Apartments	Resd	UR	2.00
High-Rise Office Building	Com	UR	2.00
Historic Structure	Dis	U	0.25
Historical Landmark	CSrv	UR	2.00
Hobby Store	Com	U	0.25
Hoover Dam	Undv	UR	3.00
Horse Race Track	Com	UR	2.00
28			
Hospital	CSrv	U	0.25
Hot Dog Restaurant	Com	U	0.25
Hotel	Com	R	1.00
Hotel	Com	C	0.10
Hotel & Casino	Com	UR	2.00
Hydroelectric Power Plant	Inds	R	1.00
Hydroelectric Power Plant	Inds	C	0.10
Hydroelectric Power Plant	Inds	C	0.10
Ice Cream Parlor	Com	C	0.10
29			
Industrial Relocation	Dis	R	1.00

Card name	Type	Rarity	Price
Industrial Supply Company	Ind	R	1.00
Inn	Com	R	1.00
InterCity Highway	CSrv	R	1.00
InterCity Station	CSrv	R	1.00
Island	Undv	R	1.00
Jewish Temple	Resd	U	0.25
Joliet Police Station	CSrv	C	0.10
Junior College	Resd	U	0.25
30			
Kennedy Space Center	Spcl	UR	3.00
Kindergarten	Resd	C	0.10
Koplow Dice	Inds	R	1.00
Labor Shortage	Dis	U	0.25
Labor Strikes Industry	Dis	R	1.00
Lake	Undv	U	0.25
Lake	Undv	C	0.10
Lake	Undv	C	0.10
Lake	Undv	C	0.10
31			
Land Fill	Spcl	R	1.00
Large Bridge	Undv	UR	2.00
Large Condominium	Resd	UR	2.00
Large Factory	Inds	UR	2.00
Large Hospital	CSrv	UR	2.00
Large Hotel	Com	UR	2.00
Large University Library	CSrv	UR	2.00
Law Office	Com	U	0.25
Le Moulin Rouge	Com	UR	3.00
32			
Liberal Arts College	CSrv	R	1.00
Lighthouse	CSrv	R	1.00
Local Cleaner	Com	U	0.25
Local Monument	Spcl	R	1.00
Logging Transport	Inds	R	1.00
London Tower Bridge	Undv	UR	3.00
Low-Income Housing	Resd	U	0.25
Lumber Mill	Inds	U	0.25
Lumber Yard	Inds	UR	2.00
33			
Lutheran Church	Resd	U	0.25
Luxor Hotel & Casino	Com	UR	2.50
Magazine	CSrv	R	1.00
Mail Proccessing Center	CSrv	UR	2.00
Major Department Store	Com	UR	2.00
Mansion	Resd	R	1.00
Marina	Com	R	1.00
Marine Base	Spcl	UR	2.00
Marsh	Undv	C	0.10
34			
Martial Arts Studio	Com	R	1.00
Mass Transit Terminal	CSrv	UR	2.00
Maxis	Com	R	1.00
Mayfair Games	Com	R	1.00
Mayor	Mayr	C	0.10
Mayor Honored	Dis	U	0.25
Mayor Recalled	Dis	U	0.25
Mayor's House	Resd	UR	2.00
Media Uncovers Bribes	Dis	U	0.25
35			
Medical Research Center	CSrv	UR	2.00
Medical Supply Center	Com	U	0.25
Mental Health Center	CSrv	R	1.00
Methodist Church	Resd	C	0.10
Metropolitan Museum	CSrv	UR	2.00
MGM Grand Hotel & Casino	Com	UR	2.50
Mobile Home	Resd	C	0.10
Mobile Home	Resd	C	0.10
Monster Attacks	Dis	R	1.00
36			
Monument Carver	Inds	R	1.00
Mount Rushmore	Undv	UR	3.00
Mountain	Undv	U	1.00

Card name	Type	Rarity	Price
Mountain	Undv	U	0.25
Mountain	Undv	C	0.10
Mountain	Undv	C	0.10
Mountain	Undv	C	0.10
Mountain	Undv	C	0.10
Movie Set	Spcl	R	1.00
37			
Movie Studio	Inds	UR	2.00
Movie Theater	Com	C	0.10
Mt. Prospect Police & Fire Station	CSrv	R	1.00
Multiple Office Building	Com	UR	2.00
Municipal Pool	CSrv	R	1.00
Museum of Anthropology	CSrv	UR	2.00
National Guard Armory	Spcl	UR	2.00
New Car Dealer	Com	U	0.25
Newspaper	Com	U	0.25
38			
Niagara Falls	Undv	UR	2.00
Nightclub	Com	U	0.25
Nuclear Power Plant	Inds	R	1.00
Office Center	Com	U	0.25
Office Equipment Plant	Inds	UR	2.00
Offshore Oil Well	Inds	UR	2.00
Oil Field	Inds	UR	2.00
Oil Refiner	Inds	U	0.25
Oil Refinery	Inds	UR	2.00
39			
Oil Storage Tanks	Inds	R	1.00
Oil Well	Inds	C	0.10
Opera House	Com	R	1.00
Optometrist	Com	R	1.00
OTB Parlor	Com	R	1.00
Outdoor Mall	Com	UR	2.00
Outdoor Stage	CSrv	UR	2.00
Outpatient Clinic	CSrv	C	0.10
Pagoda	Resd	UR	2.00
40			
Painter	Com	C	0.10
Palace	Resd	UR	2.00
Panama Canal	Spcl	UR	2.50
Paper Manufacturer	Inds	U	0.25
Park	CSrv	U	0.25
Park	CSrv	C	0.10
Park	CSrv	C	0.10
Parking Garage	Com	UR	2.00
Parking Lot	Com	U	0.25
41			
Parking Lot	Com	C	0.10
Parking Lot	Com	C	0.10
Pasture	Agri	C	0.10
Pasture	Agri	C	0.10
Pawn Shop	Com	R	1.00
Pipeline	Undv	C	0.10
Pipeline	Undv	C	0.10
Pizza Restaurant	Com	R	1.00
Plains	Undv	U	0.25
42			
Plains	Undv	C	0.10
Plains	Undv	C	0.10
Plains	Undv	C	0.10
Plane Mechanic	Com	R	1.00
Planetarium	CSrv	UR	2.00
Playground	CSrv	R	1.00
Plaza	Com	R	1.00
Pollution Alert	Dis	U	0.25
Pond	Undv	R	1.00
43			
Pool & Patio Store	Com	R	1.00
Post Office	CSrv	C	0.10
Post Office	CSrv	C	0.10
Postal Strike	Dis	U	0.25
Power Line Construction Firm	Inds	U	0.25

RARITY KEY C = Common U = Uncommon R = Rare VR = Very Rare UR = Ultra Rare F = Foil card X = Fixed/standard in all decks

Card name	Type	Rarity	Price
☐ Presbyterian Church	Resd	U	0.25
☐ Preschool	Resd	C	0.10
☐ Primitive Hut	Undv	C	0.10
☐ Printer	Inds	U	0.25
44			
☐ Prison	Spcl	R	1.00
☐ Pub	Com	C	0.10
☐ Public Library	CSrv	U	0.25
☐ Pyramid of the Sun	Spcl	UR	3.00
☐ Radio Broadcast Center	Com	U	0.25
☐ Radio City Music Hall	Com	UR	2.50
☐ Rail Construction Firm	Inds	U	0.25
☐ Railroad Offices	Com	UR	2.00
☐ Ranch House	Resd	C	0.10
45			
☐ Rapid Transit Station	CSrv	R	1.00
☐ Rapid Transit Station	CSrv	UR	2.00
☐ Real Estate Agent	Com	U	0.25
☐ Real Estate Taxes	Dis	U	0.25
☐ Recording Studio	Com	UR	2.00
☐ Regional Grade School	CSrv	UR	2.00
☐ Regional High School	CSrv	UR	2.00
☐ Regional Hospital	CSrv	UR	2.00
☐ Regional Library	CSrv	UR	2.00
46			
☐ Renovated Lofts	Resd	UR	2.00
☐ Rental Car Company	Com	U	0.25
☐ Restaurant & Saloon	Com	R	1.00
☐ Retreat Center	CSrv	U	0.25
☐ Rhine Castle	Spcl	C	0.10
☐ Rhine River	Undv	UR	2.50
☐ River	Undv	C	0.10
☐ River	Undv	C	0.10
☐ River	Undv	C	0.10
47			
☐ River	Undv	C	0.10
☐ Riverboat Casino Dock	Com	R	1.00
☐ Road Construction Firm	Inds	U	0.25

Card name	Type	Rarity	Price
☐ Roadside BBQ	Com	U	0.25
☐ Rockefeller Center	CSrv	UR	2.50
☐ Rough Coastline	Undv	U	0.25
☐ Ruins	Undv	UR	2.00
☐ Runway	Inds	UR	2.00
☐ Sandwich Shop	Com	R	1.00
48			
☐ Savings & Loan	Com	U	0.25
☐ School of Business	CSrv	R	1.00
☐ School of Law	CSrv	R	1.00
☐ School of Medicine	CSrv	R	1.00
☐ School of Science	CSrv	R	1.00
☐ Seafood Restaurant	Com	U	0.25
☐ Seaport	Inds	U	0.25
☐ Sears Tower	Com	UR	3.00
☐ Sequoia National Forest	Undv	UR	2.50
49			
☐ Ship Sinks	Dis	R	1.00
☐ Shoe Store	Com	U	0.25
☐ Shopping Mall	Com	UR	2.00
☐ Shrine Auditorium	CSrv	UR	2.00
☐ Ski Lodge	Com	U	0.25
☐ Ski Manufacturer	Inds	U	0.25
☐ Sorority House	Resd	C	0.10
☐ Soundstage	Inds	UR	2.00
☐ South Park Fire Station	CSrv	U	0.25
50			
☐ Space Needle	Com	UR	2.50
☐ Speedway	Spcl	UR	2.00
☐ Sphynx	Spcl	UR	3.00
☐ Spirits Invade	Dis	R	1.00
☐ Sporting Goods Store	Com	U	0.25
☐ St. Louis Arch	Spcl	UR	3.00
☐ Stable	Com	R	1.00
☐ State Police Headquarters	CSrv	UR	2.00
☐ Steel Distributor	Inds	U	0.25
51			
☐ Steel Processor	Inds	U	0.25
☐ Stonehenge	Spcl	UR	3.00

Card name	Type	Rarity	Price
☐ Street Festival	Com	R	1.00
☐ Street Market	Com	R	1.00
☐ Sub Station	Inds	C	0.10
☐ Suez Canal	Spcl	UR	2.50
☐ Super Store	Com	U	0.25
☐ Supermarket	Com	C	0.10
☐ Supply Company	Inds	UR	2.00
52			
☐ Surf	Undv	UR	2.00
☐ Swamp	Undv	R	1.00
☐ Sydney Opera House	Com	UR	3.00
☐ Tailor	Com	R	1.00
☐ Taj Mahal	Spcl	UR	3.00
☐ Tank Farm	Inds	UR	2.00
☐ Tavern	Com	R	1.00
☐ Telecommunications Company	Com	R	1.00
☐ Telecommunications HQ	Com	UR	2.00
53			
☐ Telephone Company	Inds	C	0.10
☐ Television Studio	Inds	UR	2.00
☐ Time Square	Com	UR	2.00
☐ Tornado Strikes	Dis	U	0.25
☐ Trading Post	Com	R	1.00
☐ Travel Agency	Com	C	0.10
☐ Truck Stop	Com	C	0.10
☐ Trucking Company	Com	U	0.25
☐ Tunnel	Undv	UR	2.00
54			
☐ TV Station A24	Com	R	1.00
☐ Union Hall	CSrv	R	1.00
☐ Union Station	CSrv	UR	2.00
☐ United Nations	Spcl	UR	2.00
☐ University Book Store	Com	U	0.25
☐ University Extension	CSrv	UR	2.00
☐ University Grounds	CSrv	C	0.10
☐ University Library	CSrv	U	0.25
☐ University of Michigan Hospital	CSrv	UR	2.00

Card name	Type	Rarity	Price
55			
☐ University Quad	Resd	U	0.25
☐ University Stadium	Com	U	0.25
☐ UNLV Stadium	Com	UR	2.50
☐ Upcountry Farmhouse	Agri	C	0.10
☐ Used Car Dealer	Com	U	0.25
☐ Vatican	Spcl	UR	2.50
☐ Video Store	Com	U	0.25
☐ Village Hall	Spcl	R	1.00
☐ Vineyard	Agri	R	1.00
56			
☐ Warehouse	Com	U	0.25
☐ Warehouse	Com	U	0.25
☐ Washington Square Park	CSrv	UR	2.00
☐ Water Purification Plant	CSrv	R	1.00
☐ Water Tower	CSrv	C	0.10
☐ Waterfall	Undv	UR	2.00
☐ Well	CSrv	R	1.00
☐ Westmore Fire Station	CSrv	C	0.10
☐ Wharf	Inds	R	1.00
57			
☐ Wheaton Police Station	CSrv	C	0.10
☐ Wholesale Warehouse	Com	UR	2.00
☐ Wildlife Park	Spcl	UR	2.00
☐ Wind Generated Power Plant	Inds	R	1.00
☐ Winter	Dis	U	0.25
☐ Woodcutter	Inds	R	1.00
☐ Work Shortage	Dis	U	0.25
☐ World Trade Center	Com	UR	2.50
☐ Yellowstone National Park	Undv	UR	2.50
58			
☐ YMCA	Resd	R	1.00
☐ YMCA	Com	U	0.25
☐ Yosemite National Park	Undv	UR	3.00
☐ Zoning Problems	Dis	U	0.25
☐ Zoo	Spcl	UR	2.00

UNION HEADQUARTERS

Convention 2. Receive 1 for each Commercial and Industrial within 10 blocks.

$ 5 ⚒ 6   ⚑ 4 ⚙ 1

Set (120 cards) — 15.00
Starter Display Box — 35.00
Starter Deck — 7.00

Card rarities are fixed.

SimCity • Chicago

Mayfair Games • Released **August 1996**
120 cards in set • **IDENTIFIER: Chicago symbol**
• Starter decks contain 120 cards; starter displays contain 6 starters

You will need **14** nine-pocket pages to store this set. (7 doubled up)

SIM CITY
THE CARD GAME™

The first expansion for **SimCity** moves the players from building a generic city to construction of **Chicago**. Many of the cards are landmarks of the city and the political cards feature famous politicians from Chicago's past, including Mayor Daley. This expansion was released only in 120-card starter decks without any booster packs.

Like future expansions, *SimCity: Chicago* gave greater scope to tournament play (Dueling Suburbs), in which each player builds a separate city, instead of constructing a common city. Instead of two generic cities, New York and Chicago, or least Elmhurst and Skokie, can vie for civic dominance. — **Michael Greenholdt**

Card name	Type	Price
1		
☐ 1 North Ave.	Resd	0.10
☐ 17 Primrose Lane	Resd	0.10
☐ 71 Elaine Pl.	Resd	0.10
☐ 347 North Ave.	Resd	0.10
☐ 514 W. Ashland	Resd	0.10
☐ 611 E. Washington	Resd	0.10
☐ 836 S. Laflin	Resd	0.10

Card name	Type	Price
☐ 910 Oak St.	Resd	0.10
☐ 1684 Lexington	Resd	0.10
2		
☐ 1722 Arlington	Resd	0.10
☐ 2773 N. Taylor	Resd	0.10
☐ 3522 S. State	Resd	0.10
☐ 4517 Hobby Ct.	Resd	0.10
☐ 7116 Caldwell	Resd	0.10
☐ Amusement Park	Spec	0.50
☐ Apartment Building	Resd	0.10
☐ Apartment Building	Resd	0.10
3		
☐ Bank	Com	0.10
☐ Beach Coastline	Undv	0.10
☐ Bridge	Undv	0.10
☐ Cathedral	Resd	0.10

Card name	Type	Price
☐ Catholic Church	Resd	0.10
☐ Cemetery	Spec	0.10
☐ Chicago Fire Station	CSrv	0.50
☐ Chicago Fire Station	CSrv	0.50
☐ Chicago Police Station	CSrv	0.50
☐ Chicago Police Station	CSrv	0.50
4		
☐ Chocolate Factory	Inds	0.50
☐ Christian Science Church	Resd	0.50
☐ City Hall	Gov	0.50
☐ Coach House	Resd	0.10
☐ College	Com	0.10
☐ Condominium	Resd	0.10
☐ Convention Center	CSrv	0.10
☐ Convention Center	CSrv	0.10

Card name	Type	Price
☐ Convention Center & Hotel	Com	0.10
5		
☐ Council Member	Cncl	0.10
☐ Council Member	Cncl	0.10
☐ Council Member	Cncl	0.10
☐ Council Member	Cncl	0.10
☐ Courthouse	Gov	0.10
☐ Crime Wave	Dis	0.10
☐ Display Company	Inds	0.10
☐ District Fire Station	CSrv	0.10
☐ District Police Station	CSrv	0.10
6		
☐ Duplex	Resd	0.10
☐ Fast Food Spot	Com	0.10
☐ Federal Office	Gov	0.10
☐ Fire!	Dis	0.10

RARITY KEY C = Common U = Uncommon R = Rare VR = Very Rare UR = Ultra Rare F = Foil card X = Fixed/standard in all decks

Card name	Type	Price
Flood	Dis	0.10
Florist	Com	0.10
Football Stadium	Spec	0.10
Forest	Undv	0.10
Forest Preserve	Undv	0.10
7		
Fountain	Spec	0.10
Funeral Home	Com	0.10
Gas Station	Com	0.10
General Aviation Airport	CSrv	0.10
Grade School	Resd	0.10
Health Club	Com	0.10
High School	Resd	0.10
Hospital	CSrv	0.10
Hotel	Com	0.10
8		
Kindergarten	Resd	0.10
Lake	Undv	0.10
Lake	Undv	0.10
Lake Coastline	Undv	0.25
Lake Coastline	Undv	0.25
Lake Coastline	Undv	0.25
Low-Income Housing	Resd	0.10
Low-Income Housing	Resd	0.10
Marina	Com	0.10
9		
Marine Training Center	Gov	0.10
Marshalling Yard	Inds	0.10
Mayor	Mayr	0.50
Monument	Spec	0.10
Movie Theater	Com	0.10
Mrs. O'Leary's	Resd	1.00
Natural History Museum	CSrv	1.00
Neighborhood Bar	Resd	0.10
Newspaper	Com	0.10
10		
Newspaper Printing Plant	Inds	0.10
North Pier	Com	1.00
Office & Condo Tower	Com	0.10
Office Center	Com	0.10
Park	CSrv	0.10
Park	CSrv	0.10
Park Building	CSrv	0.10
Parking Garage	Com	0.10
Parking Garage	Com	0.10
11		
Pawn Shop	Com	0.10
Plains	Undv	0.10
Plains	Undv	0.10
Post Office	CSrv	0.10
Power Plant	Inds	0.10
Power Plant	Inds	0.10
Power Plant	Inds	0.10
Preschool	Resd	0.10
Pub	Com	0.10
12		
Public Library	CSrv	0.10
Rapid Transit Station	CSrv	0.10
Restaurant	Com	0.10
River	Undv	0.10
River	Undv	0.10
River	Undv	0.10
Shopping Mall	Com	0.10
Showroom Mart	Com	0.10
Snow Storm	Dis	0.10
13		
St. Patrick's Day	Dis	0.10
Swamp	Undv	0.10
Technical School	Com	0.10
Telephone Company	Inds	0.10
Theater	Com	0.10
TV Station	Com	0.10
Union Headquarters	CSrv	0.10
Union Station	CSrv	0.10
Water Tower	CSrv	0.10
14		
Wetlands	Undv	0.10
Zoo	CSrv	0.10
Zoo Farm	CSrv	0.10

SimCity • Washington, D.C.

Mayfair Games • Released **May 1996**

120 cards in set • **IDENTIFIER: Capitol dome symbol**

You will need **14** nine-pocket pages to store this set. (7 doubled up)

- Starter decks contain 120 cards; starter displays contain 6 starters

The second **SimCity** expansion gave players access to the nation's capital, **Washington D.C.**

Like the **Chicago** expansion, the cards are much more specific, including street addresses. Also like *Chicago*, no boosters were released, only fixed 120-card starter decks.

While many of the *Washington* cards yield a lot of cash when placed, this is balanced by the *Washington* event cards that include demonstrations and festivals.

Also of note is the **President** card. As may be expected, the **President** has a limited influence on a city, his or her sole power being to declare a city a disaster area and so avoid an event card. — **Michael Greenholdt**

Set (120 cards)	15.00
Starter Display Box	35.00
Starter Deck	7.00

Card rarities are fixed.

Card name	Type	Price
1		
113 A Street SE	Resd	0.10
275 D Street SE	Resd	0.10
421 East Capitol St.	Resd	0.10
1185 Florida Ave. NW	Resd	0.10
1245 Pennsylvannia Ave.	Resd	0.10
1322 Constitution Ave. NE	Resd	0.10
1322 Elliott St.	Resd	0.10
2135 Cleveland St.	Resd	0.10
2144 Colorama	Resd	0.10
2		
2633 Armstrong Pl.	Resd	0.10
3442 Rhode Island	Resd	0.10
4111 Wisconsin Ave NW	Resd	0.10
Apartment Building	Resd	0.10
Apartment Building	Resd	0.10
Apartment Building	Resd	0.10
Bank	Com	0.10
Baptist Church	Resd	0.10
Bar	Com	0.10
3		
Basilica	Resd	0.10
Bed & Breakfast	Com	0.10
Blair House	Resd	0.50
Bridge	Undv	0.10
Bureau of Labor Statistics	Gov	0.50
Canal	Undv	0.10
Canal	Undv	0.10
Canal	Undv	0.10
Canal	Undv	0.10
4		
Canal Bridge	Undv	0.10
Canal Watergate	Undv	0.10
Capitol	Gov	0.10
Carousel	Com	0.10
Cemetery	Spec	0.10
Chancery	Resd	0.10
City Hall	Gov	0.10
College	CSrv	0.10
Condo	Resd	0.10
5		
Corner Grocery	Com	0.10
Corporate Office	Com	0.10
Council Member	Cncl	0.10
Council Member	Cncl	0.10
Council Member	Cncl	0.10
Custom Cake Shop	Com	0.10
DC Fire Station	CSrv	0.25
DC Fire Station	CSrv	0.25
DC Police Station	CSrv	0.25
6		
DC Police Station	CSrv	0.25
Demonstration	Dis	0.10
Department of Agriculture	Gov	0.25
Department of Commerce	Gov	0.25
Department of Education	Gov	0.25
Department of HUD	Gov	0.25
Department of Transportation	Gov	0.25
Department of Treasury	Gov	0.25
Embassy	Resd	0.10
7		
Embassy	Com	0.10
Embassy	Gov	0.10
Epidemic	Dis	0.10
Ethopian Restaurant	Com	0.10
Executive Office Building	Gov	0.10
Farmhouse	Agri	0.10
FEMA	Gov	0.50
Forest	Undv	0.10
Forest	Undv	0.10
8		
Grade School	Resd	0.10
High School	Resd	0.10
Hospital	CSrv	0.10
Hotel	Com	0.10
Ice Storm	Dis	0.10
Jefferson Memorial	Spec	1.00
Kindergarten	Resd	0.10
Library of Congress	Gov	1.00
Mall Festival	Dis	0.10
9		
Marine Police & Fire Station	CSrv	0.10
Market	Com	0.10
Mayor	Mayr	0.50
Mill	Inds	0.10
Mill Pond	Undv	0.10
Mill Pond Dam	Undv	0.10
Mosque	Resd	0.10
Mountain	Undv	0.10
Mountain Forest	Undv	0.10
10		
Mountain River	Undv	0.10
Museum	CSrv	0.10
Museum	CSrv	0.10
Museum	CSrv	0.10
Museum Restaurant	Com	0.10
National Cathedral	Resd	0.10
National Judiciary Center	Gov	0.50
Newspaper	Com	0.10
Park	CSrv	0.10
11		
Parking Lot	Com	0.10
Party Headquarters	Com	0.10
Party Headquarters	Com	0.10
Post Office	CSrv	0.10
Power Plant	Inds	0.10
Power Plant	Inds	0.10
Power Plant	Inds	0.10
Preschool	Gov	0.10
President	Cncl	0.75
12		
Public Library	CSrv	0.10
Rapid Transit Station	Com	0.10
Reflecting Pool	CSrv	0.50
River	Undv	0.10
River	Undv	0.10
River Bank	Undv	0.10
Sculpture Garden	CSrv	0.50
Spring House	Agri	0.50
Storehouse	Inds	0.10
13		
Supreme Court	Gov	1.00
Telephone Company	Inds	0.10
Theater	Com	0.10
Tunnel	Undv	0.10
TV Station	Com	0.10
Union Headquarters	CSrv	0.10
Union Headquarters	CSrv	0.10
Union Station	CSrv	0.10
Washington Monument	Spec	1.00
14		
Water Tower	CSrv	0.10
White House	Gov	1.00
Zoo	CSrv	0.10

RARITY KEY   C = Common   **U** = Uncommon   **R** = Rare   **VR** = Very Rare   **UR** = Ultra Rare   **F** = Foil card   **X** = Fixed/standard in all decks

SimCity • New York City

Mayfair Games • Released **May 1996**

120 cards in set • **IDENTIFIER: "Big Apple" symbol**

You will need **14** nine-pocket pages to store this set. (7 doubled up)

• Starter decks contain 120 cards; starter displays contain 6 starters

    New York City continues the theme of **SimCity** expansions covering actual cities. Like its predecessors, the cards are much more specific and reflect the character of New York City. Even the events are tailored to the Big Apple, including Macy's **Thanksgiving Day Parade**.

    While the money values are good, the crime rate is high — this *is* 1996 — which can really hurt a player given the right (or wrong) event cards. — ***Michael Greenholdt***

	Price
Set (120 cards)	15.00
Starter Display Box	35.00
Starter Deck	7.00

Card rarities are fixed.

Card name	Type	Price
[1]		
25 Empire Blvd.	Resd	0.10
33 Wall Street	Resd	0.10
49 Park Avenue	Resd	0.10
117 South 13th Street	Resd	0.10
129 East 11th Avenue	Resd	0.10
221 West Water	Resd	0.10
311 South 23rd Street	Resd	0.10
437 West Broadway	Resd	0.10
461 East 49th Street	Resd	0.10
[2]		
525 West 16th Avenue	Resd	0.10
562 Central Park East	Resd	0.10
617 South Adams	Resd	0.10
3743 N 5th Avenue	Resd	0.10
4418 East 4th Avenue	Resd	0.10
5421 South Harlem	Resd	0.10
Amusement Park	Com	0.50
Apartment Complex	Resd	0.10
Art Museum	CSrv	0.10
[3]		
Ball Park	Com	0.10
Bank	Com	0.10
Beach Coastline	Undv	0.10
Beach Coastline	Undv	0.10
Branch Library	CSrv	0.10

Card name	Type	Price
Bridge	Undv	0.10
Bridge	Undv	0.10
Buddhist Center	Resd	0.10
Cafe	Com	0.10
[4]		
Cathedral	Resd	0.10
Catholic Church	Resd	0.10
Cemetery	Spec	0.10
Chemical Plant	Inds	0.10
Clothing Store	Com	0.10
Coastline	Undv	0.10
Coastline	Undv	0.10
Coastline	Undv	0.10
College	CSrv	0.10
[5]		
Concert Hall	Com	0.10
Condominium	Resd	0.10
Condominium	Resd	0.10
Convention Center	Com	0.10
Council Member	Cncl	0.10
Council Member	Cncl	0.10
Council Member	Cncl	0.10
Council Member	Cncl	0.10
Dance Club	Com	0.10
[6]		
Department Store	Com	0.10
Diner	Com	0.10
Ellis Island	Gov	1.00
Empire State Building	Com	1.00
Ferry Dock	CSrv	0.10
Financial Museum	CSrv	0.50
Forest	Undv	0.10
Forest	Undv	0.10
Grand Central Station	CSrv	1.00
[7]		
Health Club	Com	0.10
High School	Resd	0.10

Card name	Type	Price
Hospital	CSrv	0.10
Hotel	Com	0.10
Hotel	Com	0.10
Investment Banker	Com	0.10
Italian Market	Com	0.10
Kindergarten & Grade School	Resd	0.10
Loft Apartments	Resd	0.10
[8]		
Loft Apartments	Resd	0.10
Low-Income Housing	Resd	0.10
Lumber Yard	Inds	0.10
Mayor	Mayr	0.50
Meltdown!	Dis	0.10
Motorcycle Club	Com	0.10
Municipal Pool	CSrv	0.10
New York Fire Station	CSrv	0.25
New York Fire Station	CSrv	0.25
[9]		
New York Police Station	CSrv	0.25
New York Police Station	CSrv	0.25
Newspaper	Com	0.10
Nuclear Power Plant	Inds	0.25
Ocean	Undv	0.10
Ocean	Undv	0.10
Ocean	Undv	0.10
Office Building	Com	0.10
Park	CSrv	0.10
[10]		
Parking Garage	Com	0.10
Pier	Inds	0.10
Pier	Inds	0.10
Plains	Undv	0.10
Plains	Undv	0.10
Plains	Undv	0.10
Playground	CSrv	0.10

Card name	Type	Price
Post Office	CSrv	0.10
Power Blackout!	Dis	0.10
[11]		
Power Plant	Inds	0.10
Power Plant	Inds	0.10
Power Plant	Inds	0.10
Preschool	Resd	0.10
Public Library	CSrv	0.10
Public Toilet	CSrv	0.10
Rapid Transit Station	CSrv	0.10
River	Undv	0.10
River	Undv	0.10
[12]		
River	Undv	0.10
Russian Restaurant	Com	0.10
Sports Arena	Com	0.10
Statue	Spec	0.10
Statue of Liberty	Spec	1.00
Steak Restaurant	Com	0.10
Stock Broker	Com	0.10
Stock Exchange	Com	0.10
Stock Exchange	Com	0.10
[13]		
Sugar Plant	Inds	0.10
Tavern	Com	0.10
Taxi Company	Com	0.10
Telephone Company	Inds	0.10
Thanksgiving Day Parade	Dis	0.25
Theater	Com	0.10
Toy Store	Com	0.10
Traffic Jams!	Dis	0.10
Trust Company	Com	0.10
[14]		
TV Station	Com	0.10
Washington Square Arch	CSrv	0.50
World Financial Center	Com	0.50

SimCity • Atlanta

Mayfair Games • Released **July 1996**

120 cards in set • **IDENTIFIER: Peach symbol**

You will need **14** nine-pocket pages to store this set. (7 doubled up)

• Starter decks contain 120 cards; starter displays contain 6 starters

    The final expansion covers ***Atlanta*** but with a twist. Both historical Atlanta (plantations, Confederate Capital, etc.) and the modern Atlanta (Martin Luther King Jr. Freedom Hall, Carter Presidential Library) are presented. A player can overlay the old with the new, or build them side by side. — ***Michael Greenholdt***

	Price
Set (120 cards)	15.00
Starter Display Box	35.00
Starter Deck	7.00

Card rarities are fixed.

Card name	Type	Price
[1]		
10 Randolph Ct.	Resd	0.10
13 Wagner Way	Resd	0.10
71 Perry Landing	Resd	0.10
101 Mountainview Ct.	Resd	0.10
317 Longs Ford Rd.	Resd	0.10
587 Peach Grove Dr.	Resd	0.10
600 Citrus Circle	Resd	0.10
817 Green Mountain Rd.	Resd	0.10
2020 Stonegate Blvd.	Resd	0.10
[2]		
3177 Morgan Trace	Resd	0.10
7110 Peachtree St.	Resd	0.10

Card name	Type	Price
Airline Headquarters	Com	0.10
Airport	CSrv	0.10
Apartment Complex	Resd	0.10
Apparel Mart	Com	0.10
Atlanta Fire Station	CSrv	0.25
Atlanta Fire Station	CSrv	0.25
Atlanta Police Station	CSrv	0.25
[3]		
Atlanta Police Station	CSrv	0.25
Bank	Com	0.10
Baptist Church	Resd	0.10
Barbecue Restaurant	Com	0.10

Card name	Type	Price
Bath House	CSrv	0.10
Broadcast Towers	Undv	0.10
Carriage House	Resd	0.10
Center For Disease Control	Gov	0.75
Cheesecake Shop	Com	0.10
[4]		
Chicken Restaurant	Com	0.10
Children's Hospital	CSrv	0.10
College	CSrv	0.10
Concrete Plant	Inds	0.10
Confederate Cemetery	Spec	0.50
Confederate Hall	CSrv	0.50

RARITY KEY   **C** = Common   **U** = Uncommon   **R** = Rare   **VR** = Very Rare   **UR** = Ultra Rare   **F** = Foil card   **X** = Fixed/standard in all decks

Card name	Type	Price	Card name	Type	Price	Card name	Type	Price	Card name	Type	Price
Convention Center	CSrv	0.10	Forest	Undv	0.10	Movie Theater	Com	0.10	Rapid Transit Police Station	CSrv	0.10
Corporate Center	Com	0.10	Forest	Undv	0.10	Museum	CSrv	0.10	Rapid Transit Station	CSrv	0.10
Corporate Headquarters	Com	0.10	Forested Plain	Undv	0.10	News Broadcast Center	Com	0.10	Rib Restaurant	Com	0.10
5			Freedom Hall	Spec	1.00	10			River	Undv	0.10
Corporate Office	Com	0.10	Grade School	Resd	0.10	Park	CSrv	0.10	River	Undv	0.10
Corporate Office	Inds	0.10	Hangar	Com	0.10	Park	CSrv	0.10	River	Undv	0.10
Cotton Exchange	Com	0.10	High School	Resd	0.10	Parking Garage	Com	0.10	River	Undv	0.10
Cotton Field	Agri	0.10	High-Rise Office Building	Com	0.10	Parking Lot	Com	0.10	Runway	CSrv	0.10
Cotton Field	Agri	0.10	8			Parson's House	Resd	0.50	13		
Council Member	Cncl	0.10	Hotel	Com	0.10	Piano Bar	Com	0.10	Science & Technology Museum	CSrv	0.50
Council Member	Cncl	0.10	Hotel	Com	0.10	Plain	Undv	0.10	Shopping Mall	Com	0.10
Council Member	Cncl	0.10	Hurricane	Dis	0.10	Plain	Undv	0.10	Skateboard Shop	Com	0.10
Council Member	Cncl	0.10	Hydroelectric Power Plant	Inds	0.10	Plain	Undv	0.10	Slave Cabin	Resd	0.10
6			Hydroelectric Power Plant	Inds	0.10	11			State Capitol	Gov	0.50
Country Doctor	CSrv	0.10	Inn	Com	0.10	Plantation House	Resd	0.10	Stone Mountain Memorial	Spec	1.00
Country Lawyer	Resd	0.10	Kindergarten	Resd	0.10	Pond	Undv	0.10	Supermarket	Com	0.10
Covered Bridge	Undv	0.10	Lake	Undv	0.10	Pond	Undv	0.10	Telephone Company	Inds	0.10
Diner	Com	0.10	Lake Coastline	Undv	0.10	Power Plant	Inds	0.10	Terminal	CSrv	0.10
Disaster Relief Center	CSrv	0.10	9			Presbyterian Church	Resd	0.10	14		
Field	Agri	0.10	Lumber Mill	Inds	0.10	Presbyterian Church	Resd	0.10	Train Station	CSrv	0.10
Field	Agri	0.10	Lumber Yard	Inds	0.10	Preschool	Resd	0.10	Water Purification Plant	CSrv	0.10
Financial Center	Com	0.10	Market	Com	0.10	Presidential Library	Gov	0.10	World Corporate Headquarters	Com	0.10
Fish Market	Com	0.10	Mayor	Mayr	0.10	Propane Distributor	Inds	0.10			
7			Moonshine Still	Dis	0.10	12					
Football Stadium	Spec	0.10	Mountain	Undv	0.10	Public Library	CSrv	0.10			

SimCity • *Promo cards*

110 cards available in packs of 10 from Mayfair

Eleven different *SimCity* promo packs (10 fixed cards each) are still available at press time from Mayfair, including many of the magazine insert cards. All of the cards were either representations of various game stores or companies, or were maxi cards, cards of greater worth and/or abilities. With a bit of luck, you can find your favorite retail store in the mix. (Hopefully, it's still there — sadly, a number of the companies and magazines listed here aren't!) — *Michael Greenholdt*

You will need **13** nine-pocket pages to store this set. (7 doubled up)

Card name	Source	Price	Card name	Source	Price	Card name	Source	Price
1			Home Office	Elfin Enterprises	2.50	Retail Game Store	Matrix Games	2.50
3270 Boggy Creek	Joe Martin Charity	2.50	House of Cards	House of Cards	2.50	Retail Game Store	Sword of the Phoenix	2.50
14117 West 56th Court	Lakefest	2.50	Ken's Creative Workshop	BenCon Charity	2.50	Retail Game Store	The Game Keeper	2.50
Adolfstrum	Ringbote Magazine	2.50	KSIM Broadcast Center	Maxis	5.00	Retail Game Store	Games People Play	2.50
A.E.G. Secret HQ	AEG	4.00	Large Bridge	Heroes World	2.50	Retail Game Store	Welt Der Spiele	2.50
Alligator Farm	Liberty Hobby	2.50	Light House	Conjure Magazine	2.50	Rosemont Expo Center	National Model/Hobby	2.50
Amphitheatre	Games Quarterly	2.50	Lighthouse (2)	Conjure Magazine	2.50	Shadis Administrative Office	AEG	2.50
Arcology	Maxis	5.00	6			10		
Beach House	Washington Island, WI	2.50	Log Cabin	TD Import	2.50	Shadis Production Department	AEG	2.50
2			Magazine Publisher	Comic Shopper	2.50	Shadis Secret HQ	Shadis	2.50
Beach House	Conjure Magazine	2.50	Mailing House	Wargames West	2.50	Sim Capitol	Maxis	5.00
Burgkirche	Spiel Pegasus	2.50	MECCA Convention Center	GenCon	2.50	Sim City	Benefit Convention	2.50
Canal Boat		2.50	Messe Essen	Essen Spielfest	2.50	Sim City Courier	Corporate Buyout	2.50
Castle	Hobbygames, Ltd.	2.50	Philidelphia Convention Center	Origins '95	2.50	Sim City Courier	The Cows Come Home	2.50
Cemetery Chapel	DC	2.50	Pickle Factory	Berkeley Games	2.50	Sim City Courier	Happy Holidays	2.50
Chessex Park	Chessex	2.50	Primitive Hut	Hobby Quarterly	2.50	Sim City Courier	Mayfair Partner	2.50
City Park	Lion Rampant	2.50	Pub	Adventures Unlimited	2.50	Sim City Courier	Pirate Raid	2.50
Civil War Smelting Furnace	Game Shop News	2.50	7			11		
Colorado Convention Center	Genghis Con	2.50	Retail Game Store	The Guard Tower	2.50	Sim City Courier	Terrorist Attack	2.50
Combo Administrative Office	Century Publishing	2.50	Retail Game Store	"Guild, Kobe, Japan "	2.50	Sim City Courier	White Christmas	2.50
3			Retail Game Store	Gamemasters	2.50	Sim Nuclear Power Plant	Maxis	5.00
Combo Headquarters	Century Publishing	2.50	Retail Game Store	Hobby Town USA	2.50	Sim Satellite Transmitter		2.50
Corporate Headquarters	Advance Comics	2.50	Retail Game Store	Games, Crafts, Hobbies	2.50	Sim Solar Power Plant	Maxis (brown)	5.00
Corporate Headquarters	Diamond Previews	2.50	Retail Game Store	All Star Games	2.50	Sim Stadium	Maxis	5.00
Corporate Office	Conjure Magazine	2.50	Retail Game Store	Silver Snail	2.50	St. Benedict Church	'95 Holy Name Mass	2.50
Corral	Heroes Westside	2.50	Retail Game Store	Phoenix Comics & Cards	2.50	Stock Exchange	1870 MFG	2.50
Crazy Egors	Crazy Egors	2.50	Retail Game Store	Riders Hobby Shop	2.50	Stone Mountain Monument	White Wolf	2.50
Crop Circles	Cosmic Encounter MFG	2.50	Retail Game Store	Pegasus Games	2.50	12		
Discount Game Warehouse	Crazy Egor's	2.50	8			Sutter's Mill	Gold Rush Games	2.50
Dream Park	Matthews-Simmons	2.50	Retail Game Store	The Screening Room	2.50	Tall Ship	999 Games, Amterdam	2.50
4			Retail Game Store	Little Shop of Magic	2.50	The Big Chicken	Game Shop News	2.50
Forgotten Heritage	White Wolf	2.50	Retail Game Store	Infinity	2.50	The World	Games & Puzzles Magazine	2.50
Friends of Peter	Peter Bromley	2.50	Retail Game Store	Game Towne	2.50	Tourist Railroad	Train Gamer's Gazette	2.50
Game Distributor	Hobby Game	2.50	Retail Game Store	Games Plus	2.50	Train Station	Empire Builder	2.50
Game Distributor & Farm	Blackhawk Distributors	2.50	Retail Game Store	Enterprise 1701	2.50	Warehouse	Wargames West	2.50
Game Masters	Game Masters	2.50	Retail Game Store	Dungeons & Starships	2.50	Warehouse	Chris Harvey Games	2.50
Game Parlor	Game Parlor	2.50	Retail Game Store	Complete Strategist	2.50	Welt der Spiele Distributors	Frankfurt	2.50
Gazebo	Wargames West	2.50	Retail Game Store	Avalon, Milano	2.50	13		
Haunted Cemetery	Chill MFG	2.50	9			Westminster Abbey	Valkyrie	2.50
Historic Depot	Bard's Quest Software	2.50	Retail Game Store	Attactix	2.50	Winter Wonderland		2.50
5			Retail Game Store	Alcove Hobbies	2.50			
Hobby Distributor	Greenfield Distributors	2.50						

RARITY KEY **C** = Common **U** = Uncommon **R** = Rare **VR** = Very Rare **UR** = Ultra Rare **F** = Foil card **X** = Fixed/standard in all decks

Spellfire

TSR • First set, *First Edition*, released **June 1994**

400 cards in set • IDENTIFIER: **"First Edition" on back; "#1-400 of 400" on face**

- Starter decks contain 110 cards; starter displays contain 6 starters
- Booster packs belong to the ***Boosters*** release

GREYHAWK — Rangers of the Hornwood

196 of 400

Spellfire: "The No Edition"

In addition to the four familiar sets, there was yet another edition of the **Spellfire** game that was never sold.

An entire run of the first 400 cards was produced without the words "First Edition" on the back, and among **Spellfire** fans this is known as the "No Edition" set.

Only produced as starter decks, these cards were used as promotional copies of the game and were given out free.

Spellfire • Promos

TSR

# Card name	Prce
☐ Pr1 Legendary Artifact	7.50
☐ Pr2 Geneva Conclave	7.50
☐ Pr3 The Wardmeister Strategy	7.50

The first CCG to reach market after ***Magic***, TSR's ***Spellfire*** achieved a level of notoriety unparalleled in the CCG industry. No other game achieved such high sales with such critical disdain. Most games that get panned disappear shortly after their release, but *Spellfire* went through four separate editions and 11 different expansions, and even now has continued to have a rather strong and devoted following, with many tournaments, promo cards, and web sites devoted to it. Credit the marketing power of TSR, which was the gaming industry up until the release of *Magic* and which brought its considerable base of *Advanced Dungeons & Dragons* players to the game.

Spellfire is different from most CCGs in that instead of conquering an opponent to win the game, the actual winner is the first to build a kingdom of six realms. In other words, the winner doesn't kill his opponent to win. *Spellfire* is also one of the few games better played multi-player than two-player, although it is certainly playable as both.

Play consists of each player "building" a realm which he now must defend from other players, while trying to "raze" or destroy the other player's realms, thereby keeping them from winning. Each turn a player may play a realm, and the first player to have six unrazed realms on the table at once is the winner. To defend the realms (and to attack other players realms) each player plays cards from a stable of fighters from the *AD&D* game; hero, wizard, cleric, thief or monster. Card symbols indicate which parts of the role-playing world the characters hail from.

Spellfire was almost never produced by TSR. After the release of *Magic*, there was considerable pressure on TSR to produce a similar game. Inside TSR, there were many who did not want to be a "copycat" company, especially considering the bad taste TSR had left over from a series of trading cards produced a few years earlier. The pressure from the distribution and retail community finally won, and TSR announced it would be producing a CCG based on the *AD&D* game worlds. After many weeks of design, the final product was thought to be too close in game play to *Magic* and was scrapped. This left, literally, only days to come up with rules, game play, and card design to make the release date. In a huge brainstorming session lasting four days, the design, card layout, and rules were developed for *Spellfire*. Card art was used from the enormous library of TSR images to compensate for the lack of time to produce the cards. So what was once the strong suit of TSR in the industry, its fantastic art, actually became a minus as retailers and consumers disliked the notion of reused art.

Spellfire marched on for more than three years until Wizards of the Coast bought TSR — which had fallen into dire straits thanks, in part, to its investment in another collectbl game, ***Dragon Dice***. Wizards chose not to keep *Spellfire* in print.

*About **First Edition**:* The **First Edition** set of 400 cards could be purchased in starter decks or booster packs. The starter decks contained two random decks of 55 cards each and the rules. This was the first CCG to come out in a configuration ready for two people to play. TSR would follow this practice with ***Blood Wars***. — *John Danovich*

SCRYE NOTES: *As with **Blood Wars**, the basic set of **Spellfire: First Edition** is treated separately from its boosters. **First Edition** starters contain cards numbered "of 400," while the boosters are a separate release, the unnamed **Boosters** expansion, which includes cards from the 400 as well as cards from a small special set "of 25." You can tell that TSR considered these first boosters a separate expansion because it numbered the first traditional expansion, **Ravenloft**, as expansion #2. **Boosters** appears on page 406.*

***Boosters** appears on page 406.*

While cards from later expansions read "First Edition" on their backs, they should not be confused with this original set. Only cards that read "of 400" and have "First Edition" on their backs are from this first starter set.

CARD NUMBERING IN CHECKLISTS: *As noted in the introduction, we try to approach checklist organization both as a collector would and as a player would, but where those preferences conflict we go with the solution more favorable to the player.*

*With **Spellfire**, there is numbering on every card, but placed in numerical order the card arrangement does not make much logical sense. (In **Magic**'s later editions, there's at least an attempt at grouping colors in alphabetical order.) While we are sure many collectors will continue to sort **Spellfire** by card number, we list the cards alphabetically here, expecting that a player is more likely to need to look for a **Fire Shield** than for "Card #379."*

We have provided the numbers, as well.

Set (400 cards)	187.50		
Starter Display Box	57.50		
Starter Deck	10.00		

You will need 45 nine-pocket pages to store this set. (23 doubled up)

#	Card name	Type	Rarity	Price
56	Adventurers	Hero	C	0.20
53	Adventurers!	Hero	C	0.20
261	Agis	Hero	U	0.50
90	Airship	Event	U	0.40
41	Alias the Sell-Sword	Hero	U	0.40
74	Allisa of the Mists	Hero	C	0.40
231	Altaruk	Holding	C	0.10
77	Amarill	Cleric	U	0.40
18	Anauroch	Realm	Rlm	0.30
262	Anavias	Hero	R	1.80
399	Ancient Curse	Event	R	1.80
383	Animate Dead	W Spell	C	0.20
345	Anti-Magic Shell	W Spell	R	1.90
36	Arabel	Holding	U	0.40
189	Arch-Druid	Cleric	R	2.40
236	Arkhold	Holding	C	0.20
58	Armies of Bloodstone	Ally	U	0.40
146	Arms of Furyondy	Holding	C	0.10
144	Arms of Greyhawk	Holding	R	1.80
143	Arms of Iuz	Holding	R	1.90
147	Arms of Nyrond	Holding	C	0.20
145	Arms of the Great Kingdom	Holding	R	2.30
142	Arms of the Horned Society	Holding	R	1.80
216	Arms of the Shield Lands	Holding	C	0.30
209	Arms of Veluna	Holding	C	0.20
271	Ashathra	Ally	C	0.20
252	Assassins	Ally	U	0.40
266	Azhul	Hero	U	0.40
158	Baba Yaga's Hut	Artifact	U	0.40
295	Baber	Ally	R	1.40
91	Bad Omens	Event	C	0.20
227	Balic	Realm	Rlm	0.30
395	Banishment	W Spell	C	0.20
102	Banner of the One-Eyed God	Item	C	0.20
268	Baqual	Cleric	C	0.20
213	Barbarian Raiders!	Event	R	2.00
356	Bark Skin	C Spell	C	0.20
31	Berdusk	Holding	U	0.40
180	Berserk Fury!	Event	R	1.80
134	Bissel	Realm	C	0.20
245	Bitter Well	Holding	C	0.20
378	Black Tentacles	W Spell	U	0.40
246	Black Waters	Holding	C	0.20
116	Blackmoor	Realm	U	0.40
352	Blade Barrier	C Spell	R	1.50
353	Bless	C Spell	C	0.20
374	Blink	W Spell	C	0.20
239	Bodach	Holding	R	1.90
198	Border Forts	Holding	C	0.20
305	Borys	Monster	R	2.30
204	Bribery!	Event	R	2.10
49	Bruenor Battlehammer	Hero	R	2.40
140	Burneal Forest	Realm	C	0.20
9	Calimshan	Realm	Rlm	0.30
400	Calm	Event	C	0.30
299	Captain Kazhal	Hero	R	2.50
141	Castle Hart	Holding	C	0.20
99	Cataclysm	Event	U	0.70
128	Celene	Realm	Rlm	0.30
287	Cha'thrang	Ally	U	0.40
390	Chain Lightning	W Spell	C	0.20
205	Charge!	Event	U	0.80
159	Chariot of Lyrx	Artifact	R	1.90
361	Chariot of Sustarre	C Spell	C	0.20

#	Card name	Type	Rarity	Price
357	Charm	W Spell	C	0.20
376	Charm Monster	W Spell	C	0.20
267	Chividal	Hero	R	2.10
282	Cistern Fiend	Monster	C	0.20
68	Cleric of Gond	Cleric	R	1.40
89	Cleric of Malar	Cleric	R	1.90
70	Cleric of Mask	Cleric	R	1.90
69	Cleric of Torm	Cleric	R	1.90
384	Cloudkill	W Spell	C	0.20
152	Codex of the Infinite Planes	Artifact	C	0.20
340	Cone of Cold	W Spell	C	0.20
396	Control Undead	W Spell	C	0.20
5	Cormyr	Realm	Rlm	0.30
138	County of Sunndi	Realm	C	0.20
55	Crime Lord	Hero	U	0.70
344	Crushing Fist	W Spell	R	1.80
153	Crystal of the Ebon Flame	Item	U	0.40
160	Cup of Al-Akbar	Artifact	U	0.40
349	Cure Light Wounds	C Spell	C	0.20
350	Cure Serious Wounds	C Spell	C	0.20
26	Daggerdale	Realm	Rlm	0.30
82	Dagrande	Hero	U	0.40
23	Damara	Realm	Rlm	0.30
27	Darkhold	Realm	Rlm	0.30
359	Darkness	C Spell	C	0.20
391	Death Fog	W Spell	C	0.20
392	Death Spell	W Spell	C	0.20
303	Defiler	Wizard	C	0.20
325	Desert Warrior	Hero	R	1.60
326	Desert Warrior	Hero	R	1.50
327	Desert Warrior	Hero	R	1.50
393	Disintegrate	W Spell	R	2.80
346	Dispel Magic	W Spell	C	0.20
358	Dispel Magic	C Spell	C	0.20
300	Dlasva	Hero	U	0.40
72	Dracolich	Monster	R	1.90
304	Dragon King	Monster	R	2.50
25	Dragonspear Castle	Realm	Rlm	0.30
221	Draj	Realm	Rlm	0.40
45	Drizzt Do'Urden	Hero	C	0.20
71	Drow Matron	Wizard	U	0.40
139	Duchy of Tenh	Realm	C	0.20
248	Dungeon of Gulg	Holding	C	0.20
79	Dwarf of Earthfast	Hero	C	0.20
94	Dwarven Hammer	Item	R	1.90
321	Elemental Cleric	Cleric	C	0.20
110	Elf Galleon	Ally	R	1.80
44	Elminster the Mage	Wizard	U	0.70
322	Elven Archer	Ally	R	1.40
207	Enlarge	W Spell	R	2.00
202	Enslaved!	Event	U	0.50
29	Evermeet	Realm	Rlm	0.50
156	Eye and Hand of Vecna	Artifact	U	0.40
186	Fairy Madness	Event	R	2.10
387	Faithful Hound	Event	C	0.20
200	Falcon Figurine	Item	U	0.40
210	Fast Talking!	Event	U	0.40
348	Fear	W Spell	R	1.80
385	Feeblemind	W Spell	C	0.20
98	Figurine of Wondrous Power	Item	C	0.20
397	Finger of Death	W Spell	C	0.20
379	Fire Shield	W Spell	U	0.40
331	Fireball	W Spell	C	0.20
367	Flame Strike	C Spell	U	0.40
97	Flameblade	Item	R	1.90
211	Flight	W Spell	C	0.20
343	Fly	W Spell	C	0.20
372	Forget	W Spell	C	0.20
247	Fort Melidor	Holding	C	0.20
149	Fortification	Holding	C	0.20

#	Card name	Type	Rarity	Price
37	Fortifications	Holding	U	0.40
38	Fortifications	Holding	U	0.40
92	Fortunate Omens	Event	C	0.20
297	Foucault	Ally	U	0.40
122	Furyondy	Realm	Rlm	0.30
274	Galek	Ally	C	0.20
394	Geas	W Spell	C	0.20
192	Giant Skeleton	Ally	R	2.10
308	Gith	Ally	U	0.40
240	Giustenal	Holding	U	0.40
257	Gladiators	Ally	U	0.90
52	Gnomes of Samek	Hero	U	0.40
100	Good Fortune	Event	U	0.40
243	Grak's Pool	Holding	U	0.20
125	Greyhawk Ruins	Realm	U	0.40
173	Griffon	Item	R	2.30
191	Griffon	Monster	R	1.90
75	Grypht the Saurial	Wizard	U	0.60
225	Gulg	Realm	U	0.60
253	Halfling Mercenaries	Ally	C	0.20
28	Haunted Hall of Eveningstar	Realm	R	1.90
190	Hell Hound	Ally	U	0.40
219	Helm of Teleportation	Item	R	2.50
264	Herminard	Hero	C	0.20
172	Hettman Tsurin	Hero	R	2.30
34	Hillsfar	Holding	U	0.40
114	Hold of the Sea Princess	Realm	Rlm	0.30
375	Hold Undead	W Spell	C	0.20
365	Holy Word	C Spell	C	0.20
154	Hordes of Castle Greyhawk	Ally	R	1.90
81	Hornhead Saurial	Ally	C	0.20
96	Horrors of the Abyss	W Spell	U	0.40
85	Hubadai	Hero	R	1.90
380	Ice Storm	Event	C	0.20
20	Icewind Dale	Realm	Rlm	0.30
19	Impiltur	Realm	Rlm	0.30
347	Improved Phantasmal Force	W Spell	C	0.20
285	Inhuman	Ally	U	0.40
86	Intellect Devourer	Ally	U	0.40
339	Invisibility	W Spell	R	2.00
370	Invisibility to Undead	C Spell	C	0.20
136	Irongate	Realm	Rlm	0.30
167	Iuz the Evil	Monster	U	0.60
218	Johydee's Mask	Artifact	R	2.10
78	Joliet the Rash	Hero	C	0.40
15	Jungles of Chult	Realm	Rlm	0.30
273	Ka'Cha	Ally	U	0.60
235	Kalidnay	Holding	C	0.20
255	Kank Lancers	Ally	U	0.50
63	Karlott the Shaman	Cleric	U	0.40
127	Keoland	Realm	Rlm	0.30
171	Kiara of Chendl	Hero	U	0.40
42	King Azoun IV	Hero	R	1.90
64	King Halvor II	Hero	U	0.40
108	Labor of Legend	Event	C	0.20
332	Lightning Bolt	W Spell	C	0.30
166	Lolth, the Spider Queen	Monster	R	2.30
242	Lost Oasis	Holding	C	0.20
386	Magic Jar	W Spell	C	0.20
334	Magic Missile	W Spell	C	0.20
206	Magic Sword	Item	C	0.20
197	Magical Barding	Item	R	2.30
234	Makla	Holding	U	0.40
43	Maligor the Red	Wizard	R	1.60
328	Marauder	Ally	C	0.20
50	Marco Volo	Hero	U	0.40
2	Menzoberranzan	Realm	Rlm	0.40
165	Mica the Wolf Nomad	Wizard	R	1.60
46	Midnight, Goddess of Magic	Wizard	R	2.30
291	Mikor	Ally	U	0.40

#	Card name	Type	Rarity	Price
183	Miles	Ally	U	0.40
83	Mind Flayer	Ally	R	1.80
175	Mist Wolf	Event	R	2.30
24				
251	Mogadisho's Horde	Ally	C	0.20
7	Moonshae Isles	Realm	Rlm	0.30
162	Mordenkainen	Wizard	R	2.30
284	Mul Savage	Monster	R	1.80
33	Mulmaster	Holding	U	0.40
168	Mutiny!	Event	R	2.10
61	Myrmidons	Ally	R	2.00
13	Myth Drannor	Realm	U	0.50
24	Narfell	Realm	Rlm	0.20
25				
259	Neeva	Hero	R	2.50
187	Nenioc	Cleric	U	0.40
217	Net of Entrapment	Item	U	0.40
226	Nibenay	Realm	U	0.40
280	Night Runners	Ally	U	0.40
84	Noble Djinni	Ally	R	2.30
256	Nomad Mercenaries	Ally	C	0.20
229	North Ledopolus	Holding	U	0.40
120	Nyrond	Realm	Rlm	0.30
26				
233	Ogo	Holding	U	0.40
104	Orb of Doom	Item	C	0.20
157	Orb of Dragonkind	Artifact	U	0.40
310	Orb of Power	Item	C	0.20
164	Otto	Wizard	R	1.90
333	Paralyze	W Spell	C	0.20
388	Passwall	W Spell	C	0.20
40	Peasant Militia	Holding	U	0.40
126	Perrenland	Realm	Rlm	0.30
27				
381	Phantasmal Killer	W Spell	R	1.80
10	Pirate Isles	Realm	Rlm	0.30
215	Potion of Fire-Breathing	Item	R	1.80
294	Powell	Ally	C	0.20
306	Preserver	Wizard	C	0.20
137	Principality of Ulek	Realm	C	0.20
360	Protection	C Spell	C	0.20
368	Protection from Lightning	C Spell	C	0.20
65	Pteranodon	Ally	C	0.20
28				
307	Punisher	Ally	C	0.20
286	Pyreen	Ally	R	1.90
177	Quagmiela the Dragon	Monster	U	0.40
222	Raam	Realm	Rlm	0.40
366	Raise Dead	C Spell	R	1.50
196	Rangers of the Hornwood	Hero	C	0.20
161	Rary the Traitor	Wizard	C	0.20
22	Rashemen	Realm	Rlm	0.30
11	Ravens Bluff	Realm	Rlm	0.30
29				
199	Ren's Crystal Ball	Artifact	C	0.20
258	Rikus	Hero	U	0.70
208	Ring of Shooting Stars	Item	R	2.30
311	Rings of All Seeing	Item	U	0.40
389	Rock to Mud	W Spell	C	0.20
220	Rod of Dispel Magic	Artifact	U	0.60
93	Rod of Shapechange	Artifact	U	0.70
269	Rowan	Ally	U	0.40
260	Sadira	Wizard	C	0.20
30				
107	Safe Harbor!	Event	R	2.10
292	Salicia	Ally	R	1.90
232	Salt View	Holding	C	0.10
237	Salt View	Holding	C	0.20
354	Sanctuary	C Spell	R	1.50
174	Sea Zombie	Ally	R	2.30
39	Selune	Holding	U	0.40
6	Sembia	Realm	Rlm	0.30
178	Seragrimm the Just	Hero	R	1.90
31				
4	Shadowdale	Realm	Rlm	0.30
87	Shandrill	Hero	C	0.20
212	Shapechange	W Spell	R	2.30
329	Shaqat Beetles	Ally	C	0.20
270	Shayira	Cleric	U	0.40
342	Shield	W Spell	C	0.20
314	Shield of Annihilation	Item	U	0.40
313	Shield of Destruction	Item	C	0.20
315	Shield of Devastation	Item	C	0.20
32				
317	Shield of Gore	Item	U	0.40
316	Shield of Wickedness	Item	C	0.20
203	Siege	Event	C	0.20
150	Siege!	Event	C	0.60
369	Silence	C Spell	C	0.50
279	Silt Stalkers	Ally	C	0.20
277	Silver Hands	Event	U	0.60
244	Silver Spring	Holding	C	0.20
155	Skeletal Horde	Monster	C	0.20
33				
193	Skeleton	Ally	C	0.20
179	Skulk	Ally	R	1.90
148	Skull Keep	Holding	C	0.20
278	Sky Singers	Event	C	0.20
341	Sleep	W Spell	C	0.20
283	Sloth	Ally	C	0.20
382	Solid Fog	Event	C	0.20
281	So-ut	Ally	R	1.80
230	South Ledopolus	Holding	U	0.40
34				
106	Spell of Formless Horror	W Spell	U	0.40
398	Spell Turning	W Spell	C	0.20
288	Spirit of the Land	Event	R	2.30
105	Staff of Conjuring	Item	C	0.20
95	Staff of Striking	Item	R	1.90
298	Stef'fa Naf'ski	Monster	R	1.50
119	Sterich	Realm	Rlm	0.30
351	Sticks to Snakes	C Spell	C	0.20
272	Stug	Ally	C	0.20
35				
362	Sunray	C Spell	R	2.00
101	Surprise Raid	Event	C	0.20
35	Suzail	Holding	U	0.40
17	Sword Coast	Realm	Rlm	0.30
169	Swordwraith	Ally	R	2.30
170	Sysania	Cleric	U	0.40
32	Tantras	Holding	U	0.40
330	Tembo	Monster	U	0.40
250	Temple	Holding	C	0.20
36				
124	Temple of Elemental Evil	Realm	U	0.50
60	Tergoz Tenhammer	Hero	C	0.20
8	Thay	Realm	Rlm	0.30
131	The Bone March	Realm	Rlm	0.30
12	The Great Rift	Realm	Rlm	0.30
80	The Black Courser	Monster	R	1.90
129	The Bright Desert	Realm	Rlm	0.30
319	The Caravan	Event	C	0.30
132	The Duchy of Urnst	Realm	Rlm	0.30
37				
111	The Free City of Greyhawk	Realm	R	1.60
66	The Gorgosaurus	Ally	R	1.90
123	The Great Kingdom	Realm	R	2.10
67	The Greater Feyr	Monster	R	1.90
51	The Harpers	Hero	C	0.20
318	The Heartwood Spear	Artifact	C	0.30
16	The High Forest	Realm	Rlm	0.30
21	The High Moor	Realm	Rlm	0.30
117	The Horned Society	Realm	Rlm	0.30
38				
59	The Iron Legion	Ally	C	0.20
57	The Jotunslayers	Hero	C	0.20
112	The Lands of Iuz	Realm	U	0.40
62	The Magister	Wizard	R	2.00
228	The Mud Palace	Holding	U	0.40
320	The Necklace	Item	U	0.40
323	The Outcast	Hero	R	1.60
48	The Pereghost	Monster	R	1.90
113	The Pomarj	Realm	Rlm	0.40
39				
135	The Scarlet Brotherhood	Realm	U	0.40
133	The Sea Barons	Realm	Rlm	0.30
30	The Trollmoors	Realm	Rlm	0.30
118	The Wolf Nomads	Realm	Rlm	0.30
115	The Yeomanry	Realm	Rlm	0.30
130	Theocracy of the Pale	Realm	Rlm	0.30
185	Thorvid	Hero	R	2.10
289	Thri-kreen	Ally	R	1.40
324	Thugs	Ally	U	0.40
40				
309	Tiger	Ally	C	0.20
301	Tithian	Hero	R	2.00
265	T'kkyl	Hero	C	0.20
47	Torg Mac Cei, the Ironlord	Hero	U	0.40
201	Transformation!	Event	C	0.20
195	Treants of the Grandwood	Ally	U	0.40
312	Treasure	Event	C	0.20
214	Treasure Fleet	Event	R	2.00
88	Triceratops	Ally	R	2.30
41				
184	Trystan	Ally	C	0.20
224	Tyr	Realm	Rlm	0.50
176	Tyrinon	Hero	U	0.40
163	Tysiln San	Wizard	U	0.40
223	Urik	Realm	Rlm	0.40
14	Vaasa	Realm	Rlm	0.30
263	Vaerhirmana	Wizard	R	1.50
73	Vasos Flameslayer	Hero	R	2.30
121	Veluna	Realm	Rlm	0.30
42				
302	Verrasi	Ally	U	0.40
103	Viperhand	Item	U	0.40
296	Wachter	Ally	C	0.20
335	Wall of Fire	W Spell	C	0.20
364	Wall of Fire	C Spell	U	0.40
371	Wall of Fog	W Spell	C	0.20
338	Wall of Force	W Spell	C	0.20
336	Wall of Iron	W Spell	C	0.20
337	Wall of Stone	W Spell	C	0.20
43				
363	Wall of Thorns	C Spell	C	0.20
109	Wand of Light	Item	U	0.40
254	War Band	Ally	C	0.20
151	War Banner	Item	C	0.20
54	War Party	Ally	C	0.20
276	Water Hunters	Event	C	0.20
1	Waterdeep	Realm	Rlm	0.30
238	Waverly	Holding	R	1.90
373	Web	W Spell	C	0.20
44				
290	Wijon	Ally	C	0.20
275	Wind Dancers	Event	U	0.60
377	Wind of Disenchantment	Event	R	1.80
355	Wind Walk	C Spell	R	1.50
194	Winged Horror	Monster	U	0.40
181	Wolf Nomads	Hero	C	0.20
76	Worden Ironfist	Hero	R	1.60
241	Yaramuke	Holding	C	0.20
188	Young Gold Dragon	Monster	C	0.20
45				
182	Zadoc	Ally	R	1.50
3	Zhentil Keep	Realm	R	1.90
249	Ziggurat	Holding	U	0.40
293	Zurn	Ally	U	0.40

RARITY KEY C = Common   U = Uncommon   R = Rare   VR = Very Rare   UR = Ultra Rare   F = Foil card   X = Fixed/standard in all decks

Spellfire • Second Edition

TSR • Released **August 1994**

420 cards in set • IDENTIFIER: "Second Edition" on back OR
"First Edition" on back AND "of 420" on face

• Starter decks contain 110 cards; starter displays contain 6 starters

TSR released the **Second Edition** of **Spellfire** immediately after **First** due to the tremendous response. Similar in that it was a double deck of 55 random cards, this set had two major differences to the first release.

The most important change was in the rules. With *First Edition* rushed to press, there was a deck construction rule that allowed up to 10 of one very powerful *First Edition*, **Caravan**, to be in each deck. The new rules changed deck construction to a maximum of two of any Event card, thereby eliminating one of the loopholes.

The second major change was in the addition of 20 cards to the end of the set, which say "First Edition" on their backs and were intended to represent surprise additions to *First Edition* "after the fact." The cards feature posed photography rather than painted art, and represent the first usage of photo art in CCGs. — ***John Danovich***

SCRYE NOTES: *We do not believe any booster packs specific to **Second Edition** came out. Such a release was announced to distributors, but it stayed on the "coming soon" list until its TSR product code was finally reassigned to the **Fourth Edition** starters.*

Aurak
Draconian Lord
If the aurak is defeated, it also forces the champion who killed it to be discarded.
418 of 420

Set (420 cards)	92.50	
Starter Display Box	40.00	
Starter Deck	6.00	

You will need 47 nine-pocket pages to store this set. (24 doubled up)

# Card name	Type	Rarity	Price
56 Adventurers	Hero	C	0.10
53 Adventurers!	Hero	C	0.10
261 Agis	Hero	U	0.50
90 Airship	Event	U	0.30
41 Alias the Sell-Sword	Hero	U	0.40
74 Allisa of the Mists	Hero	C	1.20
231 Altaruk	Holding	C	0.10
77 Amarill	Cleric	U	0.40
18 Anauroch	Realm	Rlm	0.30
262 Anavias	Hero	R	2.10
399 Ancient Curse	Event	R	2.10
383 Animate Dead	W Spell	C	0.10
411 Annulus	Artifact	R	4.80
345 Anti-Magic Shell	W Spell	R	2.20
36 Arabel	Holding	U	0.40
189 Arch-Druid	Cleric	R	1.70
236 Arkhold	Holding	C	0.20
58 Armies of Bloodstone	Ally	U	0.40
146 Arms of Furyondy	Holding	C	0.10
144 Arms of Greyhawk	Holding	R	2.10
143 Arms of Iuz	Holding	R	2.20
147 Arms of Nyrond	Holding	C	0.10
145 Arms of the Great Kingdom	Holding	R	1.60
142 Arms of the Horned Society	Holding	R	2.10
216 Arms of the Shield Lands	Holding	C	0.30
209 Arms of Veluna	Holding	C	0.20
271 Ashathra	Ally	C	0.10
252 Assassins	Ally	U	0.40
418 Aurak Draconian Lord	Monster	R	4.80
266 Azhul	Hero	U	0.40
158 Baba Yaga's Hut	Artifact	U	0.40
295 Baber	Ally	R	0.90
91 Bad Omens	Event	C	0.20
227 Balic	Realm	Rlm	0.30
395 Banishment	W Spell	C	0.20
102 Banner of the One-Eyed God	Item	C	0.10
268 Baqual	Cleric	C	0.10
213 Barbarian Raiders!	Event	R	1.50
356 Bark Skin	C Spell	C	0.10
31 Berdusk	Holding	U	0.40

# Card name	Type	Rarity	Price
180 Berserk Fury!	Event	R	2.10
134 Bissel	Realm	C	0.10
245 Bitter Well	Holding	C	0.10
378 Black Tentacles	W Spell	U	0.40
246 Black Waters	Holding	C	0.20
116 Blackmoor	Realm	U	0.40
352 Blade Barrier	C Spell	R	1.00
353 Bless	C Spell	C	0.10
374 Blink	W Spell	C	0.10
239 Bodach	Holding	R	2.20
198 Border Forts	Holding	C	0.10
305 Borys	Monster	R	1.60
204 Bribery!	Event	R	1.60
49 Bruenor Battlehammer	Hero	R	1.70
140 Burneal Forest	Realm	C	0.10
9 Calimshan	Realm	Rlm	0.20
400 Calm	Event	C	0.30
299 Captain Kazhal	Hero	R	2.00
141 Castle Hart	Holding	C	0.10
99 Cataclysm	Event	U	1.40
128 Celene	Realm	Rlm	0.20
287 Cha'thrang	Ally	U	0.40
390 Chain Lightning	W Spell	C	0.20
404 Chaos Shield	Artifact	R	4.80
205 Charge!	Event	U	0.80
159 Chariot of Lyrx	Artifact	R	2.20
361 Chariot of Sustarre	C Spell	C	0.10
357 Charm	W Spell	C	0.20
376 Charm Monster	W Spell	C	0.10
420 Chest of Many Things	Item	R	4.80
267 Chivadal	Hero	R	1.60
282 Cistern Fiend	Monster	C	0.20
68 Cleric of Gond	Cleric	R	0.90
89 Cleric of Malar	Cleric	C	0.20
70 Cleric of Mask	Cleric	R	2.20
69 Cleric of Torm	Cleric	R	2.20
384 Cloudkill	W Spell	C	0.20
152 Codex of the Infinite Planes	Artifact	C	0.10
340 Cone of Cold	W Spell	C	0.20
396 Control Undead	W Spell	C	0.20
5 Cormyr	Realm	Rlm	0.20
138 County of Sunndi	Realm	C	0.10
55 Crime Lord	Hero	U	1.40
344 Crushing Fist	W Spell	R	2.10
153 Crystal of the Ebon Flame	Item	U	0.40
160 Cup of Al-Akbar	Artifact	U	0.40
349 Cure Light Wounds	C Spell	C	0.10
350 Cure Serious Wounds	C Spell	C	0.10

# Card name	Type	Rarity	Price
26 Daggerdale	Realm	Rlm	0.30
82 Dagrande	Hero	U	0.40
23 Damara	Realm	Rlm	0.30
27 Darkhold	Realm	Rlm	0.30
359 Darkness	C Spell	C	0.20
391 Death Fog	W Spell	C	0.20
392 Death Spell	W Spell	C	0.20
303 Defiler	Wizard	C	0.20
325 Desert Warrior	Hero	R	2.10
326 Desert Warrior	Hero	R	2.00
327 Desert Warrior	Hero	R	2.00
401 Discovery of Spellfire	Event	R	4.80
393 Disintegrate	W Spell	R	2.30
346 Dispel Magic	W Spell	C	0.20
358 Dispel Magic	C Spell	C	0.20
300 Dlasva	Hero	U	0.40
72 Dracolich	Monster	R	2.20
304 Dragon King	Monster	R	1.80
25 Dragonspear Castle	Realm	Rlm	0.30
221 Draj	Realm	Rlm	1.10
45 Drizzt Do'Urden	Hero	C	0.20
71 Drow Matron	Wizard	U	0.40
139 Duchy of Tenh	Realm	C	0.10
248 Dungeon of Gulg	Holding	C	0.10
79 Dwarf of Earthfast	Hero	C	0.10
94 Dwarven Hammer	Item	R	2.20
419 Ego Coin	Item	R	4.80
321 Elemental Cleric	Cleric	C	0.10
110 Elf Galleon	Ally	R	2.10
44 Elminster the Mage	Wizard	U	1.20
322 Elven Archer	Ally	R	0.90
207 Enlarge	W Spell	R	1.50
202 Enslaved!	Event	U	0.50
29 Evermeet	Realm	Rlm	1.00
156 Eye and Hand of Vecna	Artifact	U	0.40
186 Fairy Madness	Event	R	1.60
387 Faithful Hound	Event	C	0.10
200 Falcon Figurine	Item	U	0.40
210 Fast Talking!	Event	U	0.40
348 Fear	W Spell	R	2.10
385 Feeblemind	W Spell	C	0.20
98 Figurine of Wondrous Power	Item	C	0.10
397 Finger of Death	W Spell	C	0.20
379 Fire Shield	W Spell	U	0.40
331 Fireball	W Spell	C	0.10
367 Flame Strike	C Spell	U	0.40
97 Flameblade	Item	R	2.20
211 Flight	W Spell	C	0.10

RARITY KEY C = Common U = Uncommon R = Rare VR = Very Rare UR = Ultra Rare F = Foil card X = Fixed/standard in all decks

#	Card name	Type	Rarity	Price
343	Fly	W Spell	C	0.10
372	Forget	W Spell	C	0.10
247	Fort Melidor	Holding	C	0.20
149	Fortification	Holding	C	0.10
37	Fortifications	Holding	U	0.40
38	Fortifications	Holding	U	0.40
92	Fortunate Omens	Event	C	0.10
297	Foucault	Ally	U	0.40
122	Furyondy	Realm	Rlm	0.20
274	Galek	Ally	C	0.10
394	Geas	W Spell	C	0.10
192	Giant Skeleton	Ally	R	1.60
308	Gith	Ally	U	0.40
240	Giustenal	Holding	U	0.40
257	Gladiators	Ally	U	0.90
52	Gnomes of Samek	Hero	U	0.40
100	Good Fortune	Event	U	0.40
243	Grak's Pool	Holding	C	0.20
125	Greyhawk Ruins	Realm	U	0.40
173	Griffon	Item	R	1.60
191	Griffon	Monster	R	2.20
75	Grypht the Saurial	Wizard	U	1.30
225	Gulg	Realm	U	1.40
253	Halfling Mercenaries	Ally	C	0.10
28	Haunted Hall of Eveningstar	Realm	R	1.90
190	Hell Hound	Ally	U	0.40
219	Helm of Teleportation	Item	R	1.90
264	Herminard	Hero	C	0.10
172	Hettman Tsurin	Hero	R	1.60
34	Hillsfar	Holding	U	0.40
114	Hold of the Sea Princess	Realm	Rlm	0.30
375	Hold Undead	W Spell	C	0.10
365	Holy Word	C Spell	C	0.10
154	Hordes of Castle Greyhawk	Ally	R	2.20
81	Hornhead Saurial	Ally	C	0.10
96	Horrors of the Abyss	W Spell	U	0.40
85	Hubadai	Hero	R	2.20
380	Ice Storm	Event	C	0.10
20	Icewind Dale	Realm	Rlm	0.30
19	Impiltur	Realm	Rlm	0.30
347	Improved Phantasmal Force	W Spell	C	0.20
285	Inhuman	Ally	U	0.40
86	Intellect Devourer	Ally	U	0.40
339	Invisibility	W Spell	R	1.50
370	Invisibility to Undead	C Spell	C	0.10
136	Irongate	Realm	Rlm	0.30
167	luz the Evil	Monster	U	1.30
218	Johydee's Mask	Artifact	R	1.60
78	Joliet the Rash	Hero	C	1.10
15	Jungles of Chult	Realm	Rlm	0.30
273	Ka'Cha	Ally	U	1.30
235	Kalidnay	Holding	C	0.20
255	Kank Lancers	Ally	U	0.50
63	Karlott the Shaman	Cleric	U	0.40
127	Keoland	Realm	Rlm	0.20
171	Kiara of Chendl	Hero	U	0.40
42	King Azoun IV	Hero	R	1.90
64	King Halvor II	Hero	U	0.40
108	Labor of Legend	Event	C	0.10
410	Labyrinth Map of Shucc	Artifact	R	4.80
332	Lightning Bolt	W Spell	C	0.30
408	Living Scroll	Monster	R	4.80
166	Lolth, the Spider Queen	Monster	R	1.60
242	Lost Oasis	Holding	C	0.20
386	Magic Jar	W Spell	C	0.10
334	Magic Missile	W Spell	C	0.10
206	Magic Sword	Item	C	0.20
197	Magical Barding	Item	R	1.60
402	Magical Champion	Item	R	4.80
234	Makla	Holding	U	0.40
43	Maligor the Red	Wizard	R	1.80
413	Map of Life	Event	R	4.80
415	Map to Mercenary Army	Ally	R	4.80
328	Marauder	Ally	C	0.10
50	Marco Volo	Hero	U	0.40
2	Menzoberranzan	Realm	Rlm	0.90
407	Mercenary Gold	Ally	R	4.80
165	Mica the Wolf Nomad	Wizard	R	2.10
46	Midnight, Goddess of Magic	Wizard	R	1.90
291	Mikor	Ally	U	0.40
183	Miles	Ally	U	0.40
83	Mind Flayer	Ally	R	2.10
417	Mind Flayer Lord	Monster	R	4.80
175	Mist Wolf	Event	R	1.60
251	Mogadisho's Horde	Ally	C	0.20
7	Moonshae Isles	Realm	Rlm	0.30
162	Mordenkainen	Wizard	R	1.60
284	Mul Savage	Monster	R	2.10
33	Mulmaster	Holding	U	0.40
168	Mutiny!	Event	R	1.60
61	Myrmidons	Ally	R	1.80
13	Myth Drannor	Realm	U	0.50
24	Narfell	Realm	Rlm	0.20
259	Neeva	Hero	R	1.90
187	Nenioc	Cleric	U	0.40
217	Net of Entrapment	Item	U	0.40
226	Nibenay	Realm	U	0.40
280	Night Runners	Ally	U	0.40
84	Noble Djinni	Ally	R	1.60
256	Nomad Mercenaries	Ally	C	0.10
229	North Ledopolus	Holding	U	0.40
120	Nyrond	Realm	Rlm	0.20
233	Ogo	Holding	U	0.40
104	Orb of Doom	Item	C	0.10
157	Orb of Dragonkind	Artifact	U	0.40
310	Orb of Power	Item	C	0.10
164	Otto	Wizard	R	2.20
333	Paralyze	W Spell	C	0.20
388	Passwall	W Spell	C	0.10
40	Peasant Militia	Holding	U	0.40
126	Perrenland	Realm	Rlm	0.20
381	Phantasmal Killer	W Spell	R	2.10
406	Phorbes's Scrolls	W Spell	R	4.80
10	Pirate Isles	Realm	Rlm	0.30
416	Pit Trap!	Event	R	4.80
215	Potion of Fire-Breathing	Item	R	2.10
294	Powell	Ally	C	0.10
306	Preserver	Wizard	C	0.20
137	Principality of Ulek	Realm	C	0.10
360	Protection	C Spell	C	0.10
368	Protection from Lightning	C Spell	C	0.10
65	Pteranodon	Ally	C	0.10
307	Punisher	Ally	C	0.10
286	Pyreen	Ally	R	2.20
177	Quagmiela the Dragon	Monster	U	0.40
222	Raam	Realm	Rlm	1.10
366	Raise Dead	C Spell	R	1.00
196	Rangers of the Hornwood	Hero	C	0.10
161	Rary the Traitor	Wizard	C	0.10
22	Rashemen	Realm	Rlm	0.30
11	Ravens Bluff	Realm	Rlm	0.30
409	Ren's Bell of Death	Artifact	R	4.80
199	Ren's Crystal Ball	Artifact	C	0.20
258	Rikus	Hero	U	1.40
208	Ring of Shooting Stars	Item	R	1.60
311	Rings of All Seeing	Item	U	0.40
389	Rock to Mud	W Spell	C	0.10
220	Rod of Dispel Magic	Artifact	U	1.40
93	Rod of Shapechange	Artifact	U	1.40
269	Rowan	Ally	U	0.40
260	Sadira	Wizard	C	0.20
107	Safe Harbor!	Event	R	1.60
292	Salicia	Ally	R	2.20
232	Salt View	Holding	C	0.10
237	Salt View	Holding	C	0.10
354	Sanctuary	C Spell	R	1.00
412	Scroll of 7 Leagues	Item	R	4.80
174	Sea Zombie	Ally	R	1.60
39	Selune	Holding	U	0.40
6	Sembia	Realm	Rlm	0.20
178	Seragrimm the Just	Hero	R	2.20
4	Shadowdale	Realm	Rlm	0.30
87	Shandrill	Hero	C	0.10
212	Shapechange	W Spell	R	1.60
329	Shaqat Beetles	Ally	C	0.10
270	Shayira	Cleric	C	0.10
342	Shield	W Spell	C	0.10
314	Shield of Annihilation	Item	U	0.40
313	Shield of Destruction	Item	C	0.10
315	Shield of Devastation	Item	C	0.10
317	Shield of Gore	Item	U	0.40
316	Shield of Wickedness	Item	C	0.20
203	Siege	Event	C	0.20
150	Siege!	Event	U	1.30
369	Silence	C Spell	U	0.50
279	Silt Stalkers	Ally	C	0.10
277	Silver Hands	Event	C	1.30
244	Silver Spring	Holding	C	0.20
155	Skeletal Horde	Monster	C	0.10
193	Skeleton	Ally	C	0.10
179	Skulk	Ally	R	2.20
148	Skull Keep	Holding	C	0.10
278	Sky Singers	Event	C	0.20
405	Slave Realm of Tunek	Realm	R	4.80
341	Sleep	W Spell	C	0.10
283	Sloth	Ally	C	0.10
382	Solid Fog	Event	C	0.10
281	So-ut	Ally	R	2.10
230	South Ledopolus	Holding	U	0.40
106	Spell of Formless Horror	W Spell	U	0.40
398	Spell Turning	W Spell	C	0.20
288	Spirit of the Land	Event	R	1.60
105	Staff of Conjuring	Item	C	0.10
95	Staff of Striking	Item	R	2.20
298	Stef'fa Naf'ski	Monster	R	2.00
119	Sterich	Realm	Rlm	0.20
351	Sticks to Snakes	C Spell	C	0.10
272	Stug	Ally	C	0.10
362	Sunray	C Spell	R	1.50
414	Supernatural Chill	Event	R	4.80
101	Surprise Raid	Event	C	0.10
35	Suzail	Holding	U	0.40
17	Sword Coast	Realm	Rlm	0.30
169	Swordwraith	Ally	R	1.60
170	Sysania	Cleric	U	0.40
32	Tantras	Holding	U	0.40
330	Tembo	Monster	U	0.40
250	Temple	Holding	C	0.10
124	Temple of Elemental Evil	Realm	U	0.50
60	Tergoz Tenhammer	Hero	U	0.40
8	Thay	Realm	Rlm	0.30
80	The Black Courser	Monster	R	2.20
131	The Bone March	Realm	Rlm	0.30
129	The Bright Desert	Realm	Rlm	0.20
319	The Caravan	Event	C	0.30
132	The Duchy of Urnst	Realm	Rlm	0.20
111	The Free City of Greyhawk	Realm	R	2.10
66	The Gorgosaurus	Ally	R	2.20
123	The Great Kingdom	Realm	R	1.60
12	The Great Rift	Realm	Rlm	0.30
67	The Greater Feyr	Monster	R	2.20
51	The Harpers	Hero	C	0.10
318	The Heartwood Spear	Artifact	C	0.30
16	The High Forest	Realm	Rlm	0.20
21	The High Moor	Realm	Rlm	0.30
117	The Horned Society	Realm	Rlm	0.20

RARITY KEY C = Common   U = Uncommon   R = Rare   VR = Very Rare   UR = Ultra Rare   F = Foil card   X = Fixed/standard in all decks

# Card name	Type	Rarity	Price
59 The Iron Legion	Ally	C	0.10
57 The Jotunslayers	Hero	C	0.10
112 The Lands of Iuz	Realm	U	0.40
62 The Magister	Wizard	R	1.80
228 The Mud Palace	Holding	U	0.40
320 The Necklace	Item	U	0.40
323 The Outcast	Hero	R	2.10
48 The Pereghost	Monster	R	2.20
41			
113 The Pomarj	Realm	Rlm	0.40
135 The Scarlet Brotherhood	Realm	U	0.40
133 The Sea Barons	Realm	Rlm	0.30
30 The Trollmoors	Realm	Rlm	0.30
118 The Wolf Nomads	Realm	Rlm	0.20
115 The Yeomanry	Realm	Rlm	0.30
130 Theocracy of the Pale	Realm	Rlm	0.30
185 Thorvid	Hero	R	1.60
289 Thri-kreen	Ally	R	0.90
42			
324 Thugs	Ally	U	0.40
309 Tiger	Ally	C	0.10
301 Tithian	Hero	R	1.50
265 T'kkyl	Hero	C	0.10
47 Torg Mac Cei, the Ironlord	Hero	U	0.40
403 Traitor	Event	R	4.80

# Card name	Type	Rarity	Price
201 Transformation!	Event	C	0.20
195 Treants of the Grandwood	Ally	U	0.40
312 Treasure	Event	C	0.20
43			
214 Treasure Fleet	Event	R	1.50
88 Triceratops	Ally	R	1.60
184 Trystan	Ally	C	0.10
224 Tyr	Realm	Rlm	1.30
176 Tyrinon	Hero	U	0.40
163 Tysiln San	Wizard	U	0.40
223 Urik	Realm	Rlm	0.40
14 Vaasa	Realm	Rlm	0.30
263 Vaerhirmana	Wizard	R	1.00
44			
73 Vasos Flameslayer	Hero	R	1.60
121 Veluna	Realm	Rlm	0.20
302 Verrasi	Ally	U	0.40
103 Viperhand	Item	U	0.40
296 Wachter	Ally	C	0.10
335 Wall of Fire	W Spell	C	0.20
364 Wall of Fire	C Spell	U	0.40
371 Wall of Fog	W Spell	C	0.10
338 Wall of Force	W Spell	C	0.20
45			
336 Wall of Iron	W Spell	C	0.10

# Card name	Type	Rarity	Price
337 Wall of Stone	W Spell	C	0.20
363 Wall of Thorns	C Spell	C	0.10
109 Wand of Light	Item	U	0.30
254 War Band	Ally	C	0.10
151 War Banner	Item	C	0.10
54 War Party	Ally	C	0.10
276 Water Hunters	Event	C	0.10
1 Waterdeep	Realm	Rlm	0.30
46			
238 Waverly	Holding	R	2.20
373 Web	W Spell	C	0.10
290 Wijon	Ally	C	0.10
275 Wind Dancers	Event	U	1.30
377 Wind of Disenchantment	Event	R	2.10
355 Wind Walk	C Spell	C	1.00
194 Winged Horror	Monster	U	0.40
181 Wolf Nomads	Hero	C	0.10
76 Worden Ironfist	Hero	R	2.10
47			
241 Yaramuke	Holding	C	0.10
188 Young Gold Dragon	Monster	C	0.10
182 Zadoc	Ally	R	1.00
3 Zhentil Keep	Realm	R	1.90
249 Ziggurat	Holding	U	0.40
293 Zurn	Ally	U	0.40

Spellfire • Third Edition

TSR • Released **October 1995**

440 cards in set • **IDENTIFIER:** "Third Edition" on back
OR "First Edition" on back AND "of 440" on face

- Starter decks contain 110 cards; starter displays contain 6 starters

The ***Third Edition*** of ***Spellfire*** game contains the most significant changes in the entire run of the game. While adding another 20 pseudo-***First Edition*** cards to the end of the set, ***Third Edition*** cards featured greatly edited card text and powers. This effectively created more than 200 brand new cards and powers for the game, and greatly enhanced the playability of ***Spellfire***.

In addition to the card changes, the rules were completely reworked and deck construction and card interaction was revamped and updated. This was the starter deck that ***Spellfire*** players had been hoping for. The starter decks were now playable from the box, and the rules made sense. (Though some cards were very unusual. **Hookhill** replaced **Bissel** from the *First* and *Second Edition* sets, but grew more powerful if any of those **Bissel** cards were in play.

TSR only produced this edition because of the low cost of goods. The only changes were made on one press sheet of cards, the rules booklet, a color change for the outside box, and on all the rest of the cards only the black plate was changed, thereby saving thousands of dollars in printing costs. — ***John Danovich***

Set (440 cards)	86.00
Starter Display Box	40.00
Starter Deck	5.50

> You will need **49** nine-pocket pages to store this set. *(25 doubled up)*

# Card name	Type	Rarity	Price
1			
56 Adventurers	Hero	C	0.10
53 Adventurers!	Hero	C	0.10
423 Age of Entropy	Rule	R	4.80
261 Agis	Hero	U	0.50
90 Airship	Event	U	0.30
41 Alias the Sell-Sword	Hero	U	0.40
74 Allisa of the Mists	Hero	C	1.20
231 Altaruk	Holding	C	0.10
77 Amarill	Cleric	U	0.40
2			
18 Anauroch	Realm	Rlm	0.30
146 Ancient Arms of Furyondy	Holding	C	0.10
145 Ancient Arms of the Great Kingdom	Holding	R	1.60
144 Ancient Arms of Greyhawk	Holding	R	2.10
142 Ancient Arms of the Horned Society	Holding	R	2.10
147 Ancient Arms of Nyrond	Holding	C	0.10
216 Ancient Arms of the Shield Lands	Holding	C	0.30
209 Ancient Arms of Veluna	Holding	C	0.20
399 Ancient Curse	Event	R	2.10
3			
383 Animate Dead	W Spell	C	0.10
411 Annulus	Artifact	R	4.80

# Card name	Type	Rarity	Price
345 Anti-Magic Shell	W Spell	R	2.20
36 Arabel	Holding	U	0.40
189 Arch-druid	Cleric	R	1.70
236 Arkhold	Holding	C	0.20
58 Armies of Bloodstone	Ally	U	0.40
143 Arms of Iuz	Holding	R	2.20
271 Ashathra	Ally	C	0.10
4			
252 Assassins	Ally	U	0.40
418 Aurak Draconian Lord	Monster	R	4.80
169 Avatar's Bane	Ally	R	1.60
266 Azhul	Hero	U	0.40
158 Baba Yaga's Hut	Artifact	U	0.40
295 Baber	Ally	R	0.90
91 Bad Omens	Event	C	0.20
227 Balic	Realm	Rlm	0.30
395 Banishment	W Spell	C	0.20
5			
102 Banner of the One-Eyed God	Item	C	0.10
268 Baqual	Cleric	C	0.10
213 Barbarian's Revenge	Event	R	1.50
356 Bark Skin	C Spell	C	0.10
434 Bengookee the Witch Doctor	Wizard	R	4.80
31 Berdusk	Holding	U	0.40
180 Berserker Wrath	Event	R	2.10
435 Big Chief Bagoomba	Hero	R	4.80
245 Bitter Well	Holding	C	0.10
6			
80 Black Courser	Monster	R	2.20
378 Black Tentacles	W Spell	U	0.40
246 Black Waters	Holding	C	0.20
116 Blackmoor	Realm	U	0.40

# Card name	Type	Rarity	Price
352 Blade Barrier	C Spell	R	1.00
353 Bless	C Spell	C	0.10
374 Blink	W Spell	C	0.10
239 Bodach	Holding	R	2.20
131 Bone March	Realm	Rlm	0.30
7			
198 Border Forts	Holding	C	0.10
305 Borys the Dragon	Monster	R	1.60
204 Bribery!	Event	R	1.60
203 Bruce's Revenge	Event	C	0.20
49 Bruenor Battlehammer	Hero	R	1.70
140 Burneal Forest	Realm	C	0.10
9 Calimshan	Realm	Rlm	0.20
400 Calm	Event	C	0.30
299 Captain Kazhal	Hero	R	2.00
8			
319 Caravan	Event	C	0.30
37 Castle Draw	Holding	U	0.40
141 Castle Hart	Holding	C	0.10
99 Cataclysm!	Event	U	1.40
128 Celene	Realm	Rlm	0.20
287 Cha'thrang	Ally	U	0.40
390 Chain Lightning	W Spell	C	0.20
404 Chaos Shield	Artifact	R	4.80
205 Charge!	Event	U	0.80
9			
159 Chariot of Lyrx	Artifact	R	2.20
361 Chariot of Sustarre	C Spell	C	0.10
357 Charm	W Spell	C	0.20
376 Charm Monster	W Spell	C	0.10
420 Chest of Many Things	Item	R	4.80
267 Chivdal	Hero	R	1.60

RARITY KEY C = Common U = Uncommon R = Rare VR = Very Rare UR = Ultra Rare F = Foil card X = Fixed/standard in all decks

#	Card name	Type	Rarity	Price
☐ 282	Cistern Fiend	Monster	C	0.20
☐ 68	Cleric of Gond	Cleric	R	0.90
☐ 89	Cleric of Malar	Cleric	C	0.20
☐ 70	Cleric of Mask	Cleric	R	2.20
☐ 69	Cleric of Torm	Cleric	R	2.20
☐ 384	Cloudkill	W Spell	C	0.20
☐ 152	Codex of the Infinite Planes	Artifact	C	0.10
☐ 192	Commander Skeleton	Ally	R	1.60
☐ 340	Cone of Cold	W Spell	C	0.20
☐ 396	Control Undead	W Spell	C	0.20
☐ 5	Cormyr	Realm	Rlm	0.20
☐ 138	County of Sunndi	Realm	C	0.10
☐ 55	Crime Lord	Hero	U	1.40
☐ 344	Crushing Fist	W Spell	R	2.10
☐ 153	Crystal of the Ebon Flame	Item	U	0.40
☐ 160	Cup of Al-Akbar	Artifact	U	0.40
☐ 349	Cure Light Wounds	C Spell	C	0.10
☐ 350	Cure Serious Wounds	C Spell	C	0.10
☐ 26	Daggerdale	Realm	Rlm	0.30
☐ 82	Dagrande	Hero	U	0.40
☐ 23	Damara	Realm	Rlm	0.30
☐ 27	Darkhold	Realm	Rlm	0.30
☐ 359	Darkness	C Spell	C	0.20
☐ 391	Death Fog	W Spell	C	0.20
☐ 392	Death Spell	W Spell	C	0.20
☐ 325	Desert Warrior	Hero	R	2.10
☐ 326	Desert Warrior	Hero	R	2.00
☐ 327	Desert Warrior	Hero	R	2.00
☐ 401	Discovery of Spellfire	Event	R	4.80
☐ 393	Disintegrate	W Spell	R	2.30
☐ 346	Dispel Magic	W Spell	C	0.20
☐ 358	Dispel Magic	C Spell	C	0.20
☐ 300	Dlasva	Hero	U	0.40
☐ 427	Dori the Barbarian's Cape	Artifact	R	4.80
☐ 72	Dracolich	Monster	R	2.20
☐ 25	Dragonspear Castle	Realm	Rlm	0.30
☐ 221	Draj	Realm	Rlm	1.10
☐ 45	Drizzt Do'Urden	Hero	C	0.20
☐ 71	Drow Matron	Wizard	U	0.40
☐ 139	Duchy of Tenh	Realm	C	0.10
☐ 248	Dungeon of Gulg	Holding	C	0.10
☐ 79	Dwarf of Earthfast	Hero	C	0.10
☐ 94	Dwarven Hammer	Item	R	2.20
☐ 419	Ego Coin	Item	R	4.80
☐ 321	Elemental Cleric	Cleric	C	0.10
☐ 110	Elf Galleon	Ally	R	2.10
☐ 44	Elminster the Mage	Wizard	U	1.20
☐ 322	Elven Archer	Ally	R	0.90
☐ 207	Enlarge	W Spell	R	1.50
☐ 262	Erellika	Hero	R	2.10
☐ 437	Estate Transference	W Spell	R	4.80
☐ 29	Evermeet	Realm	Rlm	1.00
☐ 156	Eye & Hand of Vecna	Artifact	U	0.40
☐ 186	Fairy Madness	Event	R	1.60
☐ 200	Falcon Figurine	Item	U	0.40
☐ 210	Fast Talking!	Event	U	0.40
☐ 348	Fear	W Spell	R	2.10
☐ 385	Feeblemind	W Spell	C	0.20
☐ 98	Figurine of Wonderous Power	Item	C	0.10
☐ 397	Finger of Death	W Spell	C	0.20
☐ 379	Fire Shield	W Spell	U	0.40
☐ 331	Fireball	W Spell	C	0.10
☐ 367	Flame Strike	C Spell	U	0.40
☐ 97	Flameblade	Item	R	2.20
☐ 211	Flight	W Spell	C	0.10
☐ 343	Fly	W Spell	C	0.10
☐ 372	Forget	W Spell	C	0.10
☐ 247	Fort Melidor	Holding	C	0.20
☐ 149	Fortification	Holding	C	0.10
☐ 38	Fortifications	Holding	U	0.40
☐ 92	Fortunate Omens	Event	U	0.10
☐ 297	Foucault	Ally	U	0.40
☐ 111	Free City of Greyhawk	Realm	R	2.10
☐ 122	Furyondy	Realm	Rlm	0.20
☐ 274	Galek	Ally	C	0.10
☐ 422	Gatekeeper	Monster	R	4.80
☐ 394	Geas	W Spell	C	0.10
☐ 421	Gelatinous Cube	Monster	R	4.80
☐ 308	Gith	Ally	U	0.40
☐ 240	Giustenal	Holding	U	0.40
☐ 257	Gladiators	Ally	U	0.90
☐ 52	Gnomes of Samek	Hero	U	0.40
☐ 100	Good Fortune	Event	U	0.40
☐ 66	Gorgosaurus	Ally	R	2.20
☐ 243	Grak's Pool	Holding	C	0.20
☐ 123	Great Kingdom	Realm	R	1.60
☐ 67	Greater Feyr	Monster	R	2.20
☐ 125	Greyhawk Ruins	Realm	R	0.40
☐ 173	Griffon	Item	R	1.60
☐ 191	Griffon	Monster	R	2.20
☐ 75	Grypht the Saurial	Wizard	U	1.30
☐ 225	Gulg	Realm	U	1.40
☐ 253	Halfling Mercenaries	Ally	C	0.10
☐ 28	Haunted Hall of Eveningstar	Realm	R	1.90
☐ 318	Heartwood Spear	Artifact	C	0.30
☐ 190	Hell Hound	Ally	U	0.30
☐ 219	Helm of Teleportation	Item	R	1.90
☐ 264	Herminard	Hero	C	0.10
☐ 172	Hettman Tsurin	Hero	R	1.60
☐ 16	High Forest	Realm	Rlm	0.20
☐ 21	High Moor	Realm	Rlm	0.30
☐ 34	Hillsfar	Holding	U	0.40
☐ 114	Hold of the Sea Princes	Realm	Rlm	0.30
☐ 375	Hold Undead	W Spell	C	0.10
☐ 365	Holy Word	C Spell	C	0.10
☐ 134	Hookhill	Realm	C	0.10
☐ 154	Hordes of Castle Greyhawk	Ally	R	2.20
☐ 81	Hornhead Saurial	Ally	C	0.10
☐ 96	Horrors of the Abyss	W Spell	U	0.40
☐ 85	Hubadai	Hero	R	2.20
☐ 380	Ice Storm	Event	C	0.20
☐ 20	Icewind Dale	Realm	Rlm	0.30
☐ 19	Impiltur	Realm	Rlm	0.10
☐ 370	Improved Invisibility to Undead	C Spell	C	0.10
☐ 347	Improved Phantasmal Force	W Spell	C	0.20
☐ 285	Inhuman	Ally	U	0.40
☐ 86	Intellect Devourer	Ally	U	0.40
☐ 339	Invisibility	W Spell	R	1.50
☐ 136	Iron Hills	Realm	Rlm	0.30
☐ 167	Iuz the Evil	Monster	U	1.30
☐ 218	Johydee's Mask	Artifact	R	1.60
☐ 78	Joliet the Rash	Hero	C	1.10
☐ 15	Jungles of Chult	Realm	Rlm	0.30
☐ 273	Ka'Cha	Ally	U	1.30
☐ 235	Kalidnay	Holding	C	0.20
☐ 255	Kank Lancers	Ally	U	0.50
☐ 63	Karlott the Shaman	Cleric	U	0.40
☐ 127	Keoland	Realm	Rlm	0.20
☐ 206	Kevin's Blade of Doom	Item	C	0.20
☐ 171	Kiara	Hero	U	0.40
☐ 42	King Azoun IV	Hero	R	1.90
☐ 64	King Halvor II	Hero	U	0.40
☐ 108	Labor of Legend	Event	C	0.10
☐ 410	Labyrinth Map of Shucc	Artifact	R	4.80
☐ 155	Lich Conclave	Monster	C	0.10
☐ 332	Lightning Bolt	W Spell	C	0.30
☐ 408	Living Scroll	Monster	R	4.80
☐ 166	Lolth the Spider Queen	Monster	R	1.60
☐ 242	Lost Oasis	Holding	C	0.20
☐ 386	Magic Jar	W Spell	C	0.10
☐ 334	Magic Missile	W Spell	C	0.10
☐ 197	Magical Barding	Item	R	1.60
☐ 402	Magical Champion	Item	R	4.80
☐ 62	Magister	Wizard	R	1.80
☐ 234	Makla	Holding	U	0.40
☐ 432	Malatra, the Living Jungle	Realm	R	4.80
☐ 43	Maligor the Red	Wizard	R	1.80
☐ 413	Map of Life	Event	R	4.80
☐ 415	Map to Mercenary Army	Ally	R	4.80
☐ 328	Marauder	Ally	C	0.10
☐ 50	Marco Volo	Hero	U	0.40
☐ 433	Mayor Charles Oliver O'Kane	Hero	R	4.80
☐ 232	Mekillot Mountains	Holding	C	0.10
☐ 2	Menzoberranzan	Realm	Rlm	0.90
☐ 407	Mercenary Gold	Ally	R	4.80
☐ 46	Midnight, Goddess of Magic	Wizard	R	1.90
☐ 165	Mika the Wolf Nomad	Wizard	R	2.10
☐ 291	Mikor	Ally	U	0.40
☐ 183	Miles	Ally	U	0.40
☐ 83	Mind Flayer	Ally	R	2.10
☐ 417	Mind Flayer Lord	Monster	R	4.80
☐ 175	Mist Wolf	Event	R	1.60
☐ 251	Mogadisho's Horde	Ally	C	0.20
☐ 7	Moonshae Isles	Realm	Rlm	0.30
☐ 162	Mordenkainen	Wizard	R	1.60
☐ 387	Mordenkainen's Faithful Hound	Event	C	0.10
☐ 284	Mul Savage	Monster	R	2.10
☐ 33	Mulmaster	Holding	U	0.40
☐ 168	Mutiny!	Event	R	1.60
☐ 61	Myrmidons	Ally	R	1.80
☐ 13	Myth Drannor	Realm	R	0.50
☐ 24	Narfell	Realm	Rlm	0.30
☐ 320	Necklace	Item	U	0.40
☐ 259	Neeva	Hero	R	1.90
☐ 187	Nenioc	Cleric	U	0.40
☐ 217	Net of Entrapment	Item	U	0.40
☐ 226	Nibenay	Realm	U	0.40
☐ 280	Night Runners	Ally	U	0.40
☐ 84	Noble Djinni	Ally	R	1.60
☐ 256	Nomad Mercenaries	Ally	C	0.10
☐ 229	North Ledopolus	Holding	U	0.40
☐ 120	Nyrond	Realm	Rlm	0.20
☐ 233	Ogo	Holding	U	0.40
☐ 104	Orb of Doom	Item	C	0.10
☐ 157	Orb of Dragonkind	Artifact	U	0.40
☐ 424	Orb of Green Dragonkind	Artifact	R	4.80
☐ 310	Orb of Power	Item	C	0.10
☐ 164	Otto	Wizard	R	2.20
☐ 323	Outcast	Hero	R	2.10
☐ 333	Paralyze	W Spell	C	0.20
☐ 388	Passwall	W Spell	C	0.10
☐ 40	Peasant Militia	Holding	U	0.40
☐ 126	Perrenland	Realm	Rlm	0.20
☐ 381	Phantasmal Killer	W Spell	R	2.30
☐ 406	Phorbes's Scrolls	W Spell	R	4.80
☐ 10	Pirate Isles	Realm	Rlm	0.30
☐ 416	Pit Trap!	Event	R	4.80
☐ 113	Pomarj	Realm	Rlm	0.30
☐ 215	Potion of Fire Breathing	Item	R	1.80
☐ 294	Powell	Ally	C	0.10
☐ 306	Preserver	Wizard	C	0.20
☐ 137	Principality of Ulek	Realm	C	0.10
☐ 431	Prismal the Outrageous	Wizard	R	4.80
☐ 360	Protection	C Spell	C	0.10
☐ 368	Protection from Lightning	C Spell	C	0.10
☐ 65	Pteranadon	Ally	C	0.10
☐ 307	Punisher	Ally	C	0.10
☐ 286	Pyreen	Ally	R	2.20
☐ 177	Quagmiela the Dragon	Monster	U	0.40
☐ 222	Raam	Realm	Rlm	1.10
☐ 366	Raise Dead	C Spell	R	1.00
☐ 196	Rangers of Hornwood	Hero	C	0.10
☐ 161	Rary the Traitor	Wizard	C	0.10
☐ 22	Rashemen	Realm	Rlm	0.30
☐ 11	Ravens Bluff	Realm	Rlm	0.30
☐ 409	Ren's Bell of Death	Artifact	R	4.80
☐ 199	Ren's Crystal Ball	Artifact	C	0.10
☐ 258	Rikus	Hero	U	1.40
☐ 208	Ring of Shooting Stars	Item	R	1.60

RARITY KEY C = Common   U = Uncommon   R = Rare   VR = Very Rare   UR = Ultra Rare   F = Foil card   X = Fixed/standard in all decks

Spellfire • Fourth Edition

SPELLFIRE Master the Magic

TSR • Released July 1996

520 cards in set • IDENTIFIER: "Fourth Edition" on back OR
"First Edition" on back AND "of 420" on face

• Starter decks contain 55 cards and one **Draconomicon** booster; starter displays contain 6 starters
Fourth Edition, a 500-card set with 20 photo chase cards, was actually a combo release with the **Draconomicon** boosters. With no starter decks available for the game (they had all sold out from TSR, **First** through **Third Edition**), there needed to be revised rules and a starter deck to help sell the remaining boosters.

With costs rising and sales slipping, TSR had decided to stop production of the **Spellfire** game unless some cost savings could make a print run of starter decks cost-effective. To this end it was decided to do a combo release, with one pack of **Draconomicon** booster cards replacing one of the 55-card starter decks in the Fourth Edition display. At the same time, the best cards from all of the first three editions and the sold-out booster expansions, as well as new cards appear in the **Fourth Edition**. Card numbering was rearranged dramatically, so while the earlier **Edition** cards lists sort of square up together, **Fourth** does not. — **John Danovich**

Dungeons & Dragons

The Throne of the Gods

The Throne of the Gods can be used by a champion of any world. It is not subject to the Rule of the Cosmos, but any champion with the Throne attached must immediately battle any other champion who also claims the Throne. The winner receives a spoils of victory.

460 of 500

Set (520 cards)	77.75	
Starter Display Box	40.00	
Starter Deck	1.60	

RARITY KEY C = Common U = Uncommon R = Rare VR = Very Rare UR = Ultra Rare F = Foil card X = Fixed/standard in all decks

SCRYE Collectible Card Game Checklist and Price Guide • **403**

#	Card name	Type	Rarity	Price
118	Airship	Event	U	0.70
280	Amaril	Cleric	C	0.60
273	Ambassador Carrague	Wizard	C	0.10
305	Amber	Cleric	C	0.60
152	Ambush	Event	U	0.70
303	Amethyst	Hero	C	0.30
415	Animal Friendship	C Spell	C	0.60
480	Annam	Cleric	R	2.30
337	Ansalong	Psionicist	C	0.30
70	Anytown, Anywhere	Realm	R	2.30
343	Apocalypse	Monster	C	0.70
306	Aquamarina	Cleric	C	0.30
60	Arak	Realm	U	0.50
285	Arch-Druid	Cleric	R	1.80
318	Arden Glimrock	Cleric	C	0.30
94	Arkhold	Holding	U	0.70
351	Arlando El-Adaba	Regent	C	0.40
208	Armies of Bloodstone	Ally	C	0.70
396	Armor	W Spell	C	0.10
200	Arrow of Slaying	Item	C	0.10
225	Ashathra	Ally	C	0.30
221	Assassins	Ally	C	0.40
146	Assault of Magic	Event	U	0.50
269	Athasian Cistern Fiend	Monster	C	0.40
230	Athasian Sloth	Ally	C	0.40
457	Axe of Dwarvish Lords	Artifact	C	0.60
187	Badge of the Wolf Nomads	Item	C	0.40
478	Bahgtru	Monster	R	2.30
145	Balance of Power	Event	U	0.70
163	Banner of the Two-Eyed God	Item	C	0.40
512	Barbaric Allies	Ally	UR	4.30
111	Barter	Holding	U	0.50
332	Beala	Psionicist	C	0.10
159	Bess's Revenge	Event	U	0.80
511	Between a Rock and a Hard Place	Event	UR	4.30
135	Black Bess	Event	U	0.50
46	Black Spear Tribes	Realm	R	2.80
375	Black Tentacles	W Spell	C	0.40
98	Black Waters	Holding	U	0.80
74	Blackstaff Tower	Holding	U	0.50
440	Blind Side!	Unarmed	C	0.40
518	Blingdenstone Symbol of Power	C Spell	UR	5.10
373	Blink	W Spell	C	0.30
57	Blood Sea of Istar	Realm	U	0.50
446	Bloodform	Ability	C	0.10
59	Bluet Spur	Realm	R	2.00
429	Body Weaponry	Psionic	C	0.10
51	Boeruine	Realm	U	0.50
105	Boeruine Trading Guild	Holding	U	0.50
434	Boot to the Head	Unarmed	C	0.70
61	Borca	Realm	R	2.00
316	Borin Moradinson	Cleric	C	0.70
268	Borys the Dragon	Monster	C	0.40
476	Brandobaris	Hero	R	2.00
153	Brave Heart	Event	U	0.50
357	Bride of Malice	Wizard	C	0.40
237	Brine Dragon	Ally	C	0.30
127	Bruce's Revenge	Event	U	0.50
141	Call to Arms	Event	U	0.70
75	Candlekeep	Holding	U	0.70
260	Captain Kazhal	Hero	C	0.30
50	Cariele	Realm	U	0.50
119	Cataclysm!	Event	U	0.70
505	Caves of Mystery	Holding	UR	4.30
482	Cegilune	Monster	R	2.00
35	Celik	Realm	U	0.50
447	Charm Aura	Ability	C	0.10
374	Charm Monster	W Spell	C	0.70
347	Chernevik	Regent	C	0.60
196	Chimes of Chelerie	Item	C	0.30
436	Choke Hold	Unarmed	C	0.10
348	Cidre Bint Corina	Regent	C	0.70
495	Circle of Life	Rule	C	0.10
247	Clay Golem	Ally	C	0.30
281	Clerics of Malar	Cleric	C	0.10
452	Codex of the Infinite Planes	Artifact	C	0.10
416	Command	C Spell	C	0.10
368	Cone of Cold	W Spell	C	0.40
477	Corellon Larethian	Wizard	R	1.80
65	Council Aerie	Realm	U	0.50
437	Counter	Unarmed	C	0.30
156	Covert Aid	Event	U	0.80
402	Creeping Doom	C Spell	U	0.50
201	Crossbow of Accuracy	Item	C	0.30
369	Crushing Fist	W Spell	C	0.30
454	Cup of Al'Akbar	Artifact	C	0.60
307	Cyclops	Monster	C	0.40
202	Dagger of Venom	Item	C	0.30
7	Daggerdale	Realm	U	0.50
6	Damara	Realm	U	0.50
112	Dance of the Red Death	Holding	U	0.50
69	Dancing Hut of Baba Yaga	Realm	U	0.50
188	Dark Haven	Item	C	0.40
136	Dead Magic Zone	Event	U	0.50
376	Death Fog	W Spell	C	0.40
381	Death Link	W Spell	U	0.70
377	Death Spell	W Spell	C	0.40
137	Deflection	Event	U	0.70
298	Diamond	Wizard	C	0.10
400	Dispel	C Spell	C	0.60
370	Dispel Magic	W Spell	C	0.60
252	Displacer Beast	Ally	C	0.30
263	Dracolich	Monster	C	0.10
198	Dragon Drums	Item	C	0.30
39	Dragon's Crown Mountains	Realm	R	2.80
519	Dragon's Eye Symbol of Power	W Spell	UR	5.10
139	Dragons Rebellious	Event	U	0.50
177	Dragonslayer	Item	C	0.60
276	Drawmij	Wizard	C	0.30
319	Drider	Monster	C	0.10
253	Drizzt Do'Urden	Hero	C	0.30
181	Drow Slippers	Item	C	0.40
20	Duchy of Tenh	Realm	R	2.80
99	Dungeon of Gulg	Holding	U	0.70
403	Earthquake	C Spell	U	0.50
470	Elemental Avatar of Air	Cleric	R	2.30
469	Elemental Avatar of Earth	Cleric	R	2.30
472	Elemental Avatar of Fire	Cleric	R	1.80
471	Elemental Avatar of Water	Cleric	R	2.80
287	Elemental Cleric	Cleric	C	0.40
442	Elemental Control	Ability	C	0.30
214	Elf Galleon	Ally	C	0.40
271	Elminster the Mage	Wizard	C	0.10
387	Elminster's Evasion	W Spell	C	0.30
232	Elven Archer	Ally	C	0.40
150	Elven Rebirth	Event	U	0.80
299	Emerald	Wizard	C	0.10
58	Enstar	Realm	R	2.00
419	Enthrall	C Spell	C	0.40
162	Escape from the Abyss	Event	U	0.50
390	ESP	W Spell	C	0.30
56	Estwilde	Realm	U	0.50
508	Ethereal Champion	Hero	UR	6.10
308	Ettin	Monster	R	1.50
30	Euripis	Realm	U	0.50
8	Evermeet	Realm	U	0.50
453	Eye and Hand of Vecna	Artifact	C	0.30
320	Eye Tyrant	Monster	C	0.30
496	Fair Fight!	Rule	C	0.60
405	Faith-Magic Zone	C Spell	C	0.10
167	Falcon Figurine	Item	C	0.30
128	Fast Talking!	Event	U	0.70
372	Fear	W Spell	C	0.30
443	Fear	Ability	C	0.10
484	Ferrix	Wizard	R	2.30
310	Fire Giant	Monster	C	0.30
420	Fire Trap	C Spell	C	0.10
363	Fireball	W Spell	C	0.10
238	Flaming Fist	Ally	C	0.40
501	Flash Flood	Event	UR	4.30
359	Fleeing Adventurers	Hero	C	0.30
235	Flesh Golem	Ally	C	0.10
361	Flight	W Spell	C	0.10
494	Forbidden Knowledge	Rule	C	0.10
160	Foreign Wars	Event	U	0.80
309	Formorian Giant	Monster	C	0.10
85	Fortification: Bailey	Holding	U	0.50
89	Fortification: Barricade	Holding	U	0.50
83	Fortification: Bastion	Holding	U	0.70
90	Fortification: Breastwork	Holding	U	0.50
88	Fortification: Bulwark	Holding	U	0.70
86	Fortification: Curtain Wall	Holding	U	0.70
87	Fortification: Inner Wall	Holding	U	0.80
84	Fortification: Parapet	Holding	U	0.70
82	Fortification: Rampart	Holding	U	0.80
22	Free and Independent City of Dyvers	Realm	U	0.50
327	Funerea	Hero	C	0.10
16	Furyondy	Realm	R	2.00
227	Galek	Ally	C	0.30
161	Gales at Sea	Event	U	0.80
473	Garl Glittergold	Hero	R	1.50
185	Gauntlets of Golem Strength	Item	C	0.40
178	Gauntlets of Swimming	Item	C	0.40
168	Ghost Crystal	Item	C	0.10
13	Giant's Run Mountains	Realm	R	2.00
183	Girdle of Storm Giant Strength	Item	C	0.40
223	Gladiators	Ally	C	0.60
314	Gloaranor	Cleric	C	0.40
120	Good Fortune	Event	U	0.70
96	Grak's Pool	Holding	U	0.70
479	Great Mother	Monster	R	2.00
18	Greyhawk Ruins	Realm	U	0.50
108	Grovnekvic Forest	Holding	U	0.80
458	Guenhwyvar	Artifact	C	0.30
29	Gulg	Realm	U	0.50
62	Gundarak	Realm	U	0.50
222	Halfling Mercenaries	Ally	C	0.40
184	Hammer of the Gods	Item	C	0.60
71	Haven of the Undead	Realm	U	0.50
444	Healing	Ability	C	0.60
421	Heat Metal	C Spell	C	0.40
21	Hell Furnaces	Realm	U	0.50
216	Hell Hound	Ally	C	0.30
255	Helm	Hero	R	2.00
441	Heroic Effort	Unarmed	C	0.60
257	Hettman Tsurin	Hero	C	0.40
207	Holy Avenger	Item	C	0.30
179	Horn of Blasting	Item	C	0.40
211	Hornhead Saurial	Ally	C	0.30
140	Hurricane!	Event	U	0.50
132	Ice Storm	Event	U	0.70
5	Icewind Dale	Realm	U	0.50
213	Intellect Devourer	Ally	C	0.70
334	Iserik	Hero	C	0.60
325	Isika	Hero	C	0.40
488	Iuz, Avatar of Evil	Monster	R	2.30
433	Jab	Unarmed	C	0.30
302	Jacinth	Hero	C	0.60
338	Jarek Halvs	Psionicist	C	0.10
203	Javelin of Lightning	Item	C	0.60
329	Jella	Psionicist	C	0.40
340	Kai'Rik'Tik	Psionicist	C	0.30
279	Kalid-na	Wizard	R	2.30
483	Kanchelsis	Wizard	R	2.30
117	Keep of the Dead	Holding	U	0.80

RARITY KEY C = Common U = Uncommon R = Rare VR = Very Rare UR = Ultra Rare F = Foil card X = Fixed/standard in all decks

#	Card name	Type	Rarity	Price
☐ 116	Kestrel's Keep	Holding	U	0.70
☐ 248	Ki-Rin	Ally	C	0.40
☐ 331	Kit'Kit'Kin	Psionicist	C	0.40
☐ 288	Klik-Ka'Cha	Cleric	C	0.30

26

#	Card name	Type	Rarity	Price
☐ 270	Korgunard the Avangion	Monster	C	0.10
☐ 122	Labor of Legend	Event	U	0.70
☐ 68	Lair of the Eye Tyrant	Realm	R	2.30
☐ 36	Lake Island	Realm	U	0.50
☐ 293	Larn	Wizard	C	0.10
☐ 143	Land Ho!	Event	U	0.50
☐ 430	Lend Health	Psionic	C	0.30
☐ 391	Leomund's Trap	W Spell	C	0.30
☐ 80	Lhespenbog	Holding	U	0.80

27

#	Card name	Type	Rarity	Price
☐ 265	Lich Conclave	Monster	C	0.40
☐ 364	Lightning Bolt	W Spell	C	0.10
☐ 382	Limited Wish	W Spell	U	0.80
☐ 294	Livekor	Monster	C	0.30
☐ 422	Locate Object	C Spell	C	0.40
☐ 489	Lolth, the Spider Avatar	Monster	R	2.30
☐ 95	Lost Oasis	Holding	U	0.50
☐ 236	Loup-Garou	Ally	C	0.30
☐ 193	Lyre of Arvanaith	Item	C	0.10

28

#	Card name	Type	Rarity	Price
☐ 204	Mace of Disruption	Item	C	0.70
☐ 109	Madding Springs	Holding	U	0.80
☐ 353	Madman Enraged	Hero	C	0.30
☐ 365	Magic Missle	W Spell	C	0.40
☐ 448	Major Resistance	Ability	C	0.40
☐ 323	Malaruat	Hero	C	0.10
☐ 324	Maleficent	Hero	C	0.60
☐ 322	Malleyahl	Hero	C	0.10
☐ 317	Mallin Dimmerswill	Cleric	C	0.10

29

#	Card name	Type	Rarity	Price
☐ 233	Marauder	Ally	C	0.40
☐ 242	Marilith Tanar'ri	Ally	C	0.10
☐ 499	Master the Magic	Rule	C	0.10
☐ 267	Mature Gold Dragon	Monster	C	0.10
☐ 1	Menzoberranzan	Realm	U	0.50
☐ 335	Merik	Hero	C	0.70
☐ 326	Merika	Hero	C	0.30
☐ 245	Mermaid	Ally	C	0.30
☐ 431	Metamorphosis	Psionic	U	0.50

30

#	Card name	Type	Rarity	Price
☐ 182	Midnight's Mask of Disguise	Item	C	0.40
☐ 487	Midnight, Goddess of Magic	Wizard	R	2.30
☐ 291	Migrane	Cleric	C	0.30
☐ 274	Mike the Wolf Nomad	Wizard	C	0.10
☐ 66	Milborne	Realm	R	2.00
☐ 212	Mind Flayer	Ally	C	0.70
☐ 426	Mindlink	Psionic	C	0.10
☐ 432	Mindwipe	Psionic	C	0.30
☐ 333	Minerva	Psionicist	C	0.60

31

#	Card name	Type	Rarity	Price
☐ 342	Minervan	Psionicist	C	0.60
☐ 386	Mirror Image	W Spell	C	0.30
☐ 392	Misdirection	W Spell	C	0.30
☐ 76	Mithral Hall	Holding	U	0.50
☐ 220	Mogadisho's Horde Marches On	Ally	C	0.30
☐ 72	Monastery of Perdien the Damned	Realm	R	2.30
☐ 148	Monstrous Intervention	Event	U	0.70
☐ 77	Moonwell	Holding	U	0.50
☐ 315	Moralin	Cleric	C	0.30

32

#	Card name	Type	Rarity	Price
☐ 339	Moraster	Psionicist	C	0.60
☐ 275	Mordenkainen	Wizard	C	0.10
☐ 73	Mulmaster	Holding	U	0.80
☐ 124	Mutiny!	Event	U	0.70
☐ 330	Myalasia	Psionicist	C	0.10
☐ 210	Myrmidons	Ally	C	0.60
☐ 517	Mystic Passage	Psionic	UR	4.30
☐ 4	Myth Drannor	Realm	U	0.50
☐ 78	Nagawater	Holding	U	0.50

33

#	Card name	Type	Rarity	Price
☐ 461	Nature's Throne	Artifact	C	0.60
☐ 261	Neeva	Hero	C	0.30
☐ 423	Negative Plane Protection	C Spell	C	0.30
☐ 284	Nenioc	Cleric	C	0.40

#	Card name	Type	Rarity	Price
☐ 313	Nernal	Cleric	C	0.60
☐ 169	Net of Entrapment	Item	C	0.10
☐ 502	Netherese Symbol of Power	W Spell	UR	5.10
☐ 31	New Giustenal	Realm	R	2.30
☐ 229	Night Runners	Ally	C	0.40

34

#	Card name	Type	Rarity	Price
☐ 64	Nightmare Lands	Realm	R	2.00
☐ 239	Ninjas	Ally	C	0.30
☐ 490	Nobody Wins!	Rule	C	0.70
☐ 15	Nyrond	Realm	U	0.50
☐ 459	Obsidian Man of Urik	Artifact	C	0.30
☐ 93	Ogo	Holding	U	0.50
☐ 244	Ogre Mage	Ally	C	0.30
☐ 170	Orb of Power	Item	C	0.30
☐ 190	Pan's Pipes	Item	C	0.40

35

#	Card name	Type	Rarity	Price
☐ 103	Peaceful Seas of Nesirie	Holding	U	0.80
☐ 304	Pearl	Cleric	C	0.70
☐ 312	Pellgrade the Inexorable	Wizard	C	0.10
☐ 262	Pereghost	Monster	C	0.40
☐ 19	Perrenland	Realm	U	0.50
☐ 450	Persuasion	Ability	C	0.30
☐ 142	Phantasmal Wolf	Event	U	0.80
☐ 428	Phobia Amplification	Psionic	C	0.30
☐ 289	Photed	Hero	C	0.40

36

#	Card name	Type	Rarity	Price
☐ 101	Points East Trading Company	Holding	U	1.20
☐ 514	Poor Man's Fort	Holding	UR	4.30
☐ 380	Power Word, Silence	W Spell	C	0.60
☐ 378	Power Word, Stun	W Spell	C	0.10
☐ 427	Precognition	Psionic	C	0.30
☐ 388	Prismatic Sphere	W Spell	C	0.70
☐ 144	Provocation	Event	U	0.50
☐ 147	Psionic Contrition	Event	U	0.50
☐ 240	Psuedodragon	Ally	C	0.30

37

#	Card name	Type	Rarity	Price
☐ 336	Pyre	Hero	C	0.60
☐ 350	Rahil the Falcon	Regent	C	0.30
☐ 401	Raise Dead	C Spell	C	0.10
☐ 438	Rake!	Unarmed	C	0.10
☐ 11	Raurin	Realm	U	0.50
☐ 393	Ray of Enfeeblement	W Spell	C	0.10
☐ 389	Re-target	W Spell	C	0.10
☐ 40	Realm of the White Witch	Realm	U	0.50
☐ 113	Red Jack	Holding	U	0.80

38

#	Card name	Type	Rarity	Price
☐ 114	Red Tide	Holding	U	0.50
☐ 481	Remnis	Monster	R	2.00
☐ 451	Ren's Crystal Ball	Artifact	C	0.10
☐ 503	Rengarth Oracle	C Spell	UR	5.10
☐ 53	Reorxcrown Mountains	Realm	U	0.50
☐ 445	Resistance	Ability	C	0.10
☐ 435	Reversal	Unarmed	C	0.30
☐ 385	Reverse Gravity	W Spell	C	0.10
☐ 52	Rhuobhe	Realm	R	2.80

39

#	Card name	Type	Rarity	Price
☐ 259	Rikus	Hero	C	0.40
☐ 171	Rings of All Seeing	Item	C	0.30
☐ 241	Roc	Ally	C	0.30
☐ 278	Rogue Defiler of Tyr	Wizard	C	0.70
☐ 321	Roper	Monster	C	0.10
☐ 224	Rowan	Ally	C	0.30
☐ 301	Ruby	Hero	C	0.40
☐ 2	Ruins of Zentil Keep	Realm	R	2.00
☐ 491	Rule Lawyer's Delight	Rule	C	0.30

40

#	Card name	Type	Rarity	Price
☐ 297	Rumples	Wizard	C	0.30
☐ 251	Rust Monster	Ally	C	0.10
☐ 277	Sadira	Wizard	C	0.40
☐ 328	Salurana	Psionicist	C	0.40
☐ 398	Sanctuary	C Spell	C	0.40
☐ 104	Sarimie's Temple of Fortune	Holding	U	0.80
☐ 199	Scarab of Protection	Item	C	0.30
☐ 205	Scimitar of Speed	Item	C	0.70
☐ 504	Sea of Dust	Realm	UR	4.30

41

#	Card name	Type	Rarity	Price
☐ 155	Secret War	Event	U	0.50
☐ 250	Selkie	Ally	C	0.40
☐ 3	Sembia	Realm	U	0.50
☐ 395	Sepia Snake Sigil	W Spell	C	0.30
☐ 346	Serpent	Regent	C	0.30

#	Card name	Type	Rarity	Price
☐ 404	Shadow Engines	C Spell	C	0.10
☐ 362	Shapechange	W Spell	U	0.80
☐ 234	Shaqat Beetles	Ally	C	0.40
☐ 110	Shark Reef	Holding	U	0.50

42

#	Card name	Type	Rarity	Price
☐ 290	Sharla	Wizard	C	0.10
☐ 33	Shault	Realm	U	0.50
☐ 286	Shayira	Cleric	C	0.70
☐ 295	Shayla	Hero	C	0.30
☐ 173	Shield of Annihilation	Item	C	0.40
☐ 172	Shield of Destruction	Item	C	0.40
☐ 174	Shield of Devastation	Item	C	0.30
☐ 175	Shield of Wickedness	Item	C	0.30
☐ 417	Shillelagh	C Spell	C	0.30

43

#	Card name	Type	Rarity	Price
☐ 54	Shining Lands	Realm	R	1.80
☐ 123	Siege!	Event	U	0.70
☐ 228	Silt Stalkers	Ally	C	0.30
☐ 97	Silver Spring	Holding	U	0.70
☐ 63	Sithicus	Realm	U	0.50
☐ 217	Skeletal Lord	Ally	C	0.30
☐ 218	Skeletal Minion	Ally	C	0.10
☐ 126	Slave Revolt!	Event	U	0.80
☐ 133	Solid Fog	Event	U	0.70

44

#	Card name	Type	Rarity	Price
☐ 92	South Ledopolus	Holding	U	0.70
☐ 379	Spell Turning	W Spell	C	0.30
☐ 189	Spellbook	Item	C	0.60
☐ 23	Spindrift Islands	Realm	U	0.50
☐ 296	Ssilcroth	Monster	C	0.70
☐ 165	Staff of Conjuring	Item	C	0.30
☐ 164	Staff of Striking	Item	C	0.30
☐ 14	Sterich	Realm	U	0.50
☐ 397	Sticks to Snakes	C Spell	C	0.40

45

#	Card name	Type	Rarity	Price
☐ 394	Stinking Cloud	W Spell	C	0.30
☐ 264	Stone Giant	Monster	C	0.30
☐ 24	Stonefist Hold	Realm	U	0.50
☐ 107	Straits of Aerele Shipping	Holding	U	0.50
☐ 226	Stug	Ally	C	0.40
☐ 425	Superior Invisibility	Psionic	C	0.10
☐ 121	Surprise Raid	Event	U	0.50
☐ 424	Switch Personality	Psionic	C	0.60
☐ 283	Sysania	Cleric	C	0.30

46

#	Card name	Type	Rarity	Price
☐ 106	Taeghan Outfitters	Holding	U	0.70
☐ 439	Tail Slap	Unarmed	U	0.80
☐ 341	Talcon	Psionicist	R	2.00
☐ 134	Tarrasque	Event	U	0.70
☐ 45	Tarvan Waste	Realm	U	0.50
☐ 17	Temple of Elemental Evil	Realm	U	0.50
☐ 138	Temporal Stasis	Event	U	0.50
☐ 352	The Ancient Dead	Monster	C	0.60
☐ 498	The Backwaters	Rule	C	0.10

47

#	Card name	Type	Rarity	Price
☐ 191	The Bagpipes of Drawmij	Item	C	0.40
☐ 129	The Barbarian's Revenge!	Event	U	0.80
☐ 41	The Battle-Fens	Realm	R	2.00
☐ 360	The Bog Monster	Monster	C	0.30
☐ 131	The Caravan	Event	U	0.50
☐ 100	The Celestial Jewel of Sarimie	Holding	U	1.20
☐ 10	The Coral Kingdom	Realm	R	1.80
☐ 151	The Death of a Hero	Event	U	0.80

48

#	Card name	Type	Rarity	Price
☐ 355	The Death Ship	Monster	C	0.40
☐ 55	The Delving	Realm	R	1.80
☐ 246	The Dreaded Ghost	Ally	C	0.30
☐ 467	The Emerald Throne	Artifact	C	0.10
☐ 497	The Event Wheel	Rule	C	0.10
☐ 49	The Five Peaks	Realm	U	0.50
☐ 34	The Forest Ridge	Realm	R	1.80
☐ 42	The Giantdowns	Realm	U	0.50
☐ 194	The Harp of Kings	Item	C	0.10

49

#	Card name	Type	Rarity	Price
☐ 254	The Harpers	Hero	C	0.10
☐ 344	The Harpy	Regent	C	0.40
☐ 209	The Iron Legion	Ally	C	0.60
☐ 67	The Isle of Beacon Point	Realm	U	0.50
☐ 37	The Jagged Cliffs	Realm	U	0.50
☐ 149	The Land Rebels	Event	U	0.80

RARITY KEY C = Common U = Uncommon R = Rare VR = Very Rare UR = Ultra Rare F = Foil card X = Fixed/standard in all decks

# Card name	Type	Rarity	Price
38 The Last Sea	Realm	U	0.50
356 The Lesser Mummy	Cleric	C	0.30
195 The Leviathan Horn	Item	C	0.30
50			
506 The Living Earth	Event	UR	4.30
345 The Magian	Regent	R	2.00
500 The Master Strategist	Rule	C	0.60
463 The Medusa Throne	Artifact	C	0.10
44 The Mistmoor	Realm	U	0.50
91 The Mud Palace	Holding	U	0.70
176 The Necklace	Item	C	0.60
507 The Painted Hills	Realm	UR	4.30
493 The Power of Faith	Rule	C	0.10
51			
455 The Ring of Winter	Artifact	C	0.10
48 The Sielwode	Realm	U	0.50
43 The Sphinx	Realm	U	0.50
513 The Sylvan Pool	Holding	UR	4.30
102 The Thorn Throne	Holding	U	0.50
460 The Throne of the Gods	Artifact	C	0.60
154 The Torments of Sisyphus	Event	U	0.50
9 The Trollmoors	Realm	U	0.50
12 The Vilhon Reach	Realm	U	0.50
52			
358 The Vulture of the Core	Monster	C	0.40
520 The Winner's Cape	Artifact	UR	7.10
256 Thorvid	Hero	C	0.60
243 Thought Eater	Ally	C	0.10
462 Throne of Bone	Artifact	C	0.30
464 Throne of Ice	Artifact	C	0.10
468 Throne of the Drow	Artifact	C	0.30

# Card name	Type	Rarity	Price
510 Throne of the Mountain God	Artifact	UR	7.10
53			
466 Throne of the Pharaohs	Artifact	C	0.10
465 Throne of the Seas	Artifact	C	0.40
47 Thurazor	Realm	U	0.50
79 Tilverton	Holding	U	0.50
492 Time of Troubles	Rule	C	0.10
383 Time Stop	W Spell	U	0.70
354 Ting Ling	Cleric	C	0.60
485 Titania	Wizard	R	2.00
158 Titans Walk the Earth	Event	U	0.50
300 Topaz	Wizard	C	0.60
54			
516 Towers of Menzoberranzan	Holding	UR	5.60
125 Transformation!	Event	U	0.80
219 Treants of the Grandwood	Ally	C	0.10
130 Treasure	Event	U	0.70
115 Treasure Vault	Holding	U	0.80
206 Trident of Fish Command	Item	C	0.30
249 Troll	Ally	C	0.40
28 Tyr	Realm	U	0.50
258 Tyrinon	Hero	C	0.30
55			
215 Tyrol	Ally	C	0.30
25 Ull	Realm	U	0.50
32 Ur Draxa	Realm	U	0.50
474 Urdlen	Monster	R	2.00
27 Urik	Realm	U	0.50
26 Valley of the Mage	Realm	R	2.00

# Card name	Type	Rarity	Price
272 Vangerdahast	Wizard	C	0.10
486 Verenestra	Cleric	R	2.00
292 Vitralis	Hero	C	0.70
56			
366 Wall of Fire	W Spell	C	0.10
371 Wall of Fog	W Spell	C	0.30
367 Wall of Force	W Spell	C	0.10
456 Wand of Orcus	Artifact	C	0.60
180 Wand of Wonder	Item	C	0.40
166 War Banner	Item	C	0.30
408 Ward of Erebus	C Spell	C	0.10
411 Ward of Freedom	C Spell	C	0.60
412 Ward of Ironguarding	C Spell	C	0.10
57			
410 Ward of Laius	C Spell	C	0.60
409 Ward of Lancoon	C Spell	C	0.10
407 Ward of Peace	C Spell	C	0.10
413 Ward of Ruin	C Spell	C	0.10
406 Ward of Sleep	C Spell	C	0.10
414 Ward of the Erinyes	C Spell	C	0.10
231 Wijon	Ally	C	0.70
399 Wind Walk	C Spell	C	0.30
186 Winged Boots	Item	C	0.40
58			
266 Winged Horror	Monster	C	0.10
384 Wish	W Spell	U	0.80
449 Wither Touch	Ability	C	0.40
157 Wrath of the Immortals	Event	U	0.80
197 Xeno-Xylophone	Item	C	0.70
475 Yondalla the Provider	Hero	R	1.80
311 Yumac the Cold	Wizard	R	1.80

Spellfire • Boosters (a.k.a. Set #1)

Halcyon

Every time Halcyon wins a round of battle, the player can return one card from the discard pile to his hand.
16 of 25

TSR • Released June 1994

25 cards in set • IDENTIFIER: "First Edition" on back, "of 25" on face

- Booster packs contain 12 cards; booster displays contain 36 boosters

The first set of boosters for **Spellfire** contain cards from the original 400-card **First Edition** set and cards from a 25-card booster-exclusive subset.

You will need **3** nine-pocket pages to store this set. (2 doubled up)

# Card name	Type	Rarity	Price
18 Alicia	Wizard	UR	3.80
24 Andra the Wise	Cleric	UR	3.80
15 Aurum, Gold Dragon	Monster	UR	5.00
6 Dagaronzie, Green Dragon	Monster	UR	4.00
14 Darbee	Hero	UR	3.80
10 Delsenora	Cleric	UR	3.80
12 Dori, the Barbarian	Hero	UR	3.80
8 Dragon Rage!	Event	UR	3.80
2 Edomira, Red Dragon	Monster	UR	4.30
23 Ember, the Red Dragon	Monster	UR	4.50
7 Fejyelsae	Hero	UR	3.80
4 Gib Ekim	Hero	UR	3.80

# Card name	Type	Rarity	Price
11 Gib Evets	Monster	UR	3.80
13 Gib Htimsen	Monster	UR	3.80
3 Gloriana	Wizard	UR	3.80
16 Halcyon	Cleric	UR	3.80
25 "Karm, Black Dragon"	Monster	UR	4.30
22 Lovely Colleen	Hero	UR	3.80
5 Neirgral, Green Dragon	Monster	UR	4.00
19 Red Zeb	Monster	UR	3.80
1 Sakornia	Hero	UR	3.80
9 Shalbaal, Red Dragon	Monster	UR	4.50
21 Smolder, Red Dragon	Monster	UR	4.30
17 Stryck	Monster	UR	3.80
20 The Avatar	Event	UR	4.00

Set (25 cards)	45.00
Booster Display Box	27.50
Booster Pack	1.80

Spellfire • Ravenloft (a.k.a. Set #2)

Timepiece of Klorr

If victorious, this champion may make one extra attack on the same realm before being put in his pool. (Def)
57 of 100

TSR • Released August 1994

100 cards in set • IDENTIFIER: Ravenloft logo "of 100" on face

- Booster packs contain 12 cards; booster displays contain 36 boosters

The first separate booster release for **Spellfire** featured card themes and art from the **Ravenloft** world in *Advanced Dungeons & Dragons*.

This horror-based world of vampires and werewolves made for an interesting-looking set of cards: **Loup-Garou** and **Flesh Golem** provided the game's first major two-card combos. But the set was overproduced and had a glaring marketing fault — no chase cards. With only 100 new cards, no major rules changes, and no chase cards, this set is today regarded as one of the worst sets for the game. — *John Danovich*

You will need **12** nine-pocket pages to store this set. (6 doubled up)

Set (100 cards)	30.00
Booster Display Box	27.50
Booster Pack	1.50

# Card name	Type	Rarity	Price
83 Adam	Monster	R	2.60
25 All Hallow's Eve	Event	C	0.30

# Card name	Type	Rarity	Price
64 Amulet of the Beast	Item	C	0.10
36 Animate Rock	C Spell	U	0.50
84 Ankhtepot	Monster	U	0.90
66 Apparatus	Artifact	R	1.70
89 Arijani	Monster	U	0.70
51 Augment Undead	W Spell	C	0.10
82 Azalin	Monster	R	2.60

RARITY KEY C = Common U = Uncommon R = Rare VR = Very Rare UR = Ultra Rare F = Foil card X = Fixed/standard in all decks

# Card name	Type	Rarity	Price
17 Azalin's Graveyard	Holding	R	2.30
1 Barovia	Realm	U	0.40
34 Binding Curse	C Spell	C	0.10
60 Blood Coin	Item	C	0.10
39 Call Lightning	C Spell	C	0.10
16 Castle Ravenloft	Holding	R	2.30
65 Cat of Felkovic	Item	C	0.10
55 Chill Touch	W Spell	C	0.10
30 City States	Rule	R	1.50
35 Conjure Grave Elemental	C Spell	R	1.90
67 Crown of Souls	Artifact	R	1.90
22 Dark Powers	Event	U	0.50
2 Darkon	Realm	R	1.90
11 Dementlieu	Realm	U	0.20
50 Detect Magic	W Spell	U	0.50
27 Disrupted Magic	Event	C	0.10
97 Dr. Mordenheim	Hero	C	0.10
86 Dr. Rudolph Van Richten	Hero	C	0.10
32 Eyes of the Undead	C Spell	C	0.10
70 Fang of the Nosferatu	Artifact	R	1.90
76 Fiend	Ally	R	1.90
73 Flesh Golem	Ally	U	0.30
93 Gabrielle Aderre	Wizard	C	0.10
74 Ghost Ship	Ally	R	1.50
38 Glyph of Warding	C Spell	C	0.10
23 Grand Conjunction	Event	C	0.10
94 Hags of Tepest	Monster	C	0.10
13 Har'Akir	Realm	C	0.10
87 Harkon Lukas	Monster	U	0.60
24 Harvest Moon	Event	R	1.90
88 Headless Horseman	Monster	R	1.50
45 Heal	C Spell	R	2.30
96 High Master Illithid	Monster	U	0.90
49 Hold Person	W Spell	R	1.50
68 Holy Symbol of Raven	Artifact	U	0.90
42 Imbue with Spell Ability	C Spell	C	0.10
43 Insect Plague	C Spell	C	0.10
9 Invidia	Realm	R	1.50
85 Ireena Kolyana	Hero	C	0.30
31 Islands of Terror	Rule	R	1.90
18 Kargat Mausoleum	Holding	C	0.10
71 Kargat Vampire	Ally	C	0.30
5 Kartakass	Realm	C	0.10
6 Keening	Realm	U	0.40
3 Lamordia	Realm	C	0.10
33 Living Ward	C Spell	U	0.50
99 Lord Soth	Monster	R	2.60
79 Loup-garou	Ally	U	0.70
21 Mists	Event	C	0.10
53 Misty Summons	W Spell	R	1.90
4 Mordent	Realm	C	0.10
81 Mysterious Stranger	Hero	C	0.10
54 Neverending Nightmare	W Spell	C	0.10
10 Nova Vaasa	Realm	C	0.10
19 Paridon	Holding	U	0.50
20 Pharaoh's Rest	Holding	C	0.10
44 Plane Shift	C Spell	R	1.90
28 Power of the Land	Event	U	0.50
40 Prayer	C Spell	C	0.10
26 Quirk of Fate	Event	R	1.50
58 Ring of Regeneration	Item	U	0.60
63 Ring of Reversion	Item	U	0.70
98 Sergei Von Zarovich	Hero	C	0.30
47 Shades	W Spell	C	0.10
46 Shadow Magic	W Spell	C	0.10
95 Sir Edmund Bloodsworth	Monster	C	0.10
92 Sir Hiregaard	Hero	C	0.10
62 Soul Searcher Medal	Item	C	0.10
14 Souragne	Realm	C	0.10
77 Spectre	Ally	U	0.50
29 Strahd Book / Drawmij	Rule	R	1.90
15 Sri Raji	Realm	U	0.40
61 Staff of Mimicry	Item	U	0.50
100 Strahd Von Zarovich	Monster	R	9.50
75 Strahd Zombies	Ally	C	0.10
52 Strahd's Malefic Meld	W Spell	U	0.70
59 Sun Sword	Item	C	0.30
69 Tapestry of Dark Souls	Artifact	U	0.70
56 Tarokka Deck	Item	U	0.50
7 Tepest	Realm	C	0.10
57 Timepiece of Knorr	Item	R	1.70
91 Tiyet	Monster	C	0.30
41 Turn Undead	C Spell	U	0.50
12 Valachan	Realm	C	0.10
48 Vampiric Touch	W Spell	C	0.10
8 Verbrek	Realm	C	0.10
78 Vistani	Ally	C	0.10
80 Werebat	Ally	C	0.10
90 Wilfred Godefroy	Monster	C	0.10
72 Wolf Pack	Ally	C	0.10
37 Word of Recall	C Spell	C	0.10

Spellfire • Dragonlance (a.k.a. Set #3)

SPELLFIRE Master the Magic

TSR • Released **Month Year**

125 cards in set • **IDENTIFIER: Dragonlance logo plus "of 25" or "of 100" on face**

- Booster packs contain 12 cards; booster displays contain 36 boosters

Correcting the mistake of **Ravenloft**, this 100-card expansion based on the *Dragonlance* world featured a 25-card bonus subset of photo chase cards.

One of the unique features of this set of cards is that it adds the element of time to **Spellfire**. Several cards have powers based on what time of day it is, so that decks could be constructed for use during day or night-time play. Another key element to this set is the addition of the Abyss, the term for the location of cards taken out of play but not out of the game. Specifically, **Takhisis's Abyssal Gateway** set up a condition that has since become an integral part of the game.

The set was very well-received, but had misleading copy on the display box, prompting TSR to overrun the chase cards and send them out to retailers to compensate for the misleading chase card odds. — **John Danovich**

You will need **14** nine-pocket pages to store this set. (7 doubled up)

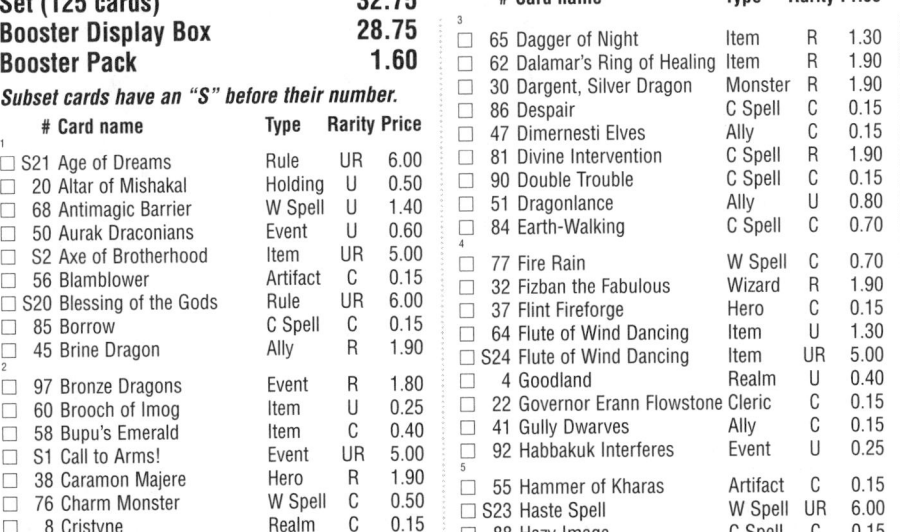

Tasslehoff Burrfoot

Set (125 cards)	32.75
Booster Display Box	28.75
Booster Pack	1.60

Subset cards have an "S" before their number.

# Card name	Type	Rarity	Price
S21 Age of Dreams	Rule	UR	6.00
20 Altar of Mishakal	Holding	U	0.50
68 Antimagic Barrier	W Spell	U	1.40
50 Aurak Draconians	Event	U	0.60
S2 Axe of Brotherhood	Item	UR	5.00
56 Blamblower	Artifact	C	0.15
S20 Blessing of the Gods	Rule	UR	6.00
85 Borrow	C Spell	C	0.15
45 Brine Dragon	Ally	R	1.90
97 Bronze Dragons	Event	R	1.80
60 Brooch of Imog	Item	U	0.25
58 Bupu's Emerald	Item	C	0.40
S1 Call to Arms!	Event	UR	5.00
38 Caramon Majere	Hero	R	1.90
76 Charm Monster	W Spell	C	0.50
8 Cristyne	Realm	C	0.15
S8 Crossed Blades	Event	UR	5.00
26 Crysania	Cleric	C	0.15

# Card name	Type	Rarity	Price
65 Dagger of Night	Item	R	1.30
62 Dalamar's Ring of Healing	Item	R	1.90
30 Dargent, Silver Dragon	Monster	R	1.90
86 Despair	C Spell	C	0.15
47 Dimernesti Elves	Ally	C	0.15
81 Divine Intervention	C Spell	R	1.90
90 Double Trouble	C Spell	C	0.15
51 Dragonlance	Ally	U	0.80
84 Earth-Walking	C Spell	C	0.70
77 Fire Rain	W Spell	C	0.70
32 Fizban the Fabulous	Wizard	R	1.90
37 Flint Fireforge	Hero	C	0.15
64 Flute of Wind Dancing	Item	U	1.30
S24 Flute of Wind Dancing	Item	UR	5.00
4 Goodland	Realm	U	0.40
22 Governor Erann Flowstone	Cleric	C	0.15
41 Gully Dwarves	Ally	C	0.15
92 Habbakuk Interferes	Event	U	0.25
55 Hammer of Kharas	Artifact	C	0.15
S23 Haste Spell	W Spell	UR	6.00
88 Hazy Image	C Spell	C	0.15
59 Inflatable Flotilla	Item	C	0.15

# Card name	Type	Rarity	Price
19 Inn of the Last Home	Holding	C	0.15
57 Irongnome	Item	U	0.25
13 Isle of Selasia	Realm	U	0.60
29 Justarian, Wizard of the Red Robes	Wizard	U	0.25
46 Kagonesti Elves	Ally	C	0.15
49 Kapak Draconians	Ally	U	0.60
25 Kaz the Minotaur	Monster	C	0.15
5 Khur	Realm	C	0.15
93 Kiri-Jolith Arrives	Event	U	0.80
S4 Knights of the Crown	Hero	UR	7.00
S6 Knights of the Rose	Hero	UR	7.00
S5 Knights of the Sword	Hero	UR	7.00
43 Krynn Minotaurs	Ally	U	0.40
28 Ladonna, Wizard of the Black Robes	Wizard	U	0.25
24 Lord Gunthar, Solamnic Knight	Hero	U	0.60
27 Maquesta Kar-Thon	Hero	R	1.90
S25 Medallion of Faith	Artifact	UR	6.50
91 Mishakal Intervenes	C Spell	C	0.15
80 Mishakal's Insistence	C Spell	R	1.30
1 Mithas	Realm	R	1.60

RARITY KEY **C** = Common **U** = Uncommon **R** = Rare **VR** = Very Rare **UR** = Ultra Rare **F** = Foil card **X** = Fixed/standard in all decks

#	Card name	Type	Rarity	Price
☐ 99	Moon Lunitari Waxes	Event	R	1.90
☐ 100	Moon Nuitari Waxes	Event	R	1.90
☐ 98	Moon Solinari Waxes	Event	R	1.90
☐ 72	Moonlight Madness	W Spell	C	0.15
☐ 95	Morgian, God of Disease, Strikes	Event	C	0.15
☐ 42	Night of the Eye	Rule	R	1.90
☐ 2	Nordmaar	Realm	C	0.15
☐ 9	Northern Ergoth	Realm	C	0.15
☐ 34	Par-Salian, Wizard of the White Robes	Wizard	U	0.50
☐ 89	Peace	C Spell	C	0.15
☐ 40	Phudge, the Great Highbulp	Hero	C	0.15
☐ 11	Plains of Dust	Realm	U	0.50
☐ 79	Protection from Draconians	W Spell	C	0.15
☐ 35	Pyrite, the Ancient Gold Dragon	Monster	U	0.60
☐ 31	Raistlin Majere, Wizard of the Black Robes	Wizard	R	1.80
☐ 74	Recall	W Spell	U	0.25
☐ 83	Reflection	C Spell	U	0.25
☐ 94	Reorx, the Forge, Walks the Land	Event	C	0.15
☐ 15	Reorxcrown Mountains	Realm	R	1.90
☐ 87	Return	C Spell	C	0.15

#	Card name	Type	Rarity	Price
☐ 7	Sancrist	Realm	C	0.15
☐ 53	Shield of Huma	Artifact	C	0.50
☐ S7	Shield of Huma	Item	UR	5.00
☐ 18	Shoikan Grove	Holding	C	0.15
☐ 3	Silvanesti	Realm	C	0.15
☐ 48	Sivak Draconians	Ally	C	0.15
☐ 21	"Skie, Blue Dragon"	Monster	C	0.15
☐ 6	Solamnia	Realm	R	1.60
☐ 61	Solamnic Armor	Item	R	1.10
☐ 44	Solamnic Knights	Ally	C	0.15
☐ 10	Southern Ergoth	Realm	U	0.40
☐ 12	Spine of Taladas	Realm	U	0.60
☐ S9	Spirit of the Que-Shu	Event	UR	5.00
☐ 52	Staff of Magius	Artifact	U	0.60
☐ 71	Steel	W Spell	C	0.15
☐ 78	Stone Water	W Spell	C	0.15
☐ 70	Strength	W Spell	C	0.15
☐ 82	Summon Griffon	C Spell	C	1.30
☐ 73	Switch	W Spell	C	0.15
☐ S3	Sword of Friendship	Item	UR	5.00
☐ S13	Takhisis's Abyssal Gateway	W Spell	UR	5.50
☐ S18	Takhisis's Helmet of Power	Item	UR	5.00
☐ S11	Takhisis's Mirror and Staff	Item	UR	5.00
☐ S12	Takhisis's Mirror and Sword	Artifact	UR	7.50

#	Card name	Type	Rarity	Price
☐ S14	Takhisis's Mirror of Life Trapping	Event	UR	5.00
☐ S16	Takhisis's Mirror of Revenge!	Item	UR	5.00
☐ S17	Takhisis's Mirror of the Abyssal Warlord	Monster	UR	5.00
☐ S15	Takhisis's Mirror of Underworld Minions	Ally	UR	5.00
☐ 33	Takhisis, Queen of Darkness	Monster	R	1.90
☐ 36	Tanis Half-Elven	Hero	C	0.15
☐ 39	Tasslehoff Burrfoot	Hero	C	0.15
☐ 75	Tenser's Transformation	W Spell	U	0.25
☐ S22	The Golden Age	Rule	UR	7.00
☐ 17	The Lost Citadel	Holding	R	1.90
☐ 54	The Nightjewel	Artifact	C	0.15
☐ S10	The Skull of Fistandantilus	Artifact	UR	8.00
☐ 14	Thorin	Realm	C	0.15
☐ 23	Tika Waylan Majere	Hero	C	0.15
☐ 67	Time Shift: Day into Night	W Spell	R	1.90
☐ 66	Time Shift: Night into Day	Item	R	1.90
☐ S19	Tower of High Sorcery	Rule	UR	5.00
☐ 16	Tower of Wayreth	Holding	R	1.90
☐ 69	Unnerving Aura	W Spell	C	0.80
☐ 63	Wand of Telekinesis	Item	R	2.00
☐ 96	Zeboim, the Sea Queen, Is Enraged	Event	C	0.15

Spellfire • Forgotten Realms (a.k.a. *Set #4*)

SPELLFIRE
Master the Magic

TSR • Released **November 1994**

125 cards in set • **IDENTIFIER: Forgotten Realms logo plus "of 25" or "of 100" on face**

• Booster packs contain 12 cards; booster displays contain 36 boosters

This expansion featured a 25-card subset of photo chase cards based on the *Forgotten Realms* world in *AD&D*. One of the most sought-after sets in *Spellfire*, this set contains many powerful cards that have become mainstays for Spellfire decks everywhere. Of special note are the cards Wish, Limited Wish, Helm, and Unusually Good Fortune. With a large segment of this set devoted to Wizard Spells, this changed the Spellfire game in a big way, allowing spell-heavy speed decks to be created. — *John Danovich*

Khelben "Blackstaff" Arunsun

Blackstaff gains +4 levels when defending Waterdeep.

94 of 100

You will need **14** nine-pocket pages to store this set (7 doubled up)

Set (125 cards)	**32.00**
Booster Display Box	**26.00**
Booster Pack	**1.30**

#	Card name	Type	Rarity	Price
☐ 84	Adon	Cleric	C	0.15
☐ 27	Aerial Servant	C Spell	C	0.15
☐ 88	Ambassador Carrague	Wizard	U	0.60
☐ 12	Apple of His Eye	Event	UR	4.30
☐ 18	Bell of Might	Item	UR	7.50
☐ 2	Black Bess	Event	R	1.60
☐ 19	Blackstaff Tower	Holding	U	0.60
☐ 63	Bloodriders	Ally	C	0.15
☐ 3	Caer Allison	Event	R	1.90
☐ 20	Candlekeep	Holding	U	0.50
☐ 2	Cold Cup of Calamity	Event	UR	7.50
☐ 11	Coral Kingdom	Realm	C	0.15
☐ 28	Creeping Doom	C Spell	U	0.80
☐ 4	Curse of Azure Bonds	Event	R	1.90
☐ 92	Cyric	Hero	R	1.90
☐ 5	Cyrinishad	Event	R	1.60
☐ 16	Dagger of Deception	Item	UR	4.30
☐ 78	Darkenbeast	Monster	C	0.15
☐ 6	Darkwalker War	Event	U	0.60
☐ 10	Day That Will Live in Infamy	Event	UR	4.30
☐ 7	Dead Magic Zone	Event	U	0.80
☐ 39	Death Link	C Spell	C	0.15
☐ 47	Deck of Many Things	Item	R	1.80
☐ 58	Dragon Throne	Artifact	R	1.90

#	Card name	Type	Rarity	Price
☐ 93	Dragonbait	Hero	C	0.15
☐ 64	Dragonclaw	Ally	R	1.90
☐ 48	Dragonslayer	Item	R	1.60
☐ 29	Earthquake	C Spell	C	0.15
☐ 8	Ebony Cup of Fate	Artifact	UR	4.30
☐ 85	Erixitl	Cleric	C	0.15
☐ 14	Feather Flight	W Spell	UR	4.30
☐ 40	Find Familiar	C Spell	C	0.15
☐ 79	Firbolg	Monster	C	0.15
☐ 49	Flametongue	Item	R	1.90
☐ 65	Flaming Fist	Ally	U	0.80
☐ 50	Frostbrand	Item	R	1.90
☐ 86	Fzoul Chembryl	Cleric	C	0.15
☐ 51	Gauntlets of Swimming	Item	C	0.15
☐ 15	Golden Barter	W Spell	UR	4.30
☐ 13	Golden Touch	W Spell	UR	4.30
☐ 41	Great Shout	C Spell	C	0.15
☐ 59	Guenhwyvar	Artifact	R	1.80
☐ 66	Halfling, Inc.	Ally	U	0.80
☐ 42	Hallucinatory Terrain	W Spell	C	0.15
☐ 12	Halruaa	Realm	C	0.15
☐ 60	Hammer of Tyr	Artifact	R	1.90
☐ 5	Hawksflight Grail	Artifact	UR	7.50
☐ 89	Helm	Hero	U	0.80
☐ 52	Helm of Water Breathing	Item	C	0.15
☐ 9	Hero's Chalice	Item	UR	4.30
☐ 21	High Horn	Holding	U	0.60
☐ 8	Horde	Event	C	0.15
☐ 53	Horn of Blasting	Item	U	0.25
☐ 30	Illusory Fortification	C Spell	C	0.15
☐ 80	Iron Golem	Monster	C	0.15
☐ 94	Khelben Arunsun	Wizard	C	0.15
☐ 13	Kozakura	Realm	C	0.15

#	Card name	Type	Rarity	Price
☐ 67	Kuo Toa	Ally	C	0.15
☐ 9	Lady Luck	Event	R	1.90
☐ 43	Limited Wish	W Spell	U	0.80
☐ 68	Locathah	Ally	C	0.15
☐ 14	Luiren	Realm	C	0.15
☐ 24	Lure of Undermountain	Rule	UR	7.50
☐ 69	Mad Monkey	Ally	R	1.60
☐ 15	Maztica	Realm	C	0.15
☐ 22	Mithril Hall	Holding	U	0.60
☐ 23	Moonwell	Holding	U	0.80
☐ 4	Mug of the Earthbound	W Spell	UR	7.50
☐ 16	Mulhorand	Realm	C	0.15
☐ 19	Muragh Brilstagg	Ally	UR	7.50
☐ 23	Netheril	Realm	UR	7.50
☐ 70	Ninjas	Ally	U	0.25
☐ 95	Ochimo	Hero	C	0.15
☐ 71	Olive Ruskettle	Ally	U	0.60
☐ 72	Orcs of Dragonspear	Ally	C	0.15
☐ 73	Orcs of the Savage Frontier	Ally	C	0.15
☐ 20	Phase Door	W Spell	UR	7.50
☐ 24	Pook's Palace	Holding	U	0.90
☐ 96	Prince Tristan	Hero	C	0.15
☐ 97	Princess Alusair	Hero	C	0.15
☐ 74	Pseudodragon	Ally	C	0.15
☐ 31	Quest	C Spell	C	0.15
☐ 32	Raise Dead	C Spell	U	0.80
☐ 98	Randal Morn	Hero	C	0.15
☐ 17	Raurin	Realm	C	0.15
☐ 75	Red Wizards	Ally	C	0.15
☐ 33	Reincarnate	C Spell	C	1.90
☐ 34	Ressurection	C Spell	R	1.90
☐ 54	Ring of Jumping	Item	C	0.15
☐ 61	Ring of Winter	Artifact	R	1.90

RARITY KEY C = Common U = Uncommon R = Rare VR = Very Rare UR = Ultra Rare F = Foil card X = Fixed/standard in all decks

	Card name	Type	Rarity	Price
11				
☐ 76	Sahuagin	Ally	C	0.15
☐ 77	Samurai	Ally	C	0.15
☐ 35	Shadow Engines	C Spell	C	0.15
☐ 18	Shou Lung	Realm	C	0.15
☐ 90	Simbul of Aglarond	Wizard	R	1.60
☐ 55	Slippers of Spider Climbing	Item	C	0.15
☐ 22	Spellblades	Item	UR	7.50
☐ 82	Stone Giant	Monster	C	0.15
☐ 81	Storm Giant	Monster	C	0.15
12				
☐ 62	Sword of Cymrych Hugh	Artifact	R	1.90
☐ 36	Symbol of Hopelessness	C Spell	U	0.60
☐ 100	Tablets of Fate	Rule	R	1.90

	Card name	Type	Rarity	Price
☐ 1	Tarrasque	Event	U	0.60
☐ 7	Teapot of the Golden Temple	Item	UR	7.50
☐ 1	Thrice Hearty Cup of Balder the Red	C Spell	UR	7.50
☐ 99	Time of Troubles	Rule	U	0.60
☐ 44	Time Stop	W Spell	U	0.80
☐ 26	Tower of Ashaba	Holding	U	0.90
13				
☐ 11	Unusually Good Fortune	Event	UR	4.30
☐ 91	Vanderdahast	Wizard	C	0.15
☐ 6	Vessel of Misty Passage	Event	UR	7.50
☐ 3	Vessel of Vaporous Stones	Event	UR	7.50
☐ 56	Vorpal Blade	Item	R	1.80

	Card name	Type	Rarity	Price
☐ 57	Wand of Wonder	Item	R	1.90
☐ 45	Water Breathing	W Spell	C	0.15
☐ 83	Werewolf	Monster	U	0.60
☐ 10	Wild Magic Surge	Event	R	1.90
14				
☐ 21	Wine of Eternity	Event	UR	7.50
☐ 46	Wish	W Spell	R	1.90
☐ 37	Word of Recall	C Spell	C	0.15
☐ 17	Wyrm of Earthwalking	Item	UR	7.50
☐ 87	Young Robyn	Cleric	C	0.15
☐ 25	Yulash	Holding	U	0.60
☐ 25	Zhentarim Intrigue	Rule	UR	7.50
☐ 38	Zone of Truth	C Spell	C	0.15

Spellfire • Artifacts (a.k.a. Set #5)

SPELLFIRE™ Master the Magic

TSR • Released May 1995

120 cards in set • **IDENTIFIER: AD&D 2nd Ed. logo plus "of 20" or "of 100" on face**

• Booster packs contain 12 cards; booster displays contain 36 boosters

Artifacts, the first set on abstract theme rather than a game world in the *Advanced Dungeons & Dragons* game, employs powerful and legendary items and characters in the *AD&D* game setting.

This set, which sold very well and still is sought after, features photo chase cards with TSR employees as characters, and (not unexpectedly) some of the most powerful cards feature TSR designers. A seven-card combo was also created for the game with the seven different **Rod of Seven Parts** cards. Each card had individual powers along with powers that interacted with the addition of the other cards. *Artifacts* also introduced a new card type, Rule Cards, which when put into play changed the basic rules of the game. — *John Danovich*

You will need **14** nine-pocket pages to store this set. (7 doubled up)

Set (120 cards)				38.75
Booster Display Box				**26.00**
Booster Pack				**1.70**

#	Card name	Type	Rarity	Price
1				
☐ 10	All-Knowing Eye Yasmin Sira	Artifact	R	2.10
☐ 18	Amelior's Restraint	Item	UR	3.80
☐ 17	Amulet of Spell Protection	Item	UR	4.40
☐ 92	Ancient Kalidnay	Realm	C	0.15
☐ 50	Ariel Anjelique	Ally	C	0.15
☐ 16	Ariel's Feather Charm	Item	UR	3.80
☐ 36	Artifact Champions	Rule	U	0.40
☐ 35	Artifact Vault	Rule	R	2.30
☐ 2	Axe of Dwarvish Lord	Artifact	C	0.15
2				
☐ 28	Bag of Holding	Item	C	0.15
☐ 5	Barab's Goblet Disolusionment	Artifact	UR	3.80
☐ 12	Bigby's Clenched Fist	W Spell	UR	3.80
☐ 88	Bluet Spur	Realm	U	0.50
☐ 96	Celik	Realm	R	2.10
☐ 11	Coin Jisan Bountiful	Artifact	C	0.60
☐ 40	Cosmic Justice	Rule	R	2.20
☐ 86	Council Aerie	Realm	U	0.50
3				
☐ 13	Crystal of Ebon Flame	Artifact	C	0.15
☐ 69	Curse Glyph	C Spell	U	0.50
☐ 29	Daern's Instant Fortress	Item	R	2.10
☐ 33	Dark Lords	Rule	U	0.20
☐ 85	Darsson Spellmaker	Wizard	C	0.15
☐ 70	Death Glyph	C Spell	C	0.15
☐ 2	Death Rock	Artifact	UR	3.80
☐ 72	Deathstream, Black Dragon	Monster	C	0.15
☐ 54	Deflection	Event	R	2.30
☐ 100	Deja Vu	C Spell	U	0.40
4				
☐ 48	Dimock the Sprite	Ally	C	0.15
☐ 20	Dragon Font	Item	UR	6.30
☐ 51	Dragon Slayer	Event	U	0.40
☐ 71	Dragon Turtle	Monster	C	0.15
☐ 43	Dragonbane	C Spell	C	0.15
☐ 76	Drawmij	Wizard	U	0.50
☐ 74	Dregoth, Undead Dragon	Monster	R	2.30
☐ 47	Erica of Dark Watch	Ally	C	0.15
☐ 81	Erital Kaan-Ipzirel	Cleric	C	0.20
5				
☐ 59	Ethereality	C Spell	C	0.20

#	Card name	Type	Rarity	Price
☐ 90	Euripis	Realm	C	0.15
☐ 13	Fire Charm	W Spell	UR	3.80
☐ 66	Fire Glyph	C Spell	R	2.10
☐ 49	Flying Carpet	Item	C	0.15
☐ 11	Forbiddance	C Spell	UR	3.80
☐ 39	Forbidden Lore	Rule	C	0.15
☐ 95	Forest Ridge	Realm	C	0.15
☐ 19	Gauntlets Ogre Power	Item	R	2.10
6				
☐ 10	Ghostly Piper	Monster	UR	3.80
☐ 17	Girdle Giant Strength	Item	C	0.15
☐ 83	Goldmoon	Cleric	C	0.15
☐ 18	Hammer of Thunderbolts	Item	R	2.10
☐ 89	Hell Furnaces	Realm	C	0.15
☐ 55	Help!	Event	R	2.30
☐ 79	Hornung the Anarch	Wizard	C	0.15
☐ 80	Invisible Stalker	Monster	U	0.40
☐ 3	Iron Flask Tuerny Merciless	Artifact	U	0.40
7				
☐ 37	Isolated Worlds	Rule	C	0.15
☐ 4	Jacinth Inestimable Beauty	Artifact	U	0.40
☐ 64	Keep of the Dead	Holding	C	0.15
☐ 63	Kestrel's Keep	Holding	U	0.50
☐ 9	Killian	Hero	UR	3.80
☐ 42	Kinsle the Druid	Ally	C	0.15
☐ 77	Klik-Ka'cha	Cleric	C	0.15
☐ 75	Korgunard the Avangion	Monster	C	0.15
☐ 97	Lake Island	Realm	C	0.15
8				
☐ 68	Lightning Glyph	C Spell	R	2.30
☐ 7	Lord Blacktree	Hero	UR	3.80
☐ 1	Mace of Cuthbert	Artifact	UR	3.80
☐ 5	Machine Lum the Mad	Artifact	R	2.10
☐ 16	Midnight's Mask Disguise	Item	C	0.60
☐ 58	Mirror Image	W Spell	U	0.50
☐ 78	Mykell, Amythest Wyrm	Monster	C	0.15
☐ 91	New Guistenal	Realm	C	0.15
☐ 38	No Funny Business	Rule	R	2.10
9				
☐ 14	Obsidian Man of Urik	Artifact	R	2.10
☐ 6	Onad the Weasel	Wizard	UR	5.00
☐ 45	Pegasus	Ally	C	0.15
☐ 31	Plentiful Psionics	Rule	R	2.10
☐ 84	Princess Amber	Hero	R	2.30
☐ 60	Prismatic Spray	W Spell	C	0.15

#	Card name	Type	Rarity	Price
☐ 3	Psychometron Nerad	Artifact	UR	3.80
☐ 6	Queen Ehlissa Nightingale	Artifact	C	0.15
☐ 56	Reverse Gravity	W Spell	U	0.40
10				
☐ 41	Roc	Ally	C	0.15
☐ 21	Rod of 7 Parts, #1	Item	U	0.50
☐ 22	Rod of 7 Parts, #2	Item	R	2.30
☐ 23	Rod of 7 Parts, #3	Item	U	0.30
☐ 24	Rod of 7 Parts, #4	Item	R	2.30
☐ 25	Rod of 7 Parts, #5	Item	U	0.60
☐ 26	Rod of 7 Parts, #6	Item	R	2.30
☐ 27	Rod of 7 Parts, #7	Item	U	0.50
☐ 15	Rod of Teeth	Artifact	U	0.40
11				
☐ 12	Seal of Lost Arak	Artifact	R	2.10
☐ 94	Shault	Realm	C	0.15
☐ 57	Shift Earth	C Spell	C	0.15
☐ 87	Shining Lands	Realm	C	0.15
☐ 44	Ship of the Sky	W Spell	R	2.30
☐ 4	Silencer of Bodach	Artifact	UR	3.80
☐ 19	Smoke Powder Pistol	Item	UR	3.80
☐ 32	Sorcerer-Kings	Rule	C	0.15
12				
☐ 15	Spectral Hand	W Spell	UR	3.80
☐ 30	Spellbook	Item	R	2.30
☐ 65	Spellfire Citadel	Holding	U	0.50
☐ 7	Sword of Kas	Artifact	U	0.50
☐ 8	Talisman of Al'Akbar	Artifact	C	0.15
☐ 52	Tanar'ri, Marilith	Ally	C	0.15
☐ 9	Teeth of Dalhvar-Nar	Artifact	U	0.40
☐ 53	Temporal Stasis	Event	U	0.50
☐ 34	The Walking Dead	Rule	U	0.50
☐ 99	Thought Eater	Ally	C	0.20
13				
☐ 14	Thunder Staff	W Spell	UR	3.80
☐ 61	Treasure Vault	Holding	R	2.30
☐ 62	Tupillil	Holding	C	0.15
☐ 93	Ur Draxa	Realm	C	0.15
☐ 1	Wand of Orcus	Artifact	R	2.10
☐ 67	Weakness Glyph	C Spell	U	0.40
☐ 46	Windrider	Ally	C	0.20
☐ 20	Winged Boots	Item	C	0.15
☐ 82	Yagno Petrovna	Cleric	C	0.15
14				
☐ 98	Year of Plenty	Event	C	0.15
☐ 8	Young Strahd	Hero	UR	3.80
☐ 73	Zielesch, Anc. Green Dragon	Monster	U	0.30

RARITY KEY C = Common   U = Uncommon   **R** = Rare   **VR** = Very Rare   **UR** = Ultra Rare   **F** = Foil card   **X** = Fixed/standard in all decks

Spellfire • Powers (a.k.a. Set #6)

TSR • Released **September 1995**

120 cards in set • **IDENTIFIER: Red AD&D logo plus "of 20" or "of 100" on face**

- Booster packs contain 12 cards; booster displays contain 36 boosters

Powers adds a new character class, Psionicist, and Psionic Ability Cards.

These mental powers changed how *Spellfire* characters interacted, and, as previous cards had no defense against them, game rules had to compensate for them. Ironically, while sales were good on *Powers*, many *Spellfire* players tended to ignore it completely in building their decks. — *John Danovich*

SPELLFIRE™
Master the Magic

You will need 14 nine-pocket pages to store this set. (7 doubled up)

Life Draining

Psionic power. Usable by psionicist champions. Automatically defeats undead champions and allies. (Off/4)

99 of 100

	Set (120 cards)	35.00
	Booster Display Box	25.00
	Booster Pack	1.50

#	Card name	Type	Rarity	Price
	2 Abhorrence of Shapechangers	Item	R	1.80
	1 Adjatha, the Spell Drinker	Item	U	0.40
	16 Antimagic Cloud	Rule	UR	3.30
	54 Aquatic Elf	Monster	U	0.40
	34 Avangion's Protection	C Spell	C	0.10
	20 Avatar's Edict	Rule	UR	4.40
	7 Bando's Whitestone	Artifact	UR	4.40
	96 Banishment	Psionic	C	0.10
	17 Bilago Lumen	Psionicist	U	0.40
	41 Bonemaster, Avatar of Nerull	Cleric	R	3.00
	10 Borah's Ring	Item	UR	3.30
	65 Brandobaris's Inversion	Rule	R	1.80
	26 Breshkll Logon	Psionicist	C	0.10
	38 Caravan Raiders	Event	C	0.10
	75 Cause Decay	Psionic	C	0.10
	64 Chameleon Power	Psionic	C	0.10
	24 Colum Calder	Psionicist	U	0.40
	67 Complete Healing	Psionic	C	0.10
	84 Control Flames	Psionic	C	0.10
	74 Control Wind	Psionic	C	0.10
	19 Cosmic Intervention	Rule	UR	4.40
	53 Crabman	Monster	U	0.40
	97 Create Object	Psionic	C	0.10
	1 Crystal Sphere	Realm	UR	4.40
	37 Dark Negation	Event	R	1.80
	9 Davron Parscall	Psionicist	U	0.40
	18 Dawn d'Ereath	Psionicist	C	0.10
	100 Dimentional Door	Psionic	C	0.10
	6 Dragonsbane	Item	U	0.40
	60 Earth Elemental	Monster	U	0.40
	66 Energy Containment	Psionic	C	0.10
	6 Fate's Promise	Item	UR	3.30
	49 Giant Space Hamster	Ally	U	0.40
	88 Gift of the Avatar	Rule	R	1.80
	52 Gith	Monster	U	0.40
	91 Graft Weapon	Psionic	C	0.10
	63 Grippli	Monster	U	0.40
	22 Havrum Riddle	Psionicist	U	0.40
	39 Icedawn, Avatar of Auril	Cleric	R	1.80
	83 Intellect Fortress	Psionic	C	0.10
	89 Intensify	Psionic	C	0.10
	55 Ixitxachitl	Monster	U	0.40
	16 Jacenelle Traen	Psionicist	C	0.10
	25 Kelaser Redbelt	Psionicist	U	0.40
	12 Kelsur Brighteye	Psionicist	C	0.10
	21 Kerm of Tyr	Psionicist	C	0.10
	79 Kiri, Avatar of Kiri-Jolith	Cleric	R	1.80
	56 Kirre	Monster	U	0.40
	42 Lady of Fate, Avatar of Istus	Cleric	R	1.80
	99 Life Draining	Psionic	C	0.10
	58 Living Wall	Monster	R	3.00
	57 Locathah Champion	Monster	U	0.40
	23 Lyr of the Mists	Psionicist	C	0.10
	94 Magnify	Psionic	C	0.10
	27 Masara d'Will	Psionicist	C	0.10
	92 Melt Stone	C Spell	C	0.10
	81 Mental Barrier	Psionic	C	0.10
	87 Mind of the Avatar	Rule	R	1.80
	72 Mind Shield	Psionic	C	0.10
	77 Mind Thrust	Psionic	C	0.10
	46 Mirror, Mirror	C Spell	C	0.10
	43 Misfortune, Avatar of Ralishaz	Cleric	R	1.80
	73 Molecular Agitation	Psionic	C	0.10
	70 Molecular Rearrangement	Psionic	C	0.10
	62 Mountain Giant	Monster	U	0.40
	31 Necromantic Wave	Event	C	0.10
	32 Night of the Blue Moon	Event	R	1.80
	40 Nightsinger, Avatar of Shar	Cleric	R	1.80
	35 Nullification	Event	C	0.10
	86 Nullify Magic	Rule	R	1.80
	51 Phase Out	W Spell	C	0.10
	19 Phridge	Psionicist	C	0.10
	17 Poisoned Water	Rule	UR	3.30
	50 Polymorph Other	W Spell	C	0.10
	7 Post-Hypnotic Suggestion	Psionic	C	0.10
	95 Probability Travel	Psionic	C	0.10
	15 Psionatrix	Rule	UR	3.30
	93 Psionic Blast	Psionic	C	0.10
	14 Psionicist Anklet	Item	UR	3.30
	13 Psionicist Bracelet	Item	UR	3.30
	98 Psychic Lock	Psionic	C	0.10
	29 Psychic Storm	Event	C	0.10
	85 Psychic Storm	Rule	R	1.80
	8 Quill Pen of the Planes	Artifact	UR	4.40
	15 Rafe Racker	Psionicist	U	0.40
	13 Rand the Bowyer	Psionicist	U	0.40
	28 Rayden Valers	Psionicist	U	0.40
	76 Repugnance	Psionic	C	0.10
	2 Rock of Bral	Holding	UR	3.30
	11 Roghal Baen	Psionicist	U	0.40
	47 Rope Trick	C Spell	C	0.10
	5 Royal Conscription/Tax Levy	Event	UR	3.30
	30 Sandstorm	Event	C	0.10
	78 Sea Queen, Avatar of Zeboim	Cleric	R	1.80
	20 Seluna Darkenstar	Psionicist	U	0.40
	14 Seveia Shadowmaster	Psionicist	C	0.10
	80 Shadair Mesker	Cleric	U	0.40
	11 Shawl of Mordenheim	Item	UR	3.30
	12 Sirrion's Brooch	Item	UR	3.30
	45 Sirrion, Avatar	Cleric	R	1.80
	61 Skriaxit, Composit Elemental	Monster	R	1.80
	48 Stasis	C Spell	C	0.10
	90 Summon Planar Creature	Psionic	C	0.10
	4 Sword of Blackflame	Item	U	0.40
	3 Sword of the Avoreen	Item	R	1.80
	8 Sword of the Black Rose	Item	R	3.00
	5 Sword of the High King	Item	R	3.00
	59 Tako	Monster	U	0.40
	71 Telekinesis	Psionic	C	0.10
	69 Teleport Trigger	Psionic	C	0.10
	44 Tempest, Avatar of Zeboim	Cleric	R	3.00
	4 The Inverter	Artifact	UR	3.30
	9 The Tantelear	Artifact	UR	3.30
	18 The Ultimate	Rule	UR	3.30
	82 Tower of Iron Will	Psionic	C	0.10
	36 Tuigan Invasion	Event	R	1.80
	3 Unipsi	Artifact	UR	3.30
	68 Wheel of Fate	Rule	R	1.80
	10 Yorgia Sandow	Psionicist	C	0.10
	33 Zepherwind	Event	R	1.80

Spellfire • The Underdark (a.k.a. Set #7)

SPELLFIRE™
Master the Magic

TSR • Released **December 1995**

125 cards in set • **IDENTIFIER: Cave frame on card faces**

- Booster packs contain 12 cards; booster displays contain 40 boosters

The Underdark, focusing on the underworld, is immediately identifiable for the cave illustration framing its cards' faces. While issuing no new card types, the set still had a certain appeal to gamers, and many cards are still popular with players. Again, many of the photo cards feature TSR employees and designers as characters. — *John Danovich*

You will need 14 nine-pocket pages to store this set. (7 doubled up)

	Set (125 cards)	36.00
	Booster Display Box	24.00
	Booster Pack	1.40

#	Card name	Type	Rarity	Price
	55 Age Dragon	C Spell	R	1.50
	28 Amulet of Protection from Artifacts	Item	R	1.50
	51 Animal Horde	C Spell	R	1.50
	98 Aquilla	Wizard	U	0.40
	29 Armor of Dispel Magic	Item	C	0.15
	73 Baelnorn	Ally	C	0.15
	95 Baldar Dwellardon	Cleric	C	0.15
	91 Belwar Dissengulp	Hero	C	0.15

RARITY KEY C = Common   U = Uncommon   R = Rare   VR = Very Rare   UR = Ultra Rare   F = Foil card   X = Fixed/standard in all decks

#	Card name	Type	Rarity	Price
35	Black Snail of Shnai	Item	U	0.40
45	Bloodstone's Spectral Steed	W Spell	C	0.15
63	Breath of Death	C Spell	C	0.15
24	Broken Arrow	Event	UR	3.50
13	Cave-in!	Event	UR	3.50
17	Cavern of the Gods	Holding	U	0.40
97	Chantal the Banshee	Monster	C	0.15
74	Chitine	Ally	C	0.15
30	Cloak of the Gargoyle	Item	C	0.15
82	Corpse Dragon	Monster	U	0.40
75	Crypt Servant	Ally	C	0.15
31	Dori's Obsidian Steed of Wondrous Power	Item	U	0.40
23	Drow Assassin	Ally	UR	3.50
21	Drow Justice	Event	R	1.50
83	Earth Weird	Monster	C	0.15
16	Echoes from the Deep	Holding	R	1.50
52	Elemental Swarm	C Spell	U	0.40
93	Ellorelloran	Wizard	C	0.15
81	Fey Dwarf	Ally	C	0.15
76	Foulwing	Ally	C	0.15
96	Fowron, the Giant	Cleric	C	0.15
86	Gibbering Mouther	Monster	C	0.15
77	Gnasher	Ally	R	1.50
19	God's Plague	Event	R	1.50
32	Goibhniu's Warhammer	Item	R	1.50
84	Gorynych	Monster	R	1.50
33	Helmet of Selnor	Item	R	1.50
38	Hornung's Baneful Deflector	W Spell	C	0.15
37	Hornung's Guess	W Spell	U	0.40
62	Hovering Road	C Spell	C	0.15
2	Inflict Pain	Psionic	UR	3.50
67	Invasion of the Undead	Rule	U	0.40
99	Iseult	Cleric	U	0.40
92	Jarlaxle	Hero	U	0.40
1	Lazarus, the Drow	Psionicist	UR	3.50
42	Locate Creature	W Spell	U	0.40
41	Lorloveim's Creeping Shadow	W Spell	C	0.15
18	Lurker in the Deep	Monster	UR	3.50
78	Magebain	Ally	R	1.50
39	Maximillian's Earthen Grasp	W Spell	C	0.15
22	Memory Moss	Event	R	1.50
26	Mika's Dragon Charm	Event	C	0.15
25	Mika's Magic Ban	Event	U	0.40
27	Mika's Undead Ward	Event	C	0.15
88	Mind Flayer	Monster	C	0.15
44	Mind Fog	W Spell	U	0.40
56	Mindkiller	C Spell	R	1.50
25	Mindshatter	C Spell	UR	3.50
90	Monster of the Lake	Monster	R	1.50
66	Moradin's Avatar	Cleric	C	0.15
89	Myconid	Monster	C	0.15
34	Necklass of Protection	Item	R	1.50
85	Noran	Monster	C	0.15
19	Oogly the Half-Orc	Hero	UR	3.50
17	Piercer	Monster	UR	3.50
53	Preservation	C Spell	C	0.15
70	Sargonnas	Cleric	C	0.15
22	Scourge of Mika	Item	UR	4.50
40	Shattered Glass	W Spell	R	1.50
36	Shovel of Gravedigging	Item	C	0.15
80	Skum	Ally	R	1.50
57	Spacewarp	C Spell	R	1.50
58	Spirit of Power	C Spell	C	0.15
49	Stalker	C Spell	R	1.50
12	Subterranean Seas	Holding	U	0.40
43	Summon Lycanthrope	W Spell	C	0.15
46	Summon Undead	C Spell	U	0.40
79	Sword Slug	Ally	C	0.15
60	Tentacle Walls	C Spell	C	0.15
72	The Avatar Shar	Cleric	U	0.40
13	The Bipolar Cavern	Holding	U	0.40
4	The Bipolar Triumvirate	Realm	U	0.40
10	The Burning Cavern	Holding	U	0.40
8	The Cavernous Hall	Realm	UR	3.00
5	The Deep	Realm	UR	3.00
15	The Demi-Lich Zyenj	Monster	UR	3.50
7	The Dispossessed	Realm	UR	3.00
18	The Dread Chamber	Holding	U	0.40
23	The East Wind	Artifact	C	0.15
65	The Faceless One, Avatar of Jubilex	Cleric	U	0.40
24	The Forest Oracle	Event	U	0.40
3	The Hoof of Auroch	Artifact	UR	3.50
14	The Mandate of Dori the Barbarian	Event	UR	3.50
20	The Marble Orb	Item	U	5.00
16	The Minotaur	Monster	UR	4.00
12	The Minotaur Attacks!	Event	UR	3.50
14	The North Wind	Artifact	C	0.15
68	The Red Death	Cleric	R	3.00
4	The Ring of Gaxx	Artifact	UR	6.00
50	The South Wind	Artifact	C	0.15
21	The Sword and Helm of Garion	Item	UR	4.50
15	The Tripolar Cavern	Holding	U	0.40
6	The Tripolar Triumvirate	Realm	R	1.50
11	The Triumphant Barbarian	Event	UR	3.50
6	The Ultimate Triumvirate	Realm	UR	3.00
71	The Uncaring, Avatar of Boccob	Cleric	R	1.50
5	The Underdark	Realm	R	1.50
11	The Unipolar Cavern	Holding	C	0.15
2	The Unipolar Triumvirate	Realm	C	0.15
64	The Unnamed, Avatar of Gruumsh	Cleric	R	1.50
10	The Way Out	Event	UR	3.50
59	The West Wind	Artifact	C	0.15
69	Things That Go Bump In The Night	Rule	U	0.40
61	Timelessness	C Spell	U	0.40
87	Umber Hulk	Monster	C	0.15
1	UnderAthas	Realm	C	0.15
9	UnderDread	Realm	C	0.15
9	Underground River	Event	UR	3.50
3	UnderKrynn	Realm	C	0.15
8	UnderOerth	Realm	C	0.15
7	UnderToril	Realm	C	0.15
47	Warband Quest	C Spell	C	0.15
54	Ward Matrix	C Spell	C	0.15
20	When God's Walk	Event	R	1.50
48	Wolf Spirits	C Spell	U	0.40
100	Xontra	Psionicist	C	0.15
94	Zaknafein the Weapons Master	Hero	C	0.15

Spellfire • Runes & Ruins (a.k.a. Set #8)

SPELLFIRE Master the Magic

The Temple of Death

The attached realm can only be attacked by clerics. Offensive spells cast in defense of the attached realm are doubled in level.

ADVANCED DUNGEONS & DRAGONS — 27 of 100

TSR • Released February 1996

125 cards in set • **IDENTIFIER: Small AD&D logo plus "of 25" or "of 100" on face**

• Booster packs contain 12 cards; booster displays contain 40 boosters

One of the more interesting expansions in **Spellfire**, **Runes & Ruins** pulls from the TSR archives old locations, items, and characters — all the old *Dungeons & Dragons* "history" that many gamers consider the golden age of role-playing.

This set introduced Unarmed Combat Cards into the game and has a great selection of high-powered chase cards. The Unarmed Combat cards retroactively made the Hero class much more powerful.

While containing many cards based on the ruins of dungeons, *Runes & Ruins* only contains one card with any runes on it, a mistake found too late to change. It also has the dubious distinction of not being a *Spellfire* set at all: the outside of the display box was misprinted with the word "Sellfire." (No, it wasn't a subliminal message to retailers.) (Remember, ask for *Sellfire: Rune & Lots of Ruins...*) — **John Danovich**

Set (125 cards)	35.00
Booster Display Box	24.00
Booster Pack	1.30

You will need 14 nine-pocket pages to store this set. (7 doubled up)

#	Card name	Type	Rarity	Price
38	Acerack the Eternal	Monster	R	1.90
69	Albruin	Artifact	C	0.15
62	Barbarian Charge!	Event	C	0.15
96	Bear Hug	Unarmed	C	0.15
79	Big Giant's Rock	Item	C	0.15
28	Bigby the Great	Wizard	R	2.10
70	Blackrazor	Artifact	R	2.10
99	Block	Unarmed	C	0.15
9	Book of the Damned	Item	UR	2.50
21	Boots of Fharlanghn	Item	UR	2.50
2	Brain Drain	Event	UR	2.50
56	Coming of the Phoenix	Event	C	0.15
53	Crystalbrittle	W Spell	C	0.15
14	Cursed Idol	Item	UR	2.50
9	Demonweb Pits	Realm	C	0.25
13	Desert of Desolation	Realm	R	1.90
94	Disarm	Unarmed	C	0.15
17	Dispel Psionics	C Spell	UR	2.50
5	Doc's Island	Realm	C	0.25
12	Dodge	Event	UR	2.50
58	Elixer of Life	Event	C	0.15

RARITY KEY C = Common U = Uncommon R = Rare VR = Very Rare UR = Ultra Rare F = Foil card X = Fixed/standard in all decks

# Card name	Type	Rarity	Price
54 Energy Drain	W Spell	U	0.30
81 Enormous Giant's Rock	Item	R	2.40
31 Falx the Silver Dragon	Monster	C	0.15
91 Flying Kick	Unarmed	U	0.15
24 Ghost Tower of Inverness	Holding	C	0.15
59 Giant Raid!	Event	U	0.30
16 Gib Kcir	Hero	UR	3.00
73 Girdle of Dwarvenkind	Item	R	2.10
36 Grimslade the Gray	Hero	C	0.15
92 Haymaker	Unarmed	R	1.90
98 Headlock	Unarmed	U	0.30
5 Holy Sword Chrysomer	Artifact	UR	5.00
10 Horn of Change	Item	UR	2.50
80 Huge Giant's Rock	Item	C	0.15
87 Hydra	Ally	C	0.15
82 Hypnosnake	Ally	C	0.15
19 Icon of Magic	Artifact	UR	5.00
48 Intercession	C Spell	U	0.30
66 Invulnerable Coat of Arnd	Artifact	U	0.30
67 Ipsissimo's Black Goose	Artifact	C	0.15
12 Isle of Dread	Realm	C	0.25
1 Isle of the Ape	Realm	R	1.90
40 Jarl the Frost Giant	Monster	C	0.40
35 Kas the Terrible	Hero	U	0.30
19 Keep on the Borderlands	Holding	R	2.90
95 Kidney Punch	Unarmed	R	1.90
41 King Snurre the Fire Giant	Monster	C	0.15
97 Knockdown	Unarmed	C	0.15
11 Kuroth's Quill	Artifact	UR	5.00
21 Labyrinth of Madness	Holding	C	0.15
32 Lord Robilar	Hero	C	0.15
4 Lost Treasure	Event	UR	2.50
6 Manshoon of the Zhentarim	Wizard	UR	3.50
46 Mordenkainen's Disjunction	W Spell	R	2.10
20 Nectar of the Gods	Artifact	UR	5.00
44 Nosnra the Hill Giant	Monster	C	0.15

# Card name	Type	Rarity	Price
23 Oasis of the White Palm	Holding	C	0.15
45 Ombi the Renegade Dwarf	Hero	C	0.15
30 Oonga the Ape	Monster	R	1.90
20 Palace of the Silver Princess	Holding	C	0.15
33 Phoebus the Lizard Man	Monster	C	0.15
25 Portal to Limbo	Event	UR	2.50
18 Psionic Reflection	C Spell	UR	3.00
63 Psionic Shield	Event	U	0.45
42 Queen Frumpy the Fire Giant	Monster	C	0.15
89 Rampaging Oni	Ally	C	0.15
88 Red Dragon	Ally	U	0.45
84 Remorhaz	Ally	U	0.30
37 Ren-O-The Blade	Hero	R	2.10
13 Runes of the Future	Item	UR	2.50
47 Slay Living	C Spell	C	0.15
78 Star Gem of Martek: Amethyst	Item	U	0.30
77 Star Gem of Martek: Clear Crystal	Item	R	2.90
74 Star Gem of Martek: Opal	Item	C	0.15
76 Star Gem of Martek: Ruby	Item	C	0.15
75 Star Gem of Martek: Sapphire	Item	U	0.45
51 Summon Air Elemental	C Spell	U	0.30
49 Summon Earth Elemental	C Spell	U	0.30
50 Summon Fire Elemental	C Spell	C	0.15
52 Summon Water Elemental	C Spell	C	0.15
18 Sunderhan, Isle of the Slave Lords	Realm	R	2.60
29 Tenser the Arch Mage	Wizard	U	0.45
26 Tenser's Castle	Holding	U	0.30
68 Tenser's Crystal Ball	Artifact	C	0.15
7 The Barrier Peaks	Realm	C	0.25
6 The City of Phlan	Realm	R	1.90
22 The Crystal Cave	Realm	UR	2.50
8 The Dark Lens	Artifact	UR	5.00
11 The Depths of the Earth	Realm	C	0.25
1 The Dream Team	Ally	UR	2.50

# Card name	Type	Rarity	Price
23 The Fair Princess	Hero	UR	3.00
2 The Forbidden City	Realm	C	0.25
57 The Forgotten King	Event	R	2.10
14 The Glacial Rift	Realm	C	0.15
10 The Hidden Shrine of Tamoachan	Realm	U	0.30
85 The Incantrix	Ally	R	2.40
43 The Keeper	Monster	U	0.30
15 The Lendore Isles	Realm	C	0.15
90 The Live Ones	Ally	R	2.40
3 The Lost Caverns of Tsojcanth	Realm	C	0.25
16 The Lost City	Realm	U	0.30
65 The Midas Orb	Artifact	C	0.15
100 The Monty Haul Campaign	Rule	R	2.10
24 The Phylactery	Item	UR	2.50
83 The Rahaisa	Ally	R	2.40
27 The Temple of Death	Holding	C	0.15
3 The Toad	Item	UR	2.50
60 The Vampire Attacks	Event	U	0.45
8 Tomb of Horrors	Realm	C	0.25
15 Tower of Spirits	Holding	UR	2.50
55 Tyranthraxus, The Possessing Spirit	Event	R	2.10
61 Undead Guardian	Event	R	2.10
7 Undead Regeneration	Event	UR	2.50
93 Uppercut	Unarmed	U	0.30
25 Vault of the Drow	Holding	C	0.15
34 Vecna the Arch Lich	Wizard	R	3.40
22 Village of Hommlet	Holding	U	0.45
17 Village of Orlane	Realm	U	0.30
64 Volcanic Eruption	Event	U	0.30
71 Wave	Artifact	U	0.30
72 Whelm	Artifact	R	2.10
4 White Plume Mountain	Realm	U	0.30
86 Winter Wolf Pack	Ally	C	0.15
39 Wulfgar	Hero	C	0.15

Spellfire • Birthright (a.k.a. Set #9)

SPELLFIRE Master the Magic

TSR • Released May 1996

125 cards in set • **IDENTIFIER: Birthright** logo plus "of 25" or "of 100" on face

• Booster packs contain 12 cards; booster displays contain 40 boosters

Following the introduction of a world of chivalry to *Advanced Dungeons & Dragons*, the *Spellfire* version of **Birthright** introduced Regent characters and Blood Ability cards.

With another new character class and ability card added into the mix, *Spellfire* became more complex, with many timing issues coming into play. Even though **Third Edition** had fixed many of the ills of the game, the increasing complexity made it necessary to do another basic edition after *Birthright* to take care of the new problems.

Birthright didn't sell as well as the previous booster set and sales as a whole were slipping for the line. This meant that, as a good set with many prized cards, the *Birthright* set was to be in short supply later on, and many of the cards continued to be sought after by players. — **John Danovich**

10

BIRTHRIGHT
Cerilian Dragon

Flyer. Can cast cleric spells. When attacking, the Cerilian Dragon may use its breath weapon to destroy any holding in the defender's formation.

71 of 100

Set (125 cards)	35.00
Booster Display Box	30.25
Booster Pack	1.20

You will need **14** nine-pocket pages to store this set. (7 doubled up)

# Card name	Type	Rarity	Price
16 Adara Addlepate	Regent	UR	3.00
35 Alertness	Ability	U	0.35
33 Amulet of Plane Walking	Item	C	0.10
36 Animal Affinity	Ability	C	0.10
80 Ankheg	Ally	C	0.10
27 Armor of the High King	Item	C	0.10
5 Avanil	Realm	U	0.35
66 Banshegh	Monster	R	2.00
97 Barak the Dark	Regent	C	0.10

# Card name	Type	Rarity	Price
9 Baruk-Azhik	Realm	R	2.00
37 Battlewise	Ability	R	2.00
22 Biding Your Time	Event	U	0.35
50 Bless Land	C Spell	U	0.35
51 Blight	C Spell	C	0.10
20 Blood Challenge!	Event	UR	2.50
60 Blood Drain	W Spell	C	0.10
7 Book of Infinite Spells	Item	UR	5.00
29 Bracers of Brachiation	Item	C	0.10
87 Caliedhe Dosiere	Regent	C	0.10
71 Cerilian Dragon	Monster	U	0.35
19 Chaos!	Event	R	2.00
22 Child's Play	Event	UR	2.50
34 Cloak of Displacement	Item	U	0.35
62 Clone	W Spell	R	2.00
53 Control Weather	C Spell	U	0.35

# Card name	Type	Rarity	Price
38 Courage	Ability	C	0.10
26 Crown of Regency	Item	C	0.10
86 Darien Avan	Regent	R	2.00
43 Death Touch	Ability	R	2.00
44 Detect Life	Ability	C	0.10
19 Diplomacy	Event	UR	2.50
73 Divine Right	Rule	C	0.10
39 Divine Wrath	Ability	C	0.10
28 Dragon's Teeth	Item	C	0.10
63 Drawmij's Instant Summons	W Spell	U	0.35
48 Emperor's Crown of Anuire	Artifact	R	2.00
18 Espionage!	Event	C	0.10
21 Festival	Event	UR	2.50
3 Forced Conscription	Event	UR	2.50
21 Forge Ley Line	Event	R	2.00
6 Ghoere	Realm	R	2.00

RARITY KEY C = Common U = Uncommon R = Rare VR = Very Rare UR = Ultra Rare F = Foil card X = Fixed/standard in all decks

# Card name	Type	Rarity	Price
82 Giant Squid	Ally	U	0.35
75 Green Slime	Ally	R	2.00
84 Grimm Graybeard	Regent	C	0.10
100 Gwenyth the Bard	Hero	U	0.35
92 High Mage Aelies	Regent	U	0.35
2 Ilien	Realm	C	0.10
12 Imperial City of Anuire	Holding	U	0.35
23 In Search of Adventure	Event	U	0.35
52 Investiture	C Spell	C	0.10
20 Investiture Ceremony	Event	C	0.10
45 Invulnerability	Ability	U	0.35
1 It's Good to be the King	Event	UR	2.50
98 Jana Orel	Regent	U	0.35
15 Kaeriaen Whiteheart	Regent	UR	3.00
15 Kal-Saitharak	Holding	R	2.00
49 Kingstopper	Artifact	R	2.00
58 Legion of Dead	W Spell	U	0.35
8 Libram of Ineffable Damnation	Item	UR	2.50
83 Lord Cronal	Regent	C	0.10
16 Magical Source	Holding	C	0.10
6 Manual of Puissant Skill at Arms	Item	UR	5.00
25 Mebhaigl Surge	Event	UR	2.50
96 Moergan	Regent	C	0.10
8 Mur-Kilad	Realm	C	0.10
95 Nadia Vasily	Regent	C	0.10
76 Nightmare	Ally	C	0.10
12 Olaf the Sly	Regent	UR	3.00
74 Orogs	Ally	C	0.10
61 Otto's Irresistible Dance	W Spell	C	0.10

# Card name	Type	Rarity	Price
55 Part Water	C Spell	C	0.10
14 Proudglaive	Holding	U	0.35
59 Raze	W Spell	R	2.00
40 Regeneration	Ability	U	0.35
24 Revolution!	Event	C	0.10
14 Rhuobhe Manslayer	Regent	UR	3.00
30 Ring of Human Influence	Item	U	0.35
31 Ring of Spell Storing	Item	R	1.00
32 Rod of Lordly Might	Item	C	0.10
1 Roesone	Realm	C	0.10
56 Speak with Monsters	C Spell	C	0.10
4 Sphere of Annihilation	Item	UR	2.50
79 Stirge Swarm	Ally	R	2.00
57 Summon Insects	C Spell	C	0.10
13 Targoth the Unclean	Regent	UR	3.00
18 Taxation	Rule	UR	2.50
85 Teodor Profiev	Regent	C	0.10
17 The Blood of Azrai	Event	UR	2.50
9 The Count of Müden	Regent	UR	2.50
89 The Elf Prince Fhileraene	Regent	R	2.00
23 The Fates	Event	UR	2.50
99 The Flower of Roesone	Hero	C	0.10
64 The Gorgon	Monster	R	2.00
4 The Gorgon's Crown	Realm	R	2.00
70 The Hag	Monster	U	0.35
13 The Heartland Outfitters	Holding	C	0.10
10 The Impregnable Heart of Haelyn	Realm	C	0.10
25 The Kraken Attacks!	Event	R	2.00
67 The Lamia	Monster	R	2.00

# Card name	Type	Rarity	Price
17 The Maze of Maalvar the Minotaur	Holding	C	0.10
91 The Noble Outlaw	Regent	R	2.00
11 The Pontifex of the Southern Coast	Regent	UR	2.50
72 The Shadow World	Rule	C	0.10
2 The Shadow World	Event	UR	2.50
68 The Siren	Monster	R	2.00
65 The Spider	Monster	U	0.35
3 The Spiderfell	Realm	U	0.35
93 The Sword Mage	Regent	C	0.10
69 The White Witch	Monster	C	0.10
94 The Wizard	Regent	U	0.35
10 The Wizardess Carrie	Regent	UR	3.00
90 Tie'skar Graecher, the Goblin King	Regent	C	0.10
46 Tighmaevril Sword	Artifact	R	2.00
88 Tomkin Dross	Regent	C	0.10
41 Touch of Decay	Ability	U	0.35
11 Tower of the Sword Mage	Realm	C	0.10
54 Transmute Metal to Wood	C Spell	C	0.10
7 Tuarhievel	Realm	C	0.10
77 Unicorn	Ally	C	0.10
42 Unreadable Thoughts	Ability	C	0.10
5 Vacuous Grimoire	Item	UR	2.50
24 War Declared!	Event	UR	2.50
47 Wintering	Artifact	R	2.00
81 Wood Nymph	Ally	C	0.10
78 Wraith	Ally	U	0.35

Spellfire • Draconomicon (a.k.a. Set #10)

SPELLFIRE Master the Magic

TSR • Released **July 1996**

125 cards in set • IDENTIFIER: **Draconomicon** logo plus "of 25" or "of 100" on face

• Booster packs contain 12 cards; booster displays contain 40 boosters

As noted on page 403, **Draconomicon** packs were included with starters for **Fourth Edition**. But the set is notable on its own for the introduction of Dragon Ability cards. As could be expected from any dragon-themed set, there are many high-powered cards.

Draconomicon was also TSR's first CCG release to be packaged in tamper-resistant foil wrapping. — **John Danovich**

Set (125 cards)	38.00
Booster Display Box	27.00
Booster Pack	1.50

# Card name	Type	Rarity	Price
99 Age of the Dragon	Rule	R	1.10
86 Amulet of the Wyrm	Artifact	U	0.35
23 Ancient Dragon Magic	Rule	UR	2.50
46 Astral Spell	W Spell	R	1.10
45 Bahamut, God of Good Dragons	Hero	U	0.35
93 Bite	Unarmed	R	1.10
58 Blessing of Bahamut	C Spell	C	0.10
57 Blessing of Tiamat	C Spell	C	0.10
25 Blessing of Zorquan	Event	C	0.10
3 Boreas	Monster	UR	3.00
94 Breath Weapon I	Unarmed	C	0.10
95 Breath Weapon II	Unarmed	U	0.35
96 Breath Weapon III	Unarmed	R	1.10
12 Charm, the Crystal Dragon	Monster	UR	5.00
13 Chimera	Ally	UR	3.00
91 Claw	Unarmed	C	0.10
52 Cold Curtain	W Spell	C	0.10
67 Combat Mind	Psionic	U	0.35
62 Confusion	C Spell	C	0.10
16 Council of Wyrms	Event	C	0.10
5 Cron the Black	Monster	UR	3.00

# Card name	Type	Rarity	Price
80 Cult of the Dragon	Ally	R	1.10
41 Cyan Bloodbane	Monster	U	0.35
11 Dark Depths	Holding	U	0.35
72 Daydream	Psionic	R	1.10
69 Death Field	Psionic	C	0.10
6 Draconic Allies	Event	UR	2.50
9 Dragon Cultist	Cleric	UR	2.50
21 Dragon Fear	Event	U	0.35
8 Dragon Hatchling	Monster	UR	2.50
17 Dragon Magic	Event	R	1.10
54 Dragon Mark	W Spell	U	0.35
2 Dragon Mountain	Realm	C	0.10
20 Dragon Raid!	Event	R	1.10
19 Dragon Skirmish	Event	UR	2.50
18 Dragon's Bones	Item	UR	2.50
22 Dragon's Breath	Rule	UR	2.50
47 Dragon's Calm	W Spell	U	0.35
15 Dragon's Crown	Holding	C	0.10
51 Dragon's Death Door	W Spell	C	0.10
18 Dragon's Graveyard	Event	U	0.35
10 Dragon's Hoard	Holding	R	1.10
25 Dragon's Scale	Item	UR	2.50
82 Dragonne	Ally	C	0.10
4 Dragonspine Mountains	Realm	R	1.10
85 Drake	Ally	C	0.10
56 Enchanted Flight	C Spell	R	1.10

You will need **14** nine-pocket pages to store this set. (7 doubled up)

Advanced Dungeons & Dragons — Maldraedior, Great Blue Wyrm

Dragon; flyer. Maldraedior can cast any spell. Phase 4 spells cast by him during combat are shuffled back into the draw pile instead of discarded.

29 of 100

# Card name	Type	Rarity	Price
98 Evade	Unarmed	C	0.10
83 Faerie Dragon	Ally	C	0.10
87 Fang of the Dragon	Artifact	U	0.35
24 Favorable Winds	Event	R	1.10
33 Fi Lendicol	Wizard	C	0.10
63 Find the Path	C Spell	C	0.10
84 Firedrake	Ally	C	0.10
50 Firetrail	W Spell	C	0.10
27 Flame	Monster	C	0.10
38 Flare	Monster	C	0.10
32 Flashburn	Hero	C	0.10
23 Forced Revolt	Event	C	0.10
74 Gauntlets of Combat	Item	C	0.10
16 Glimmer the Brass Dragon	Hero	UR	5.00
37 Greyhawk Dragon	Wizard	U	0.35
5 Griff Mountains	Realm	C	0.10
48 Humanoid Familiar	W Spell	C	0.10
66 Inertial Barrier	Psionic	C	0.10
26 Infyrana the Dragon	Monster	U	0.35
40 Khisanth	Monster	U	0.35
3 Lair of the Shadowdrake	Realm	R	1.10

RARITY KEY C = Common U = Uncommon R = Rare VR = Very Rare UR = Ultra Rare F = Foil card X = Fixed/standard in all decks

#	Card name	Type	Rarity	Price
2	Lair Raid!	Event	UR	2.50
31	Lareth, King of Justice	Wizard	R	1.10
7	Lernaean Hydra	Monster	UR	4.00
29	Maldraedior, Great Blue Wyrm	Wizard	U	0.35
79	Maul of the Titans	Item	U	0.35
55	Meteor Swarm	W Spell	U	0.35
89	Mighty Servant of Leuk-o	Artifact	U	0.35
4	Morcanth Dragontamer	Hero	UR	3.50
9	Mount Deismaar	Realm	R	1.10
7	Mount Nevermind	Realm	U	0.35
88	Orb of the Eternal Dragon	Artifact	R	1.10
8	Palanthas	Realm	C	0.10
28	Pelath the Bronze Dragon	Wizard	C	0.10
68	Phase	Psionic	C	0.10
65	Plague	C Spell	R	1.10
10	Playing to Lose	Rule	UR	2.50
12	Powers of the Land	Holding	C	0.10
73	Psychic Blade	Psionic	C	0.10
34	Rauglothgor	Monster	C	0.10

#	Card name	Type	Rarity	Price
1	Rauglothgor's Lair	Realm	C	0.10
14	Red Dragon Figurine	Item	UR	3.00
15	Saphire the Blue Dragon	Psionicist	UR	5.00
36	Shadow Dragon	Monster	R	1.10
39	Sleet	Monster	C	0.10
35	Sparkle, Crystal Dragon	Psionicist	U	0.35
53	Summon Dragon	W Spell	C	0.10
97	Swallow Whole	Unarmed	U	0.35
90	Swoop	Unarmed	U	1.10
61	Symbol of Death	C Spell	R	1.10
59	Symbol of Pain	C Spell	C	0.10
60	Symbol of Persuasion	C Spell	C	0.10
71	Synaptic Snap	Psionic	C	0.10
1	T'char, Dragon of Flame	Monster	UR	5.00
92	Tail Sweep	Unarmed	C	0.10
75	Talisman of the Beast	Item	R	1.10
30	Tamarand, Great Gold Wyrm	Cleric	C	0.10
100	The Battle Must Go On!	Rule	U	0.35
43	The Celestial Emperor	Cleric	R	1.10

#	Card name	Type	Rarity	Price
14	The Mist Caves	Holding	C	0.10
13	The Mistmarsh	Holding	C	0.10
44	Tiamat, God of Evil Dragons	Wizard	U	0.35
22	Trapped!	Event	C	0.10
17	Treasure Hoard	Event	UR	2.50
64	True Seeing	C Spell	C	0.10
70	Ultrablast	Psionic	R	1.10
81	Undead Dragonrider	Ally	U	0.35
24	Underground Lair	Realm	UR	2.50
49	Venomdust	W Spell	C	0.10
42	Verminaard the Dragonmaster	Cleric	R	1.10
6	Vesve Forest	Realm	C	0.10
76	Wand of Magic Detection	Item	C	0.10
78	Wand of Negation	Item	R	1.10
77	Well of Many Worlds	Item	U	0.35
20	Wyrmblight	Item	UR	2.50
19	Wyrm's Decree	Event	C	0.10
21	Wyrms' Conclave	Event	UR	2.50
11	Wyvern	Monster	UR	4.00

Spellfire • Night Stalkers (a.k.a. Set #11)

SPELLFIRE™ Master the Magic

TSR • Released **October 1996**

125 cards in set • **IDENTIFIER: Night Stalkers** logo plus "of 25" or "of 100" on face

• Booster packs contain 12 cards; booster displays contain 40 boosters

This set, the only one to be done *completely* with photo art featuring TSR employees in disguise, is designed around the creatures of the night: vampires, werewolves, thieves, and other non-social animals. (No reflection on the models!)

The set adds yet another new character class with the Thief and Thief Ability Cards.

Produced in very low quantities, Night Stalkers was only created as an afterthought, to try to close out the game. But with the complete sell-out of the **Fourth Edition/Draconomicon** release and the subsequent sellout of **Night Stalkers**, four more releases were put on the schedule. — **John Danovich**

The Vampire

Awnshegh: undead: earthwalker. Can use blood abilities and thief skills. All allies played with this champion are considered undead.

71 of 100

You will need 14 nine-pocket pages to store this set. (7 doubled up)

Set (125 cards)	**34.00**
Booster Display Box	**26.00**
Booster Pack	**1.30**

#	Card name	Type	Rarity	Price
74	A Sure Thing	Rule	R	1.80
91	Aging	Unarmed	C	0.20
85	Alarm	W Spell	C	0.15
9	Amulet of Undead Aura	Item	UR	2.50
81	Ancient Dracolich	Ally	R	1.80
10	Arcane Formula for a Lich	Item	UR	2.50
29	Artemis Entreri	Thief	U	0.35
14	Assassin's Guild	Holding	C	0.15
55	Back Stab	Thf Skill	C	0.15
11	Bag of Beans	Item	UR	2.50
80	Beggar	Ally	R	1.00
83	Bigby's Dexterous Digits	W Spell	C	0.15
89	Blessed Abundance	C Spell	C	0.15
51	Book of the Dead	Artifact	R	1.00
3	Busted	Event	UR	2.50
70	Caller in Darkness	Psionicist	U	0.35
78	Cat Burglar	Ally	C	0.15
92	Cause Despair	Unarmed	C	0.15
100	Cause Disease	Unarmed	C	1.80
93	Cause Fear	Unarmed	C	0.15
94	Cause Paralysis	Unarmed	C	0.15
18	Cavern of Ancient Knowledge	Holding	R	2.00
7	Celestial Lights	Event	UR	2.50
60	Climb Walls	Thf Skill	C	0.15
25	Complete Surprise	Event	R	2.00
64	Concealed Weapon	Thf Skill	U	0.35
4	Confused Hunchback	Event	UR	2.50
95	Constitution Drain	Unarmed	C	0.20
86	Corruption of the Flesh	W Spell	U	0.35

#	Card name	Type	Rarity	Price
66	Crawling Claws	Monster	C	0.15
2	Crime Does Not Pay	Rule	UR	2.50
7	Cromlin	Realm	U	0.25
46	Dancing Sword	Item	C	0.20
6	Dark Dreams	Event	UR	2.50
5	Dark Prophesy	Event	UR	2.50
30	Daryth of Calimshan	Thief	C	0.15
22	Dawn of the Dead	Event	C	0.15
24	Den of Thieves	Realm	UR	2.50
61	Detect Noise	Thf Skill	C	0.15
39	Donval	Thief	C	0.15
40	El-Hadid	Thief	U	0.35
5	Falkovnia	Realm	R	2.00
88	Find Traps	C Spell	C	0.15
13	Forgotten Crypt	Holding	C	0.15
49	Gauntlets of Dexterity	Item	U	0.35
23	Gib Aklem	Psionicist	UR	3.00
22	Gib Drawsemaj	Cleric	UR	3.00
19	Gib Hcivonad	Hero	UR	3.00
21	Gib Irod	Wizard	UR	3.00
18	Gib Lhadsemlo	Monster	UR	3.00
20	Gib Reltub	Thief	UR	3.00
1	Good Truimphs in the End	Rule	UR	2.50
84	Guardian Mist	W Spell	C	0.15
76	Guild Master	Ally	C	0.15
12	Guild Shop	Holding	C	0.20
16	Guistenal Ruins	Holding	R	2.00
11	Haunted Graveyard	Holding	R	2.00
52	Heart of Darkness	Artifact	C	0.15
17	Hellgate Keep	Holding	U	0.35
54	Herald of Mei Lung	Artifact	C	0.15
59	Hide in Shadows	Thf Skill	U	0.35
32	Jacqueline Renier	Thief	C	0.15
38	Jamlin	Thief	U	0.35
34	Julio, Master Thief of Haslic	Thief	C	0.15
75	Kaisharga	Ally	C	0.15
41	Kelda Auslawsen	Thief	C	0.15

#	Card name	Type	Rarity	Price
97	Level Drain	Unarmed	R	1.80
82	Loric the Fence	Ally	U	0.35
25	Mad Scientist's Laboratory	Realm	UR	2.50
98	Magic Resistance	Unarmed	U	0.35
45	Mask	Thief	R	2.00
3	Mintarn	Realm	C	0.15
8	Mirror of Corruption	Artifact	UR	2.50
90	Monster Mount	C Spell	C	0.15
17	Moonbeast	Monster	UR	4.00
20	Moonlight Madness	Event	C	0.15
42	Moriad	Thief	C	0.15
57	Move Silently	Thf Skill	C	0.20
73	Negative Planar Energy	Rule	R	1.80
4	Nelanther	Realm	C	0.15
67	Nemon Hotep	Cleric	C	0.15
44	Orcus	Monster	R	2.00
13	Pavlov's Bell	Item	UR	2.50
19	Paying Your Dues	Event	C	0.15
37	Phostrek	Thief	C	0.15
56	Pick Pockets	Thf Skill	C	0.15
87	Power of Faith	C Spell	R	1.00
77	Raaig	Ally	C	0.15
99	Rapid Regeneration	Unarmed	C	0.15
33	Ratik Ubel	Thief	C	0.15
62	Read Languages	Thf Skill	C	0.15
6	Richemulot	Realm	U	0.35
14	Ring of Lycanthropy	Item	UR	4.00
47	Rod of Zombie Mastery	Item	C	0.15
58	Set Traps	Thf Skill	C	0.15
12	Shadowcloak	Item	UR	2.50
68	Shera the Wise	Wizard	C	0.15
36	Simpkin The Weasel Furzear	Thief	U	0.35
31	Storm Silverhand	Thief	U	0.35
96	Strength Drain	Unarmed	C	0.20
2	The Bandit Kingdom	Realm	C	0.25
26	The Black Death	Event	C	0.15
21	The Boss Wants a Cut	Event	U	0.35

RARITY KEY C = Common U = Uncommon R = Rare VR = Very Rare UR = Ultra Rare F = Foil card X = Fixed/standard in all decks

#	Card name	Type	Rarity	Price
28	The Guildmaster	Thief	R	1.00
23	The Long Arm of the Law	Event	R	2.00
15	The Pristine Tower	Holding	U	0.35
71	The Vampire	Regent	R	2.00
9	The Vampire's Realm	Realm	U	0.25
1	The Vast Swamp	Realm	R	1.00
10	Thieve's Guild	Holding	U	0.25
27	Three Card Monte	Event	R	2.00

#	Card name	Type	Rarity	Price
53	Trumpet of Doom	Artifact	R	1.80
35	Turin Deathstalker	Thief	R	1.00
43	Uldo Dracobane	Thief	R	2.00
8	UnderCerilia	Realm	C	0.15
63	Use Poison	Thf Skill	U	0.35
16	Varney the Vampire	Wizard	UR	5.00
24	Wail of the Banshee	Event	U	0.35

#	Card name	Type	Rarity	Price
50	Wand of Bone	Item	R	1.00
65	Werebear	Monster	R	1.80
72	Wereshark	Monster	C	0.15
48	Whip of Disarming	Item	U	0.35
69	Winslow the Lich	Wizard	U	0.35
15	Zombie	Hero	UR	3.00
79	Zombie Horde	Ally	U	0.35

Spellfire • Dungeons! (a.k.a. Set #12)

Designed by **TSR**, shipped by **Wizards of the Coast** • Released **August 1997**

125 cards in set • IDENTIFIER: *Dungeons* logo plus "of 25" or "of 100" on face

• Booster packs contain 12 cards; booster displays contain 40 boosters

The last booster set from TSR, **Dungeons!** cards were conceived as "adventures" that each player could go on during the course of play that would be part of their own victory conditions. After much editing, they basically became Rules cards that only applied to the player who put the card in their deck.

An innovation was the inclusion of a subset of cards with photos of actual **Spellfire** players, taken at a special booth at Gen Con 1996. TSR took the best card designs and implemented them into the *Dungeons!* expansion. This was the first time that actual players had real input into the cards and game strategy of a CCG, beyond general suggestions. Many promo cards were produced at that Gen Con booth.

Spellfire was slower but by no means dead when TSR, in late 1996, hit the financial wall that caused the late release of *Dungeons!* and the May 1997 sale of the company to Wizards of the Coast. for late 1997, TSR had scheduled **Fiends**, based on the Planescape setting, and **Incantation**, the 14th expansion set. But Wizards of the Coast apparently already had a sword-and-sorcery CCG, and the sets were never produced. — **John Danovich**

You will need **14** nine-pocket pages to store this set. (7 doubled up)

Set (125 cards)	34.00
Booster Display Box	25.00
Booster Pack	1.20

#	Card name	Type	Rarity	Price
74	A Sure Thing	Rule	R	1.80
8	Aliki	Thief	UR	3.00
72	Amulet of Spell Turning	Item	R	1.30
68	Amulet of the Dragon King	Item	U	0.30
96	Animate Gargoyle	W Spell	R	1.80
94	Ball Lightning	W Spell	C	0.40
59	Ballista	Artifact	R	1.80
23	Bats in the Belfry	Dungeon	R	1.80
58	Battering Ram	Artifact	U	0.30
25	Beneath Castle Drawmij	Dungeon	U	0.30
5	Black Hand Thieves' Guild	Holding	UR	2.50
55	Boiling Oil	Artifact	R	1.80
31	Border Garrison	Realm	R	1.80
30	Border Post	Realm	U	0.30
61	Borer	Artifact	R	1.80
54	Bottomless Horror	Ally	U	0.30
69	Breath Charm	Item	C	0.15
85	Broad Jump	Thf Skill	R	1.80
60	Cannon Ball	Artifact	R	1.80
14	Carrock of High Magicks	Dungeon	R	1.80
62	Catapult	Artifact	C	0.15
22	Chaos Lord	Regent	UR	2.50
29	Cities of the Sun	Realm	C	0.15
92	City Shield	W Spell	C	0.40
71	Clockwork Ogre	Item	U	0.30
82	Con Game	Thf Skill	R	1.80
98	Conjure Greater Fire Elemental	W Spell	C	0.15
79	Create Minion	Ability	C	0.15
67	Crystal Dragon Figurine	Item	U	0.40
44	Dearlyn Ambersong	Wizard	C	0.15
81	Death Field	Ability	U	0.30
4	Dissolution	W Spell	UR	2.50
99	Divine Assistance	C Spell	C	0.15
4	Domain of Takhisis, Queen of Darkness	Dungeon	C	0.15
25	Dor Amberglow	Hero	UR	3.00
75	Drain Will	Psionic	U	0.30
95	Drawmij's Beneficent Polymorph	W Spell	U	0.30
2	Dungeon of the King	Dungeon	C	0.15
76	Eat Dirt!	Unarmed	C	0.15

#	Card name	Type	Rarity	Price
6	Elminster's Intuition	Event	UR	2.50
24	Elyk the Bard	Thief	UR	3.00
10	Enter Darkness Together	Event	UR	2.50
91	Extension I	W Spell	C	0.25
43	Feral Halfling	Hero	U	0.30
9	Field of the Battle Lord	Dungeon	R	1.80
3	Fighting Dirty!	Thf Skill	UR	2.50
38	Fire Dragon	Monster	R	1.00
66	Flask of Curses	Item	C	0.15
7	Fool's Paradise	Event	UR	2.50
87	Fortune Telling	Thf Skill	C	0.15
88	Gather Information	Thf Skill	C	0.15
23	Giant Troll	Ally	UR	3.00
16	Handmine	Event	UR	2.50
50	Hero Slayer	Ally	C	0.15
21	Highmaster Illithios	Psionicist	UR	3.00
86	Hijacking	Thf Skill	R	1.80
47	Hook Horror	Ally	C	0.15
89	Intimidation	Thf Skill	U	0.30
41	Jasper	Hero	U	0.30
6	Labyrinth of Castle Greyhawk	Dungeon	R	1.00
3	Lair of Dregoth, the Undead Dragon-King	Dungeon	U	0.30
83	Legal Loophole	Thf Skill	C	0.15
9	Lilac Hesabon	Hero	U	3.00
48	Lurker in the Earth	Ally	U	0.30
74	Magic Draining Field	Psionic	C	0.15
53	Master Illithid	Ally	U	0.30
1	Mausoleum of the Zombie Master	Dungeon	C	0.15
13	Maze of the Guild	Dungeon	C	0.15
80	Melt Bone	Ability	U	0.40
21	Might of the Blood Right	Dungeon	C	0.15
97	Minions of Darkness	W Spell	C	0.10
14	Necba the Wrathmaker	Thief	UR	3.00
57	Net of Ensnaring	Artifact	R	1.00
8	Palace of the Celestial Light	Dungeon	C	0.15
70	Pearl Pegasus	Item	R	1.30
11	Pit of the Mind Lord	Dungeon	C	0.15
20	Poor Oriental Lord	Thief	UR	3.00
20	Powers from the Savage Land	Dungeon	C	0.15
2	Pretty Magical Ring	Item	UR	2.50
52	Psion Sucker	Hero	C	0.15
73	Psionic Disintegration	Psionic	R	1.80
16	Purveyor of Events	Dungeon	U	0.30
19	Rary's Apprentice	Wizard	UR	3.00

#	Card name	Type	Rarity	Price
11	Recorder of Yé Cind	Artifact	UR	4.00
26	Return of the Dwarven King	Dungeon	C	0.15
15	Shan, Karate Master	Hero	UR	3.00
56	Siege Ladder	Artifact	U	0.30
63	Siege Machine	Artifact	C	0.15
40	Skulker	Thief	R	1.00
49	Skull Tumor	Ally	R	1.80
18	Slorath's Gloves	Artifact	UR	4.00
22	Song of the Dragonlance	Dungeon	R	1.80
93	Spectral Dragon	W Spell	C	0.15
19	Spells from the Grave	Dungeon	R	1.80
17	Spells of the Archmage	Dungeon	C	0.15
18	Spells of the Friar	Dungeon	C	0.15
78	Supernatural Strength	Unarmed	C	0.15
64	Sword of Sharpness	Item	C	0.15
12	Telarie Willowind	Hero	UR	3.00
24	The Azure Tower of Onad the Fallen	Dungeon	R	1.80
10	The Belly of the Beast	Dungeon	C	0.15
36	The Bitter Knoll	Realm	C	0.15
17	The Builder	Hero	UR	3.00
28	The Dragon's Refuge	Realm	U	0.30
15	The Enchanted Land	Dungeon	C	0.15
34	The Forgotten Ruins	Realm	C	0.15
27	The Guildhall	Dungeon	C	0.15
42	The Hapless Halfling	Thief	C	0.15
35	The Hidden Village	Realm	C	0.15
13	The Llama King	Hero	UR	4.00
37	The Ogre	Hero	U	0.30
32	The Ruins of Lololia	Realm	R	1.80
12	The Torture Room	Dungeon	C	0.15
65	The Triton Throne	Item	C	0.15
51	The White Weird	Ally	R	1.80
33	Tower by the Sea	Realm	C	0.15
90	Trailing	Thf Skill	C	0.15
46	Troglodyte	Ally	C	0.15
84	Tumble Out of Danger	Thf Skill	U	0.40
45	Tyvorg the Frost Giant	Cleric	C	0.15
7	Under Castle Strahd	Dungeon	C	0.15
5	Undermountain	Dungeon	C	0.15
77	Vital Blow	Unarmed	U	0.30
100	What Comes Around Goes Around	Rule	C	0.15
1	Winner's Trophy	Artifact	UR	4.00
39	Zaranda Star	Regent	C	0.15

RARITY KEY C = Common U = Uncommon R = Rare VR = Very Rare UR = Ultra Rare F = Foil card X = Fixed/standard in all decks

Star of the Guardians

Mag Force 7 • First set, *Limited*, released **April 1995**

275 cards in set

- Starter decks contain 60 cards; starter displays contain 12 starters
- Booster packs contain 15 cards; booster displays contain 36 boosters

Designed by **Don Perrin**

The **Star of the Guardians** CCG is based on the science-fiction novel series of the same name by fan-favorite author Margaret Weis. The game recreates the battles of the warlords of the galaxy who are jockeying for position and power in the crumbling Galactic Democracy.

Each player starts with 25 Power Points, which can be increased by adding more star systems under a player's control and decreased by destroying a warlord's armada and attacking his home system. Each player has a deck of 40 to 80 cards. System and Special System cards are played to increase Power and generate Influence, which is used to pay for other cards to come into play, such as Artifact, Crew, Modifier, Personality, Ship, Squadron, and Weapon cards. Ship cards are played into one of five "space lanes." Spaceplane squadrons (fighters) are used to attack or defend against bombers and fighter-bombers that can threaten the home system. Combat is between capital ships in the same space lane, although sometimes, special ships can provide support from adjacent space lanes. Each battle is resolved separately, as supporting modifiers, Crew and Personality modifiers, as well as other modifiers are taken into account. The ship with the lowest total modified attack value loses and is destroyed, along with all attending Crew, Personalities, Weapons, etc. Power is lost equal to the Influence cost of the ship, crew, and weapons lost. Successful bombers and fighter-bombers from carriers can attack the home system, and damage Power directly, as can capital ships that are not blocked.

Players quickly noted the similarities to **Magic**, and for a while it was touted as an acceptable science-fiction version of *Magic*. However, the lackluster art was a definite turnoff for many players, and the lack of expansions signed the death notice of the game shortly after it first released. Mag Force 7 went on to produce the CCG **Wing Commander** later in the year. — **James Mishler**

SCRYE NOTES: *Star of the Guardians* splits the **Scrye** Award for CCG artifact most likely to confuse archaeologists. Like **Super Nova**, only a symbol appears on the card backs.

Concept	●●●○○
Gameplay	●●○○○
Card art	●○○○○
Player pool	○○○○○

CREW

LEGENDARY
TACTICS OFFICER
Play on a ship. Ship Supports at +2.

Set (275 cards)	43.00
Starter Display Box	22.00
Booster Display Box	25.00
Starter Deck	5.00
Booster Pack	1.20

You will need **31** nine-pocket pages to store this set. (16 doubled up)

Card name	Type	Rarity	Price
Admiral Aks	Pers	R	1.30
Aerial Bombardment	Dam	R	1.30
Armored Marine Landing Barge	Wpn	U	0.30
Artifact Heist	Fate	U	0.30
Assassination	Fate	U	0.40
Asteroid Field	Mod	C	0.05
Atheism	Fate	R	1.70
Battleship: Achilles Class	Ship	C	0.10
Battleship: Chimera Class	Ship	C	0.05
Battleship: Mars Class	Ship	C	0.10
Battleship: Odysseus Class	Ship	C	0.10
Battleship: Thor Class	Ship	C	0.10
Battleship: Trajan Class	Ship	C	0.10
Black Hole	Fate	C	0.05
Bloodsword	Art	R	1.70
Boffin Turret	Wpn	C	0.05
Bombing Blitz	Tactic	U	0.30
Bribe	Fate	U	0.30
Caracole	Tactic	U	0.50
Catapult Failure	Dam	C	0.05
Civil Defense	Mod	R	1.30
Claymore Bombers: Thundering Death Squadron	Sqdn	R	1.50

Card name	Type	Rarity	Price
Codes Broken	Fate	U	0.30
Command Cruiser: Galerius Class	Ship	U	0.30
Command Cruiser: Septimus Severus Class	Ship	U	0.30
Command Cruiser: Tyr Class	Ship	U	0.30
Crisis in Command	Fate	R	1.70
Cult Following	Mod	R	1.30
Dagger Fighters: Opal Squadron	Sqdn	U	0.30
Damage Control	Dam	C	0.05
Damage Repair	Dam	U	0.40
Dark Matter Creatures	Fate	U	0.50
Deadman Switch	Wpn	C	0.05
Deep Penetration	Tactic	U	0.50
Democratic People's Medal of Honor	Art	R	1.30
Destroyer: Antiochus Class	Ship	C	0.05
Destroyer: Cyclops Class	Ship	C	0.05
Destroyer: Date Masamune Class	Ship	C	0.05
Destroyer: Florianus Class	Ship	C	0.05
Destroyer: Fofner Class	Ship	C	0.05
Destroyer: Galleinus Class	Ship	C	0.05
Destroyer: Griffin Class	Ship	C	0.05
Destroyer: Hestia Class	Ship	C	0.05
Destroyer: Minotaur Class	Ship	C	0.05
Destroyer: Nemesis Class	Ship	C	0.05
Destroyer: Nero Class	Ship	C	0.05
Destroyer: Romulus Class	Ship	C	0.05
Destroyer: Sphinx Class	Ship	C	0.05
Destroyer: Typhon Class	Ship	C	0.05
Destroyer Escort: Frey Class	Ship	U	0.30
Destroyer Escort: Loki Class	Ship	U	0.30

Card name	Type	Rarity	Price
Dirk Fighters: Mercury Squadron	Sqdn	U	0.30
Dirk Fighters: Platinum Squadron	Sqdn	U	0.30
Dirk Fighters: Ruby Squadron	Sqdn	U	0.30
Dreadnought: Odin Class	Ship	U	0.50
Dreadnought: Scipio Africanus Class	Ship	U	0.50
Dreadnought: Vulcan Class	Ship	U	0.50
Engine Failure	Dam	C	0.05
Escort Carrier: Caligula Class	Ship	C	0.05
Escort Carrier: Heimdall Class	Ship	C	0.05
Escort Carrier: Hyperion Class	Ship	C	0.05
Escort Carrier: Prometheus Class	Ship	C	0.05
Escort Carrier: Tokugawa Ieyasu Class	Ship	C	0.05
Escort Carrier: Triton Class	Ship	C	0.05
Falcata Fighters: Garnet Squadron	Sqdn	C	0.05
Fast Light Carrier: Baldur Class	Ship	U	0.50
Fast Light Carrier: Vesta Class	Ship	U	0.50
Field Promotion	Mod	R	1.30
Fighting Withdrawal	Tactic	C	0.05
Flamberge Bombers: Rolling Flame Squadron	Sqdn	R	1.30
Fleet Carrier: Tiberius Class	Ship	U	0.70
Fleet Defender: Idun Class	Ship	U	0.30
Fleet Defender: Remus Class	Ship	U	0.30
Fleet Protector: Njoerd Class	Ship	U	0.50
Fleet Support Ship: Zeus Class	Ship	U	0.70
Frigate: Hellhound Class	Ship	C	0.05
Frigate: Honda Tadatsugu Class	Ship	C	0.05
Frigate: Mercury Class	Ship	C	0.05

RARITY KEY C = Common U = Uncommon R = Rare **VR** = Very Rare **UR** = Ultra Rare **F** = Foil card **X** = Fixed/standard in all decks

416 • *SCRYE Collectible Card Game Checklist and Price Guide*

Card name	Type	Rarity	Price
Garth Pantha	Pers	R	1.30
Gatling Laser Cannon	Wpn	C	0.05
Ghost Ship	Fate	U	0.50
Glitzy Ad Campaign	Fate	U	0.40
Hangar Fire	Dam	U	0.30
Harmonic Shield Disrupter	Wpn	U	0.50
Heavy Cruiser: Atlas Class	Ship	C	0.05
Heavy Cruiser: Basilisk Class	Ship	C	0.05
Heavy Cruiser: Gorgon Class	Ship	C	0.05
Heavy Cruiser: Hades Class	Ship	C	0.05
Heavy Cruiser: Ii Naomasa Class	Ship	C	0.05
Heavy Cruiser: Joerd Class	Ship	C	0.05
Heavy Cruiser: Julius Caesar Class	Ship	C	0.05
Heavy Cruiser: Jupiter Class	Ship	C	0.05
Heavy Cruiser: Kuroda Nagamasa Class	Ship	C	0.05
Home Defense Fighters	Tactic	U	0.30
Hull Breach	Dam	U	0.30
HyperMissile	Wpn	U	0.50
Hyperspace Radio Taunt	Fate	U	0.30
James M. Warden	Pers	R	1.30
Jump Shift	Tactic	C	0.05
Jump to Hyperspace	Fate	U	0.30
Kamikaze Doom Driver Torpedoes	Wpn	C	0.05
Katana Fighters: Bloodstone Squadron	Sqdn	R	1.30
King Dion Starfire	Pers	R	1.70
Lady Maigrey Morianna	Pers	R	1.70
Laser Dazzler	Wpn	C	0.05
Last Ditch Defense	Tactic	C	0.05
Legendary Battery Commander	Crew	U	0.30
Legendary Bombardier	Crew	C	0.05
Legendary 'Bots	Crew	C	0.05
Legendary Captain	Crew	R	1.50
Legendary Chaplain	Crew	C	0.05
Legendary Engineer	Crew	U	0.50
Legendary Executive Officer	Crew	U	0.50
Legendary Flight Leader	Crew	C	0.05
Legendary Governor	Crew	U	0.50
Legendary Gunner	Crew	C	0.05
Legendary Intelligence Officer	Crew	C	0.05
Legendary Navigator	Crew	C	0.05
Legendary Reconnaisance Officer	Crew	C	0.05
Legendary Rescue Officer	Crew	C	0.05
Legendary Ship's Pilot	Crew	C	0.05
Legendary Squadron Leader	Crew	U	0.50
Legendary Squadron Maintenance Officer	Crew	U	0.50
Legendary Tactics Officer	Crew	U	0.50
Light Carrier: Augustus Class	Ship	U	0.50
Light Carrier: Dragon Class	Ship	U	0.50
Light Carrier: Neptune Class	Ship	U	0.50
Light Carrier: Poseidon Class	Ship	U	0.50
Light Cruiser: Carinius Class	Ship	C	0.05
Light Cruiser: Chimera Class	Ship	C	0.10
Light Cruiser: Cronos Class	Ship	C	0.05
Light Cruiser: Demeter Class	Ship	C	0.05
Light Cruiser: Didius Julianus Class	Ship	C	0.05
Light Cruiser: Grendel Class	Ship	C	0.05
Light Cruiser: Hera Class	Ship	C	0.05
Light Cruiser: Hippogriff Class	Ship	C	0.05
Light Cruiser: Hydra Class	Ship	C	0.05
Light Cruiser: Iapetus Class	Ship	C	0.05
Light Cruiser: Oda Nobunaga Class	Ship	C	0.05
Light Cruiser: Rhea Class	Ship	C	0.05
Light Cruiser: Unicorn Class	Ship	C	0.05
Listening Post	Mod	U	0.30
Long Range Guns	Wpn	C	0.05
Lord Derek Sagan	Pers	R	1.70
Magnetic Repeller Shields	Wpn	C	0.05
Mark of Cowardice	Art	R	1.70
Mark XXVI Smart Bombs	Wpn	U	0.50
Mass Fire	Tactic	U	0.30
Micro Jump	Tactic	C	0.05
Military Academy	Mod	R	1.70
Minefield Strength 1	Mod	C	0.05
Minefield Strength 2	Mod	U	0.30
Minefield Strength 3	Mod	R	1.30
Minesweeper Gear	Wpn	C	0.05
Missile Cruiser: Fenris Class	Ship	U	0.25
Missile Cruiser: Forseti Class	Ship	U	0.30
Missile Cruiser: Minerva Class	Ship	U	0.30
Mutiny	Fate	R	1.50
Nebula	Mod	U	0.30
Orbital Defense Platform	Mod	U	0.30
Pilot Error	Fate	U	0.30
Pilum Torpedoes	Wpn	C	0.05
Planet Buster Bomb	Wpn	C	0.05
Planetary Base	Mod	U	0.30
Planetary Defenses	Mod	U	0.30
Planetary Survey	Fate	U	0.30
Plasma Web	Wpn	U	0.40
Prayer	Fate	U	0.30
Propaganda Campaign	Tactic	U	0.30
Pulse Cannon Gun Turret	Wpn	C	0.05
Quantum Space Anomaly	Mod	U	0.30
Radiation Leak	Dam	U	0.40
Ramming Armor	Wpn	C	0.05
Ramming Shields	Wpn	U	0.30
Raoul and the Little One	Pers	R	1.50
Rapier Fighters: Amethyst Squadron	Sqdn	C	0.05
Rapier Fighters: Onyx Squadron	Sqdn	C	0.05
Rapier Fighters: Sapphire Squadron	Sqdn	C	0.05
Rebuild and Overhaul Facility	Mod	R	1.70
Recalled to Base	Tactic	U	0.50
Reconnaissance Mission	Tactic	U	0.30
Regroup	Fate	U	0.30
Revolt	Fate	C	0.05
Ripple Fire	Tactic	U	0.30
Rogar of Mooria	Pers	U	0.30
Royal Dispute	Fate	R	1.30
Ruins of the Guardian Abbey	Art	R	1.70
Running the Flank	Tactic	C	0.05
Sabotage!	Fate	R	1.70
Sacred Blade	Art	R	1.70
Salvage Base	Fate	R	1.70
Sceptre of the Goddess	Art	R	1.70
Schiavona Fighter-Bombers Jade Squadron	Sqdn	U	0.50
Schiavona Fighter-Bombers Sandstone Squadron	Sqdn	U	0.50
Scimitar (Long Range) Fighter-Bombers Diamond Squadron	Sqdn	C	0.05
Scimitar (Long Range) Fighter-Bombers Lapis Lazuli Squadron	Sqdn	C	0.05
Scimitar (Long Range) Fighter-Bombers Steel Squadron	Sqdn	C	0.05
Scimitar (Short Range) Fighters Amber Squadron	Sqdn	C	0.05
Scimitar (Short Range) Fighters Gold Squadron	Sqdn	C	0.05
Scramble	Tactic	U	0.30
Shield Booster	Wpn	C	0.05
Shield Rotation	Tactic	C	0.05
Ship Crash	Fate	R	1.70
Ship of Fools	Fate	R	1.70
Ship's Cat	Mod	R	1.70
Smart Torpedoes	Wpn	U	0.60
Snaga Ohme	Pers	R	1.30
Social Malaise	Mod	R	1.30
Solar Flares	Fate	R	1.70
Space Fungus	Dam	U	0.40
Space Rotation Bomb	Art	R	2.20
Sparafucille	Pers	R	1.30
Special System Adonia	Sys	R	1.30
Special System Canus Prime	Sys	R	1.70
Special System Capital of the Democracy	Sys	R	1.70
Special System Hell's Outpost	Sys	R	1.50
Special System Laskar	Sys	R	1.50
Special System Mescopolis	Sys	R	1.30
Special System Shiloh	Sys	R	1.70
Special System Solgarth	Sys	R	1.70
Special System TISor	Sys	R	1.30
Special System Vangelis II	Sys	R	1.30
Spinal Mount Meson Cannon	Wpn	U	0.50
Squadron Automated Launch Tubes	Wpn	U	0.90
Squadron Battle Damage	Dam	C	0.05
Star Jewel	Art	R	1.70
Stiletto Bombers: Jet Squadron	Sqdn	U	0.30
Stiletto Bombers: Zircon Squadron	Sqdn	U	0.30
Synthetic Diamond Armor	Wpn	C	0.05
System A	Sys	Sys	0.05
System B	Sys	Sys	0.05
System C	Sys	Sys	0.05
System D	Sys	Sys	0.05
System E	Sys	Sys	0.05
System F	Sys	Sys	0.05
System G	Sys	Sys	0.05
System H	Sys	Sys	0.05
System I	Sys	Sys	0.05
System J	Sys	Sys	0.05
System K	Sys	Sys	0.05
System L	Sys	Sys	0.05
System M	Sys	Sys	0.05
System N	Sys	Sys	0.05
System O	Sys	Sys	0.05
System P	Sys	Sys	0.05
System Q	Sys	Sys	0.05
System R	Sys	Sys	0.05
System S	Sys	Sys	0.05
System T	Sys	Sys	0.05
System U	Sys	Sys	0.05
System V	Sys	Sys	0.05
System W	Sys	Sys	0.05
System X	Sys	Sys	0.40
System Y	Sys	Sys	0.05
Tactical Reverse	Tactic	U	0.30
Tactical Surprise	Tactic	U	0.30
Taskforce Carrier: Aegir Class	Ship	U	0.70
The Presidential Seal	Art	U	0.30
Torpedo Bay Explosion	Dam	U	0.50
Torpedo Gunboat: Ceres Class	Ship	U	0.30
Torpedo Gunboat: Wotan Class	Ship	U	0.30
Tractor Beam	Wpn	C	0.05
Turbo Drive	Wpn	C	0.05
Underground Facilities	Mod	U	0.30
Vertical Launch Thrusters	Wpn	U	0.50
Warlord Bayne	Pers	U	0.30
Warlord Broselle	Pers	U	0.30
Warlord DiLuna	Pers	U	0.30
Warlord Fanzib	Pers	U	0.30
Warlord Kevin Murphy	Pers	U	0.30
Warlord Rykilith	Pers	U	0.30
Warlord Shagroth	Pers	U	0.30
Weapon Conduit	Tactic	U	0.40
Wild Weasel Pod	Wpn	U	0.50
Xris and Mag Force 7	Pers	R	1.80

RARITY KEY C = Common **U** = Uncommon **R** = Rare **VR** = Very Rare **UR** = Ultra Rare **F** = Foil card **X** = Fixed/standard in all decks

Star Quest

Produced and released by **Comic Images,** based on a deisgn by **White Buffalo**
First set, ***The Regency Wars***, released **August 1995**
325 cards in set

• Starter decks contain 53 cards; starter displays contain 12 starters
• Booster packs contain 15 cards; booster displays contain 36 boosters

FIREFLY 1 ✳ 2 🛡 1 ◈

2/2 | 25

GORGON HORDE WASP CLASS
FIGHTER
TROOP CAPACITY: 2
The Firefly is a lightly armed Wasp class fighter equipped with a microwave accelerator assault battery. It is identified by the aft mounted glowing orb of its drive system.
Illus. & © - Joe Petagno. TM & © 1995 White Buffalo Games. All rights reserved. Produced by Comic Images, Inc. Made in U.S.A.

Concept	●●●○○
Gameplay	●●●○○
Card art	●●●○○
Player pool	○○○○○

Art quest

Star Quest features science-fiction art from Frank Frazetta, Luis Royo, Ken Barr, Ron Waltosky, David Martin, Michael Whelan, Joe Petagno, Steve Brown, Vincent DiFate, Daerick Gross, William Stout, Karl Kofoed, and the brothers Hildebrandt, among many others.

In the far future, the Terran sphere of influence has begun a slow and painful collapse. As the once-mighty empire crumbles, other races pick at the edges of a society running toward oblivion. In ***Star Quest***, the first CCG produced by art trading-card manufacturer Comic Images, players represent either one of these four races or the weary humans.

Game play is derivative of ***Magic: the Gathering***, to a great extent. The goal is to use Resource cards (which come in three flavors: Political, Technological, or Natural) to bring into play Ships and Soldiers. Each of these has power and toughness ratings, represented as two numbers, x/y. When a ship is brought into play, it is placed in front of the base species planet. Soldiers can either be placed on ships or on planets. When attacking, players choose some ships to fly over to their opponent's planet. The opponent chooses which of his ships will block. Players compare power to toughness to see who dies. If one of the attacking ships gets through, it does damage to the opponent's planet (which can take 30 hits) and then, if the ship has troops, they land and fight it out with the troops the opponent has stationed on the planet. They slug it out until somebody dies.

There are also Effect cards that can be played as well. Some of these are Instant, taking place once, then discarded. Some of them are Sustained, which are placed on a ship, soldier, or planet, and staying there to provide a benefit (such as +2/+0).

The art is great, as could be expected from an art-card producer with a library of images from high-profile creators to draw from. *Star Quest* is, in this sense, a science-fiction relative to ***Hyborian Gates*** and ***Guardians***, released the same quarter, which gave fellow art-card producers Cardz and Friedlander Publishing Group opportunities to develop CCGs from *their* stables of card artists. The card layout is good, but the text boxes are crammed with all of the traits of a card (such as a ship class, capacity, types of armor, and types of guns), as well as game effects and flavor text. By the time all of that is in there, it is a struggle to read a solid black box block of tiny little text.

It isn't adequate to play either race, because each of the races has a casting cost in a different color. Imperial troops require Imperial resource cards to play them, therefore, there are essentially 15 different types of resource card. In each deck you get three each of six of the types. A player can get maybe two cards a turn out with these, but don't bet on it. The multiplicity of resources necessary to play makes it difficult to put together a viable deck.

Just the fact that a game is derivative of *Magic* doesn't make it a great game — it's merely... derivative. *Star Quest* quickly died, and can be found in many bargain bins, where it may find fans among collectors of the artists involved. The one announced expansion for January 1996, ***Origins***, never came out.

Comic Images may, indeed, have recoiled a bit from the *Star Quest* experience, since, while it obtained the rights to do a CCG based on the World Wrestling Federation soon after *Star Quest*, it wouldn't bring ***WWF Raw Deal*** to market until the post-***Pokémon*** CCG boom of 2000. — **Richard Weld**

Set (325 cards)	**53.00**
Starter Display Box	**20.00**
Booster Display Box	**23.00**
Starter Deck	**5.00**
Booster Pack	**1.00**

Card name	Rarity	Price
☐ Absorption Shield	R	1.00
☐ Algon	R	1.00
☐ Alpha Assassins	C	0.05
☐ Anti-Matter Beam	U	0.25
☐ Anti-Matter Storm	R	1.00
☐ Apocalypse	U	0.25
☐ Arach	C	0.05
☐ Arachnids	C	0.05
☐ Asteroid Field	U	0.25
☐ Auto Self Destruct	R	1.00
☐ Avenger	C	0.05

Card name	Rarity	Price
☐ Baleron	U	0.25
☐ Bane Worms	U	0.25
☐ Banshee	U	0.25
☐ Basilisk	R	1.00
☐ Battle Beasts	C	0.05
☐ Battle Hound	U	0.25
☐ Battle Lords	R	1.00
☐ Battle Maggots	R	1.00
☐ Battle Rage	U	0.25
☐ Battle Sphere	U	0.25
☐ Battle-masters	R	1.00
☐ Bendar	U	0.25
☐ Bendarian Night Crawlers	U	0.25
☐ Bendarian Slaver	C	0.05
☐ Berserker	U	0.25
☐ Bio Hazard	C	0.05
☐ Black Hole	U	0.25
☐ Blast Shield	R	1.00

Card name	Rarity	Price
☐ Blitzer	C	0.05
☐ Blood Star	U	0.25
☐ Blood Vermin	C	0.05
☐ Bone Breakers	U	0.25
☐ Bone Crackers	C	0.05
☐ Bone Crushers	R	1.00
☐ Bone Grinders	U	0.25
☐ Bone Manglers	C	0.05
☐ Bone Scrapers	C	0.05
☐ Bore Beetles	U	0.25
☐ Bounty Hunters	U	0.25
☐ Brain Borers	C	0.05
☐ Bug Hunters	U	0.25
☐ Carnivorous Rage	R	1.00
☐ Centurians	U	0.25
☐ Cerberus	C	0.05
☐ Challenger	U	0.25
☐ Chameleon	C	0.05

Card name	Rarity	Price
☐ Cignus	C	0.05
☐ Cignus	U	0.25
☐ Class Escape Pod	C	0.05
☐ Cloak	R	1.00
☐ Colossus	U	0.25
☐ Comet Collision	C	0.05
☐ Computer Override	U	0.25
☐ Computer Shutdown	C	0.05
☐ Computer Virus	U	0.25
☐ Conquerors	C	0.05
☐ Conscripts	U	0.25
☐ Contractual Boondoggle	R	1.00
☐ Core Breach	U	0.25
☐ Counter Measures	R	1.00
☐ Crimson Star	C	0.05
☐ Cyber Fury	U	0.25
☐ Cyborg Natural	C	0.05
☐ Cyborg Nebula	C	0.05

RARITY KEY C = Common U = Uncommon R = Rare VR = Very Rare UR = Ultra Rare F = Foil card X = Fixed/standard in all decks

Card name	Rarity	Price
Cyborg Political	C	0.05
Cyborg Technology	C	0.05
Cyclops	C	0.05
Da Vor'	C	0.05
Dark Dragons	R	1.00
Data Link	C	0.05
Death Blow	U	0.25
Death Bringers	U	0.25
Death Fang	R	1.00
Death Squad	U	0.25
Deflector Shield	C	0.05
Demolisher	C	0.05
Dervish	C	0.05
Design Flaw	U	0.25
Design Upgrade	U	0.25
Destructor	U	0.25
Devastator	U	0.25
Disband	C	0.05
Disintegrator	U	0.25
Distortion Shield	U	0.25
Doomsday	R	1.00
Draco	U	0.25
Draconian Viper	C	0.05
Dragon Star	R	1.00
Dragonfly	C	0.05
Dragoons	U	0.25
Drones	C	0.05
Electron Torpedoes	C	0.05
Emergency Life Support	R	1.00
Emergency Maintenance	U	0.25
Energy Infusion	R	1.00
Environmental Sabotage	C	0.05
Excalibur	R	1.00
Exterminator	C	0.05
Feeding Frenzy	U	0.25
Fire Slugs	C	0.05
Firefly	C	0.05
Firelancers	R	1.00
Firestorm Assault Force	R	1.00
Flame Blade	C	0.05
Flame Disk	C	0.05
Flash Dragons	R	1.00
Flesh Flayers	C	0.05
Floating Minefield	R	1.00
Galactic Barrier	R	1.00
Gamma Ray	U	0.25
Gargoyle	U	0.25
Goliath	R	1.00
Gor'	U	0.25
Gore Brutes	C	0.05
Gorgon	UR	2.50
Gorgon Hive	R	1.00
Gorgon Horde Natural	C	0.05
Gorgon Horde Political	C	0.05
Gorgon Horde Technology	C	0.05
Gorgon Nebula	C	0.05
Gorgon War Masters	U	0.25
Gorgon Warriors	U	0.25
Government Investigation	R	1.00
Gravity Boots	C	0.05
Gravity Loss	C	0.05
Grendel	R	1.00
Growlers	C	0.05
Hadrian	U	0.25
Hannibal	U	0.25
Havoc	C	0.05
Hephaestus	R	1.00
High Iron	C	0.05
Hive Creepers	U	0.25

Card name	Rarity	Price
Hive Horrors	R	1.00
Hive Masters	U	0.25
Home Guard	C	0.05
Hoplites	U	0.25
Howler	C	0.05
Hull Breachers	C	0.05
Hydra	C	0.05
Hydragris	U	0.25
Hydrus Stormers	U	0.25
Hyper Flare	U	0.25
Imperial Gladiators	C	0.05
Imperial Lions	U	0.25
Imperial Rangers	R	1.00
Imperial Templars	U	0.25
Imperium Natural	C	0.05
Imperium Nebula	C	0.05
Imperium Political	C	0.05
Imperium Technology	C	0.05
Implosion	U	0.25
Industrial Espionage	C	0.05
Insanity Swarm	U	0.25
Intrepid	C	0.05
Ion Cannon	C	0.05
Ion Storm	C	0.05
Iron Legion	R	1.00
Isis	U	0.25
J.D. Juggernauts	C	0.05
Kragg	C	0.05
Kraggot Hive	U	0.25
Kronos	U	0.25
Life Support Failure	C	0.05
Lunar Outpost	U	0.25
Maelstrom	R	1.00
Magnetic Storm	C	0.05
Major Mutiny	R	1.00
Manslayers	U	0.25
Manticore	R	1.00
Mantis Hive	R	1.00
Marto	U	0.25
Martoids	C	0.05
Maulers	U	0.25
Mech Droid Strike	C	0.05
Medical Ship	R	1.00
Melcetus	U	0.25
Mercenaries	C	0.05
Metal Storm Strike Force	R	1.00
Metalica	UR	2.50
Metallic Virus	R	1.00
Meteor Storm	C	0.05
Microwave Cannon	C	0.05
Minesweeper	R	1.00
Minor Mutiny	U	0.25
Mirror Shield	U	0.25
Munitions Ship	R	1.00
Murtok	C	0.05
Myrmidons	U	0.25
Natural Disaster	U	0.25
Neutron Charge	R	1.00
Nomads	C	0.05
Nova	U	0.25
Old Guard	U	0.25
Omaria	U	0.25
One-Eyed Terrors	U	0.25
Orbiting Defense System	U	0.25
Phalanx Laser Cannon	R	1.00
Phantom	C	0.05
Phoenix Force	U	0.25
Planet Scorcher	U	0.25
Plasma Blaster	U	0.25

Card name	Rarity	Price
Poisoned Atmosphere	U	0.25
Political Assassin	R	1.00
Political Corruption	R	1.00
Power Surge	C	0.05
Prey Slayers	C	0.05
Proton Torpedoes	C	0.05
Psionic Cannon	R	1.00
Pterasaur	U	0.25
Pulsar Cannon	C	0.05
Pulse Laser	U	0.25
Pulverizer	C	0.05
Quasar Cannon	U	0.25
Radiation Storm	C	0.05
Ragnarok	U	0.25
Raidmasters	R	1.00
Rampage	U	0.25
Razor Tooth	U	0.25
Reaper	U	0.25
Red Slayer	U	0.25
Regulas Predators	U	0.25
Repair Ship	R	1.00
Repulser Shield	C	0.05
Retaliator	R	1.00
Retrofit	U	0.25
Rogue Warriors	C	0.05
Sarto	C	0.05
Sartog	C	0.05
Sauria	UR	2.50
Saurian Natural	C	0.05
Saurian Nebula	C	0.05
Saurian Political	C	0.05
Saurian Technology	C	0.05
Saurian Thunder	U	0.25
Scanner	U	0.25
Scarlet Star	U	0.25
Scather	C	0.05
Scavenger	C	0.05
Scorcher	U	0.25
Screamer	U	0.25
Screaming Eagles	U	0.25
Screecher	U	0.25
Scurge	R	1.00
Sentries	U	0.25
Ser' Pen	R	1.00
Serpens Invaders	C	0.05
Shadow	C	0.05
Shadow Slayers	U	0.25
Shadow Strikers	U	0.25
Shock Force	C	0.05
Shredder	C	0.05
Shreiker	R	1.00
Silhouette	U	0.25
Skor	U	0.25
Slasher	C	0.05
Slavers	C	0.05
Slayers	U	0.25
Slithik	U	0.25
Solar Flare	R	1.00
Solar Wind	C	0.05
Soul Suckers	R	1.00
Southern Cross	R	1.00
Space Sickness	R	1.00
Spacedock	R	1.00
Spectre	C	0.05
Spidership	U	0.25
Spitters	U	0.25
Star Freighter	R	1.00
Star Sabre	C	0.05

Card name	Rarity	Price
Star Sabre Shock Troops	R	1.00
Steel Furies	U	0.25
Stellar Shock Wave	U	0.25
Stinger	U	0.25
Stompers	U	0.25
Strafers	C	0.05
Strike Eagle Militia	R	1.00
Strike Masters	R	1.00
Strike Troops	R	1.00
Subjugators	R	1.00
Sun Crusher	R	1.00
Sun Dagger	U	0.25
Super Nova	R	1.00
Suppressors	C	0.05
Swarm Lords	R	1.00
Sword of Damocles	R	1.00
Tactical Assimilators	C	0.05
Talon	R	1.00
Taron	R	1.00
Tarsus	C	0.05
Tarsus Darkstars	U	0.25
Technological Breakthrough	R	1.00
Technological Disaster	U	0.25
Technological Genius	R	1.00
Telepath	U	0.25
Telepathic Feedback	U	0.25
Terra	UR	2.50
Thrasher	C	0.05
Tigermoth	U	0.25
Time Warp	C	0.05
Timeportal	U	0.25
Titan	C	0.05
Trackers	C	0.05
Tramplers	C	0.05
Tu Bar'	C	0.05
Urth	R	1.00
Vindicator	U	0.25
Virus Purge	R	1.00
Vor'	UR	2.50
Vor' Pa Claws	U	0.25
Vor' Pa Command Ship	R	1.00
Vor' Pa Natural	C	0.05
Vor' Pa Nebula	C	0.05
Vor' Pa Political	C	0.05
Vor' Pa Technology	C	0.05
Vor' Pa Wrath	U	0.25
Vor' Paq	U	0.25
Vor' Paq of the Dark Grove	U	0.25
War Hammer	U	0.25
World Reapers	U	0.25
World Wrecker	R	1.00
Wormhole	U	0.25
Wraith	U	0.25

Foil cards

Star Quest has what could be called foil cards, although they are not variants and the art is, in fact, not really part of the enhancement.

Special cards for the homeworlds have a fine overlay of glitter film located on top of the art frame.

RARITY KEY C = Common U = Uncommon R = Rare VR = Very Rare UR = Ultra Rare F = Foil card X = Fixed/standard in all decks

Star Trek

Decipher • First set, *Premiere Limited*, released **November 1994** • Print run: **45.9 million cards**
363 cards in set • **IDENTIFIER: Cards have black borders and © 1994**

• Starter decks contain 60 cards; starter displays contain 12 starters
• Booster packs contain 15 cards; booster displays contain 36 boosters

Designed by **Tom Braunlich** and **Rollie Tesh**

The first CCG based on a media license, **Star Trek Customizable Card Game** was also one of the first "goal-oriented" games in the genre. Rather than trying to destroy your opponent, the objective was to gather 100 points, generally by performing various missions based on episodes of the *Next Generation* TV show.

Players first set up the "spaceline," a set of Missions. They then secretly place Dilemmas under the Missions to slow down the opponent or kill his personnel. Then Outposts, the starting points for the players, are placed. After this sometimes lengthy seed phase, play can actually begin. Players play a variety of recognizable personnel and starships from one of three affiliations (Federation, Klingon, and Romulan), as well as various non-aligned cards, which carry no affiliation. They attempt the missions and try to overcome the dilemmas their opponents have placed there. They must match skills on the personnel to the skills printed on the mission to complete it. The first player to gain 100 points from missions (or from a few other specialized "point cards") wins the game.

The strong license lured many to the game, which was previewed at GenCon in 1994. However, it had many basic mechanical flaws. Grossly overpowered cards, long set-up time, hard-to-get main characters, poorly worded cards and rules, and lack of interaction were some of the faults cited by its critics. Additionally, collation of basic cards was poor, making it tough, if not impossible, to build a basic deck from a few starters and boosters. Finally, for the first few years, players were lucky to see a new set once a year.

Despite all this, *Star Trek* won a huge following early in its life cycle. Players eager for something different than the abstract **Magic** or **Jyhad** experiences were willing to give it a try. The card images were top-notch, making it one of the most attractive games available. Top cards, such as **Jean-Luc Picard** and the **Enterprise**, went for as much as $80 early on. Incredible sales transformed Decipher, producer of *Host a Mystery* and *Pente*, from a specialty party games company into a major player in hobby gaming almost overnight.

The game was almost killed when, in 1995, due to disputes with Paramount, it was announced that it would expire at the end of 1997, and no intentions would be made to renew it. (Paramount had already shuffled off the CCG rights to the original series to Fleer/Skybox.) However, in late 1996, negotiations were restarted and, a few months later, the announcement was made that the game would remain in Decipher's hands for several more years and include the *Deep Space Nine* and *Voyager* series, as well as *First Contact* and later movies. In 1999, five years after the original release of the game, plans were announced to make sets based upon the original series show and movies, as well as an online version of the game. Despite the several bumps in the road, the CCG that wouldn't die continues to play to fanatical fans today. — *Jason Winter*

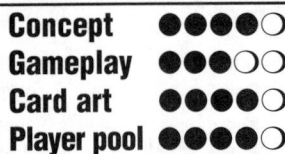

Concept	●●●●○
Gameplay	●●●○○
Card art	●●●●○
Player pool	●●●●○

Star Trek • Premiere Unlimited

Decipher • Released **December 1994** • Print run: **162 million cards**
363 cards in set • **IDENTIFIER: Cards have white borders and © 1994 OR © 1995**

• Starter decks contain 60 cards; starter displays contain 12 starters
• Booster packs contain 15 cards; booster displays contain 36 boosters

The **Unlimited** release is a white-bordered reprint of the original set. About a dozen cards were given errata. The set was vastly overprinted, leading to the "anthologies" and "enhanced" products that would be seen a few years down the line to help get rid of the excess. — *Jason Winter*

LIMITED

Set (363 cards)	387.00
Starter Display Box	120.00
Booster Display Box	162.00
Starter Deck	13.00
Booster Pack	5.00

UNLIMITED

Set (363 cards)	174.50
Starter Display Box	80.00
Booster Display Box	82.50
Starter Deck	8.30
Booster Pack	3.00

You will need **41** nine-pocket pages to store this set. (21 doubled up)

You will need **41** nine-pocket pages to store this set. (21 doubled up)

LtdPrice	Card name	Type	Rarity	UnlPrice
5.00	Albert Einstein	Per	R	4.00
1.00	Alexander Rozhenko	Per	U	0.50
4.00	Alidar Jarok	Per	R	3.00
1.00	Alien Abduction	Dil	U	0.50
3.00	Alien Groupie	Int	R	3.00
1.00	Alien Parasites	Dil	U	0.50
1.00	Alien Probe	Ev	U	0.50
4.00	Alynna Nechayev	Per	R	4.00
1.00	Alyssa Ogawa	Per	U	0.50
2.00	Amanda Rogers	Int	U	0.50
1.00	Amarie	Per	U	0.50
0.25	Anaphasic Organism	Dil	C	0.25
3.50	Ancient Computer	Dil	R	3.00

LtdPrice	Card name	Type	Rarity	UnlPrice
4.00	Anti-Time Anomaly	Ev	R	4.00
0.25	Archer	Dil	C	0.25
5.00	Armus-Skin of Evil	Dil	R	4.00
0.25	Asteroid Sanctuary	Int	C	0.25
0.25	Atmospheric Ionization	Ev	C	0.25
1.00	Auto-Destruct Sequence	Int	U	0.50
3.00	Avert Disaster	Mis	R	3.00
1.00	Ba'el	Per	U	0.50
1.00	Baran	Per	U	0.50
5.00	Barclay's Protomorphosis Disease	Dil	R	3.50
0.25	Batrell	Per	C	0.25
1.00	Benjamin Maxwell	Per	U	0.50

RARITY KEY **C** = Common **U** = Uncommon **R** = Rare **VR** = Very Rare **UR** = Ultra Rare **F** = Foil card **X** = Fixed/standard in all decks

LtdPrice	Card name	Type	Rarity	UnlPrice
6.00	Betazoid Gift Box	Art	R	4.00
10.00	B'Etor	Per	R	5.00
4				
14.00	Beverly Crusher	Per	R	8.00
0.25	B'iJik	Per	C	0.25
1.00	Birth of "Junior"	Dil	U	0.50
1.00	Bochra	Per	U	0.50
1.00	Bok	Per	U	0.50
10.00	Borg Ship	Dil	R	10.00
5.00	Bynars Weapon Enhancement	Ev	R	4.00
0.25	Calloway	Per	C	0.25
1.00	Chalnoth	Dil	U	0.50
5				
0.25	Christopher Hobson	Per	C	0.25
0.80	Cloaked Mission	Mis	U	0.50
0.25	Combat Vessal	Shp	C	0.25
1.00	Cosmic String Fragment	Dil	U	0.50
0.25	Covert Installation	Mis	C	0.25
0.80	Covert Rescue	Mis	U	0.50
7.00	Crosis	Int	R	4.00
5.00	Crystalline Entity	Dil	R	4.00
3.00	Cultural Observation	Mis	R	3.00
6				
4.00	Cytherians	Dil	R	3.00
0.25	Darian Wallace	Per	C	0.25
24.00	Data	Per	R	14.00
0.25	D'deridex	Shp	C	0.25
15.00	Deanna Troi	Per	R	9.00
1.00	Devinoni Ral	Per	U	0.50
5.50	Devoras	Shp	R	4.00
0.80	Diplomacy Mission	Mis	U	0.50
0.25	Disruptor Overload	Int	C	0.25
7				
1.00	Distortion Field	Ev	U	0.50
1.00	Distortion of Space/Time Continuum	Int	U	0.50
0.25	Divok	Per	C	0.25
0.25	Dr. Farek	Per	C	0.25
5.00	Dr. La Forge	Per	R	4.00
5.00	Dr. Leah Brahms	Per	R	4.00
1.00	Dr. Reyga	Per	U	0.50
1.00	Dr. Selar	Per	U	0.50
0.25	Dukath	Per	C	0.25
8				
8.00	Duras	Per	R	5.00
1.00	El-Adrel Creature	Dil	U	0.50
0.25	Emergency Transporter Armbands	Int	C	0.25
1.00	Energy Vortex	Int	U	0.50
0.25	Engineering Kit	Equ	C	0.25
0.25	Engineering PADD	Equ	C	0.25
1.00	Eric Pressman	Per	U	0.50
0.25	Escape Pod	Int	C	0.25
0.25	Espionage: Federation on Klingon	Ev	C	0.25
9				
0.25	Espionage: Klingon on Federation	Ev	C	0.25
0.25	Espionage: Romulan on Federation	Ev	C	0.25
0.25	Espionage: Romulan on Klingon	Ev	C	0.25
1.00	Etana Jol	Per	U	0.50
0.80	Evacuation	Mis	U	0.50
3.00	Evaluate Terraforming	Mis	R	3.00
1.00	Evek	Per	U	0.50
0.25	Excavation	Mis	C	0.25
1.00	Exocomp	Per	U	0.50
10				
3.00	Explore Black Cluster	Mis	R	3.00
3.00	Explore Dyson Sphere	Mis	R	3.00
3.00	Explore Typhone Expanse	Mis	R	3.00
0.80	Expose Covert Supply	Mis	U	0.50
3.00	Extraction	Mis	R	3.00
0.25	Federation Outpost	Out	C	0.25
0.25	Federation PADD	Equ	C	0.25

LtdPrice	Card name	Type	Rarity	UnlPrice
1.00	Fek'Ihr	Per	U	0.50
0.25	Female's Love Interest	Dil	C	0.25
11				
0.25	Fever Emergency	Mis	C	0.25
1.00	Firestorm	Dil	U	0.50
0.50	First Contact	Mis	U	0.50
1.00	Fleet Admiral Shanthi	Per	U	0.50
1.00	Full Planet Scan	Int	U	0.50
0.25	Galathon	Per	C	0.25
1.00	Gaps in Normal Space	Ev	U	0.50
1.00	Genetronic Replicator	Ev	U	0.50
18.00	Geordi La Forge	Per	R	9.00
12				
0.25	Giusti	Per	C	0.25
5.00	Goddess of Empathy	Ev	R	4.00
0.25	Gorath	Per	C	0.25
0.25	Gorta	Per	C	0.25
10.00	Gowron	Per	R	5.00
1.00	Gravitic Mine	Dil	U	0.50
5.00	Haakona	Shp	R	4.00
1.00	Hannah Bates	Per	U	0.50
1.00	Hologram Ruse	Dil	U	0.50
13				
1.00	Holo-Projectors	Ev	U	0.50
4.00	Honor Challenge	Int	R	4.00
6.00	Horga'hn	Art	R	4.50
6.00	Hugh	Int	R	4.00
4.00	Hunt for DNA Program	Mis	R	3.30
1.00	Husnock Ship	Shp	U	0.50
1.00	Hyper-Aging	Dil	U	0.50
6.00	I.K.C. Bortas	Shp	R	5.00
6.00	I.K.C. Buruk	Shp	R	5.00
14				
6.00	I.K.C. Hegh'ta	Shp	R	5.00
0.25	I.K.C. K'Vort	Shp	C	0.25
5.00	I.K.C. Pagh	Shp	R	4.00
6.00	I.K.C. Qu'Vat	Shp	R	5.00
0.25	I.K.C. Vor'Cha	Shp	C	0.25
1.00	I.K.C. Vorn	Shp	U	0.50
3.00	Iconia Investigation	Mis	R	3.00
0.25	Iconian Computer Weapon	Dil	C	0.25
0.25	Impassable Door	Dil	C	0.25
15				
1.00	Incoming Message-Federation	Int	U	0.50
1.00	Incoming Message-Klingon	Int	U	0.50
1.00	Incoming Message-Romulan	Int	U	0.50
5.50	Interphase Generator	Art	R	4.00
3.00	Investigate Alien Probe	Mis	R	3.00
0.25	Investigate Anomaly	Mis	C	0.25
3.00	Investigate Disappearance	Mis	R	3.00
3.00	Investigate Disturbance	Mis	R	3.00
3.00	Investigate Massacre	Mis	R	3.00

LtdPrice	Card name	Type	Rarity	UnlPrice
16				
3.00	Investigate Raid	Mis	R	3.00
3.00	Investigate Rogue Comet	Mis	R	3.00
3.00	Investigate Shattered Space	Mis	R	3.00
3.00	Investigate Sighting	Mis	R	3.00
3.00	Investigate Time Continuum	Mis	R	3.00
1.00	Ishara Yar	Per	U	0.50
4.00	Jaglom Shrek-Information Broker	Int	R	3.00
0.25	Jaron	Per	C	0.25
0.25	J'Ddan	Per	C	0.25
17				
30.00	Jean-Luc Picard	Per	R	20.00
1.00	Jenna D'Sora	Per	U	0.50
0.25	Jera	Per	C	0.25
1.00	Jo'Bril	Per	U	0.50
7.00	Kahless	Per	R	4.00
1.00	Kareel Odan	Per	U	0.50
4.50	Kargan	Per	R	4.00
6.00	K'Ehleyr	Per	R	4.00
1.00	Kell	Per	U	0.50
18				
2.00	Kevin Uxbridge	Int	U	0.50
6.00	Khazara	Shp	R	4.00
3.00	Khitomer Research	Mis	R	3.00
1.00	Kivas Fajo-Collector	Ev	U	0.50
0.25	Kle'eg	Per	C	0.25
4.00	Klingon Death Yell	Int	R	4.00
0.25	Klingon Disruptor	Equ	C	0.25
0.25	Klingon Outpost	Out	C	0.25
19				
0.25	Klingon PADD	Equ	C	0.25
0.25	Klingon Right of Vengeance	Int	C	0.25
1.00	K'mpec	Per	U	0.50
1.00	Konmel	Per	U	0.50
1.00	Koral	Per	U	0.50
1.00	Koroth	Per	U	0.50
1.00	Korris	Per	U	0.50
0.80	Krios Suppression	Mis	U	0.50
0.25	Kromm	Per	C	0.25
20				
1.00	K'Tal	Per	U	0.50
4.00	Ktarian Game	Dil	R	4.00
0.25	K'Tesh	Per	C	0.25
4.00	Kurak	Per	R	4.00
6.00	Kurlan Naiskos	Art	R	4.00
7.00	Kurn	Per	R	5.00
1.00	K'Vada	Per	U	0.50
5.00	Leah Brahms	Per	R	4.00
1.00	Life-Form Scan	Int	U	0.50
21				
0.25	Linda Larson	Per	C	0.25
1.00	L'Kor	Per	U	0.50
0.25	Long-Range Scan	Int	C	0.25

Star Trek • Warp Pack

Decipher • Released **March 1995**

12 cards in packs

The **Warp Pack**, a 12-card white border set, was distributed for free by Decipher. It contains seven basic missions and five cards previewing cards later seen in the **Alternate Universe** set. 500,000 packs were made.

Decipher released the set as a make-good, to provide players with enough missions and an outpost to build a deck — since many weren't getting enough basic cards in their starter decks. The other cards were "fixer" cards, designed to counter a few overpowered strategies, a tactic Decipher would adopt for all its CCGs.

At the time of its release, distribution was spotty, with the first packs made available to attendees of GenCon 1995. Since they contained "preview" cards, several saw the cards as having monetary value, and many stores that were told to distribute them for free sold them to customers desperate for new cards. But the packs have little resale value: Even today, they are available, for free, from Decipher.

RARITY KEY C = Common   U = Uncommon   R = Rare   VR = Very Rare   UR = Ultra Rare   F = Foil card   X = Fixed/standard in all decks

LtdPrice	Card name	Type	Rarity	UnlPrice
6.00	Lore Returns	Ev	R	4.00
5.00	Lore's Fingernail	Ev	R	4.00
0.25	Loss of Orbital Stability	Int	C	0.25
8.00	Lursa	Per	R	5.00
6.00	Lwaxanna Troi	Per	R	5.00
0.25	Male's Love Interest	Dil	C	0.25
1.00	Masaka Transformations	Ev	U	0.50
1.00	Matriarchal Society	Dil	U	0.50
0.25	McKnight	Per	C	0.25
0.25	Medical Kit	Equ	C	0.25
3.00	Medical Relief	Mis	R	3.00
0.25	Medical Tricorder	Equ	C	0.25
4.00	Mendak	Per	R	3.00
0.25	Mendon	Per	C	0.25
0.25	Menthar Booby Trap	Dil	C	0.25
0.25	Mercenary Ship	Shp	C	0.25
1.00	Metaphasic Shields	Ev	U	0.50
0.25	Microbiotic Colony	Dil	C	0.25
0.25	Microvirus	Dil	C	0.25
1.00	Mirok	Per	U	0.50
1.00	Morag	Per	U	0.50
4.00	Morgan Bateson	Per	R	3.00
0.50	Mot the Barber	Per	U	0.50
1.00	Movar	Per	U	0.50
4.50	Nagilum	Dil	R	4.00
1.00	Nanites	Dil	U	0.50
0.25	Narik	Per	C	0.25
1.00	Nausicaans	Dil	U	0.50
1.00	Near-Warp Transport	Int	U	0.50
4.50	Neela Daren	Per	R	4.00
1.00	Neral	Per	U	0.50
1.00	Neural Servo Device	Ev	U	0.50
3.00	New Contact	Mis	R	3.00
1.00	Nikolai Rozhenko	Per	U	0.50
1.00	Nitrium Metal Parasites	Dil	U	0.50
1.00	Norah Satie	Per	U	0.50
1.00	Nu'Daq	Per	U	0.50
1.00	Null Space	Dil	U	0.50
1.00	Nutational Shields	Ev	U	0.50
1.00	N'vek	Per	U	0.50
1.00	Ocett	Per	U	0.50
0.25	Palor Toff-Alien Trader	Int	C	0.25
0.25	Palteth	Per	C	0.25
1.00	Pardek	Per	U	0.50
1.00	Parem	Per	U	0.50
0.25	Particle Fountain	Int	C	0.25
0.25	Pattern Enhancers	Ev	C	0.25
3.00	Pegasus Search	Mis	R	3.00
0.25	Phased Matter	Dil	C	0.25
5.00	Pi	Shp	R	4.00
0.25	Plasma Fire	Ev	C	0.25
0.80	Plunder Site	Mis	U	0.50
1.00	Portal Guard	Dil	U	0.50
9.00	Q	Dil	R	8.00
1.00	Q2	Int	U	0.50
0.25	Q-Net	Ev	C	0.25
1.00	Radioactive Garbage Scow	Dil	U	0.50
1.00	Raise The Stakes	Ev	U	0.50
1.00	Rebel Encounter	Dil	U	0.50
0.25	Red Alert!	Ev	C	0.25
5.00	Reginald Barclay	Per	R	4.00
0.25	Relief Mission	Mis	C	0.25
1.00	REM Fatigue Hallucinations	Dil	U	0.50
0.25	Repair Mission	Mis	C	0.25
0.25	Res-Q	Ev	C	0.25
0.80	Restore Errant Moon	Mis	U	0.50
5.00	Richard Galen	Per	R	4.00
1.00	Riva	Per	U	0.50
6.00	Ro Laren	Per	R	4.00
6.00	Roga Danar	Per	R	4.00
0.25	Rogue Borg Mercenaries	Int	C	0.25
0.25	Romulan Disruptor	Equ	C	0.25
0.25	Romulan Outpost	Out	C	0.25
0.25	Romulan PADD	Equ	C	0.25
0.25	Runabout	Shp	C	0.25
5.00	Sarek	Per	R	4.00
3.00	Sarjenka	Dil	R	3.00
3.00	Sarthong Plunder	Mis	R	3.00
4.00	Satelk	Per	R	3.00
0.25	Scan	Int	C	0.25
0.25	Science Vessel	Shp	C	0.25
0.25	Scout Vessel	Shp	C	0.25
0.80	Secret Salvage	Mis	U	0.50
3.00	Seek Life-Form	Mis	R	3.00
8.00	Sela	Per	R	5.00
0.25	Selok	Per	C	0.25
0.80	Shaka, When the Walls Fell	Dil	U	0.50
5.00	Shelby	Per	R	4.00
0.25	Ship Seizure	Int	C	0.25
0.25	Simon Tarses	Per	C	0.25
5.00	Sir Isaac Newton	Per	R	4.00
1.00	Sirna Kolrami	Per	U	0.50
0.25	Sito Jaxa	Per	C	0.25
1.00	Soren	Per	U	0.50
0.25	Spacedock	Ev	C	0.25
0.25	Starfleet Type II Phaser	Equ	C	0.25
0.25	Static Warp Bubble	Ev	C	0.25
1.00	Strategic Diversion	Mis	U	0.50
3.00	Study Hole in Space	Mis	R	3.00
3.00	Study Lonka Pulsar	Mis	R	3.00
3.00	Study Nebula	Mis	R	3.00
0.25	Study Plasma Streamer	Mis	C	0.25
0.25	Study Stellar Collision	Mis	C	0.25
0.25	Subspace Interference	Int	C	0.25
1.00	Subspace Schism	Int	U	0.50
0.25	Subspace Warp Rift	Ev	C	0.25
6.00	Supernova	Ev	R	5.00
3.00	Survey Mission	Mis	R	3.00
0.25	Tachyon Detection Grid	Int	C	0.25
1.00	Taibak	Per	U	0.50
0.25	Taitt	Per	C	0.25
0.25	Takket	Per	C	0.25
0.25	Tallus	Per	C	0.25
4.00	Tam Elbrun	Per	R	3.50
1.00	Tarellian Plague Ship	Dil	U	0.50
0.25	Tarus	Per	C	0.25
10.00	Tasha Yar	Per	R	8.00
0.25	Taul	Per	C	0.25
0.25	Taurik	Per	C	0.25
1.00	Tebok	Per	U	0.50
1.00	Telepathic Alien Kidnappers	Ev	U	0.50
4.00	Temporal Causality Loop	Dil	R	4.00
1.00	Temporal Rift	Int	U	0.50
0.25	Test Mission	Mis	C	0.25
0.25	Tetryon Field	Ev	C	0.25
4.00	The Devil	Int	R	4.00
1.00	The Juggler	Int	U	0.50
1.00	The Traveler: Transcendence	Ev	U	0.50
0.25	Thei	Per	C	0.25
10.00	Thomas Riker	Per	R	8.00
6.00	Thought Maker	Art	R	4.00
5.00	Time Travel Pod	Art	R	4.00
0.50	Toby Russell	Per	U	0.50
0.50	Tokath	Per	U	0.50
4.50	Tomalak	Per	R	4.00
0.25	Tomek	Per	C	0.25
1.00	Toq	Per	U	0.50
1.00	Torak	Per	U	0.50
1.00	Toral	Per	U	0.50
5.00	Toreth	Per	R	4.00
0.25	Torin	Per	C	0.25
7.00	Tox Uthat	Art	R	6.00
1.00	T'Pan	Per	U	0.50
1.00	Transwarp Conduit	Int	U	0.50
0.25	Treaty: Federation/Klingon	Ev	C	0.25
0.25	Treaty: Federation/Romulan	Ev	C	0.25
0.25	Treaty: Romulan/Klingon	Ev	C	0.25
0.25	Tricorder	Equ	C	0.25
4.00	Tsiolkovsky Infection	Dil	R	3.00
1.00	Two-Dimensional Creatures	Dil	U	0.50
0.25	Type VI Shuttlecraft	Shp	C	0.25
6.00	U.S.S. Brittain	Shp	R	6.00
25.00	U.S.S. Enterprise	Shp	R	16.00
0.25	U.S.S. Excelsior	Shp	C	0.25
0.25	U.S.S. Galaxy	Shp	C	0.25
5.00	U.S.S. Hood	Shp	R	4.00
0.25	U.S.S. Miranda	Shp	C	0.25
0.25	U.S.S. Nebula	Shp	C	0.25
0.25	U.S.S. Oberth	Shp	C	0.25
6.00	U.S.S. Phoenix	Shp	R	5.00
1.00	U.S.S. Sutherland	Shp	U	0.50
7.00	U.S.S. Yamato	Shp	R	6.00
1.00	Vagh	Per	U	0.50
0.25	Varel	Per	C	0.25
5.00	Varon -T Disruptor	Art	R	4.00
5.00	Vash	Per	R	4.00
0.25	Vekma	Per	C	0.25
0.25	Vekor	Per	C	0.25
1.00	Vulcan Mindmeld	Int	U	0.50
6.00	Vulcan Stone of Gol	Art	R	5.00
5.00	Warp Core Breach	Ev	R	4.00
12.00	Wesley Crusher	Per	R	8.00
0.25	Where No One Has Gone Before	Ev	C	0.25
18.00	William T. Riker	Per	R	10.00
4.50	Wind Dancer	Dil	R	3.00
20.00	Worf	Per	R	12.00
0.25	Wormhole	Int	C	0.25
3.50	Wormhole Negotiations	Mis	R	3.00
0.25	Yridian Shuttle	Shp	C	0.25
0.25	Zibalian Transport	Shp	C	0.25

RARITY KEY C = Common   U = Uncommon   R = Rare   VR = Very Rare   UR = Ultra Rare   F = Foil card   X = Fixed/standard in all decks

Star Trek • Alternate Universe

Decipher • Released **November 1995**

122 cards in set • **IDENTIFIER: Black border AND © 1995**

• Booster packs contain 15 cards; booster displays contain 36 boosters

The first expansion to **Star Trek** came out a full year after the initial release. It was fully designed and printed months earlier, but disputes with Paramount kept it in the warehouse until November. Fans of the game desperate for new material bought it up.

Alternate Universe introduces Doorways, cards which perform a variety of functions and are usually played on the table during the seed phase. Also in the set are several "alternate universe" cards, cards conceptually from the future or past or from alternate timelines (as presented in the show) and that require a Doorway to play.

The most controversial element of the set was the **Future Enterprise**, the first ultra-rare in the game, which was found in one of every 121 packs. Many collectors were angered by the rarity of the card, which initially sold in singles markets for about $75 (compared to the $5 for most of the set's other rares). The shine wore off the set quickly, as it didn't offer much in terms of new gameplay and didn't do much to change the existing landscape of the game, which was dominated by fast Federation mission-solving decks.

It was originally announced that the set would be released in both a limited (black bordered) and unlimited (white bordered) release, but because the supply of the black bordered product was much greater than the demand, the white bordered product was never printed. The only exceptions are the white bordered cards from the set found in the **Warp Pack** and **Introductory Two-Player Game**. — *Jason Winter*

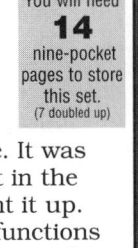

You will need **14** nine-pocket pages to store this set. (7 doubled up)

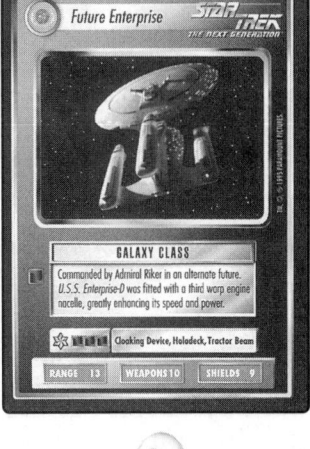

Card name	Type	Rarity	Price
Set (122 cards)			125.00
Booster Display Box			85.00
Booster Pack			2.90

Promos

Card name	Type	Rarity	Price
The Emissary	Pr		5.00
The Traveller	Pr		4.50

Card name	Type	Rarity	Price
Ajur	Per	U	1.00
Alien Labyrinth	Dil	C	0.10
Alternate Universe Door	Dwy	C	0.20
Anti-Matter Spread	Int	C	0.10
Barclay Transporter Phobia	Int	U	1.00
Baryon Buildup	Ev	C	0.10
Berlingoff Rasmussen	Per	R	4.00
Beverly Picard	Per	R	7.00
Boratus	Per	U	1.00
Brain Drain	Int	U	1.00
Brute Force	Mis	R	3.00
Captain's Log	Ev	U	1.00
Cardassian Trap	Dil	U	1.00
Coalescent Organism	Dil	R	4.00
Commander Tomalak	Per	R	4.50
Compromised Mission	Mis	R	3.00
Conundrum	Dil	C	0.10
Countermanda	Int	C	0.10
Cryosatellite	Art	R	4.00
Data's Head	Art	R	6.00
Dathon	Per	R	4.00
Dead in Bed	Int	U	1.00
Decius	Shp	R	4.00
Destroy Radioactive Garbage Scow	Int	C	0.20
Devidian Door	Dwy	R	5.00
Devidian Foragers	Int	C	0.10
Diplomatic Conference	Mis	R	3.00
D'Tan	Per	U	1.00
Echo Papa 607 Killer Drone	Equ	R	4.00
Edo Probe	Dil	U	1.00
Edo Vessel	Shp	R	4.00
Empathic Echo	Dil	C	0.10
Engage Shuttle Operations	Ev	U	1.00
Eyes in the Dark	Int	C	0.10

Card name	Type	Rarity	Price
Ferengi Attack	Dil	C	0.10
FGC-47 Research	Mis	R	3.00
Fire Sculptor	Int	C	0.10
Fissure Research	Mis	R	3.00
Frame of Mind	Dil	U	1.00
Future Enterprise	Shp	UR	60.00
Gomtuu	Shp	R	4.00
Governor Worf	Per	R	7.00
Hail	Int	C	0.10
Hidden Entrance	Dil	C	0.10
Howard Heirloom Candle	Int	C	0.10
Humuhumunu-kunukuapua'a	Int	C	0.10
Hunter Gangs	Dil	C	0.10
I.K.C. Fek'lhr	Shp	R	5.00
I.K.C. K'Ratak	Shp	C	0.20
I.P. Scanner	Equ	C	0.10
Ian Andrew Troi	Per	R	4.00
Iconian Gateway	Art	R	4.00
Incoming Message: Attack Authoriz.	Int	U	1.00
Interphasic Plasma Creatures	Dil	C	0.10
Interrogation	Ev	R	4.00
Intruder Force Field	Ev	U	1.00

Card name	Type	Rarity	Price
Isabella	Int	U	1.00
Jack Crusher	Per	R	4.00
Jamaharon	Int	C	0.10
Kevin Uxbridge: Convergence	Int	C	0.20
Klim Dokachin	Ev	U	1.00
K'mtar	Per	R	4.00
La Forge Maneuver	Int	U	1.00
Lakanta	Per	U	1.00
Latinum Payoff	Int	C	0.10
Lower Decks	Ev	U	1.00
Lt. (j.g.) Picard	Per	U	1.00
Major Rakal	Per	R	4.50
Malfunctioning Door	Dil	C	0.10
Maman Picard	Dil	U	1.00
Maques	Per	U	1.00
Mickey D.	Per	U	1.00
Montgomery Scott	Per	C	0.20
Mot's Advice	Ev	U	1.00
Neutral Outpost	Out	C	0.20
Ophidian Cane	Art	R	4.00
Outpost Raid	Dil	C	0.10
Parallel Romance	Dil	U	1.00
Particle Scattering Field	Ev	C	0.10
Paul Rice (holo re-creation)	Per	U	1.00

Card name	Type	Rarity	Price
Phaser Burns	Int	C	0.10
Punishment Zone	Dil	C	0.10
Qualor II Rendezvous	Mis	U	1.00
Quantum Singularity Lifeforms	Dil	U	1.00
Quash Conspiracy	Mis	R	3.00
Rachel Garrett	Per	R	4.50
Rascals	Dil	U	0.50
Receptacle Stones	Art	R	4.00
Rescue Captives	Int	U	1.00
Ressikan Flute	Art	R	4.00
Reunion	Mis	R	3.00
Revolving Door	Ev	R	4.00
Richard Castillo	Per	U	1.00
Risa Shore Leave	Mis	R	3.00
Rishon Uxbridge	Per	C	0.10
Romulan Ambush	Int	U	1.00
Royale Casino: Blackjack	Dil	U	1.00
Samuel Clemens' Pocketwatch	Art	R	4.00
Security Sacrifice	Int	C	0.10
Seize Wesley	Int	R	4.00
Senior Staff Meeting	Int	U	1.00
Stefan DeSeve	Per	R	4.00
Tama	Shp	U	0.80
Targ	Per	C	0.10
Tasha Yar-Alternate	Per	R	7.00
Temporal Narcosis	Ev	U	1.00
The Charybdis	Ev	U	1.00
The Gatherers	Dil	C	0.10
The Higher ... The Fewer	Dil	U	0.50
The Mask of Korgano	Ev	C	0.10
Thermal Deflectors	Ev	U	1.00
Thine Own Self	Int	C	0.10
Thought Fire	Dil	C	0.10
U.S.S. Enterprise-C	Shp	R	12.00
Vorgon Raiders	Int	R	4.00
Vulcan Nerve Pinch	Int	C	0.10
Warped Space	Mis	R	3.00
Wartime Conditions	Ev	R	4.00
Wolf	Int	U	1.00
Worshiper	Dil	C	0.10
Yellow Alert	Ev	C	0.20
Zaldan	Dil	U	1.00

Star Trek • Collector's Tin

Decipher • Released **1995**

363 cards in tins

Decipher produced a collector's tin featuring all 363 cards from **Limited** in a special, silver-bordered edition. Larger than many other CCG collector tins, the tin holds six decks in position.

The set was limited to a production run of 30,000, and a certificate bearing the number of the set can be found inside the lid. Lower numbers are presumably more valuable, and unopened tins — with the cards still in their shrinkrwrap — are more valuable than ones where the cards are loose.

Collector's Tin (unopened)	**95.00**
Collector's Tin (opened)	**55.00**

RARITY KEY C = Common   U = Uncommon   R = Rare   VR = Very Rare   UR = Ultra Rare   F = Foil card   X = Fixed/standard in all decks

Star Trek • Q-Continuum

Decipher • Released October 1996

121 cards in set • **IDENTIFIER: Black border AND © 1996**

• Booster packs contain 15 cards; booster displays contain 36 boosters

The main draw of **Q-Continuum** (featuring John deLancie's troublesome character from the series) is the two new doorways, **Q's Tent** and **Q-Flash**, which open up a variety of new and unusual strategies. **Q's Tent** serves as a sideboard of sorts, which players can access during the game, while the **Q-Flash** represents the havoc that Q could wreak on an opponent during a mission attempt.

Like **Alternate Universe**, the set came out almost a year after the last one and was delayed many times for a variety of reasons. It was somewhat back-burned because of the belief that the license would end in the near future and the success of the **Star Wars** CCG. It also lacked true "money" cards, with most rares lacking power and mainstream interest. — **Jason Winter**

You will need **14** nine-pocket pages to store this set. (7 doubled up)

Set (121 cards)	112.50
Booster Display Box	85.00
Booster Pack	3.00

Card name	Type	Rarity	Price
1			
Aldebaran Serpent	Ev	C	0.10
Amanda's Parents	Ev	C	0.10
Android Nightmares	Dil	U	1.00
Anti-Matter Pod	Eq	C	0.10
Arbiter of Succession	Int	R	4.00
Are These Truly Your Friends, Brother?	Int	C	0.10
Barber Pole	Ev	U	0.50
Bendii Syndrome	Dil	R	4.00
Blade of Tkon	Art	R	4.00
2			
Brainwash	Ev	R	4.00
Calamarain	Ev	R	4.00
Canar	Art	R	4.00
Chinese Finger Puzzle	Dil	C	0.10
Colony	St	C	0.10
Data's Body	Per	U	4.00
Data's Medals	Int	C	0.10
Discommendation	Ev	U	1.00
Door-Net	Ev	C	0.10
3			
Doppelganger	Ev	R	5.00
Dr. Q, Medicine Entity	Int	C	0.10
Drag Net	Ev	R	4.00

Card name	Type	Rarity	Price
Drought Tree	Ev	C	0.10
End Transmission	Int	C	0.10
Frigid	Ev	U	1.00
Galen	Per	R	7.00
Gibson	Per	C	0.10
Gift of the Tormentor	Int	C	0.10
4			
Go Back Whence Thou Camest	Dil	C	0.10
Guilty - Provisionally	Dil	U	1.00
Heisenberg Compensators	Ev	U	1.00
His Honor, The High Sheriff of Nottingham	Dil	U	1.00
I am not a Merry Man!	Ev	R	4.00
I.K.C. Maht-H'a	Shp	R	5.00
I.K.C. T'Ong	Shp	U	1.00
Immortal Again	Ev	U	1.00
Incoming Message - The Continuum	Int	C	0.10
5			
Into the Breach	Ev	C	0.10
Investigate Legend	Mis	R	3.00
Ira Graves	Per	R	4.00
Jealous Amanda	Ev	C	0.10
Jenice Manheim	Per	U	1.00
John Doe	Per	U	1.00
Juliana Tainer	Per	R	5.00
Kahlest	Per	U	1.00
Kareen Brianon	Per	U	1.00

Card name	Type	Rarity	Price
6			
Katherine Pulaski	Per	R	5.00
K'chiQ	Per	C	0.10
Keiko O'Brien	Per	R	5.00
Kitrik	Per	U	1.00
Klingon Civil War	Ev	R	4.00
Klingon Painstik	Int	U	1.00
K'nera	Per	U	1.00
Kova Tholl	Per	U	1.00
Lal	Per	R	5.00
7			
Lemon-Aid	Int	C	0.10
Madam Guinan	Per	R	5.00
Madred	Per	R	4.50
Mandarin Bailiff	Dil	C	0.10
Manheim's Dimensional Door	Dwy	R	5.00
Marouk	Per	U	1.00
Military Privilege	Ev	U	1.00
Mirasta Yale	Per	U	1.00
Mona Lisa	Art	R	5.00
8			
Mordock	Per	U	1.00
Mortal Q	Per	R	5.00
Mr. Homn	Per	R	5.00
Nebula	Mis	C	0.10
Nick Locarno	Per	R	5.00
Off Switch	Int	C	0.10
Parallax Arguers	Int	C	0.10
Paul Manheim	Per	R	5.00

Card name	Type	Rarity	Price
Paxan "Wormhole"	Mis	R	4.00
9			
Penalty Box	Ev	U	1.00
Plague Planet	Mis	R	4.00
Pla-Net	Dil	C	0.10
Plasmadyne Relay	Eq	C	0.10
Plexing	Int	C	0.10
Q-Flash	Dwy	C	0.10
Q's Planet	Mis	U	1.00
Q's Tent	Dwy	C	0.10
Q's Vicious Animal Things	Dil	U	1.00
10			
Rager	Per	U	1.00
Robin Lefler	Per	U	1.00
Royale Casino: Craps	Dil	U	1.00
Sakkath	Per	U	1.00
Samaritan Snare	Mis	R	4.00
Samuel Clemens	Per	U	1.00
Scottish Setter	Ev	C	0.10
Security Precautions	Dil	C	0.10
Sirol	Per	U	1.00
11			
Sonya Gomez	Per	U	1.00
Soong-Type Android	Per	C	0.10
Space	Mis	C	0.10
Subsection Q, Paragraph 10	Int	C	0.10
System-wide Cascade Failure	Dil	R	4.00
T'Pau	Shp	U	1.00
T'Shanik	Per	U	1.00
Tarchannen Study	Mis	R	4.00
Taris	Per	R	5.00
12			
Tarmin	Per	R	4.00
Telak	Per	U	1.00
Terix	Shp	R	5.00
Terraforming Station	St	R	4.00
The Higher... The Q-er	Int	C	0.10
The Issue is Patriotism	Int	U	1.00
The Naked Truth	Int	C	0.10
The Sheliak	Dil	R	5.00
Tijuana Crass	Ev	C	0.10
13			
Timicin	Per	U	1.00
Transfiguration	Ev	U	1.00
Trust Me	Ev	C	0.10
U.S.S. Stargazer	Shp	R	7.50
Ves Alkar	Per	U	1.00
Wesley Gets the Point	Int	U	1.00
Where's Guinan?	Int	U	1.00
Wrong Door	Int	U	1.00
You Will in Time	Ev	C	0.10
14			
Yuta	Dil	R	5.00
Zalkonian Storage Capsule	Ev	R	4.00
Zalkonian Vessel	Shp	C	0.10
Zon	Per	R	4.00

Star Trek • Introductory Two-Player Game

Decipher • Released December 1996

• **Klingon** and **Federation** editions

Originally announced for release and printed in 1995, this set was delayed by the disputes between Decipher and Paramount in 1995 and 1996. When the go-ahead was finally given to distribute it, demand for the product had waned to almost nil.

To combat this, six premium cards — three Klingon and three Federation — were added the set. The three Klingon cards are found only in the Klingon edition, and the three Federation cards are found only in the Federation edition. To this, Decipher added surplus **Data Laughing** cards left over from the Brady Games Strategy Guide offer. The set also included the premium **Spock** card, which had been promised since the set's initial mention in 1995.

And then there's the actual decks. Since the two decks themselves (one Federation and one Klingon) consisted of entirely common cards, the set offered little else of value, though one would be remiss not to mention the Sample Game booklet (penned by yours truly) also included in the boxed set. — **Jason Winter**

		Card name	Price	Card name	Price
Klingon Edition	**25.00**	Admiral McCoy	6.00	Gi'ral	5.00
		Admiral Picard	7.50	Ja'rod	5.00
Federation Edition	**25.00**	Commander Data	8.00	Mogh	5.00
		Commander Troi	6.00	Spock	10.00
		Data Laughing	10.00		

RARITY KEY C = Common U = Uncommon R = Rare VR = Very Rare UR = Ultra Rare F = Foil card X = Fixed/standard in all decks

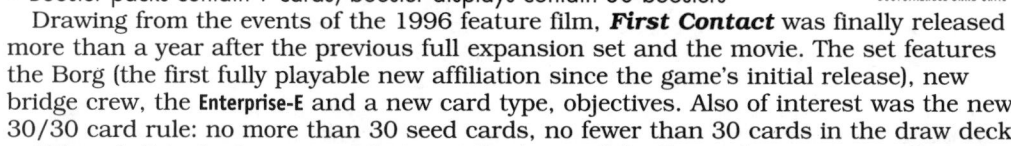
Decipher • Released **December 1997**

130 cards in set • **IDENTIFIER: 1997; movie logo; small Cube icon**

• Booster packs contain 9 cards; booster displays contain 30 boosters

Drawing from the events of the 1996 feature film, **First Contact** was finally released more than a year after the previous full expansion set and the movie. The set features the Borg (the first fully playable new affiliation since the game's initial release), new bridge crew, the **Enterprise-E** and a new card type, objectives. Also of interest was the new 30/30 card rule: no more than 30 seed cards, no fewer than 30 cards in the draw deck.

Although it took players a while to get the hang of the Borg, players eventually realized their power, specifically their ability to get around many dilemmas with ease. **First Contact** had a number of powerful cards: **Visit Cochrane Memorial**, **Assign Mission Specialists**, and **Patrol Neutral Zone** were all released for the first time in First Contact. Although nothing appeared specifically for the Romulans, many players agreed that *First Contact* was the best set yet for them.

First Contact was later repackaged in an **Enhanced First Contact** set, adding three cards not available earlier. — *Fritz Meissner*

You will need **15** nine-pocket pages to store this set. (8 doubled up)

Set (130 cards)	150.00
Booster Display Box	60.00
Booster Pack	2.50

Card name	Type	Rarity	Price
A Change of Plans	Int	C	0.25
Abandon Mission	Ev	R	3.00
Activate Subcommands	Ev	C	0.25
Adapt: Modulate Shields	Int	U	0.50
Adapt: Negate Obstruction	Int	C	0.15
Admiral Hayes	Per	R	4.00
Alas, Poor Queen	Int	R	4.00
Alyssa Ogawa	Per	R	4.00
Android Headlock	Int	R	3.00
Antique Machine Gun	Art	R	4.00
Assign Mission Specialists	Obj	C	0.25
Assimilate Counterpart	Obj	U	0.50
Assimilate Homeworld	Obj	R	4.00
Assimilate Planet	Obj	C	0.25
Assimilate Starship	Obj	U	0.60
Assimilate This!	Int	R	3.50
Assimilation Table	Equ	U	0.50
Assimilation Tubules	Int	U	0.50
Awaken	Int	C	0.15
Balancing Act	Dil	U	0.50
Beverly Crusher	Per	R	6.00
Blended	Dil	U	0.50
Borg Cube	Shp	U	0.50
Borg Kiss	Int	R	4.00
Borg Neuroprocessor	Int	R	3.50
Borg Outpost	O/P	C	0.25
Borg Queen	Per	R	12.00
Borg Scout Vessel	Shp	C	0.25
Borg Servo	Dil	U	0.50
Borg Sphere	Shp	C	0.25
Build Interplexing Beacon	Obj	R	4.00
Data	Per	R	9.00
Deactivation	Int	C	0.25
Dead End	Dil	U	0.80
Deanna Troi	Per	R	7.00
Disengage Safety Protocols	Ev	U	0.50
Don't Call Me Ahab	Dil	U	0.50
Dr. Royse	Per	C	0.15
E.M.H. Program	Per	U	0.80
Eight of Nineteen	Per	C	0.25
Eighteen of Nineteen	Per	C	0.25
Eleven of Nineteen	Per	C	0.25
Eliminate Starship	Obj	U	0.50
Espionage Mission	Mis	R	4.00

Card name	Type	Rarity	Price
Establish Gateway	Obj	C	0.25
Fifteen of Seventeen	Per	C	0.25
Five of Eleven	Per	C	0.25
Four of Eleven	Per	C	0.25
Fractal Encryption Code	Int	U	0.50
Geordi La Forge	Per	R	8.00
Hawk	Per	U	0.80
He Will Make an Excellent Drone	Int	U	0.50
I'm a Doctor, Not a Doorstop	Int	U	0.80
Inge Eiger	Per	C	0.25
Intermix Ratio	Ev	U	0.50
Jean-Luc Picard	Per	R	15.00
Joseph Travis	Per	C	0.15
Kathleen Tonell	Per	U	0.50
Lack of Preparation	Dil	C	0.25
Launch Portal	Dwy	U	0.50
Lightner	Per	U	0.50
Lily Sloane	Per	R	4.00
Lisa Azar	Per	U	0.50
Magic Carpet Ride OCD	Art	R	4.00
Maglock	Dil	C	0.15
Mercy Kill	Int	U	0.50
Mirror Image	Ev	U	0.80
Mission Debriefing	Ev	U	0.50
Montana Missile Complex	T-Loc	R	4.00
My First Raygun	Dil	R	3.00
Nine of Eleven	Per	C	0.25
Nine of Seventeen	Per	C	0.25
Obarakeh	Per	C	0.15
Ocular Implants	Ev	R	4.00
One of Eleven	Per	C	0.25
Ooby Dooby	Dil	R	4.00
Patrol Neutral Zone	Mis	U	0.50
Paul Porter	Per	R	4.00
Phoenix	Shp	R	5.00
Planet	Mis	C	0.15
Prepare Assault Teams	Obj	U	0.50
Primitive Culture	Dil	R	3.50
Queen's Borg Cube	Shp	R	10.00
Queen's Borg Sphere	Shp	R	8.00
Ready Room Door	Dwy	U	0.50
Regenerate	Ev	R	4.00
Reginald Barclay	Per	R	4.00
Remodulation	Int	U	0.50
Retask	Ev	R	4.00
Richard Wilkins	Per	C	0.15
Salvage Starship	Obj	R	4.00
Scorched Hand	Int	U	0.80

Card name	Type	Rarity	Price
Scout Encounter	Dil	R	4.00
Sense the Borg	Int	U	0.50
Sevek	Per	U	0.50
Shipwreck	Int	R	4.00
Shot in the Back	Dil	C	0.25
Six of Eleven	Per	C	0.25
Six of Seventeen	Per	C	0.25
Sixteen of Nineteen	Per	C	0.25
Solkar	Per	R	4.00
Starfleet Type III Phaser Rifle	Equ	U	0.50
Stop First Contact	Obj	R	4.00
Strict Dress Code	Dil	R	3.00
Temporal Vortex	Dwy	U	0.50
Temporal Wake	Int	R	4.00
Ten of Nineteen	Per	C	0.25
The Line Must Be Drawn Here	Ev	C	0.15
Theta-Radiation Poisoning	Dil	R	4.00
Thirteen of Nineteen	Per	C	0.25

Card name	Type	Rarity	Price
Thomas McClure	Per	U	0.50
Three of Nineteen	Per	C	0.25
Three-Dimensional Thinking	Int	R	3.00
Tommygun	Equ	U	0.50
Transwarp Network Gateway	Dwy	C	0.15
T'Shonra	Per	U	0.50
Two of Eleven	Per	C	0.25
Two of Nineteen	Per	C	0.25
Two of Seventeen	Per	C	0.25
U.S.S. Bozeman	Shp	U	1.00
U.S.S. Enterprise-E	Shp	R	15.50
Undetected Beam-In	Dil	R	4.00
Visit Cochrane Memorial	Obj	R	4.00
Vulcan Lander	Shp	U	0.60
Wall of Ships	Ev	R	3.50
Weak Spot	Int	R	4.00
William T. Riker	Per	R	10.50
Worf	Per	R	8.50
Zefram Cochrane	Per	R	5.00
Zefram Cochrane's Telescope	Art	R	4.00

Star Trek • First Anthology

Decipher • Released **April 1997**

A "filler" set released between **Q-Continuum** and **First Contact**, **First Anthology** repackaged two **Unlimited** starter decks; two booster packs each of **Unlimited**, **Alternate Universe**, and *Q-Continuum*; a **Warp Pack**; six preview cards from **Deep Space 9** and *Voyager*; and a rules supplement containing the *Alternate Universe* and *Q-Continuum* rules. The collection was packaged in an 800-card longbox.

Like the *Warp Pack*, the six new cards were seen as a bonus for players waiting for *First Contact* and many bought the set simply to get those cards. — *Jason Winter*

First Anthology (sealed)	40.00

Card name	Price
Dr. Telek R'Mor	5.00
Ensign Tuvok	6.00
Garak	6.00

Card name	Price
Orb of Prophecy & Change	5.00
Quark Son of Keldar	7.00
Thomas Paris	7.00

Star Trek • Deep Space Nine

Decipher • Released **July 1998**

277 cards in set • IDENTIFIER: © 1998; small sphere icon

You will need **31** nine-pocket pages to store this set. (16 doubled up)

- Starter decks contain 60 cards; starter displays contain 12 starters
- Booster packs contain 9 cards; booster displays contain 30 boosters

    Deep Space Nine brought the first starter decks since **Unlimited,** decks collated so that each had six missions and an outpost (making them fully playable). *DS9* was a double expansion with 276 cards plus a "twice as rare" super-rare, the white-bordered **USS Defiant.** Also included were 16 common missions only found in the starter decks.

    The set features cards from the first three years of the *DS9* TV show, including **Deep Space Nine, Terok Nor,** the **Chamber of Ministers,** and **Central Command,** and introduces two new affiliations, Cardassian and Bajoran. The Gamma Quadrant, too, appeared, leading up to the Dominion invasion in the game's next set.

    Several major rules changes were introduced with the set. Missions were no longer included in the 30-card limit for seed decks, and facilities were introduced as the general card type for all outposts, stations, and now headquarters.

    DS9 had a profound impact on the metagame. The new affiliations were all playable and competitive at tournament level. Cardassian Ore Processing decks came to the fore, and Bajoran battle decks using **Bajoran Interceptors** and **Rinnak Pire,** the "universal captain," could play extremely fast. Battle wasn't all the Bajorans were good for, with **HQ: Return Orb to Bajor** forming the backbone of many fast mission solvers. One Bajoran deck, which combined **Soong-Type Androids** and **Q-Bypass** won the 1998 World Championships. The time between *DS9* and **The Dominion**'s release was also the height of mission stealing decks, with **Plans of the Obsidian Order** and **Plans of the Tal Shiar** making espionage cards more than just binder-fodder. Other key decks to appear include the Borg Swarm archetype which ran multiples of seeded **Computer Crash** to slow other decks and scouted opponents' missions to complete **Establish Gateway** objectives. — *Fritz Meissner*

Set (277 cards)			180.00
Starter Display Box			96.00
Booster Display Box			68.00
Starter Deck			9.80
Booster Pack			2.50

Card name	Type	Rarity	Price
☐ Aamin Marritza	Per	R	4.00
☐ Access Relay Station	Mis	R	4.00
☐ Acquire Illicit Explosives	Mis	C	0.15
☐ Activate Tractor Beam	Int	C	0.10
☐ Aid Fugitives	Mis	R	4.00
☐ Airlock	Dwy	R	4.00
☐ Aldara	Shp	R	5.00
☐ Alien Gambling Device	Art	R	4.00
☐ Alter Records	Mis	U	0.50
☐ Altonian Brain Teaser	Dil	U	0.50
☐ Altovar	Per	R	4.00
☐ Amaros	Per	C	0.10
☐ Anara	Per	C	0.10
☐ Angry Mob	Dil	C	0.10

Card name	Type	Rarity	Price
☐ Aphasia Device	Dil	C	0.10
☐ Ari	Per	C	0.10
☐ Arms Deal	Dil	U	0.50
☐ Assassin's Blade	Dil	C	0.15
☐ Assault Vessel	Shp	C	0.10
☐ Automated Security System	Ev	R	4.00

Card name	Type	Rarity	Price
☐ Bajoran Civil War	Ev	R	4.00
☐ Bajoran Freighter	Shp	C	0.10
☐ Bajoran Interceptor	Shp	U	0.50
☐ Bajoran Outpost	Out	C	0.10
☐ Bajoran PADD	Eq	C	0.10
☐ Bajoran Phaser	Eq	C	0.10
☐ Bajoran Phaser Rifle	Eq	U	0.50

Card name	Type	Rarity	Price
☐ Bajoran Scout Vessel	Shp	U	0.50
☐ Bajoran Wormhole	Dwy	U	0.50
☐ Bareil Antos	Per	R	4.00
☐ Baseball	Int	R	5.00
☐ Benjamin Sisko	Per	R	14.00
☐ Beware of Q	Obj	C	0.10
☐ Boheeka	Per	R	4.00
☐ Borad	Per	R	4.00
☐ Bo'rak	Per	R	4.00
☐ Brief Romance	Dil	C	0.10
☐ Camping Trip	Mis	R	4.00
☐ Cardassian Disruptor	Eq	C	0.10
☐ Cardassian Disruptor Rifle	Eq	U	0.50
☐ Cardassian Outpost	Out	C	0.10
☐ Cardassian PADD	Eq	C	0.10
☐ Cardassian Shuttle	Shp	C	0.10
☐ Central Command	Hdq	R	4.00
☐ Cha'Joh	Shp	R	4.00
☐ Chamber of Ministers	Hdq	R	4.00
☐ Changeling Research	Mis	R	3.00
☐ Characterize Neutrino Emissions	Mis	C	0.15
☐ Clan People	Dil	C	0.10
☐ Colonel Day	Per	R	4.00
☐ Colony Preparations	Mis	U	0.50
☐ Commander's Office	Site	U	0.50
☐ Common Thief	Dil	C	0.10
☐ Computer Crash	Ev	U	0.50
☐ Coutu	Per	C	0.10
☐ Cure Blight	Mis	R	3.00
☐ Dakol	Per	C	0.15
☐ Dal'Rok	Dil	U	0.50
☐ Danar	Per	R	4.00
☐ Deep Space 9/Terok Nor	St	R	15.00
☐ Defiant Dedication Plaque	Ev	R	4.00
☐ Deliver Supplies	Mis	C	0.15
☐ Derell	Per	C	0.10
☐ D'Ghor	Per	R	4.00
☐ DNA Clues	Dil	R	3.00
☐ Docking Pads	Site	U	0.50

Star Trek • The Fajo Collection

Decipher • Released **July 1997**

    The Fajo Collection, a controversial premium set of 18 cards, was presented in the form of something one might receive from the Franklin Mint, complete with special binder and hardcover case. All of the frills, from a numbering system for each set, certificate of authenticity signed by members of the design team, to bubble gum (included with the **Roger Maris 1962 Baseball Card** card), were there.

    The cards were powerful and highly sought after simply for their names, such as **Locutus,** the long-anticipated **Guinan,** and the great collector **Kivas Fajo** himself. Each had a special element, from the bubble gum to pictures that went outside the boundary of the card; from a combination interrupt/event to a card that glowed in the dark (a printing process that was more of a headache for Decipher than anticipated).

    The set was originally announced at $80, to be sold directly by Decipher. Although a significant backlash against the product was expected from both consumers and retailers, the furor was not as great as anticipated, as most players were willing to shell out the money (and, especially in the case of overseas customers, pay significant shipping costs) — at least this one time. — *Jason Winter*

Fajo Collection	110.00

Card name	Price	Card name	Price
☐ 1962 Roger Maris Baseball Card	10.00	☐ Lore	21.00
☐ Black Hole	11.50	☐ Miles O'Brien	15.00
☐ Dixon Hill's Business Card	12.00	☐ Persistence of Memory	7.00
☐ DNA Metamorphosis	9.00	☐ Picard's Artificial Heart	8.00
☐ Dr. Soong	12.50	☐ Qapla'!	9.50
☐ Guinan	15.00	☐ Sisters of Duras	13.50
☐ I.K.C. Chang	10.00	☐ Spot	11.00
☐ Kivas Fajo	12.00	☐ Tallera	9.00
☐ Locutus of Borg	30.00	☐ U.S.S. Pasteur	13.00

RARITY KEY	**C** = Common **U** = Uncommon **R** = Rare **VR** = Very Rare **UR** = Ultra Rare **F** = Foil card **X** = Fixed/standard in all decks

426 • *SCRYE Collectible Card Game Checklist and Price Guide*

Card name	Type	Rarity	Price
Docking Ports	Site	C	0.10
Docking Procedures	Int	C	0.10
Docking Pylons	Site	U	0.50
Dr. Nydom	Per	C	0.10
Dropping In	Int	U	0.50
Dukat	Per	R	8.00
Duonetic Field Generator	Dil	U	0.50
Duranja	Ev	R	4.00
Elim Garak	Per	R	7.00
Eliminate Virus	Mis	C	0.15
Enabran Tain	Per	R	4.00
Engineering Tricorder	Eq	C	0.10
Entek	Per	R	4.00
Espionage: Bajoran on Cardassian	Ev	U	0.50
Espionage: Cardassian on Bajoran	Ev	U	0.50
Espionage: Cardassian on Federation	Ev	U	0.50
Espionage: Cardassian on Klingon	Ev	U	0.50
Espionage: Romulan on Bajoran	Ev	U	0.50
Espionage: Romulan on Cardassian	Ev	U	0.50
Establish Landing Protocols	Ev	C	0.10
Establish Station	Mis	C	0.15
Establish Tractor Lock	Obj	R	4.00
E'Tyshra	Per	U	0.50
Explore Gamma Quadrant	Obj	U	0.50
Extradition	Dil	U	0.50
Extraordinary Methods	Int	U	0.50
Fightin' Words	Dil	U	0.50
File Mission Report	Obj	U	0.50
Flaxian Assassin	Dil	U	0.50
Flaxian Scout Vessel	Shp	C	0.15
Framed for Murder	Dil	U	0.50
Galor	Shp	C	0.15
Garak Has Some Issues	Dil	R	4.00
Garak's Tailor Shop	Site	R	4.00
Garanian Bolites	Dil	C	0.10
General Krim	Per	R	4.00
Ghoren	Per	C	0.10
Gilora Rejal	Per	R	4.00
Going to the Top	Int	R	4.00
Graham Davis	Per	C	0.10
Grilka	Per	R	4.00
Groumall	Shp	R	4.00
Guest Quarters	Site	U	0.50
Harvester Virus	Dil	R	4.00
Hate Crime	Dil	U	0.50
Hidden Fighter	Int	U	0.50
Hogue	Per	U	0.50
HQ: Defensive Measures	Obj	U	0.50
HQ: Return Orb to Bajor	Obj	R	4.00
HQ: Secure Homeworld	Obj	U	0.50
HQ: War Room	Ev	U	0.50
Hypospray	Eq	U	0.50
I.K.C. Toh'Kaht	Shp	R	5.00
I Tried to Warn You	Dil	U	0.50
Incoming Message: Bajoran	Int	U	0.50
Incoming Message: Cardassian	Int	U	0.50
Infirmary	Site	U	0.50
Intercept Maquis	Mis	C	0.15
Intercept Renegade	Mis	C	0.15
Investigate Rumors	Mis	R	4.00
Isolinear Puzzle	Dil	C	0.10
Jabara	Per	U	0.50
Jace Michaels	Per	C	0.10
Jadzia Dax	Per	R	14.50

Card name	Type	Rarity	Price
Jaheel	Per	C	0.10
Jake and Nog	Per	R	10.00
Jaro Essa	Per	R	4.00
Jasad	Per	U	0.50
Julian Bashir	Per	R	11.50
Jural	Per	C	0.10
Kai Opaka	Per	R	5.00
Kalita	Per	C	0.10
Kallis Ven	Per	C	0.10
Karen Loews	Per	C	0.10
Karina	Per	R	4.00
Kidnappers	Dil	C	0.10
Kira Nerys	Per	R	10.00
Klaestron Outpost	Out	C	0.10
Korinas	Per	R	4.00
Kotran Pa'Dar	Per	U	0.50
Kovat	Per	R	4.00
Kressari Rendezvous	Mis	C	0.15
Lenaris Holem	Per	R	4.00
Lethean Telepathic Attack	Dil	U	0.50
Li Nalas	Per	R	4.00
Lockbox	Dil	C	0.10
Lojal	Per	C	0.10
Magnetic North	Int	U	0.50
Makbar	Per	R	4.00
Martus Mazur	Per	R	4.00
Medical PADD	Eq	U	0.50
Military Freighter	Shp	U	0.50
Minister Rozahn	Per	C	0.10
Miradorn Raider	Shp	U	0.50
Misguided Activist	Dil	C	0.10
Mora Pol	Per	R	4.00
Morka	Per	R	4.00
Mysterious Orb	Art	R	4.00
Nalan Bal	Per	C	0.10
Natima Lang	Per	R	4.00
Navigate Plasma Storms	Obj	U	0.50
Neela	Per	R	4.00
No Loose Ends	Dil	R	3.00
None Shall Pass	Dil	C	0.10
Nor	St	C	0.10
Odo	Per	R	15.00
Odo's Cousin	Dil	U	0.50
Oof!	Int	U	0.50
Ops	Site	C	0.10
Orb Experience	Int	U	0.50
Orb Fragment	Art	R	4.00
Orb Negotiations	Mis	U	0.50
Ore Processing Unit	Site	U	0.50
Orren Ran	Per	C	0.10
Pallra	Per	R	4.00
Parn	Per	C	0.10
Paxton Reese	Per	C	0.10
Perak	Per	C	0.10
Plain, Simple Garak	Per	R	7.00
Plans of the Obsidian Order	Obj	R	4.00
Plans of the Tal Shiar	Obj	R	4.00
Prakesh	Shp	R	4.00
Preparation	Int	U	0.50
Process Ore	Obj	U	0.50
Promenade Shops	Site	U	0.50
Protouniverse	Int	R	4.00
Prylar Mond	Per	C	0.10
Punishment Box	Dil	U	0.50
Pup	Dil	R	4.00
Rano Dake	Per	C	0.10
Rase Norvan	Per	C	0.10
Rax'Na	Per	C	0.10
Razka Karn	Per	R	4.00
Reaction Control Thrusters	Ev	C	0.10
Reclamation	Int	C	0.10

Card name	Type	Rarity	Price
Recruit Mercenaries	Ev	R	4.00
Refuse Immigration	Mis	C	0.15
Reignite Dead Star	Mis	C	0.15
Rekelen	Per	C	0.10
Relocate Settlers	Mis	C	0.25
Renewal Scroll	Ev	U	0.50
Rescue Personnel	Obj	R	4.00
Rescue Prisoners	Mis	C	0.25
Retaya	Per	R	3.00
Rhetorical Question	Dil	U	0.50
Rigelian Freighter	Shp	C	0.10
Rinnak Pire	Per	C	0.10
Rionoj	Per	C	0.15
Risky Business	Dil	U	0.50
Ruwon	Per	R	4.00
Sakonna	Per	R	4.00
Saltah'na Clock	Art	R	4.00
Science Kit	Eq	C	0.15
Science Lab	Site	U	0.50
Science PADD	Eq	U	0.50
Search and Rescue	Mis	C	0.15
Search for Survivors	Mis	C	0.15
Secret Compartment	Dwy	R	4.00
Security Office	Site	U	0.50
Seismic Quake	Dil	R	4.00
Selveth	Per	R	4.00
Shakaar Edon	Per	R	5.00
Sharat	Per	U	0.50
Skullduggery	Dil	C	0.10
Smoke Bomb	Int	U	0.50
Sorus	Per	R	4.00
Study Badlands	Mis	U	0.50
Study Plasma Storm	Mis	C	0.15
Subspace Seaweed	Dil	U	0.50
Surmak Ren	Per	R	4.00
Survey Star System	Mis	U	0.50
Symbiont Diagnosis	Mis	R	4.00
System 5 Disruptors	Ev	R	4.00
Tahna Los	Per	R	4.00
Taylor Moore	Per	C	0.10

Card name	Type	Rarity	Price
Tekeny Ghemor	Per	R	4.00
The Three Vipers	Dil	R	4.00
The Walls Have Ears	Int	R	4.00
Time to Reconsider	Int	U	2.00
T'Kar	Per	U	0.50
T'Lor	Per	C	0.10
Tora Ziyal	Per	R	4.00
Toran	Per	R	4.00
Trauma	Dil	R	4.00
Trazko	Per	U	1.80
Treaty: Bajoran/Klingon	Ev	U	0.50
Treaty: Federation/Bajoran	Ev	C	0.10
Treaty: Federation/Cardassian	Ev	C	0.10
Treaty: Romulan/Cardassian	Ev	U	0.50
Turrel	Per	R	3.50
Ty Kajada	Per	C	1.60
U.S.S. Danube	Shp	C	0.10
U.S.S. Defiant		UR	32.50
U.S.S. Yangtzee Kiang	Shp	R	6.00
Ulani Belor	Per	C	0.10
Unnatural Causes	Int	U	0.50
Untrustworthy Associate	Dil	U	0.50
Vakis	Per	R	4.00
Vantika's Neural Pathways	Dil	C	0.10
Varis Sul	Per	U	0.50
Vedek Sorad	Per	C	0.10
Vedek Winn	Per	R	5.00
Vendetta	Dil	C	0.10
Verify Evidence	Mis	C	0.15
Vole Infestation	Dil	C	0.10
Weapons Locker	Ev	C	0.10
Weld Ram	Per	C	0.10
Wormhole Navigation Schematic	Int	U	0.50
Xepolite Freighter	Shp	C	0.10
Yeto	Per	R	4.00
Zef'No	Per	R	4.00

RARITY KEY C = Common U = Uncommon R = Rare VR = Very Rare UR = Ultra Rare F = Foil card X = Fixed/standard in all decks

Star Trek • The Dominion

Decipher • Released **December 1998**

134 cards in set • **IDENTIFIER:** © 1998; small gridlike icon

• Booster packs contain 9 cards; booster displays contain 30 boosters

The fifth full expansion set for **Star Trek**, **The Dominion** consists of 130 cards plus four white-bordered previews: **Admiral Riker**, **Worf Son of Mogh**, **Seven of Nine**, and **Captain Kirk**.

The set introduces the seventh new affiliation, the Dominion. As in the TV show, Dominion personnel are divided into three major tiers: Founders, Vorta, and Jem'Hadar. Each tier lacks certain skills which the other two offset. Also introduced are infiltration mechanics for the Founders. **Empok Nor**, which could be commandeered during the game by either player, allowed races other than the Cardassians and Bajorans to use the Nor mechanics introduced in the **Deep Space Nine** set.

Although *The Dominion* had an undeniable impact on the metagame, it wasn't the new affiliation which turned heads. In theory, the Dominion was supposed to gain an edge through battle. In practice, the Klingons were better at battle. For mission solving, too, they lacked depth in key dilemma-overcoming skills. The best Dominion decks of the time kept the Jem'Hadar safely solving missions in the Gamma Quadrant while stalling opponents in the Gamma Quadrant with **Black Hole** (from **Fajo Collection**) and **Rogue Borg Mercenaries** (from **Limited/Unlimited**). The key cards of the set, as far as the older affiliations were concerned, were the headquarters for Federation, Romulan and Klingon affiliations. Also of importance were the new counters in the set: **Operate Wormhole Relays**, which hurt the prevalent Field Trip strategy and **Fair Play**, to limit the options of mission-stealing decks. — **Fritz Meissner**

Set (134 cards)			107.50
Booster Display Box			67.50
Booster Pack			2.50

Card name	Type	Rarity	Price
10 and 01	Per	R	4.00
Admiral Leyton	Per	R	3.50
Admiral Riker	Per	UR	25.00
Amat'igan	Per	R	4.00
Anya	Per	U	0.80
Arak'Taral	Per	U	0.80
Archanis Dispute	Mis	U	0.80
Atul	Per	U	0.80
Azet'izan	Per	C	0.10
Berserk Changeling	Dil	U	0.80
Betazed Invasion	Mis	R	3.50
Bioweapon Ruse	Mis	U	0.80
Borath	Per	R	4.00
Captain Kirk	Per	UR	40.00
Caught Red-Handed	Int	C	0.10
Chula: Pick One to Save Two	Dil	U	0.80
Chula: The Chandra	Dil	R	3.30
Chula: The Dice	Dil	C	0.10
Ch'Pok	Per	R	4.00
Construct Depot	Mis	C	0.10
Crew Reassignment	Ev	U	0.80
Crisis	Dil	C	0.10
Croden's Key	Art	R	4.50
Damar	Per	R	5.00
Daro	Per	U	0.80
D'deridex Advanced	Shp	R	5.00
Dejar	Per	U	0.80
Dominion PADD	Equ	C	0.10
Empok Nor	Site	R	5.50

Card name	Type	Rarity	Price
Engage Cloak	Obj	U	0.80
Eris	Per	C	0.10
Espionage: Dominion on Federation	Ev	C	0.10
Espionage: Dominion on Klingon	Ev	C	0.10
Espionage: Dominion on Romulan	Ev	C	0.10
Establish Dominion Foothold	Obj	U	0.80
Fair Play	Ev	U	0.80
Flight of the Intruder	Int	U	0.80
Founder	Per	U	0.80
Founder Leader	Per	R	5.00
Founder Secret	Dil	R	4.00
Friendly Fire	Dil	C	0.10
Garak	Per	R	5.50
General Hazar	Per	C	0.10
Goran'Agar	Per	R	4.00
Gurat'urak	Per	C	0.20
I.K.C. Rotarran	Shp	R	5.00
In the Bag	Int	C	0.10
Install Autonomic Systems Parasite	Obj	U	0.80
Intelligence Operation	Mis	U	0.80
Invasive Beam-In	Ev	C	0.10

Card name	Type	Rarity	Price
Investigate Coup	Mis	U	0.80
Issue Secret Orders	Obj	R	4.30
Jaresh-Inyo	Per	R	4.00
Jem'Hadar Attack Ship	Shp	C	0.10
Jem'Hadar Birthing Chamber	Equ	C	0.10
Jem'Hadar Disruptor	Equ	C	0.10
Jem'Hadar Disruptor Rifle	Equ	U	0.80
Jem'Hadar Sacrifice	Int	C	0.10
Jem'Hadar Warship	Shp	U	0.80
Kai Winn	Per	R	5.00
Keevan	Per	R	4.00
Keeve Falor	Per	C	0.10
Keldon Advanced	Shp	R	5.00
Keogh	Per	R	4.00
Ketracel-White	Equ	C	0.10
Kilana	Per	R	4.00
Kira Founder	Per	R	5.00
Koret'alak	Per	C	0.10
Leyton Founder	Per	R	5.00
Limara'Son	Per	C	0.10
Lovok	Per	R	4.00
Lovok Founder	Per	R	4.80
Macet	Per	U	0.80
Makla'Gor	Per	C	0.10
Martok	Per	R	5.00
Martok Founder	Per	R	5.00
Meso'Clan	Per	U	0.80
Michael Eddington	Per	R	4.30
Mining Survey	Mis	U	0.80
Mission Fatigue	Dil	U	0.80
Navigational Hazards	Dil	C	0.10
O'Brien Founder	Per	R	5.00
Office of the President	Site	R	4.00
Office of the Proconsul	Site	R	4.00
Omet'iklan	Per	R	4.00
Operate Wormhole Relays	Obj	U	0.80
Orb of Prophecy and Change	Art	R	4.00
Ornithar	Per	C	0.10
Orta	Per	U	0.80
Post Garrison	Obj	U	0.80
Primary Supply Depot	Site	C	0.10

Card name	Type	Rarity	Price
Protect Shipment	Mis	U	0.80
Quest for the Sword	Mis	U	0.80
Remata'Klan	Per	R	4.00
Remote Supply Depot	Site	C	0.10
Rescue Founder	Mis	U	0.80
Salia	Per	R	4.00
Security Briefing	Mis	U	0.80
Senator Vreenak	Per	R	4.00
Seven of Nine	Per	UR	35.00
Shape-Shift	Int	U	0.80
Silaran Prin	Per	U	0.80
Sisko 197 Subroutine	Ev	U	0.80
Sleeper Trap	Dil	R	4.00
Soto	Per	U	0.80
Strike Three	Int	C	0.10
Subjugate Planet	Obj	C	0.10
Surprise Assault	Dil	C	0.10
Tactical Console	Ev	U	0.80
Talak'talan	Per	R	4.00
Telle	Per	C	0.10
Temo'Zuma	Per	C	0.10
The Earring of Li Nalas	Art	R	4.50
The Great Hall	Site	R	4.00
The Great Link	Site	R	4.50
Toman'torax	Per	R	4.00
Trager	Shp	R	4.00
Treaty: Bajoran/Dominion	Ev	C	0.10
Treaty: Cardassian/Dominion	Ev	C	0.10
Treaty: Romulan/Dominion	Ev	C	0.10
T'Rul	Per	U	0.80
U.S.S. Defiant	Shp	R	15.00
U.S.S. Odyssey	Shp	U	0.80
U.S.S. Rio Grande	Shp	R	5.00
Uncover DNA Clues	Mis	U	0.80
Virak'kara	Per	C	0.10
Weyoun	Per	R	5.00
Worf, Son of Mogh	Per	UR	21.00
Yak'Talon	Per	C	0.10
Yelgren	Per	R	4.00
You Dirty Rat	Int	U	0.80
Young Jem'Hadar	Per	C	0.10
Zayra	Per	R	4.00
Zyree	Per	C	0.10

Star Trek • Enhanced First Contact

Decipher • Released **January 1999**

Enhanced First Contact provides a much-needed update for the Borg. Premium cards, geared towards a faster, meaner Borg, come packaged with four *First Contact* expansion packs. The premiums include four new counterparts, one each for Romulan, Klingon, Cardassian, and Bajoran affiliations as well as powerful speed cards **We Are the Borg** and **Service the Collective**.

Although there was pre-release criticism of the peculiar distribution of the new cards, players quieted as they realized the power of the new cards. While perhaps not as successful as the *First Contact* release, *Enhanced* was a quality product. — **Fritz Meissner**

"Enhanced" Deck		14.25
Add Distinctiveness		4.50
Gowron of Borg		5.00
We Are The Borg		5.00

RARITY KEY **C** = Common **U** = Uncommon **R** = Rare **VR** = Very Rare **UR** = Ultra Rare **F** = Foil card **X** = Fixed/standard in all decks

Card image caption: Young Jem'Hadar — STAR TREK DEEP SPACE NINE — CIVILIAN — Jem'Hadar youth. Typical juvenile recently emerged from birthing chamber. ❖ At end of any of your turns, may be exchanged with one of your ❖ Jem'Hadar in hand. ❂ Youth — INTEGRITY 4 CUNNING 5 STRENGTH 7

Star Trek • *Blaze of Glory*

Decipher • Released **August 1999**

130 cards in set • **IDENTIFIER: Small sword icon**

• Booster packs contain 9 cards; booster displays contain 30 boosters

The long awaited battle expansion, which Decipher had been hinting at for a number of years, was finally released in August 1999. New ship battle rules, to go with the new personnel battle rules from *First Contact* are the main feature of *Blaze of Glory*. A surprise for collectors, 18 foil cards, are inserted at random into booster packs.

The method of updating battle was a new side deck, the Battle Bridge side deck, along with Tactics, a new card type that could only be stocked in this side deck. Although players initially complained at the addition of more complicated rules, most soon realized that the change was for the better, especially as players could still battle the "old" way, without tactics.

Useful new personnel and ships, and the possibility for extremely dangerous dilemma combinations, added new vigor into the game. The metagame settled heavily into the favor of battle decks, with Patrol Neutral Zone and Borg Swarm decks taking hits from new counters. Federation Visit Cochrane Memorial, Klingon Armada, and Patrol Neutral Zone decks were the top choices of the day. — *Fritz Meissner*

You will need **15** nine-pocket pages to store this set. (8 doubled up)

Set (130 cards)		**127.50**
Booster Display Box		**57.60**
Booster Pack		**2.50**

Foil cards

	Rarity	Price
Borg Cutting Beam	VRF	5.00
Elim	URF	25.00
Fajo's Gallery	VRF	4.50
Goraxus	VRF	8.00
I.K.C. Negh'Var	VRF	8.00
Inside Operation	VRF	5.00
Jadzia Dax	URF	30.00
Kang	VRF	6.00
Koloth	VRF	7.00
Kor	SRF	10.00
Kraxon	VRF	6.50
La Forge Impersonator	SRF	14.00
Locutus' Borg Cube	URF	35.00
Maximum Firepower	SRF	10.00
Odo Founder	SRF	14.00
Riker Wil	URF	32.00
Sword of Kahless	SRF	10.00
U.S.S. Thunderchild	SRF	15.00

Card name	Type	Rarity	Price
A Good Day to Live	Mis	R	4.00
Access Denied	Inc	U	0.50
Admiral Ross	Per	R	5.00
Alpha Attack Ship	Shp	U	0.50
Ambassador Tomalak	Per	R	5.00
Attack Pattern Delta	Int	U	0.50
Attack Wing	Tac	C	0.10
Bat'leth	Eq	C	0.10
Bat'leth Tournament	Mis	U	0.50
Battle Bridge Door	Dwy	C	0.25
Blood Oath	Inc	R	4.00
Boone Impersonator	Per	R	4.00
Borg Cutting Beam	Tac	R	4.00
Captured	Inc	U	0.50
Chart Stellar Cluster	Mis	R	4.00
Chief O'Brien	Per	R	6.00
Chula: The Abyss	Dil	R	4.00
Chula: The Lights	Dil	C	0.10
Commandeer Ship	Obj	U	0.50
Counterintelligence	Int	U	0.50
Crimson Forcefield	Tac	U	0.50
Defense System Upgrade	Ev	U	0.50
Dial Martok for Murder	Ev	U	0.50
D'k Tahg	Eq	C	0.10
Dolak	Per	U	0.50
Donald Varley	Per	R	4.00

Card name	Type	Rarity	Price
Dr. Koramar	Per	U	0.50
Drumhead	Dil	U	0.50
Duran'Adar	Per	C	0.10
D'Vin	Per	C	0.10
E-Band Emissions	Ev	R	3.00
Elim	Per	R	5.00
Engage Shuttle perations: Dominion	Ev	U	0.50
Enrique Mu–iz	Per	R	4.00
Evasive Maneuvers	Tac	C	0.10
Examine Singularity	Obj	U	0.50
Fajo's Gallery	Ev	R	4.00
Ferengi Ingenuity	Dil	U	0.50
Full Phaser Spread	Tac	C	0.10
Furel	Per	U	0.50
Gelnon	Per	R	4.00
Goraxus	Shp	R	5.00
Gravimetric Distortion	Dil	C	0.10
Gul Madred	Per	R	5.00
Hazardous Duty	Dil	C	0.10
Holding Cell Door	Dwy	C	0.10
Hon'Tihl	Per	U	0.50
I.K.C. Koraga	Shp	R	5.00
I.K.C. Lukara	Shp	R	5.00
I.K.C. Negh'Var	Shp	R	5.00
Ilon Tandro	Per	R	4.00
Impersonate Captive	Obj	R	4.00
Inside Operation	Int	R	4.00
Intruder Alert!	Inc	U	0.50
Ixtana'Rax	Per	R	4.00
Jadzia Dax	Per	R	8.00
Kang	Per	R	5.00
Kar'takin	Eq	C	0.10
Kavok	Per	R	5.00
Keldon	Shp	C	0.10
Klingon Disruptor Rifle	Eq	U	0.50
Koloth	Per	R	5.00
Kor	Per	R	5.00
Kraxon	Shp	R	5.00
Kudak'Etan	Per	R	4.00
La Forge Impersonator	Per	R	5.00
Lamat'Ukan	Per	U	0.50
Locutus' Borg Cube	Shp	R	8.00
Long Live the Queen	Inc	R	4.50
Lupaza	Per	U	0.50
Maximum Firepower	Tac	R	4.00
Mek'leth	Eq	U	0.50
Miles O'Brien	Per	R	8.00
Mopak	Per	C	0.10
Navok	Per	C	0.10

Card name	Type	Rarity	Price
New Essentialists	Dil	U	0.50
N'Garen	Per	U	0.50
Odo Founder	Per	R	6.00
Oken'alak	Per	C	0.10
Outgunned	Int	R	4.00
Parthok	Per	R	4.00
Phased Polaron Beam	Tac	C	0.10
Phaser Array Power Cell	Int	C	0.10
Phaser Banks	Tac	C	0.10
Photon Torpedo	Tac	C	0.10
Picard Maneuver	Tac	R	4.00
Plasma Torpedo	Tac	C	0.10
Prepare the Prisoner	Obj	U	0.50
Primary Energy Weapon	Tac	C	0.10
Prisoner Escort	Int	C	0.10
Prisoner Exchange	Inc	U	0.50
Pulse Disruptor	Tac	C	0.10
Pulse Phaser Cannons	Tac	C	0.10
Quantum Torpedo	Tac	C	0.10
Quark Son of Keldar	Per	R	6.50
Riker Wil	Per	R	6.50
R'Mal	Per	C	0.10
Ro Laren	Per	R	5.00
Romulan Disruptor Rifle	Eq	U	0.50
Romulan Shuttle	Shp	C	0.10
Sarita Carson	Per	C	0.10
Scanner Interference	Inc	U	0.50
Security Holding Cell	Site	U	0.50

Card name	Type	Rarity	Price
Senator Letant	Per	R	4.00
Sniper	Inc	U	0.50
Spiral-Wave Disruptor	Tac	C	0.10
Starfleet Type I Phaser	Eq	C	0.10
Stellar Flare	Dil	U	0.50
Strafing Run	Tac	C	0.10
Sword of Kahless	Art	R	5.00
Tamarith	Per	U	0.50
Target Engines	Tac	C	0.10
Target Shields	Tac	C	0.10
Target These Coordinates	Tac	R	4.00
Target Weapons	Tac	C	0.10
Tharket	Per	U	0.50
The Albino	Per	R	4.00
The Big Picture	Ev	U	0.50
The Guardian	Int	U	0.50
The Wake of the Borg	Int	U	0.50
Torture	Ev	R	4.00
U.S.S. Thunderchild	Shp	R	8.00
Ultimatum	Inc	U	0.50
Umat'Adan	Per	U	0.50
Under Fire	Dil	U	0.50
Victory Is Life	Int	C	0.10
Voktak	Per	C	0.10
Wo'Din	Per	C	0.10
Worf Son of Mogh	Per	R	10.00
Zetal	Per	C	0.10

Star Trek • *Second Anthology*

Decipher • Released **December 1999**

Similar to *First Anthology*, this product contains two *Starter Deck II* decks and two expansion packs each of *First Contact*, *Deep Space Nine*, and *Dominion*. sets. Also included are six rare personnel cards, all packaged inside a box suitable for storing 800 cards.

Player response to the *Second Anthology* was good. The set was a fine entry point, and for more experienced players, the main reason to buy was for the six rares. The big complaint was its quality as a sealed deck tool. The only affiliation appearing in all the packs is the Federation, and most players had Federation cards coming out of their ears. — *Fritz Meissner*

Second Anthology (sealed)			33.00

Card name	Price
Bashir Founder	5.00
Jodmos	5.50

Card name	Price
Koval	4.50
Legate Damar	4.50
Luther Sloan	5.00
Vedek Dax	5.50

RARITY KEY C = Common   U = Uncommon   R = Rare   VR = Very Rare   UR = Ultra Rare   F = Foil card   X = Fixed/standard in all decks

EQUIPMENT — STAR TREK DEEP SPACE NINE

GOLD-PRESSED LATINUM

Valuable liquid latinum encased in relatively worthless gold dust. Standard of exchange throughout the Ferengi Alliance. Typically traded in bars, strips and slips; 1 bar = 20 strips = 2,000 slips.

Once each turn, on a Trading Post, homeworld or Quark's Bar, you may discard two Latinum (one if your Acquisition present) to download a non-Latinum Equipment card there.

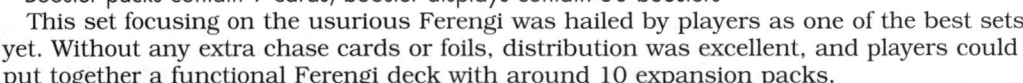

Star Trek • Rules of Acquisition

Decipher • Released **December 1999**

130 cards in set • **IDENTIFIER:** © 1999; Ferengi head symbol

• Booster packs contain 9 cards; booster displays contain 30 boosters

This set focusing on the usurious Ferengi was hailed by players as one of the best sets yet. Without any extra chase cards or foils, distribution was excellent, and players could put together a functional Ferengi deck with around 10 expansion packs.

Despite the heavy emphasis on the Ferengi, *Rules of Acquisition* has something for each affiliation: a new orb artifact for the Bajorans, a second headquarters card for the Romulans and **Cargo Bay** for any affiliation able to use a Nor. Incredible counters were another hallmark of the set. The **Writ of Accountability** awarded players a full win if their opponents abused certain strategies, while **Quark's Isolinear Rods** gave players a chance to get around their opponents' **Computer Crash** and **Wrong Door**.

The Ferengi immediately settled into their place as one of the top affiliations with their first turn downloads. The Dominion, first with Deyos and then with Founder smackdown, Romulans with dual headquarters, Bajorans on Deep Space Nine, war-like Klingons, and Borg Cube dual mission decks appeared in the first half of 2000 as the other deck types to beat. — *Fritz Meissner*

> You will need
> **15**
> nine-pocket pages to store this set.
> (8 doubled up)

Set (130 cards)			**120.00**
Booster Display Box			**65.00**
Booster Pack			**2.50**

Card name	Type	Rarity	Price
1st Rule of Acquisition	Ev	C	0.15
6th Rule of Acquisition	Ev	C	0.15
33rd Rule of Acquisition	Ev	U	0.80
34th Rule of Acquisition	Ev	U	0.80
47th Rule of Acquisition	Ev	U	0.80
59th Rule of Acquisition	Ev	U	0.80
75th Rule of Acquisition	Ev	U	0.80
211th Rule of Acquisition	Ev	C	0.15
Aluura	Per	R	4.00
Ambassador Krajensky	Per	U	0.90
Apnex	Shp	R	4.00
Arandis	Per	R	4.00
Benil	Per	U	0.80
Berik	Per	U	0.80
Birta	Per	U	0.80
Bodyguards	Inc	U	0.80
Bractor	Per	R	4.00
Breen CRM114	Eq	R	4.00
B'rel	Shp	C	0.15
Bribery	Inc	C	0.15
Brunt	Per	R	4.00
Calandra	Per	C	0.15
Cargo Bay	Site	C	0.15
Center of Attention	Dil	U	0.80
Chula: Crossroads	Dil	C	0.15
Chula: The Door	Dil	R	4.00
Collect Sample	Miss	C	0.15
Continuing Committee	F	R	4.00
Dabo	Inc	U	0.80
Dangerous Liaisons	Dil	C	0.15
Deliver Message	Miss	U	0.50
Deyos	Per	R	4.00
D'Kora Marauder	Shp	C	0.15
D'Kora Transport	Shp	C	0.15
Dr. Borts	Per	C	0.15
Edan'AtaL	Ev	C	0.15
Elizabeth Lense	Per	R	4.00
Emergency Evacuation	Inc	C	0.15
Establish Trade Route	Obj	C	0.15
Ferengi Bug	Dil	U	0.50
Ferengi Conference	Obj	U	0.80
Ferengi Credit Exchange	Inc	U	0.80
Ferengi Disruptor	Eq	C	0.15
Ferengi Disruptor Rifle	Eq	U	0.50
Ferengi Energy Weapon	Tac	C	0.15
Ferengi Outpost	F	C	0.15
Ferengi PADD	Eq	C	0.15

Card name	Type	Rarity	Price
Ferengi Shuttle	Shp	C	0.15
Forced-Labor Camp	Obj	U	0.80
Frool	Per	C	0.15
Gaila	Per	R	4.00
George Primmin	Per	R	4.00
Gold-Pressed Latinum	Eq	C	0.15
Goss	Per	U	0.80
Gral	Per	R	4.00
Grand Nagus Gint	Per	R	5.00
Grand Nagus Zek	Per	R	5.00
Gunrunning	Miss	U	0.80
Hagath	Per	R	4.00
Hanok	Per	U	0.80
Ikat'Ika	Per	R	4.00
In The Pale Moonlight	Dil	U	0.80
Incoming Message: Ferengi	Int	C	0.15
Inglatu	Per	C	0.15
Ishka	Per	R	4.00
It's Only A Game	Inc	U	0.80
Jovis	Shp	R	4.00
Karemman Vessel	Shp	C	0.15
Kasidy Yates	Per	R	5.00
Kazago	Per	U	0.80
Krajensky Founder	Per	R	4.50
Krax	Per	U	0.50
Krayton	Shp	R	4.00
Kreechta	Shp	R	4.00
Krozh	Per	C	0.15
Krunk	Per	C	0.15
Kukalaka	Eq	R	4.00
Leck	Per	R	4.00
Leeta	Per	R	5.00
Lemec	Per	R	4.00
Letek	Per	C	0.15
Lurin	Per	R	4.00
Maihar'du	Per	R	4.00
Mardah	Per	U	0.80
Margh	Per	R	4.00
Market Research	Miss	C	0.15
Morn	Per	R	5.00
Morta	Per	U	0.80
Naprem	Shp	R	4.00
Nava	Per	C	0.15
Nibor	Per	U	0.80
Nilva	Per	C	0.15
Nog	Per	R	6.00
Omag	Per	R	4.00
Orb of Wisdom	Art	R	5.00

Card name	Type	Rarity	Price
Orion Syndicate Bomb	Dil	R	4.00
Par Lenor	Per	U	0.80
Patahk	Per	R	4.00
Patrol Ship	Shp	C	0.15
Pel	Per	U	0.80
Phased Cloaking Device	Art	R	4.00
Plasma Energy Burst	Tac	C	0.20
Prak	Per	C	0.15
Protection Racket	Inc	R	4.00
Purchase Moon	Miss	U	0.80
Qol	Per	C	0.15
Quark	Per	R	8.00
Quark's Bar	Site	R	4.50
Quark's Isolinear Rods	Inc	R	4.00
Quark's Treasure	Shp	R	4.50
Reactor Overload	Inc	U	0.80
Rom	Per	R	6.00
Runabout Search	Miss	U	0.80
Scepter of the Grand Nagus	Eq	R	4.00

Card name	Type	Rarity	Price
Scientific Method	Dil	C	0.15
Senator Cretak		R	4.00
Small Cloaking Device	Eq	U	0.90
Solok	Per	C	0.15
Sovak	Per	U	0.80
Starry Night	Art	R	4.00
Strange Bedfellows	Dil	U	0.80
Taar	Per	C	0.15
The Ferengi Rules of Acquisition	Eq	U	1.00
Tog	Per	U	0.80
Tol	Per	U	0.80
Tower of Commerce	F	R	4.00
Tulaberry Wine Negotiations	Miss	U	0.50
U.S.S. Sao Paulo	Shp	R	7.00
Vacuum-Desiccated Remains	Int	C	0.15
Writ of Accountability	Inc	R	4.00

Star Trek • Enhanced Premiere

Decipher • Released **October 2000**

Appearing at DecipherCon 2000, *Enhanced Premiere* continued Decipher's trend of repackaging older products with new premium cards. It consists of six different boxes, each containing four *Unlimited* packs, one of six dual personnel cards, and a set of randomly assorted premium cards.

With it came the new sealed-deck tournament format, Warp Speed. A few of the rules changes for the Warp Speed format are: allowing players to play two cards per turn instead of one, and allowing all personnel to work together without a treaty. The format is billed as an entry point for new players, and a faster, simpler way to play the game. — *Fritz Meissner*

"Enhanced" Deck	15.00
Alien Parasites & REM Fatigue	2.30
Anaphasic Organism & Nagilum	2.30
Ancient Computer & Microvirus	2.30
Beverly and Will	4.50
Computer Weapon & Hyper-Aging	2.50
Covert Installation II	2.50
Data and Geordi	6.50
Data and Picard	6.30
Excavation II	2.30
Explore Black Cluster II	2.30
Explore Typhon Expanse II	2.30
Female's Love Interest & Garbage Scow	2.00
Investigate Anomaly II	2.30
Investigate Sighting II	2.50
Jean Luc and Beverly	6.00
Male's Love Interest & Plague Ship	2.00
Relief Mission II	2.30
Secret Salvage II	2.30
Sons Of Mogh	4.50
Test Mission II	2.50
The Trois	4.50

RARITY KEY C = Common U = Uncommon R = Rare VR = Very Rare UR = Ultra Rare F = Foil card X = Fixed/standard in all decks

430 • *SCRYE Collectible Card Game Checklist and Price Guide*

Star Trek • The Trouble With Tribbles

Decipher • Released June 2000

141 cards in set • **IDENTIFIER:** © 2000; small tribble icon

You will need **16** nine-pocket pages to store this set. (8 doubled up)

- Starter decks contain 60 cards; booster displays contain 12 boosters
- Booster packs contain 9 cards; booster displays contain 30 boosters

The Trouble With Tribbles features cards from *Deep Space Nine*'s 30th anniversary crossover with the original series. New worlds of gameplay open up, from classic bridge crew to a new Tribbles side deck. Players who disliked **Captain Kirk** could kill him using a **Tribble Bomb** — and receive impressive benefits from **Hero of the Empire** and **Stop Kirk Contact**. The ultra-rare of the set is the powerful **Dr. McCoy**, printed as a tribute to the late Deforest Kelley.

Tribbles includes something for everyone: more Ferengi, **Resistance is Futile**, and (at last) **Third of Five** for the Borg; original series personnel; **Assign Support Personnel**, **Brunt's Shuttle**, the **Bajoran Shrine** — the list goes on and on. Unfortunately, the key concepts of the set (the original personnel and the side deck) played a minimal role in the decks of the time.

Although the set was well-received, there was some controversy surrounding the ultra-rare McCoy, as there had been for the **Future Enterprise** in *Alternate Universe*. — *Fritz Meissner*

Cards marked R* below occur in special two-rare packs. Lt, Sisko and Captain Koloth appear only in starters.

Set (141 cards)	180.00
Starter Display Box	107.50
Booster Display Box	75.00
Starter Deck	10.25
Booster Pack	3.10

Card name	Type	Rarity	Price
1 Tribble (bonus)	Trib	C	0.15
1 Tribble (discard)	Trib	C	0.15
1 Tribble (go)	Trib	C	0.15
10 Tribbles (bonus)	Trib	U	0.50
10 Tribbles (go)	Trib	U	0.50
10 Tribbles (poison)	Trib	U	0.50
62nd Rule of Acquisition	Ev	C	0.15
100 Tribbles (bonus)	Trib	U	0.50
100 Tribbles (poison)	Trib	U	0.50
100 Tribbles (rescue)	Trib	U	0.50
1,000 Tribbles (bonus)	Trib	R*	5.00
1,000 Tribbles (discard)	Trib	R*	5.00
1,000 Tribbles (rescue)	Trib	R*	5.00
10,000 Tribbles (go)	Trib	VR	5.30
10,000 Tribbles (poison)	Trib	VR	5.00
10,000 Tribbles (rescue)	Trib	VR	5.00
100,000 Tribbles (clone)	Trib	VR	5.30
100,000 Tribbles (discard)	Trib	VR	5.00
100,000 Tribbles (rescue)	Trib	VR	5.50
Agricultural Assessment	Mis	U	0.50
Amet'alox	Per	C	0.15
Arne Darvin	Per	VR	5.50
Assign Support Personnel	Obj	C	0.15
B.G. Robinson	Per	U	0.50
Bajoran Phaser Banks	Tac	C	0.15
Bajoran Raider	Shp	U	0.50
Bajoran Shrine	Site	U	0.50
Barry Waddle	Per	VR	5.50
Bok'Nor	Shp	U	0.50
Breen Disruptor Burst	Tac	C	0.20
Breen Energy-Dampening Weapon	Tac	R	3.00
Breen Warship	Shp	R	4.80

Card name	Type	Rarity	Price
Broca	Per	U	0.50
Brunt's Shuttle	Shp	R	3.50
Burial Ground	Int	U	0.50
Captain Kirk	Per	VR	12.00
Captain Koloth	Per	X	3.50
Chain Reaction Pulsar	Tac	U	0.60
Chain Reaction Ricochet	Inc	R	3.50
Chula: The Drink	Dil	R	3.00
Chula: The Way Home	Dil	C	0.15
Classic Communicator	Equ	C	0.15
Classic Medical Tricorder	Equ	U	0.50
Classic Tricorder	Equ	U	0.50
Classic Type II Phaser	Equ	C	0.15
Columbus	Shp	C	0.20
Council of Warriors	Obj	R	3.00
Danderdag	Per	C	0.15
Daval	Per	C	0.15
Deep Space Station K-7	Fac	R	6.30
Defend Homeworld	Obj	U	0.50
Dominion Battleship	Shp	R	5.00
Dr. McCoy	Per	UR	57.50
Dulmer	Per	VR	5.30
Ensign Chekov	Per	VR	9.50
Ensign O'Brien	Per	VR	8.80
Executive Authorization	Dil	R	3.50
Falar	Per	C	0.15
Ferengi Infestation	Dil	R	3.00
First Minister Shakaar	Per	VR	5.30
Gal Gath'thong	Shp	R	4.00
Gem	Per	U	0.50
Grebnedlog	Per	VR	5.00
Hero of the Empire	Obj	U	0.50
Homefront	Inc	U	0.50
HQ: Orbital Weapons Platform	Inc	R	4.30
I.K.C. Gr'oth	Shp	VR	5.80
I.K.C. Ning'tao	Shp	R	5.00
... In the Engine Room	Troub	C	0.15
... In the Transporters	Troub	C	0.15
Jenok	Per	C	0.15

Card name	Type	Rarity	Price
Kalenna	Per	U	0.50
Keras	Per	VR	4.80
Kered	Per	C	0.15
Kira	Per	VR	7.00
Korax	Per	U	0.50
Kras	Per	U	0.50
Lam	Per	C	0.15
Liam Bilby	Per	U	0.50
Lineup	Dil	C	0.15
Live Long and Prosper	Int	C	0.15
Lt. Bailey	Per	VR	5.50
Lt. Bashir	Per	VR	8.50
Lt. D'Amato	Per	U	0.50
Lt. Dax	Per	VR	8.50
Lt. Grant	Per	C	0.15
Lt. Nagata	Per	U	0.50
Lt. Sisko	Per	X	7.50
Lt. Sulu	Per	VR	9.50
Lt. Uhura	Per	VR	9.50
Lt. Watley	Per	U	0.50
Lucsly	Per	VR	5.30
Lumba	Per	VR	4.80
Make It So	Inc	R	3.00
Mondor	Shp	U	0.50
Mordoc	Per	C	0.15
Mr. Scott	Per	VR	10.50
Mr. Spock	Per	VR	12.00
Nilz Baris	Per	U	0.50
Obedience Brings Victory	Int	U	0.50
Obelisk of Masaka	Inc	U	0.50
Odo	Per	VR	8.00
... On the Bridge	Troub	C	0.15
... On the Station	Troub	C	0.15
Oops!	Dil	C	0.15
Orb of Time	Art	R	3.00
Organian Peace Treaty	Ev	C	0.15
Palukoo	Dil	U	0.50
Panel Overload	Inc	C	0.15
Q Gets the Point	Dil	C	0.15

Card name	Type	Rarity	Price
Q the Referee	Inc	U	0.50
Q-Type Android	QI	U	0.50
Reginod	Per	U	0.50
Resistance is Futile	Inc	R	3.00
Sarish Rez	Per	U	0.50
Scan Cycle Check	Int	C	0.15
Sherman's Peak	T-Loc	U	0.50
Six of Thirteen	Per	C	0.15
Starship Constitution	Shp	C	0.15
Starship Enterprise	Shp	VR	12.50
Stolen Attack Ship	Shp	R	4.80
Storage Compartment Door	Dwy	C	0.15
Subspace Transporter	Ev	C	0.15
Suicidal Attack	Int	C	0.15
Temporal Investigations	Ev	C	0.15
The Centurion	Per	VR	5.30
Third of Five	Per	VR	6.00
Thopok	Per	U	0.50
Thot Gor	Per	VR	5.00
Thot Pran	Per	U	0.50
Treaty: Cardassian/Bajoran	Ev	C	0.15
Treaty: Romulan/Bajoran	Ev	C	0.15
Tribble Bomb	Inc	U	0.50
Tumek	Per	U	0.50
Varat'idan	Per	C	0.15
Velal	Per	VR	5.00
VR Headset	Equ	U	0.50
We Look for Things	Inc	U	0.50
Weyoun's Warship	Shp	R	4.50
Worf	Per	VR	10.50
Yint	Per	C	0.15

Star Trek • Mirror, Mirror

Decipher • Released December 2000

131 cards in set • **IDENTIFIER:** © 2000; small Agonizer icon

You will need **15** nine-pocket pages to store this set. (8 doubled up)

- Booster packs contain 9 cards; booster displays contain 30 boosters

Decipher's latest set at press time, *Mirror Mirror* focuses on the Mirror Universe accessed in both the original and later *Star Trek* series.

Set (131 cards)	175.00
Booster Display Box	82.50
Booster Pack	3.30

Card name	Type	Rarity	Price
35th Rule of Acquisition	Ev	U	0.50
A Fast Ship Would Be Nice	Dil	R	3.00

Card name	Type	Rarity	Price
Agonizer	Equ	U	0.50
Agony Booth	Inc	U	0.50
Alliance Galor	Shp	C	0.25
Alliance Interceptor	Shp	C	0.25
Alliance K'Vort	Shp	C	0.25
Alliance Nor	Fac	C	0.25

Card name	Type	Rarity	Price
Alliance Vor'Cha	Shp	C	0.25
Aramax	Per	C	0.25
Artillery Attack	Dil	R	3.00
Bajoran Warship	Shp	R	4.00
Bajoran Wormhole: Mirror Universe	Dwy	U	0.80

RARITY KEY C = Common U = Uncommon R = Rare VR = Very Rare UR = Ultra Rare F = Foil card X = Fixed/standard in all decks

Card name	Type	Rarity	Price
☐ Balok	Per	U	0.50
☐ Bareil	Per	R+	5.00
☐ Battle Cruiser	Shp	C	0.25
☐ Blood Screening	Ev	U	0.50
☐ Captain Bashir	Per	R+	10.00
[3]			
☐ Captain Dax	Per	R+	12.00
☐ Chief Engineer Scott	Per	R+	8.00
☐ Chief Navigator Chekov	Per	R+	10.00
☐ Chief Surgeon McCoy	Per	R+	15.00
☐ Chula: The Game	Dil	U	0.50
☐ Classic Disruptor	Equ	C	0.25
☐ Comm Officer Uhura	Per	R+	8.00
☐ Commander Charvanek	Per	R+	5.00
☐ Commander Leeta	Per	R	4.00
[4]			
☐ Construct Starship	Obj	R	4.00
☐ Crewman Wilson	Per	C	0.25
☐ Crossover	Inc	C	0.25
☐ D'vano	Per	C	0.25
☐ Defiant	Shp	R+	10.00
☐ Denevan Neural Parasites	Dil	R	3.00
☐ Disrupt Alliance	Mis	U	0.50
☐ Distraction	Dil	U	0.50
☐ Dorza	Per	C	0.25
[5]			
☐ Dr. Farallon	Per	R	3.00
☐ Dr. Roger Korby	Per	U	0.50
☐ Emblem of the Alliance	Inc	C	0.25
☐ Emblem of the Empire	Inc	C	0.25
☐ Emergency Conversion	Dil	C	0.25
☐ Enhanced Attack Ship	Shp	U	0.50
☐ Ensign Davis	Per	C	0.25
☐ Ensign Gaffney	Per	C	0.25

Card name	Type	Rarity	Price
☐ Ezri	Per	R+	4.50
[6]			
☐ Feldomite Rush	Mis	U	0.60
☐ Ferengi Whip	Equ	U	0.50
☐ Fesarius	Shp	R	3.00
☐ First Officer Spock	Per	UR	65.00
☐ Fontaine	Per	R+	4.00
☐ For Cardassia!	Obj	U	0.50
☐ Gantt	Per	C	0.25
☐ Gorn Encounter	Dil	U	0.50
☐ Gorrus	Per	C	0.25
[7]			
☐ Halkan Council	T-Loc	R	3.00
☐ Historical Research	Mis	U	0.50
☐ Horta	Dil	R	4.00
☐ Hostage Trade	Inc	C	0.25
☐ I.K.C. Ki'tang	Shp	U	0.50
☐ I'm a Doctor, Not a Bricklayer	Int	U	0.50
☐ I.S.S. Constitution	Shp	C	0.25
☐ I.S.S. Enterprise	Shp	R+	15.00
☐ Jake Sisko	Per	R+	8.00
[8]			
☐ James Tiberius Kirk	Per	R+	16.00
☐ Javek Len	Per	C	0.25
☐ Kelvan Show of Force	Dil	R	3.00
☐ Klingon Empire Outpost	Fac	C	0.25
☐ Korvek	Per	C	0.25
☐ Loreva	Per	C	0.25
☐ Lt. Kyle	Per	U	0.50
☐ Lt. Moreau	Per	U	0.50
☐ Luaran	Per	R	3.00
[9]			
☐ Marauder	Per	C	0.25

Card name	Type	Rarity	Price
☐ Marlena Moreau	Per	R+	4.80
☐ Mine Dilithium	Mis	U	0.50
☐ Mirror Dagger	Equ	C	0.25
☐ Mirror Ferengi Shuttle	Shp	U	0.50
☐ Mirror Terok Nor	Fac	R+	7.50
☐ Mr. Andrews	Per	C	0.25
☐ Mr. Brunt	Per	R+	5.00
☐ Mr. Nog	Per	R+	5.00
[10]			
☐ Mr. Quark	Per	R+	6.00
☐ Mr. Rom	Per	R+	6.00
☐ Mr. Sisko	Per	R+	8.50
☐ Mr. Tuvok	Per	R	5.00
☐ Multidimensional Transporter Device	Equ	C	0.25
☐ No Way Out	Inc	U	0.50
☐ Nurse Chapel	Per	R+	7.00
☐ Ops: Mirror Universe	Site	C	0.25
☐ Overseer Mardel	Per	U	0.50
[11]			
☐ Overseer Odo	Per	R+	6.00
☐ Professor Sisko	Per	R+	7.00
☐ Prot	Per	U	0.50
☐ Quantum Fissure	Dil	U	0.50
☐ Rebel Interceptor	Shp	C	0.25
☐ Regency 1	Shp	R	4.80
☐ Regent Worf	Per	R+	7.00
☐ Rinox	Per	U	0.50
☐ Romara Cal	Per	C	0.25
[12]			
☐ Romulan Cloaking Device	Equ	U	0.50
☐ Royale Casino: Slots	Dil	C	0.25
☐ Ruk	Per	R	3.00

Card name	Type	Rarity	Price
☐ Rukor	Per	U	0.50
☐ Search for Rebels	Mis	U	0.50
☐ Security Chief Garak	Per	R+	6.00
☐ Security Chief Sulu	Per	R+	6.00
☐ Self-Sealing Stem Bolts	Equ	C	0.25
☐ Smiley	Per	R+	4.50
[13]			
☐ Stolen Cloaking Device	Equ	U	0.50
☐ Subcommander Tal	Per	U	0.50
☐ Tagus	Per	C	0.25
☐ Tantalus Field	Art	R	3.00
☐ Taymar Bern	Per	C	0.25
☐ Telok	Per	U	0.50
☐ Terran Outpost	Fac	C	0.25
☐ Terran Rebellion HQ	Fac	R	3.00
☐ The Art of Diplomacy	Inc	R	3.00
[14]			
☐ The Emperor's New Cloak	Obj	U	0.50
☐ The Guardian of Forever	Dwy	R	3.00
☐ The Intendant	Per	R+	5.50
☐ Thomas Paris	Per	R	5.00
☐ Thrax	Per	U	0.50
☐ Transporter Chief Kyle	Per	U	0.50
☐ Transporter Mixup	Inc	U	0.80
☐ Treaty: Federation/Dominion	Ev	C	0.25
☐ T'Vor	Per	C	0.25
[15]			
☐ Type 18 Shuttlepod	Shp	U	0.50
☐ Vartoq	Per	C	0.25
☐ Vulcan "Death Grip"	Int	U	0.50
☐ Weyoun of Borg	Per	R+	5.00
☐ Wyatt Earp	Per	U	0.50

Star Trek • Reflections

Decipher • Released October 2000

105 cards in set •

- Booster packs contain 18 cards; booster displays contain 36 boosters

Reflections contains foil versions of cards from all sets from **Limited** through to **Dominion**, including hard-to-find **Two Player Game** and **Enhanced First Contact** premium cards. Surprises for players who buy entire boxes are the box and case toppers, including a foil **Seven of Nine**.

Like its Star Wars counterpart, each pack of Reflections includes 17 cards of completely random assortment, plus one random foil. It's theoretcially possible to get all rares!— **Fritz Messner**

	Price
Set (100 foil cards + 5 premium foils)	325.00
Booster Display Box	120.00
Booster Pack	5.00

Case Topper (1/case)

Card name	Type	Price
☐ Seven of Nine	Per	60.00

Display Box Topper (1/Box)

Card name	Type	Price
☐ 100,000 Tribbles (Clone)	Trib	25.00
☐ Admiral Riker	Per	25.00
☐ Dr. Telek R'Mor	Per	25.00
☐ Gowron of Borg	Per	22.00

Card name	Type	Rarity	Price
[1]			
☐ 10 and 01	Per	SRF	10.00
☐ Alas, Poor Queen	Int	VRF	5.00
☐ Armus - Skin of Evil	Dil	VRF	6.00
☐ Assimilate Homeworld	Obj	VRF	6.00
☐ Barclay's Proto-morphosis Disease	Dil	SRF	10.00
☐ Bareil Antos	Per	VRF	5.00
☐ Benjamin Sisko	Per	SRF	14.00
☐ Betazoid Gift Box	Art	VRF	5.00
☐ B'Etor	Per	SRF	9.00
[2]			
☐ Beverly Crusher	Per	SRF	10.00
☐ Beverly Picard	Per	SRF	9.50
☐ Borg Queen	Per	URF	40.00
☐ Borg Ship	Dil	SRF	12.00
☐ Bynars Weapon Enhancement	Ev	SRF	10.00

Card name	Type	Rarity	Price
☐ Central Command	Fac	SRF	8.00
☐ Cha'Joh	Shp	VRF	5.00
☐ Chamber of Ministers	Fac	SRF	8.00
☐ Cryosatellite	Art	VRF	5.00
[3]			
☐ Crystalline Entity	Dil	VRF	6.00
☐ Cytherians	Dil	SRF	8.00
☐ Damar	Per	VRF	5.00
☐ Data	Per	SRF	14.00
☐ Data's Head	Art	SRF	8.00
☐ Dathon	Per	SRF	8.00
☐ D'deridex Advanced	Shp	SRF	8.00
☐ Deanna Troi	Per	SRF	12.00
☐ Decius	Shp	VRF	6.00
[4]			
☐ Devidian Door	Dwy	SRF	10.00
☐ DNA Clues	Dil	VRF	6.00
☐ Dukat	Per	SRF	10.00
☐ Elim Garak	Per	SRF	12.00
☐ Espionage Mission	Mis	SRF	10.00
☐ Founder Leader	Per	SRF	10.00
☐ Future Enterprise	Shp	URF	40.00
☐ Galen	Per	SRF	12.00
☐ Garak	Per	VRF	6.00
[5]			
☐ Geordi La Forge	Per	SRF	10.00
☐ Gomtuu	Shp	VRF	5.00
☐ Governor Worf	Per	SRF	12.00
☐ Gowron	Per	SRF	10.00
☐ Horga'hn	Art	SRF	8.00
☐ I.K.C. Bortas	Shp	SRF	8.00
☐ I.K.C. Fek'lhr	Shp	VRF	7.00
☐ I.K.C. Hegh'ta	Shp	VRF	5.50

Card name	Type	Rarity	Price
☐ I.K.C. Rotarran	Shp	VRF	6.00
[6]			
☐ Interrogation	Ev	VRF	5.00
☐ Investigate "Shattered Space"	Mis	VRF	5.00
☐ Investigate Rumors	Mis	VRF	5.00
☐ Jadzia Dax	Per	SRF	14.00
☐ Jean-Luc Picard	Per	URF	40.00
☐ Julian Bashir	Per	SRF	14.00
☐ Kahless	Per	VRF	5.00
☐ Keldon Advanced	Shp	SRF	8.00
☐ Khazara	Shp	VRF	5.00
[7]			
☐ Kira Founder	Per	VRF	6.00
☐ Kira Nerys	Per	SRF	14.00
☐ Klingon Death Yell	Int	VRF	5.00
☐ Kurlan Naiskos	Art	VRF	5.00
☐ Kurn	Per	VRF	5.00
☐ Lursa	Per	SRF	12.00
☐ Madam Guinan	Per	SRF	10.00
☐ Magic Carpet Ride OCD	Art	VRF	5.00
☐ Major Rakal	Per	SRF	10.00
[8]			
☐ Martok	Per	SRF	10.00
☐ Montana Missile Complex	T-Loc	VRF	5.00
☐ O'Brien Founder	Per	VRF	6.00
☐ Ocular Implants	Ev	VRF	5.00
☐ Odo	Per	SRF	12.00
☐ Office of the President	Fac	SRF	8.00
☐ Office of the Proconsul	Fac	SRF	8.00
☐ Pegasus Search	Mis	VRF	5.00
☐ Plans of the Tal Shiar	Obj	VRF	5.00

Card name	Type	Rarity	Price
[9]			
☐ Prakesh	Shp	VRF	5.00
☐ Q	Dil	SRF	10.00
☐ Queen's Borg Cube	Shp	SRF	10.00
☐ Regenerate	Ev	SRF	10.00
☐ Ressikan Flute	Art	VRF	5.00
☐ Retask	Ev	VRF	5.00
☐ Revolving Door	Ev	VRF	5.00
☐ Roga Danar	Per	SRF	10.00
[10]			
☐ Scout Encounter	Dil	VRF	5.00
☐ Sela	Per	SRF	12.00
☐ Study Nebula	Mis	VRF	5.00
☐ Supernova	Ev	VRF	5.00
☐ System 5 Disruptors	Ev	VRF	5.00
☐ Taris	Per	VRF	5.00
☐ Tasha Yar-Alternate	Per	SRF	12.00
☐ The Great Hall	Fac	SRF	8.00
☐ The Great Link	Fac	SRF	8.00
☐ The Sheliak	Dil	VRF	6.00
[11]			
☐ Toreth	Per	VRF	5.00
☐ U.S.S. Defiant	Shp	URF	40.00
☐ U.S.S. Enterprise	Shp	SRF	15.00
☐ U.S.S. Enterprise	Shp	VRF	10.00
☐ Wall of Ships	Ev	VRF	5.00
☐ Weyoun	Per	SRF	10.00
☐ William T. Riker	Per	SRF	12.00
☐ Worf	Per	SRF	12.00
☐ Wormhole Negotiations	Mis	VRF	5.00
[12]			
☐ Yuta	Dil	VRF	5.00

RARITY KEY C = Common U = Uncommon R = Rare R+ = Rarer than rare VR = Very Rare SR = Super Rare F = Foil card

Star Trek: The Card Game

Fleer/Skybox • First set, *Limited*, released **June 1996**
306 cards in set

- Starter decks contain 65 cards; starter displays contain 12 decks
- Booster packs contain 15 cards; booster displays contain 36 packs

Designed by **Jeff Grubb**, **Don Perrin**, and **Margaret Weis**

How many ways can you slice a license? At times in 1990s, it seemed Paramount was determined to find out. Its comics book were published by DC — except for *Deep Space Nine*, which was published by Malibu. And with a strong CCG based on *Next Generation* characters entering its second year at Decipher, Paramount chose to send the original crew into CCG service with Fleer/Skybox. Skybox was already producing a superior line of *Star Trek* trading cards, so the connection was there. Which isn't to say that Decipher was happy about it, or that fans weren't plenty confused by it all.

In the game, which is *not* compatible with Decipher's, the mission is simple: Act out a *Star Trek* episode. Beam down to a planet, have Kirk fall in love, have Spock prove that the woman is an android energy being doomed to die, have McCoy utter a wry witticism, and see that Kirk loses his shirt and that both players lose some Red Shirts. In game terms, this means players share control of the Bridge Crew, starting with **Kirk**, **Spock**, **McCoy**, and the **U.S.S. Enterprise** itself. Each player gets a turn at sending a Landing Party to complete the Mission, Plot, and Discovery segments of an Episode. The opposing player can play Challenges, ranging from **Green Orion Slave Women** to **Gorns**.

Challenges test the crew's Combat, Humanity, and Logic. The system for determining victory consists of drawing a number of cards equal to the specific rating of the targeted crewmember. All cards drawn that have that rating symbol are tallied, and the side with the most wins, with ties going to the current player.

The game, while inelegant in play, caught the feel of the show — but couldn't catch the attention of Trek gamers, who much preferred Decipher's version. — *James Mishler*

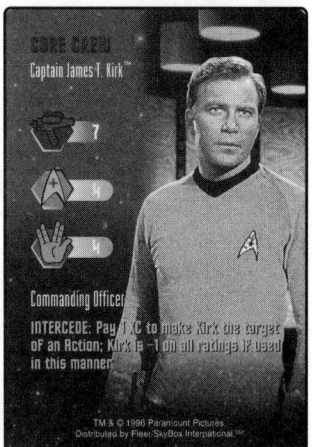

Concept	●●●●○
Gameplay	●●●○○
Card art	●●○○○
Player pool	○○○○○

Look for cards in this set autographed by Walter "Chekov" Koenig.

Set (306 cards)	75.00		
Starter Display Box	12.00		
Booster Display Box	11.00		
Starter Deck	3.30		
Booster Pack	.80		

You will need 34 nine-pocket pages to store this set. (17 doubled up)

Card name	Type	Rarity	Price
Alice in Wonderland	Chall	C	0.10
Alien Savages	Chall	C	0.10
Ambassador Robert Fox	Wild	VR	1.40
Andorians	Chall	C	0.10
Android Duplicate!	Chall	VR	1.50
Are You of the Body?	Wild	C	0.10
Ayelborne	Chall	R	0.60
Balok	Chall	R	0.60
Beam Me Up, Scotty!	Wild	U	0.25
Bele	Chall	R	0.60
Ben Childress	Chall	U	0.25
Bilar	Chall	U	0.25
Black Knight	Chall	U	0.25
Boot Scene	Wild	R	0.60
Capellans	Chall	C	0.10
Captain James T. Kirk	Crew	F	0.50
Captain John Christopher	Wild	U	0.25
Caretaker	Wild	R	0.60
Claudius Marcus	Chall	R	0.60
Colonel Green	Chall	C	0.10
Commander Spock	Crew	F	0.50
Commodore Jose Mendez	Chall	VR	1.40
Commodore Stone	Chall	U	0.25
Communicators Jammed!	Wild	C	0.10
Corbomite Maneuver	Wild	C	0.10
Court-Martial	Wild	C	0.10
Cultural Envoy	Wild	VR	1.40
Decisive Action	Wild	R	0.60
Decius	Chall	C	0.10
Default Discovery	Crew	F	0.15
Default Mission	Crew	F	0.15
Default Plot	Crew	F	0.15

Card name	Type	Rarity	Price
Deflector Shields at Maximum!	Wild	C	0.10
Denevan Neural Parasites	Chall	R	0.60
Dikironium Cloud Creature	Chall	VR	1.50
Direct Hit!	Wild	U	0.25
Disruptor Blast	Eff	U	0.25
Distraction	Wild	C	0.10
Don Juan	Chall	C	0.10
Dose of the Venus Drug	Eff	R	0.60
Dr. Brown	Chall	C	0.10
Dr. Elizabeth Dehner	Crew	U	0.25
Dr. Elizabeth Dehner	Chall	VR	1.40
Dr. Leonard H. "Bones" McCoy	Crew	F	0.50
Dr. Mark Piper	Crew	R	0.60
Dr. Roger Korby	Chall	R	0.60
Dr. Simon Van Gelder	Chall	C	0.10
Dr. Tristan Adams	Chall	U	0.25
Edge of the Galaxy	Wild	VR	1.50
Edith Keeler, 20th Century Reformer	Wild	VR	1.50
Elias Sandoval	Chall	U	0.25
Ensign Angela Martine	Crew	C	0.10
Ensign Matthews	Crew	C	0.10
Ensign Pavel A. Chekov	Crew	U	0.25
Ensign Rayburn	Crew	C	0.10
Episode: A Devil in the Dark	Disc	C	0.10
Episode: A Devil in the Dark	Miss	C	0.10
Episode: A Devil in the Dark	Plot	C	0.10
Episode: A Taste of Armageddon	Disc	R	0.50
Episode: A Taste of Armageddon	Miss	U	0.25
Episode: A Taste of Armageddon	Plot	U	0.25
Episode: Arena	Plot	C	0.10
Episode: Arena	Miss	C	0.10
Episode: Arena	Disc	U	0.25
Episode: Balance of Terror	Miss	C	0.10
Episode: Balance of Terror	Disc	C	0.10
Episode: Balance of Terror	Plot	C	0.10
Episode: Charlie X	Miss	U	0.25
Episode: Charlie X	Plot	C	0.10
Episode: Charlie X	Disc	C	0.10
Episode: Court-Martial	Miss	U	0.25

Card name	Type	Rarity	Price
Episode: Court-Martial	Plot	U	0.25
Episode: Court-Martial	Disc	R	0.50
Episode: Dagger of the Mind	Miss	R	0.50
Episode: Dagger of the Mind	Disc	U	0.25
Episode: Dagger of the Mind	Plot	U	0.25
Episode: Errand of Mercy	Disc	U	0.25
Episode: Errand of Mercy	Miss	C	0.10
Episode: Errand of Mercy	Plot	C	0.10
Episode: Miri	Disc	U	0.25
Episode: Miri	Miss	C	0.10
Episode: Miri	Plot	C	0.10
Episode: Mudd's Women	Miss	C	0.10
Episode: Mudd's Women	Plot	U	0.25
Episode: Mudd's Women	Disc	C	0.10
Episode: Operation: Annihilate!	Disc	C	0.10
Episode: Operation: Annihilate!	Miss	C	0.10
Episode: Operation: Annihilate!	Plot	U	0.25
Episode: Return of the Archons	Miss	U	0.25
Episode: Return of the Archons	Disc	U	0.25
Episode: Return of the Archons	Plot	R	0.50
Episode: Shore Leave	Miss	C	0.10
Episode: Shore Leave	Plot	U	0.25
Episode: Shore Leave	Disc	C	0.10
Episode: Space Seed	Disc	C	0.10
Episode: Space Seed	Miss	C	0.10
Episode: Space Seed	Plot	U	0.25
Episode: The Alternative Factor	Miss	C	0.10
Episode: The Alternative Factor	Plot	U	0.25
Episode: The Alternative Factor	Disc	C	0.10
Episode: The Cage	Disc	C	0.10
Episode: The Cage	Miss	C	0.10
Episode: The Cage	Plot	C	0.10
Episode: The City on the Edge of Forever	Miss	U	0.25
Episode: The City on the Edge of Forever	Plot	C	0.10
Episode: The City on the Edge of Forever	Disc	C	0.10

RARITY KEY C = Common **U** = Uncommon **R** = Rare **VR** = Very Rare **UR** = Ultra Rare **F** = Foil card **X** = Fixed/standard in all decks

Card name	Type	Rarity	Price
Episode: The Conscience of the King	Miss	U	0.25
Episode: The Conscience of the King	Plot	U	0.25
Episode: The Conscience of the King	Disc	R	0.50
Episode: The Corbomite Maneuver	Miss	C	0.10
Episode: The Corbomite Maneuver	Plot	C	0.10
Episode: The Corbomite Maneuver	Disc	C	0.10
Episode: The Enemy Within	Miss	R	0.50
Episode: The Enemy Within	Disc	U	0.25
Episode: The Enemy Within	Plot	U	0.25
Episode: The GALILEO Seven	Miss	U	0.25
Episode: The GALILEO Seven	Disc	C	0.10
Episode: The GALILEO Seven	Plot	C	0.10
Episode: The Man Trap	Disc	C	0.10
Episode: The Man Trap	Miss	C	0.10
Episode: The Man Trap	Plot	C	0.10
Episode: The Menagerie	Miss	C	0.10
Episode: The Menagerie	Plot	C	0.10
Episode: The Menagerie	Disc	C	0.10
Episode: The Naked Time	Miss	U	0.25
Episode: The Naked Time	Plot	U	0.25
Episode: The Naked Time	Disc	R	0.50
Episode: The Squire of Gothos	Miss	C	0.10
Episode: The Squire of Gothos	Disc	C	0.10
Episode: The Squire of Gothos	Plot	C	0.10
Episode: This Side of Paradise	Miss	U	0.25
Episode: This Side of Paradise	Plot	U	0.25
Episode: This Side of Paradise	Disc	C	0.10
Episode: Tomorrow is Yesterday	Miss	C	0.10
Episode: Tomorrow is Yesterday	Plot	U	0.25
Episode: Tomorrow is Yesterday	Disc	C	0.10
Episode: What Are Little Girls Made Of?	Miss	C	0.10
Episode: What Are Little Girls Made Of?	Plot	C	0.10
Episode: What Are Little Girls Made Of?	Disc	U	0.25
Episode: Where No Man Has Gone Before	Plot	C	0.10
Episode: Where No Man Has Gone Before	Miss	C	0.10
Episode: Where No Man Has Gone Before	Disc	U	0.25
Eve McHuron	Chall	U	0.25
Former Love	Chall	VR	1.50
Former Rival Finnegan	Chall	VR	1.50
Galactic High Commissioner Ferris	Chall	VR	1.50
Genghis Khan	Chall	U	0.25
Geological Technician Fisher	Crew	R	0.50
Gorn Captain	Chall	C	0.10
Great Bird of the Galaxy	Wild	C	0.10
Guardian of Forever	Wild	U	0.25
Hacom	Chall	R	0.60
Have Some Tranya	Eff	U	0.25
Heroic Sacrifice	Wild	C	0.10
Horta	Chall	U	0.25
Hostile Miners	Chall	C	0.10
HypoSpray	Wild	C	0.10
I'm a Doctor, Not a . . .	Wild	VR	1.50
IDIC	Eff	R	0.60
Insane Colonists	Chall	C	0.10
Ion Storm	Wild	U	0.25
Jahn	Chall	R	0.60
Jim - This man's a Klingon!	Wild	U	0.25
Joaquin	Chall	U	0.25
Kahless	Chall	R	0.60
Kang	Chall	U	0.25
Khan Noonien Singh	Chall	R	0.60
Klingon Arms Suppliers	Wild	R	0.60
Klingon Landing Party	Chall	C	0.10
Klingon Sniper	Chall	VR	1.40
Klingon Warrior	Chall	U	0.25
Kor	Chall	U	0.25
Landru	Chall	R	0.60
Lawgivers	Chall	C	0.10
Lay in New Course	Wild	C	0.10
Lazarus	Chall	C	0.10
Leila Kalomi	Chall	U	0.25
Lenore Karidian	Chall	R	0.60
Lethe	Chall	R	0.60
Lieutenant (j.g.) Joe Tormolen	Crew	C	0.10
Lieutenant Alden	Crew	R	0.60
Lieutenant Charlene Masters	Crew	C	0.10
Lieutenant Commander Benjamin Finney	Crew	R	0.60
Lieutenant Commander Gary Mitchell	Chall	VR	1.50
Lieutenant Commander Gary Mitchell	Crew	R	0.60
Lieutenant Commander Giotto	Crew	C	0.10
Lieutenant Commander Kelowitz	Crew	C	0.10
Lieutenant Commander Montgomery Scott	Crew	U	0.25
Lieutenant D'Amato	Crew	C	0.10
Lieutenant DePaul	Crew	U	0.25
Lieutenant DeSalle	Crew	R	0.60
Lieutenant Esteban Rodriguez	Crew	C	0.10
Lieutenant Gaetano	Crew	C	0.10
Lieutenant Hikaru Sulu	Crew	U	0.25
Lieutenant Karl Jaeger	Crew	R	0.60
Lieutenant Kevin T. Riley	Crew	R	0.60
Lieutenant Kyle	Crew	VR	1.40
Lieutenant Lang	Crew	C	0.10
Lieutenant Latimer	Crew	U	0.25
Lieutenant Lee Kelso	Crew	U	0.25
Lieutenant Leslie	Crew	U	0.25
Lieutenant Lindstrom	Crew	U	0.25
Lieutenant Marla McGivers	Crew	VR	1.50
Lieutenant Mira Romaine	Crew	R	0.60
Lieutenant O'Neil	Crew	C	0.10
Lieutenant Painter	Crew	U	0.25
Lieutenant Robert Tomlinson	Crew	C	0.10
Lieutenant Spinelli	Crew	C	0.10
Lieutenant Thom Parham	Crew	VR	1.40
Lieutenant Uhura	Crew	U	0.25
Logical Argument	Wild	C	0.10
Long-Winded Speech	Wild	C	0.10
M-113 Monster (Crewman Green Form)	Chall	VR	1.50
M-113 Monster (Natural Form)	Chall	VR	1.50
Magda Kovacs	Chall	C	0.10
Makeshift Weapons	Eff	U	0.25
Mara	Chall	U	0.25
Medical Readout	Eff	R	0.60
Medikit-Blue icon	Eff	C	0.10
Medikit-red icon	Eff	C	0.10
Melkotians	Chall	U	0.25
Metron	Chall	R	0.60
Military Officers, 20th Century	Chall	U	0.25
Mind-Sifter	Eff	R	0.60
Miraculous Recovery	Wild	R	0.60
Miri	Chall	U	0.25
Mudd's Women	Chall	U	0.25
Mugato	Chall	R	0.60
New Life and New Civilizations	Wild	C	0.10
Nomad	Chall	VR	1.50
Nurse Christine Chapel	Crew	U	0.25
Oddly Familiar Culture	Wild	R	0.60
Omicron Ceti III Spores	Wild	U	0.25
Onlies	Chall	C	0.10
Orders from Starfleet	Wild	R	0.60
Organian Council of Elders	Chall	VR	1.40
Otto	Chall	U	0.25
Personal Challenge	Wild	C	0.10
Phaser Blast -blue icon	Eff	C	0.10
Phaser Blast -yellow icon	Eff	C	0.10
Phaser on Overload	Eff	R	0.60
Phaser Rifle Fire	Eff	R	0.60
Phasers from Space	Wild	C	0.10
Photon Torpedoes	Wild	U	0.25
Planetary Guards	Chall	C	0.10
Plasus	Chall	U	0.25
Psi 2000 Virus	Wild	R	0.60
Red Alert!	Wild	U	0.25
Red Hour	Wild	R	0.60
Report to the Bridge!	Wild	R	0.60
Rojan	Chall	R	0.60
Romulan Battle Cruiser Commander	Chall	U	0.25
Romulan Bird-of-Prey	Wild	U	0.25
Romulan Bird-of-Prey Commander	Chall	C	0.10
Romulan Centurion	Chall	U	0.25
Romulan Cloaking Device	Wild	R	0.60
Romulan Disguise	Wild	U	0.25
Ruk	Chall	C	0.10
Ruth Bonaventure	Chall	C	0.10
S.S. Fesarius	Wild	VR	1.50
Samuel T. Cogley, Attorney	Wild	VR	1.40
Samurai Warrior	Chall	C	0.10
Shuttlecraft Crew Revolt	Wild	R	0.60
Shuttlecraft Galileo	Wild	C	0.10
Slingshot Effect	Wild	VR	1.50
Slug of Saurian Brandy	Eff	C	0.10
Song of a Vulcan Harp	Eff	R	0.60
Standard Procedures	Wild	U	0.25
Starbase 11	Wild	R	0.60
Starfleet Commendation	Wild	U	0.25
Talos IV	Wild	VR	1.40
Talosian Illusion	Wild	R	0.60
Talosians	Chall	U	0.25
Tantalus Chamber	Wild	VR	1.40
Tellarites	Chall	C	0.10
Thasians	Wild	VR	1.40
The Kaylar	Chall	C	0.10
The Keeper	Chall	VR	1.40
The Play's the Thing	Wild	U	0.25
Time Travel	Wild	R	0.60
Tinkering With the Engines	Wild	C	0.10
Transporter Duplicate	Chall	VR	1.40
Transporter Technician Wilson	Crew	R	0.60
Transporter, Fully Energized	Wild	R	0.60
Transporters Operational	Wild	C	0.10
Trefayne	Chall	U	0.25
Trelane	Chall	C	0.10
Tricorder Reading-red icon	Eff	C	0.10
Tricorder Reading-yellow icon	Eff	C	0.10
Turnabout Intruder	Wild	VR	1.40
U.S.S. Enterprise	Crew	F	0.50
Unknown Virus	Wild	U	0.25
Vina	Chall	U	0.25
Vina, the Orion Dancer	Chall	R	0.60
Vulcan Mind-Meld	Wild	U	0.25
White Rabbit	Chall	C	0.10
Witch	Chall	U	0.25
Wyatt Earp	Chall	U	0.25
Yarnek	Chall	R	0.60
Yeoman Janice Rand	Crew	U	0.25
Yeoman Karen Greene	Crew	C	0.10
Yeoman Martha Landon	Crew	R	0.60
Yeoman Mears	Crew	C	0.10
Yeoman Smith	Crew	C	0.10
Yeoman Teresa Ross	Crew	C	0.10
Yeoman Tina Lawton	Crew	U	0.25

RARITY KEY C = Common U = Uncommon R = Rare VR = Very Rare UR = Ultra Rare F = Foil card X = Fixed/standard in all decks

Star Trek: The Card Game •
Starfleet Maneuvers

Fleer/SkyBox • Released **January 1997**
160 cards in set • **IDENTIFIER: No identifiable difference from** *Limited*

• Booster packs contain 15 cards; booster displays contain 36 boosters

The only expansion for **Star Trek: The Card Game**, **Starfleet Maneuvers** included new episodes, crew, and wild cards. No new mechanics were included, the cards simply expanded the existing play possibilities.

Alien Encounters, announced for summer 1997, never came out, and Decipher eventually got the license to the rest of the *Star Trek* universe. — **James Mishler**

Set (159 cards)	65.00
Booster Display Box	11.00
Booster Pack	.80

You will need 18 nine-pocket pages to store this set. (9 doubled up)

Card name	Type	Rarity	Price
1			
☐ Admiral Komack	Crew	R	0.50
☐ Adrenaline	Eff	R	0.60
☐ Advanced Aging	Wild	VR	1.50
☐ Agonizer	Eff	R	0.60
☐ Agony Booth	Wild	C	0.10
☐ Ahn-Woon	Eff	C	0.10
☐ Akuta	Chall	C	0.10
☐ Alice Series Android	Chall	C	0.10
☐ Android Overload	Wild	U	0.25
2			
☐ Antigrav Units	Wild	R	0.60
☐ Apollo	Chall	R	0.50
☐ Apollo's Shrine	Wild	U	0.25
☐ Argelian Empathic Contact	Wild	R	0.60
☐ Arne Darvin	Chall	C	0.10
☐ Asteroid Yonada	Wild	C	0.10
☐ Aurora	Wild	R	0.60
☐ Botany Bay	Wild	U	0.25
☐ Bows and Arrows	Wild	R	0.50
3			
☐ Captain Koloth	Chall	C	0.10
☐ Captain Pike	Crew	VR	1.50
☐ Captain Ramart	Crew	R	0.50
☐ Captain's Chair	Wild	U	0.25
☐ Cavalry Arrives	Wild	R	0.50
☐ Central Control	Wild	R	0.60
☐ Clean Slate	Wild	VR	1.40
☐ Code 2	Wild	U	0.25
☐ Colonel Fellini	Chall	C	0.10
4			
☐ Commodore Matt Decker	Chall	U	0.25
☐ Commodore Stocker	Crew	VR	1.40
☐ Companion	Chall	C	0.10
☐ Competency Hearing	Wild	R	0.60
☐ Cultural Taboo	Wild	R	0.80
☐ Deadly Flora	Chall	U	0.25
☐ Deep Space Station K-7	Wild	U	0.25
☐ Eleen	Chall	C	0.10
☐ Engineering Room	Wild	U	0.25
5			
☐ Ensign Freeman	Crew	C	0.10
☐ Ensign Hendorf	Crew	U	0.25
☐ Ensign Montgomery	Crew	U	0.25
☐ Episode: "Amok Time"	Plot	R	0.60
☐ Episode: "Amok Time"	Disc	U	0.25
☐ Episode: "Amok Time"	Miss	U	0.25
☐ Episode: "Catspaw"	Disc	VR	1.50
☐ Episode: "Catspaw"	Miss	VR	1.50
☐ Episode: "Catspaw"	Plot	U	0.25
6			
☐ Episode: "Friday's Child"	Disc	VR	1.50
☐ Episode: "Friday's Child"	Plot	VR	1.40
☐ Episode: "Friday's Child"	Miss	U	0.25
☐ Episode: "I, Mudd"	Disc	VR	1.40
☐ Episode: "I, Mudd"	Miss	VR	1.40

Card name	Type	Rarity	Price
☐ Episode: "I, Mudd"	Plot	U	0.25
☐ Episode: "Metamorphosis"	Disc	VR	1.50
☐ Episode: "Metamorphosis"	Plot	R	0.60
☐ Episode: "Metamorphosis"	Miss	U	0.25
7			
☐ Episode: "Mirror, Mirror"	Plot	VR	1.40
☐ Episode: "Mirror, Mirror"	Disc	U	0.25
☐ Episode: "Mirror, Mirror"	Miss	C	0.10
☐ Episode: "The Apple"	Disc	VR	1.40
☐ Episode: "The Apple"	Miss	U	0.25
☐ Episode: "The Apple"	Plot	C	0.10
☐ Episode: "The Changeling"	Plot	VR	1.50
☐ Episode: "The Changeling"	Disc	R	0.60
☐ Episode: "The Changeling"	Miss	U	0.25
8			
☐ Episode: "The Deadly Years"	Plot	VR	1.40
☐ Episode: "The Deadly Years"	Disc	R	0.60
☐ Episode: "The Deadly Years"	Miss	C	0.10
☐ Episode: "The Doomsday Machine"	Disc	VR	1.50
☐ Episode: "The Doomsday Machine"	Miss	VR	1.40
☐ Episode: "The Doomsday Machine"	Plot	U	0.25
☐ Episode: "The Trouble With Tribbles"	Plot	VR	1.40
☐ Episode: "The Trouble With Tribbles"	Miss	U	0.25
☐ Episode: "The Trouble With Tribbles"	Disc	C	0.10
9			
☐ Episode: "Who Mourns For Adonais?"	Miss	VR	1.40
☐ Episode: "Who Mourns For Adonais?"	Plot	U	0.25
☐ Episode: "Who Mourns For Adonais?"	Disc	C	0.10
☐ Episode: "Wolf In The Fold"	Miss	R	0.60
☐ Episode: "Wolf In The Fold"	Plot	U	0.25
☐ Episode: "Wolf In The Fold"	Disc	C	0.10
☐ Feeders of Vaal	Chall	C	0.10
☐ Friendly Welcome	Wild	R	0.50
☐ Giant Black Cat	Chall	C	0.10
10			
☐ Highly Illogical Behavior	Eff	R	0.60
☐ I.S.S. Enterprise	Wild	R	0.60
☐ Jarvis	Chall	C	0.10
☐ Kal-If-Fee	Wild	R	0.80
☐ Kligat	Eff	C	0.10
☐ Klingon Battle Cruiser	Wild	VR	1.50
☐ Korax	Chall	C	0.10
☐ Korob	Chall	C	0.10
11			
☐ Lieutenant Carolyn Palamas	Crew	U	0.25
☐ Lieutenant Chip Carter	Crew	VR	1.50
☐ Lieutenant Hanson	Crew	U	0.25
☐ Lieutenant Jackson	Crew	C	0.10
☐ Lieutenant José Tyler	Crew	U	0.25
☐ Lieutenant Kaplan	Crew	R	0.60
☐ Lieutenant Karen Tracy	Crew	U	0.25
☐ Lieutenant Marlena Moreau	Crew	R	0.50
☐ Lieutenant Palmer	Crew	C	0.10
☐ Lieutenant Ron Perazza	Crew	VR	1.40
12			
☐ Lieutenant Rowe	Crew	U	0.25
☐ Lieutenant Singh	Crew	C	0.10
☐ Lieutenant Steve Domzalski	Crew	VR	1.50
☐ Lieutenant Tonia Barrows	Crew	VR	1.50
☐ Lieutenant Washburn	Crew	R	0.50
☐ Lirpa	Eff	C	0.10
☐ Maab	Chall	C	0.10

Card name	Type	Rarity	Price
☐ Magnesite-Nitron Tablet	Wild	R	0.60
☐ Magnetic Storm	Wild	U	0.25
13			
☐ Manual Override	Wild	R	0.60
☐ Masiform D	Wild	U	0.25
☐ Mirror Chekov	Chall	R	0.60
☐ Mirror Marlena	Chall	C	0.10
☐ Mirror Spock	Chall	R	0.50
☐ Mirror Sulu	Chall	R	0.60
☐ Native Club	Eff	C	0.10
☐ Neural Paralyzer	Wild	R	0.80
☐ Nilz Baris	Chall	C	0.10
14			
☐ Norman	Chall	C	0.10
☐ Number One	Crew	C	0.10
☐ Nurse Cheryl Thomas	Crew	VR	1.40
☐ Orion Smugglers	Wild	VR	1.40
☐ Plak-Tow	Wild	R	0.50
☐ Planet Killer	Wild	R	0.60
☐ Plate of Gems	Eff	C	0.10
☐ Plomeek Soup	Eff	C	0.10
☐ Pon farr	Wild	R	0.60
15			
☐ Quadrotriticale	Eff	C	0.10
☐ Redjak	Chall	C	0.10
☐ Redjak's Knife	Eff	C	0.10
☐ Reeducation	Wild	VR	1.40
☐ Romulan Neutral Zone	Wild	VR	1.50
☐ Science Station	Wild	U	0.25
☐ Shuttlecraft Columbus	Wild	C	0.10
☐ Sick Bay	Wild	U	0.25
☐ Sonic Pulse	Eff	C	0.10
16			
☐ Star Charts	Wild	U	0.25
☐ Stella	Chall	C	0.10
☐ Suicide Mission	Wild	R	0.80
☐ Sylvia	Chall	C	0.10
☐ Sympathetic Magic	Wild	U	0.25
☐ T'Pau	Chall	U	0.25
☐ T'Pring	Chall	VR	1.40
☐ Tantalus Field	Wild	R	0.50
☐ Taunt	Eff	C	0.10
17			
☐ Tholian Web	Wild	U	0.25
☐ Top Security Cell	Wild	VR	1.40
☐ Transmuter	Wild	U	0.25
☐ Transporter Swap	Wild	R	0.80
☐ Tribbles	Chall	U	0.25
☐ Tribbles	Chall	U	0.25
☐ Tribbles	Chall	C	0.10
☐ U.S.S. Constellation	Wild	C	0.10
☐ U.S.S. Lexington	Wild	C	0.10
18			
☐ Universal Translator	Eff	R	0.60
☐ Vaal	Chall	R	0.60
☐ Verifier	Eff	R	0.60
☐ Warning Beacon	Wild	C	0.10
☐ Yeoman Colt	Crew	C	0.10
☐ Zombie Crew	Chall	C	0.10

CREW
Captain Christopher Pike

5

5

5

Original Captain

GENERAL ORDER 7: All Challenge cards with the TELEPATHIC Attribute or TEMPT Action are at -1 to all Ratings vs. Pike.

DELEGATION: Pay 1 XC during the Final XC Segment to prevent any Crew card in Challenging Player's Complement from being a member of the next Landing Party.

TM & © 1996 Paramount Pictures
Distributed by Fleer/SkyBox International ™

RARITY KEY C = Common U = Uncommon R = Rare VR = Very Rare UR = Ultra Rare F = Foil card X = Fixed/standard in all decks

SCRYE Collectible Card Game Checklist and Price Guide • **435**

Star Wars

Decipher • First set, *Premiere Limited,* released **December 1995**
324 cards in set • **IDENTIFIER: Black border**

• Starter decks contain 60 cards; starter displays contain 12 starters
• Booster packs contain 15 cards; booster displays contain 36 boosters
Designed by **Rollie Tesh** and **Tom Braunlich**, among many others

Star Wars was the single most anticipated new release in the short history of CCGs, and little wonder. The chance to relive in CCG form the epic sequences witnessed in movie theaters years ago, such as the Battles of Yavin and Hoth, were a major draw — and with publicity building for the film rereleases and the next trilogy, *Star Wars* became the CCG everyone had to try. After numerous delays, Decipher, which had launched the **Star Trek** CCG the year before, got copies of the *Star Wars* game to market just in time for the 1995 holiday season. They didn't sit around long.

In its initial **Limited** release, the game revolved around the control of certain locations in the *Star Wars* universe. By controlling a location, players try to force their opponent to lose cards from his or her 60-card deck (termed a "Force drain" in the game). The first player to run out of cards loses. To control locations, players use the resources in their deck, such as characters and starships to fight and win over the opponents characters and starships. Battles had to be fought and won in order to win at the game. Battles can also cause an opponent to lose cards.

It soon became common knowledge that the more cards you could "Force drain" for at a single location, the more efficient your deck was. For example, Force-draining for five at one location was much more desirable and efficient than Force draining for only one at five different locations. As a result, most battles were fought only at one or two locations throughout an entire game.

Concept	●●●●●
Gameplay	●●●●○
Card art	●●●○○
Player pool	●●●●●

The most popular (and most powerful and expensive) cards were the main characters, like **Darth Vader, Luke Skywalker, Obi-Wan Kenobi,** and **Han Solo.** The *Limited Edition* versions sold for up to $50 on the singles market and still command solid prices today. Their rarity, however, was a disadvantage to some players.

Star Wars, with its enjoyable game mechanics and movie-like simulation, became a huge success. It became the #2 game behind **Magic: The Gathering** and enjoyed that position for several years, until the dawn of **Pokémon.** Even now, *Star Wars* still has a strong player base and continues to draw strong sales in a game market that gets more and more competitive every day. Some of that competition, in fact, comes from its own sister games launched by Decipher to further tap into *Star Wars* interest: **Young Jedi** in 1999 and **Jedi Knights** in 2001. — **Joe Alread**

Star Wars • Premiere Unlimited

Decipher • Released **May 1996**
324 cards in set • **IDENTIFIER: White border**

• Starter decks contain 60 cards; starter displays contain 12 starters
• Booster packs contain 15 cards; booster displays contain 36 boosters

The second printing of the **Premiere** set, the white-bordered **Unlimited** responded to the huge demand for out-of-print cards. No cards were changed or excluded from the first set except for a few text clarifications. — **Joe Alread**

Limited Set (324 cards)	375.00
Starter Display Box	110.00
Booster Display Box	134.50
Starter Deck	11.50
Booster Pack	4.50

36 nine-pocket pages to store this set. (18 doubled up)

Unlimited Set (324 cards)	225.00
Starter Display Box	95.00
Booster Display Box	89.00
Starter Deck	9.00
Booster Pack	3.00

36 nine-pocket pages to store this set. (18 doubled up)

LtdPrice	Card name	Side	Type	Rarity	UnlPrice
1.00	2X-3KPR (Tooex)	L	Dr	U1	1.00
4.00	5D6-RA-7 (Fivedesix)	D	Dr	R1	3.00
1.00	A Disturbance In The Force	D	E	U1	1.00
0.25	A Few Maneuvers	L	UI	C2	0.25
1.00	A Tremor in the Force	L	E	U1	1.00
4.00	Admiral Motti	D	Im	R2	3.00

LtdPrice	Card name	Side	Type	Rarity	UnlPrice
4.00	Affect Mind	L	E	R1	3.00
1.00	Alderaan	L	L	U2	1.00
3.50	Alderaan	D	L	R1	3.00
1.00	Alter	L	UI	U1	1.00
1.00	Alter	D	UI	U1	1.00
3.00	Assault Rifle	D	W	R2	3.00
0.25	Baniss Keeg	D	E	C2	0.25
0.80	Bantha	D	CV	U2	1.00
4.00	Beggar	L	E	R1	3.00
0.80	Beru Lars	L	R	U2	1.00
0.50	Beru Stew	L	LI	U2	1.00
5.00	Biggs Darklighter	L	R	R2	4.00
6.00	Black 2	D	SS	R1	4.00
1.00	Black 3	D	SS	U1	1.00
0.50	Blast Door Controls	D	E	U2	1.00
0.25	Blaster	L	W	C2	0.25
1.00	Blaster Rack	D	E	U1	1.00
0.25	Blaster Rifle	L	W	C1	0.25
0.25	Blaster Rifle	D	W	C2	0.25
1.00	Blaster Scope	D	D	U1	1.00

LtdPrice	Card name	Side	Type	Rarity	UnlPrice
1.00	Boosted TIE Cannon	D	SW	U1	1.00
4.00	Boring Conversation Anyway	D	UI	R1	3.00
1.00	BoShek	L	AI	U1	1.00
15.00	C-3PO (See-Threepio)	L	Dr	R1	10.50
0.80	Caller	L	D	U2	1.00
0.80	Caller	D	D	U2	1.00
4.00	Cantina Brawl	L	LI	R1	3.00
3.00	Charming to the Last	D	LI	R2	3.00
1.00	Chief Bast	D	Im	U1	1.00
0.25	Collateral Damage	D	LI	C2	0.25
0.25	Collision!	L	LI	C2	0.25
1.00	Colonel Wullf Yularen	D	Im	U1	1.00
0.25	Combined Attack	L	LI	C2	0.25
0.25	Comlink	D	D	C1	0.25
0.80	Commander Praji	D	Im	U1	1.00
1.00	Corellian Corvette	L	SS	U2	1.00
0.25	Counter Assault	D	LI	C1	0.25
1.00	Crash Site Memorial	L	E	U1	1.00
0.25	CZ-3 (Seezeethree)	L	Dr	C1	0.25

RARITY KEY C = Common   U = Uncommon   R = Rare   # = Lower #s are rarer   X = Fixed/standard in all decks   **CARD TYPES on page 438**

436 • SCRYE Collectible Card Game Checklist and Price Guide

LtdPrice	Card name	Side	Type	Rarity	UnlPrice
6					
1.00	Dantooine	L	L	U1	1.00
1.00	Dantooine	D	L	U1	1.00
4.00	Dark Collaboration	D	LI	R1	3.30
0.80	Dark Hours	D	E	U2	1.00
1.00	Dark Jedi Lightsaber	D	W	U1	1.00
5.00	Dark Jedi Presence	D	LI	R1	4.00
0.25	Dark Maneuvers	D	UI	C2	0.25
54.00	Darth Vader	D	Im	R1	41.00
1.00	Dathcha	D	AI	U1	1.00
7					
0.25	Dead Jawa	D	LI	C2	0.25
0.80	Death Star: Central Core	D	L	U2	1.00
0.80	Death Star: Detention Block Control Room	L	L	U2	1.00
0.25	Death Star: Detention Block Corridor	D	L	C1	0.25
0.25	Death Star: Docking Bay 327	L	L	C2	0.25
0.25	Death Star: Docking Bay 327	D	L	C2	0.25
1.00	Death Star: Level 4 Military Corridor	D	L	U1	1.00
4.00	Death Star Plans	L	UE	R1	4.00
1.00	Death Star Sentry	D	E	U1	1.00
8					
1.00	Death Star: Trash Compactor	L	L	U1	1.00
0.25	Death Star Trooper	D	Im	C2	0.25
0.80	Death Star: War Room	D	L	U2	1.00
4.00	Demotion	L	E	R2	3.00
15.00	Devastator	D	SS	R1	12.00
3.00	Dice Ibegon	L	AI	R2	3.00
4.00	Disarmed	L	E	R1	3.30
4.00	Disarmed	D	E	R1	3.30
3.00	Djas Puhr	D	AI	R2	3.00
9					
4.00	Don't Get Cocky	L	LI	R1	3.00
0.25	Don't Underestimate Our Chances	L	LI	C1	0.25
3.00	Dr. Evazan	D	AI	R2	3.00
0.25	Droid Detector	D	D	C2	0.25
0.25	Droid Shutdown	L	UI	C2	0.25
1.00	DS-61-2	D	Im	U1	1.00
6.00	DS-61-3	D	Im	R1	3.50
6.00	Dutch	L	R	R1	4.00
0.80	EG-6 (Eegee-Six)	D	D	U2	1.00
10					
0.25	Electrobinoculars	L	D	C2	0.25
1.00	Elis Helrot	D	UI	U2	1.00
0.25	Ellorrs Madak	L	E	C2	0.25
1.00	Emergency Deployment	D	UI	U1	1.00
0.80	Escape Pod	L	UI	U2	1.00
0.80	Evacuate?	D	UI	U2	1.00
5.00	Expand the Empire	D	E	R1	3.80
1.00	Eyes in the Dark	L	E	U1	1.00
3.00	Fear Will Keep Them In Line	D	E	R2	3.00
11					
1.00	Feltipern Trevagg	D	AI	U1	1.00
1.00	Figrin D'an	L	AI	U2	1.00
0.25	Friendly Fire	L	LI	C2	0.25
0.80	Full Scale Alert	D	LI	U2	1.00
3.00	Full Throttle	L	LI	R2	3.00
0.25	Fusion Generator Supply Tanks	L	D	C2	0.25
0.25	Fusion Generator Supply Tanks	D	D	C2	0.25
0.25	Gaderffii Stick	D	W	C2	0.25
3.00	Garindan	D	AI	R2	3.00
12					
1.00	General Dodonna	L	R	U1	1.00
5.00	General Tagge	D	Im	R2	3.00
5.00	Gift of the Mentor	L	LI	R1	4.00
4.00	Gold 1	L	SS	R2	3.00
4.00	Gold 5	L	SS	R2	3.00
20.00	Grand Moff Tarkin	D	Im	R1	14.00
0.80	Gravel Storm	D	LI	U2	1.00
3.00	Han Seeker	D	AW	R2	3.00
30.00	Han Solo	L	R	R1	21.00
13					
0.80	Han's Back	L	LI	U2	1.00

LtdPrice	Card name	Side	Type	Rarity	UnlPrice
0.25	Han's Dice	L	UI	C2	0.25
4.00	Han's Heavy Blaster Pistol	L	W	R2	3.00
0.25	Hear Me Baby, Hold Together	L	UI	C2	0.25
4.00	Help Me Obi-Wan Kenobi	L	UI	R1	3.30
0.80	How Did We Get Into This Mess	L	UI	U2	1.00
0.80	Hydroponics Station	L	D	U2	1.00
0.25	Hyper Escape	L	UI	C2	0.25
4.00	I Find Your Lack of Faith Disturbing	D	E	R1	3.80
14					
4.00	I Have You Now	D	LI	R2	3.00
0.25	Imperial Barrier	D	UI	C2	0.25
0.25	Imperial Blaster	D	W	C2	0.25
0.25	Imperial Code Cylinder	D	UI	C2	0.25
0.25	Imperial Pilot	D	Im	C2	0.25
0.25	Imperial Reinforcements	D	LI	C1	0.25
0.25	Imperial Trooper Guard	D	Im	C1	0.25
1.00	Imperial-Class Star Destroyer	D	SS	U1	1.00
3.00	Into the Garbage Chute, Flyboy	L	UI	R2	3.00
15					
1.00	Ion Cannon	D	SW	U1	1.00
0.25	It Could Be Worse	L	UI	C2	0.25
0.25	It's Worse	D	UI	C2	0.25
0.25	I've Got a Bad Feeling About This	L	UI	C2	0.25
0.25	I've Got a Problem Here	D	LI	C2	0.25
1.00	I've Lost Artoo!	D	E	U1	1.00
0.25	Jawa	L	AI	C2	0.25
0.25	Jawa	D	AI	C2	0.25
1.00	Jawa Pack	D	E	U1	1.00
16					
1.00	Jawa Siesta	L	E	U1	1.00
1.00	Jedi Lightsaber	L	W	U1	1.00
5.00	Jedi Presence	L	LI	R1	4.00
1.00	Jek Porkins	L	R	U1	1.00
3.00	Juri Juice	D	UE	R2	3.00
1.00	Kabe	L	AI	U1	1.00
5.00	Kal'Falnl C'ndros	L	AI	R1	3.50
1.00	Kessel	L	L	U2	1.00
1.00	Kessel	D	L	U2	1.00
17					
3.00	Kessel Run	L	UE	R2	3.00
0.25	Ket Maliss	D	E	C2	0.25
0.25	Kintan Strider	D	LI	C1	0.25
5.00	Kitik Keed'kak	D	AI	R1	3.80
3.00	K'lor'slug	L	E	R1	3.00
4.00	Krayt Dragon Howl	L	LI	R1	3.30
3.00	Labria	D	AI	R2	3.00
0.80	Laser Projector	D	AW	U2	1.00

LtdPrice	Card name	Side	Type	Rarity	UnlPrice
3.00	Lateral Damage	D	UE	R2	3.00
18					
3.00	Leesub Sirln	L	AI	R2	3.00
25.00	Leia Organa	L	R	R1	18.00
0.80	Leia's Back	L	LI	U2	1.00
1.00	Leia's Sporting Blaster	L	W	U1	1.00
0.80	Lieutenant Tanbris	D	Im	U2	1.00
0.25	Lift Tube	L	TV	C2	0.25
0.25	Lift Tube	D	TV	C2	0.25
4.00	Light Repeating Blaster Rifle	D	W	R1	3.50
5.00	Lightsaber Proficiency	L	E	R1	4.00
19					
0.80	Limited Resources	D	LI	U2	1.00
0.25	LIN-V8K	L	Dr	C1	0.25
0.25	LIN-V8M	D	Dr	C1	0.25
4.00	Local Trouble	D	E	R1	3.30
3.00	Lone Pilot	D	LI	R2	3.00
3.00	Lone Warrior	D	LI	R2	3.00
3.50	Look Sir, Droids	D	LI	R1	3.00
1.00	LUKE! LUUUKE!	D	UE	U1	1.00
3.00	Luke Seeker	D	AW	R2	3.00
20					
35.00	Luke Skywalker	L	R	R1	29.00
0.80	Luke's Back	L	LI	U2	1.00
1.00	Luke's X-34 Landspeeder	L	TV	U1	1.00
0.25	Macroscan	D	E	C2	0.25
3.00	Mantellian Savrip	L	E	R2	3.00
0.80	M'iiyoom Onith	D	AI	U2	1.00
25.00	Millennium Falcon	L	SS	R1	20.00
4.00	Molator	D	E	R1	3.00
0.80	Momaw Nadon	L	AI	U2	1.00
21					
3.00	Moment of Triumph	D	LI	R2	3.00
4.00	Move Along …	L	UI	R1	3.00
1.00	MSE-6 "Mouse" Droid	D	Dr	U1	1.00
3.00	Myo	D	AI	R2	3.00
0.80	Nabrun Leids	L	UI	U2	1.00
0.25	Narrow Escape	L	UI	C2	0.25
3.00	Nevar Yalnal	D	LI	R2	3.00
1.00	Nightfall	L	E	U1	1.00
3.00	Noble Sacrifice	L	LI	R2	3.00
22					
35.00	Obi-Wan Kenobi	L	R	R1	30.00
6.00	Obi-Wan's Cape	L	E	R1	4.00
8.00	Obi-Wan's Lightsaber	L	W	R1	6.50
0.80	Observation Holocam	D	D	U2	1.00
0.25	Old Ben	L	LI	C2	0.25
0.25	Ommni Box	D	UI	C2	0.25
4.00	On the Edge	L	E	R2	3.00
4.00	Organa's Ceremonial Necklace	D	UE	R1	3.50
4.00	Our Most Desperate Hour	L	UE	R1	3.50
23					
0.80	Out of Nowhere	L	UI	U2	1.00

RARITY KEY C = Common   U = Uncommon   R = Rare   # = Lower #s are rarer   X = Fixed/standard in all decks   **CARD TYPES on page 438**

LTDPRICE	Card name	Side	Type	Rarity	UNLPRICE
☐ 0.25	Overload	D	LI	C2	0.25 ☐
☐ 1.00	Owen Lars	L	R	U1	1.00 ☐
☐ 1.00	Panic	L	UI	U1	1.00 ☐
☐ 4.00	Physical Choke	D	LI	R1	3.30 ☐
☐ 0.80	Plastoid Armor	L	UE	U2	1.00 ☐
☐ 1.00	Ponda Baba	D	AI	U1	1.00 ☐
☐ 1.00	Pops	L	R	U1	1.00 ☐
☐ 0.25	Precise Attack	D	LI	C2	0.25 ☐
24					
☐ 5.00	Presence of the Force	D	E	R1	4.10 ☐
☐ 1.00	Prophetess	D	AI	U1	1.00 ☐
☐ 0.25	Proton Torpedoes	L	SW	C2	0.25 ☐
☐ 1.00	Quad Laser Cannon	L	SW	U1	1.00 ☐
☐ 0.25	R1-G4 (Arone-Geefour)	D	Dr	C2	0.25 ☐
☐ 0.25	R2-X2 (Arfour-Extoo)	L	Dr	C2	0.25 ☐
☐ 0.25	R4-E1 (Arfour-Eeone)	L	Dr	C2	0.25 ☐
☐ 0.25	R4-M9 (Arfour-Emmnine)	D	Dr	C2	0.25 ☐
☐ 0.25	Radar Scanner	L	UI	C2	0.25 ☐
25					
☐ 0.80	Reactor Terminal	D	E	U2	1.00 ☐
☐ 0.25	Rebel Barrier	L	UI	C2	0.25 ☐
☐ 0.25	Rebel Guard	L	R	C2	0.25 ☐
☐ 0.25	Rebel Pilot	L	R	C2	0.25 ☐
☐ 3.00	Rebel Planners	L	E	R2	3.00 ☐
☐ 0.25	Rebel Reinforcements	L	LI	C1	0.25 ☐
☐ 0.25	Rebel Trooper	L	R	C3	0.25 ☐
☐ 1.00	Red 1	L	SS	U1	1.00 ☐
☐ 4.00	Red 3	L	SS	R2	3.50 ☐

LTDPRICE	Card name	Side	Type	Rarity	UNLPRICE
26					
☐ 6.00	Red Leader	L	R	R1	3.50 ☐
☐ 0.25	Restraining Bolt	L	D	C2	0.25 ☐
☐ 0.25	Restraining Bolt	D	D	C2	0.25 ☐
☐ 1.00	Restricted Deployment	L	E	U1	1.00 ☐
☐ 0.80	Return of a Jedi	L	LI	U2	1.00 ☐
☐ 5.00	Revolution	L	E	R1	4.00 ☐
☐ 1.00	Rycar Ryjerd	L	E	U1	1.00 ☐
☐ 0.25	Sai'torr Kai Fas	L	E	C2	0.25 ☐
☐ 3.00	Sandcrawler	L	TV	R2	3.00 ☐
27					
☐ 3.00	Sandcrawler	D	TV	R2	3.00 ☐
☐ 0.25	Scanning Crew	D	UI	C2	0.25 ☐
☐ 0.25	Scomp Link Access	L	UI	C2	0.25 ☐
☐ 4.00	Send a Detachment Down	D	UE	R1	3.00 ☐
☐ 1.00	Sense	L	UI	U1	1.00 ☐
☐ 1.00	Sense	D	UI	U1	1.00 ☐
☐ 0.25	Set for Stun	D	LI	C2	0.25 ☐
☐ 0.25	Shistavanen Wolfman	L	AI	C2	0.25 ☐
☐ 4.00	Skywalkers	L	LI	R1	3.00 ☐
28					
☐ 3.00	Solo Han	L	LI	R2	3.00 ☐
☐ 0.25	SoroSuub V-35 Landspeeder	L	TV	C2	0.25 ☐
☐ 0.80	Spaceport Speeders	L	UI	U2	1.00 ☐
☐ 1.00	Special Modifications	L	E	U1	1.00 ☐
☐ 0.25	Stormtrooper	D	Im	C3	0.25 ☐
☐ 0.25	Stormtrooper Backpack	D	D	C2	0.25 ☐
☐ 0.25	Stormtrooper Utility Belt	D	D	C2	0.25 ☐
☐ 1.00	Sunsdown	D	E	U1	1.00 ☐
☐ 0.25	Surprise Assault	L	LI	C1	0.25 ☐
29					
☐ 3.00	Tactical Re-Call	D	UE	R2	3.00 ☐
☐ 3.00	Tagge Seeker	L	AW	R2	3.00 ☐
☐ 0.25	Takeel	D	LI	C2	0.25 ☐
☐ 0.25	Tallon Roll	D	UI	C2	0.25 ☐
☐ 0.25	Talz	L	AI	C2	0.25 ☐
☐ 1.00	Targeting Computer	L	D	U1	1.00 ☐
☐ 3.00	Tarkin Seeker	L	AW	R2	3.00 ☐
☐ 0.25	Tatooine	L	L	C2	0.25 ☐
☐ 0.25	Tatooine	D	L	C2	0.25 ☐
30					
☐ 3.00	Tatooine: Cantina	L	L	R2	3.00 ☐
☐ 3.00	Tatooine: Cantina	D	L	R2	3.00 ☐
☐ 0.25	Tatooine: Docking Bay 94	L	L	C2	0.25 ☐
☐ 0.25	Tatooine: Docking Bay 94	D	L	C2	0.25 ☐
☐ 0.25	Tatooine: Dune Sea	L	L	C1	0.25 ☐
☐ 0.25	Tatooine: Jawa Camp	L	L	C1	0.25 ☐
☐ 0.25	Tatooine: Jawa Camp	D	L	C1	0.25 ☐
☐ 0.25	Tatooine: Jundland Wastes	D	L	C1	0.25 ☐
☐ 0.25	Tatooine: Lars' Moisture Farm	L	L	C1	0.25 ☐
31					
☐ 0.80	Tatooine: Lars' Moisture Farm	D	L	U2	1.00 ☐
☐ 0.25	Tatooine: Mos Eisley	D	L	C1	0.25 ☐
☐ 0.80	Tatooine: Mos Eisley	L	L	U2	1.00 ☐
☐ 5.00	Tatooine: Obi-Wan's Hut	L	L	R1	3.50 ☐
☐ 0.25	Tatooine Utility Belt	L	D	C2	0.25 ☐

LTDPRICE	Card name	Side	Type	Rarity	UNLPRICE
☐ 3.50	Thank the Maker	L	UE	R2	3.00 ☐
☐ 0.25	The Bith Shuffle	L	UI	C2	0.25 ☐
☐ 5.00	The Circle is Now Complete	D	LI	R1	3.50 ☐
☐ 1.00	The Empire's Back	D	LI	U1	0.80 ☐
32					
☐ 4.00	The Force Is Strong With This One	L	LI	R2	3.00 ☐
☐ 1.00	This is All Your Fault	L	UI	U1	0.80 ☐
☐ 1.00	TIE Advanced x1	D	SS	U2	0.90 ☐
☐ 0.25	TIE Fighter	D	SS	C2	0.25 ☐
☐ 0.25	TIE Scout	D	SS	C2	0.25 ☐
☐ 0.25	Timer Mine	L	AW	C2	0.25 ☐
☐ 0.25	Timer Mine	D	AW	C2	0.25 ☐
☐ 5.00	Tonnika Sisters	D	AI	R1	4.00 ☐
☐ 1.00	Traffic Control	L	E	U2	1.00 ☐
33					
☐ 1.00	Trinto Duaba	D	UI	U1	1.00 ☐
☐ 0.50	Trooper Charge	D	LI	U2	1.00 ☐
☐ 3.00	Turbolaser Battery	D	SW	R2	3.00 ☐
☐ 1.00	Tusken Breath Mask	L	UE	U1	1.00 ☐
☐ 0.25	Tusken Raider	D	AI	C2	0.25 ☐
☐ 0.25	Tusken Scavengers	D	LI	C2	0.25 ☐
☐ 0.25	Ubrikkian 9000-Z001	D	TV	C2	0.25 ☐
☐ 4.00	Utinni!	L	UI	R1	3.00 ☐
☐ 4.00	Utinni!	D	UI	R1	3.00 ☐
34					
☐ 11.00	Vader's Custom TIE	D	SS	R1	9.00 ☐
☐ 4.00	Vader's Eye	D	LI	R1	4.00 ☐
☐ 10.00	Vader's Lightsaber	D	W	R1	8.00 ☐
☐ 0.25	Vaporator	L	D	C2	0.25 ☐
☐ 3.00	Warrior's Courage	L	LI	R2	3.00 ☐
☐ 3.50	WED-9-M1 "Bantha"	L	Dr	R2	3.00 ☐
☐ 3.50	WED15-1662 "Treadwell"	D	Dr	R2	3.00 ☐
☐ 4.00	We're All Gonna Be a Lot Thinner	D	LI	R1	3.50 ☐
35					
☐ 0.25	We're Doomed	L	UI	C2	0.25 ☐
☐ 1.00	Wioslea	L	AI	U1	1.00 ☐
☐ 1.00	Wrong Turn	D	E	U1	1.00 ☐
☐ 0.80	Wuher	D	AI	U2	1.00 ☐
☐ 0.25	X-wing	L	SS	C2	0.25 ☐
☐ 0.25	Yavin 4	L	L	C2	0.25 ☐
☐ 0.25	Yavin 4	D	L	C2	0.25 ☐
☐ 0.25	Yavin 4: Docking Bay	L	L	C2	0.25 ☐
☐ 0.25	Yavin 4: Docking Bay	D	L	C2	0.25 ☐
☐ 0.25	Yavin 4: Jungle	L	L	C1	0.25 ☐
36					
☐ 0.50	Yavin 4: Jungle	D	L	U2	1.00 ☐
☐ 4.50	Yavin 4: Massassi Throne Room	L	L	R1	3.50 ☐
☐ 0.80	Yavin 4: Massassi War Rm	L	L	U2	1.00 ☐
☐ 0.50	Yavin Sentry	L	E	U2	1.00 ☐
☐ 1.00	Yerka Mig	L	UE	U1	1.00 ☐
☐ 0.25	You Overestimate Their Chances	D	LI	C1	0.25 ☐
☐ 1.00	Your Eyes Can Deceive You	D	E	U1	1.00 ☐
☐ 4.00	Your Powers Are Weak, Old Man	D	LI	R1	3.30 ☐
☐ 0.25	Y-wing	L	SS	C2	0.25 ☐

Star Wars card type key

Card Type Key

AI:	Alien
AW:	Artillery Weapon
Ch:	Character
Ch W:	Character Weapon
Cr:	Creature
CV:	Creature Vehicle
D:	Device
Dr:	Droid
DSW:	Death Star Weapon
E:	Effect
EpEv:	Epic Event
IE:	Immediate Effect
Imp:	Imperial
JM:	Jedi Master
J Tst:	Jedi Test
L Int:	Lost Interrupt
L-Sec:	Location/Sector
L-Site:	Location/Site
L-Sys:	Location/System
ME:	Mobile Effect
Reb:	Rebel
SnCr:	Snow Creature
SShp:	Starship
SV:	Shuttle Vehicle
SW:	Starship Weapon
SwpCr:	Swamp Creature
Ut Ef:	Utinni Effect
Ut Ev:	Utinni Event
U Int:	Used Interrupt
U/L Int:	Used or Lost Interrupt
U/St Int:	Used or Starting Interrupt
TV:	Transport Vehicle
Veh W:	Vehicle Weapon
W:	Character Weapon
Wp:	Weapon

Star Wars • Jedi Pack

Decipher • Released February 1997

• Pack contains 11 cards

The **Jedi Pack** was given out to players in appreciation for their support. Packs were inserted in **Scrye** #18 (Feb 98). While most were hardly ever used, (many of the cards didn't even have game text!) a single card, **Gravity Shadow** makes it into a good deck every now and then. The packs are still available for free from Decipher, giving them little secondary market value. — **Joe Alread**

Jedi Pack   **5.00**

☐ Dark Forces ☐ Eriadu ☐ For Luck ☐ Gravity Shadow ☐ Han
☐ Hyperroute Navigation Chart ☐ Leia ☐ Luke's T-16 Skyhopper
☐ Motti   ☐ Tarkin   ☐ Tedn Dahai

RARITY KEY C = Common U = Uncommon R = Rare # = Lower numbers are rarer X = Fixed/standard in all decks

Star Wars • A New Hope

Decipher • Released **July 1996**

162 cards in set • **IDENTIFIER: Circle in upper right shows clashing sabers**

• Booster packs contain 15 cards; booster displays contain 36 boosters

A New Hope, the first expansion for *Star Wars*, brought the rest of the main characters from the first *Star Wars* movie. **Chewbacca**, **R2-D2**, and the **Death Star** were all big draws for the first expansion. Players could now play the epic battle of Yavin IV, with game mechanics simulating the destruction of planet systems and even the Death Star itself. Also, many of the game's powerful strategies from the first set are toned down a bit, such as playing with multiples of a single card or choking off your opponents' resources.

Unfortunately, blowing away planet systems or the Death Star never really became powerful strategies. However, the fixer cards that came out of this set still see play today and have become what this set will always be remembered for.

A white-bordered **Unlimited** edition exists and has only text changes. — **Joe Alread**

Set (162 cards)	150.00	**18** nine-pocket pages to store this set. (9 doubled up)
Booster Display Box	125.00	
Booster Pack	4.00	

Card name	Side	Type	Rarity	Price
Advance Preparation	L	UI/LI	U1	1.00
Advosze	D	Ch:Al	C2	0.25
Alternatives To Fighting	L	LI	U1	1.00
Arcona	L	Ch:Al	C2	0.25
Astromech Shortage	D	Ef	U2	0.80
Attack Run	L	EE	R2	4.00
Besieged	D	Ef	R2	3.00
Bespin Motors Void Spider THX 1138	D	SV	C2	0.25
Black 4	D	Ss	U2	1.00
Blast The Door, Kid!	L	LI	C2	0.25
Blue Milk	L	UI/LI	C2	0.25
Bowcaster	L	ChW	R2	4.00
Brainiac	L	Ch:Al	R1	6.00
Captain Khurgee	D	Ch:Imp	U1	1.00
Cell 2187	L	UEf	R1	4.00
Chewbacca	L	Ch:Al/RR	R2	15.00
Clak'dor VII	L	L	R2	3.00
Come With Me	D	Ef	C2	0.25
Commander Evram Lajaie	L	Ch:R	C1	0.25
Commander Vanden Willard	L	Ch:R	U2	0.80
Commence Primary Ignition	D	EE	R2	5.00
Commence Recharging	L	Ef	R2	3.50
Conquest	D	Ss	R1	12.00
Corellia	L	L	R1	4.00
Corellian	L	Ch:Al	C2	0.25
Corellian Slip	L	UI	C2	0.25
Dannik Jerriko	D	Ch:Al	R1	4.50
Danz Borin	D	Ch:Al	U2	0.80
Dark Waters	D	Ef	R2	3.00
Death Star	D	L	R2	12.00
Death Star: Conference Room	D	L	U1	1.00
Death Star Gunner	D	Ch:Imp	C1	0.25
Death Star Tractor Beam	D	Dv	R2	3.00
Death Star: Trench	L	L	R2	4.00
Defel	D	Ch:Al	C2	0.25
Dejarik Hologameboard	L	L	R1	4.00
Dianoga	D	SpCr	R2	3.50
Doikk Na'ts	L	Ch:Al	U2	0.80
Double Agent	L	LI	R2	3.00
DS-61-4	D	Ch:Imp	R2	4.00
Eject! Eject!	L	Ef	C2	0.25
Enhanced TIE Laser Cannon	D	SsW	C2	0.25
Evader	D	UI/LI	U1	1.00
Fire Extinguisher	L	Dv	U2	0.80
Garouf Lafoe	L	Ch:Al	U2	0.50
Ghhhk	D	LI	C2	0.25
Gold 2	L	Ss	U1	1.00
Grappling Hook	L	ImEf	C2	0.25
Greedo	D	Ch:Al	R1	8.50
Grimtaash	L	UI/LI	C2	0.25

Card name	Side	Type	Rarity	Price
Hem Dazon	D	Ch:Al	R1	4.00
Het Nkik	L	Ch:Al	U2	0.50
Houjix	L	LI	C2	0.25
Hunchback	L	Ch:Al	R1	4.50
Hyperwave Scan	D	Ef	U1	1.00
Hypo	D	Dv	R1	4.00
I Have A Very Bad Feeling About This	L	UI	C2	0.25
Ickabel G'ont	L	Ch:Al	U2	1.00
I'm Here To Rescue You	L	UI	U1	1.00
I'm On The Leader	D	LI	R1	3.60
Imperial Commander	D	Ch:Imp	C2	0.25
Imperial Holotable	D	L	R1	4.70
Imperial Justice	D	Ef	C2	0.25
Imperial Squad Leader	D	Ch:Imp	C3	0.10
Incom T-16 Skyhopper	L	SV	C2	0.25
Informant	D	UI	U1	1.00
IT-O (Eyetee-Oh)	D	Ch:D	R1	4.80
Jawa Blaster	D	ChW	C2	0.25
Jawa Ion Gun	L	ChW	C2	0.25
Kashyyyk	L	L	C1	0.25
Kashyyyk	D	L	C1	0.25
Kiffex	D	L	R1	4.00
Krayt Dragon Bones	D	Ef	U1	1.00
Laser Gate	D	Dv	U2	0.50
Leia Seeker	D	AW	R2	3.00
Let The Wookiee Win	L	LI	R1	4.00
Lirin Car'n	D	Ch:Al	U2	0.50
Logistical Delay	L	Ef	U2	0.50
Lt. Pol Treidum	D	Ch:Imp	C1	0.25
Lt. Shann Childsen	D	Ch:Imp	U1	1.00
Luke's Cape	L	Ef	R1	5.00
Luke's Hunting Rifle	L	ChW	U1	0.80
M-HYD "Binary" Droid	L	Ch:D	U1	0.80
Magnetic Suction Tube	L	Dv	R2	3.00
Magnetic Suction Tube	D	Dv	R2	3.00
Maneuver Check	D	Ef	R2	3.30
Merc Sunlet	L	Ef	C2	0.25
Mobquet A-1 Deluxe Floater	D	TV	C2	0.25
Monnok	D	UI/LI	C2	0.25
Mosep	D	Ch:Al	U2	0.50
Motti Seeker	L	AW	R2	3.00
Nalan Cheel	L	Ch:Al	U2	0.50
Ng'ok	D	UI	C2	0.25
Officer Evax	D	Ch:Imp	C1	0.25
Oo-ta Goo-ta, Solo?	D	UI	C2	0.25
Out Of Commission	L	UI	U2	0.50
Program Trap	D	Ef	U1	1.00
Quite A Mercenary	L	UI	C2	0.25
R2-D2 (Artoo-Detoo)	L	Ch:D	R2	14.00
R2-Q2 (Artoo-Kyootoo)	D	Ch:D	C2	0.25
R3-T6 (Arthree-Teesix)	D	Ch:D	R1	5.00
R5-A2 (Arfive-Aytoo)	D	Ch:D	C2	0.25
R5-D4 (Arfive-Defour)	L	Ch:D	C2	0.25
RA-7 (Aray-Seven)	L	Ch:D	C2	0.25
Ralltiir	L	L	C1	0.25
Ralltiir	D	L	C1	0.25
Rebel Commander	L	Ch:R	C2	0.25

Card name	Side	Type	Rarity	Price
Rebel Squad Leader	L	Ch:R	C3	0.10
Rebel Tech	L	Ch:R	C1	0.25
Rectenna	L	Dv	C2	0.25
Red 2	L	Ss	R1	6.00
Red 5	L	Ss	R1	9.00
Red 6	L	Ss	U1	1.00
Reegesk	D	Ch:Al	U2	0.50
Remote	L	Dv	C2	0.25
Reserve Pilot	D	Ch:Imp	U1	1.00
Retract The Bridge	D	LI	R1	4.00
Rodian	D	Ch:Al	C2	0.25
Rogue Bantha	L	CrV	U1	1.00
Sabotage	L	UI	U1	1.00
Sandcrawler: Droid Junkheap	D	L	R1	4.00
Sandcrawler: Loading Bay	L	L	R1	4.00
Saurin	L	Ch:Al	C2	0.25
Scanner Techs	L	Ef	U1	1.00
Sensor Panel	L	Dv	U1	1.00
Sniper	D	LI	U1	1.00
Solomahal	L	Ef	C2	0.25
Sorry About The Mess	L	LI	U1	1.00
Spice Mines Of Kessel	D	UEf	R1	4.00
Stunning Leader	D	LI	C2	0.25
Superlaser	D	DSW	R2	5.00
SW-4 Ion Cannon	L	SsW	R2	3.80
Swilla Corey	D	Ef	C2	0.25
Tantive IV	L	Ss	R1	12.00
Tatooine: Bluffs	D	L	R1	4.00
Tech Mo'r	D	Ch:Al	U2	0.50
Tentacle	D	ImEf	C2	0.25
There'll Be Hell To Pay	D	ImEf	U2	0.50
They're On Dantooine	L	UEf	R1	4.00
This Is Some Rescue!	D	UI	U1	1.00
TIE Assault Squadron	D	Ss	U1	1.00
TIE Vanguard	D	Ss	C2	0.25
Tiree	L	Ch:R	U2	1.00
Tractor Beam	D	Dv	U1	1.00
Trooper Davin Felth	D	Ch:Imp	R2	3.30
Tzizvvt	L	Ch:Al	R2	3.00
U-3PO (Yoo-Threepio)	D	Ch:D	R1	5.00
Undercover	L	Ef	U2	0.50
Undercover	D	Ef	U2	0.50
URoRRuR'R'R	D	Ch:Al	U2	0.50
URoRRuR'R'R's Hunting Rifle	D	ChW	U1	1.00
Victory-Class Star Destroyer	D	Ss	U1	1.00
We Have A Prisoner	D	LI	C2	0.25
WED15-I7 "Septoid" Droid	D	Ch:D	U2	0.50
Wedge Antilles	L	Ch:R	R1	15.00
What're You Tryin' To Push On Us?	L	ImEf	U2	0.50
Wookiee Roar	L	LI	R1	4.00
Yavin 4: Briefing Room	L	L	U1	1.00
Yavin 4: Massassi Ruins	L	L	U1	1.00
You're All Clear Kid!	L	UI	R1	4.00
Y-wing Assault Squadron	L	Ss	U1	1.00
Zutton	L	Ch:Al	C1	0.25

RARITY KEY C = Common   U = Uncommon   R = Rare   # = Lower #s are rarer   X = Fixed/standard in all decks   **CARD TYPES on page 438**

SCRYE Collectible Card Game Checklist and Price Guide • **439**

Star Wars • Hoth

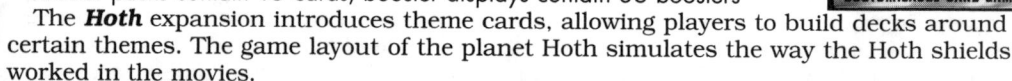

Decipher • Released **October 1996**

162 cards in set • **IDENTIFIER: Planet Hoth in circle at upper right**

• Booster packs contain 15 cards; booster displays contain 36 boosters

The **Hoth** expansion introduces theme cards, allowing players to build decks around certain themes. The game layout of the planet Hoth simulates the way the Hoth shields worked in the movies.

The cards that saw (and still see) action from the **Hoth** set are Imperial Walkers and **Echo Base Operations**. Walkers dominate on the ground, while **Echo Base Operations** gives the Rebels a new life in space. Many decks became either Hoth- or Tatooine-themed, since most players wanted to concentrate their forces on one planet, and not divide them.

This set also saw the first new persona of a main character, **Commander Luke Skywalker**. While not as useful as the original Luke, it was still sought after.

A white-bordered **Unlimited** edition exists and has only text changes. — **Joe Alread**

Set (162 cards)				150.00
Booster Display Box				123.50
Booster Pack				4.00

You will need 18 nine-pocket pages to store this set. (9 doubled up)

Card name	Side	Type	Rarity	Price
2-1B (Too-Onebee)	L	Ch: Dr	R1	4.50
A Dark Time For The Rebellion	D	LI	C1	0.15
Admiral Ozzel	D	Ch: Im	R1	6.00
Anakin's Lightsaber	L	Ch W	R1	12.00
Artillery Remote	L	D	R2	3.00
AT-AT Cannon	D	V W	U1	1.00
AT-AT Driver	D	Ch: Im	C2	0.15
Atgar Laser Cannon	L	Art W	U2	0.50
Attack Pattern Delta	L	LI	U1	0.70
Bacta Tank	L	E	R2	3.00
Blizzard 1	D	CV	R1	8.60
Blizzard 2	D	CV	R2	5.50
Blizzard Scout 1	D	CV	R1	7.90
Blizzard Walker	D	CV	U2	1.00
Breached Defenses	D	Imm E	U2	0.50
Cal Alder	L	Ch: R	U2	0.50
Captain Lennox	D	Ch: Im	U1	0.80
Captain Piett	D	Ch: Im	R2	5.00
Cold Feet	D	UI	C2	0.15
Collapsing Corridor	D	LI	R2	3.00
Commander Luke Skywalker	L	Ch: R	R1	23.75
ComScan Detection	D	UI	C2	0.15
Concussion Grenade	L	Ch W	R1	5.00
Crash Landing	D	UI	U1	0.70
Dack Ralter	L	Ch: R	R2	3.50
Dark Dissension	L	U or LI	R1	4.00
Death Mark	D	Ut E	R1	4.00
Death Squadron	D	E	U1	1.00
Debris Zone	D	UI	R2	3.00
Deflector Shield Generators	D	D	U2	0.50
Derek "Hobbie" Klivian	L	Ch: R	U1	1.00
Direct Hit	D	U or LI	U1	0.70
Disarming Creature	L	Imm E	R1	4.00
Dual Laser Cannon	L	V W	U1	1.00
Echo Base Operations	L	E	R2	4.00
Echo Base Trooper	L	Ch: R	C3	0.15
Echo Base Trooper Officer	L	Ch: R	C1	0.15
Echo Trooper Backpack	L	D	C2	0.15
EG-4 (Eegee-Four)	L	Ch: Dr	C1	0.15
Electro-Rangefinder	D	D	U1	0.90
Evacuation Control	L	E	U1	0.70
E-web Blaster	D	Art W	C1	0.15
Exhaustion	D	LI	U2	0.50
Exposure	D	LI	U1	0.90
Fall Back!	L	LI	C2	0.10
Frostbite	L	E	C2	0.15
Frostbite	D	E	C2	0.15
Frozen Dinner	D	Imm E	R1	4.00
Furry Fury	D	U or LI	R2	3.00
FX-7 (Effex-Seven)	L	Ch: Dr	C2	0.15
FX-10 (Effex-ten)	D	Ch: Dr	C2	0.15
General Carlist Rieekan	L	Ch: R	R2	4.00

Card name	Side	Type	Rarity	Price
General Veers	D	Ch: Im	R1	8.30
Golan Laser Battery	L	Art W	U1	1.00
He Hasn't Come Back Yet	D	LI	C2	0.15
High Anxiety	D	Imm E	R1	4.00
Hoth	L	L	U2	0.50
Hoth	D	L	U2	0.50
Hoth: Defensive Perimeter	L	L	C2	0.15
Hoth: Defensive Perimeter	D	L	C2	0.10
Hoth: Echo Command Center (War Room)	L	L	U2	0.50
Hoth: Echo Command Center (War Room)	D	L	U2	0.50
Hoth: Echo Corridor	L	L	C2	0.20
Hoth: Echo Corridor	D	L	U2	0.50
Hoth: Echo Docking Bay	L	L	C2	0.15
Hoth: Echo Docking Bay	D	L	C2	0.15
Hoth: Echo Med Lab	L	L	C2	0.15
Hoth: Ice Plains	D	L	C2	0.15
Hoth: Main Power Generators	L	L	U2	0.70
Hoth: North Ridge	L	L	C2	0.15
Hoth: North Ridge	D	L	C2	0.15
Hoth: Snow Trench	L	L	C2	0.15
Hoth Survival Gear	L	D	C2	0.15
Hoth: Wampa Cave	D	L	R2	3.00
I Thought They Smelled Bad On The Outside	L	UI	R1	4.00
Ice Storm	L	ME	U1	1.00
Ice Storm	D	ME	U1	1.00
I'd Just As Soon Kiss A Wookiee	D	LI	C2	0.15
Image Of The Dark Lord	D	E	R2	3.00
Imperial Domination	D	E	U1	0.70
Imperial Gunner	D	Ch: Im	C2	0.15
Imperial Supply	D	U or LI	C1	0.15
Infantry Mine	L	AW	C2	0.15
Infantry Mine	D	AW	C2	0.15
It Can Wait	L	LI	C2	0.15
Jeroen Webb	L	Ch: R	U1	0.70
K-3PO (Kay-Threepio)	L	Ch: Dr	R1	5.00
Lieutenant Cabbel	D	Ch: Im	U2	0.50
Lightsaber Deficiency	D	UI	U1	0.70
Lucky Shot	L	U or LI	U1	0.70
Major Bren Derlin	L	Ch: R	R2	3.00
Medium Repeating Blaster Cannon	L	Art W	C1	0.15
Medium Transport	L	S	U2	0.50
Meteor Impact?	D	Ut E	R1	4.00
Mournful Roar	D	Imm E	R1	4.00
Nice Of You Guys To Drop By	L	UI	C2	0.15
Oh, Switch Off	D	UI	C2	0.15
One More Pass	L	UI	U1	0.70
Ord Mantell	L	L	U2	0.50
Ord Mantell	D	L	C2	0.15
Our First Catch Of The Day	D	UI	C2	0.15
Perimeter Scan	L	UI	C2	0.10
Planet Defender Ion Cannon	L	Art W	R2	3.50
Portable Fusion Generator	D	D	C2	0.10
Power Harpoon	L	V W	U1	0.90
Probe Antennae	D	D	U2	0.60
Probe Droid	D	Ch: Dr	C2	0.15

Card name	Side	Type	Rarity	Price
Probe Droid Laser	D	Ch W	U2	0.50
Probe Telemetry	D	UI	C2	0.10
R2 Sensor Array	L	D	C2	0.15
R-3PO (Ar-Threepio)	L	Ch: Dr	R2	3.00
R5-M2 (Arfive-Emmtoo)	L	Ch: Dr	C2	0.15
Rebel Scout	L	Ch: R	C1	0.15
Responsibility Of Command	D	Ut E	R1	4.00
Rogue 1	L	CV	R1	8.00
Rogue 2	L	CV	R2	5.00
Rogue 3	L	CV	R1	7.00
Rogue Gunner	L	Ch: R	C2	0.15
Romas "Lock" Navander	L	Ch: R	U2	0.60
Rug Hug	L	LI	R1	4.00
Scruffy-Looking Nerf Herder	D	U or LI	R2	3.00
Self-Destruct Mechanism	D	UI	U1	0.70
Shawn Valdez	L	Ch: R	U1	0.70
Silence Is Golden	D	E	U2	0.50
Snowspeeder	L	CV	U2	1.00
Snowtrooper	D	Ch: Im	C3	0.15
Snowtrooper Officer	D	Ch: Im	C1	0.15
Stalker	D	S	R1	12.00
Stop Motion	D	UI	C2	0.15
Surface Defense Cannon	L	S W	R2	3.00
Tactical Support	D	LI	R2	3.00
Tamizander Rey	L	Ch: R	U2	0.50
Target The Main Generator	D	EEv	R2	4.00
Tauntaun	L	Cr V	C2	0.15
Tauntaun Bones	L	E	U1	0.70
Tauntaun Handler	L	Ch: R	C2	0.10
That's It, The Rebels Are There!	D	UI	U2	0.50
The First Transport Is Away!	L	Ut E	R1	4.00
The Shield Doors Must Be Closed	D	E	U1	0.70
This Is Just Wrong	D	Ut E	R1	4.00
Tigran Jamiro	L	Ch: R	U1	0.70
Too Cold For Speeders	D	E	U1	0.70
Toryn Farr	L	Ch: R	U1	0.70
Trample	D	I	R1	5.00
Turn It Off! Turn It Off!	D	U or LI	C1	0.15
Tyrant	D	S	R1	12.00
Under Attack	L	UI	U1	0.70
Vehicle Mine	L	AW	C2	0.15
Vehicle Mine	D	AW	C2	0.15
Walker Barrage	D	UI	U1	0.70
Walker Sighting	L	LI	U2	0.50
Wall Of Fire	D	LI	U1	0.70
Wampa	D	SnCr	R2	4.00
Weapon Malfunction	D	Ut E	R1	4.00
WED-1016 'Techie' Droid	L	Ch: Dr	C1	0.15
Wes Janson	L	Ch: R	R1	4.00
Who's Scruffy-Looking?	L	UI	R1	4.00
Wyron Serper	L	Ch: R	U2	0.50
Yaggle Gakkle	D	UI	R2	3.00
You Have Failed Me For The Last Time	L	LI	R1	4.10
You Will Go To The Dagobah System	L	LI	R1	4.00
Zev Senesca	L	Ch: R	R2	3.00

RARITY KEY C = Common U = Uncommon R = Rare # = Lower #s are rarer X = Fixed/standard in all decks **CARD TYPES on page 438**

Star Wars • Dagobah

Decipher • Released April 1997

180 cards in set • **IDENTIFIER: Yoda's eye in circle at upper right**

• Booster packs contain 9 cards; booster displays contain 60 boosters

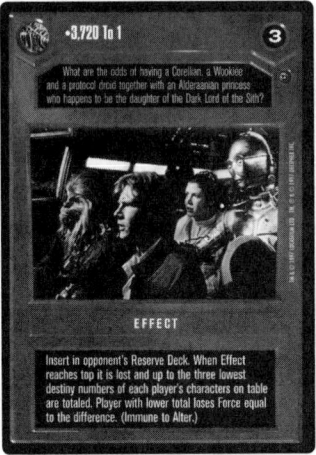

Dagobah remains the most powerful expansion ever created for **Star Wars**. Even today, when players go to make a new deck, they head for their *Dagobah* binder first.

Dagobah tended to reduce interaction in the game. Dark Side players couldn't deploy to Dagobah at all, and the new asteroid fields were risky to challenge an opponent in. Players grew afraid to fight each other, a feeling that took a number of expansions to change. Mechanics allowing a player to manipulate an opponent's cards entered the fray with this set, as well, and it's these cards that players still look to today.

High-level strategies upon *Dagobah*'s release were, as noted, low on interaction. Battles were few and far between. Because of cards that punished decks for having main characters, decks without a single main character also became viable.

A white-bordered **Unlimited** edition exists and has only text changes. — **Joe Alread**

Set (180 cards)	150.00	**You will need 20** nine-pocket pages to store this set. (10 doubled up)
Booster Display Box	142.50	
Booster Pack	2.50	

Card name	Side	Type	Rarity	Price
1				
4-LOM	D	Ch:Dr	R	7.00
4-LOM's Concussion Rifle	D	Ch:W	R	4.00
3,720 To 1	D	E	C	0.20
A Dangerous Time	D	U/L Int	C	0.20
A Jedi's Strength	L	J Tst	U	0.80
Anger, Fear, Aggression	L	E	C	0.20
Anoat	L	L-Sys	U	0.60
Anoat	D	L Sys	U	0.60
Apology Accepted	D	U Int	C	0.20
2				
Asteroid Field	L	L-Sec	C	0.20
Asteroid Field	D	L Sec	C	0.20
Asteroid Sanctuary	L	E	C	0.20
Asteroids Do Not Concern Me	L	Ut E	R	3.00
Astromech Translator	L	D	C	0.20
At Peace	L	Imm E	R	3.00
Avenger	D	S	R	12.00
Away Put Your Weapon	L	U/L Int	U	0.80
Awwww, Cannot Get Your Ship Out	D	E	C	0.20
3				
Bad Feeling Have I	D	E	R	3.00
Big One	L	L-Sec	U	0.80
Big One	D	L Sec	U	0.80
Big One: Asteroid Cave or Space Slug Belly	L	L-Site	U	0.80
Big One: Asteroid Cave or Space Slug Belly	D	L Site	U	0.80
Blasted Varmints	L	U I	C	0.20
Bog-wing	L	Cr	C	0.20
Bog-wing	D	Cr	C	0.20
Bombing Run	D	Mob E	R	3.00
4				
Bossk	D	Ch:Al	R	8.00
Bossk's Mortar Gun	D	Ch:W	R	4.00
Broken Concentration	D	E	R	3.00
Captain Needa	D	Ch:Imp	R	5.00
Close Call	D	U/L Int	C	0.20
Closer?!	L	U I	U	0.80
Comm Chief	D	Ch:Imp	C	0.20
Commander Brandei	D	Ch:Imp	U	0.80
Commander Gherant	D	Ch:Imp	U	0.80
5				
Commander Nemet	D	Ch:Imp	U	0.80
Control	L	L Int	U	1.00
Control	D	L Int	U	1.00
Corporal Derdram	D	Ch:Imp	U	0.80
Corporal Vandolay	D	Ch:Imp	U	0.90
Corrosive Damage	D	E	R	3.00
Dagobah	L	L-Sys	U	0.80
Dagobah: Bog Clearing	L	L-Site	R	4.00
Dagobah: Cave	D	L Site	R	3.50

Card name	Side	Type	Rarity	Price
6				
Dagobah: Jungle	L	L-Site	U	0.80
Dagobah: Swamp	L	L-Site	U	0.80
Dagobah: Training Area	L	L-Site	C	0.20
Dagobah: Yoda's Hut	L	L-Site	R	4.00
Defensive Fire	D	U Int	C	0.20
Dengar	D	Ch:Al	R	8.00
Dengar's Blaster Carbine	D	Ch:W	R	5.00
Descent Into The Dark	L	Imm E	R	3.00
Do, Or Do Not	L	E	C	0.20
7				
Domain Of Evil	L	J Tst	U	0.80
Dragonsnake	D	Cr	R	3.00
Droid Sensorscope	L	Dev	C	0.20
Effective Repairs	L	U/L Int	R	3.00
Egregious Pilot Error	L	L Int	R	3.00
Encampment	L	E	C	0.20
Executor	D	S	R	22.50
Executor: Comm Station	D	L Site	U	0.80
Executor: Control Station	D	L Site	U	0.80
8				
Executor: Holotheatre	D	L Site	R	4.00
Executor: Main Corridor	D	L Site	C	0.20
Executor: Meditation Chamber	D	L Site	R	4.00
Failure At The Cave	D	Ut E	R	3.00
Fear	D	L Int	C	0.20
Field Promotion	D	E	R	3.00
Flagship	D	E	R	3.00
Flash Of Insight	L	E	U	0.80
Found Someone You Have	L	L Int	U	0.80
9				
Frustration	D	L Int	R	3.00
Great Warrior	L	J Tst	C	0.25
Grounded Starfighter	L	E	U	0.80
Han's Toolkit	L	Dev	R	3.00
He Is Not Ready	D	E	C	0.20
Hiding In The Garbage	L	E	R	3.00
HoloNet Transmission	D	U/L Int	U	0.80
Hound's Tooth	D	S	R	5.00
I Have A Bad Feeling About This	L	L Int	R	3.30
10				
I Want That Ship	D	E	R	3.00
IG-88	D	Ch:Dr	R	10.00
IG-88's Neural Inhibitor	D	Ch:W	R	5.00
IG-88's Pulse Cannon	D	Ch:W	R	4.00

Card name	Side	Type	Rarity	Price
IG-2000	D	S	R	6.00
Imbalance	D	U Int	U	0.80
Imperial Helmsman	D	Ch:Imp	C	0.20
Ineffective Maneuver	L	E	U	0.80
It Is The Future You See	L	J T	R	3.00
11				
Jedi Levitation	L	L Int	R	3.00
Knowledge And Defense	D	E	C	0.20
Landing Claw	L	D	R	5.00
Lando System?	D	L I	R	3.00
Levitation	L	U/L Int	U	0.80
Lieutenant Commander Ardan	D	Ch:Imp	U	0.90
Lieutenant Suba	D	Ch:Imp	R	4.00
Lieutenant Venka	D	Ch:Imp	U	0.90
Light Maneuvers	L	U Int	R	3.00
12				
Location, Location, Location	D	E	R	3.00
Lost In Space	D	Imm E	R	3.00
Lost Relay	L	U Int	C	0.20
Luke's Backpack	L	D	R	3.00
Mist Hunter	D	S	R	6.00
Moving To Attack Position	L	L Int	C	0.20
Much Anger In Him	D	E	R	3.00
Mynock	L	Cr	C	0.20
Mynock	D	Cr	C	0.20
13				
Never Tell Me The Odds	L	E	C	0.20
No Disintegrations!	L	E	R	3.50
Nudj	L	Cr	C	0.20
Obi-Wan's Apparition	L	E	R	3.30
Order To Engage	L	E	R	3.00
Polarized Negative Power Coupling	L	E	R	3.00
Portable Fusion Generator	L	D	C	0.20
Precision Targeting	D	E	U	1.00
Proton Bombs	D	S W	U	0.80
14				
Punishing One	D	S	R	6.00
Quick Draw	L	E	C	0.20
Raithal	L	L Sys	R	3.00
Raithal	D	L Sys	U	0.80
Rebel Flight Suit	L	D	C	0.25
Recoil In Fear	L	L Int	C	0.20
Reflection	L	E	R	4.00
Report To Lord Vader	L	Ut E	R	3.00
Res Luk Ra'auf	D	L Int	R	3.50

RARITY KEY **C** = Common   **U** = Uncommon   **R** = Rare   **#** = Lower #s are rarer   **X** = Fixed/standard in all decks   **CARD TYPES on page 438**

Card name	Side	Type	Rarity	Price
15				
☐ Retractable Arm	L	D	C	0.20
☐ Rogue Asteroid	L	Mob E	C	0.20
☐ Rogue Asteroid	D	Mob E	C	0.20
☐ Rycar's Run	L	Ut E	R	3.00
☐ Scramble	L	E	U	1.00
☐ Shoo! Shoo!	L	U Int	U	0.80
☐ Shot In The Dark	D	E	U	0.80
☐ Shut Him Up Or Shut Him Down	D	U Int	U	0.80
☐ Size Matters Not	L	J T	R	4.00
16				
☐ Sleen	D	Cr	C	0.20
☐ Smuggler's Blues	L	E	R	3.30
☐ Something Hit Us!	D	U Int	U	0.80
☐ Son of Skywalker	L	Ch:Re	R	25.00
☐ Space Slug	L	Cr	R	3.00
☐ Space Slug	D	Cr	U	1.00
☐ Star Destroyer: Launch Bay	D	L Site	C	0.20
☐ Starship Levitation	L	U/L Int	U	0.80
☐ Stone Pile	L	E	R	3.00

Card name	Side	Type	Rarity	Price
17				
☐ Sudden Impact	D	E	U	0.80
☐ Take Evasive Action	D	L Int	C	0.20
☐ The Dark Path	D	E	R	3.00
☐ The Professor	L	E	R	3.00
☐ There Is No Try	D	E	C	0.20
☐ They'd Be Crazy To Follow Us	L	U Int	C	0.20
☐ This Is More Like It	L	U Int	R	3.00
☐ This Is No Cave	L	U Int	R	3.00
☐ Those Rebels Won't Escape Us	D	U/L Int	C	0.20
18				
☐ Through The Force Things You Will See	L	L Int	R	3.00
☐ TIE Avenger	D	S	C	0.25
☐ TIE Bomber	D	S	U	0.80
☐ Tight Squeeze	L	L Int	R	3.00
☐ Transmission Terminated	L	L Int	U	0.80
☐ Tunnel Vision	L	L Int	U	0.80
☐ Uncertain Is The Future	D	L Int	C	0.20
☐ Unexpected Interruption	D	L Int	R	3.00
☐ Vine Snake	L	Cr	C	0.20

Card name	Side	Type	Rarity	Price
19				
☐ Vine Snake	D	Cr	C	0.20
☐ Visage Of The Emperor	D	E	R	4.00
☐ Visored Vision	L	U/L Int	C	0.20
☐ Voyeur	D	U/L Int	C	0.20
☐ Warrant Officer M'Kae	D	Ch:Imp	U	0.90
☐ Wars Not Make One Great	L	E	U	0.80
☐ We Can Still Outmaneuver Them	L	U/L Int	R	3.00
☐ We Don't Need Their Scum	L	U/L Int	R	3.00
☐ WHAAAAAAAAAAOOOOW!	L	U Int	R	3.00
20				
☐ What Is Thy Bidding, My Master?	L	Ut E	R	3.00
☐ Yoda	L	Ch:JM	R	25.00
☐ Yoda Stew	L	U Int	U	0.80
☐ Yoda, You Seek Yoda	L	L Int	R	4.00
☐ Yoda's Gimer Stick	L	E	R	3.50
☐ Yoda's Hope	L	E	U	1.00
☐ You Do Have Your Moments	L	L Int	U	0.80
☐ Zuckuss	D	Ch:Al	R	8.00
☐ Zuckuss' Snare Rifle	D	Ch:W	R	4.00

Star Wars • Cloud City

Decipher • Released October 1997

180 cards in set • **IDENTIFIER: Twin pod cloud car in circle at right**

• Booster packs contain 9 cards; booster displays contain 60 boosters

The rules mechanics entering the **Star Wars** universe in this expansion include dueling, bounty hunting, and cloud sectors. Players were finally able to have **Darth Vader** duel **Luke** or **Obi-Wan** or have **Boba Fett** turn in **Han Solo** for a **Bounty**.

These mechanics brought new life to a game that had grown less lively with **Dagobah**. Unfortunately, it would take another expansion set to give these interactive themes the boost they needed to be viable in tournament play.

Clouds became the tournament winner with this set. With their massive Force drain potential, Cloud decks quickly became the hottest thing around. Also, multiple interrupts that affected ground battles were extremely powerful in this set, changing the way ground battles were fought for years. — **Joe Alread**

Set (180 cards)	145.00
Booster Display Box	128.50
Booster Pack	2.50

You will need 20 nine-pocket pages to store this set. (10 doubled up)

Card name	Side	Type	Rarity	Price
1				
☐ Ability, Ability, Ability	D	E	C	0.25
☐ Abyss	D	E	U	0.90
☐ Access Denied	L	DE	C	0.25
☐ Advantage	L	IE	R	3.00
☐ Aiiii! Aaa! Agggggggggg!	D	LI	R	3.00
☐ All My Urchins	L	E	R	3.00
☐ All Too Easy	D	IE	R	3.00
☐ Ambush	L	LI	R	3.00
2				
☐ Armed And Dangerous	L	LI	U	0.90
☐ Artoo, Come Back At Once!	L	UI/LI	R	3.00

Card name	Side	Type	Rarity	Price
☐ As Good As Gone	L	LI	C	0.25
☐ Atmospheric Assault	D	LI	R	3.00
☐ Beldon's Eye	L	E	R	3.00
☐ Bespin	L	L-Sys	U	1.00
☐ Bespin	D	L-Sys	U	1.00
☐ Bespin: Cloud City	L	L-Sec	U	0.90
☐ Bespin: Cloud City	D	L-Sec	U	0.90
☐ Binders	D	D	C	0.25
3				
☐ Bionic Hand	L	D	R	4.00
☐ Blasted Droid	D	UI	C	0.25
☐ Blaster Proficiency	L	UI/LI	C	0.25
☐ Boba Fett	D	Ch:Al	R	25.00
☐ Boba Fett's Blaster Rifle	D	Ch:W	R	6.00
☐ Bounty	D	E	C	0.25
☐ Brief Loss Of Control	D	LI	R	3.00
☐ Bright Hope	L	SShp	R	5.00
4				
☐ Captain Bewil	D	Ch:Imp	R	4.00

Card name	Side	Type	Rarity	Price
☐ Captain Han Solo	L	Ch:Reb	R	25.00
☐ Captive Fury	L	UI/LI	U	0.90
☐ Captive Pursuit	L	UI/LI	C	0.25
☐ Carbon-Freezing	D	E	U	0.90
☐ Carbonite Chamber Console	D	D	U	0.90
☐ Chasm	L	E	U	0.90
☐ Chief Retwin	D	Ch:Imp	R	4.00
☐ Civil Disorder	L	E	C	0.25
☐ Clash Of Sabers	L	LI	C	0.90
5				
☐ Cloud Car	L	CV	C	0.25
☐ Cloud Car	D	CV	C	0.25
☐ Cloud City Blaster	L	Ch:W	C	0.25
☐ Cloud City Blaster	D	Ch:W	C	0.25
☐ Cloud City: Carbonite	D	CL-Site	U	0.60
☐ Cloud City: Carbonite Chamber	L	L-Site	U	0.90
☐ Cloud City: Chasm Walkway	L	L-Site	C	0.25
☐ Cloud City: Chasm Walkway	D	L-Site	C	0.25
☐ Cloud City: Dining Room	D	L-Site	R	3.00
6				
☐ Cloud City: East Platform (Docking Bay)	D	L-Site	C	0.25
☐ Cloud City Engineer	D	Ch:Al	C	0.25
☐ Cloud City: Guest Quarters	L	L-Site	R	3.50
☐ Cloud City: Incinerator	L	L-Site	C	0.25
☐ Cloud City: Incinerator	D	L-Site	C	0.25
☐ Cloud City: Lower Corridor	L	L-Site	U	0.90
☐ Cloud City: Lower Corridor	D	L-Site	U	0.60
☐ Cloud City: Platform 327 (Docking Bay)	L	L-Site	C	0.25
☐ Cloud City Sabacc	L	UI	U	0.60
7				
☐ Cloud City Sabacc	D	UI	U	0.60
☐ Cloud City: Security Tower	D	L-Site	C	0.25
☐ Cloud City Technician	L	Ch:Al	C	0.25
☐ Cloud City Trooper	L	Ch:Al	C	0.25
☐ Cloud City Trooper	D	Ch:Al	C	0.25

Star Wars • First Anthology

Decipher • Released May 1997

• Set contains two **Premiere Unlimited** starter decks, a **Jedi Pack**, two **A New Hope** packs, two **Hoth** packs, and 6 promo cards

Released in a collector's box, the **Star Wars: First Anthology** is an attractive item repackaging previous releases.

The premium cards displayed art from the new **Special Edition** movies, and, with its sleek new pictures and anticipation of the Special Edition expansion in the air, the Anthology set sold well. Decipher released two more such sets in the coming years. — **Joe Alread**

First Anthology (sealed) 37.50

☐ Boba Fett	9.00	☐ Hit And Run	4.50
☐ Commander Wedge Antilles	6.00	☐ Jabba's Influence	4.50
☐ Death Star Assault Squadron	5.50	☐ X-wing Assault Squadron	5.00

RARITY KEY **C** = Common **U** = Uncommon **R** = Rare **#** = Lower #s are rarer **X** = Fixed/standard in all decks **CARD TYPES on page 438**

Card name	Side	Type	Rarity	Price
Cloud City: Upper Plaza Corridor	L	L-Site	C	0.25
Cloud City: Upper Plaza Corridor	D	L-Site	U	0.90
Clouds	L	L-Sect	C	0.25
Clouds	D	L-Sect	C	0.25
8				
Commander Desanne	D	Ch:Imp	U	0.90
Computer Interface	L	UI/LI	C	0.25
Courage Of A Skywalker	L	LI	R	4.00
Crack Shot	L	E	U	0.90
Cyborg Construct	L	D	U	0.90
Dark Approach	L	LI	R	3.50
Dark Deal	D	E	R	4.30
Dark Strike	D	LI	C	0.25
Dash	L	UI	C	0.25
9				
Despair	D	I E	R	3.80
Desperate Reach	L	UI	U	0.90
Dismantle On Sight	L	E	R	3.00
Dodge	L	LI	C	0.25
Double Back	D	LI	U	0.90
Double-Crossing, No-Good Swindler	D	LI	C	0.25
E Chu Ta	D	UI	C	0.25
E-3PO	D	Ch: Dr	R	4.00
End This Destructive Conflict	D	UI/LI	R	3.00
10				
Epic Duel	D	Ep Ev	R	6.00
Fall Of The Empire	L	LI	U	0.90
Fall Of The Legend	L	UI	U	0.90
Flight Escort	D	LI	R	3.00
Focused Attack	D	LI	R	3.00
Force Field	D	UI/LI	R	4.00
Forced Landing	D	Ut Ev	R	3.50
Frozen Assets	L	E	R	3.00
Gambler's Luck	L	LI	R	3.50
11				
Glancing Blow	L	LI	R	3.00
Haven	L	E	R	5.00
Heart Of The Chasm	D	LI	U	1.00
Hero Of A Thousand Devices	L	E	U	0.90
He's All Yours, Bounty Hunter	D	UI/LI	R	4.00
Higher Ground	L	UI/LI	R	3.30
Hindsight	L	E	R	3.50
Hopping Mad	L	E	R	3.00
Human Shield	D	UI/LI	C	0.25
12				

Card name	Side	Type	Rarity	Price
I Am Your Father	D	I E	R	4.00
I Don't Need Their Scum, Either	L	UI/LI	R	3.30
I Had No Choice	D	E	R	3.50
Imperial Decree	D	E	U	0.90
Imperial Trooper Guard Dainsom	D	Ch:Imp	U	0.90
Impressive, Most Impressive	L	LI	R	3.50
Innocent Scoundrel	L	UI/LI	U	0.90
Interrogation Array	D	D	R	3.80
Into The Ventilation Shaft, Lefty	L	LI	R	3.00
13				
It's A Trap!	L	UI/LI	U	0.90
Kebyc	L	Ch:Al	U	0.90
Keep Your Eyes Open	L	UI	C	0.25
Lando Calrissian	L	Ch:Al	R	14.00
Lando Calrissian	D	Ch:Al	R	12.00
Lando's Wrist Comlink	L	D	U	0.90
Leia Of Alderaan	L	E	R	4.50
Levitation Attack	D	UI	U	0.90
Lieutenant Cecius	D	Ch:Imp	U	0.90
14				
Lieutenant Sheckil	D	Ch:Imp	R	4.00
Lift Tube Escape	L	UI	C	0.25
Lobot	L	Ch:Al	R	7.00
Luke's Blaster Pistol	L	Ch:W	R	5.00
Mandalorian Armor	D	D	R	5.00
Mostly Armless	D	I E	R	3.50
NOOOOOOOOOOO!	L	UI/LI	R	3.00
Obsidian 7	D	SShp	R	6.00
Obsidian 8	D	SShp	R	6.00
15				
Off The Edge	L	LI	R	3.30
Old Pirates	L	LI	R	3.50
Out Of Somewhere	L	UI	U	0.90
Path Of Least Resistance	L	LI	C	0.25
Point Man	D	LI	R	3.00
Prepare The Chamber	D	UI/LI	U	0.90
Princess Leia	L	Ch:Reb	R	18.00
Projective Telepathy	D	UI	U	0.90
Protector	L	LI	R	3.50
16				
Punch It!	L	LI	R	3.50
Put That Down	L	UI	C	0.25
Redemption	L	SShp	R	9.00
Release Your Anger	D	LI	R	3.80
Rendezvous Point On Tatooine	L	LI	R	3.80

Card name	Side	Type	Rarity	Price
Rescue In The Clouds	L	UI/LI	C	0.25
Restricted Access	D	E	C	0.25
Rite Of Passage	D	UI	C	0.25
Shattered Hope	D	LI	U	0.90
17				
Shocking Information	L	UI	C	0.25
Shocking Revelation	D	UI	C	0.25
Slave I	D	SShp	R	15.00
Slip Sliding Away	D	UI	R	3.00
Smoke Screen	L	LI	R	3.00
Somersault	L	LI	C	0.25
Sonic Bombardment	D	UI/LI	U	1.00
Special Delivery	D	E	C	0.25
Surprise	D	LI	R	3.00
18				
Surreptitious Glance	L	LI	R	3.00
Swing-And-A-Miss	L	UI	U	0.90
The Emperor's Prize	D	Ut E	R	4.00
This Is Even Better	L	LI	R	3.00
This Is Still Wrong	D	UI	R	3.00
Tibanna Gas Miner	L	Ch:Al	C	0.25
Tibanna Gas Miner	D	Ch:Al	C	0.25
TIE Sentry Ships	D	LI	C	0.25
Treva Horme	L	Ch:Al	U	0.90
19				
Trooper Assault	D	UI	C	0.25
Trooper Jerrol Blendin	D	Ch:Al	U	0.90
Trooper Utris M'toc	L	Ch:Al	U	0.90
Ugloste	D	Ch:Al	R	3.50
Ugnaught	D	Ch:Al	C	0.25
Uncontrollable Fury	L	E	R	4.00
Vader's Bounty	D	E	R	4.00
Vader's Cape	D	E	R	5.00
Weapon Levitation	D	UI/LI	U	0.90
20				
Weapon Of An Ungrateful Son	D	UI/LI	U	0.90
Weather Vane	L	E	U	0.90
Weather Vane	D	E	U	0.90
We'll Find Han	L	UI	R	3.00
We're The Bait	D	Ut E	R	3.00
Why Didn't You Tell Me?	D	UI/LI	R	3.00
Wiorkettle	L	Ch:Al	U	0.90
Wookiee Strangle	L	LI	R	3.00
You Are Beaten	D	LI	U	0.90

Star Wars • Jabba's Palace

Decipher • Released March 1998

180 cards in set • **IDENTIFIER: Jabba's eye in circle at upper right**

• Booster packs contain 9 cards; booster displays contain 60 boosters

With the release of the **Jabba's Palace**, every little-known alien in the Star Wars universe got its own card. If you wanted to play with a deck designed to battle, you no longer had to rely on playing with main characters. Jabba's Palace essentially makes it possible to play the poor man's deck, and win.

New rules in this set were few and far between. Mechanics from **Cloud City** that were weak were given big boosts. **Jabba the Hutt** made his first appearance in the game.

With the heavy focus on aliens in this set, decks were made that were full of just aliens, more aliens, and nothing else. In fact, people started buying Jabba's Palace packs just so they could get more of these common and uncommon alien characters for their decks, and not the rare cards. — **Joe Alread**

		You will need
Set (180 cards)	150.00	**20** nine-pocket pages to store this set. (10 doubled up)
Booster Display Box	133.50	
Booster Pack	2.20	

Card name	Side	Type	Rarity	Price
1				
8D8	L	Ch-Dr	R	4.00
A Gift	L	IE	U	0.80
Abyssin	D	Ch-Al	C	0.25
Abyssin Ornament	D	UI	U	1.00
All Wrapped Up	D	E	U	0.80

Card name	Side	Type	Rarity	Price
Amanaman	D	Ch-Al	R	4.00
Amanin	D	Ch-Al	C	0.25
Antipersonnel Laser Cannon	D	Veh W	U	0.80
Aqualish	D	Ch-Al	C	0.25
2				
Arc Welder	L	D	U	0.80
Ardon 'Vapor' Crell	L	Ch-Al	R	3.50
Artoo	L	Ch-Dr	R	10.00
Artoo, I Have A Bad Feeling About This	L	LI	U	0.80
Attark	L	Ch-Al	R	3.00

Card name	Side	Type	Rarity	Price
Aved Luun	L	Ch-Al	R	3.50
Bane Malar	D	Ch-Al	R	6.00
Bantha Fodder	D	UI	C	0.25
Barada	D	Ch-Al	R	3.50
3				
Baragwin	L	Ch-Al	C	0.25
Bargaining Table	L	E	U	0.80
Beedo	D	Ch-Al	R	4.00
BG-J38	L	Ch-Dr	R	3.80
Bib Fortuna	D	Ch-Al	R	5.00
Blaster Deflection	L	U/L Int	R	4.00
Bo Shuda	L	E	U	0.80

RARITY KEY C = Common U = Uncommon R = Rare # = Lower #s are rarer X = Fixed/standard in all decks **CARD TYPES on page 438**

SCRYE Collectible Card Game Checklist and Price Guide • **443**

Card name	Type	Rarity	Price
☐ B'omarr Monk	L Ch-Al	C	0.25
☐ Bubo	D Cr	U	0.80
4			
☐ Cane Adiss	D IE	U	0.80
☐ Chadra-Fan	L Ch-Al	C	0.25
☐ Chevin	D Ch-Al	C	0.25
☐ Choke	L LI	C	0.25
☐ Corellian Retort	L U/L Int	U	0.80
☐ CZ-4	D Ch-Dr	C	0.25
☐ Den of Thieves	D E	U	0.80
☐ Dengar's Modified Riot Gun	D Ch-Wp	R	4.50
☐ Devaronian	L Ch-Al	C	0.25
5			
☐ Don't Forget The Droids	L U/L Int	C	0.25
☐ Double Laser Cannon	D Veh W	R	4.00
☐ Droopy McCool	L Ch-Al	R	3.00
☐ Dune Sea Sabacc	L UI	U	0.80
☐ Dune Sea Sabacc	D UI	U	0.80
☐ Elom	L Ch-Al	C	0.25
☐ Ephant Mon	D Ch-Al	R	4.00
☐ EV-9D9	D Ch-Dr	R	4.00
☐ Fallen Portal	L UI	U	0.80
6			
☐ Florn Lamproid	L Ch-Al	C	0.25
☐ Fozec	D Ch-Al	R	3.50
☐ Gailid	D Ch-Al	R	4.00
☐ Gamorrean Ax	D Ch-Wp	C	0.25
☐ Gamorrean Guard	D Ch-Al	C	0.25
☐ Garon Nas Tal	L Ch-Al	R	3.00
☐ Geezum	L Ch-Al	R	3.80
☐ Ghoel	L Ch-Al	R	3.00
☐ Giran	D Ch-Al	R	3.50
7			
☐ Gran	L Ch-Al	C	0.25
☐ Herat	D Ch-Al	R	3.50
☐ Hermi Odle	D Ch-Al	R	3.30
☐ Hidden Compartment	L D	U	0.80
☐ Hidden Weapons	D UI	U	0.80
☐ H'nemthe	L Ch-Al	C	0.25
☐ Holoprojector	L D	U	0.80
☐ Hutt Bounty	D E	R	4.00
☐ Hutt Smooch	D LI	U	0.80
8			
☐ I Must Be Allowed To Speak	L E	R	4.00
☐ Information Exchange	D E	U	0.80
☐ Ishi Tib	L Ch-Al	C	0.25
☐ Ithorian	L Ch-Al	C	0.25
☐ Jabba the Hutt	D Ch-Al	R	16.00

Card name	Type	Rarity	Price
☐ Jabba's Palace: Audience Chamber L	Lo-Si	U	1.00
☐ Jabba's Palace: Audience Chamber D	Loc Ste	U	1.00
☐ Jabba's Palace: Droid Workshop D	Loc Ste	U	1.00
9			
☐ Jabba's Palace: Dungeon	D Loc Ste	U	1.00
☐ Jabba's Palace: Entrance Cavern L	Lo-Si	U	1.00
☐ Jabba's Palace: Entrance Cavern D	Loc Ste	U	1.00
☐ Jabba's Palace: Rancor Pit	D Loc Ste	U	1.00
☐ Jabba's Palace Sabacc	L LI	U	1.00
☐ Jabba's Palace Sabacc	D LI	U	1.00
☐ Jabba's Sail Barge	D Tr Veh	R	6.00
☐ Jabba's Sail Barge: Passenger Deck	D Loc Ste	R	4.00
☐ Jedi Mind Trick	L U/L Int	R	4.00
☐ Jess	L Ch-Al	R	3.50
10			
☐ Jet Pack	D D	U	0.80
☐ J'Quille	D Ch-Al	R	3.80
☐ Kalit	L Ch-Al	R	3.80
☐ Ke Chu Ke Kukuta?	L UI	C	0.25
☐ Kiffex	L Lo-Sys	R	3.00
☐ Kirdo III	L Lo-Sys	R	3.00
☐ Kithaba	D Ch-Al	R	3.00
☐ Kitonak	L Ch-Al	C	0.25
☐ Klatooinian Revolutionary	L Ch-Al	C	0.25
11			
☐ Klatuu	D Ch-Al	R	3.00
☐ Laudica	L Ch-Al	R	3.00
☐ Leslomy Tacema	L Ch-Al	R	3.00
☐ Life Debt	L LI	R	3.80
☐ Loje Nella	L Lo-Si	R	3.50
☐ Malakili	D Ch-Al	R	3.00
☐ Mandalorian Mishap	L UI	U	0.80
☐ Max Rebo	L Ch-Al	R	4.30
☐ Mos Eisley Blaster	L Ch-Wp	C	0.25
12			
☐ Mos Eisley Blaster	D Ch-Wp	C	0.25
☐ Murttoc Yine	D Ch-Al	R	3.50
☐ Nal Hutta	D Lo-Sys	R	3.00
☐ Nar Shaddaa Wind Chimes	L UI	U	1.00
☐ Nikto	D Ch-Al	C	0.25
☐ Nizuc Bek	D Ch-Al	R	3.00
☐ None Shall Pass	D UI	C	0.25
☐ Nysad	D Ch-Al	R	3.00
☐ Oola	L Ch-Al	R	4.00
13			
☐ Ortolan	L Ch-Al	C	0.25
☐ Ortugg	D Ch-Al	R	3.00

Card name	Side Type	Rarity	Price
☐ Palejo Reshad	L Ch-Al	R	3.00
☐ Pote Snitkin	D Ch-Al	R	3.50
☐ Princess Leia Organa	L Ch-Reb	R	16.00
☐ Projection Of A Skywalker	L E	U	0.80
☐ Pucumir Thryss	L Ch-Al	R	3.00
☐ Quarren	D Ch-Al	C	0.25
☐ Quick Reflexes	D E	C	0.25
14			
☐ Rancor	D Cr	R	6.00
☐ Rayc Ryjerd	L Ch-Al	R	3.80
☐ Ree-Yees	D Ch-Al	R	4.00
☐ Rennek	L Ch-Al	R	3.00
☐ Resistance	D E	U	0.80
☐ Revealed	L LI	U	0.80
☐ R'kik D'nec, Hero Of The Dune Sea L	Ch-Al	R	4.00
☐ Saelt-Marae	L Ch-Al	R	3.50
☐ Salacious Crumb	D Ch-Al	R	5.00
15			
☐ Sandwhirl	L Mo-Eff	U	0.80
☐ Sandwhirl	D Mo-Eff	U	0.80
☐ Scum and Villainy	D E	R	5.00
☐ Sergeant Doallyn	L Ch-Al	R	3.80
☐ Shasa Tiel	L Ch-Al	R	3.00
☐ Sic-Six	L Ch-Al	C	0.25
☐ Skiff	L Tr Veh	C	0.25
☐ Skiff	D Tr Veh	C	0.25
☐ Skrilling	D Ch-Al	C	0.25
16			
☐ Skull	L UI	U	0.80
☐ Snivvian	L Ch-Al	C	0.25
☐ Someone Who Loves You	L UI	U	0.80
☐ Strangle	L LI	R	3.80
☐ Tamtel Skreej	L Ch-Al	R	7.80
☐ Tanus Spijek	L Ch-Al	R	3.80
☐ Tatooine: Desert	L Lo-Si	C	0.25
☐ Tatooine: Desert	D Loc Ste	C	0.25
☐ Tatooine: Great Pit of Carkoon	D Loc Ste	U	1.00
17			
☐ Tatooine: Hutt Canyon	L Lo-Si	U	1.00
☐ Tatooine: Jabba's Palace	D Loc Ste	U	1.00
☐ Taym Dren-garen	D Ch-Al	R	3.80
☐ Tessek	L Ch-Al	R	3.50
☐ The Signal	L U/St Int	C	0.25
☐ Thermal Detonator	D Ch-Wp	R	5.00
☐ Thul Fain	D Ch-Al	R	4.00
☐ Tibrin	L Lo-Sys	R	3.00
☐ Torture	D U/L Int	C	0.25
18			
☐ Trandoshan	D Ch-Al	C	0.25
☐ Trap Door	D LI	U	0.80
☐ Twi'lek Advisor	D U/St Int	C	0.25
☐ Ultimatum	L E	U	0.80
☐ Unfriendly Fire	L UI	R	3.50
☐ Vedain	D Ch-Al	R	3.00
☐ Velken Tezeri	D Ch-Al	R	3.50
☐ Vibro-Ax	L Ch-Wp	C	0.25
☐ Vibro-Ax	D Ch-Wp	C	0.25
19			
☐ Vizam	D Ch-Al	R	3.00
☐ Vul Tazaene	L Ch-Al	R	3.00
☐ Weapon Levitation	L LI	U	0.80
☐ Weequay Guard	D Ch-Al	C	0.25
☐ Weequay Hunter	D Ch-Al	C	0.25
☐ Weequay Marksman	D Ch-Al	U	0.80
☐ Weequay Skiff Master	D Ch-Al	C	0.25
☐ Well Guarded	D E	U	0.80
☐ Whiphid	D Ch-Al	C	0.25
20			
☐ Wittin	D Ch-Al	R	3.80
☐ Wooof	D Ch-Al	R	3.00
☐ Wortt	L Cr	U	0.80
☐ Wounded Wookiee	D LI	U	1.00
☐ Yarkora	L Ch-Al	C	0.25
☐ Yarna d'al' Gargan	L E	U	1.00
☐ You Will Take Me To Jabba Now	L UI	C	0.25
☐ Yoxgit	L Ch-Al	R	3.50
☐ Yuzzum	D Ch-Al	C	0.25

RARITY KEY C = Common   U = Uncommon   R = Rare   # = Lower #s are rarer   X = Fixed/standard in all decks   **CARD TYPES on page 438**

Star Wars • Special Edition

Decipher • Released **November 1998**

324 cards in set • **IDENTIFIER: Flaring saber in circle at upper right**

- Starter decks contain 60 cards; starter displays contain 12 starters
- Booster packs contain 9 cards; booster displays contain 30 boosters

The **Special Edition** set redefined how the **Star Wars** CCG was played, at every level. Arguably, the new cards lent themselves to almost a hundred new strategies. New card types, new main characters — it was all there. The *Star Wars* player base embraced this set, which injected new life into a game that, perhaps, had lost momentum due to its previous two somewhat lackluster expansions.

The Objectives, double-sided cards that were based on main themes from the *Star Wars* movies, make their first appearance in this set. Basically, each objective could be used as a starting point for a new deck type, and that's what happened. With 10 Objectives in the set, there was plenty of room for creativity. A glossary containingd all rules updates since the game was first introduced is included in every starter deck.

As a result, the game became much cleaner; if players had a rules problem, they could always just turn to the glossary for an answer. Out of the 10 Objectives for the set, more than half became major tournament competitors. Multiple new interrupt cards in the set were powerful enough to build decks around, as well. The potential strategy in this set was tremendous, and it could easily be argued that this was the best *Star Wars* expansion ever made. — *Joe Alread*

SPECIAL EDITION

	Price		You will need
Set (324 cards)	220.00		**36**
Starter Display Box	122.50		nine-pocket
Booster Display Box	65.00		pages to store
Starter Deck	12.00		this set.
Booster Pack	2.50		(18 doubled up)

Card name	Side	Type	Rarity	Price
2X-7KPR (Tooex)	D	Dr	C	0.25
A Bright Center To The Universe	D	E	U	0.50
A Day Long Remembered	D	E	U	0.50
A Real Hero	D	Int	R	4.00
Air-2 Racing Swoop	L	Veh	C	0.20
Ak-rev	D	AI	U	0.50
Alderaan Operative	L	AI	C	0.20
Alert My Star Destroyer!	D	E	C	0.20
All Power To Weapons	D	Int	C	0.20
All Wings Report In	L	Int	R	4.00
Anoat Operative	L	AI	C	0.20
Anoat Operative	D	AI	C	0.20
Antilles Maneuver	L	Int	C	0.20
ASP-707	L	Dr	X	0.50
Balanced Attack	L	Int	U	0.50
Bantha Herd	D	E	R	3.00
Barquin D'an	D	AI	U	0.60
Ben Kenobi	L	Reb	R	20.00
Blast Points	D	Int	C	0.20
Blown Clear	D	E	U	0.50
Boba Fett	D	AI	R	12.75
Boelo	D	AI	R	4.00
Bossk In Hound's Tooth	D	Ss	R	8.00
Bothan Spy	L	AI	C	0.20
Bothawui	L	L-Sys	X	0.45
Bothawui Operative	L	AI	C	0.25
Brangus Glee	D	AI	R	4.00
Bren Quersey	L	Reb	U	0.50
Bron Burs	L	AI	R	4.00
B-wing Attack Fighter	L	Ss	X	2.00
Camie	L	AI	R	4.00
Carbon Chamber Testing	D	Obj	R	5.00
Chyler	D	AI	U	0.60
Clak'dor VII Operative	L	AI	U	0.50
Cloud City: Casino	L	L-Site	U	0.50
Cloud City: Casino	D	L-Site	U	0.50
Cloud City Celebration	L	E	R	4.00

Card name	Side	Type	Rarity	Price
Cloud City: Core Tunnel	L	L-Site	U	0.50
Cloud City: Downtown Plaza	L	L-Site	R	3.00
Cloud City: Downtown Plaza	D	L-Site	R	3.00
Cloud City: Interrogation Room	D	L-Site	C	0.20
Cloud City: North Corridor	L	L-Site	C	0.20
Cloud City Occupation	D	E	R	4.00
Cloud City: Port Town District	D	L-Site	U	0.50
Cloud City: Upper Walkway	D	L-Site	C	0.20
Cloud City: West Gallery	L	L-Site	C	0.20
Cloud City: West Gallery	D	L-Site	C	0.20
Colonel Feyn Gospic	L	Reb	R	4.00
Combat Cloud Car	D	Veh	X	0.50
Come Here You Big Coward!	D	E	C	0.25
Commander Wedge Antilles	L	Reb	R	8.00
Coordinated Attack	D	Int	C	0.20
Corellia Operative	L	Reb	U	0.50
Corellian Engineering Corporation	L	E	R	4.00
Corporal Grenwick	D	Imp	R	3.50
Corporal Prescott	D	Imp	U	0.50
Corulag Operative	D	AI	C	0.20
Coruscant	L	L-Sys	R	4.00
Coruscant	D	L-Sys	R	4.00
Coruscant Celebration	L	E	R	3.00
Coruscant: Docking Bay	D	L-Site	C	0.25
Coruscant: Imperial City	D	L-Site	U	0.50
Coruscant: Imperial Square	D	L-Site	R	3.00
Counter Surprise Assault	D	Int	R	4.00
Dagobah	D	L-Sys	U	0.80
Dantooine Base Operations	L	Obj	R	5.00
Dantooine Operative	D	AI	U	0.20
Darklighter Spin	L	Int	C	0.25
Darth Vader, Dark Lord Of The Sith	D	Imp	R	32.50
Death Squadron Star Destroyer	D	Ss	R	7.00
Death Star	L	L-Sys	R	7.30
Death Star Assault Squadron	D	Ss	R	6.00
Death Star: Detention Block Control Room	D	L-Site	C	0.20
Death Star: Detention Block Corridor	L	L-Site	C	0.20
Debnoli	L	AI	R	4.00
Desert	L	L-Site	X	0.50
Desert	D	L-Site	X	0.50
Desilijic Tattoo	D	E	U	0.50
Desperate Tactics	L	Int	C	0.20
Destroyed Homestead	D	E	R	3.00

Card name	Side	Type	Rarity	Price
Dewback	D	Veh	C	0.20
Direct Assault	L	Int	C	0.20
Disruptor Pistol	L	W	X	0.50
Disruptor Pistol	D	W	X	0.50
Docking And Repair Facilities	L	E	R	4.00
Dodo Bodonawieedo	D	AI	U	0.50
Don't Tread On Me	L	Int	R	4.00
Down With The Emperor!	L	E	U	0.80
Dr. Evazan's Sawed-off Blaster	D	W	U	0.50
Draw Their Fire	L	E	U	0.80
Dreaded Imperial Starfleet	D	E	R	4.00
Droid Merchant	L	AI	C	0.20
Dune Walker	D	Veh	R	5.00
Echo Base Trooper Rifle	L	W	C	0.20
Elyhek Rue	L	Reb	U	0.50
Entrenchment	L	E	R	3.50
Eriadu Operative	D	AI	C	0.20
Executor: Docking Bay	D	L-Site	U	0.50
Farm	L	L-Site	X	0.50
Feltipern Trevagg's Stun Rifle	D	W	U	0.50
Firepower	D	E	C	0.20
Firin Morett	L	Reb	U	0.50
First Aid	L	Int	X	0.50
First Strike	D	E	U	0.80
Flare-S Racing Swoop	D	Veh	C	0.20
Flawless Marksmanship	D	Int	C	0.20
Floating Refinery	D	D	C	0.20
Fondor	D	L-Sys	U	0.50
Forest	L	L-Site	X	0.50
Forest	D	L-Site	X	0.50
Gela Yeens	D	AI	U	0.50
General McQuarrie	L	Reb	R	3.50
Gold 3	L	Ss	U	0.50
Gold 4	L	Ss	U	0.50
Gold 6	L	Ss	U	0.50
Goo Nee Tay	L	E	R	4.00
Greeata	D	AI	U	0.50
Grondorn Muse	L	Reb	R	3.50
Harc Seff	L	AI	U	0.80
Harvest	L	Int	R	4.00
Heavy Fire Zone	D	Int	C	0.20
Heroes Of Yavin	L	Int	R	4.00
Heroic Sacrifice	L	E	U	0.50
Hidden Base	L	Obj	R	5.00

RARITY KEY C = Common   U = Uncommon   R = Rare   # = Lower #s are rarer   X = Fixed/standard in all decks   CARD TYPES on page 438

SCRYE Collectible Card Game Checklist and Price Guide • **445**

Card name	Side	Type	Rarity	Price
☐ Hit And Run	L	Int	R	3.00
☐ Hol Okand	L	Reb	U	0.50
☐ Homing Beacon	D	D	R	3.00
☐ Hoth Sentry	L	E	U	0.50
☐ Hunt Down And Destroy The Jedi	D	Obj	R	5.00
☐ Hunting Party	D	Int	R	3.50
☐ I Can't Shake Him!	D	Int	C	0.20
☐ Iasa, The Traitor Of Jawa Canyon	D	Al	R	4.00
☐ IM4-099	D	Dr	X	0.50
☐ Imperial Atrocity	L	E	R	3.50
☐ Imperial Occupation	D	Obj	R	5.00
☐ Imperial Propaganda	D	E	R	4.00
☐ In Range	D	Int	C	0.20
☐ Incom Corporation	L	E	R	4.00
☐ Incom Engineer	L	Reb	C	0.25
☐ Intruder Missile	L	W	X	0.50
☐ Intruder Missile	D	W	X	0.50
☐ ISB Operations	D	Obj	R	5.00
☐ It's Not My Fault!	L	Int	X	0.50
☐ Jabba	D	Al	R	10.00
☐ Jabba's Influence	D	E	R	4.00
☐ Jabba's Space Cruiser	D	Ss	R	6.00
☐ Jabba's Through With You	D	Int	U	0.50
☐ Jabba's Twerps	D	Int	U	0.50
☐ Joh Yowza	L	Al	R	4.00
☐ Jungle	L	L-Site	X	0.50
☐ Jungle	D	L-Site	X	0.50
☐ Kalit's Sandcrawler	L	Veh	R	4.00
☐ Kashyyyk Operative	L	Al	U	0.50
☐ Kashyyyk Operative	D	Al	U	0.50
☐ Kessel Operative	D	Al	U	0.50
☐ Ketwol	L	Al	R	3.50
☐ Kiffex Operative	L	Al	U	0.50
☐ Kiffex Operative	D	Al	U	0.50
☐ Kirdo III Operative	L	Al	C	0.20
☐ Koensayr Manufacturing	L	E	R	3.00
☐ Krayt Dragon	D	Cr	R	5.00
☐ Kuat	D	L-Sys	U	0.50
☐ Kuat Drive Yards	D	E	R	4.00
☐ Lando's Blaster Rifle	L	W	R	4.00
☐ Legendary Starfighter	L	E	C	0.20
☐ Leia's Blaster Rifle	L	W	R	4.00
☐ Lieutenant Lepira	L	Reb	U	0.50
☐ Lieutenant Naytaan	L	Reb	U	0.50
☐ Lieutenant Tarn Mison	L	Reb	R	3.50
☐ Lobel	D	Al	C	0.20
☐ Lobot	D	Al	R	5.00
☐ Local Defense	L	Int	U	0.50
☐ Local Uprising	L	Obj	R	5.00
☐ Lyn Me	D	Al	U	0.50
☐ Major Palo Torshan	L	Reb	R	4.00
☐ Makurth	D	Al	X	0.50
☐ Maneuvering Flaps	L	E	C	0.20
☐ Masterful Move	D	Int	C	0.20
☐ Mechanical Failure	L	E	R	4.00
☐ Meditation	L	E	R	3.50
☐ Medium Bulk Freighter	L	Ss	U	0.50
☐ Melas	L	Al	R	4.00
☐ Mind What You Have Learned	L	Obj	R	5.00
☐ Moisture Farmer	L	Al	C	0.20

Card name	Side	Type	Rarity	Price
☐ Nal Hutta Operative	D	Al	C	0.20
☐ Neb Dulo	L	Al	U	0.50
☐ Nebit	D	Al	R	3.00
☐ Niado Duegad	D	Al	U	0.50
☐ Nick Of Time	L	E	U	0.50
☐ No Bargain	D	E	U	0.50
☐ Old Times	L	Int	R	3.00
☐ On Target	L	Int	C	0.20
☐ One-Arm	D	Cr	R	4.00
☐ Oppressive Enforcement	D	E	U	0.50
☐ Ord Mantell Operative	D	Al	C	0.20
☐ Organized Attack	L	Int	C	0.20
☐ OS-72-1 In Obsidian 1	D	Ss	R	5.50
☐ OS-72-2 In Obsidian 2	D	Ss	R	5.00
☐ OS-72-10	D	Imp	R	5.00
☐ Outer Rim Scout	D	Al	R	8.00
☐ Overwhelmed	D	Int	C	0.20
☐ Patrol Craft	L	Veh	C	0.20
☐ Patrol Craft	D	Veh	C	0.20
☐ Planetary Subjugation	D	E	U	0.50
☐ Ponda Baba's Hold-out Blaster	D	W	U	0.50
☐ Portable Scanner	L	D	C	0.20
☐ Power Pivot	L	Int	C	0.25
☐ Precise Hit	L	Int	C	0.20
☐ Pride Of The Empire	D	E	C	0.20
☐ Princess Organa	L	Reb	R	15.00
☐ Put All Sections On Alert	D	Int	C	0.20
☐ R2-A5	D	Dr	U	0.50
☐ R3-A2	L	Dr	U	0.50
☐ R3-T2	L	Dr	R	4.00
☐ Raithal Operative	D	Al	C	0.20
☐ Ralltiir Freighter Captain	L	Al	X	0.50
☐ Ralltiir Operations	D	Obj	R	5.00
☐ Ralltiir Operative	L	Al	C	0.20
☐ Rapid Fire	L	Int	C	0.20
☐ Rappertunie	D	Al	U	0.50
☐ Rebel Ambush	L	Int	C	0.20
☐ Rebel Base Occupation	D	E	R	4.00
☐ Rebel Fleet	L	E	R	4.00
☐ Red 7	L	Ss	U	0.50
☐ Red 8	L	Ss	U	0.50
☐ Red 9	L	Ss	U	0.50
☐ Red 10	L	Ss	U	0.50
☐ Relentless Pursuit	D	Int	C	0.20
☐ Rendezvous Point	L	L-Sys	R	5.00
☐ Rendili	D	L-Sys	X	0.50
☐ Rendili StarDrive	D	E	R	4.00
☐ Rescue The Princess	L	Obj	R	5.00
☐ Return To Base	D	E	R	4.00
☐ Roche	L	L-Sys	U	0.50
☐ Rock Wart	D	Cr	X	0.50
☐ Rogue 4	L	Veh	R	5.00
☐ Ronto	L	Veh	C	0.20
☐ Ronto	D	Veh	C	0.20
☐ RR'uruurr	D	Al	R	4.00
☐ Ryle Torsyn	L	Reb	U	0.50
☐ Rystáll	D	Al	R	4.00
☐ Sacrifice	D	Int	X	0.45
☐ Sandspeeder	L	Veh	X	0.50
☐ Sandtrooper	D	Imp	X	0.50
☐ Sarlacc	D	Cr	R	4.00
☐ Scrambled Transmission	L	E	U	0.50
☐ Scurrier	L	Cr	X	0.50
☐ Secret Plans	D	E	U	0.50
☐ Sentinel-Class Landing Craft	D	Ss	X	0.50
☐ Sergeant Edian	L	Al	U	0.80
☐ Sergeant Hollis	L	Reb	R	3.50
☐ Sergeant Major Bursk	D	Imp	U	0.80
☐ Sergeant Major Enfield	D	Imp	R	4.00
☐ Sergeant Merril	D	Al	U	0.80

Card name	Side	Type	Rarity	Price
☐ Sergeant Narthax	D	Imp	R	3.00
☐ Sergeant Torent	D	Imp	R	3.00
☐ S-foils	L	E	C	0.20
☐ SFS L-s9.3 Laser Cannons	D	W	C	0.20
☐ Short-range Fighters	D	Int	R	4.00
☐ Sienar Fleet Systems	D	E	R	4.00
☐ Slayn & Korpil Facilities	L	E	R	3.00
☐ Slight Weapons Malfunction	L	Int	C	0.20
☐ Soth Petikkin	L	Al	R	3.00
☐ Spaceport City	L	L-Site	X	0.50
☐ Spaceport City	D	L-Site	X	0.50
☐ Spaceport Docking Bay	L	L-Site	X	0.50
☐ Spaceport Docking Bay	D	L-Site	X	0.50
☐ Spaceport Prefect's Office	D	L-Site	X	0.50
☐ Spaceport Street	L	L-Site	X	0.50
☐ Spaceport Street	D	L-Site	X	0.50
☐ Spiral	L	Ss	R	6.50
☐ Star Destroyer!	L	Int	R	4.00
☐ Stay Sharp!	L	Int	U	0.50
☐ Steady Aim	L	Int	C	0.20
☐ Strategic Reserves	D	E	R	4.00
☐ Suppressive Fire	L	Int	C	0.20
☐ Surface Defense	D	Int	R	3.00
☐ Swamp	L	L-Site	X	0.50
☐ Swamp	D	L-Site	X	0.50
☐ Swoop Mercenary	D	Al	X	0.50
☐ Sy Snootles	D	Al	R	4.00
☐ T-47 Battle Formation	L	Int	R	3.50
☐ Tarkin's Bounty	D	E	U	0.80
☐ Tatooine: Anchorhead	L	L-Site	X	0.50
☐ Tatooine: Beggar's Canyon	L	L-Site	R	3.80
☐ Tatooine Celebration	L	E	R	4.00
☐ Tatooine: Jabba's Palace	L	L-Site	C	0.20
☐ Tatooine: Jawa Canyon	L	L-Site	U	0.50
☐ Tatooine: Jawa Canyon	D	L-Site	U	0.50
☐ Tatooine: Krayt Dragon Pass	D	L-Site	X	0.45
☐ Tatooine Occupation	D	E	R	3.00
☐ Tatooine: Tosche Station	L	L-Site	C	0.25
☐ Tauntaun Skull	D	Int	C	0.20
☐ Tawss Khaa	L	Al	R	4.00
☐ The Planet That It's Farthest From	L	E	U	0.50
☐ Thedit	L	Al	R	3.00
☐ Theron Nett	L	Reb	U	0.50
☐ They're Coming In Too Fast!	D	Int	C	0.20
☐ They're Tracking Us	L	Int	C	0.20
☐ They've Shut Down The Main Reactor	D	Int	C	0.20
☐ Tibrin Operative	L	Reb	C	0.20
☐ TIE Defender Mark I	D	Ss	X	2.00
☐ TK-422	L	Reb	R	12.00
☐ Trooper Sabacc	L	Int	X	0.50
☐ Trooper Sabacc	D	Int	X	0.50
☐ Uh-oh!	L	E	U	0.60
☐ Umpass-stay	D	Al	R	3.00
☐ URoRRuR'R'R's Bantha	D	Veh	R	3.00
☐ Ur'Ru'r	D	Al	R	3.00
☐ Uutkik	L	Al	R	3.00
☐ Vader's Personal Shuttle	D	Ss	R	5.50
☐ Vengeance	D	Ss	R	10.00
☐ Wakeelmui	D	L-Sys	U	0.50
☐ Watch Your Back!	D	Int	C	0.20
☐ Weapons Display	L	E	C	0.20
☐ Wise Advice	L	E	U	0.50
☐ Wittin's Sandcrawler	D	Veh	R	4.00
☐ Womp Rat	D	Cr	C	0.20
☐ Wookiee	L	Al	X	1.00
☐ Wrist Comlink	L	D	C	0.20
☐ X-wing Assault Squadron	L	Ss	R	5.00
☐ X-wing Laser Cannon	L	W	C	0.20
☐ Yavin 4: Massassi Headquarters	L	L-Site	R	4.00
☐ Yavin 4 Trooper	L	Reb	X	0.50

RARITY KEY C = Common U = Uncommon R = Rare # = Lower #s are rarer X = Fixed/standard in all decks **CARD TYPES on page 438**

Star Wars • Endor

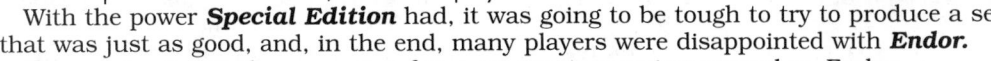

Decipher • Released April 1999

180 cards in set plus **18** foil cards • **IDENTIFIER: Shield generator in circle**

• Booster packs contain 9 cards; booster displays contain 30 boosters

With the power **Special Edition** had, it was going to be tough to try to produce a set that was just as good, and, in the end, many players were disappointed with **Endor.**

New mechanics in the expansion focus on scouts running around on Endor. Unfortunately, many game texts were weak on these characters, and few of them got used frequently. The set does manage to give some power back to weaker strategies found in *Special Edition*, and, with that, many of those weaker strategies found themselves at the top gaming tables in tournaments upon release of the set.

Endor also contains foil cards and several fixer cards which killed powerful strategies that had been hurting the game for years, a welcome addition. — *Joe Alerad*

Regular Set (180 cards)	
	147.50
Foil Set (18 cards)	250.00
Booster Display Box	72.50
Booster Pack	2.50

> **You will need**
> **20**
> nine-pocket pages to store this set
> (10 doubled up)

Foil cards

		Side	Type	Rarity	Price
☐	Biker Scout Trooper	D	Ch-Imp	CF	5.00
☐	Chewbacca Of Kashyyyk	L	Ch-R	UF	15.00
☐	Daughter Of Skywalker	L	Ch-R	UF	22.50
☐	Early Warning Network	D	E	UF	11.00
☐	Elite Squadron Stormtrooper	D	Ch-Imp	CF	5.00
☐	Endor Celebration	L	E	UF	10.00
☐	Endor: Ewok Village	L	L-Site	CF	5.00
☐	Endor: Landing Platform (Docking Bay)	D	L-Site	CF	5.00
☐	Ewok And Roll	L	UI	CF	5.00
☐	Ewok Glider	L	Tr Veh	CF	5.00
☐	General Solo	L	Ch-R	RF	40.00
☐	Hot Pursuit	D	UI/LI	UF	10.00
☐	Main Course	D	UI/LI	UF	10.00
☐	Paploo	L	Ch-Al	CF	5.00
☐	Speeder Bike	D	CV	CF	5.00
☐	Tempest 1	D	CV	RF	25.00
☐	Tempest Scout 4	D	CV	RF	25.00
☐	Threepio	L	Ch-Dr	RF	30.00

Card name		Side	Type	Rarity	Price
☐	A280 Sharpshooter Rifle	L	Ch-Wp	R	4.00
☐	Accelerate	D	UI	C	0.20
☐	Aim High	L	E	R	3.50
☐	Always Thinking With Your Stomach	D	LI	R	3.00
☐	An Entire Legion Of My Best Troops	D	E	U	1.00
☐	Aratech Corporation	D	E	R	3.00
☐	AT-ST Dual Cannon	D	Veh-W	R	4.00
☐	AT-ST Pilot	D	Ch-Imp	C	0.20
☐	Battle Order	D	E	U	1.00
☐	Battle Plan	L	E	U	1.00
☐	Biker Scout Gear	D	E	U	1.00
☐	Biker Scout Trooper	D	Ch-Imp	C	0.20
☐	Blastech E-11B Blaster Rifle	L	Ch-Wp	C	0.20
☐	Captain Yutani	L	Ch-R	U	1.00
☐	Careful Planning	L	UI/SI	C	0.20
☐	Carida	D	Lo-Sys	U	1.00
☐	Chandrila	L	Lo-Sys	U	1.00
☐	Chewbacca Of Kashyyyk	L	Ch-R	R	14.00
☐	Chewbacca's Bowcaster	L	Ch-Wp	R	5.00
☐	Chewie's AT-ST	L	CV	R	5.00
☐	Chief Chirpa	L	Ch-Al	R	4.00
☐	Closed Door	D	E	R	3.00
☐	Colonel Dyer	D	CH-Imp	R	4.00
☐	Combat Readiness	D	UI/SI	C	0.20
☐	Command Training	L	E	C	0.20
☐	Commander Igar	D	Ch-Imp	R	4.00

Card name		Side	Type	Rarity	Price
☐	Compact Firepower	D	UI	C	0.20
☐	Corporal Avarik	D	Ch-Imp	U	1.00
☐	Corporal Beezer	L	Ch-R	U	1.00
☐	Corporal Delevar	L	Ch-R	U	1.00
☐	Corporal Drazin	D	Ch-Imp	U	1.00
☐	Corporal Drelosyn	D	Ch-Imp	R	3.50
☐	Corporal Janse	L	Ch-R	U	1.00
☐	Corporal Kensaric	L	Ch-R	R	3.00
☐	Corporal Misik	D	Ch-Imp	R	3.00
☐	Corporal Oberk	D	Ch-Imp	R	3.00
☐	Count Me In	L	E	R	3.50
☐	Counterattack	D	LI	R	3.00
☐	Covert Landing	L	UI/LI	U	1.00
☐	Crossfire	D	E	R	3.00
☐	Daughter Of Skywalker	L	Ch-R	R	15.00
☐	Deactivate The Shield Generator	L	Ep E	R	4.00
☐	Dead Ewok	D	LI	C	0.20
☐	Don't Move!	D	UI	C	0.20
☐	Dresselian Commando	L	Ch-R	C	0.20
☐	Early Warning Network	D	E	R	3.00
☐	Eee Chu Wawa!	D	UI/LI	C	0.20
☐	Elite Squadron Stormtrooper	D	CH-Imp	C	0.20
☐	Empire's New Order	D	E	R	3.00
☐	Endor	L	Lo-Sys	U	0.80
☐	Endor	D	Lo-Sys	U	0.80
☐	Endor: Ancient Forest	D	L-Site	U	1.00
☐	Endor: Back Door	L	L-Site	U	1.00
☐	Endor: Back Door	D	L-Site	U	1.00
☐	Endor: Bunker	L	L-Site	U	1.00
☐	Endor: Bunker	D	L-Site	U	1.00
☐	Endor Celebration	L	UI	R	3.50

Card name		Side	Type	Rarity	Price
☐	Endor: Chief Chirpa's Hut	L	L-Site	R	3.00
☐	Endor: Dark Forest	D	L-Site	R	3.00
☐	Endor: Dense Forest	L	L-Site	C	0.25
☐	Endor: Dense Forest	D	L-Site	C	0.25
☐	Endor: Ewok Village	L	L-Site	U	1.00
☐	Endor: Ewok Village	D	L-Site	U	1.00
☐	Endor: Forest Clearing	D	L-Site	U	1.00
☐	Endor: Great Forest	L	L-Site	C	0.25
☐	Endor: Great Forest	D	L-Site	C	0.25
☐	Endor: Hidden Forest Trail	L	L-Site	U	1.00
☐	Endor: Landing Platform (Docking Bay)	L	L-Site	C	0.20
☐	Endor: Landing Platform (Docking Bay)	D	L-Site	C	0.20
☐	Endor Occupation	D	UI	R	4.00
☐	Endor Operations/Imperial Outpost	D	Obj	R	5.00
☐	Endor: Rebel Landing Site (Forest)	L	L-Site	R	4.00
☐	Endor Scout Trooper	L	Ch-R	C	0.25
☐	Establish Secret Base	D	E	R	4.00
☐	Ewok And Roll	L	UI	C	0.20
☐	Ewok Bow	L	Ch-Wp	C	0.20
☐	Ewok Catapult	L	Art W	U	1.00
☐	Ewok Glider	L	Tr Veh	C	0.20
☐	Ewok Log Jam	L	UI	C	0.20
☐	Ewok Rescue	L	LI	C	0.20
☐	Ewok Sentry	L	Ch-Al	C	0.20
☐	Ewok Spear	L	Ch-Wp	C	0.20
☐	Ewok Spearman	L	Ch-Al	C	0.20
☐	Ewok Tribesman	L	Ch-Al	C	0.20

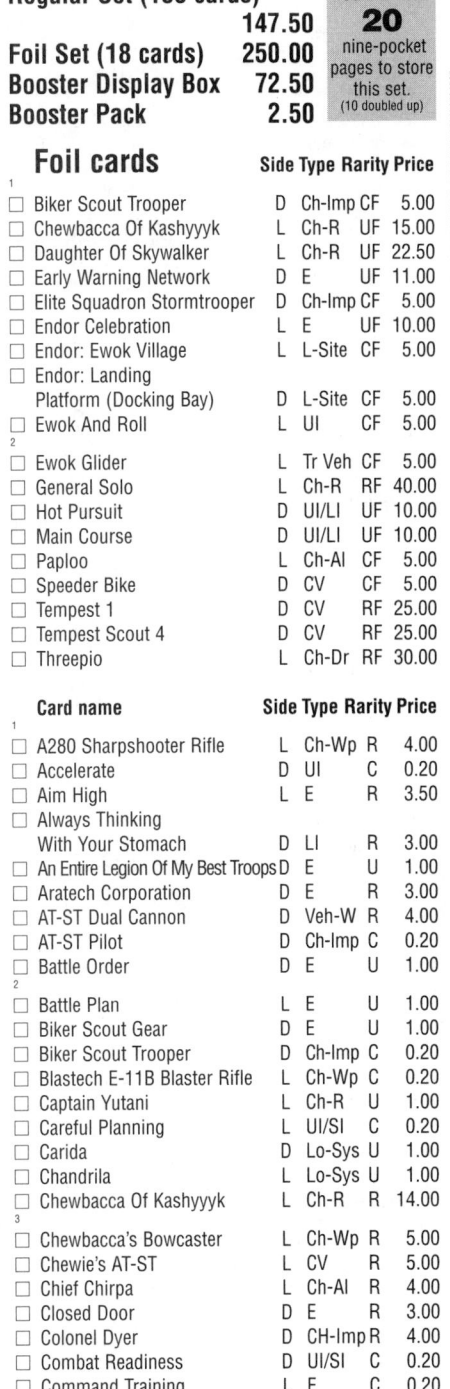

> **AT-ST Dual Cannon** ④
> High rate of fire used for anti-personnel operations.
> Enhanced design from prototype used in the Battle of Hoth.
>
> **VEHICLE WEAPON**
>
> Use 1 Force to deploy on your AT-ST. May target a character, creature or vehicle for 1 Force. Draw destiny. Add 1 if targeting a character or creature. Target hit if total destiny > defense value. May fire repeatedly for 2 Force each time.

Star Wars • Second Anthology

Decipher • Released December 1998

• Set contains eight **Premiere Unlimited** boosters, two **Cloud City** packs, two **Dagobah** packs, and 6 promo cards

This set was much like the First Anthology, except the preview cards came from the Endor and Death Star II expansions, not Special Edition. And with the much-coveted Calamari Cruiser found in every box, many players bought two or three copies of this Anthology. — *Joe Alread*

Second Anthology (sealed)   35.00

☐	Flagship Operations	4.00
☐	Mon Calamari Star Cruiser	6.00
☐	Mon Mothma	5.00
☐	Rapid Deployment	4.00
☐	Sarlacc	4.00
☐	Thunderflare	6.00

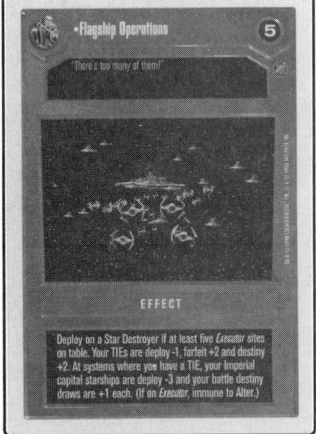

> **•Flagship Operations** ⑤
> "There's too many of them!"
>
> **EFFECT**
>
> Deploy on a Star Destroyer if at least five *Executor* sites on table. Your TIEs are deploy -1, forfeit +2 and destiny +2. At systems where you have a TIE, your Imperial capital starships are deploy -3 and your battle destiny draws are +1 each. (If on *Executor*, immune to Alter.)

RARITY KEY **C** = Common **U** = Uncommon **R** = Rare **VR** = Very Rare **UR** = Ultra Rare **F** = Foil card **X** = Fixed/standard in all decks

Card name	Side	Type	Rarity	Price
☐ Explosive Charge	L	Aut W	U	1.00
☐ Firefight	L	UI	C	0.20
☐ Fly Casual	L	UI/LI	R	3.00
☐ Free Ride	L	UI	U	1.00
☐ Freeze!	D	LI	U	1.00
☐ General Crix Madine	L	Ch-R	R	4.00
11				
☐ General Solo	L	Ch-R	R	17.50
☐ Get Alongside That One	L	UI	U	1.00
☐ Go For Help!	D	UI	C	0.20
☐ Graak	L	Ch-Al	R	3.00
☐ Here We Go Again	L	LI	R	3.00
☐ High-speed Tactics	D	UI	U	1.00
☐ Hot Pursuit	D	UI/LI	C	0.20
☐ I Have A Really Bad Feeling About This	L	UI	C	0.20
☐ I Hope She's All Right	L	E	U	1.00
12				
☐ I Know	L	LI	R	4.00
☐ I Wonder What They Found	L	E	U	1.00
☐ Imperial Academy Training	D	E	C	0.20
☐ Imperial Arrest Order	D	E	U	1.00
☐ Imperial Tyranny	D	LI	C	0.20
☐ Insurrection	L	E	U	1.00
☐ It's An Older Code	D	UI/LI	R	3.00
☐ Kazak	L	Ch-Al	R	3.00
☐ Lambda-Class Shuttle	D	S	C	0.20
13				
☐ Lieutenant Arnet	D	Ch-Imp	U	1.00
☐ Lieutenant Greeve	L	Ch-R	R	3.00
☐ Lieutenant Grond	D	Ch-Imp	U	1.00
☐ Lieutenant Page	L	Ch-R	R	4.00
☐ Lieutenant Renz	D	Ch-Imp	R	3.00
☐ Lieutenant Watts	D	Ch-Imp	R	3.00
☐ Logray	L	Ch-Al	R	4.00
☐ Lost In The Wilderness	L	LI	R	3.00
☐ Lumat	L	Ch-Al	U	1.00
14				
☐ Main Course	D	UI/LI	U	1.00
☐ Major Hewex	D	CH-Imp	R	3.50
☐ Major Marquand	D	CH-Imp	R	4.00
☐ Mon Mothma	L	Ch-R	R	5.00
☐ Navy Trooper	D	CH-Imp	C	0.20
☐ Navy Trooper Fenson	D	CH-Imp	R	3.50
☐ Navy Trooper Shield Technician	D	CH-Imp	C	0.20
☐ Navy Trooper Vesden	D	CH-Imp	U	1.00
☐ Ominous Rumors	D	E	R	4.00
15				
☐ Orrimaarko	L	Ch-R	R	5.00

Card name	Side	Type	Rarity	Price
☐ Outflank	D	UI	C	0.20
☐ Paploo	L	Ch-Al	U	1.00
☐ Perimeter Patrol	D	E	R	4.00
☐ Pinned Down	D	E	U	1.00
☐ Pitiful Little Band	D	UI	C	0.20
☐ Rabin	L	Ch-Al	U	1.00
☐ Rapid Deployment	L	LI	R	3.00
☐ Rebel Strike Team/ Garrison Destroyed	L	Obj	R	5.00
16				
☐ Relentless Tracking	D	E	R	3.00
☐ Romba	L	Ch-Al	R	3.00
☐ Scout Blaster	D	Ch-Wp	C	0.20
☐ Scout Recon	D	UI	C	0.20
☐ Search And Destroy	D	E	U	1.00
☐ Security Precautions	D	E	R	3.00
☐ Sergeant Barich	D	CH-Imp	R	4.00
☐ Sergeant Brooks Carlson	L	Ch-R	R	3.50
☐ Sergeant Bruckman	L	Ch-R	R	3.50
17				
☐ Sergeant Elsek	D	CH-Imp	U	1.00
☐ Sergeant Irol	D	CH-Imp	R	3.00
☐ Sergeant Junkin	L	Ch-R	U	1.00
☐ Sergeant Tarl	D	CH-Imp	U	1.00
☐ Sergeant Wallen	D	CH-Imp	R	3.00
☐ Sneak Attack	D	UI/LI	C	0.20
☐ Sound The Attack	L	UI/LI	C	0.20
☐ Speeder Bike	L	CV	C	0.20
☐ Speeder Bike	D	CV	C	0.20

Card name	Side	Type	Rarity	Price
18				
☐ Speeder Bike Cannon	D	Veh-W	U	1.00
☐ Surprise Counter Assault	L	LI	R	3.00
☐ Take The Initiative	L	UI/LI	C	0.20
☐ Teebo	L	Ch-Al	R	3.50
☐ Tempest 1	D	CV	R	7.00
☐ Tempest Scout	D	CV	U	1.00
☐ Tempest Scout 1	D	CV	R	5.00
☐ Tempest Scout 2	D	CV	R	5.00
☐ Tempest Scout 3	D	CV	R	5.50
19				
☐ Tempest Scout 4	D	CV	R	5.50
☐ Tempest Scout 5	D	CV	R	5.00
☐ Tempest Scout 6	D	CV	R	5.00
☐ That's One	L	E	R	3.00
☐ This Is Absolutely Right	L	UI	R	3.00
☐ Threepio	L	Ch-Dr	R	10.00
☐ Throw Me Another Charge	L	UI	U	1.00
☐ Tydirium	L	S	R	6.00
☐ Well-earned Command	D	E	R	3.00
20				
☐ Were You Looking For Me?	L	UI/LI	R	3.50
☐ Wicket	L	Ch-Al	R	4.00
☐ Wokling	L	E	R	3.00
☐ Wookiee Guide	L	UI	C	0.20
☐ Wounded Warrior	D	UI	R	3.00
☐ Wuta	L	Ch-Al	U	1.00
☐ You Rebel Scum	D	LI	R	3.00
☐ YT-1300 Transport	L	S	C	0.20
☐ Yub Yub!	L	UI/LI	C	0.20

Star Wars • Enhanced Premiere

Decipher • Released December 1998

• Box contains four **Unlimited** packs plus one of six promos

In an attempt to bring in new players and to satisfy the masses of people complaining that the game's main characters were too difficult to obtain, Decipher released **Enhanced Premiere**, repackaging **Unlimited** cards with relatively inexpensive main characters.

These characters had built-in weapons in their game text, which was fairly exciting to the game's player base at the time. Some were also better than their previous versions and, as a result, became staple cards in many powerful tournament decks. — *Joe Alread*

Enhanced Premiere Deck — 13.50

☐ Boba Fett With Blaster Rifle	8.00		☐ Leia With Blaster Rifle	14.00
☐ Darth Vader With Lightsaber	9.00		☐ Luke With Lightsaber	10.00
☐ Han With Heavy Blaster Pistol	14.00		☐ Obi-Wan With Lightsaber	10.00

Star Wars • Enhanced Cloud City

Decipher • Released October 1999

• Contains four **Cloud City** packs plus three of 12 premium cards

This set brought the game new and powerful main characters that have been included in many top-tier decks. Much like the **Enhanced Premiere** characters, many of these cards had built-in weapons. — *Joe Alread*

Enhanced Cloud City Deck — 13.50

☐ 4-LOM With Concussion Rifle	6.00		☐ Lando With Blaster Pistol	6.50
☐ Any Methods Necessary	5.00		☐ Quiet Mining Colony/ Independent Operation	5.00
☐ Boba Fett In Slave 1	9.00		☐ This Deal Is Getting Worse All The Time/ Pray I Don't Alter It Any Further	5.00
☐ Chewie With Blaster Rifle	7.00			
☐ Crush The Rebellion	5.00			
☐ Dengar In Punishing One	6.00			
☐ IG-88 With Riot Gun	6.00		☐ Z-95 Bespin Defense Fighter	4.50
☐ Lando In Millennium Falcon	7.50			

Star Wars • Enhanced Jabba's Palace

Decipher • Released December 1999

• Contains four **Jabba's Palace** packs plus three of 12 premium cards

Yet another repackaging of old stock with a few powerful new cards, these have a Jabba's Palace theme. Once again, many of these cards found their way into some very powerful tournament decks. — *Joe Alread*

Enhanced Jabba's Palace Deck — 13.50

☐ Bossk With Mortar Gun	6.00		☐ Mara Jade, The Emperor's Hand	14.50
☐ Boushh	8.00		☐ Mara Jade's Lightsaber	7.00
☐ Court Of The Vile Gangster/ I Shall Enjoy Watching You Die	5.00		☐ Master Luke	9.00
☐ Dengar With Blaster Carbine	6.00		☐ See-Threepio	6.00
☐ IG-88 In IG-2000	6.50		☐ You Can Either Profit By This/ Or Be Destroyed	5.00
☐ Jodo Kast	6.00		☐ Zuckuss In Mist Hunter	7.00

RARITY KEY C = Common **U** = Uncommon **R** = Rare **#** = Lower #s are rarer **X** = Fixed/standard in all decks **CARD TYPES on page 438**

Star Wars • Reflections: A Collector's Bounty

Decipher • Released January 2000
114 foil cards in set • **IDENTIFIER: Cards are foil versions of older cards**

• Booster packs contain 17 cards and 1 foil card; booster displays contain 36 boosters

With foil cards drawing new sales in the industry, Decipher "foiled" many of its older chase cards in this set. There were no new cards, simply a foil card in every pack along with 17 other random cards from previous sets, which included rare cards.

Four to five rares a pack was a common find when these packs were being opened, and they got opened a lot. While many players decided to stay away, since there weren't any new cards, the players and collectors who did buy into the set bought plenty, trying to complete their foil sets. — *Joe Alread*

Set (114 foil cards)	900.00
Booster Display Box	134.50
Booster Pack	5.00

You will need 13 nine-pocket pages to store this set. (7 doubled up)

Card name	Side	Set	Rarity	Price
2-1B	L	Hoth	VRF	4.50
4-LOM	D	Dag	VRF	5.00
Admiral Ozzel	D	Hoth	VRF	5.00
All Wings Report In	L	SE	VRF	4.50
Anakin's Lightsaber	L	Hoth	VRF	8.00
Artoo	L	JP	VRF	8.00
Attack Run	L	ANH	VRF	5.00
Avenger	D	Dag	VRF	7.30
Bane Malar	D	JP	VRF	5.00
Ben Kenobi	L	SE	SRF	24.50
Bib Fortuna	D	JP	VRF	4.50
Biggs Darklighter	L	Pre	VRF	4.80
Black 2	D	Pre	VRF	5.00
Blizzard 1	D	Hoth	VRF	7.00
Blizzard 2	D	Hoth	VRF	6.00
Blizzard Scout 1	D	Hoth	VRF	6.00
Boba Fett	D	CC	SRF	25.00
Boba Fett's Blaster Rifle	D	CC	VRF	5.00
Bossk	D	Dag	VRF	5.00
Bossk in Hounds Tooth	D	SE	VRF	6.00
Braniac	L	ANH	VRF	5.00
C-3PO	L	Pre	SRF	18.00
Captain Han Solo	L	CC	SRF	25.50
Chewbacca	L	ANH	SRF	20.00
Cloud City: Downtown Plaza	L	SE	VRF	5.00
Cloud City: Guest Quarters	L	CC	VRF	4.50
Commander Luke Skywalker	L	Hoth	VRF	10.00
Commence Primary Ignition	D	ANH	VRF	5.00
Conquest	D	ANH	VRF	8.00
Coruscant Celebration	L	SE	VRF	4.50
Dagobah: Yoda's Hut	L	Dag	VRF	5.00
Darth Vader	D	Pre	URF	100.00
Darth Vader, Dark Lord Of The Sith	D	SE	SRF	40.00
Death Squadron Star Destroyer	D	SE	VRF	6.00
Death Star	L	SE	VRF	7.50
Death Star	D	ANH	SRF	11.00
Death Star Plans	L	Pre	VRF	5.00
Death Star: Trench	L	ANH	VRF	5.00
Dengar	D	Dag	VRF	5.30
Devastator	D	Pre	SRF	13.50
DS-61-3	D	Pre	VRF	5.00
Dutch	L	Pre	VRF	5.00
Epic Duel	D	CC	VRF	5.00
Executor	D	Dag	SRF	25.00
Expand The Empire	D	Pre	VRF	5.00
General Veers	D	Hoth	SRF	11.00
Grand Moff Tarkin	D	Pre	SRF	15.00
Greedo	D	ANH	VRF	4.80
Han Solo	L	Pre	SRF	20.00
Haven	L	CC	VRF	5.00
IG-88	D	Dag	VRF	7.00

Card name	Side	Set	Rarity	Price
IG-2000	D	Dag	VRF	5.00
It Is The Future You See	L	Dag	VRF	5.00
IT-O	D	ANH	VRF	5.00
Jabba	D	SE	VRF	8.00
Jabba The Hutt	D	JP	SRF	19.50
Jabba's Sail Barge	D	JP	VRF	5.00
Landing Claw	L	Dag	VRF	5.00
Lando Calrissian	L	CC	SRF	13.50
Lando Calrissian	D	CC	SRF	12.00
Leia Organa	L	Pre	SRF	22.50
Lightsaber Proficiency	L	Pre	VRF	5.00
Lobot	L	CC	VRF	5.00
Lobot	D	SE	VRF	5.00
Luke Skywalker	L	Pre	URF	77.50
Mechanical Failure	L	SE	VRF	5.00
Millennium Falcon	L	Pre	SRF	20.50
Mist Hunter	D	Dag	VRF	5.30
Obi-Wan Kenobi	L	Pre	SRF	24.50
Obi-Wan's Lightsaber	L	Pre	VRF	8.00
Obsidian 7	D	CC	VRF	5.00
Obsidian 8	D	CC	VRF	5.00
Oola	L	JP	VRF	5.00
Presence of the Force	D	Pre	VRF	5.00
Princess Leia	L	CC	VRF	8.00
Princess Leia Organa	L	JP	SRF	20.00
Princess Organa	L	SE	VRF	8.50
Punishing One	D	Dag	VRF	5.00
R2-D2	L	ANH	SRF	15.00
Rancor	D	JP	VRF	5.50
Red 2	L	ANH	VRF	5.50
Red 5	L	ANH	VRF	6.00
Red Leader	L	Pre	VRF	5.50
Redemption	L	CC	VRF	6.50
Reflection	L	Dag	VRF	5.00

Card name	Side	Set	Rarity	Price
Rendezvous Point	L	SE	VRF	5.00
Revolution	L	Pre	VRF	5.50
Rogue 1	L	Hoth	VRF	6.50
Rogue 3	L	Hoth	VRF	5.00
Salacious Crumb	D	JP	VRF	5.00
Skywalkers	L	Pre	VRF	5.00
Slave I	D	CC	SRF	12.50
Slip Sliding Away	D	CC	VRF	4.50
Son Of Skywalker	L	Dag	SRF	22.00
Spiral	L	SE	VRF	6.00
Stalker	D	Hoth	VRF	7.30
Superlaser	D	ANH	VRF	5.00
Tamtel Skreej	L	JP	VRF	6.00
Tantive IV	L	ANH	VRF	7.50
The Circle Is Now Complete	D	Pre	VRF	5.00
TK-422	L	SE	VRF	10.00
Tonnika Sisters	D	Pre	VRF	5.00
Tyrant	D	Hoth	VRF	8.00
U-3PO	D	ANH	VRF	5.00
Uncontrollable Fury	L	CC	VRF	4.50
Vader's Custom TIE	D	Pre	SRF	13.50
Vader's Lightsaber	D	Pre	SRF	16.00
Vengeance	D	SE	VRF	7.30
Visage Of The Emperor	D	Dag	VRF	5.00
Wampa	D	Hoth	VRF	5.00
Wedge Antilles	L	ANH	VRF	6.00
What Is Thy Bidding, My Master?	L	Dag	VRF	4.50
Yoda	L	Dag	SRF	20.00
Zuckuss	D	Dag	VRF	5.00

Star Wars • Third Anthology

Decipher • Released April 2000

• Set contains two **Special Edition** starters, two **Jabba's Palace** packs, two **Unlimited** packs, and 6 promo cards

Another collector's box, with more new cards. The difference between this and previous Anthologies was that the new cards weren't previews, but actual premium cards available nowhere else — and fairly powerful cards, as well.

Each one introduced a new deck strategy into the tournament scene. — *Joe Alread*

Third Anthology (sealed)	27.75
A New Secret Base	5.00
Artoo-Detoo In Red 5	5.80
Echo Base Garrison	4.50
Prisoner 2187	5.00
Massassi Base Operations/One In A Million	5.50
Set Your Course For Alderaan/ The Ultimate Power In The Universe	5.00

RARITY KEY C = Common **U** = Uncommon **R** = Rare **VRF** = Very Rare Foil **SRF** = Super Rare Foil **URF** = Ultra Rare Foil

Star Wars • Death Star II

Decipher • Released **June 2000**
182 cards in set • **IDENTIFIER: Lightning blast on red in circle**
- Starter decks contain 60 cards; booster displays contain 12 boosters
- Booster packs contain 11 cards; booster displays contain 36 boosters

Featuring the climax of the original trilogy, ***Death Star II*** adds new mechanics for the turning of Darth Vader and Luke Skywalker to an opponent's side of the Force, as well as the construction of the new dreaded Death Star. Most of the new mechanics were strong enough to be competitively useful in high-level tournaments.— ***Joe Alread***

	Price
Set (182 cards)	175.00
Starter Display Box	125.00
Booster Display Box	90.00
Starter Deck	11.00
Booster Pack	3.30

Card name	Side	Type	Rarity	Price
Accuser	D	SS	R	5.00
Admiral Ackbar	L	Reb	FR	5.00
Admiral Chiraneau	D	Imp	R	4.50
Admiral Piett	D	Imp	FR	5.00
Anakin Skywalker	L	Int	R	8.00
Aquaris	L	L-Sys	C	0.20
A-wing	L	SS	C	0.20
A-wing Cannon	L	Wp	C	0.20
Baron Soontir Fel	D	Imp	R	4.50
Battle Deployment	D	Ad	R	4.00
Black 11	D	SS	R	4.30
Blue Squadron 5	L	SS	U	0.50
Blue Squadron B-wing	L	SS	R	4.00
Bring Him Before Me/ Take Your Father's Place	D	Obj	R	4.60
B-wing Attack Squadron	L	SS	R	4.50
B-wing Bomber	L	SS	C	0.20
Capital Support	L	Ad	R	4.00
Captain Godherdt	D	Imp	U	0.50
Captain Jonus	D	Imp	U	0.80
Captain Sarkli	D	Imp	R	4.00
Captain Verrack	L	Reb	U	0.50
Captain Yorr	D	Imp	U	0.50
Chimaera	D	SS	R	5.50
Close Air Support	L	Eff	C	0.20
Colonel Cracken	L	Reb	R	4.50
Colonel Davod Jon	D	Imp	U	0.50
Colonel Jendon	D	Imp	R	4.50
Colonel Salm	L	Reb	U	0.50
Combat Response	D	Eff	C	0.20
Combined Fleet Action	L	Ad	R	4.00
Commander Merrejk	D	Imp	R	4.50
Concentrate All Fire	L	Ad	R	4.00
Concussion Missiles	L	Wp	C	0.25
Concussion Missiles	D	Wp	C	0.25
Corporal Marmor	L	Reb	U	0.50
Corporal Midge	L	Reb	U	0.50
Critical Error Revealed	L	Int	C	0.25
Darth Vader's Lightsaber	D	Wp	R	6.80
Death Star II	D	L-Sys	R	9.50
Death Star II: Capacitors	D	L-Sec	C	0.20
Death Star II: Coolant Shaft	D	L-Sec	C	0.20
Death Star II: Docking Bay	D	L-Site	C	0.20
Death Star II: Reactor Core	D	L-Sec	C	0.20
Death Star II: Throne Room	D	L-Site	R	4.00
Defiance	L	SS	R	6.80
Desperate Counter	D	Eff	C	0.20
Dominator	D	SS	R	7.30
DS-181-3	D	Imp	U	0.50
DS-181-4	D	Imp	U	0.50
Emperor Palpatine	D	Imp	UR	55.00
Emperor's Personal Shuttle	D	SS	R	4.80
Emperor's Power	D	Eff	U	0.80
Endor Shield	D	Eff	U	0.50

Card name	Side	Type	Rarity	Price
Enhanced Proton Torpedoes	L	Wp	C	0.20
Fighter Cover	D	Ad	R	4.00
Fighters Coming In	D	Ad	R	4.00
First Officer Thaneespi	L	Reb	R	4.50
Flagship Executor	D	SS	R	13.50
Flagship Operations	D	Eff	R	4.00
Force Lightning	D	Int	R	4.50
Force Pike	D	Wp	C	0.20
Gall	D	L-Sys	C	0.20
General Calrissian	L	Reb	R	8.30
General Walex Blissex	L	Reb	U	0.50
Gold Squadron 1	L	SS	R	6.00
Green Leader	L	Reb	R	4.50
Green Squadron 1	L	SS	R	4.50
Green Squadron 3	L	SS	R	4.50
Green Squadron A-wing	L	SS	R	4.50
Green Squadron Pilot	L	Reb	C	0.20
Grey Squadron 1	L	SS	U	0.80
Grey Squadron 2	L	SS	U	0.80
Grey Squadron Y-wing Pilot	L	Reb	C	0.20
Head Back To The Surface	L	Int	C	0.20
Heading For The Medical Frigate	L	Int	C	0.20
Heavy Turbolaser Battery	L	Wp	C	0.20
Heavy Turbolaser Battery	D	Wp	C	0.20
Home One	L	SS	R	7.80
Home One: Docking Bay	L	L-Site	C	0.20
Home One: War Room	L	L-Site	R	4.00
Honor Of The Jedi	L	Eff	U	0.80
I Can Feel The Conflict	L	Eff	U	0.80
I'll Take The Leader	L	Ad	R	4.00
I'm With You Too	L	Eff	R	4.00
Imperial Command	D	Int	R	4.00
Inconsequential Losses	D	Eff	C	0.20
Independence	L	SS	R	6.80
Insertion Planning	L	Int	C	0.20
Insignificant Rebellion	D	Eff	U	0.80
Intensify The Forward Batteries	D	Ad	R	4.00
Janus Greejatus	D	Imp	R	5.00
Judicator	D	SS	R	7.00
Karie Neth	L	Reb	U	0.50
Keir Santage	L	Reb	U	0.50
Kin Kian	L	Reb	U	0.50
Launching The Assault	L	Eff	R	4.00
Leave Them To Me	D	Eff	C	0.20
Let's Keep A Little Optimism Here	L	Eff	C	0.20
Liberty	L	SS	R	6.00
Lieutenant Blount	L	Reb	R	4.50
Lieutenant Endicott	D	Imp	U	0.50
Lieutenant Hebsly	D	Imp	U	0.50
Lieutenant s'Too Vees	L	Reb	U	0.50
Lieutenant Telsij	L	Reb	U	0.50
Lord Vader	D	Imp	R	29.00
Luke Skywalker, Jedi Knight	L	Reb	UR	50.00
Luke's Lightsaber	L	Wp	R	7.80
Luminous	L	SS	U	0.50
Major Haash'n	L	Reb	U	0.50
Major Mianda	D	Imp	U	0.50
Major Olander Brit	L	Reb	U	0.50
Major Panno	L	Reb	U	0.50
Major Rhymer	D	Imp	U	0.50
Major Turr Phennir	D	Imp	U	0.50
Masanya	L	SS	R	5.00
Menace Fades	L	Eff	C	0.20
Mobilization Points	D	Eff	C	0.20
Moff Jerjerrod	D	Imp	R	5.00
Mon Calamari	L	L-Sys	C	0.20

Card name	Side	Type	Rarity	Price
Mon Calamari	D	L-Sys	C	0.20
Mon Calamari Star Cruiser	L	SS	R	5.50
Myn Kyneugh	D	Imp	R	5.00
Nebulon-B Frigate	L	SS	U	0.80
Nien Nunb	L	Reb	R	5.80
Obsidian 10	D	SS	U	0.50
Onyx 1	D	SS	R	5.00
Onyx 2	D	SS	U	0.50
Operational As Planned	D	Int	C	0.20
Orbital Mine	L	Wp	C	0.20
Our Only Hope	L	Int	U	0.20
Overseeing It Personally	D	Eff	R	4.00
Prepared Defenses	D	Int	C	0.20
Rebel Leadership	L	Int	R	4.00
Red Squadron 1	L	SS	R	5.00
Red Squadron 4	L	SS	U	0.80
Red Squadron 7	L	SS	U	0.80
Rise, My Friend	D	Int	R	4.00
Royal Escort	D	Eff	C	0.20
Royal Guard	D	Imp	C	0.25
Saber 1	D	SS	R	4.50
Saber 2	D	SS	U	0.90
Saber 3	D	SS	U	0.60
Saber 4	D	SS	U	0.60
Scimitar 1	D	SS	U	0.50
Scimitar 2	D	SS	U	0.50
Scimitar Squadron TIE	D	SS	C	0.20
Scythe 1	D	SS	U	0.90
Scythe 3	D	SS	U	0.90
Scythe Squadron TIE	D	SS	C	0.20
SFS L-s7.2 TIE Cannon	D	Wp	C	0.20
Sim Aloo	D	Imp	R	5.00
Something Special Planned For Them	D	Eff	C	0.20
Squadron Assignments	L	Eff	C	0.20
Staging Areas	L	Eff	C	0.20
Strike Planning	L	Eff	R	4.00
Strikeforce	L	Eff	C	0.20
Sullust	L	L-Sys	C	0.20
Sullust	D	L-Sys	C	0.20
Superficial Damage	L	Eff	C	0.20
Superlaser Mark II	D	Wp	U	0.80
Taking Them With Us	L	Ad	R	4.00
Tala 1	L	SS	R	4.50
Tala 2	L	SS	R	4.50
Ten Numb	L	Reb	R	4.50
That Thing's Operational	D	EpEv	R	4.80
The Emperor's Shield	D	SS	R	5.00
The Emperor's Sword	D	SS	R	5.00
The Time For Our Attack Has Come	L	Eff	C	0.20
The Way Of Things	L	Eff	U	0.50
There Is Good In Him/ I Can Save Him	L	Obj	R	5.30
Thunderflare	D	SS	R	5.00
TIE Interceptor	D	SS	C	0.20
Twilight Is Upon Me	L	Eff	R	4.00
Tycho Celchu	L	Reb	R	4.00
Visage	D	SS	R	5.00
We're In Attack Position Now	D	Ad	R	4.00
Wedge Antilles, Red Squadron Leader	L	Reb	R	6.50
You Cannot Hide Forever	D	Eff	U	0.50
You Must Confront Vader	L	JT	R	5.00
Young Fool	D	Int	R	4.00
Your Destiny	D	Eff	C	0.20
Your Insight Serves You Well	L	Eff	U	0.80

Star Wars • Reflections 2

Decipher • Released **December 2000**

154 foil cards in set • **IDENTIFIER: Black border cards have sun symbol**

You will need **18** nine-pocket pages to store this set. (9 doubled up)

- Booster packs contain 17 cards and 1 foil card; displays contain 36 boosters

  In addition to foils, this set has new black-bordered cards (marked as Premiere below) with new art featuring characters from the novels.

Too new for pricing! See current issues of SCRYE for the latest after-market prices!

CASE TOPPER (1/Case)	Side	Set	Rarity
☐ Darth Vader (Japanese)	D	Imp	pre

DISPLAY BOX TOPPER (1/Box)	Side	Set	Rarity
☐ Boba Fett With Blaster Rifle	D	AI	pre
☐ Han With Heavy Blaster Pistol	L	Reb	pre
☐ Leia With Blaster Rifle	L	Reb	pre
☐ Obi-Wan With Lightsaber	L	Reb	pre

Card name	Side	Set	Rarity
☐ 4-LOM With Concussion Rifle	D	ECC	SRF
☐ Abyssin Ornament & Wounded Wookiee	D	Int	pre
☐ Admiral Ackbar	L	DS2	SRF
☐ Admiral Piett	D	DS2	SRF
☐ Agents Of Black Sun/ Vengeance Of The Dark Prince	D	Obj	pre
☐ Alter & Collateral Damage	D	Int	pre
☐ Alter & Friendly Fire	L	Int	pre
☐ Arica	D	AI/Imp	pre
☐ Arleil Schous	L	OTSD	VRF
☐ Artoo & Threepio	L	Dr	pre
☐ Artoo-Detoo In Red 5	L	3rd	SRF
☐ B-wing Attack Squadron	L	DS2	SRF
☐ Bacta Tank	L	Hoth	SRF
☐ Bad Feeling Have I	D	Dag	VRF
☐ Baron Soontir Fel	D	DS2	SRF
☐ Black Squadron TIE	D	OTSD	VRF
☐ Black Sun Fleet	D	Ad	pre
☐ Blue Squadron B-wing	L	DS2	VRF
☐ Boba Fett In Slave I	D	ECC	SRF
☐ Boelo	D	SE	VRF
☐ Bossk With Mortar Gun	D	EJP	SRF
☐ Brainiac (Japanese)	L	ANH	SRF
☐ Capital Support	L	DS2	SRF
☐ Captain Gilad Pellaeon	D	Imp	pre
☐ Chall Bekan	D	OTSD	VRF
☐ Chewbacca, Protector	L	Reb	pre
☐ Chewie With Blaster Rifle	L	ECC	SRF
☐ Chief Chirpa	L	End	SRF
☐ Chimaera	D	DS2	SRF
☐ Commander Igar	D	End	VRF
☐ Control & Set For Stun	D	Int	pre
☐ Control & Tunnel Vision	L	Int	pre
☐ Corran Horn	L	Reb	pre
☐ Dark Maneuvers & Tallon Roll	D	Int	pre
☐ Darth Vader With Lightsaber	D	EP	SRF
☐ Darth Vader's Lightsaber	D	DS2	SRF
☐ Dash Rendar	L	AI	pre
☐ Death Star (Japanese)	D	ANH	SRF
☐ Death Star II	D	DS2	SRF
☐ Death Star II: Throne Room	D	DS2	VRF
☐ Defensive Fire & Hutt Smooch	D	Int	pre

Card name	Side	Set	Rarity
☐ Dengar In Punishing One	D	ECC	SRF
☐ Dengar With Blaster Carbine	D	EJP	SRF
☐ Djas Puhr	D	Pre	SRF
☐ Do, Or Do Not & Wise Advice	L	Eff	pre
☐ Don't Get Cocky	L	Pre	SRF
☐ Dr. Evazan & Ponda Baba	D	AI	pre
☐ Dreadnaught-Class Heavy Cruiser	D	OTSD	SRF
☐ Echo Base Operations	L	Hoth	SRF
☐ Emperor Palpatine	D	DS2	URF
☐ Evader & Monnok	D	Int	pre
☐ Executor: Holotheater	D	Dag	VRF
☐ Executor: Meditation Chamber	D	Dag	VRF
☐ Fighters Coming In	D	DS2	VRF
☐ Flagship Executor	D	DS2	SRF
☐ Force Lightning	D	DS2	SRF
☐ Frozen Assets	L	CC	VRF
☐ General Calrissian	L	DS2	SRF
☐ General Crix Madine	L	End	SRF
☐ Ghhhk & Those Rebels Won't Escape Us	D	Int	pre
☐ Gift Of The Mentor	L	Pre	SRF
☐ Gold Leader In Gold 1	L	RL	VRF
☐ Gold Squadron 1	L	DS2	SRF
☐ Gold Squadron Y-wing	L	OTSD	SRF
☐ Goo Nee Tay	L	SE	VRF
☐ Grand Admiral Thrawn	D	Imp	pre
☐ Green Squadron A-wing	L	DS2	VRF
☐ Guri	D	Dr	pre
☐ Home One	L	DS2	SRF
☐ Hoth: Wampa Cave	D	Hoth	VRF
☐ Houjix & Out Of Nowhere	L	Int	pre
☐ IG-88 In IG-2000	D	EJP	VRF
☐ IG-88 With Riot Gun	D	ECC	SRF
☐ Imperial Walker (Japanese)	D	E2P	SRF
☐ Independence	L	DS2	SRF
☐ Jabba's Prize	D	Reb	pre
☐ Janus Greejatus	D	DS2	VRF
☐ Jodo Kast	D	EJP	SRF
☐ Kal'Falnl C'ndros	L	Pre	SRF
☐ Kessel Run	L	Pre	SRF
☐ Kiffex	D	ANH	VRF
☐ Kiffex	L	JP	VRF
☐ Kir Kanos	D	Imp	pre
☐ Lando In Millennium Falcon	L	ECC	SRF
☐ Lateral Damage	D	Pre	VRF
☐ LE-BO2D9	L	Dr	pre
☐ Leia (Japanese)	L	Jedi	SRF
☐ Liberty	L	DS2	VRF
☐ Lone Rogue	L	E2P	VRF
☐ Lord Vader	D	DS2	URF

Card name	Side	Set	Rarity
☐ Luke Skywalker, Jedi Knight	L	DS2	URF
☐ Luke Skywalker, Rebel Scout	L	Reb	pre
☐ Luke With Lightsaber	L	EP	SRF
☐ Luke's Lightsaber	L	DS2	SRF
☐ Mantellian Savrip	L	Pre	VRF
☐ Mara Jade's Lightsaber	D	EJP	SRF
☐ Mara Jade, The Emperor's Hand	D	EJP	URF
☐ Melas	L	SE	SRF
☐ Mercenary Armor	L	Dev	pre
☐ Mirax Terrik	L	Reb	pre
☐ Moff Jerjerrod	D	DS2	SRF
☐ Myn Kyneugh	D	DS2	VRF
☐ Nar Shaddaa Wind Chimes & Out Of Somewhere	L	Int	pre
☐ No Questions Asked	L	Ad	pre
☐ Obi-Wan's Journal	L	Dev	pre
☐ Ommni Box & It's Worse	D	Int	pre
☐ Order To Engage	L	Dag	VRF
☐ Orrimaarko	L	End	SRF
☐ Out Of Commission & Transmission Terminated	L	Int	pre
☐ Outer Rim Scout	D	SE	SRF
☐ Outrider	L	SS	pre
☐ Owen & Beru Lars	L	Reb	pre
☐ Path Of Least Resistance & Revealed	L	Int	pre
☐ Prince Xizor	D	AI	pre
☐ Pulsar Skate	L	SS	pre
☐ Rebel Snowspeeder (Japanese)	L	E2P	SRF
☐ Red Leader In Red 1	L	RL	VRF
☐ Red Squadron 1	L	DS2	SRF
☐ Red Squadron X-wing	L	OTSD	SRF
☐ Run, Luke, Run	L	A2P	VRF
☐ Scum And Villainy	D	JP	VRF
☐ See-Threepio	L	EJP	SRF
☐ Sense & Recoil In Fear	L	Int	pre
☐ Sense & Uncertain Is The Future	D	Int	pre
☐ Shocking Information & Grimtaash	L	Int	pre
☐ Sienar Fleet Systems	D	SE	VRF
☐ Sim Aloo	D	DS2	VRF
☐ Smoke Screen	L	CC	SRF
☐ Sniper & Dark Strike	D	Int	pre
☐ Snoova	D	AI	pre
☐ Sorry About The Mess & Blaster Proficiency	L	Int	pre
☐ Stinger	D	SS	pre
☐ Sunsdown & Too Cold For Speeders	D	Eff	pre
☐ Talon Karrde	L	AI	pre
☐ Tawss Khaa	L	SE	VRF
☐ Tempest Scout 1	D	End	SRF
☐ The Bith Shuffle & Desperate Reach	L	Int	pre
☐ The Emperor	D	Imp	pre
☐ The Emperor's Shield	D	DS2	SRF
☐ The Emperor's Sword	D	DS2	SRF
☐ There Is No Try & Oppressive Enforcement	D	Eff	pre
☐ Trample	D	Hoth	SRF
☐ Vader's Obsession	D	A2P	VRF
☐ Vigo	D	AI	pre
☐ Virago	D	SS	pre
☐ Walker Garrison	D	E2P	SRF
☐ Watch Your Step/This Place Can Be A Little Rough	L	Obj	pre
☐ Wedge Antilles, Red Squadron Leader	L	DS2	SRF
☐ Wicket	L	End	SRF
☐ X-wing Assault Squadron	L	SE	SRF
☐ Yavin 4: Massassi Throne Room	L	Pre	SRF
☐ Yoda Stew & You Do Have Your Moments	L	Int	pre
☐ Z-95 Headhunter	L	OTSD	VRF
☐ Zuckuss In Mist Hunter	D	EJP	SRF

Star Wars • Jabba's Palace Sealed Deck

Decipher • Released **November 2000**

- Set contains six **Jabba's Palace** booster packs and 20 premium cards

  Similar to the **Official Tournament Sealed Deck**, except with a Jabba's Palace theme to it. The new fixed cards helped balance some of the more powerful strategies released in **Death Star II**. — *Joe Alread*

Jabba's Palace Sealed Deck   19.25

☐ Agents In The Court/ No Love For The Empire	2.00	☐ Mercenary Pilot	2.00	☐ Racing Skiff (Dark Side)	2.00
☐ Hutt Influence	2.00	☐ Mighty Jabba	5.00	☐ Racing Skiff (Light Side)	2.00
☐ Jabba's Palace: Antechamber	2.00	☐ My Kind Of Scum/ Fearless And Inventive	2.00	☐ Seeking An Audience	2.00
☐ Jabba's Palace: Lower Passages	2.00	☐ No Escape	2.00	☐ Stun Blaster (Dark Side)	2.00
☐ Lando With Vibro-Ax	5.00	☐ Ounee Ta	2.00	☐ Stun Blaster (Light Side)	2.00
		☐ Palace Raider	2.00	☐ Tatooine: Desert Heart	2.00
		☐ Power Of The Hutt	2.00	☐ Tatooine: Hutt Trade Route	2.00
				☐ Underworld Contacts	2.00

RARITY KEY C = Common U = Uncommon R = Rare VRF = Very Rare Foil SRF = Super Rare Foil URF = Ultra Rare Foil

Super Deck!

Card Sharks • First release, *Yellow Edition*, released **September 1994**
160 cards in set • **IDENTIFIER: Cards are © 1994**
• Starter decks contain 60 cards; starter displays contain 10 decks
Designed by **Marc Miller**

You will need
18
nine-pocket
pages to store
this set.
(9 doubled up)

The fourth CCG on the market and the first not by Wizards of the Coast or TSR, **Super Deck!** tapped into the enormous demand for CCGs and the crossover interest in comics. Designed by Marc Miller, creator of the classic role-playing game *Traveller*, *Super Deck!* enlisted a variety of mostly fan artists to create a super-hero universe for players to beat each other up in.

Each player may play a single card, or discard and draw cards, on his turn. Each player builds two opposing stacks of cards, one for heroes and one for villains. Players heroes battle opponent's villains, and vice versa. Each card has a power value or a multiplier; a base value card can be modified upward by a player or downward by an opponent. An opponent may play a minus card anytime after a player plays plus card. At the end of all this math, the first player to beat the other by 10 points in both stacks at the same time wins the battle.

As a deck must consist of at least 40 cards, no more than four of any one card, it is easy to "stack" the deck with the highest value numbers. Unfortunately, this simple design does little to capture the "feel" of super-hero action and, could, in fact, have been adapted to a game about practically anything else.

Super Deck! had its day in the moments when nothing else was out — and became the butt of jokes once more professional games became available. Still, it remains a piece of gaming Americana representing the grassroots days of CCG design. — *James Mishler*

Concept	●●●○○
Gameplay	●●○○○
Card art	●○○○○
Player pool	○○○○○

7

Mr. Fixitt™

Begin super hero stack.
Tom Fitzwich, a.k.a. Mr. Fixitt, full-time grease monkey for Roy-Boy's Good Gas, and part-time world saver has the know how to fix anything, though not even he knows how he does it.

Base

H
Copyright © 1994 CSI.
Ilio © & ™ Boldman and Bender

Set (160 cards)	**43.00**
Starter Display Box	**20.00**
Starter Deck	**5.00**

Card name	Rarity	Price
1		
☐ Alien Cure	R	1.00
☐ Alien Doctor	R	1.00
☐ Alien Emissary	U	0.25
☐ Alien Plague	R	1.00
☐ Alien Vaccine	R	1.00
☐ Alien Virus	R	1.00
☐ Amnesia 1 (photo)	U	0.25
☐ Anti-Aircraft Missile	R	1.00
☐ Anti-Tank Missile	R	1.00
2		
☐ Argus	U	0.25
☐ Artillery	U	0.25
☐ Baldwin	R	1.00
☐ Battleship	R	1.00
☐ Bearklaw	R	1.00
☐ Benny	R	1.00
☐ Blade	R	1.00
☐ Blizzard	U	0.25
☐ Breaking Dam	U	0.25
3		
☐ Brimstone	VC	0.05
☐ Bulletproof Vest	VC	0.05
☐ Captain Ostraca	C	0.10
☐ Carnivore	U	0.25
☐ Castle	VC	0.05
☐ Cattle Stampede	C	0.10
☐ Chopper	U	0.25
☐ Claw of Revenge	R	1.00
☐ Col. Calamity	R	1.00
4		
☐ Cold and Ice	VC	0.05
☐ Collapsing Bridge	R	1.00
☐ Crud	VC	0.05
☐ Dinah Mite	C	0.10
☐ Dr. Gauntlet	U	0.25

Card name	Rarity	Price
☐ Dr. Jonathan Weir	R	1.00
☐ Earth Control	U	0.25
☐ Earthquake	VC	0.05
☐ Electric Fist	R	1.00
5		
☐ Electro	R	1.00
☐ Electron Blast	U	0.25
☐ Emergency Siren	U	0.25
☐ Erupting Volcano	U	0.25
☐ Explosion	R	1.00
☐ Explosion	R	1.00
☐ Falling Airliner	R	1.00
☐ False Alarm	U	0.25
☐ Fantastic Speed	U	0.25
6		
☐ Fighter Squadron	C	0.10
☐ Fire	U	0.25
☐ First National Bank	U	0.25
☐ Fist of Flame	U	0.25
☐ Flight	C	0.10
☐ Floron	C	0.10
☐ Flygirl	C	0.10
☐ Flying Glass	U	0.25
☐ Gas Mask	U	0.25
7		
☐ Giant Asteroid	C	0.10
☐ Giant Computer	C	0.10
☐ Giant Dino-Monster	VC	0.05
☐ Giant Dinosaur	U	0.25
☐ Giant Dirigible	R	1.00
☐ Giant Fan	VC	0.05
☐ Giant Laser	U	0.25
☐ Giant Mirror	C	0.10
☐ Giant Robot	U	0.25
8		
☐ Giant Spider	U	0.25
☐ Gigant	U	0.25
☐ Goodwin	R	1.00
☐ Great White Shark	R	1.00
☐ Hidden Refuge	U	0.25
☐ Hitman	U	0.25
☐ Hydrogen Bomb	R	1.00
☐ Ice	R	1.00
☐ Intense Light	R	1.00
9		
☐ Killer Bees	U	0.25
☐ Killer Squash!	R	1.00
☐ Labyrinth	C	0.10

Card name	Rarity	Price
☐ Loss	U	0.25
☐ Magic Chant	C	0.10
☐ Magic Ring	C	0.10
☐ Magic Spell	R	1.00
☐ Magnetism	U	0.25
☐ Mantis Man	R	1.00
10		
☐ Marsman	C	0.10
☐ Mental Blast	U	0.25
☐ Mission Complete	U	0.25
☐ Mr. Fixitt tm	R	1.00
☐ Mr. Justice	R	1.00
☐ Ms. Mensa	R	1.00
☐ Mul	U	0.25
☐ Orion the Hunter	U	0.25
☐ Paladane	U	0.25
11		
☐ Partner H (Caruther)	U	0.25
☐ Partner H (Hunt)	U	0.25
☐ Partner V	U	0.25
☐ Petron	C	0.10
☐ Poison Gas	U	0.25
☐ Preying Mantis	U	0.25
☐ Pyramid Man	U	0.25
☐ Radar Sense	U	0.25
☐ Radioactive Hazard	R	1.00
12		
☐ Reptilion	C	0.10
☐ Robot Rampage	VC	0.05
☐ Robot Rider	U	0.25
☐ Rocket Blast	R	1.00
☐ Runaway Reactor	U	0.25
☐ Savage Henry	U	0.25
☐ Scalpel	R	1.00
☐ Sea Monster	R	1.00
☐ Sears Tower	C	0.10
13		
☐ Secret Base	C	0.10
☐ Secret Identity 1 (_?_)	U	0.25
☐ Secret Identity 2 (Brick)	U	0.25
☐ Semi-Auto Pistol	R	1.00
☐ Semi-Auto Rifle	VC	0.05
☐ Shadowblade tm	R	1.00
☐ Shokk	U	0.25
☐ Shrink Potion	C	0.10
☐ Shrink Ray	U	0.25
14		
☐ Sidekick V (Hunt)	U	0.25

Card name	Rarity	Price
☐ Sidekick V (Luck)	U	0.25
☐ Sinister Laboratory	C	0.10
☐ Skul	U	0.25
☐ Sleeping Gas	R	1.00
☐ Sonic Blast	U	0.25
☐ Starflare	VC	0.05
☐ Static Blast	VC	0.05
☐ Stiltmobile	R	1.00
15		
☐ Stolen Jet Bomber	U	0.25
☐ SubMachine Gun	U	0.25
☐ Submarine	U	0.25
☐ Super Pet	C	0.10
☐ Super Rigid Man	U	0.25
☐ Swarm	U	0.25
☐ Tactical Nuke	R	1.00
☐ Talonz	R	1.00
☐ Tear Gas	U	0.25
16		
☐ Teleport	U	0.25
☐ Tempest	C	0.10
☐ The Elder	U	0.25
☐ The Manifest	C	0.10
☐ The Pendulum	R	1.00
☐ The Time Triangle	R	1.00
☐ The Vizier	U	0.25
☐ Thug	U	0.25
☐ Tidal Wave	U	0.25
17		
☐ Time Bomb	C	0.10
☐ Time Warp	R	1.00
☐ Time Warp	C	0.10
☐ Tornado	U	0.25
☐ Toxon	U	0.25
☐ Trans America Bldg.	R	1.00
☐ Twin Towers	R	1.00
☐ Ultima XL-4000	U	0.25
☐ US Army Tank	U	0.25
18		
☐ Utility Knife	R	1.00
☐ Uvulo	R	1.00
☐ Vector	C	0.10
☐ Water	R	1.00
☐ Weather Control	U	0.25
☐ Wind	U	0.25
☐ Yarf the Troll	C	0.10

RARITY KEY **VC** = Very Common **C** = Common **U** = Uncommon **R** = Rare **UR** = Ultra Rare **X** = Fixed/standard in all decks

Super Deck! • Slim Decks

Card Sharks • Released **June 1995**
166 cards in set • IDENTIFIER: Cards are © 1995
• Starter decks contain 30 cards; starter displays contain 20 starters

The **Slim Decks** were the first mid-sized package in collectible card games, offering 30 cards rather than the standard 60 in starter decks or 15 in booster packs.

But the novel packaging of the *Slim Deck* did not seem to help sales, nor did others adapt the method. It may have been the cosmic karmic backlash created by including a "Legion of French Superheroes" on **Space Station**, that finally did this CCG in. — *James Mishler*

SCRYE NOTES: *Seriously, we love the French. You guys have the best fries.*
There are variant versions of several cards with different-colored backgrounds.

You will need **18** nine-pocket pages to store this set. (9 doubled up)

Set (166 cards)	40.00
Booster Display Box	20.00
Booster Pack	2.50

Promo cards	Price
☐ Amnesia 2	1.50
☐ Daemon (9)	1.50
☐ Mr. Speed	1.50
☐ Space Ship H	1.50
☐ Space Ship V	1.50
☐ Teleport (large)	1.50
☐ The Shade	1.50

Card name	Rarity	Price
☐ Achilles' Heel	VC	0.05
☐ Adamantine Armor	R	1.00
☐ Alfa	C	0.10
☐ Ancient Ring	C	0.10
☐ Ankh of Pain	C	0.10
☐ Anti-Gravity Ray	R	1.00
☐ Black Art	C	0.10
☐ Black Zenith	C	0.10
☐ Bluff (2 var)	VC	0.05
☐ Bolt	U	0.25
☐ Bonus Card 1	R	1.00
☐ Bonus Card 2	R	1.00
☐ Buff Guy	VC	0.05
☐ By Accident	U	0.25
☐ Captain California	U	0.25
☐ Carbide	VC	0.05
☐ Cavern	VC	0.05
☐ Chitin	VC	0.05
☐ Circuit	C	0.10
☐ Commando D	R	1.00
☐ Convicted	U	0.25
☐ Cosmic Blast (2 var)	U	0.25
☐ Crowd in Danger	VC	0.05

Card name	Rarity	Price
☐ Crusader	U	0.25
☐ Daemon (8)	R	1.00
☐ Dawn Horse	R	1.00
☐ Deadly Radon Gas	VC	0.05
☐ Death	R	1.00
☐ Death Hug (2 var)	U	0.25
☐ Demon Eyes (2 var)	VC	0.05
☐ Dethblo	C	0.10
☐ Dimension X	C	0.10
☐ Dismal Swamp	U	0.25
☐ Distress Call	C	0.10
☐ Diversion	U	0.25
☐ Dr. Slime	C	0.10
☐ Dream Weaver	C	0.10
☐ Drooler	VC	0.05
☐ Eiffel Tower	C	0.10
☐ Electronic Bug	C	0.10
☐ Evil Clone	U	0.25
☐ F-Stop Fitzger (2 var)	VC	0.05
☐ F1	C	0.10
☐ Falling Satellite	C	0.10
☐ False Alarm	C	0.10
☐ Fast Neutron	VC	0.05
☐ Filthy Sewer	VC	0.05
☐ Flame Thrower	VC	0.05
☐ Flying Saucers	C	0.10
☐ Foresight (2 var)	U	0.25
☐ Freeze Ray	U	0.25
☐ Gauntlets of Power	R	1.00
☐ Genius IQ	R	1.00
☐ Giant Cat	C	0.10
☐ Giant Hologram	R	1.00
☐ Giant Octopus	R	1.00
☐ Girlfriend	R	1.00

Card name	Rarity	Price
☐ Grappling Hook	VC	0.05
☐ Gunz	R	1.00
☐ Handcuffs	C	0.10
☐ Handy Math Table	VC	0.05
☐ Henchman (2 var)	VC	0.05
☐ Id Monster	C	0.10
☐ IFV	C	0.10
☐ Implosion	C	0.10
☐ Indecision	VC	0.05
☐ Integer	R	1.00
☐ Isosceles	VC	0.05
☐ Jagged Man	VC	0.05
☐ Jaws of Defeat	VC	0.05
☐ Jet Fighter	R	1.00
☐ Johnny Angel	VC	0.05
☐ Kid Lightning	C	0.10
☐ Lead Shield	VC	0.05
☐ Lightnin' Jack	R	1.00
☐ Lightning	C	0.10
☐ Luck	R	1.00
☐ Mace	R	1.00
☐ Mad Scientist	C	0.10
☐ Madness	R	1.00
☐ Magic Knife	R	1.00
☐ Mammoth	R	1.00
☐ Masque	R	1.00
☐ Mega Man	R	1.00
☐ Meteor Strike	U	0.25
☐ Motorcycle	VC	0.05
☐ Mutaton	R	1.00
☐ MX Missile	R	1.00
☐ Napoleon IV	R	1.00
☐ Neutron Bomb	U	0.25
☐ New Volcano	R	1.00

Card name	Rarity	Price
☐ Nife	U	0.25
☐ Ninja	U	0.25
☐ North Pole	U	0.25
☐ Nuclear Power	R	1.00
☐ Olympia	C	0.10
☐ Orbiting City	R	1.00
☐ Osh-Tar the Tyrant	R	1.00
☐ Paragon	U	0.25
☐ Partner V (Pallot)	U	0.25
☐ Pickpocket (2 var)	VC	0.05
☐ Plethora	C	0.10
☐ Plutonium	C	0.10
☐ Police Chief	C	0.10
☐ Police Response	VC	0.05
☐ Power of Darkness	R	1.00
☐ Prison Break	U	0.25
☐ Psychic	U	0.25
☐ Pyramids of Egypt	C	0.10
☐ Quicksand	R	1.00
☐ Radioactive Sludge	R	1.00
☐ Reality Scrambler	R	1.00
☐ Sabre Fang	VC	0.05
☐ Sahara Desert	C	0.10
☐ Sawtooth	VC	0.05
☐ Scarlet Scorpion	C	0.10
☐ Secret Plan	U	0.25
☐ Sewage Tank	R	1.00
☐ Shape Shift	U	0.25
☐ She-Bat	C	0.10
☐ Sheer Terror (2 var)	U	0.25
☐ Sidekick H (Jones)	U	0.25
☐ Sidekick H (Josh)	VC	0.05
☐ Sidekick H (Kochell)	VC	0.05
☐ Sidekick V (Alcala)	R	1.00
☐ Sinking Ship 1 (Felc)	U	0.25

Card name	Rarity	Price
☐ Sinking Ship 2 (Tutt)	U	0.25
☐ Skyscraper Fire	U	0.25
☐ Slipstream	VC	0.05
☐ Smashing Force	C	0.10
☐ SP Artillery	C	0.10
☐ Space Station	VC	0.05
☐ Spectro	R	1.00
☐ Speed Limit	U	0.25
☐ Squall	R	1.00
☐ Static	R	1.00
☐ Sumo-San	R	1.00
☐ Superhero's Pal	C	0.10
☐ Supershield	R	1.00
☐ Techno Man	R	1.00
☐ Terrakus	R	1.00
☐ The Man	VC	0.05
☐ Tidal Wave 2 (Fludd)	C	0.10
☐ Tommy Gun	C	0.10
☐ TV Crew	VC	0.05
☐ Undersea City	R	1.00
☐ Upper Cut	C	0.10
☐ Vampire	VC	0.05
☐ Veeza	R	1.00
☐ Wall of Death	C	0.10
☐ War Machine	R	1.00
☐ Warspite	C	0.10
☐ Washington	VC	0.05
☐ Well of Power	VC	0.05
☐ Westwind	C	0.10
☐ Wilde Knight	R	1.00
☐ Witness	R	1.00
☐ Wulf	R	1.00
☐ Zombie	R	1.00

Super Nova

Heartbreaker Hobbies • Released **July 1995**
165 cards in set
• Booster packs contain 18 cards; booster displays contain 36 boosters
Designed by **John Montrie**

Super Nova is only marginally a CCG by our definitions, as all play from a single deck of cards. But the game was clearly marketed as "collectible." To make sure of it, there aren't any starter decks. And just to complete the muddle, nowhere do the rules (found on cards in the packs) state when a player actually wins the game!

In this space exploration game, players "discover" worlds by playing planet cards and environment cards on those already played. Players add civilization, population, and ship cards to planets, or modifier cards to ships. Players may then trade with or attack opponents. Opponents may be attacked militarily, diplomatically, or economically.

It's slow and has no end. The winner is the player with the most population, but the rules give no guidance as to when that's settled. When the cards run out? When the sun explodes?

In all, a serious mismatch between game design and the CCG format. — *James Mishler*

You will need **19** nine-pocket pages to store this set. (10 doubled up)

Concept	●●●○○
Gameplay	●●○○○
Card art	●○○○○
Player pool	○○○○○

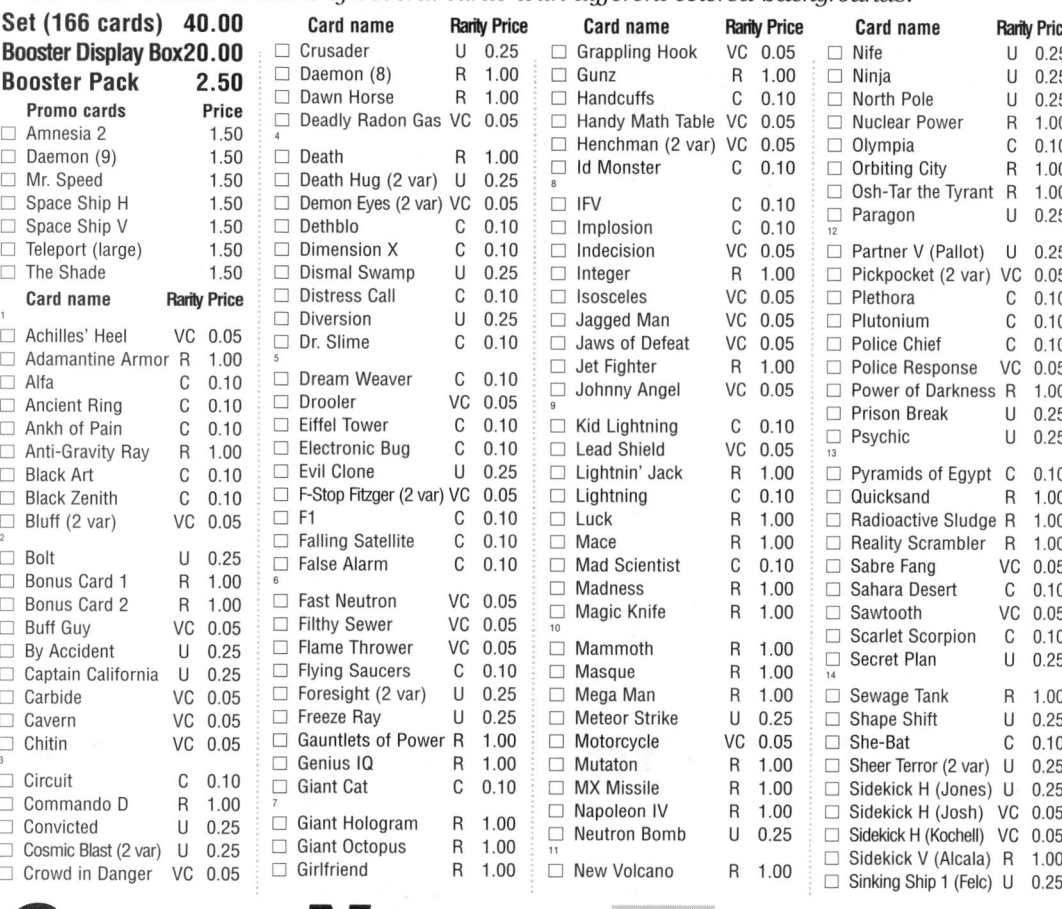

Set (165 cards)	42.75
Booster Display Box	26.00
Booster Pack	2.00

Card name	Rarity	Price
☐ Abundant Land	C	0.10
☐ Abundant Oceans	C	0.10
☐ Aldebaran	U	0.40

Card name	Rarity	Price
☐ Alien Allies	C	0.10
☐ Alien Monolith	R	1.40
☐ Alien Relic	R	1.60

Card name	Rarity	Price
☐ Altair	C	0.10
☐ Ambush	C	0.10
☐ Antares	C	0.10

RARITY KEY VC = Very Common C = Common U = Uncommon R = Rare UR = Ultra Rare X = Fixed/standard in all decks

Card name	Rarity	Price		Card name	Rarity	Price		Card name	Rarity	Price		Card name	Rarity	Price
2				☐ Drop Pods	U	0.30		☐ Long-Range Survey Ship	C	0.10		**15**		
☐ Antarian Auditors	C	0.10		☐ Eden	C	0.10		☐ Lord Faslk	C	0.10		☐ Space Traffic Control	R	1.30
☐ Antarian Brokers	R	1.10		☐ Envoy Ship	R	1.10		☐ Lost Civilization	R	1.10		☐ Spica	U	0.40
☐ Antarian Freetraders	C	0.10		☐ Epsilon Eridani	C	0.10		☐ Low Gravity	U	0.30		☐ Stan'S Star	R	1.10
☐ Antarian Kittens	C	0.10		☐ Escape Pods	C	0.10		**11**				☐ Stealth Field	U	0.30
☐ Antarian Spys	U	0.30		☐ Evac Ship	C	0.10		☐ Luxury Yacht	C	0.10		☐ Stellar Transporter	R	1.40
☐ Antarians	C	0.10		☐ Evil Clones	C	0.10		☐ Lyra	U	0.40		☐ Storm Troopers	C	0.10
☐ Apollo	U	0.40		**7**				☐ Mafia	U	0.40		☐ Suicide Attack	U	0.50
☐ Bachus	C	0.10		☐ Expert Terraformer	U	0.30		☐ Master-At-Arms	C	0.10		☐ Super Nova	R	1.40
☐ Barchan	C	0.10		☐ Extra Resources	R	1.40		☐ Matrix Cage	R	1.60		☐ Surprise Attack	C	0.10
3				☐ Factory Ship	R	1.10		☐ Megalopolis	C	0.10		**16**		
☐ Barnard'S Star	C	0.10		☐ Fast Scout Ship	C	0.10		☐ Merchant Ship	C	0.10		☐ Tactical Expert	U	0.30
☐ Battleship	C	0.10		☐ Fighter	C	0.10		☐ Military Academy	C	0.10		☐ Tan Hadron	C	0.10
☐ Beta Hydri	C	0.10		☐ Floater Colonists	R	1.10		☐ Mining Ship	U	0.30		☐ Tanker	C	0.10
☐ Binary System	C	0.10		☐ Floater Defenders	C	0.10		**12**				☐ Taurus	R	1.10
☐ Bio-Weapon	U	0.30		☐ Floater Philosophers	C	0.10		☐ Monarchy	C	0.10		☐ Teleporting Ship	C	0.10
☐ Black Hole	C	0.10		☐ Floater Psi	C	0.10		☐ Nora Lucre	C	0.10		☐ Temporal Rift	C	0.10
☐ Boarding Action	C	0.10		**8**				☐ Peace Treaty	C	0.10		☐ Terra	R	1.60
☐ Booster Engines	U	0.30		☐ Floater Researchers	U	0.30		☐ Piracy License	R	1.30		☐ Terraform	R	1.30
☐ Bureaucracy	C	0.10		☐ Floaters	C	0.10		☐ Planetary Shield	U	0.40		☐ Terran Brats	R	1.30
4				☐ Free Trade	U	0.30		☐ Poisonous Atmosphere	U	0.30		**17**		
☐ Canum	U	0.40		☐ Freya	C	0.10		☐ Pollution	U	0.30		☐ Terran Interpreters	C	0.10
☐ Capt. Twothumbs	C	0.10		☐ Garbage Scow	C	0.10		☐ Procyon	U	0.40		☐ Terran Shock Troops	U	0.30
☐ Capt. Yarnspinner	C	0.10		☐ General Bellis	C	0.10		☐ Propaganda	C	0.10		☐ Terran Traders	C	0.10
☐ Cargo Ship	C	0.10		☐ Genetic Manipulation	C	0.10		**13**				☐ Terran Weaponmaster	C	0.10
☐ Chi Draconis	C	0.10		☐ High Gravity	U	0.30		☐ Quantum Flux	C	0.10		☐ Terrans	C	0.10
☐ Chort'S Marauders	R	1.50		☐ High-G Ship	C	0.10		☐ Rebel Uprising	U	0.30		☐ Thor	C	0.10
☐ Cold Climate	C	0.10		**9**				☐ Regulus	R	1.30		☐ Tlisk	C	0.10
☐ Colony Ship	C	0.10		☐ Hostile Natives	C	0.10		☐ Relay Ship	R	1.10		☐ Tlisk Drones	C	0.10
☐ Conspiracy	C	0.10		☐ Hot Climate	C	0.10		☐ Rich Atmosphere	U	0.30		☐ Tlisk Morphers	U	0.30
5				☐ Imperial Capital	R	1.10		☐ Sabotage	C	0.10		**18**		
☐ Consul Ship	C	0.10		☐ Imperial Treasury	R	1.40		☐ Science Ship	C	0.10		☐ Tlisk Pacifists	C	0.10
☐ Cruiser	C	0.10		☐ Isis	C	0.10		☐ Scorpius	C	0.10		☐ Tlisk Scientists	R	1.30
☐ Cygni	R	1.30		☐ Ko'Ol	C	0.10		☐ Scout Ship	C	0.10		☐ Tlisk Telepaths	C	0.10
☐ Defense Contractor	U	0.30		☐ Koolian Commandos	R	1.10		**14**				☐ Trading Ship	C	0.10
☐ Delta Pavonis	C	0.10		☐ Koolian Diplomats	C	0.10		☐ Scrapman	C	0.10		☐ Transport Ship	C	0.10
☐ Dictatorship	U	0.30		☐ Koolian Explorers	U	0.30		☐ Secret Plans Stolen	C	0.10		☐ Universe Festival	C	0.10
☐ Dimension Jump	R	1.40		**10**				☐ Ship Computer	R	1.40		☐ Vega	C	0.10
☐ Diplomatic Corps	U	0.30		☐ Koolian Mob	C	0.10		☐ Ships Shields	U	0.30		☐ War And Peace	C	0.10
☐ Domed Cities	C	0.10		☐ Koolian Settlers	C	0.10		☐ Shore Leave	R	1.60		☐ Warp Cannon	C	0.10
6				☐ Koolians	C	0.10		☐ Sirius	C	0.10		**19**		
☐ Dreadnought Pt 1	C	0.10		☐ Laze Cannon	C	0.10		☐ Space Horror	C	0.10		☐ Wormhole	C	0.10
☐ Dreadnought Pt 2	C	0.10		☐ Long-Range Fighter	C	0.10		☐ Space Station Pt1	U	0.40		☐ Zerec Bloodclans	R	1.10
								☐ Space Station Pt2	U	0.40		☐ Zeta Tucanae	U	0.30

TANK COMMANDER

8 5 PzKw 9/5
12/9 IV J 6 4

THE FINAL PRODUCTION MODEL OF THE
PZKW IV WITH ANOTHER MG ADDED,
IN SERVICE 1944-45.

POINT VALUE: 29

✠ 5 7 10 5 5 ✠

Concept	●●●○○
Gameplay	●●●○○
Card art	●●○○○
Player pool	○○○○○

Set (164 cards)	40.00
Starter Display Box	20.00
Starter Deck	5.00

Tank Commander

Moments in History • First set, *The Eastern Front*, released **April 1996**
164 cards in set

• Starter decks contain 60 cards • Booster packs do not exist

At the height of World War II, tanks were a deciding factor on the German-Russian front. In *Tank Commander*, players command tanks for each side.

The mechanics appear daunting at first but are straightforward. Each unit card (tank, anti-tank emplacement, or soldier-with-a-gun) is outfitted with stacks of numbers across the top, separated by slashes. These represent all kinds of damage they can do, from long-range shelling to flame throwers at point-blank range. Along the bottom of each card are random numbers, each in a different color. There are also instants, interrupts, and terrain cards, which modify sections of the card-grid "board."

Players pick from one of nine scenarios which limit the forces in play. Some scenarios let the defender put cards into play, but not the attacker. Each turn a player may perform one action, resolve a melee, and draw. One action is cannon fire: To shoot a cannon, determine if the target is in short range (one square away) or long range (two squares away), check the tank's statistic, name a color, and draw a card from the deck. If the number of the color called on the bottom of the card drawn is equal to or less than the hit statistic on the tank, the opponent is hit.

The game has balance problems, as there are a few tanks that are nearly unstoppable. The art is functional, but uninspired: backgrounds are gray, fonts are ugly, and flavor text is just the history of each model of tank. Not as good as other military simulation CCGs, Moments in History's only CCG release is, like its subject matter, a thing of the past. The announced expansion, *North Africa* never came out. — *Richard Weld*

Card name	Rarity	Price		Card name	Rarity	Price		Card name	Rarity	Price
1				☐ 7.5 cm PaK 40	C	0.05		☐ 8.8 cm Flak 36/37	U	0.25
☐ 3.7 cm PaK 35/36	C	0.05		☐ 7.5 cm PaK 97/38	R	1.00		☐ 8.8 cm PaK 43	U	0.25
☐ 5 cm PaK 38	C	0.05		☐ 7.62 cm PaK 36 (r)	U	0.25		☐ 37 mm PtP obr.30	R	1.00

RARITY KEY C = Common U = Uncommon R = Rare VR = Very Rare UR = Ultra Rare F = Foil card X = Fixed/standard in all decks

Card name	Rarity	Price	Card name	Rarity	Price	Card name	Rarity	Price	Card name	Rarity	Price
45 mm PTP obr 42 [2]	C	0.05	JgPz VI	R	1.00	PzKw II F	U	0.25	StuPz IV	R	1.00
45 mm PTP obr.37	C	0.05	JS-2	U	0.25	PzKw II L	U	0.25	Sturmovik Air Strike	U	0.25
57 mm PTP obr.43	C	0.05	JS-2m	U	0.25	PzKw III (FI)	R	1.00	SU-100 [15]	R	1.00
76.2 mm P obr.39	C	0.05	JSU-122	R	1.00	PzKw III F	U	0.25	SU-122	U	0.25
76.2mm P obr.36	C	0.05	JSU-152	U	0.25	PzKw III G [11]	U	0.25	SU-152	U	0.25
85 mm P obr.44	U	0.25	KV-1 M39	R	1.00	PzKw III H	R	1.00	SU-57	R	1.00
100 mm PTP obr.44	U	0.25	KV-1 M41 [7]	U	0.25	PzKw III J	C	0.05	SU-76 i	R	1.00
Air Strike	U	0.25	KV-1S	R	1.00	PzKw III L	U	0.25	SU-76 M	C	0.05
Aircraft Interception	U	0.25	KV-2	R	1.00	PzKw III N	U	0.25	SU-85	U	0.25
Anti-Tank Mine	C	0.05	KV-85	R	1.00	PzKw IV F	U	0.25	Swamp	C	0.05
Anti-Tank Rifle PTRS-41 [3]	U	0.25	Leichter Panzerspaehwagen (2 cm)	U	0.25	PzKw IV G	C	0.05	T-26 M33	C	0.05
Artillery Barrage	C	0.05	Luftwaffenfeld-Squad	C	0.05	PzKw IV H	C	0.05	T-26 M39 [16]	C	0.05
BA-20	C	0.05	M3 Lee	U	0.25	PzKw IV J	C	0.05	T-28	R	1.00
Balka	C	0.05	M3A1 Scout Car	C	0.05	PzKw V D [12]	U	0.25	T-28 E	R	1.00
Breakdown	U	0.25	M3A1 Stuart III	U	0.25	PzKw V G	C	0.05	T-34 M40	U	0.25
Bridge	C	0.05	M4A2 (76) [8]	U	0.25	PzKw VI B	R	1.00	T-34 M41	C	0.05
BT-5	U	0.25	Matilda II	U	0.25	PzKw VI E	U	0.25	T-34 M43	C	0.05
BT-7	U	0.25	Mine Dogs	R	1.00	PzKw VI E P	R	1.00	T-34/85	C	0.05
BT-7A	R	1.00	Minefield	C	0.05	Recon	R	1.00	T-35	R	1.00
Bunkers [4]	C	0.05	Minefield Gap	C	0.05	Reinforcements	R	1.00	T-37	U	0.25
Churchill III	R	1.00	Mittlerer Schuetzenpanzerwagen	C	0.05	Repair	U	0.25	T-40 [17]	R	1.00
Confusion	R	1.00	OT-133	R	1.00	Rocket Artillery German	U	0.25	T-44	R	1.00
Coordination	R	1.00	OT-34	R	1.00	Rocket Artillery Soviet [13]	U	0.25	T-60	U	0.25
Counterbattery Fire	C	0.05	Panic	R	1.00	Schwerer Panzerspaehwagen (6 Rad)	R	1.00	T-70	C	0.05
Flamethrower ROKS 2	R	1.00	Panzerfaust [9]	C	0.05	Schwerer Panzerspaehwagen (8 Rad)	R	1.00	Tactical Advantage	R	1.00
Flammenwerfer 41	R	1.00	Panzerschreck	U	0.25	Sniper	R	1.00	Tank Ace	R	1.50
Flank Shot	U	0.25	Partisan Group	C	0.05	Soviet Cavalry	C	0.05	Tank Buster	R	1.50
Ford	C	0.05	Path	C	0.05	Soviet Guards Squad	C	0.05	Tank Repair Shop	UR	2.00
Forward Observer [5]	R	1.00	Pz Jg 7.5 cm PaK 40	R	1.00	Soviet Line Squad	C	0.05	Truck German	C	0.05
Foxholes	C	0.05	PzJg 38 (t) 7.5 cm PaK 40 H	R	1.00	Soviet Militia Squad	U	0.25	Truck USSR [18]	C	0.05
German Cavalry	C	0.05	PzJg 38 (t) 7.5 cm PaK 40 M	U	0.25	Soviet Paratrooper	U	0.25	Valentine II	U	0.25
German Fallschirmjaeger	U	0.25	PzJg III/IV	R	1.00	Soviet Recruits Squad [14]	C	0.05	Veteran German Squad	C	0.05
German Line Squad	C	0.05	PzJg Tiger	R	1.00	Special Ammunition	R	1.00	Village	C	0.05
German Recruits Squad	C	0.05	PzKw 35 (t) [10]	R	1.00	SPW 250	C	0.05	Waffen-SS Squad	C	0.05
Heroic Squad Leader	R	1.50	PzKw 38 (t) A	C	0.05	Stream	C	0.05	Walls	C	0.05
Hills	C	0.05	PzKw 38 (t) E	U	0.25	StuG III B	U	0.25	Weapon Malfunction	U	0.25
JgPz 38 (t)	U	0.25	PzKw II (FI)	R	1.00	StuG III G	C	0.05	Wheatfield	C	0.05
JgPz IV [6]	U	0.25	PzKw II A	R	1.00	Stuka Air Strike	U	0.25	Wire	C	0.05
JgPz IV/70	U	0.25							Withdrawal [19]	R	1.00
JgPz V	R	1.00							Woods	C	0.05

Tempest of the Gods

Black Dragon Press • Released **July 1995**

269 cards in set

- Starter decks contain 70 cards; starter displays contain 10 decks
- Booster packs contain 15 cards; booster displays contain 36 packs

Tempest of the Gods game is set in Darkurthe, a fantasy world drawn from the role-playing game of the same name. Several factions and countries war for control of territory. If this world of elves, dwarves and forces of darkness seems generic, it's easy for fantasy fans to pick out cards for which they have an affinity. The goal is to control the board by eliminating the opponent or by summoning a Deity into play.

Card types include People, including Followers, Priests, Guardians, and Champions; Spells, which only a spellcaster can use; Miracles, which anyone can use; Relics, and Temples. Each card has three statistics: Strength, Faith, and Summoning Cost. Any card with 1 Faith can "drain" itself (*i.e.*, "tap") to summon a creature with a summoning cost of 1. Normally, People cannot work together to pool their Faith and summon another card, but they can join together to summon Priests. Once a Priest is in play, other People can work together to summon expensive cards. Many basic Followers and Priests cost 0, so they are easy to get out early in the game. Relics, Temples, Spells, and Miracles are summoned in the same way.

A player can build up to the point where he has 15 Faith and a Temple in play to summon a Deity, or he can smite his opponent. Combat is quick and easy. Each player has a home "turf," and the battleground lies between the players. A player must move a Person to the battleground area in order to attack. A player will declare that his Person is attacking a Person in his opponent's turf. One of his characters in the battleground must intervene if they can. If they can't, the target Person is attacked. Combat is a very quick measure of Strength vs. Strength, and the Person with the lowest score dies. ➤

Concept	●●●○○	
Gameplay	●●●○○	
Card art	●●●●○	
Player pool	○○○○○	

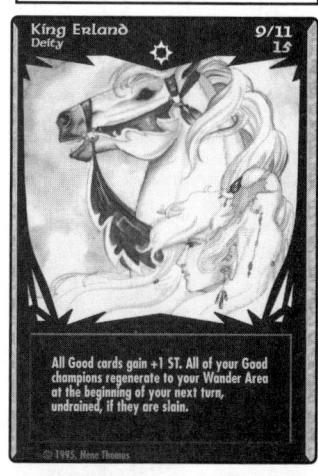

The art is fantastic, with some of 1995's best talents in fantasy art submitting the caliber of work that *Magic* used for *Legends* and *Arabian Nights*. Alas, the design brings it down. A different color for each card type would have helped.
Tempest: Egyptian Neteru never came out. Susan van Camp and Black Dragon Press went on to publish the excellent *Dragon Storm* role-playing game. — *Richard Weld*

You will need **30** nine-pocket pages to store this set. (15 doubled up)

Card name	Rarity	Price
Set (269 cards)		44.00
Starter Display Box		21.00
Booster Display Box		26.50
Starter Deck		5.00
Booster Pack		1.80

Card name	Rarity	Price
1		
Abhore, Mistress Night	U	0.35
Abol	R	4.10
Ally's Blessing	U	0.35
Alms Priest	C	0.10
Apocalypse	R	3.80
Arcanum Brotherhood	C	0.10
Archmage Mithian	U	0.35
Armored Golem	C	0.10
Avatar	C	0.10
2		
Avenging Angel	U	0.35
Azerous, The Lich King	U	0.60
Bane Blade	U	0.35
Banish	C	0.10
Basilisk	R	1.80
Battering Ram	C	0.10
Battle Fury	U	0.35
Beggar	C	0.10
Berserkers	C	0.10
3		
Besha, The Kissing Goddess	R	2.10
Bitter Frost	R	2.10
Black Gate	U	0.35
Black Orcon	R	2.80
Blasphemy	R	1.60
Blood Altar	R	2.30
Blood Covenant	U	0.35
Book of Black Magic	R	2.60
Book of Life and Death	R	2.10
4		
Breath Of Mist	R	1.80
Bull Elk	C	0.10
Burrow Worms	U	0.35
Candle of the All Father	R	1.80
Caravan	C	0.10
Catapult	U	0.35
Celestial Palace	R	2.10
Celestial Pegasus	U	0.35
Cemetary	C	0.10
5		
Changeling	R	2.10
Chaos Runes	C	0.10
Chariot Of Horne	U	0.50
Charming	U	0.35
Chimeran	R	2.30
City Of The Dead	U	0.50
Clairvoyance	C	0.10
Cloak Of Deception	U	0.35
Close Portal	C	0.10
6		
Cloud Spirit	C	0.10
Cloudwalk	U	0.35
Comet Of Fates	R	2.80
Crossed Swords	C	0.10
Crusaders Of Galadon	C	0.10
Crypt Feeder	U	0.35
Crystaltear	C	0.10
Daggers Of The Mind	U	0.35
Dark Chant	C	0.10
7		
Dark Creation	R	2.10
Dark Summons	U	0.35
Dark Walker	C	0.10
Dead Bones	U	0.35
Deadly Ichor	C	0.10
Deadwood	U	0.35
Death Cult	C	0.10

Card name	Rarity	Price
Death Knight	C	0.10
Death Vow	U	0.35
8		
Deathly Corpse	C	0.10
Deathmask	C	0.10
Defile	U	0.50
Despair	R	1.80
Destroying Angel	R	2.30
Devourer Of The Fallen	U	0.50
Disenchantment	C	0.10
Divination	R	2.10
Diviner's Mask	R	1.80
9		
Dolphin	C	0.10
Domination	R	1.80
Doom Steeds	R	2.10
Double	R	1.80
Dram The Black	R	2.10
Druine	C	0.10
Druish King	U	0.50
Drums Of Doom	R	1.80
Druna, The Protector	U	0.50
10		
Dungeons Of Thalhautma	C	0.10
Dwarven Hero	C	0.10
Dwarven Stonemasons	U	0.35
Elivari Archers	C	0.10
Enchanted Armor	U	0.35
Enchanted Weapon	U	0.35
Enigma	R	2.80
Entombment	R	1.60
Erland's Tomb	R	2.30
11		
Erodan Knight	U	0.50
Etheral Worms	R	1.80
Exodus	U	0.50
Falconer	C	0.10
False Prophet	R	1.80
Familiar	U	0.35
Famine	U	0.50
Farmer	C	0.10
Father Of Shadows	C	0.10
12		
Fathfyrn The Mighty	R	2.10
Feet Of The Jaguar	C	0.10
Fetish Shaman	C	0.10
Flash Flood	R	2.30
Forest Giant	U	0.35
Forges Of Mountainunder	R	2.30
Fortuna	C	0.10
Fountain Of Souls	R	2.30
Freeze Blast	C	0.10
13		
Frontiersman	C	0.10
Garrison	C	0.10
Giant Kin	U	0.35
Gidron The Defiler	R	1.80
Golden Lake	C	0.10
Grand Inquisitor	C	0.10
Grandmindor	R	1.80
Graveyard Of Ships	R	1.80
Great Umber Bear	C	0.10
14		
Greater Warlock	U	0.35
Grimfang The Great	R	2.30
Gryvern	U	0.50
Guard Dog	U	0.35
Gydon The Red	C	0.10
Halo	U	0.50
Harbinger Eagle	C	0.10
Harvest Season	R	2.30
Harvest Symbol	U	0.35
15		
Healers Of Southton Abbey	C	0.10
Helm Of War	R	1.80
Herb Garden Of Isa	C	0.10
Highlands Unicorn	U	0.35

Card name	Rarity	Price
Hogmuv Coven	C	0.10
Horne, God Of War	U	0.50
Hrothgar	R	1.80
Ilgit, The Great Vulne	U	0.35
Inner Sanctum	R	2.80
16		
Iron Slugs	R	2.10
Izgul, The Mad	U	0.35
Jaxx, Lord Of Ghouls	U	0.50
Karthanon, The Builder	U	0.50
Khrin Ruins	R	1.80
King Erland	U	0.50
King Erodan	R	2.30
King Ettin's Crown	R	2.30
Kings Statue	U	0.35
17		
Knights Of Three	R	2.80
Krill Vortex	R	2.60
Lawspeaker	C	0.10
Legions Of Doom	R	2.80
Living Lightning	U	0.50
Lord Dwarvendunne	U	0.50
Lord Gamrin	C	0.10
Lord Of Storms	R	2.10
Loremaster	U	0.60
18		
Lost Temple Of Baharat	U	0.35
Lurker Of The Deep	U	0.35
Mage Master	U	0.35
Maldorian Pirates	C	0.10
Martyr Massacre	U	0.35
Master Archer	R	1.80
Mazer The Misguided	R	1.80
Meld	C	0.10
Mesidian Gargoyle	C	0.10
19		
Messilist The Destroyer	R	3.30
Meteor Shower	R	1.80
Millenium	R	2.80
Minak Orb	U	0.50
Mind Shield	C	0.10
Misdirection	C	0.10
Mithra The Huntress	C	0.10
Mob Leader	U	0.50
Mokenth Charm	R	2.10
20		
Mountain Oracle	C	0.10
Mythander Thundertongue	R	2.30
Necromancer	C	0.10
Necros, Lord Of Xzulne	R	2.10
Nightfall	R	2.10
Order Of The Vanari	C	0.10
Oxylonn The Dire Worm	U	0.35
Part Water	U	0.35
Passage	C	0.10
21		
Peaseant	C	0.10
Phantasm	C	0.10
Pilgrim	C	0.10
Pillar Of Eyes	R	2.10
Pit Fighter	C	0.10
Pit Of Fire	C	0.10
Plague	R	1.80
Poison Touch	U	0.50
Pools Of Druna	R	2.10
22		
Powers On High	C	0.10
Rain Of Arrows	R	1.70
Revenant Sorcerer	U	0.35
Reverse Gravity	U	0.35
Rillobrigg	C	0.10
Ring Of Linking	U	0.50
Ring Of Many Wonders	R	2.60
Ring Of Nine Lives	R	2.10
Ring Of Water Walking	U	0.35
23		
Ringen The Valiant	U	0.35

Card name	Rarity	Price
River Of Fire	U	0.50
Rose Ossuary	U	0.35
Rose Pedal Brotherhood	C	0.10
Rumormonger	R	1.60
Sacred Earth	U	0.50
Salvation	U	0.50
Sanctuary	R	2.10
Sand Of Ages	R	2.80
24		
Savanah Monkeys	U	0.50
Scathos	U	0.35
Secret Combinations	R	2.10
Seven Seals Of Doom	R	3.30
Shadow Cat	C	0.10
Shadow Giant	U	0.35
Shadow Slayer	U	0.35
Shadowy Spirits	C	0.10
Shapeshifter	R	2.30
25		
Shield Of Shadows	C	0.10
Silandril's Salvation	U	0.50
Skaine The Vile	C	0.10
Skeleton Legions	C	0.10
Sleep	U	0.35
Soothsayer	C	0.10
Sothtis The Traveller	R	2.30
Soul Stealer	U	0.50
Southton Abbey	U	0.50
26		
Spider Plague	U	0.50
Spindlethorn	C	0.10
Staff Of The Pure Heart	R	2.60
Stairway Of The Eternities	R	2.60
Stewards Hall	U	0.50
Stewards Of Thale	C	0.10
Stones Of Drakma	R	2.30
Storm Season	R	2.30
Stormwatch	R	2.10
27		
Strong Bow	R	2.30
Swarm Skine	U	0.50
Teleport	U	0.50
Thanter Kandis	U	0.35
The Lost King	U	0.50
Thief	R	2.10
Time Sphere	R	3.30
Times Past To Present	R	2.80
Tremors	C	0.10
28		
Twin Towers	U	0.35
Urns Of Gold	U	0.35
Usher, Guardian Of Time	U	0.50
Vale Of The Sleeping Giants	U	0.50
Vasuul, Prince Of Xzulne	U	0.50
Veil Of Darkness	R	2.10
Vulne	C	0.10
Wandering Wizard	C	0.10
War Galley	U	0.35
29		
War Horse	C	0.10
War Standard	C	0.10
War Tower	U	0.35
War Wheel	R	2.10
Wargate	C	0.10
Warking Of Thrangmar	R	2.10
Warlock	C	0.10
Warp Staff	R	2.10
Whitefire Spirit	U	0.35
30		
Wild Lands	R	2.60
Witchfire	R	1.80
Witching Moon	R	2.10
Witching Season	R	2.80
Woodland Drue	C	0.10
Wyverthoom the White	U	0.50
Yunume, the All-father	R	3.60
Zealot	C	0.10

RARITY KEY C = Common   U = Uncommon   R = Rare   VR = Very Rare   UR = Ultra Rare   F = Foil card   X = Fixed/standard in all decks

Terminator

Precedence• Released **October 2000**

349 cards in set

- Starter decks contain 58 cards; starter displays contain 6 starters
- Booster packs contain 9 cards; booster displays contain 24 boosters

Based on the first *Terminator* movie, the mechanics of the **Terminator** CCG closely resemble the earlier Precedence-designed CCG, **Aliens/Predator**. In fact, the two games are compatible — something which breathed some life back into the latter.

In the basic game, one player represents Skynet, the sentient supercomputer attempting to change history via time travel in one last bid to defeat the human Resistance. The other player takes the part of the Resistance, committed to destroying Skynet.

Players alternate turns as they "build" the playing area by playing Location cards. Each character must be at a Location, which may have special properties. There are three types of victories in the basic game. Eliminate all of your opponent's main characters, safeguard/eliminate 10 Importance (to the future) points worth of supporting characters, or fulfill 10 Mission Points from Mission cards.

The CCG has a role-playing feel to it, as characters search for equipment, look for the chances to attack and comb the streets for the characters important to the future. This is another CCG in which players interested in tournaments have to maintain two decks, one for both sides. — *Michael Greenholdt*

Concept	●●●○○
Gameplay	●●●○○
Card art	●●●○○
Player pool	●●●○○

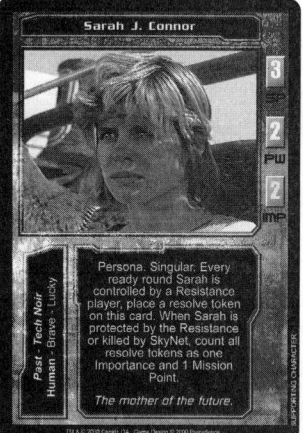

Sarah J. Connor

You will need **39** *nine-pocket pages to store this set.* (20 doubled up)

Set (349 cards)		107.50
Starter Display Box		90.00
Booster Display Box		75.00
Starter Deck		8.50
Booster Pack		2.40

Promo cards

Card name	Type	Price
☐ Beretta 92F	Item	2.50
☐ I'll Be Back	Event	3.00
☐ Skills Upgrade: Assassination	Item	3.00
☐ Target Terminated	Miss	2.50
☐ Time and Fate	Cond	2.50

Card name	Type	Rarity	Price
☐ .357 Magnum	Item	X	0.50
☐ .44 AutoMag	Item	C	0.20
☐ .45 Long-Slide	Item	X	0.50
☐ .50 cal Barrett M-82A1	Item	R	3.00
☐ .50 Desert Eagle	Item	R	2.50
☐ 12-Gauge Auto-Loader	Item	C	0.20
☐ 20-Watt Phased Plasma Rifle	Item	U	0.80
☐ 400 Rounds and Counting	Event	C	0.20
☐ 40-Watt Phased Plasma Rifle	Item	R	3.00
☐ A Learning Computer	Event	R	3.00
☐ A New Beginning	Event	R	3.50
☐ Adaptive Programming	Event	U	0.80
☐ Advanced Construction Drone	Char	U	0.90
☐ Advanced Scouting	Event	U	0.80
☐ Advanced Stealth Infiltrator	Char	R	4.00
☐ Aerial Recon Unit	Char	R	4.00
☐ Alamo Sport Shop	Loc	X	0.80
☐ Alleyway	Loc	X	0.80
☐ Ambidextrous	Event	U	0.80
☐ Ammo Cache	Event	C	0.20
☐ Anticipation	Event	C/X	0.25
☐ Apartment Complex	Loc	X	0.80
☐ AR-18 Assault Rifle	Item	R	3.50
☐ Arm-Mounted Gatling Gun	Item	R	5.00
☐ Armor-Piercing Rounds	Item	U	0.90
☐ Augmented Musculature	Item	R	3.00
☐ Automated Armory	Loc	U	0.80
☐ Automated Assembly Line	Loc	U	0.80
☐ Barred Door	Event	C	0.20
☐ Barren Wasteland	Loc	C	0.20
☐ Bartender	SChar	C	0.20
☐ Battle Fatigue	Event	C/X	0.25

Card name	Type	Rarity	Price
☐ Battlefield Repairs	Event	C/X	0.25
☐ Battlefield Shadows	Event	U	0.80
☐ Better You Than Me	Event	C/X	0.25
☐ Big Jeff's Family Restaurant	Loc	U	0.90
☐ Blending In	Event	U	0.80
☐ Blood Splatter	Event	C	0.20
☐ Blown Power Grid	Event	U	0.80
☐ Bonefields	Loc	R	4.00
☐ Braced For Impact	Event	R	3.00
☐ Bullet-Proof Vest	Item	X	0.50
☐ Castling	Event	R	3.00
☐ Caught Off Guard	Event	X	0.50
☐ Chain Link Fence	Event	C	0.20
☐ City Park	Loc	X	0.80
☐ City Ruins	Loc	U	0.80
☐ City Street	Loc	C	0.20
☐ Clean Room	Loc	R	3.00
☐ Col. Perry	Char	R	6.50
☐ Collapsed Ceiling	Event	C	3.00
☐ Combat Roll	Event	U	0.80
☐ Composite Body Armor	Item	R	3.00
☐ Compromised Stronghold	Miss	U	0.80
☐ Concealed Weapon	Event	U	0.80
☐ Concentration	Event	C	0.20
☐ Conquer	Event	U	0.90
☐ Construction Drone	Char	C	0.20
☐ Construction Site	Loc	R	3.00
☐ Coordinated Fire	Event	C	0.20
☐ Counterintelligence	Miss	R	4.00
☐ Cover Charge	Event	C	0.20
☐ Cpl. Greene	Char	U	1.00
☐ Cpl. LeBreton	Char	R	5.50
☐ Cpl. Marcus	Char	U	1.00
☐ Cpl. Pierce	Char	U	1.00
☐ Cpl. Rensey	Char	X	1.00
☐ Critical Systems Failure	Event	U	1.00
☐ Crowd Cover	Event	C	0.20
☐ Dark Alley	Loc	X	0.80
☐ Data Stream	Event	U	0.90
☐ Daybreak	Cond	C	0.20
☐ Deadly Force	Event	C	0.20
☐ Defective Ammunition	Event	C	0.20
☐ Deny Fate	Event	U	0.80
☐ Dermal Ablative Armor	Event	R	3.00
☐ Desperation	Event	C/X	0.25
☐ Destiny's Child	Miss	U	0.80
☐ Det. Lt. Ed Traxler	SChar	R	4.00
☐ Det. Sgt. Hal Vukovich	SChar	R	4.00
☐ Detachable Surveillance Module	Item	C	0.20

Card name	Type	Rarity	Price
☐ Detailed Analysis	Event	U	0.90
☐ Discipline	Event	X	0.50
☐ Disrupt Command & Control	Miss	U	0.90
☐ Distractions	Event	C/X	0.25
☐ Divine Intervention	Event	R	3.00
☐ Dr. Peter Silberman	SChar	R	8.00
☐ Drone Reconditioning Facility	Loc	U	0.80
☐ Dumpster	Loc	X	0.80
☐ Echelon Formation	Event	R	3.00
☐ Electromagnetic Rounds	Item	U	0.80
☐ Entropy	Event	U	0.80
☐ Escape Plans	Event	R	3.00
☐ Esprit de Corps	Cond	R	3.50
☐ Evasive Maneuvers	Event	R	3.00
☐ Excessive Force	Event	U	0.80
☐ Exertion	Event	C/X	0.25
☐ Extended Magazine	Event	C	0.20
☐ Extended Range	Event	C	0.20
☐ Extrapolate	Miss	C	
☐ Extreme Prejudice	Event	R	3.00
☐ Extreme Sanction	Cond	R	3.00
☐ False Sense of Security	Event	U	0.80
☐ Fearless	Event	C	0.20
☐ Field Dressing	Event	C/X	0.25
☐ Field Repairs	Event	C	0.20
☐ Firebase Delta	Loc	U	0.90
☐ First Aid Kit	Item	C	0.20
☐ Flashlight	Item	C	0.20
☐ Flight Control Facility	Loc	R	3.00
☐ For a Price	Event	R	3.00
☐ Forward Offensive	Miss	R	3.50
☐ Garbage Man	SChar	C/X	0.25
☐ Genocide	Miss	U	0.80
☐ Ginger Ventura	SChar	R	4.00
☐ Glancing Blow	Event	C	0.20
☐ Glass Shards	Event	C/X	0.25
☐ Glitch in the System	Event	C	0.20
☐ Gramps	SChar	R	4.00
☐ Gruesome Transport	Cond	U	0.80
☐ GSgt. Valdez	Char	C	0.20
☐ Guard Dogs	SChar	U	0.80
☐ Heated Fighting	Event	C/X	0.25
☐ Heavy Combat Chassis Unit	Char	U	0.90
☐ Heroic Sacrifice	Event	U	0.80
☐ Hesitation	Event	U	0.80
☐ Hidden Weapon Stash	Event	C	0.20
☐ Hide	Event	C/X	0.25

Card name	Type	Rarity	Price
☐ Hint of Things to Come	Event	R	3.00
☐ Hollow-Point Rounds	Item	C/X	0.25
☐ Holographic Array	Item	R	4.00
☐ Human Error	Event	R	3.00
☐ Human Intuition	Event	C/X	0.25
☐ Hypersonic Emitter	Item	C	0.20
☐ Inconsequential	Event	C	0.20
☐ Industrial Sabotage	Event	U	0.90
☐ Ineffective Weaponry	Event	C/X	0.25
☐ Infiltrator	Char	C/X	0.25
☐ Infiltrator Assembly Plant	Loc	R	3.00
☐ Inhuman Resilience	Event	C/X	0.25
☐ Inspiration	Event	R	3.00
☐ Interrogation Room	Loc	R	3.50
☐ Intuitive Reflexes	Event	R	3.50
☐ Investigative Reporter	SChar	X	0.50
☐ Iridium Power Cell	Item	U	0.80
☐ Isolated Side Street	Loc	X	0.80
☐ Kevlar Body Armor	Item	U	0.80
☐ Kill Shot	Event	U	0.80
☐ Kitchen	Loc	X	0.80
☐ Knight IV	Char	R	6.50
☐ Laser Defense Grid	Event	U	0.80
☐ Late Breaking Story	Event	U	0.80
☐ LCpl. Devin	Char	U	0.80
☐ Leading By Example	Miss	C	0.20
☐ Lethal Training	Event	U	0.80
☐ Light Assault Infiltrator	Char	C	0.20
☐ Limited Resources	Event	R	3.00
☐ Living Room	Loc	R	3.00
☐ Locked Storeroom	Loc	R	4.00
☐ LS-81 Laser Sight	Item	X	0.50
☐ Lt. Ryan	Char	R	6.50
☐ M-16A1 Standard Issue	Item	U	0.90
☐ M31A Phosphorous Grenade	Item	R	4.00
☐ M41 Range Finder Scope	Item	R	3.00
☐ M45 Thermal Imaging Scope	Item	U	0.80
☐ M71 Armored Tactical Helmet	Item	R	4.00
☐ Main Street	Loc	X	0.50
☐ Maj. Villalobos	Char	R	4.00
☐ Maj. Wiggs	Char	R	4.00
☐ Makeshift Barricade	Event	C	0.20
☐ Manhole	Event	U	0.80
☐ Manstopper Rounds	Item	C/X	0.25
☐ Matt McCallister	SChar	X	0.80
☐ Maximum Production	Miss	R	3.00
☐ MD301 Bio Spray	Item	R	2.50
☐ MD304 Burn Kit	Item	U	1.00

Card name	Type	Rarity	Price
☐ Medium Assault Infiltrator	Char	R	4.00
☐ Misfire	Event	C/X	0.25
☐ Mission Debriefing	Event	R	3.00
☐ Mistaken Identity	Event	C/X	0.25
☐ Mobile Assault Unit	Char	U	1.00
☐ Move It	Event	C/X	0.25
☐ Multiple Target Acquisition	Event	C	0.20
☐ Munitions Hold	Item	C	0.20
☐ Murphy's Law	Event	U	0.80
☐ Nightfall	Cond	C	0.20
☐ Nightmares	Event	C/X	0.25
☐ Oath of Allegiance: 132nd Eagle Watch	Event	R	3.00
☐ Oath of Allegiance: Black Shield Unit	Event	U	0.80
☐ Oath of Allegiance: Covert Ops	Event	U	0.80
☐ Oath of Allegiance: Delta Company	Event	U	0.80
☐ Obliteration	Event	R	3.00
☐ Observatory	Loc	C	0.20
☐ Obstruction	Event	C	0.20
☐ Ocular Implant: Infrared Optics	Item	C	0.20
☐ Ocular Implant: Retinal Laser	Item	R	3.00
☐ Ocular Implant: Targeting Matrix	Item	U	0.80
☐ On Your Feet, Soldier	Event	U	0.80
☐ Orbital Control Center	Loc	U	0.80
☐ Orphan	SChar	C	0.20
☐ Out Dancing	Event	C/X	0.25
☐ Out of Stock	Event	U	0.90
☐ Outclassed	Event	R	3.00
☐ Overproduction	Event	R	3.00
☐ Packrat	SChar	U	0.80
☐ Parking Lot	Loc	C	0.20
☐ Pawn III	Char	X	0.80
☐ Pawn Shop	Loc	X	0.80
☐ Perfect Disguise	Event	C	0.20
☐ Perimeter Patrol Dogs	SChar	C	0.20
☐ Phased Plasma Charge	Item	R	4.00
☐ Phone Book	Event	C/X	0.25
☐ Pipe Bombs	Item	C	0.20
☐ Plasma Dampening Field	Item	R	3.50
☐ Plasma Overload	Event	U	0.80
☐ Point Blank	Event	C	0.20

Card name	Type	Rarity	Price
☐ Police Officer	SChar	X	0.50
☐ Police Station	Loc	X	0.50
☐ Power Spike	Event	C	0.20
☐ Preach the Future	Miss	C	0.20
☐ Predicted Outcome	Event	U	0.80
☐ Primal Fear	Event	R	3.00
☐ Prime Directive	Miss	C	0.20
☐ Priorities Rescinded	Event	U	0.80
☐ Processor Bank	Loc	U	0.80
☐ Protection	Cond	U	0.80
☐ Puppet Strings	Event	C	0.20
☐ Pvt. Baker	Char	C	0.20
☐ Pvt. Furious	Char	U	0.90
☐ Pvt. Garcia	Char	C	0.20
☐ Pvt. Garstin	Char	C	0.20
☐ Pvt. Gentii	SChar	R	3.50
☐ Pvt. Grey	Char	U	0.90
☐ Quick Deployment	Event	C	0.20
☐ Raging Inferno	Event	R	3.00
☐ Rational Explanation	Event	C	0.20
☐ Raze	Event	C	0.20
☐ Recon Infiltrator	Char	C	0.20
☐ Reconnaissance	Miss	U	0.90
☐ Reconstructive Nanites	Item	C/X	0.25
☐ Recycling Operation	Miss	R	4.00
☐ Refractive Cloaking Armor	Item	R	3.50
☐ Reinforced Hardpoint	Event	R	3.00
☐ Reinforced Structure	Event	U	0.80
☐ Reinforcements	Cond	R	4.00
☐ Relentless	Event	C	0.20
☐ Reload	Event	C	0.20
☐ Remington 870	Item	C/X	0.25
☐ Remote Tactical Uplink	Item	U	0.80
☐ Rerouting Emergency Power	Event	R	3.00
☐ Research & Development Facility	Loc	U	0.80
☐ Resistance Private	Char	C	0.20
☐ Retractable Claws	Item	C	0.20
☐ Retroviral Engineering	Loc	R	3.00
☐ Rewriting History	Event	C	0.20
☐ Right Off The Assembly Line	Event	U	0.80
☐ Rook II	Char	U	1.00
☐ Rubber Skin	Event	R	3.00
☐ Rubble Hills	Loc	C	0.20
☐ Ruined Flesh	Event	C/X	0.25

Card name	Type	Rarity	Price
☐ Ruined Street	Loc	C	0.20
☐ Run!	Event	C/X	0.25
☐ Running Battle	Cond	U	0.80
☐ S.W.A.T. Tactical Officer	SChar	R	4.00
☐ Safehouse	Event	R	3.00
☐ Salvage Operation	Miss	R	3.50
☐ Sarah J. Connor (3/2/5)	SChar	X	1.50
☐ Sarah J. Connor (3/2/2)	SChar	R	10.00
☐ Sarah Louise Connor, Mother of Two	SChar	R	6.00
☐ Sarge	SChar	R	4.00
☐ Savagery	Event	C	0.20
☐ Scatter	Event	C	0.20
☐ Schematic Download	Event	U	0.90
☐ Scouting Mission	Event	C	0.20
☐ Search Pattern	Event	U	0.80
☐ Sentinel	Event	R	3.00
☐ Servo-Admin Drone	Char	R	5.80
☐ Sewage Tunnel Entrance	Loc	C	0.20
☐ Sewer	Loc	X	0.50
☐ Sgt. Hannum	Char	R	4.00
☐ Sgt. Kyle Reese (3/3)	Char	X	2.50
☐ Sgt. Kyle Reese (3/4)	Char	R	10.00
☐ Sgt. Maj. Jensen	Char	U	0.90
☐ Shattered Hope	Event	C/X	0.25
☐ Shifting Sands	Event	U	0.80
☐ Sixth Sense	Event	U	0.80
☐ Skills Upgrade: Basic Training	Item	U	0.80
☐ Skills Upgrade: Marksman	Item	C/X	0.25
☐ Skills Upgrade: Medical Training	Item	C	0.20
☐ Skills Upgrade: Tactical Database	Item	R	3.00
☐ Skills Upgrade: Veteran	Item	U	0.80
☐ Slagged Gear	Event	U	0.80
☐ Spread the Word	Miss	U	1.00
☐ Staff Lunchroom	Loc	C	0.20
☐ Staggered Formation	Event	U	0.90
☐ Stay Frosty	Event	C/X	0.25
☐ Steel Mill	Loc	U	0.90
☐ Storage Cell	Event	U	0.80
☐ Storm the Wires	Miss	C	0.20
☐ Street Punk	SChar	X	0.50
☐ Stronghold Mechanic	SChar	U	0.80
☐ Subdermal Armor: Level 1	Item	U	0.80
☐ Suburban House	Loc	X	0.80

Card name	Type	Rarity	Price
☐ Suburban Street	Loc	X	0.80
☐ Successful Infiltration	Miss	C	0.20
☐ Suicidal Tendencies	Event	R	3.00
☐ Sunglasses	Item	C/X	0.25
☐ Surplus Depot	Loc	R	3.00
☐ Switchblade	Item	C/X	0.25
☐ Tactical Analysis	Miss	R	3.00
☐ Tactical Command Unit	Char	R	4.00
☐ Tactical Error	Event	U	0.90
☐ Tactical Formation	Event	U	0.90
☐ Tactical Infiltrator	Char	U	1.00
☐ Target Acquired	Event	C/X	0.25
☐ Targeting System Failure	Event	C/X	0.25
☐ Tech Noir	Loc	X	0.50
☐ Technical Malfunction	Event	R	3.00
☐ The Pass	Loc	R	3.50
☐ There's a Storm Coming...	Event	R	3.00
☐ Tiki Motel	Loc	X	0.80
☐ Time Displacement Laboratory	Loc	U	0.90
☐ Time Lab Discovered!	Miss	U	0.90
☐ Toxin Coated Spikes	Item	U	0.90
☐ Trash Warrens	Loc	U	1.00
☐ Trench Warfare	Miss	C	0.20
☐ Trenchcoat	Item	U	1.00
☐ Twist of Fate	Event	C/X	0.25
☐ Underground Archives	Loc	R	3.00
☐ Unit Construction Zone	Loc	R	4.00
☐ Unit Deployment	Event	C	0.20
☐ Unpredictability	Event	U	0.90
☐ Up Close and Personal	Event	C/X	0.25
☐ Urban Ground Assault Unit	Char	R	4.00
☐ Urgency	Cond	U	0.80
☐ Uzi 9mm	Item	R	3.00
☐ Vantage Point	Loc	R	3.00
☐ Vicious Attack	Event	C	0.20
☐ Victory Through Attrition	Miss	R	3.50
☐ Viral Contamination	Event	R	3.00
☐ Walking in Shadows	Event	U	0.90
☐ Wanted	Event	R	3.00
☐ Well Rested	Event	U	0.90
☐ Wetware Processing Facility	Loc	U	0.90
☐ What Will It Be?	Event	C	0.20
☐ What's the Date?	Event	U	0.80
☐ When Animals Attack	Event	R	3.00
☐ When In Doubt	Event	C	0.20
☐ Your Clothes ...	Event	C/X	0.25

You will need **34** nine-pocket pages to store this set. (17 doubled up)

Terror

Kris Silver • First set, **Mandible**, released **1996**

305 cards in set

- Starter decks contain 60 cards; starter displays contain 10 starters
- Booster packs contain 15 cards; booster displays contain 36 packs

Designed by **Kris Silver**

Here's something few thought they'd have a chance to (or want to) to play: mutant ants.

In a post-apocalyptic earth, each player represents the queen of a hive of giant, mutant, bipedal ants. The object of the game is to expand the nest and destroy opposing hives. There is no deck. There are no hands. Each player starts with a certain number of cards in play and each turn may attempt to add more (up to the queen's Birth Number) by sorting through the rest of his cards and selecting the ones he wants.

The player rolls a 20-sided die and if it is lower than the difficulty number on that warrior or worker, the queen successfully spawns. Once enough workers are in play, they may use their Work Points to add chambers to your nest. A chamber has a Work Cost, and worker drone cards have to be dedicated to the building of it until their Work value equals the cost. Once a lot of workers get into play, the building is fairly quick. Warriors, on the other hand, participate in combat by wandering over to the other nest. When an attack is declared, each player stacks up all attacking and defending warriors in the order they will attack and die. The stacks are flipped over, the Attack values are added up, and stacks each take the other's damage. Starting with the top card, warrior cards are removed until their Defense values have absorbed the damage dealt.

MANDIBLE NEST

M-141   SPACES 4   COST 25

Concept	●○○○○
Gameplay	●●○○○
Card art	●●○○○
Player pool	○○○○○

RARITY KEY   C = Common   U = Uncommon   R = Rare   VR = Very Rare   UR = Ultra Rare   F = Foil card   X = Fixed/standard in all decks

While the art isn't bad, it is printed in red ink on a white background, so it looks pretty horrid. The cards are fortunately easy to read, as there are only four or five labeled statistics on each card. Altogether, *Terror* should have been a board game. The mechanics really look like they were designed that way, and there is no reason this should have been a collectible card game as written. — *Richard Weld*

SCRYE NOTES: *Apparently, an expansion about mutant Gorilla tribes titled* **Terror: Raiders** *was planned, but we have been unable to confirm if it has been released, or whether the card sets were intended to be compatible.*

Set (305 cards)	33.00
Starter Display Box	17.00
Booster Display Box	20.00
Starter Deck	4.25
Booster Pack	1.00

#	Card name	Price
A1	Adventure Card	0.25
A2	Adventure Card	0.25
A3	Adventure Card	0.25
A4	Adventure Card	0.25
A5	Adventure Card	0.25
A6	Adventure Card	0.25
A7	Adventure Card	0.25
A8	Adventure Card	0.25
A9	Adventure Card	0.25
A10	Adventure Card	0.25
A11	Adventure Card	0.25
A12	Adventure Card	0.25
A13	Adventure Card	0.25
A14	Adventure Card	0.25
A15	Adventure Card	0.25
A16	Adventure Card	0.25
A17	Adventure Card	0.25
M198	Build-A-Card	0.25
M168	Hazard	0.25
M169	Hazard	0.25
M170	Hazard	0.25
M171	Hazard	0.25
M172	Hazard	0.25
M173	Hazard	0.25
M174	Hazard	0.25
M175	Hazard	0.25
M176	Hazard	0.25
M177	Hazard	0.25
M178	Hazard	0.25
M179	Hazard	0.25
M180	Hazard	0.25
M181	Hazard	0.25
M182	Hazard	0.25
M183	Hazard	0.25
M184	Hazard	0.25
M185	Hazard	0.25
M186	Hazard	0.25
M187	Hazard	0.25
M188	Hazard	0.25
M189	Hazard	0.25
M190	Hazard	0.25
M191	Hazard	0.25
M192	Hazard	0.25
M193	Hazard	0.25
M194	Hazard	0.25
M195	Hazard	0.25
M196	Hazard	0.25
M197	Hazard	0.25
I1	Instruction	0.10
I2	Instruction	0.10
I3	Instruction	0.10
I4	Instruction	0.10
I5	Instruction	0.10
I6	Instruction	0.10
I7	Instruction	0.10
I8	Instruction	0.10

#	Card name	Price
I9	Instruction	0.10
I10	Instruction	0.10
I11	Instruction	0.10
I12	Instruction	0.10
I13	Instruction	0.10
I14	Instruction	0.10
I15	Instruction	0.10
I16	Instruction	0.10
I17	Instruction	0.10
I18	Instruction	0.10
M36	Mandible Assassin	0.25
M37	Mandible Assassin	0.25
M38	Mandible Assassin	0.25
M39	Mandible Assassin	0.25
M40	Mandible Assassin	0.25
M120	Mandible Council	0.25
M121	Mandible Council	0.25
M122	Mandible Council	0.25
M123	Mandible Council	0.25
M124	Mandible Council	0.25
M125	Mandible Council	0.25
M126	Mandible Council	0.25
M127	Mandible Council	0.25
M128	Mandible Council	0.25
M129	Mandible Council	0.25
M130	Mandible Council	0.25
M131	Mandible Council	0.25
M132	Mandible Council	0.25
M133	Mandible Council	0.25
M134	Mandible Council	0.25
M135	Mandible Council	0.25
M136	Mandible Council	0.25
M137	Mandible Council	0.25
M91	Mandible Destroyer	0.25
M92	Mandible Destroyer	0.25
M93	Mandible Destroyer	0.25
M94	Mandible Destroyer	0.25
M95	Mandible Destroyer	0.25
M96	Mandible Destroyer	0.25
M97	Mandible Destroyer	0.25
M98	Mandible Destroyer	0.25
M99	Mandible Destroyer	0.25
M100	Mandible Destroyer	0.25
M101	Mandible Drone	0.25
M102	Mandible Drone	0.25
M103	Mandible Drone	0.25
M104	Mandible Drone	0.25
M71	Mandible Engineer	0.25
M72	Mandible Engineer	0.25
M73	Mandible Engineer	0.25
M74	Mandible Engineer	0.25
M75	Mandible Engineer	0.25
M76	Mandible Engineer	0.25
M77	Mandible Engineer	0.25
M78	Mandible Engineer	0.25
M79	Mandible Engineer	0.25
M80	Mandible Engineer	0.25
M81	Mandible Engineer	0.25
M82	Mandible Engineer	0.25
M83	Mandible Engineer	0.25
M84	Mandible Engineer	0.25
M85	Mandible Engineer	0.25

#	Card name	Price
M86	Mandible Engineer	0.25
M87	Mandible Engineer	0.25
M88	Mandible Engineer	0.25
M89	Mandible Engineer	0.25
M90	Mandible Engineer	0.25
M61	Mandible Excavator	0.25
M62	Mandible Excavator	0.25
M63	Mandible Excavator	0.25
M64	Mandible Excavator	0.25
M65	Mandible Excavator	0.25
M66	Mandible Excavator	0.25
M67	Mandible Excavator	0.25
M68	Mandible Excavator	0.25
M69	Mandible Excavator	0.25
M70	Mandible Excavator	0.25
M105	Mandible Female	0.25
M106	Mandible Female	0.25
M107	Mandible Female	0.25
M108	Mandible Female	0.25
M109	Mandible Female	0.25
M153	Mandible Forage	0.25
M154	Mandible Forage	0.25
M155	Mandible Forage	0.25
M156	Mandible Forage	0.25
M157	Mandible Forage	0.25
M158	Mandible Forage	0.25
M159	Mandible Forage	0.25
M160	Mandible Forage	0.25
M161	Mandible Forage	0.25
M162	Mandible Forage	0.25
M163	Mandible Forage	0.25
M164	Mandible Forage	0.25
M165	Mandible Forage	0.25
M166	Mandible Forage	0.25
M167	Mandible Forage	0.25
M21	Mandible Guard	0.25
M22	Mandible Guard	0.25
M23	Mandible Guard	0.25
M24	Mandible Guard	0.25
M25	Mandible Guard	0.25
M26	Mandible Guard	0.25
M27	Mandible Guard	0.25
M28	Mandible Guard	0.25
M29	Mandible Guard	0.25
M30	Mandible Guard	0.25
M31	Mandible Guard	0.25
M32	Mandible Guard	0.25
M33	Mandible Guard	0.25
M34	Mandible Guard	0.25
M35	Mandible Guard	0.25
M138	Mandible Nest	0.25
M139	Mandible Nest	0.25
M140	Mandible Nest	0.25
M141	Mandible Nest	0.25
M142	Mandible Nest	0.25
M143	Mandible Nest	0.25
M144	Mandible Nest	0.25
M145	Mandible Nest	0.25
M146	Mandible Nest	0.25
M147	Mandible Nest	0.25
M148	Mandible Nest	0.25
M149	Mandible Nest	0.25

#	Card name	Price
M150	Mandible Nest	0.25
M151	Mandible Nest	0.25
M152	Mandible Nest	0.25
M110	Mandible Queen	0.25
M111	Mandible Queen	0.25
M112	Mandible Queen	0.25
M113	Mandible Queen	0.25
M114	Mandible Queen	0.25
M115	Mandible Queen	0.25
M116	Mandible Queen	0.25
M117	Mandible Queen	0.25
M118	Mandible Queen	0.25
M119	Mandible Queen	0.25
M1	Mandible Warrior	0.25
M2	Mandible Warrior	0.25
M3	Mandible Warrior	0.25
M4	Mandible Warrior	0.25
M5	Mandible Warrior	0.25
M6	Mandible Warrior	0.25
M7	Mandible Warrior	0.25
M8	Mandible Warrior	0.25
M9	Mandible Warrior	0.25
M10	Mandible Warrior	0.25
M11	Mandible Warrior	0.25
M12	Mandible Warrior	0.25
M13	Mandible Warrior	0.25
M14	Mandible Warrior	0.25
M15	Mandible Warrior	0.25
M16	Mandible Warrior	0.25
M17	Mandible Warrior	0.25
M18	Mandible Warrior	0.25
M19	Mandible Warrior	0.25
M20	Mandible Warrior	0.25
M41	Mandible Worker	0.25
M42	Mandible Worker	0.25
M43	Mandible Worker	0.25
M44	Mandible Worker	0.25
M45	Mandible Worker	0.25
M46	Mandible Worker	0.25
M47	Mandible Worker	0.25
M48	Mandible Worker	0.25
M49	Mandible Worker	0.25
M50	Mandible Worker	0.25
M51	Mandible Worker	0.25
M52	Mandible Worker	0.25
M53	Mandible Worker	0.25
M54	Mandible Worker	0.25
M55	Mandible Worker	0.25
M56	Mandible Worker	0.25
M57	Mandible Worker	0.25
M58	Mandible Worker	0.25
M59	Mandible Worker	0.25
M60	Mandible Worker	0.25
M199	Specialized	0.25
M200	Specialized	0.25
M201	Specialized	0.25
M202	Specialized	0.25
M203	Specialized	0.25
M204	Specialized	0.25
M205	Specialized	0.25
M206	Specialized	0.25
M207	Specialized	0.25
M208	Specialized	0.25

#	Card name	Price
M209	Specialized	0.25
M210	Specialized	0.25
M211	Specialized	0.25
M212	Specialized	0.25
M213	Specialized	0.25
M214	Specialized	0.25
M215	Specialized	0.25
M216	Specialized	0.25
M217	Specialized	0.25
M218	Specialized	0.25
M219	Specialized	0.25
M220	Specialized	0.25
M221	Specialized	0.25
M222	Specialized	0.25
M223	Specialized	0.25
M224	Specialized	0.25
M225	Specialized	0.25
M226	Specialized	0.25
M227	Specialized	0.25
M228	Specialized	0.25
M229	Specialized	0.25
M230	Specialized	0.25
M231	Specialized	0.25
M232	Specialized	0.25
M233	Specialized	0.25
M234	Specialized	0.25
M235	Specialized	0.25
M236	Specialized	0.25
M237	Specialized	0.25
M238	Specialized	0.25
M239	Specialized	0.25
M240	Specialized	0.25
M241	Specialized	0.25
M242	Specialized	0.25
M243	Specialized	0.25
M244	Specialized	0.25
M245	Specialized	0.25
M246	Specialized	0.25
M247	Specialized	0.25
M248	Specialized	0.25
M249	Specialized	0.25
M250	Specialized	0.25
M251	Specialized	0.25
M252	Specialized	0.25
M253	Specialized	0.25
M254	Specialized	0.25
M255	Specialized	0.25
M256	Specialized	0.25
M257	Specialized	0.25
M258	Specialized	0.25
M259	Specialized	0.25
M260	Specialized	0.25
M261	Specialized	0.25
M262	Specialized	0.25
M263	Specialized	0.25
M264	Specialized	0.25
M265	Specialized	0.25
M266	Specialized	0.25
M267	Specialized	0.25
M268	Specialized	0.25
M269	Specialized	0.25
M270	Specialized	0.25

RARITY KEY C = Common U = Uncommon R = Rare VR = Very Rare UR = Ultra Rare F = Foil card X = Fixed/standard in all decks

LARA CROFT ACROBAT

Tomb Raider

Precedence • First set, *Premier*, released **August 1999**
211 cards in set • **IDENTIFER: No letter before card number**

• Starter decks contain 58 cards; starter displays contain 10 starters
• Booster packs contain 8 cards; booster displays contain 48 boosters

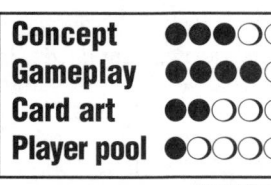

Concept	●●●○○
Gameplay	●●●●○
Card art	●●○○○
Player pool	●○○○○

You will need
24
nine-pocket
pages to store
this set.
(12 doubled up)

Based on the popular computer game of the same name, the ***Tomb Raider*** CCG pits two or more players against each other in a search for treasure. Each player has a Tomb Raider, either Lara Croft or another raider. The players then build a game board as play continues, using location cards that represent the tomb, ruin, or other location being investigated. Players move a figure representing their raider from card to card, where they encounter traps, battle viscious opponents, and search for minor treasures and items that will help their quest. The goal of the game is to be the first tomb raider to reach the target treasure chamber.

Each tomb raider card has four abilities: Fight, Move, Search, and Think. Whenever a test is called for, whether to shoot a crocodile or jump over a chasm, the player rolls a number of six-sided dice equal to the listed ability. If the total rolled is equal to or higher than the target number, the tomb raider succeeds. If not, he might take damage or he might be "stuck" at that location and have to try again next turn. Unlike most card games, if the character dies, a player simply starts over again at the entrance, or at the last place he "saved" his character. Just like in the video game.

The CCG also captures Lara's unearthly dimensions, which are, frankly, part of the video game's appeal among many of its fans. — *James Mishler*

Set (211 cards)	125.00
Starter Display Box	87.50
Booster Display Box	80.00
Starter Deck	10.00
Booster Pack	2.00

#	Promos	Price
☐ 211	Premiere Lenticular (not playable)	20.00
☐ 215	A Small Favor	4.00
☐ 214	Keep Your Cool	4.00
☐ 216	Lara Croft, Siren	11.50
☐ 217	Slippery When Wet Lenticular (not playable)	22.00

#	Card name	Rarity	Price
☐ 100	Achilles Heel	C	0.25
☐ 128	Adapt and Overcome	U	1.00
☐ 96	All or Nothing	C	0.25
☐ 83	Ambush	C	0.25
☐ 143	Ancient Glyph	U	1.00
☐ 164	Atlantean Big Boss	R	4.00
☐ 187	Atlantean DNA	R	4.00
☐ 135	Atlantean Horseman	U	1.00
☐ 113	Atlantean Lair	U	1.00
☐ 163	Atlantean Lara	R	5.00
☐ 146	Atlantean Life Amulet	U	1.00
☐ 165	Atlantean Natla	R	4.00
☐ 103	Atlantean Save	U	1.00
☐ 188	Atlantean Scion	R	4.00
☐ 118	Atlantean Treasure	U	1.00
☐ 99	Attack From Behind	C	0.25
☐ 93	Attention to Detail	C	0.25
☐ 78	Backflip	C	0.25
☐ 48	Backpack	X	0.25
☐ 122	Bait and Switch	U	1.00
☐ 10	Bat Cave	X	0.25
☐ 16	Bat Roost	X	0.25
☐ 39	Bat Shrine	X	0.25
☐ 59	Bats	C/X	0.25
☐ 22	Bear	X	0.25
☐ 14	Bend Left	X	0.25
☐ 144	Binoculars	U	1.00
☐ 43	Blind Corner	X	0.25
☐ 139	Blinding Flash Trap	U	1.00
☐ 159	Bottleneck	R	3.00
☐ 32	Boulder Passage	X	0.25
☐ 21	Bounty	X	0.25
☐ 140	Break-Away Floor	U	1.00
☐ 41	Broken Passage	X	0.25

#	Card name	Rarity	Price
☐ 124	Carpe Conundrum	U	1.00
☐ 1	Cave Entrance	X	0.25
☐ 176	Charm of the Beast	R	4.00
☐ 109	Chasm	U	1.00
☐ 70	Chute Trap	C/X	0.25
☐ 20	Claw of the Cave Bear	X	0.25
☐ 97	Collapsing Exit	C	0.25
☐ 123	Collateral Damage	U	1.00
☐ 148	Combat Knife	U	1.00
☐ 141	Compass	U	1.00
☐ 75	Concentration	C	0.25
☐ 172	Cool Shades	R	3.50
☐ 87	Coordinated Fire	C	0.25
☐ 198	Cowboy	R	4.00
☐ 116	Crawler Range	U	1.00
☐ 162	Crawling Atlantean	R	3.00
☐ 167	Crushing Stone Trap	R	3.00
☐ 82	Cursed Idol	C	0.25
☐ 65	Dark	C/X	0.25
☐ 64	Dart Trap	C/X	0.25
☐ 34	Dead End	X	0.25
☐ 160	DeathTrap?	R	4.00
☐ 150	Deep Pit Trap	U	1.00
☐ 84	Detailed Search	C	0.25
☐ 153	Difficult Slope	R	4.00
☐ 5	Dim Cavern	X	0.25
☐ 42	Dizzying Heights	X	0.25
☐ 110	Drawbridge	U	1.00
☐ 81	Drive Out	C	0.25
☐ 157	Empty Room	R	3.00
☐ 33	End of Line	X	0.25
☐ 13	End of Slide	X	0.25
☐ 35	Engraved Passage	X	0.25
☐ 137	Falling Boulder	U	1.00
☐ 24	Ferocious Attack	X	0.25
☐ 80	Flare	C	0.25
☐ 114	Fleeting Beauty	U	1.00
☐ 161	Flying Atlantean	R	4.00
☐ 88	Fool's Gambit	C	0.25
☐ 9	Fork	X	0.25
☐ 89	Fresh Start	C	0.25
☐ 50	Gap	X	0.25
☐ 6	Giant Cavern	X	0.25
☐ 104	Giant Steps	U	1.00
☐ 149	Gnashing Teeth	U	1.00
☐ 52	Good Shot	C/X	0.25
☐ 132	Gorilla	U	1.00

#	Card name	Rarity	Price
☐ 98	Guarded Attack	C	0.25
☐ 111	Hall of Revelation	U	1.00
☐ 18	Hard Right	X	0.25
☐ 15	Hidden Corner	X	0.25
☐ 71	Hidden Exit	C/X	0.25
☐ 121	I Can Do That	U	1.00
☐ 45	Idol of Fortune	X	0.25
☐ 145	Idol of Life	U	1.00
☐ 186	Idol of the Wolf	R	4.00
☐ 181	I'm Sorry	R	3.00
☐ 85	Improvise	C	0.25
☐ 189	Incan Spirit Cloak	R	4.00
☐ 177	Infrared Goggles	R	4.00
☐ 95	Insight	C	0.25
☐ 112	Jagged Cavern	U	1.00
☐ 56	Just Made It	C/X	0.25
☐ 174	Laptop Computer	R	4.00
☐ 191	Lara Croft Acrobat	R	7.50
☐ 67	Lara Croft, Adventurer	C/X	1.00
☐ 195	Lara Croft Archaeologist	R	7.50
☐ 192	Lara Croft Duelist	R	5.00
☐ 210	Lara Croft Explorer	UR	16.00
☐ 194	Lara Croft Millionaire	R	7.50
☐ 19	Lara Croft Spelunker	X	1.00
☐ 44	Lara Croft Treasure Hunter	X	1.00
☐ 193	Lara Croft Victor	R	7.50
☐ 147	Large Medi Pack	U	1.00
☐ 197	Larsen	R	5.00
☐ 117	Lava Fall	U	1.00
☐ 166	Lava Flow	R	3.00
☐ 105	Lava Straits	U	1.00
☐ 23	Leather Jacket	X	0.25
☐ 131	Lion	U	1.00
☐ 74	Loaded For Bear	C	0.25
☐ 51	Look Again	C/X	0.25
☐ 49	Lost	X	0.25
☐ 182	Luck of the Draw	R	4.00
☐ 108	Lure	U	1.00
☐ 68	Magnum Pistols	C/X	0.25
☐ 190	Map of Indiana	R	4.00
☐ 107	Maze	U	1.00
☐ 156	Meditation Chamber	R	4.00
☐ 31	Narrow Crossing	X	0.25
☐ 134	Natla	U	1.00
☐ 136	Natla's Sniper	U	1.00
☐ 79	Natla's Thug	C	0.25

#	Card name	Rarity	Price
☐ 184	No Fallback	R	3.00
☐ 38	No Return	X	0.25
☐ 91	One Slim Chance	C	0.25
☐ 7	Open Cavern	X	0.25
☐ 90	Over Encumbered	C	0.25
☐ 8	Overlook	X	0.25
☐ 196	Pierre	R	4.50
☐ 62	Pit Trap	C/X	0.25
☐ 17	Pond	X	0.25
☐ 183	Poor Aim	R	4.00
☐ 133	Pumas	U	1.00
☐ 63	Push	C/X	0.25
☐ 76	Quick Assessment	C	0.25
☐ 152	Revolving Door	R	4.00
☐ 55	Rope	C/X	0.25
☐ 58	Rough Ground	C/X	0.25
☐ 37	Rough Staircase	X	0.25
☐ 72	Run	C	0.25
☐ 142	Rusty Key	U	1.00
☐ 2	Safe Cave	X	0.25
☐ 27	Safe Chamber	X	0.25
☐ 151	Sanctuary	R	4.00
☐ 61	Save Point	C/X	0.25
☐ 129	Scent the Prey	U	1.00
☐ 180	Scope	R	4.00
☐ 201	Secret Move 1	UR	20.00
☐ 202	Secret Move 2	UR	20.00
☐ 203	Secret Move 3	UR	20.00
☐ 204	Secret Move 4	UR	20.00
☐ 205	Secret Move 5	UR	20.00
☐ 206	Secret Move 6	UR	20.00
☐ 207	Secret Move 7	UR	20.00
☐ 208	Secret Move 8	UR	20.00
☐ 209	Secret Move 9	UR	20.00
☐ 179	Secret Passage	R	4.00
☐ 155	Secret Room	R	5.00
☐ 40	Sharp Bend	X	0.25
☐ 12	Sharp T	X	0.25
☐ 120	Shotgun	U	1.00
☐ 73	Shotgun Ammo	C	0.25
☐ 199	Skateboard Kid	R	4.50
☐ 4	Skeletal Remains	X	0.25
☐ 30	Slice and Dice	X	0.25
☐ 29	Slide	X	0.25
☐ 69	Small Medi Pack	C/X	0.25
☐ 130	Snake Eyes	U	1.00
☐ 46	Snoop Ahead	X	0.25

RARITY KEY C = Common **U** = Uncommon **R** = Rare **VR** = Very Rare **UR** = Ultra Rare **F** = Foil card **X** = Fixed/standard in all decks

#	Card name	Rarity	Price
102	Sphere Room	U	1.00
169	Spied Floor	R	3.00
138	Spike Trap	U	1.00
47	Spiked Slope	X	0.25
66	Steal Item	C/X	0.25
173	Stone Tablet	R	4.00
21			
115	Storehouse	U	1.00
185	Superior Tactics	R	3.00
94	Sure Footing	C	0.25

#	Card name	Rarity	Price
57	Take Aim	C/X	0.25
200	The Bald Man	R	4.50
126	The Greater Threat	U	1.00
77	The Second Barrel	C	0.25
53	The Way Through	C/X	0.25
154	Tiger Trap	R	3.00
22			
170	TNT	R	4.00
26	Tomb Entrance	X	0.25
168	Toxic Fumes	R	4.00

#	Card name	Rarity	Price
127	Training Exercise	U	1.00
3	Treasure Cave	X	0.25
175	Treasure Map	R	4.00
28	Treasure Vault	X	0.25
54	Triggered Door	C/X	0.25
36	Uneven Corridor	X	0.25
23			
178	Unpleasant Surprise	R	4.00
125	Unstoppable	U	1.00
171	UZI	R	4.30

#	Card name	Rarity	Price
119	Uzi Clip	U	1.00
158	Waterfall	R	4.00
86	Weapon Jam	C	0.25
106	Wellspring	U	1.00
11	Wolf Bridge	X	0.25
25	Wolf Pack	X	0.25
24			
60	Wolves	C/X	0.25
92	Worst Case	C	0.25
101	Zoo	U	1.00

Tomb Raider • Slippery When Wet

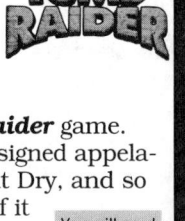

Precedence • Released **December 1999**

209 cards in set • **IDENTIFIER: 'S' before card number**

- Starter decks contain 50 cards; starter displays contain 10 starters
- Booster packs contain 8 cards; booster displays contain 48 boosters

This expansion adds several new concepts and card types to the **Tomb Raider** game.

It divides locations into Wet, Dry, and Wet/Dry locations, and similarly assigned appelations to every card. Wet obstacles could only be used at Wet locations, Dry at Dry, and so on. It also added the Air Supply Rating; every Tomb Raider starts with a 6, if it ever falls below 1... reset time!

The set also adds a new discovery card type, Companions, which gives bonuses to the Tomb Raider's ability rolls... more if the Companion actually failed his own roll and expired. "Second Banana" is obviously not a career of choice in *Tomb Raider...* — **James Mishler**

> You will need **24** nine-pocket pages to store this set. (12 doubled up)

Set (209 cards)		**95.00**
Starter Display Box		**67.50**
Booster Display Box		**67.50**
Starter Deck		**9.00**
Booster Pack		**2.00**

#	Card name	Rarity	Price
1			
S031	Abandoned Chamber	X	0.50
S059	Air Pocket	C	0.25
S068	Air Tank	C	0.25
S082	Angry Native	C	0.25
S001	Beach	X	0.50
S144	Beat Feet	U	0.80
S107	Below Decks	U	0.80
S197	Black Beard	R	4.00
S029	Blocked Passage	X	0.50
2			
S076	Blood in the Water	C	0.25
S165	Blow Gun	R	3.00
S105	Boiler Room	U	0.80
S006	Boulder Field	X	0.50
S164	Cage Trap	R	2.00
S018	Canal	X	0.50
S101	Captin's Cabin	U	0.80
S115	Cargo Hold	U	0.80
S015	Cavern Corridor	X	0.50
3			
S100	Chalk	C	0.25
S041	Channel	X	0.50
S046	Choke	X	0.50
S138	Collapsing Pillars	U	0.80
S017	Corner Room	X	0.50
S195	Cowboy, Sharp Shooter	R	4.00
S035	Crate Room	X	0.50
S038	Crawl Space	X	0.50
S063	Crocodile	C	0.25
4			
S065	Dark	C	0.25
S116	Dark Hallway	U	0.80
S181	Davy Jones' Locker	R	3.00
S049	Defensive Tactics	X	0.50
S134	Depth Gauge	U	0.80
S127	Disorientation	U	0.80
S048	Diving Flippers	X	0.50
S026	Diving Platform	X	0.50
S021	Dodge	X	0.50
5			
S133	Drain Pipe	U	0.80

#	Card name	Rarity	Price
S060	Drain Trigger	C	0.25
S179	Dread Robert's Eye	R	4.00
S152	Echo Cavern	R	2.80
S106	Engine Room	U	0.80
S122	False Trail	U	0.80
S077	First off the Line	C	0.25
S158	Floating Chamber	R	2.00
S132	Flood Gate	U	0.80
6			
S155	Flooded Fork	R	3.50
S073	Flotsam and Jetsam	C	0.25
S034	Forgotten Corridor	X	0.50
S027	Founatain Room	X	0.50
S166	Friendly Soldier	R	2.80
S061	Frogman	C	0.25
S117	Gangplank	U	0.80
S198	Gemini	R	4.00
S050	Geyser Eruption	X	0.50
7			
S047	Gigantic Eel	C/X	0.50
S080	Go in Shooting	C	0.25
S170	Grenade	R	4.00
S128	Gun Belt	U	0.80
S178	Hand of Midas	R	3.50
S120	Harpoon Gun	U	0.80
S078	Harpoons	C	0.25
S033	Hidden Back Room	X	0.50
S056	Hidden Exit	C	0.25
8			
S011	Hidden Lair	X	0.50
S097	Hidden Trap	C	0.25
S182	Horn of the Sea	R	4.00
S007	Intersection	X	0.50
S175	It Belongs in a Museum	R	3.50
S111	Keel	U	0.80
S119	Killer Whales	U	0.80
S140	King of the Hill	U	0.80
S185	Lara Croft, Athlete	R	7.00
9			
S183	Lara Croft, Code Breaker	R	7.00
S184	Lara Croft, Crusader	R	7.50
S044	Lara Croft, Mariner	X	2.00
S189	Lara Croft, Navigator	R	7.00
S069	Lara Croft, Oceanographer	C	0.25
S186	Lara Croft, Olympian	R	6.00
S019	Lara Croft, Scuba Diver	X	2.00
S187	Lara Croft, Strategist	R	8.00
S188	Lara Croft, Tactitian	R	6.00

#	Card name	Rarity	Price
10			
S190	Lara Croft, Tomb Raider	R	10.00
S193	Larsen, Master Thief	R	4.00
S087	Last Gasp	C	0.25
S169	Leather Gloves	R	3.00
S173	Limiting Options	R	3.00
S054	Look Again	C	0.25
S109	Lower Chamber	U	0.80
S053	Magnum Pistols	C	0.25
S177	Mapped Terrain	R	3.50
11			
S200	Marianis	R	3.00
S176	Maximize Resources	R	3.00
S129	Mechanical Cog	U	0.80
S139	Moment of Triumph	U	0.80
S098	Monkey	C	0.25
S084	Monkey Swing	C	0.25
S124	Mother Load	U	0.80
S095	Mud	C	0.25
S137	Mud Slide	U	0.80
12			
S042	Murkey Depths	X	0.50
S088	Native Guide	C	0.25
S118	Navigation Room	U	0.80
S028	Neptune's Sanctum	X	0.50
S045	Neptune's Trident	X	0.50
S081	No Pain, No Gain	C	0.25
S123	No Retreat	U	0.80
S162	Open Pit	R	2.80
S135	Ornate Key	U	0.80
13			
S071	Over Achiever	C	0.25
S085	Overwhelmed	C	0.25
S072	Panic Attack	C	0.25
S131	Parrot	U	0.80
S121	Passport	U	0.80
S020	Pearl of the Pacific	X	0.50
S180	Pieces of Eight	R	3.50
S194	Pierre, Renaissance Man	R	4.00
S148	Piranhas	U	0.80
14			
S199	Pisces	R	3.00
S055	Pit Trap	C	0.25
S043	Pool	X	0.50
S113	Port Side	U	0.80
S130	Propulsion Unit	U	0.80
S159	Puna	R	2.80
S141	Puzzle Trap	U	0.80
S136	Quick Sand	U	0.80

#	Card name	Rarity	Price
S004	Quiet Chamber	X	0.50
15			
S062	Rats	C	0.25
S075	Ready, Set, Go	C	0.25
S094	Recycle Resources	C	0.25
S079	Reevaluate	C	0.25
S171	Rest and Recover	R	3.50
S125	Reverse Play	U	0.80
S083	Ride the Wave	C	0.25
S160	Rig Boss	R	2.80
S150	Rig Worker	U	0.80
16			
S025	Riptide	X	0.50
S092	Roll With It	C	0.25
S168	Roman Idol	R	3.50
S058	Save Point	C	0.25
S093	Scouting Mission	C	0.25
S010	Sea Caves	X	0.50
S153	Secret Depths	R	3.50
S201	Secret Move 1	UR	15.00
S202	Secret Move 2	UR	15.00
17			
S203	Secret Move 3	UR	15.00
S204	Secret Move 4	UR	15.00
S205	Secret Move 5	UR	15.00
S206	Secret Move 6	UR	15.00
S207	Secret Move 7	UR	15.00
S208	Secret Move 8	UR	15.00
S209	Secret Move 9	UR	15.00
S172	Secrets Revealed	R	3.00
S196	Sergeant Steel	R	4.00
18			
S022	Shark	X	0.50
S066	Shark Knife	C	0.25
S167	Shark Tooth	R	3.50
S161	Shiva	R	3.50
S149	Shiva Statue	U	0.80
S040	Side Passageway	X	0.50
S191	Skateboard Kid, Mad Thrasher	R	4.00
S086	Sleight of Hand	C	0.25
S067	Slick Surface	C	0.25
19			
S142	Sliding Plates	U	0.80
S052	Small Medi Pack	C	0.25
S099	Snake	C	0.25
S023	Snorkeling Goggles	X	0.50

RARITY KEY C = Common U = Uncommon R = Rare VR = Very Rare UR = Ultra Rare F = Foil card X = Fixed/standard in all decks

DRAGON IDOL

Item Discovery

Whenever another Tomb Raider gains Life you gain an equal amount of Life (up to your maximum Life).

All of a sudden, I'm feeling much better.

TM & © 2000 Eidos and Core. Game Design © 2000 Precedence Entertainment, Big Guns.

Tomb Raider • Big Guns

Precedence • Released April 2000

159 cards in set • **IDENTIFIER: 'B' before card number**

• Booster packs contain 24 cards; booster displays contain 24 boosters

Big Guns is set in the mysterious Lost Valley, home to T-Rexes, Raptors, and Dragons. In this episode — er, expansion, Lara is searching for the legendary Dagger of Xian. She has to go through five new rival Tomb Raiders and dinosaurs as well as the usual mix of traps and dangers in order to reach her goal.

Precedence had announced a subsequent expansion, tentatively titled **Uncovered**, that would have concentrated on the darker urban, and mystically mysterious side of Lara and her adventures, for release in the summer of 2000, but it never saw the light of day. The CCG adventures of Lara Croft seem to have come to an end, as there have been no new releases for **Tomb Raider** since Big Guns. — **James Mishler**

You will need **18** nine-pocket pages to store this set. (9 doubled up)

Set (159 cards)	85.00
Booster Display Box	70.00
Booster Pack	2.50

#	Card name	Rarity	Price
21	Aftershock	C	0.25
48	Air Bubble	C	0.25
3	Alcove	C	0.25
50	All Out Attack	C	0.25
144	Amazon	R	4.00
147	Amber Fossil	R	4.00
148	Ancient Relic	R	4.00
74	Ancient Ruins	U	1.00
76	Antechamber	U	1.00
49	Aquatic Assault	C	0.25
8	Armored Vest	C	0.25
27	Bestial Rage	C	0.25
139	Black Beard, Buccaneer	R	4.00
73	Broken Bridge	U	1.00
1	Campsite	C	0.25
7	Cat Idol	C	0.25
66	Chasm	U	1.00
55	Cliff Face	U	1.00
26	Competitive Drive	C	0.25
11	Compsognathus	C	0.25
91	Cooperation	U	1.00
60	Crash Site	U	1.00
24	Crows	C	0.25
150	Dagger of Xian	R	5.00
98	Dangerous Terrain	U	1.00
59	Dark Corridor	U	1.00
30	Delaying Tactics	C	0.25
119	Detailed Study	R	4.00
41	Direct Assault	C	0.25
38	Disarm Trap	C	0.25
79	Diving Suit	U	1.00
141	Dr. Virgo	R	4.00
116	Dragon	R	4.00
111	Dragon Idol	R	4.00
107	Dream State	R	4.00
97	Drop Down	U	1.00

#	Card name	Rarity	Price
75	Dry River Bed	U	1.00
114	Earthquake	R	4.00
33	Easy Find	C	0.25
112	Faithful Butler	R	4.00
57	Firing Platform	U	1.00
120	First Aid	R	4.00
104	Flame Thrower	R	4.00
115	Flaming Pillars	R	4.00
40	Forced Draw	C	0.25
35	Forward Momentum	C	0.25
78	Fuel Tank	U	1.00
92	Future Investment	U	1.00
64	Garden	U	1.00
137	Gemini, Thrill Seeker	R	4.00
89	Giant Spider	U	1.00
110	Gold Key	R	4.00
54	Gorge	U	1.00
80	Grappling Hook	U	1.00
84	Green Dragonette	U	1.00
20	Guardian	C	0.25
72	Heartstone	U	1.00
44	Hidden Attack	C	0.25
58	Hidden Niche	U	1.00
9	Hidden Switch	C	0.25
125	Increase Threat	R	4.00
123	Infighting	R	4.00
28	Inspiration	C	0.25
146	Jade Mask	R	4.00
63	Jungle Path	U	1.00
124	Just Reward	R	4.00
85	Killer Bees	U	1.00
52	Lagoon	U	1.00
130	Lara Croft, Anthropologist	R	7.50
135	Lara Croft, Champion	R	10.00
128	Lara Croft, Commando	R	6.00
134	Lara Croft, Daredevil	R	8.00
129	Lara Croft, Gymnast	R	7.50
131	Lara Croft, Martial Artist	R	8.00
126	Lara Croft, Mercenary	R	6.00
127	Lara Croft, Scholar	R	5.00
132	Lara Croft, Survivor	R	6.00

#	Card name	Rarity	Price
133	Lara Croft, Trail Blazer	R	7.00
87	Leopard	U	1.00
83	Lightning Trap	U	1.00
143	Lord Drake	R	4.00
102	M16 Assault Rifle	R	4.00
77	M16 Clip	U	1.00
6	Machete	C	0.25
43	Malfunction	C	0.25
140	Marianis, Puppet Master	R	4.00
142	Mr. Suit	R	4.00
70	Narrow Ledge	U	1.00
39	Nine Lives	C	0.25
65	Obscured Tunnel	U	1.00
46	Old Tricks	C	0.25
145	Panthar	R	4.00
34	Perfect Shot	C	0.25
138	Pisces, Test Subject	R	4.00
105	Poison Dart	R	4.00
18	Pressure Plate	C	0.25
103	Quad Bike	R	4.00
82	Quagmire	U	1.00
94	Race to the Finish	U	1.00
90	Raptor	U	1.00
61	Raptor Nest	U	1.00
118	Raptor Pack	R	4.00
51	Ravine	U	1.00
81	Razor Disks	U	1.00
25	Razor Grass	C	0.25
47	Refresh	C	0.25
42	Reload	C	0.25
56	River Rapids	U	1.00
5	Rocket	C	0.25
101	Rocket Launcher	R	4.00
88	Rolling Blades	U	1.00
31	Search and Destroy	C	0.25
121	Secret Identity	R	4.00
108	Secret Location	R	4.00
151	Secret Move 1	SR	10.50
152	Secret Move 2	SR	10.50
153	Secret Move 3	SR	10.50
154	Secret Move 4	SR	10.50

#	Card name	Rarity	Price
155	Secret Move 5	SR	10.50
156	Secret Move 6	SR	10.50
157	Secret Move 7	SR	10.50
158	Secret Move 8	SR	10.50
159	Secret Move 9	SR	10.50
93	Secrets Betrayed	U	1.00
122	Separate Paths	R	4.00
136	Sergeant Steel, Veteran	R	4.00
149	Serpent Stone	R	4.00
95	Setbacks	U	1.00
113	Shutoff Switch	R	4.00
45	Slow Progress	C	0.25
23	Snake Pit	C	0.25
22	Spiders	C	0.25
29	Staying Ahead	C	0.25
10	Stopwatch	C	0.25
37	Stymied	C	0.25
36	Surrounded	C	0.25
69	Swamp	U	1.00
17	Switch Puzzle	C	0.25
117	T Rex	R	4.00
4	T-Rex Lair	C	0.25
16	Tar Pits	C	0.25
109	Tent	R	4.00
99	The Greater Prize	U	1.00
12	Thick Fog	C	0.25
86	Tiger	U	1.00
106	Tranquilizer Dart	R	4.00
68	Tree Canopy	U	1.00
71	Tree House	U	1.00
2	Tribal Village	C	0.25
14	Tribal Warrior	C	0.25
32	Trigger Trap	C	0.25
62	Tropical Stream	U	1.00
100	Unfair Advantage	U	1.00
53	Upper Ridge	U	1.00
96	Use the Angles	U	1.00
67	Valley Floor	U	1.00
15	Wasps	C	0.25
19	Whitewater Rapids	C	0.25
13	Witchdoctor	C	0.25

RARITY KEY C = Common • U = Uncommon • R = Rare • VR = Very Rare • UR = Ultra Rare • F = Foil card • X = Fixed/standard in all decks

462 • *SCRYE Collectible Card Game Checklist and Price Guide*

Top of the Order

Donruss/NXT Games • Released **October 1995**

360 cards in set

- Starter decks contain 80 cards; starter displays contain 10 starters
- Booster packs contain 12 cards; booster displays contain 36 boosters

Deisgned by **Duncan Macdonell**

Concept	●●●○○
Gameplay	●●○○○
Card art	●●●○○
Player pool	○○○○○

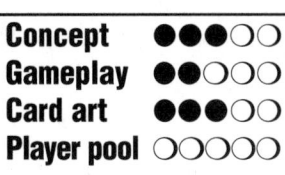

The second part of Donruss' entry into the CCG market, *Top of the Order* provided CCGs their first taste of the American pastime.

An extremely detailed baseball card game, *Top of the Order* has only one type of card, the Player card. Each card has 17 statistics, allowing them to be used for a variety of game purposes. A game begins with the managers (game players) drafting their lineup with alternating picks (each Player card is unique). Once the managers have their line-ups set, play begins. The offensive (at-bat) manager plays a card representing the type of swing the batter is using, while the defensive manager chooses the pitch with a card play. Both managers draw the top card of their deck and compare them to reveal the outcome, referring to one or more tables.

This game covers every aspect of baseball, steals, righty/lefty percentages, advancing on outs, infield depth, and even size of the ballpark. The game resemblea Strat-O-Matic baseball in its detail, with every Player rated in nine categories of performance (1994 season). It's an impressive simulation whose concept would have better suited to a non-CCG format. As such, *Top of the Order* fared slightly worse than its sister game, **Red Zone**, and did not survive to the next season.

Interesting artifacts for this game and *Red Zone* include introductory videos featuring sportscast-like presentations. — *Michael Greenholdt*

You will need **40** nine-pocket pages to store this set. (20 doubled up)

Set (360 cards)	126.00
Starter Display Box	27.00
Booster Display Box	35.00
Double Deck Game Set	12.75
Starter Deck	7.50
Booster Pack	1.50

Card name	Rarity	Price
Abbott, Jim	C	0.25
Abbott, Kurt	C	0.25
Aguilera, Rick	VC	0.10
Alicea, Luis	C	0.25
Alomar, Jr., Sandy	R	2.00
Alomar, Roberto	R	2.00
Alou, Moises	R	2.00
Anderson, Brady	C	0.25
Appier, Kevin	R	2.00
Ashby, Andy	U	0.50
Ashley, Billy	C	0.25
Ausmus, Brad	U	0.50
Avery, Steve	C	0.25
Ayala, Bobby	R	2.00
Baerga, Carlos	R	2.00
Bagwell, Jeff	U	1.00
Baines, Harold	U	0.50
Barberie, Bret	U	0.50
Bates, Jason	C	0.25
Bautista, Danny	C	0.25
Beck, Rod	U	0.50
Bell, Derek	R	2.00
Bell, Jay	C	0.25
Belle, Albert	R	2.00
Benes, Andy	U	0.50
Benitez, Armando	C	0.25
Benjamin, Mike	U	0.50
Bere, Jason	C	0.25
Berroa, Geronimo	C	0.25
Berry, Sean	U	0.50
Bichette, Dante	R	2.00
Biggio, Craig	U	0.50
Blauser, Jeff	C	0.25
Blowers, Mike	C	0.25
Boever, Joe	C	0.25

Card name	Rarity	Price
Boggs, Wade	R	3.00
Bonds, Barry	R	2.00
Bones, Ricky	C	0.25
Bonilla, Bobby	U	1.00
Boone, Bret	R	2.00
Bordick, Mike	U	0.50
Bottalico, Ricky	U	0.50
Branson, Jeff	U	0.50
Brantley, Jeff	R	2.00
Brewer, Billy	C	0.25
Brogna, Rico	C	0.25
Brosius, Scott	C	0.25
Brumfield, Jacob	C	0.25
Buhner, Jay	U	0.50
Bullinger, Jim	U	0.50
Burkett, John	C	0.25
Butcher, Mike	C	0.25
Butler, Brett	C	0.25
Caminiti, Ken	U	0.50
Candiotti, Tom	U	0.50
Canseco, Jose	U	1.50
Carr, Chuck	C	0.25
Carrasco, Hector	C	0.25
Carter, Joe	R	2.00
Castilla, Vinny	U	0.50
Cedeno, Andujar	VC	0.10
Clark, Dave	U	0.50
Clark, Will	R	2.00
Clayton, Royce	C	0.25
Clemens, Roger	C	0.25
Colbrunn, Greg	C	0.25
Cole, Alex	U	0.50
Coleman, Vince	R	2.00
Cone, David	U	0.50
Conine, Jeff	R	2.00
Cooper, Scott	C	0.25
Cora, Joey	U	0.50
Cordero, Wil	U	0.50
Cordova, Marty	C	0.25
Curtis, Chad	C	0.25
Daulton, Darren	VC	0.10
Davis, Chili	R	2.00
Dawson, Andre	VC	0.10

Card name	Rarity	Price
Deshields, Delino	C	0.25
Devereaux, Mike	U	0.50
Diaz, Alex	C	0.25
Disarcina, Gary	R	2.00
Drabek, Doug	C	0.25
Duan, Mariano	U	0.50
Dunston, Shawon	R	2.00
Durham, Ray	C	0.25
Dykstra, Lenny	U	0.50
Easley, Damion	C	0.25
Eckersley, Dennis	C	0.25
Edmonds, Jim	R	2.00
Eisenreich, Jim	U	0.50
Erickson, Scott	C	0.25
Eusebio, Tony	U	0.50
Fassero, Jeff	C	0.25
Fernandez, Alex	VC	0.10
Fernandez, Tony	C	0.25
Fetters, Mike	C	0.25
Fielder, Cecil	U	0.50
Finley, Chuck	U	0.50
Finley, Steve	R	2.00
Flaherty, John	U	0.50
Fletcher, Darrin	C	0.25
Foster, Kevin	C	0.25
Franco, John	C	0.25
Frye, Jeff	U	0.50
Fryman, Travis	U	0.50
Gaetti, Gary	C	0.25
Gagne, Greg	C	0.25
Galarraga, Andres	R	2.00
Gant, Ron	R	2.00
Garcia, Carlos	C	0.25
Gates, Brent	C	0.25
Gibson, Kirk	C	0.25
Gil, Benji	C	0.25
Gilkey, Bernard	R	2.00
Girardi, Joe	U	0.50
Glavine, Tom	U	0.50
Gomez, Chris	C	0.25
Gomez, Leo	C	0.25
Gonzalez, Alex	C	0.25
Gonzalez, Juan	C	0.25

Card name	Rarity	Price
Gonzalez, Luis	C	0.25
Goodwin, Curtis	R	2.00
Goodwin, Tom	R	2.00
Gordon, Tom	C	0.25
Grace, Mark	R	2.00
Green, Tyler	U	0.50
Greenwell, Mike	U	0.50
Greer, Rusty	C	0.25
Griffey, Jr., Ken	R	12.00
Grissom, Marquis	R	2.00
Gubicza, Mark	C	0.25
Guillen, Ozzie	R	2.00
Gwynn, Tony	R	2.00
Hamelin, Bob	C	0.25
Hamilton, Darryl	C	0.25
Hamilton, Joey	C	0.25
Hammond, Chris	R	2.00
Hammonds, Jeffrey	C	0.25
Hanson, Erik	C	0.25
Harnisch, Pete	C	0.25
Harris, Lenny	C	0.25
Hayes, Charlie	U	0.50
Henderson, Rickey	U	0.50
Henke, Tom	R	2.00
Henneman, Mike	R	2.00
Hernandez, Roberto	C	0.25
Hiatt, Phil	U	0.50
Higginson, Bob	C	0.25
Hill, Glenallen	C	0.25
Hill, Ken	C	0.25
Hoffman, Trevor	C	0.25
Hoiles, Chris	C	0.25
Hollins, Dave	C	0.25
Hudek, John	C	0.25
Hundley, Todd	C	0.25
Hunter, Brian	U	0.50
Jackson, Danny	C	0.25
Javier, Stan	C	0.25
Jefferies, Gregg	VC	0.10
Johnson, Charles	C	0.25
Johnson, Lance	U	0.50
Johnson, Mark	C	0.25
Johnson, Randy	R	2.00

Card name	Rarity	Price
Jones, Bobby	C	0.25
Jones, Chipper	C	0.25
Jones, Doug	C	0.25
Jones, Todd	R	2.00
Jordan, Brian	R	2.00
Joyner, Wally	R	2.00
Justice, David	R	2.00
Karkovice, Ron	C	0.25
Karros, Eric	R	2.00
Kelly, Roberto	C	0.25
Kent, Jeff	C	0.25
King, Jeff	C	0.25
Kingery, Mike	C	0.25
Klesko, Ryan	U	0.50
Knoblauch, Chuck	R	2.00
Langston, Mark	C	0.25
Lankford, Ray	U	0.50
Lansing, Mike	C	0.25
Larkin, Barry	R	2.00
Leius, Scott	VC	0.10
Lemke, Mark	C	0.25
Lewis, Darren	C	0.25
Liriano, Nelson	U	0.50
Listach, Pat	C	0.25
Lofton, Kenny	R	2.00
Lopez, Javy	C	0.25
Mabry, John	U	0.50
Macfarlane, Mike	C	0.25
Maddux, Greg	R	9.00
Magadan, Dave	U	0.50
Maldonado, Candy	VC	0.10
Manwaring, Kirt	C	0.25
Martin, Al	U	0.50
Martinez, Dennis	C	0.25
Martinez, Edgar	R	2.00
Martinez, Pedro	R	2.00
Martinez, Ramon	C	0.25
Martinez, Tino	R	2.00
Mattingly, Don	R	2.00
Mayne, Brent	C	0.25
McDonald, Ben	U	0.50
Mcdowell, Jack	C	0.25
Mcgriff, Fred	R	2.00

RARITY KEY **VC** = Very Common **C** = Common **U** = Uncommon **R** = Rare **UR** = Ultra Rare **X** = Fixed/standard in all decks

Card name	Rarity	Price		Card name	Rarity	Price		Card name	Rarity	Price		Card name	Rarity	Price		Card name	Rarity	Price
[24]				O'Leary, Troy	U	0.50		Reed, Steve	R	2.00		Smith, Ozzie	U	1.00		Vanlandingham, William	C	0.25
Mcgwire, Mark	R	15.00		O'Neill, Paul	U	0.50		Reynolds, Shane	C	0.25		Smoltz, John	R	2.00		Vaughn, Greg	C	0.25
Mclemore, Mark	R	2.00		Offerman, Jose	U	0.50		[31]				Snow, J.T.	U	0.50		Vaughn, Mo	R	2.00
McMichael, Greg	U	0.50		Olerud, John	VC	0.10		Rijo, Jose	U	0.50		Sorrento, Paul	C	0.25		[38]		
Mcrae, Brian	R	2.00		Oliver, Joe	U	0.50		Ripken, Jr., Cal	R	12.00		Sosa, Sammy	R	8.00		Velarde, Randy	VC	0.10
Meares, Pat	C	0.25		Ontiveros, Steve	U	0.50		Risley, Bill	R	2.00		Sprague, Ed	C	0.25		Ventura, Robin	U	0.50
Merced, Orlando	U	0.50		[28]				Roberts, Bip	R	2.00		Stahoviak, Scott	C	0.25		Veras, Quilvio	C	0.25
Mesa, Jose	U	0.50		Oquendo, Jose	C	0.25		Rodriguez, Alex	C	0.25		[35]				Vizcaino, Jose	C	0.25
Miceli, Dan	U	0.50		Orsulak, Joe	U	0.50		Rodriguez, Ivan	R	2.00		Stanley, Mike	C	0.25		Vizquel, Omar	C	0.25
Mieske, Matt	C	0.25		Owen, Spike	C	0.25		Rogers, Kenny	C	0.25		Steinbach, Terry	C	0.25		Walbeck, Matt	C	0.25
[25]				Pagnozzi, Tom	C	0.25		Rojas, Mel	U	0.50		Stocker, Kevin	C	0.25		Walker, Larry	R	2.00
Miller, Orlando	C	0.25		Palmeiro, Rafael	R	2.00		Ruffin, Bruce	U	0.50		Stottlemyre, Todd	R	2.00		Wallach, Tim	C	0.25
Molitor, Paul	C	0.25		Palmer, Dean	R	2.00		[32]				Surhoff, B.J.	U	0.50		Wegman, Bill	C	0.25
Mondesi, Raul	R	2.00		Parent, Mark	C	0.25		Russell, Jeff	C	0.25		Swift, Bill	C	0.25		[39]		
Montgomery, Jeff	C	0.25		Parrish, Lance	C	0.25		Ryan, Ken	C	0.25		Swindell, Greg	C	0.25		Weiss, Walt	C	0.25
Morandini, Mickey	U	0.50		Patterson, John	C	0.25		Saberhagen, Bret	U	0.50		Tapani, Kevin	C	0.25		Wells, David	C	0.25
Morris, Hal	C	0.25		[29]				Salmon, Tim	R	2.00		Tarasco, Tony	U	0.50		Wetteland, John	R	2.00
Mouton, James	C	0.25		Pena, Tony	C	0.25		Sanchez, Rey	U	0.50		[36]				Whitaker, Lou	R	2.00
Mulholland, Terry	C	0.25		Pendleton, Terry	U	0.50		Sanders, Deion	R	5.00		Tartabull, Danny	C	0.25		White, Devon	U	0.50
Munoz, Pedro	C	0.25		Percival, Troy	R	2.00		Sanders, Reggie	R	2.00		Taubensee, Eddie	C	0.25		White, Rondell	C	0.25
[26]				Perez, Carlos	U	0.50		Scarsone, Steve	U	0.50		Tettleton, Mickey	C	0.25		Wickman, Bob	C	0.25
Murray, Eddie	R	2.00		Perez, Melido	C	0.25		Schilling, Curt	R	3.00		Tewksbury, Bob	C	0.25		Williams, Bernie	R	2.00
Mussina, Mike	U	0.50		Phillips, J.R.	C	0.25		[33]				Thomas, Frank	R	2.00		Williams, Eddie	C	0.25
Myers, Greg	C	0.25		Phillips, Tony	U	0.50		Schourek, Pete	U	0.50		Thome, Jim	R	2.00		[40]		
Myers, Randy	R	2.00		Piazza, Mike	R	2.00		Scott, Tim	R	2.00		Thompson, Robby	C	0.25		Williams, Gerald	C	0.25
Naehring, Tim	R	2.00		Plesac, Dan	R	2.00		Segui, David	U	0.50		Thompson, Ryan	U	0.50		Williams, Matt	R	2.00
Nagy, Charles	C	0.25		[30]				Seitzer, Kevin	U	0.50		Tinsley, Lee	U	0.50		Williams, Woody	C	0.25
Navarro, Jaime	U	0.50		Plunk, Eric	R	2.00		Sele, Aaron	C	0.25		[37]				Wilson, Dan	C	0.25
Neagle, Denny	C	0.25		Polonia, Luis	C	0.25		Servais, Scott	C	0.25		Trachsel, Steve	U	0.50		Witt, Bobby	U	0.50
Nen, Robb	C	0.25		Portugal, Mark	C	0.25		Sheffield, Gary	R	2.00		Trammell, Alan	U	0.50		Wohlers, Mark	R	2.00
[27]				Puckett, Kirby	R	2.00		Sierra, Ruben	C	0.25		Trombley, Mike	C	0.25		Worrell, Todd	R	2.00
Nilsson, Dave	C	0.25		Raines, Tim	U	0.50		Slocumb, Heathcliff	U	0.50		Valdes, Ismael	U	0.50		Young, Eric	C	0.25
Nixon, Otis	U	0.50		Ramirez, Manny	R	2.00		[34]				Valentin, John	R	2.00		Zeile, Todd	C	0.25
Nomo, Hideo	R	2.00		Reed, Jody	C	0.25		Smiley, John	C	0.25		Valentin, Jose	C	0.25				
								Smith, Lee	R	2.00								

Towers in Time

Thunder Castle Games • Released **April 1995**

	Concept	●○○○○
	Gameplay	●●○○○
	Card art	●●○○○
	Player pool	○○○○○

150 cards in set

- Starter decks contain 56 cards; starter displays contain 12 starters
- Booster packs contain 8 cards; booster displays contain 60 boosters

Designed by **Mike Sager**

You will need **17** nine-pocket pages to store this set. (9 doubled up)

It's an illustration of how new a product CCGs were that **Towers in Time** was able to leave the building *without any rules*. That's right, starter decks came with cards and a phone number to call for free rules — not even toll free!

It must have been apparent even in the new and wild frontier of CCGs that players actually wanted rules, since Thunder Castle did run them in *Scrye #4*. That may not have helped its cause, as gamers found that the places where *Towers in Time* isn't that bad are the places where it's borrowing from **Magic**.

Players portray wizards warring between dimensions. (Hmmm.) Instead of trying to reduce an opponent to zero life, they try to destroy his five "shields" that keep him in this dimension. Each shield can take four points of damage. (20 points in all. Hmmm.) Minor creatures that get past "blockers" do one point, mediums do two, and large do four. There are six "schools": Fire, Water, Air, Earth, White, and Black. (Hmmm...)

OK, enough with the similarities. *Towers* does add the "Tower" concept, in which monsters in a "Tower" gain +1 to attack and defense. (Like, say, a **Magic** Castle. Oops, sorry.)

The art is not unpleasant, but the cards are a jumble of icons, many of which are not explained on the "icon explanation" card that actually is included in the starter deck!

Thunder Castle may have announced more expansions that never came out than any other CCG manufacturer, including **Greek, Zodiac, Amazon,** and **Norse** for *Towers*. Ambition may well have been the *only* thing not lacking in this effort. — **James Mishler**

Wraith Death Knights 1 8 4 4

Cannot be killed in a combat phase. Immune to white magic.
© Illus. Andrew Hale   TO 039

Set (150 cards)	36.00	
Starter Display Box	23.00	
Booster Display Box	27.00	
Starter Deck	4.50	
Booster Pack	1.00	

#	Card name	Rarity	Price		#	Card name	Rarity	Price		#	Card name	Rarity	Price
[1]					☐ TO10	Ater's Iron Golem	R	1.25		☐ TO58	Cone of Cold	U	0.25
☐ TO132	Airy Water	U	0.25		☐ TO09	Ater's Stone Golem	R	1.10		☐ TO29	Crown of Command	R	1.00
☐ TO149	Ant Lion	U	0.25		☐ TO30	Ax of Might	R	1.00		[3]			
☐ TO102	Armor	U	0.25		☐ TO48	Barbarian Raiders	U	0.25		☐ TO78	Desert	C	0.15
☐ TO100	Assault with Stone	R	1.00		[2]					☐ TO128	Destroy	R	1.25
☐ TO11	Ater's Gargoyle	R	1.25		☐ TO47	Barbarian Thralls	U	0.25		☐ TO127	Diffuse	U	0.40
					☐ TO32	Boots of Speed	U	1.00		☐ TO131	Dispel	U	0.40
					☐ TO31	Bow of the Glade	R	1.00		☐ TO59	Disrupt Transport	U	0.40
					☐ TO84	Breathe Fire	U	0.25		☐ TO65	Drown	R	1.25
					☐ TO150	Cloaker	U	0.25		☐ TO112	Dwarf Cannons	C	0.25
					☐ TO138	Cloud	C	0.15		☐ TO111	Dwarf Catapult	C	0.25
					☐ TO142	Cloud Giant	R	1.25		☐ TO109	Dwarven Dragon Flyer	R	1.00

#	Card name	Rarity	Price
[4]			
☐ TO110	Dwarven Home Guard	U	0.40
☐ TO116	Dwarven Militia	C	0.15
☐ TO114	Dwarven Riflemen	U	0.25
☐ TO3	Eagle	U	0.25
☐ TO41	Elail, Elf Prince	R	1.25
☐ TO52	Empower Tower	U	0.40
☐ TO50	Essence Enhancement	U	0.40
☐ TO1	Falcon	U	0.25
☐ TO79	Fire Ball	U	0.25
[5]			
☐ TO85	Fire Beetle	R	1.00

RARITY KEY **VC** = Very Common **C** = Common **U** = Uncommon **R** = Rare **UR** = Ultra Rare **X** = Fixed/standard in all decks

464 • SCRYE Collectible Card Game Checklist and Price Guide

#	Card name	Rarity	Price		#	Card name	Rarity	Price		#	Card name	Rarity	Price		#	Card name	Rarity	Price
TO88	Fire Drake	U	0.25		TO134	Levitate Tower	U	0.25		TO38	Mranth Troll	R	1.25		TO103	Strength of Stone	U	0.25
TO76	Fire Storm	C	0.15		TO147	Lightning Bug	R	1.00		TO87	Mroar Phoenix	R	1.00		TO123	Summon Skeletons	U	0.25
TO82	Flame Strike	R	1.25		TO130	Lightning Reflexes	U	0.25		TO86	Mroar Salamander	U	0.25		TO122	Summon Spectre	U	0.25
TO27	Flaming Sword	R	1.00		TO71	Mjorn Elemental	C	0.15		TO25	Necklace of Elements	R	1.00		TO121	Summon Wraith	U	0.40
TO81	Flare	U	0.25		TO72	Mjorn Elemental	C	0.15		TO15	Orb of Doomar	R	1.25		TO26	Sword of Swiftness	R	1.00
TO148	Flare Beetle	U	0.40		TO73	Mjorn Elemental	C	0.15		TO13	Orb of Nulification	R	1.25	15	TO33	The Assasin, Ashar	R	1.50
TO60	Flood	U	0.25		TO93	Mjorn Elemental	C	0.15	12	TO14	Orb of Power	R	1.25		TO34	The Great Strategist	R	1.50
TO133	Fly	U	0.25	9	TO94	Mjorn Elemental	C	0.15		TO16	Orb of Weakness	R	1.00		TO46	The Mad Norseman	C	0.15
6	TO17	Flying Sandals	R	1.00		TO95	Mjorn Elemental	C	0.15		TO40	Order of Light	R	1.00		TO135	Thunderhead	C	0.15
TO105	Forest	C	0.15		TO117	Mjorn Elemental	C	0.15		TO70	Pirate Ship	U	0.25		TO5	Tortoise	U	0.25
TO77	Forest Fire	C	0.15		TO118	Mjorn Elemental	C	0.15		TO69	Pirates	U	0.25		TO146	Uknek, Karak Prince	R	1.00
TO8	Frog	U	0.25		TO119	Mjorn Elemental	C	0.15		TO107	Plain	C	0.15		TO35	Ulath Healers	R	1.00
TO12	Gate to Aegea	R	1.25		TO139	Mjorn Elemental	C	0.15		TO124	Raise Dead	U	0.25		TO74	Ulathian Sea Dragon	R	1.00
TO97	Gate to Mranth	R	1.25		TO140	Mjorn Elemental	C	0.15		TO18	Ring of Stars	R	1.00		TO115	Ulgar, Dwarven Prince	R	1.25
TO51	Heal	C	0.15		TO141	Mjorn Elemental	C	0.15		TO55	River	C	0.15	16	TO108	Valley	C	0.15
TO106	Hill	C	0.15		TO42	Mjorn Elf Cavalry	U	0.25	13	TO7	Scorpion	U	0.25		TO75	Valley of Fire	C	0.15
TO20	Holy Shield	R	1.00	10	TO44	Mjorn Elf Death Dealers	U	0.25		TO62	Sea Elf Galley	U	0.25		TO83	Volcano	U	0.25
7	TO19	Holy Sword	R	1.00		TO43	Mjorn Elf Scouts	R	1.00		TO64	Sea Elf Guard	U	0.25		TO125	Walking Dead	U	0.40
TO53	Hot Spring	C	0.15		TO36	Mjorn Healers	U	0.25		TO61	Sea Elf Gunboat	R	1.25		TO80	Wall of Fire	U	0.25
TO49	Humble	U	0.25		TO98	Mountain	C	0.15		TO63	Sea Elf Marines	U	0.25		TO57	Wall of Ice	U	0.25
TO56	Iceberg	C	0.15		TO113	Mountain Dwarves	U	0.40		TO67	Sea Nymph	U	0.25		TO99	Wall of Stone	U	0.25
TO129	Invisibility	R	1.25		TO39	Mranth Death Knights	R	1.25		TO4	Seal	U	0.25		TO22	Wand of Fire	R	1.25
TO143	Karak Dive Bombers	R	1.25		TO96	Mranth Dragon	R	1.00		TO28	Shield of Protection	R	1.25		TO21	Wand of Frost	R	1.25
TO145	Karak Militia	U	0.25		TO37	Mranth Ogre	U	0.25		TO68	Siren	R	1.00	17	TO24	Wand of Lightning	R	1.00
TO144	Karak Regulars	C	0.15		TO89	Mranth Orc Boar Riders	R	1.00	14	TO2	Snake	U	0.25		TO23	Wand of Stone	R	1.25
TO126	Kill	R	1.50	11	TO90	Mranth Orc Catapult	U	0.25		TO104	Solid Ground	U	0.40		TO66	Water Breathing	U	0.25
8	TO54	Lake	C	0.15		TO92	Mranth Orc Maurauders	U	0.25		TO120	Stone Giant	R	1.00		TO137	Wind	C	0.15
TO45	Lars' Norse Raiders	U	0.25		TO91	Mranth Orcs	C	0.15		TO101	Stone Skin	R	1.00		TO6	Wolverine	U	0.25
															TO136	Zepher	C	0.15

Ultimate Combat!

Ultimate Games • First set, *Limited*, released **May 1995**

266 cards in set • **IDENTIFIER: Cards say 'Limited'**

• Starter decks contain 60 cards, rules and quickstart card; displays contain 10 starters
• Booster packs contain 15 cards; booster displays contain 36 boosters

Designed by **Dave Long**

You will need **30** nine-pocket pages to store this set. (15 doubled up)

If all CCGs are relatives of *Magic: the Gathering*, then *Ultimate Combat!* is its most direct descendent. Roughly 75% of the rules are the same. It is often easier to describe the game in how it differs from *Magic* than on its own merits.

Thematically, *Ultimate Combat!* is distinct from other CCGs, even if those who've never played confuse it with *Shadowfist* because they were released a month apart and sound similar. The genre is martial arts, but as a sport; real martial artists designed the game, which is endorsed by the U.S. Judo Association Team, the U.S. Taekwondo Team, and the U.S.A. Wrestling Team. Though realism is prevalent in the game, an important secondary theme is psychic power.

It doesn't take long to see similarities to *Magic*. Players start at 20 hit points and can lose by running out of hit points or cards. Cards are played by paying the "power" cost; power is generated by "draining" foundation, of which there are four types: knowledge, experience, fighting spirit, and conditioning. The phases of a turn are recovery (akin to untap and upkeep), draw, build (see below), activity (main), attack subphase in the middle of the activity phase, and discard. Players play one foundation during the build phase, much like *Magic*'s one land per turn, but with a key difference: instead of playing a foundation, you may discard any number of cards and draw that many cards. Attacking involves using techniques (martial arts maneuvers). An opponent may block with a technique, as well. Advantage cards may be played to increase or decrease the strength of the attack. It's possible to do 20+ damage in one attack, though this is rare.

For a simple game, *Ultimate Combat!* has strategic depth. Fast decks that attack for 4+ damage repeatedly before an opponent can set up defenses are only slightly stronger than more defensive, control-oriented decks. Sealed deck play, which is often starter versus starter without boosters, is playable and challenging. One feature is unusual in today's market: Deck construction has rarity limits. Many constructed tournaments were limited to "white belt" decks until enough players existed who wanted to try more sophisticated decks and rules for mixing different level decks were devised. — *Ian Lee*

Concept	●●●○○
Gameplay	●●●○○
Card art	●●●○○
Player pool	○○○○○

				Card name	Rarity	Price		Card name	Rarity	Price		Card name	Rarity	Price
Set (266 cards)			55.00	1				ArmLock	VR	2.80	2			
Starter Display Box			24.00	Adrenaline	C	0.15		ArmLock	R	1.50	Awareness	VR	2.80
Booster Display Box			30.00	Agony	R	2.00		ArmLock	U	0.40	AxKick	R	1.50
Starter Deck			5.00	Akiyama's Pendant	VR	3.80		Asano's Faith	VR	2.80	AxKick	U	0.40
Booster Pack			1.00	Amulet of Kwai Chang	VR	3.80		Atlas Overhead Slam	R	1.50	AxKick	C	0.15

RARITY KEY C = Common U = Uncommon R = Rare VR = Very Rare UR = Ultra Rare F = Foil card X = Fixed/standard in all decks

Card name	Rarity	Price
☐ Back Fist	R	1.50
☐ Back Fist	U	0.40
☐ Back Fist	C	0.15
☐ Bad Air	R	1.80
☐ Bad Sushi	C	0.15
3		
☐ Banana Peel	R	1.50
☐ Barrel Roll	R	3.00
☐ Barrel Roll	U	0.30
☐ Barrel Roll	C	0.25
☐ Bear's Jaw	VR	3.80
☐ Beijing Blitz	R	1.80
☐ Belly Punch	U	0.40
☐ Belly Punch	C	0.15
☐ Berserker	U	0.40
4		
☐ Bewilder	VR	2.80
☐ Body Odor	C	0.15
☐ Bojutsu Stick	VR	3.30
☐ Boken	VR	3.80
☐ Champ's Side		
Body Slam	VR	3.80
☐ Charging Front Kick	R	1.50
☐ Combination 0	C	0.15
☐ Combination 1	C	0.15
☐ Combination 2	U	0.40
5		
☐ Combination X	R	2.00
☐ Conditioning	C	0.15
☐ Confuse Foundation	R	1.50
☐ Copy Cat	U	0.40
☐ Counter 0	C	0.15
☐ Counter 1	C	0.15
☐ Counter 2	U	0.40
☐ Counter X	R	2.00
☐ Crusher's Wheel	VR	2.80
6		
☐ CupHand Ear Crush	VR	2.80
☐ Cyclone Elbow		
Smash	R	1.50
☐ Darkness	VR	3.30
☐ DeepFog	VR	3.30
☐ Depression	VR	3.00
☐ Desert Heat	VR	3.30
☐ Discipline	VR	2.80
☐ Dismay	R	1.50
☐ Double Leg Tackle	R	1.50
7		
☐ Double Leg Tackle	U	0.40
☐ Double Leg Tackle	C	0.15
☐ Double Wrist Lock	R	1.50
☐ Double Wrist Lock	U	0.40
☐ Dragon's Fire	VR	3.80
☐ DropJab	R	1.50
☐ DropJab	C	0.15
☐ Drop Spin Kick	U	0.40
☐ Drop Spin Kick	C	0.15

Card name	Rarity	Price
8		
☐ Earring of Confucius	VR	3.80
☐ Earth Mantra	U	0.40
☐ Elbow Smash	U	0.40
☐ Elephant Bracelet	VR	1.50
☐ Elixir of the Gods	VR	3.80
☐ Enduring Pain	R	1.50
☐ Enforcer's Back Kick	VR	2.80
☐ Escrema Sticks	VR	3.50
☐ Exhaustion	VR	2.80
9		
☐ Experience	C	0.15
☐ Eyes of the Ninja	R	2.00
☐ Fall Prone	U	0.40
☐ FavoriteTechnique	U	0.40
☐ Fighting Spirit	C	0.15
☐ Finger Lock	C	0.15
☐ Flexibility	VR	2.80
☐ Flooded Ground	VR	3.30
☐ Flying Double Kick	VR	2.80
10		
☐ Flying Scissors	U	0.40
☐ Flying SideKick	VR	2.80
☐ Focus	R	1.50
☐ Footsweep	R	1.50
☐ Footsweep	U	0.40
☐ Footsweep	C	0.15
☐ Freezing Cold	VR	3.30
☐ Front Kick	R	1.50
☐ Front Kick	U	0.40
11		
☐ Front Kick	C	0.15
☐ Full Nelson	VR	2.80
☐ Full Nelson	U	0.40
☐ Full Nelson	C	0.15
☐ Gi Patch-Falcon	C	0.15
☐ Gi Patch-Fox	C	0.15
☐ Gi Patch-Horse	C	0.15
☐ Gi Patch-Owl	C	0.15
☐ Great Wall Vest	VR	3.80
12		
☐ Guillotine Block	VR	2.80
☐ Hair/Elbow Strike	U	0.40
☐ Hair Grab Elbow/		
Strike	VR	2.80
☐ Hair Grab Elbow/		
Strike	R	1.50
☐ Hammer Fist/Strike	C	0.15
☐ Headband of the Ninja	R	0.50
☐ Head Butt	U	0.30
☐ Head Butt	C	0.15
☐ Head Lock	R	1.50
13		
☐ Head Lock	U	0.40
☐ Head Lock	C	1.00
☐ Healing Mantra	U	0.40
☐ Heavy Rain	VR	3.30
☐ High Altitude	VR	3.30

Card name	Rarity	Price
☐ Holy Medallion	C	0.15
☐ Hurricane Winds	VR	3.30
☐ Icy Ground	VR	3.30
☐ Inferno's Round Kick	VR	2.80
14		
☐ Inner Leg Reap	R	1.50
☐ Inner Thigh Throw	R	1.50
☐ Instant Recall	R	2.00
☐ Instant Replay	U	0.50
☐ Instep Stomp	R	1.50
☐ Instep Stomp	U	0.40
☐ Instep Stomp	C	0.15
☐ Intimidation	U	0.40
☐ Intuition	VR	2.80
15		
☐ Jump Crescent Kick	VR	2.80
☐ Jump Crescent Kick	R	1.50
☐ Jump Hook Kick	VR	2.80
☐ Jump Hook Kick	R	1.50
☐ Jump Hook Kick	U	0.40
☐ Jumping	U	0.40
☐ Kevlar Vest	R	2.00
☐ Kiai	C	0.15
☐ Kim Soon's Illusion	U	0.40
16		
☐ Knee Kick	R	1.50
☐ Knee Kick	U	0.40
☐ Knee Kick	C	0.15
☐ Knife Hand Strike	R	1.50
☐ Knife Hand Strike	U	0.40
☐ Knife Hand Strike	C	0.15
☐ Knowledge	C	0.15
☐ Leaping AxKick	VR	2.80
☐ Leaping AxKick	R	1.50
17		
☐ Leaping AxKick	U	0.40
☐ Left Hook	U	0.40
☐ Left Hook	C	0.15
☐ Leg Trap Block	VR	2.80
☐ Lifting Sleeve Throw	R	1.50
☐ Lightning Strike	U	0.40
☐ Low Round Kick	R	1.50
☐ Low Round Kick	U	0.40
☐ Low Round Kick	C	0.15
18		
☐ Mantra of Power	C	0.15
☐ Mask of Gengis Khan	VR	3.80
☐ Mental Domination	VR	2.80
☐ Morale Boost	U	0.40
☐ Moriya's Mirror	VR	3.30
☐ Move Back	C	0.15
☐ Move Front	C	0.15
☐ Move Left	C	0.15
☐ Move Left/Back	VR	2.80
19		
☐ Move Left/Front	VR	2.80
☐ Move Right	C	0.15
☐ Move Right/Back	VR	2.80
☐ Move Right/Front	VR	2.80

Card name	Rarity	Price
☐ Muddy Ground	VR	3.30
☐ Nunchaku	VR	2.80
☐ Oak Staff	VR	3.30
☐ Oblivion	VR	2.80
☐ Outer Leg Reap	U	0.40
20		
☐ Oxygen Burst	C	0.15
☐ Power Drain	R	1.50
☐ Prayer for Healing	R	1.80
☐ Primal Kiai	VR	1.40
☐ Psychic Blast	U	0.40
☐ Psychic Block	U	0.40
☐ Psychic		
Enhancement	U	0.40
☐ Psychic Freeze	R	1.50
☐ Psychic Misdirection	R	1.50
21		
☐ Psychic Nova	VR	3.80
☐ Psychic Paralysis	R	2.00
☐ Psychic Read	R	2.00
☐ Psychic Siphon	R	1.80
☐ Psychic Storm	VR	2.80
☐ Psychic Subversion	R	2.00
☐ Purity	VR	2.80
☐ Push the Pace	U	0.40
☐ Quick Jab	R	1.50
22		
☐ Quick Jab	U	0.40
☐ Quick Jab	C	0.15
☐ Reflexes	VR	2.80
☐ Regression	VR	2.80
☐ Restrict Options	U	0.40
☐ Reverse Punch	R	1.50
☐ Reverse Punch	U	0.40
☐ Reverse Punch	C	0.15
☐ RibShot	U	0.40
23		
☐ Right Cross	R	1.50
☐ Right Cross	U	0.40
☐ Right Cross	C	0.15
☐ Right Hook	R	1.50
☐ Right Hook	U	0.40
☐ Right Hook	C	0.15
☐ Ring of the Sun		
God	VR	3.50
☐ Round Kick	R	1.50
☐ Round Kick	U	0.40
24		
☐ Round Kick	C	0.15
☐ Sacrifice Foundation	R	1.50
☐ Sandy Beach	VR	3.30
☐ Shake Up	VR	2.80
☐ Shatter		
Concentration	R	1.50
☐ Shatter Foundation	R	1.50
☐ Shatter Talisman	R	1.80
☐ Shoulder Throw	VR	2.00
☐ Shoulder Throw	R	3.00

Card name	Rarity	Price
25		
☐ Shuffle	C	0.15
☐ Side Kick	R	1.50
☐ Side Kick	U	0.40
☐ Side Kick	C	0.15
☐ Single Leg Tackle	U	0.30
☐ Single Leg Tackle	C	0.25
☐ Smog Inversion	VR	3.30
☐ Snatch Talisman	R	2.00
☐ SolarPlex Strike	R	1.50
26		
☐ SolarPlex Strike	U	0.30
☐ SolarPlex Strike	C	0.25
☐ Spear Hand	R	1.50
☐ Spear Hand	U	0.30
☐ Spear Hand	C	0.25
☐ Speed1	C	0.15
☐ Speed2	U	0.50
☐ SpeedX	R	2.50
☐ Spinning Back Fist	VR	3.00
27		
☐ Spinning Back Fist	R	1.50
☐ Spinning Back Kick	VR	2.80
☐ Spinning Round Kick	VR	2.80
☐ Standing Choke	R	1.50
☐ Standing Choke	U	0.40
☐ Standing Choke	C	0.15
☐ Strength 1	C	0.15
☐ Strength 2	U	0.50
☐ Strength X	R	2.00
28		
☐ Stumble	C	0.25
☐ Sumida's		
Misdirection	R	1.50
☐ Suppress	R	1.50
☐ Sweeping Leg		
Throw	U	0.40
☐ Throat Grab	R	1.50
☐ Throat Grab	U	0.40
☐ Throat Grab	C	0.15
☐ Throat Jab	R	1.50
☐ Throat Jab	U	0.40
29		
☐ Throat Jab	C	0.15
☐ Tonfa	VR	4.30
☐ Trip	C	0.15
☐ Ukemi	C	0.15
☐ Uppercut	R	1.50
☐ Uppercut	U	0.40
☐ Uppercut	C	0.15
☐ Valerie's Sidestep	VR	2.80
☐ Warrior's Helmet	R	2.00
30		
☐ Wisdom	VR	2.80
☐ Wrist Lock	C	0.15
☐ Wrist Lock	VR	2.80
☐ Wrist Lock	R	1.50
☐ Yamashita's Belt	R	2.00

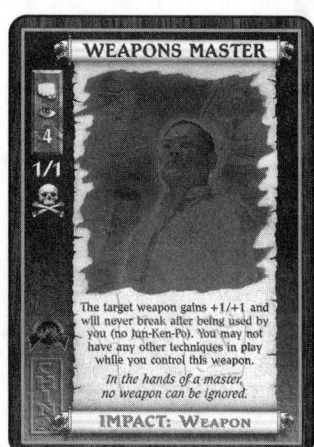

Ultimate Combat! •
Ancient Fighting Arts of China

Ultimate Games • Released **September 1995**

148 cards in set • **IDENTIFIER: Cards say 'China'**

• Booster packs contain 15 cards; booster displays contain 36 boosters

The only expansion to **Ultimate Combat!** introduces new martial art styles where all the techniques of a single style possess the same special ability. All Kung Fu techniques, for instance, have a built in combination (additional attack).

China is a mixed bag. It fixes and develops strategies from the main set well. Environment cards were weak in *Limited*; *China* has stronger environment cards as well as a card that can search for them and a card that can make them stay in play for the entire game. In fact, some action cards from the main set were by rule restricted to one per deck until the expansion was released, at which point they became unrestricted, an unusual case of foresight in the design of a CCG.

Where *China* disappoints is in the new stuff. The new theme techniques are overcosted in relation to the better techniques from the main set, even when you factor in the addi-

You will need
17
nine-pocket pages to store this set.
(9 doubled up)

RARITY KEY C = Common U = Uncommon R = Rare VR = Very Rare UR = Ultra Rare F = Foil card X = Fixed/standard in all decks

466 • SCRYE Collectible Card Game Checklist and Price Guide

tional abilities of the new cards. Impact cards, cards which could be played on other cards usually to make them better or protect them, are rarely worth playing, though the one that makes environments permanent is pretty darn good in environment decks.

China is not essential for the *Ultimate Combat!* player. It has too many cards of limited usefulness. However, for the collector, it introduced foils to the game. Ten of the gold belt cards found in *China* have foil versions. — **Ian Lee**

Set (148 cards)		46.00
Booster Display Box		27.00
Booster Pack		1.00

Card name	Rarity	Price
Alter Destiny	U	0.40
Ankle Trap Throw	C	0.10
Anticipation	VR	2.30
Attacking Palm	VR	2.30
Attacking Palm	F	4.30
Back To Basics	R	1.80
Basic Attack	C	0.10
Beast Master	U	0.40
Beginner'S Luck	C	0.10
Betrayal	R	1.80
Catch Weapon	VR	2.30
Chest Gouge	U	0.40
Clear Vision	C	0.10
Climbing Monkey Attack	R	1.80
Close The Gap	C	0.10
Coach Chung	R	1.80
Coach Jhang	R	1.80
Coach Li	R	1.80
Coach Long	VR	2.30
Coach Long	F	4.30
Coach Park	VR	2.30
Coach Weng	R	1.80
Coach Wong	R	1.80
Coach Yao	R	1.80
Confidence	C	0.10
Constriction	U	0.40
Cross Arm Body Lock	C	0.10

Card name	Rarity	Price
Crushing Power	U	0.40
Cup Strike	C	0.10
Disadvantage	U	0.10
Dislodge Armor	U	0.40
Disruption	U	0.40
Double Fist Strike	R	1.80
Double Front Jump Kick	R	1.80
Dr. Weng'S Itching Powder	R	1.80
Drop	C	0.25
Drop Kick	R	1.80
Drunken Attack	VR	2.30
Drunken Strike	U	0.40
Eagle Claw Kick	C	0.10
Earthquake	VR	2.30
Elbow Break	U	0.40
Elbow Locking Throw	R	1.80
Energy Redirection Throw	U	0.40
Enhanced Mobility	C	0.10
Environ Master	VR	2.30
Environ Master	F	4.30
Erase Memories	C	0.10
Exchange Blows	VR	2.30
Fake Attack	R	1.80
Fang Of The Viper	VR	2.30
Fang Of The Viper	F	4.30
Fetid Swamp	VR	2.30
Finger Thrust	C	0.10
Flying Instep Kick	VR	2.30

Card name	Rarity	Price
Front Hatchet Kick	C	0.10
Gi Patch: Chameleon	VR	2.30
Gi Patch: Giraffe	VR	2.30
Gi Patch: Monkey	VR	2.30
Gi Patch: Panda	R	1.80
Gi Patch: Parrot	U	0.40
Gi Patch: Phoenix	R	1.80
Gi Patch: Rat	C	0.10
Gi Patch: Rhino	U	0.40
Gi Patch: Tiger	VR	2.30
Gi Patch: Unicorn	C	0.10
Gi Patch: Wyvern	C	0.10
Ginseng	VR	2.30
Grip Of Steel	R	1.80
Hand-To-Hand Combat	R	1.80
Head Twist	C	0.10
Hesitation	C	0.10
Hot Lava	C	0.10
Ill Wind	VR	2.30
Increase Options	C	0.10
Inner Calm	C	0.10
Inner Leg Chop	U	0.40
Inspiration	VR	2.30
Intensity	R	1.80
Jarring Attack	VR	2.30
Joint Lock	VR	2.30
Jolting Force	U	0.40
Kama Chigi	C	0.10
Keep Your Distance	C	0.10
Manipulate Destiny	VR	2.30
Manipulate Destiny	F	4.30

Card name	Rarity	Price
Mark Of The Cheetah	VR	2.30
Mark Of The Cheetah	F	4.30
Master Lee	VR	2.30
Meditation	U	0.40
Mental Agility	U	0.40
Monkey Throat Gouge	C	0.10
Muscle Spasm	R	1.80
Mystic Shield	VR	2.30
Obliteration	U	0.40
Padded Armor	C	0.10
Panic	C	0.10
Permanance	U	0.40
Praying Mantis	VR	2.30
Precision Attack	U	0.40
Pressure	VR	2.30
Professor Jay	VR	2.30
Professor Uchida	VR	2.30
Protective Move	R	1.80
Psychic Boomerang	R	1.80
Psychic Delay	C	0.10
Psychic Sponge	R	1.80
Quick Thinking	R	1.80
Quicksand	VR	2.30
Rage Of The Wolf	C	0.10
Rear Kick	U	0.40
Relentless	U	0.40
Restoration	C	0.10
Retaliation	VR	2.30
Retrieval	C	0.10
Reverse Strike	U	0.40
Reverse Tactics	R	1.80
Risk Of Injury	U	0.40

Card name	Rarity	Price
Rope Dart	VR	2.30
Sai	VR	2.30
Sensei Saekow	VR	2.30
Serenity	R	1.80
Shin Guards	U	0.40
Slanting Strike	C	0.10
Snake Hand Strike	U	0.40
Snapping Throw	VR	2.30
Sneak Attack	R	1.80
Speed Kills	R	1.80
Spinning Head Kick	VR	2.30
Spinning Head Kick	F	4.30
Split Attack	VR	2.30
Stone Of Alchemy	U	0.40
Stronghold	C	0.10
Taunt	C	0.10
Three Section Staff	VR	2.30
Time Elapse	VR	2.30
Time Lapse	F	4.30
Time Shift	VR	2.30
Torque	C	0.10
Touch Of Magic	VR	2.30
Underground Waterfall	VR	2.30
Weapons Master	VR	2.30
Weapons Master	F	4.30
Whip Kick	R	1.80
Winged Sandals	U	0.40
Wooden Swords	VR	2.30
World In Chaos	VR	2.30
World In Chaos	F	4.30

Vampire: The Eternal Struggle

Wizards of the Coast/White Wolf • First set, *Unlimited*, released **August 1995**

436 cards in set

- Starter decks contain 76 cards; starter displays contain 10 starters
- Booster packs contain 19 cards; booster displays contain 36 boosters

Vampire: The Eternal Struggle, often called *V:TES*, is a reissuing of the *Jyhad* CCG, so similar that *Vampire* is called *Jyhad* as often as not. *Jyhad* may have been appropriate based on White Wolf's World of Darkness, but *Vampire: The Eternal Struggle* is a far less controversial name for the game.

Though a handful of new cards are substituted for older cards and the fronts of cards acquire new layouts, the most significant change by far is the difference in backs between the two sets. This caused quite an uproar. It also had tournament implications. An old rule was that a deck had to be all of one back or all of another or have 40-60% of each back to prevent having marked cards. The rule has become much less important, meaningless even, in the day of opaque card sleeves.

Vampire **Unlimited** boxes have a higher value than *Jyhad* boxes. Reasons range from the card backs (all the expansions have *Vampire* backs) to the overprinting of *Jyhad*.

Vampire gained new life at White Wolf on Halloween of 2000 with **Sabbat War**. — *Ian Lee*

You will need **49** nine-pocket pages to store this set. (25 doubled up)

Set (436 cards)		126.00
Starter Display Box		48.00
Booster Display Box		54.00
Starter Deck		7.50
Booster Pack		2.00

Card name	Rarity	Price
.44 Magnum	C	0.15
Aaron's Feeding Razor	R	2.00
Academic Hunting Ground	U	0.75
Aching Beauty	U	0.75

Card name	Rarity	Price
Acrobatics	C	0.15
Adrianne	V	0.25
Agrippina	V	0.25
Aid from Bats	C	0.15
Al's Army Apparatus	R	2.00
Aleph	V	0.25
Amaranth	U	0.75
Anarch Revolt	U	0.75
Anarch Troubleman	R	2.00
Anastasia Grey	V	0.25

Card name	Rarity	Price
Ancient Influence	C	0.15
Ancilla Empowerment	C	0.15
Andreas, The Bard of Crete	V	0.25
Angel	V	0.25
Angus the Unruled	V	0.25
Animalism	C	0.15
Anneke	V	0.25
Anson	V	0.25
Anvil	V	0.25
Appolonius	V	0.25

Earth Control

+1 stealth
+2 stealth

Illus. Jeff Menges
© 1995 Wizards of the Coast, Inc. All Rights Reserved.

Concept	●●●●○
Gameplay	●●●○○
Card art	●●●○○
Player pool	●●○○○

Card name	Rarity	Price
Arcane Library	R	2.00
Archon	V	0.50
Archon Investigation	U	0.75

Card name	Rarity	Price
[4]		
Arms Dealer	U	0.75
Army of Rats	C	0.15
Arson	C	0.15
Art Museum	R	2.00
Ascendance	C	0.15
Assault Rifle	U	0.75
Astrid Thomas	V	0.25
Asylum Hunting Ground	U	0.75
Aura Reading	U	0.75
[5]		
Auspex	C	0.15
Autarkis Persecution	C	0.15
Backways	U	0.75
Badger	V	0.25
Basilia	V	0.25
Bastard Sword	U	0.75
Bear Paw	V	0.25
Behind You!	R	2.00
Betrayer	R	2.00
[6]		
Bewitching Oration	C	0.15
Bianca	V	0.25
Black Cat	V	0.25
Blood Bond	U	0.75
Blood Doll	C	0.15
Blood Fury	C	0.15
Blood Hunt	U	0.75
Blood Puppy	R	2.00
Blood Rage	C	0.15
[7]		
Blur	C	0.15
Body of Sun	R	2.00
Bomb	U	0.75
Bonding	C	0.15
Boxed In	C	0.15
Brainwash	C	0.15
Brazil	V	0.25
Bribes	C	0.15
Brujah Frenzy	U	0.75
[8]		
Brujah Justicar	R	2.00
Bum's Rush	C	0.15
Burst of Sunlight	R	2.00
Business Pressure	R	2.00
Camarilla Exemplary	C	0.15
Canine Horde	C	0.15
Cardano	V	0.25
Cassandra, Magus Prime	V	0.25
Cat Burglary	R	2.00
[9]		
Cats' Guidance	C	0.15
Cauldron of Blood	C	0.15
Celerity	C	0.15
Change of Target	U	0.75
Chantry	U	0.75
Charming Lobby	U	0.75
Charnas the Imp	R	2.00
Chester DuBois	V	0.25
Claws of the Dead	C	0.15
[10]		
Cloak the Gathering	C	0.15
Colin Flynn	V	0.25
Computer Hacking	C	0.25
Conditioning	C	0.15
Conquer the Beast	R	2.00
Consanguineous Boon	C	0.15
Consanguineous Condemnation	C	0.15
Conservative Agitation	C	0.15
Courtland Leighton	V	0.25
[11]		
Crusher	V	0.25
Cryptic Mission	C	0.15
Cryptic Rider	U	0.75
Cultivated Blood Shortage	U	0.75
Cunctator Motion	R	2.00
Curse of Nitocris	R	2.00
Dancin' Dana	V	0.25
Dawn Operation	U	0.75
Day Operation	R	2.00
[12]		
Dead-End Alley	C	0.15
Deal with the Devil	C	0.15

Card name	Rarity	Price
Deer Rifle	C	0.15
Deflection	C	0.15
Delaying Tactics	U	0.75
Delilah Easton	V	0.25
Demetrius Slater	V	0.25
Democritus	V	0.25
Didi Meyers	V	0.25
[13]		
Dieter Kleist	V	0.25
Dimple	V	0.25
Disarming Presence	U	0.75
Disguised Weapon	C	0.15
Disputed Territory	C	0.15
Distraction	R	2.00
Dodge	C	0.15
Dollface	V	0.25
Domain Challenge	C	0.15
[14]		
Dominate	C	0.15
Dominate Kine	R	2.00
Don Cruez, The Idealist	V	0.25
Dorian Strack	V	0.25
Dr. Jest	V	0.25
Dr. John Casey	V	0.25
Dragon's Breath Rounds	U	0.75
Drain Essence	U	0.75
Dramatic Upheaval	V	0.25
[15]		
Drawing Out the Beast	C	0.15
Dre, Leader of the Cold Dawn	V	0.25
Dread Gaze	C	0.15
Duck	V	0.25
Eagle's Sight	U	0.75
Earth Control	C	0.15
Earth Meld	C	0.15
Ebanezer Roush	V	0.25
Ecoterrorists	R	2.00
[16]		
Effective Management	C	0.15
Elder Intervention	C	0.15
Elder Kindred Network	U	0.75
Elder Library	C	0.15
Eliott Sinclair, Virtuoso Thespian	V	0.25
Elysium: The Arboretum	U	0.75
Emerson Bridges	V	0.25
Enchant Kindred	C	0.15
Enhanced Senses	C	0.15
[17]		
Entrancement	R	2.00
Faceless Night	C	0.15
Fake Out	C	0.15
Fame	U	0.75
Far Mastery	R	2.00
Fast Hands	U	0.75
Fast Reaction	C	0.15
Felicia Mostrom	V	0.25
Fists of Death	R	2.00
[18]		
Flak Jacket	C	0.15
Flamethrower	U	0.75
Flash	C	0.15
Flesh of Marble	R	2.00
Form of Mist	U	0.75
Form of the Ghost	C	0.15
Fortitude	C	0.15
Fragment of the Book of Nod	R	2.00
Freak Drive	R	2.00
[19]		
Frenzy	C	0.15
Game of Malkav	U	0.75
Gangrel Atavism	U	0.75
Gangrel Justicar	R	2.00
Ghoul Escort	R	2.00
Ghoul Retainer	R	2.00
Giant's Blood	R	2.00
Gideon Fontaine	V	0.25
Gilbert Duane	V	0.25
[20]		
Gird Minions	C	0.15
Gitane St. Claire	V	0.25
Giuliano Vincenzi	V	0.25
Glaser Rounds	U	0.75
Gleam of Red Eyes	C	0.15

Card name	Rarity	Price
Golconda: Inner Peace	R	2.00
Govern the Unaligned	C	0.15
Graverobbing	U	0.75
Grenade	U	0.75
[21]		
Grendel the Worm-Eaten	V	0.25
Growing Fury	C	0.15
Gunther, Beast Lord	V	0.25
Gypsies	U	0.75
Hasina Kesi	V	0.25
Haven Uncovered	C	0.15
Hawg	C	0.15
Heather Florent, The Opportunist	V	0.25
Hector Sosa	V	0.25
[22]		
Helena Casimir	V	0.25
Hell Hound	R	2.00
Hidden Lurker	C	0.15
High Stakes	R	2.00
Homunculus	U	0.75
Hostile Takeover	R	2.00
Ignatius	V	0.25
Igo the Hungry	V	0.25
Illegal Search and Seizure	C	0.15
[23]		
Immortal Grapple	R	2.00
Indomitability	C	0.15
Infernal Pursuit	U	0.75
Information Highway	U	0.75
IR Goggles	U	0.75
Ivory Bow	R	2.00
J. S. Simmons, Esq.	R	2.00
Jackie Therman	R	2.00
Jazz Wentworth	V	0.25
[24]		
Jing Wei	V	0.25
Justicar Retribution	U	0.75
Justine, Elder of Dallas	V	0.25
Kallista, Master Sculptor	V	0.25
Kindred Intelligence	R	2.00
Kindred Restructure	V	0.50
Kindred Segregation	V	0.50
Kindred Society Games	R	2.00
Kine Resources Contested	C	0.15
[25]		
KoKo	V	0.25
KRCG News Radio	U	0.75
Laptop Computer	C	0.15
Lazarus	V	0.25
Legal Manipulations	C	0.15
Letter from Vienna	U	0.75
Lextalionis	V	0.50
Life Boon	U	0.75
Lost in Crowds	C	0.15
[26]		
Loyal Street Gang	U	0.75
Luccia Paciola	V	0.25
Lucian	V	0.25
Lucky Blow	C	0.15
Lucretia, Cess Queen	V	0.25
Lupo	V	0.25
Lydia Van Cuelen	V	0.25
Madness Network	R	2.00
Magic of the Smith	R	2.00
[27]		
Majesty	C	0.15
Major Boon	U	0.75
Malkavian Dementia	U	0.75
Malkavian Justicar	R	2.00
Malkavian Prank	R	2.00
Malkavian Time Auction	R	2.00
Manstopper Rounds	U	0.75
Mariel, Lady Thunder	V	0.25
Marty Lechtansi	V	0.25
[28]		
Masika	V	0.25
Mask of a Thousand Faces	U	0.75
Masquerade Endangered	U	0.75
Masquerade Enforcement	V	0.50
Melissa Barton	V	0.25
Merrill Molitor	V	0.25
Metro Underground	U	0.75
Mighty Grapple	C	0.15

Card name	Rarity	Price
Millicent Smith, Puritan Vampire Hunter	R	2.00
[29]		
Minion Tap	C	0.15
Minor Boon	U	0.75
Miranda Sanova	V	0.25
Misdirection	C	0.15
Mob Connections	U	0.75
Movement of the Mind	C	0.15
Mr. Winthrop	R	2.00
Muddled Vampire Hunter	U	0.75
Murder of Crows	R	2.00
[30]		
Natasha Volfchek	V	0.25
Navar McClaren	V	0.25
Night Moves	U	0.75
Nik	V	0.25
Nimble Feet	C	0.15
Normal	V	0.25
Nosferatu Justicar	R	2.00
Nosferatu Putrescence	U	0.75
Obedience	U	0.75
[31]		
Obfuscate	C	0.15
Open Grate	C	0.15
Outcast Mage	U	0.75
Owl Companion	U	0.75
Ozmo	V	0.25
Parity Shift	V	0.50
Patagia: Flaps Allowing Limited Flight	R	2.00
Peace Treaty	C	0.15
Police Department	U	0.75
[32]		
Political Ally	R	2.00
Political Backlash	C	0.15
Political Flux	C	0.15
Potence	C	0.15
Powerbase: Chicago	U	1.00
Powerbase: Washington, D.C.	U	1.00
Praxis Seizure: Atlanta	R	4.00
Praxis Seizure: Boston	R	4.00
Praxis Seizure: Chicago	R	4.00
[33]		
Praxis Seizure: Cleveland	R	4.00
Praxis Seizure: Dallas	R	4.00
Praxis Seizure: Houston	R	4.00
Praxis Seizure: Miami	R	4.00
Praxis Seizure: Seattle	R	4.00
Praxis Seizure: Washington, D.C.	R	4.00
Praxis Solomon	V	0.50
Presence	C	0.15
Protean	C	0.15
[34]		
Protected Resources	R	2.00
Protracted Investment	C	0.15
Psyche!	U	0.75
Psychic Projection	R	2.00
Psychic Veil	R	2.00
Pulled Fangs	R	2.00
Pulling Strings	U	0.75
Pulse of the Canaille	U	0.75
Quinton McDonnell	V	0.25
[35]		
Rake	V	0.25
Ramiel DuPre	V	0.25
Rampage	U	0.75
Rapid Healing	C	0.15
Rats' Warning	C	0.15
Raven	V	0.25
Raven Spy	U	0.75
Read Intentions	C	0.15
Regaining the Upper Hand	C	0.15
[36]		
Renegade Garou	R	2.00
Resplendent Protector	R	2.00
Restoration	C	0.15
Reversal of Fortunes	V	0.50
Ricki Van Demsi	V	0.25
Ritual Challenge	R	2.00
Ritual of the Bitter Rose	R	2.00
Roland Bishop	V	0.25
Roland Loussarian	V	0.25

RARITY KEY C = Common   U = Uncommon   R = Rare   V = Vampire Deck   UR = Ultra Rare   F = Foil card   X = Fixed/standard in all decks

468 • SCRYE Collectible Card Game Checklist and Price Guide

Card name	Rarity	Price	Card name	Rarity	Price	Card name	Rarity	Price	Card name	Rarity	Price
[37]			☐ Smudge the Ignored	V	0.25	☐ The Fourth Tradition:			☐ Unnatural Disaster	C	0.15
☐ Roman Alexander	V	0.25	☐ Social Charm	C	0.15	The Accounting	U	0.75	☐ Uptown Hunting Ground	U	0.75
☐ Roreca Quaid	V	0.25	☐ Society Hunting Ground	U	0.75	☐ The Knights	R	2.00	☐ Uriah Winter	V	0.25
☐ Roxanne, Rectrix			☐ Society of Leopold	R	2.00	☐ The Labyrinth	U	0.75	☐ Vampiric Disease	R	2.00
of the 13th Floor	V	0.25	☐ Soul Gem of Etrius	R	2.00	☐ The Rack	U	0.75	☐ Vampiric Speed	C	0.15
☐ RPG Launcher	R	2.00	☐ Spirit's Touch	C	0.15	☐ The Second Tradition: Domain	U	0.75	☐ Vanish from the Mind's Eye	C	0.15
☐ Rufina Soledad	V	0.25	☐ Sport Bike	U	0.75	☐ The Sixth Tradition: Destruction	U	0.75	[47]		
☐ Rumors of Gehenna	R	2.00	☐ Spying Mission	U	0.75	☐ The Slashers	R	2.00	☐ Vast Wealth	U	0.75
☐ Sabbat Threat	V	0.50	[41]			[44]			☐ Ventrue Headquarters	U	0.75
☐ Sabine Lafitte	V	0.25	☐ Storm Sewers	U	0.75	☐ The Spawning Pool	R	2.00	☐ Ventrue Justicar	R	2.00
☐ Sammy	V	0.25	☐ Submachine Gun	U	0.75	☐ The Third Tradition: Progeny	U	0.75	☐ Violette Prentiss	V	0.25
[38]			☐ Succubus Club	R	2.00	☐ Theft of Vitae	C	0.15	☐ Vliam Andor	V	0.25
☐ Sarah Cobbler	V	0.25	☐ Sudden Reversal	U	0.75	☐ Thomas Thorne	V	0.25	☐ Voter Captivation	U	0.75
☐ Saturday-Night Special	C	0.15	☐ Surprise Influence	C	0.15	☐ Threats	C	0.15	☐ Vulnerability	U	0.75
☐ Sawed-Off Shotgun	C	0.15	☐ Sylvester Simms	V	0.25	☐ Thrown Gate	C	0.15	☐ Wake with Evening's Freshness	C	0.15
☐ Scorn of Adonis	U	0.75	☐ Talbot's Chainsaw	R	2.00	☐ Thrown Sewer Lid	C	0.15	☐ Walk of Flame	U	0.75
☐ Sebastian Marley	V	0.25	☐ Tasha Morgan	R	2.00	☐ Tiberius, The Scandalmonger	V	0.25	[48]		
☐ Seduction	C	0.15	☐ Taste of Vitae	U	0.75	☐ Timothy Crowley	V	0.25	☐ Warzone Hunting Ground	U	0.75
☐ Selma the Repugnant	V	0.25	[42]			[45]			☐ Weather Control	U	0.75
☐ Sengir Dagger	R	2.00	☐ Tatiana Romanov	V	0.25	☐ Toreador Justicar	R	2.00	☐ Well-Aimed Car	U	0.75
☐ Shadow of the Beast	U	0.75	☐ Telepathic Counter	C	0.15	☐ Torn Signpost	U	0.75	☐ Wolf Claws	C	0.15
[39]			☐ Telepathic Misdirection	C	0.15	☐ Tragic Love Affair	U	0.75	☐ Wolf Companion	U	0.75
☐ Shattering Blow	C	0.15	☐ Telepathic Vote Counting	R	2.00	☐ Trap	C	0.15	☐ Wooden Stake	U	0.75
☐ Sheldon, Lord of the Clog	V	0.25	☐ Temptation of Greater Power	R	2.00	☐ Tremere Justicar	R	2.00	☐ Wynn	V	0.25
☐ Short-Term Investment	C	0.15	☐ Thadius Zho, Mage	R	2.00	☐ Tura Vaughn	V	0.25	☐ XTC-Laced blood	R	2.00
☐ Sideslip	C	0.15	☐ Thaumaturgy	C	0.15	☐ Tusk, The Talebearer	V	0.25	☐ Yuri, The Talon	V	0.25
☐ Sir Walter Nash	V	0.25	☐ The Barrens	C	0.15	☐ Ulugh Beg, The Watcher	V	0.25	[49]		
☐ Skin of Night	U	0.75	☐ The Embrace	R	2.00	☐ Uma Hatch	V	0.25	☐ Zack North	V	0.25
☐ Skin of Rock	C	0.15	[43]			[46]			☐ Zebulon	V	0.25
☐ Skin of Steel	C	0.15	☐ The Fifth Tradition: Hospitality	U	0.75	☐ Undead Persistence	U	0.75	☐ Zip Gun	U	0.75
☐ Slum Hunting Ground	U	0.75	☐ The First Tradition:			☐ Undead Strength	C	0.15	☐ Zoo Hunting Ground	U	0.75
[40]			The Masquerade	R	2.00	☐ Unflinching Persistence	C	0.15			
☐ Smiling Jack, The Anarch	R	2.00									

Vampire • Dark Sovereigns

Wizards of the Coast/White Wolf • Released **November 1995**

173 cards in set • **IDENTIFIER: Crown at upper right**

- Booster packs contain 15 cards; booster displays contain 36 boosters

In the first expansion for **Vampire**, the emphasis is on the European vampire world. Besides expanding on existing clans and disciplines, **Dark Sovereigns** introduces two new clans: Giovanni and Ravnos. The Giovanni are Italian bankers whose clan disciplines are potence, dominate, and necromancy (new). The Ravnos are gypsies whose clan disciplines are fortitude, animalism, and chimerstry (new).

Both of the new disciplines, necromancy and chimerstry, are weak. Chimerstry does have one extremely powerful card, **Sensory Deprivation**, which can take a vampire out of the game. The two new clans suffer from both the weakness of their respective clan-specific disciplines and because they have a much smaller assortment of vampires to choose from than the other clans.

In general, *Dark Sovereigns* has far too many cards that are laughable in their uselessness. With no rares, it isn't difficult to pick up important singles. — *Ian Lee*

You will need **20** nine-pocket pages to store this set. (10 doubled up)

Set (173 cards)		67.00
Booster Display Box		35.00
Booster Pack		2.00

Card name	Rarity	Price	Card name	Rarity	Price	Card name	Rarity	Price	Card name	Rarity	Price
[1]			[3]			☐ Fata Morgana	C2	0.20	☐ Inbase Discotek, Frankfurt	C2	0.20
☐ Acquired Ventrue Assets	U1	1.00	☐ Chandler Hungerford	V1	0.25	☐ Fear of Mekhet	U1	1.00	[8]		
☐ Aire of Elation	C3	0.15	☐ Chimerstry	C2	0.20	☐ Force of Will	C2	0.20	☐ Incriminating Videotape	C2	0.20
☐ Alexandra	V1	0.25	☐ Clan Loyalty	C2	0.20	☐ Forest of Shadows	U1	1.00	☐ Ingrid Rossler	V1	0.25
☐ Amadeo	V1	0.25	☐ Closed Session	C2	0.20	☐ Fortune Teller	C2	0.20	☐ Inveraray, Scotland	U3	1.00
☐ Anathema	U2	1.00	☐ Command of the Harpies	U2	1.00	☐ Fortune Teller Shop	C2	0.20	☐ Jar the Soul	C2	0.20
☐ Andrei Puxon	V1	0.25	☐ Compel the Spirit	U2	1.00	[6]			☐ Javier Montoya	V1	0.25
☐ Antediluvian Awakening	U2	1.00	☐ Conflict of Interests	C2	0.20	☐ Francesca Giovanni	V1	0.25	☐ Joaquina Amaya	V1	0.25
☐ Antoinette DuChamp	V1	0.25	☐ Constanza Vinti	V1	0.25	☐ Franciscus	V1	0.25	☐ Judgement:		
☐ Apparition	C2	0.20	☐ Corpse Minion	C2	0.20	☐ Francois Villon	V1	0.25	Camarilla Segregation	U1	1.00
[2]			[4]			☐ Gangrel Revel	U1	1.00	☐ Judgement: Death to the Brujah!	U1	1.00
☐ Arika	V1	0.25	☐ Cristofero Giovanni	V2	0.25	☐ Gaspare Giovanni	V1	0.25	☐ Katarina	V1	0.25
☐ Artistically Inept	U1	1.00	☐ Daliyah	V1	0.25	☐ Giovanni Acceptance	U2	1.00	[9]		
☐ Banishment	U2	1.00	☐ Darius Styx	V1	0.25	☐ Giovanni Discrimination	C2	0.20	☐ Kindred Coercion	U2	1.00
☐ Blessing of Durga Syn	C2	0.20	☐ Dartmoor, England	C2	0.20	☐ Gloria Giovanni	V1	0.25	☐ Klaus van der Veken	V1	0.25
☐ Blythe Candeleria	V1	0.25	☐ Destructive Secrets	C2	0.20	☐ Goodnight, Sweet Prince	U1	1.00	☐ Kostantin, Baro of the Caravan	V1	0.25
☐ Brujah Debate	U1	1.00	☐ Dûnal O'Connor	V1	0.25	[7]			☐ Leandro	U1	1.00
☐ Bureaucratic Overload	U2	0.50	☐ Elysium: The Palace of Versailles	U2	1.00	☐ Greger Anderssen	V1	0.25	☐ Legacy of Power	U1	1.00
☐ Burning Wrath	C2	0.20	☐ Enzo Giovanni,			☐ Guiseppe, Gravedigger	C2	0.20	☐ Legendary Vampire	U2	1.00
☐ Carlotta Giovanni,			Pentex Board of Directors	V1	0.25	☐ Gwendolyn	V1	0.25	☐ Leonardo, Mortician	U2	1.00
Necromanzatore Suprema	V1	0.25	☐ Etrius	V1	0.25	☐ Harrod	V1	0.25	☐ London Evening Star,		
			[5]			☐ Heidelburg Castle, Germany	U2	1.00	Tabloid Newspaper	U2	1.00
			☐ Eyes of the Dead	C2	0.20	☐ Horrid Reality	U1	1.00	☐ Madness of the Bard	U1	1.00
			☐ Faithful Servant	C2	0.20	☐ Horrific Countenance	C2	0.20	[10]		
			☐ Far Fatuus	C2	0.20	☐ Ignis Fatuus	C2	0.20	☐ Magdelena Schaefer	V1	0.25

RARITY KEY	C = Common	U = Uncommon	R = Rare	V = Vampire Deck	# = Lower numbers are rarer	X = Fixed/standard in all decks

Card name	Rarity	Price
Malkavian Derangement: Alternate Personality	U2	1.00
Morgue Hunting Ground	C2	0.20
Natalia	V1	0.25
Necromancy	C2	0.20
Nikolaus Vermeulen	V1	0.25
Nosferatu Hosting	U1	1.00
Nosferatu Performance Art	U1	1.00
Of Noble Blood	U2	1.00
[11]		
Order of Hermes Cabal	U1	1.00
Oxford University, England	C2	0.20
Palatial Estate	C2	0.20
Park Hunting Ground	C2	0.20
Pentex Subversion	U3	1.00
Pere Lachaise, France	U2	1.00
Playing for Keeps	U1	1.00
Possession	C2	0.20
Powerbase: Berlin	U1	3.00
[12]		
Powerbase: Rome	U2	3.00
Praxis Seizure: Amsterdam	U2	3.00
Praxis Seizure: Barcelona	U2	3.00
Praxis Seizure: Berlin	U2	3.00
Praxis Seizure: Brussels	U2	3.00
Praxis Seizure: Dublin	U2	3.00

Card name	Rarity	Price
Praxis Seizure: Frankfurt	U2	3.00
Praxis Seizure: Geneva	U2	3.00
Praxis Seizure: Glasgow	U2	3.00
[13]		
Praxis Seizure: London	U2	3.00
Praxis Seizure: Paris	U2	3.00
Praxis Seizure: Rome	U2	3.00
Praxis Seizure: Stockholm	U2	3.00
Praxis Seizure: Venice	U2	3.00
Precognizant Mobility	C2	0.20
Queen Anne	V1	0.25
Ranjan Rishi, Camarilla Scholar	V1	0.25
[14]		
Ravnos Acceptance	U2	1.00
Ravnos Cache	U1	1.00
Rebekka, Chantry Elder of Munich	V1	0.25
Regina Giovanni, The Right Hand of Augustus	V1	0.25
Release of the Shackled Soul	U2	1.00
Riposte	C3	0.15
Rom Gypsies	U2	1.00
Rudolpho Giovanni	V2	0.25
Ruins of Villars Abbey, Belgium	U1	1.00
Rutor's Hands	C1	0.20
[15]		
Sacre Cour Cathedral, France	C2	0.20

Card name	Rarity	Price
Sacrificial Lamb	C2	0.20
Salbatore Bokkengro	V1	0.25
Sasha Miklos	V2	0.25
Scapelli, The Family "Mechanic"	U2	1.00
Secure Haven	C2	0.20
Sensory Deprivation	U2	1.00
Shackles of Enkidu	U1	1.00
Shepherd's Innocence	C2	0.20
[16]		
Sigrid Bekker	V1	0.25
Soul Stealing	C2	0.20
Spectral Divination	C2	0.20
Spiritual Intervention	C2	0.20
Spiritual Protector	C2	0.20
Stanislava	V1	0.25
Stefano Giovanni	V1	0.25
Strained Vitae Supply	U2	1.00
Tara, The Hollow One (Mage)	U1	1.00
[17]		
Tereza Rost·s	V2	0.25
The Hunt Club	C1	0.20
The Louvre, Paris	C2	0.20
The Malkavian Seven Miseries	C2	0.20
The Mausoleum, Venice	U1	1.00
The Treatment	C2	0.20
The Trick of Danya	C2	0.20

Card name	Rarity	Price
Thoughts Betrayed	C2	0.20
Toreador Grand Ball	U1	1.00
[18]		
Torment the Soul	C2	0.20
Tradition Upheld	C2	0.20
Tremere Convocation	U1	1.00
Triole's Revenge	U1	1.00
Tsigane	V1	0.25
Vaclav Petalengro	V1	0.25
Veiled Sight	C2	0.20
Ventrue Directorate Assembly	C2	0.20
[19]		
Vial of Elder Vitae	U2	1.00
Vial of Garou Blood	C2	0.20
Victoria	V1	0.25
Vittorio Giovanni	V1	0.25
Volker, The Puppet Prince	V1	0.25
Wasserschloss Anif, Austria	U1	1.00
Werewolf Pack	C2	0.20
Whispers of the Nictuku	U2	1.00
Wilhelm Waldburg	V1	0.25
Wrath of the Inner Circle	U1	1.00
[20]		
Zoe	V1	0.25
Zombie	C2	0.20

You will need **20** nine-pocket pages to store this set. (10 doubled up)

VAMPIRE
THE ETERNAL STRUGGLE

Vampire • Ancient Hearts
Wizards of the Coast/White Wolf • Released February 1996
179 cards in set • **IDENTIFIER: Eye of Ra at upper right**

Set (179 cards)	86.00
Booster Display Box	30.00
Booster Pack	2.00

• Booster packs contain 12 cards; booster displays contain 45 boosters

Where **Dark Sovereigns** focused on Europe, **Ancient Hearts** focuses on the Middle East. Two new clans are added: Followers of Set (or Setites) and Assamites.

Setites are masters of corruption; one of their new cards is in fact titled **Corruption**. Their clan disciplines are Presence, Obfuscate, and Serpentis (new). Assamites are assassins. Their clan disciplines are Obfuscate, Celerity, and Quietus (new).

Ancient Hearts is reminiscent of *Dark Sovereigns* in that the new stuff is weak. Setites aren't weak because of their discipline mix, which contains two good older disciplines that work well together, but Serpentis has only one strong card, the incredibly powerful **Temptation**. Quietus lacks even that. And, like the Giovanni and Ravnos, the Setites and Assamites can use a boost in vampires to choose from. Speaking of the Giovanni and Ravnos, they do get a few more vampires, and necromancy and chimerstry get a few more cards in *Ancient Hearts*.

A few cards were made far too powerful: **Return to Innocence** first received a rewrite then was banned in tournament play.

Unlike *Dark Sovereigns*, *Ancient Hearts* has rares. Sure, 45 boosters in a box sounds like a great deal, but the rare sheet also included uncommons, so a significant portion of boosters have an uncommon in the "rare" slot. — **Ian Lee**

Card name	Rarity	Price
[1]		
Abd al-Rashid	V3	0.25
Absolution of the Diabolist	U5	0.60
Aisha	V3	0.25
Akhenaten, The Sun Pharaoh (Mummy)	R2	3.50
Akram	V3	0.25
Al-Ashrad, Amr of Alamut	V3	0.25
Alacrity	C2	0.15
Alamut	R2	3.00
Ambrosius, The Ferryman (Wraith)	R2	3.50
[2]		
Amisa	V3	0.25
Anachronism	C2	0.15
Arcanum Chapterhouse, Alexandria	U5	0.60
Arcanum Investigator	C2	0.15
Atonement	C2	0.20
Backstab	U5	0.60
Bang Nakh - Tiger's Claws	C2	0.20
Beyond Reproach	R2	3.50
Bindusara, Historian of the Kindred	V3	0.25
[3]		
Blood Agony	R2	2.00
Blood Sweat	C2	0.20
Blood Tears of Kephran	C2	0.15
Blood to Water	C2	0.15
Brachah	V3	0.25
Burnt Offerings	U5	0.60
Cairo Int'l Airport	R2	3.50
Carthage Remembered	R2	3.50
Catacombs	C2	0.15
[4]		
Children of Osiris	R2	3.50
Clan Impersonation	C2	0.15
Coagulate Blood	C2	0.15
Command	U5	0.60
Contract	C2	0.20
Cornelius Ottavio	V3	0.25
Corruption	C2	0.15
Corruption's Purge	V3	1.00
Covenant of Blood	C2	0.15

Card name	Rarity	Price
[5]		
Damaskenos, Herald of Leandro	V3	0.25
Death Pact	V3	1.00
Dedefra	V3	0.25
Depravity	V3	1.00
Disease	C2	0.20
Dog Pack	R2	2.00
Dreams of the Sphinx	R2	2.00
Elder Impersonation	C2	0.15
Elisabetta Romano	V3	0.25
[6]		
Erosion	U5	0.60
Eyes of the Serpent	C2	0.15
Faruq	V3	0.25
Foreshadowing Destruction	C2	0.15
Form of Corruption	R2	2.00
Form of the Serpent	C2	0.15
Foul Blood	U5	0.60
Grand Temple of Set	R2	3.50
Guardian Angel	C2	0.15
[7]		
Hadrian Garrick	V3	0.25
Harika Guljan	V3	0.25
Heart of Darkness	C2	0.15
Heartblood of the Clan	U5	0.60
Hidden Strength	C2	0.15

Card name	Rarity	Price
Humanitas	V3	1.00
Husamettin	V3	0.25
Iliana	V3	0.25
Illusions of the Kindred	V3	0.25
[8]		
Immaculate Vitae	C2	0.15
Imperial Decree	C2	0.15
Increased Strength	C2	0.20
Invitation Accepted	V3	1.00
Isabel de Leon	V3	0.25
Island of Yiaros	R2	3.50
Itzahk Levine	V3	0.25
Jackal	U5	0.60
Judah	V3	0.25
[9]		
Julius	V3	0.25
Kali's Fang	R2	3.50
Kalinda	V3	0.25
Kanya Akhtar	V3	0.25
Kemintiri	V3	0.25
Kephamos, High Priest of Marrakech	V3	0.25
Khalil Anvari	V3	0.25
Kherebutu (Bane Mummy)	R2	3.50
Lalitha	V3	0.25
[10]		
Laurent de Valois	V3	0.25

Card name	Rarity	Price
Lázár Dobrescu	V3	0.25
Lure of the Serpent	U5	0.60
Makarios, The Seducer	V3	0.25
Malkavian Rider Clause	R2	2.00
Marcellus	V3	0.25
Marijava Ghoul	U1/V2	1.00
Mario Giovanni	V3	0.25
Mark of Damnation	C2	0.15
[11]		
Mark of the Damned	C2	0.15
Market Square	U5	0.60
Mass Reality	C2	0.15
Mehemet of the Ahl-i-Batin (Mage)	R2	3.50
Melek	V3	0.25
Memories of Mortality	U5	0.60
Memory's Fading Glimpse	U5	0.60
Mercy for the Weak	C2	0.15
Might of the Camarilla	R2	2.00
[12]		
Mind Numb	C2	0.20
Mirembe Kabbada	V3	0.25
Muaziz, Archon of Ulugh Beg	V3	0.25
Mummify	U5	0.60
Mummy's Tongue	V3	1.00
Murat	V3	0.25

RARITY KEY **C** = Common **U** = Uncommon **R** = Rare **V** = Vampire Deck **#** = Lower numbers are rarer **X** = Fixed/standard in all decks

Card name	Rarity	Price
Mustafa Rahman	V3	0.25
Nakova, Advocate of Golconda	V3	0.25
Nepata	V3	0.25
[13] Oath of Loyalty	R2	4.00
Ohanna	V3	0.25
Opium Den	C2	0.15
Panagos Levidis	V3	0.25
Parnassus	V3	0.25
Patrizia Giovanni, Collector of Secrets	V3	0.25
Petru Sipos	V3	0.25
Phobia	U5	0.60
Praxis Seizure: Athens	R2	4.00
[14] Praxis Seizure: Cairo	R2	4.00
Praxis Seizure: Istanbul	R2	4.00
Praxis Seizure: Monaco	R2	4.00
Protect Thine Own	R2	3.50
Purity of the Beast	R2	3.50
Quietus	C2	0.20
Radeyah	V3	0.25

Card name	Rarity	Price
Rafaele Giovanni	V3	0.25
Ravnos Carnival	R2	3.50
[15] Raziya Samater	V3	0.25
Redeem the Lost Soul	R2	2.00
Regilio, The Seeker of Akhenaten	V3	0.25
Revelation of the Sire	C2	0.15
Revocation of Tyre	V3	1.00
Saqqaf, Keeper of the Grand Temple of Set	V3	0.25
Sarisha Veliku	V3	0.25
Scorpion Sting	C2	0.15
Seeds of Corruption	U5	0.60
[16] Serpentis	C2	0.20
Shadow of the Wolf	C2	0.20
Silence of Death	R2	2.00
Sins of the Cauchemar	C2	0.15
Spiridonas	V3	0.25
Suhailah	V3	0.25
Summon the Serpent	U5	0.60

Card name	Rarity	Price
Tainted Vitae	U5	0.60
Talaq, The Immortal	R2	3.50
[17] Tansu Bekir	V3	0.25
Taste of Death	C2	0.15
Temple Hunting Ground	C2	0.15
Temptation	R2	2.00
Terrorists	R2	3.50
The Ancestor's Talisman	C2	0.15
The Ankara Citadel, Turkey	U5	0.60
The Damned	C2	0.15
The Deadliest Sin	U5	0.60
[18] The Death of My Conscience	U5	0.60
The Khabar: Community	C2	0.15
The Khabar: Honor	V3	1.00
The Kiss of Ra	U5	0.60
The Parthenon	V3	1.00
The Path of Blood	C2	0.15
The Path of Typhon	C2	0.15
The Peace of Khetamon	C2	0.15
The Portrait	R2	3.50

Card name	Rarity	Price
[19] The Realm of the Black Sun	R2	2.00
The Return to Innocence	R2	3.50
The Secret Library of Alexandria	R2	3.50
The Signet of King Saul	R2	2.00
Thetmes, Calif of Alamut	V3	0.25
Tomb of Rameses III	R2	2.00
Tongue of the Serpent	C2	0.15
Treachery	U5	0.60
Treaty of Tyre Enforced	V3	1.00
[20] Uncontrollable Rage	U5	0.60
Underworld Hunting Ground	C2	0.15
Vasilis, The Traitor of Don Cruez	V3	0.25
Violation of Trust	C2	0.15
Watenda	V3	0.25
Weakness	U5	0.60
Whispers from the Dead	C2	0.15
Writ of Acceptance	C2	0.15

Vampire • The Sabbat

Wizards of the Coast/White Wolf • Released **November 1996**

411 cards in set • **IDENTIFIER: 'S' appears at upper right**

> You will need **46** nine-pocket pages to store this set. (23 doubled up)

• Booster packs contain 28 cards; booster displays contain 24 boosters

A stand-alone expansion for *Vampire*, *The Sabbat* covers the second most powerful sect in the World of Darkness (behind the Camarilla), the Sabbat. Where *Dark Sovereigns* and *Ancient Hearts* introduced two new clans each, *Sabbat* adds 10. A portion of the cards from the *Vampire* base set are reprinted.

The new cards tend to be better balanced and more playable than older cards. The emphasis is on combat over voting and bleeding. With only *Sabbat* cards, the emphasis makes sense. However, when mixing cards from all the sets, the *Sabbat* decks have a noticeable weakness in voting. And, as with all the new clans, the number of vampires per clan is far less than the original clans from the *Vampire* base set. It is a common practice to mix Camarilla clans with similar clans, the antitribu versions, from Sabbat as they often share disciplines. For example, the Brujah and the Brujah antitribu both have presence, celerity, and potence as clan disciplines.

Sabbat was very well received, so much so that a second printing sold out. One reason was that the cards have the best look in terms of layout of any Vampire cards. A stronger reason was the playability of the cards. For a while, it was possible to get boxes below retail online. But, boxes now go for a premium above retail, even online. Most of the boxes are gone, with the demand holding not only for the individual cards but for draft tournaments as well. White Wolf's **Sabbat War**, the long awaited expansion/reprint, only adds value to the *Sabbat* line of *Vampire*. — *Ian Lee*

Set (411 cards)	85.00
Starter Display Box	30.00
Booster Display Box	36.00
Starter Deck	5.00
Booster Pack	1.00

Card name	Rarity	Price
[1] .44 Magnum	C	0.20
Aaron Duggan, Cameron's Toady	V	0.35
Ablative Skin	R	2.00
Adaptability	R	2.00
Agatha	V	0.35
Aggressive Tactics	R	2.00
Alvaro, The Scion of Angelica	V	0.35
Ambush	C	0.20
Amusement Park Hunting Ground	U	0.60
[2] Anarchist Uprising	C	0.20
Angela Decker	V	0.35
Angelica, The Canonicus	V	0.35
Animalism	C	0.20
Anton	V	0.35
Antonio Delgado	V	0.35
Apportation	C	0.20
Arms of the Abyss	C	0.20
Arson	C	0.20

Card name	Rarity	Price
[3] Art Scam	R	2.00
Artemis	V	0.35
Ascendance	C	0.20
Aurora Van Brande, Paladin	V	0.35
Auspex	C	0.20
Awe	R	2.00
Ayelea, The Manipulator	V	0.35
Basil	V	0.35
Bauble	R	2.00
[4] Beast, The Leatherface of Detroit	V	0.35
Bestial Visage	R	2.00
Bewitching Oration	C	0.20
Billy	V	0.35
Black Spiral Buddy	U	0.60
Blaise	V	0.35
Blessing of Chaos	R	2.00
Blood Brother Ambush	R	2.00
Blood Doll	C	0.20
[5] Blood Feast	U	0.60
Blood of Acid	U	0.60
Bloodbath	R	3.00
Blur	C	0.20
Body Arsenal	C	0.20
Body Flare	R	2.00

Card name	Rarity	Price
Bonding	C	0.20
Bone Spur	C	0.20
Bonecraft	C	0.30
[6] Boxed In	C	0.20
Boy Toy	V	0.35
Brass Knuckles	C	0.20
Breath of the Dragon	R	2.00
Bribes	C	0.20
Bronwen	V	0.35
Brooke	V	0.35
Brujah Antitribu		
Bryan Van Duesen	V	0.35
[7] Cailean	V	0.35
Caitlin	V	0.35
Calebos	V	0.35
Call the Lamprey	U	0.60
Camarilla Threat	R	2.00
Camarilla Vitae Slave	R	2.00
Cameron	V	0.35
Campground Hunting Ground	U	0.60
Canine Horde	C	0.20
[8] Cardinal Benediction	U	0.80
Cardinal Sin: Failure of Mission	R	2.00
Cardinal Sin: Insubordination	U	0.60

Card name	Rarity	Price
Carrion Coffin	R	2.00
Carrion Crows	C	0.20
Carter	V	0.35
Catatonic Fear	U	0.60
Cats' Guidance	C	0.20
Cauldron of Blood	C	0.20
[9] Celerity	C	0.20
Changeling	C	0.20
Changeling Skin Mask	R	2.00
Channeling the Beast	C	0.35
Christine Boscacci	V	0.35
City Gangrel Connections	U	0.60
Claven	V	0.35
Cloak the Gathering	C	0.20
Code of Milan Suspended	R	2.00
[10] Coma	U	0.60
Combat Shotgun	C	0.20
Command of the Beast	U	0.60
Communal Haven: Temple	U	0.80
Computer Hacking	C	0.20
Concoction of Vitality	U	0.60
Confusion	C	0.20
Consanguineous Boon	C	0.20
Consecration Rites	U	0.60
[11] Corine Marcón	V	0.35

RARITY KEY C = Common U = Uncommon R = Rare V = Vampire Deck # = Lower numbers are rarer X = Fixed/standard in all decks

Card name	Rarity	Price
Corporate Hunting Ground	U	0.60
Creation Rites	R	2.00
Crusade: Atlanta	R	3.00
Crusade: Chicago	R	3.00
Crusade: Detroit	R	3.00
Crusade: Houston	R	3.00
Crusade: Mexico City	R	3.00
Crusade: Miami	R	3.00
Crusade: Philadelphia	R	3.00
Crusade: Pittsburgh	R	3.00
Crusade: Toronto	R	3.00
Cryptic Mission	C	0.20
Cryptic Rider	U	0.60
Cull the Herd	R	2.00
Dani	V	0.35
Dauntless Black Magician (Changeling)	R	2.00
Decapitate	U	0.60
Dementation	C	0.20
Demonstration	U	0.60
Derange	R	2.00
Detection	U	0.60
Devin Bisley	V	0.35
Direct Intervention	U	0.60
Dirty Little Secrets	U	0.60
Disarm	R	2.00
Disguised Weapon	C	0.20
Disputed Territory	C	0.20
Dissolution	U	0.60
Dodd	V	0.35
Dominate	C	0.20
Dominique	V	0.35
Donatien	V	0.35
Dragos	V	0.35
Dread Gaze	C	0.20
Dylan	V	0.35
Eldritch Glimmer	U	0.80
Elysian Fields	U	0.80
Enchanted Marionette	R	2.00
Enhanced Senses	C	0.20
Entombment	R	2.00
Escaped Mental Patient	U	0.60
Ethan Locke	V	0.35
Excommunication	U	0.60
Eyes of Chaos	C	0.20
Eyes of the Night	C	0.20
Fade from View	R	2.00
Fake Out	C	0.20
Fast Hands	U	0.60
Femur of Toomler	U	0.80
Festivo dello Estinto	U	0.60
Fetish Club Hunting Ground	U	0.60
Fire Dance	U	0.60
Fire in the Blood	R	2.00
Flamethrower	U	0.80
Flash	C	0.20
Fleshcraft	C	0.20
Forced Awakening	C	0.20
Forgotten Labyrinth	U	0.60
Fortitude	C	0.20
Fractured Armament	C	0.20
Frederick the Weak	V	0.35
Gang Tactics	R	2.00
Gang Territory	R	2.00
Gangrel Conspiracy	R	2.00
Gargoyle Slave	U	0.60
Gas-Powered Chainsaw	C	0.20
Genevieve	V	0.35
Gerard	V	0.35
Ghouled Street Thug	R	2.00
Gillian Krader	V	0.35
Gleam of Red Eyes	C	0.20
Goth Band	U	0.60
Gratiano	V	0.35
Guard Dogs	C	0.20
Guardian Ghoul	R	2.00
Guido Lucciano	V	0.35
Hand of Conrad	R	2.00
Hannibal	V	0.35
Heinrick Schlempt	V	0.35
Hidden Pathways	R	2.00
Horatio	V	0.35
Horrid Form	U	0.60
Huang, Blood Cultist	V	0.35
Hugo	V	0.35
Ian Forestal	V	0.35
Ian Wallingford	V	0.35
Ignacio, The Black Priest	V	0.35
Immortal Grapple	U	0.60
Imogen	V	0.35
Infamous Warlock	R	2.00
Infernal Familiar	R	2.00
Infernal Pact	R	2.00
Information Highway	U	0.60
Ingrid Russo	V	0.35
Innocent Bystander	R	2.00
Institution Hunting Ground	U	0.60
Intimidation	R	2.00
Investiture	R	2.00
Jacko	V	0.35
Jacob Bragg	V	0.35
Jessica	V	0.35
Jimmy Dunn	V	0.35
Josef	V	0.35
Jost Werner	V	0.35
Juan Cali	V	0.35
Kendrick	V	0.35
Kij Dansky	V	0.35
Kindred Spirits	C	0.20
Korah	V	0.35
Kurt Strauss	V	0.35
Lachlan, Noddist	V	0.35
Lambach	V	0.35
Laptop Computer	C	0.20
Lazverinus, Thrall of Lambach	V	0.35
Leather Jacket	C	0.20
Legacy of Caine	R	2.00
Legacy of Pander	R	2.00
Lena Rowe	V	0.35
Leon	V	0.35
Library Hunting Ground	U	0.60
Lightning Reflexes	R	2.00
Lisette Vizquel	V	0.35
Living Manse	R	2.00
Lolita	V	0.35
Lolita Houston	V	0.35
Lost in Crowds	C	0.20
Luther	V	0.35
Lyndhurst Estate, New York	U	0.60
Machine Blitz	R	3.00
Malkavian Derangement: Paranoia	U	0.80
Malkavian Game	U	0.60
Manstopper Rounds	U	0.60
March Halcyon	V	0.35
Marked Path	R	2.00
Marlene, The Infernalist	V	0.35
Masochism	R	2.00
Matteus, Flesh Sculptor	V	0.35
Meat Cleaver	U	0.60
Media Influence	C	0.20
Melange	R	2.00
Meshenka	V	0.35
Mind of a Child	U	0.60
Mind Rape	R	2.00
Mind Tricks	C	0.20
Mistaken Identity	U	0.60
Mitchell, The Headhunter	V	0.35
Mob Connections	U	0.60
Monique	V	0.35
Monomancy	U	0.80
Muriel Foucade	V	0.35
My Enemy's Enemy	R	2.00
Nephandus (Mage)	R	2.00
Nigel the Shunned	V	0.35
Night Moves	U	0.80
Nosferatu Kingdom	R	2.00
Obedience	U	0.60
Obfuscate	C	0.20
Obsession	R	2.00
Obtenebration	C	0.20
Olivia	V	0.35
Orgy of Blood	R	2.00
Out of Control	U	0.60
Pack Tactics	C	0.20
Palla Grande	R	2.00
Passion	C	0.20
Peace Treaty	C	0.20
Pentex Loves You!	U	0.60
Pieter	V	0.35
Plasmic Form	C	0.20
Political Antagonist	R	2.00
Political Hunting Ground	U	0.60
Political Seizure	U	0.80
Political Stranglehold	U	0.80
Political Struggle	R	2.00
Potence	C	0.20
Power Structure	R	2.00
Powerbase: Mexico City	U	1.00
Powerbase: New York	U	1.00
Precognition	C	0.20
Presence	C	0.20
Preternatural Evasion	C	0.20
Primal Instincts	C	0.20
Propaganda	U	0.80
Protean	C	0.20
Pulse of the Canaille	U	0.60
Pursuit	C	0.20
Pushing the Limit	C	0.20
Quentin	V	0.35
Quick Exit	C	0.20
Quick Meld	C	0.20
Quickness	R	2.00
Quira, The Bitch Queen	V	0.35
Ramiro	V	0.35
Rapid Change	C	0.20
Rapid Thought	U	0.60
Raptor	U	0.60
Recruiting Party	R	2.00
Recruitment	C	0.20
Redirection	C	0.20
Reform Body	R	2.00
Regaining the Upper Hand	C	0.20
Regeneration	C	0.20
Remilliard, Devout Crusader	V	0.35
Resilience	U	0.60
Restoration	C	0.20
Revelations	U	0.60
Revenant	U	0.60
Reverend Blackwood	V	0.35
Rex, The Necronomist	V	0.35
Richard Tauber, Ayelea's Puppet	V	0.35
Richter, The Templar of Du Mont	V	0.35
Rigby, Crusade Vanguard	V	0.35
Rolling with the Punches	C	0.20
Royce	V	0.35
Sabbat Inquisitor	U	0.60
Sabbat Priest	C	0.20
Sacrament of Carnage	C	0.20
Sacrifice	U	0.60
Sadie	V	0.35
Salinger	V	0.35
Samantha	V	0.35
Samson	V	0.35
Sarah Brando	V	0.35
Scouting Mission	C	0.20
Screw the Masquerade!	C	0.20
Scrying of Secrets	U	0.60
Secret Horde	C	0.20
Sela	V	0.35
Sermon of Caine	C	0.20
Shade	U	0.60
Shadow Body	C	0.20
Shadow Court Satyr (Changeling)	R	2.00
Shadow of the Beast	U	0.60
Shadow Play	C	0.20
Shadow Step	R	2.00
Shane Grimald	V	0.35
Shanty Town Hunting Ground	U	0.60
Sheila Mezarín	V	0.35
Short-Term Investment	C	0.20
Shotgun Ritual	R	2.00
Shroud of Night	C	0.20
Side Strike	C	0.20
Skin of Rock	C	0.20
Slaughtering the Herd	U	0.60
Slave Auction	R	2.00
Social Charm	C	0.20
Song in the Dark	R	2.00
Song of Serenity	C	0.20
Soul Burn	C	0.20
Speed of Thought	R	2.00
Spirit Summoning Chamber	U	0.60
Spirit's Touch	C	0.20
Sport Bike	U	0.60
Staredown	C	0.20
Steam Tunnels	U	0.60
Stravinsky	V	0.35
Submachine Gun	U	0.60
Succubus	R	2.00
Sudden Reversal	U	0.60
Summon the Abyss	R	2.00
Sunrise Service	R	2.00
Superior Mettle	C	0.20
Surprise Influence	C	0.20
Survivalist	U	0.80
Swallowed by the Night	C	0.20
Sword of Judgment	R	2.00
Telepathic Counter	C	0.20
Terror Frenzy	R	2.00
Thanks for the Donation	R	2.00
Thaumaturgy	C	0.20
The Art of Love	U	0.60
The Art of Pain	R	2.00
The Barrens	C	0.20
The Bruisers	U	0.80
The Crimson Sentinel	R	2.00
The Hungry Coyote	R	2.00
The Rumor Mill, Tabloid Newspaper	U	0.60
The Sleeping Mind	C	0.20
Theft of Vitae	C	0.20
Thelonius	V	0.35
Threats	C	0.20
Thrown Gate	C	0.20
Tier of Souls	R	2.00
Tithings	R	3.00
Tommy	V	0.35
Transfer of Power	R	2.00

RARITY KEY   C = Common   U = Uncommon   R = Rare   V = Vampire Deck   UR = Ultra Rare   F = Foil card   X = Fixed/standard in all decks

43
Card name	Rarity	Price
☐ Trap	C	0.20
☐ Tribute to the Master	C	0.20
☐ Twisted Forest	R	2.00
☐ Twisting the Knife	R	2.00
☐ Unacceptable Appearance	U	0.60
☐ Undead Persistence	U	0.60
☐ Undead Strength	C	0.20
☐ University Hunting Ground	U	0.80
☐ Unnatural Disaster	U	0.50

44
Card name	Rarity	Price
☐ Up Yours!	R	2.00
☐ Using the Advantage	R	2.00
☐ Vanessa	V	0.35
☐ Vasantasena	V	0.35
☐ Vaulderie	U	0.60
☐ Ventrue Investment	U	0.80
☐ Vicissitude	C	0.20
☐ Vicissitude Poisoning	R	2.00
☐ Victor Revell, Loyalist	V	0.35

45
Card name	Rarity	Price
☐ Violet Tremain	V	0.35
☐ Virgil	V	0.35
☐ Voter Captivation	U	0.80
☐ Walk of Flame	U	0.60
☐ Walk through Arcadia	R	2.00
☐ War Ghoul	R	2.00
☐ War Party	U	0.60
☐ Wave of Insanity	R	2.00
☐ Wendy Wade	V	0.35

46
Card name	Rarity	Price
☐ White Phosphorus Grenade	U	0.60
☐ Wolf Claws	C	0.20
☐ Wolf Companion	U	0.60
☐ Yong-Sun, Harmonist	V	0.35
☐ Yorik	V	0.35
☐ Zachary	V	0.35

Vampire • Sabbat War

White Wolf • Released **October 2000**

437 cards in set • **IDENTIFIER: Upside-down ankh at upper right**

- Starter decks contain 90 cards; starter displays contain 8 boosters
- Booster packs contain 11 cards; booster displays contain 36 boosters

After a three-year hiatus, the rights to the **Vampire** CCG went to White Wolf, on whose *Vampire: The Masquerade* story-telling game the CCG is based. On Halloween 2000, White Wolf relaunched the game with **Sabbat War**, a heavily revised edition of **The Sabbat** set.

The set included both booster packs and pre-constructed decks so that new players could get an easy introduction to the complex, strategic play of *Vampire*.

As promised, *Sabbat War* cards are compatible with all previously published editions of *Vampire*.

You will need **49** nine-pocket pages to store this set. (25 doubled up)

[Card image: Ambush]

Set (437 cards)		87.50
Starter Display Box		50.00
Booster Display Box		67.00
Starter Deck		8.50
Booster Pack		2.50

1
Card name	Rarity	Price
☐ .44 Magnum	X	0.60
☐ Aaron Duggan, Cameron's Toady	U	0.35
☐ Ablative Skin	R	3.00
☐ Acrobatics	X	0.60
☐ Adaptability	R	3.00
☐ Agatha	U	0.35
☐ Aggressive Tactics	R	3.00
☐ Alvaro, The Scion of Angelica	X	0.60
☐ Ambrosio Luis Monçada, Plenipotentiary	U	0.35

2
Card name	Rarity	Price
☐ Ambush	X/C	0.25
☐ Amelia	X	0.60
☐ Amusement Park Hunting Ground	X/U	0.75
☐ Anarchist Uprising	X/C	0.25
☐ Ancient Influence	X	0.60
☐ Angela Decker	U	0.35
☐ Angelica, The Canonicus	X	0.60
☐ Animalism	X/C	0.25
☐ Antediluvian Awakening	X	0.60

3
Card name	Rarity	Price
☐ Anton	X/U	0.25
☐ Antonio Delgado	X/U	0.25
☐ Arms of the Abyss	X/C	0.25
☐ Army of Rats	X	0.60
☐ Arson	X	0.60
☐ Art Scam	R	3.00
☐ Aurora Van Brande, Paladin	X	0.60
☐ Auspex	X/C	0.25
☐ Autarkis Persecution	X	0.60

4
Card name	Rarity	Price
☐ Awe	R	2.00
☐ Basil	U	0.35
☐ Bauble	R	3.00
☐ Beast, The Leatherface of Detroit	U	0.35
☐ Bestial Visage	R	3.00
☐ Bewitching Oration	C	0.20
☐ Billy	U	0.35
☐ Black Metamorphosis	R	2.00

5
Card name	Rarity	Price
☐ Blaise	U	0.35
☐ Blanket of Night	R	2.00
☐ Blood Brother Ambush	X/R	3.50
☐ Blood Doll	X	0.60
☐ Blood Feast	X	0.60
☐ Blood of Acid	X	0.60
☐ Blood of the Sabbat	R	2.00
☐ Blood Siege	R	2.00
☐ Bloodbath	R	3.00
☐ Bloodform	R	3.00

6
Card name	Rarity	Price
☐ Blur	X	0.60
☐ Body Arsenal	X	0.60
☐ Body Flare	R	2.00
☐ Bonding	X	0.60
☐ Bonecraft	X/C	0.25
☐ Boxed In	X	0.60
☐ Brass Knuckles	X/C	0.25
☐ Breath of the Dragon	X	0.60
☐ Bribes	X/C	0.25

7
Card name	Rarity	Price
☐ Bronwen	X	0.60
☐ Bum's Rush	X	0.60
☐ Burning Wrath	X	0.60
☐ Cailean	U	0.35
☐ Caitlin	U	0.35
☐ Calebos	U	0.35
☐ Caliban	C	0.20
☐ Camarilla Threat	R	3.00
☐ Cameron	X	0.60

8
Card name	Rarity	Price
☐ Campground Hunting Ground	U	0.50
☐ Canine Horde	X	0.60
☐ Cardinal Benediction	U	0.75
☐ Cardinal Sin: Failure of Mission	X/R	3.50
☐ Cardinal Sin: Insubordination	U	1.00
☐ Carrion Crows	X/C	0.25
☐ Carter	U	0.35
☐ Catatonic Fear	U	0.35
☐ Cats' Guidance	X/C	0.25

9
Card name	Rarity	Price
☐ Celerity	X/C	0.25
☐ Changeling	X/C	0.25
☐ Changeling Skin Mask	R	3.00
☐ Chiropteran Marauder	X/C	0.25
☐ Cicatriz	C	0.20
☐ Claven	U	0.35
☐ Cloak the Gathering	C	0.20

Card name	Rarity	Price
☐ Code of Milan Suspended	R	2.00
☐ Coma	U	0.75

10
Card name	Rarity	Price
☐ Combat Shotgun	C	0.20
☐ Command of the Beast	U	0.35
☐ Communal Haven: Temple	X	0.60
☐ Computer Hacking	X	0.60
☐ Concoction of Vitality	X	0.60
☐ Conditioning	X	0.60
☐ Consanguineous Boon	X	0.60
☐ Conservative Agitation	X/C	0.25
☐ Corine Marcón	X	0.60

11
Card name	Rarity	Price
☐ Corporate Hunting Ground	X/U	0.75
☐ Courier	U	0.50
☐ Creation Rites	R	2.00
☐ Crusade: Atlanta	R	4.00
☐ Crusade: Detroit	R	4.00
☐ Crusade: Houston	R	4.00
☐ Crusade: Mexico City	X	0.60
☐ Crusade: New York	R	4.00
☐ Crusade: Philadelphia	R	4.00

12
Card name	Rarity	Price
☐ Crusade: Pittsburgh	X	0.60
☐ Cull the Herd	R	3.00
☐ Daring the Dawn	X/R	3.50
☐ Darkness Within	U	0.35
☐ Darksight	X/C	0.25
☐ Darrel Boyce, Consul	C	0.20
☐ Dead-End Alley	X	0.60
☐ Decapitate	X	0.60
☐ Deflection	X	0.60

13
Card name	Rarity	Price
☐ Dementation	C	0.20
☐ Demonstration	X	0.60
☐ Detection	X/R	3.50
☐ Devin Bisley	X/U	0.25
☐ Direct Intervention	X	0.60
☐ Disarm	R	2.00
☐ Disguised Weapon	C	0.20
☐ Disputed Territory	X	0.60
☐ Dissolution	U	0.50

14
Card name	Rarity	Price
☐ Distraction	X	0.60
☐ Dodd	X	0.60
☐ Dodge	X	0.60
☐ Dolphin Black	C	0.20
☐ Dominate	X/C	0.25
☐ Dominique	X	0.60

Card name	Rarity	Price
☐ Donatien	U	0.35
☐ Dragos	X	0.60

15
Card name	Rarity	Price
☐ Drawing Out the Beast	X	0.60
☐ Dread Gaze	X	0.60
☐ Dylan	X	0.60
☐ Effective Management	X	0.60
☐ Elder Library	X	0.60
☐ Ellen Fence, the Tracker	U	0.35
☐ Elysian Fields	X	0.60
☐ Enchant Kindred	X	0.60
☐ Enchanted Marionette	R	3.00
☐ Enhanced Senses	X	0.60

16
Card name	Rarity	Price
☐ Entombment	X/R	3.50
☐ Escaped Mental Patient	U	0.50
☐ Eternal Vigilance	X/U	0.25
☐ Evangeline	C	0.20
☐ Excommunication	X	0.60
☐ Eyes of Chaos	C	0.20
☐ Eyes of the Night	X	0.60
☐ Fake Out	X	0.60
☐ Fame	X	0.60

17
Card name	Rarity	Price
☐ Far Mastery	X	0.60
☐ Fast Hands	X/C	0.25
☐ Femur of Toomler	X	0.60
☐ Festivo dello Estinto	X/U	1.00
☐ Fetish Club Hunting Ground	U	0.50
☐ Fire in the Blood	R	2.00
☐ Flak Jacket	X	0.60
☐ Flamethrower	X	0.60
☐ Flash	X/C	0.25

18
Card name	Rarity	Price
☐ Fleshcraft	X	0.60
☐ Forced Awakening	X/C	0.25
☐ Forgotten Labyrinth	U	0.35
☐ Fortitude	X/C	0.25
☐ Fractured Armament	X/C	0.25
☐ Francisco Domingo de Polonia	X	0.60
☐ Frederick the Weak	X/U	0.25
☐ Gang Tactics	R	3.00
☐ Gang Territory	R	3.00

19
Card name	Rarity	Price
☐ Gangrel Conspiracy	R	3.00
☐ Gas-Powered Chainsaw	X/C	0.25
☐ Gerard	X	0.60
☐ Ghouled Street Thug	R	3.00
☐ Govern the Unaligned	X	0.60

RARITY KEY C = Common   U = Uncommon   R = Rare   V = Vampire Deck   UR = Ultra Rare   F = Foil card   X = Fixed/standard in all decks

Card name	Rarity	Price
Gratiano	X/U	0.25
Greta Kircher	C	0.20
Guard Dogs	X/C	0.25
Guardian Ghoul	R	2.00
Guido Lucciano	U	0.35
Hand of Conrad	R	2.00
Hannibal	U	0.35
Haven Affinity	R	3.00
Haven Uncovered	X	0.60
Hawg	X	0.60
Hidden Lurker	C	0.20
Hidden Pathways	R	3.00
High Museum of Art, Atlanta	R	2.00
Horatio	U	0.35
Horrid Form	X	0.60
Huang, Blood Cultist	U	0.35
Hugo	X	0.60
Idalia, Prophet of Guadalajara	C	0.20
Ignacio, The Black Priest	X/U	0.25
Immortal Grapple	X/U	0.25
Information Highway	X	0.60
Ingrid Russo	X/U	0.25
Inner Essence	X/U	0.25
Institution Hunting Ground	U	0.50
Intimidation	R	2.00
Investiture	R	3.00
J. S. Simmons, Esq.	X	0.60
Jacko	U	0.35
Jacob Bragg	X	0.60
Jost Werner	U	0.35
Juan Cali	X/U	0.25
Kindred Manipulation	X/R	3.50
Kindred Spirits	C	0.20
Kite	C	0.20
Korah	U	0.35
Kraken's Kiss	X/C	0.25
Kyle Strathcona, Cardinal of Canada	X	0.60
Lambach	X/U	0.25
Laptop Computer	X	0.60
Lazverinus, Thrall of Lambach	X/U	0.25
Leather Jacket	X/C	0.25
Legacy of Caine	X/R	3.50
Legacy of Pander	R	2.00
Legal Manipulations	X	0.60
Library Hunting Ground	X/U	0.75
Life Boon	X	0.60
Lightning Reflexes	X/R	3.50
Lisette Vizquel	X	0.60
Little Tailor of Prague	U	0.35
Living Manse	R	2.00
Lobotomy	R	3.00
Lolita Houston	X	0.60
Lucita	X	0.60
Lucky Blow	X	0.60
Lunatic Eruption	R	3.00
Luther	U	0.35
Malkavian Derangement: Paranoia	R	3.00
Manstopper Rounds	X/U	0.75
March Halcyon	X	0.60
Marked Path	R	3.00
Marlene, The Infernalist	X	0.60
Masochism	R	3.00
Meat Cleaver	X/C	0.25
Media Influence	C	0.20
Melange	R	3.00
Meld with the Land	X/C	0.25
Mercy, Knight Inquisitor	C	0.20
Meshenka	X	0.60

Card name	Rarity	Price
Mighty Grapple	X	0.60
Miller Delmardigan, Teacher of Bahari	C	0.20
Mind Rape	R	2.00
Minion Tap	X	0.60
Misdirection	X	0.60
Mistaken Identity	X/R	3.50
Mitchell, The Headhunter	X	0.60
Mob Connections	X	0.60
Monomancy	U	0.75
Mr. Winthrop	X	0.60
Muriel Foucade	U	0.35
My Enemy's Enemy	R	2.00
Nigel the Shunned	U	0.35
Nosferatu Kingdom	R	3.00
Obedience	X	0.60
Obfuscate	C	0.20
Obsession	R	3.00
Obtenebration	C	0.20
Omaya	C	0.20
Open Grate	X	0.60
Orgy of Blood	R	3.00
Oubliette	X/U	0.25
Out of Control	X/R	3.50
Ox, Viceroy of the Hollows	C	0.20
Pack Tactics	C	0.20
Palla Grande	R	2.00
Patronage	U	0.75
Patterns in the Chaos	R	3.00
Peace Treaty	X	0.60
Pentex Loves You!	X/U	0.75
Personal Scourge	C	0.20
Peter Blaine	C	0.20
Pier 13, Port of Baltimore	X/U	1.00
Plasmic Form	X	0.60
Political Antagonist	R	3.00
Political Hunting Ground	X/U	0.75
Political Seizure	X/U	1.00
Political Stranglehold	X/U	1.00
Political Struggle	X/R	3.50
Potence	X/C	0.25
Power Structure	R	2.00
Powerbase: Madrid	R	2.00
Powerbase: Mexico City	X/U	1.00
Powerbase: Montreal	R	2.00
Precognition	X/C	0.25
Presence	C	0.20
Preternatural Evasion	C	0.20
Primal Instincts	X/C	0.25
Private Audience	X/C	0.25
Propaganda	U	0.75
Protean	C	0.20
Pulled Fangs	X	0.60
Pulse of the Canaille	X	0.60
Purchase Pact	X/U	0.75
Pursuit	X/C	0.25
Pushing the Limit	X/C	0.25
Quentin	X/U	0.25
Quick Exit	C	0.20
Quick Meld	C	0.20
Quickness	R	2.00
Rabble Razing	X/C	0.25
Ramiro	X	0.60
Rapid Change	C	0.20
Rapid Healing	X	0.60
Rat's Warning	X	0.60
Rave	X/C	0.25
Reality Mirror	R	2.00
Recruiting Party	R	2.00
Recruitment	X	0.60

Card name	Rarity	Price
Redirection	X/C	0.25
Reform Body	X	0.60
Regeneration	C	0.20
Regent	R	2.00
Remilliard, Devout Crusader	U	0.35
Resilience	X/U	0.75
Restoration	X	0.60
Restructure	R	3.00
Revelations	X/U	1.00
Revenant	X	0.60
Richter, The Templar of Du Mont	X/U	0.25
Rigby, Crusade Vanguard	X/U	0.25
Rolling with the Punches	X/C	0.25
Sabbat Priest	X/C	0.25
Sacrament of Carnage	X/C	0.25
Sadie	U	0.35
Salinger	X/U	0.25
Samantha	U	0.35
San Nicolás de los Servitas	R	2.00
Sarah Brando	X	0.60
Sascha Vykos, The Angel of Caine	X	0.60
Saturday-Night Special	X	0.60
Sawed-Off Shotgun	X	0.60
Scouting Mission	X/C	0.25
Scrying of Secrets	X	0.60
Secret Horde	C	0.20
Seduction	X	0.60
Sela	X	0.60
Sermon of Caine	C	0.20
Shade	X	0.60
Shadow Body	X	0.60
Shadow Court Satyr (Changeling)	R	3.00
Shadow of the Beast	U	0.50
Shadow Play	X/C	0.25
Shadow Strike	X/C	0.25
Shadow Twin	X/C	0.25
Shannon Price, the Whisperer	C	0.20
Shanty Town Hunting Ground	U	0.50
Sheila Mezarin	U	0.35
Shock Troops	R	2.00
Short-Term Investment	X	0.60
Shroud of Night	X	0.60
Side Strike	C	0.20
Sideslip	X	0.60
Skin of Rock	X/C	0.25
Skin Trap	U	0.35
Slaughtering the Herd	U	0.75
Slave Auction	R	2.00
Social Charm	X/C	0.25
Song in the Dark	R	2.00
Song of Serenity	X/C	0.25
Speed of Thought	R	2.00
Spirit's Touch	X/C	0.25
Sport Bike	X	0.60
Staredown	C	0.20
Storage Annex	X/C	0.25
Stravinsky	X	0.60
Sudden Reversal	X/U	2.00
Sunrise Service	R	3.00
Superior Mettle	X/C	0.25
Surprise Influence	X	0.60
Survivalist	X	0.60
Swallowed by the Night	C	0.20
Sword of Judgment	X	4.00
Talley, the Hound	C	0.20
Tasha Morgan	R	3.00
Taste of Vitae	X	0.60

Card name	Rarity	Price
Telepathic Counter	X/C	0.25
Telepathic Tracking	U	0.35
Telepathic Vote Counting	X	0.60
Templar	X/C	0.25
Terrence	X	0.60
Terror Frenzy	R	3.00
Thanks for the Donation	R	3.00
The Art of Pain	R	3.00
The Barrens	X	0.60
The Coven	R	2.00
The Crimson Sentinel	R	2.00
The Haunting	C	0.20
The Hungry Coyote	R	2.00
The Path of Metamorphosis	U	0.75
The Path of Night	U	0.35
The Path of the Feral Heart	U	0.50
The Rumor Mill, Tabloid Newspaper	X/U	0.75
The Sleeping Mind	C	0.20
Thoughts Betrayed	X	0.60
Threats	X/C	0.25
Thrown Gate	X	0.60
Thrown Sewer Lid	X	0.60
Tier of Souls	R	2.00
Tithings	R	3.00
Tomb of Rameses III	R	2.00
Tommy	U	0.35
Torn Signpost	X	0.60
Total Insanity	C	0.20
Transfer of Power	R	3.00
Trap	X	0.60
Tribute to the Master	X/C	0.25
Twisted Forest	R	2.00
Twisting the Knife	R	3.00
Unacceptable Appearance	R	3.00
Undead Persistence	X	0.60
Undead Strength	X/C	0.25
Unflinching Persistence	X	0.60
Unnatural Disaster	X	0.60
Up Yours!	R	3.00
Using the Advantage	R	2.00
Vagabond Mystic	U	0.75
Vanessa	X	0.60
Vasantasena	U	0.35
Vaulderie	X	0.60
Ventrue Investment	X/U	0.75
Vicissitude	X/C	0.25
Vicissitude Poisoning	X/R	3.50
Victor Revell, Loyalist	U	0.35
Victor Tolliver	X	0.60
Vincent Day, Paladin and Paragon	X	0.60
Violet Tremain	X	0.60
Voice of Madness	U	0.35
Wake with Evening's Freshness	X	0.60
Walk through Arcadia	R	3.00
War Ghoul	R	2.00
War Party	X/U	0.75
Waste Management Operation	U	0.50
Wendy Wade	U	0.35
White Phosphorus Grenade	U	0.50
Wolf Claws	C	0.20
Wolf Companion	X	0.60
Wooden Stake	X	0.60
Wren	C	0.20
Yorik	U	0.35
Zachary	U	0.35
Zip Gun	X	0.60

RARITY KEY C = Common U = Uncommon R = Rare V = Vampire Deck UR = Ultra Rare F = Foil card X = Fixed/standard in all decks

Warlords

Iron Crown Enterprises • Released September 1997

255 cards in set

You will need **29** nine-pocket pages to store this set.
(15 doubled up)

- Starter decks contain 60 cards; starter displays contain 6 starters and 24 boosters
- Booster packs contain 12 cards

Designed by **Ian Trout**

Based on the *Warlords* computer game from the early 1990s, **Warlords** depicts a fantasy battle between eight races in a Tolkienesque world.

Players take the role of one of the eight warlords and play castles, heroes, and banner cards; spend revenue; play terrain, weather, calamity, and spell cards; march their armies; engage in battles; explore ruins; and play new ruins. The game ends when the set number of castles is won, all other players lose their castles and heroes, or all players draw their "Time Passes" cards from their decks.

The battle system breaks a rule of CCG simplicity in using a Combat Resolution Table. Each Army, Hero, Ally, and Artefact [sic] card in a stack ("unit") has a Battle Value. Each player adds together the battle values of his armies, heroes, and allies that are in the stack involved in the battle. Once artifact and terrain bonuses are accounted for, the defender's total battle value is subtracted from the attacker's total combat value and then compared to the table to determine the number of cards that are lost from each stack of cards. An acceptable system for a board game, not so much for a card game.

A generic fantasy setting, lack of card rarities, complex combat system, and average artwork combined with poor marketing and lack of tournament support (for which the game seemed to be made) all contributed to *Warlords'* relatively quick demise.

A new CCG from Alderac for 2001, **Warlord**, is not related. Preview decks appear in *Scrye* 8.3 (Apr 2001) — *James Mishler*

	Rating
Concept	●●●○○
Gameplay	●●●○○
Card art	●●●○○
Player pool	○○○○○

	Price
Set (255 cards)	50.00
Display Box	25.00
Starter Deck	5.00
Booster Pack	1.00

Card name	Price
1	
Aelfwine	0.25
Ak's Archers	0.25
Alfars Leap	0.25
Ambush	0.25
Ar-Arak	0.25
Arak Treemen	0.25
Archers	0.25
Archon - Garome	0.25
Argenthorn	0.25
2	
Ariel Orcbane	0.25
Asgar's Band	0.25
Balad Naran	0.25
Bane Citadel	0.25
Barthel	0.25
Bastion #1	0.25
Bastion #2	0.25
Beast of Loremark	0.25
Beleri	0.25
3	
Boogul's Loot	0.25
Bow of Eldros	0.25
Bowmen of Mirk	0.25
Brigette	0.25
Capital	0.25
Carmel	0.25
Catapults	0.25
Cavalry of Angbar	0.25
Citadel of Fire	0.25
4	
City Curse	0.25
Cobb's Legion	0.25
Coll's Horsemen	0.25
Combat Results Oracle Help	0.25
Cragmorton	0.25
Crypt of Molok	0.25
Cup of Haste	0.25
Daric Barrows	0.25
Daric's Treasure	0.25
5	
Dark Demon	0.25

Card name	Price
Dark Forest	0.25
Dawn Stone	0.25
Dead Swamp	0.25
Demon of Iris	0.25
Derridon	0.25
Desert of Huinedor	0.25
Dhar Ghost	0.25
Dhar-Khosis	0.25
6	
Direction of Play Help	0.25
Doppelganger	0.25
Draco Ularis	0.25
Dragon of Lador	0.25
Dragon of Ungor	0.25
Dunethel	0.25
Dusk Stone	0.25
Dwarf Halls	0.25
Dwarven Bands	0.25
7	
Dwarves of Sulil	0.25
Earthquake	0.25
Elephants of Kalil	0.25
Elephants	0.25
Elvallie	0.25
Elvallie	0.25
Emerald Dragon	0.25
Emperor's Crypt	0.25
Emperor's Wizard	0.25
8	
Emrik's Wealth	0.25
Enchant	0.25
Engel's Archers	0.25
Enmouth Sqn	0.25
Enmouth	0.25
Erik's Archers	0.25
Espionage	0.25
Everful Purse	0.25
Famine	0.25
9	
Fatigue	0.25
Finger of Death	0.25
Fire Devil	0.25
Fire Elemental	0.25
Fire	0.25
Fleymark Forest	0.25
Fleymark	0.25
Forest of Sulador	0.25
Galin Giants	0.25

Card name	Price
10	
Garome Wasteland	0.25
Gemhold	0.25
Ghost of Khorfe	0.25
Giant Bats	0.25
Giant Hordes	0.25
Gildenhome	0.25
Gluk Zombies	0.25
Gol's Talisman	0.25
Gold of Ungor	0.25
11	
Gonk's Spiders	0.25
Gorag	0.25
Grail of Gold	0.25
Great Catapult	0.25
Grey Dwarves	0.25
Greyport Legion	0.25
Griffins	0.25
Gunthang	0.25
Halls of Chaos	0.25
12	
Harvest Stone	0.25
Haviel Fyrd	0.25
Haviel Ghost	0.25
Haviel's Gold	0.25
Heal	0.25
Heavy Cavalry	0.25
Heavy Infantry	0.25
Helrog's Band	0.25
Hereuth Woods	0.25
13	
Hills of Illone	0.25
Hills of Nirnoth	0.25
Hithos	0.25
Horn of Ages	0.25
Horn of Plenty	0.25
Horse Lords	0.25
Hulgar the Great	0.25
Hurricane Paramer	0.25
Ice Demon	0.25
14	
Illone Demon	0.25
Illone Pig Orcs	0.25
Ilnyr	0.25
Ilun's Griffins	0.25
Infernal Engine	0.25
Island Haven	0.25
Kabor's Jewels	0.25
Keep #1	0.25

Card name	Price
Keep #2	0.25
15	
Khamar	0.25
Knights of Fleymark	0.25
Knights of Naar	0.25
Kor	0.25
Krondana	0.25
Kyra the Slayer	0.25
Lady Arianna	0.25
Large Fleet	0.25
Leofsunu	0.25
16	
Light Cavalry	0.25
Light Infantry	0.25
Lightsword	0.25
Lord Albion	0.25
Lord Bane	0.25
Lord Khazan	0.25
Lord Melyodas	0.25
Loremark	0.25
Lurinth Wyrm	0.25
17	
M'Krum Taurs	0.25
Magic Carpet	0.25
Malikor Witch	0.25
March/Battle #1	0.25
March/Battle #2	0.25
March/Battle #3	0.25
March/Battle #4	0.25
Market Hub	0.25
Marthos Foot	0.25
18	
Marthos	0.25
Menel's Pikes	0.25
Meneloth	0.25
Minaduin Waste	0.25
Minotaurs	0.25
Mirk's Decay	0.25
Mirk's Gold	0.25
Moat #1	0.25
Moat #2	0.25
19	
Mog's Cavalry	0.25
Molok's Demon	0.25
Molok's Ghouls	0.25
Monolyth	0.25
Mordrok's Company	0.25
Morgana	0.25
Mountains of Taur	0.25

Card name	Price
Naar's Hoard	0.25
Necros' Collar	0.25
20	
Night Devil	0.25
Nik'z Orc Boyz	0.25
Nirn's Crypt	0.25
Nirn's Dwarves	0.25
Nirn's Typhoon	0.25
Nirn's Treasure	0.25
Nirnoth Dragon	0.25
Og's Giants	0.25
Ohmsmouth	0.25
21	
Okradon's Pouch	0.25
Oleg's Wolves	0.25
Orb of Loriel	0.25
Orc Mobs	0.25
Orcs of Kor	0.25
Pa-Kur	0.25
Paynor	0.25
Pegasi	0.25
Persephone	0.25
22	
Pestilence	0.25
Phantom Steed	0.25
Pikemen	0.25
Pillage	0.25
Plague	0.25
Prinz Myrkyn	0.25
Promotion	0.25
Raid	0.25
Raze	0.25
23	
Resurrection #1	0.25
Resurrection #2	0.25
Revenge	0.25
Rhojar the Sly	0.25
Ring of Power	0.25
Ruins of Kabor	0.25
Selentines	0.25
Shatter	0.25
Sir Lamerok	0.25
24	
Sirians	0.25
Small Fleet	0.25
Soul of Nob	0.25
Spear of Ank	0.25
Spiders	0.25

Card name	Price
Staff of Might	0.25
Staff of Movement	0.25
Staff of Ruling	0.25
Starlight Pegasi	0.25
25	
Stefan Fawktongue	0.25
Storm Giants	0.25
Stormheim	0.25
Sul's Spiders	0.25
Sulil Crag	0.25
Sulil Devil	0.25
Sulil Mountains	0.25
Summons	0.25
Taur Graveyard	0.25
26	
Taur Light Horse	0.25
Teleport	0.25
The Mire	0.25
Throne of Horan	0.25
Time Passes	0.25
Tome of Doom	0.25
Tower of Death	0.25
Tower of Night	0.25
Trade Port	0.25
27	
Traitor	0.25
Treachery #1	0.25
Treachery #2	0.25
Treachery #3	0.25
Ungueth Mountains	0.25
Upbourne	0.25
Vampire of Ak	0.25
Vulkir the Cruel	0.25
Wand of Flight	0.25
28	
White Mountains	0.25
Wights of Malikor	0.25
Witch's Broom	0.25
Wizard of Argenthorn	0.25
Wizard's Isle	0.25
Wolfriders	0.25
Wrath of Ohm	0.25
Wulfstan	0.25
Wyrm of Huinedor	0.25
29	
Xialla	0.25
Zaigonne Boneships	0.25
Zhoran	0.25

RARITY KEY   **C** = Common   **U** = Uncommon   **R** = Rare   **VR** = Very Rare   **UR** = Ultra Rare   **F** = Foil card   **X** = Fixed/standard in all decks

WCW Nitro

Wizard of the Coast • Released **April 2000**

169 cards in set

• Starter decks contain 82 cards; starter displays contain 12 starters
• Booster packs contain 11 cards; booster displays contain 36 boosters

Designed by **Mike Fitzgerald**

One of two werstling games to enter the CCG ring in 2000, **WCW Nitro** presents the world of World Championship Wrestling. Each player controls a specific WCW wrestler — like **Goldberg**, **Jeff Jarrett**, or **Diamond Dallas Page** — and a 60-card deck consisting mostly of various maneuvers, from **Body Slam** to the **Flying Elbow from the Top Rope**. Each maneuver does damage, which is taken directly from the other players' deck. Additional cards allow you to block damage, avoid defensive blocks, do additional damage with illegal objects (like a folding chair), bring back favorite cards from the discard pile, and much more.

The maneuvers are broken up into five categories (Hardcore, Flying, Hold, Lifting, and Maneuver), but each wrestler can only use any three of them, as indicated by color coding on the wrestler card. Some wrestlers also get damage bonuses with particular colors as well. Each player gets three Action Points per turn, and all maneuvers cost between one and three Action Points. The nastier moves cost more. Each maneuver also has a Nitro cost — you must bring **Nitro** cards into play first before you can get rolling. The first player to run out of cards loses. Frequently, a match will be decided by the luck of the draw; the player who gets his good cards into play at the right time, or draws a damage-blocking defensive card at an opportune moment, will carry the day.

WCW Nitro also has a balancing feature called Reputation. Each wrestler has a Reputation rating, and the higher the rating, the better the wrestler is likely to be. But if a full "match" is played the first player to three points wins. And while a high-Reputation wrestler only gets one point for beating a low-Rep wrestler, the low-Rep wrestler could get all three points with just a single win.

WCW Nitro suffered from the relative lack of popularity of the WCW brand of wrestling in 2000 as compared to the World Wrestling Federation. These things change, but the first *WCW* expansion, **Hardcore**, was delayed into 2001. — **Scott Haring**

Jeff Jarrett™
Height: 5'10" Weight: 230 lbs.
Once a round, you may "strut" and get 2 extra Action Points for this turn.
Jeff returned to WCW with a new attitude and quite a few guitars.
WRESTLER

Concept	●●●○○
Gameplay	●●●○○
Card art	●●●○○
Player pool	●●●○○

Set (169 cards)	102.50
Starter Display Box	80.00
Booster Display Box	80.00
Starter Deck	9.00
Booster Pack	2.80

Card name	Type	Rarity	Price
450 Splash	Move	C	0.25
Angry Fans	Thndr	U	1.00
Arm Bar	Move	C	0.25
Arm Drag and Twist	Move	U	1.00
Arm Toss	Move	C	0.25
The Artist	Move	C	0.25
Aysa at Work	Move	U	1.00
Aysa	Cornr	F	5.80
Backbreaker	Move	U	1.00
Backdrop	Move	U	1.00
Baseball Bat	Cornr	U	1.00
Bear Hug	Move	U	1.00
Belly-to-Belly Suplex	Move	C	0.25
Berlyn	Wrest	F	7.00
Berlyn's Chain	Move	R	4.50
Berlyn's Old Friend	Thndr	R	4.00
Big Block	Cornr	U	1.00
Big Splash	Move	C	0.25
Billy Kidman	Wrest	F	8.50
Block	Thndr	C	0.25
Body Slam	Move	C	0.25
Boot to the Head	Move	C	0.25
Bounce off the Ropes	Move	C	0.25
Bret Hart	Wrest	F	9.50
Bret's Sharpshooter	Move	R	4.00
Bret's the Best There Is	Thndr	R	4.00
Buff Bagwell	Wrest	F	6.50
Buff Is the Stuff	Thndr	R	4.00

Card name	Type	Rarity	Price
Buff's Fans	Cornr	R	3.50
Call for Help	Move	R	4.00
Camel Clutch	Move	U	0.90
Chae	Cornr	F	5.80
Chaos in the Ring	Move	U	1.00
Choke Hold	Move	C	0.25
Choke Slam	Move	U	1.00
Chop	Move	C	0.25
Closed Fist	Move	C	0.25
Clothesline	Move	C	0.25
Come from Behind	Move	R	4.00
Continue the Hold	Move	U	1.00
Corner Chaos	Move	U	1.00
Crowd Chants "Goldberg"	Thndr	R	4.00
DDP Gets Help from Kimberly	Thndr	R	4.00
DDP's Diamond Cutter	Move	R	4.50
DDP's Rapid-Fire Punches	Move	R	4.00
DDT	Move	U	1.00
Desperate Block	Thndr	U	1.00
Desperate Dodge	Thndr	U	1.00
Diamond Dallas Page (DDP)	Wrest	F	11.00
Disco Inferno	Wrest	F	7.50
Disco, the Gamblin' Man	Move	R	4.00
Disco's Boogie Punch	Move	R	4.00
Dive from the Top Rope	Move	U	1.00
Dodge	Thndr	C	0.25
Doug Dillinger	Cornr	R	3.50
Down but Not Out	Thndr	R	4.00
DQ	Thndr	R	4.00
Dropkick	Move	C	0.25
European Uppercut	Move	U	1.00

Card name	Type	Rarity	Price
Extra Effort	Move	U	1.00
Eye Rake	Move	C	0.25
Face Punch	Move	U	1.00
Fans Boo the Other Wrestler	Cornr	U	1.00
Fans Want Action	Cornr	R	4.00
Fast Punch	Move	C	0.25
Figure-Four Leg-Lock	Move	U	1.00
Flying Body-Press	Move	C	0.25
Flying Dropkick from the Top Rope	Move	U	1.00
Flying Elbow from the Top Rope	Move	C	0.25
Flying Forearm	Move	C	0.25
Flying Headbutt	Move	U	1.00
Flying Knee-Drop	Move	U	1.00
Folding Chair	Cornr	C	0.25
Full Stop	Cornr	U	1.00
Garbage Can	Cornr	U	1.00
Goldberg	Wrest	F	16.00
Goldberg's Jackhammer	Move	R	5.50
Goldberg's Spear	Move	R	6.00
Good Night, Everybody!	Move	U	1.00
Gouging	Move	C	0.25
Gut Check	Thndr	U	0.80
Hair Pull	Move	C	0.25
Head Stomp	Move	C	0.25
Headlock	Move	C	0.25
Heckling Fans	Thndr	U	1.00
Help	Move	U	1.00
Hidden Weapon	Move	U	1.00
Instant Replay	Move	C	0.25
Irish Whip to the Corner	Move	C	0.25
Irish Whip to the Ropes	Move	U	1.00
Jeff Jarrett	Wrest	F	6.50

Card name	Type	Rarity	Price
Jeff's Guitar	Cornr	R	4.50
Jeff's Punch	Move	R	4.00
Jimmy Hart	Cornr	U	1.00
Jump from the Top Rope	Move	C	0.25
Kevin Nash	Wrest	F	11.00
Kick	Move	C	0.25
Kidman Gets Help	Thndr	R	4.00
KidmanCam	Cornr	R	4.00
Kidman's Shooting-Star Press	Move	R	4.50
Larry Zybysko	Cornr	R	4.00
Late Nitro	Thndr	U	1.00
Loud Fans	Cornr	C	0.25
Low Blow	Move	C	0.25
Low Kick	Move	C	0.25
Making It Look Easy	Cornr	U	1.00
Mentor	Cornr	U	1.00
Missile Dropkick	Move	C	0.25
Mix In Some Nitro	Cornr	C	0.25
Moonsault	Move	C	0.25
Ms. Hancock Shows Off	Move	U	1.00
Nash's Elbow Smash	Move	R	4.50
Nash's Jackknife Power-Bomb	Move	R	6.00
Nash's nWo Support	Thndr	R	4.00
Nitro Girls	Cornr	F	6.00
Nitro Girls, Center Stage	Move	F	6.00
Nitro	Cornr	UC	0.30
No Holds Barred	Cornr	R	4.00
One on One	Move	R	3.50
Outside Interference	Cornr	R	4.00
Outta Here	Move	U	1.00
Payback	Thndr	C	0.25
Piledriver	Move	C	0.25
Pin	Move	U	1.00

RARITY KEY   **UC** = Ultra Common   **C** = Common   **U** = Uncommon   **R** = Rare   **VR** = Very Rare   **F** = Foil card   **X** = Fixed/standard in all decks

476 • *SCRYE Collectible Card Game Checklist and Price Guide*

Card name	Type	Rarity	Price
☐ Practiced Block	Cornr	C	0.25
☐ Practiced Dodge	Cornr	C	0.25
[15]			
☐ Punch	Move	C	0.25
☐ Quick Hit	Thndr	U	1.00
☐ Resistance Is Useless	Cornr	U	1.00
☐ Reversal	Thndr	R	4.00
☐ Reverse Somersault from the Top Rope	Move	U	1.00
☐ Rey Mysterio Jr.	Wrest	F	8.50
☐ Rey's Too Fast to Catch	Thndr	R	4.00
☐ Ringside Reinforcements	Cornr	R	4.00
☐ Rope Burn	Move	U	1.00

Card name	Type	Rarity	Price
[16]			
☐ Rowdy Roddy Piper Takes Charge	Move	C	0.25
☐ Running Start	Move	C	0.25
☐ Scott Hall	Wrest	F	9.50
☐ Scott's Abdominal Stretch	Move	R	4.50
☐ Scott's Outsider's Edge	Move	R	4.50
☐ Scott's Survey Time	Thndr	R	4.00
☐ Second Wind	Move	U	1.00
☐ Seeing Red	Move	U	1.00
☐ Sid Vicious	Wrest	F	8.50
[17]			
☐ Sid's Choke Slam	Move	R	4.50
☐ Sid's Rules	Thndr	R	4.50

Card name	Type	Rarity	Price
☐ Sleeper Hold	Move	C	0.25
☐ Snap Suplex	Move	C	0.25
☐ Spice	Cornr	F	5.80
☐ Spinning Kick	Move	C	0.25
☐ Stinger Splash	Move	R	4.50
☐ Sting	Wrest	F	11.00
☐ Sting's Mask	Cornr	R	4.50
[18]			
☐ Sting's Scorpion Death-Lock	Move	R	4.50
☐ Stopped Cold	Thndr	C	0.25
☐ Strong Block	Cornr	U	1.00
☐ Swinging Neckbreaker	Move	C	0.25

Card name	Type	Rarity	Price
☐ Table	Cornr	R	4.00
☐ Taking One for a Friend	Cornr	R	4.00
☐ Thrust to the Throat	Move	C	0.25
☐ Tongan Death-Grip	Move	C	0.25
☐ Top-Rope Punch	Move	U	1.00
[19]			
☐ Torrie at Work	Move	R	4.00
☐ The Total Package (TTP)	Wrest	F	9.50
☐ TTP's Flex Posedown	Move	R	4.00
☐ TTP's Torture Rack	Move	R	4.00
☐ Tygress	Cornr	F	5.80
☐ Vertical Suplex	Move	U	1.00
☐ You Can't Stop Me!	Move	U	1.00

Wheel of Time

Precedence • First set, *Premier*, released **December 1999**
297 cards in set • **IDENTIFIER: '1st ed.' appears at bottom**

- Starter decks contain 50 cards, playmat, and dice; starter displays contain 6 starters
- Booster packs contain 8 cards; booster displays contain 24 boosters

Lead designer **John Myler**

Based on the Robert Jordan fantasy book series of the same name, the **Wheel of Time** CCG presents a two-player battle between the Light and the Shadow which culminates in the "Last Battle" to decide the fate of the world.

The most distinctive features of *Wheel of Time* are the special dice, with unique symbols, which are used to resolve everything from bringing cards into play to determining who wins challenges. There are four types of dice representing the four different abilities in the game: politics, intrigue, one power, and combat. There are only seven different symbols on the dice, however, as three of the symbols can be found on multiple dice.

The Last Battle begins when the total of the Pattern reaches 20. Each side begins with two Pattern tokens on its side. Every turn, a Pattern challenge will cause either the Light, Shadow, or neutral Pattern to rise by one depending upon whether it is won by the Light or the Shadow, or whether neither wins it. Effectively, there is a sixteen-turn cap on the game because of the automatic Pattern challenge. While there are very few ways to remove Pattern tokens from the game, there are plenty of ways to add tokens, resulting in many games lasting fewer than sixteen turns. However, few games end in less than an hour. This surprising length for a two-player game comes largely from rolling numerous dice and having to track all the various results from the dice. Rolling 100+ dice towards the end of the game has been known to happen.

Up until the Last Battle, the player has several standard goals. First, having your starting character (**Rand al'Thor** for the Light, one of the Forsaken for the Dark) get killed loses you the game. Second, recruiting — playing characters and troops from hand — means that you have more dice-rolling cards in play. Rolling lots of dice wins you challenges, including the all-important Last Battle. Third, accumulating Pattern tokens on your side has a number of benefits, as does keeping your opponent's number of tokens down. The most direct benefit is that your number of tokens counts as automatic support or opposition, the terms used to determine whether a challenge succeeds or not where there must be more support than opposition for a challenge to succeed, as needed in the Last Battle.

Wheel of Time is a notable license for an unusual reason, as CCG players either were *very* familiar with the book series or knew nothing at all about it. The popularity of the books has, thereby, generated strong niche sales of the CCG in a few places. The artwork, with its slightly raised finish hasn't hurt. In addition, having lots of cards and lots of dice helps the enjoyment of the game. There are strong differences in tournament level play versus casual constructed play versus "out of the starter" play. — *Ian Lee*

You will need **33** nine-pocket pages to store this set. (17 doubled up)

Rand the King
Character, Dragon
Replace a Dragon Reborn character when you have 8 Pattern. Rand the King gains the allegiances of all characters he controls.
The Light illumine Rand al'Thor, King of Illian.

Rating					
Concept	●	●	●	○	○
Gameplay	●	●	●	●	○
Card art	●	●	●	●	○
Player pool	●	●	●	○	○

Set (297 cards)	312.50
Starter Display Box	68.00
Booster Display Box	47.50
2 player Starter Set	20.00
Starter Deck	10.00
Booster Pack	2.00

Card name	Type	Rarity	Price
[1]			
☐ A Beginning	Event	R	4.00
☐ A Murder of Ravens	Event	C	0.25
☐ A Second Chance	Adv	X	0.45

Card name	Type	Rarity	Price
☐ A Sign of Hope	Event	C	0.25
☐ A Stroke of Luck	Event	C	0.25
☐ A Time of Decision	Chall	C	0.25
☐ A Time of Peace	Event	R	4.00
☐ Advanced Scouts	Adv	U	0.80
☐ Al'cair'rahienallen	Adv	R	4.00
[2]			
☐ Amys	Char	U	0.80
☐ Andor	Adv	U	0.80
☐ Andor Cavalry	Troop	X	0.45
☐ Andor Infantry	Troop	X	0.45
☐ Andoran Spearman	Troop	U	0.80

Card name	Type	Rarity	Price
☐ Animate Stone	Event	U	0.80
☐ Asmodean	Char	R	5.50
☐ Assassination Attempt	Chall	U	0.80
☐ Aura of Death	Adv	U	0.80
[3]			
☐ Aviendha	Char	U	0.80
☐ Bain	Char	C	0.25
☐ Battle Hardened	Adv	C	0.25
☐ Be'lal	Char	R	5.00
☐ Berelain	Char	R	6.50
☐ Bitter Fighting	Event	R	4.00
☐ Blood Tide	Event	C	0.25

Card name	Type	Rarity	Price
☐ Bodyguards	Adv	X	0.45
☐ Border Clash	Chall	U	0.80
[4]			
☐ Broken Ground	Event	U	0.80
☐ Bubble of Evil	Event	C	0.25
☐ Caemlyn	Adv	R	4.00
☐ Cairhien	Adv	U	0.80
☐ Cairhien Footmen	Troop	C	0.25
☐ Cairhien Horseman	Troop	U	0.80
☐ Callandor	Chall	R	4.00
☐ Called to War	Adv	U	0.80
☐ Car'a'carn	Chall	U	0.80

Card name	Type	Rarity	Price
5			
Carpe Fatum	Event	R	4.00
Catapults	Troop	U	0.80
Charge	Event	C	0.25
Chiad	Char	U	0.80
Civil Unrest	Event	U	0.80
Combat Reserves	Adv	R	4.00
Commander	Char	X	0.45
Compulsion	Adv	R	4.00
Concealed Dagger	Adv	R	4.00
6			
Confrontation	Chall	X	0.45
Connections	Event	C	0.25
Cut Supply Lines	Chall	R	5.00
Dain Bornhald	Char	C	0.25
Dangerous Liaisons	Adv	R	4.00
Dark Dreams	Adv	R	4.00
Darkfriend	Adv	X	0.45
Darkfriend Band	Troop	U	0.80
Darkhound	Char	R	6.00
7			
Debt of Honor	Chall	X	0.45
Decisive Tactics	Event	X	0.45
Defensive Measures	Event	C	0.25
Dense Fog	Event	C	0.25
Dense Forest	Event	X	0.45
Disband	Event	C	0.25
Distractions	Event	C	0.25
Draghkar	Char	R	8.00
Dragon Banner	Adv	R	5.00
8			
Dragonsworn	Troop	R	5.00
Driven	Event	R	4.00
Duel	Event	C	0.25
Eamon Valda	Char	U	0.80
Earth Blast	Event	U	0.80
Egwene al'Vere	Char	X	0.45
Egwene the Accepted	Char	R	6.00
Elaida Sedai	Char	R	6.00
Elayne Trakand	Char	X	0.45
9			
Elyas	Char	R	6.00
Establish Contacts	Adv	U	0.80
Exiled	Chall	U	0.80
Expendable Troops	Event	C	0.25
Fade	Char	X/C	0.35
Fall Back	Event	C	0.25
Far Reaching Influence	Adv	C	0.25
Fireball	Event	X	0.45
Flanking Maneuvers	Chall	U	0.80
10			
Flowing Coffers	Chall	C	0.25
Forced Back	Chall	C	0.25
Forced March	Adv	R	4.00
Fortress of Light	Adv	R	6.00
Forward Scouts	Troop	U	0.80
From the Shadow	Chall	U	0.80
Further Demands	Adv	C	0.25
Further Goals	Event	R	4.00
Future Returns	Adv	R	5.00

Wheel of Time • Promos

Card name	Price
1	
Battle Fury	5.00
Filled With Power	4.00
Friend of the Dark	2.50
Moment of Transition	2.50
Night Raid	5.00
Pitched Battle	2.50
Power Play	2.50
Things Yet to Come	2.50
Uncontrolled Rage	2.50
2	
Unravel the Pattern	2.50

Card name	Type	Rarity	Price
11			
Gaining An Advantage	Chall	X	0.45
Galldrian su Riatin Rie	Char	R	6.00
Gareth Byrne	Char	R	5.00
Gateway	Event	U	0.80
Gather Allies	Chall	X	0.45
Gather Support	Chall	C	0.25
Gaul	Char	U	0.80
Geofram Bornhald	Char	R	5.50
Graendal	Char	R	5.00
12			
Gray Man	Char	U	0.80
Guarded by Fate	Event	R	4.00
Halfman	Char	R	5.00
Hampered	Event	C	0.25
Harassment	Event	C	0.25
Healing	Event	X	0.45
Heavy Armor	Adv	C	0.25
Heavy Fighting	Event	C	0.25
Herb Bag	Adv	U	0.80
13			
Heroic Efforts	Event	X	0.45
Heron-Mark Blade	Adv	R	4.00
Hidden Discoveries	Adv	R	4.00
Hidden Spies	Event	C	0.25
High Lady Alteima	Char	U	0.80
High Lady Estanda	Char	C	0.25
High Lord Aracome	Char	U	0.80
High Lord Geuyam	Char	C	0.25
High Lord Meilan	Char	R	6.00
14			
High Lord Samon	Adv	U	0.80
High Lord Torean	Char	C	0.25
High Lord Weiramon	Char	R	5.50
High Stakes	Event	R	4.00
Hired Agent	Char	C	0.25
Horn of Valere	Adv	R	5.00
Hostile Terrain	Event	C	0.25
House Guards	Troop	R	4.00
Human Rabble	Troop	X	0.45
15			
Hunting Trollocs	Chall	C	0.25
Illusion	Event	U	0.80
In Harm's Way	Event	C	0.25
Incentives	Event	C	0.25
Infighting	Event	C	0.25
Infiltration	Event	C	0.25
Inner Strength	Adv	U	0.80
Inspirational Leader	Adv	R	4.00
Into the Fight	Event	U	0.80
16			
Intolerance	Event	C	0.25
Ishamael	Char	R	6.00
Jaichim Carridin	Char	R	4.80
Jasin Natael	Adv	U	0.80
Juilin Sandar	Char	R	6.00
Knowledge Is Power	Event	C	0.25
Lady Aemlyn	Char	X	0.45
Lady Arathelle	Char	X	0.45
Lady Colavaere	Char	U	1.00
17			
Lady Elenia	Char	X	0.45
Lady Ellorien	Char	X	0.45
Lan Mandragoran	Char	X	0.45
Lanfear	Char	R	7.00
Learning From the Past	Chall	C	0.25
Liandrin Sedai	Char	R	5.00
Light Cavalry	Troop	X/C	0.25
Lightning	Event	U	0.80
Limit the Opposition	Chall	U	0.80
18			
Local Aid	Event	C	0.25
Loial	Char	R	6.00
Longbow	Adv	R	4.00
Lord Barthanes	Char	R	4.50
Lord Daricain	Char	U	0.80
Lord Edorian	Char	C	0.25

Card name	Type	Rarity	Price
Lord Gaebril	Adv	X	0.45
Lord Jarid	Char	X	0.45
Lord Lir	Char	X	0.45
19			
Lord Meresin	Char	U	0.80
Lord Nasin	Char	X	0.45
Lord Pelivar	Char	X	0.45
Lord Perrin	Char	R	6.00
Lord Talmanes	Char	U	0.80
Lucky Find	Event	R	4.00
Marksmen	Adv	U	0.80
Mat Cauthon	Char	X	0.45
Mat the Warrior	Char	R	6.00
20			
Min	Char	R	5.00
Misdirection	Event	C	0.25
Moghedien	Char	R	5.10
Momentum	Adv	U	0.80
Morgase Trakand	Char	R	5.00
Moiraine Sedai	Char	X	0.45
Mount	Adv	R	3.50
Naeblis	Adv	U	0.80
Narg	Char	C	0.25
21			
Narrow Escape	Event	U	0.80
Noble Allies	Chall	R	4.00
Nynaeve al'Meara	Char	R	5.00
Overrun	Event	X	0.45
Padan Fain	Char	X	0.45
Patrol	Troop	U	0.80
Pedron Naill	Char	R	5.00
Perrin Aybara	Char	X	0.45
Personal Growth	Event	X	0.45
22			
Plots	Event	X	0.45
Political Isolation	Chall	C	0.25
Political Maneuvering	Chall	C	0.25
Political Prisoner	Chall	R	4.00
Portal Stone	Event	U	0.80
Power Suppression	Event	R	4.00
Prepared Defenses	Event	C	0.25
Prolonged Campaign	Chall	R	4.50
Prophecy	Event	U	0.80
23			
Pull of the Pattern	Event	U	0.80
Queen's Guard	Troop	R	5.00
Rahvin	Char	X	0.45
Raiding Party	Troop	U	0.80
Rallying Cry	Chall	U	0.80
Rampage	Chall	X	0.45
Rand al'Thor	Char	X	1.00
Rand al'Thor	Char	R	6.00
Rand al'Thor	Char	R	10.00
24			
Rand al'Thor	Char	R	8.80
Rand the King	Char	R	8.00
Rapid Recovery	Event	C	0.25
Ravens Watching	Event	C	0.25
Raw Recruits	Adv	R	4.00
Ready Resources	Adv	R	3.80
Reducing Influence	Adv	U	0.80
Regroup	Event	C	0.25
Reinforcements	Event	C	0.25
25			
Remove Fatigue	Event	U	0.80
Request Tribute	Chall	C	0.25
Respite	Event	C	0.25
Rest and Recovery	Adv	U	0.80
Resupply	Adv	U	0.80
Rhuarc	Char	R	6.00
Rule of Power	Event	R	4.00
Rumors and Lies	Event	C	0.25
Sabotage	Event	C	0.25
26			
Saidan Angreal	Adv	R	4.50
Saidar Angreal	Adv	R	4.80
Scouting Party	Troop	U	0.80

Card name	Type	Rarity	Price
Search and Destroy	Chall	U	0.80
Seasoned Warrior	Adv	X/C	0.25
Seat of Power	Adv	R	4.00
Second Front	Event	C	0.25
Secondary Efforts	Chall	X	0.45
Secret Aid	Event	C	0.25
27			
Sentries	Troop	U	0.80
Shaidar Haran	Char	R	6.00
Shattered Dream	Chall	U	0.80
Shayol Ghul	Adv	R	5.00
Similar Ideals	Event	X	0.45
Siuan Sanche	Char	R	5.50
Skimming	Event	U	0.80
Skirmish	Chall	C	0.25
Spying	Event	X	0.45
28			
Stalemate	Chall	R	4.00
Stedding	Event	R	4.00
Strong Support	Event	C	0.25
Stymied	Event	C	0.25
Subtle Manipulations	Event	U	0.80
Superior Weaponry	Adv	C	0.25
Surprise Attack	Event	C	0.25
Surrounded	Event	C	0.25
Taking Advantage	Adv	R	4.00
29			
Tar Valon	Adv	U	0.80
Tar Valon Guards	Troop	U	0.80
Tar Valon Soldiers	Troop	U	0.80
Tear	Adv	U	0.80
Tear Lancers	Troop	R	4.00
Tear Levies	Troop	C	0.25
Tear Skirmishers	Troop	R	4.00
Tear Spearmen	Troop	C	0.25
Testing Fate	Chall	X	0.45
30			
The Art of Intrigue	Adv	U	0.80
The Dragon Revealed	Char	R	6.00
The Dying Ground	Event	U	0.80
The Great Game	Adv	R	4.00
The Ruby Dagger	Adv	R	5.00
The Stone of Tear	Adv	R	5.00
The Telling Blow	Event	C	0.25
The Tide of Battle	Chall	X	0.45
The Truth They Tell	Event	U	0.80
31			
The Way of the Leaf	Adv	C	0.25
The Wheel Turns	Event	R	4.00
The White Tower	Adv	R	4.50
Thom Merrilin	Char	R	6.00
Tight Formation	Adv	U	0.80
To The Victor	Adv	R	4.00
Training for War	Adv	C	0.25
Treaty	Chall	C	0.25
Trolloc	Char	X	0.45
32			
Trolloc Fist	Troop	R	6.00
Trolloc Footmen	Troop	X	0.45
Trolloc Horn	Adv	R	4.00
Trolloc Raiders	Troop	U	0.80
Trolloc War Band	Troop	R	4.00
Twisting Fate	Chall	R	4.50
Twists in the Pattern	Event	R	4.00
Two Rivers Archers	Troop	U	0.80
Unexpected Ally	Event	X	0.45
33			
Verin Sedai	Char	R	5.00
Wall of Fire	Event	R	4.00
Wandering Noble	Char	C	0.25
Ward of Protection	Event	R	4.00
Waygate	Event	U	0.80
Weariness	Adv	U	0.80
What Might Be	Event	R	4.00
Whispers In the Dark	Event	C	0.25
Wolves	Troop	U	0.80

RARITY KEY   C = Common   U = Uncommon   R = Rare   VR = Very Rare   UR = Ultra Rare   F = Foil card   X = Fixed/standard in all decks

Wheel of Time • *Dark Prophecies*

Precedence • Released **July 2000**
151 cards in set • **IDENTIFIER: 'DP' on card bottom**

• Booster packs contain 8 cards; booster displays contain 24 boosters

This first expansion to the *Wheel of Time* CCG has several themes. It introduces Illian cards to the game: **Council of Nine, King of Illian, City of Illian,** etc. It introduces the strongest group of cards in the game, the recruitable versions of the Forsaken. And, it even has six prophecies, a new type of card foreshadowed in the *Premier* rulebook.

Dark Prophecies is very strong. Where many CCG sets have a wide range of cards with only a minute fraction being tournament staples, *Prophecies* cards are uniformly better than similar cards from *Premier*. The game turned on its head with all the powerful effects introduced. **Mat Cauthon** and **Perrin Aybara**, main characters who were liabilities in *Premier*, receive an enormous boost from **Pull of the Ta'veren** and their new replacements (**Mat the Gambler** and **Young Bull**). Decks built around multiple allegiances receive **Dragonmount** and **Under One Banner**. Decks built around controlling a nation or nations receive **Strong Loyalties** and **A New Empire**. Illian, the new allegiance, comes out as fully formed as some of the *Premier* allegiances. Children of the Light decks become possible. Oddly, the prophecies are not generally among the strongest cards.

To compete at a tournament level requires having *Dark Prophecies*. But, this isn't the only reason the set is so highly desired among collectors and players. The most coveted cards — Faile and the seven recruitable Forsaken — are all twice as rare as the normal rares in the set. To balance the number of rares out to 50, eight of the other rares are more common than the standard rares. — *Ian Lee*

Set (151 cards)	86.50
Booster Display Box	75.00
Booster Pack	2.70

Card name	Type	Rarity	Price
1			
A New Empire	Adv	R	4.00
Advanced Maneuvers	Chall	C	0.20
Alanna Sedai	Char	U	0.60
Asmodean	Char	R	4.50
Bair	Char	U	0.60
Balefire	Event	R	4.00
Battle Plan	Adv	C	0.20
Bayle Domon	Char	R	4.50
Be'lal	Char	R	4.80
2			
Blockade Runners	Troop	U	0.60
Blood and Ashes	Adv	R	4.00
Cairhien Guard	Troop	C	0.20
Cairhien Veterans	Troop	U	0.60
Captain Caldevwin	Char	U	0.60
Charismatic Leader	Adv	C	0.20
Chesmal Sedai	Char	U	0.60
Child of the Light	Char	C	0.20
Circle of Light	Adv	C	0.20
3			
Combat Training	Adv	C	0.20
Combined Army	Troop	U	0.60
Conquest	Chall	R	4.00
Consumed by the Blight	Event	U	0.60
Couladin	Char	R	4.50
Dark Subversion	Chall	R	4.00
Deep Waters	Event	U	0.60
Defenders of the Stone	Troop	U	0.60
Dragonmount	Adv	C	0.20
4			
Draw Him Out	Chall	C	0.20
Elayne the Accepted	Char	R	6.80
Eyeless	Char	U	0.60
Faile	Char	R	7.00
Far Dareis Mai	Troop	U	0.60
First Squadron	Troop	U	0.60
Galad	Char	R	5.00
Gawyn	Char	R	4.50
Genocide	Chall	R	4.50
5			
Gholam Attack	Event	U	0.60
Graendal	Char	R	5.30
Gyldin	Adv	R	4.50

Card name	Type	Rarity	Price
Half Legion	Troop	C	0.20
Heart of the Stone	Adv	C	0.20
High Lord Hearne	Char	U	0.60
High Lord Simaan	Char	U	0.60
Hopper	Char	U	0.60
Hunting Party	Troop	C	0.20
6			
Illian	Adv	U	0.60
Illian Lancers	Troop	C	0.20
Illian Spearmen	Troop	C	0.20
Illian Traders	Troop	U	0.60
Illian Volunteers	Troop	U	0.60
Incendiary Strike	Event	U	0.60
Invasion	Chall	R	4.50
Ishamael	Char	R	7.30
Jaret Byar	Char	U1	1.30
7			
Jarette Byar	Char	U1	1.30
Kin Tovere	Char	U	0.60
King Mattin Stepaneos	Char	R	4.50
Lady Selande	Char	U	0.60
Lanfear	Char	R	5.30
Lead Them to Ruin	Chall	C	0.20
Leader of Nations	Adv	C	0.20
Leane Sedai	Char	R	4.50
Legion	Troop	R	4.00
8			
Legion of the Dragon	Troop	R	5.00
Light Brigade	Troop	C	0.20
Linked	Adv	U	0.60
Lord Argirin Darelos	Char	U	0.60
Lord Ballin Elamri	Char	U	0.60
Lord Brend	Adv	R	4.00
Lord Comar	Char	U	0.60
Lord Dobraine	Char	U	0.60
Lord Dragon	Char	R	7.50
9			
Lord Eliris Mancuri	Char	U	0.60
Lord Ershin Netari	Char	U	0.60
Lord Gregorian Panar	Char	R	6.00
Lord Jeordwyn Semaris	Char	U	0.60
Lord Kiril Drapeneos	Char	U	0.60
Lord Maringil	Char	U	0.60
Lord Spiron Narettin	Char	U	0.60
Lull in the Storm	Chall	C	0.20
Mat the Gambler	Char	R	4.90
10			
Melindhra	Char	U	0.60

Card name	Type	Rarity	Price
Military State	Adv	C	0.20
Moghedien	Char	R	5.30
Narrow Pass	Event	C	0.20
No Middle Ground	Chall	C	0.20
On All Sides	Event	C	0.20
Ordeith	Char	R	4.50
Organize Resistance	Chall	C	0.20
People of the Dragon	Adv	C	0.20
11			
Pevin	Char	U	0.60
Plans Within Plans	Event	C	0.20
Political Powerbase	Chall	C	0.20
Preemptive Strike	Adv	C	0.20
Pull of the Ta'veren	Adv	C	0.20
Questioner	Char	U	0.60
Rahvin	Char	R	6.30
Rand al'Thor (V)	Char	R	4.90
Rand al'Thor (VI)	Char	R	5.40
12			
Rand al'Thor (VII)	Char	R	6.40
Rhadam Asunawa	Char	R	4.50
Rule a Nation	Chall	C	0.20
Saboteurs	Troop	R	4.00
Sammael	Char	R	4.50
Sebban Balwer	Char	R	4.50
Second Squadron	Troop	U	0.60
Seeking Someshta	Chall	R	4.50
Selene	Adv	R	4.00
13			
Shades of Grey	Event	U	0.60
Soldier of War	Char	C	0.20
Square of Tammaz	Adv	C	0.20
Strength in Diversity	Event	C	0.20
Strength of Character	Chall	C	0.20
Strong Loyalties	Event	C	0.20
Sulin	Char	U	0.60
Take Back the Night	Adv	C	0.20
Tear Defenders	Troop	U	0.60
14			
The City of Illian	Adv	R	4.50
The Companions	Troop	R	4.00
The Dance of Spears	Event	C	0.20
The Game of Houses	Event	C	0.20
The Great Lord Comes	Adv	R	4.50
The Halls of Power	Adv	C	0.20
The Host	Troop	R	4.00
The Light Illumine	Event	C	0.20
The Lines of Loyalty	Adv	U	0.60

Card name	Type	Rarity	Price
15			
The Lion and the Rose	Event	C	0.20
The Lion Throne	Adv	C	0.20
The Lord of Chaos	Adv	R	4.50
The Pattern Decrees	Event	C	0.20
The Port of Illian	Event	C	0.20
The Prophet	Char	R	4.50
The Seals	Adv	R	4.00
The Shadows Rising	Adv	R	4.00
The Stone Shall Fall	Adv	R	4.00
16			
The Stone Still Stands	Event	C	0.20
The Sun Throne	Adv	C	0.20
The Void	Adv	U	0.60
The Younglings	Troop	U	0.60
Third Squadron	Troop	U	0.60
Trolloc Guard	Troop	C	0.20
Trolloc Horde	Troop	C	0.20
Twice Shall He Be Marked	Adv	R	4.00
Under One Banner	Adv	C	0.20
17			
United Front	Event	C	0.20
War of Attrition	Chall	C	0.20
War Party	Troop	U	0.60
Warders	Troop	U	0.60
White Lions	Troop	U	0.60
Whitecloak Spy	Char	U	0.60
Young Bull	Char	R	4.50

Spell-check

The first edition of most Precedence CCGs is known as *Premier*, not "Premiere." Perhaps "premier" has the look of "first among many."

RARITY KEY C = Common U = Uncommon R = Rare VR = Very Rare UR = Ultra Rare F = Foil card X = Fixed/standard in all decks

SCRYE Collectible Card Game Checklist and Price Guide • **479**

Wheel of Time • Children of the Dragon

Precedence • Released **January 2001**

154 cards in set • **IDENTIFIER:** 'COTD' on bottom of card

• Booster packs contain 9 cards; booster displays contain 24 boosters

The second expansion to **Wheel of Time**, **Children of the Dragon** introduces "mighty new Forsaken, **Birgette**, **Tam al'Thor**, and world-shaking Prophecies to dominate the Pattern for all time."

You will need **18** nine-pocket pages to store this set. (9 doubled up)

Set (154 cards)		85.00
Booster Display Box		72.50
Booster Pack		2.80

Card name	Type	Rarity	Price
A Crown of Swords	Adv	U	0.40
Aan'allein	Char	R1	4.00
Aiel Invaders	Troop	C	0.15
Alarys	Char	U	0.40
Alliance	Chall	C	0.15
Aludra	Char	U	0.40
Andoran Reserves	Troop	C	0.15
Aram	Char	U	0.40
Army of the Light	Troop	R	3.00
Ashandarei	Adv	R	3.00
Aviendha Apprenticed	Char	R	3.00
Ba'alzamon	Adv	R	3.00
Bael	Char	R	3.00
Balthamel	Char	R	3.00
Battle Readiness	Adv	U	0.40
Belinde	Char	U	0.40
Birgitte	Char	R1	4.00
Bruan	Char	R	3.00
Caddar	Adv	R	3.00
Cadin'sor	Adv	R	3.00
Cairhien Vanguard	Troop	C	0.15
Call Up the Reserves	Chall	C	0.15
Callbox	Event	R	3.00
Casualties of War	Adv	C	0.15
Chaelin	Char	U	0.40
Chareen Aiel	Troop	U	0.40
Chief's Chair	Adv	C	0.15
Children's Crusade	Adv	C	0.15
Codarra Aiel	Troop	U	0.40
Colinda	Char	U	0.40
Collaborators	Troop	C	0.15
Conquer and Control	Chall	C	0.15
Couladin Car'a'carn	Char	R1	4.00
Dapple	Char	U	0.40
Dark Disguises	Adv	R	3.00
Daryne Aiel	Troop	U	0.40

Card name	Type	Rarity	Price
Demetre Marcolin	Char	U	0.40
Desora	Char	U	0.40
Destroy from Within	Chall	C	0.15
Dhearic	Char	R	3.00
Doorway in Rhuidean	Event	R	3.00
Doorway in Tear	Event	R	3.00
Dream Search	Event	C	0.15
Edarra	Char	U	0.40
Enaila	Char	U	0.40
Erim	Char	R	3.00
Feast of Teven	Event	C	0.15
Fifth Squadron	Troop	R	3.00
Foolbox	Event	C	0.15
Forces of Evil	Troop	U	0.40
Fourth Squadron	Troop	R	3.00
Gai'shain	Adv	C	0.15
Goshien Aiel	Troop	U	0.40
Hadnan Kadere	Char	U	0.40
Half-moon Axe	Adv	R	3.00
Han	Char	R	3.00
He Who Comes With the Dawn	Adv	U	0.40
He Will Bind and Destroy Them	Adv	U	0.40
Herid Fel	Char	R	3.00
High Lord Darlin Sisnera	Char	U	0.40
Illian Tall Ships	Troop	C	0.15
Incite Rebellion	Chall	C	0.15
Indirian	Char	R	3.00
Isendre	Char	U	0.40
Janwin	Char	R	3.00
Jheran	Char	R	3.00
Ji'e'toh	Adv	C	0.15
Jolien	Char	U	0.40
Lady Basene	Adv	R	3.00
Lady Caraline	Char	U	0.40
Lay of the Land	Adv	C	0.15
Lead by Example	Adv	C	0.15
Liah	Char	U	0.40
Lian	Char	R	3.00

Card name	Type	Rarity	Price
Lines of Command	Adv	C	0.15
Lines of Support	Adv	R	3.00
Lord Marac den Norvin	Char	U	0.40
Lord of the Morning	Char	R1	4.00
Maiden Handtalk	Event	C	0.15
Maidens of the Spear	Adv	C	0.15
Maira	Char	U	0.40
Mandarb	Adv	C	0.15
Mandelain	Char	R	3.00
Mangin	Char	U	0.40
Manifest Destiny	Adv	C	0.15
Martyn Tallanvor	Char	U	0.40
Mat the General	Char	R1	5.00
Meira	Char	U	0.40
Melaine	Char	R	3.00
Mera'din	Troop	C	0.15
Miagoma Aiel	Troop	U	0.40
Military Dominance	Chall	C	0.15
Modarra	Char	U	0.40
Nakai Aiel	Troop	U	0.40
Nandera	Char	R	3.00
Need	Chall	C	0.15
Network of Spies	Chall	C	0.15
Nightrunner	Char	R	3.00
Omerna	Char	U	0.40
Peace of Rhuidean	Event	C	0.15
Perpetual Conflict	Chall	C	0.15
Perrin Goldeneyes	Char	R1	5.00
Rand al'Thor (IX)	Char	R	4.00
Rand al'Thor (VIII)	Char	R	4.00
Rand al'Thor (X)	Char	R	5.00
Relive the Past	Chall	C	0.15
Remnant of a Remnant	Adv	U	0.40
Reyn Aiel	Troop	U	0.40
Rhiale	Char	U	0.40
Rhuidean	Adv	U	0.40
Sammael	Char	R1	4.00
Seana	Char	R	3.00
Sept Warrior	Char	C	0.15
Sevanna	Char	R	3.00

Card name	Type	Rarity	Price
Shaarad Aiel	Troop	U	0.40
Shaido Aiel	Troop	R	3.00
Shiande Aiel	Troop	U	0.40
Shoufa	Adv	C	0.15
Siswai'aman	Troop	C	0.15
Sixth Squadron	Troop	R	3.00
Someryn	Char	R	3.00
Sorilea	Char	R	3.00
Sovereign Rule	Chall	C	0.15
Sweat Tents	Adv	C	0.15
Taardad Aiel	Troop	U	0.40
Tam al'Thor	Char	R1	5.00
Tarmon Gai'don	Event	R	3.00
Tear Regiment	Troop	C	0.15
The Bleakness	Adv	C	0.15
The Chosen	Adv	U	0.40
The Dragon Scepter	Adv	R	3.00
The Fifth	Adv	C	0.15
The Old Tongue	Chall	C	0.15
The Ta'veren	Adv	C	0.15
The Three Fold Land	Adv	U	0.40
The Traveling People	Event	C	0.15
The Waste	Adv	U	0.40
The Wheel Weaves	Event	R	3.00
The Wheel Wills	Event	R	3.00
Therava	Char	U	0.40
Time of Need	Event	C	0.15
Timolan	Char	R	3.00
Tion	Char	U	0.40
Toh	Event	C	0.15
Tomanelle Aiel	Troop	U	0.40
Trolloc Army	Troop	R	3.00
Trolloc Champion	Char	R	3.00
Urien	Char	U	0.40
Voices of the Dead	Adv	U	0.40
War Campaign	Chall	C	0.15
War Galleys	Troop	C	0.15
Wash the Spears	Chall	C	0.15
Weaken Support	Chall	C	0.15
Wolfbrother	Char	C	0.15

WildStorms

WildStorm/Aegis Entertainment • First set, released **October 1995**

350 cards in set • **IDENTIFIER:** © 1995; black borders

• Starter decks contain 60 cards; starter displays contain 12 starters

• Booster packs contain 15 cards; booster displays contain 36 boosters

Set in the WildStorm comic-book universe (then published by Image Comics), the **WildStorms** CCG features all of the heroes and villains from *WildC.A.T.S.*, *Stormwatch*, *Team 7*, *Gen13*, and *Wetworks* comic books.

Each card has a point cost and decks are built to a maximum point cost (usually 200 points), with a minimum of 50 cards. Players are free to use both heroes and villains, but a bonus is given for using characters from the same team.

The players alternate attacking each other's characters, gaining the attacked character's points when he or she is knocked out, in an attempt to capture the Battlefield card. Once a player has gained enough points to capture the Battlefield, the standard game ends. There is a campaign game with multiple battles.

RARITY KEY **C** = Common **U** = Uncommon **R** = Rare **R1** = Very Rare **UR** = Ultra Rare **F** = Foil card **X** = Fixed/standard in all decks

Combat is non-random. If a character's hand-to-hand or ranged attack is equal to or greater than the defending character's Defense, he's successful, although there are many Combat cards that can change Attack and Defense ratings.

The game mechanics capture the feel of comic-book battles nicely, although the game's real appeal is to fans of the various comics. A non-reader can get easily lost amidst the many teams and baroque art.

WildStorms produced four expansions, which eventually took in characters from other Image titles and from other comics lines entirely. The line ended before Image characters next turned up in *Image OverPower*.

Studio founder Jim Lee produced *C•23* with Wizards of the Coast in 1998 before selling his studio to DC Comics.— *Michael Greenholdt*

Concept	●●●●○
Gameplay	●●●●○
Card art	●●●○○
Player pool	●●○○○

WildStorms • Unlimited
WildStorm • Released August 1996

359 cards in set • **IDENTIFIER: © 1996; white borders**
- Starter decks contain 60 cards; starter displays contain 12 starters
- Booster packs contain 15 cards; booster displays contain 36 boosters

The *Unlimited* edition included the cards found in the *Limited* set with the addition of these nine characters: **Copycat, Evo, Alex Fairchild, Frostbite, Hardball,** Jade, **One-Eyed Jack, Rake,** and **Sublime.**

The *Unlimited* set has a white border, while the *Limited* set has a black border. — *Michael Greenholdt*

You will need **40** nine-pocket pages to store **EACH** set. (20 doubled up)

LIMITED

Set (350 cards)	89.00
Starter Display Box	35.00
Booster Display Box	41.00
Starter Deck	7.50
Booster Pack	1.50

UNLIMITED

Set (359 cards)	65.00
Starter Display Box	25.00
Booster Display Box	32.00
Starter Deck	5.00
Booster Pack	1.00

LIMITED Card name	Rarity	UNLIM
[1]		
A Doctor in the House	R	2.00 / 1.50
A Killing Moon	C	0.10 / 0.05
Achilles' Heel	R	2.00 / 1.50
Acrobatic Dodge	U	0.50 / 0.35
Act Of Mercy	C	0.10 / 0.05
Advanced Security System	C	0.10 / 0.05
Aim	C	0.10 / 0.05
Alex Fairchild	UR	3.50
Alicia Turner	U	0.50 / 0.35
[2]		
All Or Nothing	R	2.00 / 1.50
Andromache	R	2.00 / 1.50
Anti-Aircraft Fire	U	0.50 / 0.35
Armand Waering	R	2.00 / 1.50
Armor Piercing Ammo	C	0.10 / 0.05
Attica	U	0.50 / 0.35
Automatic Pistol	C	0.10 / 0.05
Avoid Obstacle	U	0.50 / 0.35
Backlash	R	3.50 / 1.50
[3]		
Bad Part Of Town	C	0.10 / 0.05
Bad Reputation	U	0.50 / 0.35
Bareknuckled Brawling	C	0.10 / 0.05
Battalion	R	2.00 / 1.50
Battlefield Flare	C	0.10 / 0.05
Beastmaster	U	0.50 / 0.35
Behemoth	R	2.00 / 1.50
Ben Santini	R	2.00 / 1.50
Biokev Bodysuit	C	0.10 / 0.05
[4]		
Black Razor	C	0.10 / 0.05
Black Razor Training	C	0.10 / 0.05
B'Lial	C	0.10 / 0.05

LIMITED Card name	Rarity	UNLIM
Blindsided	C	0.10 / 0.05
Bliss	U	0.50 / 0.35
Blitz	C	0.10 / 0.05
Block	C	0.10 / 0.05
BloodQueen	R	2.00 / 1.50
Bow & Arrows	C	0.10 / 0.05
[5]		
Breakdown	C	0.10 / 0.05
Brutus	U	0.50 / 0.35
Bullet Bike	U	0.50 / 0.35
Bulletproof Vest	C	0.10 / 0.05
Bull's Eye!	R	2.00 / 1.50
Buried Starship	R	2.00 / 1.50
Burnout	U	0.50 / 0.35
Call In A Favor	R	2.00 / 1.50
Call In The Cavalry!	R	2.00 / 1.50
[6]		
Cannon	U	0.50 / 0.35
Careful Aim	R	2.00 / 1.50
Caught in the Crosshairs	R	2.00 / 1.50
Charging Slam	R	2.00 / 1.50
Chernobyl	R	2.00 / 1.50
Clay Pigeon	C	0.10 / 0.05
Claymore	U	0.50 / 0.35
Clean Getaway	R	2.00 / 1.50
Clef Blade	C	0.10 / 0.05
[7]		
Clef Blade of the Majestrix	U	0.50 / 0.35
Clothesline	C	0.10 / 0.05
Coda Blood Ritual	U	0.50 / 0.35
Coda Cycle	U	0.50 / 0.35
Coda Discipline	C	0.10 / 0.05
Coda Mission	C	0.10 / 0.05
Coda Training	C	0.10 / 0.05
Coda Warrior	C	0.10 / 0.05
Combat Extraction	U	0.50 / 0.35
[8]		
Combat Medic	R	2.00 / 1.50
Commlink	C	0.10 / 0.05
Copycat	UR	3.00
Counterattack	C	0.10 / 0.05
Cover	U	0.50 / 0.35
Cray's Retreat, Rural Virginia	U	0.50 / 0.35
Cyber-Augmentation	U	0.50 / 0.35
Cybernary	R	2.00 / 1.50
Cyber-Resurrection	R	2.00 / 1.50
[9]		
Daemonite	C	0.10 / 0.05

LIMITED Card name	Rarity	UNLIM
Daemonite in a Flash Suit	C	0.10 / 0.05
Daemonite Keys	U	0.50 / 0.35
Daemonite Search	C	0.10 / 0.05
Dane	R	2.00 / 1.50
Deathblow	R	2.00 / 1.50
Deathtrap	U	0.50 / 0.35
Defile	R	2.00 / 1.50
Delphae's Pool	U	0.50 / 0.35
[10]		
Destine	R	2.00 / 1.50
Determination	R	2.00 / 1.50
Dinigo	C	0.10 / 0.05
Disguise	C	0.10 / 0.05
Diva	U	0.50 / 0.35
Diversity	C	0.10 / 0.05
Dodge	C	0.10 / 0.05
Doreen	U	0.50 / 0.35
Dozer	U	0.50 / 0.35
[11]		
Dramatic Pose	R	2.00 / 1.50
Dras' Adin (Vampire Nation Capital)	R	2.00 / 1.50
Dud	C	0.10 / 0.05
Electromagnetic Pulse	R	2.00 / 1.50
Emergency Evac	U	0.50 / 0.35
Emergency First Aid	R	2.00 / 1.50
Emergency Repair	R	2.00 / 1.50
Emp	R	3.50 / 2.80
Energy Blast Defense	U	0.50 / 0.35
[12]		
Escape Plan	R	2.00 / 1.50
Espionage Mission	C	0.10 / 0.05
Evo	UR	3.00
Fahrenheit	U	0.50 / 0.35
Fairchild	R	3.50 / 1.50
Fancy Flying	C	0.10 / 0.05
Feint	C	0.10 / 0.05
Fish In A Barrel	U	0.50 / 0.35
Flame-Thrower	R	2.00 / 1.50
[13]		
Flashpoint	U	0.50 / 0.35
Flawed Gen-Factor	U	0.50 / 0.35
Flying Tackle	U	0.50 / 0.35
Freefall	U	0.50 / 0.35
Frenzied Vampire	C	0.10 / 0.05
Friends In High Places	U	0.50 / 0.35
Frost Bite	UR	3.00
Fuji	U	0.50 / 0.35
Full Defense	U	0.50 / 0.35

LIMITED Card name	Rarity	UNLIM
[14]		
Fusion Detonator	R	2.00 / 1.50
Gen-Factor	U	0.50 / 0.35
Gen—Factor	R	2.00 / 1.50
Get The Goliath	C	0.10 / 0.05
Gnome	R	2.00 / 1.50
Golden Gate Bridge	U	0.50 / 0.35
Government Investigation	R	2.00 / 1.50
Grail	R	2.00 / 1.50
Grappling	U	0.50 / 0.35
[15]		
Grenade	U	0.50 / 0.35
Grifter	R	3.50 / 2.80
Grudge Match	C	0.10 / 0.05
Grunge	U	0.75 / 0.35
H.A.R.M.	U	0.50 / 0.35
Halo Enterprises	R	2.00 / 1.50
Halo Ski Lodge	U	0.50 / 0.35
Hang With The Kids	C	0.10 / 0.05
Hangfire	R	2.00 / 1.50
[16]		
Hard Training	R	2.00 / 1.50
Hardball	UR	3.00
Haze Of Battle	C	0.10 / 0.05
Heap Ammo	R	2.00 / 1.50
Heavily Defended	C	0.10 / 0.05
Helicopter: Gunship	U	0.50 / 0.35
Helicopter: Troop Transport	U	0.50 / 0.35
Hellslayer	C	0.10 / 0.05
Hellstrike	U	0.50 / 0.35
[17]		
Helmut	U	0.50 / 0.35
Helspont	R	2.00 / 1.50
Hestia	U	0.50 / 0.35
Hexon	C	0.10 / 0.05
Hidden	C	0.10 / 0.05
Hide!	R	2.00 / 1.50
High Block	C	0.10 / 0.05
Higher Powers at Work	R	2.00 / 1.50
Hightower	R	2.00 / 1.50
[18]		
Hi-Vel Ammo	R	2.00 / 1.50
Hollowpoint Ammo	C	0.10 / 0.05
Hot Spot, Georgetown, D.C.	U	0.50 / 0.35
H'Tarh	C	0.10 / 0.05
I.O. Agent	C	0.10 / 0.05
I.O. Command	R	2.00 / 1.50

RARITY KEY **C** = Common **U** = Uncommon **R** = Rare **VR** = Very Rare **UR** = Ultra Rare **F** = Foil card **X** = Fixed/standard in all decks

SCRYE Collectible Card Game Checklist and Price Guide • 481

LIMITED Card name	Rarity	UNLIM
☐ 0.10 I.O. Investigation	C	0.05 ☐
☐ 0.10 Inaccessible	C	0.05 ☐
☐ 0.10 Inconspicuous	C	0.05 ☐
[19]		
☐ 0.10 Infrared Sight	C	0.05 ☐
☐ 0.50 Ivana Baiul	U	0.35 ☐
☐ 0.10 Jab	C	0.05 ☐
Jade	UR	3.00 ☐
☐ 0.10 Jam	C	0.05 ☐
☐ 0.50 Jester	U	0.35 ☐
☐ 2.00 Jetpack	R	1.50 ☐
☐ 0.50 Jodunn	U	0.35 ☐
☐ 0.50 Johnny Savoy	U	0.35 ☐
[20]		
☐ 0.10 Join The Mercs	C	0.05 ☐
☐ 0.10 Join The WildC.A.T.s	C	0.05 ☐
☐ 0.10 Join WetWorks	C	0.05 ☐
☐ 0.50 Judgment	U	0.35 ☐
☐ 0.50 Judo Throw	U	0.35 ☐
☐ 0.10 Jump Kick	C	0.05 ☐
☐ 2.00 Jumpjet	R	1.50 ☐
☐ 0.50 Justice Stone & Staff	U	0.35 ☐
☐ 2.00 Karate Kick	R	1.50 ☐
[21]		
☐ 0.50 Karate Punch	U	0.35 ☐
☐ 0.10 Keep In Formation	C	0.05 ☐
☐ 0.10 Keep Your Distance	C	0.05 ☐
☐ 0.10 Keeper	C	0.05 ☐
☐ 0.10 Kherubim Search	C	0.05 ☐
☐ 0.10 Kidney Punch	C	0.05 ☐
☐ 0.50 Kilgore	U	0.35 ☐
☐ 0.10 Kindred Foundling Discovered	C	0.05 ☐
☐ 0.10 Knife	C	0.05 ☐
[22]		
☐ 0.10 Knockback	C	0.05 ☐
☐ 2.00 Knockout Kick	R	1.50 ☐
☐ 0.50 Knockout Punch	U	0.35 ☐
☐ 0.10 Know Someone	C	0.05 ☐
☐ 0.10 K'Rul	C	0.05 ☐
☐ 0.50 La Jolla Safehouse	U	0.35 ☐
☐ 0.10 Laser Sight	C	0.05 ☐
☐ 0.50 Leadership	U	0.35 ☐
☐ 0.10 Left Hook	C	0.05 ☐
[23]		
☐ 0.10 Leg Block	C	0.05 ☐
☐ 0.10 Link	C	0.05 ☐
☐ 0.10 Lonely	C	0.05 ☐
☐ 0.50 Luxury Ocean Liner	U	0.35 ☐
☐ 3.50 Lynch	R	1.50 ☐
☐ 0.50 Machine Pistol	U	0.35 ☐
☐ 0.10 Magick Boost	C	0.05 ☐
☐ 0.10 Major Diane LaSalle	C	0.05 ☐
☐ 2.00 Man-Portable Gatling	R	1.50 ☐
[24]		
☐ 0.50 Maul	U	0.35 ☐
☐ 0.50 Mecca, Saudi Arabia	U	0.35 ☐
☐ 2.00 Med-Evac	R	1.50 ☐

LIMITED Card name	Rarity	UNLIM
☐ 0.10 Media Circus	C	0.05 ☐
☐ 2.00 Mental Wall	R	1.50 ☐
☐ 0.10 Metal Exosheath	C	0.05 ☐
☐ 2.00 Miles Craven	R	1.50 ☐
☐ 0.50 Military Parafoil	U	0.35 ☐
☐ 2.00 Mindscape	R	1.50 ☐
[25]		
☐ 2.00 MIRV	R	1.50 ☐
☐ 0.50 Misfire	U	0.35 ☐
☐ 0.10 M'Koi	C	0.05 ☐
☐ 2.00 Mnemo	R	1.50 ☐
☐ 2.00 Mother One	R	1.50 ☐
☐ 0.50 Mr. Majestic	U	0.35 ☐
☐ 0.50 Mr. White	U	0.35 ☐
☐ 2.00 Mysterious Disappearance	R	1.50 ☐
☐ 0.50 Narrow Escape	U	0.35 ☐
[26]		
☐ 0.10 Nautika	C	0.05 ☐
☐ 0.10 Near Miss	C	0.05 ☐
☐ 2.00 Night Tribes Intervention	R	1.50 ☐
☐ 0.10 No Holding Back	C	0.05 ☐
☐ 0.10 Nychus	C	0.05 ☐
☐ 0.10 Off-Balance	C	0.05 ☐
☐ 2.00 Old Rivalry Resurfaces	R	1.50 ☐
☐ 0.10 On A Roll	C	0.05 ☐
☐ 0.10 One Shot, One Kill	C	0.05 ☐
[27]		
One-Eyed Jack	UR	3.00 ☐
☐ 0.50 One-Two Punch	U	0.35 ☐
☐ 0.50 Orb Of Aggression	U	0.35 ☐
☐ 2.00 Orb Of Excelence	R	1.50 ☐
☐ 0.50 Orb Of Fortune	U	0.35 ☐
☐ 2.00 Orb Of Healing	R	1.50 ☐
☐ 0.50 Orb Of Omniscience	U	0.35 ☐
☐ 0.50 Orb Of Protection	U	0.35 ☐
☐ 2.00 Orb Of Psi	R	1.50 ☐
[28]		
☐ 2.00 Orb Of Restoration	R	1.50 ☐
☐ 2.00 Orb Of Teleportation	R	1.50 ☐
☐ 0.50 Out Of Ammo	U	0.35 ☐
☐ 0.10 Outflank	C	0.05 ☐
☐ 2.00 Overbearing	R	1.50 ☐
☐ 0.10 Pact Of Honor	C	0.05 ☐
☐ 0.50 Pagan	U	0.35 ☐
☐ 0.10 Partial Cover	C	0.05 ☐
☐ 2.00 Personal Defense System	R	1.50 ☐
[29]		
☐ 2.00 Personal Forcefield	R	1.50 ☐
☐ 0.50 Pike	U	0.35 ☐
☐ 0.50 Pilgrim	U	0.35 ☐
☐ 0.10 Possession	C	0.05 ☐
☐ 0.50 Powered Armor (Black Razor)	U	0.35 ☐
☐ 2.00 Powered Armor (M.A.D.-1)	R	1.50 ☐

LIMITED Card name	Rarity	UNLIM
☐ 2.00 Prince Drakken	R	1.50 ☐
☐ 0.50 Prophet Of The Orb	U	0.35 ☐
☐ 2.00 Providence	R	1.50 ☐
[30]		
☐ 0.50 Providence Intervenes	U	0.35 ☐
☐ 2.00 Psi-Op Tracking	R	1.50 ☐
☐ 2.00 Purgatory Max	R	1.50 ☐
☐ 0.10 Quick Aim	C	0.05 ☐
☐ 0.10 Quickdraw	C	0.05 ☐
☐ 0.50 Rainmaker	U	0.35 ☐
Rake	UR	3.00 ☐
☐ 0.50 Razer	U	0.35 ☐
☐ 2.00 Reboot	R	1.50 ☐
[31]		
☐ 2.00 Recharge	R	1.50 ☐
☐ 0.10 Recruited by the Cabal	C	0.05 ☐
☐ 2.00 Red	R	1.50 ☐
☐ 0.50 Regent	U	0.35 ☐
☐ 0.10 Reorginize!	C	0.05 ☐
☐ 0.10 Revolver	C	0.05 ☐
☐ 0.10 Right Cross	C	0.05 ☐
☐ 0.10 Roundhouse	C	0.05 ☐
☐ 2.00 Sabatoge	R	1.50 ☐
[32]		
☐ 0.50 Satelite Uplink	U	0.35 ☐
☐ 0.50 Savant	U	0.35 ☐
☐ 2.00 Scanning the Timelines	R	1.50 ☐
☐ 0.50 SDI Astronomics	U	0.35 ☐
☐ 0.50 Second Strike	U	0.35 ☐
☐ 0.50 Second Wind	U	0.35 ☐
☐ 0.10 See the Light	C	0.05 ☐
☐ 0.10 Shoot From the Hip	C	0.05 ☐
☐ 0.10 Shotgun	C	0.05 ☐
[33]		
☐ 2.00 Shred Armor	R	1.50 ☐
☐ 2.00 Shroud Of Gloom	R	1.50 ☐
☐ 0.10 Sitting Duck	C	0.05 ☐
☐ 2.00 SkyWatch	R	1.50 ☐
☐ 0.50 Slag	U	0.35 ☐
☐ 2.00 Smoke And Mirrors	R	1.50 ☐
☐ 0.10 Snapshot	C	0.05 ☐
☐ 0.50 Sniper Practice	U	0.35 ☐
☐ 0.10 Soldier	C	0.05 ☐
[34]		
☐ 0.50 Soma	U	0.35 ☐
☐ 0.10 Spare Ammo	C	0.05 ☐
☐ 2.00 Spartan	R	1.50 ☐
☐ 0.10 Spear	C	0.05 ☐
☐ 0.50 Spinning Back Kick	U	0.35 ☐
☐ 0.50 S'Ryn	U	0.35 ☐
☐ 0.50 Statue Of Liberty	U	0.35 ☐
☐ 0.50 Strafe	U	0.35 ☐
☐ 2.00 Strength Of Will	R	1.50 ☐
[35]		
☐ 0.50 Stricture	U	0.35 ☐
Sublime	UR	3.00 ☐
☐ 0.50 Suborbital Rocket	U	0.35 ☐
☐ 0.10 Subterfuge Attack	C	0.05 ☐

LIMITED Card name	Rarity	UNLIM
☐ 0.50 Sunburst	U	0.35 ☐
☐ 2.00 Super Possession	R	1.50 ☐
☐ 2.00 Supercharge	R	1.50 ☐
☐ 0.10 Sword	C	0.05 ☐
☐ 0.50 Symbiote	U	0.35 ☐
[36]		
☐ 0.50 Synergy	U	0.35 ☐
☐ 2.00 System Crash	R	1.50 ☐
☐ 0.50 Taboo	U	0.35 ☐
☐ 2.00 Tactical Retreat	R	1.50 ☐
☐ 0.10 Tag Team	C	0.05 ☐
☐ 0.50 Take a Bullet	U	0.35 ☐
☐ 0.50 Talos	U	0.35 ☐
☐ 2.00 Tapestry Re-Draws Timeline	R	1.50 ☐
☐ 0.10 Teflon Ammo	C	0.05 ☐
[37]		
☐ 2.00 Teleport Boost	R	1.50 ☐
☐ 2.00 Teleportation Device	R	1.50 ☐
☐ 0.10 Telescopic Sight	C	0.05 ☐
☐ 0.50 The Louvre	U	0.35 ☐
☐ 2.00 The Rush	R	1.50 ☐
☐ 0.10 The UN Wants You!	C	0.05 ☐
☐ 0.50 Think Happy Thoughts	U	0.35 ☐
☐ 2.00 Threshold	R	1.50 ☐
☐ 0.50 Throat Punch	U	0.35 ☐
[38]		
☐ 0.50 Times Square	U	0.35 ☐
☐ 0.10 Toe To Toe	C	0.05 ☐
☐ 2.00 Total Cover	R	1.50 ☐
☐ 0.10 Tracer	C	0.05 ☐
☐ 0.50 Undertow	U	0.35 ☐
☐ 0.50 Union	U	0.35 ☐
☐ 0.50 Upgrade	U	0.35 ☐
☐ 0.50 Uppercut	U	0.35 ☐
☐ 2.00 VAD Hypercannon	R	1.50 ☐
[39]		
☐ 2.00 VAD PP30S	R	1.50 ☐
☐ 0.10 Vampire	C	0.05 ☐
☐ 2.00 Vampire Enclave, Transylvania	R	1.50 ☐
☐ 0.50 Virtual Bob	U	0.35 ☐
☐ 0.50 Vitals Punch	U	0.35 ☐
☐ 2.00 Void	R	1.50 ☐
☐ 2.00 Void Intervenes	R	1.50 ☐
☐ 0.75 Voodoo	U	0.35 ☐
☐ 0.50 Warblade	U	0.35 ☐
[40]		
☐ 0.10 We Don't Need No Stinkin' Armor!	C	0.05 ☐
☐ 0.10 Weatherman One	C	0.05 ☐
☐ 0.10 Werewolf	C	0.05 ☐
☐ 2.00 Wildlife Organized Research HQ, Montana	R	1.50 ☐
☐ 0.10 Will Of Iron	C	0.05 ☐
☐ 2.00 Winter	R	1.50 ☐
☐ 0.50 Wrestling Takedown	U	0.35 ☐
☐ 3.50 Zealot	R	2.80 ☐

SISTER MARY ™ C4 R4 D3
"I'll keep the demons occupied"
Mary Pittarese
Deathblow #11
Holy Faith: Add +2 D vs. Supernaturals.
TEAM Order of the Cross POINTS 4

WildStorms • Conflict

WildStorm/Aegis Entertainment • Released February 1996
152 cards in set • IDENTIFIER: 'Conflict' in copyright line
• Booster packs contain 12 cards; booster displays contain 36 boosters

This expansion stays almost entirely within the WildStorm comics universe but includes new characters and situations from those comics. — *Michael Greenholdt*

SCRYE NOTES: *We've found 12 cards not on the manufacturer's list — all 12 found in* **Conflict** *packs, identically collated. We suspect these packs were promo giveaways.*

You will need
17
nine-pocket pages to store this set.
(9 doubled up)
WILDSTORMS

Set (152 cards)	65.00
Booster Display Box	28.00
Booster Pack	1.25

Special set of 12

☐ Area Effect
☐ Attack Equipment
☐ Bumps and Bruises
☐ Condition Red
☐ High Jump
☐ "I Thought We Were Friends"
☐ Lord Entropy
☐ Serial Possession
☐ Sister Mary
☐ Spare Parts
☐ Taser
☐ Toolbox

RARITY KEY   C = Common   **U** = Uncommon   **R** = Rare   **VR** = Very Rare   **UR** = Ultra Rare   **F** = Foil card   **X** = Fixed/standard in all decks

482 • *SCRYE Collectible Card Game Checklist and Price Guide*

Card name	Rarity	Price
1		
A Mere Flesh Wound	C	0.10
Abbot O'Connor	C	0.10
Adrenaline Rush	C	0.10
Alchemy	U	0.50
And Stay There!	C	0.10
Andrew Stansfield	C	0.10
Angela	G	5.00
Anti-PSI Field Generator	C	0.10
Anti-PSI Headset	U	0.50
2		
Argos	R	2.80
Artemis	U	0.50
Ash	G	5.00
Avengelyne	G	5.00
Back From the Dead	R	2.80
Bastion	C	0.10
Belay those Orders!	U	0.50
Black Hammer	R	2.80
Blast 'em From the Sky	C	0.10
3		
Blood Moon	R	2.80
Bloodstone	R	2.80
Brass	U	0.50
Broken Sword	R	2.80
Caballito	U	0.50
Cauldron of Life	R	2.80
Celestial Balance	U	0.50
Changing the Future	R	2.80
Coda Island	R	2.80
4		
Coda Voodoo	G	5.00
Cracking Skulls	R	2.80
Crimson	R	2.80
Crossbones	C	0.10
Crusade	U	0.50
Cyberjack	C	0.10
Daemonite Cryo-pod	U	0.50
Daemonite Hovership	U	0.50
Defend With PSI	C	0.10
5		
Defensive Teleport	U	0.50
Delphe	R	2.80

Card name	Rarity	Price
Devin	C	0.10
Don't Know My Own Strength	R	2.80
Enhanced PSI	C	0.10
Evasive Acrobatics	R	2.80
Evil Laughter	C	0.10
Fairchild	UR	5.00
Fennex	C	0.10
6		
Flash Grenade	C	0.10
Flashy Fake Martial Arts Move	C	0.10
Flattop	C	0.10
Fonebone	UR	5.00
Frank Colby	C	0.10
Gabriel Newman	U	0.50
Gamorra	R	2.80
Glory	UR	5.00
Going AWOL	R	2.80
7		
Healing Spell	U	0.50
Heroic Determination	U	0.50
High Caliber Excitement	U	0.50
Hit 'em Hard!	U	0.50
Holdout Pistol	C	0.10
Holy Grail	R	2.80
Homage Studios	UR	5.00
Hostile Terrain	U	0.50
Hoverfoil	U	0.50
8		
Hunter-Killer	C	0.10
I Quit!	R	2.80
Incendiary Grenade	R	2.80
Infiltration	R	2.80
Infinate Possibilities	C	0.10
Innocent Bystanders	C	0.10
Intimidating Martial Arts Move	U	0.50
Ion	U	0.50
Jill	C	0.10
9		
Jules Newberry	C	0.10
Kaizen Gamorra	U	0.50
Kamin	C	0.10
Kanum	C	0.10
Kherubim Spaceship	R	2.80

Card name	Rarity	Price
Ladytron	U	0.50
Lancer	U	0.50
Lupo	C	0.10
Machine Shop	U	0.50
10		
Magick Ritual	C	0.10
Mess With Your Mind	C	0.10
Milo's Bistro	U	0.50
Mindblast	R	2.80
Minotaur	U	0.50
Miracle Child	R	2.80
Monkeywrench	R	2.80
Mystery Character	C	0.10
Mythos	R	2.80
11		
Necros	U	0.50
Need a Lift?	U	0.50
Neural Pacifier	R	2.80
Nicks and Scrapes	C	0.10
Nostradamus' Private Diary	R	2.80
Nunchaku	C	0.10
Offensive Teleport	R	2.80
Overkill	U	0.50
Place of Power	R	2.80
12		
Project Genesis Complex	R	2.80
Prototype BSE	U	0.50
PSI Activation	U	0.50
Psionic Overload	U	0.50
Psionic Supercharge	U	0.50
Psi-Op agent	C	0.10
PSI-Resistant Armor	C	0.10
Psychokenetic Effects	R	2.80
Psychokinetic Fury	C	0.10
13		
Qeelocke	C	0.10
Rainmaker	UR	5.00
Raithan	U	0.50
Recharging the Deck	R	2.80
Red Herring	U	0.50
Rhinnon	U	0.50
Roxy "Freefall" Spaulding	UR	5.00
Salvage Operation	R	2.80

Card name	Rarity	Price
Satchel Charge	R	2.80
14		
Savant's Bag of Tricks	R	2.80
Seedling Search	C	0.10
Shock Grenade	R	2.80
Sight Blinded	U	0.50
Slaughterhouse Smith	U	0.50
Soil Machine, San Diego	U	0.50
Spellblock	U	0.50
Spiral Eye	C	0.10
Spysat	U	0.50
15		
Stars in Alignment	C	0.10
Stonehenge	U	0.50
Stop, Thief!	R	2.80
Suicide Mission	R	2.80
Summon Vampire	U	0.50
Support Withheld	R	2.80
Tao	U	0.50
Teamwork Defense	C	0.10
Techno-Dwarf	C	0.10
16		
Telepathic Effects	C	0.10
Telepathic Force Bolt	U	0.50
The Lone One	R	2.80
The Quickness	R	2.80
Time Paradox	R	2.80
Timeline Manipulation	R	2.80
Timespan	R	2.80
Torn Costume Effect	C	0.10
Trance	U	0.50
17		
Traveller	R	2.80
U.N. Moon Base	R	2.80
Unstable Footing	C	0.10
Vendetta	C	0.10
Wilder	C	0.10
Withstand PSI Attack	U	0.50
Wreckage of Skywatch	R	2.80
Xiang	U	0.50

WildStorms • Image Universe

WildStorm/Aegis Entertainment • Released **July 1996**
216 cards in set • **IDENTIFIER: © 1996; black border**

- Booster packs contain 12 cards; booster displays contain 36 boosters

Image Universe expands **WildStorms** not just to cover other comic books published by Image (of which WildStorm Productions was one studio), but other publishers, too.

The comics from which characters are drawn include *Savage Dragon*, *The Maxx*, *Spawn*, Marvel Comics' *Fantastic Four*, and even Slave Labor's humor comic book *Milk and Cheese* ("dairy products gone bad"). The timing of the Marvel involvement coincided with WildStorm's Jim Lee taking over creative duties on the *Fantastic Four* series.

Many of the characters' power levels were out of sync with the previous releases, since they were not part of the coherent WildStorm universe. — *Michael Greenholdt*

You will need **24** nine-pocket pages to store this set. (12 doubled up)

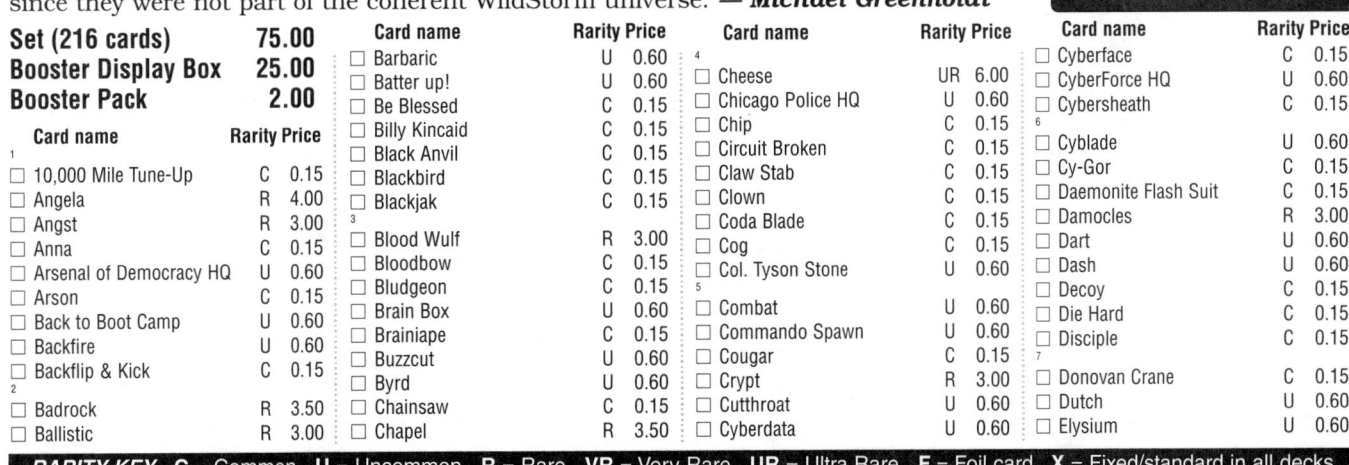

Set (216 cards)		**75.00**
Booster Display Box		**25.00**
Booster Pack		**2.00**

Card name	Rarity	Price
1		
10,000 Mile Tune-Up	C	0.15
Angela	R	4.00
Angst	R	3.00
Anna	C	0.15
Arsenal of Democracy HQ	U	0.60
Arson	C	0.15
Back to Boot Camp	U	0.60
Backfire	U	0.60
Backflip & Kick	C	0.15
2		
Badrock	R	3.50
Ballistic	R	3.00

Card name	Rarity	Price
Barbaric	U	0.60
Batter up!	U	0.60
Be Blessed	C	0.15
Billy Kincaid	C	0.15
Black Anvil	C	0.15
Blackbird	C	0.15
Blackjak	C	0.15
3		
Blood Wulf	R	3.00
Bloodbow	C	0.15
Bludgeon	C	0.15
Brain Box	U	0.60
Brainiape	C	0.15
Buzzcut	U	0.60
Byrd	U	0.60
Chainsaw	C	0.15
Chapel	R	3.50

Card name	Rarity	Price
4		
Cheese	UR	6.00
Chicago Police HQ	U	0.60
Chip	C	0.15
Circuit Broken	C	0.15
Claw Stab	C	0.15
Clown	C	0.15
Coda Blade	C	0.15
Cog	C	0.15
Col. Tyson Stone	U	0.60
5		
Combat	U	0.60
Commando Spawn	U	0.60
Cougar	U	0.60
Crypt	R	3.00
Cutthroat	U	0.60
Cyberdata	U	0.60

Card name	Rarity	Price
Cyberface	C	0.15
CyberForce HQ	U	0.60
Cybersheath	C	0.15
6		
Cyblade	U	0.60
Cy-Gor	C	0.15
Daemonite Flash Suit	C	0.15
Damocles	R	3.00
Dart	U	0.60
Dash	U	0.60
Decoy	C	0.15
Die Hard	C	0.15
Disciple	C	0.15
7		
Donovan Crane	C	0.15
Dutch	U	0.60
Elysium	U	0.60

RARITY KEY C = Common U = Uncommon R = Rare VR = Very Rare UR = Ultra Rare F = Foil card X = Fixed/standard in all decks

Card name	Rarity	Price
☐ Energy Gloves	C	0.15
☐ Exit	R	3.00
☐ Fantasticar	UR	5.00
☐ Flame On!	UR	5.00
☐ Future Spawn	U	0.60
☐ Glory	R	3.50
[8]		
☐ Gore	R	3.00
☐ Grendel	UR	8.00
☐ H.E.R.B.	C	0.15
☐ Hardedge	U	0.60
☐ Hawk's Shadow	U	0.60
☐ Heatwave	U	0.60
☐ High Pain Threshold	C	0.15
☐ High Sticking	U	0.60
☐ Hiring Freeze	U	0.60
[9]		
☐ Horde	C	0.15
☐ Hostile Takeover	U	0.60
☐ Houdini	R	3.00
☐ Hulk Smash	UR	6.00
☐ Human Torch	UR	6.00
☐ Huntsman	UR	5.00
☐ Impact	U	0.60
☐ Infiniti	U	0.60
☐ Invisible Girl	UR	6.00
[10]		
☐ Iron Man	UR	6.00
☐ Irradiated	UR	5.00
☐ Isz	C	0.15
☐ It's Clobbering Time!	UR	5.00
☐ Jamie	U	0.60
☐ Joey Finkleberry	R	3.00
☐ Johnny Redbeard	U	0.60
☐ Julie Winters	C	0.15
☐ Kenneth Irons	U	0.60
[11]		
☐ Kid Avenger	U	0.60
☐ Kid Supreme	U	0.60
☐ Kikuyo	U	0.60
☐ Kill-Cat	C	0.15
☐ Killjoy	R	3.00
☐ Killrazor	U	0.60
☐ Kimata	R	3.00

Card name	Rarity	Price
☐ Kirby	C	0.15
☐ Klone	C	0.15
[12]		
☐ Kodiak	C	0.15
☐ Lady Supreme	U	0.60
☐ Legauche	U	0.60
☐ Leopard Queen	R	3.00
☐ Liquifier	U	0.60
☐ Mace	C	0.15
☐ Mahkinot	C	0.15
☐ Make Some New Friends	C	0.15
☐ Mako	C	0.15
[13]		
☐ Malebolgia	R	4.00
☐ Manacing Mandibles	C	0.15
☐ Masada	U	0.60
☐ Maximage	R	3.00
☐ Medieval Spawn	R	5.00
☐ Mighty Man	R	3.00
☐ Milk	UR	6.00
☐ Misery	R	3.00
☐ Monster Rig	U	0.60
[14]		
☐ Mother May I	R	3.00
☐ Mr. Fantastic	UR	6.00
☐ Mr. Gone	R	3.00
☐ Mutant Strain	U	0.60
☐ Myrlu Symbiote	R	3.00
☐ Necroplasmic Blast	R	3.00
☐ Negate	C	0.15
☐ New Villian Appears	U	0.60
☐ Nottingham	C	0.15
[15]		
☐ Outback Maxx	R	4.00
☐ Overlord	U	0.60
☐ Overtkill	U	0.60
☐ Photon	R	3.00
☐ Pilot	C	0.15
☐ Pilot Spawn	C	0.15
☐ Possessed by the Fiend	R	3.00
☐ Powered Armor (Black Razor TRV)	U	0.60
☐ Powerhouse	U	0.60
[16]		
☐ Prophet	R	3.50

Card name	Rarity	Price
☐ Psi-Fire	R	3.00
☐ Psilence	U	0.60
☐ R&D Breakthrough	U	0.60
☐ Radical Mutation	U	0.60
☐ Raging Woody	U	0.60
☐ Rapture	U	0.60
☐ Redeemer	U	0.60
☐ Reign	R	3.00
[17]		
☐ Ricochet	U	0.60
☐ Ripclaw	R	3.00
☐ Riptide	C	0.15
☐ Rubble	C	0.15
☐ S.H.O.C. Trooper	C	0.15
☐ Sam Burke	C	0.15
☐ Samurai Shadowhawk	R	3.50
☐ Sara	C	0.15
☐ Savage Dragon	R	4.00
[18]		
☐ Savage Hulk	UR	6.00
☐ Sentinel	R	3.00
☐ Seoul	C	0.15
☐ Serge	C	0.15
☐ Shadowhawk	R	3.50
☐ Shaft	R	3.50
☐ She-Dragon	U	0.60
☐ Shepherd	R	3.00
☐ She-Spawn	U	0.60
[19]		
☐ Shire	C	0.15
☐ Side with Darkness	C	0.15
☐ Sigma	R	3.00
☐ Skullface	U	0.60
☐ Sneaky Trick	C	0.15
☐ Spawn	U	0.60
☐ Spawn Air Cycle	U	0.60
☐ Spawnmobile	R	3.50
☐ Spawn's Alley	U	0.60
[20]		
☐ Stalemate	C	0.15
☐ Star	C	0.15
☐ Strykeforce Submarine	U	0.60
☐ Stryker	C	0.15
☐ Summon Army of the Dead	U	0.60

Card name	Rarity	Price
☐ Superior Firepower	U	0.60
☐ Superpatriot	U	0.60
☐ Supreme	R	4.00
☐ Sword of Damocles	U	0.60
[21]		
☐ Symbiote Fragment	R	3.00
☐ T.I.M.M.I.E.	C	0.15
☐ Task	U	0.60
☐ Terry Fitzgerald	C	0.15
☐ The Baxter Building	UR	5.00
☐ The Darklands	U	0.60
☐ The Fiend	R	3.00
☐ The Freak	C	0.15
☐ The Hooly	C	0.15
[22]		
☐ The Outback	U	0.60
☐ The Thing	UR	6.00
☐ The Witchblade	R	4.00
☐ Tremor	U	0.60
☐ Trick Arrows	C	0.15
☐ Troll	C	0.15
☐ Twitch Williams	C	0.15
☐ Uncle Sam Wants You!	C	0.15
☐ Valeria & Janus	U	0.60
[23]		
☐ Vandal	C	0.15
☐ Vanguard	C	0.15
☐ Va-Va-Voom!	R	3.00
☐ Vein	U	0.60
☐ Velocity	U	0.60
☐ Vindicator	U	0.60
☐ Violator	R	4.00
☐ Violator Chopper	R	3.00
☐ Vogue	C	0.15
[24]		
☐ Volcanic	U	0.60
☐ Vort-X	C	0.15
☐ Wanda Blake	U	0.60
☐ Weapon Skill	C	0.15
☐ Witchblade	R	5.00
☐ Wylder	U	0.60
☐ You Are the Maxx!	R	4.00
☐ You're New Blood!	C	0.15
☐ Zadrok	R	3.00

NEW COSTUME

Item: EQUIPMENT. Add +1 D. Works against Psi, too.

POINTS 2

WildStorms • Legends

WildStorm/Aegis Entertainment • Released May 1997

290 cards in set • IDENTIFIER: Different card backs

• Booster packs contain 15 cards; booster displays contain 36 boosters

Legends was not an expansion set for *WildStorms*, so much as a new compatible solitaire game, based mostly on the *Limited* series cards.

The card types are different from the original game, including Heroes, Villains, Items, Sub-Plots, Events, and Trophies. The player lays out the cards in an adventure/battlescape grid and then adventures through the grid. The original *WildStorms* character cards are compatible with *Legends*, and the designers used the game as an opportunity to update many of the characters found in the original releases, bringing them into line with characters from the later expansions. — *Michael Greenholdt*

WILDSTORMS
LEGENDS
SOLITAIRE EDITION

You will need **33** nine-pocket pages to store this set. (17 doubled up)

Set (290 cards)	58.00
Booster Display Box	25.00
Booster Pack	1.50

Card name	Rarity	Price
[1]		
☐ A Clean, Well-Lit Place	U	0.35
☐ A Little Help	U	0.35
☐ A Way Around	C	0.05
☐ A Woman Scorned	U	0.35
☐ Absolom	U	0.35
☐ Act Of Mercy	U	0.35
☐ Air Strike	U	0.35
☐ Alien Invasion	U	0.35
☐ Allegra	R	2.00

Card name	Rarity	Price
[2]		
☐ An Idea!	C	0.05
☐ Anti-Magick Amulet	C	0.05
☐ Anti-Psi Headset	C	0.05
☐ Aries	U	0.35
☐ Armato	R	1.00
☐ Artemis	R	2.00
☐ Automatic Pistol	C	0.05
☐ Ax	C	0.05
[3]		
☐ Back To School	C	0.05
☐ Backlash	R	2.00
☐ Batallion	R	1.00
☐ Battle Of Wits	C	0.05
☐ Beastmaster	U	0.35

Card name	Rarity	Price
☐ Biokev Bodysuit	C	0.05
☐ Black Hammer	R	1.00
☐ Black Razor Armor	C	0.05
☐ Blackout!	U	0.35
[4]		
☐ Blast From The Past	C	0.05
☐ Bliss	R	1.00
☐ Blizzard	C	0.05
☐ Bloodqueen	R	1.00
☐ Bluff	C	0.05
☐ Bobo Del Rey	U	0.35
☐ Bomb	R	1.00
☐ Bond With Symbiote	U	0.35
☐ Bridge Out	C	0.05
☐ Building Topples	C	0.05

Card name	Rarity	Price
[5]		
☐ Bullet Bike	C	0.05
☐ Bulletproof Vest	C	0.05
☐ Burnout	R	1.00
☐ Bypass	R	1.00
☐ Call For Help!	C	0.05
☐ Casey	R	1.00
☐ Cattle Prod	U	0.35
☐ Cheap Shot	U	0.35
☐ Class 2 Cymulant	U	0.35
[6]		
☐ Claw Spell	C	0.05
☐ Claymore	R	1.00
☐ Clear Your Mind	C	0.05
☐ Clef Blade	C	0.05

Card name	Rarity	Price
☐ Clone	U	0.35
☐ Close Combat Training	C	0.05
☐ Coda Warrior	U	0.35
☐ Condition Red	R	1.00
☐ Copycat	U	0.35
[7]		
☐ Crash Course	C	0.05
☐ Crimson	R	1.00
☐ Crossbones	R	1.00
☐ Cyber Up!	C	0.05
☐ Cybernary	R	1.00
☐ Daemonite	C	0.05
☐ Daemonite in a Flashsuit	U	0.35
☐ Daemonite Spaceship	U	0.35
☐ Dane	R	1.00

RARITY KEY C = Common   U = Uncommon   R = Rare   VR = Very Rare   UR = Ultra Rare   F = Foil card   X = Fixed/standard in all decks

Card name	Rarity	Price
8		
Death Trap!	U	0.35
Deathblow	R	2.00
Deathtrap	U	0.35
Decisions, Decisions	C	0.05
Defile	R	1.00
Despot	R	1.00
Destroy Weapon	C	0.05
Diano	R	1.00
Dingo	R	1.00
9		
Discover Mystical Tome	C	0.05
Disguise	R	1.00
Domina	R	1.00
Dozer	R	1.00
Drakken	R	1.00
Drugged!	U	0.35
Earthquake	C	0.05
Emp	R	2.00
Emp Grenade	R	1.00
10		
Energy Blast Shield	U	0.35
Energy Lash Gloves	U	0.35
Er	C	0.05
Eruption!	U	0.35
Escape Plan	U	0.35
Evo	U	0.35
Exposed To Gen-Factor	R	1.00
Fahrenheit	R	2.00
Fairchild	R	2.00
11		
Find Gun	U	0.35
Fire!	C	0.05
Firehose	C	0.05
Flash Grenade	U	0.35
Flashlight	C	0.05
Flattop	R	1.00
Flint	R	1.00
Flood	R	1.00
Floor Destroyed	C	0.05
12		
Freefall	R	1.00
Frenzied Vampire	U	0.35
Friend Threatened	C	0.05
Frost Hunter	U	0.35
Frostbit	U	0.35
Fuji	R	1.00
Full Cover	C	0.05
Funhouse	C	0.05
Fusion Detonator	R	1.00

Card name	Rarity	Price
13		
Gangbanger	U	0.35
Gather Intelligence	C	0.05
Gnome	U	0.35
Grail	R	1.00
Gramalkin	R	1.00
Grenade	U	0.35
Grifter	R	2.00
Grunge	R	2.00
Hardball	R	1.00
14		
Hawksmoor	R	1.00
Hazmat Released!	U	0.35
Healing Spell	C	0.05
Heap Ammo	C	0.05
Helicopter	U	0.35
Hellstrike	R	1.00
Helmut	U	0.35
Helspont	R	1.00
Hexon	U	0.35
15		
Hightower	R	1.00
Holy Grail	U	0.35
Holy Symbol	C	0.05
Homicide	U	0.35
Hostage	U	0.35
Hunter-Killer	U	0.35
Hurricane	U	0.35
I Love It When a Plan Works	C	0.05
I'Ll Be Back	U	0.35
16		
I.O. Agent	U	0.35
Innocent Bystander	U	0.35
Inspiration	C	0.05
Interstate Pile-Up	C	0.05
Into The Sewers!	U	0.35
Investigate	C	0.05
Ivana Baiul	U	0.35
Jadon	R	1.00
Jaspar	R	1.00
17		
Jenny Sparks	R	2.00
Jester	R	1.00
Jetpack	U	0.35
Joe The Dead	U	0.35
Justice Stone & Staff	U	0.35
K.O. Gas	U	0.35
Kaizen Gamorra	R	1.00
Keeper	U	0.35
Know Your Foe	C	0.05

Card name	Rarity	Price
18		
Lady Feign	U	0.35
Ladytron	R	1.00
Large Car	C	0.05
Laser Sight	C	0.05
Le Gauche	R	1.00
Lightning Gun	U	0.35
Like A Rock!	C	0.05
Lilitu	U	0.35
Lobbing Pratice	C	0.05
19		
Lucius	R	1.00
Lucky Shot	C	0.05
Lynch	R	1.00
M.A.D.-1 Armor	U	0.35
Machine Gun	C	0.05
Machine Shop	C	0.05
Magickal Shield	U	0.35
Magickal Tome	U	0.35
Magickal Tutor	U	0.35
20		
Mahkinot	R	1.00
Majestic	R	1.00
Man-Portable Gatling	U	0.35
Maul	R	1.00
Maze	U	0.35
Medic!	C	0.05
Medikit	C	0.05
Meditate	C	0.05
Miko	R	1.00
21		
Mirv	U	0.35
Missile Command	R	1.00
Mother One	R	1.00
Mr. White	R	1.00
Murder Mystery	C	0.05
Nailgun	C	0.05
New Costume	C	0.05
Nightvision Goggles	C	0.05
Nuked!	R	1.00
22		
Nychus	U	0.35
Oil Slick	C	0.05
Omni	R	1.00
One-Eyed Jack	U	0.35
Orb Of Healing	U	0.35
Orb Of Protection	R	1.00
Orb Of Teleportation	R	1.00
Outbreak	U	0.35
Patron	U	0.35

Card name	Rarity	Price
23		
Personal Forcefield	U	0.35
Photo Op	C	0.05
Pick Up Tricks	C	0.05
Pike	U	0.35
Pilgrim	R	1.00
Police Arrive	C	0.05
Possession	U	0.35
Power Up!	C	0.05
Powerhaus	U	0.35
24		
Prayer	R	1.00
Prophet Of The Orb	U	0.35
Prototype Bse	R	1.00
Providence	R	1.00
Psi Master	C	0.05
Psi-Amp Helmet	U	0.35
Psi-Op Agent	U	0.35
Psi-Resistant Armor	U	0.35
Quickdraw	C	0.05
25		
Rainmaker	R	1.00
Raithan	U	0.35
Red	U	0.35
Repair Shop	C	0.05
Rescue Innocents	C	0.05
Revolver	C	0.05
Rifle Range	C	0.05
Robbed!	U	0.35
Rocket Launcher	U	0.35
26		
Rose Tattoo	R	1.00
Rubble	C	0.05
Run!	C	0.05
Ryka	R	1.00
Savant	R	1.00
Serge	R	1.00
Serial Killer	C	0.05
Sheba	R	1.00
Ships In The Night	C	0.05
27		
Shotgun	C	0.05
Sliver	U	0.35
Slugfest	C	0.05
Sneaky	C	0.05
Sniper Rifle	R	1.00
Sparring	C	0.05
Spartan	R	2.00
Spb Backlash	C	0.05
Speedboat	C	0.05

Card name	Rarity	Price
28		
Stay Back!	C	0.05
Storm	C	0.05
Strafe	U	0.35
Stricture	U	0.35
Stroke Of Brilliance	C	0.05
Sublime	U	0.35
Surge	R	1.00
Swift	R	1.00
Synergy	R	1.00
29		
Taboo	R	1.00
Tactical Blunder	C	0.05
Talos	U	0.35
Tank	R	1.00
Tear Gas	U	0.35
Teleportation Device	R	1.00
Terrorists Strike!	U	0.35
The Final Frontier	C	0.05
The Rush	C	0.05
30		
Threshold	R	1.00
Thug	U	0.35
Timeshift	C	0.05
Tk Flight	C	0.05
Tk Shield	C	0.05
Tunnel	C	0.05
Two-Fisted	R	1.00
Umbra	U	0.35
Union	R	1.00
31		
Vad Hypercannon	U	0.35
Vad Pp30S	C	0.05
Vad Prototype	U	0.35
Valiant Effort	C	0.05
Vampire	U	0.35
Vampirism Spell	C	0.05
Velena	R	1.00
Void	R	1.00
Volare	R	1.00
32		
Voodoo	R	2.00
War	U	0.35
Warblade	R	2.00
Weatherman One	R	1.00
Werewolf	U	0.35
Winter	R	1.00
Workout	C	0.05
Wynonna Earp	R	2.00
Zap Spell	C	0.05
33		
Zealot	R	2.00
Zen Energy Master	C	0.05

WildStorms • Best of WildStorms

WildStorm/Aegis Entertainment • Released December 1997

201 cards in set • **IDENTIFIER: 'Best of WildStorms' in copyright line; white border**

• Starter decks contain 60 cards; starter displays contain 12 starters

This condensed starter-decks-only release featured 199 of the 359 cards found in the *Limited* series, a kind of jumpstart to collecting including some of the more popular cards from *Conflict* and *Image Universe*.

Set (201 cards)	**45.00**
Starter Display Box	**20.00**
Starter Deck	**5.00**

Card name	Price
1	
Act Of Mercy	0.25
Aim	0.25
Alchemy	0.25
Anti-Aircraft Fire	0.25
Area Effect	0.25
Argos	0.25
Armand Waering	0.25
Attack Equipment	0.25
Avoid Obstacle	0.25
2	
Back From The Dead	0.25

Card name	Price
Backlash	0.50
Battalion	0.25
Beast Master	0.25
Behemoth	0.25
Belay Those Orders!	0.25
Ben Santini	0.25
Black Hammer	0.25
Black Razor	0.25
3	
Black Razor Training	0.25
Bliss	0.25
Blitz	0.25
Block	0.25
Blood Queen	0.25
Bloodstone	0.25

Card name	Price
Breakdown	0.25
Bullet Bike	0.25
Bulletproof Vest	0.25
4	
Bull's Eye	0.25
Burnout	0.25
Call In A Favor	0.25
Call In The Cavalry	0.25
Cauldron of Life	0.25
Celestial Balance	0.25
Clay Pigeon	0.25
Claymore	0.25
Clean Getaway	0.25
5	
Coda Training	0.25

Card name	Price
Combat Medic	0.25
Condition Red	0.25
Copy Cat	0.25
Counter Attack	0.25
Cover	0.25
Crimson	0.25
Crusade	0.25
Cyber-Augmentation	0.25
6	
Cybernary	0.25
Cyber-Resurrection	0.25
Daemonite	0.25
Daemonite Keys	0.25
Dane	0.25
Deathblow	0.50

Card name	Price
Defile	0.25
Despot	0.25
Disguise	0.25
7	
Diva	0.25
Diversity	0.25
Dodge	0.25
Dozer	0.25
Drakken	0.25
Dras' Adin...	0.25
Electromagnetic Pulse	0.25
Emergency First Aid	0.25
Emp	0.25
8	
Escape Plan	0.25

RARITY KEY C = Common U = Uncommon R = Rare VR = Very Rare UR = Ultra Rare F = Foil card X = Fixed/standard in all decks

Card name	Price	Card name	Price	Card name	Price	Card name	Price	Card name	Price
☐ Evil Laughter	0.25	☐ Higher Powers At Work	0.25	☐ Majestic	0.25	☐ Psi Activation	0.25	☐ Synergy	0.25
☐ Evo	0.25	☐ Holy Grail	0.25	☐ Man-Portable Gatling	0.25	☐ Psi-Op Agent	0.25	☐ Taboo	0.50
☐ Fahrenheit	0.50	☐ Hunter-Killer	0.25	☐ Maul	0.25	☐ Psi-Resistant Armor	0.25	☐ Taithan	0.25
☐ Fairchild	0.50	☐ I Quit!	0.25	☐ Med-Evac	0.25	☐ Quick Draw	0.25	☐ Take A Bullet	0.25
☐ Flashy Fake Martial Arts Move	0.25	☐ I.O. Agent	0.25	☐ Mental Wall	0.25	☐ Rainmaker	0.25	☐ Tapestry	0.25
☐ Freefall	0.25	☐ I.O. Command	0.25	☐ Miles Craven	0.25	☐ Reboot	0.25	☐ Teamwork Defense	0.25
☐ Frenzied Vampire	0.25	☐ Inconspicuous	0.25	☐ MIRV	0.25	☐ Recharging The Deck	0.25	☐ Teleport Boost	0.25
☐ Friends In High Places	0.25	☐ Infinite Possibilities	0.25	☐ Mother One	0.25	☐ Red	0.25	☐ Teleportation Device	0.25
[9]		[12]		[15]		[18]		[21]	
☐ Frostbite	0.25	☐ Infrared Sight	0.25	☐ Mysterious Disappearance	0.25	☐ Red Herring	0.25	☐ The Rush	0.25
☐ Fuji	0.25	☐ "I Thought We Were Friends..."	0.25	☐ Mystery Charater	0.25	☐ Reorganize!	0.25	☐ Threshold	0.25
☐ Full Defense	0.25	☐ Ivana Baiul	0.25	☐ Narrow Escape	0.25	☐ Revolver	0.25	☐ Time Paradox	0.25
☐ Fusion Detonator	0.25	☐ Jab	0.25	☐ Near Miss	0.25	☐ Savant	0.25	☐ Timeline Manipulation	0.25
☐ Gen-Factor	0.25	☐ Jam	0.25	☐ Need A Lift?	0.25	☐ Scanning the Timelines	0.25	☐ Toe-to-Toe	0.25
☐ Gen-Factor	0.25	☐ Jester	0.25	☐ Night Tribes Intervention	0.25	☐ Second Strike	0.25	☐ Torn Custom Effect	0.25
☐ Government Investigation	0.25	☐ Jetpack	0.25	☐ Old Rivalry Resurfaces	0.25	☐ Second Wind	0.25	☐ Union	0.25
☐ Grail	0.25	☐ Johnny Savoy	0.25	☐ One Kill	0.25	☐ Shred Armor	0.25	☐ VAD Hypercannon	0.25
☐ Grenade	0.25	☐ Justice Stone and Staff	0.25	☐ One Shot	0.25	☐ Skywatch	0.25	[22]	
[10]		[13]		[16]		[19]		☐ VAD PP30's	0.25
☐ Grifter	0.50	☐ Kaizen Gamorra	0.25	☐ Orb of Teleportation	0.25	☐ Spare Ammo	0.25	☐ Vampire	0.25
☐ Grudge Match	0.25	☐ Keeper	0.25	☐ Partial Cover	0.25	☐ Spare Parts	0.25	☐ Vendetta	0.25
☐ Grunge	0.50	☐ Kherubim Spaceship	0.25	☐ Personal Defense System	0.25	☐ Spartan	0.25	☐ Vitals Punch	0.25
☐ HALO Enterprises	0.25	☐ Knockout Punch	0.25	☐ Personal Forcefield	0.25	☐ Stop Thief!	0.25	☐ Void	0.25
☐ Hangfire	0.25	☐ Know Someone	0.25	☐ Pike	0.25	☐ Strafe	0.25	☐ Void Intervenes	0.25
☐ HEAP Ammo	0.25	☐ La Jolla Safehouse	0.25	☐ Pilgrim	0.25	☐ Strength of Will	0.25	☐ Voodoo	0.50
☐ Hellstrike	0.25	☐ Leadership	0.25	☐ Possession	0.25	☐ Sublime	0.25	☐ Warblade	0.50
☐ Helspont	0.25	☐ Lord Entropy	0.25	☐ Powered Armor (Black Razor)	0.25	☐ Subterfuge Attack	0.25	☐ Weatherman One	0.25
☐ Hide!	0.25	☐ Lynch	0.25	☐ Powerhars	0.25	☐ Super Possession	0.25	[23]	
[11]		[14]		[17]		[20]		☐ Werewolf	0.25
☐ High Jump	0.25	☐ Machine Pistol	0.25	☐ Providence	0.25	☐ Supercharge	0.25	☐ Winter	0.25
						☐ Symbiote	0.25	☐ Zealot	0.50

Wing Commander

Mag Force 7 • Released **August 1995**

312 cards in set

You will need **35** nine-pocket pages to store this set. (18 doubled up)

Concept	●●●○○
Gameplay	●●●●○
Card art	●●○○○
Player pool	○○○○○

- Starter decks contain 60 cards; starter displays contain 6 Kilrathi and 6 Terran decks
- Booster packs contain 12 cards

Designed by **Jeff Grubb** and **Don Perrin**

Based on the computer game, ***Wing Commander*** pits the Terrans against the Kilrathi (a cat-like predator-descended starfaring species). Combat takes place in the depths of space, usually between space fighters and their respective carriers.

The game recreates these battles, with each player controlling a carrier and its complement of fighters. The objective of the game is to reduce your opponent to zero Power Points by destroying his fighters or to destroy his carrier by torpedoing it twice.

The game is similar to Mag Force 7's ***Star of the Guardians***, though instead of space lanes, the game takes place upon a hexagonal grid of seven Nav Points, which fighters travel to get to the enemy location. Each player has a Ready Area, into which fighters, pilots, and weapon systems are played. Players musters fighters, pilots, and weapons from their hands to this Ready Area, then scramble them, putting together "flights" consisting of a single fighter, pilot, and weapon system. Combat takes place between opposing fighters, or fighters may attack the opposing carrier if they are at its Nav Point. Fighters have values for attack, support, bombs, maneuvering, and defense. Fighters can attack each other head-on or use their support value to assist their wingman.

The real downside of ***Wing Commander*** is the uninspired graphics and poor art. The game, while not flashy, was an improved version of Mag Force 7's *Star of the Guardians* system and showed a lot of potential. It simply got caught in the mid-1990s card game glut and disappeared. — *James Mishler*

Set (312 cards)	47.00
Starter Display Box	20.00
Booster Display Box	26.00
Starter Deck	5.00
Booster Pack	1.00

Card name	Rarity	Price	Card name	Rarity	Price	Card name	Rarity	Price
[1]			☐ Alpha	X	0.25	☐ Baron Melek	R	1.00
☐ Academy Training	C	0.05	☐ Alpha	X	0.25	☐ Battle Brothers Squadron	U	0.50
☐ Accidentally Shoot Wingman	R	1.00	☐ Alphonzo's Raiders Squadron	R	1.00	[3]		
☐ Accidentally Shoot Wingman	R	1.00	☐ Angelheart Squadron	U	0.50	☐ Beta	X	0.25
☐ Adm. Geoff Tolwyn	R	1.00	[2]			☐ Beta	X	0.25
☐ Air Mogul Squadron	U	0.50	☐ Assault the Carrier!	U	0.50	☐ Bhuk nar Hhallas	R	1.00
			☐ Assault the Carrier!	U	0.50	☐ Black Lion Squadron	R	1.00
			☐ Asteroid Field	R	1.00	☐ Black Widow Squadron	R	1.00
			☐ Asteroid Field	R	1.00	☐ Blazing Death Squadron	C	0.05
			☐ Atomic Claw Squadron	R	1.00	☐ Blazing Draptil Squadron	U	0.50
			☐ Attack My Target	C	0.05	☐ Blood Most Noble Squadron	R	1.00
			☐ Attack My Target	C	0.05	☐ Blood Rain Squadron	C	0.05

Card name	Rarity	Price
[4]		
☐ Blooded Claw Squadron	C	0.05
☐ Bloodmist's Loyal Squadron	U	0.50
☐ Blooms of the Birha Tree	U	0.50
☐ Blue Devil Squadron	C	0.05
☐ Blue Meanie Squadron	U	0.50
☐ Braxna "Minx" nar Caxki,	C	0.05
☐ Break and Attack	C	0.05
☐ Break and Attack	C	0.05
☐ Break-off	C	0.05
[5]		
☐ Break-off	C	0.05

RARITY KEY C = Common   U = Uncommon   R = Rare   VR = Very Rare   UR = Ultra Rare   F = Foil card   X = Fixed/standard in all decks

Card name	Rarity	Price
Bronze Star	C	0.05
Burma Tiger Squadron	U	0.50
Burn Out	U	0.50
Canth nar Kur'u'tak	R	1.00
Captain William Eisen	R	1.00
Capture Fighter	R	1.00
Capture Fighter	R	1.00
Capture Pilot	C	0.05
Capture Pilot	C	0.05
Capture Transport	U	0.50
Capture Transport	U	0.50
Change the Hunting Ground	R	1.00
Changing Prey	R	1.00
Chief Tech Rachel Coriolis	R	1.00
Claw Image Recognition Missile	C	0.05
Col. Christopher Blair	R	1.00
Col. Jeannette Devereaux	R	1.00
Col. Ralgha nar Hhallas	R	1.00
Communications Link Down	U	0.50
Communications Link Down	U	0.50
Court Martial	R	1.00
Crazy Diamond Squadron	U	0.50
Crimson Birha Squadron	C	0.05
Crimson Knight Squadron	U	0.50
Cruiser Shal'kuz Mang	R	1.00
Dakhath nar Caxki	R	1.00
Dark Inquisitor Squadron	R	1.00
Darkpride Squadron	C	0.05
Death from Beyond Squadron	C	0.05
Death Merchant Squadron	R	1.00
Death Reaper Squadron	R	1.00
Deathfang's Warmates Squadron	R	1.00
Deathstroke's Pride Squadron	C	0.05
Defend Listening Post	U	0.50
Defend Listening Post	U	0.50
Delta	X	0.25
Delta	X	0.25
Destroyer Bordrav	R	1.00
Destroyer Trak'hmar	R	1.00
Dewclaw	U	0.50
Dragon Master Squadron	U	0.50
Dreadnaught Vengeance of Vukar Tag	R	1.00
Dynamo Hum Squadron	C	0.05
Earth Shaker Squadron	U	0.50
Eject!	U	0.50
Eject!	R	1.00
Enslaver of Races Squadron	R	1.00
Epsilon	X	0.25
Epsilon	X	0.25
Eta	X	0.25
Eta	X	0.25
Fang Friend-or-Foe Missile	C	0.05
Fangs of Death Squadron	C	0.05
Favored by Sivar Squadron	R	1.00
Fearful Symmetry Squadron	U	0.50
Fighter Recon	U	0.50
Fighter Recon	U	0.50
Fire Birds Squadron	C	0.05
Fire Dagger Squadron	R	1.00
Fire-Eater Squadron	U	0.50
Fireball Squadron	U	0.50
Fireclaw's Avenger Squadron	U	0.50
Fish-hook	U	0.50
Forever Loyal Squadron	U	0.50
Fuel Rupture	R	1.00
Fuel Rupture	R	1.00
Furball Fever	U	0.50
Furfighter Squadron	C	0.05
Gallahad Squadron	R	1.00

Card name	Rarity	Price
Gamma	X	0.25
Gamma	X	0.25
Gawain Squadron	R	1.00
Ghostwalker Squadron	C	0.05
Going Ape	R	1.00
Gold Star	R	1.00
Golden Cheetah Squadron	C	0.05
Gray Hornet Squadron	C	0.05
Great White Squadron	C	0.05
Hadrian's Hammers Squadron	U	0.50
Hard Brake	C	0.05
Hard Brake	C	0.05
Heartbreaker Squadron	C	0.05
Heck Outa Dodge	U	0.50
Heir to the Kilrathi Throne	R	1.00
Hell's Archers Squadron	C	0.05
Hero of the H'rai Squadron	C	0.05
Hidden Dagger Squadron	R	1.00
Hit by Own Heat-Seeker!	R	1.00
Hit by Own Heat-Seeker!	R	1.00
Honor Bearer Squadron	C	0.05
Hurricane Squadron	C	0.05
Icon of Glory	R	1.00
Icon of Sivar	R	1.00
Imperial Security	U	0.50
Improved Comms	C	0.05
Improved Comms	C	0.05
Improved Shields	C	0.05
Improved Shields	C	0.05
Improved Tac Computers	C	0.05
Improved Tac Computers	C	0.05
Intel Inside	U	0.50
Iota	X	0.25
Iota	X	0.25
Jade Dragonfly Squadron	C	0.05
Kabaka Warrior Squadron	R	1.00
Kappa	X	0.25
Kappa	X	0.25
Khantahr's Snarl Squadron	U	0.50
Khitz nar Ki'ra	U	0.50
Kickstop	C	0.05
Kickstop	C	0.05
Killer Bee Squadron	C	0.05
Kilra'k Demons Squadron	C	0.05
Kramm nar Caxki	R	1.00
Kuklext Ragitagha	U	0.50
Kukubno nar Hhallas	U	0.50
Lair Master Squadron	U	0.50
Lancelot Squadron	R	1.00
Laser Fangs Squadron	C	0.05
Leatherhide Squadron	U	0.50
Lie in Wait	C	0.05
Lieutenant Laurel Buckley	U	0.50
Lightning Strike Squadron	U	0.50
Lt. Amanda Carruthers	C	0.05
Lt. Anthony Yee	U	0.50
Lt. John Hefter	C	0.05
Lt. Michael Williamson	C	0.05
Lt. Mitchell Lopez	U	0.50
Lt. Regina Ortwin	C	0.05
Lt. Robin Peters	U	0.50
Lt. Russ Wilbury	C	0.05
Lt. Simon LeDuke	C	0.05
Lt. Winston Chang	U	0.50
Lusterfur Squadron	R	1.00
Magnum Launch	R	1.00
Main Guns Damaged	U	0.50
Main Guns Damaged	U	0.50
Maj. James Taggart	U	0.50
Maj. Todd Marshall	R	1.00

Card name	Rarity	Price
Major Jace Dillon	U	0.50
Malf!	U	0.50
Malf!	U	0.50
Mandibles of Doom Squadron	C	0.05
Maneuvering Thruster Destroyed	U	0.50
Maneuvering Thrusters Destroyed	U	0.50
Maniac Solution	R	1.00
Marjak nar Kur'u'tak	R	1.00
Media Blitz	R	1.00
Merlin Squadron	R	1.00
Minefield	R	1.00
Minefield	R	1.00
Monarch Squadron	U	0.50
Monkey Hunter Squadron	C	0.05
Mr. Kat	U	0.50
Mud Shark Squadron	U	0.50
Najji Ragitagha	R	1.00
Nebula	R	1.00
Nebula	R	1.00
Night Prowler Squadron	C	0.05
Northern Lights Squadron	C	0.05
Osprey Squadron	C	0.05
Pewter Planet	R	1.00
Pilum Friend-or-Foe Missile	C	0.05
Pounce on the Prey	U	0.50
Power of the Emperor	R	1.00
Pulsar Snarls Communications	R	1.00
Pulsar Snarls Communications	R	1.00
Radio Rollins	C	0.05
Rage of Sivar Squadron	U	0.50
Ram!	R	1.00
Ram!	R	1.00
Reaper Cannon	R	1.00
Reaper Cannon	R	1.00
Recover Pilot	C	0.05
Recover Pilot	C	0.05
Red Ranger Squadron	U	0.50
Righteous Vengeance Squadron	R	1.00
Rock & Roll	R	1.00
Roll	C	0.05
Roll	C	0.05
Sabak Liegemen Squadron	C	0.05
Savage Fury Squadron	C	0.05
Scarlet Speedster Squadron	C	0.05
Seaking Squadron	R	1.00
Shake	C	0.05
Shake	C	0.05
Shake, Rattle & Roll	U	0.50
Shelton Slide	U	0.50
Shield Failure Imminent!	U	0.50
Shield Failure Imminent!	U	0.50
Shift in Battle	R	1.00
Shift in Battle	R	1.00
Show Trial	R	1.00
Show Trial	U	0.50
Silent Doom Squadron	R	1.00
Silver Star	U	0.50
Sit-'n-Kick	C	0.05
Sivar's Blessing	U	0.50
Sivar's Glory	X	0.25
Sivar's Honored H'rai Squadron	R	1.00
Skillful Use of Missile Decoys	U	0.50
Skipper Missile	R	1.00
Sky Demon Squadron	U	0.50
Sky Giant Squadron	C	0.05
Smashed Windscreen	U	0.50
Smashed Windscreen	U	0.50
Smiting Pride Squadron	C	0.05
Space Terror Squadron	U	0.50
Spaceborne Warning		

Card name	Rarity	Price
& Control Mission	U	0.50
Spaceborne Warning & Control Mission	U	0.50
Sparrowhawk Squadron	C	0.05
Speed Demon Squadron	R	1.00
Spiculum Image Recognition Missile	C	0.05
Stabilizer Destroyed	R	1.00
Stabilizer Destroyed	R	1.00
Star Pouncer Squadron	U	0.50
Stealth Technology	R	1.00
Stealth Technology	R	1.00
Steel Death Squadron	C	0.05
Storm Bringer Squadron	U	0.50
Storm Lord Squadron	U	0.50
Summons from Kilrah	R	1.00
Tachyon Gun	R	1.00
Tail	C	0.05
Tail	C	0.05
Tail Shot Off	R	1.00
Tail Shot Off	R	1.00
Taunt	C	0.05
Taunt	C	0.05
TCS Agincourt	R	1.00
TCS Coventry	R	1.00
TCS Sheffield	R	1.00
TCS Victory	X	0.25
The Emperor Speaks!	R	1.00
The Glorious Hunt	R	1.00
The Love Animals	U	0.50
The Savage Feast	U	0.50
Theta	X	0.25
Theta	X	0.25
Throat Ripper Squadron	R	1.00
Throat Wolves Squadron	U	0.50
Thundering Anger Squadron	U	0.50
Tiger Killer Squadron	U	0.50
Tight Loop	C	0.05
Tight Loop	C	0.05
TNS Publicity Tour	R	1.00
Too Much Fire Liquor	R	1.00
Too Much Vak'qu.	R	1.00
Torpedo	C	0.05
Torpedo	C	0.05
Torpedo Mount	C	0.05
Torpedo Mount	C	0.05
Traitor!	R	1.00
Traitor!	R	1.00
Transport	U	0.50
Transport	U	0.50
Tsunami Squadron	R	1.00
Turn-'n- Spin	U	0.50
Unchained Thunder Squadron	C	0.05
Unrelenting War Squadron	R	1.00
Unrepentant Rage Squadron	R	1.00
Valkyrie Squadron	R	1.00
Vengeful Pursuit Squadron	U	0.50
Vruskt nar Sihkag	U	0.50
Warrior Code	C	0.05
Well-Placed Hit	U	0.50
Well-Placed Hit	U	0.50
William Tell Squadron	C	0.05
Winterblast Squadron	C	0.05
Xilerks "Nikodaemus" Ki'ra	R	1.00
Zeta	X	0.25
Zeta	X	0.25
Zombie Wolf Squadron	R	1.00
Zrank nar Sihkag	R	1.00
Zu'kara	R	1.00

RARITY KEY C = Common U = Uncommon R = Rare VR = Very Rare UR = Ultra Rare F = Foil card X = Fixed/standard in all decks

Wizard in Training

Upper Deck • Released October 2000

142 cards in set

Concept	●●●●○
Gameplay	●●●○○
Card art	●●●○○
Player pool	●●●○○

* Starter decks contain 60 cards; starter displays contain 10 decks
* Booster packs contain 9 cards; booster displays contain 24 packs

Designed by **Kris Oprisko**

Designed as an introductory CCG for young fans of fantasy fiction, *Wizard in Training* presents a world that bears an uncanny resemblance to the world found in the *Harry Potter* series of popular child- (and adult-) oriented fantasy novels. Little wonder: Upper Deck was poised to produce the official *Potter* CCG and had a design team ready to go (although not, as has been rumored, an actual game design). When Wizards of the Coast won the bidding for that lucrative property, rather than waste its groundwork, Upper Deck developed its own game world.

The players all have character cards that represent students from the Dragontooth Academy, the last place where the ways of wizardry are taught. Every year only one student can graduate from the academy with the rank of Wizard. The game recreates the final test, the duel at the end between the two best students at the academy.

The objective is to be the first to acquire 24 Dragonteeth after attaining Level 5 as a Wizard. Each player starts with a character card, representing the student at the Dragontooth Academy. Players place Items into their Power Pools, and tally a number of Dragonteeth for each item. The player may then cast a spell of a level equal to or less than his current level. Some Spells require that the player have a specific type of Item in his Power Pool. Counterspells are included, as is a duel phase for the characters.

Wizard makes a nice introductory game for new, young gamers. An expansion, ***Professor Ploog's Prize Potions***, is scheduled for early 2001, and will add a new class of item, Potions, to the game. Other indications from the rules and cards are that additional levels of game play will be added in further expansions. And while *Wizard* was pilloried by some as a *Potter*-clone, then again, it was available right away, while fans looking for the official *Potter* CCG were still waiting in early 2001. — *James Mishler*

Set (142 cards)	65.00
Starter Display Box	46.00
Booster Display Box	52.00
Starter Deck	8.80
Booster Pack	2.50

# Card name	Type	Rarity	Price
1			
☐ 123 Acid Gargoyle	Duel	Ch3	2.50
☐ 36 All Spell Counter	Spell	R	3.30
☐ 57 Ancient Warrior (skeleton)	Duel	R	2.80
☐ 12 Anti-Gravity	Spell	C	0.10
☐ 138 Arm	Spell	Ch1	8.50
☐ 61 Banshee	Duel	C	0.30
☐ 134 Battle Axe	Item	Ch2	4.00
☐ 15 Berserker	Spell	R	2.00
☐ 69 Bo Staff	Item	C	0.30
2			
☐ 82 Bone	Item	U	0.30
☐ 68 Book of Mists	Item	C	0.30
☐ 99 Bow & arrows	Item	U	0.45
☐ 98 Breastplate	Item	U	0.45
☐ 60 Bugbear	Duel	C	0.05
☐ 142 Carapace	Spell	Ch1	8.50
☐ 112 Cauldron	Item	C	0.05
☐ 48 Centaur	Duel	C	0.05
☐ 38 Centipede	Duel	C	0.30
3			
☐ 89 Chainmail	Item	C	0.05
☐ 19 Change Form	Spell	C	0.10
☐ 74 Cloak	Item	C	0.30
☐ 103 Club	Item	R	2.00
☐ 56 Common Gargoyle	Duel	C	0.05
☐ 110 Crossbow	Item	C	0.05
☐ 66 Crystal Ball	Item	C	0.05
☐ 114 Cyclops	Duel	Ch3	2.50
☐ 33 Darkness	Spell	R	2.30
4			
☐ 25 Density	Spell	R	2.00
☐ 111 Destiny Cards	Item	C	0.05
☐ 139 Disarm	Spell	Ch1	8.50
☐ 14 Dispersal	Spell	R	2.30
☐ 73 Divining Rod	Item	C	0.30
☐ 115 Djinn	Duel	Ch3	2.50

# Card name	Type	Rarity	Price
☐ 79 Dragon's Nest	Item	U	0.30
☐ 107 Enchanted Broom	Item	C	0.30
☐ 78 Enchanted Coins	Item	U	0.30
5			
☐ 70 Enchanted Shield	Item	C	0.30
☐ 96 Energy Coil	Item	U	0.45
☐ 131 Energy Pod	Item	Ch2	4.00
☐ 7 Enlarging	Spell	C	0.05
☐ 42 Evil Arbor	Duel	C	0.30
☐ 91 Eye of Newt	Item	C	0.05
☐ 140 Fire	Spell	Ch1	8.50
☐ 118 Fire Demon	Duel	Ch3	2.50
☐ 132 Fire Wall	Item	Ch2	4.00
6			
☐ 126 Flash Pot	Item	Ch2	4.00
☐ 27 Flight	Spell	C	0.10
☐ 120 Forest Giant	Duel	Ch3	2.50
☐ 80 Fortune Board (ouija)	Item	U	0.30
☐ 94 Fossil	Item	U	0.45
☐ 24 Freeze	Spell	R	2.30
☐ 64 Ghoul Hound	Duel	C	0.05
☐ 41 Giant Anaconda	Duel	C	0.30
☐ 54 Gnome	Duel	R	2.30
7			
☐ 59 Goblin	Duel	C	0.05
☐ 52 Gorgon	Duel	R	2.30
☐ 11 Gravity	Spell	C	0.10
☐ 53 Griffin	Duel	R	2.50
☐ 28 Grounding	Spell	C	0.10
☐ 128 Halbard	Item	Ch2	4.00
☐ 113 Harpie	Duel	Ch3	2.50
☐ 23 Heat	Spell	R	2.30
☐ 88 Helmet	Item	C	0.05
8			
☐ 47 Hydra	Duel	R	2.00
☐ 67 Hypnotic Mirror	Item	C	0.05
☐ 31 Ice	Spell	R	2.80
☐ 26 Immaterial	Spell	R	2.80
☐ 135 Invisibility Cloak	Item	Ch2	4.00
☐ 17 Invisible	Spell	C	0.10

# Card name	Type	Rarity	Price
☐ 141 Juggernaut	Spell	Ch1	8.50
☐ 4 Kelli Crisp	Char	C	0.05
☐ 6 Kenzie Taylor	Char	U	0.30
9			
☐ 100 Knife	Item	U	0.45
☐ 3 Kyle Giffen	Char	C	0.05
☐ 62 Lava Gargoyle	Duel	R	2.80
☐ 76 Leather Jerkin	Item	U	0.30
☐ 32 Light Burst	Spell	R	2.30
☐ 45 Lightning Lizard	Duel	R	2.30
☐ 16 Logic	Spell	R	2.30
☐ 87 Lute	Item	U	0.30
☐ 72 Mace	Item	U	0.30
10			
☐ 105 Magic Amulet	Item	C	0.05
☐ 86 Magic Portal	Item	U	0.30
☐ 109 Magic Wand	Item	C	0.05
☐ 106 Magical Broom	Item	C	0.05
☐ 40 Mantis	Duel	U	0.30
☐ 116 Minotaur	Duel	Ch3	2.50
☐ 121 Mountain Troll	Duel	Ch3	2.50
☐ 136 Multi-Fire Wand	Item	Ch2	4.00
☐ 119 Myrmidon	Duel	Ch3	2.50
11			
☐ 29 Mystic Ore	Spell	C	0.05
☐ 77 Net	Item	U	0.45
☐ 1 Nevin Crisp	Char	C	0.05
☐ 129 Nunchuks	Item	Ch2	4.00
☐ 117 Ogre	Duel	Ch3	2.50
☐ 85 Pan Pipes	Item	U	0.30
☐ 5 Phil Yen	Char	U	0.30
☐ 50 Phoenix	Duel	R	2.00
☐ 71 Pike	Item	C	0.05
12			
☐ 104 Power Crystals	Item	C	0.05
☐ 108 Power Pod	Item	R	2.30
☐ 8 Reducing	Spell	C	0.10
☐ 101 Relic	Item	U	0.45
☐ 125 Runestone	Item	Ch2	4.00
☐ 49 Satyr	Duel	C	0.05

# Card name	Type	Rarity	Price
☐ 127 Scimitar	Item	Ch2	4.00
☐ 39 Scorpion	Duel	U	0.30
☐ 84 Scroll	Item	U	0.30
13			
☐ 93 Scythe	Item	C	0.30
☐ 2 Seetha Devi	Char	C	0.05
☐ 65 Shield	Item	C	0.05
☐ 102 Shoulder Guard	Item	U	0.45
☐ 10 Silence	Spell	U	0.30
☐ 81 Skull	Item	U	0.30
☐ 97 Smoke Bomb	Item	U	0.45
☐ 22 Solidify	Spell	R	2.00
☐ 9 Sonic	Spell	U	0.45
14			
☐ 137 Special Deal	Spell	Ch1	8.50
☐ 75 Speed Broom	Item	U	0.30
☐ 37 Spider	Duel	C	0.30
☐ 95 Stag Horn	Item	U	0.45
☐ 35 Strong Spell Counter	Spell	U	0.60
☐ 124 Swamp Creature	Duel	Ch3	2.50
☐ 13 Swarm Attack	Spell	R	2.30
☐ 90 Sword	Item	C	0.05
☐ 130 Talisman	Item	Ch2	4.00
15			
☐ 30 Targeting	Spell	C	0.05
☐ 51 Three Headed Gator	Duel	R	2.50
☐ 92 Tongue of Frog	Item	C	0.05
☐ 133 Trident	Item	Ch2	4.00
☐ 55 Troll	Duel	C	0.05
☐ 20 True Form	Spell	C	0.10
☐ 83 Tusk	Item	U	0.30
☐ 44 Unicorn	Duel	R	2.00
☐ 43 Vampire Bat	Duel	R	1.80
16			
☐ 21 Vaporize	Spell	R	2.80
☐ 18 Visible	Spell	C	0.05
☐ 122 War Goblin	Duel	Ch3	2.50
☐ 34 Weak Spell Counter	Spell	U	0.60
☐ 63 Werewolf	Duel	R	3.00
☐ 58 Yeti	Duel	R	2.80
☐ 46 Zombie	Duel	R	1.80

RARITY KEY C = Common U = Uncommon R = Rare Ch = Chase # = Lower numbers are rarer X = Fixed/standard in all decks

WWF Raw Deal

Comic Images • Released August 2000

150 cards in set

- Starter decks contain 61 cards and rulebook; starter displays contain 12 starters
- Boosters contain 12 cards; booster displays contain 36 boosters

Designed by **Mike Foley** and **Barron Vangor Toth**

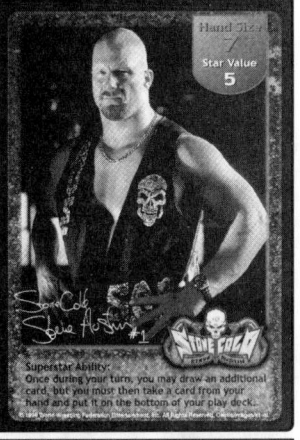

While *WCW Nitro* was first to market, *WWF Raw Deal* had the distinct advantage of being tied into the phenomenally popular World Wrestling Federation. The home of The Rock, Stone Cold Steve Austin, Triple H, and Mankind has been the clear ratings winner and fan favorite over the past several years. Comic Images, already successful with several series of WWF collector cards, presented its CCG in 2000 — after the legal wrangling with Wizards of the Coast over its game design was finally settled.

Each player controls a wrestler and has a deck filled with maneuvers, reversals, and actions. Each maneuver does a specific amount of damage, which is discarded directly from the other player's deck. The first player to turn over all the cards in his deck loses. Each maneuver has a Fortitude rating; the more devastating the maneuver, the more Fortitude you need to play it. Fortitude is built up by previous successful maneuvers, so matches start slowly with relatively weak moves, until they build up to the big finishers — just like the "sports entertainment" matches they emulate. Reversal cards not only avoid the damage of an opponent's maneuver, but they can do damage themselves.

The cards are pleasantly designed, with great photos taken directly from WWF action. If you notice a number of cards seem to feature "The Lethal Weapon" Steve Blackman and Tazz, it's because they did a special shoot to get Comic Images shots they needed that weren't otherwise available. Nice cooperation from the licensor!

An expansion, *Fully Loaded*, was in the works at press time, — *Scott Haring*

	Concept	●●●○○
	Gameplay	●●●●○
	Card art	●●●●○
	Player pool	●●●○○

Set (150 cards)	175.00
Starter Display Box	102.50
Booster Display Box	90.00
Starter Deck	10.00
Booster Pack	3.00
Stone Cold Steve Austin Boxed Set (mass market)	27.50
The Rock Boxed Set (mass market)	27.50

Boxed set and promo cards

Card name	Price
☐ Patented Austin Kick to the Gut	14.00
☐ Patented Rock Foot-stomp	14.00
☐ Piledriver	10.00

#	Card name	Type	Rarity	Price
☐ 66	Abdominal Stretch	Sub	R	4.00
☐ 57	Ankle Lock	Sub	U	1.00
☐ 51	Arm Bar	Sub	C	0.25
☐ 22	Arm Bar Takedown	Grp	C	0.25
☐ 24	Arm Drag	Grp	C	0.25
☐ 35	Atomic Drop	Grp	U	1.00
☐ 34	Atomic Facebuster	Grp	U	1.00
☐ 124	Austin Elbow Smash	HR	X	3.00
☐ 122	Ayatollah of Rock-n-Rollah	Act	UR	22.50
☐ 6	Back Body Drop	Str	C	0.25
☐ 29	Back Breaker	Grp	C	0.25
☐ 53	Bear Hug	Grp	C	0.25
☐ 38	Belly to Back Suplex	Grp	U	1.00
☐ 33	Belly to Belly Suplex	Grp	U	1.00
☐ 7	Big Boot	Str	C	0.25
☐ 28	Body Slam	Grp	C	0.25
☐ 64	Boston Crab	Sub	R	4.00
☐ 60	Bow & Arrow	Sub	U	1.00
☐ 72	Break the Hold	Rev	C	0.25
☐ 43	Bulldog	Grp	R	4.00
☐ 63	Camel Clutch	Sub	R	4.00
☐ 20	Chair Shot	Str	R	4.00
☐ 11	Cheap Shot From the Corner	Str	U	1.00
☐ 61	Chicken Wing	Sub	U	1.00
☐ 52	Chin Lock	Sub	C	0.25
☐ 55	Choke Hold	Sub	C	0.25
☐ 1	Chop	Str	C	0.25
☐ 147	Chris Jericho	Star	X	3.00

#	Card name	Type	Rarity	Price
☐ 116	Chyna Interferes	Rev	UR	25.00
☐ 77	Clean Break	Rev	U	1.00
☐ 19	Clothesline	Str	R	4.00
☐ 59	Cobra Clutch	Sub	U	1.00
☐ 49	Collar & Elbow Lockup	Sub	C	0.25
☐ 69	Combination Attack	HR	R	4.00
☐ 99	Comeback!	Act	R	4.00
☐ 10	Cross Body Block	Str	U	1.00
☐ 45	DDT	Grp	R	4.00
☐ 101	Deluding Yourself	Act	R	4.00
☐ 15	Discus Punch	Str	U	1.00
☐ 80	Disqualification!	Rev	R	4.00
☐ 94	Distract the Ref	Act	U	1.00
☐ 103	Diversion	Act	R	4.00
☐ 83	Don't Think Too Hard	Act	C	0.25
☐ 150	Don't You Never … EVER!	Rev	X	2.00
☐ 133	Double Arm DDT	Gr/Rv	X	2.00
☐ 126	Double Digits	Rev	X	2.00
☐ 30	Double Leg Takedown	Grp	U	1.00
☐ 97	Double Team	Act	U	1.00
☐ 14	Drop Kick	Str	U	1.00
☐ 100	Ego Boost	Act	R	4.00
☐ 76	Elbow to the Face	Rev	U	1.00
☐ 12	Ensugiri	Str	U	1.00
☐ 71	Escape Move	Rev	C	0.25
☐ 137	Facebuster	Rev	X	2.00
☐ 68	Figure Four Leg Lock	Sub	R	4.00
☐ 31	Fireman's Carry	Grp	U	1.00
☐ 44	Fisherman's Suplex	Grp	R	4.00
☐ 89	Flash in the Pan	Act	C	0.25
☐ 54	Full Nelson	Sub	C	0.25
☐ 98	Get Crowd Support	Act	U	1.00
☐ 65	Guillotine Stretch	Sub	R	4.00
☐ 27	Gut Buster	Grp	C	0.25
☐ 132	Have a Nice Day!	Rev	X	2.00
☐ 5	Haymaker	Str	C	0.25
☐ 3	Head Butt	Str	C	0.25
☐ 32	Headlock Takedown	Grp	U	1.00
☐ 120	Hellfire & Brimstone	Act	UR	20.00
☐ 135	HHH	Star	X	5.00
☐ 23	Hip Toss	Grp	C	0.25
☐ 82	Hmmm	Act	C	0.25
☐ 21	Hurricanrana	Str	R	4.00

#	Card name	Type	Rarity	Price
☐ 138	I Am The Game.	Act	X	2.00
☐ 36	Inverse Atomic Drop	Grp	U	1.00
☐ 88	Irish Whip	Act	C	0.25
☐ 87	Jockeying for Position	Act	C	0.25
☐ 143	Kane	Star	X	4.00
☐ 144	Kane's Chokeslam	Grp	X	3.00
☐ 145	Kane's Flying Clothesline	HR	X	3.00
☐ 146	Kane's Return!	Rev	X	2.00
☐ 119	Kane's Tombstone Piledriver	TF	UR	21.00
☐ 9	Kick	Str	U	1.00
☐ 75	Knee to the Gut	Rev	U	1.00
☐ 136	Leaping Knee to the Face	Str	X	2.00
☐ 148	Lionsault	HR	X	3.00
☐ 125	Lou Thesz Press	Rev	X	2.00
☐ 107	Maintain Hold	Act	R	4.00
☐ 79	Manager Interferes	Act	R	4.00
☐ 113	Mandible Claw	TF	UR	21.00
☐ 131	Mankind	Star	X	4.00
☐ 104	Marking Out	Act	R	4.00
☐ 114	Mr. Socko	Act	UR	20.00
☐ 81	No Chance in Hell	Rev	R	4.50
☐ 86	Not Yet	Act	C	0.25
☐ 92	Offer Handshake	Act	U	1.00
☐ 110	Open Up a Can of Whoop-Ass	Act	UR	20.00
☐ 78	Partner Interference	Rev	R	4.00
☐ 108	Pat & Gerry	Act	R	4.00
☐ 115	Pedigree	TF	UR	23.50
☐ 112	Power of Darkness	Act	UR	22.50
☐ 46	Power Slam	Grp	R	4.00
☐ 47	Powerbomb	Grp	R	4.00
☐ 48	Press Slam	Grp	R	4.00
☐ 39	Pump Handle Slam	Grp	U	1.00
☐ 2	Punch	Str	C	0.25
☐ 105	Puppies! Puppies!	Act	R	4.00
☐ 95	Recovery	Act	U	1.00
☐ 40	Reverse DDT	Grp	U	1.00
☐ 142	Rock Bottom	Gr/Rv	X	3.00
☐ 93	Roll Out of the Ring	Act	U	1.00
☐ 74	Rolling Takedown	Rev	U	1.00
☐ 4	Roundhouse Punch	Str	C	0.25

#	Card name	Type	Rarity	Price
☐ 13	Running Elbow Smash	Str	U	1.00
☐ 25	Russian Leg Sweep	Grp	C	0.25
☐ 41	Samoan Drop	Grp	R	4.00
☐ 91	Shake It Off	Act	U	1.00
☐ 106	Shane O'Mac	Act	R	4.30
☐ 8	Shoulder Block	Str	U	1.00
☐ 42	Sit Out Powerbomb	Grp	R	4.00
☐ 62	Sleeper	Sub	R	4.00
☐ 140	Smackdown Hotel	Act	X	3.00
☐ 26	Snap Mare	Grp	C	0.25
☐ 18	Spear	Str	R	4.00
☐ 17	Spinning Heel Kick	Str	R	4.00
☐ 96	Spit At Opponent	Act	U	1.00
☐ 102	Stagger	Act	R	4.00
☐ 58	Standing Side Headlock	Sub	U	1.00
☐ 70	Step Aside	Rev	C	0.25
☐ 56	Step Over Toe Hold	Sub	C	0.25
☐ 123	Stone Cold Steve Austin	Star	X	4.00
☐ 109	Stone Cold Stunner	TF	UR	25.00
☐ 16	Superkick	Str	R	4.00
☐ 84	Tag in Partner	Act	C	0.25
☐ 141	Take That Move…	Rev	X	3.00
☐ 118	The People's Elbow	TF	UR	21.00
☐ 117	The People's Eyebrow	Act	UR	21.00
☐ 139	The Rock	Star	X	4.00
☐ 127	The Undertaker	Star	X	4.00
☐ 67	Torture Rack	Sub	R	4.00
☐ 134	Tree of Woe	Grp	X	2.00
☐ 73	Trip	Rev	C	0.25
☐ 130	Undertaker Sits Up!	Rev	X	3.00
☐ 128	Undertaker's Chokeslam	Grp	X	3.00
☐ 129	Undertaker's Flying Clothesline	HR	X	3.00
☐ 111	Undertaker's Tombstone Piledriver	TF	UR	23.50
☐ 37	Vertical Suplex	Grp	U	1.00
☐ 90	View of Villainy	Act	C	0.25
☐ 121	Walls of Jericho	TF	UR	24.00
☐ 85	Whaddya Got?	Act	C	0.25
☐ 50	Wrist Lock	Sub	C	0.25
☐ 149	Y2J	Act	X	5.00

RARITY KEY C = Common U = Uncommon R = Rare VR = Very Rare UR = Ultra Rare F = Foil card X = Fixed/standard in all decks

SCRYE Collectible Card Game Checklist and Price Guide • 489

You will need
16
nine-pocket pages to store this set.
(8 doubled up)

Wyvern

U.S. Games Systems • First set, **Premiere Limited**, released **January 1995**
136 cards in set • **IDENTIFIER: No bullet before card number**

- Starter decks contain 60 cards; starter displays contain 12 starters
- Booster packs contain 12 cards; booster displays contain 36 boosters

Created by **Mike Fitzgerald**

Wyvern (wī-vern), which appeared on the CCG scene a little more than a year after *Magic*, gave players of that game something they couldn't get enough of: dragons, dragons, and more dragons. Inspired by western European, Middle Eastern, and Chinese mythology, *Wyvern* makes each player the ruler of an empire — rulers who use dragons to fight wars. Some army!

There are five types of cards used in two decks: Dragons, Terrain (Dragon Lair), Actions, Dragon Slayers, and Treasures (Treasure Horde). Each player deals out six face-down Dragon and/or Terrain cards and seven cards which may be Actions, Treasures, or Dragon Slayer cards. To win a round, a player must destroy his opponent's six Dragon/Terrain cards, which are worth points. A new round is then started and rounds continue until a player reaches a predetermined point total.

The game is straight-forward, with Treasure cards affecting one row of up to three Dragon/Terrain cards on a permanent basis, while the Action cards can modify the battle immediately upon play. The Dragon Slayer cards can destroy dragons in a separate phase, but these dragons do not count towards victory. A typical game consists of two or three rounds.

Wyvern flew for two years before being grounded. U.S. Games Systems' next CCG couldn't be further apart in topic: **Pez.— Michael Greenholdt**

Concept	●●○○○
Gameplay	●●●○○
Card art	●●○○○
Player pool	○○○○○

Set (136 cards)	150.00
Starter Display Box	25.00
Booster Display Box	25.00
Starter Deck	7.00
Booster Pack	2.00

Card name	Rarity	Price
[1]		
Ajatar	R	1.00
Amphiptere	C	0.15
Amphisbena	R	1.00
Armor	C	0.15
Avalanche	C	0.15
Azhi Dahaka	U	0.60
Basilisk	R	1.00
Battle Chaos	C	0.15
Beowulf The Dragon Slayer	C	0.15
[2]		
Brush Fire	U	0.60
Cauldron	C	0.15
Cave	C	0.15
Celestial Dragon	U	0.60
Chimera	U	0.60
Cliff	U	0.60
Clouds	U	0.60
Colchis	C	0.15
Coral Reef	C	0.15

Card name	Rarity	Price
[3]		
Crevice	U	0.60
Crystal Ball	C	0.15
Cynoprosopi	R	1.00
Desert	C	0.15
Doomsday	R	1.00
Draco	R	1.00
Dragon Egg	R	1.00
Dwarven Army	C	0.15
Earthquake	C	0.15
[4]		
Echidna	U	0.60
Fafnir	U	0.60
Fireball	C	0.15
Firebolt	C	0.15
Firebreathing	C	0.15
Flood	C	0.15
Forests	C	0.15
Forrest Fire	U	0.60
Fountain of Youth	C	0.15
[5]		
Frostbreathing	C	0.15
Frozen Lake	U	0.60
Gandarewa	U	0.60
Gani	U	0.60
Gargouille	U	0.60
Gold	C	0.15
Golden Apple	C	0.15
Golden Apples	C	0.15
Golden Fleece	R	1.00
[6]		
Grendel	R	2.00
Gryphon	U	0.60
Guivre	C	0.15
Hail Storm	C	0.15
Heatwave	C	0.15
Help	C	0.15
Hero	R	1.00
High Winds	R	1.00
Hydra	U	0.60
[7]		
Jason The Dragon Slayer	R	2.00
Jewels	C	0.15
Jormungandr	R	1.00

Card name	Rarity	Price
Kakutan	U	0.60
Kioh-Lung	U	0.60
Kiss of Le Succebe	R	1.00
Knowledge	C	0.15
Kulkulcan	U	0.60
[8]		
Lake	C	0.15
Lambton Worm	U	0.60
Leviathan	U	0.60
Lindwurm	U	0.60
Lung Wong	U	0.60
Magic Potion	C	0.15
Magic Shield	R	1.00
Magic Wand	C	0.15
Magical Healing	C	0.15
Magical Sword	C	0.15
[9]		
Magnetic Field	R	1.00
Maiden in Distress	C	0.15
Mansion in the Sky	U	0.60
Marina	C	0.15
Medea's Spell	R	1.00
Meteor Shower	C	0.15
Moat	U	0.60
Moghur	U	0.60
Mokelembembe	U	0.60
[10]		
Mountains	U	0.60
Mushussu	U	0.60
Naga	U	0.60
Night	C	0.15
Ocean	C	0.15
Oriental Princess	R	1.00
Pakawjak	U	0.60
Pan Lung	U	0.60
Pearl	C	0.15
[11]		
Phrygian	R	1.00
Pick a Treasure	C	0.15
Pit	U	0.60
Poison Breathing	C	0.15
Poison Chalice	R	1.00
Possession Spell	C	0.15
Power Switch	R	1.00
Princess Libya	C	0.15

Card name	Rarity	Price
Quicksand	R	1.00
[12]		
Rahah	U	0.60
River	C	0.15
Sacrifice	C	0.15
Scylla	U	0.60
Seaweed	C	0.15
Secret Treasure	C	0.15
Shan Dragon	U	0.60
Shapeshifter	R	1.00
Ship Wreck	C	0.15
[13]		
Sigurd The Dragon Slayer	C	0.15
Silver Chalice	R	1.00
Sir Lancelot The Dragon Slayer	C	0.15
Snow Drifts	U	0.60
Snow Storm	R	1.00
St. George The Dragon Slayer	C	0.15
Strangle Hold	R	1.00
Swamp	C	0.15
Swamp Hole	U	0.60
[14]		
Sword	C	0.15
Tarasque	U	0.60
Thuhan	R	1.00
Tiamat	U	0.60
Treasure Room	C	0.15
Tsunami	C	0.15
Tunnel	U	0.60
Turn The Tables	R	1.00
Twister	C	0.15
[15]		
Typhon	C	0.15
Underwater Cave	U	0.60
Vines	U	0.60
Vittra	U	0.60
Volcanic Eruption	C	0.15
Vouivre	R	1.00
Wall	U	0.60
Whirlpool	R	1.00
Wyvern	C	0.15
[16]		
Wyvern (gold)	UR	5.00

RARITY KEY C = Common U = Uncommon R = Rare VR = Very Rare UR = Ultra Rare F = Foil card X = Fixed/standard in all decks

Wyvern • Limited

U.S. Games Systems • Released **March 1995**
239 cards in set • **IDENTIFIER: Bullet before card number**

- Starter decks contain 60 cards; starter displays contain 12 starters
- Booster packs contain 15 cards; booster displays contain 36 boosters

The **Wyvern Limited** set reprints all of the cards in the **Premiere Limited** set and adds 104 new cards, which greatly expanded the options in the game.

Given the limited strategy involved, the initial card set of 136 cards had been considered too small by many players. — *Michael Greenholdt*

You will need **27** nine-pocket pages to store this set. (14 doubled up)

Set (239 cards)	65.00
Starter Display Box	15.00
Booster Display Box	20.00
Starter Deck	6.50
Booster Pack	1.20

Card name	Rarity	Price
Aaron's Rod	R	1.00
Abbey	U	0.50
Abraxus	U	0.50
Ajatar	R	1.00
All Bets Are Off	R	1.00
Amphiptere	C	0.05
Amphisbena	R	1.00
Ananta	U	0.50
Apep	U	0.50
Apollo	R	1.00
Archers	R	1.00
Armor	C	0.05
Avalanche	C	0.05
Azhi Dahaka	U	0.50
Bait	U	0.50
Basilisk	R	1.00
Battle Chaos	C	0.05
Behomoth	R	1.00
Beowulf	C	0.05
Black	R	1.00
Blue	R	1.00
Bride's Serpent	U	0.50
Brush Fire	U	0.50
Cadmus	C	0.05
Castle	R	1.00
Catch A Thief	C	0.05
Cauldron	C	0.05
Cave	C	0.05
Cecrops	U	0.50
Celestial	U	0.50
Chen Lung	U	0.50
Chimera	U	0.50
City	C	0.05
City In The Sky	R	1.00
Cliff	U	0.50
Clouds	U	0.50
Colchis	C	0.05
Coral Reef	C	0.05
Crevice	U	0.50
Crystal Ball	C	0.05
Cynoprosopi	R	1.00
Delphyne	U	0.50
Desert	C	0.05
Doomsday	R	1.00
Draco	R	1.00
Dracontias	R	1.00
Dragon Ashes	R	1.00
Dragon Bones	R	1.00
Dragon Egg	R	1.00
Dragon Man	R	1.00
Dragon Mother	R	1.00
Dragon Skin	R	1.00
Dragonel	U	0.50
Dwarven Army	C	0.05
Dwarven Gold Mine	R	1.00
Ea	U	0.50
Earthquake	C	0.05

Card name	Rarity	Price
Echidna	U	0.50
Fafnir	U	0.50
Feast	R	1.00
Fire Bolt	C	0.05
Fireball	C	0.05
Firebreathing	C	0.05
Flood	C	0.05
Fog	R	1.00
Forest	C	0.05
Forest Fire	U	0.50
Fountain Of Youth	C	0.05
Frost Breathing	C	0.05
Frozen Assets	R	1.00
Frozen Lake	U	0.50
Gandarewa	U	0.50
Gani	U	0.50
Gargouille	U	0.50
Geates	U	0.50
Giant	U	0.50
Giant Anteater	R	1.00
Giant Ants	R	1.00
Gold	C	0.05
Gold Find	C	0.05
Gold Shortage	C	0.05
Gold Thief	C	0.05
Golden Apple	C	0.05
Golden Apples	C	0.05
Golden Fleece	R	1.00
Grendel	R	1.00
Growth Spurt	R	1.00
Gryphon	U	0.50
Guivre	C	0.05
Gully	C	0.05
Hailstorm	C	0.05
Hall Of Chivalry	R	1.00
Hawks	R	1.00
Heatwave	C	0.05
Help	C	0.05
Help From Beyond	R	1.00
Hercules	C	0.05
Hero	R	1.00
High Winds	R	1.00
Hurricane	U	0.50
Hydra	U	0.50
Illuyankus	U	0.50
Indra	R	1.00
Indra's Spell	R	1.00
Invisibility	R	1.00
Island	U	0.50
Jason	R	1.00
Jewels	C	0.05
Jormungandr	R	1.00
Kakutan	U	0.50
Kane-Kua-Ana	U	0.50
King Arthur	R	1.00
Kioh-Lung	U	0.50
Kiss Of Le Succube	R	1.00
Knowledge	C	0.05
Kulkulcan	U	0.50
Laidly Worm	U	0.50
Lake	C	0.05
Lambton Worm	U	0.50
Leviathan	U	0.50

Card name	Rarity	Price
Library Of Ninevah	R	1.00
Lightning	C	0.05
Lindwurm	U	0.50
Loki	U	0.50
Lotan	U	0.50
Lung Wong	U	0.50
Magic Potion	C	0.05
Magic Shield	R	1.00
Magic Wand	C	0.05
Magical Healing	C	0.05
Magical Sword	C	0.05
Magnetic Field	R	1.00
Maiden In Distress	C	0.05
Mansion In The Sky	U	0.50
Marduk	C	0.05
Marina	C	0.05
Martha Of Bethany	C	0.05
Medea's Spell	R	1.00
Meteor Shower	C	0.05
Midgard Serpent	U	0.50
Mo-O	U	0.50
Moat	U	0.50
Moghur	U	0.50
Mokelembembe	U	0.50
Mount Chung	U	0.50
Mountains	U	0.50
Mushussu	U	0.50
Naga	U	0.50
Nidhoggr	U	0.50
Night	C	0.05
Ocean	C	0.05
Oriental Princess	R	1.00
Osiris	U	0.50
Pakawjak	U	0.50
Pan Lung	U	0.50
Pearl	C	0.05
Phrygian	R	1.00
Pi-Hsi	U	0.50
Pick A Treasure	C	0.05
Pirendeus Tree	C	0.05
Pit	U	0.50
Pitch	R	1.00
Place Your Bets	R	1.00
Poison Breathing	C	0.05
Poison Chalice	R	1.00
Poisonous Air	C	0.05
Possession Spell	C	0.05
Power Switch	R	1.00
Princess Libya	C	0.05
Python	U	0.50
Quicksand	R	1.00
Ra	C	0.05
Rahah	U	0.50
Ravens	R	1.00
Red	R	1.00
River	C	0.05
Ruins	U	0.50
Ryu	U	0.50
Sabra	R	1.00
Sacrifice	C	0.05
Scylla	U	0.50
Seaweed	C	0.05
Secret Treasure	C	0.05

Card name	Rarity	Price
Seth	R	1.00
Shan	U	0.50
Shapeshifter	R	1.00
Ship Wreck	C	0.05
Sigurd	C	0.05
Silver Chalice	R	1.00
Sir Lancelot	C	0.05
Sito	U	0.50
Snow Storm	R	1.00
Snowdrifts	U	0.50
St. George	C	0.05
Steal Strength	R	1.00
Strangle Hold	R	1.00
Stream	U	0.50
Subterranean Gold Mine	R	1.00
Subterranean Lair	U	0.50
Subterranean River	C	0.05
Subterranean Treasure	R	1.00
Subterranean Tunnels	C	0.05
Swamp	C	0.05
Swamp Hole	U	0.50
Sword	C	0.05
Tablets Of Destiny	R	1.00
Tarasque	U	0.50
Tatzlwurm	U	0.50
The Gambler	R	1.00
Thor	C	0.05
Thuhan	R	1.00
Tiamat	U	0.50
Town	R	1.00
Trap	U	0.50
Treasure Room	C	0.05
Treasure Thief	C	0.05
Tsunami	C	0.05
Tunnel	U	0.50
Turn The Tables	R	1.00
Twister	C	0.05
Typhon	C	0.05
Underground Avalanche	U	0.50
Underwater Cave	U	0.50
Valley	R	1.00
Vampire	R	1.00
Village	C	0.05
Vines	U	0.50
Vishnu	R	1.00
Vittra	U	0.50
Volcanic Eruption	C	0.05
Vouivre	R	1.00
Wall	U	0.50
Whirlpool	R	1.00
White	R	1.00
Windsock Banner	R	1.00
Wyvern	C	0.05
Wyvern Shadow	R	1.00
Yellow	R	1.00
Zeus	C	0.05

RARITY KEY **C** = Common **U** = Uncommon **R** = Rare **VR** = Very Rare **UR** = Ultra Rare **F** = Foil card **X** = Fixed/standard in all decks

Wyvern • Kingdom

U.S. Game Systems • Released **January 1997**

276 cards in set • **IDENTIFIER: Small dragon symbol**

- Starter decks contain 60 cards; starter displays contain 12 starters
- Booster packs contain 15 cards; booster displays contain 36 boosters

This set reprinted the **Wyvern Limited** series as an unlimited set, with the addition of a number of cards from the **Phoenix** expansion.

You will need **31** nine-pocket pages to store this set. (16 doubled up)

	Price
Set (276 cards)	50.00
Starter Display Box	15.00
Booster Display Box	20.00
Starter Deck	5.00
Booster Pack	1.00

Card name	Rarity	Price
1		
Aaron's Rod	R	1.00
Abbey	U	0.50
Abraxus	U	0.50
Adonis	X	0.25
Ajatar	R	1.00
All Bets Are Off	R	1.00
Ambrosia	X	0.25
Amphiptere	C	0.05
Amphisbena	R	1.00
2		
Ananta	U	0.50
Apep	U	0.50
Apollo	R	1.00
Archers	R	1.00
Armor	C	0.05
Atlantis	X	0.25
Avalanche	C	0.05
Avalon	X	0.25
Azhi Dahaka	U	0.50
3		
Bait	U	0.50
Banshee	X	0.25
Basilisk	R	1.00
Battle Chaos	C	0.05
Behomoth	R	1.00
Beowulf	C	0.05
Black	R	1.00
Blue	R	1.00
Bribery	X	0.25
4		
Bride's Serpent	U	0.50
Brush Fire	U	0.50
Cadmus	C	0.05
Camelot	X	0.25
Castle	R	1.00
Catch A Thief	C	0.05
Cauldron	C	0.05
Cave	C	0.05
Cecrops	U	0.50
5		
Celestial	U	0.50
Celestial Charger	X	0.25
Chen Lung	U	0.50
Chimera	U	0.50
Chronos	X	0.25
City	C	0.05
City In The Sky	R	1.00
Cliff	U	0.50
Clouds	U	0.50

Card name	Rarity	Price
6		
Colchis	C	0.05
Coral Reef	C	0.05
Crevice	U	0.50
Cricket	X	0.25
Crystal Ball	C	0.05
Cyclops	X	0.25
Cynoprosopi	R	1.00
Delphyne	U	0.50
Desert	C	0.05
7		
Doomsday	R	1.00
Draco	R	1.00
Dracontias	R	1.00
Dragon Ashes	R	1.00
Dragon Bones	R	1.00
Dragon Egg	R	1.00
Dragon Man	R	1.00
Dragon Mother	R	1.00
Dragon Of Exe Valley	X	0.25
8		
Dragon On Strike	X	0.25
Dragon Skin	R	1.00
Dragonel	U	0.50
Dwarf King	X	0.25
Dwarven Army	C	0.05
Dwarven Gold Mine	R	1.00
Ea	U	0.50
Earthly Naga	X	0.25
Earthquake	C	0.05
9		
Echidna	U	0.50
Fafnir	U	0.50
Feast	R	1.00
Fire Bolt	C	0.05
Fireball	C	0.05
Firebreathing	C	0.05
Flood	C	0.05
Fog	R	1.00
Forest	C	0.05
10		
Forest Fire	U	0.50
Fortuna	X	0.25
Fountain Of Youth	C	0.05
Frost Breathing	C	0.05
Frozen Assets	R	1.00
Frozen Lake	U	0.50
Gandarewa	U	0.50
Gani	U	0.50
Gargouille	U	0.50
11		
Geates	U	0.50
Giant	U	0.50
Giant Anteater	R	1.00
Giant Ants	R	1.00
Gold	C	0.05
Gold Find	C	0.05
Gold Shortage	C	0.05
Gold Thief	C	0.05
Golden Apple	C	0.05
12		
Golden Apples	C	0.05
Golden Dragon	X	0.25
Golden Fleece	R	1.00
Gram	X	0.25

Card name	Rarity	Price
Green Dragon	X	0.25
Grendel	R	1.00
Growth Spurt	R	1.00
Gryphon	U	0.50
Guivre	C	0.05
13		
Gully	C	0.05
Hailstorm	C	0.05
Hall Of Chivalry	R	1.00
Hawks	R	1.00
Heatwave	C	0.05
Help	C	0.05
Help From Beyond	R	1.00
Hercules	C	0.05
Hero	R	1.00
14		
High Winds	R	1.00
Hurricane	U	0.50
Hydra	U	0.50
Hypnos	X	0.25
Ida	X	0.25
Illuyankus	U	0.50
Indra	R	1.00
Indra's Spell	R	1.00
Invisibility	R	1.00
15		
Island	U	0.50
Jason	R	1.00
Jewels	C	0.05
Jormungandr	R	1.00
Kakutan	U	0.50
Kane-Kua-Ana	U	0.50
King Arthur	R	1.00
Kioh-Lung	U	0.50
Kiss Of Le Succube	R	1.00
16		
Knowledge	C	0.05
Kulkulcan	U	0.50
Labyrinth	X	0.25
Laidly Worm	U	0.50
Lake	C	0.05
Lambton Worm	U	0.50
Leviathan	U	0.50
Library Of Ninevah	R	1.00
Lightning	C	0.05
17		
Lindwurm	U	0.50
Loki	U	0.50
Lotan	U	0.50
Lung Wong	U	0.50
Magic Potion	C	0.05
Magic Shield	R	1.00
Magic Wand	C	0.05
Magical Healing	C	0.05
Magical Sword	C	0.05
18		
Magnetic Field	R	1.00
Maiden In Distress	C	0.05
Mansion In The Sky	U	0.50
Marduk	C	0.05
Marina	C	0.05
Martha Of Bethany	C	0.05
Medea's Spell	R	1.00
Medusa	X	0.25

Card name	Rarity	Price
Merlin	X	0.25
19		
Meteor Shower	C	0.05
Midas	X	0.25
Midgard Serpent	U	0.50
Minotaur	X	0.25
Mo-O	U	0.50
Moat	U	0.50
Moghur	U	0.50
Mokelembembe	U	0.50
Mount Chung	U	0.50
20		
Mountains	U	0.50
Mushussu	U	0.50
Naga	U	0.50
Nergal	X	0.25
Nidhoggr	U	0.50
Night	C	0.05
Ocean	C	0.05
Oriental Princess	R	1.00
Osiris	U	0.50
21		
Pakawjak	U	0.50
Pan	X	0.25
Pan Lung	U	0.50
Panther	X	0.25
Pearl	C	0.05
Phrygian	R	1.00
Pi-Hsi	U	0.50
Pick A Treasure	C	0.05
Pirendeus Tree	C	0.05
22		
Pit	U	0.50
Pitch	R	1.00
Place Your Bets	R	1.00
Poison Breathing	C	0.05
Poison Chalice	R	1.00
Poisonous Air	C	0.05
Possession Spell	C	0.05
Power Switch	R	1.00
Princess Libya	C	0.05
23		
Puk	X	0.25
Python	U	0.50
Quicksand	R	1.00
Ra	C	0.05
Rahah	U	0.50
Ravens	R	1.00
Red	R	1.00
Ri-Riu	X	0.25
River	C	0.05
24		
Roc	X	0.25
Ruins	U	0.50
Ryu	U	0.50
Sabra	R	1.00
Sacrifice	C	0.05
Scylla	U	0.50
Seaweed	C	0.05
Secret Treasure	C	0.05
Seth	R	1.00
25		
Shan	U	0.50
Shapeshifter	R	1.00
Ship Wreck	C	0.05

Card name	Rarity	Price
Sigurd	C	0.05
Silver Chalice	R	1.00
Sir Galahad	X	0.25
Sir Lancelot	C	0.05
Sirens	X	0.25
Sito	U	0.50
26		
Snow Storm	R	1.00
Snowdrifts	U	0.50
Steal Strength	R	1.00
Strangle Hold	R	1.00
Stream	U	0.50
Subterranean Gold Mine	R	1.00
Subterranean Lair	U	0.50
Subterranean River	C	0.05
Subterranean Treasure	R	1.00
27		
Subterranean Tunnels	C	0.05
Swamp	C	0.05
Swamp Hole	U	0.50
Sword	C	0.05
Tablets Of Destiny	R	1.00
Tarasque	U	0.50
Tatsu	X	0.25
Tatzlwurm	U	0.50
The Gambler	R	1.00
28		
Thor	C	0.05
Thuhan	R	1.00
Tiamat	U	0.50
Tor	X	0.25
Town	R	1.00
Trap	U	0.50
Treasure Room	C	0.05
Treasure Thief	C	0.05
Tsunami	C	0.05
29		
Tunnel	U	0.50
Turn The Tables	R	1.00
Twister	C	0.05
Typhon	C	0.05
Underground Avalanche	U	0.50
Underwater Cave	U	0.50
Valhalla	X	0.25
Valley	R	1.00
Vampire	R	1.00
30		
Village	C	0.05
Vines	U	0.50
Vishnu	R	1.00
Vittra	U	0.50
Volcanic Eruption	C	0.05
Vouivre	R	1.00
Wall	U	0.50
Wandering Rocks	X	0.25
Whirlpool	R	1.00
31		
White	R	1.00
Windsock Banner	R	1.00
Wyvern	C	0.05
Wyvern Shadow	R	1.00
Yellow	R	1.00
Zeus	C	0.05

RARITY KEY C = Common U = Uncommon R = Rare VR = Very Rare UR = Ultra Rare F = Foil card X = Fixed/standard in all decks

Wyvern • Phoenix

U.S. Games Systems • Released **October 1995**

90 cards in set • **IDENTIFIER: Black flying dragon symbol**

You will need **10** nine-pocket pages to store this set. (5 doubled up)

- Booster packs contain 8 cards; booster displays contain 60 boosters

The first expansion set released for **Wyvern**, **Phoenix** introduces two new Action card types, the Hidden Action and Intercept Action. The Hidden Action card is placed on an unrevealed Dragon/Terrain card and does not come into effect until the Dragon/Terrain card is revealed. If the Hidden action card applies to the situation it remains in play, making it a sort of mini-Treasure card.

The Intercept Action card allows a player to defend a Dragon being attacked with another friendly Dragon in play. This greatly increased the defensive possibilities of a deck, since one big Dragon could protect a host of weaker Dragons. — *Michael Greenholdt*

Set (90 cards)	49.00
Booster Display Box	20.00
Booster Pack	1.50

Card name	Rarity	Price
Achilles	U	0.50
Adonis	C	0.10
Agravain	U	0.50
Ajax	C	0.10
Amazons	U	0.50
Ambrosia	C	0.10
Ape	U	0.50
Atlantis	U	0.50
Atlas	U	0.50
Avalon	U	0.50
Badger	U	0.50
Banshee	C	0.10
Bifrost	U	0.50
Blinding Light	C	0.10

Card name	Rarity	Price
Bribery	U	0.50
Calypso	U	0.50
Camelot	C	0.10
Celestial Charger	C	0.10
Centaurs	C	0.10
Chronos	U	0.50
Cricket	C	0.10
Crocodile	C	0.10
Cyclops	C	0.10
Divine Naga	C	0.10
Doves	C	0.10
Dragon of Exe Valley	U	0.50
Dragon of Knucker Hole	U	0.50
Dragon on Strike	U	0.50
Dwarf King	U	0.50
Earthly Naga	U	0.50
Echo	C	0.10
Elephants	U	0.50
Ethiopian Dream	C	0.10

Card name	Rarity	Price
Firefly	U	0.50
Fortuna	U	0.50
Frey	U	0.50
Golden Dragon	C	0.10
Golden Grasshopper	U	0.50
Gram	U	0.50
Green Dragon	C	0.10
Han-Riu	C	0.10
Harpies	C	0.10
Heavenly Naga	C	0.10
Hidden Naga	C	0.10
Hippolyte	U	0.50
Hypnos	U	0.50
Ida	C	0.10
Inflation	U	0.50
Ishtar	U	0.50
Ka-Riu	C	0.10
Labyrinth	C	0.10
Lynx	U	0.50

Card name	Rarity	Price
Medusa	U	0.50
Merlin	U	0.50
Mermaid	U	0.50
Midas	U	0.50
Minotaur	C	0.10
Nectar	U	0.50
Nergal	C	0.10
O-Gon-Cho	U	0.50
Opinicus	U	0.50
Owl	U	0.50
Pan	U	0.50
Pandora	U	0.50
Panther	R	1.00
Phoenix	R	1.00
Piasa	C	0.10
Poseidon	C	0.10
Price Hike	U	0.50
Prometheus	U	0.50
Puk	C	0.10

Card name	Rarity	Price
Red Kangeroo	U	0.50
Ri-Riu	C	0.10
Roc	U	0.50
Sale	U	0.50
Seahorse	U	0.50
Sir Galahad	C	0.10
Sirens	C	0.10
Sui-Riu	C	0.10
Tatsu	C	0.10
Tengu	C	0.10
The Pathfinder	R	1.00
Tor	U	0.50
Tortoise	C	0.10
Trojan Horse	R	1.00
Trolls	C	0.10
Valhalla	U	0.50
Violet	C	0.10
Wandering Rocks	C	0.10
White-Eared Dragon	C	0.10

Wyvern • Chameleon

U.S. Games Systems • Released **April 1996**

90 cards in set • **IDENTIFIER: Gothic 'C' on cards**

You will need **10** nine-pocket pages to store this set. (5 doubled up)

- Booster packs contain 8 cards; booster displays contain 60 boosters

The **Chameleon** expansion introduces two new concepts, Native Terrain and Chameleon Reaction. A Dragon with the Native Terrain attribute for a specific Terrain can instantly destroy the Terrain card without being affected by the Terrain and gets stronger as more of that specific Terrain is in your discard pile or attached to enemy Dragon.

A Terrain with Chameleon Reaction turns into a Dragon when first attacked and remains a Dragon for as long as it remains in the game, making it a kind of booby trap. Terrain with Chameleon Reaction are immune to many Dragon Slayer Action cards, making it proof against easy kills. — *Michael Greenholdt*

Set (90 cards)	45.00
Booster Display Box	20.00
Booster Pack	1.50

Card name	Rarity	Price
Ai-Wa	C2	0.25
Alberich	U4	0.25
All Or Nothing	U3	0.50
Arctic Winds	C2	0.25
Argonauts	C2	0.25
Bellerophon	C3	0.10
Black Rainbow	C2	0.25
Bracken	U3	0.50
Brain Drain	C3	0.10
Chao-Fung	C2	0.25
Chaparral	U1	1.00
Chi-Wen	U3	0.50
Cracked Cauldron	C3	0.10
Crag	U3	0.50
Dalta	U3	0.50

Card name	Rarity	Price
Deep Freeze	U3	0.50
Drachenfels	U3	0.50
Dragon Of Deerhurst	U4	0.25
Dragon Of Nunnington	U4	0.25
Dragon Of Wells	U3	0.50
Dragonfly	C2	0.25
Dwarven Legion	U3	0.50
Enchanted Mirror	C2	0.25
Field Of Gold	C3	0.10
Fire Drake	U4	0.25
Flag Of Truce	C3	0.10
Flying Boulder	U3	0.50
Freya	C3	0.10
Fu-Tsang-Lung	U1	1.00
Gold Dig	C2	0.25
Gold Market	C3	0.10
Gold Vault	C2	0.25
Golem	U2	0.75
Grave Diggers	C3	0.10

Card name	Rarity	Price
Grotto	U3	0.50
Heavyweight Alliance	C2	0.25
Hege	U3	0.50
Helix	U3	0.50
Hidden Gold	C3	0.10
Horn Of The Unicorn	C3	0.10
Kalahari	U2	0.75
Lacustrian	U4	0.25
Last Will And Testament	C3	0.10
Lost City	C3	0.10
Lucky Strike	C3	0.10
Master Ring	U2	0.75
Megalith	U2	0.75
Mental Domination	C4	0.10
Miasma	U4	0.25
Mixcoatl	U2	0.75
Mucilinda	U2	0.75
Nebula	U3	0.50

Card name	Rarity	Price
Nibelungs	C3	0.10
Oasis	U3	0.50
Oceanus	U2	0.75
Overgrown Monument	U3	0.50
Poison Forest	C3	0.10
Possession From Beyond	C2	0.25
Precious Gems	C2	0.25
Rainbow	C3	0.10
Rebate	C3	0.10
Reclaimed Treasure	C3	0.10
Ring Of Destiny	U2	0.75
Ring Of Power	U1	1.00
Riparianm	U2	0.75
Ripplet	U3	0.50
Royal Archers	C3	0.10
Runic Tablet	C2	0.25
Rustem	C3	0.10
Sanctuary	C3	0.10

Card name	Rarity	Price
Scorpion Men	C2	0.25
Sea Goat	U4	0.25
Serpent Lance	U3	0.50
Shifting Sands	C2	0.25
Shoal	U3	0.50
Sorcerer	U1	1.00
Spectral Shift	C2	0.25
Spoils Of War	C3	0.10
Stolen Equipment	C2	0.25
Swamp Of Lernea	C2	0.25
Teuton	U4	0.25
Thor's Hammer	C2	0.25
Thunderbolt	C3	0.10
Ti-Ling	C2	0.25
Torrential Rains	C3	0.10
Tower Of Babel	C3	0.10
Treasure	U3	0.50
Treasure Fire	C3	0.10
Waterfall	U3	0.50
Windfall	C3	0.10

The X-Files

USPC Games • First set, *Premiere*, released **November 1996**

354 cards in set

- **IDENTIFIER: Black borders; cards feature 'Bureau File Number XF-96' followed by a number between 0001 and 0354, inclusive**
- Starter decks contain 60 cards; starter displays contain 12 starters
- Booster packs contain 15 cards; booster displays contain 36 boosters

Designed by **Ron Kent** and **Duncan Macdonell**

Early in its run, *The X-Files* television show was the hottest ticket in science-fiction fandom. The small number of early licensees led to runs on Topps' *X-Files* comic books and trading cards and anything else that was available. So it should have come as little surprise that the announcement in March 1995 that a CCG was in the works created much anticipation in the hobby. But a year and a half would pass before its release.

The X-Files CCG is reminiscent of Parker Brother's *Clue*, but still manages to capture the feel of the show. Each player begins the game with four Agents (drawn from the show) and an X-File card, which represents the theme or villain of an episode. You win the game by guessing which X-File card your opponent has chosen.

During a player's turn, he may play a Site card, which has a prerequisite, usually requiring an investigating Agent to possess one or more Skills at a certain level. If the prerequisite is met, the player may ask one yes or no question, usually about X-File card attributes. Each X-File Card has four unique attributes; Affiliations, Motive, Methods, and Results. Through a process of elimination, a player constructs a profile of the opponent's X-File card.

There are other card types used to aid (Equipment and Witness) or hinder (Bluff and Adversary) an investigation. Event and Combat cards can either aid or hinder depending on the card. These cards generally require the expenditure of Resource or Conspiracy points depending on whether the card aids or hinders the investigation.

The X-Files CCG release started life as a NXT Games design for sportscard maker Donruss — and when that company got out of the CCG business, the design went to the U.S. Playing Card Co. (the folks that make the *real* playing cards), which set up a special division for it, USPC Games. Delays did not help the release, and indeed *X-Files* mania may have peaked too early in the CCG's run. — *Michael Greenholdt*

You will need **40** nine-pocket pages to store this set. (20 doubled up)

Concept	●●○○○
Gameplay	●●●○○
Card art	●●●○○
Player pool	○○○○○

Set (354 cards)	**97.00**
Starter Display Box	**57.50**
Booster Display Box	**65.00**
Starter Deck	**7.50**
Booster Pack	**2.00**

Card name	Rarity	Price
A Friend In The FBI	R	1.80
Abduction	R	1.80
Access Personnel Files	C	0.10
Agent Jack Willis Shot To Death In Bank Robbery	R	1.00
Agent Janus, Trained Medic	C	0.10
Agent Karen Kossoff, Counselor	C	0.10
Agent Lamana Dies In Fatal Elevator Accident	R	1.80
Agent Moe Bocks	C	0.10
Agent Reggie Purdue Found Strangled	R	1.00
Agent Rich	C	0.10
Agent Weiss	C	0.10
Agent Weiss Killed By Unknown Toxin	R	1.50
Albert Hosteen	C	0.10
Aleister Crowley High School, Milford Haven, NH	R	1.80
Alex Krycek	UR	20.00
Alex Krycek	C	0.10
Alien Abductors	C	0.25
Alien Bounty Hunter	R	1.30
Alien Conservationist	C	0.10

Card name	Rarity	Price
Alien D.N.A Steroid Program (Project Purity Control)	C	0.10
Alien Discretion	R	1.00
Alien Experimentation	R	1.80
Alien Experimenters	C	0.10
Alien Harvester	R	1.80
Alien Listeners	C	0.10
Alien Stealth Technology	U	0.20
Ambush	C	0.10
Ancestor Spirits	C	0.10
Application For FBI Resources Approved	R	1.80
Arctic Worm	C	0.10
Arecibo, Puerto Rico	U	0.35
Arlington, VA	C	0.10
Arthur Grable	C	0.10
Assigned to the X-Files	R	1.80
Assistant Director Walter Skinner	UR	18.00
Assistant Director Walter Skinner	C	0.10
Aubrey, MO	C	0.10
Augustus Cole, a.k.a. The Preacher	C	0.10
Aura Of Invulnerability	U	0.80
Authorized Access Only	R	1.80
Autopsy	U	0.50
B.J. Morrow, Genetic Trait Recipient	C	0.10
Back Tracking Program	U	0.25
Baltimore, MD	R	1.50
Bill Mulder	R	1.80

Card name	Rarity	Price
Billy Miles	C	0.10
Binoculars	C	0.10
Blackmail	R	1.00
Block	U	0.35
Block And Attack	R	2.00
Body Armor	U	0.20
Brad Wilczek	U	0.20
Broad Street, Philadelphia, PA	C	0.10
Brother Martin, Rogue Kindred	C	0.10
Browning, MT	C	0.10
Byers	C	0.10
Cape Cod, MA	C	0.10
Car Troubles	C	0.10
Cecil Lively	C	0.10
Cellular Phone	R	1.60
Central Operating System, Artificial Intelligence	C	0.10
Central Prison, Raleigh, NC	U	0.20
Chaco House, Dudley, AR	U	0.20
Charley Tskany	R	1.00
Choke Hold	R	1.00
Church Of The Red Museum, Delta Glen, WI	C	0.50
Cigarette Butts	C	0.10
Claude Peterson	C	0.10
Clone	U	0.20
Colonel Wharton, Zombie Master	C	0.10
Commander Colin Henderson	C	0.10

Card name	Rarity	Price
Computer Access Denied	R	1.00
Containment Facility, Georgetown, MD	C	0.10
Core Training	C	0.10
Costal Northwest, OR	C	0.10
Counterintelligence Measures	UR	19.00
Covering Fire	U	0.20
Crew Cut Man	U	0.35
Crop Circles	C	0.10
Cumberland Prison, VA	C	0.10
Dana Scully	UR	30.00
Dana Scully	C	0.10
Dana Scully, Abducted	UR	15.00
Dark Forces Align	R	1.00
Darkness Falls	U	0.35
Deadhorse, AK	R	1.00
Deadly Blur	U	0.80
Decoy	U	0.35
Decreased Workload	U	0.20
Deductive Reasoning	R	1.00
Deep Throat	UR	20.00
Detective Frank Briggs	U	0.35
Detective Kelly Ryan	C	0.10
Detective Miles	U	0.80
Detective Sharon Lazard	U	0.35
Detective Thompson	U	0.20
Detective Tony Fiore	U	0.35
Disarm	R	1.00
Dissection	U	0.20
Dod Kalm	C	0.10
Dodge	U	0.20

RARITY KEY C = Common U = Uncommon R = Rare VR = Very Rare UR = Ultra Rare F = Foil card X = Fixed/standard in all decks

Card name	Rarity	Price
Donnie Pfaster, Death Fetishist	C	0.10
Doug Spinney	C	0.10
Dr. Aaron Monte	C	0.10
Dr. Banton and His Shadow	C	0.10
Dr. Berube	C	0.10
Dr. Blockhead	R	1.80
Dr. Charles Burk	C	0.10
13		
Dr. Daniel Trepkos	R	1.00
Dr. Davey	U	0.35
Dr. Diamond	R	1.80
Dr. Grissom	R	1.80
Dr. Hodge	C	0.10
Dr. Laskos	U	0.35
Dr. Nollete	R	1.00
Dr. Osborne	R	1.00
Dr. Sheila Braun	U	0.20
14		
Driving	U	0.80
Duane Barry	C	0.10
Ed Funsch, Postal Worker	C	0.10
Electron Emission Microscope	C	0.10
Ellens Air Base, ID	R	1.00
Emil And Zoe	U	0.35
Energy Strike	R	1.80
Equipment Malfunction	U	0.20
Eugene Victor Tooms	C	0.10
15		
Eurisko Building, Crystal City, VA	U	0.35
Evasive Maneuvers	R	1.00
Eve	C	0.10
Eve 7	R	1.50
Evidence Destroyed	U	0.20
Evidence Overlooked	C	0.10
Excelsis Dei Convalescent Home, Worcester, MA	U	0.20
Expedite Request For Resources	U	0.20
Expert Briefing	C	0.10
16		
Face-Off	U	0.35
Faciphaga Emasculata	C	0.10
Fairfield Zoo, Fairfield, ID	C	0.10
Farmington, NM	U	0.35
Fascination	U	0.20
Fast Draw	R	1.30
Fast Strike	R	1.00
Fingernail Scrapings	C	0.10
Fingerprints	U	0.20
17		
First Aid	C	0.10
Flaming Wall	U	0.20
Folkstone, NC	U	0.25
Fox Mulder	UR	35.00
Fox Mulder	C	0.10
Franklin, PA	C	0.10
Frohike	R	1.10
Gas Chromatograph	C	0.10
Geiger Counter	U	0.20
18		
Genetics Clinic, Marin County, CA	C	0.10
Gerd Thomas	C	0.10
Ghost In The Machine	C	0.10
Gibsonton, FL	C	0.10
Glock 19 Semi-Automatic Pistol	U	0.20
Good People, Good Food	U	0.80
Government Arrests Suspects	C	0.10
Government Car	C	0.10
Government Cover-up	C	0.10
19		
Government Mindwipe Serum	U	0.20

Card name	Rarity	Price
Government Sanctioned Pheromone Experiments	R	1.00
Grid Pattern Search	R	1.00
Gun Jammed	C	0.10
Gung Bituen	R	1.00
Hack Into Government Files	R	1.00
Handcuff	R	1.10
Hard Evidence	U	0.35
Hard Punch	C	0.10
20		
Harry Cokely	C	0.10
Hazardous Sample	C	0.10
Henry Trondheim	U	0.80
Hidden Grave	U	0.20
Hidden Transmitter	U	0.20
Hide	C	0.10
High Resolution Camera	C	0.10
High-Powered Flashlight	U	0.80
Hit And Run	U	0.35
21		
Holtzman, D.S.A.	C	0.10
Hospital Crash Cart	R	1.00
Howard Graves, The Poltergeist	C	0.10
Hunter In The Dark	C	0.10
I Want To Believe	C	0.10
Icy Cape, AK	C	0.10
Illusionary Foe	R	1.80
Improved Channels	U	0.35
In-Service Training	C	0.10
22		
Inspector Phoebe Green	C	0.10
Internal Bleeding	U	0.20
Intruder Counter-Measures Program	U	0.80
Ish-Tribal Elder	U	0.80
Jack Willis	C	0.10
Jerry Lamana	C	0.10
John Barnett	C	0.10
Kevin Morris, a.k.a. The Conduit	R	1.80
Kevlar Vest	U	0.20
23		
Kick	C	0.10
Kiss Of The Vampire	R	1.00
Knife	C	0.10
Kristen Kilar	R	1.00
Krycek, the Double Agent	R	1.30
Lake Okobogee, Campsite #53 Sioux City, IA	C	0.10
Langly	U	0.25
Laptop Computer	U	0.80
Laser Barrier	R	1.80
24		
Leonard Vance	C	0.10
Leonard, Detachable Congenital Twin	C	0.10
Lie Detector	C	0.10
Living Machine	U	0.35
Los Angeles, CA	U	0.20
Lt. Brian Tillman, Aubry Police Department	C	0.10
Lt. Colonel Marcus Aurelius Belt	R	1.00
Lucas Henry, Serial Killer	C	0.10
Lucy Kazdin	C	0.10
25		
Lula Phillips	R	1.00
Luther Lee Boggs	R	1.80
Maggie Holvey	C	0.10
Mahan Propulsion Laboratory, Colson, WA	U	0.35
Marion, VA	C	0.10
Massive Internal Damage	U	0.35
Mattawa, WA	C	0.10
Max Fenig	R	1.00
Medical Treatment	C	0.10

Card name	Rarity	Price
26		
Medi-Kit	R	1.00
Message From The Stars	R	1.80
Michael Holvey, The Evil One	C	0.10
Michelle Generoo	R	1.00
Mind Control	R	1.80
Mini-14 Assault Rifle	U	0.35
Minneapolis, MN	U	0.20
Mojo Bag	U	0.80
Mrs. Paddock, a.k.a. The Dark Angel Azazel	C	0.10
27		
Mt Avalon, WA	C	0.10
Nancy Spiller	C	0.10
NASA Mission Control, Houston, TX	U	0.20
Nasty Surprise	U	0.35
Nerve Strike	R	1.00
New York City, NY	R	1.50
Newark, NJ	C	0.10
No Place Is Safe	R	1.00
No Way Out	C	0.10
28		
Northeast Georgetown Medical Center, Washington, DC	R	1.00
Olympic National Forest, WA	C	0.10
Operation Falcon Blue Berets	R	1.00
Outskirts Of Atlantic City, NJ	U	0.35
Overwhelming Force	R	1.80
Paperwork	U	0.35
Paul Mossinger	C	0.10
Pete Calcagani	U	0.35
Peter Tanaka	U	0.35
29		
Pheromone Induced Psychosis	U	0.20
Plague Of Locusts	R	1.00
Poisonous Gases	C	0.10
Poltergeist Attack	C	0.10
Psychiatric Hospital, Richmond, VA	C	0.10
Puzzles Within Puzzles	U	0.20
Pvt. McAlpin, Zombie	C	0.10
Radioactive Area	U	0.80
Reading The Signs	U	0.80
30		
Red Tape	R	1.00
Reggie Purdue	C	0.10
Rejuvenating Caves	U	0.25
Relentless Pursuit	C	0.10
Rending Claws	U	0.80
Reporters At The Crime Scene	U	0.35
Reverse Engineers	C	0.10
Road Hazard	U	0.20
Road Trip	R	1.50
31		
Run For It!	C	0.10
Running Gun Battle	U	0.80
S.W.A.T. Training	C	0.10
Safe House	R	1.00
Samantha Mulder	R	1.80
Samuel Hartley	R	1.80
Sea Off Tildeskan, Norway	C	0.10
Section Chief Joseph McGrath	R	1.00
Section Chief Scott Blevins	C	0.10
32		
Semi-Jacketed Hollow Points	U	0.80
Senator Richard Matheson	R	1.00
Sherif Mazeroski	R	1.00
Sheriff Daniels	U	0.80
Sheriff Spencer	C	0.10
Sheriff Tom Arens, Cannibal	C	0.10
Shotgun	C	0.10
Shutting Down The X-Files	R	1.00
Sinus Cavity Implant	U	0.80
33		
Sir Malcolm Marsden	C	0.10
Skinner Adopts The Company Line	R	1.80

Card name	Rarity	Price
Skinner Chooses A Side	UR	16.50
Skyland Mountain, VA	R	1.80
Sleep Deprivation	R	1.80
Slithers In The Night	C	0.10
Smoke Screen	U	0.20
Sneak Attack	R	1.80
Spin Kick	R	1.00
34		
Spying Mission	U	0.80
Squeeze	U	0.20
Steveston, MA	R	1.00
Street Contacts	U	0.80
Stunning Blow	U	0.20
Successful Diagnosis	U	0.35
Suppressed Fury	C	0.10
Surfing The Net	R	1.80
Suspect Description	U	0.35
35		
Symbol Of Faith	R	1.00
Take Cover	C	0.10
Taped Intelligence	R	1.00
Terminal Damage	R	1.80
The Calusari	R	1.00
The Cigarette Smoking Man Strikes	R	2.00
The Cigarette-Smoking Man	C	0.10
The Conundrum	U	0.20
The Erlenmeyer Flask	R	1.80
36		
The Gregors	C	0.10
The Host	C	0.10
The Host Attacks	R	1.00
The Jersey Devil	C	0.10
The Local Law Enforcement Are Uncooperative	U	0.35
The Lone Gunmen	UR	15.00
The Manitou	C	0.10
The Manitou Stalks His Prey	R	1.80
The Mechanic	U	0.25
37		
The Overcoat Man	C	0.10
The Psychotic Attack	C	0.10
The Sandman	U	0.20
The Swarm	C	0.10
The Thinker	R	1.80
The Vampire, a.k.a. The Unholy Spirit	C	0.10
Thorough Documentation	R	1.00
Tom Colton	C	0.10
Trap	U	0.50
38		
Travel Arrangements	C	0.10
True Grit	R	1.50
Trust No One	R	1.50
U.S. Marshall Tapia	R	1.50
UFO Wreckage, Townsend, WI	R	1.50
Unexplainable Time Loss	R	1.50
University Of Maryland, Baltimore MD	R	1.80
Unnatural Aging	U	0.50
Vicious Fangs	U	0.50
39		
Volcanic Spore	C	0.10
Walther PPK 7.65 Hold Out Weapon	U	0.50
Warning From The Loa	R	1.50
Warren James Dupre, The Lazarus Man	C	0.10
Washington Monument, Washington DC	C	0.10
Watch Out	U	0.50
Webbed	R	1.50
Wire-Tap	C	0.10
Written Report	C	0.10
40		
X	UR	22.50
X-Files Research	C	0.10
You've Got A Tail	C	0.10

RARITY KEY C = Common **U** = Uncommon **R** = Rare **VR** = Very Rare **UR** = Ultra Rare **F** = Foil card **X** = Fixed/standard in all decks

X-Files • *The Truth Is Out There*

USPC Games • Released **June 1997**

354 cards in set • **IDENTIFIER: Teal borders; cards numbered 0355-0384 included**

- Starter decks contain 60 cards; starter displays contain 12 starters
- Booster packs contain 15 cards; booster displays contain 36 boosters

A reprint of the ***Premiere*** set rather than an expansion, ***The Truth Is Out There*** adds 30 new cards.

Ten ultra rare cards are added: **Spirit of the Amaru, Limited Choices, Too Close to the Truth, Nurse Owen, One Breath, Mis-Classified Case, Additional Resources, Mrs. Mulder, Margaret Scully, Melissa Scully.** Twenty rare cards are added, as well: **John Barnett Links you to Mulder, Brother Martin is Attracted to You, Leonard, F. Emasculata Outbreak, The Evil One, Injured Relative, Explosion, Lock Pick, USGS Quadrant Map, Taking Chances, A Friend in the Lab, False Leads, Witness Intimidated, Assassinated, Security Clearance, Dr. Joe Ridley, Colonel Kissell, Meet Brother Andrew, Women's Heath Clinic, Richville MD.,** and **Tracking the Killer).**

In addition, the collation problems that plagued the *X-Files Premiere* set were fixed. — *Michael Greenholdt*

> You will need
> **40**
> nine-pocket pages to store this set.
> (20 doubled up)

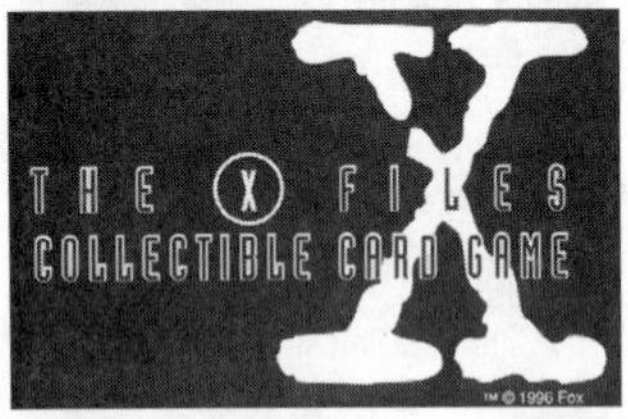

Set (354 cards)	86.00
Starter Display Box	42.50
Booster Display Box	47.50
Starter Deck	6.50
Booster Pack	1.70

Card name	Rarity	Price
A Friend In The FBI	R	1.90
A Friend in the Lab	R	2.30
Abduction	R	1.90
Access Personnel Files	C	0.05
Additional Resources	UR	15.00
Agent Alex Krycek	X/U	0.60
Agent Dana Scully	X/U	1.00
Agent Fox Mulder	X/U	1.00
Agent Jack Willis	X/U	0.60
Agent Janus, Trained Medic	X/U	0.60
Agent Jerry Lamana	X/U	0.60
Agent Karen Kosseff, Counselor	X/U	0.60
Agent Lucy Kazdin	X/U	0.60
Agent Moe Bocks	X/U	0.60
Agent Nancy Spiller	X/U	0.60
Agent Reggie Purdue	X/U	0.60
Agent Rich	X/U	0.60
Agent Tom Colton	X/U	0.60
Agent Weiss	X/U	0.60
Albert Hosteen	X/U	0.60
Aleister Crowley High School, Milford Haven, NH	R	1.90
Alien Abductors	X/U	0.60
Alien Bounty Hunter	R	1.90
Alien Conservationist	X/U	0.60
Alien D.N.A. Steroid Program (Project Purity Control)	X/U	0.60
Alien Discretion	R	1.90
Alien Experimentation	R	1.90
Alien Experimenters	X/U	0.60
Alien Listeners	X/U	0.60
Alien Stealth Technology	U	0.35
Ambush	C	0.05
Ancestor Spirits	X/U	0.60

Card name	Rarity	Price
Application For F.B.I. Resources Approved	R	1.90
Arctic Worm	X/U	0.60
Arecibo, Puerto Rico	R	1.90
Arlington, VA.	X/U	0.60
Arthur Grable	X/U	0.60
Assassinated	R	2.30
Assigned to the X-Files	R	1.90
Assistant Director Walter Skinner	X/U	0.60
Aubrey, MO.	X/U	0.60
Augustus Cole, A.K.A. The Preacher	X/U	0.60
Aura Of Invulnerability	U	0.35
Authorized Access Only	R	1.90
Autopsy	U	0.35
B.J. Morrow, Genetic Trait Recipient	X/U	0.60
Back Tracking Program	X/U	0.60
Baltimore, Maryland	U	0.35
Bill Mulder	R	1.90
Billy Miles	X/U	0.60
Binoculars	X/U	0.60
Blackmail	R	1.90
Block	U	0.35
Block And Attack	R	1.90
Body Armor	U	0.35
Brad Wilczek	U	0.35
Broad Street, Philadelphia, PA.	C	0.05
Brother Martin is Attracted to You	R	2.30
Brother Martin, Rogue Kindred	X/U	0.60
Browning, MT.	X/C	0.10
Byers	X/U	0.60
Cape Cod, MA.	C	0.05
Car Troubles	C	0.05
Cecil L'ively	X/U	0.60
Cellular Phone	R	1.90
Central Operating System, Artificial Intelligence	X/U	0.60
Central Prison, Raleigh, NC.	U	0.35
Chaco House, Dudley, AR.	U	0.35
Choke Hold	R	1.90
Church Of The Red Museum, Delta Glen, WI.	R	1.90
Cigarette Butts	C	0.05
Claude Peterson	C	0.05
Clone	U	0.35

Card name	Rarity	Price
Coastal Northwest, Oregon	X/U	0.60
Colonel Kissell	R	2.30
Colonel Wharton, Zombie Master	X/U	0.60
Commander Collin Henderson	X/U	0.60
Computer Access Denied	R	1.90
Containment Facility, Georgetown, MD.	C	0.05
Core Training	C	0.05
Covering Fire	U	0.35
Crew Cut Man	U	0.35
Crop Circles	X/U	0.60
Cumberland Prison, VA.	X/U	0.60
Dark Forces Align	R	1.90
Darkness Falls	U	0.35
Deadhorse, Alaska	R	1.90
Deadly Blur	U	0.35
Decoy	U	0.35
Decreased Workload	U	0.35
Deductive Reasoning	R	1.90
Detective Frank Briggs	U	0.35
Detective Kelly Ryan	C	0.05
Detective Miles	U	0.35
Detective Sharon Lazard	U	0.35
Detective Thompson	U	0.35
Detective Tony Fiore	U	0.35
Disarm	R	1.90
Dissection	U	0.35
Dod Kalm	X/U	0.60
Dodge	U	0.35
Donnie Pfaster, Death Fetishist	X/U	0.60
Doug Spinney	C	0.05
Dr. Aaron Monte	C	0.05
Dr. Banton And His Shadow	X/U	0.60
Dr. Berube	C	0.05
Dr. Blockhead	R	1.90
Dr. Charles Burk	X/U	0.60
Dr. Daniel Trepkos	R	1.90
Dr. Davey	U	0.35
Dr. Diamond	R	1.90
Dr. Hodge	X/U	0.60
Dr. Joe Ridley	R	2.30
Dr. Laskos	U	0.35
Dr. Sheila Braun	U	0.35
Driving	U	0.35
Duane Barry	X/U	0.60
Ed Funsch, Postal Worker	X/U	0.60
Electron Emission Microscope	C	0.05

Card name	Rarity	Price
Ellens Air Base, Idaho	X/U	0.60
Emil And Zoe	U	0.35
Energy Strike	R	1.90
Equipment Malfunction	U	0.35
Eugene Victor Tooms	X/U	0.60
Eurisko Building, Crystal City, VA.	U	0.35
Evasive Maneuvers	R	1.90
Eve	X/U	0.60
Eve 7	R	1.90
Evidence Destroyed	X/U	0.60
Evidence Overlooked	C	0.05
Excelsius Dei Convalescent Home, Worcester, MA.	U	0.35
Expedite Request For Resources	U	0.35
Expert Briefing	C	0.05
Explosion	R	2.30
F. Emasculata Outbreak	R	2.30
Face-Off	U	0.35
Faciphaga Emasculata	X/U	0.60
Fairfield Zoo, Fairfield ID.	X/U	0.60
False Leads	R	2.30
Farmington, New Mexico	U	0.35
Fascination	U	0.35
Fast Draw	R	1.90
Fast Strike	R	1.90
Fingernail Scrapings	X/U	0.60
Fingerprints	U	0.35
First Aid	C	0.05
Flaming Wall	U	0.35
Folkstone, NC.	U	0.35
Franklin, PA.	X/C	0.10
Frohike	R	1.90
Gas Chromatograph	C	0.05
Geiger Counter	U	0.35
Genetics Clinic, Marin County, CA.	X/U	0.60
Gerd Thomas	C	0.05
Ghost In The Machine	X/U	0.60
Gibsonton, FL.	X/U	0.60
Glock 19 Semi-Automatic Pistol	U	0.35
Good People, Good Food	U	0.35
Government Arrests Suspects	X/U	0.60
Government Car	X/U	0.60
Government Cover-up	C	0.05
Government Mindwipe Serum	U	0.35
Government Sanctioned Pheromone Experiments	R	1.90

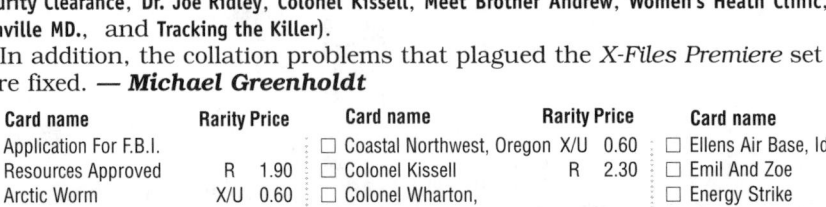

RARITY KEY C = Common **U** = Uncommon **R** = Rare **VR** = Very Rare **UR** = Ultra Rare **F** = Foil card **X** = Fixed/standard in all decks

Card name	Rarity	Price
Grid Pattern Search	R	1.90
Gun Jammed	C	0.05
Gung Bituan	R	1.90
Handcuff	R	1.90
Hard Evidence	C	0.05
Hard Punch	C	0.05
Harry Cokely	C	0.05
Hazardous Sample	C	0.05
20		
Henry Trondheim	U	0.35
Hidden Grave	U	0.35
Hidden Transmitter	U	0.35
Hide	C	0.05
High Powered Flashlight	U	0.35
High Resolution Camera	C	0.05
Hit And Run	U	0.35
Holtzman, D.S.A.	C	0.05
Hospital Crash Cart	R	1.90
21		
Howard Graves, The Poltergeist	X/U	0.60
Hunter In The Dark	U	0.35
I Want To Believe	X/U	0.60
Icy Cape, Alaska	X/C	0.10
Illusionary Foe	R	1.90
Improved Channels	U	0.35
In Service Training	C	0.05
Injured Relative	R	2.30
Inspector Phoebe Green	X/U	0.60
22		
Internal Bleeding	U	0.35
Intruder Counter-Measures Program	U	0.35
Ish-Tribal Elder	U	0.35
John Barnett	X/U	0.60
John Barnett Links You to Mulder	R	2.30
Kevlar Vest	U	0.35
Kick	C	0.05
Kiss Of The Vampire	R	1.90
Knife	C	0.05
23		
Krycek, the Double Agent	R	1.90
Lake Okobogee, Campsite #53 Sioux City, IA.	X/U	0.60
Langly	X/U	0.60
Laptop Computer	U	0.35
Laser Barrier	R	1.90
Leonard	R	2.30
Leonard Vance	X/U	0.60
Leonard, Detachable Congenital Twin	X/U	0.60
Lie Detector	X/U	0.60
24		
Limited Choices	UR	14.00
Living Machine	U	0.35
Lock Pick	R	2.30
Los Angeles, CA.	R	1.90
Lt. Brian Tillman, Aubry P.D.	X/U	0.60
Lt. Colonel Marcus Aurelius Belt	R	1.90
Lucas Henry, Serial Killer	X/U	0.60
Lula Phillips	R	1.90
Luther Lee Boggs	R	1.90
25		
M-16 (Mini-14) Assault Rifle	U	0.35
Maggie Holvey	C	0.05
Mahan Propulsion Laboratory, Colson, WA.	C	0.05
Margaret Scully	UR	16.00
Marion, VA.	C	0.05
Massive Internal Damage	U	0.35
Mattawa, WA.	C	0.05
Max Fenig	R	1.90

Card name	Rarity	Price
Medi-Kit	R	1.90
26		
Medical Treatment	C	0.05
Meet Brother Andrew	R	2.30
Melissa Scully	UR	17.00
Michael Holvey, The Evil One	X/U	0.60
Mind Control	R	1.90
Minneapolis, MN.	U	0.35
Misclassified Case	UR	14.00
Mojo Bag	U	0.35
Mrs. Mulder	UR	20.00
27		
Mrs. Paddock, A.K.A. The Dark Angel	X/U	0.60
Mt. Avalon, WA.	C	0.05
NASA Mission Control, Houston, Texas	R	1.90
Nasty Surprise	U	0.35
Nerve Strike	R	1.90
New York City, NY.	R	1.90
Newark, NJ.	X/U	0.60
No Place Is Safe	R	1.90
No Way Out	U	0.35
28		
Northeast Georgetown Medical Center, Washington DC	R	1.90
Nurse Owens	UR	16.00
Olympic National Forest, WA.	C	0.05
One Breath	UR	13.00
Operation Falcon Blue Berets	R	1.90
Outskirts Of Atlantic City, N.J.	U	0.35
Paperwork	U	0.35
Paul Mossinger	C	0.05
Pete Calcagni	U	0.35
29		
Peter Tanaka	U	0.35
Pheromone Induced Psychosis	U	0.35
Poisonous Gases	C	0.05
Poltergeist Attack	X/U	0.60
Psychiatric Hospital, Richmond, VA.	C	0.05
Puzzles Within Puzzles	U	0.35
Pvt. McAlpin, Zombie	X/U	0.60
Radioactive Area	U	0.35
Reading The Signs	U	0.35
30		
Red Tape	R	1.90
Rejuvenating Caves	U	0.35
Relentless Pursuit	C	0.05
Rending Claws	U	0.35
Reporters At The Crime Scene	U	0.35
Reverse Engineers	X/U	0.60
Road Hazard	U	0.35

Card name	Rarity	Price
Road Trip	R	1.90
Run For It	U	0.35
31		
Running Gun Battle	U	0.35
S.W.A.T. Training	C	0.05
Safe House	R	1.90
Samantha Mulder	R	1.90
Samuel Hartley	R	1.90
Sea Off Of Tildeskan, Norway	X/U	0.60
Section Chief Scott Blevins	X/U	0.60
Security Clearance	R	2.30
Semi-Jacketed Hollow Points	U	0.35
32		
Senator Richard Matheson	R	1.90
Sheriff Daniels	U	0.35
Sheriff Mazeroski	R	1.90
Sheriff Spencer	X/U	0.60
Sheriff Tom Arens, Cannibal	X/U	0.60
Shotgun	R	1.90
Shutting Down The X-Files	R	1.90
Sinus Cavity Implant	U	0.35
Sir Malcolm Marsden	C	0.05
33		
Skinner Adopts The Company Line	R	1.90
Skyland Mountain, VA.	X/U	0.60
Slithers In The Night	U	0.35
Smoke Screen	U	0.35
Sneak Attack	R	1.90
Spirit of the Amaru	UR	15.00
Spying Mission	U	0.35
Squeeze	U	0.35
Steveston, MA.	X/U	0.60
34		
Street Contacts	U	0.35
Stunning Blow	U	0.35
Successful Diagnosis	U	0.35
Suppressed Fury	X/U	0.60
Surfing the Net	R	1.90
Suspect Description	C	0.05
Symbol of Faith	R	1.90
Take Cover	U	0.35
Taking Chances	R	2.30
35		
Taped Intelligence	R	1.90
Terminal Damage	R	1.90
The Calusari	R	1.90
The Cigarette-Smoking Man	X/U	0.60
The Cigarette-Smoking Man Strikes	R	1.90
The Cigarette-Smoking Man's Solution	UR	14.00
The Conundrum	U	0.35
The Evil One	R	2.30

Card name	Rarity	Price
The Gregors	X/U	0.60
36		
The Host	X/U	0.60
The Host Attacks	R	1.90
The Jersey Devil	X/U	0.60
The Local Law Enforcement Are Uncooperative	U	0.35
The Manitou	X/U	0.60
The Manitou Stalks His Prey	R	1.90
The Mechanic	U	0.35
The Overcoat Man	C	0.05
The Psychotic Attack	X/U	0.60
37		
The Sandman	U	0.35
The Swarm	X/U	0.60
The Thinker	R	1.90
The Vampire, A.K.A. The Unholy Spirit	X/U	0.60
Thorough Documentation	R	1.90
Too Close to the Truth	UR	12.00
Tracking the Killer	R	2.30
Trap	U	0.35
Travel Arrangements	C	0.05
38		
True Grit	R	1.90
Trust No One	R	1.90
U.F.O. Wreckage, Townsend WI.	R	1.90
U.S. Marshall Tapia	X/C	0.10
U.S.G.S. Quadrant Map	R	2.30
Unexplainable Time Loss	R	1.90
University Of Maryland, Baltimore MD.	X/U	0.60
Unnatural Aging	U	0.35
Vicious Fangs	U	0.35
39		
Volcanic Spore	X/U	0.60
Walther PPK 7.65 Hold Out Weapon	U	0.35
Warren James Dupre, The Lazarus Man	X/U	0.60
Washington Monument, Washington D.C.	R	1.90
Watch Out	U	0.35
Webbed	R	1.90
Wire-Tap	X/U	0.60
Witness Intimidated	R	2.30
Women's Health Clinic, Richville, MD	R	2.30
40		
Written Report	C	0.05
X-Files Research	C	0.05
You've Got A Tail	C	0.05

X-Files • Promos

Identifiable by the letters "PR," several **X-Files** promos are highly sought after. One of the more interesting releases, **Smoke and Mirrors** appeared in *Scrye* 4.2 (Jun 97) in five slightly different versions.

Card name	Price
1	
Agent Henderson	6.00
Alien Technology	5.00
Blue Plate Special	8.00
Chester Bonaparte, The Spirit Guide	6.00
Dark Angel	7.00
Deny Everything	35.00
Die Hand Die Verletzt	10.00
Fighter Interceptor	5.00

Card name	Price
Je vois quelque chose la au dessous	10.00
2	
Mulligan	10.00
No One So Paranoid	25.00
Smoke & Mirrors 1	6.00
Smoke & Mirrors 2	6.50
Smoke & Mirrors 3	6.50
Smoke & Mirrors 4	6.50
Smoke & Mirrors 5	6.50
Teamwork	5.00

RARITY KEY C = Common U = Uncommon R = Rare VR = Very Rare UR = Ultra Rare F = Foil card X = Fixed/standard in all decks

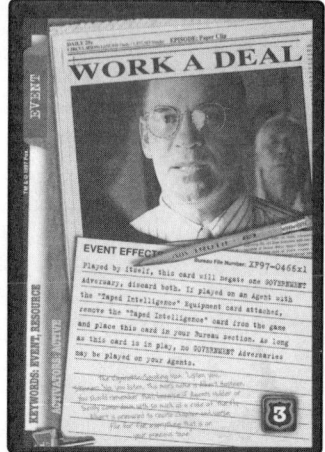

X-Files • 101361

USPC Games • Released **July 1997**

146 cards in set

IDENTIFIER: Black borders; cards feature 'Bureau File Number XF-97' followed by a number above 0384

• Booster packs contain 15 cards; booster displays contain 36 boosters

The first and only expansion for **X-Files** is sometimes known as the Mulder edition. The title refers to his birthday, 10/13/61.

The release, which covers the third season, helped solve a problem with the X-File cards. The attributes of the X-File cards were asymmetric so that certain questions would eliminate more X-Files than others would. As the number of X-File cards grew, this problem was alleviated.

A second expansion, **22364** (not a Virginia ZIP code, but Dana Scully's birthday) was never released. — **Michael Greenholdt**

> You will need
> **17**
> nine-pocket pages to store this set.
> (9 doubled up)

Set (146 cards)	**45.00**
Booster Display Box	**35.00**
Booster Pack	**2.00**

Card name	Rarity	Price
1		
☐ 2 Lux Video Camera	R	3.00
☐ 2 Shy	C	0.10
☐ A Friend in The Lab	R	2.80
☐ A Near Death Experience	UR	15.00
☐ Agent Bill Patterson	R	3.00
☐ Agent Dan Kazanjian	R	3.00
☐ Agent Danny Pendrell	R	3.00
☐ Agent Fred Nemhauser	C	0.10
☐ Agent Kreski	C	0.10
2		
☐ Alien Autopsy Video	U	0.50
☐ Alien Stiletto	UR	14.00
☐ Amaru Urn	R	3.00
☐ Ambulance	U	0.50
☐ Angry Townspeople	C	0.10
☐ Assassinated	R	3.00
☐ Avatar	R	3.00
☐ Big Blue	C	0.10
☐ Braddock Heights, Maryland	C	0.10
3		
☐ Brother Martin Is Attracted To You	R	2.50
☐ Captive Hybrid	C	0.10
☐ Carina Maywald	R	3.00

Card name	Rarity	Price
☐ Ceremony	R	3.00
☐ Cerulean Blue	R	3.00
☐ China Town, San Francisco, CA	U	0.50
☐ Circuit Board Implant	R	2.50
☐ Classified Ad	U	0.50
☐ Classified Photos	U	0.50
4		
☐ Clyde Bruckman	R	3.00
☐ Coast Guard Lieutenant	C	0.10
☐ Colonel Kissell	R	3.00
☐ Darkened Forest	C	0.10
☐ Darren Peter Oswald	R	3.00
☐ Deceiving The Flock	C	0.10
☐ Decomposing Victim	U	0.50
☐ Dental X-Ray Plate	U	0.50
☐ Desktop Computer	U	0.50
5		
☐ Detective Alan Cross	U	0.50
☐ Detective Angela White	C	0.10
☐ Detective Cline	C	0.10
☐ Detective Havez	C	0.10
☐ Detective Manners	C	0.10
☐ Detective Walter Eubanks	R	3.00
☐ Disbelief	C	0.10
☐ Dissolving Evidence	C	0.10
☐ Dr. Alexander Ivanov	R	3.00
6		
☐ Dr. Bambi Berebaum	U	0.50
☐ Dr. Bugger	U	0.50
☐ Dr. Jeff Eckerie	U	0.50
☐ Dr. Joe Ridley	R	3.00
☐ Dr. Rick Newton	C	0.10
☐ Dried Frog	C	0.10
☐ Eliminating the Source	R	3.00
☐ Ellen Kaminski	U	0.50
☐ Eric Hosteen	U	0.50
7		
☐ Escalante	C	0.10
☐ Explosion	R	3.00

Card name	Rarity	Price
☐ F. Emasculata Outbreak	R	2.50
☐ Festival of the Hungry Ghosts	R	3.00
☐ Final Repose	C	0.10
☐ Flesh Sculpting	R	2.50
☐ Foo Fighter	R	3.00
☐ Garrotte	U	0.50
☐ General Thomas Callahan	R	3.00
8		
☐ Heads Up	C	0.10
☐ Helicopter Spotter	U	0.50
☐ Hell Money	R	2.80
☐ Injured Relative	R	2.50
☐ Jerusalem, Ohio	U	0.50
☐ Jim Ullrich	C	0.10
☐ John Barnett Links You To Mulder	R	3.00
☐ John Mostow	C	0.10
☐ Jose Chung's "From Outer Space"	R	3.00
9		
☐ Joseph Patnik	U	0.50
☐ Krycek Possessed	UR	15.00
☐ Laser Targeter	U	0.50
☐ Leonard	R	3.00
☐ Lock Pick	R	2.50
☐ Lottie Holoway	R	3.00
☐ Lt. Colonel Victor Stans	C	0.10
☐ Lucy Householder	R	3.00
☐ M.R.I.	U	0.50
10		
☐ Margi Kleinjan	U	0.50
☐ Mass Grave	C	0.05
☐ Meet Brother Andrew	R	3.00
☐ Men in Black	UR	15.00
☐ Michael Kryder	C	0.10
☐ Miller's Grove, Massachusetts	U	0.50
☐ Mostow's Sketches	R	3.00
☐ Mostow's Studio, Washington, D.C.	U	0.50
☐ Murder Weapon	U	0.50
11		
☐ Navajo Elder	U	0.50
☐ No One Believes You	R	3.00
☐ One Breath	R	3.00
☐ Oubliette	R	3.00
☐ Owen Jarvis	R	3.00
☐ Parmelly	C	0.10
☐ Penny Northern	C	0.10
☐ Philosophical Question	C	0.10
☐ Positron Emission Tomography Lab	U	0.50
12		
☐ Puppet	C	0.10
☐ Queequeg	R	3.00

Card name	Rarity	Price
☐ Red-Haired Man	R	2.50
☐ Sammon Roque	U	0.50
☐ Satellite Photos	U	0.50
☐ Secret Government Files	U	0.50
☐ Secret Passage	U	0.50
☐ Security Clearance	R	3.00
☐ Sharon Kiveat	C	0.10
13		
☐ Sharon Skinner	R	3.00
☐ Sheriff John Teller	U	0.50
☐ Simon Gates a.k.a. Ferreau	U	0.50
☐ Skinner Intervenes	C	0.10
☐ Skinner's Wedding Ring	C	0.10
☐ Stan Buxton	U	0.50
☐ Stationery	U	0.50
☐ Stoner, Chick, And Dude	C	0.10
☐ Striker's Cove, Heuvalman's Lake	C	0.10
14		
☐ Strughold Mining Company, Rural	U	0.50
☐ Taking Chances	R	2.50
☐ Tape Recorder	U	0.50
☐ Teamwork	UR	13.50
☐ Terri Roberts	U	0.50
☐ Tesos Dos Bichos Excavation...	U	0.50
☐ The Evil One	R	3.00
☐ The List	R	3.00
☐ The Mailman	R	2.50
15		
☐ The Stupendous Yappi	R	2.50
☐ The Video Trap	C	0.10
☐ The Walk	U	0.50
☐ This is Not Happening	C	0.10
☐ Tong Lottery Jar	R	3.00
☐ Tracking The Killer	R	2.50
☐ U.S.G.S. Quadrant Map	R	2.50
☐ Unexpected Call	UR	15.00
☐ Veracity in Question	C	0.10
16		
☐ Victor Klemper	R	2.50
☐ Virgil Incanto's Apt., Cleveland, OH	C	0.10
☐ Visions of a Madman	R	2.50
☐ Visit From The First Elder	R	3.00
☐ War of The Coprophages	R	3.00
☐ Warden Leo Brodeur	U	0.50
☐ White Buffalo	R	2.50
☐ Witness Intimidated	R	2.50
☐ Women's Health Clinic, Richville	R	3.00
17		
☐ Work a Deal	C	0.10
☐ You're a Dead Man	R	3.00

The sets aren't out there

Before USPC Games decided in the fall of 1997 to get out of the **X-Files CCG** business, a number of remarkable releases were previewed.

In addition to the announced expansion, **22364**, USPC planned a **Two-Player Starter Kit**, a **Booster Bonus Box,** and a **Deck Bonus Box**.

Most remarkable, though, was the **Collector Set** USPC previewed at Gen Con 1997. In addition to the actual ultra-rare agent cards for **Mulder** and **Scully**, **pewter** versions of those cards would have been included in sets for those characters.

Cool, but if they came out, we haven't seen them.

RARITY KEY C = Common U = Uncommon R = Rare VR = Very Rare UR = Ultra Rare F = Foil card X = Fixed/standard in all decks

X-Men
Wizards of the Coast • Released **July 2000**

131 cards in set
- Two-player starter decks contain 61 cards, rules, playmat, counters, and dice
- Starter displays contain 6 starters
- Booster packs contain 11 cards; booster displays contain 36 boosters

The X-Men, mutants who fought to protect a world that hated and feared them, had been around in Marvel comics since 1963. They'd even appeared in CCGs as early as 1995, as part of Fleer's **OverPower**, for which they received their own expansion in 1998. But it was largely 20th Century Fox's 2000 movie that led to the licensing of a CCG all the X-Men's own.

The X-Men CCG is an indirect combat game. Each player begins play with a team of X-Men and two Villains. The object is to "kill" two Villains before an opponent does. Each turn, a player can play a Mission card which allows his X-Men to attack a Villain. After the X-Men have their move, the player may attack an opposing team with a Villain. While there are cards that can boost the X-team's attack, there are none which aid in either the Villain's or X-team's defense, making combat in the *X-Men* CCG mostly a matter of rolling dice.

Wizards of the Coast found unexpected (believe us, no one expected it) good fortune in the fact that Bryan Singer's *X-Men* movie was a surprise hit, defying all expectations based on years of bad Marvel Comics movies: *Howard the Duck, Punisher, Captain America,* and the unreleased *Fantastic Four.* But Wizards of the Coast couldn't get the booster packs out until two months after the starters, when the movie's run in theaters was already winding down. It was perceived by many as a rookie mistake, and rumored reasons ranged from cardstock being rerouted to **Pokémon** to an attack by Magneto. Whatever the reason, the game was stillborn in many stores for it, and the expansion announced for December 2000, **Generation**, had still not been released by early 2001. — *Michael Greenholdt*

> You will need **15** nine-pocket pages to store this set. (8 doubled up)

Concept	●●○○○
Gameplay	●●●●○
Card art	●●●○○
Player pool	●●○○○

Set (131 cards)		**150.00**
Starter Display Box		**67.50**
Booster Display Box		**70.00**
Starter Deck		**12.00**
Booster Pack		**2.70**

# Card name	Type	Rarity	Price
1			
☐ 81 Agility Trial	Miss	C	0.20
☐ 21 Alien Invasion	Miss	R	3.50
☐ 82 All or Nothing Battle	Miss	C	0.20
☐ 22 Ambush	Miss	R	2.90
☐ 1 Angel	X-Men	F	8.50
☐ 2 Apocalypse	Vill	F	8.00
☐ 23 Back Alley Brawl	Miss	R	3.00
☐ 83 Bad Blood	Miss	C	0.20
☐ 84 Bait and Switch	Miss	C	0.20
2			
☐ 41 Baptism by Fire	Mom	U	0.25
☐ 85 Battle Simulation	Miss	C	0.20
☐ 42 Berserker Rage	Miss	U	0.50
☐ 43 Bewilder	PwrUp	U	0.40
☐ 3 Bishop	X-Men	F	7.50
☐ 44 Blend In	PwrUp	U	0.40
☐ 45 Block	PwrUp	U	0.40
☐ 86 Blood Feud	Miss	C	0.20
☐ 46 Braindrain	PwrUp	U	0.50
3			
☐ 47 Brainwashed!	Light	U	0.40
☐ 4 Brood	Vill	F	7.50
☐ 48 Call Down the Heavens	PwrUp	U	0.40
☐ 49 Call the Cops	PwrUp	U	0.40
☐ 87 Close Call	PwrUp	C	0.20
☐ 88 Collision Course	Mom	C	0.20
☐ 89 Combat Training	Miss	C	0.20
☐ 50 Come Out Wherever You Are!	Light	U	0.40
☐ 51 Concentrate	PwrUp	U	0.40
4			
☐ 90 Controlled Burst	PwrUp	C	0.20

# Card name	Type	Rarity	Price
☐ 91 Cross-Dimensional Raid	Miss	C	0.20
☐ 24 Crossfire	Miss	R	2.60
☐ 92 Cry for Help	Miss	C	0.20
☐ 5 Cyclops	X-Men	F	15.00
☐ 122 Cyclops	X-Men	X	1.00
☐ 25 Deadly Dance	Miss	R	2.80
☐ 93 Death Trap	Miss	C	0.20
☐ 26 DMZ	Miss	R	3.00
5			
☐ 52 Dodge This!	Light	U	0.40
☐ 94 Dogfight	Miss	C	0.20
☐ 27 Don't Give Up!	Light	R	2.90
☐ 53 Double Team	PwrUp	U	0.40
☐ 95 Dramatic Confrontation	Miss	C	0.20
☐ 96 Dramatic Escape	Mom	C	0.20
☐ 97 Faceoff	Miss	C	0.20
☐ 98 Fastball Special	Mom	C	0.20
☐ 99 Fight to the Finish	Miss	C	0.20
6			
☐ 100 Finishing Blow	Mom	C	0.20
☐ 101 Firefight	Miss	C	0.20
☐ 102 First Aid!	Light	C	0.20
☐ 28 Fly Away	PwrUp	R	2.50
☐ 29 Focus	PwrUp	R	2.50
☐ 54 Follow Me!	Light	U	0.50
☐ 55 Fusillade	PwrUp	U	0.40
☐ 30 Get to the Truth!	Light	R	2.50
☐ 56 Goddess!	Light	U	0.40
7			
☐ 57 Hold Your Fire!	Light	U	0.40
☐ 103 Inferno	Miss	C	0.20
☐ 6 Jean Grey	X-Men	F	13.50
☐ 123 Jean Grey	X-Men	X	1.00
☐ 7 Juggernaut	Vill	F	8.50
☐ 58 Kiss for Luck	PwrUp	U	0.40
☐ 59 Kra-ka-thoom!	Light	U	0.40
☐ 104 Last Stand	Miss	C	0.20
☐ 31 Lend Moral Support	PwrUp	R	3.00

# Card name	Type	Rarity	Price
8			
☐ 60 Lure Them In	PwrUp	U	0.40
☐ 8 Magneto	Vill	F	8.50
☐ 124 Magneto	Vill	X	0.80
☐ 9 Marrow	X-Men	F	7.50
☐ 105 Mental Probe	Mom	C	0.20
☐ 10 Mojo	Vill	F	6.50
☐ 61 Moment of Reflection	Mom	U	0.40
☐ 32 Moment of Truth	Light	R	2.90
☐ 11 Mystique	Vill	F	7.50
9			
☐ 125 Mystique	Vill	X	1.00
☐ 33 Natural Disaster	Miss	R	2.80
☐ 62 Nice Shot!	Light	U	0.40
☐ 63 No Way Out	PwrUp	U	0.40
☐ 34 Obstacle Course	Miss	R	2.80
☐ 65 Out of Control	Miss	U	0.40
☐ 64 Outflank	PwrUp	U	0.40
☐ 106 Payback	Miss	C	0.20
☐ 107 Pounce	Mom	C	0.20
10			
☐ 66 Practical Joke	PwrUp	U	0.40
☐ 35 Practice, Practice, Practice	PwrUp	R	2.60
☐ 108 Precision Fire	Mom	C	0.20
☐ 36 Press Gang	Miss	R	2.80
☐ 12 Professor X	X-Men	F	13.50
☐ 126 Professor X	X-Men	X	1.00
☐ 109 Protection of the Innocent	Miss	C	0.20
☐ 67 Psi-Shield	Mom	U	0.40
☐ 110 Psychic Boost	Mom	C	0.20
11			
☐ 111 Psychic Showdown	Miss	C	0.20
☐ 13 Psylocke	X-Men	F	9.50
☐ 68 Read the Riot Act	PwrUp	U	0.40
☐ 37 Ready or Not	PwrUp	R	2.60
☐ 121 Reality Shift	PwrUp	X/F	5.50
☐ 69 Reprieve	PwrUp	U	0.40
☐ 112 Rescue Mission	Miss	C	0.20

# Card name	Type	Rarity	Price
☐ 14 Rogue	X-Men	F	10.75
☐ 127 Rogue	X-Men	X	0.90
12			
☐ 15 Sabretooth	Vill	F	9.00
☐ 128 Sabretooth	Vill	X	0.80
☐ 70 Scientific Solution	PwrUp	U	0.40
☐ 16 Sentinels	Vill	F	7.50
☐ 71 Shhhhh ...	Light	U	0.40
☐ 113 Showdown	Miss	C	0.20
☐ 114 Shrapnel Blast	PwrUp	C	0.20
☐ 17 Sinister	Vill	F	7.50
☐ 38 Slugfest	Miss	R	2.60
13			
☐ 39 Snikt!	Light	R	2.80
☐ 72 Spinal Tap	Mom	U	0.40
☐ 115 Stay Out of Reach	PwrUp	C	0.20
☐ 18 Storm	X-Men	F	12.25
☐ 129 Storm	X-Men	X	0.90
☐ 116 Sucker Punch	Mom	C	0.20
☐ 117 Surprise Assault	Miss	C	0.20
☐ 73 Swipe	PwrUp	U	0.40
☐ 74 Take It to the Sky	PwrUp	U	0.40
14			
☐ 75 Take the Hit	PwrUp	U	0.40
☐ 118 Take Your Best Shot	PwrUp	C	0.20
☐ 76 Teach Some Manners	PwrUp	U	0.40
☐ 77 Team Work	Miss	U	0.40
☐ 19 Toad	Vill	F	7.50
☐ 130 Toad	Vill	X	0.80
☐ 78 Ugh ... Take It!	Light	U	0.25
☐ 40 Underground Menace	Miss	R	2.80
☐ 119 Vendetta	Miss	C	0.20
15			
☐ 20 Wolverine	X-Men	F	13.50
☐ 131 Wolverine	X-Men	X	1.00
☐ 79 Work as a Team	PwrUp	U	0.40
☐ 80 Workout	Miss	U	0.40
☐ 120 You Can Make It!	Light	C	0.20

RARITY KEY C = Common U = Uncommon R = Rare VR = Very Rare UR = Ultra Rare F = Foil card X = Fixed/standard in all decks

Xena: Warrior Princess

Wizards of the Coast • Released **May 1998**

180 cards in set

- Starters contain 40 cards, and two large rules sheets
- Starter displays contain 18 starters, three each of six different theme decks
- Boosters contain 12 cards; booster displays contain 45 boosters

Designed by **Charlie Catinus**, **Mike Davis**, **Skaff Elias**, **Richard Garfield**, **Joe Grace**, **Jim Lin**, and **Joel Mick**

Based on the syndicated television series of the same name *Xena: Warrior Princess* is the second game released using the ARC System. *Xena* is compatible with **Hercules: The Legendary Journeys** as well as **C•23**, the other two ARC System releases, although it's hard to imagine Xena dropping into the comics universe of *C•23*.

The basic premise, as with the television series, is that Xena and her companions are the good guys doing battle against evil warlords, horrible monsters, and wrathful gods. The *Xena* game system accurately captures the feel of the television series, though the campiness of the series is downplayed in favor of the rock-em sock-em action.

The ARC System is a simplified Deckmaster system, similar in many respects to **Magic: The Gathering**. There are four different types of cards in the ARC System: Resource, Character, Combat, and Action cards. "Tapping" is a core game mechanism in the ARC System, as it is in Deckmaster. Unlike *Magic*, however, there are only three different "colors" in *Xena*: Red "Urban/Monetary Resources"(locations such as **Castle** and **Grand Bazaar**), Green "Rural/Supplies Resources" (**Amazon Village** and **Peasant Village**) and Blue "Mystic/Magical Resources" (**Forgotten Temple** and **Temple of Ares**).

Resources are played and then tapped to bring Characters into play or to play Combat or Action cards. Character, Combat and Action cards each are of a single color; at least one of the resources tapped to use that card must be of the same color.

Characters attack an opponent; the opponent may defend with Characters, Combat or Action cards (unlike Deckmaster, defending Characters tap). If an attacking Character is unblocked it will deal damage directly to the opponent's deck; one card discarded for every point of damage. A player that loses all cards from his deck loses the game.

All three ARC System games were released in a one-year period and found little favor with game-store customers, few of whom, in 1998, fit the description of "beginning gamers." Perhaps if the ARC System games had been released following the **Pokémon** craze, they would have met with a better reception.

Xena fared somewhat better than the other members of the ARC trio, and it was the only one to receive an expansion set. Likely, this is due to the relative popularity of *Xena* at the time, as the show was nearing the peak of its interest. — *James Mishler*

Concept	●●●○○
Gameplay	●●●○○
Card art	●●●○○
Player pool	○○○○○

Set (180 cards)	87.50
Starter Display Box	41.50
Booster Display Box	48.00
Starter Deck	7.50
Booster Pack	1.50

Card name	Rarity	Price
Acrobatic Ninjas	U	0.40
Aid from Autolycus	U	0.40
Aid from Gabrielle	U	0.40
Alert Longbow Squad	U	0.40
Altar of Ares	X	0.15
Altar Sacrifice	U	0.40
Amazon Village	X	0.15
Angered Giant	U	0.40
Angered Titan	R	2.00
Aphrodite	R	1.60
Aphrodite's Bell	U	0.40
Apprentice Swordsman	C	0.15
Ares	R	3.00
Ares Dethroned	R	2.00
Ares's Soldiers	C	0.15
Ares's Wrath	C	0.15
Argo	R	2.50
Army of Ares	R	1.10
Autolycus King of Thieves	R	2.10
Autolycus's Boast	U	0.40

Card name	Rarity	Price
Banshees	U	0.40
Bath House	X	0.25
Beauty Contest	U	0.60
Behind Bars	U	0.50
Beloved King	R	2.50
Bevy of Virgins	C	0.25
Big Ballista	R	1.90
Black Wolves	U	0.40
Border Dispute	U	0.40
Burned to the Ground	C	0.25
Caesar's Banner	C	0.25
Call the Horde	U	0.40
Captured	C	0.25
Castle	X	0.25
Catapult Siege	C	0.25
Cavalry Strike	C	0.25
Celtic Queen	U	0.50
Celtic Soldiers	C	0.25
Celtic Warrior	C	0.25
Chakram Strike	C	0.25
Charismatic Fighter	C	0.25
Charon's Tour	U	0.60
Chin Mercenary	C	0.25
Clever Defense	R	2.00
Confession	R	2.00
Corrupt Judge	R	2.00
Crossbow Archers	U	0.60

Card name	Rarity	Price
Cupid	R	3.00
Cupid's Arrows	U	0.60
Cursed to Wander	U	0.60
Cyclops Bully	U	0.60
Dagger of Helios	C	0.25
Dahak's Demon	R	3.30
Dastardly Assassin	C	0.25
Delphian Seer	C	0.25
Diversionary Tactics	U	0.40
Divination	C	0.10
Draco	R	2.50
Driven Hard by the Furies	U	0.40
Eastern Healer	C	0.10
Eastern Village	X	0.15
Elite Temple Guard	R	1.60
Enforced Peace	U	0.40
Entrance to the Underworld	X	0.15
Expert Swordsman	U	0.40
Extortionist	U	0.40
Fake Chakram	R	2.00
Fervent Warrior	U	0.40
Fighter-for-Hire	C	0.15
Flaming Arrows	C	0.15
Flying Daggers	C	0.15
Forgotten Temple	X	0.15
Frying Pan Assault	C	0.15
Furies' Madness	C	0.15

RARITY KEY C = Common U = Uncommon R = Rare VR = Very Rare UR = Ultra Rare F = Foil card X = Fixed/standard in all decks

Card name	Rarity	Price	Card name	Rarity	Price	Card name	Rarity	Price
Gabby's Little Stick	C	0.15	Nothing is Impossible	R	3.00	Temple Guards	C	0.25
Gabrielle	R	7.50	Outlying Village	X	0.50	Temple Infiltrator	U	0.25
Gabrielle Misleads	U	0.40	Overprotective Father	C	0.25	Temple of Ares	X	0.25
Gabrielle's Orders	U	0.40	Pacified	R	3.30	The Furies	R	2.00
Gallic Slave	C	0.15	Path of Morpheus	U	0.60	The Horde Attacks!	R	2.50
Gate Guard	C	0.15	Peasant Village	X	0.15	Tied to the Altar	C	0.25
Ghostly Messenger	R	1.10	Poseidon's Offer	R	3.00	To the Last Breath	R	1.20
[10]			[14]			[18]		
Giants' Burial Ground	X	0.25	Poseidon's Whirlpool	U	0.40	Tossed in Xerxes's Dungeon!	R	2.00
Gift of the Gods	C	0.25	Possession	R	2.00	Town Judge	C	0.25
Grand Bazaar	X	0.25	Priest of Esclepius	U	0.40	Trap in the Woods	C	0.25
Greek Fighter	C	0.25	Priest of Morpheus	C	0.15	Traveling Priest	C	0.25
Greek Forest	X	0.25	Priest of the Furies	C	0.15	Treasure-Trove	X	0.25
Hammer Lock	U	0.40	Priests of Dahak	U	0.40	Trojan Prince	R	3.00
Helen of Troy	R	2.50	Prometheus Bound	U	0.40	Trojan Sergeant	R	3.00
Hired Giant	U	0.40	Protege of Ares	U	0.40	Undead Warrior	U	0.60
Horde Leader	C	0.25	Rampaging Giant	R	2.00	Unstoppable Attack	U	0.60
[11]			[15]			[19]		
Horde Squad	C	0.25	Rapid Fire	C	0.15	Untrained Fighter	C	0.25
Inside Man	R	1.20	Raw Squid	U	0.40	Vengeance	R	3.50
Interior Decorators	R	2.20	Relaxing Before Battle	R	1.10	Veteran Longbow Archers	C	0.25
Jolly Ol' Toymaker	U	0.40	Releasing the Titans	R	1.10	Vigilant Sentries	C	0.25
Knight of the Pierced Heart	C	0.25	Safety in Numbers	R	1.30	Village Tough	C	0.25
Left for Dead	C	0.25	Salmoneus	R	1.30	Wall Guards	C	0.25
Legbreaker	C	0.25	Shortbow Archers	U	0.40	War	R	2.00
Liaison with Ares	U	0.40	Spartan Javelin	R	2.50	Weapon of the Gods	R	3.00
Liquor and Flame!	U	0.60	Spike Trap	U	0.40	Whim of the Fates	R	3.00
[12]			[16]			[20]		
Little Baby Godling	C	0.25	Sponsorship	R	1.10	Whip the Slaves	R	2.50
Lizard Warriors	C	0.25	Spring-Loaded Dagger	U	0.40	Witch Hunters	C	0.25
Longbow Archers	C	0.25	Straight from the Harp	R	2.00	Wounded in Battle	C	0.25
Looking for Wounds	C	0.25	Strike Team	R	2.50	Xena Brings 'Em Home	U	0.60
Lynch Mob	C	0.25	Surrounded!	R	2.00	Xena Leads the Troops	C	0.10
Major Jealousy Rage	C	0.25	Swashbuckling Swordsman	U	0.40	Xena's Bluff	U	0.40
Meleager the Mighty	R	3.00	Swing-Kick	U	0.40	Xena's Wrath	U	0.40
Merchant Port	X	0.50	Swordsman in Training	C	0.25	Xena, Warrior Princess	R	4.60
Mischief	C	0.25	Take Prisoners	R	1.20	Young Prince	C	0.10
[13]			[17]					
Mystic Priest	U	0.60	Talented Physician	C	0.25			
Mystic Tutor	R	2.00	Tattooed Fighter	C	0.25			

Xena • Battle Cry

Wizards of the Coast • Released September 1998
75 cards in set • **IDENTIFIER: 'X2' on card bottom**

- Booster packs contain 12 cards
- Booster displays contain 45 boosters

The only expansion set received by **Xena** — or any ARC system game, **Battle Cry** adds a number of cards to the mix. — *James Mishler*

You will need **9** nine-pocket pages to store this set. (5 doubled up)

Set (75 cards)	57.50
Booster Display Box	45.00
Booster Pack	1.50

Card name	Rarity	Price	Card name	Rarity	Price	Card name	Rarity	Price	Card name	Rarity	Price
[1]			[3]								
Amazon Princess	U	0.60	Cecrops	R	3.30	Ixion Centaur	R	3.00	Underworld Escapee	U	0.60
Amazon Queen	R	2.00	Cecrops's Crew	U	0.60	Jewel of Demeter	R	2.00	[8]		
Amazon Trainer	C	0.10	Centaur Charger	C	0.10	Joxer is Prepared	U	0.60	Untrained Amazon	C	0.10
Archer Attack	C	0.10	Centaur Longbow Archers	C	0.10	Joxer the Mighty	R	3.30	Velasca	R	3.30
Arm-Wrestling Contest	C	0.10	Centaur Veteran	U	0.60	King Sisyphus	R	3.00	Velasca Attacks	U	0.60
Arrows from the Woods	C	0.10	Chariot Warrior	C	0.10	[6]			Velasca's Wrath	C	0.10
Bacchae Horde	C	0.10	Cortese's Soldiers	U	0.60	Many Skills	U	0.60	War Chariots	R	2.00
Bacchae Rite	R	2.00	Devious Warrior	C	0.10	Massacre	U	0.60	Xena Puts on the Pinch	R	2.00
Bacchus	R	3.50	Ephiny, Amazon Warrior	R	2.50	Meeting of the Warlords	R	2.00	Xena's Discovery	R	1.50
[2]			[4]			Mounted Warrior	C	0.10	Xena's Graveyard Search	C	0.10
Backstabber	U	0.60	Everybody Sing!	C	0.10	Promethean Bird	C	0.10	Xena, Warrior Princess	R	7.00
Bone Dryad	U	0.60	Executioner	C	0.10	Ready for a Fight	C	0.10	[9]		
Callisto	R	7.00	Famous Duelist	C	0.10	Roman Centurion	C	0.10	YII-YII-YII-YII-YII-YII-YII!	U	0.60
Callisto Goes Overboard	R	2.00	Gabby's Scrolls	C	0.10	Sintare's Tricks	U	1.00	Young Centaur	C	0.10
Callisto Strikes	U	0.60	Gabrielle	R	5.00	Sintares	R	1.80	Young Priest	C	0.10
Callisto's Master Plan	R	2.00	Gabrielle Clears the Way	R	2.00	[7]					
Callisto's Revenge	U	0.60	Gabrielle's Sacrifice	R	2.00	Siren's Call	U	0.60			
Callisto's Wrath	C	0.10	Greedy Pirates	U	0.60	Solstice Spirit	C	0.10			
Castle Gua	C	0.10	Hades	R	4.30	Song of Orpheus	U	0.60			
			[5]			Talmadeus's Raiders	U	0.60			
			Harpies	U	0.60	Total Eclipse	R	2.00			
			Harpy	U	0.60	Transformed Bacchi	C	0.10			
			Hestian Stones	C	0.10	Trapped in Tartarus	R	2.00			
			Improvised Escape Tool	R	2.00	Treachery	R	2.00			

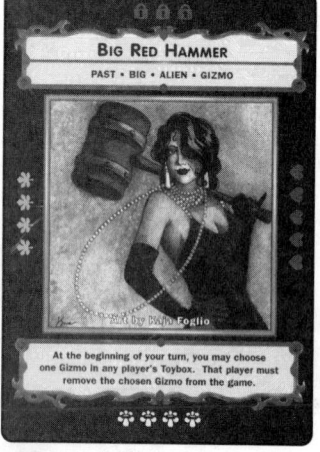

BIG RED HAMMER

PAST · BIG · ALIEN · GIZMO

At the beginning of your turn, you may choose one Gizmo in any player's Toybox. That player must remove the chosen Gizmo from the game.

Xxxenophile

Slag-Blah Entertainment • Released **July 1996**

270 cards in set

- Starter decks contain 60 cards; starter displays contain 10 starters
- Booster packs contain 15 cards; booster displays contain 24 boosters

Designed by **James Ernest**, based on a concept by **Phil Foglio**

Not every CCG was designed to make its creators a pile of money. Some are for "amusement purposes only," and none more so than ***Xxxenophile***, the only sexually-themed CCG to come down the pike.

Familiar to comics readers first through his art on *MythAdventures*, comic artist Phil Foglio became a favorite of gamers with his "What's New" comics in *Dragon*. In the late 1980s, Foglio published *Xxxenophile*, an adult comics romp, and later took an early interest in CCGs as an artist for several ***Magic*** cards. (G-rated, of course.) Foglio drew from the *Xxxenophile* world to produce a "CCG for adults." There's nudity, but it's more naughty than explicit — the comic books are racier — but it's still *definitely* not for kids, and it says so. *Xxxenophile* aspires to the lofty title of "adult party game," the monicker given to games on the top shelf at Spencer's Gifts.

The game's mechanics are understandably simple. Players (generally two to four) form a 12-card grid. Then, by flipping cards over, turning cards and matching symbols on the edges of the cards, they "pop" the cards, putting them in their score pile and sometimes following special instructions on the cards. With the exception of Gizmos, a type of card that affects gameplay after you pop it, all cards have a point value from one to ten. The winner of the game is the first player to accrue 100 points.

At the end of the game, players take turn popping cards until there are none left (during the course of the game, popped cards are replaced with cards from your hand). Cards a player pops during and after the game are his to keep, so it's not uncommon for a dozen or so cards to change hands in the course of a game. Because of this, and because all cards are mixed together in the opening grid, granting no advantage to any player, deck construction is virtually nonexistent and the cards themselves are all of equal rarity. The gameplay itself can be quite engaging and contains a surprising amount of strategy.

While nobody will mistake it for *Magic*, a game of *XXXenophile* can take some considerable thinking, but not so much that you take it seriously. If you do, just look at the pictures some more — but only if you're over 18! — *Jason Winter*

Concept	♥♥♡♡♡
Gameplay	♥♥♥♡♡
Card art	♥♥♥♥♡
Player pool	♡♡♡♡♡

Set (270 cards)	137.50
Starter Display Box	32.00
Booster Display Box	39.00
Starter Deck	8.00
Booster Pack	2.00

You will need **30** nine-pocket pages to store this set. (15 doubled up)

Card name	Era	Value	Price
1			
☐ 50s Aliens who Dig Earth Women	Pst	2	0.60
☐ AEther Bunny	Fut	4	0.60
☐ Alien Abduction Squad	Mod	9	2.90
☐ Alien Sex Mechanic	Fut	4	0.60
☐ Amelia Earhart	Pst	8	8.00
☐ Amorous Blob	Pst	2	0.60
☐ Andromeda Swain	Fut	6	0.60
☐ Anemone Mine	Fut	6	0.60
☐ Aphrodisiac of Lila	Pst	Gizmo (0)	0.90
2			
☐ Aphrodite	Pst	5	0.60
☐ Asteroid Annie	Fut	7	1.40
☐ Atlantean Witch Doctor	Pst	8	1.90
☐ Axelrod Rimthruster	Fut	5	0.60
☐ Babe Magnet	Fut	Gizmo (0)	0.90
☐ Bactram, Mad Political Scientist	Fut	7	1.40
☐ Baron Droit de Seigneur	Pst	2	0.60
☐ Bedside Manor	Pst	3	0.60
☐ Bermuda Triangle	Pst	8	1.90
3			
☐ Bernadette Sysoptrix	Fut	3	0.60
☐ Betelgeusian Pleasure Beast	Fut	4	0.60
☐ Big Book O' Forbidden Knowledge	Pst	Gizmo (0)	0.90

Card name	Era	Value	Price
☐ Big Dumb Lem	Mod	1	0.60
☐ Big Red Hammer	Pst	Gizmo (0)	0.90
☐ Bilitis the Courtesan	Pst	6	0.60
☐ Bi-Plane	Pst	7	1.40
☐ Bites-On-The-Neck	Mod	6	0.60
☐ Blow-Up Luv Panda	Pst	Gizmo (0)	0.90
4			
☐ Blue Opal	Pst	4	0.60
☐ Boolatraaca	Pst	7	1.40
☐ Bouncin' Buddy	Mod	Gizmo (0)	0.90
☐ Boy Toy	Mod	Gizmo (0)	0.90
☐ Brigid the Witch	Pst	3	0.60
☐ Brother-in-Law from Another Planet	Fut	6	0.60
☐ Buffalo Gals	Mod	1	0.60
☐ Cajun Hog-Eating Contest	Mod	7	1.40
☐ Caligula's Smarter Brother	Pst	10	2.90
5			
☐ Canned Heat	Mod	Gizmo (0)	0.90
☐ Captain Jackler	Fut	2	0.60
☐ Cat-Headed Women	Fut	5	0.60
☐ Catherine the Great	Pst	7	1.40
☐ Cernunnos	Pst	6	0.60
☐ Chain of Command	Pst	Gizmo (0)	0.90
☐ Chief Engineer Zarazewski	Fut	5	0.60
☐ Chinese Ghost	Pst	7	1.40
☐ Chronoteen, Empress of Time	Fut	0	0.90
6			
☐ Clydesdale Bob	Pst	5	0.60
☐ Colossus of Rhodes	Pst	10	2.90
☐ Control Room	Fut	4	0.60
☐ Cornelia Cannon	Mod	6	0.60

Card name	Era	Value	Price
☐ Cornelia's Double Bed	Mod	Gizmo (0)	0.90
☐ Count Pointercount	Mod	3	0.60
☐ Crash Callahan	Fut	5	0.60
☐ Crazed Cheerleader from Space	Fut	5	0.60
☐ Crop Circle Jerks	Mod	3	0.60
7			
☐ Crown of Oriana	Pst	Gizmo (0)	0.90
☐ Cult of the Jade Nipple	Fut	5	0.60
☐ Cyborg Officer Mariko Bugatti	Fut	1	0.60
☐ Cyrano de Bergerac	Pst	3	0.60
☐ Daisy Chaing	Fut	3	0.60
☐ Dark and Stormy Knight	Pst	3	0.60
☐ Death Nell	Fut	1	0.60
☐ Deep Space Incubus	Fut	6	0.60
☐ Deep Space Succubus	Fut	8	1.90
8			
☐ Deus Ex Machina Man	Fut	6	0.60
☐ Dionysus	Pst	8	1.90
☐ Dithmys the Dryad	Mod	6	0.60
☐ Doc Havoc	Pst	7	1.40
☐ Doctor Daphne Goodbody	Fut	3	0.60
☐ Earl of Sandwich	Pst	7	1.40
☐ Ecuador Jillette	Mod	5	0.60
☐ EEEAAARRGH, Prehistoric God of Love	Pst	9	2.90
☐ Elizabeth Spaceholder	Fut	5	0.60
9			
☐ Empress Wu	Pst	3	0.60
☐ Enchilada Progress	Mod	5	0.60
☐ Enid Weems	Fut	6	0.60
☐ Erotic Potato Prints	Pst	Gizmo (0)	0.90
☐ Evil Dr. Oscillator	Pst	2	0.60

RARITY KEY **C** = Common **U** = Uncommon **R** = Rare **VR** = Very Rare **UR** = Ultra Rare **F** = Foil card **X** = Fixed/standard in all decks

Card name	Era	Value	Price
Ewan McKay	Fut	6	0.60
Ex-Boyfriend	Mod	4	0.60
Ex-Girlfriend	Mod	4	0.60
Falling Skywater	Pst	6	0.60

10

Card name	Era	Value	Price
Felga Darkin	Fut	6	0.60
Finlay Hong	Fut	6	0.60
Fountain of Youth	Pst	0	0.90
French Moon Maid	Mod	7	1.40
Friendly Monolith	Fut	Gizmo (0)	0.90
Frog Prince	Pst	2	0.60
Garden of Earthly Delights	Pst	7	1.40
Gene Poole	Fut	2	0.60
Geodetic Dame	Fut	3	0.60

11

Card name	Era	Value	Price
Giant Arcturan Brain in a Jar	Fut	5	0.60
Governor Weems	Fut	6	0.60
Greased Pig	Mod	10	2.90
Green Light District	Fut	5	0.60
Headmistress Holly	Pst	3	0.60
Heemu Fee	Fut	6	0.60
Helen Highwater	Mod	4	0.60
Helen of Troy	Pst	4	0.60
Helena Handbasket	Mod	6	0.60

12

Card name	Era	Value	Price
Heroine of the Revolution	Pst	2	0.60
High-Flyin' Dirigible of Love	Pst	6	0.60
Hir-Ha-Hur-Low-Toe, Jr.	Fut	5	0.60
His Girl Tuesday	Mod	6	0.60
Home Entertainment Center	Mod	2	0.60
Huge Organ	Pst	Gizmo (0)	0.90
Huldra Maid	Pst	7	1.40
Hung Jury	Mod	9	2.90
Idyllic Planetoid	Fut	5	0.60

13

Card name	Era	Value	Price
Immel, High Priestess of Hootabix	Fut	6	0.60
Indecent Exposure Gordon	Fut	4	0.60
Iris Green, Gizmo Queen	Mod	4	0.60
Island of Lust Toys	Fut	6	0.60
Island of Mu	Pst	6	0.60
Jack Tarr	Pst	7	1.40
Jamel Ak-Kahreezistin	Pst	4	0.60
James Madison	Pst	0	0.90
Jerry Wa	Mod	7	1.40

14

Card name	Era	Value	Price
Jillian Billion	Mod	3	0.60
John of Gaunt	Pst	9	2.90
Julie Ann Frye	Mod	2	0.60
Killer B-Girl	Mod	5	0.60
King Leer	Pst	3	0.60
King Wazaromo XXIII	Mod	6	0.60
Kintu, the First Man	Pst	5	0.60
Klipshack Dragonspawn	Pst	5	0.60
Kublai Khan and Molly	Pst	8	1.90

15

Card name	Era	Value	Price
Kwai'utl	Pst	5	0.60
Lab Assistant Laurie	Fut	4	0.60
Lady Atosa	Mod	3	0.60
Lazlo, Exhibitionist from Neptune	Mod	8	1.90
Le Petit Mort	Mod	6	0.60
Leather Lads of Lomax	Fut	7	1.40
Leda and the Gecko	Fut	2	0.60
Leilani	Pst	0	0.90
Lil' Robot Buddy	Fut	Gizmo (0)	0.90

16

Card name	Era	Value	Price
Lilith	Pst	3	0.60
Lio of Ion Clan	Fut	6	0.60
Lord Thermofax	Fut	4	0.60
Lost Planet of Avalon	Fut	7	1.40
Lost Temple of Hootcheeku	Fut	6	0.60
Lovely Inga, the Milkmaid	Mod	4	0.60
Madame de Pompadour	Pst	1	0.60
Magic Whirlpool	Mod	6	0.60

Card name	Era	Value	Price
Marian Warrior	Fut	1	0.60

17

Card name	Era	Value	Price
Marital Artist	Mod	4	0.60
Marquis de Sade	Pst	7	1.40
Martian Queen	Fut	6	0.60
Marvin Teeth	Mod	7	1.40
Master of Tantric Sax	Fut	6	0.60
Master of the Cyber-Geisha	Fut	4	0.60
Mata Hari	Pst	5	0.60
Medical Officer Roytman	Fut	8	1.90
Meedrax Dragonget	Pst	9	2.90

18

Card name	Era	Value	Price
Men in Black Leather	Mod	1	0.60
Milady's Chambers	Pst	6	0.60
Mind Blower	Fut	6	0.60
Mind Control Doodad	Fut	Gizmo (0)	0.90
Minoan Bull Dancer	Pst	2	0.60
Miranda	Mod	4	0.60
Mistress Acapella House	Fut	3	0.60
Mistress of the Close Encounter	Fut	6	0.60
Moon Palace	Fut	0	0.90

19

Card name	Era	Value	Price
Mr. Right	Mod	7	1.40
Ms. Right	Mod	7	1.40
My Favorite Venusian	Mod	3	0.60
My Gazebo on Ganymede	Fut	5	0.60
Mysterious Dr. Pushtak	Fut	7	1.40
Naked City	Fut	5	0.60
Narcissus	Pst	5	0.60
Narnax, Janitor of the Jungle	Pst	5	0.60
Net Surfer	Fut	4	0.60

20

Card name	Era	Value	Price
Nether Region Nine	Fut	9	2.90
Nibbly Noo, Phone Sex Goddess	Fut	7	1.40
Nicely Curved Space	Fut	4	0.60
Nik, Fodunk of the Glass Sveege	Fut	Other	0.90
Nine Inch Neil	Fut	8	1.90
Nuclear Powered Vibrator	Fut	Gizmo (0)	0.90
Nude Ranch	Mod	6	0.60
Odeon Hammersmith	Fut	5	0.60
Officer Friendly	Mod	4	0.60

21

Card name	Era	Value	Price
Okaraska	Pst	5	0.60
One Night Stan	Mod	3	0.60
Oob the Naiad	Mod	5	0.60
Orgasm Lass	Mod	4	0.60
Pan	Pst	5	0.60
Parallel Dimension	Mod	8	1.90
Pleasure Centrifuge	Fut	Gizmo (0)	0.90
Plot Device	Fut	Gizmo (0)	0.90
Police Sirens	Mod	8	1.90

22

Card name	Era	Value	Price
Prizewinning Cucumber	Pst	Gizmo (0)	0.90
Python O'Malley	Fut	5	0.60
Queen of Sheba	Pst	3	0.60
Queen of Tarts	Pst	2	0.60
Queen of the Moon	Pst	5	0.60
Queeva Spang	Fut	7	1.40
Rashoo, Temple Maiden	Fut	7	1.40
Rising Tsar	Pst	7	1.40
Rivetts O'Reilly	Pst	2	0.60

23

Card name	Era	Value	Price
Robot Queen Rugosa	Fut	2	0.60
Robot Soldier	Fut	Gizmo (0)	0.90
Roman Bvbble Bath	Pst	6	0.60
Roxanne	Pst	5	0.60
Roxelana	Pst	1	0.60
Santa Claus	Mod	6	0.60
Scoober Spider Web	Pst	9	2.90
Seduction Pump	Mod	Gizmo (0)	0.90

Card name	Era	Value	Price
Sex Drive	Fut	Gizmo (0)	0.90

24

Card name	Era	Value	Price
Shameless Hussar	Pst	7	1.40
Shango, God of Thunder	Pst	5	0.60
Shinda Finn, International Spy	Mod	6	0.60
Sidonie Gabrielle Claudine Colette	Pst	6	0.60
Silicon Valley Girl	Fut	3	0.60
Sinbad	Pst	6	0.60
Skendo, Desert Warrior	Pst	9	2.90
Slag-Blah Priestess	Fut	7	1.40
Slumber Party	Mod	6	0.60

25

Card name	Era	Value	Price
Smokey Joe	Mod	1	0.60
Sneaky Pete	Fut	5	0.60
Sneevax, Cute But Evil Space Babe	Fut	7	1.40
Sparks Katkin	Fut	5	0.60
Squibulator	Pst	Gizmo (0)	0.90
Stan Bloon, the Man in the Moon	Pst	6	0.60
Steam Powered Love Doll	Pst	Gizmo (0)	0.90
Steamy Shower	Mod	6	0.60
Stonehenge	Pst	4	0.60

26

Card name	Era	Value	Price
Sultan Bogalaka's Harem	Pst	6	0.60
Sweet Talkin' Swan	Pst	7	1.40
Syd Krause	Mod	6	0.60
Technomage	Fut	6	0.60
Tempus Fidget, Chronovoyeur	Fut	4	0.60
Thaddeus, the Toy Builder	Fut	0	0.60
The Body Electric	Fut	Gizmo (0)	0.90
The Cartoonist	Mod	5	0.60
The Empress' Towel Boy	Pst	7	1.40

27

Card name	Era	Value	Price
The Eunuch	Mod	10	2.90
The Great Googlimoogli	Fut	4	0.60
The Hatchback of Notre Dame	Mod	7	1.40
The Little Engine That Could	Mod	Gizmo (0)	0.90
The Little Stripper	Mod	2	0.60
The Omicron	Fut	6	0.60
The Villainous Vibrator	Mod	2	0.60
Theodora, Empress of Rome	Pst	6	0.60
Thick Gloves	Fut	Gizmo (0)	0.90

28

Card name	Era	Value	Price
Three-Way Bulb	Fut	Gizmo (0)	0.90
Tia of Klim Point	Fut	4	0.60
Time Warp	Pst	7	1.40
Toby Robinson	Mod	6	0.60
TV Repairman	Mod	8	1.90
Universal Joint	Fut	6	0.60
Unnatural Axe	Pst	Gizmo (0)	0.90
Vibrator Repairman	Fut	4	0.60
Victoria Frankenstein	Pst	5	0.60

29

Card name	Era	Value	Price
Ving Tillamook	Fut	3	0.60
Vinnie V. da Vinci	Pst	3	0.60
Voin of Wukkerbee	Pst	7	1.40
Vroomhilde	Pst	4	0.60
Wand Of Pleasure	Pst	Gizmo (0)	0.90
We-Don't-Know-What-It-Is-But-We-Like-It	Fut	Gizmo (0)	0.90
Wet Blanket	Mod	Gizmo (0)	0.90
Wooden Cow of Pasiphae	Pst	Gizmo (0)	0.90
Xanadu	Pst	7	1.40

30

Card name	Era	Value	Price
XXX-Ray Specs	Fut	Gizmo (0)	0.90
Xynotreen	Pst	3	0.60
Xytina, the Lotus Eater	Pst	7	1.40
Your Own Apartment	Fut	5	0.60
Zero-G Chamber	Fut	9	2.90
Z'Gof9-7, Pyramid Builder	Pst	3	0.60
'Zilla Suit	Mod	Gizmo (0)	0.90
Zola Ching	Pst	3	0.60
Zonifax the Irradiated	Fut	6	0.60

RARITY KEY C = Common U = Uncommon R = Rare VR = Very Rare UR = Ultra Rare F = Foil card X = Fixed/standard in all decks

Young Jedi

Decipher • First set, **Menace of Darth Maul**, released **May 1999**
140 cards plus **18** foils in set
- Starter decks contain 60 cards; starter displays contain 12 starters
- Booster packs contain 11 cards; Booster displays contain 30 boosters

Part of the biggest licensing wave in history, the *Star Wars Episode I* CCG **Young Jedi** hit stores at just about the time the movie was released in the United States. Aimed at a younger crowd than Decipher's **Star Wars** CCG, *Young Jedi* is a very simple game, with few numbers on cards and no game text at all. With the success of the *Star Wars* CCG and brand new characters to play with from *Episode I*, plenty of people got in on the hype and gave the game a try.

In order to win a game of *Young Jedi*, a player needs to win two out of three of the major planets from the movie: Naboo, Coruscant, and Tatooine. To win a planet, players must fight their opponent there using a battle plan, essentially a stack of cards at a location for a game of "War." Power totals are compared when two characters come up against each other and whoever has less loses. Weapons and battle-related cards can add to the power totals.

Unfortunately, some of the main characters in the movie aren't very powerful in the CCG, and most top tournament decks upon the game's release revolved around less important characters, such as Battle Droids, Jawas, and Tusken Raiders. This would change as the game evolved in later expansions.

With its initial release, *Young Jedi* became a huge success. But subsequent expansions didn't change the game all that much, and as initial public enthusiasm for the new movie soured, *Young Jedi* took a hard hit with its second set, **The Jedi Council**. The real big ticket for kids in 1999, it turned out, was another CCG altogether, **Pokémon**. But *Young Jedi* mantains a following and new rules in new sets could bring the game back to what it once was when it first hit the shelves in 1999. Especially if *Episode II* is a better movie! **— Joe Alread**

> You will need
> **16**
> nine-pocket
> pages to store
> this set.
> (8 doubled up)

Concept	●●●●○
Gameplay	●●●○○
Card art	●●●○○
Player pool	●●●●○

Complete Set (140 cards + 18 foils)	**177.50**
Regular Set (140 cards)	**117.50**
Starter Display Box	**99.50**
Booster Display Box	**79.00**
Starter Deck	**9.50**
Booster Pack	**3.00**
Collector's Box (12 packs)	**35.00**

Foil cards	Side	Type	Rarity	Price
[1]				
☐ Anakin Skywalker's Podracer	L	Wpn	CF	4.00
☐ Battle Droid Squad, Assault Unit	D	Ch	UF	10.00
☐ Ben Quadinaros' Podracer	D	Wpn	CF	4.00
☐ Bravo 1, Naboo Starfighter	L	SS	CF	4.00
☐ C-3PO, Anakin's Creation	L	Ch	UF	11.00
☐ Darth Maul, Sith Apprentice	D	Ch	RF	40.00
☐ Darth Sidious, Sith Master	D	Ch	RF	30.00
☐ Destroyer Droid Squad, Security Division	D	Ch	UF	10.00
☐ Gasgano's Podracer	D	Wpn	CF	4.00
[2]				
☐ Jar Jar Binks, Gungan Chuba Thief	L	Ch	RF	25.00
☐ Mace Windu, Jedi Master	L	Ch	UF	15.00
☐ Mawhonic's Podracer	D	Wpn	CF	4.00
☐ Obi-Wan Kenobi, Young Jedi	L	Ch	RF	35.00
☐ Obi-Wan Kenobi's Lightsaber	L	Wpn	CF	5.00
☐ Queen Amidala, Ruler of Naboo	L	Ch	UF	10.00
☐ Republic Cruiser, Transport	L	SS	CF	4.00
☐ Sebulba's Podracer	D	Wpn	UF	8.00
☐ Teemto Pagalies' Podracer	D	Wpn	CF	4.00

Card name	Side	Type	Rarity	Price
[1]				
☐ Anakin Skywalker, Meet Obi-Wan Kenobi	L	Btl	U	0.70
☐ Anakin Skywalker, Podracer Pilot	L	Ch	R	6.00
☐ Anakin Skywalker's Podracer	L	Wpn	R	3.80
☐ Ann and Tann Gella, Sebulba's Attendants	D	Ch	U	0.60
☐ Are You An Angel?	L	Btl	U	0.70

Card name	Side	Type	Rarity	Price
☐ At Last We Will Have Revenge	D	Btl	R	3.00
☐ Aurra Sing, Bounty Hunter	D	Ch	R	5.00
☐ Aurra Sing's Blaster Rifle	D	Wpn	R	4.00
☐ Battle Droid Blaster Rifle	D	Wpn	C	0.25
[2]				
☐ Battle Droid: Infantry AAT Division	D	Ch	C	0.25
☐ Battle Droid: Infantry MTT Division	D	Ch	C	0.25
☐ Battle Droid: Officer AAT Division	D	Ch	C	0.25
☐ Battle Droid: Officer MTT Division	D	Ch	C	0.25
☐ Battle Droid: Pilot AAT Division	D	Ch	C	0.25
☐ Battle Droid: Pilot MTT Division	D	Ch	C	0.25
☐ Battle Droid: Security AAT Division	D	Ch	C	0.25
☐ Battle Droid: Security MTT Division	D	Ch	C	0.25
☐ Battle Droid Squad, Assault Unit	D	Ch	R	4.00
[3]				
☐ Battleship, Trade Federation Transport	D	SS	C	0.25
☐ Begin Landing Your Troops	D	Btl	C	0.25
☐ Ben Quadinaros' Podracer	D	Wpn	U	0.70
☐ Ben Quadinaros, Podracer Pilot	D	Ch	U	0.60
☐ Bib Fortuna, Twi'lek Advisor	D	Ch	U	0.70
☐ Blaster	L	Wpn	C	0.25
☐ Blaster	D	Wpn	C	0.25
☐ Blaster Rifle	L	Wpn	C	0.25
☐ Blaster Rifle	D	Wpn	C	0.25
[4]				
☐ Boonta Eve Podrace	D	Btl	U	0.60
☐ Boss Nass, Leader of the Gungans	L	Ch	U	0.70
☐ Bravo 1, Naboo Starfighter	L	SS	U	0.80

Card name	Side	Type	Rarity	Price
☐ Bravo Pilot, Veteran Flyer	L	Ch	C	0.25
☐ C-3PO, Anakin's Creation	L	Ch	R	4.00
☐ Captain Panaka, Protector of the Queen	L	Ch	R	3.00
☐ Captain Panaka's Blaster	L	Wpn	C	0.25
☐ Captain Tarpals, Gungan Guard	L	Ch	U	0.70
☐ Cha Skrunee Da Pat, Sleemo	L	Btl	C	0.25
[5]				
☐ Coruscant • Capital City	L	Loc	X	1.00
☐ Coruscant • Jedi Council Chamber	D	Loc	X	1.00
☐ Counterparts	L	Btl	U	0.70
☐ Da Beings Hereabouts Cawazy	L	Btl	C	0.25
☐ Darth Maul, Sith Apprentice	D	Ch	R	12.00
☐ Darth Maul, Sith Lord	D	Ch	X	3.00
☐ Darth Maul's Starfighter, Sith Infiltrator	D	SS	R	4.00
☐ Darth Sidious, Sith Master	D	Ch	R	8.00
☐ Destroyer Droid, Defense Droid	D	Ch	C	0.25
[6]				
☐ Destroyer Droid Squad, Security Division	D	Ch	R	4.00
☐ Destroyer Droid, Wheel Droid	D	Ch	C	0.25
☐ Droid Starfighter	D	SS	C	0.25
☐ Electropole	L	Wpn	C	0.25
☐ Enough Of This Pretense	L	Btl	U	0.50
☐ Eopie	L	Wpn	C	0.25
☐ Fear Attracts The Fearful	L	Btl	U	0.70

Young Jedi • Sample

First released at the *Star Wars* celebration in Denver, Colorodo, these **Young Jedi** demo decks, labelled "Sample," were the easiest way to teach people the game from the ground up.

With 20-card decks for each side, the demo games were quick, easy, and fun to play. The cards are not tournament legal, due to different numbers on the fronts and markings on the back. These decks were a major part of the massive amount of demos Decipher volunteers performed in order to get the game out into the public.

RARITY KEY **C** = Common **U** = Uncommon **R** = Rare **VR** = Very Rare **UR** = Ultra Rare **F** = Foil card **X** = Fixed/standard in all decks

Card Name	Side	Type	Rarity	Price
Flash Speeder	L	Wpn	C	0.25
Gardulla the Hutt, Crime Lord	D	Ch	U	0.70
7				
Gasgano, Podracer Pilot	D	Ch	U	0.60
Gasgano's Podracer	D	Wpn	U	0.70
Gragra, Chuba Peddler	D	Ch	C	0.25
Grueling Contest	D	Btl	U	0.70
Gungan Curiosity	L	Btl	C	0.25
Gungan Guard	L	Ch	C	0.25
Gungan Official, Bureaucrat	L	Ch	C	0.25
Gungan Soldier, Scout	L	Ch	C	0.25
Gungan Solider, Veteran	L	Ch	C	0.25
8				
Gungan Warrior, Infantry	L	Ch	C	0.25
He Was Meant To Help You	L	Btl	U	0.70
I Have A Bad Feeling About This	L	Btl	U	0.70
In Complete Control	D	Btl	C	0.25
Ishi Tib, Warrior	L	Ch	C	0.25
Ithorian, Merchant	L	Ch	C	0.25
I've Been Trained In Defense	L	Btl	U	0.70
Jabba the Hutt, Vile Crime Lord	D	Ch	R	5.00
Jar Jar Binks' Electropole	L	Wpn	U	0.70
9				
Jar Jar Binks, Gungan Chuba Thief	L	Ch	R	5.00
Jawa, Bargainer	L	Ch	X	0.80
Jawa Ion Blaster	L	Wpn	C	0.25
Jawa, Thief	L	Ch	C	0.25
Jedi Lightsaber, Constructed by Ki-Adi-Mundi	L	Wpn	C	0.25
Kaa Bazza Kundee Hodrudda!	D	Btl	U	0.70
Kaadu	L	Wpn	C	0.25
Mace Windu, Jedi Master	L	Ch	R	5.00
Mas Amedda, Vice Chancellor	L	Ch	U	0.70

Card Name	Side	Type	Rarity	Price
10				
Mawhonic, Podracer Pilot	D	Ch	U	0.60
Mawhonic's Podracer	D	Wpn	U	0.70
Multi Troop Transport	D	Wpn	U	0.70
Naboo Blaster	L	Wpn	C	0.25
Naboo Officer, Battle Planner	L	Ch	U	0.70
Naboo Security, Guard	L	Ch	C	0.25
Naboo Starfighter	L	SS	C	0.25
Naboo • Gungan Swamp	D	Loc	X	1.00
Naboo • Theed Palace	L	Loc	X	1.00
11				
Neimoidian, Trade Federation Pilot	D	Ch	X	1.00
Obi-Wan Kenobi, Jedi Padawan	L	Ch	X	3.50
Obi-Wan Kenobi, Young Jedi	L	Ch	R	10.00
Obi-Wan Kenobi's Lightsaber	L	Wpn	R	4.00
Opee Sea Killer	D	Btl	C	0.25
Padmé Naberrie, Handmaiden	L	Ch	R	4.00
Passel Argente, Senator	D	Ch	C	0.25
Pit Droid, Engineer	D	Ch	C	0.25
Pit Droid, Heavy Lifter	D	Ch	C	0.25
12				
Pit Droid, Mechanic	D	Ch	C	0.25
Podrace Preparation	D	Btl	U	0.70
Queen Amidala, Royal Leader	L	Ch	R	5.00
Queen Amidala, Ruler of Naboo	L	Ch	R	4.00
Qui-Gon Jinn, Jedi Master	L	Ch	R	6.00
R2-D2, Astromech Droid	L	Ch	R	4.00
Rabé, Handmaiden	L	Ch	U	0.60
Rep Been, Gungan	L	Ch	U	0.60
Republic Cruiser, Transport	L	SS	C	0.25
13				
Ric Olié, Ace Pilot	L	Ch	U	0.70
Royal Guard, Leader	L	Ch	C	0.25
Royal Guard, Veteran	L	Ch	C	0.25

Card Name	Side	Type	Rarity	Price
Sandstorm	D	Btl	C	0.25
Sebulba, Bad-Tempered Dug	D	Ch	R	4.00
Sebulba's Podracer	D	Wpn	R	3.00
Security Volunteers	L	Btl	C	0.25
Shmi's Pride	L	Btl	U	0.70
Sith Lightsaber	D	Wpn	R	4.00
14				
Sith Probe Droid, Spy Drone	D	Ch	C	0.25
Sniper	D	Btl	C	0.25
STAP	D	Wpn	U	0.70
Tatooine • Desert Landing Site	D	Loc	X	0.60
Tatooine • Podrace Arena	L	Loc	X	0.90
Tatooine Thunder Rifle	D	Wpn	C	0.25
Teemto Pagalies' Podracer	D	Wpn	U	0.70
Teemto Pagalies, Podracer Pilot	D	Ch	U	0.60
The Federation Has Gone Too Far	L	Btl	C	0.25
15				
The Invasion Is On Schedule	D	Btl	C	0.25
The Negotiations Were Short	L	Btl	C	0.25
The Queen's Plan	L	Btl	C	0.25
Trade Federation Tank, Armored Division	D	Ch	R	3.50
Trade Federation Tank Laser Cannon	D	Wpn	U	1.00
Tusken Raider, Marksman	D	Ch	C	0.25
Tusken Raider, Noman	D	Ch	C	0.25
Vile Gangsters	D	Btl	U	0.70
Watto, Slave Owner	D	Ch	R	3.30
16				
Watto's Wager	D	Btl	U	0.70
We're Not In Trouble Yet	L	Btl	U	0.70
Yoda, Jedi Master	L	Ch	R	6.00
You Have Been Well Trained	D	Btl	R	3.00
Yousa Guys Bombad!	L	Btl	R	3.00

Young Jedi • *The Jedi Council*

Decipher • Released **October 1999**

140 cards and **18** foils in set

- Starter decks contain 60 cards; starter displays contain 12 starters
- Booster packs contain 11 cards; booster displays contain 30 boosters

Players looked forward to **Young Jedi**'s first expansion, **The Jedi Council**, thinking about what new strategies might be available to them in the new cards. Unfortunately, there wasn't much to see.

Character cards were mostly the same as the versions from **Menace of Darth Maul**, except that they got power bonuses on Coruscant, not Tatooine.

There were new action cards in the set that introduced extremely powerful strategies into the tournament scene, strategies that went on to win the 1999 World Championships. Other than that though, the set wasn't interesting as a whole to **Young Jedi** players. — *Joe Alread*

You will need **16** nine-pocket pages to store this set. (8 doubled up)

		Price
Complete Set (140 cards + 18 foils)		**185.00**
Regular Set (140 cards)		**115.00**
Starter Display Box		**52.50**
Booster Display Box		**67.50**
Starter Deck		**10.00**
Booster Pack		**3.00**
Collector's Box (12 packs)		**25.00**

Foil cards	Side	Type	Rarity	Price
1				
Amidala's Blaster	L	Wpn	VF	5.00
Captain Panaka, Amidala's Bodyguard	L	Ch	SF	7.00
Darth Maul, Master of Evil	D	Ch	UF	38.00
Darth Maul's Lightsaber	D	Wpn	VF	6.00
Darth Maul's Sith Speeder	D	SS	VF	5.00
Darth Sidious, Lord of the Sith	D	Ch	UF	25.00
Jabba the Hutt, Gangster	D	Ch	SF	8.00
Lott Dod, Neimoidian Senator	D	Ch	VF	5.00
Mace Windu, Senior Jedi Council Member	L	Ch	SF	9.00
2				
Nute Gunray, Neimoidian Viceroy	D	Ch	SF	7.00

Foil cards	Side	Type	Rarity	Price
Obi-Wan Kenobi, Jedi Apprentice	L	Ch	UF	30.00
Padmé Naberrie, Queen's Handmaiden	L	Ch	SF	9.00
Queen Amidala, Representative of Naboo	L	Ch	VF	8.30
Qui-Gon Jinn, Jedi Protector	L	Ch	UF	25.00
Qui-Gon Jinn's Lightsaber	L	Wpn	VF	6.30
R2-D2, Loyal Droid	L	Ch	VF	7.40
Rune Haako, Neimoidian Advisor	D	Ch	VF	5.30
Watto, Junk Merchant	D	Ch	SF	8.50

Card Name	Side	Type	Rarity	Price
1				
Adi Gallia, Corellian Jedi Master	L	Ch	U	0.90
Adi Gallia's Lightsaber	L	Wpn	U	0.90
Aks Moe, Senator	D	Ch	C	0.25
Amidala's Blaster	L	Wpn	R	3.50
Anakin Skywalker, Child of Prophecy	L	Ch	R	5.50
Ascension Gun	L	Wpn	C	0.25
Balance To The Force	L	Btl	U	0.90
Battle Droid Blaster Rifle	D	Wpn	C	0.25
Battle Droid: Infantry, Assault Division	D	Ch	C	0.25

Card name	Side	Type	Rarity	Price
2				
Battle Droid: Infantry, Guard Division	D	Ch	C	0.25
Battle Droid: Officer, Assault Division	D	Ch	C	0.25
Battle Droid: Officer, Guard Division	D	Ch	C	0.25
Battle Droid: Pilot, Assault Division	D	Ch	C	0.25
Battle Droid: Pilot, Guard Division	D	Ch	C	0.25
Battle Droid: Security, Assault Division	D	Ch	C	0.25
Battle Droid: Security, Guard Division	D	Ch	C	0.25
Battle Droid Squad, Escort Unit	D	Ch	R	4.00
Battleship, Trade Federation Transport	D	SS	C	0.25
3				
Blaster	L	Wpn	C	0.25
Blaster	D	Wpn	C	0.25
Blaster Rifle	L	Wpn	C	0.25
Blaster Rifle	D	Wpn	C	0.25
Boss Nass, Gungan Leader	L	Ch	U	0.90
Brave Little Droid	L	Btl	U	0.90
Bravo 2, Naboo Starfighter	L	SS	U	0.90
Bravo Pilot, Naboo Volunteer	L	Ch	C	0.25
Captain Panaka, Amidala's Bodyguard	L	Ch	R	4.00
4				
Captain Tarpals, Gungan Battle Leader	L	Ch	U	0.90
Clegg Holdfast, Podracer Pilot	D	Ch	U	0.90

RARITY KEY C = Common U = Uncommon R = Rare VR = Very Rare UR = Ultra Rare F = Foil card X = Fixed/standard in all decks

Card Name	Side	Type	Rarity	Price
☐ Clegg Holdfast's Podracer	D	Wpn	U	0.90
☐ Coruscant • Galactic Senate	D	Loc	X	1.00
☐ Coruscant • Jedi Council Chamber	L	Loc	X	1.00
☐ Coruscant Guard Blaster Rifle	L	Wpn	U	0.90
☐ Coruscant Guard, Chancellor's Guard	L	Ch	C	0.25
☐ Coruscant Guard, Coruscant Detachment	L	Ch	C	0.25
☐ Coruscant Guard, Officer	L	Ch	C	0.25
☐ Coruscant Guard, Peacekeeper	L	Ch	C	0.25
☐ Darth Maul, Master of Evil	D	Ch	R	9.70
☐ Darth Maul, Sith Warrior	D	Ch	X	3.50
☐ Darth Maul's Lightsaber	D	Wpn	R	4.00
☐ Darth Maul's Sith Speeder	D	Wpn	R	4.00
☐ Darth Sidious, Lord of the Sith	D	Ch	R	5.70
☐ Depa Billaba, Jedi Master	L	Ch	U	0.90
☐ Destroyer Droid, Assault Droid	D	Ch	C	0.25
☐ Destroyer Droid, Battleship Security	D	Ch	C	0.25
☐ Destroyer Droid Squad, Defense Division	D	Ch	R	4.00
☐ Dos Mackineeks No Comen Here!	L	Btl	C	0.25
☐ Droid Starfighter	D	SS	C	0.25
☐ Dud Bolt, Podracer Pilot	D	Ch	U	0.70
☐ Dud Bolt's Podracer	D	Wpn	U	0.70
☐ Edcel Bar Gane, Roona Senator	D	Ch	C	0.25
☐ Eeth Koth, Zabrak Jedi Master	L	Ch	U	0.70
☐ Eirtaé, Handmaiden	L	Ch	U	0.70
☐ Electropole	L	Wpn	C	0.25
☐ Even Piell, Lannik Jedi Master	L	Ch	U	0.70
☐ Flash Speeder	L	Wpn	C	0.25
☐ Fode and Beed, Podrace Announcer	D	Ch	R	3.00
☐ Galactic Chancellor	L	Btl	C	0.25
☐ Galactic Delegate, Representative	D	Ch	C	0.25
☐ Galactic Senator, Delegate	L	Ch	X	0.50
☐ Gian Speeder	L	Wpn	C	0.25
☐ Hate Leads To Suffering	L	Btl	U	0.70
☐ Horox Ryyder, Senator	D	Ch	C	0.25
☐ I Object!	D	Btl	C	0.25
☐ I Will Deal With Them Myself	D	Btl	C	0.25
☐ I Will Not Cooperate	L	Btl	U	0.70
☐ Invasion!	L	Btl	C	0.25
☐ Jabba the Hutt, Gangster	D	Ch	R	4.50
☐ Jar Jar Binks, Gungan Outcast	L	Ch	R	3.50
☐ Kaadu	L	Wpn	C	0.25
☐ Ki-Adi-Mundi, Cerean Jedi Knight	L	Ch	R	4.00
☐ Let Them Make The First Move	D	Btl	R	3.50
☐ Lott Dod, Neimoidian Senator	D	Ch	R	3.00
☐ Mace Windu, Senior Jedi Council Member	L	Ch	R	4.50
☐ Mars Guo, Podracer Pilot	D	Ch	U	0.90
☐ Mars Guo's Podracer	D	Wpn	U	0.90
☐ May The Force Be With You	L	Btl	C	0.25
☐ Move Against The Jedi First	D	Btl	C	0.25
☐ Multi Troop Transport	D	Wpn	U	0.90
☐ Naboo • Battle Plains	D	Loc	X	0.90
☐ Naboo Blaster	L	Wpn	C	0.25
☐ Naboo • Gungan Swamp	L	Loc	X	0.90
☐ Naboo Officer, Liberator	L	Ch	C	0.25
☐ Naboo Security, Amidala's Guard	L	Ch	C	0.25
☐ Naboo Starfighter	L	SS	C	0.25
☐ Neimoidian Aide, Trade Federation Delegate	D	Ch	X	0.80
☐ Nute Gunray, Neimoidian Viceroy	D	Ch	R	4.00
☐ Obi-Wan Kenobi, Jedi Apprentice	L	Ch	R	8.00
☐ Obi-Wan Kenobi, Jedi Warrior	L	Ch	X	3.00
☐ Ody Mandrell, Podracer Pilot	D	Ch	U	0.90
☐ Ody Mandrell's Podracer	D	Wpn	U	0.90
☐ Open Fire!	D	Btl	U	0.90
☐ Oppo Rancisis, Jedi Master	L	Ch	U	0.90
☐ Padmé Naberrie, Queen's Handmaiden	L	Ch	R	4.00
☐ Plo Koon, Jedi Master	L	Ch	U	0.90
☐ Queen Amidala, Representative of Naboo	L	Ch	R	5.00
☐ Queen Amidala, Voice of Her People	L	Ch	R	4.50
☐ Qui-Gon Jinn, Jedi Protector	L	Ch	R	6.80
☐ Qui-Gon Jinn's Lightsaber	L	Wpn	R	5.00
☐ R2-D2, Loyal Droid	L	Ch	R	4.50
☐ Radiant VII, Republic Cruiser Transport	L	SS	C	0.25
☐ Ratts Tyerell, Podracer Pilot	D	Ch	U	0.90
☐ Ratts Tyerell's Podracer	D	Wpn	U	0.90
☐ Republic Captain, Officer	L	Ch	C	0.25
☐ Republic Pilot, Veteran	L	Ch	C	0.25
☐ Ric Olié, Chief Pilot	L	Ch	U	0.90
☐ Rodian, Mercenary	D	Ch	C	0.25
☐ Rune Haako, Neimoidian Advisor	D	Ch	R	3.80
☐ Saesee Tiin, Iktotchi Jedi Master	L	Ch	U	0.90
☐ Sci Taria, Chancellor's Aide	L	Ch	C	0.25
☐ Seal Off The Bridge	D	Btl	U	0.90
☐ Sebulba, Podracer Pilot	D	Ch	R	4.00
☐ Senator Palpatine	L	Btl	C	0.25
☐ Sith Infiltrator, Starfighter	D	SS	U	0.90
☐ Sith Probe Droid, Hunter Droid	D	Ch	C	0.25
☐ STAP	D	Wpn	U	0.90
☐ Start Your Engines!	D	Btl	U	0.90
☐ Switch To Bio	D	Btl	C	0.25
☐ Take Them To Camp Four	D	Btl	C	0.25
☐ Tatooine • Mos Espa	L	Loc	X	0.90
☐ Tatooine • Podrace Arena	D	Loc	X	0.90
☐ The Might Of The Republic	L	Btl	C	0.25
☐ Thermal Detonator	D	Wpn	U	0.90
☐ Trade Federation Tank, Assault Division	D	Ch	R	4.00
☐ Trade Federation Tank Laser Cannon	D	Wpn	U	1.00
☐ Valorum, Supreme Chancellor	L	Ch	C	0.25
☐ Very Unusual	D	Btl	C	0.25
☐ Vote Of No Confidence	D	Btl	C	0.25
☐ Watto, Junk Merchant	D	Ch	R	4.00
☐ We Are Meeting No Resistance	D	Btl	C	0.25
☐ We Don't Have Time For This	L	Btl	C	0.25
☐ We Have Them On The Run	D	Btl	U	0.90
☐ We Wish To Board At Once	L	Btl	C	0.25
☐ Wisdom Of The Council	L	Btl	R	3.00
☐ Wookiee Senator, Representative	L	Ch	C	0.25
☐ Yaddle, Jedi Master	L	Ch	U	0.90
☐ Yarael Poof, Quermian Jedi Master	L	Ch	U	0.90
☐ Yoda, Jedi Council Member	L	Ch	R	5.00
☐ Yoka To Bantha Poodoo	D	Btl	C	0.25
☐ Your Little Insurrection Is At An End	D	Btl	U	0.90

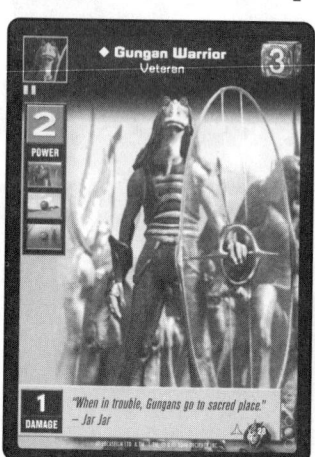

"When in trouble, Gungans go to sacred place."
— Jar Jar

Young Jedi • Battle of Naboo

Decipher • Released **April 2000**

140 cards and **18** foils in set

- Starter decks contain 60 cards; starter displays contain 12 starters
- Booster packs contain 11 cards; booster displays contain 30 boosters

With the lackluster player response to **The Jedi Council**, Decipher injected a little more strategy into **Young Jedi** with the **Battle of Naboo** expansion. Some characters actually got game text for the first time. New card types called effects were introduced. Main characters were finally getting the power that they needed to compete. It was a step in the right direction for a game that needed the help.

Player response was positive, although some argued it was still not enough. The next set, **Duel of the Fates**, would introduce several new game mechanics geared towards making Young Jedi a more complex and interesting game. — **Joe Alread**

You will need
16
nine-pocket
pages to store
this set.
(8 doubled up)

Complete Set (140 cards + 18 foils)		175.00
Regular Set (140 cards)		110.00
Starter Display Box		99.50
Booster Display Box		77.50
Starter Deck		9.00
Booster Pack		3.00

Foil cards	Side	Type	Rarity	Price
☐ Amidala's Starship, Royal Transport	L	SS	VRF	5.70
☐ Aurra Sing, Mercenary	D	Ch	URF	23.75
☐ Battle Droid Squad, Guard Unit	D	Ch	VRF	6.80

Foil Name	Side	Type	Rarity	Price
☐ Darth Maul, Dark Lord of the Sith	D	Ch	URF	30.00
☐ Darth Maul's Lightsaber	D	Wpn	VRF	6.90
☐ Destroyer Droid Squad, Guard Division	D	Ch	SRF	9.20
☐ Mace Windu's Lightsaber	L	Wpn	VRF	5.00
☐ Not For A Sith	D	Btl	VRF	5.70
☐ Nute Gunray, Neimoidian Despot	D	Ch	SRF	7.50
☐ Obi-Wan Kenobi, Jedi Knight	L	Ch	URF	30.00
☐ Queen Amidala, Keeper of the Peace	L	Ch	SRF	11.00
☐ Queen Amidala, Resolute Negotiator	L	Ch	VRF	12.00
☐ Qui-Gon Jinn, Jedi Ambassador	L	Ch	URF	30.50
☐ R2-D2, The Queen's Hero	L	Ch	SRF	10.00

Foil Name	Side	Type	Rarity	Price
☐ The Will Of The Force	L	Btl	VRF	5.90
☐ Trade Federation Tank, Guard Division	D	Ch	SRF	11.00
☐ Trade Federation Tank, Patrol Division	D	Ch	VRF	6.70
☐ Yoda, Jedi Elder	L	Ch	SRF	14.50

Card name	Side	Type	Rarity	Price
☐ A Thousand Terrible Things	D	Btl	C	0.25
☐ After Her!	D	Eff	C	0.25
☐ Alderaan Diplomat, Senator	L	Ch	C	0.25
☐ Amidala's Starship, Royal Transport	L	SS	R	3.80
☐ Anakin Skywalker, Padawan	L	Ch	R	5.00

RARITY KEY C = Common U = Uncommon R = Rare VR = Very Rare UR = Ultra Rare SR = Super Rare F = Foil card X = Fixed in all decks

Card name	Side	Type	Rarity	Price
☐ Aqualish, Galactic Senator	D	Ch	C	0.25
☐ Armored Assault	D	Btl	C	0.25
☐ Aurra Sing, Mercenary	D	Ch	R	3.00
☐ Battle Droid Blaster Rifle	D	Wpn	C	0.25
☐ Battle Droid: Infantry, Defense Division	D	Ch	C	0.25
☐ Battle Droid: Infantry, Patrol Division	D	Ch	C	0.25
☐ Battle Droid: Officer, Defense Division	D	Ch	C	0.25
☐ Battle Droid: Officer, Patrol Division	D	Ch	C	0.25
☐ Battle Droid: Pilot, Defense Division	D	Ch	C	0.25
☐ Battle Droid: Pilot, Patrol Division	D	Ch	C	0.25
☐ Battle Droid: Security, Defense Division	D	Ch	C	0.25
☐ Battle Droid: Security, Patrol Division	D	Ch	C	0.25
☐ Battle Droid Squad, Guard Unit	D	Ch	R	3.80
☐ Battleship, Trade Federation Transport	D	SS	C	0.25
☐ Bith, Musician	D	Ch	U	0.50
☐ Blaster	L	Wpn	C	0.25
☐ Blaster	D	Wpn	C	0.25
☐ Blaster Rifle	D	Wpn	C	0.25
☐ Bombad General	L	Eff	U	0.50
☐ Boss Nass, Gungan Chief	L	Ch	U	0.50
☐ Bravo 3, Naboo Starfighter	L	SS	U	0.70
☐ Bravo Pilot, Ace Flyer	L	Ch	C	0.25
☐ Captain Panaka, Veteran Leader	L	Ch	R	3.80
☐ Captain Tarpals' Electropole	L	Wpn	U	0.50
☐ Captain Tarpals, Gungan Officer	L	Ch	U	0.50
☐ Capture The Viceroy	L	Btl	C	0.25
☐ Celebration	L	Btl	C	0.25
☐ Coruscant • Capital City	D	Loc	X	0.70
☐ Coruscant • Galactic Senate	L	Loc	X	0.70
☐ Coruscant Guard, Chancellor's Escort	L	Ch	C	0.25
☐ Council Member, Naboo Governor	L	Ch	C	0.25
☐ Da Dug Chaaa!	D	Eff	U	0.50
☐ Darth Maul, Dark Lord of the Sith	D	Ch	R	8.80
☐ Darth Maul, Evil Sith Lord	D	Ch	X	1.50
☐ Darth Maul's Electrobinoculars	D	Wpn	U	0.50
☐ Darth Maul's Lightsaber	D	Wpn	R	4.00
☐ Darth Sidious, Sith Manipulator	D	Ch	R	6.00
☐ Daultay Dofine, Neimoidian Attendant	D	Ch	U	0.50
☐ Death From Above	D	Btl	C	0.25
☐ Destroyer Droid, MTT Infantry	D	Ch	C	0.25
☐ Destroyer Droid Squad, Guard Division	D	Ch	R	4.00
☐ Destroyer Droid, Vanguard Droid	D	Ch	C	0.25
☐ Diva Funquita, Dancer	D	Ch	U	0.50
☐ Diva Shaliqua, Singer	D	Ch	U	0.50
☐ Don't Spect A Werm Welcome	D	Btl	C	0.25
☐ Droid Control Ship, Trade Federation Transport	D	SS	U	0.50
☐ Droid Starfighter	D	SS	C	0.25
☐ Eeth Koth's Lightsaber	L	Wpn	U	0.50
☐ Electropole	L	Wpn	C	0.25
☐ Fambaa	L	Wpn	C	0.25
☐ Flash Speeder	L	Wpn	C	0.25
☐ Guardians Of The Queen	L	Btl	U	0.50
☐ Gunga City	L	Btl	C	0.25
☐ Gungan Battle Cry	L	Btl	U	0.50
☐ Gungan General, Army Leader	L	Ch	C	0.25
☐ Gungan Guard, Lookout	L	Ch	C	0.25
☐ Gungan Soldier, Infantry	L	Ch	C	0.25
☐ Gungan Warrior, Veteran	L	Ch	C	0.25
☐ Heavy Blaster	L	Wpn	C	0.25
☐ How Wude!	L	Btl	U	0.50
☐ I Will Make It Legal	D	Btl	C	0.25
☐ I Will Take Back What Is Ours	L	Btl	C	0.25
☐ Jabba The Hutt, Crime Lord	D	Ch	R	4.80
☐ Jar Jar Binks, Bombad Gungan General	L	Ch	R	4.50
☐ Jedi Force Push	L	Btl	U	0.50
☐ Kaadu	L	Wpn	C	0.25
☐ Kiss Your Trade Franchise Goodbye	L	Eff	U	0.50
☐ Mace Windu, Jedi Speaker	L	Ch	R	5.00
☐ Mace Windu's Lightsaber	L	Wpn	R	3.80
☐ Meeeesa Lika Dis!	L	Btl	C	0.25
☐ Multi Troop Transport	D	Wpn	U	0.50
☐ Naboo • Battle Plains	L	Loc	X	1.00
☐ Naboo Bureaucrat, Official	L	Ch	C	0.25
☐ Naboo Officer, Commander	L	Ch	C	0.25
☐ Naboo Officer, Squad Leader	L	Ch	U	0.50
☐ Naboo Security, Defender	L	Ch	C	0.25
☐ Naboo Security, Trooper	L	Ch	C	0.25
☐ Naboo Starfighter	L	SS	C	0.25
☐ Naboo • Theed Palace	D	Loc	X	1.00
☐ Neimoidian Advisor, Bureaucrat	D	Ch	X	0.35
☐ Nikto, Slave	D	Ch	C	0.25
☐ NOOOOOOOOOO!	L	Btl	R	3.00
☐ Not For A Sith	D	Btl	R	3.00
☐ Now There Are Two Of Them	D	Btl	U	0.50
☐ Nute Gunray, Neimoidian Despot	D	Ch	R	4.00
☐ Obi-Wan Kenobi, Jedi Knight	L	Ch	R	7.00
☐ Obi-Wan Kenobi, Jedi Negotiator	L	Ch	X	1.50
☐ OOM-9, Battle Droid Commander	D	Ch	U	0.70
☐ P-59, Destroyer Droid Commander	D	Ch	U	0.50
☐ Pacithhip, Prospector	D	Ch	C	0.25
☐ Padmé Naberrie, Amidala's Handmaiden	L	Ch	R	4.00
☐ Planetary Shuttle	L	Wpn	C	0.25
☐ Quarren, Smuggler	D	Ch	U	0.50
☐ Queen Amidala, Keeper of the Peace	L	Ch	R	4.00
☐ Queen Amidala, Resolute Negotiator	L	Ch	R	4.00
☐ Qui-Gon Jinn, Jedi Ambassador	L	Ch	R	6.80
☐ R2-D2, The Queen's Hero	L	Ch	R	4.80
☐ Rep Officer, Gungan Diplomat	L	Ch	X	0.45
☐ Republic Cruiser, Transport	L	SS	C	0.25
☐ Ric Olié, Bravo Leader	L	Ch	U	0.50
☐ Rune Haako, Neimoidian Deputy	D	Ch	R	4.00
☐ Sabé, Handmaiden Decoy Queen	L	Ch	U	0.50
☐ Saché, Handmaiden	L	Ch	U	0.50
☐ Sando Aqua Monster	D	Eff	C	0.25
☐ Sebulba, Dangerous Podracer Pilot	D	Ch	R	4.00
☐ Sio Bibble, Governor of Naboo	L	Ch	U	0.50
☐ Sith Force Push	D	Btl	U	0.50
☐ Sith Infiltrator, Starfighter	D	SS	U	0.80
☐ Sith Lightsaber	D	Wpn	R	4.00
☐ Sith Probe Droid, Remote Tracker	D	Ch	C	0.25
☐ STAP	D	Wpn	U	0.50
☐ Tatooine • Desert Landing Site	L	Loc	X	1.00
☐ Tatooine • Mos Espa	D	Loc	X	1.00
☐ Thanks, Artoo!	L	Btl	U	0.50
☐ The Chancellor's Ambassador	L	Btl	U	0.50
☐ The Phantom Menace	D	Btl	U	0.50
☐ The Will Of The Force	L	Btl	R	3.00
☐ There's Always A Bigger Fish	L	Eff	C	0.25
☐ They Will Not Stay Hidden For Long	D	Eff	C	0.25
☐ They Win This Round	D	Btl	C	0.25
☐ This Is Too Close!	D	Eff	U	0.50
☐ Toonbuck Toora, Senator	D	Ch	U	0.50
☐ Trade Federation Tank, Guard Division	D	Ch	R	4.00
☐ Trade Federation Tank Laser Cannon	D	Wpn	U	0.50
☐ Trade Federation Tank, Patrol Division	D	Ch	R	4.00
☐ Twi'lek Diplomat, Senator	D	Ch	C	0.25
☐ Uh-Oh!	L	Eff	C	0.25
☐ Watto, Toydarian Gambler	D	Ch	R	3.50
☐ We Are Sending All Troops	D	Btl	C	0.25
☐ We Wish To Form An Alliance	L	Eff	C	0.25
☐ Weequay, Enforcer	D	Ch	C	0.25
☐ Yané, Handmaiden	L	Ch	U	0.50
☐ Yoda, Jedi Elder	L	Ch	R	5.00
☐ Young Skywalker	L	Btl	U	0.50
☐ Your Occupation Here Has Ended	L	Btl	C	0.25

Young Jedi • Duel of the Fates

Decipher • Released **January 2001**

60 cards in set

- Booster packs contain 11 cards; booster displays contain 30 boosters
  This small expansion set comes in booster packs only and includes no foil cards.
  The next release announced by Decipher is **Boonta Eve Podrace**.

Set (60 cards)	55.00
Booster Display Box	47.50
Booster Pack	2.20

Card name	Side	Type	Rarity	Price
☐ A Powerful Opponent	L	Btl	C	0.15
☐ Anakin Skywalker, Rookie Pilot	L	Char	R	2.50
☐ Aurra Sing, Trophy Collector	D	Char	R	2.60
☐ Baskol Yeesrim, Gran Senator	D	Char	R	2.40
☐ Battle Droid Patrol	D	Btl	U	0.60
☐ Blockade	D	Eff	U	0.60
☐ Booma	L	Wpn	U	0.60
☐ Bravo Pilot, Flyer	L	Char	C	0.15
☐ Captain Panaka, Security Commander	L	Char	R	2.30

Card name	Side	Type	Rarity	Price
☐ Change In Tactics	D	Btl	C	0.15
☐ Come On, Move!	L	Btl	U	0.60
☐ Coruscant Taxi	D	Wpn	U	0.60
☐ Critical Confrontation	L	Btl	C	0.15
☐ Dangerous Encounter	D	Btl	C	0.15
☐ Darth Maul Defiant	D	Btl	C	0.15
☐ Darth Maul, Student of the Dark Side	D	Char	UR	23.50
☐ Darth Sidious, Master of the Dark Side	D	Char	R	3.50
☐ Droid Starfighter	D	SS	C	0.15
☐ End This Pointless Debate	D	Eff	U	0.60
☐ Gungan Energy Shield	L	Eff	U	0.60
☐ Gungan Mounted Troops	L	Btl	U	0.60

Card name	Side	Type	Rarity	Price
☐ He Can See Things Before They Happen	L	Eff	U	0.60
☐ Impossible!	D	Btl	C	0.15
☐ It's A Standoff!	D	Btl	U	0.60
☐ Jedi Lightsaber, Stolen by Aurra Sing	D	Wpn	U	0.60

You will need **7** nine-pocket pages to store this set. (4 doubled up)

RARITY KEY C = Common U = Uncommon R = Rare VR = Very Rare UR = Ultra Rare SR = Super Rare F = Foil card X = Fixed in all decks

SCRYE Collectible Card Game Checklist and Price Guide • 507

Card name	Side	Type	Rarity	Price
☐ Jedi Meditation	L	Eff	U	0.60
☐ Jedi Training	L	Eff	U	0.60
4				
☐ Mace Windu, Jedi Councilor	L	Char	R	2.60
☐ Mobile Assassin	D	Btl	U	0.60
☐ Naboo Fighter Attack	L	Btl	C	0.15
☐ Naboo Royal Security Forces	L	Eff	U	0.60
☐ Naboo Starfighter	L	SS	C	0.15
☐ Neimoidian Viewscreen	D	Wpn	C	0.15
☐ Obi-Wan Kenobi, Jedi Student	L	Char	R	3.60
☐ OWO-1, Battle Droid Command Officer	D	Char	R	2.30
☐ Pounded Unto Death	L	Eff	C	0.15
5				
☐ Power Of The Sith	D	Btl	C	0.15

Card name	Side	Type	Rarity	Price
☐ Queen Amidala, Young Leader	L	Char	R	2.50
☐ Qui-Gon Jinn, Jedi Mentor	L	Char	UR	23.00
☐ Qui-Gon Jinn's Lightsaber, Wielded by Obi-Wan Kenobi	L	Wpn	R	2.50
☐ Qui-Gon's Final Stand	L	Btl	C	0.15
☐ R2-D2, Repair Droid	L	Char	R	2.60
☐ Rayno Vaca, Taxi Driver	D	Char	R	2.30
☐ Ric Olie, Starship Pilot	L	Char	R	2.50
☐ Run The Blockade	L	Btl	C	0.15
6				
☐ Senate Guard	L	Eff	U	0.60
☐ Starfighter Droid, DFS-327	D	Char	R	2.30
☐ Starfighter Droid, DFS-1104	D	Char	R	2.30
☐ Starfighter Droid, DFS-1138	D	Char	R	2.30

Card name	Side	Type	Rarity	Price
☐ Starfighter Screen	D	Btl	C	0.15
☐ Tey How, Neimoidian Command Officer	D	Char	R	2.30
☐ The Duel Begins	D	Eff	U	0.60
☐ The Jedi Are Involved	D	Eff	U	0.60
☐ To The Death	D	Btl	C	0.15
7				
☐ Twist Of Fate	L	Btl	C	0.15
☐ Use Caution	D	Btl	U	0.60
☐ Valorum, Leader of the Senate	L	Char	C	0.15
☐ Where Are Those Droidekas?	D	Eff	U	0.60
☐ Yoda, Jedi Philosopher	L	Char	R	3.10
☐ You Are Strong With The Force	L	Btl	U	0.60

Young Jedi •
Enhanced Menace of Darth Maul

Decipher • Released **July 2000**

• Decks contain 4 **Menace of Darth Maul** booster packs and 1 of 6 premium cards

Along with the new premium cards, **Enhanced Menace of Darth Maul** also gave birth to the concept of the wild card. Wild cards basically allowed players to bend the game's deck-building restrictions, creating more room for creativity and strategy in deck construction. — **Joe Alread**

Starter Display Box	**185.00**
Starter Deck	**9.50**

☐ Darth Maul, Sith Assassin	9.70	☐ Qui-Gon Jinn, Jedi Protector	6.00
☐ Mace Windu, Jedi Warrior	5.50	☐ Sebulba, Champion Podracer Pilot	5.00
☐ Queen Amidala, Cunning Warrior	5.70	☐ Trade Federation Tank, Assault Leader	5.00

Young Jedi •
Enhanced Battle of Naboo

Decipher • Released **January 2001**

• Decks contain 4 **Battle of Naboo** booster packs and 3 of 12 premiums

Box	**9.50**
☐ Anakin Skywalker, Tested by the Jedi	5.00
☐ Aurra Sing, Scoundrel	5.00
☐ Captain Panaka, Royal Defender	5.00
☐ Darth Sidious, The Phantom Menace	5.00
☐ Jabba the Hutt, Tatooine Tyrant	5.00
☐ Nute Gunray, Neimoidian Bureaucrat	5.00
☐ Obi-Wan Kenobi, Jedi Avenger	5.00
☐ Padme Naberrie, Loyal Handmaiden	5.00
☐ R2-D2, Starship Maintenance Droid	5.00
☐ Rune Haako, Neimoidian Lieutenant	5.00
☐ Watto, Risk Taker	5.00
☐ Yoda, Wise Jedi	5.00

APPENDIX A: COLLECTIBLE MINIATURES GAMES
Mage Knight Rebellion

Wiz Kids • Released **November 2000**

160 figures in set

• Starter sets contain 10 figures; starter cases contain 24 sets
• Booster packs contain 5 figures; booster cases contain 48 packs

Designed by **Jordan Weisman** and **Kevin Barrett**

Attempts had been made to develop a collectible miniature game that combined the 3-D aspects of miniature wargaming with the collectability of CCGs, but no design hit the jackpot until the release of **Mage Knight Rebellion**. The difference was in the system. Jordan Weisman, one of the original creators of the highly successful **BattleTech** miniatures game, hit upon the concept of the Mage Knight Combat Dial while trying to develop a system to make miniature gaming easier for young players. The potential of the system was realized when he combined it with the starter/booster release method of CCGs.

In *Mage Knight* each player puts together an army of miniatures and battles until a specific victory goal is realized. The game ends and victory is determined by eliminating all opposing figures, or the game ends after a time limit, upon which victory is determined by calculating point values of slain, captured, and surviving figures. Each player usually has 200 points worth of figures in his army, and will be allowed two actions on his turn. Actions include movement, close combat, ranged combat, or the use of special abilities. The game is fast as miniature games go, especially as each typical army consists of only 10 to 15 figures. What makes the game fast and simple is the Combat Dial.

It's a dial attached to the base of the miniature figure. The dial can be turned by measured "clicks," each click revealing a new set of miniature statistics through holes in the base. The dial eliminates the need for any sort of record sheets. Combined with the simplicity of the system and a single sheet of color-coded combat abilities, the dial shows players all the information they need to play the game. Each miniature has a movement, attack, defense, and damage value, which changes as the miniature is damaged.

GenCon 2000 promos

☐	175 Alessi Ost	80.00
☐	164 Anunub	177.75
☐	167 Byrch	81.25
☐	171 Digger Khep	80.00
☐	162 Djakmaukar	71.00
☐	173 Fickett Townley	88.25
☐	169 Goltusep	73.00
☐	170 Kerraii	61.00
☐	161 Khujeret	70.00
☐	165 Nessa Nettle	102.50
☐	168 Oakes	60.00
☐	163 Ramkare	85.00
☐	172 Ravarshi	92.50
☐	166 Rowan	63.50
☐	174 Snow	60.50
☐	176 Torengor	68.50

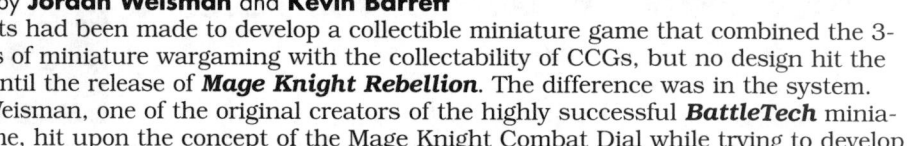

RARITY KEY **C** = Common   **U** = Uncommon   **R** = Rare   **VR** = Very Rare   **UR** = Ultra Rare   **F** = Foil card   **X** = Fixed/standard in all decks

Mage Knight Rebellion seems to have what it takes to go the distance and develop its own long-term, sustainable market. Whether an entire industry will grow up around collectible miniature games is another matter. The Combat Dial, central to the success and simplicity of *Mage Knight*, has a pending patent. Wizards of the Coast has a patent on a trading-card game "mechanism," and while that didn't seem to prevent an entire genre from springing up, competitors will be hard pressed to develop anything comparable to the Combat Dial without infringing on the pending WizKids patent.

Whether this will simply limit the potential of the collectible miniature market or inspire yet another brilliant game design has yet to be seen. — *James Mishler*

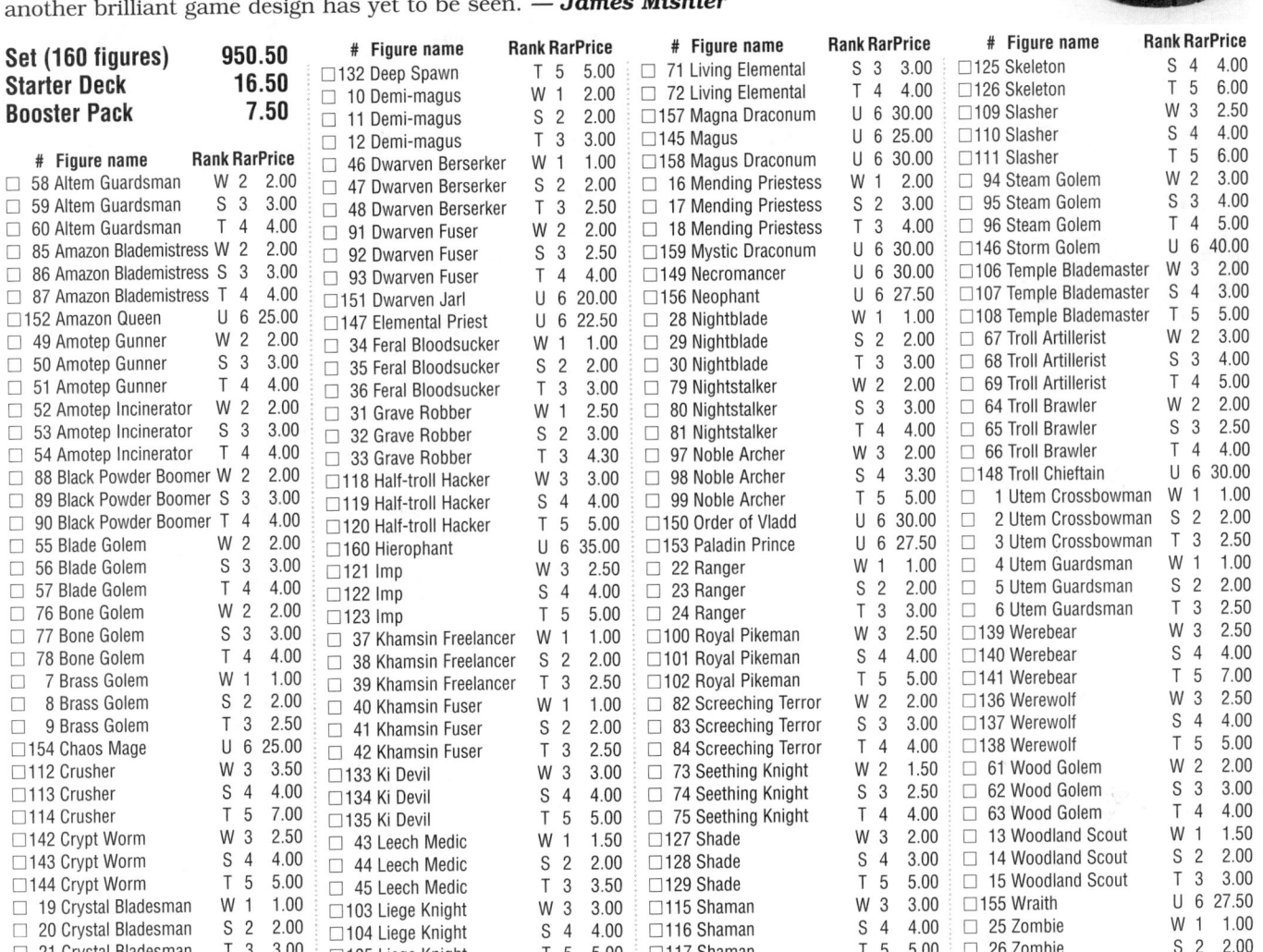

Set (160 figures)		950.50
Starter Deck		16.50
Booster Pack		7.50

#	Figure name	Rank	Rar	Price
58	Altem Guardsman	W	2	2.00
59	Altem Guardsman	S	3	3.00
60	Altem Guardsman	T	4	4.00
85	Amazon Blademistress	W	2	2.00
86	Amazon Blademistress	S	3	3.00
87	Amazon Blademistress	T	4	4.00
152	Amazon Queen	U	6	25.00
49	Amotep Gunner	W	2	2.00
50	Amotep Gunner	S	3	3.00
51	Amotep Gunner	T	4	4.00
52	Amotep Incinerator	W	2	2.00
53	Amotep Incinerator	S	3	3.00
54	Amotep Incinerator	T	4	4.00
88	Black Powder Boomer	W	2	2.00
89	Black Powder Boomer	S	3	3.00
90	Black Powder Boomer	T	4	4.00
55	Blade Golem	W	2	2.00
56	Blade Golem	S	3	3.00
57	Blade Golem	T	4	4.00
76	Bone Golem	W	2	2.00
77	Bone Golem	S	3	3.00
78	Bone Golem	T	4	4.00
7	Brass Golem	W	1	1.00
8	Brass Golem	S	2	2.00
9	Brass Golem	T	3	2.50
154	Chaos Mage	U	6	25.00
112	Crusher	W	3	3.50
113	Crusher	S	4	4.00
114	Crusher	T	5	7.00
142	Crypt Worm	W	3	2.50
143	Crypt Worm	S	4	4.00
144	Crypt Worm	T	5	5.00
19	Crystal Bladesman	W	1	1.00
20	Crystal Bladesman	S	2	2.00
21	Crystal Bladesman	T	3	3.00
130	Deep Spawn	W	3	2.50
131	Deep Spawn	S	4	4.00
132	Deep Spawn	T	5	5.00
10	Demi-magus	W	1	2.00
11	Demi-magus	S	2	2.00
12	Demi-magus	T	3	3.00
46	Dwarven Berserker	W	1	1.00
47	Dwarven Berserker	S	2	2.00
48	Dwarven Berserker	T	3	2.50
91	Dwarven Fuser	W	2	2.00
92	Dwarven Fuser	S	3	2.50
93	Dwarven Fuser	T	4	4.00
151	Dwarven Jarl	U	6	20.00
147	Elemental Priest	U	6	22.50
34	Feral Bloodsucker	W	1	1.00
35	Feral Bloodsucker	S	2	2.00
36	Feral Bloodsucker	T	3	3.00
31	Grave Robber	W	1	2.50
32	Grave Robber	S	2	3.00
33	Grave Robber	T	3	4.30
118	Half-troll Hacker	W	3	3.00
119	Half-troll Hacker	S	4	4.00
120	Half-troll Hacker	T	5	5.00
160	Hierophant	U	6	35.00
121	Imp	W	3	2.50
122	Imp	S	4	4.00
123	Imp	T	5	5.00
37	Khamsin Freelancer	W	1	1.00
38	Khamsin Freelancer	S	2	2.00
39	Khamsin Freelancer	T	3	2.50
40	Khamsin Fuser	W	1	1.00
41	Khamsin Fuser	S	2	2.00
42	Khamsin Fuser	T	3	2.50
133	Ki Devil	W	3	3.00
134	Ki Devil	S	4	4.00
135	Ki Devil	T	5	5.00
43	Leech Medic	W	1	1.50
44	Leech Medic	S	2	2.00
45	Leech Medic	T	3	3.50
103	Liege Knight	W	3	3.00
104	Liege Knight	S	4	4.00
105	Liege Knight	T	5	5.00
70	Living Elemental	W	2	2.00
71	Living Elemental	S	3	3.00
72	Living Elemental	T	4	4.00
157	Magna Draconum	U	6	30.00
145	Magus	U	6	25.00
158	Magus Draconum	U	6	30.00
16	Mending Priestess	W	1	2.00
17	Mending Priestess	S	2	3.00
18	Mending Priestess	T	3	4.00
159	Mystic Draconum	U	6	30.00
149	Necromancer	U	6	30.00
156	Neophant	U	6	27.50
28	Nightblade	W	1	1.00
29	Nightblade	S	2	2.00
30	Nightblade	T	3	3.00
79	Nightstalker	W	2	2.00
80	Nightstalker	S	3	3.00
81	Nightstalker	T	4	4.00
97	Noble Archer	W	3	2.00
98	Noble Archer	S	4	3.30
99	Noble Archer	T	5	5.00
150	Order of Vladd	U	6	30.00
153	Paladin Prince	U	6	27.50
22	Ranger	W	1	1.00
23	Ranger	S	2	2.00
24	Ranger	T	3	3.00
100	Royal Pikeman	W	3	2.50
101	Royal Pikeman	S	4	4.00
102	Royal Pikeman	T	5	5.00
82	Screeching Terror	W	2	2.00
83	Screeching Terror	S	3	3.00
84	Screeching Terror	T	4	4.00
73	Seething Knight	W	2	1.50
74	Seething Knight	S	3	2.50
75	Seething Knight	T	4	4.00
127	Shade	W	3	2.00
128	Shade	S	4	3.00
129	Shade	T	5	5.00
115	Shaman	W	3	3.00
116	Shaman	S	4	4.00
117	Shaman	T	5	5.00
124	Skeleton	W	3	2.50
125	Skeleton	S	4	4.00
126	Skeleton	T	5	6.00
109	Slasher	W	3	2.50
110	Slasher	S	4	4.00
111	Slasher	T	5	6.00
94	Steam Golem	W	2	3.00
95	Steam Golem	S	3	4.00
96	Steam Golem	T	4	5.00
146	Storm Golem	U	6	40.00
106	Temple Blademaster	W	3	2.00
107	Temple Blademaster	S	4	3.00
108	Temple Blademaster	T	5	5.00
67	Troll Artillerist	W	2	3.00
68	Troll Artillerist	S	3	4.00
69	Troll Artillerist	T	4	5.00
64	Troll Brawler	W	2	2.00
65	Troll Brawler	S	3	2.50
66	Troll Brawler	T	4	4.00
148	Troll Chieftain	U	6	30.00
1	Utem Crossbowman	W	1	1.00
2	Utem Crossbowman	S	2	2.00
3	Utem Crossbowman	T	3	2.50
4	Utem Guardsman	W	1	1.00
5	Utem Guardsman	S	2	2.00
6	Utem Guardsman	T	3	2.50
139	Werebear	W	3	2.50
140	Werebear	S	4	4.00
141	Werebear	T	5	7.00
136	Werewolf	W	3	2.50
137	Werewolf	S	4	4.00
138	Werewolf	T	5	5.00
61	Wood Golem	W	2	2.00
62	Wood Golem	S	3	3.00
63	Wood Golem	T	4	4.00
13	Woodland Scout	W	1	1.50
14	Woodland Scout	S	2	2.00
15	Woodland Scout	T	3	3.00
155	Wraith	U	6	27.50
25	Zombie	W	1	1.00
26	Zombie	S	2	2.00
27	Zombie	T	3	2.50

Rarity vs. Rank in *Mage Knight Rebellion*

The initial set of *Mage Knight* figures is made up of 64 sculptures, 48 of which are presented in ranks of Weak, Standard, and Tough, equaling 144 different characters. The last (and rarest) 16 sculptures are only presented in one form without rank, and thus are called Unique. Weak figures have Yellow highlights and are marked with one star on the combat dial, Standard figures have Blue highlights and are marked with two stars on the combat dial, Tough figures have Red highlights and are marked with three stars on the combat dial, and Unique figures have no rank markings on the figure or combat dial.

All together there are 160 different

characters in the set, ranging in rarity levels from 1 to 6 with four categories of rank (Weak, Standard, Tough, and Unique). The levels advance in a stair-step progression.

In terms of rarity, figures with collector numbers 1 to 48 are Common "A", 49 to 96 are Common "B", 97 to 144 are Rare "C", and 145 to 160 are Rare "D" Uniques. The stars of the figures' bases refer to rank only. It is important to remember that the stars only indicate whether the figure is

Weak (one star), Standard (two stars), Tough (three stars), or Unique (no stars), they do not indicate level of rarity.

Booster Packs contain a total of five figures: three common figures, one rare figure, and one variable figure. The common figures will be from rarity levels 1 to 4. The rare figures can be from levels 3 to 6. The variable figure can be from levels 2 to 6, but is guaranteed not to be a repeat of any other figure in the box.

Figure Types

Lvl			
1	Common "A" Weak (yellow)		
2	Common "A" Standard (blue)	Common "B" Weak (yellow)	
3	Common "A" Tough (red)	Common "B" Standard (blue)	Rare "C" Weak (yellow)
4		Common "B" Tough (red)	Rare "C" Standard (blue)
5			Rare "C" Tough (red)
6		Rare "D" Unique (No rank markings)	

APPENDIX B: CCGs IN OTHER LANGUAGES

While English-language CCGs are the focus of this work, we acknowledge here a **sampling** of games originally appearing in other languages, as well as foreign-language editions of English CCGs. We include checklists and pricing for **Pocket Monsters**, the only foreign-language CCG traded heavily in the United States.

Dark Forces • Germany
Schmidt Spiele GmbH/Fantasy Productions GmbH
Foreign Language Editions: **French**
Released **October 1994**

Dark Forces was the first new CCG produced outside the U.S,. The game used the classic Aventuria setting from the German role-playing game *Das Schwartze Auge*. The game system has much in common with **Magic: The Gathering**, however, there are distinct differences that set it as a game apart. While "summoned" creatures and heroes are dependent on lands, the lands are actually played as a board, rather than simply as an assortment of resources. The object of the game is to conquer your opponent's lands. The game can also end when too many points worth of creatures and heroes have died, but only so long as one player has lost a significant number more than the others.

Released originally in a 297-card set with 60-card starters and 16-card boosters. Expansions include the 72-card **Attack Pack** set and the 110-card **Captain's Pack** set, each of which were sold in 13-card booster packs.

Divine Intervention • France
October Games/Halloween Concept/Siroz Productions
Released **1995**

From what we can determine, this game seems to be about spaced out nude hippy chicks and happy little mostly-nude cherubs meeting a gruesome bloody death at the hands of vile cultists and devils obsessed with bondage and discipline. There are also some bits about Roman Catholic Cardinals and streetwalking prostitutes. We cannot tell if it has any relation to the **In Nomine** and **In Nomine Satanus** role-playing games, also designed by Croc.

Doomtrooper • Sweden
Target Games AB
Known translations include: English, **Hebrew, Swedish, German, Italian, Japanese**

Dragon's Wrath • Spain
Naipes Heraclio Fournier SA
A game that is remarkably not unlike **Magic**. Originally released only in four pre-constructed starter decks, supposedly a later booster set, **Mercuradores**, was released. It was possibly translated into French and German, though we have found no firm evidence.

Final Fantasy • Japan
Set in the world of the video game *Final Fantasy VIII*, this is a simple game designed to be played quickly. Unfortunately, it doesn't have a lot of depth, being essentially a cross between War and Tic-Tac-Toe.

Guardians • United States
Known translations include: **French**
French sets: Édition limitée, L'Île de la Dague, Drifter Nexus.

Guildes: La Quetes des Origines • France
Multisim
One of three homegrown CCGs we've seen, **Guildes** has an appearance best described as a combination between a renaissance fantasy and a Jules Verne novel.

Illuminati: New World Order • United States
Known translations include: **German**

Kabal • Sweden
Multisim
Kabal appears to be a CCG adaptation of the *Nephilim* role-playing game setting.

Magic: The Gathering • United States
These are the editions we have been able to track down with affirmative evidence, but we are certain that there are many more. Almost certainly, every set from **Fourth Edition** on has been translated into at least these seven major languages. **Renaissance** is an orginal set for the overseas market.
Known translations include: **Chinese, French, German, Italian, Japanese, Korean, Portuguese, Spanish**
Chinese sets: Revised, Fourth Edition, Fifth Edition, Stronghold, Tempest, Visions, Weatherlight
French sets: Magic: l'assemblée édition originale française, 4ème édition, 4ème version simplifiée, 5ième Édition, 6ième édition "classique", Renaissance, Terres Natales, Ère Glaciaire, Alliances, Mirage, Visions, Aquilon (Weatherlight), Tempête, Forteresse, Exode, L'Épopée d'Urza, L'héritage d'Urza, La Destinée d'Urza, Masques de Mercadia, Némésis, Prophétie, Invasion.
German sets: Revised, Fourth Edition, Fifth Edition, Renaissance, Ice Age, Mirage, Visions, Weatherlight, Tempest, Stronghold.
Italian sets: Prima edizione Italiana, Quarta Edizione, Quinta Edizione, Sesta Edizione, Leggende, L'Oscurità, Era Glaciale, Rinascimento, Origini, Alleanze, Mirage, Visioni, Cavalcavento, Tempesta, Fortezza, Esodo, Saga di Urza, Eredità di Urza, Destino di Urza, Maschere di Mercadia, Nemesis, Prophecy, Invasion.
Japanese sets: Fourth Edition, Fifth Edition, Portal Three Kingdoms, Sixth Edition, Chronicles, Mirage, Weatherlight, Tempest, Stronghold, Urza's Saga, Urza's Legacy, Urza's Destiny, Exodus, Mercadian Masques,
Korean sets: Revised, Fourth Edition, Renaissance, Visions, Weatherlight, Tempest, Stronghold, Exodus, Urza's Saga,
Portuguese sets: Revised, Fourth Edition, Ice Age, Alliances, Mirage, Visions, Stronghold, Tempest, Urza's Saga, Urza's Destiny,
Spanish sets: Revised, Fourth Edition, Mirage, Weatherlight, Tempest, Stronghold, Urza's Saga, Urza's Destiny

Middle Earth • United States
Known translations include: **French, German**
French sets: Les Sorciers, Les Dragons, Sombres Séides, L'Oeil de Sauron.
German sets: Limited, Lidless Eye.

Mythos • United States
Known translations include: **French**
Sets: Édition limitée, Expéditions de l'Université de Miskatonic, Le Réveil de Cthulhu, Légendes du Nécronomicon.

Nerve • Sweden
Nerve simulates an arcade fighting game with cards. No words appear on them, only icons. They have been found in the United States with a comic book explaining the rules in broken English.

Netrunner • United States
Known translations include: **French**

Pocket Monsters • Basic

Nintendo/Creatures/Gamefreak • Japan • **130** cards in set

- Starters and boosters available

Cards are in numerical order by their Pokémon number.

	Price
Set (130 cards)	235.00
Booster Display Box	325.00
Starter Deck	28.00
Booster Pack	8.00

You will need **12** nine-pocket pages to store this set. (6 doubled up)

キュウコン LV.31 HP80

#	Lvl	HP	Card name	Rarity	Price
1	13	40	Bulbasaur	C	0.25
2	20	60	Ivysaur	U	1.00
3	67	100	Venusaur	F	17.75
4	10	50	Charmander	C	0.25
5	32	80	Charmeleon	U	1.00
6	76	120	Charizard	F	42.50
7	8	40	Squirtle	C	0.25
8	22	70	Wartortle	U	1.00
9	52	100	Blastoise	F	22.50
10	13	40	Caterpie	C	0.25
11	21	70	Metapod	C	0.25
13	12	40	Weedle	C	0.25
14	23	80	Kakuna	U	1.00
15	32	80	Beedrill	R	5.00
16	8	40	Pidgey	C	0.25
17	36	60	Pidgeotto	R	5.00
19	9	30	Rattata	C	0.25
20	41	60	Raticate	U	1.00
25	12	40	Pikachu	C	0.35
26	40	80	Raichu	F	15.25
27	12	40	Sandshrew	C	0.25
32	20	10	Nidoran (M)	C	0.25
33	25	60	Nidorino	U	1.00
34	48	90	Nidoking	F	13.00
35	14	40	Clefairy	F	15.00
37	11	50	Vulpix	C	0.25
38	32	80	Ninetales	F	11.00
50	8	30	Diglett	C	0.25
51	36	70	Dugtrio	R	5.00
58	18	60	Growlithe	U	1.00
59	45	100	Arcanine	U	1.00
60	13	40	Poliwag	C	0.25
61	28	60	Poliwhirl	U	1.00
62	48	90	Poliwrath	F	12.00
63	10	30	Abra	C	0.25
64	38	60	Kadabra	U	1.00
65	42	80	Alakazam	F	15.00
66	20	50	Machop	C	0.25
67	40	80	Machoke	U	1.00
68	67	100	Machamp	F	12.00
77	10	40	Ponyta	C	0.25
81	13	40	Magnemite	C	0.25
82	28	60	Magneton	F	10.00
83	20	50	Farfetch'd	U	1.00
84	10	50	Doduo	C	0.25
86	12	60	Seel	U	1.00
87	42	80	Dewgong	U	1.00
92	8	30	Gastly	C	0.25
93	22	60	Haunter	U	1.00
95	12	90	Onix	C	0.25
96	12	50	Drowzee	C	0.25
100	10	40	Voltorb	C	0.25
101	40	80	Electrode	R	4.50
107	33	70	Hitmonchan	F	12.75
109	13	50	Koffing	C	0.25

#	Lvl	HP	Card name	Rarity	Price
113	55	120	Chansey	F	15.00
114	8	50	Tangela	C	0.25
120	15	40	Staryu	C	0.25
121	28	60	Starmie	C	0.25
124	23	70	Jynx	U	1.00
125	35	70	Electabuzz	R	5.00
126	24	50	Magmar	U	1.00
129	8	30	Magikarp	U	1.00
130	41	100	Gyarados	F	12.50
137	12	30	Porygon	U	1.00
145	64	90	Zapdos	F	15.00
147	10	40	Dratini	U	1.00
148	33	80	Dragonair	R	5.00
150	53	60	Mewtwo	F	12.50
Bill				C	0.25
Clefairy Doll				R	3.30
Computer Search				R	3.50
Defender				U	1.00
Devolution Spray				R	3.00
Energy Removal				C	0.25
Energy Retrieval				U	1.00
Full Heal				U	1.00
Gust of Wind				C	0.25
Impostor Professor Oak				R	3.00
Item Finder				R	3.00
Lass				R	3.00
Maintenance				U	1.00
PlusPower				U	1.00
Pokédex				U	1.00
Pokémon Breeder				R	3.40

#	Lvl	HP	Card name	Rarity	Price
Pokémon Center				U	1.00
Pokémon Flute				U	1.00
Pokémon Trader				R	3.00
Potion				C	0.25
Professor Oak				U	1.00
Revive				U	1.00
Scoop Up				R	3.00
Super Energy Removal				R	3.50
Super Potion				U	1.00
Switch				C	0.25
Double Colorlesss Energy				U	1.00
Colorless Energy				C	0.25
Fighting Energy				C	0.25
Fire Energy				C	0.25
Grass Energy				C	0.25
Lightning Energy				C	0.25
Psychic Energy				C	0.25
Water Energy				C	0.25

Pocket Monsters • Jungle

Nintendo/Creatures/Gamefreak • **Japan** • **48** cards in set

- Boosters available

	Price
Set (48 cards)	199.50
Booster Display Box	325.00
Booster Pack	7.00

You will need **6** nine-pocket pages to store this set. (3 doubled up)

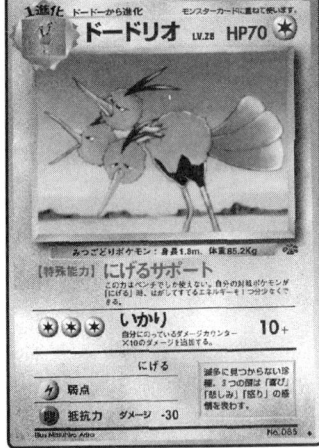

ドードリオ LV.28 HP70

#	Lvl	HP	Card name	Rarity	Price
12	28	70	Butterfree	U	1.00
18	40	80	Pidgeot	F	10.00
21	13	50	Spearow	C	0.25
22	27	70	Fearow	U	1.00
25	14	50	Pikachu	C	0.30
29	13	60	Nidoran (F)	C	0.30
30	24	70	Nidorina	U	1.00
31	43	90	Nidoqueen	F	10.00
36	34	70	Clefable	F	10.50
39	14	60	Jigglypuff	C	0.25
40	36	80	Wigglytuff	F	12.00
43	8	50	Oddish	C	0.25
44	22	60	Gloom	U	1.00
45	35	80	Vileplume	F	10.00
46	8	40	Paras	C	0.25
47	28	60	Parasect	U	1.00
48	12	40	Venonat	C	0.25
49	28	70	Venomoth	F	10.00
52	15	50	Meowth	C	0.25
53	25	70	Persian	U	1.00
56	7	30	Mankey	C	0.25
57	35	70	Primeape	U	1.00
69	11	40	Bellsprout	C	0.25
70	28	70	Weepinbell	U	1.00
71	42	80	Victreebel	F	10.00
78	33	70	Rapidash	U	1.00
85	28	70	Dodrio	U	1.00
101	42	90	Electrode	F	10.00
102	14	50	Exeggcute	C	0.25

#	Lvl	HP	Card name	Rarity	Price
103	35	80	Exeggutor	U	1.00
104	13	40	Cubone	C	0.25
105	26	60	Marowak	U	1.00
108	26	90	Lickitung	U	1.00
111	18	70	Rhyhorn	C	0.25
112	48	100	Rhydon	U	1.00
115	40	90	Kangaskhan	F	12.00
118	12	40	Goldeen	C	0.25
119	28	70	Seaking	U	1.00
122	28	40	Mr.Mime	F	13.00
123	25	70	Scyther	F	14.25
127	24	60	Pinsir	F	11.75
128	32	60	Tauros	U	1.00
133	12	50	Eevee	C	0.25
134	42	80	Vaporeon	F	10.50
135	29	70	Jolteon	F	12.00
136	28	70	Flareon	F	12.00

Snorlax

#	Lvl	HP	Card name	Rarity	Price
143	20	90	Snorlax	F	10.00
Pokéball				C	0.25

Pocket Monsters • Fossil

Nintendo/Creatures/Gamefreak • **Japan** • **48** cards in set

- Booster available

	Price
Set (48 cards)	214.50
Booster Display Box	475.00
Booster Pack	9.00

You will need **6** nine-pocket pages to store this set. (3 doubled up)

#	Lvl	HP	Card name	Rarity	Price
23	10	40	Ekans	C	0.25
24	27	60	Arbok	U	1.00
26	45	90	Raichu	F	15.00
28	33	70	Sandslash	U	1.00
41	10	40	Zubat	C	0.25
42	29	60	Golbat	U	1.00
54	15	50	Psyduck	C	0.25
55	27	70	Golduck	U	1.00
72	10	30	Tentacool	C	0.25

#	Lvl	HP	Card name	Rarity	Price
73	21	60	Tentacruel	U	1.00
74	16	50	Geodude	C	0.25
75	29	60	Graveller	U	1.00
76	36	80	Golem	U	1.00
79	18	50	Slowpoke	C	0.25
80	26	60	Slowbro	U	1.00

#	Lvl	HP	Card name	Rarity	Price
82	35	80	Magneton	F	10.00
88	17	50	Grimer	C	0.25
89	34	70	Muk	F	10.25
90	8	30	Shellder	C	0.25
91	25	50	Cloyster	U	1.00
92	17	50	Gastly	U	1.00

RARITY KEY C = Common U = Uncommon R = Rare VR = Very Rare UR = Ultra Rare F = Foil card X = Fixed/standard in all decks

#	Lvl	HP	Card name	Rarity	Price
93	17	50	Haunter	F	10.00
94	38	80	Gengar	F	12.00
97	36	90	Hypno	F	10.00
98	20	50	Krabby	C	0.25
99	27	60	Kingler	U	1.00
106	30	60	Hitmonlee	F	14.25
110	27	60	Weezing	U	1.00

#	Lvl	HP	Card name	Rarity	Price
116	19	40	Horsea	C	0.25
117	23	60	Seadra	U	1.00
126	31	70	Magmar	U	1.00
131	31	80	Lapras	F	11.75
132	20	50	Ditto	F	12.50
138	19	40	Omanyte	C	0.25
139	32	70	Omastar	U	1.00

#	Lvl	HP	Card name	Rarity	Price
140	9	30	Kabuto	C	0.25
141	30	60	Kabutops	F	11.50
142	28	60	Aerodactyl	F	14.50
144	35	70	Articuno	F	15.00
145	40	80	Zapdos	F	15.00
146	35	70	Moltres	F	15.00
149	45	100	Dragonite	F	17.00

#	Lvl	HP	Card name	Rarity	Price
151	23	50	Mew/Myuu	F	40.00
			Energy Search	C	0.25
			Fossil of Something	C	0.25
			Gambler	C	0.25
			Old Man Fuji	U	1.00
			Recycle	C	0.25

Pocket Monsters • Team Rocket

Nintendo/Creatures/Gamefreak • Japan • 65 cards in set

- Boosters available

You will need **8** nine-pocket pages to store this set. (4 doubled up)

#	Lvl	HP	Card name	Rarity	Price
8	21	60	Dark Wartortle	U	1.00
9	28	70	Dark Blastoise	F	20.00
19	12	40	Rattata	C	0.25
20	25	50	Dark Raticate	C	0.25
23	15	50	Ekans	C	0.25
24	25	60	Dark Arbok	F	10.50
41	9	40	Zubat	C	0.25
42	25	50	Dark Golbat	F	10.00
43	21	50	Oddish	C	0.25
44	21	50	Dark Gloom	U	1.00
45	29	60	Dark Vileplume	F	11.00
50	15	40	Diglett	C	0.25
51	18	50	Dark Dugtrio	F	10.00
52	10	40	Meowth	C	0.25
53	28	60	Dark Persian	F	10.00
54	16	50	Psyduck	C	0.25
55	23	60	Dark Golduck	U	1.00
56	14	40	Mankey	C	0.25
57	23	60	Dark Primeape	U	1.00
63	14	40	Abra	C	0.25

#	Lvl	HP	Card name	Rarity	Price
64	24	50	Dark Kadabra	U	1.00
65	30	60	Dark Alakazam	F	14.00
66	24	50	Machop	C	0.25
67	28	60	Dark Machoke	U	1.00
68	30	70	Dark Machamp	F	10.25
77	15	50	Ponyta	C	0.25
78	24	60	Dark Rapidash	C	0.25
79	16	50	Slowpoke	C	0.25
80	27	60	Dark Slowbro	F	10.00
81	12	40	Magnemite	C	0.25
82	26	60	Dark Magneton	F	10.00
88	10	40	Grimer	C	0.25
89	25	60	Dark Muk	U	1.00
96	10	50	Drowzee	C	0.25
97	26	60	Dark Hypno	F	10.00
100	13	40	Voltorb	C	0.25
101	24	60	Dark Electrode	U	1.00
109	12	40	Koffing	C	0.25
110	24	60	Dark Weezing	F	10.25
129	6	30	Magikarp	C	0.25
130	31	70	Dark Gyarados	F	11.50

#	Lvl	HP	Card name	Rarity	Price
133	9	40	Eevee	C	0.25
134	28	60	Dark Vaporeon	U	1.00
135	23	50	Dark Jolteon	U	1.00
136	23	50	Dark Flareon	U	1.00
137	20	40	Porygon	C	0.25
147	12	40	Dratini	C	0.25
148	28	60	Dark Dragonair	U	1.00
149	33	70	Dark Dragonite	F	14.50
			Boss's Way	U	1.00
			Challenge!	U	1.00
			Digger	C	0.25
			Full Heal Energy	C	0.25
			Goop Gas Attack	C	0.25
			Here Comes Team Rocket!	URF	39.50
			Imposter Oak's Revenge	U	1.00
			Nightly Garbage Run	C	0.25
			Potion Energy	C	0.25
			Rainbow Energy	F	14.50
			Rocket's Sneak Attack	F	10.00
			Sleep!	C	0.25

Set (65 cards) 220.00
Booster Display Box 477.50
Booster Pack 9.00

#	Lvl	HP	Card name	Rarity	Price
4	9	40	Charmander	C	0.25
5	23	50	Dark Charmeleon	U	1.00
6	38	80	Dark Charizard	F	35.00
7	16	50	Squirtle	C	0.25

Pocket Monsters • Gym Leaders

Nintendo/Creatures/Gamefreak • Japan • 94 cards in set

- Boosters and theme deck starters available

You will need **11** nine-pocket pages to store this set. (6 doubled up)

#	Lvl	HP	Card name	Rarity	Price
35	16	50	Erica's Clefairy	U	1.00
36	35	70	Erica's Clefable	F	9.00
37	10	40	Brock's Vulpix	C	0.35
37	16	50	Brock's Vulpix	U	1.00
38	30	70	Brock's Ninetales	F	10.00
39	13	50	Erica's Jigglypuff	C	0.35
41	11	40	Brock's Zubat	C	0.35
42	30	70	Brock's Golbat	U	1.00
43	10	40	Erica's Oddish	C	0.35
43	15	50	Erica's Oddish	C	0.35
44	24	60	Erica's Gloom	U	1.00
45	34	80	Erica's Vileplume	F	9.90
46	17	50	Erica's Paras	C	0.35
50	13	40	Brock's Diglett	C	0.35
54	18	60	Misty's Psyduck	C	0.50
55	32	70	Misty's Golduck	F	7.60
56	12	40	Brock's Mankey	C	0.35
57	32	70	Brock's Primeape	U	1.00
60	16	50	Misty's Poliwag	C	0.35
61	37	70	Misty's Poliwhirl	U	1.00
69	13	40	Erica's Bellsprout	C	0.35
69	15	50	Erica's Bellsprout	C	0.35
70	26	60	Erica's Weepinbell	U	1.00
71	37	80	Erica's Victreebel	R	7.00
72	16	50	Misty's Tentacool	U	1.00
73	30	70	Misty's Tentacruel	F	9.00
74	13	40	Brock's Geodude	C	0.35
74	15	50	Brock's Geodude	C	0.35
75	32	70	Brock's Graveler	U	1.00
81	10	30	Lt. Surge's		

#	Lvl	HP	Card name	Rarity	Price
			Magnemite	U	1.00
81	12	40	Lt. Surge's Magnemite	C	0.25
82	30	70	Lt. Surge's Magneton	F	8.00
86	14	50	Misty's Seel	C	0.35
87	40	80	Misty's Dewgong	U	1.00
95	41	100	Brock's Onix	C	0.35
100	12	40	Lt. Surge's Voltorb	C	0.35
102	15	50	Erica's Exeggute	U	1.00
103	31	70	Erica's Exeggutor	U	1.00
107	29	60	Team Rocket's Hitmonchan	F	10.50
108	24	80	Brock's Lickitung	U	1.00
111	29	70	Brock's Rhyhorn	C	0.35
112	38	80	Brock's Rhydon	F	9.90
114	21	60	Erica's Tangela	C	0.35
116	10	40	Misty's Horsea	C	0.35
116	16	50	Misty's Horsea	C	0.35
117	30	70	Misty's Seadra	F	7.60
118	10	40	Misty's Goldeen	C	0.35
120	16	40	Misty's Staryu	C	0.35
123	23	60	Team Rocket's Scyther	F	11.00
125	28	70	Lt. Surge's Electabuzz	F	10.00
129	5	30	Misty's Magikarp	C	0.35
130	42	100	Misty's Gyarados	F	10.00
133	10	40	Lt. Surge's Eevee	U	1.00
135	32	70	Lt. Surge's Jolteon	R	7.50
146	26	60	Team Rocket's Moltres	F	10.00
147	14	40	Erica's Dratini	U	1.00

#	Lvl	HP	Card name	Rarity	Price
148	32	80	Erica's Dragonair	F	9.90
			Brock	R	5.00
			Brock's Training Method	U	1.00
			Brock's Protection	R	4.00
			Celadon City Gym	U	1.00
			Cerulean City Gym	U	1.00
			Charity	R	4.50
			Derangement Gym	R	5.00
			Energy Flow	C	0.50
			Erica	R	5.00
			Erica's Kindness	R	4.00
			Erica's Maids	U	1.00
			Erica's Perfume	U	1.00
			Good Manners	U	1.00
			Vermilion City Gym	U	1.00
			Lt. Surge	R	5.00
			Lt. Surge's Secret Operation	R	4.00
			Lt. Surge's Treaty	U	1.00
			Misty	R	4.90
			Misty's Duel	C	0.50
			Misty's Selfishness	R	4.00
			Misty's Tear	C	0.50
			Misty's Wrath	U	1.00
			Narrow Gym	C	0.25
			No Removal Gym	R	4.50
			Pewter City Gym	U	1.00
			Recall	U	1.00
			Rocket's Training Gym	R	4.30
			Secret Mission	U	1.00
			The Rocket's Trap	F	8.50

Brock's Deck (orange) 29.00
Misty's Deck (blue) 30.00
Lt. Surge's Deck (yellow) 30.00
Erica's Deck (green) 30.00
Sabrina's Deck (purple) 30.00
Blaine's Deck (red) 38.00
Booster Set (94 cards) 249.00
Booster Display Box 487.50
Booster Pack 8.00

#	Lvl	HP	Card name	Rarity	Price
1	15	50	Erica's Bulbusaur	U	1.00
19	7	30	Lt. Surge's Rattata	C	0.35
20	33	60	Lt. Surge's Raticate	U	1.00
21	17	50	Lt. Surge's Spearow	C	0.35
22	30	70	Lt. Surge's Fearow	F	8.00
25	10	40	Lt. Surge's Pikachu	C	0.45
27	20	50	Brock's Sandshrew	C	0.35
28	34	70	Brock's Sandslash	U	1.00

RARITY KEY C = Common U = Uncommon R = Rare VR = Very Rare UR = Ultra Rare F = Foil card X = Fixed/standard in all decks

Pocket Monsters • Gym Leaders 2: Challenge from the Darkness

Nintendo/Creatures/Gamefreak • Japan • 98 cards in set

• Boosters available

Set (98 cards) 235.00
Booster Display Box 450.00
Booster Pack 9.00

#	Lvl	HP	Card name	Rarity	Price
2	22	60	Erika's Ivysaur	U	1.00
3	45	90	Erika's Venusaur	F	16.50
4	16	50	Blaine's Charmander	C	0.40
5	29	70	Blaine's Charmeleon	U	1.00
6	50	100	Blaine's Charizard	F	35.00
13	13	40	Koga's Weedle	C	0.30
14	21	60	Koga's Kakuna	U	1.00
15	34	80	Koga's Beedrill	F	11.50
16	9	40	Koga's Pidgey	U	1.00
16	15	50	Koga's Pidgey	C	0.30
17	34	60	Koga's Pidgeotto	R	5.00
23	17	50	Koga's Ekans	C	0.30
24	44	90	Koga's Arbok	R	5.00
26	38	80	Lt. Surge's Raichu	F	13.00
29	11	50	Giovanni's Nidoran (F)	C	0.30
30	35	80	Giovanni's Nidorina	U	1.00
31	51	100	Giovanni's Nidoqueen	R	5.00
32	14	40	Giovanni's Nidoran (M)	C	0.30
33	32	70	Giovanni's Nidorino	U	1.00
34	58	120	Giovanni's Nidoking	F	12.00
37	9	40	Blaine's Vulpix	C	0.30
38	27	60	Blaine's Ninetales	R	5.00
41	14	40	Koga's Zubat	C	0.30
42	27	60	Koga's Golbat	U	1.00
48	13	40	Sabrina's Venonat	C	0.30
49	24	60	Sabrina's Venomoth	R	5.00
51	27	60	Brock's Dugtrio	R	5.00
52	12	40	Giovanni's Meowth	U	1.00
52	17	50	Giovanni's Meowth	C	0.30
53	23	60	Giovanni's Persian	F	12.00
54	16	50	Sabrina's Psyduck	C	0.30
55	33	70	Sabrina's Golduck	R	5.00
56	14	40	Blaine's Mankey	C	0.30
58	15	50	Blaine's Growlithe	C	0.30
59	42	90	Blaine's Arcanine	F	18.00
62	43	90	Misty's Poliwrath	R	5.00
63	11	40	Sabrina's Abra	C	0.30
64	41	70	Sabrina's Kadabra	U	1.00
65	44	80	Sabrina's Alakazam	F	15.00
66	18	50	Giovanni's Machop	C	0.30
67	36	80	Giovanni's Machoke	U	1.00
68	50	100	Giovanni's Machamp	F	11.50
77	13	50	Blaine's Ponyta	C	0.30
78	31	70	Blaine's Rapidash	U	1.00
79	15	50	Sabrina's Slowpoke	C	0.30
80	29	70	Sabrina's Slowbro	U	1.00
84	15	50	Imakuni's Doduo	UR	28.00
84	17	50	Blaine's Doduo	C	0.30
88	19	50	Koga's Grimer	C	0.30
89	38	80	Koga's Muk	R	5.00
92	10	40	Sabrina's Gastly	U	1.00
93	20	50	Sabrina's Haunter	U	1.00
94	39	80	Sabrina's Gengar	F	12.50
96	15	50	Sabrina's Drowzee	C	0.30
97	31	70	Sabrina's Hypno	U	1.00
109	10	40	Koga's Koffing	C	0.30
109	15	50	Koga's Koffing	U	1.00
110	31	70	Koga's Weezing	U	1.00
111	26	60	Blaine's Rhyhorn	C	0.30
113	38	90	[Your name]'s Chansey	UR	16.50
114	16	50	Koga's Tangela	C	0.30
115	36	80	Blaine's Kangaskhan	U	1.00
122	20	50	Sabrina's Mr. Mime	C	0.30
124	21	60	Sabrina's Jynx	U	1.00
126	29	60	Blaine's Magmar	U	1.00
127	27	70	Giovanni's Pinsir	R	5.00
128	34	70	Blaine's Tauros	C	0.30
129	9	30	Giovanni's Magikarp	C	0.30
130	40	90	Giovanni's Gyarados	F	12.25
132	12	40	Koga's Ditto	F	9.90
137	17	40	Sabrina's Porygon	C	0.30
143	40	90	Team Rocket's Snorlax	R	5.00
145	34	70	Team Rocket's Zapdos	F	15.00
146	44	90	Blaine's Moltres	F	15.00
150	35	70	Team Rocket's Mewtwo	F	13.25
			Blaine	R	5.00
			Blaine's Gamble	C	0.25
			Blaine's Last Resort	U	1.00
			Blaine's Quiz #3	U	1.00
			Giovanni	F	6.00
			Giovanni's Trump Card	R	4.00
			Gurentown Gym	U	1.00
			Invisible Wall	C	0.30
			Koga	R	5.00
			Koga's Secret Transformation Act	U	1.00
			Minion of Team Rocket	U	1.00
			Sabrina	R	5.00
			Sabrina's ESP	U	1.00
			Sabrina's Eye	C	0.30
			Sabrina's Psychic Control	U	1.00
			Sekichiku City Gym	U	1.00
			Team Rocket Experiment	U	1.00
			Team Rocket's Explosive Gym	U	1.00
			Tickling Machine	U	1.00
			Tokiwa City Gym	R	3.00
			Trash Exchange	C	0.30
			Warp Point	C	0.25
			Yamabuki City Gym	U	1.00

Pocket Monsters • Neo

Nintendo/Creatures/Gamefreak • Japan • 96 cards in set

• Boosters available

Set (96 cards) 274.50
Booster Display Box 50.00
Booster Pack 10.00

#	Lvl	HP	Card name	Rarity	Price
25	15	50	Pikachu	C	0.60
35	19	50	Clefairy	U	1.20
43	7	40	Oddish	C	0.50
44	26	60	Gloom	U	1.00
79	20	50	Slowpoke	C	0.50
95	22	60	Onix	C	0.50
116	22	50	Horsea	C	0.50
117	36	70	Seadra	U	1.00
125	38	70	Electabuzz	U	1.20
126	37	70	Magmar	U	1.20
152	12	40	Chikoreeta	C	0.50
153	39	80	Bayleaf	U	1.00
154	57	100	Meganium	F	12.00
155	21	50	Cyndaquil	C	0.50
156	35	70	Quilava	U	1.00
157	55	100	Typhlosion	F	12.00
158	20	50	Totodile	C	0.50
159	34	70	Croconaw	U	1.00
160	56	100	Feraligatr	F	12.00
161	13	40	Sentret	C	0.50
162	27	60	Furret	U	1.00
163	17	50	Hoot Hoot	C	0.50
164	23	60	Noctowl	U	1.00
165	19	40	Ledyba	C	0.50
166	32	60	Ledian	U	1.00
167	15	40	Spinarak	C	0.50
168	29	60	Ariados	U	1.00
170	12	50	Chinchou	C	0.50
171	26	70	Lanturn	U	1.00
172	5	30	Pichu	F	20.00
173	6	30	Cleffa	R	7.30
175	14	40	Togepi	U	1.30
176	31	60	Togetic	F	18.00
177	10	30	Xatu	C	0.50
178	45	80	Xogo	U	1.00
179	12	40	Mareep	C	0.50
180	26	60	Flaaffy	U	1.00
181	40	80	Centerity	F	12.00
182	36	70	Bellossom	F	12.00
183	9	40	Marill	C	0.50
184	29	70	Azumarill	F	15.00
185	29	60	Sudowoodo	C	0.50
187	21	50	Hoppip	C	0.50
188	28	60	Skiploom	U	1.00
189	35	70	Jumpluff	F	12.00
190	18	40	Aipom	U	1.00
191	16	40	Sunkern	C	0.50
192	36	70	Sunflora	U	1.00
194	18	50	Amphoros	C	0.50
195	33	70	Quagsire	U	1.00
198	25	50	Murkrow	R	6.50
199	39	80	Slowking	F	14.50
203	30	60	Girafarig	C	0.50
207	60	60	Gligar	C	0.50
208	64	110	Steelix	F	12.50
209	19	50	Snubbull	C	0.50
210	33	70	Granbull	U	1.00
213	32	50	Shuckle	C	0.50
214	28	60	Heracross	F	12.00
215	34	60	Misdreavus	R	5.50
220	8	40	Swinub	C	0.50
221	36	80	Torvado	U	1.00
226	31	60	Mantine	C	0.50
227	30	60	Wooper	F	12.00
230	50	90	Kingdra	F	12.00
231	11	40	Phanpy	U	1.00
232	34	70	Donphan	R	5.00
234	29	60	Stantler	C	0.50
239	6	30	Elekid	R	5.00
240	5	30	Magby	R	5.00
241	32	70	Miltank	U	1.00
249	45	90	Lugia	F	23.50
			Card Flip Game	U	1.00
			Dark Energy	R	5.00
			Double Switch	C	0.50
			Ecologym	R	3.50
			Energy Charge	R	4.00
			Gold Nut	U	1.50
			Kiai Head Band	R	3.50
			Kurumi	R	4.00
			Masaki's Transportation Machine	U	1.50
			Miracle Nut	U	1.00
			Moo Moo Milk	C	0.50
			New Pokémon Illustrated Book	U	1.00
			Nut	C	0.50
			Pokémon Gear	R	3.30
			Pokémon March	C	0.40
			Professor Utsugi	U	1.00
			Recycle Energy	R	4.00
			Slot Game	R	4.00
			Steel Energy	F	12.00
			Super Energy Collection	R	4.00
			Super Pokémon Collection	U	1.00
			Terrific Fishing Pole	C	0.50
			Time Capsule	R	4.00
			Tower of Madatsubomi	U	1.00

Pocket Monsters • Special Sets

ANA Promo folder 1998	50.00
ANA Promo folder #1 1999	67.50
ANA Promo folder #2 1999	72.75
CD single w/Lapras Misty Trainer	16.50
CD single w/Meowth	12.75
Neo Premium File (9 cards)	15.00
Neo 2 Premium File (9 cards)	20.00
Neo two-card promo Dark set	12.25
Pikachu CD w/10 cards sealed	100.00
Promo Card Intropack sealed (82 cards w/Video)	50.00
Promo Card Intropack Sealed (82 cards)	45.00
Quick Starter Set (Red & Green decks)	55.00

RARITY KEY C = Common U = Uncommon R = Rare VR = Very Rare UR = Ultra Rare F = Foil card X = Fixed/standard in all decks

Pocket Monsters • Neo 2: Beyond the Ruins

Nintendo/Creatures/Gamefreak • Japan • 56 cards in set

• Boosters available

#	Lvl	HP	Card name	Rarity	Price
11	70	23	Metapod	U	1.00
12	80	38	Butterfree	F	10.00
13	40	14	Weedle	C	0.25
14	70	22	Kakuna	U	1.00
15	80	36	Beedrill	F	10.00
26	70	31	Raichu	F	15.00
60	40	14	Poliwag	C	0.25
61	70	35	Poliwhirl	U	1.00
62	90	45	Poliwrath	F	11.50
81	40	16	Magnemite	F	10.50
123	60	24	Scyther	U	1.70
133	50	14	Eevee	U	1.00
138	50	21	Omanyte	C	0.25
139	80	39	Omastar	U	1.00
140	50	21	Kabuto	C	0.25
141	90	42	Kabutops	F	12.00
161	50	18	Sentret	C	0.25
167	50	19	Spinarak	C	0.25
174	30	6	Igglybuff	U	1.00

#	Lvl	HP	Card name	Rarity	Price
177	40	13	Xatu	C	0.25
178	70	38	Xogo	U	1.00
179	50	18	Mareep	C	0.25
186	100	53	Politoed	F	12.00
187	30	8	Hoppip	C	0.25
193	60	32	Dunsparce	F	10.00
194	50	17	Ampharos	C	0.25
196	80	45	Espeon	F	12.00
197	80	40	Umbreon	F	12.00
201	40	14	Unown D	U	1.30
201	40	16	Unown F	U	1.00
201	40	14	Unown M	U	1.00
201	40	16	Unown U	U	1.00
201	40	15	Unown A	F	11.75
202	90	46	Sonansu	F	11.75
204	40	15	Skarmory	C	0.25
205	80	40	Forrestress	F	12.25
206	30	9	Duglari	C	0.25

#	Lvl	HP	Card name	Rarity	Price
212	80	43	Scizor	F	13.50
216	40	12	Himeguma	C	0.25
217	80	42	Ursaring	F	11.75
222	50	27	Corsola	U	1.00
228	40	15	Houndour	U	2.00
228	50	22	Houndour	F	10.00
229	70	37	Houndoom	F	12.00
235	50	27	Ebeagle	F	11.75
236	30	7	Baruki	C	0.25
237	60	31	Hitmontop	F	12.00
246	40	10	Tarvitar	C	0.25
247	70	32	Pupitar	U	1.00
248	100	54	Tyranitar	F	12.50
			Egg Fossil	U	1.00
			Energy Ark	C	0.50
			Hyper Devolution Spray	U	1.00
			Stone Board Remains (ver. 1)	U	1.00
			Stone Board Remains (ver. 2)	U	1.00

Set (55+1 variant cards) 211.50
Booster Display Box 450.00
Booster Pack 10.00

#	Lvl	HP	Card name	Rarity	Price
10	50	16	Caterpie	C	0.25

Pocket Monsters • Promo and Special Cards

SOUTHERN ISLAND (palm tree icon)

Southern Island Set in binder **48.75**
Southern Island Set **54.00**

#	Lvl	HP	Card name	Price
			Beach set of 3	13.00
	36	70	Slowking (Yadoking)	6.90
8	20	60	Wartortle	4.20
103	27	70	Exeggutor	4.20
			Field of Flowers set of 3	14.25
	12	40	Ledyba (Rediba)	9.00
12	37	80	Butterfree	3.00
39	10	50	Jigglypuff	4.00
			Jungle set of 3	14.00
45	30	70	Vileplume	5.90
57	26	60	Primeape	3.00
108	25	70	Lickitung	3.00
			Riverside set of 3	15.00
	10	40	Togepi	14.50
2	23	60	Ivysaur	3.00
20	25	60	Raticate	3.00
			Sea set of 3	17.50
	10	40	Marrill	14.75
73	30	60	Tentacruel	3.00
131	30	70	Lapras	3.00

SKY set of 3 **20.00**

#	Lvl	HP	Card name	Price
18	39	70	Pidgeot	3.00
95	40	90	Onix	3.00
151	5	30	Mew	12.00

JUMBO VENDING (Pokéball Icons)

	Price
Jumbo 1 Set	50.00
Jumbo 2 Set	97.50
Jumbo 3 Set	77.50
Jumbo promo sheet (00 on back)	50.00
Jumbo 1 unpeeled sheet (red counters)	6.30
Jumbo 2 unpeeled sheet (colored counters)	7.50
Jumbo 3 unpeeled sheet (4 cards/page)	8.00

COLOSSAL CARDS

#	Lvl	HP	Card name	Rarity	Price
25	13	50	Pikachu	F	15.00
150	30	60	Mewtwo	F	17.50
151	25	50	Mew	F	25.00
6	76	120	Charizard		43.75
25		50	Pikachu Summer Holiday		10.00
150		100	MewTwo's Counterattack		11.50
			Girarudan		5.50
		60	Pikachu/Clefairy/Jigglypuff		10.00
			Pokémon Park		6.00
			Pokémon Valley		20.00
		120	Zapdos/Articuno/Moltres		9.90

PROMO CARDS

#	Lvl	HP	Card name	Rarity	Price
3	67	100	Venusaur (lightning icon)	F	15.00
6	76	120	Charizard (lightning icon)	F	45.00
9	52	100	Blastoise (lightning icon)	F	20.00
25	16	60	Pikachu (leaves in background)		60.00

#	Lvl	HP	Card name	Rarity	Price
25	17	50	Birthday Pikachu	F	250.00
25	17	50	Birthday Pikachu w/calendar	F	350.00
25	13	50	Surfing Pikachu		160.00
25	12	40	Flying Pikachu		160.00
25	9	40	Pikachu Snap (camera icon)		20.00
34	50	100	Giovanni's Nidoking (Gym 2)		19.75
76	37	80	Golem (Jumbo 3 mail-in)	F	15.00
94	40	80	Gengar (Jumbo 3 mail-in)	F	15.00
137	15	50	Cool Porygon (N64)	F	15.00
143	50	100	Gluttonous Snorlax (N64)	F	15.00
149	41	100	Dragonite (Game Boy)	F	6.50
149	43	90	Dragonite (ANA Promo)		150.00
151	8	40	Mew (on lilypad)		33.75
151	8	30	Ancient Egypt Mew - glitter	F	80.00
151	8	30	Ancient Egypt Mew - sparkle	F	80.00
154	54	100	Meganium (Neo Premium File)	F	7.50
157	57	100	Typhlosion (Neo Premium File)	F	8.30
160	69	120	Feraligatr (Neo Premium File)	F	7.50
173	6	30	Cleffa (Neo)		8.00
(na)	8	30	Togepi (Neo, glossy)		12.00
(na)	17	50	Marill (Neo, glossy)		15.00
199	40	80	Slowking (Neo)	F	8.70
208	57	100	Steelix (Neo fan club mag)	F	12.00
212	36	70	Scizor (Neo 2, glossy)		11.00
			Dark Energy (Neo, glossy)		3.00
			Koga's Ninja Gym (Gym 2)		11.50

Pokémon • United States
Known translations include: **Dutch, French, German**
French sets: Base, Jungle, Fossil
German: Base, Dschungel, Fossil, Team Rocket

Spellfire • United States
Known translations include: **French**
French sets: Maitrisez la magic

Star Wars • United States
Known translations include: **Japanese**

Ultragate • Japan
Based on the Ultraman television character, **Ultragate** was supposedly available in 1997 or even earlier. We have found no solid evidence that it actually existed.

Yu-Gi-Oh Duel Monsters • Japan
Konami

The hottest CCG in Japan since **Pocket Monsters**, **Yu-Gi-Oh** strikes a middle ground between **Magic** and **Pokémon**, both in gameplay and setting. Each player can summon one monster each turn. There are no "casting costs," except that higher level monsters can only be brought in with the sacrifice of lower-level monsters.

Yu-Gi-Oh is based on the manga and anime series of the same name, in which Yugi Mutou, a bullied student in high school, is given an ancient Egyptian puzzle by his grandfather. When solved, the puzzle makes the student strong, confident, and able to defeat anyone at any game, notably the popular "Magic and Wizards" trading card game. The "Magic and Wizards" card game of the manga and anime was eventually developed as a real game, with the "Duel Monsters" subtitle coming from the second Yu-Gi-Oh anime series, "Duel Monsters."

The odds are good *Yu-Gi-Oh* will never be seen in the United States unless licensed through Wizards of the Coast, as the game play is too similar to *Magic* to go without a legal response.

Expansions: There are currently six main sets out, plus a number of basic pre-constructed deck sets, and a whole legion of offshoot games and toys.

RARITY KEY C = Common U = Uncommon R = Rare VR = Very Rare UR = Ultra Rare F = Foil card X = Fixed/standard in all decks

APPENDIX C: PSEUDO-COLLECTIBLE CARD GAMES

This volume covers CCGs, but there are many games which are occasionally assumed to be "collectible card games," which do not meet the definition described on page 12. We acknowledge a **sampling** here, as well as a selection of other products directly inspired by CCGs, such as collectible dice and disk games. **Warning:** We may change our minds on some of these.

Age of Heroes
Renegade Mage • Released 1997

Age of Heroes is a non-collectible "character-adventure" style card game, similar in many respects to **Dragon Storm**, **Fantasy Adventures**, and **Ruins World**. The deck is a fixed set of 70 cards, and includes characters, monsters, weapons, armor, magic treasures, and spells. The game can be played solitaire or in multi-player games, where players do not compete but cooperate instead. The object is to have the highest ratio of points of Monsters slain to points of Heroes lost.

The artwork and layout are good for a first-time production, but three additional, unnamed sets were planned for 1998 were never released.

Anime Madness
Matthew Johnston Games • Released 1996

Anime Madness brings together characters from many different anime series, including *Bubblegum Crisis*, *Bubblegum Crash*, *Riding Bean*, *AD Police Files*, *Genesis Survivor Gaiarth*, and *Scramble Wars*. Each player represents an anime production company attempting to either eliminate the competition or move their own anime shows to the hottest spots in the industry — by having the anime characters battle in virtual reality!

The system is the same basic system as **Magic**. This is not a coincidence, as the designer started the game as an "underground expansion to *Magic*." Animator cards provide resources to bring out cards. Animators are found in the Bullpen Deck, while all other cards, Characters, Tools, Plot Devices, and Maneuvers, are found in the Studio Deck. Characters have Hand Damage, Ranged Damage, and Hit Point statistics, used in combat just like in *Magic*.

Anime Madness was released in limited editions at around the same time **Ani-Mayhem** was released. There was apparently confusion as to the relationship between the two games, and *Anime Madness* lost out in the competition. *Anime Madness* was originally designed to be a full-fledged collectible card game, with boosters and later expansions. However, only one set, the *Preview Edition Starter Set*, was ever released, and as all cards in the set are available through the purchase of one starter it does not qualify as a true CCG.

Battlecards
Merlin Publishing International • Released 1993

Known as the "Scratch & Slay" game, *Steve Jackson's BattleCards* was a combination card game and lottery game. First released in England, an edition was also published in America as the **Magic** craze was starting. Each card had different portions that could be scratched off, as on a lottery ticket, underneath which were symbols that told the player if he hit the opposing card.

As the game is not played with a deck and the collectibility of used cards is zero, *BattleCards* does not qualify as a CCG.

The "Steve Jackson" of **BattleCards** is the English Steve Jackson of Fighting Fantasy Novels, not the American Steve Jackson of Steve Jackson Games.

Beer: The Card Game
Stupendous Games

The goal of this non-collectible card game by Stuart John Bernard is to drink as much beer as possible before you run out of money or before the "Last Call" card is drawn. The card set features images from 63 different microbrewery beers. Released as a standard style card game in a single deck, **Beer** is listed here as some have erroneously believed it to be a CCG.

Brawl
Cheapass Games • Released Summer 1999

A stand-alone card game by James Ernest, Brawl comes in several pre-constructed character decks, each based on a single fighter in a brawl. A player's own speed and dexterity are as important as the cards in hand. Each player uses a single fighter deck, with each card representing a different move. Players create stacks of cards representing the different portions of the Brawl between the two fighters. A game lasts no longer than a minute. The winner is the player that collects the most stacks (i.e., beats up the opponent more than he himself was beaten up).

More decks were added with *Brawl: Club Foglio*, a set of six fighters illustrated by Phil Foglio.

Chaos Progenitus
Destination Games • Released 1996

Another collectible dice game designed by Lester Smith, designer of **Dragon Dice**, **Chaos Progenitus** differs from its cousin in that each set of dice represents a single monster rather than an army.

Each player has his own monster, made up of 13 dice. The players fight with their monsters until one or the other is destroyed. Unlike *Dragon Dice*, *Chaos Progenitus* only came with six-sided dice.

The game was regarded as a good beer-and-pretzels game, but the images on the plain-colored dice were bland, if functional, and the name has been described by some as among the worst ever chosen for a game.

Chaos Progenitus was released with a single starter set and had a single booster set, **Plague Beasts**.

ChronX
Genetic Anomalies • Launched June 1997

ChronX is an Internet-based "collectible digital card" game. It's set in the year 2091, after the United States has collapsed into feudal corporate states and the United Nations teeters as it tries to keep the whole world from collapsing into a new dark age. Players take on the roles of warlords in the global conspiracy known as "The Body," seeking to destroy opposing warlords and wrest control of The Body, and thus the world, from all others.

The game takes place entirely on the Internet. "Cards" are digital representations, as is all play action. "Cards" can be bought in digital booster packs and even traded digitally. There are currently 650 different cards in the game, spanning three main editions and three expansions (*Overture*, *Ascension*, and *Defiance*). Nothing new has been released for *ChronX* from Genetic Anomalies since its acquisition by THQ in December 1999.

Dino Hunt
Steve Jackson Games • Released 1996

Dino Hunt is a board game with expansion cards. Players take the part of time travelers in the age of the Dinosaurs; the object is to capture the most or best dinosaurs for your zoo back in your own time.

A release of randomly-sorted cards expands the number of dinosaur and playing cards available, but with no deck design by each player, it is not a classic CCG.

Diskwars
Fantasy Flight Games • Released 1999

Diskwars, like *Dragon Dice* before it, initiated a whole new genre of games in the "collectible" category. Unlike *Dragon Dice* and collectible dice games, however, *Diskwars* and collectible disk games have created a firm if small niche in the market that lasts to this day. Like collectible dice games, collectible disk games have as much in common with war games and board games as they do with collectible card games.

Players of *Diskwars* each have their own fantasy-based "army" of collectible disks, much like a deck in a collectible card game, except that each army is built according to a number of points, and disks are arranged in order on the stack ("deck") as the player wishes. Disks are moved on a table as though in a miniatures battle. When Disks meet, they attack each other. The objective is usually to capture the "home disk" of the opposing players. To date, *Diskwars* has spawned two major licensed games (**Legend of the Five Rings Diskwars** and **Range Wars**) and a third, **Heavy Gear Diskwars**, is planned for release in 2001 as of press time.

Expansions include **Moon over Thelgrim**, **The Wastelands, Legions**, and **Waiqar's Path**. *Moon over Thelgrim* and *Waiqar's Path* are available in faction-based Starters that are part fixed, part random, while *The Wastelands* was offered in an experimental random Booster format. The *Legions* set is a starter set that includes four fixed-content, dual-army boxes.

Doomtown: Range Wars
Fantasy Flight Games • Released 2000

Doomtown: Range Wars is a *Diskwars* game set in the same setting as the *Deadlands* role-playing game from Pinnacle and the *Doomtown* collectible card game from Alderac. Instead of factions there are Outfits, such as the Sweetrock Mining Company, The Collegium, and the infamous Whateley Clan. Play is similar to Diskwars, though there are additional rules due to the prevalence of six-shooters over sorcery and weird ghost rock devices rather than magical items.

Dragon Dice
TSR • Released 1995

Designed by Lester Smith, **Dragon Dice** was the first and best collectible dice game. Detractors claimed it was a ploy to cash in on the "collectible" side of gaming, but players regarded it as a new genre.

The game combines aspects of CCGs with wargame and board game concepts. Each player fields an army of dice, usually of a single race or of a few allied races. Dice include 4-, 6-, 8-, 10-, and 12-sided dice, each with different mixes of images on each side. Each move, attack, or action calls for a number of dice to be rolled. The level of success depends on the number of proper images rolled. The game requires strategy and planning, as much as if not more so than most collectible card games. Fan-sponsored *Dragon Dice* tournaments can still be found at conventions to this day.

Several expansions ("kicker" rather than "booster" packs) were released from 1995 through 1998. Wizards of the Coast halted the hideously expensive production of *Dragon Dice* game when it purchased TSR in 1998. Similar *Hercules: The Legendary Journeys* and *Xena: Warrior Princess* dice games were planned in 1998, based on the two popular television series, but were never released. SFR Inc., a start-up company formed in

2000, purchased the rights to the *Dragon Dice* game and setting from Wizards of the Coast in October 2000, and plans to release the long-awaited *Treefolk* expansion in 2001.

Kicker Pack expansions include **Amazons & Monsters, Firewalkers, Undead, Feral, MageStorm, Swamp Stalkers, Frostwings,** and **Scalders**.

DragonElves
Fast Forward Entertainment • Launched 2000

Designed by Tim Brown, with Lester Smith and Jim Ward, *DragonElves* is billed as the first "E-card" game. E-card games are a cross between standard collectible card games and completely web-based card games, with a twist. Players buy points from Fast Forward, with which they can design their own cards from a set number of options on the *DragonElves* web site. Players can also use points for standard cards from the web site. They then print out the cards and play with them like a standard CCG, designing their own decks from cards they designed themselves. The cards are thus designed on the web, but played in the real world.

There are two factions, DragonElves and BronzeMen. Each is offered in a "starter set," a tin containing 32 plastic card sleeves, a rulebook (including 32 tear-out cards), and a code worth 1,000 to 100,000 points.

As there is no collectible value to the cards (each player can print out as many of each as he wishes) and the cards are not sold in random boosters and starters, the E-card concept is a new animal. Pinnacle Entertainment worked out a deal with Fast Forward Entertainment to create eight **Lost Colony** cards using the same format, mixing E-cards and CCGs together for the first time. Time will tell whether the format is a viable game type.

Dragon Storm
Black Dragon Press • Released 1996

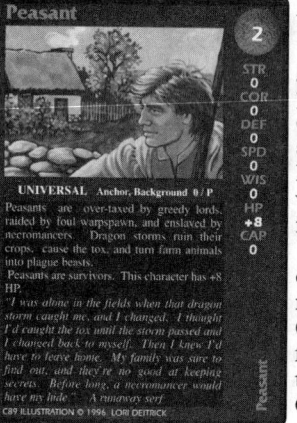

Designed by Susan Van Camp with Mark Harmon, *Dragon Storm* is actually a role-playing game that uses cards during play. The only successful game of its type, *Dragon Storm* has a small and loyal following that has kept the game going strong while other CCGs and role-playing games have languished.

Each player designs his own character based on a specific number of points of cards. Cards represent everything from abilities and skills to treasures and mundane items. One player then puts together an adventure using monster, treasure, encounter, and region cards. Players run their characters as a standard party of role-playing game adventurers and go forth and adventure in a game moderated by the game master. The cards are used for ease of play; the rules are simple yet elegant.

Kanchaka Valley is the only "traditional" random booster pack expansion for the game, while cut out cards are found in the *Kanchaka Valley, Haskalad Empire, Valarian Champions*, and *Necromancer's Manifesto* sourcebooks. Numerous cards and five character sets are available directly from Black Dragon Press at conventions or through mail order.

Emmerlaüs: Duel of Mages
Creations Chaos • Released 1996 (1st Edition), 1999 (2nd Edition)

Designed by Frederic Dumas and Jean-Francois Hamel, *Emmerlaüs* allows two to ten players take the

part of dueling wizards. Comparisons to **Magic** are common, but play is much different. There is only one deck from which all players draw; each player has a hand of five to seven cards. Players start out with 50 hit points. The goal is to use the spells and items from the deck to reduce opponents to zero. Dice are used with many spells to determine damage. The number of dice rolled are often dependent upon the Power Level of the player, which is determined by the magic items he has in play as well as spells he has cast. It can be a lethal game.

Emmerlaüs has been released in a First Edition available only in French. The Second Edition is available in both French and English versions, and will eventually have at least four 50-card expansion sets. The first, *Communion*, was already out as of press time, while the other three, *Power*, *Destiny*, and *Abundance*, were planned for release by mid-2001.

Fluxx
Looney Labs

Fluxx is often mistaken for a CCG due to the nature of its release. There are only two rules: Draw one card, play one card. That is, until the card you play changes the rules. How does one win? Well, no one knows until someone plays a Goal card.

There have been several "Convention Special" expansion cards offered at Gen Con and Origins by Looney Labs, but as the game is still played with only one deck shared among the players, it's not a classic CCG.

Gangland
Corglenburg • Released 1996

Gangland was intended to be an "expandable" single-deck card game, with later releases adding new cards. The setting was the gritty prohibition era streets of Chicago, where players would try to build the biggest and most powerful gang and defeat the other players.

The Great Dalmuti
Wizards of the Coast • Released 1995

The Great Dalmuti is a classic "college drinking game," adapted and expanded by Richard Garfield into a family game. As it was a Wizards of the Coast release, some considered this basic card game a CCG, especially after the release of a *Dilbert* version.

Groo: The Card Game
Archangel Entertainment

Based on the comic misadventures of Sergio Aragonés' barbarian, this game allows four to six players to re-enact the devastation wrought by Groo as he wanders his way across the land — preferably in the opponent's villages.

The first to successfully build a village to a total of seven victory points wins, which is not as easy as it sounds with Groo hanging around. The basic set of 60 cards allows for up to four players, while a 55-card expansion allows for six player games.

Havic: The Bothering
PGI • Released 1998

Designed by Peter Gray and Frank Martell as a parody of **Magic: The Gathering**, *Havic: The Bothering* (the first set subtitled *Skool Daze*) expressly forbade players to "construct a deck from a pooled set of cards" lest the players infringe on Wizard of the Coast's rights. Otherwise the game was startlingly similar to *Magic*, with

the exception that there were **Chain Smoker**, **Farmer's Daughter**, and **Vengeful Resident Assistant** "Minion" cards rather than creature cards, and **Hangover**, **Term Paper**, and **Detox** cards instead of instant and sorcery cards. Minions were "coerced" to do players bidding by using resources generated from **Convenience Stores (Smokes)** and **Breweries (Booze)**. The humor degenerated from there.

It was regarded as the "Animal House" parody of *Magic*. A planned booster set expansion, *Spring Break*, was never released.

The rules specifically state that it's not a CCG.

Heavy Gear Fighter
Dream Pod 9 • Released 1995

The *Heavy Gear Fighter* card game, designed by Jean Carrières, is based in the same setting as the *Heavy Gear* miniature war game and role-playing game. *Heavy Gear Fighter* is an expandable card game in which each player uses a Gear (Mecha) card while all players are dealt play cards from one deck. Each different Gear has a number of actions it may perform during one turn. Offensive and defensive moves are color-coded; a Gear must have the same color capability and requisite number of actions left. Range between Gears is also taken into account. The game is entirely strategy, as there are no random elements.

The initial set of 116 cards includes eight Gear cards. Expansion sets include a *Weapons & Equipment* set of 72 cards, and three 12-card sets, *Mishaps, Fortune, and Booster Set 1*.

Illuminati
Steve Jackson Games • Released 1982

The original I*lluminati* game, based in part on the conspiracy novels by Robert Shea and Robert Anton Wilson, remains one of the greatest card games to come out of hobby gaming. Three expansion sets came out in the 1980s, each adding a fixed set of new cards to the single-deck game.

Jackson relased a CCG version, **Illuminati: New World Order**, in 1994. Since that game wound down, new releases of the original version of *Illuminati* have come out using the better "look" of the CCG cards.

Legend of the Five Rings Diskwars
Alderac Entertainment Group • Released 2000

Based on the card game and role-playing game of the same name, **Legend of the Five Rings Diskwars** is compatible with the standard **Diskwars** game produced by Fantasy Flight games. The *Legend of the Five Rings* editions are being produced in the same order as the card game was produced, allowing new players to join in the story line at the beginning. The story line of the *Diskwars* edition, however, is determined by *Legend of the Five Rings Diskwars* story line tournaments, and thus may eventually diverge from the classic story line.

One expansion, **Shadowlands**, has been released.

Lost Worlds Fantasy Cards
Greysea LLC/Flying Buffalo/Chessex

The *Lost Worlds* combat picture book game was developed more than 20 years ago by Alfred Leonardi and may be best remembered from its incarnation as *Ace of Aces*. Each player has his own combat book, featuring a warrior, dragon, mummy, centaur, or other character or creature from fantasy or legend. Each book has a combat matrix. Players' exchange their books but keep their own matrix for reference. They then battle each other using the matrices to cross reference maneuvers pictured in the books; each player sees his opponent's character in the book he has in hand, and a full view of what occurs as the combat ensues.

The Fantasy Cards were added to the mix after the

CCG craze started. Cards include tactics, spells, magic weapons, magic items, and other things that can modify a combat book character's abilities or otherwise alter the game. The cards cannot be used except as supplementary game aids to the combat book game.

Lunch Money
Atlas Games • Released 1995

Designed by Charlie Wiedman, *Lunch Money* is a simple card game, in that each player uses cards drawn from a common deck to beat up the other players. There are attack cards like **Hail Mary**, **Headbutt**, **Pimp Slap**, **Knife**, and **Hammer**, as well as defense cards such as **Dodge**, **Block**, and **Disarm**. The objective is to be the last player standing, the theme that of a brawl in the sand lot over lunch money. It's a fine beer and pretzels game, though the imagery, that of a young girl perpetrating mayhem with a grin on her face, might be disturbing for younger players.

The game is not by any means or design a CCG, but has often been mistaken by such by those who only knew Atlas from **On the Edge**.

Magic Poker Deck
Wizards of the Coast • Released 1998

The *Magic Poker Deck* is just that — a poker deck with art from **Magic: The Gathering**. Two decks with Magic backs, not the same as the CCG, are included in the set.

Monster Magic
Trio Toys • Released 1995

A mass-market game designed by J. D. Crowe, little is known of this card game. It was targeted at a younger crowd than the typical **Magic: The Gathering** market, and died out long before **Pokémon** came on the scene.

Mystick
Anoch Games Systems • Released 2000

An expandable tarot-card based card game, **Mystick** is thus far available in two sets, the **Domination** set and the **Companion** set.

Each set has a Basic Deck and a Power Deck, with each deck containing 78 cards. A role-playing game based on the background is also planned.

Nuclear War
Flying Buffalo • Designed 1965

Nuclear War is the classic off-color game of, well, nuclear war, using up "people" the way other games use money. Flying Buffalo's version was originally released in the late 1970s, and had two expansion box sets, *Nuclear Escalation* and *Nuclear Proliferation*.

During the height of the CCG craze, Flying Buffalo released a set of 47 new cards in a randomized booster pack format, actually just shrinkwrapped with a title card. The limited number of cards combined with the fact that they were quickly available as a complete set separately limited the "collectability" of the cards, and the game itself is not a CCG.

While its popularity has slacked off over the last decade, it's still one of the best card games out there.

Once Upon a Time
Atlas Games • Released 1993

Designed by Richard Lambert, Andrew Rilstone, and James Wallis, *Once Upon a Time* is a storytelling card game in which players try to build a fairy tale using the cards from the set deck. Players try to win the place of Storyteller by playing their cards in such a way as to advance the story. The first player to play out all their cards and end the story "Happily Ever After" wins the game. The game is in its second edition.

Again, it has been mistaken as a CCG by those who only knew Atlas from **On the Edge**.

Quest for the Faysylwood
Faysylwood Press • Released August 1993

Designed by David Shaw, *Quest for the Faysylwood* did not do as well as that other card game released at the 1993 Gen Con Game Fair, **Magic: The Gathering**.

Quest, though released in what appears to be a starter deck, is a traditional card game, in which players try to get their characters to the Faysylwood by travelling through lands represented by cards, where they encounter monsters, bandits, and wizards. Opponents play the bad guys against each other trying to slow down the opposing character. The down side of playing monsters is that if they are defeated the winning player can play treasures from his hand.

Quest was a nice little card game that was unfortunately drowned in the collectible card game flood.

Shadow Raven
Destiny Horizons Inc.

Billed as a "combat card game" rather than as a collectible card game, *Shadow Raven* has the look and feel of a CCG but it is available only in a single, pre-constructed deck. The game system would be familiar to any fan of **Magic**, as the system is essentially the same.

The game adds "levels" to the characters, wherein by stacking a copy of the same card on top of another the base card rises in "level," achieving higher attack and defense values as well as access to special abilities. The endgame also is different, as it is a decking game rather than a life point game. A player loses when his "base" (deck) is depleted and he has no cards in hand. There is an alternate endgame, wherein a player must acquire five "Battle Cards," which represent massive attacks in the various territories of the Shadow Raven universe.

Spammers
Atlas Games

Designed by Jeff Tidball, *Spammers* is another non-CCG offering from Atlas. It is a humorous take on the Internet, wherein players "spam," or blindly e-mail, various groups in order to run scams, make money, and become known as the biggest jerk on the Internet.

Star Trek Collectible Dice Game
Five Rings Publishing • Released 1996

More an "expandable" dice game than a collectible dice game like **Dragon Dice**, the **Star Trek Collectible Dice Game** uses dice as the core system for representing the various elements of starships during combat simulations.

Each player places his own set of dice on a layout resembling the controls of the *Enterprise* or the Borg Sphere. Dice represent Command, Movement, Repair, Special, and Weapons systems on the ship. Each turn a player decides which systems to power up, then combat occurs. A ship is eliminated when its warp core is breached. Designed to be a one-on-one game, some players developed rules for multi-player games (official rules were planned but apparently never released). It's a good ship combat game, though not a fast-playing one.

Borg Sphere starter and boosters and **U.S.S. Enterprise NCC-1701-E** starter and boosters came out. Each starship comes with a fixed starter box that contains everything needed to play. The booster packs are fixed sets of dice in five different combinations.

Five Rings planned to release starter sets for the **Klingon Vor'cha Attack Cruiser** and the **Federation Galaxy Class Starship**, and there have been reported sightings of the sets. However, we have not been able to confirm whether or not they were released. There were also plans for a Romulan ship set.

Star Wars Episode 1 CCG Boxed Set
Decipher • Released 1999

Designed for play by two to four players, this game is a highly simplified version of the *Young Jedi* CCG that Decipher also publishes. In fact, the game system used in this card game was originally planned to be the system for *Young Jedi*, but last minute changes were made when it was determined that the system was not complex enough. The four decks in the box can be adjusted, but no further cards can be brought into the mix, so it's not often considered a CCG — but the cards can be confused with *Young Jedi* cards, hence its listing here.

Darth Maul
Leader Bonus: +5
1

Stratego Legends
Avalon Hill/Hasbro • Released 1999

Designed by Craig van Ness, *Stratego Legends* combines classic *Stratego* with *Magic* elements. In place of Napoleonic armies and bombs, each player fields a force of fantasy creatures and magical traps and items.

Game play is essentially the same as the classic *Stratego*, except the power ratings on figures are reversed. In classic *Stratego*, the most powerful piece is a "1," and the weakest the "10". It's the reverse in *Stratego Legends*, which also introduces special powers for just about every figure, as well as piece types (as in Giant, Dragon, Wizard, Elf, and so forth). There are six different major factions, divided into two major groups of three each, Good and Evil. The board is made up of four random boards, which have the grids divided into land types, such as forests, deserts, and swamps, which tie in with special abilities on the pieces.

The *Starter Set* contains 60 random plastic playing pieces with metallic character stickers, four random battle boards with borders, six reference cards (one for each major faction), storage tray, and rulebook with game setting legend. There are also randomized booster packs, each of which contain 15 pieces with stickers (plus an extra plastic piece), which are further divided into Good and Evil army packs (*Landor's Legion* and *Kralc's Horde*, respectively). There are more than 200 different pieces, plus 24 different battle boards. There are thus far also four ultra-rare pieces, available from Avalon Hill only at conventions: one pair in 1999, the other in 2000.

The Three Stooges
Archangel Entertainment

Imagine *Lunch Money* with the Three Stooges instead of the scary little girl. Got it? OK, you know this game. It adds a few twists, notably the "Cheese" phase, which is an opportunity to totally go nuts with attack cards, but other than that the game is pretty much the same.

A fine little game, *Three Stooges* did not survive the downfall of Archangel Entertainment.

Tribbles: The Card Game
Decipher • Released 2000

When Decipher published the *Trouble with Tribbles* Expansion for the *Star Trek CCG*, it included a sub-game within the game, simply called *Tribbles*. It later went on to publish *Tribbles* as a separate card game, with its own decks and box.

Similar in ways to other traditonal card games, the object of *Tribbles* is to collect as many of the furry little

critters as possible. There are cards that can reverse the order of play, collect a series of cards early, and so forth.

WWF: With Authority!
Genetic Anomalies

Cousin to the other Genetic Anomalies offering, *ChronX*, *WWF: With Authority* is planned to be another Internet-based game. As of press time the game was still in beta testing, but with this new game, Genetic Anomalies is moving away from the CCG appellation and has created a new term for the Internet based collectible card game genre, "online collectible strategy gaming," which more accurately reflects the card-less environment of the Internet.

Zoon
Humanoids/Yeti/West End Games

Zoon was originally a French game that was translated and developed for an American audience. It can best be described as a combination between chess and *Stratego*, played with cards. Tribes of mutant humanoid animals, each humorously based on a classical or medieval human culture, dominate the imaginary world of Zoon. Each player has an army made up of a single nation. The cards are played face down then moved like chess pieces. When one card invades the space of another, each card is spun, then a corner is picked. The numbers under the corners picked are compared, and the highest number wins, with the loser being killed. The object of the game is to capture the flag of the opposing army.

Expansion deck sets available in French and English include *Europa* and *Bigear*. Sets so far only available in French are *U.Z.A.*, *Zyatik*, and *Gandent*.

NOTABLE ALMOST-WERE CCGs

Apocalyptica

This had a brief life as a possible game with an unfinished background and story line. No details are known about this almost-was game save for the name of the would-have-been and that it was going to be produced in Aberdeen. For all we know it still might be in development.

Arcanus

Zach Weiner's **Arcanus** premiered in conceptual and playtest design form on the web with some small fanfare in June 1998, was briefly bandied about as a potential winner if ever published in paper form, and disappeared quietly in August 1998. There was a brief resurgence in March 1999, but nothing ever came of it. *Arcanus* belongs among the "urban legends" of CCGs as the card game that never was. At press time the playtest rules and images still existed at: *www.geocities.com/SiliconValley/Campus/2436/arcanus*.

Magic: Ysgarth Expansion

Before **Magic: The Gathering** became a hit, Wizards of the Coast signed a deal with Ragnarok Press, makers of the *Ysgarth Role-Playing Game*, for Ragnarok to develop a **Magic** expansion based on the Ysgarth setting. The design team developed and playtested a set with more than 400 cards, along with several new mechanics. The expansion was put on hold after Wizards decided that the *Ysgarth* expansion as developed was too similar to its own impending **Ice Age** set. Wizards killed the deal shortly thereafter and no further **Magic** licensing deals were made between Wizards and other manufacturers. Most of the creative team behind the *Ysgarth* expansion later went on to develop the **Quest for the Grail** CCG, and released it through their new company, Stone Ring Games.

Realms Arcana

Though promo cards do exist, Knight Press has confirmed that 1995's announced *Realms Arcana* CCG never came out.

War

We have promo cards for Deity Games' *War*, but we cannot confirm its existence as a released CCG.

SUBSCRYEBE TODAY!

Don't let this vital vault of game knowledge go unopened. Start your **SCRYE** subscription now. **Just $27.98** brings you the next 8 big issues, packed with brand-new, tournament-winning strategies, information on new games and expansions, and the latest on games in development. **PLUS**, you'll find special tips on building better decks and starting one from scratch, current prices on cards from a variety of sets, the most recent banned or restricted cards, and a built-in marketplace of advertisers that can help you get the cards you need.

Let your games continue...and make them better than ever by starting your **SCRYE** subscription today.

To place a credit card order Call

800-258-0929 Offer ABA39N

M-F, 7 am - 8 pm • Sat, 8 am - 2 pm, CST